ISBN 978-0-331-12283-1
PIBN 11098073

English
Français
Deutsche
Italiano
Español
Português

www.forgottenbooks.com

Mythology Photography **Fiction**
Fishing Christianity **Art** Cooking
Essays Buddhism Freemasonry
Medicine **Biology** Music **Ancient**
Egypt Evolution Carpentry Physics
Dance Geology **Mathematics** Fitness
Shakespeare **Folklore** Yoga Marketing
Confidence Immortality Biographies
Poetry **Psychology** Witchcraft
Electronics Chemistry History **Law**
Accounting **Philosophy** Anthropology
Alchemy Drama Quantum Mechanics
Atheism Sexual Health **Ancient History**
Entrepreneurship Languages Sport
Paleontology Needlework Islam
Metaphysics Investment Archaeology
Parenting Statistics Criminology
Motivational

FORSYTH REST CURE, BERWYN, ILLINOIS.

For Ladies Only.   Accessible by the Chicago, Burlington & Quincy and Illinois Central Railroads.

viii

ix

THE

CHICAGO BLUE BOOK

OF

SELECTED NAMES

OF

CHICAGO AND SUBURBAN TOWNS

CONTAINING THE

Names and Addresses of Prominent Residents, arranged Alphabetically
and Numerically by Streets; also Ladies' Shopping Guide,
Street Directory, and other Valuable Information.

FOR THE YEAR ENDING 1895.

THE CHICAGO DIRECTORY COMPANY.
PUBLISHERS,
ROOMS 2, 3 and 4 LAKESIDE BUILDING.

To Get the Best......

ICE

xiv

PREFACE.

WE herewith present the Sixth issue of the CHICAGO BLUE BOOK. We wish to thank our lady patrons for the appreciation they have shown our efforts, and trust that this volume will retain the high place in their favor, which we have won, and will endeavor to hold.

Neither time nor money have been spared to make the work as complete and valuable as possible; notwithstanding this, the difficulty attending the compiling of such a book can be easily appreciated. We therefore trust that any omissions will be brought to our notice, that they may be corrected in future. We keep the entire work standing in type, that such corrections can be made promptly ; and in this way we hope to make the Chicago Blue Book as nearly perfect as it is possible to make such a volume.

The title, "BLUE BOOK," is simply a name given the work on account of its *blue* cover. It does not refer to blue blood, as many people suppose. Webster's definition of Blue Book is as follows: "BLUE BOOK—A parliamentary publication, so called from its blue paper cover, such being commonly used; *also, a book containing a list of fashionable addresses.*"

We do not claim the BLUE BOOK to be either a City Directory or absolutely an Elite Directory ; neither do we pretend to pass upon the social or financial standing of the parties whose names are contained therein. It is simply a compilation of thirty thousand names of the most prominent householders of Chicago, and suburbs within a radius of thirty miles, published in the most convenient form for reference by our lady patrons.

While retaining all the old features, such as Calling Days in the Street List, and Summer Residences in Alphabetical List, we have added very materially to our Miscellaneous Information, Club Lists, Churches, etc.

We shall always be pleased to receive any suggestions from our lady patrons whereby we can enhance the value of this work to them, or any

xv

815841

information regarding Social or Literary Clubs and Associations, which
we have not already incorporated in our volume. The data of this work
has not been compiled from circulars or information out of other Directories, but experienced men, particularly adapted for such work, have been
assigned to each locality, and the greatest care has been used in selecting
these names. In order to issue the book before the Holidays, it is neces-
sary for us to commence our canvass early in September. We would
therefore deem it a great favor if those absent from their homes after
October 1st would send us the information which they wish inserted, as it
is not safe to take it from servants, or anyone except the parties interested.

THE PUBLISHERS.

xvii

xviii

GENERAL INDEX.

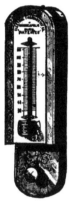

INDEX TO ADVERTISERS.

NICHOLAS AUW.....
STEAM DYE WORKS

Ladies' and Gentlemen's Garments Dyed,
Cleaned and Repaired........

Dyeing and Cleaning in all its Branches.

GARMENTS CLEANED
WITHOUT RIPPING OR
REMOVING TRIMMINGS

SUPERIOR WORK DONE

Telephone South-803.

141 E. 20th Street

THE GREAT AMERICAN STEAM....
CARPET AND LACE CLEANING WORKS.....

**Carpets Taken Up, Cleaned and Laid.
Carpets Renovated on the Floor.
Rugs and Drapery a Specialty.**

The Latest Improved Carpet Cleaning Machine....

Hair Mattresses Made Over and Renovated.
DO ONLY FIRST-CLASS WORK.

NICHOLAS AUW

141 E. 20th St., Bet. State St. and Wabash Ave.   Tel. South-803.

INDEX TO STREETS.

8

GEO. B. CARPENTER ---& CO...

MISCELLANEOUS INFORMATION.

CORPORATION OF THE CITY.

Mayor—John P. Hopkins, office, 2d floor, City Hall.

City Clerk — Charles D. Gastfield, office, 1st floor, City Hall.

Comptroller—Hiram J. Jones, office, 1st floor, City Hall.

Board of Public Works—John McCarthy Commissioner, 2d floor, City Hall.

Treasurer—M. J. Bransfield, office,1st floor, City Hall.

Corporation Counsel — John Mayo Palmer, office, 2d floor, City Hall.

City Attorney—Geo. A. Trude, office, 3d floor, City Hall.

Prosecuting Attorney—W. C. Asay, office, 3d floor, City Hall.

Health Commissioner — Arthur R. Reynolds, M.D., office, basement City Hall.

City Physician—James F. Todd, office, 22d cor. Wabash av.

Supt. House of Correction—Mark L. Crawford,S.California av.nr.W.Twenty-sixth.

Supt. Public Schools—Albert G. Lane, office, 12th floor, Schiller bldg., 109 Randolph.

School Agent— C. C. Chase, office, 1103 Chamb. Com. bldg.

City Sealer of Weights and Measures —Robert E. Burke, office, 29 City Hall.

Fire Marshal—Denis J. Swenie, office, City Hall, basement.

Gen'l Supt. Police—M. J. Brennan, office, room 32, City Hall.

Gas Inspector—H. F. Donovan,office, basement City Hall.

Inspector of Oils—Wm. Mangler, office, 79 Dearborn.

Inspector of Steam Boilers—John H. Pickham, City Hall.

BOARD OF ALDERMEN.
Meets every Monday evening.

First Ward—Louis I. Epstean, Rep., John J. Coughlin, Dem.

Second Ward—Martin Best, Rep., Addison Ballard, Rep.

Third Ward—Eli Smith, Rep., Edward Marrener, Rep.

Fourth Ward—John W. Hepburn, Rep., M. B. Madden, Rep.

Fifth Ward—Patrick J. Wall, Dem., David Deist, Dem.

Sixth Ward—Thomas Reed, Dem., Charles Martin, Dem.

Seventh Ward — Wm. J. O'Neill, Dem., John A. Cooke, Rep.

Eighth Ward — Martin Morrison, Dem., Frank Slepicka, Dem.

Ninth Ward—Jos. E. Bidwell, Rep. Fred Rohde, Dem.

Tenth Ward—John F.Dorman, Dem., Fred C. Engel, Rep.

Eleventh Ward—Wm. D. Kent, Rep., Alex H. Watson, Rep.

Twelfth Ward—Conrad Kahler, Rep., James L. Campbell, Rep.

Thirteenth Ward—Martin Knowles, Dem., Edward W. Stanwood, Rep.

Fourteenth Ward — James Keats, Rep., L. Kamerling, Rep.

Fifteenth Ward — Michael Ryan, Dem., Joseph Lammers, Rep.

Sixteenth Ward—Stanley H. Kunz, Dem., John Scherman, Rep.

Seventeenth Ward—Stephen M. Gosselin, Dem., M. F. O'Connor, Dem.

Eighteenth Ward—William F. Mahoney, Dem., John J. Brennan, Dem.

Nineteenth Ward — John Powers, Dem., Thos. Gallagher, Dem.

Twentieth Ward — Otto Hage, Rep., Chas. E. Ehlert, Rep.

Twenty-first Ward—John McGillen, Dem., Anton J. Brachtendorf, Dem.

Twenty-second Ward—E.Muelhoefer, Rep., Henry C.Schendorf, Rep.

Twenty-third Ward—John A. Larson, Rep., Wm. J. Kelly, Dem.

Twenty-fourth Ward—Zara C. Peck, Rep., Thomas H. Currier, Rep.

Twenty-fifth Ward—Albert H. Kleinecke, Rep.,William P. Chapman, Rep.

Twenty-sixth Ward — William Finkler, Rep., William E. Schlake, Dem.

24

Twenty-seventh Ward—M. J. Conway, Rep., Hubert W. Butler, Rep.

Twenty-eighth Ward—Thomas Sayle, Rep., John Bigane, Dem.

Twenty-ninth Ward—Robert Mulcahy, Dem., Thomas Carey, Dem.

Thirtieth Ward—Walter Merchant, Rep., John W Utesch, Rep.

Thirty-first Ward—Edward J. Noble, Rep., James L. Francis, Rep.

Thirty-second Ward—Wm. R. Kerr, Rep., James R. Mann, Rep.

Thirty-third Ward—Cyrus H. Howell, Rep., George W. Shepherd, Rep.

Thirty-fourth Ward—John O'Neill, Rep., Oliver L. Chadwick, Rep.

MAYOR'S DEPARTMENT.

2d floor, City Hall.

r Mayor—John P. Hopkins; Secretary, Felix Senff.

BOARD OF ELECTION COMMISSIONERS, 3D FLOOR, CITY HALL.

Chairman P. H. Keenan, Henry Schomer and John J. Badenoch, W. A. Taylor, chief clerk.

BUILDING DEPARTMENT.

1st floor, City Hall.

Commissioner of Buildings—James McAndrews; Chief Clerk — William Edgar.

CITY CLERK'S DEPARTMENT.

1st floor, City Hall.

City Clerk—Charles D. Gastfield; Deputy—John G. Neumeister; Chief Clerk—Wyatt McGaffey

CITY COLLECTOR'S DEPARTMENT.

1st floor, City Hall.

Collector—F. X. Brandecker.

CITY TREASURER'S DEPARTMENT.

1st floor, City Hall.

Treasurer—M. J. Bransfield.

COMPTROLLER'S DEPARTMENT.

1st floor, City Hall.

Comptroller—W.K. Ackerman; Chief Clerk—Francis M. Barrett.

DEPARTMENT OF PUBLIC WORKS.

2d floor, City Hall.

Commissioner—Hiram J. Jones; Dep. Commissioner — John A. Moody; Sec.—J.W.Touhy; CityEngineer—Samuel G. Artingstall; 3d floor; Superintendent of Sewerage — A. W. Cooke, Superintendent of Streets—John McCarthy; Assistant Superintendent of Streets—Patrick .McCarthy; Chief Engineer of Streets—J. H. Flagg; Assistant

Engineers—R. P. Brown, George F. Samuels, J. B. Hittel, L. A. Meyers, D. W. Maher, George K. Wheelock, H. A. Stevens, A. M. Hirsch, P. L. Benton; Superintendent of Map Dept.—Wm. Reisennegger; Superintendent of Water Dept.—W. E. Crossette; Assessor of Water Rates—Frank Dvorak ; Special Assessments—J. Samuel Sheahan.

HEALTH DEPARTMENT.

Basement, City Hall.

Commissioner—Arthur R. Reynolds, M,D.; Asst. Commissioner and Secretary—J F. McCarty; Clerk — E. L. Haynes; Registrar of Vital Statistics — W. A. Kimmitt; Clerk to Registrar—J. J. Dillon.

LAW DEPARTMENT.

3d floor, City Hall.

Corporation Counsel—Harry Rubens City Attorney—George A. Trude; Prosecuting Attorney—W. C. Asay.

PARK COMMISSIONERS.

Lincoln Park — President, Andrew Crawford; v. pres., John S. Cooper; sec., Geo. W. Weber; auditor, Bernard F. Weber; F. H. Winston, Martin Becker. Office, Lincoln Park.

West Chicago Park—President, Carl Moll; Treasurer, E. S. Dreyer; Secretary, Harry Wilkinson; Commissioners, Walter S. Bogle, Andrew J. Graham, Carl Moll, John Milton Oliver, Edward G. Uihlein, Charles J. Vopicka, Harvey T. Weeks. Office, Union Park.

South Park—Pres., Joseph Donnersberger; Auditor, William Best; Treas., John R. Walsh; Jefferson Hodgkins, John B. Sherman, J. W. Ellsworth.

POST-OFFICE.

Government Building, Clark, cor, Adams.

Postmaster—Washington Hesing.

Assistant Postmaster—John M. Hubbard.

Supply Clerk—J. W. Ward. Record Clerk—John Matter.

Superintendent Mails—John A. Montgomery.

Private Secretary—Daniel P. Cahill Cashier—Henry R. Green jr.

Bookkeeper—Thomas R. Melody.

Supt. of City Delivery—M. J. McGrath.

Supt. of Money Order Division — Joseph B. Schlossman.

Supt. of Registry Division — Perry H. Smith.

OFFICE HOURS.

Postmaster's office from 9 a. m. to 4 p. m.

Superintendent of Mails, from 9 a. m. to 5 p. m.

Cashier and Accountant, from 9 a. m. to 4.30 p. m.

Money Order Division, 9 a.m. to 5 p.m.

Registered Letter Division, 8 a. m. to 6 p. m.

Wholesale Stamp Division, 9 a. m. to 4.30 p. m.

Retail Stamp Division,7a.m. to 10p.m.

Carrier's Division for Delivery of Mail, 7:15 a. m. to 6 p. m.—Sundays, 11:30 a. m. to 12:30 p. m.

General Delivery, 7:30 a. m. to 10 p. m. —Sundays, 11:30 a. m. to 12.30 p. m.

CARRIER STATIONS.

Post Office—Clark and Adams
A—355 N. Clark. To remove to 575 and 577 N. Clark.
B—1353 Diversey av.
C—N.W.cor. Washington and Halsted. To remove to 416 and 418 W. Madison.
D—981 W. Madison.
E—2021 W. Madison.
F—517 Milwaukee av.
G—1551 Milwaukee av.
H—543 Blue Island av.
J—3217 State
K—4193 Halsted.
L—2224 Cottage Grove av.
M—3729 Cottage Grove av.
N—324, 55th.
O—528, 63d.
P—630, 79th. To remove to 606, 79th.
R—1143, 75th.
S—234-236, 91st.
T—2370, 115th
V—1058 Millard av.
W—3155 Archer av.
X—1250 E. Ravenswood Park
Y—4775 N. Clark.

SUB-STATIONS,

1—405 Larrabee
2—1072 Lincoln av.
3—117 Wells.
4—1249 N. Clark.
5—511 Lincoln av.
6—1061-1063 Milwaukee av.
7—530 W. Indiana.
8—2601 S. Halsted.
9—409 S. Western av.
10—3815 Archer av.
11—1324 Ogden av.
12—675 W. Lake.
13—525 W. Vanburen.
14—572 W. Madison.
15—1355 Wabash av.
16—5001 State.
17—143, 35th

18—3801 State.
19—48, 43d.
20—245, 57th.
21—2904 Archer av.
22—360 Ogden av.
23—108. 53d.
24—2127 Archer av.
25—1273 W. Vanburen
26—5100 Ashland av.
27—601 Garfield boul.
28—260 S. Halsted.
29—To be established at 200 W. Randolph.
30—63d and Woodlawn av.
31—Masonic Temple.
32—S.W. cor. Evanston & Bryn Mawr avs., Edgewater.
33—Lincoln av. and North 59th, Bowmanville.
34—Discontinued October 1, 1894
35—1168 Douglas, Irving Park.
36—Kedzie and Belmont avs., Avondale.
37—255 Hoffman av., Maplewood.
38—999 Kimball av., Simons.
39—1085 Keeney av., Hermosa.
40—87 N. West 48th, Moreland
41—6764 S, Chicago av , Park Manor.
42—7102 Cottage Grove av., Brookline Park.
43—7500 Ford av., Windsor Park.
44—7900 Commercial av., Cheltenham.
45—8683 Vincennes av,. South Englewood.
46—9332 Cottage Grove av., Burnside.
47—95th and Wood, Rock Isl. Depot, Longwood.
48—N.E. cor. 103d and Vincennes av., Washington Hts.
49—614, 102d, Fernwood
50—11154 Michigan av., Roseland.
51—11600 Dearborn, Gano.
52—10554 Torrence av., Cummings.
53—10301 Avenue K, Colehour.
54—26 Robinson av., Linden Park.

SUB STATIONS—BRANCH POST OFFICES.

Pullman—25 Arcade bldg.
Forest Glen—Cor. Elston and Forest Glen avs.
Jefferson—N.E. cor. Milwaukee av. and Short.
Mayfair—Railroad av., near St. James.
Dunning—Railroad Station, C.M. & St.P.R.R.
Montclare—Railroad Station, C.M. & St.P.RR.
Elsdon—S.E, cor. 51st and Trumbull av.
Chicago Lawn—63d near St. Louis av.
South Lynne—S.E.cor.64th and Cooper
Clarkdale—Central Park av.; near 83d Place.
Forest Hill—7900 S. Robey.

28

Riverdale—13565 Indiana av.
Hegewisch—13500 Hegewisch av.
West Pullman—752, 120th.
Norwood Park—Chicago and Central
avs.

FOREIGN MAILS.

Mails for Great Britain and Ireland,
Sundays, Mondays and Thursdays, and
Tuesdays during summer via New
York, close at 4 p. m.

For Denmark, Norway and Sweden,
Sundays, Mondays and Thursdays, via
New York, close at 4 p. m.

For Germany via New York, Mondays
and Thursdays.

For China, Japan, New Zealand, Australia, Sandwich Islands, Fiji Islands,
Samoa and specially addressed addressed matter for Siam, mails close daily at
2 a. m. sent to San Francisco for dispatch in direct bags from that office.

Note—Mails for countries not named
above close daily at 4 p.m. and are sent
to New York for dispatch in the closed
bags from that office.

For Canada—Provinces Ontario and
Quebec, close at 9.30 a.m. and 8.30 p. m.
daily except Sunday, and Sunday 5 p.m.,
Hamilton, Toronto, Montreal, London,
special dispatch closes daily at 2:30
p. m.

For Nova Scotia, New Brunswick,
Prince Edward's Island and Newfoundland, close daily at 7:45 and 10 a.m. and
3:30 and 8.15 p. m. and are dispatched
(except for Newfoundland) at 2.30 p.
m. daily.

For British Columbia and Manitoba,
dispatched via St. Paul, closing daily at
2 a.m.

Foreign postage tables will be found
in the public lobbies of the main and
branch offices.

For Mexico close daily at 8.15 a. m.,
and 8 p.m.

UNIVERSAL POSTAL UNION.

The rates of postage to the countries
and colonies composing the Universal
Postal Union (except Canada and
Mexico) are as follows:

Letters, per 15 grams (½ ounce,) 5
cents; postal cards each, 2 cents; newspapers and other printed matter, per 2
ounces, 1 cent; commercial papers,
packets not in excess of 10 ounces, 5
cents, packets in excess of 10 ounces,
for each 2 ounces or fraction thereof, 1
cent; samples of merchandise, packets
not in excess of 4 ounces 2 cents, packets in excess of 4 ounces, for each 2
ounces or fraction thereof, 1 cent;
registration fee on letters or other articles, 10 cents.

Ordinary letters for countries of the
Postal Union (except Canada and
Mexico) will be forwarded, whether
any postage is prepaid on them or not.
All other mailable matter must be prepaid, at least partially.

Argentine Republic, Australia, Austria-Hungary, Babamas, Barbadoes,
W. I., Belgium, Bermudas, Bolivia,
Brazil, British Colonies on West coast
of Africa and in West Indies, British
Guiana, British Honduras, British India, Bulgaria, Canada, Ceylon, Chili,
Colombia U. S. of, Congo, Costa Rica,
Cyprus, Cuba, Danish Colonies of St.
Thomas, St. Croix and St. John; Denmark, Dominica, Ecuador, Egypt,
Falkland Islands, Fiji Islands, France,
French Colonies, in Asia, Africa,
America and Oceanica; Germany, German Protectorates, Great Britain and
Ireland, Greece, Greenland, Guatemala, Hawaii, Sandwich Islands; Hayti,
Honduras, Hong Kong, Italy, Jamaica,
Japan, Labuan, Liberia, Luxemburg,
Malta, Mauritius, Mexico, Montenegro,
Netherlands, Netherland Colonies in
Asia, Oceanica and America, Newfoundland, New South Wales, New
Zealand, Nicaragua, Norway, Paraguay, Persia, Peru, Porto Rico, Portugal, Portuguese Colonies in Asia and
Africa, Queensland, Roumania, Russia,
Salvador, Servia, Siam, South Australia, Spain, Spanish Colonies in
Africa, Oceanica and Asia; Singapore,
Penang and Malacca; St. Vincent, W.
I., Sweden, Switzerland, Tasmania,
Trinidad, W. I., Regency of Tunis,
Uruguay, Venezuela, West Australia.

RATES OF POSTAGE.

The letter rate of postage is two
cents for each ounce or fraction thereof
throughout the United States and Dominion of Canada and Mexico. The
postage on letters dropped in the office
for delivery in the city is two cents per
ounce.

All letters must be fully prepaid by
stamps.

The following Classes of Letters are
not Advertised: Drop Letters. Box
Letters. Letters directed and sent to
hotels, and thence returned to the post
office as unclaimed. Letters returned
from the dead letter office to writers,
and card request letters. Circulars,
free packets, containing printed documents, speeches and other printed matter. N.B.—A request for the return of
a letter to the writer if unclaimed within
thirty days or less, written or printed
with the writer's name, post-office and
State, across the left hand side of the
envelope, on the face side, will be com-

plied with. Such letters will be returned to the writer free of postage.

MAIL MATTER OF THE SECOND CLASS.

This class embraces newspapers and other periodical publications, issued not less than four times a year, from a known office of publication, and bearing a date of issue, and which have no cloth, leather, or other substantial binding. Such publications must have a legitimate list of subscribers and must not be designed primarily for advertising purposes or for free circulation. The rate of postage on second-class matter when sent from the office of publication (including sample copies), or when sent from a news agent to actual subscribers, or to other news agents, is one cent per pound or fraction thereof; but if sent by any other than the publisher or a news agent is one cent for each four ounces or fraction thereof.

MAIL MATTER OF THE THIRD CLASS.

This class embraces transient newspapers and periodicals, books (printed), photographs, circulars, proof sheets.and corrected proof sheets with manuscript copy accompanying the same, and all matter of the same general character, as above enumerated. The rate of postage is one cent for each two ounces or fractional part thereof, except on transient newspapers and periodicals of the second-class, which will be one cent for each four ounces or fraction thereof.

MAIL MATTER OF THE FOURTH CLASS.

This class embraces labels, patterns, playing cards, visiting cards, address tags, paper sacks, wrapping paper and blotting pads, with or without printed advertisements thereon, bill heads, letter heads, envelopes with printed addresses thereon, ornamented paper, and all other matter of the same general character. This class also includes merchandise, and samples of merchandise, models, samples of ores, metals, minerals, seeds, etc., and any other matter not included in the first, second, or third classes, and which is not in its form of nature liable to damage the contents of the mail bag, or harm the person. Postage rate thereon, one cent for each ounce or fractional part thereof.

U. S. POSTAL MONEY ORDER SYSTEM.
FEES FOR MONEY ORDERS.

On orders not exceeding $5 . . 5 cts.
Over $5, and not exceeding $10. . 8 cts.
Over $10 and not exceeding $15, 10 cts.
Over . 15 " " .30, 15 cts.

Over $30 and not exceeding $40, 20 cts.
Over 40 " " 50, 25 cts.
Over 50 " " 60, 30 cts.
Over 60 " " 70, 35 cts.
Over 70 " " 80, 40 cts.
Over. 80 " " 100, 45 cts.

No fraction of cents to be introduced in the order.

No single orders issued for more than $100.

Parties desiring to remit larger sums must obtain additional money orders.

No applicant, however, can obtain in one day more than three orders payable at the same office and to the same payee.

INTERNATIONAL MONEY ORDER SYSTEM.

Orders can be obtained upon any money order office in Great Britain and Ireland, Germany, Austria, Belgium, Holland, Denmark, Sweden, Norway, Switzerland, Italy, Canada, France, Algeria, Japan, Portugal, The Hawaiian Kingdom, Jamaica, New Zealand, New South Wales, Hungary, Egypt and Hong Kong, India and Tasmania, Queensland, Cape Colony, The Windward Islands and The Leeward Islands, for any sum not exceeding $50 in United States currency.

No single order issued for more than $50.

Parties desiring to remit larger sums must obtain additional money orders. There is no limit to the number of orders in the International Money Order System.

FEES FOR ALL INTERNATIONAL MONEY ORDERS.

On orders not exceeding $10 . . $ .10
Over $10 and not exceeding $20 . .20
" 20 " " 30 . .30
" 30 " " 40 . .40
" 40 " " 50 . .50

POSTAL NOTES.

Postal Notes for sums not exceeding $4.00 will be issued on payment of a fee of three cents each. These notes are made payable to bearer at any money order office in the United States which the purchaser may designate.

REGISTRY DEPARTMENT.

Letters can be registered to all parts of the United States upon payment of a fee of eight cents, in addition to the regular postage.

RAILWAY POST-OFFICES.

Railway post-offices are established on all lines from Chicago. These offices

run upon nearly all trains, and letters may be mailed at the cars up to the moment prior to the departure of the trains. Stamps of the denominations of two cents may be had at the cars.

ACADEMIES AND SEMINARIES.

ARMOUR INSTITUTE — Armour av. sw. cor. 33d.

BAPTIST UNION THEOLOGICAL SEMINARY—Morgan Park.

BIBLE INSTITUTE FOR HOME AND FOREIGN MISSIONS OF THE CHICAGO EVANGELIZATION SOCIETY—80 Institute pl. and 228 to 240 Lasalle av.

CHICAGO KINDERGARTEN COLLEGE—10 Vanburen. Director, Mrs. J. N. Crouse; Prin. Miss Elizabeth Harrison.

CHICAGO MANUAL TRAINING SCHOOL—Michigan av. nw. cor. 12th.

CHICAGO MUSICAL COLLEGE—3d floor Central Music Hall.

CHICAGO THEOLOGICAL SEMINARY—81 Ashland boul.

CHRISTIAN SCIENCE THEOLOGICAL SEMINARY—72 Auditorium

DE LA SALLE INSTITUTE—Wabash av. ne. cor. 35th

GARRETT BIBLICAL INSTITUTE—Evanston.

GERMAN LUTHERAN THEOLOGICAL SEMINARY—437 N. Ashland av.

ILLINOIS INDUSTRIAL SCHOOL FOR GIRLS—South Evanston.

McCORMICK THEOLOGICAL SEMINARY OF THE PRESBYTERIAN CHURCH—1060 N. Halsted.

NORTHWESTERN UNIVERSITY —Evanston.

NORTHWESTERN UNIVERSITY LAW SCHOOL—7th floor, Masonic Temple.

ST. IGNATIUS COLLEGE—413 W. 12th.

ST. PROCOPIUS COLLEGE—704 Allport.

ST. VIATEUR'S COLLEGE—Bourbonnais Grove.

THEOLOGICAL SEMINARY OF THE EVANGELICAL LUTHERAN CHURCH—1301-1311 Sheffield av. n. of Addison, Lake View.

UNIVERSITY OF CHICAGO — Located bet. 57th and 59th and Ellis and Lexington avs. W. R. Harper, Pres. of University; Martin A. Ryerson, Pres. of Board; C. L Hutchinson, Treas.; T. W. Goodspeed, Sec.; Harry P. Judson, Dean of Faculty; F. F. Abbott, University Examiner; C. R. Henderson, Chaplain; H.B.Grose, Recorder and Registrar; Geo. N. Carmen, Dean of Morgan Park Academy; Nath'l Butler jr., Acting Director Univ. Extension.

WESTERN THEOLOGICAL SEMINARY OF THE PROTESTANT EPISCOPAL CHURCH—1113 Washlugton boul.

WOMEN'S COLLEGE OF LITERATURE AND ART—Evanston

ASYLUMS.

CHICAGO HOME FOR INCURABLES (THE)—Ellis av. ne. cor. 56th.

CHICAGO INDUSTRIAL SCHOOL FOR GIRLS—49th and Indiana av.

CHICAGO NURSERY AND HALF ORPHAN ASYLUM—855 N. Halsted and 175 Burling.

CHICAGO ORPHAN ASYLUM — 2228 Michigan av.

CHURCH HOME FOR AGED PERSONS—4327 Ellis av.

CHURCH HOME FOR ORPHANS —4331 Ellis av.

COOK COUNTY INSANE ASYLUM—Located at Dunning, Ill.

COOK COUNTY POOR HOUSE—Dunning P. O.

DANISH LUTHERAN ORPHANS' HOME—Maplewood

ENGLEWOOD NURSERY OF CHILDREN'S HOME SOCIETY—6516 Perry av.

EPWORTH CHILDREN'S HOME —2297 Commercial (L.V.)

ERRING WOMAN'S REFUGE—5024 Indiana av.

FOUNDLINGS HOME—114 S.Wood nr. W. Madison.

GERMAN OLD PEOPLE'S HOME —Harlem. (Altenheim P.O.) Cook Co.

GERMAN ORPHAN ASYLUM—Rose Hill.

GUARDIAN ANGEL GERMAN (R.C.) ORPHAN ASYLUM—Located at Rose Hill (Havelock P.O.) Cook Co.

Rosehill Cemetery

SITUATED on exceptionally high rolling ground 7 miles from Chicago, on Milwaukee Division Chicago and Northwestern Railway. Good carriage drives from the city to the ground.

GEO. H. SCOTT, Acting Supt.   EUGENE C. LONG, Sec'y & Treas.
Post-Office Address, HAVELOCK, ILL.   WM. H. TURNER, Prest.

City Office, National Life Building, Rooms 90 and 92

157 to 163 La Salle Street

TELEPHONE DIRECTIONS—If City is wanted, ask for Main-615
If Cemetery is wanted ask for Lake View-101
When it answers ask for Rosehill Cemetery.

HOLY FAMILY ORPHAN ASY-LUM—136 W. Division.

HOME FOR AGED AND DIS-ABLED RAILWAY MEN – 45 N. Washtenaw av.

HOME FOR THE AGED—W. Harrison cor. Throop.

HOME FOR THE AGED—Sheffield av. sw. cor. Fullerton av.

HOME FOR CRIPPLED CHIL-DREN—Park av. cor. Paulina

HOME FOR MISSIONARIES' CHILDREN—Morgan Park.

HOME FOR UNEMPLOYED GIRLS—Market and Elm.

HOME FOR THE FRIENDLESS—1926 Wabash av.

HOUSE OF MERCY (for young women)—Adjoining Mercy Hospital, Calumet av. cor. Twenty-sixth.

HOUSE OF THE GOOD SHEP-HERD—N. Market cor. Hill.

ILLINOIS INDUSTRIAL SCHOOL FOR GIRLS—South Evanston.

ILLINOIS MASONIC ORPHAN'S HOME—447 Carroll av. cor. Sheldon.

ILLINOIS SCHOOL OF AGRI-CULTURE AND MANUAL TRAIN-ING SCHOOL FOR BOYS—Glenwood Park.

ILLINOIS STATE HOME FOR FEMALE JUVENILE OFFEND-ERS—3111 Indiana av.

INDUSTRIAL SCHOOL FOR GIRLS—49th cor. Indiana av.

INDUSTRIAL SCHOOL FOR GIRLS (POLISH)—130 W. Division

JEWISH OLD PEOPLE'S HOME—62d and Drexel av.

MARTHA WASHINGTON HOME—Graceland av. cor. Western av., Lake View.

NEWS-BOYS' & BOOT-BLACKS' HOME—1418 Wabash av.

OLD PEOPLE'S HOME—Indiana av. nw. cor. Thirty-ninth.

SCHOOL FOR THE DEAF AND DUMB—433 W. 12th.

SERVITE SISTERS' INDUSTRIAL HOME FOR GIRLS—1396 W. Vanburen.

SOLDIERS' HOME—South Evanston.

ST. JOSEPH PROVIDENT OR-PHAN ASYLUM—Crawford av. bet. W. Diversey av. and W. Belmont av.

ST. JOSEPH'S HOME FOR THE FRIENDLESS—409 S. May.

ST. JOSEPH'S ORPHAN ASYLUM—Thirty-fifth cor. Lake av.

ST MARY'S MISSION HOUSE—215 Washington boul.

ST. MARY'S TRAINING SCHOOL FOR BOYS—Feehanville, Cook Co., Ill.

ST. VINCENT'S INFANT ASYLUM AND MATERNITY HOSPITAL—191 Lasalle av.

UHLICH EVANGELICAL LU-THERAN ORPHAN ASYLUM—221 Burling nw. cor. Centre.

WASHINGTONIAN HOME—566 to 572 W. Madison.

WORKING BOYS' HOME AND MISSION OF OUR LADY OF MERCY—363 W. Jackson.

WORKING WOMEN'S HOME—21 S. Peoria.

CEMETERIES.

CALVARY—Ten miles n. of city. Office at Cemetery and 19 Reaper blk.

CONCORDIA—Five miles west of city limits on Madison. Office 2, 173 Randolph.

FOREST HOME CEMETERY—Office 92 Washington.

GERMAN LUTHERAN OF ST. PAUL AND EMANUAL CHURCHES—N. Clark cor. Graceland av.

GRACELAND—N. Clark ne. cor. Graceland av. five miles n. of court house, on Chicago & Evanston R.R. Open every day (Sundays to lot owners only). Office, room 56 Montauk blk.

HEBREW BENEVOLENT SO-CIETY—S. of Graceland cemetery.

MOUNT GREENWOOD CEME-TERY—One-half mile w. of Morgan Park. Office, room 33, 95 Washington.

MOUNT HOPE CEMETERY—Washington Heights. Office, 305, 138 Jackson.

MOUNT OLIVE CEMETERY—Dunning Station, C. M. & St. P. Ry. 9 miles w. of city hall. Office, 409 Milwaukee av.

MOUNT OLIVET CEMETERY—One-half mile w. of Morgan Park, on Grand Trunk R. R. Office, 19 Reaper blk.

OAKWOODS—Sixty-seventh st. cor. Cottage Grove av., Hyde Park. Office, room 102, 187 Dearborn.

RIDGELAWN CEMETERY—Crawford av. cor. Peterson av. (J.)

ROSEHILL—Seven miles from city, on Mil. div. C. & N.W.Ry. City office, 90 and 92, 159 Lasalle.

ST.BONIFACE—(German Catholic) N. Clark cor. Lawrence av.

WALDHEIM—Ten miles from court house, on Galena div. C.H.& B. and C. & Wis.Cent.Ry. Office, 161 Randolph.

ZION CONGREGATION CEMETERY—Rosehill.

CHURCHES.

Baptist.

AUBURN PARK—622,79th. Pastor, Rev. W. A. Waldo

AUSTIN—Pastor, Rev. J. F. Bartlett

AUSTIN SWEDISH—Pastor, Rev. J. Samuelson.

BELDEN AVENUE—N. Halsted cor. Belden av. Pastor, Rev. J. S. Kennard.

BERWYN—Pastor, Rev. B. F. Martin

BETHANY—Hoyne av. nr. 35th. Pastor, Rev. E. A. Orr.

BETHEL (Colored)—72d cor. Champlain av. Pastor, Rev. J. W. Cabeen.

BETHESDA(Colored)—34th se. cor. Armour av. Pastor, Rev. W. A. Birch.

CALVARY—Wabash av. cor. 38th. Pastor, Rev. W. B. Riley.

CENTENNIAL—W. Jackson cor. Lincoln. Pastor, Rev. Alonzo K. Parker, D.D.

CENTRAL—316 Clark, Pastor, Rev. T. L. Smith.

CHELTENHAM—Coles av. and Cheltenham pl. Rev. J. T. Proctor.

COLEHOUR GERMAN—Pastor, Rev. A. Peterson.

COVENANT—Maple cor. Wright. Pastor, Rev. Gilbert Frederick.

ELSDON—52d cor. Bonney av. Pastor, Rev. J. M. Griswell.

ENGLEWOOD FIRST—Englewood av. cor. Stewart av. Pastor, Rev. Myron W. Haynes.

ENGLEWOOD SWEDISH—Princeton av. nr. 57th. Pastor, C. Rosen.

EVANGEL—Dearborn nr. 47th. Pastor, Rev. Charles Henry.

EVANSTON FIRST SWEDISH—Pastor, Rev. Charles Palm.

FERNWOOD—Murray st. Fernwood. Pastor, Rev. T. W. Heyland

FIRST DANISH—Tolman av. cor. Lemoyne. Pastor, Rev.C.Henningsen.

FIRST EVANSTON—Pastor, Rev. H. A. Delano.

FIRST—South Park av.cor. 31st. Pastor, Rev. P. S. Henson, D.D.

FIRST GERMAN—Superior cor. Paulina. Pastor, Rev. J. L. Meier.

FIRST SWEDISH—Elm cor. Milton av. Pastor, Rev. A. Hjelm.

FOURTH—Ashland boul. cor. Monroe. Pastor, Rev. Kittredge Wheeler.

FOURTH SWEDISH—111th and Curtis av. Pastor, Rev. E. J. Nordlander.

GRACE—Sacramento av. and Lake. Pastor, Rev. W. Carey MacNaul.

HIGHLAND PARK—Pastor, Rev. L. A. Gould.

HUMBOLDT PARK—Humboldt cor. Cortland. Pastor, Rev. J. F. McNamee.

HUMBOLDT PARK SWEDISH—Rockwell cor. Wabansia av. Pastor, Rev. M. Carlson.

HYDE PARK—Madison av. cor. 54th. Pastor, Rev. John R. Gow.

IMMANUEL—ws. Michigan av. nr. 23d. Pastor, Rev. O. P. Gifford.

IRVING PARK—Pastor, Rev. A. J. Stedman

LAGRANGE—Pastor, Rev. G. M. Daniels.

LAKE VIEW—Otto nr. Southport av, Pastor, Rev. Robert Carrol

LAKEVIEW SWEDISH—Noble nr. Clifton. Pastor, Rev. C. W. Anderson.

LASALLE AVENUE—Lasalle av. nr. Division. Pastor, Rev. H. O. Rowlands, D.D.

MAPLEWOOD—Fullerton av. cor. Greenwood av. Pastor, Rev. H. H. Hurley

MAYWOOD—Pastor, Rev. A. W Wishart.

MEMORIAL—Oakwood boul. nr. Drexel boul. Pastor, Rev. L. A. Crandall, D.D.

MESSIAH—Flournoy cor. Washtenaw av. Pastor, Rev. Howland Hanson.

MILLARD AVENUE—Millard av. se. cor. W. 24th. Lawndale. Pastor, Rev. Geo. McGinnis.

MORGAN PARK—Crescent av. Pastor, Rev. W. D. Fuller.

Knickerbocker Ice Company

SUCCESSORS TO E. A. SHEDD & CO.

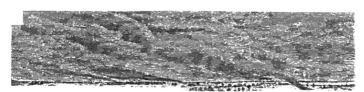

Showing the Ice Houses at **Wolf Lake, Ind.**, the Largest in the World.

OWNED AND OPERATED BY

THE KNICKERBOCKER ICE COMPANY,

PRINCIPAL OFFICE,

134 VAN BUREN ST., CHICAGO. Tel. Main-1789 and Main-1796

BRANCH OFFICES,

Corner 22d Street and Stewart Avenue, - -	Tel. South-403
" Sangamon and Lake Streets, - - - -	" Main-4001
" Ogden Avenue and West 14th Street, - -	" West-132
" 38th Street and Western Avenue—Brighton Park,	" Yards-505
" 40th Street and Stewart Avenue—Oakland, - Tel. Oakland-877
" 43d Street and Stewart Avenue—Town of Lake, " Yards-660
" 61st Street and Lexington Avenue, - - " Oakland-479
" 63d St. and Wentworth Ave.—Englewood Tel. 38, " Wentworth-526
" 75th Street and Dobson Avenue—Grand Crossing.
" 93d Street and Anthony Avenue—South Chicago.
" 115th Street and Stephenson Avenue—Pullman.

PRINCIPAL STORAGE,

CRYSTAL LAKE, ILLINOIS. OCONOMOWOC, WISCONSIN. WOLF LAKE, INDIANA.

NORMAL PARK—Stewart av. cor. 70th.

OAK PARK—Pastor, Rev. T. H. Rowley.

OAK PARK GERMAN—Pastor, Rev. Jacob Fellman

OGDEN AVENUE—633 Ogden av. Pastor, Rev. J. J. Ashby.

OLIVET (Colored)—Harmon ct. cor. Holden pl. Pastor, Rev. J. F. Thomas.

PILGRIM TEMPLE—824 N. Leavitt. Pastor, Rev. J. P. Thoms.

PROVIDENCE (Colored)—26 N. Irving pl. Pastor, Rev. A. W. Newsome.

PULLMAN—Pastor, Rev. Fred. Berry.

PULLMAN SWEDISH—Pastor, Rev. E. J. Nordlander.

RAVENSWOOD—Pastor, Rev. F. E. Weston.

ROGERS PARK—Pastor, Rev. C. Braithwaite.

SALEM SWEDISH—Ambrose cor. Lincoln. Pastor, Rev. C. W. Sundmark.

SCANDINAVIAN PILGRIM—N. Carpenter cor. Ohio. Pastor, Rev. E. L. Myrland.

SECOND—Morgan sw. cor. W. Monroe. Pastor, Rev. W. M. Lawrence, D.D.

SECOND EVANSTON (Colored)— Pastor, Rev. G. M. Davis.

SECOND GERMAN—Burling cor. Willow. Pastor, Rev. Christian Dippel.

SECOND SWEDISH—3018 and 3020 5th av. nr. 31st. Pastor, Rev. O. John Engstrand.

SOUTH CHICAGO—Houston av. and 90th. Pastor, Rev. A. C. Kelly.

SOUTH CHICAGO GERMAN— Pastor, Rev. Grasenick.

SOUTH CHICAGO SWEDISH— Fourth av. and 98th. Pastor, Rev. A. Xallgren.

TABERNACLE SWEDISH—Erie and Ninetieth. Pastor, Rev. David Myrhman

THIRD GERMAN—Johnson cor. Henry. Pastor, Rev. Carl Bruckmann.

TRINITY—Ohio nr. Robey.

WESTERN AVENUE—Warren av. nw. cor. S. Western av. Pastor, Rev. C. Perren, Ph. D.

WOODLAWN PARK —Lexington av. and 62d. Pastor, Rev. W. R. Wood

Baptist Missions.

BOHEMIAN MISSION—Throop s. 16th. Rev. John Kejr, missionary.

HOPE MISSION—Noble nw. cor. Ohio.

RAYMOND MISSION—Poplar av. nr. 30th.

Christian.

CHURCH OF CHRIST—W. Jackson cor. Oakley av. Pastor, Elder Carnduff.

CENTRAL—Indiana av. cor. 37th. Pastor, Rev. W. F. Black.

CHRISTIAN (Colored)—2811 Dearborn. Pastor, ——.

ELSMERE—15 Ballou nr. North av.

ENGLEWOOD—Dickey s. of 64th. Pastor, Rev. N. S. Haynes.

GARFIELD PARK—W. Monroe cor. Francisco. Pastor, ——.

HYDE PARK—Masonic hall 57th e. Washington av. Pastor, Rev. H. L. Willett.

NORTH SIDE—Sheffield av. and Montana, nr. Lincoln av. Pastor, Rev. W. B. Taylor.

RAVENSWOOD—Leland av. and Lyman. Pastor, ——.

WEST SIDE—W. Jackson cor. S. Western av. Pastor, Rev. John W. Allen.

Congregational.

ARMOUR MISSION—33rd cor. Armour av. Pastor, Rev. C. T. Wyckoff.

ASHLAND AVENUE—S. Ashland av. cor. W. 20th. Pastor, Rev. William Cochran.

AUBURN PARK—77th and Wright. Pastor, Rev. H. T. Sell.

AUSTIN — Pastor, Rev. Thomas Westerdale.

AVONDALE (GERMAN)—205 Belmont av. Pastor, Rev. Wm. Boetcker.

BETHANY—Superior cor. Lincoln. Pastor, Rev. —. Beddoes.

BETHESDA—235 Division. Pastor, Rev. E. K. Fisher.

BETHLEHEM CHAPEL—709 to 713 Loomis. Pastor, Rev. E. A. Adams.

BLUE ISLAND—Pastor, Rev. J. R. Smith.

BOWMANVILLE — Bowmanville. W. Peterson, S. S. Supt.

BRIDGEPORT (SWEDISH)— Bloom cor. 35th. Aug. Hamrin, S. S. Supt.

Jewel Gas Stoves...

ARE UNEQUALED

106 STYLES,

75 Cents to $68.00

Endorsed by the leading
demonstrators of cooking.

INVESTIGATE the JEWEL.

SALESROOM:

Cor. Monroe and Michigan Ave.

GEORGE M. CLARK & COMPANY,

MAKERS, CHICAGO.

R. W. CROSS & CO.,

22 VAN BUREN ST.

....ATHENÆUM BUILDING....

Western Representative
...OF THE...
CELEBRATED

USED BY.....

Anton Seidel, Julia Rive-King

AND SEVENTY-TWO OTHER ARTISTS
DURING THE PAST SEASON.

- - - **22** Van Buren St., ATHENÆUM BLDG.

BRIGHTON—34th ct. nr. Lincoln. Pastor, Rev. W. J. Marsh.

CALIFORNIA AVENUE—California av. cor. W. Monroe. Pastor, Rev. D. F. Fox.

CENTRAL PARK—W. 40th pl. cor. Park av. Pastor, Rev. S. C. Haskins.

CORTLAND ST.—913 N. Robey. Pastor, Rev. O. C. Grauer.

COVENANT—W. Polk nw. cor. Claremont av. Pastor, Rev. J.W.Fifield.

CRAGIN—Armitage av. nr. Grand av. Pastor, Rev. C. H. Corwin.

DOREMUS—Butler nr. 31st. Pastor, Rev. J. H. Clark.

DOUGLAS PARK—903 Sawyer av. Pastor, Rev. F. T. Lee. ·

DUNCAN AVENUE—Duncan av. cor. 77th. Pastor, Rev. G. H. Grannis.

ELMHURST—Pastor, Rev. M. L. Williston.

EVANSTON—Pastor, Rev. J. F. Loba.

EWING STREET—241 and 243 Ewing. Pastor, Rev. B. S. Winchester.

FIRST—Washington boul. sw. cor. Ann. Pastor, Rev. E. P. Goodwin, D.D.

FIRST SCANDINAVIAN — Point. cor Chaney. Pastor, Rev. C. T. Dyrness.

FOREST AV. (Oak Park)—F. Milligan, S. S. Supt.

FORESTVILLE—Chaplain av. cor. 46th. Pastor, Rev. W. A. Lyman.

GLEN ELLYN—Pastor, Rev. J. S. Rood.

GLENCOE—Pastor, Rev. M. Smith G. Johnson.

GRACE —Powell av. cor. Cherry pl. Pastor, Rev. W. J. Warner.

GRACELAND—Jansen av. cor. Waveland av. Pastor, Rev. W. W. Newell.

GRAND AV.—Grand and Lawndale avs. Pastor, Rev. J. U. Stotts.

GREEN STREET—56th cor. Green. Pastor, Rev. J. P. Burling.

GROSS PARK—1865 N. Hoyne av. Pastor, Rev. W. H. Hopkins.

HERMOSA—Howard av. nr. Cortland. Pastor, Rev. C. H. Corwin. ·

HINSDALE— Rev. J. O. Morris, S. S. Supt.

HUMBOLDT PARK— W. Chicago av. cor Fairfield av. Pastor, Rev. A. Lenox.

JEFFERSON—Jefferson Park. Pastor, Rev. A. M. Thome.

JEFFERSON PARK (German)— Pastor, Rev. John Block.

JOHANNES GERMAN — Franklin nr. Eugenie. Pastor, Rev. G. A. Zimmerman.

LA GRANGE—Pastor, Rev. H. A. Bushnell.

LAKE VIEW — Seminary av. cor. Lill av. Pastor, Rev. P. Krohn.

LAKESIDE (Winnetka)—W. Merrilies, S. S. Supt.

LEAVITT STREET—S. Leavitt sw. cor. W. Adams. J. K. Allen, S. S. Supt.

LINCOLN PARK—Garfield av. cor. Mohawk. Pastor, Rev. David Beaton.

LOMBARD — Pastor, Rev. H. F. Goodwin.

MAPLEWOOD—Maplewood nr. Fullerton av. Pastor, Rev. E. B. Smith.

MAYFLOWER CHAPEL —Sacramento av. cor. Fillmore. Pastor, Rev. F. G. Wilcox.

MAYWOOD—Pastor, Rev. G. H. Kemp.

MILLARD AVENUE — S. Central Park av. se. cor. W. Twenty-third. Pastor Rev. J. C. Cromer.

MONT CLARE — Pearl cor. Vine. Pastor, Rev. E. S. Chandler.

MORGAN PARK—Pastor, Rev. J. M. Campbell.

MORTON PARK—Pastor, Rev. C. E. Watson.

NEW ENGLAND — Dearborn av. cor. Delaware pl. Pastor, Rev. James G. Johnson.

NORTH ENGLEWOOD — Lasalle cor. 59th. Pastor, Rev. Chas. Reynolds.

OAKLEY BRANCH—W. Indiana nr. Oakley av. Pastor, Rev. C. K. Westfall

OAK PARK—R. S. Thain, S.S.Supt.

PACIFIC — Cortland cor. Ballou. Paul V. Throop. S. S. Supt.

PARK MANOR—71st and Rhodes av. G. S. Osborn, S. S. Supt.

PILGRIM—Harvard cor. 64th. Pastor, Rev. A. L. Smalley.

PILGRIM GERMAN — Avers av. cor. Emory av. Pastor, Rev. H. W. Heinzelmann.

PLYMOUTH—Michigan av.nr. 26th. Pastor, Rev. Frank W. Gunsaulus,D.D.

PORTER MEMORIAL BRANCH —Paulina nr. Taylor. Pastor, Rev. G. L. Smith.

PULLMAN (Swedish) — T. Tronstadt, S. S. Supt.

RAVENSWOOD -- Commercial and Sulzer. Pastor, Rev. Charles H. Keays.

REDEEMER—School nr. Evanston av.

RIDGELAND—Pastor, Rev. W. A. Bartlett.

ROGERS PARK—

ROSEHILL—Rosehill. Pastor, ——.

ROSELAND (Swedish)—Indiana av. sw. cor. 113th. Pastor, Rev. C. E. Stadshang.

SARDIS WELSH — 143 S. Peoria. Pastor, Rev. R. T. Evans.

SECOND SCANDINAVIAN—Butler nr. 31st. Pastor, Rev. B. C Bjuge.

SEDGWICK BRANCH—Sedgwick nr. Blackhawk. Pastor, Rev. W. H. Day.

SOUTH — Drexel boul. nw. cor. 40th. Pastor, Rev. W. Scott.

SOUTH CHICAGO — Ontario nr. 91st. Pastor, Rev. G. H. Bird.

SOUTH GERMAN—Ullman cor. James av. Pastor, Rev. John Sattler.

ST. MATTHEW EVANGELICAL GERMAN—51st nr. Western av. Pastor, Rev. G. L. Albrecht.

SUMMERDALE — E. Ravenswood Park nr. Walnut. Pastor, Rev. E. B. Wylie.

SWEDISH MISSION (Moreland) Pastor, Rev. L. Akeson

TABERNACLE — W. Indiana se. cor. Morgan. Pastor, Rev. B. F. Boller.

TRINITY—Wright cor. 71st. Pastor, ——.

UNION PARK — Cor. S. Ashland av. and Washington boul. Pastor, Rev. Frederick A. Noble, D.D.

UNIVERSITY—56th and Madison av. Pastor, Rev. N. I. Rubinkam.

WARREN AVENUE — Warren av. sw. cor. Albany av. Pastor, Rev. J. A. Adams.

WASHINGTON PARK—1010, 51st nr. Indiana av. Pastor, Rev. S. Fisher.

WICKER PARK—615 Davis. Pastor, Rev. H. F. Josephson.

WILMETTE—Pastor, Rev. E. B. Dean.

WINNETKA—Pastor, Rev. Q. L. Dowd.

Cumberland Presbyterian.

CHURCH OF PROVIDENCE — Sheffield av. nr. Cornelia. Pastor, Rev. A. H. Stephens.

FIRST—Stewart boul. opp. 66th pl. Pastor, Rev. Hugh Spencer Williams.

SECOND—Oakley av. and 68th st. Pastor, W. C. Logan.

MEMORIAL CHURCH—64th nr. Madison av. Pastor, Rev. A. Allison.

Episcopal.

DIOCESE OF CHICAGO—Bishop, Rt. Rev. William E. McLaren, D.D., D.C.L. Office 510 Masonic Temple; res. 64 Astor. Dean, Rev. Clinton Locke, D.D.; Rev. Luther Pardee, Sec. and Treas., The Walton; F. F. Ainsworth, Treas. Board of Missions, 2302 Indiana av. City Hissionary, Rev. Jos. Rushton, 103 Adams.

ALL ANGELS (for the deaf)— State nr. 20th. Rev. A. W. Mann.

ALL SAINTS'—701 Leland av. Rev. C. R. D. Crittenton.

ANNUNCIATION — Auburn Park. Rev. George B. Pratt.

CATHEDRAL SS. PETER AND PAUL — cor. Washington boul. and Peoria. Bishop, Rt. Rev. William E. McLaren. D.D., LL.D. Priests, Revs. George D. Wright and G. S. Todd, 18 S. Peoria.

CALVARY—Western av. cor. Monroe. Rector, Rev. W. B. Hamilton.

CHRIST—64th cor. Woodlawn av. Rector, Rev. A. L. Williams.

CHRIST— (Winnetka) Rector, Rev. R. H. Neely.

CHURCH OF ATONEMENT— Edgewater. Priest, F. W. Keator.

CHURCH OF THE ASCENSION —Lasalle av. se. cor. Elm. Rector, Rev. Edward A. Larrabee.

CHURCH OF THE EPIPHANY— Ashland boul. cor. W. Adams. Rector, Rev. T. N. Morrison.

CHURCH OF THE GOOD SHEPHERD—1057 Bonney, av. Priest, Rev. J. Wynne Jones.

CHURCH OF THE HOLY COMMUNION — Maywood. Rector, Rev. C. C. Tate.

CHURCH OF THE MEDIATOR— Morgan Park. Rector, Rev. J. M. McGrath.

CHURCH OF THE HOLY NA-. TIVITY — 699 W. Indiana. Rector, Rev. G. B. Pratt.

CHURCH OF THE HOLY TRIN-
ITY—Stock Yards. Rector, Rev. H. C.
Kinney.

CHURCH OF OUR SAVIOR —
700 Fullerton av. Rector, Rev. W. J.
Petrie.

CHURCH OF THE REDEEMER
—56th cor. Washington av. Rev. F. B.
Dunham.

CHURCH OF THE TRANSFIGU-
RATION—43d nr. Cottage Grove av.
Rector, Rev. Walter Delafield, S. T. D.

EMMANUEL—LaGrange. Rector,
Rev. Morton Stone.

GRACE—Oak Park. Rector, Rev.
C. P. Anderson.

GRACE—1445 Wabash av. nr. 16th.
Rector, Rev. Clinton Locke; D.D.;
Asst. Rev. E. M. Stires.

GRACE—Hinsdale. Rector, Rev. H.
W. Perkins.

HOLY CROSS—State nr. 20th.

SEMINARY CHAPEL—1113 Washington boul. Rector, Rev. W. J. Gold,
S.T.D.

ST. ALBAN'S—4336 Prairie av.
Rector, Rev. Geo. W. Knapp.

ST. ALBAN'S—Norwood Park.

ST. ANDREW'S—Washington boul.
cort Robey. Rector, Rev. W. C. De-
wit.

ST. ANSGARIUS' — Sedgwick nr.
Chicago av. Rector, Rev. Herman
Lindskog.

ST. AUGUSTINE—(Wilmette).

ST. BARNABAS'—West 40th, Rector, Rev. L. Pardee

ST. BARTHOLOMEW'S—65th cor.
Stewart av. Rector, Rev. B.F.Matrau.

ST. CHRYSOSTOM—544 Dearborn
av, Rector, Rev. T. A. Snively.

ST. GEORGE'S—Grand Crossing.
Priest, Rev. T. Cory Thomas.

ST. JAMES'—Cor. Cass and Huron.
Rector, Rev. James S. Stone.

ST. JOHN'S — Irving Park. Rev.
E. M. Thompson.

ST. JOHN'S CHAPEL—26 and 28
Clybourn pl. Rev. Irving Spencer.

ST. LUKE'S—388 S. Western av.
Rector, Rev. C. E. Bowles.: Asst. Rev.
E. B. Streator.

ST. LUKE'S — Evanston. Rector,
Rev. D. F. Smith.

ST. MARGARET — Windsor Park.
Rev. T. Cory Thomas.

ST. MARK'S—Evanston. Rector,
Rev. A. W. Little.

ST. MARK'S—Cottage Grove av.
cor. 36th. Rector, Rev. W. W. Wilson.

ST. MARY'S—Morton Park. Rector, Rev. J. C. Sage.

ST. MATTHEW'S—Evanston. Rector, Rev. H. R. Neely.

ST. MATTHIAS—(Chicago Lawn)
Rev. H. G. Moore.

ST. MICHAEL AND ALL
ANGELS—(Berwyn) Rev. J. C. Sage.

ST. PAUL THE APOSTLE—Aus-
tin. Rev. L. Pardee.

ST. PAUL'S—4928 Lake av. Rector,
Rev. C. H. Bixby.

ST. PAUL'S CHURCH—Riverside.
Rector, Rev. George D. Adams.

ST. PAUL'S—Rogers' Park. Rector, Rev. J. O. Ferris.

ST. PETER'S — 1737 Belmont av.
Rector, Rev. S. C. Edsall.

ST. PHILIP THE EVANGELIST—
Brighton Park. Rector, Rev. Henry
G. Moore.

ST. STEPHEN'S—Johnson nr. W.
Taylor. Rev. C. N. Moller.

ST. THOMAS' - (colored) — Dearborn nr. 30th. Rector, Rev. James E.
Thompson.

TRINITY—Michigan av. cor. 26th.
Rector, Rev. John Rouse. Asst., Rev.
J. Hollister Lynch.

TRINITY—Highland Park. Rector,
Rev. P. C. Wolcott.

TRINITY—Wheaton. Rector, ——.

Missions and Chapels).

CHAPEL OF ST. LUKE'S HOS-
PITAL,1430 Indiana av. Chaplain,Rev.
Edward Warren.

SISTERS OF ST. MARY CHAPEL
—Washington boul. nr. Peoria.

Episcopal (Reformed).

(Synod of Chicago.)

Bishop, Rt. Rev. Chas. E. Cheney,D.D.

CHRIST—Michigan av. and 24th.
Rector, Rt. Rev. Charles E. Cheney,
D. D.

EMANUEL — Hanover cor. 28th.
Rector. Rev. Geo. W. Bowne.

ST. JOHN'S—37th cor. Langley av.
Rector, Rev. H. F. Milligan.

ST. LUKE'S HUMBOLDT PARK
—Humboldt Park. Minister in Charge,
Rev. Chas. J. Millar.

ST. MARK'S—Maplewood. Rector, Rev. C J. Millar.

ST. MATTHEW'S—Larrabee cor. Kemper pl. Minister in Charge, Rev. Frederick Shelley.

TRINITY—Yale av. cor. 70th. Rector, Rev. Fred J. Walton.

TRINITY—Oak Park, Rector, Rev. W. C. Sheppard.

TYNG MISSION—Archer av. cor. 21st. Supt., Robert J. Martin.

EPISCOPAL (REFORMED) MISSIONARY JURISDICTION OF THE NORTHWEST AND WEST—Bishop, Rt. Rev. Samuel Fallows, D. D.

ST. PAUL'S—W. Adams sw. cor. Winchester av. Rector, Rt. Rev. Samuel Fallows. D. D.

Evangelical Association.

Board of Bishops—Bishop J. J. Esher, 745 W. Jackson; Bishop Thomas Bowman. 232 Winchester av.; Bishop S. C. Breyfogel, Reading, Pa., Bishop William Horn, Cleveland, O.

CHICAGO DISTRICT—Presiding Elder, William Schmus, 658 Sheffield av.

CENTENNIAL—W. Harrison sw. cor. Hoyne av. Pastor, Rev. G. C. Knobel.

EBENEZER—Sangamon nr. 67th (Englewood). Pastor, Rev. F. C. Stierle.

EMANUEL—Sheffield av. ne. cor. Marianna. Pastors, Revs. J. C. Kiest. and J. A. Giesse.

FIRST—35th cor. Dearborn. Pastors, Revs. A. J. Voegelen and W. Klingbiel.

LANE PARK—Roscoe cor. Bosworth. Pastors, Revs. J. C. Kiest and J. A. Giesse.

SAINT JOHN'S—W. Huron cor. Noble. Pastor, Rev. J. Zipperer.

SALEM—W. 12th cor. Union. Pastors, Revs. A. J. Vogelin and W. Klingbeil.

SECOND—Wisconsin cor. Sedgwick. Pastor, Rev. H. Hoehn.

SOUTH CHICAGO—6th av. nr. 98th. Pastor, Rev. W. A. Schultz.

Evangelical Lutheran.

ENGLISH.

CHRIST—269 W. Erie. Pastor, Rev. H. F. G. Bartholomew.

CHRIST—Hoyne av. cor. Augusta. Pastor, Rev. H. J. Bartholomew.

CHURCH OF THE HOLY TRINITY—398 Lasalle av. Pastor, Rev Charles Koerner.

GRACE—Belden av. cor. Larrabee. Pastor, Rev. Lee M. Heilman.

ST. PAUL'S LUTHERAN—Fairfield av. cor. Hirsch. Pastor, Rev. R. F. Weidner.

WICKER PARK—N. Hoyne av. nw. cor. LeMoyne. Pastor, Rev. H. W. Roth, D. D.

GERMAN.

BETHANIA—Humboldt cor. Rockwell. Pastor, Rev. E. Pardieck.

BETHLEHEM—N. Paulina cor. McReynolds. Pastor, Rev. Augustus Reinke.

BETHLEHEM—103d cor. Av. G. Pastor, Rev. J. Feiertag.

CHRIST—cor. Humboldt and Byron av. Pastor, Rev. E. Werfelmann.

CHURCH OF THE HOLY CROSS—Ullman nw. cor. James av. Pastor, Rev. W. Uffenbeck.

CONCORDIA—N. California nr. Centre av. Pastor, Rev. P. Brauns.

EMMAUS—California av. cor. Walnut. Pastor, Rev. M, Fuelling.

GETHSEMANE—Dearborn and 49th. Pastor, Rev. J. G. Nuetzel.

IMMANUELS—527 Ashland boul. Pastors, Rev. L. Holter and J. Seidel.

IMMANUELS—9031 Houston av. Patsor, Rev. Carl Eisfeldt.

ST. ANDREAS—37th cor. Honore. Pastor, Rev. W. Kohn.

ST. JACOBI—Fremont sw. cor. Garfield av. Pastor, Rev. Wm. Bartling.

ST. JOHANNES—Montrose boul. and Sampson av., Jefferson. Pastor, Rev. P. Lucke.

ST. JOHANNES—W. Superior cor. Bickerdyke. Pastor, Rev. H. Succop.

ST. LUCAS—Belmont av., Lake View. Pastor, Rev. J. G. A. Mueller.

ST. MARCUS—California av. cor. Moore. Pastor, Rev. Th. Kohn.

ST. MARTINI—51st cor. Ashland av. Pastor, Rev. F. C. Leib.

ST. MATTHEW'S—Hoyne av. bet 20th and 21st. Pastor, Rev. H. Engelbrecht.

ST. PAUL'S—Superior cor. N. Franklin. Pastor, Rev. Henry Wunder. Asst. Rev. H. Brauns.

ST. PAUL'S—Madison av. nr. 76th. Pastor, Rev. August Frederking.

ST. PETER'S—Dearborn s. of 39th. Pastor, Rev. F. P. Merbitz.

ST. STEPHANUS — Englewood av. and Winter. Pastor, Rev. A. J. Buenger.

TRINITY (U. A. C.)—S. Canal cor. 25th pl. Pastor, Rev. Louis Lochner.

TRINITY—Hegewisch. Pastor, Rev. W. Brauer.

WASHINGTON HEIGHTS—Winston nr. 99th. Pastor, Rev. R. P. Budach.

ZION—W. 19th ne. cor. Johnson. Pastors, Revs. Anton Wagner and A. Lange.

ZION'S—Winston av. and 99th. Pastor, Rev. Paul Bubach.

ZION'S—113th and Curtis av. Pastor, Rev. G. Sievers.

NORWEGIAN.

BETHANIA—W. Indiana se. cor. Carpenter. Pastor, Rev. John Z. Torgersen.

BETHLEHEM—W. Huron cor. N. Centre av. Pastor, Rev. J. N. Kildahl.

EMANUEL—Perry av. cor. Cherry pl. Pastor, Rev. I. I. Breidablick.

NORWEGIAN EVANG. LUTHERAN CHURCH OF CHICAGO (The)—Baxter cor. Roscoe. Pastor, Rev. O. E. Brandt.

OUR SAVIOR'S—May cor. W.Erie. Pastor, Rev. Christian K. Preus.

ST. PAUL'S—W. North av. bet. Leavitt and Shober. Pastor, Rev. I. B. Torrson.

TRINITY—W. Indiana av. sw. cor. Peoria. Pastor, Rev. C. O. Broehaugh.

SWEDISH.

BETHANIA—Houston av. nr. 91st. Pastor, Rev. G. Lundhal.

BETHEL — Sangamon nr. 66th. Pastor, Rev. A. S. Becklund.

BETHLEHEM—58th cor. Atlantic. Pastor, Rev. G. E. Youngdahl.

ELIM—113th cor. Calumet av. Pastor, Rev. H. O. Lindeblad.

GETHSEMANE—May cor. W. Huron. Pastor, Rev. Matthew C. Ranseen.

IMMANUEL—Sedgwick cor. Hobbie. Pastor, Rev. C. A. Evald; Asst. Rev. J. Mellander.

SALEM—Portland av. bet. 28th and 29th. Pastor, Rev. L. G. Abrahamson.

SARON—Humboldt cor. Shakespeare av. Pastor, Rev. Eric J. A. Rosenquist.

TRINITY—Seminary av. cor. Noble av. Pastor, Rev. S. A. Sandahl.

ZION—Rice pl. nr. 22d. Pastor. Rev. C. Granath.

Evangelical United.

BETHLEHEM'S—Diversey av. cor. Lewis. Pastor, Rev. J. G. Kircher.

CHURCH OF PEACE—52d cor. Justine. Pastor, Rev. K. J. Freitag.

IMMANUELS—46th nr. Dearborn. Pastor, Rev. W. Hattendorf.

JOHANNES — North Park av. nr. Eugenie. Pastor, Rev. G. A. Zimmermann.

PETRI — Chicago av. cor. Noble. Pastor G. Lambrecht.

SALEMS—25th nr. Wentworth av. Pastor. Rev. T. Krafft.

ST. CHRISTUS—Lexington av. cor. Francisco. Pastor, Rev. C. W. Locher.

ST. JOHANNIS—Moffatt nr. Western av. Pastor, Rev. H. Stamer.

ST. LUKAS—62d cor.Green. Pastor, Rev. A. Schmidt.

ST. MARKUS — 35th cor. Dashiel. Pastor, Rev. L. Kohlmann.

ST. NICOLAS—Avondale. Pastor, Rev. K. C. Struckmeier.

ST. PAUL'S—Lasalle av. cor. Ohio. Pastor, Rev. R. A. John.

ST. PETRI—103d cor. Av. J. Pastor, Rev. F. Werhahn.

TRINITY—Ambrose cor. So. Robey. Pastor, Rev. Julius Kircher.

ZION'S—14th cor. Union. Pastor, Rev. Paul Foerter.

ZION'S—Auburn Park. Pastor, Rev. J. Holz.

Friends.

FRIENDS' MEETING (Orthodox) 26th bet. Indiana and Prairie avs.

FRIENDS' MEETING—Athenaeum bldg., 18 Vanburen.

Free Methodist.

CRAWFORD—N. Crawford av. nr. W. Lake. Pastor, Rev. F. O. Lewis.

FIRST—16 N. May. Pastor, Rev. J. D. Kelsey.

HUMBOLDT PARK — Mozart nr. Armitage av. Pastor, Rev. G. W. Whittington.

SANGAMON STREET—72d cor. S. Sangamon. Pastor, Rev. W. E. Bardell.

SECOND—547 Ogden av.

SOUTH SIDE—5251 Dearborn. Pastor, Rev. W. E Bardell.

SOUTH CHICAGO—South Chicago. Pastor, Rev. E. G. Creyer.

THIRD CHURCH—701 W. Lake. Pastor, Rev. B. J. Brown.

Holland Christian Reformed.

HOLLAND CHRISTIAN RE-FORMED—524 W. 14th. Pastor, John Riemersma.

HOLLAND CHRISTIAN RE-FORMED—Roseland. Pastor, Rev. J. Robberts.

HOLLAND CHRISTIAN RE-FORMED—63d ne. cor. S. Green. Pastor.——

Independent.

CHICAGO AVENUE—Chicago av. nw. cor. Lasalle av. Pastor, Rev. R. A. Torrey.

CENTRAL—Central Music Hall, State se. cor. Randolph. Pastor, Rev. N. D. Hillis.

KIRKLAND MISSION—111 S. Halsted. Morris E. Hulbert, supt.

PEOPLE'S—McVicker's Theater. Pastor, Rev. H. W. Thomas, 535 W. Monroe.

Jewish.

ANSHE EMETH—349 Sedgwick. Pres. Harry Cohn; Sec. Robert Saltiel; Treas. Herman Kohn; Minister, —— Services Friday at 6:30 p. m.; Saturday 9:30 a. m.

ANSHE K'NESSETH ISRAEL—Judd se. cor. Clinton. Pres. L. Pishofsky; Sec. J. Cohn; Minister, K. Kleinowitz; Rabbi, Rev. B. Bernstein, Services 5 a. m., 3 p. m. and 8 p. m. daily.

ANSHE RUSSIA-POLE-TZEDEK—S. Clinton cor. W. 12th.

CONGREGATION ANSHE SU-WALK—576½ S. Canal.

CONGREGATION AQUDATH ACHIM—Maxwell cor. Newberry av. Rabbi, Rev. Herman Yursky; Sec. N. Neurman.

CONGREGATION BETH HAME-DRASH—134 Pacific av. Pres. W. Goldstein; Sec. Israel Wolfson; Rabbi, Rev. A.J. G. Lesser, 138 Pacific av. Services daily at 7 a. m. and 6 p.m.; Saturday 7:30 a. m. and 4:30 p. m.

CONGREGATION BETH HAME-DRASH HACHODOSCH—439 Clark. Pres. R. Goldstein; Sec. H. Levi; Rabbi, L. Arnichster. Services daily 7 a. m. and 6 p. m.; Saturday 7.30 a. m. and 5 p. m.

CONGREGATION B'NAI ABRA-HAM—509 Marshfield av. Pres. C. Klausner; Sec., L. Levy; Treas. D. Goldstein; Minister, Dr. A. R. Levy. Services Saturday 10 a.m.

CONGREGATION EMANUEL—280 and 282 N. Franklin. Pres. E. Redlich; Treas. Henry Beck: Sec. Abe Stern; Rabbi, L. Darmstedter. Services Saturday 10 a. m.; Sabbath School Saturday and Sunday at 9 a. m.

CONGREGATION OHAVEH EM-UNAH—386 Clark. Pres. Adolph Ascher; Sec. M. Golliner; Minister, Services Friday at 7. p. m.; Saturday 10 a.m. Sabbath-school Saturday 2 p.m.

CONGREGATION OHAVEH-SHOLOM—582 S. Canal. Pres. Carl Listner; Sec. H. Etchoken; Rabbi, —— Brody. Services daily at 6 a. m.; Saturday 7.30 a. m. and 6. p. m.

CONGREGATION OF THE NORTH SIDE—Lasalle av. cor. Goethe. Pres. A. I. Frank; Minister, Rev. Dr. A. Norden. Services Saturday 10 a. m.; Sabbath-school Saturday 9.30 a.m.

CONGREGATION MOSES MON-TEFIORE—130 Augusta. Pres. Adolph Chaim; Sec. Leopold Fuchs. Services Friday evening and Saturday at 8 a.m.

CONGREGATION BETHEL—N. May nr. W. Huron. Pres. A. Kaufman; Sec. Ignatz Gottlieb; Treas. Morris Friend; Minister, Julius Rappaport. Services Saturday 10 a.m.

KEHILATH ANSHE MAARIV—(Congregation of the Men of the West)—Indiana av. cor. Thirty-third. Pres. Henry N. Hart; Minister, Rev. Isaac S. Moses. Services Saturday 10 a. m. Sabbath school Saturday 10 a. m.

KEHILATH B'NAI SHOLOM—(Sons of Peace)—Twenty-sixth cor. Indiana av. Pres. S. Richter; Sec. Charles Cohen; Minister, Rev. Dr. J. A. Messing. Services Saturday 10 a. m. Sabbath-school Saturday 9 a. m.; and Sunday 9;30 a. m.

SINAI CONGREGATION—Indiana av. cor. Twenty-first. Pres. J. L. Gatzert; Lecturer, Dr. E. G. Hirsch. Services Sunday 10.30 a. m. Sabbath-school Sunday 9 a. m.

ZION CONGREGATION—Ogden av. se. cor. Washington boul. Pres, Jacob Schramm; Minister, Rev. Jos. Stolz. Services Saturday 10.30 a. m.; Sunday 11 a. m. Sabbath-school Saturday 9. a. m.; Sunday 9.30 a. m.

Methodist Episcopal.

Bishop—Rev. S. M. Merrill, 1138 Washington boul. Office 57 Washington.

Presiding Elders—Chicago District, Rev. William H. Burns; North Chicago District, Rev. Henry G. Jackson.

Cor. Sec. Chicago Home Missionary and Church Extension Society—A. D. Traveller, 57 Washington.

ADA STREET—Ada bet. W. Lake and Fulton. Pastor, Rev. N. J. Harkness.

ADAMS STREET — Adams cor. West 42d. Pastor, Rev. C. A. Kelly.

ARLINGTON HEIGHTS—Supply, Rev. D. C. McLean.

ASBURY—3120 to 3122 Fifth av. Rev. Joseph Odgers

ASHLAND BOUL.—Ashland boul. cor. W. Harrison. Pastor, Rev. W. W. Diehl.

AUBURN PARK—Auburn Park. Pastors, Revs. T. R. Strobridge and W. R. Goodwin.

AUSTIN—Pastor, Rev. M. W. Satterfield.

AVONDALE — Avondale. Supply F. H. Chamberlain.

BERWYN—Pastor, Rev. W. E. McLennan.

BETHANY—W. Jackson ne. cor. Francisco.

BRIGHTON PARK — Washtenaw av. nw. cor. 38th. Supply, Rev. Herbert Hunt.

CENTENARY—295 W. Monroe nr. Morgan. Pastor, Rev. H. W. Bolton.

CENTRAL AVENUE—Evanston. Pastor, Rev. A. S. Haskins.

CHICAGO AVENUE—Chicago and Lasalle avs. Pastor, Rev. D. M. Farson.

CHICAGO LAWN—Chicago Lawn. Rev. C. S. Moore.

CUMMINGS—Cummings. Rev. D. C. Clancy.

CUYLER—Byron cor. Perry, Pastor, Rev. D. D. Canfield.

DEERING — Dunning nw. cor. Ward. Supply, Rev. J. H. Alling.

DOUGLAS PARK—624 and 626 S. Washtenaw av. Pastor, Rev. L. A. Rockwell.

ELSMERE—Mead sw. cor. Waubansia av. Pastor, Rev I. Linebarger

EMMANUEL — Evanston.

ENGLEWOOD FIRST—6410 Stewart av. Pastor, Rev. C. E. Mandeville.

EPWORTH—Kenmore av. cor. Berwyn av. Pastor Rev. W. A. Burch.

ERIE STREET—W. Erie nr. N. Robey. Pastor, Rev. J. S. Wilson.

FERNWOOD—Pastor, Rev. H. M. Stokes

FIRST—Cor. Clark and Washington, Methodist Church blk. Pastor, Rev. H. D. Kimball.

FIRST — Evanston. Pastor, Rev. F. M. Bristol.

FORT SHERIDAN—Pastor, Rev. J. O. Foster.

FORTY-SEVENTH STREET—47th cor. Dreyer. Pastor, Rev. M. H. Plumb.

FOWLER—Millard av. ne. cor. W. 23d. Pastor, Rev. M. M. Bales.

FULTON STREET—891-893 Fulton w. of Oakley av. Pastor, Rev. J. P. Brushingham.

GARFIELD BOUL.—Garfield boul. cor. Emerald av. Pastor, Rev. J. H. Odgers.

GARFIELD PARK—W. Lake. cor. Homan av. Pastor, Rev. J. Clayton Youker.

GRACE—Lasalle av. cor. Locust. Pastor, Rev. W. A. Phillips.

GRAND CROSSING—Grand Crossing. Pastor, Rev. C. A. Bucks.

GROSS PARK—Gross Park (L.V.) Pastor, Rev. John Nate.

HALSTED STREET—778 to 784 S. Halsted. Pastor, Rev. D. J. Holmes.

HAMLIN AVENUE—Pastor, Rev. R. H. Wilkinson.

HEGEWISCH—Hegewisch av. s. 133d. E. M. Pillow.

HEMENWAY—Evanston. Pastor, Rev. W. E. Wilkinson.

HERMOSA—Hermosa (J.) Pastor, Rev. C. D. Wilson.

HUMBOLDT PARK—Pastor, Rev. James Rowe.

HYDE PARK—Pastor, Rev. H. G. Leonard.

IRVING PARK—Irving Park. Pastor, Rev. A. C. Wakeman

KENWOOD—83, 43d. Pastors, Revs. R. B. Kester and J. J. Rapp.

KENSINGTON—Michigan av. cor. Kensington av. Pastor. Rev. G. B. Millar.

LAGRANGE—Pastor, Rev. E. E. McKay,

LEAVITT AND DEKALB STREETS—nr.Ogden av. Pastor,Rev. R. H. Pate.

LINCOLN STREET—S. Lincoln se. cor. Ambrose. Pastor, Rev. J. T. Ladd.

LOOMIS STREET—Pastor, Rev. T. K. Gale.

LUKE HITCHCOCK—Homer w. Milwaukee av.Pastor,Rev.G.P.Sturges.

MAYWOOD — Supply, Rev. J. W. Welsh.

MONTROSE—Pastor, Rev. J.' W. Lee.

MORELAND — Moreland. Pastor, Rev. M. B. Williams

MORGAN PARK — Pastor, Rev. W. F. Atchison.

NORMAL PARK—Normal Park. Pastor, Rev. G. M. Bassett.

NORWOOD PARK—Supply, Rev. M. C. Cooper.

OAK PARK—Pastor, Rev. R. H. Pooley.

OAKLAND—Oakland boul. sw. cor. Langley av. Pastor, Rev. P. H. Swift.

PARK AVENUE—Park av. se. cor. Robey. Pastor, Rev. W. W. Painter.

PARK MANOR—6758 S. Chicago av. Supply L. E. Dennis.

PARK RIDGE—Pastor, Rev. R. H. Dolliver.

PARK SIDE—Supply, Rev. H. B. DeBra.

PAULINA STREET—3342 S. Paulina nr. Archer av. Pastor, Rev. Wm. J. Libberton.

PULLMAN—Pullman. Pastor, Rev. W. H. Carwardine.

RAVENSWOOD—Commercial cor. Sunnyside av. Pastor, Rev. N. H. Axtell.

RIVER FOREST—Pastor, Rev. U. S. Villars.

ROGERS PARK — Pastor, Rev. R. W. Bland.

SACRAMENTO AVENUE—Sacramento av. head of Adams st. Pastor, Rev. J. A. Matlack.

SECOND ENGLEWOOD—62d cor. S. May. Pastor, Rev. B. W. Marsh.

SHEFFIELD AVENUE—Sheffield av. cor. George. Pastor, Rev. H. R. Calkins.

SIMPSON—Lasalle cor. 59th. Pastor, Rev. O. E. Murray.

SOUTH CHICAGO—Superior av. ne. cor. 91st. Pastor, Rev. Ray Harker'

SOUTH ENGLEWOOD — Murray cor. 87th. Pastor, Rev. M. G. Wenz.

SOUTH PARK AVENUE — South Park av. cor. 33d. Pastor, Rev. J. M. Caldwell. Asst., Rev. Wm. Fawcett.

STATE STREET — 4637 State. Pastor, Rev. G. S. Young.

ST. PAUL'S — Center av. nr. W· Taylor. Pastor, Rev. W. B. Leach.

TRINITY — Indiana av. nr. 24th. Pastor, Rev. T. J. Leake.

WABASH AVENUE — Cor. 14th and Wabash av. Pastor, Rev. J. J. Tobias.

WASHINGTON PARK—47th cor. Champlain av. Pastors, Revs. R. B. Kester and J. J. Rapp.

WESLEY — 1003-1009 N. Halsted. Pastor, Rev. A. M. White.

WEST PULLMAN—Supply, J. P. McCarthy.

WESTERN AVENUE — Cor. W. Monroe and Western av. Pastor, Rev. R. S. Martin.

WHEADON, EVANSTON — Pastor, Rev. John Lee.

WICKER PARK—N. Robey cor. Evergreen av. Pastor, Rev. W. H. Holmes.

WILMETTE — Pastor, Rev. H. S. Atchison.

WINTER STREET — Winter cor. 44th. Pastor, Rev. Edward W. Drew.

WOODLAWN PARK — Woodlawn Park. Supply, Rev. W. E. Tilroe.

AFRICAN.

ALLEN CHAPEL—Avondale. Pastor, Rev. R. Knight.

BETHEL—Dearborn ne. cor. 30th. Pastor, Rev. D. A. Graham.

QUINN CHAPEL—Wabash av. se. cor. 24th.Pastor, Rev. James. M. Townsend

ST. JOHNS—333, 63d. Pastor, Rev. J. C. Anderson.

ST. STEPHEN'S — 682 Austin av. Pastor, Rev. George W. Gaines.

WAYMAN CHAPEL—214 Chicago av. Pastor, Rev. S. McDowell.

WRIGHT STREET MISSION— Wright cor. 54th. Pastor, Rev. George W. Slater.

ZION—3736 Armour av. Pastor, Rev. D. J. Donlhoo.

ZION MISSION — 5914 S. Morgan. Pastor, Amos D. Howard.

BOHEMIAN.

FIRST — 778 S. Halsted. Pastor, Rev. F. J. Hrejsa.

JAN HUSS—24th nw. cor. Sawyer av. Pastor, Rev. Vaclav Vanek.

SECOND—S. Halsted cor. W. 12th. Pastor, Rev. J. Froula.

GERMAN.

Presiding Elder Chicago District, German Conference — Rev. B. Lampert, 306 Maxwell.

ASHLAND AVENUE—485 N. Ashland av. Pastor, Rev. B. Becker.

CENTENNIAL MISSION — Cor. Wellington and Sheffield avs., Lake View. Pastor, Rev. C. H. Abells.

CENTER STREET — Center nw. cor. Dayton. Pastor, Rev. William W. Weber.

CLYBOURN AVENUE—51 and 53 Clybourn av. Pastor, Rev. William Keller.

EBENEZER—Ullman sw. cor. 31st. Pastor, ——.

FULLERTON AVENUE—W. Fullerton av. ne. cor. N. Western av. Pastor, Rev. F. F. Klenzky.

IMMANUEL—832 and 834 W. 22d. Pastor, Rev. Henry Wegner.

McLEAN STREET—McLean cor. Hencock. Pastor, Rev. Charles H. Hedler.

MAXWELL STREET—308 and 310 Maxwell. Pastor, Rev. Wm. Keller. Asst. Pastor, Rev. J. Kluesner.

PORTLAND AVENUE—Portland av. se. cor. 28th. Pastor, Rev. Charles Weinreich.

ROBEY STREET—Robey nr. W. 12th. Pastor, Rev. H. C. Apfelbach.

SOUTH MORGAN STREET—54th cor. S. Morgan. Pastor, Rev. J. D. Meyn.

WENTWORTH AVENUE—Wentworth av. s. 37th. Pastor, Rev. A. Mulfinger.

SWEDISH.

Presiding Elder Chicago District, Swedish Conference—Rev. A. Anderson, Ravenswood.

·· AUSTIN—Austin av. cor. Augusta. Pastor, Rev. S. B. Newman.

BRIGHTON PARK—Pastor, Rev. George Swift.

EMANUEL—Marvin nr. Blue Island av. Pastor, Rev. A. Sallen.

ENGLEWOOD — 66th ct. cor. Wright. Pastor, Rev. Isaac Anderson.

FIFTH AVENUE — Fifth av. ne. cor. 33d. Pastor, Rev. C. O. Karlson.

FIRST—N Market and Oak. Pastor, Rev. K. H. Elinstrom.

FOREST GLEN — Jefferson. Pastor, Rev. C. W. Bloomquist.

HUMBOLDT PARK—Fairfield av. nr. North av. Pastor, Rev. P. M. Alfvin.

LAKE VIEW — Cor. Baxter and Noble av. Pastor, Rev. A. J. Anderson.

MELROSE PARK AND OAK PARK—Pastor, Rev. J. B. Anderson

MORELAND—Indiana cor. W. 48th. Pastor. Rev. C. O. Sherman.

PULLMAN—113th cor. Indiana av. Pastor, Rev. J. O. Nelson.

RAVENSWOOD CHURCH — Ravenswood. Pastor, Rev. A. N. Sollin.

SECOND—May bet. Ohio and Erie. Pastor, Rev. John Bendix.

SOUTH CHICAGO—Exchange av. cor. 91st. Pastor, Rev. Reese.

WESTERN SPRINGS — Pastor, Rev. G. A. Hillberg.

NORWEGIAN AND DANISH.

Presiding Elder Chicago District. Norwegian Conference — Rev. Frederick King, 798 Dania av.

FIRST—W. Indiana se. cor. Sangamon. Pastor, Rev. J. H. Johnson.

IMMANUEL—232 W. Huron. Pastor, Rev. Paul Haugan.

MAPLEWOOD AVENUE—Maplewood av. cor. LeMoyne av. Pastor, Rev. L. C. Knudson.

MORELAND — Pastor, Rev. H. Danielsen.

PARK SIDE — Pastor, Rev. E. Gierding.

New Jerusalem (Swedenborgian).

NEW-CHURCH HALL—274 Van Buren. Pastors, Rev. L. P. Mercer and Rev. Thomas A. King.

ENGLEWOOD—Revs. L. P. Mercer and Thomas A. King, Pastors.

Presbyterian.

AUSTIN FIRST—Lake and Central av. Pastor, Rev. James Clarke Hill.

AVONDALE — Avondale. Pastor, Rev. W. W. Smith.

BELDEN AVENUE — Belden av. cor. Seminary av. Pastor, Rev. Robert D. Scott.

BETHANY — Humboldt Park boul. cor. Cortland. Pastor, Rev. Joseph D. Cherry.

BRIGHTON PARK—Pastor, Rev. James MacLaughlin.

BROOKLINE — 73d cor. Storm. Pastor, Rev. J. A. Gray.

CALVARY—W. Harrison cor. W. 40th. Rev. G. A. Mitchell.

CAMPBELL PARK — S. Leavitt cor. Harrison. Pastor, Rev. William G. Clarke.

CENTRAL PARK — Warren av. cor. Sacramento av. Pastor, Rev. H. H. Van Vranken.

CHICAGO HEIGHTS — Chicago Heights. Pastor, Rev. E. F. Hoke.

CHICAGO LAWN—Chicago Lawn. Pastor, ——.

CHRIST CHAPEL — Orchard and Center. Pastor, ——.

COVENANT—N. Halsted se. cor. Belden av. Pastor, ——.

EIGHTH — Washington boul. nw. cor. Robey. Pastor, Rev. Thos. D Wallace, D.D.

ELEVENTH — 384 W. Division. Pastor, Rev. Geo. B. Laird.

EMERALD AVENUE — Emerald av. and 67th. Pastor, Rev. S. M. Campbell.

ENDEAVOR — Melrose cor Wood. Pastor, Rev. Herbert A. Bradford.

EVANSTON — Evanston. Pastor, ——.

FIFTH—Indiana av. cor. 30th. Pastor, Rev. LeRoy Hooker.

FIRST CHURCH OF ENGLE- WOOD—64th cor. Yale. Pastor, Rev. W. H. Robinson, D.D.

FIRST—Indiana av. cor. 21st. Pastor, Rev. John H. Barrows, D.D.

FIRST GERMAN—Willow cor. Orchard. Pastor, Rev. Daniel Volz.

FORTY-FIRST STREET — Grand boul. cor. 41st. Pastor, Rev. Howard A. Johnston.

FOURTH—Rush cor. Superior. Pastor, Rev. Thos. C. Hall.

FULLERTON AVENUE—Fullerton av. nw. cor. Larrabee. Pastor, Rev. John Rusk,

GRACE (colored) — Dearborn s. 34th. Pastor, Rev. M. H. Jackson.

HIGHLAND PARK—Highland Park. Pastor, Rev. Henry Neill.

HINSDALE FIRST — Hinsdale. Pastor, Rev. C. F. Moore.

HYDE PARK—Washington av. cor. 53d. Pastor, Rev, H. C. Herring.

IMMANUEL—2835 Keeley. Pastor, Rev. E. B. Hubbell.

ITALIAN—W. Ohio cor. Milwaukee av. Pastor, Rev. Fillipo Grille.

JEFFERSON PARK—W. Adams cor. Throop. Pastor, Rev. Fred Campbell.

LA GRANGE FIRST—La Grange. Pastor, Rev. Chas. J. Howell.

LAKE FOREST — Lake Forest. Pastor, Rev. J. G. K. McClure.

LAKE VIEW—Evanston av. cor. Addison. Pastor, Rev. J. M. Fulton.

MAYWOOD — Maywood.

MORELAND—Fulton cor. W. 48th.

MORGAN PARK—Morgan Park.

NINTH—Ashland av. cor. Hastings. Pastor, Rev. Charles E. Morse.

NORMAL PARK—69th cor. Yale. Pastor, Rev. Wm. M. Hindman.

OAK PARK—Oak Park. Pastor, Rev. Charles S. Hoyt.

OLIVET — Larrabee cor. Vedder. Pastor, Rev. N. B. W. Gallwey.

ONWARD—Hoyne av. and W. Indiana. Pastor, James E. Foster.

PULLMAN — Pastor, Rev. G. R. Pike.

RAILROAD CHAPEL—3825 Dearborn. Pastor, Rev. S. M. Johnson.

RIDGEWAY AVENUE — Ridgeway av. and W. Huron. Pastor, Rev. D. A. McWilliams.

RIVER FOREST——River Forest. Pastor, Rev. W. H. Reynolds.

RIVERSIDE — Riverside. Pastor, Rev. Chas. E. Snyder.

SCOTCH—S. Sangamon cor. W. Adams. Pastor, Rev. H. S. Jenkinson.

SECOND—Michigan av. cor. 20th. Pastor, Rev. Simon J. McPherson, D.D.

SEVENTH—South Englewood. Pastor, Rev. Martin Luther.

SIXTH — Vincennes av. cor. 36th. Pastor, Rev. Carlos Martyn.

SIXTIETH STREET—60th and Princeton av. Pastor, Rev. Joseph E. Elliott,

SOUTH CHICAGO—Houston av. cor. 92d. Pastor, Rev. L. A. Mitchell.

SOUTH EVANSTON—Evanston. Pastor, Rev. John N. Mills.

TENTH—42d cor. Winter. Pastor, Rev. Joseph N. Boyd.

THIRD—S. Ashland av. cor. Ogden av. Pastor, Rev. John L. Withrow, D. D.

WELSH—W. Monroe ne. cor. Sangamon.

WEST DIVISION STREET—W. Division cor. Maplewood av. Pastor, Rev. C. H. Currens.

WESTMINSTER—S. Peoria cor. W. Jackson.

WOODLAWN PARK — 64th cor. Sheridan. Pastor, Rev. J. G. Iuglis.

MISSIONS.

ADA STREET MISSION—68th cor. Ada.

BETHLEHEM MISSION—51st and Atlantic.

BROOKDALE MISSION—73d and Greenwood av.

ELSTON AV. MISSION—519 Milwaukee av.

ERIE CHAPEL—Erie cor. Noble.

FOSTER MISSION—Peoria and Jackson.

HOPE MISSION—691 Augusta.

MOSELEY MISSION—2539 Calumet av.

SYRIAN MISSION—406 Clark.

(Services are held in all these missions at 3 p. m.)

Reformed Churches.

BETHANY—111th w. of State (Roseland). Pastor, Rev. G. J. Hekhuis.

IRVING PARK—Irving Park. Pastor, Rev. Jesse W. Brooks, Ph.D.

NORWOOD PARK—Norwood Park. Pastor, Rev. J. S. Joralmon.

TRINITY—440 Marshfield av. Pastor, Rev. P. Moerdyke.

HOLLAND.

ENGLEWOOD — 62d cor. Peoria. Pastor, Rev. L. Dykstra.

FIRST—Hastings nr. Ashland av. Pastor, Rev. R. Bloemendal.

FIRST CHURCH OF GANO—Clark cor. 117th. Pastor, Rev. J. Warnshuis.

FIRST ROSELAND—Michigan av. sw. cor. 107th (Roseland). Pastor, Rev. B. VanEss.

NORTHWESTERN — W. Superior bet. N. Robey and Hoyne av. Pastor, Rev. J. H. Vanden Hook.

Roman Catholic.

Archbishop of Chicago—Most Rev. Patrick A. Feehan, D. D.

Vicar-General—Very Rev. D. M. J. Dowling.

Chancellor and Secretary—Rev. P. J. Muldoon.

CATHEDRAL OF THE HOLY NAME—Cor. Superior and N. State. Most Rev. Patrick A. Feehan, D. D.; Rector, Rev. M. J. Fitzsimmons; Assts., Rev. J. M. Scanlan, Rev. J. S. Finn, Rev. N. J. Mooney, Rev. J. P. Dore and Rev. F. Barry.

ALL SAINTS'—Wallace sw. cor. 25th pl. Pastor, Rev. J. C. Gillan; Assts. Rev. Alex McGavick and Rev. Thomas Walen.

CHAPEL OF OUR LADY OF MERCY—St. Paul's Home, 383 W. Jackson. Pastor, Rev. D. S. A. Mahoney.

CHURCH OF NOTRE DAME DE CHICAGO (French)—Vernon Park pl. cor. Sibley. Pastor, Rev. Achille L. Bergeron.

CHURCH OF OUR LADY OF GOOD COUNSEL (Bohemian)—Western av. cor. Cornelia. Pastor, Rev. J. F. Jedlicka.

CHURCH OF OUR LADY OF LOURDES—N. Ashland av. cor Leland av. Pastor, Rev. F. N. Perry.

CHURCH OF OUR LADY OF LOURDES (Bohemian)—Crawford av. nr. 16th. Attended from St. Procopius.

CHURCH OF OUR LADY OF MOUNT CARMEL—Wellington and Blucher. Pastor, Rev. P. O'Brien; Asst., Rev. E. J. Fox.

CHURCH OF OUR LADY OF SORROWS—1406 W. Jackson. Vicar-General of the Order in the U. S., Very Rev. B. Baldi, O. S.; Rev. Hugh Crevier, O. S., Pastor; Assts., Rev. F. Gagnon, O. S., Rev. A. Quigley, O. S., and Rev. A. Dourche, O. S.

CHURCH OF THE ANNUNCIATION B. V. M.—N. Paulina sw. cor. Wabansia av. Pastor, Rev. Hugh O'Gara McShane; Asst., E. M. Griffin.

CHURCH OF THE ASSUMPTION B. V. M. (Italian)—Illinois nr.

N. Market. Rev. Thos. Moreschini, O. S. Asst., Rev. Joachim Tonissi, O.S. Rev. Fredericus Angelucii, O.S.;

CHURCH OF THE BLESSED SACRAMENT—W. 22d and Central Park av. Rev. J. M. Dunne; Asst., Rev. J. F. Bennet.

CHURCH OF THE HOLY AN-GELS—281 Oakwood boul. Pastor, Rev. Dennis A. Tighe; Assts., Rev. H. Wills, Rev. J. Welsh, and Rev. M. S. Gilmartin.

CHURCH OF THE HOLY CROSS—6604 Maryland av., Park Manor. Rev. D. Hishen.

CHURCH OF THE HOLY FAM-ILY—W. 12th cor. May. Pastor, Rev. M. J. Dowling, S. J.; Assts., Rev. F. L. Weinmann, S. J., Rev. J. D. Condon, S. J., Rev. John L. Setters, S. J., Rev. A. O'Neill, S. J., Rev. C. Lagae, S. J., Rev. M. Van Agt, S. J., Rev. Henry Baselmans, S. J., Rev. James M. Hayes, S. J., Rev. F. X. Schulak, S. J. Rev. J. J. Corbley, S. J., Rev. P. Ponziglione, S. J., Rev. H. M. Calmer, S. J., Rev. J. P. Hogan, S.J.

CHURCH OF THE HOLY ROS-ARY—113th sw. cor. South Park av. (Roseland). Pastor, Rev. P. J. Tinan; Asst., Rev. W. M. Foley

CHURCH OF THE IMMACU-LATE CONCEPTION—N. Franklin n. of Schiller. Pastor, Rev. P. T. Butler; Asst., Rev. J. H. Crowe.

CHURCH OF THE NATIVITY OF OUR LORD—37th cor. Union av. Pastor, Rev. Joseph M. Cartan; Assts., Rev. J. C. McCormick and Rev. M. O'Sullivan and Rev. P. Scanlan.

CHURCH OF THE SACRED HEART—se. cor. W. 19th and Johnson. Pastor, Rev. Michael J. Corbett, S. J.; Assts., Rev. P. Tshieder, S. J., Rev. Walter Hill, S.J., Rev. F. Bondreaux, S. J., Rev. J. Masterson, and Rev. C. J. Ward, S. J.

CHURCH OF THE SACRED HEART OF MARY—Longwood. Pastor, Rev, P. S. McDonnell.

CHURCH OF ST. CATHERINE OF SIENNA—Austin. Pastor, Rev. L. Campbell.

CHURCH OF THE VISITATION—53d and Sangamon. Pastor, D. F. McGuire; Asst., Rev. Thomas Feeley.

HOLY TRINITY (German)—S.Lincoln cor. W. Taylor. Pastor, Rev. Joseph W. Hausser. Asst. Rev. J. Suerth.

HOLY TRINITY (Polish) — 540 Noble. Pastor Rev. C. Truszynski, C.S.C.

IMMACULATE CONCEPTION B. V. M. (German)—2944-2946 Bonfield nr. Archer av. Pastor, Rev. W. F. Verhalen; Asst., Rev. P. L. Biermann.

IMMACULATE CONCEPTION B. V. M. (Polish)—Commercial av. nw. cor. 88th. Pastor, Rev. V. Zaleski.

NOTRE DAME LEO VICTOIRES—135 Springfield av. Pastor, Rev. U. Martel.

ST. ADELBERT'S (Polish)—cor. W. 17th and Paulina. Pastor, Rev. J. Radziejewski; Assts. Rev. B. Pawlowski and Rev. I. Rothe.

ST. AGATHA—627 S. Albany av. Pastor Rev. M. Bonfield.

ST. AGNES—S. Washtenaw av. nr. 38th, Brighton Park. Pastor, Rev. N. Hitchcock; Asst., F. Carraber.

ST. AILBE — 9150 Washington av. Pastor, Rev. W. S. Hennessy.

ST.ALOYSIUS' (German)—Thompson cor. Davis st. Pastor, Rev. A. J. Thiele; Asst., Rev. F. J. Haarth.

ST. ALPHONSUS' (German)—Lincoln av. cor. Southport av. Pastor, H. Weber, C.SS.R.; Assts., Revs. Chas. Hahn, C.SS.R., J. B. Neu, C.SS.R., Nich. Franzen, C.SS.R.

ST.ANN'S—cor. 55th and Wentworth av. Pastor, Rev. P. M. Flannigan; Assts., Rev. F. Renolds, Rev. D. J. Crimmins and Rev. J. O'Shea.

ST. ANTHONY OF PADUA (German)—Hanover se. cor. 24th pl. Pastor, Rev. Peter Fisher; Asst., Rev. J. Schulte.

ST. AUGUSTINE'S (German)—Laflin and 49th. Rev. S. Forstman, O. S. F.; Asst., Revs. Paulinus Weiss, O. S. F., Paschalis Nolte, O. S. F., and Pius Niermann, O. S. F.

ST. BERNARD'S—66th and Stewart av. Pastor, Rev. Bernard P. Murray; Asst., Rev. J. J. Dennison.

ST. BONIFACE'S (German)—Cornell cor. Noble. Pastor, Rev. Clement Venn; Asst., Rev. A. Wolfgarten.

ST. BRENDAN'S—67th and Bishop. Rev. M. T. Macken.

ST. BRIDGET'S—Archer av. cor. Church pl. Pastor, Very Rev. Daniel M. J. Dowling, V. G.; Asst., Rev. P. R. Bulfin.

ST. CASIMIR'S (Polish)—22d and Little. Pastor, Rev. A. Furman.

ST. CECELIA'S—Bristol nr. Wentworth av. Pastor, Rev. E. A. Kelly;

Assts., Revs. J. P. O'Reilly and T. Ryan.

ST. CHARLES BORROMEO'S—87-91 Cypress. Pastor, Rev. Patrick D. Gill; Assts., Rev. J. Kearney, and J. J. Jennings.

ST. COLUMBA'S—Mackinaw av. s. 133d, Hegewisch. Attended from St. Kevins.

ST. COLUMBKILL'S—Cor. N. Paulina and W. Indiana. Pastor, Rev. Thomas Burke; Assts., Rev. William Lynch, Rev. Denis O'Brien and Rev. E. M. Dunne, D. D.

STS. CYRIL AND METHODIUS (Bohemian)—50th cor Page. Pastor, Rev. Thomas Bobal.

ST. DIONYSIUS'—Hawthorne. Pastor, Rev. D. Konen.

ST. ELIZABETH'S—41st ne. cor. State. Pastor, Rev. D. J. Riordan; Assts., Rev. James McGavick and Rev. D. Croke.

ST. FRANCIS OF ASSISIUM (German)—W. 12th cor. Newberry av. Pastor, Rev. D. M. Thiele. Assts. Rev. Peter Faber and Rev. John Shikowski.

ST. FRANCIS DE SALES—Ewing av. cor. 102d. Rector, Rev. J. Diekman.

ST. FRANCIS XAVIER (German)—Avondale. Rev. E. Goldschmidt.

ST. FRANCIS XAVIER—LaGrange. Pastor, Rev. John M. Hagen.

ST. GABRIEL'S—45th se. cor. Wallace. Pastor, Rev. M. J. Dorney; Assts., Rev. J. Healey and Rev. J. E. Madden.

ST. GEORGE'S (German) — 3924 Wentworth av. Pastor, Rev. J. Dettmers.

ST. GEORGE'S (Lithuanian)—33d and Attica, Pastor. Rev. M. Krawczunes.

ST. HEDWIG'S (Polish)—n. s. Kosciusco bet. N. Hoyne av. and St. Hedwig. Pastor, Rev. Joseph Barzynski, C. R.

ST. HENRY'S—High Ridge. Pastor, Rev. J. Rutershoff.

ST. JAMES'—Wabash av. and 30th. Pastor, Rev. Hugh McGuire; Assts., Rev. P. Gildea, Rev. B. Swanson and Rev. H. G. Van Pelt.

ST. JARLATH'S — Hermitage av. cor. W. Jackson. Pastor, Rev. T. F. Cashman; Assts., Rev. P. J. O'Connor and Rev. Thomas E. Cox.

ST. JOHN BAPTIST—1006, 50th ct. Pastor, Rev. F. Quimet.

ST. JOHN CAUTIUS (Polish)—Carpenter and Chicago av. Pastor, J. Kasprzcki, C.R.

ST. JOHN THE BAPTIST (Cyrian-Arabian) 323 Franklin. Pastor, Rev. B. Souaya.

ST. JOHN'S—18th cor. Clark. Rector, Very Rev. Thaddeus J. Butler, D. D.; Assts., Rev. E. Kramer, Rev. W. Hackett.

ST. JOHN NEPOMUCENE'S (Bohemian)—25th cor. Portland av. Pastor, Rev. Francis Bobal.

ST. JOSEPH'S (German Priory)—N. Market cor. Hill. Pastor. Rev. C. Stratmann, O.S.B.; Assts., Rev. Lucius Wimmer, O. S. B., Rev. R. Schremps, O. S. B., and Theobald Mueller, O. S. B.

ST. JOSEPH'S (French)—Brighton Park. Rev. J. C. Lasage

ST. JOSEPH'S (Polish)—48th and Paulina. Rev. M. Pyplatz.

ST. JOSAPHAT'S (Polish)—Belden av. nw. cor. Ward. Pastor, Rev. J. Lange.

ST. KEVIN'S—Cummings. Pastor, Rev. Timothy Sullivan.

ST. LAWRENCE—75th nr. Brooks av., Grand Crossing. Pastor, Rev. S. Maloney; Asst., Rev. P. A. Byrne.

ST. LEO'S—Wright cor. Schorling av., Auburn Park. Pastor, Rev. P. A. L. Egan.

ST. LOUIS' — Pullman. Pastor, Rev. J. B. Bourassa.

ST. LUDMILLA'S—W. 24th and Albany av. Rev. M. Farnik.

ST. MALACHY'S — Walnut cor. Western av. Pastor, Rev. Thomas P. Hodnett; Assts., Rev. J. Cody, Rev. S. Woulfe and Rev. J. Luttrell.

ST. MARTIN'S (German)—59th and School. Pastor, Rev. J. Schaefers.

ST. MARY'S—Wabash av. cor. Eldridge ct. Rector, Rev. E. A. Murphy; Asst., Rev. P. C. Conway.

ST. MARY'S (German)—Riverdale. Attended from St. Joseph's.

ST. MARY'S OF PERPETUAL HELP (Polish)—32d and Mosspratt. Pastors, Rev. S. Nawrocki and Rev. F. S. Byrgier.

ST. MATHIAS—Bowmanville, Pastor, Rev. M. E. Erz.

ST. MATTHEW'S — 611 Walnut. Pastor. Rev. J. Flood.

ST. MAURITIUS'—Thirty-sixth and Hoyne av. Pastor, Rev. G. J. Blatter.

THE CHICAGO NATIONAL BANK

Dearborn and Monroe Streets.

CAPITAL_____$500,000.
SURPLUS_____ 500,000

CURRENT ACCOUNTS kept in conformity with the practice of Chicago Banks. Parties keeping current accounts can have approved commercial paper discounted and can obtain loans on negotiable securities.

DEPOSIT ACCOUNTS. Money in sums of fifty dollars and upward received from the public generally, repayable on demand. If deposited for a fixed term, interest is allowed according to the state of the money market. Parties keeping current accounts can transfer any part of their balance to deposit account.

LETTERS OF CREDIT FOR TRAVELERS issued available in the principal cities of the world. Foreign Exchange bought and sold.

CORRESPONDENCE or a personal interview with a view to business relations respectfully invited.

DIRECTORS.

F. MADLENER,	FERD. W. PECK,
C. K. G. BILLINGS,	WILLIAM BEST,
ANDREW McNALLY,	J. R. WALSH,
MAURICE ROSENFELD.	

J. R. WALSH, President.
ANDREW McNALLY, Vice-President.
F. M. BLOUNT, Cashier.
T. M. JACKSON, Ass't-Cashier.

ST. MICHAEL'S (German)—Eugenie cor. Cleveland av. Pastor, Rev. A. Herz,C.S.S.R.; Assts., Rev. August Troisdorf, C. SS. R.; Rev. Martin Gruener, C. SS. R.; Rev. A. Ebel, C. SS. R. Rev. Peter Heller, C. SS. R., Rev. Geo. Thomas, C. SS. R., Rev. Jos. Biel, C. SS. R.

ST. MICHAEL'S (Polish)—83d cor. Bond av. Pastor, Rev. A. Nawicki.

ST. MONICA'S (Colored)—448, 36th, Rector, Rev. D. J. Riordan.

ST. NICOLAS' (German) — 113th Place and State. , Pastor, Rev. Theodore A. Bonifas.

ST. PATRICK'S—Commercial av. nr. Ninety-fifth, So. Chicago. Pastor, Rev. M. Van de Laar; Asst., Rev. J. Aylward.

ST. PATRICK'S—S. Desplaines cor. W. Adams. Pastor, Rev. Thomas F. Galligan; Asst., Rev. E. Byrnes.

ST. PAUL'S (German)—S. Hoyne av. cor. Ambrose. Pastor, Rev. Geo. Heldman; Asst. Rev. J. Wanner.

ST. PETER'S (German)—Clark cor. Polk. Rev. Paulinus Tolksdorf, O. S. F,; Rev. I. Gey, O. S. F.

SS. PETER AND PAUL—91st cor. Exchange av., So. Chicago. Pastor, Rev. F. Burelbach.

ST. PHILLIP'S—Park av. cor. W. 43d. Pastor. Rev. P. J. McDonnel; Asst., Rev. Thomas Smith.

ST. PIUS'—S. Ashland av. se. cor. W. 19th. Pastor, Rev. F. S. Henneberry; Assts., Rev. D. J. McCaffery and Rev. J. W. Melody,

ST. PROCOPIUS' (Bohemian) — Allport cor. W. 18th. Pastor, Rev. Nepomuck Jaeger, O. S. B.; Assts., R..v. Wenceslaus Kozarnik, O. S. B., Rev. Valerian Haolovic, O. S. B., Rev. Procop Neuzil, O. S. B., Rev. Ildephonse Wittman, O. S. B., and Rev A. Rebec, O. S. B.

ST. ROSE OF LIMA—Ashland av. nr. 48th. Pastor, Rev. Dennis Hayes. Asst. Rev. P. Dwyer.

ST. STANISLAUS KOSTKA'S(Polish)—Noble cor. Ingraham. Superior, Very Rev. Simon Chas. Kobrzynski, C. R.; Rector, Rev. Vincent Barzynski, C. R.; Assts., Rev. L. Machdzicki, C. R., Rev. John Kasprzycki, C. R., Rev. Theophil Szypkowski, C. R., Rev. Bernard Zimjewski, C. R., Rev. J. Piechowski, C. R., Rev. J. LeGrand, C. R. Rev. E. Sedlaczek, C. R., Rev. Joseph Gehurowski, C. R., and Rev. F. Matuszewski, C. R.

ST. STEPHEN'S—N. Sangamon cor. W. Ohio. Pastor, Dominic Egan; Asst., Rev. H. Quinn.

ST. SYLVESTER'S—California av. and Shakespeare av. Pastor, Rev. P. J. Agnew; Asst., A. J. Hines.

ST. TERESA'S (German)—Centre cor. Clyde. Pastor, Rev. Mathias W. Barth; Asst., Rev. C. A. Erkenswick.

ST. THOMAS'—55th and Kimbark av. Pastor, Rev. J. J. Carroll; Assts., Rev. J. Glennon, and Rev. J. Callaghan.

ST. VIATEUR'S—Cor. Belmont and Crawford avs. Pastor, Very Rev. C. Fournier, P. S. V.; Asst. Rev. T. Dugart, P. S. V.

ST. VINCENT DE PAUL'S—Webster av. cor. Osgood. Pastor, Rev. E. Smith, C. M.; Assts., Rev. F. X., Antil, C. M., Rev. J. E. Hennelly, C. M.

ST. VITUS—Paulina and VanHorn. Attended from St. Procopius by Rev. Valerian Havlovic, O. S. B.

ST. WENCESLAUS' (Bohemian) —173 DeKoven. Pastor, Rev. Joseph Molitor.

The Salvation Army.

DIVISIONAL HEADQUARTERS —Princess Rink, 558 W. Madison. Brigadier. Edward Fielding, chief divisional officer.

CHICAGO 1—Princess Rink, 558 W. Madison.

CHICAGO 2—39th and Langley av.

CHICAGO 3—999 W. Lake.

CHICAGO 4—Harvey, Ill.

CHICAGO 5—1682 Milwaukee av.

CHICAGO 6—Music Hall, 6221 Wentworth av. Englewood.

CHICAGO 7—(Swedish)1721N.Clark.

CHICAGO 8—2948 State.

CHICAGO 9—4029 State.

CHICAGO 10—(Swedish) 9115 Erie av. South Chicago.

CHICAGO 11—2932 Wentworth av.

CHICAGO 12—Evanston, Ill.

CHICAGO 13—(Swedish) 17 Milton av. (north side.)

CHICAGO 15— (Swedish) 5428 LaSalle.

CHICAGO 16—(Swedish) 6116 Aberdeen.

CHICAGO 17— 723, 47th (L.)

CHICAGO 18—Calumet Hall bldg. Grand Crossing.

CHICAGO 19—La Grange.

CHICAGO 20—Austin.

CHICAGO 21—5345 Lake av. (H.P.)

CHICAGO 22—W. Harrison e. of Halsted.

Union Evangelical.

BETHANY UNION—Prospect av. cor 103d. Pastor Rev. Geo. E. Hunt.

KENWOOD EVANGELICAL—Greenwood av. and 46th. Pastor, Rev. John P. Hale.

LAKE AVENUE UNION—Lake av. nr. 45th. Pastor, ——.

OAKWOODS UNION—Champlain av. and 65th. Pastor, Rev. C. E. Hulbert.

ST. PAUL'S EVANGELICAL—Prospect av. and 94th. Pastor, Rev. William Russell Scarritt.

Unitarian.

ALL SOULS'—Oakwood boul. se. cor. Langley av. Pastor, Rev. Jenkin Lloyd Jones.

CHURCH OF THE MESSIAH—Michigan boul. se. cor. 23d. Pastor, Rev. W. W. Fenn.

THIRD UNITARIAN—Monroe se. cor. Laflin. Pastor, Rev. James Vila Blake.

UNITY—Dearborn av. se. cor. Walton pl. Pastor, Rev. B. R. Bulkeley.

United Evangelical.

Bishop, Rudolph Dubs, D.D. LL.D., office 911 Chicago Opera House blk. Presiding Elder, Rev. John Schneider, 938 Haugan av.

ADAMS STREET—Adams cor Robey. Pastor, Rev. W. H. Foulke,

DEARBORN STREET — Armour av. bet. 36th and 37th. Pastor, Rev. Frederick Busse.

NORTH ASHLAND AV.—N. Ashland av. cor. Noble av. Pastor, Rev. C. A. Fuesele.

ZION'S—N. Hoyne av. cor. Iowa. Pastor, Rev. W. F. Schmalle.

United Presbyterian.

FIFTH—Ravenswood. Pastor, Rev. Ralph Atkinson.

FIRST—W. Monroe sw. cor. S. Paulina. Pastor, Rev. Wm. T. Meloy.

FOURTH—1080 W. Polk. Supply, Rev. J. A. Collins, D. D.

SECOND—Honore cor. 63d. Pastor, Rev. J. A. Duff.

THIRD—Indiana av. cor. 35th. Pastor, ——.

Universalists.

BLUE ISLAND—Pastor. Rev. W. R. Libby.

CHURCH OF THE REDEEMER—Warren av. ne. cor. Robey. Pastor, Rev. M. H. Harris, D.D.

ST. PAUL'S—Prairie av. cor. 30th. Pastor, Rev. A. J. Canfield, D.D.

THIRD UNIVERSALIST — 80 Hall nr. Diversey av and N. Clark. Pastor, Rev. L. J. Dinsmore.

UNIVERSALIST MISSION — 54th cor. State. Pastor, Rev. R. A. White.

STEWART AVENUE — 65th st., and Stewart av. Pastor, Rev. R. A. White.

RYDER CHAPEL—Woodlawn Park. Pastor, Rev. C. A. Garst.

UNITY—Oak Park. Pastor, Rev. R. F. Johonnot

Miscellaneous.

APOSTOLIC CATHOLIC—Ss. Locust, w. Franklin. Pastor, Rev. E. R. W. Bersch.

ARMOUR MISSION—33d se. cor. Armour av. Pastor, Rev. Charles T. Wyckoff.

CHURCH OF CHRIST — Pastor, Rev. F. S. Van Eps, Auditorium Bldg. Services every Sunday morning at 10:45 o'clock.

DISCIPLES OF CHRIST—Meet every First Day at 10:30 a. m. and 7:30 p. m. at 23 and 25 Kendall.

PACIFIC GARDEN MISSION—100 E. Vanburen, Supt. Mrs. Geo. R. Clarke; Asst. Supt. Harry Monroe. Meetings every evening.

PEOPLE'S INSTITUTE — (Undenominational) Vanburen cor. Oakley av.

REORGANIZED CHURCH OF LATTER-DAY SAINTS—Franklin Hall, 70 Adams.

CONSULS IN CHICAGO.

ARGENTINE REPUBLIC—193 Vanburen. Consul, P. S. Hudson.

AUSTRO-HUNGARIAN — 1637 Michigan av. Consul, Franz Von Sponer; Vice-Consul, F. Freyesleben.

BELGIUM—539, 108 Lasalle. Consul, Charles Henrotin.

BRAZIL—406, 19 Wabash av. Consul, Stuart R. Alexander.

CHILE—57, 22d, Consul, Mathew J. Steffens.

DENMARK — 34, 70 Lasalle. Consul, Otto A. Dreier.

FRANCE—600, 56, 5th av. Consul G. André Mondehare; Chancellor, A. Jowe.

GERMAN EMPIRE—501, 120 Randolph. Consul, Carl Buenz; Vice-Consul, F. Bopp.

GREAT BRITAIN—4, 72 Dearborn. Consul, James Hayes Sadler; Vice-Consui, W. H. Bankes-Price.

GREECE — Corn Exchange Bank. Consul, General Charles L.Hutchinson:

HONDURAS — 1, 124 Dearborn. Consul, Edward E. Day.

ITALY—500, 56, 5th av. Consul, Count Girolamo Marazzi

MEXICO—30, 126 Washington. Consul, Felipe Berriozabal, jr.

NETHERLANDS—85 Washington. Consul, Geo. Birkhoff, jr.

PERU—301, 358 Dearborn. Consul. Charles H. Sergel.

RUSSIA — Chicago Beach Hotel. Consul, M. H. de Thal.

SPAIN—42, 115 Monroe. Consul, Hobart Chatfield Chatfield-Taylor.

SWEDEN & NORWAY—Lasalle cor. Lake. V. Consul, John R. Lindgren; Sec. Count C. A. Wachtmeister.

SWITZERLAND—167 Washington. Consul, A. Holinger.

TURKEY—539, 108 Lasalle. Consul, Chas. Henrotin.

URUGUAY REPUBLIC—193 Vanburen, Consul C. C. Turner.

EDUCATIONAL.

BOARD OF EDUCATION.

12th floor, 109 Randolph.
Office open—From 9 a. m. to 5 p. m.

OFFICE HOURS OF SUPERINTENDENT AND SUPERVISORS.

Superintendent and Assistant Superintendents—From 9 a.m. to 5 p.m.
Supervisor of Vocal Music, Grammar Department—Monday, Tuesday, Wednesday, Thursday, 4 p.m. to 5 p.m., Saturday, 10 a.m. to 12 m.
Supervisor of Drawing—Monday and Friday, from 4 to 5 p.m.
Supervisor of German — Monday, Wednesday and Friday, from 4 to 5 p.m.

Business Manager—Daily, from 4 to 5 p.m.
Chief Engineer—From 4 to 5 p.m.

OFFICERS OF THE BOARD.

President—Alfred S. Trude.
Vice-President—Daniel R. Cameron.
Secretary—W. A. S. Graham; Superintendent—Albert G. Lane.
Assistant Superintendents of Schools —Edward C. Delano, Albert R. Sabin, Ella F. Young, Elizabeth L. Hartney, Leslie Lewis, James Hannan, A. F. Nightingale, A. Kirk.
Supervisor of EveningSchools—James H. Brayton.
Business Manager—John A. Guilford.
Auditor—George G. Custer.
Attorney—Donald L. Morrill.
School Agent — Charles C. Chase, 1103 Chamber of Commerce bldg.
Chief Engineer—Thomas J. Waters.

COOK COUNTY BOARD OF EDUCATION.

Room 320, Court House.
Henry F. Donovan, Pres't., 302 Webster av.; O. T. Bright, Sec'y., 320 Court House; Henry Biroth, 485, 25th St.; S. D. Walden, 1206 Titie & Trust bldg.; Nelson A. Cool, Blue Island; Geo. Struckman, 203 Court House; John R. Lindgren, 154 Lake; C. S. Cutting, 812 Cham. Com. bldg.
O. T. Bright, sec. and superintendent.

Free Kindergartens.

FREE KINDERGARTEN ASSOCIATION—Armour av. cor. 33d. H. H. Higinbotham, Pres.; W. E. Kelley, Treas.; Hon. Thos. C. MacMillan, Sec.; Mrs. L. A. Hagans, Cor. Sec.

NORMAL AND TRAINING DEPARTMENT.

Faculty—Miss Eva B. Whitmore, General Superintendent and Instructor in Occupations; Miss Alice Temple, Assistant Superintendent; Miss Anna E. Bryan, Principal of Normal and Training Department, and Instructor in Theory and Gifts; Miss Margaret Morley, Natural Sciences, Psychology, Physical Culture and Methods; Dr. F. W. Gunsaulus, Education and Christianity; Miss Mari-Ruef Hofer, Music.

THE KINDERGARTENS.

ADA STREET—Ada cor. Fulton.
ALUMNÆ—Ewing nr. S. Halsted.
ARMOUR—Thirty-third and Armour av.
BETHESDA—406 S. Clark.
ELEANOR REID—2541 Calumet av.
ERIE CHAPEL—Erie st. nr. Noble
FORWARD MOVEMENT—Halsted cor. Congress.

..STREETER HOSPITAL..

2646 CALUMET AVENUE.

For the Treatment of Diseases of Women.

The Finest Private Hospital in the World: Rooms, Board and Nursing, from $30.00 to $50.00 per week.

G. L. HARVEY,
Manager.

JOHN W. STREETER, M. D.,
Chief Surgeon.

58

GERMAN—Locke and Bonaparte.

HALSTED STREET—784 S. Halsted.

HOME FOR THE FRIENDLESS —Twentieth and Wabash av.

LINCOLN PARK—Garfield av. and Mohawk.

LINCOLN STREET — Ambrose cor. Lincoln.

MARIE CHAPEL—Wentworth av. and Bushnell.

PATRIOTIC ORDER DAUGHTERS OF AMERICA—Chicago av. cor. Lasalle av.

PLYMOUTH—3027 Butler.

RAILROAD CHAPEL—3825 Dearborn.

RAYMOND MISSION—Poplar av. cor. 30th.

SIXTH PRESBYTERIAN — Vincennes av. cor. 36th.

ST. PAUL'S—Thirtieth and Prairie av.

TABERNACLE—Morgan and Indiana.

TALCOTT—169 W. Adams.

UNION AV.—Union av. cor. 44th.

UNIVERSITY CONGREGATIONAL CHURCH—Madison av. cor. 56th.

HOSPITALS.

ACACIA MASONIC HOSPITAL—369 Washington boul.

ALEXIAN BROTHERS HOSPITAL—539 to 569 N. Market.

AUGUSTANA HOSPITAL — 480 Cleveland av.

BENNETT HOSPITAL—Ada nw. cor. Fulton.

CHICAGO BAPTIST HOSPITAL —32 and 34 Centre av.

CHICAGO CHARITY HOSPITAL — 2407 Dearborn.

CHICAGO EMERGENCY HOSPITAL—194 Superior.

CHICAGO HOMEOPATHIC HOSPITAL—S. Wood se. cor. York.

CHICAGO HOSPITAL—Champlain av. cor. Fortieth.

CHICAGO HOSPITAL FOR WOMEN AND CHILDREN—W. Adams nw. cor. Paulina.

CHICAGO OPHTHALMIC HOSPITAL—607 W. Vanburen.

CHICAGO POLICLINIC HOSPITAL — 174 and 176 Chicago av.

COOK COUNTY HOSPITAL—W. Harrison cor. Wood.

DETENTION HOSPITAL—Wood nw. cor. Polk.

GERMAN HOSPITAL—754 and 756 Larrabee.

HAHNEMANN HOSPITAL—2811 to 2815 Groveland av.

ILLINOIS CHARITABLE EYE AND EAR INFIRMARY—227 W. Adams.

LINNAEAN HOSPITAL—1732 Diversey

MARINE HOSPITAL—N. Halsted nr. Graceland av. five miles north of court house, on lake shore. Office, Custom House bldg. room 20.

MAURICE PORTER MEMORIAL FREE HOSPITAL FOR CHILDREN —606 Fullerton av.

MERCY HOSPITAL—Calumet av. cor. Twenty-sixth.

MICHAEL REESE HOSPITAL—Twenty-ninth ne. cor. Groveland av.

POST-GRADUATE HOSPITAL—(Under direction of Post-Graduate Medical School). 819 W. Harrison

PRESBYTERIAN HOSPITAL—300 S. Wood.

PROVIDENT HOSPITAL AND TRAINING SCHOOL—2900 Dearborn.

ST. ELIZABETH'S HOSPITAL—Davis se. cor. Lemoyne.

ST. JOSEPH'S HOSPITAL—360 Garfield av. nw. cor. Burling.

ST. LUKE'S HOSPITAL—1420 to 1434 Indiana av.

STREETER HOSPITAL—2646 Calumet av.

WESLEY HOSPITAL—2459 Dearborn

WOMAN'S HOSPITAL OF CHICAGO—Thirty-second nw. cor. Rhodes av.

LIBRARIES AND READING ROOMS.

ARMOUR MISSION—Thirty-third se. cor. Butterfield.

CHICAGO ATHENÆUM LIBRARY—18 to 26 Vanburen. Open week days from 8 a.m. to 9 p.m.

CHICAGO BRANCH OF THE INTERNATIONAL TRACT AND

MISSIONARY SOCIETY, 51 Ashland boul.

CHICAGO HISTORICAL SOCIETY LIBRARY—Dearborn av. nr. cor Ontario.

CHICAGO LAW INSTITUTE—Room 414 County bldg.

CHICAGO PUBLIC LIBRARY—4th floor. City Hall. Open week days from 9 a.m. to 10 p.m. Sundays 9 a.m. to 6 p.m. Regular meetings of the Board 2d and 4th Saturdays of each month, at 3 p.m.

CHICAGO THEOSOPHICAL SOCIETY LIBRARY—Room 48 Athenaeum bldg. 26 Vanburen.

HAMMOND LIBRARY—81 Ashland boul.

HYDE PARK LYCEUM READING ROOM AND LIBRARY-136, 53d.

NEWBERRY LIBRARY—Walton pl. bet. Clark and Dearborn av.

PULLMAN PUBLIC LIBRARY—73 and 75 Arcade bldg. (P.)

RAVENSWOOD PUBLIC LIBRARY—2517 Commercial

SOUTH CHICAGO PUBLIC LIBRARY—Bowen School bldg. 93d cor. Houston av.

UNION CATHOLIC LIBRARY ASSOCIATION—94 Dearborn. Open from 12.30 to 5 p.m.

WESTERN NEW CHURCH UNION BOOK ROOM—17 Vanburen. Open 9 a.m. to 5 p.m.

WHEELER THEOLOGICAL LIBRARY—1113 Washington boul.

YOUNG MEN'S CHRISTIAN ASSOCIATION READING ROOM—Open daily from 9 a.m. to 10 p.m. except Sundays, 153 Lasalle; 542 W. Monroe; Wilson av., Ravenswood; 250, 92d (S. C.); Larrabee cor. Grant pl.; Garfield boul. and Shields av.; Canal, W. Kinzie, Pullman, 34 Arcade bldg.

YOUNG MEN'S CHRISTIAN ASSOCIATION READING ROOM (Scandinavian)—Reading room and library open every evening from 7 to 10:30.

YOUNG MEN'S LIBRARY (Colored)—400 Dearborn. Open daily from 7:30 a.m. to 10:30 p.m.

MILITARY.

United States Army.

Stationed at Headquarters, Dept. of the Missouri, Pullman bldg., southwest cor. Michigan av. and Adams st.

Major General Thomas H. Ruger, U. S. Army, room No. 406.

Lieutenant Chas. G. Lyman, 2d Cavalry, Aide-de-Camp, room No. 407.

Lieutenant Colonel James P. Martin, A. G. Dept., Assistant Adjutant General, room No. 403.

Colonel Edward M. Heyl, Inspector General, room No. 401.

Major Stephen W. Groesbeck, J. A. G. Dept., Judge Advocate, room 610.

Brevet Lieutenant Colonel Jeremiah H. Gilman, Sub. Dept., Chief Commissary of Subsistence, room 417.

Lieut. Colonel Albert Hartsuff, Medical Department, Medical Director, room No. 404.

Brevet Brigadier General Judson D. Bingham, Assistant Quartermaster General, Chief Quartermaster, room No. 415.

Lieutenant Colonel George W. Candee, Pay Department, Chief Paymaster, room No. 506.

Captain William L. Marshall, Corps Engineers, Engineer Officer, room 411.

Captain Jesse M. Lee, 9th Infantry, Assistant to I. G., room 401.

Major Forrest H. Hathaway, Q. M. Dept. Disbursing Officer, room No. 416.

Major George W. Baird, Pay Dept., Paymaster, room 405.

First Lieutenant Henry Jervey, Corps Engineer. In charge of River and Harbor Improvements, 2258 Wabash av.

Lieutenant Colonel Thomas C. Sullivan, Subsistence Department, Depot Commissary of Subsistence, 248-250 Illinois.

Captain Louis S. Tesson, Med. Dept., Attending Surgeon, 511 Pullman bldg.

First Lieut. Joseph A. Gaston. 8th Cavalry, Recruiting Officer, 10 S.Clark.

Captain Philip Reade, 3d Infantry, Recruiting Officer, 82 W. Madison and 427 State.

Illinois First Brigade National Guard.

Stationed at Chicago Headquarters, 712 to 715 Old Colony bldg., Brigadier General HarrisA. Wheeler, Commanding. Personal Staff: Aides-de-Camp, First Lieut. Gilbert M. Weeks and First Lieut. Wm. J. McNally; Brigade Staff: Asst. Adjt. General, Lieutenant Colonel Wm. N. Pelouze; Lieutenant Colonel LeRoy T. Steward, Asst. Inspector General; Lieutenant Colonel Frank H. Ray, Inspector Small Arms Practice; Lieutenant Colonel . M. Oliver, Judge Advocate; Major James

H. Etheredge, Surgeon; Captain Joseph Leiter. Quartermaster; Captain Chas. A. Stevenson, Commissary of Subsistence; Captain R. H. Aiken, 6th Inf. Range Officer; First Lieut. Wm. J. Lloyd. 2d Inf. Signal Officer.

First Regiment Infantry.

Armory 1542 Michigan av. Field and Staff Officers—Colonel, Henry L. Turner; Lieut. Col. George V. Lauman; Majors, Joseph B. Sanborn and Edgar B. Tolman; Adjutant, Captain W. L. De Remer; Surgeon, Major Chas. Adams, M.D.; Assistant Surgeon, John W. Streeter; Quartermaster, First Lieut. A. L. Bell; Inspector of Rifle Practice, Captain Eugene R. Cox; Chaplain, Captain Hiram W. Thomas. Company A—Captain Benj. F. Patrick jr. Company B—Captain W. J. Sanderson. Company C—Captain Anson L. Bolte. Company D—Captain J. H. Barnett. Compauy E—Captain William F. Knoch. Company F—Captain J. M. Eddy jr., Company G—Captain G. W. Bristol. Company H—Captain Chas. G. Bolte. Company I—Captain F. W. Chenoweth. Company K—Captain Willis J. Wells. Company L—Captain John S. Beeler, Company M—Captain Edward H. Switzer.

Second Regiment Infantry.

Armories Washington boul. ne. cor. Curtis. and 135 Michigan av. Field and Staff Officers—-Colonel, George M. Moulton; Lieutenant Colonel, W. D. Hotchkiss; Majors, Frank B. Logan, W. P. Dusenberry and James E. Stewart; Adjutant, Captain Holman G. Purinton; Inspector of Small Arms Practice, Captain J. P. Sherwin; Quartermaster, First Lieutenant Fred W. Laas; Surgeon, Major G. F. Lydston; Assistant Surgeon, Captain Malcolm Gunn; Chaplain, Captain H. W. Bolton.

Company A—Captain Philip Samuels. Company B—Captain George Meehan. Company C—Captain T. I. Mair. Company D--Captain W. A. Chadwick. Company E--Captain M.L. Vanderkloot. Company F—Captain Joseph I. Kelly. Company G—Captain Willis McFeely. Company H—Captain John J. Garrity. Company I—Captain Wm. E. Hoinville. Company K—Captain E. G. Brown. Company M—Captain Wm. B. Alexander.

Chicago Zouaves meet Monday at Battery D Armory. Captain, T. J. Ford; First Lieutenant, Benj. A. Case; Second Lieutenant, F. L. Huguelet.

Seventh Regiment Infantry.

Headquarters and Armory 23 Lake. Field and Staff Officers: Commanding Colonel, Francis T. Colby; Lieut. Col., Marcus Kavanagh: Major, Garrett J. Carroll; Surgeon, Major Michael E. McGrath; Adjutant, Captain Thomas L. Hartigan; Inspector of Small Arms Practice, Captain Jeremiah S. Hyland; Chaplain, Captain Edward A. Kelly. Company A—Captain Daniel T. McGraw. Company B—Captain Michael Punch; Company C—Captain Michael D. Sullivan. Company D—Captain Edmund P. Burke. Company E—Captain Daniel Moriarty. Compauy F—Captain J. J. Sisk. Company G—Captain Thos. Garry. Company H—Captain William J. Carroll.

First Battalion Illinois Naval Militia.

Armories 135 Michigan av. and Battle Ship Illinois. Lieut. Com., B. M' Shaffner; Staff: Adjutant, Lieutenant Raymond B. Swigart; Ordnance Officer, Lieutenant William J. Wilson; Paymaster, Lieutenant Horatio L. Wait; Surgeon, Lieutenant Samuel J. Jones. Divisions — First Division: Lieutenant Henry A. Allen, Commanding; Lieutenant John R. Eldred, jr., grade; Ensign, George F. Jewett; Ensign, Henry Dolese. Second Division: Lieutenant William M. Robinson, Commanding; Lieutenant John A. Ubsdell, jr., grade; Ensign, William H. Kirkland. Third Division: Lieutenant Herbert McNulty, jr., grade; Ensign, Norman B. Holdane; Ensign, Clarence B. Shaffner. Fourth Division: Lieutenant Frank H. Kochersperger, Commanding; Lieutenant, J. B. Marshall; Ensign, Charles B. Wilmarth; Master at Arms, Victor B. Strelitz; Chief Gunner's Mate, William J. Warner; Signal Quartermaster, R. B. Moore; Engineer, E. H. Kenny.

Battery D First Artillery.

Armory 145 Michigan av. Captain, First Lieutenant, Alfred Russell; Senior Second Lieutenant, William Austin; Junior Second Lieutenant, Axel Lindman.

Cavalry Troop A.

Armory 135 Michigan av. Captain, Paul B. Lino; First Lieutenant, G. C. Lenke; Second Lieutenant, J. Howard Ireland.

Chicago City Troop.

Commissioned Officers—Captain, M. L. C. Funkhouser, 414 The Temple;

First Lieutenant, Joseph B. Keen; Second Lieutenant, Frank B. Alsip.

Non-Commissioned Officers— First Sergeant, L. F. Brown; Second Sergeant, O. W. McMichael; Third Sergeant, W.R. Toppan; Fourth Sergeant, Leo Wampold (Quartermaster); First Corporal, A. L. Bournique; Second Corporal, E. J. Gaston; Third Corporal, S. S. Baker; Fourth Corporal, I. F. Laing.

Board of Directors—M. L. C. Funkhouser, Joseph B. Keen, Frank R. Alsip, Will H. Clark, W. R. Toppan, S. S. Baker, H. N. Morris.

Chicago Hussars.

Commissioned Officers—Captain Edwin L. Brand, 1610 Michigan av.; First Lieutenant, Thomas S. Quincy; Second Lieutenant, J. J. Murray.

Staff—Adjutant, P. R. McLeod; Judge Advocate, J. W. Duncan; Inspector, Matt Pinkerton; Quartermaster, Charles Kern; Surgeon, Stewart Johnstone, M.D.; Chaplain, Rev. O. P. Gifford.

Non-Commissioned Officers—First Sergeant, Waldo H. Howe; Second Sergeant, J. S. Townsend; Third Sergeant, Sol Wolf; Fourth Sergeant, F. K. Higbee; Fifth Sergeant, Roland J. Crandal; Sixth Sergeant, F. H. Russ; Seventh Sergeant, Joseph Horer; Color Sergeant, Maurice Hecht; Chief Trumpeter, Lieutenant James R. Thacker; Troop Veterinary, Chas. E. Sayre; First Corporal, George Getz; Second Corporal, F. W. McIntosh; Third Corporal. Harry W. Kern; Fourth Corporal, George Miller.

Civic Department—Board of Directors, 1893—Edwin L. Brand, M. L. C. Funkhouser, Joseph B. Keen, J. J. Murray, Will H. Clark, Matt W. Pinkerton, J. F. Latham.

Recruiting Committee—F.H.Higbie, Louis F. Brown, O. W. McMichael.

MUSEUMS.

CHICAGO ACADEMY OF SCIENCES—Matthew Laflin Memorial Bldg., Lincoln Park. Pres. S. H. Peabody; Sec. Frank C. Baker; Rec. Wm. H. Knap.

FIELD COLUMBIAN MUSEUM—Jackson Park. Pres. Edward E. Ayer; 1st Vice-Pres. Martin A. Ryerson; 2d Vice-Pres. Norman B. Ream; Secretary, George Manierre; Secretary, Byron L. Smith; Trustees—Ed. E. Ayer, Owen F. Aldis, G. R. Davis C. H. McCormick, Martin A. Ryerson,

H. N. Higinbotham, Watson F. Blair, H. W. Jackson, George Manierre, Edwin Walker, G. E. Adams, W. J. Chalmers Arthur B. Jones, Norman B. Ream, N. Williams; Director F. J. V. Skiff; Curator Anthropology, W. H. Holmes; Curator Botany, C. F. Milspaugh; Curator Zoology except Ornitholog, D. G. Elliott; Hon. Curator Ornithology, C. B. Cory; Curator Geology, O. C. Farrington; Curator Economic Geology, H. W. Nichols; Recorder and Librarian, E. L. Burchard; Accountant, D. C. Davies; Gen. Supt. of Building, J. B. Goodman.

PARKS.

DOUGLAS—W. 12th, Fairfield av. W. Nineteenth and Albany avs.

DOUGLAS MONUMENT SQUARE—Foot 35th.

ELLIS—fr. Prospect pl. to Thirty-seventh w. of Cottage Grove av.

GARFIELD—W. Madison, S.Homan av. W. Lake, etc.

HUMBOLDT — W. North av. S. California av. W. Division, etc.

JACKSON—The Lake, 56th, Stony Island av. 67th

JEFFERSON—W. Adams, Throop, W. Monroe, Loomis.

LAKE FRONT — Michigan av. fr. Jackson to Lake Park pl.

LINCOLN—The Lake, North av. N. 'lark, N. Park av. Diversey av.

MIDWAY PLAISANCE — Cottage Grove av. to Stony Island av. bet. 59th and 60th.

SOUTH—See Jackson and Washington Parks.

UNION—Ogden av. Warren av. Ashland av. W. Lake, Bryan pl.

VERNON—Lytle, Sibley, Gilpin pl. Macalister pl.

WASHINGTON—Cottage Grove av. 51st, South Park av. 60th

WASHINGTON SQ. — N. Clark, Washington pl. Dearborn av. Walton pl.

WICKER—Park, Fowler, N. Robey.

PUBLIC HALLS, BLOCKS, AND BUILDINGS.

Adams Express bldg,—185 to 189 Dearborn.

Alabama Flats—Prairie av. cor. 31st.

Allen Flats—143 and 145 Oakwood boul.

American Express Co.'s Bldg—72 to 78 Monroe.

Apollo Hall—5th floor, 69 State.

Arcade Bldg.—156 to 164 Clark.

Arcade Bldg.—Pullman.
Argyle Bldg.—Jackson nw. cor. Michigan av.
Arizona The—Greenwood av., 42d and Lake av.
Armour Flats—33d and Dearborn.
Art Institute The—Michigan av. opp. Adams
Ashland Blk.—53 to 65 Clark.
Ashland The—213 Ashland boul.
Association Bldg.—153 and 155 Lasalle.
Athenæum Bldg.—18 to 26 Vanburen.
Atlas Blk.—45 to 61 Wabash av.
Auditorium Bldg. — Congress, Michigan av. and Wabash av.
Audubon The—63 and 65 E. Pearson
Avon Flats—99, 33d.
Ayer's Bldg.—166 to 172 State
Bay State Bldg. —State se. cor. Randolph.
Belden Flats—295 and 297 Belden av.
Belvidere Flats—3100 Cottage Grove av.
Benton Flats—Ohio sw. cor. Pine.
Berkshire Flats—2505 Michigan av.
Board of Trade—Head of Lasalle.
Borden Blk. — Randolph nw. cor. Dearborn.
Bort Bldg.—19 and 21 Quincy.
Boyce Bldg.—112 and 114 Dearborn.
Boylston Block—265 to 273 Dearborn.
Brand's Hall—160 to 170 N. Clark.
Brother Jonathan Bldg. — 2 and 4 Sherman.
Bryan Blk.—160 to 174 Lasalle.
Calumet Bldg.—187 to 191 Lasalle.
Calumet Flats—248 Erie.
Cambria Flats—290 and 292 Rush
Cambridge Flats—39th nw. cor. Ellis av.
Canterbury Flats—6034 and 6036 Park End av.
Carleton Flats—63, 18th.
Caxton Bldg.—328 to 334 Dearborn.
Central Market—State ne. cor. South Water.
Central Mnfrs. Blk—74 to 88 Market.
Central Music Hall — State se. cor. Randolph.
Central Union Blk—Madison nw. cor. Market.
Chamber of Commerce Bldg.—Washington se. cor. Lasalle.
Champlain Bldg.—State nw. cor. Madison
Charlevoix Flats—87 Rush.
Chemical Bank Bldg.—85 and 87 Dearborn.
Chicago Herald Bldg—154 to 156 Washington.
Chicago Opera House Bldg.—Clark sw. cor. Washington.
Chicago Stock Exch. Bldg. — Lasalle sw. cor. Washington
Chicago. Title and Trust Co. Bldg.—98 to 102 Washington.

Chickering Hall—241 Wabash av.
Cisco Bldg.—84 Washington.
Citizen's Bank Bldg. — 119 and 121 Lasalle.
City Hall—Washington cor. Lasalle.
Clarendon Hotel—152 N. Clark
Cleveland Flats—659 to 665 Cleveland av.
Clinton The—1423 to 1429 Michigan av.
Cobb's Bldg.—120 to 128 Dearborn.
Columbia Theatre—104 to 110 Monroe.
Columbus Memorial Bldg. —State se. cor. Washington
Commerce Bldg.—14 and 16 Pacific av.
Commercial Nat. Bank Bldg.—Dearborn se. cor. Monroe.
Como Bldg.—323 and 325 Dearborn.
Corinthian Hall—187 Kinzie.
Continental Bank Bldg.—218 Lasalle.
Counselmah Bldg.—Lasalle cor. Jackson.
County Bldg.—Clark cor. Washington.
Covenant Hall—36 Lasalle.
Criminal Ct. Bldg. — Michigan cor. Dearborn av.
Criterion Theater—274 Sedgwick.
Custom House.—Clark cor. Adams.
Dakota Flats.—3025 Prairie av.
Dale Bldg.—308 to 316 Dearborn.
Dearborn Hall—40 Dearborn.
DeSoto Flats—3663 Wabash av.
Dexter Bldg.—80 and 82 Adams.
Dickey Bldg.—34 to 46 Dearborn.
Donohue & Henneberry's Bldg.—407 to 425 Dearborn.
Ely Bldg.—Wabash av. sw. cor. Monroe.
Empire Blk.—128 and 130 Lasalle.
Equitable Bldg.—106 to 110 Dearborn.
Erie Flats—Lake av. sw. cor. 37th.
Erie The—148 N. State.
Evaline Flats—5902 Michigan av.
Evening Post Bldg.—162-164 Washington.
Exchange Bldg.—Union Stock Yards.
First Cavalry Armory—Foot Monroe st.
First Inf. I. N. G. Armory—Michigan av. nw. cor. 16th.
First Nat. Bank Bldg.—Dearborn nw. cor. Monroe.
Florence Flats—16 to 22 Bellevue pl.
Foote Blk.—Clark sw. cor. Monroe.
Forbes Blk.—193 Washington.
Franklin Bldg.—341 to 349 Dearborn.

FREIBERG'S OPERA HOUSE—
180, 182 and 184, 22d.
Fullerton Blk.—90 to 96 Dearborn.
Gaff Bldg.—230 to 236 Lasalle.
Gault House—W. Madison cor. Clinton
Girard Bldg.—298 to 306 Dearborn.
Glencoe Flats—344 Michigan av.
Grand Opera House—87 Clark.
Greenebaum Bldg.—72 to 82 Fifth av,

Halsted St. M. E. Ch. Blk.—778 S. Halsted.
Hampden Flats—39th ne. cor. Langley av.
Hampshire Blk. — Lasalle se. cor. Monroe.
Hartford Bldg.—134 to 146 Dearborn.
Haymarket Theatre.—161 to 169 W. Madison.
Hodge's Bldg.—Indiana av. ne. cor. Twenty-second.
Home Insurance Bldg.—Lasalle ne. cor. Adams.
Hotel Alvard—Cottage Grove av. cor. Oakwood boul.
Hotel DeLincoln.—60 and 62 Wisconsin.
Hotel LaVita—211 and 213 Dearborn av.
Hotel Rutland—282 Indiana.
Hotel Vendome—780 North Park av.
Hotel Windham—52 and 54 Rush.
Hotel Worth—435 Washington boul.
Houghton Flats—584 Dearborn av.
Howland Blk.—174 to 192 Dearborn.
Illinois Bank Bldg. — 111 to 117 Dearborn.
Imperial Bldg.—252 to 260 Clark.
Ingleside Flats.—1 to 5 Park av.
Insurance Exchange Bldg. — Lasalle sw. cor. Adams.
Inter-Ocean Bldg. — Dearborn nw. cor. Madison.
Isabella Bldg.—48 Vanburen.
Ivanhoe Flats.—Thirty-sixth cor. Cottage Grove av.
Ivar Flats. — Thirtieth cor. Cottage Grove av.
Jaeschke Flats—296 Ohio.
Journal Bldg.—159 and 161 Dearborn.
Kedzie Bldg.--120 and 122 Randolph.
Kenilworth Flats. — Thirty-sixth nw. cor. Ellis av.
Kenosha Flats—2976 South Park av.
Kimball Hall.—243 to 249 Wabash av.
Kinzie Flats—144 Pine.
Klare's Hall—72 N. Clark.
Knickerbocker Flats—4160 Ellis av.
Lakeside Bldg. — Clark sw. cor. Adams.
Lakeside The—1839 Indiana av.
Lasalle Blk.—Lasalle nw. cor. Madison.
Lasalle Flats.—204 and 206 Cass.
Leamington Flats—94 to 98, 37th.
Lenox Bldg.—88 and 90 Washington.
Locust Apartment Bldg.—113 and 115 Locust.
Loomis Bldg.—2 to 6 Clark.
Loraine Flats—Thirty-sixth ne. cor. Ellis av.
Lumber Exchange. — South Water nw. cor. Franklin.
Lumberman's Exchange. — 238 South Water.

Majestic The—Walton pl. sw. cor. Rush.
Major Blk.—139 to 151 Lasalle.
Mallers Bldg.—226 and 228 Lasalle.
Manhattan Bldg. 307 to 321 Dearborn.
Marine Bldg.—152 to 158 Lake.
Marion Flats—248 Ohio.
Marquette Bldg. — Dearborn nw. cor. Adams.
Marquette Flats.—85 Rush.
Martine's Halls. — 55 S. Ada and 22d nw. cor. Indiana av.
Mason Blk.—92 and 94 Washington.
Masonic Temple—State ne. cor. Randolph.
McCormick Blk.—67 to 73 Dearborn.
McCormick J. L. Bldg.—15 to 27 Wabash av.
McNeil Bldg.—128 and 130 Clark.
McVicker's Theatre Bldg.—78 to 84 Madison.
Medinah Temple—Fifth av. ne. cor. Jackson.
Melrose The—3756 Ellis av.
Mentone Flats.—146 Dearborn av.
Mentor Blk.—163 State.
Mercantile Bldg.—112 to 118 Lasalle.
Merchants' Bldg.—Lasalle nw. cor. Washington.
Methodist Church Blk. — Clark se. cor. Washington.
Metropolitan Blk.—159 to 165 Randolph.
Milano Flats.—338 Ohio.
Monadnock Bldg.—Jackson cor. Dearborn.
Monon Blk.—320 to 326 Dearborn.
Montauk Blk.—111 to 117 Monroe.
Morton Flats.—203 and 205 Ontario.
Morton Flats.—Michigan av. cor. 18th.
Mueller's Hall—356 to 364 North av.
National Life Ins. Bldg. — 159 to 163 Lasalle.
Needham Flats—49 and 51 Thirty-second
Newberry The—225 to 231 Dearborn av.
Newport Flats—77 to 83 Pine.
New York Life Ins. Bldg.—Lasalle ne. cor. Monroe.
Normandy Flats—2300 and 2302 Indiana av.
Norwood Flats—3000 Indiana av.
Ogden Bldg.—Clark sw. cor. Lake.
Ohio Flats.—344 Ohio.
Old Colony Bldg.—Vanburen se. cor. Dearborn.
Omaha Bldg.—Vanburen se. cor. Pacific av.
Oneida The—5100 Hibbard av.
Ontario Flats.—N. State sw. cor. Ontario.
Open Board Bldg.—18 to 24 Pacific av.
Oriental Bldg. and Hall—122 Lasalle.
Ormonde The—49 to 55 Astor.
Otis Bldg.—Madison sw. cor. State.

C. JEVNE & Co.

......Importing
Grocers.

**Wholesale and Retail Purveyors of Choicest Edibles
and Food Products.**

110-112 MADISON ST.

109-111 WABASH AVE.

66

Otis Blk.—138 to 158 Lasalle.
Owings Bldg.—215 Dearborn.
Oxford Bldg.—84 and 86 Lasalle.
Ozark Flats—3501 Wabash av.
Parker Bldg.—95 and 97 Washington.
Pelham Flats—544 to 552 Garfield av.
Phenix Bldg.—See W. U. Bldg.
Pickwick Bldg. — Michigan av. cor. 20th.
Plaza The—N. Clark se. cor. North av.
Pontiac Bldg.—Dearborn nw. cor. Harrison.
Portland Blk.—103 to 109 Dearborn.
Post-Office.—Clark se. cor. Adams.
Potomac The—3000 to 3012 Michigan av.
Powers Bldg.—Madison nw. cor. Michigan av.
Prairie Flats.—3031 Prairie av.
Pullman Bldg. — Adams sw. cor. Michigan av.
Quincy Bldg.—Clark ne. cor. Adams.
Quinlan Bldg.—81 and 83 Clark.
Rand-McNallyBldg.—162 to 182 Adams.
Rawson Bldg.—149 and 151 State.
Real Estate Board Bldg.—Dearborn ne. cor. Randolph.
Reaper Blk.—Clark ne. cor. Washington.
Recital Hall—Auditorium Bldg.
Reliance Bldg.—State sw. cor. Washington
Renfost The—Cottage Grove av. cor. 52d.
Rialto Bldg. — 135 to 153 VanBuren, rear Board of Trade.
Rookery Bldg. — Lasalle se. cor. Adams.
Rosalie Music Hall—Rosalie ct. sw. cor. 57th.
Royal Insurance Bldg. — 165 to 173 Jackson and 108 to 116 Quincy.
Ryerson Bldg.—45 to 49 Randolph.
St. Agnes Flats—4448 and 4450 St. Lawrence av.
St. Benedict's Flats.—Cass ne. cor. Chicago av.
Schiller Bldg.—103 to 109 Randolph.
Schloesser Blk.—200 to 210 Lasalle.
Sears Bldg.—99 and 101 Washington.
Second Regt. Armory. — Washington boul. ne. cor. Curtis.
Seville Flats.—159 and 161 Locust.
Sherwood Flats.—105 to 109, 37th.
Shreve Blk.—91 and 93 Washington.
Sibley Bldg.—2 to 16 N. Clark.
Sorento—Clark ne. cor. Kinzie.
Staats Zeitung Bldg.—91 to 99 Fifth av.
Stewart Bldg.—State nw. cor. Washington.
Stock Exchange Bldg.—167 to 171 Dearborn.
Stratford Flats—93, 33d.
Superior Blk.—75 to 79 Clark.

Tacoma Bldg.—Lasalle ne. cor. Madison.
Taylor Bldg.—140 to 146 Monroe.
Telephone Bldg.—203 Washington.
Temple Ct.—217 to 225 Dearborn.
The Temple—Lasalle sw. cor. Monroe.
Times Bldg.—Washington nw. cor. Fifth av.
Title and Trust Bldg.—98 to 102 Washington.
Torino Flats.—337 Indiana.
Traders' Bldg.—6 to 12 Pacific av.
Traynor Bldg.—182 State.
Tribune Bldg. — Dearborn se. cor. Madison.
Tudor The—4300 to 4316 Ellis av.
Union Bldg.—100 to 110 Lasalle.
Unity Bldg.—75 to 81 Dearborn.
University Club Bldg.—116 and 118 Dearborn.
U. S. Express Co.'s Bldg.—87 and 89 Washington.
VanDyke The—3953 Michigan av.
Vendome Club Hotel—Oglesby av. sw. cor. 62d.
Vendome Flats.—Ogden av. ne. cor. W. Madison.
Victoria Flats.—52 and 54 Rush.
Wacousta Flats.—275 Erie.
Wadsworth Bldg.—175 to 181 Madison.
Walton Flats.—307 N. Clark sw. cor. Locust.
Warren Apartment Bldg. — Warren av. sw. cor. Ogden av.
Western Bank Note Bldg.—Madison sw. cor. Michigan av.
Western Union Bldg—138 Jackson.
Westminster Flats—6050 and 6052 Park End av.
Westminster Hotel—462 N. Clark.
Wheeler Bldg.—6 and 8 Sherman.
Willard Hall — Monroe sw. cor. Lasalle.
Willoughby Bldg.—Franklin nw. cor. Jackson.
Windsor Theater. — 466 and 468 N. Clark.
Woodstock The—2728 Wabash av.
Yale Flats—Yale ne, cor. 66th.
Yorkshire Hotel—1837 Michigan av.

THEATRES AND PLACES OF AMUSEMENT.

ACADEMY OF MUSIC — Halsted near Madison.

ALHAMBRA THEATRE—State cor. 20th.

AUDITORIUM, THE — Congress cor. Wabash av.

CASINO—Wabash av. and Jackson.

CENTRAL MUSIC HALL — State cor. Randolph.

CHICAGO OPERA HOUSE—Washington sw. cor. Clark.

COLUMBIA THEATRE — 108 and 110 Monroe.

CRITERION THEATRE — 274 Sedgwick.

EMPIRE THEATRE — 152 W. Madison.

GRAND OPERA HOUSE — 87 Clark.

HAVLIN'S THEATRE — Wabash av. and Nineteenth.

HAYMARKET THEATRE—Madison east of Halsted.

HOOLEY'S THEATRE—149 Randolph.

JACOBS' CLARK ST. THEATRE —Kinzie and N. Clark.

KIMBALL HALL—243 to 249 Wabash av.

LINCOLN THEATRE — 468 N. Clark

McVICKER'S THEATRE—82 Madison.

SOCIETIES, CLUBS AND ASSOCIATIONS.

ACACIA CLUB—105 S. Ashland av. See p. 381.

ÆOLUS CYCLING CLUB — 174 Evergreen av. H. L. Krinker, Sec.

ALBION CRICKET CLUB—Pres. W. B. Pearn, Sec. H. A. Watson, 774 Warren av.

ALTERNATE CLUB — 515 Fullerton av. Pres. Miss Rebecca S. Rice; V. Pres. Mrs. J. B. Hobbs and Mrs. L. C. Grosvenor; Sec. Mrs. L. N. Grosvenor, 928 Kenmore av.

AMATEUR MUSICAL CLUB — Meets alternate Mondays at Athenaeum bldg. See p. 382.

AMERICAN BAPTIST HOME MISSION SOCIETY — Gen'l Supt. Rev. Wm. M. Haigh, D.D. 177 Wabash av.

AMERICAN BAPTIST MISSIONARY UNION—Dist. Sec. Rev. C. F. Tolman, D.D. 49, 69 Dearborn, Home Sec. Rev. Henry C. Mabie, Boston, Mass.

AMERICAN BAPTIST PUBLICATION SOCIETY—Department and

Depository for the Northwest, 177 Wabash av. Depositary,Rev.F.G.Thearle; Dist. Sec. Rev. J. W. Harris.

AMERICAN BOARD OF COMMISSIONERS FOR FOREIGN MISSIONS—151 Washington. Dist. Sec. Rev. A. N. Hitchcock.

AMERICAN MISSIONARY ASSOCIATION—151 Washington. Western Sec. Rev. J. E. Roy, D.D.

AMERICAN SUNDAY-SCHOOL UNION—808, 153 Lasalle. Supt. F. G. Ensign.

AMERICAN TRACT SOCIETY— 211-213 Wabash av. Manager, Josiah Cox; Dist. Sec. Rev. E. M. Wherry, D.D.

AMERICUS CLUB — 536 Garfield av. Pres. James D. Morrison; Treas. Andrew Sullivan; Rec. Sec. N. T. Whitty; Fin. Sec. J. F. Norton

APOLLO MUSICAL CLUB—Meets at Recital Hall, Auditorium; Pres. Samuel A. Lyne; Sec. Frederick J. Wessels; Musical Director, William L. Tomlins.

ARCHITECTURAL SKETCH CLUB—274 Michigan av. Pres. Hugh M. Garden; 1st V. Pres. Stephen M. Wirts; 2d V. Pres. Alfred R. Schlesinger; Sec. Edward G. Garden

ARGONAUTS—Foot of Randolph. See p. 383.

ASHLAND CLUB.—575 Washington boul. See p. 383.

BANKER'S CLUB—See p. 385.

BAPTIST CITY MISSION SOCIETY OF CHICAGO — 122 Wabash av. Pres. Frances W. Parker; V. Pres. C. R. Henderson; Treas. Richard Street; Sec. Louis K. Gillson

BAPTIST GENERAL ASSOCIATION OF ILLINOIS—Supt. of Missions, Rev. H. C. First, Upper Alton, Ill.

BAPTIST MISSIONARY TRAINING SCHOOL—2411 Indiana av. Mrs. C. D. Morris, Preceptress. Miss M. G. Burdette, Cor. Sec.

BAPTIST PASTOR'S CONFERENCE—Meet every Monday at Y. M. C. A. bldg. at 10.30 a. m.

BAPTIST THEOLOGICAL UNION — (Sustaining the Divinity School of the University of Chicago). Pres. E. Nelson Blake; Treas. Edward Goodman, 69 Dearborn: Fin. Sec. Rev. C. E. Hewitt, D.D. 5535 Lexington av.

BAPTIST YOUNG PEOpLE'S UNION OF AMERICA—Headquarters at 122 Wabash av. Pres. John A. Chapman; Gen. Sec. Rev.F.L.Wilkins; Treas. Frank Moody.

BAPTIST YOUNG PEOPLE'S UNION OF THE CHICAGO ASSN.— Pres. Norman G. Lenington, 308 Dearborn; V. Pres. Henry Abrens; Treas. A. Braithwaite; Sec. L. T. Austermell.

BOARD OF FOREIGN MISSIONS OF THE PRESBYTERIAN CHURCH IN THE U. S. A.—Field Sec. Rev. Thomas Marshall, D.D., 48 McCormick blk.

BROTHERHOOD OF ST. ANDREW (Chicago Local Council)— 707, 59 Dearborn. Pres. W. R. Stirling; Sec. Burton F. White.

BRYN MAWR CLUB—7149 Jeffery av. See p. 386.

CALUMET CLUB—Michigan av. ne. cor. Twentieth. See p. 386.

CARLETON CLUB — 3800 Vincennes av. See p. 388.

CATLIN BOAT CLUB—Lake shore ft. Pearson. Pres, Chas. Catlin; Sec. G. S. Dixon; Capt. J. J. Griffiths.

CENTRAL ART ASSOCIATION OF AMERICA—1408 Auditorium Tower. Pres. Hamlin Garland; Ex. Sec. T. Vernette Morse; Treas. Franklin H. Head.

CHICAGO ACADEMY OF SCIENCES—Lincoln Park. Pres. S. H. Peabody; Sec. Frank C. Baker; Rec. Wm. H. Knap.

CHICAGO ART INSTITUTE — Michigan av. opposite Adams. Pres. C. L. Hutchinson; V. Pres. James H. Dole; Treas. L. J. Gage; Sec. N. H. Carpenter; Director, W. M. R. French.

CHICAGO ASTRONOMICAL SOCIETY—Pres. Elias Colbert; Sec. H. C. Ranney, 160 Lasalle; Treas. Murry Nelson; Director, Prof. G. W. Hough.

CHICAGO ATHENÆUM—18 to 26 Vanburen. Pres. Ferd W. Peck; 1st V. Pres. Wm. R. Page; 2d V. Pres. Harry G. Selfridge; Sec. and Treas. Franklin H. Head; Supt. E. Charles R. Barrett

CHICAGO ATHLETIC ASSOCIATION—Michigan av. bet. Madison and Monroe. See p. 389.

CHICAGO BAPTIST CITY MISSION SOCIETY—87, 161 Randolph. Pres. Francis W. Parker; Treas. R. Street; Sec. Louis K. Gilson.

CHICAGO BAPTIST SOCIAL UNION—Pres. Andrew McLeish; Sec. Louis K. Gilson, 87 Metropolitan blk.; Treas. Geo. A. Holloway.

CHICAGO BAR ASSOCIATION— Meets at 100 Washington. Pres. Thomas Dent; V. Pres. Horace K. Tenney and Howard Henderson;Treas. Thomas Taylor jr.; Sec. Wm. B. McIlvaine.

CHICAGO BIBLE SOCIETY — Office and Depository, 817 to 820, 155 Lasalle. Rev. J. A. Mack, Gen. Sec. and Agt.

CHICAGO CANOE CLUB—foot of 37th. Commodore, L. J. Marks; Purser, D. H. Crane, 200 Adams.

CHICAGO CENTRAL WOMEN'S CHRISTIAN TEMPERANCE UNION—1101 The Temple. Pres. Mrs. Matilda B. Carse; V. Pres. Margaret Howell; Cor. Sec. Mrs. M. B. Horning; Rec. Sec. Mrs. R. L. Lake.

CHICAGO CERAMIC ASSOCIATION—274 Michigan av. Pres. Mrs. John W. Marsh; 1st V. Pres. Mrs. Victoria B. Jenkins; 2d V. Pres. J. E. Zeublin; Treas. Mrs. Anna P. Harrison; Rec. Sec. Mrs. E. L. Humphrey.

CHICAGO CHRISTIAN ENDEAVOR UNION—P. O. Box 1013. Pres. F. E. Page; V. Pres. Dr. S. A. Wilson; Sec. Miss Jessie Williams.

CHICAGO CITY MISSIONARY SOCIETY—Supt. Rev. J. C. Armstrong, 24, 151 Washington

CHICAGO CLUB—Michigan av. sw. cor. Vanburen. See p. 397.

CHICAGO CONGREGATIONAL CLUB—Regular meetings third Monday in each month, October to May inclusive, at the Auditorium Hotel. Pres. E. D. Redington; Sec. J. H. Tewksbury, 175 Wabash av.; Treas. J. R. Chapman.

CHICAGO CONTINENTAL GUARD, THE—Captain, Samuel E. Gross; Lieutenant, Frederick C. Pierce; Ensign, John C. Long; Adjutant Seymour Morris, 142 Lasalle; Paymaster, John S. Sargent; Quartermaster, Horace T. Currier; Surgeon, H. Newberry Hall.

CHICAGO CRICKET ASSOCIATION—Pres. J. P. Jaffray; Sec. and treas. J. Duke, 221 Adams.

CHICAGO CYCLING CLUB—3016 Lake Park av. Pres. H. P. Walden; V. Pres; W. F. Bode; Sec. and Treas. Geo. K. Barrett. Directors: H. P. Walden, W. F. Bode, Geo. K. Barrett, C. W. Davis, C. P. Root, H. A. Githens, N. H. VanSicklen, I. N. VanPelt.

CHICAGO DAILY NEWS FRESH-AIR FUND—C. M. Faye, mngr. 123, 5th av.

CHICAGO DEACONESSES' HOME—Supt. Miss Mary Jefferson, 227 Ohio.

CHICAGO DIOCESE ORGANIZATION OF GIRLS FRIENDLY SOCIETY—Pres. Miss Fanny Groesbeck; Sec. Mrs. Rudolph Williams, 258 Ontario.

CHICAGO DIOCESAN CHOIR ASSOCIATION—Patron, Rt.Rev.Wm. Edward McLaren, D.D., D.C.L.; Pres. Rev. William White Wilson; Secretary, S. Henry.

CHICAGO EXCHANGE FOR WOMEN'S WORK—109 Wabash av. Pres. Mrs. J. B. Lyon; Cor. Secs. Mrs. T. F. Withrow, Miss King, Mrs. Clinton J., Warren; Treas. Mrs. N. M. Chittenden.

CHICAGO GOLF CLUB—J. C. Sterling, pres.; E. W. Cramer, sec.; 643 Rookery bldg.

CHICAGO HISTORICAL SOCIETY —Open daily from 9 a. m. to 5 p. m Free to theypublic. Pres. Edward G. Mason; V. Pres. A. C. McClurg; Geo. W. Smith; office Dearborn av. n.w. cor. Ontario.

CHICAGO HOME MISSIONARY AND CHURCH EXTENSION SOCIETY—Cor. Sec. Rev. A. D. Traveller, 35, 57 Washington.

CHICAGO KINDERGARTEN CLUB—Meets at 10 Vanburen 4th Saturday of every month. Pres. Miss Katherine Beebe

CHICAGO LITERARY CLUB—200 Michigan av. See p. 400.

CHICAGO MECHANICS' INSTITUTE—23, 129 Madison. Pres. George C. Prussing; 1st V. Pres. John Wilkinson; 2d V. Pres. J. W. Hosmer; Treas. Amos Grannis; Sec. and Librarian, J. Silvers.

CHICAGO METHODIST PREACHERS' MEETING—Sessions Mondays 10.30 a. m. in lecture room, Methodist Church blk. Pres. Rev. P. H. Swift; Sec. and Treas. Rev. R. W. Bland.

CHICAGO PRAYER BOOK SOCIETY—Treas. Charles A. Street, 510 Masonic Temple,

CHICAGO RELIEF AND AID SOCIETY—51 and 53 Lasalle. Office hours 8 a. m. to 5 p. m. Pres. Henry W. King; Chairman Executive Committee, T. W. Harvey; Treas. Ernest A. Hamill; Sec. Wm. H. Hubbard; Gen.

Supt. Rev. C. G. Trusdell. Directors meet first Monday of every month. Provident Wood Yard, 395 N. Clark.

CHICAGO SOCIETY OF ARTISTS —274 Michigan av. Pres. Ernest Albert; V. Pres. Dr. J. E. Colburn; Sec. L. J. Millet; Fin. Sec., E. Boutwood; Treas. Ernest J. Wagner.

CHICAGO SOCIETY OF DECORATIVE ART—34 and 36 Washington. Business Manager, Mrs.M. E. Pode.

CHICAGO THEOLOGICAL BOOK CLUB—Pres. Rev. F. J. Hall, 510 Masonic Temple.

CHICAGO TRACT SOCIETY—211 Wabash av. Sec. Rev. E. M. Wherry.

CHICAGO TRAINING SCHOOL FOR CITY, HOME AND FOREIGN MISSIONS—Dearborn av. cor. Ohio. Prin. Mrs. Lucy Rider Myer, M.D.; Sec. Wm. E. Blackstone; Treas. George D. Elderkin; Supt. Rev. J. Shelley Meyer.

CHICAGO WHIST CLUB— Western Bank Note bldg. Pres. G. G. Willard; V. Pres. L. D. Hammond; Treas. H. A. Blair; Sec. Irving T. Hartz.

CHICAGO WOMEN'S CLUB— 15 Washington. See p. 401.

CHICAGO WOMEN'S PRESS LEAGUE—Pres. Miss Mary H. Krout; Rec. Sec. Miss Jennie Van Allen; Cor. Sec. Mrs. Laura D. Fessenden, Highland Park; Treas. Mrs, A. V. H. Wakeman.

CHILDREN'S AID SOCIETY OF CHICAGO— 712, 167 Dearborn. Sec. and Financial Agt. Mrs. Jennie L. Wood; Asst. Sec. Ernest Wood; Gen'l Supt. Rev. Geo. K. Hoover.

CHILDREN'S HOME SOCIETY— (National) 712, 167 Dearborn. Pres. Hon. John Woodbridge; V. Pres. Lyman J. Gage; Supt. Rev. Geo. K. Hoover; Fin. Sec. Rev. Jacob Hartman; Asst. Gen. Supt. Mrs. M. V. B. Van Arsdale; Treas. Edward F. Lawrence; Gen l Organizer, Rev. F. M. Gregg.

CHURCH CLUB OF CHICAGO, THE—510 Masonic Temple. Pres. W. R. Stirling: V. Pres. Jos. T. Brown; Treas. H. J. Jones.

CHURCH HOME FOR AGED PERSONS—4327 Ellis av. Visitor ex-officio, Rt. Rev. Wm. E. McLaren, D.D., D.C.L.; Pres. Rev. Dr. Walter Delafield; Treas. O. W. Ballard; Matron, Mrs. A. S. Field.

CHURCH HOME FOR ORPHANS —4331 Ellis av. Pres. Rev. Walter Delafield; Treas. Ira P. Bowen

CICERO CRICKET CLUB—Ridgeland. Pres. A. W. Giles; Sec. Benj. Lockyear; Treas. E. C. K. Davies.

CITIZEN'S ASSOCIATION OF CHICAGO—33 Merchants' bldg. 94 Lasalle. Pres. Melville E. Stone; V. Pres. Francis Beidler;Sec.J.C.Ambler; Treas. Geo. Schneider; Executive Committee, —J. J. Glessner, Francis B. Peabody, O. S. A. Sprague, Wm. A. Fuller, Christoph Hotz, J. Harley Bradley, Murry Nelson, I. K. Boyesen, H. N. Higinbotham, Francis Beidler, Melville E. Stone, Josiah L. Lombard, R. J. Smith. Julius Stern, H. H. Kohlsaat. Office, open daily. Executive committees meet Tuesdays.

CITIZEN'S LEAGUE OF CHICAGO—(For the suppression of the sale of liquors to minors) — 45, 113 Adams. Meets 1st Friday, at 4 p. m.; office open daily. Pres. I. P. Rumsey; Cor. and Rec. Sec. F. P. Fisher; Treas. A. L. Coe; Gen. Agt. H. J. Hayward.

CIVIL SERVICE REFORM LEAGUE OF CHICAGO—Pres. John W. Ela; Sec. and Treas. Edward J. Phelps, 207 Herald bldg.

COLUMBUS CLUB—43-45 Monroe. See p. 405.

COMMERCE CLUB, THE--25 Auditorium bldg. S. Fred Howe, mngr.

COMMERCIAL CLUB—Meets last Saturday in each month, October to April inclusive. See p. 408.

CONCORDIA CLUB—3140 Indiana av. See p. 408.

CONGREGATIONAL CHURCH BUILDING SOCIETY—Office 26, 151 Washington. Sec. Rev. C. H. Taintor.

CONGREGATIONAL EDUCATION SOCIETY—26. 151 Washington. Western Sec. Geo. M. Herrick.

CONGREGATIONAL S.S. AND PUB. SOCIETY—Mgr. J. H. Tewksbury, 175 Wabash av.

CONTRIBUTORS' CLUB—Editor, Arthur J. Eddy, 618 The Rookery. See p. 409.

COOK COUNTY SUNDAY SCHOOL ASSOCIATION—30. 132 Lasalle. Pres. Mrs. R. B. Preuszner; V. Pres. J. A. Russell; Sec. W. B. Jacobs; Treas. R. E. Brownell.

CORPORATION FOR RELIEF OF WIDOWS AND ORPHANS OF DECEASED CLERGYMEN — Pres. Henry Keep; Sec. and Treas. Mrs. Wm. G. Hibbard, 1701 Prairie av.

COSMOPOLITAN ART CLUB— Sec. George L.Schreiber, 1741, 47th (L.)

COUNTRY CLUB OF EVANSTON —See p. 410.

DAUGHTERS OF THE AMERICAN REVOLUTION—See p. 413.

DEARBORN CLUB—200 Michigan av. Pres. N. K. Fairbank; Treas. George H. Wheeler; Sec. Austin A. Burnham.

DELAWARE BOAT CLUB — Pres. John M. Schaack; Treas. Fred J. Ringley; Sec. John T. Reilly; Capt. Arthur Franz.

DELTA KAPPA EPSILON NORTHWESTERN ASSN. — Pres. Frank M. Larned; V. Pres. Albert P. Goodwin; Sec. and Treas. Edward Hurd Smith, 107 Dearborn. Headquarters, Grand Pacific Hotel.

DIOCESAN BRANCH OF THE WOMAN'S AUXILIARY—Pres. Mrs. O. V. S. Ward, 1701 Prairie av.; Treas. Mrs. Frances M. Barrett.

DOUGLAS CLUB—3518 Ellis av. See p. 414.

DOUGLAS PARK CLUB—911 S. Kedzie av. See p. 415.

EDGEWATER CASINO — Edgewater. See p. 416.

ENGLEWOOD WHEELMEN — Stewart av. cor. 67th (L.) Sec. O. V. Mueller.

EVANSTON BOAT CLUB—Sheridan Road n. of Greenleaf. Evanston. Chas. B. Congdon, pres.; C. M. Carr, sec.; C. B. Ide, treas.; W.D.Hess, capt.

EVANSTON CLUB—See p. 416.

FELLOWSHIP CLUB—See p. 417.

FIELD COLUMBIAN MUSEUM —See Museums.

FORTNIGHTLY CLUB — Meets Fridays at 2.30 p. m., at 10 Vanburen. See p. 418.

FORTY CLUB—See p. 419.

FOX LAKE SHOOTING AND FISHING CLUB—Meets at Grand Pacific Hotel. Pres. R. B. Miller; Sec. Victor D. Gowan, 154, 5th av.; A. V. Hartwell, manager.

FRENCH LITERARY CLUB — See p. 420.

FRIDAY CLUB—See p. 420.

GERMANIA MÆNNERCHOR — Club Room N. Clark nw. cor. Grant. See p. 421.

GRANT CLUB—Pres. L. L. Bond; Treas. M. E. Cole; Sec. Dr. Liston H. Montgomery, 200, 70 State.

HAMILTON CLUB—21 Groveland Park. . See p. 424.

HARVARD CLUB — Harvard and Sixty-third. See p. 425.

HELIADES CLUB—90 Warren av. See p. 425.

HIGHLAND PARK CLUB—Highland Park. See p. 426.

HINSDALE CLUB—See p. 426.

HOME CLUB—6737 Wentworth av. See p. 427.

HOME FOR DESTITUTE AND CRIPPLED CHILDREN—Park av. se. cor. Paulina. Rec. Sec. Mrs. H. A. Delano.

HOME FOR SELF-SUPPORTING WOMEN—275 and 277 Indiana. Pres. Mrs. J. R. Key; Treas. Mrs. H. P. Crowell; Rec. Sec Mrs. E. W. Cramer; Matron, A. M. Rugby.

HYDE PARK CLUB. Washington av. nw. cor. 51st. See p. 427.

IDEAL CLUB—531 N.Wells. See p. 429.

ILLINOIS CLUB—154 S. Ashland av. See p. 429.

ILLINOIS CYCLING CLUB—1063 Washington boul. Pres. F. B. Davidson; V. Pres. Fred Gerlach; Sec. W. A. Davis; Treas. W. Eisenberg; Asst. Sec., E. J. Porter; Directors—E. M. Blaine, E. P. Richardson, R. W. Knisely, Jr., J. A. Barkey, J. P. Pomeroy, E. A. Chisholm, C. R. Street, T. L. Sloan, E. G. Richardson.

ILLINOIS HOME MISSIONARY SOCIETY — Office 151 Washington. Supt. Rev. James Tompkins; Treas. A. B. Mead.

ILLINOIS HUMANE SOCIETY—560 Wabash av. Complaints received at office from 8 to 6. Pres. John G. Shortall; Treas. George Schneider; Sec. Belden F. Culver.

ILLINOIS SOCIETY SONS OF THE AMERICAN REVOLUTION—Pres. Josiah L. Lombard; Sec. John D. Vandercook, 111, 185 Dearborn.

ILLINOIS ST. ANDREWS SOCIETY—Meets 1st Thursday in February, May, August and November at 7, 81 Clark. Pres., John J. Badenoch; Treas., Duncan Cameron; Sec., John F. Holmes.

ILLINOIS STATE SUNDAY SCHOOL ASSOCIATION—Pres., Henry Augustine; Treas., R. W. Hare; Gen. Sec. W. B. Jacobs, 30, 132 Lasalle.

ILLINOIS WOMAN'S CHRISTIAN TEMPERANCE UNION — Women's Temple. Pres. Mrs. L.S. Rounds, Chicago; V. Pres. Mrs. Carrie L. Grout, Rockford, Ill.; Cor. Sec. Miss Helen Walker; Rec. Sec. Miss Maud Rittenhouse, Cairo, Ill.; Treas. Mrs. A. E. Sanford, Bloomington, Ill.

ILLINOIS WOMAN'S HOME MISSIONARY UNION—26, 151 Washington. Cor. Sec. Mrs. C. H. Taintor.

ILLINOIS WOMEN'S PRESS ASSOCIATION—See p. 431.

INDIANA CLUB—3349 Indiana av. See p. 432.

INTERNATIONAL YOUNG WOMEN'S CHRISTIAN ASSN.—1301, 34 Washington. Chairman, Mrs. J. V.Farwell jr.; Sec. Mrs. F. F. West; Treas. Mrs. L. W. Messer.

IROQUOIS CLUB —Michigan av. nw. cor. Adams. See p. 433.

IRVING CLUB—Irving Park. See p. 434.

JOSEPH JEFFERSON DRAMATIC CLUB—1411 Unity Building. John Rosenberg, Mngr.

KENEITHA CLUB—837, 61st, Englewood. Pres., Lewis S. Browere, V.-Pres., Thurman Gerard; Sec., Pierre E. Miller, Treas., Harry L. Lindquist. Meets 2d and 4th Wednesdays of each month.

KENWOOD CLUB—47th cor. Lake av. See p. 435.

KLIO CLUB, THE—210 Masonic Temple. See p. 437.

LA GRANGE CLUB—See p. 437.

LAKE VIEW CYCLING CLUB—401 and 403 Orchard. Pres., W. J. Parsons; Sec., C. E. Gamet ; Treas. G. L. Weaver.

LAKESIDE CLUB—3138 and 3140 Indiana av.

LAKOTA CLUB—4111 Grand boul. see p. 438.

LEAGUE AMERICAN WHEELMEN, ILLINOIS DIVISION—Sec. A. J. Marrett, 509 Cleveland av.

LEGENSIA CLUB— Evanston. Pres., Fleming H. Revell; V.-Pres., Miss M. A. Childs; Sec. and Treas., Miss M. A. Phelps.

LESSING CLUB—447 W. Taylor.

LINCOLN CLUB—531 W. Adams. See p. 439.

LINCOLN CYCLING CLUB — 1 Ogden Front. See p. 440.

LINWOOD CLUB—Irving Park. Pres. L. Thomas; Sec.W.H. Brown.

MARQUETTE CLUB — 365 Dearborn av.: See p. 441.

MARGARET ETTER CRECHE— Pres., Mrs. I. A. Perkins; Treas., Mrs. H. M. Starkey; Sec, Mrs. Philander Pickering

MARY NOBLE CLUB—Meets at Kenwood Club House. Pres. Mrs. Edwin H. Keen; V. Pres. Mrs. J. C. Stirling; Sec. and Treas. Mrs. Wm. H. Ray; Executive Committee, Mrs. E. R. Shumway. Mrs. E. F. Bayley, Mrs. Wm. T. Brown, Mrs. I. Henry Long.

MENOKEN CLUB—1196 Washington. See p. 442.

MORTON PARK CLUB—Morton Park. See p. 444.

MUSCODA CLUB—1115 Lawndale av. Pres. Lawton C. Bonney; Sec. and Treas. H. L. Burnette, 511 Tacoma bldg.

NATIONAL PRESS LEAGUE— Pres. Miss Mary H.Krout, Inter-Ocean; V.-Pres., Mrs. Frank Davidson, La Grange; Rec. Sec., Miss Jennie VanAllen, Ravenswood; Cor. Sec., Mrs. B. A. Fessenden, Highland Park; Treas., Mrs. A. V. H. Wakeman.

NATIONAL WOMAN'S CHRISTIAN TEMPERANCE UNION—The Temple. Pres. Miss Frances E.Willard, 732 Chicago av., Evanston, Ill.; Cor. Sec. Mrs. Catherine Lents Stevenson; Treas. Miss Helen M. Barker.

NORTH END TENNIS CLUB—N. State and Burton pl. Pres. F. W. Gookin; Treas. Fred A. Fish.

NORTH SHORE CLUB—1835 Wellington av. See p. 444.

NORTHWESTERN BAPTIST EDUCATION SOCIETY—Sec. Rev. C. E. Hewitt, D.D. University of Chicago.

OAK PARK CLUB—Oak Park, Ill. See p. 445.

OAKLAND CLUB—22 Oakwood av. See p. 446.

OAKS, THE—Austin. See.p. 447.

OLIO CLUB—See p. 447.

PARK CLUB—57th cor. Rosalie ct. See p. 448.

PHOENIX CLUB—104 to 110 Monroe. See p. 449.

POWHATTAN CLUB—1782 Wrightwood av.

PRAIRIE CLUB—Prairie av. cor. Railroad boul.. Oak Park. Pres. John Farson; V. Pres. W. R. Patterson; Treas. H. L. Jewell; Sec. Orin L. Cox.

PRESBYTERIAN BOARD OF AID FOR COLLEGES AND ACADEMIES—30, 115 Monroe. Pres. Rev. Herrick Johnson; V. Pres. Rev. S. J. McPherson; Sec. Mrs. W. B. Jacobs; Clerk Rev. J. G. K. McClure; Treas. Charles M. Charnley. .

PRESBYTERIAN LEAGUE THE —Pres. George F. Bissell; 1st V. Pres. James E. Downs; 3rd V. Pres. Rev. Thomas D. Wallace, D. D.; Treas. Charles S. Holt; Act. Sec. James Frothingham.

PRESBYTERIAN MINISTERIAL ASSOCIATION — Meets Mondays, 10:30 a.m. at 155 Lasalle. Rev. James Clark Hill, D. D. chairman.

PRESBYTERIAN SOCIAL UNION—Meets monthly from October to April. Pres. Judge Henry V. Freeman; Sec. Fred B. Mason, 301, 225 Dearborn; Treas. William H. Brintnall.

PROGRESSIVE CLUB—3800 Vincennes av. Pres. George E. Van Hagen; Sec. Charles J. Dash; Treas. H. G. Howard.

PROTECTIVE AGENCY FOR WOMEN AND CHILDREN — 808 Chicago Opera House bldg. Mrs. Lilian Johnstone Dreier, agt,

PSYCHEON CLUB—Sheridan av. cor. 61st. See p. 452.

PULLMAN ATHLETIC CLUB— Grounds Athletic Island, Pullman, Ill. Pres. Alex. McLauchlan; V. Pres. Geo. A. Martin; Sec. B. D. Blakeslee; Treas. J. Wiley Dennison.

PULLMAN CRICKET CLUB — Grounds Pullman, Ill. Pres. John Dixey; Sec.and Treas.Edward Butcher.

QUEEN ISABELLA ASSOCIATION OF CHICAGO—70 State. Pres. Miss Eliza A. Starr; Sec. Dr. Frances Dickinson.

RYDER CLUB—Pres. Oliver Sollitt; V. Pres. Wm. E. Lamb; Sec Mrs. F. N. Gage; Treas. Miss Francelia Colby.

SHERIDAN CLUB—4100 Michigan av. See p. 453.

SISTERS OF ST. MARY—Mission houses at Cathedral, Washington boul. cor. S. Peoria.

SOCIETY FOR ETHICAL CULTURE —Lectures every Sunday, at 11 a.m., at Grand Opera House. Ethical School, 40 Dearborn Sundays 10 a.m. Pres. F. B. Tobey; Treas. C. A. Brown; Sec. E. C. Wentworth; Lecturer, M. M. Mangasarian.

SOCIETY FOR THE RELIEF OF WIDOWS AND ORPHANS— Pres. Henry Keep; Sec. Mrs. Lydia B. Hibbard, 1701 Prairie av.

SONS OF MAINE — Pres. Charles F. Kimball; Treas. Roswell Z. Herrick; Sec. Charles P. Mattocks, New York Life bldg.

SONS OF NEW YORK — Pres. DeWitt C. Cregier; sec. John E. Davis, 12, 154 Lake; Treas. Charles E. Leonard.

SONS OF VERMONT— Pres. Austin Clement; Treas. William H. Gleason; Sec. Seymour Edgerton, 802, 171 Lasalle.

SOUTH SIDE CYCLING CLUB— 749, 46th. Pres. W. A. Manning; Fin. Sec. W. B. Neyenesch; Rec. Sec. C. A. Jensen; Cor. Sec. William L. Loos; Treas. G. J. Duffett.

ST. GEORGE'S BENEVOLENT ASSOCIATIGN—Meets 1st Mondays in St. George's Hall. Pres. W. B. Jackson; Sec. C. J. Burroughs, 859 Washington boul. Treas. Wm. L. Tapson.

ST. GEORGE'S ATHLETIC ASSN. — Grounds Fullerton av. cor. North Park av. Pres. W. J. Fleming; V. Pres. S. Piggott; Treas. Wm. H. Bullen; Sec. W. Lovegrove.

STANDARD CLUB—Michigan av. sw. cor. Twenty-fourth. See p. 454.

SUNSET CLUB — Sec. Philip S. Post jr,

SYMPHONY CLUB ORCHESTRA —Meets at Athenæum Hall, Monday evenings. Shea Smith, Pres., H. M. Lay, Sec. 46 Jackson

TACOMA CLUB—1134 Melrose. H. F. Pottgether, Pres.; W.P. Hildebrand, V. Pres.; H. J. Schuette, Sec.; F. P. Dudenhoeffer, Treas.

TOLLESTON CLUB—Pres. F. A. Howe; Sec. George Manierre, 214 The Temple.

TRUSTEES OF THE ENDOWMENT FUND OF THE DIOCESE OF CHICAGO—Pres. Francis B. Peabody; Treas. Wm. Kelsey Reed, 78 Lasalle; J. W. Doane, William C. Hibbard, Albert E. Neeley, Emory Cobb, Collins H. Jordan, Nelson A. Steele, John DeKoven.

TWENTIETH CENTURY CLUB —See p. 456.

UM-ZOO-ELL CLUB—Meets semimonthly at Lincoln Park Refectory, first and third Tuesdays. Pres. E. J. Brundage; Sec. M. Stoddard.

UNION CLUB—Washington pl. sw. cor. Dearborn av. See p. 457.

UNION LEAGUE CLUB—Jackson sw. cor. Custom House pl. See p. 459.

UNION PARK CHORAL SOCIETY—Louis Falk, director. Meets Union Park Congreg. ch. Saturday evenings.

UNITED HEBREW CHARITIES —223, 26th. Office hours 8 a.m. to 4 p.m. Pres. I. Greensfelder; Rec. Sec. Julian W. Mack; Fin. Sec. Chas. Hefter; Supt. Francis Kiss; Supt. Employment Bureau, S. Bartenstein.

UNIVERSITY CLUB — 118 Dearborn. See p. 464.

VETERAN UNION LEAGUE—6 Madison. Pres. E. C. Hamburgher; Treas. W. H. King; Sec. Theo. F Brown.

WAHPANSEH WHIST AND CHESS CLUB—3828 Ellis av. Pres. W. D. Anderson; V. Pres. W. H. Colvin; Sec. George C. Fry; Treas. A. E. Matteson.

WANDERER'S CRICKET AND ATHLETIC CLUB—Grounds 39th cor. Wentworth av. Sec. Fred Sansome.

WASHINGTON PARK CLUB — Office, 32 Palmer House. Pres. Geo. Henry Wheeler; V. Prests. Samuel W. Allerton, Columbus R. Cummings, Henry J. Macfarland, Charles D. Hamill; Treas. John R. Walsh; Sec. James Howard.

WEST CHICAGO CLUB—48 and 50 Throop. See p. 466.

WEST END WOMAN'S CLUB— 542 W. Monroe. See p. 467.

WOMAN'S AUXILIARY OF THE BOARD OF MISSIONS—Pres. Mrs. O. V. S. Ward; Treas. Mrs. Frances M. Barrett.

WOMAN'S BOARD OF MISSIONS OF THE INTERIOR—Room 603, 59 Dearborn. Pres. Mrs. Moses Smith; V. Pres. Mrs. Lyman Baird; Secs. Mrs. E. W. Blatchford, Mrs. J. F. Temple,

WILL W. MILLNER   JESSIE PAT?

Mr. and Mrs. Will W. Mil

--- ELOCUTIONISTS ---

*TEACHERS OF ELOCUTION, ORATORY
DRAMATIC ART*

*MAY BE ENGAGED FOR PUBLIC AND PRIVA
RECITALS*

INSTRUCTION GIVEN   STUDIO
TO A LIMITED NUMBER
OF PRIVATE PUPILS   **76 KIMBALL H**

243 WABAS

Mrs. G. B. Wilcox, Miss M. D. Wingate, Mrs. H. M. Lyman and Mrs. George M. Clark; Rec. Sec. Miss M. D. Wingate; Treas. Mrs. J.B.Leake. Office hours, 9 a. m. to 5 p. m. Illinois branch of W. B. M. I., Sec. Mrs. W. A. Montgomery, 407 N. State.

WOMAN'S PRESBYTERIAN SOCIETY FOR HOME MISSIONS— 369 Chicago av. Pres. Mrs. H. P. Merriman; Rec. Sec. Mrs. George M. Eckels. 5313 Washington av.; Treas. Mrs. John P. Yale.

WOMAN'S PRESBYTERIAN BOARD OF MISSIONS OF THE NORTHWEST—48 McCormick blk. Meets every Friday morning at 10 o'clock. Pres. Mrs. H. D. Penfield, 2456 Prairie av.; Rec. Sec. Mrs. W. B. Jacobs, Chicago; Treas. Mrs. C. B. Farwell, 48 McCormick blk.

WOMAN'S TEMPERANCE BUILDING ASSOCIATION—214 The Temple. Pres. Mrs. Matilda B. Carse; Sec. and Treas. George Manniere.

WOMEN'S BAPTIST HOME MISSION SOCIETY — 2411 Indiana av. Pres. Mrs. J. N. Crouse; Cor. Sec. Miss M. G. Burdette, 2411 Indiana av.; Treas. Mrs. A. H. Barber, 3715 Langley av.

WOMEN'S BAPTIST HOME MISSION UNION—2411 Indiana av. Pres. Mrs. Norman T. Gassette; Treas. Miss Kittie F. Taylor; Sec. Mrs. Joseph Bond.

WOMEN'S BAPTIST FOREIGN MISSION QUARTERLY—Pres. Mrs. Galusha Anderson; V. Pres. Mrs. J. R. Gow; Treas. Miss Mary W. Ranney, 122 Wabash av.

WOMEN'S BAPTIST FOREIGN MISSIONARY SOCIETY OF THE WEST—122 Wabash av. Pres. Mrs. L. Everingham; Rec. Sec. Mrs. E. W. Brayman; Treas. Miss Mary W. Ranney.

WOMEN'S FOREIGN MISSIONARY SOCIETY of the Methodist Episcopal Church, Northwestern Branch—Meets 2d and 4th Fridays at 57 Washington. Headquarters, 114 Dearborn av. Pres. Mrs. I. R. Hitt: Cor. Sec. Mrs. F. P. Crandon; Rec. Sec. Mrs. W. H. Henkle.

WOODLAWN MATINEE MUSICALE. See p. 468.

WOODLAWN PARK CLUB— Woodlawn av. cor 64th. See p. 469.

WORKING WOMAN'S HOME ASSOCIATION—21 S. Peoria. Pres. Andrew Chaiser; V. Pres. Dr. Odelia Blinn; 2d V. Pres. Lewis Melander; Sec. Mrs. R.A.Emmons; Treas.Geo. P. Bay; Auditor, Frank E. Brown; Manager Home, Laura G. Fixen.

WYANDOT TENNIS CLUB—Superior and Pine. Pres. Robt. F. Shonklin; V. Pres; Miss Helen Jones; Capt. Louis V. LeMoyne; Treas. William A. McLaren; Sec. John A. Ryerson.

YOUNG MEN'S CHRISTIAN ASSOCIATION—General office, 153-155 Lasalle. Pres. John V. Farwell jr.; Treas. James L. Houghteling; Gen. Sec. L. Wilbur Messer; Asst. Gen. Sec. W. T. Hart. Central Dept. 153-155 Lasalle. Chairman, H. M. Hubbard; Dept. Sec. Daniel Sloan. West Side Dept. 542 W. Monroe, Chairman, J. W. Hedenburg; Dept. Sec. A. D. Mackey. Ravenswood Dept. 610 Wilson av. Ravenswood. Chairman, R. J. Bennett; Dept. Sec. H. W. Mixsell. Pullman Dept. Pullman, Ill., Chairman, A. S. DeWitt; South Chicago Dept. 250 Ninety-second, Chairman, A. I. Blackwood, M.D.; Dept. Sec. H. M. Finch. Kinzie St. Railway Dept. 17 W. Kinzie, Chairman, E. H. Duff; Dept. Sec. Wm. Cook. Garfield Boul. R.R. Dept. Garfield boul. and Shields av. Chairman, A. H. Somers; Dept. Sec. O. A. Young. German Dept. 758 Larrabee, Chairman, A. Kurz; Dept. Sec. L. A. Horlacher. Intercollegiate Dept. 542 W. Monroe, Chairman. H. R. Miner; Dept. Sec. J. L. Maltby.

YOUNG MEN'S CHRISTIAN ASSOCIATION — Evanston, 1576 Sherman av. open daily 9 a. m. to 10 p. m. Sundays 3 to 5 p. m. Gen. Sec. Wm. Boyd.

YOUNG WOMEN'S CHRISTIAN ASSOCIATION—291 Michigan av. Pres. Mrs. Leander Stone; Treas. Miss M. E. True; Rec. Sec. Mrs. A. S. Chamberlin; Supt. Employment Bureau, Mrs. A. L. Fitch; Supt. Boarding House (288 Michigan av.) Mrs. H. W. Lafayette.

FROM ANYWHERE EAS

-----BY-----

TO EVERYWHERE WES

REMEMBER THAT....... THROUGH CARS

 and   FINEST EQUIPMENT

BEST DINING CAR SERVICE IN THE WORLD

Are Some of
Its------ Specialties

THE magnificent modern train **BIG 5** leaves Chicago at 10 p. m. an
running via Des Moines, Omaha and Lincoln arrives at Denver 7:2
a. m., Colorado Springs 7:35 a. m., Pueblo 9:10 a. m. second morning
The Foothill Cities reached with one day out.

JOHN SEBASTIAN, G. P. A

E. ST. JOHN, Gen'l Manager.   ....Chicago....

REFERENCES.

<table>
<tr><td>Hotel Metropole,</td><td>Ogden J. Armour Residence,</td></tr>
<tr><td>Annex Auditorium Dining Hall,</td><td>Marshall Field, Jr., Residence,</td></tr>
<tr><td>Spalding's Jewelry Store,</td><td>Watson Blair Residence,</td></tr>
<tr><td>Woman's Temple,</td><td>Geo. A. Fuller Residence,</td></tr>
<tr><td>H. H. Kohlsaat's, on State St.,</td><td>S. E. Gross Residence.</td></tr>
</table>

Mr. Staak has designed and modeled all Ornamental Bronze Work on the Columbus Memorial Building.

Varallo's ·· Mandolin ·· Orchestra

SUITE 616, SCHILLER BUILDING, 103-109 EAST RANDOLPH ST.

Also
Violin
Music
for
Balls
and
Parties
Season
1894-95

Engage-
ments

for...
Concerts
Receptions
Dinners
Weddings
Banquets
Etc....

VARALLO BROS., Directors

PART FIRST.

SOUTH DIVISION.

THE BLUE BOOK.

*ARRANGED ACCORDING TO STREETS AND NUMBERS,
NUMERICALLY, WITH OCCUPANTS' NAMES,
GIVING THE ODD NUMBERS IN
LEFT COLUMN, AND EVEN
IN THE RIGHT.*

STANTON & CO.

Table...
Delicacies

FRUIT
  WINES
    LIQUORS
      CIGARS

54 AND 56
MADISON STREET

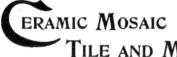

SOUTH DIVISION.

ALDINE SQUARE.

1 Mr. & Mrs. Henry A. Rust
1 Miss Mary C. Rust
1 Mr. & Mrs. James W. Johnston
2 Mr. & Mrs. Charles E. Bliven
Receiving day Tuesday
3 Mr.& Mrs.Thomas Brown jr.& dr.
3 Everett C. Brown
4 Mrs. Henry E. Meleney & dr.
Receiving day Monday
4 George B. Meleney
4 Miss Katharine C. Innis
5 Mr. & Mrs. Wm. A. Moulton
6 Mr. & Mrs. Thos. E. Milchrist & drs.
6 Wm. A. Milchrist
7 Mr. & Mrs. Charles H. Hildreth
7 Miss Grace Chappelle
8 Mr. & Mrs. Alex. P. Moore
8 Clarence E. Moore
8 Mr. & Mrs. John S. Sargent
9 Mrs. R. H. Kelly
9 Mrs. A. W. Freeman
9 L. H. Freeman
10 Mr. & Mrs. Geo. R. Walker
10 Mr. & Mrs. Samuel K. Dow
11 Mr. & Mrs. Henry C. F. Zeiss
12 Mr. & Mrs. John W. Marsh & dr.
12 John P. Marsh
13 Mr. & Mrs. S. B. Gafford & dr.
14 Mr. & Mrs. Tho. E. Aspden & drs.
14 William Aspden
15 Mr. & Mrs. Abner Smith
16 Mr. & Mrs. Frank P. Waters
17 Mr. & Mrs. Daniel C. Osmun
18 Mrs. E. C. Bassett
Receiving day Friday
18 Miss Sara Horton
19 Mr. & Mrs. Thos. Cadwallader
20 Dr. & Mrs. Charles F. Bassett
21 Rev. & Mrs. Wm. White Wilson
Receiving day Monday
21 Louis W. Wilson
21 Miss Elizabeth Wilson
22 Mr. & Mrs. Sidney M. Jenkins

24 Mr. & Mrs. Alexander Forbes
24 George S. Forbes
24 Allen B. Forbes
24 Robert R. Forbes
24 John A. Forbes
25 Mr. & Mrs. John C. Hatch
25 Edwin H. Hatch
25 Luelus J. Ennis
26 J. Montgomery Johnston
26 Miss Victoria M. Johnston
26 Miss Agnes E. Johnston
26 J. Frank Johnston
26 Fred. H. Johnston
26 Mrs. Joseph H. Hall
27 Mr. & Mrs. John H. Purdy
27 Charles S. Purdy
28 James P. Black
30 Mr. & Mrs. Edward A. Mulford
31 Mr. & Mrs. John D. Parker
31 John Wills
32 Mr.& Mrs.Augustus O. Hall & dr.
Receiving day Tuesday
32 William A. Hall
32 Newman G. Hall
34 Mr.&Mrs.JosephW.Helmer&drs
34 Harry Helmer
35 Mr. & Mrs. Alonzo Blossom & dr.
36 Mr. & Mrs. Mifflin E. Bell & drs.
36 Miss Anna Van Hoff
37 Mr. & Mrs. William S. Jackson
37 William C. Jackson
37 Arthur S. Jackson
37 Harry H. Jackson
38 Mr. & Mrs. Wm. G. Jerrems & dr.
38 Arthur W. Jerrems
41 Mrs. Myrtle W. Thayer & dr.
41 Mrs. Myrtilla Wilkins
41 Mrs. May W. Arms
41 Frank D. Arms
41 Charles H. Wilkins
41 Edwin P. Wilkins
41 William A. Wilkins
42 Mr. & Mrs. H. D. Smith
42 George B. Smith
42 Harry B. Smith

BERKELEY AVENUE.

4117 Mr. & Mrs. H. A. Shourds
4119 Mrs. P. A. Barton & dr.
4119 Jesse B. Barton
4121 Mr. & Mrs. Charles D. Steele
4125 Mr. & Mrs. John P. Neal
        Receiving day Thursday
4131 Mr. & Mrs. J. C. Thurston
4133 Mr. & Mrs. O. A. Skinner
4143 Mr. & Mrs. Albert Steinke
4149 Mr. & Mrs. W. B. Greene
4159 Mr. & Mrs. Albert B. Porter
4161 Dr. & Mrs. W. A. Fisher
4167 Mr. & Mrs. George G. Yeomans
4169 Mr,& Mrs.Frederick W. Becker
        Receiving day Wednesday
4227 Mr. & Mrs. J. W. Simmons
4311 Dr. & Mrs. Chas. F. Wright
4311 G. B. Brigham
4315 Mr. & Mrs. James H. Teller
4317 Mr. & Mrs. Henry A. Pope
4319 Mrs. M. E. Magee & dr.
4319 George Magee
4321 Mr. & Mrs. L. D. Wright
4323 Mrs. Margaret Turner
4325 Mr. & Mrs. John S. Palmer
4327 Mr. & Mrs. I. T. Hartz
4329 Mr. & Mrs. A. B. Sloan
4331 Mr. & Mrs. Arthur Schiller
4335 Mr. & Mrs. E. H. Griffiths
4337 Mr. & Mrs. J. W. Simpson
4343 Mr. & Mrs. Reuben Wright
4343 G. E. Robins
4347 Mr. & Mrs. L. B. Converse
4353 Mr. & Mrs. H. E. Adams
4353 Mr. & Mrs. W. H. Shellman
4355 Mr. & Mrs. Palmer L. Randall
4359 Mr. & Mrs. E. A. Calkins
4401 Dr. & Mrs. Albert S. Gray
4405 Mr. & Mrs. D. Alexander
4405 Mr. & Mrs. John W. Ayers
4409 Mr. & Mrs. Louis Heilprin
4411 Mr. & Mrs. Edward Rector
4413 Harry Wilkinson
4413 Miss J. P. Wilkinson
4415 Mr. & Mrs. Hamlin M. Spiegel
4417 Willis V. Myers
4425 Mrs. A. M. Topping & drs.
4429 Mr. & Mrs. M. E. Mead
4429 Mrs. E. L. Olmstead
4431 Mr. & Mrs. S. H. Kahn & dr.
4433 Mr. & Mrs. W. W. Gill & dr.
        Receiving day Thursday
4433 Mr. & Mrs. F. W. Millar
        Receiving day Thursday

4120 Mr. & Mrs. Edgar A. Gardner
4120 Mr. & Mrs. W. H. Batterson
4122 Mrs. Celia Karatosky
4126 Mr. & Mrs. W. B. Hibbard
4126 Mr. & Mrs. M. A. Ford
4128 Dr. E. R. Carpenter
4128 Mr. & Mrs. W. P. J. DeLand
4130 Mr. & Mrs. C. P. Boorn
4130 W. C. Boorn
4132 Mr. & Mrs. Julius Hunt
4138 Mr. & Mrs. J. S. Putney
4140 Mrs. C. Webster
4140 Mr. & Mrs. Henry Lawrie
4140 William Lawrie
4142 Mr. & Mrs. R. G. Mullen
4144 Mr. & Mrs. Dwight N. Howe
        Receiving day Wednesday
4146 Mr. & Mrs. L. B. Shephard
4146 Mr. & Mrs. John A. Fulton
4148 Mr.& Mrs. Orson E. Merrill
4148 Henry H. Merrill
4150 Mr. & Mrs. Byron D. Adsit
4154 Mr. & Mrs. Samuel Laib
4154 Mrs. P. Frank
4154 Mr. & Mrs. A. Wettengel
4156 Mrs. Mary M. Hill
4156 John H. Hill
4200 Mr. & Mrs. C. J. Horton
4200 Dr. & Mrs. Winthrop Girling
4200 Mr. & Mrs. S. H. Peabody & dr.
        Receiving day Friday
4200 Mr. & Mrs. George W. DeMaid
        Receiving day Tuesday
4202 Mr. & Mrs. J. H. Farwell
4202 J. Charles Farwell
4206 Mr. & Mrs. Charles T. Williams
4206 Dr. Wm. Carver Williams
4206 Day Williams
4206½ Mr. & Mrs. Geo. N. Pogue
4208 Mrs. M. J. Maxwell
4210 Mrs. Mary S. Foulke
4210 Mr. & Mrs. Fred. H. Sammis
4212 Mr. & Mrs. C. C. Russell
4214 Mr. & Mrs. E. P. Foreman
4216 Mr. & Mrs. G. A. Douglass
4216 Leonard B. Douglass
4216 F. A. Ingails
4216 Morton A. Hosford
4222 Mr. & Mrs. C. B. Holmes
4222 Mrs. E. H. Osborn
4222 Mrs. M. E. Ellsworth
4222 Miss Eva H. Brodlique
4314 Mr. & Mrs. C. B. Rule
4314 Mr. & Mrs. W. R. H. Crump

4435 Mr. and Mrs. F. W. Preston
Receiving day Thursday
4441 Mr. & Mrs. Charles J. Dodgshun
4443 Rev. & Mrs. L. A. Crandall &
dr.
4443 B. V. Bruce
4453 Mr. & Mrs. Carlos C. W. Platt
4453 Mr. & Mrs. C. M. Nichols
4455 Rev. & Mrs. John P. Hale
4455 Mr. & Mrs. J. N. Hobb
4455 Mr. & Mrs. W. P. Elliott

———

4416 Mr. & Mrs. W. H. Sills
4422 Mr. & Mrs. S. Ostheimer
4424 Mr. & Mrs. J. L. Barclay
4426 Mr. & Mrs. Wm. H. Cooper
4430 Mr. & Mrs. A. C. Hooke
4432 Mr. & Mrs. Marc S. Holmes
4434 Mr. & Mrs. Frank Reed
4436 Mr. & Mrs. George F. Schilling
4438 Mr. & Mrs. William J. Thorne
4438 Arthur W. Hardy
4438 Dr. & Mrs. I. A. Freeman
4440 Mr. & Mrs. Henry Eddy
4440 Mr. & Mrs. S. Wolf
4440 Mrs. F. F. Engle
4442 Mr. & Mrs. George E. Marcy
4444 Mr. & Mrs. Albert H. Meads
4446 Mr. & Mrs. Henry H. Windsor
4450 Mr. & Mrs. R. Delos Martyn
Receiving day Friday
4456 Mr. & Mrs. Clift B. Wise
4460 Dr. & Mrs. Charles E. Kurtz
4460 Mr. & Mrs. J. R. Peachy
4462 Mr. & Mrs. Frank L. Danforth
4464 Mr. & Mrs. J. B. Pollard
Receiving day Thursday

4314 Mr. & Mrs. Lewis Cole
4316 Mr. & Mrs. Joseph H. Hayden
4318 Mr. & Mrs. Calvin Dunning
4322 Mr. & Mrs. H. H. Drew & dr.
4324 Mr. & Mrs. Wm. C. Drew
4326 Wm. E. Trainer
4328 Mr. & Mrs. Charles H. Smith
4328 W. T. Smith
4330 W. M. Hitt
4332 Mr. & Mrs. Louis Faithorn
4334 Mr. & Mrs. C. H. Southard
4336 Mr. & Mrs. A. C. Mace
4338 Charles E. Parkhill
4338 Mr. & Mrs. George M. Peale
4338 George M. Peale jr.
4338 Fred Peale
4340 Mr. & Mrs. Archibald Cattell
4340 Mr. & Mrs. E. A. Parker
4346 Mr. & Mrs. Frank S. Davis
4348 Mr. & Mrs. G. E. Downe
4348 W. Emil Kugemann
4350 Mr. & Mrs. A. H. Van Vliet
4350 Mr. & Mrs. Clifford F. Andrews
4356 Mr. & Mrs. Wm. D. Scott
4356 Dr. Eliza R. Morse
4358 Mr. & Mrs. M. F. Mogg
4400 Mr. & Mrs. S. G. Hinckley
4400 E. G. Hinckley
4402 Dr. & Mrs. John T. Binkley, jr.
4404 Mrs. David Emerick
4406 Mr. & Mrs. B. M. Douglas
4408 Mrs. A. D. Barrett & dr.
Receiving day Wednesday
4408 Mr. & Mrs. Frederick B. Barrett
4410 Mr. & Mrs. George Bristol
4412 Mr. & Mrs. B. F. Patrick jr.
Receiving day Wednesday
4414 Mr. & Mrs. Isaac Hartman

BOULEVARD PLACE.

573 Mr. & Mrs. James M. Smith
575 Mr. & Mrs. Thos. J. Leonard
575 Mr. & Mrs. C. P. Swigert
613 Mr. & Mrs. George M. Lovejoy
625 Mr. & Mrs. D. N. Stearn & drs.
635 Mr. & Mrs. A. P. O'Bryan

634 Miss Mabel E. Goodwin
634 Karl H. Goodwin
636 Mr. & Mrs. Horace E. Wells
640 Mrs. L. C. Patterson & drs.
640 George K. Patterson
640 C. Edgar Patterson

560 Mr. & Mrs. Joseph C. Cohen
562 Mr. & Mrs. Edward C. Bates
568 Mr. & Mrs. Fred P. Sherman
574 Mrs. N. E. Ross
574 William J. Ross
574 Mr. & Mrs. Asa Q. Reynolds
576 Mr. & Mrs. Gustave Myren
624 Mr. & Mrs. Frank C. Randall
626 Mr. & Mrs. H. S. Grose
628 Mr. & Mrs. Rudolph Eiseman
634 Mr. & Mrs. J. H. McCartney
634 Mr. & Mrs. Joseph W. Swain
634 Mrs. Carrie A. Goodwin

BOWEN AVENUE.

61 Mrs. Josephine Burnett
61 Frank Burnett
61 Albert L. Burnett
61 George W. Burnett
73 Mr.& Mrs. Deloss N.Gould& dr.
73 Miss Emma Lang
75 Mr. & Mrs. Herbert Hedges
77 Miss Fannie Schwartz
77 Mrs. S Zuckerman & dr.
79 Mr. & Mrs. Alfred R. Urion
91 Mr. & Mrs. Frank A. Bingham
93 Mr. & Mrs. David L. Druliner
193 Mr. & Mrs. B. P. Mackey & drs.
     Receiving day Thursday
261 Mr. & Mrs. F. A. La Monte
261 E. C. Thurber
263 Mr. & Mrs. A. E. Frankland
269 Mrs. Emma Kissell & dr.
305 Mr. & Mrs. Thos. J. Hartigan
315 John E. Kehoe
325 Dr. & Mrs. George H. Andrews
327 Mr. & Mrs. W. W. Wyatt
327 Miss Louise Mosher
329 Mr. & Mrs. S. VanKirk
333 Mr.& Mrs.Thomas C.Boyd & dr.
333 William Boyd
339 Mrs. Mary C. Taylor & dr.
343 Mr. & Mrs. R. E. Ismond
349 Mr.& Mrs. Fred Flynn
355 Mr. & Mrs. S. Kundtstadter & dr
357 Mr. & Mrs. Lawrence Bayor
359 Mr. & Mrs. Andrew P. Daly
363 Mr. & Mrs. F. H. Holden
363 Miss Abbie L. Howe   ·
367 Mr. & Mrs. Wm. Fulghum
371 Mr. & Mrs. M. C. Scobey & drs
371 Mr. & Mrs. H. G. Hopkins
373 Mr. & Mrs. J. G. Hester
     Receiving day Wednesday.
373 Miss Nancy H. Hester
373 Chas. R. Hester
375 Mr. & Mrs. Michael Herbert
399 Mr. & Mrs. Michael Ash
403 Mr. & Mrs. J. S. Hartmann
405 Mr. & Mrs. H. E. Howard
     Receiving day Friday
411 A. M. Burch
411 Miss Louise M. Dunning
411 Miss Ella M. Hannah
413 Mr. & Mrs. H. J. Pollak
413 Mrs. H. Goldberg & dr.
415 Mr. & Mrs. Alvin Westcott
417 Mr. & Mrs. Chas. A. Stonehill
417 Chas. E. Hyman

80 Mr. & Mrs. John M. Allen
182 Mr. & Mrs. Harry M. Turner
182 Mrs. S. A. Turner
188 Mr. & Mrs. Wm. S. Fell
190 Mr. & Mrs. C. G. Shepard
194 Mr. & Mrs. Alfred Daniels
196 Mr. & Mrs. Louis Hasbrouck
198 Dr. B. A. Cottlow
272 Mr. & Mrs. Frank A. Putnam
278 Mr. & Mrs. Chas. F. Roush
292 Mr. & Mrs. John Hosbury & dr.
298 Miss Anna M. Taylor
298 Miss Susan Taylor
302 Mrs. Mary S. Holloway & dr.
     Receiving day Wednesday
302 Charles Halloway
320 Dr. & Mrs. Morey L. Reed
332 Mr. & Mrs. George F. Morgan
     & drs.
     Receiving day Tuesday
332 Mr. & Mrs. Chas. A. Hetich
332 Mrs. L. C. Upton & dr.
348 Mrs. F. A. Gordon & dr.
350 Mr. & Mrs. Wm. Robyn & dr.
362 Mr. & Mrs. E. P. Rodgers
364 Mrs. E. A. Bain
376 Mr. & Mrs. George S. Finney
378 Mr. & Mrs. Christian Bergerson
378 Mr. & Mrs. Louis Bergerson
390 Mr. & Mrs. William Harpole
390 Mr. & Mrs. Enoch Harpole
394 Samuel J. Litt
402 Mr. & Mrs. W. I. T. Brigham
408 Dr. & Mrs. A. L. Van Patten
410 Mr. & Mrs. J. F. Randolph
410 Miss Ruth F. Randolph
414 Mrs. Kenyon Green
416 Mrs. Ann Green & dr.
416 Mr. & Mrs. A. P. Green
418 Mr. & Mrs. B. Shoninger
444 Mr. & Mrs. W. L. Parrotte
448 Mr. & Mrs. John Spencer
448 Mr. & Mrs. Charles T. Byrne
456 Mrs. Oswin Mayo
460 Mr. & Mrs. MaxyOhnstein
460 Mrs. A. E. Greenhood
460 Mr. & Mrs. Chas. Brunswick
462 Mr. & Mrs. J. E. Strader
464 Mr. & Mrs. Neil McMillan
472 Mr. & Mrs. L. L. Adams
472 E. Clinton Adams
482 Dr. & Mrs. W. C. Stone
486 Mr. & Mrs. C. R. Pfeiffer
494 Mr. & Mrs. John S. Chichester

451 Mrs. Elizabeth S. Grant
451 Mr. & Mrs. W. J. Miller
457 Mr. & Mrs. Harry Gardner
457 W. Herbert O'Connell
457 Mrs. Asahel Pierce & drs.
  Receiving day Friday
457 William F. Pierce
459 Mr.& Mrs. Burke Stone
459 Mr. & Mrs. S. G. Puterbaugh
459 Mr. & Mrs. Harry Gay
459 Rev. & Mrs. Edward C. Ray
463 Mr. & Mrs. Alfred Chichester
463 Mr. & Mrs. John E. Ennis
467 Mr. & Mrs. George Newhaus
467 Mr. & Mrs. A. M. Kitchen
469 Mr. & Mrs. J. C.Considine & drs.
469 Miss Frances Considine
471 Mr. & Mrs. Martin Jonas & dr.

471 James M. Jonas
475 Mr. & Mrs. Robert S. Ross
475 Miss Christina M. Ross
475 Miss Catherine Ross
477 Mrs. O..H. Cheney
479 Mr. & Mrs. J. C. Beifeld
481 Mr. & Mrs. M. Stern
481 Mr. & Mrs. M. Joseph
481 M. B. Joseph
483 Mr. & Mrs. James W. Stevens
485 Mr. & Mrs. James Hood
485 John D. Hood
485 Mr. & Mrs. John G. Boess
489 Rev. & Mrs. Howard A. Johnston

495 Mrs. Mary Kilgour & dr.
495 Harry B. Kilgour
495 Arthur W. Kilgour

BRYANT AVENUE.

19 John B. Adams
19 Nellie M. Adams
21 Mr. & Mrs. William J. Marks
21 Mrs. Dennis C. Graham & drs.
21 Dennis C. Graham
35 Mr. & Mrs. A. D. Hayward
39 Mrs. Martha A. Walker
39 Mrs. Jessie M. Tucker
45 Mr. & Mrs. Eugene C. McCune
57 Mr. & Mrs. Elli A. Beach & dr.
57 Henry L. Beach
57 Clinton S. Beach
59 Mr. & Mrs. O. D. Pillsbury
61 Mr. & Mrs. Jos. G. Talbot
65 Mr. & Mrs Wm. B. Jacobs & drs.
67 Mr. & Mrs. Edward T. Glennon
67 Mrs J. H. Slavin
69 Mrs. Caroline H. Cotton & dr.
69 Charles H. Cotton
77 Mr. & Mrs. Herbert V. Richards
77 Mr. & Mrs. Charles A. Crell
81 Mr. & Mrs. Joseph S. Shaw
83 Dr. & Mrs. S. G. Bailey

80 M. R. Healy
80 Mr. & Mrs. C. A. Orvis & dr.
82 Samuel C. Sargeant
86 Mrs. Mary C. Low & dr.
86 Charles H. Low

12 Mr. & Mrs. David J. Bard
14 Miss Charlotte Murch
14 Mrs. Addie S. Cornell
18 Mr. & Mrs. William S. Bates
22 Mr. & Mrs. Albert H. Barber
26 Mr. & Mrs. Frederick Dickinson
26 John R. Dickinson
30 Mr. & Mrs. Louis P. Herzog
30 Mrs. Mina Degen
32 Mr. & Mrs. Edward J. Merimee
32 I. G. Levy
32 Louis M. Hopkins
34 Mr. & Mrs. Herman Prenzlauer
38 Mrs. E. Goodwin
40 Mr. & Mrs. T. P. Murray
44 Mrs. Mary C. Clark
44 J. S. Clark
44 Frank L. Davis
46 Mr. & Mrs. John L. Jones.
54 Mr. & Mrs. W. S. Goodhue & drs.
54 Homer Goodhue
56 Mr. & Mrs. Louis Hornthal
58 Dr. & Mrs. I. S. Moses
64 Mr. & Mrs. Geo. A. Hastreiter
66 Mr. & Mrs. Frank B. Griffing
68 Mr. & Mrs. Thomas Ackers
74 Mr. & Mrs. Orrin S. Cook & dr.
74 Robert S. Cook
80 Mrs. Elicia F. Sargeant & dr.

CALUMET AVENUE.

1929 George W. Reid
1931 Mr. & Mrs. Charles S. Holt
2101 Mrs. Moses Gunn
2101 Walter C. Gunn

1830 Dr. & Mrs. Wm. E. Casselberry
1832 Mr. & Mrs. John Buckingham
1836 Mr. & Mrs. Norman Williams
1836 Miss Laura Williams

2101 Dr. Malcolm Gunn
2107 Mr. & Mrs. Arthur B. Meeker
& dr.
2115 Mr. & Mrs. John A. Hamlin &
dr.
2115 Fred. R. Hamlin
2115 Herbert W. Hamlin
2119 Mr. & Mrs. Geo. M. Moulton &
dr.   *Receiving day Friday*
2119 Mrs. M. A. Garland
Receiving day Friday
2125 Mr. & Mrs. John A. Markley
2125 Mr. & Mrs. W. Vincent Baker
2129 Mr. & Mrs. William E. Kelley
Receiving day Friday
2129 Wm. R. Kelley
2129 Mrs. Ellen P. Vail
2131 Mr. & Mrs. John Alling & dr.
2131 John Alling jr
2133 Mr. & Mrs. John R. Walsh &
drs.
2141 Mr. & Mrs. D. V. Purington
2141 Miss Sarah Barnes
2201 Mr. & Mrs. B. F. Jacobs
2203 Mr. & Mrs. G. S. McReynolds
2205 J. A. Cassidy & dr.
2205 Harry C. Cassidy
2205 Mrs. V. W. Kay
2207 Mr. & Mrs. John M. Cutter
2207 Miss Mell Campbell
2209 Mr. & Mrs. Albert H. Farnum
2209 Harry W. Farnum
2213 Mr. & Mrs. Lazarus Silverman
& dr.
2217 Mr. & Mrs. M. Bensinger
2217 B. E. Bensinger
2217 Mr. & Mrs. Joseph Fish
2223 Noel S. Munn
2223 Edmund V. Church
2223 R. D. Lyon
2223 Dr. C. J. Swan
2223 Frederick W. Perkins
2227 Dr. & Mrs. Robt. G. Marriner
2229 Mr. & Mrs. Joseph Rosenbaum
Receiving day Friday.
2231 E. P. Tobey & drs.
2233 Mr. & Mrs. O. W. Barrett
2235 Judge & Mrs. Kirk Hawes
2239 Mr. & Mrs. C. L. Raymond
2241 Mr. & Mrs. Frank Hall Childs
2241 Miss Clara Hunt
2241 Clement M. Hunt
2241 A. Lucas Hunt
2243 Mr. & Mrs. Leopold Simon
Receiving day Friday
2243 Miss Bertha Simon

1840 Charles E. Fargo
1900 Judge John D. Caton
1910 Mr. & Mrs. Arthur J. Caton
1922 Mr. & Mrs. Henry Dibblee
1928 Mr. & Mrs. H. N. Greene
Receiving day Friday
1928 Dr. Frank C. Greene
1928 D. Russell Greene
1932 Mr. & Mrs. Leon Mandel
Receiving day Wednesday
1932 Fred L. Mandel
1932 Robert I. Mandel
2000 Mr. & Mrs. Henry Crawford &
dr.
Receiving day Wednesday
2000 William R. Crawford
2000 Miss E. L. Kent
2004 Mr. & Mrs. W.H. Mitchell & drs.
2004 Guy H. Mitchell
2004 Mrs. Louise Stevens
2008 Mrs. P. C. Hanford & dr.
2016 Mr. & Mrs. C. H. Starkweather
2018 Mr. & Mrs. J. A. Kohn & dr.
Receiving day Saturday
2032 Mr. & Mrs. Otto Young
2032 Miss Cecile Young
2032 William Young
2032 Baroness Marie VonUntzer
2100 Mrs. D. B. Fisk
2100 Mr. & Mrs. B. B. Botsford & dr.
2100 Mr. & Mrs. D. M. Fisk
2100 Miss M. B. Fisk
2100 Henry E. Fisk
2106 Mr. & Mrs. A. C. Badger
2106 Miss Ada C. Badger
2114 Mr. & Mrs. John B. Drake & dr.
2114 John B. Drake jr.
2124 Mr. & Mrs. Theodore A. Shaw
2124 Theodore A. Shaw jr.
2128 Mr. & Mrs. John A. Davidson
2140 Mrs. Daniel A. Jones
Receiving day Friday
2220 Mrs. Chas. Gilman Smith
2220 Miss Katherine Hammond
2222 Mrs. A. DeGraff
2222 Robert M. Fair
2222 Miss A. M. Fair
2222 Joseph B. Fair
2238 Mr. & Mrs. Chas. J. Barnes
Receiving day Tuesday
2238 Miss Bertha L. Barnes
2238 Nelson L. Barnes
2240 H. A. Kohn
2240 Mrs. James Springer
2240 Abe Kohn
2240 Mr. & Mrs. Joseph Frank

2244 Mrs. Asa P. Kelley
2244 Mr. & Mrs. W. B. E. Shufeldt
2252 Mrs. Wm. F. Coolbaugh & drs.
2300 Mr. & Mrs. Charles D. Irwin
   Receiving day Thursday
2306 Mr. & Mrs. Augustus W. Green
   Receiving day Friday
2310 Mr. & Mrs. John S.Gould & drs.
2312 Mr. & Mrs. John B. Mayo
   Receiving day Friday
2316 Mrs. Henry L. Hill
2316 Russell D. Hill
2320 Mr. & Mrs. P. J. Roche & drs.
2320 Frank J. Roche
2320 William C. Roche
2328 W. Jarvis Jones
2340 Mr. & Mrs. W. J. L'Engle
2342 Mr. & Mrs. Franklin Nichols
2342 Mrs. Edwin Lee Brown
2342 Mr. & Mrs. James A. Harvey
2346 Dr. & Mrs. Stanley P. Black &
   dr.
2346 Mr.& Mrs. Chas. W.Thompson
2346 Miss Fanchon H. Thompson
2346 Fred Ware Thompson
2346 C. Frederick Livermore
2346 Mrs. Rachael A. I. Pancoast
2346 Mr. & Mrs. J. Cameron Pancoast
2346 Dr. & Mrs. Wm. F. Fowler
2346 F. R. Donahue
2348 Mr. & Mrs. E. S. L. Bacheldor
2348 Mr. & Mrs. Hunter W. Finch
2348 Mr. & Mrs. Willard T. Orr
2354 Mrs. J. E. Cross & dr.
2522 Mr. & Mrs.A.W.Windett & drs.
2522 Victor Windett
2600 Dr. & Mrs. F. W. Mercer
   Receiving day Thursday.
2602 Mr. & Mrs. Asa E. Briggs
2604 Mr. & Mrs. N. W. Campbell
2606 Mr. & Mrs. Chester M. Clark
2606 Mr. & Mrs. William H.Clark
2608 Mr. & Mrs. H. P. Colegrove
2608 Dr. T. Jay Robeson
2616 Mrs. Jennie Hall Aiken
2616 Frank Hall
2616 Miss Mary J. Carrigan
2624 Charles H. Randall
2624 Clarence A. Randall
2624 Mr. & Mrs. T.D. Randall & dr.
2624 Mrs. Charlotte Breese
2632 E. A. Burbank
2646 Dr. & Mrs. John W. Streeter
2704 Mrs. James Stenson
2704 Miss Nellie Stenson

3123 Mrs. Bernard Steele .
3123 Maurice Steele
3127 Mr. & Mrs. Isaac Wedeles
        Receiving day Tuesday
3133 Mr.&Mrs.Benj.Hagaman & dr.
3139 Mr. & Mrs. Lyman Blair jr.
3139 Norman Peck Cooley
3141 Mr. & Mrs. Joseph Deimel
3141 Mr. & Mrs. Rudolph Deimel
3143 Mr. & Mrs. Guy C. Ledyard
3143 Guy C. Ledyard jr.
3147 Mr. & Mrs. Levi B. Bane
3151 Mr. & Mrs. Oswald Lockett
3153 Mr. & Mrs. S. Strauss & drs.
3155 Mr. & Mrs. Melvin J. Neahr
3155 George H. Neahr
3157 Mr. & Mrs. Malcom C. Mitchell
3201 Dr. & Mrs. Ernest Lackner
3201 Mr. & Mrs. J. Grossenheider
3203 Mr. & Mrs. Thomas Kent
3203 Miss Isabella E. Westlake
3207 Mrs. Samuel M. Fleishman
3207 Mrs. Jacob May
3207 Henry Heyman
3211 Mr. & Mrs. John A. Orb
3221 Mr. & Mrs. Francis A. Hayden
        Receiving day Thursday
3221 Miss Mae E. Hayden
3221 James C. Sinclair
3223 Mr. & Mrs. Chas. H. Shriner
3223 Mr. & Mrs. P. Fred Harting
3233 Mr. & Mrs. D. Mayer & dr.
3233 Nathan Mayer
3233 Moses E. Mayer
3245 Mr. & Mrs. Stephen Healy&dr.
3247 Mr. & Mrs. D. H. Baker
3251 Mr. & Mrs. Isaac Dessau
3253 Mr. & Mrs. Henry Kerber & dr.
3255 Mr. & Mrs. Charles Clayton
3305 Mr. & Mrs. Isa Monheimer
3307 Mr. & Mrs. Edw. S. Goodwin
3307 Henry O. Goodwin
3309 Mr.& Mrs. J. Loewenstein & dr.
3309 Harry Loewenstein
3311 Mr. & Mrs. Hiram A. Hanson
3311 Charles H. Hanson
3313 Miss M. L. McAuley
3315 Mr. & Mrs. August Binswanger
        & dr.
3317 Mr. & Mrs. Leopold Seaman
3319 Mr. & Mrs. E. Starr Lloyd
3319 Mrs. C. H. Young
3321 Mr. & Mrs. Morris Cohn
3327 Dr. G. L. Morgenthau
3327 Lewis Morgenthau
3327 Sidney Morgenthau

2710 Mr. & Mrs. W. A. McClelland
2712 Mr. & Mrs. M. C. Hickey & drs.
2712 Charles M. Hickey
2712 Joseph V. Hickey
2714 Mr. & Mrs. E. L. Tabor
2714 Mr. & Mrs. Thos. J. Qualey
2714 Miss Laura Hoover
2716 Mrs. Geo. W. Adams & dr.
2716 Mr. & Mrs. Harry H. Fisher
2718 M . & Mrs. Jacob Schroder &
        drs.
2718 Milton Schroder
2718 Albert Schroder
2728 Mr.& Mrs. William H. Peeke jr
2732 Mr. & Mrs. C. L. Willey
2804 Mr. & Mrs. John Soames
2804 Arthur F. Soames
2818 Mrs. Margaret S. Perine
2818 Josiah W. Perine
2818 Mr. & Mrs. Henry H. Munger
2920 Mrs. Ransom Dexter & dr.
2950 Mr. & Mrs. Edwin Sturtevant
2950 Mr. & Mrs. J. H. Whitman
2954 Mr. & Mrs. James E. Taylor
2954 Mrs. D. W. Sawin
2954 William A. Baack
3010 Mr. & Mrs. J. Manvel & drs.
3010 Dr. R. W. Hardon
3020 Mr. & Mrs. O. D. Wetherell
3020 Albert P. Wetherell
3024 Mr. & Mrs. G. L. Magill
3028 Mr. & Mrs. A. S. Weinsheimer
3032 Mr. & Mrs. George M. Gray
3034 Mr. & Mrs. Thos. Ambrose &
        dr.
3040 Mrs. J. M. Colwell
3040 Dr. Ben. L. Colwell
3040 Ray M. Colwell
3040 Clyde B. Colwell
3044 Mr. &. Mrs. Thomas Dorwin
3048 Mr. & Mrs. Horace S. Hubbard
3050 Mr. & Mrs. L. D. Doty
3058 Mr. & Mrs. Wm. Warren Ab-
        bott
3058 Edwin B. Frank
3058 Mr. & Mrs. Henry M. Sexton
3058 Dr. Chas. W. Klinetop
3058 Dr. & Mrs. Harvey H. Bates
3058 Mr. & Mrs. William R. Everett
3104 Mr. & Mrs. Ira S. Younglove
3118 Mr. & Mrs. William Mueller
        & dr.
3120 Mr. & Mrs. D. K. Tenney
3120 Miss Mary S. Tenney
3120 Mrs. Emily A. Sanborn
3122 Mr. & Mrs. Milton B. Miller

3327 Milton Morgenthau
3327 Miss Morgenthau
3331 Mr. & Mrs. S. Parliament
  Receiving day Wednesday
3331 Mrs. S. J. Ela
3333 Mr. & Mrs. F. W. Holder
3333 C. N. Reynolds
3335 Dr. & Mrs. Mendle A. Cohen
  & drs.
3335 David M. Cohen
3335 Dr. Samuel A. Cohen
3335 Henry A. Cohen
3335 Joseph J. Cohen
3337 Mr. & Mrs. Jordan Hofeld & dr.
3341 Mrs. Marion Goldschmidt &
  drs.
3341 Moses Goldschmidt
3347 Mr. & Mrs. Samuel C. Wing
3347 Mr. & Mrs. D. C. Higley
3351 Dr. & Mrs. A. M. Rivenburgh
3359 Miss Annie Dooling
3359 Miss Ellen Dooling
3361 Mrs. Charles Packer
3363 Mr. & Mrs. Oscar Rosenberg
3369 Mr. & Mrs. Thos. M. Hoyne
3401 Mr. & Mrs. Leo A. Loeb
  Receiving day Thursday
3403 Mr.& Mrs.Frank H. Markham
  Receiving day Thursday
3405 Mr. & Mrs. M. S. Rosenfield
  Receiving day Wednesday
3407 Mr. & Mrs. Henry Klopfer
3409 Mr. & Mrs. T. H. Watson
3409 Thomas Watson
3411 Mr. & Mrs. J. B. Stubbs & dr.
  Receiving day Wednesday
3411 James H. Stubbs
3411 William Stubbs
3413 Mr. & Mrs. Fred F. Day
3415 Mr. & Mrs. S. N. Swan
3435 Mr. & Mrs. David A. Levy
3437 Mr. & Mrs. L. G. Wolff
3441 Mr. & Mrs. J. F. Edgeworth
3515 Mr. & Mrs. Alvin P. Gaylord
3517 Rev. & Mrs. W. W. Fenn
3517 Mrs. H. M. Fenn
3519 Mr. & Mrs. Wm. T. Hall
3523 Rev. & Mrs. S. Feilchenfeld &
  drs.
3523 Bismark Feilchenfeld
3523 Arthur Feilchenfeld
3523 Isaac E. Feilchenfeld
3523 Alex Feilchenfeld
3525 Mr. & Mrs. Frank Beard
3525 George A. Kates
3529 Mr. & Mrs. Alex Goodman

3122 Charles B. Miller
3122 Mr. & Mrs. Edwin G. Forman
3126 Mr. & Mrs. William H. Russell
3126 Mrs. Elizabeth C. White
3132 Mr. & Mrs. John J. Fay jr.
3138 Mr. & Mrs. Aaron Rosenblatt
3140 Carl D. Bradley
3140 Mrs. Barbara O. Bradley
3140 Frank B. Bradley
3140 Howard E. Perry
3140 Mr. & Mrs. James Nellis
3140 Mr. & Mrs. A. H. Tyner
3146 Mrs. Elissette Miller
3146 Louis K. Miller
3146 Mr. & Mrs. Jacob Keim
3150 Mrs. A. Liebenstein & dr.
  Receive 2d and 4th Wednesday
3150 A. M. Liebenstein
3152 Mr. & Mrs. G. L. Stonehill
3152 Mr. & Mrs. Julius Rosenwald
3154 Mr. & Mrs. Henry W. Bryant
3202 Mr. & Mrs. Herman Bornstein
3208 Mr. & Mrs. Alexander Barth
3210 Mr. & Mrs. Leopold Eisenstaedt
3212 Mr. & Mrs. L. B. Dixon
  Receiving day Friday
3212 Lawrence B. Dixon
3212 Mrs. E. D. Smith
3216 Mrs. Anna Wedeles
3216 Edward Wedeles
3216 Sigmund Wedeles
3218 Alfred Despres
3218 Emil M. Despres
3218 Miss Anaise Despres
  Receiving day Friday
3222 Mr. & Mrs. R. H. Countiss &
  drs.
3222 Fred D. Countiss
3224 Mrs. A. R. St. John
3224 James S. Park
3226 Mr. & Mrs. Selden Fish
3228 Mr. & Mrs. N. W. Lyman
3230 Mr. & Mrs. John R. Barrett
3230 George K. Barrett
3232 Mr. & Mrs. S. W. Wyatt
3236 Mr. & Mrs. Benjamin W. Root
3238 Mr. & Mrs. J. D. Sheahan & dr.
3240 Mr. & Mrs. Geo. S. Blakeslee
  & dr.
3242 Mr. & Mrs. Wm. J. Manning
3304 Mr. & Mrs. Joseph Beifeld
  Receiving day Monday
3304 Alexander Beifeld
3304 Morris Hirsch
3306 Mr. & Mrs. Jos. Schaffner

3529 Mrs. R. Deitsch
3533 Mr. & Mrs. Jos. Kaufmann
3535 Mr. & Mrs. Geo. L. Rood
3541 Mrs. Isabelle Wormer
Receiving day Friday
3831 Geo. W. Anderson
3833 Mr. & Mrs. L. D. Powers
3833 Mrs. M. Watkins
3835 Mrs. M. L. Livingston & drs.
3835 Howard W. Livingston
3835 Thomas Livingston
3841 Mr. & Mrs. E. C. Richardson
3843 Mr. & Mrs. E. Pfaelzer
3847 Mr. & Mrs. H. S. Raymond
4101 Mr. & Mrs. James A. Baldwin
4209 Herbert A. Pierce
4209 Mr. & Mrs. Addison S. Pierce
4215 Mr. & Mrs. Paul F. Knefel
4233 Mrs. K. Moran
4233 J. A. Hinsey
4241 Mr. & Mrs. W. G. Anthony
4243 Mr. & Mrs. John W. Walsh
4247 Mr. & Mrs. H. W. Forward
4247 W. Blanchard Moore
4309 Mr. & Mrs. Frank D. Patterson
4309 Mr. & Mrs. C. Earl Patterson
4333 Mr. & Mrs. F. Bending & drs.
4341 Mr. & Mrs. Thos. F. Harvey
Receiving day Wednesday
4343 Mr. & Mrs. Opie Read
Receiving day Friday
4351 Mr. & Mrs. Millard J. Sheridan
4351 Mr. & Mrs. J. H. Breckenridge
4353 Mr. & Mrs. George W. Bittinger
Receiving day Wednesday
4355 Mr. & Mrs. Hugo Brady
4355 Miss Lillie Schoenfeld
4405 Mr. & Mrs. J. H. Wilson
4407 Mrs. Daniel Wilkins
4407 Mr. & Mrs. D. W. Higbie
4409 Mr. & Mrs. W. S. Johnson
4411 Dr. & Mrs. A. V. Park
Receiving day Wednesday
4429 Mr. & Mrs. J. A. Loranger
4749 Mr. & Mrs. M. Fleming
4749 Mr. & Mrs. D. Cromelien
4749 Mr. & Mrs. Charles A. Allen
4751 Mrs. C. Payen & drs.
4757 Frank B. Hall
4901 Dr. W. K. Foote
4901 H. A. Jones

———

3528 Mr. & Mrs. B. F. Stewart & dr.
Receiving day Tuesday

3306 Miss Rachael Schaffner
3308 Mr. & Mrs. James P. Sherwin
3308 Mr. & Mrs. V. P. Sherwin
3308 Charles E. Clifton
3312 Mr. & Mrs. B. Lindauer & dr.
Receive Monday afternoon
3312 Julius B. Lindauer
3316 Mr. & Mrs. L. Loewenstein & dr.
3316 Emanuel L. Loewenstein
3316 Sidney Loewenstein
3320 Mr. & Mrs. Harry Hart
Receiving day Thursday
3322 Mr. & Mrs. Clarence A. Knight
3326 Mr. & Mrs. Frank Behrens
3330 Mr. & Mrs. Paul Brown
3332 Mr. & Mrs. Joseph Bond
3336 Mr. & Mrs. Silas Huntley
3336 Mr. & Mrs. Jas. H. Gilbert & dr.
3338 Mr. & Mrs. Edmund Pendleton
3338 Henry Clarke
3342 Mr. & Mrs. Wm. D. Stein
3344 Mrs. Orvil S. Abbott
3348 Mrs. J. E. Hebard
3350 Mr. & Mrs. E. Saltsman
3352 Mr. & Mrs. Charles J. Furst
3356 Mr. & Mrs. George A. Gilbert
3358 Mr. & Mrs. George F. Bunday
3358 Miss Blanche Bunday
3358 George J. Bunday
3360 Mr. & Mrs. Chauncey E. Seaton
3362 Mr. & Mrs. O. S. Caspary
Receiving day Monday
3364 David Witkowsky
3364 Leopold Witkowsky
3364 Miss Esther Witkowsky
3400 Mr. & Mrs. Geo. Atwell Hamlin
3402 Mr. & Mrs. Louis Eisendrath
3408 Dr. & Mrs. R. A. Clark
3412 Edward A. Moore
3412 Mr. & Mrs. E. F. Moore & drs.
3412 James B. Smith
3414 Mr. & Mrs. M. A. Weinberg & dr.
3422 Mr. & Mrs. Joseph Baer
3424 Mr. & Mrs. Amson Stern
3430 Joseph Kline & drs.
3430 Mrs. Kline
3430 Julius Kline
3432 Mr. & Mrs. Geo. Braham & dr.
3512 Mr. & Mrs. Wellington Leavitt
3514 Mrs. C. Sumerfield & dr.
3516 Mr. & Mrs. David Thompson
3518 Mr. & Mrs. W. M. Baker
3522 Mr. & Mrs. Edward J. Judd
3524 Prof. & Mrs. Frank C. Hatch

4120 Herman U. Hitt
4122 Mr. & Mrs. Chas. E. Hayward
4126 Mr. & Mrs. George H. Rugg
4132 Mr. & Mrs. I. D. Richards
    & dr.
4156 Mr. & Mrs. M. R. Moses
4158 Mr. & Mrs. John A. Doherty
4158 Mr. & Mrs. J. H. W. Bride
4158 Mr. & Mrs. S. C. Johnstone
4200 Dr. O. W. McMichael
4200 Mr. & Mrs. S. B. McMichael
4202 Mr.&Mrs. S. Mendelsohn&drs.
    Receiving day Friday
4202 Jacob S. Mendelsohn
4202 Samuel S. Mendelsohn
4202 Max S. Mendelsohn
4204 Mr. & Mrs. S. D. Witkowsky
4210 Mr. & Mrs. Ethel Edwin Wilson
4210 Thomas E. Wilson
4210 Moses Wilson & drs.
4212 Mr. & Mrs. Thomas S. Norton
4216 Mr. & Mrs. Saul Shoninger
4216 Mr. & Mrs. Julius Speyer
4220 Mr. & Mrs. C. F. McVeigh
4226 Mr. & Mrs. Ferdinand Langbein & drs.
    Receiving day Friday
4228 Mr. & Mrs. Edward J.Queeney
4234 Mr. & Mrs. Morris Mayer
4234 Abe Hart
4236 Mr. & Mrs. M. Ruben & drs.
    Receiving day Friday
4236 Charles Ruben
4306 Mrs. Evelyn Leckie & drs.
4306 Mr. & Mrs. George T. Morgan
4306 Mrs. E. Mack
4324 Charles Friend
4338 Mr. & Mrs. W. H. Hennessey
4338 Miss Isabel McEnerny
4352 Mr. & Mrs. Thomas M.Norton
4354 Mr. & Mrs. Wm. H. Wood
4356 Mr. & Mrs. Abner Piatt & dr.
4500 Mr. & Mrs. J. K. Cady
4500 Jacob T. Foster
4852 Mr. & Mrs. Louis H. Marston

(ENGLEWOOD).

326 Mr. & Mrs. W. D. Kennedy
332 Mr. & Mrs. John Mies
334 Rev. & Mrs. Chas. Reynolds

CHAMPLAIN AVENUE.

4215 Mr. & Mrs. William Garnett jr.
4227 Mrs. Caroline H. Lutz & dr.
4227 Mrs. Margaret D. Howard
4227 Harry G. Davis
4243 Mr. & Mrs. W. K. Haynes
4315 Mrs. Sarah W. Booth
4319 Mr. & Mrs. N. H. Carpenter
4321 Mrs. L. H. Carpenter
4401 Dr. & Mrs. N. H. Henderson
4405 Mr. & Mrs. Samuel Dietrick
4417 Mr. & Mrs. O. W. Hinckley
4419 Mr. & Mrs. W. H. Moore
4421 Mr. & Mrs. A. L. Potter
4421 Irving B. Potter
4421 Allen L. Potter
4421 Augustus E. Potter
4427 Mr. & Mrs. Edward S. Meloy
4427 Mrs. Jenny Mitchell
4427½ Mr. & Mrs. OrrenV.Stookey
4433 Fred L. Ryder
4437 Mr. & Mrs. John Vosburgh &
     dr.
4437 Frank Ilse
4437 Mr., & Mrs. Raymond Lipe
4441 Edmond S. Holbrook & drs.
4451 Mr. & Mrs. G. W. Chandler
4455 Mr. & Mrs. O. S. Gaither
4541 Mr. & Mrs. F. H. Wolford
4551 Mrs. C. E. Page
     Receiving day Wednesday
4551 Edgar Pope
4613 Mr. & Mrs. James Buchanan
4613 Thomas Kirby
4613 Mr. & Mrs. John F. Mathews
4629 Mr. & Mrs. Wm. Murray & dr.
4715 Mr. & Mrs. R. W. Playford jr.
4717 Mr. & Mrs. Edward G. Gilbert
4717 Mr. & Mrs. Wm. M. Thacher
     & dr.
4723 Mr. & Mrs. Wm. M. Miller
4729 Mr. & Mrs. W. W. Taberner
4733 Mr. & Mrs. O. H. Bardwell
4737 Mr. & Mrs. John J. Van Nos-
     trand & dr.
4739 Mr. & Mrs. Alfred C. Bryan
4743 Mr. & Mrs. G. W. Conover
4749 Mr. & Mrs. G. P. Vosbrink
4749 Mr. & Mrs. J. E. Shaughnessy
4815 Mr. & Mrs. George A. Emery
4821 Mrs. Shirley Wetmore
4821 Mr. & Mrs. Eugene Briot
4821 Lillie Briot
4823 Mr. & Mrs. J. P. Beal
4921 Mr. & Mrs. Richard S. Walsh

4240 Mrs. W. H. Edgar & dr.
4240 William H. Edgar
4240 Mrs, James F. Wallace
     Receiving day Thursday
4316 Mr. & Mrs. M. K. Stewart
     & drs.
4342 Mr. & Mrs. Charles L. Reed
4356 Mr. & Mrs. Wm. A. Fulton
4404 John A. Moody
4404 Miss Susan I. Moody
4418 Mr. & Mrs. J. J. Farrelly
4420 Mr. & Mrs. F. C. Penniman
4420 Mr. & Mrs. C. T. Zahringer
4422 Mr. & Mrs. G. F. Geist
4444 Mr. & Mrs. Alfred E. Harper
4448 Mr. & Mrs. John C. Ilse
4518 Mr.&Mrs. William J.Reynolds
4532 Mr. & Mrs. D. C. Paxson
4552 Mr. & Mrs. W. H. Duffield
4608 Mr. & Mrs. Robert J. Hill
     Receiving day Thursday
4610 Mr. & Mrs. Daniel Boyle
4620 Mr. & Mrs. Geo. Brill & dr.
     Receiving day Friday
4620 Miss Carrie Brill
4626 Mr. & Mrs. Thomas B. Seavey
4724 Mr. & Mrs. Truman D. Gore
4726 Mr. & Mrs. John E. Day & dr.
4730 Mr. & Mrs. P. Noonan
4734 Mr. & Mrs. L. W. Allenberg
4736 Mr.& Mrs. Hiram H. Newhall
4738 Mr. & Mrs. Charles H. Doane
4738 William W. Doane
4740 Mr. & Mrs. Horace L. Cooper
4742 Mr. & Mrs. George O. Gordon
4744 Mr. & Mrs. Charles B. Thomp-
     son
4744 Frederick A. Liscombe
4748 Mr. & Mrs. Willard A.Roberts
4748 Mrs. Sarah C. Whiteman
4750 Mr. & Mrs. John J. Rogers&dr.
4752 Mrs. Clara F. Miller
     Receiving day Friday
4752 Mrs. Elizabeth T. Means & dr.
4756 Mr. & Mrs. John Coulter
     Receiving day Tuesday
4758 Mr. & Mrs. Frederick J. Hamill
     Receiving day Friday
4806 Mr. & Mrs. A. C. Thomas
4808 Mr. & Mrs. E. C. Shankland
4814 Mr. & Mrs. William H. Hop-
     kins   *Receiving day Friday*
4834 Mr. & Mrs. Robert L. Grady
4920 Mr. & Mrs. Jacob F. Doerr

4923 Mr. & Mrs. Frederick Rex-
    inger & dr.
4923 Mr. & Mrs. George W. Carr

4924 Mr. & Mrs. John Doerr
    Receiving day Thursday
4924 William P. Doerr

CHESTNUT STREET (ENGLEWOOD).

315 Mr. & Mrs. J. A. Dunn
317 Mr. & Mrs. Edward Larkin&dr.
317 John A. Larkin
321 Mr. & Mrs. Albert Fisher & drs.
321 Albert Fisher jr.
325 Mr.&Mrs.I.LeGrand Lockwood
    Receiving day Thursday
335 Mr. & Mrs. E. R. Merrell
427 Mr. & Mrs. J. L. Schureman
427 Mr. & Mrs. J. L. Schureman jr.
533 Mr. & Mrs. Samuel G. Goss
535 Rev. & Mrs. N. S. Haynes
549 Mr. & Mrs. A. A. Fox
559 Mrs. Lucy E. Sisson & drs.
603 Mr. & Mrs. W. W. Robinson
607 Mrs. C. E. Sloan & drs.
607 Mr. & Mrs. Wolsey A. Sloan
607 J. Richard Sloan
611 Mr. & Mrs. C. E. Green
615 Mrs. H. L. Byrne & drs.
735 Mr. & Mrs. R. N. Youngblood
737 Mr. & Mrs. Charles W. Taylor
—
638 Mr. & Mrs. George W. Baker
640 L. Bartholomew
640 Mr. & Mrs. G. W. Atterbury
646 Mr. & Mrs. James B. Crummey
650 Mr. & Mrs. Samuel Russell
708 William B. Rice & dr.
708 Mr. & Mrs. P. B. Harrison
732 Mr. & Mrs. Willard C. Smith

318 Mr. & Mrs. W. D. Nicholes
318 I. Ellsworth Nicholes
318 Miss Anna E. Nicholes
318 Miss S. Grace Nicholes
318 Mr. & Mrs. C. W. Braithwaite
340 Mr. & Mrs. F. A. Woodbury
340 Mrs. S. D. Moore
340 C. H. Moore
350 Rev. & Mrs. O. E. Murray
    Receiving day Thursday
356 Mr. & Mrs. P. W. George
402 Mr. & Mrs. F. F. Porter
522 Mr. & Mrs. James Baynes
524 Mrs. E. A. Lockart & dr.
528 Mr. & Mrs. A. J. Cutler
532 Mr. & Mrs. W. J. Hoag
540 Mr. & Mrs. Robert J. Roulston
544 Mr. & Mrs. Wm. H. Garrett
548 Mr. & Mrs. J. H. Lehner
558 Mr. & Mrs. Ely Bliss
600 Allen Gregory
606 Mr. & Mrs. Charles S. Beach
608 Mr. & Mrs. E. T. Evans
608 R. H. Evans
608 B. C. Evans
610 Mr. & Mrs. H. L. Phelps
610 Miss Maud Burhance
614 Mr. & Mrs. Robert Ansley
    Receiving day Thursday
630 Mrs. N. E. Hutchins & dr.
630 Earl A. Hutchins

COLLEGE PLACE.

34 Mr. & Mrs. Chas. W. McCluer
34 Mrs. Kittie Munger

34 Mrs. Glendora Bidwell

CORNELL AVENUE.

5115 Mr. & Mrs. J. F. Barney
5115 Mr. & Mrs. J. E. Amos jr.
5125 Mr. & Mrs. J. S. Carpenter
5125 W. P. Griswold
5127 Mr. & Mrs. C. A. Weaver
5147 Frederic D. Ware
5149 Mr. & Mrs. J. Austin Brown
    Receiving day Friday
5313 Mr. & Mrs. Frank Wood
5327 Mr. & Mrs. S. L. Underwood
5327 Mr. & Mrs. S. F. Underwood

5106 Mr. & Mrs. Adam Armstrong
5130 Mrs. Junius Mulvey
    Receiving day Thursday
5130 Arthur B. Mulvey
5200 Mr. & Mrs. E. T. Root & drs.
5204 Mr. & Mrs. Alfred Wayte
5206 Mr. & Mrs. H. C. M. Thomson
5214 Mr. & Mrs. W. L. Robinson
5238 Mr. & Mrs. Walter J. Gray
5316 Mrs. E. D. Jameson & dr.
5316 Franklin Denison

5333 Mr. & Mrs. F. W. Root & dr.
5335 Mrs. H. E. Hubbard
5339 Mr. & Mrs. J. A. Phillips & dr.
5401 Mr. & Mrs. F. W. Sanger
        Receiving day Thursday
5401 Mrs. M. C. Sanger
5451 Mr. & Mrs. G. L. Paddock & dr.
5461 Mrs. George Driggs
5461 Miss Josephine C. Griffing
5461 Frank L. Douglas
5473 Mr. & Mrs. H. B. Johnson
5473 Mr. & Mrs. Edward L. Dennis
5473 R. L. Parsons
5477 Mrs. J. N. Smart
5495 Mr. & Mrs. R. W. Hyman jr.
        Receiving day Wednesday
5501 Mr. & Mrs. C. D. Rogers
5503 Mr. & Mrs. A. G. Wellington
5505 Mr. & Mrs. J. C. Fleming
5511 Mr. & Mrs. Henry Phillips
5517 Mr. & Mrs. Arthur Kirke
        Baldwin
5533 Mr. & Mrs. M. G. Sterrett
5535 Mr. & Mrs. John Wooley
5539 Mr. & Mrs. Frank W. Smith

———

5538 Mr. & Mrs. Gilbert E. Porter
5540 Mrs. I. McWhinney
5540 Mr. & Mrs. Edward Lowy

5326 Mr. & Mrs. Frederick R.Lamb
5326 Walter J. Feron
5334 Mr. & Mrs. H. Schuhmann
5334 David H. Schuhmann
5340 George R. Mitchell
5402 Mr. & Mrs. R. W. Bridge
5402 Miss A. E. Allison
5420 Mrs. E. H. Hall & dr.
5422 Mrs. M. G. Dow
5422 Mr. & Mrs. George H. French
5448 Mr. & Mrs. E. Listenwalter
5450 Mr. & Mrs. D. M. Lord
5458 Mr. & Mrs. A. E. Dyer
5476 Mr. & Mrs. George Miller
5476 Mr. & Mrs. James McLean
5480 Mr. & Mrs. J. H. Ware
5484 Dr. & Mrs. E. E. Smith
5504 Mr. & Mrs. F. C. Lewis
5508 Mr. & Mrs. Charles S. Mason
5510 Mr. & Mrs. J. S. Hendrickson
5510 Ernest Hendrickson
5530 Mr.& Mrs.Edwin Burritt Smith
5530 Miss S. E. Dauman
5534 Frank L. Eastman
5538 Mr. & Mrs. C. B. Brown
5538 Mr. & Mrs. George Lorimer
5538 Mr. & Mrs. J. C. Conrad
5538 Mr. & Mrs. Wm. Brooks Covell
        Receiving day Monday
5538 Miss Mae Kimball
        Receiving day Monday

COTTAGE GROVE AVENUE.

3269 Dr. & Mrs. H. I. Davis
3311 Mr. & Mrs. D. Blackman
3311 Mr. & Mrs. Wm. Dodds
4201 Mr. & Mrs. W. P. Gorsline
4313 Mr. & Mrs. Harry D. Hollister
cor. 52d The Renfost
        Mr. & Mrs. E. J. Adair
        Mr. & Mrs. Robert C. Adams
            & dr.
        Mr. & Mrs. T. H. Arnold
        Mr. & Mrs. Geo. S. Atterbury
        John C. Barr
        Mr. & Mrs. D. C. Beard
        Mr. & Mrs. Edward Benedict
        Mr. & Mrs. Harry Bitner
        Mr. & Mrs. B. F. Bruce jr.
        Mr. & Mrs. C. C. Bruckner
        Mr. & Mrs. E. W. Burdick
        Mr. & Mrs. Calvin L. Cole
        Mrs. Margaret Collins
        Mrs. Carrie R. Crane
        Mr. & Mrs. R. O. Evans

2304 Dr. H. T. Murphy
3000 Mr. & Mrs. August Newhouse
3030½ Mr. & Mrs. C. Louis Amberg
3300 Dr. J. A. Dinwoody
3312 Dr. & Mrs. D. D. Richardson
        Receiving day Wednesday
3638 Arthur W. Bigelow M.D.
3720 J. B. Cahill
3948 Mrs. Dr. M. A. Bowerman
3976 Dr. Theron Bradford
4102 Dr. & Mrs. F. M. Stringfield
4136 Mr. & Mrs. Henry D. Field
4136 Mr. & Mrs. Lew Rothschild
4136 P. H. Keenan
4136 Llewellyn B. Lesh
4154 Dr. Laura L. Randolph
4154 Dr. Richard Randolph
4338 Mr. & Mrs. J. H. Eastburn &dr.
4338 Arthur Eastburn
4458 Dr. A. Ralph Johnstone
4458 Evan L. Lloyd
4516 Mr. & Mrs. M. C. Stender

Mr. & Mrs. Frederic A. Hamilton
Mr. & Mrs. Geo. A. Hamilton
Mr. & Mrs. E. A. Henderson
Mr. & Mrs. Harry Langle
Mr. & Mrs. S. A. Mallory
Mr. & Mrs. J. I. Marshall
Mr. & Mrs. John A. Mohler
Mrs. Anna Owens
Dr. Henry J. Reynolds
Miss Elizabeth Reynolds
Mrs. F. F. Schroder
Mr. & Mrs. A. J. Sharpe
Mr. & Mrs. B. D. Southard
Mr. & Mrs. George N. Terry
Mrs. H. Treadwell
Mr. & Mrs. C. C. Valentine
Mr. & Mrs. K. E. Valentine
Watts Valentine
Mr. & Mrs. A. C. Van Duyne
Mr. & Mrs. Thomas Vetter
Dr. & Mrs. B. Whelan

5415 Dr. & Mrs. M. J. Jones
5415 Mrs. Florence Chapman
5415 Mr. & Mrs. S. C. Hayes
5415 Mr. & Mrs. M. V. Gannon
5415 Mr. & Mrs. K. C. Pardee & dr.
5415 F. J. Pardee
5415 Mr. & Mrs. Edwin Hasbrouck
5415 Alliger Hasbrouck
5415 Mrs. S. N. Lilienthal
5415 Miss Luella Kerr
5415 Mrs. E. J. Mostyn
5415 Wellington Cobb
5415 Arthur Cobb
5425 Mr. & Mrs. E. D. McConnell
5425 Mr. & Mrs. M. Rogers
5429 Mr. & Mrs. Clement L. Clapp
5429 Mrs. R. C. Hilgard & drs.
5429 Mr. & Mrs. A. W. Shults & dr.
5429 Mr. & Mrs. E. T. Keim
5431 Mr. & Mrs. Jules Girardin

DICKEY STREET.

5931 Mr. & Mrs. William Gately
6257 Mr. & Mrs. F. E. Jack
6457 Mr. & Mrs. J. H. Wyman
6459 Mr. & Mrs. F. M. Carsley
6459 Mr. & Mrs. Frank H. Noble

5930 Mr. & Mrs. Chas. A. Warren
5944 Jos. H. Schneider & drs.
5944 Henry Schneider
6434 Mr. & Mrs. Wm. Sigler
6434 S. Sigler
6438 Mr. & Mrs. Wm. H. Tatge

DREXEL AVENUE

5201 Mr. & Mrs. Austin J. Doyle
5201 Austin J. Doyle jr.
5541 Mr. & Mrs. Wm. F. Axtman
6413 Mr. & Mrs. P. L. Simpson
6547 Mr. & Mrs. William O. Wolfe
6631 Mr. & Mrs. J. H. Symeson
6633 Mr. & Mrs. M. O'Sullivan
———
6338 Mr. & Mrs. F. D. Hoag
6340 Mr. & Mrs. Augustus Hussey
6352 Mr. & Mrs. G. C. Miller
6422 H. S. Browne

5836 Mr. & Mrs. Edward W. Bemis
6316 Mr. & Mrs. P. M. Murphy
6316 Dr. & Mrs. C. R. Rowley
6318 Mr. & Mrs. R. Findlay
6320 Mrs. A. Flook
6320 Mr. & Mrs. George S. Barry
6320 W. E. Barry
6322 Mr. & Mrs. Charles E. Bartley
6328 Mr. & Mrs. George P. Mills
6330 Mr. & Mrs. John Byrne
6336 Mrs. F. D. Porter & drs.

DREXEL BOULEVARD.

3961 Mr. & Mrs. Telford Burnham
  Receiving day Tuesday
3963 Mr. & Mrs. George Hackney
3965 Mr. & Mrs. W. J. Edbrooke
3975 Dr. E. B. Weston
3975 Miss M. E. Weston
3977 Mr. & Mrs. P. Kuntz
  Receiving day Wednesday

3946 Dr. F. B. Ullery
3946 Dr. J. D. McGowan
3958 Mr. & Mrs. Henry B. Dodge
3960 Dr. & Mrs. T. R. Potter
3960 Mr. & Mrs. N. MacMillan
  Receiving day Wednesday
3960 Miss H. Fish Taylor
3960 Miss H. Newton Taylor

3979 Mrs. L. V. Maull
3981 Mr. & Mrs. J. C. Thomas
3983 Mr. & Mrs. W. W. McCarty
3985 Mr. & Mrs. E. B. Sherman
3985 B. W. Sherman
3987 Mr. & Mrs. Daniel H.Kochers-
  perger
    Receiving day Friday
3987 Mr. & Mrs. Arthur J. Morrison
3989 Mr. & Mrs. Robt. E. Jenkins &
  dr. *Receiving day Thursday*
3989 George R. Jenkins
3993 Mr. & Mrs. C. H. Crawford
3995 Mr. & Mrs. D. W. Potter
  & dr.
3995 Mr. & Mrs. F. M. Smith
4001 Mr. & Mrs. J. H. McFarland
    Receiving day Wednesday
4001 Mr. & Mrs. Cres Smith
4003 Mrs. R. H. Fleming
4007 Mrs. Ellery C. Spinney
4011 Miss M. E. Brookings
4013 Mr.& Mrs. C. Middleton Smith
4013 Mr. & Mrs. Arthur J. O'Leary
4025 Mr. & Mrs. William A. Bond
4033 Mr. & Mrs. N. T. Read
4037 Mr. & Mrs. J. H. Bell
4045 Hiram A. Gooch
4045 Carolus Brenner
4101 Mr. & Mrs. W. H. Starbuck
4101 Miss Jessie Kerr
4101 Mr. & Mrs. Henry W. Cook
4105 Mrs. Thomas Dunne
4105 Mr. & Mrs. William H. Hoops
4109 Mr. & Mrs. Albert H. Thacker
4111 Mr. & Mrs. J. Robert Thacker
4111 R. F. Edgecomb
4111 C. Edward Thacker
4115 Mr. & Mrs. Geo. L. Pratt
    Receiving day Wednesday
4115 Mr. & Mrs. Clinton B. Pratt
4119 Baroness Von Reichert
4121 Mr. &. Mrs. Jacob H. Gregory
4121 A. W. Gregory
4123 Mr. & Mrs. W. E. Hennessy
    Receiving day Wednesday
4123 W. B. Hennessy
4123 C. M. Hennessy
4125 Dr. & Mrs. Joseph B. Bacon
4127 Dr. & Mrs. Willoughby Walling
4129 Mrs. R. Lancaster
4129 Dr. & Mrs. F. A. Emmons
4241 Mr. & Mrs. J. A. Gauger
4243 Mr. & Mrs. S. H. Hunt

3960 David W. Blair
3960 Dr. J. M. Sleicher
3974 Dr. & Mrs. W. H. Schrader
4000 Mr. & Mrs. A. N. Linscott
4000 Harry F. Linscott
4000 Dr. & Mrs. D. B. Freeman
4004 Mr. & Mrs. Horace W. Soper
4008 Mr. & Mrs. Harry Hoffman
4008 Miss Sylvia Garrity
4012 Mr.& Mrs.Thos. C.Pennington
4012 Charles R. Pennington
4014 Miss Juliette McLaughlin
4014 Mr. & Mrs J. A. McCartney
4014 Joseph A. McCartney jr.
4020 Mr. & Mrs. Egerton Adams
    Receiving day Friday
4020 Mrs. Frances M. Steele
4024 Mrs. M. F. Coe
4024 Dr. & Mrs. A. H. Hiatt
4026 Dr. & Mrs. W. M. Harsha
4106 Mrs. L. M. Wilson
4124 Mr. & Mrs. C. Engstrom
4124 Luther C. Young
4128 Harry C. Head
4130 Mr. & Mrs. James M. Smith
4130 Mrs. J. E. Whitney
4148 Mr. & Mrs. A. G. Cone
4148 Mr. & Mrs. W. S. Bond
4166 Mr. & Mrs. John W. Iliff
4168 Mr. & Mrs. G. F. Cram
  & drs.
4200 Mr. & Mrs. Charles C. Landt
4202 Mr. & Mrs. S. A. Humiston
4204 Mr. & Mrs. Francis Beidler
4206 Dr. & Mrs. O. W. F. Snyder
4212 Mr. & Mrs. Jno. Blair Robertson
4212 Gordon S. Robertson
4246 Mr. & Mrs. J. L. Bobo
4246 S. J. Mowen
4342 Mr. & Mrs. Chauncey J. Blair,
  after May 1st, 1895, 4830
  Drexel boul.
    Receiving day Tuesday
4346 Mr. & Mrs. William H. Keogh
  & dr.
    Receiving day Thursday
4346 James B. Keogh
4346 Chester H. Keogh
4346 John W. Keogh
4450 Mr. & Mrs. James Stinson
4450 Henry Stinson
4450 Miss Cornelia Stinson
4450 Miss Margaret Stinson
4508 Mr. & Mrs. S. T. Fish
    Rec. days 2d and 4th Wednesdays

4245 Mr. & Mrs. E. Sidney Lunt
  Receiving day Wednesday
4247 Dr. & Mrs. L. L. McArthur
4247 Mrs. M. A. Walker
4313 Mr. & Mrs. C. W. Powell & dr.
4313 Clifford Powell
4315 Mr. & Mrs. Adolph Kraus &
  dr.
4325 Mr. & Mrs. M. Rieman
  Receiving day Wednesday
4329 Mr. & Mrs. J. M. Gartside
  Receiving day Friday
4337 Mr. & Mrs. David S. Googins
  & dr.
4337 Joseph B. Googins
4345 Mr. & Mrs. George D. Holton
4353 Mr. & Mrs. George A. Fuller
4353 Miss Grace BeatriceFuller
4415 Mr. & Mrs. Franklin C. Jocelyn
4419 Mr. & Mrs. John H. Weiss
4425 Mr. & Mrs. Henry C. Levi
4427 Mr. & Mrs. Charles Netcher
  Receiving day Thursday
4433 Mr. & Mrs. Henry Falker & dr.
4501 Mr. & Mrs. C. H. Smith
4537 Mr. & Mrs. Anthony Schmitt
  & dr.
  Receiving day Thursday
4537 Eugene J. Schmitt
4545 Mr. & Mrs. W. E. Hale
4545 Mr. & Mrs. George E. Hale
4545 George W. Hale
4605 Mr. & Mrs. John A. Roche &
  dr.
4613 Mr. & Mrs. E. Crane Wilson
4613 Dr. & Mrs. Luke Hitchcock
4613 Luke I. Wilson
4613 Miss Adelaide Wilson
4623 Mr. & Mrs. Everett W. Brooks
4623 Miss Evelyn Brooks
4623 Miss Janet Robertson
4637 Mr. & Mrs. C. E. Gifford
4637 Mr. & Mrs. I. C. Gifford
4651 Mr. & Mrs. Warren F. Leland
4651 Charles W. Leland
4825 Mr. & Mrs. Albert Wisner
  Receiving day Tuesday

4520 Mr. & Mrs. N. W. Harris
  Receiving day Friday
4520 N. Dwight Harris
4650 Mr. & Mrs. H. P. Darlington
  Receiving day Tuesday
4650 Frank Floyd
4700 Mr. & Mrs. James W. Oakley
  Receiving day Friday
4700 Miss Bertha Oakley
4700 Miss Annie Oakley
4700 Mrs. M. Oakley-Carson
4724 Mr. & Mrs. Geo. T. Williams
4724 Grant Williams   ·
4724 Mrs. M. J. Eggleston
4730 Mr. & Mrs. Caleb H. Marshall
  *Receive Monday afternoons and
  evenings.*
4730 Benj. H. Marshall
4730 Miss Carrie L. Phillips
4730 Edmund R. Phillips
4736 Wm. Fleming
4736 Misses Sarah & Dierdre Fleming
4740 Mr. & Mrs. S. B. Walton &
  drs.
4742 Mr. & Mrs. Henry E. Weaver
4902 Harlan Kent Bolton
4902 James Bolton
4938 Dr. & Mrs. J. A. McGill
4938 Miss Elizabeth Coonley
4938 Walter D. Ball
4960 Mr. & Mrs. A. S. Trude & dr.
  Receiving day Thursday
4960 George A. Trude
4960 Alfred Percy Trude
4960 Mrs. A. P. Dana
  Receiving day Thursday
5012 Mr. & Mrs. Siegfried M. Fischer
5016 Mr. and Mrs. Adolph Nathan
  Receiving day Wednesday

———

4851 Mr. & Mrs. Martin A. Ryerson
  Receiving day Tuesday
4917 Mr. & Mrs. C. H. Matthiessen
4941 Mr. & Mrs. John H. Nolan

EAST END AVENUE.

5110 Mr. & Mrs. Horace R. Hobart
5120 Mr. & Mrs. Robert Law
5126 Mr. & Mrs. W. F. Hunt
5126 Arthur S. Peebles
5126 William S. Peebles
5200 Mr. & Mrs. James Morgan

5200 Dr. & Mrs. H. H. Frothingham
5220 Mr. & Mrs. A. R. Porter
5334 Mrs. E. Edwards
5406 Mr. & Mrs. R. S. Thompson & dr.
5420 C. B. Wood
5420 Webster Wood   ·

5420 Miss Julia Wood
5420 Miss Caroline Wood
5420 Miss Harriet Wood
5482 Mrs. L. P. Perry
    Receiving day Thursday
5484 Mr. & Mrs. D. Johnston
    Receiving day Thursday
5488 Mr. & Mrs. Joseph Roster
5488 Mr. & Mrs. C. L. Pierce
5488 Mr. & Mrs. F. H. Atkinson

5488 Mr. & Mrs. M. Strauss
5488 Mr. & Mrs. Munson T. Case
5488 Mr. & Mrs. Nelson Burchard
5490 Fred S. Ackerman
5496 Mr. & Mrs. C. W. Smith
5498 Mr. & Mrs. J. Stockly Cary
5518 Mr. & Mrs. W. B. Conkey
5522 Mr. & Mrs. N. Anderson & dr.
5530 Mr. & Mrs. E. S. Rice

EDGERTON AVENUE.

6039 Mr. & Mrs. E. S. Sibley
6045 Mr & Mrs. Frank I. Bennett
6049 Mr. & Mrs. L. D. Cortright
6071 Mr.& Mrs. Lawrence C. Moore

6020 Mr. & Mrs. Ralph R. Crocker
6020 Hubert D. Crocker
6046 Mr. & Mrs. James Rosenthal
6048 Harry S. Updike

EGGLESTON AVENUE.

6929 Mr. & Mrs. I. O. Harsh
6929 J. Irving Harsh
6953 Mrs. Henrietta Fowler
7111 Mr. & Mrs. C. H. Tabor
7525 Stewart Moore & drs.
7529 Mr. & Mrs. Chas. L. VanDoren
7833 Mr. & Mrs. A. T. Olmstead
7849 Mr. & Mrs. H. Brown
———
7526 Mrs. I. F. Dillon
7620 Mr. & Mrs. Waldo H. Marshall
7620 Mrs. Margaret Marshall
7648 Mr. & Mrs. S. W. Earle
7716 Mr. & Mrs. Chas. A. Birney
7720 Mr. & Mrs. H. A. Ferguson
7726 Mr. & Mrs. W. Roulet
7726 Miss Florence Spence
7730 Mr. & Mrs. E. R. Ealy
7816 Mr. & Mrs. Z. D. Scobey

6920 Mr. & Mrs. Fred K. Higbie
    Receiving day Wednesday
7024 Mr. & Mrs. Henry H. Davis &
    dr.
7100 Mr. & Mrs. E. J. Hill & dr.
7100 Fred. W. Hill
7112 Dr. & Mrs. Joseph DeSilva
    Receiving day Tuesday
7114 Mr. & Mrs. Alex. McDouall
7114 John D. McDougall
7120 Mrs. Emeline Monroe
7120 Wilmer D. Monroe
7120 Mrs. Emma Crist
7120 William D. Crist
7130 Mr. & Mrs. D. H. Glover
7436 Mr. & Mrs. W. N. Abbott
7522 Mr. & Mrs. E. L. Kendall
7526 Dr. & Mrs. E. Lathrop
7526 Mr. & Mrs. E. D. Seaton

EIGHTEENTH STREET.

63 Mr. & Mrs. W. S. Jenks
65 Dr. W. L. Chamberlin
81 Charles F. Bryant
81 Harry L. Bryant
87 Dr. & Mrs. W. H. Rumpf

66 Bernard Neu
———
87 Dr. & Mrs. Olof Schwarzkopf
89 Mr. & Mrs. Harry V. Hoffman

ELLIS AVENUE.

3517 Mr. & Mrs. Horace Tucker
3517 Fred W. Tucker
3521 Mrs. E. P. Harley & dr.
3521 Mr. & Mrs. C. A. Harley
3523 D. W. Chalmers
3523 Mr. & Mrs. George M. Aykroyd
3525 Mrs. E. M. Wheeler

3508 Mr. & Mrs. Edward F. Stearns
    Receiving day Monday
3528 Mr. & Mrs. Joseph G. Lane & dr.
    Receiving day Friday
3528 Richard B. Langdon
3530 Mr. & Mrs. David M. Cochrane
    & dr. *Receiving day Wednesday*

3525 J. K. Wheeler
3525 George V. Crawford
3529 Mr. & Mrs. Albert D. Pickering
3529 Mr. & Mrs. J. Lincoln Pfaff
3537 Mr. & Mrs. Alexander Boetti
3537 Joseph Boetti
3541 Isaac A. Kohn
3541 Simon A. Kohn
3541 Louis A. Kohn
3541 Miss Henrietta A. Kohn
3543 Mr. & Mrs. Dankmar Adler
3545 Mr. & Mrs. Emanuel Bach
3549 Mr. & Mrs. Simeon E. Sylvester & dr.
3549 Richard T. Sylvester
3549 Mr. & Mrs. Fred Schwantke
3555 Dr. & Mrs. T. R. Potter
3555 Mr. & Mrs. Wm. C. O'Kane
3555 J. B. Winstandley
3555 Hoyt King
3601 Mr. & Mrs. T. G. Warden
3605 Mr. & Mrs. Wm. Morris Booth
Receiving day Tuesday
3605 Harvey W. Loper
3609 Mr. & Mrs. Charles L. Miller
3611 Mrs. B. Eisendrath & dr.
Receiving day Friday
3611 Simeon B. Eisendrath
3611 Sam Eisendrath
3611 Oscar Eisendrath
3615 Mr. & Mrs. Jacob Newman jr.
3615 Miss Pauline Bauland
3615 Jacob H. Bauland
3617 Mr. & Mrs. Eugene Vallens
3619 Mr. & Mrs. Jacob Keller
Receiving day 1st & 3d Thursdays
3619 Louis Keller
3621 Mr. & Mrs. Samuel Bierly
3625 Mr. & Mrs. Geo. E. Halsey & dr.
3627 Mr. & Mrs. Frederick A. Brodhead & drs.
3627 Collins F. Huntington
3631 Mr. & Mrs. E. A. Casey
3633 Mr. & Mrs. A. J. W. Copelin & dr.
3635 Mr. & Mrs. Mark Morton
3641 Miss V. E. Day
3641 Mr. R. C. Millard
3641 Wallace D. Millard
3701 Dr. & Mrs. F. O. Pease
3703 Mr. & Mrs. William B. Candee
3703 Dr. & Mrs. Harry Williamson
3705 Mr. & Mrs. Thomas S. Temple
3705 Mr. & Mrs. E. Doul
3707 Timothy S. Fitch

3530 D. K. Cochrane
3530 William H. Cochrane
3530 Robert M. Cochrane
3532 Mr. & Mrs. John S. Snyder
3532 Frank M. Snyder
3532 Mrs. Annie Hall
3532 Manton Maverick
3532 John Wade
3534 Mr. & Mrs. Archibald Winne & dr.
3534 John Winne
3536 Mr. & Mrs. S. D. Ward & drs.
3538 Mrs. Eda Holzheimer
3538 Levi A. Eliel
3538 Mr. & Mrs. Gustav Eliel & dr.
3540 Mr. & Mrs. Chas. W. Van Benschoten & dr.
3540 Geo. W. Van Benschoten
3544 Mr. & Mrs. Chas. E. Cox & drs.
Receiving day Friday
3544 Eugene R. Cox
3546 Mr. & Mrs. Charles D. Stone
3546 Miss Lou A. Bellows
3548 Mr. & Mrs. I. H. Mayer
3550 Mr. & Mrs. B. R. Cahn
3552 Mr. & Mrs. S. H. Kirchberger
3610 Mr. & Mrs. George W. Best
3612 Mr. and Mrs. Wm. R. Bascom & dr.
3614 Mr. & Mrs. H. Edward Cobb
3616 Mrs. John Beers
3618 Mr. & Mrs. Alex. Gardner
3624 Mrs. M. Rider
3624 William H. Rider
3626 Frank H. Dickey
3626 Miss Belle Dickey
3700 Mr. & Mrs. E. W. Fergusou
3700 Mrs. Clarissa Ferguson
3700 John Q. Ferguson
3702 R. E. Edmonson
3702 Samuel B. Edmonson
3704 Mr. & Mrs. L. Bach
3704 Benj. Kauffman
3704 Morris J. Einstein
3706 Mrs. G. Newburger & dr.
3706 E. Newton Newburger.
3706 William S. Newburger
3706 Frank D. Newburger
3706 James M. Newburger
3706½ Mrs. A. S. Temple
3706½ Thomas Tobey
3708 Mr. & Mrs. Geo. Karnes & dr.
3708 William Karnes
3710 Mr. & Mrs. Ernest D. Owen
3712 Mrs. L. B. Root & dr.
3712 Mr. & Mrs. Willis C. DeMar

3707 Miss Mary A. Fitch
3707 Miss Beatrice Fitch
3709 Mrs. Dr. C. E. Weilhart
3709 Mrs. Amelia Meyer
3713 Mr. & Mrs. Geo. W. Mowbray
& dr.
Receiving day Wednesday
3715 Moses Willner
3721 Mr. & Mrs. D. S. Low & dr.
3727 Mr. & Mrs. Wm. F. Kellogg &
drs.
3729 Mr. & Mrs. Paul K. Richter
3731 Henry C. Hullinger
3733 Mr. & Mrs. Louis W. Rennard
3733 Robert L. Gifford
3735 Mr. & Mrs. Herman Landauer
3737 Mr. & Mrs. Edward D. Kimball
3737 Mrs. O. S. Hough & dr.
3737 Albert J. Hough
3737 Charles H. Hough
3739 Mrs. M. P. Patterson & drs.
3739 Frank H. Patterson
3739 J. E. Barnard
3743 Mr.& Mrs.Wm. G. Ewing&drs.
3745 Mr. & Mrs. Bernard Scovel &
drs.
3747 Mr. & Mrs. Wm. B. Purple
3747 Mr. & Mrs. Adlai T. Ewing
3749 Mrs. L. G. McFarland
Receiving day Thursday
3749 Miss Ariel Nichols
3749 Miss Lida Shogren
3749 Ralph Meriman
3753 Mr. & Mrs. Willis J. Wells
3757 Mr. & Mrs. Anson L. Bolte
3757 Edward M. Endicott
3763 Mr. & Mrs. J. E. Forsyth
3767 Mr. & Mrs. Edwin H. Ellett &
dr.
3767 Harry L. Ellett
3767 Mrs. Diantha Stockton
3801 Mr. & Mrs. Harry J. Conners
3801 Mr. & Mrs. Silas W. Blodgett
3801 Mr. & Mrs. Austyn W. Granville
3815 Mr. & Mrs. Frederick M. Steele
3815 Mrs. Roxana Pratt
3819 Mr. & Mrs. M. C. Noyes & drs.
Receiving day Tuesday
3821 Mrs. Urilla Clark & dr.
3821 Frank H. Clark
3823 Mr. & Mrs. William K. Sidley
& dr.
3823 William P. Sidley
3823 Fred K. Sidley

3718 Mr. & Mrs. Shubael Park
3718 Miss Louise Neel
3718 Samuel R. Neel
3718 Carr B. Neel
3722 Mrs. E. C. Dodsworth & drs.
3724 Mr. & Mrs. Ward B. Sherman
& drs.
3724 Frank C. Sherman
3724 Miss Annette Cole
3724 Mrs. Phoebe Cole
3728 Mr. & Mrs. J. S. Bloomingston
3736 Mr. & Mrs. Robt. G. Dwen
Receiving day Saturday
3736 James G. Dwen
3736 Mrs. L. A. Davies & dr.
3740 Mr. & Mrs. Louis Halle & dr.
3742 Mr. & Mrs. Henry S. Tiffany
3742 Mrs. H. C. Tiffany
3756 The Melrose
Mr. & Mrs. S. G. Rosekrans
Mr. & Mrs. J. P. Barnes
A. Bowen
Mr. & Mrs. M. Liebher
Mrs. Rose Sonnenschein & dr.
Dr. & Mrs. Julius Wise
Mr. & Mrs. F. L. Rumble
Dr. & Mrs. E. M. Rosekrans
Mr. & Mrs. Fred Derbyshire
Mr. & Mrs. J. S. Spitzer
Mr. & Mrs. M. Kleinhans
Mr. & Mrs. J. R. Lynn, jr.
Mrs. L. A. Bevens & dr.
Mr. & Mrs. Frank C. Lake
Mr. & Mrs. F. W. Smith
Mr. & Mrs. John McLelland
Mr. & Mrs. F. B. Fellows
Mr. & Mrs. L. T. Bodine & drs.
Mrs. H. N. Foley
Mr. & Mrs. D. R. Coover
Mr. & Mrs. Frank M. Utt
Mr. & Mrs. A. W. Reid
Mr. & Mrs. W. E. Cameron
Mrs. M. J. Ross & drs.
Mr. & Mrs. W. S. Kelsey
Mr. & Mrs. W. H. Umstot
Mr. & Mrs. L. G. Hoyt
Mrs. D. E. Beardsley
Mr. & Mrs. Geo. A. Neafus
Mrs. Catherine Thomas
Mr. & Mrs. C. C. Babcock
Mr. & Mrs. H. P. Hart
Mr. & Mrs. D. P. Anthony
Mrs. Harry W. Aldis
Mrs. O. Wheeler
Mr. & Mrs. H. P. Hatch
Mr. & Mrs. N. B. Ingersoll

3827 Mr. & Mrs. Josiah W. Wight
3827 Mr. & Mrs. Edwin W. Wight
3827 Mrs. M. L. Newbury
3831 Mr. & Mrs. T. C. Williams jr.
3831 Miss Estella Meyer
3831 John M. Meyer
3833 Mr. & Mrs. C. M. McCormick
3833 W. A. Tolley & dr.
3833 Elmer W. Tolley
3833 Harry R. Tolley
3835 Mrs. Sarah A. Methven & drs.
3835 Walter J. Methven
3835 Samuel L. Methven
3835 Huston F. Methven
3837 Mr. & Mrs. John Brison & drs.
3839 Cornelius Callahan & dr.
3845 Mr. & Mrs. D. W. Gale & drs.
3845 Mrs. George Evans
3845 Mr. & Mrs. Henry J. Blake
3845 Mrs. Fred L. Smith
3845 Lemuel Hitchcock
3845 Frank Sweet
3845 James H. Neilson
3845 Walter Blake
3847 Mr. & Mrs. Robert A. Scovel
3847 Mr. & Mrs. Benj. F. Troxell
3849 Mr. & Mrs. M. L. Wade
3851 Mr. & Mrs. Noyes Jackson
3853 Mr. & Mrs. Aaron S. Nichols
 & drs.
3853 Mr. & Mrs. William Burton
3861 Mr. & Mrs. Dean Bangs
3861 Mr. & Mrs. John D. Bangs
3861 Harrie L. Bangs
3869 Mr. & Mrs. Jeremiah Leaming
 & drs.
3929 Mr. & Mrs. J. R. Bensley & dr.
 Receiving day Wednesaay
3929 John R. Bensley jr.
3929 Miss Kate W. Bensley
3931 Mr. & Mrs. C. H. Tregu
3933 Mr. & Mrs. I. N. Simons & dr.
3933 Robert Simons
3933 Louis E. Simons
3933 Leonard Simons
3935 Mr. & Mrs. Harry G. Wilson
3935 Maj. & Mrs. A. W. Clancy
3937 Mr. & Mrs. Sidney W. Rice
 Receiving day Wednesaay
3937 Mrs. Jane Bruce & drs.
 Receiving day Wednesday
3939 Mr. & Mrs. A. H. Wolf
 Receive Saturday afternoon
3939 Henry M. Wolf
3939 Moses Wolf
3941 Mr. & Mrs. Wm. W. Bell & dr.

 Mr. & Mrs. W. G. Woodruff &
 dr.
3816 Mr. & Mrs. W. H. Davis & dr.
3816 Mrs. A. H. White
3820 Henry I. Harmon
3822 Mr. & Mrs. S. H. Crane & dr.
3822 Marcus L. Barrett
3822 Miss Anna Hendricks
3824 Mr. & Mrs. Festus B. Cole
 & dr.
3824 Mr. & Mrs. J. R. Vincent
3834 Mr. & Mrs. Alfred D. Eddy
3834 Mr. & Mrs. Edward Silvey
3836 Mr. & Mrs. James A. Stuart &
 dr.
3840 Mr. & Mrs. George M. Dugan
 & dr.
3840 Rees H. Dugan
3842 Mr. & Mrs. J. H. Swinarton
3852 Mr. & Mrs. VanBuren Ruth
3852 Henry Thackray
3858 Dr. & Mrs. U. G. Latta
3908 Mr. & Mrs. Samuel Pike & drs.
3908 Charles S. Pike
3916 Mr. & Mrs. Charles M. Hardy
 & drs.
3916 William Hardy
3916 Guy Hardy
3942 Mr. & Mrs. E. O. Hills & dr.
3942 Mr. & Mrs. Wm. E. Hills
3946 Mr. & Mrs. Dennison F. Groves
3946 George M. Groves
3946 Mr. & Mrs. Allan M. Clement
3952 Mr. & Mrs. S. O. Blair
3982 Mr. & Mrs. Frank E. Barnard
 & dr.
3998 Mr. & Mrs. Alex. C. Soper
3998 Miss Polly Pope
4000 Mr. & Mrs. Arthur Crandall
4002 Dr. & Mrs. Wm. H. Wilder
4004 Mr. & Mrs. Albert E. Hutchins
4012 Dr. & Mrs. James Burry
4014 Dr. & Mrs. M. H. Lackersteen
4016 Mr. & Mrs. A. Judson Heath
 Receiving day Wednesday
4016 Miss J. A. Cool
4018 Mr. & Mrs. Charles W. Beeman
 & dr.
4018 Charles H. Beeman
4020 Mrs. Elizabeth Newell
4020 Mr. & Mrs. L. Bernard Kilbourne
4024 Mr. & Mrs. Charles E. Morrison
4024 Ezekiel Morrison
4028 Mr. & Mrs. Frank N. Gage
4032 Mr. & Mrs. A. M. Thomson

3943 Mr. & Mrs. Simeon Straus
3945 Mr.& Mrs. John W. MacFarlane
3945 Henry J. MacFarlane
3945 Miss Mabel M. Brown
3949 Mr.&Mrs. Wm. N. Eisendrath
3963 Mr. & Mrs. Chas. C. Lay
3963 Frederick C. Lay
3963 Robert D. Lay
3963 Mr. & Mrs. H. M. Wright & dr.
3963 Miss Mamie Wright
3965 Mr. & Mrs. S. S. Whitehouse
3971 Mr. & Mrs. Shea Smith
3975 Mr. & Mrs. C. W. Merriam
3991 Mr. & Mrs. S. W. Lamson & dr.
3991 Mr. & Mrs. Harry H. Lobdell
3995 Mr.& Mrs. Samuel Baker & drs.
3995 James R. Baker
4003 W. H. Colvin & drs.
4013 Mr. & Mrs. J. C. Hately & drs.
4013 J. George Hately
4021 Mr. & Mrs. John Roper & dr.
4037 Mr. & Mrs. Alex. Dunlop & dr.
4037 Sydney H. Dunlop
4037 Mr. & Mrs. Geo. M. Pennoyer
4043 Thomas Orton
4043 Mr. & Mrs. M. Newman
4043 Edward B. Grossman
4043 Mr. & Mrs. Nathan W. Rath-
　　　bun & dr.
4043 Mr. & Mrs. Charles G. Wicker
4045 Mr. & Mrs. Louis Fernbach
4045 Mr. & Mrs. William A. Ross
4045 Mrs. Rose M. Knickerbocker
　　　& dr.
4045 Charles K. Knickerbocker
4047 Mr.&Mrs. Benj. H. Rosenblatt
4047 Mr. & Mrs. P. S. DeGraff
4049 Mr. & Mrs. Walter B. Phister
4049 Mr. & Mrs. Marcus Lake
4049 W. H. Lake
4049 Mr. & Mrs. J. H. Leyonmarck
4049 Mr. & Mrs. Louis A. Cornelius
4051 Mr.& Mrs. Solon D. Wilson
4201 Mr. & Mrs. J. L. McDaniel
4201 M. Delaplaine McDaniel
4201 Mr. & Mrs. Theo. Weil
4201 Mr. & Mrs. Henry F. Leopold
4201 G. Ebert Kline
4201 Lee Kline
4201 Mr.& Mrs. Albert Lineaweaver
4201 Dr. P. B. Saur
4201 Mrs. Alice Houghton
4203 Mrs. H. C. Smith & drs.
4203 Howard P. Smith
4203 Fred A. Smith
4203 Mrs. Alice Meyer

4032 Mr. & Mrs. L. E. Burr
　　　　　　　Receiving day Tuesday
4036 Mr. & Mrs. Lucius G. Fisher &
　　　dr.
4036 L. G. Fisher jr.
4036 Miss Frances M. Eddy
4040 Mrs. Lucy W. Messer
4040 Charles Messer
4044 Mr. & Mrs. Wm. M. Johnston
4050 Mr. & Mrs. R. Kennicott
4050 Mr. & Mrs. Cass L. Kennicott
4050 Lynn S. Kennicott
4058 Mr. & Mrs. Wm. H. Brown
4058 Mr. & Mrs. Charles M. Blair
4058 Mr. & Mrs. John C. Harmon
4060 Mr. & Mrs. Leonard P. Wood-
　　　bury
4060 Mrs. Laura A. King
4060 Mrs. Grace Haviland
4060 Dr. Bond Stowe
4060 Mrs. E. S. McHenry
4060 Mrs. E. Scollay
4100 Mr. & Mrs. A. B. Davis
4100 Mr. & Mrs. Fred M. Bliss
4102 Mr. & Mrs. Mathias Walker
4104 Mr. & Mrs. C. R. Brown
4104 Mr. & Mrs. J. Frederick Brown
4106 Mr. & Mrs. W. E. Morgan
4108 Mr. & Mrs. Henry A. Thayer
4108 Mr. & Mrs. Wm. A. Bither
4110 Mr. & Mrs. Lewis Viele
4114 Mr. & Mrs. A. C. Vander-
　　　burgh
4116 Mr. & Mrs. Daniel Mayer
4116 Richard Norman
4118 Mr. & Mrs. James H. Hinman
　　　& dr.
4118 John M. Hinman
4120 Mr. & Mrs. E. R. Rosenthal
4122 Mrs. Bertha Leopold
4122 Joseph Leopold
4124 Mr. & Mrs. Wm. B. Holton
4126 Mr.& Mrs. William M. Dunham
4128 Mr. & Mrs. D. M. Slocum
4130 Mr. & Mrs. Robert E. Payne
4130 Mrs. Abbie M. Kingman
4132 Mr. & Mrs. Iver C. Zarbell & dr.
4136 Mrs. Leretta M. Crandal & dr.
4136 Frederick E. Crandal
4136 Mr. & Mrs. William B. Ewing
4138 Mr. & Mrs. James D. Tuohy
4138 David W. Tuohy
4138 Stephen P. Tuohy
4138 John D. Tuohy
4140 Mr. & Mrs. John C. Lewis & dr.
4140 Chas. Ray Lewis

4203 Victor Barothy
4207 Mr. & Mrs. James F. Wangbop
4207 Miss Ella Cassell
4211 Mrs. F. S. Emmons
4211 Mr. & Mrs. Joseph F. Titus
4211 Calvin W. Titus
4211 Miss S. M. Titus
4213 Mrs. Mary E. Munger
4213 Mr. & Mrs. S. O. Adams
4213 Mr. & Mrs. George K. Lowell
4215 Mr. & Mrs. Albert D. Stone &
    drs.
4215 Robert Cady
4215 Howard Finley
4215 Mr. & Mrs. Robert Bliss
4217 Mrs. G. P. Herrick & dr.
4217 Dr. M. J. Creighton
4305 Mr. & Mrs. Chas. F. Thompson
4307 Mr. & Mrs. Thos. A. Bowden
    & drs.
4309 Mr. & Mrs. Bert S. Church
    Receiving day Wednesday
4311 Mr. & Mrs. David Anderson
    Receiving day Tuesday
4313 Mr. & Mrs. Chas. T. Allyn
4313 Mr. & Mrs. Jesse Scribner
4315 Mr. & Mrs. John F. Wallace &
    dr.
4315 Harold U. Wallace
4317 Mr. & Mrs. John H. Hartog
    Receive Wednesday afternoon
4319 Mrs. Harriet H. Burleson & drs.
4319 Mr. & Mrs. Charles E. Burleson
4319 George A. Eaton
4321 Mr. & Mrs. Laurence A. Carton
4325 Mr. & Mrs. Edwin A. Warfield
    & dr.
4325 Edwin A. Warfield jr.
4333 Rev. & Mrs. Walter Delafield
    & drs.
4333 Mrs. Charles Delafield
4335 Mr. & Mrs. Sigmund Kahn
4335 Mrs. S. G. Norman
4335 Charles E. Norman
4335 Mr. & Mrs. Edward J. Wright
4337 Mr. & Mrs. Theo. Podolski
    Receiving day Wednesday
4337 Mr. & Mrs. W. J. Cook
4339 Mr. & Mrs. Bert Bettelheim
    Receiving day Friday
4339 Mrs. Elizabeth Stevenson & dr.
    Receiving day Friday
4339 Miss Elizabeth B. Stevenson
4341 Mr. & Mrs. Chas. I. Humphrey
    Receiving day Monday
4343 Mr. & Mrs. A. W. Sproehnle

4146 Mr. & Mrs. Fred M. Bailey
4148 Mr. & Mrs. O. W. Mitchel
4148 Herman Myers
4154 Mrs. Victorine Wolf
4156 Mrs. Esther A. McDougall
4156 William McDougall
4156 Mr. & Mrs. Carlton R. Wheeler
4160 The Knickerbocker
    Mr. & Mrs. Duff Porter
    John Albert Porter
    Mrs. Mary E. Benedict
    Mr. & Mrs. Caleb Clapp
    Mr. & Mrs. M. I. Cohen
    Receive Tuesday
    Mr. & Mrs. Martin W. Emer-
    son
    Mr. & Mrs. A. B. Fagan
    Miss B. Grabbe
    Miss Rose Heller
    Wilson O. Martin
    Mr. & Mrs. August Schiffer
    & dr.
    Mr. & Mrs. L. D. Vose
    Miss H. J. Weld
4200 Mrs. Rossiter Kehoe & dr.
    Receiving day Thursday
4200 Mr. & Mrs. John Blanchfield
    Keogh
    Receiving day Thursday
4200 James Clowry
4202 Mr. & Mrs. John P. Byrne
    Receiving day Thursday
4204 Mr. & Mrs. William S. Thomas
4204 Mr. & Mrs. Edward S. Thomas
4206 M . & Mrs. Caleb Goodwin &
    dr.
4206 Leonard R. Goodwin
4206 William Warren
4206 Mr. & Mrs. C. W. Robinson
4206 Miss E. S. Warren
4206 Mr. & Mrs. Frank L. Wilder
4206 Walter L. Wilder
4212 Mrs. Margaretta E. Burnap
4212 Mr. & Mrs. A. Nellis
4212 Miss Annie DeFlow
4214 Mr. & Mrs. Harris Russell &
    drs.
4214 Mr. & Mrs. James M. Hadley
4214 Edwin M. Hadley
4214 Mr. & Mrs. S. H. Greeley
4214 Mr. & Mrs. H. M. Carle
4216 Mr. & Mrs. Edward P. Barry
    & dr.
4216 Fred Barry
4220 Mr. & Mrs. John A. Yakel
4220 J. Stephen Soden

4345 Dr. & Mrs. C. Gurnee Fellows
 Receiving day Thursday
4347 Mr. & Mrs. Jay Morton
4347 Col. & Mrs. A. C. Babcock
4347 Charles D. Babcock
4347 Sheldon E. Babcock
4347 Frank C. Babcock
4347 Pitt K. Babcock
4349 Mr. & Mrs. Edwin O. Excell
4349 Wm. Alonzo Excell
4349 Harry Cartwright
4401 Mr. & Mrs. L. J. Carter
4403 Mr. & Mrs. G. H. Martin
4405 Dr. & Mrs. Edwin C. Williams
4407 Mr. & Mrs. C. V. Banta jr.
4409 Mr. & Mrs. John Sebastian
 Receiving day Tuesday
4409 Don B. Sebastian
4413 Abraham Lipman & drs.
4413 August Lipman
4415 Mr. & Mrs. W. F. Newberry
4417 Mr. & Mrs. C. H. McConnell
 & dr. *Receiving day Tuesday*
4419 Mr. & Mrs. Brice Worley
4421 Mr. & Mrs.Geo.F. Montgomery
4423 Mr. & Mrs. H. H. Handy
4423 Mrs. C. C. Cole
4425 Mr. & Mrs. John D. Besler
4425 Mrs. Laura B. Bassett
4427 Mr. & Mrs. George Michaelson
 Receiving day Tuesday
4429 Mr. & Mrs. Wm. B. Forsyth
4429 John G. Hicks
4429 E. Spencer Sturges
4431 Mr. & Mrs. Christopher J. Hess
 Receiving day Wednesday
4431 Howard A. Hess
4433 Mr. & Mrs.W. P. Johnson & drs.
4435 Mr. & Mrs. James F. Lewis
4437 Dr. & Mrs. J. P. Morrison
4439 Mr. & Mrs. William Renshaw
 Receiving day Tuesday
4441 Mr. & Mrs. Richard Walsh
4443 Mrs. M. Eliel
4443 Miss Clara D. Eliel
4443 Alexander B. Eliel
4443 Walter R. Eliel
4443 Eugene D. Eliel
4445 Mr. & Mrs. George E. King
4447 Mr. & Mrs. Charles S. Bateman
 &dr. *Receiving day Tuesday*
4449 Mr. & Mrs. Jas. E. Fellows
4451 Miss Annie M. Boggs
4451 Albert W. Boggs
4451 A. Emmet Boggs
4453 Gen'l & Mrs.C.S.Bentley & drs.

4300-4316 The Tudor
 Mr. & Mrs. Paul O. Bakke
 Receiving day Thursday
 Mr. & Mrs. John J. Berne
 Mr. & Mrs. John C. Bosworth
 Mr. & Mrs. Gustaf H. Carlson
 Mr. & Mrs. Robert E. Casey
 Mr. & Mrs. Frank R. Cooke
 Receiving day Thursday
 William D. Cravens
 Mr. & Mrs. Henry Crossley
 Mr. & Mrs. Simeon W. Croy
 Mr. & Mrs. William Cum-
 mings
 William H. Cummings
 Mr. & Mrs. Henry Ray Dering
 Mrs. James R. Doolittle & dr.
 Mr. & Mrs. Charles E. Felton
 Receiving day Friday
 Mr. & Mrs. Leonard Ficklen
 William Ficklen
 Dion Geraldine
 Mr. & Mrs. Frank B. Gifford
 Mr. & Mrs. George B. Hoit
 Mr. & Mrs. W. C. Hoyer
 Mr. & Mrs. John Arthur Lane
 & dr.
 David S. Lasier
 Mr. & Mrs. George L. Lavery
 Mr. & Mrs. Bradley Mahanna
 Mr. & Mrs. Travers J. Mason
 Mr. & Mrs. Wm. G. Neimeyer
 Mr. & Mrs. Henry E. Palmer
 Mr. & Mrs. D. P. Peck
 Mrs. J. R. Stow
 Mr. & Mrs. Wm. Henry
 Thompson
 Receiving day Tuesday
 Mr. & Mrs. John A. D. Vickers
 Harry C. Wade
 Mr. & Mrs. Henry P. Wade &
 drs.
 Dr. & Mrs. Albert H. Wales
 Dr. & Mrs. Frederick M. Wales
 H. W. Wales jr.
 Mr. & Mrs. Charles E. Willard
 Mr. & Mrs. Alfred J. Wright
4320 Mr. & Mrs. Henry L. Green
4322 Mr. & Mrs. J. C. Wallace
4322 Clyde H. Wallace
4322 J. T. Ohlheiser
4324 Mr. & Mrs. Myron W. Atwood
4324 Mrs. E. A. Swazey
4330 Mrs. Mary A. Clark
4330 Mr. & Mrs. Arthur R. Clark
4330 Wallace G. Clark

4455 Mr. & Mrs. F. O. Boylan
  Receiving day Thursday
4457 Mr. & Mrs. Ralph Gates
4457 Harry E. Church
4459 Mr. & Mrs. S. Howe & dr.
4459 Wm. R. Hemphill
4459 E. F. Hemphill
4461 Mr. & Mrs. S. M. Emmons
4463 Mr. & Mrs. B. E. Kinslow
4465 Mr. & Mrs. G. E. VanWoert
  Receiving day Wednesday
4503 Mr. & Mrs. Frank O. Butler
4503 Mr. & Mrs. J. W. Butler
4505 Mr. & Mrs. Wallace Heckman
4505 Jean J. Heckman
4515 Mr. & Mrs. Chas. E. Follansbee
4521 Mr. & Mrs. I. Block
4523 Mr. & Mrs. F. Rosenthal
4523 Alex. Rosenthal
4525 Mr. & Mrs. James H. Hiland
4527 Mr. & Mrs. Isaac M. Mayer
  Receiving day Friday
4527 Mrs. R. Mayer & dr.
4529 Mr. & Mrs. L. J. Odell
4531 Mr. & Mrs. H. Schwabacher jr.
4531 Mr. & Mrs. J. A. Odell
4533 Mr. & Mrs. Magnus Goodman
4535 Mr. & Mrs. F. E. A. Wolcott
4537 Mr. & Mrs. John A. Colby
4543 Mr. & Mrs. W. Northup
4543 Martin S. Rowley
4545 Mr. & Mrs. Frederick M. Smith
  & drs. *Receiving day Friday*
4547 Mr. & Mrs. John M. Low
4549 Mr. & Mrs. E. G. Shumway
4551 Mr. & Mrs. E. C. Ferguson
4551 William G. Ferguson
4553 Mr. & Mrs. Chas. E. Gill & dr.
4553 Preston Gill
4553 Mrs. Mary Mitchell
4555 Mrs. T. G. McLaury
4557 Mr. & Mrs. C. G. Ortmayer
4559 Mr. & Mrs. M. Gottfried
4559 Carl M. Gottfried
4611 Mr. & Mrs. D. Regensburg
4613 Mr. & Mrs. Albert Sauveur
4615 Mr. & Mrs. H. W. Seymour
4617 Mr. & Mrs. A. G. Wheeler & dr.
4617 Mrs. Catherine Taylor
4619 Mrs. Jessie S. Moss
4619 Mr. & Mrs. W. F. Heikes
4619 Milton Moss
4621 Mr. & Mrs. Wm. H. Brintnall
4623 Mr. & Mrs. F. W. Jackson
4625 Mr. & Mrs. Milo B. Randall
4625 Benj. G. Randall

4332 Mr. & Mrs. Charles M. Fay
4332 Mrs. Frances McIntire
4334 Mr. & Mrs. F. W. C. Hayes
4334 Mr. & Mrs. John H. Rood
4334 Dr. & Mrs. W. K. Jaques
4336 Mr. & Mrs. S. A. Harvey & dr.
4336 Edwin F. Harvey
4338 Mr. & Mrs. R. M. Critchell
4338 L. Wilcox
4340 Mr. & Mrs. Geo. H. Martin &
  dr. *Receiving day Friday*
4342 Mr. & Mrs. Gordon Valentine
4342 Lewis Nowlin
4348 Mr. & Mrs. I. H. Rea
4348 Albert Mendel
4356 Mr. & Mrs. Edward S. Jenison
  & dr.
4400 Mr. & Mrs. J. L. Chance & dr.
4400 M. B. Clancy
4402 Mr. & Mrs. William M. White
4402 Harley C. White
4402 Mr. & Mrs. H. G. Chamberlain
4404 Mr. & Mrs. Merrill C. Clancy
4404 Miss Belle Leslie
4406 Mr. & Mrs. J. D. Derby
  Receiving day Monday
4406 Mrs. C. A. Davis
4408 Mr. & Mrs. Wm. Clancy
4410 Mr. & Mrs. Moses Baker & dr.
4412 Mrs. Julius Bauer & dr.
4412 Richard Bauer
4412 A. O. Mueller
4420 Mr. & Mrs. C. B. Shefler
4422 Mr. & Mrs. G. W. Simpson & drs.
4422 Joseph A. Simpson
4422 John H. Jones
4424 Mr. & Mrs. John R. LeVally
4424 John S. Scoville
4430 Mr. & Mrs. Oliver Jackson &
  drs. *Receiving day Thursday*
4430 Paul Jackson
4430 Oliver A. Jackson
4430 Miss Hattie Jackson
4432 Mr. & Mrs. Robert Mather
  Receiving day Friday
4434 Mr. & Mrs. Gardner McGregor
  & dr.
4436 Mr. & Mrs. E. B. Lathrop
4438 Edward Ellicott
4438 Mr. & Mrs. Chester D. Crandall
4440 Mr. & Mrs. Frank Matthiesen
4442 Mrs. B. Bremner
4442 Mr. & Mrs. Edward A. Bremner
4442 James W. Bremner

4625 Miss Julia A. Rust
4669 Percy B. Herr
4727 Mr. & Mrs. John A. Tolman
4731 Mr. & Mrs. O. F. Lindman
4731 Mrs. Harriet Tallmadge
4737 Mr. & Mrs. David N. Hanson
4933 Mr. & Mrs. J. L. Higgie & drs.
4933 Noble K. Higgie
4933 Arthur M. Higgie
4933 Miss M. L. Higgie
　　　　Receiving day Wednesday
4933 Archibald A. Higgie
4945 S. W. Rawson
4945 F. H. Rawson
5401 Mr. & Mrs. Theodore Oehne
5401 Mrs. T. Schell & dr.
5401 Louis Schell
6511 Rev. & Mrs. Joseph Rushton
6511 Joseph A. Rushton
6517 Mr. & Mrs. David Chambers
6519 Elliott Flower
6619 Mr. & Mrs. Joseph H. Craig

————

5006 Mr. & Mrs. P. B. Palmer
5006 George R. Palmer
5012 Mr. & Mrs. Henry W. Har-
　　　　wood
5330 Mr. & Mrs. Albert D. Elmers
5330 Mr. & Mrs. Robert Ennis
5336 Mr. & Mrs. Francis F. Browne
　　　　& dr.
5336 Francis G. Browne
5400 Mr. & Mrs. Wm. J. Moore
5406 Mr. & Mrs. Elbert S. Young &
　　　　dr.
5412 Mr. & Mrs. A. McIntosh & dr.
5422 Mr. & Mrs. Frederick Keppler
5444 Mr. &Mrs. J. R. Hansell
5514 Mr. & Mrs. J. M. Detrick
5614 Prof. & Mrs. Starr W. Cutting
5620 Mr. & Mrs. Wells H. Hurlbutt
　　　　jr.
6320 Mr. & Mrs. R. Colvin
6328 Mr. & Mrs. S. Nicholson
6332 Mr. & Mrs. E. G. Ahern
6404 Dr. & Mrs. H. Claflin
6404 Mr. & Mrs. Walter H. Latimer
6404 Mr. & Mrs. David C. Grant
6414 Mr. & Mrs. W. W. Crosby
6440 Mr. & Mrs. J. C. Sherer
6440 Mr. & Mrs. S. N. Howard
6522 Mr. & Mrs. Curtis Dunham
6552 Mr. & Mrs. Emil Ufer
6552 Mr. & Mrs. Cornelius B. Hayes
6600 Mr. & Mrs. M. Leonard

4444 Mr. & Mrs. J. G. Bodenschatz
4450 Mr. & Mrs. Frank B. Orr
　　　　Receiving day Monday
4454 Mr. & Mrs. J. Dreyfus
4456 Mr. & Mrs. Henry W.Wolseley
4458 Mr. & Mrs. M. Lewis Swift
4500 Mr. & Mrs. Jacob S. Smith
4502 Mr. & Mrs. H. R. Graham
4502 Miss Laura B. Eckfeldt
4504 Mrs. M. A. Greeley
　　　　Receiving day Tuesday
4506 Mr. & Mrs. Percy G. Ullman
　　　　Receive 1st & 3d Tuesdays
4508 Mr. & Mrs. Louis M. Dillman
4510 Mr. & Mrs. H. Felsenthal &
　　　　drs.
　　　　Receive Friday afternoon
4510 Mrs. H. Schwarz
4514 Mr. & Mrs. Theo. Holman
4514 Edward Holman
4516 Mr. & Mrs. Marshall W.George
4516 Charles P. Franklin
4516 Mrs. Percy R. Franklin
4520 Mr. & Mrs. William H. Eaton
4520 Mr. & Mrs. Isaac I. Eaton
4524 Mr. & Mrs. E. H. Sedgwick
4550 Mr. & Mrs. DeWitt P. Ballard
4552 Mr. & Mrs. Wilber Wait & drs.
4554 Mr. & Mrs. Frank Hardy
4556 Mr. & Mrs. Robert Stobo
4558 Mr. & Mrs. A. N. Reece & drs.
4600 Mr. & Mrs. E. T. Williams
4600 John R. Williams
4600 Mrs. H. E. Whipple
4628 Mr. & Mrs. John G. Shedd
4800 Mr. & Mrs. E. C. Potter
4812 Mr. & Mrs. J. C. Hutchins
4822 Mr. & Mrs. A. C. Buttolph
4832 Mr. & Mrs. Alonzo M. Fuller
4840 Mr. & Mrs. Frank Hoyt Fuller
4908 Mr.&Mrs.Anthony J. Hageman
4918 Mr. & Mrs. Theo Starrett
4920 S. Wedeles
4920 Mrs. Celia Wedeles
4920 Miss Babetta Wedeles
4924 Mrs. S. Becker & dr.
4924 Benj. F. Becker
4928 Mr. & Mrs. James B. Collins
　　　　Receiving day Tuesday
4938 Mr. & Mrs. A. L. Nestlerode
4940 Mr. & Mrs. L. T. Dickason &
　　　　dr.
4942 Mr. & Mrs. Benjamin Thomas
4942 Mrs. Henry Gaylord
4944 Mr. & Mrs. Ferdinand Gun-
　　　　drum & drs.

ELLIS PARK.

3601 Mr. & Mrs. T. M. Turner & dr.
3601 J. Lyle Turner
3601 Thomas M. Turner jr.
3605 Enos M. Cowles
3605 Mr. & Mrs. Frederick S.Cowles
3607 Frank W. Ruffner
3607 Will R. Ruffner
3615 Mr. & Mrs. Meyer Wheeler & dr.
3621 Dr. John G. Trine & dr.
3621 Mrs. A. C. Burgess
3623 Mrs. Rose Forrester
3623 Mr. & Mrs. S. E. Davis
3623 Robert E. Sturgeon
3625 Mr. & Mrs. John E. Henning
3625 Mrs. W. F. Bischoff
3627 Mrs. Blanch R. Smith

3606 Mr. & Mrs. John M. Dandy
3608 Mr. & Mrs. J. G. Cozzens
3610 Lewis F. Fell
3610 E. G. Low
3612 Mrs. Myra Medbery
3616 Mrs. Elizabeth Shermer
3616 John S. Stanley
3624 Mr. & Mrs. Henry D. Deam
3626 Mr. & Mrs. Edward Lowy

3627 Frederick H. Christy
3629 Mr. & Mrs. C.W.Barbour & drs.
3629 Rev. & Mrs. Moses Barker
3633 Mr. & Mrs. Jesse T. Greene
3633 Charles K. Greene
3641 Mr. & Mrs. Fred F. Daggett
3641 Mrs. E. A. Marsh

ELMWOOD PLACE.

3731 Mr. & Mrs. Gustav Goodkind
3823 Mr. & Mrs. J. B. Wiggins &drs.
3841 Mr. & Mrs. William Pound
3841 Thomas A. Pound
3841 Alfred N. Pound

3810 Mr. & Mrs. E. H. Reynolds
3832 Mr. & Mrs C. D. Stone
3842 Mr. & Mrs. A. J. White

3704 Mervin H. Lobdell
3704 Thomus L. Brunk
3716 Mr. & Mrs. E. A. Whipple
3726 Mr. & Mrs. George C. Vining
3740 Mrs. D. C. Jackson
3740 Darius C. Jackson
3740 Howard B. Jackson
3746 Mr. & Mrs. T. S Casey
3808 Mr.& Mrs.G.A. M. Liljencrantz

EMERALD AVENUE.

4335 Mr. & Mrs. J. F. Waugh
4335 Allen Middleton
4341 Mr. & Mrs. Washington Mc-Nair
4361 Mr. & Mrs. A. M. Plant
4361 J. D. Burris
4443 Mr. & Mrs. H. L. Goodall
4453 Mr. & Mrs. Charles H. Crosby
4453 Mr. & Mrs. William E. Watt
4457 Mr. & Mrs.W.H. Thompson jr.
4457 Mrs. Esther Churchill
4515 Mr. & Mrs. Samuel Cozzens
4515 D. G. Gray
4515 T. A. Hovey
4553 Mr.&Mrs.R.N.Tomlinson & dr.
4553 H. S. Tomlinson
4561 Mr. & Mrs. Arnold Henn
4601 Mr. & Mrs.William W. Shearer
4625 Mr. & Mrs. H. C. Burquedel
4635 Mr. & Mrs. A. B. Butler
4635 Mrs. Marie Lamb & dr.
6401 Charles L. Safford

4304 Mrs. Maria S. Cornwell
4304 C. D. Hurd
4310 Mr. & Mrs. A. B. Edwards
4310 Mr. & Mrs. Geo. E. Adams
4312 Mr. & Mrs. J. F. Humphreys & dr.
4316 Mrs. Mary McConville & drs.
4316 Edward McConville
4320 Mr. & Mrs. Hiram Holmes
4328 Mr. & Mrs. J. C. Bone
4414 Bartholomew Healy
4430 Mr. & Mrs. J. C. Bohart
4430 J. J. McRoberts
4436 Dr. & Mrs. W. H. Bohart
4440 Mr. & Mrs. Abraham Rosenberg
4442 Mr. & Mrs. J. A. Monroe & drs.
4442 J. Allen Monroe jr.
4452 Mr. & Mrs. G. F. Swift
4452 Mr. & Mrs. Charles H. Swift
4506 Dr. & Mrs. W. R. Parsons
Receiving day Saturday

6751 Mr. & Mrs. Malcom McNab
7733 Mr. & Mrs. J. W. Callahan
7733 Miss Emma N. O'Neil
7737 Mr. & Mrs. Chas. E. Baker & dr.
7737 Chas. Baker jr.
7749 Mr. & Mrs. C. H. Wheeler
7751 Mr. & Mrs. W. A. Colvin

4624 Mr. & Mrs. D. E. Hartwell
     Receiving day Friday

4506 Mr. & Mrs. Charles Perks
4506 Mr. & Mrs. Samuel M. Mc-Kibbin
4514 Mr. & Mrs. Henry T. Higgins
     Receiving day Wednesday
4520 Dr. & Mrs. W. B. Clark
4544 Mr. & Mrs. Augustus Hirsh
4552 Mr. & Mrs. Charles J. Coe
4554 Mr. & Mrs. George Dennis
4554 Mr. & Mrs. Charles H. Bean
4612 Mr. & Mrs. Edward Tilden
4614 Mr. & Mrs. W. W. Copley

ENGLEWOOD AVENUE.

435 Mr. & Mrs. William B. Oxnam
439 Mr. & Mrs. C. H. Hathaway
441 Dr. & Mrs. J. P. Webster & drs.
441 Mrs. Caroline Higgins
443 Dr. & Mrs. J. F. Oaks
443 Mrs. Mary Blanding & dr.
445 Mr. & Mrs. Baxter A. Dickinson
447 Mrs. Nellie A. Bryan
447 Omer G. Bryant
453 Mr. & Mrs. Philip C. Miller
457 Mrs. C. A. Baker
457 Mr. & Mrs. Fred G. Thearle jr.
517 Mr. & Mrs. Chas. E. Vaughan
519 Mrs. Amanda Pettet
519 Freeman E. Pettet
519 Miss Anna May Pettet
525 Mr. & Mrs. Jas. Hyde Forbes
533 Mr. & Mrs. J. C. Kilgore
533 Mrs. M. Noble & dr.
537 Mr. & Mrs. S. T. Lewis
541 Mr. & Mrs. James E. Farrell
551 Mr. & Mrs. Walter H. Miller
555 W. S. Hancock
623 Mr. & Mrs. Pearce C. Kelley
627 Mr. & Mrs. Wm. W. Schatz
627 Mr. & Mrs. J. Stoltz

634 Mr. & Mrs. Wm. W. Backman & drs.
636 Mr. & Mrs. John A. Morgan
754 Mr. & Mrs. Louis Rathje

432 Mr. & Mrs. G. W. I. Cole
432 Mrs. Hannah Bloom
432 Jacob C. Bloom
432 Mr. & Mrs. Nathan Friedman
438 Mr. & Mrs. H. C. Washburn & dr.
438 Mr. & Mrs. Charles Washburn
438 Mr. & Mrs. F. W. James
440 Dr. & Mrs. J. E. DeWolf
440 Mr. & Mrs. Thos. Smyth & dr.
444 Mr. & Mrs. Frank Marshall
444 Mr. & Mrs. E. A. Watson
456 Mr. & Mrs. John W. Burdette
500 Mr. & Mrs. S. M. Sutherland
500 Ralph E. Sutherland
504 Mrs. George Pigott & drs.
508 Mr. & Mrs. H. A. Swanzey
512 Mrs. B. G. Carpenter
512 Mr. & Mrs. H. H. Carpenter
526 Mr. & Mrs. Jonathan Periam & drs.
534 Mr. & Mrs. William H. Reid jr.
538 Mr. & Mrs. Asa A. Kile & dr.
542 Mr. & Mrs. H. C. Darlington
556 Mr. & Mrs. R. H. Patterson & dr.
600 Mr. & Mrs. C. H. Timmerman
606 Mr. & Mrs. James A. Hinson
614 Mr. & Mrs. Elisha C. Field & dr.
614 Robert L. Field
614 Mr. & Mrs. Charlas E. Field
618 Rev. & Mrs. Myron W. Haynes
620 Mr. & Mrs. Edmond A. Wood

EVANS AVENUE.

4331 Mr. & Mrs. C. B. Slade
4337 Mr. & Mrs. Lincoln Eastburn
4429 Mr. & Mrs. Herman T. White
4435 Mr. & Mrs. W. H. Walker
4439 Mr. & Mrs. George W. Connell
4441 Mr. & Mrs. Melville J. Wendell

4332 Mr. & Mrs. W. D. Snyder
4424 Mr. & Mrs. John Sundin & dr.
4436 Mr. & Mrs. B. F. Cronkrite
4444 Mr. & Mrs. Charles Farquhar
4522 Mr. &. Mrs. John J. Brady
4522 Mr. & Mrs. Clyde DeWitt
4546 Dr. & Mrs. Alfred Dahlberg

4449 Mr. & Mrs. H.C. Wolfe
4449 Mr. & Mrs. J. H. Skaggs
4449 Mr.·& Mrs. Walter C. Huling
4459 Mr. & Mrs. H C. Adcock
4551 Mr. & Mrs. John K. Yarnell
4559 Mr. & Mrs. Samuel M. Rieser
4559 Mr. & Mrs. F. J. Fadner
4559 Miss Lovetta B. Agin
4625 Dr. & Mrs. M. Schycker
4705 Dr. & Mrs. C.G. McCullough
4705 Mr. & Mrs. Chas. J. Anderson
4709 Dr. Wm. A. Campbell
4709 J. G. Campbell
4711 George L. Hastings

4744 Mr. & Mrs. Frank M. Trissal
4748 Mrs. Sarah C. Anderson & drs.
4818 Mr. & Mrs. F. R. Powell
4818 Mrs. Emma McCalley & drs.
4830 Mr. & Mrs. Samuel E Watson
4836 Mr. & Mrs. T. H. Howland
4838 Mr. & Mrs. J. F. Sturdy
4850 Dr. & Mrs. W. O. Cheeseman
4858 Mr. & Mrs. Frank Schlegel

4558 Dr. & Mrs. Elgin MaWhinney
4558 Mr. & Mrs. L. S. Bailey
4620 Mrs. Kuni Miller & dr.
4640 Mr. & Mrs. T. M. Hammond
4642 Dr. & Mrs. Leon Miesse
4642 Mr. & Mrs. Wm. H. Lintz
4644 Mr. & Mrs. Charles H. Thule
4714 Dr. & Mrs. Charles A. Kersey
4714 Mr. & Mrs. David S. Baird
4714 Mr. & Mrs. J. G. Taylor
4714 Mr. & Mrs. N. S. Hitchcock
4716 Mr. & Mrs. Kent K. Baldwin
4720 Mr. & Mrs. Joseph Herz
4720 Arthur Herz
4722 Mr. & Mrs. M. B. Custard & drs.
4724 Mrs. M. L. Graham
4724 R. A. Wells
4724 E. L. Wells
4726 Rev. & Mrs. W. M. Howie
4732 Mr. & Mrs. R. L. Garth
4732 Miss Maggie A. Waggener
4738 Mr. & Mrs. E. C. Webster
4742 William C. Childs
4742 Miss Minnie C. Childs

FIFTIETH STREET (HYDE PARK).

389 Mr. & Mrs. Edward Burnham
397 Mr. & Mrs. B. C. Strehl

150 Mr. & Mrs. H. G. Northrop
154 Mr. & Mrs. F. A. White
156 Mr. & Mrs. G. H. Lussky
156 E. A. Lussky
466 Mr. & Mrs. C. E. Bunker
466 Mr. & Mrs. C. T. Hass
468 Mrs. Annie Dean
728 Mr. & Mrs. Chas. W. Greenfield

76 Mr. & Mrs. John Morey
76 Dr. & Mrs. William B. Hunt
78 Mr. & Mrs. J. Franklin Worth-
       ington
78 Mr. & Mrs. W. W. Curtis
       Receiving day Wednesday
132 Mr. & Mrs. Edwin F. Simonds
134 Mr. & Mrs. Lucius Wakeley
142 Mr. & Mrs. Richard F. Clark
144 Mr. & Mrs. H. S. Hyman
148 Mr. & Mrs. E. F. H. Krause

FIFTY-FIRST STREET (HYDE PARK).

95 Mr. & Mrs. James Smith
97 Mr. & Mrs. William H. Spear
97 Harry E. Spear
97 Mrs. Mary M. Raper
101 Mr. & Mrs. C. C. Shepard
121 Mr. & Mrs. Martin H. Bennett & dr.
121 Carroll M. Bennett
123 Dr. & Mrs. John H. R. Bond
       Receiving day Friday
125 Prof. & Mrs. A. A. Michelson
       Receiving day Thursday
127 Mr. & Mrs. R. M. Rogers jr.
127 Mr. & Mrs. R. M. Rogers
129 Mr. & Mrs. Barton Sewell
129 G. M. Wilson

158 Mr. & Mrs. E. E. Smith
210 Mr. & Mrs. J. H. Gates
212 Mr. & Mrs. J. J. Hattstaedt
248 Mr. and Mrs. E. E. Amory
252 Mr. & Mrs. James F. May
252 Franklin W. Kohler
252 G. A. Edward Kohler
258 Mr. & Mrs. A. F. Merrill
260 Mr. & Mrs. James M. Curtiss
264 Mr. & Mrs. Homer D. Russell
264 Mr. & Mrs. A. F. Shiverick

169 Mr.& Mrs. John Cameron & drs.
169 William F. Cameron
169 Gordon Cameron

171 Mr. & Mrs. Edwin C. Loomis
171 Mr. & Mrs. John E. Amos
171 Miss Elizabeth S. Stewart
171 Mrs. Jane Shirra
171 Mr. & Mrs. N. C. Chase
171 Richard B. Chase
171 Robert D. Chase
171 Harry E. Bosseller
171 Mr. & Mrs. Henry Curtis
171 Mr. & Mrs. C. A. Tousey
171 Thomas E. Tousey
177 Mr. & Mrs. A. M. Githens
      Receiving day Thursday
177 Herbert A. Githens
569 to 575 The Vermont Flats
  . Mr. & Mrs. Charles O. Barles
    Mr. & Mrs. M. K. Boyd

Mr. & Mrs. Lewis E. Chipman
Mrs. A. Clark
Prof. & Mrs. Solomon. H. Clark
Maj. & Mrs. David T. Corbin
Mr. & Mrs. Romulus A. Cox
Mrs. Mary F. Deane
Mr. & Mrs. F. L. Dougherty
Mrs. A. Reeves Jackson
Mr. & Mrs. F.W. Matthiessen jr.
Mr. & Mrs."C. McLennan
Mr. & Mrs. George H. Nesbett
Mr. & Mrs. Aaron J. Newby
Mrs. H. S. Pond
Mr. & Mrs. Edward D. Sniffen
Mr. & Mrs. Charles W. Taylor
Mr. & Mrs. Justin Wetmore

FIFTY-SECOND STREET (HYDE PARK).

225 Mr. & Mrs. William A. Burrows
227 Mr. & Mrs. Ulich Young
227 Frank Young
273 Mrs. Nellie Hunneman
275 Rev. & Mrs. J. R. Gow
581 Mr. & Mrs. Thomas Davies

228 Mr. & Mrs. Theodore E. Hayes
230 Mr. & Mrs. Arthur Dole
232 Mr. & Mrs. Wm. G. Carlisle
232 Mr. & Mrs. Chas. W. Schaberg

FIFTY-THIRD STREET (HYDE PARK).

35 Mr. & Mrs. Charles S. Baker
     Receiving day Saturday
35 Mrs. A. V. H. Wakeman
39 Mr. & Mrs. Ernest R. Graham
     Receiving day Monday
39 Mrs. George C. Jackson
41 Mrs. Emily Hertell
41 Mr. & Mrs. Andrew Brown
41 Frederick Lovedridge
41 Henry Dennis
51 Mr. & Mrs. Charles R. Henderson
53 Mr. & Mrs. James T. Harahan
53 Mr. & Mrs. James B. Sherlie
157 Dr. & Mrs. H. W. Gentles
169 Mr. & Mrs. Charles W.Melcher
179 Dr. & Mrs. L. F. Dayan
181 Mr. & Mrs. Hubert C. Herring
     Receiving day Friday
205 Mr. & Mrs. F. M. Atwood
205 Mr. & Mrs. James E. Baker
213 Frederick D. Hills
213 Mrs. Abigail M. Hills
213 Mrs. A. M. Hunn
217 Dr. & Mrs. Denslow Lewis
247 Mr. & Mrs. John J. Clark & drs.
247 W. Odell Clark

42 Mr. & Mrs. E. H. Kellogg & dr.
42 E. B. Kellogg
44 Mr. & Mrs. Warner E. Jones
48 Mr. & Mrs. Geo. W. Binford
52 Mr. & Mrs. Lester A. Talcott
54 Fred Rothschild
68 W. Dix Webster
136 H. D. Jones
192 Mr. & Mrs. James Inglis
192 Mr. & Mrs. John Inglis .
224 Frank Gardner Perkins
228 Mr. & Mrs. James J. West
228 Mr. & Mrs. James A. Hair
228 Mr. & Mrs. George M. Eckles
236 Mr. & Mrs. S. F. Fogg
238 Dr. & Mrs. F. E. Wadhams
240 Mr. & Mrs. Charles A. Mifflin
244 Mrs. G. T. McMurray
244 Geo. N. McMurray
244 C. H. McMurray
244 A. M. McMurray
248 Mr. & Mrs. Albert O. Parker &
     dr. *Receiving day Thursday*
248 Mr. & Mrs. N. A. Parker
248 B. M. Parker
248 A. H. Parker
248 M. B. Parker

263 Mr. & Mrs. Rudolph H. Gar-
    rigue
271 Mr. & Mrs. John A. Cole
271 Mrs. Mary E. W. Cole
271 Arthur W. Cole
271 Mrs. M. M. Alvord
275 Mr. & Mrs. Charles E. Morrill
279 Mr. & Mrs. Allan M. Hays
289 Mr. & Mrs. J. F. Sanders
289 Miss Ethel J. Magee
295 Mr. & Mrs. W. H. Palmer
297 Mr. & Mrs. J. J. Clark
299 Mrs. Mary J. C. Morrison
301 Mr. & Mrs. S. L. Tompkins
    Receiving day Thursday
305 Mr. & Mrs. N. W. Hacker
305 Mrs. A. P. Hacker

252 Mr. & Mrs. Frederick A. Bowles
262 Mr. & Mrs. Geo. Willard & drs.
262 George R. Willard
284 Mr. & Mrs. Robert D. Ferris
300 Mr. & Mrs. Charles H. Randle
300 Mrs. M. E. Hanson
310 Mr. & Mrs. G. H. Mack
316 Mr. & Mrs. Andrew McAdams

———

307 Mr. & Mrs. Arthur A. Crosby
309 Mr. & Mrs. Charles F. Drew
335 Mrs. Louisa H. Adams
335 Mrs. Melancthon Smith
339 Mr. & Mrs. Edward Allen
339 Mr. & Mrs. Arthur G. Allen
341 Mr. & Mrs. Louis J. Reedy

FIFTY-FOURTH STREET (HYDE PARK).

191 Mr. & Mrs. Wm. C. Davenport
191 Mrs. Anna Whitman
191 Mr. & Mrs. Washington I. Terry
221 Mr. & Mrs. H. P. Blair
223 Prof. & Mrs. C. O. Whitman
307 Mr. & Mrs. J. T. Geraty
    Receiving day Thursday

———

304 Mr. & Mrs. Chas. P. Jennings

144 Dr. & Mrs. Edward Malcolm
    Bruce
    Receiving day Thursday
146 Mr. & Mrs. Walter Wardrop &
    drs.
146 Walter Wardrop jr.
188 Mr. & Mrs. W. C. Robinson
190 Mr. & Mrs. Edwin S. Tice
    Receiving day Thursday

FIFTY-FOURTH PLACE (HYDE PARK).

189 Mr. & Mrs. Oscar H. Ward
193 Mr. & Mrs. Erasmus D. Steen
193 Mrs. Laura Rabb
225 L. M. Dougherty

228 Mr. & Mrs. Frank M. Sessions
230 Mr. & Mrs. Chas. W. Kersteter
232 Mr. & Mrs. D. W. Cooke

FIFTY-FIFTH STREET (HYDE PARK).

129 Colonies Hotel
129 Prof. Richard G. Moulton
129 Mr. & Mrs. Ernest R. Sharpe
137 Chauncey Kelsey
277 Dr. Albert Peacock

268 Dr. J. O'Sullivan
560 Dr. & Mrs. H. A. Cross

———

277 Dr. Samuel R. Peacock
291 Dr. & Mrs. Wm. B. McCord

FIFTY-SIXTH STREET (HYDE PARK).

301 Rev. & Mrs. Nathaniel I. Rub-
    inkam
307 Mr. & Mrs. Charles E. Lane
309 Mr. & Mrs. F. M. Taylor
309 Henry C. Taylor

356 Mr. & Mrs. J. S. Mayou

———

347 Mr. & Mrs. Ephraim Hewitt
1211 Mr. & Mrs. Frank H. Graham

FIFTY-SEVENTH STREET (HYDE PARK).

Rev. S. S. Matthews & drs.
cor. Madison av. Mrs. Zella A. Dixson
415 Mr. & Mrs. C. P. Dawley
425 Mr. & Mrs. P. J. Daemicke
433 Mr. & Mrs. C. A. Jerman
437 Mr. & Mrs. J. Fred Waggoner
441 Mr. & Mrs. Logan F. Moore

438 Mr. & Mrs. Henry Parry

244 Mrs. Walter F. Moring & dr.
244 G. Race Moring
244 Dr. J. W. MacLachlan
248 Mr. & Mrs. Samuel Nelson
248 Mr. & Mrs. Van R. Livingston
322 Mr. & Mrs. James C. Beeks &dr.
322 Edward C. Beeks
322 McCarty W. Beeks
326 Mr. & Mrs. Andrew L. Smith
416 Mr. & Mrs. George Wragg

FIFTY-EIGHTH STREET (HYDE PARK).

315 Mr. & Mrs. T. W. Hamill & dr.
351 Miss Louise Dickinson
351 Miss Jennie Dickinson
357 Prof. & Mrs. George Baur

361 Mr. & Mrs. Wm. C. Wilkinson
363 Mrs. Reliance Bowman & dr.
363 Blake A. Bowman

FIFTY-NINTH STREET (ENGLEWOOD).

621 Freeman DeWolfe
621 Miss Eda DeWolfe

540 Mr. & Mrs. W. G. Limbocker
542 Mr. & Mrs. James E. Plew
600 Dr. & Mrs. S. A. Lundgren

FOREST AVENUE.

3107 Mr. & Mrs. Edw. E. Wendell
3113 Mr. & Mrs. W. K. Forsyth
3117 Mrs. Philo G. Dodge
3117 Edmond F. Dodge
3123 Mr. & Mrs. Jerry Knowles
3131 Mr. & Mrs. Wm. W. Crooker & drs.
3131 Miss Elizabeth M. Buckley
3135 Mr. & Mrs. B. F. Horton
3135 Mr. & Mrs. J. G. Slafter
3137 Mrs. W. B. Jenks & dr
3137 John G. Jenks
3139 Mr. & Mrs. Geo. H. Cole & dr
3143 Mr. & Mrs. M. C. Isaacs
3149 Mr. & Mrs. J. C. Manheimer
3149 Wm. Manheimer
3151 Mr. & Mrs. Leon Klein
3153 Mr. & Mrs. H. H. Heimerdinger
3157 Mr. & Mrs. Philip A. Auer
3157 Miss Lizzie Fraser
3157 Miss May C. Fraser
3159 Mr. & Mrs. Joseph H. Dimery
3159 Thomas W. Gilmore
3231 Mrs. F. B. Miles & drs.
3231 Fred S. Miles
3231 H. D. Miles
3233 Mrs. Hattie S. Boyd
3233 E. T. Shedd

3122 W. I. Neely
3130 Dr. & Mrs. F. Montrose Weller
3134 Mr. & Mrs. George Marienthal
3204 Mr. & Mrs. Wm. Busby
3206 Prof. Julius Neumann
3206 I. D. Neumann
3210 Mr. & Mrs. A. Fontayne & drs.
3210 Albert Fontayne jr.
3224 Mrs. F. Herbst
3224 Mr. & Mrs. Victor M. Barbour
3232 Mr. & Mrs. J. W. Scofield
3238 Mr. & Mrs. John W. Nicholson
3246 Mr. & Mrs. N. Martin
3258 Mr. & Mrs. S. R. Howell
3316 Mr. & Mrs. Henry A. Leland
3332 Mrs. Emanuel Strauss & drs.
3332 Raphael Strauss
3332 Samuel Strauss
3334 Mr. & Mrs. Samuel Engel
3340 Mr. & Mrs. I. L. Hamburger
Receive 1st & 3d Friday
3342 Mr. & Mrs. Leopold Heller
3342 Gustav Heller
3346 Mr. & Mrs. Isaac Lichtstern
3348 Mr. & Mrs. Samuel C. Peiser
3362 Mr. & Mrs. Sigmund Stein
3364 Mr. & Mrs. Wm. T. Collins
Receiving day Thursday

3237 Mr. & Mrs. Sumner Hopkins
3237 Mr. & Mrs. H. R. Vandercook
3239 Mr.& Mrs. Morris Brown &drs.
3243 Mrs. James Hennessy & dr.
3245 Mrs. W. H. Sanders
3245 Dr. H. B. Sanders
3251 Mr. & Mrs. Nicoll Halsey
3253 Mr. & Mrs. Clifford Williams
Ne. cor. 33d Dr. & Mrs. Frank H.
    Gardiner
3301 Dr. & Mrs. Marcus P. Hatfield
3301 Benjamin S. Levy
3303 Mr. & Mrs. W. F. Goodwin
3305 Mr. & Mrs. N. Strauss
3307 Mr. & Mrs. Ambrose Risdon
    Receiving day Tuesday
3309 Mr. & Mrs. W. N. Evans
3311 Mr. & Mrs. George F. Bodwell
3313 Mr. & Mrs. Emanuel Lederer
3313 M. Oppenheimer & dr.
3315 Mr. & Mrs. Eric Winters
3317 Mr. & Mrs. George N. Stone
3323 Mr. & Mrs. Frederick Crum-
    baugh
3333 Mr. & Mrs. S. Lester Burton
3339 Mr. & Mrs. Mark Simons & dr.
    Receiving day last Wednesday
3341 Mr. & Mrs. W. L. Wright & drs.
3343 Mr.& Mrs. Henry Herbert Carr
    & dr.
3345 Mr. & Mrs. Joseph Harron
3349 Mr. & Mrs. Levi Strouss & dr.
3349 Joseph Strouss
3349 Emil Strouss
3349 Aaron Strouss
3351 Mr. & Mrs. John D. Stowell &
    drs.
3351 Miss Louise M. Farnham
3353 Mr. & Mrs. B. F. Chase & dr.
3353 B. F. Chase jr.
3359 Nat Stone
3363 Mr. & Mrs. S. M. Cantrovitz
    Receiving days 1st & 3d Fridays
3403 Mr. & Mrs. J. Freudenthal
3405 Mr. & Mrs. Joseph C. Lamm
    Receiving days 2d & 4th Wednes.
3407 Mr. & Mrs. Henry Heppner
    Receiving day Wednesday
3409 Mr. & Mrs. Simon L. Rubel
3411 Mr. & Mrs. W. Solomon
3413 Mr. & Mrs. F. Rothschild
3419 Mr. & Mrs. Henry Myer
3423 Mr. & Mrs. G. Lehrberg
3563 Mr. & Mrs. M. B. Madden
    Receiving day Thursday
3565 Mr. & Mrs. John O'Connor

3364 James T. Collins
3400 Mr. & Mrs. F. M. Solomon
3402 Mr. & Mrs. M. P. Rosenheim
3404 Mrs. Jacob Peiser
3404 Mrs. H. J. Metz & dr.
3406 Mr. & Mrs. Charles Joseph
    Receiving day Wednesday
3408 Mr. & Mrs. Isadore Eisen-
    staedt & drs.
    Receiving days 1st & 3d Wednesdays
3408 A. L. Eisenstaedt
3428 Judge & Mrs. D. J. Lyon
3518 Mr. & Mrs. Frank Foreman
3520 Mr. & Mrs. E. A. Buzzell
3520 Mr. & Mrs. J. H. Gibson
3524 Mr. & Mrs. Arthur W. Gray
3526 Wm. J. Burdsall
3526 Miss Marion C. Burdsall
3526 Miss Mary J. Burdsall
3546 Mr. & Mrs. Wm. Wolff
3562 Mr. & Mrs. Wm. Davis
3600 Benjamin Kronthal
3602 Mr. & Mrs. Jacob Fass
    Receiving day Thursday
3604 Mr. & Mrs. Herman Heine
    Receive 1st Wednesday
3604 Albert Heine
3604 Oscar Heine
3648 Joseph L. Lyons
3700 Mr. & Mrs. Max Ellbogen
3702 Dr. & Mrs. S. Eisenstaedt
3702 Mrs. N. Gatzert & dr.
3706 Mr. & Mrs. S. Leppel & dr.
    Receive 1st Friday
3706 Maurice Leppel
3712 Mr. & Mrs. L. Myers
3716 Mr. & Mrs. Osbourne J. Shan-
    non & dr. *Receiving day Tuesday*
3716 Mrs. Mary E. Holt
3722 Mr. & Mrs. M. De Lee & drs.
3722 S. T. De Lee
3722 Dr. Joseph B. De Lee
3724 Mr. & Mrs. J. H. Myers & dr.
    Receiving day Friday
3726 Mrs. Clara Mandelbaum
3726 M. H. Mandelbaum
3730 Mr. & Mrs. C. A. Garcelon
3732 Mr. & Mrs. Geo. Sunderland
3736 D. J. Young
3736 Mr. & Mrs. W. P. Carey
3736 Charles N. Carey
3738 Mr. & Mrs. Joseph T. Carey
3740 Mr.& Mrs. Sol. H. Eisenstaedt
3742 Mr. & Mrs. David Wasserman
3742½ Mr. & Mrs. Emil Rothschild
3744 Mr. & Mrs. Joseph A. Kramer

8

3631 Mrs. S. Hyman & drs.
3633 Mr. & Mrs. Henry Kahn
3635 Mr. & Mrs. S. M. Rothschild &
   dr. *Receiving day Thursday*
3635 I. D. Rothschild
3635 Wm. L. Rothschild
3637 Mr. & Mrs. Henry Spitz
3639 Mr. & Mrs. H. Simons
3643 Mr. & Mrs. Henry S. Schlossman
   Receiving day 1st Wednesday
3647 Mr. & Mrs. Samuel Flower
3649 Mr. & Mrs. Julius Cone
3651 Mr. & Mrs. L. W. Austermell
   & dr.
3651 Lewis T. Austermell
3655 Mr. & Mrs. G. Felsenthal
3655 Henry Felsenthal
3657 Mr. & Mrs. B. Boice
3715 L. J. Hettich
3715 H. L. Hettich
3721 Mrs. Fannie Schaffner & drs.
3721 Abraham Schaffner
3723 Mr. & Mrs. Hugh Shiells
   Receiving day 3d Tuesday
3725 Mr. & Mrs. James H. Northup
3725 Walter G. Seeley
3727 Mr. & Mrs. Wm. Dillon
3731 Mr. & Mrs. Wm. O. Stanley
3733 Mr. & Mrs. Thos. W. Wilmarth
3735 Mr. & Mrs. William F. Senour
3737 Dr. & Mrs. T. B. Swartz
3741 Mr. & Mrs. George J. Hutt
3747 Mr. & Mrs. P. Peterson
3751 Mr.& Mrs. Harry C. Hilbourne

3744 Mrs. Julius Rosenberger
3746 Mrs. Wm. D. Dee
3746 William E. Dee
3746 George W. Dee
3748 Mr. & Mrs. Ernst Puttkammer
3748 Mr. & Mrs. C. H. Ingwersen
3748 Marvin Ingwersen
3754 Mrs. H. H. Conover
3754 Mrs. Addie C. Keiller
3656 P. J. McIntyre

3801 Mr. & Mrs. F. G. Springer &
   dr.
3805 Mr. & Mrs. James C. Simm
3811 Mr. & Mrs. H. F. Billings
3813 Mr. & Mrs. L. Kussner & dr.
3813 Albert J. Kussner
3813 Matthew E. Magill
3815 Mr. & Mrs. Edwin A. Armstrong
3817 Mr. & Mrs. E. L. Tufts
   Receiving day Wednesday
3817 Mr. & Mrs. M. S. Nichols
3821 Mr. & Mrs. J. T. Menefee & drs.
3821 Mr. & Mrs. Henry M. Paynter
3823 Mr. & Mrs. F. S. Armstrong
   & dr.
3827 Mr. & Mrs. O. W. Richardson
   & drs.
3827 Orlo D. Richardson
3829 Mr. & Mrs. Edward Browne
3833 Mr. & Mrs. Edward F. Keebler
   Receive Wednesday 3 to 5
3841 H. L. Carpenter

FORRESTVILLE AVENUE.

4319 Mr. & Mrs. A. G. Jewell & dr.
4319 Edwin S. Jewell
4323 Mr. & Mrs. George S. Sutton
4331 Mr. & Mrs. Charles H. Evans
4333 Mr. & Mrs. Isaac Wolff & dr.
4335 Mr. & Mrs. Charles D. Cox
4337 Mr. & Mrs. Charles W. Meeker
4339 Mr. & Mrs. Leopold Price
4527 Mr. & Mrs. Buel R. Hopkins
4545 Mr. & Mrs. Ralph T. Sollitt
4553 Dr. & Mrs. J. P. McGill
4555 Mr. & Mrs. Byron M. Fellows
   Receiving day Thursday
4837 Mr. & Mrs. A. Cummings
4839 Mr. & Mrs. E. R. Dillingham
4841 Mr. & Mrs. M. O. Tremaine
4845 Mr. & Mrs. Albert C. Arnold

4314 Mr. & Mrs. Wm. J. Martin
4318 Jerome Hewitt & drs.
4320 J. P. Moran
4528 Mr. & Mrs. Thos. S. Howell
4528 Louis B. Howell
4534 Mr. & Mrs. J. H. Lenehan
4534 Mr. & Mrs. John Clinton Wood
4534 Mr. & Mrs. Calvin C. Johnson
4534 Mr. & Mrs. A. A. Angustus
4536 Mr. & Mrs. Charles H. King
4536 Mr. & Mrs. F. L. Beveridge
4538 Mr. & Mrs. Franklin G. Aver
4552 Mr. & Mrs. H. F. Vehmeyer
4916 Mr. & Mrs. John G. Tait
4916 Mr. & Mrs. Frank J. Hurney
4948 Mr. & Mrs. Samuel J. Howe
4954 Mr. & Mrs. John K. Blatchford

4909 Mr. & Mrs. Frank C. Hageman
4909 Dr. & Mrs. Frederiek C. Hageman
4911 Harry H. Doggett
4911 William F. Doggett

4958 Mr. & Mrs. N. P. Cummings
_____
4911 Mrs. Mary E. Doggett
4935 Mr. & Mrs. Herbert B. Leavitt

FORTIETH STREET (HYDE PARK).

1 Mr. & Mrs. C. A. Barker
17 Mr. & Mrs. W. M. Sage & dr.
17 W. G. Sage
17 C. F. Sage
187 Thomas C. Bowen
213 Mr. & Mrs. C. H. Bradley
213 Mr. & Mrs. Loring Bradley
371 Dr. & Mrs. Charles P. Pruyn
373 Judge & Mrs. John Gibbons
391 Mr. & Mrs. Lewis Defoe
391 Thomas Defoe
395 John D. Adair
401 Mr.& Mrs. J. G. Earle
_____
368 Byron T. Collingbourne
418 Mr. & Mrs. Nicholas C. Miller
420 Mrs. A. M. Patten

96 Mr. & Mrs. M. Eisenberg & dr.
98 Mr. & Mrs. H. D. Post
104 Dr. & Mrs. Bayard Holmes
192 Mr. & Mrs. W.H. Robinson &dr.
192 W. B. Robinson
196 Mr. & Mrs. Wm. D. Clark & dr.
218 William B. Elmore
220 Mrs. May Anderson Trestrail
Receiving day Wednesday
220 Goethe G. Faust
224 Mr. & Mrs. A. S. Loeb
358 Thomas B. Livingstone & drs.
Receiving day Thursday
358 Archie T. Livingstone
358 John K. Livingstone
360 Mr. & Chas. T. Farson
368 Albert B. Collingbourne

FORTY-FIRST STREET (HYDE PARK).

93 Mr. & Mrs. C. Frank Jobson
195 Mrs. Margaret Boyd & drs.
195 Robert H. Boyd
305 Mrs. Louise B. Kilbourne
305 Walter F. Kilbourne
305 Edwin D. Kilbourne
305 Charles H. Dutro
307 Rev. & Mrs. P. H. Swift
313 Mr. & Mrs. Levi Salomon
319 Mr. & Mrs. M. D. Hays
319 Mr. & Mrs. Albert H. Dix
343 Mr. & Mrs. A. E. Whitaker
351 Mr. & Mrs. W. A. Lowell & drs.
353 Mrs. A. R. Abbott & drs.
355 Mr. & Mrs. William Cleaver
355 Arthur W. Cleaver
359 Mr. & Mrs. A. E. Crowley
361 Mr. & Mrs. Ferry A. Gardner
393 Mr. & Mrs. Benjamin F. Methven *Receiving day Thursday*
393 Mr. & Mrs. J. C. Ryan
405 Mr. & Mrs. W. A. Howe
407 Mr. & Mrs. H. C. Bunn
409 Mr. & Mrs. O. G. Green
427 Mr. & Mrs. J. Austin Dunn
Receiving day Tues
429 Mr. & Mrs. George S. Bridge
435 Mr. & Mrs. C. H. Durand
451 Mr. & Mrs. C. E. White

184 Mr. & Mrs. L. M. Barber & drs.
186 Mr. & Mrs. June Barrett
206 N. D. Soper
226 Mr. & Mrs. Charles A. Folsom
292 Mr. & Mrs. W. P. Hoit & dr.
302 Mr. & Mrs. A. M. Kendrick
302 Mrs. Flora M. Carson
306 Mr. & Mrs. J. H. Smith
314 Mr. & Mrs. W. S. Proudfit & dr.
314 James M. Proudfit
320 Mr. & Mrs. E. L. Wilson
320 Thomas S. Wilson, U. S. N.
324 Mr. & Mrs. R. H. Washburne
326 Mr. & Mrs. James M. Cobham
330 Mr. & Mrs. S. J. Moss
336 Mr. & Mrs. Dahiel G. Bardon
350 Mr. & Mrs. Alfred Fortin
354 Mr. & Mrs. John Bagley
358 Mr. & Mrs. T. H. Williams
360 Mr. & Mrs. R. O. Cassell
362 Mr.& Mrs. Benjamin Brunswick
364 Mr. & Mrs. H. M. Quackenbos
408 Mr. & Mrs. George Fortin
420 Mrs. S. L. Jenks
442 Miss Abbie A. Birdsall
442 Miss Nettie Birdsall
_____
599 Mr. & Mrs. Donald R. Fraser

FORTY-SECOND STREET (HYDE PARK).

147 Mrs. S. L. Jacques
149 Mr. & Mrs. A. Pearson & drs.
149 Dr. Wm. H. Warder
151 Mr. & Mrs. Charles Stewart
153 Mr. & Mrs. J. O. Davidson
155 Mr. & Mrs. D. E. Kenyon
157 Mrs. J. E. Morrison
157 Mrs. E. B. Kellogg
  Receiving day Friday
219 Mr. & Mrs. Wm. Blyben & dr.
225 Mrs. Emily E. Calder & drs.
289 Mr. & Mrs. Peter B. Wight
295 Mrs. Andrew Wight
295 Mr. & Mrs. J. S. Beck
303 Mr. & Mrs. Albert Joseph
327 Mr. & Mrs. William M. Barrett
327 Charles W. Barrett
327 Mrs. Mary F. Nebeker
333 Mr. & Mrs. D. H. Fletcher & drs.
335 Dr. Lindley Murray Moore
375 Mr. & Mrs. Ben R. Hyman
375 Miss Settie Reinganum
375 Miss Lena Reinganum
475 Mrs. M. Holmes & dr.
475 Mrs. P. W. Raber
487 Mr. & Mrs. Amos Lakey
489 Mr. & Mrs. Joseph Jones
489 Dr. Bertha VanHoosen
491 Mr. & Mrs. Walter Chapman
567 Dr. & Mrs. William C. Wise

———

492 Mr. & Mrs. C. W. Huggins
496 Mrs. L. A. Palmer
496 C. M. Palmer
708 Mrs. Martha E. Young & dr.
710 Mr. & Mrs. Ernest Dresher

32 Mr. & Mrs. J. J. Howard
36 Mr. & Mrs. J. A. Conly
36 Harry F. Conly
se. cor. Lake av.
  Mr. & Mrs. W. H. D'Lisle
  Mr. & Mrs. H. W. Hart jr.
  Mr. & Mrs. A. H. Williams
96 Mr. & Mrs. John H. Cook
140 Mr. & Mrs. Ira T. Eaton
142 Mr. & Mrs. F. D. Helmer
142 Samuel A. Johnson
148 Mr. & Mrs. Garson Myers
  Receiving day Wednesday
148 Mr. & Mrs. P. G. Burns
148 Mr. & Mrs. Jacob C. Dietz
154 Mr. & Mrs. F. A. Menge
154 Dr. Frederick Menge
214 Mr. & Mrs. George W. Manning
220 Mr. & Mrs. Jacob Kahn & dr.
  Receiving day Wednesday
224 Mr. & Mrs. F. B. Munsell
228 Mr. & Mrs. Geo. W. Teel & dr.
286 Mr. & Mrs. W. R. Mooney & dr.
208 Joseph B. Schnadig
350 Mr. & Mrs. Herman Hefter
356 E. B. Everard
364 G. W. Collins
368 George F. Brown
410 Mr. & Mrs. Anthony Beck
464 Dr. & Mrs. H. S. Tucker
464 Mrs. C. Whitley
472 Mr. & Mrs. T. S. Quincey
472 Miss Franc C. Morrison
484 Mr. & Mrs. C. H. Bunker
490 Mr. & Mrs. G. L. Marchand
492 Mr. & Mrs. A. J. King

FORTY-SECOND PLACE (HYDE PARK).

215 Mr. & Mrs. H. C. Johnson
223 Mr. & Mrs. M. W. Dyer
229 Dr. & Mrs. Fitch C. E. Mattison
229 Mr. & Mrs. Charles H. Storm
425 Mr. & Mrs. H. A. Howland
427 T. W. Browning
429 Mr. & Mrs. F. Stewart Smith
477 Mr. & Mrs. John Blum & dr.
477 Benjamin Blum
477 Edgar C. Blum
477 Louis J. Blum
477 Mr. & Mrs. Morris Jacobson
479 Dr. & Mrs J. R. Richardson
481 Henry L. Roecker

214 Mr. & Mrs. J. Schnadig
216 Rev. & Mrs. Willard Scott
426 Mr. & Mrs. Edward L. Wallwork
482 Mr. & Mrs. G. C. Morgan
482 C. K. Morgan
482 Mr. & Mrs. J. M. Van Nest
484 Mrs. Ella L. Marx
484 M. P. Duhig
484 Mr. & Mrs. Edward Beach & dr.
484 Miss Katharine M. Beach
490 Mr. & Mrs. Charles Hefter
492 Mr. & Mrs. G. B. Chamberlin
492 Mrs. May G. Rubel

485 Mr. & Mrs. J. J. Kearney
    Receiving day Thursday
485 T. P. Connell
485 Mrs. Margaret Sullivan
491 Mr. & Mrs. S. P. Carter
497 Mr. & Mrs. J. J. Doctor
507 Mr. & Mrs. J. Aagard

498 Mr. & Mrs. W. M. Northrup
498 S. W. Conger
498 Mr. & Mrs. I. A. Fleming
500 Mr. & Mrs. Jas. H. Birmingham
500 Mrs. A. Thomas & drs.
    Receiving day Friday

FORTY-THIRD STREET (HYDE PARK).

5 Dr. & Mrs. Henry A. Costner
11 Mr. & Mrs. L. S. Tiffany
13 Mr. & Mrs. Wm. R. Mason
17 Mr. & Mrs. John F. Kingwill
75 Dr. & Mrs. M. H. Cazier
81 Mr. & Mrs. S. S. Dickey
83 Mr. & Mrs. Arthur D. Sage
83 Mr. & Mrs. Wm. J. Smyth
91 Mrs. V. H. Wheat
91 Joseph Caldwell
161 Mr. & Mrs. Wesley J. Clizbe
245 Dr. & Mrs. T. S. Huffaker
331 Dr. John A. Kirkpatrick
497 Dr. W. F. Nutt
525 Dr. Emmet L. Smith

48 Dr. & Mrs. William A. J. Mann
58 Dr. J. C. Hoag
106 J. B. Bradford
106 Dr. Robert C. Wilson
108 Mr. & Mrs. D. Frederick Hurd
108 Mr. & Mrs. E. J. Scott
114 Mr. & Mrs. James Love
116 Mr. & Mrs. Wesley Merritt
116 Dr. H. R. Wallace
116 Mr. & Mrs. C. H. Ingram
116 Miss M. J. Eddy
156 Mr. & Mrs. George F. Ebert
296 Miss Julia P. Leavens
568 Mr. & Mrs. Frank M. Morris
576 W. L. Eldred

FORTY-FOURTH STREET (HYDE PARK).

79 Mr. & Mrs. T. W. Blatchford
81 Mr. & Mrs. J. P. Flersheim
81 Geo. B. Flersheim
87 Mr. & Mrs. C. E. Fowler
89 Mr. & Mrs. C. F. Vent
91 Mr. & Mrs. E. T. Doyle
91 Mrs. M. R. Woods
93 Mr. & Mrs. A. R. Russell
97 Mrs. Susan Keen & dr.
97 Mrs. E. H. Keen
195 Mr. & Mrs. W. A. Combs
196 Mr. & Mrs. Geo. D Whitcomb
197 Mr. & Mrs. E. F. Skinner
197 Mr. & Mrs. E. H. Skinner
205 Dr. & Mrs. Garrett Newkirk
207 Mr. & Mrs. Edward M. Adams
207 Mr. & Mrs. Elmer E. Black
345 Mr. & Mrs. Paul Shniedewend
369 Dr. & Mrs. Edwin F. Rush
535 Mr.& Mrs. John E.Murphy&drs.
535 James S. Murphy
535 Daniel Duffin

24 Mr. & Mrs. Mark R. Sherman
30 Mr. & Mrs. J. T. Nickerson
40 Mr. & Mrs. J. C. F. Royer
72 Mr. & Mrs. Belton Halley
78 Miss Georgianna Springer
78 Miss Adele Springer
78 Mrs. James S. Smale & drs.
200 Mr. & Mrs. Gordon MacLeod
200 Mr. & Mrs. Henry R. Kaiser
208 Mr. & Mrs. Frank E. Pettit
208 Mrs. G. M. Smith
338 Mrs. R. G. Stevens & drs.
338 Dr. & Mrs. James Robertson
342 Mr. & Mrs. James S. Barker
360 Dr. & Mrs. Norman Teal
380 Mr. & Mrs. Asa G. Adams
470 Dr. & Mrs. G. E. Willard
606 Mr. & Mrs. O. W. Folsom
608 Mr. & Mrs. J. M. Hoadley & dr
724 Miss N. B. Roll

FORTY-FOURTH PLACE (HYDE PARK).

527 Miss Anna L. Boyce

484 Mr. & Mrs. W. H. Forbes

FORTY-FIFTH STREET (HYDE PARK).

105 Dr. & Mrs. Edgar D. Swain
231 Mr. & Mrs. G. W. Brandt
235 Mr. & Mrs. Charles F. Harding
377 Samuel J. Marks
495 Mr. & Mrs. John W. Keys
515 Mr. & Mrs. K. J. W. Featherstone
517 Mr. & Mrs. M. J. Benson

---

320 Mr. & Mrs. S. M. Dille
434 Mr. & Mrs. C. G. Thomas
440 Mr. & Mrs. Peter Fish
450 Mrs. Nellie E. Fowler
460 Mr. & Mrs. George E. Croppe
554 Dr. & Mrs. Merrill G. Pingree
554 J. Kemper Dering

108 Mr. & Mrs. C. B. Shourds
108 James L. Shourds
112 Mr. & Mrs. Anson Low
116 Mr. & Mrs. Robert Richards
172 Mr. & Mrs. C. E. Scribner
190 Mr. & Mrs. C. H. Wilson
230 Mr. & Mrs. D. A. Southworth & dr.
234 Mr. & Mrs. Jay Dwiggins
234 Guy Arbogast
236 Mr. & Mrs. B. F. Paine
236 Mrs. Mary A. Cobb
240 Mr. & Mrs. E. B. Campbell
242 Mr. & Mrs. John Craig
316 Mr. & Mrs. C. C. Prest
316 Harry R. Prest
318 Mr. & Mrs. H. F. Moyer

FORTY-SIXTH STREET (HYDE PARK).

15 Mr. & Mrs. Thomas Crouch & dr.
   Receiving day Wednesday
15 Albert W. Crouch
17 Mr. & Mrs. E. H. Haines
17 Mr. & Mrs. Norman W. Kellogg
25 Mr. & Mrs. Thomas Miller
31 Mr. & Mrs. Robert S. Buchanan
35 Dr. & Mrs. W. A. McDowell
41 Mr. & Mrs. J. M. Bennett & dr.
41 Mr. & Mrs. Frank I. Furber
41 Mrs. M. V. Wheeler & dr.
41 Ralph M. Shankland
45 Mr. & Mrs. Edmund L. Mansure
45 Mrs. Susan T. Forsman
47 Mr. & Mrs. Samuel B. Cadow
47 George E. Harmon
49 Mr. & Mrs. Francis B. Hooker
49 Mr. & Mrs. George P. Perkins
201 Mr. & Mrs. R. J. Wilson
205 Mr. & Mrs. James A. Clark
205 Mr. & Mrs. W. H. Little

20 William S. Stewart & dr.
22 Mr. & Mrs. John Millar
22 Mrs. Theresa Barcal & dr.
148 Mr. & Mrs. W. S. Seaverns
148 L. H. Ash
206 Mr. & Mrs. Frank H. Baker
220 Mr. & Mrs. T. C. Keller
220 Mr. & Mrs. Nathan Smith
464 Mr. & Mrs. M. J. Cragin
514 Mr. & Mrs. Adam Ortseifen

---

205 Mr. & Mrs. T. A. Rittenhouse
219 Mr. & Mrs. R. W. Cross
221 Mr. & Mrs. Stuart F. Marchant
275 Mr. & Mrs. Douglass Smith
353 Mr. & Mrs. John Boomer & drs.
353 John B. Boomer
399 Mr. & Mrs. Charles C. Leonard
437 Mr. & Mrs. C. H. Newbre
619 Rev. & Mrs. Frank W. Gunsanlus

FORTY-SEVENTH STREET (HYDE PARK).

25 Dr. O. J. Stein
81 Mr. & Mrs. Frederick L. Fake
   Receiving day Thursday
81 Frederick L. Fake jr.
81 Miss A. E. Scammon
83 Dr. & Mrs. Charles W. Crary & dr.
85 Mr. & Mrs. C. W. Lapham
   Receiving day Tuesday
99 Mr. & Mrs. W. H. Burnet & dr.
109 Mrs. Walter Proby & dr.
109 James W. Proby

56 Mr. & Mrs. Joseph B. Lewis
90 Mr. & Mrs. G. R. Thorne
90 George A. Thorne
90 Robert J. Thorne
90 James W. Thorne
124 Mr. & Mrs. Orvin L. Fox
124 Mrs. Mary E. Faunce
126 Mr. & Mrs. James S. Cummins
126 Miss Mary L. Byllesby
128 Mr. & Mrs. William Alton jr.
130 Mr. & Mrs. Wm. S. Shaw
130 Edward R. Shaw
132 Mr. & Mrs. Elmer Dwiggins

109 Miss Jennie L. Proby
111 Gen. & Mrs. Geo. M. Guion & dr.
111 Leroy P. Guion
113 Mr. & Mrs. Ben. L. Cook & dr.
125 Mr. & Mrs. William C. Niblack
Receiving day Tuesday
135 Mr. & Mrs. Milo G. Kellogg
143 Mr. & Mrs. E. M. Barton
175 Mr. & Mrs. C. H. Phillips
191 Mr. & Mrs. N. S. Bouton
197 Dr. & Mrs. Geo. F. Washburne
Receiving day Thursday
197 Mr. & Mrs. Oscar Washburne
205 Mr. & Mrs. Charles Murray
205 Miss Jean Murray
221 Mr. & Mrs. I. N. Ash
227 Mr. & Mrs. Edward A. Turner
267 Mr. & Mrs. L. Pratt & dr.

140 Mr. & Mrs. Wm. C. Thorne
152 Mr. & Mrs. Robert Strahorn
164 Mr. & Mrs. J. J. Dau
174 W. M. Alister
174 Miss Anna Carleton
244 Mr. & Mrs. Leslie D. Thomas
246 Mr. & Mrs. S. W. Stone
250 Mr. & Mrs. W. Adolphus
254 Mr. & Mrs. C. D. Osborn
434 Dr. & Mrs. Thomas W. Combs

267 Rodney K. Pratt
267 Clayton A. Pratt
299 Dr. & Mrs. Sydney Walker
453 Dr. Orrin L. Smith
455 Mr. & Mrs. Richard R. Trench
529 Mr. & Mrs. Charles D. Lusk
Receiving day Wednesday p.m.
657 Wm. C. Spafford

FORTY-EIGHTH STREET (HYDE PARK).

69 Mr. & Mrs. George O. Knapp
211 Mr. & Mrs. Albert W. Walburn
215 Mrs. G. A. Coburn
215 Mr. & Mrs. Thomas Foster & dr.
291 Mr. & Mrs. E. J. Harkness & dr.
419 Mr. & Mrs. Roland A. Crandall
419 Mrs. Mary E. Ballard
421 Mr. & Mrs. Chas. B. Niblock
425 Mr. & Mrs. W. H. Colvin
477 Mr. & Mrs. Geo. W. Swigart
Receiving day Thursday
677 Mr. & Mrs. George W. Fretts

70 Walter I. Cleverdon
220 Rev. & Mrs. Louis P. Mercer
282 Mr. & Mrs. Frederic Ullmann
284 Mr. & Mrs. C. H. Morse & dr.
286 Mr. & Mrs. Henry Martyn Bacon
290 Mr. & Mrs. D. O. Strong & dr.
290 Charles R. Strong
492 Mr. & Mrs. G. A. Claussenius
492 Mr. & Mrs. Frank W. Bennett
Receiving day Friday

FORTY-NINTH STREET (HYDE PARK).

47 Mr. & Mrs. Paul Morton
249 Mr. & Mrs. W. H. Newman
257 Mr. & Mrs. Stephen N. Hurd
317 Mr. & Mrs. S. S. Beman
321 Clinton B. Wiser & drs.

118 Frederick B. Buss
120 Mr. & Mrs. Chas. W. Hall
122 Mr. & Mrs. G. S. Norton
124 Mr. & Mrs. J. P. Hubbell
302 Mr. & Mrs. Chas. H. Marshall
306 Mr. & Mrs. Charles Denham
366 Mr. & Mrs. A. T. Newhall

GARFIELD BOULEVARD.

113 Dr. & Mrs. C. Korssell
119 Dr. & Mrs. Francis G. Arter
129 Mr. & Mrs. C. F. Kinnally
129 John Kinnally
133 Mrs. Catherine White & dr.
133 William White
135 Dr. & Mrs. Frank M. Steward
139 Mrs. T. H. Headly & dr.
139 Howard Headly

112 Mr. & Mrs. E. D. Colvin
130 Mr. & Mrs. Louis Merki & drs.
Receiving day Thursday
130 George Merki
130 Maitland J. Merki
138 Mr. & Mrs. M. A. Hickey
138 H. E. Spieker
138 G. D. Steere
140 Mr. & Mrs. Wm. Schneider

139 Mr. & Mrs. P. M. Ottman
143 Mr. & Mrs. L. Fagersten & dr.
335 Mr. & Mrs. P. J. Doyle & drs.
337 Mr. & Mrs. L. H. Burdick
341 Mr. & Mrs. W. F. Peterson
351 Mr. & Mrs. G. H. Casler
401 Dr. & Mrs. P. S. Dougherty
411 Mr. & Mrs. P. J. Flynn & dr.
417 Mr. & Mrs. L. M. Bonheim
421 Mr. & Mrs. J. C. Rolle
421 Mrs. D. Hyde
425 Mr. & Mrs. Don J. Barnes
425 S. H. Putnam
429 Dr. & Mrs. Peter B. Anton
551 Mr. & Mrs. M. Coghlan & dr.
551 H. D. Coghlan
557 Dr. A. E. Kroening
557 Mr. & Mrs. Albert Kroening
601 Dr. R. H. Moffitt
601 Mr. & Mrs. John McNally
609 Dr. & Mrs. John D. Parker
609 Harley Parker
609 Jay D. Parker
633 Dr. & Mrs. F. M. Richardson
719 Mr. & Mrs. Matt Welsh
743 Mr. & Mrs. Aaron Miller
743 Mrs. Mary K. Drennan & dr.
751 Mr. & Mrs. P. J. Long
845 Dr. & Mrs. Henry James

140 Mr. & Mrs. L. W. Conover
142 Capt. & Mrs. J. F. Nelson
        Receiving day Friday
142 Mrs. Edward Lee
144 Mr. & Mrs. Peter Wolter & dr.
144 Peter Wolter jr.
148 Mr. & Mrs. L. Groh
244 Mr. & Mrs. S. C. Kenyon
        Receiving day Thursday
302 Dr. & Mrs. W. O. Nance
302 Dr. L. A. Kelley
314 Mr. & Mrs. Chas. Nielsen
314 Mrs. Louise Nelson
610 Mr. & Mrs. C. E. Clark
820 Mr. & Mrs. Louis H. Mahnke
1044 Mr. & Mrs. F. D. Cummings
1044 William C. Cummings
1048 Mr. & Mrs. A. Z. Olson
1048 Mr. & Mrs. C. Olson
1110 Mrs. Magdalene Jung
ne. cor. Laflin Mr. & Mrs. John
        Griffin
ne. cor. Laflin James W. Griffin
        James Meade

845 Mr. & Mrs. A. D. Hill
847 Dr. & Mrs. John Allison
909 Mr. & Mrs. Thomas Byrne
1001 Mrs. C. Kotzenburg & drs.

GOLDSMITH AVENUE.

7519 Mr. & Mrs. James W. Morton
7525 Mr. & Mrs. Herbert Tweedie

7715 Mr. & Mrs. Nelson F. Stowell

GRACE AVENUE.

6429 Mr. & Mrs. A. R. Oughton

6445 Mr. & Mrs. H. B. Jackson

GRAND BOULEVARD.

3515 Dr. Joseph E. R. Hawley
3515 Samuel F. Hawley
3515 Mr. & Mrs. Wm. E. Hawley
3515 Mr. & Mrs. Chas. A. Hawley
3517 Mr. & Mrs. George Davis
3517 George H. Davis
3517 Mortimer A. Davis
3517 Ernest A. Davis
3521 Dr. & Mrs. Ambrose Breese
3521 Stanley Marshall
3523 Mr. & Mrs. R. S. Dement & dr.
        Receiving day Monday
3523 Mr. & Mrs. James D. Packard
3525 Mrs. M. E. Byrne & drs.

3558 Mr. & Mrs. Arthur G. Wells
3560 Mr. & Mrs. Jonas Goldenberg
        & drs.
3562 Mr. & Mrs. John F. Finerty
        Receiving day Wednesday
3564 Mr. & Mrs. H. S. Rosenthal
3564 Elias Rosenthal
3564 Lubin L. Rosenthal
3568 J. F. Whiting
3568 Robert Whiting
3568 David Whiting
3602 William J. Neebes & dr.
3602 William J. Neebes jr.
3602 George Neebes

3525 R. H. Byrne
3525 Miss Marietta Sisson
3529 Mr. & Mrs. J. Joseph & dr.
3529 S. L. Joseph
3537 Mr. & Mrs. J. Aron
3539 Mr. & Mrs. George E. Cole
3541 Mr. & Mrs. Francis W. Walker
  Receiving day Friday
3543 Mr. & Mrs. Charles Jouvenat & dr.
3545 Mr. & Mrs. J. L. Kesner
Receiving days 1st & 3d Wednesdays
3547 Mr. & Mrs. Bernard Pollock & dr. *Receiving day Friday*
3547 Arthur Pollock
3547 Albert Pollock
3565 Mr. & Mrs. John N. Faithorn
  Receiving day Thursday
3565 John N. Faithorn jr.
3565 Miss Maude Faithorn
3611 Mr. & Mrs. William Lowe
3611 Mr. & Mrs. A. E. Gilbert
  Receiving day Wednesday
3611 A. J. Fish
3623 Mr. & Mrs. Horace C. McConnell
3625 Mr. & Mrs. A. B. Cody
3625 Mr. & Mrs. Hiram H. Cody
3627 Mr. & Mrs. Frank I. Pearce
  Receiving day Thursday
3627 Mr. & Mrs. Robert T. Pearce
  Receiving day Thursday
3629 Mr. & Mrs. Chas. H. ReQua
3631 Mr.&Mrs. Morris Epstein& dr.
3631 Hugo Epstein
3631 Max Epstein
3633 Mr. & Mrs. M. Stern
3639 Mrs. H. C. Burgie
3639 Edmo Pattison
3639 Miss Jennie A. Moore
3645 Mr. & Mrs. Sol Levy
  Receiving day Friday
3645 Miss Henrietta Levy
3647 Mr. & Mrs. T. H. Wickes
3651 Mr. & Mrs. Max Mendel
3653 Mr. & Mrs. Louis Bauer & drs.
3653 Gustav T. Bauer ·
3655 Mr. & Mrs. M. J. LaBounte
  Receiving day Wednesday
3655 Miss Genevieve Longevin
3657 Mr. & Mrs. L. B. Lehman
  Receiving day Thursday
3657 Max Dembufsky
3659 Mr. & Mrs. F. E. Morse & dr.
3659 J. F. Morse
3735 Mr. & Mrs. S. Leonard Boyce

3604 Judge and Mrs. Gwynn Garnett & dr.
3604 Eugene Garnett
3608 Mr. & Mrs. J. J. Hill
3612 Dr. & Mrs. Emil G. Hirsch
  Receiving day Friday
3614 Mr. & Mrs. John Tait
3614 Martin Roche
3616 Mr. & Mrs. John McCormick
  Receiving day Thursday
3616 George J. McCormick
3622 Mr. & Mrs. Adolph Loeb & drs. *Receiving day Thursday*
3624 Mr.& Mrs. Martin Meyer&drs.
 Receiving days 1st & 3d Fridays
3624 Fred Meyer
3626 Mr. & Mrs. Herman F. Hahn & dr.
3626 Harry W. Hahn
3626 Edmund J. Hahn
3628 Mr. & Mrs. J. L. Gatzert & dr.
  Receiving day Tuesday
3630 Mr. & Mrs. Charles H. Nichols
3630 Miss Carrie B. Macalister
3642 Mr. & Mrs. Moses Adams
  Receiving day Wednesday
3644 Mr. & Mrs. Max Eichberg&dr.
  Receiving day Friday
3646 Mr. & Mrs. Samuel Shoyer
3648 Mr. & Mrs. Tobias Oberfelder
3650 Mr. & Mrs. J. S. Kimmelstiel
3650 Mrs. Y. Ballenberg
3656 Mr. & Mrs. R. L. Henry
  Receiving day Tuesday
3656 Fidelio S. Henry
3720 Mr. & Mrs. L. J. Lamson
3736 Mr. & Mrs. Charles R. Crane
3740 Mr. & Mrs. B. Israel & dr.
  Receive 1st & 3d Tuesdays
3742 Mr. & Mrs. John W. Smith
  Receiving day Thursday
3744 Mr. & Mrs. Louis H. Salomon & drs.
3744 August J. Salomon
3924 Mr. & Mrs. H. Grossman
  Receiving day Friday
3926 Mr. & Mrs. Herman Lehman
3928 Mr. & Mrs. Jacob R. Custer
3930 Mr. & Mrs. Edward C. Huling
3930 Mr. & Mrs. Edward B. Huling
3932 Mr. & Mrs. Charles R. Cave
3932 Philip W. Raber
3938 Mr. & Mrs. P. J. Ryan
3938 Edwin J. Ryan
4018 Mr. & Mrs. James F. O'Brien
4018 Frank O'Brien

3741 Mr. & Mrs. W. H. Moorhouse
    Receiving day Thursday
3741 Wm. R. Moorhouse
3741 L. C. Merrick
3741 Miss Zella Merrick
3811 Mr. & Mrs. S. P. Parmly
3811 Samuel P. Parmly jr.
3811 Mr. & Mrs. H. C. Parmly
3811 Mrs. R. B. Sumner
3911 Mrs. J. E. Allen
    Receiving day Thursday
3911 J. Shirlock Allen
3913 Mr.&Mrs. Simon M. Silverman
3915 Mr. & Mrs. Wm. H. Godair
3915 Floyd J. Godair
3917 Mrs. Harriet Palmer & dr.
3917 Frank E. Baker
3917 C. M. Palmer
3921 Mr. & Mrs. Jas. Wright & drs.
3923 Mr. & Mrs. S. B. Foster
3925 Mr. & Mrs. Norris G. Dodge
3925 Harry A. Dodge
3931 Mr. & Mrs. F. A. Howe
3933 Mr. & Mrs. Frank A. Devlin
    Receiving day Thursday
4001 Mr. & Mrs. George S. Middle-
    brook
4001 Mr. & Mrs. W. A. McLean
4001 Mr. & Mrs. Frederick W. Lee
4001 David J. Mitchell
4001 Mr. & Mrs. Edward L. Will-
    marth
4001 Bertrand H. Mitchell
4001 John D. Mitchell
4043 Mrs. Emily Coonley
4043 Mr. & Mrs. N. L. Barmore
4045 Mr. & Mrs. Fred C. Tyler
4101 Dr. & Mrs. J. G. Sinclair
4101 W. Sarsfield York
4101 The Misses York
4101 Mr. & Mrs. Frank B. Draper
4103 Mr. & Mrs. W. G. Roberts
4105 Mr. & Mrs. Frank S. Loomis
4107 Mrs. S. B. Collins & drs.
4107 Miss Helen A. Bearup
4107 Miss Marium A. Bearup
4109 Mrs. H. E. Henderson & dr.
    Receiving day Saturday
4109 Howard Henderson
4117 Mr. & Mrs. Solomon Hirsh &
    drs.
4117 Manuel Hirsh
4117 Morris G. Hirsh
4119 Mr. & Mrs. Henry C. Jacobs
    & dr.
4119 Mr. & Mrs. Joseph Wright

4018 Miss Catherine Quinn
4013 Miss Anna Quinn
4022 Dr. & Mrs. P. I. Mulvane &
    dr.
4022 Miss Elizabeth Mulvane
4024 Mrs. James Sullivan
4026 Mr. & Mrs. William Straw-
    bridge & drs.
4026 Charles H. Strawbridge
4028 Mr. & Mrs. B. M. Davies
4028 Mr. & Mrs. J. M. LeRoy
4030 Mr. & Mrs. Charles Kern
4050 Mr. & Mrs. J. L. Allen & dr.
    Receiving day Tuesday
4052 Mr. & Mrs. Richard W. Barger
4054 Mr. & Mrs. J. A. Hill
4054 Fred M. Hill
4054 Bert C. Hill
4056 Mr. & Mrs. Edward H. Elwell
    Receiving day Thursday
4108 Mr. & Mrs. E. B. Felsenthal
    Receiving day Wednesday
4112 Mr. & Mrs. Orr Sang
4114 Mr. & Mrs. L. R. Norton
4122 Mr. & Mrs. Ralph E. Pratt
4122 Miss Ella Shockey
4124 Mr. & Mrs. Milton J. Palmer
4124 Mrs. Wm. H. Atwood
4218 Mr. & Mrs. W. J. Carney
4220 Mr. & Mrs. Andrew M. Lynch
    & dr.
    Receiving day Thursday
4222 Mr. & Mrs. William R. Selleck
    Receiving day Wednesday
4224 Mr. & Mrs. J. H. Campbell
4224 Mr. & Mrs. Otis F. Hall
4224 Robert J. Hall
4226 Mr. & Mrs. William Mida
4226 Walter Mida
4226 Lee Mida
cor. 43d Dr. Emmet L. Smith
4318 Mr. & Mrs. Geo. T. Houston
4318 Miss M. Eleanor Brown
4322 Mr. & Mrs. G. Lang
4342 Mr. & Mrs. Gustave D. Glaser
4346 Mr. & Mrs. Max L. Falk
4346 Mr. & Mrs. Louis Leopold
4346 Maurice Leopold
4348 Mr. & Mrs. William H. West
4348 Charles F. Hippach
4350 Mr. & Mrs. D. A. Hyman
    Receiving day 1st & 3d Friday
4350 Miss Clara Hyman
4352 Mr.& Mrs. Norris Cochran&dr
4354 Edward Baggot
4354 George Baggot

4167 Mr. & Mrs. S. C. Nessling & dr.
4201 John W. Conley
4201 Mrs. Sarah A. Gilbert
4201 Miss M. A. Sturges
4203 Henry Regensburg
4203 Miss Fannie Regensburg
4203 O. H. Regensburg
4205 Mr. & Mrs. James F. Meagher
4205 Mr. & Mrs. Edward Kendrick
Grant
Receiving day Tuesday
4207 Mr. & Mrs. Daniel S. Stern
4217 Mr. & Mrs. Byron Z. Terry
4217 Mr. & Mrs. Albert C. Terry
4219 Mr. & Mrs. Chas. B. Gilbert
4223 Mr. & Mrs. F. A. Hibbard
4223 Mrs. John Hibbard
4235 Mr. & Mrs. James E. McElroy
4237 Mr. & Mrs. James A. Armour
4237 E. G. Beach
4239 Mr. & Mrs. Nelson B. Record
4241 Mr. & Mrs. George P. Lee
4241 Miss Anna W. Lee
4243 Mr. & Mrs. Morris Cassard
4245 Mr. & Mrs. N. P. Richman
4257 Mr. & Mrs. A. W. Taft
4257 Mr. & Mrs. N. L. Clement
Receiving day Friday
4257 Mr. & Mrs. George E. Wright
4259 Judge & Mrs. Peter S. Grosscup
4337 Mr. & Mrs. Frank J. Barnes
4337 Mr. & Mrs. Elwood H. Hipple
4337 Mrs. Mary A. Gaylord
4339 Mr. & Mrs. J. Straus
4341 Mr. & Mrs. F. MacKenzie
4341 Mrs. Joel Ellis
4341 Mrs. L. Pinney
4343 Mr. & Mrs. George A. H. Scott
4345 Mr. & Mrs. Joseph Pajeau
4345 Mrs. M. A. Cochrane
4347 Mr.&Mrs.Sol.Hamburger & dr.
4349 Mr. & Mrs. W. N. Sattley
4445 Mr. & Mrs. H. M. Shepard
4445 Mrs. Charles B. Stuart
4455 Mrs. Phebe A. Osborne
4455 Mr. & Mrs. Frank Sayre Osborne

4354 Mr. & Mrs. John D. Baggot
4354 Miss Margaret Kelly
4400 Frederick R. Barnheisel
4400 Charles H. Barnheisel
4400 Mrs.Henrietta Barnheisel&dr.
4404 Mr. & Mrs. M. Stumer
4404 Louis M. Stumer
4404 A. R. Stumer
4406 Dr. & Mrs. A. J. Baxter & dr.
Receiving day Friday
4406 A. Lawson Baxter
4406 Miss Virginia M. Tauble
4426 Mr. & Mrs. John Trayner & dr.
Receiving day Tuesday
4428 Judge & Mrs. Wm. G. Mann
4434 Mrs. Emeline C. Thurston
4434 Frank W. Thurston
4630 Mr. & Mrs. F. W.Hunerberg & drs.
4800 Mr. & Mrs. R. N. Baylies
Receiving day Tuesday
4800 Mr. & Mrs. F. A. Poor
4816 Mrs. Mary C. Wilson
4816 John Gaynor
4840 Mr. & Mrs. Patrick McManus & drs. *Receiving day Sat.*
5134 Mr. & Mrs.James Hannan&dr.
5156 Mr. & Mrs. Chas. A. Mallory
5156 Mr. & Mrs. W. H. Stanton

4455 Henry S. Osborne
4509 Mrs. C. Schoenman & drs.
4509 Charles S. Schoenman
4509 Byron Schoenman
4509 Emil L. Schoenman
4511 Mr. & Mrs. Samuel J. Kline
Receiving day Friday
4545 Mr. & Mrs. Charles W. Leeming
4545 Frank Leeming
4547 Mr. & Mrs. Horatio R. Wilson
4635 Mr. & Mrs. W. C. Foley
4709 Mr. & Mrs. W. S. Booth
4717 Mr. & Mrs. George T. Smith
4725 Mr. & Mrs. Fred W. Smith
4731 Mr. & Mrs. T. P. Smith
4847 Mr. & Mrs. George W. Pierce

GRANT PLACE (ENGLEWOOD).

6901 Dr. & Mrs. L. Schwarz

6901 Herbert E. Schwarz

GREEN STREET.

7807 Mr. & Mrs. T. Jeffrey & drs.
7807 Robert G. Jeffrey

7740 Rev. & Mrs. G. J. Johnson & dr.

GREENWOOD AVENUE.

4323 Mr. & Mrs. Wm. L. Church jr.
4325 Mrs. Gerald T. Tully
4325 Mr.& Mrs.Phillip De Q. Mesny
4327 Dr. & Mrs. W. P. MacCracken
4331 Mr. & Mrs. J. H. Keating
4331 Mr. & Mrs. E. C. Keating
4331 E. C. Keating jr.
4365 Mr. & Mrs. A. M. Smith
4407 Mrs. A. F. McCormick
4407 Mr. & Mrs. Daniel B. Nuss-
    baum *Receiving day Monday*
4409 Mr. & Mrs. J. D. Caldwell
4439 Mr. & Mrs. Jacob O. Curry & dr.
4447 Mr. & Mrs. Edwin F. Daniels
4455 Mr. & Mrs. R. S. Critchell & dr.
4515 Mr. & Mrs. A. F. Fisher
4519 Mr. & Mrs. Horace G. Bird&dr.
4523 Eugene S. Kimball
4531 Mr. & Mrs. M. Swenson
4533 Mr. & Mrs. Frederick Fox
4535 Mr. & Mrs. B. W. May
4537 Dr. & Mrs. C. R. E. Koch
4539 Mr. & Mrs. John Haveron
4541 Mr. & Mrs. D. Cohen
4545 Mrs. S. M. Follansbee
    Receiving day Wednesday
4545 Mrs. J. Van Olinda
4549 Mr. & Mrs. Schauweker
    Receiving day Tuesday
4623 Mr. & Mrs. W. E. Higley & dr.
4625 Dr. & Mrs. Milton Barker
4627 Mr. & Mrs. C. L. Hammond
4633 Mr. & Mrs. F. W. Barker
4637 Mr. & Mrs. W. T. Brown
4637 Mrs. H. I. Spalding
4727 Mr. & Mrs. H. S. Smith & dr.
4729 Mr. & Mrs. James W. Janney
4741 Mr. & Mrs. Charles L. Allen
4741 Miss Annie Hitchcock
4803 Mr. & Mrs. James P. Gardner
4803 Mrs. L. A. Barnum
4819 Mr. & Mrs. H. B. Bogue
4819 Hamilton B. Bogue jr.
4849 Mr. & Mrs. W. B. Kniskern
4849 Charles A. Kniskern
cor. 49th Mr. & Mrs. O. C. Ely
4929 Mr. & Mrs. L. H. Turner
4929 Mr. & Mrs. Edward H. Turner
4935 Mr. & Mrs. A. W. Green
    Receiving day Thursday
5035 Mr.&Mrs.Charles Counselman
5329 Mr. & Mrs. Charles W. Gore
5331 Mrs. F. Lazelle

cor. 42d The Arizona
A1 Mr. & Mrs. E. P. Howell
A2 F. O. Bartlett
A3 Mr. A. S. Moffett
A4 Mr. & Mrs. W. H. Powers
A5 Mr. & Mrs. W. H. Holway
A6 Dr. & Mrs. L. T. Potter
A7 Mr. & Mrs. G. H. Kelsey
A8 Mr. & Mrs. S. P. Wiley
B1 Mr. & Mrs. William G.
    Phyall
B2 Mr. & Mrs. H. C. Jackson
B3 Mr. & Mrs. J. M. Wood
B4 Mr. & Mrs. W. W. Palmer
B6 Mr. & Mrs. G. S. Newsome
B7 George H. Bliss
B7 Ernest W. Bliss
B8 Mrs. Dr. C. J. French & drs.
C2 Mrs. E. D. Hill
C2 Mrs. M. K. Reid
C3 Mr. & Mrs. S. G. Chard
C5 Capt. & Mrs. H. T. Coffee
    & drs.
C5 John L. Kerr
C6 F. B. Clarke
C7 Mr. & Mrs. R. E. McCowie
C8 Mr. & Mrs. Irving H. Rich
D2 Mr. & Mrs. D. S. Geer
D3 Mr. & Mrs. G. W. Cass
D4 Mr. & Mrs. L. Perfitt
D5 Mr. & Mrs. Jerome F. Wares
D7 Mr. & Mrs. J. H. Reid
    Receiving day Wednesday
D8 Mr. & Mrs. G. H. Love
E1 Mr. & Mrs. R. E. Slagle
    Receiving day Thursday
E3 Mrs. John A. Davis
E4 Mrs. H. B. Saxton
E5 Mr. & Mrs. C. H. Rhoades
E7 Mr. & Mrs. F. H. Tibbits
E7 Mrs. Flora V. Tibbits
E8 Mr. & Mrs. A. L. Eaton
F2 Mr. & Mrs. C. J. Sterling
F3 Mr. & Mrs. D. H. Harris
F4 Mr. & Mrs. F. G. Stevens
F5 Mr. & Mrs. Chas. Barton
    Darling
F6 Mrs. Lillie P. Miller
    Receiving day Thursday
F8 Mr. & Mrs. D. L. Murray
G1 Mr. & Mrs. John O'Keefe
G2 Mr. & Mrs. T. F. Bowes
G3 Mr. & Mrs. Ernest Rayfield

5345 Mr. & Mrs. J. L. Burke & dr.
Receiving day Thursday
6323 Mr. & Mrs. James Stroud
6345 Mr. & Mrs. E. M. Miller

4438 Mrs. R. Lawton
4444 Mr. & Mrs. Munson P. Buel
4446 Mr. & Mrs. James Mullen & dr
4446 Frederick Mullen
4500 Mr. & Mrs. Benj. F. DeMuth
Receiving day Friday
4504 Mr. & Mrs. J. F. Thacker
Receiving day Wednesday
4504 Miss Emma Rommeiss
4510 Mr. & Mrs. M. J. Fitch
4522 Mr. & Mrs. Charles Squires
4522 Mr. & Mrs. Edward Rosing
4526 Mr. & Mrs. J. B. Nellegar
4534 Mr. & Mrs. William Jones
4540 Mr. & Mrs. Thomas Parker
4544 Mr. & Mrs. C. H. Thorne
4612 Mr. & Mrs. A. H. Hanson
4612 Mrs. M. A. Osgood
4620 Dr. & Mrs. Alfred W. Hoyt
4620 Dr. A. L. Hoyt
4624 Mr. & Mrs. E. A. Schoyer
4630 Mr. & Mrs. A. W. Glessner
4634 Mr. & Mrs. Edwin F. Bayley
4700 Mr. & Mrs. Wm. Lathrop Moss
Receiving day Thursday
4700 Miss Edith Helen Moss
Receiving day Thursday
4726 Mr. & Mrs. W. L. Catherwood
4728 Mr.& Mrs.Charles Loughridge
4734 Mr. & Mrs. Dexter G. Brown
4754 Mr. & Mrs. C. B. Vankirk
4754 Mrs. S. A. Vankirk
4820 Mr. & Mrs. E. T. Cushing
4820 Mrs. Margaret S. Bross
4826 Miss L. B. Merritt
4830 Mr. & Mrs. William Cuthbert
4830 Mrs. Carrie Cuthbert
4850 Mr. & Mrs. E. K. Butler
4850 Miss Lilian B. Weide
4918 Mr. & Mrs. A. R. Bremer
4924 Mr.&Mrs.I..Everingham &drs.
4924 Edward L. Everingham
4924 H. Dick Everingham
4950 Mr. & Mrs. John C. Welling
4950 Miss Mary Paul
5000 Mr. & Mrs. J. N. Barker
5000 Mrs. W. N. Hibbard
5008 Mr. & Mrs. G. T. Williamson
5016 Mr.& Mrs.Charles H.Hawkins
• *Receiving day Thursday*

G4 Mr. & Mrs. F. J. Wall
G5 Mr. & Mrs. George A.Stickney
G6 Mr. & Mrs. W. C. Whitcomb
G7 Mrs. J. L. Fitzhugh
G8 Mr. & Mrs. J. E. Roemheld
Receiving day Tuesday
4228 Mr. & Mrs. T. W. Harford
4228 Mr. & Mrs C. E. Allstadt
4302 Dr. & Mrs. H. B. Carriel
4304 Samuel J. Sullivan
4306 Mr. & Mrs. M. Hogan .
4312 Mr. & Mrs. K. Barnhart
Receiving day Friday
4314 Mr. & Mrs. J. S. Jacobus
4316 Mr. & Mrs. F. C. N. Robertson
Receiving day Thursday
4318 Mr.&Mrs.Frederick L.Merrick
4322 Mr. & Mrs. E. E. Adams
4324 Mr. & Mrs. E. L. Becker
Receiving day Thursday
4324 Mrs. Emma A. Jones
4330 Miss Eva J. Peck
4332 Mr. & Mrs. George F. Fisher
Receiving day Wednesday
4332 G. F. Fisher, jr.
4334 J. R. Walls
4334 Mrs. M. L. Walls
4334 Miss Emma Walls
4336 Mr. & Mrs. S. J. Grimes & drs.
4338 Mrs. E. J. Parke & drs.
4338 Mr. & Mrs. H. Wilder
4338 C. S. Keown
4338 S. T. A. Loftis
4340 Mr. & Mrs. E. L. Ayres
Receiving day Friday
4342 Mr. & Mrs. Isaac N. Isham
4342 Mrs. C. M. Warren
4344 Mr. & Mrs. A. R. Townsend
4344 Dr. S. N. Chapin
4346 Mr. & Mrs. Thomas F. Vaughn
4348 Mr. & Mrs. F. E. Hayne
4350 Dr. & Mrs. H. H. Deming
4354 Mr. & Mrs. F. E. Hayne
4400 Mrs. E. A. Keeler & dr.
4400 Mrs. A. K. Ryland
4400 William S. Ransom
4414 Dr. & Mrs. A. W. Harlan & dr.
Receiving day Thursday.
4420 Mr.& Mrs. Geo. W.Chamberlin
4420 Edward C. Chamberlin
4420 Mr. & Mrs. W. Morton Brown
4434 Mr. & Mrs. J. W. Fernald & dr
4434 Mrs. P. C. Ruggles
4438 Mr. & Mrs. L. C. Lawton

5022 Mr. & Mrs. Geo. A. Tripp
5026 Mr. & Mrs. William O. Goodman *Receiving day Tuesday*
5316 Mrs. Henry W. Clark
5316 Mrs. Elizabeth Underhill
5330 Mrs. E. Wadlow
5330 Dr. & Mrs. J. T. Lave
5400 Mr. & Mrs. G. E. Cave

5418 Dr. & Mrs. John Dewey
5450 Mr.&Mrs.Charles Eaton & drs.
Receiving day Wednesday
5474 Mr. & Mrs. Hugo Hoffmann
5474 Arthur Hoffmann
5478 Mrs. Harriet A. McConnell
5478 Willard M. McConnell
5478 Miss Dean McConnell

GROVELAND AVENUE.

2907 Mr. & Mrs. F. K. Morrill
2907 Mr. & Mrs. Wesley Morrill
2909 Mr. & Mrs. Edward F. Dyke
2915 Mr. & Mrs. James J. Egan
2917 Mr. & Mrs. Dwight S. Bryant
2919 Mr. & Mrs. Harry B. Lyford
2921 Mr. & Mrs. Will H. Lyford
Receiving day Tuesday
2927 Mr. & Mrs. D. S. Vilas
2929 Mr. & Mrs. Theodore G. Janssen
Receive 2d and 4th Wednesdays
2929 Dr. & Mrs. F. Kreissl
2931 Mr. & Mrs. E. H. Miller
2933 Mr. & Mrs. W. H. Hosmer
2937 Mr. & Mrs. D. E. Gillingham
2939 Mr. & Mrs. W. L. Stenberger
& dr.
Receiving day Wednesday
2947 Mr. & Mrs. James Bowlan
2951 Alexander Simmons
2951 Mr. & Mrs. A. B. Albaugh
2953 Mrs. T. M. Humphrey
2953 W. B. Lavinia
2955 Mrs. Flora Madden
2957 Mr. & Mrs. Samuel W. Rosenfels & drs.
2959 Mr. & Mrs. Morris Kohn
2959 Simon Kohn
2961 Mr. & Mrs. D. Lepman
2963 Mr. & Mrs. M. Weinschenk
2963 Lucius Weinschenk
2965 Mr. & Mrs. John F. Linscott
Receiving day Friday
2967 Mrs. R. F. McComas
Receiving day Tuesday
2967 Eugene McComas
2967 Duke McComas
2967 Rufus F. McComas
2969 Mr. & Mrs. William Harbridge
2971 Mrs. H. Tallert
2973 Mr. & Mrs. C. H. Baker
2973 William D. Cooper
3001 Mr. & Mrs. Joseph Pfirshing
3009 Mr. & Mrs. J. C. Morganthau

2900 Mr. & Mrs. B. F. Nourse
Receiving day Thursday
2902 George I. Gibbs
2904 Mr. & Mrs. A. C. Farnsworth
2908 Mr. & Mrs. J. H. Brown & dr
2912 Mr. & Mrs. L. J. Wolf
2914 Miss Mary E. Booth
2914 Miss Ellen H. Williams
2918 Mrs. L. W. Holt
2920 Mr. & Mrs. A. Riegelman
2922 Ferdinand Zeug
2922½ Mr.& Mrs.Brian Philpot
2922½ B. F. Philpot
2924 Mr. & Mrs. Henry Rogers
2924 Mrs. Elizabeth Davenport
2928 Mr. & Mrs. W. A. Knapp
2930 Mr. & Mrs. Hamilton Frazer
2930 Mr. & Mrs. Charles Slayback
2942 John A. McCormick
2944 Mr. & Mrs. Geo.B.Cruickshank
2944 Mr. & Mrs. W. T. Carey
2946 Mr. & Mrs. A. H. Cook & dr.
2946 A. H. Cook jr.
2946 Mr. & Mrs. W. C. Gartside
2948 Mr. & Mrs. Samuel Friend
2948 Mr. & Mrs. Jas. A. McDonald
2952 Robert B. Cooper
2956 Mr. & Mrs. E. L. Barber
2956 S. M. Parish
2962 Mrs. A. Kallman
2962 J. Westenberger
2962 S. L. Strauss
2964 Mr. & Mrs. Isaac Meyer
2970 Mrs. C. H. Brainard
3002 Mr. & Mrs. T. L. Kelly
3002 H. L. D. Kelly
3006 Mr. & Mrs. Jay V. Northam &
dr.
3008 Mr. & Mrs. Fred H. Marsh
3018 Mr. & Mrs. Emanuel Hirsh
3018 Mr. & Mrs. David Neumann
& dr.
3018 Alexander Neumann
3018 Louis Neumann
3020 Mrs. Chas. Duffield & drs.

3013 Mr. & Mrs. A. H. Buel
3015 Mr. & Mrs. O. M. Parsons
3025 Mrs. Lillian H. Parish & dr.
  Receiving day Tuesday
3025 Miss Lucile M. Parish
  Receiving day Thursday
3027 Mr. & Mrs. William Phillips
3027 Miss Grace Hiltz
3029 Mr. & Mrs. Lyman B. Glover
3033 Mr. & Mrs. R. R. Buchanan
  Receiving day Tuesday
3039 Mr. & Mrs. N. N. Cronholm
3043 Mr. & Mrs. Jonas Hutchinson
3045 L. P. Bannister
3047 Mr. & Mrs. M. McFarlin & dr.
3047 W. W. McFarlin
3107 Mr. & Mrs. Nathan Mayer
3111 Mr. & Mrs. I. H. Fry
3111 Mr. & Mrs. C. L. Glass
3129 Mrs. Hannah Clark
3129 R. G. Telfer
3131 Mr. & Mrs. H. McCloy
3145 Mrs. Franklin Lester & dr.
3145 Leon M. Lester
3145 Charles M. Haft
3161 Mr. & Mrs. W. Scott Thurber
  & drs.
3165 Mr. & Mrs. F. Warner
3167 Mr. & Mrs. M. R. Hall
3169 Dr. & Mrs. Frank T. Andrews
3213 Mr. & Mrs. H. E. Southworth
3213 Mr. & Mrs. James B. Watt
3217 Mr. & Mrs. H. Baldwin & dr.
3219 Mr. & Mrs. Harlan D. Cook
3223 Mr. & Mrs. Matson Hill & dr.
3227 Mr. & Mrs. Edward Marrenner
3227 Mr. & Mrs. Edw. S. Marrenner
  Receiving day Tuesday
3229 Mr. & Mrs. C. E. Frankenthal
3231 Mr. & Mrs. Geo. B. Clason
3235 Mr. & Mrs. J. Spiegel
3241 Mrs. N. V. Reynolds
3241 Walter L. Johnson
3243 Mr. & Mrs. F. G. Hoyne
  Receiving day Thursday
3245 Mr. & Mrs. A. Blum
3247 Dr. & Mrs. Henry H. Schuhmann
3249 Mr. & Mrs. H. R. Vynne
3249 W. B. Cunningham
3249 Miss Catharine Cunningham
32.5 Mr. & Mrs. C. R. Hopkins & dr.
3257 Mr. & Mrs. A. W. Beidler
3257 Mr. & Mrs. Samuel R. Moore
  Receiving day Tuesday
3259 Mr. & Mrs. Edward A. James

3020 A. Howard Duffield
3022 Mr. & Mrs. Alfred Denyes
3030 Mrs. E. Harrison
3034 Mr. & Mrs. M. M. Day
3034 W. B. Day
3038 Mr. & Mrs. W. K. Reed
3042 Mr. & Mrs. J. G. Crosby
3042 Mr. & Mrs. James R. Terhune
3100 Henry Schneewind
3106 Jules Frank
3118 Mr. & Mrs. Samuel Elsner
3120 Mr. & Mrs. F. W. Bedee & dr.
3142 Mr. & Mrs. F. C. Bush
3142 Mrs. Edgar H. Montgomery &
  dr.
3142 Dr. B. F. Kerns
3144 Mr. & Mrs. W. G. Adkins
3148 Mr. &. Mrs. Amasa Orelup
3150 Albert C. Wenban
3152 Mr. & Mrs. A. R. Hicks
3158 Mr. & Mrs. Albert Schindler
  & drs. *Receiving day Friday*
3158 Alfred Schindler
3160 Mr. & Mrs. M. C. Bristol
3160 Mrs. Agnes J. Scott
3162 Mr. & Mrs. Charles D. Hoard
3164 Mrs. Mary E. Woodruff &
  dr.
3166 Dr. & Mrs. Joseph Matteson
3168 Mr. & Mrs. L. B. Cox
3170 Leopold Mayer
3170 Mrs. Flora M. Kahn
3216 Mr. & Mrs. E. H. Goodrich
3216 Miss Edna Goodrich
3218 Mr. & Mrs. A. P. Upham
3222 Mr. & Mrs. Thomas J. Dixon
  Receiving day Wednesday
3226 Mrs. Nellie Carpenter
3226 Mrs. Flora Fraser
3228 Mr. & Mrs. James Johnston
3230 Mr. & Mrs. John Barton Payne
3230 Mrs. D. A. Bunker
3232 W. L. Hagans
3232 Misses H. J. & C. E. Hagans
3232 Dr. L. A. L. Day
3234 Mr. & Mrs. Albert F. Dexter
3238 Mr. & Mrs. J. W. Robertson
3240 Mr. & Mrs. Samuel Freeman
3242 Mr. & Mrs. G. S. Baer
3242 Joseph C. Stettheimer
3244 Mr. & Mrs. George V. Harvey
3244 Mrs. Isabelle C. Buckingham
3248 Mr. & Mrs. J. H. Milne & dr.
3248 George H. Milne
3250 Mr. & Mrs. J. E. Greenebaum
3252 Mr. & Mrs. M. C. Mayer

3261 Mr. & Mrs. J. B. Stubbs
3261 Mr. & Mrs. C. H. Warner
3263 Mr. & Mrs. J. S. Buhrer
3269 Mrs. C. F. Brown
3269 Mrs. S. A. Vincent

3258 Mr. & Mrs. Wm. H. Sherwood
Receiving day Friday
3260 Dr. & Mrs. R. Dewey
3262 Mr. & Mrs. F. G. Frank
3264 Mr. & Mrs. W. S. Forrest

GROVELAND PARK.

1 Mr. & Mrs. J. T. Moulton
1 Mr. & Mrs. L. D. Kneeland
3 Mr. & Mrs. Frederic Archer&drs.
3 Harry B. Archer
3 Richard M. Archer
3 E. J. Napier
5 Mrs. Robert Warren
7 Mr. & Mrs. F. H. Wachsmuth
7 H. F. Wachsmuth
7 L. C. Wachsmuth
9 Dr. & Mrs. W. E. Hall
9 Mr. & Mrs. C. E. Hall
11 Mr. & Mrs. R. B. Miller & dr.
11 E. Olmstead
15 Mr. & Mrs. Joy Morton
19 Mr. & Mrs. Frank Wells

42 Mr. & Mrs. F. E. Gould & drs.
48 Dr. & Mrs. John S. Marshall
Receiving day Thursday

2 Dr. & Mrs. H. Alfred Gunther
Receiving day Wednesday
2 Elias Colbert
6 Mr. & Mrs. H. F. Starbuck
6 John L. Hughes
8 Mrs. Mary E. Mills
10 Mrs. Electa L. Thayer
10 Miss Florence A. Redway
Receiving day Friday
12 Mr. & Mrs. H. Borden & drs.
14 Mr. & Mrs. Walter C. McKinlock
16 Mr. & Mrs. John W. Carrington
20 David Mayer
26 Mr. & Mrs J. W. Green & dr.
28 Mr. & Mrs. F. M. Sproehnle
32 Mr. & Mrs. C. L. Hunter
34 Mr. & Mrs. Edward S. Hunter
36 Mr. & Mrs. John B. Mallers
36 Mr. & Mrs. Edward B. Mallers
40 Mr. & Mrs. Arba N. Waterman

HARVARD STREET.

6353 Mr. & Mrs. Fred Malkow & dr.
6409 Dr. & Mrs. F. E. Minor
6409 Miss Eva Gagnon
6409 Miss Edith Gagnon
6431 Mr. & Mrs. L. K. Scotford
6437 Mr. & Mrs. G. L. Carman & dr.
6501 Mr. & Mrs. J. F. Olmsted
6505 Mr. & Mrs. Geo. H. Owen&dr.
6515 Mr. & Mrs. O. T. Bright
6521 Mr. & Mrs. G. L. Purinton
Receiving day Friday
6525 Rev. & Mrs. C. A. Capwell &
dr.
6525 Mr. & Mrs. James A. Stoddard
6531 Mr. & Mrs. J. A. Ball
6537 Mr. & Mrs. E. M. Condit
6537 James A. Bell
6537 Miss Florence M. Perfect
6559 Mr. & Mrs. Theo. P. Day
6559 Mr. & Mrs. A.A. Hutchison & dr.
6559 James Hutchison
6565 Mr.& Mrs. George Middendorf
6601 Mr. & Mrs. C. H. Caldwell
6605 Mr. & Mrs. W. W. Ramsey
Receiving day Wednesday

6314 Dr. & Mrs. E. E. Holman
Receiving day Thursday
6328 Mr.&Mrs. Jesse Sherwood&dr.
6336 Dr. & Mrs. James G. Entwistle
6336 James McCall
6346 Mr. & Mrs. Samuel Thompson
6346 Samuel R. Thompson
6350 Mr. & Mrs. Allen Waters
6356 Mr. & Mrs. L. A. Patterson &
dr.
6356 Mrs. M. R. Allen & drs.
6400 Dr. & Mrs. A. Y. McCormick
6410 Mr. & Mrs. L. P. Maynard
6410 Mr. & Mrs. Geo. L. Maynard
6416 Mr. & Mrs. C. H. Vehmeyer
6426 Mr. & Mrs. John McKeand &
dr.
6438 Mr. & Mrs. Joseph P. Card
6438 Miss Grace B. Bard
6438 Joseph B. Card
6500 Mr. & Mrs. A. D. Rich & dr.
6516 Mr. & Mrs. H.W.K.Cutter&dr.
6522 Mr. & Mrs. D. J. Hubbard
6536 Mr. & Mrs. H. L. Kent
6536 Mrs. Helen M. Kent

6613 Mr. & Mrs. H. B. Thearle
    Receiving day Thursday
6617 Mr. & Mrs. C. H. Knights
6617 Mr. & Mrs. Wm. H. Daniel
6621 Mr. & Mrs. Edwin J. Noble
6627 Mr. & Mrs. Edwin Bebb
6629 Dr. & Mrs. A. B. Spach
6629 Mrs. M. A. Brown
6631 Mr. & Mrs. Jesse R. Embree
6631 W. R. Clayton
6643 Mr. & Mrs. William Law jr.
    Receive Wednesday evg.
6647 Mrs. Thomas Thombs
6657 Mr. & Mrs. J. E. Deakin
7237 Mr. & Mrs. O. D. Frary
7241 Mr. & Mrs. J. M. Pennington
7241 M. P. Pennington

———

7320 Mr. & Mrs. Alfred Owen
7524 Mr. & Mrs. George Jackson & drs.
7534 Mr. & Mrs. F. T. Haynes & dr.
7534 George M. Haynes
7534 Joseph R. Haynes

6536 Mr. & Mrs. Fred I. Kent
6544 Mr. & Mrs. S. D. Walden & dr.
6560 Mr. & Mrs P. S. Hudson
    Receiving day Friday
6564 Mr. & Mrs. G. W. Kelly
6610 Mr. & Mrs. J. J. Nichols
6616 Mr. & Mrs. John D. Vail & dr.
6616 U. G. Vail
6620 Mr. & Mrs. W. T. Eaton
6626 Mr. & Mrs. P. E. Lane & drs.
6630 Mrs. T. C. Ledward
6636 Mr. & Mrs. William Macklem
6642 Mr. & Mrs. John M. Young
6648 Mr. & Mrs. T. B. Galbraith
6652 Mr. & Mrs. F. E. Moore
    Receiving day Thursday
7120 Mrs. Mary E. Potter & dr.
7120 James S. McKenney
7130 Mr. & Mrs. F. H. Preston
7142 Mr. & Mrs. A. D. Morrison
7216 Mr. & Mrs. M. A. Garrett
7216 Carlton M. Garrett
7310 Mr. & Mrs. Howard McEldowney
7320 Mr. & Mrs. Wm. Owen

HAWTHORNE AVENUE (ENGLEWOOD).

Mr. & Mrs. Joseph L. P. Arnold
Mrs. Elizabeth Boyd
Randall W. Burns
Mr. & Mrs. J. M. Heath
Mr. & Mrs. Charles Herendeen
Mr. & Mrs. G. F. McKnight
    Receiving day Wednesday
S. C. McKnight
Mr. & Mrs. George E. McFadden
Mrs. R. J. Melchard

Mr. & Mrs. E. H. Rood & dr.
    Receiving day Wednesday
Dwight H. Rood
Mr. & Mrs. William Root
W. T. Root
Miss Tettie Root
Mr. & Mrs. Wm. B. Shute
Dr. & Mrs. Hiram F. Smiley
Marvin Dight Smiley

HIBBARD AVENUE.

5101 C. H. Hunt
5101 Mrs. H. W. Hunt & dr.
    Receiving day Wednesday
5103 Mr. & Mrs. A. G. Farr
5103 Mr. & Mrs. William Snow
5111 Mr. & Mrs. George Catlin
5117 Mr. & Mrs. Wm. Seymour
5127 Mrs. William C. Ritchie
5127 Thomas W. Ritchie
5127 Robert H. Ritchie
5127 Miss Nora Fisher
5131 Mr. & Mrs. John B. Daniels
5131 Alexander M. Daniels
5131 Mr. & Mrs. Amory E. Taylor
5135 Mr. & Mrs. John H. Cameron
5141 Mr. & Mrs. Gideon N. Caleb

5100 The Oneida
    Mr. & Mrs. C. E. Ware
    Mr. & Mrs. Edward Niles Hill
    Mr. & Mrs. W. C. Sommer
    Mr. & Mrs. W. S. Sheppard & dr.
    Mr. & Mrs. Alfred F. Pashley
    Mr. & Mrs. Jas. Bowen Wheatley
    Mrs. Anna W. Knight
5106 Mr. & Mrs. Frederick H. Trude
5108 Mr. & Mrs. E. W. Spencer
5110 Mr. & Mrs. William J. White
    Receiving day Friday
5110 Mrs. John Forman
5112 Mr. & Mrs. Thomas J. Hudson

9

5201 Mr. & Mrs. F. G. Ranney
5203 Mr. & Mrs. John W. Alvord
5205 Mr. & Mrs. Frederic Vinal
5207 Mr. & Mrs. H. W. Boyd
       Receiving day Monday
5209 Mr. & Mrs. James W. Jordan
5211 Mr. & Mrs. Thos. B. James
5213 Mr. & Mrs. Harvey C. Olin
5213 Miss Nora L. Olin
5215 C. A. Cairns
5215 Misses Cairns
5217 Mr. & Mrs. H. W. Boyd
5217 James A. Boyd

5222 Mr. & Mrs. W. Irving Beman
5228 Mr. & Mrs. Edward Grant

5114 Mr. & Mrs. William D. McKey
5116 Mrs. Harriet McKey
5116 Mr. & Mrs. Richard M. McKey
5120 Mr. & Mrs. George L. Warner
5120 Dr. Caroline Smith
5130 Mr. & Mrs. T. G. McCulloh
5140 Mr. & Mrs. William Chalmers
5206 Mr. & Mrs. J. C. Brown
5206 Mr. & Mrs. Ernest Anderson
5206 Mr. & Mrs. Charles E. Calkins
5210 Mr. & Mrs. Geo. W. Hoyt
       Receiving day Monday
5210 Mr. & Mrs. Morris W. Hartwell
       Receiving day Monday
5214 Mr. & Mrs. Henry Gower
5218 Mr. & Mrs. Charles E. Pope

HONORE STREET (ENGLEWOOD).

5907 Mr. & Mrs. Henry Gray
5911 Mr. & Mrs. John C. Huggett
6315 Mr. & Mrs. Jno. C. Woodworth
6315 Mr. & Mrs. Joseph Buker
6317 Mr. & Mrs. Warren E. Foskett
6331 Mrs. J. S. Barnes
6351 Dr. & Mrs. J. W. Meek
6351 Mr. & Mrs. Amasa L. Aller
6411 Mr. & Mrs. Chas. Pugh
6437 Mrs. Catherine J. Bloss
6437 Roy S. Bloss
6441 Mr. & Mrs. S. H. Campbell
6511 Mr. & Mrs. Selden Thayer
6547 Mr. & Mrs. F. B. Cook
6617 Mr. & Mrs. J. J. Byrne
6619 Mr. & Mrs. Frank W. Hadfield
6635 Mr. & Mrs. J. C. McFarland
6635 Mr. & Mrs. T. W. McFarland
6639 Mr. & Mrs. Ralph W. Clayton
6641 Mr. & Mrs. D. Freeman
6643 Mr. & Mrs. W. G. Gurnett
6655 Mr. & Mrs. F. E. Carsley
6659 Walter C. McCallum
6711 Mrs. C. W. Culliton
6715 Mr. & Mrs. James Penhallegon
6717 Mr. & Mrs. F. A. Griffith
6721 Mr. & Mrs. Chas. I. Westerfield
6759 Dr. & Mrs. Wm. J. Arnold
6839 Dr. & Mrs. C. A. Lambert
6847 Mr. & Mrs. J. Louis Smith
6851 Mr. & Mrs. Edward Korte
6851 Mrs. M. Donohue
6927 Mr. & Mrs. J. R. Trenton & dr.
6933 Mr. & Mrs. H. J. Russell

5918 Mr. & Mrs. Fred'k W. Weiss
5918 Mr. & Mrs. Chas. D. Gasaway
5926 Mr. & Mrs. F. B. Howland
5932 Mr. & Mrs. M. B. Derrick
5932 Mrs. H. N. Nourse
5938 Mr. & Mrs. W. B. Kennedy & dr.
6328 Mr. & Mrs. Henry Ocorr
6346 Mr. & Mrs. S. A. Dean
6404 Mr. & Mrs. A. H. Waggener
6404 John N. Driver
6424 Mr. & Mrs. R. S. Iles
6434 Mr. & Mrs. H. D. Safford & dr.
6434 W. H. Safford
6500 Mr. & Mrs. John S. Ward
6504 Rev. & Mrs. J. A. Duff
6512 Mr. & Mrs. J. C. Church
6634 Dr. & Mrs. George W. Miller
6640 Mr. & Mrs. F. W. Parker & drs.
6738 Mr. & Mrs. F. W. Werneburg &
       drs.
6738 Alex E Werneburg
6744 Mr. & Mrs. Leroy Hanna
6956 Mr. & Mrs. Charles H. Emery
7402 Mr. & Mrs. W. H. Dietz
7408 Mr. & Mrs. Geo. Sutherland
7506 Mr. & Mrs. William S. Love

7037 Mr. & Mrs. C. S. Tewksbury
7037 W. W. Tewksbury
7047 Mr. & Mrs. W. W. Janery
7425 Mr. & Mrs. Geo. M. Reed
7425 Miss Grace C. Dillon
7435 A. J. Underhill & drs.
7455 Mr. & Mrs. Fred'k Steere

HOPE AVENUE.

6617 Mr. & Mrs. Rollin F. Wiley·   6619 Mr. & Mrs. T. George Hislop

INDIANA AVENUE.

1609 Henry Sayers
1619 Dr. & Mrs. E. C. Dudley
1619 John H. Dudley
1623 Mr. & Mrs. Murry Nelson & dr.
1637 Mr. & Mrs. George Smith
1637 George Hall Smith
1641 Mr. & Mrs.C.R. Cummings
1641 Mrs. J. P. Cummings
1641 Mrs. H. T. Robinson
1703 Mr. & Mrs. E. M. Phelps
1703 George E. P. Dodge
1713 Mr. & Mrs. C. D. Peacock & drs.
1801 Mr.& Mrs. J. M. Gillespie &drs.
1801 Jos. M. Gillespie
1805 James Wright
1805 Miss Martha Wright
1809 Mr. & Mrs. Joseph C. Theurer
1813 Mrs. George C. Cook
1813 Mrs. H. W. Cook & drs.
1813 J. O. Cottrell
1815 Mrs. A. C. McHenry
1815 Mr. & Mrs. Arthur W. Driggs
1819 Mr. & Mrs. Isaac G. Lombard
1819 Ernest B. Lombard
1819 Mr. & Mrs. Herman E. Haass
1821 Mr. & Mrs. John C. Schubert
1825 Mr.&Mrs. Frederick M. Talbot
1829 Mr. & Mrs. B. Loewenthal
Receiving day Saturday
1829 Julius W. Loewenthal
1833 Dr. & Mrs. T. S. Hoyne
1833 Mr. & Mrs. Chas. C. Buell
1839 The Lakeside
    Mr. & Mrs. Irving A. Leonard
     & dr.
    Mr. & Mrs. Thomas Eustace
     & drs.
    Mrs. Winslow Wright
    Miss Bertha Dewey
    Walter E. Dewey
    J. A. Duggan
    W. A. Tucker
    J. Derry
    M. J. Bixby
1901 James F. Lord
1901 Edgar A. Lord
1913 Mr. & Mrs. L. B. Kuppen-
    heimer
Receive 1st and 3d Friday
1915 Mr. & Mrs. Charles Silverman
1915 Max Grabfield
1915 David S. Simon
1915 Dr. Joseph P. Grabfield
1915 Jacob Grabfield

1602 Mr. & Mrs. C. F. Gunther
1602 Burnell Gunther
1602 Whitman Gunther
1610 Mrs. William C. Grant
1610 Mrs. Ira P. Nudd
1610 Charles E. Grant
1610 Louis Moen Grant
1610 Miss C. A. Baker
1612 Mr. & Mrs. H. M. Curtis & dr.
1612 Mrs. A. Murison
1612 George W. Murison
1616 Miss Janet R. Perkins
1618 Mr. & Mrs. Henry N.Hart & dr.
Receive 1st & 3d Thursday
1618 Herbert L. Hart
1620 Mr. & Mrs. Arthur G. Burley
1624 Mrs. Marie Lehmann
1624 Mr. & Mrs. Oscar A. Lehmann
1624 Fred Lehmann
1624 Alfred A. Lehmann
1624 Edmund Lehmann
1628 Mr. & Mrs. Williard T. Block
1628 Miss Anna Larrabee
1630 Mr. & Mrs. Charles F. Pierce
1630 Carl H. Pierce
1640 Mr. & Mrs. Charles B. Sawyer
1640 Mr. & Mrs. Charles A. Sawyer
1706 Mr. & Mrs. Henry K. Elkins
1710 Mr. & Mrs. B. E. Gallup & drs.
1710 Mr. & Mrs. Stephen Laskey
1718 Mr. & Mrs. H. H. Gallup
Receiving day Thursday
1718 Mr. & Mrs. James Mix & dr.
1718 James T. Mix
1800 Dr. & Mrs. E. Russell Ogden
1800 J. M. Wright
1800 Mr. & Mrs. P. A. McEwan
1806 Mrs. Ella Spaulding
1822 Mrs. M. Mannheimer.
1822 Miss M. Norton
1826 Mr. & Mrs. C. Price & dr.
1826 Mr. & Mrs. James S. Price
1826 Samuel C. Price
1826 M. Wallace Price
1826 Miss Delia Price
1826 O. W. Stoughton
1826 Miss Abbie Benson
1838 Mr. & Mrs. Wm. H. Swift
1838 David Campbell
1840 Mr. & Mrs. George Lomax
Receiving day Friday
1840 George Lomax jr.
1842 Mr.&Mrs. B. W. Thomas & drs.
Receiving day Friday

1919 Mr. & Mrs. E. Fullem & drs.
1921 Mr. & Mrs. C. A. Morgan
1923 Mrs. Therese Falkenau
1923 Louis Falkenau
1923 Mr. & Mrs, Louis Danziger
1927 Myron McGee
1927 Harry L. McGee
1927 Wilford J. McGee
1927 Mme. J. Wolf
1931 Mr.& Mrs.Morris Schwabacher
1933 Mr. & Mrs. F. A. Delano
2001 Mrs. Cyrus Bentley & dr.
2003 Mr. & Mrs. A. Courtney Campbell
2007 Mr. & Mrs. Walter B. Mitchell
2009 Mrs. L. V. Comer
       Receives Tuesday eve.
2009 Mr. & Mrs. P. Benson
2011 Mrs. S. M. Case & dr.
       Receiving day Friday
2011 Francis M. Case
2011 John E. Case
2013 Mr. & Mrs. Wm. Crocker
2013 Miss Mary R. Hayes
2019 Mr. & Mrs. Wm. D. Adams
2023 Mrs. H. G. Sutherland & dr.
2023 Mrs. Henry Fuller
2023 Henry W. McClellan
2023 Fuller McClellan
2027 Mr. & Mrs. A. J. Crippen
       Receiving day Thursday
2027 Mr. & Mrs. R. L. Rainbow
2107 Mr. & Mrs. C.F. Blakeslee & dr.
2107 John W. Gary
2115 Mr. & Mrs. Alfred L. Holman
       Receiving day Wednesday
2115 Miss Frances S. Dickerman
2115 Miss Ellen W. Collins
2311 Mr. & Mrs. Hiram Tompkins
2311 Mrs. M. L. Hinckley
2311 Mr. & Mrs. J. B. Rayner
2317 Dr. Louise A. Dickerson
2317 James A. Davis
2327 Mr. & Mrs. F. E. Buddington
2331 Mr.& Mrs.E. P. Griswold & dr.
2335 Mr.& Mrs.J.C. Richberg & drs.
2339 Mr. & Mrs. Alfred H. Gross
2415 Miss Hattie Benedict
2419 Dr. & Mrs. John E. Gilman
2419 Wm. T. Gilman
2421 Mr. & Mrs. J. R. Barker & drs.
       Receiving day Wednesday
2421 Mrs. E. H. Mott
2427 Mrs. O. B. Phelps
2427 W. B. Reddon
2437 Mr. & Mrs. Thomas Whitfield

1842 Lloyd Washington
1842 Wilberforce Veitch
1904 Mr. & Mrs. Herman Nathan
1904 Louis M. Cohen
1906 Mr. & Mrs. Charles Schaffner
1914 Mrs. Estella Harps
       Receiving day Thursday
1920 Mrs. A. S. Piper
1920 Anson Piper
1920 Allen A. Piper
1920 Mr. & Mrs. James T. Wells
1922 Dr. & Mrs. George W. Webster
1926 Mr. & Mrs. F. M. Thomas
1926 Mr. & Mrs. George P. Gore
2000 Mr. & Mrs. C. D. Peacock jr.
2000 Mr.& Mrs. Arthur F. McArthur
2014 Mr. & Mrs. Ceo. A. Gibbs
2022 Mr. & Mrs. A. R. Warner
2022 Harry D. Warner
2022 Mrs. F. R. Warner
2022 Fred Keeler
2022 Mr. & Mrs. E. W. Pardridge
2024 Mr. & Mrs. Aug. R. Gray
2024 Chas. H. Gray
2024 Mr. & Mrs. Jas. B. Heth
2024 Henry S. Heth
2028 Mr. & Mrs. Chas. E. Murison
2028 Mr. & Mrs. Adolph Lewis
2028 Harry B. Gilbert
2028 Miss F. E. Gilbert
2028 Miss Maud Gilbert
2030 Dr. Robison Tripp
2030 Waldemar T. Hansen
2030 Chas. W. Hansen
2030 Mr. & Mrs. Weston G. Kimball
2034 Mr. & Mrs. Chas. W. Webster
       & drs.
       Receiving day Wednesday
2034 Frank B. Webster
2034 Mr. & Mrs. J. C. Maslin
       Receiving day Thursday
2034 Mrs. R. F. Parker
2034 Miss C. E. Maslin
2034 R. D. Parker
2034 Dr. & Mrs. Frank W. Reilly
2034 Leigh Reilly
2034 R. K. Reilly
2034 R. R. Reilly
2034 H. M. Hyde
2034 E. S. Beck
2036 Dr. & Mrs. A. H. Burr
       Receive Wednesday p. m. and eve.
2036 Mr. & Mrs. E. G. Minnemeyer
       Receiving day Wednesday
2036 Walter T. Chandler
2036 L. Hamilton Chandler

2441 Mr. & Mrs. J. H. Van Vlissen-
gen
2441 Miss Ella Parrette
2449 Mr. & Mrs. Howard E. Laing
2449 Harold A. Laing
2449 F. P. Kellogg
2453 Mr. & Mrs. Nelson Morris
2453 Herbert N. Morris
2453 Ira Morris
2509 Mr. & Mrs. Eli M. Straus
Receive 1st & 3d Friday
2509 Morton E. Straus
2511 Mrs. Michael Walsh
2511 Mrs. Ann Riley
2519 Rev. Dr.& Mrs. T. J. Leak &dr.
Receiving day Thursday
2523 Mr. & Mrs. Joseph Wahl & drs.
2525 Mr. & Mrs. John F. Ryan
2535 Mrs. Hugh Riddle
2539 Mr. & Mrs. Cyrus Dupee &
drs.
2539 Mrs. Charles Dana
2545 Mrs. James Couch
Receiving day Friday
2545 Dr. Richard S. Curtiss
2547 Mr. & Mrs. Chas. Yondorf
Receiving day Saturday
2613 Mr. & Mrs. H.W.Dudley & drs.
2613 Dr. Lewis W. Dudley
2613 Arthur H. Dudley
2613 Mrs. Mary A. Darrow
2613 Raymond Dudley
2619 Mr. & Mrs. John C. Neely & dr.
2619 John C. Neely jr.
2633 Dr. & Mrs. J. H. Stowell
2633 Miss Ida M. Stowell
2705 Mrs. Elizabeth S. Farwell
2705 Francis W. Farwell
2705 George E. Farwell
2705 Mr. & Mrs. James R. Chapman
2709 Mr. & Mrs. M. W. Powell
2713 Mr. & Mrs. M. Rosenthal & dr.
2713½ Dr. & Mrs. A. L. Lundgren
2721 Mr. & Mrs. D. W. Pomeroy &
dr.
2729 Dr.& Mrs.Charles Krusemarck
2735 Mr. & Mrs. J. G. Clinnen
2809 Mr. & Mrs. Gustave G. Shauer
Receiving day Thursday
2809 Miss Grace Lidy
2809 Byron W. New
2813 Maj. & Mrs. J. H. McArthur
2815 Mr. & Mrs.L.Ottenheimer&dr.
Receive 2d and 4th Friday
2815 Mr. & Mrs. L. S. Ottenheimer
2815 Henry L. Ottenheimer

2036 N. E. Chandler
2114 Mr. & Mrs. H. T. Pitt
2114 Mr. & Mrs. W. W. Pitt
2126 Mrs. Alice Peterson
2126 Soren Mathison
Receiving day Wednesday
2300 and 2302 The Normandy Flats
1 Mr. & Mrs. A. A. Spencer
2 Mr. & Mrs. Chas. H. Collins
3 Dr. & Mrs. H. V. Halbert
Receiving day Thursday
4 Mrs. S. G. Smith
4 S. Fred Smith
6 Mr. & Mrs. Wm. Castle
7 Miss Fannie Blinn
7 Dr. Louise Montague Blinn
7 Miss Nellie Jewett
7 Mr. & Mrs. George W. Marsh
Receiving day Thursday
8 Mr. & Mrs. F. F. Ainsworth
2306 Dr. & Mrs. T. T. Oliver
2306 Mr. & Mrs. John L. Yocum
2310 Mrs. J. M. Van Osdel
2310 Miss Martha Van Osdel
2320 Mr. & Mrs. W. D. Preston
2320 Mrs. J. C. Roberts
2320 Charles S. Roberts
2322 Mr.& Mrs. Leroy Payne
2322 Mr. & Mrs. William Mueller jr.
Receiving day Thursday
2326 Mrs. Isabella L. Jones & drs.
2326 Mr. & Mrs. Edward W. Jones
2330 Mr. & Mrs. H. S. Wilson
2328 Mrs. E. W. Densmore & dr.
2330 Mr. & Mrs. H. M. Sallee & drs.
2334 Dr. W. W. Stafford
2340A Dr. S. D. Ebersole
2342 Mr. & Mrs. G. A. Follansbee
2342 M. D. Follansbee
2342 Miss Blanche D. Follansbee
2342 Mrs. M. M. Davis
2400 Dr. & Mrs. Daniel T. Nelson
2400 Miss Electa Gifford
2400 Miss Anna Millar
2406 Francis C. Nelson
2424 Mr. & Mrs. Samuel Powell
2426 Mr. & Mrs. J. W. Richards
2426 O. K. Richards
2426 Miss Hattie N. Marshall
2428 Mrs. D. A. Hewes
2428 Chas. H. Foster
2428 Walter H. Remwick
2428 J. B. Chandler
2428 Miss Mamie A. Lewis
2428 Irving W. Rosenstein
2430 Mr. & Mrs. Oliver C. Nelson

2825 Rev. Dr. & Mrs. Clinton Locke
2825 Mr. & Mrs. John K. MacKenzie
2825 Mrs. A. Douthitt
2829 Dr. & Mrs. Peter S. MacDonald
2829 James M. MacDonald
2829 Raymond J. McDonald
2839 Mr. & Mrs. Henry Hyman
2919 Mrs. Sarah Wilder Pratt
　　　　Receiving day Thursday
2919 Miss E. A. Wilder
2921 Mr. & Mrs. Wm. J. Clarke
2921 Mr. & Mrs. Wm. C. Johnson
2921 Mrs. E. J. Henderson
2921 Mr. & Mrs. A. J. F. McBean
2923 Mr. & Mrs. Lee Roy Pontious
2925 Mr. & Mrs. George L. Brown
2925 Mrs. G. A. Harmount
2927 Mr. & Mrs. James M. Barden
2927 H. R. Barden
2927 Mr. & Mrs. Harrison Kelley & dr.
2927 Tracy H. Clark
2927 Miss Almeda Mann
2927 Miss Harriet Johnson
2927 Charles S. Cole
2931 Mr. & Mrs. W. H. Andrews
2931 Otto Gresham
2935 Dr. & Mrs. Frank Cary
2935 Mrs. Ellen Cary
2937 Mr. & Mrs. J. B. Woodruff
2937 Albert H. Buck
2937 Miss Grace P. Buck
2943 Mrs. F. M. Conlee
2943 Miss H. I. Kingsbury
2943 Mr. & Mrs. W. H. Pettibone
　　　　Receiving day Wednesday
2945 Mrs. Sarah Danziger
2945 Samuel S. Danziger
2945 Edward Danziger
2945 Mr. & Mrs. Israel Stein
2947 Mrs. Alice Bickel & dr.
2947 Mr. & Mrs. C. H. Hinman
2947 Capt. & Mrs. J. G. Milligan
2947 Mr. & Mrs. Edgar Wells
2951 Mrs. J. Freedman
2951 Mr. & Mrs. L. Goodman
2955 Mr. & Mrs. Henry M. Ralston
2957 Rev. Dr. & Mrs. John Henry Barrows
2963 Mr. & Mrs. E. R. Bliss
　　　　Receiving day Tuesday
2967 Mr. & Mrs. Alfred Hammer
2969 Dr. & Mrs. H. B. Fellows
2971 Mr. & Mrs. Edgar A. Clark
　　　　Receiving day Tuesday

2438 Mr. & Mrs. S. L. Soule
　　　　Receiving day Thursday
2446 Mrs. Mary Espert
2450 Dr. & Mrs. J. H. Low
2450 Mr. & Mrs. Jos. Couthoui & dr.
2450 Mr. & Mrs. Frank D. Tobey
2454 Dr. & Mrs. Chas. W. Leake
　　　　Receiving day Wednesday
2454 Mrs. M. M. Foster
2454 W. M. Foster
2454 Mr. & Mrs. H. L. Smithson
2458 Mr. & Mrs. Samuel R. Wells
2458 Mrs. Ida N. Smythe & dr.
2458 Milo J. Chase
2458 Mr. & Mrs. Charles Busby
2458 Mr. & Mrs. Wm. S. Smithson
2500 Mme. R. Horwitz
2502 Mrs. M. Ettlinger
2502 Carl Wolfsohn
2506 Mrs. Irene B. Roney & dr.
2506 Henry B. Roney
2506 Charles J. Roney
2510 Dr. & Mrs. Milton Jay
2510 Dr. Frank W. Jay
2512 E. Bruce Chandler
2512 George M. Chandler
2512 Miss Alice Chandler
2520 H. N. Wheeler & drs.
2520 Mr. & Mrs. Arthur J. Singer
2528 Mr. & Mrs. J. H. Strong
　　　　Receiving day Friday
2532 Mr. & Mrs. Geo. W. Mathews
2532 Miss Clara Louise Mathews
2532 Fred W. Mathews
2532 Miss Clara Wardwell
2536 G. F. Harding & dr.
2536 Geo. F. Harding jr.
2542 Dr. & Mrs. S. Chas. DeVeny
2548 Mr. & Mrs. F. R. Hilger
2548 Mr. & Mrs. Albert Pike
2548 Harry D. Jenkins
2548 Frederick A. Ray
2548 Mrs. V. B. Jenkins
2548 Mrs. Marian VanDuyn
2548 Irving C. Black
2600 Dr. C. E. Paddock
2600 Mr. & Mrs. C. S. Winn
2600 Rev. C. A. Allen
2600 Mr. & Mrs. Wm. A. Myer
2602 Mr. & Mrs. S. P. Herron
2602 Mr. & Mrs. Albert Coakley
2602 Mr. & Mrs. F. J. Greene
2604 Mr. & Mrs. Horace C. Frost
2604 Mrs. A. R. Milligan
2604 James A. Mahon
2606 Albert I. Newton

2973 Mr.& Mrs. J. A. Robbins & dr.
2973 Mrs. Ann Owens
2979 Mr. & Mrs. Ernest Werner
2979 Mr. & Mrs. Frederick Noth
3025 Dr. & Mrs. Albert Weil
 Receiving day Thursday
3025 Miss Lottie E. Johnson
3029 Dr. A. L. Thomas
3029 J. P. Thomas
3029 A. S. Thomas
3029 Mrs. M. I I. Perkins
3029 Miss Mattie Thomas
 Receiving day Wednesday
3031 Dr. & Mrs. G. M. Chamberlin
3031 George M. Chamberlin jr.
3131 Mr. & Mrs. Patrick Burke & drs.
3131 Mr. & Mrs. W. Cullen Bryant
3131 Mr. & Mrs. Albert Levison & drs.
3131 Mrs. Elizabeth Hennessy & dr.
3131 Mrs. C. Ruarc
3131 Mr. & Mrs. Wm. P. Morgan
 Receiving day Thursday
3131 Mr. & Mrs. E. H. Ayer
3131 Mrs. J. M. Bromley
3135 Mr. & Mrs. Siegel Hess & drs.
 Receive 1st Friday
3135 Leo Hess
3139 Mr. & Mrs. B. F. Michael
3141 Mr. & Mrs. J. H. Thompson & dr.
3145 Mrs. John Hutchinson & dr.
3147 Dr. & Mrs. D. B. Eaton
 Receiving day Tuesday
3147 Miss Anna Abel
3157 Prof. & Mrs. Wm. Schmidt
3159 Mrs. Jane L. Fitch
 Receiving day Friday
3159 Mr. & Mrs. H. M. Ayres
3201 Dr. & Mrs. A. L Freund
 Receive 2d & 3d Friday
3201 Mrs. Dora Korsoski
3205 Mrs. H. S. Kohn & drs.
3205 Louis H. Kohn
3205 Simon H. Kohn
3207 J. M. Perry & dr.
3229 Mrs. J. Corrigan & drs.
3229 R. E. Corrigan
3233 Mr. & Mrs. H. W. Zemansky
 Receiving day Wednesday
3233 Nathan J. Zemansky
3233 Mrs. Mary E. Holmes & dr.
3233 Rev. David E. Holmes
3233 Edward I. Holmes
 Receiving day Monday

2606 Wm. G. Newton
2606 Dr. S. T. Burke
2606 Miss Rachael Burke
2606 Mrs. A. S. Newton
2606 Mrs. C. E. Ryder
2614 Mr. & Mrs. Albert W. Kohn
 Receiving day Thursday
2616 William Fitzgerald
2616 Miss M. F. Fitzgerald
2616 W. H. Fitzgerald
2616 Miss M. Corbett
2640 Mr. & Mrs. M. A. Allen
2644 Mr. & Mrs. Geo. L. Gray
2704 Mr.&Mrs.J. D. Goodman &drs.
2704 Mr. & Mrs. L. F. Minzesheimer
2712 Mr. & Mrs. Jacob Reinach
 Receive 2d and 4th Thursday
2712 Jacob Ullman
2712 Gustave S. Ullman
2714 Mr. & Mrs. Isaac Rubel
2714 Mrs. Sarah Haas
2714 Mrs. Bertha Pollak
2724 Miss H. L. Blackman
2724 Mrs. Lucinda Rounsevell
2724 Judson Blackman
2728 Mr. & Mrs. Myron A. Pearce
2732 Mr. & Mrs. Louis Busch
2804 Mr. & Mrs. J. H. Willets & drs.
2806 Mr. & Mrs. Dyer N. Burnham & dr.
2808 Mrs. George E. Blish & drs.
2814 Mr. & Mrs. M. M. Levison
2818 Rev. & Mrs. Arthur Edwards & drs.
2818 Dr. Arthur R. Edwards
2826 Mr. & Mrs. Hugh Heron & dr.
2832 Mr. & Mrs. Ira W. Buell
2836 Mr. & Mrs. Chas. A. McLean
2836 C. F. McLean
2838 Mr. & Mrs. A. H. Downs
2838 Mr. & Mrs. Theodore Emery
2840 Mr. & Mrs. Tracy C. Drake
2910 Dr. & Mrs. W. W. Jaggard
2910 Mrs. J. S. Newberry
2916 Mr. & Mrs. Amos Grannis
2916 Albert A. Grannis
2916 Harry A. Grannis
2916 Frank L. Grannis
2916 Mrs. C. Eldredge & dr..
2920 Dr. & Mrs D. A. K. Steele
2920 Joseph S. Tomlinson
2932 Mr. & Mrs. James Viles jr.
2934 Mr. & Mrs. E. F. Robbins
 Receive Friday afternoon
2934 J. D. Cory
2938 Mr. & Mrs. W. F. Burrows

3233 Mrs. S. Collins & dr.
3233 Mrs. K. C. Reynolds
3233 Frank W. Reynolds
3233 Mr. & Mrs. Walter Upp
3235 Mr. & Mrs. G. W. Shepard & drs.
3237 Dr. & Mrs. Charles Caldwell
    Receiving day Thursday
3239 Dr. & Mrs. Elmer E. Babcock
    Receiving day Thursday
3241 Mrs. A. S. Cook
3241 Horatio J. Jacoby
3251 Mr. & Mrs. Ira J. Mix
    Receiving day Wednesday
3253 Mr. & Mrs. Harry E. Blood
3255 Harry C. Solomon
3255 Leopold Kahn
3257 Mr. & Mrs. Alverson E. Morley
3257 Mr. & Mrs. N. F. Hart
3259 John E. Dean & dr.
3259 Mr. & Mrs. John E. Wood
3325 Mr. & Mrs. A. J. Hewlings
3327 Mr. & Mrs. B. D. Slocum
3329 Mr. & Mrs. L. C. Straight
3331 Mrs. E. P. Broughton
3333 Miss May Buckingham
3333 Frank E. Burley
3335 Mr. & Mrs. Isaac J. Lewis
3339 Mr. & Mrs. Leon Hirshman
3341 Mr. & Mrs. J. R. Robinson
    Receiving day Thursday
3343 Mr. & Mrs. H. P. Hansell
3345 Mr. & Mrs. Thos. H. Brown & drs.
3351 Mr. & Mrs. F. E. Halle
3351 Arnold Halle
3353 Albert Schwartz
3353 Dr. Rosa Engelmann
3353 Miss Lily Engelmann
3353 Jacob Block
3353 Mme. C. Fey
3359 Mrs. Daniel Goodman & dr.
3361 Mr. & Mrs. Louis F. Collins
3363 Mr. & Mrs. David Rosenfeld
3363 Maurice B. Rosenfeld
3363 Louis J. Rosenfeld
3365 Mr. & Mrs. Albert E. Snow
3401 Mr. & Mrs. W. R. Hill
3401 Mrs. E. Hausmann
3401 Edward Hausmann
3403 Mr. & Mrs. George W. Watson
3403 Frank Watson
3407 Henry Keller & dr.
3411 Mme. Marie Biro de Marion
3421 Mrs. M. Wallace
3423 Dr. & Mrs. Wilson H. Davis

2940 Mrs. Henry D. Warner & dr.
2942 Mr. & Mrs. W. W. Sherman
2942 Francis J. Hill
2942 Charles R. Smith
2944 Mr. & Mrs. T. A. Broughton
2946 Mr. & Mrs. C. W. Bryant
2946 Mrs. C. A. Van Slyck
    Receiving day Friday
2948 Dr. Maurice L. Goodkind
2950 Dr. & Mrs. A. H. Ferguson
    Receiving day Wednesday
2952 Mr. & Mrs. M. B. Lydon & drs.
2952 William A. Lydon
2952 Harry C. Lydon
2956 Mrs. E. S. Reilly &'drs.
2956 John J. Reilly
2958 Miss Henrietta Brooks
2958 Lorenzo C. Brooks
2958 J. Henry Brooks
2958 Miss Sarah A. Brooks
2962 Mrs. Bernard Callaghan & dr.
2962 Mr. & Mrs. J. E. Callaghan
2966 Miss M. J. O'Brien
2966 Miss M. V. O'Brien
2968 Mr. & Mrs. Mandred A. Morton
    Receiving day Wednesday
2968 Mrs. F. B. Morton
2972 Mr. & Mrs. J. H. Wilcox
2974 Mr. & Mrs. William Marvin
2978 Mrs. Martha Foote Crow
3000 The Norwood Flats
   1 Dr. W. Edgar Ervin
   2 Dr. & Mrs. Louis A. Greens-felder
   5 Dr. & Mrs. Chas. A. Canfield
   7 Mrs. M. McCreery
    Receiving day Thursday
   7 A. H. Baldwin
   8 Dr. & Mrs. Emil Kjellberg
   9 Mr. & Mrs. J. M. Davis
  10 Mr. & Mrs. H. A. Seymoure
  11 Mr. & Mrs. J. B. Henry
  12 Mrs. G. R. Blodgett
  13 Mrs. C. A. Woolley & dr.
  14 Mrs. Kate G. Smith
  18 Mrs. Addie Adams Hull
  18 Oliver W. Hull
  18 Miss Gertrude S. Rose
  19 Miss Ella Doyle
3012 Mr. & Mrs. Gilbert W. Barnard
3018 Dr. & Mrs. E. H. Thurston & dr.
    Receiving day Thursday
3020 Miss Nancy D. Mitchell
3020 Lucien C. Mitchell
3020 Mrs. Maria E. Smith

3427 Mr. & Mrs. Lumley Ingledew
   & drs.
3427 Lumley Ingledew jr.
3429 Mr. & Mrs. Geo. W. Getchell
   Receiving day Wednesday
3431 Mr. & Mrs. Jas. L. Chapman
3431 Mrs. D. S. Thompson
3431 Mrs. Emily M. Smythe
3449 Dr. & Mrs. Charles W. Ward
3449 Mr. & Mrs. Leon J. Jacobs
   Receiving day Friday
3449 Ludwig Loeser
3505 Dr. Isaac A. Abt
3505 Mr. & Mrs. John M. Ray
3505 John A. Wiemer
3505 F. E. Olinger
3505 Mr. & Mrs. John P. Olinger
   Receiving day Thursday
3505 Jean Prosper Olinger
3517 Mr. & Mrs. Edward P. Murray
3517 Wm. E. O'Neill
3519 Mrs. V. M. Logan
3519 Mrs. E. M. Fleming
3519 Mr. & Mrs. Isaac Rosenthal
3519 Joseph Siegel
3519 Mr. & Mrs. Louis D. Heusner
3519 Mrs. Kate Owen & dr.
3519 Ole Owen
3531 Mr. & Mrs. James McNaughton
3531 Mr. & Mrs. W. B. Schwartz
3531 Nathan Engel
3531 Meyer Lippman
3533 F. R. Johnson
3535 Mr. & Mrs. J. R. Taylor
3537 Dr. & Mrs. Jacob Wile
3537 Mrs. Helen A. Remick
3537 Mr. & Mrs. E. E. Evans
3537 Mr. & Mrs. L. E. McPherson
3537 Mr. & Mrs. J. L. Davenport
   Receiving day Thursday
3601 Wm. Friedman
3601 Louis Friedman
3601 Miss Pauline Friedman
3601 Mrs. Kate Grossman
3619 Michael Lawler & drs.
   Receiving day Thursday
3619 John Lawler
3619 Michael Lawler jr.
3625 Dr. & Mrs. T. J. Watkins
   Receiving day Friday
3643 Mr. & Mrs. M. P. Taylor & drs.
3645 Mr. & Mrs. Charles F. Smith
3645 Miss Harriet P. Clapp
3651 Mr. & Mrs. W. Cohn
3651 Elias Cohn
3657 Henry A. Lovell

3024 Dr. Catharine J. Wells
3024 Dr. Vida A. Saunders
3128 Mr. & Mrs. Michael Espert
3130 Dr. & Mrs. G. F. Shears
   Receiving day Thursday .
3130 Dr. James B. Miner
3134 Dr. & Mrs. Chas. H. Lodor
   Receiving day Tuesday
3146 Dr. Marie White
3146 Dr. Anna M. Braunwarth
3148 Dr. & Mrs. Alfred E. Thomas
3150 Mr. & Mrs. I. L. Cox & dr.
3150 William J. Cox
3150 Mr. & Mrs. Charles A. Corwin
3150 Mrs. Clarence N. Millerd
3150 Miss Alice Biglow
3154 Dr. & Mrs. J. R. Kippax
3156 Dr. & Mrs. J. P. Cobb
3156 Dr. W. O. Forbes
3160 Dr. & Mrs. William E. Quine
3200 Mr.& Mrs. Thos. Montgomery
3202 Mr. & Mrs. M. D. Witkowsky
3210 Edward A. Rosenthal
3218 Mr. & Mrs. H. M. Elliott & dr.
3226 Mr. & Mrs. Geo. M. Fadner
   Receiving day Wednesday
3230 Mr. & Mrs. James T. Healy &
   drs.
3244 Mr. & Mrs. James M. Reddy
3300 Mrs. S. H. Clark
3300 Dr. & Mrs. Horace M. Starkey
3300 Miss M. Ella Starkey
3302 Dr. & Mrs. Charles H. Thayer
3306 Mr. & Mrs. James A.Lawrence
   Receiving day Wednesday
3306 Mr. & Mrs. J. O. Hinkley
3306 Mr. & Mrs. M. E. Swart
3312 Mr. & Mrs. Henry Hefter & dr.
3312 C. H. Hefter
3312 Charles Hefter
3316 Mr. & Mrs. George P. Smith
   Receiving day Friday
3316 Mrs. H. M. Sherman & dr.
3316 Mrs. Isabel Morgan
3316 Mr. & Mrs. Lile Sharpneck
3318 Mr. & Mrs. D. E. Sibley
3318 James W. Sibley
3320 Mr. & Mrs. Isaac Kuh
   Receiving day Wednesday
3320 Dr. Sidney Kuh
3322 Mr. & Mrs. Arnold Cohn
3322 Mr. & Mrs. Godfrey Harris
3326 Mr. & Mrs. M. A. Cheney
3328 Mr. & Mrs. John Tyrrell
3330 Mr. & Mrs. Charles S. Frost
3332 Mr. & Mrs. H. R. McCullough

3659 Mr. & Mrs. Bryant Moseley
Receiving day Thursday
3659 Mrs. Jennie Clark
3807 Dr. & Mrs. D H. Sullivan
3807 Mrs. Eliza J. Powers
3835 Mrs. M. Follette
3835 H. A. Follette
3919 Mrs. M. W. Bromley
3929 Mr. & Mrs. D. H. Perkins
3939 Mr. & Mrs. A. Rheinstrom
Receiving day Monday
3939 Mrs. R. Dexter
4013 F. P. Puterbaugh
4015 Mr. & Mrs. J. B. Kennedy
4019 Mr. & Mrs. R. B. Organ
4021 Mr. & Mrs. Edward G. Fish
4021 Mrs. S. Huckins
4021 Percy Smith
4023 Mr. & Mrs. Wm. J. Fleming & drs.
4025 Mr. & Mrs. M. P. Metcalf
4027 Mr. & Mrs. H. J. O'Brien
4029 Mr. & Mrs. M. C. Follansbee
4029 Miss Annie Eckstadt
4035 Mr. & Mrs. A. P. Brainard
4037 Mr. & Mrs. H. S. Tobey
4037 Miss Carrie B. Watkins
4039 Benjamin Auerbach
4039 Mr. & Mrs. Frank S. Rolfe
4043 Mrs. E. S. Hamilton
4047 Mr. & Mrs. Joseph Duncan
4051 Mr. & Mrs. Herbert E. Goodman
4101 Thomas D. Walsh
4103 Mr. & Mrs. J. E. Defebaugh
4109 Mr. & Mrs. Walter Scates & dr.
4207 Mr. & Mrs. B. J. Young & drs.
4207 Harry Young
4229 Mr. & Mrs. George W. Crawford
Receiving day Thursday
4229 Mr. & Mrs. Wm. M. Bolles
4341 Mr. & Mrs. Sylvester Marshall
4341 Mr. & Mrs. Charles Pulham & dr.
4345 Mr. & Mrs. George H. Liberty
4351 Mrs. H. R. Koehler & drs.
4357 Mr. & Mrs. Edgar J. Hunter
4417 Mr. & Mrs. Nathan B. Higbie
Receiving day Wednesday
4417 Mr. & Mrs. W. B. Ingwersen
4501 Mr. & Mrs. P. Nacey & drs.
4503 Mr. & Mrs. James Moore
4505 Mr. & Mrs. S. V. Hill & dr.
4519 Mr. & Mrs. Wm. Conroy
4739 Mr. & Mrs. P. H. Dobbins
4743 Mr. & Mrs. Phil. Kopf & dr.

3336 Mr. & Mrs. Chas. B. Eggleston
Receiving day Thursday
3336 Chas. E. Eggleston
3350 Mr. & Mrs. C. Edward Baker
3352 Mrs. Leander Stone & drs.
Receiving day Friday
3400 Dr. & Mrs. John Leeming
3400 R. W. Leeming
3402 Mr. & Mrs. W. R. Manlove
Receiving day Thursday
3402 L. A. Mitchell
3404 Mr. & Mrs. Leopold Fried & dr.
3406 Mr. & Mrs. Ferdinand Neuberger
Receiving day 1st & 3d Friday
3408 Mr. & Mrs. A. E. Neuberg & drs.
3426 Mr. & Mrs. Philip Maher
3428 Mr. & Mrs. Sam'l Shoeneman
3428 Mr. & Mrs. Henry Dewitz
3438 Dr. & Mrs. M. J. Moth
3438 Trueman Franklin
3440 Mr. & Mrs. R. Eisenstaedt
Receive 1st and 3d Thursday
3444 Mr. & Mrs. Julius M. Crane
3444 Miss Celestine Metzger
3450 Mr. & Mrs. F. V. Fitzsimmons
3506 Dr. & Mrs. Andrew J. Coey
3528 Mr. & Mrs. J. L. McCluer
3528 Mrs. Sarah A. Dolph
3528 William S. Dolph
3530 Mr. & Mrs. W. W. Wilkins
3632 Mr. & Mrs. Louis Eggers
3634 Mr. & Mrs. H. F. Buettner
3638 Mrs. Timothy Upton
3638 Mr. & Mrs. Fred Schrauder & dr.
3640 Dr. G. E. Rollins
3640 John Rollins
3640 Miss Georgia Rollins
3646 Frank L. Honore
3646 Mr. & Mrs. James A. Cowles
3648 Mr. & Mrs. Henry Fleischman
Receiving day 1st & 3d Wednesday
3666 Mrs. Barbara Neumann
3666 Ignatz Hasterlik
3666 Henry Hasterlik
3670 Mr. & Mrs. Jacob Williams
3670 James Davy Williams
3756 Mr. & Mrs. Louis Morris & dr.
Receiving day first Tuesday
3756 Henry Morris
3758 Mrs. A. Levi & dr.
3758 David Levi
3758 Henry Levi
3760 Miss Clara J. Vierling
3760 Robert Vierling

4743 Wm. P. Kopf
4809 Mr. & Mrs. John Hickey
5609 Mr. & Mrs. Orrin Lee Evans
5721 Mr. & Mrs. Joseph B. Bettles
5735 Elmer E. Kilmer
5735 Dr. Anna Kilmer
5737 Mr. & Mrs. A. C. Clark
5813 Mr. & Mrs. N. C. Thayer
5843 B. H. Vreeland
5855 Mr. & Mrs. N. A. Lauer
5901 Emanuel P. Barnet
5901 M. P. Barnet
5919 Mr. & Mrs. F. P. Kennedy
5919 Mrs. Sarah Slayton
5927 Mr. & Mrs. Wm. M. Hughes
6001 Mr. & Mrs. H. H. Gross
6015 Mr. & Mrs. H. R. Stebbings & drs. *Receiving day Thursday*
6015 Walter L. Stebbings
6027 Mrs. E. S. Bliss
6033 Dr.& Mrs.Horace P. Stebbings *Receiving day Thursday*
6125 Mr. & Mrs. A. C. Mann & dr. *Receiving day Thursday*

4512 Mr. & Mrs. Austin A. Canavan
4516 Mr. & Mrs. T. G. McElligott
4564 Mr. & Mrs. L. J. Hanchett
4626 Mrs. M. C. Bell
4628 C. E. Dobbins
4630 Mr. & Mrs. H. Wilson & drs.
4630 A. T. Wilson
4634 Mr. & Mrs. Nathaniel Bacon
4638 Mr. & Mrs. O. A. Mathison
4656 Mrs. Agnes E. Foss & dr. *Receiving day Tuesday*
5140 Mr. & Mrs. Nelson Young
5172 Rev. & Mrs. Chas. E. Blodgett
5334 Mr. & Mrs. Moses S. Greenebaum
5610 Mr. & Mrs. O. S. Baylies
5846 Mr. & Mrs. Almer Coe *Receive 2d and 4th Wednesday*
5910 Mrs. S. L. McDowell
5910 Mrs. A. B. Huson
5918 W. H. Parish
6012 Mr. & Mrs. Henry B. Lewis
6012 Mr. & Mrs. Will W. Carter *Receiving day Friday*
6020 Mr. & Mrs. Thos. Cunningham
6020 Wm. Cunningham
6020 Miss Helen B. O'Neil
6034 Mr. & Mrs. C. J. Riley
nw. cor. 63d Mr. & Mrs. Isaac T. Sunderland
nw. cor. 63d Mrs. Ida T. Rankin

3760 Louis Vierling
3764 Mr. & Mrs. J. Jos. Hoffman
3764 Mrs. P. Landman
3764 Fred C. Bryan
3766 Mr. & Mrs. Sig. Welter
3766 Bela Welter
3800 Mr. & Mrs. Charles Livingston *Receiving day 3d Wednesday*
3804 Mr. & Mrs. A. W. Becker
3804 Isaac J. Becker
3804 Mrs. M. Heinrich
3806 Mr. & Mrs. Isaac Meyer
3808 Dr. & Mrs. F. H. Honberger
3810 Mr. & Mrs. H. B. Wheelock
3926 Mr. & Mrs. Wm. Rothschild
3932 Mr. & Mrs. John O'Rourke
3944 Mr. & Mrs. D. Eugene Brush *Receiving day Thursday*
3952 Mr. & Mrs. Thos. H. Treacy & drs.
3952 Hugh T. Treacy
4016 Mr. & Mrs. John M. Kulms
4022 Mr. & Mrs. William A. Purcell
4048 Mr. & Mrs. Albert H. Loeb
4048 Edward Slattery
4056 Dr. & Mrs. L. R. Eichberg *Receiving day Thursday*
4100 Allen L. Howard
4104 Mr. & Mrs. Ransom Richards & drs.
4104 Charles R. Richards
4110 Miss M. Jennie Kinsella
4110 Miss Annie F. Kinsella
4110 F. D. Kinsella
4110 J. J. Kinsella
4110 J. E. Kinsella
4112 Mr. & Mrs. C. L. Dougherty *Receiving day Tuesday*
4114 Mr. & Mrs. T. A. Stevens
4136 Mrs. Wm. R. Berger *Receiving day Thursday*
4136 Morris Berger
4140 Mr. & Mrs. L. E. Campbell
4144 Mr. & Mrs. E. K. Herrick
4226 Dr. & Mrs. N. C. Kemp
4228 Mr. & Mrs. J. J. Burns
4232 Mr. & Mrs. R. Ettlinger
4240 Mr.& Mrs.James T.Young &dr.
4310 Mr. & Mrs. John W. Paxson
4322 Mr. & Mrs. James Galvin
4400 Mr.& Mrs.John H.Martin & dr.
4400 Wallace R. Martin
4400 Robert P. Martin
4412 Mr. & Mrs. Roswell Z. Herrick
4412 Mrs. N. B. Thurston
4446 Mr. & Mrs. Fred H. Koehsel

INGLESIDE AVENUE.

5309 Mr. & Mrs. John R. Bour

5723 Mr. & Mrs. Charles M. Moore

IONE PLACE.

690 Dr. & Mrs. Twing B. Wiggin

JACKSON AVENUE.

5425 Mr. & Mrs. Edward T. Lincoln
5425 Walter D. Lincoln

5316 Mr. & Mrs. W. R. Rose
     Receiving day Wednesday
5422 Mr. & Mrs. Max May

JACKSON PARK TERRACE.

223 Mr. & Mrs. M. Felsenthal
223 Mrs. A. Wooley & dr.

301 Mr. & Mrs. J. W. Forsinger

JEFFERSON AVENUE.

5031 Mr. & Mrs. Francis J. Schulte
5031 L. F. Armstrong
5039 Mr. & Mrs. Wm. Irvine
5117 Mr. & Mrs. E. H. Noyes
5119 Mr. & Mrs. John B. Lord
5125 Mr. & Mrs. R. J. O. Hunter
5125 Mrs. Robert Hunter
5125 Miss Ethel Hunter
5129 Mrs. J. H. Miles & dr.
5129 Miss Clara B. Miles
5129 Thomas D. Miles
5131 Mr. & Mrs. E. C. Ware
5137 Dr. & Mrs. W. H. Buck
5201 Mr. & Mrs. L. W. Starbird
5201 Beecher E. Starbird
5201 Rupert N. Starbird
5203 Mr. & Mrs. W. H. Jenkins & dr.
5203 Robert M. Jenkins
5221 Mrs. Rowland Longmire & drs.
5223 Dr. & Mrs. B. S. Arnulphy
5225 Mr. & Mrs. T. S. E. Dixon
5229 Mr. & Mrs. James Taylor
5237 William B. Main
5317 Mr. & Mrs. Wm. H. Henkle
5319 Mr. & Mrs. Charles A. Knorr
5321 Mr. & Mrs. Gurden Bingham
5335 Mr. & Mrs. H. N. Hibbard & drs.
5407 Mr. & Mrs. J. H. Stevison & dr.
     Receiving day Thursday
5409 Mr. & Mrs. C. A. Reed & dr.
5409 C. S. Reed
5411 Mr. & Mrs. Jerome B. Wilkinson
5423 Mr. & Mrs. E. E. Abrams
5427 Mr. & Mrs. Wm. Lewis
5467 Mr. & Mrs. W. R. Head & drs.

5000 Mr. & Mrs. Edward Johnson
5012 Mr. & Mrs. E. A. S. Clarke
5016 Mr. & Mrs. C. Harlan Canby
     Receiving day Wednesday
5036 Mr. & Mrs. T. G. Butlin
5036 Mr. & Mrs. Clement L. Eaton
5046 Mr. & Mrs. Noah Barnes
5046 Mr. & Mrs. B. H. Bingham
5104 Mr. & Mrs. Paul Cornell & dr.
5104 George K. Cornell
5104 Mr. & Mrs. Henry C. Speer
5110 Mr. & Mrs. R. G. Clarke
5112 George S. Knapp
5112 Mrs. C. S. Knapp
5112 Miss C. A. Knapp
5112 Miss J. D. Knapp
5112 Charles H. Knapp
5114 Mr. & Mrs. H. W. Hoyt
5120 Mr. & Mrs. Walter C. Nelson
5124 Mr. & Mrs. Byron W. French & dr.
5124 Charles B. French
5146 Mr. & Mrs. W. C. Ott & drs.
5216 Dr. & Mrs. Robt. L. Beaumont
5216 Mr. & Mrs. Lewis Payne
     Receiving day Thursday
5216 Mr. & Mrs. John C. Craft
5218 Mrs. Helen M. Carlile
5218 Mr. & Mrs. A. M. Nichols
5220 Mr. & Mrs. Ben Williams
5222 Mr. & Mrs. Charles L. Krum
5228 Mr. & Mrs F. I. Moulton
5230 Mr. & Mrs. Geo. C. Bailey
5232 Mr. & Mrs. Robert Boyd
5232 Alexander Boyd
5232 William S. Boyd

5467 Richard Head
5467 Paul Head
5471 Mr. & Mrs. Fitzhenry McClure
5471 Mrs. Cornelius K. Martin

5432 Mr. & Mrs. S. H. Stevens & drs.
5432 Russell H. Stevens
5432 S. H. Stevens jr.
5436 Mr. & Mrs. F. W. Wood
5436 Thomas R. Wood
5440 Mr. & Mrs. H. E. R. Wood
5458 Mr. & Mrs. George W. Dexter
5464 Mr. & Mrs. M. L. Beers
5470 Mr. & Mrs. Henry A. Porter
5470 F. D. Porter
5474 Mr. & Mrs. L. A. Parker
5488 Mr. & Mrs. Edward P. Skene
5508 Mr. & Mrs. Frank R. Bagley
5516 Dr. Charles Berrien Hall
5516 Mrs. Amos T. Hall
5516 Mrs. R. T. Bacon
5526 Mr. & Mrs. Geo B. Parkins
5556 Mr. & Mrs. A. V. Daegling

5238 Mrs. Hannah Rosing
5238 Miss Kate Rosing
5316 Mr. & Mrs. W. F. Sargent
5318 Dr. J. Eugene Tremaine
5318 Mr. & Mrs. M. J. Tremaine
5320 Dr. & Mrs. J. Ramsay Flood &
    dr.   *Receiving day Friday*
5320 Samuel D. Flood
5320 Robert D. Flood
5324 Mr. & Mrs. W. H. Richardson
    & dr.
5328 Mr. & Mrs. A. D. Philpot
5330 Mr. & Mrs. W. Fay Tuttle
5330 John A. S. Tuttle
5344 Mr. & Mrs. T. M. Fulton
5400 Mr. & Mrs. Albert Marshall
5400 Mr. & Mrs. J. M. Marshall
5406 Mr. & Mrs. C. Robinson
5406 W. C. Robinson
5406 A. E. Robinson
5406 Mr. & Mrs. C. M. Capen
5410 Dr. & Mrs. C. M. Oughton
5416 Mr. & Mrs. O. M. Powers
5426 Mr. & Mrs. A. G. Mason

KENWOOD AVENUE.

4717 Mr. & Mrs. John Nichol
4719 Mr. & Mrs. L. P. Morehouse
    & dr.
4719 George G. Morehouse
4733 Mr. & Mrs. J. M. Neuburger
4733 John M. Neuburger
4737 Charles T. Lawton
4739 Mr. & Mrs. Chas. B. Whipple
    Receiving day Wednesday
4741 Mr. & Mrs. W. A. Shaw
4741 Godfrey Harold Atkin
4801 Mr. & Mrs. C. Henry Cutler
4815 Mr. & Mrs. J. R. Putnam
    & dr.
4815 Mr. & Mrs. F. S. Wheeler
4827 Mr. & Mrs. Horace K. Tenney
4831 Mrs. E. N. Ludington
4831 Mr. & Mrs. C. H. M. Tobey
4837 Mr. & Mrs. C. H. Tobey
4839 Miss E. M. Tobey

4830 Mr. & Mrs. Chas. E. Matthews
4852 Mr. & Mrs. Warren McArthur
4852 Mrs. Olive E. Weston
4858 Mr. & Mrs. Geo. W. Blossom

4714 Mr. & Mrs. Francis Etheridge
4716 Mr. & Mrs. C. J. Northup
4718 Mr. & Mrs. Geo. H. Cook
4720 Mr. & Mrs. W. A. Green
4720 Mrs. M. E. Hanford
4722 Mr. & Mrs. M. D. Downs jr.
4724 Mr. & Mrs. J. H. Ives
    Receiving day Wednesday
4726 Robert B. De L'Armitage
4726 Mme. Arabella Root De L'Ar-
    mitage
4726 Mr. & Mrs. George E. Arndt
4726 Mrs. Wm. H. King & drs.
4725 Mr. & Mrs. Walter G. Taylor
4726 Miss Mary B. Hill
4730 Mr. & Mrs. J. C. Shand
4744 Mr. & Mrs. Frank Fairman
4748 Mr. & Mrs. Chas. W. Winslow
4756 Mr. & Mrs. William H. Low
4756 Dr. Julia R. Low
4756 Arthur Wray Street
4800 Mrs. Augustus Evans Walker
    & drs.
4810 Mr. & Mrs. John S. Miller
    Receiving day Wednesday
4822 Mr. & Mrs. E. H. Sargent
4822 Mr. & Mrs. Thos. P. Smith jr.

KENWOOD PLACE.

559 Mr. & Mrs. Charles Gross
561 Mr. & Mrs. Jacob Slimmer
569 Mr. & Mrs. Joseph M. Baggot

———

568 Wm. M. McMillan
568 Mr. & Mrs. William Austin
570 Mr. & Mrs. W. W. Bowers
570 Mr. & Mrs. John E. Shields

558 Mrs. C. L. Waldron
558 Henry S. Waldron
558 Mr. & Mrs. Arthur R. Jones
558 Mr. & Mrs. Albert Elwell
560 Mr. & Mrs. Edward H. Hill
560 Mr. & Mrs. Clayton O. Billow
566 Mr. & Mrs. Wm. T. Holly
566 Mr. & Mrs. Edw. L. Burchard
568 Mr. & Mrs. Wm. McMillan &
    dr. *Receiving day Wednesday*

KIMBARK AVENUE.

4711 Mr. & Mrs. L. R. Doty
4711 Wilson K. Doty
4713 Mr. & Mrs. C. M. Armstrong
4717 Mr. & Mrs. Charles P. Parish
4721 Mr. & Mrs. Samuel C. Tobin
4721 Mrs. Rosamond P. Parish
4725 Mr. & Mrs. C. L. Currier
    Receiving day Monday
4725 C. L. Currier jr.
4725 Miss E. B. Currier
4729 Mr. & Mrs. Alex Bishop
4729 Walter H. Bishop
4729 Miss Alice Bowman
4735 Mr. & Mrs. James H. Long
4737 Mr. & Mrs. F. C. Osborn
4747 Mr. & Mrs. W. R. Page & dr.
4747 Ralph Page
4801 Mr. & Mrs. Joseph H. Howard
4805 Mr. & Mrs. J. Finley Barrell
4811 Mr. & Mrs. Willard Wiley
4811 W. R. Wiley
4811 Miss Dorothy Frink
4819 Mr. & Mrs. Frank F. Wood
    Receiving day Tuesday
4819 Chas. W. Hillard
4823 Mr. & Mrs. D. J. Wile
4829 Mrs. L. O. Downs
4829 A. O. Downs
4829 C. S. Downs
4833 Mr. & Mrs. Edw. C. Hale
4847 Mr. & Mrs. E. J. Edwards
4853 Mr. & Mrs. Robert McMurdy
    Receiving day Wednesday
4853 Mr. & Mrs. Maurice F. Harter
4857 Mr. & Mrs. C. E. Woodruff
5101 Dr. & Mrs. John Pilsbury
5101 Miss Beatrice Wilcox
5101 Mr. & Mrs. Robert S. Smith
5101 Mr. & Mrs. Joseph D. Wade
5101 Mr. & Mrs. Walter L. Githens
5101 A. L. Pacaud

4700 Mr. & Mrs. A. Montgomery
    Ward
4714 Mr. & Mrs. Calvin DeWolf
4726 Mr. & Mrs. Geo. R. T. Ward
4730 Mr. & Mrs. H. G. Willard
4734 Mr. & Mrs. Reynolds Fisher
4740 Mr. & Mrs. J. H. Swan
4740 Miss Annie L. Morrison
4744 Mr. & Mrs. R. B. Boak
4752 Mr. & Mrs. W. G. Coolidge & dr.
4752 Winthrop Coolidge
4800 Mr. & Mrs. Geo. W. Stahl
4808 Mr. & Mrs. Nathan Manasse
4812 Mr. & Mrs. Clarence T. Morse
4820 Mr. & Mrs. Platt P. Gibbs
4824 Mr. & Mrs. J. J. Lindman
4826 Mr. & Mrs. H. H. Field
4826 Judson L. Field
4828 Mr. & Mrs. W. F. Parish
4828 W. F. Parish jr.
4828 Harry F. Parish
4830 Mr. & Mrs. A. W. Sullivan
    Receiving day Tuesday
4840 Mr. & Mrs. Chas. F. Listman
4846 Mr. & Mrs. T. W. Letton
4846 Harold Letton
4850 Mr. & Mrs. Norman Carroll
5112 Mr. & Mrs. William Kent
5116 Mr. & Mrs. Julius S. Grinnell
5120 Mr. & Mrs. C. S. Dennis
5126 Mr. & Mrs. E. B. Myers & dr.
    Receiving day Thursday
5132 Mr. & Mrs. Walter C. Hately
    Receiving day Wednesday
5136 Mrs. Henry McKey
5136 Mrs. W. S. Parkhurst
5200 Mrs. Atwood Vane & dr.
5200 Augustus S. Vane
5202 Mr. & Mrs. James Darlow
5206 Mr. & Mrs. Geo. A. Soden
5208 Mrs. Fletcher S. Bassett

5101 A. D. Pacaud
5101 Mr. & Mrs. Chas. G. L. Kelso
5105 Mr. & Mrs. Charles S. Brainard
  Receiving day Tuesday
5105 Miss Mabel Brainard
5107 Mr. & Mrs. Eaton G. Osman
5109 K. V. R. Lansingh & drs.
5109 V. R. Lansingh
5109 Mrs. A. L. Tichenor
5121 Mr. & Mrs. C. E. Conover
  Receiving day Wednesday
5125 Mr. & Mrs. I. K. Boyesen
5125 Miss Austa Boyesen
5137 Mr. & Mrs. Wm. H. Sterling
5141 Dr. & Mrs. C. A. Williams
5207 Mr. & Mrs. A. S. Hopkins
5209 Mr. & Mrs. A. A. Morrill
5211 Mr. & Mrs. George W. Korn
5213 Mr. & Mrs. R. W. Rathborne
5215 Mr. & Mrs. Emil Rudert
5225 Mr. & Mrs. Joseph Fulton
5233 Mr. & Mrs.Edmund F.Schwarz
5235 Mr. & Mrs. James May

5208 Wilbur W. Bassett
5224 Dr. & Mrs. J. E. Hinkins
5226 Mr. & Mrs. Wm. Howe Hess
5226 Robert H. Given jr.
5470 Rev. John J. Carroll
5602 Mr. & Mrs. William Metzger &
  dr.
5602 Charles Metzger
5602 Mrs. F. P. Handtmann
5630 Rev. & Mrs. Thos. W. Goodspeed
5630 Edgar J. Goodspeed
5630 Chas. T. Goodspeed
5630 Stephen Goodspeed
5630 Mrs. Jane Ten Broeke
5700 Dr. & Mrs. Geo. M. Emrick
5722 Mr. & Mrs. David H. Stapp &
  dr.
5734 Mr. & Mrs. V. L. Cunningham
5756 Mr. & Mrs. Wm. A. Pridmore

5733 Mr. & Mrs. F. A. Lorenz

LAFAYETTE AVENUE.

6509 Mrs. C. N. Brisco
  Receiving day Wednesday
6537 Mr. & Mrs. Fred Johnston
6541 J. F. Atwood
6543 Mr. & Mrs. C. F. Baum
6551 Mr. & Mrs. Marvin Judd & drs.
6601 Mr. & Mrs. F. W. Meckes&dr.
6621 Mr. & Mrs. W. J. Black
6637 Mr. & Mrs. Julian Kunc
6639 Mr. & Mrs. W. S. Anderson
  & drs.
6643 Mr. & Mrs. Thos. H. Winters
6701 Mrs. M. E. Drown
6701 Miss Maude White
6701 David White
6705 Mr. & Mrs. W. S. Bielfeldt
6731 Mr. & Mrs. Edw. J. McGowen
6733 Mr. & Mrs. David Moore
  & drs.
6735 Mr. & Mrs. C. D. Armstrong
6801 Mr. & Mrs. H. Eschmeyer

6754 Mr. & Mrs. A. G. Scott
6820 Mr. & Mrs. John Lawrie
6826 Mr. & Mrs. G. W. Rigler
6830 F. D. Hellman
6832 Mr. & Mrs. George W. Wells

6500 Mr. & Mrs. F. C. Vehmeyer
6506 Mr. & Mrs. F. B. Badt
6506 Miss Eleanor O'Donnell
6514 Mr. & Mrs. L. A. Hamlin
6516 George W. Frosch
6522 Mr. & Mrs. F. S. Thompson
6522 D. S. Thompson
6526 Mr. & Mrs. J. N. Eulette
6526 C. H. Eulette
6526 F. I. Eulette
6526 George W. Eulette
6534 Mr. & Mrs. A. T. Whitman
6542 Mr. & Mrs. L. A. Walton
6542 W. S. Woodworth
6544 Mr. & Mrs. J. C. Craig
6550 Rev. & Mrs. Rufus A. White
6600 Mr. & Mrs. Geo. E. Marshall
6602 Mr. & Mrs. F. J. Martin
6618 Mr. & Mrs. T. F. Indermille
  Receiving day Tuesday
6618 W. M. Chase
6618 Frank R. Davis
6620 Mr. & Mrs. John B. Fay
6642 Mr. & Mrs. R. B. Jones
6704 Mrs. J. G. Richardson
6704 Mr. & Mrs. Calvin Smith & dr.
  Receiving day Thursday
6730 Mr. & Mrs. W. L. Sharp

LAKE AVENUE.

3543 Judge & MrsFrank Baker&drs.
 Receiving day Saturday
3601 Mr. & Mrs. Adolph Sutter
3601 Edwin A. Sutter
3603 Mr. & Mrs. Jacob Sutter
3603 Raymond C. Sutter
3603 Clarence B Sutter
3603 Walter C. Sutter
3605 Mrs. A. Burgoyne & drs.
3605 Mr. & Mrs. C. C. Fuller
3605 Miss M. E. Gilman
3605 Frank Gilman
3605 George G. Emerson
3605 H. A. Wise
3605 Harry A. Mead
3605 Louis P. Hoyt
3605 A. L. Millery
3605 Edward Guion
3611 Mrs. Grace Patton
3611 Judge B. F. Friedley
3611 Frank F. Patton
3615 Mr. & Mrs. Edward C. Cleaver
3615 Frederick C. Cleaver
3615 James M. Cleaver
3619 Mr. & Mrs. E. A. Everett
3619 Mrs. W. E. Tascott
3619 Mr. & Mrs. R. A. Wilson
3619 Mr. & Mrs. L. G. Johnson
3623 C. E. Boynton
3709 Mr. & Mrs. Wm. G. Curtis
3727 Robert Rintoul
3751 Mr. & Mrs. Gustav Hiller
3751 Mr. & Mrs. Edward E. Roehl
3755 Mr. & Mrs. J. C. Tucker
3761 Mr. & Mrs. Charles H. Morse
3761 Mr. & Mrs. Fred'k J. Knight
3769 Mr. & Mrs. F. A. Price
3769 Mr. & Mrs. W. M. Hodge
3769 Mr. & Mrs. D. U. Crockett
3769 Dr. & Mrs. W. C. Brinkerhoff
3769 Mr. & Mrs. C. H. Gillespie
3769 Mr. & Mrs. Edmund H. Blair
 & dr. *Receiving day Monday*
3769 Mr. & Mrs. Edwin Raftery
 Receiving day Tuesday
3807 Mr. & Mrs. J. W. Bloom
3807 Miss Lila Baily
3811 Mr. & Mrs. N. B. Boyden & dr.
3811 C. M. Boyden
3815 Mr. & Mrs. T. H. McCoy & drs.
3815 M. Max McCoy
3829 Mr. & Mrs. W. J. Jefferson & dr.
3829 W. T. Jefferson
3829 Ralph J. Jefferson

3506 Dr. & Mrs. John Pischczak
3506 Mrs. C. P. Morgan
3510 Mr. & Mrs. E. S. Eldredge
3510 Charles J. Eldredge
3530 Mr. & Mrs. J. S. Russ
3530 Robert H. Magee
3530 Mr. & Mrs. Frank Drebing
3530 Miss Tina Drebing
3532 Mr. & Mrs. George A. Hyers
3536 Mr. & Mrs. William W. Watkins
3536 A. Beardsley
3538 Mrs. E. E. Spence
3538 J. F. Brookes
3538 Miss Mary J. Brookes
3600 Mr. & Mrs. E. Nusbaum & drs.
 Receive 1st & 3d Mondays
3600 A. E. Nusbaum
3602 Roy D. Johnson
3604 Mr. & Mrs. T. S. Donahue
3604 Mr. & Mrs. H. R. Gillette
3604½ Mrs. N. L. Buckbee
3604½ Walter Buckbee
3606 Mr. & Mrs. Frank J. Crawford
3608 Mrs. S. A. Dutton
3618 Mr. & Mrs. John W. Clover
3618 Mrs. Wm. Boalch
3626 L. Gaston Gottschalk
3630 Mr. & Mrs. L. O. Goddard &
 dr.
3630 Sterling Goddard
3636 Mr. & Mrs. Samuel E. Bliss
3638 Mr. & Mrs. George C. Fry
3640 Mr. & Mrs. Frank E. Johnson
3652 Mr. & Mrs. James B. Galloway
3652 Mr. & Mrs. A. J. Galloway
3652 Mrs. M. G. Fogg
3700 Mr. & Mrs. Daniel E. Root
3700 Chas. H. Foster
3700 Dr. & Mrs. W. Franklin Coleman
3700 Miss Margaret Kinnear
3702 Mrs. W. D. McLain & drs.
3702 William T. McLain
3702 Mr. & Mrs. Waite Bliven
3702 Mr. & Mrs. Vittorio Carpi
3706 Miss E. A. Brown
3706 Miss Lulu Brown
3706 W. F. Brown
3706 Mr. & Mrs. Henry Gilbert
3706 Mrs. C. M. Gould
3706 Mr. & Mrs. Thomas Knapp
3706 Mr. & Mrs. F. Moore
3708 C. H. Blakely
3708 Mr. & Mrs. H. F. Dousman

3829 Mrs. E. Dennis
3831 Mrs. M. Pollard & drs.
    Receiving day Thursday
3835 Mr. & Mrs. Alexander Cook & dr.
3835 Archibald Cook
3849 Mr. & Mrs. Oscar Schleiter
    Receiving day Wednesday
3859 Mr. & Mrs. Robert P. Brown
3861 Mr. & Mrs. C. W. Lobdell
3861 Miss Marion Lobdell
3865 Mr. & Mrs. E. P. Baker & dr.
3877 Mr. & Mrs. H. S. Hayden
3877 Mrs. M. V. Downer
3879 Mr. & Mrs. George Carr
    Receiving day Thursday
3901 Mr. & Mrs. Max Steele & dr.
Receiving days 2d & 4th Thursdays
3935 Mr. & Mrs. C. T. Trego & dr.
3935 Mr. & Mrs. Wm. T. Trego
3935 Frank Trego
3937 Mr. & Mrs. Wm. H. Rand & dr.
3937 Mr. & Mrs. Charles E. Rand
3945 Mr. & Mrs. J. G. McWilliams
    Receiving day Thursday
3945 Mrs. M. L. Pardridge .
3945 Charles R. Lee
3949 John Borden & dr.
3961 Mr. & Mrs. L. McWilliams
3965 Mr. & Mrs. Charles E. Brown
3965 Miss M. Isabella Brown
3965 Miss Bessie B. Brown
3967 Mr. & Mrs. Charles Howe
4035 Mr. & Mrs. C. S. Harmon
4035 Mr. & Mrs. J. W. Harmon
4039 Mr. & Mrs. G.W. Thomas & dr.
4043 Mr. & Mrs. Washington Porter
4049 Mrs. E. C. Sumner
4049 Miss P. Owens
4049 Miss M. L. Hawkins
4053 Mr. & Mrs. J. M. Starbuck
4053 Mr. & Mrs. F. A. Dennison
4053 J. R. Godman
4059 O. P. Curran
4059 Mr. & Mrs. D. B. Curran
4059 Samuel H. Curran
4155 Mr. & Mrs. A. A. Dewey & drs.
4155 Allen A. Dewey
4163 Mr. & Mrs. D. W. Wilkins
4163 Mr. & Mrs. Frank W. Goodman
4163 Mrs. Helen M. Burton
4165 John G. Egan
4201 Mr. & Mrs. D. A. Griffiths
4201 Mr. & Mrs. Thomas Allen
4201 E. M. Gage

10

3716 Mr. & Mrs. Charles H. Wright
3716 Mr. & Mrs. Robert Goldie
3716 Mr. & Mrs. William Goldie jr.
3716 Mr. & Mrs. John Oliver Plank
    Receiving day Thursday
3716 Mrs. Susan Zeller
3716 John O. Plank jr.
3716 Mr. & Mrs. R. P. Walker
3716 Mr. & Mrs. E. S. Heyman
    Receiving day Friday
3716 Mr. & Mrs. Edward A. Fargo
3716 Mrs. R. Feibelman
3716 Dr. & Mrs. D. O. Fruth
3716 Mr. & Mrs. George M. Forman
3716 Mr. & Mrs. R. W. Hamill
3716 Mr. & Mrs. Eli S. Hart
3716 Mr. & Mrs. D. B. Stedman
3716 Capt. E. M. Stedman
3716 Josiah Stedman
3716 E. M. Stedman jr.
3724 Mr. & Mrs. Wm. E. Larned
3730 Mr. & Mrs. F. H. Warren
3732 Mr. & Mrs. A. B. Cook
3736 Mr. & Mrs. Geo. H. Hess & drs.
3752 Mr. & Mrs. Maurice Watkins & dr.
3756 A. B. Jenks
3756 Miss Hattie Lyons
    Receiving day Friday
3756 Charles L. Jenks
3762 Mr. & Mrs. Chester B. Davis
3762 Mr. & Mrs. B. F. Harris
3764 Mr. & Mrs. F. S. Bagg
3766 Mr. & Mrs. Charles H. Engel
    Receiving day Thursday
3802 Strickland Hotel
    Ben Bartlett
    Dr. & Mrs. W. T. Chambers
    E. A. Doolittle
    Mr. & Mrs. H. C. Foster
    Mr. & Mrs. W. H. Habbeler
    Mr. & Mrs. O. C. Jaquith
    Mr. & Mrs. J. F. Jordan & dr.
    Bud Jordan
    Mr. & Mrs. W. C. Luce & dr.
    Mr. & Mrs. James H. Miles
    Mr. & Mrs. D. J. Mugridge
    O. J. Delmarle
    Frank W. Somers
    S. Chapman Sims
    Mr. & Mrs. F. E. Wagner
3820 Mr. & Mrs. Charles C. Ruggles
3830 Mr. & Mrs. Henry J. Thayer
3834 Mrs. M. J. Morgan
3834 Miss Anna Morgan

4201 Mrs. Louise J. Matkin
4201 John I. Matkin
4201 Otho F. Matkin
4203 Mr. & Mrs. T. E. King
4211 Mr. & Mrs. Jas. McDevitt
4211 Mr. & Mrs. Chas. Vories
4211 Harry F. Vories
4219 Mr. & Mrs. J. K. Seifert
4221 Mr. & Mrs. Oliver S. Ross
4223 Mr. & Mrs. E. G. Simms & dr.
4319 Mr. & Mrs. B. Billings
4319 Mrs. Jennie Pursell
4319 Dr. E. J. George
4321 Mr. & Mrs. Oscar F. Schmidt
4321 Mr. & Mrs. D. L. Taylor
4323 Mr. & Mrs. E. F. Lapham
4327 Mr. & Mrs. J. P. Haire & drs.
4329 Dr. & Mrs. Edwin H. Dorland
      Receive Friday evening
4333 Mr. & Mrs. D. J. Canary
4333 Robert D. Carter
4333 Charles B. Carter
4333 Henry W. Carter
4335 C. J. Knight & dr.
4335 Samuel Knight
4337 Mr. & Mrs. John W. Skeele
4359 Mr. & Mrs. Frederick K. Paris
4343 Mr. & Mrs. E. H. Tharp
4345 Mr. & Mrs. William S. Adams
4349 Mr. & Mrs. C. H. Blackman
      Receiving day Friday
4351 Mr. & Mrs. A. I. Valentine
4351 P. A. Valentine
4351 Mrs. A. J. Valentine
4357 Mr. & Mrs. E. H. Lewis
4359 Mr. & Mrs. Jas. S. McConnell
4359 Mr. & Mrs. E. P. McConnell
4359 Mrs. E. W. Pike
4363 Mrs. E. L. Browne & dr.
4363 Mr. & Mrs. H. A. C. Mathew
4365 Mr.& Mrs. James Allison & drs.
4367 Dr. & Mrs. Calvin S. Case
4403 Mr. & Mrs. Lewis T. Moore
4405 Mr. & Mrs. Robert C. Moore
4407 Mr. & Mrs. T. H. Smith
4407 Miss Ellen C. Smith
4411 Mr. & Mrs. Joseph Spies & dr.
4415 Mr. &Mrs.H.H.Chandler&drs.
      Receiving day Wednesday
4415 Edwin W. Chandler
4417 Samuel G. Hair & drs.
4417 Mrs. E. S. Hair
4417 Mrs. Margaret McHatton
4427 Mr. & Mrs. W. W. Dudley
4429 Mr. & Mrs. E. P. Fassett
4433 Mr. & Mrs. John D. Sherman

3834 Mrs. Addison J. Trunkey
3838 Mr.& Mrs.JonathanC. Mitchell
3844 Mr. & Mrs. L. Hiller
3844 Martin Frank
3846 Mrs. S. B. Packard
3846 Miss Madge Myers
3848 Mrs. James McArthur & dr.
3848 Rev. Augusta J. Chapin
3850 Mr. & Mrs. B. S. White
3852 Mr. & Mrs. John A. Baldwin
3852 Mrs. John Baldwin
3852 Harry H. Baldwin
3854 Mr. & Mrs. Thomas B. Smith
3856 Mr. & Mrs. John T. Shayne
3856 Ray M. Shayne
3860 Mr. & Mrs. Spoor Mackey
3866 Mr. & Mrs. Jacob Mayer
3866 Mr. & Mrs. G. R. French
3870 Ransom W. Dunham
3900 Mr. & Mrs. J. L. McKeever
3900 Buell McKeever
3902 Mr. & Mrs. H. J. Page
      Receiving day Monday
3902 Mr. & Mrs. E. C. Page
3906 Mr. & Mrs. Edward J. Phelps
3916 J. P. Hoit & dr.
3916 Charles S. Hoit
3918 Mr. & Mrs. J. S. Ford
3918 Mrs. Rita E. Ford
3920 Mrs. Wm. G. Wilson
3936 Mr. & Mrs. Simon Steiniger
3938 Mr. & Mrs. W. S. Rothschild
      Receiving day Thursday
3940 Mr. & Mrs. J. H. Conrad
3940 Charles H. Conrad
3942 Mr. & Mrs. W. H. Rogers
3942 Mr. & Mrs. E. B. Greenleaf
3946 W. H. Forrest
3978 Mrs. Henry Provost
3978 Mr. & Mrs. J. W. Maxwell
3980 Mr. & Mrs. E. E. Maxwell
3982 Mr. & Mrs. Calvin S. Smith
3984 Mr. & Mrs. Wm. A. Merigold
      & dr.
4008 Mr. & Mrs. Lyman Trumbull
4008 Henry Trumbull
4008 Mrs. Walter Trumbull
4016 Mrs. George Trumbull
4016 Mr. & Mrs. J. P. Underwood
4026 Mr. & Mrs. J. H. Trumbull
4028 Mr. & Mrs. Godfrey H. Ball
4030 Mr. & Mrs. John Clay
      Receive Friday
4030 Mr. & Mrs. John Clay jr.
4030 Charles H. Dalgleish
4058 Mr. & Mrs. W. J. Lavery

4435 Mr. & Mrs. O. H. Brooks
4439 Mr. & Mrs. G.W. Prickett & dr.
4449 Mr. & Mrs. Alexander F. Greig
4449 Miss Mabelle Lucille Greig
4461 Mr. & Mrs. W. D. Oliver
4463 Mr. & Mrs. G. W. Traer
4465 Mr. & Mrs. W. W. Young
4465 Thomas Clements
4467 Dr. & Mrs. H. G. Wildman
  Receiving day Thursday
4469 Mr. & Mrs. William Blair
4471 Mr. & Mrs. C. F. Love
  Receiving day Wednesday
4507 Dr. & Mrs. A. J. Roe
4507 Charles Roe
4507 Edward Roe
4507 Mr. & Mrs. Geo. Merrill Doe &
  dr.
4507 Ormand P. Doe
4507 George H. Baird
4515 Mr. & Mrs. C. H. Smith
4515 Fred A. B. Smith
4519 Mr. & Mrs. W. A. Pfaff
4519 John L. Pfaff
4523 John Herson
4533 Mr. & Mrs. Joseph Gregg & dr.
4535 Mr. & Mrs. S. D. Hathaway &
  drs.
4535 Stephen J. Hathaway
4537 Mr. & Mrs. C. W. Wells
4539 J. Dunlap & dr.
4539 Mrs. Minerva Ross & dr.
4539 William J. Ross
4541 Mr. & Mrs. W. B. Biddle
4545 Mr. & Mrs. J. E. Hopkins
4545 Charles Hopkins
4545 Robert Hopkins
4547 Mr. & Mrs. J. M. McGill & dr.
4547 Miss Mary Irwin
4557 Mr. & Mrs. H. A. Callan
4559 Mr. & Mrs. J. Arnold Brecher
  & dr.
  Receiving day Wednesday
4559 Emanuel A. Brecher
4561 Mr. & Mrs. Edward P. Buchanan
4561 Mr. & Mrs. Bernard Fowler
4561 Miss Harriet Fowler
4561 Miss Martha Fowler
4561 Miss Blanche Fowler
4565 Mrs. M. E. Dean
4565 Miss Adelaide Leckie
4567 Mr. & Mrs. C. M. Bragg
4569 Mrs. Henry Rogers
4569 Mr. & Mrs. D. W. Buchanan
4571 Dr. & Mrs. Edward F. Wells

4060 Mr. & Mrs. H. Solomon
  Receiving day 1st & 3d Thursdays
4060 Mrs. F. Peyser
4062 Mr. & Mrs. J. N. Eisendrath
  Receiving day Wednesday
4066 Mr. & Mrs. A. Silberman
  Receiving day Wednesday
4068 Mr. & Mrs. James P. Barrett
4068 Louis Barrett
4070 Mr. & Mrs. Lucien H. Green
4072 Mr. & Mrs. Thos. C. Goodman
4074 Mr. & Mrs. H. Lamberton
4076 Mrs. I. P. Gibson & dr.
4076 G. G. Gibson
4100 Rev. & Mrs. Peter Wallace
4102 Mr. & Mrs. S. M. Pray
4106 Mr. & Mrs. Walter E. Miller
4108 J. C. Cox
4108 Mrs. S. J. Wardner
4118 Mr. & Mrs. Samuel Dally & drs.
4118 A. Harry Dally
4120 Mr. & Mrs. J. C. Ellis & dr.
4120 William Ellis
4126 Mr. & Mrs. Abner Strawn
4126 Mr. & Mrs. C. C. Foord
4126 Silas H. Strawn
4126 Alf. M. Shaw
4130 Mr. & Mrs. Wm. H. Reed
  Receiving day Friday
4130 Chester B. Reed
4132 Mr. & Mrs. Edwin D. Scott
4132 Mrs. Maria B. Scott
4132 William H. Scott
4140 Mr. & Mrs. C. R. Rothwell
4142 Mr. & Mrs. H. E. Dick
  Receiving day Wednesday
4150 Mr. & Mrs. Adolph Jacobs
4150 Mr. & Mrs. Louis Sincere
4152 Mr. & Mrs. Charles Frink
4154 Mr. & Mrs. H. T. Scranton
4154 J. T. Plumsted
4156 Mr. & Mrs. A. J. Wampler
4158 Mr. & Mrs. George H. Reynolds
4160 Mr. & Mrs. C. H. Brittan
4162 Mr. & Mrs. L. M. French
4164 Mrs. F. R. Stevens & dr.
4204 George W. Davis
4304 Dr. S. C. Plummer
4306 Mr. & Mrs. Frank H. Brown
4320 Mr. & Mrs. John E. Cowles &
  dr.
4340 W. H. Chappell & dr.
4400 Mr. & Mrs. Wm. M. Wright
  Receiving day Thursday
4400 Warren Wright
4402 Mr. & Mrs. F. P. Stone

4571 Michael B. Wells
4573 Mr. & Mrs. I. Giles Lewis
4573 Louis H. Sullivan
4577 Dr. Kate E. MacRae
4577 Norman MacRae
4619 Mrs. L. W Frost & dr.
4619 Mrs. H. W. Harmon
4621 Mr. & Mrs. Chas. L. McMahon
4625 A. Thomas
4625 Miss Harriet E. Thomas
4625 Mr. & Mrs. James Linden
4627 Mr. & Mrs. G. P. Titus
　　Receiving day Tuesday
4627 James M. Stryker
4627 Mrs. E. M. Stryker & dr.
4627 Mrs. M. J. Miller & dr.
4627 Mrs. M. W. Brooks
4643 Dr. & Mrs. A. Brooks & drs.
　　Receiving day Monday
4643 Dr. Frank Brooks
4665 Mr. & Mrs. Wm. W. Hunter
4669 Mr. & Mrs. Hiero B. Herr & dr.
4669 Mr. & Mrs. Percy B. Herr & dr.
4669 Percy Herr
4725 Miss M. A. Walsh
4735 Mr. & Mrs. H. C. Fisher
4735 Miss Josie Anderson
4737 Mr. & Mrs. J. J. Parker
4737 Mrs. A. F. Parker
4737 J. J. Parker jr.
4747 Mr. & Mrs. Charles P. Packer
4747 Mr. & Mrs. Wm. F. Carroll
4801 John Lane
4801 George C. Wilson
4805 Mr. & Mrs. Joseph G. Parkinson
4811 Warren G. Purdy & drs.
4811 Miss Sarah E. Purdy
4811 W. Fred Purdy
4815 Mr. & Mrs. O. W. Norton
4815 Miss Ida M. Lane
4827 Mrs. E. Remmer & dr.
4835 Mr. & Mrs. Chas. T. Atkinson
4853 Mr. & Mrs. B. R. Wells
4853 Miss Louise Wells
4861 Mr. & Mrs. C. W. Clingman
4901 Mr. & Mrs. J. T. Nicholson
4901 W. A. Nicholson
4905 Mr. & Mrs. E. C. Long & dr.
4919 J. E. L. Frasher
4919 John S. Frasher
4919 Mr. & Mrs. Wm. R. Gwinn
4923 Mr. & Mrs. Geo. W. Little
4939 Miss N. A. Wait
4939 Miss Isabella Wait
4945 Mr. & Mrs. F. W. Norwood & dr.
　　Receiving day Thursday

4402 Dr. & Mrs. J. W. Hanson
4408 Mr. & Mrs. G. M. Schmidt
4412 Mr. & Mrs. S. P. Douthart
　　Receiving day Tuesday
4422 Mr. & Mrs. George Wright
4422 Frank G. Wright
4424 F. W. Douglas
4424 Miss Alice Douglas
4426 Dr. & Mrs. Henry F. Lewis
4432 Mrs. T. S. Wright
4432 Mr. & Mrs. W. H. Merritt
4434 Mr. & Mrs. A. J. Toolen
　　Receiving day Wednesday
4438 Mr. & Mrs. A. S. Berry & drs.
　　Receiving day Friday
4438 F. C. Berry
4440 Mr. & Mrs. H. B. Evans
4440 Miss Linnie M. Jellison
4440 W. W. Harless
4440 C. D. Harless
4500 Mr. & Mrs. Henry S. Downe
4504 Mrs. A. Otis & drs.
4508 Mr. & Mrs. Thomas G. Otis & dr.
4514 Rev. & Mrs. Conrad Haney
4516 Mr. & Mrs. A. B. Farwell
4520 Mr. & Mrs. James N. Steele &
　　drs.
4524 H. T. Willson
4524 C. C. Willson
4522 Walter Hudnall
4524 Edgar Patterson
4524 Mrs. M. A. Carlin
4524 Miss Dell Fulton
4526 Mr. & Mrs. Courtlandt Bab-
　　cock *Receiving day Friday*
4526 Miss Emily R. Babcock
4526 Miss Lillian Babcock
4526 Dr. T. Melville Hardie
4528 Mr. & Mrs. George H. Bliss &
　　dr.
4528 Julian P. Bliss
4528 Mrs. James S. Dickinson &
　　dr.
4530 Mr. & Mrs. F. H. Foote
4532 Mr. & Mrs. L. K. Scofield & dr.
4532 Mrs. A. L. Morse
4534 Mr. & Mrs. James B. Fraley
4536 Mr. & Mrs. Francis E. Rew
4536 George C. Rew
4536 Miss Frances Rew
4538 Mr. & Mrs. H. N. Jackson
4540 Mr. & Mrs. Alexander Ber-
　　gevin
4542 Mr. & Mrs. J. H. Wheeler
4542 Mrs. F. C. Greene
4544 Mr. & Mrs. I. V. Mettler

4945 Mrs. Vina N. Jones
4965 Mr. & Mrs. J.L. VanUxem & dr.
  Receiving day Friday
4969 Mr. & Mrs. John J. Silberhorn
5001 Mrs. Emily W. Butts
5001 Miss Kathryn Butts
5001 Miss Annie E. Butts
5001 Miss Cynthia L. Stone
5001 Miss Elizabeth Schmidt
5025 Mr. & Mrs. W. H. H. Peirce
5027 Mr. & Mrs. C. N. Holmes
5029 Mr. & Mrs. George G. Standart & dr.
5035 Mr. & Mrs. C. E. Gifford jr.
5037 Mr. & Mrs. J. H. Rhodes
5039 Mr. & Mrs. Frank Douglas
5039 Frank L. Douglas
5039 Mr. & Mrs. A. J. Smith
5039 Miss Mary Calkins
5067 Mr. & Mrs. Edward F. Carry
  Receiving day Monday
5069 Mr. & Mrs. J. R. Hoagland
5101 Mr. & Mrs. W. S. Noyes

4808 Mr. & Mrs. Everett M. Warren
4808 William C. Warren
4808 Miss K. J. McMullen
4812 Mr. & Mrs. S. H. Wright
4818 Mr. & Mrs. Julius Steele
  Receiving day Tuesday
4822 Mr. & Mrs. W. H. Drake
4824 Mr. & Mrs. Arthur G. Jones
4824 Tappan Halsey
4830 Mr. & Mrs. A. S. White
4926 Rev. & Mrs. C. H. Bixby & drs.
  Receiving day Wednesday

4544 Dr. L. Harrison Mettler
4546 Mr. & Mrs. Luther C. Marley
4548 Mrs. A. E. Brandt
4548 Mr. & Mrs. Henry E. Lowe & dr.
4550 Mr. & Mrs. J. A. Coleman & drs.
4552 Mr. & Mrs. James Fanning
  Latham
4558 Mr. & Mrs. Edward S. Blackall
4608 Dr. Philo L. Holland
4614 Mr. & Mrs. W. K. Ackerman
4634 Mr. & Mrs. Penoyer L. Sherman
4634 Lucius B. Sherman
4634 Penoyer L. Sherman jr.
4634 Samuel Sherman
4634 Roger Sherman
4670 Dr. & Mrs. C. M. Prentice
  Receiving day Wednesday
4736 Mr. & Mrs. Wm. E. Spencer &
  dr.
4736 Mrs. Wm. B. Pierce
4738 Mrs. M. M. Whitney & dr.
4744 Mrs. Carl Dreier
4756 Mr. & Mrs. J. T. Robison
4758 Mr. & Mrs. E. H. Reed
4762 Mr. & Mrs. Geo. M. Hord
  Receiving day Tuesday
4762 Charles S. Hord
4762 Miss Lillian Hord
4762 Allen D. Ives
4762 Jewett Wilcox
4800 Mrs. F. S. Rowe
4800 Edward R. Shaw
4802 Mr. & Mr. John C. Irwin
4802 Henry L. Irwin
4802 Edward A. Irwin

LAKE PARK AVENUE.

2924 J. I. Kopperl
2930 Dr. & Mrs. G. S. Thomas
2930 Dr. Mary W. Thomas
2930 Dr. Richard U. Piper
2930 Miss H. B. Wright
2932 Dr. & Mrs. Joseph Zeisler
  Receiving day Wednesday
2940 Mr. & Mrs. Charles Kinsman
2968 Mr. & Mrs. O. S. Lyford
2968 Oliver Lyford
2968 Miss Laura A. Thyng
3000 Mr. & Mrs. Morris Beifield
3002 Mrs. Emma Milbury
3002 Philip Potter
3008 Mr. & Mrs. A. W. Fellows &
  dr.
3008 Alfred Fellows

3010 Mr. & Mrs. F. W. S. Brawley
3010 Charles F. Haynes
3014 Mr. & Mrs. Geo. A. Hamilton
3024 Mr. & Mrs. J. R. Kester
  Receiving day Wednesday
3024 Mr. & Mrs. John D. Furlong
3026 Mr. & Mrs. August M. Schilling
3028 Mr. & Mrs. C. D. Otis
3028 Henry B. Otis
3028 Mr. & Mrs. Otto Lang
3030 Mrs. M. Dubois
3030 Henry Baldwin
3036 Mr. & Mrs. Joseph Ruff & dr.
3038 Mr. & Mrs. Charles Eppinghou-
  sen & dr.
3042 Mr. & Mrs. Gilbert Simonds & dr.
3046 Mr. & Mrs. Victor Erich

3046 Miss Johanna Erich
3050 Mrs. Margaret E. Horton & drs.
3116 Louis E. Winchell
3136 Mrs. J. V. D. Wright
3136 William V. D. Wright
3136 F. K. Dunn
3138 Mr. & Mrs. Thomas Bennett
3138 James Bennett
3140 Mr. & Mrs. E. P. Bailey
3142 Mr. & Mrs. A. W. Mitchell & dr.
3142 A. W. Mitchell jr.
3142 Mr. & Mrs. David C. Mitchell
3146 Mr. & Mrs. Fletcher W. Rockwell
3150 Mr. & Mrs. Alfred Ennis & drs.
   Receiving day Wednesday
3154 Mr. & Mrs. F. G. Whiting
3158 Mr. & Mrs. O. Reynolds
3158 Mr. & Mrs. Joseph H. Troyer
   Receiving day Monday
3160 Mr. & Mrs. J. M. Martin
3162 Mrs. Ellen Quinlan
3164 Mr. & Mrs. Granville Gross
3166 Mr. & Mrs. F. P. Gerow & dr.
3200 Mr. & Mrs. C. A. Beck
3200 Raymond A. Beck
3200 Burt A. Beck

3208 Mr. & Mrs. Edward A.Packard
   Receiving day Wednesday
3208 John Wheeler
3210 Dr. & Mrs. Franklin H. Martin
3216 Mr.& Mrs.J.Frederick Wallach
3220 Dr. & Mrs. Thos. L. Gilmer
3222 Mrs. Geo. B. Carpenter & dr.
   Receiving day Wednesday
3224 Mr. & Mrs. C. B. Evans
3226 Mr. & Mrs. William C. Ervin
   Receiving day Wednesday
3228 Mr. & Mrs. Robert B. Miller
   Receiving day Thursday
3230 Mr. & Mrs. John C. Cantner
3232 Mr. & Mrs. J. W. D. Kelley
3232 Miss Annie S. Kelley
3232 J. Frank Kelley
3232 W. D. Kelley
3236 Mr. & Mrs. B. W. Phillips
3240 Mr. & Mrs. Wm. T. Hughes & drs.
3240 E. J. Hughes
3242 Mr. & Mrs. G. W. Borland
3244 Mr. & Mrs. J. C. Pennoyer
3246 Mr. & Mrs. Julius Schnering
3246 Miss Julia Curtis
3266 Mr. & Mrs. C. P. Dewey
3266 Fred L. Jewett
3266 Harry M. Jewett

LANGLEY AVENUE.

3715 Mr. & Mrs. John H. Parr
3717 Mr. & Mrs. C. L. Miller
3719 Mr. & Mrs. Jacob Beiersdorf
3719 Arthur Beiersdorf
3725 Mr. & Mrs. D. Levi
3727 Mr. & Mrs. David Robinson & drs.
3731 Mr.& Mrs. Chas. A.Hasbrouck
3731 Mrs. G. Douglas Johnson
3731 Mrs. T. K. Watson
3733 Mr. & Mrs. Henry L. Miller
3743 Mr. & Mrs. Geo. Green
3743 Miss Lilian Randolph
3745 Mr. & Mrs. Albert Felsenthal
3747 Mr. & Mrs. A. M. Finney
3747 Mrs. E. M. Finney
3747 Elmer E. Finney
3747 Mrs. Mary H. Ford
3751 Mr. & Mrs. George M. Porter & dr.
3751 Wilfred L. Porter
3801 Mr. & Mrs. T. M. Caliger & dr.
3801 T. D. Caliger
3803 Mr. & Mrs. Ezra S. Bodge

3708 Mr. & Mrs. Charles B. Simons
3714 Mr. & Mrs. C. E. Sweep
3716 Peter Daggy
3716 Mr. & Mrs. J. J. Daggy
3724 Mr. & Mrs. Richard M. Gardner
3724 George Cadogan Gardner
3726 Mr. & Mrs. John F. Thompson & dr.
3728 Mrs. E. Murray & dr.
3730 Mr.& Mrs. A. Livingston & drs.
3730 Samuel Livingston
3730 Emanuel Livingston
3730 Milton Livingston
3730 G. Livingston
3732 Mr. & Mrs. A. Moses
3732 Mrs. E. Levy
3736 Mr. & Mrs. John Wade & dr.
3738 Mr. & Mrs. James Irvin
3738 Charles Allen Bourne
3738 Mrs. E. M. Bourne
3740 Mr. & Mrs. Bernhart Simon
3748 Dr. & Mrs. Edgar M. Reading
3750 Mrs. Edgar Reading

3805 Mr. & Mrs. W. T. Burgess
3805 Miss Jennette E. Paul
3807 Mr. & Mrs. F. A. Johnson
3809 Mr.&Mrs. Henry C. Noyes&dr.
3811 Mr. & Mrs. Isaac Degen & dr.
3813 Mrs. Addison H. Storer
3813 Mr. & Mrs. George B. Storer
3813 Rex S. Storer
3815 Mr. & Mrs. Raymond Gregg & dr.
3819 Mr. & Mrs. R. Forman & dr.
3829 Mr. & Mrs. R. Metcalf
3843 Mr. & Mrs. Ed. T. Lloyd & dr.
3845 Mr. & Mrs. H. L. Kochersperger
3847 Mr. & Mrs. Wm. A. Buttolph
3847 Mrs. Mary B. Russell
3915 Mr. & Mrs. Charles L. Munger
3917 E. S. Skillen
3917 Mrs. E. C. Howland
3917 E. A. Howland
3921 Mr. & Mrs. B. R. Nickerson
3921 Mrs. W. W. Dickson
3939 Rev.& Mrs. Jenkin Lloyd Jones
3943 Miss Lulu Frame
3943 Dr. Robert Dodds
3943 Dr. Jessie B. Dodds
3943 Mr. &Mrs. Harry Benedict
4139 Mr. & Mrs. A. J. Vaughan
4145 Luther Smith
4145 Mrs. J. L. Day
4145 Henry P. Heyzer
4147 Mrs. W. W. Day
4147 Mr. & Mrs. Frank H. Roberts
4149 Mr. & Mrs. F. A. Gregory
4149 F. A. Gregory jr.
4153 Frank H. Morice
4153 Mr. & Mrs. F. B. Lawson
4157 Mr. & Mrs. A. Pardridge
4207 Mr. & Mrs. E. Loeb
4215 Mr. & Mrs. Chas. E. Gregory
4215 Mr. & Mrs. A. P. Farrington
4223 Mrs. Amy B. Sheldon & dr.
4223 Oliver R. Stratton
4311 Mrs. S. B. Davis
4313 Mrs. Charlotte Trude
4313 Dr. Frank M. Trude
4313 Mark W. Trude
4313 Dr. & Mrs. Albert S. Core
4331 Mr. & Mrs. W. S. Hefferan
4333 George W. Becker
4333 Mrs. M. A. Becker
4333 Mrs. Kate C. Buddendorff
4335 Mr.&Mrs.Jacob Richman&drs
4443 Mr. & Mrs. R. H. Ismon
4445 Mr. & Mrs. C. W. Hodges

3750 Miss H. E. Coolidge
3806 Dr. Melancthon Stout
3810 Mr. & Mrs. Walter H. Lum
3810 Mrs. Mary H. Lum
3818 Mr. & Mrs. John Greig & dr.
3822 Dr.&Mrs. A.E. Matteson &drs.
3822 Dr. Murray G. Matteson
3824 Mr. & Mrs. B. H. Cohn
3826 Mr. & Mrs. Louis Newton
3832 Mr. & Mrs. George Bensley
3834 Mr. & Mrs. P. F. Wolff & dr.
3840 Charles E. Starr
3840 Mrs. Mary Starr & dr.
3840 Robert Starr
3844 Mr. & Mrs. P. R. Chandler
3848 Samuel T. Alexander
3910 Frederick W. Hill
3910 Mrs. James M. Hill & drs.
3918 Mr. & Mrs. Charles M. Day
3918 Charles C. Day
3922 Mr. & Mrs. Herbert E. Cleaver
3924 Mrs. S. H. Sieg
3924 Miss Emily L. Sieg
3924 D. E. Groesbeck
3926 Joshua W. Carr & drs.
3926 Albert J. Carr
3958 Mr. & Mrs. Chas. F. Robinson
3958 Mr. & Mrs. G. Tafel
3958 Rev. & Mrs. Matthew Clarke
3960 Mr. & Mrs. Frank W. Miller
3960 Mr. & Mrs. Albert J. Henry
3960 William J. Henry
3962 Mrs. D. E. Lindsay
3962 Miss Clair Austin
3962 Mr. & Mrs. B. F. Monroe
3966 Mr. & Mrs. G. E. Rood & dr.
3968 Mr. & Mrs. John Clemenger
4200 Mr. & Mrs. George A. Hook
4206 Dr. C. E. Bentley
4210 Mr. & Mrs. John Roberts
4224 Mr. & Mrs. Lyman M. Paine
4232 Harry A. Cronin
4242 Julian W. Mack
4250 Mr. & Mrs. A. C. Speed
4314 Mr. & Mrs. D. B. Woodbury
4316 Mr. & Mrs. Wm. E. Dewey
4316 Mr.& Mrs. Daniel W. Williams
4320 Mr. & Mrs. H. W. Christian
4326 Dr.&Mrs. Chas. F. Waterhouse
4328 Mr. & Mrs. H. C. Munch
4342 Mr. & Mrs. Richard Melcher
4346 Mr. & Mrs. Henry B. Wilson
4346 Mrs. Agnes Irons & dr.
4406 Frank G. McCracken
4406 Mrs. Margaret McCracken
4410 Mr. & Mrs. E. T. Pearce

4447 Mrs. Kate Stuart
4449 John Morava
4617 Dr. & Mrs. Lewis S. Eastlake
4715 Mr. & Mrs. Nathan Burwell
4719 Mr. & Mrs. Fred'k U. Haines
4721 Mr. & Mrs. J. J. Rust
4721 Mr. & Mrs. C. F. Silvester
4721 Mr. & Mrs. Maxwell M. Jones
4721 Mr. & Mrs. Charles T. Sisloff
4727 Mr. & Mrs. Frazier W. Hurl-
       burt & dr.
4727 Mr. & Mrs. Charles E. Lund
4727 Harry O. Day
4727 Mr. & Mrs. Louis E. Bloch
4729 Mrs. A. G. Heitman
4729 Mr. & Mrs. J. P. Ferre
       Receiving day Thursday
4729 Mr. & Mrs. Nelson Fortin
4743 Mr. & Mrs. A. W. Kitchin
4743 Mr. & Mrs. Vernon W. Behel
4743 Mr. & Mrs. Frank Dart
4811 Edwin B. Jennings
4811 Mrs. A. E. Jennings
4819 Miss Bessie Ayers
4823 Mr. & Mrs. David Sullivan
4823 Edward B. Healy
4831 Mr. & Mrs. B. C. Payne
4833 Mr. & Mrs. T. C. Mosely & dr.
4833 George H. Mosely
4835 Mr. & Mrs. A. E. Frost
4835 Mrs. S. E. Hand
4835 Oliver H. Hand

4820 Harrison F. Howard
4822 Mr. & Mrs. August D'Ancona
4826 Mr. & Mrs. Israel Altman
4830 Mr. & Mrs. A. D. Jones
4830 B. W. Jones
4832 Mr. & Mrs. L. C. Springer & dr.
4834 Mr. & Mrs. L. Connart & drs.
4836 Mr. & Mrs. Newton Hatch
4840 Mr. & Mrs. J. Hafner
4840 Mrs. A. W. Fitch
4840 Mrs. Sarah Bonnell
4844 Mr. & Mrs. Henry J. Lange
4846 Mr. & Mrs. William Craig
4850 Mr. & Mrs. Henry F. Elliott &
       drs.

4410 Ray A. Pearce
4410 Mr. & Mrs. Wm. W. Richardson
4414 Mr. & Mrs. M. Foster & drs.
4416 Mr. & Mrs. S. Wolfe
4418 Mr. & Mrs. E. V. Wendell
4420 T. A. Gehrmann
4420 Dr. Adolph A. Gehrmann
4432 H. E. Wilson
4432 Mr. & Mrs. George Wilson & dr.
4444 Mr. & Mrs. John W. Betts
4444 Isaac S. Lederer
4450 Mrs. E. A. Dorcey & drs.
4450 Charles H. Dorcey
4450 Frank E. Dorcey
4714 Mr. & Mrs. W. T. Rankin
4716 Mr. & Mrs. H. D. Bogardus
4716 Harry Bogardus
4716 Charles Bogardus
4718 Mr. & Mrs. S. L. Bailey & dr.
4726 Mr. & Mrs. R. Watts
4726 George C. Watts
4728 Mr. & Mrs. E. C. Murphy
4734 Mr. & Mrs. R. H. Middleton
4734 R. J. Middleton
4736 Mr. & Mrs. A. H. Lund
4736 H. W. Hale
4740 Mr. & Mrs. H. R. Ford
4742 Mrs. H. Ford
4742 Mr. & Mrs. Edmund H. Stevens
4744 Mr. & Mrs. L. C. Ball
4744 S. Willis Ball
4744 Charles T. Ball
4750 Mr. & Mrs. E. W. Ruhe
4752 Mr. & Mrs. J. W. Stevens
4752 C. N. Stevens
4754 Mr. & Mrs. E. C. Powell
       Receiving day Tuesday
4758 Dr. & Mrs. John E. Walsh
cor. 48th Mr. & Mrs. D. M. McKindley
4808 Mr. & Mrs. Henry Bonn
       Receiving day Friday
4808 Miss Emma Bonn
4808 Henry Bonn jr.
4808 Wm. Bonn
4816 Mr. & Mrs. Frederick L. Wiley
4816 Mrs. Alvira Gilman
4820 Dr. & Mrs. John A. McGaughey
4820 Mrs. Matilda C. Howard

LANGLEY PLACE.

5 Mr. & Mrs. Fred H. Brown
5 Mrs. T. B. Brown
9 Mr. & Mrs. George Bell

6 Miss Mary E. Gale

4 Mr. & Mrs. J. E. Perryman
4 Mr. & Mrs. H. S. Park
4 Dr. & Mrs. Wm. J. Laurence
6 Mr. & Mrs. S. K. Jackson
6 Mr. & Mrs. Marmaduke Bates
6 Mr. & Mrs. Robert Crothers

LEXINGTON AVENUE.

5127 Mr. & Mrs. M. W. Nichols
5137 Mr. & Mrs. L. P. Bauer
5247 R. P. Smith & drs.
5247 Jacob B. Smith
5247 L. K. Smith
5307 Mr. & Mrs. Geo. P. Barton
5307 Mrs. James Wood
5471 Mr. & Mrs. Chas. E. McDowell
5471 Mr. & Mrs. F. Berriozabel
5479 Dr. & Mrs. Julius Stieglitz
5535 Rev. & Mrs. Charles E. Hewitt & dr.
5535 Henry Harwood Hewitt
5535 Herbert E. Hewitt
5551 Rev. & Mrs. John R. Effinger
5551 John R. Effinger jr.
5551 H. Gerard Effinger
6221 Mr. & Mrs. Wm. F. Hobbs
6317 Mr. & Mrs. James Wadsworth
6335 Mr. & Mrs. D. B. Fairman
6351 Mr. & Mrs. J. H. Standring
6351 Frank C. Standring
6351 Thomas J. Standring
6351 Walter Standring
6361 Mrs. Cyrus S. Wilcox

5142 Mr. & Mrs. J. C. Robinson
5212 Mr. & Mrs. Pliny F. Munger
5222 J. P. Smith
5244 Mr. & Mrs. J. A. Edwards
5300 Mr. & Mrs. D. F. Burke
5316 Mr. & Mrs. Granville M. Holt
5326 Mr. & Mrs. James S. Casey
6156 H. L. Barnet
6156 Mr. & Mrs. Henry L. Barnet jr.
6156 Miss Annie Barnet
6246 Mrs. M. J. Whitney & dr.
6348 Mr. & Mrs. E. T. Nicholas
6354 Mr. & Mrs. Wm. H. Leonard
6400 W. S. James
6454 Mr. & Mrs. Thos. H. Mitchell
6506 Mr. & Mrs. Charles J. Bour
6510 Mr. & Mrs. Geo. J. M. Porter
6520 Mr. & Mrs. John M. Storrow
6528 Mr. & Mrs. John Boller
6528 Claude B. Boller
6600 Mr. & Mrs. George S. English

———

6415 Mr. & Mrs. Walter R. B. Lewis
6415 Albert W. Lewis
6421 Mr. & Mrs. Ernest J. Spierling

MADISON AVENUE.

4759 Mr. & Mrs. F. S. Stelling
4763 Mr. & Mrs. Wm. P. Byrne
4809 Mr. & Mrs. E. A. Jewett
4809 Mr. & Mrs. D. C. Mallory
4817 Mr. & Mrs. Franklin A. Miller
4819 Mr. & Mrs. H. M. Wright & dr.
4821 Mr. & Mrs. Henry C. French
4827 Mr. & Mrs. Harry Mills
      Receiving day Friday
4829 Mr. & Mrs. Wm. Aiken
4831 Mr. & Mrs. Edward Woodruff
4831 Richard Snowdon
4833 Mr. & Mrs. John Norcott
4835 Mr. & Mrs. C. C. Whitacre
4835 Mr. & Mrs. Geo. H. Harlow
4839 Mr. & Mrs. C. H. Deethmann
4845 Mr. & Mrs. G. Hardie & dr.
4849 Mr. & Mrs. Edwin S. Douglas
4849 Mrs. Robert Douglas
4901 Mr. & Mrs. M. J. Dunne & dr.
4913 Mr. & Mrs. William A. Amory
4919 Mr. & Mrs. Horatio L. Wait
4919 Henry Heileman Wait
4919 Mr. & Mrs. Jas. J. Wait
4921 Mr. & Mrs. A. H. Trotter & dr.

4710 Dr. & Mrs. J. G. Reid
4712 Mr. & Mrs. N. Sherwood & dr.
      Receiving day Wednesday
4712 Mrs. L. A. Ware
4718 Mr. & Mrs. Jerome G. Steever
4720 Mr. & Mrs. John M. Hamilton
4736 Mr. & Mrs. John C. Neemes & dr.
4802 Mr. & Mrs. Frederic Grant Gleason
4802 Mrs. Marie A. Kennicott & dr.
4830 Mr. & Mrs. Wm. M. Jones
4830 William M. Jones jr.
4830 Mr. & Mrs. Chas. S. Painter
4832 Mr. & Mrs. Edwin A. Potter
5000 Mr. & Mrs. A. P. Callahan
5100 Mr. & Mrs. William G. Lewis
5114 Mr. & Mrs. Williston Fish
5120 Mrs. C. L. Vanderlip
5126 Frank A. Vanderlip
5140 Mr. & Mrs. E. F. Osborne
5142 Mr. & Mrs. J. S. Hair
5142 J. W. Hair
5206 Mr. & Mrs. Robert Stuart
5324 Mr. & Mrs. H. P. Knapp
5328 Mr. & Mrs. George F. Wessels

4927 Dr. & Mrs. Archibald Church
5003 Mr. & Mrs. Thos. S. Cruttenden
5015 A. A. Kevan
5027 Mr. & Mrs. A. T. Armstrong
5027 Mr. & Mrs. H. W. Simmons
5029 Mr. & Mrs. Henry H. Courtright
5031 Mr. & Mrs. Wm. Allen Markee
5031 Mr. & Mrs. P. R. Earling
5033 Mr. & Mrs. J. F. Curtis
5033 J. F. L. Curtis
5033 Ludlow LeFurgy
5037 Mr. & Mrs. David Quigg & dr.
5041 Prof. & Mrs. T. C. Chamberlin
5201 Mr. & Mrs. Joseph Powell
5203 Mr. & Mrs. Hale L. Flint
5205 Mr. & Mrs. Herbert M. Paddon
    Receiving day Wednesday
5207 Dr. & Mrs. A. E. Garceau
    Receiving day Tuesday
5209 Mr. & Mrs. W. T. Fenton
5211 Mr. & Mrs. Charles Esson
5217 Mrs. L. E. Loveday
5217 Mrs. A. R. Cockrill
5219 Mr. & Mrs. A. E. Campbell
5223 Mr. & Mrs. G. E. Harris
5241 Mr. & Mrs. Samuel Delamater
    & dr. *Receiving day Friday*
5311 Mr. & Mrs. Holton F. Miles
5311 Mr. & Mrs. Alfred H. Smith
5311 Charles P. Smith
5313 Mr. & Mrs. J. E. Grubb
5313 Mrs. J. B. Chapin
5313 Mr. & Mrs. Wm. Morgan
5319 Mr. & Mrs. C. A. Johnson
5327 Mr. & Mrs. J. Clifford Gould
5401 Dr. & Mrs. C. B. Rockwell
5401 Dr. & Mrs. Gordon C. Rockwell
5403 Gilbert Hubbard
5403 Miss Edna R. Hubbard
5407 Mr. & Mrs. M. L. Helpman
5413 Mr. & Mrs. C. L. Nelson
5429 Rev. R. B. Foresman
5429 Robert Foresman
5429 Hugh A. Foresman
5433 H. L. Whittlesey
5441 Mr. & Mrs. Henry Choate
5443 Mr. & Mrs. J. W. Riley & dr.
5495 Dr. & Mrs. H. N. Day
5511 Mr. & Mrs. R. M. Thomas
5511 Dr. & Mrs. James E. Child
5515 Mr. & Mrs. John E. Shea
5517 Miss Anna E. Trimingham
5523 Mr. & Mrs. Wm. E. Holland
5603 Mr. & Mrs. E. K. Boyd
5605 Mr. & Mrs. Leslie Lewis & drs.

5328 Frederick J. Wessels
5328 Robert S. Wessels
5398 Mr. & Mrs. D. H. Champlin
5406 Mr. & Mrs. E. C. Hibbard & dr.
5410 Mr. & Mrs. F. J. Miller
5412 Mr. & Mrs. D. E. Evans
5414 Mr. & Mrs. E. L. Jayne
5414 Sam. R. Jenkins
5426 Mr. & Mrs. George G. McRoy
5524 Mr. & Mrs. Charles G. Page
5526 Mrs. Daniel Shepard
5528 M. L. Willard
5528 G. G. Willard
5528 Mrs. P. H. Willard
5528 Mr. & Mrs. W. A. Pope
5532 Mr. & Mrs. A. H. Caryl
5536 Mr. & Mrs. Samuel E. Dunham
5542 Mr. & Mrs. Theodore P. Bailey
5546 Mr. & Mrs. Theodore Valentine
5604 Dr. & Mrs. E. V. McDonald
5604 William H. V. McDonald
5610 Mr. & Mrs. Thomas A. Banning
5610 Samuel Banning
5614 Mr. & Mrs. Newton A. Partridge
5622 Horace P. Taylor
5622 John H. Telford
5642 Mr. & Mrs. W. A. Olmstead
5648 Mrs. A. McPherran
5648 Benjamin McPherran
5648 Samuel H. McPherran
5660 Mr. & Mrs. E. B. Tolman
5704 Major & Mrs. T. TenEyck & dr
5704 Mr. & Mrs. C. G. Sholes & dr.
5704 Mr. & Mrs. W. P. Campbell
5708 Mr. & Mrs. M. D. Wilber
5708 Mrs. Mary E. Drake
5710 Mr. & Mrs. J. D. Wilber
5714 Mrs. John C. Parsons
5714 J. C. Parsons
5720 Dr. & Mrs. L. D. Gorgas
5720 Mrs. E. F. Stewart & dr.
5726 Mr. & Mrs. John Osborn & dr.
5728 Mr. & Mrs. Edward I. Galvin
5728 Carroll D. Galvin
5752 E. Hoyt & dr.
5752 Mrs. C. J. Ferguson
5752 E. J. Jenness
5752 Albert Ferguson
6110 Dr. & Mrs. A. T. Buchanan
6114 Mr. & Mrs. Michael J. Enright
    Receiving day Thursday
6156 Mr. & Mrs. J. S. Vaughn
6238 Dr. & Mrs. F. A. Amerman
    Receiving day Tuesday
6340 Mr. & Mrs. H. C. Overman & dr.

5607 Mr. & Mrs. J. U. Morgan
5617 Mr. & Mrs. T. W. Gilson
5619 Mrs. M. C. Brown
5727 Mr. & Mrs. C. H. Rice
5729 Mr. & Mrs. E. R. Woodle
5731 Mr. & Mrs. C. P. Van Inwegen
5733 Mr. & Mrs. F. W. Stephenson
5735 Mr. & Mrs. C. W. Dickerson
5737 Rev. & Mrs. F. B. Dunham
5745 Prof. & Mrs. Wm. D. McClintock
5747 Mr.& Mrs. James Peabody & dr.
5747 Earl W. Peabody
5749 Mr. & Mrs. B. F. Quimby & dr.
5751 Mr. & Mrs. George C. Bates
  Receiving day Thursday
5751 Fred G. Bates
5753 Mr. & Mrs. Alexander Stewart
5753 Charles C. Stewart
5755 Mr. & Mrs. H. E. Finney & dr.
5755 Harry Finney
5759 Mr. & Mrs. Joseph Twyman &
  dr. *Receiving day Thursday*
5761 Mr. & Mrs. Chas. S. Roberts

6340 W. C. Overman
6340 Mr. & Mrs. E. J. Wilber jr.
6416 Mrs. S. W. Pike & dr.
6426 Dr. & Mrs. Henry P. Loomis
6446 Mr.& Mrs. P.F. McGoorty&drs.
6530 Mrs. Susan O. Wyles
6530 Miss Fannie A. Harrington
6538. Mr. & Mrs. Chas. F.Whitmarsh
_____
5803 Mr. & Mrs. Harry W. Getz
5815 Amos B. George :
5821 E. E. Cornell
5821 Mrs. D. D. Cornell & dr.
5831 Mr. & Mrs. Charles Hughes
5833 Mr. & Mrs. Thomas Hancock
5841 Mr. & Mrs. Robert Kirkland
5845 Mr. & Mrs. H. S. Hawley
6011 Mr. & Mrs. C. P. Root
6049 Dr. & Mrs. Louis M. Turbin
6051 Dr. & Mrs. Thomas Winston
6051 Edward M. Winston
6107 Mr. & Mrs. J. P. McGoorty
6209 Mr. & Mrs. Charles H. Shaver

MADISON PARK.

1 Mr. & Mrs. O. S. Favor & dr.
1 Moses T. Miles.
5 Mr. & Mrs. Wm. L. Moyer
7 Mr. & Mrs. Rufus P. Jennings
9 Mr. & Mrs. C. D. Marquardt
17 Mr. & Mrs. R. Bell & dr.
29 Mr. & Mrs. Roderick Nevers
47 Dr. & Mrs. Samuel J. Jones
53 Mr. & Mrs. A. A. Kennard & dr.
53 Alexander D. Kennard
55 Mr. & Mrs. Edwin D. Wheelock
55 Mrs. Edward Sheldon
67 Mr. & Mrs. Angelo De Prosse
  Receiving day Thursday
99 Mr. & Mrs. W. E. Ritchie

2 Mr. & Mrs. Fred C. Swett
16 Mr. & Mrs. James B. Thorsen
24 Mr. & Mrs. K. B. Cook
24 N. B. Cook
24 Mrs. L. B. Turrill
24 John F. Turrill
34 Mr. & Mrs. George K. Kinney
36 Mr. & Mrs. Arthur M. Heath
38 Mr. & Mrs. C. D. Ballard
40 Mr. & Mrs. L. S. Boomer
68 Mr. & Mrs. A. E. Spink
70 W. Nelson Burritt
70 Miss Florence Castle

MAPLE STREET (ENGLEWOOD).

317 Mr. & Mrs. C. F. Smith
  Receiving day Wednesday
327 Mr. & Mrs. Otto Kalteich
327 Emil Hoeppner
331 Dr. & Mrs. J. Dittmann
333 Mrs. Mary E. Reed
333 Carlos L. Reed
333 George W. Reed
333 W. Albert Reed
339 Mr. & Mrs. John Taylor

330 Mr. & Mrs. James R. Dickey
332 Dr. & Mrs. M. H. Garland
340 Mrs. M. J. Tubbs
342 Mr. & Mrs. Charles L. Saylor
348 Mr. & Mrs. M. B. Hughson
352 Mr. & Mrs. F. H. Tuthill
354 Mrs. R. W. Doyle
416 Mr. & Mrs. Henry Blum & dr.
416 Mr. & Mrs. Henry Blum jr.
612 Mr. & Mrs. Ira W. Allen

353 Mr. & Mrs. Homer Bevans
415 Mr. & Mrs. William Owen & dr.
433 Mrs. A. D. Sawyer
507 Mr. & Mrs. Frank D. Blish
529 Mr. & Mrs. E. S. Swift
529 Mr. & Mrs. Charles Swift

612 Mr. & Mrs. Ira W. Allen jr.

541 Mr. & Mrs. W. J. Terpenny & drs.
609 Mr. & Mrs. D. J. Ireland
609 Francis M. Ireland
623 Rev. & Mrs. G. Fuchs & dr.

MICHIGAN AVENUE.

cor. Adams street, Pullman bldg.
700A J. R. Hald
701 Charles S. Roe
704 George E. McHie
705 Mr. & Mrs. Wm. C. Asay
706 J. H. Dearing
706 H. N. Nichols
707 Mr. & Mrs. E. D. Comings
708 W. S. Keith
713 E. W. Eldridge
714 W. A. R. Mitchell
716 J. H. Garner
717 H. Nelson
719 Mr. & Mrs. J. B. Griffin
719 W. F. Griffin
721 W. C. Bailey
722 C. H. Gibson
723 Mrs. N. R. Deyo
724 Charles M. Faye
800A E. C. Way
800B Mr. & Mrs. C. W. Trow-
      bridge
801 Urban H. Broughton
801 F. A. Marsh
802 Preston C. Maynard
803 F. M. Larned
806 Louis Eckstein
813 Charles Field
814 L. Wuichet
815 J. C. Davison
817 I. K. Pond
817 A. B. Pond
819 H. E. Hooper
819 George Clarke
820 R. E. Lidgerwood
821 H. J. Jones
822 J. Berr
823 Miss Mary Dillon
824 N. P. Smith
903 W. Ferguson
907 Alex. Euston
909 Mr. & Mrs. L. B. Crumbaugh
910 F. S. Cowgill
910 H. F. Baldwin
914 Otto Schaefer
919 R. C. Warde
920 H. F. Pushman

921 Victor Garwood
921 J. Nathan Coxe
225 E. Greble Killen
226 Mr. & Mrs. L. E. Ford
228 Mr. & Mrs. George C. Walker
229 Mrs. Stiles Burton
229 Mr. & Mrs. Ira Holmes
229 E. Burton Holmes
229 Ira G. Holmes
229 Mrs. H. A. Sherman
230 Mr. & Mrs. William Blair
232 Col. & Mrs. M. H. Alberger
232 Clarence Eddy
232 Mrs. Sara Hershey Eddy
232 Mrs. Josephine Minor
233 Mrs. J. H. Dunham & dr.
235 Mr. & Mrs. Washington Hesing
235 Mr. & Mrs. James E. Gross
235 Douglass Hoyt
235 C. Fred Kimball
235 Mr. & Mrs. A. G. Pettibone
235 Burton Hanson
235 Mrs. Ella Young
235 Mr. & Mrs. Chas. L. Patterson
235 Charles Scates
235 Charles E. Booth
235 Charles Catlin
235 Mrs. Susan G. Cook
235 Miss Alice G. Cook
235 E. P. Edwards
235 Miss Celia Galoglee
235 Mrs. Louise Ferson
235 Stanley Field
235 Mrs. S. Llewington
235 Miss Mary Freeman
235 Miss Libbie Freeman
235 Henry W. Hill
235 Mr. & Mrs. Henry J. Furber
235 Mr. & Mrs. Henry J. Furber jr.
235 William E. Furber
235 Mrs. Helen Cross & dr.
235 Dr. Florence Hunt
235 E. M. Woodson
235 A. D. Currier
235 Miss Grace V. Corneau
235 R. P. Marks
235 Edgar Holt

235 George A. Kittridge
235 Peter Lapp
235 Mrs. Martha J. Boardman
241 Mrs. Jerome Beecher
243 Mrs. L. E. Young
243 Mr. & Mrs. Oliver B. Jackson
243 Thomas H. Haley
243 Charles W. Shippey
243 Mr. & Mrs. S. Ferd. Howe
243 George Chandler
243 Henry Lindsay
247 Mrs. L. C. P. Freer
247 Mr. & Mrs. Oliver K. Johnson
247 Mrs. W. H. Wilber
252 Mr. & Mrs. T. B. Blackstone
258 Mr. & Mrs. James McKindley
Receiving day Tuesday
258 Mrs. Mary A. Beall
262 Mr. & Mrs. John B. Lyon
Receiving day Tuesday
262 Mrs. William P. Conger
262 William C. Lyon
265 Mr. & Mrs. H. E. Bucklen
265 Col. Cuthbert W. Laing
265 David R. Laing
265 Miss Anna Latta
265 Miss Edna Heckerthorne
267 Mr. & Mrs. H. L. Andrews
270 Mr. & Mrs. William B. Pettit
271 L. B. Eaton
276 D. A. Clippinger
276 Mr. & Mrs. William J. Knight
276 Guiseppe Valisi
276 Cesare Valisi
276 Mr. & Mrs. Albert E. Ebert & dr.
276 Benj. F. Stauffer
276 Mrs. Clara Murray
276 Miss B. Blair
276 Mr. & Mrs. Merton B. Thrift
276 Mr. & Mrs. E. R. Walsh
Receiving day Monday
287 Mrs. Joseph Peacock

287 Miss Alice M. Peacock
287 George C. Peacock
287 Miss Margaret Perry
302 Dr. & Mrs. Charles H. Gant
Receiving day Thursday
306 Mrs. E. L. Gillette
306 Edwin F. Gillette
309 Mrs. E. J. Lehmann
313 Mrs. Marcus C. Stearns
313 Mr. & Mrs. Richard I. Stearns
313 George R. Stearns
321 Mr. & Mrs. A. Tracy Lay & drs.
321 Mr. & Mrs. R. Floyd Clinch
323 Dr. John S. Ranney
323 Mr.& Mrs. Frank B. Knowlton
323 Mr.&Mrs. Edward J. Goldberg
325 Mr. & Mrs. Seth Gage
325 Harry S. Allen
329 Mr. & Mrs. W. A. Jenkins & dr.
329 Charles W. Jenkins
329 Mr. & Mrs. James R.VanCleave
329 Mr. & Mrs. Arthur L. Clarke
329 Mr. & Mrs. W. A. Burch
329 Isaac Powell
337 Chas. H. Cougle
344 Glencoe Flats
2 Mr. & Mrs. D. D. Cougle
Receiving day Wednesday
4 Mr. & Mrs. J. G. Caravatti
Receiving day Wednesday
5 Mr. & Mrs. Chas. Parmelee
5 Mr. & Mrs. Geo. W. Cleaveland
Receiving day Thursday
6 Mr. & Mrs. R. D. Buckingham
7 Mr. & Mrs. Frank Ely
8 Dr. & Mrs. J. G. Marbourg
8 Mr. & Mrs. M. Fleming
9 Mr. & Mrs. C. B. Orvis
10 James L. Onderdonk
10 Mr. & Mrs. Daniel J. Kelly

1217 Mr. & Mrs. Frederick Freiberg
1217 Mr. & Mrs. Julius Freiberg
1217 Miss Otilie H. Hallersleben
1217 Miss Martha A. Hallersleben
1245 Dr. Mary S. Winter
1249 Mr. & Mrs. John Oothout
1255 Dr. & Mrs. H. E. Macdonald
1311 Mr. & Mrs. Herbert T. Clark
1311 Dr. & Mrs. L. A. Stillman
1311 Miss E. Ada Danks
1311 Mr. & Mrs. Fred F. Danks
1311 Mrs. Jennie Burnett

1200 Mr. & Mrs. Edward G. Mason
1200 Edward H. Mason
1246 Mr. & Mrs. C. E. Sayre
1246 Dr. James A. Bovett, jr.
1250 Mrs. Dell Chamberlin & dr.
Receiving day Wednesday
1250 A. L. Chamberlin
1250 Mrs. May Gibbs
1254 Dr. James H. Reed
1316 Mr. & Mrs. George W. Brandt
1340 Mr. & Mrs. P. J. Sexton
Receive Wednesday afternoon

1311 Isaiah Danks
1313 Dr. & Mrs. J. C. Kennedy
1313 Mr. & Mrs. Wm. R. Wilson
1313 Mrs. Anna A. McCreary
1313 Miss Mary McHugh
1315 George H. Glover
1315 Miss F. M. Glover
1321 Mr. & Mrs. James H. Rice
1321 Miss Helen L. Tucker
1331 Mr. & Mrs. DeForest W. Saxe
1337 Mr. & Mrs. Z. R. Winslow
　　　Receiving day Thursday
1337 Mr. & Mrs. James M. Winslow
1337 James Magner
1341 Isaac Lowenberg
1341 Mr. & Mrs. Carl Dernburg
1343 Mrs. Marcus A. Farwell
1347 Mr. & Mrs. M. Clayburgh
　　　Receiving day Saturday
1347 Joseph Clayburgh
1347 Morris Clayburgh
1347 Mrs. M. C. Mayer
1409 Mr. & Mrs. M. Hanlon & dr.
1409 William J. Hanlon
1411 Mr. & Mrs. Fred. B. Hildreth
1423 to 1429 The Clinton
　　　Hideh Fushike
　2 Mrs. Mary E. Williams
　2 Miss Carrie E. Williams
　2 Mrs. Eliza Paddock
　2 Wilburn E. Paddock
　5 Mr. & Mrs. C. D. DuBois
　6 Mrs. Elizabeth Wheelhouse
　　　& dr.
　6 C. C. Thompson
　9 Mrs. Lydia A. Lawrence
　9 Mrs. Gertrude L. Kytka
　C Ernest Hermenhous
　F Mr. & Mrs. P. B. Shaffner
Receive Tuesday and Thursday
　F Miss May Doran
　H Rev. & Mrs. J. Wm. Van Ingen
　J William J. Buckley
　J James Dalton
1459 John M. L. Sexton
1465 Mr. & Mrs. A. E. Rawson
1465 Charles E. Fizette
1467 Mr. & Mrs. H. F. Leopold & dr.
　　　Receiving day Thursday
1467 Edward F. Leopold
1501 Mr. & Mrs. Henry F. Royce
　　　Receiving day Monday
1501 Mr. & Mrs. S. D. Haskell
1501 L. Green Munford
1503 Mr. & Mrs. J. Parker Smith
1503 Mr. & Mrs. A. D. Joslin

1420 Mr. & Mrs. John Ford
1420 William Ford
1426 James J. Healy
1428 Judge J. B. Bradwell
1428 Mr. & Mrs. Frank A. Helmer
1436 Mr. & Mrs. Chas. M. Kipp
1436 Mrs. J. Tennant
1452 Donald A. MacDonald
1454 Mr. & Mrs. W. J. Root
　　　Receiving day Thursday
1456 Mr. & Mrs. J. C. Smith
1458 Mr. & Mrs. Lewis H. Davis
1468 Mr. & Mrs. Charles F. Keeler
1474 Mrs. A. E. Goodrich
1474 Mr. & Mrs. A. W. Goodrich
1506 J. Heiland
1506 Mr. & Mrs. S. A. Ryder
1508 Mr. & Mrs. Wm. J. Morden
1508 F. L. Houston
1510 Mrs. G. W. Norton
1510 Mr. & Mrs. J. F. Farrell
1514 Mr. & Mrs. Addison Ballard
1516 Mr. & Mrs. Charles Haynes
1516 Mrs. Jennie Haynes
1528 Dr. & Mrs. Henry Merckle
1612 Mr. & Mrs. Elias Greenebaum
1612 Mr. & Mrs. Nathan S. Gutman
1614 Mr. & Mrs. George H. Laflin
1614 Arthur K. Laflin
1620 J. Rosenberg
1620 Mr. & Mrs. Maurice Rosenfeld
1634 Dr. & Mrs. J. H. Etheridge
　　　& dr.
1636 Dr. & Mrs. E. J. Ogden & dr.
1636 Mr. & Mrs. Chas. P. Ogden
1638 A. Booth
1638 Mr. & Mrs. Willard S. Gaylord
1702 I. L. Lake
1704 Mr. & Mrs. Caryl Young
1704 Caryl B. Young
1706 Dr. & Mrs. M. H. McKillip & dr.
1710 Mr. & Mrs. George L. Otis & dr.
1714 Mr. & Mrs. Chas. L. Willoughby
1720 Mr. & Mrs. F. S. Hanson & dr.
1722 Mr. & Mrs. Philo A. Otis
1722 James Otis
1728 Dr. & Mrs. Horatio F. Wood
1728 Dr. A. O. Howe
1728 Mr. & Mrs. O. F. Fischer
1732 Mr. & Mrs. C. T. Boal & dr.
1732 Miss Anna Boal
1732 Enos Ayres
s.w. cor. 18th Morton Flats
　　　Mrs. Geo. C. Morton
　　　Mr. & Mrs. Percy C. Hamilton
　　　Mr. & Mrs. W. P. Cowan

1509 Mr. & Mrs. D. Mergentheim & dr.
Receive Mon. & Thurs. eve's.
1509 Mr. & Mrs. A. D. Mergentheim
1521 Mr. & Mrs. J. G. Weeks
1547 Mr. & Mrs. Chas. B. Kirtland
1557 T. A. French
1601 Mr. & Mrs. Augustus N. Eddy
1601 Spencer F. Eddy
1607 Mrs. C. E. Barker
1611 Mrs. John J. Borland
1635 Mr. & Mrs. John Poole
Receiving day Thursday
1637 Franz DeSponer
1637 Ferdinand Freyesleben, LL.D.
1639 Mr. & Mrs. Aaron Stern & dr.
1641 Mr. & Mrs. Chas. C. Godman & dr.
1641 Raphael M. Skelton
1703 Mr. & Mrs. Henry Melhuish
1703 Frank Melhuish
1705 Mrs. Henry Horner
Receives 1st and 3d Friday
1705 Mrs. D. Levy
1705 Mr. & Mrs. Albert Horner
1705 Isaac Horner
1705 Angel Horner
1705 Charles Horner
1709 Mr. & Mrs. Charles H. Schwab
1709 Henry C. Schwab
1709 Jerome C. Schwab
1709 Levi Monheimer
1717 Mr. & Mrs. Morris Selz
Receiving day Thursday
1717 Emanuel F. Selz
1717 Miss Theresa Kohn
1719 Mrs. James L. Trumbull
1729 Mr. & Mrs. M. J. Clifford & drs.
1729 Judge Richard W. Clifford
1729 James M. Clifford
1801 Mr. & Mrs. N. K. Fairbank & dr.
1801 Kellogg Fairbank
1801 Wallace Fairbank
1805 Mr. & Mrs. Alfred Cowles
1805 William H. Cowles
1815 Mr. & Mrs. Benj. Allen & dr.
1815 Benjamin C. Allen
1815 Lewis D. Allen
1819 Mr. & Mrs. Lewis L. Coburn
1819 Mrs. Olivia S. Swan
1823 Dr. & Mrs. R. Ludlam
1823 Dr. R. Ludlam jr.
1825 Mr. & Mrs. T. S. Dobbins & dr.
1825 Mr. & Mrs. Chas. S. Purington
1827 Mr. & Mrs. Chas. D. Seeberger

Mr. & Mrs. B. E. Holladay
Dr. & Mrs. Casey A. Wood
1806 Dr. & Mrs. J. E. Owens
Receiving day Friday
1806 Miss Marie G. Owens
1810 C. H. Killough
1812 Mr. & Mrs. Arthur E. Hull
1814 Patrick McTerney & drs.
1816 Mr. & Mrs. J. M. Greenebaum
1820 James W. Ellsworth
1826 Mr. & Mrs. Ferdinand W. Peck
1826 Ferdinand W. Peck jr.
1826 Miss Buda M. Peck
1826 Mrs. Wm. Spaulding
1836 Mr. & Mrs. A. A. Parker
1836 Frank A. Parker
1838 Mr. & Mrs. Leopold Strauss
Receive Monday eve.
1838 Miss Jennie Strauss
Receives 1st and 2d Wednesday
1838 A. L. Strauss
1842 Mr. & Mrs. J. H. McVicker
1902 Mr. & Mrs. James R. Owen
1906 Mrs. X. L. Otis & dr.
1912 Mr. & Mrs. Hugh T. Birch
1918 Mr. & Mrs. Edwin L. Brand
Receiving day Tuesday
1918 Edwin L. Brand jr.
1922 Mr. & Mrs. Geo. Wm. de Smet
Receive 1st and 3d Saturday
1922 Prof. J. C. Grant
1924 Mr. & Mrs. J. S. Boyer
1924 Mrs. Adelaide L. Nellis
2000 Mr. & Mrs. George Schneider
2010 Mr. & Mrs. Albert Keep
2014 Mr. & Mrs. Henry Keep
2018 Mr. & Mrs. Albert J. Averell
2022 Frederick B. Tuttle
2026 Mr. & Mrs. A. A. Bigelow & dr.
2028 Mr. & Mrs. Edward Harvey Waldron
2108 Mr. & Mrs. J. Russell Jones & dr.
2116 Mr. & Mrs. Eben Lane
2116 Miss F. G. Lane
2118 Mr. & Mrs. H. M. Sherwood
2118 Miss Grace Sherwood
2120 Mr. & Mrs. R. H. Day
Receiving day Thursday
2124 Mr. & Mrs. Chas. B. Sears
2124 Mr. & Mrs. John G. Elliott
2124 Robert McLeod
2124 Albert R. Warner
2124 Frank J. Fanning
2124 Mr. & Mrs. Samuel Redfern
2124 Mr. & Mrs. Theo. O. Fraenkel
2124 John F. Holland

1837 Hotel Yorkshire
    Mr. & Mrs. A. Berger
    Mr. & Mrs. W. Butterfield
    Mrs. M. J. Codd
    Mr. & Mrs. Sidney Cohen
    Mrs. George Conrad
    J. I. Cooper
    Mr. & Mrs. J. L. Dorsett
    F. Drummond
    Miss Giselle D'Unger
    D. L. Feibelman
    Linton T. Floyd-Jones
    Thomas Floyd-Jones
    A. S. Guggenheimer
    Mr. & Mrs. Geo. W. Leighton
    L. L. Loveridge
    Mme. E. Luneau
    Mr. & Mrs. C. E. Mabie
    Mr. & Mrs. R. Mansfield
    Mr. & Mrs. R. E. McDonald
    Mr. & Mrs. W. L. Moore
    Mr. & Mrs. F. M. Pease
    Miss Mary C. Pratt
    Mr. & Mrs. Frank Reilly
    Mrs. A. A. Roberts
    Mr. & Mrs. A. P. Schack
    Miss Della Stoner
    George E. Swartz
    Mr. & Mrs. John M. Sweeney
    Mr. & Mrs. C. H. Tebbetts
    J. Tomlinson
    H. Vistendahl
    A. F. Warner
    Miss Minnie Wehmer
    Mr. & Mrs. G. K. Wheeler
    Miss Anna Williams
    Miss Edna York
    Mrs. H. York
1839 Mr. & Mrs. Joseph Horner
1843 R. H. Park
1843 Miss A. E. Sampson
1907 Mr. & Mrs. E. L. Eaton & dr.
    Receiving day Monday
1907 Mr. & Mrs. Geo. A. Hayes
1907 Miss M. L. Bentley
1911 Dr. A. E. Brown
1911 Dr. L. Read Brown
1911 Miss E. M. Brown
1911 Dr. & Mrs. J. O. Ely
1911 Mr. & Mrs. Wilmer Wright
1911 Stuart B. Andrews
1913 Mr. & Mrs. George W. Henry
1915 Mr. & Mrs. J. Forsyth & drs.
1915 Oliver O. Forsyth
1915 George W. Forsyth
1915 John J. Forsyth

2210 Dr. & Mrs. Hugh Blake Williams
2216 Mr. & Mrs. Charles W. Drew
2218 Mr. & Mrs. C. W. Butterfield
2222 Mr. & Mrs. John Beggs
2222 Pliny B. Smith
2240 G. M. Hollstein
2240 Albert M. Hollstein
2240 Sidney A. Loth
2242 Mr. & Mrs. John J. Janes
2246 Mrs. H. Williams
2246 Miss Gwendolyn Williams
2246 H. E. Williams
2246 Leverett Thompson
2248 Mrs. M. A. Field
2248 John S. Field
2248 George D. Field
2250 Mrs. Grange Sard
2250 William H. Sard
2250 Mrs. Anna Sard Simpson
2250 Howard Sard Simpson
2254 Mr. & Mrs. Clarence I. Peck
2254 Mrs. P. F. W. Peck
2330 Mrs. H. Sprague & dr.
2330 Charles W. Sprague
2330 Miss Frances Cooke
2330 Miss Jessamine Cooke
2334 Mr. & Mrs. Joseph O'Hare & dr.
2338 Mr. & Mrs. J. H. Short
2420 Mr. & Mrs. J. H. Clough & dr.
2428 Jacob Strader & dr.
2428 Miss Florence I. Strader
2428 J. Louis Strader
2428 Mrs. Kate R. Tichenor
2430 Mr. & Mrs. William McLain & dr.
2430 Mrs. Mary E. McLain
2430 Andrew J. McLain
2438 Mr. & Mrs. M. H. Maher
2440 Mr. & Mrs. J. W. Gates
2440 C. G. Gates
2446 Mr. & Mrs. L. E. Crandall
2450 Mrs. D. E. Crane
2454 Mr. & Mrs. Charles W. ReQua
2454 William B. ReQua
2458 Mr. & Mrs. Lucius B. Otis
2458 Mrs. Carrie O. Meacham
2502 Mr. & Mrs. James K. Murphy
2506 Mr. & Mrs. John A. Farwell
2506 John A. Farwell jr.
2508 Mrs. A. F. Chambers
2512 Mr. & Mrs. I. Greensfelder & dr.
    Rec. days 1st & 3d Wednesday
2512 Adolph Greensfelder
2512 Julius Greensfelder
2512 Nathan Greensfelder
2518 Mrs. S. G. Spaulding

1919 Mr. & Mrs. Edward T. Jeffery
    Receiving day Thursday
1923 Henry J. Macfarland
1923 Mr. & Mrs. A. G. Newell
1925 Austin Bierbower
1925 Miss Alida Varena
1925 Mrs. J. A. Myers & dr.
1925 Mr. & Mrs. Wm. Gillingham
1925 Robert M. Elliott
2001 The Pickwick
    Mrs E. W. Crawford
    O. W. Crawford
    A Mr. & Mrs. H. A. Hubbard
    A Eugene Guthman
    B Mr. & Mrs. Malcom Mc-
      Neill & drs.
    B Malcom McNeill jr.
    C Mrs. Wm. Bross
    C Miss Jennie A. Bross
    D Mr. & Mrs. J. N. Raymond
2007 Mr. & Mrs. E. C. Morton
2007 Charles H. Ferguson
2007 George Miller Ferguson
2007 James L. Ferguson
2013 Mrs. Luther Stone & dr.
2013 Mrs. J. L. Corthell
2017 Mr. & Mrs. A.F. Seeberger &dr.
2019 John F. Wilson
2019 Mrs. J. D. Gardiner
2023 Mr. & Mrs. Seymour Coleman
2027 Mr. & Mrs. W. C. D. Grannis
2027 George H. Curtis
2103 Mr. & Mrs. Henry H. Honoré
2103 Adrian C. Honoré
2103 Lockwood Honoré
2103 Nathaniel K. Honoré
2107 Mr. & Mrs. W. W. Miltner
2125 Mr. & Mrs. Charles French
2209 Mr. & Mrs. Frank A. Crandall
    & dr.
2211 Dr. Georgia S. Ruggles
2211 Mr. & Mrs. Frank A. Wunder
2215 Mrs. J. R. Winterbotham
2215 Mrs. E. S. Houghteling & drs.
2231 Mr. & Mrs. Chas. W. Dumont
2235 Mr. Harriet J. Loomis
2237 Mrs. Peter Smith
2239 Dr.& Mrs. H. P. Merriman
2239 Mrs. P. A. Avery
2241 Mr. & Mrs. H. G. Allen & drs.
2243 Mr. & Mrs. H. Arms
2243 William A. Yager
2247 Mr. & Mrs. Charles Fargo &
    dr.
2247 Mrs. I. F. Andrews
2247 Livingston W. Fargo
11

2522 Mrs. Godfrey Snydacker & dr.
    Receiving day Saturday
2522 Joseph G. Snydacker
2522 Emanuel F. Snydacker
2544 Mr. & Mrs. Marx Wineman
2544 Joseph M. Wineman
2544 Mr. & Mrs. A. S. Lowenthal
2544 Jacob R. Wineman
2544 Simon R. Wineman
2544 Milton R. Wineman
2550 Mr. & Mrs. M. D. Wells
2600 Mr. & Mrs. S. K. Martin & dr.
2600 Wilton B. Martin
2600 S. K. Martin jr.
2612 Mr. & Mrs. Edwin Walker
2612 Miss Alma L. Kimball
2612 Miss Louise E. Kimball
2618 Mrs. J. J. Gore & dr.
2622 Mr. & Mrs. J. Franklin Keeney
    Receiving day Friday
2626 Mr. & Mrs. T. J. Lefens
2702 Mr. & Mrs. H. H. Honore jr.
2704 Dr. & Mrs. W. N. Reeves & dr.
2704 William O. Reeves
2704 L. Claude Reeves
2706 Mr. & Mrs. George Enger
2710 Miss Nellie M. Weibezahn
2712 Mr. & Mrs. S. H. Ives
    Receiving day Thursday
2712 John Streight
2714 Miss Anna E. Fraeser
    Receiving day Monday
2714 Mr. & Mrs. E. D. Scott
    Receiving day Monday
2724 Mr. & Mrs. Joseph Shepard
2724 Harry W. Treat
2724 James D. Stone
2804 Mr. & Mrs. J. S. McClelland
2804 Will S. McClelland
2808 Mr. & Mrs. M. S. Davis & dr.
2810 Mr. & Mrs. Robert T. Martin
    & dr.
2810 George S. Martin
2816 Mr. & Mrs. C. W. Brega
2816 Miss Louise E. Brega
2816 Miss Margaret Enders
2822 Mr. & Mrs. George Adams
2822 Miss Lizzie Adams
2826 Mr. & Mrs. C. E. Kohl
2838 Mr. & Mrs. H. N. Higinbotham
2838 Harry M. Higinbotham
2838 Harlow D. Higinbotham
2838 Miss Florence Higinbotham
2900 Mr. & Mrs. J. H. S. Quick
2900 William F. Quick
2900 George A. Quick

2255 Mr. & Mrs. W. T. Baker & dr.
2255 Henry D. Baker
2313 Mr. & Mrs. Wm. B. Clark
2313 J. T. Augur
2317 Mr. & Mrs. J. B. King
2317 Mr. & Mrs. J. D. Dezendorf
2317 James L. King
2317 Carlton King
2317 Frank M. Eddy
2317 Mrs. L. B. Stoddart & dr.
2317 Dr. Rufus W. Bishop
2317 Mrs.Genevra JohnstoneBishop
3317 Mr. & Mrs. Charles H. Sergel
2317 Mr. & Mrs. D. T. Hunt
2321 Mrs. Joseph Frank & dr.
    Receiving day Wednesday
2321 Emanuel J. Frank
2323 Mr. & Mrs. J. Firmenich & dr.
2323 George F. Firmenich
2325 Mr. & Mrs. Josiah Stiles & dr.
2325 George N. Stiles
2325 Miss Emily Nichols
2333 Mr. & Mrs. W. Moseback
2335 Matthew Laflin
2335 Miss Grovene P. Barbour
2339 Mr. & Mrs. James A. Todd
    Receiving day Wednesday
2339 Miss Marion Miles
2339 Mr. & Mrs. Wm. H. Gleason
2343 Mrs. Clara Mayer & dr.
2347 Mr. & Mrs. F. C. Vierling
2359 Mr. & Mrs. Charles H. Bogue
2409 Dr. & Mrs. James Nevins Hyde
    Receiving day Monday
2409 Charles Cheney Hyde
2409 Rt.Rev.& Mrs.Charles Edward
    Cheney *Receiving day Mon.*
2411 Mr. & Mrs. Orestes Brownson
    Tennis
    Receiving day Wednesday
2413 Mr.& Mrs.Philander Pickering
2413 L. E. Overman
2413 Charles R. Overman
2415 Dr. & Mrs. J. N. Banks
2415 Mr. & Mrs. John Benham
2415 Mrs Sidney Fairlee
2417 Mrs. F. S. Fisher & drs.
2417 Mrs. Jane W. Wiswell
2417 Franklin V. Chamberlain & dr.
2417 Mr. & Mrs. Geo. S. Frink
2417 Mrs. George Field
2419 Arthur Woodcock
2419 Mr. & Mrs. F. P. Fisher
2419 Isaac H. Pedrick
2421 Mr. & Mrs. John S. Cooke&dr.
2421 George J. Cooke

2902 Mrs. J. F. Heyworth
2902 James O. Heyworth
2902 Lawrence Heyworth
2908 Mr. & Mrs. J. F. Gillette & dr.
2908 Howard F. Gillette
2918 Mr. & Mrs. James Barrell
    Receiving day Thursday
2918 Stewart E. Barrell
2918 Albert M. Barrell
2922 Mr. & Mrs. William H. Moore
    Receive Thursday
2926 Mrs. F. Sidney Papin
2926 Miss Pamilla W. Thompson
2934 Mr. & Mrs. D. E. Corneau
2938 Mr. & Mrs. J. P. Dalton
2944 Mr. & Mrs. S. A. Kent
2954 Mr.& Mrs.Joseph Austrian&dr.
    Receiving day Wednesday
2956 Mr. & Mrs. Bernhard Kuppen-
    heimer
2956 Albert B. Kuppenheimer
2962 Mrs. Hiram Wheeler
2962 Mr. & Mrs. Eugene Wheeler
2962 Arthur Wheeler
2968 Mr. & Mrs. Hiram B. Peabody
3000 to 3012 The Potomac
    Mr. & Mrs. J. A. Agee
    William Allore
    Mrs. Franc P. Hawes-Allore
    Mr. & Mrs. E. A. Benson & dr.
        Receiving day Thursday
    Mr. & Mrs. I. B. Cougle
        Receiving day Thursday
    Miss Minnie Daly
    Mrs. D. H. Dunn & dr.
    Theo. G. Fischel
    Dr. Arthur E. Genius
    Miss Ethel L. Genius
    Dr. Richard M. Genius
    Mrs. C. Goetz
    Miss Margaret Goetz
    Miss Emma Grubb
    Mrs. Elizabeth Haughey
    Mr. & Mrs. L. C. Haughey
        Receiving day Monday
    Mr. & Mrs. Harry Holland
    Mr. & Mrs. F. J. Kennedy &
    dr.
    D. R. Levy
    Mrs. S. H. McCabe
    Mrs. F. A. McCoy
    Fred B. McCoy
    Mrs. G. G. Melcher
    Mr. & Mrs. C. B. Moore & drs.
    Mr. & Mrs. F. S. Mooneland
    Dr. & Mrs. D. T. Phillips

2421 John R. Cooke
2427 Mr. & Mrs. J. B. Clarke
2427 Fred R. Clarke
2427 Winthrop H. Clarke
2429 Mr. & Mrs. G. F. Baldwin
2435 Mr. & Mrs. F. R. Emerson
2441 Charles J. Mauran & dr.
 Receiving day Thursday
2441 Charles S. Mauran
2441 Miss Jennie Gray
2451 Mr. & Mrs. A. A. Spear
2451 Clarence M. Converse
2451 Mr. & Mrs. George Bass
 Receiving day Thursday
2453 Mr. & Mrs. Wm. Gilman
2453 Mrs. Reuben Frame
2453 Mrs. Sarah S. Davidson
2455 Mrs. Mary A. Holman
2455 Miss Harriet Holman
2455 Miss Maria H. Holman
2459 Mr. & Mrs. E. Rothschild & dr.
2501 Mr. & Mrs. A. G. Leonard
 Receiving day Thursday
2501 George A. Leonard
2505 The Berkshire
 1 Mr. & Mrs. Harry H. Cooper
 2 Mr. & Mrs. J. A. Adams
  Receiving day Thursday
 2 Miss E. L. Adams
 2 William T. Adams
 3 Mr. & Mrs. Geo. J. Volland
 4 Mr. & Mrs. D. I. Lufkin
 5 Mrs. Mary Fuller Manning
 5 Miss Kate A. White
 7 Mrs. Horace Reed & dr.
 8 Mr. & Mrs. Geo. F. Stitch
  Receiving day Thursday
 9 Mr. & Mrs. Carl D. Stone
  Receiving day Tuesday
 10 Mr. & Mrs. Wm. T. Angell
 10 Miss Eugenia Price
 12 Miss Lizzie E. Downs
 12 Arthur W. Downs
2511 Mr. & Mrs. Lyman M. Newton & dr.
2511 Jervis O. Newton
2513 Robert S. McMillan
2537 Mr. & Mrs. W. A. Giles & dr.
2537 William F. Giles
2537 Mrs. C. F. Hill
2541 Mr. & Mrs. R. T. Crane & dr.
2541 Dr. Frances Crane
2541 Richard T. Crane jr.
2541 Mr. & Mrs. Edmund A. Russell
.2559 Mr. & Mrs. D. K. Hill
 Receiving day Wednesday

Mr. & Mrs. Thos. Riley & drs.
Frank Riley　.
Dr. & Mrs. M. M. Ritter
Mr.& Mrs. Geo. W. Sturdevant
Mr. & Mrs. H. S. Von Gigeh
Mr. & Mrs. A. Winklebleck
 dr.
Mr. & Mrs. H. C. Winklebleck
Dr. & Mrs. Geo. W. Winslow
 Receiving day Thursday
Mr. & Mrs. P. L. Wright
3014 Mr. & Mrs. O. B. Taft
3014 Harry L. Taft
3014 Miss Ina M. Taft
3014 Mrs. J. B. Gallagher
3018 Mr. & Mrs. Henry McCall
3018 Harry E. McCall
3020 Mr. & Mrs. James C. Carlisle
3024 Mrs. M. Cunningham
3024 James E. Cunningham
3028 Mr. & Mrs. I. S. Smith
3030 Mr. & Mrs. Peachey Malden
 Receiving day Thursday
3030 Mr. & Mrs. R. J. Walker
3030 Ralph S. Walker
3030 Harry Walker
3032 Mrs. Thomas G. Bowles
3032 Frank Goodwin Bowles
3034 Dr. E. Stillman Bailey
3034 Dr. H. R. Chislett
3034 Dr. Daniel H. Williams
3116 Judge & Mrs. Elbridge Hanecy
3122 Mr. & Mrs. A. J. Earling
 Receiving day Friday
3122 Mrs. M. S. Peebles
3124 Mr. & Mrs. S. B. Chapin
 Receiving day Wednesday
3138 Mr. & Mrs. Michael Cudahy
 & drs.
3142 Mr.& Mrs.A.O.Slaughter & dr.
 Receiving day Friday
3142 A. O. Slaughter jr.
3142 Mrs. J. B. Tilden
3148 Mr. & Mrs. James Swan
 Receiving day Tuesday
3150 Mr. & Mrs. Francis P. Owings
 Receiving day Tuesday
3154 Mr. & Mrs. J. Brandt Walker
3154 Miss Florence Gilson
3154 Mr. & Mrs. Archibald McNeill
 Receiving day Thursday
3200 Mr. & Mrs. C. W. Pardridge
3200 A. J. Pardridge
3200 Miss May A. Pardridge
3200 C. A. Pardridge
3200 Mrs. Evelyn P. Clayton

2559 Mrs. Lucretia P. Tracy
2559 Mr. & Mrs. James Tracy Hill
2613 Dr. & Mrs. T. A. Kimmell
  Receiving day Wednesday
2613 Mrs. Maud Lord Drake
2619 Mr. & Mrs. E. Sondheimer &
  drs.
  Receive 1st & 3d Thursdays
2619 Max Sondheimer
2619 Edward A. Sondheimer
2619 Henry Sondheimer
2621 Mrs. Harry W. Phillips
  Receiving day Tuesday
2621 Mrs. Matilda C. Dinsmore
2621 George H. Taylor
2623 Wilbur F. Henderson
2623 Mr.&Mrs.Wilbur S.Henderson
2631 Mrs. W. Scott Linn
2631 Walter A. Rapp
2633 Mrs. J. A. Rothschild & drs.
  Receiving day Monday
2633 Benjamin Rothschild
2633 Leo J. Rothschild
2635 Herbert P. Crane
2637 John Robson
2643 Mr. & Mrs. V. A. Watkins
  Receiving day Wednesday
2701 Mr. & Mrs. Chas. F. Babcock
2703 Dr. & Mrs. Edward Prentice
2709 Mr. & Mrs. William R. Linn
2709 Mrs. M. L. Andrews
2715 Mr. & Mrs. George W. Cass
2729 Frank J. D'Episy
2729 Mme. Lucie D'Episy
2733 Col. & Mrs. J. S. Cooper
2735 Mr.& Mrs. Philip D.Armour jr.
2801 Mr. & Mrs. W. D. Ewart & dr.
2801 Miss Julia D. Ewart
2805 Mr. & Mrs. L. Schlesinger
2807 Mr. & Mrs. J. G. Miller
  Receiving day Friday
2811 Mr. & Mrs. Charles H. Knapp
2819 Mr. & Mrs. Geo. A. Seaverns
  & dr.
2825 Mr. & Mrs.EdwardP.Hastings
2825 Cyrus A. Hardy
2825 B. Frank Hardy
2825 Frederick B. Fuller
2825 Mrs. Anna V. Lynn
2827 Mr. & Mrs. H. S. Fitch & dr.
2829 Mr. & Mrs. Henry S. Stebbins
2835 Mrs. Charles B. Pope
2837 Mr. & Mrs. H. Botsford & dr.
2841 J. H.Witbeck & dr.
2841 Mrs. M. E. Guernsey
2901 Gerhard Foreman

3200 Mrs. T. Gannon
3206 Mr.& Mrs.Simon Mandel & dr.
  Receiving day Friday
3206 Frank S. Mandel
3206 Leonard Jas. Mandel
3210 Mrs. Mary C. Frazer
3210 Mrs. S. W. Cook
3212 Mr. & Mrs. Philip Lichtenstadt
  Receiving day Saturday
3212 Miss Susie Lichtenstadt
3212 Harry Lichtenstadt
3214 Mr. & Mrs. F. J. Mackey
3218 Mr. & Mrs. Wm.H. McKinlock
  Receiving day Monday
3222 Mr. & Mrs. J. P. Marsh & drs.
3230 Miss Caroline L. Williamson
3230 Mr. & Mrs. I. K. Hamilton
3232 Mr. & Mrs. W. Henry McDoel
3236 Dr. Lester Frankenthal
3236 M . & Mrs. E. Frankenthal &
  dr.
3236 Oscar E. Frankenthal
3254 Mr. & Mrs. John Cudahy
3300 Mrs. Conrad Seipp & drs.
  Receiving day Tuesday
3322 Mr. & Mrs. George Middleton
  Receiving day Wednesday
3322 Miss Rilla Kelby
3322 Miss Bessie Middleton
3328 Edwin L. McCallay
3328 Mr. & Mrs. D. McCallay
3334 Mr. & Mrs. E. W. Gillett
3334 Miss Lillian May Gillett
3334 Charles W. Gillett
3336 Mr. & Mrs. Wm. W. Miller
  Receiving day Wednesday
3336 Wm. Yates Miller
3340 Mr. & Mrs. D. A. Kohn
  Receiving day Thursday
3340 Alfred D. Kohn
3340 Mr. & Mrs. Irving S. Bernheimer
3344 Mrs. M. Chapin
  Receiving day Monday
3344 Miss Alice Chapin
3358 Mr. & Mrs. C. P. Libby
  Receiving day Friday
3358 Miss Una Libby
3400 Mr. & Mrs. Emanuel Mandel
  Receiving day Tuesday
3400 Frank Mandel
3408 Mr. & Mrs. E. B. Butler
3408 Mr. & Mrs. A. T. Evans
3416 E. R. Wadsworth
3416 F. T. Wheeler
3420 Mr. & Mrs. Alfred H. Sellers

2901 Jules Ballenberg
2901 Mr. & Mrs. J. L. Rosenberg
2901 Mr. & Mrs. N. F. Leopold
2901 Mr. & Mrs. A. C. Schwab
2909 Mr. & Mrs. A. Byram & dr.
2909 Charles F. Byram
2913 Mr. & Mrs. Leroy W. Fuller
2913 William A. Fuller & dr.
2917 Mr. & Mrs. M. H. Wilson
2923 Mr. & Mrs. R. B. Crouch
2929 Mr. & Mrs. D. G. Hamilton
Receiving day Wednesday
2937 Mr. & Mrs. Cyrus D. Roys
2939 Mr. & Mrs. Frank L. Stevens
Receiving day Thursday
2941 Mr. & Mrs. N. T. Wright & dr.
2949 Mrs. L. M. Koenigsberg
2949 Mr. & Mrs. Wm. A. Waterbury
2951 Mr. & Mrs. Felix Kahn
Receiving days 1st & 3d Wed.
2951 Mark Kahn
2951 Mr. & Mrs. Lewis Kaufman
2953 Mr. & Mrs. James F. Hervey
Receiving day Tuesday
2953 Mr. & Mrs. W. C. Duell
2953 Miss Belle H. Jones
2957 Mr. & Mrs. Chas. H. Hoops
2959 Mr. & Mrs. Roswell Miller
Receiving day Tuesday
2961 Anson Gorton & dr.
2965 Mr. & Mrs. DeW. C. Leach
2969 Mr. & Mrs. E. B. Sackett
2969 W. C. Potter
2971 Mrs. M. A. Harper & drs.
2973 Mr. & Mrs. J. B. Collins
2973 Henry M. Peck
2977 Mr. & Mrs. Joseph Cahn
Receiving day Tuesday
2977 Bertram J. Cahn
3011 Mr. & Mrs. Edw. Bauman&dr.
Receive last Thursday
3011 Joseph Bauman
3017 Dr. & Mrs. W. S. Maxwell
3017 Dr. & Mrs. J. A. Swasey
3017 Calvin Tuck
3017 Miss Alice L. Tuck
3017 Dr. & Mrs. C. M. Thompson
3019 Mr. & Mrs. E. J. Quinlan
3019 E. J. Quinlan jr.
3019 James M. Quinlan
3019 Wm. A. Quinlan
3019 Arthur D. Quinlan
3027 Mr. & Mrs. Alexander Stelle
Receiving day Thursday
3027 Mrs. Julia H. Coe
3027 Harry I. Coe

3420 Frank H. Sellers
3426 Mr. & Mrs. C. L. Shattuck
3426 Mr. & Mrs. John Brown
3428 Mr. & Mrs. George Howard
3430 Mr. & Mrs. Jacob Hirsh
Receiving day Thursday
3430 Solomon J. Hirsh
3430 Mr. & Mrs. J. H. Schmaltz
Receiving day Thursday
3432 Mr. & Mrs. R. Rubel
3432 Miss Rose Rubel
Receiving day Thursday
3432 Isaac F. Rubel
3432 Milton Rubel
3434 Mr. & Mrs. H. M. Marks
Receiving day Tuesday
3440 Mr. & Mrs. Frederick W.
Straus & drs.
Receive 1st and 3d Tuesdays
3456 Dr. & Mrs. S. A. McWilliams
3456 Miss Mary Scheibel
3522 Mr. & Mrs. J. E. Kimball
3522 Miss M. B. Kimball
3524 Mr. & Mrs. Vernon Shaw-Kennedy
3538 Mr. & Mrs. W. F. Neil
3600 Dr. & Mrs. J. R. Zaring
4600 Mr. & Mrs. J. Ellsworth Gross
3604 Mr. & Mrs. Robt. H. Van-Schaack
3608 Mr. & Mrs. Joseph Donnersberger & drs.
3638 Mr. & Mrs. Zimri Dwiggins & dr.
3642 Mr. & Mrs. Fred Siegel
3642 Frank E. Vogel
3646 Mr. & Mrs. Moses Gimbel & dr.
3646 Jacob W. Gimbel
3646 Horace B. Gimbel
3646 Charles A Gimbel
3650 Mr. & Mrs. A. Hart
3650 Harry R. Hart
3650 Milton R. Hart
3652 Mr. & Mrs. Louis Stein
Rec. days 1st & 3d Fridays
3652 Lawrence Stein
3656 Mr. & Mrs. Madison B. Kennedy
3658 Marcus Marx
3658 Miss Hattie Marx
3660 Mr. & Mrs. W. O. Hoffman
3660 Mrs. William McKindley
3662 Mr. & Mrs. A. R. Wilson
3662 Mr. & Mrs. E. M. Underwood
3668 Mrs. James Leonard

3027 James R. Coe
3031 Mr. & Mrs. T. P. Moody & dr.
3033 Mr. & Mrs. H. W. Gifford
3035 George M. Shaw
3113 Mr. & Mrs. Wilbur Rude Davis
3113 Mr. & Mrs. J. R. Davis & dr.
3121 Clarence W. Marks
3123 Mr .& Mrs. B. Engel & drs.
3125 Dr. & Mrs. Edwin J. Kuh
3127 Mr. & Mrs. Max Hart
        Receiving day Tuesday
3129 Mrs. Julia R. Austrian & drs.
3129 Alfred S. Austrian
3131 Mr. & Mrs. Arthur Dixon&drs.
        Receiving day Friday
3131 Arthur A. Dixon
3131 George W. Dixon
3133 Mr. & Mrs. Julius Schwabacher
3133 Henry H. Schwabacher
3133 Mr. & Mrs. M. L. Horner
3139 Mr. & Mrs. Harry H. Fuller
3139 Mrs. M. B. Raymond
3139 Mrs. Lillian C. Davis
3139 Mr. & Mrs. N. C. Thrall
3139 Jefferson A. Greer
3139 Mr. & Mrs. E. J. Dimmick
3141 Mr.& Mrs. Abraham Kuh
        Receiving day Tuesday
3141 Julius S. Kuh
3141 Mr. & Mrs. Emanuel Buxbaum
3143 Mr.&Mrs.Siegmund Florsheim
        & dr.
        . Receive 1st and 3d Fridays
3143 Felix Florsheim
3155 Mr. & Mrs. Albert Hayden
3159 Mr. & Mrs. David Kelley
3159 Addison D. Kelley
3201 Mr. & Mrs. Charles T. Yerkes
3207 Mr. & Mrs. G. C. Benton
3207 Clarence A. Tuttle
3211 Mr. & Mrs. Geo. G. Felton
        Receiving day Tuesday
3213 Mr. & Mrs. John Angus
3213 Miss Margaret C. Drake
3215 Mr. & Mrs. Eugene O'Reilly
        & drs. *Receiving day Thursday*
3215 Eugene F. O'Reilly
3219 Mr. & Mrs. Louis E. Frank
3223 Mr. & Mrs. E. J. Kohn
        Receiving day Wednesday
3223 Martin B. Cahn
3223 Bernard Cahn
3229 Mr.&Mrs.LouisWampold & dr.
        Receiving day Friday
3229 Leo Wampold
3229 Frederick C. Cahn

3672 Mr. & Mrs. Leopold Bloom
        *Receive 1st & 3d Thursdays
        of every month*
3672 Aaron L. Bloom
3672 Miss Hulda B. Bloom
3724 Mr. & Mrs. J. Ogden Armour
3736 Mr. & Mrs. A. J. Lichtstern
3740 Mrs. B. Lichtstern & drs.
3742 Mr. & Mrs. Benj. Arnheim
3806 Mr. & Mrs. John Griffiths & dr.
3816 Mr. & Mrs. Wm. M. Crilly
        Receiving day Monday
3820 Mr. & Mrs. Daniel F. Crilly
3820 Frank L. Crilly
3924 Dr. & Mrs. S. E. Wood
3924 Samuel Kay Wood
3924 Miss S. Ella Wood
3934 Mr. & Mrs. Irus Coy
3934 Lincoln M. Coy
3934 Mrs. J. M. Mahaffey
4016 Mr. & Mrs James Wood & dr.
4016 Dr. George A. Wood
4042 William E. Keenan
4042 Joseph L. Keenan
4042 Mr. & Mrs. W. T. Keenan&dr.
        Receiving day Thursday
4114 Mr. & Mrs Thomas English
4136 Mr.& Mrs. W. L.Tamblyn & dr.
4200 Mrs. Mary Updike
4202 Mr. & Mrs. C. L. Porter
4202 Mr. & Mrs. Fred P. Updike
4202 Mr. & Mrs. J. W. Merriam
4202 Mr. & Mrs. Seth C. Earl
4204 Mr. & Mrs. Albert Llewellyn
        Barnett
4204 Mr. & Mrs. Wm. B. McCollum
4204 Mr. & Mrs. Alex Bateson &drs.
4206 Charles Matthias
4206 Mrs. Mary M. Mathias
4206 Mr. & Mrs. Parker M. Lewis
4300 Mr.& Mrs. John H.Wood & dr.
4316 Mr. & Mrs. L. W. Stone
        . . Receiving day Friday
4346 Mr. & Mrs. H. C. Walker
4346 Henry W. Walker
4346 H. Edwin Walker
4346 Clarence M. Walker
4400 Mr. & Mrs. John P. Barrett
4404 Mr. & Mrs. M. Ederheimer
        Receiving day Monday
4406 Mr. & Mrs. Sol. Kaiser
        Receiving day Monday
4544 Dr. & Mrs. C. C. Beery
4544 Mrs. Louise Leppelman
4800 Mr. & Mrs. Simon Hasterlik
        Receiving day Thursday

3233 Mr.&Mrs.C.M.Fegenbush & dr.
Receiving day Wednesday
3233 Mr. & Mrs. J. W. Michie
3237 Dr. & Mrs. Alexander Loew
3237 Ignace Loew
3237 Leo Tuska
3239 Mr. & Mrs. Loring A. Pease
3241 John W. Dickerson
3241 John A. Knisely
3251 Mr. & Mrs. C. L. Adams & dr.
3253 Mr. & Mrs. C. A. Kerfoot
3257 Mr. & Mrs. L. B. Doud
3305 Isaac Woolf
3311 Mr. & Mrs. Morris Rosenbaum
&dr. *Receiving day Wed.*
3317 Mr. & Mrs. A. D'Ancona & dr.
Receive Friday aft'n & Sun. eve.
3317 Mr.& Mrs.Alfred E. D'Ancona
3317 Edward N. D'Ancona
3317 Clarence P. D'Ancona
3319 Mrs. H. H. Hayden & dr.
3319 Charles E. Hayden
3319 H. H. Hayden jr.
3323 Dr. & Mrs. O. L. Schmidt
3327 Mr. & Mrs. Frank Hall
3329 Mr. & Mrs. J. Harry Selz
3333 Mr. & Mrs. Harry D. Kohn
3335 Mr. & Mrs. Edwin D. Kohn
3337 Mr. & Mrs. H. E. Greenebaum
Receiving day Friday
3339 Mr. & Mrs. S. F. Leopold & dr.
Receiving day Friday
3339 Alfred F. Leopold
3341 Mr. & Mrs. George F. Kimball
Receiving day Tuesday
3347 Mr. & Mrs. J. H. Shepard
3347 Miss Laura J. Shepard
3347 Henri E. Shepard
3357 Mr. & Mrs. A. A. Libby
3357 Miss Mabel V. Libby
3357 Miss Pearl G. Libby
3401 Mr. & Mrs. H. G. Chase
3401 Miss Bessie L. B. Chase
3401 Miss Lucy B. Chase
3401 Samuel M. Chase
3423 Mr. & Mrs. Gilbert B. Shaw
3427 Mr. & Mrs. Chas E. Maxwell
3427 Mr. & Mrs. Solomon Hirsch ﹗
Receiving day Monday
3427 Harry S. Hirsch
3427 Dwight S. Hirsch
3429 Mr. & Mrs. H. M. Loomis
3431 Mr. & Mrs. O. H. Manning
3433 Mr. & Mrs. Moses Born
3435 Mr. & Mrs. Samuel Gregsten
Receiving day Tuesday

4800 Mr. & Mrs. David Brede
4912 Mr. & Mrs. Edward G. Elcock
Receive 1st Wednesday
4914 Mr. & Mrs. Thos. Gahan
5156 Mr. & Mrs. W. P. Hayes
5156 Miss Nannie V. Hayes
5168 Mr. & Mrs. Seymour S. Borden
5168 Mrs. S. A. Andrews
5234 Mr. & Mrs. James J. Wade
5234 Miss Katherine Wade
5234 Thomas P. Wade
5238 Mr. & Mrs. David Coey
5238 Samuel B. Coey
5238 Grant Coey
5242 Mr. & Mrs. Isaac Bowen
5242 Chas. Roy Bowen
5242 Miss Helene M. Bowen
5648 Mr. & Mrs. Frank Schell
5812 Mr. & Mrs. Walter S. Maher
Receiving day Thursday
5900 to 5904 Evaline Flats
Mr. & Mrs. Wm. E. Barnum
Mr. & Mrs. C. Hamontree&dr.
Mr. & Mrs. Wm. J. McGovern
Mr. & Mrs. James Reeve
Mr. & Mrs. E. G. Wright
H. C. Wright
6100 Mr. & Mrs. Wm. T. Keck
6100 Rev. W. A. Sadtler
6100 A. S. Kleppinger
6106 Mr. & Mrs. Hugh Harding
6106 Dr. & Mrs. F. D. Rogers
6116 Mr. & Mrs. A. B. Elliott & dr.
Receiving day Thursday
6120 Mrs. L. H. Diffenderfer
6120 Mr. & Mrs. J. J. Armstrong
6122 Mr. & Mrs. Walter E. Harris
6144 Mrs. G. C. Thompson & dr.
Receiving day Wednesday
6210 Mr. & Mrs. M. E. McGregor
6210 Miss Nellie D. Butler
6218 Mr. & Mrs. D. W. Miller

3435 Harry Speer
3435 Mr. & Mrs. Chas. W. Nicholes
3437 Mr. & Mrs. Morris M. Hirsh
3439 Mr. & Mrs. Horatio O. Stone
3441 Mr. & Mrs. J. D. Allen & dr.'
3537 Mr. & Mrs. G. W. Maxfield
3537 Mr. & Mrs. H. C. Hackney
3539 Mr. & Mrs.R.Pennington &drs.
3539 Mrs. Theresa Spiering
3539 Theodore B. Spiering
3539 Louis C. Spiering
3539 Mr. & Mrs. J. V. Watson
3543 Mr. & Mrs. T. A. Webb

3543 Mrs. Hannah C. Madden
3545 Mr. & Mrs. Secor Cunningham
  Receiving day Tuesday
3601 Mr. & Mrs. Thomas A. Wright
3639 Mr.& Mrs. Moses Waixel & dr.
  Receiving day Tuesday
3639 M. Sol. Waixel
3639 Mr. & Mrs. Fred Hirsch
  Receiving day Tuesday
3647 Mr. & Mrs. G. W. Wiggs & dr.
3647 Mrs. Luelle White & dr.
3651 Mr. & Mrs. Jacob Levi
3653 Mrs. Esther Nast & dr.
3653 Samuel Nast
3653 Alexander D. Nast
3661 Mr. & Mrs. S. Karger & dr.
  Receive 1st Saturday
3661 Lessing Karger
3661 Samuel I. Karger
3663 Mr. & Mrs. Lipman Glick
3667 Mr. & Mrs. J. F. Parker
3667 William C. Parker
3725 Mr. & Mrs. A. M. Rothschild
3801 Mr. & Mrs. Thos. A. Pearce
3803 Mr. & Mrs. Thos. Kearney
3805 Mr. & Mrs. J. I. Solomon
  Receiving day Thursday
3805 Julius Furth
3805 Miss Ella Furth
3811 Mr. & Mrs. Walter C. Trott
3811 Mrs. Belle Bowditch & dr.
3813 Mr. & Mrs. Henry L. Bristol
3813 Miss Kate Cohen
  Receives Saturday p.m.
3813 Charles W. Thompson
3813 Emery J. Nichols
3817 Judge & Mrs. M. R. M. Wallace & drs.
3819 Mr. & Mrs. J. L. Curtis
  Receiving day Thursday
3819 Miss Belle Stevens
3831 Mr. & Mrs. George A. Seavearns jr.
3847 Mr. & Mrs. Chas. D. Ettinger & dr.
3849 Mrs. A. C. Baldwin
3849 Willis M. Baldwin
3907 Dr. F. R. Webb
3907 Charles Webb & drs.
3925 Benjamin B. Lamb
3925 Augustus D. Lamb
3933 Mr. & Mrs. N. A. Kaufmann
  Receiving day Thursday
3953 The Van Dyke
  A Mr. & Mrs. P. H. Bettman
  B Mr. & Mrs. W. S. Hills

The Van Dyke (cont'd.)
200 Mrs. Emma L. Pulford
200 Mrs. Helen Sevant
202 Mr. & Mrs. Valentine Lapham
204 Mr. & Mrs. J. J. Grafton
206 John D. Evans
208 Mr. & Mrs. C. G. Hixson
212 Mr. & Mrs. A. S. Houston
216 Mrs. Almira J. Chase
300 Theodore Egersdorff & dr.
302 Mr. & Mrs. Bernard O'Neill
306 Mr. & Mrs. Octavius Pierce
310 Mr. & Mrs. Finley Scruggs
312 A. Devin Duvivier
312 Mrs. Jenny Eddison Duvivier
314 Mrs. Julia M. Dodge
314 Mrs. Lottie E. Gillespie
314 Walter E. Gillespie
316 William B. McVicker
316 Miss O. Violia McVicker
318 Mr. & Mrs. J. T. MacCoun
400 Mrs. Peter White
402 Mr. & Mrs. F. Austin Kerr
404 Mrs. M. W. Thompson
404 Miss M. Ellen Thayer
406 Mr. & Mrs. W. S. Corning
406 William B. Blackman
408 Mr. & Mrs. Chas. C. Bulkley
410 Mr. & Mrs. John A. Tobey
412 Dr. & Mrs. J. H. Prothero
414 Mr. & Mrs. C. T. Edwards
414 Mr. & Mrs. John Mills
4225 Mr. & Mrs. J. A. Hayes & dr.
4231 Mr. & Mrs. W. B. Judson
4237 Mr.&Mrs. Sam'lH.Regensburg
4239 Mr.&Mrs.H.C.Ingwersen & dr.
4239 G. J. Ingwersen
4239 Miss Ella C. Ingwersen
4409 Mr. & Mrs. Fred Howard
4415 Mr. & Mrs. Daniel E. Brush
4415 H. J. Brush
4417 Mr. & Mrs. Albert Pick, jr.
4425 Dr. & Mrs. C. P. Caldwell
4445 Dr. & Mrs. Frank T. McMahon
4631 Mr. & Mrs. Henry Hafer & drs
  Receive 2d Thursday
4635 Mr. & Mrs. Chas. R. Calkins
4643 Mr. & Mrs. C. C. Harder& dr.
4859 Mr. & Mrs. M. Clarkson
4859 Miss Kate Henneberry
4927 Mr. & Mrs. Joseph Osher & dr.
4927 Mrs. S. C. Brown
5045 Mr. & Mrs. J. J. Dunn
5045 Frank Dunn
5113 Mr. & Mrs. F. W. Connelly
5121 Mr. & Mrs. J. C. Griffin

5137 Mr. & Mrs. John E.Norton&dr.
5137 Fay Norton
5203 Mr. & Mrs. E. J. McArdle
5203 P. L. McArdle
5349 Mr. & Mrs. Robert Muehleisen
5349 Emile M. Gross

5623 Mr. & Mrs. George Beldam & drs.
5623 George C. Beldam
5627 Mr. & Mrs. Allen McCullough
5943 Mr. & Mrs. James Phillips
6215 Mrs. Margaret Krause & dr.

MICHIGAN TERRACE.

4024 Mrs. W. A. Weed
4024 William Weed
4024 Dr. & Mrs. Chas. Morgan
4024 John R. Morgan
4054 Mr. & Mrs. George E. West
4054 Mr. & Mrs G. H. Canniff
4054 T. H. Miles
4056 Mr. & Mrs. J. R. Cochrane & dr.
4056 Mr. & Mrs. Chas. C. Griswold
4058 Mrs. N. L. Potter & dr.
4058 Mrs. F. Cooper & drs.
4058 Charles A. Fitch
4058 Mr. & Mrs. Arthur E. Lumsden
4058 Mr. & Mrs. Thos. A. Maclean

4060 Mr. & Mrs. H. J. Williams&dr.
4060 Mr. & Mrs. Wm. C. Blauvelt
4060 Mr. & Mrs. Lewis S. Taylor
4060 Charles Armstrong
4062 Mr. & Mrs. Charles Corby
4062 Mr. & Mrs. Robert H. Pugh
4062 J. P. Claddo
4062 Mr. & Mrs. Chester J. McPherson
4064 Mr. & Mrs. John W. Higgins
4064 Mr. & Mrs. Royal H. Doud
4064 Benj. S. Doud
4064 Arthur S. Midlam
4064 Mr. & Mrs. Charles Jenkins

MONROE AVENUE.

5401 Mrs. Belle DesGranges
5407 Mr. & Mrs. Fred Harper
5455 Mr. & Mrs. C. E. Crandall
5471 Mr. & Mrs. W. T. Dix
5527 Mr. & Mrs. C. L. Moulton
5535 Dr. & Mrs. Wm. F. Waugh
5543 Mr. & Mrs. S. A. Hyers
5545 Mr. & Mrs. Frank N. Hayden
5545 Mr. & Mrs. J. B. Cutler
5551 Mrs. I. S. Mahan
5553 Mr. & Mrs. Chas. H. Mehagan
5555 Mrs. Ellen M. Buchanan
5555 Miss S. M. Paine
5555 T. G. Day
5557 Mr. & Mrs. Frank B. Felt
5617 Mrs. Joseph B. Doggett
5617 Miss Eunice S. Doggett
5621 Mr. & Mrs. W. Morava
5625 Mr. & Mrs. M. Butler
5627 Mr. & Mrs. Frank B. Stone
5627 Mrs. Lucy E. Stone
5727 Mr. & Mrs. Henry W. Chappell
5735 Mr. & Mrs. G. W. Northrup. jr.
5737 Mr. & Mrs. W. H. Boice
5813 Mrs. C. O. Tobin
5813 A. W. Tobin
5813 Mr. & Mrs. H. W. Richard
     Receiving day Thursday
5831 Rev. & Mrs. Wm. Goodfellow
5833 Prof. & Mrs. Wm. Gardner Hale
     Receiving day Thursday

5420 Mr. & Mrs. J. G. Pratt & dr
5420 Mr. & Mrs. W. W. Dunnigan
5420 Mr. & Mrs. W. H. Woodward
5422 Mr. & Mrs. Joseph G. Pratt
5422 Grafton H. Pratt
5422 M. Elizabeth Pratt
5426 Mr. & Mrs. R. H. Pierce
5430 Mr. & Mrs. Julius Kluefer
5434 Mr. & Mrs. C. C. Heldmann
5436 Mr. & Mrs. H. C. Stacey
5438 Mr. & Mrs. J. H. Husted
5440 Prof. & Mrs. C. F. Castle
5440 Mr. & Mrs. C. Minot
5466 Mr. & Mrs.. Chas. H. Avery
5466 Mr. & Mrs. Wm. H. Brodnax
5468 J. H. Hagenbuck
5468 Mr. & Mrs. Albert H. Tolman
5468 Mr. & Mrs. Theo. Behr
5484 Mr. & Mrs. J. S. Washburn
5484 Mr. & Mrs. C. M. Anderson
5484 Mrs. S. L. Beach
5484 Mr. & Mrs. Geo. M. Barbour
5484 Mrs. G. E. Bartlett
5496 Mr. & Mrs. Gilbert Wilson
5506 Mr. & Mrs. Wm. S. Colwell
5506 Mr. & Mrs. C. W. Moore
5506 Mrs. J. P. Jackson
5506 Mr. & Mrs. Jas. VanCraenenbroeck
5514 Mr. & Mrs. Robt. C. Garrabrant
5520 Mr. & Mrs. Albert C. Hawes

5524 Mr. & Mrs. W. B. Clancy
5524 Mr. & Mrs. L. B. Mason
5528 Dr.&Mrs. H. Hamilton Forline
 Receiving day Wednesday
5528 Mrs. Henry F. Miller
5528 Miss G. A. Howard
5528 Miss Emma Howard
5528 Julius F. Brower
5532 Mr. & Mrs. H. W. Mahan
5538 Kenneth S. Walbank
5538 Mrs. E. J. Walbank
5540 Mr. & Mrs. George S. Terry
5540 Prof. R. D. Sailsbury
5544 Mr. & Mrs. W. S. Whiteside
5548 Mr. & Mrs. W. O. Johnson
5552 Mr. & Mrs. Joseph M. Miller
5552 Raymond J. Miller
5554 Mr. & Mrs. J. F. Brine
5556 Mrs. L. P. Miller
5600 Dr. & Mrs. L. Hulbert Fuller
5600 Mr. & Mrs. Jules M. Gaspard
5600 Mr. & Mrs. Joseph Crisand
5602 Mr. & Mrs. Frank Upman
5616 Mr. & Mrs. F. G. Cobb
5620 Mr. & Mrs. Samuel Lyon
5624 Mr. & Mrs. James Dalzell

5624 Walter Dalzell
5624 Mr. & Mrs. C. R. Dickerson
5628 Mr.& Mrs. Chas. B. Allen & dr.
5628 J. F. MacKenzie
5642 Mr. & Mrs. J. L. Hotchkin & dr.
5646 Mr.& Mrs.George E.Robertson
5652 Mr. & Mrs. George E. Griggs
5656 Mr. & Mrs. Walter W. Hilton
5656 J. Ranney Hilton
5700 Mr. & Mrs. John Lally & dr.
5708 Mr. & Mrs. Homer G. Fordyce
5712 Mr. & Mrs. Alpheus W. Smith
5726 J. Mason Jackson
5730 Mr. & Mrs. W. R. Patterson
5738 Mr. & Mrs. Frank Ransford
5738 Mr. & Mrs. J. B. McGregor
5738 Mr. & Mrs. A. C. Stinson
5740 Mr. & Mrs. W. H. McWatters
5740 Mr. & Mrs. W. L. Smith
5748 Mr. & Mrs. I. E. Roll
5754 Mr. & Mrs. Chas. F. Pearce
 Receiving day Thursday
5754 Mrs. Jane W. Merriam
5756 Mr. & Mrs. J. F. Kent
5756 Miss Ada M. Kent
5810 Mrs. J. Young Scammon

MYRTLE AVENUE.

6439 Mr. & Mrs. John F. Crow & dr.
6445 Mr. & Mrs. Charles G. Bowen
6449 Dr. & Mrs. Eugene Vigneron
6453 Mr. & Mrs. Charles Erickson
 ———
6428 Mr. & Mrs. J. G. King
6428 Harry V. King.
6432 Mr. & Mrs. R. J. Breckenridge
6460 Mr.& Mrs. S. M.Biddison & dr.
6500 Mr. & Mrs. Edward W. Nason
6500 Albert H. Kinkaid
6500 Mr. & Mrs. L. A. Sandmeyer

6504 Mr.& Mrs. Herbert F. Seymour
6532 Mr. & Mrs. Rufus J. Haight
6532 Mrs. Nellie E. Stewart
6346 Fred W. Green
6346 Miss Julia A. Green
6352 Mr. & Mrs. F. B. Stowell
6362 Mr. & Mrs. James H. Atwood
6402 Mr. & Mrs. Archie C. Cracraft
6418 Mrs. Mary Moore
6418 Mr. & Mrs. M. L. Campbell
6422 Mr.&Mrs.George W. Coolidge
6424 Dr. Chas. E. Austin

NORTH NORMAL PARKWAY.

402 Mr. & Mrs. Augustus F. McKay
412 Mr. & Mrs. James L. Gates
416 Mr. & Mrs. J. D. Dymond
436 Mr. & Mrs. Marshall Holmes
448 Mr. & Mrs. A. B. Crossman
452 Mr. & Mrs. John J. McDonald
 Receiving day Wednesday

456 Mr. & Mrs. Chas. Mather
512 Rev. & Mrs. B. F. Matrau
528 Mr. & Mrs. E. H. Ericson
532 Mr. & Mrs. A. F. Walther
542 Mr. & Mrs. Julian C. Jones
548 Mr. & Mrs. P. Osborn
550 Mr. & Mrs. H. A. Rubidge

SOUTH NORMAL PARKWAY.

451 Rev. & Mrs. John B. Hutton
533 Mr. & Mrs. A. Fox
533 Will A. Fox
533 Mrs. L. M. Wilms

535 Rev. & Mrs. Homer J. Vosburg
539 Mr. & Mrs. J. J. Mogg
539 Millard E. Mogg
539 Clayton W. Mogg

OAK AVENUE.
(See Thirty-sixth.)

OAKENWALD AVENUE.

4201 Mr. & Mrs. A. M. McKinney & dr.
4207 Mr. & Mrs. Percy F. Webster
4209 Mr. & Mrs. Thos. Sanford & dr.
4209 H. T. Sanford
4221 Mr. & Mrs. Norville Wheaton
4225 George A. Wright
4229 Mr. & Mrs. Alfred Kirk
4301 Mr. & Mrs. Henry C. Elliot
    Receive 1st and 3d Wednesdays
4301 Dr. & Mrs. C. M. Burrows
4301 Theodore B. Myers
4301 W. E. Woodward
4307 Mr. & Mrs. Herbert G. Teed
4307 Mr. & Mrs. H. O. Whitaker & drs.
4307 Mrs. Marie A. Young
4311 Mr. & Mrs. A. P. Spencer
4323 Mrs. L. L. Rapp
4323 W. J. Elwell
4327 Mr. & Mrs. Edward P. Sills
4327 Mrs. E. J. Lamplugh
4329 Mr. & Mrs. A. W. Becker
4335 Mrs. B. C. Poitras
4335 Frank L. Linden
4335 Ernest J. Wagner
4339 Mrs. J. B. Follett
4339 L. H. Wilson
4339 Miss Gertrude Gibson
4339 Miss Helen Marrh
4341 James T. Hall & drs.
4347 Mr. & Mrs. James G. Davis
4347 Graham Davis
4349 Mr. & Mrs. H. T. Sidway
4349 L. B. Sidway
4349 Mrs. D. E. Milner
4351 Mrs. S. Strelitz & dr.
    Receiving day Friday
4351 David Strelitz
4351 Victor Strelitz
4355 Mr. & Mrs. W. W. Chandler
4355 Dr. & Mrs. Eugene W. Sawyer
    Receiving day Wednesday eve.
4367 Mr. & Mrs. Louis Manasse
4401 Mr. & Mrs. Porter Deardoff
4403 Mr.&Mrs.Edward W.Andrews
4415 Mr. & Mrs. J. A. Shepard
4415 Mrs. Wm. W. Hunter
4455 Mr. & Mrs. R. L. Wilson
4455 Mrs. C. C. Hawley
4455 Mrs. G. A. Boyd

4200 Mr. & Mrs. D. B. Sweet
4204 Mr. & Mrs. Chas. E. Adams
4204 Mrs. Lois A. Goodwin
4206 Mr. & Mrs. George Watkins
4210 Mrs. Helen Shufeldt & drs.
4208 Mr. & Mrs. A. H. Massey
4212 Mr. & Mrs. J. F. Beals
    Receiving day Wednesday
4212 A. R. Thomas
4214 Mr. & Mrs. W. F. Wylie
4216 Mr. & Mrs. N. B. Koontz
4218 Mr. & Mrs. J. P. Bishop
4218 Frank Bishop
4220 Mr. & Mrs. W. D. Anderson
4224 Mr. & Mrs. M. H. McCarthy
4228 Mr. & Mrs. Francis Squair
4232 Mr. & Mrs.William Allen & dr.
4306 Mr. & Mrs. W. H. A. Brown
4310 Mr. & Mrs. C. D. Warren
4310 Allyn D. Warren
4310 Mrs. Phineas Parker
4314 Mr. & Mrs. Chas. Leyenberger & dr. *Receiving day Tuesday*
4318 Mr. & Mrs. John M. Fiske
4328 Mr. & Mrs. Herbert Hammond
4330 Mr. & Mrs. A. A. Turner
4338 Mr. & Mrs. C. F. Livermore
4338 Cornelius M. Trowbridge
4340 Mr. & Mrs. William F. White
4344 Mr. & Mrs. Henry Mills
4344 Mr. & Mrs. M. E. Mills
4346 Mr. & Mrs. C. L. Bingham
4350 Mrs. Mary M. Patterson & dr.
4350 Ralph C. Seymour
4350 John P. Seymour
4350 Granville H. Howard
4354 Mr. & Mrs. John J. Grey
4356 Mr. & Mrs. George D. Milligan
4358 Mr. & Mrs. M. A. Myers
4360 Mr. & Mrs. E. R. Shurly
4360 Bert Shurly
4362 Mr. & Mrs. W. D. Wyman
    Receiving day Thursday
4364 Mr. & Mrs. C. G. Armstrong
4366 Mr. & Mrs. Lewis E. Pennington
4368 Mr. & Mrs. George Thomas
4406 Mr. & Mrs. Charles O. Robinson
4408 Mrs. Martha I. Alward & dr.
4408 Emmet C. Gibson

4459 Mr. & Mrs. A. A. Rolf
4459 Mr. & Mrs. D. Norton
4461 Horace Howell & drs.
4461 Mr. & Mrs. R. A. Hall
4465 Mr. & Mrs. Chas. E. Braden
4465 Mr. & Mrs. Henry Erkins
4467 Mr. & Mrs. E. G. Carlisle
4467 Dr. & Mrs. T. H. Rockwell
4469 Mr. & Mrs. John S. Murray
4469 Edward A. Sutter
4483 Mr. & Mrs. A. H. Pickering
4483 Miss Mary Lee Bufkin
4519 Mr. & Mrs. J. B. Wilson
4533 Mr. & Mrs. J. G. Hartigan
4535 Mr. & Mrs. H. W. Griswold
4539 James P. Hankey
4539 Luther Williams
4539 Frank Birkin
4539 George B. White
4561 Joseph B. Marshall
4567 Mr. & Mrs. C. S. Hartley & dr.
4577 Dr.&Mrs. Robt. W. McMahan
4577 Miss Una McMahan
4577 Miss Florence L. McMahan
4585 Mr. & Mrs. Isaac F. Dickson
4585 Mrs. Lizzie B. Kellogg
4589 Dr. & Mrs. Robert Jessup
4591 Mr. & Mrs. A. A. Paddon
4595 Mr. & Mrs. A. B. Southard
4597 Mr. & Mrs. C. F. Eiker
4599 Mr. & Mrs. Harold Henderson

4558 Mr. & Mrs. Eugene Capelle
4558 Miss Harriet Tafft
Receiving day Tuesday
4558 Mr.&Mrs.Hampden F.Thomas
4558 R. C. Van Bokkelen
4360 Mr. & Mrs. Frank J. Reed
4560 Mr. & Mrs. Geo. H. Heafford
4560 Mr. & Mrs. F. T. West
4560 Mr. & Mrs.Rudolph R.Magnus
4560 C. H. Mecum
4564 Mr. & Mrs. John H. Ferris
4564 James W. Ferris
4564 William J. Ferris
4564 Mrs. Rosina Tyler
4576 Mr. & Mrs. J. C. Sampson& dr.
4576 Mr. & Mrs. W. H. Sampson
4578 Mr. & Mrs. A. W. Hutchins
4580 Mr. & Mrs. Albert D. Sheridan
4584 Mr. & Mrs. C. L. Wilson

4410 Mr. & Mrs. Robert Nicholas
4416 Mr. & Mrs. Charles Morris
Receiving day Thursday
4418 Mr. & Mrs. J. Grafton Parker
4418 Mr.&Mrs. J. Grafton Parker jr.
4420 Mr. & Mrs. George P. Benton
4422 Mr. & Mrs. Geo. H. Curtiss
4450 Mr. & Mrs. Wm. P. Huguenin
4450 Mr. & Mrs. George A. Coe
4450 Mr. & Mrs. C. C. Morton
4454 Mr. & Mrs. Leon C. Welch
4454 Mr. & Mrs. Frank B. Clark
4454 Mr. & Mrs. Edwin G. Chase
4454 Mr. & Mrs. Edwin C. Veasy
4454 Mrs. Wm. Aldrich
4458 Mr. & Mrs. John M. Dodson
4458 Mr. & Mrs. Edwin L. Wagner
4460 Mr. & Mrs. E. R. Baker
4460 Mr. & Mrs. Charles G. James
4460 Mr. & Mrs. A. C. Balch
4462 Mrs. Isaac Lincoln jr.
4462 Mrs. Josephine S. Strait
4466 Mr. & Mrs. George F. Bartlett
4466 George F. Bartlett jr.
4470 Mr. & Mrs. George B. Bartlett
4514 Mr. & Mrs. August Pollak
4518 Mrs. Almira Abbott
4518 Frederick Abbott
4526 Mr. & Mrs. Ezra Holden &drs.
4526 E. Wallace Holden
4528 Mr. & Mrs. Otis O. Hall
4528 Miss Rose Richardson
4530 Mr. & Mrs. A. C. Keebler
4530 Miss Nettie Keebler
4532 Mr. & Mrs. Wm. McLain
4540 Mr. & Mrs. W. H. Welch
4540 Miss Josie King
4540 Miss Tillie King
4540 Albert Welch
4542 Mr. & Mrs. F. H. Jones
4544 Mr. & Mrs. Morris Trumbull
4546 Mr. & Mrs. W. F. Bode
4548 M. S. Woodward
4552 Mr. & Mrs. E. S. Frasher
4552 Mr. & Mrs. Hugh D. Bowker
4552 Mr. & Mrs. Oscar Remmer
4554 Mr. & Mrs. E. F. Hinckley
4554 Mrs. A. G. Bagg
4558 C. V. Gwin & drs.
4558 James M. Gwin
4558 Mr. & Mrs. H. E. McNeil

OAKLAND CRESCENT.

3 Mrs. Grace R. Sheldon
7 Mr. & Mrs. George Gregg

2 Dr. & Mrs. C. Stoddard Smith
6 Walter B. Kelby

OAKWOOD AVENUE.

23 Mr. & Mrs. William Hoagland

58 George C. Bailey
60 Mr. & Mrs. Albert L. Smith
60 Mr. & Mrs. B. C. Ernst
98 Mr.& Mrs.Samuel Faulkner&drs.

50 Mr. & Mrs. C. H. Schaeffer
50 Mr. & Mrs. Wm. Irvin & dr.
50 William Johnson
50 Dr. & Mrs. N. B. Delamater
52 Mrs. Esther Marion
58 Mr. & Mrs. E. W. Bailey

OAKWOOD BOULEVARD.

143 and 145 The Allen
　　F. M. Wood
　　Miss Martha Fleming
1 Mr. & Mrs. H. M. Hunt
2 Dr. & Mrs. O. G. Tremaine
3 Mr. & Mrs. G. C. Campbell
3 Douglas Campbell
4 Mrs. A. B. Crane
6 Mr. & Mrs. Wm. Best
8 Mrs. S. B. Pease
8 Mr. & Mrs. Jno. B. Viets
9 Mr. & Mrs. C. W. Allen
11 Mr. & Mrs. J. St. Hiliare
12 J. R. Brooks
13 Mrs. John W. Foster
13 Mrs. C. M. Thompson
14 Mr. & Mrs. C. C. Gebhart
15 Miss M. M. Tait
15 Miss J. A. Tait
15 Miss M. Eveline Stack
16 Mr. & Mrs. G. W. Darrow
17 Mrs. S. G. Higgins
17 W. G. Higgins
17 Miss Marion Higgins
18 Mr. & Mrs. I. H. Waggoner
19 E. J. Sherwin
20 Mrs. A. B. Barnes
20 Willard E. Shandrew
20 D. Monroe Barnes
21 Mr. & Mrs. Lewis Fuess &
　　drs.
22 Mr. & Mrs. Geo. C. Skidmore
　　Receiving day Thursday
24 Mr. & Mrs. John P. Kochers-
　　perger   *Rec. day Tuesday*
26 Mr. & Mrs. Thomas Hoops
　　Receiving day Tuesday
27 Mr. & Mrs. W. O. Brewster
　　Receiving day Tuesday
28 Mr. & Mrs. O. C. Gay
29 Mr. & Mrs. Thomas Carr
　　Receiving day Tuesday
30 Miss Martha Fleming
30 Miss Helen Fleming
31 Mr. & Mrs. D. Henry Sheldon

144 Dr. L. S. Tenney
156 Mr. & Mrs. D. D. McKillip
160 Mrs. E. F. Miner
160 Miss A. J. French
160 Miss Maud Miner
162 Mrs. M. L. Sheldon
162 George H. Nawn
164 Dr. & Mrs. G. F. Wetherell
166 Mr. & Mrs. Wm. Mayor & dr.
170 Dr. & Mrs. Charles S. Jones
170 Dr. & Mrs. A. C. Fruth
170 Dr. R. B. Miller
172 Mr. & Mrs. L. M. Smith
172 Mr. & Mrs. G. P. Richardson
172 Mr. & Mrs C. B. McKibbin
174 Mrs. F. P. VanValkenberg
174 M. A. Stacy
174 John H. Ahern
194 Mr. & Mrs. William Stewart
194 R. M. Orr
194 Dr. Henry Stewart
198 Mr. & Mrs. H. D. Patton
198 A. M. Prentiss
198 Mr. & Mrs. I. W. Blood
200 Mr. & Mrs. Charles H. Sieg
　　Receiving day Thursday
200 Mr. & Mrs. O. W. Ellis
202 Mr. & Mrs. S. Strauss
202 Mr. & Mrs. J. T. White
　　Receiving day Tuesday
202 Mr. & Mrs. William H. Berger
204 Mr. & Mrs. James A. Burhans
204 Mr. & Mrs. R. H. Cherry
206 H. H. Bowen
206 Mrs. L. C. Bowen & drs.
226 Mr. & Mrs. J. D. James
232 Mr.& Mrs.Charles S.Burkholder
234 Mrs. J. M. Beverly
236 Mr. & Mrs. Samuel Slade
238 Mr. & Mrs. Julian C. Burdick
240 Mrs. V. Sutter & dr.
240 Victor Sutter
242 Mr. & Mrs. Clarence Preston
　　Eyre   *Rec. day Thursday*
244 Mr. & Mrs. C. M. Clark

 32 Mr. & Mrs. L. A. Haseltine
        & dr.
 32 Frank R. Haseltine
 32 Fred W. Haseltine
167 Dr. & Mrs. L. B. Hayman
185 Mr. & Mrs. G. S. Bush
185 Mr. & Mrs. Edward B.McCleary
187 Mr. & Mrs. E. J. Milligan
189 Mr. & Mrs. J. McDowell
189 R. P. McDowell
191 Mr. & Mrs. Foster Stone
        Receiving day Thursday
191 Kenneth Stone
191 Mr. & Mrs. A. E. Frear & dr.
191 A. Edward Frear
195 Mrs. L. A. Munger
195 A. Page Munger
195 Frank S. Munger
195 Mrs. Mary E. Hitchcock & dr.
195 William Hitchcock
197 Mr. & Mrs. J. S. McClure
223 Joseph Dion & dr.
223 Dr. Delvina Dion
225 J. B. Armijo
225 Miss Josefina C. Armijo
229 Mr. & Mrs. F. W. Flint
231 Mr. & Mrs. T. C. Smith & drs.
        Receiving day Thursday
233 Mrs. M. V. Collins
233 Mr. & Mrs. J. Nycum
237 Mr. & Mrs. A. E. Forrest
239 Mr. & Mrs. Cummings Cherry
241 Mr. & Mrs. M. D. Davis
245 Mr. & Mrs. Samuel Barnum
245 Mr. & Mrs. Albert C. Barnum
245 E. S. Barnum
245 Mr. & Mrs. W. W. Thacher
245 Mrs. Jennie B. Williams
255 Mr. & Mrs. W. Roberts
257 Mr. & Mrs. Charles J. C. Will
261 Mrs. H. A. Donly
261 John G. Donly
263 Mr. & Mrs. Franklin S. Eberhart
265 Mr. & Mrs. George H. Sidwell
271 Mrs. I. W. Boardman
271 Mr. & Mrs. J. R. Morron
271 Mrs. M. F. Pierce
271 Mrs. L. H. Cone
271 Mr. & Mrs. Wm. H. Browning
271 Mr. & Mrs. W. A. Dunshee
        Receiving day Thursday
271 Charles F. Hills
271 Mrs. E. O. Read
271 J. J. Knickerbocker
271 Eugene M. Farr
271 George D. Farr

246 Mr. & Mrs. H. M. Wilcox
246 Mrs. L. Thacker
248 Mrs. Harriet E. Munger
248 H. B. Munger
248 Mrs. L. Munger Jones
252 Mr. & Mrs. P. Leonard
314 Mrs. J. W. Houston & drs.
314 Frank B. Houston
314 James S. Houston
316 Mr. & Mrs. G. O. Garnsey
320 Mr. & Mrs. A. N. Warner
320 Mr. & Mrs. C. H. Brand
322 Mr. & Mrs. Frank Shepard
326 Mr. & Mrs. Allen F. Murray
330 Mr. & Mrs. W. D. S. Anderson
320 Mrs. J. A. Perkins
332 Mrs. C. M. Stokes
332 C. F. Stokes
334 Mr. & Mrs. James R. Mann
336 Mr.& Mrs. Martin C. Kehoe
338 Mr. & Mrs. R. C. Morrison
340 Mr. & Mrs. W. R. Toppan
344 Mr. & Mrs. D. P. Perry
346 Mrs. Elizabeth Stevens & dr.
346 Mrs. Ella L. Aldrich
348 Mr. & Mrs. W. E. Rogan
        Receiving day Wednesday
350 Mr. & Mrs. L. E. Steinmann
350 E. A. Steinmann
352 Mr. & Mrs. Benjamin Bruce &
        dr.   *Receiving day Friday*
352 Edward I. Bruce
352 Frank A. Bruce
354 Mr. & Mrs. Almon W. Bulkley
358 Mr.& Mrs. M. L. C. Funkhouser
360 Mr. & Mrs. J. Schoenfeld
378 Mr. & Mrs. David Mayer & drs.
378 Toby Mayer
380 Mr. & Mrs. H. N. Stephens
380 Mrs. A. L. Ruth
382 Mr. & Mrs. N. Morganroth
386 Mr. & Mrs. E. D. Murray jr.
386 Miss Jennie Murray
386 E. B. Murray

        ———

323 Miss Emily J. Smith
337 Mr. & Mrs. Robert Excell
339 Mr. & Mrs. Henry Sandmeyer
        &dr.*Receiving day Wednesday*
341 Mr. & Mrs. S. Daniels & drs.
        Receiving day Friday
343 Mr. & Mrs. John J. Sherman
347 Mr. & Mrs. Willard L. Cobb
347 Mr. & Mrs. Joseph C. Field
353 Mrs. B. Powell
        Receiving day 1st Friday

353 Henry Hirsch
353 I. Hirsch
353 M. Hirsch
355 Mrs. & Mrs. George Woodland
355 Fred B. Woodland
361 Mr. & Mrs. I. N. W. Sherman
361 W. B. Sherman
361 Charles K. Sherman
365 Mr. & Mrs. A. L. Patterson

367 Mr. & Mrs. Morris Barbe
367 Miss Gertrude Snowden
373 Mr. & Mrs. Arthur W. Allyn
377 Mr. & Mrs. J. W. Byers & drs.
385 Mr. & Mrs. H. C. Buhoup
   Receiving day Wednesday
387 Mr. & Mrs. W. M. Morrill
389 Mr. & Mrs. J. B. Conlin
389 S. H. Finch

OGLESBY AVENUE.

6033 Mr. & Mrs. C. D. Beale & drs.
6033 Warren A. Beale
6033 Roland R. Beale
6037 Mr. & Mrs. John Roper
6037 Miss Jessie Roper
6041 Mr. & Mrs. Carl D. Buck
6045 Mr. & Mrs. W. H. Potter & dr.
   Receiving day Thursday
6049 Mr. & Mrs. L. M. Smith
6053 Mr. & Mrs. P. Carhart
6059 Mr. & Mrs. W. H. Mooney
6179 Mr. & Mrs. Wm. H. Stewart
6137 Mrs. M. M. Atwood
6137 Fred G. Atwood
6237 Mr. & Mrs. Louis Danne
   Receiving day Friday
6237 Mr. & Mrs. William H. Ford
6249 Mr. & Mrs. J. W. Boyd
6303 Dr. Harry W. Cheney
6307 J. E. McDowell
6321 Mr. & Mrs. A. J. Mills
6325 Spencer A. Brown
6325 C. P. Hurlbut
6341 Mr. & Mrs. M. E. Dayton & dr.
6341 Charles Dayton
6403 Mr. & Mrs. S. W. Straub
6403 Arthur M. Straub
6403 Mrs. C. Bowling
6405 Mr. & Mrs. T. J. Holton
6411 Mrs. L. S. Sherer & dr.
6417 Mr. & Mrs. Robert W. Hall
6417 William Hall
6443 Mrs. S. L. Bell & drs.
6501 Mr. & Mrs. W. Irving Midler
6505 Mr. & Mrs. Paul Henson
6519 Mr. & Mrs. W. E. Bond
6519 Mr. & Mrs. Robert Fawcett

6352 Dr. Helen M. Buchanan & drs.
6352 Mrs. N. D. Arnold
6352 Mahlon Barron & dr.
6352 Mr. & Mrs. Elbert D. Weyburn
6352 Ned C. Weyburn
6356 Mr. & Mrs. Daniel B. Hubbard

6032 Mr. & Mrs. H. W. Coolidge &
   drs.
6032 Mr. & Mrs. Benj. Hoskins
   Receiving day Thursday
6036 Dr. & Mrs. Howard Crutcher
nw. cor. 61st Dr. Frances Dickinson
nw. cor. 61st Dr. Lucy Waite
nw. cor. 61st Judge & Mrs. C. B.
   Waite
nw. cor. 61st Dr. & Mrs. F. B. Robinson
nw. cor. 61st Mr. & Mrs. Edgar F.
   Russell
6110 Mr. & Mrs. Charles Peck & drs.
6146 Mr. & Mrs. C. H. Hillman
6150 Mr. & Mrs. Geo. W. Spencer
6158 Mr. & Mrs. E. A. Hughes & dr.
6158 Robert E. Hughes
6206 Vendome Club Hotel
   Mr. & Mrs. Geo. W. Lilley
   Mr. & Mrs. Henry Knight
   Mr. & Mrs. Samuel M. Parker
   Stephen Hexter
   Mr. & Mrs. J. A. Wilkens
   Wm. J. English
   Mrs. C. H. Bailey
   Mr. & Mrs. Phil Ryan & drs.
   Receiving day Wednesday
   Mr. & Mrs. John G. Hale
   Mr. & Mrs. Ossian Guthrie
   Clarence M. LaShelle
   Mr. & Mrs. T. W. Magill
   O. A. Olmsted
6212 Mr. & Mrs. W. B. Davidson
6214 Mr. & Mrs. Edwin W. Cobb
6220 Mr. & Mrs. Silas T. Hawthorne
6222 Mrs. J. Baird & dr.
6228 Mr. & Mrs. Thomas Scanlan
6230 Mr. & Mrs. Chas. B. Helfen-
   stein & dr.
6240 Mr. & Mrs. R. V. Hayes
6320 Mr. & Mrs. Frank Pearson
6334 Mr. & Mrs. D. V. Keedy
6336 Mr. & Mrs. E. A. Beeks

6400 Dr. R. E. L. Rodgers
6400 George W. Rodgers
6400 John L. Rodgers
6404 Mr. & Mrs. Harry Dolling & dr.
6410 Mr. & Mrs. F. A. Braymer
6410 Mrs. H. Story
6416 Mr. & Mrs. T. G. Northrup & dr
6420 Mr. & Mrs. Hugh Irvine
6424 Augustus J. Burbank
6436 Mr. & Mrs. George C. Fairman
6436 F. W. Disbrow
6438 Mr. & Mrs. Frank J. Smith

6456 Mr. & Mrs. S. V. Cornish
6460 Mr. & Mrs. Jacques Loeb
6462 Mr. & Mrs. C. A. Guernsey
Receiving day Thursday
6502 Mr. & Mrs. John Quinn
6506 Mr. & Mrs. A. E. Buisseret
6510 Mr. & Mrs. J. Claude Hill
6530 Mr. & Mrs. G. W. Ford
6534 Mr. & Mrs. W. J. Mullen
6616 Mr. & Mrs. G. N. VanHouten
6620 Mr. & Mrs. Samuel Leland
6620 Mr. & Mrs. Charles F. Tuttle
6640 Mr. & Mrs. J. E. Zimmerman

PARK END AVENUE.

6016 Mr. & Mrs. Pulaski J. Bryan
6020 Mr. & Mrs. Lincoln Brooke
6024 Mr. & Mrs. S. B. Lamberson
6028 Mr. & Mrs. H. E. Shean
Receiving day Tuesday
6030 Dr. & Mrs. C. H. Beard

6030 Harry A. Clark
6040 Mr.& Mrs.Geo.W.McKee & dr.
6050 Mr. & Mrs. Frank E. Brady
6050 Mr. & Mrs. W. Bancroft Jarvis
6052 Mr. & Mrs. Robt. H. Countiss
jr.

SOUTH PEORIA STREET.

7719 Mr. & Mrs. Frank A. Henshaw

5534 Mr. & Mrs. C. W. Gross
7752 Mr. & Mrs. John L. Manning

ORCHARD STREET.

24 Dr. & Mrs. E. R. Kellogg
Receiving day Tuesday

24 Mr. & Mrs. J. B. Tower
24 G. W. Hern

PERRY AVENUE.

6537 Mr. & Mrs. Lyman Lewis & dr.
6539 Mr. & Mrs. L. E. Keil
6541 A. P. Miller
6545 Mrs. A. E. Sinclair & dr.
6549 Mr. & Mrs. M. H. Wagar & dr.
6557 Mr. & Mrs. F. Salter & dr.
6633 Mr. & Mrs. W. M. Alexander
6633 Miss L. Alexander
6641 Mr. & Mrs. Wm. H. Dunn
6641 K. E. Dunn
6647 Mr. & Mrs. James Norman
6651 Mr. & Mrs. W. M. Bartlett
6659 Mr. & Mrs. W. H. Sharp
6707 Mr. & Mrs. W. H. Lain
6711 Mr. & Mrs. Abe S. Smith
6731 Mr. & Mrs. John A. Bartlett
6731 Mr. & Mrs. Charles A. Bartlett
6749 Mr. & Mrs. F. W. Croft & dr.
6749 F. L. Croft
6801 Mr. & Mrs. S. H. Moore
6817 Mr. & Mrs. A. C. Halliwell
6837 Mrs. B. De Bey
6837 Mr. & Mrs. H. Vanderploeg

6500 Mrs. M. J. Robinson
6528 Mr. & Mrs. Chas. E. DaShiell
& dr.
6532 Mr. & Mrs. Charles D. Dunann
6602 Mr. & Mrs. E. R. O'Hara
6606 Mr. & Mrs. H. C. Draper
6620 Mr. & Mrs. B. F. Butler
6624 Mr. & Mrs. C. A. McKelvey
6628 Mr. & Mrs. P. R. Hilton
6636 Mr. & Mrs. Myron H.Tichenor
6640 Mr. & Mrs. J. K. Hooper
6646 Mr. & Mrs. Ervin A. Rice
6700 Mr. & Mrs. Chas. H. Mitchell
6716 Mr. & Mrs. H. Y. Lazear
6738 Mr. & Mrs. Leonard C.Snyder
6738 Mr. & Mrs. D. Gilday
6740 Mr. & Mrs. D. Welling
6744 Mr. & Mrs. Thomas Day & dr.
6748 Mr. & Mrs. Ed. R. Price
6752 Mr. & Mrs. Francis M. Buck
6800 Mr. & Mrs. W. F. Sargent
6800 Mrs. R. A. Preble
6800 Glenwood Preble

6939 Mr. & Mrs. Dayton E. Jones
6943 Mr. & Mrs. James H. Davis
6947 Mr. & Mrs. R. W. Faulkner
6951 Mr. & Mrs. F. E. Brown
6959 Mr. & Mrs. Joseph Keene
7007 Mr. & Mrs. Chas. W. Jackson

6946 Miss Frances L. Goodwin
6950 Mr. & Mrs. Willis Smith
7056 Mr. & Mrs. August Tidholm

6816 Dr. & Mrs. H. W. Hemingway
6816 Mr. & Mrs. Jerome P. Stevens
6826 Mr. & Mrs. Chas. Salmon
6832 Mr. & Mrs. C. E. Nason
6912 Mr. & Mrs. L. J. Sergel
6912 Mrs. L. W. Clark & dr.
6914 Rev. & Mrs. W. M. Hindman
6916 Mr. & Mrs. Wilbur S. Jackman
6930 Mr. & Mrs. Thos. Edwards
6940 Mr. & Mrs. Geo. Stuart
6946 Mr. & Mrs. Wm. Porter & dr.

PRAIRIE AVENUE.

1601 Wm. Morton Payne
1615 Mr. & Mrs. Lyman Wilson
1615 Mr. & Mrs. D. W. Greig
1619 Mr. & Mrs. George Alexander
  McKinlock
  Receiving day Tuesday
1621 Mr. & Mrs. John H. Hamline
1621 George A. Mead
1623 Mr. & Mrs. J. M. Allan
1625 Mr. & Mrs. Hugh J. McBirney
  Receiving day Tuesday
1635 Mr. & Mrs. Warren Springer
1637 Mr. & Mrs. Jesse Spalding
1637 Miss Jessie Spalding
1701 Mrs. O. Van Schaack Ward
  Receiving day Monday
1701 Mr. & Mrs. William G. Hibbard
  Receive Monday afternoon
1701 William G. Hibbard jr.
1701 F. V. S. Hibbard
1721 Mrs. Wirt Dexter
1729 Mr. & Mrs. Geo. M. Pullman &
  dr.   *Receiving day Friday*
1729 W. Sanger Pullman
1801 Mr. & Mrs. W. W. Kimball
  Receiving day Tuesday
1801 Mrs. M. M. Cone
1811 Rev. Loren C. Collins
1811 Judge & Mrs. Lorin C. Collins jr
  Receiving day Tuesday
1823 Mr. & Mrs. Thomas Dent
1827 Mr. & Mrs. J. W. Doane
1827 Mr. & Mrs. John Edwin Doane
1901 Mr. & Mrs. Norman B. Ream
1905 Mr. & Mrs. Marshall Field
1919 Mr. & Mrs. Marshall Field jr.
1923 Mrs. Sarah H. Kellogg & dr.
1923 Mr. & Mrs. Pierrepont Isham
1945 Mrs. Henry Corwith
1945 Charles R. Corwith
1945 John W. Corwith
1945 Mr. & Mrs. Alfred L. Baker

1600 John G. Shortall
1604 Mr. & Mrs. John L. Shortall
1608 Mr. & Mrs. Henry L. Frank
1612 Mr. & Mrs. P. E. Studebaker
1616 Mr. & Mrs. William R. Stirling
1620 Dr. & Mrs. Lyman Ware
1620 Robert H. Law
1620 Robert Law
1626 Mr. & Mrs. Abraham Longini
1628 Mr. & Mrs. Morris Einstein
  Receiving day Thursday
1628 Benjamin Einstein
1628 Mrs. Emma Beirs
1630 Mrs. Peter Brust & drs.
1634 Mrs. E. Foote
1634 Erastus Foote jr.
1634 Mr. & Mrs. T. H. Bellas
1636 Mr. & Mrs. H. Morris Johnston
1636 H. McB. Johnston
1636 Morris L. Johnston
1638 Mr. & Mrs. Robert B. Gregory
1638 Mrs. Elizabeth Gregory
1702 Mr. & Mrs. T. W. Harvey
1702 Turlington W. Harvey jr.
1702 Robert H. Harvey
1712 Albert Sturges & dr.
1712 Washington Sturges
1712 Solomon Sturges
1720 Mrs. James M. Walker
  Receives Tuesday afternoon
1720 Wirt D. Walker
1726 Mr. & Mrs. James R. Walker
  Receiving day Tuesday
1730 Mr. & Mrs. Joseph E. Otis
1730 Ralph C. Otis
1736 Mr. & Mrs. Hugh McBirney
1800 Mr. & Mrs. John J. Glessner
  Receive Tuesday afternoon
1800 J. G. M. Glessner
1808 Mr. & Mrs. O. R. Keith
1808 Miss Alice Keith

2001 Mr. & Mrs. J. L. Lombard
2003 Mr. & Mrs. George F. Bissell
2003 Richard M. Bissell
2003 Arthur G. Bissell
2009 Mrs. M. A. Meyer & drs.
Receiving day Thursday
2009 E. F. Meyer
2009 Albert Meyer
2009 Carl Meyer
2011 Mrs. E. Camille Storey
2013 Mr. & Mrs. William H. Reid
2021 Mr. & Mrs. James L. High & dr.
2027 Mr. & Mrs. William B. Walker
2027 Charles Cobb Walker
2027 Silas B. Cobb
2031 Mr. & Mrs. Samuel A. Tolman
2033 Mr. & Mrs. F. R. Otis & drs.
2033 Charles T. Otis
2033 Lucius J. Ot's
2035 Mrs. H. O. Stone
2035 Robert E. Stone
2101 Mrs. Helen Rockwell
2101 Mr. & Mrs. Eugene S. Pike
Receive Tuesday afternoon
2101 Charles B. Pike
2101 William W. Pike
2109 Mr. & Mrs. Robert W. Roloson
Receive Tuesday 2 to 5 p. m.
2109 Mrs. Judith L. Marshall
2115 Mr. & Mrs. Phillip D. Armour
Receive Tuesday afternoon
2115 Mrs. Alice A. Sloan
2123 Thomas M. Avery
2123 Mr. & Mrs. Frank M. Avery
2123 Mrs. Ella S. Clark
2125 Mr. & Mrs. C. H. Wheeler
2201 Mr. & Mrs. Eugene Rockwell Pike
2207 Mr. & Mrs. Samuel C. Comstock
Receiving day Tuesday
2207 Miss Mae E. Comstock
2207 Mrs. Emma A. Beebe
2209 Mr. & Mrs. A. B. Meeker
2209 Dr. & Mrs. F. S. Coolidge
2211 Samuel Insull
2211 Martin J. Insull
2213 Mr. & Mrs. N. P. Bigelow
2219 Mr. & Mrs. Abner Price & dr.
2221 Mr. & Mrs. John J. Herrick
Receiving day Tuesday
2223 Mrs. Hosmer A. Johnson
Receiving day Tuesday
2223 Miss M. F. Seward
Receiving day Tuesday

1812 Mr. & Mrs. George Henry Wheeler
Receive Tuesday afternoon
1812 Dr. Henry L. Wheeler
1816 Mr. & Mrs. Charles M. Henderson & drs.
1828 Mr. & Mrs. Daniel B. Shipman
Receiving day Friday
1834 Mr. & Mrs. Fernando Jones
Receiving day Sunday
1834 Graham Jones
1900 Mr. & Mrs. Elbridge G. Keith & dr.
1900 Elbridge B. Keith
1900 Clarence B. Hall
1906 Mr. & Mrs. Edson Keith
1906 Walter W. Keith
1912 Mr. & Mrs. M. T. Greene & dr.
1936 Mr. & Mrs. S. W. Allerton
Receiving day Monday
1936 Robert H. Allerton
2000 Bruce Clark
2000 Mr. & Mrs. John M. Clark
2010 Mr. & Mrs. W. L. Grey & drs.
2010 Walter Grey
2018 E. Walter Herrick
2018 Mrs. L. A. Herrick
2018 Miss Louise Herrick
2018 Mrs. A. H. DeTeresa
2026 Mrs. Levi Rosenfeld
2026 Mr. & Mrs. D. Stettauer & dr
2026 Mr. & Mrs. Charles S. Stettauer
2026 James Stettauer
2026 Harry Rosenfeld
2036 E. Buckingham & drs.
2036 Clarence Buckingham
2100 Mr. & Mrs. James H. Ashby
2100 John B. Sherman
2108 Mr. & Mrs. Alex. H. Seelye
2108 Mrs. Miner T. Ames
2110 Mr. & Mrs. Edson Keith jr.
Receive Tuesday 3 to 6 p.m.
2112 Mr. & Mrs. Levy Mayer
2120 Mr. & Mrs. Frank S. Gorton
Receiving day Friday
2126 Mr. & Mrs. Chas. D. Hamill
2126 Charles H. Hamill
2126 Paul Hamill
2126 Miss Alice W. Page
2126 Miss Eleanor H. Page
2130 Thomas Murdoch
2130 Miss Jane Murdoch
2140 Mr. & Mrs. Byron L. Smith
Receiving day Friday
2200 Dr. & Mrs. Edwin M. Hale
2200 Dr. & Mrs. Albert B. Hale

2227 Mr. & Mrs. Archie J. McBean
2227 George B. McBean
2227 Mr. & Mrs. John McBean
2231 Miss Elizabeth Harrison
2231 Dr. & Mrs. John N. Crouse
    Receiving day Tuesday
2231 D. H. Crouse
2233 Mr. & Mrs. Wilton C. Roosevelt
2233 Dr. & Mrs. Charles W. Blend
2237 Mr. & Mrs. Warren Gibbs & dr.
2407 Mr. & Mrs. F. J. Schroter
    Receiving day Wednesday
2409 Mr. & Mrs. James J. Reilly
    Receiving day Thursday
2409 Mr. & Mrs. Samuel Brown
2411 Mr. & Mrs. D. F. Garland
2413 Mr. & Mrs. George Harvey
2443 Mr. & Mrs. O. D. Orvis
2443 Miss Edith E. Orvis
2447 Dr. & Mrs. James F. Todd
2449 Mr. & Mrs. Joel Bigelow
2453 Thomas S. Robinson
2453 Mrs. E. L. Whitaker
2457 J. W. Waughop & drs.
2521 Dr. & Mrs. Frank S. Johnson
2535 Mrs. Stella D. Loring & drs.
    *Receive Tuesday afternoon
    and Friday evening*
2601 Mr. & Mrs. D. W. Keith
2601 Miss J. L. Keith
2603 Mr. & Mrs. Charles A. Coolidge
2607 Mrs. G. C. Campbell & dr.
2607 Otis R. Glover
2607 Henry T. Glover
2619 Mr. & Mrs. Henry C. Rew
2619 Irwin Rew
2623 Mr. & Mrs. J. W. Donohue
    Receiving day Thursday
2625 Mr. & Mrs. John E. Jenkins
2631 Mr. & Mrs. Albert B. Dewey
2631 Miss Alma H. Shufelt
    Receiving day Friday
2637 Mr. & Mrs. Ernest A. Hamill
2637 Miss Anna Hamill Clarke
2641 Mr. & Mrs. A. F. Gartz
2701 Mr. & Mrs. Noble B. Judah
2703 Mr. & Mrs. E. A. Lancaster
2703 Mrs. B. P. Hutchinson
2709 Mr. & Mrs. C. L. Hutchinson
    Receiving day Tuesday
2713 Mrs. Louisa B. Stephens & drs.
    Receiving day Tuesday
2713 R. D. Stephens
2719 Mr. & Mrs. E. M. Doolittle
2719 Mrs. H. P. Crane
2723 Mrs. Henry W. Hoyt

2200 Mrs. Frances Hale Gardiner
2204 Mr. & Mrs. Franklin Ames
2204 Miss Eleonora Cowen
2206 Mr. & Mrs. Edward Forman
2206 Mrs. Robert Clark
2208 Mr. & Mrs. James T. Hoyne
2210 Mr. & Mrs. M. W. Mix
2210 H. E. Herbert
2212 Rev. & Mrs. John Rouse
    Receiving day Wednesday
2216 Mrs. Nathaniel Goold
2216 Mr. & Mrs. John E. Goold
2226 John H. Steiner
2228 Henry C. Flonacher
2228 Edward Flonacher
2340 Dr. James C. Valentine
2340 Dr. Sara L. Valentine
2342 Mr. & Mrs. C. J. Tanner
2352 Mr. & Mrs. Charles B. McCoy
2400 Mrs. George A. Hall
2400 Mrs. Lodema Sherman
2404 James L. Mahan
2406 Dr. & Mrs. J. S. Perekhan
2408 Mrs. Melvine M. Scovil
2408 Mr. & Mrs. George A. Foster
2410 Mr. & Mrs. George S. Miller
2410 Mr. & Mrs. A. E. Silverthorne
2412 Mr. & Mrs. H. Temple Bel-
    lamy *Receiving day Tuesday*
2414 Mr. & Mrs. Chas. E. Brown
2414 George F. Brown
2414 George F. Brown jr.
2432 Mr. & Mrs. Henry T. Murray
2448 Mr. & Mrs. Joshua Smith & dr.
2450 John G. McMurtry & dr.
2450 John G. McMurtry jr.
2450 Mr. & Mrs. J. W. Rood & dr.
2450 Louis Rood
2452 Mr. & Mrs. Frederick P. Taylor
2456 Mr. & Mrs. H. D. Penfield
2456 E. W. Penfield
2458 Mr. & Mrs. John O'Hara & dr.
2458 John O'Hara jr.
2510 Mr. & Mrs. Carl Buehl
2512 Dr. & Mrs. E. Wyllys Andrews
    Receiving day Monday
2514 Mrs. C. B. McGenniss
2518 Mrs. William W. Phelps
2518 Mrs. Lucina C. Zelie
2518 Brayton Saltonstall
2520 Dr. & Mrs. E. Andrews & dr.
2520 Miss Miriam Barrett
2520 Miss Laura T. Barrett
2522 Mr. & Mrs. William Alton
2522 Davis C. Alton
2522 Mr. & Mrs. Jesse B. Alton

2725 Mr. & Mrs. Lewis W. Pitcher
2729 Mrs. J. C. Walter
2729 Alfred M. Walter
2735 Mr. & Mrs. Henry A. Blair
2801 Mr. & Mrs. George E. Wood
2801 Miss Maud M. Kelley
2801 Mr. & Mrs. John Fitzslmmons
2807 Mr. & Mrs. F. D. Gray & dr.
2811 Mrs. Thos. H. Sheppard
2811 Miss Louise Sheppard
2815 Mr. & Mrs. S. B. Barker & dr.
2821 Mr. & Mrs. Geo. H. Webster
2821 Mr. & Mrs. Geo. H. Webster jr.
2821 Stuart Webster
2825 Mr. & Mrs. Chauncey Keep
2825 Mrs. Lyman Blair
2829 Thomas F. Keeley
2829 E. M. Keeley
2829 Miss Clara Keeley
2831 Mrs. Geo. W. Fuller
2831 Miss Mary Fuller
2831 Henry B. Fuller
2909 Charles H. Blair
2909 Mr. & Mrs. L. D. Warren
2911 Mrs. B. F. Murphey & drs.
2911 F. E. Murphey
2915 Mr. & Mrs. Henry Stern
 Receive 2d and 4th Tuesday
2917 Mr.&Mrs.John H.Wrenn & drs.
2917 Benton Sturges
2919 Mr. & Mrs. Frank G. Logan
2925 Mr. & Mrs. Charles R. Barrett
 Receiving day Thursday
2925 Miss Blanche L. Barrett
2925 Mrs. S. M. Baldwin
 Receiving day Friday
2935 Mr. & Mrs. Henry Hyams
2939 Mr. & Mrs. Leonard M. Leon.
2947 John C. Everett
2947 Judge & Mrs. William S. Everett
2947 Coleman S. Everett
2953 Mr. & Mrs. P. F. Gillespie
2953 Charles M. Gillespie
2953 John P. Gillespie
2955 Mr. & Mrs. Leo. Straus
 Receiving day Friday
2963 Mr. & Mrs. Samuel Stern & dr.
 Receive 1st & 3d Tuesdays
2965 Mr. & Mrs. Elisha P. Whitehead
2969 Mr. & Mrs. Germaine G. Alvord & dr.
2971 Mrs. William G. Mead & dr.
2975 Mr. & Mrs. B. R. DeYoung
 Receive Wednesday
2975 Miss Sadie De Young

2528 Mrs. Rosa Beiersdorf
2528 Joseph R. Beiersdorf
2532 Mr. & Mrs. Walter H. Wilson
2536 Mr. & Mrs. Eugene Cary
2548 Mr.& Mrs.Myron L.Pearce&dr.
2600 E. L. Powers
2602 Mr. & Mrs. James O. Claghorn
 Receiving day Thursday
2602 Mr. & Mrs. George E. Hall
2602 Mrs. Elizabeth Meeker
2602 Mrs. Sarah Howland
2604 Mr. & Mrs. S. D. Hinman & dr.
2604 Miss Lenore Wood
2604 Miss Edith Wood
2606 Dr. & Mrs. Joel R. Gore
2606 George R. Day
2620 Mr. & Mrs. L. B. Doggett & drs.
2620 O. J. Doggett
2620 William L. Doggett
2620 H. E. L. Doggett
2620 Arthur M. Doggett
2622 Mr. & Mrs. Chas. A. Chapman
2622 Walter A. Chapman
2622 Clarence C. Chapman
2626 Mr. & Mrs. Morton B. Hull
2628 Bruce B. Barney
2628 Mr. & Mrs. Edwin F. Getchell
2628 Mrs. B. B. Barney
2632 Mr. & Mrs. Walter W. Ross
2638 Mr. & Mrs. B. W. Kendall
2640 Mr. & Mrs. William J. Watson
2700 Mr.&MrsO.S.A.Sprague & drs.
2700 Albert Sprague 2d
2710 Mr. & Mrs. A. A. Sprague
2716 Mrs. Hiram Kelly
2720 Mr. & Mrs. A. C. Bartlett
2730 Mrs. E. F. Dore & drs.
2730 Walter J. Dore
2734 Mrs. A. M. H. Ellis
 Receiving day Monday
2802 Mr. & Mrs. Conrad Witkowsky & drs.
2802 James Witkowsky
2804 Rev. & Mrs. S. J. McPherson
2808 Mr. & Mrs. Edwin Pardridge
2808 Miss Florence Pardridge
2808 Fred C. Pardridge
2808 Frank R. Pardridge
2808 Mrs. Elizabeth Bailey
2808 Mrs. Melissa Roberts
2822 Mr. & Mrs. Geo. B. Phelps jr.
2824 Mr.& Mrs.FrederickT.Haskell
2828 Mr. & Mrs. Marvin Hughitt
2828 Marvin Hughitt jr.
2832 Mr.& Mrs. Joseph E. Otis jr.
2834 Mr. & Mrs. A. Williams & dr.

2979 Arthur H. Pierce
3011 Mrs. Charles Hutchinson
3011 Arthur Hutchinson
3011 J. William Hutchinson
3015 Mr. & Mrs. Charles B. Shedd
3015 Edward A. Shedd
3025 Charles Cromwell
3025 Mrs. Caroline Cromwell & dr.
3025 Mrs. John Y. Fuller
3031 Mr. & Mrs. Thomas D. Cottrell
    Receiving day Thursday
3031 Mrs. H. S. Clark
3031 Mrs. S. J. Clark
3031 Mr. & Mrs. William A. Foster
3031 Mr. & Mrs. Charles W. Newton
3113 Mr. & Mrs. Edward Iverson
3117 Mr. & Mrs. C. A. Paltzer
3133 Mr. & Mrs. Jos. Smart & drs.
3133 Joseph Smart jr.
3133 John Smart
3141 Mr. & Mrs. Joseph S. Smith
3143 Mr. & Mrs. I. Lockey
3149 Mr. & Mrs. Thos. E. Sullivan
3151 Mrs. Aaron Cahn
    Receiving day Thursday
3151 Miss Susie Cahn .
    Receiving day Thursday
3153 Mr. & Mrs. T. H. Walker
3157 Mr. & Mrs. Martin Barbe & drs.
    Receive 2d & 4th Tuesday
3209 Mr. & Mrs. Edward Hanff
3221 Mr. & Mrs. T. D. Hurley
3231 Mr. & Mrs. D. E. Livermore
3241 Mr. & Mrs. Jerry Sullivan
3249 Mr. & Mrs. Henry P. Harned
3251 Mr. & Mrs. David Mayer
3337 Mr. & Mrs. B. Schram
    Receiving day Friday
3337 David L. Schram
3341 Mr. & Mrs. D. M. Hillis
3343 Mr. & Mrs. M. Wilmersdorf
3345 Mr. & Mrs. Fred Myer
    Receiving day Friday
3345 Mr. & Mrs. Moses Myer
3347 Mr. & Mrs. Isaac Keim
3359 Mr. & Mrs. Chas. S. Babcock
3403 Mr. & Mrs. David Pfaelzer
3407 Mrs. H. Danziger & dr.
3407 Benjamin Danziger
3407 Abraham Danziger
3407 Emanuel Danziger
3409 Mr. & Mrs. D. Herrick
3409 Dr. Jacob Rosenthal
3411 Mr. & Mrs. Sigmond Frank
3411 D. L. Frank
3413 Mr. & Mrs. Julius Guettel

2842 Mrs. Mary Corigan
2842 Miss Kate Casey
2900 Miss Mary Little
2900 Isaac N. Perry
2902 Mr. & Mrs. Edmund Adcock
2904 Mr. & Mrs. Milton R. Wood
2904 Miss Ida M. Wood
2912 Dr. & Mrs. J. A. Manning
2914 Mr. & Mrs. F. Kramer & dr.
    Receiving day Friday
2914 A. F. Kramer
2914 Charles Stein
2922 Mr. & Mrs. Marshall J. Wilson
2922 Henry K. Wilson
2936 Mr. & Mrs. W. Dempster & dr.
2936 Charles W. Dempster
2940 Mr. & Mrs. S. H. Sweet & dr.
2940 Hiram Sweet
2940 Mrs. J. H. Winslow
2946 Mr. & Mrs. Morris Bauland & dr.
2946 Mr. & Mrs. Ernest Hofheimer
    Receiving day Monday
2948 Mrs. J. Keegan
2952 Mrs. Erwin E. Wood & dr.
    Receiving day Thursday
2952 Miss Evelyn Frisbie
2954 Dr. & Mrs. J. Sidney Mitchell
    & dr.
2960 Mr. & Mrs. Simon Yondorf
2960 Miss Maude Yondorf
2962 Daniel Ullman & dr.
2964 M. W. Murphy & dr.
2964 Miss Anna W. Synon
2968 Mr. & Mrs. Archibald Shaw
2968 John Shaw
2978 Mr. & Mrs. H. H. Kohlsaat
    Receiving day Tuesday
3000 Mr. & Mrs. Wm. E. Frost & dr.
3002 Rev. & Mrs. A. J. Canfield
    Receiving day Monday
3002 John B. Canfield
3004 Mr. & Mrs. L. S. Owsley
3004 C. R. Guerin
3004 Harry J. Kendig
3004 Henry M. Young
3004 Mrs. Lavinia G. Calkins
3004 Miss Evelyn L. Calkins
3004 Walter J. Calkins
3004 Mr. & Mrs. John M. Phelps
3004 Charles B. Phelps
3004 Harrison Musgrave
3004 Miss Mae Musgrave
3004 Mrs. M. S. Musgrave
3004 Mr. & Mrs. Henry L. Hollis
3004 John T. Sickel
3006 Mr. & Mrs. L. A. Goddard

3415 Mr. & Mrs. Oscar Rosenthal
3417 Mr.& Mrs.HenryForeman&dr.
   Receiving day Monday
3417 Mr. & Mrs. David H. Foreman
3417 Isaac H. Foreman
3419 Mr. & Mrs. A. L. Stone
3421 Mr. & Mrs. Samuel Spitz
3439 Mr. & Mrs. Herman Cohn
3441 Mr. & Mrs. M. Longini
   Receive 2d & 4th Friday
3443 Mr. & Mrs. John McCoy
3445 Mr. & Mrs. Eugene S. Weil
   Receive Thursday evening
3447 Mrs. Nina B. Leland
3447 Mr. & Mrs. John M. Hoon
3449 Mrs. A. B. Dunne
   Receiving day Tuesday
3449 Mrs. Margaret Lynch
   Receiving day Tuesday
3449 Mr. & Mrs. Earl M. Seitz
3449 John F. Blackburn
3449 Mrs. F. R. Anderson
3539 Lewis M. Hammond
3541 Dr. & Mrs. Horatio Keeler
3549 Mr. & Mrs. S. Ruben
   Receive 1st & 3rd Fridays
3549 Jacob Franks
3553 Dr. & Mrs. Edwin B. Tuteur
   Receiving day Wednesday
3553 Mrs. I. Tuteur
   Receiving day Thursday
3559 Mr. & Mrs. Benj. F. Harrison
3561 Mr.& Mrs.Bernhard Wolf & dr.
3563 Mr. & Mrs. Henry Mayer & drs.
3601 Mr. & Mrs. Chas. Leopold
3603 Mrs. S. C. Lamm & drs.
   Receiving day Tuesday
3603 Arthur G. Lamm
3603 Edgar Lamm
3605 Mr. & Mrs. L. B. Seligman
   Receiving day Wednesday
3607 Mr. & Mrs. G. A. Kantrowitz
3609 Mr. & Mrs. P. Wallace
3611 Mr. & Mrs. I. F. Brown
3613 Mr. & Mrs. Simon L. Marks
3617 Dr. & Mrs. W. E. Dodds
3617 Mr. & Mrs. Charles M. Barnes
3617 William R. Barnes
3617 Samuel D. Barnes
3617 Romulus E. Barnes
3627 Mr. & Mrs. J. H. Romaine
3629 Mr. & Mrs. D. C. DeWolf
   Receiving day Tuesday
3631 Mr. & Mrs. Ernest Cuthbert
3633 Mr. & Mrs. Rockwell Sayer
   Receiving day Thursday

3006 Mr.&Mrs. C. Marion Hotchkin
3006 Mr. & Mrs. John R. Butler
3010 Miss Marion M. Inness
3016 Mrs. A. Ryder
3016 Dr. & Mrs. W. C. Dyer
3018 Mrs. Ann A. Gaylord & drs.
3018 E. L. Gaylord
3018 Robert Gaylord
3020 Mr. & Mrs. H. F. Chappell
3022 Mr. & Mrs. P. L. Underwood &
   drs.
3030 Dr. Helen M. Hannah
3118 Mr. & Mrs. Thos. R. Melody
3128 Dr. & Mrs. Herman Oberndorf
3130 Mr. & Mrs. Jacob Hess
3132 Mr. & Mrs. Edgar White Kirk
3132 Mrs. Elizabeth A. Ely
3136 Mr. & Mrs. Ira A. Heath
3148 Mr. & Mrs. M. L. Kaiser
3148 Mrs. H. Auerbach
3150 Mr. & Mrs. Aaron Boehm
3152 Mr. & Mrs. J. A. Thain
3152 Mr. & Mrs. R. N. Clarke
3154 Mr. & Mrs. DeWitt C. Clapp
3156 Mr. & Mrs. G. H. Fox
3158 Mrs. Julia A. Colton
3158 Charles S. Colton
3158 Mr. & Mrs. F. E. Drake
3158 Mr. & Mrs. Wm. C. Miller
3158 Mr. & Mrs. W. H. Scott
3158 Mr. & Mrs. John W. Ulm
3158 Mr. & Mrs. Wm. P. Anderson
3158 Miss L. Johnson
3208 Dr. Charles C. Lipe
3212 Mr. & Mrs. R. Warner Hare
   Receiving day Thursday
3218 S. Klein
3218 Nathan Klein
3220 Mr. & Mrs. H. Baum
3224 Mr. & Mrs. Isaac Hess
3226 Mr. & Mrs. S. Mossler
   Receive 2d & 4th Friday
3226 Miss G. Mossler
3228 Mr. & Mrs. John F. Reid
3228 Harry M. Reid
3236 David VanWinkle
3236 A. L. VanWinkle
3236 Miss G. A. Shute
3242 Jacob Leserman
3326 Mr. & Mrs. George H. Bowen
   Receiving day Wednesday
3336 Mr. & Mrs. Samuel Lyser
3338 Mr. & Mrs. Joseph.T. Anthony
3340 Mr. & Mrs. M. F. Rittenhouse
3342 Mr. & Mrs. Chas. B. Pierce
3346 Mr. & Mrs. Gilbert Montague

3635 Mr. & Mrs. Percy W. Palmer
 Receiving day Thursday
3639 Mr. & Mrs. Max Leopold
3641 Mr. & Mrs. J. H. Hoadley
3645 Mr. & Mrs. D. E. McCurdy
3647 Mr. & Mrs. George L.McCurdy
3649 Mr. & Mrs. William Lilienfeld
3651 Mr. & Mrs. James I. Bradburn
3655 Mr.& Mrs.Adolph Reichenfeld
3657 Mr. & Mrs. Wm.Haskell & drs.
3657 William H. Haskell
3707 Mr. & Mrs. Francis T. Murphy
3707 Mr. & Mrs. G. R. Burgess
3707 Mr. & Mrs. John J. Duffy
3723 Mr. & Mrs. A. O. Mason
3725 Mr. & Mrs. John Schlacks
3727 Mr. & Mrs. Samuel Despres
3729 John Gilcreest
3733 Mr. & Mrs. J. H. Bowers
3735 Mr. & Mrs. M. F. Moss
3737 Mr. & Mrs. Charles D. Rubel
 Receive 3d & 4th Wednesdays
3739 Mr. & Mrs. C. Weatherson
3745 Mr. & Mrs. Charles W.Gindele
3747 Mr. & Mrs. Fred Honkamp
3753 Mr. & Mrs. John W. Merriman
3757 Mr. & Mrs. C. Francis Davies
3801 Mr. & Mrs. R. Guthmann
3805 Mr. & Mrs. M. Jacob Daube
 Receive 3d Thursday
3809 Mr. & Mrs. E. T. Towler
3813 Mr. & Mrs. C. W. Pierce & dr.
3819 Mr. & Mrs. G. A. Springer
 Receiving day Tuesday
3819 Miss A. E. Springer
3819 Miss Gertrude Springer
3819 Miss Cornelia Springer
3819 Charles E. Springer
3819 Edward L. Springer
3907 Mr. & Mrs. Chas. Philbrick
3907 Mr. & Mrs. F. O. Mills
3907 John A. Bender
3907 John R. Bender
3913 Mr. & Mrs. Harvey Bentley
3913 Rev. George W. Knapp
3913 William T. Dickson
3913 James McArthur
3913 J. W. Shields
3915 Mrs. A. W. Clark
3917 Mr. & Mrs. F. J. Rappal & drs.
3917 Lawrence L. Rappal
3917 Frederick J. Rappal jr.
3921 J. H. Holbrook
3931 Mr. & Mrs. Joseph C. Braden
3933 Mr. & Mrs. Geo. W. Stone&dr.
3943 Mr. & Mrs. Thomas B. Lee

3348 Mr. & Mrs. L. E. Lebolt
 Receive 1st and 3d Friday
3348 M. H. Lebolt
3348 J. Y. Lebolt
3350 Mr. & Mrs. Eugene Harbeck
3352 Mr. & Mrs. Winfield S. Haggard
3360 Mr. & Mrs. Henry Kuh
3362 Mrs. A. J. Unna
 Receives 1st and 2d Saturday
3362 Miss Adele Herrnheiser
3362 Julius A. Unna
3364 Mr. & Mrs. James W. Duncan
 & dr.
 Receiving day Wednesday
3400 Dr. & Mrs. L. D. McMichael
3400 Miss Addie L. McMichael
3406 Mr. & Mrs. H. H. Boyington
3408 Mr. & Mrs. J. B. McFatrich
3412 Dr. & Mrs. C. G. Lumley
3416 Mr. & Mrs. Daniel T. McGraw
3418 Mr. & Mrs. Dennis O'Connell
3420 Mr. & Mrs. Thomas A. Dean
3422 Mr. & Mrs. Spencer Johnson
3422 August Gatzert
3424 Mr. & Mrs. Gilbert J. Garraghan
3436 Mr. & Mrs.George A.Holloway
3442 Mr. & Mrs. M. Hirsch
3446 Mr. & Mrs. Charles R. Anderson
3528 Arthur H. Stevenson
3552 Mr. & Mrs. H. F. Kett
3554 Mrs. M. F. Hine
3556 Mr. & Mrs. R. S. Hopkins
3558 Mr. & Mrs. Henry Best
3558 Miss Minnie Best
3560 Mrs. J. Keefe & drs.
3564 Mr. & Mrs. Abraham Wertheimer
3566 Mr. & Mrs. M. S. Fleishman
3600 Mr. & Mrs. Henry Barnet
3602 Mr. & Mrs. A. G. Becker
3602 Joseph Friedman
3602 Isaac K. Friedman
3602 Oscar J. Friedman
3602 H. C. Friedman
3604 Mr. & Mrs. Solomon Freehling
3606 Mr. & Mrs. B. Rosenberg
3606 Mr. & Mrs. Harry Lazarus
3608 Mr. & Mrs. Charles Sax
3608 Mr. & Mrs. E. E. Levy
3610 Mr. & Mrs. S. Harmon
3612 Mr. & Mrs. John A. Knapp
3614 Mr. & Mrs. Louis Frank
3616 Mr.& Mrs. Nathan Hoffheimer

3945 Mr. & Mrs. Wm. J. McMullen & drs.
3949 Mr. & Mrs. Thomas Kelly
4023 Mr. & Mrs. Chester L. Root
4023 Mr. & Mrs. J. I. D. Westerwelt
4319 Mr. & Mrs. P. H. Sullivan
4323 Dr. & Mrs. W. E. Schroeder
Receiving day Friday
4325 Mr. & Mrs. M. Wormser
4327 Mr. & Mrs. Robert Liston
4327 D. Grant Liston
4329 Mr. & Mrs. C. W. Dameier
4331 Mr. & Mrs. A. M. Cobb
4339 Mr. & Mrs. Chas. E. Bloch
4343 Mr. & Mrs. W. R. Hornbaker
4343 Mr. & Mrs. L. H. Towler
4343 Mr. & Mrs. W. G. Harvey
4427 Mr. & Mrs. W. C. Ilette
4439 Mr. & Mrs.William H.Mallory
4441 Mr. & Mrs. R. H. Lee
4523 Mr. & Mrs. John O'Brien
4525 Mr. & Mrs. Joseph Stein
4547 Mr. & Mrs. J. P. Bowes
4547 Mrs. Joseph Nash & drs.
4549 Mr. & Mrs. S. P. Buchanan
4549 Mr. & Mrs. S. Rosenthal
4819 Mr. & Mrs. Wm. H. Leckie
4819 Miss Elizabeth Stephenson
4917 Mrs. Elizabeth C. Bodle
4953 Mr. & Mrs. H. Liberman
4953 Mr. & Mrs. Daniel W. Cole
4953 Charles R. Cole
4955 Mr. & Mrs. H. H. Lyon
4955 Mr. & Mrs. J. W. Hunter
4955 Thomas B. Hunter
4957 Mr. & Mrs. John A. Peppard
4957 Mr. & Mrs. Wm. E. Foster
4957 Mr. & Mrs. Chas. O. Albertson
4959 Mr. & Mrs. E. E. Billow
Receiving day Wednesday
4959 Mr. & Mrs. Harry E. Harper
4959 Mr. & Mrs. Frank P. Epps
Receiving day Thursday

4008 Nathan Eiseman
4020 Mr. & Mrs. Thos. Sollitt & drs.
4020 Oliver Sollitt
4020 Sumner Sollitt
4024 Mr. & Mrs. L. B. Kent
4030 Mr. & Mrs. Charles N. Gillette
4030 Mr. & Mrs. T. S. Gillette
4032 Mr. & Mrs. Henry G. Young
4036 Mr. & Mrs. R. Frank Quick
4036 Francis A. Hopkins
4104 Mr. & Mrs. Samuel Muir
4104 Lorenzo E. Dow

3616 Mrs. Ada Wolf
3626 Mr. & Mrs. Charles Kaufman
Receive 1st and 4th Thursday
3628 Dr. & Mrs. J.Clarence Lindsay
3632 Mr. & Mrs. I. Livingston
3632 Mr. & Mrs. C. G. Livingston
3632 David Livingston
3634 Mr. & Mrs. Jonas Kuppenheimer
3636 Mr. & Mrs. N. B. Rappleye & dr.
3640 Mr. & Mrs. Duncan S. McBean
3642 Mr. & Mrs. Orville W. Ballard
3642 George S. Ballard
3644 Mr. & Mrs. Maurice Hecht
3650 Mr. & Mrs. Aaron Rosenblatt
3652 Mr. & Mrs. H. Hart & dr.
3652 Leo Hart
3654 Mr. & Mrs. Herbert Hess
3658 Mr. & Mrs. Julius Starrett
3802 Mr.& Mrs. Edw. C.Wentworth
3804 Mr. & Mrs. Judson A. Tolman
3820 Mrs. F. L. Dickey
3830 Mr. & Mrs. John Smith
3842 Mr. & Mrs. Benjamin Myer
3846 Mr. & Mrs. C. P. Monash
Receive Wednesday evenings
3862 A. M. Polack
3910 Mr. & Mrs. Louis Keefer
3912 Mr.&Mrs. Sigmund Guthmann
3914 Mr. & Mrs. Samuel Nathan
3916 Mr. & Mrs. Max Oberfelder
3918 Mr. & Mrs. B. Mergentheim
Receiving day Friday
3918 Miss Ella Mergentheim
Receives 1st and 2d Friday
3920 Mr. & Mrs. Julius Loeb
3922 Mr. & Mrs. A. Kleinert & dr.
3924 Mrs. Johanna Loeb
3924 Sidney Loeb
3924 Jacob M. Loeb
3926 Mr. & Mrs. H. Scarborough
3926 Mrs. E. E. Scarborough
3928 Mr. & Mrs. L. H. Meyers
3930 Mr. & Mrs. George T. Ward
3936 Dr. & Mrs. Chas. M. Emmart
3946 Mr. & Mrs. L. O. Tomlinson
3946 John L. Tomlinson
3946 C. Frederick Warren
3946 N. P. Winchell
3950 Mr. & Mrs. John W. Morrison
4004 Mr. & Mrs. John M. Follinger
Receiving day Thursday
4008 Mr. & Mrs. M. Eiseman & drs.
Receive 1st Friday in mo.
4008 Max Eiseman

4104 Joseph Cummings
4112 Mr. & Mrs. Wm. B. Quinn
4112 Charles Quinn
4120 Mr. & Mrs. T. H. Ingwerson
4136 Mr. & Mrs. Wm. Maurer
4136 R. B. Swigart
4144 Mr. & Mrs. E. H. Ingwerson
4208 Mr. & Mrs. M. M. Ritterband
4210 Mrs. Florence C. Dodson
4210 James McElroy
4216 Henry H. Matthews,
4230 Mr. & Mrs. Wm. R. Forbes
4230 Mr. & Mrs. C. E. Bortell
4232 Mr. & Mrs. William W. Yeates
4234 Mr. & Mrs. Robert T. Lunham
4236 Mr. & Mrs. W. Parker Wright
    & dr.
4316 Mr. & Mrs. Samuel Ayers
4318 Dr. & Mrs. B. Rel VanDoozer
4324 Mrs. L. Smith
4324 Mr. & Mrs. Chauncy W.Foster
4326 W. B. Ecton
4328 Mr. & Mrs. J. W. Winkler
4328 John C. Stetson
4334 Mr. & Mrs. Charles A. Neal
4334 Mr. & Mrs. A. W. Burnham
4418 Mr. & Mrs. O. A. Wells
4418 Mrs. L. C. Milhous
4418 Mr. & Mrs. A. L. Kesner
4420 Mr. & Mrs. Horace M. Keenan
4420 Mrs. C. E. Plato
4422 Mr. & Mrs. D. P. House
4422 Mr. & Mrs. Charles Coonley
4422 Mr. & Mrs. John E. Zeltner
4422 Mrs. E. Reiner

4430 Albert J. Cronin
4432 Mr. & Mrs. Philip Angsten
4432 Mr. & Mrs. B. Rosenheim
4432 Mr. & Mrs. Henry Rosenfield
4438 Mr. & Mrs. A. G. Zulfer
4500 Mr. & Mrs. Peter A. Newton
4506 Mr. & Mrs. Allan C. Story
4512 John G. Willden
4512 Mrs. Ellenor S. Lateer
4520 Mr. & Mrs Wm. H. Ebbert
4526 Mr. & Mrs. Alfred Vernon
    Booth
4526 Mr. & Mrs. L. A. Barry
4526 Mr. & Mrs. R. S. Bauer
    Receiving day Tuesday
4528 Mr. & Mrs. John J. Cashin
4528 Mr. & Mrs. Thomas Gibson
4536 Mr. & Mrs. Alexander Sqnair
4536 Mr. & Mrs. Frederick Giest
4540 Mr. & Mrs. George Wood
4608 Mr. & Mrs. Melville T. Roberts
4610 Mr. & Mrs. James Hannan
4616 Mr. & Mrs. Edward A. Bern
4628 Mr. & Mrs. Albert W. Landon
4706 Mr. & Mrs. R. H. Chamberlin
4706 Mr. & Mrs. B. R. Chamberlin
4720 Mr. & Mrs. Wm. B. French
4720 Mr. & Mrs. Will A. French
4808 Mr. & Mrs. F. M. Celley & dr.
4820 Mr. & Mrs. John A. Nourse
4950 Rev. & Mrs. Thomas Towler
4950 Mr. & Mrs. F. A. Fowler
    Receiving day Thursday
4950 Mr. & Mrs. A. Nelson
4950 C. W. Hotchkin

PRINCETON AVENUE.

5729 Mr. & Mrs. J. T. Webber & dr.
5935 Mr. & Mrs. John Berg
5935 Mr. & Mrs. John S. Berg
5941 Mr. & Mrs. Wm. H. Mitchell
    & drs.
5945 Mr. & Mrs. Wm. H. James
5945 Miss Minnie Lewis
5949 Mr. & Mrs. J. J. Hannahan

6210 Mr. & Mrs. D. E. Mitchell
6210 Mrs. M. S. Moss
6210 E. S. Moss
6216 Mrs. A. B. Finefield

5934 J. S. Wolfe & dr.
5934 A. W. Wolfe
5950 Mr. & Mrs. George Barr
6008 Mr. & Mrs. James Strachan
6008 Mr. & Mrs. James Strachan jr.
6008 Mrs. M. Edwards
6042 Mr. & Mrs. C. W. Lane & drs.
6042 William C. Lane
6044 Mr.& Mrs. Jos. W.Ebersol &dr.
6044 Mr. & Mrs. W. D. Pearne
6100 J. W. Barney
6100 Mr. & Mrs. F. N. Barney
6110 Mr. & Mrs. Chas. H. Crofut

RAY STREET.

39 Dr. N. J. Nielson
49 Mr. & Mrs. D. Gordon Wells
49 George W. Packard

36 Mr. & Mrs. H. C. Ranney & dr.
    Receiving day Thursday
36 George A. Ranney

51 Mr. & Mrs. Wm. John Cox
51 Mr. & Mrs. Chas. B. English &
    dr.
53 Mr. & Mrs. Geo. W. Manley
53 John E. Nelson
─────
44 Prof. & Mrs. N. Gray Bartlett

38 Mr. & Mrs. Edwin L. Lobdell
38 Miss Eleanor Lawlor
40 Mr. & Mrs. Wm. A. Magie
    Receiving day Thursday
40 Frank O. Magie
40 Edward A. Magie

RHODES AVENUE.

3119 Mrs. Louisa N. Goyette
3133 Mr. & Mrs. John McKeough
3135 Mr. & Mrs. C. A. VanAnden
3135 Miss Mary B. Lichter
3137 Mr. & Mrs. Otto E. Hennig
3137 Mr. & Mrs. Joseph B. Dillon
3141 Mr. & Mrs. Wm. E. Crossette
3141 Dr. & Mrs. Heman Spalding
    Receiving day Tuesday
3145 Mr. & Mrs. William W. Clay
3147 Mr. & Mrs. Chas. Reitler &
    drs.
3151 Mr. & Mrs. Albert M. Docter
3155 Mr. & Mrs. A. C. Harding
3201 Mr. & Mrs. M. E. Greenebaum
3203 Mr. & Mrs. Harry A. Miller
3207 Mr. & Mrs. John P. Owen
3209 Mr. & Mrs. Ben Steinfeld
3213 Mr. & Mrs. M. H. Berg & dr.
3215 Mr. & Mrs. Nathan Friedman
    &. dr. *Receiving day Tuesday*
3215 Joseph N. Friedman
3215 Abraham B. Friedman
3217 Mr. & Mrs. A. M. Einstein
3219 Mr. & Mrs. J. Simonson & dr.
3321 Mr. & Mrs. Chas. W. Hubbell
3223 Mr. & Mrs. Thomas Davies
    Receiving day Friday
3225 Mr. & Mrs. James Angunes
3229 Mr. & Mrs. Julius Strelitzer
3231 Mr. & Mrs. E. G. Ewart
3233 Mr.&Mrs. Abraham A. Devore
3233 Miss Carrie Long
3235 Mr. & Mrs. John Belknap
3235 Miss Addie M. Belknap
3235 Charles C. Belknap
3235 William S. Kenny
3237 Mr. & Mrs. Fred F. Haigh
3237 Raymond C. Haigh
3237 Mrs. M. E. Colton
3239 Mr. & Mrs. Edw. G. Wiggin
3239 Mr. & Mrs. Herbert C. Metcalf
3241 Mr. & Mrs. Joseph Guckenhei-
    mer
3243 Mr. & Mrs. Harry Barnard
3245 Mr. & Mrs. Henry G. Foreman

3132 Mrs. Jennie E. Shaffner
    Receiving day Monday
3140 Mr. & Mrs. Isaac Cohen
3146 Mr. & Mrs. Marcus I. Sloman
3200 Mrs. Elizabeth Porter
3200 J. T. Geltmacher
3204 Mrs. S. F. Duncan & drs.
3214 Mrs. Louis Ullrich
3214 William A. Ullrich
3218 Mr. & Mrs. Charles B. Orr
3220 Mr. & Mrs. James W. Cecil
3222 Mr. & Mrs. Frank VanVoorhis
3222 Mr. & Mrs. Apollos D. Foote
3224 Mr. & Mrs. Myron H. Beach
3224 Harry L. Beach
3228 Mr. & Mrs. Frank D. Rubel
3230 Mr. & Mrs. A. J. Deniston
    Receiving day Wednesday
3236 Mr. & Mrs. C. H. MacDonald
3238 Mr. & Mrs. T. F. Andrews
3242 Mr. & Mrs. David Van Ness
    Person
3244 Mr. & Mrs. Henry Leopold, jr.
3246 Mr. & Mrs. Carl Appel
3248. Mr. & Mrs. L. W. Reiss & dr.
3248 William Reiss
3250 Mrs. Jennie E. Lane
3250 Mr. & Mrs. J. T. McRoy
3252 Mr. & Mrs. John Mayo Palmer
3254 Mr. & Mrs. D. M. Pollack &
    dr.
3256 Mr. & Mrs. Willard A. Smith
3260 Mr. & Mrs. William E. Smith
3260 Mr. & Mrs. Bruce Chamberlain
3302 Mr. & Mrs. Edwin R. Wooley
3302 Dr. Henry P. Wooley
3304 Mr. & Mrs. George A. Ogle
3310½ Wm. D. Schmidt
3336 Mr. & Mrs. S. C. Knight
3340 C. E. Rothschild
3342 Mrs. W. W. Everts
3342 Miss Grace T. Smith
3344 Mr. & Mrs. John H. Leslie
3348 Mr. & Mrs. H. G. McCartney
3348 Mrs. A. Miller
3350 Mr. & Mrs. A. W. Merrill & dr.

3247 Mr. & Mrs. Morris Mayer
Rec. days 2d & 4th Wednesdays
3249 Mr. & Mrs. Frank Lewald
3263 Mr. & Mrs. Atlee V. Coale
3307 Mrs. Alice E. Silke & drs.
3307 William F. Smith
3307 Mr. & Mrs. Edwin A. Munger
3309 Mr. & Mrs. Wm. D. Washburn
Receiving day Thursday
3311 Mr. & Mrs. I. Swabacker
3311 A. A. Ballenberg
3339 Mr. & Mrs. Bonham M. Fox
3339 Dr. Harriet Magee Fox
3441 Mr. & Mrs. Daniel G. Garnsey
3815 C. G. Muehlmann

3352 Mr. & Mrs. Willis H. Gale
3354 Mr. & Mrs. W. R. Perrin
3356 Mr. & Mrs. J. W. Prindivilie
Receiving day Thursday
3356 Egbert B. Clark & dr.
3430 Dr. & Mrs. John H. Hollister
3430 Judge & Mrs. M E. Hollister
3432 Mr. & Mrs. J. T. Richards
3434 Mr. & Mrs. Charles M. Gates
3438 Mr. & Mrs. Geo. Pitkin & dr.
3520 Prof. & Mrs. Gabriel Bam-
bérger
3534 Edward Van Dalson
3616 Ms. & Mrs. Albert E. Croft
3822 Mr. & Mrs. J. J. Palmer & drs.
3824 Dr. & Mrs. John B. Palmer

RIDGEWOOD COURT.

5411 Mr. & Mrs. A. Burgland & drs.
5413 Mr. & Mrs. C. S. Wheeler
5423 Mr. & Mrs. Charles B. Post
5463 Mr. & Mrs. B. W. Wright
5475 Mr. & Mrs. S. C. Goss
5475 Ivan C. Waterbury

5456 Dr. A. Frank Allen
5470 Mr. & Mrs. A. C. Stevens
5486 Mr. & Mrs. M. Y. Campbell

5402 Mr. & Mrs. Charles Carr
5404 Mr. & Mrs A. F. McMillan
5420 Mr. & Mrs. Franklin Wyman
5420 C. Sherman Bouton
5422 Mr. & Mrs. George W. James
5430 Mr. & Mrs. E.S. Hawley & drs.
5430 F. R. Hawley
5440 Mr. & Mrs. John W. Allgire
5442 Mr. & Mrs. Henry Goldmark
5450 Mr. & Mrs. A. S. Bradley & drs.
5450 A. S. Bradley jr.

ROBERTSON AVENUE.

297 Mr. & Mrs. A. Annan

280 Mr. & Mrs. John Darby & drs.
280 Benjamin L. Darby

ROSALIE COURT.

5713 Mr. & Mrs. B. F. Carr
5713 Mr. & Mrs. F. N. Kimberly
5721 Mr. & Mrs. C. H. Whiting
5725 Mr. & Mrs. H. S. Manning
5725 Mr. & Mrs. Charles E. Banks
5735 Mr. & Mrs. S. H. Richardson
5735 Mr. & Mrs. J. L. Rynearson
5745 Ralph W. Webster
5751 Mr. & Mrs. Edward P. Miller
5755 Rev. James H. Bourns
5755 Arthur P. Bourns
5759 Dr. Lizzie P. James
5803 Mr. & Mrs. F. M. Reynolds
5807 Mr. & Mrs. Wm. P. Ogden
5809 Mr. & Mrs. J. W. Rickey

5810 John J. Magee
5812 Mr. & Mrs. Uzziel P. Smith
5816 Capt. & Mrs. F. A. Smith

5708 Dr. & Mrs. John C. Cook
5712 Mr. & Mrs. Elliott Durand
5716 Mr. & Mrs. George M. Shirk
5720 Mr. & Mrs. Wm.H.Chesbrough
5724 Mr. & Mrs. A. H. Beardsley
5728 Mr. & Mrs. Chas. G. Field & dr.
5728 Robert Hunter Patton
5732 Mr. & Mrs. William B. Ottman
5736 Mr. & Mrs. Wm. F. Fox & drs.
5740 Henry T. Chace & dr.
5744 Mr. & Mrs. Ernest W. Heath
5744 J. H. Hamilton
5752 Mr. & Mrs. Charles Bonner
5758 Mr. & Mrs. Chas. Smalley
5762 Mrs. C. E. Watson & dr.
5800 Mr. & Mrs. John L. Martin
5806 Mr. & Mrs. John H. Wood
5810 Mr. & Mrs. William Waterman
5810 Mrs. Ella Warren Waterman

5822 Mr. & Mrs. Byron J. Parker
5824 Gen. & Mrs. Israel N. Stiles
5832 Mr. & Mrs. Wm. H. Christman
5834 Mr. & Mrs. Charles T. Mason

5838 Mr. & Mrs. Warner Smeenk
5838 Mr. & Mrs. Cassius M. Lewis
5854 Mr. & Mrs. Hart Rawson
5854 Charles A. Rawson

ROSENMERKEL STREET.

624 Mr. & Mrs. Roy O. West

624 Mr. & Mrs. C. Porter Johnson

ROSS AVENUE.

6510 Mr. & Mrs. C. G. Drake
6510 Mr. & Mrs. E. T. Skinkle

6516 Col. & Mrs. Thos. E. Maley
6536 Mr. & Mrs. Albert J. Mitchell
6554 Mr. & Mrs. Fred L. Chase

SOUTH SANGAMON STREET.

7728 Mr. & Mrs. J. W. Crow
7748 Mr. & Mrs. J.,H. Long

7750 Rev. & Mrs. T. M. Colwell
7804 Mr. & Mrs. G. A. Clark

SEVENTY-EIGHTH STREET (AUBURN PARK).

611 Mr. & Mrs. H. B. Chichester
615 Mr. & Mrs. H. A. Smith
619 Mr. & Mrs. E. N. Lessey
621 Mr. & Mrs. Clifford Lake

629 Miss Julia H. Thayer
610 Mr. & Mrs. C. E. Fowler
626 Mr. & Mrs. Walter E. Bliss
     Receiving day Wednesday

SEVENTY-NINTH STREET (AUBURN PARK).

507 Mr. & Mrs. J. J. Monahan

730 Dr. & Mrs. S. A. Waterman

SHERIDAN AVENUE.

6123 Mr. & Mrs. Geo. L. Andrew
6123 Mr. & Mrs. Victor Heinze
6147 Mr. & Mrs. J. M. Dennis
6149 Mr. & Mrs. Carleton Moseley
6149 Mr. & Mrs. E. Ramsdell
6219 Mr. & Mrs. Charles H. Leach
6231 Rev. & Mrs. William R. Wood
     Receiving day Wednesday
6241 Mrs. F. E. Owens & drs.
6241 Guy Owens
6311 Mr. & Mrs. F. W. Wheeler
6335 Mr. & Mrs. Isaac Anderson
6341 Mr. & Mrs. C. A. Baudouine
6407 Dr. & Mrs. A. W. McCandless
6407 Mr. & Mrs. F. Compton & dr.
     Receiving day Monday
6413 Dr. & Mrs. R. M. Barrows
6417 Mr. & Mrs. William A. Fowler
6417 Frank H. Wolcott
6427 Mr. & Mrs. John M. Levis
6441 Mr. & Mrs. G. W. McMillin
     Receiving day Thursday
6445 Mr. & Mrs. Adelbert DeLand
6451 Mr. & Mrs. Charles E. Bragdon
6451 W. L. Bragdon

6014 Mr. & Mrs. S. E. Magill
6016 Mr. & Mrs. C. E. Atwater
6018 Mr. & Mrs. James F. Pershing
     Receiving day Thursday
6046 Mr. & Mrs. Edwin M. Ashcraft
     Receiving day Wednesday
6052 Mr. & Mrs. John E. Zeublin
6052 Prof. & Mrs. Charles Zeublin
6054 Mr. & Mrs. A. J. Hirschl
6116 Mr. & Mrs. Edmond G. Otton
6134 Mr. & Mrs. B. F. Tilden
6140 Mr.& Mrs. Charles H. Spencer
6144 Mrs. W. S. Sparrow & dr.
6144 John S. Beattie
6148 Prof. & Mrs. Wm. K. Higley
6154 Mr. & Mrs. W. G. Press
6200 Col. & Mrs. W. B. Keeler
     Receiving day Wednesday
6200 Capt. & Mrs. G. M. Farnham
6200 Mr. & Mrs. Chas. S. Sargeant
6204 Mr. & Mrs. Jasper G. Gilkison
6210 Joseph Jellyman
6210 Miss M. Jellyman
6220 Mr. & Mrs. C. B. VerNooy
6224 Mr. & Mrs. W. F. Keenan

6507 Mrs. Helen M. Avery & dr.
6519 Henry H. Northrop
6537 Mr. & Mrs. J. W. Harrison
6557 Mr.& Mrs. Herman J.Trumbull

6520 Mrs. A. L. Hall
6538 Mrs. C. S. Dunscombe & drs.
6538 W. E. Dunscombe
6542 Mr. & Mrs. A. F. Chamberlain
6542 Mr. & Mrs. M. H. McChesney
6550 Mrs. H. C. Long
6626 Mr. & Mrs. Julius Stern & dr.
6230 Henry J. Kirk

6230 Mrs. S. K. Elmore
6244 Mr. & Mrs. John R. Towle
6412 Mr. & Mrs. W. J. Lafferty
        Receiving day Friday
6416 Mr. & Mrs. T. W. Parshall &
        dr. *Receiving day Tuesday*
6420 Mr. & Mrs. S. J. Stewart
6426 John Manington & drs.
6436 Mrs. Laura J. Tisdale
6510 Mrs. Martha S. Coman
6516 Mr. & Mrs. Wm. B. Fiske
6518 Mr. & Mrs. N. C. Wheeler
6520 Mr. & Mrs. F. E. Crawford
        Receiving day Thursday

SHERMAN STREET.

6559 Mr. & Mrs. P. J. Murray
7711 Mr. & Mrs. F. A. Schlieper
7715 Mr. & Mrs. C. E. Harding
7721 Mr. & Mrs. Chas. H.Beckwith
7729 Mr.& Mrs. C. B. Kinney
7733 Mr. & Mrs. A. E. Race
7737 Mr. & Mrs. C. A. Jay
7737 Herbert Jay
7741 Charles H. Palmer
7745 Mr. & Mrs. J. F. Earl
7745 Fred C. Earl
7745 Mr. & Mrs. C. W. Challis
7749 Mr. & Mrs. C. J. Larson
7757 Mr. & Mrs. J. L. Francis
7757 Mrs. Agnes Bauer
7819 Mr. & Mrs. L. G. Gerrish & dr.
7819 Mrs. M. C. Gleason

7804 Mr. & Mrs. Geo. W. Merchant
7810 Mr. & Mrs. George A. Leslie
7812 Mr. & Mrs. S. T. Webber
7832 Mr. & Mrs. G. B. Stock

6632 Mr. & Mrs. C. W. Lanz
6714 Mr. & Mrs. O. C. Harrower
6736 Mrs. Abbie F. Heywood
6736 Reuben H. Heywood
6746 Mr. & Mrs. Stephen Tucker
6758 Mr. & Mrs. O. R. Thompson
6758 Mr. & Mrs. M. L. Gruber
6800 Mr. & Mrs. Geo. Thompson
6800 Mr. & Mrs. Garret V. Weart
6814 Mr. & Mrs. Alfred Grossmith
6820 Mr. & Mrs. H. Strube
6830 Mr. & Mrs. Hiram Palmer
7000 Mrs. William Cromwell
7000 Mr. & Mrs. Frank M. McIntyre
7640 Mr. & Mrs. Joshua Stevens
7646 Mr. & Mrs. J. N. Bixby
7736 Mr. & Mrs. Olin T. Wilson
7738 Mr. & Mrs. S. Penepacker
7742 Mr. & Mrs. D. C. Woods
7748 Dr. & Mrs. G. H. Carder
        Receiving day Wednesday
7748 Mrs. M. J. Roberts
7754 Mr. & Mrs. C. E. Ferreira

SIDNEY AVENUE.

4405 Mr. & Mrs. Edward J. Goit
4407 Maj.& Mrs.Chas.Northup & dr.
4407 Mr. & Mrs. Milton Northup
4433 Mr. & Mrs. Nelson H. Town
        Receiving day Thursday
4437 Mr. & Mrs. Otis H. Waldo
4441 Mr. & Mrs. G. H. Jenkins
4443 Mr. & Mrs. Adolph Lund
4445 Mr. & Mrs. George B. Horr
4449 Mr. & Mrs. Robt. J. Randolph
4449 Frank J. Howell

4456 Mr. & Mrs. Chas. L. Dering
4458 Mr. & Mrs. E. W. Syer
        Receiving day Wednesday

4404 Mr. & Mrs. A. M. Burns
4406 Mr. & Mrs. F. H. Waterbury
4408 Mr. & Mrs. Edward Copland
4430 Mr. & Mrs. Horace W. Nich-
        ols *Receiving day Friday*
4438 Mr. & Mrs. Hamilton Dewar
4440 Mrs. J. Thomas & drs.
4442 Mr. & Mrs. Charles B. Ross
4442 Warner C. Ross
4448 Mr. & Mrs. G. Frank Watts
4450 Mr. & Mrs. James T. Fulton
4452 Mr. & Mrs. James D. Bradley
4454 Mr. & Mrs. Charles M. Brooks
4456 Mr. & Mrs. T. S. Cunningham
        & dr.

SIXTIETH STREET (HYDE PARK).

296 Mr. & Mrs. J. Carolus Stirling
sw. cor. Washington av. Ingram
    Hotel
    Mr. & Mrs. D. J. Haynes
    Victor L. Haynes

    Mr. & Mrs. H. J. Smith
320 Mr. & Mrs. H. W. Greenwood
588 Mr. & Mrs. John H. Copeland
600 Mr. & Mrs. R. Chester Frost

SIXTIETH STREET (ENGLEWOOD).

339 Mr. & Mrs. B. F. Peters
341 Mr. & Mrs. J. J. Hayes
343 Mr. & Mrs. A. J. Scheveis
347 Mr.& Mrs.Henry Wheeler & dr.
353 Mrs. W. I Howard & dr.
353 W. M. Howard
433 Mr. & Mrs. F. A. Stone
525 Mr. & Mrs Patrick Henry Flan-
    ley *Receiving day Thursday*
529 Mr. & Mrs. W. P. Browne
529 Mr. & Mrs. E. C. Frantz
539 Mr. & Mrs. F. D. Thomason
543 Mr. & Mrs. C. W. Carr
543 W. O. Carr
551 Mrs. B. T. Sample & dr.
555 Mr. & Mrs. J. F. Quigg & drs.
    Receiving day Friday
611 Mr. & Mrs. Wm. P. Haight
611 Mr. & Mrs. W. S. Edson
611 J. M. Edson
615 Mr. & Mrs. T. Merrill Watson
617 Mr. & Mrs. Chas. Taylor Harris

322 Mr. & Mrs. J. B. Moulton
326 Alden S. Darrow
326 Mrs. Caroline H. Darrow & dr.
518 Mr. & Mrs. John Shoemaker
520 Mr. & Mrs. O. A. Matthews
524 Mr. & Mrs. C. J. Beattie
550 Mr. & Mrs. W. O. Budd
556 Mr. & Mrs. A. H. Ebersold
620 Mr. & Mrs. H. P. Tiffany
620 Miss Mary J. Tiffany
642 Mr. & Mrs. George L. Dow
654 Mr. & Mrs. A. Levin & drs.

621 Mr. & Mrs. James C. Davis
711 Mr. & Mrs. P. B. Brown
713 Mr. & Mrs. Chas. R. Murray &
    dr.
715 Mr. & Mrs. F. M. Fender
719 Mr. & Mrs. P. Demers & drs.
731 Mr. & Mrs. F. Prosch & drs.
731 E. Prosch
739 Mr. & Mrs. F. P. Rosback & dr.

SIXTY-FIRST STREET (HYDE PARK).

225 Mr. & Mrs. George W. Riggs
251 Mr. & Mrs. Albert E. Ruff
251 Louis P. Ruff
435 Mr. & Mrs. Charles W. Hoff
437 Prof. & Mrs. C. W. Votaw
    Receiving day Tuesday

222 Mr. & Mrs. William L. Shepard
    & dr.
222 George P. Shepard
240 Mr. & Mrs. George A. Yuille
254 Mr. & Mrs. Max Young
272 Mr. & Mrs. F. C. Nicholas

SIXTY-FIRST STREET (ENGLEWOOD).

321 Mrs. M. R. Kesler
321 A. E. Kesler
321 Mrs. S. C. Kesler
321 Albert W. Riggle
323 Mrs. E. W. True
325 Mr. & Mrs. Ralph E. Lidster
327 Mr. & Mrs. J. T. Peck
335 Mr. & Mrs. D. C. Stebbins
335 Charles P. Doerr
339 Mr. & Mrs. O. N. Smith
345 Mr. & Mrs. G. M. Stackpole
353 Mr. & Mrs. A. S. Green & drs.

318 Mr. & Mrs. James D. Marston
332 Mr. & Mrs. Samuel T. Johnston
336 Mr. & Mrs. Walter French
344 Mr. & Mrs. Chas. D. Clapp
350 Dr. & Mrs. A.H. Champlin & dr.
406 Mr. & Mrs. C. C. Denton
410 Mr. & Mrs. P. Ackerman
410 Mr. & Mrs. Herbert Hutchins
418 Rev. & Mrs. Gibert Frederick
418 Mr. & Mrs. Amasa Mann
434 Mrs. Alfred Clark
514 Dr. & Mrs. A. F. Harris

615 Mr. & Mrs. W. E. W. Johnson
617 Mr. & Mrs. C. S. Deneen
623 Mr. & Mrs. T. C. Janisch
627 Mr. & Mrs. A. L. Whitehall
639 Mr. & Mrs. David A. Preston & dr.
645 Mr. & Mrs. E. Wright
645 Charles S. Wright

528 Mr.& Mrs.MiltonT.Zimmerman
536 Mr. & Mrs. Emanuel R. Boyer
548 Mr. & Mrs. H. M. Henderson
548 Mrs. M. Lyon
552 Mr. & Mrs. James D. Neilson
558 J. E. Eaton
620 Mr. & Mrs. Frank M. Hill
640 Mr. & Mrs. Ansel Hales
718 Mr. & Mrs. N. G. Lenington

SIXTY-FIRST PLACE (HYDE PARK).

296 Mr. & Mrs. George L. Beman

SIXTY-SECOND STREET (HYDE PARK).

341 Mr. & Mrs.E. A. Young & dr.
347 Mr. & Mrs. F. D. Mack
347 Mrs. Frances D. Mack

436 Mr. & Mrs. Francis M. Bradshaw
Receiving day Thursday

SIXTY-SECOND STREET (ENGLEWOOD).

505 Lee F. English
513 Mrs. E. G. Simmons
513 Frank A. Simmons
513 Robert S. Padan
513 Miss Nettie Goddard
515 Mr. & Mrs.Charles Breasted
515 Mrs. May B. Powell
517 Dr. & Mrs. John Sumney & drs.
521 Mr. & Mrs. M. A. Lawrence
525 Mr. & Mrs. J. H. Forsyth & dr.
525 Mr. & Mrs. George Tramel
529 Mr. & Mrs. J. E. Armstrong
533 Mr. & Mrs. David Ward Wood
539 Mr. & Mrs. W. W. Doolittle
539 Mrs. L. H. Doolittle
545 Mr. & Mrs. Josiah C. Fleming
547 Mr. & Mrs. J. H. Brown
551 Mr. & Mrs. L. H. Heinz
553 Mrs. W. C. Westerfield & dr.
555 Mr. & Mrs. F. B. Hanchett
601 Mr. & Mrs. F. G. Thearle & dr.
617 Mr. & Mrs. A. H. Whitley

328 Mr. & Mrs. M. G. Tousley & dr.
332 Mr. & Mrs. H. D. Fulton & dr.
524 Mr. & Mrs. James B. Kellogg
Receiving day Thursday
528 Mr. & Mrs. W. G. Brimson
534 Mr. & Mrs. Wm. A. DuBreuil
548 Mr. & Mrs. John F. Pearce
550 Mr. & Mrs. E. W. Gregory
558 Mr. & Mrs. J. C. Denison
558 Mrs. Lucy W. Gifford
612 Mr. & Mrs. C. S. VanDeursen
620 Mrs. M. Knight
630 Mr. & Mrs. N. C. Keeran
634 Mr. & Mrs. W. M. Darlington
640 Mr. & Mrs. Roger W. Atwood & dr.
650 Mr. & Mrs. J. R. Sommers

———

627 Mr. & Mrs. E. J. Chamberlin
627 Mr. & Mrs. A. Bundy
633 Mr. & Mrs. Warren S. Palm

SIXTY-THIRD STREET (HYDE PARK).

325 Mr. & Mrs. Wm. B. Harvey
455 Mr. & Mrs. David Graham
Receiving day Thursday
455 Mr. & Mrs. G. D. Thompson
455 Mr. & Mrs. T. A. Lockwood
703 Mr. & Mrs. P. K. Hardin
721 Dr. & Mrs. Chas. W. Morrow

224 Mr. & Mrs. Gay Dorn
338 Dr. & Mrs. L. A. Shultz
Receiving day Tuesday
340 Dr. & Mrs. C. W. Courtright
450 Mr. & Mrs. C. G. Brommer
510 Mr. & Mrs. A. S. Delaware
522 Mr. & Mrs. Samuel W. Dripps

SIXTY-THIRD STREET (ENGLEWOOD).

305 Dr. Henry R. Boettcher
603 Dr. & Mrs. A. G. Hayden
603 Dr. O. B. Hayden
———
656 Miss Linnie Dietz

420 J. E. Weed
518 Dr. & Mrs. J. J. Cornelius
656 Dr. & Mrs. J. Pettet & dr.
656 Ormsby E. Pettet
656 Miss Delia Dietz

SIXTY-THIRD COURT (ENGLEWOOD).

727 Mr. & Mrs. Manning Hunt&drs.
741 Mr. & Mrs. F. Felker
749 Mrs. A. F. Estey
753 B. E. Tilden
755 Mrs. A. M. Sturges
757 Mr. & Mrs. D. C. Gregg
761 Mrs. Anna Easton
763 Mr. & Mrs. George R. Peare
775 Mr. & Mrs. W. J. Brownell
———
806 Dr. Ernestine Hicks

726 Albert T. Myers
728 Mr. & Mrs. J. I. McCauley
730 Mr. &. Mrs. J. W. Taylor
732 Mr. & Mrs. Ernest Reckitt
734 Mr. & Mrs. C. Rose
738 Mr. & Mrs. E. H. Robinson
754 Mr. & Mrs. Elmer Granger
756 Mr. & Mrs. Wm. Harrington &
    dr.
756 Mr. & Mrs. Wm. Phelps.
762 Dr. & Mrs. J. T. Musick

SIXTY-FOURTH STREET (HYDE PARK).

401 Mr. & Mrs. Wm. H. Taft
401 Miss Olivia M. Taft
403 Mr. & Mrs. Riley Darnell
405 Mr. & Mrs. Wm. H. Bean
    Receiving day Monday

246 Dr. & Mrs. Warner P. Cary
250 Mr. & Mrs. S. E. Shogren
256 Mr. & Mrs. Waldo H. Spencer
    Receiving day Thursday
260 Dr. & Mrs. John W. White

SIXTY-FOURTH STREET (ENGLEWOOD).

321 Mr. & Mrs. H. Worthington
    Judd
361 Mr. & Mrs. Frank F. Douglass
401 Mr. & Mrs. Vinal F. Hatch&drs.
403 Mr. & Mrs. A. B. Hadden
403 Mr. & Mrs. S. E. Whitley
405 Mr. & Mrs. J. B. Chapin
441 Mr. & Mrs. R. S. Smith
443 Mr. & Mrs. E. W. Maynard
445 Mr. & Mrs. Arthur B. Wilson
445 Mr. & Mrs. George A. Clark
———
804 Mrs. Linda A. Dent

410 Mr. & Mrs. William Jenkinson
440 Mr. & Mrs. Henry Veeder
440 Mr. & Mrs. H. E. Slaught
442 Mr. & Mrs. Homer H. Peters
726 Mr. & Mrs. G. Z. T. Kenyon
730 Mrs. Ida Z. Lemon & dr.
732 Mr. & Mrs. Simon F. Mann
734 Mr. & Mrs. H. S. McCracken
740 Mr. & Mrs. Arthur Blackmarr
744 Mr. & Mrs. John Weir & dr.
746 Mr. & Mrs. Cyrus Boggs
762 Mr. & Mrs. B. B. Dow
804 Lewis D. Dent

SIXTY-FIFTH STREET (HYDE PARK).

485 Mr. & Mrs. J. D. Mendenhall &
    dr.
485 Mr. & Mrs. Thos. Greig Burton
    & dr.

680 Mr. & Mrs. E. R. Olds
———
603 Mr. & Mrs. Cyrus Kitching

SIXTY-FIFTH STREET (ENGLEWOOD).

243 Dr. E. O. Gratton
249 Mr. & Mrs. J. A. Ahrens
249 Henry Ahrens
359 Mr. & Mrs. C. J. Morehouse
359 Mr. & Mrs. Julius A. Johnson
359 Rev. James R. Boise
361 Mr. & Mrs. L. E. DeGarmo
361 Mr. & Mrs. Edgar H. Nichols
361 Mr. & Mrs. A. D. Rogers & dr.
361 Mr. & Mrs. Henry C. Rogers
403 Mr. & Mrs. Walter O. Smith
      Receiving day Wednesday
403 Mrs. John Little & drs.
445 Mr. & Mrs. E. Rich
449 Mrs. Elizabeth McKelvey & drs.
451 Mr. & Mrs. L. C. Noble
515 Dr. & Mrs. Alfred J. Oakey
517 Mr. & Mrs. Oliver C. Pugh
527 Mr. & Mrs. Ishi Smith
537 Mr. & Mrs. I. L. Woods & dr.
553 Mr. & Mrs. J. V. Avent & dr.
557 Mr. & Mrs. Wm. M. Sherwood
559 Mr. & Mrs. Wm. F. Mondschein
559 Charles A. Mondschein
559 Wm. H. Mondschein
601 Mr. & Mrs. R. G. Martin & dr.
601 Edward Martin
601 Frank C. Martin
605 Mr. & Mrs. F. M. Timms

140 Mr. & Mrs. Geo. W. Hotaling
140 Mr. & Mrs. Chas. A. Hendricks
222 Mr. & Mrs. Geo. M. Sterne
230 Dr. & Mrs. W. W. Wentworth
      Receiving day Thursday
230 Mrs. C. M. Monfort & dr.
358 Mrs. Lucy M. C. Rolfe
358 Clark C. Rolfe
360 Mrs. Emma L. Sheer
360 Mrs. Lucina F. Smith
360 Miss M. P. Raymond
400 Mr. & Mrs. H. A. McCord
402 Mrs. Annie W. Block
402 Thomas Marr
402 Mr. & Mrs. F. P. Crane
402 Mrs. Emma J. Hahn
438 Mr. & Mrs. A. B. St. John
440 Mr. & Mrs. W. B. Fish
440 Mr. & Mrs. Albert L. McCoy
442 Mr. & Mrs. J. B. Johnston
442 Mr. & Mrs. Charles F. Bane
444 Mr. & Mrs. Wm. Foster & drs.
450 Mr. & Mrs. Edward Maher
466 Mr. & Mrs. H. L. Blakeslee
510 Rev. & Mrs. J. S. Hughes & drs.
614 Rev. & Mrs. Stanley E. Kellar
618 Mr. & Mrs. H. H. Hitchcock
622 Mr. & Mrs. Hiram Colby

613 Mr. & Mrs. J. Moss

SIXTY-FIFTH COURT (ENGLEWOOD).

516 Mr. & Mrs. Fred H. Walther

526 Mr. & Mrs. Paul Schulz

SIXTY-SIXTH STREET (HYDE PARK).

253 Mr. & Mrs. Frank E. Bell
301 Mr. & Mrs. S. P. Adams

307 Mr. & Mrs. H. M. Harvey
s.w. cor. Sheridan av. Mr. & Mrs. John D. Tash

SIXTY-SIXTH STREET (ENGLEWOOD).

119 Mr. & Mrs. Alonzo Colt
441 Mr. & Mrs. C. W. Jackson
529 Mr. & Mrs. Edward Stemp & dr.
609 Mr. & Mrs. L. T. Regan
611 Rev. & Mrs. Edwin B. Graham
613 Rev. & Mrs. A. J. Colwell
613 Mrs. S. M. Alexander & dr.
615 Mr. & Mrs. Horace R. Hurlbut

120 Mr. & Mrs. S. Pomeroy

627 Mr. & Mrs. Lewis C. Thompson
629 Mrs. V. F. Betts
747 Mr. & Mrs. Henry M. Dunne
747B Col. & Mrs. Michael Dunne
755 Mr. & Mrs. Theodore Kenyon
757 Mr. & Mrs. Chas. R. McLain

13

SIXTY-SIXTH PLACE (HYDE PARK).

235 Mr. & Mrs. E. P. Marum
259 Mrs. Julia E. Brown & dr.
297 Mr. & Mrs. Wm. A. Coleman

cor. Hope av. The Lafayette
    Chas. C. Shepherd
    Robert J. Gunning
    C. H. Israel
    W. L. Israel

SIXTY-SEVENTH STREET (ENGLEWOOD).

315 Mrs. Dr. Viola H. Ludden
347 Asahel F. Bennett
415 Mr. & Mrs. E. L. Paterson
421 Mr. & Mrs. E. J. Noblett
423 Mr. & Mrs. James J. Kelly
427 Dr. & Mrs. H. E. Whitford
515 Mr. & Mrs. Orson Potter & dr.
    Receiving day Tuesday
515 Mr. & Mrs. E. R. Nourse
    Receiving day Tuesday
525 Mr. & Mrs. Albert Trebilcock
539 Mr. & Mrs. A. S. Cullum
557 Mr. & Mrs. F. C. Doran
613 Mr. & Mrs. Geo. Hildebrandt .

———

610 Mr. & Mrs. John Gascoigne
742 Mr. & Mrs. David Sloan
758 E. Norton White
762 Rev. & Mrs. S. M. Campbell

122 Mr. & Mrs. George A. Hubbard
168 Dr. & Mrs. Joseph F. O'Neal
168 Mrs. Ann Wharton
238 Mr. & Mrs. C. Lindsay Ricketts
400 Mr. & Mrs. A. W. McCornack
    dr.
516 Mr. & Mrs. Henry H. Nickerson
518 Rev. & Mrs. M. B. VanArsdale
    & drs.
518 Miss Anna McCormick
522 Mr. & Mrs. Michael J. Clark
534 D. C. Smith
534 John U. Smith
538 Mr. & Mrs. Frank Leland
538 Miss E. M. Bickle
538 Miss M. A. Bickle
542 Mr. & Mrs. F. C. Clements
562 Mr. & Mrs. J. A. Smith
600 Mr. & Mrs. J. P. Holland
602 Mr. & Mrs. R. E. Kehl

SIXTY-EIGHTH STREET (ENGLEWOOD).

734 Mrs. Emma Pollard & dr.

SIXTY-NINTH STREET (ENGLEWOOD).

559 Mr. & Mrs. Albert G. Ferree

SOUTH PARK AVENUE.

2253 J. E. Slocum
2253 Mrs. Mary E. Slocum
2253 Mrs. Anna L. Stouffer
2359 Mr. & Mrs. Chas. E. Field
2359 Oscar P. Erskine
2403 H. Waldo Howe
2403 Warren Phipps
2409 Mr. & Mrs. Harry W. Miller
2411 Mr. & Mrs. John Summerfield
2411 Mr. & Mrs. J. L. Baugh
2413 Mr. & Mrs. J. M. Lewey
2417 Mr. & Mrs. Herbert L. Whiting
2417 Mr. & Mrs. A. C. Whiting
2427 Mr. & Mrs. George P. Upton
2725 Mr. & Mrs. N. Rosenthal

2300 Mr. & Mrs. W. N. Thompson
    & drs.
2400 Mr. & Mrs. Harmon Spruance
    & dr.
2400 L. J. C. Spruance
2448 Mr. & Mrs. George Dickinson
2458 Mr. & Mrs. Fred H. Russ
2458 Mr. & Mrs. F. W. Jaros
2714 Mrs. M. L. Keith & dr.
2972 Mr. & Mrs. David J. Lines
2976 Kenosha Flats
    Mrs G. C. VanDriesen
    Mr. & Mrs. Robert O. Law
    Mr. & Mrs. W. F. Turner
3010 John R. Geary

2725 Louis Rosenthal
2809 Mrs. F. H. Avers
2941 Dr. & Mrs. Herman Kirschstein
2973 Mr. & Mrs. Joseph P. Emery
2973 Mr. & Mrs. George W. Underwood
2977 Mr. & Mrs. Jas. H. Fisk & drs.
Receiving day Thursday
3017 Mrs. L. H. Flershem
3017 Mr. & Mrs. G. T. Flershem
Receiving day Wednesday
3035 Dr. & Mrs. Wellman M. Burbank
3035 Dr. Charles W. McIntyre
3123 Mrs. M. Blackman & dr.
3125 Mr. & Mrs. L. H. Arnold
3141 Mr. & Mrs. Jno. B. Jeffery
3141 Harry B. Jeffery
3141 Dr. & Mrs. A. K. Crawford
Receiving day Friday
3145 Mrs. Levi Cline
3147 Mr. & Mrs. J. P. Katz & dr.
3147 Aber L. Katz
3159 Mr. & Mrs. Geo. Fisher & dr.
3159 Mrs. W. J. Walker
3159 Wm. R. Walker
3159 Mrs. M. W. Tripp
3201 Mr. & Mrs. Edward F. Newton
3203 Dr. & Mrs. James E. Stubbs
3203 Dr. F. Gurney Stubbs
3207 Mr. & Mrs. Jonas Brown
3209 Mr. & Mrs. Thomas Bradwell
3213 Mrs. B. Rosenthal & drs.
Receiving day Friday
3213 Joseph M. Schnadig
3215 Mr. & Mrs. D. Wormser
3215 Louis Wormser
3219 Mr. & Mrs. C. A. Raggio
3219 John G. Raggio
3221 Mr. & Mrs. P. A. Hull & dr.
Receiving day Friday
3223 Mr. & Mrs. Simon W. Straus
3225 Mr. & Mrs. Sidney B. Cahn
3227 Mr. & Mrs. Ezra D. Brown
3227 Mr. & Mrs. Milroy H. Gibson
3229 Mr. & Mrs. Louis Kaufman
3231 Mr. & Mrs. Conrad Steinmetz
3231 John H. Steinmetz
3231 D. Henry Steinmetz
3233 Mr. & Mrs. Myer Neumann
3233 Mr. & Mrs. Emil Hart
3235 Mr. & Mrs. Willis H. Page
3235 Mr. & Mrs. L. Felsenthal
3237 Mrs. Benne Kurz & drs.
3237 Adolph Kurz
3239 Mr. & Mrs. Leo B. Newburgh

3010 Thomas F. Geary
3010 W. T. Geary
3014 Mr. & Mrs. William Parker
3022 Mr. & Mrs. Emanuel Rosenheim
3114 Mr. & Mrs. S. S. Riesenfeld
3116 Mr. & Mrs. W. E. Poulson
3116 Mrs. A. B. Pierce
3118 Mr. & Mrs. E. J. Stransky
3122 Mr. & Mrs. Edwin G. Foreman
3126 Mr. & Mrs. Fred Uhlmann
3128 Mr. & Mrs. Max Frank
3130 Mrs. C. A. Josephi & drs.
3132 Mr. & Mrs. Joseph Basch
3136 Dr. L. J. Isaacs
3136 M. J. Isaacs
3138 Mr. & Mrs. Maurice Weill
3140 Mr. & Mrs. George T. Loker & dr.
3140 Harry A. Loker
3142 Mr. & Mrs. C. A. Whyland
3144 Mr. & Mrs. T. N. Donnelly
3152 Mr. & Mrs. John W. Green
3154 Mr. & Mrs. Edward Hoffman
3156 Mr. & Mrs. D. S. Greenebaum
3200 Mr. & Mrs. Louis Hutt & dr.
3214 Mr. & Mrs. J. L. Cahn & dr.
3218 Mrs. Bertha Cowen
3218 Israel Cowen
3218 Carlos Cowen
3222 Mr. & Mrs. Julius Glaser & dr.
Receiving day 1st & 3rd Fri.
3222 Byron Z. Glaser
3222 Mrs. J. G. Myers
Receiving day 1st & 3d Friday
3224 Mr. & Mrs. W. J. Leadbeater
3226 Mrs. Horace W. Chase
3226 Mrs. Elizabeth M. Odlin
3228 Mr. & Mrs. Charles N. Perry
3230 Mr. & Mrs. Gus N. Greenebaum
3232 Mr. & Mrs. L. M. Wurzberger
3234 Mr. & Mrs. E. Leger
3234 Harry B. Leger
3236 Mr. & Mrs. W. L. Kerber
3238 Mr. & Mrs. Milton L. Strauss
3240 Mr. & Mrs. Max Glaser & dr.
3240 George Glaser
3242 Mr. & Mrs. Samuel A. Wilson
3250 Mr. & Mrs. E. H. Payne
3250 Miss Ella Olson
3250 Mr. & Mrs. A. A. Anderson
3252 Mr. & Mrs. Richard Nash
3252 Mr. & Mrs. Nelson Shaul & drs.
3252 H. A. Wrenn
3254 Mr. & Mrs. M. Byron Rich
3256 Dr. & Mrs. J. Harvey Bates

3245 Mr. & Mrs. J. Harry Theobald
3247 Mr. & Mrs. Henry F. Googins
3249 Rev.& Mrs. P. S. Henson & dr.
3249 Mrs. Hudson L. Henson
3249 Mr. & Mrs. Wilmer Y.Henson
     Receiving day Thursday
3249 Mr.& Mrs. Charles W. Henson
3249 Horace Henson
3251 Mrs. A. F. Risser & dr.
3311 Mr. & Mrs. Sol. S. Sulzberger
3313 Mr. & Mrs. James B. Friedlander
3315 Mrs. Marion J. Schmaltz
3315 Nathan J. Schmaltz
3315 Joseph Schmaltz
3317 Dr. & Mrs. H. Bak & dr.
3321 Mr.& Mrs. Chas. F. Cooke
3325 Mr. & Mrs. Adolph Moses
3325 Joseph W. Moses
3327 Mr. & Mrs. Levi Abt
     Receiving day 1st & 3d Wed.
3327 Dr. Arthur I. Abt
3327 Sol. L. Abt
3327 Herman H. Abt
3327 Jacob J. Abt
3329 Mr. & Mrs. A. Hirsch
     Receiving day Wednesday
3329 Oscar Hirsch
3331 Mr. & Mrs. Charles Haas
     Receiving day Friday
3333 Mr. & Mrs. Sol Guthman
3335 Mr. & Mrs. George W. Ristine
3343 Mr. & Mrs. William A. Ranney
3345 Mr. & Mrs. H. M. Rosenblatt
     Receiving day Friday
3347 Mr. & Mrs. M. L. Rothschild
3347 Mr. & Mrs. Philip Opper
3349 Mr. & Mrs. W. F. Behel
     Receiving day Thursday
3351 Mr. & Mrs. Leon Hartman
3353 Mr. & Mrs. George E. Challacombe
3355 Mr. & Mrs. Leo Fox
3361 Mr. & Mrs. Emanuel Hartman & drs.
3363 Mr. & Mrs. George G. Pope & dr.
3363 Henry Pierce Pope
3365 Mr. & Mrs. J. G. Cella
3365 J. G. Cella jr.
3365 Angelo S. Cella
3365 Andrew Cella
3417 Mr. & Mrs. Rogers Porter
     Receiving day Thursday
3419 Mr. & Mrs. P. H. Linneen & dr.
3419 David F, Linneen

3314 Rev. & Mrs.John M. Caldwell
3326 Mrs. N. C. Fay
3326 Mr. & Mrs. Albert R. Fay
3328 Mr. & Mrs. H. H. Kennedy
3330 Mr. & Mrs. Robert Hart & dr.
3336 Mr. & Mrs. Morris Weil
3338 Mr. & Mrs. J. D. Robertson
3340 Mr. & Mrs. Selig Greenbaum
3340 Mr. & Mrs. Jos. Lowenbach
3340 William L. Lowenbach
3342 Mr. & Mrs. Samuel Rosenwald & dr.
3342 Morris S. Rosenwald
3342 Julius E. Weil
3344 Mr. & Mrs. Joseph Spiegel
3344 S. M. Spiegel
3344 M. J. Spiegel
3346 Mr. & Mrs. Raphael Stern
3348 Mr. & Mrs. G. H. Cassard & drs.
3348 Vernon Cassard
3350 Mr. & Mrs. Charles F. Thompson jr.
3352 Mr. & Mrs. Samuel Herman
3354 R. B. Appleby
3354 Addison S. Appleby
3354 William R. Appleby
3354 Mrs. Anna Dickson
3356 Mr. & Mrs. M. S. Flersheim
     Receive 1st & 3d Thursday
3358 Mr.& Mrs.Edward H.Foreman
3358 Isaac J. Bloom
3366 Mrs. M. M. Judson
3400 Walter A. Frost
3400 Mr. & Mrs. John Livingston
3402 Simon Ettlinger
3402 Mrs. Sam Schram
3402 Dr. H. J. Wallin
3404 Mr. & Mrs. M. Varrell
3408 Mr. & Mrs. J. H. Cohn
     Receiving days 1st & 2d Friday
3408 Miss Ida Cohn
     Receiving day Friday
3412 Mr. & Mrs. Henry Guth & dr.
3412 Charles Herbertz
3414 Mr. & Mrs. L. J. Friedman
3414 Mrs. Belle Lesen
3420 Mr. & Mrs. S. Lindauer
3424 Mrs. Sophia Sulzberger & drs
3426 Mr. & Mrs. Moses Goodman & drs.
3426 Milton F. Goodman
3428 Mr. & Mrs. Isaac Rosenfield
3440 Mr. & Mrs. B. F. Nell
     Receiving day Wednesday
3440 Miss Lilly Newman

3419 William P. Linneen
3421 Mr. & Mrs. William J. Bulger
  Receiving day Wednesday
3423 Mr. & Mrs. W. H. Thacher
  Receiving day Tuesday
3423 Mr. & Mrs. Leon M. Herman
3425 Mr. & Mrs. Jacob Strauss
3425 Louis E. Strauss
3427 Mr. & Mrs. Morris Adler

3540 Mr. & Mrs. Geo. A. Graves
  ———
3429 Mr. & Mrs. A. L. Simons
  Receiving day Friday
3429 Harry Simons
3431 Mr.& Mrs.Chas. C. Jerome
  Receiving day Wednesday
3433 Mr. & Mrs. A. P. Starr
3433 Arthur D. Dana

SAINT LAWRENCE AVENUE.

4201 Mrs. M. E. Moylan
4203 Mr. & Mrs. John P. Watson
4205 Mr. & Mrs. J. A. Mussenden
4209 Mr. & Mrs. L. B. Dutton
4223 Mr.& Mrs.Cyrus Thomas & dr.
4227 Mrs. S. J. Neeson & drs.
4227 Mr. & Mrs. John E. Link
4231 Mrs. O. C. Jenner
  Receiving day Thursday
4231 Mr.& Mrs. Chauncey D.Morse
4233 Mrs. Letitia Boulter & drs.
4233 Mr. & Mrs. George W. Pierce
4235 Mr. & Mrs. J. I. Eichman
4239 Mr. & Mrs. Oscar E. Anderson
4241 Mr. & Mrs. Wm. A. Merriam
4341 Mr. & Mrs. G. D. Barrett
4341 Mr. & Mrs. W. J. Sanderson
4345 Mr. & Mrs. W. L. Gregson
4349 Mr. & Mrs. C. F. Hinman
4357 Mr. & Mrs. A. F. Brooks & drs.
  Receiving day Wednesday
4359 Mr. & Mrs. John B. Murphy
4429 Mr. & Mrs. George S. Snider
4431 Mr. & Mrs. W. H. Hollister
4519 Mr. & Mrs. Arthur S. Wells
4519 Mr. & Mrs. John H. Brison
4543 Mr. & Mrs. William Ritchie
4543 Mr. & Mrs. John G. Cook
4543 Mr. & Mrs. Henry L. Cook
4543 Albert A. Cook
4545 Mrs. M. E. Lees
4545 Alison E. Mosier
4545 Mr. & Mrs. James M. Doud
4731 Mr. & Mrs. William Kirby
4731 Mr. & Mrs. George O. Roberts
4733 Mr. & Mrs. Robert F. Wilson
4801 Mr. & Mrs. Chas. S. Spencer &
  dr.
4803 Mr. & Mrs. George V. Wells
4825 Frank H. Dimock
4825 Mrs. Sarah Dimock
4825 Mr. & Mrs. Geo. S. Savage
4827 Mr. & Mrs. S. Goodman
4831 Mr. & Mrs. Herman Daniels

4236 Dr. & Mrs. Albert M. Markle
4238 Mr. & Mrs. W. S. Harpole
4242 Mr. & Mrs. Gerritt W.Madison
4244 Mr. & Mrs. George F. Johnston
4246 Mr. & Mrs. Charles W. Cohn
4250 Mr. & Mrs. James Dibb
4250 William P. Prentiss
4320 Dr. & Mrs. Solomon Ellias
4320 Mr. & Mrs. Edward B. Ellias
4320 Charles W. Holmes
4320 Mr. & Mrs. John A. Eppinger
4322 Mr. & Mrs. John Lancaster
4324 Mr.& Mrs. Jacob B. Hammond
4326 Mr. & Mrs. Albert Benedict
4328 Mr. & Mrs. W. Watkins
  Receiving day Wednesday
4344 Mr. & Mrs. M. Guettel & drs.
  Receiving day Friday
4344 Nathan M. Guettel
4346 Mr. & Mrs. Lee Rubens
  · *Receive 2d Wednesday*
4400 Mrs. F. C. Hieronimus
4400 Julius Hieronimus
4416 Mr. & Mrs. Charles M. Peale
4418 Mr. & Mrs. Edgar H. Clark
4418 Mr. & Mrs. Arthur W. O'Neill
4422 Mr. & Mrs. William Groh
4424 Mr. & Mrs. W. B. Miller
4434 Mr. & Mrs. Elwood G. Ladd
4444 Mr. & Mrs. Will T. Davies
4448-4450 St. Agnes Flats
 D Mr. & Mrs. B. Horwitz
 M Mr. & Mrs. Wm. D. Howard
 N Mr. & Mrs. M. Sommer
 O Mr. & Mrs. John Shaw
4510 Mr. & Mrs. A. E. Finnemore
4510 Mr. & Mrs. E. C. Francis
4514 Mr. & Mrs. Chas. C. Miller
4524 Mr. & Mrs. N. F. Pierce
4530 Mr. & Mrs. Wm. H. Martwell
4530 Mr. & Mrs. James H. Latter
4530 Mr. & Mrs. Wm. M. Bright
4540 Mr. & Mrs. W. E. Polhemus
4540 Mr. & Mrs. Wm. E. Newbern

4833 Mr. & Mrs. Duncan Campbell
4851 Mr. & Mrs. N. H. Fairbanks
4853 Mr. & Mrs. Henry Russell Platt
———
4810 Adolph Dernburg
4812 Mr. & Mrs. Benj. A. Fowler
4812 Mr. & Mrs. Benj. F. Quinby
4812 Mr. & Mrs. Eugene A. Weeks
    Receiving day Friday
4812 Charles D. Weeks
4812 Mr. & Mrs. John W. Blanchard
4828 Mrs. L. E. Brayton
4828 Mr. & Mrs. John E. Brayton
    Receiving day Tuesday
4828 Mr. & Mrs. John Asher

4544 Mr. & Mrs. R. Wolfner
4546 Mr. & Mrs. Wm. B. McCurdy
4800 Rev. & Mrs. Reese B. Kester
    Receiving day Friday
4800 L. A. Bell
4800 Mr. & Mrs. Ordell H. Powers
4800 Mr. & Mrs. Frank C. Wintrode
4802 Mr. & Mrs. Seneca J. Chadwick
    Receiving day Thursday
4804 Mr. & Mrs. Jos. T. Kilgour
4804 Mr. & Mrs. Jos. D. Porter
4806 Mr. & Mrs. Wallace L. Serrell
4806 Mr. & Mrs. Wm. H. Foote
4806 Stanley C. Foote
4810 Mr. & Mrs. F. W. Menhennitt

STAR AVENUE.

6351 Mr. & Mrs. William H. Foulke
6351 Edward Foulke
6359 Mrs. Hannah R. Foster
6359 Frank S. Foster
6401 Mr. & Mrs. Richard S. King.
6439 Mr. & Mrs. Robert Larkins

6336 William H. Burch
6400 Mrs. Lou Hoyt
6408 Mr. & Mrs. John W. Brown
———
6441 Mr. & Mrs. J. H. Snyder

STEWART AVENUE.

6111 Mr. & Mrs. H. W. Fairbank
6143 Mr. & Mrs. J. T. Ustick
6213 Mr. & Mrs. J. G. Thomas
6213 Mr. & Mrs. Frederick J. Sansome
6309 Rev. & Mrs. K. W. Benton
6341 Mr. & Mrs. A. O. Kendall
6341 Mrs. R. B. Winslow
6345 Mr. & Mrs. C. B. McDonald & dr.
6349 Dr. & Mrs. Wm. H. Ensminger & dr.
6349 Mrs. Emma M. Elliott & dr.
6349 James D. Elliott
6351 Dr. & Mrs. H. W. Pierson
6351 Mrs. Lucy D. Wiseman & drs.
6351 Mrs. Laura M. Early
6357 Mr. & Mrs. Albert Russell
    Receiving day Thursday
6401 Dr. & Mrs. M. J. Lyman & drs.
6409 Mr. & Mrs. Benj. Holbrook & drs.
6409 Benjamin Holbrook jr.
6415 Mr. & Mrs. E. M. Overbaugh
6417 Rev. & Mrs. J. R. Berry

6104 Mr. & Mrs. Jesse D. Janes
6104 Rev. & Mrs. Squire Rice
6104 Roland P. Rice
6106 Mr. & Mrs. Frank E. Stearns
6108 Mr. & Mrs. J. A. Barnes & dr.
6108 Charles E. Barnes
6122 Mrs. Lizzie A. McFarland
6122 Charles I. McFarland
6138 Mr. & Mrs. C. E. Tibbles & dr.
6314 Mr. & Mrs. John Tredwell
6314 Dr. & Mrs. F. K. Stanley
6314 Mr. & Mrs. Chas. F. Jordan
6316 Dr. & Mrs. D. Brix
6326 Mr. & Mrs. George W. Simpson
6340 Mr. & Mrs. B. F. Lewis
6348 Mr. & Mrs. George W. Wylie
6352 Mr. & Mrs. D. C. Smith
6352 C. D. Smith
6352 W. B. Smith
6356 Rev. H. S. Taylor & drs.
6356 Dr. Cora E. Taylor
6356 Dr. Rachel E. Hollingsworth
6410 Rev. & Mrs. C. E. Mandeville & dr.
6410 Mrs. Mary C. Brouse

6421 L. LaRue Smith
6429 Mr. & Mrs. E. S. Evarts
6435 Mr. & Mrs. H. Wangeman
6517 Mr. & Mrs. J. T. Cook
6521 Mr. & Mrs. R. P. Shields & dr.
6527 Mr. & Mrs. N. N. Nay
6533 Mr. & Mrs. T. Logan
6533 Mrs. Ann Williams
6535 Mr. & Mrs. John A. Campbell
6547 Mr. & Mrs. Charles H. Palmer
6601 Mr. & Mrs. J. A. Henry & dr.
6605 Mr. & Mrs. Henry C. Hicks
6609 Mr. & Mrs. Geo. N. Chase & dr.
6617 Mr. & Mrs. B. C. Hicks
6617 John Parker
6617 Mrs. Mary Parker
6621 Rev. & Mrs. Hugh S. Williams
     & dr.
           Receiving day Thursday
6621 Dr. Helen S. Williams
6637 Mr. & Mrs. John J. Fenn & dr.
6643 Mr. & Mrs. Fred R. Mitchell
6651 Mr. & Mrs. S. C. Mason
6655 James D. Pierce
6657 Eugene W. Whipple
6701 Mr. & Mrs. D. R. Smart
6711 Mr. & Mrs. John S. Batkin
6715 Mr. & Mrs. Charles N. Coen
6911 Mr. & Mrs. G. F. Anderson &
     dr.
6911 Mr. & Mrs. Frederick Layton
     & dr.
6913 Judge & Mrs. H. T. Helm &
     dr.
6915 Mr. & Mrs. Arnold H. Heine-
     mann
6915 Henry E. O. Heinemann
6923 Dr. & Mrs. E. J. Parkison
6925 Mr. & Mrs. E. Allen Dorrance
6929 Mr. & Mrs. F. G. Reynolds
6937 Mrs. M. F. Temple & dr.
6947 Mr. & Mrs. E. A. Thearle
6949 Mr. & Mrs. H. H. Lawrence
6951 Dr. C. H. L. Souder
6951 Dr. Ellen Starr Souder
7001 Mr. & Mrs. C. D. Colson & dr.
7329 Mrs. Sarah K. Terry
7523 Mr. & Mrs. A. E. Wagner
7523 Charles P. Wagner
7523 George A. Gary
7525 Mr. & Mrs. W. H. Duder
7525 Frank Bogan

     ———

7120 Mr. & Mrs. A. D. Lord
7334 Mr. & Mrs. T. M. Wright

6416 Mr. & Mrs. J. H. Pendry
6418 Dr. & Mrs. E. T. Allen
6418 Rev. Thomas Allen
6420 Mr. & Mrs. J. R. Harman
6426 Mr. & Mrs. James S. Daniel
6426 Miss Sadie J. Doty
6426 John M. Doty
6428 Dr. & Mrs. Wm. C. Stubbs
6428 Mr. & Mrs. A. P. Zeller
6442 Mr. & Mrs. C. C. Church
6446 Mr. & Mrs. E. M. Waterbury
6450 Mr. & Mrs. William H. Frink
6450 Mr. & Mrs. William T. Meech
6450 W. R. Meech
6554 Mr. & Mrs. L. J. Rice & dr.
          Receive Wednesday and Friday
6508 Mr. & Mrs. J. C. Hallenbeck
6512 Mr. & Mrs. M. H. Collins & dr.
6512 George M. Collins
6534 Mr. & Mrs. Parker Saunders &
     drs.
6534 Walter P. Saunders
6538 Mr. & Mrs. S. C. Glover & dr.
6538 Benjamin R. Howell
6542 Mr. & Mrs. John A. Lashar
6542 Mr. & Mrs. A. W. Specht
6546 Mr. & Mrs. E. MacPhetridge &
     dr.
6550 Mr. & Mrs. J. N. Radle & dr.
6554 Mr. & Mrs. J. J. Corcoran
          Receiving day Wednesday
6558 Mr. & Mrs. Charles Howard
6562 Mr. & Mrs. C. T. Page
6636 Mr. & Mrs. Robt. S. Smith
6636 Mme. A. D. Roszelle
6636 Mr. & Mrs. Darius Water-
     house & dr.
6638 A. J. Hoagland & dr.
6638 Mrs. Daisy H. Reed
6638 Mr. & Mrs. Samuel Roberts &
     drs.
6700 Dr. & Mrs. D. W. McNeal
6704 Mr. & Mrs. Fred A. Wells
6710 Mr. & Mrs. C. C. Smith & dr.
6922 Mr. & Mrs. Edw. G. Binz
6924 Mr. & Mrs. Will B. Moak
6932 Mr. & Mrs. H. B. Bates
6946 Mr. & Mrs. Carl Plum & drs.
7026 Mr. & Mrs. Charles A. McLagan
7026 Charles J. McLagan
7046 Mr. & Mrs. A. B. Baker
7046 A. Emmett Baker
7048 Mr. & Mrs. George Umsted
7048 Frank A. Umsted
7048 Harry C. Umsted
7052 Mr. & Mrs. Walter N. Beecher

7336 Mr. & Mrs. Francis A. Smith
7504 Mr. & Mrs. John J. Rugg
7506 Mr. & Mrs. Sidney D. Terry
7600 Mr. & Mrs. C. S. Thornton
7600 Mr. & Mrs. S. Thornton
7708 Mrs. E. H. Gadsden

THIRTIETH STREET.

49 Mr. & Mrs. J. Klassen
73 Mrs. R. E. Morey
73 C. S. Blackman
73 F. O Blackman
73 Harry L. Blackman
75 Mr. & Mrs. B. A. Blair & dr.
159 Mrs. A. E. Cochrane & drs.
163 Miss E. McDonnell
       Receiving day Wednesday
163 Miss H. McDonnell
       Receiving day Wednesday
163 Thomas Brenan
191 Mr. & Mrs. E. E. Moberly
193 Mr. & Mrs. A. P. Pendleton & dr
195 Michael F. Driscoll
197 Mr. & Mrs. Frank Jacobson
201 Mr. & Mrs. M. Farrell & dr.

96 Mr. & Mrs. Charles H. Blanch-
       ard
96 Mrs. M. Sutliff
98 Mrs. Frances T. Bowen & drs.
98 Mr. & Mrs. E. B. Allis
98 Mr. & Mrs. Thomas E. Diamond
134 Pierce Smiddy & drs.
134 Richard P. Smiddy
160 Mr. & Mrs. A. C. Anson
306 Mrs. Susan Cummings
310 Mr. & Mrs. N. H. Morgan
310 Mrs. J. H. Roberts

203 Mr. & Mrs. E. Von Hermann
       Receiving day Tuesday
263 Mr. & Mrs. Hugh P. Moran
305 Mr. & Mrs. W. B. Wanzer

THIRTY-FIRST STREET.

1 Mrs. Fannie Cottle
1 Murray G. Haskins
3 George N. Lee
3 Miss Kate Richards
5 Mrs. J. H. Manny
51 Dr. & Mrs. E. H. Sammons
51 Miss Sarah E. Hanson
219 Dr. & Mrs. Charles F. Stewart
       Receiving day Wednesday

96 Mr. & Mrs. Wm. Longhurst
208 Mr. & Mrs. Chas. J. Jones
214 Mr. & Mrs. Walter Davis
214 Mrs. Charles S. Frink
214 Mr. & Mrs. S. S. Buckley
214 Mr. & Mrs. W. H. Morrow
214 Miss Meta Wellers
300 Dr. & Mrs. C. Pruyn Stringfield
       Receiving day Wednesday
300 Dr. W. Bonnar

THIRTY-SECOND STREET.

53 Mr. & Mrs. M. Wolfe
83 Mr. & Mrs. Gabriel Wolf
89 Mr. & Mrs. Max Philipsborn
93 Joseph M. Wilson
95 Mrs. Louis Snydacker & dr.
95 Joseph L. Snydacker
95 Morris L. Snydacker
113 Mr. & Mrs. N. Rosenthal & dr.
113 Louis Rosenthal
191 Mr. & Mrs. C. S. Peacock
191 Mrs. T. E. Webb
217 Gus Hoffstadt
233 Mr. & Mrs. Louis Lepman

116 Dr. & Mrs. Boerne Bettman
       Receive Wednesday eve.
168 Mr. & Mrs. W. W. Dewees
190 Mr. & Mrs. D. Yondorf
212 Mr. & Mrs. Wm. Fairfax Wood
232 A. S. Lower
276 Mr. & Mrs. A. I. Marcus
278 Mr. & Mrs. William Goodkind
284 Dr. & Mrs. C. J. Simons
284 F. P. Simons
       ————
237 Mrs. Dora Marcuse & dr.

THIRTY-THIRD STREET.

15 Mr. & Mrs. Peter Wolf & dr.
19 J. Roy Robertson & dr. .
19 M. A. Fountain

116 Mr. & Mrs. George Coones
122 Mr. & Mrs. Levi Sprague
122 Herbert A. Sprague

29 Mr. & Mrs. D. H. Keyes
35 M. B. Williams
37 Mrs. Veronica McCarthy
37 Mr. & Mrs. E. S. Peaslee
37 Mrs. L. M. Peaslee
39 Mr. & Mrs. Jas. M. Hubbard
55 The Rainer
   J. K. Cohen
   G. K. Cohen
   S. K. Cohen
   Dr. E. K. Bennington
   George T. Mason
   Dr. Elbert Wing
   Mr. & Mrs. B. F. Tobin
71 Mr. & Mrs. Geo. W. Davis
85 Mr. & Mrs. John P. Wolf
85 Miss Augusta Morton
87 Mrs. Blanche Shirey
89 Mr. & Mrs. Justus M. Krauss
93 Stratford Flats—
  1 Miss Kittie Neather
  1 J. Pearce Neather
  3 Mr. & Mrs. Chas. L. Sullivan
  7 Mr. & Mrs. J. W. McBride
99 Avon Flats—
  A Harry G. Sommers

126 Mr. & Mrs. Edward J. Painter
146 Mr. & Mrs. Nathan Eisendrath
150 Mr. & Mrs. C. S. Shepherd
212 Miss Ellen C. Alexander
214 Mr. & Mrs. A. W. Fulton
216 Mr. & Mrs. Samuel H. Trude
     Receiving day Friday

A Miss Lilian Sommers
D Mr. & Mrs. George Ellison
D Charles Ellison
G Mr. & Mrs. A. B. Decker
G Mr. & Mrs. W. R. Hoagland
115 Mr. & Mrs. M. C. Markham
117 Mr. & Mrs. Andrew J. Farley
147 Mr. & Mrs. Edward L. Glaser
     Receiving day Thursday
149 Mr. & Mrs. T. Lilienfeld
151 Mrs. N. Friend & dr.
153 Mr. & Mrs. A. Reinhard
155 Mr. & Mrs. Monroe J. Friedman
399 Mr. & Mrs. Fred U. Smith
399 Mrs. M. C. Moore
407 Mr. & Mrs. E. C. Dodge

THIRTY-FOURTH STREET.

139 Mr. & Mrs. Eugene Hunt
163 Mr. & Mrs. R. Temple-Vriedberg
293 Mr. & Mrs. I. Katzauer & drs.
329 Amos C. Dean
329 J. Clark Dean
331 Mr. & Mrs. Charles Marks & dr.
331 M. M. Marks
331 Louis C. Marks
333 Mrs. A. W. Herr & drs.

134 Mr. & Mrs. S. L. Eisendrath
162 Mrs. L. Adler
168 Mr. & Mrs. Thos. Nicholson
168 James Nicholson
422 Mr. & Mrs. J. P. Butterfield
426 Mrs. Mary F. Jameson
426 Mrs. Jennie M. Jameson

365 Mr. & Mrs. George Holden
     Receiving day Wednesday

THIRTY-FIFTH STREET.

19 Mrs. A. W. Holbrook
21 Mrs. E. M. Tully & drs.
21 John W. Tully
23 Mr. & Mrs. Dempster Ostrander
25 Mr. & Mrs. D. Howard
29 Mr. & Mrs. George Stearns & drs.
29 Marcus Stearns
se. cor. Ellis av. Mr. & Mrs. G. A.
   Spicer
se. cor. Ellis av. S. S. Davis jr.
143 Dr. Samuel L. Weber
251 Dr. Ralph H. Wheeler
251 Dr. & Mrs. C. S. Bigelow

36 Dr. & Mrs. Herman F. Ratte
40 Mr. & Mrs. A. F Sauer
42 Mr. & Mrs. H. S. Parkhurst
42 Miss Ethel Mosby
42 Frank Markoe
42 William Mosby
44 Mrs. O. M. Sheldon
44 Miss Jennie Woodman
46 Mr. & Mrs. H. H. Blake
46 Mrs. Fannie Hicks
46 Miss Althea Ogden
46 Mr. & Mrs. C. C. Swinborne
48 Mr. & Mrs. C. M. Wilbur
48 Miss Mary Nesbitt

50 E. C. Chapman
50 Dr. C. F. Matteson
52 Dr. & Mrs. James I. Tucker
54 Mr. & Mrs. A. J. Phillips
56 Mr. & Mrs. Frederick W. Phillips

74 Mr. & Mrs. Gaylord S. Hull
190 Mr. & Mrs. James Burke
190 Frank Burke
192 Mr. & Mrs. John Burke
270 Dr. & Mrs. James M. Brydon

THIRTY-SIXTH STREET. ·

55 Mr. & Mrs. KennethMcLennan
59 B. L. Moore
145 Robert Sharp
145 Mr. & Mrs. Louis L. Sharp
163 Mrs. Mary F. Kellogg
165 Mr. & Mrs. George H. Francis
167 Mrs. William V. Randall & drs.
175 Mr. & Mrs. Isaac Bond
175 William H. Bond
179 Mr. & Mrs. George Brockway
179 Guy Brockway
185 Mr. & Mrs. Alexander S. Leib
Receiving day Tuesday
195 Harriet Straith-Miller
195 Fred Straith-Miller
197 Mr. & Mrs. Charles A. Stevens
201 Mr. & Mrs. Chas. J. Merritt
449 Mr. & Mrs. J. Edmund Jones

___

164 Ralph C. Stevens
170 Mrs. Jane De Mary
170 Mr. & Mrs. Donald M. Stevenson
174 Mr. & Mrs. Charles N. Black
184 Mrs. Harriet F. Spooner
184 Thomas F. Spooner
188 Mrs. Jane Wood
188 Miss Irene E. Wood
190 Mr. & Mrs. F. P. Leffingwell
192 Mrs. Sophia S. Kenfield & dr.
192 H. J. Kenfield
192 Fred. S. Kenfield
194 Mr. & Mrs. W. K. Hilton & drs.
196 Mr. & Mrs. Henry H.McDuffee
200 Mr. & Mrs. R. F. Peyton
200 T. Dade Peyton
200 R. F. Peyton jr.

ne. cor. Ellis av. The Lorraine
   Mr. & Mrs. John W. Hepburn
   Mr.& Mrs. A. W. Mullien
   Mr. & Mrs. N. B. Dewey
   Mr. & Mrs. Chas. W. Rice
   Harry Peters
   Mrs. Louise Leyman
   Dr. W. C. Carroll
   Nat Jacobson
nw. cor. Ellis av. Kenilworth Flats
   Mr. & Mrs. John W. Blaisdell
 1 Miss Elizabeth Jamieson
ne. cor. Cottage Grove av. Ivanhoe
   Flats
 B Dr. Rachael H. Carr
 C Dr. & Mrs. JohnW.Montrose
 E Mr. & Mrs. W. H. Leech
 F Mr. & Mrs. Francis H. Day
 98 Mr. & Mrs. Geo. Schlesinger
106 Mrs. E. Strickland
106 Miss Kathrine Strickland
   Receiving day Thursday
108 Mr. & Mrs. Isaac S. Dement
140 Mr. & Mrs. T. Middleton & drs.
142 Mr. & Mrs. Robt. W. Ransom
150 Mrs. Charles H. Hayden
152 Mr. & Mrs. Frank Mears
152 Mr. & Mrs. R. T. Perry
152 John Stirlen
152 Theodore Kempf
152 Mr. & Mrs. James Lightner
152 Mr. & Mrs. Frank Mather
152 Mr. & Mrs. Romyn Hitchcock
152 Dr. J. W. Williamson
152 Mr. & Mrs. Luther N. Doty & dr.
152 Mr. & Mrs. E. F. Wheeler & drs.
162 Mr. & Mrs. R. Barnard
164 Mr. & Mrs. E. D. Stevens

THIRTY-SEVENTH STREET.

23-25 Erie Flats
   A Mr. & Mrs. H. B. Ely
   D Mr. & Mrs. Edward M. Fitzsimons
      Receiving day Friday
   G Mr. & Mrs. Wm. G. Leonard
29 Mr. & Mrs. L. J. Mason

64 Mr. & Mrs. E. M. Scott
94 to 98 The Leamington
   1 Mr. & Mrs. H. B. Williams
   2 Mr. & Mrs. Wm. A. Ball
   4 Mr. & Mrs. A. L. McCombs
13 Dr. & Mrs. H. W. Case
17 Mr. & Mrs. S. Ford

31 Mr. & Mrs. W. H. Nicolet
31 A. J. Nicolet
33 Mr.& Mrs.William P.Penhallow
57 Mr. & Mrs. J. W. Taylor
65 Mr. & Mrs. John B. Delbridge
65 Mr. & Mrs. John L. Laughlin
67 Mr. & Mrs. Edward F. West
67 Mr.& Mrs.Archibald McClellan
67 Mr. & Mrs. F. C. Seymour
67 Mr. & Mrs. Charles H. Sampson
91 Mrs. C. B. Gilbert
91' Mrs. S. A. Boyington
95 George T. Dale
95 Dr. H. C. Dale
97 Mr. & Mrs. H. T. VanDenbergh
   & dr.
99 Mrs. Elizabeth B. Ballard
101 Mr. & Mrs. F. A. Wixon
101 Mrs. C. Frank Wixon
101 Mr. & Mrs. J. B. McChesney
103 Mr. & Mrs. Daniel V. Samuels
105 Mr. & Mrs. S. J. Sherwood & dr.
105 Philip Sherwood
105-111 The Sherwood
   C. E. Phelps
2 Mr. & Mrs. Benj. F. Smith
3 Mr. & Mrs. Philip S. Kingsland
5 John F. Carnegie
5 Mrs. Barbara Carnegie
5 Mrs. Annie De Vore
7 Mr. & Mrs. George R. Lewis
8 Mr. & Mrs. John D. Jones
10 Mr. & Mrs. William G.Howe
11 Mr. & Mrs. J. T. Townes
12 Mr. & Mrs. E. A. Benson
14 Mrs. E. M. Edwards
14 Mrs. Harriet Ely
15 Mr. & Mrs. B. F. Wedgewood & dr.
16 Mrs. M. Lela Dame
135 Mr. & Mrs. E. D. Herdman
137 Mr. & Mrs. James McKinney
139 Mr. & Mrs. D. W. Burry & drs.
141 Mr. & Mrs. John Smith & dr.
173 Mr. & Mrs. S. H. Southwick &
   dr.
179 Mrs. Mary C. Vaughan
181 Mr. & Mrs. Charles L. Russ
181 Mr. & Mrs. Alamando B. Russ
183 Lincoln A. Brown
183 Miss Ella W. Brown
187 Mr. & Mrs. A. T. Gannon & dr.
187 Henry Gannon
195 Rev. & Mrs. H. F. Milligan
209 Mr. & Mrs. W. F. Bixby & drs.

19 Mr.&Mrs. Atwood Cummins
148 Dr. & Mrs. Sheldon Leavitt
   Receiving day Wednesday
148 Mr. & Mrs. C. Frank Leavitt
176 Mr. & Mrs. H. C. Wilcox
176 Mrs. M. A. Wilcox
176 C. S. Wilcox
176 Mrs. Christiana Wehrli
176 Mr. & Mrs. George W. Robinson
176 Mrs. Lina Wohlgemuth
176 Julius Wohlgemuth
176 Mrs. M. B. Egbert
176 D. W. Baker
176 Mr. & Mrs. E. P. Webster
178 Mr. & Mrs. John V. Steger & dr.
184 Dr. & Mrs. J. Mitchell Taylor
   Receiving day Wednesday
184 J. Howard Taylor
190 Mrs. N. Bennett
   Receiving day last Saturday
190 Miss Rose Herzog
194 Mr. & Mrs. T. H. Patterson
206 Mrs. Jacob Liberman & dr.
210 Mrs. Wallace Warren & dr.
210½ Mr. & Mrs. Nathaniel Croft
210½ Horace I. Croft
210½ Herbert J. Croft
210½ Mr. & Mrs. Edgar H. Croft
218 Mr. & Mrs. W. R. Robbins & dr.
218 Miss E. C. Munro
228 Mr. & Mrs. Joseph H. Ely & drs.
228 George Ely
254 Mrs. Emma S. Mandel & drs.
258 Mrs. Alfred C. Titus & dr.
258 Miss Manna Pflaum
260 Mr. & Mrs. E. A. Bensinger
Receiving days 2d & 4th Thursdays
260 Albert Wise
286 Benj. A. Watson
286 Mr. & Mrs. Charles H. Bradley
   Receiving day Thursday
286 Miss E. B. Shumway
   Receiving day Friday
294 Mr. & Mrs. C. M. Bradley
318 Mr. & Mrs. T. Stern
320 Mr. & Mrs. Charles M. Updike
322 Henry Strauss
322 Mr. & Mrs. Jacob Berolzheim
344 Mr. & Mrs. Henry Kaufman
580 Mr. & Mrs. John Wiese
584 Dr. & Mrs. Peter H. Vesterborg

   ———

325 Mr. & Mrs. Geo. W. Bouton
447 Dr. J. W. Dostal
549 Dr. & Mrs. A. J. Sprague

THIRTY-EIGHTH STREET.

138 Mr. & Mrs. M. M. Jacobs
138 Mr. & Mrs. Henry C. Tell & drs.
140 Mr. & Mrs. T. DeWitt Ganse
140 Mr. & Mrs. E. W. Tillotson
140 Benjamin H. Hellen
140 Louis A. Farnsworth

298 Mr. & Mrs. Harry Branch
298 Mr. & Mrs. Louis B. Shaw
438 Dr. & Mrs. C. E. Caldwell
438 Mr. & Mrs. J. C. Page
450 Mr. & Mrs. Jacob Goodman & dr.
450 Mr. & Mrs. Edmund L. Gallauner

THIRTY-NINTH STREET.

15 Mr. & Mrs. Chas. H. Compton
15 Mrs. Sarah B. MacDonald
15 Cornelius J. MacDonald
15 Mr. & Mrs. Thaddeus H. Howe
15 Mr. & Mrs. Franklin E. Jordan
17 Mr. & Mrs. L. A. Hagerty
17 Mr. & Mrs. A. Fletcher Brown
17 Mrs. Ellen B. Shepard
143 Mr. & Mrs. Frank A. Cummings
143 Walter D. Cummings

———

607 Mr. & Mrs. F. R. VanDoozer
613 Mr. & Mrs. H. L. Burnette
704 Mr. & Mrs. George Sparks
n.e. cor. Langley av. The Hampden
Will E. Coman
Mr. & Mrs. Wm. S. Gould
Mr. & Mrs. Odell E. Lansing
Roscoe U. Lansing
Mr. & Mrs. E. C. Moderwell
Miss Louisa F. Moderwell
Miss Mary W. Moderwelll
Dr. & Mrs. Wyllys Moore
Charles E. Patrick
Mr. & Mrs. Geo. W. Shannon
164 Otis P. Swift
164 Harry A. Swift.
176 Mr. & Mrs. Walter Scott Hull
     Receiving day Tuesday
176 Mrs. Henrietta W. LaFayette

42 The Cambridge
B   Dr. and Mrs. G. P. Doyle
C1 H. J. Gould
C2 Mr. & Mrs. A. H. Potter
E   Thomas W. Evers
E   Frank P. Brown
F   Mr. & Mrs. W. H. Estep
G1 Mr. & Mrs. P. C. Gaynor
G2 Mr. & Mrs. C. H. Schultz
H   Mr. & Mrs. Chas. H. Peck
I1 Mr. & Mrs. H. C. Cunliffe-Owen
I2 Mr. & Mrs. J. G. McMichael
K2 Mr. & Mrs. Ralph H. Drake
M   Mrs. M. Christian
Q1 John H. Blocher
R1 Mr. & Mrs. J. C. Wood
304 Mr. & Mrs. B. N. Gartsin
310 Harry Mugridge
311 Mr. & Mrs. H. M. Miller
402 Mr. & Mrs. J. W. Wilson
404 Robert C. Burchell
407 Mr. & Mrs. E. C. VanWagenen
411 Mr. & Mrs. Hugh McMinn
502 Mr. & Mrs. A. F. Brown
506 John E. Parrott
507 Mr. & Mrs. W. C. Holmes
509 Mr. & Mrs. J. F. Porterfield
511 H. L. Omerod
602 Mr. & Mrs. A. E. Hallett
606 P. S. Twells

TWENTIETH STREET.

53 Mr. & Mrs. A. S. Badger
55 Mr. & Mrs. C. H. Hall
57 Dr. & Mrs. Charles W. Purdy
83 Mrs. Anna D. Sottrup & dr.
83 Ella C. Anable
83 James B. Safford
83 Mr. & Mrs. R. H. Opdyke

54 Mrs. M. J. Willing & dr.
54 Julian V. Wright

———

83 V. H. Surghnor
85 Mr. & Mrs. Arthur M. Warrell
85 Mr. & Mrs. E. P. Crooker

TWENTY-FIRST STREET.

117 T. D. Lawther
119 Mr. & Mrs. Madison H. Ferris
119 Mr. & Mrs. J. R. Cameron
121 Mr. & Mrs. John V. Hess
123 Mr. & Mrs. Harry E. Daggett

66 Mr. & Mrs. Douglas Westervelt
90 Mr. & Mrs. Frank R. Greene
90 Mrs. Norman T. Gasette
92 Mr. & Mrs. John J. Simmons
126 Mrs. J. Ames

TWENTY-SECOND STREET.

17 Mr. & Mrs. John J. McDermid
35 Mr. & Mrs. Frank K. Root.
37 Mr. & Mrs. Peter VanSchaack
37 Joseph Rathborne
39 Mrs. L. C. Wheeler
39 D. O. Arnold

43 Mr. & Mrs. G. Edwin Jones
45 Dr. & Mrs. Frank Billings
45 Charles L. Billings
55 Mr. & Mrs. M. J. Steffens
69 Mr. & Mrs. Leopold Moss
Rec. day 1st & 2d Wednesday

TWENTY-THIRD STREET.

19 Mr. & Mrs. C. W. Pulsifer
21 Mr. & Mrs. C. P. VanSchaack
23 Mr. & Mrs. W. O. King
51 Mr. & Mrs. A.E. Bournique & dr.
51 Alvar L. Bournique
51 Lyman G. Bournique
67 Dr. George Silver

64 Dr. & Mrs. Samuel French
70 Mrs. W. M. Derby
70 Mr. & Mrs. W. M. Derby jr.
Receiving day Friday

71 Mr. & Mrs. J. E. Eastes
71 Mr. & Mrs. John A. Chisholm

TWENTY-FOURTH STREET.

103 Mr. & Mrs. David R. Crego
325 Mr. & Mrs. L. W. Framhein
335 Mr. & Mrs. J. S. Rydell

68 Fred L. Brown
68 Miss Alice R. Brown
68 Miss Minnie Clay Luxton
68 J. P. Brown
68 Chas. B. Orendorff
100 Mr. & Mrs. Charles W. Hinkley
100 Mr. & Mrs. George E. Dawson
100 Mrs. Julia A. Dawson
100 Miss Kate Manierre

48 Mr. & Mrs. J. Q. Hoyt
50 Mr. & Mrs. Albert H. Larned
50 Ezra R. Larned
52 Mrs. A. F. Vollmer
Receiving day Thursday
52 Thomas Brown
52 Prof. E. Alfieri
64 Mr. & Mrs. George P. Whitcomb
& drs.
64 Miss Adele Whitcomb
68 Mr. & Mrs. Julius N. Brown
Receiving day Wednesday

TWENTY-FIFTH STREET.

33 Mr. & Mrs. Robert Hervey
123 Mr. & Mrs. E. D. Anderson
Receiving day Thursday
127 Mr. & Mrs. L. Deutsch
129 Mr. & Mrs. Louis Marks
153 Mrs. Ada B. Jarvis
153 Mrs. Nancy P. Coburn
153 Mrs. Mary C. Holmes
161 Mr. & Mrs. Walter A. Barker
181 Mr. & Mrs. John H. York
185 Mr. & Mrs. L. Polacheck

82 Mr. & Mrs. Andrew Hallen
82 Mrs. B. Berlin
84 Stephen D. May
88 Mr. & Mrs. J. Gillespie Moore
126 Mr. & Mrs. Oscar M. Stern
156 Dr. Marie J. Mergler
162 Mrs. M. A. McCalla & dr.
162 Miss Alice DeWitte
164 Mr. & Mrs. A. T. Willett
166 Mr. & Mrs. A. F. Williams
192 Mrs. Esther Sackerman

189 Dr. & Mrs. E. P. B. Wilder
199 Mr. & Mrs. M. T. Jones
201 Mr. & Mrs. Frank C. Butze
201 Dr. & Mrs. J. W. Fowler
201 William A. Carney

200 Mr. & Mrs. William Herbst

201 Edward A. Carney
201 Robert R. Manners

TWENTY-SIXTH STREET.

45 Mr. & Mrs. Oscar E. Flint
45 Dr. & Mrs. H. R. Sackett
47 Mr. & Mrs. George H. Beebe
93 Mr. & Mrs. Wm. C. Snell
99 Henry Butterworth
99 Miss Sydney Butterworth

88 Mr. & Mrs. J. Slocum
88 Dr. J. K. Smith
88 Walter F. Slocum
92 Mr. & Mrs. Watson S. Hinkley

TWENTY-EIGHTH STREET.

207 S. E. Moore
209 Mr. & Mrs. T. H. Keefe
       Receiving day Wednesday
211 Mr. & Mrs. W. D. Moone
225 Mr. & Mrs. A. C. Driggs
225 Mr. & Mrs. Robert H. Marston
225 Thos. B. Marston
225 Mrs. A. W. Straw
225 Mrs. J. A. Cherry
225 W. E. Keily
225 Mr. & Mrs. David W. Reed
225 Mr. & Mrs. Geo. H. Clark & dr.
225 Mr. & Mrs. Francis Redmond

206 Dr. & Mrs. Charles Adams
208 Mr. & Mrs. John Koch
212 Charles S. Steel
216 Mrs. L. B. Manning
216 Wm. F. Manning

229 W. O. Pringle
229 R. Pringle
229 Mr. & Mrs. J. E. Shawhan
229 Dr. & Mrs. W. R. Hillegas
229 Mr. & Mrs. C. A. Bryant
229 Miss Nellie Crimmins
229 Mr. & Mrs. J. O. Twichell

TWENTY-NINTH STREET.

31 Mr. & Mrs. F. Keeler
       Receiving day Tuesday
31 Dr. & Mrs. F. E. Blackman
       Receiving day Wednesday
35 Mr. & Mrs. John H. Bogue
       Receiving day Wednesday
35 Mrs. M. Frailey
221 Mr. & Mrs. C. D. Newbury
221 Mrs. Flora Messenger & dr.
223 Mrs. A. E. Bacon
223 Geo. H. Campbell & dr.

32 Mr. & Mrs. James D. Watson
       Receiving day Wednesday
34 Dr. William E. Morgan
34 Mrs. C. W. Jamieson
       Receiving day Wednesday

227 Mrs. Margaret Prophet & dr.
227 Edward Prophet
237 Mr. & Mrs. J. A. Westlake & dr.
237 Mr. & Mrs. S. F. Miller

UNION AVENUE.

6721 Mr. & Mrs. C. Wainwright
       Receiving day Thursday
6747 W. B. Fitch
6749 Mr. & Mrs. Gus Homan
6755 Mr. & Mrs. F. R. Stone
6821 Mr. & Mrs. H. Coombs & drs.
6829 A. W. Sterrett
6845 Mr. & Mrs. W. F. Madlung
6847 Mr. & Mrs. G. D. Stevenson
7613 Mr. & Mrs. Wm. Bishop

6546 Mr. & Mrs. M. H. Hoey.
6704 Mr. & Mrs. J. B. Leake & dr.
       Receiving day Wednesday
6724 Mr. & Mrs. T. W. Witwer
6734 Mr. & Mrs. J. F. Mosser
6740 Mrs. Theo. W. Kennedy & dr.
6748 Mr. & Mrs. J. W. Marshall
6752 Dr. & Mrs. A. W. Freeman
6814 Mr. & Mrs. J. H. Zies
6820 Mr. & Mrs. J. D. Bacon & drs.

7613 Thomas R. Bishop
7621 Mr. & Mrs. James Jackson&dr.
7631 Mr.& Mrs.Howard H. Fielding
7637 Mr. & Mrs. Milton Bayne
7713 Mr. & Mrs. F. M.Kirkham & dr.
7713 Miss Mamie Carpenter
7721 Mr. & Mrs. John W. Smith
7905 Mr. & Mrs. E. V. Davis

7734 Mr. & Mrs. George T. Halla
7746 Mr. & Mrs. H. H. Glidden
7754 Mr. & Mrs. M. A.Donohue&dr.
        Receiving day Friday
7754 William F. Donohue
7802 Mr. & Mrs. Peter Carpenter
7808 Mr. & Mrs. Oscar Oldberg
7814 E. A. Barnes
7814 Miss Myra Barnes

6840 Mr. & Mrs. C. G. Settergren
        Receiving day Wednesday
6850 J. G. Teller
6946 Mr. & Mrs. G. A. Redman
7534 Mrs. George M. Jennings & dr.
7534 Mr. & Mrs. George F. Jennings
7546 Mr. & Mrs. W. E. Danner
7614 Mr. & Mrs. Jules DeHorvath &
        dr. *Receiving day Tuesday*
7614 Mrs. M. DeJankovitz
7624 Mr. & Mrs. Peter H. Peck
7628 Mr. & Mrs. O. J. Buck
7630 Mr. & Mrs. G. A. Poppelbaum
7636 Mr. & Mrs. A. M. Garland
7700 Miss Alta E. Wilmot
7708 Mr. & Mrs. W. Irving Carpenter
7722 Mr. & Mrs. H. W. Magee

UNIVERSITY PLACE.

7 Mr. & Mrs. G. A. Lepper
        Receiving day Wednesday
7 Mrs. W. D. Hatten
9 W. H. Pearson
11 Mr. & Mrs. Stephen C. Holland
11 Capt. & Mrs. Ezra W. Kingsbury
11 Mr. & Mrs. John W. Kingsbury
11 Mrs. L. K. Anderson
11½ Mr. & Mrs. John A. Richardson
23 Mrs. James M. Bell
23 Mrs. C. W. Rose
25 Mr. & Mrs. J. B. Chandler
25 Miss Gertrude Roberts
25 Miss Flora Roberts
29 Mr. & Mrs. Jos. S. Woodruff
35 Dr. Lester Curtis
39 Mr. & Mrs. W. G. Sherer

39 Mrs. S. E. O. Howe
41 Rev. & Mrs. C. F. Tolman & dr.
43 Mr. & Mrs. Noah C. Brower
43 Mr. & Mrs. Robert Ellis
53 Mrs. Lucy Shinn & drs.
53 Mr. & Mrs. Fred W. Buescher
59 Mr. & Mrs. W. H. Thomas &drs.
61 Mr. & Mrs. D. R. Thomas
61 Mrs. Norah Gridley-Gridley
65 Mr. & Mrs. Ernest M. Bowman
65 Mr. & Mrs. John A. Devore
65 Miss Emma Long
65 Mr. & Mrs.Wm. Carpenter Camp
67 Mr. & Mrs. John F. Hoke
67 Mr. & Mrs. William Hill
69 Mr. & Mrs. Edwin C. Ulrich
71 Mr. & Mrs. Wm. K. Copenhaver

VERNON AVENUE.

2931 Mr. & Mrs. Jos. M. Crennan
2935 Mr. & Mrs. S. C. Smith & dr.
2943 Stephen S. Conway
2967 Mr.& Mrs. D.W.Jackson & drs.
        . *Receiving day Thursday*
2967 The Misses Bacon
2967 Mrs. W. F. Myrick
3005 Mrs. H. H. McLane & drs.
3005 James A. McLane
3005 Charles W. Hubbard
3007 Mr. & Mrs. J. Parsons & dr.
3009 Mr. & Mrs. Edwin E. Hills
3009 Alfred K. Hills
3009 Gage Hills
3011 Mrs. Ida Gardner

2832 Mr & Mrs. Charles A. Story
2944 Mrs. A. E. Hall
2944 George Bohner
2944 Miss Mary A. Bohner
        Receiving day Wednesday
2964 Mr. & Mrs. J. E. Neiswanger
2964 Mr. & Mrs. Wm. J. Seib
2966 Mr. & Mrs. William Goldie
2968 Dr. Walter S. Barnes
2968 Miss Lillian Barnes
2968 Mr. & Mrs. A. B. Sherwood
2970 Mr. & Mrs. R. E. Farnham
2970 Mr. & Mrs. Leon Klain
2970 Gustave Cure
2970 Adams A. Goodrich

3015 Mr. & Mrs. J. D. Milliken & dr.
3017 Rev. & Mrs. LeRoy Hooker & drs.
3017 George F. Hooker
3019 Mr. & Mrs. L. Summerfield & dr.
3019 Mr. & Mrs. Benj. Schneewind
3021 Mrs. M. C. Palmer & dr.
3027 Mr. & Mrs. W. B. Henion
3029 Mr. & Mrs. C. L. Harper
3121 Mr. & Mrs. T. H. Flood & dr.
3121 Frank J. Flood
3123 Mr. & Mrs. J. H. Hogey
3125 Mrs. M. Levie & dr.
3125 Jerome M. Levie
3125 Charles M. Levi.
3125 Oliver M. Levi
3127 Samuel J. Loeb
3129 Mr.&Mrs. David Frank & drs.
3129 Morris Frank
3129 D. Frank
3131 Mrs. Simon Joseph & dr.
3131 Herbert L. Joseph
3131 Henry M. Joseph
3133 Mr. & Mrs. S. L. Joseph
3135 Mrs. Henrietta Childs & drs.
3137 Mr. & Mrs. Samuel Goldsmith
3139 Mr. & Mrs. L. B. Meyer & dr.
3139 Sigmund Meyer
3141 Mr. & Mrs. S. Silberman
3143 Mr. & Mrs. M. Keating
3145 Mr. & Mrs. D. J. Harris
3147 Mr. & Mrs. Eli Smith
3147 Edwin M. Smith
3211 Mr. & Mrs. D. C. Barringer & dr.
3211 Walter M. Barringer
3213 Mr. & Mrs. Louis Newberger
3221 Mr. & Mrs. Gustavus Freund
3223 Mr. & Mrs. Jos. Rosenthal
3225 Mr. & Mrs. Leopold Freiberger
3227 Mr. & Mrs. N. Ernst
3229 Mr. & Mrs. Henry P. Caldwell
3231 Mr. & Mrs. C. R. Stouffer &dr.
3233 Mr. & Mrs. William Manson
3235 Mrs. Bertha Greenhoot & dr.
3237 Mr. & Mrs. F. E. Anderson
3239 Mr. & Mrs. Joseph Shoninger
3241 Mr. & Mrs. Alfred Kohn
3243 Mr. & Mrs. A. F. Slyder
Receiving day Friday
3245 Mr. & Mrs. Henry Herman
3247 Mr. & Mrs. Leopold Wolf
3249 Mr. & Mrs. Edward Hirsch
3251 Mr. & Mrs. L. Lebensberger
Receive 1st and 3d Friday

2970 Frank I. Cords
3000 Mr. & Mrs. Charles A. Crane
3002 Mrs. J. L. Hewitt
3002 Mr. & Mrs. F. L. Miner
3002 Mrs. I. M. Wheeler
3012 Mr. & Mrs. W. W. Wilcox & dr.
3024 Mr. & Mrs. Philip Ringer & dr.
3024 Jacob Ringer
3026 Mr. & Mrs. Noel Brosseau
3028 Mr. & Mrs. J. A. Sibley & dr.
3028 G. M. Sibley
3112 Mr. & Mrs. A. P. Burland
3118 Mr. & Mrs. J. M. Mills
3130 Mr. & Mrs. O. L. American & dr.
3132 Mrs. Joseph Foreman & dr.
3132 Milton J. Foreman
3140 Mr. & Mrs. A. Batchelder
3142 Mrs. E. P. Hall
3142 Miss Mollie Hahn
3144 Mr. & Mrs. Samuel B. Lingle
3146 Dr. & Mrs. W. W. Lazear
3146 Mrs. Ann Davies
3152 Frederick N. Mills
3152 Miss Jennie M. Mills
3152 Miss Katherine L. Mills
3156 Mr. & Mrs. Thomas R. Lynas
3200 Dr. & Mrs. A. J. Park & dr.
3200 Mr. H. S. Peck & dr.
3202 Mr. & Mrs. R. W. Beckwith
3202 Mr. & Mrs. C. Lazarus
3206 Mr. & Mrs. Louis Benjamin
3210 Mr. & Mrs. John T. Pratt
3212 Mr. & Mrs. Leopold Daube
3214 Mr. & Mrs. Joseph Berolzheim
3218 Mr. & Mrs. J. P. Ahrens
3218 Mrs. M. J. Hamblin & dr.
3220 Dr. & Mrs. F. B. Ives
3220 Mrs. L. Cailcott & drs.
3222 Mrs. John W. Peck& drs.
3222 Mr. & Mrs. Walter Ramsey
3224 Mrs. Catherine Schwahn
3234 Mr. & Mrs. C. T. Whitgreave
3236 Mr. & Mrs. Isaac Michaels
3238 Mr. & Mrs. J. E. Levy
3242 Dr. & Mrs. Ed. Bert
Receive last Tuesday in mo.
3242 Dr. & Mrs. G. Krieger
3244 Mrs. M. L. Clancy
3244 William M. Clancy
3246 Mr. & Mrs. L. Benjamin & drs.
3248 Mr. & Mrs. Charles Hasterlik
3248 Samuel Hasterlik
3250 Mr. & Mrs. Morris Goodman
3250 Mrs. Adeline Neuman
3252 Mr. & Mrs. W. B. Wrenn

3253 Mr. & Mrs. M. A. Meyer
3257 Mr. & Mrs. Joseph Hyman
3257 Miss Frances Hyman
3259 Mr. & Mrs. Robert G. Hall
3261 Mr. & Mrs. M. Schwarz
3261 Aibert Schwarz
3263 Mr. & Mrs. J. N. Strauss
3265 Mr. & Mrs. J. R. Anthony
3265 Samuel Rosenthal
3267 Mr. & Mrs. Wm. Rosenbaum
3267 David Waixel
3301 Mrs. H. B. Benjamin & drs.
3303 Mr. & Mrs. Edward Sincere
3305 Dr. & Mrs. S. Cole
   Receiving day Tuesday
3307 Mr. & Mrs. S. Hartman
3313 Mr. & Mrs. David A. Stein
3313 Max L. Lindheimer
3315 Mr. & Mrs. Louis Kaufman
3317 Mr. & Mrs. J. J. Epstein
3319 Mr. & Mrs. M. Joel
3321 Mr. & Mrs. S. Schlesinger
3323 Mr. & Mrs. Leon Friedlander
3325 Mr. & Mrs. Simon Butler
3327 James F. Coyle
3329 A. C. Hesing
3329 Mr. & Mrs. M. Werkmeister
3331 Mr. & Mrs. W. H. Phelps
   Receiving day Thursday
3333 Mr. & Mrs. J. M. Joseph
3339 Mr. & Mrs. James Jay Smith
3339 Mrs. S. C. Avy
3401 Dr. & Mrs. J. Priestman & drs.
3405 Mr. & Mrs. H. W. Hendrick
3405 Miss Hallie Rives
3405 Miss Mamie Tabb
3411 Mr. & Mrs. G. W. Stone
3411 Harry W. Stone
3413 Mr. & Mrs. W. E. Frost & drs.
3421 Mr. & Mrs. E. S. Walker
3423 Mr. & Mrs. W. L. Schaub
3425 Mrs. K. B. Davis
3427 Mr. & Mrs. Daniel J. Schuyler
3427 Daniel J. Schuyler jr.
3431 Mr.&Mrs.Charles S.Dickinson
3439 Mr. & Mrs. Andrew Wallace
  & drs.
3519 Mr. & Mrs. J. Musselwhite&dr.
3521 Mr. & Mrs. Geo. A. S. Wilson
3523 Mr. & Mrs. William Lehman
3527 Mr. & Mrs. S. Eppstein
3529 Mr. & Mrs. H. Stern
   Receive 1st & 3d Thursday
3531 Mr. & Mrs. Aaron Straus
3531 Mrs. Therese Eliel & dr.
3533 Mr. & Mrs. L. Hartman

14

3254 Mr. & Mrs. J. J. Herman
3256 Mr. & Mrs. David Witkowsky
 & dr.
3258 Mr. & Mrs. E. A. Josephi
3260 Mr. & Mrs. Geo. C. Sumerfield
3262 Mr & Mrs. B. Whyland
3264 Mr. & Mrs. B. W. Eisendrath
 & dr.
3266 Mrs. Emanuel Levi
3266 Walter C. Levi
3266 Leon Levi
3300 Mr. & Mrs. C. K. Nims
3300 O. L. Nims
3304 Frank Drake
3304 Mr. & Mrs. W. R. Raymond
3320 Mr. & Mrs. William Brackett
3322 Mr. & Mrs. L. D. Davis
   Receiving day Wednesday
3322 Mr. & Mrs. J. Baum
3324 Mr. & Mrs. Jesse Holdom
3326 Mr. & Mrs. James G. McBean
3326 Leroy H. McBean
3332 Mr. & Mrs. N. J. Ullman
   Receive 1st & 3d Friday
3334 Mr. & Mrs. Jonathan Abel
3334 Mr. & Mrs.Wesson Macomber
3338 Mr. & Mrs. William Levy
3338 Louis Rosenfield
3340 Mr. & Mrs. Sidney W. Sea
3346 Maurice W. Kozminski
3346 Mrs. Charles Kozminski
3348 Mr. & Mrs. W. A. Prior
3348 Mrs. Martha E. Hayes
3350 Mr. & Mrs. D. Berlizheimer
3352 Mr. & Mrs. Henry Oberndorf
3352 Joseph Oberndorf
3352 Louis Oberndorf
3354 Mr. & Mrs. William Hirsch
3356 Mr. & Mrs. Anthony Burke
3400 Mr. & Mrs. John K. Prindiville
3404 Mr. & Mrs. Carl Joseph
3406 Mr. & Mrs. Samuel Hirschbein
3408 Mr. & Mrs. D. Osterman
3408 W. A. Nye
3410 Mr. & Mrs. S. L. Frazer
3412 Mr. & Mrs. J. T. McAuley
3414 Mr. & Mrs. B. Rosenberg
3416 Mr. & Mrs. Jacob Cohn & dr.
3418 Mr. & Mrs. S. H. Foreman
3420 Mrs. A. Gottlieb
3420 Richard D. Gottlieb
3422 Mr. & Mrs. Wm. Garnett & dr.
3422 John L. Garnett
3422 Eugene Garnett
3424 Mr. & Mrs. Charles P. Montgomery

3551 Mr. & Mrs. Michael Altman
      Receiving day Wednesday
3553 Mr. & Mrs. Fred Oberndorf
3557 Mr. & Mrs. D. Launder
3609 Mr. & Mrs. Bernhard Pfaelzer
3625 Mr. & Mrs. B. J.McCleary & dr.
      Receiving day Thursday
3627 Mrs. J. Truax & dr.
3627 Miss Nellie Chaffee
3627 G. Frank White
3631 Mrs. R. O'Connell & dr.
3633 Mr. & Mrs. Jos. M. Hirsh & dr.
      Receiving day Wednesday
3633 Arthur Hirsh
3635 Mr. & Mrs. Marcy F. Minden
      Receiving day Thursday
3635 Mr. & Mrs. Albert Hoefeld
3639 Mr. & Mrs. Emil Guthmann &
      drs.
3643 Mr. & Mrs. William Spier
      Receive 1st & 3d Friday
3645 Mrs. E. A. King
3645 Vere B. King
3739 Mr. & Mrs. E. E. Johnson
3743 Mr. & Mrs. L. Rubel
3745 Mr. & Mrs. Wm. Pickett & dr.
3745 Mrs. W. S. Pickett
3753 Mr. & Mrs. Geo. W. Hancock
3753 Mrs. L. C. Layton
3759 Mr. & Mrs. Philip Keller & dr.
3761 Mr. & Mrs. John W. Turner
3763 Mr. & Mrs. J. H. Kowalski
3819 Mr. & Mrs. Benjamin F. Chase
      Receiving day Wednesday
3821 Mr. & Mrs. J. Emery Tate
3823 Mr. & Mrs. Fred Holmes
3825 Mr.& Mrs. Edwin F. Masterson
3827 Mr. & Mrs. E. G. McCurdy
3829 Mr. & Mrs. James M. Dawson

3426 Mr. & Mrs. James K. Burtis
3428 Mrs. M. S. Andrus
3430 Mr. & Mrs. F. W. Parker
3430 Mrs. D. W. Chapman
3432 Mr. & Mrs. F. W. Tourtellotte
3432 Frederick J. Tourtellotte
3434 Mr. & Mrs. C. E. Cook
3438 Mr. & Mrs. J. T. Richards
3440 Mr. & Mrs. Thomas D. O'Brien
3440 Samuel Rosenbaum
3442 Mr. & Mrs. Bernard Mayer
3532 Mr. & Mrs. J. C. Schwartz
3532 Mr. & Mrs. Olof G. Olson
3538 Sidney Simon
3542 Mr. & Mrs. Patrick McMahon
      & drs.
3542 A. J. McMahon
3548 Mr. & Mrs. Wm. M. Morrison
3552 Mr. & Mrs. Sidney T. Emerson
3554 Mr. & Mrs. C. L. Schaar
3560 Mr. & Mrs. Jacob Mayer
3564 Mr. & Mrs. Samuel Polkey
3604 Mr. & Mrs. James L. Ross
3624 Mr. & Mrs. A. Weiskopf
3626 Mr. & Mrs. A. H. Cohn
3628 Mr. & Mrs. Fred Boyden
3628 Mr. & Mrs. Burton W. Stadden
3628 Mrs. Woodbury M. Taylor
3630 Mr. & Mrs. Isaac Van Hagen
3630 George E. Van Hagen
3632 Charles J. Dash
3634 Mr. & Mrs. Henry H. Heaford
3824 Mr. & Mrs. Louis Vehon
3826 Mr. & Mrs. E. S. Hyman
3828 Mr. & Mrs. Ralph M. Leo-
      pold
3936 Mr. & Mrs. Louis Becker
3982 Mr. & Mrs. John V. Hair

VINCENNES AVENUE.

3555 Mrs. Angelica Kuehne
3555 Mrs. Ida Sporlein
3555 Otto Kuehne
3555 Clemens Kuehne
3559 Mr. & Mrs. Wm. R. Omohun-
      dro. *Receiving day Friday*
3559 Riley C. Omohundro
3559 Mr. & Mrs. Alfred L. Jones
      Receiving day Tuesday
3559 Miss Clara A. Jones
3549 Richard W. Jordan
3559 J. Mabbett Brown & dr.
3559 Frank C. Brown
3559 Edward O. Brown

3548 Mr. & Mrs. Frank C. Rutan
3552 Mr. & Mrs. Thomas V. Conner
      Receiving day Tuesday
3560 Isaac Freeman & drs.
3560 Benjamin Freeman
3560 William Freeman
3566 Mr. & Mrs. Fitzallen B. Wil-
      liams & dr.
3566 Waldo A. Williams
3566 Frank B. Williams
3568 Mr. & Mrs. Frank A. Upham
3570 Mr. & Mrs. T. G. Younglove
3580 Dr. & Mrs. John E. Harper
3580 Mrs. G. B. Walker

3601 The Vincennes—
Mrs. Alice H. Blackstone
   Receiving day Tuesday
Mrs. Tarasa Azalia Dodge-
   Bowron
   Receiving day Wednesday
Mr. & Mrs.Chas.Turner Brown
Mrs. Margaret T. Clarke
Mrs. L. DeBennette
   Receiving day Thursday
Mr. & Mrs. Walter S. Jones
   Receiving day Wednesday
Mrs. M. J. Kilbourne
Mr. & Mrs. E. N. Lapham
Mrs. M. B. MacDonald
Miss Grace G. MacDonald
Mr. &. Mrs. Edward H. Mc-
   Pherran
   Receiving day Tuesday
Mr. & Mrs. Charles T. Merritt
   Receiving day Thursday
E. J. Nally
Mr. & Mrs. Herman J. Reiling
Mrs. A. V. Shorey & dr.
   Receiving day Wednesday
Mr. & Mrs. Howard L. Smith
Mrs. Emma Weiland
   Receives Tuesday evening
3625 Mrs. Marrie Harrold Garrison
3625 Allan C. Wilde
3629 Mr. & Mrs. Edwin B. Durno
3629 Miss Nettie Durno
3637 Mr. & Mrs. L. B. Nichols
   Receiving day Tuesday
3639 Mr. & Mrs. Edwin W. Wile
3639 Aaron E. Rosenthal
3641 Mr. & Mrs. John W. Shute & dr.
3643 Mr. & Mrs. Chas. A. Sturges &
   dr.
3645 Mr. & Mrs. Geo. B. Flanders
3647 Mr. & Mrs. S. W. Burnham
3701 Mrs. Kate Fuller
3705 Mr.& Mrs.Chas. Homer Miller
3707 Mr. & Mrs. Hiram B. Johnson
3707 Mr. & Mrs. I. I. Scofield
3707 Charles Jones
3717 Mr. & Mrs. Jacob Lindheimer
3717 Samuel Sonnenberg
3719 Mrs. Roxana Millard
3719 George M. Millard
3721 Mr. & Mrs. Wm. A. Sommers
3725 Mr. & Mrs. C. L. Ely & dr.
3725 A. G. Ely
3731 Mr. & Mrs. Maurice Landsberg
3733 Dr. & Mrs. Edward W. Sawyer
3735 Mr. & Mrs. W. A. Denny & dr.

3632 Mr. & Mrs. J. Wilber Stott
3632 Mr. & Mrs. Henry Pollak&drs.
3632 Mr. & Mrs. Geo. W. Hatter
3634 Mrs. Mary Alison
3634 John M. Alison
3634 Rowland H. Alison
3644 Mr. & Mrs. S. J. Bellamy
3646 Mr. & Mrs. W. F. Wood
3650 Mrs. S. E. Moore
3650 Miss Mary J. Moore
3652 Mr. & Mrs. Lucius D. Tuttle
3658 Dr. & Mrs. W. W. Hester
3658 Miss Jennie Harrison
3658 Thomas E. Harrison
3658 Philip D. Norcom
3658 Mr. & Mrs. George E. Cook
3658 Horace G. Davis
3806 Mr. & Mrs. Peter H. Witt & dr.
   Receiving day Thursday
3806 Andrew Witt
3826 S. E. Smith & dr.
3826 Henry W. Smith
3834 Mr. & Mrs. J. K. Joice
3836 Dr. & Mrs. J. A. Hemsteger
   Receiving day Thursday
3840 Mr. & Mrs. John W. Morse
3846 Mr. & Mrs. William H. Underwood & dr.
3846 William A. Underwood
3848 Dr. & Mrs. Amos L. Lennard
3848 Lewis L. Lennard
3848 Miss Susan Dillon
3912 Mr. & Mrs. L. H. Bisbee & dr.
3920 Mr.& Mrs.Thomas Hutchinson
   & drs.
3972 Mr. & Mrs. Hugh Martin
3976 Mr. & Mrs. Adam Craig
4002 Mr. & Mrs. Max Goldman
4008 Mr. & Mrs. E. C. J. Cleaver
4016 Mr. & Mrs. Wm. J. Graham
4018 Mr. & Mrs. Matthew J. Brennan
4020 Mr. & Mrs. Thomas Conlin
4022 Dr. & Mrs. H. S. Barnard
4102 Mr. & Mrs. H. P. Elliott
4104 Mr. & Mrs. George B. Kerr
4106 Mr. & Mrs. Charles E. Crone
   Receiving day Tuesday
4116 Mr. & Mrs. R. T. Barton
4120 Mr. & Mrs. Hollis W. Field
4122 Mr.&Mrs. W.H.Murdock&drs.
4200 Mr. & Mrs. James C. Miller
4202 Mr. & Mrs. John Kelly
4208 Mr.&Mrs.Lawrence Honkomp
4214 Mr. & Mrs. Thos. F. Williamson & drs.

3735 Nathan R. Denny
3743 Mr. & Mrs. Levi A. Fretts
3743 J. Frank Edwards
3751 Mr. & Mrs. C. L. Caswell & dr.
3751 C. L. Caswell jr.
3753 Mrs. Caroline Green & drs.
3757 Henry B. Ford
3801 Mr. & Mrs. James M. Aubery
    Receiving day Thursday
3801 Mr. & Mrs. James M.Aubery jr.
3805 Mr. & Mrs. Charles Berg
3807 Mr. & Mrs. C. W. Fairrington
3807 Warren M. Fairrington
3807 Frank E. Eaker
3807 Miss H. A. Manny
3811 Arthur W. Newton
3813 Mrs. I. Schrimski & dr.
3813 Israel Schrimski
3815 Mr. & Mrs. M. D. Flavin
3817 Col. & Mrs. Geo. K. Brady
3819 Mr. & Mrs. J. R. Laing
    Receiving day Thursday
3819 William G. Laing
3823 Mr. & Mrs. Martin Cummings
3825 Mr. & Mrs. Harry C. Adams
3827 Mr. & Mrs. H. C. Champlain
    & drs.
3835 Mr. & Mrs. David Lelewer
3835 Miss Philipene Hoefeld
3839 Mr. & Mrs. Adolph Sinks
3839 B. H. Sinks
3843 Mr. & Mrs. Fred A. Paddleford
3843 Mr. & Mrs. John M. Hubbard
3845 Mr. & Mrs. H. Y. Rowley
3905 Mr. & Mrs. John W. Moore
3907 Mr. & Mrs. Thos. N. Jamieson
3915 Mr. & Mrs. C. H. Gillette
3917 Mr. & Mrs. Henry Gillette
3927 Mr. & Mrs. I. N. Conroy & drs.
3927½ Mr. & Mrs. Levi G. Rabel
3929 Mr. & Mrs. John A. Waterman
4001 Mr. & Mrs. Chas. F. Simonson
4001 Mr. & Mrs. C. C. Colby
4001 Mr. & Mrs. G. L. Clausen
4001 Mr. & Mrs. Frank W. Harvey
4007 John Hallett
4007 Harvey J. Hallett
4007 Mr. & Mrs. J. W. Rust
4009 Mr. & Mrs. George A Dunlap
4009 Ernest Dunlap
4015 Mr.&Mrs.J.W.McDonald&drs.
    Receiving day Thursday
4015 Mrs. Anna Downing
4017 Mrs. George Wright
4017 George W. Wright
4019 Mrs. Mary C. Mevelle & drs.

4220 Mr. & Mrs. Theodore Butter-
    worth
4220 Theodore A. Butterworth
4226 Mr. & Mrs. Louis Rueckheim
4320 Mr. & Mrs. Moses Cohn
4322 Mr. & Mrs. R. A. Canterbury
    Receiving day Thursday
4350 Mr. & Mrs. Frank A. Coker
4436 Mr. & Mrs. E. A. Wood & drs.
4500 Mr. & Mrs. John T. Garm
4500 Mr. & Mrs. J. M. Treadway
4500 Mr. & Mrs. John B. Roach
4500 Mr. & Mrs. George A. Gill
4500 Mr. & Mrs. Thomas J. Duffy
4500 Mr. & Mrs. Wm. H. Alcock
4500 Mr. & Mrs. Henry B. Sauve
4504 Mr. & Mrs. Edward I. Field
4504 Mr. & Mrs. F. W. Zeddies
4504 Mr. & Mrs. S. D. Andrus
4504 Mr. & Mrs. Henry F. Hawes
4504 Mr. & Mrs. Thos. C. Roney
4504 Mr. & Mrs. P. L. Inglis
4506 Mr. & Mrs. John S. Collman
4510 John A. Brown
4512 Mr. & Mrs. David J. Pfaelzer
4546 Philip C. Bauer
4550 Mr. & Mrs. Thos. F. McAvoy
4550 Mrs. Minerva M. Sawyer
4632 Mr. & Mrs. Alva V. Shoemaker
4632 Mr. & Mrs. A. L. Utz
4632 Mrs. E. H. Beck
4634 Mr. & Mrs. John F. Brock
    Receiving day Wednesday
4634 Mr. & Mrs. Wm. H. Marsh
4636 Mr. & Mrs. Charles O. Goss
4648 Mr.&Mrs.Joseph H. Steele
    Receiving day Thursday
4710 Judge & Mrs. Thos. A. Moran
    Receiving day Tuesday
4802 Mr. & Mrs. Samuel J. Nash
4804 Mr. & Mrs. H. Boore
4808 Mr. & Mrs. W. T. Nash
4812 Mr. & Mrs. James Mowatt &
    dr.
4842 Mr. & Mrs. A. H. Veeder & dr.
    Receiving day Thursday
4842 Albert H. Veeder jr.
4930 Mr. & Mrs. Wm. J. Brachvogel
4930 Mr. & Mrs. Hugh A. Kelso
4930 H. A. Kelso jr.
4930 Mrs. May Donnally Kelso
4950 Mr. & Mrs. M. C. Harris
4950 Mr. & Mrs. C. J. Dunlap
4950 W. P. Dunlap
4952 Mr. & Mrs. C. E. Woolley
4952 Mr. & Mrs. Walter S. Isaacs

4019 Chas. W. Mevelle
4021 Mr. & Mrs. James P. Lott
4023 Mr. & Mrs. Charles Schimel
4027 Mrs. Delina Kepner & drs.
4029 Mr. & Mrs. Henry O. Nourse
4033 Rev. & Mrs. Carlos Martyn
    Receiving day Tuesday
4101 John B Heeney
4101 Miss Frances Heeney
4103 Mr. & Mrs. James. E. Baggot
4119 Mr. & Mrs. Thos. A. Dean
    Receiving day Wednesday
4125 Mr. &Mrs. JoelM Longenecker
4201 Mr. & Mrs. F. W. Rueckheim
4207 Mr. & Mrs. John P. Bowles
4211 Mr. & Mrs. Wm. J. Byrnes
4211 Mrs. Mary K. Collins
4211 Mr. & Mrs. Thos. C. Clifford
4211 Mr. & Mrs. Charles L. Will
4213 Mr. & Mrs. Isidor A. Rubel
4217 Mr. & Mrs. Jacob Thorne &drs.
4219 Mr. & Mrs. Clarence S. Darrow
4225 Mr. & Mrs. Blanford R. Peirce
4235 Mr. & Mrs. James O'Callaghan
4235 Mr. & Mrs. John R. O'Callaghan
4239 Mr. & Mrs. David F. Haskell
4239 Reuben L. Haskell
4239 Lester A. Haskell
4243 Mr. & Mrs. Robert S. Hill
4317 Mr. & Mrs. Leon Cline
4319 Mr. & Mrs. Maurice Strauss
4321 Mr. & Mrs. A. Florsheim & dr.
4329 Mr. & Mrs. Albert Hyman
4329 David Hyman
4419 Mr. & Mrs. Frank A.Anderson
4419 Mr. & Mrs. Frank Bixby
4421 Mr. & Mrs. Henry G. Eckstein
4423 Mr. & Mrs. John A. Thomas
4425 Mr. & Mrs. Robert Russell
4425 Mrs. Margaret A. Humble & dr.
4425 Mr. & Mrs. Henry N. Poirer

4525 Mr. & Mrs. J. L. Parrotte & dr.
4525 Mr. & Mrs. Edwin A. Behan
4525 Warren P. Behan
4525 George H. Behan
4525 Mr. & Mrs. Emanuel Loeb
4527 Chester H. Martin
4527 Miss Addie T. Martin
4527 Miss Florence Martin
4527 Mr. & Mrs. James F. Broderick
4529 Mr. & Mrs. J. C. Christman
4529 Mr. & Mrs. James F. Shields
4529 Mr. & Mrs. A. B. Clampet
4531 Mr. & Mrs. Frank W. Himrod
4531 Mr. & Mrs. David H. Salinger
4549 Mr. & Mrs. John Maher & dr.
4611 Dr. & Mrs. W. W. Coker
4615 Mr. & Mrs. Richard J. Murphy
    Receiving day Tuesday
4615 Joseph Sherwin
4617 Mr. & Mrs. David B. Gann
    Receiving day Tuesday
4617 Howard E. Nicholas
4647 Mr. & Mrs. William C. Stevens & drs.
4647 Theron Fay Stevens
4647 Miss Geneva I. Willard
4707 Mr. & Mrs. William H. Cunningham & drs.
4725 Mr. & Mrs. Thomas E. Wells
4821 Mr. & Mrs. Henry J. Cox
4827 Mr. & Mrs. Chas. H. Brachvogel
4829 Mr. & Mrs. Oliver W. Marble
    Receiving day Thursday
4831 August Wies
4831 Charles A. Wies
4839 Mr. & Mrs. John Q. McAdams
4919 Mr. & Mrs. Sylvester J. Fitzpatrick
4919 Mr. & Mrs. William E. Brown
4919 Thomas J. Norton
4919 Mr. & Mrs. John Brady & dr.
4919 John A. Brady

WABASH AVENUE.

1301 Mrs. Harriet G. Brainard
1731 Mr. & Mrs. C. H. White
1827 Louis Shissler
2033 Dr. Mary Shaffer
2125 B. C. Gelder
2125 W. B. Hunnewell
2231 Dr. & Mrs. R. E. Woodward
2233 Mr. & Mrs. C. A. Hancock
2303 Adolph Neubauer

1204 Mr. & Mrs. James T. Vickery
1204 Thomas G. Vickery
1204 John R Vickery
1318 Dr. & Mrs. W. W. Buchanan
2236 Mr. & Mrs. E. C. Quarles
2424 Willis Shaw
2426 Harry White
2450 Mr. & Mrs. P. M. Cleary & drs.

2415 Dr. Ira D. Isham
2425 Mr. & Mrs. A. Sweger & dr.
2427 Mr.& Mrs.W. H. Hafner
2427 W. H. Hafner jr.,
2439 Mr. & Mrs. T. H. Miller
2439 Thomas' H. Miller jr.
2441 Alf. M. Snydacker
2443 Mr. & Mrs. Charles Stein
2445 Mrs. M. Hayes & drs.
2501 Mrs. Elizabeth Marks
2501 Louis J. Marks
2501 Kossuth Marks
2501 Joseph E. P. Marks
2501 Edward C. Marks
2509 Mr. & Mrs. Louis Mayer
2509 Edwin L. Mayer
2513 Mr. & Mrs. Kaufman Hexter & drs.
2513 Miss Rose Lebold
2515 Mrs. F. M. Wilder & dr.
Receiving day Wednesday
2525 George B. O'Reilly
2541 Henry Cherrie & drs.
2541 Robert M. Cherrie
2541 Mrs. M. J. Dolph
2541 Henry C. Dolph
2541 Mrs. Sarah C. Adams
2541 Miss Eva E. Adams
2621 Mr. & Mrs. M. Kanter & dr.
2621 Louis Kanter
2623½ Mr. & Mrs. F. E. Rose
2625 Mr. & Mrs. Samuel C. Kanter
2631 Dr. & Mrs. W. A. Stevens
2703 Mr. & Mrs. Jacob Weil & dr.
2703 Mr. & Mrs. J. S. Meyer
2707 Mr. & Mrs. J. C. Starr & dr.
2707 Western Starr
2715 Dr. & Mrs. I. H. Hopkins
2719 Mr. & Mrs. C. D. Austin
2723 Mr. & Mrs. Anthony Lichtenheim & dr.
2727 Mr. & Mrs. S. M. McConnell
2727 Mr. & Mrs. W. S. McConnell
2923 Mrs. M. Pieser
2923 Mrs. L. Frank
2959 Mrs. A. Sanders & dr.
2959 John P. Sanders
2963 Mrs. John O'Neill & drs.
2973 Mr. & Mrs. S. Heidweyer & drs.
2973 Moses Florsheim
2975 Mrs. H. Cowan & drs.
3011 Dr. & Mrs. N. Rowe
3017 Mrs. F. B. Gilbert
3017 Rev. George W. Bowen
3113 Mr. & Mrs. M. M. Bardon
3115 Dr. & Mrs. J. R. Kewley

2450 Edward E. Cleary
2458 Mr. & Mrs. A. S. Moore
2512 Mrs. L. C. Dyer
2512 Judge Randall H. White
2522 Mr. & Mrs. Samuel Stiefel &dr.
2532 Mr. & Mrs. S. J. Cooke
2556 David R. Riddell
2618 Mr. & Mrs. Oliver R. Nelson
2622 Mr. & Mrs. C. S. Baker & drs.
2622 A. H. Baker
2628 Mr. & Mrs. George W. Palmer
2630 Mr. & Mrs. David W. Cressler
2630 Joseph A. Cressler
2712 Meyer Meyer
2714 Mrs. C. W. Chaffee
2716 Samuel H. Adams jr.
2720 Mr. & Mrs. S. C. Fish
2728 The Woodstock
   Mr. & Mrs. Wm. A. Stanton
2 Mrs. Antoinette L. Woods
5 Mrs. H. E. Lowdermilk
5 A. W. Lowdermilk
5 Mrs. Hattie Copeland
7 Dr.&Mrs.E.J.Nickerson&drs
8 Mr. & Mrs. John A. May
9 Mrs. C. Satterthwaite & drs.
18 Mr. & Mrs. S. W. Fargo
21 Mr. & Mrs. T. P. Sherborne
27 Mr.& Mrs.Francis V.Putnam
2956 Mr. & Mrs. A. B. Perrigo
2964 Mr. & Mrs. Albert Heller
2964 J. Heller
2964 Mrs. I. I. Herzfeld
2974 Dr. & Mrs. E. Sincere & dr.
2978 Mr. & Mrs. A. Cummings
3018 Mr. & Mrs. Andrew Ritter
3018 E. S. Craig
3032 D. W. Mason & drs.
3032 George Allen Mason
3122 Mr. & Mrs. C. L. Epstein & drs.
3138 Mrs. Martin Crowe & drs.
3138 P. J. Hillary
3138 Mr. & Mrs. E. C. Smith
3152 Mr. & Mrs. E. Heller
3156 Mr. & Mrs. M. W. Wolf.
3158 E. C. Klauber
3210 Mr. & Mrs. S. Minchrod & dr.
   Receiving day Thursday
3210 Miss Ada B. Minchrod
3210 Louis Newmark
3212 John F. Clare
3216 Clinton Briggs & drs.
3022 Mr. & Mrs. Sidney Wanzer
3228 Mr. & Mrs. Adolph Grossman & drs. *Receive Monday*
3228 George Grossman

3117 Dr. & Mrs. Martin Matter
3121 Mr. & Mrs. J. E. Beaver
3121 Mr. & Mrs. C. E. Fargo jr.
3125 Mrs. Jane Beaver
3125 Mr. & Mrs. J. S. Bassett
3125 J. Eugene Bassett
3131 Mr.&Mrs.William Walsh&drs.
3133 Mr. & Mrs. N. Davis & dr.
3137 Mr. & Mrs. L. Schoenbrun & drs.
3137 Irving Schoenbrun
3137 Sampson Schoenbrun
3139 Mr. & Mrs. Molesworth King
3153 Mrs. Annie Gitzgibbon
3155 Mrs. Florence A. Camp
3201 Mr. & Mrs. Edw. Hudson & dr.
    Receiving day Tuesday
3201 Edward Hudson jr.
3211 Mr. & Mrs. J. Kahn
    Receiving day Friday
3211 Louis Kahn
3211 Harry Kahn
3211 Mr. & Mrs. J. S. Wolbach
3213 Mr. & Mrs. Leo D. Mayer & dr.
    Receiving day Friday
3213 Edgar J. Mayer
3217 Mrs. H. Schaffner
3217 Mr. & Mrs. N. Becker
3219 Mr. & Mrs. B. J. Wertheimer
3221 Mr. & Mrs. Jacob Schnur
3223 Mr. & Mrs. C. D. Hancock
3225 Mr. & Mrs. M. E. Lindauer
3227 Mr. & Mrs. James Smith
3229 Mr. & Mrs. M. H. Mayer
    Receiving day Tuesday
3231 Mr. & Mrs. W. C. Ross
3231 Alexander Bell
3231 Clement Bell
3241 Mr. & Mrs. Edward Rose & dr.
    Receiving day Monday
3241 Mr. & Mrs. H. L. Swarts
3247 Mr.&Mrs.Julius Rosenthal&dr.
    Receiving day Friday
3247 Lessing Rosenthal
3251 Mr. & Mrs. Marvin S. Chase & dr. *Receiving day Thursday*
3255 Mr. & Mrs. Max Schlesinger
3255 Mr. & Mrs. Joseph Reitler
3255 Mr. & Mrs. Charles Schuster
3255 Mr. & Mrs. U. Rosenheim
3255 Mr. & Mrs. L. Schamberg
    Receiving day Tuesday
3255 Mr. & Mrs. Max Wolf
3255 Mr. & Mrs. I. Orschel
3255 Mrs. Eva Singer
3255 J. H. Weil

3230 Mr. & Mrs. David B.Falter&dr.
    Receive Tuesday
3232 Mr. & Mrs. I. G. Schwarz & drs.
3236 Mr. & Mrs. A. Florsheim & dr.
3238 Mr. & Mrs. Chas. Liebenstein & dr.
    Receive 1st & 3d Thursday
3246 Thomas F. Barry
3248 Mr. & Mrs. C. L. Smith & drs.
3248 S. H. Smith
3250 Mr. & Mrs. Lee Mayer & dr.
    Receiving day Thursday
3250 Harry L. Mayer
3250 Joseph Mayer
3250 Edward Mayer
3252 Mrs. L. Glaser
3252 Victor L. Glaser
3252 Mrs. L. Monheimer
3252 Milton L. Monheimer
3254 Mr. & Mrs. Max C. Eppenstein
    Receiving day Saturday
3254 S. C. Eppenstein
3254 T. W. Duncan
3308 Mr. & Mrs. G. F. Trask
3308 Miss Blanche Stephens
3312 Mr. & Mrs. P. H. Rice
    Receiving day Thursday
3312 Miss Angeline C. Walsh
3326 Mr. & Mrs. Eugene Arnstein
3336 Mr. & Mrs. T. F. DeVeney
3338 Mr. & Mrs. M. Dunne
3344 Mrs. S. A. Dowling
3344 R. A. Dowling
3350 Mr. & Mrs. A. H. Bliss
3350 Mr. & Mrs. George B. Moore
3354 Mr. & Mrs. A. W. Wright
    Receiving day Thursday
3402 Mr. & Mrs. J. McDermott
3404 E. W. Peeke
3408 Mr. & Mrs. Reuben L. Sidwell
3410 Mr. & Mrs. Geo. Weise & dr.
3412 Mengo Morgenthau
3414 Mr. & Mrs. J. Dolese & drs.
3414 John Dolese jr.
3420 Mr.& Mrs.Henry Waixel & dr.
    Receiving day Thursday
3420 Sol H. Waixel
3420 Isaac H. Waixel
3420 Mr. & Mrs.Hy.Schwabacher jr.
    Receiving day Thursday
3424 Mr. & Mrs. Alfred D. Plamondon
3438 Mr. & Mrs. Solva Brintnall
3438 Mrs. O. F. Woodford
3438 Charles A. Woodford

3255 Mrs. S. Stern
3255 Mr. & Mrs. Louis Ullman
3255 Frank R. Strauss
3333 Mrs. H. Goodman & dr.
 Receiving day Thursday
3333 Maurice Goodman
3333 Miss Hannah Miers
 Receiving day Thursday
3333 Mr. & Mrs. Jacob Newman
3337 Mr. & Mrs. A. Strauss
 Receiving day Friday
3337 Leon A. Strauss
3337 Henry X. Strauss
3337 Milton A. Strauss
3341 Mr. & Mrs. Isaac Rubel
3341 Benjamin F. Rubel
3343 Mr. & Mrs. S. Florsheim & drs.
 Receiving day Monday
3343 Norman Florsheim
3343 Sidney Florsheim
3347 Mr. & Mrs. C. C. Chandler
3349 Mrs. Joseph Bee & dr.
3349 Harry Bee
3349 R. Addison Bee
3353 Mrs. Wallace C. Barker
3359 Mr. & Mrs. Thomas D. Hastings
3401 J. C. McCord
3409 Mr. & Mrs. Hyman Levy & drs.
 Receiving day Thursday
3411 Mr. & Mrs. Jacob F. Ritter
 Receiving day Thursday
3417 Mr. & Mrs. Henry Herschman
 & drs.
3417 Charles Herschman
3421 Mr. & Mrs. Isaac Schloss & dr.
3421 Samuel B. Schloss
3421 Benjamin I. Schloss
3431 James Leahy & drs.
 Receiving day Wednesday
3431 Miss Helen Gartlan
3441 Mr. & Mrs. Herman Elson
 Receive 1st & 3d Thursday
3443 Mr. & Mrs. Max Weinberg
3443 Meyer J. Hollander
3443 Mr. & Mrs. David Berg
3449 Mr. & Mrs. Thos. Kelly & drs.
3509 Mr. & Mrs. Herbert T. Sterling
3509 Mrs. John Long
3517 Mr. & Mrs. Jacob Steiner & drs.
3517 Mrs. H. B. Falk
3519 Mr. & Mrs. Harry Byrne
3519 Mrs. Rose Boland
3521 Mrs. Annie Moffatt & dr.
 Receiving day Wednesday
3525 Mrs. W. Klinger & drs.

3440 Mr. & Mrs. J. C. Nickerson
3440 Wilbur Nickerson
3442 Mr. & Mrs. Freeman Nickerson
3442 Mr. & Mrs. W. S. Smith
3446 Rev. & Mrs. A. J. Messing
3446 Herman J. Messing
3446 Sigmund J. Messing
3448 Mr. & Mrs. Albert Fishell
 Rec. days 2d & 4th Thursday in mo.
3448 E. W. Fishell
3450 Mr. & Mrs. W. J. Bigley
3450 W. L. Bigley
3516 John L. Nelson
3516 N. J. Nelson
3516 T. E. Nelson
3518 Mr. & Mrs. Samuel C. Nessler
3520 Mr. & Mrs. J. B. Long
3524 Mr. & Mrs. Morris Mitchell &
 dr. *Receiving day Wednesday*
3524 Henry H. Mitchell
3528 Mr. & Mrs. Michael McDermott
3530 Mr. & Mrs. Charles Long & drs.
 Receive first and last Friday
3530 Louis Long
3530 Lee Long
3530 Sidney Long
3532 Mr. & Mrs. Charles Pick
 Receiving day Wednesday
3532 Mr. & Mrs. Max Brede
 Receiving day Wednesday
3534 Mr. & Mrs. John T. Martin
 Receiving day Thursday
3542 Mrs. Eliza Corbidge
3542 Wm. H. Corbidge
3646 Mr. & Mrs. Samuel Beers & drs.
3648 Mr. & Mrs. W. G. Nutsford
3648 Mr. & Mrs. J. H. Wilson
3662 Mr. & Mrs. Harry S. Thornton
3666 Dr. & Mrs. James G. Berry
3668 Mr. & Mrs. Robt. Peacock &
 drs.
3670 Mr. & Mrs. John Patterson
 & dr.
3708 Mrs. Hannah Livingston & dr.
 Receiving day Thursday
3708 Sigmund Livingston
3708 Nathan Livingston
3708 Mr. & Mrs. Isaac Pieser
3710 Mr. & Mrs. Louis Livingston
3712 Mr. & Mrs. Tobias Rubovits
3712 Mrs. Max Goodkind
3716 Prof. & Mrs. Wm. F. Black
3716 Mr. & Mrs. J. H. Ibsen
3720 Mr. & Mrs. Simon O'Donnell
3720 Mrs. W. H. Luby
3728 Dr. & Mrs. Edwin Pynchon

3525 William Klinger
3525 Mr. & Mrs. L. Uhlendorf
3531 Mrs. Louis Hefter & drs.
3531 Caesar L. Hefter
3535 Mrs. Mary Wilson & niece
   Receiv'g day Tuesday
3661 Mrs. Dr. Louise Goertz
3663 De Soto Flats
 2 Mr. & Mrs. R. B. Belden
 9 Mr. & Mrs. Edgar Franklin
 10 Mrs. Jos. Bissicks & drs.
 11 Mr. & Mrs.DanielH.Church
 12 Mr. & Mrs. Lucius M. Hall
3669 Mr. & Mrs. Patrick Farrell .
3745 Mr. & Mrs. W. M. Cave
3805 Dr. & Mrs. M. G. Hart
3809 Mr. & Mrs. Walter Krouskup
3809 Henry F. Ehrhorn
3811 Mr. & Mrs. August Dosch
3816 Mr. & Mrs. James Ralston
3833 Mr. & Mrs. Jos. H. Patrick
3833 Mrs. Mary A. Patrick
4039 Rev. D. J. Riordan
4223 Thomas F. Delaney
4237 Mr. & Mrs. N. T. Jones
4313 Mr. & Mrs. D. O. Thompson
4501 Dr. & Mrs. W. Harrison Hipp
4511 William P. Minteer
4547 Mr. & Mrs. W. J. Strickland
4553 Mr. & Mrs. James McEnerney
   Receiving day Thursday
4807 Mr. & Mrs. J. J. McKenna
5007 Mr. & Mrs. C. R. Jaynes
5119 Mr. & Mrs. H. W. Smith
5145 Mrs. Eliza Gunther
5147 Mr. & Mrs. John Kennedy
5163 C. E. Pardridge
5303 Mr. & Mrs. T. J. Prendergast
5403 Mr. & Mrs. H. H. Seaverns
5405 Mr. & Mrs. Edward Milan
5407 Mr. & Mrs. Geo. A. Gindele
5853 Dr. & Mrs. M. A. Colman
5855 Mr. & Mrs. Edward S. Fogg
5911 Mr. & Mrs. B. W. Bradley

    ———

5822 Mr. & Mrs. J. L. Collins
5822 Mrs. H. L. Prentice
5856 Mr. & Mrs. F. J. Demling
5856 Mr. & Mrs. E. Claussenius
5900 Mr. & Mrs. John O'Neill
5924 Mr.& Mrs.C. H.Schlacks & dr.
   Receiving day Thursday

3738 Mr. & Mrs. David Moog
   Receiving day 1st Tuesday
3742 Mr. & Mrs. M. Klein & drs.
3744 Mr. & Mrs. Thos. Murphy
  & drs.
3744 Thomas J. Murphy
3744 Edward J. Murphy
3744 John P. Murphy
3746 Mr. & Mrs. John W. Geist
3748 Mrs. C. Ludden & drs.
3748 John H. Ludden
3752 Mr. & Mrs. Joseph Mayer
3752 Capt. & Mrs. John D. Shea
3800 Mrs. Louise de Wedig
3802 Dr. & Mrs. E. O. Christoph
3804 Mr. & Mrs. John MacDonald
   Receiving day Tuesday
3810 Mr. & Mrs. A. Junge
   Receive 1st Wednesday
3812 Mr. & Mrs. H. R. Henry
3834 Mr. & Mrs. Julius Levi
3838 Mr. & Mrs. Joseph Bryne
3838 Myer M. Freeman
4136 Dr. & Mrs. A. L. Cory
   Receiving day Thursday
4136 V. P. Cory
4212 Mr. & Mrs. Jacob Spizer
4226 Mr. & Mrs. W. W. Gilmore&dr.
4232 Mr. & Mrs. Frank E. Patterson
4238 Mrs. J. F. Kelling
4240 Mr. & Mrs. Frank H. Bishop
4248 Mr. & Mrs. A. Vanderkloot
4412 Mr. & Mrs. David Weber
   Receiving day Thursday
4444 Mr. & Mrs. Robt Masterson
4448 Mr. & Mrs. S. G. McCausland
4550 R. J. Hercock
4562 Dr. & Mrs. H. I. Nance
4656 Mrs. A. M. Fogg
   Receiving day Thursday
4712 Dr. & Mrs. Arthur W. Slaught
5112 Mr. & Mrs. John Farren
5112 Dr. John A. Farren
5132 Mr. & Mrs. John MacMahon
5138 Mr. & Mrs. T. B. Skeeles
5138 Harry Skeeles
5140 L. Jackson
5160 Mr. & Mrs. Mathias Ross & dr.
5300 Mr. & Mrs. Wm. Feil
5646 Mr. & Mrs. C. Christensen
5746 Mrs. Marie Hickey & drs.
5746 J. J. Hickey
5754 Mr. & Mrs. John M. Hubbard jr·

WALLACE STREET.

6956 Mr. & Mrs. E. S. Metcalf   6956 Guido Metcalf

WASHINGTON AVENUE.

5011 Mr.& Mrs. Christian Eigenman	4842 Mr. & Mrs. Charles H. Foote
5011 Christian Eigenman jr.	4846 Mr. & Mrs. E. Williamson
5021 Mr. & Mrs. W. H. Benton & drs.	4858 Mr. & Mrs. Edgar G. Barratt
5021 W. H. Benton jr.	4860 Mr. & Mrs. Chas. B. Kelley
5037 Mr. & Mrs. O. A. Bogue	4862 Mr. & Mrs. B. J. Soper & dr.
5037 Miss Agnes Belden	4900 C. V. Marsh & dr.
5037 Miss Grace Belden	4904 Mr. & Mrs.George M.Benedict
5039 Mr. & Mrs. James Hayes & dr.	4904 Mr. & Mrs. H. J. Boyer
5041 Mr. &. Mrs. F. B. Davis	4904 Allen Boyer
5045 Dr. & Mrs. J. Oscar Campbell	4906 H. B. Bach
5045 Mr. & Mrs. F. H. Lord	4906 A. C. Bach
5121 Mr. & Mrs. R. M. Whipple&dr.	4906 Harry C. Waters
5121 John P. Whipple	4906 Thomas Ashley
5131 Mr. & Mrs. Thos. B. Brougham	4906 Walter J. Ambrose
5131 Seymour Edgerton	4908 Mr. & Mrs. J. M. Gwinn & dr.
5135 Judge & Mrs. M. F. Tuley	4908 Russell S. Gwinn
5139 Mr. & Mrs. A. W. Wheeler	4916 Mr. & Mrs. W. F. Gorrell
5211 Mr & Mrs. William C. Lawson	4916 W. C. Gorrell
5213 Mr. & Mrs. J. J. Holland	4916 Miss A. C. Elliott
5215 Mrs. E. Frederickson	4956 Karleton Hackett
5215 Mrs. Jane Bradley	5004 Mr. & Mrs. Howard G. Loomis
5215 W. J. Frederickson	*Receiving day Tuesday*
5227 Mr. & Mrs. G. W. Ayer	5006 Mr.& Mrs. Wm. O. Swett & dr.
5311 Mr. & Mrs. John P. Roberson	5006 Wm. O. Swett jr.
5311 Mr. & Mrs. John E. Parke	5026 Mr. & Mrs.Wilfred T.Caldwell
5311 Mr. & Mrs. Amory W.Sawyer	5026 George T. Caldwell
5311 Mrs. Harriet A. Phelps	5026 E. F. Caldwell
5315 E. E. Noyes	5030 Robert F. Goodman
5315 Mrs. Mary M. Noyes	5030 Charles Goodman
5315 Miss Clara M. Noyes	5030 Robert B. Goodman
5315 Mr. & Mrs. M. S. Bradley	5030 James Goodman
5317 Dr. & Mrs. Ernest W. Keith	5034 Dr. & Mrs. Irwin Simpson
5319 Mr. & Mrs. James H. Moore	5036 Mr. & Mrs. J. V. Allen & dr.
5319 Fred W. Moore	5038 Mr. & Mrs. Chas. M. Pepper
5321 Mr. & Mrs. Jas. R. Hethering-ton	5038 Mrs. E. Rose
	5040 Mr. & Mrs. James Hewitt
5325 Mr. & Mrs. W. H. Dodge	5040 Mr. & Mrs. Henry W. Price
5325 W. R. Dodge	5126 Mr. & Mrs. William R. Kerr
5409 Mr. & Mrs. Martin J. Russell	5128 Mr. & Mrs. S. G. Wilkins
5413 Mr. & Mrs. Eben Byron Smith	5132 Mr. & Mrs. Will H.Moore & dr.
5417 Ralph W. King	5132 I. Preston Rice
5417 Mrs. Anna King	5142 Dr. & Mrs. Henry C. Allen
5417 Sam B. King	5142 Frank L. Allen
5423 Dr. & Mrs. G. W. Whitfield	5142 Helen Marian Allen
Receiving day Thursday	5142 Edward L. Goold
5423 Albert Whitfield	5200 Mr. & Mrs. A. V. Hartwell
5425 Mr. & Mrs. R. A. Emmons	5200 Mr. & Mrs. A. B. Emery
5425 Dr. C. A. Emmons	5210 Mr. & Mrs. F. B. Perry
5435 Mr. & Mrs.W.Harrison French	5216 Mr. & Mrs. Geo. B. Stoddard
5451 Mr. & Mrs. W. Bodemann	5220 Mr. & Mrs. A. V. Powell
5463 Mr.& Mrs.R. K. Hitchens & dr.	5224 Mr. & Mrs. James F. Brown
5465 Mr. & Mrs. David J. Lindsay	5226 Dr. & Mrs. T. Frank Keys
5465 Miss Louisa Milner	5314 Dr. P. E. Minckler
5517 Mr. & Mrs. Chas. A. Wear & dr.	5324 Mr. & Mrs. R. H. Kerr

5517 Mrs. Maria P. Hunter
5517 Fritz O. Andrear
5531 Mr. & Mrs. Dixon Bean & dr.
5533 Mr. & Mrs. F. D. Brown & dr.
5533 L. E. Brown
5533 Berlyn B. Brown
5533 F. Junior Brown
5545 Mr. & Mrs. Herman J. Hall
5545 Mrs. S. W. Wade
5547 Mr. & Mrs. M. R. Doty & dr.
5547 C. Edwin Doty
5601 Mr. & Mrs. Frank Harlow
5611 Mr. & Mrs. G. E. Highley
5611 Mr. & Mrs. C. B. Hauk
5611 Charles D. Hauk
5617 Mr. & Mrs. F. W. Porter
5621 Mr. & Mrs. Wm. Zimmerman
5623 Dr. & Mrs. F. E. Cheeseman
5625 Mr. & Mrs. Edward Donker
5625 Mr. & Mrs. W. W. Walls
5639 Mrs. Ella M. Burns
        Receiving day Wednesday
5639 Charles A. Marsh
5639 J. Gorton Marsh
5639 Fred A. Marsh
5649 Mr. & Mrs. M. F. Gallagher
5657 Mr. & Mrs. Wm. R. Harper
        Receiving day Thursday
5661 Mrs. E. F. Cannon & drs.
5661 Carleton White
5663 Dr. Kate I. Graves
5663 Arthur Graves
5725 Mr. & Mrs. Fred. K. Root
5729 Mr. & Mrs. L. W. Messer
5729 Miss Frances Garcelon
5731 Mr. & Mrs. Albion W. Small
        Receiving day Thursday
5731 Miss F. Von Masow
5735 Mr. & Mrs. Charles W. French
5735 George Carter Howland
5739 Mr. & Mrs. Chas. L. Jenks
5761 Mr. & Mrs. Thomas H. Murray
5809 Mrs. M. M. Woods
5809 Mr. & Mrs. Frank B. Lines
5813 Mr. & Mrs. Joseph G. Simpson
5813 Mrs. J. H. Eoff
5827 Mr. & Mrs. Fred Bode
5831 Mr. & Mrs. Wm. E. Webbe & dr.
5837 Mr. & Mrs. Frank Riedle & dr.
5859 Mr. & Mrs. Otis Jones
5859 Mr. & Mrs. John Edwards & dr.
6101 Mr. & Mrs. W. L. Hazen
6117 Dr. & Mrs. Curtis T. Fenn
6125 Mr. & Mrs. J. C. Behrer

5722 Mr. & Mrs. H. F. Pennington

5324 Mrs. M. Gibson
5326 Judge & Mrs. C. M. Hawley
5332 Dr. & Mrs. W. S. Johnson & dr.
5332 Miss Hattie Mason
5338 Mr. & Mrs. Arthur H. Rugg
5338 Mr. & Mrs. John C. Long
5338 Mrs. I. H. Parish & dr.
5338 James A. Farovid
5338 Mr. & Mrs. W. R. Scribner
5338 Mr. & Mrs. James W. Phillips
5338 Mrs. M. A. Bowman & dr.
5338 Mr. & Mrs. Harry L. Ashton
5338 Mr. & Mrs. Harmon Hurlbut
5338 Mr. & Mrs. J. A. Jackman jr.
5338 Mr. & Mrs. E. S. Skinner
5344 Mr. & Mrs. Jesse P. Lyman
5400 Mrs. James M. Gilchrist
5400 John F. Gilchrist
5408 Mr. & Mrs. Abner T. Hinckley
5408 Abner T. Hinckley jr.
5408 Mrs. Sarah Ritchie
5410 Mr. & Mrs. Charles H. Arms
5412 Mr. & Mrs. O. L. Munger
5418 Mr. & Mrs A. W. Hayward
5420 Mr. & Mrs. Chas. F. Forster
5420 Miss Elizabeth Reid
5424 Mr. & Mrs. J. P. B. Brown
5426 Mr. & Mrs. W. L. Bosworth
5426 Mr. & Mrs. F. F. Bosworth
5430 Mr. & Mrs. John A. Murphy
5454 Mr. & Mrs. Charles A. Wilson
5460 Mr. & Mrs. Charles Brewer & dr.
5460 Mrs. Julia Shaul
5464 Mr. & Mrs. D. A. Peirce
5486 Mr. & Mrs. J. B. Whitney
5520 Mrs. Granville S. Ingraham
5520 Mrs. W. H. Reynolds
5520 Mrs. Ella R. Wager
5534 Mr. & Mrs. James P. Root & dr.
5534 Clarence J. Root
5534 J. H. Baldwin
5550 Mr. & Mrs. Robert W. Parker
5550 Mrs. Amelia S. Parsons
5610 Mr. & Mrs. L. C. Kuhnert
5616 Mr. & Mrs. John S. Ford
5616 William A. Simpson
5620 Mr. & Mrs. H. M. Norton
5620 Mrs. T. C. Fanning
5642 Mr. & Mrs. E. O. Lanphere
5656 M. E. Sanford
5656 Mrs. E. H. Griffith
5714 Mr. & Mrs. A. B. Lapham & drs.
        Receiving day Tuesday
5714 A. B. Lapham jr.
5716 Mr. & Mrs. Eugene A. Hatch
5720 Mr. & Mrs. D. W. Chapman

5722 Mr. & Mrs. H.F.Pennington jr.
5722 F. A. Pennington
5724 Mr. & Mrs. Wm. L. Pierce
5726 Mrs. John I. Bennett
5726 George R. Bennett
5726 John I. Bennett jr.
5726 William Bennett
5732 Mr. & Mrs. Edward Rubovits
5732 Frank E. Rubovits
5738 Mr. & Mrs. Henry H. Belfield
5738 Mr. & Mrs. Harry M. Bates
5744 Mr. & Mrs. A. A. Adams
5748 Mr. & Mrs. P. F. Cameron
5752 Mr. & Mrs. H. N. Field
5752 Mr. & Mrs. W. T. Field
5754 Mr. & Mrs. R. E. Barrett
5806 Mrs. L. P. Cross & dr.

5806 David C. Templeton
5810 Mrs. M. A. Goodman
5810 Mr. & Mrs. A. L. Bell
5816 Dr. & Mrs. Harrison Withrow
5822 Mr. & Mrs. R. A. Shailer
5826 Mr. & Mrs. E. D. Sniffin
5830 Dr. W. S. Foote
5830 Dr. & Mrs. W. M. Stearns
5830 G. W. Stearns
5830 Clyde D. Lee
5832 Mr. & Mrs. E. D. Weary.
6018 Mr. & Mrs. W. W. Ingram
6018 Lawrence T. Ingram
6108 Mr. & Mrs. C. J. McGary
6016 Mr. & Mrs. Oscar S. Bass
6026 Mr.& Mrs. Chas. V. Barrington
6108 J. W. Meeker

WEBSTER AVENUE (ENGLEWOOD).

6949 Mr. & Mrs. J. M. Towers
6955 Mr. & Mrs. James Pittaway&dr.
7039 Mr. & Mrs. E. Hicks & dr.
7043 Mr. & Mrs. E. U. Smith
7047 Dr. & Mrs. J. S. Beaudry
7051 Mr. & Mrs. Thomas D. Snyder
7051 Miss Alice Snyder
7105 Mr. & Mrs. Thomas J. Eulette
7105 Mrs. E. Heath
7131 Mr. & Mrs. D. R. Patterson
7141 Mr. & Mrs. Fred A. Jones
7141 Mrs. Maggie W. Hyde
      Receiving day Thursday
7153 Mr. & Mrs. W. Forman Collins
      Receiving day Thursday
7157 Mrs. T.Baker
7157 F. R. Baker
7201 Mr. & Mrs. Walter D. Hodson
7201 Mr. & Mrs. Clark T. Northrop
      Receiving day Friday
7201 Mrs. M. A. Ballou

6952 Mrs. Annie E. Plimley
6952 Thomas Yates
6956 Mr. & Mrs. C. Morgan
7010 Mr. & Mrs. Charles R. Fuller
7100 Mr. & Mrs. Robert Rae jr.
7100 Miss L. Wolff
7110 Mr. & Mrs. G. G. Spencer & dr.
7116 Mr. & Mrs. Charles R. Harsh-
      berger
7214 Mr. & Mrs. Wm. E. Davis
7226 Mr. & Mrs. James G. Campbell
7240 Mr. & Mrs. F. E. Turner
7240 Mrs. J. M. Connell
7330 Mr. & Mrs. J. A. Wentz
7404 Mr. & Mrs. W. W. Hayne
7408 Mr. & Mrs. Alex Murison
7412 Mr. & Mrs. R. H. Herring

7207 Mr. & Mrs. J. E. G. Scott
7207 Mrs. Barclay Felch
7211 Mr. & Mrs. R. Ransom

WELLINGTON PLACE.

1 Mr. & Mrs. W W. Jackson
7 A. C. McClaughery
9 Mr. & Mrs. Jerome D. Steere

4 Mr. & Mrs. James A. Warren
8 Mr. & Mrs. G. E. Watson

WENTWORTH AVENUE.

6059 Mr. & Mrs. Wm. Graver & dr.
6059 James S. Graver
6059 William F. Graver
6059 Philip S. Graver
6323 Mr. & Mrs. J. J. Horning
6331 Mr. & Mrs. George Muirhead
6545 Mr. & Mrs. Alvin L. Ringo
6557 Dr. & Mrs. Geo. T. Greenleaf

5552 Mr. & Mrs. E. W. Adkinson
5814 Mr. & Mrs. F. A. Wheeler
6058 Dr. & Mrs. C. H. Lovewell
6058 C. H. Lovewell jr.
6320 Dr. & Mrs. G. J. Wilder
6400 Mr. & Mrs. G. P. Bay & dr.
6636 Mr. & Mrs. B. E. Hoppin
6648 Dr. & Mrs. M. M. Leahy

6615 Mr. & Mrs. Robert Craig
6629 Mr. & Mrs. Geo. L. Thompson
6635 Mr. & Mrs. J. C. Church
6707 Mr. & Mrs. H. F. Rohde
6719 Mr. & Mrs. W. C. Brown
6719 E. L. Brown
6719 A. S. Brown
6727 Mr. & Mrs. Edward S. Jones
6743 Col. & Mrs. J. S. Crane
6749 Mr. & Mrs. H. C. Dickinson
6757 Mr. & Mrs. A. R. Swift
6757 H. C. Swift
6817 Dr. & Mrs. M. W. Bacon & dr.
6843 Mr. & Mrs. J. P. Seymour
6843 J. A. Seymour
6901 Mr. & Mrs. Chas. Tinley & dr.
6927 Mr. & Mrs. W. A. Patterson
7001 Mrs. Mary Forbes & drs.

6706 Mr. & Mrs. J. Hodgkins
6716 Mr. & Mrs. E. Kirk jr.
6732 Mr. & Mrs. D. W. Storrs
6750 Mr. & Mrs. Geo. C. Langford
6750 Ed. G. Langford
6840 J. H. Earl
6846 Mr. & Mrs. E. H. Norton
6936 Mr. & Mrs. Edward Addy
6948 Mr. & Mrs. George P. Bent
7116 Mr. & Mrs. Emil Danne
7226 Mr. & Mrs. Thos. H. Fitzgerald
7236 Mr. & Mrs. Hart J. Fitzgerald

7117 Mrs. Fred W. Porter
7121 Mr. & Mrs. A. W. Stuart
7127 Mrs. M. W. Farmer & drs.
7127 Charles H. True
7147 Mr. & Mrs. A. A. Abbott

WHARTON AVENUE.

6337 Mr. & Mrs. Edward Jones
6455 Mr. & Mrs. C. D. Mosher
6517 Mr. & Mrs. Frederick French

6150 Mr. & Mrs. Theodore M. Hammond
6504 Mr. & Mrs. Taylor E. Brown
6518 Mrs. Joanna Trainor & dr.
6522 Mr. & Mrs. Henry Lesch

WINNECONNA AVENUE.

7805 Mr. & Mrs. James H. Gaffrey
 Receiving day Thursday
7811 Dr. E. M. Harrison
7817 Mr. & Mrs. J. W. Ross
7829 Mr. & Mrs. H. D. Booge

7831 Mr. & Mrs. Frank H. Mealiff
7855 Mr. & Mrs. Duncan Macmillan
 & dr.
7855 Lincoln Macmillan

WOODLAND PARK.

5 Dr. & Mrs. J. F. Campbell
5 A Mr. & Mrs. Harry E. Bradt
13 M. E. Cook
13 John F. Corbly
25 Dr. & Mrs. Z. E. Patrick & drs.
29 Mr. & Mrs. James A. Moffett
35 Mr. & Mrs. Gaius S. Merwin
39 M. A. O. Packard
47 Mr. & Mrs. A. Baldwin & dr.

60 Mr. & Mrs. Ambrose L. Thomas
60 Mr. & Mrs. Abner Crossman
 Receiving day Wednesday
60 Mr. & Mrs. Frank H. Thomas
 Receiving day Wednesday
62 Mr. & Mrs. Henry B. Wall
 Receiving day Friday

14 Mr. & Mrs. William H. Flagg
14 Mr. & Mrs. Elmer T. Flagg
14 Mrs. Sarah M. Tyler
28 T. C. Fetrow
28 Mr. & Mrs. John S. Huey
30 Mr. & Mrs. John T. Roberts
32 Dr. & Mrs. Louis E. Ireland
36 Mr. & Mrs. James G. Wright & dr.
36 J. Joseph Wright
42 Mr. & Mrs. Noble Hill Howe
 Receiving day Thursday
44 Mr. & Mrs. Albert S. Tyler
44 Mr. & Mrs. Frank A. Merriam &
 dr.
44 James T. Edwards
56 Mr. & Mrs. G. Herbert Jones

WOODLAWN AVENUE.

4513 Mr. & Mrs. Anson H. Law-
      rence
4515 Mr. & Mrs. Robert Thin
4517 Mr. & Mrs. E. C. Hatheway
4519 Mr. & Mrs. J. H. Hinckley
4523 Warren C. Anderson
4551 Mr. & Mrs. W. M. Wilson
4559 Mr. & Mrs. Elmer Washburn
      & drs.
            Receiving day Friday
4609 Mr.& Mrs.R.R.Donnelley & dr.
4609 Mr. & Mrs. Reuben H. Don-
      nelly
4609 T. E. Donnelley
4609 B. S. Donnelley
4613 Mr. & Mrs. Harlan W. Cooley
4613 Mrs. S. Sibley
4613 Sylvester Chase Sibley
4613 Dr. & Mrs. John S. Marsh&dr.
4615 Mr. & Mrs. Walter C. Hough
4619 Mr. & Mrs. Orville M. Truman
4619 Mr. & Mrs. W. G. Bruen
4621 Mr.& Mrs. Wallace L. DeWolf
            Receiving day Thursday
4621 Mr. & Mrs. H. B. Cook
4629 Mr. & Mrs. P. W. Snowhook
            Receiving day Wednesday
4629 Wm. B. Snowhook
4705 Mr. & Mrs. Wm. W. Michener
4709 Mr. & Mrs. Lyman A. Wiley
4723 Mr. & Mrs. A. E. Bingham
4723 Mrs. George W. Whitney
4729 Mr. & Mrs. H. M. S. Mont-
      gomery
4733 Mr. & Mrs. E. N. Wiley
4733 S. M. Moore
4737 Mr. & Mrs. Marvin A. Farr
4747 Mr. & Mrs. John W. Cloud
5127 Mr. & Mrs. Jacob Mansar
5515 Mr. & Mrs. Eugene Bergeron
5515 Dr. & Mrs. Clifford Mitchell
            Receiving day Thursday
5515 Mr. & Mrs. Chester C. Broomell
5515 Mr.& Mrs.Frederick Johnstone
5515 Prof. & Mrs. F. I. Carpenter
5545 Mr. & Mrs. Hugo O. von Hof-
      sten   *Receiving day Friday*
5555 Rev. & Mrs. Henry Willard
      & drs.
5555 Dr. Rose Willard
5555 Norman P. Willard
6111 William C. Malley
6115 Mr. & Mrs. T. C. Havens
6205 Mr. & Mrs. Howard K. Brooks

4444 Dr. & Mrs. Robert Challoner
            Receiving day Wednesday
4446 James D. Hurd
4446 Mrs. Chas. E. Hayward
4454 Mr. & Mrs. F. E. Walker & dr.
4454 F. A. Walker
4454 E. L. Walker
4520 Albert L. Deane
4520 Miss Lillie A. Deane
4520 Miss Margaret Deane
4526 Mr. &·Mrs. Albert M. Graves
            Receiving day Tuesday
4532 Mr. & Mrs. Jesse Tipman
4532 Mr. & Mrs. George B. Tipman
4534 Mr. & Mrs. James H. Keeler
4536 Mr. & Mrs. Wm.W. Bridgeman
4552 Mr. & Mrs. L. D. Condee & dr.
4552 Mrs. H. J. Johnson
4614 Mr. & Mrs. M. L. Wheeler
            Receiving day Tuesday
4614 Miss Lotta Wheeler
4614 Charles F. White
4620 Mr. & Mrs. W. A. Thrall
4620 Mr. & Mrs. S. E. Thrall
4620 Mrs. Maria Boyce
4626 Mr. & Mrs. F. G. Kammerer
4722 Mr. & Mrs. J. S. Belden
4722 Miss A. W. Pool
4726 Mr. & Mrs. E. E. Crepin
4726 Mrs. Delia Pierce
4738 J. B. Knight
4738 Mr. & Mrs. Fred H. Andrus
4738 Philip L. Marshall
4744 Mr. & Mrs. E. A. Sherburne
4744 Mrs. C. W. Dunkley
4750 Mr. & Mrs. John Marder & dr.
4750 John W. Marder
4750 Clarence Marder
4812 Mr. & Mrs. C. B. Bouton & dr.
4812 Sherman H. Bouton
4820 Mr. & Mrs. H. M. Dupee
4820 Leroy C. Dupee
4850 Mr. & Mr. John Davis
4850 Mr. & Mrs. John S. Hibbard
4912 Mr. & Mrs. J. W. Brooks jr.
4924 Mr. & Mrs. A. G. Spalding
            Receiving day Thursday
4924 Keith Spalding
4948 Mrs. Van H. Higgins
4948 Mrs. W. E. Pinney
5012 Mr. & Mrs. John J. Mitchell
            Receiving day Tuesday
5020 Mr. & Mrs. Edward A. Kimball
            Receiving day Monday

6211 Mr. & Mrs. George Wagner
6217 Mrs. Isidore G. Smith
6217 Sewell Smith
6221 Mr. & Mrs. G. S. Hardenbrook
6223 Mr. & Mrs. E. G. Hardenbrook
6307 Dr. W. D. Herriman
6315 Mr. & Mrs. H. D. Bowling
6325 Mr. & Mrs. E. A. Erickson
6327 Dr. & Mrs. G. V. Hilton
6327 H. H. Hilton
6329 Timothy G. Hallinan
6335 Mr. & Mrs. John T. Sweetland
6337 Mr. & Mrs. Russell C. Rose
6337 Mr. & Mrs. Rudolph E. Schultz
6427 Mr. & Mrs. Joseph W. Hill
6453 Rev. & Mrs. Arthur L. Will-
    iams   *Receive Monday eve.*
6627 Mr. & Mrs. Henry E. Scholle
6641 Mr. & Mrs. R. F. Green

6200 Mr. & Mrs. E. J. Wilber
6212 Mr. & Mrs. J. H. Lobdell
6230 Mr. & Mrs. Frank E. Brown &
    dr.
6246 Mr. & Mrs. J. J. Patchen
6320 Dr. & Mrs. F. A. Barber
6324 Mr. & Mrs. T. A. Evoy & dr.
6430 Mr. & Mrs. W. Y. Barnett
6430 Miss H. Huff

5020 Mrs. Elvira Kimball
5034 Mr. & Mrs. T. M. Bigelow &dr.
5046 Mr. & Mrs. L. F. Swift
    Receiving day Tuesday
5046 Miss Mary Avis Scott
5114 W. R. Donnelly
5116 Mr. & Mrs. George F.Hughson
    Receiving day Thursday
5134 Mr. & Mrs. M. Hamburger
.   *Receiving day Friday*
5140 Mr. & Mrs. George D. Cook &
    dr. *Receiving day Tuesday*
5222 Mr. & Mrs. Geo. W. Hunt
5222 Mr. & Mrs. F. H. Madden
5234 Mr. & Mrs. H. T. Gilbert
5234 Mrs. M. B. Leland
5238 Mr. & Mrs. Chas. G. French
5300 Mr. & Mrs. L. B. Shattuck
5300 George B. Shattuck
5516 Prof. Paul Shorey
5520 Mr. & Mrs. D. L. Shorey & dr.
5554 Mr. & Mrs. Theo. F. Rice
5554 Miss Elizabeth Price
5760 Judge & Mrs. Henry V. Free-
    man
6104 Mr. & Mrs. A. D. Ensign & dr.
    Receiving day Thursday
6104 Harry A. Ensign
6106 Mr. & Mrs. C. F. A. Spencer
6146 Mr. & Mrs. C. G. Bogart

WOODLAWN TERRACE.

220 Mr. & Mrs. Theophile Maher
    & drs.
220 Walter S. Maher
230 Mr. & Mrs. Lyman A. White

230 Frank White
304 Mr. & Mrs. E. T. Martin
312 Mr. & Mrs. Albert J. Maher

WRIGHT STREET.

6337 Mr. & Mrs. Jacob Rodatz
6341 Mr. & Mrs. John B. McGinty
6343 Mr. & Mrs. J. W. Hunter
6361 Mr. & Mrs. J. F. Mick & drs.
6361 Mrs. J. C. McLachlan
6401 Mr. & Mrs. James G. Elsdon
6419 Mrs. A. A. Barker
6423 Mr. & Mrs. W. A. Heusner
6429 Mr. & Mrs. H. E. Vale
6449 Mr. & Mrs. C. H. Reese
6453 Mr. & Mrs. W. G. Boulton
6639 Mr. & Mrs. M. A. Thompson
6641 Mr. & Mrs. F. F. Ryther
6713 Mrs. M. A. Rowe
7051 Mr. & Mrs. W. A. Adams
7051 W. H. Adams

5718 Mr. & Mrs. Harry E. Fox
5918 Mr. & Mrs. W. H. Dudgeon
6208 Dr. & Mrs. H. W. Burnard
6334 Mr. & Mrs. C. M. Reynolds
6340 Mrs. Geo. W. Foss
6410 Rev. & Mrs. F. A. Hardin
6420 Mr. & Mrs. H. Chittick & drs.
6420 John H. Chittick
6440 Mr. & Mrs. D. E. Terrierre
6446 Mr. & Mrs. S. B. Herron
6618 Mr. & Mrs. Frank E. Mick
6624 Mr. & Mrs. T. W. Sharon
6636 Rev. & Mrs. W. H. Robinson
6638 Mr. & Mrs. Gates A. Ryther
    Receiving day Tuesday
6722 Mr. & Mrs. W. C. Shaw & dr.

7305 Mr. & Mrs. R. J. Watt
7343 Mr. & Mrs. Joseph Kurtz
7343 Miss Gertrude Myers
7355 Mr. & Mrs. A. L. Jones
7413 Mr. & Mrs. Charles Smith .
7601 Mr. & Mrs. C. R. Hough & dr.
7629 Mr. & Mrs. Irving Hall
7657 Rev. & Mrs. H. T. Sell
7659 Mr. & Mrs. G. Huston
7715 Mr. & Mrs. D. W. Andrews
7715 Ellis C. Andrews
7719 Mr. & Mrs. P. J. Boyle
7731 Mr. & Mrs. James Ingram
7735 Mr. & Mrs. J. Watts & dr.
7747 Mr. & Mrs. E. B. Boyd
7751 Mr. & Mrs. C. C. Letts
7761 Mr. & Mrs. G. G. Ogden
7753 Dr. & Mrs. D. G. Allinder
7847 Dr. & Mrs. H. H. Mather
7849 Dr. & Mrs. Wm. B. Porter
———
7738 George Weber
7804 Dr. & Mrs. B. H. Birney.
7738 Mr. & Mrs. Henry Weber

6738 Mrs. Frances A. Smith
6738 Mrs. E. K. Currier
6756 Mr. & Mrs. E. F. Stevens
6808 Mr. & Mrs. L. D. Bristol
6818 Mr. & Mrs. W. P. Keeler
6918 Mr. & Mrs. George B. Inger-
    soll
6920 Mr. & Mrs. William Lichten-
    walter
7020 Dr. & Mrs. Charles D. Camp
7030 Mr.& Mrs.James B.McCracken
7410 Mr. & Mrs. James C. Lynch
7508 Mr. & Mrs. W. A. Hawkins
7528 Mrs. C. E. Brigham
7528 Mrs. M. M. Straight
7536 Mrs. Mary Forsythe & dr.
7614 Mr. & Mrs. J. Edward Triller
7614 Mrs. A. T. Newcomb
7614 H. D. Newcomb
7620 Mr. & Mrs. H. S. Folger
7620 Mrs. Alice Stewart
7624 Mr. & Mrs. J. P. Haynes
7626 Mr. & Mrs. C. L. Cline
7732 Mr. & Mrs. Wm. H. Weber

YALE STREET.

6315 Dr. & Mrs. J. M. Foster
6319 Mr. & Mrs. James H. Brayton
6323 Mr. & Mrs. Robert Weir
6333 Dr. Franklin Chavett
6339 Mr. & Mrs. J. M. Warner
6343 Mr. & Mrs. Frank L. Robinson
6351 Mr. & Mrs. Frederick F. Judd
6353 Mr. & Mrs. F. H. McAdow
    Receiving day Thursday
6357 Mr. & Mrs. C. W. Benedict
6357 Mrs. E. C. Baldwin
6357 Joseph C. Baldwin
6405 Mr. & Mrs. L. H. Fluke
6429 Mr. & Mrs. Joseph Badenoch
6429 Joseph Badenoch jr.
6429 Roland N. Badenoch
6439 Andrew Drysdale
6439 Mr. & Mrs. T. B. Wisdom
6505 Mr. & Mrs. Charles H. Smith
6515 Mr. & Mrs. George B. Watson
6519 Mr. & Mrs. F. E. Baker
6519 Mr. & Mrs. Geo. A. McClellan
    Receiving day Thursday
6519 Mr. & Mrs. W.W. McCullough
6521 Mr. & Mrs. Charles Dunlap
6521 Mrs. John F. Hall
6521 John A. Hall
6521 Mrs. Emma F. Beardsley
6525 Mr. & Mrs. Geo. E. Smith

6320 Mrs. L. S. Bushnell & dr.
6324 Mr. & Mrs. F. W. Jones
6324 Harry P. Jones
6334 Mr. & Mrs. John Whitley & dr.
6334 William G. Holbrook
6342 Dr. & Mrs. C. D. Fairbanks
6350 Mr. & Mrs. George F. Davie
6418 Mr. & Mrs. Charles F. Berg
6422 Mr. & Mrs. B. B. Redfield
6436 H. E. Tinsman
6442 Mr. & Mrs. R. E. Barrett
6446 Mr. & Mrs. H. C. Staver
6446 Charles S. Clark
6500 Mr. & Mrs. E. W. Sproul
6500 Mr. & Mrs. Isaac Drake
6510 Mr. & Mrs. John Moore
6514 Mr. & Mrs. Charles W. Jones
6524 Mr. & Mrs. A. H. Reeves
6534 Mr. & Mrs. John W. Munday
6540 Mr. & Mrs. William J. Smith
6558 Mr. & Mrs. C. J. Roberts
6560 Mr. & Mrs. Joseph Uhrig
6564 Mr. & Mrs. Frank Nowak
6600 Mr. & Mrs. P. T. Barry
    Receiving day Wednesday
6600 Miss Kathryn Barry
6606 Mr. & Mrs. J.M. Johuson & dr.
6610 Mr. & Mrs. Geo. T. French
6616 Mr. & Mrs.CharlesA.Buell&dr.

6527 Mr. & Mrs. W. H. Whiteside
6531 Mr. & Mrs. Eugene E. Loomis
6539 Mr. & Mrs. J. E. Sanford
6545 Mr. & Mrs. E. C. Green
6549 Mr. & Mrs. N. C. Smith
6551 Mr. & Mrs. J. F. Edgington
6557 Mr. & Mrs. C. B. Pfahler
6557 Mr. & Mrs. D. M. Stevens
6565 Mrs. C. R. Rogers
6565 Mr. & Mrs. H. A. Morgan
"The Yale," ne. cor. 66th
    Mr. & Mrs. W. B. Cooper
    Burton W. Cooper
2 Prof. & Mrs. Robert Stronach
    Receiving day Thursday
7 Mr. & Mrs. Floyd T. Logan
21 Mr. & Mrs. H. B. Speed & drs.
21 Kellogg Speed
25 Mr. & Mrs. John P. Fowler
    Receiving day Tuesday
26 Mr. & Mrs. Jno. McDonald & dr.
31 Mr. & Mrs. J. S. Davis
32 Mr. & Mrs. J. L. Holbrook
42 Mr. & Mrs. S. T. Rowley
45 Mr. & Mrs. Geo. W. Martin
54 Mr. & Mrs. W. A. Carroll
56 Mrs. R. O. Sinclair
56 Miss Zaidee Mitchell
56 Mr. & Mrs. Geo. K. Maltby
57 Mr. & Mrs. Wm. F. Braun
62 Mrs. A. E. Hill
62 C. Edward Hill
63 Rev. & Mrs. Albert L. Smalley *Receiving day Friday*
65 Mr. & Mrs. John Cullen
6601 Mr. & Mrs. Chas. J. Fellows
6605 Mr. & Mrs. G. N. Henry
6611 Mr. & Mrs. James G. Everest & dr.
6611 D. J. Pratt
6617 Mr. & Mrs. W. O. Mumford
6621 Mr. & Mrs. J. C. Walters
6629 Mr. & Mrs. Franklin P. Simons
6633 Mr. & Mrs. Wm. Lichtner
6635 Mr. & Mrs. C. J. Moore
6645 Mr. & Mrs. C. B. Woodruff
6647 Mr. & Mrs. Charles A. Chase
6653 Mr. & Mrs. Albert B. Pine
6737 Dr. & Mrs. Ellis H. Sparling
6825 Mr. & Mrs. John D. Vail jr.
6847 Mrs. Eliza Patterson
6907 Mr. & Mrs. E. C. Leach
6907 Mr. & Mrs. Clarence L. Dakin
6911 Mr. & Mrs. W. H. Haskell
6915 Rev. & Mrs. William M. Haigh
6919 Mr. & Mrs. Chas. D. Snapp

6620 Mr. & Mrs. R. N. Woodworth & dr.
6626 A. Harshberger
6636 Mr. & Mrs. Oscar Crandall
6642 Mr. & Mrs. William K. Mitchell
6812 Mr. & Mrs. Frederick B. Baird
6826 Dr. & Mrs. H. O'Brien
6846 Mr. & Mrs. D. H. Hayes
6922 Mr. & Mrs. James Durham
6930 Mr. & Mrs. F. F. Dickinson
6934 Mr. & Mrs. Walter Metcalfe
6942 Mr. & Mrs. Walter H. Furlong
7024 Mr. & Mrs. Frank L. Porter
7026 Mr. & Mrs. W. S. Barbee
7040 Mr. & Mrs. E. N. Weart
7044 Mr. & Mrs. Jerome G. Abbott
7052 Mr. & Mrs. James A. Rankin
7100 Mr. & Mrs. R. E. Brownell
7106 Mrs. J. S. Kinkaid
7106 C. F. Kinkaid
7106 Rev. & Mrs. Frederick J. Walton
7110 Mr. & Mrs. F. B. Wyckoff
7116 Mr. & Mrs. E. W. Whitcomb & dr.
7120 Mr. & Mrs. Bayard E. Hand
7124 Mr. & Mrs. G. T. Robie
    Receiving day Wednesday
7128 Mr. & Mrs. E. C. Burr
7130 Mr. & Mrs. W. J. Allen
7140 Mr. & Mrs. J. M. Norris
7216 Mr. & Mrs. J. P. Mallette
7220 Mr. & Mrs. George H. Crosby
7226 Mr. & Mrs. C. D. Ellis
7236 Mr. & Mrs. C. L. Thomas
7236 Miss Edith Thomas
7330 Mr. & Mrs. George Young

—————

6939 Mr. & Mrs. E. U. Griffith
6945 Mrs. J. F. Johnson
6951 Mr. & Mrs. Frank L. Wean
6955 Mr. & Mrs. John Critchell & dr.
    Receiving day Thursday
6955 Miss Nellie M. Critchell
6955 J. H. Critchell
6957 Mr. & Mrs. A. G. Robinson
7001 Mr. & Mrs. T. Fenlon
    Receiving day Wednesday
7009 Mr. & Mrs. Joseph VanHorn
7015 Mr. & Mrs. H. H. Horr
7023 Mr. & Mrs. S. M. Dowst
7025 Mr. & Mrs. James M. Connell
7045 Dr. & Mrs. J. C. Nichols
7111 Mr. & Mrs. Charles A. S. McCracken
7117 Mr. & Mrs. James T. Brink

15

7127 Mrs. A. C. Smith
7127 Miss Anna Walbridge
7201 Mr. & Mrs. Charles E. Davis
    Receiving day Tuesday
7211 Mr. & Mrs. W. B. Mather
    Receiving day Friday
7231 Mr. & Mrs. G. F. Wadsworth

7241 O. A. Baker
7241 Mr. & Mrs. Edwin S. Lemoine
7301 Mr. & Mrs. J. B. Thompson
7305 Mr. & Mrs. H. C. Wilkinson
    Receiving day Friday
7311 Dr. & Mrs. A. M. Kinkaid
7315 Mr. & Mrs. W. Braggins

227

PART SECOND.

NORTH DIVISION.

THE BLUE BOOK.

ARRANGED ACCORDING TO STREETS AND NUMBERS,
NUMERICALLY, WITH OCCUPANTS' NAMES,
GIVING THE ODD NUMBERS IN
LEFT COLUMN, AND EVEN
IN THE RIGHT.

R. E. Rhode's Pharmacy

504 North Clark St., corner Goethe

Drugs and Chemicals of the highest grade and purity dispensed by competent Pharmacists. Select line of TOILET REQUISITES. Manufacturer of

RHODE'S KUMYSS

Eau de Quinine, a Hair Tonic; Cleopatra's Lotion, Etc.

GEO. L. ROOD

HEATING AND VENTILATING

ROYAL AND PRINCE
ROYAL FURNACES

TIN AND SHEET IRON JOB WORK
MANUFACTURER OF EVERYTHING IN SHEET METAL

FACTORY AND WAREHOUSE
111 AND 113 LAKE STREET

79 LAKE STREET, CHICAGO
TELEPHONE MAIN-4251.

NORTH DIVISION.

ADDISON STREET.

1408 Dr. & Mrs. E. A. Bergstrom
1710 Mr. & Mrs. Augustus Newman

1740 Mr. & Mrs. F. W. Holbrook & drs.
1740 William G. Holbrook

ALDINE AVENUE.

1521 Mr. & Mrs. Chas. H. Ripley
1535 Mr. & Mrs. C. M. Netterstrom & dr.
Receiving day Thursday
1535 Mr. & Mrs. John N. Lawson
1817 Mr. & Mrs. John F. Bacon
1817 Mr. & Mrs. Robert L. Davis
1817 Mr. & Mrs. J. J. Monaghan
1819 Mr. & Mrs. James L. Kellogg
1819 Mr. & Mrs. Sam'l H. Williams
1821 Mr. & Mrs. A. B. Towers
1823 Mr. & Mrs. Peter George
1823 Mr. & Mrs. J. F. Talbot

1508 Dr. & Mrs. L. W. Whitmer
1546 Mr. & Mrs. H. Behrens
1554 Mr. & Mrs. J. A. Modin & dr.
1650 Mr. & Mrs. Carl Schneider
1650 Mr. & Mrs. J. W. Dietz
1824 Mr. & Mrs. A. Lotz
1838 Mr. & Mrs. J. Wm. Helm
1838 Mrs. George H. Kettelle
1842 Mrs. Caroline Stenbeck
1850 Mr. & Mrs. Robert L. North
1850 Robert L. North jr.
1850 Miss Ada C. Sweet

ALEXANDER AVENUE.

1545 Mr. & Mrs. T. W. Alges
1551 Mr. & Mrs. David E. Platter
1583 Mr. & Mrs. George M. Eddy
Receiving day Monday
1613 Mr. & Mrs. George Bryant
1671 Mr & Mrs. Everett B. Deming
1687 Mr. & Mrs. Wm. Pottle
1693 Mr. & Mrs. J. E. Roberts
Receiving day Wednesday
1729 P. P. Pease
1729 P. P. Pease jr.
1729 Mrs. Clara E. Head
Receiving day Thursday
———
1728 Miss Harriette Lutz

1540 Mr. & Mrs. C. W. Dingman
1546 Mr. & Mrs. J. E. Rouse
1558 Mr.&Mrs. Chas. A. Rolfe & dr.
1574 Mr. & Mrs. B. J. Fitzgerald
1688 Mrs. I. D. M. Lobdell
1698 Mr. & Mrs. Chas. E. Lake
Receiving day Wednesday
1698 Fred Irving Lake
1698 Charles H. Lake
1706 Mr.& Mrs. George Warrington
Receiving day Wednesday
1718 Mr. & Mrs. Arthur J. Eddy
1728 Mr. & Mrs. Theodore W. Buhmann
Receiving day Thursday

ARLINGTON PLACE.

23 Mr. & Mrs. Wm. P. Powers
27 Mr. & Mrs. Gustav Hessert jr.

22 Mr. & Mrs. Hans J. Lystad

ARLINGTON STREET.

3227 Mr. & Mrs. George Hipplé
3227 Mr. & Mrs. George I. Hipple
3180 Mr. & Mrs. L. P. Shriver
3281 Mr. & Mrs. C. H. Beyer

ASHLAND AVENUE.

2271 Mr. & Mrs. Otto E. Pietsch
2301 Mrs. S. J. Dressler
2301 Mr. & Mrs. W. M. Dressler
2301 Miss M. E. McCormick
2543 Mr. & Mrs. John A. G. Roberts
2555 Mr. & Mrs. L. C. Kiefer
2565 Simon Simon & drs.
2565 Robert M. Simon
2565 George Simon
2565 Henry E. Simon
2569 Mr. & Mrs. August Ziesing
2569 Miss Helene Ziesing
2575 Mr. & Mrs. George W. Rogers
   & drs.
2579 Mrs. Laura V. Hendley &
   drs.
2595 Mr. & Mrs. T. Herbert Morgan
2607 Miss Georgie E. Shores
2607 Mr. & Mrs Squire Dingee
2607 Squire Dingee jr.
2607 Miss Minnie Dingee
2629 Mr. & Mrs. B. H. Rogers
2637 Mrs. Rosa Hirshfield
2645 Rev. & Mrs. Chas. H. Keays
   Receiving day Monday

2292 Mr. & Mrs. E. J. Ostling
2546 Mr. & Mrs. B. F. Weber
2566 Mr. & Mrs. Washington J.
   Irvin
2570 Mr. & Mrs. Wm. G. Stephens
2580 James W. Newell
2580 Mrs. Charles B. Newell
2580 James B. Newell
2580 William S. Newell
2596 Mrs. H. J. Sprague
   Receiving day Wednesday
2596 Mrs. C. J. Ferris   •
   Receiving day Wednesday
2596 Miss Georgia Ferris
2596 Mrs. Grace G. Houston
2600 Mr. & Mrs. Freeman A. Mann

2663 Mr. & Mrs. Charles W. Bassett
   Reeeiving day Wednesday
2667 Mr. & Mrs. Otto Igle
2667 Theodore F. Igle
2679 Col. & Mrs. Emery S. Bond
2687 Mr. & Mrs. H. W. Fischer
2691 Mr. & Mrs. George L. Lero w
2703 Mr. & Mrs. E. R. Glasscock

ASTOR STREET.

7 Mr. & Mrs. Horace F. Waite & dr.
9 Mr. & Mrs. L. W. Bodman & dr.
9 Mrs. A. A. Smith
11 Mr. & Mrs. H. J. Fitzgerald
13 Mrs. Theodore Neubarth & dr.
15 Mr. & Mrs. George E. Newlin
17 Mr. & Mrs. John H. Colvin
23 Dr. & Mrs. John H. Chew
23 Walter Meadowcroft
23 William Meadowcroft
25 Mr. & Mrs. Edward G. Pauling
27 Mr. & Mrs. Edward F. Cragin
47 Mr. & Mrs. Fred L. Foltz
47 Mr. & Mrs. S. Corning Judd
49 to 55 The Ormonde
   Mr. & Mrs. Chas. F. Mason
   Mr. & Mrs. M. W. Phalen
   William J. Phalen
   Frank J. Phalen
   Mr. & Mrs. Thos. A. Dillon

14 Mr. & Mrs. C. H. Summers&drs.
   Receiving day Friday
14 Mr. & Mrs. A. W. Towsley
14 Mr. & Mrs. H. L. Burgess
14 Leland L. Summers
14 Bertrand S. Summers
14 Mr. & Mrs. Edward Wright
20 Mr. & Mrs. Frank R. Fuller
   Receiving day Monday
20 Miss Mary V. Hayes
22 Mr. & Mrs. Emil Liebling
22 Miss Florence Jones
26 Mr. & Mrs. John G. Garibaldi
30 Mrs. Eliphalet Cramer & dr.
30 Frank Cramer
32 Mr. & Mrs. Thos. Taylor jr.
34 Mr. & Mrs. Charles A. Street
34 Harry L. Street
36 Mr. & Mrs. F. P. Schmitt & drs.
36 Charles S. Schmitt

Mr. & Mrs. Wm. O. Manson
Frank M. Manson
Mr. & Mrs. A. Obermann
Mr. & Mrs. Edw. M. Samuel
Mr. & Mrs. Chas. T. A. Mc-
  Cormick
Mr. & Mrs. Geo. W. Cobb
Mr. & Mrs. Harold O. Crane
Mrs. L. A. Frankelyn
85 Dr. & Mrs. E. J. Gardiner
85 Mrs. John F. Clements
87 Mr. & Mrs. William H. Warren
89 Mr. & Mrs. Chas. H. Hodges
99 Mr. & Mrs. James Charnley
99 John M. Douglas jr.
125 Mr. & Mrs. George Farnsworth
  & dr.
131 Rensselaer W. Cox
131 William A. Angell
131 Mrs. Electra R. Cox
131 Miss J. E. Cox
133 Mr. & Mrs. E. R. Hutchins
141 Otto W. Meysenburg
141 Carr Meysenburg
147 Mr. & Mrs. Horatio N. May

———

140 Mr. & Mrs. Geo. Frederic Westover
    Receiving day Tuesday
140 Mr. & Mrs. Harry S. Channon
    Receiving day Tuesday
142 Mr. & Mrs. Harry B. Owsley
148 Mr. & Mrs. C. Vallette Kasson
  & dr.
150 Mr. & Mrs. Chas M. Webber
154 Mr. & Mrs. Hempstead Washburne
    Receiving day Monday
154 Elihu B. Washburne
166 Mr. & Mrs. R. W. Patterson jr.

38 Mr. & Mrs. E. M. Ehrlich
44 Mr. & Mrs. Charles D. Dana &
  dr.
46 Mr. & Mrs. William J. Goudy
50 Mr. & Mrs. Lewis B. Mitchell &
  drs.
50 Clarence A. Burley
52 Mr. & Mrs. Ernest Langrishe
  Allen
    Receiving day Monday
54 Mr. & Mrs. H. B. Butler
56 Mr. & Mrs. Lindon W. Bates
    Recciviug day Monday
58 Miss Mary A Prescott
62 Mr. & Mrs. David B. Jones
62 Miss Annie Bayley
62 Thomas D. Jones
64 Rt. Rev. & Mrs. W. E. McLaren
  & dr.
64 W. A. McLaren
66 Mr. & Mrs. Frank S. Weigley
    Receiving day Monday
70 Mrs. Mary F. Maguire
70 Mrs. Grant Goodrich
72 Mr. & Mrs. Thomas R. Lyon
72 Mrs. Emily S. Rice
82 Mr. & Mrs. William H. Hubbard
84 Mr. & Mrs Conrad Furst
84 Mr. & Mrs. Leo Ernst
86 Mr. & Mrs. Charles F. Clarke
88 Mr. & Mrs. George S. Payson
96 Mr. & Mrs. G. W. Sheldon &
  dr.
106 Mr. & Mrs. Clyde de V. Hunt
    Receiving day Monday
110 Mr. & Mrs. Wm. E. Baker
    Reeeiving day Monday
112 Mr. & Mrs. E. J. Martyn
118 Mr. & Mrs. Thomas Woodnutt
  Hinde
136 Mr. & Mrs. J. T. Bowen
138 Mr. & Mrs. B. E. Sunny

BANKS STREET.

1 Mr. & Mrs. Edw. E. Ayer
27 Mr. & Mrs. J. L. Houghteling
    Receiving day Monday
31 Mr. & Mrs. E. L. Ryerson
    Receiving day Monday
37 Mr. & Mrs. E. A. Ferguson
41 Mr & Mrs. John Maynard Harlan

2 Franklin H. Head & drs.
    Receiving day Tuesday
32 Mr. & Mrs. Charles I. Sturgis
40 Mr. & Mrs. William Waller

———

43 Mr. & Mrs. Wm. A. Vincent

BARRY AVENUE.

1649 Mr. & Mrs. Henry Wichert
1649 Hugo Franz
1677 Mr. & Mrs. J. L. Rippey
1677 Mr. & Mrs. Walter Lockwood
1683 Mrs. Mary Thiesing & drs.
1683 Mr. & Mrs. W. T. Carpenter
1691 Joseph Dietzgen
1707 Conrad L. Elm
1707 Mrs. Minnie Anderson
1805 Mr. & Mrs. Henry V. Pierpont
1805 Mr. & Mrs. S. B. Brunaugh
1807 Mr. & Mrs. Fitz-William Sargent
1807 Mrs. C. B. Lawrence
1817 Mrs. Harry Fox & dr.
1817 Fred H. Fox
1821 Mr. & Mrs. Edward F. Comstock
1825 Mr. & Mrs. W. M. Knight
1831 Mr. & Mrs. Theodore Freeman
1843 Mr. & Mrs. John Stillwell & drs.
1849 Mr. & Mrs. Alex. M. Ross & dr.
1849 Arthur J. Ross
1851 Mr. & Mrs. Chas. Atherton Clarke
1851 Mr. & Mrs. Walter P. Whiting
1853 Mr. & Mrs. Gustav Riebe
1855 Mr. & Mrs. C. R. Schniglau & dr.
1905 Mr. & Mrs. John C. Durgin

1932 Mr. & Mrs. Albert Magnus
1942 Mr. & Mrs. E. A. Beauvais
1942 Joseph H. Bourassa
1950 Mr. & Mrs. Z. P. Brosseau

1630 Mr. & Mrs. H. F. Sawford
1632 Mr. & Mrs. McP. Chamberlin
1640 Mr. & Mrs. C. F. Weber & dr.
1642 Richard G. Schmid
1662 Rev. & Mrs. Carl A. Evald
1684 Mr. & Mrs. Daniel Johnson
1686 Mr. & Mrs. Wm. B. Hopkins
1686 Dr. & Mrs. Ira B. Crissman
1686 Mrs. A. Y. McDonald
1686 Miss Mary Messner
1690 Mr. & Mrs. Walter H. Smith
1690 Mr. & Mrs. James McDonald
1694 Mr. & Mrs. Eugene Dietzgen
1708 Mr. & Mrs. Chas. J. Stratton
1804 Mr. & Mrs. J. W. Kee & dr.
1812 Mr. & Mrs. John B. Meyer
1812 Christian B. Meyer
1828 Mr. & Mrs. Wm. L. Roseboom
1828 Miss Evelyn M. Roseboom
1834 Mr. & Mrs. Adolph Heile
1834 Louis Heile
1834 Chas. Dyer Heile
1848 Mr. & Mrs. Wm. H. Redington
1856 Mr. & Mrs. Frank Yott
1864 Mr. & Mrs. W. H. Ross-Lewin & dr.
1912 Mr. & Mrs. Daniel O. Hill
1918 Mr. & Mrs. Charles E. Hurd & dr.
        Receiving day Tuesday
1918 Charles A. Hurd
1918 Walter W. Hurd
1918 Miss Mae Morgan
1922 Mr. & Mrs. George Parker
1926 Mr. & Mrs. Wm. Campbell & dr.
1928 Mr. & Mrs. Frank A. Arend
1928 Mr. & Mrs. J. Spencer Butterfield

BEACON STREET.

3127 Mr. & Mrs. Edward Carqueville
3127 Edgar H. Carqueville
3127 Alex. Carqueville
3165 Mr. & Mrs. Frank J. Gallagher
3165 Frank H. Gallagher
3165 Miss Annie Gallagher
3203 Mr. & Mrs. Samuel Brown jr.
3203 Jamot Brown
3247 Mr. & Mrs. Theodore Krueger
3247 Mrs. Antoinette Rrueger
3247 Miss Johanna Rendtorff

3222 Mr. & Mrs. B. B. Jones
3232 Mr. & Mrs. Geo. Heicher

3267 Mr. & Mrs. Salvatore Tomaso
        Receiving days Monday and Thursday
3267 E. W. Petesch
3267 Miss Charlotte Petesch
3283 Mr. & Mrs. Herman Zitzewitz
3297 Mrs. Catherina Haustetter & dr.

BEETHOVEN PLACE.

47 August Blumenthal

54 Mr. & Mrs. Henry Buschmeyer
54 Mr. & Mrs. Otto Schrader

22 Mr. & Mrs. Julius Ehlers
24 Dr. & Mrs. Theodore Stretz
36 Mr. & Mrs. W. B. Clifford
46 Mr. & Mrs. G. Langhenry

BELDEN AVENUE.

207 Mrs. H. A. Kroeschell
209 Mr. & Mrs. C. Kroeschell
211 Mr.& Mrs.John Gertenrich & dr.
215 Mr. & Mrs. T. Pfister
217 Mr. & Mrs. W. N. Wilson
217 Mr. & Mrs. L. M. Blanton
217½ Mr. & Mrs. F. Clapp
217½ Mr. & Mrs. Chas. E. Jones
219 Mrs. Richard H. Watson
219 Mr. & Mrs. Henry W. Deuel
219 Mr. & Mrs. H. L. Meyer
221 Mr. & Mrs. P. B. Fitzgerald
223 Mr. & Mrs. J. G. Klais
225 Mr. & Mrs. Atwood H. Huff
227 Dr. & Mrs. G. M. Illingworth
249 Mr. & Mrs. F. W. Ganse
251 Mrs. H. D. Ganse & drs.
253 Mr. & Mrs. W. C. Seavey
255 Mr. & Mrs. F. A. Doolittle & dr.
255 Oliver S. Doolittle
259 Mr. & Mrs. J. M. Hardy
265 Mr. & Mrs. Theo. Gottmann
269 Mr. & Mrs. F. L. Grunewald
271 Mr. & Mrs. J. P. Boyle
273 Mr. & Mrs. J. B. Patterson
275 Mr. & Mrs. J. H. Johnson
295 and 297 The Belden Flats
    A Mr. & Mrs. James B. Carney
       Receiving day Friday
    A Mr. & Mrs.William A. Kreid-
      ler   *Receiving day Friday*
    B Mrs. M. E. S. Cooper
    B Mr. & Mrs. Wm. H. Mc-
      Glashon
    C Mr. & Mrs. Thomas E. Fry
    D Mr.& Mrs. T. M. Luce
    F Mr. & Mrs. Morris L. Greeley
301 Rev. & Mrs. L. J. Halsey
301 Edward A. Halsey
307 Dr. & Mrs. E. J. Mellish
309 Mr. & Mrs. Louis Schlesinger
311 Mrs. S. B. Newell
311 Frederick O. Swannell
317 Mr. & Mrs. J. H. Manny
317 Dr. Harvey H. Manny
317 J. Y. Bergen & dr.
321 Mr. & Mrs. Robt. T. Howard

224 Mr. & Mrs. J. W. McLean &
    drs.
232 Mr. & Mrs. Geo. W. Todd
232 L. M. Todd
236 Mr. & Mrs. F. W. Kinney
238 Mr. & Mrs. L. Wilson
270 Mr. & Mrs. H. I. Morris
272 Mr. & Mrs. Robt. Bluthardt
276 Mr. & Mrs. S. Velie
276 Miss Mae Varges
276 Charles Varges
278 Mr. & Mrs. B. Williams & dr.
      Receiving day Wednesday
278 Mrs. Clara E. Shilton
280 Mr. & Mrs. Andrew Weber
280 Miss Lizzie Pinter
284 Mr. & Mrs. Frank S. Hereth
284 Mr. & Mrs. Franc Gardner
286 Mrs. Cora K. Adams
286 Mrs. C. C. King
288 Mr. & Mrs. Alfred P. Bigelow
290 Mr. & Mrs. H. J. Thompson &
    drs.   *Receiving day Friday*
292 Mr. & Mrs. Onward Bates
294 Mr. & Mrs. G. F. Steele
294 Miss Clara S. Steele
296 Mr. & Mrs. W. Cochran & dr.
300 Mr. & Mrs. Morris P. Carroll
302 Mr. & Mrs. Alfred Noble
304 Mr. & Mrs. S. S. Warne & dr.
304 Mr. & Mrs. H. D. Warne
306 Mr.& Mrs. Charles C. Cox & drs.
308 Mrs. C. A. Voris
308 Floy T. Voris
308 Miss Jessie Carpenter
308 Miss Mary Squire
312 Mr. & Mrs. Delevan S. Foote
314 Mr. & Mrs. Charles F. Noyes
314 Mrs. Sarah B. Moore
316 Mr. & Mrs. Amos Pettibone
320 Rev.& Mrs.David R.Breed&drs.
      Receiving day Tuesday
344 Dr. & Mrs. J. W. Oswald
344 Mr. & Mrs. Dwight Brown
344 Mr. & Mrs. J. B. Alexander
346 Mr. & Mrs. Chas. Hartoch & drs.
346 Sigmund Hartoch

321 Mrs. Leonard Swett
323 Mr. & Mrs. I. J. Mason & drs.
323 Fred Mason
325 Dr. & Mrs. Cyrenies A. David
325 Miss Rilla A. David
399 Mrs. M. J. Boyington
399 Mr. & Mrs. J. T. Weber
401 Mr. & Mrs. Frank L. Thorpe
403 Mr. & Mrs. H. R. Weber
407 Mr. & Mrs. W. K. Mills & dr.
407 Mrs. E. M. Guinea & dr.
409 Mr. & Mrs. Geo. J. Reed
411 Mr. & Mrs. T. B. Cutts
413 Mr. & Mrs. C. H. Crantz
413 Mr. & Mrs. Samuel A. Gould
417 Mr. & Mrs. Peter Mattes
417 Mr. & Mrs. Wm. C. Hovey
435 Mr. & Mrs. Archibald L. Doherty
435 Mr. & Mrs. C. S. DeMorest
435 Dr. & Mrs. J. J. Temple
435 Mr. & Mrs. Geo. H. Spoor
435 Mr. & Mrs. C. W. Beggs
437 Mr. & Mrs. Robt. A. Forsyth
       jr.
437 Mr. & Mrs. F. H. Peak
437 Mr. & Mrs. Wm. Hock jr.
437 Mr. & Mrs. W. B. Dunton
437 Mr. & Mrs. John H. Johnson
439 Mr. & Mrs. Fred G. Wessling
439 Mr. & Mrs. John Gormley
443 Mr. & Mrs. F. E. Lockwood
445 Mr. & Mrs. Samuel D. Stoll
447 Mr. & Mrs. Edward Keir & dr.
       Receiving day Thursday
447 Miss Mary Melody
453 Mr. & Mrs. J. D. C. Whitney
475 Mr. & Mrs. W. C. Harrah
475 Mrs. H. Lilja
479 Mr. & Mrs. John R. Lilja & drs.
479 Mr. & Mrs. David W. Miller
481 Mr. & Mrs. Charles Catlin
481 Mrs. Henry Martin Hobart
483 Mr. & Mrs. Edward G. White
483 Beverly T. White
483 Mr. & Mrs. R. C. Campbell
485 Mr. & Mrs. Oscar Mueller
485 Mrs. J. I. Adler
       Receiving day Tuesday
485 Sidney Adler
487 Mr. & Mrs. W. N. Arend & dr.
487 Mr. & Mrs. Alphonse Fritsch
489 Mr. & Mrs. S. L. Robinson &
       dr.
493 Mrs. S. K. Trorlicht
       Receiving day Friday
493 Adolph Nickelsen

346 Mr. & Mrs. Moritz Krembs &
       drs.
348 Mr. & Mrs. G. G. Congdon & dr.
348 Mr. & Mrs. W. A. Arms
348 Mr. & Mrs. Emil Gerber
352 Mr. & Mrs. James Hart
352 Rev. & Mrs. H. D. Wiard
356 Mr. & Mrs. S. F. Fritze
356 Mrs. Heman Allen & drs.
360 Mr. & Mrs. Edward B. Martin
392 Mr. & Mrs. Frank H. Berry
392 Hugo Benedix
396 Dr. & Mrs. H. M. Goodsmith
396 Mr. & Mrs. William Goodsmith
398 Mr. & Mrs. George Foster
402 Mr. & Mrs. Henry E. Shattock
402 Mr. & Mrs. E. P. Warner
404 Mr. & Mrs. C. A. Morrill & dr.
406 Mrs. Charles Ohm
406 Mr. & Mrs. Curt Ohm
408 Mr. & Mrs. Louis S. Hays
408 Mr. & Mrs. L. Mattern
408 Mr. & Mrs. Otto A. Dreier
412 Mr. & Mrs. Otto Peltzer
       Receiving day Thursday
416 Mr. & Mrs. S. A. Jenks
418 Mr. & Mrs. Henry Turner
420 Mr. & Mrs. O. G. Wiley
420A Mr. & Mrs. Jonas Johnson &
       drs.
422 Mr. & Mrs. M. Kahn & drs.
422 Julius Kahn
422 Mr. & Mrs. Frederick A. Hoyer
424 Dr. & Mrs. F. A. Sieber
424 Mr. & Mrs. Frederick J. Patter-
       son
430 Mr. & Mrs. S. L. Anable
430 Courtland W. Anable
430 Mr. & Mrs. Albert Phalen
430⅙ Mr. & Mrs. Wilfred F. Boosey
430½ Mr. & Mrs Charles Falls
432 Mr. & Mrs. Frank N. James
434 Mrs. M. A. Farish
434 Mrs. J. H. Bethune
436 Mr. & Mrs. W. P. Stearns
440 Mr. & Mrs. John D. Schrock
440 Mr. & Mrs. Emil Hamilton
442 Mr. & Mrs. H. B. Prudden
442 Mr. & Mrs. Fletcher Randolph
442 Mr. & Mrs. A J. Hobon
444 Mr. & Mrs. Alex Krauss
444 Mr. & Mrs. Richard Clayton
444 T. W. Clayton
444 Mr. & Mrs. James C. Miller
446 Mr. & Mrs. C. E. Sayler
446 Mrs. Ida Gillman & dr.

507 Mr. & Mrs. H. M. Grandin
  Receiving day Friday
507 Mr. & Mrs. W. H. Pettengill
519 Mr. & Mrs. John Tellιng & dr.
519 John E. Telling
519 H. I. Telling
521 Mr. & Mrs. Elwood McGrew
521 Mr. & Mrs. W. Taylor
521 Miss Minnie Wigeland
523 Mr. & Mrs. E. F. Thompson
525 Mr. & Mrs. John A. Pettigrew
  & drs.
527 Mr. & Mrs.George M.Clute & dr.
527 George F. Clute
527 Paul B. Warner
527 James N. Fort
529 Mr. & Mrs. J. B. Carter
531 Mr. & Mrs. B. Bicknell Young
531 Mme. Mazzucato Young
531 Miss Late Young
533 Mr. & Mrs. Oscar Cobb
535 Mrs. Charles S. Carter
  Receiving day Thursday
537 Mr. & Mrs. T. A. Hagerty
537 Miss P. Himrod
  ————
508 Mr. & Mrs. Chas. W. Davenport
  Receiving day Monday
508 Mr. & Mrs. C. P. Porter
530 Mr. & Mrs. George E. Adams

446 William Gillman
446 Mrs. W. S. Hawthorne
446 Miss Purda Tuppler
446 Mrs. M. E. Deacon & drs.
446 Fred A. Deacon
446 C. B. Deacon
448 Mr. & Mrs. W. J. Henderson
448 C. F. Jones
448 F. J. Hommes
450 Mr. & Mrs. Walter S. Allen
450 Mr. & Mrs. B. Henderson
450 F. H. Henderson
456 Mr. & Mrs. E. L. Huntley
456 Lightner Henderson
464 Mr. & Mrs. Otto C. Butz
464 Emil C. Butz
478 Mr. & Mrs. H. H. Hurlbut
478 Mr. & Mrs. A. E. Hurlbut
480 Mr. & Mrs. W. L. Potter
488 Mr. & Mrs. Harry B. Smith
488 Mr. & Mrs. Wm. Reed
494 Mr. & Mrs. O. Benson & drs.
494 Alfred S. Benson
502 Mr. & Mrs. C. E. Fulton
502 Mr. & Mrs. E. L. Oppermann
502 Mr. & Mrs. Thos. J. Hughes
502 Mr. & Mrs. Harry B. Shaw
508 Mr. & Mrs. E. C.Willison
508 Mr. & Mrs. Chas. I. Patterson
508 Mr. & Mrs. A. E. Mathews

BELDEN PLACE.

12 Mr. & Mrs. Louis Muench

BELLE PLAINE AVENUE.

931 Mr. & Mrs. Carroll C. Prentiss   936 Mr. & Mrs. Wm. G. Wheelock

BELLEVUE PLACE.

11 Mrs. D. Watterson
11 Mr. & Mrs. T. C. Hammond
11 Fred Hammond
15 Mr. & Mrs. F. B. Smith
17 Mrs. E. A. Chesbrough
  Receiving day Monday
17 Mr. & Mrs.Ellis S.Chesbrough jr.
  Receiving day Monday
19 Mr. & Mrs. Arthur D. Wheeler
21 Mr. & Mrs. Edward O'Brien
21 Mrs. Agnes D. Smith
23 Dr. & Mrs. Marvin E. Smith
23 Ross T. Parshall
27 Mrs. L. P. Smith & dr.
29 Mr. & Mrs. J. S. Dunham

14 R. M. Fay
14 I. B. Williams
14 Mr. & Mrs. C. H. Kirkham & dr
16 C. N. Fessenden
16 Mr. & Mrs. Grant D. Dial
16 Mr. & Mrs. J. J. Reynolds
16 Mr. & Mrs. E. H. Campbell
18 Mr. & Mrs. C. A. Storer
18 Miss Mary L. Card
18 Warren H. Pierce
18 Mr. & Mrs. E. B. Lewis
18 George A. Lewis
18 Mr. & Mrs. E. J. Gibbons
20 Mr. & Mrs. Henry J. Bate
20 Mr. & Mrs. H. M. Grandin

31 Mr. & Mrs. W. Vernon Booth
33 Mr. & Mrs. Theodore Sheldon
35 Mrs. David F. Waller
35 Miss M. E. Waller
39 Dr. & Mrs. Howard N. Lyon
   Receiving day Monday
39 Dr. Ellen F. Hancock
39 Mrs. Bradford Hancock
41 Mr. & Mrs. Orson Smith
43 Mr. & Mrs. Theodore Thomas
45 Mr. & Mrs. Henry B. Stone
47 Mr. & Mrs. A. P. Richardson
49 Mr. & Mrs. F. C. Austin
   Receiving day Monday
57 Mr. & Mrs. A. L. Coe
59 Mr. & Mrs. Arthur Ryerson
61 Mr. & Mrs. George Manierre
65 Mr. & Mrs. George R. Peck
67 Mr. & Mrs. P. E. Stanley & dr.
   Receiving day Monday
69 Mr. & Mrs. Robert H. Parkinson *Receiving day Monday*
73 Mr. & Mrs. Geo. M. Clark & dr.
77 Mr. & Mrs. Bryan Lathrop
77 O. F. Aldis
89 Mr. & Mrs. William Borden

72 Mr. & Mrs. J. B. Wilbur
   Receiving day Wednesday
72 Benjamin Wilbur
74 Mr. & Mrs. C. F. Arms
74 Mr. & Mrs. A. J. Cross
76 I. S. Collins
78 Mr. & Mrs. E. W. Cramer
88 Gen. Joseph T. Torrence

22 Mr. & Mrs. Alexander Marshall
22 Mrs. M. Louise Mason & dr.
22 Mr. & Mrs. John G. Miller
22 Mr. & Mrs. Fred G. Stanley
   Receiving day Tuesday
34 Mr. & Mrs. J. H. Curtis
36 Mr. & Mrs. Joseph D. Hubbard
38 Mr. &. Mrs. Henry Hathaway
38½ Dr. J. W. Bate & dr.
38½ Miss Margaret Cameron
40 Mrs. F. W. Christoph & drs.
   Receiving day Thursday
40 William H. Christoph
40 Edward G. Christoph
42 Mrs. Mary A. Curran & drs.
   Receiving day Thursday
42 M. W. Diffley
44 Mr. & Mrs. J. W. Hosmer
44½ Dr. & Mrs. G. E. Richards
48 Mrs. Julia A. Ray & drs.
52 Mr. & Mrs. H. P. Field & dr.
52 William A. Field
52 Willis P. Dickinson
54 Mr. & Mrs. B. W. Sayers
54 Mrs. Caroline Cottier
54 A. E. Cottier
56 Mr. & Mrs. F. Eberlein
60 Samuel S. Greeley
60 Louis M. Greeley
60 Miss L. M. Greeley
60 Miss Ethel M. Greeley
64 Dr. & Mrs. George S. Isham
66 Mr.& Mrs.Albert Antisdel
70 Mr. & Mrs. A. F. Bullen
   Receiving day Wednesday
70 G. R. Bullen

BELMONT AVENUE.

1531 Dr. & Mrs. E. N. Elliott
1623 Mr. & Mrs. James Pease
1631 Mr. & Mrs. H. Dittmann
1639 Mr. & Mrs. H. P. Victor
1643 Dr. & Mrs. Edward Otto
1719 Mr. & Mrs. F. J. Flinn
1719 Mr. & Mrs. James Blair
1723 Mr. & Mrs. W. E. Crmpbell
1723 R. Seidel
1725 Mr. & Mrs. C. H. Squire
1725 Mrs. Mary L. Southard
   Receiving day Thursday
1725 Miss Nellie Estelle Southard
1725 Edward C. Southard
1727 Mr. & Mrs. Gust Meyer & drs.
1731 Dr. & Mrs. F. H. Ihne
1731 Mrs. P. Dausch

1446 Mr. & Mrs. Oscar Blomgren
1624 Mr. & Mrs. Kirk Nimrod
1648 Mr. & Mrs. Ernst Stock
1656 Mr. & Mrs. Gustav Segersten
   & dr.
1704 Mr. & Mrs. John A. Mayer
1718 Mr. & Mrs. James Thomson
1812 Mr. & Mrs. James W. Steele
1812 Mrs. Mary Bland Fowlei
1812 A. Lester Fowler
1814 Mr. & Mrs. Wm. H. Chadwick
1824 Mr. & Mrs. Henry P. Klein
1832 Mr. & Mrs. S. E. Dale & drs.'
1832 Walter Dale
1832 Fred Dale
1846 Mr. & Mrs. C. C. Chase
1922 Mr. & Mrs. Edward E. Gray

1733 Mr. & Mrs. F. H. Atwood
1817 Mr.& Mrs. O. A. Ruthenberg &
    dr.
1817 Dr. Erich B. Ruthenberg
1833 Mr. & Mrs. Wm. O. Tegt-
    meyer
1847 Mr. & Mrs. W. C. Pease & dr.
1849 Mr. & Mrs. James J. Hoch

1928 Mr. & Mrs. Hugh McFarlane
    & drs.
    Receiving day Thursday
1928 Miss Helen McFarlane
1946 S. B. Chase & drs.

1849 Paul E. Held

BEST AVENUE.

21 Dr. & Mrs. Leo Galitzki
21 Mr. & Mrs. Benjamin R. Steel
21 Mr. & Mrs. Geo. M. Stevens
21 William M. Blue
23 Mr. & Mrs. Walter L. Cossar
25 Mr. & Mrs. W. L. DeBeck
25 Frank B. DeBeck
29 Mr. & Mrs. John M. Stevens
31 Mr. & Mrs. E. A. Wright & drs.

8 Rev. & Mrs. Philip Krohn
26 Mr. & Mrs. Hugh R. Ritchie
28 Mr. & Mrs. A. D. Berry
46 Mr. & Mrs. James Malcolm
54 Henry F. Walliser

31 Mr. & Mrs. Robert C. Peters
35 Mr. & Mrs. G. Wittmeyer
35 Gustave Wittmeyer jr.

BISSELL STREET.

239 Mr. & Mrs. Aug. Zander
261 Mr.& Mrs.Augustus Berlin & dr.
261 Mr. & Mrs. Robert C. Berlin
261 Henry Berlin
263 Dr. & Mrs. E. M. S. Fernandez
263 Mr. & Mrs. Wm. H. Rattray
267 Mr. & Mrs. J. M. Scott
269 Mr. & Mrs. William R. Guile
275 Mrs. H. McGee & drs.
275 Ray C. Lyon
277 Dr. & Mrs. W. C. Wermuth
281 Mr. & Mrs. George K. Rix
283 Mr.&Mrs.W.Bellinghausen&drs.
353 Mr. & Mrs. John F. Walsh & dr.
353 Miss B. M. Kennett
375 Mr. & Mrs. Theodore Stroble
377 Mr. & Mrs. John E. Rogerson
381 Mr. & Mrs. John S. Dixon
381 Miss Henrietta Dupuy

384 Sam Brown & dr.

236 Mr. & Mrs. J. Stamsen
240 Mr. & Mrs. Robert B. Palmer
240 Mr. & Mrs. C. H. Graves
276 Mr. & Mrs. A. Druiding
278 Dr. James F. Graham
278 Capt. F. H. Farrell
282 Mr. & Mrs. George A. Coffin
290 Mr. & Mrs. Edward A. Davis
300 Mr. & Mrs. David Schnitzer
354 Mr. & Mrs. Herman Kroeschell
    & dr.
354 Mr. & Mrs. Albert Kroeschell
358 Mrs. B. Burns
358 Nicholas T. Burns
362 Mr. & Mrs. Geo. B. Boardman
380 Mr. & Mrs. J. C. Bolter
382 Mr. & Mrs. D. M. Ring
382 Mr. & Mrs. Robert J. Reed
382 Mr. & Mrs. William J. Reed
382 Mr. & Mrs. F. J. Kron
384 Mrs. Jennie A. Shaw

BITTERSWEET PLACE.

23 Mr. & Mrs. M. A. Seymour
23 Mr. & Mrs. H. C. Seymour
35 Mr. & Mrs. J. M. Fulton

60 Mr. & Mrs. W. L. B. Jenney
60 C. L. Marsh

BRADLEY PLACE.

19 Mr. & Mrs. Julius Gebhard

27 Mr. & Mrs. Arthur R. Neimz

BRIAR PLACE.

1615 Dr. & Mrs. Wm. H. Cook
1641 Mr. & Mrs. Wm. D. Hoffman
1641 Dr. & Mrs. W. D. Clark
1643 Mr. & Mrs. Wm. N. Danks
1651 Mr. & Mrs. C. E. Cleveland
1651 Mr. & Mrs. Edwin Grant Crist
1651 Mr. & Mrs. A. H. Winslow
1653 Mr. & Mrs. H. M. Clarke
1657 Mrs. John G. Reid
1657 Mr. & Mrs. J. J. Drake
1657 Mr. & Mrs. Grant W. Eschen-
　　　burg
1707 Mr. & Mrs. Frank Lehmpuhl

1622 Mr. & Mrs. F. M. Richardson
1658 Mr. & Mrs. Henry C. Critten-
　　　den
1712 Mr. & Mrs. Wliliam H. Bennett
1726 Mr. & Mrs. Paul Beattie
1728 Mr. & Mrs. Frank N. Williams
1734 Mrs. S. Givins & dr.
1742 Mr. & Mrs. Theo. A. Heineman
　　　————
1721 Mr. & Mrs. Edward Seifert
1741 Mr. & Mrs. C. F. Julin
1741 Mr. & Mrs. Robert W. Pettitt

BROMPTON AVENUE.

1629 Mr. & Mrs. Wm. Wernecke
1629 Richard Wernecke

1635 Mr. & Mrs. Robert Illing

BRYAN AVENUE.

804 Mr. & Mrs. Louis Dederick
804 Miss Frances A. Roles
1046 Mr. & Mrs. Louis H. Jennings

1120 Mrs. Amelia Erpelding
1120 Mr. & Mrs. George B. Erpelding
1120 John N. Erpelding

BRYN MAWR AVENUE.

1330 Mr. & Mrs. A. T. H. Brower

1350 Mr. & Mrs. F. C. Schoenthaler
　　　Receiving day Thursday

BUCKINGHAM PLACE.

1728 Mr. & Mrs. H. W. Hanson & drs.

1732 Mr. & Mrs. A. W. Ring & dr.

BUENA AVENUE.

95 Mr. & Mrs. Alexander Zeese &
　　drs.
95 Albert Zeese
117 Mr. & Mrs. O. S. Richardson
117 W. C. B. Richardson
129 Mr. & Mrs. Earl L. Hambleton
131 Dr. & Mrs. Geo. F. Hawley & dr.
　　　Receiving day Thursday
141 Mr. & Mrs. Walter A. Daniels

ne. cor. Evanston av. Mr. & Mrs.
　　W. E. Clow
76 Mr. & Mrs. Joseph M. Rogers
76 Joseph M. Roberts jr.
76 J. Gamble Rogers
76 John A. Rogers
80 Mr. & Mrs. B. F. Rogers
　　　————
169 Mr. & Mrs. W. J. Bryson

BUENA PARK TERRACE.

40 Mr. & Mrs. R. G. Waggener

40 Mrs. H. A. Tonnas

BURLING STREET.

185 Mr. & Mrs. W. F. Yagle
195 Mr. & Mrs. Ernst H. Knoop
257 Mr. & Mrs. G. A. Bischoff
259 Mr. & Mrs. Frank T. Peterson

324 Mr. & Mrs. F. J. Sanchez
338 Mr. & Mrs. J. H. Leonard
344 Mr. & Mrs. A. Rauch & dr.
344 Wm. A. Rauch

333 Mrs. L. Wurzburger
333 Jonas Wurzburger
333 Mr. & Mrs. Wm. Hammerstroem
337 Mrs. Augusta Mayer
337 Albert Mayer
339 Mr. & Mrs. W. J. Weinsheimer
339 Mr. & Mrs. Wm. F. Lambach
365 Mr. & Mrs. Peter Jung
369 Mr. & Mrs. R. G. Uhlemann
373 Mr. & Mrs. G. D. Phelps & dr.
373 A. H. Phelps
373 E. L. Phelps
509 Mrs. Emma L. Jackman
513 Mr. & Mrs. H. L. Palmer
519 Mr. & Mrs. Charles E. Pain
519 Mrs. B. Smith & dr.
523 Mr. & Mrs. C. F. Congleton
525 Mr. & Mrs. Charles Kotz
531½ Mrs. L. H. Weil
543 Mr. & Mrs. Carl Becker
547 Mr. & Mrs. Julius Speyer
549 Mr. & Mrs. O. W. Mayer
563 Mr. & Mrs. Henry Hoffmann
567 Mr. & Mrs. E. F. Wagner
569 Mr. & Mrs. John Hanssen
571 Mr. & Mrs. Charles E. Bateman
573 Mr. & Mrs. A. W. Barlow
577 Mr. & Mrs. H. E. Synwolt
579 Mr. & Mrs. E. S. Curtis
579 Mr. & Mrs. Peter McLean
581 Mr. & Mrs. Charles Mauch
591 Mr. & Mrs. Gustav G. Kaufmann
953 Mr. & Mrs. A. F. Hussander
643 Mr. & Mrs. George Jenkins
645 Mr. & Mrs. Adolf Haerle & dr.
657 Mr. & Mrs. Andrew F. Wanner
659 Mr. & Mrs. Fred Buchholz
693 Mr. & Mrs. Max Kortum
695 A. E. Anderson
695 Mr. & Mrs. Peter Anderson

346 Mr. & Mrs. J. Wright
348 Mr. & Mrs. C. J. Roe
350 Mr. & Mrs. M. E. Morrison
352 Mr. & Mrs. Moritz Keil
354 Mr. & Mrs. Walter Butler
356 Mr. & Mrs. Otto C. Ericson
360 Mr. & Mrs. J. H. Steele
364 Mr. & Mrs. Franklin Hatheway
510 Mrs. F. C. Dye & dr.
514 Mr. & Mrs. R. H. Duryee
520 Mrs. Peter Eckes
520 John Eckes
522 Mr. & Mrs. J. A. Boland
526 Mr. & Mrs. J. Knecht
538 Mr. & Mrs. Wm. Pietsch & dr.
546 Mrs. Jacob Burkhart & dr.
546 George Burkhart
546 Mr. & Mrs. J. Linton Graff
548 Mr. & Mrs. F. H. Ehlen
550 Mr. & Mrs. A. P. Williams & drs.
550 Mrs. Daisy D. Ure
558 Mr. & Mrs. Thomas Purdon
560 Dr. & Mrs. C. B. Reed
562 Mr. & Mrs. J. Manz & drs.
562 Paul Manz
568 Mr. & Mrs. Edward W. Synwolt
576 Mrs. P. J. Hussander & dr.
598 Mr. & Mrs. Wm. Eckart
602 Mr. & Mrs. Adolf Berger
606 William R. Schick
606 Albert H. Schick
678 Mrs. Louis Dressel
698 Mr. & Mrs. Charles Hild

695 Mr. & Mrs. George E. Willis
705 Mr. & Mrs. Horace F. Hardy & dr.
705 Tucker Hardy
705 H. Florville Hardy

BURTON PLACE.

7 Mrs. Gertrude Woodwell
7 Mr. & Mrs. George Lyons
9 Mr. & Mrs. Charles S. Terry
9 Mr. & Mrs. Jabez Brewster
9 Mr. & Mrs. A. T. Harrington
11 Mrs. E. Germer & dr.

4 Mr. & Mrs. Geo. Edwin Boothroyd
8 Mr. & Mrs. J. Edward Wynne
16 Mr. & Mrs. F. S. Martin
16 Miss Lizzie Sands
44 J. A. Lynch
44 J. D. Lynch

BYRON STREET.

529 Mr. & Mrs. Chas. W. Spalding

538 Mr. & Mrs. Abraham Mitchell

512 Mr. & Mrs. Chas. M. Jackson
518 Mr. & Mrs. Chas. R. Spalding
522 Alex Lozo

CARL STREET.

19 Mr. & Mrs. A. Schoepflin
19 Mr. & Mrs. Peter Meyer
19 Mr. & Mrs. Louis Brodhay & dr.
19 Louis R. Crodhay
19 Otto C. Brodhay

12 Mr. & Mrs. Alfred·C. Kemper
16 Mr. & Mrs. Charles Emmerich
16 Edward Emmerich
20 Mr. & Mrs. Peter H. Bolten
22 Mr. & Mrs. C. Birchmeier
    Receiving day Thursday
22 Miss Sophie M. Birchmeier

CASS STREET.

67 Mr. & Mrs. E. B. McCagg
67 Miss Caroline McCagg
83 Mr. & Mrs. A. A. Carpenter &dr.
83 A. A. Carpenter jr.
87 Mr. & Mrs. Nathan Mears
101 Joseph Medill
101 Mr. & Mrs.Robert S.McCormick
113 Dr. & Mrs. Robert H. Babcock
113 Mr. & Mrs. A. M. Barnhart
113 Mr. & Mrs. Roswell Mason
113 Mr. & Mrs. William Borner
113 Mrs. J. B. Sullivan
113 A. C. Crane
113 Mr .& Mrs. Lockwood Brown
113 Mr. & Mrs. E. R. Nichols
113 Edward Crist
113 Miss L. L. Brownley
113 Miss E. E. Lumm
113 Mr. & Mrs. Samuel Rodman
113 Mr. & Mrs. Frank Wright
113 George Love
113 Mr. & Mrs. E. A. Shepley
113 Miss Emma S. Blood
113 William R. Betham
147 J. Hamilton & dr.
157 Mr. & Mrs. Edward T. Blair
159 Mrs. Louisa C. Barnard
159 Mr. & Mrs. John B. Skinner
163 Mr. & Mrs. M. Sullivan
167 Mrs. Margaret Denison & drs.
167 Andrew J. Denison
183 Mr. & Mrs. LeBaron Loring
    Austin
    Receiving day Tuesday
183 Mr. & Mrs. Wm. S Walker & dr.
183 Mr. & Mrs. John M. Russell
183 Miss E. J. Saunders
187 Mr. & Mrs. Thomas Jordan
187 Mr. & Mrs. W. T. Casgrain & dr.

94 Mr. & Mrs. Lambert Tree
    Receiving day Wednesday
94 Mr. & Mrs. Arthur M. Tree
108 Leslie Carter
108 Miss H. L. Carter
108 Miss Margaret Carter
126 Mrs. John S. Reed
180 Mrs. J. P. Chapin
180 Henry C. Chapin
180 Miss Ella D. Chapin
180 Miss Fanny Chapin
182 Mr. & Mrs. W. S. Willard
200 Dr. F. H. Lockwood
200 Mr. & Mrs. James R. Lockwood
202 Mr. & Mrs. John S. Sexton
204 Mr. & Mrs. Myer Emrich
206 Mr. & Mrs. Samuel Finneron
206 Mr. & Mrs. C. W. Cook
208 Mr. & Mrs. G. H. Stanbury
210 C. H. Whalen
212 Mrs. Mary May & dr. ·
214 Mr. & Mrs. A. E. Griffin
214 Mrs. J. Barlow Clark
216 Mr. & Mrs. H. J. Bonney & drs.
218 General & Mrs. Joseph B. Leake
220 Mr. & Mrs. Wm. Rapp & dr.
220 William J. Rapp
230 G. Charles Koch & drs.
234 Mrs. Elizabeth M. Hoffman
234 Mrs. C. M. Komans

187 George D. Casgrain
189 Mr. & Mrs. J. P. Agnew
205 Harry P. Tomlin
205 Allan R. Tomlin
209 W. W. Rathborne
209 Robert F. Shanklin
209 Frank Hamlin

CATALPHA STREET.

935 Mr. & Mrs. Wm. Twick

964 Mr. & Mrs. George E. Gall

930 John F. Gall
930 Mrs. Barbara Gall
930 Charles H. Gall

CEDAR STREET.

43 Mr. & Mrs. Chas. S. Winslow
Receiving day Tuesday
45 Mr. & Mrs. C. H. Wilmerding
45 Chas. Norman Fay
47 Thomas Dougall & drs.
53 Mr. & Mrs. Rudolph Brand
55 Mr. & Mrs. E. K. Beach & drs.
55 C. B. Beach
57 Mr. & Mrs. Eugene Vincent Robbin
Receiving day Wednesday
57 Mrs. Harriet Mabrey
59 Mr. & Mrs. Geo. Meeker High
59 Gilbert Trufant Spilman
59 Mrs. T. J. Spilman
61 Mr. & Mrs. Wallace Kirk
61 Mrs. Alfred A. Arrick
63 Mr. & Mrs. P. Cavanagh
65 Mr. & Mrs. D. Mark Cummings
Receiving day Monday
65 Mrs. Chas. P. Dexter & dr.
65 Miss Edith Dexter
67 James E. Deering

16 Mr. & Mrs. Hugo Timm
16 John Magnus
16 Mrs. J. A. Gauer
18 Mrs B. Heller & dr.
32 Michael Brand
32 Horace L. Brand
36 Mr. & Mrs. L. A. Prindiville
Receiving day Thursday
36 Mr. & Mrs. August H. Reinke
44 Mr. & Mrs. A. T. Whiting
50 Mr. & Mrs. Benj. Carpenter
52 Mr. & Mrs. Azel F. Hatch
58 Col. & Mrs. B. J. D. Irwin
58 Miss A. de H. Irwin
60 Mr. & Mrs. J. Harper Poor
Receiving day Wednesday
62 Mr. & Mrs. Henry C. McLeod
64 Mr. & Mrs. Merle Middleton
66 Mr. & Mrs. John Whitcomb Cotton
Receive Monday afternoon
68 Mr. & Mrs. Roswell P. Fish

CENTER STREET.

161 Mr. & Mrs. F. L. Schellenberg
163 Mr. & Mrs. B. Straessle
165 Mr. & Mrs. George Kuehl
263 Dr. F. Fuhrmann
323 Dr. & Mrs. Joseph Krost
371 Mrs. Jennie W. Cameron & drs.
373 Mrs. Mary Cahill
373 Edward T. Cahill
407 Dr. & Mrs. E. E. Gwynne
Receiving day Friday
411 Mr. & Mrs. Cyrus H. Sinclair
413 Mr. & Mrs. S. Day
415 Mr. & Mrs. William H. Stickney
417 Mrs. E. J. Maxwell
419 Mr. & Mrs. T. L. Forrest & dr.
419 T. Lawrence Forrest jr.
421 Mr. & Mrs. Udo Brachvogel
423 Mr. & Mrs. C. F. Collott & dr.
427 Dr. & Mrs. J. F. Williams
431 Dr. Augusta Linderborg
433 Mr.&Mrs.GeorgeC.Kober & drs.
Receiving day Thursday
435 Dr. & Mrs. Paul R. Welcker
437 Mr. & Mrs. C. C. Housel

140 Mr. & Mrs. F. Wirth
142 Mrs. Catherine Barry
156 Dr. & Mrs. E. E. Vaughan
194 Mr. & Mrs. E. Katz
200 Rev. & Mrs. W. J. Weber
202 Dr. & Mrs. R. Ulrich
202 Miss Emma Sauter
342 Mr. & Mrs. C. O. Hansen
342 Mr. & Mrs. D. Weyl
402 Dr. Frederick Everett
404 Mr. & Mrs. Sam'l Gillespie&dr.
404 Miss Marie Gillespie
406 Mr. & Mrs. L. P. Converse
408 Dr. & Mrs. W. Christopher
408 Walter Shield Christopher
412 Mrs. Patrick Joyce & dr.
412 Harry Joyce
416 Mr. & Mrs. Charles H. Curtis
416 Mrs. F. A. Curtis
420 Dr. & Mrs. Oscar O. Baines
420 Mrs. Alice Bellows
420 Miss Bertha Christie
422 Dr. & Mrs. Henry Dietrich
426 Mr. & Mrs. Charles C. Holton
426 Ethan Allen Holton

CENTRE STREET (ARGYLE PARK).

1027 Mr. & Mrs. Albert Tuerk
16

1080 Mr. & Mrs. Daniel Hesly

CHALMERS PLACE.

1 Rev. & Mrs. D. C. Marquis
1 Dr. George P. Marquis
3 Mr. & Mrs. L. M. Hamline
5 Mr. & Mrs. John Woodbridge
7 Mr. & Mrs. F. O. Wyatt & dr.
9 Mr. & Mrs. John S. Barrow
11 Rev. & Mrs. J. S. Kennard & drs.
13 Mrs. C. E. Mussey
17 Mr. & Mrs. B. T. Van Allen
19 Mr. & Mrs. C. H. Bolster
19 J. Frank Smith

2 Rev. & Mrs. Andrew C. Zenos
4 Mr. & Mrs. C. M. Osborn
4 Mr. & Mrs. Chas. M. Osborn jr.
6 Mr. & Mrs. N. J. Goll
8 Rev. & Mrs. A. H. Huizinga
8 Rev. J. R. Stevenson
10 Mr. & Mrs. A. R. Brandt
10 Oscar E. Brandt
12 Mr. & Mrs. Wm. D. Nelson
14 Mr. & Mrs. John T. Crocker
16 Mr. & Mrs. Charles E. Wilcox

CHARLTON AVENUE.

2647 Dr. & Mrs. L. H. Phipps
2673 Mr. & Mrs. A. E. Mayer
2687 Mr. & Mrs. Henry C. Hansen
2717 Mr. & Mrs. Frank Voigtmann
———
2712 Mr. & Mrs. O. M. Packard

2640 Mr. & Mrs. F. Reusch
2668 Mr. & Mrs. F. S. Baker
2670 Mr. & Mrs. Henry L. Smith
2686 Mrs. M. A. Watson
2686 O. H. Watson
2690 Mr. & Mrs. A. L. Buswell

CHASE AVENUE.

721 Mr. & Mrs. Walter L. Sempill
723 Dr. & Mrs. William W. Hinish
723 Mr. & Mrs. Carl W. Hinish
749 Mr. & Mrs. Robert M. Scholes
819 Mrs. Sarah G. Redfield
819 Mr. & Mrs. David W. Redfield
823 Mr. & Mrs. Daniel D. Bathrick
917 Mr. & Mrs. Zeno C. Spencer
1065 Mr. & Mrs. Lloyd G. Kirkland

820 Mr. & Mrs. Joseph A. Diede-
ricl¹
828 Mrs. E. Laubenheimer & dr.
912 Mrs. Catherine Coons
1040 Mr. & Mrs. David B. McMehan
1128 Mr. & Mrs. Edwin S. Bush
———
1069 Judge & Mrs. John P. Hand
1125 Mr. & Mrs. Seward H. Little

CHESTNUT STREET.

265 Mrs. M. L. Deane
267 William J. Mize
305 Mr. & Mrs. George J. Klein
333 Mr. & Mrs. Eric Bernstein
335 Mrs. Charles Harding
361 Dr. & Mrs. Oren J. Watters
379 John C. Harrington

444 Mr. & Mrs. A. B. Newell
446 Dr. DeLaskie Miller
446 Mr. & Mrs. Charles C. Curtiss

268 Mrs. Florence H. Ives
300 Mr. & Mrs. E. F. Dellano
306 Mr. & Mrs. Clinton B. Carpenter
306 Miss Carrie T. Kingman
308 Mr. & Mrs. P. B. Bradley jr.
372 Mr. &. Mrs. Nathaniel Faxon
386 Mr. & Mrs. Henry R. Green jr.
386 Mrs. Josephine Bruning
408 James J. Moore
440 Mr. & Mrs. Ernest F. Smith
442 Mr. & Mrs. George W. Meeker

CHICAGO AVENUE.

207 Dr. & Mrs. A. H. Gordon
293 Mrs. N. E. Brown
293 Mrs. E. L. Wilder
301 Mr. & Mrs. Chas. S. Eveland

298 Mr. & Mrs. Henry Schoellkopf
& dr.
298 Henry Schoellkopf jr.
300 Mr. & Mrs. F. A. Waidner

301 Mr. & Mrs. Charles H. Kehl
307 Dr. & Mrs. D. H. Stern
307 Adolph Zeisler
313 Dr. J. E. Smedley
345 Mr. & Mrs. Henry F. Jones
349 Mr. & Mrs. Thos. J. Duggan
349 D. W. Hawkins & dr.
351 Mr. & Mrs. G. W. Emerson
351 Mrs. C. Hentrich
353 Mrs. Chas. Rache
355 Mr. & Mrs. George Gilbert
355 Mr. & Mrs. J. Stemberg
355 Mr. & Mrs. G. Dougall
369 Mr. & Mrs. John W. Dickinson
369 Mr. & Mrs. Arthur L. Farwell
369 Mr. & Mrs. Arthur Taylor Aldis
369 Mr. & Mrs. J. A. Yale
369 Mr.& Mrs. John Van A. Weaver
369 Mr. & Mrs. John Vance Cheney

302 Mr. & Mrs. Fred Bartling
302 Mr. & Mrs. Fred H. Herhold
302 Miss Matilda Grannis
346 Mr. & Mrs. C. L. Epps
348 Mr. & Mrs. G. D. Bennett
352 Mrs. J. W. Stearns
352 Mr. & Mrs. J. C. Whitmarsh
378 Mr. & Mrs. Albert Varty
382 Mr. & Mrs. R. J. Embleton
390 Mrs. W. K. H. Fetter
410 Mr. & Mrs. R.Grigsby Chandler
412 Frank J. LeMoyne
412 Louis V. LeMoyne
412 William M. LeMoyne
416 Mr. & Mrs. H. E. Stump
420 Mr. & Mrs. J. S. Sheahan
424 Mr. & Mrs. A. M. F. Colton
424 Samuel K. Colton
424 Simeon C. Colton
424 Miss S. S. Kirk
424 Fred Sutton

CLAREMONT AVENUE.

1240 Mr. & Mrs. W. F. Quinlan
1340 Mr. & Mrs. Howard Greer&dr.

1340 Paul E. Greer

CLARENCE AVENUE.

127 Mr. & Mrs. R. E. O'Donnell

194 Mr. & Mrs. John M. Armstrong

130 Mr. & Mrs. H. R. Pollow
130 Mr. & Mrs. L. R. Boyington
142 Rev. & Mrs. E. N. Heimann

NORTH CLARK STREET.

103 Edward O'Brien
103 Mr. & Mrs. Edward O. Towne
103 Mr. & Mrs. J. F. Gookins
237 Dr. Chas J. Whalen
237 Dr. A. G. Johnson
307 The Walton
  1 Mr. & Mrs. Robert W. Patton
  2 Nathan Dickinson
  2 Charles Dickinson
  2 Albert Dickinson
  2 Miss M. Dickinson
  2 Charles D. Boyles
  3 Mr. & Mrs. John P. Roberts
  4 Mr. & Mrs. Stephen B.Weber
  5 T. C. Edwards
  5 Charles E. Deane
  6 Robert Forsyth
  8 Mrs. A. E. Lull & dr.
  8 Mr. & Mrs. Newton Lull
  9 Mr. & Mrs.Horace H. Martin
  10 Mrs. Theron Pardee
  10 Harry T. Pardee

102 Mr. & Mrs. Henry F. Russell
102 William L. French
152 Clarendon Hotel
    Charles A. Andrews
    Mr. & Mrs. Frank G. Baker
    Mr. & Mrs. Chas. T. Hotchkiss
    G. E. Burgesser
    H. G. Saylor
    Frank M. Taber
186 Mr. & Mrs. Joseph Waldhauser
260 Mr. & Mrs. Chas. G. Bennett
256 Dr. Rush E. Crissman
380 Maurice Collat
382 Dr. & Mrs. Irwin F. Upson
388 Dr. E. L. Knapp
390 Dr. & Mrs. Wm. Lett Bain
            Receiving day Friday
390 Dr. & Mrs. H. H. Brown
462 Westminster Hotel
    Charles Waller
    Mr.&Mrs.Theodore Kantney
    Frederick G. Kissam

339 Mr. & Mrs. John C. W. Rhode
   & drs.
    Receiving day Wednesday
339 Paul J. C. Rhode
343 Dr. & Mrs. Ph. D. Paul
345 Mr. & Mrs. Alfred R. Edwards
353 Mrs. C. A. Church
    Receiving day Wednesday
353 Dr. H. G. Anthony
375 Dr. & Mrs. Henry O. Redlich
375 Alexander E. Redlich
445 Dr. John L. Bingham
451 Henry Koenker
499 Mr. & Mrs. John Tempel & drs.
505 Mr. & Mrs. E. L. Negley
515 Mr. & Mrs. Louis Weber
525 William Wilson
547 Dr. & Mrs. Rudolph Menn
    Receive 3d Thursday in mo.
571 Mr. & Mrs. Julius Wegmann
579 Mr. & Mrs. A. Muehlbauer
591 Dr. & Mrs. Henry Geiger & dr.
593 Mr. & Mrs. Valdemar Michaelsen
599 Mr. & Mrs. Jas. W. Maxwell
699 Mr. & Mrs. Henry Eder
699 Charles H. Eder
741 Mr. & Mrs. Oliver W. Nixon
741 Mr. & Mrs. Charles E. Nixon
    Receiving day Friday
743 Mr.&Mrs.William Penn Nixon
   & drs.
763 Mrs. R. M. Frisbie
769 Mr. & Mrs. George S. Willis
771 Mr. & Mrs. Julius Heineman
771 Mr. & Mrs. E. Kaeseberg
779 Mr. & Mrs. L. W. Campbell
    Receiving day Thursday
781 Mrs. C. J. Dyer & drs.
781 Ernest E. Dyer
783 Mr. & Mrs. James C. Essick
783 Mrs. Eva Smith
823 Dr. Emilie Siegmund
829 Mr. & Mrs. John Blocki & dr.
    Receiving day Wednesday
829 Frederick W. Blocki
833 Mrs. Emma Mueller
833 Mrs. Minna Feldkamp & dr.
    Receiving day Friday
835 Mr. & Mrs. Henry Borsch
835 Mr. & Mrs. G. Park Kinney
    Receiving day Wednesday
899 Mr. & Mrs. Fred Griewisch
957 Mrs. Sarah Moulding
957 Thomas C. Moulding
957 Dr. & Mrs. Wm. P. Goodsmith

   C. N. Lobdell
   Edward Lyon
   A. H. Lawrence
   Dr. & Mrs. N. P. Pearson
   Mr. & Mrs. H. N. Thomas
482 Dr. Charles E. Rennebaum
482 Mr. & Mrs. Wm. L. Best & dr.
526 Henry A. Foster
526 Edward Grass
554 Mr. & Mrs. W. H. Grant
578 Mr.& Mrs.HenryThorwart&dr.
620 Mr. & Mrs. Millard S.Denslow
622 Mr. & Mrs. Robert McCleery
630 Mr. & Mrs. Benj. W. Merrill
se. cor. North av. The Plaza
100 Dr. Fenton B. Turck
200 Mrs. George H. Kettelle
200 George H. Kettelle
201 Mr. & Mrs. Cyrus Henry
   Clarke
201 Mrs. Margaret McKay
202 Mr. & Mrs. Willis Counselman
    Receiving day Friday
204 Mr. & Mrs. Winfield Scott
205 Mrs. Susan H. Philles
206 Rev. & Mrs. F. E. Shearer
   & dr.
208 Sam. C. Bachman
210 Mr. & Mrs. Edward Koch
212 Mr. & Mrs. F. Dangerfield
213 E. S. Keeley
214 Mr. & Mrs. Charles J. Blair
    Receiving day Thursday
216 Mr. & Mrs. Chas. Pember-
   ton Wurts
217 Mr. & Mrs. Frank S.
   Wheeler
221 Mr. & Mrs. Wm. F. White
221 Miss Virginia Adams
222 Mrs. Cynthia Ludlow
222 Fred D. Ludlow
300 Mr.& Mrs.Schiller Hosford
301 Mr. & Mrs. G. R. Blanchard
302 Mr. & Mrs. Christian Lee
302 Miss Cora Anderson
305 Herbert Noyes
308 Mr. & Mrs. W.'J. Snyder
310 Mr. & Mrs. DavidA.Noyes
314 Mr. & Mrs. Rufus P. Pattison
    Receiving day Thursday
316 Mr.&Mrs.EdwardMcKeon
317 Mr. & Mrs. P. J. Phelps
318 Mr. & Mrs. Edw. P. Buss

1029 Mr. & Mrs. Albert Hinds jr.
1031 Mr. & Mrs. H. A. Swanson
1035 Mr. & Mrs. Amos G. Sears
  Receiving day Thursday
1043 Mr. & Mrs. T. Frank Hull
  Receiving day Friday
1047 Mrs. Vista Rolfe
1049 Mr. & Mrs. Herman Meyer
1049 Mr. & Mrs. Theo. Karls
1053 Mr. & Mrs. Wm. R. Swinford
1055 Mr. & Mrs. Henry B. Hellman
1059 Mrs. M. E. Koons
  Receiving day Wednesday
1059½ Mr.& Mrs.Geo.P.Allmendinger
1065 Mr. & Mrs. Chas. L. Gamer & drs. *Receiving day Thursday*
1065 George W. Gamer
1067 Mrs. M. S. Wolcott
1067 J. D. Spear
1071 Dr. & Mrs. T. W. Miller & drs.
1097 Mr. & Mrs. F. E. Brookman
1103 Mr. & Mrs. Gebhardt W. Zeiger
1107 Mr. & Mrs. Edmund G. Fiedler
1115 Dr. & Mrs. E. M. Landis
1117 Mr. & Mrs. Ralph Modjeski
1121 Daniel W. Maher
1123 Mr. & Mrs. L. D. Thoman
1123 Miss Melissa M. Thoman
1127 Mr.&Mrs.Charles L.Feldkamp
1127 Dr. James M. C. Potts
1127 Mr. & Mrs. Herbert D. Jones
1143 Will I. Saunders
1143 Mr. & Mrs. Austin Saunders
1143 Miss Clara Swarthout
1147 Mr. & Mrs. George Oberne
1147 George N. Oberne
1155 Mr. & Mrs. James Charlton & drs.
1157 Mr. & Mrs. Edward Schultz
1157 Mr. & Mrs. Wm. D. Morris
1157 Mr. & Mrs. Miles H. Morris
1159 Mr. & Mrs. J. Henry Zitt
1159 Mr. & Mrs. F. J. Schmidt
1159 Moritz W. Boehm
1161 Mr. & Mrs. Howard N. Wagg
1161 Mr. & Mrs. Victor Troendle
1161 Mr. & Mrs. Gustav Riel
1163 Mr. & Mrs. Frank Deppe & drs.
1163 Mr. & Mrs. Proctor M. Wilson & drs.
1171 Mr. & Mrs. John Fischback
1181 Mr. & Mrs. R. A. Meiswinkel & dr.

The Plaza (continued.)
319 Mr. & Mrs. H. Wadsworth
320 Mr. & Mrs. George Bowles
321 Mr. & Mrs. Henry C.Wood
322 Mrs. C. A. Sykes
  Receiving day Friday
400 Mr. & Mrs. J. S. Brewer
401 Mr. & Mrs. E. S. Matthews
403 Mr.&Mrs.Edward G.Halle
403 Mr.&Mrs. Robert B. Cotter
405 Robert T. Brewer
405 Howard Throckmorton
406 Mr. & Mrs. A. M. Wright
408 Mr.& Mrs.Wilson G.Baker
410 Mr.& Mrs. Henry J. Rogers
413 Mr. & Mrs. Lawrence Proudfoot
414 Mr. & Mrs. Hepburn Johns
415 Mr. & Mrs. Geo. A. Hart
416 Mr. & Mrs. Robt. H. McArthur
419 Mr. & Mrs. J. P. Bacon
420 Mr. & Mrs. Edward List
  Receiving day Friday
421 Mr. & Mrs. Chas. Walsh
422 Mr. & Mrs.Wm.Wrigley jr.
500 Mr. & Mrs J. R. Chapman
501 Col. & Mrs. E. B. Williston
503 Mr. & Mrs. H. B. Twyford
504 Mr. & Mrs. Robt.H.Walch
505 Mr.& Mrs.Walter A.Mayer
  Receiving day Friday
506 Mr. & Mrs. A. K. McRae
508 Mrs. C. W. Hempstead
508 Charles G. Perkins
510 Mr. & Mrs. Clark Varnum
513 Mr. & Mrs. F.W. Matthews
515 Mr. & Mrs. A. C. Stitely
516 Mr. & Mrs. J. I. Booge & drs.
518 Mr.& Mrs. Robt. F. Palmer
  Receiving day Friday
519 Mr. & Mrs. Wm. M. Peters
521 Mr. & Mrs. J. W. Moulton
522 Mr. & Mrs. C. W. Battell
600 J. K. Harmon
600 A. C. Harmon
600 F. H. Harmon
600 Miss Lydia Harmon
601 Mr. & Mrs. D. G. Drake
603 Mr. & Mrs. John M. Locke
604 Mr. & Mrs. C. E. Mosley
605 Mr.& Mrs.Arthur G. Fuller
606 Mr. & Mrs. Geo. H. Ross
  Receiving day Thursday
608 Mr. & Mrs. E. G. Sugg

1253 Mr. & Mrs. John G. Davies
1255 Mr. & Mrs. Edward C. Lines
1273 Mr. & Mrs. H. H. Hoffmann & dr.
1273 Benjamin Hoffmann
1275 Mr. & Mrs. Henry W. d'Evers
1373 Dr. & Mrs. N. E. Oliver
1457 Mrs. Mary A. J. Parker & dr.
1457 DeWitt C. Morrill
4691 Mrs. Amanda A. Carroll & dr.
4773 Dr. & Mrs. A. D. Lowell
4915 Mrs. Della Benner & dr.

819 Mr. & Mrs. A. W. Maltby
821 Mr. & Mrs. B. F. Culver & drs.
922 Dr. Effie T. Straub
940 Mrs. Edward Burkhardt
954 Dr. & Mrs. Frederick Van Ackeren
956 Mr. & Mrs. Louis Kurz
958 Mr. & Mrs. Adolph Hartman
958 Mr. & Mrs. Frederick Brooks
962 Mr. & Mrs. Leo Kabell
1024 Mr. & Mrs. Wm. H. Mather
1038 Mr. & Mrs. C. D. Millis
1040 Rev. & Mrs. David Beaton
1112 Mr. & Mrs. George C. Chapman & dr.
 Receiving day Wednesday
1112 Dr. George L. Chapman
1146 Mr. & Mrs. David Goodwillie & drs.
1146 Willis L. Goodwillie
1186 Mr. & Mrs. John B. Brosseau
1186 Mr. & Mrs. Eugene Seeger
1220 Mr. & Mrs. Henry Kleine
1238 Mr. & Mrs. Geo. M. McKenzie
1246 Dr. & Mrs. P. M. Woodworth
 Receiving day Thursday
1246 Dr. John Teare
1314 Mr. & Mrs. M. J. Tillmann & drs.
1314 Charles F. Tillmann
1326 Mrs. E. J. Lehmann
1326 Miss Tillie Preasant
1326 Charles Preasant
1380 Dr. & Mrs. F. H. Bowman
1380 Dr. Wm. E. Kramer
1474 Mr. & Mrs. Edmund Knauer & dr.
1620 Mrs. John Spelz & drs.
1620 Frederick W. Spelz
ne. cor. Thome av. Robins S. Mott

The Plaza (continued.)
610 Mr. & Mrs. Wm. D. McIlvaine
612 Mr. & Mrs. Theo. P. Shonts
 Receiving day Friday
613 Miss Josephine Locke
615 Mr. & Mrs. Chas. H. Baldwin
617 Mr. & Mrs. Edw. W. Spurr
618 Mrs. N. H. Barnes & dr.
619 Mr. & Mrs. Hartley D. Harper
621 Mr. & Mrs. Wm. H. Finney
622 Mr. & Mrs. E. W. Copelin
701 Mr. & Mrs. B. L. Honore
702 James C. Clow
702 Mr. & Mrs. Jas. B. Clow
702 Charles R. Clow
703 Maj. & Mrs. S. W. Groesbeck
705 Mr. & Mrs. Chas. W. Jenks
708 Mr. & Mrs. Hubert M. Russell
710 Mr. & Mrs. Walter Ferrier
 Receiving day Friday
712 Mr. & Mrs. James H. Sullivan
713 Mr. & Mrs. Fred C. Wheeler
714 Rev. Thaddeus A. Snively
715 Mr. & Mrs. J. C. Rand
716 Mr. & Mrs. John A. Drake
717 Mrs. E. C. Brown
718 Mr. & Mrs. Frederick Meadowcraft
 Receiving day Thursday
718 Mrs. L. K. Platt
719 Mr. & Mrs. J. A. Miner
801 Mr. & Mrs. Clinton J. Warren
801 Mrs. N. M. Chittenden
801 George W. Chittenden
801 Fred W. Chittenden
801 Harry W. Chittenden
802 Mrs. Wm. E. Strong & dr.
 Receiving day Monday
806 Mrs. O. E. Babcock
 Receiving day Wednesday
806 Orville E. Babcock
806 Campbell E. Babcock
808 Mr. & Mrs. E. A. Wanner
810 Mr. & Mrs. S. M. Fargo & dr.
813 Mr. & Mrs. Lysander E. Stone
815 Mr. & Mrs. Chas. S. Hannan
816 Mr. & Mrs. A. A. Jannotta
 Receiving day Tuesday

4298 Mr. & Mrs. Chas. Hitchcock
5008 Mr. & Mrs. P. L. Touhy & drs.
5008 Edmund R. Touhy

5008 Joseph Touhy
5008 Stephen R. Touhy
5138 Mr. & Mrs. John F. Ure

CLEVELAND AVENUE.

57 Dr. & Mrs. A. H. Wimermark
145 Mr. & Mrs. O. B. Roberg
167 Charles Edelmann & drs.
167 John Melchior Edelmann
401 Mr. & Mrs. S. Goldsmith
401 Mr. & Mrs. J. Back
401 Harry Steinfeld
401 Mr. & Mrs. Fred. Seigmund
411 Mr. & Mrs. N. M. Plotke
427 Mr. & Mrs. Charles Werno
427 Mrs. B. Scherr
451 Mr. & Mrs. William G. Apfel
451 Louis E. Weick
455 Mr. & Mrs. D. M. S. Cohen
455 Abraham L. Cohen
457 Mr. & Mrs. A. S. Anderson
457 Mr. & Mrs. George G. May
463 Mr. & Mrs. Nicholas Gerten
463 Mrs. M. E. Welcher
467 Mr. & Mrs. W. O. Buttner
475 Mr. & Mrs. F. Meurer
475 Mr. & Mrs. A. L. Smith
481 Mr. & Mrs. Charles Schumann
481 Mr. & Mrs. Peter Hand
487 Mr.&Mrs. A. D. Wilmanns&drs.
497 Dr. & Mrs. William A. Zeno
509 Dr. S. H. Bottomley
515 Dr. & Mrs. G. J. Schaller
517 Mr. & Mrs. John Clifford
519 Dr. & Mrs. A. Goldspohn
519 Mr. & Mrs. Samuel Schneider
523 Mr. & Mrs. Joachim Saehn
523 August Saehn
525 Mr. & Mrs. J. B. Hurlbut
525 Mrs. A. J. Allen
525 Mr. & Mrs. C. P. Allen
529 Mr. & Mrs. James J. Casey
533 Mr. & Mrs. Jacob Retterer
    Receiving day last Thurs. in mo.
533 Mr. & Mrs. H. Rehtmeyer
535 John McGillen
537 Mr. & Mrs. M. A. Delany & dr.
541 Mr. & Mrs. C. J. Sauter & drs.
541 L. E. Sauter
541 C. Frank Sauter
543 Mr. & Mrs. Julius Blum
545 John Booth & drs.
549 Mr. & Mrs. Otto Wasmansdorff
    Receiving day 2d Sat. in mo.
551 Mr. & Mrs. Jacob Thein & drs.

412 Mr. & Mrs. Charles Mills
424 Mr. & Mrs. D. Sander
428 Mr. & Mrs. Wm. R.Hildebrand
448 Mr.& Mrs. H.N.Elkington & dr.
448 Charles S. Elkington
448 Mrs. M. L. King & drs.
456 Mr. & Mrs. C. P.Holenberg & dr.
456 Mr. & Mrs. H. Bishop & dr.
456 Herman H. Bishop
456 Mr. & Mrs. W. Miloslewsky
458 Mr. & Mrs. Paul Bracht
458 Mr. & Mrs. Otto C. Fischer
460 Mrs. M. E. Briggs & dr.
466 Mr. & Mrs. F. J. Pischel & dr.
466 Irvin J. Lewis
466 Mrs. Harriet M. Lewis
470 Mr. & Mrs. J. M. Johnson
470 Mr. & Mrs. George Kennedy
472 Dr. Elise Berwig
472 Mrs. Margaret Schumm & dr.
508 Mr. & Mrs. S. J. Harris
510 Mrs. Kate A. Mayer & dr.
528 Mr. & Mrs. Wm. L. Schrader &
    dr.
530 Mr. & Mrs. Lee Fellows
532 Mr. & Mrs. M. Newfield
538 Mrs. W. Maxwell & dr.
538 D. G. Maxwell
540 Mr. & Mrs. John G. Roland
542 Mr. & Mrs. Wm. Washburn
546 Mr. & Mrs. Samuel Friedlander
548 Dr. & Mrs. J. Simpson & drs.
592 Mrs. M. A. Porter
594 Mr. & Mrs. E. T. Keyes
594 Mrs. Lucy Keyes
596 Mr. & Mrs. E. B. Bacon & dr.
628 Mr. & Mrs. B. D. Anguish
630 Mr. & Mrs. Jos. Brucker & dr.
634 Mr. & Mrs. Paul Boyton
634 Mr. & Mrs. Cornelius Connolly
636 Mr. & Mrs. J. S. Clarke
640 Mrs. Mary Morrow & dr.
640 Robert J. Morrow
646 Mr. & Mrs.John Anderson & dr.
654 Mr. & Mrs. W. J. Fleming
654 Mrs. P. A. Reed

553 Mr. & Mrs. M. Kaufman & dr.
555 Mr. & Mrs. John Schoen & dr.
565 Mrs. Elizabeth Engberg & dr.

565 Martin J. Engberg
569 Rev. & Mrs. Philip Klein
575 Mr. & Mrs. Nelson Chesman
575 Mr. & Mrs. R. H. Stewart & drs.
575 George R. Stewart
587 Mr. & Mrs. A. Chaiser & drs.
591 Charles F. Miller
597 Rev. & Mrs. J. M. Williams
597 Mr. & Mrs. Frederick A. Lester
603 Mr. & Mrs. J. Petersen
603 Nicholas Hand
609 Mr. & Mrs. C. R. Matson
        Receiving day Friday
615 Mr. & Mrs. Joseph M. Watte

619 Mr. & Mrs. Arthur G. Jukes
621 Mr. & Mrs. Hermann Mueller
625 Mr. & Mrs. Charles Heinemann
631 Mr. & Mrs. George Finney
631 Harry P. Finney
649 Miss Emma Engleman
659-665 Cleveland Flats
  2 Reginald G. Smith
  2 Miss Alice M. Smith
  5 Irving L. Gould
  5 Mrs. E. I. Gould
  6 Mr. & Mrs. Douglas H. Howe
  9 Mr. & Mrs. A. E. Eggert
 13 Mr. & Mrs. H. B. Armstrong

CLIFTON AVENUE.

 65 Dr. & Mrs. G. G. Praetorius
183 Mr. & Mrs. J. J. Dolan

90 Mr. & Mrs. Charles E. Ehlert
90 Mrs. B. Gegenheimer

COMMERCIAL STREET.

2293 Mrs. August Lang
2303 Mr. & Mrs. Julius H. Zeitner
2339 Mrs. Eva S. Miller
        Receiving day Thursday
2339 Miss Ella B. Stewart
2433 Mr. & Mrs. Hugh Wrightson
2439 Mr. & Mrs. Charles A. Vail
2443 Mr. & Mrs. S. F. Champlin
2447 Mr. & Mrs. Lloyd Canaday
2453 Mr. & Mrs. J. H. Norton
2453 Mrs. H. Goodfellow & dr.
2475 Mr. & Mrs. John W. Salladay
2485 Mr. & Mrs. J. A. Hornsby
2485 Mr. & Mrs. H. G. Cilley
2493 Mrs. Nicholas R. Cozzens
2505 Mr. & Mrs. John H. Haake
2515 Mr. & Mrs. Edwin M. Clark
2541 Dr. & Mrs. Thomas A. Broad-
        bent
2547 Miss Ellen Reedy
2571 Dr. & Mrs. LeRoy C. Hedges
2577 Mr. & Mrs. Wm. A. Trowbridge
2577 Mrs. Julia Sinclair
2577 Miss Sara Watt
2585 Rev. & Mrs. William A. Lloyd
        & dr.
2585 Ray N. Lloyd
2585 Robert C. Lloyd
2585 Wm. W. Lloyd
2629 Mr. & Mrs. Albert Galloway
2629 Mr. & Mrs. W. E. Miles
2667 Mr. & Mrs. Charles W. Slosson
2667 Mrs. Elizabeth Kirk
2671 Mr. & Mrs. George F. Koester

2410 Mr. & Mrs. Oliver R. Trow-
        bridge
2412 Mr. & Mrs. Chas. C. Linthicum
2430 Miss May E. Gates
2430 Frank H. Frost
2430 Alonzo F. Cooley
2434 Mr. & Mrs. H. P. Decker
2444 Mr. & Mrs. A. S. Terrill
2478 Mr. & Mrs. Geo. A. Wrisley
2478 Mrs. A. B. Thompson
2486 Mr. & Mrs. Volney C. Chase
2490 Mr. & Mrs. Oscar J. Bersbach
2548 Mr. & Mrs. Samuel Powell
2558 Mr. & Mrs. L. F. Koehn jr.
2564 Mr. & Mrs. B. V. Emery
2568 Mr. & Mrs. Alfred J. Bersbach
2574 Mr. & Mrs. William A. Gardner
2578 Mr. & Mrs. J. E. Martin
2582 Mrs. M. H. Crosby
2582 Frederick W. H. Rogers
2584 Dr. & Mrs. Harry Parsons
2610 Mrs. W. B. Holcomb
2610 Mr. & Mrs. David N. Holcomb
2614 Mr. & Mrs. James W. Andrews
2614 J. Roy Andrews
2620 Mr. & Mrs. Albright Griffeth
2620 Abraham L. Griffeth
2620 Cuyler D. Rees
2024 Mr. & Mrs. George H. Bryant
2636 Mr. & Mrs. DeWitt Van Evera
2644 Mr. & Mrs. James Gilchrest
2654 Mr. & Mrs. Edward S. White
2666 Dr. & Mrs. Wallace C. Abbott
2698 Rev. & Mrs. C. R. D. Crittenden

2691 Mr. & Mrs. Franklin S. Hal-
    lock
2719 Mr. & Mrs. Perry Krus & dr.
2809 Mr.&Mrs. George R. Thomson

2754 Mr. & Mrs. Charles G. Mackin
2840 Mr. & Mrs. William C. Bieden-
    weg
2844 Mr. & Mrs.Joseph E.Flanagan
    Receiving day Thursday
2908 Mr. & Mrs. John A. Witty

CORNELIA STREET.

1611 Mrs. J. W. Krause
1611 Mr. & Mrs. Fred S. Rogers
1715 John F. Brady
1715 Mrs. Archie A. Anderson
1721 Mr. & Mrs. S. M. Eisendrath
1721 Mr. & Mrs. John M. Chappell
1721 Mrs. M. L. Wilcox
1721 Mr. & Mrs. Gustav C. Priebe
1723 Mr. & Mrs. Rufus C. Hall
1723 Mr. & Mrs. Robt. J. Thompson
1723 Mr. & Mrs. Paul W. Lange

1438 Mr. & Mrs. Marcus A. Miller
1438 Mr. & Mrs. Preston K. Law-
    rence
1438 Mr.& Mrs. Frederick H.Jacobs
1440 Mr. & Mrs. Wm. S. Palmer
1440 Mr. & Mrs. Frank B. Modica
1442 Mr. & Mrs. Walter Lockwood
1442 Mr. & Mrs Earl P. Sedgwick
1442 Rev. & Mrs. Armstead H.
    Stephens
1624 Mrs. E. J. Wilson
1624 Frank R. Wilson
1624 Mr. & Mrs. Louis Duquette

CRILLY PLACE.

1 Mr. & Mrs. Wm. L. Lindsey
3 Mr. & Mrs. August Spielmann
5 Mr. & Mrs. Geo. W. Claussenius
7 Mr. & Mrs. S. Sinsheimer
7 Max N. Epstein
7 N. M. Epstein
9 Mr. & Mrs. David M. Kirton
11 Mr. & Mrs. Jacob Spielmann

13 Mr. & Mrs.H.M.Lindenthal & dr.
17 Mr. & Mrs. Louis Kohn
19 Mr. & Mrs. John V. May
23 Mr. & Mrs. John C. Kessler
    Receiving day Thursday
23 Mrs. Abbie Strasburger

CUYLER AVENUE.

424 Mr. & Mrs. Lewis B. Scott

DAKIN STREET.

1439 Mr. & Mrs. John B. Johnson
1441 Mr. & Mrs. H. E. Smith
1459 Mr. & Mrs. Wm. Seiffe

———

1518 Mr. & Mrs. Ira L. Gifford

1438 Mr. & Mrs. Olin C. Eastman
1438 Mr. & Mrs. L. D. Eastman
1446 Dr. & Mrs. Wm. P. Richards
1448 Mr. & Mrs. F. W. McLean
1448 Mrs. Sarah Laffrinier
1452 Mr. & Mrs. G. Bergman

DAYTON STREET.

351 Mr. & Mrs. L. Popper
355 Mr. & Mrs. Albert Breitung
365 Mr. & Mrs. Michael Brennan
443 Mr. & Mrs. George H. Nolte
451 Mr. & Mrs. W. Glasser
457 Mr. & Mrs. W. L. Kroeschell
    Rec. day last Thursday in mo.
459 Mr. & Mrs. C. G. Stowell

330 Mr. & Mrs. E. C. Sloan
330 Miss L. Stephens
330½ Mr. & Mrs. C. F. M. Allen
338 Mr. & Mrs. Wm. E. Spangen-
    berg
344 Mr. & Mrs. C. T. Wilt & dr.
    Receiving day Thursday
344 Elmer E. Wilt

360A Mr. & Mrs. I. B. Hammond
370 Mr. & Mrs. C. Louis Niehoff
380 Mr. & Mrs. E. R. Van Buren
392 Mr. & Mrs. Moses Meyer
442 Mr. & Mrs. J. W. Walker
442 Mr. & Mrs. E. Jepson
450 Mr. & Mrs. Otto Kroeschell
452 Mr. & Mrs. Met L. Saley & dr.
452 Mr. & Mrs. H. H. Daw

456 Mr.& Mrs. Aug. Moeckel
456 Mr. & Mrs. Louis Marden
456 The Misses Marden
460 Mr. & Mrs. J. P. Hettinger
462 Mr. & Mrs. Frank A. Knipschild
462 Mr. & Mrs. John L. Street
462 A. W. Street
462 Mrs. S. R. Taylor & drs.
462 Mr. & Mrs. B. M. Justice

DEARBORN AVENUE.

131 Dr. & Mrs. C. D. Bradley & dr.
   Receiving day Monday
133 George Keller
147 David S. Mackay
151 Mr. & Mrs. L. P. Stickney
161 Mr. & Mrs. W. H. McLean
169 Mr. & Mrs. A. A. Sample
181 Dr. Cornelia S. Stettler
189 Mr. & Mrs. D. Frank Dearborn
189 Henry F. Brown
189 Charles J. Dorrance
201 Mr. & Mrs. Michael J. Teehan
211-213 Hotel La Vita
   Mrs. G. Allen
   William Coakley
   Mr. & Mrs. Thos. J. Martin
   Mr. & Mrs. St. Eyre Powell
217 Dr. J. S. Christison
225-231 The Newberry
   E. J. Abel
   Mr. & Mrs. Geo. S. Acker
   George Acker jr.
   Louis R. Adams
   Mr. & Mrs. Morgan Bates
   Miss Lora Beck
   Dr. Leila G. Bedell
   Mrs. Wm. Burke & dr.
   John C. Campbell
   Wm. Fennimore Cooper
   Mr. & Mrs. Edward L. Cregier
   William F. Crowley
   Mr. & Mrs. Thos. H. Doane&dr
   Barrett Eastman
   Mr. & Mrs. T. A. Evans
   Miss Isadore Fanning
   Mrs. S. A. Floyd & dr.
   John I. Floyd
   O. G. Formhals
   Mr. & Mrs. Henry L. Foster&dr.
   Philip H. Gaspard
   Mr. & Mrs. Henry E. Hamilton
   Mrs. Henry L. Hatch & dr.
   Miss H. R. Howard
   Miss Sadie Hurd

148 The Mentone
   Mrs. Mary Christianson
   Capt. John Cliff
   Mrs. E. A. Funk
   Mr. & Mrs. Philip Greene
   Edward L. Hicks
   Mr. & Mrs. H. Heiman
   Miss Julia Jorgenson
   Mr. & Mrs. C. W. Monroe
   Mr. & Mrs. Byron H. Newell
   Mr. & Mrs. O. S. Pew
   A. C. Powers
   C. H. Roehrig
   Mr. & Mrs. H. C. Shinnick
      Receiving day Wednesday
   A. R. Tressler
   George Weatherbee
   Mr. & Mrs. A. G. Webster
   Miss Emma Webster
   Mr. & Mrs. Chas. Woodward
156 Mr. & Mrs. C. J. Wood
156 Mr. & Mrs. William C. Gallaway
156 Mr. & Mrs. Wm. T. Gallaway
156 Mrs. Susan Jacques
156 F. Carey Smith
178 Mr. & Mrs. John Addison
178 Mr. & Mrs. Edward N. Camp
180 Dr. J. L. Irwin
190 Dr. Emanuel J. Senn
192 Mr. & Mrs. M. Otis Hower
      Receiving day Wednesday
208 Mr. & Mrs. Geo. Gulick
216 Dr. A. Melville Tully
216 William Burry
216 John W. Lowe
220 Mrs. J. H. Wilson
222 Mr. & Mrs. Leverett E. Fitts
226 William F. DeWolf
226 Mrs. Albert Erskine
226 Albert DeW. Erskins
226 James D. Erskine
226 Miss Margaret Erskine
230 Mr. & Mrs. Frank Headen

Mr. & Mrs. Wm. J. Irvin
Mrs. Catherine Lonsdale
Harry B. Mair
A. J. McCausland
Mr. & Mrs. Jos. McDonald
Mr. & Mrs. E. M. McMillan
Miss Floy McMullan
Fred P. Morrill
Miss Julia E. Officer
John H. Patterson
Mrs. M. I. Pitts
Mr. & Mrs. John Reid
John C. Richardson
Mr. & Mrs. Charles Rines
Mr. & Mrs. Isaac M. Sowers
William Y. Stafford
Mr. & Mrs. John C. Stuart
Frederick Swift
Mr. & Mrs. Erwin M. Thomas
George K. Thompson
William K. Thompson
Mr. & Mrs. Edward C. Towslee
John R. Vansant
Mrs. Annie B. Wakefield
Mrs. Lydia M. Waldron
L. Whitworth
Thomas H. Wilcox
Wm. S. Wilkinson
Wm. J. S. Williams
235 Mr. & Mrs. James C. Brooks
235 Miss Alice Brooks
237 Louis G. Beers
237 Mr. & Mrs. Wells Isbell
237 John H. Hume
239 Thomas D. Drake
239 Mr. & Mrs. Wm. Marshall
239 John K. Hanes
241 Mrs. Josephine Taylor
245 Mr. & Mrs. Wm. K. Carlisle
247 The Misses Mineah
Receiving day Friday
251 Mr. & Mrs. Thomas Lynch
253 Mrs. P. A. Spurlock
253 Mr. & Mrs. Henry B. Spurlock
Receiving day Wednesday
255 Lowrie McClurg
257 Mr. & Mrs. P. Quitman
259 Mrs. Samuel Kitson
259 Marion May jr.
259 Miss Lucia Gale
263 Dr. & Mrs. Robert N. Tooker
Receiving day Monday
263 Robert N. Tooker jr.
285 Mrs. J. H. Thompson
285 Watts C. Thompson
285 Payson Thompson

234 Dr. & Mrs. A. H. Cooke
234 Dr. John M. Cooke
234 Alexander W. Cooke
238 Dr. & Mrs. S. Newton Schneider
238 Mrs. H. E. Tucker
244 Mr. & Mrs. A. J. Marble & dr.
250 Mr. & Mrs. Richard I. Field
250 George W. Field
250 Arthur C. Field
254 Mr. & Mrs. Augustus H. Burley
256 Mr. & Mrs. Aldace F. Walker
328 Mr.&Mrs. Albert M.Gilbert&dr.
328 H. K. Gilbert
332 Mr. & Mrs. M. W. Kerwin
332 Miss Mary E. Kerwin
336 Mr. & Mrs. James W. Ferry
336 Mrs. J. H. Ferry
344 J. Lawrence McIntyre
346 Mrs. A. F. Lewis
348 Mr. & Mrs. W. D. Kerfoot
348 C. Stewart Kerfoot
350 Mr. & Mrs. J. S. Runnells &dr.
356 Mrs. Edward Waller & dr.
356 Edward Waller
370 Mr. & Mrs. William M. Hoyt
370 Mr. & Mrs. N. Landon Hoyt
370 Phelps B. Hoyt
370 Miss H. J. Landon
374 Mr. & Mrs. L. B. Mantonya
374 Mr. & Mrs. Fred J. Hoyt & dr.
374 Mr. & Mrs. T. Barbour Brown
374 Mr. & Mrs. Ward Stockton
374 Frank E. Scott
376 Mr. & Mrs. Theo. Springer
376 Fred W. Eldredge
376 Mr. & Mrs. Robt. A. Irving
376 Mr. & Mrs. Geo. W. Brayton
376 Mrs. Joseph Breed
376 Mr. & Mrs. Carlos A. Cook & dr.
376 Carlos E. Cook
378 Mr. & Mrs. M. L. Thackaberry
378 Dr. & Mrs. Wm. S. Fowler
Receiving day Thursday
378 Mr. & Mrs. Clarence B. Bishop
378 Mrs. S. A. St. John
378 Mr. & Mrs. Elliott T. Monett
378 Mr. & Mrs. Wesley M. Lowrie
400 Mrs. J. M. Adsit & drs.
400 Mrs. Ezra I. Wheeler
400 James M. Adsit jr.
402 Mr. & Mrs. John DeKoven
408 Mrs. J. E. Siem
412 Mr. & Mrs. John N. Jewett
414 Dr. & Mrs. R. D. MacArthur
426 Mr. & Mrs. F. B. Peabody
432 Egbert C. Fuller

285 Benj. F. C. Thompson
293 Mr. & Mrs. George B. Carpen-
     ter
321 Dr. & Mrs. R. N. Isham
325 Mr. & Mrs. O. F. Fuller
325 Henry M. Fuller
337 Mr. & Mrs. James H. Dole & dr.
337 Miss Julia F. Dole
343 Mr. & Mrs. Albion Cate
     Receiving day Tuesday
337 Mr. & Mrs. Henry W. Leman
337 George S. Dole
345 Mr. & Mrs. James H. Walker
345 James H. Walker jr.
345 Miss Annie C. Walker
347 Mrs. T. S. Phillips & drs.
349 Mr. & Mrs. Fred A. Warren
351 Mrs. G. S. Carmichael
355 Dr. & Mrs. John W. Niles
357 Mr. & Mrs. Thomas F. Ander-
     son
357 Mr. & Mrs. Wm. M. Smith
359 Mr. & Mrs. Franklin C. Taylor
359 Hamilton B. Dox
361 Mr. & Mrs. T. C. Oakman
375 Miss Mabel Collins
375 E. O. Fitch
375 Mr. & Mrs. J. C. Ambler
375 Henry Pieters
375 P. A. Pincoffs
377 Mr. & Mrs. M. R. Davis
377 Mrs. P. R. Poole & dr.
377 W. H. Mullen
377 Miss Dora Mullen
377 T. F. Mullen
377 Miss Elizabeth Parkes
377 Mr. & Mrs. W. F. Turney
377 Grosvenor A. Harper
377 J. Mullen
379 Mr. & Mrs. John Johnston
379 Mr. & Mrs. Harrison Rosa
379 Mr. & Mrs. I. G. Garner
379 Mrs. Anna B. Atkins
381 Mr. & Mrs. Geo. S. Searing
381 Mr. & Mrs. Geo. M. Ayer
383 Mr. & Mrs. Julius Harris & drs.
     Receiving day Tuesday
385 Mrs. O. K. A. Hutchinson & dr.
385 Otis King Hutchinson
387 William F. Keep
387 Frederick A. Keep
387 Miss Frances Keep
389 Mr. & Mrs. W. S. Potwin
393 W. J. Cannon
393 H. T. Griffin
399 Mr. & Mrs. E. C. Coulter

434 Dr. Harry L. Walker
440 Mrs. Annie Forstall
444 Mr. & Mrs. Wiley M. Egan
444 Charles W. Egan
444 Miss Lizzie Egan
444 Mr. & Mrs. Lucian P. Cheney
446 Allen R. Vinnedge
446 Mr. & Mrs. Mahlon A. Vinnedge
448 Mr. & Mrs. C. A. Spring jr.
450 Mr. & Mrs. Peter Britten & dr.
452 Mr. & Mrs. Wm. E. Boynton
     Receiving day Monday
454 Mrs. George Payson & dr.
460 Dr. & Mrs. George W. Newton
460 Mr. & Mrs. Rudolph Ortmann
460 Mr. & Mrs. Rudolph Matz
476 Mr. & Mrs. Peter L. Yoe
476 Mr. & Mrs. L. G. Yoe & drs.
480 Mr. & Mrs. J. M. W. Jones & drs.
480 E. Lee Jones
480 Miss M. Katherine Jones
480 Miss Helen Snow Jones
484 Henry S. Monroe
484 Miss Harriet S. Monroe
484 Miss Lucy B. Monroe
484 William S. Monroe
484 Mrs. J. W. Root
486 Mr. & Mrs. Charles A. Dupee & dr.
486 Eugene H. Dupee
486 George W. Dupee
486 Arthur Dupee
488 Mrs. Christian Lichtenberger
490 Mr. & Mrs. W. H. Gray
492 Mr. & Mrs. Henry Tifft
496 Mr. & Mrs. Andrew Ortmayer
     & dr.
496 Albert Kuhlmey
502 Mr. & Mrs. C. O. Harz
502 Henry Brockman
508 Mr. & Mrs. Adolph Shakman
512 Mr. & Mrs. Albert F. Borcherdt
512 Miss Martha Starkie
516 Mr. & Mrs. H. Kaufman
518 Mr. & Mrs. F. O. Baumann
518 Mr. & Mrs. Frank Linsenbarth
520 Mr. & Mrs. D. M. Ruggles
520 Mr. & Mrs. Geo. G. Lewis
520 Miss Beatrice Clow
522 August Magnus
522 Mr. & Mrs. H. F. Williams
524 Mr. & Mrs. R. C. Clowry
528 Mr. & Mrs. Adolph Loeb
528 Mr. & Mrs. Henry N. Green-
     baum
532 Dr. & Mrs. Nicholas Senn
536 Mr. & Mrs. Jesse Holladay & drs.

405 Mr. & Mrs. C. R. Larrabee & drs.
405 Rev. Edward A. Larrabee
405 Miss Caroline R. Larrabee
405 Miss E. Wood
407 Mr. & Mrs. H. B. Sherman ,
409 Mr. & Mrs. P. L. Garrity
    Receiving day Thursday
409 Miss Blanche de Chantell Garrity
409 Miss Grace Garrity
409 Dr. Joseph Garrity
411 Mrs. A. Hixson
413 Mrs. M. L. Stern & drs.
413 Daniel Stern
415 Joseph Woodward
415 Mrs. J. K. Woodward
415 Mr. & Mrs. Herbert C.DeCamp
417 Mr. & Mrs.William Troost & dr.
433 George P. Gilman
433 Miss Mary Gilman
433 George P. Gilman jr.
435 Mr. & Mrs. Richard F. Redell
437 Mr. & Mrs. W. H. Parsons
439 Mr. & Mrs. H. B. Franklin & dr.
441 Dr. & Mrs. L. D. Rogers.
445 Mr.& Mrs.Edmund Loewenthal
445 Mr. & Mrs. Bernard Mandl
451 Mrs. M. J. Egan & drs.
453 Mr. & Mrs. M. Wolff
453 Samuel Wolff
453 Benjamin Wolff
453 Nathan Wolff
455 Mr. & Mrs. E. R. Schlick & drs.
    Receiving day Thursday
457 Mr. & Mrs. J. H. Batterman & dr.
459 Mr. & Mrs. R. Philip Gormully
463 N. J. Sandberg
463 Charles Sandberg
463 George Sandberg
465 Mr. & Mrs. Victor Falkenau
465 Mr. & Mrs. Lyman Baird & dr.
465 Max Baird
465 William C. Moulton
465 Rudolf Hasselgren
465 Mr. & Mrs. Homer S. Chandler
465 Mr. & Mrs. W. A. Cissna
    Receiving day Wednesday
467 Paul Rothbarth
467 Mrs. Mary Weichmann
469 Mr. & Mrs. George W.Reessing
473 Mr. & Mrs. John Fanning & drs.
473 Mr. & Mrs. F. C. Hotz
477 Mr. & Mrs. Harold A. Howard

538 Mr. & Mrs. D. H. Tolman
538 Elmer E. Tolman
538 Miss Lucy Bull
540 Mr. & Mrs. J. P. Hand
550 Mr. & Mrs. A. T. Galt
550 Mason Bross
552 Mr. & Mrs. Philo R. King & dr.
554 Mr. &. Mrs. Frank McCauley
556 Mr. & Mrs. J. B. Lynch & drs.
556 Thomas G. Lynch
556 Andrew G. Lynch
558 Mr. & Mrs.C.J.Hambleton & dr.
560 Mr. & Mrs. James S. Norton
564 Mr. & Mrs.John P.Wilson & drs.
568 J. C. Bullock & dr.
568 Carl C. Bullock
572 Mr. & Mrs. Geo. E. Rickcords
584 Mr. & Mrs. Fred K. Maus & dr.
584 Dr. & Mrs. Francis G. Bonynge
584 Mr. & Mrs. Percival Fuller
584 Mr. & Mrs. Frank M. Luce
586 Mr. & Mrs. Horace E. Hurlbut
586 Dr. J. D. Kales
586 Mrs. Frances Kales
586 William R. Kales
588 Mr. & Mrs. George C. Prussing
599 Mr. & Mrs. Fred W. Upham
592 Mr. & Mrs. Louis Stern
592 E. J. Gutmann
594 Mr. & Mrs. Henry Elkan
594 Mr. & Mrs. Jos. Gutmann
596 Mr. & Mrs. Arnold Tripp
600 Mr. & Mrs. A. H. Dainty
600 Mr. & Mrs. Henry C. Bellamy
606 Mr. & Mrs. Matthew J. Swatek
608 Mrs. J. S. Barnes
608 Mr. & Mrs. F. G. Barnes
610 Mr. & Mrs. Truman Penfield
616 Mr. & Mrs. J. B. Grommes
620 Mr. & Mrs. W. C. Egan
626 Mr. & Mrs. S. E. Egan
626 Miss Jennie Egan
628 Charles W. Fullerton
628 Mrs. J. E. Fullerton
628 Miss Mattie S. Hill ·

481 Miss Rebecca S. Rice
481 Miss Mary E. Beedy
483 Dr. & Mrs. Francis A. Henning
    Receiving day Friday
483 Mrs. Maria Anna Heyer
485 Mr. & Mrs. R. L. Davis
    Receiving day Wednesday
487 Mr. & Mrs. John Johnston jr.
    Receiving day Tuesday
487 Henry L. Gay

489 Mr. & Mrs. Joseph C. Ficklin
489 C. A. Underwood
491 Mr. & Mrs. Ulrich Duehr & dr.
491 Mr. & Mrs. Fred T. Evans jr.
491 Mr. & Mrs. W. L. Bush
491 Mr. & Mrs. Wm. L. Haskell
493 Mr. & Mrs. John Miehle jr.
493 Mr. & Mrs. Wm. Inglis
493 Miss Clara Inglis
497 Mr. & Mrs. Chas E. Johnson
497 Mr. & Mrs. Fred'k D. Mont-
      gomery
497 Mr. & Mrs. K. R. Owen
499 Mr. & Mrs. Wm. V. O'Brien
499 Mrs. M. Hand & drs.
499 Mr. & Mrs. Jesse Lowe
501 Dr Ward Greene Clarke
501 Mr. & Mrs. E A. Bigelow
503 Mr. & Mrs. Augustus Warner
505 Mr. & Mrs. John Irwin & drs.
505 John B. Irwin
507 Mr. & Mrs. J. C. Nyman
507 John E. Nyman
507 Fay Nyman
507 Fred Nyman
507 Mr. & Mrs. Louis Bliss
509 Mr. & Mrs. LeGrand W. Perce
      & dr.
509 H. Wallace Perce
513 A. H. Blackall & dr.
515 Mr. & Mrs. R. T. Whelpley
515 Miss Zaidee Gorham
517 Mr. & Mrs. Herman Herbst
519 Mr. & Mrs. DeLancey H. Louder-
      back
519 Mr. & Mrs. Frederic J. Squibb
      Receiving day Tuesday
521 Miss M. E. Harrison
521 Miss Annie Harrison
525 Mr. & Mrs. Albert Cahn
525 Mrs. N. Nathanson
525 Martin Nathanson
527 Mrs. Henrietta Schiff
529 Mr. & Mrs. Thos. C. Haynes
531 Mr. & Mrs. Luther W. McCon-
      nell
533 Mr. & Mrs. Wm. P. Forbush
533 Rev. & Mrs. T. B. Forbush
533 Harry R. Forbush
535 Mr. & Mrs. Charles C. Wallin
535 Mr. & Mrs. Thomas S. Wallin
537 Mr. & Mrs. William Sprague & dr.
537 Fred W. Sprague
541 Mr. & Mrs. George W. Hale & drs.
541 Miss Isabelle H. McKindley
541 Miss Harriet M. McKindley

543 Mr. & Mrs. Eben M. Betts
545 Mr. & Mrs. Elden C. DeWitt
545 Sidney C. Sladden
545 Mrs. M. G. Meech
545 Mr. & Mrs. Jas. S. Woodruff
545 Mr. & Mrs. August W. Rietz
545 Mr. & Mrs. C. W. Farr
545 Mr. & Mrs. Chas. C. Brown
551 John J. Whaley
551 William Swannell
551 Mr. & Mrs. Jos. J. Monahan
551 Mrs. James S. Farrar
551 Roy Farrar
553 Mr. & Mrs. Highland H. Parker
553 Mr. & Mrs. Morris St. P. Thomas
553 Gen. & Mrs. J. D. Bingham
553 William M. Bingham
553 Mr. & Mrs. Fred W. McKinney
555 Mr. & Mrs. Thos. Parker jr.
555 Miss Ella G. Parker
557 Mr. & Mrs. Hugh L. Mason
559 Mr. & Mrs. J. J. Rardon
561 Mr. & Mrs. Graham H. Harris
567 E. A. Matthiessen & drs.
571 Mrs. Caroline E. Stanley
571 Miss Harriet E. Stanley
573 Mr. & Mrs. M. Shields
575 Louis C. Huck
575 Henry Huck
579 Mr. & Mrs. Francis Lackner
585 Mr. & Mrs. J. J. McGrath & dr.
585 Charles H. McGrath
585 J. J. McGrath jr.
587 Mrs. Wm. S. Mellen
587 Miss Gertrude Mellen
589 Mrs. H. D. Colvin
589 Miss Emma Preston
589 Miss L. F. Colvin
589 D. F. Cameron
595 Mr. & Mrs. Ransom J. Morse
595 B. Morse
595 W. D. Morse
597 Mr. & Mrs. C. R. Corbin
597 Frank N. Corbin
597 C. Dana Corbin
599 Mr. & Mrs. Max Morgenthau &
      drs.
      Receive Monday afternoon
599 Mrs. R. Ehrich
601 Mr. & Mrs. Hermann Petersen
      Receiving day 1st Saturday
601 Miss Adelaide Petersen
603 Mr. & Mrs. Emil Petersen & dr.
      Receiving day 2d Tuesday
603 Hugo T. Petersen
603 Miss Freda Petersen

609 Mr. & Mrs. Wm. H. Grubey
609 George W. Grubey
619 Mr. & Mrs. Jacob Rehm & dr.
　　Receive last Friday in mo.
619 William H. Rehm

619 Frank Rehm
623 Mr. & Mrs. Wm. Stewart & drs
627 Mr. & Mrs. T. F. Withrow & dr
627 Mrs. L. J. Tilton
627 Miss Catherine P. Tilton

DELAWARE PLACE.

17 Mrs. R. M. Hooley & dr.
17 Mrs. R. F. Hurlburt
19 Mr. & Mrs. E. B. Preston
19 Miss Marguerite Preston
25 Mr. & Mrs. E. E. Prussing
27 Geo. M. Trowbridge
27 Mrs. J. H. Trowbridge
27 Miss Cornelia Trowbridge
27 Mr. & Mrs. Henry G. Miller
27 Mr. & Mrs Edwin White Moore
29 Mr. & Mrs. Henry B. Mason
49 George S. Morrison
51 Mr. & Mrs. Geo. A. Carpenter
55 Mr. & Mrs. Herman Pabst
57 Mr. & Mrs. Frank L. Hill
57 Mrs. M. E. Stockdale & dr.
57 Mr. & Mrs. W. W. Reid

18 Mrs. Charlotte Nórris & dr.
18 Robert A. Norris
18 Mr. & Mrs. W. E. Heywood
20 Mr. & Mrs. Kimball C. Haycock
24 Mr. & Mrs. Edward Barbour
26 Mr. & Mrs. Wm. A.·Otis
26 G. S. Thurber
26 Wilson L. Mead
26 Ernest W. Morrison
28 Mr. & Mrs. R. T. Brydon
28 Mr. & Mrs. Edward P. Russell
32 Capt. & Mrs. A. A. Dennie
32 Mr. & Mrs. R. E. Rispin
32 Mrs. G. E Dunne
————
95 Mr. & Mrs. A. Collender.

DEMING COURT.

1705 Mr. & Mrs. Henry Rieke & drs.
1713 Mr. & Mrs. H. A. Haugan
1719 Mr. & Mrs. F. A. Powers
1723 Mr. & Mrs. J. W. Kindt
1725 Mr. & Mrs. Jacob Liebmann
1737 Mr. & Mrs. William Sieck
1741 Mr. & Mrs. George Meller
1745 Mr. & Mrs. John C. Schiess
1745 Mr. & Mrs. Edw. R. Eisner
1749 Mr. & Mrs. M. Johnson & dr.
1769 Mr. & Mrs. H. E. Bullock
1773 Mr. & Mrs. E. Gerstenberg & dr.
1907 Dr. & Mrs. R. B. Preble
1907 Mr. & Mrs. C. G. Boldenweck
1907 Mr. & Mrs. H. C. Niblock　·
1907 Mr. & Mrs. D. A. Molton
1911 Mr. & Mrs. O. F. Greifenhagen
1913 Mr. & Mrs. H. H. Rountree
1921 Mr. & Mrs. Geo. R. English
1921 Mr. & Mrs. Benj. Green
1923 Mr. & Mrs. W. Irving Way
1923 Miss Kate Way
1923 Mr. & Mrs. Edward J. Blake

1710 Mr. & Mrs. James Hayde
1720 Mr. & Mrs. Adam Miller
1720 Fred Miller
1730 Mr. & Mrs. Jacob Gross
1732 Mr. & Mrs. C. Husche
1734 Mr. & Mrs. H. W. Meyer
1734 Mr. & Mrs. Carl H. Meyer
1738 Mr. & Mrs. Wm. Schmidt
1754 Mr. & Mrs. C. E. Ernst
1758 Mr. & Mrs. August Heuer
1774 Mr. & Mrs. L. F. Nonnast
1778 Henry Ackhoff
1778 Miss L. Ackhoff
1788 Mr. & Mrs. Horace A. Goodrich
1794 Mr. & Mrs. E. Boettcher
1800 Mr. & Mrs. John Glenn Collins
　　Receiving day Wednesday
1804 Mr. & Mrs. W. J. Rardon
1804 Dr. & Mrs. B. M. Behrens
————
1923 Mr.&Mrs. Douglas Dyrenforth
1953 Mrs. Jennie V. Scherenberg
1953 Henry A. Beneke
1953 Miss Lottie C. Beneke

DIVERSEY STREET.

1607 Dr. & Mrs. C. V. Massey
1911½ Mr. & Mrs. James R. Ward
1911½ Miss Grace Cumett

1534 Mr. & Mrs. R. W. Campion & drs.
1610 George Sugg

1915 Mr. & Mrs. D. A. Devine
1917 Mrs. E. E. L. Woodward
   Receives 1st & 3d Fridays

1742 Dr. & Mrs. G. S. Smith & drs.
   Receiving day Thursday
1742 W. M. Smith
1742 M. L. Smith
1824 Mr. & Mrs. C. E. Affeld
1840 Mr. & Mrs. Thomas Boyle
1852 Mrs. P. J. Maginnis & dr.
1880 Mr. & Mrs. Thomas W. Wing
1884 Mr. & Mrs. P. O'Malley
1932 Mr. & Mrs. Joseph Stockton
2004 Mr. & Mrs. E. S. Dreyer
2004 Mrs. Charlotta Billegman

1610 Mr. & Mrs. Eugene Sugg
1624 Mr. & Mrs. Alfred J. Cox
1624 Alexis J. Cox
1624 Alfred W. Cox
1628 Mathias Thome
1628 Miss Victoria Thome
1628 Leo Thome
1704 Mr. & Mrs. Gustaf Stieglitz
1712 Mrs. Catherine Kane
1712 Mrs. M. Mack
1712 Mrs. Maud Wilmot
1722 Mr. & Mrs. A. Maritzen
1724 Mrs. E. Heidleberger
   Receiving day Thursday
1726 Miss Ella Sullivan
1740 Mr. & Mrs. Arthur G. Morey
1740 Mr. & Mrs. Charles J. Morey

DIVISION STREET.

305 Dr. & Mrs. A. H. Lane
305 Dr. E. M. Smith
305 Dr. & Mrs. E. D. Smith
307 Dr. & Mrs. C. W. Swank
451 Dr. & Mrs. Robert Eckart
537 Mr. & Mrs. J. Fred Studley
557 Mr. & Mrs. George A. Mayo
557 Mr. & Mrs. Franz Peterson
561 Mr. & Mrs. Moulton J. Cross &
   dr.
563 Mr. & Mrs. Geo. Bingham
563 Miss Alice Mitton
565 M. J. Keane
565 Miss Laura J. Keane
567 Mr. & Mrs. G. K. Shoenberger
569 Mrs. Theodore Phillips & dr.
569 Charles W. Phillips
571 Mr. & Mrs. Louis Adler
573 Mrs Kate Phelizot
573 George Phelizot
573 James A. Hemingway
575 Mr. & Mrs. David L. Barnes
577 Mr. & Mrs. John West & drs.
607 Mr. & Mrs. George D. Rumsey
609 Mr. & Mrs. A. S. Littlefield
613 Mr. & Mrs. Frederick T. West

598 Mr. & Mrs. E. J. Strong
600 Mr. & Mrs. M. W. Welles
600 E. P. Welles
600 Fred W. Welles
602 Mrs. R. F. Bower
602 Miss Annie T. Bower
604 Charles D. Bickford
604 Mr. & Mrs. Wm. S. Crosby
604 Mr. & Mrs. J. Henry Norton

376 Dr. & Mrs. William J. Webb
462 Dr. John Bartlett
554 Dr. & Mrs. F. A. Hess
558 Mrs. Josephine Albert & drs.
558 Charles W. Albert
560 Mrs. Ida Manchester & dr.
560 Mr. & Mrs. Wm. Warren Case
564 Mr. & Mrs. Joseph R. Wilkins
   & dr.
566 Mr. & Mrs. Richard C. Crawford
568 Mr. & Mrs. Sigmund Zeisler
568 Miss Rosa Kanner
568 August Jouve
570 Mr. & Mrs. H. P. Robinson
572 Mr. & Mrs. James C. Bishop .
572 H. R. Bishop jr.
574 Mr. & Mrs. H. W. Chandler
574 Col. & Mrs. Stephen W. Stryker
   & dr.
578 Mr. & Mrs. Howard O. Edmonds
578 Mr. & Mrs. Lewis H. Falley
580 Dr. Thomas G. Corlett
580 M. M. Boddie
580 John T. Boddie
582 Mrs. W. Green & drs.
586 Mrs. Elizabeth W. Morse & dr.
586 Charles Fleetwood
588 Thomas W. Yardley
588 Mr. & Mrs. Robert W. Hunt
592 Mrs. M. J. VanKeuren
   Receiving day Wednesday
592 Dr. & Mrs. Joseph Little
594 Mr. & Mrs. William Dunn
594 Miss Alida Leavenworth
596 Mr. & Mrs. Alexander W. Pond

604 Colin C. H. Fyffe
604 William J. Fyffe
604 Dr. Edith A. H. Fyffe
608 Maj. & Mrs. Geo.W.Baird & drs.
608 George H. Baird
608 Mr. & Mrs. J. P. Dabney
608 Mrs. E. S. Adams & dr.

608 Samuel Adams
608 Mr. & Mrs. Ira C. Wood
610 Mr. & Mrs. Samuel G. Taylor
612 Mr. & Mrs. Chas. H. Ferry
614 J. Devereux York
614 Mrs. E. J. T. Brooke
620 Mrs. John C. Coonley

DOVER STREET.

3177 Mr. & Mrs. Edward A.Saalfeld
3179 Mr. & Mrs. Walter V. Hayt

3207 Mr. & Mrs. M. O'Shaughnessy

DUNNING STREET.

1131 Mr. & Mrs. W. H. Hackett
1131 Mrs. M. J. Laing
1337 Mr. & Mrs Cyrus A. Hull
1401 Mr. & Mrs. Milo D. Matteson

1314 Mrs. M. A. Walsh & dr.
1516 Dr. & Mrs. John A. Tomhagen

EARLY AVENUE.

1043 Mr. & Mrs. G. F. Mills
1111 Mr. & Mrs. L. B. Bishop
1111 Paul Bishop
1115 Mr. & Mrs. A. D. Williston
1117 Mr. & Mrs. H. A. Dayton

1086 Mr. & Mrs. A. Stewart
Receiving day Wednesday
1096 Mr. & Mrs. Patrick Tyrrell
1110 Mr. & Mrs. M. N. Simons

EDGECOMB COURT.

1423 Mr. & Mrs. T. Drummond Gray
1423 Mrs. D. L. Boone
1423 H. C. Boone
1423 S. O. Boone
1425 Mr. & Mrs. Louis E. Woodbury
Receiving day Wednesday
1425 Mr. & Mrs. W. H. Woodbury
1447 Mr. & Mrs. H. W. Nicholson
1471 Mr. & Mrs. Pierre Funck

1444 Mr. & Mrs. Thomas Harrison & dr.
1444 Miss Gertrude Harrison
1444 C. Thomas Harrison
1454 Mr. & Mrs. George H. Wessling
1464 Mr. & Mrs. J. C. Finch
1466 Mr. & Mrs. J. C. Freeman

1471 Dr. & Mrs. H. B. Kaufman

ELAINE STREET.

49 Mr. & Mrs. Frederick Liese & drs.

50 Mr. & Mrs. John Chiville

ELM STREET.

345 J. P. Lauth
369 Dr. Norval Pierce
369 Mrs. S. J. Wethrell
369 James B. Wethrell
369 Edward H. Wethrell
371 Mrs. B. A. Branch
383 Mr. & Mrs. H. P. Ide
385 Mr. & Mrs. John Miller
389 Mr. & Mrs. Gustav A. Kirchner

408 Mr. & Mrs. George D. Cobb
408 Mr. & Mrs. W. H. Thomson
424 Mr. & Mrs. Hugh W. Montgomery
426 Mr. & Mrs. Geo. A. Hellman & dr. *Receiving day Tuesday*
426 George A. Hellman jr.
428 Mr. & Mrs. R. G. Calder
428 George W. G. Calder

17

407 Mrs. Edward Corse
407 Charles Prindiville
407 Thomas W. Prindiville
407 Miss Marguerite Prindiville
433 Mr. & Mrs. H. J. Porter
433 Miss Annie Riddell
437 Mr. & Mrs. William S. Warren
437½ Mr. & Mrs. Chas. J. Haines
437½ John Allen Haines
441 Mr..& Mrs. Lloyd Milnor
447 Mr. & Mrs. J. C. F. Brocklebank
447 Miss Barbara Durell
455 Mr. & Mrs. Charles C. Adsit
455 Mr. & Mrs. Charles E. Dole
455½ Mr. & Mrs. Rodney D. Bradley
455½ Mr. & Mrs. Ed. F. Bradley
461 Mrs. George W. Culver
461 Frank H. Culver
465 Mr. & Mrs. Moses J. Wentworth
469 Mr. & Mrs. DeWitt C. Cregier
        Receiving day Thursday
469 DeWitt C. Cregier jr.
469 Washington R. Cregier
471 Mr. & Mrs. L. H. Boldenweck
        & drs.
471 Peter Busch
473 Mr. & Mrs. Arthur J. Magnus
———
474 Frank M. Andrews
474 Louis Carpenter
474 Hamlin Garland
476 Mr. & Mrs. Chas. L. Strobel
478 Mr. & Mrs. Cherles H. Conover
    Receiving day Monday afternoon
478 Miss Olive Rumsey

436 Mr. & Mrs. Wm. R. Voshell
440 Mr. & Mrs. George D. Gregory
440 James C. Gregory
444 Dr. & Mrs. M. R. Brown
446 Mr. & Mrs. Francis Keeling
446 Mrs. Louisa Leonard
448 Mr. & Mrs. Oscar Charles
450 Mr. & Mrs. Robert H. Bulkeley
452 Judge & Mrs. George Evans
452 Lynden Evans
454 Mrs. T. J. Marsh
454 Henry W. Marsh
456 David L. Gallup
456 Miss Agnes Gallup
456 Miss Lila Gallup
458 Mr. & Mrs. J. D. Springer
460 Mr. & Mrs. James B. Forgan
460 Mrs. Donald Murray & dr.
462 Mrs. Samuel J. Walker & drs.
462 Dr. Samuel J. Walker
462 Wm. Ernest Walker
464 Mrs. U. S. Harper
464 Mrs. Joseph S. Sharp
464 Edward F. Sharp
466 Mr. & Mrs. W. F. Merrill
466 Miss S. S. Fessenden
468 Mr. & Mrs. Ovington Ross
468 Mrs. George P. Ross
468 William Hulin
470 Mr. & Mrs. James E. Eagle
472 Mr. & Mrs. F. A. Luce
472 A. S. Luce
472 Mrs. E. A. Prindle
474 Mr. & Mrs. Wilbur G. Bentley
474 Mrs. Juliette Watters

ERIE STREET.

243 Dr. & Mrs. W. A. Hawley & dr.
        Receiving day Thursday
243 N. G. Hawley
267 Dr. & Mrs. G. Hessert
269 Mr. & Mrs. S. M. Henderson & dr.
        Receiving day Thursday
269 Mr. & Mrs. Chas. W. Rhodes &
    dr.   *Receive 1st Thursday*
269 William Rhodes
269 Miss Katharine Rhodes
281 Dr. & Mrs. N. J. Dorsey & dr.
299 Mrs. James A. Hutchison & drs.
299 Stanton Hutchison
301 Mr. & Mrs. Ambrose Cramer
311 Mr. & Mrs. H. H. Porter
317 Mr. & Mrs. S. M. Nickerson
        Receiving day Wednesday p.m.
317 Mr. & Mrs. R. C. Nickerson

266 James H. Pierce
266 Edgar A. Bancroft
266 Alex. A. McCormick
268 Mr. & Mrs. W. R. Hartley
268 Mrs. C. C. Parker
272 Frank Vail
272 William W. Hook
272 J. Frank Upham
272 Mrs. J. Upham & drs.
272 Miss L. Upham
276 Mrs. C. Dummert & drs.
282 R. W. Lloyd
282 C. B. McMullen
282 Adolph Traub
294 Mr. & Mrs. Charles S. McEntee
296 Mrs. M. W. Drew
296 Fred L. Drew
296 Frank M. Byron

317 Mrs. A. C. Crosby
363 Henry I. Sheldon
363 Miss Sheldon
369 Mr. & Mrs. George SpencerWillits
Receiving day Wednesday
399 Gen. Walter C. Newberry & drs.
405 Mr. & Mrs. Edward Stanley Worthington *Rec. day Wed.* 3 *to* 6
407 Mr. & Mrs. T. W. Wadsworth
421 Robert Fergus
421 B. F. Fergus
421 Miss Jessie Fergus
423 Dr.& Mrs.W.G.Cummins & drs.
427 Commodore & Mrs. Robert Rae
Receiving day Wednesday
427 Harry Heisel Rae
_____
412 Dr. & Mrs. Frederick D. Owsley

298 Mr. & Mrs. G. W. Roe
298 Mr. & Mrs. John F. R. Robie
298 Mrs. Thomas Burrows
302 Frederick W. Bleike
304 Mr. & Mrs. W. R. Sears & dr.
312 Mr. & Mrs. R. R. Cable & drs.
378 Mr. & Mrs. John T. Noyes
380 Mrs. B. C. Davy
380 H. G. Davy
380 Harry Vincent
380 Mr. & Mrs. M. W. McReynolds
382 Mr. & Mrs. T. E. Copelin
384 Mr. & Mrs. W. J. Quan & drs.
384 James E. Quan
384 Henry W. Quan
384 T. Albert Quan
404 Mr. & Mrs. V. K. Spencer
406 Mr. & Mrs. Russell Whitman
408 Mr. & Mrs. Heaton Owsley

EUGENIE STREET.

157 Dr. & Mrs. Wm. C. Sanford
157 Mr. & Mrs. Robt. J. Halle
157½ Mr. & Mrs. J. Kasper
157½ Mr. & Mrs. Walter V. Kasper
159 Mr. & Mrs. T. M. Knox
159½ Mr. & Mrs. Frank E. Nellis
Receiving day Friday
161 Mr. & Mrs. Jas. H. Adams & dr.
161 Orlando Ware
163 Mr. & Mrs. W. J. Davis
165 Mr. & Mrs. John F. Jelke

122 Mrs. Kate Birren
170 Mr. & Mrs. A. Holinger
170 Mr. & Mrs. W. Haggerman
170 Mr. & Mrs. D. H. Rust
172 Mr. & Mrs. Julius Ascher
172 Mr. & Mrs. Albert Stern
174 Dr. & Mrs. Carl Beck
_____
171 Mr. & Mrs. Julius Wagner&drs.
173 Mr. & Mrs. John C. Ender
173 Eugene H. Ender

EVANSTON AVENUE.

95 Mrs. A. Alfonso Oldfield
95 Dr. & Mrs. J. K. Winer
103 Mr.&Mrs.Wm.VanBenthuysen
Receiving day Thursday
105 Mr. & Mrs. E. William Kalb
Receiving day Wednesday
107 Mr. & Mrs. Charles M. White
115 Mr. & Mrs. Lloyd J. Smith
119 Mr. & Mrs. R. S. Elder
147 Mr. & Mrs. Robt. Sommers & dr.
Receiving day 1st & last Wednesday
149 Mr. & Mrs. C. F. Jacobs
175 Mr. & Mrs. L. B. Hitchings
Receiving day Thursday
175 Mrs. C. B. Allen
Receiving day Thursday
179 Mr. & Mrs. Tabor P. Randall
179 Mrs. A. S. Randall
225 Mr. & Mrs. G. A. Fleischer
283 Mr. & Mrs. F. F. Henning

88 Mrs. Janette Dessauer & dr.
96 Mr. & Mrs. Granville Bates & drs.
162 Mr. & Mrs. Samuel Taussig
296 Mr. & Mrs. George F. Blanke
488 Mr. & Mrs. T. Howard
488 W. H. Howard
514 Dr. & Mrs. Louis L. Gregory
534 Mr. & Mrs. James Payne & dr.
580 Mrs. H. F. Spread
Receiving day Wednesday
614 Mrs. Ida Jordan
Receiving day last Wednesday in mo.
614 Carl W. Jordan
664 Mr.& Mrs.William Ristow&dr.
664 Mr. & Mrs. John Wischover
664 Mr. & Mrs. James Young
890 Dr. & Mrs. Samuel P. Hedges
900 Mr. & Mrs. J.Wyndham-Quinn Channer
Receiving day Thursday

285 Mr. & Mrs. John L. Flannery
    Receiving day Thursday
385 Mr. & Mrs. John Koch & drs.
395 Mr. & Mrs. J. C. Morper
395 Lawrence J. Morper
427 Mr. & Mrs. William S. Young
437 Mr. & Mrs. William Hudson
453 Mr. & Mrs. J. D. McIlvaine
457 Mr. & Mrs. Edward A. Blake
543 Mr. & Mrs. J. E. Tilt & drs.
693 Mr. & Mrs.OliverColborne&dr.
699 Mr. & Mrs. Edw. L. Smith&drs.
699 Henry Smith
739 Mr. & Mrs. Dwight B. Heard
901 Mr. & Mrs. Henry E.Longwell
    Receive Wednesdays
905 Mr. & Mrs. Noah F. Gorsuch
    & dr.
907 Mrs. Eliza Mize
907 Mrs. Hattie A. Bischoff
917 Mr. & Mrs. James Nicol
921 Mr. & Mrs.Jas. Stuart Temple-
    ton
921 James E. Templeton
sw. cor. Buena av. Mrs. James B.
    Waller & drs.

906 Mr. & Mrs. Thomas B. Dohan
912 Mr. & Mrs. W. W. White
1026 Mr. & Mrs. F. Geudtner
    Receiving day 1st Saturday in mo.
1026 Charles P. Geudtner
1050 Mrs. E. H. McDermitt
1050 Miss J. H. McDermitt
1088 Mr. & Mrs. C. A. Spoehr
2664 Mr. & Mrs. A. Brisboit
2678 Mr. & Mrs. C. D. Lunceford
2682 Mr. & Mrs. Oscar M. Smith &
    drs.
2704 Mr. & Mrs. T. J. Sellinger

———

1031 Mr. & Mrs. C. F. Dunderdale
    & drs.
1033 Mr. & Mrs. Eugene Field
    & dr.
1033 Mrs. Ida B. Below
1035 Mr. & Mrs. R. Evans
1037 Mr. & Mrs. J. W. Hiltman
1039 Mr. & Mrs. Hart Tayler
1039 Mrs. Julia H. Taylor
1039 E. H. Taylor
2653 Mr. & Mrs. Cyrus M. Avery

FARGO AVENUE.

811 Mr. & Mrs. Harry C. Edwards
915 Mr. & Mrs. William I.McMaster

924 Mr. & Mrs. Ben M. Smith
930 Mr. & Mrs. William H. Harman
936 Mr. & Mrs. Thomas W. Kava-
    nagh

FARWELL AVENUE.

467 Rev. & Mrs. RegestreW.Bland
471 Mr. & Mrs. Jacob Snyder & dr.
545 Mr. & Mrs. Merrick B. Dean
715 Mr. & Mrs. Frederic D. Gifford
729 Mr. & Mrs. Geo.M.MacDonald
811 William H. Titus
811 Mrs. M. A. Titus & dr.
827 Mr. & Mrs. Jacob P. Easter &
    drs.
827 Joseph H. Easter
907 Mr. & Mrs. James Markey

464 Mr. & Mrs. Henry C. Foster &
    dr.
464 William H. Foster
726 Mr. & Mrs. Cyrus B.McDonald
808 Mr. & Mrs. Jay J. Read
1028 Rev. & Mrs. Charles Braith-
    waite

———

907 James B. Markey
915 Mr. & Mrs. Gilbert C. Pryor
1005 Mr. & Mrs. Claude C. Hill

FAY AVENUE.

4128 Mr. & Mrs. James J. Barbour
nr. Pratt av. John L. Patterson

nr Pratt av. Mr. & Mrs. James W.
    Patterson

NORTH FIFTY-NINTH STREET.

1109 Mr. & Mrs. Dennis Ward&drs.

FLORENCE COURT.

nr. Indian Boundary rd. Mr. & Mrs.
William E. Hatterman

FOREST AVENUE.
(Rogers Park.)

4284 Mrs. Mary E. Thomas & dr.
4284 Mr. & Mrs. James G. Redfield
4364 Rev. & Mrs. John O. Ferris

FREDERICK STREET.

1715 Mr. & Mrs. P. O. Fiedler
1717 Mr. & Mrs. Peter Rinderer
1727 Mr. & Mrs. James Miles
1727 Mr. & Mrs. H. A. Kasten
1731 Mr. & Mrs. C. F. Baseler
1751 Mr. & Mrs. William Schick
1751 Charles E. Schick
1807 Mr. & Mrs. Sidney C. Eastman
1807 Mrs. Z. Eastman
1809 Mr. & Mrs. D. L. Morrill
1809 Mrs. Ellen V. Eaton
1809 Mr. & Mrs. Lawrence Hessel-
    roth
1815 Mrs. Louis Reinach
1817 Mr. & Mrs. John C. Windheim
1829 Mr. & Mrs. Herman Hartwig
1831 Mrs. L. W. Golding & drs.
1833 Mr. & Mrs. C. Lotz
1835 Mrs. E. E. Bromilow
1851 Mr. & Mrs. D. B. Elliott & drs.
1851 Charles G. Blake
1853 Mrs. Mary Jackson
1853 Amzi W. Strong
1855 Mr. & Mrs. Duncan O. Welty
1855 Mr. & Mrs. Edwin S. Jennison
1855 Mr. & Mrs. Edward Dickinson
1857 Mr. & Mrs. C. P. Stacy

1716 Mr. & Mrs. Fred Deecken
1744 Mr. & Mrs. H. C. Dovenmuehle
1760 John W. Gibbons
1808 Mr. & Mrs. Chas. C. Holton
1808 Ethan A. Holton
1808 Mr. & Mrs. K. E. Morgan
1808 Mr. & Mrs. G. E. Keasel
1810 Mr. & Mrs. E. B. Humphrey
1810 Mr. & Mrs. Samuel M. Rich-
    ardson
1810 Mr. & Mrs. L. M. Richardson
1816 Mr. & Mrs. Louis Schroeder
1818 Mr. & Mrs. E. A. Furst
1822 Mr. & Mrs. David R. Shively
1832 Mr. & Mrs. Ferdinand Schap-
    per
1834 Dr. & Mrs. G. C. Paoli
1838 Mr. & Mrs. G. B. Newman
1838 Mr. & Mrs. Matthew P. Gilbert
1838 Clarence Runals
1840 Mr. & Mrs. Geo. Roehling
1850 Mr. & Mrs. George W. Linn
1854 Mr. & Mrs. Fred'k J. Tucker
1854 Mr. & Mrs. R. L. Thornton
1856 Mr. & Mrs. Morris H. Crapser

FREMONT STREET.

183 Rev. Wm. Bartling & dr.
195 Dr. & Mrs. William Thies & dr.
    Receive Thursday
197 Mr. & Mrs. Harold Zimmerman
201 Mrs. George Will
201 Henry F. Martin
203 Mr. & Mrs. J. K. Sutton
203 Mr. & Mrs. Harry B. Sutton
205 Mr. & Mrs. R. P. Fruer & drs.
207 William Kreicker
209 Mr. & Mrs. Gustav Pick
211 Mr. & Mrs. Ernest B. Stuart & dr.
213 Mr. & Mrs. Henry Spain & dr.
213 Mr. & Mrs. Charles Dasenbrook

158 Mr. & Mrs. Isidore Levy & drs.
158 Max Levy
166 Mr. & Mrs. Edward Zipf
168 Mr. Henry W. Heuermann & drs.
168 James C. McNaughton
168 Guy McNaughton
170 Mr. & Mrs. Alex. Klappenbach
174 Mr. & Mrs. Michael F. Mahony
174 Mr. & Mrs. John C. Wright
202 Mr. & Mrs. C. D. Shoemaker
224 Mrs. Charlotte Cohen
226 Mr. & Mrs. Leopold Sonnen-
    schein
228A Mr. & Mrs. Adolph Kraus

215 Mr. & Mrs. William D. Meeker
217 Mr. & Mrs. Charles Roberts & dr.
221 Mr. & Mrs. Judson F. Going
221 Mr. & Mrs. A. J. Monat
225 Mr. & Mrs. William Harms
227 Mr. & Mrs. Joseph A. Sauter
229 Miss Louise Bauer
229 Miss Julia Bauer
229 Miss Alma Bauer
259 Mr. & Mrs. John Bradford
261 Mr. & Mrs. C. A. Jordan
261 Mr. & Mrs. Uriah W. Weston
265 Mr. & Mrs. Adolph Graeff & dr.
265 Otto Graeff
267 Mr. & Mrs. Albert Bunte
271 Mr. & Mrs. Geo. E. Zimmerman
271 Mr. & Mrs. A. P. Davis

228B Mrs. Jacob Danek
228B Miss Rosa Keller
256 Mr. & Mrs. G. C. Patterson
258 Mr. & Mrs. David Burr & dr.
260 Mr. & Mrs. H. H. Hirschfield & dr.
266 Mr. & Mrs. Charles Steinbeiss
268 Mr. & Mrs. Wm. C. Pfister
276 Fritz Frillman & dr.
276 Mrs. Josephine Bateman
278 Mr. & Mrs. John Baur
Receive Wednesday

277 Mr. & Mrs. Jacob Lengacher
277 Oscar F. Lengacher
279 Mr. & Mrs. Joseph Shaw
281 Mr. & Mrs. W. C. Dayton

FULLERTON AVENUE.

465 Mr. & Mrs. Charles H. Cowan
465 Harry R. Cowan
465 Wm. K. Cowan
469 Mr. & Mrs. F. M. Trask
469 Mrs. M. P. Hopkins
473 Mr. & Mrs. J. Doyle
475 Mr. & Mrs. A. Thornton
475 E. L. Thornton
475 E. A. Thornton
481 Mr. & Mrs. Geo. O. Fairbanks
481 Mr. & Mrs. R. L. Brown
483 Mrs. F. B. Hosmer
485 Mr. & Mrs. Wm. Moerecke & dr.
485 Otto C. Moerecke
485 Frederick Moerecke
487 Mr. & Mrs. H. B. Merritt
489 Mr. & Mrs. G. B. Dickinson
489 W. W. Dickinson
491 Mr. & Mrs. Charles R. Kappes
491 Mr. & Mrs. J. Henry Kappes
Receiving day Tuesday
493 Mr. & Mrs. Wm. C. Nichols
493 Francis H. Nichols
495 Mr. & Mrs. Ernest L. Ransome & dr.
497 Mr. & Mrs. B. L. Hobson
499 Mr. & Mrs. Frank Price
501 Mr. & Mrs. J. B. Moll
503 Mr. & Mrs. William Gregg
503 Dr. Mary E. Gregg
507 Mrs. E. P. Judd
507 Miss Anna E. Potwin
509 Mr. & Mrs. R. S. Benham & dr.
511 Mr. & Mrs. James L. Rowe & dr.
513 Mr. & Mrs. Fred. H. Hall

274 Mr. & Mrs. Albert J. Ward
280 Mr. & Mrs. John McDonald & dr.
280 Harry J. McDonald
280 Joseph N. McDonald
328 Mr. & Mrs. Louis C. Spooner
332 Mr. & Mrs. Gustave A. Bunte
336 Mrs. Chas. F. Hatterman & dr
336 Mrs. C. O. Becker
338 Dr. J. Harry Haiselden
338 Mr. & Mrs. George Haiselden
338 Mr. & Mrs. G.H.Harlacher&dr.
342 Dr. & Mrs. J. Johnston Bell
342 Mrs. Hattie Myers
342 Miss Lottie Bell
344 Mr. & Mrs. Archibald D. Browne
364 Mr. & Mrs. Michael Cahill & drs.
368 Dr. & Mrs. Gerald Edmunds
454 Mr. & Mrs. John M. Evans
456 Mr. & Mrs. James Andrews & dr.
456 John J. Healy
456 George H. Pratt
464 Mrs. Cynthia E. Ferry & dr.
468 Mr. & Mrs. S. L. Hopper
468 Mr. & Mrs. R. F. Maxwell
472 Mr. & Mrs. Chas.H.Chapin&dr.
474 Mr. & Mrs. M. A. Hawkes
478 Mr. & Mrs. William Ostatag
480 Mr. & Mrs. John Gilliam
480 Mr.&Mrs. Frederick C. DeLong
Receiving day Wednesday
484 Mr. & Mrs. Leander Sawyer
486 Dr. J. G. Forrester
486 Mr. & Mrs. Frederick F. Cain
490 Mrs. V. A. Boyer

515 Dr. & Mrs. J. E. Hequembourg
629 Edward H. Kemper
631 Mr. & Mrs. A. Schweitzer
631 Dr. & Mrs. C. Rutherford
 Receiving day Tuesday
631 Dr. & Mrs. C. L. Clancy
635 Mr. & Mrs. Howard V. Tobey
635 Mrs. S. Hirsch
635 Mr. & Mrs. Albert D. Morris
637 Mr. & Mrs. Henry T. Miller
637 Mr. & Mrs. Alfred R. Varian
639 Mrs. Margaret Revell & dr.
 Receiving day Wednesday
639 J. T. Revell
639 D. J. Revell
639 Mr. & Mrs. W. H. Ryan
639 Mr. & Mrs. Alfred F. Edler
641 Mr. & Mrs. P. Peterson
643 Mr. & Mrs. Ernest Ammon & dr.
643 Frederick E. Ammon
645 Mr. & Mrs. Simon Blum
647 Rev. & Mrs. John Rusk
647 Miss Nellie B. Rusk
649 Mr. & Mrs. Albert Miller
649 Mrs. Herman Kirchstein
651 Mr. & Mrs. Sam A. Hofeld &dr.
651 Felix S. Hofeld
657 Mr. & Mrs. Frederick Hauck
657 Mr. & Mrs. Otto W. Hauck
669 Mr. & Mrs. Adolph Karpen
669 Mrs. Anna Swanson
679 Mrs. M. I. Lidell
679 Mr. & Mrs. W. E. Wills
681 Dr. & Mrs. J. J. Thompson
681 Mr. & Mrs. Charles B. Prouty
683 Mr. & Mrs. J. Henry Pank
685 Mr. & Mrs. Herman Vollner
685 Dr. Ivo Bernauer
695 Mr. & Mrs. Henry Schaller
715 Mr. & Mrs. George Wolff
717 Mr. & Mrs. John C. Barker &dr.
717 Miss Agnes Carpenter
719 Mr.& Mrs.H.Hemmelgarn
719 Mr. & Mrs. A. von Glahn
725 Mr. & Mrs. R. T. Goode
725 Mrs. George Stade
727 Mr. & Mrs. Charles Daniels
727 Mr. & Mrs. F. H. Tubbs
727 Mr. & Mrs. C. A. Servoss
727 Mr. & Mrs. James F. McChesney
729 Mr. & Mrs. Edward A. Parker
729 Mr. & Mrs. Willis J. Abbott
729 Mr. & Mrs. Nelson A. White
731 Mr. & Mrs. Harry Ward Maxwell
731 Mr. & Mrs. A. I. Wittman

490 Miss Caroline Specht
490 Mrs. Robert Miller & dr.
494 Mrs. Marie J. Morgan
494 Mrs. Eliza A. Hawkes
494 Mr. & Mrs. E. Frobenius
496 Mr. & Mrs. Benj. C. Chambers
496 Mr.& Mrs.Charles W.McCorkle
498 M . & Mrs. George Newkirk &
 drs.
500 Mr. & Mrs. Edward Cheetham
500 Edward L. Cheetham
504 Mr. & Mrs. Martin Howard
508 Mr. & Mrs. W. R. Morrison
516 Mr. & Mrs. Ernest C. Cook
518 Mr. & Mrs. H. C. Grosse & drs.
522 Mrs. W. W. Younglove & dr.
526 Mr. & Mrs. Wm.F.Zimmermann
566 Mr. & Mrs. H. Hudler
568 Mr. & Mrs. William Brace
570 Dr. & Mrs. J. R. Waldmeyer
570 Mr. & Mrs. A. Gilbert Heron
574 Mr. & Mrs. Thos. P. Hallinan
 Receiving day Wednesday
574 Harry J. Hallinan
576 Dr. E. I. Kerlin
576 Miss Melissa A. Kerlin
576 Miss Lizzie M. Kerlin
578 Mr. & Mrs. Justice Wilson
584 Mr. & Mrs. Arthur Hawxhurst
588 Mr. & Mrs. Frederick Wallis
592 Mr. & Mrs. Max Tonk
616 Mrs. E. Holzwarth
624 Mr. & Mrs. Leon Wolf
628 Mr. & Mrs. Zero Marx
638 C. A. Tinkham
638 Mr. & Mrs. S. B. Titcomb& drs.
638 Arthur B. Titcomb
640 Mr. & Mrs. W. P. Dunn & dr.
640 Robert W. Dunn
640 Mrs. A. A. Pettengill
642 Mr. & Mrs. Ernest Hecht
642 Walter Hecht
644 Mr. & Mrs. F. H. Guhl
644 Walter F. Guhl
646 Mr. & Mrs. Leo Austrian
 Receive 2d Thursday
650 Mr. & Mrs. L. O. Kohtz
652 Mr. & Mrs. L. Wolff
654 Mr. & Mrs. Eugene Lipkau
656 Mr. & Mrs. L. Schaffner & drs.
674 Mrs. Daniel Jackson & dr.
674 Miss M. E. Philbrick
676 A. W. Stewart
676 Miss M. H. Stewart
676 Miss S. J. Stewart
678 Mr. & Mrs. Anthony Freeman

747 Mrs. C. P. Buckingham
747 E. H. Buckingham
789 Mrs. Julia F. Porter
789 James W. Porter
789 James F. Porter
789 Mrs. N. S. Foster
——
726 Mr. & Mrs. Edward Kreut-
      zinger
750 Mr. & Mrs. Fred L. Rossbach
750 Mr. & Mrs. Hugh E. Bayle
752 Mr. & Mrs. Stephen C.Walkerje
754 Dr. & Mrs. Abram J. Moore
754 Mrs. J. B. Vaughan

686 Mr. & Mrs. B. Edwards
690 Mr. & Mrs. J. D. Zernitz
690 John P. Zernitz
690 Julius C. Zernitz
698 M. W. Robinson
698 Miss Ethel Robinson
698 Walter B. Robinson
700 Rev. Wm. J. Petrie
710 Mr. & Mrs. A. Bigelow
710 Norman Hapgood
712 Mr. & Mrs. C. M. Staiger
716 Dr. & Mrs. Gustav Futterer
720 Mr. & Mrs. Robt. Schmeling
720 Mr. & Mrs. S. A. Swanson

GARFIELD AVENUE.

423 Mr. & Mrs. E. Keefe & dr.
423 E. F. Keefe
445 Mr. & Mrs. Dennis W. Sullivan
525 Mr. & Mrs. Olaf Vider & drs.
537 Mr. & Mrs. Augustus C. Barler
——
532 Peter Van Vlissingen
532 Mr. & Mrs. Louis K. Waldron
532 Dr. W. T. Belfield
544 to 552 Pelham Flats.
     2 Mr. & Mrs. Chas. C. Glazier
     3 Mr. & Mrs. Essington N.
         Gilfillan
     4 Mrs. M. L. Lamb
     6 Mr. & Mrs. D. F. Danforth
     8 Miss L. A. Dimon
     8 Miss B. Montgomery
    10 Mr. & Mrs. Wm. W. Porter
    10 G. M. Porter
    15 Mr. & Mrs. P. A. B. Kennedy
    22 Mr. & Mrs. Wm. G. Forrest
    28 Mr. & Mrs. F. W. Hamilton
568 Mr. & Mrs. S. Wilmer Cannell

228 Mr. & Mrs. Henry C. Bartling
266 Mr. & Mrs. S. J. Hallock & dr.
268 Mr. & Mrs. Samuel Piggott
270 Mr. & Mrs. Anton Pfeiffer
290 Mr. & Mrs. Charles T. Wilt jr.
396 Mr. & Mrs. Sam. B. Chase & dr.
398 Mr. & Mrs. Albert G. Schmidt
442 Mr. & Mrs. E. C. Jager & drs.
446 Mr. & Mrs. M. E. Page jr.
450 Dr. & Mrs. W. P. Verity
486 Mr. & Mrs. Philip Apfel & dr.
486 Philip Apfel jr.
524 Mr. & Mrs. N. Banks Cregier
524 Mrs. Anna Stearns
524 Mrs. Margaret Schwender
526 Mr.& Mrs.Chas. Henry Thomp-
      son
530 Mr. & Mrs. August Heinze
530 Hermann Heinze
530 Max Heinze
530 William Heinze
530 August Heinze jr.
530 Mr. & Mrs. Albert Heimann

GARY PLACE.

1741 Dr. & Mrs. A. G. Schloesser

1718 Mr. & Mrs. Arthur Labes

GEORGE STREET.

1503 Mr. & Mrs. W. B. Getty
1521 Mr. & Mrs. George W. Reed

1236 Mr. & Mrs. B. A. L. Thomson

GEORGE AVENUE.

1905 Mr. & Mrs. John G. Smyth
1905 Martin R. Smyth
——
1910 Mr. & Mrs. M. S. Bacon & drs
1926 Mr. & Mrs. Anton Boenert

1824 Mr. & Mrs. Geo. Brauckmann
1844 Mrs. F. W. Passmore
1844 Miss Alice Williams
1844 Miss Helen R. Williams
1908 Mr. & Mrs. E. R. Bacon

GOETHE STREET.

151 Mrs. E. Rhode
151 Rudolph E. Rhode
151 Otto Rhode
151 Oswald Von Lengerke
171 Mr. & Mrs. E. A. Valentine
    Receiving day Monday
171 Mrs. J. H. McAvoy
173 Mr. & Mrs. Wm. A. Parker
175 Mr. & Mrs. Geo. Higginson jr.

240 Mrs. Wm. C. Goudy
240 Mr. & Mrs. Ira J. Geer
240 Seymour Coman

122 Mr. & Mrs. Andrew L. Williams
180 Mrs. E. H. Shotwell & drs.
180 J. C. Thomson
184 Mr. & Mrs. E. Caubert
196 Mr. & Mrs. Fred A. Cary
198 Dr. & Mrs. H. Newberry Hall
202 Mr.& Mrs.George Merryweather
204 Mr. & Mrs. C. F. Spalding
206 Mr. & Mrs. J. B. Parsons
208 Mr. & Mrs. Chas. E. Rector
210 Mr. & Mrs. E. H. Brush
212 Mr. & Mrs. H. R. Durkee
    Receiving day Tuesday
214 Mr. & Mrs. Dwight W. Graves

GORDON TERRACE.

7 Mr. & Mrs. Wm. H. Coen
7 Sterling H. Coen
17 Mr. & Mrs. W. L. Garey
27 Mr. & Mrs. Wm. B. Mundie
27 James B. Mundie
41 Mr. & Mrs. Chas. A. Adams
41 William B. Mann
47 Mr. & Mrs. G. E. Foss
    Receiving day Friday

8 Mr. & Mrs. F. T. Simmons
8 Miss Mary K. Busch
48 Mr. & Mrs. T. Deykes Whitney
    Receiving day Thursday
48 George B. Whitney
48 Charles U. Gordon

47 G. Edmund Foss

GRACE STREET.

733 Dr. & Mrs. Walter H. Marble
741 Dr. & Mrs. Lancaster F. Scott
1229 Mr. & Mrs. Harry C. Koechel
1235 Mr. & Mrs. H. P. Schwennesen
1323 Mr. & Mrs. Albert B. Brunk
1523 Mr. & Mrs. Leo Kasehagen

720 Mr. & Mrs. John W. Lanehart

1615 Mr. & Mrs. Jno. E. P. Wicks
1615 Rev. & Mrs. John Wicks
1619 Mr. & Mrs. Henry Suder

GRACELAND AVENUE.

1450 Mr. & Mrs. Elijah C. Harpold
    & dr.
1450 Harry W. Harpold
1478 Mr. & Mrs. David S. Anderson
    Receiving day Wednesday

1478 Miss Theresa M. Anderson
1486 Frederick F. Fazzie
1486 Miss Camella Fazzie
ne. cor. N. Halsted Mr. & Mrs. Luther Laflin Mills

GRAND AVENUE (ROGERS PARK).

nr. Pratt av. Mr. & Mrs. W. H. Chamberlin
4139 Mr.&Mrs.Carroll S. McMillan
4143 Mr. & Mrs. George G. Bottum
4143 Hudson G. Bottum
4165 Mr. & Mrs. David J. Braun & drs.
4179 Mr. & Mrs. Harry F. Harvey
4185 Miss Emma A. King
sw. cor. Farwell av. Mr. & Mrs. Jacob A. Eiffert & dr.

4118 Mr.& Mrs. Amos B. King & drs.
4260 Mr. & Mrs. Robert W. Vasey

4223 Mr.&Mrs. Edward R. Foerster
sw. cor. Morse av. Mr. & Mrs. Ed- R. Harmon
4267 Mr. & Mrs. Ed. R. Gale
4279 Mr. & Mrs. Henry Hiestand
4307 Mr. & Mrs. Samuel M. Grimes
4355 Mr. & Mrs. Allan T. Stearns
4355 Mrs. Elizabeth Norawa

GRANT PLACE.

45 Mr. & Mrs. Dietrich Kahn
49 Mr. & Mrs. L. S. Berry
57 Mr. & Mrs. Thos. E. O'Brien
57 Mr. & Mrs. Eli J. August

69 Mr. & Mrs. W. C. Scupham
69 Mr. & Mrs. Theo. C. Thielepape
73 Mr. & Mrs. G. L. Reimann

GREENLEAF AVENUE.

47 Mr. & Mrs. Alvah B. Mathews
203 Mr. & Mrs. Frank W. Loomis
447 Mr. & Mrs. William R. Bond
517 Mr. & Mrs. Henry G. Wright
523 Mr. & Mrs. Cephas H. Leach
539 Mr. & Mrs. Francis P. Sullivan
703 Dr. & Mrs. Edward L. Webb
703 Dr. Walter M. Wilkins
805 Charles F. Bunte
933 Mr. & Mrs. Elmer E. Beach

———

602 Mr. & Mrs. Geo. R. Hinners
630 Mrs. Celia A. Nelson
804 Mr. & Mrs. Joel Pratt
818 Mr. & Mrs. Raymond W. Beach
818 Mrs. N. C. Healy
928 Mr. & Mrs. William S. Warren
948 Dr. & Mrs. Frank L. Browne

Forest Hotel nw. cor. Forest av.
Mrs. Robert Hill
Edwin Hill
D. W. Johnson
Mr. & Mrs. F. A. Lathrop
Mr. & Mrs. P. S. Leland
A. P. Clark Matson
Charles E. Merry
Mr. & Mrs. E. A. Patton
Mr. & Mrs. J. R. Spicer
Mr. & Mrs. Benj. P. Van Court.
Mr. & Mrs. J. B. Watson
504 Mr. & Mrs. Charles R. Adams
512 Mr. & Mrs. Charles S. Lowe &
  drs.
528 Mr. & Mrs. Chester McNeil
532 Mr. & Mrs. Chas. W. Hallman
538 Mr. & Mrs. Albert O. Swift & dr.
538 Mrs. Mary Swift

HALL STREET.

25 Mr. & Mrs. Justus Loehr
29 Mr. & Mrs. L. F. Hussander

43 Mr. & Mrs. Charles E. Simon

NORTH HALSTED STREET.

695 Mr. & Mrs. Louis Diesel
701 Mr. & Mrs. Frank Diesel
701 John Diesel
1011 Mr. & Mrs. Rupert Coleman
1011 Mrs. Samuel Thorpe & dr.
1013 Mr. & Mrs. E. U. Roper
1047 Mr. & Mrs. Carl Mueller
1049 Mr. & Mrs. John W. White & dr.
1049 John J. Metzler & dr.
1055 Mr. & Mrs. George W. Wilbur
1267 Dr. Oscar A. Tiedt
1267 Mr. & Mrs. John Tiedt
1271 Dr. & Mrs. Alfred F. Sprosser
1375 Mr. & Mrs. William H. Peacock
1377 Mr. & Mrs. Francis W. Savage
  & dr.
1377 Mr. & Mrs. Edward P. Savage
1383 Mr. & Mrs. John C. Scales
1405 Mr. & Mrs. Christopher Johnson
  & dr.

916 Mrs. Wm. Griener & dr.
936 Dr. Wm. H. Wood
936 Dr. John A. Diestelow
954 Dr. & Mrs. Chas. C. Bernard
980 Ezra F. Hazell
1000 Mrs. R. Boylston Hall
1004 Dr. & Mrs. W. D. Barber
1022 Mrs. A. Schupp & dr.
1038 Mr. & Mrs. James M. Hills
1042 Dr. & Mrs. A. S. Carrier
1048 Rev. & Mrs. Willis G. Craig &
  dr.
1048 Mr. & Mrs. Bryan Y. Craig
1070 Rev. & Mrs. Herrick Johnson
1102 Dr. & Mrs. Richard Herrmann
1130 Mrs. M. J. Shrock
1170 Mr. & Mrs. F. W. Kasehagen
1348 Dr. & Mrs. Lawrence H. Prince
1390 Mr. & Mrs. Felix J. Schweisthal

1413 Mrs. Edward Rummel & dr.
1483 Dr. Vincent Cole
1483 Mr. & Mrs. Ellis P. Cole
1511 Andrew Bolter
1511 Mrs. A. Schneider
1525 Mrs. Evelyn Eugenia Presstman *Receiving day Tuesday*
1547 Mr. & Mrs. Robert R. Clarke
1547 Mrs. Daniel Elston
1547 Miss Blanche Bassett
1635 Mr. & Mrs. Charles Mueller
1661 Mr. & Mrs. Arthur Schroeder
1681 Mr. & Mrs. Wm. Boldenweck
1767 Mr. & Mrs. C. R. Browder
1799 Mr. & Mrs. Theo. Even
2339 Mr. & Mrs. Louis Hillman
2339 Mrs. Louisa Klineofen
2383 Mr. & Mrs. Henry T. Fry
2501 Mrs. V. Q. Umlauf

1518 Mr. & Mrs. Carl Roehl & drs.
1594 Dr. & Mrs. F. D. Porter
1614 Mr. & Mrs. Edward J. Walsh
1634 Mr. & Mrs. J. S. Cram
1634 LeRoy T. Cram
2122 Mr. & Mrs. George A. Wait
nr. Gordon Terrace, Dr. S. R. Ingalls
nr. Gordon Terrace, Dr. & Mrs. S. D.
Brooks
nr. Gordon Terrace, Dr. & Mrs. J. B.
Hamilton
2354 Mr. & Mrs. B. Robbins & dr.
2354 Burnett W. Robbins

2501 Louis C. Umlauf
2501 William Umlauf
2501 Mr. & Mrs. A. W. Marston

HAMMOND STREET.

81 Mrs. Annie C. Buckie & drs.
109 Mr. & Mrs. F. H. Prince & dr.

92 Mr. & Mrs. Martin A. Fiedler
102 Mr. & Mrs. L. Marcuse
102 Miss Jessie H. Marcuse
108 Mr. & Mrs. F. H. O'Connor

HAMPDEN COURT.

221 Mr. & Mrs. Frank P. Schmitt jr.
221 Mr. & Mrs. Hugh W. Dyar
221 Mr. & Mrs. Wm. A. Sittig
227 Mr. & Mrs. Louis Bartling &
drs.
231 Mrs. Marie C. Freeman & dr.
233 Mr. & Mrs. J. H. Frank
239 Mr. & Mrs. F. A. Winslow
241 Mr. & Mrs. Carl Koelling
241 John Koelling
241 Mr. & Mrs. George N. Niese
315 Mr. & Mrs. G. Douglas Potter
323 Mr. & Mrs. F. C. Lang & drs.
Receiving day Thursday
325 Mr. & Mrs. Geo. F. Schwarz
331 Mark F. Madden
331 James A. Madden
331 Mr. & Mrs. Hugh M. Wilson
331 Mr. & Mrs. Chas. E. Gilbert
335 Mr. & Mrs. J. E. Martine
335 Mr. & Mrs. Archer C. Stiles
335 Mr. & Mrs. Geo. W. Mathison
345 Mr. & Mrs. Philip Maas
345 Fred Maas

234 Mr. & Mrs. Benjamin Hyde
234 Mr. & Mrs. Francis H. Treat
234 Mr. & Mrs. Jno. Kerr George
234 Mr. & Mrs. F. J. Schaub
240 Mr. & Mrs. Davis G. Mellor
240 Mrs. John D. Boyd
240 Mr. & Mrs. Henry C. Voute
242 Mr. & Mrs. Adolph Stark
242 Mr. & Mrs. C. Augustus Ebert
242 Mr. & Mrs. James C. McMath
244 Mr. & Mrs. Fred Woltz
320 Mr. & Mrs. Wm. P. Hussey
320 Mr. & Mrs. Henry D. Sturtevant
328 Mr. & Mrs. Arthur Leask
330 Mr. & Mrs. C. E. Brown
332 Mr. & Mrs. Chas. S. Bartholf
334 Mr. & Mrs. Henry E. C. Peterson
334 Mr. & Mrs. Chas. H. Dennis

349 William Heinemann jr.
349 Mr. & Mrs. Chas. N. Strotz
349 Mr.& Mrs. William Heinemann
& dr.

HAWTHORNE PLACE.

17 Mr. & Mrs. R. Granger
27 Mr. & Mrs. Philip C. Dyrenforth
27 Arthur Dyrenforth
37 Mr. & Mrs. H. H. Hettler
63 Mr. & Mrs. Rockwell King

10 Mr. & Mrs. Willis F. Johnson
10 Miss A. Blanche Johnson
30 Mr. & Mrs. George E. Marshall
30 Mrs A. J. Marshall
36 Mr. & Mrs. B. F. McConnell
60 Mr. & Mrs. John McConnell
60 Edward D. McConnell

HOLLYWOOD AVENUE.

1327 Mr. & Mrs. Thomas Balmer

846 Mr. & Mrs. Wm. Prettyman
1328 Mr. & Mrs. Jos. Lyman Silsbee

HOWE STREET.

61 Mr. & Mrs. Geo. J. Schmidt
163 Mr. & Mrs. A. C. Schmidt
    Receiving day Wednesday
165 Mr. & Mrs. J. M. Hitchcock
173 Mr. & Mrs. A. J. Anderson
181 Mrs: Johanna Kohn & drs.

184 Mr. & Mrs. Marcus Levy & drs.
    Receive Friday eve.

158 Mr. & Mrs. Lincoln E. Clark &
    dr.
168 Mr. & Mrs. W. McQuigg
170 Mr. & Mrs. Charles N. Hale
172 Mrs. W. Hegert & drs.
176 Mr. & Mrs. DeWitt C. Bonham
180 Mr. & Mrs. Samuel Hecht
182 Mr. & Mrs. Herman Jacobson

HURON STREET.

271 Mr. & Mrs. C. A. Winship
289 Mr. & Mrs. W. M. Devine & drs.
    Receiving day Tuesday
289 J. A. Devine
289 W. P. Devine
291 Dr. & Mrs. N. S. Davis
295 Mr. & Mrs. Henry C. Bannard
299 Miss Eliza Allen Starr
    Receiving day Wednesday
299 Mrs. C. W. W. Wellington
    Receiving day Wednesday
301 Mr. & Mrs. F. W. Crosby
301 Mrs. Warren Norton
303 Mr. & Mrs. J. P. Bell & drs.
    Receiving day Tuesday
303 J. P. Bell jr.
303 C. F. Bell
303 Cyrus F. Cook
303 William F. Hoig
305 Mr. & Mrs. C. F. Pietsch
307 Mr. & Mrs. Harris Pomeroy
309 Mr. & Mrs. James C. Peasley
313 Mrs. J. S. Rumsey & drs.
313 J. M. Rumsey
313 Mr. & Mrs. Treat Campbell
321 Mr. & Mrs. Cyrus Hall McCor-
    mick
405 Mr. & Mrs. L. G. Hallberg

270 Dr. & Mrs. F. A. Leusman
    Receiving day Thursday
270 Louis Campbell Tipton
272 Dr. & Mrs. R. L. Rea
    Receiving day Thursday
272 Mrs. Mary F. Manlove
276 Mr. & Mrs. Peter Adler
    Receiving day Thursday
284 Mr. & Mrs. John M. Kranz & drs.
286 Lewis Edward Dickinson
288 Dr. Otto T. Freer
288 Mrs. Catherine Freer
292 Mrs. Francis Agnew & drs.
292 Mr. & Mrs. Chas. P. Monahan
294 Mr. & Mrs. E. A. Otis
294 Miss Marion Otis
330 Dr. & Mrs. Peter P. Lobig
354 Mr. & Mrs. Percy L. Fearn
382 Ernest C. Johnson
422 Mr. & Mrs. Eugene H. Fishburn
422 Randolph E. Fishburn
422 Mr. & Mrs. Samuel S. Fowler

407 Mr. & Mrs. James S. Sharp
409 Mr. & Mrs. John Mountain &
    drs.
411 Mr. & Mrs. Arthur A. Maclean

411 Henry Memory & dr.
413 Mr. & Mrs. O. Chanute & drs.
413 Mrs. A. E. Boyd
415 Mr. & Mrs. F. W. Coler
419 Mr. & Mrs. Hulburd Dunlevy
419 John C. Dunlevy

421 Mr. & Mrs. W. Irving Babcock
423 Mr. & Mrs. Charles P. McAvoy
425 Mr. & Mrs. Ullman Strong
    Receiving day Tuesday
427 Mr. & Mrs. G. F. Gail
429 Judge & Mrs. S. P. McConnell

INDIAN BOUNDARY ROAD.

780 Mr. & Mrs. Edward Henderson
    & dr.

789 Edwin A. Henderson

INDIANA STREET.

283 Leonard Gould
297 Dr. & Mrs. L. H. Watson
305 Mr. & Mrs. H. V. Raymond
307 Mr. & Mrs. Thomas Raymond
337 Rev. & Mrs. E. J. Alden
351 Dr. & Mrs. Benj. F. Tolson

292 Mr. & Mrs. H. C. Hinman
312 Mr. & Mrs. George Lane
312 Miss May Brink
    ————
363 Samuel Glickauf

JACKSON AVENUE (ROGERS PARK).

501 Mr. & Mrs. James F. Morton
501 Mr. & Mrs. James B. S. Morton
505 Mr. & Mrs. George Q. Allen
505 Miss Eva Viola Allen
747 Mr. & Mrs. John R. Bruce
751 Mr. & Mrs. Thomas B. Gault
751 George M. Gault
751 Dr. & Mrs. James D. Craig
767 Mr. & Mrs. James F. Pratt
803 Mr. & Mrs. Abel L. Allen
809 Mr. & Mrs. Parker Scholes
817 Mr. & Mrs. Josiah T. Hair

504 Mr. & Mrs. John W. Mills & dr.
540 Mr. & Mrs. Harvey H. Mellen
620 Mr. & Mrs. George W. Greig
758 Mr. & Mrs. George W. Hamil-
    ton
762 Mr. & Mrs. Thos. H. Coleman
828 Mr. & Mrs. Richard W. Faux
    ————
821 Mr. & Mrs. Charles Adams
831 Mr. & Mrs. John H. Brown
929 Mr. & Mrs. Jacob M. Dice
941 Mr. & Mrs. Wm. J. Maxwell

KEMPER PLACE.

17 Mr. & Mrs. Geo. F. Francis

19 Mrs. Sage G. Halla & dr.

KENMORE AVENUE.

347 Mr. & Mrs. Henry Frankfurter
357 Mrs. M. H. Bovee & dr.
357 Rev. Wm. A. Burch
363 Mr. & Mrs. J. W. Robertson
    & dr.
377 Miss May Faron
377 Mr. & Mrs. A. F. Portman
401 Mr. & Mrs. L. G. Stiles
415 Mr. & Mrs. John F. Lambert-
    son
435 Mr. & Mrs. T. C. Massey
445 Mr. & Mrs. F. M. Chapman
449 Mr. & Mrs. Chas. V. Peckham
    Receiving day Wednesday
455 Mr. & Mrs. Wm. A. Vawter

338 Mr. & Mrs. G. O. Evans
338 Mrs. C. Stattman & dr.
354 Mrs. C. A. Hoover
378 Mr.& Mrs. Edward C. Portman
402 Mr. & Mrs. P. Herdien & dr.
408 Mr. & Mrs. Alex. Hofflund
414 Mr. & Mrs. A. W. Pulver
418 Mr. & Mrs. James Flanigan
426 Mr. & Mrs. William N. Taylor
426 Mrs. E. F. Taylor
430 Mrs. E. A. Ingalls & dr.
430 A. R. Ingalls
436 Mr. & Mrs. Napoleon C.
    Fisher
446 Mr. & Mrs. L. T. M. Slocum

461 Mr. & Mrs. William McDon-
      nell
665 Mr. & Mrs. Joseph N. Brown
665 Mr. & Mrs. George J. Brine
667 Mr. & Mrs. George I. Jones
677 Mr. & Mrs. J. P. Meyer
683 Mr. & Mrs. Jesse K. Farley
691 Mr. & Mrs. A. A. Thomas
699 Mr. & Mrs. Wm. R. Collins
699 Harry B. Collins
723 Mr. & Mrs. Robert Clark & dr.
727 Mr. & Mrs. H. L. Angell
729 Mr. & Mrs. O. B. Osborne
733 Dr. & Mrs. B. L. Hotchkin
747 Mr. & Mrs. George A. Mason
747 Mr. & Mrs. E. J. Cusack
757 Mr. & Mrs. W. Edward Fallon
797 Mrs. C. S. Brown
797 Mrs. Caroline A. Spencer
797 Mr. & Mrs. G. W. Powell
797 Mr. & Mrs. Myron H. Powell
805 Mr. & Mrs. Wayman C. Budd
815 Mr. & Mrs. E. R. Wheeler
825 Mrs. Fred A. Heath
825 Mrs. L. L. Ormsby
873 Mr. & Mrs. Perry Trumbull
893 Mrs. M. H. Church
893 Frank W. Church
925 Mr. & Mrs. Louis Lange
935 Mr. & Mrs. George P. Jones
935 Graham P. Jones
945 Mr. & Mrs. Fred S. Comstock
945 S. F. Comstock
979 Mr. & Mrs. Walter C. Gillett
      Receiving day Tuesday

452 Mr. & Mrs. Eli P. Chatfield
486 Mr. & Mrs. Frank A. B. Moore
668 Mrs. Loraine J. Pitkin
682 Mr. & Mrs. J. B. Chesney
682 William P. Chesney
684 Mr. & Mrs. Howard N. Elmer
698 Mr. & Mrs. H. J. Lowery
744 Mr. & Mrs. Fritz Glogauer
756 Mr. & Mrs. Edward T. Ander-
      son
756 Mr. & Mrs. Wm. B. Anderson
756 Mr. & Mrs. Lyman Feltus &
      dr.
798 Mr. & Mrs. Arthur T. Howe
798 Mr. & Mrs. D. F. Flannery
812 Mr. & Mrs. John Wardlow
874 Mr. & Mrs. Harrison J. Glas-
      pell
928 Dr. & Mrs. Lorenzo N. Gros-
      venor
      Receiving day Thursday
1034 Mr. & Mrs. Albert B. Hunt
1052 Mr. & Mrs. A. W. Greene
1068 Mr. & Mrs. J. F. Steward
1116 Mr. & Mrs. Charles C. Wheeler
1132 Mr. & Mrs. B. C. Caldwell
1152 Mr. & Mrs. R. L. Duvall
1214 Mr. & Mrs. J. W. Sullivan

1035 Mr. & Mrs. Edward W. Curtis
1035 Edward W. Curtis jr.
1047 Mr. & Mrs. E. C. Smith
1071 Mr. & Mrs. George F. Lang
1129 Mr. & Mrs. B. C. Rogers
1145 Mrs. Albert Prescott & dr.

KING PLACE.

1431 Mr. & Mrs. Frank R. Jackson

LAKE SHORE DRIVE.

18 Mr. & Mrs. Charles Pope
19 Mr. & Mrs. Alfred Henry Mulli-
      ken
21 Mr. & Mrs. Albert Blake Dick
      Receiving day Monday
22 Mrs. Allen Manvel & drs.
22 Mrs. Emily Sheldon
48 Mr. & Mrs. S. E. Gross
      Receiving day Monday
48 Miss Minnie Campbell
55 Col. & Mrs. John Mason Loo-
      mis   *Receiving day Monday*
57 Mr. & Mrs. Edward F. Lawrence
57 Dwight Lawrence

60 Mr. & Mrs. S. D. Kimbark
60 Charles A. Kimbark
60 Walter Kimbark
60 Miss Grace Kimbark
60 Miss Marie Kimbark
60 Mrs. Thomas Church
63 Mr. & Mrs. Geo. Henry High
      Receiving day Monday
64 Mrs. J. Whitney Farlin
      Receive Monday afternoon
64 Myron Whitney Farlin
65 Mr. & Mrs. Carl C. Heisen
      Receiving day Monday
65 G. B. Heisen

65 Maj. George C. Waddill
66 Mrs. Henry Starring
66 Mr. & Mrs. Mason B. Starring
100 Mr. & Mrs. Potter Palmer
 Receiving day Mon. 4 to 6 p.m.
100 Honore Palmer
100 Potter Palmer jr.
103 Mr. & Mrs. Franklin MacVeagh
 Receiving day Mon. 4 to 6 p.m.
103 Eames MacVeagh
109 Mr. & Mrs. S. E. Barrett & dr.
 Receiving day Monday
109 Robert D. Barrett

111 Mr. & Mrs. M. D. Ogden
111 Bernon Ogden
112 Mr. & Mrs. V. C. Turner
 Receiving day Monday
112 Edward Craft Green
117 Mrs. Barbara Armour
117 Allison V. Armour
120 Mr. & Mrs. George A. Armour
125 Mr. & Mrs. Alex. C. McClurg
 Receiving day Monday
130 Mr. & Mrs. O. W. Potter
 Receiving day Monday 3 to 6 p.m.

LAKE VIEW AVENUE.

5 Mr. & Mrs. Andrew E. Leicht
 Receiving day Thursday
5 Miss Stella Leicht
5 John Seba
11 Mr. & Mrs. Edward A. Leicht
 Receiving day 1st Friday
17 Mr. & Mrs. F. Madlener
31 Mr. & Mrs. R. Lothholz
71 Mr. & Mrs. J. M. O'Grady
 Receiving day Thursday
71 W. G. Tuller
71 Miss E. Eugenia Bower
73 Dr. & Mrs. F. H. Foster
75 Mr. & Mrs. A. S. Maltman & drs.
 Receiving day Wednesday

75 Stewart A. Maltman
 cor. Deming ct.
 Dr. & Mrs. Francis D. Holbrook
 Dr. C. A. Weirick
207 M. A. Johnson
251 Mr. & Mrs. John J. Philbin
251 John Mackin
265 Mr. & Mrs. R. Schloesser & dr.
 Receiving day Tuesday
269 Mr. & Mrs. Lem W. Flershem
 & dr.
269 Rudolph Flershem
321 Mr. & Mrs. A. L. Sercomb

LANE PLACE.

11 Mrs. C. L. Kaub
11 Mr. & Mrs. John Sexton
 Receiving day Wednesday
13 Mr. & Mrs. Adolph Sturm
15 Mr. & Mrs. W. D. Avery
15 Mr. & Mrs. F. W. Gerould
17 Mr. & Mrs. Carlton H. Prindiville
19 James Lane
21 Mr. & Mrs. John E. Lewis
 Receiving day Friday
25 Mrs. C. Simon
25 John G. Simon
25 Charles W. Simon
25 Mr. & Mrs. Clayton F. Summy

10 Mr. & Mrs. John P. Miller
14 Mr. & Mrs. S. Birkenstein
14 Louis Birkenstein
14 David Birkenstein
16 Mr. & Mrs. W. C. Becker
16 W. J. Becker
16 Mr. & Mrs. Frank J. Stern
20 Mr. & Mrs. M. Gaensslen
20 Walter Gaensslen
24 Mr. & Mrs. L. B. Schaefer

29 Mr. & Mrs. Frederick Goetz
35 Mr. & Mrs. I. F. Kearns
37 Mrs. Lucy L. Stitt
49 Mr. & Mrs. Charles Ehman & dr.

LARRABEE STREET.

543 Mr. & Mrs. Henry W. Frische
543 Mr. & Mrs. C. Frische & dr.
545 Mr. & Mrs. M. Schmitz
545 Mr. & Mrs. N. J. Schmitz

774 Mr. & Mrs. M. Bartelme & drs.
774 E. J. Bartelme
782 Rev. & Mrs. L. M. Heilman
 Receiving day Thursday

595 Mr. & Mrs. Ernst H. Fischer
599 Mr. & Mrs. Joseph Hacek jr.
599 Mr. & Mrs. Anton Tempel
767 Mrs. A. Weyl
767 Mr. & Mrs. John L. Crosley
769 Dr. & Mrs. Frederick Roesch
771 Mr. & Mrs. M. A. Scholbe
775 Mr. & Mrs. D. O. Gallear
825 Mr. & Mrs. E. P. Learned &drs.
825 Richard Learned
827 Mr. & Mrs. Henry Vocke
869 Mr. & Mrs. Vincent S. Boggs
   Receiving day Wednesday
869 Mr. & Mrs. A. V. Julin
873 Mr. & Mrs. C. Murphy
901 Mr. & Mrs. P. F. Eckstorm&dr.
901 Christian A. Eckstrom

858 Mr. & Mrs. John Devore
864 Mr. & Mrs. A. H. Apfel
864 Mrs. H. Gerstenberg & dr.
868 Mrs. Cornelia Berry
868 Mr. & Mrs. Clement E. Ireland
868 Dr. and Mrs. Joseph Watry
   Receiving day Tuesday
910 Mr. & Mrs. E. P. McNaughten
   Receiving day Wednesday
912 Mr. & Mrs. E. F. Heinze
914 Mr. & Mrs. F. G. Heinze
916 Mr. & Mrs. Peter Emmel
   Receiving day Wednesday
916 William Emmel
916 Robert Emmel
—
903 Mr. & Mrs. John Jucker

LA SALLE AVENUE.

207 Mr. & Mrs. J. F. Birdsall
209 Mr. & Mrs. August Eckle
223 Mr. & Mrs. E. C. Hamburgher
Receiving days 1st & 3d Saturdays
223 Miss Ray Hamburgher
227 Mr. & Mrs. H. Ratzek
227 Mrs. S. Weil
227 Mr. & Mrs. R. M. Berlizheimer
229 Dr. & Mrs. B. C. Elms
229 Mr. & Mrs. C. K. Herrick
299 Adolph Henrotin
229 Mrs. Mary C. Grosse
233 Dr. & Mrs. Sven Windrow
   Receiving day Wednesday
233 Miss Mia Windrow
235 Frank Paxton
235 Mr. & Mrs. C. Mandeville
241 Mrs. Charles Gee
245 George E. Purington & drs.
   Receiving day Monday
247 Mr. & Mrs. Simon Levy
249 Mr. & Mrs. Emil Petersen
259 Mrs. F. M. Cragin
259 Miss Frances M. Cragin
259 Mr. & Mrs. J. G. Hall
   Receiving day Tuesday
259 Miss Nina Willson
263 Mr. & Mrs. G. W. Nye
265 Mr. & Mrs. Thomas Callahan
267 Mr. & Mrs. R. H. Peters
269 Dr. & Mrs. Christian Fenger
269 Dr. W. S. Brown
271 Mr. & Mrs. John H. Johnson
   & dr.
275 Mr. & Mrs. Daniel Loeser
277 Dr. & Mrs. J. Fisher

158 Mr. & Mrs. Armand F. Teefy
158 Miss Hattie E. Wolfe
172 Mr. & Mrs. J. Schmidt & dr.
172 E. C. Schmidt
246 Mr. & Mrs. Adolph Berg
246 Max A Berg
246 Isidor Berg
250 Mr. & Mrs. John C. Uhrlaub
260 D. V. Gallery
260 D. J. Gallery
260 J. J. Gallery
268 Mr. & Mrs. Albert E. Roof
270 Mr. & Mrs. H. K. Macdonald
270½ Miss Sarah Gleason
274 Mr. & Mrs. E. E. Hartwell
290 Mr. & Mrs. James Harrison
   Channon
290 Dr. & Mrs. John D. Andrews
290 Mr. & Mrs. Iver Lawson
290 Mr. & Mrs. Henry F. Billings
290 Mr. & Mrs. Alfred Mortensen
290 Mr. & Mrs. D. F. Kelly
290 William T. Carrington
300 Mr. & Mrs. J. McGregor Adams
300 Miss L. L. King
300 Miss L. A. King
314 Mrs. Robert E. Moss
314 Miss M. Smith
314 Earl C. Moss
316 Mrs. Sarah C. McMillen
320 Mr. & Mrs. C. J. Hurlbut
320 H. W. Rogers
320 Miss S. M. Rogers
322 Mr. & Mrs. Wm. A. Elmendorf
322 Willard Elmendorf
328 Mr. & Mrs. Thos. W. Lewis&dr.

277 Mrs. J. B. Smalley & dr.
    Receiving day Tuesday
277 J. H. Smalley jr.
279 Mr. & Mrs. I. Ettelson
283 Mr. & Mrs. Joseph Rudolph
283 Charles Rudolph
283 Franklin Rudolph
285½ Miss Jennie McLaughlin
285½ Miss Reita McLaughlin
285½ J. Wilbur Sutton
289 Mrs. E. G. Kriechbaum
289 Miss Viola M. Smith
299 Mr. & Mrs. O. F. Geeting
299 Adolph Henrotin
303 Mr. & Mrs. D. Y. McMullen
    Receiving day Tuesday
305 Mr. & Mrs. L. N. Sawyer
307 Mr. & Mrs. A. C. Brackebush
317 Mr. & Mrs. Victor F. Lawson
323 Mr. & Mrs. Maurice Pincoffs
335 Mrs. S. F. Oliphant
337 Mr. & Mrs. W. A. Hammond &
    dr.
339 Mrs. W. G. Pigman
339 Mr. & Mrs. Thomas J. Staley&dr.
339 David W. Staley
343 Mr.& Mrs. James B. Hobbs
    Receiving days 2d & 3d Mon.
345 Mr. & Mrs. Ph. Jaeger & drs.
    Receive last Friday in mo.
345 George J. Jaeger
353 Dr. & Mrs. F. Henrotin
353 Mrs. Charles Prussing
359 Mr. & Mrs. George K. Dauehy
359 Samuel O. Dauchy
359 Otis B. Dauchy
361 Mr. & Mrs. Walter Peek
363 Mrs. J. T. Schofield & dr.
363 William E. Schofield
367 Mr. & Mrs. N. H. Blatchford
375 Mr. & Mrs. E. W. Blatchford
    Receiving day Monday
381 Ralph Isham
383 Mr. & Mrs. J. H. Prentiss
387 Harry M. Hubbard
387 Mrs. Abijah Keith
387 Mrs. Max Hjortsberg
403 Mr. & Mrs. Oliver B. Green& dr.
403 Andrew Hugh Green
415 Mr. & Mrs. C. N. Davis
    Receiving day Friday
415 Mrs. Agnes Barker
415 Clyde Barker
415 Mr. & Mrs. Hiram Baker
417 Dr. E. J. Warren
417 Mr. & Mrs. George P. Everhart
18

328 Miss S. E. Chart
328 Mrs L. A. Richardson
330 Dr. & Mrs. Charles A. Pusheck
    Receiving day Thursday
330 Miss Edna Pusheck
330 Miss Emily Christopher
330 John T. Mitchell
330 Mrs. J. E. Dougherty & drs.
330 John Quincy Adams
336 Mr. & Mrs. Edward Moll
340 Mr.&Mrs.George H.Rozet&drs.
342 Mr. & Mrs. Zack Hofheimer
342 Albert Ellinger
342 Morris Ellinger
356 Mr. & Mrs. August Beck
356 Mr. & Mrs. Otto C. Schneider
360 Misses E. H. & Lillie J. Smith
360 Wm. D. Smith
362 Mr & Mrs. J. F. Wollensak
366 Mr. & Mrs. Fred Griesheimer
366 Mr.& Mrs.Benjamin Englehard
370 Mr. & Mrs. W. H. Purcell
372 Mr.&Mrs.DavidFranklin Kenly
372 F. Corning Kenly
372 Mr. & Mrs. Chas. P. Treat
376 Mrs. C. S. Peerstone & dr.
376 Mrs. C. A. Pratt
378 Col. & Mrs. A. F. Stevenson
    & dr.
380 Dr. Charles White & dr.
382 Miss E. Hosmer
382 R. W. Hosmer
384 Henry Bausher
386 J. H. Roseboom
388 Mrs. C. B. Blakemore & dr.
388 F. T. Blakemore
388 W. R. Blakemore
388 Paul Clayton
388 Mrs. James W. Clayton
390 Mr. & Mrs. Robt. T. T. Spence
392 Mr. & Mrs. Charles M. Walker
396 Mr. & Mrs. Peter Willems
402 C. C. Moeller
402 Mr. & Mrs. Augustus Bauer
404 Mr. & Mrs. Wm. Goodrich
408 Mrs. J. M. Bryant
410 Mr. & Mrs. W. S. Wilkins
    Receiving day Tuesday
410 Miss Emma Wilkins
412 Wm. Loeb & dr.
412 Jacob W. Loeb
414 Mrs. August Schrenk
416 Mr. & Mrs. H. S. Kelsey
416 Mr. & Mrs. J. W. Taylor
418 Mrs. Mathias Grass & drs.
418 J. P. Buck M. D.

425 Mr. & Mrs. T. G. Springer
    Receiving day Thursday
425 Mr. & Mrs. C. W. Doton
425 Mr. & Mrs. G. W. Marquardt jr.
    Receiving day Friday
425 Mr. & Mrs. E. H. Carmack
425 Mr. & Mrs. T. F. Gane & drs.
425 David R. Carrier
425 Miss K. M. Shippen
425 Mr. & Mrs. O. T. Wharton & dr.
425 George C. Wharton
425 Granville W. Browning
435 Mrs. Louise Crocker
443 Mr. & Mrs. F. A. Winship
445 Judge & Mrs. Theodore Brentano
447 Mr. & Mrs. Otto Reiss
449 Mr. & Mrs. Moses S. Eisendrath
449 Mr. & Mrs. E. R. Weil
453 Dr. & Mrs. T. J. Bluthardt
455 Mrs. F. Hecht
457 Dr. & Mrs. F. W. Rohr
459 Dr. & Mrs. M. L. Harris
459 Emery S. Walker
459 Mr. & Mrs. Wm. K. Kenly
461 C. W. Colehour & drs.
461 Mr. & Mrs. Fred Muench
    Receiving day 3d Wednesday
463 Mr. & Mrs. August Fiedler
465 Mr. & Mrs. Francis Worcester
465 Theodore Worcester
467½ Mr. & Mrs. Louis Schott
    Receiving day Friday
471 Mr. & Mrs. Bernard Berlizheimer
    Receiving day Friday
471 Mrs. Johanna Kunreuther
471 Mrs. E. Lazare
485 Mrs. Jennie Mullin & drs.
485 Mrs. S. Eber Oberholtzer
487 F. C. O'Day
495 Mr. & Mrs. Theodore Ascher
495 Martin Ascher
497 Mr. & Mrs. E. Witkowski
497 Isadore Witkowski
501 Mrs. Eliza DeClerque-Rabing
501 Mr. & Mrs. Henry DeClerque
501 Prof. R. Fischer
503 Mrs. R. Mendelson
    Receiving day Saturday
503 Mr. & Mrs. W. Wetzler
    Receiving day Saturday
505 Mr. & Mrs. Warren Keeler
505 Oliver E. Jenkins
507 Mrs. Joseph Deschauer
507 Dr. & Mrs. George A. Christmann
509 Mrs. E. J. Blachford
511 Christian Temple & drs.

420 Mrs. Wilhelmina Schwarz
    Receiving day Thursday
420 John J. Schwarz
420 Mrs. Rose Schwarz
424 Mr. & Mrs. Joseph S. Phillips &
    dr. *Receiving day Saturday*
424 J. S. Phillips jr.
424 Abraham Phillips
426 Dr. Augusta Hinz
428 Mrs. Katie Kohn & drs.
428½ Mr. & Mrs. Wm. C. Furst
430 Thos. Ritchie & drs.
430 Thomas Ritchie jr.
432 Mr. & Mrs. Henry L. Regensburg
    Receiving day Thursday
432 Mrs. S. M. Rosenthal
434 Mr. & Mrs. William Hammer-
    miller & dr.
436 Mr. & Mrs. H. A. Kirchhoff
    Receiving day 3d Saturday
436 Miss E. Standinger
438 Dr. & Mrs. Geo. F. Fiske
    Receiving day Thursday
440 Mrs. John McVoy & dr.
440 John A. McVoy
440 Eugene J. McVoy
448 Mr. & Mrs. Malcolm McNeil
450 Mr. & Mrs. D. Murphy
450 Mr. & Mrs. M. B. Herely
454 Mr. & Mrs. Nicholas Koch & dr.
456 Dr. H. Banga
456 Miss Emily Banga
458 Mr. & Mrs. Adolph Felsenthal
462 Mr. & Mrs. Herman Weber
464 Gilbert Witters
464 W. A. Follette
466 Mrs. J. M. Bell
468 Mr. & Mrs. J. P. Reynolds
470 Mr. & Mrs. Wm. Dickinson
472 Mr. & Mrs. Victor D. Gowan
474 A. G. Cox
482 Mr. & Mrs. Jno. Wilkinson
488 Mr. & Mrs. Paul Juergens & drs.
    Receiving day 2d Wed. in mo.
488 William F. Juergens
490 Mr. & Mrs. J. A. Clybourn & dr.
490 F. T. Clybourn
492 Dr. Julia Holmes Smith
492 Sabin Smith
496 Mr. & Mrs. John Wynne
498 Mr. & Mrs. Chas. Bachrach
504 Mr. & Mrs. Fred W. Wolf & dr.
506 Mr. & Mrs. A. J. Featherstone
506 Miss Mary E. Mills
508 Mr. & Mrs. Morris Griesheimer
508 Mrs. M. Dernham

508 Mr.& Mrs. Arnold Gundelfinger
512 Mr. & Mrs. John McEwen
512 Miss Eleanor McEwen
    Receiving day Monday
512 Paul J. McEwen
512 John McEwen jr
512 Alfred McEwen
514 Mr. & Mrs. Morris Sellers & dr.
514 John M. Sellers
520 Mr. & Mrs. Wm. Vocke
520 Fred W. Vocke
520 Frank Bopp
528 Mr. & Mrs. Wm. Grus & drs.
528 Wm. Grus jr.
530 Mr. & Mrs. F. M. Atkinson
532 Mrs. J. O'Connell
    Receiving day Wednesday
532 John J. O'Connell
532 William J. O'Connell
534 Mrs. Fred Keller
542 Mr. & Mrs. Wm. Zellmann .
542 Misses Amelia & Adelia Blauer
552 Dr. & Mrs. Charles E. Manierre
558 Dr. J. S. Clark
558 Dr. J. S. Clark jr.
576 Dr. & Mrs. D. J. Rush
    Receive Thursday
576 Judge & Mrs. Arthur H. Chet-
    lain
576 Mr. & Mrs. Geo. W. Critchfield
580 Mr. & Mrs. George Barnard
580 Mr. & Mrs. Albert Schultz
580 Martin Schultz
580 Mr. & Mrs. James H. Caswell
580 Mr. & Mrs. G. F. Fischer
580 Mr. & Mrs. H. J. Powers
580 John H. Thayer
580 Mrs. M. F. Solomon
580 Mr. & Mrs. George P. Rinn
582 Mrs. E. E. Stelle
582 O. M. Lemon
586 Rev. & Mrs. H. O. Rowlands
588 Mr. & Mrs. A. H. Crocker
588 Mr. & Mrs. Samuel Cohn
592 Mr. & Mrs. Chas. Halla
    Receiving day Thursday
596 Mrs. E. G. Klaner & dr.
596 Mr.& Mrs.Anton H. Rintelman
602 Mr. & Mrs. Ernest Hess
604 Mr. & Mrs. Charles E. Hess
606 Mr. & Mrs. S. Eichberg
606 Mrs. J. Florsheim
608 Mr. & Mrs. W. H. Flentye
620 J. J. Holdsworth
622 Mr. & Mrs. J. J. Epstein
624 Mr. & Mrs. M. F. Pardee

591 Mr. & Mrs. Jos. W. Merriam
601 Mr. & Mrs. J. Metzler & dr.
611 Mr. & Mrs. A. B. Fiedler
611 A. B. Fiedler jr.
611 Mr. & Mrs. Frank W. Hess
615 Mr. & Mrs. Philip Rinn & drs.
   Receiving day 2d Thursday
621 W. O. George
621 Mr. & Mrs. William E. George
621 Mrs. L. Troyer & dr.
625 Mr. & Mrs. Chas. S. Waller&drs.
657 Mr. & Mrs. Edward Allen
657 John R. Wilson
663 Dr. & Mrs. Theo. W. Heuchling
   & drs. *Receiving day Friday*
665 Mr. & Mrs. Wm. Hunneman &
   dr.
669 Mrs. George P. Schumann
669 Mr.& Mrs.J.W.Eschenburg& dr.
669 H. A. Eschenburg

———

670 Miss Mary H. Krout
674 Mr. & Mrs. George P. Braun
674 Miss Lizzie Vail
678 Mr. & Mrs. Robert Lindblom
   Receive 1st and 3d Tuesdays
678 Miss Lenore Lindblom
678 Mrs. M. D. Lewis

628 Mr. & Mrs. Herman Paepcke
   Receiving day 1st Friday
632 Mr. & Mrs. Frank L. Bellows
632 Mr. & Mrs. Virgil Bogue
632 Mr. & Mrs. E. A. Dorner
634 Mr. & Mrs. Henry L. Dahl & dr.
640 Mr. & Mrs. C. Jevne & drs.
640 Henry M. Jevne
646 Mr. & Mrs. Gottleib Merz & drs.
646 Edward G. Merz
652 Mr. & Mrs. B. Gradle & dr.
   Receiving day 1st & last Sat. in mo.
654 Mr. & Mrs. Jacob Meyer
656 Mr. & Mrs. Ernest Wienhoeber
658 Mr. & Mrs. Nicholas Strotz &
   dr.
660 Mr. & Mrs. Harry Hargis
   Receiving day Tuesday
660 Olive A. Houghton
662 Mr. & Mrs. William Weadley
   Receiving day Wednesday
662 J. L. Weadley
666 Dr. B. Louise Heegaard
666 Mr. & Mrs. W. H. Heegaard &
   dr.   *Receiving day Monday*
666 Mr. & Mrs. Ralph Wm. Sprague
   Receive Monday
670 Mr. & Mrs. Chas. C. Cummings
670 Morris C. Cummings

LELAND AVENUE.

503 Mr. & Mrs. Charles W. Turner
507 Mr. & Mrs. Joseph P. Tracy
511 Mr. & Mrs. Cuthbert Warner
   Receiving day Tuesday

316 Mr. & Mrs. Spencer Ward
526 Mr. & Mrs. George W. Hoof
   Receiving day Wednesday

LILL AVENUE.

1549 Mr. & Mrs. Thos. I. Lovdall &
   drs.
1549 N. Harry Lovdall
1549 Thomas H. Lovdall
1559 Mr. & Mrs. John S. Cook
1559 John M. Anderson
1571 Mr. & Mrs. C. J. Whitney & dr.
1575 Mr. & Mrs. Otho D. Swearingen

1214 Mr. & Mrs. S. Wilson
1214 Merrill Spalding
1510 Dr. & Mrs. M. Herzog
1526 Mr. & Mrs. A. J. Cornell
1560 Mr. & Mrs. Thomas Ball
1572 Mr. & Mrs. Robert Cameron
1574 Mr. & Mrs. Frank M. Power
1578 Mrs. Harriet Jackson
1578 Mr. & Mrs. G. W. Barnett

LINCOLN AVENUE.

13 Mr. & Mrs. John W. White
15 Mr. & Mrs. Theodore A. Kochs
15 Miss Amelia Kochs
17 Dr. & Mrs. J. Frank
25 Mr. & Mrs. Thos. Carney & drs.
27 Mr. & Mrs. D. Rothschild

14 Mr. & Mrs. N. Hosmer
16 C. W. Utley & drs.
20 Mr. & Mrs. S. Goodman & dr.
20 Joseph Goodman
26 Mr. & Mrs. D. Jacobson
28 Mr. & Mrs. George L. Bottum

35 Mr. & Mrs. J. C. Spills
37 Mr. & Mrs. Eugene W. Blocki
51 Mrs. Charles T. Parkes & dr.
51 C. Herbert Parkes
59 Henry McKay & dr.
59 Miss Norah McKay
61 Miss Elizabeth L. Hartney
61 Miss Mollie Hartney
61 M. P. Hartney
63 Mr. & Mrs. William Greiner jr.
Receiving day last Fri. in mo.
63 Miss M. Frasch
71 Mr. & Mrs. John Thomlinson
73 Mrs. C. L. Kriete
75 Mr. & Mrs. Clarence Porter
75 Mr. & Mrs. James F. Bowers
77 D. J. Powers
79 M. S. Brady & drs.
83 Mr. & Mrs. C. P. Schaad
85 Mr. & Mrs. J. M. Armstrong
85 Thomas A. Armstrong
85 John J. Armstrong
87 Mrs. V. Scheppers
89 Mr. & Mrs. George W. Haines
91 Mrs. M. E. Owen
119 Mr. & Mrs. G. H. Stevens
133 Dr. & Mrs. J. N. Bartholomew
141 Miss Emma Rudowsky
143 Mr. & Mrs. W. A. Hinkins
143 Mr. & Mrs. J. Woltz
173 Mr. & Mrs. Charles Roth
Receive 1st Friday
173 Miss Matilda Roth
177 Mr. & Mrs. C. R. McCabe
177 John J. McCabe
185 Dr. & Mrs. L. C. Grosvenor
185 Wallace F. Grosvenor
193 Mr. & Mrs. F. B. Edelmann
193 Miss Lillian Folz
193 Miss Carrie Folz
205 Dr. & Mrs. Herbert J. Tarr & dr.
Receiving day Tuesday
205 Herbert J. Tarr jr.
205 Dr. William W. Tarr
239 Arthur G. Thome M.D.
239 Miss Hattie S. Thome
281 D. C. Bacon D.D.S.
281 Marie Thompson-Bacon D.D.S.
297 Mrs. Dorothea Tresselt & dr
313 Mr. & Mrs. John Wallace & drs.
315 Isadore L. Green M.D.
315 Mr. & Mrs. S. Edenheim
317 Mr. & Mrs. W. J. Lamb
319 Mr. & Mrs. T. F. Weber
319 Mrs. Barbara Stucker & drs.
319 Mr. & Mrs. E. L. Ross

46 Mr. & Mrs. Louis Gathmann
48 Mr. & Mrs. Philip Henrici&dr.
50 Augustus I. Lewis
58 Mr. & Mrs. Ferdinand Hincelot
60 Mr. & Mrs. C. Ramm
66 Mr. & Mrs. A. J. Press & dr.
66 Adam J. Press jr.
68 L. Vorderbrugge
68 Miss Minnie Schilling
68 Miss Annie Schilling
68 William Schilling
68 John Schilling
70 Mr.& Mrs. Christopher Pfeiffer
& dr.
74 Mr. & Mrs. George Frank
80 Mr. & Mrs. C. H. Gates
82 Mr.&Mrs.Leopold Becker&dr.
86 Miss J. Daly
88 Mrs. Edna Mason
88 J. A. Stolba
90 Mr. & Mrs. H. Ender
94 Dr. May H. Warren
94 Dr. W. E. Warren
98 Dr. T. M. Smith, D.D.S.
138 Dr. & Mrs. A. L. Farr
140 Mr. & Mrs. Hiram Barber & dr
144 Mr. & Mrs. John Soderberg
146 Mrs. Caroline Mehrle & dr.
146 Richard O. Mehrle
146 Henry A. Mehrle
146 H. W. Mehrle
214 Mr. & Mrs. H. F. Alborn
244 Dr. Coresta T. Canfield
294 Mr. & Mrs. Louis Kroth
598 Dr. & Mrs. J. A. Printy
600 Dr. & Mrs. C. H. Ludwig
Receiving day Thursday
600 Miss Martha Ludwig
602 Mr. & Mrs. John Bell
602 Miss Lottie Bell
602 Mr. & Mrs. Willis H. Towne
612 Dr. & Mrs. J. Vinton Bacon
642 Dr. & Mrs. Henry Ehrlich
886 E. C. Scholer M. D.

359 Mr. & Mrs. Hermann J. Becker
& drs.
411 Dr. J. G. Ames
695 Dr. Grant J. Roberts
695 Phillips C. Vaughan M. D.
721 Dr. & Mrs. A. E. Palmer
Receiving day Tuesday
721 Miss Violet N. Palmer
729 Dr. & Mrs. A. Buttner
945 Dr. & Mrs. N. E. Lentes

LINCOLN AVENUE (ROGERS PARK).

4117 Mr. & Mrs. Henry Newgard
4131 Mr. & Mrs. Morris Salmonson
4131 Alexander Salmonson
4132 Mr. & Mrs. Peter R. Carlson
4142 Mr. & Mrs. Hans C. Rixon
4142 Albert W. Rixon

LINCOLN PLACE.

5 Dr. & Mrs. W. W. Cook
7 Mr. & Mrs. Emanuel Weinberger
9 Mr. & Mrs. Simon J. Bloch
11 Mr. & Mrs. E. B. Smith
23 Mr. & Mrs. Carl Stein
37 Mr. & Mrs. J. A. Mayer
39 Mr. & Mrs. M. Franzen & dr.

12 Hugo W. Schmidt
12 Mr. & Mrs. F. W. Schmidt
12 Mr. & Mrs. F. C. Dammerau
   Receiving day Monday
18 Mrs. B. Gruenewald
22 Mrs. Michael Bauer
26 Mr. & Mrs. Joseph Staab
34 Mr. & Mrs. Alex. White
46 Mr. & Mrs. F. J. Loesch

LINDEN PLACE.

15 Mrs. N. B. Buford
15 Mr. & Mrs. Wm. T. Egan
21 Mr. & Mrs. Carl M. Mohr
21 Mr. & Mrs. W. D. Smith
21 Mr. & Mrs. Henry T. Brown

26 Mrs. Wm. H. Lotz
28 Mr. & Mrs. Martin O.Brien
28 Mr. & Mrs. E. R. Wetmore
30 Mr. & Mrs. Nathan Corwith

LOCUST STREET.

137 Rev. James Grundy
159 Mr. & Mrs. H. M. Smith
159 Mr. & Mrs. Henry Newton
161 Mr. & Mrs. John D. White
161 Mr. & Mrs. T. E. Chandler
161 George D. Chandler
165 William C. Oakley
165 Miss Carrie I. Oakley

138 Mr. & Mrs. John W. Connorton
142 Rev. & Mrs. W. A. Phillips
166 Mr. & Mrs. N. F. Olson
168 Mr. & Mrs. A. M. Neymann
    Receiving day 3d Friday

165 Mr. & Mrs. Wm. Bayne
165 T. F. Ransford

LUNT AVENUE.

519 Mr. & Mrs. Wallis K. Cook
771 Dr.& Mrs. Charles H. Burbank
813 Mr.& Mrs.Albert J. Grosswiller
1035 Mr. & Mrs. Charles H. Stiles
1125 Mr.& Mrs. Charles H. Prescott
1137 Mr. & Mrs. Emil Yung
1167 Mr. & Mrs. Wilmer K. Roberts

910 Mr. & Mrs. Frederick J. Doni-
    · hoo
930 Dr. & Mrs. Resegu C. Knox

236 Mr. & Mrs. Julius Mark
306 Mr. & Mrs. Isaac S. Pine
538 Mr. & Mrs. Hyman Levin
602 Mr. & Mrs. John S. Ziegler
624 Mr. & Mrs. Eugene M. Nichols
730 Dr. Bertha E. Bush
754 Mr. & Mrs. Edward D. Coxe
754 Charles B. Coxe
770 Mr. & Mrs. Oscar F. Herren
820 Mr. & Mrs. Joseph H. Servatius
820 Herbert H. Reed

MAGNOLIA AVENUE.

2501 Mr. & Mrs. G. F. Starkweather

2576 Mr. & Mrs. Max Henius

MALDEN STREET.

3133 Mr. & Mrs. Thomas B. Jeffery
3170 Mr. & Mrs. Parker A. Jenks
3183 Mr. & Mrs. E. A. Morris
    Receiving day Thursday
3183 Leo Meyers

3170 Mr. & Mrs. G. R. Murray
3170 H. W. Murray
3270 Mr. & Mrs. R. W. Clough

3287 Mr. & Mrs. Austin O. Sexton

MAPLE AVENUE.

4105 Mr. & Mrs. Edward C. Hammond
4127 Mr. & Mrs. James T. Caldwell
4313 Mr. & Mrs. Lawrence Mouat & dr.
4313 Mr. & Mrs. G. Harvey Bliss
4361 Mr. & Mrs. Albert J. Gates

4108 Mr. & Mrs. Joseph B. Noelle
4112 Mr. & Mrs. M. G. Stimmel
4112 C. Harrold Stimmel
4122 Mr. & Mrs. Plato G. Emery
4128 Mr. & Mrs. Chas. E. Browne

MAPLE STREET.

67 Mr. & Mrs. William P. Dickinson & dr.
71 Mrs. L. M. Meyer
73 Mr. & Mrs. Theodor Schrader
77 Mr. & Mrs. F. Campe
———
74 Mr. & Mrs. R. J. Zorge
76 Mr. & Mrs. Julius H. Huber

12 Mr. & Mrs. W. P. Wincher
12 Mr. & Mrs. Wm. Rossiter
12 Mr. & Mrs. Louis H. Lyford
22 Mr. & Mrs. Charles Fass
24 Mr. & Mrs. James Arnold & drs.
70 Mr. & Mrs. George Schmid
70 Mr. & Mrs. Godfrey Schmid
72 Mr. & Mrs. Wm. H. Johnson

MARQUETTE TERRACE.

23 Mr. & Mrs. C. M. Walworth
23 Mrs. M. L. Cheney
23 G. P. Taylor

14 Mr. & Mrs. F. A. Libbey

MAYFAIR STREET.

945 Charles West
947 Mr. & Mrs. Lewis Reynolds

964 Mr. & Mrs. H. Henderson
980 Mr. & Mrs. Theodore Corten

MELROSE STREET.

1825 Mr.& Mrs.Adolph Schoeninger
1847 Mr.&Mrs. Herrmann B.Washington
1849 Mr. & Mrs. Alfred Swadkins
    Receiving day Thursday
1855 Mr. & Mrs. S. P. Pugsley & dr.
1857 Mr. & Mrs. W. R. Jones
1857 Mr. & Mrs. G. H. Welton & dr.

1718 Jerome Probst
1816 Mr. & Mrs. R. Boericke
1838 Mr. & Mrs. W. L. Butterfield
1842 Mr. & Mrs. John M. Bredt
1860 Mr. & Mrs. F. P. Woollen & dr.
1866 Mr. & Mrs. Edward R. Jewett
———
1857 Mr. & Mrs. Chas. G. Welton

MENOMONEE STREET.

39 Mr. & Mrs. Frank W. Engers
43 Mr. & Mrs. Louis T. Starkel
43 Mr. & Mrs. Jul Buehler
———
14 Dr. & Mrs. B. B. Maydwell

8 Mr. & Mrs. W. A. Coit
    Receiving day Thursday
10 Mr. & Mrs. J. L. Goldsmith
12 Mrs. A. Rosenberg
12 Philip J. Magevney
12 J. C. Rosenberg

MOHAWK STREET.

337½ Mr. & Mrs. George W. Weber
363 Edward Melchior
367 Miss Margaret H. Syme
367 Mr. & Mrs. George A. Gregg
371 Mr. & Mrs. Charles Lenz
381 Dr. & Mrs. S. Kunz
385 Mr. & Mrs. Fred Volger & dr.

192 Mr. & Mrs. Henry Schomer
266 Daniel Sloan
354 Mr. & Mrs. F. W. Brenckle
360 Mr. & Mrs. C. J. Stone
368 Mr. & Mrs. George Kersten
370 Mr. & Mrs. H. B. Cady
372 Mr. & Mrs. J. W. Cones

MONTROSE BOULEVARD (LAKE VIEW).

1431 Mr. & Mrs. O. C. Simonds
1431 Mrs. H. N. Simonds
1507 Mr. & Mrs. M. M. Dutton
       Receiving day Thursday

1507 Kirk Avery Dutton
1617 Mr. & Mrs. Charles G. Ludlow

MORSE AVENUE.

471 Mr. & Mrs. Wm. A. Doolittle
471 William H. Doolittle
533 Mr. & Mrs. Jedediah H. Smith
727 Dr. & Mrs. Samuel V. Romig
731 Rev. & Mrs. Augustus W. Williams & dr.
811 Mr. & Mrs. John L. Healy
813 Mr. & Mrs. Thomas S. Wild
813 Mr. & Mrs. Jumes I. Ennis
817 Mr. & Mrs. Cornelius H. Ceperly
823 Mr. & Mrs. Robert Irvine & drs.

462 Mr. & Mrs. Andrew T. Hodge
462 Thomas Hodge
506 Mr. & Mrs. Albert E. Dickerman
548 Mr. & Mrs. William M. Welch
830 Mr. & Mrs. Harrison M. Wild
932 Mr. & Mrs. Jesse E. Smith
1020 Mr. & Mrs. George B. Simpson
1122 Mr. & Mrs. William T. Little

823 Mr. & Mrs. William Black
1225 Mr. & Mrs. Otto E. Freund

NEVADA STREET.

1823 Mr. & Mrs. James H. Smith
1825 Rev. & Mrs. Samuel C. Edsall

1859 Mr. & Mrs. Louis Behring
1859 Mr. & Mrs. Henry Behring
1871 Mr. & Mrs. W. H. O'Brien

NEWPORT AVENUE.

15 Mr. & Mrs. William Nash
15 Mrs. G. Schoen
27 Mr. & Mrs. Louis O'Neill
27 Mr. & Mrs. Benj. F. Bush
31 Mr. & Mrs. Frank P. Jackson
35 Mr. & Mrs. Edwin S. Hartwell
35 Joseph Lane
41 Mr. & Mrs. E. R. Mead & drs.
41 E. A. Mead

36 Mr. & Mrs. George M. Harvey
38 Mr. & Mrs. Egbert Jamieson
50 Mr. & Mrs. M. M. Jamieson
68 Mr. & Mrs. Edward L. Canfield
68 George H. Jenney

47 Dr. & Mrs. R. M. Paine
65 Mr. & Mrs. S. S. Gregory

NORTH AVENUE.

445 Dr. & Mrs. Albert G. Seeglitz
459 Mr. & Mrs. Chas. W. Reen
———
se. cor. N. State Most Rev. P. A. Feehan

454 Dr. & Mrs. Paul Kreye
458 Dr. H. E. Welcker
514 Mr. & Mrs. A. Schrader
516 Mr. & Mrs. J. W. Buell
516 Karl Demmler

NORTH PARK AVENUE.

631 Mr. & Mrs. Louis H. Schafer
    Receiving day Wednesday
631 Mr. & Mrs. Leo Strauss
681 Mr. & Mrs. Frank Hoefner
681 Mr. & Mrs. Geo. G. Thompson
    Receiving day Wednesday
681 Mr. & Mrs. Isador Berkenfield
691 Mr. & Mrs. Louis Chatroop
693 Mr. & Mrs. Wm. Hebel & drs.
693 Otto W. Hebel
695 Mr. & Mrs. B. J. Nockin
699 Mr. & Mrs. Jacob Henrich & dr.
703 Mr. & Mrs. D. I. Morris
703 Mr. & Mrs. Henry L. Forsyth
705 Mr. & Mrs. J. A. Bishop
    Receiving day Thursday
709 Otto F. Nau
713 Mrs. Elizabeth Walpole
743 Dr. & Mrs. C. N. Johnson
745½ Mr. & Mrs. J. Tuchband & dr.
751 Mr. & Mrs. Aaron Mossler

836 Mr. & Mrs. Fred. G. McNally
838 Mr. & Mrs. Theodore Schintz & dr.
842 Mr. & Mrs. Wm. K. Gillett
846 Mr. & Mrs. Marcus R. Williams
848 Mr. & Mrs. George B. Reeve
852 H. M. Hosick

682 Mr. & Mrs. Geo. W. Renners
    Receiving day Thursday
686 Dr. & Mrs. David M. Rankin &
    drs. *Receiving day Monday*
686 Mrs. Fannie Alcot Davis
688 Mr. & Mrs. Wm. Nethercot&dr.
688 S. G. Nethercot
688 Mr. & Mrs. M. A. Smith
696 Mr. & Mrs. James F. Pomeroy
698 Mrs. C. F. Wagner & dr.
704 Mr. & Mrs. Simon H. Baum
706 Mr. & Mrs. Fred Puff
708 Mr. & Mrs. Julius Eisendrath
710½ Mr. & Mrs. Holger de Roode
712 John H. Glade
714 Mr. & Mrs. C. H. Wacker
720 Mrs. Carrie Wangersheim
720 Mr. & Mrs. Fred Lowenheim
720 Emil Frank
750 Mr. & Mrs. John Macauley & dr.
750 Mr. & Mrs. Elmer C. Hill
758 Mr. & Mrs. Charles Woelffer
810 Mr. & Mrs. A. W. Olds & dr.
818 Mr. & Mrs. J. B. Cuyler
820 Mr. & Mrs. John Stevenson
822 Mr. & Mrs. R. A. Bower
824 Mr. & Mrs. Andrew McNally
824 Mr. & Mrs. Harry B. Clow
832 Mr. & Mrs. Alexander Belford

OAK STREET.

229 Edward McGurrin
269 Mr. & Mrs. W. H. Bush
269 Mr. & Mrs. George A. Bush
279 Mr. & Mrs. Thomas Cratty
295 Mrs. Frank R. Smith
295 C. H. Antes
333 Johannes Gelert
381 Mr. & Mrs. H. M. Love & dr.
    Receiving day Thursday
385 Mrs. C. Gallagher & dr.
397 Mrs. L. W. M. Abbott
401 Mr. & Mrs. Henry J. Spruhan
401 Jas. Cary Evans
401 Frederick W. Lamport
403 Mr. & Mrs. E. F. Heywood
403 Mr. & Mrs. George W. Beck
    Receiving day Monday
405 Miss C. A. Shattock
405 Miss Hannah Widerstrom
407 Mr. & Mrs. Geo. B. Hammond
407 Mr. & Mrs. Harry J. Hearn
411 Mrs. J. V. Knapp

248 Louis J. Millet
276 Mr. & Mrs. Wm. Flood & drs.
276 Russell H. Curtis
370 Mrs. K. C. Harrington
374 Mr. & Mrs. S. Glickauf
376 Mr. & Mrs. J. C. Burns
376 John S. Cooper & dr.
376 Robert W. Cooper
376 Mrs. H. W. Smith
378 Mr. & Mrs. Alexander Sullivan
380 Mr. & Mrs. R. A. Bowman
384 Mr. & Mrs. John Hitt
388 Mr. & Mrs.W. S. Chapman & dr.
388 Robert C. Chapman
390 Mr. & Mrs. Jacob Johnson
394 Mr. & Mrs. Charles Harpel
394 Mr. & Mrs. Charles J. Harpel
396 Mr. & Mrs. Thomas L. Dillon
410 Mr. & Mrs. Frank M. Bingham
410 Mr. & Mrs. Chas. T. Ravenal
410 Mrs. M. L. Ewing
410 Geo. B. Lathrop

411 Kemper K. Knapp
413 Mr. & Mrs. Jacob Engel
413 Miss Hattie Engel
417 Mr.&Mrs.HenryRuethling & dr.
419 Mr. & Mrs. Miles Barry
419 Henry J. Merceret
423 Mrs. W. A. Taylor
423 Rev. & Mrs. William Fawcett
425 Mr. & Mrs. Marshall Lapham
        Receiving day Wednesday
427 Mr. & Mrs. John J. Warde
        Receiving day Thursday
431 Mr. & Mrs. Otto H. Matz
        Receiving day Tuesday

410 John L. Lathrop
410 Joseph Lathrop
412 Miss Martha Murray
414 Mr. & Mrs. A. W. Browne
424 Mr. & Mrs. D. Frank Baxter
424 Mr. & Mrs. John H. Reardon
426 Mr. & Mrs, John T. Donaldson
428 Mr. & Mrs. John G. Frick
428 Wm. S. Powers
428 Mr. & Mrs. S. A. Freeman
————
431 Mr. & Mrs. Herman L. Matz
431 Miss Evelyn Matz

OAKDALE AVENUE.

1501 Mr. & Mrs. E. J. Henry
1747 Mr. & Mrs. C. A. Burton
1747 A. G. Burton
1749 Mr. & Mrs. Henry B. Ferris
1757 Mr. & Mrs. C. M. Smith
1757 Miss M. S. Sanford
1761 Mr. & Mrs. C. S. Hallberg
1761 Mr. & Mrs. F. T. Crittenden
1761 Mr. & Mrs. James Rowan
1765 Mr. & Mrs. Fred L. Miller
1765 Mr. & Mrs. J. M. Hoffman
1821 J. W. Finkler
1831 Mr. & Mrs. James White
1845 Mr. & Mrs. C. A. Gerold
1849 Mr. & Mrs. W. H. Bullen
1851 Mrs. Sarah E. Wheeler
1859 Mr. & Mrs. H. S. Tufts

1722 Mr. & Mrs. P. F. Groll
1750 Mr. & Mrs. Victor J. Petersen
1782 Mr. & Mrs. Wm. F. Lubeke
1784 Mr. & Mrs. John R. True
1810 Jesse M. Watkins
1814 Mr. & Mrs. J. B. Moos
1832 Mr. & Mrs. John M. Mott
1832 Mr. & Mrs. George P. Hoover
1842 Mr. & Mrs. John H. Behrens
1846 Mr. & Mrs. John Agar & dr.
        Receiving day Tuesday
1846 Woodbury S. Agar
1928 Mr. & Mrs. B. A. Ulrich
1928 B. A. Ulrich jr.
1928 A. Louis Ulrich
1932 Mr. & Mrs. Chas. Schonlau
1940 Mr. & Mrs. Richard Letsche
1944 Mr.&Mrs.CharlesSeegers&drs.
1944 George F. Seegers

OHIO STREET.

211 Mr. & Mrs. A. H. Perkins
213 Merritt D. Cobb
227 Miss Mary Jefferson
253 Mr. & Mrs. Chas. D. Moyer
255 Miss Josie Heath
255 Mrs. Emma E. Efner
259 Edward P. Carter & dr.
265 Mr. & Mrs. A. B. Brinkerhoff
267 Dr. & Mrs. Wm. C. Rohu
333 Mr. & Mrs. B. A. E. Landergren
333 Dr. Fred H. Wallace
333 Miss K. M. Regan
333 Mr. & Mrs. John W. C. Smith &
        drs.
333 Dr. M. W. Horine
337 Mr. & Mrs. George Gates & dr.
339 Mr. & Mrs. W. H. Barrett
339 Miss Jennie Griffith

210 Mr. & Mrs. W. Levy & dr.
        Receiving day Tuesday
210 Morris F. Levy
210 Mrs. Beckie Oppenheimer
216 James M. Maggart
216 Miss Kate A. Titlow
218 John Heron
220 Mr. & Mrs. G. A. Stanley & dr.
220 John J. Arney
240 Jethro D. Brown & dr.
240 Milton S. Shepler
262 Mr. & Mrs. C. E. R. Mueller
280 David Lanagan & drs.
282 Mr. & Mrs. S. Swartchild
284 Mrs. Rosa Kraus
284 Mr. & Mrs. Henry Leeb
284 Adolph Uhrlaub
286 Mr. & Mrs. Albert S. Evans

345 Mr. & Mrs. Charles Mears
345 Miss Ella Middleton
365 Mr. & Mrs. Egbert B. Mack
377 Mr. & Mrs. Garrett Burns
379 Rev. & Mrs. Elijah S. Fairchild
 Receiving day Thursday
379 Edward W. Fairchild
379 Meredith H. Fairchild
379 Arthur E. Fairchild

———

 10 Augustus Arend & dr.
 11 Mr. & Mrs. F. D. Hyde
 12 Mr. & Mrs. Wm. O. Chase
308 Charles Engle
308 C. S. Engle
308 Albert A. Munger
344 Mr. & Mrs. C. S. Rosenthal
344 Mr. & Mrs. E. M. Woodridge
358 Mr. & Mrs. Henry N. Mann
364 Mr. & Mrs. Patrick H. Shinners

286 Mr. J. D. Jones & dr.
288 Mr. & Mrs. John McKechney
288 John McKechney jr.
288 Mrs. Caroline Hill
290 Mr. & Mrs. J. R. McKay
 Receiving day Wednesday
290 Mr. & Mrs. Stuyvesant Leroy jr
 Receiving day Wednesday
290 J. M. McKay
292 Mr. & Mrs. Jonathan Slade
292 Henry Slade
296 Jaeschke Flats
 1 Mrs. Adolph L. Jaeschke
 1 G. A. Jaeschke
 2 Mr. & Mrs. W. S. Cotes
 4 Mr. & Mrs. E. D. Parmelee
 5 Mr. &. Mrs. W. G. Arnold
 6 Mr. & Mrs. John M. Berry
 7 Mr. & Mrs. Henry E. Mason
 8 Mr. & Mrs. Eugene Klapp
 9 Dr. & Mrs. Joseph W. Wassall
 Receiving day Monday

ONTARIO STREET.

227 Mr. & Mrs. J. A. B. Waldo
227 J. B. Waldo
227 Mrs. M. A. Ayers
253 Mr. & Mrs. M. J. Driscoll
255 Mr. & Mrs. E. V. Hitch
255 Edward Moore
261 Mr. & Mrs. J. B. Evans
263 Mrs. H. G. Holden
263 Samuel Chandler
267 George Burritt
267 Mrs. M. J. Burritt
271 Mr. & Mrs. Thomas Allen
273 Mrs. Anna Armstrong
275 Mr. & Mrs. Ezra T. Sturtevant
279 Mrs. A. Graham
287 Mrs. J. G. Forsyth
289 Mr. & Mrs. Allan P. Millar
289 Earl B. Millar
289 George B. Arnold
289 Henry L. Arnold jr.
291 Mr. & Mrs. C. V. Stockdale
297 Mr. & Mrs. Arthur C. Ely
297 J. C. Morse
301 Mr. & Mrs. Sidney Sawyer
301 Mr. & Mrs. T. M. Garrett
357 Mr. & Mrs. John R. Key & drs.
359 Mrs. Mary B. Rogers & dr.
363 Mrs. M. E. Williams
365 Mr. & Mrs. C. N. Hammond & drs.
365 Wm. P. Martin
365 George Weidig

226 Dr. & Mrs. G. Beecher Malone
252 Mr. & Mrs. S. P. Melander
254 Mr. F Mrs. Harris Bull
256 Mr. & Mrs. Milo George
256 Mrs. A. S. Ferris
256 Miss Winona A. Hohmann
256 Horace H. Thomas
258 Mrs. L. W. Ferris
258 Mr. & Mrs. Rudolph Williams
258 Mrs. Helen P. Wilbur
260 Mrs. N. K. Sherwin
266 Mr. & Mrs. Huron A. Ells
266 Thomas E. Liday
336 Mrs. H. K. Buel & dr.
336 Ira P. Bowen
336 Mrs. James H. Bowen
336 John R. Bowen
336 Mr. & Mrs. F. G. Draper
338 Mrs. Katherine S. Cooley &
 dr.
348 Mrs. John Newell & dr.
350 Abbot L. Adams
350 Misses H. L. & C. D. Adams
352 Mrs. J. H. Forrester
352 J. Lee Mahin
356 Mrs. J. S. McIlvaine & drs.
356 Lewis Spahn
358 Mr. & Mrs. R. M. Parker & dr.
360 Mr. & Mrs. H. H. Tilton
362 Mr. & Mrs. E. Earnshaw
362 Charles Earnshaw

369 Judge & Mrs. J. E. Gary & drs.
373 Mr. & Mrs. Edwin C. Harmon
373 Charles J. Harmon
373 Walter R. Harmon
375 Mr. & Mrs. Charles Higgins
379 Mr. & Mrs. Stuart R. Alexander
385 Mr. & Mrs. A. McIntyre
385 Percy H. Smith jr.
387 Mrs. G. P. A. Healy
389 Mrs. H. A. Hurlbut
389 Miss S. E. Hurlbut
389 Walter W. Edsall
399 C. H. Besly
399 Mrs. Oliver Besiy
401 Mr. & Mrs. W. W. Augur
403 Mr. & Mrs. P. H. Early
_____
410 Mr. & Mrs. George W. Haskell
410 Miss Georgina Haskeil
410 Mr. & Mrs. David Rutter
410 Lynn R. Rutter

362 Mr. & Mrs. A. A. Putnam
362 John A. Putnam
366 Dr. & Mrs. J. H. Buffum
368 Miss Jennette Beal
368 Miss May Page
368 Mrs. J. A. Maltby
370 Mr. & Mrs. Edward K. Rogers
372 Mr. & Mrs. R. Kenny
372 J. S. Kenny
372 Mr. & Mrs. John W. Hagerty
374 Mr. & Mrs. Chas. Blair Mac-
      donald
376 Mr. & Mrs. Charles Henrotin
378 Mr.& Mrs. Frederick S.Winston
380 Mr. & Mrs. Charles H. Coffin
      Receiving day Thursday
390 Mr. & Mrs. C. W. Boynton
396 Mr. & Mrs. Lawrence M. Wil-
      liams
398 Mr. & Mrs. S. A. Lynde
400 Mr. & Mrs. R. H. McElwee

ORCHARD STREET.

277 Mr. & Mrs. James G. Kendrick
301 Mr. & Mrs. W. S. Bartholomew
303 Mr. & Mrs. Elisha S. Bottum
313 Mr. & Mrs. Joseph Edmunds
341 Mr. & Mrs. Hugo Schmoll
381 Mr. & Mrs. Albion B. Lynch &
      drs.
385 Mr. & Mrs. F. C. Kramer
389 Mr. & Mrs. Fred Klaner
391 Mr. & Mrs. Philip Halla
391 Mr. & Mrs. W. Eugene Peck
397 Mr. & Mrs. Christopher Strass-
      heim
399 Mr. & Mrs. Emil Mannhardt
407 Mr. & Mrs. William Kuecken
      & dr.
407 Charles Kuecken
417 Mr. & Mrs. William E. Furness
417 James T. Furness
417 Miss Elizabeth M. Furness
417 Miss Grace E. Furness
417 Miss Margaret Furness
423 Mr. & Mrs. Henry M. Elliott
463 Mr.&Mrs. Frederick Y. Gookin
      & dr.
463 Frederick W. Gookin
473 Mr.& Mrs.William C. Dow
523 Mr. & Mrs. Charles W. Newman
      Receiving day Wednesday
527 Mr. & Mrs. Gustav Newman
529 Mrs. John A. Newman
531 Mr. & Mrs. Oscar Affeld

368 Prof. & Mrs. Aaron G. Dundore
392 Mrs. M. V. Brayton
404 Mrs. E. D. Seavey
404 Mrs. Juliet M. Seavey
456 Mr. & Mrs. Henry Goetz
460 Mr. & Mrs. Henry Baade
462 Mr. & Mrs. John M. Roach
462 Fred L. Roach
518 Mr. & Mrs. E. P. Clarkson
      Receiving day Thursday
520 Mrs. H. M. Hamill
524 Mr.&Mrs.Frederick Kleine&drs.
524 Louis H. Kleine
526 Mr. & Mrs. John A. Bryant
526 Miss Susan Bornhofen
528 Mr. & Mrs. J. S. Rossiter
532 Mr. & Mrs. James Chisholm
534 Mr. & Mrs. J. W. Ackermann
536 Mr. & Mrs. A. M. Mothershead
      & drs.
536 H. B. Lusch
612 Mr. & Mrs. Milton Jones
614 Mr. & Mrs. A. F. Hussander
614 Mr. & Mrs. A. M. Mayhew
626 Mr. & Mrs. W. E. Lewis
626 Mr. & Mrs. Charles Ackhoff
650 Mr. & Mrs. P. E. Nelson
_____
535 Mrs. A. L. Wood
535 E. D. Wood
535 P. P. Wood
535 Ralph Wood

569 Mr. & Mrs. John S. Farrel & drs.
569 John E. Farrel
569 William J. Farrel
575 Mr. & Mrs.Edmund Furthmann
 Receiving day Thursday
577 Mr. & Mrs. John P. Anderson

579 Mrs. Frederick Koehler & drs.
663 Mr. & Mrs. William G. Weigle
663 Mr. & Mrs. Charles J. Swanson
697 Mr. & Mrs. J. T. Smith
701 Mr.& Mrs. Fred. W. Foehringer
709 Mrs. Eliza Barrett & drs.

OSGOOD STREET.

113 Mr. & Mrs. John Carden
151 Mr. & Mrs. John Weber
171 Mr. & Mrs. Ernest P. Heinze
187 Mr. & Mrs. P. Dougherty
215 Mr. & Mrs. M. H. Hereley
245 Mr. & Mrs. Frank Amman&drs.

280 Mr. & Mrs. Andrew J. Pruitt
286 Mr. & Mrs. Alfred Graeff
———
247 Mr. & Mrs. W. M. Sullivan
253 Mr. & Mrs. Joseph J. Duffy

PALMER STREET.

1177 Mr. & Mrs. P. W. Gray
1211 Mr. & Mrs. James E. Keith
 Receiving day Wednesday
1245 Mr. & Mrs. M. VanAllen & drs.
1259 Mr. & Mrs. H. B. Barnes
1265 Mr. & Mrs. Joseph S. Miles
1271 Mr. & Mrs. Frank E. Baker
1279 Mr. & Mrs. E. E. Hutchins
1279 Dr. & Mrs. H. Rivenburgh
1283 Mr. & Mrs. William Miller
1337 Mr. & Mrs. Edmund O. Sewall
1341 Mr. & Mrs. H. S. Schwind
1341 Mr. & Mrs. Douglas McCallum

1230 Rev. & Mrs. James V. Lucas
1282 Mr. & Mrs. Martin C. Meader
1352 Mr. & Mrs. J. S. Seaverns
1378 Mr. & Mrs. Edmund D. Brigham
1384 Mr. & Mrs. E. V. Adkins
1398 Mr. & Mrs. Francis W. Percival
1412 John F. Hack
———
1383 Mr. & Mrs. Robert T. Regester
1397 Mr. & Mrs. Irving I. Stone
1469 Mr. & Mrs. W. E. Peckham

PARK AVENUE (Lake View).

107 Mr. & Mrs. William Grace
109 Mr. & Mrs. B. C. Barnes
109 Mr. & Mrs. T. G. Milsted
109 Mr. & Mrs. Andrew Crawford
 & dr.
 Receiving day Thursday

88 Mr. & Mrs. Sol Lande
90 Mr. & Mrs. John Fay
92 Mrs Helen Ryan & drs.
94 Mr. & Mrs. Harry C. Sawyer
96 Mr. & Mrs. W. C. Groetzinger
100 Mr. & Mrs. P. L. A. Schwarz
100 Miss Mahlie E. Weigle

PAULINA STREET.

2305 Mr. & Mrs. J. A. Roberts & drs.
2305 Walter A. Roberts
2337 Mr. & Mrs. H. Hochbaum & dr.
2397 Dr.&Mrs. Edw. B. Fetherston
2403 Mr. & Mrs. Charles M. H. Vail
2421 Mr. & Mrs. John McLauchlan
2429 Judge & Mrs. Nathaniel C.
 Sears
2429 Hale Knight
2433 Mr. & Mrs. John Trelease
2449 Mr. & Mrs. Robt. J. Bennett
2469 Mr. & Mrs. Arthur G. Bennett
 Receiving day Thursday
2573 Mr. & Mrs. James McWilliams

2288 Mrs. Jane N. Sulzer
2288 Mr. & Mrs. Charles M. Bowen
2302 Mr. & Mrs. Chas. S. Norris
2312 Mr. & Mrs. John A. Kreutzberg
2354 Mr. & Mrs. Edward H. Robinson
2384 Mr. & Mrs. P. J. Perry
2388 Mr. & Mrs. F. A. Munson
2402 Dr. & Mrs. Samuel C. Taylor
2402 Dr. Anna B. Taylor
2402 Burton J. Taylor
2410 Mr. & Mrs. Robert Matheson
2424 Mr.& Mrs.Chester F.Hall & dr.

2619 Mrs. James Wallace & dr.
2625 Mr. & Mrs. George A. Du Puy
2641 Mr. & Mrs. Frank Field
2641 Harry Field
2641 Charles Field
2645 Mr. & Mrs. Thos. E. Barrett
2653 Mr. & Mrs. Thomas E. Barrett
2665 Mr. & Mrs. Hervey H. Anderson
2681 Mr. & Mrs. J. K. Livesey
2685 Mr. & Mrs. Charles F. Persch
2705 Mr. & Mrs. F. A. Tripp
2731 Mr. & Mrs. E. F. Angell
2755 Mr. & Mrs. E. R. Newman
2771 Mr. & Mrs. William L. Wood
2781 Mr. & Mrs. G. P. Vance
2821 Mr. & Mrs. Francis J.Gillespie
2821 Mr. & Mrs. Augustine V. Gillespie

2684 Mr.& Mrs. James L. Batchelder
2706 Mr. & Mrs. Charles J. Dale
2736 Dr. & Mrs. Galloway Truax & dr.
2742 Mr.& Mrs.William Richardson

2430 Mr. & Mrs. Chas. N. Ettinger
2440 Mr. & Mrs. Frank D. Huth
2440 Mrs. Isabella Huth
2450 Mr. & Mrs. G. N. Ackley
2450 William E. Ackley
2454 Mrs. W. K. McAllister & dr.
2454 Mrs. Ellen Spencer
2486 Mr.&Mrs. Frederick T. Morris
2510 Mr.& Mrs. E. S. Lloyd
2560 Mr. & Mrs Frederick D. Stevens
2586 Mr. & Mrs. P. Spielmann
2586 Mr. & Mrs. Charles Spielmann
2586 Jacob Spielmann
2614 Mr. & Mrs. William F. Kienzle
2620 Mr. & Mrs. Luther C. Burgess
2624 Mr. & Mrs. Aaron M. McKay
2654 Mr. & Mrs. Charles H. Truax
2666 Mr. & Mrs. Daniel J. Murphy
2672 Mr. & Mrs. W. J. Pettitt
2672 Edward K. Pettitt
2678 Mr. & Mrs. Geo. E. Milligan
2678 Mrs. Patience Milligan
2682 Mr. & Mrs. D. H. McDaneld
Receiving day Tuesday

EAST PEARSON STREET.

27 Mr .& Mrs. H..H. Kellogg
35 Mr. & Mrs. George H. Taylor
35 Mr. & Mrs. Chas. H. Remien
35 Charles H. Remien jr.
39 J. J. Doyle
39 James H. Boyle
57 Mr. & Mrs. Thomas Minchin
57 Mr. & Mrs. Arthur Davis
63 and 65 The Audubon
   A Mr. & Mrs. C. Stevens
   B Mr. & Mrs. Robert M. Kerr
   C Mr. & Mrs. Jas. L. Benner
   D Miss K. E. Patrie
   E Mr. & Mrs. E. H. Brown
   F Miss E. Frenz
   G Miss P. Frenz
   G Franklin Remington
   H Mr. & Mrs. L. W. Burtis

38 Mr. & Mrs. G. P. English
38 Dr. J. Edward Slayter
42 Mr. & Mrs. John R. Bisland&dr
42 William A. Bisland

99 Mr. & Mrs. Charles B. Farwell
99 Mr. & Mrs. H. C. Chatfield-Taylor
99 Mr. & Mrs. Dudley Winston
99 Walter Farwell
109 Mr. & Mrs. John V. Farwell
125 Mrs. Bertha S. Flesh
125 Mr. & Mrs. Geo. W. Bryson
129 Mr. & Mrs. Vincent H. Perkins
131 Mr. & Mrs. N. Cohen & drs.
131 Reuben S. Cohen
137 Mr. & Mrs. J. M. Dowling

PERRY STREET.

sw. cor. Cosgrove av. Mr. & Mrs. John Logeman & drs.
   John H. Logeman
1369 Mr. & Mrs. Wm. Eastman
1475 Mr.&Mrs. Rudolph W.Gronow
1491 Mr. & Mrs. Washington Van Horn
1491 James H. Van Horn

1306 Mrs. M. Sulzer & drs.
1450 Mr. & Mrs. D. S. Scoville
1452 Mr. & Mrs. Louis H. Semper
1462 Mrs. A. Eugene Little
1462 William P. Little
1512 Mr. & Mrs. Joseph Johnson

1491 Charles E. Sinclair

PINE STREET.

51 Mr. & Mrs. Charles R. Barrett
55 Dr. & Mrs. C. E. Peck
55 J. R. Bowman
77 to 83 Newport Flats
   Cyrus Libby
   A Dr. & Mrs. Lloyd T. Dorsey
   B Mr.& Mrs. Joseph G. Carson
   C Mr.&Mrs. Jno.M. Hagar &dr.
   C Edward Mc. Hagar
   D Mr. & Mrs. Herbert Walker
   E Mrs. Franklin H. Beckwith
   E S. H. Kerfoot
   F Mr. & Mrs. Dudley A. Tyng
   H Mr. & Mrs. James L. Archer
89 Mr. & Mrs. A. Poole & drs.
99 Mr. & Mrs. B. F. Ayer & dr.
99½ Mr. & Mrs. M. J. Power
107 Mrs. George Sturges & drs.
115 Mr. & Mrs. W. F. Dummer
135 Edward J. Stokes
135 Miss S. L. Stokes
141 Mrs. C. Conlan
141 John A. Ryerson
147 Mrs. Alice Sullivan & dr.
147 Victor Elting
149 Miss Emily Wakem

184 Mrs. M. F. Hunkins & dr.
186 Mr. & Mrs. George Keen
188 Mr. & Mrs. Trusdale & dr.
   Receiving day Monday
190 Mrs. Marian A. Mulligan
190 Miss Allie Mulligan
190 Miss Alice Nugent
190 Mr. & Mrs. J. C. Carroll
   Receiving day Monday
220 John Dullaghan & dr.
220 Stephen M. Dullaghan
220 John P. Dullaghan
220 Edward P. Dullaghan
224 Dr. & Mrs. Geo. H. Bentley
236 Mr. & Mrs. John Miller & drs.
   Receiving day Thursday
238 Mr. & Mrs. J. N. Anderson
238 Miss Anna Wingreen

16 Mrs. J. P. Ferns & drs.
104 Mrs. I. N. Arnold & dr.
104 Miss Elizabeth Foote
106 Mrs. W. M. Scudder & dr.
106 J. Arnold Scudder
nw. cor. Huron Mrs. Mary Coleman
   Stuckert
   Receive 1st and 3d Mondays
nw. cor. Huron Miss Lily Stuckart
nw. cor. Huron A. M. Stuckert
108 Mr. & Mrs. Edwin D. Hosmer
118 Mr. & Mrs. James Fentress
120 Mr. & Mrs. S. F. Andrews
122 Mr. & Mrs. Willey S. McCrea
132 Mr. & Mrs. Henry Wischemeyer
132 Miss Mary C. Meyer
134 Mr. & Mrs. H. P. Crowell
   Receiving day Thursday
136 Mr. & Mrs. W. G. Scott
136 E. N. Scott
138 Dr. & Mrs. H. B. Favill
144 to 150 Kinzie Flats
   Mr. & Mrs. Chas. Cavaroc jr.
   Mr. & Mrs. R. L. Woodrough
   Receiving day Monday
   Mrs. Perry H. Smith
   Receiving day Monday
   Mrs. F. A. Sawyer
   Receiving day Monday
   Charles C. Cook
   Mr. & Mrs. B. F. Hadduck
   Receiving day Monday
   Mrs. O. P. Morton
   Mr. & Mrs. Percy L. Shuman
   Receive 1st Monday
   Oliver T. Morton
   Mr. & Mrs. C. W. Ware
   Mrs. J. M. Love & dr.
   Sidney C. Love
   Mrs. S. C. Gill
   Edward S. Adams
   Mrs. John E. Chapman & dr.
   John Adams Chapman
   Mr. & Mrs. Edward H. Davis
   Benjamin H. Campbell jr.
184 Mr. & Mrs. James W. Scott

PINE GROVE AVENUE.

297 Mr. & Mrs. John M. Bryant
303 Mr. & Mrs. Chas. F. Rietz
307 Mr. & Mrs. Frederick Rietz
595 Mr. & Mrs. Geo. L. Peterson
599 Mr. & Mrs. H. M. Hansen&drs.
   Receiving day Wednesday
605 Mr. & Mrs. Wm. R. Dawson

607 Mr. & Mrs. Henry G. Dawson
653 Mr. & Mrs. Otto A. Wolff
657 Dr. & Mrs. Wallace A. Bonniwell
663 Mr. & Mrs. Leonard S. Mulford
667 Mr. & Mrs. Julius H. Thunack
717 Mr. & Mrs. J. J. Mendelsohn

PRATT AVENUE.

901 Mr. & Mrs. Irvin E. Rockwell
923 Mr. & Mrs. Edward A. King
947 Mr. & Mrs. George S. Cook
1023 Mr. & Mrs. Christian L.Benson
1055 Mr. & Mrs. John M. Carlson
1137 Mr. & Mrs. Charles M. Bickford

808 Mr. & Mrs. Horace C. B. Alexander
812 Mrs. A. E. Dicks & drs.
948 Mr. & Mrs. Charles V.Muehlke
————
1221 Miss Josephine E. Rust
1231 Mr. & Mrs. John W. Sweet

RACINE AVENUE.

59 Mr. & Mrs. George R. Thamer
163 Dr. & Mrs. T. J. Lockie
271 Mrs. W. G. Reichwald
305 Mr. & Mrs. R. T. Stanton
305 John W. Stevens & dr.
305 Mrs. John J. McLinden
327 Mr. & Mrs. Thomas Goode
337 Mr. & Mrs. J. D. Mackie
357 Mr. & Mrs. R. J. Lewis
435 Mr. & Mrs. J. A. Seebaum
451 Mr. & Mrs. E. L. Abbott
455 Mr. & Mrs. W. L. Abbott
455 Mr. & Mrs. E. F. DeWalsh
517 Mr. & Mrs. George M. Boyd
521 Dr. & Mrs. W. S. Walker
525 Mr. & Mrs. A. E. Gamet & dr.
525 Clayton E. Gamet
527 Daniel Gamet

72 Mr. & Mrs. John Taubmann
74 Mr. & Mrs. E. Riegert
100 Dr. Geo. L. Stubinger
180 Mrs. Frederick Busse
202 William Hutton
260 Mr. & Mrs. Oscar A. Reum
268 Mr. & Mrs. James F. Bushnell
346 Mr. & Mrs. William G. Nourse
346 Miss Georgia Anna Nourse
350 Mr. & Mrs. G. L. Barrell
356 Mr. & Mrs. Otto Pressprich jr.
358 Dr. & Mrs. Fred B. Merrill
462 Mr. & Mrs. G. B. Schwarz
466 Mr. & Mrs. R. Hudson & dr.
666 Mr. & Mrs. J. W. Schmid
780 Mr. & Mrs. J. E. Webb
780 Mr. & Mrs. W. F. Stoll

EAST RAVENSWOOD PARK.

1240 Dr. Peter H. Pursell
1248 Dr. & Mrs. J. A. Carlstein

1462 Mr. & Mrs. Thomas B. Walton
1470 Mr. & Mrs. J. B. Washburne

WEST RAVENSWOOD PARK.

1209 Mr. & Mrs. John Fishleigh sr.
1219 Mrs. Cornelia Howard
1223 Dr. & Mrs. John Boynton

1241 Mr. & Mrs. Louis Semper & dr.
1241 Harry O. Buell
1361 Mr. & Mrs. Thomas C. Goudie

RETA STREET.

1829 Mr. & Mrs. Wm. A. Carlson
1837 Mr. & Mrs. Chas. Spangenberg
1837 Mr. & Mrs. Nathan VanDenburgh

1832 Mr. & Mrs. Louis Carson
1844 Mr. & Mrs. Geo. Thompson
1844 Mr. & Mrs. John R. Shellberg
1870 Mr. & Mrs. Albert D. Wentz
1872 Mr. & Mrs. Paul Kinze

RIDGE AVENUE (ROGERS PARK).

3742 Mr. & Mrs. William Richmond

3824 Mr. & Mrs. Levi H. Thomas
3824 Mr. & Mrs. Edgar S. Foote

RITCHIE PLACE.

5 Mr. & Mrs. James Van Inwagen
  Receiving day Monday
5 James Von Inwagen jr.
5 Arthur Van Inwagen
7 Rev. & Mrs. Jas. Gibson Johnson
  & dr.
9 J. L. Yale
9 Mrs. Madeline G. Wynne
11 Mr. & Mrs. Lloyd W. Bowers
13 Mr. & Mrs. Graeme Stewart
15 Mr. & Mrs. LeGrand Burton

10 Mr. & Mrs. Amos R. Smith
  Receiving day Tuesday
10 Lawrence W. Smith
10 Edward Page Smith
12 Mr. & Mrs. John A. Spoor
14 Mr. & Mrs. H. H. Forsyth
14 H. H. Forsyth jr.
14 W. Holmes Forsyth
14 George H. Forsyth
18 Mr. & Mrs. J. G. Coleman
20 Mr. & Mrs. E. M. Switzer
24 Mr. & Mrs. J. H. Swart

NORTH ROBEY STREET.

2567 Mr. & Mrs. Edw. C. Merrick
2601 Mr. & Mrs. Alexander Smith
2605 Rev. & Mrs. Joseph Adams
2605 Mrs. Julia Adams, M.D.
2615 Mr. & Mrs. L. R. Ermeling
2619 Mr. & Mrs. G. D. Dunham
2637 Mr. & Mrs. T. E. Mathews
2647 Mr. & Mrs. David Frost jr.
2665 Mr. & Mrs. Charles R. Haws

2673 Mr. & Mrs. Joseph Norton
2677 Mr. & Mrs. Joseph Patoille
2701 Mr. & Mrs. Clemens Oscamp
2703 Mr. & Mrs. Earl A. Pettigrew
2707 Mr. & Mrs. Chas.W.Cleveland
2707 Mr. & Mrs. Sam'l G.Cleveland
2719 Mr. & Mrs. Wm. G. Berger
2741 Mr. & Mrs. Wm. Gibson
2749 Mr. & Mrs. E. W. Zander

ROKEBY STREET.

1195 Mr. & Mrs. Walter E. Benson
1195 Mrs. E. J. Gamet & dr.
1207 Mr. & Mrs. Henry S. Schmitt

1220 Mr. & Mrs. Samuel Badgley

ROSCOE STREET.

733 Mr. & Mrs. Wm. I. Reedy
1621 Dr. & Mrs. A. G. Haerther
1633 Mr. & Mrs. Calvin K. Austin
1633 Mr.&Mrs.C. E. Corrigan & drs.
1633 Mr. & Mrs. Jeremiah J. O'Donnell
1633 Charles E. Corrigan
1633 George F. Corrigan
1645 Mr. & Mrs. W. R. Paige

1414 Mr. & Mrs. John C. Paul
1736 Mr. & Mrs. Henry Strassheim
1744 Mr. & Mrs. Frederick Kaehler
  & dr.
1746 Mr. & Mrs. Harry Hartt & dr.
———
1717 Mr. & Mrs. Charles Evans
1735 Mr. & Mrs. Edw. P. Ederer
1741 Mr. & Mrs. W. J. Haerther

ROSLYN PLACE.

9 Mr. & Mrs. A. W. Barnard
11 Mr. & Mrs. Wm. J. Bartholf
15 Mr. & Mrs. Frank H. Scott
15 Mr. & Mrs. Henry Drucker
17 Mrs. John Woollacott
23 William G. Webster
23 Mr. & Mrs. G. Martin Gunderson
23 Mrs. Ellen D. Driver
  Receiving day Thursday
23 Mrs. E. M. Rogers

42 Mr. & Mrs. F. L. Chapman
46 Mr. & Mrs. Brice A. Miller
46 Miss Blanche M. Hutton
———
31 Mrs. J. C. Garretson
31 Mr. & Mrs. I. C. Ketcham
33 Mr. & Mrs. O. W. Ruggles
33 Miss A. Roberta Ruggles
33 L. A. Cobb
35 Mr. & Mrs. H. Vernon Seymour

19

37 Mr. & Mrs. John W. Buehler
39 Mr. & Mrs. G. D. Searle
41 Mr. & Mrs. D. A. Ranck & dr.
43 Mr. & Mrs. D. McGuire

45 Mr. & Mrs. E. Rudolph
47 Mr. & Mrs. Butler Lowry
49 Mr. & Mrs. Ernest A. Shanklin
51 Mr. & Mrs. F. S. Cable

RUSH STREET.

77 Mr. & Mrs. J. P. Greene
85 Marqnette Flats
  Mr. & Mrs. T. H. Hawks
  Miss Helen E. Snow
  Miss Emma C. Kellogg
  Miss Anna C. Thaw
  Miss Josephine Stockton
  Mr. & Mrs. E. K. Punnett
    Receiving day Monday
  Dr. & Mrs. W. H. Allport
  Mr. & Mrs. Edw W. Russell &
    drs.
  Frank Russell
  Mr. & Mrs. Robt. A. Burton
87 Charlevoix Flats
  Mr. & Mrs. W. C. E. Seeboeck
    Receive Monday p. m.
  Mrs. W. S. Johnston
    Receiving day Friday
  Mr. & Mrs. E. St. John
  Mr. & Mrs. J. Jackson Todd
  Mrs. C. P. Abbott & dr.
  Mr. & Mrs. W. J. Head
    Receiving day Thursday
  Mrs. George Fisher & dr.
  Elbert C. Fisher
  Fred G. Fisher
  Mr. & Mrs. W. D. Baker
97 Mr. & Mrs. W. F. McLaughlin
  & drs.   *Receive Friday*
97 George D. McLaugblin
135 Mrs. Cyrus H. McCormick
135 Mrs. Emmons Blaine
151 Mr. & Mrs. Henry W. King
155 Mr. & Mrs. Cyrus H. Adams
157 Mr. & Mrs. W. G. McCormick
159 Charles B. King
159 Charles G. King
159 Miss Alice G. King
161 Mrs. Joseph Kirkland & drs.
    Receiving day Wednesday
161 John W. Kirkland
163 Mr. & Mrs. Dudley P. Wilkinson
    Receiving day Monday
163 Dudley P. Wilkinson jr
167 Mr. & Mrs. Sydney Williams &
  dr. *Receiving day Saturday*
169 Mr. & Mrs. Albert Hall
169 A. Percival Hall

76 Mr. & Mrs. La Verne W. Noyes
100 Miss E. Skinner
100 Miss F. Skinner
110 Mr.& Mrs. Henry J.Willing&dr.
    Receive Monday 3 to 6 p.m.
110 Miss Evelyn Pierrepont Willing
122 Mrs. J. V. Clarke & dr.
122 J. V. Clarke
122 Henry B. Clarke
122 Louis B. Clarke
124 Mr. & Mrs. R. Hall McCormick
124 Miss Henrietta H. McCormick
124 Miss Elizabeth D. McCormick
134 Mrs. Charles H. Hunt
136 Mr. & Mrs. S. H. Kerfoot & dr.
    Receiving day Wednesday
138 Mr. & Mrs. Walter F. Cobb
148 Mr. & Mrs. E. T. Watkins
156 Mr. & Mrs. W. K. Nixon
    Receiving day Monday
156 W. W. K. Nixon
158 Mr. & Mrs. F. Meredyth Whitehouse *Receiving day Monday*
162 Mrs. Edward S. Stickney
    Receiving day Monday
164 Mr. & Mrs. W. F. Blair
182 Mr. & Mrs. F. R. Chandler
    Receiving day Wednesday
182 Mr. & Mrs. Harry G. Selfridge
    Receiving day Wednesday
290-292 Cambria Flats
  Mrs. A. J. Brooks
  Mr. & Mrs. Robt W. Gray
  Mr. & Mrs. J. R. Hesslein
  Mr. & Mrs. H. R. Heaton
  Mr. & Mrs. Chas. S. Wilson
  John G. Watson
  Chas. U. Stuart
  Wm. R. Farquhar

173 Mr. & Mrs. A. H. Gates
177 Mr. & Mrs. P. L. Elder & dr.
177 P. L. Elder, jr.
179 Mr. & Mrs. E. H. Roche
181 Mr. & Mrs. Wm. McFadon
183 Mrs. Robert D. McFadon
185 C. N. Lauman
185 George V. Lauman

185 Mrs. J. G. Lauman
187 Mr.& Mrs. Edward A. Meysenburg
253 Mr. & Mrs. J. D. Higgins & dr.
253 James E. Higgins
291 Mrs. Bertha Fouts & dr.
291 Mr. & Mrs. Henry P. Taylor &
dr.
291 Benjamin Taylor
291 Mr. & Mrs. J. D. Fleming

293 Mr. & Mrs. J.A.Henderson &dr.
293 William Henderson
293 Walter Henderson
333 Mr. & Mrs. E. M. Watkins
333 Frederick A. Watson
345 Mr. & Mrs. Charles W. Johnson
Receiving day Friday
345 Mr. & Mrs. R. V. Wade
347 Mr. & Mrs. N. J. Gauer
347 A. H. Gauer

SCHILLER STREET.

169 C. William Alt jr.
191 J. W. Dyrenforth
215 Dr. Marie E. Reasner
295 Mr. & Mrs. Carter H. Harrison
jr. *Receiving day Monday*
299 Mr. & Mrs. A. C. Bodman
301 Mr. & Mrs. Andrew Peters
301 Mrs. Henrietta Cowles
303 Mr. & Mrs. William A. Mason
303 Sheridan Mason
305 Mr. & Mrs. Russell Ulrich

214 Mr. & Mrs. Leo Canman
220 Mr. & Mrs. Julius Goldzier
222 Mr. & Mrs. Max Stern
224 Mr. & Mrs. S. G. Pitkin & dr.
244 Mr. & Mrs. Maier Rosenthal
246 Mrs. Hannah Rosenfield & drs.
302 Mr. & Mrs. Wm. D. C. Street
306 Mr.&Mrs.Henry A.Towner&dr.

---

307 Benjamin M. Shaffner
309 C. M. Charnley

SCOTT STREET.

9 Mrs. Robt. Mercer Sheridan
9 Mrs. William H. Whiteside
9 Mr. & Mrs. J. R. Gay
13 Gen. & Mrs. Augustus L. Chetlain
13 Miss Virginia Freeman
13 Miss Ada M. Lowrie
15 Mrs. Anna Fleetwood
15 Mrs. Emma D. January
15 Mr. & Mrs. Stanley Fleetwood
17 Dr. William J. Hawkes & dr.
19 Mr. & Mrs. William B.McKinley
19 Miss Helen B. Gregory
19 Mrs. P. W. Frisbee
21 Mr. & Mrs. L. Mendelsohn & drs.
21 Abram Mendelsohn
21 Jacob Mendelsohn
23 Mr. & Mrs. Gregory Vigeant
23 Mr. & Mrs. George F. Ross
23 Herman B. Wickersham
23 George D. Holmes
25 Mr. & Mrs. John W. Ela
25 Miss Alice M. Neale

10 Henry W. King
10 Miss Katherine D. Kriegh
10 Miss Belle Davison
22 Mr. & Mrs. William D. Allen
24 Porter P. Heywood
24 John P. Heywood
24 Mr. & Mrs. Frank S. Heywood
24 Miss Marion B. Heywood
26 Mr. & Mrs. Richard Waterman
26 Richard Waterman jr.
42 Dr. & Mrs. Omer C. Snyder
42 Mr. & Mrs. Allen T. Prentice
44 Miss Mary J. Holmes
46 Alfred H. Wittstein
46 August Wittstein
46 Charles T. Wittstein
46 Miss Emma Wittstein
48 Mr. & Mrs. Bernt Moe & dr.
50 W. A. Paulsen
50 Mr. & Mrs. Edmund Swayer

---

27 Mr. & Mrs. Charles S. Crain

SEDGWICK STREET.

473 Mr. & Mrs. Wm. Mangler
473 Miss Emma Roelle
621 Dr. & Mrs. L. W. Case

526 Ferdinand Goss
636 Dr. Frederick A. Karst
642 Mr. & Mrs. Charles Barnes

625 Mr. & Mrs. J. Harry Ballard
625 Mr. & Mrs. C. Heimbrodt
657 Dr. & Mrs. Geo. E. Hawkins
665 W. H. Smith
.665 Dr. Jennie E. Smith
667 Mr. & Mrs. Goswin Hummel
681 Mr. & Mrs. C. E. Frizelle
683 Mr. & Mrs. G. A. Zimmerman
687 Mr. & Mrs. S. R. Ireland
689 Mr. & Mrs. Bernard Herbst
        Receiving day Wednesday
697 Mr. & Mrs. L. G. Kunze
735 Mr. & Mrs.Charles Waldschmidt
735 August W. Waldschmidt
739 Mrs. Ella M. Adams
747 Mrs. Amelia Holland & dr.
755 Mr. & Mrs. Fred G.Jungblut&dr.

———

780 Edward D. Cooke
780 Wilson H. Cooke
780 George Lanz

644 Mr. & Mrs. George Force
648 F. X. Brandecker
678 Mr. & Mrs. Samuel Custer
710 Dr. A. G. Ochsner
716 Rev. & Mrs. A. Norden & dr.
716 Dr. H. A. Norden
716 Felix A. Norden
718 Mr. & Mrs. Adolph Ascher & dr.
718 Julius Ascher
718 Henry Ascher
728 Mr. & Mrs. William White
        Receiving day Friday
730 Mr. & Mrs. Charles Sparre
738 Mr. & Mrs. A. H. Grunewald
738 Mrs. Dorothea Grunewald
740 Mr. & Mrs. F. Jager
744 Mr. & Mrs. George W. Kellner
756 Mr. & Mrs. K. G. Schmidt
778 Mr. & Mrs. H. Mueller
778 Mr. & Mrs. O. F. Mueller
778 Mr. & Mrs. Paul F. Lobanoff
780 Mrs. Cynthia Cooke

SEMINARY AVENUE.

85 Mr. & Mrs. J. M. Schoen
85 Mr. & Mrs. W. J. Lee
91 Mr. & Mrs. John C. Ramcke
107 Mr. & Mrs. Fred Klein
107 Mr. & Mrs. R. E. Harrsch
135 Mr. & Mrs. John C. Parkes
135 John C. Parkes jr.
209 Mr. & Mrs. H. H. Levis
211 Mr. & Mrs. E. B. Dyer
211 Mr. & Mrs. E. A. Bolten
221 Mr. & Mrs. A. H. Sime
221 Mr. & Mrs. S. M. Hastings
227 Mrs. Margaret S. Fitch & dr.
247 James Lyman & dr.
263 Mr. & Mrs. Robert Thompson
269 Mr. & Mrs. Rufus H. Sage
271 Mrs. Jacob J. Burbach
277 Mr. & Mrs. Duncan Cameron
279 Rev. & Mrs. Robert D. Scott
289 Mr. & Mrs. Peter Kraner
291 Mr. & Mrs. Paul Dilg
405 James Ford
425 Mr. & Mrs. John Northen & drs.
425 Thomas Northen
439 Mrs. E. B. Charles & dr.
439 Robt. B. Charles   .
439 Harry C. Charles
441 Mr. & Mrs. E. L. Waterman
        & drs.
445 Mr. & Mrs. James Dale

122 Dr. & Mrs. G. F. Zaun
178 Dr. & Mrs. John F. Runnells
206 Mr. & Mrs. J. D. Morrison
208 Mr. & Mrs. O. H. Kraft
208 Mr. & Mrs. Henry Sottmann
216 Mr. & Mrs. D. H. Carden
224 Mr. & Mrs. G. W. Williams
254 Mr. & Mrs. E. J. Birk
256 Mr. & Mrs. Fred H.Hildebrandt
256 Mr. & Mrs. Charles Eckstein
268 Mrs. Elizabeth Bryant
268 Fred L. Bryant
268 Mr. & Mrs. F. G. Bishop
280 Mr. & Mrs. Thomas Rankin
280 Mrs. John Lish   •
282 Mr. & Mrs. Lewis Jones
282 Mr. & Mrs. L. H. Noel
406 Mr. & Mrs. Jacob Harth
448 Dr. & Mrs. E. R. Bennett
498 Mr. & Mrs. Michael Kunkel
500 Mr. & Mrs. Charles Raiser

———

447 Mr. & Mrs. S. S. Jackman
        & dr.
479 Mr. & Mrs. Jno. A. Mahoney
555 Mr. & Mrs. M. Kaufman
579 Dr. & Mrs. R. S. Dubs
579 Mr. & Mrs. Fred A. Petersen
1151 Mr. & Mrs. Otto L. Wullweber

SEMINARY PLACE.

1203 Mr. & Mrs. Henry J. Samson
1205 William W. Lill
1205 Mr. & Mrs. George Lill & dr.

1218 Mr. & Mrs. Mathias Mueller & dr.
1222 Mr. & Mrs. Herman Metzger

SHEFFIELD AVENUE.

245 Mr. & Mrs. Martin Loescher
249 Mr. & Mrs. George J. Barth
399 Mr. & Mrs. Thomas P. Culloton
401 Mr. & Mrs. Jacob Volkmann
401 Mr. & Mrs. Jay Ingersoll
523 Mr. & Mrs. S. J. Verhalen
605 Wilhelm Griesser
641 Mr. & Mrs. Wm. H. Loehde
927 Rev. & Mrs. L. D. Dinsmore
929 Rev. & Mrs. Frederick Rinder
& dr.

678 Rev. & Mrs. W. F. Walker
& drs.
680 Rev. & Mrs. W. L. Walker
686 Dr. & Mrs. C. M. Downs
734 Mr. & Mrs. F. Bergman
912 Dr. Frank H. Skinner
914 Dr. & Mrs. F. E. Chandler
1194 Mr. & Mrs. Thos. A. Quinlan
& dr.

SHERIDAN ROAD.

1501 Mr. & Mrs. James C. Haskin
1563 Mr. & Mrs. Chas. A. McDonald
1563 Gabriel F. Slaughter
1609 Mr. & Mrs. Otis W. Bruner
1617 Mr. & Mrs. Wm. Treese Smith
1617 William C. Stone
1627 Mr. & Mrs. A. D. Winslow
1629 Mr. & Mrs. E. D. Winslow
1635 Mr. & Mrs. F. S. James & dr.
1635 W. P. James
1665 Mr. & Mrs. Robert A. Waller
1677 Mr. & Mrs. Henry A. Knott
1691 Mr. & Mrs. Ralph Stebbins Greenlee
1691 Mr. & Mrs. Jas. Allen Lounsbury
1691 Mrs. Emily Abbott Brooks
1701 Mr. & Mrs. Henry J. Peet
1711 Mr. & Mrs. James B. Waller
2151 Mr. & Mrs. Joseph W. Slayton
2155 Mr. & Mrs. Wm. D. Owen
2175 Mr. & Mrs. A. F. Nightingale
& drs.
Receiving day Thursday
2175 Rev. C. H. Chase
2175 Harry Nightingale

1224 Mr. & Mrs. Hudson W. Harper
1448 Mr. & Mrs. D. Sauer & drs.
1518 Mr. & Mrs. Joseph D. Bray
1522 Mr. & Mrs. Robt. Griffith
1530 Mr. & Mrs. John A. Graham
1542 Mr. & Mrs. John S. Stromberg
1548 Mr. & Mrs. Thos. W. Wrixon
1680 Henry C. Eddy & drs.
1684 Mr. & Mrs. Eliada B. Mallory
& drs.
1754 Mr. & Mrs. Edward A. Renwick
1764 Mr. & Mrs. A. P. Brink & dr.
Receiving day Friday
1764 Percy A. Brink
3660 Mr. & Mrs. Hervey E. Keeler
3660 Mr. & Mrs. Oscar T. Harroun

2211 Mr. & Mrs. Albert W. Rogers
2219 Mrs. Charles W. Campbell
2223 Mr. & Mrs. Edward S. Judd
2229 Mr. & Mrs. V. S. Woolley
2229 Mrs. Frances C. Wolley
2233 Mr. & Mrs. F. B. Townsend
2233 Mrs. J. R. Barstow
2237 Mr. & Mrs. B. B. Anderson
3229 Mr. & Mrs. John B. Fergus
3229 William L. Fergus

SHERWIN AVENUE.

903 Mr. & Mrs. John F. Bruckner
935 Mr. & Mrs. Schuyler F. Smead

844 Miss Kate Gallaher

808 Mr. & Mrs. Joseph A. Christoph
822 Mr. & Mrs. Harry T. Grundt
832 Mr. & Mrs. Charles H. Johnson
832 Miss Jennie Johnson
844 Mr. & Mrs. Charles Higgins

SIDNEY COURT.

15 Mr. & Mrs. E. A. Sittig & dr.
        Receiving day Thursday
17 Mr. & Mrs. C. Kollenberg
19 Mr. & Mrs. Adolph Seckel
29 Mr. & Mrs. Herman C. Buechner
33 Mr. & Mrs. J. G. Neumeister
49 Mrs. C. Frommann & dr.
        Receiving day Friday
49 E. H. Frommann

————

42 Mrs. John Wells Hubbard
42 Arthur O. Probst
44 Mr. & Mrs. H. S. Morgan
46 Mr. & Mrs. Ernest M. Dickey

16 Mrs. H. Spiel & dr.
18 Mr. & Mrs. J. W. Thorp
18 Charles Lederer
18 Mrs. Frank I. Jervis
18 Mrs. J. W. Crawford
32 Mr. & Mrs. Herman Kiper
34 Mr. & Mrs. P. Hardcastle
34 Mr. & Mrs. Jos. Barnhurst
36 Mr. & Mrs. M. J. Faherty
38 Mr. & Mrs. L. Jerome Baldwin
        Receiving day Wednesday
38 Lewis J. Baldwin
40 Mr. & Mrs. J. C. Bartlett
40 Miss Julia Sampson
42 Mr. & Mrs. S. Ross Stevens
        Receiving day Thursday

SOUTHPORT AVENUE.

4035 Mr. & Mrs. John Friemann
4061 Mr. & Mrs. Lionel E. Bush

4127 Mr. & Mrs. Jesse D. Marmaduke
4137 Mr. & Mrs. C. A. Eddy & dr.

ST. CLAIR STREET.

55 Mr. & Mrs. W. N. D. Winne & dr.
57 Mr. & Mrs. Wm. O. Green

52 Mr. & Mrs. Foree Bain
52 Miss Mary Allen

ST. JAMES PLACE.

9 Mr. & Mrs. W. L. Trowbridge
9 Mr. & Mrs. David Wylie
17 Mr. & Mrs. S. H. Lea
15 Mr. & Mrs. James A. Duthie
25 Mr. & Mrs. C. H. Murray
27 Mrs. J. H. Truman & dr.
27 Mrs. R. E. Cowdery
29 Mr. & Mrs. Frank Peters
29 Frank M. Peters
37 Wm. V. R. VanKleek
37 Mr. & Mrs. J. Almon Austin
        Receiving day Wednesday
43 Mr. & Mrs. E. W. Davv
53 Mr. & Mrs. Edmund R. Krause
        Receiving day Friday
55 Mrs. Augusta Erwin
55 Miss Emily Anderson
55 Mrs. Ida Martin
57 Mrs. L. P. McDaid
59 Mr. & Mrs. J. F. McGuire

8 Dr. & Mrs. George A. Baynes
8 Mrs. Sarah Gregory & dr.
8 M. S. Gregory
8 Mr. & Mrs. Charles D. Church
10 Mr. & Mrs. Chas. A. Higgins
10 Mr. & Mrs. Arthur R. Brown
16 Mr. & Mrs. Philip R. Smith
16 Mr. & Mrs. Henry C. Burbank
16 Mr. & Mrs. Russell N. Rogers
18 Mr. & Mrs. Lucian M. Williams
18 Mr. & Mrs. Wm. W. Vernon
22 Mr. & Mrs. Theo H. Purple
24 Mr. & Mrs. Chas. P. Miller
24 Mr. & Mrs. Lorenzo B. Roland
24 Mr. & Mrs Wilfred Massey
24 Mr. & Mrs. W. H. Cairnduff
28 Miss Netta Nixon
30 Mr. & Mrs. A. Weinberg
38 Mr. & Mrs. Chas. H. Nix
40 Mr. & Mrs. Jacob Friedman
42 W. Meyer & drs.

NORTH STATE STREET.

175 Mr. & Mrs. J. J. Barkley
175 W. H. Hannah
177 Mrs. M. E. Gould & dr.

148 J. Wilson
148 The Erie
        Mr. & Mrs. A. A. Blanchard

177 Mr. & Mrs. John Gattie
205 Mr. & Mrs. John R. Coleman
211 John W. Diggles
219 John Corse Howard
219 William H. Duval
237 Dr. & Mrs. A. W. Baėr
297 Dr. & Mrs. John Flood
297 Mr. & Mrs. H. C. Muhlke
299 Mr. & Mrs. Joseph H. Muhlke
299 Mr. & Mrs. J. Tiedemann
307 Mrs. Catharina Muhlke & dr.
307 George F. Muhlke
359 H. N. Taylor
383 Andrew Scherer
385 Mrs. Marion W. Butler
387 Mr. & Mrs. Frederick T. Vaux
387 Mr. & Mrs. Geo. W. Gould
387 Mr. & Mrs. Charles Hempstead
387 Mr. & Mrs. J. R. Manning
391 Dr. & Mrs. C. C. Higgins & dr.
391 Charles F. Higgins
399 H. F. Jaeger
399 Mrs. Caroline Jaeger
401 J. G. Dudley
401 G. T. Burrows
401 Charles Wilson
401 E. H. Stroud
401 Mrs. J. W. Kennicott
401 Mrs. C. Walker
401 W. H. Comstock
401 Frederick Merritt
403 J. Edmund Holland
405 Mr. & Mrs. Wm. H. Beebe
407 Mr. & Mrs. W. A. Montgomery
407 John R. Montgomery
415 Mr. & Mrs. Herman Benze
   Receiving day 2d Thursday
423 Mr. & Mrs. Chas. H. Hulburd
425 Rev. & Mrs. T. C. Hall
427 Mr. & Mrs. Nelson Thomasson
429 Mrs. Charles Dennehy
429 Thomas C. Dennehy
439 Mr. & Mrs. Robert Berger
449 Mr. & Mrs. Edw. H. Valentine
449 Mr. & Mrs. John Valentine
463 Mr. & Mrs. Walter L. Fisher
463 Howard Fisher
467 Mr. & Mrs. Samuel R. Jewett
469 Mr. & Mrs. H.E. Southwell&dr.
483 Mr. & Mrs. J. J. P. Odell & dr.
485 Mr. & Mrs. Sherburn Sanborn
495 Mr. & Mrs. Stewart Spalding
   Receiving day Monday
497 Mr. & Mrs. G. P. Fisher
499 Mr. & Mrs. W. B. Lewis

Mr. & Mrs. F. E. Crain
H. M. Davis
Thomas Duncan
Prof. C. H. Hathaway
Mr. & Mrs. L. N. Lord
Edward Maidment
Mr. & Mrs. S. Mandeville
E. Moore
Mr. & Mrs. Geo. L. Myers
Frank F. Oviatt
J. A. White
J. Wilson
166 Mr. & Mrs. John O. Blake
166 Harry J. Blake
168 Edwin Brainard
180 Mr. & Mrs. Alex. F. Beattie
180 Dr. W. A. D. Montgomery
180 John Alston
190 Mr. & Mrs. Joseph Martin
194 Mr. & Mrs. Wm. Auer & dr.
194 George E. Waldo
214 Mrs. J. Blanchard & drs.
214 Dr. Wallace Blanchard
216 Mr. & Mrs. J. Barrett
224 Mrs. J. M. Dillon
226 Mr. & Mrs. Wm. Sharpe
228 Edward J. Hoyer
230 Mr. & Mrs. A. W. Engel
266 Emil G. Harz
312 Dr. Marie A. Olsen
314 Mr. & Mrs. Thos. W. Johnstone
   Receiving day Wednesday
314 Thatcher W. Johnstone
314 Dr. William P. Adams
320 Mrs. Sarah Fouse
320 Robert E. Fouse
322 Mrs. Dr. Sarah Hackett Stevenson
384 Dr. & Mrs. R. R. Campbell
384 Dr. & Mrs. Robert Good
386 Mr. & Mrs. L. Spiesberger
388 Mr. & Mrs. John Prindiville & dr.
388 Redmond Prindiville
390 Mrs. J. E. Davidson
392 Mrs. Phebe B. Gehr & dr.
   Receiving day Thursday
392 Arthur C. Gehr
392 S. Whipple Gehr
394 Mrs. Almira M. Gilbert & drs.
396 Mr. & Mrs. Edward W. Bangs
400 Mr. & Mrs. E. O. Brown
406 Mr. & Mrs. Wm. K. West
410 Mr. & Mrs. James McNally
412 Mr. & Mrs. Charles F. Quincy
414 Mr. & Mrs. Henry S. Robbins

499 Mr. & Mrs. John A. Post
499 Mr. & Mrs. John E. Lloyd
501 Mr. & Mrs. Chester M. Dawes
503 Mrs. W. H. Estey
503 Mr. & Mrs. E. B. Hawley
507 Mrs. Wilson Cary
507 Wilson Cary jr
527 Mr. & Mrs. W. W. Gurley
531 Mr. & Mrs. A. C. Mather
533 Mr. & Mrs. Wm. C. Seipp
537 Mr. & Mrs. H. S. Durand & dr.
541 Dr. & Mrs. Henry Hooper
543 Mr. & Mrs. George B. Harris
545 Mr. & Mrs. S. S. Sherman & dr.
545 Mr. & Mrs. Fred S. Sherman
553 Mr. & Mrs. J. B. Inderrieden
553 John L. Inderrieden
553 Joseph S. Inderrieden
555 B. F. Felix
555 Mr. & Mrs. Ben Bates Felix
557 Mr. & Mrs. C. S. Kirk
565 Mr. & Mrs. Frank W. Stanley

———

514 Miss Catharine Smith
518 Mr. & Mrs. C. T. Wheeler & dr.
528 Mr. & Mrs. Christopher Watrous & dr.
534 Mr. & Mrs. Thomas S. Chard
536 Mr. & Mrs. John Lewis Cochran
538 Gen. & Mrs. M. D. Hardin
540 Mr. & Mrs. George A. Weiss
544 Mr. & Mrs. C. K. Miller & dr.
550 Mr. & Mrs. A. M. Pence & drs.
552 Mr. & Mrs. Jacob A. Wolford
556 Mr. & Mrs. Augustus A. Engle
556 Walter J. Engle
560 Mr. & Mrs. A. Mackay
600 Mr. & Mrs. Daniel Goodwin
Receive Tuesdays, afternoon
606 Mr. & Mrs. William Bush
606 Misses Clara & Emma Bush
608 Mr. & Mrs. Auguste Brosseau
Receiving day Monday

418 Mr. & Mrs. Adolph Cudell
Receiving day Saturday
418 Mr. & Mrs. Joseph Fleischmann
420 Mrs. J. Schmall & dr.
Rec. day 1st & 3d Wed. in mo.
420 H. W. Heinrichs
420 Miss C. L. Heinrichs
422 Mrs. Malvina Davidson
422 Mr. & Mrs. H. E. Davidson
424 Dr. & Mrs. Ernest Schmidt
424 Fred M. Schmidt
426 R. S. Emmett
426 Mrs. Eliza Talbot
426 Miss Laura Talbot
426 Dr. Hugh T. Patrick
426 Warren L. Beckwith
428 Lieut.-Col. & Mrs. Geo. W. Candee
428 Mrs. J. H. Hiebler
428 Capt. & Mrs. Jesse M. Lee & dr.
432 Mr. & Mrs. H. W. Henshaw
434 Mr. & Mrs. John R. Wilson
438 Mr. & Mrs. Max Newhouse & dr.
438 Mr. & Mrs. Leopold Newhouse
440 Rev. & Mrs. R. A. Torrey
450 Leonard Schmidt & dr.
460 Mr. & Mrs. Edward Engle
470 Mr. & Mrs. Lyman J. Gage
474 Mr. & Mrs. Horace E. Fisk
476 Mr. & Mrs. John K. Stearns
Receive Wednesdays, afternoon
476 Mr. & Mrs. Arthur B. Wells
480 Mr. & Mrs. S. C. Payson
482 Mr. & Mrs. Walter Morton Howland
502 Mr. & Mrs. W. B. McIlvaine
504 Mr. & Mrs. Ruthven Deane
506 Mr. & Mrs. John Russell Adams
Receiving day Thursday
508 Mrs. E. D. Bement
510 Mr. & Mrs. David S. Wegg
510 Mrs. J. Wegg
514 Mr. & Mrs. George W. Smith
514 Kinney Smith

STONE STREET.

39 Mr. & Mrs. Wm. C. Davis & drs.

SUNNYSIDE AVENUE.

237 Mr. & Mrs. Joseph C. Brompton
281 Mr. & Mrs. John A. Winters

———

346 Mr. & Mrs. Thomas Moore
346 Mr. & Mrs. W. L. Wait
346 Mr. & Mrs. W. Warner Fuller

214 Mr. & Mrs. Irving Washington
230 Mr. & Mrs. Oscar A. Beyer
236 Dr. & Mrs. Frank L. Peiro & dr.
236 Mr. & Mrs. John Wycoff
Reciving day Thursday
236 Miss Eva Emmet Wycoff

490 Dr. & Mrs. J. F. Berry
496 Mr. & Mrs. Felix Canda & drs.
528 Mr. & Mrs. Charles Walton
532 Mr. & Mrs. M. L. Paddock

534 Mr. & Mrs. Thomas L. Wolf
538 Dr. & Mrs. T. A. Keeton
538 Mrs. S. M. Frases
690 Rev. & Mrs. N. H. Axtell

SUPERIOR STREET.

269 Mr. & Mrs. Harry Meyering
273 Mr. & Mrs Nicholas J. Neary
273 Mrs. D. Quirk
273 James E. Bourke
277 Dr. J. J. Muldoon
313 Mr. & Mrs. E. B. Strong
    Receiving day Tuesday
315 Col. & Mrs. P. J. Hennessy
317 Mr. & Mrs. M. C. Newkirk
319 Mr. & Mrs. Russell Tyson
319 John Dorr Bradley
361 Mr. & Mrs. J. M. Flower
    Receiving day Monday
361 Mr. & Mrs. Louis B. Flowey
363 Mr. & Mrs. L. Meyering & dr.
365 Mr. & Mrs. William I. Howland
369 F. H. Winston
369 Miss Marie Winston
371 W. H. Thorne
373 William E. Strong
373 Miss Carrie M. Strong
373 Miss M. B. Laughton
377 Mr. & Mrs. Fred A. Smith
381 George M. Lyon
383 Mr. & Mrs. Joseph O. Morris
383 Mr. & Mrs. B. M. Winston
383 Mr. & Mrs. Charles C. Finkler
383 William R. Odell
385 Mrs. J. W. Sheahan & dr.
385 W. D. Sheahan
385 G. H. Sheahan
391 Miss H. V. Folsom
395 Miss A. Nolan
397 Mrs. A. S. Hibbard
399 Mr. & Mrs. Wm. R. Manierre
401 Mr. & Mrs. Jewett E. Ricker
407 Mr. & Mrs. John S. Hannah
411 Mr. & Mrs. S. Haughton Graves
417 Mr. & Mrs. Thos. S. McClelland
419 Mr. & Mrs. Thomas J. Shay

272 Mr. & Mrs. Thos. E. Doyle
294 Mrs. Bartley Langan
296 Mrs. Mary Ratty
296 Wm. Dent Beall
304 Mr. & Mrs. John Worthy & dr.
306 Mr. & Mrs. James Walsh
320 Miss Mary M. Anderson
320 Miss Josephine Large
322 John L. Lincoln
322 Chas. Wilson Goodrich
324 Mr. & Mrs. T. H. Harney
326 Dr. & Mrs. N. S. Davis jr.
328 Mr. & Mrs. Slason Thompson
396 Mr. & Mrs. E. W. Miller
400 Mr. & Mrs. James S. Gibbs
404 Judge James Goggin
404 Miss M. Goggin
406 Mr. & Mrs. Robert T. Newberry
408 Mr. & Mrs. E. L. Humphrey
408 Mrs. G. W. Stevens
408 Miss H. N. Davol
408 S. W. Stevens
408 Mr. & Mrs. Harry D. Stevens
412 Mrs. W. Floto
416 Mr. & Mrs. Oscar Marggraf & dr.
    Receiving day Thursday
416 Frank O'Donnell
418 Mrs. S. Garthe & dr.
418 Henry Garthe
422 John George Graue
424 Mr. & Mrs. Hugh MacMillan & dr.
    Receiving day Wednesday
426 Mr. & Mrs. Nathan K. Good-
    rich
426 Mr. & Mrs. H. F. Perkins
430 Mr. & Mrs. Calvin B. Cady
430 Mr. & Mrs. C. J. Gorton

---

421 Mr. & Mrs. Alfred L. Tetu
423 Mr. & Mrs. H. R. Campbell

SURF STREET.

2007 Gustav Hofmann & drs.

1860 Mr. & Mrs. Charles G. Muller & dr.
1904 Mr & Mrs. Luther H. Peirce & dr.
1910 Mr. & Mrs. C. C. Merriman
    Receiving day Thursday

1824 Mr. & Mrs. Wm. Marshall & dr.
1824 Irvin Marshall
1824 Alvah Marshall
1836 Mr. & Mrs. Wm. A. Wieboldt
1844 Mr. & Mrs. Nels Johnson
1848 Mr. & Mrs. C. H. Hanson
1852 Mr. & Mrs. Otto Ernst

SURREY COURT.

27 Mr. & Mrs. John Millar
33 Mr. & Mrs. W. S. Menger

37 Mr. & Mrs. E. R. Moffat
41 Mr. & Mrs. C. H. Barstow

TOUHY AVENUE.

467 Mr. & Mrs. George Addy & dr.
517 Mr. & Mrs. Waldo E. Dennis
531 Rev. & Mrs. Oliver E. Burch &
  drs.
743 Mr. & Mrs. Harlow W. Phelps
  & dr.
749 Mr. & Mrs. Ernest S. Smith
771 Mr. & Mrs. John Horn
807 Mr. & Mrs. Henry P. Daly & dr.
807 Mrs. E. R. Krebaum
817 Mr. & Mrs. Ashlin J. Beckler
817 Mrs. Eliza Beckler

532 Rev. & Mrs. Festus P. Cleveland
532 Mr. & Mrs. John D. Cleveland
768 Mr. & Mrs. Henry Newman
776 Dr. & Mrs. William D. Gentry
776 Carroll C. Hughes
812 Mr. & Mrs. Wm. G. Diederich
828 Dr. & Mrs. Jabez B. Burns
852 Mr. & Mrs. Franklin H. Doland
904 Mr. & Mrs. Wm. L. Crawford
———
839 Mr. & Mrs. Lyman H. Partridge

TOWER PLACE.

1 Edward S. Isham
1 E. S. Isham jr.
1 Miss A. E. Isham
1 Miss Frances Isham
  Receiving day Monday
3 Hon. & Mrs. A. S. Northcote
5 Mr. & Mrs. Francis King

4 Mr. & Mrs. Levi Z. Leiter & drs.
4 Joseph Leiter
  Receiving day Sunday, 12 to 2 p. m.
6 Mr. & Mrs. Geo. C. Eldredge
6 Mr. & Mrs. Geo. J. Hamlin
10 Mr. & Mrs. Sartell Prentice
10 E. Parmelee Prentice
10 H. P. Isham
10 Mrs. Pierrepont Isham

VILAS AVENUE.

217 Mr. & Mrs. Alfred T. Smith

WALTON PLACE.

9 Mr. & Mrs. J. C. Black
15 Mr. & Mrs. S. H. Wheeler
19 Mr. & Mrs. C. M. Smith & dr.
19 Miss Mary Rozet Smith
19 Francis Drexel Smith
21 Mr. & Mrs. Chas. F. Smith
39 Mr. & Mrs. Peter J. Biegler
61 Frank S. Pagin
63 Dr. M. B. Pine
65 Mr. & Mrs. Hart Conway
69 Mr. & Mrs. Joseph Paul & drs.
97 Miss Juniata Stafford
103 Mrs. Pauline Nathan
103 Albert Nathan
103 Edward Higgins & drs.
111 Mr. & Mrs. Elwyn A, Barron
111 Mr. & Mrs. W. J. Applegate

F. H. Armstrong
Mrs. John H. Avery

16 Mr. & Mrs. Frank Gilbert
18 Mr. & Mrs. M. J. Carney
20 Mr. & Mrs. F. A. Thomas
22 Mr. & Mrs. Lewis T. Hall
22 George F. Wright
22 Mrs. George F. Wright
24 Mr. & Mrs. H. Sherman Boutell
24 Mrs. Charles Horatio Gates
26 Mr. & Mrs. Wm. S. North
28 Mr. & Mrs. John B. Lee
28 Mrs. C. H. Perry
30 Dr. & Mrs. A. Belcham Keyes
30 Mrs. Edward Byam Martin
32 Mrs. A. M. Payne
34 Mrs. Laura Gibson
36 Mrs. E. DeLuce
36 S. H. Hubbard
38 Mr. & Mrs. Thos. J. Finney
Sw. cor. Rush, The Majestic
  Mr. & Mrs. A. V. Abbott

Baron & Baroness Curt von
  Biedenfeld
Mr. & Mrs. Wirt K. Gassette
Dr. & Mrs. Wallace K. Harrison
Dr. & Mrs. A. B. Hosmer
Mr. & Mrs. Edwin Jaquith
   Receiving day Monday
Mr. & Mrs. W. C. Kidder
Mr. & Mrs. Wm. H. Klapp
Mr. & Mrs. I. Kraft
Mr. & Mrs. J. B. Langan

Mr. & Mrs. C. E. Loss
Mr. & Mrs. G. W. Ogelvie
Capt. & Mrs. Philip Reade
Mr. & Mrs. Geo. Mills Rogers
Mr. & Mrs. Warren Salisbury
Mrs. Josephine M. Stewart
Col. & Mrs. Henry L. Turner
62 Mrs. Ada Brues & dr.
62 William Armstrong
76 E. E. Turner
106 Mr. & Mrs. M. J. Naghten

WASHINGTON PLACE.

1 James Bryson
3 Miss A. C. Fuller
5 Mrs. R. G. Bogue
5 Dr. & Mrs. O. N. Huff
5 Charles H. McKnight
7 Judge & Mrs. B.D. Magruder&dr.
7 Henry Latham Magruder

2 Mrs. Gordon Hall
2 Dr. & Mrs. Junius M. Hall
2 Dr. Alfred M. Hall
2 Dr. John Chester Lyman
4 Miss C. S. Durfee
4 E. H. Pease
6 Dr. & Mrs. L. H. Montgomery

WAUBUN AVENUE.

221 Mr. & Mrs. Herman Mueller

WAVELAND AVENUE.

1730 Mr. & Mrs. Henry Tewes

WEBSTER AVENUE.

231 Mr. & Mrs. Homer A. Squires
   Receiving day Thursday
283 Mr. & Mrs.Robert F. Goldsmith
285 Mr.& Mrs.George Thurber&drs.
285 Mr. & Mrs. James Heald
287 Mr. & Mrs. Gilbert L. Grant
289 Mrs. A. Heylmann & drs.
289 Mr. & Mrs. C. A. Flanders
289 Dr. C. J. Heylmann
291 Mr. & Mrs. John T. Long
293 T. B. Allen
305 Mr. & Mrs. O. Curtis & dr.
307 Mr. & Mrs. R. M. Hennessey
309 Mr. & Mrs. W. A. McGuire
309 Mrs. C. Grogan
311 Mr. & Mrs. Joseph Hodgson
311 J. H. Hodgson
315 Dr. & Mrs. G. W. Reynolds
321 Mr. & Mrs. Otto Guenther
401 Prof. Louis Kretlow
401 Miss Emma Kretlow
483 Mr. & Mrs. Martin Larsen
491 Mr.& Mrs.Charles Schotte & dr.
493 Mr. & Mrs. Albert Fredrich
497 Mr. & Mrs. John A. Hand&drs.

196 Mr. & Mrs. J. T. Quinn
202 Mr. & Mrs. John S. Butler
202 Mr. & Mrs. Fred Plotke
206 Mr. & Mrs. Charles Herrman
210 Mr.& Mrs.Anton Hellmich&drs.
264 Mr. & Mrs. B. T. Kennedy
264 Mrs. S. Rosenfeldt
274 Mr. & Mrs. Austin O'Malley
274 Mr. & Mrs. F. O. Kettering
286 Mr. & Mrs. Charles A. Dean
294 Mr. & Mrs. F. M. Charlton
294 Mr. & Mrs. L. N. Smith
296 Mrs. John Q. Delihant & drs.
298 Dr. & Mrs. J. H. Hoelscher
300 Mr. & Mrs. Stephen G. Hooker
300 George Hooker
302 Mr. & Mrs. Harry F. Donovan
308 Mr. & Mrs. E. G. Sheckler
308 Albert H. Hettich
312 Mr. & Mrs. John Seiler & dr.
312 Alfred Seiler
314 Mr.&Mrs.T.H.Glassbrook&drs.
318 Mr. & Mrs. J. Roth
320 Mr. & Mrs. Carl Huncke
324 Mr. & Mrs. Henry Lampert&dr.

499 Mr. & Mrs. C. Dickinson
499 Mr. & Mrs. Fred J. Casterline
499 Paul Dickinson
503 Mr. & Mrs. Carl Schmidt
505 Herman Liebman
509 Mr. & Mrs. T. J. Callinan
511 Mr. & Mrs. James D. Sturges
555 Mr. & Mrs. C. Jeanneret
555 Harry G. Jeanneret
555 J. Sidney Browne
557 Mr. & Mrs. C. W. Jeanneret
563 Mr. & Mrs. E. Harland & dr.

---

510 Mr. & Mrs. H. I. Howland
510 Mrs. J. E. Howland
512 Mr. & Mrs. G. Dengler
514 Mr. & Mrs. M. Freehling
516 Mr. & Mrs. H. Kollmorgen
520 Mr. & Mrs. James A. Grimes
522 Mr. & Mrs. F. Lewis

326 Mr. & Mrs. A. W. Peck
350 Dr. & Mrs. C. S. Bacon
356 Dr. & Mrs. Charles Storck
356 Mr. & Mrs. William H. Storck
360 Mrs. Sophia De Miller & drs.
360 William Rutlinger
372 Mr. & Mrs. W. C. Hollister
372 Mr. & Mrs. Emil H. Geudtner
374 Mr. & Mrs. T. J. Milholland
374 Mr. & Mrs. August E. Eckle
386 Mr. & Mrs. A. L. Brown
386 Miss Louise B. Brown
392 Mr. & Mrs. John M. Humlid
488 J. Hamilton Farrar
494 Mr. & Mrs. C. Stromberg
496 Mr. & Mrs. Chas. Canisius
504 Mr. & Mrs. R. C. DeLap
504 Mr. & Mrs. F. W. Childs
508 Mr. & Mrs. John Stoddard
508 Dr. & Mrs. Geo. C. Sanderson
510 Mr. & Mrs. H. P. Daw

WELLINGTON STREET.

1467 Mr. & Mrs. Robert M. Jaffray
1467 Mr. & Mrs. E. A. Filkins
1469 Dr. & Mrs. A. Grant Hopkins
1469 Mr. & Mrs. Chas. von Helmolt
1473 Mr. & Mrs. H. H. Davis
1473 Mr. & Mrs. John Koenig
1503 Mr. & Mrs. John A. Qualey
1503 Mr. & Mrs. W. T. Mason
1505 Mr. & Mrs. Edmund H. Striker
1505 Mr. & Mrs. George I. Burrell
1509 Mr. & Mrs. George Beaumont
1701 Mr. & Mrs. Frederick W. Freer
1705 Mr. & Mrs. W. M. Watson
1709 Mr. & Mrs. Walter Butz
1841 Mr. & Mrs. Chas. N. Holden
1847 Mr. & Mrs. Geo. Rounsavell
1847 Miss Isabella Rounsavell
1847 Miss Maude K. Rounsavell
1901 Mr. & Mrs. Jacob Birk & dr.
1901 William A. Birk
1915 Mr. & Mrs. Wyllys W. Baird

1854 Miss F. A. Barber
1900 Mr. & Mrs. C. W. Lasher
1920 Mr. & Mrs. Charles T. Messinger
1924 Mr. & Mrs. Dunlap Smith
1928 Mr. & Mrs. August F. Richter

1456 Mr. & Mrs. Wm. G. Wasmans-
      dorff
1456 Mr. & Mrs. A. E. Hultin
1480 Mr. & Mrs. Justus Chancellor
1644 Mr. & Mrs. Geo. Messersmith
1668 Mr. & Mrs. Nicholas Watry
1674 Mr. & Mrs. George Diehl
1678 Mr. & Mrs. Clarence Boyle
1694 Mr. & Mrs. Louis Hummel
1698 Mr. & Mrs. Emil Freise
1698 Mr. & Mrs. E. C. Ritsher
1700 Mr. & Mrs. Paul Merker
1710 Mr. & Mrs. John Shutts & dr.
1710 Mr. & Mrs. Adelbert J. Shutts
1806 Mr. & Mrs. F. E. Walther
1808 Dr. & Mrs. E. A. Gray
1810 Mr. & Mrs. J. W. Buschwah
1810 Gustav A. Brecher
1810 Mr. & Mrs. Charles Waller
1820 Mr. & Mrs. David Williams
1826 Mr. & Mrs. Herman Arnold
1830 Mr. & Mrs. Arthur J. Kirkwood
      & dr.
1844 Mr. & Mrs. Frederick Baumann
      & dr.
1844 Edward S. Baumann
1854 Mr. & Mrs. George M. Barber

NORTH WELLS STREET.

321 Mrs. Mary C. Hild
321 Frederick H. Hild
381 Mr. & Mrs. Daniel Schneider

332 Dr. & Mrs. C. O. Dorchester
362 Mrs. Annie Dieden
362 Dr. & Mrs. J. Muller

395 Dr. Edmund A. Boas
397 Dr. & Mrs. H. L. Lemker
455 Harry Pflaum
457 Dr. & Mrs. S. Schlesinger
515 Mr. & Mrs. Adolph Sturm
617 Mr. & Mrs. John Hirt
617 Mr. & Mrs. Henry Piper & dr.
679 Dr. Julia R. Howe
713 Mr. & Mrs. Harry Levy & drs.
719 Mr. & Mrs. Moses M. Fletcher
721 Dr. & Mrs. A. H. Peck
721 Miss Clara E. Schau
721 Mr. & Mrs. Christian Kussel
723 Mr. & Mrs. Fred Heide sr.
723 Mr. & Mrs. Hubert C. N. Press
725 Dr. & Mrs. W. F. Coy
727 Mr. & Mrs. Louis Schutt
727 Louis Schutt jr

———

710 Mr. & Mrs. Fayette C. Hall
    Receiving day 1st Tuesday
720 Mr. & Mrs. H. Schneck
722 Mr. & Mrs. Thomas H. Dwyer
732 Mr. & Mrs. L. E. Murphey

364 Mrs. Amelia Arnold & dr.
398 Dr. & Mrs. Carl Klein
398 Dr. William S. Orth
456 Mr. & Mrs. George Heppe &drs.
460 Mr. & Mrs. William Freund &dr.
460 Herman Freund
460 Charles Freund
486 Mr. & Mrs. H. E. Horn & dr.
486 Mr. & Mrs. Joseph Fitzek
500 Mr. & Mrs. Henry G. Emmel
    Receiving day first Tues. of mo.
500 Miss Martha Siefert
506 Dr. & Mrs. A. Decker
528 Mr. & Mrs. A. J. Boerlin
584 Dr. & Mrs. Felix Behrendt
622 Mrs. Henry Eisert
628 Mr. & Mrs. W. Niemeyer & dr.
676 Mr. & Mrs. Robert Klatz
678 Mr. & Mrs. Gust Loebman
678 Fred Loebman
682 Mr. & Mrs. August Gross & dr.
696 Mr. & Mrs. Frank Tempel & dr.
700 Mr. & Mrs. Moritz Freytag
708 Mrs. Peter Cunningham & drs.
708 Miss Sarah L. Cunningham

WEST COURT.

297 Mr. & Mrs. Conrad J. Gundlach
301 Mr. & Mrs. Isaac A. Grassie
301 Mr. & Mrs. Norbert Becker
301 Mr. & Mrs. Chas. W. Rogers
307 Mr. & Mrs. Gustav Fuchs

306 Mr. & Mrs. Charles B. Hull
306 Mr. & Mrs. John H. Free
308 Mr. & Mrs. Fred D. Shaver

———

307 Mr. & Mrs. Charles P. Noble

WILSON AVENUE.

237 Mr. & Mrs. S. E. Ockerlund
303 Mrs. Miranda Ballou
545 Mr. & Mrs. M. F. Ferry

214 Mr. & Mrs. John A. Thompson

WILTON AVENUE.

1187 Mr. & Mrs. Jas. S. McCoy & dr.
1191 Mr. & Mrs. John H. Murphy
1195 Mr. & Mrs. Felix E. McHugh
1199 Mr. & Mrs. Wm. Mitchell
1207 Mr. & Mrs. Louis Young
1215 Mr. & Mrs. Henry W. Wagner
1219 Mr. & Mrs. Martin Holst
1261 Mr. & Mrs. Dixon C. Williams
1261 Mr. & Mrs. Seymour Walton
1273 Mr. & Mrs. A. G. Wigeland
1287 Mr. & Mrs. Chas. A. Weber
1293 Mr. & Mrs. Sylvester J. Post
1297 Mr. & Mrs. Max P. Portman
1299 Mr. & Mrs. J. W. Edmonson

1286 Mr. & Mrs. Wm. Kennedy
1330 Mr. & Mrs. Karl F. Keppler
1334 Mr. & Mrs. Earl W. DeMoe
1344 Mr. & Mrs. Chas. H. Pfeil

———

1323 Mr. & Mrs. Wm. H. Dorothy
1327 Mr. & Mrs. Patrick O'Donnell
1327 James V. O'Donnell
1329 Mr. & Mrs. Elbridge H. Beck-
     ler
1331 Mr. & Mrs. Wm. P. Chapman
1369 Mr. & Mrs. Thos. F. Dow

WINONA STREET.

1015 Mr. & Mrs. G. C. Otterson
1069 Mrs. John Shepherd & dr.
1069 Chester H. Freeman
1069 Miss Emma B. Freeman
1089 Mr. & Mrs.Walter Hannington
1093 Mr. & Mrs. W. S. Pease

918 Mr. & Mrs. Albert L. Brown

———

1093 Mrs. L. S. Pease
1109 Mr. & Mrs. Cicero Hine
1169 Milton Hine

WINTHROP AVENUE.

419 Rev. & Mrs. Gustav Zollmann
    & dr.
419 John Zollmann
425 Mr. & Mrs. Paul Pitzgerald &
    drs.
441 Mrs. R. B. Caldwell & dr.
441 J. B. Caldwell
609 Mr. & Mrs. Willis G.Stoughton
869 Mr. & Mrs. Robert L. Morley
875 Mr. & Mrs. W. J. Ammen
883 Mr. & Mrs. John C. Scovell
891 Mr. & Mrs. S. H. Littlefield
1049 Mr. & Mrs. E. L. Burrell
1199 Mr. & Mrs. Albert W. Crane

———

1136 Ernest Dalton
1210 Mr. & Mrs. S. W. Belknap &
    drs. *Receiving day Thursday*
1210 Dr. & Mrs. J. P. Henderson
1220 Mr. & Mrs. Charles P. Whitney
1220 Mrs. Kate A. Whitney

368 Mr. & Mrs. N. Lederer
368 Mrs. E. D. Edwards
412 Mr. & Mrs. Stewart Galbraith
426 Mr. & Mrs. G. Nelson
430 Mr. & Mrs. E. P. Haven
430 Mrs. S. M. Haven
432 Dr. & Mrs. Wm. W. Hartman
502 Mr. & Mrs. George J. Rawll
668 Mr. & Mrs. James K. Cullen
688 Mr. & Mrs. E. S. Jackman
742 Mr. & Mrs. Martin Andrews
802 Mr. & Mrs. H. H.Osgood&drs.
812 Mr. & Mrs. James John
    Receiving day Tuesday
822 Mr. & Mrs. J. C. Gerstetter
822 Mrs. John Gerstetter
888 Mr. & Mrs. J. F. Muchmore
894 Mr. & Mrs. E. E. Dick
    Receiving day Thursday
1030 Mr. & Mrs. Robert Wahl
1126 Mr. & Mrs. R. G. Tennant
1136 Mr. & Mrs. Samuel Dalton

WISCONSIN STREET.

9 Mr. & Mrs. William McNeil &dr
9 Mr. & Mrs. William R.Strehl
15 Mr. & Mrs. C. Smith
23 Mr. & Mrs. John Druecker
    Receiving day Thursday
25 Mr. & Mrs. A. I. Frank
27 Mrs. W. C. Andrus
27 Mr. & Mrs. William H. Andrus
    Receiving day Friday
29 Mr. & Mrs. R. Phillipson
33 Mr. & Mrs. John Willson
35 Mrs. E. B. Hanna
35 Mr. & Mrs. Edmund Hanna
37 Mr.& Mrs.Robert G.Lucas & drs.
45 Dr. & Mrs. Frederick J. Leimer
57 Dr. & Mrs. Philip H. Matthei
    Receiving day last Wed. in mo.
57 Dr. & Mrs. Wm. Doepp

———

6 Reinhold Dresler & drs.

18 Mr. & Mrs. Charles Himrod
22 Roland Butterfield
22 Mr. & Mrs. Peter Lerch & dr.
22 Mr. & Mrs. Franklin L. Chase
46 Mr. & Mrs. Fritz Sontag
50 Mrs. J. B. Fox & drs.
50 Thomas E. Fox
50 J. V. Fox
50 Mr. & Mrs. Cornelius McAuliff
54 Mr. & Mrs. Edward Ruehlow
56 Mr. & Mrs. David W. Rowlands
56 William D. Rowlands
60 and 62 Hotel De Lincoln
    Mrs. P. C. Curtin & drs.
    Mr. & Mrs. John W. Prussing
    Mr. & Mrs. Henry A. Ritter
2 Mr. & Mrs. R. R. Knapp
3 Mr. & Mrs. D. L. Wheeler
5 William J. Louderback
5 Mrs. S. A. Louderback

6 Fred R. Dresler
7 Mr. & Mrs. Otto J. Weidner
Receiving day Tuesday

64 Mr. & Mrs. Andrew Nelson
66 Mr. & Mrs. Peter Loeffel
118 Mr. & Mrs. Max E. Wild

WOLCOTT STREET.

1209 Mr. & Mrs. Chas. A. Jennings
1215 Mr. & Mrs. Henry J. Mallernee
1219 Mr. & Mrs. Thos. C. Thompson
1219 Mr. & Mrs. Thos. W. Hibbard
1221 Mr. & Mrs. Charles A. Hurst
1221 Mrs. Mary Shubert
1225 Mrs. George M. Grannis
1255 Mr. & Mrs. Alonzo Stephens
1261 Mr. & Mrs. Theo. Pohlman
1265 Mr. Edwin J. Cubley & dr.
1277 Mr. & Mrs. David P. Brown
1269 Mr. & Mrs. Peter K. Rayner &
     dr.
1279 Dr. & Mrs. Wm. S. Gates
1279 Mrs. Harriet Pillsbury
1285 Mr. & Mrs. Chas. A. Stewart
1285 Charles H. Stewart
1291 Mr. & Mrs. Geo. H. Austin
1305 Mr. & Mrs. Peter F. Kaehler
1309 Mr. & Mrs. John Y. Sawyer
1309 Benjamin Sawyer

1210 C. Rich
1220 Mr. & Mrs. Burr A. Kennedy
1268 Mr. & Mrs. Henry Sumpter
1270 Mr. & Mrs. Wm. Thompson
1272 Mr. & Mrs. Henry Spangenberg
1290 Mr. & Mrs. John C. Hoof
1308 Mr. & Mrs. Wm. Dole
1318 Mr. & Mrs. D. R. Anderson
1358 Mr. & Mrs. Edmond J. Cadwell
1362 Mr. & Mrs. P. P. Porter
1362 Dr. P. B. Porter
———
1309 Frank S. Sawyer
1317 Mr. & Mrs. M. V. Montgomery
1321 Mr. & Mrs. John Taggart & dr.
1331 Dr. & Mrs. Henry H. DePew
1341 Mr. & Mrs. John M. Johnson
1347 Mr. & Mrs. H. Eschenburg
1351 Mr. & Mrs. P. H. Eschenburg
1351 Mrs. C. A. May & dr.
1397 Mr. & Mrs. Harry L. Harmount

WOLFRAM STREET.

1511 Mr. & Mrs. Alvin J. Butz
1511 Mr. & Mrs. Fred Heinberg
1523 Mr. & Mrs. Alfred A. Hirsch
1525 Mr. & Mrs. C. G. Stromberg
1535 Mrs. C. Christy & dr.
1535 Mr. & Mrs. Fred C. Christy
1543 Mr. & Mrs. Chas. Harms & dr.

1458 Mr. & Mrs. Philip Hillinger &
     drs.
1506 Mr. & Mrs. Wm. H. Weckler
1510 Mr. & Mrs. Chas. Anwander
1516 Mr. & Mrs. F. L. Frenke
1528 Mr. & Mrs. Chas. J. Stromberg

WRIGHTWOOD AVENUE.

1217 Mr. & Mrs. Julius Solomon
1233 Mr. & Mrs. Rudolph C. Radtke
1239 Mr. & Mrs. Nicholas Druecker
1239 Mrs. Ida Altsheler
1245 Mr. & Mrs. John G. Tenney
1247 Mr. & Mrs. J. C. Redheffer & dr.
1247 Dr. Charles F. Adams
1247 Mrs. Martha A. Adams
1325 Mr. & Mrs. C. H. Niemann
1437 Mr. & Mrs. A. C. Baker
1439 Ludwig Brown
1453 Mr. & Mrs. J. C. Coveny
1501 Mrs. A. C. Friese & dr.
1529 Mr. & Mrs. Lawrence J. Walsh
1715 August C. Swarth & dr.
1725 Mr. & Mrs. Oscar J. Hansen
1737 Mr. & Mrs. C. C. Wetherell
     Receiving day Thursday

1222 Mr. & Mrs. R. M. Hitchcock
1232 Mr. & Mrs. Edward C. Band
1254 Mr. & Mrs. Perley A. Russell
1256 Mr. & Mrs. C. Alfred Smith
1312 Mr. & Mrs. Charles Vergho
1312 Mr. & Mrs. Charles Vergho jr.
1312 Mr. & Mrs. A. C. Gondring
1316 Mr. & Mrs. Joseph Teven
1324 J. F. Reifsnider
1402 Dr. & Mrs. W. D. Storer
1436 Dr. & Mrs. Edwin Cross
1450 Mr. & Mrs. Henry Best
1450 Mr. & Mrs. Max Rehfeld
1456 Mr. & Mrs. Francis J. McCabe
1456 Mr. & Mrs. H. E. Mertens
1458 Mrs. Arthur Mackie & drs.
1506 Mr. & Mrs. Joseph W. Errant
1512 Mrs. T. J. Kinsella

1741 Mr. & Mrs. Arthur Dawson
1741 Mr. & Mrs. J. A. McDonald
1743 Mr. & Mrs. Julius Kiper
1761 Mr. & Mrs. G. A. Misch & dr.
1765 Mr. & Mrs. Henry Schultz
sw. cor. Hampden ct. Mr. & Mrs.
    Francis J. Dewes
1901 Mr. & Mrs. L. R. Williams
1917 Mr. & Mrs. Chas. E. Bleyer
1919 Mr. & Mrs. Charles E. Graves
1919 Mr. & Mrs. Thomas Mayhew
1921 Mr. & Mrs. George J. Williams

1784 Mr. & Mrs. Zel F. Windes
1784 Mr. & Mrs. T. H. Chamberlin
1814 Mr. & Mrs. Edwin A. Wood-
    ward
1814 Mr. & Mrs. Chas. W. Fischer
1820 Mr. & Mrs. C. H. Gottig
1850 Mr. & Mrs. W. D. Boyce
1938 Mr. & Mrs. August Wilkie

1512 Joseph F. Kinsella
1512 Daniel P. Kinsella
1620 Mr. & Mrs. Wm. P. Henderson
1728 Mr. & Mrs. F. A. Bischoff
1732 Robert White
1736 Mr. & Mrs. Solomon Karpen
1742 Mr. & Mrs. John P. Nissen
1746 Mr. & Mrs. E. W. Bromilow
1746 John B. Hittel
1746 Dr. Chas. E. Meerhoff
1750 Mr. & Mrs. Wm. C. Titcomb
1752 Mr. & Mrs. H. A. Noble
1760 Mr. & Mrs. Oscar F. Kosche
1760 Mr. & Mrs. A. J. White
1768 Mr. & Mrs. Elwyn B. Gould
1774 Burton Johnson
1776 Charles Swain
1776 Mr. & Mrs. L. P. Hugel
1784 Mr. & Mrs. E. S. Shockey
    Receiving day Thursday
1784 Mr. & Mrs. Frank D. Turner

YORK PLACE.

1727 Mr. & Mrs. E. H. Popper
    Receive 1st and 3d Thursdays

1738 Mr. & Mrs. F. A. Fritze

1722 Mrs. Robert Morrow
1722 Louis R. Morrow
1724 Mr. & Mrs. Jarve Platt
1732 Mr. & Mrs. H. O. Clausen &
    drs.

THE ONLY ONE.

Chicago, Milwaukee & St. Paul Railway is the only
nning solid Vestibuled, Electric Lighted and Steam
d trains between Chicago, Milwaukee, St. Paul
inneapolis.

Chicago, Milwaukee & St. Paul Railway is the only
nning solid Vestibuled, Electric Lighted and Steam
d trains between Chicago, Council Bluffs and Omaha.

berth reading lamp feature in the Pullman Sleeping
run on these lines is patented, and cannot be used
y other Railway Company. It is the greatest im-
ment of the age. Try it and be convinced,

further particulars apply at Ticket Office, 207-209
Street, Chicago, or at Passenger Station, Canal
, between Madison and Adams.

PART THIRD.

WEST DIVISION.

THE BLUE BOOK

ARRANGED ACCORDING TO STREETS AND NUMBERS,
NUMERICALLY, WITH OCCUPANTS' NAMES,
GIVING THE ODD NUMBERS IN
LEFT COLUMN, AND EVEN
IN THE RIGHT.

WEST DIVISION.

ABERDEEN STREET.

51 Dr. & Mrs. C. I. Thacher
59 Mrs. S. L. Brown
59 Miss C. Addie Brown
59 Edward C. Delano
95 Dr. & Mrs. R. G. Walker
157 Mrs. W. J. Moody

14 Mr. & Mrs. Lemuel J. Swift
20 Mr. & Mrs. Chas. C. P. Holden

167 Mr. & Mrs. Jonathan Clark
171 Mrs. Mary Elmes
175 Mr. & Mrs. Thos. Clark & dr.

NORTH ADA STREET.

19 Mr. & Mrs. F. W. Wilcox
55 James W. Twohig

86 Mrs. Calvin Stone
86 Mr. & Mrs. Fred K. Stone

WEST ADAMS STREET.

263 Mr. & Mrs. Addison E. Shaffner
267 Mr. & Mrs. M. C. Dean
267 Bradley Dean
269 Mr. & Mrs. J. S. Harvey
275 Mr. & Mrs. S. T. Alling
279 Mrs. B. Schwarz & dr.
279 Dr. A C. Brendecke
281 John T. Ripley
283 Mrs. Julia Richards & dr.
283 Mr. & Mrs. A. T. Graham
285 Mrs. W. B. Wilcox
285 Robert B. Wilcox
285 Thomas Turner
287 Mr. & Mrs. Peter Schuttler
    Receive 1st & 2d Friday in mo.
287 Peter Schuttler jr.
301 Mr. & Mrs. Christoph Hotz
    Receiving day 3d Friday in mo.
301 Miss Clara J. Hotz
301 Robert S. Hotz
345 Chas. E. Barker
345 George F. Barker
385 Mr. & Mrs. William B. Lord
389 Mr. & Mrs. David Bradley
    Receiving day Monday
389 Mr. & Mrs. G. Cadogan Morgan
    Receiving day Monday
389 Mr. & Mrs. Byron C. Bradley
389 B. Harley Bradley
393 Mrs. L. Bersback & dr.

300 Mr. & Mrs. John M. Smyth
300 Thomas Smyth
354 Mrs. Helen J. Stannard
354 Harry W. Stannard
354 Dr. Frank D. Stannard
354 Mrs. Jane P. Fittz
372 Dr. & Mrs. P. J. Rowan
374 Mr. & Mrs. Chas. W. Lewis
374 George E. Lewis
378 Mrs. M. Barrett
378 John T. McLeish
384 Mr. & Mrs. C. Shackleford
388 Mr. & Mrs. John F. Wright &
    dr.
392 Mr. & Mrs. E. S. Shepherd
392 Mrs. Fred Reed
398 M. F. Donoghue & drs.
398 Frank Donoghue
402 Mr. & Mrs. O. H. Hall
404 Mrs. R. W. Sinclair
428 Mr. & Mrs. J. G. Peters
430 Mr. & Mrs. Albert G. Lane
434 Dr. H. N. Moyer
434 Mr. & Mrs. W. Moyer
434 Mr. & Mrs. W. J. Moyer
434 Mr. & Mrs. E. A. West
434 Hugh Huleatt
434 Miss Helen Robinson
436 Mr. & Mrs. George B. Whitman
    & dr.

393 Otto Bersback
393 Mr. & Mrs. Ashley McDonald
395 Mr. & Mrs. Charles H. Slack
399 Mr. & Mrs. J. B. Campbell
477 Mr. & Mrs. B. T. VanHousen
479 Mr. & Mrs. Daniel Delaney
481 Mr. & Mrs. Francis Adams
481 Fred Adams
483 Dr. & Mrs. W. S. Harvey
485 Mr. & Mrs. D. J. Avery & dr.
487 Mrs. G. W. Newton
487 Miss Gertrude Newton
489 Mr. & Mrs. A. W. McDougald
491 Dr. & Mrs. A. C. Hewett & dr.
　　　　Receiving day Wednesday
491 Miss Henrietta H. Waring
495 Mrs. James Irons & drs.
　　　　Receiving day Thursday
501 Dr. & Mrs. F. Ziegfeld
501 F. Ziegfeld jr.
501 Carl Ziegfeld
501 William Ziegfeld
503 Mr. & Mrs. Irby W. Poor
　　　　Receiving day Tuesday
503 Mr. & Mrs. J. C. Ross
505 Dr. & Mrs. G. Horace Somers
505 Mr. & Mrs. George W. Ross
505 Miss Bertha F. Kohlsaat
505 Miss Anna M. Kohlsaat
507 Dr. & Mrs. E. Fletcher Ingals
509 Mrs. O. E. Benedict
509 Mr. & Mrs. Jno. Zimmerman
509 Mr. & Mrs. Jno. S. Mitchell
513 Mr. & Mrs. H. R. Pearson
515 Mr.& Mrs. G. W. Champlin
　　　　Receiving day Thursday
515 William R. Champlin
515 F. L. Champlin
515 Charles P. Champlin
517 Mr. & Mrs. W. O. Carpenter
521 Mr. & Mrs. Plowdon Stevens
533 Dr. & Mrs. W. M. Tomlinson
535 Mr.& Mrs.George G. Knox & dr.
535 Mr. & Mrs. Charles M. Knox
535 Miss Mary E. Knox
537 Mrs. B. Stein
537 Sydney Stein
537 S. Arthur Stein
539 Mrs. Calista E. Bigelow
541 Mr. & Mrs. F. K. Bowes
541 Chas. Lane Bowes
541 Mrs. C. B. Lane
541 William H. Lane
543 A. C. Durborow
543 A. C. Durborow jr.
543 Mr. & Mrs. C. E. Durborow

438 Philip N. Carter
438 Wallace Carter
440 Mr. & Mrs. G. H. Farrell
440 J. C. Hathaway
448 E. T. Mason
448 Frank B. Tobey
450 Mr. & Mrs. Chas. P. Abbey
454 Mr. & Mrs. D. G. Sawyer
454 C. P. Sawyer
464 Rev. & Mrs. E. R. Davis
464 Mrs. L. H. Palmer & drs.
464 Mrs. Tott L. Walker
464 Dr. Andrew Stewart
464 Miss Mary L. Sargeant
464 Mr. & Mrs. George T. Link
464 Mr. & Mrs. Albert Moffat
464 Mrs. Mary T. Reed
464 Mr. & Mrs. William Hall
464 M. A. Lane
464 Miss Sallie Lane
464 Miss Josie Lane
468 Mr. & Mrs. W. P. Smith
470½ Mr. & Mrs. Mark Phelps
470½ Mrs. Belle Reed
470½ Mr. & Mrs. J. Harris
474 Mr. & Mrs. H. W. McKewin
474 J. S. Connell
476 Mr. & Mrs. Michael Cohen & drs.
478 Mr. & Mrs. F. A. Bergman
478 George A. Bergman
492 Dr. & Mrs. Wm. A. Tichenor
496½ Mr. & Mrs. Melville Clark
498 Mr. & Mrs. Henry A. Gray
500 Mr. & Mrs. R. S. Lyon
504 Mr. & Mrs. William C. Pullman
506 Dr. & Mrs. J. Edwin Rhodes
508 Dr. Effa V. Davis
510 Mr. & Mrs. B. S. Crocker
510 H. P. Reigart
512 Dr. & Mrs. Chas. S. Taylor
　　　　Receiving day Tuesday
514 Mr. & Mrs. John H. Roy & dr.
514 Miss Hazel Campbell
514 R. Bulmer
514 Mr. & Mrs. Charles H. Merrill
514 Frederick L. Merrill
514 Mr. & Mrs. Robert C. Newton
516 Mr. & Mrs. Newton Andrews
516 Mr. & Mrs. Edward M. Hough
518 Dr. & Mrs. J. P. Mills
　　　　Receiving day Friday
518 Mr. & Mrs. Philip B. Harley
520 Rev. & Mrs. H. M. Scott
522 Mr. & Mrs. E. M. Teall

543 Conrad B. Durborow
545 Mr. & Mrs. Charles W. Mann
    Receiving day Thursday
545 Milo G. Derham
545 Ben M. Jaquish
565 Mrs. J. N. Lonergan
565 Mrs. L. Silk
567 M. Cunningham & drs.
575 Mr. & Mrs. George Birkhoff jr.
577 Mr. & Mrs. Geo. Birkhoff & drs.
577 Wm. G. Barfield
579 Mr. & Mrs. J. H. Bryant
    Receiving day Tuesday
581 Mr. & Mrs. S. B. Johnson & dr.
581 M. B. Rutt
583 Mr. & Mrs. L. F. Daly & dr.
    Receiving day Wednesday
627 William H. Snow
627 C. R. Jacobs
629 Mrs. E. M. Little
635 Mr. & Mrs. H. I. Morgan & dr.
635 Rev. Rudolph Dubs
637 Mr. & Mrs. William Craig
639 Mrs. Jane Holden & dr.
639 Henry P. Holden
641 Mr. & Mrs. R. A. Williams
    Receiving day Thursday
643 Mrs. M. H. Favor
645 Mr. & Mrs. A. R. Carrington & dr.
647 Mr. & Mrs. W. S. Elliott & dr.
647 E. E. Elliott
649 Rev. & Mrs. Henry G. Jackson
649 Charles H. Jackson
651 Mr. & Mrs. S. B. Cochran
651 Dr. A. W. Hartupee
655 Dr. & Mrs. Nelson Edmunds
655 J. Stephens
655 Mrs. F. R. Maher
657 Mrs. Sarah Nichols
677 Mr. & Mrs. H. S. Burkhardt & dr. *Receiving day Tuesday*
679 Mr. & Mrs. C. H. Magoon
679 Henry A. Magoon
683 Dr. & Mrs. G. M. Hammon
683 James R. Lane
685 Mrs. Caroline Solbery
685 Mr. & Mrs. Charles C. Reed
685 Elam L. Clarke
687 Mr. & Mrs. Ingram F. Glover
689 Mr. & Mrs. A. S. Devendorf & drs.
689 C. A. Devendorf
691 Mr. & Mrs. W. J. Rogan
691½ Mrs. Adelaide Lemon
691½ George S. Lemon
691½ Herbert L. Lemon

526 Mr. & Mrs. Jonas Z. Werst & dr.
530 Dr. E. L. Holmes & drs.
530 Dr. Rudolph W. Holmes
532 Pres. & Mrs. Franklin W. Fisk
    Receiving day Saturday
532 Mr. & Mrs. Henry E. Fisk
534 Mr. & Mrs. H. J. Coon & drs.
534 Thomas H. Coon
536 Mr. & Mrs. J. Roemheld & drs.
    Receiving day Sunday
536 Mr. & Mrs. C. F. Martens
538 Dr. & Mrs. O. J. Price
540 Mr. & Mrs. William Martin
576 Mr. & Mrs. John Walker & drs.
578 Mr. & Mrs. John R. Trimmer
578 William A. Trimmer
582 Dr. & Mrs. A. G. Beebe
584 Dr. & Mrs. N. B. Rice
    Receive 3d Saturday in mo.
584 Miss Louise Brown
586 Mr. & Mrs. Joseph Rothschild & dr.
590 Dr. & Mrs. T. C. Duncan
590 Mrs. John Osborn
592 Mr. & Mrs. James Lynch & drs.
592 Mr. & Mrs. L. J. Walsh
638 Mrs. Jerusha A. Webster & dr.
638 Mr. & Mrs. George Webster
642 Mrs. William Ilett
642 Edward P. Ilett
644 Mr. & Mrs. J. B. Peabody
644 Mr. & Mrs. J. A. Peabody
646 Mr. & Mrs. E. A. Hartwell & dr.
650 Mrs. Edward Twitty & drs.
652 R. Wilson More
652 Miss S. More
652 Mrs. N. B. Jones
654 Mr. & Mrs. Henry Rang
654 Eugene A. Rang
656 Mr. & Mrs. C. A. Davies
656 Mr. & Mrs. W. B. Everingham
660 Mrs. M. J. Forsyth & dr.
664 Mr. & Mrs. F. Hutchison
664 J. F. Hutchison
666 Mr. & Mrs. Lewis T. Jones
668 Mr. & Mrs. D. H. Henderson
668 Miss Ida Williams
672 Mrs. Catheriue A. Sheldon & drs.
672 H. D. Sheldon
676 Mr. & Mrs. Frank W. Young
678 Mrs. Mary Fullenwider & drs.
678 James A. Fullenwider
680 Mr. & Mrs. Emil Berger
680 Nathan Green
682A Mrs. M. A. Brackett
684 Mr. & Mrs. W. H. Iliff & dr.

691½ Mr. & Mrs. W. A. Baker
695 Mr. & Mrs. B. C. Prentiss
697 Mr. & Mrs. George D. Eddy
697 Albert Eddy
705 Dr. & Mrs. Chas. G. Davis
 Receiving day Wednesday
707 Mrs. E. E. Rennels
711 Mr. & Mrs. M. A. True
713 Mr. & Mrs. D. W. Baker & dr.
713 Mrs. Julia R. Sherwood
713 Henry Baker
713 Digory W. Baker jr.
715 Mr. & Mrs. T. C. Nash
717 Mr. & Mrs. A. J. Mitchell
719 Dr. & Mrs. S. S. Bishop
719 Mrs. P. Butlen
721 Col. & Mrs. J. H. Wood
721 T. C. Erlanger
729 Mr. & Mrs. J.C. McMullin & dr.
729 Mr. & Mrs. F. R. McMullin
733 Mr. & Mrs. J. C. Magill
735 Mr. & Mrs. N. A. Skinner
 Receiving day Wednesday
735 Mrs. A. Crandall
735 Miss Nellie Lonergan
737 Mr. & Mrs. John Wain
747 Mr. & Mrs. S. G. Lonsdale & dr.
751 Mr. & Mrs. R. B. Arnold
757 Mr. & Mrs. W. S. Tucker & dr.
757 William R. Tucker
759 Judge & Mrs. E. W. Burke
759 William V. Webster
763 Mr. & Mrs. W. S. Elliott jr.
 Receiving day Friday
765 W. E. Williams
771 Mr. & Mrs. C. R. Williams
771 Mrs. E. A. Judson
821 Mr. & Mrs. James K. McGill jr.
825 Mr. & Mrs. B. F. Underwood
837 Mrs. W. C. Dunning
839 Mr. & Mrs. Henry A. Osborn
839 Mrs. Susan Osborn
843 Mr. & Mrs. J. W. Hersey & dr.
843 Mr. & Mrs. James A. Hart
843 Mr. & Mrs. D. A. Arnold
855 Mr. & Mrs. J. H. Huyck & drs.
 Receiving day Thursday
873 Mrs. S. E. Cleveland
873 Mrs. Marian Guthrie
875 A. Lewis Edgarton
877 Mr. & Mrs. C. T. Chandler
891 Mr. & Mrs. Geo. F. Whidden
899 Mr. & Mrs. J. B. Rogan
901 Mr. & Mrs. W. F. Rollo
903 Mr. & Mrs. G. W. Huddleston
 Receiving day Friday

692 Dr. Sarah A. Conrad
692 Louis W. Conrad
692 Warren J. Anderson
696 Mrs. C. S. Butterfield
698 Mrs. J. C. Perrett
710 Mrs. M. H. Moore & dr.
 Receiving day Tuesday
710 Miss C. E. Davenport
710 Miss E. Cavanagh
712 Mr. & Mrs. L. Lloyd & drs.
714 Mr. & Mrs. T. A. Cantwell & dr.
 Receiving day Thursday
716 Rev. & Mrs. K. Wheeler
718 Mr. & Mrs. A. E. Ruger
718½ Mr. & Mrs. Claude S. Synder
718½ Mrs. Elizabeth D. Linney
720 Mr. & Mrs. B. F. Crosby & drs.
720 David K. Crosby
720 Mr. & Mrs. J. C. Moore
726 Mrs. M. A. Rood & dr.
726 John W. Rood
726 Dudley H. Rood
726 Mr. & Mrs. N. F.Valentine & dr.
728 Mr. & Mrs. Charles G. Davis
730 Mrs. Margaret Timberlake
730 Prof. E. T. Harper
730 Miss Lucina Harper
730 Miss Eva Stevens
732 Mr. & Mrs. W. H. Gibson
734 Mr. & Mrs. Richard Street & dr.
736 Mr. & Mrs. F. S. Young
736 Mr. & Mrs. J. S. Sawin
738 Mr. & Mrs. A. B. Smith
 Receiving day Thursday
738 Prof. Claire A. Orr
748 Mrs. Catherine Boyle & drs.
748 W. H. Boyle
752 Dr. & Mrs. E. B. Murdock
758 Dr. & Mrs. G. Frank Lydston
760 Mr. & Mrs. C. H. Bohanon
762 Mr. & Mrs. H. E. Metzger
 Receiving day Thursday
764 Mr. & Mrs. Albert F. Dean
764 Walter M. Dean
766 Mr. & Mrs. G. P. Brown
794 Mr. & Mrs. Albert R. Sabin
794 Mr. & Mrs. E. K. Symonds & dr.
800 Dr. & Mrs. W. J. Martin
800 Mr. & Mrs. H. R. Josselyn
808 Mr. & Mrs. Joseph B. Edwards
808 Frank L. Edwards
808 Miss Susie Cocroft
812 Mrs. D. B. Roman & dr.
816 Mr. & Mrs. T. C. MacMillan
816 Miss Margaret R. Goudie
820 Mr. & Mrs. R. M. Birdsall

903 Miss Sara Lacy
905 Mr. & Mrs. Eben A. Delano
907 Dr. & Mrs. J. R. Corbus & dr.
   Receiving day Tuesday
911 Mr. & Mrs.Louis Chester Rollo
   Receiving day Thursday
913 Mr. & Mrs. Morris Haber
915 Mr. & Mrs. J. F. Golding
927 Mr. & Mrs. I.W.Litchfield & dr.
927 Mr. & Mrs. James McGraw
935 Rev. & Mrs. F. L. Wilkins
937 Mr. & Mrs. J. H. Chapman
939 Mr. & Mrs. W. G. Jackson
983 Mr. & Mrs. James L. Board
987 Mr. & Mrs. E. Erskine McMillan
1043 Dr. & Mrs. O. Gibbs
1149 Mrs. Frances R. Francis & dr.
1149 Charles R. Francis
1167 Mr. & Mrs. H. C. Bennett
1185 Mr. & Mrs. W. H. Lamson
1185 Dr. C. St. Clair Drake
1227 Mr. & Mrs. F. C. Morley
1301 Mr. & Mrs. E. B. Howard
   Receiving day Thursday
1307 Mr. & Mrs. Alfred Barker
1313 Mr. & Mrs. Frank D. Rogers
1497 Mr. & Mrs. Thos. A. Leach
1535 Mr. & Mrs. I. W. Pierson
1541 James M. Hunter
1587 Mr. & Mrs. John L. Jackson
1603 Mr. & Mrs. Geo. L. Ayres
1635 Sidney H. Warner

946 Dr. & Mrs. Matthew Faloon
946 Miss Emma Faloon
952 Mr. & Mrs. W. J. Sherwood
974 Mr. & Mrs. E. W. Aldrich
   Receiving day Friday
978 Rev. & Mrs. C. Perren
   Receiving day Wednesday
978 Charles Perren
978 Frederick Perren
982 Dr. & Mrs. J. H. Salisbury
982 Miss Laura Thomson
992 Dr. & Mrs. C. Todd Hood
992 Miss Grace Chandler
1020 Mr. & Mrs. Francis Murphy & dr.
1020 Edward J. Murphy
1164 Dr. & Mrs. Henry S. Whitney
1200 Mr. & Mrs. Harvey C. Vernon
1206 Dr. G. H. Edgerton
1224 Mr. & Mrs. T. G. Farmer
1236 Mr. & Mrs. E. C. Chambers

820 Miss Louise Andrew
822 Mr. & Mrs. Arthur Burnam
822 Mr. & Mrs. Robert Bowie
824 Mr. & Mrs. Junius R. Sloan
828 Dr. & Mrs. A. E. Baldwin
836 Mr. & Mrs. B. F. Baker & dr.
   Receiving day Monday
838 Mr. & Mrs. A. D. Skillman & dr.
838 Dr. Fred B. Skillman
840 Mr. & Mrs. T. F. Dunton
842 Mr. & Mrs. John D. Clarke
842 J. N. Hunt
844 Dr. & Mrs. H. A. Phillips
844 James B. Muir
846 Mr. & Mrs. W. N. Alley
846 Mr. & Mrs. Fred M. Alley
862 Mr. & Mrs. Lee Wilson
864 Mr. & Mrs. W. R. Cleveland
866 Mr. & Mrs. C. B. Wilson
868 Mr. & Mrs. L. B. Ong
872 Mrs. A. Bielman
872 Mr. & Mrs. M. C. Paradise
874 Mr. & Mrs. Geo. G. Robinson & dr.
876 Mr. & Mrs. Charles B. Merrill
876 Rev. & Mrs. Stephen M. Merrill
878 Dr. & Mrs. G. W. Newton
880 Mr. & Mrs. Albert Schwarz & dr.
880 Edward Schwarz
882 P. A. Cavanna
884 Mr. & Mrs. Job Webb
886 Mr. & Mrs. H. H. Scoville & dr.
886 Mrs. E. M. Scoville
888 Mr. & Mrs. F. E. Sagendorph
888½ Mr. & Mrs. I. Hoffert
890 Mr. & Mrs. Rudolph Born
890 Victor Born
890 Julius Born
892 Mr. & Mrs. L. Oberndorf & dr.
   Receiving day Wednesday
892 Max L. Oberndorf
896 Mrs. Kate A. Wise
896 William Johnston
904 H. S. Dale
904 Miss Caroline H. Dale
904 Miss Jeannette Dale
908½ Mr. & Mrs. C. A. Barnard
922 James Vaughan
922 Mr. & Mrs. F. H. Morrison
922 Mr. & Mrs. A. J. Perry
928 Mr. & Mrs. L. D. Hammond
928 Luther S. Hammond
936 Mr. & Mrs. B. C. Miller
938 Mr. & Mrs. S. M. Hall
942 Mr. & Mrs. David Straus

1276 Dr. & Mrs. Richard Lull
1278 Mr. & Mrs. Stewart B. Sabin
1280 Dr. & Mrs. Cassius D. Wescott
1302 Mr. & Mrs. E. L. McAdams
1304 Mr. & Mrs. G. H. Johnston
1304 James E. Park
1310 Stephen Griffin

1312 Mr. & Mrs. Edward A. Davis
1334 Dr. & Mrs. W. H. Amerson
1532 Mr. & Mrs. Robt. H. Gillespie
1556 Dr. James A. Lydston
1616 Mr. & Mrs. George Lindon
1638 Mr. & Mrs. R. J. Puster
1642 Mr. & Mrs. Edw. S. Bristol

ARTHINGTON STREET.

96 Mr. & Mrs. T. N. Bell

ASHLAND BOULEVARD.

15 Mr. & Mrs. Allen B. Safford
17 Mr. & Mrs. Joseph W. Cowley
17 Mr. & Mrs. Chester E. Lapham
17 Arthur C. Lapham
17 Mr. & Mrs. H. H. Decker
19 Mr. & Mrs. N. M. Simonds
19 Miss Helen H. Hill
19 Mr. & Mrs. Wm. A. Glasner
    Receiving day Tuesday
21 Mr. & Mrs. Samuel Ehrlich
21 Mr. & Mrs. Moses Ehrlich
27 John J. Townsend & drs.
27 John J. Townsend jr.
27 James J. Townsend
27 Charles D. Townsend
29 Mr. & Mrs. Walter B. Godfrey
31 Miss Helen Culver
31 Miss Emma French
35 Mrs. Lydia J. Cadwill
35 Frederick D. Doty
35 G. S. Doty
35 G. S. Doty jr.
35 Harry E. Doty
37 Mr. & Mrs. Abner M. Lewis &
    drs.
131 The Ashland
    C. L. Adams
    Dr. P. Adolphus
    Mr. & Mrs. B. F. Ayers & drs.
    William G. Baxter
    Frank P. Dean
    A. J. Elliott
    H. A. Forbes
    Daniel J. Gallagher
    John C. Gallagher
    Mr. & Mrs. James Grassie
    Mr. & Mrs. Arthur Gustorf
    Mr. & Mrs. F. L. Lloyd
    Mr. & Mrs. F. L. Riggs
    Mr. & Mrs. L. C. Riggs
    John L. Sefton
    Mr. & Mrs. T. P. Sorenson

118 Mr. & Mrs. J.B.Overmeyer&drs.
120 Mr. & Mrs. Henry Agnew
122 Mr. & Mrs. J. M. Horton & dr.
122 Mrs. F. R. Duck
124 Mr. & Mrs. W. W. Wait & dr.
130 Mr. & Mrs. Samuel Carson
130 Dr. Alfred W. Woodward
132 Mr. & Mrs. Jas. W. Hedenberg
132 Mr. & Mrs. James B. Tascott
142 Mr. & Mrs. Joseph Deutsch
142 Mr. & Mrs. Obed Dann
142 Mrs. Edith J. Fisher
142 Joseph Fowler
144 Mr. & Mrs. John W. Thomas
144 Mr. & Mrs. A. B. Ellithorpe
144 Mr. & Mrs. Albert Shaw
146 Mr. & Mrs. Warren A. Wells
160 Mrs. J. J. Hankins
160 Mr. & Mrs. A. C. Paterson
    Receiving day Monday
160 Miss Maibelle Justice
160 J. Howard Wilson
162 Mr. & Mrs. D. B. Hutchinson
    & dr.
162 Mrs. E. E. Sprague
164 William Maxwell
166 Mr. & Mrs. Henry C. Storey
    Receiving day Wednesday
170 Mrs. Jane Armstrong
170 Joslyn Johnson
172 Mr. & Mrs. Ward S. Minkler
172 Dr. & Mrs. Adam Miller
174 J. Carrington Dunn
174 Nathan B. Dunn
174 Marion Thomas
176 Dr. & Mrs. Truman W. Brophy
    & drs.
176 Carlisle Mason
192 William J. Wilson
192 Miss Maggie V. Wilson
192 Mrs. Allen H. King
196 Mr.& Mrs.Wm.A.Pinkerton&dr.

Mr. & Mrs. S. Springer
Mr. & Mrs. R. H. Thomas
Mr. & Mrs. C. H. Wilcox
145 Mr. & Mrs. J P. Hart
145 Mr. & Mrs. Arthur E. Lane
145 Mr. & Mrs. John C. Deacon
145 H. V. Conine
145 Mr. & Mrs. C. T. Sisson & dr.
147 Mrs. Lenora S. Diller & dr.
147 Mr.& Mrs. Howard C. Pettibone
147 Rev. & Mrs. E. S. Williams
147 Miss Floy H. Miner
147 Mr. & Mrs. Fred H. Morrison
147 Miss Kate Morrison
147 Miss Belle Morrison
147 Frank P. Potter
147 Mr. & Mrs. E. B. Cobb
149 William H. French
149 Miss Mary French
149 Rev. & Mrs. J. L. Withrow
149 Miss Mary Jones
153 Mr. & Mrs. Wm. P. Rend
        Receiving day Wednesday
153 Joseph P. Rend
161 Mr. & Mrs. Charles FitzSimons
171 Mr. & Mrs. H. S. Dwight
171 Wm. J. McNally
171 Mr. & Mrs. F. A. Thayer
171 Miss Maria Sayward
171 W. G. Zoller
173 Mr. & Mrs. M. J. Scrafford
179 Mr. & Mrs. Thomas Chalmers
179 Thomas Chalmers jr.
201 Mr. & Mrs. Charles H. Case
209 Mr. & Mrs. John C. Polley & dr.
209 John C. Polley jr.
209 Mr. & Mrs. Frank R. Spear
211 Mr. & Mrs. Thomas L. Haynes
213 Mr. & Mrs. William Ridgway
215 Mr. & Mrs. Henry H. Aldrich
• 215 Edwin B. Harts
215 Clarence B. Hale
217 Mrs. Matilda B. Carse
        Receiving day Saturday
217 John B. Carse
217 David B. Carse
231 Mr. & Mrs. E. W. Kohlsaat &
        dr.
231 Philemon B. Kohlsaat
231 Mr & Mrs. Forest W. Hammon
237 Mr. & Mrs. H. Lee Borden
237 Gerald M. Borden
239 Judge & Mrs. C. C. Kohlsaat &
        dr.
241 Mr. & Mrs. Albert L. Sweet
241 Charles A. Sweet

200 Dr.& Mrs.Henry M.Lyman & dr.
200 Mr. & Mrs. Howard Greer jr.
204 Mr. & Mrs. Addison E. Wells
206 Miss Ora S. Gibbs
206 Mr. & Mrs. Henry H. Brown
210 Mr. & Mrs. E. A. Robinson &drs
222 Miss Virginia Sayre
        Receiving day Monday
224 Mr. & Mrs. Ulric King & dr.
224 Miss M. G. Jenkins
226 Mr. & Mrs. S. A. Scribner
230 Mr. & Mrs. E. F. Gobel & dr.
230 H. Elias Gobel
230 Miss Harrietta M. Gobel
234 Mr. & Mrs. William James Chal-
        mers
238 Mr. & Mrs. Charles F. Elmes
        Receive 1st & 4th Tuesday
238 Carleton L. Elmes
238 C. Warren Elmes
242 Mr. & Mrs. John W. Midgley
248 Mr. & Mrs. B. M. Hair & dr.
248 G. Ridgway
254 Mr. & Mrs. George H. Taylor
254 John S. Taylor
258 Mr. & Mrs. George A. Cobb
258 Mr. & Mrs. D. S. Lovejoy
258 D. L. Watkins
258 Miss Carrie Louise Watkins
260 Rev. & Mrs. Theo. N. Morrison
260 Miss Louise Swazey
262 Mrs. Carrie E. Hall
262 George Essig
272 Mr. & Mrs. Charles L. Rising
272 Frederick H. Rising
272 Henry W. Prouty
274 Mr. & Mrs. A. W. Eckert
276 Mr. & Mrs. John A. King
276 Mrs. Lorina Stevens
276 Miss Gertrude L. Stevens
284 Mrs. Emma Fick & dr.
        Receiving day Thursday
284 B. W. Fick
284 Mead Moore
286 Mr. & Mrs. Murdoch Campbell
        & dr. *Receiving day Thursday*
286 J. Albert Campbell
288 Mrs. Mary V. Haines & dr.
288 Fred H. Haines
290 Mrs. Frank DeVerna
290 Mr. & Mrs. Anson Mark
290 E. W. Hucksoll
290 D. C. Hucksoll
290 Miss Minnie Schultz
292 Mr. & Mrs. Lewis M. Prentiss
292 Lewis R. Prentiss

243 Mr. & Mrs. Marshall D. Talcott
    & dr.
245 Mrs. Henrietta Owsley
245 Mr. & Mrs. George K. Owsley
245 J. Guy Owsley
251 Mr. & Mrs. I. Stein
        Receive 2d Saturday in mo.
251 Mrs. B. Baumgartl
259 Mr. & Mrs. Bruno H. Goll
        Receiving day Wednesday
259 Bruno H. Goll jr.
261 Mr. & Mrs. Henry H. Hill
        Receiving day Thursday
261 Mr. & Mrs. George L. Shuman
        Receiving day Thursday
269 Mr. & Mrs. Oscar Burdick & drs.
269 Munson Burdick
273 Mr. & Mrs. Henry C. Hayt
275 Julius Petersen & drs.
277 Mrs. Ruth A. Featherstone
Receives 1st & last Tuesday in mo.
277 Edward A. Featherstone
277 Mrs. Lorina C. Furris
281 Mr. & Mrs. E. B. Holmes & dr.
281 Harvey A. Holmes
281 Mr. & Mrs. A. M. Campbell
287 Mr. & Mrs. Solon D. Stanbro
289 Mr. & Mrs. Clayton Mark
        Receiving day Tuesday
291 Mr. & Mrs. James M. Pyott
291 James M. Pyott jr.
291 William C. Pyott
291 George W. Pyott
293 Mr. & Mrs. Henry Detmer & drs.
293 J. Henry Detmer
293 Julian F. Detmer
293 Martin J. Detmer
295 Mr.&Mrs.D.M.Goodwillie & drs.
        Receiving day Thursday
295 Douglas M. Goodwillie jr.
297 Dr. & Mrs. John A. Robison
299 Mr. & Mrs. Charles R. Ruggles
301 Mrs. Frances L. Rickcords
303 Mr. & Mrs. Morrell O. Brown
305 Mr. & Mrs. Charles N. Post
305 Junius S. Post
307 Mr. & Mrs. J. A. Bingham
307 Mrs. Jane M. Bingham
317 Mr. & Mrs. F. H. Hayes
319 Mr. & Mrs. J. Edward Downs
319 Hubert C. Downs
325 Mr. & Mrs. Walter M. Pond
325 Walter E. Pond
327 Mr. & Mrs. George R. Nichols
329 Mr. & Mrs. Charles T. Nash
329 Mr. & Mrs. Hollis M. Thurston

292 Mr. & Mrs. J. D. Couffer
294 Mr. & Mrs. Chas. Stein
310 Mr. & Mrs. Thomas Kane
310 Miss Theo. Kane
314 Mr. & Mrs. Phillip L. Auten
322 Mr. & Mrs. F. G. Jordan
322 Mr.&Mrs. Augustine W. Wright
326 Thomas Templeton
326 Miss M. Templeton
330 Mr. & Mrs.G.C. Hutchinson&dr.
        Receiving day Tuesday
330 George A. Hutchinson
332 Mr. & Mrs. D. B. Scully
342 Mr. & Mrs. Jefferson L. Fulton
    & dr.
342 Lester B. Fulton
346 Mr. & Mrs. Lewis Russ
346 Bert S. Russ
348 Mr. & Mrs. Lyman L. Barbour
348 Ernest Barbour
348 Mr. & Mrs. E. L. Thompson
348 Mrs. E. Reddish
350 Mrs. G. F. Watt & dr.
350 George F. Watt
350 Mr. & Mrs. Robt. J. Goodwillie
        Receiving day Tuesday
350 Mrs. Carrie A. Hill
350 Miss Irene N. Hill
352 Mr. & Mrs. R. H. Piratzky
        Receive 2d Wednesday in mo.
352 Miss Alma E. Piratzky
        Receives 2d Wednesday in mo.
356 Mr. & Mrs. George B. Kane
356 William D. Kane
360 Mr. & Mrs. Louis Woltersdorf &
    dr. *Receiving day Wednesday*
360 Arthur F. Woltersdorf
364 Mr. & Mrs. Simon Klein
        Receiving day Friday
368 Mrs. Wm. Matthei
        Receive 1st Tuesday in mo.
368 Mrs. Meta Dore
368 Gustave P. Matthei
368 Charles A. Matthei
368 William H. Matthei
390 Mr. & Mrs. James W. Sheridan
394 Mr. & Mrs. F. V. Gindele & drs.
        Receive 2d Wednesday in mo.
394 George W. Gindele
398 Mr. & Mrs. James Dunne & dr.
        Receiving day Wednesday
406 Mr. & Mrs. Gabriel Franchere
        Receiving day Tuesday
406 Miss Tillie Franchere
408 Mr. & Mrs. John B. Scott
410 Mr. & Mrs. Jens L. Christensen

333 Mr. & Mrs. John H. Bradshaw
    & dr.
339 Mr. & Mrs. John McLaren
339 J. Loomis McLaren
343 Mr. & Mrs. Alonzo G. Fisher
    Receiving day Wednesday
345 Mr. & Mrs. John Kummer
347 Mr. & Mrs. William J. Mayer
347 Mrs. Eva M. Greene
349 Mr. & Mrs. Edward G. Clark
    Receiving day Tuesday
349 James Neff
351 Mr. & Mrs. Arthur Gray
353 Mr. & Mrs. M. Mullaney & drs.
353 T. F. Mullaney
355 Mr. & Mrs. G. Friedlander
357 Mr. & Mrs. Eugene H. Pearson
359 Mr. & Mrs. Robert J.Smith & dr.
359 R. Earl Smith
359 Alonzo D. Smith
361 Mrs. Edwin P. Wilce
    Receiving day Tuesday
361 Earle P. Bodley
363 Mr. & Mrs. John C. Spry jr.
    Receiving day Tuesday
363 Edwin W. Chandler
365 Mr. & Mrs. Henry B. Maxwell
365 Mrs. Fannie E. West
367 Mr. & Mrs. James Maxwell
    Receiving day Wednesday
369 Mr. & Mrs. Adolph Stein
    Receive 1st Saturday in month
369 Miss Rose K. Stein
373 Mr. & Mrs. Oliver W. Holmes
363 Mr. & Mrs. Harry Woolf
    Receive 1st Saturday in mo.
379 Mr. & Mrs. Charles K. Offield
385 Mr. & Mrs. Wm. W. Shaw
385 Mr. & Mrs. Robert Shaw
385 E. B. Shaw
389 Mr.& Mrs.John L. Haverkampf
391 Mr. & Mrs. Charles G. Ricklefs
393 Mr. & Mrs. W. B. Crane
395 Mr. & Mrs. W. P. Ketcham
395 Mr. & Mrs. Edwin J. Bowes jr.
399 Mrs. James P. Ketcham
399 Mr. & Mrs. F. D. Ketcham
    Receive 1st Friday in mo.
419 Mr. & Mrs. Louis Levy
419 Mr. & Mrs. Wm. Z. Johnson
419 Harry Kahn
423 Mr. & Mrs.Adolph Goldschmidt
423 Mrs. A. R. Hurd
443 Mr. & Mrs. Henry Scherer &dr.
443 Louis H. Scherer
445 Mr. & Mrs. Frank Alsip & drs.

410 Mr. & Mrs. W. W. Salmon
    Receiving day Tuesday
410 Mr. & Mrs. F. L. Foster
420 Mr. & Mrs. Charles Richardson
420 Mr. & Mrs. Adolph Karpen
420 Mr.& Mrs. Magnus A. Hess
422 Dr. & Mrs. E. L. Morehead
424 Mr & Mrs. Louis Martens
424 Mr. & Mrs. G. Eisenstadt
424 Mr. & Mrs. S. Baer
426 Mr. & Mrs. Isidore Jonas
    Receiving day Thursday
428 Mrs. G. A. Hoffman & dr.
428 Charles G. Hoffmann
430 Mr. & Mrs. A. Ragor & dr.
430 Joseph A. Ragor
436 Mr. & Mrs. Max Eberhardt &dr.
436 Waldemar Eberhardt
438 Mr. & Mrs. Victor Jacobs
440 John J. McDonnell
442 Mr. & Mrs. James E. Baggot
442 Mr. & Mrs. Chas. H. Stone
444 Mr. & Mrs. Edward Fleming
444 Patrick H. Fleming
444 Maurice F. Fleming
444 Lloyd Fleming
444 Edward J. Fleming
466 Dr. & Mrs. J. J. Larkin
468 Mrs. Anne Gilmore & drs.
470 Mr. & Mrs. Jacob Hart
472 Mr. & Mrs. John Rawle
474 Mr. & Mrs. Sol Klein
476 Mr. & Mrs. William W. Lufkin
476 Mr. & Mrs. M. Carlton
478 Mr. & Mrs. A. L. Suesman
478 Walter P. Suesman
478 Asa B. Suesman
478 Mr. & Mrs. John O. Batterman
478 Paul Stamsen
482 Dr.& Mrs. Theo. S. Bidwell&dr.
502 Patrick Brennan & drs.
502 William F. Brennan
510 Mr. & Mrs. Frank Slavik
510 Henry A. Slavik
510 Frank Slavik jr.
510 William M. Slavik
512 Mr. & Mrs. David Walsh
512 Thomas J. Walsh
512 Mr. & Mrs. David Torofsky
514 Dr. & Mrs. G. A. Fischer
514 Mr. & Mrs. Patrick Canfield &
    dr.
516 Mr. & Mrs. John Tatge
530 Mr. & Mrs. A. Menge
530 William Menge & dr.
534 Mr. & Mrs. Edward Roos

445 Charles H. Alsip
449 Mr. & Mrs. August Rietz
    Receiving day 1st Wednesday
449 Harry F. Rietz
473 Mr. & Mrs. Joseph Turk & drs.
475 Mr. & Mrs. Frank Wenter
481 Mr. & Mrs. Leon Klein
483 Mr. & Mrs. Saul G. Harris & dr.
485 Mr. & Mrs. Charles Crede
489 Mr. & Mrs. Traugott C. Diener
489 Wm. J. Diener
503 William Ruehl & dr.
503 Harry A. Ruehl

534 Otto A. Roos
534 Mr. & Mrs. Joseph C. Chapeck
538 Dr. & Mrs. F. W. E. Henkel

———

505 Mr. & Mrs. Henry Furst
505 Mr. & Mrs. Henry Furst jr.
511 Mr. & Mrs. F. C. Schoenstedt
527 Rev. & Mrs. H. L. Hoelter
527 Rev. Jacob Seidel
527 Miss Clara Seidel
657 Rev. C. E. Morse
657 Miss Gertrude Morse

BISHOP COURT.

14 Mr. & Mrs. R. S. Maulsby
14 John H. Minges

14 Mr. & Mrs. Hugh McIndoe
14 Mr. & Mrs. C. W. Rilling

BONNEY AVENUE.

1119 Mr. & Mrs. Leon Silverman
1121 Mr. & Mrs. L. J. Colburn
1165 Mr. & Mrs. Wm. D. Evans

1142 Mr. & Mrs. A. W. Ewing
1144 Mr. & Mrs. W. L. Minton
1148 Mr. & Mrs. R. H. Ewing
1188 Mrs. Martha M. White

BRYAN PLACE.

19 Mr. & Mrs. G. McCracken
23 Mr. & Mrs. George W. Metzger

31 Mr. & Mrs. George Tapper

SOUTH CALIFORNIA AVENUE.

25 Mr. & Mrs. Wm. F. Albright
115 S. G. Many

135 Mr. & Mrs. Frank Soltow

SOUTH CAMPBELL AVENUE.

149 Mr. & Mrs. A. H. Darrow
187 Mr. & Mrs. Arthur T. Rice & dr.
187 George A. Rice
193 Dr. & Mrs. M. B. Blouke
195 Mr. & Mrs. Alex. C. Martin
213 Charles D. Wilkinson
223 Mrs. J. E. Willits
223 Ward W. Willits
235 Dr. H. T. Roop
307 Henry Kerr
307 Mr. & Mrs. E. J. Bulkley
371 Dr. & Mrs. E. L. Clifford
377 Dr. & Mrs. Edward L. Stahl
379 William H. Edward

260 Mrs. M. J. Frawley & dr.
278 Mr. & Mrs. Francis T. Colby
    Receiving day Wednesday
308 Mr. & Mrs. A. A. Rawson
308 Mr. & Mrs. Harry Earl North-
    way   *Receive Wednesday*
340 Dr. & Mrs. P. J. Kester
360 Mr. & Mrs. Walter Brown
362 Mrs. Hannah Hazen
    Receiving day Wednesday
362 Frank A. Hazen
366 Mrs. Sarah E. Lightfoot

CAMPBELL PARK.

3 Mr. & Mrs. J. N. Staples & drs.
3 John M. Staples
29 Mr. & Mrs. Wm. H. Maple & dr.

2 Mr. & Mrs. Samuel Taylor
12 Mr. & Mrs. Thomas Wilson & dr.
30 Mr. & Mrs. H. H. Henshaw

39 Mr. & Mrs. George K. Hazlitt
39 Mr. & Mrs. George H. Hazlitt
43 Mr. & Mrs. James C. Patterson
45 Mr. & Mrs. A. Ransom
47 Mr. & Mrs. John W. Voorhees

52 Dr. V. A. Brockway
52 Mr. & Mrs. Ricbard M. Peare jr.
54 Rev. & Mrs. W. G. Clarke

55 Mr. & Mrs. Chas. H. Harraden

CARROLL AVENUE.

427 Maurice Rothschild
427 Benjamin Rothschild
429 Rev. & Mrs. J. W. Marcusson
429 Dr. W. B. Marcusson

722 Charles H. Barmm
722 Frank H. Barmm

429 Elmore W. Dreher

SOUTH CENTRAL PARK AVENUE.

861 Mr. & Mrs. Thos. McEnerny
863 Mr. & Mrs. Samuel A. Cooper
947 Mr. & Mrs. John Hunter & drs.
955 Mr. & Mrs. James L. Meriam
969 Mr. & Mrs. R. J. Stone
981 Mr. & Mrs. W. P. Hatfield
993 Rev. John M. Dunne
1067 Mr. & Mrs. Wm. H. Hays
    Receiving day Thursday
1089 Mr. & Mrs. John Wood
1089 Mrs. Jane Reynolds
1103 Mrs. H. A. Truax & dr.
1165 Miss E. L. Perkins
1165 Mrs. E. J. Trudeau
1175 Mr.&Mrs. W. H. Andrews&dr.
1191 Mr. & Mrs. David Hitchcock

934 Mr. & Mrs. Edw. D. Fried-
    lander
936 Mr. & Mrs. Jacob H. Wilson
940 Mr. & Mrs. John A. Downey
948 Mr. & Mrs. S. M. Gilmore
948 Ephraim Gilmore
960 Dr. & Mrs. David Rose
964 Mrs. E. E. Lanterman & dr.
984 Mr. & Mrs. C. S. Dwight
1044 Mr. & Mrs. Charles H. McAfee
1050 Mrs. Chester Wright
1058 Dr. & Mrs. A. C. Hiester
1060 Mr. & Mrs. Z. O. Jackson
1064 Dr. & Mrs. Richard F. Worth
1066 Mr. & Mrs. W. H. Worth
1120 Mr. & Mrs. P. T. Platt
1128 Mr. & Mrs. William R. Smith
1128 Mrs. Elizabeth Glaspell

CENTRE AVENUE.

37 Mr. & Mrs. George Furst
43 Mr. & Mrs. John York & dr.
43 John B. York
77 John Hoggins
167 Mr. & Mrs. L. J. Eastland
169 Mr. & Mrs. Chas. S. Sawyer
203 Daniel J. McElherne
343 Mrs. Ella Connell & dr.
343 James A. Connell

318 Mr. & Mrs. S. Sinsheimer
322 Dr. & Mrs. J. G. Wolfe
326 Mr. & Mrs. John Fitzpatrick

72 Mr. & Mrs. R. Neely & drs.
72 Joseph C. Neely
78 Orville V. Thompson
78 George C. Lowell
78 Mr. & Mrs. E. L. Bartholomew
82 Mr. & Mrs. C. J. Tilton
84 Mr. & Mrs. George Plamondon
    Receiving day Thursday
88 Mr. & Mrs. I. H. Holden & drs.
90 Mr. & Mrs. Eugene Keogh
104 William W. Wheelock
316 Mr. & Mrs. Elidoro de Campi
    & dr.

CLAREMONT AVENUE.

293 W. D. Sager
301 Mr. & Mrs. Wm. L. Snell

296 Mr. & Mrs. Geo. R. Daley
366 Chester T. Drake
382 Mr. & Mrs. Charles J. Magee

CLIFTON PARK AVENUE.

947 Mr. & Mrs. A. W. Nohe
947 Frank C. Nohe
947 Mrs. A. E. Sargent

1066 Mr. & Mrs. H. P. Sipe
1070 Mr. & Mrs. R. S. Bixby

WEST CONGRESS STREET.

365 Frank Crowe
365 Miss Genevieve Crowe
427 Mr. & Mrs. Napoleon Picard
       Receiving day Tuesday
439 Mr. & Mrs. L. A. Lange
441 Mr. & Mrs. C.G.Lichtenberger
445 Mr. & Mrs. W. J. Moxley
447 Mrs. John Young & dr.
449 Mr. & Mrs. Arthur Harris
455 Mr. & Mrs. W. F. Swissler
455 Mr. & Mrs. F. L. Gerwig
461 Mr. & Mrs. Isadore Baumgartl
463 Mr. & Mrs. Thomas Sealor
463 Mr. & Mrs. I. G. Loeber
467 Mr. & Mrs. Wm. Henderson
469 Mr. & Mrs. C. E. Edwards
477 Dr. & Mrs. F. G. Mason
477 Mr. & Mrs. Judd E. Wells
491 Mr. & Mrs. Lewis R. Bain
493 Mr. & Mrs. John N. Dole
499 Mr. & Mrs. J. B. Carter
503 Mrs. Mary Murray
503 Joseph R. Murray
503 Mr. & Mrs. J. W. Walsh
       Receiving day Tuesday
503 E. W. Cullen
505 Mrs. G. E. Lloyd
505 Mr. & Mrs. James Fraser
505 Edward C. Williams
507 Mr. & Mrs. James T. Milner
509 Mr. & Mrs. J. W. Patrick
517 Mr. & Mrs. Joseph Pomeroy
519 Dr. & Mrs. Wm. McCarthy
523 Mr. & Mrs. Henry Simons
525 Mr.& Mrs. James C. O'Brien &
       dr.
567 Dr. & Mrs. W. T. Montgomery
569 Mr. & Mrs. G. E. Griswold
571 Mr. & Mrs. Joseph Barstow
575 Mr. & Mrs. Chas. H. Mitchell
583 Mr. & Mrs. G. W. Miley
585 Mr. & Mrs. Frank Porter
587 Mr. & Mrs. John Sargent &dr.
591 Dr. & Mrs. T. J. Shaw & dr.
591 Dr. & Mrs. D. Lee Shaw
635 Dr. & Mrs. H. B. Stehman
635 Miss Emma R. Miller
657 Mr. & Mrs. Frederick Carlisle

252 Mr. & Mrs. Edwin Thompson
252 William Thompson
360 Mr. & Mrs. George Duddleston
394 Mr. & Mrs. O. R. Erwin
406 John T. Boyle
444 Mr.& Mrs.G.N.Archibald & dr.
444 George S. Ault
446 Dr. N. S. Davenport
446 Edward A. Davenport
450 Mr. & Mrs. Wm. D. Kent
452 Mrs. Doris Butzow
452 Robert C. Butzow
452 Mr. & Mrs. I. Schuchat
452 Henry Schuchat
460 Mr. & Mrs. John Meyer
468 Mrs. Charlotte Hartmann
468 Mrs. Charlotte Hingst
472 Mr. & Mrs. A. J. Murphy
478 Mr.& Mrs. Albert M. Eddy&dr.
       Receiving day Thursday
478 Miss Lina A. Eddy
482 Mr. & Mrs. P. H. Fitzpatrick &
       drs.
496 Mr. & Mrs. M. Finlayson
504 Mr. & Mrs. J. C. Wintermeyer
504 Mr. & Mrs. Harry Kraus
506 Mr. & Mrs. George C. Ball
508 Mr. & Mrs. H. W. Caldwell
508 Oliver N. Caldwell
510 Mr. & Mrs. F. G. Hartwell
514 Mr. & Mrs. J. M. Oliver
514 J. W. Showalter
520 Mr. & Mrs. J. F. Brabrook & dr.
520 W. A. Brabrook
522 Mr. & Mrs. M. Weill
522 Mr. & Mrs. Frank Strasser
524 Mr. & Mrs. Fred C. Storey
524 Mr. & Mrs. J. F. McIntosh
524 Mr. & Mrs. R. S. Grant
568 Mr. & Mrs. Harvey T. Weeks
568 Gilbert M. Weeks
570 Mr. & Mrs. J. S. Sosman
       Receiving day Thursday
578 Mr. & Mrs. D. A. Starrett
582 Mr. & Mrs. C. C. Haskins
582 Frank C. Haskins
582 Mrs. S. C. Chapman
584 Mr. & Mrs. B. Behrend & dr.

657 H. W. Carlisle
657 Alfred W. Carlisle
657 Mrs. E. M. Stevens
707 Mr. & Mrs. James S. Hubbard
719 Mr. & Mrs. T. H. Gault
719 Mrs. L. Hughes
835 Mr. & Mrs. Sam Freudenthal
837 Edward A. Arcouet
839 Mr. & Mrs. Robert VanSands
889 Mr. & Mrs. Wm. Thomas
989 Mr. & Mrs. A. C. Wood
1159 Mr. & Mrs. A. C. Laing
1259 George Frederick Lyman

586 Mr. & Mrs. N. B. Holden
594 Dr. & Mrs. A. W. Gray
594 Louis A. Gray
606 Mr. & Mrs. W. H. Crump
612 Mr. & Mrs. John J. Hart
614 Mr. & Mrs. S. Witkowsky
616 Mr. & Mrs. Joseph Stein
616 Mr. & Mrs. Wm. Wilhartz
624 Mr. & Mrs. Fred A. Parker
630 Mr. & Mrs. E. L. Messer
632 Mr. & Mrs. Eli Payn
736 Mayer H. Eichengreen
1158 Mr. & Mrs. Peter McAdam
1186 Mr. & Mrs. C. B. Stone

DE KALB STREET.

57 Mr. & Mrs. Louis I. Blackman
61 Mr. & Mrs. A. J. Haight
75 Dr. & Mrs. I. W. Brown
83 Mrs. T. E. Flowers
99 Mr. & Mrs. J. L. Campbell
103 Mr. & Mrs. F. O. Wakeley
107 Mr. & Mrs. I. P. Poinier
107 Edward W. Poinier

46 Dr. & Mrs. Fitz Bullen
102 Mr. & Mrs. Stephen R. Wilson
106 Mr. & Mrs. S. D. Simpson
108 Mr. & Mrs. Frank R. Swift
120 Mr. & Mrs. John N. Cunning
142 Mr. & Mrs. A. H. Lord
146 Dr. & Mrs. E. C. Fortner
146 Mrs. Sophia R. Tuthill

EVERGREEN AVENUE.

113 Mr. & Mrs. Max Mickel
113 Mr. & Mrs. Henry Hanson
———
140 Dr. & Mrs. K. F. M. Sandberg
142 Dr. & Mrs. J. Dal
172 Mr. & Mrs. Emil A. Holmes
196 Mrs. A. J. Johnson & drs.
220 Edward Mee
222 Mr. & Mrs. David D. Mee
222 Wm. J. Dobson

28 Mrs. Charles Heinze & dr.
32 Rev & Mrs. I. W. Higgs
42 Mrs. Peter Thompson
56 Mr. & Mrs. F. Paysen
58 Mr. & Mrs. F. R. Moles
114 Mr. & Mrs. John Stut & dr.
114 Mr. & Mrs. E. Vantwood
128 Mr. & Mrs. T. Tollakson
134 Dr. & Mrs. Nils E. Remmen
140 Mr. & Mrs. P. O. Stensland

EWING PLACE.

9 Mr. & Mrs. John Buehler
17 Mr. & Mrs. Chas. S. Petrie
27 Mr.& Mrs.A. F.Weinberger &dr.
27 George A. Weinberger
27 Felix Weinberger
33 Mr. & Mrs. George Rahlfs & dr.
33 George Rahlfs jr.
73 Mr. & Mrs. Herman Mueller
79 Mr. & Mrs. H. D. Runge
85 Mr. & Mrs. Kickham Scanlan
85 Mr. & Mrs. M. W. Conway
89 Mr. & Mrs. John C. Horn

20 Dr. & Mrs. James B. Williams
24 Mr. & Mrs. John P. Hanson&drs.
34 Mr. & Mrs. Edward G. Uihlein
70 Mr. & Mrs. Fred C. Mueller
72 Mr. & Mrs. J. Schuldt
72 Mr. & Mrs. Charles H. Fleischer
76 Mr. & Mrs. H. Weinhardt
———
89 Mr. & Mrs. Wm. Legner
93 Mr. & Mrs. August Lenke
93 Mr. & Mrs. Geo. J. Sayer

FLOURNOY STREET.

39 Col. & Mrs. R. F. Taylor & dr.	100 Mr. & Mrs. Chas. A. Homrig
59 Mr. & Mrs. Edward S. Hunt	102 Mrs. M. A. Horn & dr.
69 Mr. & Mrs. W. T. Cushing	106 Mr. & Mrs. S. C. Postlewait
111 Mr. & Mrs. J. I. Straw & dr.	114 Mr. & Mrs. C. V. Osborn
315 Mr. & Mrs. Frederick Peake	116 Mr. & Mrs. Thos. H. Webster
543 Mr. & Mrs. Frank W. Hoyt	118 Mr. & Mrs. L. T. Minehart
———	124 Mr. & Mrs. Frank T. Bentley
336 Raymond K. Thatcher	124 Mr. & Mrs. S. E. Patterson
574 Dr. & Mrs. Konrad Schaefer	126 Dr. & Mrs. James P. Prestley
574 C. Bryant Schaefer	288 Mr. & Mrs. Oscar Dudley

FOWLER STREET.

93 Mr. & Mrs. A. C. Lausten	8 Mr. & Mrs. Charles E. Meyer
93 Charles Lausten	*Receiving day 1st Thursday*
93 W. H. Lausten	10 Mr. & Mrs. James Keats & dr.
95 Mr. & Mrs. Fred Grimsell	10 Arthur S. Keats
101 Mr. & Mrs. H. Dresselhaus	12 Mr. & Mrs. Alex. Dierkes
	26 Mr. & Mrs. Solomon Weil
———	42 Mr. & Mrs. H. Cohn
92 Ernst A. Erickson	52 Dr. & Mrs. N. T. Quales
94 Mr. & Mrs. Wm. J. Hamilton	60 Dr. & Mrs. B. I. Meyer
96 Mr. & Mrs. T. H. Marshall	62 Mr. & Mrs. Halvor Michelson
98 Mr. & Mrs. Hans L. Anderson	86 Mr. & Mrs. Charles F. Elsner
102 Mr. & Mrs. Anton Johnson	92 Mr. & Mrs. C. Erickson & dr.

FULTON STREET.

481 Mr. & Mrs. John B. Rogers&dr.	424 Mr. & Mrs. C. C. Bonney & dr.
481 Mr. & Mrs. E. E. Speed	424 Lawton C. Bonney
483 Mr. & Mrs. Melville Burke	430 Mr. & Mrs. L. Pfaelzer & dr.
625 Mr. & Mrs. James Frake	430 Mr. & Mrs. J. Felsenthal
667 Mr. & Mrs. J. J. Swenie	430 David Pfaelzer
681 Mr. & Mrs. John O'Callaghan	452 Mr.&Mrs. John H.VanHousen
& drs.	458 Mr. & Mrs. F. W. Munson
695 Mr. & Mrs. H. Bradshaw &drs.	460 Mr. & Mrs. Thomas Goodman
705 D. C. Eddy & drs.	& dr.
711 Mr. & Mrs. A. Murray & drs.	460 Mr. & Mrs. W. A. Goodman
717 Mrs. E. J. Halsted & dr.	466 Mr. & Mrs. W. E. Ray
735 Mr. & Mrs. W. F. Wolff	500 Mr. & Mrs. J. H. Tallmadge
873 Miss L. M. Freeman	518 Mr. & Mrs. Frank M. Lamb
881 Mr. & Mrs. A. Ober & drs.	528 Mrs. S. A. Michaels & drs.
895 Rev. & Mrs. J. P. Brushingham	*Receiving day Thursday*
Receiving day Monday	528 Charles D. Michaels
915 Mrs. I. M. Bray	662 Mr. & Mrs. John H. Whipple
1335 Mr. & Mrs. D. L. Lapointe	682 D. Walsh & drs.
1355 Mr. & Mrs. John L. Adams	878 Dr. J. Spafford Hunt
1357 Mr. & Mrs. Edgar A. Hall	878 Ferd S. Hunt
1447 Mr. & Mrs. T. W. Eaton & drs.	1336 Mr. & Mrs. Charles S. Brown
1447 E. W. Eaton	1342 Mr. & Mrs. John C. Satterlee
1455 Mr. & Mrs. O. S. Ward	1386 Dr. J. E. Hayner
1475 Mr.&Mrs.William H. Coolidge	1404 Mr. & Mrs. A. W. Smith
1477 Mr. & Mrs. John Robertson	1404 Mr. & Mrs. John Cordes
1493 Mr. & Mrs. William League	1408 J. P. Esmay
1493 Dr. W. M. Brown	1456 Mr. & Mrs. M. Levinson

1493 John S. Brown
1495 Mr. & Mrs. C. E. Wyman
1495 Miss Florence Wells
1523 Mr. & Mrs. Wm. Cook & dr.
1525 Mr. & Mrs. E. L. Sadler
1533 Mrs. F. A. Funk & dr.
1535 Mr. & Mrs. Charles Carpenter
1537 Mr. & Mrs. E. W. Stanwood
1543 Mr. & Mrs. Samuel S. Parks
1551 Mr. & Mrs. E. C. Brown
1553 Mr. & Mrs. E. A. Osbornson
1613 Mr. & Mrs. W. W. Klock
1623 Mr. & Mrs. W. H. Dymond
1629 Mr. & Mrs. E. T. Sederholm

1580 Mr. & Mrs. H. S. Brackett

1458 Mr. & Mrs. T. T. Loomis jr.
1484 G. P. Bartelme
1484 Miss Adeline T. Bartelme
1484 Miss May M. Bartelme
1524 Mr. & Mrs. Frank M. Heggie
1526 Mr. & Mrs. Marshall L.Browne
1526 Mr. & Mrs. F. C. Ralston
1542 Mr. & Mrs. A. H. Foskett
1544 G. C. Otis
1556 Mr. & Mrs. E. P. Beach
1556 Miss Mary E. Beach
1556 Mr. & Mrs. P. Bird Price
1562 Mrs. Emma C. Winslow
1564 Mr. & Mrs. George W. Trout
Receiving day Thursday
1564 Mrs. Annie B. Wilbur

GILPIN PLACE.

12 Mr. & Mrs. M. Miniter
16 Mr. & Mrs. Joseph Magee

18 Dr. & Mrs. G. V. Bachelle
106 Andrew J. Ryan

HAMILTON AVENUE.

11 H. Burgheim & dr.
11 Gus Burgheim
13 Mr. & Mrs. Samuel G. Artingstall
    & dr.
23 Mr. & Mrs. Frank W. Sweet
43 Mr. & Mrs. Joseph W.Daugherty
49 Mr. & Mrs. J. J. Brewis
49 Mrs. S. Brewis
51 Mr. & Mrs. Albert Jack

12 Harry J. Wyman
16 Mrs. S. J. Crane & drs.
22 Mr. & Mrs. Julien Smith & drs.
    Receiving day Wednesday
44 Mr. & Mrs. O. J. Pierce & drs.
50 T. W. Gilmore
50 Miss Mary E. Gilmore
52 Mr. & Mrs. J. R. Preston
66 Mr. & Mrs. H. C. Christensen
66 Mr. & Mrs. J. P. Preis & dr.
66 Mr. & Mrs. Otto Heper

WEST HARRISON STREET.

387 Mr. & Mrs. W. M. Sherman
597 Mr. & Mrs. P. D. Rathbone
649 Mr. & Mrs. J. H. Synon
649 Miss Kate M. Foy
663 Mr. & Mrs. Wm. F. Kyle
689 Mr. & Mrs. Charles W. Davis
689 Miss L. D. Clark
691 Dr. & Mrs. A. M. Corwin
703 Charles A. Thayer
717 Mr. & Mrs. Jesse Cox
743 Rev.& Mrs. J.C.Armstrong&dr.

708 Mr. & Mrs. Thomas E. Wilce
Receiving day Tuesday
708 George C. Wilce
708 E. Harvey Wilce
872 Mr. & Mrs. J. Hubert Smith
946 Mr. & Mrs. John G. Rick
1084 Dr. & Mrs. D. Duncan

875 Mr. & Mrs. Cesaire Gareau
949 James S. Gadsden
951 Dr. & Mrs. G. H. Cleveland

HERMITAGE AVENUE.

221 Mr. & Mrs. John Graham &drs.
221 Eugene Graham
233 Mrs. James Dunne & drs.
233 Romeo Dunne
233 Otho Dunne
247 Dr. & Mrs. T. O. Butler
265 Mr. & Mrs. D. B. Parker

338 Mrs. E. A. Challacombe & dr.

265 Mr. & Mrs. J. F. Alexander
323 Mr. & Mrs. A. Campbell & dr.
363 Mr. & Mrs. Alexander Rodgers
445 Joseph J. Shannessy

21

SOUTH HOMAN AVENUE.

941 Dr. & Mrs. John B. Woodruff
————
280 John J. Kahler

24 Mrs. John Oliver
230 Mr. & Mrs. Thomas S. Keirnan
280 Mr. & Mrs. Conrad Kahler

HONORE STREET.

158 Mr. & Mrs. Seaward Foster
200 Mr. & Mrs. Squire Rush Harris

238 Mr. & Mrs. Filmore Weigley

NORTH HOYNE AVENUE.

613 Mr. & Mrs. Henry Schroeder
    Receive last Thursday in mo.
610 Mr. & Mrs. S. D. Thorson
625 Mr. & Mrs. John Heinsen
631 Mr. & Mrs. Herman Kirchhoff
637 Mr. & Mrs. Morris Schlesinger
637 T. R. Schlesinger
643 Dr. & Mrs. D. G. Moore
697 Mr. & Mrs. Henry Grusendorf
697 Edward Grusendorf
703 Mr.& Mrs. Kolben Johnson&dr.
721 Dr. & Mrs. H. J. Burwash
    Receiving day Thursday
727 Mr. & Mrs. George C. Mages
731 Mr. & Mrs. C. H. Plautz
735 Mr. & Mrs. Phil Rosenberg
739 Mr. & Mrs. Henry T. Kley

492 Mr. & Mrs. Harry Levy
572 Dr. & Mrs. D. C. Stillians
632 Mr. & Mrs. Henry Rieper
632 Mr. & Mrs. Henry L. Hertz
640 Mr. & Mrs. E. E. Granquist
654 Mr. & Mrs. John H. Rapp
666 Mr.&Mrs.William Johnson&drs.
672 Mr. & Mrs. Nels Arneson & drs.
692 Mr. & Mrs. Fred Faber
700 Mr. & Mrs. Adolph Borgmeier
    & dr.
724 Mr. & Mrs. F. P. Schreiber
732 Mrs. Albin Greiner & drs.
736 Mr. & Mrs. Saul Moses & dr.
746 Mr. & Mrs. Charles Bodach

SOUTH HOYNE AVENUE.

 35 Mr. & Mrs. John J. Chase & dr.
107 Mr. & Mrs. Foster W. Lamb
143 Mr. & Mrs. John Skelton
143 Mark Bangs
143 Mr. & Mrs. Fred A. Bangs
151 Mrs. F. A. Shoyer & drs.
163 Mr. & Mrs. Henry Cordes
163 Lewis Cordes
181 Mr. & Mrs. Chas. Deming & dr.
181 William B. Deming
183 Mr.&Mrs.James Buchanan
183 Mr. & Mrs. Wm. Francis jr.
195 Mr.&Mrs.William Hafner&drs.
197 Mr. & Mrs. F. K. Ream
197 Mr. & Mrs. W. J. Jewell
207 Mr. & Mrs. John A. J. Kendig
213 Mr. & Mrs. O. F. Gaines & dr.
215 Mr. & Mrs. Thos. E. Archibald
215 Mr. & Mrs. R. A. Hurxthal

104 Mr. & Mrs. Chas. M. Weaver
110 Mr. & Mrs. North West
152 Mr. & Mrs. James McMillan
226. Mr. & Mrs. Fred W. Griffin
312 Mr. & Mrs. Milton Kellogg

————

217 Mr. & Mrs. Wm. A. Browne
219 Mr. & Mrs. John Roberts
219 Mrs. Belle Keuthan & drs.
237 Dr. & Mrs. J. M. Patton
241 Mr. & Mrs. S. B. Boynton
275 Col. Thomas Pattison
295 Mr. & Mrs. Philip Benz
307 Mr. & Mrs. F. F. Jones
339 Mr. & Mrs. Michael W. Connery
347½ Mr. & Mrs. T. G. Owen & dr.
377 Mr. & Mrs. J. Swartz

IRVING AVENUE.

191 Mr. & Mrs. F. E. Gibbs
219 Mr. & Mrs. David Blair & drs.
223 Mr. & Mrs. M. H. Buzzell
227 Mr. & Mrs. P. A. Niebergall & dr.
233 Mr. & Mrs. O. W. Snyder
235 Mr. & Mrs. E. P. Benz
271 Mr. & Mrs. Chas. Van Sickel
271 Mrs. Catharine Watson
273 Mr. & Mrs. Edward Rueb
    Receiving day Thursday
275 Mr. & Mrs. Charles D. Bull
283 Mr. & Mrs. L. C. Jacqnish
    Receiving day Wednesday
283 Mr. & Mrs. Frank C. Baker
285 Mr. & Mrs. Fred S. Smith
287 Mr. & Mrs. J. F. Ahles
    Receiving day Wednesday
295 Mr. & Mrs. E. W. Fowler & dr.
295 George J. Fowler
295 Samuel W. Fowler
303 Mr. & Mrs. E. R. Paige
305 Mr. & Mrs. George S. Miles
307 Mr. & Mrs. W. C. Leiferman
423 Mr. & Mrs. A. H. White & dr.
437 Mr. & Mrs. John H. Tyler
447 Mr. & Mrs. Frank C. Roundy
451 Mr. & Mrs. H. C. Cox & dr.
453 Mr. & Mrs. Peter Milroy
459 Mr. & Mrs. J. M. Nockin & dr.
461 Mr. & Mrs. Ernest Woltersdorf
    Receiving day Tuesday

152 Dr. & Mrs. Lewis H. Cass & dr.
222 Mr. & Mrs. H. H. Hubbard
228 Mr. & Mrs. W. S. Bogle & dr.
    Receiving day Thursday
230 Mr. & Mrs. O. H. Jewell & dr.
    Receiving day Tuesday
230 Ira H. Jewell
234 Gen. & Mrs. J. H. Stibbs & dr.
234 Mr. & Mrs. Thomas Stibbs
236 Mrs. Sarah F. Cozens & drs.
266 Mrs. Waldo Abeel & drs.
272 Mr. & Mrs. John D. Osgood
274 Mr. & Mrs. L. W. Winchester
276 Mr. & Mrs. W. J. Davies
276 Mr. & Mrs. Edward C. Davies
278 Mr. & Mrs. Thomas W. Prior
280 Mr. & Mrs. J. Eugene Smith & dr.
282 Mr. & Mrs. Edward Hennessy
    Receiving day Tuesday
288 Mr. & Mrs. J. A. Wilson
290 Mr. & Mrs. Charles Brodie & dr.
296 Mrs. C. M. Lumley
296 Mr. & Mrs. G. R. Ingram & drs.
296 Edward L. Ingram
298 Mr. & Mrs. Chas. P. Whetston
300 Mrs. Lottie J. Groshon
452 Mr. & Mrs. H. R. Woodley
454 Mr. & Mrs. O. E. Haman
———
463 Mr. & Mrs. A. O. Whitcomb
463 Mrs. C. P. Tuttle
465 Mr. & Mrs. Theo. C. Paulsen
473 Mr. & Mrs. Geo. F. Trevette & dr.

JACKSON BOULEVARD.

313 Mr. & Mrs. W. Rankin
313 Mr. & Mrs. James Rankin
351 Mr. & Mrs. Geo. Harper
365 Dr. & Mrs. M. W. Borland & dr.
365 Mr. & Mrs. C. H. McDowell
369 Mr. & Mrs. Hugh Mason
391 Mrs. Herman Raster & dr.   .
391 Edwin Raster
391 Walter Raster
393 Mrs. M. McDonald
393 Mr. & Mrs. M. McDonald jr.
401 Mr. & Mrs. O. W. Bond
403 Mr. & Mrs. A. H. Loomis & dr.
    Receiving day Thursday
403 Philip A. Loomis
409 Mr. & Mrs. W. B. Davidson
411 Henry C. Fuller
417 Mr. & Mrs. Charles J. White

270 Mr. & Mrs. W. H. Beidler
    Receiving day Friday .
272 Mr. & Mrs. A. B. Camp
314 Mr. & Mrs. M. W. Williamson
396 Mr. & Mrs. J. H. Gutches
400 Charles O'Donnell
402 Dr. & Mrs. John Alderson
406 Thomas F. O'Brien
408 Mr. & Mrs. A. Sparr
412 Mr. & Mrs. E. D. Ellis
412 John F. Ellis
416 E. R. Letterman
418 Mr. & Mrs. A. W. Martin
426 Mr. & Mrs. J. S. Conger
426 Mr. & Mrs. E. L. Stewart
434 Mr. & Mrs. James R. Willett
444 Dr. George L. Beach
450 John Murray

423 George W. Cox
459 Mr. & Mrs.George F.Wetherell
461   Mr. & Mrs. H. S. Purchase
467 Mr. & Mrs. Frank S. Wright &
      dr.
469 Mr. & Mrs. F. D. Meacham
469 Mrs. E. Weatherhead
471 Mr. & Mrs. J. Anderson
483 Mrs. Sarah C. King
483 Mr. & Mrs. Frank B. Alsip
485 Mr. & Mrs. J. R. Graves
487 Mr. & Mrs. H. C. Bennett
487½ Mr. & Mrs. A. W. Johnston
489 Mr. & Mrs. R. J. Mason
491 Mr. & Mrs. Ira Tomblin & dr.
493 Mr. & Mrs. F. C. Taylor & dr
493 W. C. Hale
495 Mr. & Mrs. F. H. Lamb
497 Mr. & Mrs. Charles A. Lamb
499 Mr. & Mrs. Scott Jordan
501 Mr. & Mrs. George G. Parker
501 Mrs. O. L. Parker
503 Mr. & Mrs. J. P. Soper
505 Mr. & Mrs. A. E. Barnhart &dr.
505 Mrs. Harriet French
509 Mr. & Mrs. J. H. Pearson
509 Arthur L. Pearson
511 Mr. & Mrs. Obadiah Sands & dr.
513 Mr. & Mrs. George Fritze & dr.
515 Mr. & Mrs. John Sollitt
519 Mr. & Mrs. Walter Shoemaker
519 Chas. W. Shoemaker
519 Miss May E. Shull
521 Mr. & Mrs. W. T. Bussey
523 Mr. & Mrs. James L. Clark
525 Mr. & Mrs. J. D. Marshall
527 Mr. & Mrs. George Titus
527 Mrs. Wm. P. Hewitt
529½ Mr. & Mrs. George Mendsen
531 Mr. & Mrs. J. W. McCauley
533 Mr. & Mrs. A. F. Doremus
535 Mr. & Mrs. R. E. Shimmin
537 Mr. & Mrs. Alonzo Wygant
539 Mr. & Mrs. George Ross
           Receiving day Thursday
541 Mr. & Mrs. M. N. Moyer & dr.
541 H. Clayton Moyer
541 Herbert P. Moyer
543 Mr. & Mrs. W. P. Henneberry
549 A. M. Henderson & dr.
551 Mr. & Mrs. E. Wiley Taylor
553 Dr. & Mrs. R. N. Foster & drs.
553 Miss N. Halsted
557 Mr. & Mrs. Adolph Shire
579 Mr. & Mrs. E. H. Baird
585 Mr. & Mrs. H. J. Armstrong

452 Dr. & Mrs. J. O. Hobbs
454 Dr. & Mrs. W. H. Morgan
458 Mr. & Mrs. J. D. Wallace
464 Mr. & Mrs. H. L. Thornburgh
           Receiving day Thursday
494 Mr. & Mrs. A. N. Eastman
494 Mr. & Mrs. H. A. Eastman
494 Edward P. Eastman
496 Mr. & Mrs. G. H. Green
496 Dr. & Mrs. Rufus H. Bartlett
498 Mr. & Mrs. J. L. Pattison & dr.
500 Mr. & Mrs. James A. McMahon
502 Mr. & Mrs. William Hinchliff
504 Mr. & Mrs. C. W. Storey
           Receiving day Wednesday
504 Mrs. E. W. Westfall
           Receiving day Wednesday
508 Mr. & Mrs. P. J. Healy
510 Mr. & Mrs. G. V. Drake
510 Mrs. S. Sheppard
512 Mr. & Mrs. F. A. Riddle
514 Mr. & Mrs. S. A. Low
518 Mr. & Mrs. G. S. Carrington
522 Capt. & Mrs. J. G. Keith & dr.
524 Mr. & Mrs. James H. Ward
           Receiving day Thursday
526 Mr. & Mrs. John Fortune
526 William J. Fortune
530 Mr. & Mrs. B. F. Ferguson
532 Judge & Mrs. R. S. Tuthill & drs
534 Judge R. Prendergast
536 Mr. & Mrs. F. L. Welles
536 Miss Katherine Welles
538 Mr. & Mrs. W. S. Edwards
538 Mrs. C. S. Clark
540 Mrs. Margaret Hastie
542 Mrs. H. C. Morey
544 Mrs. A. Cox
546 Mrs. Luella Barnes Thatcher
548 Mr. & Mrs. W. D. Messinger
550 Dr. & Mrs. W. S. Downey
552 Mrs. C. C. Fisher
552 Mrs. W. P. Chisholm
554 Mr. & Mrs. Charles M. Foskett
556 Mr. & Mrs. Wm. H. Mortimer
558 David Reed
596 Mr. & Mrs. Frank E. Stanley
622 Mr. & Mrs. P. Finn
622 Nicholas R. Finn
624 Mr. & Mrs. David Pyott
626 Mr. & Mrs. E. G. Stearns
628 Mr. & Mrs. D. A. Pyott
628 Mrs. C. E. DeLuce
630 Mr. & Mrs. F. A. Arnold
630 Dr. Samuel C. Beach
632 Mr. & Mrs. J. C. Winn

587 Mr. & Mrs. H. Saunders
589 Mr. & Mrs. R. Hart
593 Mr.& Mrs.Stalham L.Williams
593 Stalham L. Williams jr.
597 Dr.& Mrs. Daniel R. Brower &
    dr.
597 Daniel R. Brower jr.
599 Mr. & Mrs. Humphrey Fall
601 Mr. & Mrs. Charles E. Hyde
603 Mr. & Mrs. C. H. Jordan
603 Mr. & Mrs. Cady M. Jordan
    Receiving day Tuesday
603 Mrs. J. A. Griffith
605 Miss M. A. Keefe
607 Mrs. P. Casey & drs.
607 Edward P. Casey
607 Thomas P. Casey
617 Mr. & Mrs. Adam Schaaf
617 John Schaaf
619 William Phelon
619 Dr. & Mrs. W. P. Phelon
619 Mr. & Mrs. J. E. Ingram
619 Joshua Reeves
625 Mr. & Mrs. J. H. Mather
627 Mr. & Mrs. E. C. Ward
631 Dr. & Mrs.John M. Dodson
631 Mrs. Dexter N. Kasson & dr.
635 Mr. & Mrs. C. H. Simmons
637 Mr. & Mrs. G. H. Williams
639 Mr. & Mrs. Frank A. Hecht
639 Miss Pauline Hecht
661 Mr. & Mrs. E. B. Stone
667 Dr. & Mrs. J. D. Shugart
677 Dr. & Mrs. Alfred C. Cotton
695 Mr. & Mrs. P. H. Putnam & dr.
695 R. Mitchell
699 Mr. & Mrs. J. M. VanOsdel 2d
    & dr.
699 F. M. VanOsdel
703 Mrs. Willard Woodard
705 Dr. & Mrs. J. M. Auld
713 Mr. & Mrs. J. W. Enright
731 Dr. & Mrs. Fred D. Marshall
745 Rev. & Mrs. J. J. Esher
755 Mr. & Mrs. J. D. Robertson
761 Mr. & Mrs. T. K. Edwards
761 Mrs. E. K. Edwards
761 Harry D. Edwards
767 Mr. & Mrs. S. Salomon
767 Moses Salomon
767 Joseph Salomon
767 William Salomon
767 A. D. Salomon
769 Mr. & Mrs. Harry Berger
779 Mr. & Mrs. C. DuB. Howell
821 Walter H. Munroe

638 Dr. Mary H. Thompson
644 Mr. & Mrs. J. E. Swartz
658 Rev. Thomas F. Cashman
658 Rev. P. J. O'Connor
658 Rev. T. E. Cox
694 Mr. & Mrs. D. B. Salisbury
700 Mr. & Mrs. A. K. Tappan
706 Mr. & Mrs. James R. Bowie
706 H. T. Bowie
708 Mr. & Mrs. F. S. Butler
710 J. W. Millington
720 Mrs. Cora B. Pierce
720 Mr. & Mrs. A. Arthur Banks
738 Judge & Mrs. E. A. Fisher
    Receiving day Thursday
754 Mr. & Mrs. G. F. Alward
768 Mr. & Mrs. W. H. Hawes
770 Mr. & Mrs. E. L. Cox
774 Mr. & Mrs. John A. Duncan
780 Mr. & Mrs. Thos. Kimball
786 Mr. & Mrs. F. R. Van Hamm
788 Mr. & Mrs. W. E. Marble
792 Mr. & Mrs. J. J. Johnston
792 Mrs. Anna Hiltabidell
818 Mr. & Mrs. E. R. Bullard
820 Dr. & Mrs. John C. Webster &
    dr.
822 Mr. & Mrs. A. Hosking
824 Mr.&Mrs. A. J. C. Ledgerwood
872 Mr.& Mrs. Francis E.Halligan
878 Mr. & Mrs. Presly M. Heron
880 Mr. & Mrs. F. C. Foster
896 Mrs. Kittie Armstrong
900 Leon Hornstein
922 Mr. & Mrs. E. C. Fitts
922 Mrs. Augusta Scofield
926 Mrs. Harry C. Linn
928 Mr. & Mrs. F. A. Barnes
936 Dr. & Mrs. J. L. Mulfinger
942 Mr. & Mrs. J. W. Slosson
942 Mr. & Mrs. Elias C. Greenlee
944 Mr. & Mrs. Leopold Gans
946 Mr. & Mrs. Henry Simon
948 Mr. & Mrs. E. W. Thompson
950 Dr. & Mrs. E. P. Rice
952 Mr. & Mrs. Charles M. Rogers
966 Mr. & Mrs. Frank Jerome
    Receiving day Wednesday
970 Thomas S. Hogan
970 Michael W. Hogan
972 Dr. Mary A. Dearlove
972 George Dearlove
974 Mr. & Mrs. J. Stellwagen
1040 Mr. & Mrs. Daniel Donahoe
1048 Mr. & Mrs. H. A. Beard
1074 Mr. & Mrs. E. B. Martin

823 Mr. & Mrs. R. C. Demarest
831 Mr. & Mrs. John M. Dunphy
831 John M. Dunphy jr.
843 Dr. & Mrs. E. L. Hayford
847 Mr. & Mrs. John Kiley
851 Dr. & Mrs. G. F. Butler
853 Mr. & Mrs. J. C. Crow
857 Mr. & Mrs. F. Mackay & dr.
857 Albert H. Tyrrell
857 James B. Pope
859 Mrs. A. J. Carbery
861 Mrs. M. D. Barnard & dr.
861 Henry Barnard
865 Dr. Samuel Willard & drs.
889 R. H. Munger
901 Dr. & Mrs. S. S. Baker
907 Mr. & Mrs. William Smillie & dr.
907 Thomas B. Smillie
907 J. Oliver Smillie
909 Mr. & Mrs. Wm. L. Newman
    & drs.
913 Mr. & Mrs. O. H. Allen
915 Mr. & Mrs. George Raymond
919 Mr. & Mrs. Albert Raymond
923 Mr. & Mrs. Charles Kaestner
    Receive 3d Friday in mo
925 Mr. & Mrs. Thos. H. McNeill
927 Mr. & Mrs. H. M. Lemon
929 Mr. & Mrs. George Rockwood
937 Wm. R. Northway
945 Mr. & Mrs. Samuel Harris
949 W. G. Williamson
953 Mr. & Mrs. J. A. Davidson
955 Dr. & Mrs. Charles Davison
955 Mrs. Martha Davison
961 Mr. & Mrs. Samuel Gans
963 Mr. & Mrs. J. H. McCorkle
965 Mr. & Mrs. Thomas McCann
967 Mr. & Mrs. S. Wheelock
969 Mr. & Mrs. H. Gross & drs.

1152 Mr. & Mrs. John S. Stevens
1158 Mr. & Mrs. W. A. Wigley
1190 Mr. & Mrs. Louis E. Randall
1214 Mr. & Mrs. John E. Patterson
1268 Mr. & Mrs. F. C. Russell
1322 Mr. & Mrs. Charles B. Moore
1380 Mr. & Mrs. E. Greenburg
1388 Mr. & Mrs. H. H. Hammond
1390 Mr. & Mrs. Wm. H. Baker
1644 Mr. & Mrs. H. M. Soper
1644 W. P. Graves
1852 Mr. & Mrs. Geo. W. McLester

969 George G. Gross
969 Edgar J. Gross
979 Mr. & Mrs. J. T. Gill
981 Mr. & Mrs. C. N. Ford
981 Miss M. A. Allinder
981 S. H. Allen Adams
983 Mr.&Mrs.B.Frank Howard&dr
987 Dr. & Mrs. T. A. Davis
989 Mr. & Mrs. Charles P. Kidd
1001 Mr. & Mrs. Thos. N. McCauley
1003 Dr. & Mrs. E. M. Northcott
1005 Mr. & Mrs. J. B. Stafford
1007 Mrs. W. Lester
1009 Mr. & Mrs. W. B. Howe
1011 James T. Ganson
1013 James C. Strain
1015 Mr. & Mrs. S. J. Clarke
1017 Mr. & Mrs. A. T. Hardick
1021 Mr. & Mrs. John Knox
1025 Merritt B. Austin
1149 Mr. & Mrs. Eugene Smith
1245 Mr. & Mrs. O. E. Chapin
1343 Mr. & Mrs. W. F. Thomas
    Receiving day Wednesday
1359 Dr. & Mrs. P. B. Hayes
1359 Mr. & Mrs. Robt. D. Wardwell
1361 Mr. & Mrs. W. S. Fox & drs.

NORTH KEDZIE AVENUE.

98 Mr. & Mrs. O. S. Hinds

136 Mr. & Mrs. Byron A. Baldwin

SOUTH KEDZIE AVENUE.

107 Mr. & Mrs. Delos W. Champlin
    & dr.
625 Dr. & Mrs. F. W. Fitzgerald
865 Mr. & Mrs. A. W. Miller
883 Mr. & Mrs. D. H. Kirkpatrick
891 Mr. & Mrs. Kirk N. Eastman &
    dr.
891 Kirk J. Eastman
933 Mr. & Mrs. Robert H. Cowdrey
995 Allen L. Schryver

80 Mr. & Mrs. H. Clarence Ambler
120 Mr. & Mrs. Edw. E. Mallory
144 Dr. & Mrs. C. Bruce Walls
886 Mr. & Mrs. C. E. Ruggles & dr.
888 Mr. & Mrs. H. C. Kline
890 Mr.&Mrs.JamesA.Calbrick&dr.
894 Mr. & Mrs. Charles G. Wink
898 Mr. & Mrs. William M. Gunton
904 Mr. & Mrs. John J. Lane
904 Mr. & Mrs. Wm. L. Craig

LAFLIN STREET.

55 Mr. & Mrs. Wm. A. Dodge
55 T. E. Woodley
55 Mr. & Mrs. L. M. Hubbard
61 Mr. & Mrs. H. E. Bennett
61 Mr. & Mrs. G. A. Marshall
65 Mr. & Mrs. C. S. Blackman
69 Mr. & Mrs. W. H. Taylor
71 Mrs. A. M. Walter
91 Miss F. W. Rowland
121 Mr. & Mrs. Leigh H. Jackson

70 Mr. & Mrs. Thos. E. Courtney
   & dr.
92 Mr. & Mrs. John Lamb
94 William H. Haas
94 Mr. & Mrs. H. Hayman
170 Mr. & Mrs. F. H. Henrici
———
121 Mr. & Mrs. Abram Jackson
191 Mr. & Mrs. T. R. Richardson
191 Mr. & Mrs. S. M. Lederer

WEST LAKE STREET.

504 Mr. & Mrs. A. M. Billings

LAWNDALE AVENUE.

641 Mr. & Mrs D. D. Campbell
817 Mrs. Julia A. Moore & dr.
817 William A. Moore
817 Mr. & Mrs. George A. Blume
855 Mr. & Mrs. Martin J. Kraus
1039 Mr. & Mrs. James A. Windsor
1043 Mr. & Mrs. O. A. Riggle
1043 Mr. & Mrs. Charles F. Riggle
1075 Mr. & Mrs. Geo. W. Straight
1127 Mr. & Mrs. Chas. L. Bonney
1137 Edwin A. Bennett
1143 Mr. & Mrs. Nelson J. Bennett
1153 Rev. Norman A. Millerd & dr.
1153 Mrs. Laura M. Millard
1173 Mr. & Mrs. J. M. Abell
1173 J. E. Abell

610 Mr. & Mrs. Hollis M. Chase
612 Mr. & Mrs. Frank Posta
800 Mr. & Mrs. Frank D. Hyde
1078 Mr. & Mrs. James L. Gregorie
1102 Mr. & Mrs. T. Oliver Stokes
1112 Mr. & Mrs. Wm. P. Northcott
1140 Mr. & Mrs. Chas. H. Beckler
1142 Mr. & Mrs. John V. Brown
1152 Mr. & Mrs. S. F. Symonds
1156 Mr. & Mrs. Wm. G. Rattray
1242 Mr. & Mrs. J. B. Benson
———
1177 D. Fuller Hayes & dr.
1193 Mrs. F. F. White & dr.
1195 Mr. & Mrs. C. F. Shepard&dr.
1227 Mr. & Mrs. E. B. Blinn

SOUTH LEAVITT STREET.

111 Mr. & Mrs. C. A. Dibble
117 Mrs. A. G. Ormsbee
145 Mr. & Mrs. Geo. A. Mason
145 G. W. Livingston
159 Mr. & Mrs. Wm. Scott & dr.
207 Mr. & Mrs. Adam Short
209 Mr. & Mrs. T. D. Wayne
209 Mrs. M. P. Lyon
213 Mr. & Mrs. John H. Williams
217 Mr. & Mrs. H. J. Luders
       Receiving day Wednesday
225 Mrs. John Sherman jr.
229 Mrs. A. Paul
229 Richard Brown
233 Miss M. E. Hamilton
237 Mr. & Mrs. C. A. Vosburgh
245 Mr. & Mrs. James M. Banks&dr.

108 William Lamb & dr.
114 Mr. & Mrs. Daniel A. Allen
116 Mr. & Mrs. C. B. Wilson
118 Mr. & Mrs. R. Manly
152 Mr. & Mrs. A. H. Bradish
154 George T. Belding
154 Mrs. C. Belding & drs.
156 Mr. & Mrs. J. N. Adams
156 Mr. & Mrs. N. B. Webster
158 W. S. McLean
234 Mr. & Mrs. Thos. Sutton
234 Judge & Mrs. F. Scales & dr.
278 Mr. & Mrs. Wm. Steppelman
282 Mr. & Mrs. John Gillespie
282 Albert E. Mortimer
400 Mr. & Mrs. E. S. Pratt & dr.
       Receiving day Thursday

283 Mr. & Mrs. Samuel Lowden&dr.
287 Mr. & Mrs. A. P. Redfield & dr.
    Receiving day Friday
289 Mr. & Mrs. W. E. Wilcox
289 Mr. & Mrs. E. H. Pifer
291 Mr. & Mrs. J. R. Coulter
293 Mr. & Mrs. N. E. Dillie
295 Mr. & Mrs. H. D. Hatch
295 Mr. & Mrs. A. J. Keefe
299 Mr. & Mrs. Harry S. Haines
303 Mr. & Mrs. Fred. A. Lindquist
387 Dr. & Mrs. P. Chester Madison
393 Dr. & Mrs. S. Perkey
395 Mr. & Mrs. A. Coulter & dr.

400 Harry E. Pratt
414 Mrs. O. S. Maxfield
414 Miss Margaret Bowman
414 William Hayden
418 Mr. & Mrs. O. A. Smith
422 Mr. & Mrs. F. R. McKee
428 Mr. & Mrs. S. W. Bassett

397 Mr. & Mrs. W. O. Wann & drs.
425 Mr.& Mrs.W.P.Fitzpatrick & dr.
435 Mr. & Mrs. A. G. Dayton
459 Mr. & Mrs. J. C. King
479 Mr. & Mrs. Fred D. Peirce
479 Dr. & Mrs.William Rittenhouse

LEXINGTON AVENUE.

1413 Mr. & Mrs. R. E. Pendarvis

1481 Mr. & Mrs. A. M. Chamberlin

SOUTH LINCOLN STREET.

12 Mr. & Mrs. A. L. Shepard
83 Mrs. Adeline Lempkey
161 Mr. & Mrs. Fred C. Rojahn
215 Mr. & Mrs. N. B. Richards
227 Miss Sarah Hanna
227 Miss Lucy Hanna
227 Mr. & Mrs. James Crighton
229 Mr. & Mrs. E. C. Barnard
229 Albert E. Barnard
229 Mr. & Mrs. J. W. Rogers
267 Mr. & Mrs. J. P. Ferrell
275 Mr. & Mrs. F. W. Collins
275 Mr. & Mrs. John W. Heller

112 Mr. & Mrs. J. G. Holden
114 Mr. & Mrs. Z. T. Griffin
188 Mr. & Mrs. J. Fieldhouse
206 G. B. Halliday & dr.
208 Mr. & Mrs. Charles Lester
210 Mr. & Mrs. Daniel G. Trench
    Receiving day Thursday
244 Mr. & Mrs. Thomas F. Judge
244 John M. Duffy

277 Mr. & Mrs. L. O. Whitman
277 Dr. V. A. Latham
277 Mr. & Mrs. B. H. Worrall

LOOMIS STREET.

13 Mrs. E. Webb Haskett
83 George R. Allen
89 Mr. & Mrs. C. J. Shields
89 Miss Lillian Shields
97 Mr. & Mrs. Geo. H. Vrooman
97 W. A. Shaw
97 Mrs. K. A. Shaw
105 Mr. & Mrs. F. L. Eastman
107 Mr. & Mrs. B. F. Richolson
109 Dr. & Mrs. A. H. Brumback
111 Mr. & Mrs. P. Hickcox
111 Mr. & Mrs. W. D. Bradshaw
111 Mrs. A. M. Wright
125 Mr. & Mrs. G. W. A. Biddle&dr.
125 Noble L. Biddle
127 Mrs. Mary G. Bowen & drs.
127 Eugene K. Bowen
127 Claude G. Bowen
211 Miss Josie Anderson
215 Dr. & Mrs. Chas. L. Webster

14 Dr. Henrietta K. Morris
14 Dr. J. L. Morris
14 James C. Morris
40 Mr. & Mrs. J. R. Francis
40 Mr. & Mrs. V. F. Mashek
44 Judge & Mrs. Phillip Stein
46 Mrs. J. W. Tuohy
46 Dr. W. S. Haines
48 Mr. & Mrs. William M. Dandy
50 Mrs. Robert Owens & dr.
50 J. O. Watkins
52 Mr. & Mrs. Geo. B. Swift & dr.
52 Brown F. Swift
52 Herbert B. Swift
54 Mr. & Mrs. Mathias Benner
84 Mr. & Mrs. J. H. Kingwill
86 Mr. & Mrs. D. S. Munger & dr.
88 Mr. & Mrs. E. J. Rogerson
    Receiving day Wednesday
92 Mr. & Mrs. J. H. MacDonald

217 Mr. & Mrs. A. S. True
223 Mr. & Mrs. H. Hazelton
225 Mr. & Mrs. Michael Hanley
229 Mr. & Mrs. C. H. Moody
235 Mr. & Mrs. Jeremiah Murphy
237 Mr. & Mrs. John F. McCarthy
241 Mr. & Mrs. John T. Donlan&dr.
241 J. P. Donlan
285 Dr. & Mrs. W. J. Nolan
305 Mr. & Mrs. Edwin J. Stubbs
305 Mr. & Mrs. Chas. T. Picard&dr.
        Receiving day Friday
305 Arthur Picard
325 A. Harris
325 Mr. & Mrs. Moses Harris & dr.
327 Mr. & Mrs. P. Gleeson & dr.

318 Mr. & Mrs. M. McNellis

96 Mr. & Mrs. George Robins
102 Mr. & Mrs. M. S. Lansing
104 Mr. & Mrs. G. A. Fellows
120 Mr. & Mrs. J. C. Harper
124 Mrs. Belle Valentine
124 G. F. Valentine
140 Mrs. M. E. Crane & dr.
140 George E. Crane
144 Mr. & Mrs. E. M. Sperbeck
154 Mrs. Wm. Henry
154 F. W. Holmes.
222 Mr. & Mrs. O. J. Franchere
230 Mr. & Mrs. B. Curtis
240 Mr. & Mrs. D. F. Bremner & dr.
258 Dr. & Mrs. O. G. Wernicke
276 Mr. & Mrs. Thomas Connelly
300 Mr. & Mrs. J. P. Bowler
318 Mr. & Mrs. M. Horan

LYTLE STREET.

151 Mr. & Mrs. W. W. Summers

60 Mr. & Mrs. John W. Garvy & dr.
        Receiving day Tuesday

52 Dr. & Mrs. C. P. Harrigan
52 Mr. & Mrs. Edward J. Coleman
56 Mr. & Mrs. John T. McEnery
56 F. C. Peyraud
56 Mr. & Mrs. Matthew Wallace

MACALISTER PLACE.

19 Mrs. E. Ragor
29 Mr. & Mrs. John Brenock & drs.
29 William Brenock
31 Mr. & Mrs. John Coughlan
31 T. E. Coughlan
33 Mr. & Mrs. J. A. Koenig & dr.
37 Mr. & Mrs. W. J. Onahan & dr.
39 Mr. & Mrs. Peter S. Haywood
41 Mr. & Mrs. Chas. F. Goodwillie
        Receiving day Thursday
43 Mr. & Mrs. Edward Powell & drs.
43 Edward L. Powell
43 George J. Powell
43 W. H. Powell
45 Mr. & Mrs. D. W. Mitchell & dr.
45 Mr. & Mrs. John Williamson
59 Mr. & Mrs. M. Considine & dr.

16 Mr. & Mrs. T. H. Gilmore

59 Michael J. Considine
59 John Considine
79 Mr. & Mrs. Frank Bartholomae
81 Mr. & Mrs. Morton W. Kelly
85 Mr. & Mrs. Thos. O'Connell &dr.
        Receiving day Tuesday
85 A. J. O'Connell
85 Thos. F. O'Connell
85 Theo. W. O'Connell
93 Mrs. A. L. Amberg
93 Mrs. Elizabeth Breuer
97 Mr. & Mrs. M. J. Corboy
99 Mr. & Mrs. Andrew Stamm & drs.
99 Dr. J. Carl Stamm
99 Mr. & Mrs. William Stamm

WEST MADISON STREET.

Gault house. D. S. Place
247 Dr. R. B. Treat
437 Dr. & Mrs. J. M. Auld
1037 Dr. & Mrs. C. R. Warren
1373 Dr. & Mrs. C. P. Donelson
1393 Dr. & Mrs. F. Brooks

1016 William Utting

220 Winfield S. Coy
382 Dr. L. L. Skelton
528 Mr. & Mrs. R. H. Fish
582 Mr. & Mrs. Chas. E. Jones
688 Dr. C. M. Glass
734 Mrs. A. M. Putnam & dr.
734 C. G. Evans
822 Stella E. Jacobi M.D.
874 Mr. & Mrs. W. L. Cook

MARSHFIELD AVENUE.

223 Mr. & Mrs. George S. Sloan
223 Howard J. Sloan
223 Mrs. Mary Whitford
229 Mr. & Mrs. Alonzo Snider & dr.
231 Mr. & Mrs. Howard Hill
231 Mrs. Sarah Hill
235 Mr. & Mrs. Hill C. Smyth
Receiving day Tuesday
237 Mr. & Mrs. Francis B. Lane
337 H. H. Moran
353 Mr. & Mrs. John E. Mullaly & dr.
Receiving day Thursday
355 Mr. & Mrs. Julius Loeser
363 Mr. & Mrs. C. C. Barrett
363 Mr. & Mrs. Frank J. Hanchett
Receiving day Friday
367 Mrs. A. C. Curtis
367 Dr. J. H. Curtis
375 Mr. & Mrs. Joseph B. Vergho
375 Mr. & Mrs. W. G. Outerbridge
375 Mrs. Wm. Steinman
383 Mr. & Mrs. W. F. Clark
401 Dr. & Mrs. A. Schirmer
407 Mr. & Mrs. M. W. Doty
406 Mr. & Mrs. T. F. Rooney
407 Thomas E. Rooney
409 Mr. & Mrs. Herman Tripp
411 Mr. & Mrs. Luke Clarke & dr.
413 Mr. & Mrs. Seymour Swarts
Receiving day Thursday
415 Mr. & Mrs. H. G. Underwood & dr.
415 H. M. Underwood
417 Mr. & Mrs. Joseph Hirsch
419 Mr. & Mrs. William B. Oliphant
425 Mr. & Mrs. John Wilson jr.
427 Mr. & Mrs. S. Kraus
429 Mr. & Mrs. D. O'Leary
433 Mr. & Mrs. E. E. Merz
433 Mr. & Mrs. S. Franklin
435 Mr. & Mrs. A. Merz
443 Dr. & Mrs. Edmund Christie
445 Mr. & Mrs. S. H. Myers & drs.
445 Mr. & Mrs. H. Rosenthal & dr.
447 Mr. & Mrs. S. G. Frank
449 Mr. & Mrs. John McSorley
449 Mr. & Mrs. S. A. Diamond
449 Henry A. Aronson
455 J. J. Morrison
455 Richard W. Morrison
455 Mrs. E. G. Snow
455 B. P. Smith
475 Mr. & Mrs. C. R. Lynch & drs.
Receiving day Thursday

214 Robert Slade & dr.
222 A. Brookins
224 Mrs. R. Frost
224 Mr. & Mrs. L. H. Goodrich
230 Mr. & Mrs. George J. Harrison
Receiving day Thursday
270 Mr. & Mrs. A. J. Oliver
272 Mr. & Mrs. R. M. Barber
276 Mr. & Mrs. Charles J. McNellis
276 Mrs. E. Weldon & dr.
278 Dr. & Mrs. H. O. Bates
278 Morley Bates
288 Mr. & Mrs. Murdock MacLeod
290 Mr. & Mrs. F. W. McFarland
292 Mr. & Mrs. Chas. E. Higbee & drs.
296 Mr. & Mrs. A. Pyott
298 Mr. & Mrs. M. R. Cobb
300 Mr. & Mrs. George V. DeForest
306 Mr. & Mrs. Jas. Keough & dr.
310 Mr. & Mrs. J. C. Vaughan
310 Miss Gussie Linquist
312 Mr. & Mrs. Walter T. Clark
Receiving day Wednesday
316 Mr. & Mrs. V. W. Dashiell
318 Mr. & Mrs. A. Weil
Receiving day Friday
320 Albert W. True
320 Charles J. True
320 Miss M. E. True
320 Miss Ella P. True
322 Mr. & Mrs. H. Weil
Receive 2d & 4th Friday
322 Miss Yetta May
326 Mrs. M. A. Monroe
326 W. F. Monroe
328 Mr. & Mrs. Thomas W. Sennott
330 Mr. & Mrs. Chas. F. Lammert
332 Mr. & Mrs. L. T. Alton
332 Ralph Alton
332 Mr. & Mrs. Alex S. Robertson
332 Thomas Robertson
408 Dr. & Mrs. David Birkhoff
410 Mr. & Mrs. Paul Boas
412 Mr. & Mrs. Max Aaron
422 Mr. & Mrs. John Dunlap
422 Mrs. Maggie Gray
428 Mr. & Mrs. Mark Torofsky
Receiving day Thursday
428 Mr. & Mrs. Louis Jacobson
Receive 1st & 3d Thursday
442 Mrs. Sarah Fleming
446 Rev. & Mrs. P. Moerdyke
448 Mr. & Mrs. John McCarthy

495 Mr. & Mrs. Aug. Thiele & dr.
495 Edward Thiele
495 Louis Theile

500 P. O'Neil Byrne

448 Mr. & Mrs. Frank Fox
454 Mr. & Mrs. Henry Wolf & dr.
454 Samuel Wolf
458 Dr. & Mrs. S. L. McCreight
482 Mr. & Mrs. James C. Dooley

MILLARD AVENUE.

975 Dr. & Mrs. H. W. Scaife
993 Mr. & Mrs. Frederick J. Peare
1085 Mr. & Mrs. C. H. Smith
1105 Mr. & Mrs. Dana Slade
1139 Mr. & Mrs. Edmund A. Curtis
1145 Mrs. George E. Bliss
1145 Arthur Bliss
1161 Mr. & Mrs. G. S. Needham
1161 Rev. & Mrs. Jeremiah C. Cromer *Receiving day Tuesday*
1225 Mr. & Mrs. Harry C. Cooper
1227 Mr. & Mrs. Charles A.Cox&dr.
1383 Mr. & Mrs. J. C. Tebbetts

1330 Mr. & Mrs. Geo. J. Needham
1358 Mrs. Chas. A. Pardee
1406 Mr. & Mrs. James E. Cross

978 Mr. & Mrs. Geo. A. Wegener
978 George A. Wegener jr.
994 Mr. & Mrs. William S. Jackson
1092 Mr. & Mrs. T. P. Rogers & dr.
1092 Harry L. Rogers
1092 Mrs. Caroline Bacon
1102 Mr. & Mrs. Edwin J. Decker
    & dr.
1108 Mr. & Mrs. J. C. Sieh & drs.
1126 Mr. & Mrs. Frederick Hawkins
1166 Mr. & Mrs. J. V. A. Hasbrook
1166 Mr.&Mrs. EdwardF.Hasbrook
1170 Mr. & Mrs. George R. Elliott
1174 Mr. & Mrs. W. W. Ingraham
1176 Dr. Julia D. Godfrey & drs.
1182 Mr. & Mrs. Charles A. Baldwin
1186 Mr. & Mrs. H. L. Billings & dr.
1326 Mr. & Mrs. H. H. Hart

WEST MONROE STREET.

289 Dr. & Mrs. T. P. Seeley
305 W. C. Donle
307 Mr. & Mrs. S. W. Crandall
311 Mrs. John P. Almquist & dr.
313 Mr. & Mrs. M. A. Wells
327 Mr. & Mrs. H. R. Shaffer
327 Mr. & Mrs. F. M. Gray
335 Mr. & Mrs. Charles Barnes
335 Frank J. Baker
335 E. M. Carson
341 Mrs. Virginia Hartley
341 Mrs. Thos. Gannon
341 Miss Jennie Baylis
341 Miss Charlotte Baylis
341 H. A. Barber jr.
343 Dr. J. A. Stansbury
345 Mr. & Mrs. E. Kirchberg
355 A. J. Arata
377 A. J. Brock
395 Mr. & Mrs. S. I. Curtis
397 Prof. & Mrs. Graham Taylor
399 Mr. & Mrs. R. M. Outhet
399 John C. Outhet
405 Miss Louise M. Summerfield
409 Rev. & Mrs. H. W. Bolton
411 Mr. & Mrs. John H. Amberg
413 Mr. & Mrs. Chas.A.Plamondon
    Receiving day Tuesday

294 Mrs. S. P. Walker & dr.
296 Dr. T. D. Fitch
296 Dr. C. Fred Fitch
300 Mr. & Mrs. A. Flower
324 J. C. Gould
328 Mr. & Mrs. Bernard Roesing
412 Mr. & Mrs. William H. McKee
492 Rev. & Mrs. W. M. Lawrence
    Receiving day Wednesday aft.
494 Mr. & Mrs. Romaine M. Conger
494 Richard Fennimore
494 William Fennimore
496 Mr. & Mrs. George D. Broomell
496 George D. Broomell jr.
496 Francis E. Broomell
496 Mrs. Maria W. Babcock
498 Mr. & Mrs. C. H. Chappell
498 C. H. Chappell jr.
500 Mr. & Mrs. William H. Holden
504 Mr. & Mrs. John McArthur & dr.
504 John McArthur jr.
506 Mr. & Mrs. W. H. Aldrich
510 Mr. & Mrs. E. A. Blodgett & drs.
510 Coles Veeder
512 Mr. & Mrs. Lester L. Bond
512 Mrs. Laura D. Ayres
516 Dr. George A. Jett
516 R. S. Shannon

433 Mrs. E. A. Talcott
447 Mr. & Mrs. John P. Foss
447 Fred D. Foss
459 Mr. & Mrs. William H. Alsip
 Receiving day Wednesday
461 Mr. & Mrs. C. E. Hambleton
461 Mr. & Mrs. Charles A. Dew
463 Mrs. Helen J. Bremner
 Receiving day Thursday
463 B. E. Bremner
463 Edw. H. Llewellyn
465 Mr. & Mrs. George Betts
467 Mr. & Mrs. Lewis M. Reed
467 Mr. & Mrs. Frank A. Place
467 Mr. & Mrs. L. D. Harkness
469 Mr. & Mrs. George K. Barnes
475 Mrs. Eliza Foss
475 Horace B. Foss
481 Mrs. John Spry
 Receiving day Wednesday
481 Mr. & Mrs. S. A. Spry
487 William J. Pope
487 Mr. & Mrs. August C. Magnus
489 Jerome Root
489 Dr. Eliza H. Root
489 J. Sherman Root
493 Mr.& Mrs.Rodney S.Whitcomb
493 Mr. & Mrs. W. C. B. Palmer
499 Mr. & Mrs. B. A. Eckhart
503 Mrs. Henrietta Cornell
503 Mr. & Mrs. G. W. Blanchard
505 W. H. Nichols
505 J. W. Hatch
507 W. T. Keener
507 Mrs. Sarah F. Nicholas
507 Miss Eunice A. Martin
507 Mrs. C. M. Lewis
507 Miss Emma M. Lewis
507 Mr. & Mrs. T. N. Bond
507 Mr. & Mrs. George W. Thacher
507 Edwin Wynn
507 Clarence M. Kelsey
507 Rev. & Mrs. Fred'k Campbell
507 H. Y. Williamson
507 Mrs. E. M. Bedell
509 Mr. & Mrs. M. A. Bartlett
511 Mr. & Mrs. Charles Mackie
 Receiving day Thursday
511 George Mason
519 Mr. & Mrs. Joseph Hogan
 Receiving day Thursday
521 Mrs. David Boyle
521 Henry J. Boyle
525 Miss Lizzie M. Russell
525 Mr. & Mrs. R. L. Wyman
525 Mr. & Mrs. A. P. White

518 Mr. & Mrs. R. N. Pearson & dr.
518 Mr. & Mrs. F. H. Shannon
518 Mr. & Mrs. C. E. Brush
520 Mr. & Mrs. Robert Smale & dr.
520 W. R. Smale
522 James A. Doane
522 Mr. & Mrs. B. F. Baldwin
522 H. C. Baldwin
528 Mr. & Mrs. Henry Towne & dr.
530 Mr. & Mrs. J B. Sherwood & dr.
532 Mrs. Chas. E. Strong & dr.
534 Mrs. W. W. Farwell
534 J. W. Farwell
616 Mr. & Mrs. Chas. T. Marsh
626 Dr. & Mrs. H. J. Treat
628 Mrs. M. Salomon & dr.
628 Dr. Gottfried S. Salomon
632 Mrs. P. B. Knokes
632 Mrs. S. A. Able
640 Mr. & Mrs. J. B. Myers
644 Mr. & Mrs. S. B. Kimball
644 A. S. Kimball
644 Ernest M. Kimball
644 Mr. & Mrs. H. D. French
646 Mrs. H. E. Morton
646 Mrs. S. F. Hinckley .
648 Mr. & Mrs. I. R. Krum
648 Mrs. R. A. Brett
650 Mr. & Mrs. A. M. Forbes & drs.
652 Mr. & Mrs. H. A. Wheeler
652 Mrs. L. A. Small
654 Mr. & Mrs. George W. Warvelle
 Receiving day Wednesday
656 Mrs. S. E.W. Martin & dr.
660 Daniel Gregory
660 Walter D. Gregory
660 Mr. & Mrs. William Rodiger
672 Dr. & Mrs. D. W. Graham
672 Mrs. S. A. Pratt
672 Mr. & Mrs. A. F. Campbell
674 Mrs. D. B. Cheney
674 Dr. & Mrs. F. S. Cheney
676 Mrs. C. E. Benson
676 John L. Wilkin
678 Mr. & Mrs. Christopher Wright
 & dr.
680 Mr. & Mrs. Geo. S. Mackenzie
 & dr.
684 Mr. & Mrs. C. C. Hilton
688 Mr. & Mrs. Joseph Landis
688 Mr. & Mrs. L. K. Tucker
690 Dr. & Mrs. William E. Clarke
 & dr.
690 Glenn E. Plumb
692 Mr. & Mrs. William McGregor
694 Mrs. E. A. Bell & dr.

525 Dr. Mary H. Bowen
531 Rev. & Mrs. J. Vila Blake
531 Clinton F. Blake
533 Dr. & Mrs. Albert B. Strong
533 Mr. & Mrs. T. G. Carroll
535 Rev.& Mrs. HiramW. Thomas
 Receive Wednesday p.m.
539 Dr. L. St. John
539 Fred St. John
539 Mrs. Jennie Booth
543 Mr. & Mrs. J. H. Bacon & dr.
543 William R. Morse
543 J. H. Golden
545 Mr. & Mrs. J. P. Wathier
547 Mrs. N. Lamport
547 Mrs. Mary Dunn
547 Mr. & Mrs. Isaac W. Nichols
547 Dr. E. Rauch
549 Mr. & Mrs. Isaac N. Camp
 Receiving day Tuesday
551 Mr. & Mrs. Simeon F. Leonard
555 Mr. & Mrs. J. Howard Jones&dr.
555 Mr. & Mrs. Frank L. Jones
555 Harry P. Jones
555 Miss L. M. Higgins
591 Mrs. S. E. Patterson
591 James W. Patterson
591 Mr. & Mrs. J. A. Corwin
593 Mr. & Mrs. C. A. Fitch & dr.
595 Mr. & Mrs. A. D. Swain
601 Mrs. Amanda Tallman
601 W. D. Tallman
603 Mr. & Mrs. A. Cossman
603 Meyer Cossman
605 Miss Jennie Roberts
613 Dr. & Mrs. E. C. Sweet
625 Mr. & Mrs. L. W. Hess
627 Mr. & Mrs. A. D. Edgeworth
627 Dr. & Mrs. E. W. Roe
631 Mr.& Mrs. William Jauncey&dr.
631 Mrs. M. W. Chase
633 Dr. & Mrs. Richard J. Piper
633 Mr. & Mrs. George Duffy
633 W. H. Slack
639 Miss Bertha Clark
641 Mr. & Mrs. Nicholas Bernard
643 Mr. & Mrs. J. Dell
643 Mrs. E. Clarke
643 Mr. & Mrs. Howard Watson
645 Dr. & Mrs. C. M. Fitch
645 Dr. & Mrs. Walter M. Fitch
647 Mr. & Mrs. Chas. W. Bard & drs.
649 Mr. & Mrs. R. E. Haskett
649 Miss M. D. Wingate
649 Miss Rebecca Kerr
655 Mr. & Mrs. Wm. E. Best & drs.

694 Leonard F. Bell
694 F. H. Bell
694 Mr. & Mrs. Albert F. Solberg
698 Mr. & Mrs. Simon Wolf & dr.
698 Alphonso S. Wolf
698 Morris E. Wolf
698 Benjamin Wolf
700 Dr. & Mrs. Eugene Marguerat
 & dr.
712 Mrs. E. L. Martin
 Receiving day Thursday
712 Miss Lilian Cary
714 Dr. & Mrs. W. H. Burt
714 J. A. Burt
716 Mr. & Mrs. John W. Eckhart
722 Mr. & Mrs. S. D. Thompson
726 Mr. & Mrs. B. T. Hosking
728 Dr. & Mrs. Amos J. Nichols
728 Eliot Cobb
730 Mr. & Mrs. Charles Brooks&dr.
730 Arthur S. Abbott
732 Mr. & Mrs. J. Loewenthal
738 Mr. & Mrs. J. B. McDonald
740 Mr. & Mrs. Thos. Shaughnessy
 & drs.
742 Mr. & Mrs. W. L. Kehr
744 Mr. & Mrs. Moritz Hofman
744 Henry Hofman
744 Samuel Hofman
746 Mr. & Mrs. J. H. Hildreth
752 Mrs. Jacob Armstrong
752 Miss Clara Hall
754 Miss Emma Enslee
754 Dr. Charles L. Enslee
754 Mr. & Mrs. Robert Barlow
754 Mr. & Mrs. G. W. Clark & dr.
770 Rev. & Mrs. R. F. Parshall
770 Mr. & Mrs. W. W. Beaty
772 Mrs. Ella Graham
772 Mrs. E. B. Scarritt
778 Mr. & Mrs. Thomas J. Wheeler
780 Dr. & Mrs. H. H. Jackson
786 Mr. & Mrs. G. G. Benedict
786 Edwin P. Benedict
788 Mr. & Mrs. A. Eddy & dr.
788 G. S. Eddy
788 Thomas H. Eddy
790 Mr. & Mrs. I. W. McCasky&dr.
792 Mr. & Mrs. J. G. Aldridge
794 Mrs. Catherine Russell & drs.
796 Mrs. Lucy Haywood & drs.
798 Mr. & Mrs. J. K. Allen
802 Mrs. Elizabeth Holden
802 Mr. & Mrs. Andrew J. Wood
804 Mr. & Mrs. Silas L. Wood
804 Mr. & Mrs. D. F. Holman & dr.

661 Mr. & Mrs. J. W. Benham
663 Mrs. Nettie A. Yates
663 A. F. Smith
663 Miss Libby Baldwin
665 Mr. & Mrs. John Dadie
    Receiving day Wednesday
667 Mr. & Mrs. H. J. Franks
669 Dr. & Mrs. Lisle Cummins
    Waters
    Receiving day Thursday
669 Mrs. Fannie T. Waters
671 Mr. & Mrs. Albert Willey & dr.
677 Mr. & Mrs. R. L. Greenlee & dr.
    Receiving day Tuesday
681 Mrs. C. N. Holden
683 Mr. & Mrs. A. W. Patterson
    Receiving day Thursday
683 Mr. & Mrs. N. L. Lenham
685 Mr. & Mrs. G. M. Whitney
    Receiving day Wednesday
689 Mr. & Mrs. Addison L. Gardner
695 Mr. & Mrs. Paul C. Eilers
695 Mr. & Mrs. D. C. Jones
695 Fred H. Jones
697 Louis E. Hart
699 Miss S. J. Grace
699 Mrs. I. Baker
701 Mr. & Mrs. A. H. Waterman
703 Mr. & Mrs. Martin E. Cole
703 Mr. & Mrs. Daniel K. Boughton
705 Dr. & Mrs. W. C. Cox
707 Mr. & Mrs. John C. Ford
707 Mr. & Mrs. F. A. Gabriel
709 Mr. & Mrs. William H. Kane
715 Mr. & Mrs. Benj. F. McNeill
719 Mr. & Mrs. A. J. Walker & dr.
721 Mrs. Elizabeth Plattenburg
721 C. B Plattenburg D. D. S.
721 C. S. A. Plattenburg
725 Mr. & Mrs. D. Munroe
729 Mr. & Mrs. H. B. Galpin
729 Mr. & Mrs. Homer K. Galpin
733 Mr. & Mrs. A. Pam & drs.
733 Max Pam
733 Hugo Pam
735 Mr. & Mrs. George I. Hicks
739 Mr. & Mrs. E. P. Johnston & drs.
741 Mr. & Mrs. T. W. Slattery
743 Mr. & Mrs. D. J. Tobias & drs.
745 Mr. & Mrs. F. H. Hill
749 Mrs. Charles Holmes
753 Mr. & Mrs. E. M. Gardiner
779 Dr. & Mrs. A. H. Foster
781 Mr. & Mrs. G. W. Stanford
785 Mrs. O. W. Barrett & dr.
787 Mrs. S. A. Hitchcock

808 Mr. & Mrs. W. H. Austin
810 Mr. & Mrs. L. T. Woodcock
812 Mr. & Mrs. Chas. F. Judd
    Receiving day Wednesday
814 Mr. & Mrs. J. C. Grant
820 Mr. & Mrs. L. M. Habel & dr.
824 Mr. & Mrs. W. H. Price
824 Mrs. Alice Rutherford
830 Mr. & Mrs. N. R. Wakefield & dr.
    Receiving day Tuesday
832 Mr. & Mrs. Cornelius Quinlan
834 Mr. & Mrs. W. G. Twitty
840 Mr. & Mrs. James Q. Baird & dr.
840 Mr. & Mrs. A. Y. Stebbins
846 Dr. & Mrs. A. H. Tagert
848 Mr. & Mrs. W. H. Vehon
850 Dr. & Mrs. George J. Tobias
856 Dr. & Mrs. C. J. Adams
858 Dr. & Mrs. Stephen G. West
860 Mr. & Mrs. A. P. Dodge
862 Mr. & Mrs. J. A. Ewing & dr.
862 Mr. & Mrs. Wm. O. Emery
862 Mr. & Mrs. Fred Sturtevant
866 Dr. & Mrs. W. L. Copeland
868 Mr. & Mrs. J. C. Banks
870 Mrs. Ella Hall & dr.
870 Shirley C. Hall
870 Mrs. Florence Bacon & dr.
878 Mr. & Mrs. C. S. Gurney
878 Mrs. T. T. Gurney
882 Mr. & Mrs. L. L. Troy
882 C. L. Miles
902 Mr. & Mrs. Duncan Cameron
906 Mrs. Rebecca A. Johnson
908 Mr. & Mrs. W. H. Tyler
910 Dr. & Mrs. Joseph Rogers & dr.
912 Mr. & Mrs. Thomas Collins &
    dr.
916 Mr. & Mrs. A. Levine
918 Mr. & Mrs. Joseph Vehon & dr.
918 Morris Vehon
920 Mr. & Mrs. Samuel Levy
930 Mr. & Mrs. Isidore Heller
932 Mr. & Mrs. C. H. Rawlins
932 Mr. & Mrs. F. A. Cobb
938 Mr. & Mrs. G. W. VanZandt
938 O. C. Van Zandt
940 Mr. & Mrs. A. J. Miksch
944 Mr. & Mrs. Geo. C. Farnum
946 Mr. & Mrs. E. C. Thomas
958 Mr. & Mrs. T. W. Draper
958 Mr. & Mrs. Arthur W. Draper
962 Mrs. M. A. Kavanagh
962 Charles J. Kavanagh
964 Dr. & Mrs. A. V. Hutchins
968 Mr. & Mrs. W. F. Van Olinda

787 E. J. Hitchcock
789 Mr. & Mrs. William J. Hack
789 Mr. & Mrs. Basil Dunstan
793 Mr. & Mrs. Samuel I. Pope&dr.
793 George A. Pope
797 Mr. & Mrs. John F. Wolff
799 Mr. &Mrs. Louis A. Podrasnik
799 Mr. & Mrs. B. F. Ryer
805 Mr. & Mrs. Mark M.Thompson
831 Mr. & Mrs. C. J. Wolff
Receiving day Thursday
833 Mr. & Mrs. David Vernon & drs.
841 Mr. & Mrs. William Curran
849 Mr. & Mrs. David Oliver
853 Mr. & Mrs. H. B. Utley
855 Mr. & Mrs. J. M. Carroll
857 Mr. & Mrs. W. J. Aiken
859 Mrs. S. C. Schultz & drs.
859 James M. Schultz
859 Alex J. Schultz
861 Mr. &Mrs. I. Van Baalen & dr.
861 Mr. & Mrs. J. S. Lit
865 Mr. & Mrs. R. C. Christy
867 Mr. & Mrs. H. C. Odell
869 Mr. & Mrs. Charles A. Allen
871 Mr. & Mrs. T.S. Albright & dr.
871 Miss Belle Steen
871 Mr. & Mrs. Frank H. Rice
875 Miss Emma Webb
877 Dr. & Mrs. R. B. Tuller
877 Mrs. Emma S. Pribyl
883 Mr. & Mrs. George Van Zandt
883 Mr. & Mrs. Edgar E. Hunt
895 Mr. & Mrs. A.E. Havens &drs.
895 Mrs. Kate Havens
897 Mr. & Mrs. W. C. Hickox
899 Mr. & Mrs. Austin Clement
903 Dr. & Mrs. I. N. Danforth
905 Mr. & Mrs. John McCully
907 Mr. & Mrs. James A. Mason
907 Mrs. J. H. Cleveland
911 Mrs. M. Newgass
917 Mr. & Mrs. James M. Wanzer
921 Mr. & Mrs. Morris Silverstone
921 Mr. & Mrs. F. V. Newell
923 Mr. & Mrs. J. S. Fifield
923 F. W. Brainerd
923 E. T. Brainerd
929 Mr. & Mrs. M. Polachek & drs.
933 Miss Adelaide McMillan
933 Louis S. McMillan
933 Mrs. M. J. Montfort & drs.
933 William Montfort
937 Ithiel P. Farnum
939 Dr. & Mrs. Harvey A. Tyler
941 Mr. & Mrs. E. B. Friedman

996 Mr. & Mrs. J. W. Swafford
1010 Mr. & Mrs. John Myers
1010 Dr. O. P. Hatheway
1016 Mrs. Richard Butcher & drs.
1016 Nelson Butcher
1028 Dr. & Mrs. S. K. Falls
1054 Mr. & Mrs. Edwin C. Tagg
1070 Mr. & Mrs. W. M. Campbell
1390 Mr. & Mrs. E. C. Berg
1406 Mr. & Mrs. George Marsh
1410 Mr. & Mrs. B. L. Ames
1472 Mr. & Mrs. W. N. Van Matre
1472 Mr.&Mrs.Geo. E.W. De Clercq
1424 Mr. & Mrs. George Oliver
1444 Mr. & Mrs. H. W. Mallen
1520 Mr. & Mrs. William Meredith
1522 Mr. & Mrs. John Ganson
1534 Mr. & Mrs. John B. Scully
1534 Dr. & Mrs. J. M. Fleming
1538 Mr. & Mrs. H. S. Duncombe
1544 Dr. & Mrs. A. W. Smith
1552 Mr. & Mrs. G. R. Bocher
1554 Mr. & Mrs. T. J. Bolender
1556 Mr. & Mrs. William H. Price
1566 Mr. & Mrs. John F. Higgins
1566 Mr. & Mrs. Chas. Rowan
1566 Mrs. J. F. Warner
1570 Mr. & Mrs. L. M. Walters
1572 Mr. & Mrs. W. H. Pettee
1670 Mr. & Mrs. F. O. Griffin & dr.

---

943 Mr. & Mrs. Joseph B. David
945 Mr. & Mrs. S. B. Miles
961 Dr. & Mrs. Frank Branen
963 Dr. & Mrs. H. P. Skiles
965 Mr. & Mrs. James H. Johnson
967 Rt. Rev.& Mrs.Sam'l Fallows&
drs. *Receiving day Monday*
1017 Mr. & Mrs. A. O. Humphrey
1023 Mrs. Louise Dilley
1023 Mr. & Mrs. William Dilley
1077 Mr. & Mrs. J. W. Ostrander
1093 Frank J. Kilcrane
1193 Miss Rachel M. Booth
1201 Mrs. Katherine Loding
1205 Mr. & Mrs. R. B. Swift
1315 Mr.& Mrs. Chas. F. Felthousen
1331 Mr. & Mrs. O. N. Carter
1393 Mr. & Mrs. Alfred E. Barr
1423 Mr. & Mrs. J. M. Leet
1471 Mr. & Mrs. A. B. Sherwin & dr.
1471 Aug. G. Sherwin
1473 Mr. & Mrs. John E. Williams
1473 Mr. & Mrs. J. H. Whiteside
1489 Mr. & Mrs. S. H. Harris
1491 Mr. & Mrs. G. W. Haskins

1491 Miss Lucy Hannah
1525 Mr. & Mrs. Frank M. Nichols
1527 William J. Nye
1531 Mr. & Mrs. W. M. Terriberry
1531 Mr. & Mrs. John Oliver jr.
1543 Mr. & Mrs. W. G. Oliver
1543 Mr. & Mrs. Charles Baltz
1543 Mr. & Mrs. Wm. Gardner
1545 Mr. & Mrs. W. T. Goss
1551 Mr. & Mrs. P. H. McLaughlin
1555 E. C. Meinel
1555 F. A. Meinel

1555 William Meinel
1619 Mr. & Mrs. A. C. Perrill
1651 Mr. & Mrs. N. A. Williams
1651 Mr. & Mrs. M. D. Williams
1657 Mr. & Mrs. Geo. F. Featherstone
1659 Mr. & Mrs. John Naghten
1659 James J. Naghten
1659 Frank A. Naghten
1665 Mr. & Mrs. Chas. E. Matthews
1669 Mr. & Mrs. John Memhard &
    dr. *Receiving day Tuesday*
2189 Mr. & Mrs. Thos. P. Thompson

SOUTH MORGAN STREET.

133 Mr. & Mrs. Rollin Sherman
133 Dr. & Mrs. J. Bassett

218 Louis Adams
133 R. J. Bassett

NORTH OAKLEY AVENUE.

79 Rev. Henry G. Perry

SOUTH OAKLEY AVENUE.

109 Mrs. Mary E. Potwin
109 Homer Potwin
109 Miss Mary L. Potwin
153 Mrs. Charles H. Brower & drs.
155 Mark H. Salt
155 John Saltar jr.
157 Mrs. E. S. Rice & drs.
157 H. J. Snell
159 Mr. & Mrs. C. I. Bewley
159 A. A. Bewley
161 J. D. Okes
183 Mrs. J. C. Maxfield
183 Mr. & Mrs. Wm. L. Connon
183 Mr. & Mrs. H. R. Alborn
    Receiving day Thursday
187 Mrs. John Lovely
219 Mr. & Mrs. M. Weston & dr.
219 Mr. & Mrs. George A. Baker jr.
219 Mr. & Mrs. George Mehring
225 Mrs. Addie M. Jordan
225 Miss Ella M. Jordan
225 Mr. & Mrs. F. B. Davidson
    Receiving day Thursday
227 Mr. & Mrs. John A. McKay
229 Mr. & Mrs. Floyd E. Jennison
231 Rev. & Mrs. John W. Allen
235 Mr. & Mrs. Samuel Ruth
275 Mr. & Mrs. George Gregson
279 Mr. & Mrs. William H. Sloan &
    dr.
287 Dr. & Mrs. E. W. Olcott & dr.
289 Aaron Williams

80 James Hagan
102 Mrs. F. H. Green
110 Dr. & Mrs. D. A. Payne
112 Mr. & Mrs. Michael Blumenthal
112 William Blumenthal
114 Mr. & Mrs. J. S. Meister
116 Dr. & Mrs. S. J. Boyd
118 Mr. & Mrs. Rivers McNeill
120 Mrs. Emily Corby & drs.
120 Ralph B. Corby
148 G. S. Zschech
150 Mr. & Mrs. L. Erstein
    Receiving day Tuesday
152 Mrs. C. R. Dennett
220 Mr. & Mrs. C. W. Ellsworth
222 Mr. & Mrs. A. Newton
224 Mr. & Mrs. Chas. E. Bonnell
    Receiving day Wednesday
230 Mr. & Mrs. L. A. Hamblen
234 Mr. & Mrs. C. L. Gray
236 Mr. & Mrs. A. M. Searles
236 Willard G. Searles
266 Mr. & Mrs. F. A. Wadsworth
268 Mr. & Mrs. A. H. Halleman
276 Mr. & Mrs. Robt. McMullen &
    drs.
276 R. A. McMullen
278 Mr. & Mrs. John Gately
294 Dr. & Mrs. J. D. Tuthill
302 Dr. F. J. Dewey
310 Mr. & Mrs. A. Desjardins
348 Dr. & Mrs. A. M. Stout

289 Miss Annie E. Williams
305 Mr. & Mrs. Joseph Trienens
307 Dr. & Mrs. J. H. Creer
355 Mr. & Mrs. J. H. McCormick
355 Frank P. McCormick
357 Mr. & Mrs. G. M. Lovelock
  Receiving day Thursday
359 Mr. & Mrs. O. E. Whitcomb
361 Mr. & Mrs. George W. Hicks & dr.
361 Mr. & Mrs. Henry E. Marble
363 Mr. & Mrs. E. I. Sutfin
365 Mr. & Mrs. Thomas Greig
371 Mr. & Mrs. E. D. Powell
383 Mrs. Elizabeth Adams
385 Mr. & Mrs. J. C. Craig
389 Mr. & Mrs. A. Jacobson
403 Mrs. Arabella Mollan
403 John F. Mollan
403 Charles G. Mollan
411 Mr. & Mrs. James A. S. Reed
431 Mr. & Mrs. P. R. McLeod
433 Mrs. C. L. Wann
433 Mrs. Kittie Van Allen

348 Mr. & Mrs. Jas. S. Robinson
376 Mr. & Mrs. O. W. Dean
  Receiving day Wednesday
390 Mr. & Mrs. J. F. Moore
394 J. V. McAdam
394 Charles V. McAdam
394 Miss May Rose McAdam
414 Mr. & Mrs. J. A. Winter & drs.
414 E. J. Winter
414 R. W. Winter
422 Mrs. J. A. Edington & dr.
434 Mrs. S. H. Cady
434 George W. Cady
454 Mr. & Mrs. George Edmanson
460 Dr. Henry J. Way
460 Dr. & Mrs. J. E. Reynolds
464 Mr. & Mrs. J. William Allen
468 Mr. & Mrs. J. E. Richardson
532 Mr. & Mrs. C. Hammond
—————
435 Mr. & Mrs. W. D. Hall & dr.
437 Mrs. Eliza Lawrence
451 Mrs. L. K. Woodbridge
451 Mrs. Louisa Percy

OGDEN AVENUE.

597 Mr. & Mrs. O. C. Mattern
685 Dr. L. C. Borland
1353 Mr. & Mrs. John A. Bickford
1417 Mr. & Mrs. C. F. Schultz
1441 Mr. & Mrs. Z. R. Carter

26 Mrs. A. H. Field & dr.
64 Mr. & Mrs. George Rosa
66 Mr. & Mrs. Charles R. Holden
78 Mr. & Mrs. Benton Warder
98 Dr. W. G. Willard
348 James L. Higgie jr.

PARK AVENUE.

The Ingleside Flats
 1 Mr. & Mrs. Louis Schram
 5 Mrs. L. M. Dunn
  Receiving day Thursday
17 Miss I. Honora Swartz
19 Henry Meiselbar
21 Mr. & Mrs. Thomas Walls & dr.
21 Dr. Frank X. Walls
23 Dr. & Mrs. Orrison B. Damon
27 Mr. & Mrs. Lester H. Robinson
35 Mrs. F. L. Peck
35 Mr. & Mrs. E. F. Bosley
37 Dr. & Mrs. John R. McCullough
47 Prof. & Mrs. Jas. G. Leonard
47 Harry L. Van Housen
55 Dr. Emanuel Friend
55 Alexander Friend
57 Mr. & Mrs. Charles Green
59 Mrs. M. E. Cunningham

18 Mr. & Mrs. J. M. Sherman
26 Mrs. Fannie English
36 Mr. & Mrs. John P. Larkins
48 Mr. & Mrs. Charles G. Singer
48 Mrs. H. A. Singer
50 Miss Lillian May Rapp
  Receiving day Wednesday
50 Lee S. Rapp
58 Mrs. E. Morgan
58 Mrs. B. E. Morgan
60 Mr. & Mrs. Joseph A. Roe
62 Mr. & Mrs. J. F. Murray
64 Mr. & Mrs. R. W. Day
72 Mr. & Mrs. Robert Tarrant
72 Mr. & Mrs. F. W. Brodie
82 Mr. & Mrs. H. Humiston
82 William H. Humiston
88 Mr. & Mrs. R. I. Marr
88 Robert H. Ure
90 Mr. & Mrs. J. W. Strackbein

22

61 J. W. Low
69 Mr. & Mrs. E. B. Bennett
71 Mr. & Mrs. P. C. Sears & dr.
71 Mr. & Mrs. J. E. Young & dr.
73 Mr. & Mrs. S. A. Moffett
73 William B. Moffett
73 Walter H. Moffett
73 Mr. & Mrs. B. L. Coolidge
75 Mr. & Mrs. Franklin Sawyer
75 Robert F. Sawyer
79 Mrs. J. P. Emmert
79 Mr. & Mrs. J. W. Brockway
79 Mr. & Mrs. B. F. Jenks
83 Mr. & Mrs. Frank Busch & drs.
83 John Busch
85 Mr. & Mrs. Arthur W. Masters
91 Mr. & Mrs. Albert Dow
91 Walter K. Dow
95 Mrs. H. N. Bishop & drs.
95 Charles N. Bishop
97 Mr. & Mrs. G. O. Wentworth
97 A. Lansing Hurdle
99 Mr. & Mrs. Chas. Hayward &dr.
107 Mr. & Mrs. A. D. O'Neill & dr.
107 A. D. O'Neill jr.
117 Mr. & Mrs. Louis Sievers
117 Alexander Sievers
123 Mr. & Mrs. F. C. Wilson & drs.
127 Mr. & Mrs. Henry Warrington
127 James N. Warrington
127 William H. Warrington
131 Mr. & Mrs. B. Wygant & dr.
       Receiving day Thursday
131 Hugh Cunningham
135 Mr. & Mrs. G. T. Gould
139 Mr. & Mrs. Geo. W. W. Perkins
141 Mr. & Mrs. W. G. Wood
145 Dr. & Mrs. James A. Egan
175 Mr. & Mrs. P. F. Bryce & dr.
175 Robert Bryce
177 Mrs. D. G. Smith
177 Burton M. Smith
179 Mr. & Mrs. B. W. Veirs
       Receiving day Wednesday
179 Mrs. L. F. Bowyer
181 Mr. & Mrs. J. F. Slocum
181 Mr. & Mrs. John Graham jr.
185 Mr. & Mrs. William T. Maypole
201 Mr. & Mrs. J. F. Balkwill
201 Mrs. A. M. Garner
203 Mr. & Mrs. James A. Hitchcock
213 Mr. & Mrs. Edw. H. Boehne &
       dr.
213 Miss Pearl Schofield
223 Mrs. Isabella Christian & drs.
227 Mrs. M. Gallagher

92 Mr. & Mrs. Adolph Sorg jr.
92 Mr. & Mrs. Edward J. Lewis
106 Mr. & Mrs. G. B. Fritts
108 Mr. & Mrs. W. J. Ellinwood
114 Mr. & Mrs. Thomas Charles
122 Dr. W. M. Gray & dr.
128 Dr. & Mrs. M. E. Conger
132 Mr. & Mrs. Edward M. Hough
132 Miss Ella Campbell
134 H. J. Jones & drs.
134 Ford Jones
134 Robert Bailey
136 Dr. & Mrs. Henry Hemingway
136 Howard E. Hall
138 Mr. & Mrs. W. W. Wheeler
144 Mr. & Mrs. W. H. Bunge
146 Mr. & Mrs. I. V. Edwards
148 Mr. & Mrs. J. Edwards Fay & dr.
148 B. W. Fay
150 Mr. & Mrs. F. H. Hall
150 Dr. & Mrs. J. R. Buchan
158 Mr. & Mrs. J. M. Cyrus & dr.
158 Mr. & Mrs. C. E. Collins
160 Mr. & Mrs. J. A. Ruth & dr.
160 Mrs. Fannie Ruth
162 H. A. Hurlburd &dr.
162 Mrs. M. A. Kelly
162 L. C. Parker
166 Mr. & Mrs. Wm. Kilpatrick
166 Charles Kilpatrick
180 Mr. & Mrs. M. T. Cole
182 Dr. & Mrs. J. W. Meek
186 Mr. & Mrs. S. M. Meek
186 Mr. & Mrs. Thomas M. Meek
194 Mr. & Mrs. Alvin Hulbert & drs.
       Receiving day Thursday
198 Mr. & Mrs. A. W. Cooper
200 Mr. & Mrs. J. B. Storey
210 Mr. & Mrs. Theodore H. Elmer
       & dr.
       Receiving day Thursday
214 Dr. Elmer E. Prescott
216 Mr. & Mrs. Daniel Reiley & dr.
218 Mr. & Mrs. George V. Frye
224 Mr. & Mrs. A. W. Hadfield
230 Mr. & Mrs. Theo. Arnold & drs.
       Receiving day last Friday in mo.
238 Dr. & Mrs. J. Brown Loring
244 Mr. & Mrs. H. B. Chandler
250 Mr. & Mrs. J. L. Beckwith
258 Peter Fortune
258 Miss Josie Fortune
262 Mrs. A. M. Cook & dr.
264 Mr. & Mrs. Franz Gindele & dr.
264 Frank L. Gindele
276 Mr. & Mrs. J. L. Geraghty

227 William Gallagher
227 Mr. & Mrs. J. E. Birtwistle
233 Mr. & Mrs. D. H. Fritts
239 Mr. & Mrs. George Gillespie
241 Mr. & Mrs. James Kirkle & dr.
247 Dr. & Mrs. J. B. Walker
249 Dr. & Mrs. A. K. Smith
255 Mr. & Mrs. William M. Dayton
259 Rev. & Mrs. W. W. Painter
267 Rev. & Mrs. Chas. K. Westfall
Receive Thursday and Friday
267 William Sundermeaer
267 Mr. & Mrs. Peter Smith & dr.
277 Mr. & Mrs. Rufus King & dr.
277 William King
283 Dr. & Mrs. J. F. Burkholder
285 Mr. & Mrs. J. J. Murray
287 Mr. & Mrs. W. C. C. Lartz
287 Mr. & Mrs. D. P. Johnston
293 Mr. & Mrs. DeWitt C. Palmeter & dr.
299 Mr. & Mrs. A. A. Burnham
Receiving day Thursday
301 Mrs. A. R. Atkins & dr.
303 Mr. & Mrs. Will C. Rood
303 Mrs. S. E. Walworth
305 Mr. & Mrs. W. R. Daniels
311 Mr. & Mrs. John O. Dunn
315 Mr. & Mrs. Edw. E. Todd
315 Wellington Weigley
319 Mrs. M. E. Ward & drs.
321 Mr. & Mrs. J. Wolfenstetter
Receiving day Thursday
333 Mrs. Mary S. Gore & dr.
333 Alfred W. Gore
339 Mr. & Mrs. George W. Strell
341 Mr. & Mrs. G. W. Wilson & dr.
343 Mr. & Mrs. W. Cummings & dr.
345 Mr. & Mrs. J. H. White
347 Mr. & Mrs. Levi Shepard
355 Mr. & Mrs. W. W. Hewitt
357 Mr. & Mrs. M. M. Warner
361 Mr. & Mrs. F. G. Bradley
363 Mrs. Frank McAvoy
365 Mr. & Mrs. P. S. Dingey
367 Mr. & Mrs. S. B. Mills
367 Walter Mills
373 Mr. & Mrs.Louis Rubens &drs.
Receiving day Friday
373 Charles Rubens
373 Mrs. E. Cohn
391 Miss Frances Le Barron
593 Mr. & Mrs. W. H. Vallas
651 Dr. & Mrs. J. N. Ranger
661 Mr. & Mrs. James Martin&drs.
661 Mr. & Mrs. Elbert Battershall

280 Mr. & Mrs. C. F. Swigart
282 Mr. & Mrs. J. G. McCarthy
284 Mr. & Mrs. C. P. Gilkison
288 Mr. & Mrs. Theo. J. Amberg
290 Mr. & Mrs. Charles W. Wright
290 John E. Wright
292 Mrs. M. A. Barnes & dr.
292 H. H. McPherson
294 Mr. & Mrs. D. T. Jack
298 Mr. & Mrs. Edwin D. Wilder
310 Mr. & Mrs. Frank B. Furniss
312 Mr. & Mrs. Walter Lister & drs.
Receiving day Monday
318 Dr. & Mrs. E. Honsinger
318 Miss Hulda L. Seeley
324 Mr. & Mrs. J. L. Hathaway
328 Mr. & Mrs. Samuel Metz
330 Mr. & Mrs. K. S. McLennan
346 Mr. & Mrs. H. D. Smith
346 Mrs. Maria Barron
358 Mr. & Mrs. J. H. Bradley & dr.
360 Mr. & Mrs. James M. Short
360 B. J. Short
364 Mr. & Mrs. T. H. Pease & dr.
364 Albert E. Pease
408 Charles S. Thomas
420 Mr. & Mrs. T. H. Blair
420 Mrs. G. K. Krigger
600 Mr. & Mrs. L. G. Kniffin
602 Mr. & Mrs. John Archer
602 Mrs. Addie E. Heron
626 Mr. & Mrs. E. DeVolt
634 Mrs. E. H. Tuttle & drs.
634 Dr. Sterling D. Tuttle
634 Dr. O. H. Tuttle
636 Mr. & Mrs. Edwin S. Rooks
670 Mr. & Mrs. David C. Dewey
672 Mr. & Mrs. W. F. Taylor
672 John S. Taylor
674 Mr. & Mrs. Oscar Dubois
678 Mrs. M. E. Barstow & dr.
680 A. J. Sands
682 Mrs. M. H. Ogden & dr.
938 Mr. & Mrs. M. D. Tillotson & dr.
938 Mr. & Mrs. H. H. Marcusson
942 Mr. & Mrs. Harry L. Jacobs
944 Mrs. E. Jones & dr.
944 David P. Jones
948 Mr. & Mrs. E. B. Benbow
968 Mr. & Mrs. R. H. Spurgeon
970 Mr.&Mrs. Richard W. Knisely
1018 Mr. & Mrs. Alfred Rohn
Receiving day last Thur.in mo.
1020 Mr. & Mrs. G. A. Martin
1022 Mr. & Mrs. John J. A. Dahmke

663 Mr. & Mrs. Fred M. Taylor
671 Mr. & Mrs. C. E. Cruikshank
673 Mr. & Mrs. Earl Preble
673 Mrs. M. Abrahams
677 Mr. & Mrs. Monroe A. Swift
943 Mr. & Mrs. C. Waller Pank ⁻
943 Mr. & Mrs. D. W. Hunt
943 Mr. & Mrs. E. R. Greene
955 Mr. & Mrs. H. C. Latus
957 Mrs. M. E. Morris & dr.
961 Mr. & Mrs. W. H. Wright
961 Mr. & Mrs. E. Van DeMark
967 Mr. & Mrs. M. P. Brady

1028 Mr. & Mrs. John Marr
1028 Wiilliam Marr
1028 Mr. & Mrs. J. H. Sayle

971 Mr. & Mrs. E. A. Grimm
971 Mr. & Mrs. J. H. Wilson
1005 Mr. & Mrs. F. C. Neagle & drs.
   Receiving day Wednesday
1007 Mr. & Mrs. J. J. Hyland
   Receiving day Wednesday
1009 Mr. & Mrs. M. W. Hyland
1025 Mr. & Mrs. T. O. Perry
1027 Mr. & Mrs. Chas. A. Fanning

SOUTH PAULINA STREET.

21 Mrs. Emma Bell
149 Rev. & Mrs. W. T. Meloy
149 J. Y. Meloy
161 Mr. & Mrs. H. N. Harris
233 Mr. & Mrs. A. S. Ross
331 Miss Hattie Beynon
331 Mrs. Clara Caratu
349 Mr. & Mrs. C. J. Luck
357 Mr. & Mrs. Joseph H. Lawler
359 J. P. McMahon
367 Mr. & Mrs. Thomas J. Waters
369 Mrs. S. Frank & dr.
   Receiving day Friday
375 Mr. & Mrs. W. T. Tate
377 Rev. & Mrs. LeGrand Smith
   Receiving day Tuesday
397 Mr. & Mrs. B. Simon
397 Otto Wollner
399 Mr. & Mrs. J. J. Hanlon & dr.
399 J. W. Hanlon
399 Leo Hanlon
405 Mr. & Mrs. J. H. Simon
415 Mr. & Mrs. Joseph Kahn
419 Mr. & Mrs. J. J. Best
419 Mrs. Mary Best
425 Dr. & Mrs. E. F. Buecking
   Receiving day Friday
435 Mrs. Abraham Oppenheimer

222 Mr. & Mrs. Alfred Hall & dr.
226 Mr. & Mrs. W. E. Hall
228 Mr. & Mrs. J. Barnett & dr.
334 Mr. & Mrs. Simon Ex
340 Mr. & Mrs. J. M. Vernon & dr.
344 Mr. & Mrs. George J. Dorr
344 Melvin L. Dorr
344 Mrs. Rodney L. Taylor
354 Bernard Quinn
358 Mr. & Mrs. L. P. Rittenhouse
360 Mr. & Mrs. William L. Arnold
364 Mr. & Mrs. Charles F. Noll
370 Mr. & Mrs. Julius Butts
372 Mr. & Mrs. G. E. Emery
374 Mr. & Mrs. D. May
392 Mr. & Mrs. J. P. Cline
394 Mr. & Mrs. John J. McGrath
394 Mr. & Mrs. W. P. Cowen
396 Mr. & Mrs. Edward B. Gallup
402 Dr. & Mrs. C. N. Ballard
418 Mr. & Mrs. Alexander F. Swander
450 Mr. & Mrs. Fred Stolba & dr.

———

443 Mr. & Mrs. S. Lazarus
447 Mr.&Mrs.Rudolph von Bachelle
487 Mr. & Mrs. J. Phillipson

WEST POLK STREET.

832 Mr. & Mrs. Wm. H. Cameron

974 Dr. Espy L. Smith

WEST RANDOLPH STREET.

391 Mr. & Mrs. John J. Badenoch
463 Mr. & Mrs. Bradford Sherman
   Receiving day Wednesday
463 Miss S. A. Platt

284 Dr. & Mrs. F. S. Dart
450 Rev. & Mrs. Bernhard Felsenthal & drs.
450 Edwin I. Felsenthal
468 Mr.& Mrs. J. E.Woodhead & dr.

NORTH ROBEY STREET.

411 Mr. & Mrs. Joseph Hermann
469 Rev. & Mrs. H. J. G. Bartholo-
      mew
        Receiving day Thursday
469 Dr. J. K. Bartholomew
485 Mr. & Mrs. M. J. Seifert
        Receiving day Thursday
499 Dr. & Mrs. J. W. Dal
593 Mr. & Mrs. Maurice S.Lindholm
597 Mr. & Mrs. F. W. McIntosh
639 Mr. & Mrs. M. D. Stecher
647 Mr. & Mrs. F. W. Belz
667 Mr. & Mrs. R. Gottlieb
667 Mr. & Mrs. John Grosse
675 Mr. & Mrs. Fred. Herhold &
      drs
683 Mr. & Mrs. Jacob Gottlieb

482 Mr. & Mrs. H. Apple
        Receive 2d & 4th Thursday
482 Mr. & Mrs. Wm. Meyne
626 Mr. & Mrs. John Ott
632 Mr. & Mrs. Erik L. Vognild
720 Mr. & Mrs. M. Schulz
———
685 Dr. & Mrs. Merritt W. Thomp-
      son
685 Mrs. J. Tausig
689 Mr. & Mrs. Oswald F. Kropf
695 Mr. & Mrs. Andrew P. Johnson
697 Dr. & Mrs. Theo. Wild & dr.
697 Theo. Wild jr.
707 Mr. & Mrs. John Mohr
707 Joseph Mohr
717 Mr.& Mrs.Frank Patzack & drs.

SOUTH ROBEY STREET.

 81 Walter S. Holden
145 Dr. & Mrs. E. B. Loomis
145 Louis Davis
155 Mr. & Mrs. Archibald Johnson
161 James K. Lake & dr.
163 Mr. & Mrs. Lewis H. Mitchell
165 Mrs. Abby Gilbert
165 Mrs. A. J. Spicer
237 Mr. & Mrs. R. S. Hazen

194 Mr. & Mrs. F. M. Blount
198 J. M. Deane
198 Mrs. Eloise A. Deane
380 Dr. & Mrs. E. A. Phillips
———
319 Mr. & Mrs. I. A. Watson
367 Mr. & Mrs. C. A. MacDonald
403 F. J. Keogh

SOUTH SANGAMON STREET.

 95 Mr. & Mrs. M. R. Harris
113 Mr. & Mrs. Elmer A. Rich
167 Mr. & Mrs. Jacob Beidler

167 Augustus F. Beidler
167 George Beidler
221 Mr. & Mrs. William McCoy

SAWYER AVENUE.

635 Mr. & Mrs. A. F. Rusy
801 Mr. & Mrs. John Fucik
813 Mr. & Mrs. Frank Fucik
817 Dr. & Mrs. A. V. Bergeron
859 Mr. & Mrs. James Cairns & dr.
871 Dr. George R. Bassett
871 Dr. Susan A. Bassett
871 George H. Bassett
879 Mr. & Mrs. Cuthbert McArthur
881 Mr. & Mrs. B. M. Gray
887 Mr. & Mrs. George W. Ferris
901 Mr. & Mrs. I. C. Wilson & dr.
907 Mr. & Mrs. Wm. Harlev
909 Mrs. S. Spreine & drs.
911 W. B. Towles
915 Mr. & Mrs. Chas. A. Myers
        Receiving day Thursday
·915 Mr. & Mrs. Henry Tibbits

740 Mr. & Mrs. F. H. Hammond
866 Mr. & Mrs. S. M. Randolph
870 Mr. & Mrs. N. K. Sheibley
872 Mr. & Mrs. John J. Coburn
876 J. H. Spears
882 Mrs. Cora M. Hane
884 Mr. & Mrs. J. C. Hyde
934 William F. Dunham

917 Mr. & Mrs. Edwin McLinden
921 Mr. & Mrs. E. P. Peacock & drs.
923 Mr. & Mrs. J. F. Lyon
933 Mr. & Mrs. Cyrus J. Ward
941 Mr. & Mrs. Chas. Emmons
943 Mr. & Mrs. O. F. Wood
949 Mrs. H. Huebner & drs.
957 Mr. & Mrs. John Craib

SEELEY AVENUE.

13 Mr. & Mrs. G. B. Townsend &
    dr.
15 Mr. & Mrs. Perry A. Moxley
23 Mr. & Mrs. F. Pardee
37 Mr. & Mrs. J. C. Newcomb&dr.
39 Mr. & Mrs. P. Hartwell
41 Mr. & Mrs. H. V. Reed
    Receiving day Tuesday
41 Miss Myrtle Reed
43 Mr. & Mrs. G. M. Vanzwoll
    Receiving day Tuesday
43½ Rev. A. K. Parker
45 Mr. & Mrs. A. C. Selleck
    Receiving day Thursday
47 Mr. & Mrs. H. J. Whitcomb
47 Mr. & Mrs. J. C. Whitcomb
51 Mr.& Mrs.Albert M.Osgood&dr.
51 Albert T. Osgood
51 Harry S. Osgood
51 George B. Osgood
71 Mr. & Mrs. W. H. Kose
73 Mrs. E. J. White
85 Mr. & Mrs. E. E. Hooper

48 T. W. Brennan
80 Mr. & Mrs. B. Woodworth
82 Mrs. Elizabeth Penny
82 Frank O. Penny
84 E. C. Austin
84 Mrs. Clara Hurley
106 Mr. & Mrs. F. E. Degenhardt
106 C. Degenhardt
108 Mr. & Mrs. Rudolph Rohn
108 Robert Rohn
112 Mr. & Mrs. A. T. Packard
114 Mr. & Mrs. F. D. Austin
120 Joseph West & dr.
120 George E. Clark
124 Mr. & Mrs. Franklin Emery
126 Mr. & Mrs. I. D. Johnston &
    drs

_____

85 Dr. & Mrs. H. S. Hahn
93 Mr. & Mrs. C. M. Smith
93 James G. Smith
115 Mr. & Mrs. C. E. Ross

NORTH SHELDON STREET.

39 Frank E. Hayner
51 Mr. & Mrs. F. T. Morgan
_____

62 J. Ward Amberg

58 Rev. & Mrs. N. J. Harkness
62 Mr. & Mrs. Wm. A. Amberg &
    drs.   *Receive Wednesday*

SOUTH SHELDON STREET.

43 Mrs. M. E. Hess

48 Dr. & Mrs. John H. Byrne & dr.
    Receiving day Thursday
48 Dr. John G. Byrne

SIBLEY STREET.

61 Mr. & Mrs. Samuel H. Smith
    Receiving day Friday
63 Mr. & Mrs. Robert A. Smith
65 Gen. & Mrs. J. C. Smith
    Receiving day Friday

65 Mr. & Mrs. J. C. Smith jr.
    Receiving day Friday
65 Miss Ruth A. Smith

SPAULDING AVENUE.

877 Mr. & Mrs. Chas. Hohlfeld
879 Dr. & Mrs. C. W. Hawley
879 Mr. & Mrs. W. B. Spence
881 Mr. & Mrs. E. M. Craig
885 Mr. & Mrs. Oscar Weinmann
907 Mr. & Mrs. Charles W. Clark
909 Mr. & Mrs. W. V. Smith
909 Mr. & Mrs. W. S. Abbott

911 Mr. & Mrs. W. D. Patterson
913 Mr. & Mrs. John Triggs & dr.
913 Charles W. Triggs
919 Mr. & Mrs. T. E. McCormack
949 Mr. & Mrs. Herman Spitz
951 Mr. & Mrs. J. H. McNamara
953 Mr. & Mrs. John T. Hanna

ST. JOHN'S PLACE.

13 Mr. & Mrs. Eli J. Carpenter
15 Mr. & Mrs. Frederick A. Muncey
21 Mr. & Mrs. B. N. Foster
23 Mr. & Mrs. B. Burr & dr.
23 J. M. Hupp
23 W. C. C. Gillespie

20 Mr. & Mrs. L. Sonnenschein
26 Dr. & Mrs. Robt. H. Lowry
30 Mr. & Mrs. John C. Mayer
36½ Mr. & Mrs. Philip Kaufman

27 Mr. & Mrs. R. T. Sill & drs.

ST. LOUIS AVENUE.

819 Mr. & Mrs. Richard Voge
865 Mr. & Mrs. F. M. Kluge
871 Mr. & Mrs. Wm. Kluge
871 Mr. & Mrs. Thomas Trigg
879 Mrs. Wm. Stewart
1023 Mr. & Mrs. Lucius Lanterman

834 Mrs. Minnie A. Phelps
882 Mr. & Mrs. Edward Fielding
896 Mr. & Mrs. Walter Oliphant

1023 Miss Alice Hardy

WEST TAYLOR STREET.

399 Mr. & Mrs. John P. Barron
439 Dr. George S. Gfroerer
439 Dr. Frank M. Tebbetts
625 Dr. & Mrs. Gustave Schirmer
641 Mr. & Mrs. C. W. Grassly
675 Dr. & Mrs. F. J. Patera
1079 Mr. & Mrs. E. J. H. Wright

452 Mr. & Mrs. Thomas Coughlan
454 Mr. & Mrs. John Bermingham
644 J. Frank Higgins
976 Mr. & Mrs. William S. Camp-
     bell

1079 Frederick Hainsworth

THROOP STREET.

75 Mr. & Mrs. S. H. Dempsey & dr.

58 Mrs. O. W. Goit & dr.
58 Frank H. Goit
76 Mr. & Mrs. R. H. Liddell & dr.
76 Alfred R. Liddell
78 Mr. & Mrs. A. H. Arnold
80 William W. Nutting
164 Dr. & Mrs. J. D. Phillips
176 Mr. & Mrs. William Phillips

34 Dr. E. Ingals & drs.
34 Dr. & Mrs. H. M. Thomas & dr.
36 Mr. & Mrs. Ambrose Plamondon
40 Mr. & Mrs. M. W. Ryan
40 George Cochrane
40 Miss Lizzie Gately
42 Mr. & Mrs. Theodore Snell & drs.
44 Dr. & Mrs. J. B. Murphy
52 Mr. & Mrs. R. C. Gannon
54 Mr. & Mrs. T. H. Jones
56 Mr. & Mrs. W. E. V. Holland

TURNER AVENUE.

725 Dr. & Mrs. John C. Spray
849 Dr. & Mrs. Samuel J. Watson
921 Mr. & Mrs. Walter Cambridge
923 Mr. & Mrs. J. P. Cadieux
937 Mr. & Mrs. Frank E. Rainier

954 Mr. & Mrs. Lawrence M. Ennis
     Receive Friday

710 Mr. & Mrs. John C. Wilson
894 Mr. & Mrs. J. A. Schoenthaler
908 Mr. & Mrs. Ralph H. Coshun
942 Mr. & Mrs. W. J. Ennisson
950 Mrs. Elizabeth Gorton & dr.
950 Miss Belle L. Gorton

WEST TWENTY-SECOND STREET.

1767 Mr. & Mrs. Cyrus Bixby
1817 James Kerby
1853 Mr. & Mrs. James F. Lee
———
1834 Mrs. Elizabeth Benton & dr.
1834 George E. Benton
1834 Miss Gertrude D. Briggs

1790 Mr. & Mrs. W. C. H. Keough
1790 William Keough
1804 Mr. & Mrs. Jno. S. Stiles & dr.
1804 George S. Stiles
1806 Mr. & Mrs. J. S. Stiles jr.
1820 Mr. & Mrs. E. S. Albro & drs.
1820 Clarence Albro
1828 Mr. & Mrs. F. L. Mercer

UNION PARK PLACE.

55 Mr. & Mrs. Hugh Watt & drs.
55 Archibald M. Watt

60 Mr. & Mrs. J. P. McGrath

WEST VAN BUREN STREET.

549 Mrs. C. H. Rice
549 J. Brainard Kerr
549 Miss Anna J. Kerr
549 Charles Babson Soule
551 Mr. & Mrs. Hugh Templeton
563 W. H. Lacey
605 Dr. & Mrs. H. P. Nelson
719 Mr. & Mrs. Robert L. Martin
735 William M. McRae

426 Dr. John B. Ewing
538 Dr. H. N. Small
594 Mrs. Rebecca Appleton & dr.
594 Ernest Appleton
596 Mr. & Mrs. Alfred Russell
934 Mr. & Mrs. Walter M. Plantz
———
1155 William H. Matthews

VERNON PARK PLACE.

19 Mr. & Mrs. J. D. Pickham
———
52 Mr. & Mrs. Leo A. La Rocque
66 Mr. & Mrs. J. T. Coughlan
86 Mr. & Mrs. George Lewis
86 Mr. & Mrs. William Dietz

26 Mr. & Mrs. P. Hines & drs.
26 Edward M. Hines
26 Mr. & Mrs. D. Sattler & drs.
26 D. S. Sattler
34 Mr. & Mrs. Joseph Chalifoux
50 Dr. & Mrs. Jos. Bergeron

WALNUT STREET.

17 Mr. & Mrs. E. E. Lee
293 Mr. & Mrs. William R. Mumford
345 Rev. Thomas P. Hodnett
593 Mr. & Mrs. R. J. Tugwell
635 Mr. & Mrs. W. F. Osgood
655 W. S. Felton
679 Mr. & Mrs. J. F. Ager
    Receiving day Tuesday
697 Mr. & Mrs. T. P. Hicks
713 Mr. & Mrs. F. D. Champlin
713 Mr. & Mrs. W. A. Field
731 Mr. & Mrs. Frederick M. Fish
    Receiving day Wednesday
731 Rev. J. W. Fish
739 Mr. & Mrs. E. P. Burroughs
749 Mr. & Mrs. O. M. Brady
751 Mr. & Mrs. Robert M. Littler

162 Mr. & Mrs. Thos. M. Wignall & dr.
164 Mr. & Mrs. J. F. O'Neil
314 Mr. & Mrs. W. C. Lyman & drs.
314 Benj. K. Lyman
314 Wilfred C. Lyman jr.
594 Mr. & Mrs. J. P. Trenter
652 Mr. & Mrs. John W. Tindall
658 Dr. & Mrs. W. M. W. Davison
682 Mr. & Mrs. Sherman W. Smith
694 Mr. & Mrs. J. M. Coughlin
698 Mr. & Mrs. Harry McKee
758 Mr. & Mrs. F. S. Baird
762 Mrs. A. M. Pratt
762 Dr. H. P. Pratt
764 Dr. & Mrs. J. S. Wilkin & dr.
774 Mr. & Mrs. E. J. Piggott
780 Dr. & Mrs. S. J. Avery

757 Mr. & Mrs. T. D. Smith
791 Mr. & Mrs. C. C. Campbell
    Receiving day Wednesday
829 Mr. & Mrs. Bayard E. Taylor
853 Mr. & Mrs. C. E. Reed
859 Mr. & Mrs. C. H. Brown & drs.
859 Otto Koehler
873 Mr. & Mrs. Lucius Clark
877 Mr. & Mrs. S. P. McKelvey
901 Mr. & Mrs. A. C. Johnson
901 Mr. & Mrs. Chas. P. Braslan
915 Dr. & Mrs. J. H. Mellinger
917 Mr. & Mrs. W. E. Mellinger
935 Mr. & Mrs. J. C. Phillips
985 Mr. & Mrs. Joseph A. Painter
1029 Mr. & Mrs. S. W. Roth·
1037 Mr. & Mrs. Wm. T. Lesher

———

912 Mr. & Mrs. C. E. Smith
926 Mr. & Mrs. Alexander Rietz
928 Dr. & Mrs. Jas. D. Higgins
928 Dr. & Mrs. Robert Steele
930 Mr. & Mrs. A. J. Fisher
938 Mr.&Mrs. Eugene J. McCarthy
1030 Miss L. Blanche Fearing

790 Mr. & Mrs. A. W. Jones
    Receiving day Thursday
798 Mr. & Mrs. W. G. Lemay
816 Dr. & Mrs. A. S. Everett
818 Mr. & Mrs. A. W. Ovitt
    Receiving day Thursday
820 Mr. & Mrs. E. E. Palmer
    Receiving day Thursday
832 Mrs. T. Adams & dr.
832 James J. Adams
834 Mrs. R. M. Leedy
834 John C. Leedy
836 Mr. & Mrs. Robert Austin
842 Mr. & Mrs. Roger C. Sullivan
856 Mr. & Mrs. C. E. Cable
    Receiving day Wednesday
866 Mr. & Mrs. F. X. Daul
866 Mr. & Mrs. Joseph B. Toohy
    Receiving day Wednesday
874 Mr. & Mrs. F. T. Kinnare
874 Mr. & Mrs. Ed. S. Cummings
880 Mr. & Mrs. Frank H. Fogarty
900 Mr. & Mrs. John P. Woods
904 Mr. & Mrs. Albert J. Koch
906 Mrs. T. Forch
906 Mr. & Mrs. S. C. Pashley

WARREN AVENUE.

1 Mrs. M. Conboy
47 Mr. & Mrs. J. D. Williams
47 Mr. & Mrs. A. Winchester
49 Mrs. L. J. Campbell & drs.
51 Mr. & Mrs. E. H. Humphrey
51 Orrin P. Chase & dr.
51 Mrs. L. P. Owings
53 Anna M. Parker, M. D.
53 Helen M. Parker, M. D.
53 Mr. & Mrs. C. M. Harris
61 Mr. & Mrs. William K. Thomas
61 William K. Thomas jr.
65 Mrs. Shepard Johnston
65 Mrs. L. A. Morris
67 Dr. & Mrs. L. J. Davis
69 Mrs. J. C. Clement & dr.
71 Mr. & Mrs. A. W. Brickwood
73 Mr. & Mrs. Edward M. Greene
73 Mr. & Mrs. L. Eberhart
77 Mr. & Mrs. Grant Carpenter
77 Mr. & Mrs. Frederick H. Hamlin
79 Mr. & Mrs. J. A. Ulrich
81 Mr. & Mrs. Fergus Campbell
81 E. B. Noyes
89 J. F. Smith & dr.
    Receiving day Tuesday

14 Dr. & Mrs. A. C. Cowperthwaite
54 Mr. & Mrs. Louis F. Burrell
64 S. B. French
66 Mr. & Mrs. E. Hopkins jr.
70 Mr. & Mrs. R. B. Merriam
88 Mr. & Mrs. J. Berry
90 Dr. & Mrs. Joseph Haven
98 A. L. Goodman
98 G. B. Reid
100 Mr. & Mrs. Lloyd G. Spencer
104 Mr. & Mrs. A. L. Norton
104 Mr. & Mrs. J. B. Willoughby
110 Mr. & Mrs. Alfred F. Scott
110 Mrs. B. Smith
134 Miss M. Elizabeth Farson
144 Mr. & Mrs. B. Hallinstein
    Receive 2d and 4th Thursdays
164 Mr. & Mrs. Horace W. Beek
164 Stephen Thorne
168 Mr.& Mrs. R. M. Buckman&drs.
168 Mr. & Mrs. Victor Arnold
174 Mrs. Ora V. Coffman
174 Mr. & Mrs. James R. May
180 Mr. & Mrs. H. H. Ring
182 Mr. & Mrs. R. T. Clark
188 Mr. & Mrs. A. E. Clark
    Receive Tuesday afternoon

89 Mr. & Mrs. William W. Wells
95 Mr. & Mrs. H. S. Newton
97 Mr. & Mrs. M. Bachman
97 Mrs. E. C. Nain & drs.
99 A. D. Pitcher
103 Mr. & Mrs. Horace H. Stoddard
111 Mrs. Lloyd Wheaton
111 Mrs. Mary J. Greene
Receiving day Thursday
149 Mr. & Mrs. Geo. F. Wisshack
155 Mr. & Mrs. R. S. Pettibone
155 Mr. & Mrs. R. F. Pettibone
159 Mr. & Mrs. P. F. Pettibone
165 Mr. & Mrs. George Heimbrodt
165 Mr. & Mrs. Jos. H. Wilson
171 Mr. & Mrs. W. Gray Brown
171 Miss Florence Brown
175 Mrs. L. A. Bushnell
177 Mr. & Mrs. Francis B. Little
Receiving day Wednesday
181 Mrs. M. G. Doan
183 Col. & Mrs. M. D. Birge
185 Mr. & Mrs. A. A. Hall
199 Mr. & Mrs. L. J. Blades
203 Mr. & Mrs. J. Louis Pfau jr. & dr.
205 Rev. & Mrs. T. D. Wallace
205 Walter Hill
205 Wm. Shermay Hay
207 Mr. & Mrs. Wm. Baldwin
215 Mr. & Mrs. John H. Cowper
215 George E. Allcock
225 A. De Camp
227 Mr. & Mrs. George T. Clark
231 Mr. & Mrs. F. W. Clark
237 Miss Cecilia Richardson
237 George W. Parke
245 Dr. & Mrs. Chauncy F. Chapman
245 Dr. John A. Benson
245 Mrs. Mary Benson
259 Dr. & Mrs. V. C. McClure & drs.
261 Mr. & Mrs. J. C. Knowles & dr.
261 George H. Knowles
261 William T. Alden
263 Mr. & Mrs. W. R. White & dr.
265 Mrs. S. A. Patterson
267 Mr. & Mrs. B. Loewenthal
269 Mr. & Mrs. S. V. Shipman & dr.
Receiving day Thursday
271 Mr. & Mrs. S. N. Brooks
271 D. K. Cornwell
273 Mr. & Mrs. A. H. Vanzwoll
273 H. B. Vanzwoll
275 Mr. & Mrs. Edwin B. Pease
275 Mrs. B. M. Pease & dr.

188 A. S. Clark
188 Edwin H. Clark
190 Mr. & Mrs. James H. Moore
196 Mr. & Mrs. L. F. Macomber
196 Mr. & Mrs. F. P. Macomber
198 Mr. & Mrs. A. M. Ray
Receiving day Thursday
200 Mr. & Mrs. John S. Zimmerman
204 Mr. & Mrs. L. Wangersheim
204 Mrs. J. H. Friedman
206 Mr. & Mrs. Samuel Angel
218 Mr. & Mrs. Edward Seyfarth
220 Mr. & Mrs. Lawrence Ostey
222 Mr. & Mrs. Sidney Bear
Receiving day 1st & 3d Thursday
226 Alexander M. Stewart
226 Mr. & Mrs. John Stewart
226 John P. Stewart
226 R. M. Stewart
230 Mr. & Mrs. James A. Hart
232 Mr. & Mrs. Charles H. King
232 Miss Jennie King
236 G. W. Newcomb & drs.
236 William H. Newcomb
244 Mr. & Mrs. L. E. Robertson
246 Mr. & Mrs. H. G. Brooks
248 Mrs. Mary E. Dickinson
248 Mr. & Mrs. S. H. Mooney
254 Mr. & Mrs. W. G. Miller
254 Mrs. F. H. Northway
256 Mr. & Mrs. F. A. Oswald & drs.
258 Miss Elizabeth Thumser
Receiving day Wednesday
258 Wm. W. Thumser
260 Mr. & Mrs. T. E. Dougherty
260 Irving Davis
262 Mr. & Mrs. C. V. L. Peters
272 Mrs. Charles A. Taylor & drs.
276 Mr. & Mrs. W. H. Mosher & dr.
276 Miss Belle Mosher
278 Dr. H. Boyd-Snee
278 Mrs. A. H. Buck
284 Mr. & Mrs. E. C. Reichwald
286 A. B. Boughan
306 Mrs. A. Patten
306 Mr. & Mrs. J. A. Patten
308 Harry L. Brooks
322 Mr. & Mrs. Thomas B. Rice
322 Mr & Mrs. Waldo F. Miller
322 D. P. Lee
322 Louis J. Block
328 Mrs. J. Hopkins & dr.
328 Forest B. Hopkins
328 Mr. & Mrs. T. E. D. Bradley
330 Mr. & Mrs. T. J. Sammons
334 Mr. & Mrs. S. Lyon

279 Dr. & Mrs. A. J. Harris & dr.
281 Dr. & Mrs. C. C. P. Silva
281 Miss L. Walcott
293 Mrs. Mary Baird & drs.
297 Mrs. Mary E. Studley
301 Mr. & Mrs. H. L. Brown
303 Mr. & Mrs. Frank Binne & dr.
317 Mr. & Mrs. E. A. Hill
327 Mr. & Mrs. A. W. Adcock
327 Mrs. E. L. Young
333 Mr. & Mrs. Arthur E. Wilcox
335 Mr. & Mrs. N. A. Phillips
339 Dr. & Mrs. R. N. Hall
343 Mr. & Mrs. Allan Waterhouse
343 Mr. & Mrs. E. W. Farnham
345 Mr. & Mrs. W. M. Wright
359 Dr. & Mrs. Franklin C. Wells
375 Mr. & Mrs. Jas. A. Gaynor & dr.
377 Mr. & Mrs. Frank S. Waters
381 Mr. & Mrs. John A. Sweet
385 Mr. & Mrs. T. C. Baldwin
387 Mr. & Mrs. F. A. Winkelman
389 Mr. & Mrs. Fred Conover
391 Mr. & Mrs. J. H. Beers
391 W. J. Mendenhall
391 Walter L. Hixon
395 Mr. & Mrs. J. A. Eagle & drs.
395 W. H. Eagle
395 T. D. Eagle
397 Mr. & Mrs. W. B. Coit
      Receiving day Thursday
403 Mr. & Mrs. Burns L. Newman
405 Mr. & Mrs. Harry S. Rich
409 Mr. & Mrs. W. R. Kellogg
413 Mr. & Mrs. Wm. P. Frailey
413 Mr. & Mrs. James S. Watson
415 Mrs. W. W. Wilcox
415 Mr. & Mrs. George Wilcox
419 Mrs. Joanna O. Winter
425 Miss Mary E. Vaughan
427 Herschel W. Dryer
427 Mrs. P. K. Dryer
431 Mr. & Mrs. M. Unger & dr.
433 Mr. & Mrs. J. F. Tenney
437 Mr. & Mrs. James Parker & dr
439 Mr. & Mrs. Julius Marcus & drs.
443 Mr. & Mrs. Henry Duncan &drs.
447 Mr. & Mrs. E. C. Roush
451 Mr. & Mrs. W. F. Merle
457 Mr. & Mrs. John W. Kilmare
461 Mr. & Mrs. John Young & drs.
461 Mr. & Mrs. Albert Mathers
465 Dr. & Mrs. J. W. Martin
465 Mr. & Mrs. Leon Sykes
469 Mr. & Mrs. Louis Nau
507 Joseph A. Peale

336 Mr. & Mrs. Isaac Borg
338 Mr. & Mrs. Theodore G. Case
340 Mr. & Mrs. J. A. Reichelt
342 Mr. & Mrs. W. B. Ayers
342 Mr. & Mrs. James L. Mallory
350 Mrs. Daniel Scully & drs.
352 Mr. & Mrs. C. W. Austin
356 Mr. & Mrs. C. F. Dexter
356 Miss Fannie A Tobey
366 Mr. & Mrs. E. F. Rennacker
368 Mr. & Mrs. Frank M. Jones
368 Mrs. M. Haber
368 Mrs. Honora Brown & drs.
368 John F. Brown
370 Mr. & Mrs. Charles H. Fuller
376 Gen. John E. Smith
376 Mr. & Mrs. Benjamin M. Smith
376 Mrs. Adelaide Bascom
378 Mrs. Ira Blanchard
378 T. F. Blanchard
384 A. L. Patterson
384 S. P. Patterson
384 Charles A. Patterson
386 Mr. & Mrs. B. F. Morse & dr.
390 Mr. & Mrs. H. J. Hoffman
394 Mr. & Mrs. M. Cornhauser
      Rec. day 1st & 2d Friday in mo.
406 William C. Dunwell
408 Mr. & Mrs. E. S. Johnson
      Receiving day Wednesday
408 Mr. & Mrs. L. H. Johnson
      Receiving day Wednesday
410 Rabbi & Mrs. J. Stolz
      Receiving day Tuesday
414 Mr. & Mrs. Joseph Rogerson
418 Mr. & Mrs. George T. Giles
418 Mr. & Mrs. L. R. Kimberly
420 Mr. & Mrs. S. Mendelsohn
426 Mr. & Mrs. Fred M. Gale
426 Fred Gale
426 Miss Belle G. Scribner
428 Dr. E. E. Tull
428 Rev. & Mrs. J. D. Tull
430 Mr. & Mrs. W. S. Decker
434 Mr. & Mrs. J. Bernhard
434 Mr. & Mrs. E. Woolf
434 B. Wolff
436 Mr. & Mrs. W. B. Smith
      Receiving day Thursday
438 Mr. & Mrs. W. S. Cameron
438 Mrs. N. C. Safford
438 Miss Dorethea Palm
438 Miss Ida Skidmore
440 Mrs. A. Douglas
440 Dr. Percy E. Douglas
440 Clyde Douglass

569 Mr. & Mrs. Wm. B. Bangs
569 Oscar R. Smith
569 R. E. Smith
569 Dr. O. R. Bluthardt
665 Dr. & Mrs. C. H. Boughton & dr.
665 Fred J. Boughton
679 Mr. & Mrs. W. L. Aborn
679 Everett A. Aborn
679 Walton C. Aborn
703 Mrs. F. K. Bowen
705 Mr. & Mrs. J. L. Johnson
707 Mr. & Mrs. B. L. Bevington
735 Mr. & Mrs. J. G. Frank
743 S. M. Baum
745 Mr. & Mrs. John D. Murphy
747 Mrs. G. M. Ingersoll
747 Edward O. Ray
749 Mr. & Mrs. George H. Clark
751 Dr. & Mrs. J. B. Herrick
751 Mr. & Mrs. J. G. Evenden
789 Dr. & Mrs. E. H. Deyoe
789 Dr. & Mrs. L. E. Miley
791 Mrs. F. M. Lovedale & drs.
793 Mr. & Mrs. Robert L. Chapin
795 Mr. & Mrs. F. E. Coyne
797 Mr. & Mrs. Thos. F. Crosby
797 Mr. & Mrs. W. D. Young
803 Mrs. C. E. Benson
807 Mr. & Mrs. J. Stewart
809 Joseph E. Hardy
815 Mr. & Mrs. H. Saunders
815 Mr. & Mrs. Thos. H. Saunders
819 Capt. & Mrs. A. Allen
819 Mr. & Mrs. Edward Sholes
821 Dr. Annette S. Richards
821 Mr. & Mrs. S. J. Stewart
821 Rev. J. P. Richards
825 Mr. & Mrs. Marc Sherwood
829 Mr. & Mrs. G. B. Fern
831 Mr. & Mrs. H. S. Fassett
833 Mr. & Mrs. John L. Burnside
Receiving day Thursday
837 Mr. & Mrs. A. H. Dunham
837 Frederick M. Sisson
839 Mr. & Mrs. J. C. Benedict
841 Mr. & Mrs. D. W. Wells & dr.
843 Mr. & Mrs. G. W. Giroux
845 Mr. & Mrs. H. W. Stroker
847 Mr. & Mrs. Nathan Herzog
847 Mr. & Mrs. C. R. Street
853 Dr. & Mrs. Eli Wight
871 Mr. & Mrs. W. O. H. Moore
875 Dr. A. P. Sawyer
875 H. Sawyer
879 W. A. Taylor
879 J. S. L. Taylor

442 Mr. & Mrs. Geo. W. Stanton
442 Mrs. H. W. Dobson & dr.
Receiving day Thursday
442 Robert Dobson
448 Mr. & Mrs. E. A. Holroyd
448 E. H. Rosenthal
452 Mr. & Mrs. Silas Palmer
460 Dr. & Mrs. Adam Barber
462 Mr. & Mrs. H. A. Meyer
Receiving day Friday
468 Mr. & Mrs. C. J. Pettibone
470 Mr. & Mrs. Geo. A. Binford
482 Max Guthman
580 Mr. & Mrs. D. H. Wilkie
704 Mr. & Mrs. W. B. Laparle
712 Mr. & Mrs. E. M. Blakeslee
716 Mr. & Mrs. H. L. Childs
716 Gilman T. Chadwick
716 M. E. Ames
726 Mrs. I. T. Stevens
730 Dr. & Mrs. Chas. H. Evans & dr.
736 Mr. & Mrs. T. H. Simmons
742 George P. Blair
758 Mr. & Mrs. William A. Doyle
762 Mr. & Mrs. J. Schafer
762 Mr. & Mrs. E. W. Nash & dr.
766 Mr. & Mrs. Theodore I. Wilson
766 Mr. & Mrs. Walpole Wood
768 Mr. & Mrs. D. R. Anderson
770 Mr. & Mrs. J. C. Holenshade
772 Mrs. J. D. Johnson
780 Mr. & Mrs. A. Hurd
782 Mr. & Mrs. J. W. Sykes
784 Dr. Thomas Faith
800 Mr. & Mrs. J. H. Brewster
802 Mr. & Mrs. Thos. W. Cole
804 Mr. & Mrs. David Whiteford
810 Dr. & Mrs. E. L. Graves & dr.
810 Dr. Samuel P. McKinney
812 Mr. & Mrs. Aaron F. Walcott
812 Mrs. O. Hatterman
818 Mr. & Mrs. J. E. Grassie
824 Mr. & Mrs. R. J. Kroff
824 Mr. & Mrs. S. H. Brand
826 Dr. & Mrs. G. W. Wolgamott
826 Samuel H. Bloom
832 Mr. & Mrs. Herbert Goodridge
832 Mrs. J. W. Cobb & dr.
834 Mr. & Mrs. J. E. Jennings
844 Dr. & Mrs. A. E. Halsted
848 Mr. & Mrs. H. E. Pitkin
858 Mr. & Mrs. R. E. Spangler
860 Mr. & Mrs. D. L. Carver
860 Mr. & Mrs. Gilman W. Smith
862 Mrs. Lena Emmerton
862 Mr. & Mrs. H. M. Meyers

887 Mr. & Mrs. F. W. Bryan
887 Miss Grace Bryan
891 Mr. & Mrs. Wm. J. Walker
891 Mr. & Mrs. Stephen L. Walker
891 George L. Walker
905 Mr. & Mrs. J. Hainsworth
925 Dr. J. W. Ross
949 Mr. & Mrs. R. C. Haskins
949 Mrs. Mary A. Haskins
953 Mr. & Mrs. Charles H. Smith
953 Mr. & Mrs. C. Y. Lucas & drs.
965 Mr. & Mrs. David T. Devin
965 Mr. & Mrs. Frank F. Holmes
973 Mr. & Mrs. H. B. Eaver
975 Mrs. A. Swenson & drs.
983 Mr. & Mrs. George S. Hunt
983 Mr. & Mrs. Charles Barrett
987 Mr.& Mrs.CharlesA.L.Kramer
997 Mr. & Mrs. J. T. Webner & drs.
999 Mr. & Mrs.HenryF. Band & dr.
Receiving day Thursday
999 Mr. & Mrs. Isaac R. Mansfield
1007 Mrs. Mary Hayes
1009 Mr. & Mrs. Thomas Davis&dr.
1015 Mr. & Mrs. Frederick F. Bullen
1023 Mr. & Mrs. Henry Rice
1025 Mr. & Mrs. George W. Rice
1025 Mrs. Josephine Spring & dr.
1025 Charles E. Spring
1027 Mrs. Elizabeth Mouat
1029 Mr. & Mrs. Eugene Cowan
1029 Herbert B. Cowan
1029 Miss Julia Cowan
1029 Mr. & Mrs. Geo. B. Grosvenor
1033 Mr. & Mrs. T. C. H. Wegeforth
1033 Mr. & Mrs. Warren F. Holden
& drs.
1035 Dr. & Mrs. J. E. Hetherington
1037 Mr. & Mrs. E. G. T. Colles
1059 Mr. & Mrs. Geo. Herrmann
1065 Mrs. Sarah Granger
1065 Mrs. Mary Tryon
1067 Mr. & Mrs.John L. Hoffman
1067 Mrs. John Hoffman
1069 Mr. & Mrs. A. D. MacGill
Receiving day Thursday
1071 Mr. & Mrs. J. H. Liversey
1071 Mrs. N. E. Stevens
1081 Mr. & Mrs. A. Mouns jr.
1081 Miss M. Connelley

870 Dr. & Mrs. James C. Gill
876 Fred O. Streich
880 Mrs. M. D. Downs & drs.
884 Mr. & Mrs. Geo. A. Cameron
886 Mr. & Mrs. G. E. Palmer
888 Mr. & Mrs. H. B. Harden
904 Mr. & Mrs. John Buckley & drs.
908 Mr. & Mrs. E. A. Dicker
914 Mr. & Mrs. William Lang
914 Miss Nellie Van Loon
916 Mr. & Mrs. H. B. Cook
918 Rev. & Mrs. J. A. Adams
Receiving day Tuesday
920 Mrs. J. N. Clark
920 Mr. & Mrs. Frank E. Clark
922 Mr. & Mrs. Charles E. Fisher
924 Mrs. B. Reidell
956 Mr.& Mrs.David W.Clark&dr.
958 Mr. & Mrs. M. McAuley
960 Herbert E. Bell
972 Mr. & Mrs. Henry Lovi & dr.
974 Mr.& Mrs. Andrew Stark & dr.
976 Mr. & Mrs. W. H. Durant
982 Mr. & Mrs. Edward H. Brown
990 Mr. & Mrs. E. J. Molloy
Receiving day Thursday
1006 Joseph Berg & drs.
1006 E. A. Berg
1010 Capt. & Mrs. Thos. Ledden
1010 Thos. H. Ledden
1010 Mr. & Mrs. J. C. Alling
1010 Mr. & Mrs. F. H. Kilbourn
1014 Mr. & Mrs. H. D. Golbeck
1018 Mr. & Mrs. C. W. Gray
1030 Mr. & Mrs. A. D. Kennedy
1058 Mr. & Mrs. H. W. Pardey
Receiving day Friday
1060 Mr. & Mrs. Chas. T. Patterson
1066 Rev. & Mrs. E. Corwin & dr.
1066 Cecil S. Corwin
1074 Dr. & Mrs. Peter Fahrney
1074 W. H. Fahrney
1076 Mr. & Mrs. G. B. Coffin & dr.

1089 Mr. & Mrs. J. A. Schafer & dr.
Receiving day Wednesday
1089 Frank Schafer
1089 Louis Schafer
1089 Emil Schafer

WASHINGTON BOULEVARD.

287 Dr. & Mrs. G. VanZandt
317 Mrs. Mahala Jones
317 Harry W. Jones

300 Dr. S. J. Beeson
306 Dr. & Mrs. Z. P. Hanson
308 William H. Condon

319 Mrs. A. S. Barnett
319 Mr. & Mrs. Frank L. Fuller
335 Dr. & Mrs. G. W. Reynolds
341 Dr. & Mrs. J. S. Young
341 Miss Edith G. Young
361 Mr. & Mrs. L. R. Hall
361 Mrs. N. G. Morgan & dr.
369 Dr. & Mrs. E. E. Page
381 Mr. & Mrs. George E. White
  Receiving day Friday
409 Mr. & Mrs. D. H. Curtis & dr.
409 George P. Curtis
409 C. H. Curtis
413 Mrs. Mary L. Groesbeck & dr.
  Receiving day Wednesday
413 Mr. & Mrs. Augustus VanBuren
415 Mr. & Mrs. W. W. Wallace
417 Mr. & Mrs. Albert Wahl
419 Mr. & Mrs. S. Herzog & drs.
421 Mr. & Mrs. C. M. Story
423 Mr. & Mrs. M. L. Hawks
425 Mrs. A. J. Snell
427 Mr. & Mrs. C. E. Rollins
429 Edward C. F. Dolle
429 Clark B. Samson
431 Mr. & Mrs. A. J. Stone
435 Hotel Worth
  Mr. & Mrs. W. H. Worth
  Mr. & Mrs. Geo. E. Andro
  vette
  Mr. & Mrs. H. Gratton Don·
  nelly
  Joseph J. Duffy
  Mr. & Mrs. M. J. Slattery
  E. C. Cooper
  G. A. Ganser
  J. Roy Ickes
  Mrs. S. G. Ingham
  H. H. Ingham
  Mr. & Mrs. Cabell Clifford
  Dr. E. J. Farnum
  Daniel McKenzie
  Dr. E. D. Messinger
  Dr. Celestia D. Messinger
  Mr. & Mrs. F. R. Millard
  A. F. Musgrave
  Mrs. D. R. Newell & dr.
  Mr. & Mrs. N. M. Nusley
  A. W. Parkhurst
  George W. Sloat
  Mr. & Mrs. John Y. Smith
  Stuart Smith
  Mr. & Mrs. I. Springer
  Mr. & Mrs. Geo. H. Stephens
  H. R. Williams
  Mr. & Mrs. N. L. Young

316 Mr. & Mrs. Ezra A. Cook & dr.
316 Maurice Langhorne
316 Verner V. Snook
338 E. C. Cole
342 G. Harry Stallman
346 H. D. Hunter
346 G. A. Williams
348 T. Mitchell Campbell
354 Mrs. C. C. Newell
354 Rev. & Mrs. E. P. Goodwin
354 Albert P. Goodwin
376 Prof. W. W. Dresden
376 Mrs. Dot Thompson
376 John C. Lundberg
376 Alfred J. Youngdahl
376 Mr. & Mrs. J. C. Snyder
376 Mr. & Mrs. John Fulton
376 W. H. Fisk
390 Mr. & Mrs. Tho. Appleton
390 Robert L. Wyatt
392 Mr. & Mrs. Lucas P. Miller
398 Hon. Edward T. Noonan
398 Mrs. Mary H. Noonan
400 Mr. & Mrs. Thos. Carbine
400 Mr. & Mrs. F. F. Bluhm
402 M. P. Alford
408 Mr. & Mrs. B. F. Hales
408 Mr. & Mrs. R. E. Cruzen
408 Mr. & Mrs. W. E. Bell
410 Dr. & Mrs. J. E. Low
410 Mr. & Mrs. John W. Weston
410 Mrs. M. L. Bangs
414 Dr. & Mrs. J. C. Frey
414 Miss Harriet E. Winchell
414 John M. Brown
414 Frank Pyatt
416 P. R. Judkins
416 Mr. & Mrs. John Shepherd
416 S. M. Little
418 Miss Agnes Henderson
420 Mr. & Mrs. A. Roberts
422 Dr. & Mrs. J. H. Plecker & dr.
428 Mrs. Joseph P. Ross & dr.
428 Robert E. Ross
428 Miss Bessie G. Ross
432 Mrs. Emma Rosenfeld
432 Sidney Rosenfeld
434 Mr. & Mrs. C. H. Solomon
436 Mr. & Mrs. W. W. Cheney
444 Mrs. A. R. Briggs & dr.
444 J. R. Briggs
448 Mr. & Mrs. Louis Karcher
456 Mr. & Mrs. A. H. Woodruff
456 Mr. & Mrs. M. W. Brownlee
462 Mrs. W. H. Wells & drs.
464 Mr. & Mrs. A. B. Hay & dr.

445 Mr. & Mrs. I. R. Rowland
Receiving day Wednesday
445 B. F. Martin
445 Mrs. Virginia McGee
445 Mrs. Esther M. Orton
445 Chas. O. Wetmore
449 Mrs. Adelaide L. Harding
449 Mr. & Mrs. A. E. Macdonald
449 Mr. & Mrs. Frank D. Abbott
451 Mr. & Mrs. Wm. W. Green
451 Mrs. Mary Hopkinson
451 Mr. & Mrs. Wm. S. Johnson
453 Mr. & Mrs. William W. Strong
453 Clair E. More
455 Dr. & Mrs. W. B. Hanna
Receiving day Wednesday
457 Mr. & Mrs. C. C. Wheeler
457 C. M. Wheeler
457 Miss Josephine E. Orvis
459 Mr. & Mrs. Geo. W. Pitkin
459 Josiah R. Pye
463 Mr. & Mrs. W. E. Rollo & drs.
465 Mrs. M. G. Merrill
465 Fred G. Merrill
469 Judge & Mrs. C. D. F. Smith&dr.
469 Mr. & Mrs. Wm. E. Smythe
469 Mr. & Mrs. A. W. McClure
469 Mrs. C. A. Phelps
469 Miss Julia Phelps
471 Mrs. Mary Barnhart
471 William J. Barnhart
471 Dr. & Mrs. John A. McDonell
479 Charles F. Kimball
479 Willard P. Alward
481 Galusha Emigh
485 Mr. & Mrs. M. J. Richards
485 Mr. & Mrs. Jacob Deardorff
505 Mrs. A. Farrar & drs.
513 Rev. & Mrs. W. F. McMillen
517 Mr. & Mrs. C. N. Cutler
517 Frank T. Cutler
521 Mr. & Mrs. J. E. Haskell
535 Mrs. C. W. Earle & dr.
535 Dr. & Mrs. Frank B. Earle
545 Samuel H. Adler
549 Mr. & Mrs. Wm. H. Ford
555 Mr. & Mrs. Henry Kerwin
557 Mr. & Mrs. J.W.C. Haskell&dr.
569 Mr.& Mrs. H. M. Hooker & dr.
571 Mr. & Mrs. C. E. Waters
571 Charles W. Waters
585 Mrs. John A. Tyrrell
585 Charles T. Tyrrell
585 Mr. & Mrs. Fred S. Tyrrell
587 Mr. & Mrs. Willey B. Waters
591 Oran Ott

468 C. H. Ruddick
468 Miss Harriet M. Farnsworth
470 Mr. & Mrs. C. K. G. Billings
482 Mr. & Mrs. George E. Spry
502 Mr. & Mrs. B. W. Ellis & dr.
512 Prof. & Mrs. G. B.Willcox & drs.
512 A. B. Willcox
516 Mr. & Mrs. J. H. Ohlerking &
drs.
518 Dr. & Mrs. G. E. Zinn
518 Frank M. Hicks
518 Miss Nettie Churchill
520 Mrs. E. F. Vogel
Receiving day Thursday
520 Mrs. L. M. Glenney
524 Mr. & Mrs. David Thresher
524 William D. Thresher
528 Mr. & Mrs. E. C. Thurber & dr.
530 Mrs. R. A. Haines
532 Rev. & Mrs. F. A. Noble
Receiving day Tuesday
532 Frederic P. Noble
534 Prof. & Mrs. Geo. H. Gilbert
536 W. Wallace Clark
538 D. W. Bosley & dr.
540 Mr. & Mrs. E. F. Bosley
Receiving day Tuesday
544 Dr. & Mrs. Wm. G. Willard
Receiving day Tuesday
544 Mrs. Ellen W. Carpenter
550 Mr. & Mrs. George R. Filer
552 Mr.& Mrs.Charles Heper & dr.
552 Mr. & Mrs. John Milloy
Receiving day Tuesday
558 Mrs. Harriet M. Blake
560 Alexander H. Peters & drs.
562 Mr. & Mrs. William W. Evans
564 Mr. & Mrs. L. H. Evans
564 Mrs. E. W. Evans & dr.
566 Mr. & Mrs. E. T. Marshall & dr.
566 Randall E. Marshall
568 Mr. & Mrs. W. H. Salisbury
570 Mr. & Mrs. J. F. Talbot
574 Mr. & Mrs. A. L. Singer & drs.
576 Dr. & Mrs. Ira E. Marshall
576 Mr. & Mrs. M. R. M. Sherry
576 Dr. Arthur B. Freeman
576A Mr. & Mrs. O. C. DeSouchet
576A Mr. & Mrs. J. T. DeSouchet
576A Mr. & Mrs. John A. Gunn
576A Mrs.Mary W. Fuarey
578 Mr. & Mrs. J. W. Herbert
578 Mr. & Mrs. J. F. Phillips
582 Dr. & Mrs. F. C. Schaefer
604 Mr. & Mrs. E. T. Harris
604 Mrs. M. J. Little & drs.

591 Mrs. Katherine Ott
595 Mrs. Nony R. Williams & drs.
599 Mr. & Mrs. Perley Lowe
603 Mr. & Mrs. T. F. Farrell
607 Charles M. McCrea
609 Mr. & Mrs. J. A. Guilford & dr.
611 Dr. & Mrs. W. H. Woodbury
611 Miss Carrie E. Hill
617 Mr. & Mrs. G. H. Bynum
619 Dr. & Mrs. Curtis M. Beebe
619 Dr. & Mrs. James R. Dewey
619 Miss Lucy L. Wilson
621 Mrs. P. B. Merwin
621 Jos. B. Redfield & dr.
625 Mrs. J. Sherman Hall & drs.
625 E. Sherman Hall
625 Louis J. Hall
625 Miss Rebecca M. Oakes
631 Dr. & Mrs. Byron S. Palmer
633 Mr. & Mrs. L. Friedman
  Receiving day Tuesday
633 Maurice Friedman
633 William Friedman
633 Miss Jennie Friedman
635 Mr. & Mrs. Chester Warner
637 Mr. & Mrs. A. B. Carson
  Receiving day Wednesday
639 Mr. & Mrs. M. D. Temple & dr.
643 Rev. & Mrs. John Willard & dr.
645 Mr. & Mrs. J. H. Tewksbury
645 Mr. & Mrs. S. O. Webster
647 Mr. & Mrs. John E. Wright & dr.
647 Frank P. Wright
647 Dr. Clarence H. Wright
649 Mr. & Mrs. G. D. Pease & dr.
649 Mrs. S. J. Osgood
651 Mr. & Mrs. D. H. Dickinson &
  dr.
651½ Mr. & Mrs. J. E. Loomis & dr.
663 Mr. & Mrs. Chas. Perkins & dr.
663 Mr. & Mrs. C. H. Robinson
663 Mrs. L. M. Grassie
663 Henry Grassie
667 Mrs. Anna M. White
667 Halsey B. G. White
667 Mr. & Mrs. D. T. Duncombe
667 Mr. & Mrs. Otto von Bachelle
667 Mrs. Marcia M. Hardy
681 Dr. & Mrs. J. D. Skeer & drs.
681 Charles H. Skeer
681 Geo. M. Skeer
683 Dr. A. E. Hoadley
683 Dr. Richard Fyfe
683½ Mr. & Mrs. E. Wisdom & dr.
683½ Edward Wisdom jr.
683½ Harry E. Wisdom

606 Mr. & Mrs. J. S. Meckling & dr.
608 Mr. & Mrs. H. L. Marshall &drs.
  Receiving day Wednesday
610 Mr.&Mrs. George A. Head&drs.
612 Mrs. L. W. Foley
  Receiving day Thursday
612 Mr. & Mrs. Wm. C. Heinroth
614 Mr. & Mrs. L. D. Collins
616 Mr. & Mrs. Roger S. Pitkin
616 Mr. & Mrs. Jerome M. Chapman
616 Arthur W. Chapman
616 Miss Harriet M. Adams
618 Mr. & Mrs.W.H.Anderson & dr.
620 Mrs. A. L. Ashley
620 Thomas White
622 Mrs. Catherine Clinton & dr.
622 Mrs. Julia C. Howe
622 Mr. & Mrs. Morris Friedman
622 Miss Clara L. K. Strauss
622 Mr. & Mrs. J. L. Livingston
624 Mr. & Mrs. Sigfried Langbein
624 Mrs. T. Oesterreicher & dr.
624 Leopold Oesterreicher
626 Mr. & Mrs. Edgar French
626 Mr. & Mrs. Ira Stover
628 Rev. & Mrs. G. S. F. Savage
630 D. R. Cameron
630 Miss Caroline I. Cameron
630 Miss Sadie J. Cameron
630 Miss Flora I. Cameron
632 Mr. & Mrs. A. B. Mead & dr.
632 Mrs. J. B. Packard
632 Miss Lizzie McDonald
634 Mr. & Mrs. L. R. Harsha
634 Mrs. J. L. Burns
636 Dr. & Mrs. R. T. Isbester
636 Mrs. M. A. VonKetel
638 Mr. & Mrs. F. A. Mitchell
638 Mrs. Abbie Mott
642 Mr. & Mrs. H. A. Winter
  Receiving day Friday
642 Miss Grace L. Winter
642 Frank F. Winter
644 Mr.&Mrs.C.M. Linington & dr.
644½ Mr. & Mrs. Charles R. Clark
646 Mr. & Mrs. G. T. Burroughs
646 Frank C. Burroughs
646 Edward R. Burroughs
648 C. H. Schub
650 Mr. & Mrs. F. A. Crane
650 Miss Elizabeth J. Nichols
654 Miss Harriet A. Farrand
654 Miss Mary L. Butler
656 Mrs. Rosanna Caldwell & drs.
658 Mr. & Mrs. T. J. Cochrane
  Receiving day Wednesday

685 Mr. & Mrs. E. Banning
    Receiving day Tuesday
687 Mrs. Geo. P. Holmes.
687 George J. Holmes
689 Mr. & Mrs. Robert L. Tatham
691 Dr. & Mrs. T. D. Palmer
691½ Mr. & Mrs. Henry O. Shepard
    Receiving day Tuesday
695 Mr. & Mrs. Frank T. Fowler
695 George H. Hill
697 Mr. & Mrs. C. A. Weare
699 Dr. & Mrs. E. M. P. Ludlam
699 Mr. & Mrs. C. F. Fessenden
    Receiving day Tuesday
699 Mr. & Mrs. J. F. Nachbour
701 Mr.& Mrs.Thomas Hood & drs.
703 Mr. & Mrs. J.W. Eisenberg & dr.
703 Wm. P. Eisenberg
709 Mr. & Mrs. O. W. Wallis & drs.
711 Mr. & Mrs. Fred G. Brooks
711 Mrs. Julia A. Brooks
713 Mr. & Mrs. C. B. Morrow
713 Dr. A. W. Morrow
713 Mrs. C. Belle Vickers
715 Mr. & Mrs.W.R. England & dr.
    Receiving day Wednesday
715 Mr. & Mrs. H. F. Streich
715½ Mr. & Mrs. H. R. Kent
    Receiving day Tuesday
715½ Miss Libbie J. McMillan
719 Mr. & Mrs. Frank E. Hale
719 Prescott G. Hale
721 Dr. & Mrs. E. A. Royce
721 Mrs. E. A. Matthews
723 Mr. & Mrs. J. W. Corlies & dr.
725 Mr. & Mrs. B. O. Price & dr.
725 George W. Price
727 Mr. & Mrs. J. T. Rawleigh
727 Miss Ava F. Rawleigh
731 Mr. & Mrs. J. Harry Rawleigh
733 Mrs. William Heap
737 Mr. & Mrs. H. C. Goodrich
    & drs.
737 Mr. & Mrs. A. C. Fordham
739 Mr. & Mrs. Thos. Sharp
739 Henry Waller
745 Mrs. W. D. Gibson & dr.
745 Miss Belle Gibson
751 Dr. & Mrs. E. Garrott
757 Mr. & Mrs. H. A. Christy
757 Dr. & Mrs. Sanger Brown
763 Mr. & Mrs. F. H. Adams & drs.
765 Rev. & Mrs. M. H. Harris
    Receiving day Monday
767 Mr. & Mrs. W. H. Busbey & dr.
767 L. White Busbey

660 Mr. & Mrs. N. H. Curtis
678 Alexander Vaughan
678 Mr. & Mrs. S. S. Vaughan
678 Mr. & Mrs. Frank S. Atherton
682 Mr. & Mrs. Edward Nevers
682 Mrs. E. G. Francis
682½ Mr. & Mrs. P. R. Wright
686 Mr. & Mrs. W. A. Golder & dr.
686½ Mr. & Mrs. C. H. Weaver
686½ Arthur C. Weaver
686½ Dr. & Mrs. G. L. Bennett
690 Mr. & Mrs. J. K. Stevens
690 Mrs. Jacob S. Cater
692 Mr. & Mrs. Geo. R. Davis &drs.
692 Benjamin Davis
696 Mr. & Mrs. L. M. Bushnell
696 Charles E. Bushnell
708 Mrs. C. H. Safford & dr.
708 Lewis B. Safford
708 Bigelow T. Safford
708 Mr. & Mrs. H. W. French
710 Mr. & Mrs. Calvin F. Taylor
712 Mr. & Mrs. J. F. Mendsen
714 Mr. & Mrs. Chester P. Cory
716 Mr. & Mrs. J. W. Kiser
718 Dr. & Mrs. A. W. Hinman
718 Miss Annie L. Glidden
718 Dr. Chester C. Dodge
724 Mr. & Mrs. E. G. W. Rietz & drs.
    Receiving day Wednesday
726 Hon.Cyrus&Mrs.Dr.Wellington
    & drs.
726 Dr. Gertrude G. Wellington
730 Mr. & Mrs. A. H. McClurg & dr.
732 Mr. & Mrs. W. L. Tapson & drs.
732 John L. Tapson
734 Rev. & Mrs. R. A. Jernberg
734 Mrs. Prudence E. Libby
738 Mr. & Mrs. George A. Rose
738 John Rose
738 Miss Lenore Fancher
738 Dr. & Mrs. A. I. Bouffleur
    Receiving day Thursday
740 Mr. & Mrs. A. H. Hart
742 Mr. & Mrs. H. King Smith
742 Mrs. Margaret Smith
744 Mr. & Mrs. James F. Griffin
754 Mr. & Mrs. F. P. Stone
756 Lucius A. Steveley
756 Thad H. Quick
756 Mr. & Mrs. John F. Steveley
756 Mrs. C. F. Grow & dr.
756 Mr. & Mrs. J. B. Allan
756 A. N. Marquis
756 Mrs. Walter Windsor
760 Mr. & Mrs. J. K. Barry

769 Mr. & Mrs. Chàs. S. MacCarty
 Receiving day Wednesday
769 Mrs Catherine McMorrine
777 Miss Mollie E. Moody
777 Frank A. Moody
783 Mr. & Mrs. Wm. Ripley
783 Mr. & Mrs. B. W. Ripley
793 Rev. & Mrs. H. D. L. Webster
 & dr.
811 Mrs. Rose Scully
811 Michael Scully
811 Maurice H. Scully
811 Bartel Yarr
813 Mr. & Mrs. Chas. W. Richards
815 Dr. & Mrs. Wells Andrews
815 Jay A. Andrews
817 Mr. & Mrs. Sydney S. Date
821 Mr. & Mrs. Alonzo Weston
821 Mr. & Mrs. Reuben Hatch
823 Mr. & Mrs. J. W. Gehrig
823 Miss Anna Guetschow
831 Mr. & Mrs. Frank Hayes
833 Dr. & Mrs. A. W. Burnside
833 Mr.& Mrs. V.Wallace Burnside
833 Dr. & Mrs. Wm. S. White
865 Mr. & Mrs. D. T. Helm
877 Mr. & Mrs. Simeon Cobb
887 Dr. & Mrs. E. E. Holroyd
969 Mr. & Mrs. J. A. Benner
969 Mrs. A. E. Skinner
975 Dr. & Mrs. J. C. Geary
1017 Mr. & Mrs. James H. Clark
1017 Mr. & Mrs. H. H. Good
1019 Mr. & Mrs. L. G. Peloubet
1019 Jarvis Peloubet
1019 Mrs. Sophia H. Wardell
1061 Mr. & Mrs. Robert B. Campbell
1065 Mr. & Mrs. Wm. D. Fitch
1065 Dr. & Mrs. P. L. Clark
1067 Mrs. Daniel P. Murphy
1067 Joseph G. Murphy
1067 Mr. & Mrs. J. D. Murphy
1069 Mr. & Mrs. Geo. H. Bishop
1077 Mr. & Mrs. A. Rose & drs.
1077 William H. Rose
1079 Dr. & Mrs. J. C. Bryan
1081 Mr. & Mrs. Wm. S. Tillotson
 & dr.
1083 Mr. & Mrs. Wm. K. Sullivan
1093 Mr. & Mrs. F. W. Morgan
1093 Miss Josephine L. Wright
1101 Mr. & Mrs. H. A. Williams
1101 Miss M. F. Hoag
1113 Rev. William Jason Gold S.T.
 D. & drs.

762 Mr. & Mrs. Alex. J. Hodge
768 Mr.& Mrs.M.F.Bingham & drs.
 Receiving day Thursday
786 Mr. & Mrs. Henry Cohn & drs.
788 Mr. & Mrs. A. Longstreet
790 Rev. & Mrs. W. C. DeWitt
792 Mr. & Mrs. D. A. Price
794 Miss Emma S. Brett
794 Theodore F. Brett
806 Mr. & Mrs. B. Subert & dr.
806 Charles Subert
806 Max Subert
806 Mr. & Mrs. Alexander White
806 Mr. & Mrs. J. J. Byrne
806 Miss Mary Byrne
.810 Mr. & Mrs. G. W. Plummer
810 Ralph W. Plummer
812 A. B. Scully
812 Miss Mary Scully
812 Miss Agnes L. Scully
812 Mr. & Mrs. C. E. Newton
832 Mr. & Mrs. F. A. White & dr.
832 Burton F. White
834 Mr. & Mrs.William Barker&dr.
834 William Barker jr.
844 Mr. & Mrs Charles Noyes
846 Mr. & Mrs. H. P. Thompson
848 Mrs. R. S. Johnson
850 Mr. & Mrs. Edward Harzfeld
850 Mr. & Mrs. Jacob W.Strauss &
 dr.
854 Mr.&Mrs. C. F. Hamilton&dr.
854 Miss M. O. Barnes
856 Mr. & Mrs. W. W. Irish & dr.
860 Mr. & Mrs. Wm. G. Metzger
868 Mr. & Mrs. Jas. J.Sullivan &dr.
878 Mr. & Mrs. Wm. F. MacLachlan
880 Mr. & Mrs. W. R.Clark
880 Mr. & Mrs. F. S. Frost
880 Mr. & Mrs. Chas. W. Ralph
882 Mrs. Elizabeth Smeeth & dr.
882 George S. Smeeth
882 Alfred T. Smeeth
882 Mrs. Edith S. Weaver
890 Mrs.JamesC. McAndrews& dr.
890 James McAndrews jr.
890 Joseph R. McAndrews
970 Miss Frances B. Smith
970 Mrs. Elizabeth J. Bertch
1004 Rev. & Mrs. W. M. Claybaugh
1006 Mr. & Mrs. Robert A. Dwyer
1010 Mr. & Mrs. J. H. Ritter
1010 Mr. & Mrs. W. B. Wyne
 Receiving day Thursday
1010 Mrs. Joel Lee

1113 Mrs. S. E. E. Chamberlin
1133 Mr. & Mrs. H. F. Brand
1135 Mr. & Mrs. T. J. Rice
1139 Mrs. A. B. Rundell & drs.
1139 Miller H. Rundell
1141 Mrs. Mary L. Atkins
1143 Mr. & Mrs. C. H. Ball
  Receiving day Wednesday
1145 Mr. & Mrs. Henry Reuter &
  drs.
1165 Mr. & Mrs. J. T. Matthews
1173 Mr. & Mrs. Uri Weaver
1177 Mrs. W. L. May
1177 H. C. Kittredge & dr.
1177 Mr. & Mrs. J. E. Keating
1177 Miss Ida M. Benke
1179 Mr. & Mrs. Frank R. Grout
1179 Charles R. Grout
1179 Mr. & Mrs. H. F. Chandler
1181 Mr. & Mrs. H. P. Murphy&drs.
1181 Austin J. Murphy
1183 Mrs. Nettie E. Gunlock & dr.
1183 Col. & Mrs. B. VanBuren
1187 Mr. & Mrs. M. C. Bullock & dr.
1195 Mrs. M. M. McCourtie
1195 Mrs. M. E. Bell
1197 Mr. & Mrs. A. B. McCourtie
1199 Mr. & Mrs. S. L. Burrows & dr.
1205 Mr. & Mrs. M. D. Lamoreaux .
1229 Mr. & Mrs. F. J. Dennis
  Receiving day Tuesday
1231 Mr. & Mrs. John Featherstone
  Receiving day Wednesday
1237 Mr. & Mrs. N. D. Fraser
1239 Mr.&Mrs. S.T. Gunderson&dr.
  Receiving day Wednesday
1239 Mr. & Mrs. G. O. Gunderson
1239 Mr. & Mrs. S. M. Gunderson
1241 Mr. & Mrs. Adam Kolb & dr.
  Receiving day Wednesday
1241 Mr. & Mrs. Oscar E. Kolb
1257 Mr. & Mrs. Wm. Sollitt
1261 Mr. & Mrs. W. E. Mortimer
1261 Frank G. Mortimer
1271 Mr. & Mrs. Henry J. Evans
  Receiving day Wednesday
1271 Sidney J. Evans
1271 Mr. & Mrs. Chas. J. Mortimer
1285 Mr. & Mrs. J. G. Harlow
1287 Mr. & Mrs. F. I. Wilson
1287 Dr. A. Bromley Allen
1295 Mr. & Mrs. F. F. Whitman
  Receiving day Tuesday
1295 John M. Whitman
1319 Mr. & Mrs. L. Wolff
1319 Ludwig Wolff jr.

1010 Mr. & Mrs. L. K. Stevens
1010 Robert W. Stevens
1010 Mr. & Mrs. Charles L. Stevens
1012 Mr. & Mrs. M. H. Buckley
1016 Mr. & Mrs. Walter Wrigley
1020 Mr. & Mrs. J. A. Brophy
1020 Miss Mary Brophy
1022 Mr. & Mrs. A. A. Stewart
  Receiving day Tuesday
1050 Mrs. C. H. Clancy
1050 Edwin M. Clancy
1050 Mr. & Mrs. A. C. Leebrick
1052 J. M. Hoskins & dr.
1052 Mr. & Mrs. J. H. Little & dr.
1054 Mrs. Alice Willis & dr.
1054 M. J. Comerford
1056 Mr. & Mrs. Wm. H. Riddiford
1058 Mr. & Mrs. L. A. Morey
1058 Charles F. Craig
1060 Mr. & Mrs. A. W. Neff
1076 Rev. & Mrs. J. A. Mackelvey
1076 Dr. & Mrs. Wm. J. Stewart
1076 George W. Stewart
1076 Dr. Harry J. Stewart
1080 William A. Shaw
1100 Mr. & Mrs. Geo. S. Fergus
1100 Mrs. Isabelle M. George & dr.
1100 Mr. & Mrs. Louis Bloch
1102 Mrs. Sarah S. Potter
1102 Selah R. Potter
1102 Mr. & Mrs. Chas. F. Cole
1102 Mr. & Mrs. A. J. Davis
1110 Mr. & Mrs. H. C. Stewart
1110 Mrs. Helen M. Johnson
1110 Miss Tillie McAuley
1118 Mrs. Julia G. Colson
1118 Harry G. Colson
1118 Mr. & Mrs. J. W. Hart
1120 Mr. & Mrs. H. E. Patrick
1122 Mrs. R. A. Drummond
1122 Mr. & Mrs. D. M. Reynolds
1122 Mr. & Mrs. George B. Merrill
1124 Mr. & Mrs. John J. Rigney
1126 Mr. & Mrs. H. Z. Lewis
1128 Mr. & Mrs. J. B. Brady
1128 James T. Brady
1128 Mr. & Mrs. James Quirk
1128 Dr. James P. Quirk
1130 Mrs. Emily Ahles
1130 William Ahles
1130 Edward Ahles
1136 Mr. & Mrs. J. L. Kneisly
1138 Mrs. Amelia E. Green
1138 Mr. & Mrs. E. D. Miller
1142 Mr. & Mrs. J. C. Henderson &
  dr.

1319 Herman M. Hoelscher
1319 Edward C. Hoelscher
1323 Mr. & Mrs. Samuel Kerr
1323 Robert J. Kerr
1371 Mr. & Mrs. F. S. Atkin
1371 Mrs. Mary E. Edgell
1371 Miss Emma L. Wilson
1371 Mr. & Mrs. W. B. Pearson
1373 Dr. & Mrs. J. Leggett
    Receiving day Tuesday
1373 Mrs. Thomas Leggett
1373 George J. Ryan
1379 Mr. & Mrs. Daniel Forbes
1383 Mr. & Mrs. L. J. Reed
    Receiving day Thursday
1383 Charles A. Roberts
1383 Mr. & Mrs. B. Quirk & dr.
1389 Mr. & Mrs. John McMahon
1399 Miss Mary J. Fish
    Receiving day Friday
1399 Miss Sarah C. Fish
1399 Mr. & Mrs. P. F. Ryan & dr.
    Receiving day Thursday
1401 Mrs. Nathan F. Merrill
1403 Mrs. N. D. Cooper
    Receiving day Tuesday
1403 Dr. & Mrs. A. G. Bond
1411 Mr. & Mrs. A. J. Graham
1423 Mr. & Mrs. Arnold Heap
    Receiving day Thursday
1427 Mr. & Mrs. Carl Moll
1427 Mr. & Mrs. J. C. Witte & dr.
1473 Mr. & Mrs. D. M. Farson
1479 Mr. & Mrs. Wm. E. Mason
1487 Mr. & Mrs. John Eiszner
1487 Frank J. Eiszner
1491 Mr. & Mrs. A. H. Sanders
1497 Mr. & Mrs. Elisha W. Case
1499 Mr. & Mrs. Joseph E. Shipley
    & dr.
1499 J. Cheshire Shipley

1316 Mrs. Ada M. F. Atkins
1316 Mrs. Venetia M. G. Heron
1316 Mrs. Mary E. Carr & dr.
1318 Mr. & Mrs. Wm. Taussig
1328 Mr. & Mrs. Maurice von Platen
    Receiving day Tuesday
1328 Mr. & Mrs. E. N. Bowes & dr.
1328 Frederick M. Bowes
1328 Mr. & Mrs. J. P. Marsh
1330 Mr. & Mrs. Elmo J. Johnson
1330 Mrs. Annie E. Leekley & dr.
1330 Harlow A. Leekley
1330 Mr. & Mrs. Wm. A. Wallace
1332 Mrs. Emma Backus

1144 Mr.&Mrs. Wm. E. Janes & drs.
1146 Mr. & Mrs. E. H. Hoagland
1146 Edward H. Hoagland
1146 Jay S. Hoagland
1170 Rev. & Mrs. Wm. E. Holyoke
1170 Mr. & Mrs. Wm. D. Fischer
1172 Mr. & Mrs. E. R. Ozias & dr.
1172 Mr. & Mrs. F. L. Jacobs
1174 Mr. & Mrs. John Gilbert
1176 Mr. & Mrs. George Fyfe & dr.
1176 John Holland
1176 Arthur Fulton
1176 John W. Foster
1178 Mr. & Mrs. E. B. Merritt
1178 Mr. & Mrs. John C. Bauer
1180 Mr. & Mrs. Chauncey M.
    Stokes & dr.
1180 Mrs. Mary Kenny & drs.
1188 Mr. & Mrs. Otto Foerster
1188 Miss Prema Rhea
1192 Mr. & Mrs. A. E. Nickerson
    Receiving day Friday
1192 Mr. & Mrs. Wm. E. Ottie
1212 Mr. & Mrs. M. A. Richardson
    & dr.
    Receiving day Thursday
1212 M. Arthur Richardson
1212 Dr. & Mrs. B. H. Chamberlin
1218 Mr. & Mrs. F. M. Woods
1220 Mr. & Mrs. John Mullin
1220 Mr. & Mrs. John J. Naghten
1234 Mr. & Mrs. R.F.Conway & drs.
1234 Mrs. Mary A. Reed
1236 Mr. & Mrs. Wallace Casler
1242 Mr. & Mrs. W. Fred Main
1248 Mr. & Mrs. C. A. Hallam
1250 Mr. & Mrs. Wm. T. Hill
1268 Mr. & Mrs. James A. Sackley
1270 Mr. & Mrs. R. D. Huszagh
    Receiving day Wednesday
1272 Mr. & Mrs. G. P. Harris & dr.
    Receiving day Wednesday
1274 M . & Mrs. Chas. Champion &
    dr.
1276 Mrs. Chas. Munson & dr.
    Receiving day Thursday
1276 Charles W. Munson
1276 Mrs. Elizabeth Kelly & dr.
1286 Mr. & Mrs. Albert J. Danz
1286 C. A. Danz
1286 Mrs. Margaret Danz
1288 Mr. & Mrs. Michael Hayes
1304 Mr. & Mrs. Francis M. Barrett
1304 Miss Nora Buckley
1314 Mr. & Mrs. Wm. R. Daniels
1316 Mrs. Maria G. Carr

1336 Mr.& Mrs. HenryB.Mathews jr
1336 Henry B. Mathews
1338 Mr. & Mrs. G. M. Richardson
1338 E. Perrin Richardson
1356 Mr. & Mrs. W. George Morris
1364 Mrs. Henry Van Buren
1364 Mr. & Mrs. Geo. F. Knisely
1364 Miss Ella E. Rearick
1364 Mr. & Mrs. Geo. W. Nolan
1482 Mrs. Eliza J. Crane

1482 Mr. & Mrs. Frank R. Crane
1492 Mr. & Mrs. C. H. Chamberlain
1494 Mr. & Mrs. Edward Horan
1510 Mr. & Mrs. Daniel W. Mills
     Receiving day Thursday
1520 Mr. & Mrs.G.W.Spofford & dr.
     Receiving day Thursday
1520 Percy M. Spofford
1520 Mrs. E. Alexander
1520 H. Arthur Rice

WAVERLY PLACE.

23 R. A. Baker
23 Mrs. C. E. Brown
25 Mr. & Mrs. Henry L. Slayton

16 Dr. & Mrs. J. B. Armstrong
16 Guy N. Armstrong
18 Miss Mary Young
24 Mr. & Mrs. R. J. Taylor
32 Mr. & Mrs. George H. Benedict

WILCOX AVENUE.

993 Mr. & Mrs. James J. White
999 Mr. & Mrs. M. F. Yates
1001 Mr. & Mrs. Stephen B. Jones
1031 Mr. & Mrs. B. F. Davison
1043 Mr. & Mrs. Jos. K. C. Forrest
1045 Mr. & Mrs. T. Addison Busby
1045 Mrs. Wm. T. Coggeshall
1131 Mr. & Mrs. G. E. Kelly
1131 W. A. Kelly
1173 Mr. & Mrs. Wm. C. Clark
1175 Mr. & Mrs. John W. Lyke
1225 Mr. & Mrs. George W. Salter
1225 Mr. & Mrs. Frank H. Zinn
1239 Mrs. E. A. Chapman
1243 Mr. & Mrs. C. W. Walduck
1259 Mr. & Mrs. L. J. Hammell

1280 Rev. and Mrs. D. F. Fox
1286 Harry S. Mecartney
1298 Mr. & Mrs. M. D. Madigan
1300 Mr. & Mrs. F. A. Barnard
1308 Mr. & Mrs. O. D. Bond
1310 Mr. & Mrs. Joseph Short

1034 Mrs. M. A. Perce
1034 Charles F. Perce
1054 Mr. & Mrs. Jas. L. Hampton
1058 Mr. & Mrs. N. Beecher Place
1058 Lewis N. Piace
1132 J. J. LeFevre
1138 Joseph F. Peacock
1138 Mr. & Mrs. Jos. J. Peacock&dr
1184 Mr. & Mrs. B. S. Elmendorf
1220 Mr. & Mrs. F. B. Pettibone
1222 Mr. & Mrs. Charles D. Cole
1226 Mr. & Mrs. F. B. Stevenson
1232 Mr. & Mrs. Seth Riford
1236 Mr. & Mrs. Arthur W. Conna-
     ble
1236 Mr. & Mrs. Walter S. Baldwin
1242 Mr. & Mrs. W. N. Treleaven
1244 Mr. & Mrs. F. M. Lew
1258 Mr. & Mrs. D. S. Bain
1260 Dr. & Mrs. W. F. Haley
1262 Mr. & Mrs. Joseph R. Payson
1274 Mr. & Mrs. J. A. Sperry
1276 Mr. & Mrs. H. B. Douville

WINCHESTER AVENUE.

105 Dr. & Mrs. Chas. C. O'Byrne
105 Mr. & Mrs. H. E. Hunt
105 Mr. & Mrs. W. H. Cuyler & dr.
151 Mr. & Mrs. A. Meyer
163 F. F. Overlook
197 John I. Spafford
213 Mr. & Mrs. George D. Brown
215 Mr. & Mrs. Theodore B. Wells
217 Mrs. Augusta Pomeroy

112 Mr. & Mrs. Jarvis Blume
160 Mr. & Mrs. James A. Sheehan
160 Edward L. Bailey
200 Mr. & Mrs. Robt. E. Cantwell
204 Mrs. M. E. Gamble & dr.
204 William C. Gamble
228 Mr. & Mrs. Chas. F. Halbe
232 Bishop & Mrs. T. Bowman
     Receiving day Thursday

227 Mr. & Mrs. John Parker & drs.
231 Mr. & Mrs. Wm. B. Richards
235 Mr. & Mrs. Frank H. Hebard
241 Mr. & Mrs. Ernest T. Ross
247 Mrs. N. J. Mitchell
247 Mr. & Mrs. Joseph L. Locke
247 William J. Locke
247 C. C. Bartlett
267 Mrs. H. T. Wynkopp
    Receiving day Thursday
299 Mrs. Elizabeth Butler & drs.
301 Rev. & Mrs. R. W. French
353 Mr. & Mrs. W. H. Nagle
353 Mrs. Margaret Nagle & drs.
423 Mr. & Mrs. Cornelius Van Bezey
425 James VanBezey
439 Mr. & Mrs. Samuel R. Zwetow
445 Mr. & Mrs. Wm. G. Ruehl
453 Mr. & Mrs. Peter Reder
457 Mr. & Mrs. Peter Bernard
457 John F. Bernard

234 Mr. & Mrs. E. B. Esher
    Receiving day Wednesday
238 Simon Vehon
240 Mr. & Mrs. John H. Mueller
302 Mr. & Mrs. Wm. G. Kriegsman
342 Mr. & Mrs. Nath'l Cameron & dr.
342 Hiram K. Cameron
520 John White
520 Thos. M. White
520 Miss Ellen C. White
520 Miss Elizabeth V. White

———

499 Mr. & Mrs. J. W. Ashbury
501 Mr. & Mrs. John Geringer
507 Mr. & Mrs. Charles J. Vopicka
515 Mr. & Mrs. Otto Kubin
525 Mr. & Mrs. Walter Tehle
531 Mr. & Mrs. J. G. Riel
531 Mr. & Mrs. J. Wartman
535 Mr. & Mrs. L. A. Ruehl

WINTHROP PLACE.

23 Mr. & Mrs. M. J. Breen

SOUTH WOOD STREET.

117 Mr. & Mrs. P. M. Bobb
157 F. W. Metz
163 Mr. & Mrs. J. H. Chamberlin
163 James F. Criswell
163 Mrs. F. McLindon
165 Mr. & Mrs. Eugene Bassler
199 Mrs. A. Smith
203 Mr. & Mrs. Jas. M. Doyle
211 Mr. & Mrs. W. E. Hall
215½ Mr. & Mrs. F. C. Traver
215½ Mr. & Mrs. T. H. Cranston
217 John M. H. Burgett

30 Mr. & Mrs. H. M. Lewis
36 Mr. & Mrs. Henry Sierks
162 Mr. & Mrs. N. Atchison
162 John D. Atchison
162 James A. Atchison
164 Mrs. E. Tiffany
164 Mr. & Mrs. W. A. Alden
408 Mr. & Mrs. Thomas J. Tierney
416 Mr. & Mrs. John McGovern

———

217 Mr. & Mrs. Charles A. Brown

360

PART FOURTH.

THE HOTELS.

THE BLUE BOOK.

CONTAINING LISTS OF THE PERMANENT BOARDERS
OF THE PROMINENT HOTELS.

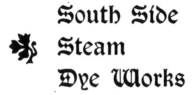

THE HOTELS.

AUDITORIUM HOTEL.

Michigan Avenue nw. cor. Congress.

Mr. & Mrs. Milward Adams
Mr. & Mrs. Oscar F. Bane
Webster Batcheller
Mr. & Mrs. P. A. Brady
D. C. Briggs
Mr. & Mrs. John B. Brown
J. S. Buckley
Mr. & Mrs. Henry C. Clement
Mr. & Mrs. W. B. Coleman
A. Conkling
Mr. & Mrs. W. Corliss
Miss Sarah E. Crowell
Walter Cullerton
Mr. & Mrs. J. L. Day
Thaddeus Dean
Mrs. Sarah Robinson Duff
E. S. Everets
A. Featherstone
W. B. Gibbs
Harry L. Hamlin
David Henderson
Eugene Hogue
Mrs. L. F. Jenks

Samuel Kayzer
J. Edward Kennedy
A. S. Laflin
Mr. & Mrs. L. Laflin
Chas. E. Leonard
Capt. Charles G. Lyman
Mr. & Mrs. R. B. Marten
Mr. & Mrs. J. W. Merriam & dr.
William Monroe
F. Tennyson Neely
F. A. Palmer
J. W. Parmelee
Gen.& Mrs.Thos. H. Ruger &dr.
C. H. Savage
Mr. & Mrs. J. J. Shafer
Mr.&Mrs. R. H. Southgate&drs.
R. E. Starkweather
W. F. Studebaker
Mr. & Mrs. Wm. J. Sutherland
Abner Taylor
Mr. & Mrs. S. R. Udell
Mrs. C. W. Wallace

AUDITORIUM ANNEX.

Michigan Avenue sw. cor. Congress.

Mr. & Mrs. L. S. Allen
Walter C. Anderson
Mr. & Mrs. C. W. Barnes & dr.
A. Bowersaux
Ed. R. Brainerd
Henry W. Brackett
E. L. Brewster
I. Raleigh Burns
Walter F. Burns
Arthur C. Butts
Mr. & Mrs. DeiWtt C. Butts

Siragan S. Costikyan
Mr. & Mrs. J. S. Given jr.
Dr. & Mrs. Carl T. Gramm
Dr. Jabez D. Hammond
William J. Hayne
Francis Hinton
Mrs. Anna Holton
Huntington W. Jackson
Mr. & Mrs. John Kroeger jr.
Mr. & Mrs. Alex. H. Levy
I. C. Lindley

Wm. O. Lindley
Mr. & Mrs. A. W. Longley
Mrs. Nelson Ludington
Charles A. Mair
W. D. Munhall
William Munro
John A. Neal
Mrs. Juan A. Neal
B. F. Norris
Mr. & Mrs. H. S. Pickands
Lee Price
Mrs. Martin Ryerson

G. A. Schwartz
Mr. & Mrs. Frederick C. Smith
Mr. & Mrs. D. S. Taylor
George W. Tewksbury
Mr. & Mrs. F. S. Van Eps
Mr. & Mrs. Chas. J. Wenderoth
Frank Wenderoth
Mr. & Mrs. C. W. Wheeler
Mrs. F. E. Whitney
Mrs. H. M. Wilmarth
Mr. &. Mrs. George W. Young

CHICAGO BEACH HOTEL.

Fifty-First Street and the Lake.

F. E. A. Acker
Mr. & Mrs. J. Frank Aldrich
Mrs. K. C. Anderson
Col. H. C. Ayer
Mrs. Charles J. Ball
W. J. Banghart
Frank Barbour
P. H. Barker
Mrs. A. R. Barnett
Dr. W. L. Baum
Mrs. F. D. Beall
F. W. Beall
P. D. Beard
Henry H. Brooks
Mr. & Mrs. R. D. Buchanan
Mr. & Mrs. W. S. Caleb
Mr. & Mrs. J. A. Campbell & dr.
Mr. & Mrs. W. D. Carnahan
A. B. Carpenter
Mrs. J. F. Cone
W. E. Cooke
Mr. & Mrs. C. W. Cowes
Mr. & Mrs. E. C. Day
Mr. & Mrs. H. S. Denison
Mr. & Mrs. P. DeThal
Mr. & Mrs. O. P. Dickinson
A. H. Dodge
Mr. & Mrs. C. H. Douglass
Gail Dray
Mrs. W. S. Dray
Mr. & Mrs. H. L. Earle & dr.
Mr. & Mrs. W. H. Epply
Mrs. A. H. Everet & dr.
P. D. Fenn
Dr. & Mrs. C. E. Fisher
E. J. Fowler
Mr. & Mrs. H. W. Fowler
Mr. & Mrs. C. O. French
C. A. Funk

Mrs. A. E. Gates
Mr. & Mrs. P. W. Gates
Mr. & Mrs. W. B. Gates
Mr. & Mrs. C. C. Germain
Mr. & Mrs. H. M. Gilbert
E. A. Graff
H. D. Graff
Mr. & Mrs. W. H. Henchman
D. Henning
Mr. & Mrs. Edward Henning
H. R. Hickson
Mr. & Mrs. John N. Hills
J. A. Hopkins
Mr. & Mrs. F. W. Horne
Mr. & Mrs. George H. Hovey
Mr. & Mrs. Benjamin Ives
Mr. & Mrs. Wm. V. Kelley
Rev. & Mrs. M. G. Knight & dr.
Mr. & Mrs. J. B. Lapham
Mr. & Mrs. C. D. Lathrop
L. H. Lermit
Mr. & Mrs. Henry Lockwood & dr.
Mr. & Mrs. H. N. Loomis
Mr. & Mrs. J. L. Loose
Mrs. E. W. Lynch
Mr. & Mrs. C. E. P. Lyon
Mr. & Mrs. Sandford Makeever
Count G. Marazzi
Mr. & Mrs. F. D. Markee
Col. & Mrs. J. P. Martin
Mr. & Mrs. A. C. Mason
W. K. McClintock
Mrs. J. E. McElroy & dr.
M. A. Mead
A. L. Mills
Mrs. H. E. Morrison
Mr. & Mrs. C. T. Morse
Mr. & Mrs. F. D. Muir

Mrs. L. P. Myers
M. C. Myers
Mr. & Mrs. W. R. Mygatt
Mr. & Mrs. W. A. Newell
Mrs. A. S. Newhouse
Mr. & Mrs. D. W. Norton
A. W. Paige
S. K. Palmer
Mr. & Mrs. A. Patton
Mr. & Mrs. R. S. Peale
W. S. Peasley
Alfred Peats
C. M. Peeples
Mr. & Mrs. J. M. Peeples & dr.
Miss Josephine D. Pfeifer
Dr. Charles P. Pinckard
H. E. Platt
H. C. Poillon
William Poillon
Mrs. M. A. Pritchard
Dr. & Mrs. W. A. Pusey
F. H. Rapley
Mr. & Mrs. Alanson H. Reed
A. L. Reid
Mrs. H. T. Reid
Mr. & Mrs. A.P.Robertson&drs.
Mr. & Mrs. J. Rollin
Mr. & Mrs. L. H. Russell

Mr. & Mrs. W. D. Salisbury&dr.
Receive Monday afternoon
Everett T. Schuler
Mr. & Mrs. F. M. Scofield
Miss A. S. Sherman
Mr. & Mrs. E. W. Shirk
Mr. & Mrs. L. W. Shively & dr.
Mr. & Mrs. L. G. Smith
Mr. & Mrs. E. M. Snow & dr.
Mr. & Mrs. F. E. Spooner & drs.
Mr. & Mrs. W. F. Steele
D. D. Streeter
J. Benson Thomas
Mr. & Mrs. W. D. Tilden
Mr. & Mrs. George H. Tousey
Mr. & Mrs. S. R. Udell
Mr. & Mrs. W. H.Wamsley&dr.
B. R. Watson
Mr. & Mrs. George L. Webb
G. A. Webster
Mr. & Mrs. F. Wheeler
Mr. & Mrs. B. C. White
Mr. & Mrs. J. Wilcox & drs.
Dr. J. D. Willoughby
W. J. Woods
Mrs. James L. Woodward
T. H. Woodward

CLIFTON HOUSE.
Monroe nw. cor. Wabash Avenue.

Mr. & Mrs. H. P. Barber
Ellis Brooks
F. M. Burroughs
Miss Rose E. Burroughs
Miss Louisa Burns
DeWitt W. Campbell
George Cummings
Mr. & Mrs. Chas. W. Dabb
J. C. Donnelly
Mr. & Mrs. Rush H. Field
George R. Ford
David B. Gerrett
A. G. Greenwood
A. N. King
George D. Knab

Albert W. Kohler
Miss Amy Lesslie
Henry C. Logan
Mr. & Mrs. M. A. Loring
P. B. Mason
R. M. Patterson
H. C. Porter
Mr. & Mrs. P. Ramond
G. A. Rollins
S. Rosenberg
Dr. & Mrs. F. R. Sherwood
Stanley S. Stout
Mr. & Mrs. M. J. Thompson
Edwin Wallace

GRANADA HOTEL.
70 to 76 Rush.

J. S. Barnum
O. H. Barnum
Mr. & Mrs. J. H. Barry
Thomas W. Berry
D. Bevier

H. R. Bishop
Richard T. Cammack
H. F. Chester
Mr. & Mrs. M. C. Connelly
Mr. & Mrs. F. M. DeRivas

W. J. Diggs
Case Edwards
G. S. Ellinger jr.
Mr. & Mrs. A. L. Ensign
Mr. & Mrs. W. M. Ford
Miss Lizze Forsythe
Miss Mollie Forsythe
Mr. & Mrs. C. L. Furey
W. H. Gardner
T. N. Gibbs
F. L. Gilbert
G. Goward
Mr. & Mrs. S H. Helm
L. M. Henoch
G. Leland Hunter
Mr. & Mrs. W. J. Hynes
Mr. & Mrs. J. W. Kepler
Mr. & Mrs. A. H. Koach
Blewett Lee
Mr. & Mrs. Thomas R.Lombard
Eugene R. Lyons
Mr. & Mrs. F. D. Manahan

Mr. & Mrs. J. L. Millard
W. D. Miller
H. C. Mowray
Mr. & Mrs. LaVerne W. Noyes
J. D. O'Riley
Mr. & Mrs. F. S. Pixley
Mr. & Mrs. Frank D. Ray
Frank D. Ray jr.
Horton S. Ray
A. R. Sainte Croix
Mr. & Mrs. David J. Smith
Col. T. C. Sullivan
Mr. & Mrs. J. C. Taylor
Mr. & Mrs. Dwight K. Tripp
E. W. Wagner
Theodore Wagner
Mr. & Mrs. T. Waterbury
T. E. Wayman
Capt. Wells Willard
Gen. J. A. Williamson
E. L. Young

GRAND PACIFIC HOTEL.

Clark nw. cor. Jackson.

John Crerar
E. A. Drummond
J. Ensign Fuller
Fred Gaylord
Dr. Vincent L. Hurlbut
Mr. & Mrs. J. Frank Lawrence
Dr. R. MacMartin
L. E. Myers
Samuel W. Parker
Mr. & Mrs. Frank Parmelee
Lewis S. Perry

D. A. Robinson
H. B. Shaw
W. H. Shaw
Mrs. Elizabeth A. Straut
John R. Tanner
D. W. Trotter
Joseph F. Tucker
Henry H. Walker
F. K. Whittemore
George Woodford

GREAT NORTHERN HOTEL.

Dearborn ne. cor. Jackson.

W. M. Babcock
Miss H. Marie Burkart
Horace N. Claxton
Mr. & Mrs. W. S. Eden
R. Clarke Forsyth
W. E. Foy
L. C. Garrabrant
Mr. & Mrs. N. P. Glann
Mrs. J. N. Griffith
L. B. Jackson
E. V. Johnson

H. D. Laughlin
G. L. McGregor
J. W. Newcomer
T. W. Phinney
Mr. & Mrs. Chas. W. Rand
Dr. Robert W. Steger
W. B. Strong
Dr. & Mrs. W. I. Tallman
Mr. & Mrs. E. H. Ullman
Dr. S. Wickersham

HOTEL BARRY.

59th Street cor. Washington av.

Mr. & Mrs. F. H. Barry
F. H. Barry jr.
Mr. & Mrs. W. H. Barry
Miss Florence Beardsley
W. D. Beaty
A. G. Beaunisne
Mr. & Mrs. J. A. Blakely
Mr. & Mrs. James N. Buchanan
  & dr.
George Burry
Prof. E. D. Burton
William Caldwell
Charles Chappell
Mr. & Mrs. M. D. Clare
Mr. & Mrs. E. W. Cook
Mr. & Mrs. Chas. S. Corning
F. H. Dow
Mr. & Mrs. E. T. Ellicott
Mr. & Mrs. Geo. E. Farrington
C. H. Fowler
Prof. E. Freund
C. H. Gallion
Mr. & Mrs. A. H. Goode
Prof. & Mrs. G. S. Goodspeed
Mr. & Mrs. W. S. Grubb
Mr. & Mrs. Wm. H. Hagedorn
Mr. & Mrs. J. C. Hanauer
K. M. Hardy
Prof. R. F. Harper
Mr. & Mrs. Edward C. Hart
O. H. Hicks
Prof. E. B. Hulbert
C. A. Hyde
C. H. Irwin
Mr. & Mrs. W. H. Jarvis
Prof. & Mrs. Franklin Johnson
Dr. F. Johnson
Prof. & Mrs. H. P. Judson
Mr. & Mrs. W. E. Keepers
W. M. Kelso
Mr. & Mrs. McIlvain King
C. Kochi
Miss Emma Livezey
Miss Sadie Livezey
W. K. Lowrey

E. M. Lund
Mr. & Mrs. M. J. Lyman
Mr. & Mrs. R. G. Lyons
Prof. & Mrs. S. Mathews
Miss Jennie McIntosh
J. M. McIntosh
Miss Mary McIntosh
H. W. Meehan
Prof. H. C. Miller
Miss H. K. Mills
Mr. & Mrs. A. J. Minard
F. H. Minard
M. T. Moody
E. D. Murray
J. F. Nickerson
Mr. & Mrs. H. G. Niles jr.
Mr. & Mrs. A. T. Otto
Mr. & Mrs. H. Parden
Mr. & Mrs. C. F. Park
S. A. Perry
Mr. & Mrs. F. L. Pettee
Mr. & Mrs. M. W. Pinckney
Mr. & Mrs. W. H. Rowe
E. B. Rowland
Dr. & Mrs. George B. Salter
Mr. & Mrs. Geo. E. Scranton
Mr. & Mrs. Harry Scull
Mr. & Mrs. E. L. Somers
E. M. Sprague
Mr. & Mrs. E. B. Springer.
Mr. & Mrs. H. Stursberg
Prof. F. B. Talbel
C. S. Tarbox
Miss Nettie Tollason
Mr. & Mrs. E. D. Townsend
Miss Helen Townsend
W. C. Vaughan
G. B. Walker
Dr. & Mrs. L. P. Walters
Dr. G. N. West
B. H. White
Carl White
Mr. & Mrs. H. W. White
E. D. Wooster

HOTEL GROVELAND.

Groveland Avenue sw. cor. 31st Street.

W. S. Baker & dr.
J. W. Breen
Mr. & Mrs. E. H. Briggs
Harry Butler
George S. Cheeseman
Ernest A. Chowan
Miss Lizzie M. Crane
Mr. & Mrs. C. G. Cutter & dr.
C. H. Dalgleish
Mr. & Mrs. J. P. Dugger
C. J. Esterly
Mr. & Mrs. F. E. Fernald
George Fernald
Mr. & Mrs. George W. G. Ferris
John Foreman
Mr. & Mrs. G. Edward Fuller
Miss L. O. Green
E. C. Greenbaum
Mr. & Mrs. S. Greenbaum
Mr. & Mrs. J. J. Hackney & dr.
Miss H. N. B. Johnson
Mr. & Mrs. T. V. Leeson & dr.
Mrs. W. C. Lyman
M. G. Magill
Mrs. S. Martin
Mr. & Mrs. E. J. McPhelim
John S. Morris
Mrs. Annie Neils
Arthur Nester
Mr. & Mrs. Timothy Nester & drs.
Mr. & Mrs. Frederick C. Osgood
Mr. & Mrs. B. E. Pike

Mr. & Mrs. Harry C. Powell
George Rannenberg
Mr. & Mrs. H. W. Rannenberg
Frank H. Ray
George A. Reynolds
Albert W. Ryan
Charles L. Ryan
J. W. Ryan
Miss Kate Ryan
Oswald E. Ryan
H. E. Seemueller
F. E. Sergeant
Mr. & Mrs. Lester W. Stevens
William H. Smith
Mr. & Mrs. C. H. Somes
Frederick M. Somes
Will W. Somes
Mr. & Mrs. Charles A. Stephenson & dr.
Mr. & Mrs. L. W. Stevens
Mr. & Mrs. W. R. Stewart, jr.
Mr. & Mrs. M. Straus
John W. Sturtevant
Mr. & Mrs. W. E. Sutherland
Mr. & Mrs. W. A. Waide
H. Winston Walker
Mr. & Mrs. Sheldon W. Warner
William H. Weber
Carl H. Weil
Mr. & Mrs. Ernest Welisch
Mr. & Mrs. H. G. White
H. E. Whitney

HOTEL IMPERIAL.

Michigan Avenue se. cor. 12th.

James H. Barnard
J. L. Bloom
Mr. & Mrs. J. P. Cameron
Miss Harriet Cronkhite
Mr. & Mrs. Louis Curtice
Mr. & Mrs. Horace Fletcher & dr.
J. L. Gerry
Mr. & Mrs. C. C. Grannis
John Harrison
Mr. & Mrs. H. S. Haven
Mr. & Mrs. E. J. Hopson

Miss Frances H. Hopson
Joseph A. Hopson
Julius Kessel
Horace J. Koetser
Mr. & Mrs. W. E. McHenry
Mr. & Mrs. John W. Northrop & dr.
B. Oppenheimer
A. S. Patterson
Theodore Pine
Mr. & Mrs. H. I. Pinney
Mr. & Mrs. J. P. Read

Mr. & Mrs. J. W. Rochlitz
Miss Annie M. Rose
George E. Rose
Mrs. Edith Sexton & drs.
Miss Maude Alison Shaw
Dr. C. F. Smith
C. E. Smithman

Dr. Lot Snoddy
Mr. & Mrs. Joseph Somers
Mrs. H. H. Thorpe
James T. Wall
Mr. & Mrs. Stanley Waterloo
Mr. & Mrs. L. R. Wright
August Yunker

HOTEL METROPOLE.

Michigan Avenue sw. cor. 23d.

John J. Abbott
George J. Adam
Joseph Adams
G. M. Alexander
Miles Almy & dr.
Miss J. E. Ames
Miss V. T. Artz
Mrs. A. B. Barclay
Mrs. D. B. Barnum
Mr. & Mrs. J. H. Bauland
Mr. & Mrs. Thomas M. Baxter
Miss Edith Baxter
Mr. & Mrs. F. J. Berry
Dr. A. D. Bevan
Miss N. G. Bevan
Mr. & Mrs. Eugene Bournique
Lawrence P. Boyle
J. B. Breese
E. W. Brown
Miss Jessie Brown
Mr. & Mrs. J. H. Brown
Mr.&. Mrs. Henry H. Browning
Mr. & Mrs. F. R. Buell
Mr. & Mrs. J. T. Burgess
Mr. & Mrs. J. S. Carter
Miss Kathryn Carter
J. R. Case
George F. Chase
C. C. Clark
C. C. Clark jr.
Mrs. A. Comfort
Samuel C. Curtis
George De Bruyn
Miss H. Dennis
Col. & Mrs. J. T. Dickinson
Dr. & Mrs. E. J. Doering
Dr. & Mrs. W. A. Dunn
Walter Dupee
Mr. & Mrs. John Dupee
Mr. & Mrs. J. M. Durand
Samuel D. Eldridge
Mr. & Mrs. E. Y. Eltonhead
E. Engalitcheff
Mrs. J. M. Eyster

Mr. & Mrs. George Fabyan
Mr. & Mrs. S. G. Field
W. G. Field
G. M. Fisher
Mrs. M. Gage
F. C. Gibbs
F. S. Giles
Mr. & Mrs. J. B. Hart
E. S. Heaton
Col. & Mrs. E. M. Heyl
C. E. Hill
Judge&Mrs. Lysander Hill & dr.
Nelson Hiss
Mrs. J. S. Hodgson
Mrs. L. S. Hood
F. H. Hopkins
T. H. Hulbert
Dr. & Mrs. Stuart Johnstone
J. N. Kalff
Mr. & Mrs. George Keen
William B. Keen jr.
J. A. Kelsey
Mr. & Mrs. F. J. Kennett
R. A. Kettle
Miss Sallie C. King
Mr. & Mrs. G. H. Leatherbee
Charles H. Lester
M. G. Linsley
E. H. Lyons
Miss L. Maddox
J. E. Mann
Mr. & Mrs. A. F. McArthur
J. McCarthy
Mrs. E. McClellan
A. C. McNeill
G. A. Mead
Mrs. S. J. Medill
T. J. Monahan
Mrs. F. H. Murphy
Mr. & Mrs. G. G. Newbury
Mrs. E. L. Nicholson
E. P. Palmer
Miss Mame Palmer
Mr. & Mrs. Williard Pardridge

Mr. & Mrs. ·T. E. Patterson
E. O. Perry
Miss L. Pike
Mr. & Mrs. M. B. Pike
William P. Porter
Mr. & Mrs. Fred K. Pulsifer
Mr. & Mrs. A. N. Raymond
Mr. & Mrs. H. Raymond
Mr. & Mrs. B. J. Rosenthal
Miss Fannie Rothschild
Mrs. M. M. Rothschild
E. Ryder
John Schwender
Mrs. R. S. Scott
Sylvan Siegel
Franklin P. Smith
Mr. & Mrs. Fred A. Smith
Judge & Mrs. Sidney Smith
Miss Fannie Smith
Miss J. Smith
Sidney W. Smith
Theo. Smith
Mrs. W. J. Smith
Mr. & Mrs. F. P. Snyder
Mr. & Mrs. J. L. Stagg

L. R. Stagg
G. S. Steere
Mrs. J. F. Studebaker
Mrs. B. Sumner
Mrs. L. Tewksbury
John M. Thacher
Miss Sarah A. Thacher
Mr. & Mrs. Copeland Townsend
Miss Edith W. Vail
B. A. Walker
Mr. & Mrs. E. C. Walker
H. H. Walker
J. M. Wallingsford
Miss J. Wallingsford
Mrs. H. Weil
Mr. & Mrs. L. Weis
Miss B. Whiting
Mr. & Mrs. C. H. Whiting
Mrs. E. T. Whiting
Miss L. Whiting
Mr. & Mrs. S. T. Williams
J. E. Wisiner
Mr. & Mrs. W. H. Wood
A. S. Work

HOTEL NORMANDIE.

339-341 Michigan Avenue.

C. S. Belden
S. P. Butler
William W. Charles
Eugene D. Cohn
Mr. & Mrs. J. B. Cox
Mr. & Mrs. Wm. A. Delenoy
M. Dupuis
Miss Amaroy Eskridge
Frank G. Gardner
Frederick W. Gardner
Felix Hiller
Charles W. Hyde
Mr. & Mrs. Geo. Jackson
Mr. & Mrs. J. S. A. Judson

Edward F. Leland
Arthur T. Marix
F. G. McCurdy
Frank J. Mulcahy
Mr. & Mrs. F. L. Noble
Dr. J. C. Oakshette
Mr. & Mrs. Geo. Randall
J. F. Rock
L. deB. Spiridon
Mrs. R. C. Stout
Mr. & Mrs. S. D. Thompson
Samuel B. Thompson
Mr. & Mrs. Clarence T. Williams

HOTEL RICHELIEU.

Michigan Avenue bet. Jackson and Van Buren.

Isaac E. Adams
Walter C. Arnold
Mr. & Mrs. Henry V. Bemis .

Mr. & Mrs. T. A. Griffin
Edgar F. Henderson
William B. Keep

HOTEL WINDERMERE.

56th nw. cor. Cornell av.

Prof. & Mrs. F. F. Abbott
Bradford L. Ames
Dr. W. V. B. Ames
Mr. & Mrs. J. K. Andrews
Miss Marie Andrews
C. L. Bartlett
A. C. Battelle
Adolph Bernard
Mr. & Mrs. Robert Bines
Mr. & Mrs. Benjamin Bissinger
Mr. & Mrs. E. J. Blossom
Addison Booth
Mr. & Mrs. Eben Brewer
F. F. Brodix
Mr. & Mrs. E. S. Card
George P. Cary
Mr. & Mrs. Wm. E. Cash
Mr. & Mrs. E. G. Chamberlain
Miss Maude Corbett
Mr. & Mrs. Edward F. Cost
Herbert Cost
Mr. & Mrs. Walter H. Craig
Mr. & Mrs. B. F. Cummins
Mr. & Mrs. Joseph H. Defrees
Mr. & Mrs. Simon Donau
Miss Fidele Donlan
Mr. & Mrs. L. C. Ehle
Edward S. Elliott
Capt. J. W. Evans
Mr. & Mrs. B. M. Freese
Mr. & Mrs. S. R. Fuller & dr.
Beekman Grah'am
Miss Gertrude Guilbert
O. H. Guilbert
Mrs. George R. Haines
E. M. Hardin
Mr. & Mrs. W. P. Healey
Mr. & Mrs. M. O. Higgins
Mr. & Mrs. James M. Hill
L. Hitchcock
Mr. & Mrs. Marshall K. Howe
Mr. & Mrs. A. S. Huey
Clinton Hunter
G. T. Jennings
Merwyn E. Johnston
George B. Jordon
Mr. & Mrs. W. B. Keene jr.
Miss Ethel Keene
A. H. Kennedy
Mr. & Mrs. E. Louis Kuhns
R. P. LaMonte

Walter H. Lee
Mr. & Mrs. G. Russell Leonard
Miss Marion Lowery
T. E. May
Mr. & Mrs. L. D. Mayhew
Mr. & Mrs. James McCabe
Mr. & Mrs. J. J. McClellan
Mr. & Mrs. Herbert C. Metcalf
Thomas Metcalf
Mr. & Mrs. Walter L. Milliken
Prof. E. R. Moulton
Prof. J. U. Nef
Mr. & Mrs. James W. Nye &
   drs.
Lee Olds
Judge & Mrs. Walter Olds
J. A. Ostrom
Mr. & Mrs. Chas. T. Peavey
Miss Eva Pierce
Mr. & Mrs. James A. W. Pine &
   dr.
Miss Lucille M. Potvan
Mr. & Mrs. L. H. Prentice & drs.
Mrs. Eva L. Prescott & dr.
Lieut. & Mrs. Hugh T. Reed
Mr. & Mrs. Chas. K. Reynolds
Russell Reynolds
Mr. & Mrs. George P. Ross
H. B. Sawyer
J. D. Shatford
Prof. & Mrs. F. J. V. Skiff
True L. Sloan
Mrs. M. J. Smith
T. W. Sprague
E. R. Stettinius
J. Q. Symes
Mr. & Mrs. H. G. Thornton
R. F. Vogt
Arthur H. Walker
Mr. & Mrs. E. P. Warner
John E. Waters
Mr. & Mrs. M. D. Watson
Miss Mary Watson
Thomas Watson jr.
Mr. & Mrs. C. O. Webster
Mrs. R. W. Winslow
Mr. & Mrs. Homer Wise
T. F. Woodman
C. K. Wooster
Henry Work
Clinton S. Zimmerman

24

HYDE PARK HOTEL.

Fifty-first sw. cor. Lake Avenue.

Mr. & Mrs. William Amos
Mrs. E. M. Andrews
Dr. & Mrs. A. G. Bailey
F. H. Boynton
F. M. Brinkerhoff
H. M. Brinkerhoff
Mr. & Mrs. E. Carrington & dr.
J. W. Carruth
Mr. & Mrs. C. J. Clark
Mrs. S. C. Clark
Mr. & Mrs. John E. Cornell
Mr. & Mrs. W. D. Cram
Mrs. E. E. Crampton
Mr. & Mrs. A. W. Crawford
Mr. & Mrs. L. M. Crump
G. C. K. Culmer
Mr. & Mrs. G. F. Culmer
Mr. & Mrs. Thos. Cunningham
Miss Bessie Darling
Mrs. Ira C. Darling
J. T. Davis
Miss Rena De Camp
Mr. & Mrs. Nathan Deutsch
Mr. & Mrs. W. H. Drake
D. C. Franche
F. C. Giddings
Robert Gordon
T. Gorman
Mr. & Mrs. A. M. Grose
Paul J. Healey
Raymond J. Healey
Mr. & Mrs. J. W. Hiner
Mr. & Mrs. J. M. Hodge
S. J. Holland
I. W. Holman
Mr. & Mrs. Thos. D. Knight
Mr. & Mrs. H. M. Lane
Mr. & Mrs. J. W. Leis

Mr. & Mrs. Mark T. Leonard
Mr. & Mrs. E. N. Lewis
H. C. Lewis
William Lewis
Mr. & Mrs. Albert Liebenstein
J. E. Lukins
Capt. & Mrs. W. L. Marshall
Irving G. McCall
W. B. McElevey
Sanford McKeeby
J. T. Mercier
F. A. Miller
C. F. Milligan
Mrs. Harry Morgan
Mr. & Mrs. H. A. Morse
Mr. & Mrs. J. R. Norton
Miss H. O'Callahan
G. A. P. Oliver
J. B. Oliver
Richard Oliver
E. E. Perley
Mr. & Mrs. L. E. Pollock
Mr. & Mrs. E. H. Salisbury
Mr. & Mrs. G. S. Scofield
Mr. & Mrs. C. F. Scovill
Mr. & Mrs. S. Sharp & dr.
Mr. & Mrs. Joseph B. Simpson
Miss Edna Smith
Mr. & Mrs. S. T. Smith
Miss L. E. Smythe
Mr. & Mrs. C. Stickney
Mr. & Mrs. R. H. Talbott
Mrs. A. G. Thayer
C. G. Thayer
C. H. Thayer
Miss E. VandeVenter
P. T. White
T. S. Wilmarth & dr.

JULIEN HOTEL.

Cor. Sixty-third and Stewart Avenue.

Mr. & Mrs. J. T. Alexander&drs.
F. E. Armour
A. W. Axtell
F. A. Baux
Mr. & Mrs. S. H. Bechtole
Thomas Boesch
Mr. & Mrs. M. A. Boles
J. K. Brittain
Mr. & Mrs. A. W. Campbell

Mrs. S. E. Cougle
Mrs. M. E. Crissey
J. Danner
M. H. Dey
Mrs. M. J. Glass
Miss G. Hauk
Mr. & Mrs. J. B. Hill
C. S. Jones
Dr. F. A. Larkin

Mr. & Mrs. O. J. May
George E. Nichols
H. M. North
Frank Nunamaker
H. C. Orem
T. P. Scott
T. Shellenback
Mr. & Mrs. W. A. Sumner

P. Thomson
William Tillinghast
Mr. & Mrs. B. Timmerman
Mr. & Mrs. J. M. Warner
R. G. Watt
Miss E. L. Webb
R. E. Wood

LAKOTA HOTEL.

Michigan av. se. cor. 30th

George J. Adams
R. H. Austin
Fred R. Babcock
Mr. & Mrs. W. L. Barnum
Mr. & Mrs. N. W. Beidler
Mrs. C. W. Belden & dr.
Mrs. L. S. Belding
Mr. & Mrs. A. O. Bradley
Mr. & Mrs. Geo. S. Bullock
Mr. & Mrs. M. Burke
Frank W. Buskirk
Mrs. John B. Carson
Mr. & Mrs. G. S. Chapin
Miss K. Chapin
Mrs. J. D. Chapman
Mrs. H. D. Compton
O. C. Cleave
Mrs. Ira Couch
Ira J. Couch
Count & Countess DeBrazza
Dr. George J. Dennis
A. L. Dillenbeck
H. S. Downs
Mr. & Mrs. Calvin M. Favorite
Mrs. W. M. Ford
Mr. & Mrs. O. G. Foreman
George F. Getz
J. Haines
Mr. & Mrs. J. E. Hall
Mr. & Mrs. D. H. Hammer
W. H. Harper & drs.
W. J. Haynes
James E. Healy
Mr. & Mrs. Chas. C. Hilton
George L. Hilton
Mr. & Mrs. Jno. R. Hoxie & dr.
Mr. & Mrs. C. S. Hutchins
Miss Martha Johnstone
Mr. & Mrs. J. S. Jones
W. H. Kaufman
Mr. & Mrs. E. D. Kenna
Mrs. Mark Kimball
Mr. & Mrs. C. E. Kremer

C. F. Langdon
Denis Leahy
Miss E. Long
J. B. Long
Miss F. M. Lund
Mr. & Mrs. Godfrey MacDonald
H. W. Magill
Mr. & Mrs. Geo. W. Mathews
T. S. McInerney
Dr. & Mrs. John McKinlock
Mr. & Mrs. J. W. Merriam & dr.
Mr. & Mrs. Geo. L. Miller
Judge & Mrs. Jas. Hobart Moore
Mr. & Mrs. Edward Morris
Judge Joseph A. Murphy
Mrs. H. H. Nash
Mr. & Mrs. W. P. Nelson
Gen. Thomas O. Osborne
Mr. & Mrs. Malcolm D. Owen
Mrs. J. A. Parish
Col. & Mrs. W. N. Pelouze
Mr. & Mrs. J. P. Primley
Dr. A. R. Reynolds
Mr. & Mrs. Geo. L. Rhodes
Mr. & Mrs. J. Foster Rhodes
Mr. & Mrs. R. J. Richardson
R. W. Richardson
Mr. & Mrs. D. B. Robinson & dr.
H. H. Robinson
J. B. Robinson
Mr. & Mrs. J. K. Robinson & drs.
Miss Lena Robinson
Harry Rockwood
Mr. & Mrs. W. H. Rockwood
E. O. Seymour
Henry Siegel & dr.
Mr. & Mrs. D. J. Simpson & dr.
Mr. & Mrs. J. O. Smith
E. A. Still
Mr. & Mrs. E. F. Swift
Gale Thompson
Mrs. M. G. Thompson
W. H. Thompson

Mr. & Mrs. James S. Toppan
Mr. & Mrs. S. A. Treat
Mr. & Mrs. W. P. Tuttle
Mrs. T. Underwood
W. T. Underwood

Morris E. Ward
Phil Wechsler
Mr. & Mrs. C. B. White
Mr. & Mrs. L. G. Willner
Mr. & Mrs. E. E. Worthington

LELAND HOTEL.

Michigan Avenue sw. cor. Jackson Street.

T. H. Brigg
Mr. & Mrs. Samuel Burdett
George Carroll
Mr. & Mrs. J. M. Connelly
C. J. Crawford
John F. Crisp
John S. Cowan
Mrs. K. Davidson
M. A. Eddy
J. A. Gaston
L. J. Gilbert
W. C. Gregory
Mrs. Florence Huntley

Mr. & Mrs. Samuel Johnson
Mr. & Mrs. H. F. Kittredge
Mr. & Mrs. L. A. Kittredge
George H. Lally
H C. Logan
James Lyons
Mr. & Mrs. W. B. Miller
B. S. Packard
Mr. & Mrs. C. H. Platt
Mr. & Mrs. E. V. Price
Mrs. O. C. Russell
H. A. Wambold
H. H. Whitney

LEXINGTON HOTEL.

Michigan Avenue ne. cor. Twenty-second.

Mrs. M. N. Abbott
Albert M. Adams
Capt. James Allen
J. H. Andrews
Mr. & Mrs. E. A. Bacheldor
C. E. Barnes
Miss Catherine Bass
Mr. & Mrs. Frank E. Bird
Mr. & Mrs. Harry St. Francis
　Black
S. Block
Lieut. & Mrs. George P. Blow
Mr. & Mrs. Charles E. Borden
Mr. & Mrs. J. Harley Bradley &
　drs.
Gordon Buchanan
Mr. & Mrs. M. D. Buchanan
Miss Daisy Buchanan
Miss Mary Buchanan
H. W. Buckingham
George E. Buell
J. A. Bunnell
J. E. Burke
Miss J. B. Chappel
Mr. & Mrs. J. T. Chumasero
K. P. Chumasero
Townsend V. Church
Mr. & Mrs. E. A. Clark

Thomas C. Clark
Clinton Collier
Mrs. N. Corwith & dr.
Mr. & Mrs. R. S. Cox
Mr. & Mrs. W. N. Craine
H. C. Crawz
J. C. Curtis
W. J. Dee
E. John Degge
John C. DeMille
Mr. & Mrs. J. M. Denniston
Mr. & Mrs. J. J. Driscoll
Mr. & Mrs. Martin Emerich
Joseph Fels
Joseph M. Garson
Mrs. C. H. Gibbs
Col. & Mrs. J. H. Gilman & dr.
Mr. & Mrs. H. K. Gilman
E. R. Gilman
Mr. & Mrs. R. C. Givins
R. S. Givins
J. B. Goodman
Mrs. Artie Goodwin
Hugh Goodwin
Mr. & Mrs. H. C. Gray
Mr. & Mrs. S. C. Griggs & dr.
Miss Carolyn A. Griggs
Mr. & Mrs. C. H. Gurney

Mrs. G. M. Haller
Mr. & Mrs. Joseph Harris
Dr. & Mrs. A. Hartsoff & dr.
Mr. & Mrs. C. S. Hartwell
Mr. & Mrs. Chas. T. Haughey
Benjamin Hillman
Edward Hillman
Louis Hillman
Miss Sarah Hillman
R. A. Hitchcock
Mr. & Mrs. Seth B. Howes
Dr. & Mrs. Joseph Hughes
Dr. J. D. Hunter
Mr. & Mrs. Laurin Ingles
E. B. Jennings
G. F. Jennings
Mrs. E. L. Johnson
C. S. Kahn
Fred Kauffman
Mr. & Mrs. J. B. Ketcham
C. A. Knight
Mr. & Mrs. W. S. Knight
Mr. & Mrs. C. L. Lancaster
C. H. Lane
Fred W. Lipe
Frank O. Lowden
Mrs. M. E. Lutz
Dr. J. Grant Lyman
Mr. & Mrs. Louis Manheimer
Walter Mattocks
C. R. McCorkle
James C. McShane
Mr. & Mrs. J. H. Michener
Mr. & Mrs. George Miller
John Morris
Mr. & Mrs. M. Neumann & dr.
Mrs. John F. Nichols
Mr. & Mrs. Walter L. Peck
Mr. & Mrs. E. H. Phelps
Mr. & Mrs. H. E. Pitkin
Mr. & Mrs. J. B. Reeme & dr.
Mr. & Mrs. F. Willis Rice

A. A. Riley
Mr. & Mrs. O. H. Roche
Dr. & Mrs. E. O. F. Roler
W. L. Roloson
G. A. Rose
H. H. Rose
L. C. Rose
J. R. W. Sargent
Mrs. L. C. Rose
Miss A. Sawyer
Charles H. Scott
Mr. & Mrs. Washington M. Shaddinger
Mr. & Mrs. Horace M. Singer
H. J. Slater
Burton Smith
Edward L. Smith
Mr. & Mrs. O. C. Smith
Rev. & Mrs. E. M. Stires
Mr. & Mrs. A. S. Strauss
Mrs. Marian Strong
W. H. Sweet
Mrs. D. Thornton
Dr. R. Tilley
Mrs. J. C. Turner
Dr. & Mrs. R. T. VanPelt
A. H. Walker
J. F. Watson
Mr. & Mrs. A. Weil
M. Wendell
Mr. & Mrs. C. Gilbert Wheeler
L. E. Wheeler
F. M. Whitbeck
William M. Whitehead
J. C. Whitney
L. K. Whiton
W. S. Whiton
William B. Wirt
Mr. & Mrs. Theron R. Woodward
Miss Harriet V. Woodward

NEW HOTEL HOLLAND.

Lake Avenue nw. cor. Fifty-third.

J. Lewis Alabaster
Mr. & Mrs. Frank B. Bort
   Receiving day Wednesday
Miss Mabel E. Bort
Mr. & Mrs. George Burgess .
Mr. & Mrs. L. Clark
Mr. & Mrs. R. G. Clymer
Mr. & Mrs. Wm. Culbertson
George L. Dyer

Mr. & Mrs. G. W. Fitch
James S. Graham
T. J. Heller
Mr. & Mrs. Edgar M. Madden
Mr. & Mrs. J. J. Marshall
Mr. & Mrs. R. W. McCann
Dr. & Mrs. Louis Ottofy
Mr. & Mrs. S. Q. Perry & dr.
Mr. & Mrs. R. C. Reed

Charles E. Rollo
B. H. Rose
Edward H. Sanford
Miss Ella R. Sanford
Mr. & Mrs. C. W. Scott
Mr. & Mrs. S. P. Smith

Charles M. Stratton
Mr. & Mrs. C. T. Trueheart
Mr. & Mrs. John Turnbull & dr.
Mr. & Mrs. F. C. Willis
Mr. & Mrs. W. J. Wisdom

THE ONTARIO.
118 North State.

Mr. & Mrs. A. W. Allen
Miss May Allport
H. W. Berg
Charles Buford
Mrs. J. L. Clark
Hugh Crabbe
Mr. & Mrs. Wm. Dickinson
A. I. Freeman
Mr. & Mrs. Paul Gores
Frederick S. Hebard
G. C. Hempstead
F. Horton
Mr. & Mrs. J. H. McConnell
C. J. Miller

Maynard Miller
Mr. & Mrs. W. T. Morgan
Mr. & Mrs. H. L. Norton
Horace S. Oakley
Mr. & Mrs. John R. Pruyn
Mr. & Mrs. Carver Remington
Alex. Robertson
Alphonso B. Shubert
George M. Wallace
Mr. & Mrs. T. B. Wilcox
Simeon B. Williams & drs.
J. E. Woodbridge
Kimball Young
Miss Nellie Young

PALMER HOUSE.
State se. cor. Monroe.

Mr. & Mrs. J. M. Arnold
 Receiving day Tuesday
Samuel S. Barlow
Dr. Robert D'Unger
Mr. & Mrs. Joseph R. Dunlop
Mr. & Mrs. H. F. Eames
Dr. & Mrs. C. S.Eldredge
Dr. A. E. Evans
 Receiving day Thursday
Charles F. Foskett
Miss Sara T. Hallowell
Herman J. Huiskamp
George A. Lederle

Dr. Elmer Lee
Dr. M. D. Ogden
Miss Florence Olmsted
Mr. & Mrs. Benj. P. Price
Mr. & Mrs. C. M. Ratzel
R. C. Rounsville
Mr. & Mrs. H. L. Seixas
Mr. & Mrs. T. P. Tallman
Mr. & Mrs. Wm. H. Turner &
 dr.
William Vierbuchen
Mr. & Mrs. J. N. Wetherill

REVERE HOUSE.
N. Clark se. cor. Michigan st.

John H. Barnett
Ernest F. Bunn
Miss Emma Cassing
Mr. & Mrs. James Conlan
James Conlan jr.
Joseph P. Conlan
John A. Cooper
Mr. & Mrs. J. H. Currier

Robert Hooley
Mr. & Mrs. W. J. Maxwell
J. McFadden
Mr. & Mrs. E. A. Potter
Mr. & Mrs. James E. Purnell
Mr. & Mrs. H. T. Russell
George A. Sperry

SHERMAN HOUSE.
Clark nw. cor. Randolph.

Harry L. Allen
J. A. Andregg
C. C. Barrett
H. S. Cantrovitz
S. Cantrovitz
Mr. & Mrs. M. Conrad
E. W. Denaby
Mr. & Mrs. S. E. Douglas
Frank Hart
D. Ferguson Jennings
Mr. & Mrs. Bernard H. Kemper
James C. King

W. E. Parsons
Mr. & Mrs. John Irving Pearce jr
Mr. & Mrs. J. Irving Pearce
Myron Pearce
William C. Pierce
N. E. Platt
S. D. Prouty
W. J. Richardson
Judge S. P. Shope
J. E. Sturges
William Wyles

SOUTHERN HOTEL.
Wabash ave. nw. cor. 22d

Thomas Baird
Dr. & Mrs. W. C. Clarke
Mr. & Mrs. Walter Elfelt
James H. Ferguson
Dr. E. W. Hunter
J. Francis Lee

David F. Reid
Marc Reynolds
W. A. Thompson
Mr. & Mrs. B. Waterloo
A. C. Wilkie

STAMFORD HOTEL.
1254 Michigan ave.

S. Z. Akamatsaa
Mr. & Mrs. Wm. Ambridge
H. J. Bardwell
Eugenc C. Bianchini
F. W. Bleuchyndell
R. Bleuchyndell
D. L. Clinch

Albert E. Jessurum
Carl Levi
Prof. G. Mantellini
Prof. A. Patricolo
Hardwick Peres
G. VonReinholts
Frederick N. Williams

TREMONT HOUSE.
Dearborn se. cor. Lake.

C. W. Angell
B. M. Callender
Mr. & Mrs. L. H. Clark
Martin Dawson
Dr. & Mrs. C. A. Logan

Mr. & Mrs. C. H. Matthews
A. W. Paige
Charles F. Rapp
F. F. Toynton

VICTORIA HOTEL.
Michigan Avenue nw. cor. Vanburen

Walter Barnes
H. M. Cable
L. H. Eames
Mr. & Mrs. H. E. Felton

Mrs. F. Haskell
Charles A. Munson
J. C. Walker

THE VIRGINIA HOTEL.

Rush and Ohio.

Mrs. A. W. Bailey
Frank T. Baird
Mrs. William D. Brall
Mr. & Mrs. Arthur Britton
Miss C. A. Britton
Mr. & Mrs. E. A. Burdette
K. Buenz
Mr. & Mrs. J. H. Chandler & dr.
Mr. & Mrs. S. S. Chisholm
Mr. & Mrs. W. D. Cole
W. G. Collins
Mr. & Mrs. Charles S. Colton
Mrs. Geo. N. Culver
C. H. Cutting
Mr. & Mrs. F. S. Delafield
Mr. & Mrs. F. C. Donald
Mr. & Mrs. Frank M. Douglass
Mr. & Mrs. R. P. H. Durkee
Mrs. C. H. Dyer
George T. Dyer
Mr. & Mrs. R. D. Eakin
Mr. & Mrs. E. T. Earl
Miss Mella Everhart
Mr. & Mrs. J. I. Farish
Mr. & Mrs. Robert B. Farson
Mr. & Mrs. Edward Inglis Frost
M. S. Frost
Mr. & Mrs. Fred E. Goodhart
John R. Gott
F. F. Greene
John F. Harris
Mrs. Rachael A. Harris
Miss Laura M. Harris
Mr. & Mrs. John R. Harvey
Dr. A. W. Hebert
Mr. & Mrs. C. M. Hewitt
Mrs. G. F. Hillman
Mr. & Mrs. R. G. Holmes
Jarvis Hunt
Eustace Jaques
Col. & Mrs. H. M. Kidder
W. T. Kirk
Mrs. Mary J. Larned
Miss Frances Larned
Mr. & Mrs. E. S. Lenox
Mr. & Mrs. Henry V. Lester
Mr. & Mrs. Robert T. Loomis
Mr. & Mrs. A. M. Loring

Mr. & Mrs. S. F. McCall
Mr. & Mrs. Leander J. McCormick
H. S. Mecartney
A. Meinrath
N. W. Meserole
Mr. & Mrs. Gurdon G. Moore
Miss Mullholland
Mr. & Mrs. C. H. Mulliken
Mr. & Mrs. Edwin Norton
Mr. & Mrs. Andrew Onderdonk
Mr. & Mrs. C. E. Palmer
Mr. & Mrs. James H. Parker
Mr. & Mrs. P. P. Paxton
Mrs. R. T. Peck
Mr. & Mrs. J. P. Perrish
Mrs. Charles Pope
Dr. & Mrs. E. H. Pratt
Mr. & Mrs. W. G. Randall
Mr. & Mrs. Samuel B. Raymond
Lowry B. Raymond
William W. Raymond
Mr. & Mrs. Wm. H. Bankes Rice
Mr. & Mrs. W. F. Roos
Col Ralph H. Hayes Sadler
Mr. & Mrs. Walter A. Scott
Mr. & Mrs. M. L. Shoemaker
Mr. & Mrs. LeGrande Smith
F. B. Stephenson
Mr. & Mrs. B. H. Thomas
Mr. & Mrs. John D. Thompsoa
Mr. & Mrs. J. A. Wakefield
Miss Marion F. Wales
Mrs. Peter Walker
Mr. & Mrs. Franklin Watriss
Mr. & Mrs. Lewis D. Webster
Mr. & Mrs. L. W. Wellington
Mr. & Mrs. James P. Whedon
Mr. & Mrs. George W. White
Mr. & Mrs. P. R. Whitridge
Mr. & Mrs. H. C. Wicker & dr.
Mr. & Mrs. B. M. Wilson
Mrs. John Wilson
Clarence M. Woolley
Mr. & Mrs. George Z. Work
George R. Work
Mr. & Mrs. H. T. Wright
Mr & Mrs. C. C. Yoe

THE WELLINGTON.

Wabash Avenue ne. cor. Jackson.

Mr. & Mrs. S. Ansbach
Charles C. Carhart
Mr. & Mrs. C. E. Cass
B. W. Dawley
Miss L. C. Feeser
Mr. & Mrs. Albert S. Gage
Mr. & Mrs. E. J. M. Hale
Miss Josephene Holden
N. S. Jones
Benjamin H. Kaufman
Abraham Lamm

Miss Mary McMahon
Mrs. L. K. Norton
Mr. & Mrs. D. S. Pate
Dr. G. A. Ransom
W. H. Schimpferman
W. H. Singer
L. L. Smith
Mr. & Mrs. Edgar Terhune
C. F. Whiting
Joseph Wolf

Chicago Directory Company

ROOMS 2, 3 & 4 LAKESIDE BUILDING,
CLARK, S. W. COR. ADAMS STREETS.

Publishers......

"Lakeside" City Directory of Chicago.

Containing full, General and Classified Lists. Street Guide, Miscellaneous Information, etc. Issued annually, July 15. Price $7.50.

"Lakeside" Business Directory of Chicago.

Containing Alphabetical and Classified Lists of all Persons and Firms doing business in Chicago; Street Guide, Miscellaneous Information, etc. Issued annually, August 1st. Price $2.50.

Chicago Blue Book.

Containing 25,000 names and addresses of Prominent residents of Chicago and Suburbs, arranged alphabetically and numerically by streets; also containing full list of Members of all the Prominent Clubs, Ladies' Shopping Guide, and much other valuable information. Issued annually in December. Price $3.00.

Chicago Securities.

A Digest of Information relative to Stocks, Bonds, Banks and Financial Institutions of Chicago. Issued annually in April. Price $2.00.

"Lakeside" Street and Ave. Guide of Chicago.

A complete List of all Streets, Avenues, Boulevards, Street Numbers and how to find them. Issued annually. Price 25 cts.

Chicago Directory Company's Maps of Chicago.
25 cts., 50 cts., $1.00, $2.00 and $3.00.

A full file of the Latest Directories of all the other Large Cities can be found at our office for use of the public.

378

HAZEN'S MANDOLIN ORCHESTRA

MUSIC FURNISHED FOR WEDDINGS, RECEPTIONS, ENTERTAINMENTS, ETC.
THE LARGEST AND MOST SELECT REPERTOIRE IN THE CITY.

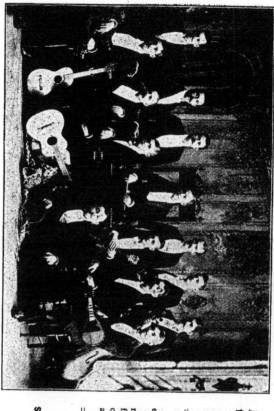

**Music arranged
for Clubs.**

*Songs Transposed
and Copied.*

The Orchestra is available
either in or out of town.
A specialty is made of furnishing a complete programme,
furnishing in addition to orchestra, Vocal and Instrumental Soloists.

W. L. Hazen, Director.

STUDIO--------
ROOM 74 KIMBALL HALL,
243 WABASH AVE.

379

S AND SOCIETIES.

BLUE BOOK.

TORS, AND ACTIVE MEMBERS OF
INENT CLUBS AND SOCIETIES
HICAGO AND SUBURBS.

CLUBS.

ACACIA CLUB.

105 ASHLAND BOULEVARD.

OFFICERS.

JOHN CORSON SMITH, - - - - - - President.
D. J. AVERY, - - - - First Vice-President.
CYRUS B. PLATTENBURG, - Second Vice-President.
C. S. GURNEY, - - - - - - - Secretary.
S. T. GUNDERSON - - - - - Treasurer.

DIRECTORS.

John Corson Smith	Wm. Johnston	F. C. Roundy
Hugh Mason	G. W. Warvelle	Cyrus B. Plattenburg
D. J. Avery	L. C. Riggs	Daniel A. Arnold
Gorham B. Coffin	Henry Baker	Chester T. Drake

MEMBERS.

Arnold D. A.	Franks H. J.	McDonnell Chas.	Salter Allen
Avery D. J.	Furst Henry jr.	McIntosh J. F.	Sampson C. B.
Baker Henry	Galpin H. B.	McPherson H. H.	Saunders E.
Baldwin C. W.	Griffin Z. T.	Miller T. E.	Shepard H. O.
Bassler E.	Gunderson S. T.	Moore Jas. A.	Sheridan W. G.
Beckley W. G.	Gurney C. S.	Moore W. J.	Sherrard F. R.
Beusch John	Halbe C. F.	Morey A. G.	Shoemaker C. W.
Blanchard G. W.	Halpin T. P.	Moulton Geo. M.	Shoemaker Walter
Brock A. J.	Hammond J. D.	Muns A.	Simpson S. D.
Butler G. F.	Harper George	Nason W. T.	Simsrott W. A.
Clarke W. W.	Harris G. P.	Offerman C. C.	Smith John C.
Coffin G. B.	Harris S. R.	Onderdonk Jas.	Smith W. A.
D'Allmaine Chas.	Haskins C. C.	Overmeyer John B.	Smith W. R.
Dart William	Henriques J. E.	Painter J. A.	Sweet E. C.
Donley W. E.	Holzman L. J.	Passmore J. E.	Tenney J. F.
Drake C. T.	Hunter H. D.	Plattenburg C. B.	Thornburg H. L.
Drewett R. J.	Hupp J. M.	Quanstrom J. F.	Tobey John D.
Dryer H. W.	Jackson G. W.	Randolph S. M.	Varnum Clark
Duddleston Geo.	Johnston John	Rankin C. W.	Voltz D. W.
Eastland L. J.	Johnston William	Reiss Otto	Walduck C. W.
Eddy G. D.	LeRoy E. W.	Rice N. B.	Warvelle G. W.
Eddy A. M.	Livingston J. C.	Riggs L. C.	Weidig Geo.
Edmanson Jas.	Lydston G. Frank	Rogers F. D.	Wethey J. R.
Ellis E. D.	Lyke J. W.	Root J. Sherman	Wilder Nathan
Evans H. J.	Lyman W. C.	Ross C. E.	Williams G. A.
Fennimore Wm.	Many S. G.	Rothe C. W.	Williams James
Forsyth W. K.	Mason Hugh	Roundy F. C.	Wolff J. F.
Framhein L. W.	McClurg A. H.	Rydell J. S.	Wyman H. J.

AMATEUR MUSICAL CLUB.

OFFICERS.

MRS. GEO. B. CARPENTER, - - - -	President.
MRS. FRANK GORTON, - - - -	Vice-President.
MISS KATHARINE D. KRIEGH, - - - -	Secretary.
MISS EDA F. SYMONDS, - - - -	Treasurer.

EXECUTIVE COMMITTEE.

Mrs. Hugh Birch   Miss Frances D. Gould
Mrs. J. A. Farwell   Miss Neuberger
Mrs. E. H. Brush

MEMBERS.

Abbott Miss Anna K.
Adams Miss Harriet M.
Addison Mrs. J.
Adsit Miss Jeanie M.
Allinson Mrs. L. W.
Allport Miss May
Ayer Mrs. E. E.
Bagg Mrs. F. S.
Balfour Mrs. J.
Bangs Mrs. Fred. A.
Barbour Mrs. Edward
Barrett Miss M.
Bartlett Mrs. J. C.
Batcheldor Mrs. O. R.
Beardslee Miss
Benter Miss A. S.
Bigelow Mrs. E. A.
Bingham Mrs. A. E.
Birch Mrs. Hugh T.
Bradley Mrs. Philip
Bragg Miss A. P.
Brauckman Miss M.
Bremner Mrs. Benj. E,
Brouse Mrs. M. C.
Brush Mrs. E. H.
Buck Miss Grace
Bulkley Miss Helen E.
Burnet Miss Anna L.
Burr Mrs. L. E.
Burton Mrs. H. M.
Butterfield Mrs.
Cable Mrs. H. D.
Cameron Mrs. Margaret
Campbell Mrs. Courtney
Campbell Mrs. D. W.
Campbell Mrs. Treat
Canfield Miss Nellie
Carpenter Mrs. Geo. B.
CarpenterMrs.G.Benedict
Carpenter Miss
Castle Miss Florence
Chappell Mrs. H.
Clark Mrs. J. M.
Clark Mrs. Melville
Clarke Miss C. N.
Clarke Miss J. A.
Clarke Mrs. Robert G.
Coburn Mrs. L. L.
Cones Mrs. N.
Coolbaugh Miss W.

Coolidge Mrs. F. S.
Cornell Mrs. John E.
Crow Miss F. G.
Cruttenden Miss Ada
Cudahy Miss C.
Custer Mrs. J. R.
Davis Mrs. W. L.
Driver Miss H.
Duruo Miss Nettie
Eddy Miss F. M.
Eisendrath Mrs. J. N.
Ely Mrs. C. F.
Englemann Dr. Rosa
Farwell Mrs J. A.
Fordham Miss L.
Frank Mrs. Henry L.
Frasher Mrs. Edw.
Freer Mrs.
Fuller Mrs. E. M.
Gardner Mrs. H. H.
Gibbs Mrs. James S.
Gilman Miss Catherine
Gilpin Mrs. T. E.
Gorton Mrs. E. F.
Gorton Mrs. F. S.
Gould Miss F. D.
Gray Miss Anna M.
Green Miss E. C.
Groff Miss A. K.
Haass Mrs. H. E.
Hackney Miss Mae
Haines M s. C. J.
Hale Miss H.
Hale Miss Mary
Hall Mrs. F. G.
Harding Miss A.
Harvey Mrs G. V.
Hawley Miss J. M.
Hickox Mrs. C. V.
Hiner Mrs. J. W.
Hinkley Mrs. J. O.
Hinman Miss
Hoagland Miss J.
Horst Mrs. Louis
Howard Mrs. F. A.
Hoyt Mrs. A. W.
Hubbard Mrs. W. H.
Hudson Mrs. Charles
Hunkins Miss Virginia
Hunt Mrs. James A.

Hurr Miss Ruby
Hutchins Mrs. A. E.
Hypes Mrs. W. F.
Jenks Mrs. W. S.
Jennings Miss Maud
Johnson Mrs. O. K.
Jones Mrs. Ben C.
Kelley Miss A. S.
Kennard Miss
Kimball Mrs. M. D.
King Mrs. Ella
King Mrs. Francis
King Miss Fanny
King Miss Jennie
Knickerbocker Mrs. H.
Knickerbockei Miss
Knott Miss Marie
Kreigh MissKatharine D
Krum Mrs. C. L.
Large Miss J.
Larrabee Miss C.
Lawson Mrs. W. C.
Leidigh Miss C.
Leonard Mrs. Mark T.
Lord Mrs. Geo. S.
Lynde Mrs. S. A.
Magnus Mrs. Rudolph
Markee Mrs. Wm.
Mason Mrs. A. O.
Matz Mrs. Rudolph
McClure Mrs. F. H.
McGrath Mrs. John
McIlvaine Mrs. W. D.
McLane Miss Marie
McLaughlin Mrs. R.
Means Mrs. Joseph O.
Medill Mrs. Sam
Meeker Miss Katheryn
Merrick Miss Gertrude
Methot Mrs. M. D.
Miner Miss H. H.
Mitchell Miss W.
Mockridge Mrs. Whitney
Moore Mrs. James H.
Moore Mrs. James S.
Morse Miss May
Moss Miss F. W.
Murphy Miss Veronica
Nellis Miss C. B.
Neuberger Miss

Newton Mrs. H. S.
Noyes Mrs. G. E.
Noyes Mrs. W. S.
Officer Miss
Olcott Miss Grace
Packard Mrs. H. D.
Palmer Miss Helen
Phillips Miss Daisy
Pinckard Miss
Pincoffs Mrs. M.
Prickett Mrs. G. N.
Pulsifer Mrs. G. R.
Purdy Mrs. Chas. W.
Putnam Miss Alice
Rasmus Miss S.
Remmer Mrs. Oscar B.
Rexford Miss L.
Richards Miss May L.
Richardson Mrs. R. E.
Robb Mrs. A. M.
Roelle Miss Emma
Roman Miss Louisa

Rommeiss Mrs. Pauline
Root Miss Jessie F.
Root Miss Grace
Rust Miss Mary
Seeboeck Mrs. W. C. E.
Selfridge Mrs. H. G.
Shippen Miss K. M.
Smith Miss A. M.
Smith Mrs. A. P.
Smith Mrs. Frank M.
Sperry Mrs. Elmer A.
Starr Mrs. Chandler
Starr Miss Flora
Stearns Mrs. R. I.
Steever Mrs. J. G.
St. John Miss E.
Sturckow Miss T.
Summy Mrs. C. F.
Swabacher Mrs. I.
Symonds Miss E. F.
Temple Miss Grace
Thacker Mrs. J. Frank

Thomas Mrs. Theodore
Thomson Miss Mary P.
Trego Mrs. C. H.
Trimble Mrs. C. G.
Troost Miss Louise
Ullmann Mrs. F.
Underwood Mrs. A. W.
Vaughan Mrs. Thomas
Wadsworth Miss G.
Walker Mrs. W. S.
Warren Mrs. Wm. S.
Wheeler Mrs. Frances G.
Wheeler Miss Helen D
Whiting Miss Olive
Wicker Mrs. Charles
Wood Miss S. E.
Wood Mrs. W. F.
Yoe Miss C. W.
Zeisler Mrs. Joseph
Zeisler Miss
Zimmerman Mrs. O.

THE ARGONAUTS.

THE ARGO, RANDOLPH STREET VIADUCT.

OFFICERS.

FRANKLIN H. WATRISS, - - - - - Skipper.
J. HENRY NORTON, - - - - - - - First Mate.
FRANK H. RAY, - - - - - Jack o' the Dust.
JAMES DEERING, }
JOSEPH LEITER, } - - - - - Mates.

MEMBERS.

Armour Allison V.
Barnes Charles H.
Beale William G.
Blair Watson F.
Burnham Dan'l H.
Caton Arthur J.
Chalmers Wm. J.
Chatfield - Taylor
  Hobart
Deering Charles
Deering James
Dodge Geo. E. P.
Eames Frederic S.
Ely Arthur C.

Fish Stuyvesant
Fisher Archie J.
FlemmingRob't D.
Forsythe Robert
Gorton Frank S.
Howe James T.
Hunt Robert R.
Insull Samuel
Johnson Clifford P.
Keep Frederic A.
Kirk Milton W.
Leiter Joseph
Macdonald Chas.B.
McFarlandHenryJ.

McKay James R.
McNally Andrew
Morse Jay C.
Norton J. Henry
OnderdonkAndrew
PattersonRobertW
  jr.
Parmelee John W.
Phelps Erskine M.
Ray Frank H.
Raymond Sam'l B.
Ryerson EdwardL.
Schwartz Gust. A.

Scott James W.
Stevenson Chas. A.
Stone Henry B.
Switzer Edward M.
Tracy William W.
WatrissFranklinH.
Wheeler Chas. W.
Wheeler George H.
Wheeler H. A.
Willits George S.
Worthington Ed-
  ward S.
Yale Julien

ASHLAND CLUB.

575 WASHINGTON BOULEVARD.

OFFICERS.

FREDERICK W. GRIFFIN, - - - - President.
EDWARD M. SPERBECK, - - First Vice-President.
GEORGE F. BARKER, - - Second Vice-President.
EDWIN W. CHANDLER, - - - - Treasurer.
PHILIP M. BOBB, - - - - - Secretary.

DIRECTORS.

Fred J. Dennis
George L. Shuman

Charles P. Abbey
Edward J. Rogerson

George O. Gunderson
Joseph H. Chamberlain

Abbey Charles P.	Butler J. Fred.	Driggs Arthur W.	Hubbard L. Myers
Adams S. H. Allen	Butzow Robert C.	Duffy Geo.	Humphrey A. O.
Alden Wm. T.	Caile John E.	Duhn J. Carrington	Hunt J. N.
Allcock Geo. E.	Campbell A. M.	Dunwell Wm. C.	Hurdle A. Lansing
Allen George R.	Campbell Colin C.	Durborow A. C. jr.	Ikett George W.
Allen H. W.	Campbell Fergus	Durborow C. E.	Ingalls Henry A.
Alling James C.	Campbell John D.	Durborow C. B.	Jacobs C. R.
Allyn Chas. T.	Carpenter Grant	Earle Dr. Frank B.	Jennings E. B.
Ambler H. C.	Carter Henry W.	Eaton E. W.	Johnson Andrew
Archibald Thos. E.	Carter Samuel P.	Eilers Paul C.	Johnson E. H.
Armbrecht W. H.	Chamberlain J. H.	Eldred John R.	Johnston J, J.
Arnold Alvin H.	Chandler C. T. jr.	Ellicott Edward	Jones Ford
Ault Geo. S.	Chandler E. W.	Ellithorpe A. B.	Jones Harry P.
Ault Percy B.	Chase Orrin P.	Emery J. H.	Judkins Putnam R.
Austin M. B.	Cheeseman F. E.	Evans Louis H.	Kent Heury R.
Bailey J. F.	Chrisinger J. I.	Fanning Frank J.	Kent Wm. D.
Bailey R. R.	Chrystal W. L.	Fish F. M.	Killmer Fred A.
Baker Frank J.	Clark Chas. H.	Fisk W. H.	Killough CharlesH.
Baker Geo. A. jr.	Clark Geo. E.	Fiske William B.	Kilmore John W.
Baker Dr. S. S.	Clark John V.	Ford Charles N.	Kilpatrick Chas.H.
Bangs Fred A.	Clarke Elam L.	Fordham Albert C.	Kimball A. S.
Bangs Wm. B.	Clarke E. G.	Foreman Grant	Kimball E. M.
Banks J. C.	Clement Allan M.	Foskett Andrew H.	Kimbark E. H.
Banning E.	Cleveland W. R.	Fowler Frank F.	Kimberly E. E.
Barber H. A. jr.	Cobb Eliot	Frazer Wm. E.	King Charles H.
Barber R. M.	Cobb Thos. A.	Freeman A. B.	Kiser J. W.
Barden Gerald M.	Codman Chas. F.	Frem John B.	Knight Thomas D.
Barfield Wm. G.	Cole Martin E.	Gallie Don M.	Knowles Geo. H.
Barker Alfred	Collins J. D.	Galpin Homer K.	Lange Leonard A.
Barker Chas. E.	Conine H. V.	Gibbs F. E.	LeMessurier John
Barker Geo. F.	Conyne E. A.	Goodridge A. E. G.	Lewis E. J.
Barnes Alfred J.	Coon T. H.	Goodman Alf. L.	Lloyd Arthur H.
Baxter A. Lawson	Coons J. H.	Gordon Edsie E.	Ludlow Fred D.
Baxter Wm. G.	Copley Ira C.	Gray Charles W.	Lull Dr. Richard
Beadles Charles H.	Cox George	Gross Geo. G.	Lundberg John C.
Bell F. H.	Coy Winfield S.	Griffin Fred W.	Lydston G. Frank
Bell Herbert E.	Crandall S. W.	Griffin G. W.	MacHatton B. R.
Bell L. A.	Crane Fred A.	Gunderson Geo. O.	MacLeod M.
Berg E. A.	Craw Henry F.	Gunderson S. M.	McCrea Charles M.
Berry John	Criswell James	Gutchus H. B.	McDowell C. H.
Bersback Ernest	Crosby David K.	Hale John F.	McMullan Robt. A.
Biddle Noble L.	Cunningham Hugh	Hall E. Sherman	McMullin F. R.
Bishop Chas. N.	Cunningham Percy	Hall Frank W.	McNally W. J.
Bobb P. M.	Currier C. L. jr.	Hamilton Frank A.	McRae W. M.
Bond Lester L.	Curtis Dr. J. H.	Harlow J. G.	Magill Arthur W.
Borland Dr. L. C.	Dale H. S.	Harris E. T.	Marcusson DrW.B.
Bosley E. F.	Daley Geo. R.	Hatch Henry D.	Marder John W.
Boughton Danl. K.	Danz Albert J.	Hayner Frank E.	Marquis A. N.
Bowes Edwin J. jr.	Danz Chas. A.	Hazen Frank A.	Marshall Frank B.
Boyles Chas. D.	Debus Jacob P.	Heckard M. O.	Marshall Dr. Ira E.
Boynton S. D.	Dennis Fred J.	Heron Lester G.	Marshall Joseph B.
Bradley B. Harley	DeProft Louis C.	Heron Presley M.	Martin A. W.
Briggs Richard C.	Dewes Francis J.	Hickey A. C. B.	Mason E. T.
Brooks Fred G.	Dietrick H. W. R.	Hicks George I.	Masters Arthur W.
Brooks Harry L.	Dodge Chester C.	Hill George H.	Matthes John F.
Brower Dr. D. R.	Dodson Dr. J. M.	Hill W.	Matthews Chas. E.
Brown Thomas L.	Donahue E.	Hogan J. H.	Maypole Wm. T.
Brown Walter	Donlan John T.	Hoggins John	Mehring George
Browne Wm. A.	Donle W. C.	Hohman Jno. B.	Meiselbar Henry
Buckman R. M.	Doty Fred D.	Holden J. S.	Meloy J. Y.
Bunges Albert J.	Dougherty T. E.	Holden W. S.	Mendenhall W. J.
Burdick Munson	Doyle W. A.	Hooper E. E.	Metz F. W.
Burrell John F.	Drake C. St. Clair	Hopkins Forest B.	Meyers John
Buss William	Dreher Elmore W.	Howard E. B.	Millard Frank R.

Milloy John	Plumb Glenn E.	Slade Dana jr.	Tuttle Louis F.
Mitchell Arthur J.	Poor Irby W.	Sloat George W.	Tyrrell A. H.
Moffett B. B.	Pope James B.	Smith Fred E.	Tyrrell Charles T.
Moir Alex.	Price Wm. H.	Smith Fred S.	Van Derkloot A.
Moir James	Quirk John J. Dr.	Smith Hudson	VanDerSlice W. J.
MontgomeryDrLH	Rapp Lee S.	Smith H. H.	Van Zandt O. C.
Mooney F. A.	Rawleigh J. H.	Smith J. F.	Vanzwoll H. B.
More R. Wilson	Ray Ned Osgood	Smith J. G.	Vette John F.
Morley W. J.	Reed L. J.	Smith N. G. C.	Waddle James
Morris J. L.	Reeves Joshua	Smith Robert C.	Wagner W. L.
Morrison Fred. H.	Rice H. A.	Smith R. E.	Wakefield J. G.
Mortimer Chas. J.	Richolson B. F.	Smyth John M.	Walker Geo. L.
Muldoon J. A.	Riggs Fred L.	Snell Harry J.	Walker J. A.
Munroe Walter H.	Robertson H. E.	Soltow Frank	Warner Samuel R.
Musgrave A. F.	Rodgerson Edw. J.	Somers Frank W.	Weakley J. A.
Nate J. J.	Ross George W.	Spear T. R.	Weaver C. A.
Newcomb Wm. H.	Ross Ovington	Sperbeck E. M.	Weaver Dr. Geo.H.
Newman B. L.	Roth S. W.	Spofford Geo. W.	Weeks G. M.
Nichols Dr. A. J.	Rounds Charles H.	Spofford P. M.	Wells Theo. B.
Nichols Wm. H.	Sager W. D.	Stahl Frank A.	WentworthGeo. O.
Nickerson J. F.	Salisbury D. B.	Stannard Dr. F. D.	West Edward A.
Noble W. L.	Sandham Chas. B.	Stannard Harry W.	Wetmore Chas. O.
Noonan Ed. T.	Sanford E. H.	Stevens Charles L	Wheelock W. W.
Norton Joel H.	Saunders Thos. H.	Stewart Edward L.	Whipple John H.
Nye Wm. J.	Sawyer Carlos P.	Streich Fred O.	White George E.
Olson George T.	Schmid Richard G.	Stubbs Edwin J.	Whiting Geo. B.
Osgood A. T.	Schultz Alex. J.	Swift Brown F.	Wilcox R. B.
Overlock F. F.	Schultz Jas. M.	Swift H. B.	Wilkin Jno. L.
Page Fred H.	Scully D. B.	Tapper Geo. F.	Wilkinson C. D.
Palmer B. S.	Scully Morris H.	Taylor Frank W.	Williams J. D.
Patrick H. E.	Sefton J. L.	Taylor H. C.	Williams W. E.
Patterson C. A.	Senour W. F.	Thatcher Raymond	Wilson A. B.
Paynter Henry M.	Shaw Dr. D. Lee	Thompson Orvl. V	Wilson John C.
Pearson W. E.	Sheldon H. D.	Thompson T.	Wilson Joseph H.
Peloubet Jarvis	Shipman S. V.	Thornburgh H. L.	Wilson J. Howard
Perce Hiram W.	Shuman Geo. L.	Tilden Edward	Wisshack Geo. F.
Perkins Harry S.	Shumway N. C.	Traver F. C.	Worth W. P.
Perry J. G.	Simmons C. H.	True Albert W.	Wright Clarence H.
Phelps Herbert T.	Skeen J. C.	True Charles J.	Wright Frank P.
Pitcher A. D.	Slack W. H.	Tryren Albert H.	Youngdahl A. J.
Pitt Dr. H. N.	Sladden S. C.	Tuttle A. M.	Zoller W. G.

BANKERS' CLUB.

OFFICERS.

EDWARD S. LACEY, - - - - - President.
JAMES B. FORGAN, - - - - Vice-President.
W. D. C. STREET, - - Secretary and Treasurer.

EXECUTIVE COMMITTEE.

William T. Fenton   Edward S. Lacey   John C. Neely
W. D. C. Street   James B. Forgan

MEMBERS.

Baker W. V.	Brintnall Wm. H.	Dewey D. B.	Forgan James B.
Berger Robert	Brown Frank E.	Doud Levi B.	Forman Edward G.
Billings H. F.	Bryant Edw. F.	Dummer W. F.	Foreman Oscar G.
Black John C.	Chapman James R.	Farson John	Gage L. J.
Blair C. J.	Coman Seymour	Farwell C. B.	Getty H. H.
Blount Ferd M.	Craft John C.	Farwell Granger	Gibbs James S.
Blum Aug.	Crosby F. W.	Fenton Wm. T.	Goddard L. A.
Bowen Ira P.	Dewar A. L.	Field Henry D.	Gookin F. W.

25

Hall E. R.	Kirk John B.	Palmer Percy W.	Stone S. W.
Hamill Ernest A.	Lacey Edward S.	Pearsons Henry A.	Street R. J.
Hammond Wm. A.	Lathrop E. B.	Perry Isaac N.	Street W. D. C.
Hankey F. L.	Lawrence E. F.	Phelps Erskine M.	Sturges J. D.
Harris N. W.	Lobdell E. L.	Preston W. D.	Taft O. B.
Haskell Fred T.	Lynch John A.	Rawson S. W.	Tilden Edward
Henrotin Chas.	May H. N.	Reid Charles C.	Wacker C. H.
Herrick R. Z.	Mayer N. A.	Ryther Gates A.	Walsh John R.
Hipwell W. O.	McLeod H. C.	Schneider Geo.	Wetherell O. D.
Hoge Holmes	Mitchell John J.	Seipp Wm. C.	WhitacreCharlesC.
Hurtley Arthur	Moll Carl	Shaw G. B.	Wilbur James B.
Hutchinson C. L.	Morton Joy	Slaughter A. O.	Wilson G. M.
Keith E. G.	Moulton D. A.	Smith Byron L.	Witbeck J. H.
Kelley David	Neely John C.	Smith Orson	Woodland George
Kent H. R.	Odell J. J. P.	Stone Melville E.	Worthy John
King John A.	Orr R. M.		

HONORARY MEMBERS.

Malott V. F., Indianapolis, Ind. Tracey W. W., Springfield, Ill.
Northrup B. B., Racine, Wis. Talcott C. H., Joliet, Ill.
Reed L. E., St. Paul, Minn. Waldron E. D., Elgin, Ill.
Wendell Emory, Detroit, Mich.

BRYN MAWR CLUB.

7149 JEFFERY AVENUE.

OFFICERS.

HON. HENRY V. FREEMAN, - - - - President.
GEORGE BEST, - - - - - - - Vice-President.
CHARLES A. BARKER, - - - - - - Secretary.
LUTHER N. FLAGG, - - - - - - Treasurer.

DIRECTORS.

Henry V. Freeman	Frank I. Bennett	John Lundie
George Best	George C. Bour	George A. Otis
Charles A. Barker	George F. Clingman	H. L. Sayler.
Luther N. Flagg	E. Lee Heidenreich	John I. Sauther
Milton I. Beck	L. B. Langworthy	Oscar Remmer

MEMBERS.

Barker Charles A.	Flagg Luther N.	Hume S. W.	Remmer Oscar
Beck Milton I.	Freeman Henry V.	Hyde James D.	Ricker F. K.
Bennett Frank I.	Frothingham Jas.	Langworthy L. B.	Sauther John I.
Best George	Harvey John H.	Lundie John	Sayler H. L.
Bour Frank	Heidenreich E. Lee	McGill William	Swan Dr. C. F.
Bour George C.	Holt Alfred E.	Otis George A.	Wait James J.
Cassidy H. J.	Howell C. H.	Peckham Chas. L.	Winger O. E.
Clingman Geo. F.			

CALUMET CLUB.

MICHIGAN AVENUE, CORNER TWENTIETH STREET.

OFFICERS.

N. K. FAIRBANK, - - - - - - - President.
OSBORNE R. KEITH, - - - - First Vice-President.
CHARLES FARGO, - - - - Second Vice-President.
JOHN M. CUTTER, - - - - - - - Secretary.
CHAS. C. ADSIT, - - - - - - - Treasurer.

DIRECTORS.

J. H. Andrews	Clinton Collier	A. F. Kimball
Walter Mattocks	R. A. Kettle	Frank O. Lowden
A. W. Goodrich	Wm. H. Moore	J. C. Whitney

MEMBERS.

Adam A. B.	Cranz H. C.	Herrick E. Walter	McVicker J. H.
Adsit Chas. C.	Crawford Wm. R.	Hibbard Wm. G.	Macfarland H. J.
Adsit Jas. M. jr.	Cromwell Chas.	Higinbotham H. N.	Mackey Frank J.
Alexander G. M.	Crouse John N.	Hill Lysander	Marten R. B.
Allen Benj.	Cummings C. C.	Hills C. F.	Martin S. K.
Allerton Sam'l W.	Cummings C. R.	Howard Wm. B.	Mattocks Walter
Andrews Jos. H.	Cutter John M.	Hoyt Douglas	Mayo John B.
Armour J. O.	Dexter A. F.	Hughitt Marvin	Meinrath Ariel
Armour P. D.	Dick A. B.	Hughitt Marvin jr.	Miller John G.
Armour P. D. jr.	Dickson L. T.	Hulbert Thos. H.	Mitchell M. C.
Austin F. C.	Dickey Ernest M.	Hutchinson C. L.	Mitchell W. B.
Averell A. J.	Dillman L. M.	Insull Samuel	Mixer C. H. S.
Avery Frank M.	Doane J. W.	Isham E. S.	Moore J. H.
Avery T. M.	Dodge G. E. P.	Jackson H. W.	Moore Wm. H.
Baker A. L.	Drake John B.	Jay Milton	Munger A. A.
Baker Wm. T.	Drew Chas. W.	Jeffery E. T.	Murdoch Thos.
Baldwin Geo. F.	Eiker Chas. F.	Jenkins J. E.	Murison Geo. W.
Ballard D. P.	Evans Walter N.	Jenkins T. R.	Olmstead E.
Barber O. C.	Fairbank N. K.	Jones J. Edmund	Otis Chas. T.
Barker John H.	Fargo Chas.	Jones J. Russell	Otis Geo. L.
Barnes Chas. J.	Farnum A. H.	Judah Noble B.	Otis Joseph E.
Barrett Chas. C.	Ferguson Chas. H.	Judson C. E.	Otis Philo A.
Barrett O. W.	Field John S.	Keen George	Overman L. E.
Bartlett A. C.	Field Marshall	Keen W. B. jr.	Owens John E.
Baxter T. M.	Fitch Henry S.	Keep Albert	Parker Sam'l W.
Bigelow A. A.	Fleetwood Chas.	Keep Chauncey	Peacock C. D.
Bigelow N. P.	Fleming Robt. H.	Keep Henry	Pearce J. Irving
Bishop R. W.	Frost Chas. S.	Keep Wm. B.	Peck C. I.
Blackstone T. B.	Fuller Leroy W.	Keith D. W.	Peck Ferd. W.
Bogue Chas. H.	Fuller Wm. A.	Keith Edson	Peck Walter L.
Booth A.	Gage Albert S.	Keith Edson jr.	Perry L. S.
Borden J. U.	Gary J. W.	Keith O. R.	Phelps E. M.
Breese J. B.	Gaylord W. S.	Kelley A. D.	Phillips C. H.
Brewster E. L.	Getty H. H.	Kelley David	Pitcher L. W.
Bryant H. W.	Gibbs F. C.	Kelley Wm. E.	Pitkin H. E.
Burley Frank E.	Gibbs W. B.	Kennedy M. B.	Porter H. H.
Case John E.	Giles Wm. A.	Kent S. A.	Powell Samuel
Cass George W.	Glessner J. J.	Ketcham Jas. B.	Preston Wm. D.
Cassidy J. A.	Goodman J. B.	Kettle R. A.	Price James S.
Caton Arthur J.	Goodrich A. W.	Kimball C. Fred	Pullman Geo. M.
Champlin Fred L.	Gore George P.	Kimball W. W.	Pulsifer Fred. K.
Champlin Wm. R.	Gorton Frank S.	Knickerbocker J. J.	Purcell Wm. A.
Chandler E. B.	Grannis W. C. D.	Knight W. S.	Purdy Chas. W.
Chandler E. E.	Graves W. M.	Laflin Albert S.	Ream N. B.
Chapin Simeon B.	Gray Franklin D.	Laflin A. K.	Reibold L. E.
Chapman C. A.	Green A. W.	Laflin Geo. H.	ReQua Chas. H.
Chumasero John T.	Gresham Otto	Laflin Jno. P.	Rew Henry C.
Chumasero K. P.	Grey Wm. L.	Lane Ebenezer	Robinson J. K.
Clark John M.	Griswold H. F.	Lapp Peter	Roloson R. W.
Clark Chas. E.	Hagaman B.	Ledyard Guy C.	Roney H. B.
Cobb Silas B.	Hale Clinton B.	Lefens T. J.	Rowe N.
Coburn Lewis L.	Hamill Chas. D.	Leiter Levi Z.	Rutter David
Coleman Seymour	Hamline John H.	Loomis J. M.	Sard Wm. H.
Collier Clinton	Harper W. H.	Lord Edgar A.	Schimpferman W.H
Cooper John S.	Hayden Albert	Lowden Frank O.	Schneider Geo.
Corwith C. R.	Heaton E. S.	Ludlam R.	Seeberger A. F.
Cottrell J. O.	Henderson C. M.	McCullough H. R.	Seeberger C. D.
Cowles Alfred	Henderson E. F.	McCrea W. S.	Shaw G. B.
Crandall Arthur	Henderson W. S.	McDoel W. H.	Shedd E. A.

Shepard J. H.
Shipman D.B.
Shirk E. W.
Shissler Louis
Silverthorne A. E.
Smith Byron L.
Starkweather C. H
Stephens H. N.
Stevens F. L.
Stiles George N.
Stiles Josiah
Stone C. B.
Stone H. O.

Streeter John W.
Studebaker P. E.
Surghnor V. H.
Swinarton J. H.
Thomas Fred M.
Thomson A. M.
Thrall W. A.
Towne Arthur F.
Tuttle Fred'k B.
Tyrrell John
Vierling Frank C.
Wachsmuth L. C.

Wadsworth E. R.
Walker Edwin C
Walker Geo. C.
Walker Wm. S.
Walsh John R.
Ward Morris E.
Warner E. Percy
Wells M. D.
Wentworth M. J.
Wheeler F. T.
Wheeler G. H.
Wheeler H. N.

Whitney H. H.
Whitney J. C.
Willey C. L.
Williams Abram
Williams Norman
Willoughby C. L.
Wood Geo. E.
Work A. S.
Wrenn John H.
Wyatt S. W.
Young Caryl
Young Otto

CARLETON CLUB.

3800 VINCENNES AVENUE.

OFFICERS.

ALLEN B. FORBES,   -   -   -   -   -   President.
WILLIAM A. MOULTON,   -   -   - First Vice-President.
C. EARL PATTERSON,   -   -   - Second Vice-President.
ROSCOE U. LANSING,   -   -   -   -   -   Secretary.
D. FREDERICK HURD,   -   -   -   -   Treasurer.

DIRECTORS.

J. W. Morse   Graham Davis   Edwin H. Hatch
L. O. Goddard   L. H. Freeman   Robert S. Wessels

MEMBERS.

Adams S. H. jr.
Allen Guy L.
Aspden Wm.
Atwood J. F.
Augustus A. A.
Baker J. J. W.
Barrett Charles W.
Barrett James W.
Bassett J. E. H.
Bayor W. A.
Beck Raymond A.
Beek H. W.
Beeks E. C.
Beeks M. W.
Bell G. H.
Bell M. E.
Bergerson C.
Best William W.
Black Elmer E.
Bliven C. E.
Bliven Howard O.
Boorn W. C.
Brigham Fred
Bruce Edwin I.
Bryant Harry L
Bushnell Jas. F.
Bushnell S.Morgan
Byrnes Edward
Caliger T. D.
Canfield A. J.
Card Joseph B.
Castle Robert M.
Caswell C. L., jr.
Chamberlin A. M.

Clark Wm. E.
Clippinger D. A.
Coman W. E.
Cook Geo. E.
Cook Robert S.
Dash Charles J.
Davies Charles F.
Davis George H.
Davis Graham
Davis Horace G.
Dean Amos C.
Dean J. Clark
Dinwoody Dr. J. A.
Disbrow Frank W.
Divine Frank L.
Doggett William F.
Dolese Henry
Dolese John, jr.
Doty C. Edward
Dougherty L. M.
Dresher E. J.
Dutch J. Flemming
Eldred W. L.
Eldredge C.
Elmore William B.
Ennis L. J.
Everard E. B.
Fell Lewis F.
Fisher E. B.
Fitch T. S
Follette H. A.
Forbes Allen B.
Forbes Geo. S.
Forbes John A.

Forbes Robert R.
Fowler A. F.
Freeman L. H.
French D. A.
Gilchrist John F.
Gillett Frank P.
Goddard L. O.
Gorman Wm. H.
Greathead E. E.
Greeley S. H.
Grier H. B.
Gunther Dr. H. A.
Hall Frank B.
Hall Thomas C.
Harbeck Jerome S.
Harris Robert M.
Harrison Geo., jr.
Harrison T. E.
Haseltine Frank R.
Hatch Edwin H.
Hatch Eugene A.
Hatch L. S.
Haughton E.
Hays William
Helmer H.
Henning J. E.
Hercock R. J.
Hester Charles R.
Hettich Harry L.
Hettich L. J.
Hill Bert C.
Hill Fred M.
Hilton John R.
Hitt Herman U.

Holbrook J. H.
Houston Frank B.
Houston J. S.
Howland E. A.
Huling Walter C.
Hunt Robert I.
Hunter T. B.
Huntington C. F.
Hurd D F.
Jackman A. C.
Jackson Arthur S.
Jackson Harry H.
Jackson F. G.
Jerrems Arthur W.
Jerrems W. G.
Jerrems W. G. jr.
Kates George A.
Keys E. W.
King Vere B.
Knapp Thomas
Kopp W. P.
Laing John R.
Laing Wm. G.
Leslie O. G.
Lansing Roscoe U.
Lester Leon
Lathrop J. F.
Lipe Fred W.
Lobdell Harry H.
Logan B. F.
Loker Harry A.
Low E. G.
Lyon James A.
Marsh John P.

Mason George T.	Olinger F. E.	Roberton D. C.	Swigart R. B.
Maurer J. E.	Orem Harry C.	Robins Frank G.	Templeton Phelps
McBride J. H.	Osmun Daniel C.	Robinson W. C.	Thomas J. Benson
McCall Harry	Osmun R. A.	Ruffner Will R.	Thompson W. H.
McClaughery A. C.	Parish Wm. H.	Seeley Walter G.	Tinsley J. Harry
McComas Duke	Parker Robert W.	Senns Otto	Tobin Arthur W.
McComas Eugene	Parsons C. T.	Sherman Chas. K.	Troyer J. H.
McCombs A. L.	Parsons R. L.	Sherman W. B.	Updike Harry S.
McConnell W. S.	Patterson C. Earl	Skidmore Geo. C.	VanHagen Geo. E.
McKeand C. A.	Peckenpaugh V. C.	Skillinger W. C.	Vreeland B, H.
McKeand Edw.	Penfield J. H.	Smith Abner	Waddell F. W
McKeand H. A.	Pennington C. R.	Smith B. E.	Waters E. D.
McMechan J. E. D.	Peyton R. F. jr.	Smith Charles P.	Watson F. L.
McVeigh C. F.	Pfaff J. L.	Smith E. M.	Wessels R. S.
Methven W. J.	Pillsbury O. D.	Smith H. D.	Wilkins C. H.
Miller A. P.	Playford R. W.	Smith H. D., jr.	Wilkins David W
Miller R. J.	Poor Fred A.	Spohn Zeno	Wilkins E. P.
Mitchell B. H.	Pope Henry Peirce	Steel Charles S.	Wilkins W. A.
Morse J. W.	Quarles E. C.	Steinmetz D. Harry	Wilson J. Malcom
Mott R. S.	Randall P. L.	Steinmetz J. H.	Wilson Wm. White
Moulton Wm. A.	Randolph E. C.	Stirlen John	Winchell L. E.
Mulford E. O.	Ransford T. F.	Stone Richard R.	Wood T. R.
Nethercot S. G.	Reiter A. P.	Stoner George	Wright H. H.
Newton Arthur W.	Rhodes J. Foster	Strawn Silas H.	Zeiss Henry C. F
Norcum P. D.	Richards H. W.		

CHICAGO ATHLETIC ASSOCIATION.

Michigan Ave., bet. Madison and Monroe.

OFFICERS.

C. K. G. Billings, ...	President.
E. E. Prussing, ...	Vice-President.
Joseph Adams, ...	Secretary.
Jas. S. Gibbs, ...	Treasurer.

DIRECTORS.

M. C. Lightner	William M. Booth	J. G. Steever
W. Vernon Booth	B. F. Cummings	Wm. H. Hubbard
R. A. Kettle	Charles P. Whitney	Randolph E. Fishburn
James R. McKay	E. A. Potter	Wm. Henry Burke
W. S. McCrea	E. Walter Herrick	J. Parker Smith
F. L. Champlin	Charles B. VanKirk	

MEMBERS.

Abbott Willis J.	Allen Ernest L.	Ash L. H.	Banghart W. J.
Abbott A. H.	Allerton Robert H.	Atkin G. Harold	Banks A. F.
Acker Chas. E.	Alling John jr.	Auten P. L.	Barbour Frank
Acker F. E.	Almy Miles	Avery Frank M.	Barge W, D.
Ackhoff Henry W.	Amberg J. W.	Ayer B. F.	Barnard Jas. H.
Adam George J.	Amberg W. A.	Ayer Ed. E.	Barnes Burdette C.
Adams Abbott L.	Ames W. V. B.	Ayer H. C.	Barnes Chas. J.
Adams A. A.	Anderson A. E.	Babcock Fred. R.	Barnes David L.
Adams Cyrus H.	Anderson David	Bacheldor E. A.	Barnes Nelson L.
Adams George E.	Andrews E. W.	Bacon Henry M.	Barnett A. L.
Adams Geo. J.	Andrews Dr. F. T.	Bacon Dr. J. B.	Barnum E. D.
Adams Isaac E.	Andrews Joseph H.	Bailey Theo. P.	Barothy Victor
Adsit J. M. jr.	Andrews S. F.	Baker Alfred L.	Barrell J. F.
Aiken W. E.	Andrews Wm. H.	Baker Jas. R.	Barrell S. E.
Akin Henry F.	Ansley Robert	Baker Wm. V.	Barrett E. E.
Alberger M. H.	Archer J. L.	Baldwin A. H.	Barrett S. E.
Aldis Owen F.	Armour Allison V.	Baldwin Geo. F.	Bartlett Geo. F. jr.
Allen D. A.	Armsb J. K. jr.	Baldwin Willis M.	Batchelder A.
Allen Chas. W.	ArnoldyFred'k A.	Ball W. D.	Bates L. W.

Baumann Edward
Bayley E. F.
Beach C. B.
Beach E. G.
Beale Wm. G.
Beardsley C. B.
Beatty Wm. R.
Becker B. F.
Beckwith W. L.
Beers L. G.
Beidler A. W.
Beidler Francis
Belding H. H.
Belford Alex
Belknap C. C.
Bell A. L.
Bell K. H.
Bellows Frank L.
Beman S. S.
Benedict Geo. H.
Benner Adolph L.
Bennett A. F.
Bennett Thomas
Bensinger M.
Bentley Harry G.
Berg Henry W.
Besley C. H.
Betham W. R.
Bevans A. D.
.Bevier Dubois
Bigelow A. A.
Bigelow R. A.
Billings Frank
Billings Harry F.
Bills Geo. D.
Binder Carl
Birch Hugh T.
Bishop Chas. Nelson
Bishop Jas. A.
Black H. S.
Black John D.
Blackman Carlos H.
Blackman Chas. S.
Blair Chauncey J.
Blair Henry A.
Blair Lyman
Blair Watson F.
Blakely C. H.
Blanchard Wm.
Blatchford T. W.
Blayney T. C.
Bleyer C. E.
Bliss Chas. L.
Bliss E. Raymond
Blood H. E.
Blood Jas. A.
Blount F. M.
Boal Chas. T.
Boddie M. M.
Bode Fred'k.
Bodman A. C.
Bodman L. W.
Bogue Hamilton B. jr.

Bogert W. B.
Bohner Geo.
Bond Joseph
Bonney Chas. L.
Bonney Lawton C.
Booth Chas. E.
Booth W. M.
Booth Wm. S.
Borden Jas. U.
Borner Wm.
Botsford Bennet B.
Boulton Geo. D.
Bourke Jas. E.
Bournique Alva L.
Bournique August-us E.
Bournique Eugene A.
Bowen A. P.
Bowen Joseph T.
Bower Robert A.
Bowes Frank B.
Boyce S. Leonard
Boyce W. D.
Boyden Geo. D.
Boynton C. T.
Brackett Henry W.
Braden C. E.
Bradley C. B.
Bradley Jas. D.
Brainard Edwin
Brega Chas. W.
Brewster Edw. L.
Brocklebank J. C.
Brooks C. M.
Brooks Jas. C.
Brooks John H.
Brooks J. W. jr.
Brophy Dr. T. W.
Bross Mason
Brown Albert L.
Brown A. L.
Brown C. E.
Brown D. G.
Brown Edwin
Brown Everett C.
Brown Geo. D.
Brown Geo. F. jr.
Brown H. F.
Brown J. Mabbitt
Brown Lincoln A.
Brown Paul
Brown Dr. Sanger
Brown Taylor E.
Brown W. C.
Brown W. H. A.
Bryant C. F.
Bryson Wm. J.
Buchanan Gordon
Buchanan Robt. S.
Buckingham H. W.
Buehler Edward H.
Bullen A. F.
Bullen Fred F.
Bullen G. R.
Bullen W H.

Bullock C. C.
Bunnell J. A.
Burdett Samuel M.
Burgesser G E.
Burke W. H.
Burley Frank E.
Burnham D. H.
Burnham Walter
Burr Louis E.
Burrows Daniel W.
Burrows W. F.
Burry Geo.
Butler H. B.
Buttolph A. C.
Byford Dr. H. T.
Caldwell J D.
Caldwell O. N.
Callan Henry A.
Camburn J. C.
Cameron D. R.
Cameron J. P.
Camp Edward N.
Campbell Chas. W.
Campbell J. W.
Campbell L. W.
Campbell Treat
Campbell W. J.
Cannell S. Wilmer
Cantlie Geo.
Capelle Eugene
Carhart Chas.
Carlisle E. G.
Carmack E. H.
Carnegie Jno. F.
Carpenter A. A. jr.
Carpenter E. F.
Carroll Norman
Carse Jno. Bradley
Carse David B.
Carson Samuel
Carter Leslie
Carter Jas. S.
Carter Wm. J.
Caty Frank
Carey Geo. P.
Cary Paul V.
Casey Edward A.
Cassady H. J.
Cassidy Harry C.
Cassard Morris
Cassard Vernon
Case Edward B.
Case J. E.
Cass Geo. W.
Catlin George
Caton Arthur J.
Cavaroc Chas. jr.
Chalmers Thos. jr.
Chalmers Wm. J.
Chamberlin G. M.
Champlin D. H.
Champlin Fred L.
Champlin Wm. R.
Chandler H. W.
Channer J. W.
Channon H. S.

Channon Jas. H.
Chapin Gardner S.
Chapin Henry C.
Chapin S. B.
Charlton Geo. J.
Chase Harry G.
Chase Horace G.
Chattell B. M.
Cheeney C. C.
Childs R. A.
Christian H. W.
Chumasero John T.
Chumasero Kennett P.
Church Edmund V.
Clark Alfred C.
Clark Bruce
Clark Frank B.
Clark George T.
Clark John M.
Clark Robt. G.
Clark Robert S.
Clark Dr. W. C.
Clark Walter T.
Clarke George
Clarke Henry B.
Clarke J. V.
Clarke Louis B.
Cleave O. C.
Clement Thos.
Clifton Chas. E.
Clinch R. Floyd
Clow Chas. R.
Clow H. B.
Cobb A. W.
Coe Schuyler M.
Coen W. H.
Colburn Frank D.
Colby Charles C.
Cole W. H.
Coler Frank
Collins H. B.
Collins I. S.
Collins W. G.
Colton Samuel K.
Colvin W. H. jr.
Coman Seymour
Comstock L. K.
Congdon Chas. B.
Conkey W. B.
Conkling Allen
Conover Chas. H.
Cook C. F.
Cook Geo. T.
Cook H. D.
Cook W. J.
Cooke Edward H.
Cooke H. H.
Cooley Norman P.
Cooper J. I.
Cooper Jno. S.
Cooper Wm. D.
Cooper W. F.
Copeland F. K.
Corbin C. D.
Corbin F. N.

Corby R. B.
Cordo F. I.
Corneau D. E.
Corwith Chas. R.
Cost E. F.
Cotton J.Whitcomb
Couch Ira J.
Counselman Chas.
Cowles Alfred
Cox A. G.
Cox Chas. D.
Crabb C. C.
Crandall L. E.
Crane C. R.
Crane H. P.
Crane R. T.
Crane T. R. jr.
Crankshaw C. W.
Cranz H. C.
Craw Henry F.
Crawford H. jr.
Crawford W. R.
Creighton Thos. S.
Critchell John
Critchell R. M.
Crocker Jno. T.
Cromwell Chas.
Cronin Harry A.
Crosby C. H.
Crosby Henry A.
Crosby Thomas F.
Crosette C. H.
Crowell H. P.
Cruttenden Thos.S.
Cudahy John
Cummings Martin
Cummins B. F.
Cummins Wm. G.
Cunningham Secor
Curtis E. W.
Curtis Jas. C.
Curtis J. H.
Cutter Jno. M.
Dabney John P.
Dadie John
Daggett H. E.
Dainty A. H.
Dalgleish Chas. H.
Danforth Frank L.
Daniels E. F.
Darlington Herbert
Darlow James
Darrow C. S.
Davidson John A.
Davis Chester B.
Davies Colby
Davis Geo. W.
Davis Graham,
Davis J. M.
Davis Simon S. jr.
Davis Wm. J.
Davis Wm. L.
Dawson Martin
Day Robert W.
Dayan L. F.
Deane Chas F.

DeCamp A. L.
Delaney Henry
Deering Joseph H.
Deeves G. H.
Defrees Joseph H.
DeKoven John
Demmler Karl
Dempster C. W.
Dennehy Thos. C.
Dennis Gwynne
Dering C. L.
Dering J. Kemper
DeTamble E. R.
Deveney Thos. F.
Dick A. B.
Dickerson C. W.
Dickey Ernest M.
Dickinson Albert
Dickinson Charles
Dickson H. M.
Dillingham E. R.
jr.
Dillman L. M.
Dixon Geo. W.
Dixon Thomas J.
Doggett W. L.
Donker Edward
Donnelley Reuben
H.
Dore Walter J.
Doty L. R.
Dougherty T. E.
Douglas F. L.
Douglass Frank M.
Dovenmuehler H.
C.
Downe Geo. E.
Downe H. S.
Downs A. O.
Downs J. Edward
Drake John A.
Drake John B. jr.
Drake Tracy C.
Driscoll M. F.
Driggs A. C.
Driver John S.
Duddleston George
Duffy James J.
Dumont C. W.
Dungan Thomas A.
Dunlap Chas. M.
Dunlevy Hulburd
Dunn A. E.
Dunn Frank K.
Dunn John
Dupuis Modeste
Durand Elliott
Durand Henry Cal-
vin
Dwelle A. D.
Dwiggins Jay
Eagle J. E.
Eames John H.
Eastland L. J.
Ebeling Geo.
Eckel John C.

Eckstrom C. A.
Eddy A. D.
Eddy Augustus N.
Eder C. H.
Edson J. T.
Edwards E. P.
Filer Chas. F.
Ellis E. D.
Ellis Jno. C.
Ellsworth E. S.
Elmendorf Willard
Ely Arthur C.
Enger George
Ennis R. B.
Ensign Harry A.
Ernst Leo
Erskine Oscar P.
Eschenburg G. W.
Essig George
Eustis Percy S.
Evans Dr. A. E.
Everhart Geo. P.
Ewart W. D.
Ewen J. M.
Fair Joseph B.
Fairbank Geo. O.
Fairbank Kellogg
Fairbank N. K.
Fargo Charles E.
Fargo Edw. A.
Fargo F. M.
Farley A. J.
Farnum A. H.
Farr Marvin A.
Farson John
Farson Robert B.
Farwell John A.
Farwell .Walter
Faurot Henry
Fay C. N.
F J. J. jr.
Fay R. Morse
Fell Wm. S.
Fellows Dr. C. G.
Fellows James E.
Ferguson C. H.
Ferguson E. A.
Ferguson Geo. M.
Ferguson Jas. L.
Ferguson Walton,
jr.
Feron Walter J.
Ferris Heury B.
Field Chas. E.
Field John S.
Field Marshall
Field Stanley
Field Wentworth
G.
Finkler J. W.
Fischer O. F.
Fischer S. M.
Fischer Wm. D.
Fish S. C.
Fishburn Eugene
H.

Fishburn Randolph
E.
Fisher Francis P.
Fisher G. M.
Fisher L. G.
Fisk, F. P.
Fiske Geo. F.
Flagg W. H.
Flannery J. L.
Fleming P. H.
Flershem L. W.
Force F. L.
Forman Edwd.
Forrest Wm. H.
Forsyth Robert
Foster Chas. H.
Foster Dr. F. H.
Foster Henry A.
Fowler C. I.
Fowler W. S.
Fox John V.
Frasher J. S.
Frederick F. S.
Freer Nathan M.
Freer Otto T.
Frost Walter A.
Frothingham H. H.
Fuller Chas. H.
Fuller E. C.
Fuller George A.
Fuller Henry H.
Fuller P. S.
Fullerton Chas. W.
Fulton Harry S.
Funk Chas. A.
Funkhouser M. L.
C.
Fyffe Colin C. H.
Fyffe Jno. L.
Fyffe Wm. J.
Gage A. S.
Gage Frank N.
Gallear D. O.
Gallup Howard H.
Gardiner E. J.
Gardiner Frank H.
Gardner Frank G.
Gardner F. A.
Gardner F. W.
Gardner Geo. C.
Gardner Jas. P.
Gartz Adolph F.
Gaspard P. H.
Gates J. H.
Gates J. W.
Gates P. W. jr.
Gates W. D.
Gaylord A. P.
Gaylord Edw.
Gaylord W. S.
Geltmacher J. T.
Gentry Chas. H.
George E. J.
Geraldine Dion
Gibbons Wm. M.
Gibbs F. B.

Gibbs Fred'k C.	Haines Geo. B.	Henry E. J.	Hulin William
Gibbs Jas. S.	Halbert Dr. H. V.	Hepburn John W .	Huling Edward B.
Gifford I. C.	Hale Albert B.	Herrick E. Walter	Huling E. C.
Gifford W. L.	Hall Henry G.	Hesing Washingt'n	Huling Walter C.
Gilbert A. M.	Hall Rich'd C.	Hessert Gustav jr.	Humiston S. A.
Gilbert Chas. T.	Halsey Tappan	Hettler H. H.	Hunt Chas. H.
Gilbert Henry D.	Hamill Chas. D.	Hewitt Herbert H.	Hunt Dr.Sam'lHall
Gilbert Hiram T.	Hamill Ernest A.	Heywood Edwin F.	Hunt Geo. W.
Gilbert H. K.	Hamilton J. H.	Hibbard Frank V.S	Hunter Chas. L.
Gilbert James H.	Hamilton Percy C.	Hibbard Wm. G.	Hunter Edw. S.
Gilkison J. G.	Hamlin Geo. A.	Hibbard Wm. G. jr.	Hunter R. J. O.
Gill Charles E.	Hamlin Geo. J.	Hicks Edward L.	Hunter William C.
Gillett W. C.	Hamline John H.	Hicks John G.	Hurd Jas. D.
Gillette Edwin F.	Hammond Thos. C.	Hicks O. H.	Hurlbut Horace E.
Gilman Dr. J. E.	Hanecy Elbridge	Higinbotham H. D.	Hurbut Dr. Vincent
Gilmore Thos. W.	Hanes J. K.	Higinbotham H. M.	L.
Gilmore Dr. A. P.	Hankey F. L.	Hild F. H.	Hutchins E. R.
Givins Robert C.	Hankey James P.	Hill R. D.	Hyde Charles W.
Glade John H.	Hardie T. Melville	Hill W. T.	Hyde James Nevins
Glennon E. T.	Harding Geo. F.	Hilliard C. W.	Hyman R. W.
Goldie Robert A.	Hardy Cyrus A.	Hincelot F.	Hynes Wm. J.
Goodman Wm. O.	Harlan Dr. A. W.	Hinde Thos. W.	Ingals E. Fleteher
Goodrich Edson H.	Harlow Frank	Hiner Joseph W.	Ingalls F. A.
Goodridge A. E. G.	Harmon Edw. C.	Hinkley Jas. O.	Insull Martin J.
Gookin F. W.	Harmon Geo. E.	Hitchcock R. A.	Insull Samuel
Gordon Thos. S.	Harris Geo. B.	Hoard Charles D.	Ireland Louis E.
Gore George P.	Harris Jno. F.	Hodge Andrew T.	Irvine Hugh
Gores Paul s	Harrison Carter H.	Hoefer Thos. J.	Irving Robert A.
Gormley Ja . H.	jr.	Hofmann George	Isham Pierrepont
Gormully R. Philip	Harrison Wm. Pres-	Hogue Eugene	Isham Ralph
Gorton F. S.	ton	Holman Alfred L.	Ives Frank
Gottfried Carl M.	Hart E. C.	Holman Dr. E. E.	Izard E. M.
Graham Beeckman	Hartwell C. S.	Holmes E. Burton	Jackman E. S.
Graham W. A. S.	Hartwell D. E.	Holmes Geo. J.	Jackson Howard B.
Granger Rodney	Hartwell E. S.	Holt Geo. H.	Jackson Hunting-
Grannis W. C. D.	Hartwell F. G.	Homer F. V.	ton W.
Grassie Henry	Harvey F. W.	Hook W. W.	Jackson O. B.
Graue John Geo.	Harvey Geo. M.	Hooper H. E.	Jaggard Dr. W.
Graves Chas. E.	Harvey Geo. V.	Hoops C. H.	Wright
Gray A. W.	Harvey Dr. W. S.	Hopkins Anson S.	Jaquith E. P.
Gray Louis A.	Hasbrouck L.	Hopkins John P.	James Edw. A.
Green H. L.	Haskell Fred'k T.	Hopkins Marcellus	James Fred S.
Greene D. R.	Haskell Geo. W.	Horne F. W.	Jamieson Egbert
Greene J. P.	Haskell Jno. W. C.	Hosford M. A.	Jamieson M. M.
Gregory F. A. jr.	Hately John C.	Hosmer Dr. A. B.	Jeffery E. T.
Gregory J. H.	Hately J. Geo.	Hotz Robert S.	Jenkins Geo. R.
Gregory S. S.	Haughey Chas. T.	Howard H. A.	Jenks John G.
Gregory W. D.	Havemeyer Wm.A.	Howard H. E.	Jenks Wm. S.
Grepe Hamilton E.	Havron John	Howe A. O.	Jerrems A. W.
Grey Walter C.	Hawxhurst J. M.	Howe Chas. M.	Jevne Heury M.
Gresham Otto	Hay W. S.	Howe Thad. H.	Jewell Ira H.
Griffin Fred'k W.	Hayden Frank N.	Howell Frank J.	Jewett Samuel R.
Grinnell Julius S.	Hayes James	Howland Geo. Car-	Jobson C. Frank
Griswold H. S.	Haynes T. C.	ter	Johnson A. J.
Griswold Watson P	Healy George L.	Hoyt Douglas	Johnson Burton
Gross S. E.	Healy James E.	Hoyt George W.	Johnson Ernest C.
Guerin Craig R.	Heath Ernest W.	Hoyt Phelps B.	Johnson E. V.
Gunn Walter C.	Hebard Fred'k S.	Hoyt W. M.	Johnson Wm. H.
Gunning Robert J.	Hellyer Fred'k	Hoyne Frank G.	Johnson W. O.
Gunther Burnell	Hemphill R. W.	Hubbard H. A.	Jones Frank Her-
Gunther C. F.	Henderson David	Hubbard Will	bert
Gunther Whitman	Henderson W. F.	Hubbard Wm. H.	Jones Fred. B.
Gurney Chas. H.	Henkle Wm. H.	Huck L. C.	Jones Hiram J.
Hadduck B. F.	Henrotin Adolph	Hudson Thos.	Jones Harry J.
Hagenbuck E. L.	Henrotin Dr. Fer-	Hulbert Thos. H.	Jones John H.
Hames E. H.	nand	Hulbert W. M.	Jordan Cady M.

Jordan Scott
Joslin A. D.
Judson C. E.
Kammerer Frank G.
Karpen Adolph
Kasten Herman A.
Keeley Thomas F.
Keen Edwin H.
Keen Wm. B. jr.
Keene George
Keep F. A.
Keep William B.
Keith Edson jr.
Keith H. A.
Kelley Addison D.
Kelley Edward B.
Kelley J. Frank
Kelley Wm. E.
Kelley W. V.
Kelly D. F.
Kelsey Chauncey
Kelsey H. N.
Kelsey J. A.
Keogh James B.
Keogh John W.
Kennard Alex. D.
Keunedy W. B.
Kenny Wm. S.
Kent William
Kent William B.
Kenyon D. E.
Kerfoot Chas. A.
Kerr George B.
Kerr Robert G.
Ketcham Frank D.
Ketcham John B. 2d.
Kettle R. A.
Keyes Eben W.
Kidder D. S.
Kilbourne L. Bernard
Kilgour J. T.
Killen E. G.
Kimball Charles F.
Kimball C. Fred.
Kimball Weston G.
Kimbark Chas. A.
Kimbark Walter
King Francis
King John C.
King McIlvain
King Rockwell
Kirk John B.
Kirk Wallace F.
Kirkman W. B.
Knapp Geo. O.
Knapp Geo, S.
Kneeland L. D.
Knight Clarence A.
Knisely Harry C.
Knisely John A.
Knott Henry A.
Kochersperger D. H.

Kraus Adolph
Kremer Charles E.
Kroger John jr.
Kussner Albert J.
Laflin Arthur King
Laflin A. S.
Laflin Geo. H.
Laflin John P.
Laflin Lycurgus
Laing C. W.
Lake I. L.
Lake Wm. H.
Lamb B. B.
Lamb Chas. A.
Lamb Frank H.
Lane Ebenezer
Lane Francis B.
Lapp Peter
Larned Francis M.
Lartz W. C. C.
Lathrop Bryan
Lathrop Geo. B.
Lawrence Dwight
Laws F. B.
Lawson Victor F.
Lawton L. C.
Lay Chas. C.
Leach Thomas A.
Leask Arthur
Lederer Charles
Leeming Chas. W.
Lefens T. J.
Lehman Edmund
Leibhart Frank C.
Leigh E. B.
Leiter Joseph
Leland E. F.
Lenehan J. H
Lester C. H.
Lester H. V.
Levis John M.
Levy Alex H.
Lewis A. I.
Lewis Dr. Denslow
Lewis D. R.
Lewis H. C.
Lewis I. J.
Libby C. P.
Lidgerwood J. M.
Liggett Howard J.
Lightner Milton C.
Lindgren John R.
Lindsay David J.
Listman C. F.
Livermore C. F.
Lloyd A. H.
Lloyd H. R.
Lobdell H. H.
Loker Geo. T.
Long J. B.
Longley Albert W.
Longwell H. E.
Loose J. L.
Loper W. H.
Lord Daniel M.
Lord Geo. S.

Loss Chas. E.
Louderback W. J.
Love S. C.
Lovejoy Geo. M.
Lowe J. W.
Lusch Harry B.
Lusk Wm. H.
Lyford O. S. jr.
Lyford W. H.
Lyman J. P.
Lynch Jas. D.
Lynch J. A.
Lyon Fred'k D.
Lyon R. S.
McArt1ur A. F.
McArthur Dr. L. L.
McArthur Warren
McCauley T. N.
McCartney H. G.
McCleery Robert
McClurg A. C.
McConnell John
McCormick A. J.
McCormick W. G.
McCullough H. R.
McEwen John jr.
McEwen Paul
McFarlin F. M.
McFatrick Jas. B.
McGann L. E.
McGuire Edward A.
McHie Geo. E.
McHugh P.
McIntosh H. M.
McKay A. A.
McKay Jas. R.
McKechney John jr.
McKinlock Wm. H.
McKnight H. P.
McMurray Geo. N.
McNally Fred G.
McNeill Archibald
McNeill Malcolm
McPherran Samuel H.
McVoy John A.
McWilliams J. G.
MacDonald Chas.
Macdonald C. A.
Macfarland Henry J.
MacGregor Edward
Mackay J. M.
Maclean A. A.
Maclean George A.
MacMartin Dr. R. D.
Madden M. F.
Magill H. W.
Magill Matthew E.
Magnus Arthur J.
Magnus A. C.
Magnus R. R.
Magoon C. H.
Mahin J. Lee

Main Wm. B.
Main W. F.
Mallory C. A.
Maltby A. W.
Manierre Dr. Chas E.
Manners R. R.
Mansure E. L.
Marks Kossuth
Marks L. J.
Marks R. P.
Marrenner E.
Marsh Henry W.
Marshall C. H.
Marshall Geo. E.
Marshall Philip
Marston W. L.
Marten R. B.
Martin A. C.
Martin Fred'k S.
Martin G. H.
Martin Wm.
Martin William A.
Mason Sheridan F.
Mason W. A.
Mathews Geo. W. jr.
Matile Herman O.
Matthews Wm. H.
Maxwell Chas. E.
Maxwell Edw. E.
Mayer E. J.
Maynard E. Percy
May F. E.
May Horatio N.
Mead W. L.
Meeker Chas. W.
Mehring George
Memory Henry
Merigold W. A.
Merrick Fred'k L.
Merritt Wesley
Michmer W. W.
Millard G. M.
Miles Erasius M.
Miles Gen. Nelson A.
Millard Sylvester M.
Miller B. C.
Miller E. W.
Miller Jas. A.
Miller Jas. H.
Miller J. M.
Miller Robert B.
Mills Albert J.
Mills F. N.
Mills J. M.
Milner Jas. T.
Milnor Lloyd
Moberly E. E.
Montgomery F. D.
Montgomery Geo. W.
Moore J. H.
Moore Jas. J.

Moore Lawrence C.
Moore S. M.
Moore W. H.
Morava John
Morford T. T.
Morgan A. C.
Morgan Fred W.
Morgan K. E.
Morgan O. H.
Morgan W. P.
Morrill C. A.
Morrill Fred K.
Morris F. M.
Morrison Chas. E.
Morron J. R.
Moseley Carleton
Moulton F. l.
Moulton Geo. M.
Moxley Wm. J.
Mueller J. H.
Mueller Wm. jr.
Muir John
Mulford E. A.
Mulford Robert
Mundy N. W.
Munger P. F.
Munn Noel S.
Murison C. E.
Murphey D. J.
Murphy F: M.
Murphy Jos. J.
Murphy J. B.
Murray Charles R.
Musgrave Harrison
Myers E. B.
Myers Sam'l
Nachbour J. F.
Nash Geo.
Nawn Geo. H.
Neely John C.
Neely W. I.
Nellegar J. B.
Nelson C. L.
Nelson Eric J.
Nelson John L.
Nelson N. J.
Nelson W. P.
Neumeister John G.
Nevins Roderick
Newton Chas. E.
Niblock F. W.
Nickerson RolandC
Nixon Miles G.
Normile John T.
Norris C. S.
Norton D. W.
Norton I. Henry
Noyes David A.
Noyes L. W.
Oakley Horace S.
O'Brien Edward
O'Brien Thomas D.
O'Brien W. V.
O'Connor T. G.
O'Heir A. J.
Ogden Dr. M. D.

Oliver Frederick S.
Oliver Jas. B.
Olmsted O. A.
Orde George F.
Orb John A.
Orr Rob't M.
Ortmann Rudolph
Orvis Orland D.
Osborn Clark D.
Ostrom J. A.
Otis Chas. T.
Overman L. E.
Owen K. R.
Owen Wm. D.
Owings F. P.
Owsley Dr. F. F.
Pacand A. Lincoln
Page J. C.
Page Wm. R.
Palmer J. F.
Pardee H. T.
Pardey H. W.
Pardridge C. W.
Pardridge F. C.
Pardridge F. R.
Parker Lewis W.
Parks Jno. C.
Parmelee Ed. D.
Patrick B. F. jr.
Patrick Chas. E.
Patterson Chas. L.
Paul C. R.
Pauling E. G.
Paulson W. A.
Pavey M. E.
Payne Jno. Barton
Payson Geo. S.
Payson S. C.
Peabody F. F.
Peabody F. S.
Peacock C. D.
Peacock C. D. jr.
Pearson W. H.
Pease Edw. H.
Pease James
Peasley J. C.
Peats Alfred
Peck Clarence I.
Peck Ferd. W.
Peck Ferd. W. jr.
Peck Walter L.
Pellet C. S.
Pelouze Frederick
Pelouze Wm. N.
Penhallow Wm. P.
Pennington M. P.
Pennoyer Geo. M.
Perkins C. G.
Perkins Dwight H.
Perkins Fred'k W.
Peters U. G.
Pettet F. E.
Pettibone A. G.
Phalen M. W.
Phelps C. E.
Phelps Erskine M.

Phelps E. H.
Phillips W. G.
Pickering AlbertD.
Pickett M. B.
Pierce Arthur H.
Pieters Henry
Pike Eugene S.
Pilsbry F W.
Pincoffs Maurice
Pincoffs P. A.
Pinkerton W. A.
Pittman C. K.
Plows Edward
Poor J. H.
Pope Wm. J.
Porter Gilbert E.
Porter Washington
Porter Wm. P.
Potter Edwin A.
Potter J. A.
Potwin Homer
Poucher Barent G.
Poucher Morris R.
Powell G. W.
Powell Myron H.
Powers Harry J.
Powers L. D.
Prentice Dr. Chal-
mer
Prentice Leon H.
Preston E. B.
Pringle Robert
Probst Jerome
Pulsifer Fred. K.
Pullman W. C.
Pullman W. Sanger
Purington C. S.
Purinton H. G.
Purple T. H.
Putnam A. A.
Putnam F. W.
Quan Henry W.
Quincy C. F.
Raftery Edmond
Rand Chas. E.
Rankin Wm. T.
Rathbone Wm. W.
Rawson A. E.
Raymond Lawry B.
Rector Chas. E.
Redington W. H.
Reddon W. B.
Reed Frank
Reed Frank F.
Reese Harvey H.
Rehm W. H.
Reid Alan L.
RevellAlexanderH.
Rew Irwin
Rhodes J. Foster
Rice Chas B.
Rice Erwin A.
Rice Frank L.
Rice T. F.
Rich Elmer A.
Richards G. E.

Richardson DanlE.
Richardson R.Jul's.
Richardson R. W.
Richter Paul K.
Riddle Francis A.
Riggs George W.
Rintoul Robert
Ripley B. W.
Ritchie T. W.
Roberts C. A.
Roberts C. J.
Roberts John T.
Robertson F. C. N.
Robertson las. P.
Robertson J. W.
Robinson Chas. O.
Robinson Elisha A.
Robinson J. K.
Rockwood FrankB.
RockwoodHarveyT
Roddin E. V.
Rodiger Wm.
Rogers Charles D.
Rogers J. E.
Rogers R. M. jr.
Rollo L. C.
Ross Edward F.
Ross Edwin
Ross G. F.
Rounds Chas. H.
Rountree Harri-
son H.
Rubens Harry
Ruddock C. H.
Rudolph Franklin
Ruffner F. W.
Ruggles Chas. R.
Ruh F. E.
Ruhstrat Fred'k
Rumph W. H.
Rumsey Julian M.
Rush J. W.
Russell A. R.
Russell Edward W.
Russell E. A.
Ruxtan Wm.
Ryerson Arthur
Ryerson Edw. L.
Ryerson Martin A.
Sage C. F.
Salisbury W. D.
Salisbury W. H.
Samuel Edward M.
Sands A. J.
Sargent Wm. D.
Sattley W. N.
Sawyer H. C.
Sayler C. E.
Schaub F. J.
Schaub Wm. L.
Schilling G. F.
Schimpferman WH
Schnur Jacob
Schmidt Fred. M.
Schmidt Leonard
Schmidt LeonardF.

Schmidt Dr. O. L.
Schmitt Anthony
Schmitt Chas. S.
Schmitt E. J.
Schultz Albert
Schultz M. M.
Schuttler Peter jr.
Schwab A. C.
Schwarz Herbert E.
Scott E. N.
Scott Geo. A. H.
Scott James W.
Scott Walter A.
Scoville C. B.
Scudder John A.
Scull Harry
Seaverns Geo. A. jr
Seckel Albert
Seifert Edward
Seifert Maurice
Seipp W. C.
Sellers F. H.
Sellers John M.
Seymour Herbert V.
Sharp E. F.
Sharp J. S.
Sharp Wm. N.
Sharpe C. A.
Shaw Edward R.
Shaw Howard V. D.
Shaw-Kennedy Vernon
Shaw T. A. jr.
Shayne J. T.
Shearson John
Sheed Edward A.
Sheldon Geo. W.
Sheldon Theodore
Shepard Edward S.
Shepard Harry E.
Sherwood Marc
Shinners P. H.
Shonts T. P.
Shortall John L.
Shubert A. B.
Shuman Percy L.
Sidway H. T.
Sills Edward P.
Sills W. H.
Silverthorne A. E.
Simmons Chas. H.
Simon Charles W.
Simpson T. S.
Sittig W. A.
Skillen E. S.
Skinner Richard
Slack Chas. H.
Slade C. B.
Sloan T. L.
Smalley Chas. M.
Smith Chas. F.
Smith C. S.
Smith Dunlap
Smith E. E.
Smith Franklin P.
Smith Frederick C.

Smith F. A. B.
Smith F. M.
Smith F. Stewart
Smith Gilbert A.
Smith Granger
Smith Jay H.
Smith J. Frank
Smith Loyal L.
Smith Lutellus
Smith Marven E.
Smith Orson
Smith R. K.
Snow A. E.
Soden G. A.
Sontag Frederick
Soper Jas. P.
Spalding Chas. F.
Spencer Earl W.
Spiegel Hamlin L.
Spoor John A.
Sproehnle A. W.
Sproehnle F. M.
Spry Samuel A.
Stanley Frank W.
Stanley P. E.
Stanton Edgar
Stanton W. A.
Starkweather Ch. H.
Starkweather Fk. H.
Starrett Theo.
Stedman E. M.
Stedman Josiah
Steele Dr. A. K.
Steele S. B.
Steele Julius
Stephens W. C.
Stevens Harry D.
Stevens Lester W.
Stevens S. H. jr.
Stevenson Chas. A.
Stevenson D. M.
Stevenson H. M.
Stewart A. A.
Stewart A. M.
Stewart Will T.
Stokes Chas. F.
Stone Geo. F.
Stone Geo. N.
Stone Henry B.
Street Richard J.
Streeter Allen R.
Streeter D. L.
Streeter Dr. J. W.
Streeter W. C.
Stuart Robert
Studebaker W. F.
Sturges Benton
Sturges Lee
Sullivan J. W.
Sullivan Louis H.
Sullivan T. E.
Surghnor V. H.
Sunny B. E.
Sutherland W. J.
Sutter Edwin A.
Swanson S. A.

Swannell Wm.
Sweet Jno. W.
Swift Edward F.
Swift Frederick
Swift L. F.
Syer E. W.
Taber Frank M.
Tabnall Wm. F.
Taft A. W.
Tanner John B.
Taylor Geo. H.
Taylor F. H.
Taylor H. A.
Taylor H. N.
Taylor Thomas jr.
Teeple F. W.
Tenney H. W.
Tewsbury Geo. W.
Tewksbury Wm. J.
Thacker J. F.
Theurer Joseph
Thoman Leroy D.
Thomas A. L.
Thomas Benj.
Thomas Frank H.
Thomas F. M.
Thomas H. A.
Thomas Homer M.
Thompson John F.
Thompson Slason
Thompson S. B.
Thomson H. C. M.
Thorne Chas. H.
Thorne Wm. C.
Thorsen J. B.
Thrall Sam E.
Thurber Geo. S.
Thurston F. W.
Tilley Dr. Robert
Tilt J. E.
Titcomb W. C.
Titus Virgil E.
Todd Chas. C.
Todd James A.
Totten Harry
Towers A. B.
Townsend Copland
Townsend J. J.
Toynton F. E.
Traer Glenn W.
Tripp F. A.
Trube G. A.
Trude F. H.
Trumbull John H.
Turner A. A.
Turner E. E.
Turner Henry L.
Turrill J. F.
Tuttle F. B.
Tuttle Wm. P.
Twitchell J. O.
Twitty Walt r G.
Udell S. R.
Ullman Herbert J.
Ullmann Frederic
Ullrich Michael

Underwood J. P.
Upham Abel P.
Ure Robert H.
Utz A. L.
Valentine E. A.
Valentine Jno.
Vail H. S.
VanCleave Jas. R. B.
Vanderslip Fra'k A.
VanHamm F. R.
VanInwagen Jas.
VanSicklen N. H.
VanVlissingen J. H.
VanVlissingen P.
VanVoorhis Frank
Veitch Wilberforce
Vent R. T.
Vinnedge Allen H.
Vinnedge Mahlon
VonGlahn August
Voorhees John W.
Vories H. F.
Vrooman George H.
Wachsmuth Fr'd H.
Wachsmuth L. C.
Wacker Chas. H.
Waggoner I. N.
Wagner George
Wagner Wm. L.
Wait George A.
Walbank Kenneth S
Waldschmidt Aug.
Walker George B.
Walker Geo. C.
Walker Francis W.
Walker W. B.
Wakem J. Wallace
Walker Henry H.
Walker H. W.
Walker Jas. R.
Walker Robert P.
Walker Wm. B.
Walker W. S.
Waller Jas. L.
Waller J. B.
Waller Wm.
Waller R. A.
Walsh R. D.
Walter Alfred M.
Wampler A. J.
Warden T. G.
Wardlow John
Wardwell Robt. D.
Wares J. F.
Warner A. R.
Warrell A. M.
Warren Clinton J.
Warren Paul
Washburn E. B.
WashburneH'mstd
Wassall Jos. W.
Waters F. S.
Waters H. S.
Watson G. E.
Watson S. E.
Watt Jas. B.

Weaver Chas. A.
Webber Chas. M.
Webster George W.
Webster G. A.
Webster Lewis D.
Weddell J. Robson
Weeks Harvey T.
Weeks J. G.
Wegner W. A.
Weidig Geo.
Wells Brenton R.
Wells M. D.
Wenderoth Chas. T.
Wenderoth Frank
Wentworth Frank W.
Wentz A. D.
Werner P. E.
West Fredk. T.
West Geo. E.
Weston W. S.
Whedon Geo. H.
Whedon James P.
Wheldon, J. P.
White A. J.
White A. S.
White Harry
White Sam T.

White W. J.
Whitehead E. P.
Whitehead Percy D
Whitehead Wm. M.
Whitehouse S. S.
Whitgreave C. T.
Whiting Chas. H.
Whiting F. G.
Whitney Chas. P.
Whitney J. C.
Whittemore C. L.
Wilce E. Harvey
Wilce George C.
Wilde Wm. A.
Wiley Edward N.
Wiley Lyman A.
Wiley Sterling P.
Wiley W. R.
Wilkins Jos. R.
Wilkins S. G.
Willard F. E.
Williams Benj.
Williams Chas. S.
Williams Ch'ncy L.
Williams Edward C.
Williams H. F.
Williams John

Williams Norman
Williams S. L'wrnce
Williams Walter
Williamson John
Williamson W. G.
Willits George S.
Willits Ward W.
Willoughby Chas. L.
Wilson Geo. A. S.
Wilson H. R.
Wilson H. S.
Winston Dudley
Winston F. S.
Wirts Stephen M.
Winne Archibald
Wise H.
Wolf Henry M.
Wolford J. A.
Wood C. A.
Woodbury S. H.
Woodle Edwd. R.
Woodrough R. L.
Woods Wm. J.
Woodward E. A.
Woodward T. R.
Woodward M. S.

Woolley C. M.
Wooster C. K.
Work A. S.
Work Geo Z.
Worthington E. E.
Wren Wm. B.
Wrenn H. A.
Wright Chas. H.
Wright Geo. C.
Wright Geo. E.
Wright H. M.
Wright Thos. A.
Wurts C. P., jr.
Wygant A.
Wylde Edward
Wyman Wm. D.
Yager W. A.
Yerkes Chas. T.
Yoe Lucien G.
Young George W.
Young Henry M.
Young Otto,
Young W. W.
Young Luther C.
Younglove Ira S.
Ziegfeld Dr. F.
Zimmerman, Jos.

LIFE MEMBERS.

Adams Joseph
Andrus Fred H.
Armour J. O.
Armour P. D.
Armour P. D. jr.
Barnhart A. M.
Billings C. K. G.
Booth A.
Booth W. Vernon
Brown Charles E.
Brown William T.
Buchanan Milford D.
Cavanagh Patrick
Chatfield-Taylor H. C.
Cobb Henry Ives
Crawford R. C.
Derby W. M. jr.
DeWolf Wallace L.
Diffley M. W.
Downs Charles S.
Fraser Norman D.
Gerould Frank W.
Goodrich A. W.
Greeley Frederick

Griffin T. A.
Gross Howard H.
Halbach J. Fred'k A.
Hamburger L. M.
Hannah William H.
Harlan Jno. Maynard
Hately Walter C.
Hutchinson Chas. L
Jones G. Edwin
Jones William
Kimball Eugene S.
Kirby R. D.
Kirk Milton W.
Kirkman M. M.
Lancaster C L.
Leake James B.
McCormick C. H.
McCrea W. S.
McNally A.
Mackey F. J.
Martin Joseph S.
Mayer David
Mayo J. B.
Merriam J. W.

Mitchell O. W.
Monroe W. F.
Nickerson Sam'l M.
Pearson John B.
Peasley J. C.
Pike Charles B.
Pike Eugene R.
Porter H. H.
Porter James W.
Porter Rogers
Preston W. D.
Prussing E. E.
Prussing Geo. C.
Ray Frank H.
Ream Norman B.
Reed Isaac N.
Rew Henry C.
Richardson A. P.
Smith Byron L.
Smith J. Parker
Smith Wyllys K.
Spalding A. G.
Spalding Stewart
Steele H. B.
Steever J. G.

Stewart Graeme
Stockton Richard
Strobel C. L.
Thompson Gale
Thompson Wm. Hale
Thorne George A.
Thorne George R.
Thrall W. A.
Torrence Joseph T.
Trude A. S.
Urson Frank J.
VanKirk Charles B.
Vierling Louis
Ward A. Montgomery
Waters W. B.
Weary E. D.
Wheeler A. W.
Wheeler E. R.
White George E.
Wilbur J. B.
Williams George J.
Williams L. R.
Willing Henry J.

NON-RESIDENT MEMBERS.

Abbott A. C.
Alden I. C.
Allen George H.
Ames J. C.
Anderson Reddick
Andree Julius
Arnold G. L.

Arundell A. L.
Bacon D. H,
Baker Charles H. jr.
Baker Edward L.
Baker E. E.
Balke Julius
Ball Howard J.

Bardeen George E.
Baumann Gustav
Benz George G.
Bissell Julius B.
Boland John
Bowers L. H.
Brewer O. W.

Broenniman E. G.
Brown Charles S.
Brown Francis A.
Bullock F. W.
Cairness J. J.
Calhoun William J.
Callahan A. F.

Campbell Arch. M.
Carlisle C. A.
Carroll James F.
Catlin Charles
Cavanah James
Christie James
Church S. M.
Clark C. Everett
Clarke James
Claxton H. N.
Coan C. C.
Coleman R. L.
Comstock J. H.
Conley James
ConnollyAndrewC.
Corbin L. P.
Corning F. T.
Coryell George R.
Crawley Edwin F.
Crerar John
Crosby W. H.
Cunningham Alex.
Cunningham L. S.
Davis Warren J.
Dawes E. C.
Dayton H. F.
Dearborn W. L.
DeMott Howard
Donovan W. F.
Downs Hubert C.
Dreier Carl
Elkins W. L.
Farwell Jno.Arthur
Fay Louis E.
Finch George R.
Fish Frederick S.
Flershem R.Byford
Fort Robert B.
Frankel Henry U.
Fraser Robert G.
Fuller Edward M.
Funk Deane N.
Garrison O. L.
Gibson Charles B.
Gill Thomas H.
Goodfellow Bruce

Gordon Charles W.
Gray Willis E.
Green Edw. H. R.
Gribbel John
Griffiths G. R.
Hackney W. S.
Hall Eugene
Hamlin Robert A.
Hanford C. W.
Harris John C.
Harris Newton M.
Hastings F. S.
Heenan D.
HendersonWemyss
Hersey R. F.
Hixon William L.
Hodgson I. jr.
Hollister T. H.
Hood A. N.
Huber Otto
Huhn George A.
Huiskamp H. J.
Hulbert S. S.
Humphreys H. D.
Hutchinson J. W.
Jenkins Silas H.
JermanowskiBaron
  E. J.
Johnson Arthur
Johnston L. G.
Johnstone W. H.
Kent Carrol C.
Kenyon W. J. C.
Kilvert Max Alex.
Kimberly J. A.
Kirkham GeorgeD.
Kissam George
Kittson J. C.
Kramer H. L.
Kuhns E. Louis
Laflin Louis E.
Labee E. H.
Lamb Chancy R.
LanahanCharlesM.
Lanahan Samuel J.
Lathrop George H.

Law Charles D.
Leiter T. Benton
Lemoine E. S.
Lindsley F. B.
McBride George J.
McCanna C. B.
McClellan E. W.
McCullough Dan'l
Marr D. C.
Martin A. D.
May Charles H.
Merriam R. H.
Mills M. B.
Morris Howard
Morrison A. Cresey
Myers W. B.
Newton G. H.
Nichols H. N.
Norton H. C.
Nye Ray
O'Bannon John W.
Oglesbee R. B.
Orendorf U. G.
Osborn Charles S.
Osborn Robert A.
Osborn William
Pages Almeric
Patterson Wm. jr.
Penfield George F.
Plant F. W.
Pratt H. T.
Remer Clarence
Rivet Albert
Robinson Frank
  DeH.
Ross William K.
Rouse H. G.
Rumsey J. Turner
Russell Frank H.
Russell Walter S.
Rust R. E.
Ruttan W. E.
Sanger Frank M.
Schmidt F. W.
Scott Thomas B.

Sheldon C. E.
Sherwin W. W.
Sladden Sidney C.
Smith G. M.
Smith Walter M.
Sprague Seth
StachelbergCharles
  G.
Stack J. L.
Stephenson Fred
  M.
StephensonIsaac jr.
Stocking C. J.
Stone J. F.
Stott F. L.
Studebacker Clem
  jr.
Studebacker Geo.
  M.
Tarbell Gage E.
Townsend H. C.
Tracey F. M.
Trimble A.J.
Tuttle E. D.
UnderwoodEugene
  jr.
Underwood H. W.
Vorhees Fred'k N.
Walker Lyman T.
Wells W. H.
Wells W. H. jr.
Whaling John A.
Wheelock W. G.
Whitcomb F. L.
Whitman Geo. A.
Wickes William J.
Widener P. A. B.
Winship E. T.
Wood D. E.
Wright Rufus
Wright Walter C.
Yates Blinn
Young W. J. jr.
Yule George A.
Yule William L.

THE CHICAGO CLUB.

MICHIGAN AV. SW. COR. VANBUREN.

OFFICERS.

HENRY W. BISHOP. - - - - - - President.
HENRY B. STONE, - - - - Vice-President.
ALLISON V. ARMOUR, - - Secretary and Treasurer.

EXECUTIVE COMMITTEE.

Allison V. Armour
Robert Forsyth,
Edward M. Switzer
Norman Williams ·
John M. Clark

Edward T. Blair
George A. Armour
Henry B. Stone
Arthur J. Caton
William G. Beale

George S. Morison
William W. Kimball
James VanInwagen
Frederick S. Eames

MEMBERS.

Ackerman Wm. K.
Adam AlexanderB.
Adams Abbott L.
Adams Edward S.
Adams George E.
Adams J.McGregor
Adams Joseph
Adams John R.
Adsit Charles C.
Adsit James M. jr.
Aldis Arthur T.
Aldis Owen F.
Alexander StuartR.
Alexander Wm. A.
Allen Benjamin
Alling John
Antisdel Albert
Armour Allison V.
Armour George A.
Armour Philip D.
Atwood Charles B.
Ayer Benjamin F.
Ayer Edward E.
Babcock W. Irving
Baker William T.
Baker William V.
Baldwin Henry F.
Ball George C.
Bangs Edward W.
Bannard Henry C.
Barber Ohio C.
Barker Samuel B.
Barnes Charles J.
Barrell James
Bartlett A. C.
Bartlett Benjamin
Bartlett Wm. H.
Bausher Henry
Beale William G.
Bellas Thomas H.
Beman Solon S.
Bigelow Anson A.
Bigelow Nelson P.
Biglow Anson K.
Billings Albert M.
Billings C. K. G.
Billings Frank
Birch Hugh T.
Bishop Henry W.
Black John C.
Blackstone T. B.
Blair Chauncey J.
Blair Edward T.
Blair Henry A.
Blair Watson F.
Blanchard Geo. R.
Blatchford E. W.
Boal Charles T.
Borden William
Botsford Henry
Boutell Henry S.
Bowen Joseph T.
Boyce S. Leonard
Boyden George D.

Bradley J. Harlen
Breese Jacob B.
Brega Chas. W.
BrewsterEdwardL.
Brosseau August
Broughton UrbanH
Brown FrancisC.
Brown William L.
Budd Wayman C.
Buffum Joseph H.
Bullen George
Burley Arthur G.
Burley Frank E.
Burnet William H.
Burnham DanielH.
Burrows Daniel W.
Burry William
Burton LeGrand
Butler Edward B.
Butterfield C. W.
Cable Ransom R.
Campbell Treat
Campbell Wm. J.
Campbell Wm. N.
Carpenter Aug. A.
Carpenter August-
  us A. jr.
Carpenter Benj.
Carpenter Myron J.
Carrington Wm. T.
Carter Leslie
Cary Eugene
Caton Arthur J.
Cavaroc Chas. jr.
Chalmers Wm. J.
Chandler JosephH.
Chatfield - Taylor
  H. C.
Chisholm Sam'l S.
Chumasero John T.
Church Townsend
  V.
Clark John M.
Clark Alson E.
Clarke EdwardA.S.
Clay John jr.
Clay Wm. W.
Clowry Robert C.
Cobb Albert W.
Cobb Henry I.
Cobb Walter F.
Collins Charles C.
Collins Lorin C. jr.
Collins Wm. A.
Colvin William H.
Comstock Wm. C.
Connell Charles J.
Conover Chas. H.
Coolidge Chas. A.
Coolidge Fred. S.
Corwith Chas. R.
Counselman Chas.
Cox Rensselaer W.
Cramer E. W.

Crane Chas. R.
Crane Richard T.
CrosbyChaunceyH.
Crosby Fredk. W.
Cudahy John
Cummings C. R.
Cummings D. M.
Curran Orville P.
Cutter John M.
Dau J. J.
Davis George R.
Davis Lewis H.
Day Albert M.
Deering Charles
Deering James
DeKoven John
Dibblee Henry
Dickey Ernest M.
Dickinson Edward
Doane John E.
Doane John W.
Dodge George E.P.
Dole Charles S.
Douglas John M. jr.
Dows David jr.
Drake John B.
Driver Edward A.
Ducat Arthur C.
Dunlap George L.
Dunn Frank K.
Dupee John
Durkee R. P. H.
Dwight John H.
Eames FrederickS.
Easton Charles L.
Eddy Augustus N.
Eldredge Geo. C.
Elkins William L.
Ellsworth JamesW.
Elmer Howard N.
Ely Arthur C.
Eustis Percy S.
Evans James C.
Ewen John M.
Fair Robert M.
Fairbank Kellogg
Fairbank N. K.
Fargo Charles
Fargo Livingston
  W.
Farwell Charles B.
Farwell Granger
Farwell John V. jr.
Farwell Walter
Fay Charles N.
Fearn Percy L.
Fentress James
FergusonWalter jr.
Ferry Chas. H.
Field Marshall
Field Marshall jr.
Fisher Archie J.
Fisher Lucius G.
Fitch Henry S.

Fitzhugh Carter H.
Fleming John C.
Fleming Robert H.
Flint Edward E.
Flower James M.
Floyd Frank
Forrest William H.
Forsyth Robert
Frost Edward I.
Fuller Charles G.
Fuller Leroy W.
Fuller Melville W.
Fuller William A.
Fullerton Chas. W.
Gage Albert S.
Gage Eliphalet B.
Gage Lyman J.
Gardner HoratioH.
Gates John W.
Geddes Alexander
Getty Henry H.
Gibbs James S.
Gilbert Albert M.
Gillett Wm. K.
Glessner John J.
Glover Otis R.
Goodheart Fred. E.
Goodman James B.
Goodrich AlbertW.
Gorton Frank S.
Grannis Wm. C. D.
Graves S.Haughton
Green AdolphusW.
Greene Wm. M.
Grepe J. Stanley
Gresham Otto
Griffin Thomas A.
Grinnell Julius S.
Gross Samuel E.
Hale Wm. E.
Hamill Charles D.
Hamill Ernest A.
Hamilton David G.
Hamline John H.
Hammond Jabez
Hannah John S.
Hapgood Chas. H.
Harahan James T.
Harding George F.
Harper Wm. R.
Harris George B.
Harris John F.
Harvey Joel D.
Harvey T. W.
Haskell Fred. T.
Havemeyer Wm.A.
Hayden Albert
Head Franklin H.
Hellyer Frederick
HendersonChas.M.
Henderson W. S.
Henrotin Charles
Herrick John J.
Hibbard Wm. G.

High Geo. H.
Higinbotham H. N.
Hill Robert
Holt George H.
Honore Nathaniel K.
Hosmer R. W.
Hotz Christoph
Howard Harold A.
Howard William B.
Howe James T.
Howland WilliamI.
Hubbard Henry M.
Hubbard Wm. H.
Hughitt Marvin
Hulburd Chas. H.
Hunt Robert W.
Hutchins James C.
Hutchinson C. L.
Insull Samuel
Isham Edward S.
Isham Edward S.jr.
Isham Henry P.
Isham Pierrepont
Jackson H. W.
Jacobson Augustus
James Frederick S.
Janes John J.
Jeffery Edward T.
Johnston CliffordP.
Johnston John
Jones Samuel J.
Jones Samuel M.
Judson Charles E.
Keep Albert
Keep Frederic A.
Keep William B.
Keep William F.
Keith Edson
Keith Edson jr.
Keith Walter W.
Keith W. Scott
Kennedy V. Shaw
Kennett Francis J.
Kent Sidney A.
Kerfoot WilliamD.
Ketcham Frank
Ketcham John B.
Key John R.
Keyes Rollin A.
Kimball C. Fred.
Kimball Wm. W.
Kimbark Seneca D.
King Francis
King Henry W.
Kirk Wallace F.
Kirk John B.
Kirk Milton W.
KirkmanM'sh'll M.
Kirkwood William
Kirkwood Thos. S.
Kitchen John B.
Kneeland Lorenzo D.
Knott Henry A.
Kohlsaat H. H.

Lamb Benjamin B.
Larned Walter C.
Lathrop Bryan
Lathrop Chas. D.
Lawrence E. F.
Lawson Victor F.
LeBaron William
Lee Blewett
Leiter Joseph
Leiter Levi Z.
Leman Henry W.
Lightner Milton C.
Lincoln Robert T.
Linn William R.
Lloyd Henry D.
Loomis John M.
Loose Jacob L.
Lyman David B.
Lyon George M.
Lyon John B.
Lyon Thomas R.
Lyon William C.
Macdonald Chas.B.
Macfarland H. J.
Mackay Alexander
MacVeagh Franklin
Mair Charles A.
Manierre George
Marsh Frank A.
Marten Robert B.
Martin Thomas J.
Martyn Edward J.
Mason Edward G.
May Horatio N.
Maynard PrestonC.
McAuley John T.
McAvoy Chas. P.
McBean Archie J.
McCagg Ezra B.
McCallay Daniel
McClurg Alex. C.
McCormick C.H.
McCormick Robert S.
McCormick R. Hall
McCormick Wm.G.
McHenry Wm. E.
McKay Henry
McKay James R.
McMullin James C.
McVicker James H.
McWilliams J. G.
Meagher James F.
Meeker Arthur
Merrill William F.
Merryweather Geo.
Meserole Nicholas W.
MeysenburgOttoW
Miller J S.
Miller Roswell
Mitchell John J.
Montgomery G. W.
Moore Gurdon G.
Moore James H.

Moore William H.
Morison George S.
Morse Charles H.
Morse Jay C.
Morton Joy
Morton Paul
Moss Jesse L.
MudgeD.Archibald
Mulliken A. Henry
Mulliken Chas. H.
Mundy Norris W.
Munger Albert A.
Munn Charles A.
Munro William
Murdoch Thomas
Mygatt William R.
Nelson Murry
Newell Wm. A.
Newman Wm. H.
Nickerson R. C.
Nickerson Sam'l M.
Noble Alfred
Northcote AmyasS.
Norton J. Henry
Norton James S.
Noyes John T.
Odell James W.
Odell John J. P.
Onderdonk Andrew
Orr Arthur
Otis George L.
Overman Linnæus E.
Palmer Potter
Parkinson Rob't H.
Parker Samuel W.
Parkes John C.
ParkhurstJossiahJ.
Parmelee Chas. K.
Parmelee John W.
Patterson R. W. jr.
Payson George S.
Peasley James C.
Peck Clarence I.
Peck Ferd W.
Peck George R.
Peters Roswell A.
Pettibone Asa G.
Phelps Erskine M.
Pickands Henry S.
Pike Eugene S.
Pope Arthur W.
Pope Charles
Pope William J.
Porter Henry H.
Porter William D.
Potter Orrin W.
PrenticeEParmelee
Prentiss John H.
Preston Wm. D.
Pretyman William
Pullman George M.
Pullman Wm. C.
Ray Frank H.
Raymond Chas. L.
Raymond Sam'l B.

Ream Norman B.
Reid Alan L.
Rhodes J. Foster
Rice F. Willis
Richardson Aug. P.
Ripley Edward P.
Robbins Henry S.
Robinson DanielB.
Robinson John K.
Roloson Robt. W.
Roloson Walter L.
Rood James jr.
Roper John
Rozet George H.
Runnells John S.
Runnion James B.
Russell Edward P.
Rust Henry A.
Ryan Thomas J.
Ryerson Arthur
Ryerson Edward L.
Ryerson Martin A.
Salisbury W. M.
Sard William H.
Schimpferman WH
Schmidt Max E.
Schoyer Ernest A.
Schwartz G. A.
Scott George A. H.
Scott James W.
Scudder M. L. jr.
Sears Joseph
Seaverns Geo. A.
Seaverns Geo.A. jr.
Seeberger A. F.
Seeberger Chas. D.
Selfridge Harry G.
Shortall John G.
Shufeldt Philp S.
Singer Charles J.
Slaughter ArthurO.
Smith Byron L.
Smith Dunlap
Smith Ernest F.
Smith George
Smith George T.
Smith Horace S.
Smith LeGrand
Smith Orson
Smith Perry H. jr.
Smith WilliamSooy
Southgate R. H.
Spalding Jesse
Spencer Earl W.
Spoor John A.
Sprague Albert A.
Sprague Otho S. A.
Springer James D.
Stauffer Benj. F.
Stephens Henry N.
Stevenson Chas. A.
Stevenson D. M.
Stirling John C.
Stirling William R.
Stockton Richard
Stone Henry B.

Stone Melville E.
Strobel Chas. L.
Studebaker P. E.
Sullivan Louis H.
Switzer Edward M.
Thomas Theodore
Traer Glenn W.
Tree Arthur M.
Tree Lambert
Tripp Dwight K.
Trumbull Perry
Tufts Eugene L.
Tuttle Emerson B.
Tuttle Fred. B.
Ullrich Michael
ValentineAlastairI.
Valentine Ed. A.
Van Inwagen Jas.
Viles James jr.
Vincent Wm A.
Waggoner IrvingH.
Walker Aldace F.

Walker Charles C.
Walker Edwin
Walker George C.
Walker Henry H.
Walker James H.
Walker James H.jr.
Walker James R.
Walker William B.
Walker William R.
Walker Wm. S.
Walker Wirt D.
Waller James B.
Waller Robert A.
Waller William
Wallop Oliver H.
Walsh John R.
Ward Geo. R. T.
Warner Ezra J.
Warren Robert
Warren Clinton J.
Washburne Hemp-
stead

Watriss FranklinH.
Watson John G.
Weare Portus B.
Webster Lewis D.
Wellington John C.
Wells Moses D.
Wells Thomas E.
Wheeler Arthur
Wheeler Arthur D.
Wheeler Chas. W.
Wheeler Eugene
Wheeler Geo. H.
Wheeler Harris A.
Wheeler SamuelH.
White A. Stamford
Whitehouse F. M.
Whiting Alex. T.
Whitney Geo. B.
Wicker Henry C.
Wickes Thomas H.
Widener PeterA.B.

Williams Abram
Williams Lawrence
Williams Nelson B.
Williams Norman
Willing Henry J.
Willits George S.
Wilmerding Chas.
H.
Wilson Benj. M.
Wilson Walter H.
Wilson Wm. M.
Winslow D.
Winston Fred'k.H.
Winston Fred'k S.
Worthington E. S.
Wrenn John H.
Wright Joseph
Wright Thomas A.
Yale Julian L.
Yoe Charles C.
Young George W.

CHICAGO LITERARY CLUB.

116 AND 118 DEARBORN STREET.

OFFICERS.

WILLIAM ELIOT FURNESS, - - - - President.
ABRAM M. PENCE. ⎫
FRANK GILBERT, ⎬ - - - Vice-Presidents.
JOHN J. GLESSNER, ⎭
JOHN H. BARROWS, - Corresponding Secretary.
FREDERICK W. GOOKIN, - Recording Sec. and Treas.
The above officers constitute the Board of Directors.

MEMBERS.

Ackerman Wm. K.
Adams Charles
Adams Geo. E.
Adams Joseph
Aldis Owen F.
Aldrich Charles H.
Allen Chas. L.
Anderson Galusha
Andrews Edmund
Andrews E. Wyllys
Andrews Frank T.
Armour George A.
Ayer Benj. F.
Bailey Edward P.
Bancroft Edgar A.
Barnum Wm. H.
Barron Elwyn A.
Barrows John H.
Bartlett A. C.
Belfield Henry H.
Belfield Wm. T.
Bentley Cyrus
Billings Frank
Bissell Richard M.
Blair Edward T.
Blatchford E. W.
Block Louis J.

Blodgett H. W.
Boutell Henry S.
Boutell Lewis H.
Boyesen Ingolf K.
Bradley Charles F.
Brittan Chas. H.
Brown Edward O.
Burley Clarence A.
Burnham DanielH.
Canfield Andrew J.
Case William W.
Cass George W.
Charnley James
Chatfield - Taylor
Hobart C.
Cheney Chas. E.
Clark John M.
Cobb Henry Ives
Coolidge Fred'c S.
Corbin David T.
Curtiss Chas. C.
Dauchy Geo. K.
Davis N. S. jr.
Dawson George E.
Denison Franklin
Dent Thomas
Dudley Emilius C.

Dupee Chas. A.
Durkee Henry R.
Eastman Sidney C.
Elliott Frank M.
Fairbank N. K.
Fales David
Farr Marvin A.
Farwell J. V. jr.
Fay Chas. Norman
Fenn Wm. W.
Fisher Walter L.
Fiske Geo. F.
Fleming Robt. H.
Freeman Heury V.
French W. M. R.
Fuller Chas. G.
Fuller M. W.
Fullerton Chas. W.
Furber Henry J., jr.
Furness Wm. Eliot
Gage Lyman J.
Galvin Edward I.
Gardiner Edwin J.
Gilbert Frank
Glessner John J.
Goodwin Daniel
Gookin Fred'k W.

Grant John C.
Greeley Fred'k
Greeley S. S.
Green Oliver B.
Gregory Stephen S.
Hale John P.
Hall Thomas C.
Hamill Chas. D.
Hamline John H.
Hapgood Norman
Hardin Martin D.
Harding Geo. F.
Harmon Chas. S.
Harper William R.
Hatch Azel F.
Head Franklin H.
Hendricks Robt. J.
Herrick John J.
Heywood Porter P.
Hibbard Homer N.
High James L.
Hild Fred'k H.
Hirsch Emil G.
Holt Chas. S.
Holt Geo. H.
Horton Oliver H.
Hosmer E. D.

Houghteling J. L.
Howland W. M.
Hubbard Joseph D.
Hubbard Wm. H.
Hulburd Chas. H.
Hunt James A.
Hunter George L.
Hutchinson C. L.
Hyde James Nevins
Isham Edward S.
Jackson H. W.
Jacobson Aug.
Jenuey W. L. B.
Johnson Frank S.
Johnson Herrick
Johnson Jas.Gibson
Jones David B.
Jones Thos. D.
Jones Samuel M.
Kales John D.
Keep Wm. B.
Keith Edson jr.
Keith Elbridge G.
Kerfoot S. H. jr.
King Henry W.
Larned Walter C.
Lathrop Bryan
Leake Joseph B.
Lee Blewett
Lewis Leslie
Lincoln Robert T.
Little Charles J.
Lloyd Henry D.
Locke Clinton
Long James H.

Lowden Frank O.
Lyman David B.
Lynde Samuel A.
McCagg Ezra B.
McClure J. G. K.
McClurg Alex. C.
McConnell S. P.
McCormick Alex.A.
McCormick C. H.
McIlvaine Wm. B,
McPherson S. J.
Mack Julian W.
MacVeagh F.
Manierre Geo.
Marston Thos. B.
Martin Horace H.
Mason E. G.
Mason Henry B.
Mason Roswell H.
Matz Herman L.
Matz Rudolph
Merriman Henry P.
Messer Loring W.
Miller Henry G.
Miller James A.
Montgomery W. A.
Nelson Murry
Nelson Murry, jr.
Nixon W. W. K.
Norton James S.
Noyes John T.
Oakley Horace S.
Oppenheim Wm. S.
Otis Ephraim A.
Paddock Geo. L.

Paige Alonzo W.
Payne John Barton
Peabody F. B.
Peabody Selim H.
Peirce James H.
Pence Abram M.
Perkins Herbert F.
Petrie Wm. J.
Phelps George B.jr.
Pickett Charles C.
Pond Allen B.
Pond Irving K.
Poole Charles C.
Prentice Sartell
Rogers Joseph M.
Root Frederic W.
Rosenthal Julius
Roys Cyrus D.
Runnels John S.
Ryerson Martin A.
Schneider George
Schobinger J. J.
Scott Frank H.
Sheldon Theodore
Sheppard Robt. D.
Shorey Daniel L.
Shorey Paul
Shortall John G.
Shortall John L,
Silsbee Jos. L.
Smith Edwin B.
Smith Fred'k B.
Smith Geo. W.
Smith Perry H.
Smith Pliny B.

Smith William H.
Sprague Albert A.
Sprague O. S. A.
Starr Merritt
Stirling J. Carolus
Stirling Wm. R.
Stone George F.
Stone Henry B.
Sullivan Louis H.
Taft Lorado
Taylor Graham
Taylor Thomas, jr.
Thacher John M.
Thomas Alfred A.
Thompson Lever'tt
Thompson Slason
Wait Horatio L.
Wait James J.
Walker Aldace F.
Walker Wirt D.
Waterman Arba N.
Wegg David S.
Wells Arthur B.
Wheeler Arthur D.
Wight Peter B.
Wilkinson D. P.
Wilkinson John
Williams Edw'd F.
Williams Norman
Wilmerding C. H.
Wilson John P.
Young A. V. E.
Young Kimball
Zeisler Sigmund

CHICAGO WOMEN'S CLUB.

15 WASHINGTON STREET.

OFFICERS.

SARAH HACKETT STEVENSON, - - - - President.
MARY H. WILMARTH, - First Vice-President.
FRANCES B. SMITH, - Second Vice-President.
KATE G. HUDDLESTON, - Corresponding Secretary.
SARAH J. WHEELER, - - - Recording Secretary.
LUCY F. FURNESS, - - - - - - Treasurer.

DIRECTORS.

Isadore Taylor
Mary E. Lewis
Alice W. Putnam
Hannah G. Solomon
Louise D. Sherman
Charlotte C. Holt

Emma C. Mann
Isabelle C.Buckingham
Mary E. Bundy
Maria C. Remick
Matilda L. Ware
Janie S. Boyesen

Harriet H. Cary
Helen L. Gridley
Helen W. Affeld
Hannah T. Vollner
Mary K. Bartlett
Celia P. Wooley

MEMBERS.

Abbott Mrs. A. C.
Abbott Mrs. A. R.
Adam Mrs. Alexander B.
Adams Mrs. Chas. A.
Adams Mrs. Egerton
Adams Mrs. Elvira H.

Adams Mrs. E. S.
Adams Mrs. G. E.
Adams Mrs. J. R.
Addams Miss Jane
Addis Mrs. Arthur T.
Adkinson Mrs. Elmer W.

Affeld Mrs. C. E.
Aldrich Mrs. J. Frank
Alexander Miss Ellen C.
Alexander Dr. H. C. B.
Altgeld Mrs. John P.
Andrews Mrs. James

26

Annis Mrs. F. M.
Atkins Mrs. F. L.
Ayer Mrs. Edward
Babcock Mrs. H. H.
Babcock Miss Mabel K.
Bacon Mrs. Georgiana R.
Badger Mrs. H. H.
Bagley Mrs. Frederick P.
Baker Mrs. Frank H.
Baker Mrs. Wilson G.
Baldwin Miss Annie B.
Ball Mrs. Farlin Q.
Bangs Mrs. John D.
Barker Mrs. Cyrus A.
Barnes Mrs. Nelson H.
Barnum Mrs. Wm. L.
Bartlett Mrs. Geo. F.
Bassett Mrs. F. S.
Bates Mrs. Lindon W.
Bayley Mrs. Edwin F.
Bedell Leila G., M.D.
Beebe Mrs. Emma A.
Beedy Miss Mary E.
Belden Mrs. J. S.
Belfield Mrs. H. H.
Bennett Mrs. Will H.
Bigelow Mrs. Edward A.
Billings Mrs. C. K. G.
Billings Mrs. Henry F.
Blackman Mrs. Edwin
Blackwelder Mrs. I. S.
Blood Miss Emma S.
Bloomingston Mrs. J. S.
Bodman Mrs. Albert C.
Bodman Mrs. Luther W.
Bolté Mrs. Charles Guy
Booth Miss Rachel M.
Borland Mrs. John J.
Boyesen Mrs. I. K.
Brainard Mrs. Harriet C.
Brayton Mrs. G. W.
Brayton Dr. Sarah H.
Brewer Mrs. John S.
Bright Mrs. Orville T.
Brine Mrs. George J.
Brodlique Miss Eva H.
Brooks Mrs. Almon
Brooks Mrs. James C.
Brooks Miss Laura H.
Broomell Mrs. Geo. D.
Brown Mrs. E. O.
Brown Mrs. T. H. jr.
Brown Mrs. Wm. T.
Brown Mrs. W. L.
Bryant Mrs. John J.
Buckingham Mrs. John
Buckingham Mrs. Jno. H.
Bundy Mrs. John C.
Burnham Mrs. Telford
Burrows Mrs. Thomas
Burt Miss Mary E.
Bush Mrs. W. H.
Butler Mrs. A. O.
Butts Miss Annie E.
Callender Mrs. B. M.
Camp Mrs. I. N.

Campbell Mrs. W. J.
Carmon Mrs. George N.
Carpenter Mrs. A. A.
Carpenter Mrs. Geo. B.
Carpenter Mrs. Wm. O.
Carr Rachel H., M.D.
Carse Mrs. Matilda B.
Carton Mrs. Laurence A.
Cary Mrs. Frank
Chalmers Mrs. W. J.
Chapin Rev. Augusta J.
Chapin Dr. Elizabeth L.
Chapman Mrs. W. S.
Chappell Mrs. H. W.
Chisholm Mrs. James
Chittenden Mrs. Nellie M.
Clapp Mrs. George
Clark Mrs. Alson E.
Clark Mrs. George M.
Clark Mrs. Andrew G,
Clark Miss Hannah B.
Clinton Mrs. George O.
Clowry Mrs. R. C.
Coffin Mrs. C. F.
Coffin Mrs. C. H.
Colby Mrs. John A.
Coleman Mrs. W. Franklin
Collins Mrs. Lorin C. jr.
Colvin Miss Katharine
Coman Mrs. Martha S.
Conant Mrs. Luther
Conger Mrs. Wm. Perry
Cooke Mrs. A. H.
Cooley Mrs. Harlan W.
Coolidge Mrs. F. S.
Coonley Mrs. John C.
Cooper Mrs. Harry H.
Corby Mrs. Emily
Corey Mrs. G. J.
Coulter Miss Hortense
Cox Mrs. Charles E.
Cox Mrs. LeRoy B.
Coy Mrs. Reuben D.
Crane Mrs. C. R.
Crane Mrs. Frances
Crane Mrs. Harbert P.
Crane Mrs. R. T.
Crepin Mrs. Ernest E.
Cropp Mrs. Carl
Crouse Mrs. J. N.
Crowe Mrs. Martha F.
Cummings Mrs. C. C.
Curtis Mrs. J. LaFayette
Cutler Mrs. C. H.
Dainty Mrs. Albert H.
Danforth Mrs. I. N.
Davidson Mrs. S. Frank
Davis Mrs. Charles W.
Delano Mrs. F. A.
Dennis Mrs. Charles S.
Dickinson Dr. Frances
Dietz Mrs. Jacob C.
Dingee Miss Gertrude P.
Dixon Mrs. L. B.
Dixson Mrs. Zella A.
Donald Mrs. F. C.

Doud Mrs. L. B.
Dow Mrs. Wm. Cary
Dreier Mrs. Carl
Driver Mrs. Edward A.
Duncanson Mrs. H. W.
Dunlap Mrs. George L.
Dupee Mrs. E. W.
Dye Mrs. Mary I.
Eastman Mrs. S. C.
Eaton Mrs. C. L.
Eckhardt Mrs. Thomas
Edwards Mrs. Arthur
Effinger Mrs. John R.
Ela Mrs. John W.
Ellis Mrs. Sumner
Emery Mrs. Theodore
Engleman Miss Emma
Ewing Miss Edith C.
Fairbanks Mrs. Geo. Otis
Farnham Mrs. R. E.
Farson Mrs. R. B.
Fearing Miss L. Blanche
Ferry Mrs. James W.
Fessenden Mrs. Benj. A.
Finch Mrs. Hunter W.
Fischer Mrs. A. C.
Fiske Mrs. George F.
Fitch Mrs. H. S.
Fitz Simons Mrs. Chas.
Flemming Miss Martha
Flower Mrs. James M.
Follansbee Mrs. Geo. A.
Foote Mrs. Sarah V
Forsyth Mrs. Wm.
Fox Miss Harriett A.
Fox Dr. Harriet Magee
Frank Mrs. H. L.
Freeman Mrs. Henry V.
Fry Mrs. Henry T.
Fry Mrs. Thomas E.
Fulton Mrs. J. L.
Furber Mrs. H. J.
Furness Mrs. W. E.
Furness Miss E. M.
Galvin Mrs. E. I.
Gary Miss Fannie E.
Gilbert Mrs. A. M.
Gilbert Mrs. Frank
Gilbert Mrs. James H.
Girling Mrs. Winthrop
Glaspell Mrs. Albert
Gorton Miss Belle L.
Granger Mrs. Wm. S.
Graves Kate I., M.D.
Graves Mrs. Dwight W.
Graves Mrs. Sara L.
Greele Miss L. M.
Green Mrs. A. W.
Greenleaf Mrs. Walter G.
Gridley Mrs. Nelson C.
Gross Mrs. Samuel E.
Gwinn Mrs. J. Morris
Hageman Mrs. Anthony J.
Hagerty Mrs. Thomas A.
Hale Mrs. Geo. W.
Hall Mrs. Frederick H.

Halsted Miss N.
Hamilton Mrs. Henry E.
Hammer Mrs. D. Harry
Hammond Mrs. L. D.
Hancock Mrs. Bradford
Hancock Miss Ellen F.
Handy Mrs. Henry H.
Harding Mrs. Addie C.
Harding Mrs. George F.
Harmon Mrs. Edwin C.
Harmon Miss Mary L.
Harris Mrs. Rachel A.
Harrison Miss Elizabeth
Harvey Mrs. J. D.
Harvey Mrs. Wm. P.
Harwood Mrs. Henry W.
Haskell Mrs. Geo. W.
Hastings Mrs. T. D.
Haworth Mrs. Geo. D.
Hayt Mrs. Henry C.
Haythorne Miss Florence
Heard Mrs. D. B.
Hedenberg Miss Cecilia
Henderson Mrs. C. R.
Henrotin Mrs. Charles
Heilé Mrs. Adolf
Hequembourg Mrs. J. E.
Heywood Mrs. F. S.
Hibbard Mrs. W. N.
Hicks Mrs. Oliver H.
Hiestand Mrs. Mary
Higgins Mrs. Milton O.
Higginson Mrs. C. M.
Higginson Mrs. Geo., jr.
Hill Mrs. J. M.
Hill Mrs. Lysander
Himrod Mrs. Charles
Himrod Miss Phebe
Hinckley Mrs. Chas. W.
Hobart Mrs. Horace R.
Hobbs Mrs. J. B.
Hodges Mrs. Walter E.
Holbrook Mrs. A. W.
Holden Mrs. T. N.
Holmes Mrs. Bayard
Holt Mrs. G. M.
Holton Mrs. E.
Hood Miss Helen L.
Hoppin Mrs. Bush E.
Horton Mrs. H. B.
Hosmer Miss Eliza
Hosmer Mrs. F. B.
Hosmer Mrs. J. W.
Hough Mrs. Sheldon L.
Howard Mrs. Thomas
Howe Mrs. F. S.
Howell Mrs. S. R.
Howells Miss Theodora W.
Hoyt Mrs. Henry W.
Hoyt Mrs. Wm.
Huddleston Mrs. Geo. W.
Hughes Mrs. John B.
Hunt Dr. Florence W.
Hutchins Mrs. James C.
Hutchinson Miss F. C.
Ingals Mrs. E. Fletcher

Jenney Mrs. H. W.
Johnson Mrs. Francis A.
Johnson Mrs. Willis F.
Johnston Mrs. Jas. B.
Jones Mrs. Graham
Jones Mrs. J. L.
Judah Mrs. Noble B.
Judd Miss S. Alice
Judson Mrs. W. B.
Keen Mrs. Edwin H.
Keen Mrs. W. B. jr.
Keepers Mrs. Wm. E.
Kempton Madame Jenny
Kendall Mrs. B. w.
Kendig Mrs. J. A. J.
Kett Mrs. H. F.
Keyes Mrs. Rollin A.
King Mrs. Philo R.
Kingman Mrs. Chas H.
Kirkland Miss Elizabeth
Kirtland Mrs. India U.
Kohlsaat Mrs. Herman H.
Kretschmar Mrs. H. S.
Kretzinger Mrs. G. W.
Krout Miss Mary H.
Kuh Mrs. Edwin J.
Kuh Mrs. Henry
Lacy Miss Sara
Lane Mrs. A. G.
Lane Miss Ida M.
Lapham Mrs. Joseph
Lasher Mrs. C. W.
Lathrop Miss Julia C.
Lawrence Mrs. E. F.
Leavens Miss Julia P.
LeBaron Miss Frances
Leekley Miss Charlotte A.
Leman Mrs. H. W.
Leopold Mrs. Max
Lewis Mrs. Leslie
Lloyd Mrs. Henry D.
Long Mrs. James H.
Loomis Mrs. M. B.
Loring Mrs. M. A.
Loveday Mrs. Fanny M.
Low Dr. Julia Rossy
Lumm Miss Emma G.
Lunt Mrs. E. M.
Lyford Mrs. Will Hartw'l
MacArthur Mrs. A.
MacLeish Mrs. Andrew
Magee Mrs. Henry W.
Mann Mrs. James R.
Manierre Mrs. Wm. R.
Marquerat Mrs. Eugene
Marsh Mrs. George
Marsh Mrs. James P.
Marshall Mrs. Geo. E.
Martin Miss Ellen A.
Martin Mrs. Franklin H.
Martin Mrs. S. K.
Marvin Mrs. William
Mason Mrs. M. Louise
Mason Mrs. Wm. A.
Mather Mrs. Alonzo C.
Matson Mrs. Canute R.

Matz Mrs. Otto H.
Maxwell Mrs. E. E.
Maxwell Mrs. S. A.
Mayer Mrs. L.
McBean Mrs. A. J.
McConnell Mrs. Luther M.
McCrea Mrs. James
McCulloch Mrs. C. W.
McDoel Miss Mary A.
McDougall Miss Isabel
McEntee Mrs. Chas. S.
McGraw Mrs. J. W.
McKinlock Mrs. Wm. H.
McMahan Mrs. R. W.
Mead Miss Marian
Meadowcroft Miss F. M.
Mergler Dr. Marie J.
Merrill Mrs. A. F.
Metcalf Mrs. H. C.
Middendorf Mrs. Geo.
Millard Mrs. S. M.
Miller Mrs. A. C.
Miller Mrs. C. P.
Millington Mrs. L. B.
Mitchell Mrs. J. Sidney
Mitchell Mrs. L. B.
Mixer Dr. Mary A.
Montgomery Mrs. Wm. A.
Morford Mrs. T. T.
Morgan Miss Anna
Morley Miss Margaret W.
Morris Mrs. Thomas G.
Murray Mrs. L. W.
Nagle Mrs. A. F.
Neale Miss Alice E.
Nelson Mrs. Walter C.
Nixon Mrs. Wm. Penn
Nolan Mrs. John H.
North Mrs. C. A.
North Mrs. R. L.
Norton Mrs. Edwin
O'Connor Mrs. John
Odell Mrs. J. J. P.
Olson Mrs. N. F.
Ostrander Mrs. D.
Packard Mrs. George
Page Mrs. C. L.
Palmer Mrs. Potter
Parker Mrs. Francis W.
Parker Mrs. J. J.
Parker Mrs. Lewis W.
Peabody Mrs. S. H.
Peck Mrs. Walter L.
Peirce Mrs. Arthur H.
Peirce Mrs. L. H.
Penfield Mrs. Truman
Perry Mrs. Frederick B.
Peters Mrs. Wm. Morgan
Pettibone Mrs. A. G.
Pettibone Mrs. P. F.
Phelps Mrs. E. M.
Pierce Mrs. Chas F.
Pierce Mrs. Henry A.
Pittman Mrs. Clement K.
Plummer Mrs. G. W.
Plummer Mrs. J. W.

Porter Mrs. Edward C.
Potter Mrs. Edwin A.
Potter Mrs. O. W.
Potter Mrs. W. L.
Pratt Mrs. J. H.
Pratt Mrs. Sarah W.
Preston Mrs. E. B.
Prindle Mrs. Jason R.
Prussing Miss Linda M.
Pryor Mrs. Gilbert
Purdy Miss Sara C.
Putnam Mrs. Joseph R.
Rand Mrs. John C.
Rand Mrs. W. H.
Rawson Mrs. Hart
Raynolds Mrs. James D.
Reasner Dr. Marie E.
Reed Mrs. George J.
Reed Mrs. Robert C.
Remick Mrs. Marie C.
Rice Miss Rebecca S.
Richardson Mrs. A. P.
Richardson Mrs. D. E.
Rickcords Mrs. Geo. E.
Ripley Mrs. E. P.
Robbins Mrs. Walter R.
Rogers Mrs. John G.
Rogers Mrs. J. C.
Rohde Mrs. H. F.
Rowe Mrs. Chas. H.
Rowe Mrs. James L.
Ryerson Mrs. Martin A.
Sawyer Mrs. C. B.
Sawyer Mrs. Francis A.
Saxton Mrs. Hester B.
Scho er Mrs. Ernest A.
ScottyMrs. J. W.
Sears Mrs. Nathaniel C.
Seaton Mrs. Chauncey
Seaverns 'Mrs. Geo. A. jr.
Seavey Mrs. D. H.
Seeberger Mrs. Louis A.
Seeley Mrs. T. P.
Shackelton Mrs. A.
Sharpe Mrs. Ernest R.
Shattuck Mrs. L. B.
Shears Mrs. G. F., M.D.
Shepard Mrs. Daniel
Sheppard Mrs. Thos. H.
Sheridan Mrs. W. A.
Snively Miss Anna M.
Solomon Mrs. Henry
Somerville Mrs. Robert
Soper Mrs. James
Southwell Mrs. H. E.
Spalding Mrs. A. G.
Spicer Mrs. G. A.
Spicer Mrs. V. K.
Sprague Mrs. A. A.
Springer Miss Ada E.
Sprague Mrs. O. S. A.
Squire Miss Mary E.
Stafford Miss Juniata
Stanley Mrs. C. E.
Stanton Mrs. Edgar
Stanton Mrs. S. Cecil

Starkey Mrs. Horace M.
Starin Mrs. Wm. A.
Starr Miss Ellen
Starr Mrs. Merritt
Starrett Mrs. Helen E.
Steele Mrs. D. A. K.
Steiniger Mrs. S.
Sterling Mrs. Chas. J.
Stevens Mrs. Plowdon
Stevenson Sarah H.,M.D.
Sherman Mrs. John jr.
Sherman Mrs. John D.
Sherman Mrs. P. L.
Sherwood Mrs. John B.
Sherwood Mrs. M.
Sherwood Miss T. L.
Shorey Mrs. D. L.
Shorey Miss Martha H.
Shortall Mrs. John L.
Sill Mrs. Robert T.
Silsbee Mrs. J. L.
Simmons Mrs. F. T.
Simonds Mrs. John C.
Smith Mrs. Byron L.
Smith Mrs. Calvin S.
Smith Miss Clara A.
Smith Mrs. C. C.
Smith Mrs. Frederick A.
Smith Mrs. George W.
Smith Dr. Julia Holmes
Smith Miss Mary Roset
Smith Mrs. Perry H.
Smith Mrs. Proctor
Smyth Mrs. J. G.
Stiles Miss Lucy Goddard
Stirling Mrs. J. Carolus
Stirling Mrs. Wm. R.
St. John Mrs. E.
Stone Mrs. Henry B.
Stout Mrs. Melancthon S.
Strauss Mrs. Michael
Strong Mrs. E. B.
Sturckow Mrs. F. L.
Sturges Mrs. George
Sturges Miss Marion D.
Sullivan Dr. Margaret E.
Summers Miss Maud
Swan Mrs. James H.
Swan Mrs. O. S.
Sweet Miss Ada C.
Talbot Mrs. Eugene
Taylor Mrs. Homer S.
Taylor Mrs. S. G.
Temple Miss Alice
Temple Miss Grace
Tenney Miss Mary S.
Thayer Mrs. Nathaniel C.
Thomas Mrs. C. G.
Thomas Mrs. Herbert A.
Thompson Mrs.Wm.Hale
Thorne Mrs. George R.
Tilton Miss Catherine P.
Tilton Mrs. Lucian
Tisdale Mrs. Laura J.
Travers Mrs. R. P.
Treat Mrs. Chas. P.

Tripp Mrs. Mattie W.
Tucker Mrs. L. K.
Tuley Mrs. M. F.
Turner Mrs. Edward H.
Twyman Mrs. Joseph
Tyler Mrs. Wm. H.
Ullman Mrs. Frederick
Underhill Mrs. Elizabeth
Upton Mrs. E. L.
VanBenschoten Mrs.M.C.
VanNortwick Miss Louise
Van Voorhis Mrs. Frank
Vaughan Mrs. J. C.
Vaughan Miss Mary E.
Vollmer Mrs. A. F.
Wagg Mrs. Howard N.
Wait Mrs. Horatio L.
Wakemann Mrs. A. V. H.
Waldron Mrs. Louis K.
Wallace Mrs. James
Wallace Mrs. M. R. M.
Walsh Mrs. John R.
Walter Mrs. J. C.
Wanzer Mrs. James M.
Ware Mrs. John M.
Warner Mrs. W. C.
Washburne Mrs. Geo. F.
Watrous Mrs. C.
Watson Mrs. I. A.
Wegg Mrs. D. S.
Weide Miss Lillian B.
Wells Mrs. C. H.
West Mrs. James J.
Weston Mrs. Olive E.
Wetherell Mrs. O. D.
Wheeler Mrs. C. G.
Wheeler Mrs. Sarah E.
Whidden Mrs. Geo. F.
Whitcomb Miss Adele
White Mrs. W. R.
White Miss W. T.
Whiteford Mrs. David
Whiting Miss Fannie
Whitman Mrs. Russell
Whitney Mrs. Charles P.
Whitney Mrs. John B.
Wiles Mrs. Robert H.
Wilkinson Mrs. John
Willard Mrs. C. E.
Willard Miss Frances E.
Willard Miss May F.
Wilmarth Mrs. H. M.
Wilson Mrs. John P.
Wilson Mrs. John R.
Withrow Mrs. Thomas F.
Withrow Miss Bonnie
Wood Mrs. Casey A.
Wood Mrs. Milton R.
Woodward Mrs. Geo. W.
Woodward Mrs. James L.
Woodyatt Mrs. W. H.
Woolley Mrs. J. H.
Worthy Mrs. John
Wright Mrs. Charles H.
Wygant Mrs. Alonzo
Young Mrs. Ella F.

COLUMBUS CLUB.

43 AND 45 MONROE STREET.

OFFICERS.

WM. A. AMBERG, - - - - - - - -	President.
ZENOPHILE P. BROSSEAU, - - - - -	First Vice-President.
JNO. GUERIN, - - - - - - - -	Second Vice-President.
WILLIAM E. O'NEILL, - - - - - - -	Secretary.
WILLIAM P. HENNEBERRY, - - - - -	Treasurer.

DIRECTORS.

. David F. Bremner	Charles S. Winslow	Morris H. P. Thomas
Thomas A. Moran	Alex. W McDougal	Daniel B. Scully

MEMBERS.

Abbott Wm. N.	Boyle Daniel	Campbell Rev.L.A.	Cooper J. S.
Adjutor Rev. Bro.	Boyle James H.	Campbell Wm. L.	Corboy M. J.
Agnew John P.	Boyle John T.	Canavan Austin A.	Corkery Charles
Agnew Rev. P. J.	Boyle J. P.	Cannon E. H.	Coughlin Thomas
Allen Chas. F. M.	Boyle L. P.	Cannon W. J.	Coughlan T. E.
Allen Wm. H.	Bradley Dr. C. P.	Carey Wm. P.	Cox Thomas
Alt C. William, jr.	Brady J. B.	Carpenter Grant	Coyne D. J.
Amberg C. Louis	Brady J. T.	Carroll John C.	Cratty Thomas
Amberg John H.	Brandecker F. X.	Carroll John M.	Cremin Jno. F.
Amberg J. Ward	Bransfield M. J.	Casey Thomas S.	Crennan Joseph M.
Amberg Theo. J.	Breen J. B.	Caubert Eugene	Crennan W. A.
Amberg W. A.	Breen Martin J.	Cavanagh Patrick	Croarkin FrancisE.
Ames M. E.	Breen Thomas	Christoph E. G.	Cronin A. J.
Armstrong HenryJ.	Breen T. B.	Clarke H. B.	Crowe Dr. J. J.
Bagley Frank R.	Bremner D. F.	Clear M. E.	Crowley W. F.
Bailey M. B.	Bremner D. F. jr.	Cleary J. J.	Cudahy Michael
Bardon Michael M.	Bremner R. J.	Cleary P.	Cudahy John
Barrett John F.	Brenan Thos.	Clifford John	CullenyE. W.
Barrett John P.	Brennan J. J.	Clifford R. W.	Cummings Andrew
Barrett Thomas E.	Brennan Michael	Clifford T. H.	Cummings Ed. S.
Barrington Chas.V.	Brennan T. W.	Clohery T. B.	Cunningham W. H.
Barrington P. F.	Brennock John	Clowry James	Cusack Thomas
Barry James L.	Brent W. L.	Coakley Wm.	Dalton Jno. E.
Barry Miles	Broduer H. J.	Cochrane Geo. H.	Daly A. D.
Barry P. T.	Brosseau Aug.	Cochrane Thos J.	Daly Dennis S.
Barry Thomas F.	Brosseau Z. P.	Coffey J. J.	Dean O. W.
Bauerle Michael	Brown Edward O.	Colby F. T.	Dean T. A.
Beauvais Elzear A.	Brueckner J. F.	Coleman M. J.	Delaney Daniel
Becker A. W.	Buford Charles	Collins M. A.	Delaney ThomasF.
Bedard Antoine J.	Bulger W. J.	Condon W. H.	Delany Martin A.
Benzinger M. V.	Burke James H.	Conlan James	Delihant W. T.
Bergeron Rev.A.L.	Burns James	Conlau J. A. jr.	Demers Phedime
Bergeron J.Z.,M.D.	Burns James M.	Conlan J. F.	Dennehy Thos. C.
Bergevin Alex. M.	Butler B. F.	Conley C. E.	Dent T. A.
Bergevin Daniel	Butler John R.	Conley Dr. P. H.	DeParadis P. A.
Berry Thomas W.	Byrne John	Conley Thomas	DeTamble M.
Bessems Paul	Byrne J. P.	Conley T. J.	Detmer J. F.
Bigley W. L.	Byrne P. O'Neil	Connell Geo. W.	Deveney J. H.
Birmingham J. H.	Byrne William P.	Connell J. A.	Devlin Frank A.
Blanc N. F.	Caffrey P. F.	Connell T. P.	Devlin John
BonfieldRev. Michael	Cahill E. T.	Connelly Thomas	Diggles J. W.
	Caldwell Chas. P.	Connolly C. C.	Dillon Wm.
Boughan A. B.	Callahan A. P.	Cook P. J.	Dolan J. J.
Boughan John	Callahan M. C.	Cooke C. F.	Donnersberger Jos.
Bourassa J. H.	Callinan Thos. J.	Cooke J. S.	Donoghue M. F.
Bowen Patrick K.	Cameron D. R.	Cooke W. J.	Donohue J. W.
Bowers J. F.	Campbell J. F. jr.	Cooney P. H.	Donohue M. A.

Donohue Wm. F.
Dooley J. C.
Downey Nicholas J.
Doyle Austin J.
Doyle Austin J. jr.
Doyle James
Doyle J. J.
Doyle J. M.
Doyle Wm. A.
Drant Jno. W.
Druiding Adolphus
Duffy Jno. M.
Duffy Thomas J.
Duncan J. W.
Dunne Edward F.
Dnnne E. M.
Dunne Jas.
Dunne Michael J.
Dupuis Modeste
Durgan C. P.
Duvall W. H.
Dyrenforth J W.
Eagle Harry R.
Early Patrick H.
Ebbert W. H.
Ederer E P.
Egan J. J.
English Wm. J.
Enright J. W.
Ernst C. E.
Evoy Thomas A.
Fay J. L.
Ferguson L. A.
Fitzgerald Henry J.
Fitzgerald W. H.
Fitzpatrick Bern'rd
Fitzpatrick H. J.
Fitzpatrick John
Fitzpatrick Peter
Fitzsimmons John
FixKlen . C.
Fleming J. D.
Foley W. C.
Foltz Fritz
Fortin J. T.
Fortune Peter
Fortune Wm. J.
Foster George P.
Fox John V.
Franchere G. F.
Franchere O. J.
Gahagan Dr. H. J.
Gahan Thomas
Gallagher Daniel
Gallagher M. F.
Gallery Daniel J.
Gallery D. V.
Gannon Richard
Gareau Cesaire
Garrity P. L.
Garvey Jno. W.
Gateley John
Gaynor John
Gaynor J. A.
Gfrorer Dr. G. S.
Gibbons John

Gill P. D.
Gillespie P. F.
Glassbrook T. H.
Glennon E. T.
Goggin James
Goodwin P. H.
Graham A. J.
Graham Eugene
Green A. W.
Green G. P.
Green H. R. jr.
Griffin H. T.
Griffin M. J.
Griffin S. D.
Guerin Dr. Jno.
Guerin M. Henry
Guerin Thomas E.
Hagan J. M.
Halla Charles
Halligan Frank E.
Hallinan T. G.
Hallinan T. P.
Hannan James
Harbour P. C. ;
Hart John J.
Hartnett J. jr.
Hayes C. B.
Hayes David
Hayes E. J.
Hayes H. V.
Hayes John
Hayes John J.
Hayes J. J.
Hayes Louis
Hayes P. D.
Hayne W. J.
Healy J. J.
Healy J. R.
Healy J. T.
Healy P. J.
Heany James B.
Hefferan W. D.
Hellman H. B.
Helmholz Fred.
Henneberry Rev FS
Henneberry W. P.
Hennessey S. A.
Herbert C. J.
Herel M. B.
Heron John
Herson John
Hickey A. C.
Higgins J. Frank
Higgins J. F.
Hilly H. T.
Hilly M. B.
Hines Edward
Hodnett Rev. T. P.
Hoey M. H.
Hogan Thomas S.
Holland J. J.
Honan M. W.
Hoops Wm. H.
Hopkins John P.
Hudson Edward
Hughes Jos.

Hurley F. J.
Hurley T. D.
Hutchings W. A.
Hut?hinson Thos.
Hutchinson W. H.
Hyland J. S.
Hyland M. D.
Hynes W. J.
Jacksou O. A.
Jennings C. P.
Judge T. F.
Kanes T. C.
Kasper A. J.
Kasper Peter J.
Kavanaugh M.
Keane M. J.
Kearney Joseph
Kearney J. J.
Kearns H. J.
Keating J. F.
Keating M.
Keefe A. J.
Keefe Dr. Jas. F.
Keeler Charles E.
Keeley Eugene M.
Keeley Thos. F.
Kehoe J. E.
Kelly D. F.
Kelly Rev. E. A.
Kelly Jas. J.
Kelly John
Kelly J. W.
Kelly M. R.
Kelly M. W.
Kelly Thomas
Kelly Thomas
Kelly William
Kennedy Edw. F.
Kent W. D.
Keogh F. J.
Keogh J. B.
Keogh James B.
Kerwin M. W.
Kiernan Thos. S.
Kilcrane F. J.
Kiley John
Kinnare F. T.
Kinsella F. D.
Kinsella J. E.
Kinsella J. J.
Kiolbassa Peter
Kreer John J.
Kyle W. F.
Lackey P.
Lally J. J.
Lambert J. A.
Lantry T. B.
Lapoint D. A.
Larkin Dr. J. J.
Larney John
Lauth J. P.
Leahy James
Leonard T. J.
Linneen P. H.
Lloyd Evan
Lloyd Wm. G.

Loftus S. T. A.
Long Edward
Loomis E. E.
Luken Wm. M.
Lydon Wm. A.
Lynch Andrew M.
Lynch C. R.
Lynch Daniel
Lynch John
Lynch T. R.
Ly J. J.
Macksn John
Madden Mark F.
Madden M. S.
Madden P. J.
Magee Charles J.
Mages Geo. C.
Maginn B. B.
Maher D. W.
Maher James
Maher Philip
Mahon Bernard
Mair Chas. A.
Mair Henry B.
Maloy B. J.
Mandable M. L.
Marum E. .
Mayer Joseph
Mayer Levy
Mayer R. H.
McAdam C. V.
McAdam John V.
McAdam Peter
McArdle P. L.
McCabe John
McCaffery D. J.
McCarthy Florence
McCarthy John
McCarthy John J.
McCarthy J. F.
McCarthy J. G.
McCarthy Dr. Wm.
McCausland A. J.
McCoy Wm.
McDonald J. A.
McDonnell B. A.
McDonnell Wm.
McDougall A. W.
McElherne D. J.
McEnery John T.
McEvoy Robert M.
McFarland F. W.
McGee M. J.
McGoey John
McGoorty J. P.
McGowan J. D.
McGrath Chas. H.
McGrath John J.
McGrath J. P.
McGrath J. T.
McGrath Dr. P. J.
McGuire Rev. Hugh
McGuire John F.
McGuire Wm. A.
McGurrin Edward
McHugh Patrick

McKindley D. M.
McLaughlin Geo.D
McMahon John
McMahon J. P.
McMahon M. J.
McNamara Jere-
miah
McNamara J. H.
McNamee Rev.W.J
McNamee P. F.
McNulty T. J.
McShane James
McVoy John
Meagher James F.
Melody Rev. J. W.
Melody Thomas R.
Miller G. S.
Minnehan R. M.
Mollan C. G.
Molloy Edward
Monaghan J. J.
Moody C. H.
Moody J. A.
Moore C. M.
Moran J. P.
Moran R. H.
Morun Thomas
Moran T. M.
Moran T. W.
Morrison J. D.
Morrison R. W.
Mudd Frank X.
Mulcahy F. J.
Muldoon Rev. P. J.
Mullaney T. F.
Mullay T. H.
Mullen John A.
Mullin J. J.
Munhall Wm. D.
Murphy Chris.
Murphy Daniel J.
Murphy F. T.
Murphy Jeremiah
Murphy John B.
Murphy John E.
Murphy Joseph G.
Murphy J. H.
Murphy J. P.
Murphy N. J.
Murphy P. M.
Murphy R. J.
Murphy W. H.
Murphy M. W.
Murray Rev. B. P.
Naghten Frank A.
Naghten James J.
Naghten John
Naghten J. J.
Naghten M. J.
Nagle J. F.

Nally E. J.
Neary N. J.
Nelson L. A.
Nelson John L.
Nelson N. J.
Nelson Wm. P.
Niehoff Frank J.
Niehoff Otto E.
Nolan J. F.
Nolan Louis E.
O'Brien Bernard
O'Brien Frank
O'Brien T. E.
O'Brien Wm. H.
O'Connell A. J.
O'Connell H. C.
O'Connell James
O'Connell John
O'Connell J. A.
O'Connell Thomas
O'Connor J. J.
O'Day F. C.
O'Donnell FrankA.
O'Dwyer Robt.
O'Garn T. J.
Ohearne W. F.
O'Heir A. J.
Ohlhesier J. T.
O'Keefe P. J.
O'Keeffe Patrick
O'Laughlin James
O'Leary Daniel
O'Leary M. J.
Olinger F. E.
O'Malley John
Onahan W. J.;
O'Neil J. F.
O'Neill Richard
O'Neill Wm. E.
O'Reilly G. B.
O'Shea Dr. David
Phalen M. W.
Philbin J. J.
Phinney T. W.
Pickham J. D.
Piper Dr. R. J.
Plamondon A.
Plamondon A. D.
Plamondon C. A.
Plamondon Geo.
Plantz Walter M.
Pound N. D.
Powell J. J.
Powell W. H.
Powers Harry J.
Prendergast Rich-
ard
Prindeville C. H.
Quinlan Thos. A.
Quinn W. A.

Quinn W. E.
Raggio C. A.
Ralston J. S.
Reddy Jas. M.
Reed Lawrence J.
Reilly George
Rend Wm. P.
Reynolds Geo. W.
Rice Patrick H.
Rice T. J.
Rigney Jno. J.
Riordan Rev. D. J.
Roach J. T.
Roche E. H.
Rock D. J.
Rock J. F.
Rockbin Rev. L. A.
Roe Joseph A.
Roemheld J. E.
Rogan W. E.
Rooney Thos. E.
Rowan James :
Rowan Peter J.
Russell M. J.
Ryan Andrew J.
Ryan E. J.
Ryan G. J.
Ryan John F.
Ryan John J.|
Ryan J. M.
Ryan M. W.
Ryan P. F.
Ryan P. J.
Ryan T. E.
Ryan T. J.
Ryan Wm. W.
Sackley James A.
Sattler D. S.
Sauter C. J.
Sawyer C. S.
Sayer G. J.
Scales Frank
Schaub F. J.
Schaub Wm. L.
Schomer Henry
Scully Daniel B.
Sennott T. W.
Sexton John
Sexton Patrick J.
Shanahan J. P.
Shanahan M. W.
Shannon N. J.
Shay Thomas J.
Shea J. B.
Shea J. E.
Sheahan J. S.
Sheehy J. J.
Slattery T. W.
Smith Geo. W.
Smith J. Charles

Smith Wm. H.
Smith W. H.
Smith W. M.
Smyth Rev. H. P.
Smyth Jno. M.
Snowhook P. W.
Spelz F. W.
Sullivan C.
Sullivan D.
Sullivan James
Sullivan Jo . W.
Sullivan MSC.
Sullivan R. C.
Sweitzer R. W.
Swenie Dennis J.
Swenie J. J.
Synon J. H.
Teehane M. J.
Thatcher A. P.
Thomas M. H. P.
Thomas R. H.
Thompson J. D.
Thorne W. H.
Tighe Rev. D. A.
Tobin F. W.
Turnbull G. T.
Vernon C. S.
Vosbrink G. P.
Vowrie H. J.
Wade John J.
Wade Thos. P.
Walls Dr. F. X.
Walls Thomas
Walls T. P.
Walsh E. E.
Walsh E. J.
Walsh James
Walsh John W.
Walsh Richard
Walsh Wm. J.
Walsh W. C.
Ward Albert J.
Ward J. H.
Waters J. E.
Waters T. J.
Weadley Wm.
Welch Dr. P. H.
Wetterer Herman
Whalen Chris.
White Patrick
White T. M.
Wigham T. A.
Winslow C. S.
Winslow E. D.
Wolfe R. W.
Wolford J. A.
Wright Frank S.
Wrightson Hugh
Young F. W.
Zahringer C. T.

THE COMMERCIAL CLUB.

OFFICERS.

WILLIAM T. BAKER, - - - - - President.
JOHN B. DRAKE, - - - - - Vice-President.
JOHN J. JANES, - - - - - Secretary.
HENRY J. MACFARLAND, - - - - Treasurer.

EXECUTIVE COMMITTEE.

F. B. Peabody.　　　　H. B. Stone.　　　　O. S. A. Sprague.

MEMBERS.

Armour P. D.
Ayer Edward E.
Baker Wm. T.
Bartlett A. C.
Blatchford E. W.
Bradley J. Harley
Carpenter A. A.
Cary Eugene
Clark John M.
Crane R. T.
DeKoven John
Doane J. W.
Drake John B.
Fairbank N. K.
Fargo Charles

Farwell C. B.
Field Marshall
Fuller W. A.
Gage L. J.
Glessner J. J.
Grannis W. C. D.
Harvey T. W.
Head Franklin H.
Henderson C. M.
Hibbard W. G.
Higinbotham H. N.
Hotz Christopher
Houghteling J. L.
Hughitt Marvin
Hutchinson C. L.

Janes John J.
Keith Edson
Keith E. G.
King H. W.
Kohlsaat H. H.
MacFarland H. J.
MacVeagh F.
McClurg, A. C.
McCormick C. H.
Munro William
Murdock Thomas
Nelson Murry
Oakley J. W.
Peabody F. B.
Phelps E. M.

Porter H. H.
Potter O. W.
Pullman Geo. M.
Rand W. H.
Ream Norman B.
Ryerson Martin A.
Seeberger A. F.
Sprague A. A.
Sprague O. S. A.
Stone H. B.
Stone Melville E.
Walker George C.
Walker J. H.
Wampold Louis
Watkins E. T.

CONCORDIA CLUB.

3140 INDIANA AVENUE.

OFFICERS.

LOUIS EISENDRATH, - - - - - President.
A. FRESHMAN, - - - - - - Vice-President.
JOSEPH G. STRAUS, - - - - - Secretary.
MICHAEL ALTMAN, - - - - - Treasurer.

GOVERNORS.

H. Schopflocher,
Ralph Strauss,
Louis Kahn,

J. Spiegel,
A. Michaels,
I. Altman,
Ben Steinfeld,

Dan Guthman.
M. Simons,
Robert Hart.

MEMBERS.

Adler Morris
Adler S. S.
Altman I.
Altman M.
Auerbach J. C.
Baer Ike
Baernstein D. S.
Bamberger Prof.G.
Barnett H.
Bauman E.
Bauman Joseph
Berlizheimer D.
Black I.
Black Morris

Blum Leon
Childs William
David Sol.
Davis Samuel
DeLee Charles
Drom Lee
Eiseman Max
Eisendrath Louis
Emerich Martin
Eppenstein E. C.
Epstein Sam
Ettlinger S.
Fass Jacob
Frank N. L.

Freeman H.
Freshman A.
Gattman Hy.
Getz Dan
Getz Meier
Goldschmidt M.
Greenbaum J. M.
Guggenheim Harry
Guggenheim Jos.
Guthman Dan
Guthman E.
Guthman L.
Hart R.
Hasterlick Sam

Hepburn John W.
Herman Ben
Herrick I.
Hess Jacob
Hexter K.
Hirsch Rev. E. G.
Hirsh Fred
Hirsh M.
Hoexter J. N.
Hofheimer Isa
Jacobson Harry
Jesselson Isaac
Jesselson Max

Joseph Charles
Joseph Jacob
Joseph L.
Kahn L.
Kahn M.
Kaiser J. M.
Katz Abe L.
Kaufman Aaron
Kaufman Louis
Klein G. L.
Kohn Milton M.
Kramer Leon
Landauer Fred
Lemberg L.
Leppel M.
Leppel S.
Levy A. M.
Levy I. D.
Levy J. B.
Lichtenstadt P.
Lilienfeld Harry
Loebenstein Rud
Lubliner S.
Lyons J. L.

Macdonald W. A.
Madden M. B.
Marks Charles
Marks M.
Mayer Isaac M.
Mayer Jacob
Mayer L. L.
Mayer Morris
Mayer M. H.
Mayer Simon
Michaels A.
Michaels Joseph
Minzesheimer L.F.
Moses Rev. I. S.
Myers C.
Myers Ed.
Neuberger J. Ed.
Neuman A.
Neumann Ig.
Olff Max
Ottenheimer D. M.
Picard Lehman
Piviansky L. H.
Podolski Theo.

Powell Adolph
Regensberg S. H.
Reitler Joseph
Rice I. M.
Rosenberg A.
Rosenberg S. A.
Rosenheim S.
Rosenthal Isaac
Rothschild Harry
Rothschild Justin
Rothschild William
Sahlin Max
Samuel Leo
Samuels M.
Sattler David
Schamberg L.
Schlesinger B.
Schlesinger Max
Schneewind Sam.
Schopflocher H.
Schwarzschild S.
Schyke H. W.
Simon David
Simons Mark

Spiegel J.
Steiner Jacob
Steinfeld B.
Stern A.
Stern Ike
Sternberg E.
Strauss Henry
Strauss J. G.
Strauss Ralph
Strauss Sam
Strouss Emil
Waixel Henry
Waixel Moses
Weber Dr. S. L.
Weil Carl
Weinberg M.
Weingarten J.
Weinschenk Lucius
Weiskopf A.
Wertheimer M.
Wilmersdorf M.
Wolf Sigmund B.
Wolff Charles
Wolfstein I. N.

THE CONTRIBUTORS' CLUB.

OFFICERS.

Mr. Franklin H. Head, - - - - President.
Mrs. H. M. Wilmarth, - - - Vice-President.
Mr. John W. Ela, - - - - - Treasurer.
Miss Caroline Kirkland, - - - - Secretary.
Mrs. Alexander F. Stevenson, - - Manager.
Mr. Arthur J. Eddy, - - - - - Editor.

MEMBERS.

Abbott Mrs. Charles P.
Bates Mrs. Clara Doty
Brainard Mrs. Harriet G.
Buell Miss May
Caton Mr.& Mrs.ArthurJ.
Chatfield-Taylor Mr. &
Mrs. H C.
Clark Mr. & Mrs. John M.
Cochran Mr. & Mrs. J. L.
CramerMr. & Mrs. Ambrose
Crow Mrs. Martha Foote
Eames Mr. & Mrs. Frederick S.
Eddy Mr. & Mrs. Arthur Jerome
Eddy Mr. & Mrs Augustus N.
Ela Mr. & Mrs. John W.
Field Mr. & Mrs. Eugene
Fuller Mr. Henry B.
Gardiner Mrs.FannyHale
Glessner Mr. & Mrs. J. J.
Harlan Mr. James S.
Harlan Mr. & Mrs. John
Maynard

Head Mr. Franklin H.
Heaton Mr. Harold R.
Henrotin Mr. & Mrs.
Charles
Hill Miss M. S.
Holmes Mr. E. Burton
Jones Mr. Thomas D.
Kirkland Major & Mrs.
Joseph
Kirkland Miss Caroline
Larned Mr. & Mrs. Walter
Cranston
Macdonald Mr. & Mrs.
Charles Blair
MacVeagh Mr. & Mrs.
Franklin
Mason Mr. & Mrs. Alverin
A.
Martin Miss Maud
McClurg Gen. & Mrs. A.
C.
McCormick Mr. & Mrs.
Robt.
McEwen Mr. Walter
Monroe Miss Harriet
Monroe Miss Lucy

Morton Mr. Oliver T.
Moss Mr. & Mrs. Jesse L.
Moulton Prof. Richard G.
Palmer Mr.& Mrs. Potter
Peabody Mr. & Mrs. Stuyvesant
Ryerson Mr. & Mrs. Arthur
Scott Mr. & Mrs. James
W.
Smith Mr. Delavan
Stevenson Col. and Mrs.
Alexander F.
Taber Mr. & Mrs. Sydney
Richmond
Thompson Mr. & Mrs.
Slason
Upton Mr. & Mrs. Geo. P.
Wakem Miss Emily
Walker Mr. & Mrs. Wm.
Bentley
Waller Mr. & Mrs. James
Breckinridge
Willing Mr. & Mrs. Henry
J.
Wilmarth Mrs. H. M.

THE COUNTRY CLUB OF EVANSTON.

OFFICERS.

MARSHALL M. KIRKMAN, ... President.
FREDERICK ARND, . . . First Vice-President.
BENJAMIN F. ADAMS, . . Second Vice-President.
NICHOLAS G. IGLEHART, ... Treasurer.
EDWIN F. BROWN, ... Secretary.

DIRECTORS.

Marshall M. Kirkman	Benjamin F. Adams	T. S. Creighton
Frederick Arnd	John W. Scott	Charles H. Matthews
Edwin F. Brown	Hanson McDowell	William Holabird
Arthur Orr	Nicholas G. Iglehart	

MEMBERS—GENTLEMEN.

Adams Benj. F.	Carman Alex. R.	Gardner Bert M.	Johnston W. J.
Aldrich Charles H.	Carpenter Edw. F.	Gates William W.	Jones W. H.
Allen John M.	Carr Clyde M.	Gifford Archer	Kedzie J. R. jr.
Allen A. P.	Case Edward B.	Goffe Louis K.	Kendall R. R.
Anthony C. E.	Catlin W. W.	Gorham J. D.	Kennedy H. C.
Anthony W. M.	Chandler C. H.	Gould Frank M.	Kerr H. H.
Aplin F. A.	Chapin Fred S.	Grafton Murray L.	Kimball Dorr A.
Armsby Geo. N.	Childs John A.	Graham W. A. S.	Kimberly S. A.
Armsby James K.	Clark Stewart	Grant-Schaefer G.	Kirk John B.
Armsby Jas. K. jr.	Coburn E. A.	Alfred	Kirk Milton W.
Arnd Charles	Comstock Charles	Grepe Hamilton E.	Kirk Walter T.
Arnd Frederick	Congdon Chas B.	Grepe J. Stanley	Kirkman A. T.
Ayars H. M. ,.	Connell Chas. J.	Grev Charles F.	Kirkman Marshall
Balding W. T.	Cook David S.	Gridley Martin M.	J.
Bancroft Allen R.	Crampton J. N.	Gridley Nelson C.	Kirkman W. Bruce
Bartlett Wm. H.	Creighton Thos. S.	Grimstead Wm. W.	Klock John H.
Bass Perkin B.	Currier Albert D.	Gunnell Frank	Lacey E. S.
Bates Thomas	Dakin H. W.	Hamilton E. F.	Lake Richard C.
Battle J. A.	Dakin Richard L.	Hamilton W. A.	Lane Maurice T.
Bayless Benjamin	Dalgleish Chas H.	Hammond Wm. A.	Lawrence Chas.H.
Bayless Charles T.	Dean Charles R.	Harbert A. B.	Lewis Charles G.
Bayless George W.	Deering Chas. W.	Hardin J. H.	Lewis D. R.
Beach Franklin G.	DeGolyer L. N.	Hardy F. A.	Lewis Thos H.
Beard Thomas	DeGolyer Nelson	Harper William H.	Lindgren John R.
Beebe A. A.	Dewey David B.	Haskin Charles G.	Littlejohn W. J.
Belknap Edwin C.	Dickinson Clarence	Hazlehurst Andrew	Lord Alonzo B.
Belknap Fred. W.	Dixon J. Arthur	Hertle Louis	Lord Benjamin W.
Blunt John E.	Donelson D. P.	Hess Winter D.	Lord Frank E.
Blunt John E., jr.	Doran George H.	Hill Calvin H.	Lord Geo. S.
Bogert W. B.	Downs Lewis C.	Hillman C. W.	Lord Thos.
Bond James M.	Dunlap Chas. M.	Hitchcock W. D.	Lord Wm. S.
Boynton C. T.	Dwight Walter T.	Hoag Wm. G.	Lunt George
Brelsford C. E. H.	Dyche William A.	Hoge Holmes	Lynch Richard W.
Brooks W. C.	Elliot Frank M.	Holabird R. G.	Maltman Stewart A.
Brown Andrew J.	Elphicke C. W.	Holabird William	Mann Dr. O. H.
Brown Edwin F.	Eversz Ernest H.	Hotchkiss E. Dougl.	Marsh William D.
Brown W. L.	Ewen John M.	Howard O. McG.	Matthews C. H.
Buckley Chas. W.	Fabian W. J.	Hubbard Joseph D.	McCarrell A. F.
Buckner Thomas A.	Farwell Harry S.	Hubbard Will	McDowell Hanson
Buehler E. H.	Farwell Simeon	Hubbart J. Roy	McDowell Irving
Buehler William	Ferguson L. A.	Hutchinson N. Mil-	McLeod Robert L.
Buell Augustine C.	Foster Adelbert M.	ler	McMullen R. B.
Burch Charles S.	Foster Albert V.	Ide Charles B.	McWilliams Chas.
Burnham Daniel H.	Foster Volney W.	Ide W. K.	D.
Burt Wm. Griswold	Frazier F. P.	Iglehart Nicholas G.	Mears Charles H.
Cable Herman D.	French Fred. E.	Jacobsen Rud'ph C.	Metcalf John S.
Caldwell B. D.	Fuller Charles G.	Jenkins Geo. R.	Meyrick Chas. W.

Miller Benjamin L.
Miller F. C.
Moore B. J.
Moseley Alex W.
Moseley Geo. V. H.
Mudge Daniel A.
Noyes David A.
Noyes Herbert
Noyes Paul
Noyes Thomas S.
Onderdonk W. H.
Orr C. F.
Paterson J. H.
Peabody F. S.
Pearsons Henry A.
Pearsons H. P.
Pettibone H. C.
Phillips Dr. W. A.
Pitman S. Kemp
Poole W. Fred
Post Henry R.
Poucher B. G.
Powers George E.
Quan James E.
Raeder Henry
Raymond JamesH.

Read Gardner
Reimers Charles D.
Remy Curtis H.
Rice Calvin F.
Rice L. S.
Rickards Wm. T.
Ridlon Dr. John
Rogers Emery H.
Sargent Geo. H.
Sargent Geo. M.
Sargent W. D.
Savage F. M.
Sawyer Ward B.
Scott Charles F.
Scott John Wm.
Sheldon F. P.
Sherman Edwin
Shumway P. R.
Simmons Park E.
Smith F. W.
Smith Gilbert A.
Smith Herbert S.
Spencer Robert
Spining Chas. P.
Stacey Thomas I.
Stanford Arthur L.

Stanford George E.
Starr William E.
Stockton Wm. E.
Talbot Hugh
Throckmorton
Howard
Tiernan John
Tilghman Wm.
Toogood Ernest T.
Towne Arthur F.
Tyson Will S.
Underwood A. W.
VanArsdale Wm.T.
VanBenschoten W.
C.
Vance W..L.
Vandercook R. O.
VanVoorhis Chas.
E.
Wallingford H. J.
Walrath Wm. B.
Ward J. F.
Warner Albert R.
Waterbury T. O.
Weaver Chas. S.

WebsterDr.Edw.H
Wells Wm. L.
Wendell J. A.
White Sheldon F.
Whitehead Harry
W.
Whitfield Geo. W.
Whittemore C. L.
Wickes Roscoe L.
Wilcox G. G.
Wilfolk Clinton S.
Willard E. R.
Williams Chas. E.
Williams C. L.
Williams E. J.
Williams Frank J.
Williams John A.
Wilson Hugh M.
Wilson Hugh R.
Winchell Harley C.
Wing Luman R.
Winne Frank N.
Zang William
Zimmerman Chas.
H.

MEMBERS—LADIES.

Adams Mrs. Benjamin F.
Aishton Miss Catherine
Aishton Miss Elizabeth
Aldrich Mrs. Charles H.
Anderson Miss Maria
Andreas Miss Eulalie
Anthony Mrs. C. E.
Anthony Mrs. W. M.
Aplin Mrs. F. A.
Armsby Mrs. James K.
Armsby Mrs. Jas. K. jr.
Arnd Miss Carlena
Arnd Mrs. Frederick
Ayars Mrs. Charles G.
Ayars Mrs. Lucy M.
Balding Mrs. Thomas E.
Bartlett Mrs. W. H.
Bass Miss Stella
Bates Mrs. Thomas
Bates Miss Rosa C.
Battle Mrs. J. A.
Bayless Mrs. Benjamin
Bayless Miss Wilhelmine
Beach Mrs. Franklin G.
Beebe Miss Katherine E.
Belknap Mrs. Edwin C.
Blanchard Miss Alice
Bliss Miss Bertha
Bliss Miss Jessie
Blunt Mrs. John E.
Blunt Miss M. E.
Blye Miss Fannie E.
Bogert Mrs. W. B.
Bond Mrs. James M.
Boteler Miss Virginia
Boynton Mrs. C. T.
Brayton Dr. Sarah H.

Brelsford Mrs. C. E. H.
Brooks Mrs. William C.
Brown Mrs. A. J.
Brown Mrs. Edwin F.
Brown Miss Jennie E.
Brown Mrs. W. L.
Buckley Mrs. Chas. W.
Buckner Mrs. Thomas A.
Buehler Miss Katharine B.
Buehler Mrs. E. H.
Bueil Mrs. Augustine C.
Burch Mrs. Charles S.
Burch Miss Grace
Burnham Mrs. Daniel H.
Butler Mrs. Rebecca N.
Cable Mrs. Herman D.
Caldwell Mrs. B. D.
Carpenter Mrs. Edw. F.
Carr Mrs. Clyde M.
Case Mrs. Edward B.
Catlin Mrs. W. W.
Chandler Mrs. C. H.
Chapin Miss Betsey C.
Chapin Mrs. Jennie
Chapin Miss Marietta P.
Chapman Mrs Belle B.
Cheatle Miss Gertrude A.
Childs Mrs. John A.
Clark Mrs. Stewart
Coburn Mrs. E. A.
Comstock Mrs. Charles
Comstock Miss Fanny
Congdon Mrs. Charles B.
Connell Mrs. Chas. J.
Cook Mrs. David S.
Creighton Mrs. Thos. S.
Crie Miss Kate B.

Cushing Miss Anna F.
Dakin Miss Catharine A.
Dakin Miss Florence A.
Dale Miss C. P.
Deering Miss Abby M.
Deering Mrs. Charles W.
DeGolyer Mrs. Nelson
Dewey Mrs. David B.
Dingee Miss May
Donelson Mrs. D. P.
Dwight Mrs. Mary B.
Dwight Mrs. Walter T.
Eddy Mrs. Clara H.
Elliot Mrs. Frank W.
Elphicke Mrs. C. W.
Ely Miss Lou S.
Everts Miss Blanche
Ewen Mrs. John M.
Fabian Mrs. W. J.
Farwell Mrs. Harry S.
Farwell Miss Pearl
Farwell Miss Ruth
Farwell Mrs. Simeon
Ferguson Mrs. L. A.
Field Mrs. Howard
Fletcher Miss Bessie
Fletcher Mrs. F. A.
Foster Mrs. Adelbert M.
Foster Miss Eva C.
Frazier Mrs. F. P.
French Mrs. Frederick E.
French Miss Josephine
Fuller Mrs. Charles G.
Gallup Miss Stella H.
Gardner Miss Eleanor
Gifford Mrs. Archer
Goffe Mrs. Louis K.

Grafton Miss Fanny R.
Graham Mrs. Wm. A. S.
Grant-Schaefer Miss Marie S.
Grepe Mrs. J. Stanley
Grey Mrs. Charles F.
Gridley Mrs. Nelson C.
Gunnell Mrs. Frank
Hallam Miss Alice B.
Halliday Miss Adelia
Halliday Mrs. W. P.
Hammond Mrs. Wm. A.
Handford Miss Alice E.
Harbert Miss Corinne B.
Hardin Miss Gertrude
Hardin Miss Geraldine
Hardin Mrs. I. N.
Hardy Mrs. F. A.
Harper Mrs. Wm. H.
Hartshorn Miss Grace E.
Haskin Mrs. Chas. G.
Hazlehurst Mrs. Andrew
Hempstead Miss Mary
Hertle Mrs. Louis
Hess Miss Grace
Hill Mrs. E. N.
Hillman Mrs. C. W.
Hitchcock Miss Anna L.
Hitchcock Miss Emma
Hitchcock Mrs. W. D.
Hoge Mrs. Holmes
Hoge Miss Louise
Holabird Miss Cornelia B.
Holabird Mrs. William
Hotchkiss Mrs. Anna I.
Hotchkiss Mrs. E. D.
Hotchkiss Miss Florence
Hubbard Mrs. Joseph D.
Hughes Miss Blanche
Ide Miss Helen M.
Ide Mrs. Helen M.
Iglehart Mrs. Nicholas G.
Jenkins Miss Anna E.
Jenkins Mrs. George R.
Johnston Mrs. W. J.
Jones Miss Katharine
Jones Mrs. W. H.
Judd Mrs. George T.
Kedzie Miss Margaret F.
Kennedy Mrs. H. C.
Kidder Mrs. Henry M.
Kimball Mrs. Dorr A.
Kimberly Mrs. Samuel A.
Kirk Mrs. John B.
Kirk Mrs. Milton W.
Kirkman Miss Minnie S.
Kirkman Mrs. Wm. Bruce
Lacey Miss E. M.
Lacey Mrs. E. S.
Lacey Miss J. P.
Lake Miss Amy
Lake Miss Jessie
Lake Mrs. Richard C.
Lane Miss Ella
Lane Miss Irene
Lane Mrs. Maurice T.

Larimer Mrs. J. M.
Lawrence Miss Mabel
Lewis Mrs. D. R.
Lewis Miss Mary
Littlejohn Mrs. W. J.
Lord Miss Annie W.
Lord Miss Catherine
Lord Miss Cornelia F.
Lord Mrs. Geo. S.
Lord Miss Jennie W.
Lord Miss Mary W.
Lord Mrs. Wm. S.
Lunt Mrs. George
Lunt Miss Nina G.
Lynch Mrs. Richard W.
Marsh Miss Josie E.
Marsh Mrs. William D.
Matteson Miss Jean McN
Matthews Mrs. C. H.
McCarrell Mrs. A. F.
McCabe Miss
McDowell Mrs. Gordon
McMullen Mrs. R. B.
Mears Mrs. Chas. H.
Metcalf Mrs. John S.
Metcalf Miss T. A.
Meyrick Mrs. Chas. W.
Moore Mrs. B. J.
Morse Miss Mina
Mudge Mrs. Daniel A.
Noyes Mrs. David A.
Noyes Mrs. E. E.
Onderdonk Mrs. W. H.
Parker Miss Lillian M.
Parker Mrs. Maud D.
Parkhurst Mrs. J. J.
Paterson Mrs. J. H.
Peabody Mrs. F. S.
Pearsons Mrs. Henry A.
Pearsons Miss Louise M.
Pettibone Mrs. H. C.
Phillips Mrs. W. A.
Post Mrs. Henry R.
Poucher Mrs. B. G.
Powers Miss Sarah F.
Pratt Miss Elizabeth A.
Raeder Mrs. Henry
Raymond Mrs. James H.
Redfield Miss Louise R.
Reed Miss Alice
Remy Mrs. Curtis H.
Rice Mrs. Calvin F.
Rice Miss Louise
Rice Miss May Louise
Rice Mrs. L. S.
Rickards Miss Frances C.
Rickards Mrs. Wm. T.
Ridlon Mrs. John
Rogers Mrs. E. H.
Rogers Miss Nettie
Rowe Miss Emily D.
Rowe Miss Susanna L.
Sargent Miss Annie C.
Sargent Mrs. Geo. M.
Scott Miss Lida G.

Sheldon Mrs. F. P.
Sherman Mrs. Edwin
Sherman Mrs. M. E.
Shumway Mrs. Mary R.
Simmons Miss G. E.
Simpson Miss Anna M.
Smith Mrs. Gilbert A.
Smith Mrs. Herbert S.
Smith Miss Winifred E.
Spalding Miss Alice H.
Spalding Miss Grace
Spencer Mrs. Robert
Spencer Mrs. Sarah A.
Spining Mrs. Chas. P.
Stanford Miss Mary E.
Stockton Miss Martha E.
Stockton Mrs. William E.
Stone Miss Eliza Atkins
Talbot Miss Mae
Tiernan Miss Bessie
Towle Miss May E.
Towne Mrs. Arthur F.
Underwood Mrs. Arthur W.
VanAlstine Miss Emma
VanAlstine Mrs. Maria A.
Vance Mrs. W. L.
VanVoorhis Mrs. C. E.
Wallingford Mrs. H. J.
Ward Miss Edith C.
Ward Miss Estelle F.
Ward Miss Jessie C.
Ward Mrs. J. F.
Ward Miss Rosella
Ward Miss Sadie G.
Watson Mrs. Julia M.
Watson Miss Margaret S.
Weaver Mrs. Chas. S.
Webster Mrs. Edward H.
Wells Miss Dora L.
Wells Miss Mabel
Wells Mrs. W. L.
Wendel Miss
Wendel Mrs. J. A.
White Miss Elizabeth
White Miss J. H.
White Miss Susan
Whitely Mrs. C. J.
Whitely Miss Elizabeth
Whittemore Mrs. C. L.
Wilcox Miss Anna J.
Wilcox Mrs. G. G.
Williams Mrs. C. L.
Williams Miss Edith
Williams Miss Irene
Williams Miss Jessica
Williams Mrs. John A.
Williams Miss Madelaine A.
Williams Mrs. Walter S.
Wilson Mrs. Hugh M.
Wilson Mrs. Hugh R.
Wilson Miss Mary T.
Wing Mrs. Luman R.
Winne Mrs. Frank N.
Woodyatt Mrs. Clara L.

DAUGHTERS OF THE AMERICAN REVOLUTION.

CHICAGO CHAPTER.

OFFICERS.

MRS. SAML. H. KERFOOT, - - - State Regent of Illinois.
MRS. JOHN N. JEWETT, 412 Dearborn av. - Chapter Regent.
MRS. P. L SHERMAN, 4634 Lake av. - - - - Vice-Regent.
MRS. FREDERICK A. SMITH, The Metropole, - - Registrar.
MRS. FREDERICK W. BECKER, 4169 Berkeley av. - Secretary.
MRS. FREDERICK DICKINSON, 26 Bryant av. - Corresponding Sec'y.
MRS. JOHN C. BUNDY, Sheridan Square, Evanston, - Treasurer.

MEMBERS.

Adams Mrs. Edgerton
Anthony Mrs. C. E.
Arnold Mrs. C. C.
Ayer Mrs. B. F.
Barber Mrs. J. O.
Beckwith Mrs. F. H.
Block Mrs. Willard T.
Brown Mrs. Wm. Thayer
Bundy Mrs. John C.
Burke Mrs. Edmund
Barnes Mrs. Charles J.
Brown Mrs. Charles F.
Brooks Mrs. James C.
Barker Mrs. Frank W.
Bailey Mrs
Bartlett Mrs. Geo. F.
Baker Miss Ethel
Baker Miss Nora
Bryant Mrs. Thomas B.
Barker Mrs. Joseph N.
Bradley Mrs. A. O.
Buschwah Mrs. N.
Bryan Miss Jennie Byrd
Becker Mrs. Frederick W.
Barry Mrs. George
Boyeson Mrs. I. K.
Bloomingston Mrs. John S.
Bradley Mrs. M. S.
Bradford Mrs. David G.
Burchard Mrs. Mortimer Nelson
Beach Mrs. Myron H.
Bodman Mrs L. W.
Coe Mrs. A. L.
Corbin Mrs. C. R.
Cooke Mrs. N. F.
Cooke Miss Mary Gertrude
Claflin Mrs. A. St. M.
Chapin Mrs. Simeon
Cleaveland Miss Josephine
Conover Mrs. Charles H.
Cole Miss Emma Sylvia
Cole Miss Lillie E.
Corthell Miss Alice E.
Chard Mrs. Thomas
Card Miss Grace Barton
Crane Mrs. T. H.
Curtis Mrs. J. LaFayette
Clinch Mrs. Richard Floyd

Durburrow Mrs. A. C.
Dickerman Miss Frances A
Dickinson Mrs. Frederick
Dainty Mrs. A. H.
Dunning Mrs. S. W.
Doud Mrs. Levi B.
Duell Mrs. Wm. Comstock
Durgin Mrs. John Cooper
Day Mrs. Albert Morgan
Duval Mrs. Louis Alphonse
Durand Mrs. Elliott
Eggleston Mrs. Nicholas S.
Everhart Miss Mella D.
Everett Mrs. W. S.
Eurich Mrs. E. F.
Ewing Mrs. Adlai T.
Ely Mrs. Oliver C.
Ely Miss Marian A.
English Mrs. Gustavus Percy
Elliott Mrs. Lizzie N. McL.
Farson Mrs R. B.
Ferry Mrs. Abby Farwell
Frank Mrs. Monroe
Fullerton Mrs. Thos. C.
Farr Mrs. M. A.
Fisher Mrs. George
Freeman Mrs. Henry
Galt Mrs. A. T.
Goodwin Mrs. Daniel
Glessner Mrs. J. J.
Goss Mrs. Chas. O.
Gustorf Miss Harriet M.
Guthrie Mrs. Ossian
Gwinn Mrs. John Morris
Graves Mrs. Dwight W.
Goodhart Mrs. F. E.
Hart Mrs. J. P.
Hamilton Mrs. H. H.
Hayes Miss Laura
Hopkins Mrs. A. H.
Hubbard Miss Laura M.
Howe Mrs. F. S.
Holman Mrs. S. C.
Hopkins Mrs. A. W.
Haskell Mrs. George W.
Hynes Mrs. Wm. J.
Hervey Mrs. James Fred'k

Hosmer Miss Eliza
Hardy Mrs. Charles M.
Hurlbut Miss Sarah Elizabeth
Hunt Mrs. R. M.
Hutchinson Miss Matilda
Hutchinson Mrs. Jonas
Huling Mrs. E. B.
Husted Mrs. William H.
Haven Mrs. Joseph
Jewett Mrs. John N.
Johnson Mrs. Frank A.
Johnston Mrs. John jr.
Jameson Miss Mary
Jameson Miss Alice W.
Judson Mrs. Edwin
Jones Mrs. Robert H.
Judd Mrs. N. B.
Jones Mrs. Cassius Clay
Judd Mrs. Edward James
Jameson Mrs. John Alexander
Knight Mrs. Wm.
Kerfoot Mrs. S. H.
Krout Miss Mary
Kimball Miss Alma L.
Kimball Miss Louise E.
Karner Mrs. Wm. J.
Kirkland Miss Elizabeth Stansbury
Kirkland Miss Cordelia Stansbury
Kennedy Mrs. Madison B.
Lay Mrs. A. T.
Lay Miss Margaret
Lewis Mrs. E. R.
Lewis Mrs. James
Loose Mrs. Jacob L.
Martin Miss Ellen A.
Manning Miss Josephine Nelson
Manning Mrs. E. N.
Marsh Mrs. Wm. D.
McCormick Miss Elizabeth D.
McCormick Miss Henrietta H.
McCormick Mrs. Leander
Meeker Miss Sarah W.

Murphy Mrs. H. C.
Murphy Mrs. Caroline C.
Meeker Miss Margaret Beekman
Moore Miss·Nena
Mather Mrs. A. C.
Matlock Mrs. Chas. P.
Metcalf Mrs. Ralph
Marshall Mrs. John A.
Mills Mrs. James M.
Marsh Mrs. John W.
McCalla Miss Helen Wayne
McClelland Mrs. Thos. S.
Moss Mrs. Wm. Lathrop
Munson Mrs. Fred W.
Nelson Mrs. Walter C.
Noyes Mrs. Oliver J.
Nichols Mrs. M. E.
Osborn Mrs. F. S.
Ogden Dr. Emma K.
Owens Mrs. John E.
Owens Miss Maria Gervia
Otis Mrs. Ephraim A.
Ogden Mrs. Mahlon D.
Payne Mrs. Olive
Pittman Miss Cora Helen Knowles
Porter Mrs. M. H.
Pynchon Mrs. Daniel
Prentiss Miss Emma Catherine
Pajeau Mrs. Joseph
Phelps Miss Mary Pearce
Pettibone Mrs. A. G.
Peck Mrs. Walter L.

Page Miss Florence Ethel
Ramage Mrs. George
Rozet Mrs. George H.
Rozet Miss Marie Josephine
Reed Mrs. C. W.
Robbins Mrs. Walter R.
Ranney Mrs.AlfredEdgar
Reed Miss Julia Lyle
ReQua Mrs. Charles Howard
Rice Mrs. Fletcher C.
Rappleye Miss Maud Minerva
Shepard Mrs. H. M.
Sherman Mrs.PennoyerL.
Sinclair Miss Judith P.
Smith Mrs. Frederick A.
Smith Mrs. Earnest L.
Smith Mrs. Perry H.
Stone Mrs. Leander
Stuart Mrs. Charles B.
Shumway Mrs. Noble C.
Sinclair Miss Mattie P.
Schmidt Mrs. Max
Shumway Miss Mary
Simmons Mrs. F. T.
Salmon Mrs. Charles
Sawyer Mrs. Francis A.
Stone Miss Isabella
Stone Mrs. Melville E.
Stone Mrs. Newton R.
Stuart Mrs. Chas. F.
Smith Miss Elizabeth Brockway

Strobel Mrs. Chas. Louis
Simms Mrs. Wm. Edward
Scammon Mrs. J. Y.
Shaw Miss Helen L.
Smith Mrs. Marvin
Satterlee E. T.
Sherman Mrs. W. W.
Tibbetts Mrs. Elisha
Trumbull Mrs. Lyman
Trippe Mrs. Sylvanus
Turner Mrs. Volentine
Underwood Mrs. I. Platt
Vandercook Mrs. John D.
Wait Mrs. Horatio L.
Wait Miss Maria A.
Willard Miss Frances E.
Wilson Mrs. John P.
Wilson Miss Margaret C.
Walker Mrs. James H.
Walker Miss AnnieCampbell
Williams Mrs. G. T.
Williams Mrs. G. S.
Williams Miss Helen
Wiles Mrs. Robert
Wheeler Miss Mabel
Watson Mrs. John
Winslow Mrs. John H.
White Miss Emma Gertrude
Williams Mrs. Frank
Warren Mrs. Mary Ann
West Frederick T.
Wilson Mrs. John R.
Yoe Mrs. Charles C.

DOUGLAS CLUB.

3518 ELLIS AVENUE.

OFFICERS.

W. W. WATKINS,	President.
J. FRANK EDWARDS,	First Vice-President.
THOMAS B. ACKERS,	Second Vice-President.
W. H. FLAGG.	Third Vice-President.
RUDOLPH G. GEISLER,	Secretary.
J. RUSSELL VINCENT,	Treasurer.

DIRECTORS.

George H. Hovey   George L. Magill   A. H. Barber   A. E. Forrest
E. D. Stevens   Charles R. Carroll   C. C. Swinborne

MEMBERS.

Ackers T. B.
Ahern J. H.
Albright W. B.
Alford M. P.
Amos J. E. jr.
Armour W. L.
Arnold W. G.
Baker Frank
Baldwin Abraham
Baldwin A. H.

Barber A. H.
Beach H. L.
Beardsley A.
Beebe W. H.
Bell George H.
Best Wm.
Bishopp W. D.
Black E. F.
Blake H. H.
Blatchford T. W.

Bliss E. W.
Bliss S. E.
Bloomingston J. S.
Bogue J. H.
Booth Wm. M.
Borden Hamilton
Bour J. R.
Boyden Byron
Boyington H. H.
Bradley D. E.

Buchanan E. P.
Buchanan J. N.
Bulkley Almon W.
Burkholder C. D.
Burnham S. W.
Cadwallader J.
Carroll C. R.
Casey E. A.
Cherry R. H.
Christy F. H.

Clapp C. L.
Clarke Arthur L.
Clarke E. B.
Clay W. W.
Cleaver H. E.
Clizbe W. J.
Clover John W.
Coen H. C.
Coghlan Henry D.
Colbert Elias
Connor T. V.
Cook H. W.
Copelin Alex. J. W.
Cowles W. D.
Cox Eugene R.
Crapser J. H.
Crawford A. W.
Curtis W. G.
Cutter C. G.
Davis Georg W.
Deitz C. J. Dr.
Delbridge J. B.
Dennis G. J.
Dick William F.
Doolittle E. A.
Douglass W. A.
Dugger J. P.
Edwards J. Frank
Ehle Louis C.
Elliott Robert L.
Ennis L. J.
Ervin Dr. W. E.
Ewing W. G.
Farrington Geo. E.
Fellows B. M.
Fenn P. D.
Fischer George T.
Flagg Elmer T.
Flagg W. F.
Flagg W. H.
Flood S. D.
Forrest A. E.
Fountain A. M.
Fox B. M.
Frederickson Wm.
Fretts Geo. W.
Fretts L. A.
Fry G. C.
Gage F. N.
Gardner F. G.
Gassette W. K.
Geisler Rudolph G.
Gifford R. L.
Gilmer Thos. L. Dr.

Glennie A. E.
Glennon E. T.
Goddard L. O.
Goodhue W. D.
Gorman W. H.
Gray A. S.
Green John W.
Guion E. L.
Haines Fred N.
Harvey S. A.
Hascall M. S.
Hepburn J. W.
Hern G. W.
Hester C. R.
Hitchcock Frank
Holton Geo. D.
Hood J. D.
Hopkins F. A.
Hopkins L. M.
Hosbury John
Hoskin M. G.
Hovey Geo. H.
Hubbard J. M. jr.
Huey J. S.
Huntington C. F.
Hurlbut C. P.
Ingersoll N. B.
Jerrems W. G. Jr.
Johnson R. D. jr.
Jones Wm. J.
Jones W. S.
Jouvenat Charles
Kelley J. W. D.
Kelley W. D.
Kerr George B.
Keyes D. H.
King Hoyt
Lake W. H.
Langsdorf C. L.
Lapham A. B.
Lapham A. B. jr.
Lapham E. N.
Launder D.
Lee Geo. N.
Leger H. B.
Leib A. S.
Lesh L. B.
Liday T. C.
Linden F. L.
Logan C. A.
Ludlam R. jr.
Magee R. H.
Magill George L.

Makeever Sanford
Marsh J. W.
McPherran E. H.
Mead H. A.
Merrill A. W.
Merritt C. T.
Milchrist T. E.
Mix Melville W.
Moffett J. A.
Moulton Wm. A.
Muehlmann C. G.
Myers M. A.
Myers W. L.
Niles H. G. jr.
Norris Robt. A.
Noyes E. E.
Noyes Hy. C.
Ogden W. L.
Omohundro W. R.
Paddleford F. A.
Palmer E. P.
Pardridge C. E.
Parkhurst C. C.
Parkhurst H. S.
Penhallow W. P.
Peyton R. F.
Phelps C. E.
Pike E. C.
Platt C. A. W.
Platt Henry R.
Plumsted J. T.
Rheem W. M.
Rice C. W.
Richardson G. P.
Rose W. R.
Ross J. L.
Ruff Joseph
Rumsey J. Frank
Russ J. S.
Ryder Fred L.
Schmidt R. E.
Scovel Robert A.
Selleck W. E.
Senour W. F.
Shaw John
Shaw L. B.
Shayne J. T.
Sheldon T. P.
Shute J. W.
Sibley G. M.
Sibley J. A.
Simny John C.
Simm J. C. jr.

Simpson J. W.
Smith Howard L.
Snyder Dr. O.W.F.
Somers E. L.
Spooner Thomas
Sproehnle F. M.
Stevens Chas. A.
Stevens E. D.
Stone G. W.
Sutter A.
Sutter J.
Swift O. P.
Swinborne C. C.
Tate J. E.
Thomas A. L.
Thomas C. G.
Thompson J. F.
Tillotson E. W.
Timmerman W. M.
Tobey Thomas
Torrey A. C.
VanBenschoten C. W.
VanDalson Edward
Vierbuchen Wm.
Vincent J. R.
Wade Jno.
Wagner Ernest J.
Wall F. J.
Wallin Dr. H. J.
Warden T. G.
Waterbury W. A.
Watkins W. W.
Weaver Burr
Weaver C. A.
Wells W. J.
Wheeler C. S.
White G. B.
White H. W.
White Dr. J. W.
Wicker C. G.
Wiggins J. B.
Wilkin J. L.
Wilson H. S.
Wilson L. H.
Wing Dr. E.
Winne Archibald
Winstandley J. B.
Wise H. A.
Wood F. M.
Wood J. C.
Woods W. J.
Young Max

DOUGLAS PARK CLUB.

911 SOUTH KEDZIE AVENUE.

OFFICERS.

F. E. RAINIER, - - - - - - - President.
J. J. COBURN, - - - - - First Vice-President.
JOHN CRAIB, - - - - Second Vice-President.
A. L. COAKES, - - - - - - Secretary.
HERMAN SPITZ, - - - - - - Treasurer.

DIRECTORS.

Wm. Harlev
Lawrence M. Ennis
S. M. Randolph
Charles Wink

MEMBERS.

Barker George G.	Dunham W. F.	Keough W. C. H.	Schryver A. L.
Bassett Geo.R.MD.	Eastman Kirk N.	Lombard Josiah L.	Spears J. H.
Bickford J. A.	Ennis Lawrence M.	McNamara J. H.	Spitz Herman
Coakes A. L.	Gruger E. R.	Pratt E. H.	Towles W. B.
Coburn J. J.	Halverson A. A.	Rainier F. E.	Wink Charles
Cowdrey R. H.	Harlev William	Randolph S. M.	Wood O. F.
Craib John	Hudnall Walter		

EDGEWATER CASINO.

OFFICERS.

W. C. GILLETT, - - - . - - President.
W. N. TAYLOR, - - - - - Vice-President.
JOHN WARDLOW, - - - - - - Secretary.
JULIUS P. MEYER. - - - - - - Treasurer.

MEMBERS.

Angell H. L.	Jones Graham P.	Keator F. C.	Silsbee J. L.
Balmer Thomas	Farley J. K.	Lange Louis	Slayton J. W.
Chesney Wm. P.	Flannery D. F.	Lunceford C. D.	Smith H. L.
Clark Robert	Gillette W. C.	Mason G. A.	Stiles L. G.
Cochran J. L.	Glaspell H. J.	Meyer J. P.	Taylor W. N.
Collins H. B.	Grosvenor L. N.	Muchmore J. F.	Thomas A. A.
Collins Wm.	Hotchkin B. L.	Powell George W.	Vawter W. A.
Cullen James K.	Howe A. S.	Powell M. H.	Wardlow John
Cusack E. J.	Hunt A. B.	Schoenthaler F. C.	Wheeler E. R.
Dalton Saml.	Jones George P.	Scovel John C.	Williston A. D.
Dick E. E.			

EVANSTON CLUB.

OFFICERS.

MARSHALL M. KIRKMAN, - - - - - President.
W. H. BARTLETT, - - - First Vice-President.
NELSON C. GRIDLEY, - - Second Vice-President.
N. G. IGLEHART, - - - - - - Secretary.
WILLIAM J. FABIAN, - - - - - - Treasurer.

DIRECTORS.

Curtis H. Remy
Nicholas G. Iglehart
Nelson C. Gridley
D. A. Mudge
William Holabird
Marshall M. Kirkman
Francis A. Hardy
William H. Bartlett
Henry A. Pearsons
William J. Fabian

MEMBERS.

Adams Benj. F.	Beach F. G.	Brown William L.	Church Edmund V.
Aldrich Charles A.	Blanchard William	Buehler Edward H.	Clapp Dr. E. P.
Aldrich Chas. H.	Bogart William B.	Buell Augustine C.	Clark Stewart
Allen John M.	Boltwood Prof.H.L.	Burch C. S.	Clayton A. B.
Anthony Walter M.	Boynton C. T.	Burnham D. H.	Cleveland Chas. B.
Arnd Charles	Bradley David E.	Cable H. D.	Coe David A.
Arnd Frederick jr.	Bragdon Dr. M. C.	Calkins G. G.	Congdon Chas. B.
Baker George S.	Bretsford C. E. H.	Campbell J. W.	Connell C. J.
Barhydt Frank	Brook Noah W.	Case Edw. B.	Cook David S.
Bartlett William H.	Brooks Chas. D.	Charles Joseph J.	Creighton Thos. S.
Bayless Benj.	Brown William H.	Childs John A.	Cumnock Robt. L.

Cutler William H.
Dakin Richard L.
Daniels H. E. C.
Deering Chas. W.
DeGolyer Nelson
Dewey David B.
Donnell Jas. W.
Donnell W. H.
Dunn A. E.
Dwight Walter T.
Elliott Frank M.
Elphicke Chas. W.
Engelhard Geo. P.
Eyer C. B.
Fabian William J.
Farwell Harry S.
Farwell Simeon
Foster A. M.
Foster Volney W.
Fowler E. H.
Frazier F. P.
Fuller Charles G.
Fullerton Wm. D.
Fyffe John L.
Garwood Wm. C.
Gilbert Charles J.
Gould Frank
Graham W. A. S.
Grepe J. Stanley
Gridley Martin M.
Gridley Nelson C.
Grover Frank R.
Hall Ed. R.
Hamilton Wm. A.
Hammond Wm. A.
Harbert Charles H.
Harding Amos J.
Harding Lucien J.

Hardy Francis A.
Harper H. M.
Harper Wm. H.
Harpham E. L.
Hazlehurst A.
Hill Calvin H.
Hillman Chas. W.
Hitchcock Wm. D.
Hoge Holmes
Holabird William
Hubbard Will
Hurd Harvey B.
Hurlbut E. J.
Hurlbut J. H.
IglehartNicholasG.
Insull Martin J.
Insull Samuel
Jenkins George R.
Jernegan Charles
Jones William H.
Judson Frank P.
Kedzie John H.
Kimball Dorr A.
Kimbark E. N.
Kimbark E. V.
Kirk Milton W.
Kirk John B.
Kirkman M. M.
Kirkman W. Bruce
Lacey Edw. S.
Lake Richard C.
Lawrence Chas. H.
Lewis Charles G.
Lindgren John R.
Littlejohn W. J.
Lord Alonzo B.
Lord Frank E.
Lord George S.

Lyon Jesse R.
Magill Wm. C.
Manchester Geo. O.
Mann Oscar H.
Marsh Marshall S.
Marsh Wm. D.
Matthews Chas. H.
McCormick A. J.
Mears Charles H.
Merrick Geo. P.
Merwin O. H.
Miller H. H. C.
Mitchell Charles P.
Moore Birney J.
Mudge D. A.
Murray James S.
Norton Lemuel D.
Olmsted W. B.
Onderdonk W. H.
Orr Arthur
Osborn Eugene
Parker James O.
Parkhurst Josiah J.
Peabody F. S.
Pearsons Henry A.
Pearsons H. P.
Pittman C. K.
Post Henry R.
Prentiss Wm.
Raymond Jas. H.
Reed Edward H.
Remy Curtis H.
Rice Calvin F.
Rickards Wm. T.
Rogers Henry W.
Rowe Mrs. Chas.H.
Sargent George M.
Sargent Wm. D.

Scripps G. B.
Sheldon Frank P.
SheppardR.D.Rev.
Sherman Edwin
Shumway Philip R.
Simmons Park E.
Simpson Andrew
Stanford Arthur L.
Stevens Harry S.
Stockton Wm. E.
Taylor Edward S.
Turner John C.
Vance W. H.
Walcott C. P.
Walworth Mrs. H.
  H.
Ward Mrs. Ellen C.
Ward Joseph F.
Webster C. R.
Webster Dr. E. H.
Webster Edw. H.
Webster T. K.
Wells Wm. L.
Wentworth W. C.
Wheeler Chas. P.
Whittemore C. L.
Wicks Roscoe L.
Wightman Chas.A.
Wilcox George G.
Wilder John E.
Williams C. L.
Williams J. M.
Wilmeroth C. W.
Wilson Hugh R.
Winne Frank N.
Woodbridge J. R.
Woodford P. R.
Young Aaron N.

THE FELLOWSHIP CLUB.

OFFICERS.

JAMES W. SCOTT, - - - - - - President.
M. E. STONE, - - - - - - Vice-President.
F. WILLIS RICE, - - - - - - Secretary.
H. G. SELFRIDGE, - - - - - - Treasurer.

MEMBERS.

Adams Milward
Baumann Gustav
Beale William G.
Blanchard Geo. R.
Burnham Daniel H.
Butler E. B.
Chalmers William J
Chatfield-TaylorH.
  C.
Counselman Chas.
Davis George R.
Davis Will J.
Deering James E.
Ellsworth JamesW.
Field Eugene

Field Marshall
Gage Lyman J.
Handy M. P.
Hatch Azel F.
Head Franklin H.
Higinbotham H. N.
Hoard W. D.
Hutchinson Chas.L
Keep William B.
Keyes Rollin A.
Kirk Milton W.
Kirkman M. M.
Kohlsaat H. H.
Lawson Victor F.
Lederer Charles

MacVeaghFranklin
MacFarland H. J.
McDonald Chas. B.
Millet F. D.
Norton James S.
Nye James W.
Palmer Thos. W.
Peck Ferd W.
Peck George R.
Preston William D.
Ray Frank H.
Raymond S. B.
Revell Alex. H.
Rice F. Willis

Runnels John S.
Salsbury N.
Scott James W.
Selfridge Harry G.
Skiff F. J. V.
Stone Melville E.
Switzer Edward M
Wacker Charles H.
Waller R. A.
Washburne Hemp-
  stead
Wheeler Harris A.
Willits George S.
Winston F. S.

27

THE FORTNIGHTLY OF CHICAGO.

10 VANBUREN STREET.

OFFICERS.

MRS. H. M. WILMARTH, - - - - -	President.
MRS. MORGAN BATES, - - -	1st Vice-President.
MRS. C. GILMAN SMITH. - - -	2d Vice-President.
MRS. CHARLES M. HENDERSON, Corresponding Secretary.	
MRS. JAMES R. OWEN, - - - Recording Secretary.	
MRS. M. BYRON RICH, - - - - - Treasurer.	

DIRECTORS.

Mrs. Charles D. Hamil	Mrs. O. W. Potter	Mrs. John M. Ewen
Mrs. Joseph Kirkland	Mrs. B. D. Magruder	Mrs. Alice Kerfoot

MEMBERS.

Abbott Mrs. A. R.
Adams Mrs Milward
Alling Mrs. John
Allport Miss May
Armour Mrs. Geo. A.
Ayer Mrs. B. F.
Babcock Mrs. Henry H.
Baldwin Mrs. Abraham
Barrett Mrs. Samuel E.
Bates Mrs. Morgan
Becker Mrs. Fred'k W.
Bentley Mrs. Cyrus jr.
Blackstone Mrs. T. B.
Blair Mrs. William
Bliss Mrs. Samuel
Bodman Mrs. L. W.
Brainard Mrs. Harriet G.
Brackett Mrs. William
Brayton Dr. Sarah H.
Brown Mrs. Wm. Thayer
Buffum Mrs. Joseph H.
Burke Mrs. Edmund
Burrows Mrs. Thomas
Butler Mrs. William P.
Campbell Mrs. N. W.
Carpenter Mrs. Geo. B.
Chapin Dr. Elizabeth
Cheney Mrs. Chas. Edw.
Coleman Mrs. Mary W.
Compton Mrs. Helen D.
Conover Mrs. O. M.
Coolidge Mrs. Chas. A.
Coonley Mrs. John C.
Crowe Mrs. M. F.
Day Mrs. Albert M.
Dexter Mrs. Wirt
Donelson Mrs. K. H.
Doty Miss Eliza
Dudley Mrs. E. C.
Eames Mrs. Henry F.
Eames Mrs. Fred.
Ela Mrs. John W.
Ellis Mrs. Sumner
Emerson Mrs. Ralph
Emerson Mrs. Joseph
Ewen Mrs. John M.

Fairbank Mrs. N. K.
Farwell Mrs. C. B.
Ferry Mrs. Abbie Farwell
Flower Mrs. James M.
Frank Mrs. Henry L.
Fuller Mrs. Chas. G.
Galt Mrs. A. T.
Gane Mrs Thomas
Gardiner Mrs. Frances H.
Gilbert Mrs. Frank
Glessner Mrs. John J.
Goan Mrs. Orrin S.
Grant Mrs. George R.
Gregory Mrs. Robert B.
Griggs Mrs. S. C.
Hallowell Miss Sara T.
Halsted Miss Nellie
Hamill Mrs. Charles D.
Hammond Miss Katharine
Hannah Mrs. John
Harding Mrs. George F.
Harvey Mrs. T. W.
Haven Mrs. Joseph
Hays Miss Mary
Henderson Mrs. Chas. M.
Henrotin Mrs. Charles.
Herrick Mrs. John J.
Hitchcock Mrs. Charles
Howe Miss Grace T.
Hubbard Mrs. James M.
Hunt Mrs. James A.
Hutchinson Mrs. Chas L.
Hyde Mrs. James Nevins
Jackson Mrs. A. Reeves
Jewett Mrs. John N.
Johnson Mrs. Herrick
Johnson Mrs. H. A.
Kendig Mrs. J. A. J.
Kerfoot Miss Alice
Kimball Mrs. Edward A.
Kimball Mrs. W. W.
Kirkland Mrs. Joseph
Kirtland Mrs. Chas. B.
Klenze Mrs. Clara von
Kretzinger Mrs. Geo. W
Larned Mrs. W. C.

Lathrop Mrs. Bryan
Lawrence Mrs. C. B.
Leake Mrs. Joseph B.
Lloyd Mrs. Henry D.
Locke Mrs. Clinton
Lockwood Mrs. Walter
Loomis Mrs. William
Loomis Mrs. John M.
Lord Mrs. George
Loring Mrs. Stella Dyer
. Lunt Miss Nina Grey
MacVeagh Mrs. Franklin
Magruder Mrs. B. D.
Martin Miss Kate B.
Mason Mrs. Henry
Mason Mrs. Alverin A.
Matz Mrs. Otto H.
Matz Mrs. Rudolph
Matz Miss Evelyn
McClurg Mrs. A. C.
McCormick Mrs. Robert
McCormick Mrs. R. Hall
McCormick Mrs. Wm. G.
McMurray Mrs. E. B.
Merrill Mrs. Kate M.
Mitchell Mrs. J. S.
Monroe Miss Harriet S.
Moore Mrs. Gurdon G.
Mott Mrs. John Grenville
Mulliken Mrs. Chas. H.
Nixon Mrs. Wm. Penn
Owen Mrs. James R.
Palmer Mrs. Potter
Parker Mrs. Frank W.
Peirce Mrs. L. H.
Perkins Miss Janet R.
Phelps Mrs. Erskine M.
Potter Mrs. O. W.
Pretyman Mrs. Wm.
Ray Mrs. Julia A.
Reith Mrs. Julia
Rice Miss Rebecca S.
Rich Mrs. M. Byron
Rogers Mrs. Henry W.
Root Mrs. John W.
Scammon Mrs. J. Y.

Sheldon Mrs. Theodore
Shorey Mrs. Daniel L.
Silsbee Mrs. J. L.
Smith Mrs. Chas. G.
Smith Mrs. Sabin
Starrett Mrs. Helen E
Stevenson Mrs. A. F.
Stevenson Dr. Sarah H.
Stickney Mrs. Edward
Stone Mrs. H. O.

Stone Mrs. Henry B.
Swan Mrs. James H.
Talbot Miss Marion
Thompson Mrs. Slason
Tilton Mrs. Lucretia J.
Trimingham Miss A. E.
Underhill Mrs. Elizabeth
Walker Mrs. J. M.
Walker Mrs. Wm. B.
Walker Mrs. Marie A.

Waller Mrs. Edward
Ward Mrs.O Van Schaack
Watson Mrs. L. H.
Wilkinson Mrs. Dudley
Williams Mrs. Stalham
Willits Mrs. Geo. S.
Wilmarth Mrs. H. M.
Withrow Mrs. Thomas F.
Wright Mrs. Edward
Wynne Mrs. Madeline G.

THE FORTY CLUB.

OFFICERS.

W. T. HALL, -   -   -   -   -   -   - President.
H. C. CHATFIELD-TAYLOR, -   -   - Vice-President.
EDWARD FREIBERGER, -   -   -   -   - Secretary.
HARRY G. SOMMERS, -   -   -   -   -   - Treasurer.

MEMBERS OF EXECUTIVE COMMITTEE.
Gen. H. A. Wheeler   E. W. Kohlsaat   Montgomery Gibbs

MEMBERS.

Akin H. F.
Allen James Lane
Barron Elwyn A.
Chatfield – Taylor
  H. C.
Clayton C. B.
Cone G. W.
Crawford S. A.
Defrees J. H.
Dew Charles A.
Ewing Judge W. G.

Freiberger Edward
Gibbs Montgomery
Glover Lyman B.
Hall W. T.
Hamlin George J.
Hancock GeorgeW.
Horton Judge O. H.
Jenks E. W.
Jenney George H.
Kayzer Samuel
KohlsaatJudgeC.C.

Kohlsaat E. W.
Kuhns E. L.
MacMillan Newton
Morris Frank M.
Powers Harry J.
Powers L. D.
Root Frederick W.
Scales Judge Frank
Smith Harry B.
Sommers Harry G.

Stevenson Chas. A.
Stires Rev. Ernest
  M.
Stone Melville E.
Taylor Wm. A.
Thomas Dr. Homer
Turner Col. Henry
  L.
Wallace Genio
Wheeler Gen. H. A.

NON-RESIDENT MEMBERS.
French George H., St. Louis
Gardiner Cornelius, Washington
Hayman Alf, New York
Lashelle Kirke, New York
MacIntosh Burr, New York
Murray Frank, New York
Reade Capt. Philip H., U. S. A.

Richardson Leander, New York
Salsbury Nate, New York
Shuman A. F., Los Angeles, Cal.
Unitt E. G., New York
Wallace I. Laurie, Omaha
Wilkie John E., London
Williams Walter, New York

HONORARY MEMBERS.
Barnabee Henry C.
Barrymore Maurice
Clay Cecil
Dixey Henry E.
Goodwin Nat C.
Hoff Edwin W.
HollandEdward M.

Karl Tom
Lackaye Wilton
MacDonald W. H.
Morris Felix
Morris Ramsay
Nye Bill
O'Neill James

O'Rell Max
Page Thomas N.
Paulding Frederick
Reed Roland
Root Dr. George F.
Russell Edmund

Skinner Otis
Smith F. Hopkin-
  son
Sweatnam Willis
Willard Edward S.
Wilson Francis

FRENCH LITERARY CLUB.

OFFICERS.

W. T. UNDERWOOD, - - - - - President.
R. D. WARDWELL, } - - - Vice-Presidents.
MRS. C. A. SYKES, }
MISS LILY ROEMHELD, - - - - Secretary.
ARTHUR WOODCOCK, - - - - - Treasurer.
A. GOUERE, - - - - Directeur Dramatique.

MEMBERS.

Barclay Mrs. J. C.
Beckmann Fritz
Bennett J. L.
Benoit Miss M. L.
Bequet Mrs. M.
Bideleux Edward
Bideleux W. E.
Blitz Albert
Bonet L.
Brosseau Noel
Burdick Miss M.
Burdick Miss Nina
Burton LeGrand
Charlton Miss May
Choquet Leon
Conmert E.
Crane Charles R.
Crocker Miss An-
   nette
Danidis A. V.
Davis F.
Delinotte Miss M.
DeLuce Mrs. A. E.
Denison T. S.
Douglass Mrs. F.
Douglass Grace S.
Dubois Wm.
Dubois Mrs. W.
Dutton Miss K.

Edwards W. H.
Emery Miss A. M.
Friend C. E.
Friend Mrs. C. E.
Gottschalk L. G.
Guertin V.
Gunther C. F.
Grehier Leon
Hannah W. H.
Harphand E. L.
Hawxhurst Arthur
Hennebery Moses
Holmes E. B.
Howard Mrs. Chas.
Janocha Leo
Jenks Arthur W.
Kaufman Theo.
Keehn Geo. W.
Kenand J. E. A.
Knowles Miss K.
Knowles Mrs. M.H.
Kozminski M. W.
Mackey Mrs. F. J.
Mantellini Sig. G.
Marguerat Mrs. C.
Marshall Mrs. L. E.
Mason George
Matthey C.

Mayer R.
McDonald Miss I.
McFadden E. R.
McMichael Dr.
Mellen Henry J.
Meyer Herman
MeyerMrs.Herman
Mulliken Mrs. C.H.
Mysenberg O. W.
Nyland A. C. H.
Officer Miss Julia
Payne William M.
Pettibone A. G.
Pettibone Mrs.A.G.
Phillips W. G.
Picard Arthur
Picard C. F.
Pincoffs P. A.
Planchamp C. C.
Probst A. O.
ReynoldsMissM.D.
Roemheld Jules
Roemheld Louis
Roemheld Miss L.
Roemheld Mrs. J.
Ryhiner F. C.
Sadouski Leon de
Saltonsall Bryaton

Sommer Waldemar
Spencer Mrs. A. P.
Stetani A. J.
Stevely Lucius
Stone M. E.
Stone Mrs. M. E.
Streeter Mme. R.
Strong Mrs. E. B.
Syer E. W.
Sykes Mrs. C. A.
Tallert Jacques
Tanty Mrs. A.
Tanty Jean C.
Tanty Paul
Taylor Hobart C.
Teal Miss Anna C.
Townsend Mrs. J.S.
Underwood W. T.
Varesi Miss E.
Von Holland Miss
   H.
Von Krzisch K. R.
Wardwell R. D.
Wegman Jules T.
Wessman Axel J.
Wheeler C. Gilbert
Winslow C. S.
Woodcock Arthur

THE FRIDAY CLUB.

OFFICERS.

MISS CAROLINE KIRKLAND, - - - - President.
MRS. H. B. BUTLER, - - - First Vice-President.
MRS. DUNLAP SMITH, - - Second Vice-President.
MISS E. M. FURNESS, - - Corresponding Secretary.
MRS. EDMOND BURKE, - - Recording Secretary.
MRS. J. B. WALLER, JR., - - - - Treasurer.

EXECUTIVE COMMITTEE.

Mrs. L. W. Bates
Mrs. Ambrose Cramer
Miss E. P. Head

Miss Kathleen Healy
Miss M. S. Hill
Miss J. L. King

Mrs. H. H. Martin
Miss E. W. Towner

MEMBERS.

Aldis Mrs. Arthur T.
Alward Mrs. Herbert
Andrews Mrs. W. H.

Atkinson Mrs. Chas.
Augur Mrs. Wheaton
Baldwin Mrs. Charles H.

Bates Mrs. Lindon W.
Bentley Miss Anna
Bentley Mrs. Cyrus jr.

Blaine Mrs. Emmons
Blatchford Miss F. M.
Blatchford Mrs. Paul
Bryan Miss Jennie B.
Burke Mrs. Edmund
Butler Mrs. Hermon B.
Carpenter Mrs. G. A. .
Carpenter Miss Nellie
Chandler Mrs. E. E.
Chappell Mrs. Howard F.
Chatfield-Taylor Mrs.H.C
Cochrane Mrs. J. Lewis
Coolidge Mrs. Frederic
Cox Miss Jennie E.
Cramer Mrs. Ambrose
Cramer Mrs. E. W.
Cramer Miss May
Crowell Mrs. Henry P.
Davis Mrs. N. S. jr.
Davis Mrs. R, L.
Dawes Mrs. C. M.
Deane Mrs. Ruthven
Delano Mrs. F. A.
Douglas Mrs. Frank M.
Enders Miss Margaret
Ewen Mrs. J. M.
Farwell Mrs. F. C.
Farwell Mrs. J. V. jr.
Ferry Mrs. A. F.
Ferry Mrs. Charles H.
Fisher Mrs. George P. jr.
Fuller Mrs. F. R.
Furness Miss E. M.
Garret Mrs. T. Mauro
Goudy Mrs. William J.
Gray Miss I. C.
Greely Mrs. Morris L.
Griggs Miss Caroline
Hale Miss Mary B.
Head Miss E. P.
Head Miss Katharine
Healy Miss Edith
Healy Miss Kathleen
Henrotin Mrs. Charles
Herrick Miss Louise
Hill Miss M. S.

Hooper Mrs. Heury
Houghteling Mrs. J. L.
Hubbard Mrs. William H.
Hunt Mrs. C. du Vernet
Isham Miss A. E.
Isham Mrs. George
Isham Miss Katherine
Jaggard Mrs. W. W.
Jewett Mrs. E. R.
Jewett Mrs. Samuel R.
Johnson Mrs. Frank S.
Jones Miss M. K.
Kales Miss Frances
Keep Miss Frances
Kellogg Miss Emma C.
King Mrs. Francis
King Miss J. L.
King Mrs. Rockwell
Kirkland Miss Caroline
Knott Mrs. H. A.
Laflin Mrs. Louis E.
Landon Miss H. J.
Lynde Mrs. S. A.
Martin Mrs. Horace H.
Martin Miss Maud
McCormick Mrs. Cyrus H.
McCormIck Mrs.Hamilton
McCormick Miss Henrietta
McGenniss Mrs. Charles
Meeker Mrs. George W.
Miller Mrs. Roswell
Monroe Miss Lucy B.
Moss Mrs. Jesse L.
Nixon Miss M. S.
Northcote Mrs. Amyas S.
Otis Mrs. William A.
Packard Mrs. George
Payson Mrs. George
Peabody Mrs. F S.
Pomeroy Mrs. S. H.
Ryerson Mrs. E. L.
Ryerson Miss Eleanor
Sanborn Mrs. Victor C.
Sawyer Mrs. Francis A.

Shufeldt Mrs. W. B. E.
Skeele Mrs. H. B.
Skinner Miss Elizabeth
Skinner Miss Frederika
Smith Mrs. Dunlap
Smith Mrs. Ernest F.
Smith Miss Mary Rozet
Snow Miss Helen
Spicer Mrs. V. K.
Straus Mrs. Michael
Street Mrs. Charles A.
Sturges Mrs. H.
Sturges Miss Mary D.
Thompson Mrs. Slason
Towner Miss E. W.
Troost Miss Louise S.
Trowbridge Miss Cornelia R.
Tuttle Mrs. Henry M.
Wadsworth Miss Georgiana
Wadsworth Miss Helen
Waite Miss Ella R.
Walker Mrs. Charles M.
Walker Miss Marguerite
Waller Mrs. James B. jr.
Waller Mrs. Robert A.
Waller Mrs. William
Webster Mrs. Louis D.
Wentworth Mrs. Moses J.
West Mrs. Frederic T.
Wheeler Mrs. Arthur D.
Wheeler Mrs. Frank S.
Whitman Mrs. Russell
Williams Miss Annie
Williams Miss Cora B.
Williams Miss Laura
Williams Mrs. Lawrence
Willing Mrs. Henry J.
de Windt Mrs. H. A.
Winston Mrs. Dudley
Winston Mrs. F. S.
·Withrow Miss Bonnie
Wood Mrs. I. C.
Worthington Mrs. E. S.

GERMANIA MÆNNERCHOR.

Northwest Corner Clark Street and Germania Place.

OFFICERS.

THEODOR BRETANO,	- - - - -	President.
GUSTAV A. HOFMANN,	- - - -	Vice-President.
AD. UHRLAUB,	- - - - - -	Secretary.
E. S. DREYER,	- - - - -	Treasurer.

TRUSTEES.

Dr. T. J. Bluthardt   Albert Kuhlmey   Dr. H. C. Welcker
George W. Claussenius   Otto C. Schneider

MEMBERS.

Abel E. J.   Adams Geo. E.   Alexander J. B.   Amberg Franz
Ackhoff H. W.   Affeld C. E.   Altgeld J. P.   ·Ammon E.

Andersen S.
Andrae Arnold O.
Apfel W. G.
Arend Aug.
Arend W. N.
Arnold Herm.
Babo Alexander V.
Baggot E.
Ball W. T.
Barothy Victor
Baseler C. F.
Baumann Ferd O.
Beck Aug.
Becker Norbert
Berger Ad.
Berger Rob.
Bert Dr. E.
Biegler Louis
Binder Carl
Birk Wm. A.
Blanke Geo. F.
Blocki E. W.
Blocki John
Blum Simon S.
Blumenthal Aug.
Bluthardt G. A.
Bluthardt R. E.
Bluthardt Dr. T. J,
Bluthardt T. J. jr.
Boas Dr. E. A.
Bobsin Julius
Boerricke R.
Boittcher Paul O.
Boldenweck C. G.
Boldenweck L. H.
Boldenweck W.
Booth Geo. B.
Borcherdt A. F.
Brackenbush A. C.
Bradish A. H.
Brand Friedrich
Brand Horace
Brand M.
Brand Rud.
Brandecker F. X.
Brandt Carl
Braun Geo. P.
Bredow A. A.
Bredt J. M.
Brentano Theo.
Brinkman C.
Bromilow E. W.
Brookman FrankE.
Brucker Jos.
Buck Dr. J. P.
Buehl Carl
Buehler John
Buehler J. W.
Buenz Dr. Carl
Bumiller Emil
Calder Geo. W. G.
Calder R. G.
Campe Frank
Carqueville E.
Chase Sam. B.
ChristmannDrG.A.

Christoph E. G.
Christy F. C.
Clark J. S.
Claussenius Ed.
Claussenius G. W.
Coith Emil
Collot C. F.
Crapser MauriceH.
Crawford R. C.
Cudell A.
Davis Will J.
Deecken F.
Demmler Carl
Dennehy T. C.
Detmer Henry
Dewes Aug. J.
Dewes Carl J.
Dewes F. J.
Diehl F.
Diehl George
Dierkes Alex.
Dietrich Dr. H.
Dietzgen Eugene
Dietzsch Emil
Doepp Dr. W.
Dressbach Phil.
Dreyer E. S.
Druding A.
Eckart Wm.
Eder H.
Edler Francis
Egersdorff Theo F.
Ehlen J. C.
Ehmann Chas.
Eitel Carl
Eitel Emil
Elich F. W.
Emmel Henry G.
Emmerich Charles
Engelsmann Franz
Engers Frank W.
Engle August
English Wm. J.
Ernst C. Emil
Ernst Leo.
Eschenburg A. W.
Eschenburg HansA
Eschenburg J. W.
Faulhaber J. M.
Fecker Ernest jr.
Ferguson Chas. H.
Fiedler A.
Fiedler Anton B. jr.
Fiedler M. A.
Finkler Adolf
Finkler Gustav
Finkler Wm.
Fischer Chas. W.
Fiske Dr. G. F.
Fleischmann J.
Fleming P. H.
Forch John L.
Foster Henry A.
Freise Emil
Freund Chas. E.
Freund Herm. W.

Freund Wm.
Freytag Moritz
Fricke Max
Friedel J Daniel
Fritz C. W.
Fromann E. H.
Fuchs Gustav
Fuehring Wm. A.
Fuerst Conrad
Fuerst Edward A.
Fuetterer Dr. G.
Fuller G. Edward
Funck Peter
Furthmann Edmd.
Gaensslen Walter
Gail G. Ferd
Garthe Emil
Gartz A. F
Gehrig Jos. W.
Gerold C.
Gerstenberg E.
Geudtner Charles.
Geudtner Francis
Gilsdorff Edw. W.
Gindele Geo. A.
Glade John H.
Glasser W.
Glennie Albert E.
Gloeckler Chas. S.
Glogauer Fritz
Goetz Fred.
Goldzier Julius
Gormully P. R.
Gottfried Carl
Gottfried M.
Gowan Victor D.
Grass Ed.
Graue J. George
GreenshieldABates
Gregory Geo.
Greiner Wm. jr.
Griesheimer F.
Griewisch F.
Grommes J. B.
Gundrum Fred.
Haerther Wm. J.
Hahne Wm.
Halla Ch.
Hallberg L. G.
Halle E. G.
HammermillreWm
Hand J. P.
Hand Peter
Hansen Oscar J.
Harbers Ch.
Hartmann Ad.
Hartmann S. E.
Harz Emil G.
Harz Theo.
Haverkamp F.
Hecht Ernst
Hecht Frank A.
Hecht Walter
Heinemann Wm.
Heinemann W. C.
Heinrichs H. W.

Heissler Jac.
Helmolt C. von
Henius Dr. Max
Henne Phil.
Henning Dr. Francis A.
Henrici Phil.
Henrotin Adolph
Henrotin Ch.
Herbert Herman
Herbert M. B.
Herbst Hermann
Hertel F.
Herz Arthur
Hesing A. C.
Hesing Wash.
Hess E.
Hess Frank W.
Hettich W. A.
Heuchling H. A.
HeuchlingDr.T.W.
Hild Fred. H.
Hill Henry W.
Hirsch Dr. Emil G.
Hirt J. C.
Hobein Edward
Hobein Fritz
Hoffbauer Wm.
Hoffman J. Jos.
Hofmann Gust. A.
Holinger Arnold
Hotz Dr. C. F.
Huber Julius
Huck L. C.
Huefner William
HummelGoswin jr.
Huncke Carl
Hutchings W. A.
Ingwersen C. H.
Jaeger Ph.
Jansen H.
Jannss Dr. Peter
Johnson A. G.
Johnson Chas. J.
Juergens Paul
Jummell Paul
Junker A.
Kaestner Ad.
Kaestner Chas.
Kandeler Theo.
Karls T.
Kasper Jos.
KatzenbergerGeoA
Kee J. W.
Keeley Thomas
Kehl Charles H.
Keil Moritz
Keller G.
Kelley A. D.
Kellner F. G.
Kellner Dr. Max
Kemper Alfr.
Kerfoot W. D.
Kern Chas.
Kern Jacob J.
Kersten Geo.

Kilian Justus
Kiolbassa Peter
Kirchhoff H. Aug.
Klaner Fred.
Klein Albert S.
Klemm Walter
Kny Lothar
Koch Arthur
Koch Edw.
Koch Henry
Koch Otto
Kochs Theo. A.
Koehne H. L.
Kohlhammer R.W.
Kohlsaat Peter N.
Kohtz Louis O.
Kollmorgen Herm.
Kranz John
Krause Edm. R.
Krause O. K.
Kreismann P.
Kroeschell Herman
Kroeschell Otto
Kroeschell Wm.
Kroth Louis
Kuecken Wm.
Kuhlmey Alb.
Langan J. B.
Lange F. J.
Langewisch L.
Laux John
Leake Jos. B.
Lederer Chas.]
Lee Dr. Ed.
Leeb Henry
Lefens T. J.
Lehmann Ed.
Lehmann E. J.
Lehrkind Paul
Leman Henry W.
Leutz C. F. W.
Lewandowski Theo
Lindbloom Rob.
Lotholz Oscar
Lotholz R.
Lotz Arthur C.
Lubeke Wm. F.
Maas Fred.
Maas Phil.
Macdonald Chas.B.
Madlener Albert F.
Madlener F.
Magnus Albert
Magnus Arthur J.
Magnus Aug.
Magnus Aug. C.
Maltby A. W.
Mann Henry N.
Manstein R. Avon
Maritzen Aug.
Martin Edward B.
Matthai Dr. P. H.
Matthiessen E. D.
Mauch Max
Maus F. K.
May Horatio

Mayer David
Mayer Henry
Mayer Levi
Mayer Oscar F.
Mayer W. J.
McCarthy J. G.
McCrea W. S.
McDonald H. K.
McGillan John
Meagher J. F.
Meinshausen O.
Mendius H.
Menn Dr. Rudolph
Merckle Dr. H.
Messersmith Geo.
Metzler J. Jacob
Meyenschein F. A.
Meyer Adam J.
Meyer Jacob
Meyer Magnus
Meyer Martin
Meysenburg O. W.
Michaelis W. R.
Miller B.
Miller Dr. Truman
Mitchell Otto W.
Moeller C. C.
Mohl O. C.
Moll E.
Morrill Donald L.
Mueller Alf. O.
Mueller Herman
Mueller Hermann R.
Mueller Val.
Muffat Dr. M.
Neymann A. M.
Nickelsen A.
Nockin Bernhard jr
Nockin Edward
Obermann Ad.
Olsen A. G.
Orb John A.
Paepcke H.
Paffrath Casper
Pank J. Henry
Parker Th. jr.
Parsons J. B.
Pauling E. G.
Peabody F. S.
Peak F. H.
Peters F.
Peters F. M.
Petersen Emil
Petersen George L.
Petersen Hermann
Petersen Hugo T.
Petersen Victor J.
Petersen W. A.
Peterson P. S.
Petri M.
Petrie Nic.
Pietsch Carl
Pietsch Dr. Carl
Piper Henry
Plautz C. H.

Poppenhusen Conrad H.
Porter Hibbard
Powers Henry J.
Prager Eugen
Probst H.
Pruessing Geo. C.
Rang Henry
Raster Edwin
Rehm Jacob
Reimann G. L.
Revell A. H.
Rhode Rud. E.
Rice John C.
Richberg J. C.
Richter Aug. F.
Riebe Gustav
Riel Gustav
Rinn Ph.
Rintelman Anton
Roehling Geo.
Roesch Frank
Roessler F. Herm.
Rohr Dr. F.
Romer Max
Roof A. E.
Rosenthal Jul.
Rosenthal Oscar
Roth Charles
Rothbart Paul
Rothe Aug.
Rubens Harry
Rudolph C.
Rudolph Emil
Ruehl Dr. L. A.
Ruh Frank E.
Ruhstrat Ad.
Ruhstrat Fred.
Scales Frank
Schaller Henry
Schapper Ferd. C.
Schaub F. J.
Schilling George F.
Schlachter J.
Schlesinger L.
Schlick E. R.
Schloesser Dr.A.G.
Schloesser Rud.
Schlogl J.
Schlotthauer G. H.
Schmetzer J. A.
Schmid Geo.
Schmid Godfrey
Schmidgall F. L.
Schmidt Hugo
Schmidt K. G.
Schmidt Leo
Schmidt Richard G.
Schmidt Wm.
Schneider George
Schneider Otto C.
Schoenfeld Henry
Schoeninger Ad.
Schoepflin A.
Scholbe M. A.
Scholl J. B.

Schonlau Carl
Schotte Mrs. Chas.
Schrader Th.
Schrader Wm. L.
Schubert John C.
Schuettler Peter
Schultz Alb.
Schultz Martin M.
Scott James W.
Seckel Adolph
Seiffert Rudolph
Seipp W. C.
Sheldon George W.
Shields Michael
Sierks H.
Simon Chas. W.
Simon John G.
Sittig Eug. A.
Sittig Wm. A.
Smith C. A.
Sommer Otto A.
Sontag Fritz
Spalding C. F.
Spelthahn Leo
Spicker Dr. M.
Spielmann Arthur
Spirkil Dr. J.
Spirkel Dr. L. C.
Stein Carl
Stern Frank J.
Stern Max
Stevenson Alex. F.
Stieglitz Gust
Strassheim C.
Strotz Chas N.
Strotz Nicholas
Sturges Jas. D,
Sturm Adolph
Tempel John
Thaler A. G.
Theurer J.
Thielemann Carl
Thielemann Franz
Thielen Jacob
Thome M.
Thompson M. B.
Thorwarth H.
Thurber Geo. S.
Tiedemann Jacob H
Tosetti Ernst
Tripp Arnold
Tripp Dwight K.
True J. R.
Uhlemann R. G.
Uhlendorf L.
Uhrlaub Ad.
Uhrlaub John C.
Uihlein Ed. G.
Ullrich Michael
Unzicker H.
Unzicker Otto
Valy Ernest
VanDame C.
VanVlissingenP,H.
Vocke Wm.
Voelcker John J.

Vogelsang John
Vogler Hermann
Vogler W. H.
Volger Fred.
Vollmer Herman
Vouwie H. J.
Wacker Chas. H.
Wagner Dr. Carl
Wagner Dr. C. B.
Wagner E. W.
Wagner Fritz
Wallis H. H.
Walsh John R.
Walter T.
Washburn H.

Wassmansdorff O.
Wassmansdorrf W.
G.
Weaver Chas. S.
Weber Andr.
Weber P. I.
Wegmann Julius
Wegmann Julius F.
Wehrheim A. S.
Weidner O. J.
Weinsheimer Wm.
J.
Weiss G. A.
Weiss John H.

Welcker Dr. H. C.
Welcker Dr. P. R.
Wertheim Edw.
Wetterer Dr. Her-
mann
Wichert Henry
Wiedel E.
Wilke Gust.
Williams H. F.
Willits Geo. S.
Winston F. S.
Winter Phil.
Wittmeyer Gust
Wittstein A. H.

Wohlhuetter C. V.
Wolff Geo.
Wollensak J. F.
Woltersdorff Louis
Woltz J.
Wuthmann Ad.
Zeiger Geb. W.
Yerkes Chas. T.
Zander Aug.
Zeiger Geb. W.
Ziegfeld Dr. F.
Zimmerman Dr.GA
Zitt J. H.
Zschuppe C. jr.

HAMILTON CLUB.

21 GROVELAND PARK.

OFFICERS.

ARTHUR DIXON, ...	President.
JOHN S. MILLER, , . . .	First Vice-President.
FRANK WELLS, . . .	Second Vice-President.
EDWARD S. ELLIOTT, ...	Secretary.
RALPH METCALF, ...	Treasurer.

DIRECTORS.

H. H. Boyington
George W. Dixon
A. F. Risser

W. P. Penhallow
John C. Everett
Fred A. Smith
M. H. Gibson

S. F. Hawley
M. W. Kozminski
J. R. Terhune

MEMBERS.

Aldrich J. Frank
Allerton Samuel W.
Ashcraft E. M.
Bancroft Edgar A.
Barnes Albert C.
Beach H. L.
Beam W. T.
Best Henry
Bliss E. R.
Boyington H. H.
Bradley C. H.
Brainerd Edw. R.
Brand E. L.
Browne Edward
Bruner Charles E.
Cameron John M.
Chase B. F.
Clark Frank H.
Clark James L.
Crocker H. D.
Defrees Jos. H.
Deneen Chas. S.
Dixon Arthur
Dixon Arthur A.
Dixon George Wm.
Dixon Thos. J.
Dyke Edward F.
Egan John G.
Elliott Edward S.
Engelhard Geo. P.

Everett John C.
Foreman Henry G.
Foster Wm. Elmore
Fuller H. H.
Gibson Milroy H.
Glennie Albert E.
Goodman Herbert
E.
Graves George A.
Gunning Robt. J.
Hamilton E. F.
Hamline John H.
Hanecy Ellbridge
Harlow George H.
Harmon Chas. S.
Harpham Edwin
L.
Hart Harry
Hawley S. F.
Helmer Frank A.
Hirschl A. J.
Holdom Jesse
Horton B. F.
Hughes Chas.
Hull Perry A.
Ireland Dr. L. E.
Jenkins Robt. E.
Jones Chas. J.
Judd Edward J.
Kerr Wm. R.

Kozminski Maurice
W.
Laing John R.
Leyenberger Chas.
Mann James R.
Marrenner E.
Mather Robert
Matthews Henry M.
McAuley J. T.
McDonald R. J.
McKendry W. H.
McMurdy Robt. H.
McRoy John L.
Metcalf Herbert C.
Metcalf Ralph
Milchrist W. A.
Miller John S.
Mills C. W.
Miner William R.
Moderwell E. C.
Moulton F. I.
Newman Jacob
Nickerson D. W.
Orr Charles F.
Parish S. M.
Penhallow W. P.
Pollasky Marcus
Preston W. D.
Purington D. V.
Reed Alanson H.

Reynolds C. N.
Ringer Jacob
Risser A. F.
Rosenthal James
Rubovitz Edward
Sattley Winfield N.
Schuyler D. J.
Sheldon Hervey
Sherman Marky R.
Smith Eli
Smith Frederick A
Strong Joseph H.
Swartz George E.
Swett W. H.
Tenney D. K.
Terhune James R.
Underwood Geo. W.
Vallette Frank H.
Van Meter H. H.
Vierling Louis
Vierling Robert
Wallace Jno. F.
Warren Charles D.
Wells Frank
West Roy O.
White Randall H.
White Wm. F.
Williams Daniel H.
Woodward W. E.

THE HARVARD CLUB.

HARVARD AND SIXTY-THIRD STREETS.

OFFICERS.

JOHN B. FAY, - - - - - - - - President.
W. O. BUDD, - - - - - - Vice-President.
GEORGE H. OWEN, - - Secretary and Treasurer.

DIRECTORS.

J. B. Fay	George H. Owen	I. L. Lockwood
W. O. Budd	H. H. Peters	F. E. Jack
J. G. Everest		B. Timmerman

MEMBERS.

Abbott A. A.	Foster J. M. Dr.	Metcalf Walter	Smith C. H.
Adams H. C.	Frink Wm. H.	Miller W. H.	Smith O. N.
Axtell A. W.	Frosch George	Mitchell Fred. R.	Snapp Chas. D.
Baker Wm.	Goss Samuel G.	Moak W. B.	Sommers J. R.
Ball J. A.	Green A. S.	Morgan H. A.	Speed H. B.
Barry P. T.	Gregory E. W.	Muirhead George	Spencer H. Frank
Berg Chas. F.	Gross J. W.	Munday Jno. W.	Spencer I.L'wrence
Blackman W. B.	Hall Jno. A.	Nay N. N.	Staver H. C.
Blakeslee H. L.	Hallenbeck Jno. C.	Neilson J. D.	Stebbins D. C.
Boettcher Dr. H. P.	Hellman F. D.	Nellis C. S.	Stebbins O. B.
Bowlby D. Roy	Henry Jno. A.	Newman C. S.	Stevens Jerome P.
Bradley B. W.	Hildebrandt Geo.	Noble E. J.	Stoddard J. A.
Brittain Joseph K.	Hoag Wm. J.	Noble L. C.	Stone F. A.
Brown Edwin	Hooper J. K.	Olmsted J. F.	Swett Wm. O.
Budd W. O.	Howard J. F.	Ottofy Louis	Teller J. G.
Card J. B.	Hubbard D. J.	Owen Geo. H.	Terriere D. E.
Clark C. S.	Irwin Harry L.	Page Chas. T.	Thearle H. B.
Colt Alonzo	Jack F. E.	Patterson W. A.	Thomas J. G.
Cutter H. W. K.	Johnson C. Porter	Peters Homer H.	Thompson Sam'l
Daniel W. H.	Jones Edward S.	Pettet F. E.	Tichnor M. H.
Darling C. S.	Jones F. E.	Porter F. L.	Timms F. M.
Davidson W. M.	Juneau E. L.	Preston D. A.	Timmerman Benj.
Davie Geo. F.	Keeran N. C.	Preston F. A.	Uhrig Jos.
Deakin J. E.	Kent Henry L.	Ramsey W. W.	Walbridge H. B.
Drake Isaac	Lewis H. B.	Reed Carl L.	Warner J. M.
Dudgeon W. H.	Lockwood J. Le-	Rich A. D.	Waterbury E. M.
Eaton W. T.	Grand	Robinson W. W.	Watson Geo. B.
Embree J. R.	Loomis E. E.	Rockhold F. A.	Weed J. E.
Eulete George W.	Maher Edward	Rollo C. E.	Wentz J. A.
Eulette C. H.	McKelvey Chas. A.	Roovart Wm.	Whitford H. E. Dr.
Eulette I. F.	McKeand W. B.	Rowland E. F.	Willard Frank
Everest J. G.	Marston Jas. D.	Ryther G. A.	Woodbury F. A.
Fay Jno. B.	Macphetridge E.	Safford Chas. L.	
Ferguson H. A.	Marshall Geo. E.	Sherwood Jesse	
Field E. C.	Meech W. R.	Sloan J. R.	
Fitch W. B.	Meech W. T.	Sloan W. A.	

HELIADES CLUB.

90 WARREN AV.

OFFICERS.

MRS. MARY E. HAVEN, - - - - - President.
MRS. MASON B. LOOMIS, - - - - Vice-President.
MRS. MARC SHERWOOD, - - - - - Secretary.

MEMBERS.

Boughton Mrs. D. F.	Harkness Mrs. E. J.	Price Mrs. A. D.
Camp Mrs. I. N.	Haven Mrs. Jos.	Sherwood Mrs. Jno. B.
Chapman Mrs. J. M.	Haven Mrs. Mary E.	Sherwood Mrs. Marc
Collins Mrs. L. D.	Loomis Mrs. Mason B.	Temple Mrs. M. D.
Fitz Simons Mrs. Chas. F.	Lyman Mrs. H. M.	Willcox Mrs. G. B.
Hall Mrs. J. S.	Polley Mrs. J. C.	

HIGHLAND PARK CLUB.

HIGHLAND PARK.

OFFICERS.

CHARLES W. KIRK, - - - - - President.
P. A. MONTGOMERY, - - - First Vice-President.
F. D. EVERETT, - - - Second Vice-President.
DANIEL COBB, - - - - - - - Secretary.
H. S. VAIL, - - - - - - - - Treasurer.

DIRECTORS.

Charles W. Kirk	S. M. Coe	F. W. Cushing
P. A. Montgomery	C. W. Rice	F. D. Everett
E. E. Prussing	H. S. Vail	J. H. Shields

MEMBERS.

Adams J. McG.	Conger Dr. T. H.	Hawkins R.	Schumacker B. W.
Alexander W. A.	Cummings G. B.	Hemstreet W. J.	Shields J. H.
Anderson J. F.	Cunningham W. S.	Howard Dr. E. G.	Sites G. L.
Babcock R. H.	Cushing F. W.	James S. W.	Small E. A.
Ball G. C.	Cushing L.	Jennings John	Smith Mrs. C. R.
Ball J. L.	Emerson W. H.	Jones Mrs. B. C.	Smoot K. R.
Basye A. A.	Erskine D. M. jr.	Jones B. F., U.S.A.	Snow E. M.
Basye H. C.	Everett C. J.	Kip A. L.	Spencer Clinton J.
Bennett G. L.	Everett F. D.	Kirk Chas. W.	Spencer T. H.
Bergen Dr. L. M.	Everingham G. S.	Knox S. F.	Stockton John L.
Bingham B. C.	Fargo F. M.	Lasher W. S.	Street H. C.
Bingham S. R.	Fessenden B. A.	Lightner M. C.	Street R. H.
Boulton G. D.	Farrar W. G.	Middleton John	Street R. J.
Boyington Edgar	Fischer Fred	Mihills M. A.	Street R. P.
Boyington F. P.	Fletcher A. W.	Millard S. M.	Stubbs W. C.
Boyington W. W.	Flinn C. J.	Montgomery P. A.	Sweetland Dr. W.
Brown E. H.	Flinn W. W.	Morgan A. C.	M.
Brown F. C.	Floyd Mrs. H. C.	Morgan Elisha	Taylor Dr. G. O.
Campbell A. S.	Fullerton Chas. W.	Morgan O. H.	Thorn Francis
Carver H. C.	Gifford R. L.	Myers S. N.	Vail H. S.
Chandler E. W.	Goodridge W. M.	Neall Rev. Hy.	VanSchaick H.
Chandler H. H.	Gray Elisha	Patton R. W.	Wakem J. W.
Childs W. F.	Green C. M.	Phillips C. G.	Watson Miss Lyda
Clark T. M.	Gump B. F.	Prall J. S.	Winchester C. J.
Clow F.	Hall F. P.	Prussing E. E.	Winchester F. W.
Cobb Daniel	Hammond C. G.	Requa H. L.	Wolcot Rev. P. C.
Coe S. M.	Haskins Dr. H. S.	Rice Chas. B.	Yoe L. G.
Colburn Dr. J. E.	Hawkins F. P.	Rice John F.	

THE HINSDALE CLUB.

HINSDALE.

OFFICERS.

CHAS. A. ALLEN, ... President.
M. L. RAFTREE . . . . . . Vice-President.
F. E. AYERS, ... Secretary and Treasurer.

DIRECTORS.

Chas. A. Allen	C. D. Bird	F. J. Schuyler
M. L. Raftree	R. R. Bradley	L. K. Hildebrand
	F. E. Ayres	

MEMBERS.

Allen Charles
Allen C. A.
Allen J. E.
Ayers F. E.
Bassett O. P.
Bird C. D.
Blackman W. L.
Blayney George W.
Blood J. A.
Bogue Geo. M.
Bradley J. C. F.
Bradley J. H.
Bradley R. R.
Carleton W. B.
Cary G. P.
Cary J. W.
Cary Paul V.
Childs R. A.
Coffeen W. C.
Colburn H.
Colburn W. R.
Cole Harry
Cole W. H.
Cole W. O.

Conover L. P.
Cooke H. H.
Courter D. A.
Crossette C. H.
Cushing C. H.
Dana H. C.
Danforth Jerome J
Dennison C. G.
Duncan Wm.
Earle J. E.
Ellsworth F. R.
Eustis T. M.
Fairchild E. J.
Fayerweather E.E.
Fulton H. A.
Gardner Geo. C.
Gardner H. A.
Gordon Wm. G.
Grabo H. F.
Groff Carl
Hawtin F. W.
Heaphy A. T.
Heineman S.
Hench J. B.

Hildebrand L. K.
Hinds C. E.
Hinds E. P.
Hinds E. P. jr.
Hines A. G.
Hudson Charles
Irvine F. R.
Jackson Horace
Jourdan E. F.
Knight W. H.
Kniseley H. C.
Landis J. W.
Linsley T. H.
McClintock Jas.
McCredie William
McGee W. E.
Merrill J. C. F.
Middaugh H. C.
Muller L. jr.
Payne W. C.
Pearsall A. L.
Preston D. H.
Raftree M. L.
Redfern J. N.

Richie Bruce E.
Ridgway J. V.
Robbins George B.
Roberts C. M.
Robinson A. R.
Ross J. C.
Ruth L. C.
Schuyler F. J.
Shaw Edward E.
Smith Donald
Smith George E.
Stevens W. T.
Stuart Charles
Taylor F. T.
Thayer C. H.
Thayer H. R.
Townsend P. S.
Wadington John
Wait W. W.
Walker A. E.
Washburn C. L.
Williams Geo. H.
Wismer George C.
Zimmerman Jos.

HOME CLUB.

6737 WENTWORTH AVENUE.

OFFICERS.

J. A. BARTLETT, - - - - - - - President.
GEORGE MIDDENDORF, - - - Vice-President.
C. W. WALTERS, - - Secretary and Treasurer.

DIRECTORS.

J. A. Bartlett
C. W. Walters
C. H. Caldwell

Aug. Tidholm
G. A. Erhart
W. H. Dunn

F. L. Salisbury
J. P. Mallette
George Middendorf

MEMBERS.

Baker O. A.
Bartlett Chas. A.
Bartlett J. A.
Beek H. W.
Bent Geo. P.
Brink J. T.
Caldwell C. H.
Croft F. W.
Crosby Geo. H.
Cullum A. S.
Eddy Geo. S.

Eddy H. C.
Erhart Geo. A.
French Geo. T.
Garrett M. A.
Hemingway H. W.
Hendricks P. C.
Hodgkins J.
Hodgkins W.
Hoppin B. E.
Hudson P. S.
Johnson J. M.

Kendall John S.
Kirk E. jr.
Mallette Jas. P.
McKnight G. F.
Middendorf G.
Morton E. C.
Nason C. E.
Norris J. M.
Robie Geo. T.
Salisbury F. L.
Salmon Chas.

Storrs D. W.
Swift A. R.
Swift H. C.
Thompson Geo. L.
Tidholm August
Tracy L. M.
Walters C. W.
Wheelock Geo. K.
Whitman A. T.
Young Alex. C.

HYDE PARK CLUB.

WASHINGTON AVENUE NW. COR. FIFTY-FIRST.

OFFICERS.

EUGENE B. MYERS, ... President.
J. S. GRINNELL, ... Vice-President.
EDWARD R. SHAW, ... Secretary.
BEN WILLIAMS, ... Treasurer.

DIRECTORS.

Will. H. Moore	George A. E. Kohler	J. P. Smith, jr.
James A. Edwards	A. P. Callahan	M. J. Dunne
George C. Bailey		T. S. Cruttenden

MEMBERS.

Aldrich J. F.	Douglas E. S.	King S. B.	Sewell Barton
Allen Henry C.	Dunne M. J.	Kneeland L. D.	Shaw Ed. R.
Asay W. C.	Dupee H. M.	Kohler Frank W.	Sheridan A. D.
Bailey G. C.	Eaton C. L.	Kohler G. A. E.	Smith A. J.
Baker C. S.	Edwards Jas. A.	Krum Charles L.	Smith Edward E.
Baker F. E.	Edwards W. H.	Lamb Fred. R.	Smith Jacob S.
Ballard C. D.	Emery A. B.	Lawson W. C.	Smith James M.
Beatty W. R.	Evans D. E.	LeValley J. R.	Smith J. B. jr.
Bell W. E.	Everett John C.	Lewis Denslow Dr.	Smith J. P.
Beman W. I.	Farovid Jas. A.	Lewis Wm. G.	Smith L. K.
Bennett F. I.	Fellows J. E.	Lindsay D. J.	Smith R. G.
Biglow T. M.	Felt Frank B.	Loose J. L.	Smith R. P.
Bisbee L. H.	Fenton W. T.	MacLachlan J. W.	Smith S. A.
Blood H. E.	Ferguson G. M.	Madden F. H.	Soden G. A.
Blossom E. J.	Feron Walter G.	Main W. B.	Spencer Earl W.
Blossom G. W.	Flint H. L.	Mann James R.	Starrett Ralph
Bogue H. B.	French C. G.	Marcy George E.	Sterling W. H.
Bowes J. P.	Gary John W	Marder John	Stuart Robert
Boyd Robert	Gates J. W.	Mason A. C.	Swanitz A. W.
Bremer A. R.	Germain C. C.	Matkin O. F.	Swift L. F.
Brougham T. B.	Gilbert H. T.	McKey R. M.	Thomas B.
Brower J. F.	Gordon Robert	McKey W. D.	Tousey C. A.
Brown F. D.	Green A. W.	Miller A. L.	Tousey Thos. E.
Brown J. F.	Grinnell J. S.	Miller J. H.	Trude F. H.
Buchanan Robt. S.	Griswold W. P.	Miller Thomas	Udell S. R.
Bunnell John A.	Grubb J. E.	Milligan C. F.	Ulrich Russell
Burchard M. N.	Hale Edward C.	Mitchell F. D.	Underwood S. L.
Caleb G. N.	Hancock Thomas	Mitchell J. J.	Valentine P. A.
Callahan A. P.	Harahan J. T.	Moore Will H.	Vories H. F.
Cameron John	Hartwell A. V.	Morrill C. E.	Ware J. H.
Campbell A. E.	Hartwell M. W.	Munger P. F.	Warner G. L.
Campbell D. W.	Hately Walter	Murray T. H.	Warren C. D.
Campbell J. A.	Hawley E. S.	Myers E. B.	Weaver Charles A.
Case C. C.	Henderson E. K.	Newhall A. F.	Wells B. R.
Catlin George	Hinkins Dr. J. E.	Nicholas F. C.	Wheeler A. W.
Chalmers William	Holman I. W.	Nichols H. N.	Wheelock W. G.
Clark C. J.	Hoyt G. W.	Norton J. R.	Whelan Dr. Bion
Clark T. C.	Hudson T. J.	Palmer W. H.	Whipple R. M.
Clark Dr. W. C.	Huffman R. M.	Parker L. A.	White A. J.
Cooke S. J.	Hunt Charles H.	Porter A. R.	White C. E.
Cooper A. J.	Hunter R. J. O.	Potwin Homer	White Frank A.
Cortright L. D.	Hyman R. W. jr.	Rawson S. W.	White Wm. J.
Crawford C. H.	Jayne E. L.	Ray B. F.	Wilkins S. G.
Crews Seth F.	Jenkins S. R.	Reed Chas. A.	Williams Ben.
Cruzen R. E.	Jennings R. P.	Reid Dr. J. G.	Williams Dr. C. A.
Cruttenden T. S.	Jocelyn F. C.	Rice E. S.	Williams E. C.
Danks I.	Jocelyn R. M.	Robinson J. C.	Winchell N. P.
Darnall H. A.	Johnson W. O.	Robinson W. L.	Wise C. B.
Davis F. B.	Jones A. G.	Russell Martin J.	Woodman T. F.
Davis George W.	Kennard A. D.	Salisbury E. H.	Woodruff C. E.
Davis John	Kent Wm. M.	Sampson J. C.	Wright Geo. C.
DeMuth B. F.	Kerr R. H.	Sattley W. N.	Wyman W. D
Dickason L. T.	Kerr William R.	Schimpferman W H	

IDEAL CLUB.

531 - 533 N. WELLS.

OFFICERS.

JOSEPH GOODMAN, - - - - - -	President.
F. SILBERMAN, - - - - -	Vice-President.
LAMBERT O. WILE, - - - - -	Secretary.
ADOLPH BERG, - - - - - -	Treasurer.

DIRECTORS.

A. Marks	M. Jonas	A. Yondorf
S. Rosenthal	Geo. Frank	H. Pflaum
F. Silberman		

MEMBERS.

Alschuler Arthur	Frank A. I.	Jonas M.	Rothschild C. F.
Alschuler Harry	Frank George	Kaufman M.	Rothschild D.
Bacharach I.	Frank Dr. J.	Klee A.	Saxe Dan A.
Baer Louis	Frank J. H.	Lanz George	Schneider S.
Baer S.	Friedlander S.	Leiser D.	Shakman A.
Becker Leon V.	Geickauf E. S.	Loeb William	Silberman F.
Berg A.	Goldsmith M.	Maas M.	Spiesberger L.
Berg M.	Gombrig A.	Marks Al.	Stern L.
Bloch C. S.	Goodman Jos.	Mayer M. S.	Stern L.
Caumann Dave L.	Gradle B.	Metzler J.	Swartschild S.
Cohen B. M.	Griesheimer F.	Norden Dr. A.	Taussig S.
Cohn Louis	Greisheimer M.	Norden F. A.	Wangersheim D.
Cohn Sam.	Gutman E. J.	Nusbaum M.	Wangersheim Wm
Collat M.	Hamburgher E. C.	Pflaum H.	Weil Irving
Eichberg D.	Hecht E. S.	Plotke N. M.	Weil Joseph
Eichberg F.	Hecht S. P.	Regensburg H. L.	Weinreb Jos.
Eichberg L.	Hofheimer Z.	Reinach A. A.	Wile Lambert O.
Eisendrath S.	Horner Harry	Rosenfeld Maurice	Williams H. L.
Elkan H.	Jacobs C. F.	Rosenthal M.	Windmuller L.
Fass C.	Jonas James	Rosenthal Sam	Yondorf A.
Felsenthal A.			

THE ILLINOIS CLUB.

154 ASHLAND AVENUE.

OFFICERS.

WALTER SHOEMAKER, - - - - - -	President.
HOMER M. THOMAS, - - - - -	Vice-President.
CHARLES SHACKLEFORD, - - - - -	Secretary.
H. J. JONES, - - - - - -	Treasurer.

TRUSTEES.

W. H. Mortimer	A. E. Clark	H. S. Burkhardt
Alonzo Wygant	W. F. Main	W. J. Pope
W. J. Wilson	F. D. Meacham	Homer M. Thomas

MEMBERS.

Adcock A. W.	Barnard D. Elroy	Bogle W. S.	Brown H. H.
Avery Daniel J.	Beek H. W.	Bond L. L.	Brown M. O.
Aldrich W. H.	Beidler W. H.	Bond Thomas N.	Brown Sanger
Aldrich H. H.	Benner Mathias	Booth Harvey W.	Bishop Chas. N.
Alsip Wm. H.	Berg Henry W.	Bosley Daniel W.	Billings C. K. G.
Artingstall S. G.	Blodgett Edward A	Bradshaw Jno. H.	Burkhardt H. S.
Auten P. L.	Blount F. M.	Brower Dr. D. R.	Burdick Oscar

Banning E.
Birkhoff George jr.
Borland Dr. M. W.
Borland L. C. Dr.
Bremner D. F.
Blackman C. S.
Baldwin L.
Burgett J. M. H.
Brown E. C.
Brophy Dr. T. W.
Badenoch John J.
Bidwell Thos. S.
Brooks H. G.
Blair Geo. P.
Barr A. E.
Brown W. Gray
Bushnell L. M.
Burke Edmund W.
Busbey L. W .
Bussey W. T .
Bryan F. W.
Camp I. N.
Carpenter W. O.
Clark A. E.
Christy H. A.
Champlin Wm. R.
Cobb E. B.
Cobb Martin R.
Coffin G. B.
Conger R. M.
Cox E. R. •
Carson Samuel
Clark J s. L.
Clark Walter T.
Chalmers W. J.
Champlin F. L.
Chalmers Thos. jr.
Chappell C. H.
Clark E. G.
Chalmers Thomas
Cowperwaite Dr.
  A. C.
Crawford Mark L.
Crocker BenjaminS
Crossman F. M.
Crow John C.
Dalton John E.
Danforth I. N.
Davis C. G.
Davis George R.
Darrow A. H.
Dickinson D. H.
Dole John N.
Doremus A. .
Downey Joseph
Downey W.Stewart
Dougherty T. E.
Duncanson H. W.
Durborow A. C. jr.
Elmer T. H.
Elmes Chas. F.
Eckhart B. A.
Emigh G.
Evans W. W.
Fay J. Edward
Forbes A. M.

Foster Addison H.
Foster Dr. R. N.
Ferguson B. F.
Fisher A. G.
Fisk Franklin P.
Farwell J. W.
Farrell Thos. F.
Flannery D. F.
French Cyrus O.
Fulton J. L.
Fitz Simons Chas.
Fritze Geo.
Frake James
French W. H.
Fraser Norman D.
Foskett Chas. M.
French Edgar
Fraser D. R.
Garrott Dr. E.
Gates P. W.
George C. H.
Graham Dr. D. W.
Gregory W. D.
Golder W. A.
Gadsden Jas. S.
Gobel E. F.
Grant Robert S.
Grassie Henry
Grassie Jas.
Griswold Geo. E.
Hambleton C. E.
Harsha Leslie R.
Harvey W. S. Dr.
Hayt Henry C.
Head George A.
Helm D. T.
Holden I. H.
Holden Wm. H.
Hosking Anthony
Hosking B. T.
Hotz Chris.
Hewett Dr. A. C.
Hyde C. E.
Holden N. B.
Hammond L. D.
Hall L. R.
Healy P. J.
Hutchinson G. C.
Henneberry W. P.
Hartwell A. V.
Hill Edgar E.
Hayes Frank
Ingalls Dr. E. F
Jackson W. G.
James Fred S.
Jones H. J.
Jordan C. H.
Johnston Wm
Jordan Scott
Kane Thomas
King Ulric
Kohlsaat C. C.
Keeler Jos. B.
Keith John G.
King John A.
Kingwill J. H.

Kendig John A. J.
Kerr Samuel
Ketcham Wm. P.
Kent W. D.
Kohlsaat Ernest
Knowles J. C.
Kralovec John
Krum Iretus R.
Lacey W. H.
Lane W. H.
Lane Francis B.
Lane James R.
Lansing M. S.
Lawrence J. Frank
Lasier D. S.
Leonard Simeon F.
Linington C. M.
Landis Perry
Lamb Chas. A.
Loomis A. H.
Loomis Mason B.
Loomis Dr. E. B.
Lyon R. S.
McCourtie A. B.
McCarthy J. G.
McCarty Chas. S.
McCauley Thos. N.
McDonald J. B.
McGill J. K.
McLaren John
McMahon James
McMullin J.C.
McMullin F. R.
McGregor A.
McKeebe Sanford
McMillan T. C.
Martin E. B.
Morgan Wm.
Mortimer Wm. H.
Mortimer W. E.
Miller Jas. A.
Messinger W. D.
Meacham F. D.
Meek S. M.
Montgomery W. T.
Mason George
Mason Jas. A.
Marshall H. L.
Mark Clayton
Main W. F.
Mason Carlile
Marshall Geo. A.
Martin A. W.
Martin Robt. L.
Marshall Jas. D.
Magill J.C.
Maxwell Henry B.
Maxwell James
Mitchell A. J.
Moxley W. J.
Moyer M. N.
Mullany T. F.
Murphy H. P.
Murphy John B.Dr.
Murray John
Nash Chas T.

Newton H. S.
Newcomb J. C.
Nutting Wm. W.
Nichols Geo. R.
Nichols Frank M.
North Chas. A.
Norris W. W.
Offield C. K.
Oliver J. M.
Outhet R. M.
Overmeyer J. B.
Pond Walter M.
Pope Wm. J.
Pitkin Geo. W.
Parsons John B.
Pashley A. F. .
Palmer W. C. B.
Patten James A.
Peters Chas. V. L.
Pearson Eugene H.
Post Charles N.
Price Dr. O. J.
Pyott Albert E.
Parker Thos. jr.
Potter F. P.
Parker Geo. G.
Price P. Bird
Pettibone P. F.
Peters Joseph G.
Rawleigh Jas. T.
Riddle Francis A.
Richolson Benj. S.
Ripley B. W.
Roberts F. E.
Rodgers George W.
Rollo Charles E.
Rollo William F.
Royce E. A.
Ruddock Chas. H.
Roche John A.
Reed C. C.
Rogerson E. J.
Rollins Charles E.
Ross George
Rog J. B.
Rodager William
Rising C. L.
Rodgers John L.
Russ Louis
Salisbury W. H.
Sennott Thos. W.
Shoemaker Walter.
Smith C. H.
Smith R. J.
Stanford Geo. W.
Strong Wm. H.
Spry John C.
Spry S. A.
Shepard Henry O.
Sherwood Marc
Shaw W. A.
Slack Chas. H.
Sloan Geo. S.
Stewart A. M.
Schuttler Peter
Showalter J. W.

Scully D. B.
Solberg A. F.
Smyth John M.
Sands O.
St.John Dr.Leon'rd
Strong Dr. A. B.
Samson C. B.
Strong C. E.
Spry Geo. E.
Stover Ira
Sosman J. S.
Stone A. J.
Soper James P.
Shaw W. W.
Shoemaker C. W.
Stearns Edgar G.
Stehman Dr. H. B.
Stevens J. K.
Shackleford Chas.
Stroker H. W.

Swift George B.
Tatham R. L.
Teall E. M.
Thurston H. M.
Tichenor Wm. A.
Trimmer Wm. A.
Thomas H. M.
Tomblin Ira
Tapper George
Tobey Frank B.
Tuthill R. S.
Taylor W. H.
Taylor Geo. H.
Tuttle W. P.
Talbot J. F.
Thomas John W.
Taylor F. C.
Taylor E. Wiley
Thomas William
Talcott M. D.

Thompson Harvey L.
Vanderkloot A.
Van Zandt Geo.
Vaughan J. C.
Vrooman Geo. H.
Waller Henry jr.
Wallis O. W.
Washburne Geo. F. Dr.
Waters C. E.
Waters W. B.
Watkins J. O.
Wilce E. Harvey
Willett Jas. R.
Wilson F. C.
West E. A.
Williams J. D.
Wilson Wm. J.
Wheeler H. A.

Wells W. A.
Wells A. E.
Wallace Jas. D.
Wood Joseph H.
Woods F. M.
Williams Frank B.
Williamson John
Wright A. W.
Wright Frank S.
Weeks Harvey T.
Wygant Alonzo
Wood Walpole
Weigley Fillmore
Williams G. H.
Whitcomb R. S.
Weaver C. H.
Wenter Frank
Wells M. A.
Woodward T. R
Zimmerman J. S

ILLINOIS WOMAN'S PRESS ASSOCIATION.

OFFICERS.

ELIZABETH A. REED, - - - - - - - President.
GRACE DUFFIE-ROE,
JULIA A. BARNES, }- Vice-Presidents.
HARRIET B. KELLS,
SALLIE M. MOSES, - - - - Recording Secretary.
IDA A. NICHOLS, - - - - Asst. Rec. Secretary.
E. JEANNETTE ABBOTT, - Corresponding Secretary.
ANNNA N. KENDALL, - - - - Asst. Cor. Secretary.
MRS. FRANCES E. OWENS, - - - - Treasurer.
FANNY M. HARLEY, - - - - - Librarian.

MEMBERS.

Abbott Mrs. E. Jeannette
Adams Mrs. Crosby
Ahrens Mrs. Mary A.
Anderson Mrs.HelenVan
Arnold Mrs. Josie M.
Ashley Jessie W.
Ashton Mrs. Mary J.
Auten Esther R.
Avery Mrs. Rosa Miller
Barnes Mrs. Julia K.
Bass Miss Ella S.
Bell Mrs. Esther Crane
Bittinger Mrs. Geo. W.
Blinn Odelia, M. D.
Bogg Mrs. Ada B.
Bohn Mrs. Grace Green
Bowman Miss Eliza W.
Brinkman Mrs. A. P.
Campbell Mrs. Theo. C.
Candee Mrs. Isabelle L.
Carpenter Mrs. Alice D.
Catherwood Mrs. Mary H.
Chandler Mrs. Lucinda B.
Chapin Mrs. C. C.
Colburn Mrs. Elizabeth T.
Conant Mrs. Frances E.

Crane Mrs. Hannah W.
DeGraff Mrs. Ellen D.
DeReimer Mrs. Emily True
D'Unger Miss Giselle
Dunn Mrs. Julia Mills
Dusenberry Miss Frances L.
Dye Mrs. Mary Irene
Emmons Mrs. R. A.
English E. E.
Fake Mrs. Lucy D.
Fowler Miss Almira M.
Gallagher Miss Marion C.
Gardner Ida M.
Gilbert Miss Gertrude F.
Glass Mrs. Adeline Rowe, M.D.
Gordon Miss Anna A.
Gorton Miss Belle L.
Gridley Mrs. Nora
Grout Mrs. Carrie L.
Hanchett Emma E.
Harley Mrs. Fannie M.
Heath Mrs. Louisa B.
Heegaard B. Louise
Heron Mrs. Addie E.

Hesse Marie J.
Holbrook Mrs. Ellye G.
Hoover Miss Olive M.
Huling Caroline A.
Jeffery Mrs. Isadore G.
Johnson Belle C. Miss
Johnson Mrs. Carrie Ashton
Kells Mrs. Harriet B.
Kendall Mrs. Anna N.
Kennedy Mrs. Inez A.
Law Mrs. Dorothy N.
Leavens Miss Julia P.
Lee Mrs. Mary U.
LeFavre Mrs. Carrica
Light Mrs. Ellen M.
Locke Miss Josephine
Logan Mrs. John A.
Lull Mrs. Virginia T.
Madden Mrs.LauraChamberlain
Marchant Mrs.AdelaideG.
McGinnis Mrs. Grace C.
Metcalf Mrs. Ada P.
Meyer Mrs. Lucy R.
Morley Miss Margaret
Moses Mrs. Sallie M.

Nichols Mrs. Ida A.
Nottingham Mrs.CarrieC.
Ogilvie Mrs. Carolyn M.
Orcutt Miss Harriet E.
Orr Mrs. Lucy J.
Orwig Mrs. Maria S.
Owens Mrs. Francis E.
Palmer Mrs. Mate
Partridge Miss Carrie T.
Perry Mrs. Marie T.
Phelon Mrs. M. M.
Power Mrs. Marie
Pratt Mrs. Sarah Wilder
Rae Mrs. M. E.
Reed Mrs. Elizabeth A.
Reed Miss Myrtle
Robertson Mrs. Charlotte C.

Roe Mrs. Grace Duffie
Romney Mrs. Caroline W.
Sandes Mrs. Margaret I.
Sawyer Mrs. C. B.
Sergel Mrs. Annie Myers
Smith Mrs. Eva Munson
SmithMissJenny Fairman
Smith Julia Holmes,M.D.
Somerset Lady Heury
Starrett Mrs. Helen E.
Stephenson Mrs. K. L.
Stockham Alice B.
Stockham Miss Cora L.
Strickland Mrs. Martha
Strong Mrs. Mary F.
Swarthout Mrs. M. F.

Talbot Mrs. Lida H.
Taylor Mrs. Florence Montgomery
VanBenschoten Mrs.M.C.
VanEps Mrs. Marion B.
Voss Mrs. Hedwig
Wallace Mrs. M. R. M.
Wardner Mrs. Louise R.
Webster Mrs. H. Effa
Weeks, Mrs. Anna R.
White Mrs. A. Hungerford
Will Miss Kate
Willard Mrs. A. C.
Willard Miss Frances E.
Wood Mrs. J. A.
Yarnall Mrs. Jane W.

INDIANA CLUB.

3349 INDIANA AVENUE.

OFFICERS.

GEORGE L. McCURDY, - - - - - - President.
B. R. DeYOUNG, - - - - - - - Vice-President.
W. A. FROST, - - - - - - - Secretary.
J. B. STUBBS, - - - - - - - Treasurer.

DIRECTORS.

W. A. Purcell,
J. E. Taylor
L. D. Huesner

J. B. Stubbs
B. R. DeYoung
W. A. Frost

J. E. Taylor
Geo. L. McCurdy
A. H. Stevenson

MEMBERS.

Babcock Charles S.
Ballard Orville W.
Bliss E. R.
Bowen George H.
Brush H. J.
Burley F. E.
Carr H. H.
Clark R. M.
Clark E. A.
Curtis J. Lafe
Davis Dr. W. H.
Dennis Geo. J.
DeYoung B. R.
Eaton D. B.
Foster W. A.
French W. B.
Frost W. A.
Fuller Harry H.
Fuller S. R.

Gilbert Geo. A.
Googins David S.
Harper Wm. H.
Hough F. A.
Howell S. R.
Huesner L. D.
Huntley S.
Jenkins O. E.
Kimball Josiah E.
Krouskup Walter
Lavinia W. B.
Leeming Chas. W.
Leeming Frank
Leeming Dr. John
Marsh J. B.
Mathews G. W. jr.
McCord J. C.
McCullough H. R.
McCurdy D. E.

McCurdy Geo. L.
McWilliamsDrS.A
Mills F. N.
Mitchell L. A.
Mix I. J.
Moseley B.
Nash John F.
Norton J. H.
Partridge E.
Partridge W. E.
Peacock Robert
Petty C. J.
Phelps J. M.
Pingree M. G.
Purcell W. A.
Pomeroy D. W.
Reid John F.
Reid William H.

Robbins J. A.
Russell H. D.
Seaton ChaunceyE.
Sibley D. E.
Sibley J. M.
Somes Fred
Stevenson A. H.
Stewart B. F.
Straight L. C.
Stubbs J. B.
Sturtevant Edward
Taylor John
Taylor J. E.
Tenney Dr. L. L.
Thain J. A.
Vierling Louis
Vierling Robert
Whiting J. F.

IROQUOIS CLUB.

MICHIGAN AVENUE, N.W. COR. ADAMS.

OFFICERS.

LAMBERT TREE, - - - - - - - President.
FRANKLIN MACVEAGH, ⎫
JOHN S. COOPER, ⎮
JAMES A. MINER, ⎮
WM. T. BAKER, ⎮
SPOOR MACKEY, ⎬ - - - Vice-Presidents.
J. HENRY CONRAD, ⎮
FRANK WENTER, ⎮
SAMUEL H. HARRIS, ⎮
ALONZO D. SMITH, ⎭
WILLIAM D. BARGE, - - - Recording Secretary.
GEORGE W. CASS. - - - Corresponding Secretary.
HERBERT DARLINGTON, - - - - - - Treasurer.

MEMBERS.

Ackhoff Henry W.	Brown Taylor E.	Darrow C. S.	Garland Solomon
Adams Louis	Buchanan Robt. S.	Dawson George E.	Gatzert J. L.
Addison John	Budd W. O.	Defebaugh Jas. E.	Gaulter Frank J.
Altgeld John P.	Burnam Frank	Dennehy Thos. C.	Gehr Arthur C.
Althrop Thomas	Burry Jas.	Devine Wm. M.	Getty Henry H.
Avers Herbert M.	Burry William	Dimery Joseph H.	Gibbons J. W.
Babcock C. F.	Bushy William H.	Doane John W.	Gilbert Hiram T.
Bailey Sterling L.	Butterfield J. P.	Doggett Herb E. L.	Gilmore Arnold P.
Baker William T.	Byrne John J.	Doggett Wm. L.	Goddard Lester O.
Barbe Morris	Callahan James E.	Dougherty Chas.L.	Goddard L. A.
Barge William D.	Cameron D. R.	Doyle Austin J.	Goldzier Julius
Barnhart A. M.	Camp Edward N.	Doyle Wm. A.	Goodrich Adam A.
Barton Jesse B.	Campbell D. A. ⁻	Dreyer Edward S.	Grannis W. C. D.
Baxter A. Lawson	Carqueville Ed.	Duncan James W.	Gray Edward E.
Bemis Henry V.	Carroll John C.	Dunlop Joseph R.	Green A. W.
Bermingham John	Cary George P.	Dunne Fdward F.	Gregory Stephen S.
Best William	Cary John W.	Durborow Allan C.	Grinnell Julius S.
Black John C.	Casey James J.	Eckhart John W.	Gross S. E.
Blood Harry E.	Cass George W.	Eddy Arthur J.	Guerin John
Blum August	Catlin Wm. W.	Ela John W.	Gunther Charles F.
Boddie M. M.	Champlin Geo. W.	Eliel Levi A.	Gwin Cornelius V.
Bogle Walter S.	Chandler Geo. M.	Emerich Martin	Hackney W. D.
Bolte Charles G.	Chase Samuel B.	EngelmannChas.P.	Hamburger L. M.
Bonner Andrew W.	Chumasero J. T.	English Wm. J.	Hanes John K.
Bonney Charles C.	Clark W. Irving	Ennis Alfred	Harris Samuel H.
Bonney C. L.	Clifford R. W.	Ernst Leo	Haskell Geo. W.
Bonney Lawton C.	Clinch D. L.	Ewing Adlai T.	Hatch H. D.
Bort Frank B.	Coler F. W.	Ewing Wm. G.	Henry R. L.
Bowers L. W.	Conrad . Henry.	Favor Otis S.	Hesing Washingt'n
Boyesen Ingolf K.	Cooper John S.	Field Rush	Heth Henry S.
Boyle Lawrence P.	Cooper J. S.	Fisher Benj. G.	Hexter Kaufman
Bradwell Thomas	Couch Ira J.	Flanders John J.	Higgins C. W.
Brady John B.	Courtney Thos. E.	Florez Genaro	Hitchcock Wm. D.
Brand Michael	Cox Eugene R.	Ford Henry B.	Hofheimer Zach.
Brandt Geo. W.	Crafts Clayton E.	Foreman Oscar G.	Hopkins John P.
Brandt John R.	Crain Chas. S.	Forrest Wm. S.	Hornstein Leon
Brega Charles W.	Crane Chas. R.	Foster George P.	Hoyne Frank G.
Brine George J.	Cregier DeWitt C.	Foster Volney W.	Hoyne James T.
Brosseau Zen P.	Crilly Wm. M.	Fox Harry E.	Hoyne Thos. M.
Broughton H. E.	Crosby Wm. S. ⁻	Franche D: C.	Hurlbut Horace E.
Brown Charles E.	Cummins Wm. G.	Franklin Lesser	Huston Albert C.
Brown Edward O.	Curry L. M. ´ `	Gahan Thos.	Hutchinson Jonas
Brown Paul	Darlington H.	Gallagher M. F.	Hyman R. W. jr.

28

Ibsen J. H.
Jackson Benj. V.
Job Fred W.
Johnson C. Porter
Johnson W. S.
Jones Warner E.
Karpen Benno
Keeley Thos. F.
Keenan Wilson T.
Keirnan Thos. S.
Kelly Thos.
Kendig J. A. J.
Kern Charles
Kerwin Mich'l W.
Kidder George B.
Kiolbassa Peter
Kirkman M. M.
Kirton David M.
Knight Clarence A.
Kraus Adolph
Lancaster Chas. L.
Lane C. E.
Lanehart John W.
Lartz W. C. C.
Lasier D. S.
Lawrence Ed. F.
Leaming Jos. F.
Leiter Levi Z.
Lindsey Wm. L.
Linneen P. H.
Loss C. E.
Lynde S. A.
MacDonald H. K.
Mack Julian W.
Mackey Spoor
MacVeagh Franklin
Mahoney Jos. P.
Maltby A. W.
Mamerow Geo.
Manasse L.
Mandel Emanuel
Mann Joseph B.
Mann W. G.
Marble Henry E.
McArthur A. F.
McConnell S. P.
McCormick C. H.
McCoull Neill
McCulloch F. H.
McDonald M. jr.
McElligott T. G.
McFarland J. C.

McGann Lawr. E.
McGrath John J.
McHugh P.
McKay Henry
McKelvey S. P.
McLester Geo. W.
McNeill Alex. C.
McNeill Malcolm
McNeill Rivers
Mendelsohn J. S.
Merrick Geo. P.
Miles Hazen T.
Miller Thos.
Miner James A.
Minzesheimer L. F.
Mitchell Charles P.
Monroe Wm. F.
Moran Thos. A.
Morford Thos. T.
Morrill Donald L.
Morrison R. W.
Morton Joy
Moses Adolph
Moss Leopold
Murdock Wm. H.
Neuberger J. M.
Newberry W. C.
Newberry W. F.
Niblack William C.
Noonan Edward T.
Oakley Horace S.
Oberndorf Fred'ick
Olsen Olof G.
Onahan Wm. J.
O'Neill W. E.
Oppenheim Wm.S.
Page Samuel S.
Palmer John Mayo
Palmer Potter
Paxson D. C.
Payne W. R.
Peabody F. B.
Phelps E. M.
Powers W.S.
Prendergast R.
Prentiss William
Price Cornelius
Prindiville John K.
Queeny Edward J.
Quick J. H. S.
Rawson S. W.
Ray Frank H.

Reiling H. J.
Richards Jacob W.
Richberg John C.
Robinson Thos. S.
Robson John
Rogers George M.
Rogers Henry W.
Rhode H. F.
Rollins Charles E.
Rolston H. M.
Rosenthal Benj. J.
Rosenthal Edw. A.
Rubens Harry
Ruehl L. H.
Russell Martin J.
Russell Wm. H.
Sanborn Joseph B.
Scales Frank
Schubert John C.
Schwab Chas. H.
Scott James W.
Scully A. B.
Seeberger A. F.
Seipp William C.
Seixas Hyman L.
Shackleford Chas.
Shayne John T.
Shepard Henry M.
Sherwood Jesse
Shields James H.
Shipman D. B.
Shubert A. B.
Sibley J. A.
Siegel Ferdinand
Simonson Julius
Slaughter A. O.
Smith Alonzo D.
Smith Byron L.
Smith Fred M.
Smith Howard L.
Smith P. H. jr
Smith Robt J.
Smith R. Earle
Sniffen E. D.
Snowhook P. W.
Somerville Robert
Spangler J. E.
Squibb Fred J.
Steever J. G.
Stein Philip
Stensland Paul O.
Stone Melville E.

Story Allan C.
Strauss M.
Streeter Allen R.
Streeter David L.
Sullivan Roger C.
Taber Frank M.
Taberner W. W.
Taylor Wm. A.
Thomas M. St. P.
Thompson W.H.jr.
Thornton Chas. S.
Thornton H. W.
Tolman E. B.
Tree Lambert
Tuley Murray F.
Twohig James W.
Ullrich Michael
Vaughan J. C.
Veitch Wilberforce
Vincent W. A.
Wacker Chas. H.
Wadhams H. P.
Walker Chas. M.
Walker Frank W.
Walker Geo. C.
Wallace Andrew
Waller Henry jr.
Waller Robt. A.
Walsh John R.
Warren C. S.
Washington Lloyd
Watkins W.
Wells W. J.
Wenter Frank
Weston U. W.
Westover Geo. F.
Whitney Jas. D. C.
Wilkinson Harry
Wilkinson H. C.
Willden John G.
Wilt Charles jr.
Winchester L. W.
Windes Thos. G.
Winston Fred'k H.
Wolf Joseph
Woodbury S. H.
Wright Austin W.
Young Frank W.
Yunker E. J.
Zeisler Joseph
Zeissler Sigmund
Zuber George

IRVING CLUB.

IRVING PARK, ILL.

OFFICERS.

F. A. CREGO, - - - - - - - President.
T. G. PALMER, - - - - - - - Vice-President.
W. C. JORDAN, - - - - - - - Secretary.
H. E. TURNER, - - - - - - - Treasurer.

DIRECTORS.

C. E. Martin	F. E. Larson	T. G. Palmer
F. A. Crego	A. H. Hill	W. C. Toles
	D. D. Mee	

MEMBERS.

Allison J. A.	Goven Ed.	Lusted W.	Snyder D. G.
Atkins M. D.	Hacker N. W.	Mamerow Geo. T.J.	Stark J. E.
Barrett A. A.	Hartwell Miss Mary	Martin C. E.	St. Clair S. M.
Barrett Henry	Haywood Miss E.A.	McCormack S. J.	Stevens A. C.
Barstow C. F.	Heath J. S.	McEwen W. M.	Stevens C. W.
Bautz R. A.	Herman John	McNett C. S.	Stokes Frank E.
Berry A. V.	Hilands C. E.	Mee D. D.	Sumner Smith
Binyon L. D.	Hill A. H.	Mee Ed	Swartz John
Boerlin L. J.	Hollis F.	Milburn E. L.	Talman J. B.
Brown H. A.	Hollis J. F.	Millard W. K.	Telfer R. G.
Brown W. H.	Hollis L. L.	Monk J. S.	Thomas L.
Buzzell D. L.	Hopping Mrs. Allie	Moore Dr. M. T.	Toles W. C.
Calhoun Mrs. M. R.	M.	Myers A. T.	Tracy D. M.
Campbell Geo.	Hotchkiss E. S.	Nichols Amos J.	Tryon L. C.
Carlin F. E.	Israel Mrs. A. H.	Okeson W. H.	Turner H. E.
Chapin E. M.	Israel C. H.	Osborn A. C.	Van Harlingen H.C.
Christianson S. J.	Israel W. L.	Oswald J. I.	Van Ness G. B.
Colby e . E.	Jacobs W. B.	Owens J. P.	Van Ness L. T.
Condon Jo J.	Johnson A.	Palmer T. G.	VanOstrand A.
Coyle P. W.	Jordan W. C.	Parsons W. R.	Wallis A. O.
Crego F. A.	Julien W. N.	Paulson O. L.	Wallis W. H.
Cross A. M.	Kane J. A.	Peters H. V.	Walmsley A. H.
Curtis W. H.	Kellogg W. R.	Peterson J. A.	Walter G. E.
Cushing Frank	Kendrick W. J.	Rehwoldt E. H.	Washburn A. T.
Davis P. J.	Ketchum S. C.	Reynolds E. W.	Webster C. L.
Day C. A.	Ketchum W. N.	Reynolds F. H.	Weise Theodore
DeVos A. J.	Kimbell M. N.	Rice M. W.	Wells J. C.
Dixon L. J.	Kimbell S. S.	Richey A. D.	White J. W.
Dobson W. J.	Kingsley F. W.	Richey F. L.	Whitman C. M.
Drissbach C. E.	Lane A. M.	Roberts R. L.	Wickersham J. A.
Dunlop S. A.	Larson F. E.	Ropp Silas	Wilcox W. D.
Duvall P. H.	Lear C. H.	Sayler W.	Wilcox W. L.
Dyer Geo. W.	Lewis A. B.	Schmidt J. C.	Williams J. W.
Esdohr H.	Lewis F. C.	Sethness C. O.	Wilson F. J.
Fisher A. J.	Livesey H. B.	Shepard H. V.	Wilson S. R.
Foote M. A.	Lobdell B. S.	Skinner Clarence	Wolfinger C. I.
Garratt L. D.	Loucks C. N.	Smith Dr. D. A.	Wulff Henry
Geise J. A.	Longfellow F. M.	Smith E. G.	Wulff Robert
Goodridge A. G.			

KENWOOD CLUB.

FORTY-SEVENTH STREET AND LAKE AVENUE.

OFFICERS.

SILAS M. MOORE,	President.
WILLIAM A. THRALL,	Vice-President.
E. K. BUTLER,	Second Vice-President.
GEO. B. SHATTUCK,	Secretary.
EDWARD ROSING,	Treasurer.

DIRECTORS.

W. C. Niblack	Walter C. Nelson	E. G. Shumway
W. C. Thorne	Chas. C. Whitacre	John B. Knight
Samuel H. Wright	A. J. Hageman	

MEMBERS.

Adolphus W.	Fairman F.	Letton Theo. W.	Ritchie Robert H.
Aldrich J. Frank	Farr M. A.	Le Valley J. R.	Ritchie W. E.
Andrus F. H.	Fellows Dr. C.	Lewis Dr. D.	Roberts Chas. S.
Armstrong C. M.	Gurnee	Lewis H. F.	Root F. W.
Ash I. N.	Field Heman H.	Lewis I. G.	Rosing Edward
Ash L. H.	Fisher Dr. C. E.	Lindman O. F.	Schmitt A.
Atwood M. W.	Fisher Hart C.	Listman Charles F.	Schoyer E. A.
Barker F. W.	Fisher R.	Little George W.	Schuler E. T.
Barker J. N.	Fiske Jno. M.	Little W. H.	SeavernsWilliam S.
Bayley E. F.	Follansbee C. E.	Long J. H.	Sebastian John
Belden J. S.	Foote Chas. H.	Lord D. M.	Shankland Ralph
Bennett F. I.	Fowler H. W.	Loughridge Chas.	M.
Bigelow T. M.	Frasher E. S.	McArthur Warren	Shattuck George B.
Bingham A. E.	Frasher John S.	McClellan J. J.	Sherman J. D.
Bissell J. H.	Frasher J. E. L.	McKey Richard M.	Sherman L. B.
Blackman C. H.	French C. G.	McMurdy R. H.	Sherman P. L.
Boak Robert B.	Frothingham DrH.	McMurray Geo. N.	Sherwood N.
Bogue H. B.	Fuller Alonzo M.	McNeil H. E.	Shourds Clayton B.
Bond John H. R.	Furber Frank I.	McReynolds Geo.S.	Shumway E. G.
Bouton C. B.	Gates William B.	Mallory Chas. A.	Sibley E. S.
Bouton N. S.	Gifford C. E. jr.	Marcy George E.	Smale J. S. Mrs.
Bremer A. R.	Gifford I. C.	Marder Clarence	Smith Horace S.
Bridge R. W.	Glessner A. W.	Marder John	Spalding A. G.
Brooks Dr. A.	Graves A. M.	Marder John W.	Spooner F. E.
Brooks C. M.	Griffin ThomasA.	Marsh C. V.	Springer Miss G.
Brooks J. W. jr.	Gwinn J. M.	Marshall Philip L.	Squires Chas.
Brown W. T.	Gwinn W. R.	Mason L. B.	Steele Julius
Burrows Chas. M.	Hageman A. J.	Mathews Charles	Steever J. G.
Butler E. K.	Halsey Tappan	Mettler L.Harrison	Stinson James
Butlin T. G.	Hamilton J. M.	Miller John S.	Stobo Robert
Buttolph A. C.	Hammond C. L.	Mills A. L.	Strong Charles R.
Cameron John	Hanson A. H.	Mitchell Geo. R.	Strong D. O.
Capelle Eugene	Harding Chas. F.	Moore S. M.	Swett F. C.
Carton L. A.	Harlan Alison W.	Morehouse L. P.	Tenney H. K.
Cheverton Edward	Harris Norman W.	Morgan James	Thompson R. S.
G.	Hattstaedt John J.	Morse C. H.	Thorne C. H.
Clancy W. B.	Hawkins Chas. H.	Moss W. L.	Thorne George A.
Clingman Chas. W.	Heckman Wallace	Nash Sam'l J.	Thorne Geo. R.
Cloud John W.	Henning E.	Nellegar J. B.	Thorne James W.
Condee L. D.	Hibbard John D.	Nelson W. C.	Thorne W. C.
Cook H. B.	Higgie·James L.	Newhall Arthur T.	Thrall S. E.
Coolidge W. G.	Higley W. E.	Newman W. H.	Thrall W. A.
Cornell J. E.	Hitchcock Mrs. A.	Niblack W. C.	Tobey C. H.
Cowles J. E.	Hoagland Jno. R.	Nichols C. M.	Tobey C. H. M.
Crary Dr. C. W.	Howard J. H.	Nolan J. H.	Trowbridge C. M.
Critchell R. S.	Hunter W. W.	Norton C. L.	Turner A. A.
Cruttenden T. S.	Ives John H.	Norton Oliver W.	Turrill John F.
Cummins B. F.	Jackson F. W.	Norwood F. W.	Ullmann Frederic
Cunningham W.H.	Johnstone M. E.	Oppenheim Wm. S.	Underwood S. F.
Currier Chas. L.	Jones H. D.	Osborn Clark D.	Valentine A. J.
Cushing E. T.	Jones John H.	Packer C. P.	VanKirk C. B.
Daniels E. F.	Jones Wm.	Page W. R.	VanUxem J. L.
Dau J. J.	Kelley W. V.	Palmer Geo. R.	Viets John B.
Davis John	Kellogg M. G.	Palmer Percival B.	Wait H. L.
DeWolf C.	Kellogg Norman	Park Mrs. Mary W.	Wales Albert H.
DeWolf W. L.	Kimball E. S.	Peale R. S.	Walker A. E. Mrs.
Donnelley R. H.	Kirkland Robt.	Perkins F. W.	Ward A. M.
Donnelley R. R.	Knapp George O.	Phillips C. H.	Ware E. C.
Doty Levi R.	Knight J. B.	Plummer Sam'l C.	Warren A. D.
Douglas Frank	KniskernWarrenB.	Potter E. A.	Warren C. D.
Drake Geo. H.	Lane Henry M.	Pratt L.	Washburne Dr. G.
Drake W. H.	Lawton Lyndon C.	Proby J. W.	F.
Dupee H. M.	Lee ClydeyD.	Purdy W. G.	Waters Harry C.
Eaton C. L.	Leland W. F.	Putnam Joseph R.	Welling J. C.

Wells B. R.	Wiley E. N.	Wilson E. Crane	Woodruff Chas. E
Whitacre C. C.	Willard H. G.	Winslow C. W.	Woodruff Dr. T. A.
White A. S.	Williams Ezra T.	Wiser Clinton B.	Wright S. H.
White William F.	Williamson G. T.	Woodle E. R.	

KLIO CLUB.

210 MASONIC TEMPLE.

OFFICERS.

EVA H. BAKER, - - - - - - - President.
CARLOTTA V. GRAHAM, - - - - Vice-President.
LAURA M. THOMAS, - - - - Second Vice-President.
MISS MARY SHUMWAY, - - - - - Treasurer.
MARY W. MOWBRAY, - - - Corresponding Secretary.
MRS. IDA W. MORGAN, - - Recording Secretary.

DIRECTORS.

Je W. Sherwood		Jennie Clark Hutchins
Louise B. Marston	Mary E. Palmer	Lillian Davis Duncanson

MEMBERS.

Allen Miss M. L.	Hutchins Mrs. Herbert	Pynchon Mrs. Edwin
Archibald Mrs. G. A.	Husragh Mrs.	Rathbone Mrs. P. D.
Baker Mrs. Hiram	Innes Miss Kathrine	Robinson Mrs. Mary
Ballou Mrs. George H.	Jaquish Mrs. Clarence	Louise
Bangs Mrs. Fred	Jennison Mrs. Floyd E.	Sherman Mrs. W. M.
Barker Mrs. Agnes	Johnstone Mrs. Stuart	Sherwood Mrs. J. B.
Bigelow Mrs. E. A.	King Mrs. Charles	Shourds Mrs. Clayton B.
Bliss Mrs. N. E.	LaBarre Madame	Shumway Miss Mary
Bowen Mrs. F. K.	Landis Mrs. Percy	Shumway Mrs. Noble C.
Calt Mrs. A. J.	Lindon Mrs. George	Slosson Mrs. A. H.
Chase Mrs. Mary A. C.	Loomis Mrs. A. H.	Smith Mrs. Fred M.
Crandall Mrs. Lyman E.	Madden Mrs. Edgar	Smith Mrs. J. Hubert
D'Unger Miss Griselle	Marston Mrs. J. D.	Smith Miss Ruth A.
Duncanson Mrs. H. W.	Mattioli Miss Eugenia	Snider Miss Harriet
Dunn Mrs. J. O.	Milchrist Mrs. Thos. E.	Stevens Mrs. Plowden
Eastman Mrs. J. C.	Miles Mrs. George S.	Stewart Mrs. B. F.
Eilers Mrs. Paul	Morgan Mrs. Harry A.	Stoddard Mrs. H. H.
Fay Mrs. J. B.	Morse Mrs. F. L.	Swartz Miss I. Honora
Fessler Miss Ada G.	Mowbray Mrs. George	Talcott Mrs. Elva
Fifield Miss Katharine L.	Newbury Mrs. Mary	Temple Mrs. T. S.
Follett Mrs. J. D.	Wright	Thomas Mrs. J. W.
Goodall Mrs. H. P.	Newton Mrs. H. S.	Thornburgh Mrs. H. L.
Graham Mrs. E. R.	Nourse Mrs. E. R.	Thule Chas. H. Mrs.
Gray Mrs. Phebe S.	Palmer Mrs. T. D.	Webb Miss Emma
Groner Mrs. George	Parker Mrs. Fred A.	Wells Miss Florence
Grosvener Mrs. G. B.	Phillips Mrs. N. A.	Westfall E. W. Mrs.
Haskett Mrs. E. W.	Prescott Miss Mary	Woodbury Mrs. Louis E.
Hill Miss Helen Hoyt		

LA GRANGE CLUB.

OFFICERS.

D. W. MUNN, ... President.
E. R. NEELY, ... First Vice-President.
J. R. GILBERT, ... Second Vice-President.
H. BEARSE, ... Treasurer.
O. B. MARSH, ... Secretary.

DIRECTORS.

Jas. Kidston		H. P. Burkholder
G. A. Moncur	Chas. F. Parker	W. H. Wall

Allison John T.
Ashley A. M.
Babbitt C. M.
Bearse H.
Blakely L. P.
Beecroft F. W.
Blount S. P.
Boisot E. K.
Brainard E. C.
Brydon J. A.
Burkholder H. P.
Bushnell E. B.
Bourgoise O. F.
Bunker W. I.
Butler F. H.
Cadwallader B.
Carpenter M. J.
Clark W. I.
Collins W. A.
Cooley E. G.
Cooper H. N.
Cossitt F. D. jr.
Dunne G. R.
Edwards Chas.

Fogarty W. A.
Fox Dr. G. M.
Freer L. H.
Gardner P. G.
Gilbert J. R.
Goodwin H. E.
Haight Frank
Hall Ferd.
Hallowell P. M.
Hill Tremont
Horton Richard
Howe D. N.
Kellogg M. L.
Kidston James
Kidston Will.
Laubenstein G. H.
Leckie A. S.
Ludwig Dr. R. F.
Lyman D. B.
Lyon D. A.
Mandel Fred
Marsh O. B.
Marshall J. A.
McCoy George

McDonald Harley C.
McGregor D. P.
McGrew J. H.
Moncur Geo. A.
Morgan Geo. C., jr.
Moses Chas. A.
Munn D. W.
Murray Donald
Neely E. R.
Newman J. B.
Packer John F.
Pagin L. A.
Palmer E.
Parker C. F.
Parker H. B.
Rice John F.
Rich E. A.
Rogers J. W. R.
Rogerson E. J.
Rossman C.
Rothwell A. S.
Rothwell H. L.
Rothwell R. E.

Sacriste L. J.
Scott W. A.
Shordiche P. R.
Skidmore G. C.
Slocum L. W.
Smith F. C.
Snyder E. D.
Stevens Fred H.
Stiles C. L.
Swisher S. G.
Turner J. W.
Unold Geo. D.
Walbridge W. P.
Walbridge W. H.
Walker Dudley
Walker H.
Walker J. R.
Walker M. B.
Wall W. H.
Werno Henry
Wheat C. L.
Whitney C. A.
Wright Wm.

LAKOTA CLUB.

4111 Grand Boulevard.

S. Marshall, - - - - . - - - President.
W. F. Steele, - - - - - First Vice-President.
C. W. Foster, - - - - Second Vice-President.
C. L Will, - - - - - - - Secretary.
C. S. Jones, - - - - - - - Treasurer.

H. M. Keenan
C. Gross
B. T. Collingbourne

E. D. Anderson
F. Mackenzie
G. H. Liberty
A. L. Cory

L. Bartholomew
J. A. Bender
W. S. York

Aagaard J.
Adams E. C.
Agnew J. H.
Anderson E. D.
Arnold A. C.
Arnold B. J.
Bartholomew L.
Bender J. A.
Bernard A.
Bortell C. E.
Brainard A. P.
Brown J.
Burdick L. H.
Burrows F. R.
Cahill J. B.
Carpenter H. L.
Carr A. J.

Chandler G. W.
Christian H. W.
Cobb A. M.
Cohenenour C.
Collingbourne A.B.
Collingbourne B.T.
Conover L. W.
Cory A. L.
Cory V. P.
Craig E. S.
Crawford G. V.
Crawford G. W.
Cummins J.
Damcier G. A.
Davis C. E.
Day W. B.
Dostal J. W.

Eager A. M.
Ecton W. B.
Ehrhorn H. F.
Eichberg L. R.
Elliot H. R.
Elwell A.
Elwell W. J.
Emmat C. M.
Folsom O. W.
Forbes W. R.
Foster C. W.
Grassell J.
Griffith K. F.
Green O. S.
Gross Charles
Gross C W.
Hanchett L. J.

Hancock T.
Hannaford C.
Higgins H. T.
Hilbourne H. C.
Hoffman J. D.
Hoffman J. J.
House P. D.
Houston A. S.
Ingwersen E. H.
Ingwersen G. J.
Ingwersen H. C.
Ingwersen J. H.
Ingwersen T. H.
Ingwersen W. B.
Jerome C. F.
Jevne C. G.
Johnson F. R.

Johnson S. J.
Jones A. R.
Jones C. S.
Jones E. L.
Jones H. A.
Keenan H. M.
Keenan H. F.
Keenan J. L.
Kelly J. H.
Kemp N. C.
Kennedy J. B.
Knapp G. W.
Leavitt W.
Lee R. H.
Liberty G. H.
Liston D. G.
Long J. B.
Mackenzie F.
Mallory W. H.
Mann J. R.
Marshall S.
Martin J. H.

Martin J. T.
Maurer W.
McDowell J. E.
McIntyre P. J.
Meyers G.
Mills F. O.
Minteer W. P.
Minteer William P.
Moore B. L.
Moore W. B.
Morris E.
Nash W. T.
Newton P. A.
Nichols S. J.
Norton T. S.
Osher J.
Perrine H. R.
Philbrick C.
Piatt A.
Pierce B. A.
Porter E. A.
Proctor G. C.

Pullman C.
Quick R. T.
Quinn Chas.
Quinn W. B.
Rappal L. L.
Redman G. A.
Reynolds W. J.
Richards F.
Richards I. D.
Richman N. P.
Ross F. R.
Sang O.
Schroeder W. E.
Sears C. B.
Selleck W. A.
Shannon G. W.
Shannon O. J.
Shattuck W. F.
Smith C. E.
Smith G. E.
Smith J. W.
Smith T.

Sollitt O.
Steele W. F.
Stewart C. F.
Strader J. E.
Swift C. H.
Thompson C. W.
Traquair W. M.
Uebele B.
Wallwork E. L.
Ward W. M.
Warde G. T.
Watkins T. J.
White E. C.
Will C. J. C.
Will C L.
Wilson T. E.
Wolford F. H.
Wood J. H.
Woods J. G.
Yates W. W.
York W. S.

LINCOLN CLUB.

531 W. ADAMS STREET.

OFFICERS.

WILLIAM W. WHEELOCK, - - - - President.
JOHN R. PARKER, - - - First Vice-President.
W. L. NOBLE, - - - - Second Vice-President.
GUY A. RICHARDS, - - - - - Secretary.
ALBERT WAHL, - - - - - - Treasurer.

DIRECTORS.

William Henderson
Charles A. Brown
William W. Wheelock
John R. Parker

W. L. Noble
Guy A. Richards
Albert Wahl
A. P. Goodwin

Breck D. Porter
A. J. Elliott
H. S. Dale
W. S. Minkle

MEMBERS.

Abbott E. O.
Almquist J. F.
Alsip W. H.
Anderson L. N.
Bagby George M.
Ball Farlin Q.
Banning Ephriam
Barrett E. E.
Barrett P. W.
Bassett R. J.
Beckwith S. J.
Bergey T. Sam
Betts George
Blodgett E. A.
Blount F. M.
Blume Jarvis
Bollinger I. W.
Boyce G. W.
Brickwood Albert
Brown Charles A.
Brown D. Green
Burkhart Harvey

Butler Geo. F., M.D.
Campbell D. D.
Carrier P. J.
Carter Henry
Carter James B.
Carter O. N.
Carter Zina R.
Case Theodore G.
Casper A. O.
Chapin O. E.
Chase Hollis M.
Clark A. B. Dr.
Clement E. L.
Clement Leonard A.
Cole M. E.
Colson Robert K.
Corbus J. W.
Cotton A. C. Dr.
Coy W. S.
Coyne Fred E.
Cranston T. H.
Crowe Frank

Cummings J. E.
Curtis D. H.
Curtis Geo. P.
Dale H. S.
Dale Russell
Davison Chas. Dr.
Deming Gail E.
DeVarney W. D.
Dickson Wm. R.
Dixon Arthur
Donle W. C.
Doremus A. F.
Drake Marshall
Dudley Oscar
Dunne N. O.
Eastman A. N.
Eastman Edward R.
Eastman R. A.
Eckhart B. A.
Edwards Joseph B.
Eilers P. C.
Elliott A. J.

Elliott H. J.
Feldman David L.
Fenn P. D.
Fitz-Simons Chas.
Fortner Dr. E. C.
Francoeur A.
Friedman Wm.
Frink Dr. F. L.
Gaines O. F.
Geddes Robt. jr.
George C. H.
Gifford H. B.
Gillespie John
Gindele George W.
Goodwin A. P.
Goss S. A.
Graham D. W. Dr.
Greenlee E.
Gregson George
Gunderson S. T.
Halbe Charles F.
Hale Clarence B.

Hail Howard E.
Hamilton E.
Hamilton W. J.
Harper Thomas S.
Harraden Chas. H.
Hart Jno. J.
Haskins Frank E.
Hathaway J. C.
Hay William H.
Henderson William
Holden H. P.
Holden Walter S.
Hudson J. E.
Ingram J. E.
Jefferson Fred'k A.
Johnson J. M.
Jones DeWitt C.
Kaufman W. S.
Keller David M.
Kent W. D.
Kester Dr. P. J.
Kimball A. S.
Kimball C. F.
Kohler Conrad
Kohlsaat C. C.
Lee D. C.
Lee E. E.
Leigh C. A.
Letterman E. R.
Liddell R. H.
Llewellyn Ed'wdH.
McAdam J. V.

McIudoe Hugh
McMillan E. E.
McNichols Thos. J.
Martin A. W.
Martin R. L.
Mason George
Mason James
Mason William E.
Mattern Otto
Maulsby R. S.
Meyers H. B.
Midgeley T.
Minkle W. S.
Mitchell R.
Moir James F.
Monroe W. T.
More Clark E.
More R. Wilson
Nechootal F.
Nicholas H. E.
Nichols Dr. Amos
Nichols Frank E.
Noble W. L. Dr.
Nohren John E.
Northcott E.M. Dr.
Noyes E. B.
O'Donnell Charles
O'Donnell P. H.
O Shaughnessy
Parker John R.
Patterson R. M.

Payne Wm. R.
Pendarvis R. E.
Penner Gus A. ·
Perkins H. S.
Piper Charles E.
Plummer Geo. W.
Pomeroy Joseph,
Porter Breck D.
Reid G. B.
Rennacker E. F.
Rhodes Joseph
Richards Guy A.
Richolson B. F.
Riderberg S. W.
Roberts F. E.
Robinson E. A.
Robinson Thomas
Roop H. T. Dr.
Ross Alexander
Rowe Peter A.
Salt M. H
Schock L. S.
Scroogs C. L.
Sennott Thos. W.
Shaunessy Jqs. J.
Shea Arthur J.
Sherwood Harold
Simmons C. H.
Sitts Lewis D.
Slavik Frank jr.
Smart W. F.

Smith Horace E.
Smith W. R.
Smyth John M.
Snow George
Stevens W. A.
Stewart E. L.
Stone E. B.
Stowe A. J.
Swift Geo. B.
Tucker W. S.
Tuttle C. S.
Tuttle Dr. O. H.
Tuttle Dr. S. D.
VandervireLouisD.
Wade C. A.
Wahl Albert
Ward W. A.
Watson A. H.
Weaver Charles M.
Wells J. S.
Wheeler H. A. Gen
Wheelock W. W.
White George E.
Wilk Fred L.
Winchester A.
Wood A. C.
Wood Dr. Kent T.
Wright J. F.
Wright J. G.
Wygant Alonzo
Zinn Dr Frank H.

LINCOLN CYCLING CLUB.

1 OGDEN FRONT.

OFFICERS.

W. D. MORRIS, ... President.
DR. C. W. BAKER, ... Vice-President.
GRO. E. HANSELMAN, ... Secretary.
E. M. NEWMAN, ... Treasurer.
F. B. BIGELOW, ... Quartermaster.
W. H. BRAUN, ... Librarian.

DIRECTORS.

Chas. T. Wittstein   H. G. Zander
H. L. Pound   J. M. Miller

MEMBERS.

Almgren E.
Altman W. M.
Anderson C. J.
Baird E. P.
Baker C. W., M.D.
Berg I. D.
Bigelow F. B.
Bills John
Blake C. H.
Blake J. O.
Bonney N. J.
Bottomley H. A.
Bottomley S.H. Dr.
Braum W. H.
Brewster A. D.

Bruhn D. J.
Calrow J. G. jr.
Canfield E. L.
Catto George R.
Chase F. L.
Chase Phil A.
Church H. C.
Coffey E. E.
Cooke A. G.
Cross E. J.
Cross E. L.
Curtis C. R.
Day George E.
Deem W. M.
Dirr F. L.

Donohoe F. E.
Ernzen John
Erskine J. D.
Erwin J. M.
Fairchild C. M.
Featherstone A.
Fleischer T. E.
Fritze F. A. jr.
Gerould F. W.
Getchell Louis
Goss Ferd
Gould E. L.
Griffith A. N.
Gunther J. F.
Hanback C. T.

Hanford Harry
Hanselman George
Henderson F. B.
Herrick C. K.
Herrick Wm.
Hochkirk W. F.
Horn A. B.
Hosford M. L.
Huhn S. N.
Hynson C.
Inskeep E. A.
Jackson A. V. jr.
Jaffray R. M.
Jennings M. H.
Johnson F. K.

Kosche O. F.
Kustner O.
Larsen C. W.
Lee C. L.
Lennie R. C.
Lobig P. P.
Loescher M. E.
Long F. H.
Marrett A. J.
Marsh John
Matthei Walter
May George W.
McEwen F. E.
Miles Samuel A.
Miller J. M.
Morris F. M.
Morris W. D.
Morrison G. W.
Moxam C.

Munger L. D.
Napier C. R.
Newman Edgar M.
Olds C. B.
Overman C. R.
Pagin F. S.
Pease J. M.
Peck A. P.
Pendery H. C.
Pendley H. C.
Pine M. B.
Pound Harry L.
Pound Harvey L.
Pratt George H.
Radell A. H.
Rainer A. L.
Raux A. G.
Richardson W. J.

Schmidgall F. A.
Schmidt Hugo
Searle R. P.
Sears I. N.
Servoss C. A.
Shorb Rutledge
Slusser A. W.
Smith A. T.
Smith F. H.
Smith W. A.
Spielman A.
Spooner F. Ed.
Stephens C. D.
Stephens J. Q.
Stevenson F. C.
Stevenson J. R. D.
Sues Gustave
Swarthout J. F.

Templeton J. E.
Tilt Fred
Tuttle H. B.
Volkman F. J.
Walton C. C.
Walter John P.
Warman J. I.
Westerman F.
Whitney C. P.
Wilson H. C.
Wilson F. S.
Wimmersteadt O.
Winship H. R.
Wittstein A. W.
Wittstein Chas. T.
Zahn J. H.
Zander H. G.
Ziegler Chas.

MARQUETTE CLUB.

CORNER DEARBORN AVENUE AND MAPLE STREET.

OFFICERS.

CHAS. U. GORDON, - - - - - - - President.
L. J. SMITH, - - - - - First Vice-President.
JOHN M. ROACH, - - - Second Vice-President.
JOHN J. ARNEY, - - - - - - - Secretary.
EDWARD G. PAULING, - - - - - Treasurer.

DIRECTORS.

J. H. Curtis.   C. H. Gentry.   W. N. Pelouze.
Elder C. Dewitt.   John H. Johnson.   Edward A. Bigelow.

MEMBERS.

Adams E. J.
Adams Geo. E.
Adkinson E. W.
Ahern John H.
Alexander Wm. A.
Allerton Samuel W
Anderson A. E.
Andrae Arnold O.
Anning H. M.
Anthony Chas. E.
Anthony G. D.
Armstrong J. M. jr.
Arney John J.
Babcock C.
Baldwin C. W.
Baldwin R. R.
Ball Wm. T.
Barber Hiram
Barbour Frank
Barnes Burdette C.
Baum W. L.
Becker David
Beckerman W. H.
Beers L. G.
Belfield Wm. T.
Belmont Jno. W.
Bent E. M.
Bentley W. G.

Bigelow E. A.
Bique N. J.
Blake Chas. C.
Bletsch A. L.
Boldenweck Wm.
Brace Wm.
Bradford S. W.
Brandt Hy.
Brentano Theo.
Broadbent T. A.
Brooks John H.
Bullen George R.
Burmeister Chas.
Busse Fred A.
Cahill E. T.
Chandler Geo. H.
Channon J. H.
Chapman F. M.
Chapman W. P.
Charles A. N.
Chatfield E. P.
Clemence D D.
Chetlain A. H.
Chytraus Axel
Colby C. C.
Collins Chas. H.
Cook J. L.
Corlett Thos. G.

Cotton S. K.
Crissman Ira B.
Cummings Wm. J.
Curtis John H.
Daniels W. K.
Denell R. A.
DeWitt Elden C.
Dickinson Wm.
Dickson W. H.
Dodge A. H.
Doherty D. J.
Dorrance Chas J.
Dovale Arthur
Earnshaw Chas.
Easley R. M.
Elwes F. P.
Erickson Sam'l E.
Farrill Henry Baird
Farrington Geo. E.
Farringtou W. E.
Farwell H. C.
Feldkamp C. L.
Ferguson G. M.
Filkins Ed. A.
Finkler Wm.
Finney H. P.
Fishleigh J.
Flannery John L.

Flavelle Arthur
Foley Jno. B.
Forhan S. J.
Forrest T. L. jr.
Foss Geo. E.
Frankenstein W.B.
Friel Wm. T.
Frohn Jno. B.
Fuller H. M.
Furbeck W. F.
Gentry Chas. H.
Gerwig F. L.
Going J. F.
Goldy H. I.
Gordon C. U.
Gormully R. P.
Goss Ferd
Gould Elwyn B.
Graves C. E.
Gray W. H.
Gregg Geo. A.
Gross S. E.
Hall Junius M.
Hambleton C. J.
Hamburger E. C.
Hamilton I.B. Gen.
Hamilton R. A.
Hamlin Frank

Harrison Jas. H.
Hartford Peter
Hatch J. A.
Healy John J.
Hebel Oscar
Heckman A. R.
Heegard W. H.
Hellen Benj. H.
Helm J. W.
Hess F. A.
Heywood E. F.
Heywood J. P.
Heywood P. P.
Hirsch James H.
Hirth Aug.
Hoefer R. A.
Hogland Chas. H.
Holmboe A
Hohn O. F. H.
Huber Julius H.
Huehl Harris W.
Huhn Jno. H.
Hume J. H.
Hussander W. S.
Illingworth Geo. M.
Jenney G. H.
Johnson C. N.
Johnson John H.
Johnson Victor W.
Johnson Wm. Herbert
Johnson W. F.
Jones C. S.
Judd Edward J.
Kasper Joseph
Kavanagh Marcus jr.
Kehler C. S.
Keith J. S.
Kerr Robert G.
Kimball C. V.
Kleinecke A. H.
Kohlsaat H. H.
Krzminski C. R.
Laird F. G.
Lamson Wm. A.
Lange Paul W.
Langhenry G.
Latham H. I.
Lauman G. V.
Lederer Nathan
Lee A. V.
Lemon O. W.
Lewis G. A.
Linn G. W.

Linn Jno. A.
Littlefield A. S.
Loeb Adolph
Loesch Frank J.
Lovejoy Geo. T.
Luce F. M.
Luehr Arthur
Lundahl J.
Lundell John P.
Lusch Harry B.
McConoughey O. H.
McCrea W. S. ,
McNally Jas.
Mahin J. L.
Mandeville Samuel
Mangson E. W.
Marsland George H.
Mason W. A.
Mather R. H.
Matson C. R.
Maxwell D. G.
May Horatio N.
Mayer Simon
Mayer Solomon
Mettenheimer W.
Meyers W. L.
Millard S. M.
Moore Fredk. W.
Moore James S.
Money A. G.
Morgan K. E.
Morrill Chas. A.
Morris Jos. O.
Morrison E. W.
Morse E. D.
Morse M. A.
Muhlke Jos.
Murray P. P.
Myers L. E.
Nelson William D.
Netterstrom Chas.
Newberry R. T.
Niblock C. B.
Nigg C.
Norton A. L.
Obermeyer C. B.
O'Brien Edward
Ogden E. W.
Olsen Harry
Olson Nils F.
Olson O. C. S.
Oswald Julius W.
Palmer A. E.
Parkhurst J. J.
Pauling E. G.

Paulsen W. A.
Pease E. H.
Pease James
Peats Alfred
Peck Z. C.
Pelouze Wm. N.
Perkins Thos. L.
Perley E. E.
Pettit F. W.
Pierce W. H.
Pollasky Marcus
Potis S. jr.
Powell Geo. W.
Power M. J.
Powers M. J.
Pulver A. W.
Putnam A. A.
Redieske Paul
Remick A. E.
Rennocker W. R.
Revell A. H.
Revell D. J.
Rhode John C. W.
Rhodes Wm. M.
Riggles M. F.
Ring A. W.
Rinn G. P.
Ritchie J. W.
Ritter H. A.
Roach F. P.
Roach J. M.
Rogers Jas. E.
Roney J. W.
Runnells J. S.
Sandberg Geo. N.
Sanford W. C.
Schaefer Paul
Schneider E. C.
Schnell J. B.
Sears N. C.
Seeley J. S.
Seeman Emil H.
Severin Henry W.
Sexton James A.
Shean Henry E.
Shepler E. A.
Sherman C. M.
Sherman E. W.
Shields S. P.
Simmons F. T.
Simon R. M.
Simpson T. S.
Smith B. M.
Smith F. A.
Smith F. E.

Smith H. T.
Smith Jay H.
Smith Lloyd J.
Sperling Isaac D.
Stacy John
Stanley G. A.
Stave Louis Q.
Stevens P. D.
Stevenson A. F.
Strong A. W.
Struckmann W. F.
Studley J. F.
Sundell Chas F.
Swatek John W.
Swatek M. J.
Taylor L. D.
Taylor S. G.
Timmermann W.E.
Thompson W.H.jr.
Thurber G. S.
Traub Adolph
Treedy W. J.
Tucker F. J.
Turner H. L.
Turner J. W.
Upham Fred W.
Vigeant Gregory
Vinnedge A. R.
Vinnedge M. A.
Vocke Wm.
Waide W. Arthur
Wait Geo. A.
Walker C. R.
Washburne E. B.
Washburne H.
Webster W. G.
Welles Edward P.
Wells F. K.
West John
Whaley J. J.
Wheadon Jas. P.
White John D.
Whitman John L.
Wickersham H. B.
Williams G. W.
Williams H. L.
Williams I. B.
Williams J F.
Willits Geo. S.
Wittstein A. H.
Woodruff F. N.
Worley D. A.
Worthy John
Wynne J. Edward

MENOKEN CLUB.
1196 WASHINGTON BOUL.

OFFICERS.

F. M. WOODS, - - - - - - President.
F. E. COYNE, - - - - - - Vice-President.
J. A. PAINTER, - - - - - - Secretary.
FRANK F. HOLMES, - - - - Treasurer.

TRUSTEES.

Samuel Kerr   F. W. Bryan   D. W. Mills
F. E Coyne   F. S. Baird   F. M. Woods
Frank F. Holmes   H. J. Evans   Ludwig Wolff
J. A. Painter   S. T. Gunderson   Wm. E. Mortimer
E. W. Stanwood

MEMBERS.

Allen John K.	Esmay J. P.	Knisely John L.	Rice T. J.
Arnold Theo.	Evans H. J.	Kroff R. J.	Richards C. D.
Ayres Geo. L.	Faith Thomas Dr.	Lamoreaux M. D.	Richardson G. M.
Baird F. S.	Fassett W. H.	Lamson W. H.	Robinson T. F.
Baldwin B. A.	Featherstone John	LeFevre J. J.	Rogers C. M.
Baldwin Walter S.	Felthousen C. S.	Leggett Dr. John	Rojahn F. C.
Barr A. E.	Felton W. S.	Lemay W. G.	Rollo L. C.
Bartholomew I. N.	Fern G. B.	Locke J. L.	Ross C. S.
Biglow J.	Fletcher R. C.	Loomis J. E.	Ross G. W.
Blount F. M.	Foster J. W.	Loomis T. T· jr.	Rundell M. H.
Brackett H. S.	Fulton A. W.	Lydston J. A.	Russell D. E.
Bradshaw T. F.	Gardiner E. F.	McClurg A. H.	Sammons T. J.
Brewster J. H.	Gardner D. B.	McCourtie A. B.	Sanborn G. C.
Brown C. H.	Gardner F.	McGill J. K.	Sanders A. H.
Brown E. C.	Gillespie R. H.	McIndoe Hugh	Sargent F. R.
Brown W. E.	Giroux Geo. W.	McKee H.	Sawyer C. S.
Bryan F. W.	Golden J. H.	McNiell T. H.	Seymour G. F.
Bullen Fred F.	Gunderson S. T.	Mansfield I. R.	Shaw W. A.
Bullock M. C.	Hainsworth J.	Many S. G.	Sherwood M.
Burroughs E. P.	Hall E. A.	Marshall H. L.	Sholes E.
Cable C. E.	Hallam C. A.	Martin R. L.	Simmons T. H.
Carter O. N.	Harris Geo. P.	Mason Wm. E.	Sisson F. M.
Chamberlain C. H.	Hayes S. C.	Meinel E. C.	Sollitt Wm.
Chambers E. C.	Helm Daniel T.	Meinel F. A.	Spofford G. W.
Clark D. W.	Henderson John C.	Meinel William	Spry S. A.
Clark F. E.	Herrick J. B. Dr.	Miller B. C.	Stanwood E. W.
Clark G. T.	Hewitt John	Mills D. W.	Steker F. J.
Coffin G. B.	Hicks T. P.	Moll Carl	Stokes C. M.
Cole C. D.	Higgins G. W.	Mortimer A. E.	Street C. R.
Conway R. F.	Hoadley A. E.	Mortimer C. J.	Stroker H. W.
Cook E. G.	Hoelscher E. C.	Mortimer F. G.	Strong G. W.
Cook W. H.	Hoelscher H. M.	Mortimer Wm. E.	Strong M. H.
Cowan Eugene	Hoffman John	Moxley P. A.	Sullivan W. K.
Cox E. R.	Holland J. E.	Munson C. W.	Thompson H. L.
Coyne F. E.	Holmes Frank F.	Murphy H. P.	Tillotson W. S.
Crane F. R.	Holroyd Dr. E. E.	Newton Chas. E.	Utting Wm.
Crocker B. S.	Hopkins R. N.	Nickerson A. E.	VanBuren B.
Cruikshank C. E.	Hostetter J. N.	Norton L. A.	VanMatre W. N.
Cummings F.	Howard J. H.	Oliver John jr.	Verhoeff J. R.
Danz C. A.	Hoy James	Oliver Wm. G.	Warner S. W.
DeClercq G. E. W.	Huszagh R. D.	Osbornson E. A.	Warner S. H.
Dennis F. J.	Hutchinson J. F.	Ozsias E. R.	Wells W. H.
Dicker E. A.	Jackson J. L.	Painter J. A.	Wengler M.
Donelson C. P. Dr.	Johnson C. J.	Palmer G. E.	White Alexander
Downey Joseph	Johnston J.	Palmer S.	Whiteside J. H.
Doyle W. A.	Kahler Conrad	Patterson John E.	Whitman F. F.
Duncombe H. S.	Karcher L. H.	Peak F. H.	Whitman J. M.
Dunham A. H.	Keating Arthur	Perry T O.	Wight Eli Dr.
Durant W. H.	Kendall G. W.	Piggott E. J.	Wilson F. J.
Dymond W. H.	Kenning R. H.	Place D. S.	Wolff C. J.
Eaton E. W.	Kennedy R. B.	Pope Samuel I.	Wolff J. F.
Eaton T. W.	Kerr Samuel	Price D. A.	Wolff Ludwig
Eckhart B. A.	Kerstein G. T.	Reed Charles E.	Woods F. M.
Eckhart J. W.	Klink A. F.	Reitz G. C.	Young J.
Eiszner John			

MORTON PARK CLUB.

MORTON PARK.

OFFICERS.

CHAS. C. RUBINS, - - - - - - - President.
JOHN E. GARDIN, - - - - - - Vice-President.
DR. J. H. COULTER, - - - - - - Secretary.
WM. W. WEARE, - - - - - - - Treasurer.

DIRECTORS.

John E. Gardin   Dr. J. H. Coulter   William Gebhardt
Wm. W. Weare   C. C. Rubins   Lot Brown

MEMBERS.

Bennett N. J.	Coulter J. H.	Hancock Albert	Rubins C. C.
Bensing N. J.	Curtis E. A.	Higgs E. B.	Rubins H. W.
Blowney H. E.	Darrow H. C.	Johnson J. F.	Rubins W. F.
Broadway C. H.	Drummond E. M.	McDowell Edw. B.	SchantzO. M.
Broadway M. D.	Dutton B. B.	McNamee H. R.	Smith J. P.
Brown Lot	Edgerly D. G.	Moore J. L.	Walters Chas. A.
Brown S. H. C.	Flagler S. A.	Moore W. A.	Weare P. B.
Bruce Chas.	Flagler W. B.	Needham Geo. J.	Weare Wm. W.
Bushnell G. W.	Gardin J. E.	Pardee Frank	Wegener G. A.
Chapman S. J.	Gebhardt W. C.	Radford J. W.	Wolf O. F.
Corris J. F.	Gilbert A. L.	Richardson L. B.	

NORTH SHORE CLUB.

1835 WELLINGTON AVENUE.

OFFICERS.

R. A. BOWER, - - - - - - President.
JOHN L. FLANNERY, - - - First Vice-President.
WILLIAM H. REDINGTON, - - Second Vice-President.
ADOLPH HEILE, - - - - - - Treasurer.
DEWITT C. MORRILL, - - - - - Secretary.

DIRECTORS.

W. Grace   John McConnell   George M. Barber
R. M. Paine   A. L. Sercomb   William D. Boyce
C. A. Clarke   F. H. Fox

MEMBERS.

Affeld C. E.	Chadwick Wm. H.	Engle Walter J.	Hester A. W.
Agar John	Clark George	Flannery J. L.	Hill Daniel O.
Altgeld J. P.	Clarke Chas A.	Fox Fred H.	Himrod Kirk
Anguish B. D.	Comstock E. F.	Gerould F. W.	Holbrook Francis
Arend Frank	Counselman Willis	Goodrich H. A.	W.
Baldwin L. Jerome	Cram LeRoy T.	Grace Wm.	Holden Chas N.
Barber Geo. M.	Crawford Andrew	Graves Charles E.	Holmes Wm. E.
Bower R. A.	CrittendenHenryC.	Gregory L. L.	Hosick Henry M.
Boyce W. D.	Diehl G.	Gregory Miles S.	Johnson McM. A.
Brauckmann Geo.	Dreyer E. S.	Haerther W. J.	Kee Jas. W.
Brecker Gustav A.	Dunn W. P.	Hagerty Thos. A.	Ketcham I. C.
Brocklebank J. C.	Durgin J. C.	Harrison Thos.	Kirkwood A. J.
Brosseau Z. P.	Dyrenforth Doug-	Harvey Geo. M.	Knight Wm. M.
Butterfield J. S.	las	Heile Adolph	KramerWilliam E.
Butz Alvin J.	Dyrenforth Ph. C.	Heile Louis L.	Krause Edmund R.
Cannell S. Wilmer	Eastman Sidney C.	Hequembourg J. E.	Landis E. M.

Lange Fred J.
Lasher C. W.
McConnell B. F.
McConnell Edw.D.
McConnell John
McFarlane Hugh F.
McNally Andrew
Marshall Geo. E.
Matteson M. D.
Messersmith Geo.
Messinger Chas. T.

Miller Truman W.
Mitchell Abraham
Morey Chas. J.
Morrill Dewitt C.
Morrill Donald L.
Mott John M.
Pagin Frank S.
Paine R. M.
Peirce Luther H.
Porter Fred D.
Redington W. H.
Reed Geo. L.

Richardson O. S.
Richardson W.C.B.
Roseboom W. L.
Sauer D.
Sawyer H. C.
Sercomb A. L.
Seymour H. V.
Shockey E. S.
Smith Dunlap
Smith L. J.
Smith W. D.
Smyth Martin R.

Stratton C. J.
Telling John
Thoman Judge L.D.
True John R.
VonGlahn A.
Watkins Jesse M.
Weinberg A.
Whitney Edward S
Wichert Henry
Williams J. F.
Woodworth P. M.

THE OAK PARK CLUB.

115 PARK PLACE.

OFFICERS.

S. R. Ainslie, ...	President.
C. E. Bolles, ...	First Vice-President.
C. S. Pellet, ...	Second Vice-President.
Arthur R. Metcalfe, ...	Treasurer.
B. L. Dodge, ...	Secretary.

DIRECTORS.

D. D. Garcelon
H. D. Pierce

F. B. Gibbs
Wm. N. Sharp

A. O. Butler
George W. Woodbury

MEMBERS.

Abbott A. H.
Ackert Chas. H.
Ainslie S. R.
Ames C. L.
Austin H. W.
Ayers C. B.
Baker Fred G.
Baker J. M.
Baldwin C. M.
Ball Farlin O.
Ballard F. E.
Banks A. F.
Bartlett Earle B.
Barto Daniel O.
Bassett H. W.
Bentley Harry G.
Beye Wm.
Blatchford Paul
Bliss C. L.
Bliss Theo. F.
Bolles C. E.
Boyd R. L.
Broughton Jno. W.
Brown Isaac W.
Bryant A. W.
Burton E. F.
Butler A. O.
Butler F. M.
Butler J. Fred
Butters Geo.
Carleton Stanley
Charlton Geo. J.
Cheney Augustus J.
Claflin Wm.
Clapp Geo.

Cook Edward
Cook Geo. F.
Cooke W. J.
Coombs Hiram
Conyne C. B. S.
Cratty Josiah
Cribben W. H.
Curtis H. Rolland
Davidson Geo. M.
Dodge B. L.
Dorsey R. M.
Draper A. W.
Dunlop Jos. K.
Emery Elwood A.
Everett J. D.
Fargo James L
Farson John
Fitch A. L.
Flinn Charles B.
Freer Nathan M.
Furbeck Geo. W.
Furbeck Warren F.
Gale E. Vincent
Garcelon D. D.
Gates Ryerson D.
Gerts Geo. E.
Gerts W. S.
Gibbs F. B.
Gilbert Lawson A.
Gile D. H.
Gilmore Wm.
Goodwillie R. W.
Griffen Felix J.
Gustorf Arthur
Hamilton Henry R.

Harvey James
Harvey Wm. R.
Hascall Milo S.
Hatch Wm. H.
Hayden James T.
Heald James H.
Hennegen R. H.
Herrick D. C.
Heurtley Arthur
Hoffman GeorgeW.
Horton Ben. P.
Horton Henry B.
Hull Delos
Hutchinson W. A.
Ingalls Emerson
Ingersoll Geo. W.
Ingman Lucius S.
Ingram Jos. S.
Jackson Dwight
Jaicks Andrew
James Austin F.
Jenkins Chas. E.
Johnson Edwin T.
Jones John I.
Jones Willis S.
Kavana L. J.
Kennedy D. J.
Ketcham M. W.
King Edw.
Larwill L. J.
Leach F. W.
Lenox John P.
Lewis John
Lord Nathaniel
Lovett L. M.

Loveland W. L.
Lunsford Louis
Lunsford Todd
MacDonald W. J.
McClary N. A.
McConnell W. A.
McCready E. W.
McGregor James
McHugh C. R.
McMynn J. C.
Malone E. T.
Martin E. P.
Mathews Allan A.
Melville Geo. W.
Metcalfe Arthur R.
Miller Andrew A.
Moore N. G.
Morley Thos.
Morris Thos. G.
Morris T. Gardner
Moser Geo. W.
Nash O. W.
Nelson John E.
Nichols Edward C.
Nickerson Jos. F.
Niles S. S.
Noyes Harry B.
Noyes M.
Noyes M.
Orr G. H.
Owen W. R.
Palmer J. H.
Patch G. M.
Patrick Henry E.
Patterson W. R.

Patton N. S.
Pebbles H. R.
Pebbles S. E.
Pellet Clarence S.
Perkins Frank G.
Pierce H. D.
Rattle Thos. S.
Ray Allen S.
Richardson Harry B
Ripley Gordon
Roberts C. E.
Roberts T. E.
Robertson Wm. A.
Rogers James C.
Roser E. A.
Rothermel S. A.
Schroyer Chas. A.

Seaman John A.
Searing Aaron B.
Sharp George P.
Sharp J. P.
Sharp Wm. N.
Sharpe Caswell A.
Sheridan W. A.
Shuey William H.
Sinden Henry P.
Skeen J. C.
Skillin Thomas J.
Smith H. K.
Standish A. H.
Talbot E. S.
Taylor H. A.
Thatcher Geo. L.
Thomas Cyrus P.

Todd Charles C.
Tomlinson E. S.
Tope J. W.
Towle H. S.
Townsend W. R.
Tristram J. E.
Ullmann Albert I.
Ullmann H. J.
Updike F. D.
VanVlietLeonardS.
Vilas A. H.
Wales Harry A.
Walker C. F.
Walker Geo. H.
Waller Edward C.
Waller J. D.
Ward Jas. L.

Warner W. C.
Weage Collins A.
White Horace F.
Williams Chauncey
  L.
Wilson Geo.Landis
Winslow W. H.
Winslow W. P.
Wood F. H.
Wood Martin E.
Wood Wm. H.
Woodbury Geo. W.
Worthington G. H.
WorthingtonHarry
  C.
Worthington R. S.
Young H. P.

OAKLAND CLUB.

OAKWOOD AVENUE N.E. COR. ELLIS AVENUE.

OFFICERS.

JOHN R. BENSLEY, - - - - - President.
A. W. CLANCY, - - - - First Vice-President.
A. H. MEADS, - - - - Second Vice-President.
B. W. SHERMAN, - - - - - - Secretary.
F. D. HELMER, - - - - - Treasurer.

DIRECTORS.

E. C. Moderwell
Dr. H. P. Woley
Robert Thacker

N. Cochran
F. T. Bliss
Dr. Wyllys Moore

Simeon Straus
Andrew Pearson

MEMBERS.

Abel Jonathan
Anderson W. D. S.
Bailey Fred'k M.
Bailey E. W.
Banghart W. J.
Bannister L. P.
Barger R. W.
Barnard J. E.
Barrett M. L.
Bensley John R.
Beverly J. M. Mrs.
Bisbee L. H.
Blair C. M.
Bliss F. T.
Blood I. W.
Bovett J. A.
Boynton C. E.
Bowen T. C.
Clancy A. W. Maj.
Clark F. H.
Clark Wallace G.
Clark W. D.
Cochran Norris
Colvin W. H. jr.

Conner F. F.
Conroy I. N.
Cook George E.
Cooper A. J.
Crawford Hon.C.H.
Cronkrite B. F.
Dille S. M.
Donohue M. A.
DunhamHon.R.W.
Dunlop Alexander
Eisendrath W. N.
Eldridge Dr. C. S.
Ellett E. H.
Everett E. A.
Farson Chas. T.
Fretts L. A.
Gardner Frank G.
Gunther H. A. Dr.
Harvey J. H.
Helmer Fred'k D.
Herrick R. Z.
Hill James M. Mrs.
Huey J. S.
Hunt Henry M.

Iones Alfred L.
Kimball Charles F.
Kline George E.
KocherspergerD.H
KocherspergerH.L
Lamb A. D.
Landt Charles C.
Larned W. E.
Lovett T. J.
Mann James R.
Maull Mrs.Dr.W.C.
Mayer Daniel
Meade Abert H.
Moderwell E. C.
Moore Wyllys Dr.
Morrison Arthur J.
Norton Joel H.
Pearson Andrew
Quincey T. S.
Rand William H.
Randolph J. F.
Rice Sidney W.
Schmidt W. D.

Sea Sidney W.
Shandrew W. E.
Shannon Geo. W.
Sherman J'dgeE.B.
Sherman B. W.
Shissler Louis
Sidwell Geo. H.
Skidmore G. C.
Sommers F. W.
Soper N. D.
Straus Simeon
Tanner John R.
Thacker Robert
Thomas J. C.
Weston E.B., M.D.
Wheeler Martin L.
White William M.
Wilson H. G.
Wilson Mrs. L. M.
Woley Dr. H. P.
Wood F. W.
Woods S. E.

THE OAKS CLUB.

AUSTIN.

OFFICERS.

GEORGE M. DAVIS, ... President.
R. H. TRAILL, ... First Vice-President.
D. OLIPHANT, . . . Second Vice-President.
E. D. ROBINSON, ... Secretary.
H. H. REARDEN, ... Treasurer.

DIRECTORS.

F. R. Schock,   C. W. Hatch,   R. A. Jampolis,
Fred C. Beeson   D. R. McAuley.   Thomas Hunter
C. C. Murray,   J. J. McCarthy,

MEMBERS.

Abbott Edwin F.	Crafts Will	Kretzinger G. W.	Potwin Henry A.
Austin H. W.	Cummings E. A.	Lacy Daniel	Powell F. M.
Baker E. O.	Davis Geo. M.	Leland E. F.	Price John P.
Ballard C. W.	Davis W. E.	Lendrum Alex.	Price R. P.
Barnett Joseph H.	Davis W. G.	Lew C. H.	Purvis John
Bartelme A. E.	Decker Jacob E.	Lindgren C. J.	Ray W. F.
Bartelme F. E.	Denison George R.	Lloyd W. G.	Rearden H. H.
Bassett N. M.	Dunham H. J.	Luedders John	Roberts A. L.
Beeson F. C.	Eveleth S. H.	MacLean J. D.	Roberts L. C.
Beeson Walter	Fitch Ellis B.	MacLean J. D. jr.	Robertson Howard
Bennett J. W.	Frink H. F.	McAuley D. R.	Robinson E. D.
Bennett W. H.	Frost Z. J.	McCarthy J. J.	Rooklidge H. E.
Briggs B. P.	Frost Z. J. jr.	McFarland W. W.	Schlecht C. F.
Bonney C. F.	Gardner W. W.	McNeal S. D.	Schlecht O. G.
Bowes John R.	Garner J. P.	Martin Arthur H.	Schock Fred'k. R.
Brooks H. B.	Giles W. A.	Martin Jas. A.	Shepard A. A.
Buck B. F.	Hall L. E.	Martin J. H.	Snow T. A.
Bush E. E.	Hatch Chas. W.	Matthews WalterC.	Stratford H. K.
Campbell H. O.	Hathaway J. N.	Meredith M. M.	Strom A. A.
Carson E. M.	Hecox J. F.	Miller J. J.	Thorndyke J. E.
Castle Chas. S.	Hill Fred. A.	Miller M. G.	Thurber W. E.
Castle Percy V.	Hobler E. J.	Milanmow J. F.	Traill R. H.
Chapell George E.	Hood Thomas C.	Moore A. G.	Vanderkloot M. L.
Church Geo. W	Hulbert W. M.	Moore E. B.	Walker E. S.
Cody H. R.	Hunter Thos. M.	Morrill John W.	Wallace F. P.
Collins A. C.	Huston Phil W.	Murray C. C.	Walser J. J.
Cone George W.	Jampolis Robert R.	Murray M. F.	Wayt Edw.
Corrigan C. E.	Johnson A. A.	Nelson E. J.	Weston Walter
Crafts A. A.	Johnson A. B.	Norton L. A.	Williams Wm.
Crafts Clayton E.	Johnson F. L.	Oliphant David	Wills S. S.
Crafts Miles B.	Judkins E. F.	Park Geo. H.	Woodbury S. H.
Crafts Sigel J.	Knowlton E. R.	Pole Robert G.	Wyman J. D.
Crafts Stanley C.	Kreis G. A.	Potwin Harry	Wyman W. L.

OLIO CLUB.

OFFICERS.

MRS. AMELIA WEED HOLBROOK, - - - - - President.
MRS. EDWARD A. MEYSENBURG, - - - - - Vice-President.
MRS. ALICE E. GOODALL, Princeton Hotel, - Recording Secretary.
MRS. EVA M. HUGHES, 75, 43d st. Flat C - - Corres. Secretary.
MRS. CHAS. F. MITCHELL, 430 E. 47th St. - - - Treasurer.

MEMBERS.

Ahrens Mrs. Mary A.
Anderson Mrs. J. C.
Baker Mrs. Hiram
Blount Mrs. S. P.
Brinkman Mrs. Alonzo
Barker Mrs. Agnes
Bower Miss E. Eugenia
Brown Mrs. Moreau R.
Borland Mrs. Emily
Baldwin Mrs. William
Crane Mrs. J. S.
Colt Mrs. A. J.
Chandler Mrs. J. N.
Chamberlain Mrs. M. J.
Carroll Mrs. Lester Scott
Crane Mrs. F. P.
Craig Mrs. J. C.
DeGraff Mrs. Ellen E.
Eskridge Mrs. Belle C.
Evald Mrs. Carl A.
Fussell Miss Helen
Ferriss Mrs. Francis
Foote Mrs. Edgar S.
Francis Mrs. J. L.
Flemming Mrs. Minnie
Furgeson Mrs. Adelaide
Fowler Mrs. C. H.
Guthrie Mrs. Seymore

Goodall Mrs. Alice E.
Gielesman Mrs. J.
Gartlain Mrs. Adelaide
Holbrook Mrs. Amelia Weed
Hughes Mrs. Eva M.
Haskett Mrs.EmmaWebb
Hamlin Mrs. L. A.
Huling Miss Caroline
Hayden Miss Anna
Judson Mrs. M. M.
Johnson Mrs. E. C.
Jenks Mrs. S. L.
Keeton Mrs. T. A.
Kloeber Mrs. J. V.
Keepus Mrs. W. E.
Leahy Miss
Lancaster Mrs. Rosalie
Mitchell Mrs. Chas. F.
Mowqray Mrs. Geo.
Meysenburg Mrs. Edward A.
Morgan Mrs. Ida W.
Murphey Mrs. Henry
Millard Mrs. S. M.
Melander Mrs. L. M.
McDowell Mrs. Janet B.

Olson Mrs. N. F.
Orr Mrs. Frank Barrington
Prentice Mrs. V. E.
Putney Mrs. J. C.
Powers Mrs. W.
Prescott Miss Mary M.
Phillips Mrs.
Robertson Mrs. Charlotte C.
Richardson Mrs. D. W.
Springer Mrs. Callie
Saxton Mrs. H. B.
Severinghaus Miss Vesta E.
Scull Mrs. Heury
Springer Mrs. T. C.
Spellman Mrs. E.
Shourds Mrs. C. B.
Stuckert Mrs. Mary Coleman
Temple Mrs T. C.
Tracy Mrs. F. K.
Thomas Mrs. J. W.
White Mrs. J. Harrison
White Miss Minnie
Williams Mrs. J. P.

PARK CLUB.

FIFTY-SEVENTH STREET AND ROSALIE COURT.

OFFICERS.

ELLIOTT DURAND, - - - - - - President.
HERMAN J. HALL, - - - - First Vice-President.
E. W. HEATH, - - - - Second Vice-President.
CHARLES R. DICKINSON, - - - - Secretary.
J. J. MAGEE, - - - - - - - Treasurer.

DIRECTORS.

Berlyn B. Brown
Otis Jones
Cornelius Curtis

E. K. Boyd
F. M. Reynolds
Samuel E. Dunham
T. H. Murray

M. R. Poucher
R. A. Shailer
B. W. Wight

MEMBERS.

Baldwin J. H.
Banks Charles E.
Berry F. A. jr.
Bowes J. P.
Boyd E. K.
Bradley M. S.
Brower J. F.
Brown B. B.
Brown F. D.
Brown L. E.
Campbell W. P.
Chandler P. R.
Chesebro W. H.
Conkey W. B.
Cook J. C., M. D.

Curtis Cornelius
Dalzell Walter
Davenport W. C.
Dickerson Chas. R.
Dickerson C. W.
Dow F. H.
Dunham Saml. E.
Durand Elliott
Eastman Frank L.
Ensign H. H.
Field C. G.
Fuller L. H., M. D.
Garrigue R. H.
Gilchrist John F.
Gilson T. W.

Githens W. L.
Graham E. R.
Hall H. J.
Hamill T. W.
Hamilton J. H.
Harlow F.
Hawley H. S.
Heath Ernest W.
Hilton W. W.
Holmes E. S.
Jackson J. Mason
Jones Otis
Lane C. E.
Lines F. B.

Magee J. J.
March C. A.
Marston L. H.
Martin John L.
Mayou J. S.
Meade H. B.
Murphy John A.
Murray Thos. H.
Nelson W. C.
Northrup G. W. jr.
Norton Chas. L.
Page C. G.
Parry Henry
Partridge N. A.
Pierce W. L.

Porter F. W.
Poucher Morris R.
Randle C H.
Reynolds F. M.
Rogers C. D.
Root C. P.

Root F. K.
Schaberg C. W
Scott A. F.
Shailer Robert A.
Shepard George P.
Simpson J. G.

Smeenk Warner
Stone F. B.
Stone J. R.
Tolman E. B.
Webster Ralph W.
Webster W. Dix

Wight B. W.
Willard G. G.
Wood J. H.
Woodle E. R.
Zimmerman Wm.

THE PHOENIX CLUB.

104-110 MONROE.

OFFICERS.

MARTIN EMERICH, - - - - - - - President.
BENJAMIN F. RUBEL, - - - - - - Vice-President.
ALBERT S. LOUER - - - - Recording Secretary.
GUS. M. GREENEBAUM, - - - - - Treasurer.
HUGO PAM, - - - - - Financial Secretary.
B. C. GELDER, - - - - - - Superintendent.

DIRECTORS.

Jacob H. Bauland
M. J. Einstein
Wm. S. Manheimer

Simeon B. Eisendrath
Max Frank
Henry C. Flonacher
S. Franklin

Alfred D. Kohn
Jacob Ringer
Dr. H. H. Schuhmann

MEMBERS.

Aaronson Henry A.
Adler Sidney
Alexander A.
Altman M.
Arnheim Benj.
Arnstein Eugene
Bach L.
Bacharach B. C.
Bak Dr. H.
Ballenberg A. A.
Barbe Martin
Barnard Harry
Barnett M. P.
Basch Joseph
Bauland Jacob H.
Bauland Joseph H.
Baum S. M.
Bear Sidney
Becker Louis
Beifeld Alex
Beifeld Joseph
Beifeld M.
Benjamin Louis
Bensinger Benj. A.
Berg Morris H.
Binswanger Augustus
Bissinger Benj.
Block Isaac
Bloom M. J.
Blumenthal I.
Bodenheimer Simon
Cohen Benj.
Cohen G. K.
Cohen Jacob H.
Cohen J. K.

Colat M.
Cornhauser M.
D'Ancona Edw. M.
Daniels Samuel
Daube Jos. L.
Daube Jacob M.
DeCosta H. A.
Dembufsky Max
Dernburg Adolph
Dernburg A.
Dreyfus Moise
Eckstein Louis
Einstein Morris J.
Eisendrath S. B.
Eisenstaedt A. L.
Elkin Mark
Ellbogen Max
Emerich Martin
Emrich Myer J.
Eppenstein M. C.
Eppenstein Sol C.
Epstein Max N.
Falkenau Louis
Fass Charles
Fechheimer E. S.
Fels Joseph
Felsenthal Eli B.
Felsenthal Herman
Fessenden Charles F.
Fishell Albert
Flonacker Edw.
Flonacker Hy. C.
Florsheim N.
Foreman Frank
Foreman Isaac H.
Foreman Milton J.

Foreman Oscar G.
Frank Jos.
Frank Louis
Frank Max
Frankel Jos.
Franklin Sol
Franks Jacob
Freund Isaac
Friedman Abe B.
Friedman Oscar J.
Friend Chas.
Gans Samuel
Gatzert August
Gatzert J. L.
Glaser Geo. M.
Goodkind M. L.
Goodman Jos.
Goodman M. F.
Green Jacob J.
Greenbaum Gus M.
Griesheimer Morris
Grossman Ed
Guckenheimer Joseph
Gundelfinger Arnold
Haber M.
Hahn H. W.
Harris Jos.
Harris Saml H.
Hart Emil
Hartman Leon
Hartman Louis
Hartman Milton L.
Heilbron Jos.
Herbst Benj.
Herrick Chas.

Hersig Leo S.
Hexter Stephen
Heymann Emanuel S.
Hillman Ben
Hillman Edw.
Himes Isidore H.
Hirsch Henry
Hirsch Isaac
Hirsch L. K.
Hirsch Morris
Hirsch Moses
Hirsch William
Hofeld S. A.
Hoffstadt Gus
Hollenstein B.
Horner Chas. H.
Hyman E. S.
Hyman Joseph
Israel Harry W.
Jacobs Jos. W.
Jacobson Nat.
Joseph Herbert L.
Joseph S. L.
Kahn Leopold
Kantrowitz G. A.
Kaufman Adolph
Kaufman Ben
Kauffman Fred
Kauffman Theo.
Kesner J. L.
Klauber E. C.
Klein I. L.
Klien Isaac
Kline Samuel J.
Kline Solomon
Kohn Abe H.

29

Kohn Alfred D.
Kohn Louis A.
Kopperl Ira J.
Kramer A. F.
Kramer J. A.
Kronthal B.
Langbein S.
Lazarus Harry
Lebolt J. Y.
Lebolt M. H.
Lefi William H.
Lehman Wm.
Leopold Sam. F.
Lepman David
Leubrie Lou
Levi Carl
Levie Oliver M.
Levinson I. N.
Levy D. R.
Levy Morris F.
Liebenstein A. M.
Liebenstein Chas.
Lilienfeld W.
List Edward
Loeb Adolph
Loeb A. H.
Loeb Jacob W.
Loeb Leo A.
Loeb M.
Loeb Samuel J.
Loeb Sidney
Loeb William
Loeser Julius
Lowenthal B.
Lowenthal J. W.
Long Louis
Loth Sidney A.
Louer A. S.
Lowenbaum R.
Lowy Edw.
Lyons Jos. L.
Mandel Frank E.
Mandel Fred L.
Mandel Robert
Mandel Leonard J.
Manheimer Louis
Manheimer William
Marcus M. H.
Marks Jul M.

Marks Samuel J.
Mayer H. L.
Mayer Isaac
Mayer Jacob
Mayer Jos.
Mayer Lee
Mayer M. Harry
Mergenthain A. D.
Meyer E. F.
Meyer Fred
Morgenthau G. L.
Morgenthau J. C.
Morgenthau Mengo
Morgenthau M.
Morris Herbert N.
Moses Jos. W.
Myer Albert
Nathan Herman
Nessler S. C.
Neu B.
Newberger Eli M.
Newgrass Wm.
Newhouse H. L.
Newman Jacob jr.
Newman Morris
Newmark Louis
Nye William A.
Oberndorf Herman
Oberndorf M. L.
Oster Lawrence
Ottenheimer L. S.
Pam Hugo
Pam Max
Peckham Chas. V.
Pflaum Harry
Phillips J. S.
Polack A. M.
Pollak August
Polocheck Max
Popper E. H.
Reiss Otto
Rice Isaac M.
Riegelman A.
Ringer Jacob
Ritter M. M., M.D
Rosenbaum Morris
Rosenbaum Sam
Rosenberg Benj.
Rosenberg Sig. A.
Rosenthal A. E.

Rosenthal B. J.
Rosenthal L. L.
Rosenthal Samuel
Rosenthal S. H.
Rothschild A. M.
Rothschild Lew
Rubel Ben F.
Rubel Frank D.
Rubel Isaac
Rubel Isaac M.
Rubel L. G.
Rubel Milton
Rubel S. L.
Ruben Charles
Rubovits E.
Rubovits Frank E.
Rubovits Toby
Scheuer Jack J.
Schlesinger T.
Schneewind Hy.
Schnodig Joseph B.
Schoenbrun Irving
Schoenbrun Sam
Schram Harry
Schram Samuel
Schuhmann Dr. H. H.
Schwab Al. C.
Schwab Chas.
Schwabacker H. H.
Schwabacker H. H. jr.
Shire Adolph
Siegel Sylvan
Simonds L. B.
Simons A. L.
Simons H. S.
Simonson Julius
Siegel Fred
Smyth John M.
Snydacker Jos.
Solomon H. C.
Solomon J. I.
Solomon L. H.
Sommers Chas.
Sondheimer Max
Spiegel H. W.
Spiegel M. J.
Spiegel S. M.
Stein Adolph

Stein Arthur
Stein Arthur
Stein Charles
Ssein Ignatz
Stern David
Stern D. S.
Stern Julius
Stern Oscar M.
Stettauer C. S.
Stone Nat
Stonehill Charles
Straus Eli M.
Straus Julius
Strauss A. L.
Strauss Frank R.
Strauss Henry X.
Strauss Leo
Strauss Leo J,
Strauss M. A.
Strauss S. L.
Strelitz V. B.
Strons Aaron
Strum Max A.
Stumer A. R.
Stumerx Louis M.
Tuska Leo
Ullman E. H.
Vallens Eugene
Wasserman D.
Wechsler Phil
Weil Eugene S.
Weil Harry
Weil Morris
Weil Theodore
Wendell Edw. E.
Wile D. J.
Wilharz William
Willner L. J.
Wilson Jos. M.
Wineman M. R.
Wolf J. M.
Wolff Max
Woolf Benj.
Woolf Harry
Woolf Isaac
Wormser Louis
Wurzburger J
Wurzburger Louis
Zwetow Samuel R.
Zwilling Isidor

PRESS CLUB.

133 SOUTH CLARK STREET.

OFFICERS.

FRANK A. VANDERLIP,	President.
M. B. GIBBS,	First Vice-President.
I. A. FLEMING,	Second Vice-President.
FRED G. RAE,	Third Vice-President.
W. H. FREEMAN,	Recording Secretary.
FRANK E. JOHNSON,	Financial Secretary.
GEORGE SCHNEIDER,	Treasurer.
LEROY ARMSTRONG,	Librarian.

DIRECTORS.

A. S. Leckie   Chas. L. Rhodes   A. L. Clarke
W. G. Nicholas   E. M. Lahiff

MEMBERS.

Abbott F. D.	Busby W. H.	Erwin J. M.	Hollman Joseph C.
Abbott Willis J.	Cahill Daniel P.	Etten W. J.	Holmes Frank
Adams A. B.	Campbell Quintin	Faraday Walter	Hough Clarence A.
Adams F. U.	Canman Leo.	Fargo H. D.	Housman L. M.
Ade George	Cannon Thos. H.	Fay John	Hubbard L. C.
Almy C. D.	Carpenter H. H.	Faye C. M.	Hull P. C.
Anderson F. S.	Carr H. J.	Finerty John F.	Hunt H. M.
Andrews Byron	Cassidy Bert	Finnegan F. X.	Hunter W. B.
Andrews O. F.	Carus Paul, M.D.	Flanders A. R.	Hutton N. D.
Armstrong H. A.	Chaiser A.	Fleming I. A.	Hyde Harry M.
Armstrong Leroy	Champion T. J.	Flynn J. J.	Hyde W. T. C.
Armstrong Wm.	Chandler W. G.	Forker Harry G.	Iglehart William
Atwell Benj. H.	Chapin W. E.	Forrester George	Insley Edw.
Ayers S. P.	Clark A. L.	Freeman W. H.	Jacobsen R. C.
Ayme Louis H.	Cleveland H. I.	Frieberger Ed.	Jeffery J. B.
Babbitt Geo. A.	Clover Sam T.	Frizelle Charles E.	Johnson B. A.
Bailey W. W.	Cobb W. R.	Fuller J. J.	Johnson Charles C.
Baird Thomas	Colbert Elias	Fulton A. W.	Johnson F. E.
Baker E. J.	Connelly M. W.	Gardiner C.	Johnson H.
Baker R. S.	Conwell James W.	Gardner H. G.	Jones Alex J.
Banks C. E.	Cornell William P.	Gay H. Lord	Jones H. Leroy
Barnes David	Cossar Walter L.	Gesswein A. J.	Jones R. H.
Barron E. A.	Costello John J.	Gibbs M.	Jones R. R.
Barry P. T.	Crane Jonathan M.	Giveene R. F.	Kalheim O. M.
Batey J. F.	Crawford C. E.	Glenn W. M.	Keeley James
Beach Henry L.	Crissey Forrest	Glover L. B.	Keily John
Beachel George D.	Crowell C. H.	Goodspeed Charles	Keough H. E.
Beck E. D.	Curtis Fred D.	L.	Kerr C. H.
Bemis H. V.	Curtis W. E.	Granville Austym	Ketchum R. L.
Benham P. D.	Daley J. R.	Gray F. S.	Kimball E. R.
Bennett F. O.	Dame Asa	Gregory W. C.	Kimball M. B.
Bennett James O'D.	Dandy J. M.	Grover Chester A.	Knight H. W.
Bentham George	Davis Augustine	Halbert D. M.	Knox W. M.
Benzinger Fred	Davis J. D.	Hall Dr. C. B.	Kochersperger H.L
Bernard E. M.	Davis J. M.	Hall H. P.	Kohlsaat H. H.
Berry Thomas P.	Dean Clarence L.	Haller W. J.	Lahiff Edward M.
Blakely Charles F.	DeFoe Louis	Halloran John	Lamb Louis A.
Bloomingston J. S.	DeKraft S. I.	Hamilton John B.,	Landers H. O.
Bloss H. H.	Deming O. L.	M. D.	Lane J. J.
Bloss William L.	Denison T. S.	Handy M. P.	Lane Marcus
Bogart R. D.	Denslow W. W.	Harden E. W.	Langland James
Bohn H. J.	Dickson M. E.	Harding Victor M.	LaShelle Kirke
Bolling George W.	Dillabough Joseph	Harkness A. H.	Lawson Victor
Bowen Wm. A.	Dillingham E. R.	Harper W. H.	Layton Harry B.
Boyd James	Dixon John Arthur	Harris F. B.	Leckie A. S.
Bradley C. H.	Donaldson Henry F	Harrison John H.	Lederer Sam
Bradwell J. B.	Donnelly Ignatius	Harrison William P.	LeWis Irving
Bramhall John	Dowst Chas.	Hatch A. F.	Lewis W. E.
Brenne Richard	Duncan Thomas	Hays C. L.	Link D. M.
Brewer John A.	Dunlop Joseph R.	Hazard Eugene J.	Linthicum Richard
Bronson Leonard	Dunne Finley P.	Hector Eugene	Lloyd B. F.
Brooks Frank H.	Durand Elliott	Heineman A. H.	Lonergan L. F.
Brown E. B.	Easley Ralph M.	Heinemann H.E.O.	Lower Elton
Browne Ray	Eastman Barrett	Henderson David	Lowrie Harrie R.
Bryan I. J.	Eastman John C.	Henderson J. F.	Lush Chas. K.
Buchanan R. B.	Eaton W. D.	Hendrickson Prof.P	Macbetn W. H.
Bunting Harry D.	Eddy M. Allen	Henius Dr. Max	Mackenzie Fred
Burdette Samuel M.	Eggleston W. G.,	Hesing Washingt'n	Mac Millan Lincoln
Burrelle F. A.	M. D.	Hitchcock C. I.	Mac Rae W. G.
Busby L. W.	Emerson Willis G.	Holden R. H.	Maitland James

Malkoff M.	Packard A. T.	Rollins C. E.	Thompson T. O.
Manning Harry	Palmer Thos. W.	Rose Robert F.	Tobin Frank W.
Mansfield J. B.	Park W. H.	Rowe Dr. N.	Tozer A. B.
Marble Earl	Patterson A. L.	Sass L.	Tracey F. K,
Martin Riley P.	Patterson R. W.	Sasseen D. E.	Turner H. O.
Martin W. J.	Payne Frank C.	Sayler H. L.	Underwood Kings-
Matthias Chas.	Payne J. Edward	Schneider Geo.	ley
Maxwell John	Peck F. N.	Schulte F. J,	Upton George P.
McCutchon John T.	Peck F. W.	Scott J. W.	VanBenthuysen W.
McEldowney J. H.	Pepper Charles	Scovel H. M.	Vanderlip F. A.
McEnnis John C.	Perce C. F.	Senff Felix	Visscher W. S.
McGaffey Ernest	Perkins Charles G.	Shanks W. J.	Vos J. Hubbard
McGovern John	Perkins George O.	Shepard H. O.	Vynne Harold R.
McGrath George B.	Phinney Warren	Sheridan Ed.	Waldo J. B.
McHugh J. P.	Pickard E. W.	Sherman John D.	Walker W. S.
McKay C. P.	Pierce H. A.	Shields G. O.	Walsh John R.
McKay W. K.	Pixley Frank S.	Shuman A. F.	Walton L. R.
McKenzie E. S.	Place R. M.	Shuman Ed.	Waterloo Stanley
McLaughlin D. J.	Pollard J. P.	Sittig E. A.	Waterman Nixon
McNeil August	Pomeroy P. P.	Sittig W. A.	Weddell T. R.
McQuilkin A. H.	Powers C. J.	Smith C. W.	Weed C. E.
Medill Joseph	Powers T. E.	Smith W. V.	Weigley Frank S.
Mercier David I.	Pratt George W.	Smyth Hill C.	Weippiert G. W.
Meredith W. M.	Price T. J.	Smythe J. H.	Welch F. B.
Michels C. D.	Priest J. L.	Snyder H. W.	Wellman Walter
Miller Hubert F.	Prime S. T. K.	Soustcheffsky R.	Weston J. W.
Mitchell H. B.	Pritchard E. R.	Sparks Clinton	Whitford C. B.
Moody O. E.	Rae F. G.	Steele S. V.	Wight George H.
Morrill F. K.	Ransom Robert	Steiger Charles H.	Wilkie A. C.
Mullaney B. J.	Ray Wm. E.	Stone Edwin P.	Wilkie J. E.
Murphy R. J.	Raymond Sam M.	Stone M. E.	Wilmarth J. C.
Nathanson Martin	Read O. P.	Stromme P. O.	Willy John
Newell A. G.	Reed N. A. jr.	Strong C. E.	Wood George S.
Nicholas W. G.	Reilly Leigh	Strong J. W.	Woodridge H. B.
Nicholl T. J.	Reiwitch Herman	Strong W. H.	Woodward F. R. E.
Nixon Chas. E.	L.	Suesman A. L.	Woodward T. R.
Nixon Wm. P.	Rhodes Charles	Sullivan M. L.	Wright C. G.
Norton S. F.	Rice F. W.	Sullivan W. K.	Wright Herbert C.
Nye Fred	Rice Wallace DeG.	Sweeney Paul DeH.	Wright John L.
O'Connor John C.	Richardson Fred	Taylor C. W.	Wright J. E
O'Neill A. W.	Richardson John S.	Taylor W. A.	Wright Nat ᴗ
O'Neill Thomas J.	Ritchie John	Terbush L. F.	Wright W. C.
O'Sullivan Daniel	Robinson H. P.	Thomas J. C.	Wyatt Frank T.
Oviatt F. C.	Rockwell R. K.	Thompson Slason	Yount A. H.
Owen E. E.	Rogers L. W.		

THE PSYCHEON CLUB.

OGLESBY AVENUE, COR. SIXTY-FIRST STREET.

OFFICERS.

JAMES W. MEEKER,	President.
CLARENCE A. PERRY,	Vice-President.
NED C. WEYBURN,	Secretary.
LEWIS H. DODD,	Treasurer.

DIRECTORS.

Dr. A. G. Miller	John S. Beattie	Geo W. Rodgers
Harry G. Hurd	Lloyd M. Faulkner	Philip S. Brown

MEMBERS.

Beattie John S.	Breckenridge Wil-	Brown Philip S.	Fallow James D.
Beeks Edward C.	liam M.	Dodd Lewis H.	Faulkner Lloyd M.
Bragdon Walter L.	Bronson Leonard E.	Doty Benonie S.	Frear Allen E.

Gammons James A.
Golden John
Hardenbrook Burt C.
Hurd Harry G.
Jacoby F. Leslie

Lafferty Charles C.
Loring George F.
Maher Walter S.
Meeker James W.
Miller Dr. A. G.

Nay William G.
Northrup Earle J.
Perry Clarence A.
Rodgers Geo. W.
Roper John

Sloan Ernest G.
Stevenson John S.
Stewart John P.
Weyburn Ned C.
Weyburn Ralph B.

SHERIDAN _ CLUB.

4100 MICHIGAN AVENUE.

OFFICERS.

MICHAEL CUDAHY, ... President.
EDWARD BAGGOT, ... Vice-President.
ED. J. MURPHY, ... Secretary.
JOSEPH C. BRADEN, ... Treasurer.

DIRECTORS.

James Bradburn
Michael Espert

Michael McDermott
Thomas F. Keeley

John J. Cashin

MEMBERS.

Alexander S. T.
Alexander W. W.
Baggot E.
Baggot James E.
Baggot Joseph
Baggot J. D,
Ball J. M.
Bardon D. G.
Bauer Richard
Beattie L. M.
Bern E. A.
Birmingham J. H.
Bowen J. F.
Bowles J. P.
Boyle J. P.
Boyle L. P.
Bradburn James
Braden J. C.
Bremner D. F.
Bremner James W.
Bulger W. J.
Burke A.
Burke D. F.
Byrne Chas. T.
Byrne Harry
Calahan James E.
Caldwell Dr. C. P.
Canavan A. A.
Carey C. N.
Carey Jos. T.
Carey W. P.
Carney Thos.
Carney W. J.
Carroll D. J.
Carroll W. F.
Casey James J.
Cashin J. J.
Cella A. S.
Christian H. W.
Clare James
Clare John F.
Clare J. J.
Clarkson J. F.

Cleary J. J.
Clifford John
Clinnen J. G.
Clowry James
Clowry W. J.
Coleman E. J.
Collins L. F.
Colnou J. E.
Conlan James jr.
Connolly F. W.
Conway S. S.
Cook John F.
Cooke Chas F.
Cooke Geo. J.
Cooke John R.
Cooke J. S.
Cooper John S.
Corboy M. J.
Corigan R. E.
Cox Thos.
Coyle James F.
Cragin M. J.
Crennan J. M.
Crilly D. F.
Crilly Wm. M.
Cronin A. J.
Crowe F.
Cudahy John
Cudahy Michael
Cummings A.
Cummings F. H.
Cummings W. A.
Cummins M.
Davis Z. T.
Dee George W.
Dee Wm. E.
DeVeney T. F.
Devlin F. A.
Dimery J. H.
Dixon Arthur
Doerr J. F.
Doerr J. P.
Donnelly T. N.

Donnersberger Jos.
Donohue J. W.
Donohue M. A.
Donohue W. F.
Dowling R. A.
Downey N. I.
Doyle Edward
Duffy John J.
Duggan P. H.
Duffin Dan'l
Duncan James W.
Dunn J. J.
Egan Edward
Eagle H. R.
Ebbert W. H.
Elcock E. G.
Enger Geo.
English R. R.
Enright Wm. J.
Espert Michael
Everett John C.
Fitzgerald H. J.
Fitzpatrick Dr. J. H.
Flavin M. D.
Flood Frank J.
Foley W. C.
Fortune W. J
Foster George P.
Foster M.
Fox G. H.
Fox Harry E.
Fox John V.
Gahan Thomas
Gallagher Daniel
Gallagher Jos. P.
Galvin James
Gaulter Frank J.
Geary A. J.
Geary W. T.
Geary John R.
Geary T. F.
Gibbons John
Gillice Hugh

Glennon E. T.
Goldie Robert
Goldie William jr.
Graham F. H.
Greenfield C. W.
Gregory J. H.
Griffin James
Griffin S. D.
Griffith John
Griffith K. F.
Hagan J. H.
Haley P.
Hanrihan S. J.
Hardin D.
Hardin P. K.
Hayne W. J.
Healy James T.
Healy J. J.
Healy M. R.
Heenan D.
Heeney J. B.
Henneberry W. P.
Hennessy P. J.
Hennessey W. E.
Hickey C. M.
Hickey M. A.
Higbie Fred K.
Hines Edward
Hoffman Andrew
Hogan James A.
Honan M. A.
Hopkins J. P.
Horan Dennis J.
Hudson E.
Hudson E. jr.
Hughes Joseph
Hutchinson Thos.
Jenkins J. B.
Jones John L.
Keeley E. M.
Keeley T. F.
Keenan P. H.
Keenan W. T.

Kelley James J.
Kelley Thomas F.
Kelly John
Kelly Joseph I.
Kelly Samuel
Kelly Thomas
Kenney J. J.
Kerber W. L.
Kern Jacob J.
Keys John W.
Kiley D. T.
Kinsella F. D.
Kinsella J. E.
Kinsella J. J.
Knisely John
Lawless Dr. James
Leahy D.
Leahy James
Leonard P.
Ludden J. H.
Lydon H. C.
Lydon W. A.
Lynch C. P.
Madden M. B.
Madden M. F.
Maher Phillip
Mahoney James
Maloney M. T.
Manning Geo. W.
Martin E. H.
McAdams John
McArdle E. J.
McArdle P. L.
McBride GeorgeW.
McCarty Dr. C. H.
McCormick J. A.
McDermott M.
McDermott Wm.
McDonald J. W.
McElherne D. J.
McGoorty J. P.

McGrath J. P.
McGraw D. T.
McGuire W. A.
McKenna W. J.
McKernan J.
McMahon F. T.
McMahon J. P.
McManus J. B.
McMullen John H.
McMullen J. H.
McShane James
McVoy Eugene
McVoy John H.
Mealiff F. H.
MellenW. P.
Melody T. R.
Minehan R. M.
Mix Ira J.
Moore C. M.
Moore James
Moore James H.
Moran Hugh P.
Moran T. A.
Morrison Wm. M.
Mulcahy F. T.
Munhall W. D.
Murphy E. J.
Murphy F. T.
Murphy James S.
Murphy John E.
Murphy Jos. J.
Murphy M. W.
Naghten Frank
Neil W. F.
Nelson J. L.
Nelson N. J.
Nelson T. E.
Nelson W. P.
Nicholson J. J
Nolan T. J.
Noonan E. T.

Noonan P.
Nortman W. T.
O'Brien Frank
O'Brien John
O'Brien M. G.
O'Brien T. F.
O'Donnell F. A.
O'Donnell J. V.
O'Donnell J. S.
O'Malley John
O'Malley W. J.
O'Meara James E.
O'Neill Wm. E.
O'Reilly E. jr.
O'Rourke John
Ortmayer C. G.
Ortseifen Adam
Palmer C. M.
Perkins H. A.
Perrigo A. B.
Plamondon A. D.
Plant George D.
Plantz W. M.
Powell E. J.
Powers Harry J.
Pratt George L.
Prindiville J. K.
Quinlan D. B.
Quinlan W. A.
Reddy James M.
Reed W. S.
Reilly John J.
Rend Joseph P.
Rend W. P.
Rice P. H.
Roach Martin
Roughan M. J.
Rutherford James
Ryan P. J.
Sanders J. P.
Scales Frank

Schaar C. L.
Schaub W. L.
Shayne J. T.
Shea John E.
Simpson D. J.
Slattery Edward
Smith E. C.
Smith W. H.
Smyth Dr. J. P.
Solon D. A.
Strickland W. J.
Stringfield C. P.
Sullivan J.
Sullivan J. D.
Sunderland George
Tait John
Tait John G.
Thackeray W. O.
Thompson Jo T
Tomlinson Hhß.
Toolen A. J.
Trainor J. W.
Trayner C. J.
Trayner O. R.
Treacy Hugh T.
VonHerman E.
Wade Thomas P.
Walsh John R.
Walsh Richard
Walsh T. D.
Walsh W. C.
Ward James P.
Weadly J. L.
Welch Dr. P. H.
Whitney H. E.
Wilcox L. P.
Wild H. C.
Wright George A.
Wright G. K.
Young D. J.
Young Jas. T.

STANDARD CLUB.

CORNER TWENTY-FOURTH STREET AND MICHIGAN AVENUE.

OFFICERS.

MOSES BENSINGER,	President.
MILTON J. FOREMAN,	Vice-President.
A. GATZERT,	Treasurer.
G. M. HOLLSTEIN,	Financial Secretary.
ALFRED S. AUSTRIAN,	Recording Secretary.

TRUSTEES.

A. M. Snydacker
Leo Straus
Louis A. Kohn

J. H. Foreman
H. M. Rosenblatt
Simon Yondorff
M. R. Wineman

H. B. Gimbell
Norman Florsheim
Felix Kahn

MEMBERS.

Abt H. H.
Abt J. J.
Abt Sol L.
Adams Moses
Adler Dankmar

Adler Henry
Altman Michael
Appel Carl
Arnstein Eugene
Arnold Walter C.

Arnheim Benj.
Austrian A. S.
Austrian Joseph
Bach Emanuel
Ballenberg A. A.

Ballenberg Jules
Barth Alex.
Bauland Jacob H.
Bauland Joseph H.
Becker A. G.

Becker Louis
Beifeld Alexander
Beifeld Joseph
Beirsdorf A. J.
Benjamin Louis
Bensinger Moses
Bensinger Ben. E.
Berg Morris H.
Bernheimer I. S.
BettmanBoerneDr.
Block Samuel
Bloom Leopold
Bloom Isaac J.
Born Moses
Buxbaum Emanuel
Cahn Ben. R.
Cahn Bernard
Cahn Fred C.
Cahn Joseph
Cahn Sidney B.
Cahn Martin
Clayburgh M.
Cohen S. K.
Cohn J. H.
D'Ancona Abr.
D'Ancona Alf. E.
D'Ancona E. N.
Deimel Joseph
Deimel Rudolf
Dernburg Carl
Eckstein L. E.
Ederheimer Max
Eichberg Max
Einstein Morris
Einstein B. M.
Einstein Arthur
Eisendrath Jos. N.
Eisendrath L.
Eisendrath Sig. L.
Eisendrath Wm. N.
Eliel Levi A.
Elkan Henry
Elson Herman
Engel Bernard
Ettlinger Simon
Falk M. L.
Falkenau Louis
Fechheimer E. S.
Feibelman D. L.
Felsenthal Eli B.
Fischer S. M.
Fish Joseph
Flonacher H. C.
Florsheim August
Florsheim Felix
Florsheim MiltonS.
Florsheim Moses
Florsheim Norman
Florsheim Sidney
Florsheim Simon
Foreman Edw'd H.
Foreman Edwin G.
Foreman Frank
Foreman Gerhard
Foreman Henry G.
Foreman Isaac H.

Foreman Milton J.
Foreman Oscar G.
Foreman Rudolph
Foreman S. H.
Fox Leo.
Frank Daniel
Frank D. L.
Frank Louis
Frank Louis E.
Frank Joseph
Frank F d. G.
Frankenthal C. E.
Frankenthal E.
FrankenthalDrLE.
Freudenthal Jos.
Friedman Oscar J.
FriedmanMonroeJ.
FriedmanJosephN.
Friedman J.
Friend Ed.
Gatzert J. L.
Gatzert August
Gimbel M.
Gimbel Jacob W.
Gimbel Horace B.
Gimbel Charles A.
Glaser B. Z.
Glaser Victor L.
Glaser G. D.
Glaser Edward L.
Glick Lipman
Goldsmith Sam.
Gottlieb A.
Grabfield Jacob
Grabfield Max
Greenebaum M. E.
Greenebaum H. E.
Greenebaum James
Greenebaum Selig
Greensfelder Isaac
Greensfelder N.
Grossman Edw'dB.
Grossman George
Grossman Herman
Grossman Adolf
Guckenheimer Jos.
Guthman Sol.
Haas Charles
Hahn Harry W.'
Hahn H. F.
Hamburger Scl.
Hart A.
Hart Henry N.
Hart Harry
Hart Max
Hart M, R.
Hart Herbert L.
Hartman Leon
Heilprin L.
Heppner Henry
Herman Leon M.
Heyman E. S.
Hillman Edward
Hirsch Adolph
Hirsch E. G. Rev.
Hirsch Fred

Hirsch Ike
Hirsch L. K.
Hirsch Morris G.
Hirsh Jacob
Hirsh Solomon
Hirsh Manuel
Hirsh Sol. J.
Hirsh Harry J.
Hirsh Harry S.
Hirsh Dwight S.
Hirsh Morris G.
Hirsh Morris M.
Hoffman E.
Hollander Myer J.
Hollstein A. M.
Hollstein G. M.
Horner Albert
Horner Maurice L.
Horner Jos.
Horner Isaac
Horner Angell
Hyman Ed. S.
Israel Bern.
Joseph Sam. L.
Kaiser Sol.
Kahn Harry
Kahn Jacob
Kahn Felix
Kahn Mark
Kahn Henry
Kantrowitz G. A.
Katz Henry
Kaufman Wm. H.
Keefer Louis
Kirchberger S. H.
Kline Sam. J.
Kohn Simon A.
Kohn Simon H.
Kohn D. A.
Kohn Abraham H.
Kohn Edwin D.
Kohn H. A.
Kohn Albert W.
Kohn Alfred
Kohn E. J.
Kohn Harry D,
Kohn Isaac A.
Kohn Louis A.
Kohn Louis H.
Kohn A. D.
Kozminsky M.
Kraus Adolf
Kuh Julius S.
Kuh Abraham
KuppenheimerA.B
Kuppenheimer J.
Kuppenheimer B.
Kuppenheimer L.B
Lamm Abram
Lamm Joseph C.
Lamm Arthur G.
Landauer Herman
Lebolt M. H.
Lehman H.
Lehman Judah
Lehman L. B.

Lehman William
Leopold Alfred F.
Leopold Henry
Leopold H. F.
Leopold Maurice
Leopold S. F.
Leopold Chas. M.
Leopold Nathan F.
Leopold Henry jr.
Leopold Max
Leon Leonard M.
Levi Jacob
Levi Henry C.
Levie Jerome M.
Levy Ben S.
Levy Wm.
Lewald Frank
Lichtstern A. J.
Liebenstein Chas.
Lilienfeld Wm.
Lindauer Ben.
Lindauer M. E.
Lindauer Seligman
Lindheimer MaxL.
Loeb Adolph
Loeb Adolph
Loeb A. H.
Loeb Julius
Loeb Leo. A.
Loeb Sidney
Loeb Wm.
Loewenthal B.
Loewenthal J. W.
Long Lee
Long Sidney
Longini Abr.
Lowenbach Wm.L.
Lowenberg Isaac
Lowenstein Sidney
Lowenthal Berth'ld
Lyons Elias H.
Mandel E.
Mandel Frank E.
Mandel Frank S.
Mandel Fred L.
Mandel Leon
Mandel Robert
Mandel Simon
Manheimer W. S.
Marks H. M.
Marks Simon L.
Marx M.
Mayer Leopold
Mayer M. H.
Mayer Nathan
Mayer N. A.
Mayer Isaac H,
Mayer Bernard
Mergentheim B.
Mergentheim D.
Mergentheim A. D.
Meyer Isaac
Meyer Edwin F.
Miller Chas. L.
Miller I. H.
Miller Louis K.

Minchrod Simon	Rosenwald Julius	Siegel Joseph	Stumer Louis M.
Monheimer Levi	Rothschild A. M.	Siegel Sylvan	Sulzberger Sol. L.
Monheimer Isa	Rothschild Ben	SilbermanSigmund	Sutton Wm. H.
Morgenthau M.	Rothschild C. E.	Silverman Chas.	Swabacher Isa
Morris H. N.	Rothschild Eman-	Simon David S.	Uhlmann Fred
Morris Nelson	uel	Simon L.	Ullman Gus
Morris Edward	Rothschild Felix	Smith Samuel H.	Ullman Louis
Moses Adolph	Rothschild Fred	Snydacker Alf. M.	Ullman Nathan
Moss Moses F.	Rothschild I. D.	Snydacker . G.	Ullman Percy G
Nathan Herman	Rothschild Leo J.	Snydacker Jos. L.	Vogel Frank E.
Nathan Sam.	Rothschild M. L.	Sondheimer Em'l	Waixel David
Nathan Sidney S.	Rothschild S. M.	Spiegel Modie J.	Waixel M. S.
Nathan Adolph L.	Rothschild W. L.	Spiegel Sidney M.	Wampold Louis
Nessler S. C.	Rothschild W. S.	Spitz Samuel	Wampold Leo.
Neu Bernard	Rubel I. F.	Steele H. B.	Weil Jacob
Neuman Maier	Rubel Isidore	Steele Maurice B.	Weil Julius E.
Newman Jacob	Rubel Levi G.	Steele S. B.	Weil Morris
Nusbaum Aaron E	Rubel Chas. D.	Stein Louis	Weil Theodore
Oberfelder Max	Salomon Dr. G. S.	Stein Sydney	Wedeles EdwardL.
Oberfelder Tobias	Sax Charles	Stein D. A.	Wendell M.
Oppenheimer B.	Schaffner Charles	Steiniger Simon	Wertheimer B. J.
Opper Philip	Schaffner Joseph	Stern Aaron	Wertheimer A.
Pam Max	Schmaltz JosephH.	Stern D. S.	Willner L. J.
Pfaelzer Louis	Schmaltz Nathan J.	Stern Henry	Wineman M.
Prenzlauer Herman	Schnadig Jacob	Stern Herman	Wineman J. R.
Price Leopold	Schnadig JosephM.	Stern Louis	Wineman MiltonR.
Regensburg Sam.	Schoenbrum Sam'l	Stern Oscar M.	Wise Maurice
Rose Edward	Schoenbrun L.	Stern Sam	Witkowsky Conrad
Rosenbaum Joseph	Schoenman C. S.	Stettauer David	Witkowsky James
Rosenbaum Morris	Schwab Alfred C.	Stettheimer Jos. C.	Wolbach J. S.
Rosenberg Ben.	Schwab Chas. H.	Straus Leo.	Wolf A. H.
Rosenberg Oscar	Schwab Henry C.	Straus Aaron	Wolf Henry M.
Rosenberg Jacob	Schwabacher H. H.	Straus F. W.	Wolf L. J.
Rosenberg Julius	Schwabacher Julius	Straus Eli M.	Wolf Aaron
Rosenblatt H. M.	Schwabacher M.	Straus Simon W.	Wolff Isaac
Rosenblatt Aaron	Selz J. Harry	Strauss Albert L.	Woolf Benjamin
Rosenfield Maurice	Selz E. F.	Strauss Henry	Woolf Isaac
Rosenfield Isaac	Selz M.	Strauss Milton A.	Wormser Louis
Rosenfeld Maurice	Shoninger Jos.	Strauss Milton L.	Wormser David
Rosenfield Louis	Siegel Ferdinand	Strauss Jacob N.	Yondorf Chas.
RosenfieldMorrisS.	Siegel Henry	Strauss Leopold	Yondorf S.
Rosenthal Oscar			
Rosenwald M. S.			

THE TWENTIETH CENTURY CLUB.

OFFICERS.

GEORGE E. ADAMS, - - - - - President.
L. C. COLLINS, JR., } - - Vice-Presidents.
MRS. FERNANDO JONES, }
WILLIAM MORTON PAYNE, - Secretary and Treasurer.
1601 Prairie Avenue.

GENERAL COMMITTEE.

Elwyn A. Barron	William R. Harper	Mrs. O. H. Matz
Hugh T. Birch	William Morton Payne	Mrs. Fernando Jones
Charles W. Brega	James W. Scott	Mrs. C. L. Raymond
Mrs. Fredk. W. Becker	A. A. Sprague	Mrs. N. B. Ream
George E. Adams	Mrs. L. L. Coburn	Mrs. G. M. Pullman
L. C. Collins jr.	Mrs. J. J. Glessner	Mrs. H. O. Stone
Charles D. Hamill	Mrs. John Wilkinson	Mrs. H. M. Wilmarth
LeGrand Burton	Martin Ryerson	Mrs. Harriet C. Brainard

MEMBERS.

* after a name signifies Mr. & Mrs.

AdamsCyrus H. *
Adams George E. *
Alexander Stuart R. *
Allen Charles L. *
Andrews Sidney F. *
Baldwin Miss Annie
Barron Elwyn A. *
Bartlett A. C.
Becker Frederick W. *
Birch Hugh T.
Blair Chauncey J. *
Blakeway Mrs. Charles
Block Louis J.
Bodman Luther W. *
Brainard Mrs. Harriet C
Brega Charles W. *
Bross Mason
Brush Emerson H. *
Burton LeGrand *
Carlisle Chas. A. *
CarmichaelMrs.George·S.
Carolan Mrs. Frank J.
Carpenter George B. *
Case Mrs. Emma W.
Chatfield-Taylor H. C. *
Clark Clinton C.
Coburn Lewis L. *
Collins Judge L. C. jr. *
Cooley Harlan W. *
Coolidge FrederickS.Mrs.
Coonley Mrs. John C.
Dent Thomas *
Dewey Albert B. *
Dunham M. V. Miss
Ellis Mrs. A. M. H.
Enders Miss Margaret
Fargo Miss Florence B.
Fargo Livingston W.
Field Marshall
Fiske Dr. Geo. F. *
Fitch Henry S. *
Fitch Miss Julia
Fitch Winchester
Fullerton Charles W.
Galt Mrs. A. T.
Gane Thomas F. *
Gilmore Thomas W.
Glessner J. J. *
Goodman James B.
Gookin F. W.
Green Augustus W. *

Grey Miss Jessie
Griggs Miss Carolyn A.
Gross S. E. *
Hamill Charles D. *
Harper Pres. Wm. R. *
Hawes Judge Kirk *
Heard Dwight B. *
Herrick Miss Louise
Hervey James F. *
Higinbotham H. N. *
Hitchcock Mrs. Chas.
Honoré Adrian C.
Hoyne Mrs. Frank G.
Hutchinson Charles L. *
Hutchinson Dr. Mahlon *
Hutchinson Miss Florence
Izard Edward M.
Jackson Mrs. A. Reeves
Jones Fernando *
Jones Grahame
Judah Noble D. *
Keep Chauncey*
Keep W. B.
Keith Elbridge G. *
Kent William *
Ketcham Frank D. *
Ketcham John Berdan *
Kirk Wallace F. *
Kirkland Miss E. S.
Kohlsaat H. H. *
Lancaster E. A. *
Larned Miss Emily B.
Larned Francis M.
Lawrence Edward F. *
Leighton George W.
Lunt Miss N. G.
MacVeagh Franklin *
Manierre William R. *
Manners Robert R.
Mason A. A. *
Matthiessen E. A.
Matz Mrs. O. H.
McKay James R. *
McKindley Mrs. James
McKinlock Dr. John *
Medill Mrs. S. J.
Miller James A.
Mitchell Dr. Clifford *
Mitchell L. B. *
Moore Wm. H. *
Nixon Mrs. W. K.

Norton J. Henry *
Otis George L. *
Paige Alonzo W.
Palmer Potter Mrs.
Parker Augustus A. *
Payne William Morton
Peck Clarence I. *
Peck Ferd. W. *
Pierce Dr. Norval H.
Pincoffs Maurice *
Pincoffs P. A.
Pullman Miss Florence
Pullman George M. *
Raymond Charles F. *
Ream Norman B. *
Reed Earl H. *
Rodman Thomas J.
Root Miss Frances A.
Ross Miss Bessie G.
Ross Mrs. Joseph P.
Runnels John S. *
Ryerson Martin A. *
Scott James W. *
Seeberger Charles *
Sellers Alfred H. *
Sellers Frank
Sherman E. B. *
Smith Byron L. *
Smith Dr. Julia Holmes
Sprague Albert A. *
Sprague Miss C. A.
Sprague O. S. A. *
Steele Julius *
Stevenson Dr. Sarah H.
Stone H. B. *
Stone Mrs. H. O.
Switzer Edward M. *
Tuttle F. B.
Van Inwagen James *
Vilas Dr. C. H.
Walker H. H.
Walker Jam H. *
Walker W. Ss*
Watson Mrs. Lewis H.
Wheeler Arthur
Wilkinson John *
Wilmarth Miss Anna
Wilmarth Mrs. H. M.
Winterbotham Miller
Wolfsohn Carl

UNION CLUB.

WASHINGTON PLACE AND DEARBORN AVENUE.

OFFICERS.

GEORGE S. WILLITS, - - - - - -	President.
JOSEPH R. WILKINS, - - - - -	Vice-President.
HENRY F. BILLINGS, - - - - -	Treasurer.
STUYVESANT LEROY JR. - - - -	Secretary.

DIRECTORS.

George M. Pynchon	Charles P. Yoe	Fred W. Crosby
Augustus Jacobson	C. P. Willard	Chester M. Dawes
Robert W. Hunt ·	Thomas C. Hammond	LeGrand Burton

MEMBERS.

Adams Abbott L.	Cochran J. Lewis	Goodrich C. W.	Kirk James A.
Adams Cyrus H.	Coleman J. G.	Goodwin Newton	Kirk W. F.
Adams Edward S.	Comstock W. H.	Gott John R.	Kitchen J. B.
Adams George E.	Conover Chas. H.	Gormully R. Philip	Koch Edw.
Adams John R.	CookeAlex'nderW.	Goudy W. J.	Laflin A. K.
Adams Joseph	Cotton J. W.	Gray John	Lamb B. B.
Adams J. McGregor	Corwith C. R.	Gregory Stephen S.	Lamport F. W.
Aldis Owen F.	Cramer E. W.	Gross Sam'l E.	Lathrop B.
Alston John	Cramer Frank	Hale G. W.	Lathrop Jos.
Armour A. V.	Crawford R. C.	Hammill Caleb W.	Lawrence E. F.
Armour Geo. A.	Crerar John	Hammond T. C.	Lawson V.F.
Atwood Charles B.	Crosby Fred W.	Handy Moses P.	Leake J. B.
Barbour Edward ·	Culver F. H.	Hannah W. H.	Leiter Joseph
Barron Gregor	Cummings C. R.	Hardy Cyrus A.	Leiter Levi Z.
Beach E. Kellogg	Davis James A.	Harrison W. P.	LeRoy S.
Beale William G.	Dawes Chester M.	Hartwell E. S.	Lightner M. C.
Beall William Dent	Deane Chas. E.	Havermeyer Henry	Lincoln J. L.
Belford A.	Deane R.	Hawkes W. J.	Lincoln R. T.
Bevier Dubois	Deering James E.	Hempstead G. C.	Littlefield A. S.
Billings H. F.	DeKoven John	Henrotin A.	Loomis J. Mason
Bishop Henry W.	Dick Albert B.	Henrotin Chas.	Louderback D. H.
Bishop H. R. jr.	Dickey Ernst M.	Henrotin F.	Lowe J. W.
Black J. C.	Dole James H.	Hettler H. H.	Lynch J. D.
Blair F. M.	Dox Hamilton B.	Heisen C. C.	Lynch J. A.
Blair Watson F.	Drake T. D.	Higgins Chas.	MacArthur R. D.
Blythe J. H.	Dunlap G. L.	Hooper Henry	Macdonald Charles
Booth W. Vernon	Eames F. S.	Hosmer E. D.	A.
Borden William	Eddy A. N.	Hosmer R. W.	MacDonaldCharles
Boynton Wm. E.	Edward Thos. C.	Howard H. A.	B.
Brainerd Edwin	Ely Arthur C.	Howard W. B.	MacKay Alex.
Brewster E. L.	Emmet R. S.	Howland W. I.	MacVeagh F.
Brooks James C.	English G. P.	Hubbard S. H.	Manierre W. R.
Brown Charles A.	Ernst Leo	Hunt Clyde deV.	Marble A. J.
Browning G. W.	Evans Ellicott	Hunt Jarvis	Marsh H. W.
Bryan C. Page	Evans James Carey	Hunt Robert W.	Mason H. B.
Burley Aug. H.	Farnsworth Geo.	Hurlbut Horace E.	Mason J. A. C.
Burley Clarence A.	Farwell A. L.	Hutchins E. R.	Matthieson E. A.
Burry Geo.	Farwell Walter	Hutchinson M.	May Horatio N.
Burry Wm.	Fenner W. H.	Isham E. S.	McClurg Alex. C.
Burton LeGrand	Ferguson E. A.	Isham G. S.	McCormick C.H.
Burrows D. W.	Ferry Chas. H.	Isham H. P.	McCormick W. G.
Bullen A. F.	Ferry James W.	Isham Pierrepont	McCrea W. S.
Cable Ransom R.	Fessenden Chas.N.	Izard E. M.	McKay Henry
Cameron Daniel R.	Field Marshall	Jacobson Aug.	McKay James R.
Campbell Benj. H.	Fisher Archibald J.	Jewett John N.	McKnight C. H.
Campbell Wm. N.	Fishburn E. H.	Johnson Burton	McLaughlin G. D.
Carrington W. T.	Fiske Redington	Johnson W. H.	Mead Wilson L.
Carter Leslie	Flower James M.	Johnston C. P.	Merryweather Geo.
Cavaroc Chas. jr.	Forsyth Robt.	Jones S. J.	Middleton Merle
Chamberlain C. C.	Foster Henry A.	Kasson C. V.	Millard S. M.
Chapin E. F.	Fuller Geo. A.	Keen George	Miller A. P.
Chatfield – Taylor	Fuller P. S.	Keep F. A.	Miller Maynard
H. C.	Fullerton Chas. W.	Keep W. F.	Miller Truman W.
Cheney L. P.	FurthmanEdmund	Kenly D. F.	Mitting E. K.
Chesbrough E.S.jr.	Gage Lyman J.	Kerfoot S. H. jr.	Mix James T.
Christoph E. G.	Garrett T. M.	King Henry W.	Moore Gurdon G.
Cobb H. Ives	Gibbs J. S.	King J. C.	Morrison Geo. S.
Cobb Walter F.	Gilbert A. M.	King Rockwell	Morton Oliver T.
Coburn Lewis L.	Goodrich Albert W.	Kirk C. S.	

Munger Albert A.
Munro Wm.
Nickerson Sam'lM.
Nickerson R. C.
Norton Edmund
Norton James S.
Norton J. Henry
Noyes J. T.
Odell James W.
Odell J. J. P.
Odell W. R.
Onderdonk Andrew
Osborne Chas. M.
Paige Alonzo W.
Parker James H.
Parmlee John W.
Parsons J. B.
Patterson R. W. jr.
Pavy M. E.
Peabody Francis B.
Peck George R.
Pierce N. H.
Pond Alex. W.
Poor J. Harper
Pope Charles
Porter Henry H.
Porter Wm. D.
Prentice Sartell
Preston EverettB.
Probst Arthur O.
Pullman George M.
Pynchon G. M.
Quan Henry W.
Quan James E.
Quincy C. F.

Ray F. H.
Raymond Sam'l B.
Rathborne W. W.
Reed S. A.
Rhea Foster A.
Richardson A. P.
Robbins Henry S.
Robertson Alexander
Robinson H. P.
Rogers E. K.
Rozet George H.
Rumsey G. D.
Runnells J. S.
Russell Edward P.
Russell Edgar F.
Ryerson Edward L.
Salisbury W. M.
Schmitt Frank P.
Scott E. N.
Scott J. W.
Selfridge H. G.
Sellers Morris
Sharpe E. F.
Sharpe J. S.
Sheldon Henry I.
Sherman Chas. M.
Sherman Fred'k S.
Sherman H. B.
Smith Douglass
Smith Ernest F.
Smith Frederick B.
Smith George W.
Smith LeGrand
Smith Orson

Smith Dunlap
Sprague Wm.
Spoor J. A.
Springer James D.
Stanley F. W.
Stanley PhileskyE.
Stevenson C. A.
Stevenson F. B.
Stewart Graeme
Stockton Richard
Stone Henry B.
Street Chas. A.
Strobel Chas. L.
Swift Fred'k
Switzer E. M.
Taylor Geo. H.
Thomasson Nelson
Thurber George L.
Tooker R. N.
Torrence J. T.
Tree Lambert
Tuttle E. B.
Tully A. Melville
Ullrich M.
Vilas Chas. H.
Vincent W. A.
Wacker C. H.
Wakem J. Wallace
Walker Aldace F.
Walker Chas. M.
Walker H. H.
Walker James H.
Walker Wirt D.
Waller James L.

Waller R. A.
Walsh James
Ward Geo. R. T.
Warren Paul
Washburn Hempstead
Wassall Jos. W.
Watkins Elias M.
Watriss F. H.
Watson John G.
Webber Chas. M.
Webster Lewis D.
Wheeler Frank S.
Wheeler G. Henry
Wheeler Sam'l H.
Wicker Henry C.
Wickersham H. B
Wilkins Jos. R.
Wilkinson D. P.
Willard Chas. P.
Williams S. L.
Willing Henry J.
Willits Geo. S.
Wilmerding C. H.
Wilson Benj. M.
Winston Fredk. S.
Winston F. H.
Winston Dudley
Winston B. M.
Woodbridge J. E.
Worthington Ed.S
Yale J. L.
Yoe Chas. C.
Young George W.

UNION LEAGUE CLUB.

CORNER JACKSON STREET AND CUSTOM HOUSE PLACE.

OFFICERS.

JOHN P. WILSON,	President.
CHRISTIAN C. KOHLSAAT,	First Vice-President.
JAMES H. MOORE,	Second Vice-President.
WALTER H. WILSON,	Secretary.
EDWARD B. LATHROP	Treasurer.
ALBERT E. GLENNIE,	Superintendent.
W. A. ROOT,	Asst. Treasurer.
E. E. NOYES,	Asst. Secretary.

DIRECTORS.

Edwin F. Bagley
Warren G. Purdy
R. G. Chandler

William A. Bond
Harry G. Selfridge
John Barton Payne

William E. Kelley
Alex. H. Revell
Henry E. Weaver

MEMBERS.

Ackert C. H.
Ackhoff H. W.
Adams A. Egerton
Adams Cyrus H.
Adams Edward S.
Adams George E.
Adams J. McG.

Adler Dankmar
Affeld Chas. E.
Aldis Owen F.
Aldrich Chas. H.
Aldrich J. Frank
Alexander Wm. A.
Allen Benjamin

Allen Charles L.
Allen E. L.
Allen W. D.
Allerton S. W.
Alling John
Alsep William H.
Ames Franklin

Anderson James C.
Andrews W. H.
Angell Wm. A.
Angus John
Ansley Robert
Anthony Elliott
Archer J. L.

Armour Philip D.
Armstrong F. H.
Arnold Fred'k A.
Avery Daniel J.
Ayer E. E.
Babcock Cortlandt
Babcock Fred R.
Bacheldor E. A.
Bacon Henry M.
Badenock J. J.
Bagley FrederickP.
Bailey Edward P.
Baird Lyman
Baird Wyllys W.
Baker Frank H.
Baker Samuel
Baldwin Jesse A.
Baldwin Willis M.
Ballard Frank E.
Ballard Thomas P.
Bancroft Edgar A.
Bane Levi B.
Bane Oscar F.
Banning Epbraim
Banning Thos. A.
Barker James
Barnes Albert R.
Barnes David L.
Barnhart A. M.
Barnum Wm. H.
Barnum Wm. L.
Barrett Elmer E.
Barrett Marcus L.
Barrett Samuel E.
Bartlett Alvin C.
Bartlett William H.
Barton E. M.
Barton George P.
Bass George
Bates Lindon W.
Bayley Edwin F.
Beach M. H.
Beale William G.
Beardsley C. B.
Beaunisne AlbertG.
Beidler Francis
Belden John S.
Bell J. H.
Beman S. S.
Benham John
Bennett Frank I.
Bensley John R.
Bentley Wilber G.
Besly Chas. H.
Bettman Boerne
Bigelow E. A.
Billings C. K. G.
Bingham Arthur E.
Bird A. C.
Birkhoff George jr.
Bissell George F.
Blackman C. H.
Blackstone T. B.
Blackwelder I. S.
Blair Chauncey J.
Blair Henry A.

Blair William
Blakely C. H.
Blatchford E. W.
Blatchford N. H.
Bleyer C. E.
Bliss Chas. L.
Bliss George H.
Bliven Charles E.
Block Willard T.
Blossom Geo. W.
Blount F. M.
Bode Fred.
Bodman Luther W.
Bogert W. B.
Bond Lester L
Bond Wm. A.
Boorn W. C.
Borden Hamilton
Borden James U.
Botsford Henry
Boutell Henry S.
Bouton C. B.
Boyce W. D.
Boyden Geo. D.
Boyesen I. K.
Bradley A. O.
Bradley Carl D.
Bradley F. B.
Bradley J. Harley
Bradley John H.
Bradley P. B. jr.
Bradwell Jas. B.
Brainerd Ed. R.
Bridge Reuel W.
Brooks J. W.
Brophy TrumanW.
Brower A. T. H.
Brown Chas. A.
Brown C. S.
Brown Geo. F.
Brown M. O.
Brown Sanger M.D.
Brown Spencer A.
Brownell R. E.
Brucker Joseph
Brush Emerson H.
Bryan Thos. B.
Bryant H. W.
Bryant John J.
Buck F. M.
Buckingham C.
Buckingham E.
Buell A. C.
Buell Ira W.
Bullock Geo. S.
Bullock Milan C.
Burchard M. N.
Burhans Jas. A.
Burkhardt H. S.
Burley Clarence A.
Burley Frank E.
Burnham D. H.
Burrows W. F.
Butler E. B.
Butler E. K.
Butler J. W.

Butters Daniel
Cable Herman D.
Cable R. R.
Cahn Bernard
Cairnduff W. H.
Callahan A. P.
Cameron D. F.
Camp A. B.
Camp Isaac N.
Campbell Robt. B.
Campbell Wm. J.
Carpenter Geo. B.
Carr H. H.
Cary Eugene
Cary W. P.
Case Chas. H.
Case E. B.
Chadwick Wm. H.
Chalmers Thos. jr.
Chalmers Wm. J.
Chamberlin Dr. G.
M.
Chamberlin G. W.
Chandler Frank R.
Chandler PeytonR.
Chandler R. G.
Chandler W. T.
Chappell C. H.
Chard Thos. S.
Charnley James
Cheney ClarenceC.
Chumasero J. T.
Clark F. W.
Clark Geo. M.
Clark John M.
Clark Jonathan
Clark Will H.
Clement Henry C.
Cleveland Chas B.
Cloud John W.
Clowry Robert C.
Coburn Lewis. L.
Coe Albert L.
Coffin Charles H.
Cole Geo. E.
Cole William O.
Collier Clinton
Collins Joseph B.
Collins L. C. jr.
Colvin W. H.
Colvin W. H. jr.
Cone Albert G.
Congdon Chas. B.
Conkey W. B.
Conover Charles H.
Conway E. S.
Cook George D.
Cook Wm. H.
Cooke Edward D.
Coolidge Walter G.
Coombs Hiram
Cooper John S.
Cooper Wm. D.
Corbin C. R.
Corneau D. E.
Cortright L. D.

Cost E. F.
Coulter John M.
Cox Charles D.
Cox R. W.
Cragin Edward F.
Crandall L. E.
Crane H. P.
Crane Richard T.
Crane Simeon H.
Craver Charles F.
Crawford Andrew
Crilly Daniel F.
Critchell Robert S.
Cronkrite B. F.
Cross Clarence L.
Crowell H. P.
Cruttenden T. S.
Cudahy Michael
Culver Belden F.
Cummings E. A.
Cummins B. F.
Cunningham T. S.
Cunningham W.H.
Curry J. O.
Curtiss Chas. C.
Cushing E. T.
Cushing F. W.
Custer J. R.
Dainty Albert H.
Dale J. T.
Dana Charles D.
Daniels E. F.
Dauchy Geo. K.
Davidson John A.
Davies B. M.
Davies C. F.
Davis Chester B.
Davis Geo. R.
Davis John
Davis Lewis H.
Davis William J.
Dayton M. E.
Dean A. F.
Defrees Joseph H.
De Golyer Nelson
Dent Charles W.
DeMuth B. F.
Dering C. L.
deRoode Holger
Devore John A.
Dewey Albert B.
Dewey David B.
DeWolf Wallace L.
DeYoung Benj. R.
Dickason L. T.
Dickerson J. S.
Dickey Ernest M.
Dickinson Albert
Dickinson John W.
Dickson H. M.
Dixon Arthur
Dixon Geo. Wm.
Dixon Thos. J.
Doane J. W.
Dodge Edmond F.

Donald F. C.
Donnell James W.
Donnelley R. H.
Donnelley R. R.
Dorrance Chas. J.
Doud Levi B.
Douglas F. L.
Douglass Wm. A.
Downey Joseph
Downs J. Edward
Drake John B.
Drew Chas. W.
Dreyer E. S.
Driscoll M. F.
Dudley W. W.
Dummer Wm. F.
Dunham J. S.
Dunham R. W.
Dunn F. K.
Dunn William
Dupee Chas. A.
Durand C.
Duval R. L.
Dwight John H.
Eames John H.
Earling A. J.
Eastman Sidney C.
Eaton William H.
Eckhart BernardA.
Eddy H. C.
Edwards J. A.
Elliott John G.
Ellsworth Jas. W.
Engelhard Geo. P.
Enger Geo.
Etheridge Jas. H.
Ettinger Chas. D.
Eustis Truman W.
Evans Clinton B.
Everingham L.
Ewart W . D.
Ewen John M.
Fairbank N. K.
Falkenau Victor
Fargo Chas. E.
Fargo Edward A.
Fargo Frank M.
Farr Albert G.
Farr Marvin A.
Farson John
Farson Robert B.
Farwell Chas. B.
Farwell J. A.
Farwell John V.
Fauntleroy T. S.
Fay R. M.
Felsenthal Eli B.
Ferguson Chas. H.
Ferguson Elbert C.
Ferry Chas H.
Fessenden Benj. A.
Field Eugene
Field John S.
Field Marshall
Fishburn Randolph
E.

Fisher Geo. M.
Fisher L. G.
Fisher Reynolds
Fiske Dr. GeorgeF.
Fitz Simons Chas.
Fleming John C.
Flinn Wm. W.
Flower James M.
Follansbee Chas E.
Follansbee Geo. A.
Foote Erastus
Foreman Henry G.
Foreman Oscar G.
Forgan James B.
Foster George A.
Foster Sam'l B.
Foster V. W.
Fowler E. M.
Fraser Norman D.
French W. M. R.
Frost Chas. S.
Frost Wm. E.
Fuller Charles H.
Fuller George A.
Fuller G. Edward
Fuller Henry C.
Fuller Wm. A.
Fulton J. I..
FunkhouserM.L.C.
Furbeck W. F.
Garnett Gwynn
Gartside J. M.
Gartz A. F.
Gary Elbert H.
Gelert Johannes
Gerow Floyd P.
Getchell Edwin F.
Getty Henry H.
Gilbert C. B.
Gilbert James H.
Giles Wm. A.
Gillette E. W. ·
Gilman E. R.
Gilman Stephen W.
Glessner John J.
Glidden H. H.
Gobel E. F.
Goddard L. O.
Goodman Wm. O.
GoodwinWarren F.
Gordon Charles U.
Gormully R. P.
Gould Chas. H.
Gould John
Grace Wm.
Grannis Amos
Graves A. M.
Gray Elisha
Gray W. H.
Green A. W.
Green E. H. R.
Green J. W.
Greenlee R. I..
Greenlee R. S.
Gregory Robert B.
Grey Chas. F.

Grey William L.
Griffin Thos. A.
Griffin Chas. F.
Griffiths John
Grinnell Julius S.
Griswold E. P
GunsaulusRev.FW
Gunther Chas. F.
Gurley Wm. W.
HackerNicholasW.
Hagar John M.
Halbach J. F. A.
Hale Geo. W.
Hale Wm. E.
Hall Augustus O.
Hall Frank G.
Hall James T.
Halle E. G.
Hambleton Earl L.
Hamill Ernest A.
Hamilton D. G.
Hamilton Percy C.
Hamlin John A.
Hamline John H.
Hammer D. Harry
Hammond W. A.
Handy Henry H.
Hanecy Elbridge
Hannah Wm. H.
Harbeck Eugene
Harding Abner C.
Harding Amos J.
Harding Geo. F.
Hare R. W.
Harkness E. J.
Harmon John K.
Harper Wm. H.
Harper Wm. R.
Harris Albert W.
Harris Elijah T.
Harris N. W.
Harvey Geo. V.
Harvey S. A.
Haskell Fred. T.
Hatch Azel F.
Hately John C.
Hately Walter
Haugan H. A.
Hauk Charles D.
Hawes Kirk
Hayden Albert
Hayt Henry C. ·
Head Franklin H.
Healy James E.
Healy P. J.
Heath Ernest W.
Hecht Frank A.
Heckman W.
Hedenberg J. W.
Heisen C. C.
Henderson C. M.
Henderson W. S.
Hendricks R. J.
Henion W. B.
Henkle William H.
Henry Robert L.

Hewett C. M.
Hewitt H. H.
Heywood P. P.
Heyworth Jas. O.
High Geo. Henry
Higinbotham H.D.
Higinbotham H.M.
Higinbotham H. N.
Hill Calvin H.
Hill D. K.
Hill Edgar A.
Hill James T.
Hill Lysander
Hillis David M.
Hills Chas. F.
Himrod Charles
Hinkley Watson S.
Hirsch EmilG.Rev.
Hitt John
Hobbs J. B.
Hodgkins J.
Hoffman Geo. W.
Holabird William
Holdom Jesse
Hole L. H.
Hollis H. L.
Holmes Ira
Holt Chas. S.
Holt Geo. H.
Hooker F. B.
Horne F. W.
Horton Horace E.
Horton Oliver H.
Hosmer Jos. W.
Howard J. H.
Howell C. D. B.
Hubbard Harry M.
Hubbard Wm. H.
Hubbell CharlesW.
Huck Louis C.
Hughes J. B.
Hughitt Marvin
Huiskamp H. J.
Hulburd Chas. H.
Hull Morton B.
Hunter W. W.
Hurd Harvey B.
Hutchins E. R.
Hutchins Jas. C.
Hutchinson C. L.
Hyman Robt. W.jr.
Irwin C. D.
Jacobs Wm. V.
Jacobson Aug.
Janney James W.
Jefferson W. J.
Jeffery John B.
Jelke John F.
Jenkins George H.
Jenkins John E.
Jenkins Robt. E.
Jenkins T. R.
Jenney Wm. L. B.
Jerrems Wm. G.
Jocelyn F. C.
Johnson Ernest V.

Johnson J. M.
Jones George P.
Jones Otis
Jones J. S.
Jones William H.
Judd E. J.
Judson Wm. B.
Kane Thomas
Keeler Chas.Butler
Keep Chauncey
Keith Edson
Keith E. G.
Keith O. R.
Kelley David
Kelley Wm. E.
Kellogg Milo G.
Kelsey J. A.
Kendall Benj. W.
Kennedy David J.
Kent Sidney A.
Kent William
Kent William D.
Kerfoot W E. D.
Kerr Wm. R.
Ketcham W. P.
Keyes Rollin A.
Kimball Chas. F.
Kimball Geo. F.
Kimbark Chas. A.
Kimbark S. D.
Kimbell Spencer S.
King J A.
King Rockwell
Kirk John B.
Kirk M. W.
Knapp Homer P.
Knapp M. A.
Kneeland L. D.
Knickerbocker J. J.
Knight John B.
Knott Henry A.
Kohlsaat C. C.
Kohlsaat H. H.
Kreidler W. A.
Kultchar M. R.
Lacey Edward S.
Lackner Francis
Lake Richard C.
Landt Chas. C.
Lane C. E.
Lane Eben
Lasher Chas W.
Lathrop E. B.
Lavery Geo. L.
Lawrence E. F.
Lawson Victor F.
Lay A. Tracy
Lay Chas. C.
Leach Thomas A.
Leake Joseph B.
Lefens Thies J.
Leffingwell F. P.
Leigh E. B.
Leiter Levi Z.
Leonard Charles E.
Letton T. W.

Lewis David R.
Libby C. P.
Lindblom Robt.
Lindgren John R.
Linn Wm. R.
Listman Chas. F.
Littlefield A. S.
Littlejohn W. J.
Lobdell C. W.
Lobdell E. L.
Lockett Oswald
Logan Frank G.
Lombard Isaac G.
Lombard Josiah L.
Long James H.
Longenecker C. S.
LongeneckerJoelM
Lord Geo. S.
Lord John B.
Louderbach D. H.
Lowden Frank O.
Lowry Butler
Lundie John
Lyman D. B.
Lyman Edson W.
Lynas Thomas R.
Lynch Richard W.
Lyon Richard S.
Lyon Thomas R.
Macdonald C. A.
MacMillan Hugh
Mallette J. P.
Manasse L.
Mann Henry N.
Mann James R.
Manning Wm. J.
Markley John A.
Marsh Chas. Allen
Marsh Wm. D.
Marshall Geo. E.
Marshall Dr.JohnS.
Marshall Thos. H.
Martin Horace H.
Martin J. E.
Mason Ira J.
Mason Roswell H.
Mather Alonzo C.
Mather Robert
Mathews Geo. W.
Matthiessen C. H.
Matthiessen E. A.
Maxwell Chas. E.
Maxwell Ed. E.
Mayer David
Mayer Isaac H.
Mayer Levy
Mayo E. A.
Mayo John B.
McBean LeRoy H.
McBirney Hugh
McClellan John J.
McConnell L. W.
McCord Alvin C.
McCormick A. J.
McCrea Willey S
McCullough H. R.

McDoel W. Henry
McDonald J. J.
McGrath John J.
McKay A. A.
McKay Geo. A.
McKindley James
McKinlock G. A.
McKinlock Wm.H.
McLaren John
McLeish Andrew
McLennan J. A.
McMullen J. C.
McNally Andrew
McVoy John A.
McWilliams J. G.
McWilliamsL.
Mead Aaron B.
Mecum C. H.
Medill Joseph
Mehring George
Merigold W. A.
Merwin G. S.
Metcalf H. C.
Meysenburg O. W.
Millard S. M.
Miller Chas. K.
Miller H. H. C.
Miller James A.
Miller John G.
Miller J S.
Miller Robert B.
Mills A. L.
Mitchell John J.
Mitchell Lewis B.
Mitchell W. B.
Modjeski Ralph
Moll Carl
Montgomery P. A.
Moore B. J.
Moore George H.
Moore Jas. Hobart
Moore James H.
Moore Nathan G.
Moore Silas M.
Moore Will H.
Moore Wm. H.
Morford T. T.
Morgan O. H.
Morganthau Max
Morrill C. E.
Morse Chas. H.
Morse Francis E.
Morse John F.
Moseback Wm.
Moss Wm.Lathrop
Moulton D. A.
Moulton Geo. M.
Mundie Wm. Bryce
Murphy J. B.
Myers Eugene B.
Nash William
Neely John C.
Nelson Walter C.
Newman Jacob
Nissen John P.
Nixon Wm. Penn

Nolan John H.
Northup Willet
Norton Edwin
Norton John L.
Norton O. W.
Noyes E. H.
Noyes LaVerne W.
Oakley W. C.
Offield Chas. K.
Olds Walter
Oliver John Milton
Oppenheim W. S.
Orr Arthur
Orr Frank B.
Ortmann Rudolph
Osborne E. F.
Osmun Daniel C.
Overman L. E.
Owen James R.
Packard EdwardA.
Packer Chas. P.
Paden Joseph E.
Page S. S.
Page William R.
Palmer John W.
Palmer Percival B.
Palmer Percy W.
Parker F. W.
Parker H. A.
Parkhurst J. J.
Parkinson Robt.H.
Parmly Henry C.
Partridge N. A.
Pashley Alfred F.
Patrick H. E.
Patterson R. W. jr.
Patton Normand S.
Patton Robt. W.
Payne John Barton
Peacock Chas. D.
Pearson Eugene H.
Pearsons Henry A.
Peck Clarence I.
Peck Ferd. W.
Peck Oliver D.
Peck Walter L.
Pence Abram M.
Penny Arthur W.
Penny Chas. H.
Perce L. W.
Perry David P.
Perry Howard E.
Perry Isaac N.
Peterson Andrew
Peterson P. S.
Petterson Wm. A.
Pettet Freeman E.
Pettibone Asa G.
Pettibone P. F.
Phelps Elliott H.
Phelps Geo. B. jr.
Pickering P.
Pike Eugene S.
Pitkin E. H.
Poole Abram
Porter James W.

Porter Rogers
Post Charles N.
Potter Edward C.
Potter Edwin A.
Potter Orrin W.
Pratt N. D.
Preble Glenwood
Prentice Leon H.
Preston David A.
Preston Wm. D.
Price E. R.
Price Dr. V. C.
Primley J. P.
Prussing E. E.
Prussing Geo. C.
Pullman C. L.
Pullman Geo. M.
Purdy Warren G.
Purington D. V.
Rand Wm. H.
Ransome Ernest L
Raymond Chas. L.
Raymond James N.
Raymond Jas. H.
Ream Norman B.
Redington W. H.
Remy Curtis H.
Rend William P.
Revell Alex. H.
Revell John T.
Rew Henry C.
Rice F. Willis
Rice Theodore F.
Rich Henry S.
Richardson G. P.
Richardson R. J.
Rickards W. T.
Rickcords Geo. E.
Riddle Francis A.
Robinson J. K.
Roche John A.
Rockwood FrankB.
Rogan John B.
Rogers Bernard F.
RogersHenryWade
Rogers R. M. jr.
Rogers Sam'l S.
Roloson R. W.
Rosenthal Julius
Rowe James L.
Roys Cyrus D.
Rubens Harry
Ruggles O. W.
Rumsey Israel P.
Rumsey J. F.
Runnells John S.
Russell E. A.
Rust Henry A.
Ryerson Martin A.
Sage Wm. M.
Samuel E. M.
Sanborn G. E.
Sargent Geo. M.
Sargent H. E.
Sargent Wm. Dun-
  ham

Savage H. G.
Schlesinger L.
Schmitt Anthony
Schneider Geo.
Schniglau C. R.
Schumacher B. W.
Schwab Chas. H.
Scott F. H.
Scott James W.
Scott Robert
Scoville Chas. B.
Scribner Chas. E.
Seaverns Geo. A.
Seaverns G. A. jr.
Sebastian John
Seckel Adolph
Seckel Albert
Seipp W. C.
Selfridge Harry G.
Selleck Wm. E.
Sellers A. H.
Selz Morris
Sercomb Albert L.
Shaffer J. C.
Shailer Robert A.
Shaver C. H.
Shaw Gilbert B.
Shayne J. T.
Shedd Chas. B.
Shedd Edward A.
Shedd John G.
Sheldon Geo. W.
Shepard J. H.
Shepherd E. S.
Sherman Elijah B.
Sherman James M.
Sherwood H. M.
Sickel John T.
Sickles Frank
Sidway LeveretteB.
SimmonsFrancisT.
Simonds Edwin
Simpson Joseph B.
Singer A. L.
Singer Edward T.
Singer Horace M.
Singer W. H.
Smith Abner
Smith Byron L.
Smith Calvin S.
Smith C. H.
Smith C. M.
Smith Frank J.
Smith Fred'k A.
Smith Frederick B.
Smith Geo. W.
Smith Granger
Smith H. D.
Smith H. S.
Smith J. P.
Smith Robert J.
Smith Shea
Smith Thos. H.
Smith Willard A.
Smith W. Sooy
Smith Wm. Treese

Smyth John M.
Soper Alex. C.
Soper Horace W.
Soper James P.
Spalding A. G.
Spalding Jesse
Spicer George A.
Spooner F. E.
Sprague O. S. A.
Sprague William
Springer Edw. B.
Springer J. D.
Stagg John L.
Stanton Wm. A.
Starbuck J. M.
Starr Merritt
Starrett Julius
Staver H. C.
Stearns John K.
Stearns R. I.
Stebbins L. C.
Steever J. G.
Stevens James W.
Stiles Geo. N.
Still E. A.
Stirling J. C.
St. John Everitte
Stobo Robt.
Stokes Chas. F.
Stone Frank B.
Stone Melville E.
Straight Hiram J.
Streeter A. R.
Streeter David L.
Strong Joseph H.
Stuart Robert
Studebaker P. E.
Sturges Solomon
Suesman A. L.
Sullivan A. W.
Sullivan Louis H.
Sunny B. E.
Sweet S. H.
Swift George B.
Swift Wm. H.
Taft O. B.
Taylor Abner
Templeton Thos.
Terry Franklin S.
Tewksbury G. W.
Thacher John M.
Thoman Leroy D.
Thomas A. A.
Thomas Benjamin
Thomas Herbert A.
Thomasson N.
Thompson R. S.
Thorn Frank
Thorne George R.
Tilt J. E.
Timmerman B.
Tobey Frank B.
Towle Henry S.
Towne W. H.
Treat Chas. P.
Treat Samuel A.

Trego Chas. T.
Tripp Chas. E.
Tripp Dwight K.
Trowbridge C. W.
Truax Charles
Trumbull John H.
Turner E. H.
Turner L. H.
Turner Wm. H.
Tuthill Richard S.
Ullmann Frederic
Underwood J. Platt
Underwood P. L.
Underwood Wm.T.
Upham Fred W.
Upton Geo. P.
Valentine E. H.
VanCleave J. R. B.
Vanderkloot A.
Vanderlip FrankA.
VanKirk Chas. B.
Van VlissingenJ.H.
Van Voorhis Frank
Van Woert G. E.
Vaux Frederick T.
Vierling Louis
Vierling Robert
Viles James jr.
Vocke Wm.
Wachsmuth L. C.
Wacker Charles H.
Wagner W. L.
Wait J. J.
Walker Edwin
Walker E. S.
Walker F. E.
Walker H. H.
Walker James R.
Walker J. H.
Walker Robt. P.
Wallace John F.
Wallach John F.
Waller E. C.
Waller Robt. A.
Wallin Thomas S.
Walsh John R.
Wampold Louis
Warner Geo. L.
Warren Charles D.
Warren Wm. S.
Washburn Wm. D.
Waterman Arba N.
Watkins Wm. W.
Watson Wm. J.
Watson Wm. jr.
Weare Portus B.
Weare William W.
Weary E. D.
Weaver Henry E.
Webster Thos. H.
Webster T. K.
Wegg D. S.
Weigley Frank S.
Weinsheimer A. S.
Weiss Geo. A.
Welling J. C.

Wells Frank
Wells Geo. S.
Wells R. M.
Wetherell O. D.
Wheeler Geo. A.
Wheeler H. A.
Whelpley R. T.
Whitacre C. C.
White Horace F.
Whitehead W. M.
Whittemore C. L.
Wilbur J. B.
Wilcox Geo. G.
Wilcox J. Fred

Wilkinson Harry
Wilkinson John
Willard George
Williams Ben.
Williams E. T.
Williams Geo. T.
Williams John A.
Williams Wm. P.
Willing Henry J.
Willits Ward W.
Wilson C. H.
Wilson E. Crane
Wilson Hugh R.
Wilson John P.

Wilson John R.
Wilson M. J.
Wilson Milton H.
Wilson Walter H.
Wilson W. M.
Winslow E. D.
Winslow FrancisA.
Winslow W. H.
Wiser Clinton B.
Witbeck John H.
Wolff J F.
WolseleyhilenryW.
Wood George E.

Wood Ira C.
Wood Wm. H.
Wood W. F.
Woodward Arthur H.
Worthy John
Wyman W. C.
Wyman W. D.
Yaggy L. W.
Yerkes C. T. jr.
Young Otto
Younglove I. S.
Zimmerman W.

UNIVERSITY CLUB.

118 DEARBORN STREET.

OFFICERS.

OWEN F. ALDIS, - - - - - - - President.
BRYAN LATHROP, - - - - - - Vice-President.
LAWRENCE WILLIAMS, - - - - - Secretary.
GRANGER FARWELL, - - - - - - Treasurer.

DIRECTORS.

T. B. Marston
H. S. Boutelle

C. P. Bryan
A. B. Newell
O. H. Waldo

H. C. French
G. S. Isham

MEMBERS.

Abbott Edward H.
Ackerman F. S.
Adams Edward S.
Adams George E.
Aldis Arthur T.
Aldis Owen F.
Aldrich Charles H.
Allen Charles L.
Alley Wm. H.
Allport W. H. Dr.
Alton William jr.
Andrews E. W.
Andrews J. H.
Anthony Elliott
Armour Allison V.
Armour George A.
Armour P. D. jr.
Augur Walter W.
Babcock Chas. S.
Bacon Edward R.
Bacon Henry M.
Bacon Roswell B.
Baird Max
Barber Joel Allen
Barnum A. W.
Bartlett Josiah C.
Bartlett Wm. H.
Bentley Cyrus
Bentley Fred'k J.
Bigelow Nelson P.
Billings Caddingt'n
Billings Frank

Bissell Richard M.
Blatchford E. W.
Blatchford Paul
Boddie John T.
Booth Wm. T.
Boutell Henry S.
Boutell Lewis H.
Bowers Lloyd W.
Boyce Leo S.
Boyle Clarence
Bradley David E.
Bradley Wm. H. jr.
Bross Mason
Brower Jule F.
Brown Edward O.
Brown Frank T.
Brown George W.
Browning G. W.
Bryan Chas. P.
Burley Clarence A.
Burnham DanielH.
Burry George
Burry William
Burton LeG. S.
Butler Hermon B.
Cady Jeremiah K.
Campbell Treat
Carpenter Benj.
Carpenter Geo. A.
Case William W.
Cass George W.
Caton Arthur J.

Chandler Samuel
Charnley C. M.
Charnley James
Chase Charles A.
Chumasero Ken-neth P.
Clark John M.
Cobb Henry I.
Cochran John L.
Coffin Charles P.
Cooley Harlan W.
Corwith Charles R.
Corwith J. W.
Cowles Alfred
Cramer Ambrose
Curtis Russell H.
Dauchy Samuel
Davis N. S. jr.
Deering James
Delano F. A.
deWindt H. A.
Dinwiddie J. H.
Doane John E.
Donelson D. P.
Douglas J. M. jr.
Douglass Frank M.
Dudley Emilius C.
Dunlevey Hulburd
Durand Scott S.
Durkee Heury R.
Dyche Wm. A.
Elliot Frank M.

Elting Victor
Etheridge Jas. H.
Evans Lynden
Ewen John M.
Fales David
Fargo L. W.
Farwell Arthur L.
Farwell F. C.
Farwell Granger
Farwell John V. jr.
Farwell Walter
Fay Charles N.
Ferry Charles H.
Field Marshall jr.
Fisher G. P. jr.
Fisher Walter L.
Fiske George F.
Flower Louis B.
Follansbee M. D.
ForsythHenryH.jr.
Forsyth Robert
Forsyth W. H.
Freeman Henry V.
French Charles B.
French Henry C.
French S. Tenney
Fuller Charles G.
Fuller P. S.
Fullerton Chas. W.
Furness Wm. E.
Fyffe Colin C. H.
Galloway Jas. B.

Gamble William C.
Gardiner Edwin J.
Gardner Henry A.
Gardner James P.
Giles Wm. F.
Gillette Edwin F.
Greely Louis M.
Green Adolphus W
Gridley Martin M.
Griffing Edward S
Hall Ford P.
Hall Thos. C.
Halsey Edward A.
Hamilton Wm. A.
Hamlin Frank
Hamlin Fred R.
Hamlin H. L.
Hamline John H.
Hapgood Norman
Harding Chas. F.
Harlan James S.
Harlan John M.
Harmon Charles S.
Harper William R.
Harris Graham H.
Harrison C. H. jr.
Hatch Azel F.
Head Franklin H.
Helmer Frank A.
Henderson Howard
Henderson W. F.
Herr Hiero B.
Herrick John J.
Hibbard Wm. G. jr.
High James L.
Higginson Geo. jr.
Holabird William
Holt C. S.
Honore Adrian C.
Honore Lockwood
Hosmer Edward D.
Hotz Robert S.
Houghteling J. L.
Howland Walter M.
Hubbard Chas. W.
Hubbard Wm. H.
Hubbard Joseph D.
Hull Morton D.
Hutchins E. R.
Hutchinson Geo. A.
Hutchinson M.
Hyde James N.
Isham George S.
Isham Ralph
Isham Ralph N.
Jackson H. W.
Jaggard W. W.
Jewett Samuel R.
Johnson Frank S.
Johnston John jr.
Jones David B.
Jones Thomas D.
Kales John D,
Kales William R.
Kasson Chas. V.

Keene Francis B.
Keep William B.
Keith Edson jr.
Keith Walter W.
Kendig Harry J.
Kent William
Ketcham F. DeH.
King Francis
Knott Henry A.
Kurtz Charles M.
Laflin Arthur K.
Laflin L. E.
Lamb Benj. B.
Lanehart John W.
Larned Francis M.
Larned Walter C.
Lathrop Barbour
Lathrop Bryan
Lawrence Chas. H.
Lederle George A.
Leiter Joseph
LeMoyne Louis V.
LeMoyne Wm. M.
Lewis Charles G.
Lewis David R.
Lincoln John L. jr.
Lord Frank E.
Lowrey Wm. K.
Lyman David B.
Lyman Francis O.
Lynde Samuel A.
MacVeagh F.
Magill Henry W.
Magruder H. L.
Manierre George
Marsh C. L.
Marsh Henry W.
Marston Thos. B.
Martin F. S.
Mashek V. F.
Mason Edward G.
Mason Henry B.
Mason Henry E.
Matz Herman L.
Matz Rudolph
McArthur Arthur F
McBirney H. J.
McCluer Wm. B.
McClurg Alex. C.
McClurg Walter L.
McConnell B. F.
McConnell S. P.
McCormick C. H.
McFadon William
McIlvaine Wm. B.
McLane James A.
McLaren Wm. A.
Meeker Geo. W.
Merrill Wm. F.
Mills Luther L,
Montgomery John R
Montgomery W. A.
Moore Nathan G.
Morse Clarence T.

Murphy John A. jr.
Musgrave H.
Nixon Miles G.
Nixon W. K.
Nixon Wm. W. K.
Noble Philip S.
Northcote A. S.
Norton James H.
Norton James S.
Oakley Horace S.
Osborn Chas. M. jr.
Osborn E. E.
Otis Chas. T.
Otis Ephraim A.
Otis J. E. jr.
Otis Philo Adams
Otis Wm. A.
Owsley Heaton
Paddock George L.
Page Wm. R.
Palmer E. C. jr.
Payson Geo. S.
Peabody F. B.
Peabody S. H.
Peet Henry J.
Penfield E. W.
Perkins A. T.
Pike Eugene R.
Pillsbury William F
Pond Irving Kane
Prentice Ezra P.
Prentice Sartell
Putnam Jos. R.
Raeder Henry
Rand Charles E.
Raynolds J. D.
Reynolds Wm. C.
Rice Frank Leon
Richter Paul K.
Ridlon John
Ritsher Edward C.
Rodman Thos. J.
Rogers Geo. M.
Rogers J. G.
Rogers Joseph M.
Rose Hiram H.
Ryerson Arthur
Ryerson E. L.
Ryerson John A.
Sargent J. R. W.
Sargent Wm. D.
Schuyler D. J.
Scott Frank H.
Scott Geo. A. H.
Scott James W.
Sears Nathaniel C.
Sellers Frank H.
Shankland E. C.
Shanklin Robt. F.
Sheldon Henry I.
Sheldon Theodore
Shepard Henry M.
Sheppard Robt. D.
Shorey Daniel L.

Shumway Philip R.
Sidley Wm. P.
Silsbee Joseph L.
Skinner John B
Smith Byron L.
Smith Delavan
Smith Dunlap
Smith Ed, Barritt
Smith LeGrand
Spalding Chas. W.
Sprague Albert A.
Sprague Fred'k W.
Starkweather R. E.
Stevens Harry S.
Strobel Charles L.
Strong Henry
Sturges Solomon
Sturgis Chas. I.
Taylor Thos. jr.
Thompson Leverett
Thompson Slason
Tilton John Neal
Todd John Jackson
Treat Charles P.
Trowbridge Geo. M.
Tuttle Emerson B.
Tuttle Henry N.
Tyson Russell
Waite H. G.
Waldo Otis H.
Walker J. R.
Walker Wirt D.
Waller Edward
Waller James B.
Waller James Lees
Waller Robert A.
Waller William
Warrington J. N.
Webster Hosea
Wells Chas. W.
Wentworth M. J.
Wertheimer Benj. J
Wheeler Arthur D.
Wheeler Chas. P.
Wheeler Sam'l H.
Whitman Russell
Whitney Geo. B.
Willard G. G.
Willard M. L.
Willard Norman P.
Williams Norman
Williams S. L.
Willits George S.
Wilson John P.
Wolf Albert H.
Wolf Henry M.
Wood Charles B.
Wood H.
Wood Kay
Wright Julian V.
Yoe L. G.
Young Frank O.
Young George W.
Young Kimball

30

WEST CHICAGO CLUB.

50 THROOP STREET.

OFFICERS.

HARRY KRAUS, - - - - - - - President.
DAVID STRAUS, - - - - - - - Vice-President.
WM. WILHARTZ, - - - - - - - Secretary.
JULIUS LOEWENTHAL, - - - - - Treasurer.

DIRECTORS.

David Straus,   Harry Kraus   Adolph Stein
Julius Loewenthal   M. Cornhauser   Philip Stein
William Wilhartz   Fred Oberndorf   Leo Gans
                     Jacob Schram.

MEMBERS.

Aarons Ed	Hefter Louis B.	Norden Meyer	Schuchat P.
Aarons Louis	Hennoch Sol	Oberndorf Fred	Shire A.
Aarons Max	Herzog Nathan	Oberndorf Jos.	Simon Henry
Abraham Nathan	Hirsch William	Oberndorf L.	Simon Sidney
Adler Sam H.	Jacobs Harry	Oberndorf Max F.	Sinsheimer Samuel
Bach Julius	Johnson W. Z.	Oberndorf M. L.	Sinsheimer Sol.
Bachman Sam	Kahn Harry	Olff Abe	Sommers Charles
Baer Sidney	Kahn Ludwig	Olff Lee	Son Sol.
Baumgartl Isidore	KahnweilerAlexan-	Oppenheimer B.	Sonnenberg Sam
Beck Arthur	der	Oppenheimer H.	Sonnenschein Leo-
Benjamin Alex	Kaiser Alex	OppenheimerLouis	pold
Berger Harry	Karpen Leopold	Oppenheimer Na-	Sonnenschein Otto
Biers Isaac	Karpen Will	than	Stein Adolph
Blau William	Katz B.	Pam Hugo	Stein Adolph
Bloom Sol	Klee A.	Pam Max	Stein Bernhard
Burgheim Gus	Klee Nathan	Pfaelzer David	Stein Chas.
Cohen Michael	Klee Simon	Pfaelzer Ely	Stein Ignatz
Cohn Sam	Klein Simon	Pfaelzer Louis	Stein Louis
Cornhauser M.	Klein Sol.	Plout A.	Stein Philip
Daube Abe	Kohn E.	Polachel Max	Stein Samuel
Daube L.	Kraus Harry	Pollak Anton	Stolz Jos. Rev.
DeLee Nat	Lange Charles	Rice J.	Stone Max
Dernburg Adolph	Lederer Isaac	Ringer Jacob	Straus David
Eichengreen Mayer	Lederer S. M.	Rosenbaum S.	Straus Ed E.
EichengreenMorris	Levy Harry	Rosenfeld Sidney	Straus Joe
Erstein L.	Levy Isidor	Rosenthal Alex.	Straus Maurice
Farber E. S.	Lewis Henry	Rothchild I.	Straus Sieg
Felsenthal B. Rev.	Lindheimer Jacob	Rothschild Al.	Strausser Frank
Fensenthal Julius	Litt Sam	Rothschild B.	Taussig William
Freudenthal Sam	Loeffler William	Rothschild E.	Unger M.
Fridkyn P. B.	Loewenthal B.	Rothschild M.	VanOsten Charles
Friend Alex	Loewenthal J.	Rubel Frank D.	Vehon M. H.
Gans Leo	Louis H. S.	Rubens Chas.	Vehon Simon
Gans Samuel	Mandl B.	Salomon A. D.	Vehon William
Goldsmith M. L.	Mandl Emanuel	Salomon Ben	Wedeles E.
Goldstine Harry	Mandl Joseph	Salomon L.	Wedeles Leo.
Goldstine Louis	Marcus Maurice	Salomon Moses	Weinfield E.
Grossman M.	May Albert	Schiller Arthur	Weisenbach C. A.
Gutwillig Ernest	Mayer David	Schimmelpfenig	Wilhartz S.
Haber M.	Meyer Meyer	Moses	Wilhartz Wm.
Haber Sol.	Mayer Toby	Schlesinger T.	Wolf A. S.
Hanauer Gus	Meyers A.	Schram Harry	Wolf Louis
Harris Samuel	Neufeld N.	Schram Jacob	Wollner Otto
Hart A. H.	New Aaron	Schram Lewis	Woolf Ben
Hart Harry H.	New E. L.	Schuchat H,	Woolf Harry
Harzfeld E.	Newberger Sol		

WEST END WOMAN'S CLUB.

542 WEST MONROE STREET,

OFFICERS.

SARRH M. CLARK, - - - - - - President.
ADELINE C. SHERWOOD, - - First Vice-President.
AGNES V. SHERWOOD, - - Second Vice-President.
FANNIE B. HAVEN, - - - Recording Secretary.
EVELYN A. FRAKE, - - - Corresponding Secretary.
ELLEN M. LOOMIS, - - - - - Treasurer.

DIRECTORS.

Ellen C. Broomell	Augusta R. FitzSimons	Helen M. Scott
Joan Chalmers	Ida B. Graham	Adeline B. Kane

MEMBERS.

Adcock Mrs. A. W.	Cobb Mrs. E. B.	Harris Mrs. M. H.
Aldrich Mrs. H. H.	Cobb Mrs. M. R.	Harsha Mrs. L. R.
Aldrich Mrs. W. H.	Cole Mrs. M. E.	Hart Mrs. J. P.
Alsip Mrs. Wm.	Collins Mrs. L. D.	Hartwell Mrs. A. V.
Ashley Mrs. A. L.	Collins Mrs. S. J.	Hartwell Mrs. F. G.
Auten Mrs. P. L.	Conger Mrs. J. S.	Haven Mrs. Jos.
Ayers Mrs. L. D.	Cook Mrs. Chas. E.	Hayes Mrs. Frank
Barbour Mrs. Lyman L.	Cornell Mrs. H. W.	Hayt Mrs. Henry C.
Barnhart Mrs. A. E.	Crane Mrs. Charles	Hewitt Mrs. A. O.
Beers Mrs. J. Hobart	Crane Mrs. Frank R.	Hedenberg Mrs. J. W.
Benham Mrs. Jas. W.	Cushing Mrs. W. T.	Higgins Mrs. G. W.
Benson Mrs. C. E.	Danforth Mrs. I. N.	Hill Mrs. Carrie A.
Bigelow Mrs. H. D. P.	Dashiell Mrs. V. W.	Holden Mrs. W. H.
Billings Mrs. C. K. G.	Davis Mrs. C. W.	Holmes Mrs. G. P.
Bingham Mrs. Jane M.	Davis Mrs. G. R.	Holmes Mrs. Oliver W.
Bingham Mrs. J. A.	Dennis Mrs. Fred J.	Hooker Mrs. H. M.
Birkhoff Mrs. George jr.	Dickinson Mrs. D. H.	Hotz Mrs. Christoph
Blackman Mrs. Chester	Dole Mrs. John N.	Howells Mrs. Cornelius
Blades Mrs. L. J.	Downs Mrs. J. E.	DuB.
Blodgett Mrs. Edw. A.	Dunn Mrs. Jno. O.	Hutchinson Mrs. G. C.
Bradshaw Mrs. J. H.	Dunton Miss Nellie	Ingals Mrs. E. F.
Brooks Miss Maria	Earle Mrs. C. W.	Ingals Miss Mary E.
Broomell Mrs. Geo.	Earle Mrs. Frank B.	James Mrs. Fred S.
Brower Mrs. D. R.	Eckhart Mrs. B. A.	Janney Mrs. J. W.
Brown Mrs. Sanger	Eddy Mrs. Azariah	Jordan Mrs. Cady
Bullock Mrs. M. C.	Elmes Mrs. C. W.	Jordan Mrs. Scott
Burdick Mrs. Oscar	Evans Mrs. W. W.	Kane Mrs. Geo. B.
Burkhardt Mrs. Alice S.	Farson Miss M. E.	Kane Mrs. Thomas
Burkhardt Mrs. H. S.	FitzSimons Mrs. Chas.	Keeler Mrs. J. B.
Burt Miss Mary E.	Flannery Mrs. D. F.	Kelsey Mrs. Horatio
Busbey Mrs. Wm. H.	Fordham Mrs. O. C.	Kendig Mrs. J. A. J.
Bushnell Mrs. L. M.	Foster Mrs. R. N.	Ketcham Mrs. J. P.
Camp Mrs. I. N.	Frake Mrs. Jas.	Ketcham Mrs. W. P.
Carpenter Mrs. Grant	Fulton Mrs. J. L.	Kilmore Mrs. J. W.
Carpenter Mrs. W. O.	Gardner Miss Jessie S.	King Mrs. A. H.
Chalmers Mrs. W. J.	Gates Mrs. P. W.	King Mrs. John A.
Chandler Mrs. H. H.	Gibson Miss Belle	King Mrs. Ulric
Chapman Mrs. J. M.	Golder Mrs. W. A.	Kohlsaat Mrs. C. C.
Chappell Mrs. C. H.	Graham Mrs. D. W.	Kohlsaat Mrs. Ernest W
Cheney Mrs. W. W.	Gray Mrs. Arthur	Krum Mrs. J. R.
Christy Mrs. H. A.	Greenlee Mrs. Ralph S.	Lamb Mrs. Chas.
Clark Mrs. A. B.	Greenlee Mrs. R. L.	Lamb Mrs. Frank
Clark Mrs. A. E.	Hall Mrs. Grace W.	Lansing Mrs. Mark S.
Clark Mrs. E. G.	Hall Mrs. J. Sherman	Lawrence Mrs. W. M.
Clark Mrs. Jas. L.	Hall Mrs. L. R.	Leonard Mrs. S. F.
Clement Mrs. Austin	Halsted Miss Nellie	Linington Mrs. C. M.

Little Mrs. F. B.
Loomis Mrs. M. B.
Lounsbury Mrs. J. A.
Lull Mrs. Richard
Lyon Mrs. R. S.
Martin Mrs. A. W.
Mathews Mrs. G. L.
Maxwell Mrs. Henry B.
Maxwell Mrs. Jas.
McClenthan Mrs. F. C.
McCrea Mrs. S. H.
McLaren Mrs. John
Meacham Mrs. F. D.
Mead Mrs. A. B.
Mergler Dr. Marie J.
Mills Mrs. J. P.
Mitchell Mrs. M. A.
Montgomery Mrs. W. S.
Morgan Mrs. G. C.
Moyer Mrs. W.
Mulfinger Mrs. J. Leonard
Munger Mrs. D. S.
Murphy Mrs. J. B.
Nevers Mrs. Edward
Newton Mrs. Robb C.
Nichols Mrs. G. R.
Parker Mrs. Thos. jr.
Pearson Mrs. E. H.
Pearson Mrs. J. H.
Peters Mrs. Joseph
Pettibone Mrs. P. F.
Pettibone Mrs. R. S.
Pinkerton Mrs. W. A.
Plamondon Mrs. C. A.
Polley Mrs. J. C.
Pond Mrs. Walter M.
Post Mrs. C. N.
Prentiss Mrs. L. M.
Price Mrs. O. J.
Price Mrs. W. H.
Pullman Mrs. W. C.

Randall Tabor P.
Rawleigh Mrs. Ja . T.
Reece Mrs. A. N.s
Rend Mrs. W. P.
Richolson Mrs. Benj. F.
Ripley Mrs. William
Rising Mrs. C. L.
Robison Mrs. Jno. A.
Roche Mrs. J. A.
Rockwood Mrs. G. H.
Rodiger Mis. Wm.
Rollings Mrs. Chas. E.
Ross Mrs. Geo.
Royce Mrs. E. A.
Ruggles Mrs. C. R.
Russ Mrs. Lewis -
Salisbury Mrs. Eugene F
Salisbury Mrs. W. H.
Sands Mrs. O.
Sayre Miss Virginia
Schuttler Mrs. Peter
Scott Mrs. H. M.
Scribner Mrs. S. A.
Sherwood Mrs. Geo.
Sherwood Mrs. Jno.
Sherwood Mrs. Marc
Shoemaker Mrs. Walter
Simonds Mrs. N. M.
Singer Mrs. Chas.
Skelton Mrs. J. W.
Slack Mrs. Charles
Sloan Mrs. G. S.
Small Mrs. L. A.
Smith Mrs. R. J.
Smith Mrs. Wm. Penn
Soper Mrs. J. P.
Sosman Mrs. Jos,
Spry Mrs. J. C.
Stehman Mrs. H. B.
Stevens Mrs. J. K.

Stevens Mrs. Plowdon
Stoddard Mrs. H. H.
Stone Mrs. A. J.
Talbot Mrs. J. F.
Talcott Mrs. Marshall
Tatham Mrs. Robt. L.
Taylor Mrs. Eleanor M.
Taylor Mrs. F. C.
Taylor Mrs. G. H.
Temple Mrs. Morris
Thatcher Mrs. A. T.
Thatcher Mrs.Solomon jr.
Thomas Mrs. H. W.
Thomas Mrs. John W.
Thompson   Dr.   Mary
   Harris
Tomblins Mrs. I.
True Miss Mary E.
Tuttle Mrs. W. P.
Tyrrell Mrs. F. S.
VanHook Mrs. Weller
Vaughn Mrs. J. C.
Wallace Mrs. T. D.
Walworth Mrs. C. M.
Warner Mrs. Chester
Waters Mrs. W. B.
Weeks Mrs. H. T.
Wells Mrs. Addison E.
Wells Mrs. T. B.
Wells Mrs. W. W.   .
West Mrs. E. A.
Wheeler Mrs. H. A.
Williams Miss Anna R.
Williams Mrs. Jno.
Williams Mrs. N. A.
Wilson Mrs. F. I.
Wilson Miss M. V.
Winchell Miss H. N.
Withrow Mrs. J. L.
Woodbury Mrs. W. H.

WOODLAWN MATINEE MUSICALE.

OFFICERS.

Mrs. W. A. Fowler, - - - - - - President.
Mrs. Thos. Hall, - - - - - Vice-President.
Mrs. Frank Compton, 6407 Sheridan av., Secy. and Treas.

EXECUTIVE COMMITTE.

Mrs. Julius Stern   Mrs. Arthur L. Chamberlain   Miss Grace Wilson

MEMBERS.

Atwood Mrs. Harry A.
Barrows Mrs. Dr. R. M.
Bell Miss Cora
Bell Miss Maude
Bogart Mrs. C. G.
Coulter Mrs. Edward
Chamberlain Mrs. A. L.
Compton Mrs. Frank
Compton Miss Grace F.
Crawford Mrs. Fred E.
Fowler Mrs. Wm. A.

Graham Mrs. David
Jones Mrs. M. M.
Haskell Mrs. W.
Hall Mrs. Thos.
Irvin Mrs. Hugh
Kendrick Mrs. Henrietta
Keenan Mrs. Walter F.
Kurtz Mrs. Melvin G.
McCandless Mrs. Dr.A.W
Mitchell Mrs. Chas.
Matteson Mrs. W. F.

Nicholas Mrs. Edmund T.
Peabody Mrs. Arthur
Pierpont Mrs. Robt. B.
Powers Mrs. Percy
Press Mrs. Whiting G.
Pierce Miss Julia
Ruff Mrs. Albert E.
Sbolle Mrs. Henry E.
Smith Miss Lottie
Stern Mrs. Julius
Wilson Miss Grace

WOODLAWN PARK CLUB.

WOODLAWN AVENUE COR. 64TH STREET.

OFFICERS.

J. G. KING, - - - - - - -	President.
GEORGE WAGNER. - - - - - -	Secretary.
R. W. HALL, - - - - - - -	Treasurer.

DIRECTORS.

Thomas A. Evoy	W. J. Lafferty	R. W. Hafl
George J. M. Porter	H. H. Northrop	E. T. Nicholas
	James Baird	

MEMBERS.

Allen C. W.	Dennis J. M.	Hirschl A. J.	Rose Russell C.
Ashcraft Edwin M.	Dorn Guy	Holton Thos. J.	Rushton Joseph A.
Atwood Fred G.	Dripps Samuel W.	Irvine Hugh	Salisbury Nathan
Atwood James H.	Enright Michael J.	Jackson H. B.	Sandmeyer Louis A
Austin Dr. Chas.E.	Erickson Edw. A.	James W. S.	Schultz Rudolph E.
Baird James	Evans John	Jellyman Joseph	Seymour Herbert F.
Barrows Dr. R. M.	Evoy Thomas A.	Keenan W. F.	Simpson P. L.
Barber Dr.Frank A.	Fairman Clarence	King Harry V.	Sparrow Wm. S.
Beattie John S.	Fairman Dan'l B.	King Jesse G.	Spencer C. H.
Bogart Clarence G.	Ford George W.	Kirk Henry J.	Spencer Geo. W.
Boller C. V.	Ford William H.	Lafferty Wm. J.	Springer Edward B.
Bour Charles J.	Forsinger J. W.	Levis John M.	Staley William C.
Boyd J. W.	Fowler Wm. A.	Lockwood Thos. A.	Stern Julius
Bragdon Chas. E.	Frost E. R.	Loomis Dr.Henry P	Stewart Samuel J.
Breckenridge R. J.	Gilkison Jasper G.	Magill Samuel E.	Storrow John
Brommer C. G.	Graham David	Maher Albert J.	Straub A. M.
Bryant E. F.	Green Fred. W.	Malley Wm. C.	Sweetland John T.
Chamberlain Arth'r	Green Robert F.	Manington John	Tash John D.
F.	Hall Robert W.	McCandless A. W.	Thompson Glenn D
Coleman Wm. A.	Hallinan Timothy	McKnight H. P.	Towle John R.
Colt James D.	G.	McMillin Geo. W.	Travis James A.
Michler H. Capt.	Hardenbrook Ed-	Meeker J. W.	Vigneron Eugene
Newell John	win G.	Miller E. M.	Wagner George
Giffin James D.	Hardenbrook G. S.	Mills Albert J.	Weyburn Elbert D.
Coolidge'GeorgeW.	Harrison Jas. W.	Nicholas Edmd. T.	Weyburn Ned C.
Cortright Lewis D.	Harvey H. M.	Northrup HenryM.	Wheeler F. W.
Courtright C. W.	Harvey Wm. B.	Oughton A. R.	Wheeler Martin L.
Crawford Fred. E.	Herriman W. D.,	Pershing James F.	Wheeler Newton C.
Darby Benj. L.	M. D.	Porter Geo. J. M.	White Chas. F.
Darnell Riley	Hill Joseph W.	Press Whiting G.	Wilber E. J. jr.
Delaware Ambrose	Hilton Dr. Geo. V.	Riggs George W.	Williams Wm. H.
S.	Hilton H. H.	Rodgers Dr.R.E.L.	

The Chicago Academy of Dramatic Art

470

Mr. and Mrs. McKee

Residence, 698 Walnut Street,
CHICAGO.

Academy of Dancing...

WEST SIDE	LA GRANGE
Van Buren Opera House,	Conservatory Hall.
Cor. California Ave. and Madison St.	
CLASSES	**CLASSES**
Monday, Friday, Saturday.	Tuesday.

ARTISTIC SINGING

✤ ✤ ✤ CONCERT, CHURCH AND ORATORIO..........

MRS. L. M. DUNN

The oldest exponent of Madam Cappiani, and familiar with the methods of the best teachers in Europe. Pupils received at 1 Park Avenue, Ingleside–5.

Mrs. Dunn will be at the Isabella Building, 46 East Van Buren Street, Suite 405, Mondays, Wednesdays and Fridays at 9 a. m. Voices tried free.

"Oh! Mamma!

See the dirt under this mat."

PART SIXTH.

ALPHABETICAL LIST.

THE BLUE BOOK.

*CONTAINING THE NAMES OF PROMINENT HOUSE-
HOLDERS OF CHICAGO AND SUBURBS, AR-
RANGED IN ALPHABETICAL ORDER
ACCORDING TO NAMES,
GIVING ALSO THE SUMMER RESIDENCE.*

ALPHABETICAL LIST.

AAGAARD J. 507, 42d pl.
    Aaron Marks, 412 Marshfield av.
Abbott Almira Mrs. 4518 Oakenwald av.
Abbott Arthur S. 730 W. Monroe
Abbott A. A. 7147 Wentworth av.
Abbott A. H. 59 Madison
Abbott A. R. Mrs. 353, 41st
Abbott A. V. Walton pl. sw. cor. Rush
Abbott C. F. Oak Park
Abbott C. P. Mrs. 87 Rush
Abbott Edwin F. Austin
Abbott E. L. 451 Racine av.
Abbott Frank D. 449 Washington boul.
Abbott Frank E. LaGrange
Abbott Frederick, 4518 Oakenwald av.
Abbott F. F. Prof. Hotel Windermere
Abbott F. J. Berwyn
Abbott Jerome G. 7044 Yale
Abbott John J. Hotel Metropole
Abbott L. Berwyn
Abbott L. W. M. Mrs. 397 Oak
Abbott M. N. Mrs. Lexington hotel
Abbott Orvil S. Mrs. 3344 Calumet av.
Abbott Wallace C. Dr. 2666 Commercial
Abbott William Warren, 3058 Calumet av.
Abbott Willis J. 729 Fullerton av.
Abbott Wilson N. 7436 Eggleston av.
Abbott W. L. 455 Racine av.
Abbott W. S. 909 Spaulding av.
Abeel Waldo Mrs. 266 Irving av.
Abel Anna Miss, 3147 Indiana av.
Abel E. J. Newberry hotel
Abel Jonathan, 3334 Vernon av.
Abell James E. 1173 Lawndale av.
Abell James M. 1173 Lawndale av.
Abercrombie John J. 3632 Calumet av.
Able S. A. Mrs. 632 W. Monroe
Aborn Everett A. 679 Warren av.
Aborn Walton C. 679 Warren av.
Aborn W. L. 679 Warren av.
Abrahams M. Mrs. 673 Park av.
Abrams E. E. 5423 Jefferson av.
Abt Arthur I. Dr. 3327 South Park av.
Abt Herman H. 3327 South Park av.
Abt Isaac A., M.D. 3505 Indiana av.
Abt Jacob J. 3327 South Park av.
Abt Levi, 3327 South Park av.
Abt Sol L. 3327 South Park av.
Acker F. E. A. Chicago Beach hotel
Acker George S. Newberry hotel
Acker George S. jr. Newberry hotel
Ackerman Fred S. 5490 East End av.

Ackerman George H. Austin
Ackerman Peter, 410, 61st Englewood
Ackerman William K. 4614 Lake av.
Ackermann John W. 534 Orchard
Ackers Thomas, 68 Bryant av.
Ackert C. H. Oak Park
Ackhoff Charles, 626 Orchard
Ackhoff Henry W. 1778 Deming .
Ackhoff Louisa Miss, 1778 Deming ct.
Ackley G. Newton, 2450 N. Paulina
Ackley William E. 2450 N. Paulina
Adair A. A. Oak Park
Adair A. B. Evanston
Adair E. J. The Renfost
Adair John D. 395, 40th
Adam A. B. 2249 Calumet av.
Adam E. B. Miss, 2249 Calumet av.
Adam George J. Hotel Metropole
Adams Abbot L. 350 Ontario
Adams Asa G. 380, 44th
Adams A A. 5744 Washington av.
Adams A. H. Oak Park
Adams A. M. Lexington hotel
Adams Benjamin F. Evanston
Adams Charles, 821 Jackson av.
Adams Charles, M.D. 206, 28th
Adams Charles A. 41 Gordon Terrace
Adams Charles E. 4204 Oakenwald av.
Adams Charles F., M. D. 1247 Wright
    wood av.
Adams Charles L. 3251 Michigan av.
Adams Charles P. 450 W. Adams
Adams Charles R. 504 Greenleaf av.
Adams Cora K. Mrs. 286 Belden av.
Adams Cyrus H. 155 Rush
Adams C. D. Miss, 350 Ontario
Adams C. J., M.D. 856 W. Monroe
Adams C. L. The Ashland
Adams Edward A. Austin
Adams Edward M. 207, 44th
Adams Edward S. 150 Pine
Adams Egerton, 4020 Drexel boul.
Adams Elizabeth Mrs. 383 S. Oakley av
Adams Ella M. Mrs. 739 Sedgwick
Adams Elmer J. 148 Dearborn av.
Adams Emma L. Miss, 2505 Michigan
    av.
Adams Eugene E. 4322 Greenwood av.
Adams Eva E. Miss, 2541 Wabash av.
Adams E. Clinton, 472 Bowen av.
Adams E. S. Mrs. 608 Division
Adams Francis, 481 W. Adams

Adams Francis H. 763 Washington boul.
Adams Fred, 481 W. Adams
Adams George, 2822 Michigan av.
Adams George D. Rev. Riverside
Adams George E. 4310 Emerald av.
Adams George E. 530 Belden av.
Adams George G. Highland Park
Adams George J. Lakota hotel
Adams George W. Evanston
Adams George W. Mrs. 2716 Calumet av.
Adams Hannah Mrs. Evanston
Adams Harriet M. Miss, 616 Washington boul.
Adams Henry E. Irving Park
Adams H. C. 3825 Vincennes av.
Adams H. E. 4353 Berkeley av.
Adams H. L. Miss, 350 Ontario
Adams Isaac E. Hotel Richelieu
Adams James H. 161 Eugenie
Adams James J. 832 Walnut
Adams John B. 19 Bryant av.
Adams John L. 1355 Fulton
Adams John N. 156 S. Leavitt
Adams John Quincy, 330 Lasalle av.
Adams John Russell, 506 N. State
Adams Joseph, Hotel Metropole
Adams Joseph Rev. 2605 N. Robey
Adams Julia M.D. 2605 N. Robey
Adams J. Aaron, 2505 Michigan av.
Adams J. A. Rev. 918 Warren av.
Adams J. E. River Forest
Adams J. McGregor, 300 Lasalle av.
    Sum. res. "Yarrow," Highland Park
Adams Lizzie Miss, 2822 Michigan av.
Adams Louis, 218 S. Morgan
Adams Louis R. Newberry hotel
Adams Louisa H. Mrs. 335, 53d
Adams Lyman L. 472 Bowen av.
Adams Martha A. Mrs. 1247 Wrightwood av.
Adams Milward, Auditorium hotel
Adams Moses, 3642 Grand boul.
Adams Nellie M. 19 Bryant av.
Adams Richard K. Evanston
Adams Robert C. The Renfost
Adams Samuel, 608 Division
Adams Samuel H. jr. 2716 Wabash av.
Adams Sarah C. Mrs. 2541 Wabash av.
Adams S. H. Allen, 981 Jackson boul.
Adams S. O. 4213 Ellis av.
Adams S. P. 301, 66th
Adams T. Mrs. 832 Walnut
Adams Virginia Miss, 221 The Plaza
Adams William D. 2019 Indiana av.
Adams William P. Dr. 314 N. State
Adams William P. 856, 72d pl. (H.P.)
Adams William R. Evanston
Adams William S. 4345 Lake av.
Adams William T. 2505 Michigan av.
Adams W. A. 7051 Wright
Adams W. G. Oak Park
Adams W. H. 7051 Wright
Adcock A. W. 327 Warren av.
Adcock Edmund, 2902 Prairie av.
Adcock H. C. 4459 Evans av.
Addams Jane Miss, 335 S. Halsted

Addison John, 178 Dearborn av.
Addy Edward, 6936 Wentworth av.
Addy George, 467 Tuohy av.
Adkins E. V. 1384 Palmer
Adkins W. G. 3144 Groveland av.
Adkinson E. W. 5552 Wentworth av.
Adler Dankmar, 3543 Ellis av.
Adler Henry, 2625 Calumet av.
Adler J. I. Mrs. 485 Belden av.
Adler Liebman Mrs. 162, 34th
Adler Louis, 571 Division
Adler Morris, 3427 South Park av.
Adler Peter, 276 Huron
Adler Samuel H. 545 Washington boul.
Adler Sidney, 485 Belden av.
Adolphus Philip Dr. The Ashland
Adolphus William, 250, 47th
Adsit Byron D. 4150 Berkeley av.
Adsit Charles C. 455 Elm
Adsit James M. Mrs. 400 Dearborn av.
Adsit James M. jr. 400 Dearborn av.
Adsit Jeanne M. Miss, 400 Dearborn av.
Affeld Charles E. 1824 Diversey
Affeld Oscar, 531 Orchard
Agar John, 1846 Oakdale av.
Agar Woodbury S. 1846 Oakdale av.
Agee J. A. 3000 Michigan av.
Ager J. Frank, 679 Walnut
Agin Lovetta B. Miss, 4559 Evans av.
Agnass Jean E. C. Norwood Park
Agnew Francis Mrs. 292 Huron
Agnew Henry, 120 Ashland boul.
Agnew J. P. 189 Cass
Ahern Elliott G. 6332 Ellis av.
Ahern John A. River Forest
Ahern John H. 174 Oakwood boul.
Ahles Edward, 1130 Washington boul.
Ahles Emily Mrs. 1130 Washington boul.
Ahles J. F. 287 Irving av.
Ahles William, 1130 Washington boul.
Ahrens C. H. L. Washington Heights
Ahrens Henry, 249, 65th, Englewood
Ahrens John A. 249, 65th, Englewood
Ahrens J. P. 3218 Vernon av.
Aiken Jennie Hall Mrs. 2616 Calumet av.
Aiken Mayhew P. Evanston
Aiken Rose T. Miss, Evanston
Aiken William A. 4829 Madison av.
Aiken William J. 857 W. Monroe
Aikin Charles, Evanston
Ainslie S. R. Oak Park
Ainsworth Franklin F. 2300 Indiana av.
    Sum. res. Bethel, Vt.
Aishton Richard H. Evanston
Akamatsaa S. Z. Stamford hotel
Aken John Mrs. Glencoe
Akin Abel, Maywood
Akin Henry F. Maywood
Alabaster J. Lewis, New Holland hotel
Albaugh A. B. 2951 Groveland av.
Albee George J. Evanston
Albee P. Mrs. Lombard
Alberger M. H. Col. 232 Michigan av.
Albert Charles W. 558 Division
Albert Christopher J. Prof. Elmhurst
Albert Josephine Mrs. 558 Division

Albertson Charles Q. 4957 Prairie av.
Alborn Hilton R. 183 S. Oakley av.
Alborn H. F. 214 Lincoln av.
Albright T. S. 871 W. Monroe
Albright W. F. 25 S. California av.
Albro Charles B. Oak Park
Albro Clarence, 1820 W. 22d
Albro Emelius S. 1820 W. 22d
Alcock Wm. H. 4500 Vincennes av.
Alden E. J. Rev. 337 Indiana
Alden Frederick H. Austin
Alden William T. 261 Warren av.
Alden W. A. 164 S. Wood
Alderson John J. Dr. 402 Jackson boul.
Aldis Arthur Taylor, 369 Chicago av.
Aldis Harry W. Mrs. 3756 Ellis av.
Aldis Owen F. 77 Bellevue pl.
Aldrich Charles H. Evanston
Aldrich Ella L. Miss, 346 Oakwood boul.
Aldrich E. W. 974 W. Adams
Aldrich F. C. Lake Forest
Aldrich Henry H. 215 Ashland boul.
Aldrich J. Frank, Chicago Beach hotel
Aldrich William Mrs. 4454 Oakenwald av.
Aldrich W. H. 506 W. Monroe
Aldridge J. G. 792 W. Monroe
Alexander A. Grace hotel.
Alexander Charles A. Austin
Alexander David 4405 Berkeley av,
Alexander Ellen C. Miss, 212, 33d
Alexander E. Mrs. 1520 Washington boul.
Alexander George M. 1583 Alexander av.
Alexander G. M. Hotel Metropole
Alexander Henry M. Austin
Alexander Horace C. B. 808 Pratt av.
Alexander John F. 265 Hermitage av.
Alexander J. B. 344 Belden av,
Alexander J. T. Julien hotel
Alexander L. Miss, 6633 Perry av.
Alexander Samuel T. 3848 Langley av.
Alexander Stuart R. 379 Ontario
Alexander S. M. Mrs. 613, 66th, Engle-
    wood.
Alexander W. M. 6633 Perry av.
Aley F. W. Lake Forest
Alfieri E. Prof. 52, 24th
Alford M. P. 402 Washington boul.
Algeo Thomas W. 1549 Alexander av.
Alison John M. 3634 Vincennes av.
Alison Mary Miss, 3634 Vincennes av.
Alison Rowland H. 3634 Vincennes av.
Alister W. M. 174, 47th
Allan John B. 756 Washington boul.
Allan J. M. 1623 Prairie av.
Allcock George E. 215 Warren av.
Allen Abel L. 803 Jackson av.
Allen Anna M. Mrs. Highland Park
Allen Arthur G. 339, 53d
Allen A. Capt. 819 Warren av.
Allen A. Brom. Dr.1287 Washington boul.
Allen A. Frank Dr. 5456 Ridgewood ct.
Allen A. J. Mrs. 525 Cleveland av.
Allen A. W. The Ontario
Allen Benjamin, 1815 Michigan av.
Allen Benjamin C. 1815 Michigan av,
Allen Charles A. 869 W. Monroe

Allen Charles A. 4749 Calumet av.
Allen Charles B. 5628 Monroe av.
Allen Charles B. Mrs. 175 Evanston av.
Allen Charles E. Riverside
Allen Charles L. 4741 Greenwood av.
Allen Charles W. 145 Oakwood boul.
Allen Clark P. 525 Cleveland av.
Allen C. A. Hinsdale
Allen C. A. Rev. 2600 Indiana av;
Allen C. F. M. 330½ Dayton
Allen Daniel A. 114 S. Leavitt
Allen Edmund T., M.D., Ph.D. 6418
    Stewart av.
Allen Edward, 657 Lasalle av.
Allen Edward A. 339, 53d (H.P.)
Allen Ernest L. 52 Astor
Allen Eva Viola Miss, 505 Jackson av.
Allen Ford J. Evanston
Allen Frank L. 5142 Washington av.
Allen George Q. 505 Jackson av.
Allen George R. 83 Loomis
Allen G. Mrs. Hotel LaVita
Allen Harry K. Riverside
Allen Harry L. Sherman house
Allen Harry S. 325 Michigan av.
Allen Helen Marian Miss, 5142 Washing-
    ton av.
Allen Heman Mrs. 356 Belden av.
Allen Heman G. 2241 Michigan av.
Allen Henry C. Dr. 5142 Washington av.
Allen Ira W. 612 Maple, Englewood
Allen Ira W. jr. 612 Maple, Englewood
Allen James Capt. U. S. A. Lexington
    hote
Allen James Lane, 4050 Grand boul.
Allen John K. 798 W. Monroe
Allen John M. 80 Bowen av.
Allen John W. Rev. 231 S. Oakley av.
    Sum. res. Macatawa Park, Mich
Allen Joseph D. 3441 Michigan av.
Allen J. E. Hinsdale
Allen J. E. Mrs. 3911 Grand boul.
Allen J. M. Oak Park
Allen J. Shirlock. 3911 Grand boul.
Allen J. V. 5036 Washington av.
Allen J. William, 464 S. Oakley av.
Allen Lewis D. 1815 Michigan av.
Allen L. S. Auditorium Annex
Allen Mary Miss, 52 St. Clair
Allen M. A. 2640 Indiana av.
Allen M. R. Mrs. 6356 Harvard
Allen O. D. Oak Park
Allen O. H. 913 Jackson boul.
Allen Sarah C. Mrs. Riverside
Allen Thomas, 271 Ontario
Allen Thomas, Glencoe
Allen Thomas. 4201 Lake av.
Allen Thomas Rev. 6418 Stewart av.
Allen T. B. 293 Webster av.
Allen Walter S. 450 Belden av.
Allen William, 4232 Oakenwald av.
Allen William D. 22 Scott
Allen William H. Columbus Club
Allen W. J. 7130 Yale
Allenberg Lew W. 4734 Champlain av,
Aller Amasa L. 6351 Honore ·

Allerton Robert H. 1936 Prairie av.
Allerton Samuel W. 1936 Prairie av.
Alles John, Winnetka
Alles John jr. Winnetka
Alley Fred M. 846 W. Adams
Alley William H. Highland Park
Alley W. N. 846 W. Adams
Allgire John W. 5440 Ridgewood ct.
Allinder Daniel G. Dr. 7753 Wright
Allinder M. A. Miss, 981 Jackson boul.
Alling John, 2131 Calumet av.
Alling John jr. 2131 Calumet av.
Alling Joseph H. Rev. Evanston
Alling J. C. 1010 Warren av.
Alling S. T. 275 W. Adams
Allis E. B. 98, 30th
Allison A. E. Miss, 5420 Cornell av.
Allison James, 4365 Lake av.
Allison John Dr. 847 Garfield boul.
Allison John T. LaGrange
Allison J. Albert, 2341 Park av. (J.)
Allmendinger George P. 1059½ N. Clark
Allore Franc P. Hawes Mrs. 3000 Michigan av.
Allore William, 3000 Michigan av.
Allport May Miss, The Ontario
Allport W. H. Dr. 85 Rush
Allstadt C. E. 4228 Greenwood av.
Allyn Arthur W. 373 Oakwood boul.
Allyn Charles T. 4313 Ellis av.
        Sum. res. Delavan Lake, Wis.
Almberg S. Th. Forest Glen (J.)
Almquist John P. Mrs. 311 W. Monroe
Almy Miles, Hotel Metropole
Alsip Charles H. 445 Ashland boul.
Alsip Frank, 445 Ashland boul.
Alsip Frank B. 483 Jackson boul.
Alsip William H. 459 W. Monroe
Alston John, 180 N. State
Alt C. William jr. 169 Schiller
Altgeld John P. Hon. Springfield, Ill.
Altman Israel, 4826 Langley av.
Altman Michael, 3551 Vernon av.
Alton Davis C. 2522 Prairie av.
Alton Jesse B. 2522 Prairie av.
Alton Leo T. 332 Marshfield av.
Alton Ralph, 332 Marshfield av.
Alton William, 2522 Prairie av.
Alton William jr. 128, 47th.
Altsheler Ida Mrs. 1239 Wrightwood av.
Alvord Germaine G. 2969 Prairie av.
Alvord John W. 5203 Hibbard av.
Alvord M. M. Mrs. 271, 53d
Alward G. Florus, 754 Jackson boul.
Alward Martha I. Mrs. 4408 Oakenwald av.
Alward Willard P. 479 Washington boul.
Amberg A. L. Mrs. 93 MacAlister pl.
Amberg C. Louis, 3030½ Cottage Grove av.
Amberg John H. 411 W. Monroe
Amberg J. Ward, 62 N. Sheldon
Amberg Theodore J. 288 Park av.
Amberg William A. 62 N. Sheldon
        Sum. res. Mackinac Island
Ambler H. Clarence, 80 S. Kedzie av.

Ambler J. C. 375 Dearborn av.
Ambridge William, Stamford hotel
Ambrose Thomas, 3034 Calumet av.
Ambrose Walter J. 4906 Washington av.
American F. A. Dr. 6238 Madison av.
American Oscar L. 3130 Vernon av.
Amerson William, Austin
Amerson Wm. H. Dr. 1334 W. Adams
Ames Alfred A. Edison Park
Ames Benj. L. 1410 W. Monroe
Ames Bradford L. Hotel Windermere
Ames Charles L. Ridgeland
Ames Franklin, 2204 Prairie av.
Ames J. Mrs. 126, 21st.
Ames J. E. Miss, Hotel Metropole
Ames J. G. Dr. 411 Lincoln av.
Ames Miner T. Mrs. 2108 Prairie av.
Ames M. E. 716 Warren av.
Ames W. V. B. Dr. Hotel Windermere
Amman Frank, 245 Osgood
Ammen William J. 875 Winthrop av.
Ammon Ernest 643 Fullerton av.
Ammon Frederick E. 643 Fullerton av.
Amory Eugene E. 248, 51st
Amory William A. 4913 Madison av.
Amos John E. 171, 51st
Amos John E. jr. 5115 Cornell av.
Amos William, Hyde Park hotel
Anable Courtland W. 430 Belden av.
Anable Ella C. Mrs. 83, 20th
Anable S. L. 430 Belden av.
Anderman Frederick H. Lake Forest
Anderson Alexander E. 695 Burling
Anderson Andrew J. 173 Howe
Anderson Andrew S. 457 Cleveland av.
Anderson Archie A. Mrs. 1715 Cornelia
Anderson A. A. 3250 South Park av.
Anderson Benjamin B. 2237 Sheridan rd.
Anderson Benjamin L. Norwood Park
Anderson Charles J. 4705 Evans av.
Anderson Charles R. 3446 Prairie av.
Anderson Cora Miss, 302 The Plaza
Anderson C. M. 5484 Monroe av.
Anderson C. P. Rev. Oak Park
Anderson David R. 768 Warren av.
Anderson David R. 1318 Wolcott
Anderson David S. 1478 Graceland av.
Anderson Edward T. 756 Kenmore av.
Anderson Emily Miss, 55 St. James pl.
Anderson Ernest V. 5206 Hibbard av.
Anderson Eugene D. 123, 25th
Anderson Frank A. 4419 Vincennes av.
Anderson F. E. 3237 Vernon av.
Anderson F. R. Mrs. 3449 Prairie av.
Anderson Galusha Prof. Morgan Park
Anderson George F. 6911 Stewart av.
Anderson George H, Berwyn
Anderson George W. 3831 Calumet av.
Anderson Georgie C. Miss, Evanston
Anderson Hans L. 98 Fowler
Anderson Hervey H. 2665 N. Paulina
Anderson Isaac, 6335 Sheridan av.
Anderson James, Lake Forest
Anderson James C. Highland Park
Anderson James F. Highland Park
Anderson John, 646 Cleveland av.

Anderson John, Evanston
Anderson John G. Wilmette
Anderson John M. 1559 Lill av.
Anderson John N. 238 Pine
Anderson John P. 577 Orchard
Anderson Joseph, Morgan Park
Anderson Josie Miss, 4735 Lake av.
Anderson Josie Miss, 211 Loomis
Anderson J. 471 Jackson boul.
Anderson J. L. Oak Park
Anderson K. C. Mrs. Chicago Beach hotel
Anderson L. K. Mrs. 11 University pl.
Anderson Maria Miss, Evanston
Anderson Mary M. Miss, 320 Superior
Anderson Minnie Mrs. 1707 Barry av.
Anderson N. 5522 East End av.
Anderson Oscar E. 4239 St. Lawrence av.
Anderson Peter, 695 Burling
Anderson Sarah B. Miss, Mo gan Park
Anderson Sarah C. Mrs. 4748 Evans av.
Anderson Sebastian, 515 Lasalle av.
Anderson Theresa M. Miss, 1478 Graceland av.
Anderson Thomas F. 357 Dearborn av.
Anderson Walter C. Auditorium Annex
Anderson Warren C. 4523 Woodlawn av.
Anderson Warren J. 692 W. Adams
Anderson William B. 746 Kenmore av.
Anderson William G. 515 Lasalle av.
Anderson Wm. H. 618 Washington boul.
Anderson William P. 3158 Prairie av.
Anderson W. D. 4220 Oakenwald av.
Anderson W. D. S. 330 Oakwood boul.
Anderson W. S. 6639 Lafayette av.
Andrear Fritz O. 5517 Washington av.
Andreas A. T. French House, Evanston
Andregg J. A. Sherman house
Andrew Edward, Austin
Andrew George L. 6123 Sheridan av.
Andrew George W. Evanston
Andrew Louise Miss, 820 W. Adams
Andrews A. H. Lombard
Andrews Bertha M. Miss, Lombard
Andrews Charles A. 152 N. Clark
Andrews Clifford F. 4350 Berkeley av.
Andrews D. W. 7715 Wright
Andrews Edmund Dr. 2520 Prairie av.
Andrews Edward W. 4403 Oakenwald av.
Andrews Ellis C. 7715 Wright
Andrews E H. Oak Park
Andrews E. M. Mrs. Hyde Park hotel
Andrews E. Wyllys Dr. 2512 Prairie av.
Andrews Frank M. 474 Elm
Andrews Frank T. Dr. 3169 Groveland av.
Andrews George H. Dr. 325 Bowen av.
Andrews Herbert L. 267 Michigan av.
Andrews Irene F. Mrs. 2247 Michigan av.
Andrews James, 456 Fullerton av.
Andrews James D. Oak Park
Andrews James K. Hotel Windermere
Andrews James S. Riverside
Andrews James W. 2614 Commercial (L.V.)
Andrews Jay A. 815 Washington boul.
Andrews John D., M.D., 290 Lasalle av.

Andrews J. H. Lexington hotel
Andrews J. Roy, 2614 Commercial (L.V.)
Andrews J. W. 943 72d pl. (H.P.)
Andrews Margaret L. Mrs. 2709 Michigan av.
Andrews Marie Miss, Hotel Windermere
Andrews Martin, 742 Winthrop av.
Andrews Newton, 516 W. Adams
Andrews Sarah A. Mrs. 5168 Michigan av.
Andrews Sarah R. Mrs. Hinsdale
Andrews Sidney F. 120 Pine
Andrews Stuart B. 1911 Michigan av.
Andrews Theodore F. 3238 Rhodes av.
Andrews Wells Dr. 815 Washington boul.
Andrews Wm. H. 1175 S. Central Park av.
Andrews William J. Evanston
Andrews W. H. 2931 Indiana av.
Androvette George E. 435 Washington boul.
Andrus Fred H. 4738 Woodlawn av.
Andrus M. S. Mrs. 3428 Vernon av.
Andrus Sherwood D. 4504 Vincennes av.
Andrus W. C. Mrs. 27 Wisconsin
Angel Harry A. Oak Park
Angel Samuel, 206 Warren av.
Angell Charles W. Tremont house
Angell Edward F. 2731 N. Paulina
Angell Henry L. 727 Kenmore av.
Angell William A. 131 Astor
Angell William T. 2505 Michigan av.
Angole O. D. Evanston
Angsten Philip, 4432 Prairie av.
Anguish Benjamin D. 628 Cleveland av.
Angunes James, 3225 Rhodes av.
Angus John, 3213 Michigan av.
    Sum. res. Hartland, Wis.
Annan A. 297 Robertson av.
Ansbach S. The Wellington
Ansley Robert, 614 Chestnut, Englewood
Anson Adrian C. 160, 30th
Antes C. H. 295 Oak
Anthony C. E. Evanston
Anthony D. P. 3756 Ellis av.
Anthony E. Judge, Evanston
Anthony George D. Evanston
Anthony Henry G. Dr. 353 N. Clark
Anthony Joseph T. 3338 Prairie av.
Anthony J. R. 3265 Vernon av.
Anthony Walter M. Evanston
Anthony Willard G. 4241 Calumet av.
Antisdel Albert, 66 Bellevue pl.
Antoine Charles, 38, 16th
Anton Peter B. Dr. 429 Garfield boul.
Anwander Charles, 1510 Wolfram
Apfel Arthur H. 864 Larrabee
Apfel Philip, 486 Garfield av.
Apfel Philip jr. 486 Garfield av.
Apfel William G. 451 Cleveland av.
Aplin Frank A. Evanston
Appel Carl, 3246 Rhodes av.
Apple Herman 482 N. Robey
Appleby Addison S. 3354 South Park av.
Appleby Richard B. 3354 South Park av.
Appleby William R. 3354 South Park av
Applegate William J. 111 Walton pl.
Appleton Ernest, 594 W. Vanburen

Appleton Rebecca Mrs. 594 W.Vanburen
Appleton Thomas, 390 Washington boul.
Arata A. J. 355 W. Monroe
Arbogast Guy, 234, 45th
Archer Frederic, 3 Groveland Park
Archer Harry B. 3 Groveland Park
Archer James L. 81 Pine
Archer John, 602 Park av.
Archer J. J. Berwyn
Archer Richard M. 3 Groveland Park
Archibald George N. 444 W. Congress
Archibald Thos. E. 215 S. Hoyne av.
Arcouet Edward A. 837 W. Congress
Arend Augustus, 296 Ohio
Arend Frank A. 1928 Barry av.
Arend William N. 487 Belden av.
Armbruster F. P. Oak Park
Armijo Josefina Miss, 225 Oakwood boul.
Armijo Joseph B. 225 Oakwood boul.
Armitage A. Oak Park
Armour Allison V. 117 Lake Shore Drive
Armour Barbara Mrs. 117 Lake Shore
    Drive
Armour F. E. Julien hotel
Armour George A. 120 Lake Shore Drive
Armour James A. 4237 Grand boul.
Armour J. Ogden, 3724 Michigan av.
    Sum. res. Oconomowoc, Wis.
Armour Philip D. 2115 Prairie av.
Armour Philip D. jr. 2735 Michigan av.
Arms Charles H. 5410 Washington av
Arms C. F. 74 Bellevue pl.
Arms Frank D. 41 Aldine sq.
Arms Harrison, 2243 Michigan av.
Arms May W. Mrs. 41 Aldine sq.
Arms W. A. 348 Belden av.
Armsby George N. Evanston
Armsby James K. Mrs. Evanston
Armsby James K. jr. Evanston
Armstrong Adam, 5106 Cornell av.
Armstrong Anna Mrs. 273 Ontario
Armstrong A. T. 5027 Madison av.
Armstrong Charles, 4060 Michigan Ter-
    race
Armstrong Charles G. 4354 Oakenwald
    av.
Armstrong Charles M. 4713 Kimbark av.
Armstrong Clyde D. 6735 Lafayette av.
Armstrong Edwin A. 3815 Forest av.
Armstrong Edwin R. T. Evanston
Armstrong Frank S. 3823 Forest av.
Armstrong F. H. Walton pl. sw. cor.
    Rush
Armstrong Guy N. 16 Waverly pl.
Armstrong H. B. 665 Cleveland av.
Armstrong H. J. 585 Jackson boul.
Armstrong Jacob Mrs. 752 W. Monroe
Armstrong James E. 529, 62d, Englewood
Armstrong Jane Mrs. 170 Ashland boul.
Armstrong John B. Dr. 16 Waverly pl.
Armstrong John J. 85 Lincoln av.
Armstrong John M. 194 Clarence av.
Armstrong J. C. Rev. 743 W. Harrison
Armstrong J. J. 6120 Michigan av.
Armstrong J. M. 85 Lincoln av.
Armstrong Kittie Mrs. 896 Jackson boul.

Armstrong Lafayette F. 5031 Jefferson
    av.
Armstrong Thomas A. 85 Lincoln av.
Armstrong Wm. 62 Walton pl.
Arnd Charles, French house, Evanston
Arnd Frederick, Evanston
Arndt George E. 4726 Kenwood av.
Arndt John, Wilmette
Arneson Nels, 672 N. Hoyne av.
Arney John J. 220 Ohio
Arnheim Benjamin, 3742 Michigan av.
Arnison Herbert, Evanston
Arnold Albert C. 4845 Forrestville av.
Arnold Amelia Mrs. 364 N. Wells
Arnold A. H. 78 Throop
Arnold Charles, Austin
Arnold Charles C. Winnetka
Arnold Daniel A. 843 W. Adams
Arnold D. O. 39, 22d
Arnold F. A. 630 Jackson boul.
Arnold George B. 289 Ontario
Arnold Henry L. jr. 289 Ontario
Arnold Herman, 1826 Wellington
Arnold Irving L. Austin
Arnold Isaac N. Mrs. 104 Pine
Arnold James, 24 Maple
Arnold James M. Palmer house
Arnold Joseph L. P. 7822 Hawthorne av.
    Englewood
Arnold Llewellyn W. LaGrange
Arnold L. H. 3125 South Park av.
Arnold N. D. Mrs. 6352 Oglesby av.
Arnold R. B. 751 W. Adams
Arnold Theodore, 230 Park av.
Arnold T. H. The Renfrost
Arnold Victor, 168 Warren av.
Arnold Walter C. Hotel Richelieu
Arnold William G. 296 Ohioe
Arnold William H. Lagrange
Arnold William J. Dr. 6759 Honore
Arnold William L. 360 S. Paulina
Arnstein Eugene, 3326 Wabash av.
Arnulphy Bernard S., M.D. 5223 Jeffer-
    son av.
Aron Jacob 3537 Grand boul.
Aronson Henry A. 449 Marshfield av.
Arrick Alfred A. Mrs. 61 Cedar
Arter Francis G. Dr. 119 Garfield boul.
Arthur Lemuel J. Evanston
Artingstall Samuel G. 13 Hamilton av
Artz V. T. Miss, Hotel Metropole
Asay William C. 705 Pullman bldg.
Ascher Adolph, 718 Sedgwick
Ascher Henry, 718 Sedgwick
Ascher Julius, 172 Eugenie
Ascher Julius, 718 Sedgwick
Ascher Martin, 495 Lasalle av.
Ascher Theodore, 495 Lasalle av.
Ash Chester C. Evanston
Ash I. N. 221, 47th
Ash L. H. 148, 46th
Ash Michael, 399 Bowen av.
Ash M. L. 399 Bowen av.
Ashbury John W. 499 Winchester av.
Ashby G. W. Berwyn
Ashby James H. 2100 Prairie av.

Ashcraft E. M. 6046 Sheridan av.
Ashelman Laura Mrs. Oak Park
Asher John, 4828 St. Lawrence av.
Ashford Joseph B. 7214 Cottage Grove
    av.
Ashley Albert B. LaGrange
Ashley A. L. Mrs. 620 Washington boul.
Ashley Thomas, 4906 Washington av.
Ashton Harry L. 5338 Washington av.
Ashton Matilda Mrs. Evanston
Ashton William, Longwood
Ashton William jr. Longwood
Aspden Thomas, 14 Aldine sq.
Aspden William, 14 Aldine sq.
Aspinwall M. H. Dr. Oak Park
Atchison Hugh Rev. Wilmette
Atchison James A. 162 S. Wood
Atchison John D. 162 S. Wood
Atchison N. 162 S. Wood
Atchison W. F. Rev. Morgan Park
Atherton Frank S. 678 Washington boul.
Atkin Godfrey H. 4741 Kenwood av.
Atkin Ferdinand S.1371Washington boul.
        Sum. res. Roxbury, Mass.
Atkins Ada M. F. Mrs. 1316 Washington
    boul.
Atkins Anna B. Mrs. 379 Dearborn av.
Atkins A. R. Mrs 301 Park av.
Atkins Mary L. Mrs. 1141 Washington
    boul.
Atkinson Charles T. 4835 Lake av.
Atkinson Frank H. 5488 East End av.
Atkinson F. M. 530 Lasalle av.
Atkinson George W. P. Evanston
Atkinson G. Clarence, Evanston
Atkinson John W. Highland Park
Atkinson Pearce, Evanston
Atterbury George S. The Renfost
Atterbury G. W. 640 Chestnut, Engle-
    wood
Attridge Samuel D. Ridgeland
Atwater A. J. Morgan Park
Atwater Mary Miss, 70 Astor
Atwater Rhoda Miss, 70 Astor
Atwell Charles B. Evanston
Atwood Charles B. Union Club
Atwood Clarence E. 6016 Sheridan av.
Atwood Fred. G. 6137 Oglesby av.
Atwood Fred H. 1733 Belmont av.
Atwood F. E. Evanston
Atwood F. M. 205, 53d
Atwood James H. 6362 Myrtle av.
Atwood J. F. 6541 Lafayette av.
Atwood Myron W. 4324 Ellis av.
Atwood M. M. Mrs. 6137 Oglesby av.
Atwood Roger W. 640, 62d, Englewood
Atwood William H, Mrs. 4124 Grand
    boul.
Aubery James M. 3801 Vincennes av.
        Winter res. Cala. Nevada
Aubury James M. jr. 3801 Vincennes av.
Auer Philip A. 3157 Forest av.
Auer William, 194 N. State
Auerbach Benjamin, 4039 Indiana av.
Auerbach H. Mrs. 3148 Prairie av.
Augur J. T. 2313 Michigan av.
    31

Augur W. W. 401 Ontario
August Eli J. 57 Grant pl.
Augustus A. A. 4534 Forestville av.
Auld John M. Dr. 705 Jackson boul.
Ault George S. 444 W. Congress
Austermell Lewis T. 3651 Forest av.
Austermell Lewis W. 3651 Forest av.
Austin Alexander, Oak Park
Austin A. O. Mrs. Park Ridge
Austin Calvin K. 1633 Roscoe
• Austin Catherine Mrs. Oak Park
Austin Charles E. Dr. 6424 Myrtle av.
Austin Charles W. Oak Park
Austin Clair Miss, 3962 Langley av.
Austin C. D. 2719 Wabash av.
Austin C. W. 352 Warren av.
Austin E. C. 84 Seeley a .
Austin Frederick C. 49 Bellevue pl.
Austin F. D. 114 Seeley av.
Austin George H. 1291 Wolcott
Austin H. W. Oak Park
Austin H. W. Mrs. Oak Park
Austin J. Almon, 37 St. James pl.
Austin LeBaron L. 183 Cass
        Sum. res. Boston, Mass.
Austin Merritt B. 1025 Jackson boul.
Austin Robert, 836 Walnut
Austin R. H. Lakota hotel
Austin William, 568 Kenwood pl.
Austin Willis A. Oak Park
Austin W. H. 808 W. Monroe
Austrian Alfred S. 3129 Michigan av.
Austrian Joseph, 2954 Michigan av.
Austrian Julia R. Mrs. 3129 Michigan av.
Austrian Leo, 646 Fullerton av.
Auten Phillip L. 314 Ashland boul.
Avent John V. 553, 65th, Englewood
Averell Albert J. 2018 Michigan av.
Avers Franklin G. 4538 Forrestville av.
Avers F. H. Mrs. 2809 South Park av.
Avers Herbert M. Riverside
Avery Charles H. 5466 Monroe av.
Avery Cyrus M. 2653 Evanston av.
Avery D. J. 485 W. Adams
Avery Frank M. 2123 Prairie av:
Avery Helen M. Mrs. 6507 Sheridan av.
Avery John Hazard Mrs. Walton pl. sw.
    cor. Rush
Avery Phoebe A. Mrs. 2239 Michigan av.
Avery Samuel J., M.D. 780 Walnut
Avery Thomas M. 2123 Prairie av.
Avery W. D. 15 Lane pl.
Avy S. C. Mrs. 3339 Vernon av.
Axtell A. W. Julien hotel
Axtell J. L. Miss, Lake Forest
Axtell N. H. Rev. 690 Sunnyside av.
Axtman W. F. 5541 Drexel av.
Ayars Charles G. Avenue house, Evans-
    ton
Ayars Henry M. Evanston
Ayars James Mrs. Evanston
Ayer Benjamin F. 99 Pine
Ayer Edward E. 1 Banks
        Sum. res. Lake Geneva, Wis.
Ayer Edward H. 3131 Indiana av.
Ayer George M. 381 Dearborn av.

Ayer G. W. 5227 Washington av.
Ayer Herbert C. Col. Chicago Beach hotel
Ayers Bessie Miss, 4819 Langley av.
Ayers B. F. The Ashland
Ayers Charles B. Oak Park
Ayers John W. 4405 Berkeley av.
Ayers M. A. Mrs. 227 Ontario
Ayers Samuel, 4316 Prairie av,
Ayers W. B. 342 Warren av.
Aykroyd George M. 3523 Ellis av.
Ayres Anson, Mrs. Hinsdale
Ayres Edgar, Morgan Park
Ayres Edward L. 4340 Greenwood av.
Ayres Elizabeth Miss, Evanston
Ayres Enos, 1732 Michigan av.
Ayres Frank E. Hinsdale
Ayres George L. 1603 W. Adams
Ayres Harry Melville 3159 Indiana av.
Ayres Laura D. Mrs. 512 W. Monroe

BAACK WILLIAM A.2954 Calumet av.
Baade Henry, 460 Orchard
Babbitt Clarence M. LaGrange
Babbitt Lewis, Evanston
Babcock A. C. Col. 4347 Ellis av.
Babcock Campbell E. 806 The Plaza
Babcock Campbell S. 806 The Plaza
Babcock Charles D. 4347 Ellis av.
Babcock Charles F. 2701 Michigan av.
Babcock Charles S. 3359 Prairie av.
Babcock Courtlandt, 4526 Lake av.
Babcock C. C. 3756 Ellis av,
Babcock Elmer ..., M.D. 3239 Indiana av.
Babcock Emily H. Miss, 4526 Lake av.
Babcock Frank C. 4347 Ellis av.
Babcock Fred R. Lakota hotel
Babcock F. J. Mrs. Oak Park
Babcock Lillian Miss, 4526 Lake av.
Babcock Maria W. Mrs. 496 W. Monroe
Babcock Mary Keyes Mrs. Kenilworth
Babcock Orville E. 806 The Plaza
Babcock O. E. Mrs. 806 The Plaza
Babcock Pitt K. 4347 Ellis av.
Babcock R. H., M.D. Highland Park
Babcock Sarah L. Mrs. Evanston
Babcock Sheldon E. 4347 Ellis av.
Babcock William H. Hinsdale
Babcock W. Irving, 421 Huron
Babcock W. M. Great Northern hotel
Babeuf C. R. 6909 Vernon av.
Bach A. C. 4906 Washington av.
Bach Emanuel, 3545 Ellis av.
Bach H. B. 4906 Washington av.
Bach Leopold, 3704 Ellis av.
Bacheldor E. A. Lexington hotel
Bacheldor E. S. L. 2348 Calumet av.
Bachelle G. V., M.D., 18 Gilpin pl.
Bachelle Otto von, 667 Washington boul.
Bachman M. 97 Warren av.
Bachman Sam C. 208 The Plaza
Bachrach Charles, 498 Lasalle av.
Bachrach Isidor, 529 Lasalle av.
Back Joseph 401 Cleveland av.
Backman William W. 634 Englewood av.
Backus Emma Mrs.1332 Washington boul.

Bacom Caroline Mrs. 1092 Millard av.
Bacon A. E. Mrs. 223, 29th
Bacon C. S. Dr. 350 Webster av.
Bacon D. C., D.D.S. 281 Lincoln av.
Bacon E. B. 596 Cleveland av.
Bacon E. R. 1908 George av.
Bacon Florence Miss, 870 W. Monroe
Bacon George L. Maywood
Bacon Henry Martyn, 286, 48th
Bacon Jennie G. Miss, 2967 Vernon av.
Bacon Jeremiah D. 6820 Union av.
Bacon John Foster, 1817 Aldine av.
Bacon Joseph B. Dr. 4125 Drexel boul.
Bacon J. H. 543 W. Monroe
Bacon J. M. Mrs. 7442 Bond av.
Bacon J. P. 419 The Plaza
Bacon J. Vinton Dr. 612 Lincoln av.
Bacon Lillian F. Miss, 2967 Vernon av.
Bacon Marie Thompson D. D. S. 281 Lincoln av.
Bacon M. S. 1910 George av.
Bacon M. W. Dr. 6817 Wentworth av.
Bacon Nathaniel, 4634 Indiana av.
Bacon Roswell B. 71 Monroe
Bacon R. T. Mrs. 5516 Jefferson av.
Badenoch John J. 391 W. Randolph
Badenoch Joseph, 6429 Yale
Badenoch Joseph jr. 6429 Yale
Badenoch Roland N. 6429 Yale
Bader C. A. Berwyn
Badger Ada C. Miss, 2106 Calumet av.
Badger Alpheus C. 2106 Calumet av.
Badger A. S. 53, 20th
Badger Carlton S. Riverside
Badger Edward, Riverside
Badger Horace H. Riverside
Badgley Samuel, 1220 Rokeby
Badt F. B. 6506 Lafayette av.
Baer A. W., M.D., 237 N. State
Baer G. S. 3242 Groveland av.
Baer Joseph, 3422 Calumet av.
Baer Loms, 573 LaSalle av.
Baer Samuel, 424 Ashland boul.
Baer Sol, 573 LaSalle av.
Bagg A. G. Mrs. 4554 Oakenwald av.
Bagg F. S. 3764 Lake av.
Baggot Edward, 4354 Grand boul.
Baggot George, 4354 Grand boul.
Baggot James E. 442 Ashland boul.
Baggot John, 4354 Grand boul.
Baggot John D. 4354 Grand boul.
Baggot Joseph M. 569 Kenwood pl.
Baggott James E. 4103 Vincennes av.
Bagley Frank R. 5308 Jefferson av.
Bagley Frederick P. Hinsdale
Bagley John, 354, 41st
Bailey A. G. Dr. Hyde Park hotel
Bailey A. W. Mrs. Virginia hotel
Bailey Brunot, River Forest
Bailey C. H. Mrs. Vendome Club hotel
Bailey C. M., Maj. Fort Sheridan
Bailey Edward L. 160 Winchester av.
Bailey Edward P. 3140 Lake Park av.
Bailey Edward W. 58 Oakwood av.
Bailey Elizabeth Mrs. 2808 Prairie av.
Bailey E. Stillman Dr. 3034 Michigan av

Bailey Fred M. 4146 Ellis av.
Bailey George C. 58 Oakwood av.
Bailey George C. 5230 Jefferson av.
Bailey Isaac, Evanston
       Winter res. Pasadena, Cal.
Bailey L. S. 4558 Evans av.
Bailey Robert, 134 Park av.
Bailey Samuel G. Dr. 83 Bryant av.
       Sum. res. Cushing's Island, Me.
Bailey Sarah Mrs. Evanston
Bailey Sterling L. 4718 Langley av.
Bailey Theodore P. 5542 Madison av.
Bailey W. C. 721 Pullman bldg.
Baily Lila Miss, 3807 Lake av.
Bain David S. 1258 Wilcox av.
Bain E. A. Mrs. 364 Bowen av.
Bain Foree, 52 St. Clair
Bain Lewis R. 491 W. Congress
Bain Wm. Lett Dr. 390 N. Clark
Baines Oscar O. Dr. 420 Centre
       Sum. res. Bear Lake, Mich.
Baird C. A. Norwood Park
Baird David S. 4714 Evans av.
Baird Frank T. Virginia hotel
Baird Frederick B. 6812 Yale
Baird Frederick S. 758 Walnut
Baird George H. 4507 Lake av.
Baird George W.Maj. U.S.A.608 Division
Baird James Mrs. 6222 Oglesby av.
Baird James Q. 840 W. Monroe
Baird Lyman, 465 Dearborn av.
Baird Mary Mrs. 293 Warren av.
Baird Max. 465 Dearborn av.
Baird P. E. Mayfair
Baird Robert Prof. Evanston
Baird Thomas, Southern hotel
Baird Wyllys W. 1915 Wellington av.
Bak H., M.D. 3319 South Park av.
Baker Addison B. 7046 Stewart av.
Baker Albert C. 1437 Wrightwood av.
Baker Alfred L. 1949 Prairie av.
Baker Arthur G. Evanston
Baker A. Emmett, 7046 Stewart av.
Baker A. H. 2622 Wabash av.
Baker A. H. Mrs. 6419 Wright
Baker B. F. 836 W. Adams
Baker Charles jr. 7737 Emerald av.
Baker Charles E. 7737 Emerald av.
Baker Charles H. Highland Park
Baker Charles S. 35, 53d (H.P.)
Baker C. A. Mrs. 457 Englewood av.
Baker C. A. Miss, 1610 Indiana av,
Baker C. Edward, 3350 Indiana av.
Baker C. H. 2973 Groveland av.
Baker C. S. 2622 Wabash av.
Baker Digory W. 731 W. Adams.
       Sum. res. Hinsdale, Ill.
Baker D. H. 3247 Calumet av.
Baker D. W. 176, 37th
Baker D. W. jr. 713 W. Adams
Baker Edward, Longwood
Baker Edwin R. 4460 Oakenwald av.
Baker Emily Mrs. Washington Heights
Baker E. Darwin, Hinsdale
Baker E. F. Dr. Evanston
Baker E. P. 3865 Lake av.

Baker Frank Judge, 3543 Lake av.
Baker Frank C. 283 Irving av.
Baker Frank E. 3917 Grand boul.
Baker Frank E. 1271 Palmer
Baker Frank G. 152 N. Clark
Baker Frank H. 206, 46th (H.P.)
Baker Frank J. 335 W. Monroe.
Baker Frederick S. 2668 Charlton av.
Baker F. E. 6519 Yale
Baker F. G. Oak Park
Baker F. R. 7157 Webster av. Eng.
Baker George. Winnetka
Baker Geore A. jr. 219 S. Oakley av.
Baker George S. Evanston
Baker George W. 638 Chestnut, Eng.
Baker Henry, 713 W. Adams
Baker Henry D. 2255 Michigan av.
Baker Hiram, 415 Lasalle av.
Baker H. D. Evanston
Baker J. Mrs. 699 W. Monroe
Baker James E. 205, 53d (H.P.)
Baker James R. 3995 Ellis av.
Baker John F. 331 Cedar, Englewood
Baker John M. Oak Park
Baker J. E. Evanston
Baker L. H. Dr. Oak Park
Baker Mary Mrs. Washington Heights
Baker Milton H. jr. Highland Park
Baker Moses, 4410 Ellis av.
Baker M. H. Mrs. Highland Park
Baker O. A. 7241 Yale
Baker R. A. 23 Waverly pl.
Baker Samuel, 3995 Ellis av.
Baker Samuel E. River Forest
Baker Selby S. 7015 Oglesby av.
Baker S. S. Dr. 901 Jackson boul.
Baker T.Mrs.7157 Webster av. Eng.
Baker William E. 110 Astor
Baker William H. 1390 Jackson boul.
Baker William H. La Grange
Baker William T. 2255 Michigan av.
Baker W. A. 691½ W. Adams
Baker W. D. 87 Rush
Baker W. G. 408 The Plaza
Baker W. M. 3518 Calumet av.
Baker W. S. Hotel Groveland
Baker W. Vincent, 2125 Calumet av.
Bake Paul O. The Tudor
Balch N. C. 4460 Oakenwald av.
Balding Wm. T. Evanston
Baldwin Abraham, 47 Woodland Park
Baldwin Adelia C.Mrs.3849 Michigan av.
Baldwin Annie Miss, 47 Woodland Park
Baldwin Arthur Kirke, 5517 Cornell av.
Baldwin A. E. Dr. 828 W. Adams
Baldwin A. H. 3000 Indiana av.
Baldwin Benson D. Evanston
Baldwin Byron A. 136 N. Kedzie av.
Baldwin B. F. 522 W. Monroe
Baldwin Charles A. 1182 Millard av.
Baldwin Charles H. 615 The Plaza
Baldwin Charles M. Dr. Oak Park
Baldwin C. C. Berwyn
Baldwin David S. Oak Park
Baldwin E. C. Mrs. 6357 Yale
Baldwin George F. 2429 Michigan av.

Baldwin Harry H. 3852 Lake av.
Baldwin Heman, 3217 Groveland av.
Baldwin Henry, 3030 Lake Park av.
Baldwin H. C. 522 W. Monroe
Baldwin H. F. 910 Pullman bldg.
Baldwin James A. 4101 Calumet av.
Baldwin John Mrs. 3852 Lake av.
Baldwin John A. 3852 Lake av.
Baldwin Joseph C. 6357 Yale
Baldwin J. A. Oak Park
Baldwin J. H. 5534 Washington av.
Baldwin Kent K. 4716 Evans av.
Baldwin Libbie Miss 663 W. Monroe
Baldwin L. Jerome 38 Sidney ct.
Baldwin L. S. 38 Sidney ct.
Baldwin Myron T. La Grange
Baldwin S. M. Mrs. 2925 Prairie av.
Baldwin T. C. 385 Warren av.
Baldwin Walter S. 1236 Wilcox av.
Baldwin William, 207 Warren av.
Baldwin Willis M. 3849 Michigan av.
Balfour Harry, Riverside
Balfour John, Riverside
Balfour Walter E. Riverside
Balfour William K. La Grange
Balkwill J. F. 201 Park av.
Ball Charles H. 1143 Washington boul.
Ball Charles J. Mrs. Chicago Beach hotel
Ball Charles T. 4744 Langley av.
Ball David M. Norwood Park
Ball F. Q. Oak Park
Ball George C. 506 W. Congress
Ball Godfrey H. 4028 Lake av.
Ball Jane H. Mrs. Evanston
Ball J. A. 6531 Harvard
Ball Lysander C. 4744 Langley av.
Ball Mary J. Mrs. Evanston
Ball S. Willis, 4744 Langley av.
Ball Thomas, 1560 Lill av.
Ball Walter D. 4938 Drexel boul.
Ball William A. 94, 37th
Ballagh James H. Hinsdale
Ballard Addison, 1514 Michigan av.
Ballard Charles D. 38 Madison Park
Ballard Charles H. Ridgeland
Ballard C. N. Dr. 402 S. Paulina
Ballard Clarence W. Austin
Ballard DeWitt P. 4550 Ellis av.
Ballard Elizabeth B. Mrs. 99, 37th
Ballard F. E. Oak Park
Ballard George S. 3642 Prairie av.
Ballard J. Harry, 625 Sedgwick
Ballard Mary E. Mrs. 419, 48th
Ballard Orville W. 3642 Prairie av.
Ballard Thomas P. Evanston
Ballenberg Abraham A. 3311 Rhodes av.
Ballenberg Jules, 2901 Michigan av.
Ballenberg Yette Mrs. 3650 Grand boul.
Ballou Miranda Mrs. 303 Wilson av.
Ballou M. A. Mrs. 7201 Webster av. Eng.
Balmer Thomas, 1327 Hollywood av.
Baltz Charles, 1543 W. Monroe
Bamberger Gabriel Prof. 3520 Rhodes av.
Bancroft Allen R. Evanston
Bancroft Edgar A. 266 Erie
Bancroft George, Evanston

Bancroft J. D. Oak Park
Band Edward C. 1232 Wrightwood av.
Band Henry F. 999 Warren av.
Bane Chas. F. 442, 65th, Englewood
   Sum. res. Lake Geneva, Wis.
Bane Levi B. 3147 Calumet av.
Bane Oscar F. Auditorium hotel
Banga Emily Miss, 456 Lasalle av.
Banga H., M.D. 456 Lasalle av.
Banghart William J. Chicago Beach hotel
Bangs Dean, 3861 Ellis av.
Bangs Edward W. 396 N. State
Bangs Fred A. 143 S. Hoyne av.
Bangs Harrie L. 3861 Ellis av.
Bangs John D. 3861 Ellis av.
Bangs Mark, 143 S. Hoyne av.
Bangs Maude L. Mrs. 410 Washington boul.
Bangs William B. 569 Warren av.
Banks A. Arthur, 720 Jackson boul.
Banks A. F. Oak Park
Banks Charles E. 5725 Rosalie ct.
Banks James M. 245 S. Leavitt
Banks J. C. 868 W. Monroe
Banks J. C. LaGrange
Banks J. N. Dr. 2415 Michigan av.
Bannard Henry C. 295 Huron
Banning Ephraim, 685 Washington boul.
Banning Sam. 5610 Madison av.
Banning Thomas A. 5610 Madison av.
Bannister L. P. 3045 Groveland av.
Banta Cornelius V. jr. 4407 Ellis av.
Barbe Martin, 3157 Prairie av.
Barbe Morris, 367 Oakwood boul.   •
Barbeau James, Ridgeland .
Barbee W. S. 7026 Yale
Barber Adam Dr. 460 Warren av.
Barber Albert H. 22 Bryant av.
Barber Arthur E. Evanston
Barber Eliza C. Mrs. Evanston
Barber E. L. 2956 Groveland av.
Barber Fanny A. Miss, 1854 Wellington av.
Barber F. A., M.D. 6320 Woodlawn av
Barber George M. 1854 Wellington
Barber Hiram, 140 Lincoln av.
Barber H. A. jr. 341 W. Monroe
Barber H. P. Clifton house
Barber Joel Allen, Galena
Barber L. M. 184, 41st
Barber Russell M. 272 Marshfield av.
Barber W. D., M.D. 1004 N. Halsted
Barbour Charles W. 3629 Ellis Park
Barbour Edward, 24 Delaware pl.
Barbour Ernest, 348 Ashland boul.
Barbour Frank, Chicago Beach hotel
Barbour George M. 5484 Monroe av.
Barbour Grovene P. Miss, 2335 Michigan av.
Barbour James J. 4128 Fay av.
Barbour Lyman L. Mrs. 348 Ashland boul.
Barbour Victor M. 3224 Forest av.
Barbour William T. River Forest
Barcal Teresa Mrs. 22, 46th (H.P.)
Barclay A. B. Mrs. Hotel Metropole
Barclay Jacob L. 4424 Berkeley av.

Bard Charles W. 647 W. Monroe
Bard David J. 12 Bryant av.
Barden H. R. 2927 Indiana av.
Barden James M. 2927 Indiana av.
Bardon Daniel G. 336, 41st (H.P.)
Bardon M. M. 3113 Wabash av.
Bardwell H. J. Stamford hotel
Bardwell Orsamus H. 4733 Champlain av.
Barfield Wm. G. 577 W. Adams
Barge William D. Iroquois Club
Barger Richard W. 4052 Grand boul.
Barhydt Frank, Evanston
Barker Agnes Mrs. 415 Lasalle av.
Barker Alfred, 1307 W. Adams
          Sum. res. Lake Bluff
Barker Charles A, 7149 Euclid av. (H.P.)
Barker Charles E. 345 W. Adams
Barker Clyde, 415 Lasalle av.
Barker Cordelia E. Mrs. 1607 Michigan
    av.
Barker C. A. 1, 40th
Barker David E. Mrs. Evanston
Barker Frank W. 4633 Greenwood av.
Barker Geo. F. 345 W. Adams
Barker James, 134, 50th
Barker James S. 342, 44th (H.P.)
Barker John C. 717 Fullerton av.
Barker John R. 2421 Indiana av.
Barker J. N. 5000 Greenwood av.
Barker Milton Dr. 4625 Greenwood av.
Barker Moses Rev. 3629 Ellis Park
Barker M. E. Wilmette
Barker O. B. Oak Park
Barker P. H. Chicago Beach hotel
Barker R. Alice Miss, Evanston
Barker Samuel B. 2815 Prairie av.
Barker Wallace C. Mrs. 3353 Wabash av.
Barker Walter A. 161, 25th
Barker William, 834 Washington boul.
Barker William jr. 834 Washington boul.
Barkley J. J. 175 N. State
Barler Augustus C. 537 Garfield av.
Barles Charles O. 573, 51st (H.P.)
Barlow Arthur W. 573 Burling
Barlow Catherine N. Mrs. Evanston
Barlow Napoleon B. Evanston
Barlow Robert, 754 W. Monroe
Barlow Samuel S. Palmer house
Barmm Charles H. 722 Carroll av.
Barmm Frank H. 722 Carroll av.
Barmore Nathaniel L. 4043 Grand boul.
Barnard Albert E. 229 S. Lincoln
Barnard Alice L. Miss, Tracy
Barnard A. W. 9 Roslyn pl.
Barnard Charles J. River Forest
Barnard C. A. 908½ W. Adams
Barnard Daniel, Tracy
Barnard Elizabeth Miss, Tracy
Barnard Erastus A. Tracy
Barnard Eugene E. Evanston
Barnard E. C. 229 S. Lincoln
Barnard Frank A. 1300 Wilcox av.
Barnard Frank E. 3982 Ellis av.
Barnard Fred, Oak Park
Barnard F. G. Park Ridge
Barnard Gilbert W. 3012 Indiana av.

Barnard George, 580 Lasalle av.
Barnard Harry, 3243 Rhodes av.
Barnard Hayden S. Dr. 4022 Vincennes av.
Barnard Henry, 861 Jackson boul.
Barnard James H. Hotel Imperial
Barnard J. E. 3739 Ellis av.
Barnard Louisa C. Mrs. 159 Cass
Barnard Moses R. Evanston
Barnard M. D. Mrs. 861 Jackson boul.
Barnard Richard, 162, 36th
Barnes Albert R. Evanston
Barnes A. B. Mrs. 145 Oakwood boul.
Barnes A. C. Riverside
Barnes Bertha L. Miss, 2238 Calumet av.
Barnes B. C. 109 Park av. (L.V.)
Barnes Charles, 335 W. Monroe
Barnes Charles, 642 Sedgwick
Barnes Charles E. 6108 Stewart av.
Barnes Charles J. 2238 Calumet av.
Barnes Charles M. 3617 Prairie av.
Barnes Charles W. Auditorium Annex
Barnes C. E. Lexington hotel
Barnes David L. 575 Division
Barnes Don J. 425 Garfield boul.
Barnes D. Monroe, 145 Oakwood boul.
Barnes Erastus A. 7814 Union av.
Barnes Francis W. Wilmette
Barnes Frank J. 4337 Grand boul.
Barnes Frederick M. 7554 Bond av.
Barnes F. A. 928 Jackson boul.
Barnes F. G. 608 Dearborn av.
Barnes Geo. K. 469 W. Monroe
Barnes Henry B. 1259 Palmer
Barnes James M. Evanston
Barnes John A. 6108 Stewart av.
Barnes J. P. 3756 Ellis av.
Barnes J. S. Mrs. 608 Dearborn av.
Barnes J. S. Mrs. 6331 Honore
Barnes Lillian Miss, 2968 Vernon av.
Barnes M O. Miss, 854 Washington
    boul. ary
Barnes Myra Miss, 7814 Union av.
Barnes M. Augusta Mrs. 292 Park av.
Barnes Nelson H. Mrs. 616 The Plaza
Barnes Nelson L. 2238 Calumet av.
Barnes Noah, 5046 Jefferson av.
Barnes Romulus E. 3617 Prairie av.
Barnes Samuel D. 3617 Prairie av.
Barnes Sarah Miss, 2141 Calumet av.
Barnes Walter, Victoria hotel
Barnes Walter S. Dr. 2968 Vernon av.
Barnes William R. 3617 Prairie av.
Barnet Annie Miss, 6156 Lexington av.
Barnet Emanuel P. 5901 Indiana av.
Barnet Henry, 3600 Prairie av.
Barnet Henry L. 6156 Lexington av.
Barnet Henry L. jr. 6156 Lexington av.
Barnett Albert Llewellyn, 4204 Michi-
    gan av.
Barnett A. R, Mrs. Chicago Beach hotel
Barnett A. S. Mrs. 319 Washington boul.
Barnett G. W. 1578 Lill av.
Barnett John, 228 S. Paulina
Barnett John H. Revere house
Barnett Joseph H. Austin
Barnett M. P. 5901 Indiana av.

Barnett W. Y. 6430 Woodlawn av.
Barney Bruce B. 2628 Prairie av.
Barney B. B. Mrs. 2628 Prairie av.
Barney F. N. 6100 Princeton av.
Barney J. F. 5115 Cornell av.
Barney J. W. 6100 Princeton av.
Barnhart Arthur M, 113 Cass
Barnhart A. E. 505 Jackson boul.
Barnhart K. 4312 Greenwood av:
Barnhart Mary Mrs.471 Washington boul.
Barnhart Wm. J. 471 Washington boul.
Barnheisel Charles H. 4400 Grand boul.
Barnheisel Frederick R. 4400 Grand boul.
Barnheisel Henrietta Mrs. 4400 Grand
   boul.
Barnhurst Joseph, 34 Sidney ct.
Barnum Albert C. 245 Oakwood boul.
Barnum Albert W. Riverside
Barnum D. B. Mrs. Hotel Metropole
Barnum Edward S. 245 Oakwood boul.
Barnum J. S. Granada hotel
Barnum L. A. Mrs. 4803 Greenwood av.
Barnum O. H. Granada hotel
Barnum Samuel, 245 Oakwood boul.
Barnum William E. 5904 Michigan av.
Barnum W. H. Riverside
Barnum W. L. Lakota hotel
Barothy Victor, 4203 Ellis av.
Barr Alfred E. 1393 W. Monroe
Barr George 5950 Princeton av.
Barr John C. The Renfost
Barr Oliver M. River Forest
Barr William T. Hinsdale
Barratt Edgar G. 4858 Washington av.
Barrell Albert M. 2918 Michigan av.
Barrell G. L. 350 Racine av.
Barrell James, 2918 Michigan av.
Barrell J. Finley, 4805 Kimbark av.
Barrell Stewart E. 2918 Michigan av.
Barrett Ancil D. Mrs. 4408 Berkeley av.
Barrett Blanch L. Miss, 2925 Prairie av.
Barrett Charles, 983 Warren av.
Barrett Charles C. Sherman House
Barrett Charles R. 51 Pine
Barrett Charles R. 2925 Prairie av.
Barrett Charles W. 327, 42d
Barrett Clyde E. Maywood
Barrett C. C. 363 Marshfield av.
Barrett Elmer E. Western Springs
Barrett Eliza Mrs. 709 Orchard
Barrett Francis M.1304 Washington boul.
Barrett Frederick B. 4408 Berkeley av.
Barrett George D. 4341 St. Lawrence
   av.
Barrett George K. 3230 Calumet av.
Barrett James P. 4068 Lake av.
Barrett John F. River Forest
Barrett John P. Prof. 4400 Michigan av.
Barrett John R. 3230 Calumet av.
Barrett June, 186, 41st (H. P.)
Barrett J. 216 N. State
Barrett Laura T. Miss, 2520 Prairie av.
Barrett Louis, 4068 Lake av.
Barrett Marcus L. 3822 Ellis av.
Barrett Miriam Miss, 2520 Prairie av.
Barrett M. Mrs. 378 W. Adams

Barrett O. W. 2233 Calumet av.
Barrett O. W. Mrs. 785 W. Monroe
Barrett Robert D. 109 Lake shore drive
Barrett R. E. 5754 Washington av.
Barrett R. E. 6442 Yale
Barrett R. G. jr. 7230 Vernon av.
Barrett S. E. 109 Lake shore drive
Barrett T. E. 2653 N. Paulina
Barrett William C. Highland Park
Barrett William M. 327, 42d (H. P.)
Barrett W. H. 339 Ohio
Barrie Mary L. Miss, Evanston
Barringer D. C. 3211 Vernon av.
Barringer Walter M. 3211 Vernon av.
Barrington Charles V. 6026 Washington
   av.
Barron Elwyn A. 111 Walton pl.
Barron John P. 399 W. Taylor
Barron Mahlon, 6352 Oglesby av.
Barron Maria Mrs. 346 Park av.
Barrow John S. 9 Chalmers pl.
Barrows John Henry Rev., D.D. 2957
   Indiana av.
      Sum. res. Mackinac Island, Mich.
Barrows R. M., M.D. 6413 Sheridan av.
Barry Catherine Mrs. 142 Center
Barry Edward P. 4216 Ellis av.
Barry Frank H. Hotel Barry
Barry Frank H. jr. Hotel Barry
Barry Fred. 4216 Ellis av.
Barry George, Wilmette
Barry George F. Wilmette
Barry George S. 6320 Drexel av.
Barry James H. Granada hotel
Barry Joseph K. 760 Washington boul.
Barry L. A. 4526 Prairie av.
Barry Kathryn Miss, 6600 Yale
Barry Miles, 419 Oak
Barry P. T. 6600 Yale
      Summer res. Lake Geneva
Barry Samuel S. Kenilworth
Barry Thomas F. 3246 Wabash av.
Barry W. E. 6320 Drexel av.
Barry William H. Hotel Barry
Barstow C. F. Irving Park
Barstow C. H. 41 Surrey ct.
Barstow H. D. Mrs. Irving Park
Barstow Jane R. Mrs. 2233 Sheridan rd.
Barstow Joseph, 571 W. Congress
Barstow M. E. Mrs. 678 Park av.
Barstow-Pike Rhoda Dr. Irving Park
Bartelme Adeline T. Miss, 1484 Fulton
Bartelme E. J. 774 Larrabee
Bartelme Ferdinand E. Austin
Bartelme George P. 1484 Fulton
Bartelme May M. Miss, 1484 Fulton
Bartelme M. 774 Larrabee
Barth Alexander, 3208 Calumet av.
Barth George J. 249 Sheffield av.
Bartholf Charles S. 332 Hampden ct.
Bartholf William J. Roslyn pl.
Bartholomae Frank, 79 MacAlister pl.
Bartholomew E. L. 78 Centre av.
Bartholomew H. J. G. Rev. 469 N. Robey
Bartholomew J. K. Dr. 469 N. Robey
Bartholomew J. N. Dr. 133 Lincoln av.

Bartholomew L. 640 Chestnut, Englewood
Bartholomew W. S. 301 Orchard
Bartlett A. C. 2720 Prairie av.
Bartlett Benjamin, 3802 Lake av.
Bartlett Charles A. 6731 Perry av.
Bartlett Charles T. Evanston
Bartlett C. C. 247 Winchester av.
Bartlett C. L. Hotel Windermere
Bartlett E. B. Oak Park
Bartlett F. O. The Arizona
Bartlett George B. 4470 Oakenwald av.
Bartlett George F. 4466 Oakenwald av.
Bartlett George F. jr. 4466 Oakenwald av.
Bartlett G. E. Mrs. 5484 Monroe av.
Bartlett Harry A. Austin
Bartlett John M.D. 462 Division
Bartlett John A. 6731 Perry av.
Bartlett Joseph F. Rev. Austin
Bartlett Josiah C. 40 Sidney ct.
Bartlett M. A. 509 W. Monroe
Bartlett N. Gray, Prof. 44 Ray
      Sum res. Belvidere Park, Lake
      Geneva, Wis.
Bartlett Rufus H. Dr. 496 Jackson boul.
Bartlett S. C. Mrs. Winnetka
Bartlett William Rev. Ridgeland
Bartlett William H. Evanston
Bartlett W. M. 6651 Perry av.
Bartley Charles E. 6322 Drexel av.
Bartling Fred. 302 Chicago av.
Bartling Henry C. 228 Garfield av.
Bartling Louis, 227 Hampden ct.
Bartling William Rev. 183 Fremont
Barto D. O. Oak Park
Barton Charles A. Evanston
Barton E. M. 143, 47th (H. P.)
Barton George F. Austin
Barton George P. 5307 Lexington av.
Barton Jesse B. 4119 Berkeley av.
Barton Paulina A. Mrs. 4119 Berkeley av.
Barwick John, Tracy
Basch Joseph, 3132 South Park av.
Bascom Adelaide Mrs. 376 Warren av.
Bascom William R. 3612 Ellis av.
Baseler Carl F. 1731 Frederick
Baskin O. L. Evanston
Bass Catherine Miss Lexington Hotel
Bass George, 2451 Michigan av.
Bass George A. Evanston
Bass James K. Evanston
Bass M. H. Mrs. Evanston
Bass Oscar S. 6116 Washington av.
Bass Perkins B. Evanston
Bassett Andrew J. Austin
Bassett Arthur J. 7520 Nutt av.
Bassett Blanche Miss, 1547 N. Halsted
Bassett Charles F. Dr. 20 Aldine sq.
Bassett Charles W. 2663 N. Ashland av.
Bassett E. C. Mrs. 18 Aldine sq.
Bassett Fletcher S. Mrs. 5208 Kimbark av.
Bassett George H. 871 Sawyer av.
Bassett George R. Dr. 871 Sawyer av
Bassett H. W. Dr. Oak Park
Bassett J. Dr. 133 S. Morgan
Bassett J. Eugene, 3125 Wabash av.
Bassett J. S. 3125 Wabash av.

Bassett Laura B. Mrs. 4425 Ellis av.
Bassett Nelson M. Austin
Bassett Orlando P. Hinsdale
Bassett R. J. 133 S. Morgan
Bassett Samuel W. 428 S. Leavitt
Bassett Susan A. Dr. 871 Sawyer av.
Bassett Wilbur W. 5208 Kimbark av.
Bassler Eugene 165 S. Wood
Batchelder A. 3140 Vernon av.
Batchelder James L. 2684 N. Paulina
Batchelder John H. Winnetka
Batcheller Webster, Auditorium hotel
Bate Henry J. 20 Bellevue pl.
Bate J. W., M.D. 28½ Bellevue pl.
Bateman Charles E. 571 Burling
Bateman Charles S. 4447 Ellis av.
Bateman Josephine Mrs. 276 Fremont
Bates Edward C. 562 Boulevard pl.
Bates Emma Miss, Hinsdale
Bates Fred. G. 5751 Madison av.
Bates Frederick H. Dr. Elmhurst
Bates George C. 5751 Madison av.
Bates Granville, 96 Evanston av.
Bates Harry B. 6932 Stewart av.
Bates Harry M. 5738 Washington av.
Bates Harvey H. Dr. 3058 Calumet av.
Bates H. O. Dr. 278 Marshfield av.
Bates J. Harvey Dr. 3256 South Park av.
Bates Lindon W. 56 Astor
Bates Marmaduke, 6 Langley pl.
Bates Morgan, Newberry hotel
Bates Morley, 278 Marshfield av.
Bates Onward, 292 Belden av.
Bates Thomas, Evanston
Bates Walter N. Riverside
Bates William S. 18 Bryant av.
Bateson Alexander 4294 Michigan av.
Bathrick Daniel B. 823 Chase av.
Batkin J. S. 6711 Stewart av
Battams Walter J. Evanston
Battell C. W. 522 The Plaza
Battelle A. C. Hotel Windermere .
Battelle Joel A. Evanston
Batterman John H. 457 Dearborn av.
Batterman John O. 478 Ashland boul.
Battershall Elbert, 661 Park av.
Batterson W. H. 4120 Berkeley av.
Baudouine Charles A. 6341 Sheridan av.
Bauer Agnes Mrs. 7757 Sherman
Bauer Alma Miss, 229 Fremont
Bauer Augustus, 402 Lasalle av.
Bauer Gustav T. 3653 Grand boul.
Bauer G. H. Irving Park
Bauer John C. 1178 Washington boul.
      Sum. res. Warrenville, Ill.
Bauer Julia Miss, 229 Fremont
Bauer Julius Mrs. 4412 Ellis av.
Bauer Louis, 3653 Grand boul.
Bauer Louise Miss, 229 Fremont
Bauer L. P. 5137 Lexington av.
Bauer Michael, Mrs. 22 Lincoln pl.
Bauer Philip C. 4546 Vincennes av.
Bauer Richard, 4412 Ellis av.   ·
Bauer R. S. 4526 Prairie av.
Baugh J. L. 2411 South Park av.
Bauland Jacob H. 3615 Ellis av.

Bauland Joseph H. Hotel Metropole
Bauland Morris, 2946 Prairie av.
Bauland Pauline Miss, 3615 Ellis av.
Baum C. F. 6543 Lafayette av.
Baum H. 3220 Prairie av.
Baum J. 3322 Vernon av.
Baum Simon H. 704 North Park av.
Baum S. M, 743 Warren av.
Baum William L., M.D. Chicago Beach hotel
Bauman Edward, 3011 Michigan av.
Bauman Joseph, 3011 Michigan av.
Bauman Edward S. 1844 Wellington
Baumann Frederick, 1844 Wellington
Baumann F. O. 518 Dearborn av.
Baumgartl B. Mrs. 251 Ashland boul.
Baumgartl Isadore, 461 W. Congress
Baur George Prof. 357, 58th (H. P.)
Baur John, 278 Fremont
Bausher Henry, 384 Lasalle av.
Baux F. A. Julien hotel
Baxter A. J., M.D. 4406 Grand boul.
Baxter A. Lawson, 4406 Grand boul.
Baxter D. Frank, 424 Oak
Baxter Edith Miss, Hotel Metropole
Baxter Robert Y. Winnetka
Baxter Thomas M. Hotel Metropole
Baxter Wm. G. The Ashland
Bay G. P. 6400 Wentworth av.
Bayless Benjamin, French house, Evanston
Bayless Charles T. French house, Evanston
Bayless Farmer D. Ridgeland
Bayless George W. Evanston
Bayley Annie Miss, 62 Astor
Bayley Edwin F. 4634 Greenwood av.
Baylies Oscar S. 5610 Indiana av.
Baylies R. N. 4800 Grand boul.
Baylis Charlotte Miss, 341 W. Monroe
Baylis Jennie Miss, 341 W. Monroe
Bayliss J. H. Mrs. Evanston
Bayne Milton, 7637 Union av.
Bayne William, 165 Locust
Baynes George A. Dr. 8 St. James pl.
Baynes James, 522 Chestnut, Eng.
Bayor Lawrence, 357 Bowen av.
Beach Chandler B. Riverside
Beach Chas. S. 606 Chestnut, Eng.
Beach Clinton S. 57 Bryant av.
Beach C. B. 55 Cedar
Beach Edmund G. 4237 Grand boul.
Beach Edward, 484, 42d pl. (H.P.)
Beach Edward P. 1556 Fulton
Beach Elli A. 57 Bryant av.
Beach Elmer E. 933 Greenleaf av.
Beach E. K. 55 Cedar
Beach Franklin G. Evanston
Beach George, Hinsdale
Beach George L. Dr. 444 Jackson boul.
Beach Harry L. 3224 Rhodes av.
Beach Henry L. 57 Bryant av.
Beach James A. Tracy
Beach Katharine M. Miss, 484, 42d pl. (H.P.)
Beach Mary E. Miss, 1556 Fulton

Beach Myron H. 3224 Rhodes av.
Beach Raymond W. 818 Greenleaf av.
Beach Samuel C. 630 Jackson boul.
Beach S. L. 5484 Monroe av.
Beal Jennette Miss, 368 Ontario
Beal John P. 4823 Champlain av.
Beale Charles D. 6033 Oglesby av.
Beale Roland R. 6033 Oglesby av.
Beale Warren A. 6033 Oglesby av.
Beale Wm. G. Union Club
Beall F. D. Mrs. Chicago Beach hotel
Beall F. W. Chicago Beach hotel
Beall Mary A. Mrs. 258 Michigan av.
Beall William D. 296 Superior
Beals J. F. 4212 Oakenwald av.
Beam Rudolph R. Hinsdale
Bean Charles H, 4554 Emerald av.
Bean Dixon, 5531 Washington av.
Bean William H. 405, 64th (H.P.)
Bear Sydney, 222 Warren av.
Beard C. H. Dr. 6030 Park End av.
Beard D. C. The Renfost
Beard Frank, 3525 Calumet av.
Beard Herbert A. 1048 Jackson boul.
Beard P. D. Chicago Beach hotel
Beard Richard, Oak Park
Beard Thomas, Evanston
Beardsley Addison H. 5724 Rosalie ct.
Beardsley A. 3536 Lake av.
Beardsley D. E. Mrs. 3756 Ellis av.
Beardsley Emma F. Mrs. 6521 Yale
Beardsley Florence Miss, Hotel Barry
Bearse Hiram, LaGrange
Bearson Olive Mrs. Evanston
Bearup Andrew C. Evanston
Bearup Helen A. Miss, 4107 Grand boul.
Bearup Marium A. Miss, 4107 Grand boul.
Beaton David, Rev. 1040 N. Clark
Beattie Alex F. 180 N. State
Beattie Chas. J. 524, 60th, Eng.
Beattie C. S. Oak Park
Beattie John S. 6144 Sheridan av.
Beattie Paul, 1726 Briar pl.
Beatty Frank E. LaGrange
Beatty Harry B. LaGrange
Beatty James T. LaGrange
Beatty Sarah J. Mrs. LaGrange
Beatty William R. LaGrange
Beaty W. D. Hotel Barry
Beaty W. W. 770 W. Monroe
Beaudry J. S., M.D. 7047 Webster av. Eng.
Beaumont George, 1509 Wellington
Beaumont Robert L. Dr. 5216 Jefferson av.
Beaunisne Albert G. Hotel Barry
Beauvais E. A. 1942 Barry av.
Beaver Jane Mrs. 3125 Wabash av.
Beaver J. E. 3121 Wabash av.
Beazley John G. Evanston
Bebb Edwin, 6627 Harvard
Bechtole S. H. Julien hotel
Beck Anthony, 410, 42d (H.P.)
Beck August, 356 Lasalle av.
Beck Burt A. 3200 Lake Park av.
Beck Carl A. Dr. 174 Eugenie
Beck Charles A. 3200 Lake Park av.

Beck Edward Scott, 2634 Indiana av.
Beck E. H. Mrs. 4632 Vincennes av.
Beck George W. 403 Oak
Beck J. S. 295, 42d (H.P.)
Beck Lora Miss, Newberry hotel
Beck M. I. 7120 Euclid av. (H. P.)
Beck Raymond A. 3200 Lake Park av.
Becker A. G. 3602 Prairie av.
Becker A. W. 4329 Oakenwald av.
Becker A. W. 3804 Indiana av.
Becker Benjamin F. 4924 Ellis av.
Becker Carl, 543 Burling
Becker C. O. Mrs. 336 Fullerton av.
Becker Edwin L. 4324 Greenwood av.
Becker Frederick W. 4169 Berkeley av.
Becker George W. 4333 Langley av.
Becker Hermann J. 339 Lincoln av.
Becker Isaac J. 3804 Indiana av,
Becker Leopold, 82 Lincoln av.
.Becker Louis, 3936 Grand boul.
Becker Mary A. Mrs. 4333 Langley av.
Becker Norbert, 301 West ct.
Becker N. 3217 Wabash av.
Becker S. Mrs. 4924 Ellis av.
Becker William C. 16 Lane pl.
Becker William J. 16 Lane pl.
Beckler Ashlin J. 817 Tuohy av.
Beckler Charles H. 1140 S. Lawndale av.
Beckler Elbridge H. 1329 Wilton av.
Beckler Eliza Mrs. 817 Tuohy av.
Beckley Major H. E. Riverside
Beckwith Charles H. 7721 Sherman
Beckwith Franklin H. Mrs. 77 Pine
Beckwith J. L. 250 Park av.
Beckwith R. W. 3202 Vernon av.
Beckwith Warren L. 426 N. State
Bedard Antoine J. Oak Park
Bedee Frank W. 3120 Groveland av.
Bedell E. M. Mrs. 507 W. Monroe
Bedell Leila G., M.D. Newberry hotel
Bee Harry, 3349 Wabash av.
Bee Joseph Mrs. 3349 Wabash av.
Bee R. Addison, 3349 Wabash av.
Beebe Albert G., M.D. 582 W. Adams
Beebe Archibald A. Evanston
Beebe Curtis M., M.D. 619 Washington boul.
Beebe Emma A. Mrs. 2207 Prairie av.
Beebe George H. 47, 26th
Beebe Ralph E. Wilmette
Beebe Thomas H. Evanston
Beebe William H. 405 N. State
Beecher Jerome Mrs. 241 Michigan av.
Beecher Walter N. 7052 Stewart av.
Beecroft F. W. La Grange
Beedy Mary E. Miss, 481 Dearborn av.
Beek Horace W. 164 Warren av.
Beeks Edward C. 322, 57th (H.P.)
Beeks E. A. 6336 Oglesby av.
Beeks James C. 322, 57th (H.P.)
Beeks Mack W. 322, 57th (H.P.)
Beeks McCarty W. 322, 57th (H.P.)
Beeman Charles H. 4018 Ellis av.
Beeman Charles W. 4018 Ellis av.
Beers John Mrs. 3616 Ellis av.
Beers J. H. 391 Warren av.

Beers Louis G. 237 Dearborn av.
Beers M. L. 5464 Jefferson av.
Beers Samuel, 3646 Wabash av.
Beery C. C. Dr. 4544 Michigan av.
Beeson Frederick C. Austin
Beeson S. J. Dr. 300 Washington boul.
Beeson Walter G. Austin
Beggs C. W. 435 Belden av.
Beggs John, 2222 Michigan av.
Behan Edwin A. 4525 Vincennes av.
Behan George H. 4525 Vincennes av.
Behan Warren P. 4525 Vincennes av.
Behel Vernon W. 4743 Langley av.
Behel Wilbur F. 3349 South Park av.
Behr Theo. 5468 Monroe av.
Behrend B. 584 W. Congress
Behrendt Felix Dr. 584 N. Wells
Behrens B. M. Dr. 1804 Deming ct.
Behrens Frank, 3326 Calumet av.
Behrens H. 1546 Aldine av.
Behrens John H. 1842 Oakdale av.
Behrens John H. Morton Park
Behrer J. C. 6125 Washington av.
Behring Henry, 1859 Nevada
Behring Louis, 1859 Nevada
Beidler Augustus F 167 S. Sangamon
Beidler A. W. 3257 Groveland av.
Beidler Francis, 4204 Drexel boul.
Beidler George, 167 S. Sangamon
Beidler H. A. Evanston
Beidler Jacob, 167 S. Sangamon
Beidler N. W. Lakota Hotel
Beidler W. H. 270 Jackson boul.
Beiersdorf Arthur, 3719 Langley av.
Beiersdorf Jacob, 3719 Langley av.
Beiersdorf Joseph R. 2528 Prairie av.
Beiersdorf Rosa Mrs. 2528 Prairie av.
Beifeld Alexander, 3304 Calumet av.
Beifeld Jacob C. 479 Bowen av.
Beifeld Joseph, 3304 Calumet av.
Beifeld Morris, 3000 Lake Park av.
Beirs Emma Mrs. 1628 Prairie av.
Beisel George W. Riverside
Beldam George, 5623 Michigan av.
Beldam George C. 5623 Michigan av.
Belden Agnes Miss, 5037 Washington av.
Belden C. S. hotel Normandie
Belden C. W. Mrs. Lakota hotel
Belden Grace Miss, 5037 Washington av.
Belden J. S. 4722 Woodlawn av.
Belden Reuben B. 3663 Wabash av.
Belding Caroline Mrs. 154 S. Leavitt
Belding George T. 154 S. Leavitt
Belding H. H. Longwood
Belding L. S. Mrs. Lakota hotel
Belfield Henry H. 5738 Washington av
Belfield Wm. T. Dr. 532 Garfield av.
Belford Alexander, 832 North Park av.
Belknap Addie M. Miss, 3235 Rhodes av.
Belknap Augustus L. Evanston
Belknap Charles C. 3235 Rhodes av.
Belknap Fred W. Evanston
Belknap Giles F. Oak Park
Belknap John, 3235 Rhodes av.
Belknap John S. Wilmette
Belknap S. W. 1210 Winthrop av.

Bell Alexander, 3231 Wabash av.
Bell A. L. 5810 Washington av.
Bell Clement, 3231 Wabash av.
Bell Cornelius F. 303 Huron
Bell Emma Mrs. 21 S. Paulina
Bell E. A. Mrs. 694 W. Monroe
Bell Frank E. 253, 66th (H.P.)
Bell F. H. 694 W. Monroe
Bell George, 9 Langley pl.
Bell Herbert E. 960 Warren av.
Bell James A. 6537 Harvard
Bell James M. Mrs. 23 University pl.
Bell John, 602 Lincoln av.
Bell Joseph P. 303 Huron
Bell Joseph P. jr. 303 Huron
Bell J. H. 4037 Drexel boul.
Bell J. Johnston, M.D. 342 Fullerton av.
Bell J. M. Mrs. 466 Lasalle av.
Bell Leonard F. 694 W. Monroe
Bell Lilian Miss, 3941 Ellis av.
Bell Lottie Miss, 342 Fullerton av.
Bell Lottie Miss, 602 Lincoln av.
Bell L. A. 4800 St. Lawrence av.
Bell Mifflin E. 36 Aldine sq.
Bell M. C. Mrs. 4626 Indiana av.
Bell M. E. Mrs. 1195 Washington boul.
Bell Robert, 17 Madison Park
Bell Robert, Lake Forest
Bell S. L, Mrs. 6403 Oglesby av.
Bell Thomas W. Evanston
Bell T. N. 96 Arthington
Bell William W. 3941 Ellis av.
Bell W. Edward, 408 Washington boul.
Bellamy Henry C. 600 Dearborn av.
Bellamy H. Temple, 2412 Prairie av.
Bellamy Samuel J. 3644 Vincennes av.
Bellas Thomas H. 1634 Prairie av.
Bellinghausen W. 283 Bissell
Bellows Alice Mrs. 420 Centre
Bellows F. L. 632 Lasalle av.
Bellows Lou A. Miss, 3546 Ellis av.
Below Ida C. Mrs 1033 Evanston av.
Belz Frederick W. 647 N. Rohey
Beman George L. 296, 61st pl. (H.P.)
Beman S. S. 317, 49th (H.P.)
Beman W. Irving, 5222 Hibbard av.
Bement E. D. Mrs. 508 N. State
Bemis Edward W. 5836 Drexel av.
Bemis Henry V. Hotel Richelieu
Benbow E. B. 948 Park av.
Bender John A. 3907 Prairie av.
Bender John R. 3907 Prairie av.
Benedict Albert, 4326 St. Lawrence av.
Benedict C. W. 6357 Yale
Benedict Edward, The Renfost
Benedict Edwin P. 786 W. Monroe
Benedict Geo. H. 32 Waverly pl.
Benedict George M. 4904 Washington av.
Benedict G. G. 786 W. Monroe
Benedict Harry 3943 Langley av.
Benedict Hattie Miss, 2415 Indiana av.
Benedict J. C. 839 Warren av.
Benedict Mary E. Mrs. 4160 Ellis av.
Benedict O. E. Mrs. 509 W. Adams
Benedix Hugo, 392 Belden av.
Beneke Henry A. 1953 Deming ct.

Beneke Lottie C. Miss, 1953 Deming ct.
Benham James W. 661 W. Monroe
Benham John, 2415 Michigan av.
Benham R. S. 509 Fullerton av.
Benight J. McD. Wilmette
Benjamin Henry S. 3916 Calumet av.
Benjamin H. B. Mrs. 3301 Vernon av.
Benjamin Louis, 3206 Vernon av.
Benjamin L. 3246 Vernon av.
Benke Ida M. Miss, 1177 Washington
  boul.
Benner Della Mrs. 4915 N. Clark
Benner James L. 63 E. Pearson
Benner Mathias, 54 Loomis
Bennett Annette Dr. Park Ridge
Bennett Arthur G. 2469 N. Paulina
Bennett Ashael F. 347, 67th
Bennett Caroline M. Mrs. Evanston
Bennett Carroll M. 121, 51st (H.P.)
Bennett Charles G. 260 N. Clark
Bennett Charles S. Evanston
Bennett Edwin A. 1137 Lawndale av.
Bennett E. B. 69 Park av.
Bennett E. R. Dr. 448 Seminary av.
Bennett E. W. Longwood
Bennett Frank I. 6045 Edgerton av.
Bennett George A. Evanston
Bennett George R. 5726 Washington a
Bennett G. D. 348 Chicago av.
Bennett G. L. Dr. 686½ Washington boul.
Bennett Henry C. 1167 W. Adams
Bennett Horace C. 487 Jackson boul.
Bennett H. E. 61 Laflin
Bennett I. M. 41, 46th (H.P)
Bennett Frank W. 492, 49th (H.P.)
Bennett James, 3138 Lake Park av.
Bennett John I. Mrs. 5726 Washington av.
Bennett John I. jr. 5726 Washington av.
Bennett J. C. Dr. Evanston
Bennett J. W. Austin
Bennett Martin H. Mrs. 121, 51st (H.P.)
Bennett Mary E. Dr. Norwood Park
Bennett Nelson J. 1145 Lawndale av.
Bennett N. Mrs. 190, 37th
Bennett Robert J. 2449 N. Paulina
Bennett Thomas, 3138 Lake Park av.
Bennett Willard, Evanston
Bennett Wilham, 5726 Washington av.
Bennett William H. 1712 Briar pl.
Bennington E. K. Dr. 55 33d (H.P.)
Bensinger B. E. 2217 Calumet av.
Bensinger E. A. 260, 37th
Bensinger M. 2217 Calumet av.
Bensley George, 3832 Langley av.
Bensley John R. 3929 Ellis av.
Bensley John R. jr. 3929 Ellis av.
Benson Abbie Miss, 1826 Indiana av.
Benson Alfred S. 494 Belden av.
Benson Christian L. 1023 Pratt av.
Benson C. E. Mrs. 676 W. Monroe
Benson C. E. Mrs. 803 Warren av.
Benson Edwin A. 3000 Michigan av.
Benson E. A. 107, 37th
Benson John A. Dr. 245 Warren av.
Benson Joseph B. 1242 Lawndale av.
Benson Mary Mrs. 245 Warren av.

Benson M. J. 517, 45th (H.P.)
Benson O. 494 Belden av.
Benson Paul, Evanston
Benson Peter, 2009 Indiana av.
Benson Walter E. 1195 Rokeby
Bent Geo. P. 6948 Wentworth av.
Bentley Charles E. Dr. 4206 Langley av.
Bentley Cyrus, Elmhurst
Bentley Cyrus Mrs. 2001 Indiana av.
Bentley C. S. Gen. 4453 Ellis av
Bentley Frank T. 124 Flournoy
Bentley George H. Dr. 224 Pine
Bentley Harvey, 3913 Prairie av.
Bentley H. G. Oak Park
Bentley M. L. Miss, 1907 Michigan av.
Bentley Oscar F. Ravinia
Bentley Thomas D. 7636 Ford av.
Bentley Thomas D. jr. 7636 Ford av.
Bentley Walter G. Ridgeland
Bentley Wilber G. 474 Elm
Benton Elizabeth Mrs. 1834 W. 22d
Benton E. L. Hinsdale
Benton George C. 3207 Michigan av.
Benton George E. 1834 W. 22d
Benton George P. 4420 Oakenwald av.
Benton Kendrick R. Rev. 6309 Stewart av.
Benton William H. 5021 Washington av.
Benton W. H. jr. 5021 Washington av.
Benz E. P. 235 Irving av.
Benz Philip, 295 S. Hoyne av.
Benze Herman, 415 N. State
Berens August Rev. Elmhurst
Berg Adolph, 246 Lasalle av.
Berg Charles, 3805 Vincennes av.
Berg Charles F. 6418 Yale
Berg David 3443 Wabash av.
Berg E. A. 1006 Warren av.
Berg E. C. 1300 W. Monroe
Berg Henry W. The Ontario
Berg Isidore, 246 Lasalle av.
Berg John, 5935 Princeton av.
Berg John S. 5935 Princeton av.
Berg Joseph, 1006 Warren av.
Berg Max A. 246 Lasalle av.
Berg Morris H. 3213 Rhodes av.
Bergen Joseph Y. 317 Belden av.
Bergen Lloyd M. Dr. Highland Park
Bergen Theodore L. LaGrange
Berger Adolph, 602 Burling
Berger A. 1837 Michigan av.
Berger Emil, 680 W. Adams
Berger Harry, 769 Jackson boul.
Berger Morris, 4136 Indiana av.
Berger Robert, 439 N. State
Berger William G. 2719 N. Robey
Berger William H. 202 Oakwood boul.
Berger William R. Mrs. 4136 Indiana av.
Bergeron A. V. Dr. 817 Sawyer av.
Bergeron Eugene Prof. 5515 Wood-
    lawn av.
Bergeron Jos., M.D., 50 Vernon Park pl
Bergerson Christian, 378 Bowen av.
Bergerson Louis, 378 Bowen av.
Bergevin Alexander 4540 Lake av.
Bergman Frank A. 478 W. Adams
Bergman F. 734 Sheffield av.

Bergman George A. 478 W. Adams
Bergman G. 1452 Dakin
Bergstrom E. A. Dr. 1408 Addison av.
Berkenfield Isador, 681 North Park av.
Berlin Augustus, 261 Bissell
Berlin B. Mrs. 82, 25th
Berlin Henry, 261 Bissell
Berlin Robert C. 261 Bissell
Berlizheimer Bernard, 471 Lasalle av.
Berlizheimer David, 3350 Vernon av.
Berlizheimer R. M. 227 Lasalle av.
Bermingham John, 454 W. Taylor
Bern Edward A. 4616 Prairie av.
Bernard Adolph, Hotel Windermere
Bernard Charles C. Dr. 954 N. Halsted
Bernard John F. 457 Winchester av.
Bernard Nicholas, 641 W. Monroe
Bernard Peter, 457 Winchester av.
Bernauer Ivo, M.D., 685 Fullerton av.
Berne John J. The Tudor
Bernhard J. 434 Warren av.
Bernheimer Irving S. 3340 Michigan av.
Bernstein Eric, 333 Chestnut
Berolzheim Jacob, 322, 37th
Berolzheim Joseph, 3214 Vernon av.
Berr J. 822 Pullman bldg.
Berriozabal Felipe, 5471 Lexington av.
Berry Alexander D. 28 Best av.
Berry A. S. 4438 Lake av.
Berry A. V. Irving Park
Berry Cornelia Mrs. 868 Larrabee
Berry Frank, Wilmette
Berry Frank H. 292 Belden av.
Berry F. C. 4438 Lake av.
Berry F. J. Hotel Metropole
Berry John, 88 Warren av.
Berry John M. 296 Ohio
Berry Joseph, Evanston
Berry Joseph R., D.D. 6417 Stewart av.
Berry J. F., M.D. 490 Sunnyside av.
Berry J. G. Dr. 3666 Wabash av.
Berry Lafayette S. 49 Grant pl.
Berry Thomas W. Granada hotel
Bersbach Alfred J. 2568 Commercial
    (L.V.)
Bersbach Oscar J. 2490 Commercial
    (L.V.)
Bersback L. Mrs. 393 W. Adams
Bersback Otto, 393 W. Adams
Bert E., M. D. 3242 Vernon av.
Bertch Elizabeth J. Mrs. 970 Washing-
    ton boul.
Bertsch W. H. Lieut. Fort Sheridan
Berwig Elise Dr. 472 Cleveland av.
Besler John D. 4425 Ellis av.
Besly C. H. 399 Ontario
Besly Oliver Mrs. 399 Ontario
Bessems Paul, LaGrange
Best George, 7126 Euclid av. (H.P.)
Best George W. 3610 Ellis av.
Best Henry, 1450 Wrightwood av.
Best Henry, 3558 Prairie av.
Best Jacob J. 419 S. Paulina
Best Mary Mrs. 419 S. Paulina
Best Minnie Miss, 3558 Prairie av.
Best William, 145 Oakwood boul.

Best William E. 655 W. Monroe
Best William L. 482 N. Clark
Betham William R. 113 Cass
Bethune J. H. Mrs. 434 Belden av.
Bettelheim Bert, 4339 Ellis av.
    Sum. res. Babylon, L. I.
Bettles Joseph B. 5721 Indiana av.
Bettman Boerne, M. D. 116, 32d
Bettman P. Henry, 3953 Michigan av.
Betts Charles H. Evanston
Betts Eben M. 543 Dearborn av.
Betts George, 465 W. Monroe
Betts John W. 4444 Langley av.
Betts Norman C. Oak Park
Betts Virginia F. Mrs. 629, 66th, Eng.
Bevan A. D. Dr. Hotel Metropole
Bevan N. G. Miss, Hotel Metropole
Bevans Homer, 353 Maple, Eng.
Bevens L. A. Mrs. 3756 Ellis av.
Beveridge F. L. 4536 Forrestville av.
Beverly J. M. Mrs. 234 Oakwood boul.
Bevier Dubois, Granada hotel
Bevington B. L. 707 Warren av.
Bewley A. A. 159 S. Oakley av.
Bewley C. I. 159 S. Oakley av.
Beye William, Oak Park
Beyer Conrad H. 3281 Arlington
Beyer Mary Mrs. Evanston
Beyer Oscar A. 230 Sunnyside av.
Beynon Hattie Miss, 331 S. Paulina
Beynon James, 7425 Nutt av.
Bianchine Eugene C. Stamford hotel
Bickel Alice Mrs. 2947 Indiana av.
Bickford Charles D. 604 Division
Bickford Charles M. 1137 Pratt av.
Bickford John A. 1353 Ogden av.
Bickford R. K. Oak Park
Bickle Edith M. Miss, 538, 67th, Englewood
Bickle Mabel A. Miss, 538, 67th, Englewood
Bicknell E. Dean, Oak Park
Bicknell F. W. Oak Park
Bicknell O. L. Oak Park
Bicknell W. W. Oak Park
Biddison Samuel M. 6460 Myrtle av.
Biddle G. W. A. 125 Loomis
Biddle Noble L. 125 Loomis
Biddle W. B. 4541 Lake av.
Bideleux Edward F. Kenilworth
Bidwell Glendora Mrs. 34 College pl.
Bidwell Theo. S., M.D. 482 Ashland boul.
Biedenfeld Baron Curt von, Walton pl.
    sw. cor. Rush
Biedenweg William C. 2840 Commercial
    (L.V.)
Biegler Peter J. 39 Walton pl.
Bielfeldt W. S. 6705 Lafayette av.
Bielman A. Mrs. 873 W. Adams
Bierbower Austin, 1925 Michigan av.
Bierly Samuel, 3621 Ellis av.
Bigelow Alfred P. 288 Belden av.
Bigelow Anson A. 2026 Michigan av.
Bigelow Arthur W., M.D., 3638 Cottage
    Grove av.
Bigelow A. 710 Fullerton av.

Bigelow Calista E. Mrs. 539 W. Adams
Bigelow C. S. Dr. 251, 35th
Bigelow Edward A. 561 Dearborn av.
Bigelow Joel, 2449 Prairie av.
Bigelow Nelson P. 2213 Prairie av.
Bigelow T. M. 5034 Woodlawn av.
Biggs Albert, Longwood
Biggs Bert P. Austin
Biggs Foster H. Evanston
Biggs Paul G. Austin
Bigley W. J. 3450 Wabash av.
Bigley W. L. 3450 Wabash av.
Biglow Alice Miss, 3150 Indiana av.
Billegman Charlotta Mrs. 2004 Diversey
Billings A. M. 504 W. Lake
Billings B. 4319 Lake av.
Billings Charles L. 45, 22d
Billings Cornelius K. G. 470 Washington
    boul.   Sum. res. Geneva Lake
Billings Frank Dr. 45, 22d
Billings Henry F. 290 Lasalle av.
Billings Henry F. 3811 Forest av.
Billings H. L. 1186 Millard av.
Billingslea A. Evanston
Billingslea Claud, Evanston
Billingslea Edward, Evanston
Billow Clayton O. 560 Kenwood pl.
Billow Elmer E. 4959 Prairie av.
Bills George D. Ridgeland
Bines Robert, Hotel Windermere
Binford George A. 470 Warren av.
Binford George W. 48, 53d (H.P.)
Bingham A. E. 4723 Woodlawn av.
Bingham B. H. 5046 Jefferson av.
Bingham C. L. 4346 Oakenwald av.
Bingham Frank A. 91 Bowen av.
Bingham Frank M. 410 Oak
Bingham George, 563 Division
Bingham Gurden, 5321 Jefferson av.
Bingham James A. 307 Ashland boul.
Bingham Jane M. Mrs. 307 Ashland boul.
Bingham John L. Dr. 445 N. Clark
Bingham Judson D. Gen. U. S. A. 553
    Dearborn av.
Bingham J. T. 6747 Prairie av.
Bingham Millard F. 768 Washington
    boul.   Sum. res. Pittsfield, Mass.
Bingham Stillman R. Highland Park
Bingham William M. 553 Dearborn av.
Binkley John T. Dr. 4402 Berkeley av.
Binne Frank, 303 Warren av.
Binswanger August, ___ Calumet av.
Binz Edward G. 6922 Stewart av.
Birch Edward A. Evanston
Birch Hugh T. 1912 Michigan av.
Birchmeier Celestin, 22 Carl
Birchmeier Sophie M. Miss, 22 Carl
Bird Alberta Miss, Evanston
Bird A. C. Evanston
Bird Curtis D. Hinsdale
Bird Frank E. Lexington hotel
Bird Horace G. 4519 Greenwood av.
Birdsall Abbie A. Miss, 442, 41st (H.P.)
Birdsall J. F. 207 Lasalle av.
Birdsall Nettie Miss, 442, 41st (H.P.)
Birdsall Robert, Evanston

Birdsall R. M. 820 W. Adams
Birdsall William Y. Evanston
Birge M.D. Col. 183 Warren av.
Birk E. J. 254 Seminary av.
Birk Jacob, 1901 Wellington
Birk William A. 1910 Wellington
Birkenstein David, 14 Lane pl.
Birkenstein Louis, 14 Lane pl.
Birkenstein S. 14 Lane pl.
Birkhoff D., M.D. 408 Marshfield av.
Birkhoff George, 577 W. Adams
Birkhoff George jr. 575 W. Adams
Birkin Frank, 4539 Oakenwald av.
Birmingham James H. 500, 42d pl.
Birney B. H. Dr. 7804 Wright
Birney Charles A. 7716 Eggleston av.
Birren Kate Mrs. 122 Eugenie
Birtwistle J. E. 227 Park av.
Bisbee Lewis H. 3912 Vincennes av.
Bischoff Fred. A. 1728 Wrigl wood av.
Bischoff Gustav A. 257 Burling
Bischoff Hattie A. Mrs. 907 Evanston av.
Bischoff Wilhelm F. Mrs. 3625 Ellis Park
Bishop Alex, 4729 Kimbark av.
Bishop Charles Nelson, 95 Park av.
Bishop Clarence B. 378 Dearborn av.
Bishop Edwin R. Mrs. La Grange
Bishop Frank 4218 Oakenwald av.
Bishop Frank H. 4240 Wabash av.
Bishop F. G. 268 Seminary av.
Bishop Genevra Johnstone Mrs. 2317
    Michigan av.
Bishop George H. 1069 Washington boul.
Bishop Henry W. Chicago Club
            Sum. res. Pittsfield, Mass.
Bishop Herman, 456 Cleveland av.
Bishop Herman H. 456 Cleveland av.
Bishop H. N. Mrs. 95 Park av.
Bishop H. R. Granada hotel
Bishop H. R. jr. 572 Division
Bishop James C. 572 Division
Bishop J. A. 705 North Park av.
Bishop J. P. 4218 Oakenwald av.
Bishop L. Brackett, 1111 Early av.
Bishop Paul, 1111 Early av.
Bishop Rufus W. Dr. 2317 Michigan av.
Bishop S. S. Dr. 719 W. Adams
Bishop Thomas, Maywood
Bishop Thomas R. 7613 Union av.
Bishop Walter H. 4729 Kimbark av.
Bishop William, 7613 Union av.
Bishop William S. LaGrange
Bishopp Weller D. 3652 Calumet av.
Bisland John R. 42 E. Pearson
Bisland William A. 42 E. Pearson
Bissell Arthur G. 2003 Prairie av.
Bissell Frank R. Evanston
Bissell George F. 2003 Prairie av.
Bissell Richard M. 2003 Prairie av.
Bissett C. N. Evanston
Bissett H. P. Mrs. Evanston
Bissicks Joseph, 3663 Wabash av.
Bissinger Benjamin, Hotel Windermere
Bither William A. 4108 Ellis av.
Bitner Harry, The Renfost
Bittinger George W. 4353 Calumet av.

Bixby Charles H. Rev. 4926 Lake av.
Bixby Cyrus, 1767 W. 22nd.
Bixby Frank, 4419 Vincennes av.
Bixby John N. 7646 Sherman
Bixby M. J. 1839 Indiana av.
Bixby Rufus S. 1070 Clifton Park av.
Bixby W. F. 209, 37th
Bixel Charles F. Irving Park
Blachford E. J. Mrs. 509 Lasalle av.
Black Annie W. Mrs. 402, 65th, Eng.
Black Charles N. 174, 36th
Black C. A. Mrs. Austin
Black Elmer E. 207, 44th
Black Harry St. Francis, Lexington hotel
Black Irving C. 2548 Indiana av.
Black James P. 28 Aldine sq.
Black J. C. 9 Walton pl.
Black Stanley P. Dr. 2346 Calumet av.
Black William, 823 Morse av.
Black William F. Prof. 3716 Wabash av.
Black William P. Capt. Park Ridge
Black W. J. 6621 Lafayette av.
Blackall Alfred H. 513 Dearborn av.
Blackall Edward S. 4558 Lake av.
Blackburn John F. 3449 Prairie av.
Blackler Samuel, Lake Forest
Blackman Carlos H. 4349 Lake av.
Blackman C. S. 65 Laflin
Blackman C. S. 73, 30th
Blackman Daniel, 3311 Cottage Grove av.
Blackman Edwin, Austin
Blackman F. E., 31, 29th
Blackman F. O. 73, 30th
Blackman Harry L. 73, 30th
Blackman H. L. Miss, 2724 Indiana av.
Blackman Judson, 2724 Indiana av.
Blackman Louis I. 57 Dekalb
Blackman M. Mrs. 3123 South Park av.
Blackman William B 3983 Michigan av.
Blackman Willis L. Hin da
Blackmarr Arthur, 740, 64th, Eng.
Blackmarr Frank, 5429 Cottage Grove av.
Blackmarr Mary C. Mrs. 5429 Cottage
    Grove av.
Blackmer O. C. Oak Park
Blackstone Alice H. Mrs. 3601 Vincennes
    av.   Sum. res. Lynn, Mass.
Blackstone Andrew P. Oak Park
Blackstone James H. Oak Park
Blackstone T. B. 252 Michigan av.
Blackstone W. E. Oak Park
Blackwelder I. S. Morgan Park
Blackwell M. J. Evanston
Blades L. J. 109 Warren av.
Blaikie W. E. Park Ridge
Blaine Emmons Mrs. 135 Rush
Blair B. Miss, 276 Michigan av.
Blair B. A. 75, 30th
Blair Charles H. 2909 Prairie av.
Blair Charles J. 214 The Plaza
Blair Charles M. 4058 Ellis av.
Blair Chauncey J. 4342 Drexel boul.
    After May 1st, 1895, 4830 Drexel boul.
Blair David, 219 Irving av.
Blair David, Irving Park
Blair David W. 3960 Drexel boul.

Blair Edmund H. 3769 Lake av.
Blair Edward T. 157 Cass
Blair Gardiner C. Irving Park
Blair George P. 742 Warren av.
Blair Henry A. 2735 Prairie av.
Blair H. P. 221, 54th (H. P.)
Blair James, 1719 Belmont av.
Blair Lyman Mrs. 2825 Prairie av.
Blair Lyman jr. 3139 Calumet av.
Blair Orval G. 871 Warren av.
Blair S. O. 3952 Ellis av.
Blair T. H. 420 Park av.
Blair Watson F. 164 Rush
Blair William, 230 Michigan av.
Blair William, 4469 Lake av.
Blair William, S. Evanston
Blaisdell John W. 36th nw. cor. Ellis av
Blake Charles G. 1851 Frederick
Blake Clinton F. 531 W. Monroe
Blake Edward A. 457 Evanston   .
Blake Edward J. 1923 Deming ctav
Blake Evans, 468 Kenwood Terrace
Blake Harriet M. Mrs. 558 Washington
    boul.
Blake Harry J. 166 N. State
Blake Henry H. 3845 Ellis av.
Blake H. H. 46, 35th
Blake James Vila Rev. 531 W. Monroe
Blake John O. 166 N. State
Blake Wallace H. Evanston
Blake Walter, 3845 Ellis av.
Blakelidge George W. LaGrange
Blakely C. H. 3708 Lake av.
Blakely J. A. Hotel Barry
Blakely L. P. LaGrange
Blakemore C. B. Mrs. 388 Lasalle av.
Blakemore F. T. 388 Lasalle av.
Blakemore W. R. 388 Lasalle av.
Blakeslee C. F. 2107 Indiana av.
Blakeslee E. M. 712 Warren av.
Blakeslee George S. 3240 Calumet av.
Blakeslee H. L. 446, 65th, Eng.
Blakeslee Levi, LaGrange
Blanchard A. A. 148 N. State
Blanchard Charles H. 96, 30th
Blanchard C. R. Oak Park
Blanchard Geo. R. 301 The Plaza
Blanchard G. W. 503 W. Monroe
Blanchard Ira Mrs. 378 Warren av.
Blanchard John W. 4812 St. Lawrence av.
Blanchard Julius M. Austin
Blanchard J. Mrs. 214 N. State
Blanchard Lewis, Evanston
Blanchard T. F. 378 Warren av.
Blanchard Wallace, M.D. 214 N. State
Blanchard William, Evanston
Bland R. W. Rev. 467 Farwell av.
Blanden Charles, Berwyn   ·
Blanding Mary, 443 Englewood av.
Blanke George F. 296 Evanston av.
Blanton L. M. 217 Belden av.
Blatchford E. W. 375 Lasalle av.
Blatchford John K. 4954 Forrestville av.
    Sum. res. Paw Paw Lake, Mich.
Blatchford N. H. 367 Lasalle av,
Blatchford Paul, Oak Park

Blatchford T. W. 79, 44th (H.P.)
Blatherwick Charles W. Austin
Blauer Adelia Miss, 542 Lasalle av.
Blauer Amelia Miss, 542 Lasalle av.
Blaurock C. A. Oak Park
Blauvelt William C. 4060 Michigan Ter-
    race
· Blauvelt W. F. Lieut. Fort Sheridan
Blayney George W. Hinsdale
Blayney Louise Mrs. Riverside
Blayney Thomas C. Riverside
Bleike Frederick W. 302 Erie
Blend Charles W. Dr. 2233 Prairie av.
Bluchyndell F. W. Stamford hotel
Bleuchyndell R. Stamford hotel
Bleyer Charles E. 1917 Wrightwood av.
Blick Walter H. La Grange
Blinn Edmund B. 1227 Lawndale av.
Blinn Fannie Miss, 2300 Indiana av.
Blinn Louise Montague Dr. 2300 Indi-
    ana av.
Blish Frank D. 507 Maple, Eng.
Blish George C. Mrs. 2808 Indiana av.
Bliss Arthur, 1145 Millard av.
Bliss A. H. 3350 Wabash av.
Bliss Charles, Berwyn
Bliss Charles L. Oak Park
Bliss Edgar B. Riverside
Bliss Elizabeth S. Mrs. Evanston
Bliss Ely, 558 Chestnut, Eng.
Bliss Ernest W. The Arizona
Bliss E. R. 2963 Indiana av.
Bliss E. S. Mrs. 6027 Indiana av.
Bliss Frank T. Evanston
Bliss Fred M. 4100 Ellis av.
Bliss George F. Mrs. 1145 Millard av.
Bliss George H. 4528 Lake av.
Bliss George H. The Arizona
Bliss George J. Oak Park
Bliss G. Harry. 4313 Maple av.
Bliss Julian P. 4528 Lake av.
Bliss Louis 507 Dearborn av.
Bliss Robert, 4215 Ellis av.
Bliss Samuel E. 3636 Lake av.
Bliss T. F. Oak Park
Bliss Walter E. 626, 78th, Auburn Park
Bliven Charles E. 2 Aldine sq.
Bliven Waite, 3702 Lake av.
Bloch Charles E. 4339 Prairie av.
Bloch Jacob, 3353 Indiana av.
Bloch Louis, 1100 Washington boul,
Bloch Louis E. 4729 Langley av.
Bloch Simon J. 9 Lincoln pl.
Blocher John H. 42, 39th
Block Isaac, 4521 Ellis av.
Block Louis J. 322 Warren av.
Block S. Lexington hotel
Block Williard T. 1628 Indiana av.
    Sum. res. Green Lake, Wis
Blocki Eugene W. 37 Lincoln av.
Blocki Frederick W. 829 N. Clark
Blocki John, 829 N. Clark
Blodgett Chas. E. Rev. 5172 Indiana av.
Blodgett E. A. 510 W. Monroe
Blodgett G. R. Mrs. 3000 Indiana av,
Blodgett Silas W. 3801 Ellis av.

Blomgren Oscar N. 1446 Belmont av.
Blood Emma S. Miss, 113 Cass
Blood Harry E. 3253 Indiana av.
Blood I. W. 190 Oakwood boul.
Blood James A. Hinsdale
Blood John H. Colonies hotel
Bloom Aaron L. 3672 Michigan av.
Bloom Hannah Mrs. 432 Englewood av.
Bloom Hulda B. Miss, 3672 Michigan av.
Bloom Isaac J. 3358 South Park av.
Bloom Jacob C. 432 Englewood av.
Bloom J. L. Hotel Imperial
Bloom J. W. 3807 Lake av.
Bloom Leopold, 3672 Michigan av.
Bloom Samuel H. 826 Warren av.
Bloomingston John S. 3728 Ellis av.
Bloss C. J. Mrs. 6437 Honore
Bloss Harry H. 855, 69th (H.P.)
Bloss L. K. Mrs. 855, 69th (H.P.)
Bloss Roy S. 6437 Honore
Blossom Alonzo, 35 Aldine sq.
Blossom E. J. Hotel Windermere
Blossom George W. 4858 Kenwood av.
Blouke Milton B.,M.D.193 S.Campbell av
Blount Frederick M. 194 S. Robey
Blow George P. Lieut. Lexington hotel
Blow W. N. Lieut., Fort Sheridan
Blowney H. E. Morton Park
Blue William M. 21 Best av.
Bluhm Frederick F. 400 Washington
    boul.
Blum August, 3245 Groveland av.
Blum Benjamin, 477, 42d pl. (H.P.)
Blum Edgar C. 477, 42d pl. (H.P.)
Blum Henry, 416 Maple, Englewood
Blum Henry jr. 416 Maple, Englewood
Blum John, 477, 42d pl. (H.P.)
Blum Julius, 543 Cleveland av.
Blum Louis J. 477, 42d pl. (H.P.)
Blum Simon, 645 Fullerton av.
Blume George A. 817 S. Lawndale av.
Blume Jarvis, 112 Winchester av.
Blumenthal August, 47 Beethoven pl.
Blumenthal Michael, 112 S. Oakley av.
Blumenthal William, 112 S. Oakley av.
Blunt John E. Evanston
Blunt John E. jr. Evanston
Bluthardt O. R. Dr. 569 Warren av.
Bluthardt Robert E. 272 Belden av.
Bluthardt T. J. Dr. 453 Lasalle av.
Blyben William, 219, 42d (H.P.)
Blye Fannie E. Miss, Evanston
Boak Robert B. 4744 Kimbark av.
Boal Anna Miss, 1732 Michigan av.
Boal C. T. 1732 Michigan av.
Boalch William Mrs. 3618 Lake av.
Board E. M. Evanston
Board James L. 983 W. Adams
Board Nathaniel, Oak Park
Boardman George B. 362 Bissell
Boardman I. W. Mrs. 271 Oakwood boul.
Boardman Martha J. Mrs. 235 Michigan
    av.
Boas Edmund A. Dr. 395 N. Wells
Boas Paul, 410 Marshfield av.
Bobb Philip M. 117 S. Wood

Bobb Samuel A. Grayland
Bobo J. L. 4246 Drexel boul.
Boche Louis, Irving Park
Bocher George R. 1552 W. Monroe
Bockius Eisen, M.D. Mayfair
Bockius Joseph A. Wilmette
Bodach Charles, 746 N. Hoyne av.
Boddie John T. 580 Division
Boddie Malcolm M. 580 Division
Bode Fred, 5827 Washington av.
Bode W. F. 4546 Oakenwald av.
Bodemann W. 5451 Washington av.
Bodenschatz G. A. Oak Park
Bodenschatz John G. 4444 Ellis av.
Bodey E. F. Oak Park
Bodge Ezra S. 3803 Langley av.
Bodine A. H. Evanston
Bodine Jacob, Evanston
Bodine Jacob jr. Evanston
Bodine Lewis T. 3756 Ellis av.
Bodinghouse Richard, Wilmette
Bodle Elizabeth C. Mrs. 4917 Prairie av.
Bodley Earle P. 361 Ashland boul.
Bodman Albert C. 299 Schiller
Bodman Luther W. 9 Astor
Bodwell George F. 3311 Forest av.
Boehm Aaron, 3150 Prairie av.
Boehm Moritz W. 1159 N. Clark
Boehne Edward H 213 Park av.
Boenert Anton, 1926 George av.
Boericke Richard 1816 Melrose
Boerlin A. J. 528 N. Wells
Boerlin Louis J. Irving Park
Boerner Gustav R. Ravinia
Boerner Wunibald R. Ravinia
Boesch Thomas, Julien hotel
Boess John G. 485 Bowen av.
Boettcher Ernest, 1794 Deming ct.
Boettcher Henry R. Dr. 305, 63d (L.)
Boetti Alexander, 3537 Ellis av.
Boetti Joseph, 3537 Ellis av.
Bogardus Charles E. 4716 Langley av.
Bogardus Harrison D. 4716 Langley av.
Bogardus Harry F. 4716 Langley av.
Bogart C. G. 6146 Woodlawn av.
Bogert William B. Evanston
Boggs Albert W. 4451 Ellis av.
Boggs Annie M. Miss, 4451 Ellis av.
Boggs A. Emmet, 4451 Ellis av.
Boggs Cyrus, 746, 64th, Eng.
Boggs Vincent S. 869 Larrabee
Bogle W. S. 228 Irving av.
Bogue Charles H. 2359 Michigan av.
Bogue Elias, Hinsdale
Bogue George M. Hinsdale
Bogue Hamilton B. 4819 Greenwood av.
Bogue Hamilton B. jr. 4819 Greenwood av.
Bogue John H. 35, 29th
Bogue O. A. 5037 Washington av.
Bogue R. G. Mrs. 5 Washington pl.
Bogue Virgil G. 632 Lasalle av.
Bohanon C. H. 760 W. Adams
Bohart James C. 4430 Emerald av.
Bohart William H., M.D., 4436 Emerald
    av.
Bohl G. Mrs. Fort Sheridan

Bohlander J. Maywood
Bohn Henry J. Morgan Park
Bohner George, 2944 Vernon av.
Bohner Mary A. Miss. 2944 Vernon av.
Boice Benjamin 3657 Forest av.
Boice Hugh M. Evanston
Boice William H. 5737 Monroe av.
Boise James R. Rev. 359, 65th, Eng.
Boisot Emil K. LaGrange
Boland John A. 522 Burling
Boland Rose Mrs. 3519 Wabash av.
Boldenweck C. G. 1907 Deming ct.
Boldenweck Louis H. 471 Elm
Boldenweck William 1681 N. Halsted
Bolender T. . 1554 W. Monroe
Boles M. A. Julien hotel
Boller Claude B. 6528 Lexington av.
Boller John, 6528 Lexington av.
Bolles C. E. Oak Park
Bolles William M. 4229 Indiana av.
Bolster Charles H. 19 Chalmers pl.
Bolte Anson L. 3757 Ellis av.
Bolte Charles Guy, Winnetka
Bolten E. A. 211 Seminary av.
Bolten Peter H, 20 Carl
Bolter Andrew, 1511 N. Halsted
Bolter J. C. 380 Bissell
Bolton Harlan Kent, 4902 Drexel boul.
Bolton H. W. Rev. 409 W. Monroe
Bolton James, 4902 Drexel boul.
Boltwood H. L. Evanston
Bonbright Daniel Mrs. Evanston
Bond A. G. Dr. 1403 Washington boul.
Bond Emory S. Col. 2679 N. Ashland av.
Bond E. T. Evanston
Bond Isaac, 175, 36th
Bond James, M. Evanston
Bond John H. R. Dr. 123, 51st (H. P.)
Bond Joseph, 3332 Calumet av.
Bond Lester L. 512 W. Monroe
Bond Orville D. 1308 Wilcox av.
Bond O. W. 401 Jackson boul.
Bond Thomas S. Dr. Evanston
Bond T. N. 507 W. Monroe
Bond William A. 4025 Drexel boul.
Bond William H. 175, 36th
Bond William R. 447 Greenleaf av.
Bond W. E. 6519 Oglesby av.
Bond W. S. 4148 Drexel boul.
Bone John C. 4328 Emerald av.
Bonham De Witt C. 176 Howe
Bonheim Lee M. 417 Garfield boul.
Bonn Emma Miss, 4808 Langley av.
Bonn Henry, 4808 Langley av.
Bonn Henry jr. 4808 Langley av.
Bonn William, 4808 Langley av. .
Bonnar W. Dr. 300, 31st
Bonnell Charles E. 224 S. Oakley av.
Bonnell David, Evanston
Bonnell Sarah Mrs. 4840 Langley av.
Bonner Andrew W. 831 Ernst av.
Bonner Charles, 5752 Rosalie ct.
Bonney Charles C. 424 Fulton
Bonney Charles F. Austin
Bonney Charles L. 1127 Lawndale av,
Bonney E. A. Mrs. Austin

Bonney H. J. 216 Cass
Bonney Lawton C. 424 Fulton
Bonniwell Wallace A. Dr. 657 Pine Grove av.
Bonynge Francis G., M. D. 584 Dearborn av.
Booge H. D. 7829 Winneconna av.
Booge John I. 516, The Plaza
Boomer John, 353, 46th (H. P.)
Boomer John B. 353, 46th (H. P.)
Boomer L. S. 40 Madison Park
Boone D. L. Mrs. 1423 Edgecomb ct.
Boone H. C. 1423 Edgecomb ct.
Boone S. O. 1423 Edgecomb ct.
Boore H. 4804 Vincennes av.
Boorn Charles P. 4130 Berkeley av.
Boorn William C. 4130 Berkeley av.
Boosey Wilfrid F. 430½ Belden av.
Booth Addison, Hotel Windermere
Booth Alfred Vernon, 4526 Prairie av.
Booth Charles E. 235 Michigan av.
Booth George C. Rev. Evanston
Booth Jennie Mrs. 539 W. Monroe
Booth John, 545 Cleveland av.
Booth Mary E. Miss, 2914 Groveland av
Booth Rachel M. Miss, 1193 W. Monroe
Booth Sarah W. Mrs. 4315 Champlain av.
Booth William Morris, 3605 Ellis av.
Booth William S. 4717 Grand boul.
Booth W. H. Evanston
Booth W. Vernon, 31 Bellevue pl.
Boothroyd Geo. Edwin, 4 Burton pl.
Bopp Frank, 520 La Salle av.
Borcherdt Albert F. 512 Dearborn av.
Borden Charles E. Lexington hotel
Borden Gerald M. 237 Ashland boul.
Borden Hamilton, 12 Groveland Park
Borden Henry Lee, 237 Ashland boul.
Borden James U. Calumet club
Borden John, 3949 Lake av.
Borden Seymour S. 5168 Michigan av.
Borden William, 89 Bellevue pl.
Borg Isaac, 336 Warren av.
Borgmeier Adolph, 700 N. Hoyne av.
Boring C. O. Evanston
Borland George W. 3242 Lake Park av
Borland John J. Mrs. 1611 Michigan av.
Borland J. J. Morgan Park
Borland L. C. Dr. 685 Ogden av.
Borland M. W., M.D. 365 Jackson boul.
Born Julius, 890 W. Adams
Born Moses, 3433 Michigan av.
Born Rudolph, 890 W. Adams
Born Victor, 890 W. Adams
Borner William, 113 Cass
Bornhofen Susan Miss, 526 Orchard
Bornstein Herman, 3202 Calumet av.
Borsch Henry, 835 N. Clark
Bort Frank B. New Hotel Holland
          Sum. res. Waukesha, Wis.
Bort Mabel E. Miss, New Hotel Holland
Bortell Charles E. 4230 Prairie av.
Borton F. L. Evanston
Bortree Franklin S. 84 Robinson av.
Bortree Herbert W. 94 Robinson av.
Bortree H. L. Mrs. 54 Robinson av,

Bortree M. R. 54 Robinson av.
Borwell E. B. Mrs. Oak Park
Borwell Frank, Ridgeland
Borwell Frank L. LaGrange
Bosler E. H. Longwood
Bosley Daniel W. 538 Washington boul.
Bosley Edward F. 35 Park av.
Bosley Edward F. 540 Washington boul
Bosseller Harry E. 171, 51st (H.P.)
Bostedo Alfred L. Oak Park
Bostedo Louis G. River Forest
Bosworth Albert O. Evanston
Bosworth F. F. 5426 Washington av.
Bosworth John C. The Tudor
Bosworth W. L. 5426 Washington av.
Botsford Bennett B. 2100 Calumet av.
Botsford Henry, 2837 Michigan av.
Bottomley S. H. Dr. 509 Cleveland av.
Bottum Elisha S. 303 Orchard
Bottum George G. 4143 Grand av.
Bottum George L. 28 Lincoln av.
Bottum Hudson G. 4143 Grand av.
Bouer Charles Prof. Elmhurst
Bouffleur Albert I., M.D. 738 Washington
    boul.
Boughan A. B. 286 Warren av.
Boughan John. 1249 Newport av.
Boughton C. H. Dr. 665 Warren av.
Boughton Daniel K. 703 W. Monroe
Boughton Fred J. 665 Warren av.
Boulter Letitia Mrs.4233 St. Lawrence av.
Boulton George D. Highland Park
Boulton W. G. 6453 Wright
Bour Charles J. 6506 Lexington av.
Bour F. F. 472 Kenwood Terrace
Bour George C. 440 Kenwood Terrace
Bour John R. 5309 Ingleside av.
Bourassa Joseph H. 1942 Barry av.
Bourgeois Oscar F. LaGrange
Bourke James E. 273 Superior
Bourne Charles Allen, 3738 Langley av.
Bourne Emma M. Mrs. 3738 Langley av.
Bournique Alvar L. 51, 23d
Bournique Augustus E. 51, 23d
Bournique Eugene A. Hotel Metropole
Bournique Lyman G. 51, 23d
Bourns Arthur P. 5755 Rosalie ct.
Bourns James H. Rev. 5755 Rosalie ct.
Boutell Henry Sherman, 24 Walton pl.
    Sum. res. Kennebunkport, Me.
Boutelle Caroline Miss, Evanston
Boutelle J. P. Evanston
Boutelle Lewis H. Evanston
Bouton C. B. 4812 Woodlawn av.
Bouton C. Sherman, 5420 Ridgewood ct.
Bouton George W. 325, 37th
Bouton N. S. 191, 47th
Bouton Sherman H. 4812 Woodlawn av.
Bovee Mary H. Mrs. 357 Kenmore av.
Bovett James A. jr. Dr.1246 Michigan av.
Bowden Thomas A. 4307 Ellis av.
Bowditch Belle Mrs. 3811 Michigan av.
Bowen Arthur P. Riverside
Bowen A. 3756 Ellis av.
Bowen Charles M. 2288 N. Paulina
Bowen Charles Roy, 5242 Michigan av.
32

Bowen Claude G. 127 Loomis
Bowen Eugene K. 127 Loomis
Bowen Frances T. Mrs. 98, 30th
Bowen T. K. 703 Warren av.
Bowen George H. 3326 Prairie av.
Bowen George W. 3017 Wabash av.
Bowen Handy H. 206 Oakwood boul.
Bowen Helene M. Miss,5242 Michigan av.
Bowen Ira P. 336 Ontario
Bowen Isaac, 5242 Michigan av.
Bowen James H. Mrs. 336 Ontario
Bowen John R. 336 Ontario
Bowen J. T. 136 Astor
Bowen L. C. Mrs. 206 Oakwood boul.   .
Bowen Mary G. Mrs. 127 Loomis
Bowen Mary H. Dr. 525 W. Monroe
Bowen S. T. 7140 Euclid av. (H.P.)
Bowen Thomas C. 187, 40th (H.P.)
Bower Annie T. Miss, 602 Division
Bower E. Eugenia Miss, 71 LakeView av.
Bower Robert A. 822 North Park av.
Bower R. F. Mrs. 602 Division
Bowerman M. A. Mrs. Dr. 3948 Cottage
    Grove av.
Bowers Elbran S. Evanston
Bowers James F. 75 Lincoln av.
Bowers John, LaGrange
Bowers J. H. 3733 Prairie av.
Bowers Lloyd W. 11 Ritchie pl.
Bowers Mary L. Mrs. Evanston
Bowers W. Wallace, 570 Kenwood pl.
Bowersaux A. Auditorium Annex
Bowes Chas. Lane, 541 W. Adams
Bowes Edwin J.¹jr. 395 Ashland boul.
Bowes Edwin N. 1328 Washington boul.
Bowes Frederick M. 1328 Washington
    boul.
Bowes F. K. 541 W. Adams.
Bowes Jerome P. 4547 Prairie av.
Bowes John R. Austin
Bowes T. F. The Arizona
Bowie H. T. 706 Jackson boul.
Bowie James R. 706 Jackson boul.
Bowie Robert R. 822 W. Adams
Bowker Hugh D. 4552 Oakenwald av.
Bowlan James, 2947 Groveland av.
Bowler J. P. 300 Loomis
Bowles Frank Goodwin 3032 Michigan av.
Bowles Frederick A. 252, 53d (H.P.)
Bowles George, 320 The Plaza
Bowles John P. 4207 Vincennes av.
Bowles Joseph B. La Grange
Bowles Thos. G. Mrs. 3032 Michigan av.
Bowling C. Mrs. 6403 Oglesby av.
Bowling H. D. 6315 Woodlawn av.
Bowman Alice Miss, 4729 Kimbark av.
Bowman Benjamin F.6814 South Park av.
Bowman Blake A. 363, 58th (H.P.)
Bowman Ernest M. 65 University pl.
Bowman Frederick H. Dr. 1380 N. Clark
Bowman John A. 6902 Anthony av.
Bowman Johnston R. 55 Pine
Bowman Margaret Miss, 414 S. Leavitt
Bowman M. A. Mrs. 5338 Washington av.
Bowman Reliance Mrs. 363, 58th (H.P.) .
Bowman R, A, 380 Oak

Bowman Thomas Rt.Rev.232 Winchester av.
Bowron Tarasa Azalia Dodge, The Vincennes
Bowyer L. F. Mrs. 179 Park av.
Boyce Anna L. Miss, 527, 44th pl. (H.P.)
Boyce Maria Mrs. 4620 Woodlawn av.
Boyce S. Leonard, 3735 Grand boul.
Boyce William D. 1850 Wrightwood av.
Boyd Alexander, 5232 Jefferson av.
Boyd Alice E. Mrs. 413 Huron
Boyd Edward B. 7747 Wright
Boyd Elizabeth Mrs. Hawthorne av. Auburn Park
Boyd E. K. 5603 Madison av.
Boyd George M. 517 Racine av.
Boyd G. A. Mrs. 4455 Oakenwald av.
Boyd Hattie S. Mrs. 3233 Forest av.
Boyd H. W. 5217 Hibbard av.
Boyd James A. 5217 Hibbard av.
Boyd John, Elmhurst
Boyd John D. Mrs. 240 Hampden ct.
Boyd John W. 6249 Oglesby av.
Boyd Margaret Mrs. 195, 41st (H.P.)
Boyd M. K. 569, 51st (H.P.)
Boyd Robert, 5232 Jefferson av.
Boyd Robert H. 195, 41st (H.P.)
Boyd R. L. Oak Park
Boyd-Snee H. Dr. 278 Warren av.
Boyd S. J. Dr. 116 S. Oakley av.
Boyd Thomas C. 333 Bowen av.
Boyd William, 333 Bowen av.
Boyd William, Evanston
Boyd William S. 5232 Jefferson av.
Boyden Byron, 225, 74th pl. (H.P.)
Boyden Charles M. 3811 Lake av.
Boyden Fred, 3628 Vernon av.
Boyden George D. Union League Club
Boyden N. B. 3811 Lake av.
Boyden William C. 3005 Calumet av.
Boyer Allen, 4904 Washington av.
Boyer Emanuel R. 536, 61st. Eng.
Boyer Frank N. River Forest
Boyer H. J. 4904 Washington av.
Boyer J. S. 1924 Michigan av.
Boyer V. A. Mrs. 490 Fullerton av.
Boyesen Austra Miss, 5125 Kimbark av.
Boyesen I. K. 5125 Kimbark av.
Boyington Arthur M. Highland Park
Boyington George B. Highland Park
Boyington H. H. 3406 Prairie av.
Boyington Levi R. 130 Clarence av.
Boyington M. J. Mrs. 399 Belden av.
Boyington S. A. Mrs. 91, 37th
Boyington W. W. Highland Park
Boylan F. O. 4455 Ellis av.
Boyle Catherine Mrs. 748 W. Adams
Boyle Clarence, 1678 Wellington
Boyle Daniel, 4610 Champlain av.
Boyle David Mrs. 521 W. Monroe
Boyle Henry J. 521 W. Monroe
Boyle Hugh E. 750 Fullerton av.
Boyle James H. 39 E. Pearson
Boyle John T. 406 W. Congress
Boyle J. P. 271 Belden av.
Boyle Lawrence P. Hotel Metropole

Boyle Peter J. 7719 Wright
Boyle Thomas, 1840 Diversey
Boyle W. H. 748 W. Adams
Boyles Charles C. Riverside
    Sum. res. Lake Geneva
Boyles Charles D. 307 N. Clark
Boyles Charles D. Riverside
Boyles Thomas D. Riverside
Boynton Charles T. Evanston
Boynton C. E. 3623 Lake av.
Boynton C. W. 390 Ontario
Boynton Edgar S. Highland Park
Boynton F. H. Hyde Park hotel
Boynton John R. Dr. 1223 W. Ravenswood Park
Boynton S. B. 241 S. Hoyne av.
Boynton Wm. E. 452 Dearborn av.
Boyton Paul, 634 Cleveland av.
Brabrook J. F. 520 W. Congress
Brabrook W. A. 520 W. Congress
Brabrook William F. Morgan Park
Brabrook W. Fred jr. LaGrange
Brace William, 568 Fullerton av.
Bracht Paul, 458 Cleveland av.
Brachvogel Charles H. 4827 Vincennes av.
Brachvogel Udo, 421 Center
Brachvogel William J. 4930 Vincennes av.
Brackebush A. C. 307 Lasalle av.
Bracken James O. LaGrange
Brackett Henry W. Auditorium annex
Brackett H. S. 1580 Fulton
Brackett M. A. Mrs. 682 W. Adams
Brackett William, 3320 Vernon av.
Bradburn James I. 3651 Prairie av.
Bradbury J. H. jr. Evanston
Braden Charles E. 4465 Oakenwald av.
Braden Joseph C. 3931 Prairie av.
Bradford Anna E. Mrs. Austin
Bradford Edwin R. Evanston
Bradford Jesse B. 142 (H.P.)
Bradford John, 259 Fremont
Bradford Theron D. 3976 Cottage Grove
Bradish Albert H. 152 S. Leavitt
Bradley A. O. Lakota hotel
Bradley A. S. 5450 Ridgewood ct.
Bradley A. S. jr. 5450 Ridgewood ct.
Bradley Barbara O. Mrs. 3140 Calumet av.
Bradley Byron C. 389 W. Adams
Bradley B. Harley, 389 W. Adams
Bradley B. W. 5911 Wabash av.
Bradley Carl D. 3140 Calumet av.
Bradley Charles D. Dr. 131 Dearborn av.
Bradley Charles H. 286, 37th
Bradley Charles M. 294, 37th
Bradley C. B. Evanston
Bradley C. F. Prof. Evanston
Bradley C. H. 213, 40th
Bradley David, 389 W. Adams
Bradley D. E. Avenue house, Evanston
Bradley Edward E. Evanston
Bradley Edward L. Riverside
Bradley E. L. Mrs. Hinsdale
Bradley E. F. 455½ Elm
Bradley Francis Mrs. Evanston
Bradley Frank A. Mrs. Evanston

Bradley Frank B. 3140 Calumet av.
Bradley F. G. 361 Park av.
Bradley James D. 4452 Sidney av.
Bradley James P. 3734 Calumet av.
Bradley Jane Mrs. 5215 Washington av.
Bradley John Dorr, 319 Superior
Bradley John H. Hinsdale
Bradley J. Harley, Lexington hotel
Bradley J. H. 358 Park av.
Bradley Kate Miss, Oak Park
Bradley Loring, 213, 40th
Bradley M. S. 5315 Washington av.
Bradley P. B. 308 Chestnut
Bradley P. B. jr. 308 Chestnut
Bradley Ralph R. Hinsdale
Bradley Rodney D. 455½ Elm
Bradley Seth E. Wilmette
Bradley Street, Riverside
Bradley T. E. D. 328 Warren av.
Bradley Wm. Dr. Evanston
Bradshaw Hugh, 695 Fulton
Bradshaw John H. 333 Ashland boul.
Bradshaw T. F. Oak Park
Bradshaw W. D. 111 Loomis
Bradstreet J. Edwin, Winnetka
Bradt A. Schuyler, 7235 Cottage Grove av.
Bradt Harry E. 5A Woodland Park
Bradt Schuyler B. 7235 Cottage Grove av.
Bradwell J. B. Judge, 1428 Michigan av.
Bradwell Thomas, 3209 South Park av.
Brady Frank E. 6050 Park End av.
      Sum. res. Lakewood, N. Y.
Brady George K. Col. 3817 Vincennes av.
Brady Hugo, 4355 Calumet av.
Brady James T. 1128 Washington boul.
Brady John, 4919 Vincennes av.
Brady John A. 4919 Vincennes av.
Brady John B. 1128 Washington boul.
Brady John F. 1715 Cornelia
Brady John J. 4522 Evans av.
Brady M. P. 967 Park av.
Brady M. S. 79 Lincoln av.
Brady Oscar M. 749 Walnut
Brady P. A. Auditorium hotel
Bragdon Charles E. 6451 Sheridan av.
Bragdon M. C. Dr. Evanston
Bragdon S. C. Mrs. Evanston
Bragdon W. L. 6451 Sheridan av.
Braggins William, 7315 Yale
Braham George, 3432 Calumet av.
Brainard A. P. 4035 Indiana av.
Brainard C. H. 2970 Groveland av.
Brainard C. S. 5105 Kimbark av.
Brainard Edward C. La Grange
Brainard Edwin, 168 N. State
Brainard Harriet G. Mrs. 1301 Wabash av.
Brainard Mabel Miss, 5105 Kimbark av.
Brainerd Ed. R. Auditorium annex
Brainerd E. T. 923 W. Monroe
Brainerd F. W. 923 W. Monroe
Braithwaite Charles Rev. 1028 Farwell av.
Braithwaite Charles W. 318 Chestnut, Eng.
Brall William D. Mrs. Virginia hotel
Brammer Frederick H. Evanston

Brammer Matilda Miss, Evanston
Branch A. E. Oak Park
Branch B. A. Mrs. 371 Elm
Branch Harry, 298, 38th
Branch John W. Evanston
Brand C. H. 320 Oakwood boul.
Brand Edwin L. 1918 Michigan av.
      Sum. res. Richfield Springs, N. Y.
Brand Edwin L. jr. 1918 Michigan av.
Brand Harry F. 1133 Washington boul.
Brand Horace L. 32 Cedar
Brand Michael, 32 Cedar
Brand Rudolph, 53 Cedar
Brand Silas H. 824 Warren av.
Brand William E. Highland Park
Brandecker F. X. 648 Sedgwick
Brandt A. E. Mrs. 4548 Lake av.
Brandt A. R. 10 Chalmers pl.
Brandt George W. 1316 Michigan av.
Brandt G. W. 231, 45th (H. P.)
Brandt Oscar E. 10 Chalmers pl.
Branen Frank Dr. 961 W. Monroe
Braslan Charles P. 901 Walnut
Brauckmann George, 1824 George av.
Braun David J. 4165 Grand av.
Braun George P. 674 Lasalle av.
Braun Wm. F. 57 The Yale
Braunwarth Anna M. M.D. Miss, 3146 Indiana av.
Brawley Francis W. S. 3010 Lake Park av.
Bray I. M. Mrs. 915 Fulton
Bray Joseph D. 1518 Sheridan road
Bray Justin L. Evanston
Braymer F. A. 6410 Oglesby av.
Brayton George W. 376 Dearborn av.
Brayton James H. 6319 Yale
Brayton John E. 4828 St. Lawrence av.
Brayton Lydia E. Mrs. 4828 St. Lawrence av.
Brayton Sarah H. Miss, M.D. Evanston
Breakwell S. Fort Sheridan
Breasted Charles, 515, 62d, Eng.
Brecher Emanuel A. 4559 Lake av.
Brecher Gustav A. 1810 Wellington
Brecher J. Arnold, 4559 Lake av.
Breckenridge J. Howard, 4351 Calumet av.
Breckenridge R. J. 6432 Myrtle av.
Breckenridge Stephen L. Dr. Riverside
Breckinridge W. L. Mrs. Evanston
Brede David, 4800 Michigan av.
Brede Max, 3532 Wabash av.
Bredt John M. 1842 Melrose
Breed Charles L. La Grange
Breed David R. Rev. 320 Belden av.
Breed Joseph Mrs. 376 Dearborn av.
Breen J. W. Hotel Groveland
Breen Martin J. 23 Winthrop pl.
Breese Ambrose Dr. 3521 Grand boul.
Breese Charlotte Mrs. 2624 Calumet av.
Breese J. B. Hotel Metropole
Breese Sidney H. Hinsdale
Breeze Leland, Wilmette
Brega Charles W. 2816 Michigan av.
Brega Louise E. Miss. 2816 Michigan av.
Breitling John, Oak Park
Breitung Albert, 355 Dayton

Brelsford C. E. H. Avenue house, Evanston
Bremer Albert R. 4918 Greenwood av.
Bremner B. E. 463 W. Monroe
Bremner B. Mrs. 4442 Ellis av.
Bremner D. F. 240 Loomis
Bremner Edward A. 4442 Ellis av.
Bremner Helen J. Mrs. 463 W. Monroe
Bremner James W. 4442 Ellis av.
Brenan Thomas, 163, 30th
Brenckle F. W. 354 Mohawk
Brendecke A. C. Dr. 279 W. Adams
Brennan Matthew J. 4018 Vincennes av.
Brennan Michael, 365 Dayton
Brennan Patrick, 502 Ashland boul.
Brennan T. W. 48 Seeley av.
Brennan William F. 502 Ashland boul.
Brenner Carolus, 4045 Drexel boul.
Brenock John, 29 MacAlister pl.
Brenock William, 29 MacAlister pl.
Brentano Theodore Judge, 445 Lasalle av.
Brethvold C. H. Wilmette
Brett Emma S. Miss, 794 Washington boul
Brett R. A. Mrs. 648 W. Monroe
Brett Theodore F. 794 Washington boul.
Breuer Elizabeth Mrs. 93 MacAlaster pl.
Brewer Charles, 5460 Washington av.
Brewer C. S. Evanston
Brewer Eben, Hotel Windermere
Brewer Edwin P. Lieut. Fort Sheridan
Brewer Frank B., M.D. Evanston
Brewer Frank M., M.D. Evanston
Brewer J   S. 400 The Plaza
Brewer Robert T. 405 The Plaza
Brewis J. J. 49 Hamilton av.
Brewis S. Mrs. 49 Hamilton av.
Brewster Benjamin, Glencoe
Brewster Edward L. Auditorium annex
Brewster Jabez, 9 Burton pl.
Brewster James P. Glencoe
Brewster J. H. 800 Warren av.
Brewster William O. 143 Oakwood boul.
Brickwood Albert W. 71 Warren av.
Bride J. H. W. 4158 Calumet av.
Bridge George S. 429, 41st (H. P.)
Bridge R. W. 5402 Cornell av.
Bridgeman William W. 4536 Woodlawn av.
Bridges Emily C. Mrs. Oak Park
Bridgman Walter R. Prof. Lake Forest
Brigg T. H. Leland Hotel
Briggs Anna R. Mrs. 444 Washington boul.
Briggs Asa E. 2602 Calumet av.
Briggs Clinton, 3216 Wabash av.
Briggs David C. Auditorium Annex
Briggs E. H. Hotel Groveland
Briggs George M. La Grange
Briggs Gertrude D. Miss, 1834 W. 22d
Briggs J. Rogers, 444 Washington boul.
Briggs L f yette, Hinsdale
Briggs Ma E. Mrs. 460 Cleveland av.
Briggs Nathan E. La Grange
Briggs S. W. Oak Park
Brigham C. E. Mrs. 7528 Wright
Brigham Edmund D. 1378 Palmer
Brigham Gustavus B. 4311 Berkeley av.

Brigham Willard T. 402 Bowen av.
Bright John B. Evanston
Bright O. T. 6515 Harvard
Bright William M. 4530 St. Lawrence av.
Brill Carrie Miss, 4620 Champlain av.
Brill George, 4620 Champlain av.
Brimson W. Geo. 528, 62d, Eng.
Brinckerhoff Leslie, Kenilworth
Brine George J. 665 Kenmore av.
Brine John F. 5554 Monroe av.
Brink Arthur P. 1764 Sheridan rd.
Brink Edwin D. Ridgeland
Brink James T. 7117 Yale
Brink Mary Miss, 312 Indiana
Brink Percy A. 1764 Sheridan rd.
Brinkerhoff A. B. 265 Ohio
Brinkerhoff F. M. Hyde Park hotel
Brinkerhoff Henry R. Capt. Fort Sheridan
Brinkerhoff H. M. Hyde Park hotel
Brinkerhoff William C., M. D. 3769 Lake av.
Brinkmann Clemens, 585 Lasalle av.
Brintnall Solva, 3438 Wabash av.
Brintnall Wm. H. 4621 Ellis av.
Briot Eugene, 4821 Champlain av.
Briot Lillie, 4821 Champlain av.
Brisbois A. 2664 Evanston av.
Brisco C. N. Mrs. 6509 Lafayette av.
Brison John, 3837 Ellis av.
Brison John H. 4519 St. Lawrence av.
Bristol Angeline B. Mrs. Evanston
Bristol Edward S. 1642 W. Adams
Bristol Frank M. Rev. Evanston
Bristol George 4410 Berkeley av.
Bristol Henry L. 3813 Michigan av.
Bristol L. D. 6808 Wright
Bristol Merritt C. 3160 Groveland av.
Brittain J. K. Julien hotel
Brittan Arthur, Virginia hotel
Brittan C. A. Miss, Virginia hotel
Brittan Charles H. 4160 Lake av.
Britten Peter, 450 Dearborn av.
Brix Dominicus Dr. 6316 Stewart av.
Broadbent Thomas A. Dr. 2541 Commercial (L. V.)
Brock A. J. 377 W. Monroe
Brock John F. 4634 Vincennes av.
Brock Lizzie Miss, Winnetka
Brock Martin R. Highland Park
Brocklebank J. C. F. 447 Elm   Sum. res. Geneva Lake
Brockman Henry, 502 Dearborn av.
Brockway George, 179, 36th
Brockway Guy, 179, 36th
Brockway James W. 79 Park av.
Brockway Vira A. Dr. 52 Campbell Park
Broderick James F. 4527 Vincennes av.
Brodhay Louis, 19 Carl
Brodhay Louis R. 19 Carl
Brodhay Otto C. 19 Carl
Brodhead Frederick A. 3627 Ellis av.
Brodie Charles, 290 Irving av.
Brodie F. W. 72 Park av.
Brodix F. F. Hotel Windermere
Brodlique Eve H. Miss, 4222 Berkeley av.

Brodnax William H. 5466 Monroe av.
Brodt Herman, Prof. Elmhurst
Bromilow E. E. Mrs. 1835 Frederick
Bromilow E. W. 1746 Wrightwood av.
Bromley J. M. Mrs. 3131 Indiana av.
Bromley M. W. Mrs. 3019 Indiana av.
Brommer C. G. 450, 63d (H. P.)
Brompton Joseph C. 237 Sunnyside av.
Bronson E. V. Mrs. Oak Park
Brook Ida Bell Miss, Evanston
Brooke E. J. T. Mrs. 614 Division
Brooke Lincoln, 6020 Park End av.
Brookes J. F. 3538 Lake av.
Brookes Mary J. Miss, 3538 Lake av.
Brookings M. E. Miss, 4011 Drexel boul.
Brookins A. 222 Marshfield av.
Brookman Frank E. 1097 N. Clark
Brooks Albert J. Mrs. 290 Rush
Brooks Alice Miss, 235 Dearborn av.
Brooks Almon Dr. 4643 Lake av.
Brooks A. F. 4357 St. Lawrence av.
Brooks Carrie I. Miss, 4357 St. Lawrence
  av.
Brooks Charles, 730 W. Monroe
Brooks Charles M. 4454 Sidney av.
Brooks Ellis, Clifton house
Brooks Emily Abbott Mrs. 1691 Sheridan
  rd.
Brooks Evelyn Miss, 4623 Drexel boul.
Brooks Everett W. 4623 Drexel boul.
Brooks Fannie Miss, 4357 St.Lawrence av.
Brooks Frank Dr. 4643 Lake av.
Brooks Fred G. 711 Washington boul.
Brooks Frederick, 958 N. Clark
Brooks Harry L. 308 Warren av.
Brooks Henrietta Miss, 2958 Indiana av.
Brooks Henry H. Chicago Beach hotel
Brooks H. G. 246 Warren av.
Brooks H. K. 6205 Woodlawn av.
Brooks James C. 235 Dearborn av.
Brooks John W. Kenilworth
Brooks Julia A. Mrs.711Washington boul.
Brooks J. Henry, 2958 Indiana av.
Brooks J. R. 145 Oakwood boul.
Brooks J. W. 4912 Woodlawn av.
Brooks J. W. jr. 4912Woodlawn av.
Brooks Lorenzo C. 2958 Indiana av.
Brooks M. W. Mrs. 4627 Lake av.
Brooks Noah W. Evanston
Brooks O. H. 4435 Lake av.
Brooks Sarah A. Miss, 2958 Indiana av.
Brooks S. D. Dr. U. S. Marine hospital
Brooks S. N. 271 Warren av.
Brooks William A. Hinsdale
Brooks William C. French house, Evans-
  ton
Broomell Chester C. 5515 Woodlawn av.
Broomell George D. 496 W. Monroe
Broomell George D. jr. 496 W. Monroe
Brophy James A. 1020 Washington boul.
Brophy Mary Miss, 1020 Washington
  boul.
Brophy Truman W.Dr. 176 Ashland boul.
Bross Jennie A. Miss, 2001 Michigan av.
Bross Margaret S. Mrs. 4820 Greenwood
  av.

Bross Mason, 550 Dearborn av.
Bross William Mrs. 2001 Michigan av.
Brosseau Auguste, 608 N. State
Brosseau Jo B. 1186 N. Clark
Brosseau Noel, 3026 Vernon av.
Brosseau Zenophile P. 1950 Barry av.
Brothers William E. Evanston
Brougham Thos. B. 5131 Wahsington av.
Broughton E. P. Mrs. 3331 Indiana av.
Broughton Henry E. River Forest
Broughton John W. River Forest
Broughton T. A. 2944 Indiana av.
Broughton Urban H. 801 Pullman bldg.
Brouse Mary C. Mrs. 6410 Stewart av.
Browder C. R. 1767 N. Halsted
Brower A. T. H. 1330 Bryn Mawr av.
Brower Charles H. Mrs. 153 S. Oakey av.
Brower D. R., M.D. 597 Jackson boul.
Brower D. R. jr. 597 Jackson boul.
Brower Julius F. 5528 Monroe av.
Brower Noah C. 43 University pl.
Brown Adelbert E. Dr. 1911 Michigan av.
Brown Albert L. 918 Winona
Brown Alice R. Miss, 68, 24th
Brown Alma L. Miss, River Forest
Brown Andrew, 41, 53d (H.P.)
Brown Andrew J. Evanston
Brown Annie Miss, Lake Forest
Brown Arthur L. Evanston
Brown Arthur R. 10 St. James pl.
Brown A. Fletcher, 17, 39th
Brown A. L. 386 Webster av.
Brown A. S. 6719 Wentworth av.
Brown Berlyn B. 5533 Washington av.
Brown Bessie B. Miss, 3965 Lake av.
Brown Charles A. 217 S. Wood
Brown Charles C. 545 Dearborn av.
Brown Charles E. 2414 Prairie av.
Brown Charles E. 3965 Lake av.
Brown Charles J. Austin
Brown Charles S. 1336 Fulton
Brown Charles T. 3601 Vincennes av.
Brown Clarence S. Riverside
Brown C. Addie Miss, 59 Aberdeen
Brown C. B. 5538 Cornell av.
Brown C. E. 330 Hampden ct.
Brown C. E. Mrs. 23 Waverly pl.
Brown C. F. Mrs. 3269 Groveland av.
Brown C. H. 859 Walnut
Brown C. R. 4104 Ellis av.
Brown C. S. Mrs. 797 Kenmore av.
Brown David, Austin
Brown David P. 1277 Wolcott
Brown Dexter G. 4734 Greenwood av.
Brown Dwight, 344 Belden av.
Brown Edward H. 982 Warren av.
Brown Edward Houghton,Highland Park
Brown Edward O. 3559 Vincennes av.
Brown Edwin F. Evanston
  Sum. res. Lake Geneva, Wis.
Brown Edwin Lee Mrs. 2342 Calumet av.
Brown Eleanor M.Miss,1911 Michigan av.
Brown Ella A. Miss, 3706 Lake av.
Brown Ella W. Miss, 183, 37th
Brown Emma E. Miss, Irving Park
Brown Everett C. 3 Aldine sq.

Brown Ezra D. 3227 South Park av.
Brown E. C. 1551 Fulton
Brown E. C. Mrs. 717 The Plaza
Brown E. H. 63 E. Pearson
Brown E. L. 6719 Wentworth av.
Brown E. O. 400 N. State
Brown E. W. Hotel Metropole
Brown Finley D. 5533 Washington av.
    Sum. res. Diamond Lake, Mich.
Brown Florence Miss, 171 Warren av.
Brown Francis C. Highland Park
Brown Frank C. 3559 Vincennes av.
Brown Frank E. 6230 Woodlawn av.
Brown Frank H. 4306 Lake av.
Brown Frank P. 42, 39th
Brown Fred H. 5 Langley pl.
Brown Fred L. 68, 24th
Brown Frederick I. Dr. Irving Park
Brown F. E. 6951 Perry av.
Brown F. Junior, 5533 Washington av.
Brown F. S. Evanston
Brown F. W. Evanston
Brown George D. 213 Winchester av.
Brown George F. 368, 42d (H.P.)
Brown George F. jr. 2414 Prairie av.
Brown George L. 2925 Indiana av.
Brown George P. 766 W. Adams
Brown G. H. Evanston
Brown Henry, 7849 Eggleston av.
Brown Henry F. 189 Dearborn av.
Brown Henry H. 206 Ashland boul.
Brown Henry T. 21 Linden pl.
Brown Honora Mrs. 368 Warren av.
Brown H. H. Dr. 390 N. Clark
Brown H. L. 301 Warren av.
Brown H. W. Morgan Park
Brown Isaac W. Oak Park
Brown Isidore F. 3611 Prairie av.
Brown I. E. Oak Park
Brown I. W. Dr. 75 DeKalb
Brown James C. 5206 Hibbard av.
Brown James F. 5224 Washington av.
Brown Jamot, 3203 Beacon
Brown Jessie Miss, Hotel Metropole
Brown John, 3426 Michigan av.
Brown John A. 4510 Vincennes av.
Brown John B. Auditorium hotel
    Sum. res. Ipswich, Mass.
Brown John F. 368 Warren av.
Brown John G. Evanston
Brown John H. 2908 Groveland av.
Brown John H. 547, 62d, Eng
Brown John H. 831 Jackson av.
Brown John M. 414 Washington boul.
Brown John M. Evanston
Brown John M. La Grange
Brown John S. 1493 Fulton
Brown John V. 1-42 Lawndale av.
Brown John W. 6408 Star av.
Brown John W. Evanston
Brown Jonas, 3207 South Park av.
Brown Joseph Mrs. Evanston
Brown Joseph N. 665 Kenmore av.
Brown Julia E. Mrs. 259, 66th pl. (H.P.)
Brown Julius N. 68, 24th
Brown J. Austin, 5149 Cornell av.

Brown J. D. 240 Ohio
Brown J. D. Wilmette
Brown J Frederick, 4104 Ellis av.
Brown J. H. Hotel Metropole
Brown J. Mabbett, 3559 Vincennes av.
Brown J. P. 68, 24th
Brown J. P. B. 5424 Washington av.
Brown J. W. Oak Park
Brown Lincoln A. 183, 37th
Brown Lockwood, 113 Cass
Brown Lot, Morton Park
Brown Louis F. Evanston
Brown Louise Miss, 584 W. Adams
Brown Louise B. Miss. 386 Webster av.
Brown Ludwig, 1439 Wrightwood av.
Brown Lula Miss, 3706 Lake av.
Brown L. Cass, LaGrange
Brown L. D. Oak Park
Brown L. E. 5533 Washington av.
Brown L. G. Washington Heights
Brown L. Read Dr. 1911 Michigan av.
Brown Mabel M. Miss, 3945 Ellis av.
Brown Minnie F. Miss, French house,
    Evanston
Brown Morrill O. 303 Ashland boul.
Brown Morris, 3229 Forest av.
Brown M. A. Mrs. 6629 Harvard
Brown M. C. Mrs. 5619 Madison av.
Brown M. Eleanor Miss, 4318 Grand boul.
Brown M. Isabella Miss, 3965 Lake av.
Brown M. R. M. D. 444 Elm
Brown N. E. Mrs. 293 Chicago av.
Brown Paul, 3330 Calumet av.
Brown Pliny B. 711, 60th, Eng
Brown Richard, 229 S. Leavitt
Brown Richard, Evanston
Brown Robert C. River Forest
Brown Robert P. 3859 Lake av.
Brown R. L. 481 Fullerton av.
Brown Sam, 384 Bissell
Brown Samuel jr. 3203 Beacon
Brown Samuel, 2409 Prairie av.
Brown Sanger Dr. 757 Washington boul.
Brown Sarah C. Mrs. 4927 Michigan av.
Brown Scott, Oak Park
Brown Spencer A. 6325 Oglesby av.
Brown S. L. Mrs. 59 Aberdeen
Brown Taylor E. 6504 Wharton av.
Brown Thomas, 52, 24th
Brown Thomas Mrs. River Forest
Brown Thomas jr. 3 Aldine sq.
Brown Thomas H. 3345 Indiana av.
Brown T. Barbour, 374 Dearborn av.
Brown T. B. Mrs. 5 Langley pl.
Brown Walter, 360 S. Campbell av.
Brown Walter Lee, Evanston
Brown William, Morton Park
Brown William C. Evanston
Brown William E. 4919 Vincennes av.
Brown William H. 4058 Ellis av.
Brown William H. Evanston
Brown William Liston, Evanston
Brown William S. Dr. 269 Lasalle av.
Brown Wm. Thayer, 4637 Greenwood av.
Brown W. C. 6719 Wentworth av.
Brown W. C. Mrs. Oak Park

Brown W. F. 3706 Lake av.
Brown W. Gray, 171 Warren àv.
Brown W. H. Irving Park
Brown W. H. A. 4306 Oakenwald av.
Brown W. Morton, 4420 Greenwood av.
    Sum. res. Lake Beulah, Wis.
Brown W. M. Dr. 1493 Fulton
Browne Archibald D. 344 Fullerton av.
Browne A. W. 414 Oak
Browne Charles E. Glencoe
Browne Charles E. 4128 Maple av.
Browne Edward, 3829 Forest av.
Browne E. L. Mrs. 4363 Lake av.
Browne Francis F. 5336 Ellis av.
Browne Francis G. 5336 Ellis av.
Browne Frank L. Dr. 948 Greenleaf av.
Browne H. S. 6422 Drexel av.
Browne Josiah M. LaGrange
Browne J. Sidney, 555 Webster av.
Browne Malcolm J. LaGrange
Browne Marshall L. 1526 Fulton
Browne William A. 217 S. Hoyne av.
Browne William P. 529, 60th, Eng.
Browne Willis W. LaGrange
Brownell Albert S. Elmhurst
Brownell R. E. 7100 Yale
Brownell William J. 775, 63d ct. Eng.
Browning Granville W. 425 Lasalle av.
Browning Henry H. Hotel Metropole.
Browning William H. 271 Oakwood boul.
Browning T. W. 427, 42d pl. (H.P.)
Brownlee Mungo W. 456 Washington
    boul.
Brownley L. L. Miss, 113 Cass
Bruce Benjamin, 352 Oakwood boul.
Bruce B. F. jr. The Renfost
Bruce B. V. 4443 Berkeley av.
Bruce Charles, Morton Park
Bruce Edward I. 352 Oakwood boul.
Bruce Edward Malcolm Dr. 144, 54th (H.
    P.)
Bruce Frank A. 352 Oakwood boul.
Bruce Jane Mrs. 3937 Ellis av.
Bruce John R. 747·Jackson av.
Bruce M. Ervin, Ridgeland
Brucker Joseph, 630 Cleveland av.
Bruckner C. C. The Renfost
Bruckner John F. 903 Sherman av.
Bruen William G. 4619 Woodlawn av.
Brues Ada Mrs. 62 Walton pl.
Brumback A. H. Dr. 109 Loomis
Brunaugh Samuel B. 1805 Barry av.
Bruner A. C. Oak Park
Bruner Charles E. 2337 Calumet av.
Bruner Otis W. 1609 Sheridan rd.
Bruner Stanley C. 2337 Calumet av.
Bruning Josephine Mrs. 386 Chestnut
Brunk Albert B. 1323 Grace
Brunk Thomas L. 3704 Elmwood pl.
Bruns Francis F. 579 Lasalle av.
Bruns Louis Wilkens, 579 Lasalle av.
Brunson F. M. Morgan Park
Brunswick Benjamin, 362, 41st
Brunswick Charles, 460 Bowen av.
Brush C. E. 518 W. Monroe
Brush Daniel E. 4415 Michigan av.

Brush D. Eugene, 3944 Indiana av.
Brush E. H. 210 Goethe
Brush H. J. 4415 Michigan av.
Brushingham J. P. Rev. 895 Fulton
Brust Peter Mrs. 1630 Prairie av.
Bryan Alfred C. 4739 Champlain av.
Bryan C. Page Col. Elmhurst
Bryan E. H. Mrs. Austin
Bryan E. S. Maywood
Bryan Fred C. 3764 Indiana av.
Bryan F. W. 887 Warren av.
Bryan Grace Miss, 887 Warren av.
Bryan John C. Dr. 1079 Washington
    boul.
Bryan Pulaski J. 6016 Park End av.
Bryan Thomas B. Elmhurst
Bryant A. W. Oak Park
Bryant Charles F. 81, 18th
Bryant Clifford Wellington, 2946 Indiana
    av.
Bryant C. A. 229, 28th
Bryant Dwight S. 2917 Groveland av.
Bryant Edward F. Pullman
Bryant Elizabeth Mrs. 268 Seminary av.
Bryant Fred L. 268 Seminary av.
Bryant George, 1613 Alexander av.
Bryant George H. 2624 Commercial
    (L.V.)
Bryant Harry L. 81, 18th
Bryant Henry W. 3154 Calumet av.
Bryant John A. 526 Orcbard
Bryant John H. 579 W. Adams
Bryant John J. Riverside
Bryant John J. jr. Riverside
Bryant John M. 297 Pine Grove av.
Bryant J. M. Mrs. 408 Lasalle av.
Bryant Nellie A. Mrs. 447 Englewood av.
Bryant Omer G. 447 Englewood av.
Bryant W. Cullen, 3131 Indiana av.
Bryce P. F. 175 Park av.
Bryce Robert, 175 Park av.
Brydon James M. Dr. 270. 35th
Brydon J. A. LaGrange
Brydon Robert T. 28 Delaware pl.
Bryne Joseph, 3838 Wabash av.
Bryson George W. 125 E. Pearson
Bryson James, 1 Washington pl.
Bryson Wm. J. 169 Buena av.
Buchan J. R. Dr. 150 Park av.
Buchanan A. T. Dr. 6110 Madison av.
Buchanan Daisy Miss, Lexington hotel
Buchanan D. W. 4569 Lake av.
Buchanan Edward P. 4561 Lake av.
Buchanan Ellen M. Mrs. 5555 Monroe
    av.
Buchanan Gordon, Lexington hotel
Buchanan Helen M. Dr. 6352 Oglesby av.
Buchanan James, 183 S. Hoyne av.
Buchanan James, 4613 Champlain av.
Buchanan James N. Hotel Barry
Buchanan Mary Miss, Lexington hotel
Buchanan M. D. Lexington hotel
Buchanan R. D. Chicago Beach hotel
Buchanan Robert S. 31, 46th (H.P.)
Buchanan R. R. 3033 Groveland av.
Buchanan S. P. 4549 Prairie av.

Buchanan Walter W. Dr. 1318 Wabash
   av.
Buchholz Frederick, 659 Burling
Bucholz Fred W. 6818 St. Lawrence av.
Buck Albert H. 2937 Indiana av.
Buck A. H. Mrs. 278 Warren av.
Buck B. F. Austin
Buck Carl D. 6041 Oglesby av.
Buck Francis M. 6752 Perry av.
Buck Grace P. Miss, 2937 Indiana av.
Buck Harry R. Austin
Buck J. P., M.D. 418 Lasalle av.
Buck Orlando J. 7628 Union av.
Buck W. H., M.D. 5137 Jefferson av.
Buckbee Julian E. Col. Winnetka
Buckbee N. L. Mrs. 3604½ Lake av.
Buckbee Walter, 3604½ Lake av.
Buckie Annie C. Mrs. 81 Hammond
Buckingham Clarence, 2036 Prairie av.
Buckingham C. P. Mrs. 747 Fullerton av.
Buckingham E. 2036 Prairie av.
   Sum. res. Lake Forest
Buckingham E. H. 747 Fullerton av.
Buckingham H. W. Lexington hotel
Buckingham Isabelle C. Mrs. 3244 Grove-
   land av.
Buckingham Jo , 1832 Calumet av.
Buckingham May Miss, 3333 Indiana av.
Buckingham R. D. 344 Michigan av.
Buckius A. O. LaGrange
Bucklen H. E. 265 Michigan av.
Buckley Charles W. Evanston
Buckley Elizabeth M. Miss 3131 Forest av.
Buckley John, 904 Warren av.
Buckley J. S. Auditorium hotel
Buckley Mead H. 1012 Washington boul.
Buckley Nora Miss, 1304 Washington boul.
Buckley S. S. 214, 31st
Buckley William J. 1429 Michigan av.
Buckman R. M. 168 Warren av.
Buckner Thomas A. Evanston
Budach P. H. Rev. Washington Heights
Budd Wayman C. 805 Kenmore av.
Budd William O. 550, 60th, Englewood
Budde Alfred, Ridgeland
Buddendorff Kate C. Mrs. 4333 Langley
   av.
Buddington F. E. 2327 Indiana av.
Buechner Herman C. 29 Sidney ct.
Buecking Edward F., M.D. 425 S. Paulina
Buehl Carl, 2510 Prairie av.
Buehler Edw. H. Evanston
Buehler John, 9 Ew g pl.
Buehler John W. 37 Roslyn pl.
Buehler Jul. 43 Menomonee
Buehler William, 1241 Hinman av.
Buel A. H. 3010 Groveland av.
Buel H. K. Mrs. 336 Ontario
Buel M. P. 4444 Greenwood av.
Buell Augustine C. Evanston
Buell Charles A. 6616 Yale
Buell Charles H. 1833 Indiana av.
Buell F. R. Hotel Metropole
Buell George E. Lexington hotel
Buell Harry O. 1241 W. Ravenswood
   Park

Buell Ira W. 2832 Indiana av.
Buell James W. 516 North av.
Buell K. D. Mrs. River Forest
Buenz K. Virginia hotel
Buescher Fred W. 53 University pl.
Buettner H. F. 3634 Indiana av.
Buffum J. H. Dr. 366 Ontario
Bufkin Mary Lee Miss, 4483 Oakenwald
   av.
Buford Charles, The Ontario
Buford N. B. Mrs. 15 Linden pl.
   Win. res. St. Augustine, Fla.
Buhmann Theodore W. 1728 Alexander
   av.
Buhoup H. C. 385 O   boul.
Buhrer John S. 3263 Greenwood av.
Buisseret A. E. 6506 Oglesby av.
Buker Joseph, 6315 Honore
Bulckens Isabel, Austin
Bulckens Louise Miss, Austin
Bulger William J. 3421 South Park av.
Bulkeley Robert H. 450 Elm
Bulkley Almon W. 354 Oakwood boul.
Bulkley Charles C. 3953 Michigan av.
Bulkley Egbert J. 307 S. Campbell av.
Bull Charles D. 275 Irving av.
Bull Harris, 254 Ontario
Bull Lucy Miss, 538 Dearborn av.
Bullard Charles W. Maywood
Bullard E. R. 818 Jackson boul.
Bullen A. F. 70 Bellevue pl.
Bullen Fitz Dr. 46 DeKalb
Bullen Frederick F. 1015 Warren av.
Bullen George, Oconomowoc, Wis.
Bullen G. R. 70 Bellevue pl.
Bullen W. H. 1849 Oakdale av.
Bullock Carl C. 568 Dearborn av.
   Sum. res. Lake Geneva
Bullock George S. Lakota hotel
Bullock Henry E. 1769 Deming ct.
Bullock J. C. 568 Dearborn av.
Bullock Milan C. 1187 Washington boul.
Bullock Seth Mrs. Evanston
Bulmer R. 514 W. Adams
Bunday Blanche M. Miss, 3358 Calumet
   av.
Bunday George F. 3358 Calumet av.
Bunday George J. 3358 Calumet av.
Bundy Asahel, 627, 62d, Eng.
Bundy John C. Mrs. Evanston
Bunge W. H. 144 Park av.
Bunker C. E. 466, 50th (H.P.)
Bunker C. H. 484, 42d (H.P.)
Bunker D. A. Mrs. 3230 Groveland av.
Bunker William I. LaGrange
Bunn Ernest, F. Revere house
Bunn H. C. 407, 41st (H.P.)
Bunnell J   A. Lexington hotel
Bunte Albert, 267 Fremont
Bunte Charles F. 805 Greenleaf av.
Bunte Ferdinand, 805 Greenleaf av.
Bunte Gustave A. 332 Fullerton av.
Burbach Jacob J. Mrs. 271 Seminary av.
Burbank Augustus J. 6424 Oglesby av.
Burbank Charles H. Dr. 771 Lunt av.
Burbank E. A. 2632 Calumet av.

Burbank Henry C. 16 James pl.
Burbank Wellman M. Dr.3035 South Park
　　av.
Burch Albert M. 411 Bowen av.
Burch Charles S. Evanston
Burch Oliver E. Rev. 531 Touhy av.
Burch William, 3816 Calumet av.
Burch William A. 329 Michigan av.
Burch William A. Rev. 357 Kenmore av.
Burch William H. 6336 Star av.
Burch Wirt, Berwyn
Burchard Edward L. 566 Kenwood pl.
Burchard G. W. Evanston
Burchard Nelson, 5488 East End av.
Burchell Robert C. 42, 39th
Burchmore John H., M.D. Evanston
　　　　　　Win. res. Daytona, Fla.
Burden William E. Evanston
Burdett Samuel, Leland hotel
Burdette E. A. Virginia hotel
Burdette John W. 456 Englewood av.
Burdick Elford W. The Renfost
Burdick Julian C. 238 Oakwood boul.
Burdick L. Henrique 337 Garfield boul.
Burdick Munson, 269 Ashland boul.
Burdick Oscar, 269 Ashland boul.
Burdsal Frances A. Mrs. Evanston
Burdsal George B. Evanston
Burdsal John W. Evanston
Burdsal John W. jr. Evanston
Burdsall Marian C. Miss, 3526 Forest av
Burdsall Mary J. Miss, 3526 Forest av.
Burdsall Wm. J. 3526 Forest av.
Burgard Lilian Miss, Evanston
Burge Edward A. Wilmette
Burgess A. Oak Park
Burgess A. C. Mrs. 3621 Ellis Park
Burgess Frank A. Evanston
Burgess Frank A. Highland Park
Burgess George, New Hotel Holland
Burgess G. R. 3707 Prairie av.
Burgess H. L. 14 Astor
Burgess I. S. Morgan Park
Burgess J T. Hotel Metropole
Burgess Luther C. 2620 N. Paulina
Burgess William T. 3805 Langley av.
Burgesser G. E. 152 N. Clark
Burget Mark, LaGrange
Burgett John M. H. 217 S. Wood
Burgheim Gus. 11 Hamilton av.
Burgheim Herman, 11 Hamilton av.
Burghoffer J. J. G. 1549 Michigan av.
Burgie Henry C. Mrs. 3639 Grand boul.
Burgland Andrew, 5411 Ridgewood ct.
Burgoyne A. Mrs. 3605 Lake av.
Burguedel H. C. 4625 Emerald av.
Burhance Maud Miss, 610 Chestnut, Eng.
Burhans James A. 204 Oakwood boul.
Burhans Robert B. Evanston
Burkart George, 546 Burling
Burkart H. Marie Miss, Great Northern
　　hotel
Burkart Jacob, 546 Burling
Burke Anthony, 3356 Vernon av.
Burke Daniel F. 5300 Lexington av.
Burke E. W. Judge, 759 W. Adams

Burke Frank, 190, 35th
Burke James, 190, 35th
Burke John C. 192, 35th
Burke John E. Lexington hotel
Burke J. L. 5345 Greenwood av.
Burke Melville, 483 Fulton
Burke M. Lakota hotel
Burke Patrick, 3131 Indiana av.
Burke Rachael Miss, 2606 Indiana av.
Burke Richard, Austin
Burke Richard H. Rev. Austin
Burke S. T. Dr. 2606 Indiana av.
Burke Thomas M. Rev. Evanston
Burke William Mrs. Newberry hotel
Burke William H. Evanston
Burke W. H. Chicago Athletic assn.
Burkhardt Edward Mrs. 940 N. Clark
Burkhardt H. S. 677 W. Adams
Burkholder Charles S. 232 Oakwood boul.
Burkholder Henry, LaGrange
Burkholder Henry P. La Grange
Burkholder J. F. Dr. 283 Park av.
Burkholder R. Cortland, Evanston
Burkitt Charles H. Evanston
Burland A. P. 3112 Vernon av.
Burleigh William R. La Grange
Burleson Charles E. 4319 Ellis av.
Burleson Harriet H. Mrs. 4319 Ellis av.
Burley Arthur G. 1620 Indiana av.
Burley Augustus H. 254 Dearborn av.
Burley Clarence A. 50 Astor
Burley Frank E. 3333 Indiana av.
Burling W. S. Evanston
Burlingham E. P. Mrs. 3905 Calumet av.
Burlingham Frederick W. 3005 Calumet
　　av.
Burnam Arthur, 822 W. Adams
Burnam Frank, Iroquois Club
Burnap Margaretta E. Mrs. 4212 Ellis av.
Burnard H. W. Dr. 6208 Wright
Burnet W. H. 99, 47th (H.P.)
Burnett Albert L. 61 Bowen av.
Burnett C. H. Maywood
Burnett Frank E. 61 Bowen av.
Burnett George W. 61 Bowen av.
Burnett Jennie Mrs. 1311 Michigan av.
Burnett Josephine Mrs. 61 Bowen av.
Burnette Harry L. 42, 39th
Burnham A. A. 299 Park av.
Burnham A. W. 4334 Prairie av.
Burnham Daniel H. Evanston
Burnham Dyer N. 2806 Indiana av.
Burnham Edward, 389, 50th (H.P.)
Burnham E. Mrs. 2729 Calumet av.
Burnham Frank, Iroquois Club
Burnham Franklin P. Kenilworth
Burnham John P. Oak Park
Burnham Oliver G. Longwood
Burnham Sherburne W. 3647 Vincennes
　　av.
Burnham Telford, 3961 Drexel boul.
Burns A. M. 4404 Sidney av.
Burns B. Mrs. 358 Bissell
Burns Garrett, 377 Ohio
Burns J. Raleigh, Auditorium annex
Burns Jabez B. Dr. 828 Touhy av.

Burns James, 747 W. Superior
Burns J. C. 376 Oak
Burns J. J, 4228 Indiana av.
Burns J. L. Mrs. 634 Washington boul.
Burns Louisa Miss, Clifton house
Burns Nicholas T. 358 Bissell
Burns P. G. 148, 42d (H.P.)
Burns Randall W. Hawthorne av. Eng.
Burns Robert M. Pullman
Burns Walter F. Auditorium annex
Burns William H. Rev. Evanston
Burns William M. Austin
Burns W. Foster, Evanston
Burns W. T. Mrs. 5639 Washington av.
Burns W. W. Park Ridge
Burnside A. W. Dr. 833 Washington boul.
Burnside John L. 833 Warren av.
BurnsideV.Wallace833Washington boul.
Burr Albert H. Dr. 2036 Indiana av.
Burr Bradley, 23 St. Johns pl.
Burr Chauncy S., M.D. Longwood
Burr David, 258 Fremont
Burr E. C. 7128 Yale
Burr Louis E. 4032 Ellis av.
Burrell E. L. 1049 Winthrop av.
Burrell George I. 1505 Wellington
Burrell Louis F. 54 Warren av,
Burris J. D. 4361 Emerald av.
Burritt George, 267 Ontario
Burritt M. J. Mrs. 267 Ontario
Burritt Wm. Nelson, 70 Madison Park
Burroughs Edward R. 646 Washington
    boul.
Burroughs E. P. 739 Walnut
Burroughs FrankC.646Washington boul.
Burroughs F. M. Clifton house
Burroughs Geo. T. 646 Washington boul.
Burroughs Rose E. Miss, Clifton house
Burrows A. E. Rev. Evanston
Burrows C. M., M.D. 4301 Oakenwald av.
Burrows Daniel W. Union Club
Burrows Frederick R. 4035 Indiana av.
Burrows G. T. 401 N. State
Burrows Samuel L.1199Washington boul.
Burrows Thomas Mrs. 298 Erie
Burrows William A. 223, 52d (H.P.)
Burrows W. F. 2938 Indiana av.
Burry D. W. 139, 37th
Burry George, Hotel Barry
Burry James, M.D. 4012 Ellis av.
Burry Wm. 216 Dearborn av.
Burt Ada L. Mrs. Evanston
Burt J. A. 714 W. Monroe
Burt William, Evanston
Burt Wm. Griswold, Evanston
Burt W. H., M.D. 714 W. Monroe
Burtis James K. 3426 Vernon av.
Burtis Lewis W. 65 E. Pearson
Burton A. G. 1747 Oakdale av.
Burton Charles G. Oak Park.
Burton C. A. 1747 Oakdale av.
Burton C. S. Oak Park
Burton Edmund F. Oak Park
Burton E. D. Prof. Hotel Barry
Burton H. M. Mrs. 4163 Lake av.
Burton John, Hinsdale

Burton LeGrand, 15 Ritchie pl.
Burton Robert O. 85 Rush
Burton Stiles Mrs. 229 Michigan av.
Burton S. Lester, 3333 Forest av.
Burton Thomas Greig, 485, 65th (H.P.)
Burton William, 3853 Ellis av.
Burtt Frederick P. Hinsdale
Burtt George H. Hinsdale
Burtt George N. Hinsdale
Burwash H. J. Dr. 721 N. Hoyne av.
Burwell Nathan, 4715 Langley av.
Busbey L. White, 767 Washington boul.
Busbey T. Addison. 1045 Wilcox av.
Busbey W. H. 767 Washington boul.
Busby Charles, 2458 Indiana av.
Busby William, 3204 Forest av.
Busch Frank, 83 Park av.
Busch John, 83 Park av.
Busch Louis, 2732 Indiana av.
Busch Peter, 471 Elm
Buschmeyer Henry, 54 Beethoven pl.
Buschwah J. W. 1810 Wellington av.
Bush Benjamin F. 27 Newport av.
Bush Bertha E. Dr. 730 Lunt av.
Bush Clara Miss, 606 N. State
Bush Edwin E. Austin
Bush Edwin S. 1128 Chase av.
Bush Emma Miss, 606 N. State
Bush F. C. 3142 Groveland av.
Bush George A. 269 Oak
Bush G. S. 185 Oakwood boul.
Bush I. S. Hinsdale
Bush Lionel E. 4061 Southport av.
Bush Lorenzo Dr. LaGrange
Bush Mary K. Miss, 8 Gordon Terrace
Bush Ross. L. Lieut. Fort Sheridan
Bush William, 606 N. State
Bush W. H. 269 Oak
Bush W. L. 491 Dearborn av.
Bushnell Charles E. 696 Washington
    boul.
Bushnell Edmund B. LaGrange
Bushnell George W. Morton Park
Bushnell H. A. Rev. LaGrange
Bushnell James F. 268 Racine av.
Bushnell Lemuel M. 696 Washington
    boul.
Bushnell Lewis H. Evanston
Bushnell L. A. Mrs. 175 Warren av.
Bushnell L. S. Mrs. 6320 Yale
Buskirk Frank W. Lakota hotel
Buss Edward P. 318 The Plaza
Buss Edward W. Norwood Park
Buss Frederick B. 118, 49th (H.P.)
Busse Frederick Mrs. 180 Racine av.
Bussey W. T. 521 Jackson boul.
Buswell Albert L. 2690 Charlton av.
Butcher Nelson, 1016 W. Monroe
Butcher Richard Mrs. 1016 W. Monroe
Butlen P. Mrs. 719 W. Adams
Butler Andrew O. Oak Park
Butler A. B. 4635 Emerald av.
Butler A. L. Evanston
Butler Benjamin M. Evanston
Butler B. F. 6620 Perry av.
Butler Edward B. 3408 Michigan av.

Butler Elizabeth Mrs. 299 Winchester av.
Butler E. K. 4850 Greenwood av.
Butler Frances Mrs. Austin
Butler Frank D. River Forest
Butler Frank M. Oak Park
Butler Frank O. 4503 Ellis av.
Butler Fred H. LaGrange
Butler F. S. 708 Jackson boul.
Butler George F. Dr. 851 Jackson boul.
Butler Harry, Hotel Groveland
Butler Herman B. 54 Astor
Butler H. W. Jefferson Park
Butler John R. 3006 Prairie av.
Butler John S. 202 Webster av.
Butler Joseph H. Evanston
Butler J. Fred, Oak Park
Butler J. H. Park Ridge
Butler J. W. 4503 Ellis av.
Butler Marion W. Mrs. 385 N. State
Butler MaryL.Miss,654 Washington boul.
Butler Minnie H. Miss, Winnetka
Butler Morton, Evanston
Butler N. 5625 Monroe av.
Butler Nellie D. Miss, 6210 Michigan av.
Butler Simon, 3325 Vernon av.
Butler S. P. Hotel Normandie
Butler Thomas H. Ridgeland
Butler T. O. Dr. 247 Hermitage av.
Butler Walter, 354 Burling
Butler W. P. Lake Forest
Butlin T. G. 5036 Jefferson av.
Butterfield Charles W. 2218 Michigan av.
Sum. res. The Maples, Otsego Lake,N.Y.
Butterfield C. S. Mrs. 696 W. Adams
Butterfield Joseph P. 422, 34th
Butterfield J. Spencer, 1928 Barry av.
Butterfield Roland 22 Wisconsin
Butterfield W. 1837 Michigan av.
Butterfield W. L. 1838 Melrose
Butters Daniel, Union League Club
Butters George, Ridgeland
Butterworth Harry, 99, 26th
Butterworth Sydney Miss, 99, 26th
Butterworth Theodore, 4220 Vincennes av.
Butterworth Theodore A, 4220 Vincennes av.
Buttner A. Dr. 729 Lincoln av.
Buttner W. O. 467 Cleveland av.
Buttolph A. C. 4822 Ellis av.
Buttolph William A. 3847 Langley av.
Butts Annie E. Miss, 5001 Lake av.
Butts Arthur C. Auditorium annex
Butts De Witt C. Auditorium annex
Butts Emily W. Mrs. 5001 Lake av.
Butts Julius, 370 S. Paulina
Butts Katharyn Miss, 5001 Lake av.
Butz Albert M. Oak Park
Butz Alvin J. 1511 Wolfram
Butz Emil C. 464 Belden av.
Butz Otto C. 464 Belden av.
Butz Walter, 1709 Wellington av.
Butze Frank C. 201, 25th
Butzow Doris Mrs. 452 W. Congress
Butzow Robert C. 452 W. Congress
Buxbaum Emanuel, 3141 Michigan av.

Buzzell Delos L. Irving Park
Buzzell E. A. 3520 Forest av.
Buzzell M. H. 223 Irving av.
Byam John W. Evanston
Byers J. W. 377 Oakwood boul.
Byford Genevieve Miss, 3021 Calumet av.
Byford H. T. Dr. 3021 Calumet av.
Byllesby Mary L. Miss, 126, 47th (H.P.)
Bynum Guy H. 617 Washington boul.
Byram Augustus, 2909 Michigan av.
Byram Charles F. 2909 Michigan av.
Byrne Charles T. 448 Bowen av.
Byrne Harry, 3519 Wabash av.
Byrne H. L. Mrs. 615 Chestnut, Eng.
Byrne John, 6330 Dickey
Byrne John G. Dr. 48 S. Sheldon
Byrne John H. Dr. 48 S. Sheldon
Byrne John J. 806 Washington boul.
Byrne John J. 6617 Honore
Byrne John P. 4202 Ellis av.
Byrne Mary Miss, 806 Washington boul.
Byrne Mary E. Mrs. 3525 Grand boul.
Byrne P. O'Neil, 500 Marshfield av.
Byrne Ralph H. 3525 Grand boul.
Byrne Thomas, 909 Garfield boul.
Byrne William P. 4763 Madison av.
Byrnes William J. 4211 Vincennes av.
Byron Frank M. 296 Erie
Byus J. E. Evanston

CABEREY H. R. Longwood
Cable Charles E. 856 Walnut
Cable Fayette S. 51 Roslyn pl.
Cable Herman D. Evanston
Cable H. M. Victoria hotel
Cable Ransom R. 312 Erie
Cade Robert, Park Ridge
Cadieux Joseph P. 923 Turner av.
Cadman Mary Miss, River Forest
Cadow Samuel B. 47, 46th
Cadwallader Bassett LaGrange
Cadwallader Thos. 19 Aldine sq.
Cadwell Edmond J. 1358 Wolcott
Cadwell Edward S. LaGrange
Cadwill Lydia J. Mrs. 35 Ashland boul.
Cady Calvin B. 430 Superior
Cady George W. 434 S. Oakley av.
Cady H. B. 370 Mohawk
Cady Jeremiah K. 4500 Calumet av.
Cady Robert, 4215 Ellis av.
Cady S. H. Mrs. 434 S. Oakley av.
Cady S. P. Morgan Park
Cahill Edward T. 373 Center
Cahill J. B. 3720 Cottage Grove av.
Cahill Mary Mrs. 373 Center
Cahill Michael, 364 Fullerton av.
Cahn Aaron Mrs. 3151 Prairie av.
Cahn Albert, 525 Dearborn av.
Cahn Benjamin R. 3550 Ellis av.
Cahn Bernard, 3223 Michigan av.
Cahn Bertram J. 2977 Michigan av.
Cahn Frederick C. 3229 Michigan av.
Cahn Jacob L. 3214 South Park av.
Cahn Joseph, 2977 Michigan av.
Cahn Martin B. 3223 Michigan av.
Cahn Sidney B. 3225 South Park av.

Cahn Susie Miss, 3151 Prairie av.
Cain Frederick F. 486 Fullerton av.
Cairnduff William H. 28 St. James pl.
Cairns C. A. 5215 Hibbard av.
Cairns James, 859 Sawyer av.
Calahan J. Y. Kenilworth
Calais F. W. Irving Park
Calbrick James A. 890 S. Kedzie av.
Calder Emily E. Mrs. 225, 42d
Calder George W. G. 428 Elm
Calder Robert G. 428 Elm
Caldwell Boyd C. 1132 Kenmore av.
Caldwell B. D. Evanston
Caldwell Charles, M.D. 3237 Indiana av.
Caldwell Charles E., M.D. 438, 38th
Caldwell Charles P., M.D. 4425 Michigan av.
Caldwell C. H. 6601 Harvard
Caldwell Ernest L. Morgan Park
Caldwell E. F. 5026 Washington av.
Caldwell Frank C. Oak Park
Caldwell George T. 5026 Washington av.
Caldwell Henry A. Oak Park
Caldwell Henry P. 3229 Vernon av.
Caldwell H. W. 508 W. Congress
Caldwell James B. 441 Winthrop av.
Caldwell James T. 4127 Maple av.
Caldwell John D. 4409 Greenwood av.
Caldwell John M.Rev.3314 South Park av.
Caldwell Joseph, 91, 43d
Caldwell Oliver N. 508 W. Congress
Caldwell Rebecca B. Mrs. 441 Winthrop av.
Caldwell Rosanna Mrs. 656 Washington boul. Sum. res. Chicago Heights
Caldwell Wilfred T. 5026 Washington av.
Caldwell William, Hotel Barry
Caleb Gideon N. 5141 Hibbard av.
Caleb W. S. Chicago Beach hotel
Calhoun F. C. S. Oak Park
Calhoun George Mrs. Irving Park
Caligar Thomas D. 3801 Langley av.
Caligar Thomas M. 3801 Langley av.
Calkins Charles E. 5206 Hibbard av.
Calkins Charles R. 4635 Michigan av.
Calkins Elias A. 4359 Berkeley av.
Calkins Evelyn L. Miss, 3004 Prairie av.
Calkins George A. Evanston
Calkins G. G. Evanston
Calkins Lavinia G. Mrs. 3004 Prairie av.
Calkins Mary Miss, 5039 Lake av.
Calkins Walter J. 3004 Prairie av.
Callaghan Bernard Mrs. 2962 Indiana av.
Callaghan J. E. 2962 Indiana av,
Callaghan Simon, Austin
Callahan Andrew P. 5000 Madison av.
Callahan Cornelius, 3839 Ellis av.
Callahan James, 7108 Vernon av.
Callahan John W. 7733 Emerald av.
Callahan Thomas, 265 Lasalle av.
Callan H. A. 4557 Lake av.
Callender B. M. Tremont house
Calligan John B. Evanston
Callinan T. J. 509 Webster av.
Calrow Harriet E. Mrs. Winnetka
Calrow J. G. Winnetka

Calvert Edgar S. Lake Forest
Calvert Frank, Lake Forest
Cambridge Walter, 921 Turner av.
Cameron Caroline I. Miss, 630 Washington boul.
Cameron Daniel R. 630 Washington boul.
Cameron Daniel R. 630 Washington boul.
Cameron Duncan, 277 Seminary av.
Cameron Duncan, 902 W. Monroe
Cameron Dwight F. 589 Dearborn av.
Cameron Flora I. Miss, 630 Washington boul.
Cameron George A. 884 Warren av.
Cameron Gordon, 169, 51st (H.P.)
Cameron Hiram K. 342 Winchester av.
Cameron Jennie W. Mrs. 371 Center
Cameron John, 169, 51st (H.P.)
Cameron John H. 5135 Hibbard av.
Cameron John M. 6829 Prairie av.
Cameron John K. 119, 21st
Cameron J. P. Hotel Imperial
Cameron Margaret Miss,38½ Bellevue pl.
Cameron Nancy Mrs. 874, 71st pl. (H.P.)
Cameron Nathaniel, 342 Winchester av.
Cameron P. F. 5748 Washington av.
Cameron Robert 1572 Lill av.
Cameron Sadie J. Miss, 630 Washington boul.
Cameron William F. 169, 51st (H.P.)
Cameron William H. 832 W. Polk
Cameron W. E. 3756 Ellis av.
Cameron W. S. 438 Warren av.
Camp A. B. 272 Jackson boul.
Camp Charles D. Dr. 7020 Wright
Camp C. N. 7918 Edwards av.
Camp Edward N. 178 Dearborn av.
Camp Florence A. Mrs. 3155 Wabash av.
Camp Isaac N. 549 W. Monroe
Camp William C. 65 University pl.
Campbell Archibald 323 Hermitage av.
Campbell Archibald M. 281 Ashland boul.
Campbell August S. Highland Park
Campbell A. E. 5219 Madison av.
Campbell A. F. 672 W. Monroe
Campbell A. W. Julien hotel
Campbell Benjamin H. jr. 144 Pine
Campbell Charles P. Longwood
Campbell Charles W. Mrs. 2219 Sheridan rd.
Campbell Coler, Evanston
Campbell Colin C. 791 Walnut
Campbell Courtney, 2003 Indiana av.
Campbell David, 1838 Indiana av.
Campbell DeWitt W. Clifton house
Campbell Douglas, 143 Oakwood boul.
Campbell Duncan, 4833 St. Lawrence av.
Campbell D. C. Longwood
Campbell D. D. 641 Lawndale av.
Campbell Ella Miss, 132 Park av.
Campbell E. B. 240, 45th
Campbell E. H. 16 Bellevue pl.
Campbell Fergus, 81 Warren av.
Campbell Frank W. 3538 Calumet av.
Campbell Frederick Rev. 507 W. Monroe
Campbell George. Evanston
Campbell George C. 143 Oakwood boul.

Campbell Geo. H. 223, 29th
Campbell G. C. Mrs. 2607 Prairie av.
Campbell Hazel Miss, 514 W. Adams
Campbell Herbert O. Austin
Campbell H. R. 423 Superior
Campbell H. S. Miss, Riverside
Campbell James A., M.D. Austin
Campbell James B. 399 W. Adams
Campbell James G. 7226 Webster av. Eng.
Campbell James G. Evanston
Campbell James H. 4224 Grand boul.
Campbell James L. 99 DeKalb
Campbell John, Hinsdale
Campbell John A. 6535 Stewart av.
Campbell John C. Newberry hotel
Campbell John P. Norwood Park
Campbell J. Albert, 286 Ashland boul.
Campbell J. A. Chicago Beach hotel
Campbell J. F. Dr. 5 Woodland Park
Campbell J. F. jr. 403 Blue Island av.
Campbell J. G. 4709 Evans av.
Campbell J. McDougal, Evanston
Campbell J. Oscar Dr. 5045 Washington a .
Campbell J. W. Evanston
Campbell Leonard W. 779 N. Clark
Campbell Louis A. Rev. Austin
Campbell Lucius E. 4140 Indiana av.
Campbell L. J. Mrs. 49 Warren av.
Campbell Malcolm Y. 5486 Ridgwood ct.
Campbell Mell Miss, 2207 Calumet av.
Campbell Minnie Miss, 48 Lake Shore Drive
Campbell Murdoch, 286 Ashland boul.
Campbell M. L. 6418 Myrtle av.
Campbell Nathan W. 2604 Calumet av.
Campbell Robert B. 1061 Washington boul.
Campbell Robert C. 483 Belden av.
Campbell R. R. Dr. 384 N. State
Campbell Samuel H. 6441 Honore
Campbell S. M. Rev. 762, 67th Eng.
Campbell Treat, 313 Huron
Campbell T. Mitchell, 384 Washington boul.
Campbell William, 1926 Barry av.
Campbell William A. Dr. 4709 Evans av.
Campbell William J. Riverside
Campbell William L. 976 W. Taylor
Campbell W. E. 1723 Belmont av.
Campbell W. M. 1070 W. Monroe
Campbell W. P. 5704 Madison av.
Campe Frank, 77 Maple
Campion R. W. 1534 Diversey
Canaday Lloyd, 2447 Commercial (L.V.)
Canary D. J. 4333 Lake av.
Canavan Austin A. 4512 Indiana av.
Canby C. Harlan, 5016 Jefferson av.
Canda Felix, 496 Sunnyside av.
Candee Fred J. Hinsdale
Candee G. W. Col. U. S. A. 428 N. State
Candee Henry W. Hinsdale
Candee William B. 3703 Ellis av.
Candee William S. Evanston
Canfield A. J. Rev. Dr. 3002 Prairie av.
Canfield Charles A., M.D. 3000 Indiana av.

Canfield Coresta T. Dr. 244 Lincoln av.
Canfield Edward L. 68 Newport av.
Canfield Francis, Austin
Canfield George, 7206 Euclid av. (H.P.)
Canfield John B. 3002 Prairie av.
Canfield Patrick, 14 Ashland boul.
Canfield William J. Evanston
Canisius Charles, 496 Webster av.
Canman Leo, 214 Schiller
Cannell S. Wilmer, 568 Garfield av.
Caniff G. H. 4054 Michigan Terrace
Cannon E. F. Mrs. 5661 Washington av.
Cannon W. J. 393 Dearborn av.
Canterbury R. A. 4322 Vincennes av.
    Sum. res. Franklin Grove, Ill.
Cantlie George, Chicago Athletic Assn.
Cantner John C. 3230 Lake Park av.
Cantrovitz H. S. Sherman house
Cantrovitz S. Sherman house
Cantrovitz S. M. 3363 Forest av.
Cantwell Robert E. 200 Winchester av.
Cantwell T. A. 714 W. Adams
Capelle Eugene, 4558 Oakenwald av.
Capen Charles M. 5406 Jefferson av.
Capper Charles W. Longwood
Capper Henry, Longwood
Capper John S. Longwood
Capron Allyn Capt. Fort Sheridan
Capron A. B. Winnetka
Capron Edward F. Evanston
Capron Fred S. Evanston
Capwell C. A. Rev. 6525 Harvard
Caratu Clara Mrs. 331 S. Paulina
Caravatti J. G. 344 Michigan av.
Carbery A. J. Mrs. 859 Jackson boul.
Carbine Thomas, 400 Washington boul.
Card E. S. Hotel Windermere
Card Grace B. Miss, 6438 Harvard
Card Joseph B. 6438 Harvard
Card Joseph P. 6438 Harvard
Card Mary L. Miss, 18 Bellevue pl.
Carden D. H. 216 Seminary av.
Carden John, 113 Osgood
Carder G. H. Dr. 7748 Sherman
Carey Charles N. 3736 Forest av.
Carey Joseph T. 3738 Forest av.
Carey M. T. Oak Park
Carey Warren Dr. LaGrange
Carey William P. 3736 Forest av.
Carey W. T. 2944 Groveland av. ·
Carhart Charles, Wilmette
Carhart Charles C. The Wellington
Carhart David W. Riverside
Carhart P. 6053 Oglesby av.
Carle H. M. 4214 Ellis av.
Carleton Anna Miss, 174, 47th
Carleton Welby B. Hinsdale
Carlile Helen M. Mrs. 5218 Jefferson av.
Carlin M. A. Mrs. 4524 Lake av.
Carlisle Alfred W. 657 W. Congress
Carlisle E. G. 4467 Oakenwald av.
Carlisle Frederick, 657 W. Congress
Carlisle H. W. 657 W. Congress
Carlisle James C. 3020 Michigan av.
Carlisle William G., 232, 52d (H.P.)
Carlisle William K. 245 Dearborn av.

Carlson Axel, Evanston
Carlson Carl O. Wilmette
Carlson Gustaf H. The Tudor
Carlson John M. 1055 Pratt av.
Carlson Peter R. 4132 Lincoln av.
Carlson William A. 1829 Reta
Carlstein John A. Dr. 1248 E. Ravenswood Park
Carlton C. C. Mrs. Austin
Carlton Lewis F. Austin
Carlton M. 476 Ashland boul.
Carmack E. H. 425 Lasalle av.
Carman A. R. Evanston
Carman Geo. L. 6437 Harvard
Carman George N. Prof. Morgan Park
Carman Rufus Mrs. Evanston
Carmichael G. S. Mrs. 351 Dearborn av.
Carnahan W. D. Chicago Beach hotel
Carne Edgar W. Ridgeland
Carne John, Ridgeland
Carnegie Barbara Mrs. 107, 37th
Carnegie John F. 107, 37th
Carney Edward A. 201 25th
Carney James B. 295 Belden av.
Carney M. J. 18 Walton pl.
Carney Thomas, 25 Lincoln av.
Carney William, Evanston
Carney William A. 201 25th
Carney William J. 4218 Grand boul.
Carolan Henry, Evanston
Carpenter Agnes Miss, 717 Fullerton av.
Carpenter A. A. 83 Cass
Carpenter A. A. jr. 83 Cass
Carpenter A. B. Chicago Beach hotel
Carpenter Benjamin, 50 Cedar
Carpenter Benjamin J. LaGrange
Carpenter B. G. Mrs. 512 Englewood av.
Carpenter Charles, 1535 Fulton
Carpenter Charles C. LaGrange
Carpenter Clinton B. 306 Chestnut
Carpenter Eli J. 13 St. John's pl.
Carpenter Ellen W. Mrs. 544 Washington boul.
    Sum. res. Honey Creek, Wis.
Carpenter E. F. Evanston
Carpenter Elliott R. Dr. 4128 Berkeley av.
Carpenter F. I. Prof. 5515 Woodlawn av.
Carpenter F. S. Dr. Berwyn
Carpenter George A. 51 Delaware pl.
Carpenter George B. 293 Dearborn av.
    Sum. res. Park Ridge
Carpenter George B. Mrs. 3222 Lake Park av.
Carpenter Grant, 77 Warren av.
Carpenter H. H. 512 Englewood av.
Carpenter H. L. 3841 Forest av.
Carpenter Jessie Miss, 308 Belden av.
Carpenter J. S. 5125 Cornell av.
Carpenter Louis, 474 Elm
Carpenter Lucina H. Mrs. 4321 Champlain av.
Carpenter Mamie Miss, 7713 Union av.
Carpenter Miron J. LaGrange
Carpenter Nellie Mrs. 3226 Groveland av.
Carpenter Newton H. 4319 Champlain av.

Carpenter Orrin F. Evanston
Carpenter Peter, 7802 Union av.
Carpenter W. Irving, 7802 Union av.
Carpenter William O. 517 W. Adams
Carpenter W. T. 1683 Barry av.
Carpi Vittorio, 3702 Lake av.
Carqueville Alexander, 3127 Beacon
Carqueville Edgar H. 3127 Beacon
Carqueville Edward, 3127 Beacon
Carr Albert J. 3926 Langley av.
Carr B. F. 5713 Rosalie ct.
Carr Charles, 5402 Ridgewood ct.
Carr Charles W. 543, 60th, Eng.
Carr Clyde M. Evanston
Carr George, 3879 Lake av.
Carr George W. 4923 Champlain av.
Carr Henry Herbert, 3343 Forest av.
Carr Joshua W. 3926 Langley av.
Carr Maria G. Mrs. 1316 Washington boul
Carr Mary E. Mrs. 1316 Washington boul.
Carr Oliver K. Dr. 2425 Calumet av.
Carr Rachel H., M.D. 36th n. e. cor. Cottage Grove av.
Carr Richard B. Evanston
Carr Richard B. jr. Evanston
Carr Thomas, 145 Oakwood boul.
Carr William O. 543, 60th, Englewood
Carriel Henry B., M. D. 4302 Greenwood av.
Carrier Augustus S. Dr. 1042 N. Halsted
Carrier David R. 425 Lasalle av.
Carrigan Mary J. Miss. 2616 Calumet av.
Carrington A. R. 645 W. Adams
Carrington E. Hyde Park hotel
Carrington G. S. 518 Jackson boul.
Carrington John W. 16 Groveland Park
Carrington W. T. 290 Lasalle av.
Carroll Amanda A. Mrs. 4691 N. Clark
Carroll D. J. 31 Miller
Carroll George, Leland hotel
Carroll James, Austin
Carroll John C. 190 Pine
Carroll John J. Rev. 5470 Kimbark av.
Carroll John M. 855 W. Monroe
Carroll Margaret Miss, Evanston
Carroll Morris P. 300 Belden av.
Carroll Norman, 4850 Kimbark av.
Carroll T. G. 533 W. Monroe
Carroll William F. 4747 Lake av.
Carroll W. A. 54 The Yale
Carroll W. C. Dr. 36th ne. cor. Ellis av.
Carruth J. W. Hyde Park hotel
Carruthers James, Oak Park
Carry Edward F. 5067 Lake av.
Carse David B. 217 Ashland boul.
Carse John B. 217 Ashland boul.
Carse Matilda B. Mrs. 217 Ashland boul.
Carsley Frank E. 6655 Honore
Carsley F. M. 6459 Dickey
Carson Adolphus B. 637 Washington boul.
Carson Edwin M. 335 W. Monroe
Carson Flora M. Mrs. 302, 41st
Carson John B. Mrs. Lakota hotel
Carson Joseph G. 79 Pine
Carson Louis, 1832 Reta
Carson Oliver M. Evanston

Carson Samuel, 130 Ashland boul.
Carter Byron B. Hinsdale
Carter Charles B. 4333 Lake av.
Carter Charles S. Mrs. 535 Belden av.
Carter Edward C. Evanston
Carter Edward P. 259 Ohio
Carter Henry W. 4333 Lake av.
Carter H. L. Miss, 108 Cass
Carter J. B. 499 W. Congress
Carter J. B. 529 Belden av.
Carter J. S. Hotel Metropole
Carter Kathryn Miss, Hotel Metropole
Carter Leslie, 108 Cass
Carter Lionel J. 4401 Ellis av.
Carter Margaret Miss, 108 Cass
Carter Merritt T. Wilmette
Carter O. N. 1331 W. Monroe
Carter Philip N. 438 W. Adams
Carter Robert D. 4333 Lake av.
Carter S. P. 491, 42d pl.
Carter Thomas B. Evanston
Carter Wallace, 438 W. Adams
Carter William W. 6012 Indiana av.
Carter Zina R. 1441 Ogden av.
Carton Laurence A. 4321 Ellis av.
Cartwright Harry, 4349 Ellis av.
Carver Anna A. Mrs. Highland Park
Carver D. L. 860 Warren av.
Carver F. R. Evanston
Carver Henry C. Highland Park
Carver J. Winchester, Highland Park
Cary Ellen Mrs. 2935 Indiana av.
Cary Eugene, 2536 Prairie av.
Cary Frank, M.D. 2935 Indiana av.
        Sum. res. Mackinac Island
Cary Fred A. 196 Goethe
Cary George P. Hotel Windermere
Cary John W. Hinsdale
Cary J. Stockly, 5498 East End av.
Cary Lilian Miss, 712 W. Monroe
Cary Paul V. Hinsdale
Cary Warner P. Dr. 246, 64th (H.P.)
Cary Wilson jr. 507 N. State
Cary Wilson Mrs. 507 N. State
Caryl A. H. 5532 Madison av.
Case Calvin S. Dr. 4367 Lake av.
Case Charles H. 201 Ashland boul.
Case Edward B. Evanston
Case Edwin R. Austin
Case Elisha W. 1497 Washington boul.
Case Francis M. 2011 Indiana av.
Case George J. Glencoe
Case H. W. Dr. 98, 37th
Case John E. 2011 Indiana av.
Case John R. Elmhurst
Case J. R. Hotel Metropole
Case Lafayette W., M.D. 621 Sedgwick
Casen Munson T. 5488 East End av.
Case S. M. Mrs. 2011 Indiana av.
Case Theodore G. 338 Warren av.
Case Ward H. Mrs. Evanston
Case Wm. Warren, 560 Division
Casey Edwin A. 3631 Ellis av.
Casey Edward P. 607 Jackson boul.
Casey James J. 529 Clexeland av.
Casey James S. 5326 Lexington av,

Casey Kate Miss, 2842 Prairie av.
Casey P. Mrs. 607 Jackson boul.
Casey Robert E. The Tudor
Casey Thomas P. 607 Jackson boul.
Casey T. S. 3746 Elmwood pl.
Casgrain George D. 187 Cass
Casgrain W. T. 187 Cass
Cash William E. Hotel Windermere
Cashin John J. 4528 Prairie av.
Cashman Thomas F. Rev. 658 Jackson
    boul.
Casler George H. 351 Garfield boul.
Casler Wallace, 1236 Washington boul.
Caspary O. S. 3362 Calumet av.
Cass C. E. The Wellington
Cass George W. 2715 Michigan av.
Cass G. W. The Arizona
Cass Lewis H. Dr. 152 Irving av.
Cassady H. J. 7137 Euclid av. (H.P.)
Cassard George Carleton, Evanston
Cassard George Carleton Mrs. Evanston
Cassard Gilbert H. 3348 South Park av.
Cassard Margaret Mrs. French House,
    Evanston
Cassard Morris, 4243 Grand boul.
Cassard Vernon, 3348 South Park av.
Casselberry William Evans Dr. 1830 Calu-
    met av.
Cassell Ella Miss, 4207 Ellis av.
Cassell R. O. 360, 41st
Cassidy Harry C. 2205 Calumet av.
Cassidy J. A. 2205 Calumet av.
Cassing Emma Miss, Revere house
Casterline Fred J. 499 Webster av.
Castle Charles S. Austin
Castle C. F. Prof. 5440 Monroe av.
Castle Florence Miss, 70 Madison Park
Castle L. B. Mrs. Oak Park
Castle Percy V. Austin
Castle Perley D. Austin
Castle William, 2300 Indiana av.
Caswell Charles L. 3751 Vincennes av.
Caswell C. L. jr. 3751 Vincennes av.
Caswell James H. 580 Lasalle av.
Cate Albion, 343 Dearborn av.
        Sum. res. Winchester, Mass.
Cater Jacob S. Mrs. 690 Washington boul.
Catherwood William L. 4726 Greenwood
    av.
Catlin Charles, 235 Michigan av.
Catlin Charles, 481 Belden av.
Catlin George, 5111 Hibbard av.
Catlin W. W. Evanston
Caton Arthur J. 1910 Calumet av.
Caton John D. Judge, 1900 Calumet av.
Cattell Archibald, 4340 Berkeley av.
Caubert E. 184 Goethe
Cavanagh E. Miss, 710 W. Adams
Cavanagh Patrick, 63 Cedar
Cavaroc Charles jr. 150 Pine
Cave Charles R. 3932 Grand boul.
Cave G. E. 5400 Greenwood av.
Cave W. M. 3745 Wabash av.
Cavey Thomas J. Austin
Cayzer A. L. Evanston
Cazier M. Howard Dr. 75, 43d

Cecil James W. 3220 Rhodes av.
Cella Andrew, 3365 South Park av.
Cella Angelo S. 3365 South Park av.
Cella . G. 3365 South Park av.
Cella J. G. jr. 3365 South Park av.
Celley F. M. 4808 Prairie av.
Ceperly Cornelius H. 817 Morse av.
Chace Henry T. 5740 Rosalie ct.
Chadwick Gilman T. 716 Warren av.
Chadwick Seneca J. 4802 St. Lawrence av.
Chadwick William H. 1814 Belmont av.
Chaffee C. W. Mrs. 2714 Wabash av.
Chaffee Nellie Miss, 3627 Vernon av.
Chaisfer Andrew, 587 Cleveland av.
Chalifoux Joseph, 34 Vernon Park pl.
Challacombe E.A. Mrs.338 Hermitage av.
Challacombe Geo. E. 3353 South Park av.
Challis Charles W. 7745 Sherman
Challoner Robert Dr. 4444 Woodlawn av.
Chalmers David W. 3523 Ellis av.
Chalmers James, 879, 71st pl. (H.P.)
Chalmers Thomas, 179 Ashland boul.
Chalmers Thomas jr. 179 Ashland boul.
Chalmers William, 5140 Hibbard av.
Chalmers William J. 234 Ashland boul.
   Sum. res. Lake Geneva, Wis.
Chamberlain A. F. 6542 Sheridan av.
Chamberlain B. F. Maywood
Chamberlain Bruce, 3260 Rhodes av.
Chamberlain Charles C. 2259 Calumet
 av.
Chamberlain Charles H.1492 Washington
 boul.
Chamberlain E. G. Hotel Windermere
Chamberlain Franklin V. 2417 Michigan
 av.
Chamberlain H. G. 4402 Ellis av.
Chamberlain W. B. Oak Park
Chamberlin A. L. 1250 Michigan av.
Chamberlin A. M. 1481 Lexington
Chamberlin Barney H. Dr. 1212 Washing-
 ton boul.
Chamberlin Barney R. 4706 Prairie av.
Chamberlin Dell Mrs. 1250 Michigan av.
Chamberlin Edward C.4420Greenwood av.
Chamberlin Elmer J. 627,62d, Englewood
Chamberlin George M. ,M.D. 3031 Indi-
 ana av.
Chamberlin George M. jr. 3031 Indiana av
Chamberlin George W.4420Greenwood av
Chamberlin G. B. 492, 42d pl.
Chamberlin Joseph H. 163 S. Wood
Chamberlin Lou Miss, LaGrange
Chamberlin McP. 1632 Barry av.
Chamberlin R. H. 4706 Prairie av.
Chamberlin Sarah E. E. Mrs. 1113 Wash-
 ington boul.
   Sum. res. Wentworth, N. H.
Chamberlin T. C. Prof. 5041 Madison av.
Chamberlin T. H. 1784 Wrightwood av.
Chamberlin Walter H. Grand av. nr.
 Pratt av.
Chamberlin W. L. Dr. 65, 18th
Chambers Alice F. Mrs.2508 Michigan av.
Chambers Benjamin C. 496 Fullerton av.
Chambers Charles, Riverside

Chambers David, 6517 Ellis av.
Chambers E. C. 1236 W. Adams
Chambers George, Riverside
Chambers William E. Evanston
Chambers Wm. T. Dr. 3802 Lake av.
Champion Charles,1274Washington boul.
   Sum. res. Fox Lake, Ills.
Champlain H. C. 3827 Vincennes av.
Champlin Alfred H. Dr. 350, 61st, Eng.
Champlin Charles P. 515 W. Adams
Champlin Delos W. 107 S. Kedzie av.
Champlin D. H. 5398 Madison av.
Champlin Fred L. 515 W. Adams
Champlin F. D. 713 Walnut
Champlin G. W. 515 W. Adams
Champlin S. F. 2443 Commercial (L.V.)
Champlin William R. 515 W. Adams
Chance J. L. 4400 Ellis av.
Chancellor Justus, 1480 Wellington
Chandler Alice Miss, 2512 Indiana av.
Chandler Charles H. Evanston
Chandler C. C. 3347 Wabash av.
Chandler C. T. 877 W. Adams
Chandler C. W. C. Oak Park
Chandler Edwin W. 4415 Lake av.
Chandler Edwin W. 363 Ashland boul.
Chandler E. Bruce, 2512 Indiana av.
Chandler Fremont E. Dr. 914Sheffield av.
Chandler F. R. 182 Rush
Chandler George, 243 Michigan av.
Chandler George D. 161 Locust
Chandler George M. 2512 Indiana av.
Chandler Grace Miss, 992 W. Adams
Chandler G. W. 4451 Champlain av.
Chandler Henry E. Evanston
Chandler Homer S. 465 Dearborn av.
Chandler H. B. 244 Park av.
Chandler H. F. 1179 Ashland boul.
Chandler H. H. 4415 Lake av.
   Sum. res.Highland Park
Chandler H. W. 574 Division
Chandler Joseph B. 25 University pl.
Chandler J. B. 2428 Indiana av.
Chandler J. H. Virginia hotel
Chandler L. Hamilton 2036 Indiana au.
Chandler Norborne E. 2036 Indiana av.
Chandler Peyton R. 3844 Langley av.
Chandler R. Grigsby, 410 Chicago av.
Chandler Samuel, 263 Ontario
Chandler T. E. 161 Locust
Chandler Walter T. 2036 Indiana av.
Chandler W. W. 4355 Oakenwald av.
Channer J. Wyndham-Quinn, 900 Evans-
 ton av.
Channon Harry S. 140 Astor
Channon Henry, 571 Lasalle av.
Channon J Harrison, 290 Lasalle av.
Chanute Octaers, 413 Huron
Chapeck Joseph C. 534 Ashland boul.
Chapell E. P. Austin
Chapell George E. Austin
Chapin Alice Miss, 3344 Michigan av.
Chapin Augusta J. Rev. 3848 Lake av.
Chapin Betsey C. Miss, Evanston
Chapin Charles O. Lombard
Chapin Edward F. Lake Forest

Chapin Ella D. Miss, 180 Cass
Chapin E. S. Capt. Fort Sheridan
Chapin Fanny Miss, 180 Cass
Chapin Frederick S. Evanston
Chapin G. S. Lakota hotel
Chapin Henry C. 180 Cass
Chapin Jennie Mrs. Evanston
Chapin Joel B. 405, 64th, Englewood
Chapin J. B. Mrs. 5313 Madison av.
Chapin J. P. Mrs. 180 Cass
Chapin K. Miss, Lakota hotel
Chapin Marietta P. Miss, Evanston
Chapin M. A. Mrs. 3344 Michigan av.
Chapin O. E. 1245 Jackson boul.
Chapin Robert L. 793 Warren av.
Chapin Simeon B. 3124 Michigan av.
Chapin Staley N. Dr. 4344 Greenwood av.
Chapin W. M. Mrs. Evanston
Chapman Addie T. Miss, Evanston
Chapman Almon, Ridgeland
Chapman Arthur W. 616 Washington
boul.
Chapman Belle B. Mrs. Evanston
Chapman Charles A. 2622 Prairie av.
Chapman Chauncy F. Dr. 245 Warren av.
Chapman Clarence C. 2622 Prairie av.
Chapman D. W. Mrs. 3430 Vernon av.
Chapman D. W. 5720 Washington av.
Chapman E. A. Mrs. Evanston
Chapman Emelie A. Mrs. 1239 Wilcox av.
Chapman E. C. 50, 35th
Chapman Florence Mrs. 5415 Cottage
Grove av.
Chapman Francis M. 445 Kenmore av.
Chapman Frederick L. 42 Roslyn pl.
Chapman George C. 1112 N. Clark
Chapman Geo. H., M.D. 7510 Greenwood
av.
Chapman George L. Dr. 1112 N. Clark
Chapman James R. 500 The Plaza
Chapman James R. 2705 Indiana av.
Chapman Jerome M. 616 Washington
boul.
Chapman John A. 150 Pine
Chapman John E. Mrs. 150 Pine
Chapman J. D. Mrs. Lakota hotel
Chapman J. H. 937 W. Adams
Chapman J. L. 3431 Indiana av.
Chapman Robt. Clowry, 388 Oak
Chapman S. C. Mrs. 582 W. Congress
Chapman Walter, 491, 42d
Chapman Walter A. 2622 Prairie av.
Chapman William P. 1331 Wilton av.
Chapman Wilson S. 388 Oak
Chapman W. B. 3217 Vernon av.
Chappel J. B. Miss, Lexington hotel
Chappell Charles, Hotel Barry
Chappell C. H. 498 W. Monroe
Chappell C. H. jr. 498 W. Monroe
Chappell Henry W. 5727 Monroe av.
Chappell Howard F. 3020 Prairie av.
Chappell John M. 1721 Cornelia
Chappell Richard W. Wilmette
Chappell W. H. 4340 Lake av.
Chappelle Grace Miss, 7 Aldine sq.
Chard Charles, 4950 Prairie av.
33

Chard S. G. The Arizona
• Chard Thomas S. 534 N. State
Charles E. B. Mrs. 439 Seminary av.
Charles George B. Dr. Austin
Charles Harry C. 439 Seminary av.
Charles John J. Evanston
Charles Oscar, 448 Elm
Charles Robert B. 439 Seminary av.
Charles Thomas, 114 Park av.
Charles William W. Hotel Normandie
Charlton Francis M. 294 Webster av.
Charlton George J. Ridgeland
Charlton James, 1155 N. Clark
Charnley Charles M. 309 Schiller
Charnley James, 99 Astor
Chart S. E. Miss, 328 Lasalle av.
Chase Almira J. Mrs. 3953 Michigan av.
Chase Benjamin F. 3819 Vernon av.
Chase Benjamin·F. 3353 Forest av.
Chase Benjamin F. jr. 3353 Forest av.
Chase Bessie L.B.Miss,3401 Michigan av.
Chase Charles A. 6647 Yale, Englewood
Chase Charles C. 1846 Belmont av.
Chase Charles H. Rev. 2175 Sheridan rd.
Chase Dudley, Riverside
Chase Edwin G. 4454 Oakenwald av.
Chase Egbert, LaGrange
Chase E. W. Highland Park
Chase Franklin L. 22 Wisconsin
Chase Fred. L. 6554 Ross av.
Chase George N. 6609 Stewart av.
Chase George F. Hotel Metropole
Chase Harry G. Riverside
Chase Henry I. Riverside
Chase Hollis M. 610 Lawndale av.
Chase Horace G. 3401 Michigan av.
Sum. res. Hopkinton, N. H.
Chase Horace W.Mrs.3226 South Park av.
Chase John J. 35 S. Hoyne av.
Chase Lucy B. Miss, 3401 Michigan av.
Chase Marvin S. 3251 Wabash av.
Chase Milo J. 2458 Indiana av.
Chase M. W. Mrs. 631 W. Monroe
Chase N. C. 171, 51st (H.P.)
Chase Orrin P. 51 Warren av.
Chase Philander F. Riverside
Chase Richard B. 171, 51st (H.P.)
Chase Robert D. 171, 51st (H.P.)
Chase Sam B. 396 Garfield av.
Chase Samuel B. 1946 Belmont av.
Chase Samuel M. 3401 Michigan av.
Chase Volney C. 2486 Commercial (L.V.)
Chase Wayland J. Prof. Morgan Park
Chase William M. 6618 Lafayette av.
Chase William O. 296 Ohio
Chatfield Eli P. 452 Kenmore av.
Chatfield-Taylor Hobart Chatfield, 99 E.
Pearson
Chatroop Louis, 691 North Park av.
Chattell Bertram M. La Grange
Chatterton W. A. Wilmette
Chavett Franklin Dr. 6333 Yale
Cheal William H. Oak Park
Cheatle A. Evanston
Cheeseman F. E. Dr. 5623 Washington
av.

Cheeseman George S. Hotel Groveland
Cheeseman W.O. Dr. 4850 Evans av
Cheetham Edward, 500 Fullerton av.
Cheetham Edward L. 500 Fullerton av.
Cheney A. J. Oak Park
Cheney Charles Edward, Rt. Rev. 2409 Michigan av.
 Sum. res. Prouts Neck, Me.
Cheney Clarence C. LaGrange
Cheney D. B. Mrs. 674 W. Monroe
Cheney F. S. Dr. 674 W. Monroe
Cheney Harry W. Dr. 6303 Oglesby av.
Cheney John Vance, 369 Chicago av.
Cheney Lncian P. 444 Dearborn av.
Cheney Maynard A. 3326 Indiana av.
Cheney M. L. Mrs. 23 Marquette Terrace
Cheney Orlando H. Mrs. 477 Bowen av.
Cheney William W.436 Washington boul.
 Sum. res. Lake Geneva, Wis.
Cherrie Henry, 2541 Wabash av.
Cherrie Robert M. 2541 Wabash av.
Cherry Cummings, 239 Oakwood boul.
Cherry J. A. Mrs. 225, 28th
Cherry Robert H. 204 Oakwood boul.
Chesbrough Ellis S. jr. 17 Bellevue pl.
Chesbrough E. A. Mrs. 17 Bellevue pl.
Chesbrough William H. 5720 Rosalie ct.
Chesman Nelson, 575 Cleveland av.
Chesney James B. 682 Kenmore av.
Chesney William P. 682 Kenmore av.
Chester Harry G. Riverside
Chester H. F. Granada hotel
Chetham S. C. Irving Park
Chetlain Arthur H. Judge, 576 Lasalle av.
Chetlain A. L. Gen. 13 Scott
Chew John H., M.D. 23 Astor
Chichester Alfred, 463 Bowen av.
Chichester Henry B. 611, 78th, Eng.
Chichester John S. 494 Bowen av.
Chidister W. J. Sherman house
Chilcott L. Mrs. 3220 Vernon av.
Child James E., M.D., 5511 Madison av.
Childs A. C. Oak Park
Childs A. H. Evanston
Childs A. S. Dr. Wilmette
Childs E. W. Evanston
Childs Frank Hall, 2241 Calumet av.
Childs F. W. 504 Webster av.
Childs Harry K. 73d, nw. cor. Lake av.
Childs Henrietta Mrs. 3135 Vernon av.
Childs H. L. 716 Warren av.
Childs John A. Evanston
Childs Mary A. Mrs. Evanston
Childs Minnie C. Miss, 4742 Evans av.
Childs Robert A. Hinsdale
 Sum. res. Belvidere Park, Lake Geneva
Childs William C. 5742 Evans av.
Childs W. Fred, Highland Park
Chipman Lewis E. 573, 51st (H.P.)
Chisholm James, 532 Orchard
Chisholm John A. 71, 23d
Chisholm S. S. Virginia hotel
Chisholm W. P. Mrs. 552 Jackson boul.
Chislett Howard R. Dr. 3034 Michigan av.

Chittenden Fred W. 801 The Plaza
• Chittenden George W. 801 The Plaza
Chittenden Harry W. 801 The Plaza
Chittenden N. M. Mrs. 801 The Plaza
Chittendon George C. Park Ridge
Chittick H. 6420 Wright,
Chittick John H. 6420 Wright
Chiville John, 50 Elaine
Choate Henry, 5441 Madison av.
Chowan Ernest A. Hotel Groveland
Christensen C. 5646 Wabash av.
Christensen Henry C. 66 Hamilton av.
Christensen Jens L. 410 Ashland boul.
Christensen Sophia A. Mrs. Irving Park
Christensen S. J. Irving Park
Christian Henry W. 4320 Langley av.
Christian Isabella Mrs. 223 Park av.
Christian M. Mrs. 42, 39th
Christianson Mary Mrs. 148 Dearborn av.
Christie Bertha Miss, 420 Center
Christie Edmund, M.D., 443 Marshfield av.
Christison J. S. Dr. 217 Dearborn av.
Christman J. C. 4529 Vincennes av.
Christman William H. 5832 Rosalie ct.
Christmann George A. Dr. 507 Lasalle av.
Christoph Edward G. 40 Bellevue pl.
Christoph F. W. Mrs. 40 Bellevue pl.
Christoph Joseph A. 808 Sherwin av.
Christoph William H. 40 Bellevue pl.
Christopher Emily Miss, 330 Lasalle
Christopher J. Irving, LaGrange
Christopher Theodore D. LaGrange
Christopher Walter Shield, 408 Center
Christopher W. Dr. 408 Center
Christy C. Mrs. 1535 Wolfram
Christy Fred C. 1535 Wolfram
Christy Frederick H. 3627 Ellis Park
Christy Harry A. Elmhurst
Christy Henry A. 757 Washington boul.
Christy R. C. 865 W. Monroe
Chumasero John T. Lexington hotel
Chumasero K. P. Lexington hotel
Church Archibald Dr. 4927 Madison av.
Church Bert S. 4309 Ellis av.
Church C. A. Mrs. 353 N. Clark
Church Charles C. 6442 Stewart av.
Church Charles D. 8 St. James pl.
Church Cleveland E. Longwood
Church Daniel H. 3663 Wabash av.
Church Edmund V. 2223 Calumet av.
Church Edward, Austin
Church Frank W. 893 Kenmore av.
Church Freeman S. Longwood
Church George W. Austin
Church Harry E. 4457 Ellis av.
Church Jared C. 6512 Honore
Church J. C. 6635 Wentworth av.
Church M. H. Mrs. 893 Kenmore av.
Church Rollin, Evanston
Church Thomas V. 60 Lake Shore Drive
Church Townsend V. Lexington hotel
Church William E. Evanston
Church William L. 4423 Greenwood av.
Church William L. Mrs. Evanston

Church William T. Longwood
Churcher C. A. Mrs. Evanston
Churchill Esther Mrs. 4457 Emerald av
Churchill Frank H. LaGrange
Churchill Nettie Miss, 518 Washington boul.
Cihlar Thomas, Austin
Cilley Horatio G. 2485 Commercial(L.V.)
Cissna Walter A. 465 Dearborn av.
Claddo John P. 4062 Michigan Terrace
Claflin Hebern Dr. 6404 Evans av.
Claflin Isaac, Lombard
Claflin J. F. Oak Park
Claflin Mack A. Oak Park
Claflin W. Lombard
Claghorn James O. 2602 Prairie av.
Clampert A. B. 4529 Vincennes av.
Clancy A. W. Maj. 3935 Ellis av.
Clancy Caroline H. Mrs. 1050 Washington boul.
Clancy Cornelius L. Dr. 631 Fullerton av.
Clancy Edwin M. 1050 Washington boul.
Clancy Merrill C. 4404 Ellis av.
Clancy M. B. 4400 Ellis av.
Clancy M. L. Mrs. 3244 Vernon av.
Clancy William, 4408 Ellis av.
Clancy William B. 5524 Monroe av.
Clancy William M. 3244 Vernon av.
Clapp Amelia E. Mrs. Evanston
Clapp Caleb, 4160 Ellis av.
Clapp Charles D. 344, 61st, Eng.
Clapp Clement L. 5429 Cottage Grove av.
Clapp DeWitt C. 3154 Prairie av.
Clapp Eben P. Dr. Evanston
Clapp F. 217½ Belden av.
Clapp George, Oak Park
Clapp Harriet P. Miss, 3645 Indiana av.
Clapp Irvine E. Evanston
Clare John F. 3212 Wabash av.
Clare M. D. Hotel Barry
Clark Albert B. Dr. Evanston
Clark Alexander, Evanston
Clark Alfred Mrs. 434, 61st, Eng.
Clark Alfred C. 5737 Indiana av.
Clark Arthur R. 4330 Ellis av.
Clark A. Mrs. 573, 51st (H.P.)
Clark A. B. Austin
Clark A. E. 188 Warren av.
    Sum. res. Comfort Island, Alexandria Bay, N. Y.
Clark A. S. 188 Warren av.
Clark A. W. Mrs. 3915 Prairie av.
Clark Bertha Miss, 639 W. Monroe
Clark Bruce, 2000 Prairie av.
Clark Charles E. Calumet Club
Clark Charles M. 244 Oakwood boul.
Clark Charles R. 644½ Washington boul.
Clark Charles W. 907 Spaulding av.
Clark Chester M. 2606 Calumet av.
Clark C. C. Hotel Metropole
Clark C. C. jr. Hotel Metropole
Clark C. J. Hyde Park hotel
Clark C. M. Longwood
Clark C. S. 6446 Yale
Clark C. S. Mrs. 538 Jackson boul.
Clark C. S. Wilmette

Clark David W. 956 Warren av.
Clark Edgar A. 2971 Indiana av.
Clark Edgar H. 4418 St. Lawrence av.
Clark Edward G. 349 Ashland boul.
Clark Edward S. Evanston
Clark Edwin H. 188 Warren av.
Clark Edwin M. 2515 Commercial av. (L.V.)
Clark Egbert B. 3356 Rhodes av.
Clark Elizabeth Mrs. Maywood
Clark Ella S. Mrs. 2123 Prairie av.
Clark E. A. Lexington hotel.
Clark Frank Burchard, 4454 Oakenwald a.
Clark Frank E. 920 Warren av.
Clark Frank H. 3821 Ellis av.
Clark F. W. 231 Warren av.
Clark George A. 7804 S. Sangamon
Clark Geo. A. 445, 64th, Englewood
Clark George E. 120 Seeley av.
Clark George H. 225, 28th
Clark George H. 749 Warren av.
Clark George M. 73 Bellevue pl.
Clark George T. 227 Warren av.
Clark George W. River Forest
Clark G. W. 754 W. Monroe
Clark Hanna Mrs. 3129 Groveland av.
Clark Harry, Maywood
Clark Harry A. 6030 Park End av.
Clark Henry W. Mrs. 5316 Greenwood av.
Clark Herbert T. 1311 Michigan av.
Clark H. S. Mrs. 3031 Prairie av.
Clark James A. 205, 46th
Clark James A. Ridgeland
Clark James H. 1017 Washington boul.
Clark James J. 297, 53d (H.P.)
Clark James L. 523 Jackson boul.
Clark Jennie Mrs. 3659 Indiana av.
Clark John C. Oak Park
Clark John J. 247, 53d (H.P.)
Clark John M. 2000 Prairie av.
                Sum. res. Marion, Mass.
Clark John S. 44 Bryant av.
Clark John V. LaGrange
Clark Jonathan, 167 Aberdeen
Clark J. Barlow, Mrs. 214 Cass
Clark J. L. Tracy
Clark J. L. Mrs. The Ontario
Clark J. N. Mrs. 920 Warren av.
Clark J. Scott, Prof. Evanston
Clark J. S., M.D. 558 Lasalle av.
Clark J. S. jr. Dr. 558 Lasalle av.
Clark Lincoln E. 158 Howe
Clark Lucius, 873 Walnut
Clark Luke, 7850 Bond av.
Clark L. New Hotel Holland
Clark L. D. Miss, 689 W. Harrison
Clark L. H. Tremont house.
Clark L. W. Mrs. 6912 Perry av.
Clark Mary A. Mrs. 4330 Ellis av.
Clark Mary C. Mrs. 44 Bryant av.
Clark Melville, 496½ W. Adams
Clark Michael J. 522 67th, Englewood
Clark Nelson C. LaGrange
Clark Percy L. Dr. 1065 Washington boul.
Clark Richard F. 142, 50th (H.P.)

Clark Robert, 723 Kenmore
Clark Robert Mrs. 2206 Prairie av.
Clark Robert S. Evanston
Clark Robert T. 182 Warren av.
Clark R. A. Dr. 3408 Calumet av.
Clark Solomon H. Prof. 573, 51st (H.P.)
Clark Stewart, Evanston
Clark S. C. Mrs. Hyde Park hotel
Clark S. H. Mrs. 3300 Indiana av.
Clark S. J. Mrs. 3031 Prairie av.
Clark Theodore M. Highland Park
Clark Thomas, 175 Aberdeen
Clark Thomas C. Lexington hotel
Clark Tracy H. 2927 Indiana av.
Clark Urilla Mrs. 3821 Ellis av.
Clark Wallace G. 4330 Ellis av.
Clark Walter T. 312 Marshfield av.
Clark William B., M.D. 4520 Emerald av.
Clark William B. 2313 Michigan av.
Clark William C. 1173 Wilcox av.
Clark William D. 196, 40th
Clark William H. 2606 Calumet av.
Clark William R. 880 Washington boul.
Clark W. D. Dr. 1641 Briar pl.
Clark W. F. 383 Marshfield av.
Clark W. Irving, La Grange
Clark W. Odell, 247, 53d
Clark W. Wallace, 536 Washington boul.
Clarke Anna H. Miss, 2637 Prairie av.
Clarke Arthur L. 329 Michigan av.
Clarke Charles Atherton 1851 Barry av.
Clarke Charles F. 86 Astor
Clarke Cyrus Henry, 201 The Plaza
    Sum. res. Lombard, Ill.
Clarke Ed A. LaGrange
Clarke Elam L. 685 W. Adams
Clarke E. Mrs. 643 W. Monroe
Clarke E. A. S. 5012 Jefferson av.
Clarke Francis B., M.D. Ridgeland
Clarke Fred R. 2427 Michigan av.
Clarke F. B. The Arizona
Clarke George, 819 Pullman bldg.
Clarke George R. Mrs. Morgan Park
Clarke Harry M. 1653 Briar pl.
Clarke Henry, 3338 Calumet av.
Clarke Henry B. 122 Rush
Clarke John B. 2427 Michigan av.
    Sum. res. "Oakhurst," Waukegan
Clarke John D. 842 W. Adams
Clarke John E. Washington Heights
Clarke John S. 636 Cleveland av.
Clarke John W. Prof. Washington Heights
Clarke J. B. Washington Heights
Clarke J. V. Mrs. 122 Rush
Clarke J. V. 122 Rush
Clarke Louis B. 122 Rush
Clarke Luke, 411 Marshfield av.
Clarke Margaret T. Mrs. 3601 Vincennes
    av.
Clarke Matthew Rev. 3958 Langley av.
Clarke Robert G. 5110 Jefferson av.
Clarke Robert R. 1547 N. Halsted
Clarke Robert W. Hinsdale
Clarke R. N. 3152 Prairie av.
Clarke S. J. 1015 Jackson boul.
Clarke Ward G. Dr. 215 Dearborn av.

Clarke William E., M.D. 690 W. Monroe
Clarke William G. Rev. 54 Campbell Park
Clarke William J. 2921 Indiana av.
Clarke Winthrop H. 2427 Michigan av.
Clarke W. C. Dr. Southern hotel
Clarkson E. P. 518 Orchard
Clarkson Michael, 4859 Michigan av.
Clarkson William H. Morton Park
Clason George B. 3231 Groveland av.
Clausen Gustav L. 4001 Vincennes av.
    Sum. res. Bluff Lake, Lake Co. Ill.
Clausen Hans O. 1732 York pl.
Claussenius Edward 5856 Wabash av.
Claussenius George W. 5 Crilly pl.
Claussenius G. A. 492, 48th (H.P.)
Clausson J. F. Washington Heights
Claxton Horace N. Great Northern hotel
Clay John, 4030 Lake av.
Clay John jr. 4030 Lake av.
Clay John B. Wilmette
Clay William W. 3145 Rhodes av.
Claybaugh William M. Rev. 1004 Wash-
    ington boul.
Clayberg George M. Oak Park
Clayburgh Joseph, 1347 Michigan av.
Clayburgh Martin, 1347 Michigan av.
Clayburgh Maurice, 1347 Michigan av.
Clayton Allen B. Dr. Evanston
Clayton Charles, 3255 Calumet av.
Clayton Evelyn P. Mrs. 3200 Michigan av.
Clayton James W. Mrs. 388 Lasalle av.
Clayton Paul, 388 Lasalle av.
Clayton Ralph W. 6639 Honore
Clayton Richard, 444 Belden av.
Clayton T. W. 444 Belden av.
Clayton W. R. 6631 Harvard
Clear M. E. Austin
Cleary Edward E. 2450 Wabash av.
Cleary John J. Ridgeland
Cleary P. M. 2450 Wabash av.
Cleave O. C. Lakota hotel
Cleaveland Frank A. Norwood Park
Cleaveland Frederick B. Norwood Park
Cleaveland George W. 344 Michigan av.
Cleaver Arthur W. 355, 41st (H.P.)
Cleaver Charles S. 7251 Jeffery av.
Cleaver C. A. 7251 Jeffery av.
Cleaver Edward C. 3615 Lake av.
Cleaver E. C. J. 4008 Vincennes av.
Cleaver Frederick C. 3615 Lake av.
Cleaver Herbert E. 3922 Langley av.
Cleaver James M. 3615 Lake av.
Cleaver Mary Miss, 7251 Jeffery av.
Cleaver P. F. 7251 Jeffery av.
Cleaver S. C. 4731 St. Lawrence av.
Cleaver William, 355, 41st (H.P.)
Clegg Robert, 3828 Calumet av.
Cleland A. T. 3007 South Park av.
Clemenger John, 3968 Langley av.
Clement Allan M. 3946 Ellis av.
Clement Austin, 809 W. Monroe
Clement E. Miss, Oak Park
Clement F. M. Dr. Longwood
Clement Henry C. Auditorium hotel
Clement J. C. Mrs. 69 Warren av.
Clement N. L. 4257 Grand boul.

Clementi George V. Glencoe
Clements Frederick C. 542, 67th, Eng.
Clements John F. Mrs. 85 Astor
Clements Thomas, 4465 Lake av.
Clendennen I. Dr. Maywood
Cleveland Charles W. 2707 N. Robey
Cleveland C. B. Evanston
Cleveland C. E. 1651 Briar pl.
Cleveland Festus P. Rev. 532 Touhy av.
Cleveland Festus W. Evanston
Cleveland G. H., M.D. 951 W. Harrison
Cleveland John D. 532 Touhy av.
Cleveland J. F. Oak Park
Cleveland J. H. Mrs. 907 W. Monroe
Cleveland Samuel G. Mrs. 2707 N. Robey
Cleveland S. E. Mrs. 873 W. Adams
Cleveland Willard R. 864 W. Adams
Clevenger S. V. Dr. Riverside
Cleverdon Walter I. 70, 48th
Cliff John Capt. 148 Dearborn av.
Clifford Cabell, 435 Washington boul.
Clifford E. L. Dr. 371 Campbell av.
Clifford Hannah D. Mrs. Evanston
Clifford James M. 1729 Michigan av.
Clifford John, 517 Cleveland av.
Clifford Martin J. 1729 Michigan av.
Clifford Richard W. Judge, 1729 Michigan av.
Clifford Thomas C. 4211 Vincennes av.
Clifford William B. 36 Beethoven pl.
Clifford Winchester E. Evanston
Clifton Charles E. 3308 Calumet av.
Clinch D. L. Stamford hotel
Clinch R. Floyd, 321 Michigan av.
        Sum. res. Highland Park
Cline C. L. 7626 Wright
Cline James P. 392 S. Paulina
Cline Leon, 4317 Vincennes av.
Cline Levi Mrs. 3145 South Park av.
Clingman Charles W. 4861 Lake av.
Clingman George, 7210 Euclid av. (H.P.)
Clinnen J. G. 2735 Indiana av.
Clinton Catherine Mrs. 622 Washington boul.
Clippinger D. A. 276 Michigan av.
Clissold H. R. Morgan Park
Clizbe Wesley J. 161, 43d (H.P.)
Cloud John W. 4747 Woodlawn av.
Clough John H. 2420 Michigan av.
Clough John L. La Grange
Clough R. W. 3270 Malden
Clover John W. 3618 Lake av.
Clow Beatrice Miss, 520 Dearborn av.
Clow Catherine S. Mrs. Evanston
Clow Charles R. 702 The Plaza
Clow Harry B. 824 North Park av.
Clow James B. 702 The Plaza
Clow James C. 702 The Plaza
Clow William E. Buena Park av. ne. cor. Evanston av.
Clowry James, 4200 Ellis av.
Clowry Robert C. 524 Dearborn av.
Clute George F. 527 Belden av.
Clute George M. 527 Belden av.
Clybourn F. T. 490 Lasalle av.
Clybourn James A. 490 Lasalle av.

Clymer R. G. New Hotel Holland
Coakley Albert, 2602 Indiana av.
Coakley William, Hotel LaVita
Coalaman Emanuel, 2443 Wabash av.
Coale Atlee V. 3263 Rhodes av.
Coates George R. Austin
Coates Philip M. LaGrange
Coates Robert W. LaGrange
Coates Thomas R. Austin
Coats J. G. 6720 Rhodes av.
Cobb Arthur, 5415 Cottage Grove av.
Cobb A. M. 4331 Prairie av.
Cobb A. W. Lake Forest
Cobb Daniel, Highland Park
Cobb Edwin W. 6214 Oglesby av.
Cobb Eliot, 728 W. Monroe
Cobb Emmons B. 147 Ashland boul
Cobb F. G. 5616 Monroe av.
Cobb George A. 258 Ashland boul.
Cobb George D. 408 Elm
Cobb George W. 53 Astor
Cobb Henry Ives, Lake Forest
Cobb H. Edward, 3614 Ellis av.
Cobb John D. Highland Park
Cobb Joseph P. Dr. 3156 Indiana av.
Cobb J. W. Mrs. 832 Warren av.
Cobb Luther A. 33 Roslyn pl.
Cobb Mary A. Mrs. 236, 45th
Cobb Merritt D. 213 Ohio
Cobb M. L. Miss, Highland Park
Cobb M. R. 298 Marshfield av.
Cobb Oscar, 533 Belden av.
Cobb Silas B. 2027 Prairie av.
Cobb Simeon, 877 Washington boul.
Cobb Thomas A. River Forest
Cobb Walter F. 138 Rush
Cobb Welden J. LaGrange
Cobb Wellington, 5415 Cottage Grove av.
Cobb Willard L. 347 Oakwood boul.
Cobham James M. 326, 41st
Coble N. Arthur, Evanston
Coburn E. A. Evanston
Coburn G. A. Mrs. 215, 48th
Coburn John J. 872 Sawyer av.
Coburn Lewis Larned, 1819 Michigan av.
Coburn Nancy P. Mis. 153, 25th
Cochran A. W. Park Ridge
Cochran Garris Mrs. 6825 Anthony av.
Cochran J. Lewis, 536 N. State
        Sum. res. Edgewater
Cochran Norris, 4352 Grand boul.
Cochran Samuel, Park Ridge
Cochran S. B. 651 W. Adams
Cochran W. 296 Belden av.
Cochrane A. E. Mrs. 159, 30th
Cochrane David M. 3530 Ellis av.
Cochrane D. K. 3530 Ellis av.
Cochrane George, 40 Throop
Cochrane J. R. 4056 Michigan Terrace
Cochrane Mary A. Mrs. 4345 Grand boul.
Cochrane Robert M. 3530 Ellis av.
Cochrane Thomas J.658Washington boul.
Cochrane William H. 3530 Ellis av.
Cockrill A. R. Mrs. 5217 Madison av.
Cocroft Susie Miss, 808 W. Adams
Codd M. J. Mrs. 1837 Michigan av.

Codey Norman Peck, 3139 Calumet av.
Cody Arthur B. 3625 Grand boul.
Cody Hiram H. 3625 Grand boul.
Cody Hope Reed, Austin
Coe Albert L. 57 Bellevue pl.
Coe Almer, 5846 Indiana av.
Coe Charles J. 4552 Emerald av.
Coe D. A. Evanston
Coe George A. 4450 Oakenwald av.
Coe George A. Prof. Evanston
Coe Harry I. 3027 Michigan av.
Coe James R. 3027 Michigan av.
Coe Julia H. Mrs. 3027 Michigan av.
Coe Milton F. Mrs. 4024 Drexel boul.
Coe Schuyler M. Highland Park
Coe Wilbur E. Evanston
Coen Charles N. 6715 Stewart av.
Coen Sterling H. 7 Gordon Terrace
Coen William H. 7 Gordon Terrace
Coey Andrew J., M.D. 3506 Indiana av.
Coey David, 5238 Michigan av.
Coey Grant, 5238 Michigan av.
Coey Samuel B. 5238 Michigan av.
Coffee H. T. Capt. The Arizona
        Winter res. Memphis, Tenn.
Coffeen Helen E. Mrs. Hinsdale .
Coffeen M. Lester, Kenilworth
Coffeen William R. Hinsdale
Coffin Charles H. 380 Ontario
Coffin Charles P. Evanston
Coffin George A. 282 Bissell
Coffin Gorham B. 1076 Warren av.
Coffin John, Evanston
Coffman Ora V. Mrs. 174 Warren av.
Cogdal George B. Austin
Coggeshall Charles P. Irving Park
Coggeshall Wm. T. Mrs. 1045 Wilcox av.
Coghlan Henry D. 551 Garfield boul.
Coghlan Michael, 551 Garfield boul.
Cohen Abraham L. 455 Cleveland av.
Cohen Charlotte Mrs. 224 Fremont
Cohen David M. 3335 Calumet av.
Cohen David M. S. 455 Cleveland av.
Cohen D. 4541 Greenwood av.
Cohen G. K. 33d cor. Cottage Grove av.
Cohen Henry A. 3335 Calumet av.
Cohen Isaac, 3140 Rhodes av.
Cohen Joseph C. 560 Boulevard pl.
Cohen Joseph J. 3335 Calumet av.
Cohen J. K. 33d cor. Cottage Grove av.
Cohen Kate Miss, 3813 Michigan av.
Cohen Louis M. 1904 Indiana av.
Cohen Mendel A. Dr. 3335 Calumet av.
Cohen Michael, 476 W. Adams
Cohen Morris I. 4160 Ellis av.
Cohen Nathan, 131 E. Pearson
Cohen Reuben S. 131 E. Pearson
Cohen Samuel A. Dr. 3335 Calumet av.
Cohen Sidney, 1837 Michigan av.
Cohen S. K. 55, 33d
Cohn Arnold, 3322 Indiana av.
Cohn A. H. 3626 Vernon av.
Cohn Benjamin H. 3824 Langley av.
Cohn Charles W. 4246 St. Lawrence av.
Cohn Elias, 3651 Indiana av.
Cohn E. Mrs. 373 Park av.

Cohn Eugene D. Hotel Normandy
Cohn Harris, 42 Fowler
Cohn Henry, 786 Washington boul.
Cohn Henry, Prof. Evanston
Cohn Herman, 3439 Prairie av.
Cohn Ida Miss, 3408 South Park av.
Cohn Jacob, 3416 Vernon av.
Cohn J. H. 3408 South Park av.
Cohn Morris, 3321 Calumet av.
Cohn Moses, 4320 Vincennes av.
Cohn Samuel, 588 Lasalle av.
Cohn William 3651 Indiana av.
Coit W. A. 8 Menomonee
Coit W. B. 397 Warren av.
Coker Frank A. 4350 Vincennes av.
Coker W. W. Dr. 4611 Vincennes av.
Colbert Elias, 2 Groveland Park
Colborn Alice J. Miss, Oak Park
Colborne Oliver, 693 Evanston av.
Colburn Frank D. Evanston
Colburn Harry, Hinsdale
Colburn Joseph E. Dr. Highland Park
Colburn Josiah E. Glencoe
Colburn Levi J. 1121 Bonney av.
Colburn S. A. Mrs. Hinsdale
Colburn William, Hinsdale
Colby Charles C. 4001 Vincennes av.
Colby C. H. 4537 Ellis av.
Colby Francis T. 278 S. Campbell av.
Colby Hiram, 622, 65th, Englewood
Colby J. A. 4537 Ellis av.
Colby Sarah Miss, Austin
Coldwell George G. Morgan Park
Cole Annette Miss, 3724 Ellis av.
Cole Arthur W. 271, 53d (H.P.)
Cole Blanche E. Miss, Hinsdale
Cole Calvin L. The Renfost
Cole Charles D. 1222 Wilcox av.
Cole Charles F. 1102 Washington boul.
Cole Charles R. 4953 Prairie av.
Cole Charles S. 2927 Indiana av.
Cole Charles W. Winnetka
Cole C. C. Mrs. 4423 Ellis av.
Cole Daniel W. 4953 Prairie av.
Cole Ellis P. 1483 N. Halsted
Cole E. S. 338 Washington boul.
Cole Festus B. 3824 Ellis av.
Cole George E. 3539 Grand boul.
Cole George H. 3139 Forest av.
Cole G. W. I. 432 Englewood av.
Cole Harry A. Hinsdale
Cole Henry A. Oak Park
Cole John A. 271, 53d (H.P.)
Cole Lewis, 4314 Berkeley av.
Cole Martin E. 703 W. Monroe
Cole Mary E. W. Mrs. 271, 53d (H.P.)
Cole Moses T. 180 Park av.
Cole M. T. Oak Park
Cole Phoebe Mrs. 3724 Ellis av.
Cole S., M.D. 3305 Vernon av.
Cole Thomas W. 802 Warren av.
Cole Vincent D. 1483 N. Halsted
Cole William H. Hinsdale
Cole William O. Hinsdale
Cole W. D. Virginia hotel
Colegrove H. P. 2608 Calumet av.

Colehour C. W. 461 Lasalle av.
Colekin Richard jr. Oak Park
Coleman Edward J. 52 Lytle
Coleman John R. 205 N. State
Coleman J. A. 4550 Lake av.
Coleman J. G. 18 Ritchie pl.
Coleman Rupert, 1011 N. Halsted
Coleman Seymour, 2023 Michigan av.
Coleman Thomas H. 762 Jackson av.
Coleman William A. 297, 66th pl.
Coleman W. B. Auditorium hotel
Coleman W. Franklin, M.D. 3700 Lake av.
Coler Francis W. 415 Huron
Collat Maurice, 380 N. Clark
Collender A. 95 Delaware pl.
Colles E. G. T. 1037 Warren av.
Collier A. C. Austin
Collier Clinton, Lexington hotel
Colling George, Evanston
Collingbourne Albert B. 368, 40th (H.P.)
Collingbourne Byron T. 368, 40th (H.P.)
Collins A. C. Austin
Collins Charles H. 2300 Indiana av.
Collins C. C. River Forest
Collins C. E. 158 Park av.
Collins Ellen W. Miss, 2115 Indiana av.
Collins F. W. 275 S. Lincoln
Collins George M. 6512 Stewart av.
Collins George W. 364, 42d
Collins Harry B. 699 Kenmore av.
Collins I. S. 76 Bellevue pl.
Collins James B. 4928 Ellis av.
Collins James T. 3364 Forest av.
Collins Jessie B. Mrs. 63, 18th
Collins John Glenn, 1800 Deming ct.
Collins John L. 5822 Wabash av.
Collins Joseph B. 2973 Michigan av.
Collins Levi D. 614 Washington boul.
Collins Lorin C. sr. 1811 Prairie av.
Collins Lorin C. jr. Judge, 1811 Prairie
   av.
Collins Louis F. 3361 Indiana av.
Collins Mabel Miss, 375 Dearborn av.
Collins Margaret Mrs. The Renfost
Collins Martin H. 6512 Stewart av.
Collins Mary K. Mrs. 4211 Vincennes av.
Collins Mary V. Mrs. 233 Oakwood boul.
Collins S. Mrs. 3233 Indiana av.
Collins S. B. Mrs. 4107 Grand boul.
Collins S. T. Hinsdale
Collins Thomas, 912 W. Monroe
Collins V. T. Mrs. Evanston
Collins William A. Western Springs
Collins William R. 699 Kenmore av.
Collins William T. 3364 Forest av.
Collins W. Forman, 7153 Webster av.
Collins W. G. Virginia hotel
Collman John S. 4506 Vincennes av.
Collott C. F. 423 Center
Colman Martin A. Dr. 5853 Wabash av.
Colson Charles D. 7001 Stewart av.
Colson Harry G. 1118 Washington boul.
Colson Julia G. Mrs. 1118 Washington
   boul.
Colt Annie Miss, 6825 Anthony av.
Colt Alonzo, 119, 66th, Eng.

Colton A. M. F. 424 Chicago av.
Colton Charles S. 3158 Prairie av.
Colton Julia A. Mrs. 3158 Prairie av.
Colton Mary E. Mrs. 3237 Rhodes av.
Colton Samuel K. 424 Chicago av.
Colton Simeon C. 424 Chicago av.
Colvin E. D. 112 Garfield boul.
Colvin Harvey D. Mrs. 589 Dearborn av.
Colvin John H. 17 Astor
Colvin Katharine Miss, 4003 Ellis av.
Colvin Libbie F. Miss, 589 Dearborn av
Colvin R. 6320 Ellis av.
Colvin William A. 7751 Emerald av.
Colvin W. H. 4003 Ellis av.
Colvin W. H. jr. 425, 48th (H.P.)
Colwell A. J. Rev. 613, 66th, Eng.
Colwell Ben L. Dr. 3040 Calumet av.
Colwell Clyde B. 3040 Calumet av.
Colwell John D. Ridgeland
Colwell J. M. Mrs. 3040 Calumet av.
Colwell Ray M. 3040 Calumet av.
Colwell T. M. Rev. 7750 S. Sangamon
Colwell William S. 5506 Monroe av.
Coman Martha Mrs. 6510 Sheridan av.
Coman Seymour, 240 Goethe
Coman Will E. 39th ne. cor. Langley av.
Combs Thomas W., M.D. 434, 47th
Combs W. A. 195, 44th
Comer L. V. Mrs. 2009 Indiana av.
Comerford M. J. 1054 Washington boul.
Comfort A. Mrs. Hotel Metropole
Comings Edward D. 707 Pullman bldg.
Comley Fred, Oak Park
Compton Charles H. 15, 39th
Compton Frank, 6407 Sheridan av.
Compton H. D. Mrs. Lakota hotel
Comrad George Mrs. 1837 Michigan av.
Comstock Alphonso S. Evanston
Comstock Charles, Evanston
Comstock Edward F. 1821 Barry av.
Comstock Fanny Miss. Evanston
Comstock Fred S. 945 Kenmore av.
Comstock J. A. Evanston
Comstock Levi M. Ravinia
Comstock Louis K. Evanston
Comstock Mae E. Miss, 2207 Prairie av.
Comstock Samuel C. 2207 Prairie av.
Comstock Samuel F. 945 Kenmore av.
Comstock W. H. 401 N. State
Comstock W. R. Oak Park
Conant Luther, Oak Park
Conant William C. Oak Park
Conboy M. Mrs. 1 Warren av.
Condee L. D. 4552 Woodlawn av.
Condict Wallace R. Evanston
Condict Wallace R. jr. Evanston
Condit E. M. 6537 Harvard
Condon William H. 308 Washington
   boul.
Cone A. G. 4148 Drexel boul.
Cone George W. Austin
Cone Julius, 3649 Forest av.
Cone J. F. Mrs. Chicago Beach hotel
Cone L. H. Mrs. 271 Oakwood boul.
Cone M. M. Mrs. 1801 Prairie av.
Cones Joseph W. 372 Mohawk

Congdon B. Mrs. Oak Park
Congdon Carrie Mrs. Riverside
Congdon Charles B. Evanston
Congdon G. G. 348 Belden av.
Congdon J. Lyman, M.D. Riverside
Congdon Willis R., M.D. Riverside
Conger J. S. 426 Jackson boul.
Conger M. E. Dr. 128 Park av.
Conger Romaine M. 494 W. Monroe
Conger S. W. 498, 42d pl.
Conger Theodore H. Dr. Highland Park
Conger William P. Mrs. 262 Michigan av.
Congleton Charles F. 523 Burling
Conine H. V. 145 Ashland boul.
Conkey Lucius W. Evanston
Conkey W. B. 5518 East End av.
Conlan James, Revere house
Conlan J. F. Revere house
Conklin G. D. Mrs. Oak Park
Conklin William B. Austin
Conklin W. F. Oak Park
Conkling Allen, Auditorium hotel
Conlan C. Mrs. 141 Pine
Conlan James, Revere house
Conlan James jr. Revere house
Conlan Joseph P. Revere house
Conlee F. M. Mrs. 2943 Indiana av.
Conley John W. 4201 Grand boul.
Conlin John B. 389 Oakwood boul.
Conlin Thomas, 4020 Vincennes av.
Conly Harry F. 36, 42d
Conly J. A. 36, 42d
Connable Arthur W. 1236 Wilcox av.
Connard Isaac N. Oak Park
Connart Louis, 4834 Langley av.
Connell Ella Mrs. 343 Centre av.
Connell Charles J. Evanston
Connell George W. 4439 Evans av.
Connell James A. 343 Centre av.
Connell James M. 7025 Yale
Connell John S. 474 W. Adams
Connell Joseph A. LaGrange
Connell J. M. Mrs. 7240 Webster av.Eng.
Connell Theodore P. 485, 42d pl. (H.P.)
Connelley M. Miss, 1081 Warren av.
Connelly Francis W. 5113 Michigan av.
Connelly J. M. Leland hotel
Connelly M. C. Granada hotel
Connelly Thomas, 276 Loomis
Conner Thomas V. 3552 Vincennes av.
Conners Harry J. 3801 Ellis av.
Connery Michael W. 339 S. Hoyne av.
Connolly Cornelius, 634 Cleveland av.
Connon William L. 183 S. Oakley av.
Connor J. C. Mrs. Evanston
Connor Thomas E. Evanston
Connorton John W. 138 Locust
Conover Charles E. 5121 Kimbark av.
Conover Charles H. 478 Elm
Conover Fred. 389 Warren av.
Conover George W. 4743 Champlain av.
Conover H. H. Mrs. 3754 Forest av.
Conover Lawrence P. Hinsdale
Conover Luther W. 140 Garfield boul.
Conpropst Thomas M. Riverside
Conrad Charles H. 3940 Lake av.

Conrad C. H. Capt. Fort Sheridan
Conrad J. C. 5538 Cornell av.
Conrad J. Henry, 3940 Lake av.
Conrad Louis W. 692 W. Adams
Conrad M. Sherman house
Conrad Sarah A. Dr. 692 W. Adams
Couroy I. N. 3927 Vincennes av.
Couroy William, 4519 Indiana av.
Considine Frances Miss, 469 Bowen av.
Considine John, 59 Macalister pl.
Considine J. C. 469 Bowen av.
Considine Michael J. 59 Macalister pl.
Considine M. 59 Macalister pl.
Converse Clarence M. 2451 Michigan av.
Converse E. A. Evanston
Converse James W. Irving Park
Converse Lucius B. 4347 Berkeley av.
Converse L. P. 406 Center
Convis Alonzo P. Wilmette
Convis A. A. Mrs. Hinsdale
Convis James E. Hinsdale
Conway Edwin S. Oak Park
Conway Hart, 65 Walton pl.
Conway M. W. 85 Ewing pl.
Conway Richard F.1234 Washington boul
Conway Stephen S. 2943 Vernon av.
Conyne Charles B. S. Oak Park
Cook Albert A. 4543 St. Lawrence av.
Cook Alexander, 3835 Lake av.
Cook Alice G. Miss, 235 Michigan av.
Cook Archibald, 3835 Lake av.
Cook A. B. 3732 Lake av.
Cook A. H. 2946 Groveland av.
Cook A. H. jr. 2946 Groveland av.
Cook A. M. Mrs. 262 Park av.
Cook A. S. Mrs. 3241 Indiana av.
Cook Ben L. 113, 47th
Cook Carlos A. 376 Dearborn av.
Cook Carlos E. 376 Dearborn av.
Cook Charles A. Irving Park
Cook Charles C. 150 Pine
Cook C. E. 3434 Vernon av.
Cook C. W. 206 Cass
Cook David S. Evanston
Cook Edward, Oak Park
Cook Ernest C. 516 Fullerton av.
Cook Ezra A. 316 Washington boul.
            Sum. res. Wheaton. Ill.
Cook E. C. Oak Park
Cook E. W. Hotel Barry
Cook Frank B. 6547 Honore
Cook Frank L. Irving Park
Cook F. W. Oak Park
Cook George C. Mrs. 1813 Indiana av.
Cook George D. 5140 Woodlawn av.
Cook George B. 3658 Vincennes av.
Cook George F. Oak Park
Cook George H. 4718 Kenwood av.
Cook George M. 3640 Lake av.
Cook George S. 947 Pratt av.
Cook George T. Evanston
Cook Harlan D. 3219 Groveland av.
Cook Henry L. 4543 St. Lawrence av.
Cook Henry W. 4101 Drexel boul.
Cook H. B. 916 Warren av.

Cook H. B. 4621 Woodlawn av.
Cook H. W. Mrs. 1813 Indiana av.
Cook John C., M.D. 5408 Rosalie ct.
Cook John G. 4543 St. Lawrence av.
Cook John H. 96, 42d
Cook John S. 1559 Lill av.
Cook John T. 6517 Stewart av.
Cook K. B. 24 Madison Park
Cook Marcus E. 13 Woodland Park
Cook Nathan H. 24 Madison Park
Cook N. B. 24 Madison Park
Cook Orrin S. 74 Bryant av.
Cook Owen D. Hinsdale
Cook Robert S. 74 Bryant av.
Cook Sarah W. Mrs. 3210 Michigan av.
Cook Susan G. Mrs. 235 Michigan av.
Cook Wallis K. 519 Lunt av.
Cook William, 1523 Fulton
Cook William H. Dr. 1615 Briar pl.
Cook W. J. 4337 Ellis av.
Cook W. L. 874 W. Madison
Cook W. W. Dr. 5 Lincoln pl.
Cooke Alexander W. 234 Dearborn av.
Cooke A. H., M.D. 234 Dearborn av.
Cooke Charles F. 3321 South Park av.
Cooke Cynthia Mrs. 780 Sedgwick
Cooke D. W. 232, 54th pl. (H.P.)
Cooke Edward D. 780 Sedgwick
Cooke Frances Miss, 2330 Michigan av.
Cooke Frank R. The Tudor
Cooke George J. 2421 Michigan av.
Cooke Harry H. Hinsdale
Cooke Jessamine Miss, 2330 Michigan av.
Cooke John M., M.D. 234 Dearborn av.
Cooke John R. 2421 Michigan av.
Cooke John S. 2421 Michigan av.
　　　　Sum. res. Lake Geneva, Wis
Cooke S. J. 2532 Wabash av.
Cooke Wilson H. 780 Sedgwick
Cooke W. E. Chicago Beach hotel
Cooke W. J. Oak Park
Cookingham Theron W. Irving Park
Cool J. A. Miss, 4016 Ellis av.
Coolbaugh W. F. Mrs. 2252 Calumet av
Cooley Alonzo F. 2430 Commercial(L.V.)
Cooley Edwin G. La Grange
Cooley Harlan W. 4613 Woodlawn av.
Cooley Katherine S. Mrs. 338 Ontario
Cooley Norman P. 3139 Calumet av.
Cooley Proctor P. Evanston
Coolidge Ben L. 73 Park av.
Coolidge Charles A. 2603 Prairie av.
　　　　Sum. res. Marion, Mass.
Coolidge Frederic S. Dr. 2209 Prairie av.
Coolidge George W. 6422 Myrtle av.
Coolidge Henry W. 6032 Oglesby av.
Coolidge H. E. Miss, 3750 Langley av.
Coolidge Sidney, La Grange
Coolidge Walter G. 4752 Kimbark av.
Coolidge William H. 1475 Fulton
Coolidge Winthrop, 4752 Kimbark av.
Coombs Hezekia, 6821 Union av.
Coombs Hiram, Ridgeland
Coon Hiram J. 534 W. Adams
Coon Marietta Miss, Irving Park
Coon Thomas H. 534 W. Adams

Coones George, 116, 33d
Coonley Charles, 4422 Prairie av.
Coonley Elizabeth Miss, 4938 Drexel
　boul.
Coonley Emily Mrs. 4043 Grand boul.
Coonley John C. Mrs. 620 Division
Coons Catherine Mrs. 912 Chase av.
Cooper Arthur W., D.D.S. Evanston
Cooper A. J. Evanston
Cooper A. W. 198 Park av.
Cooper Burton W. The Yale
Cooper B. E. LaGrange
Cooper C. B. The Yale
Cooper Edward C. 435 Washington boul.
Cooper Edward M. Evanston
Cooper Erva Miss, Evanston
Cooper F. Mrs. 4058 Michigan Terrace
Cooper Harry C. 1225 Millard av.
Cooper Harry H. 2505 Michigan av.
Cooper Henry N. LaGrange
Cooper Horace L. 4740 Champlain av.
Cooper John A. Revere house
Cooper John S. Col. 2733 Michigan av.
Cooper John S. 376 Oak
Cooper Joseph I. 1837 Michigan av.
Cooper J. Edward, La Grange
Cooper Mary E. Stethen Mrs. 295 Belden
　av.
Cooper Nellie D. Mrs. 1403 Washington
　boul.
Cooper Robert B. 2952 Groveland av.
Cooper Robert W. 376 Oak
Cooper Samuel A. 863 S. Central Park
　av.
Cooper William D. 2973 Groveland av.
Cooper Wm. Fenimore, Newberry hotel
Cooper Willam H. 4426 Berkeley av.
Coover D. R. 3756 Ellis av.
Copeland Frederick K. Winnetka
Copeland Hattie Mrs. 2728 Wabash av.
Copeland John H. 588, 60th (H.P.)
Copeland Lowell, Winnetka
Copeland W. L. Dr. 866 W. Monroe
Copelin A. J. W. 3633 Ellis av.
Copelin Eudolphus W. 622 The Plaza
Copelin Thomas, Winnetka
Copelin Thomas E. 382 Erie
Copenhaver William K. 71 University
　pl.
Copland Edward, 4408 Sidney av.
Copley William W. 4614 Emerald av.
Corbett Maude Miss, Hotel Windermere
Corbett M. Miss, 2616 Indiana av.
Corbidge Eliza Mrs. 3542 Wabash av.
Corbidge William H. 3542 Wabash av.
Corbin Calvin R. 597 Dearborn av.
Corbin C. Dana, 597 Dearborn av.
Corbin David T. 569, 51st
Corbin Frank N. 597 Dearborn av.
Corbly John F. 13 Woodland Park
Corboy M. J. 97 Macalister pl.
Corbus J. R., M.D. 907 W. Adams
Corby Charles, 4062 Michigan Terrace
Corby Emily Mrs. 120 S. Oakley av.
Corby Ralph B. 120 S. Oakley av.
Corcoran John J. 6554 Stewart av.

Cordes Henry, 163 S. Hoyne av
Cordes John, 1404 Fulton
Cordes Lewis, 163 S. Hoyne av.
Cordo Frank I. 2970 Vernon av.
Core Albert S. Dr. 4313 Langley av.
Corey Francis W. Highland Park
Corey George J. LaGrange
Corey Ray Webster, LaGrange
Corigan Mary Mrs. 2842 Prairie av.
Corlett Thomas G., M.D. 580 Division
Corlies John W. 723 Washington boul.
Corlies William, Evanston
Corliss W. Auditorium hotel
Corneau D. Ellis, 2934 Michigan av.
Corneau Edwin G. Ridgeland
Corneau Grace V. Miss, 235 Michigan av.
Cornelius J. J. Dr. 518, 63d, Eng.
Cornelius Louis A. 4049 Ellis av.
Cornell Addie S. Mrs. 14 Bryant av.
Cornell A. J. 1526 Lill av.
Cornell D. D. Mrs. 5821 Madison av.
Cornell E. E. 5821 Madison av.
Cornell Geo. K. 5104 Jefferson av.
Cornell Henrietta Mrs. 503 W. Monroe
Cornell John E. Hyde Park hotel
Cornell Paul, 5104 Jefferson av.
Cornhauser M. 394 Warren av.
Corning Chas. S. Hotel Barry
Corning Winfield S. 3953 Michigan av.
Cornish G. A. Capt. Fort Sheridan
Cornish Robert H. Prof. Morgan Park
Cornish S. V. 6456 Oglesby av.
Cornwell D. K. 271 Warren av.
Cornwell Maria S. Mrs. 4304 Emerald av.
Corrigan Charles E. 1633 Roscoe
Corrigan Charlotte Mrs. 1633 Roscoe
Corrigan C. E. 1633 Roscoe
Corrigan Geo. F. 1633 Roscoe
Corrigan J. Mrs. 3229 Indiana av.
Corrigan R. E. 3229 Prairie av.
Corris J. F. Morton Park
Corse C. J. Longwood
Corse Edward Mrs. 407 Elm
Corson George D. Evanston
Corten Theodore, 980 Mayfair
Corthell J. L. Mrs. 2013 Michigan av.
Cortright L. D. 6049 Edgerton av.
Corwin Arthur M. Dr. 691 W. Harrison
Corwin Cecil S. 1066 Warren av.
Corwin Charles A. 3150 Indiana av.
Corwin Eli Rev. 1066 Warren av.
Corwin J. A. 591 W. Monroe
Corwith Charles R. 1945 Prairie av.
Corwith Henry Mrs. 1945 Prairie av.
Corwith John W. 1945 Prairie av.
Corwith Nathan jr. 30 Linden pl.
Corwith Nathan Mrs. Lexington hotel
Cory Alfonzo L. Dr. 4136 Wabash av.
Cory Chester P. 714 Washington boul.
Cory J. D. 2934 Indiana av.
Coryell George, M.D. Riverside
Coshun Ralph H. 908 Turner av.
Cossar Walter L. 23 Best av.
Cossitt Franklin D. LaGrange
Cossitt F. D. jr. LaGrange
Cossman A. 603 W. Monroe

Cossman Meyer, 603 W. Monroe
Cost EdwardyF. Hotel Windermere
Cost Herbert, Hotel Windermere
Cost Jacob A. River Forest
Costikyan Siragan S. Auditorium annex
Costner Henry A. Dr. 5, 43d
Cotes W. S. 296 Ohio
Cotter J. Lieut. Fort Sheridan
Cotter Robert B. 404 The Plaza
Cottier A. E. 54 Bellevue pl.
Cottier Caroline Mrs. 54 Bellevue pl.
Cottle Fannie Mrs. 1, 31st
Cottlow Benjamin A. Dr. 198 Bowen av.
Cotton Alfred C. Dr. 677 Jackson boul.
Cotton Caroline H. Mrs. 69 Bryant av.
Cotton Charles H. 69 Bryant av.
Cotton J. Whitcomb, 66 Cedar
Cottrelf J. O. 1813 Indiana av.
Cottrell Thomas D. 3031 Prairie av.
          Sum. res. Hillsdale, Mich.
Couch Ira Mrs. Lakota hotel
Couch Ira J. Lakota hotel
Couch James Mrs. 2545 Indiana av.
Couffer J. D. 292 Ashland boul.
Coughlan John, 31 Macalister pl.
Coughlan J. T. 66 Vernon Park pl.
Coughlan Thomas, 452 W. Taylor
Coughlan T. E. 31 Macalister pl.
Coughlin James M. 694 Walnut
Cougle Charles H. 337 Michigan av.
Cougle Daniel Depue, 344 Michigan av.
Cougle Irvin B. 3012 Michigan av.
Cougle S. E. Mrs. Julien hotel
Coulter Adrian, 395 S. Leavitt
Coulter Eugene C. 399 Dearborn av.
Coulter John, 4756 Champlain av.
Coulter John M. Dr. Lake Forest
Coulter John R. 291 S. Leavitt
Coulter J. Homer Dr. Morton Park
Coulter W. G. Tracy
Council W. H. LaGrange
Counselman Charles, 5035 Greenwood av.
Counselman Willis, 202 The Plaza
Countiss Frederick D. 3222 Calumet av.
Countiss Robert H. 3222 Calumet av.
Countiss Robert H. jr. 6052 Park End av.
Courter David A. Hinsdale
Courtney Thomas E. 70 Laflin
Courtright C. W. Dr. 340, 63d (H.P.)
Courtright Henry H. 5029 Madison
Couthoui Joseph, 2450 Indiana av.
Covell Marias C. LaGrange
Covell Wm. Brooks, 5538 Cornell av.
Coveny J. C. 1453 Wrightwood av.
Covert M. Mrs. Oak Park
Cowan Charles H. 465 Fullerton av.
Cowan Eugene, 1029 Warren av.
Cowan Harry R. 465 Fullerton av.
Cowan Herbert B. 1029 Warren av.
Cowan H. Mrs. 2975 Wabash av.
Cowan John S. Leland hotel
Cowan Julia L. Miss, 1029 Warren av.
Cowan William K. 465 Fullerton av.
Cowan William P. 1800 Michigan av.
Cowdery Hiram C. W. 7034 Addison av.
Cowdery R. E. Mrs. 27 St. James pl.

Cowdrey Robert H. 933 S. Kedzie av.
Cowen Bertha Mrs. 3218 South Park av.
Cowen Carlos, 3218 South Park av.
Cowen Eleonora Miss, 2204 Prairie av.
Cowen Israel, 3218 South Park av.
Cowen William P. 394 S. Paulina
Cowen W. H. Dr. Morgan Park
Cowes C. W. Chicago Beach hotel
Cowgill F. S. 910 Pullman bldg.
Cowles Altred, 1805 Michigan av.
    Sum. res. York Harbor, Me.
Cowles Enos M. 3605 Ellis Park
Cowles Frederick S. 3605 Ellis Park
Cowles Henrietta Miss, Evanston
Cowles Henrietta Mrs. 301 Schiller
Cowles James A. 3646 Indiana av.
Cowles John E. 4320 Lake av.
Cowles John T. Morgan Park
Cowles William H. 1805 Michigan av.
Cowles W. D. Douglas club
Cowley Joseph W. 17 Ashland boul.
Cowling J. G. Evanston
Cowper Charles H. Evanston
Cowper John H. 215 Warren av.
Cowperthwaite A. C. Dr. 14 Warren av
Cox Agnes Mrs. 544 Jackson boul.
Cox Alexis J. 1624 Diversey
Cox Alfred J. 1624 Diversey
Cox Alfred W. 1624 Diversey
Cox A. G. 474 Lasalle av.
Cox Charles, Oak Park
Cox Charles A. 1227 Millard av.
Cox Charles C. 306 Belden av.
Cox Charles D. 4335 Forrestville av.
Cox Charles E. 3544 Ellis av.
Cox Cornelius, Tracy
Cox Edward L. 770 Jackson boul.
Cox Electra R. Mrs. 131 Astor
Cox Eugene R. 3544 Ellis av.
Cox George W. 423 Jackson boul.
Cox Harry N. Glencoe
Cox Henry J. 4821 Vincennes av.
Cox H. C. 451 Irving av.
Cox I. L. 3150 Indiana av.
Cox Jennie E. Miss, 131 Astor
Cox Jesse, 717 W. Harrison
Cox J. B. Hotel Normandie
Cox J. C. 4108 Lake av.
Cox LeRoy B. 3168 Groveland av.
Cox Lewis H. Glencoe
Cox Rensselaer W. 131 Astor
Cox Richard S. Lexington hotel
Cox Romulus A. 569, 51st (H.P.)
Cox T. E. Rev. 658 Jackson boul.
Cox William H. Glencoe
Cox William John, 51 Ray
Cox William J. 3150 Indiana av.
Cox W. C., M.D. 705 W. Monroe
Coxe Charles B. 754 Lunt av.
Coxe Edward D. 754 Lunt av.
Coxe J. Nathan. 921 Pullman bldg.
Coy Irus, 3934 Michigan av.
Coy Lincoln M. 3934 Michigan av.   ·
Coy R. D. Glencoe
Coy Winfield S. 220 W. Madison
Coy W. F. Dr. 725 N. Wells

Coyle James F. 3327 Vernon av.
Coyne F. E. 795 Warren av.
Cozens Sarah F. Mrs. 236 Irving av.
Cozzens James G. 3608 Ellis Park
Cozzens N. R. Mrs. 2493 Commercial
    (L.V.)
Cozzens Samuel, 4515 Emerald av.
Crabbe Hugh, The Ontario
Cracraft Archie C. 6402 Myrtle av.
Craft John C. 5216 Jefferson av.
Crafts Arthur A. Austin
Crafts Clayton E. Austin
Crafts Miles B. Austin
Crafts Stanley C. Austin
Crafts Siegel J. Austin
Crafts William C. Austin
Cragin Edward F. 27 Astor
Cragin Frances M. Miss, 259 Lasalle av.
Cragin F. M. Mrs. 259 Lasalle av.
Cragin Henry B. Evanston
Cragin Morgan J. 464, 46th (H.P.)
Craib John, 957 Sawyer av.
Craig Adam, 3976 Vincennes av.
Craig Alexander, Bond av. nr. 75th
Craig A. Dewes, Riverside
Craig Bryan Y. 1048 N. Halsted
Craig Charles F. 1058 Washington boul.
Craig E. M. 881 Spaulding av.
Craig E. S. 3018 Wabash av.
Craig James C. 6544 Lafayette av.
Craig James D. Dr. 751 Jackson av.
Craig John, 242, 45th
Craig Joseph C. 385 S. Oakley av.
Craig Joseph H. 6619 Ellis av.
Craig Robert, 6615 Wentworth av.
Craig Walter H. Hotel Windermere
Craig William, 637 W. Adams
Craig William, 4846 Langley av.
Craig William L. 904 S. Kedzie av.
Craig Willis G. Rev. 1048 N. Halsted
Crain Charles Mrs. Evanston
Crain Charles S. 27 Scott
Crain F. E. 148 N. State.
Crain George H. Evanston
Crain Osro A. Evanston
Craine W. N. Lexington Hotel
Cram George F. 4168 Drexel boul.
Cram John S. 1634 N. Halsted
Cram LeRoy T. 1634 N. Halsted
Cram W. D. Hyde Park hotel
Cramer Ambrose, 301 Erie
Cramer Charlie D. Wilmette
Cramer E. Mrs. 30 Astor
Cramer E. W. 78 Bellevue pl.
Cramer Frank, 30 Astor
Crampton E. E. Mrs. Hyde Park hotel
Crampton J. N. Evanston
Crampton R. L. Oak Park
Crandal Frederick E. 4136 Ellis av.
Crandal Leretta M. Mrs. 4136 Ellis av.
Crandall Arthur, 143 Oakwood boul.
Crandall A. Mrs. 735 W. Adams
Crandall Chester D. 4438 Ellis av.
Crandall C. E. 5455 Monroe av.
Crandall Frank A. 2209 Michigan av.
Crandall Lyman E. 2450 Michigan av.

Crandall L. A. Rev. 4453 Berkeley av.
Crandall Miles, Oak Park
Crandall Oscar, 6636 Yale
Crandall Roland A. 419, 48th
Crandall R. S. Mrs. 47, 77th
Crandall S. W. 307 W. Monroe
Crandon Frank P. Evanston
Crane Albert W. 1199 Winthrop av.
Crane A. B. Mrs. 145 Oakwood boul.
Crane A. C. 113 Cass
Crane Carrie R. Mrs. The Renfost
Crane Charles A. 3000 Vernon av.
Crane Charles R. 3736 Grand boul.
    Sum. res. Lake Geneva, Wis.
Crane D. E. Mrs. 2450 Michigan av.
Crane Eliza J.Mrs. 1482 Washington boul.
Crane Frances Dr. 2541 Michigan av.
    Sum. res. Lake Geneva, Wis.
Crane Frank P. 402, 65th, Englewood
Crane Frank R. 1482 Washington boul.
    Sum. res. Escanaba, Mich
Crane Frederick A. 650 Washington boul.
Crane George E. 140 Loomis
Crane Harold O. 55 Astor av.
Crane Henry A. Wilmette
Crane Herbert P. 2635 Michigan av.
    Sum. res. Lake Geneva, Wis.
Crane H. P. Mrs. 2719 Prairie av.
Crane Julius M. 3444 Indiana av.
Crane J. S. Col. 6743 Wentworth av.
Crane Lizzie M. Miss, Hotel Groveland
Crane L. Mrs. Austin
Crane M. E. Mrs. 140 Loomis
Crane Richard T. 2541 Michigan av.
    Sum. res. Lake Geneva, Wis.
Crane Richard T. jr. 2541 Michigan av.
Crane Simeon H. 3822 Ellis av.
Crane S. J. Mrs. 16 Hamilton av.
Crane Willis E. Wilmette
Crane W. B. 393 Ashland boul.
Cranshaw Charles W. Avenue house,
    Evanston
Cranston T. H. 215½ S. Wood
Crantz C. H. 413 Belden av.
Cranz H. C. Lexington hotel
Crapser Morris H. 1856 Frederick
Crary Charles W. Dr. 83, 47th
Cratty Josiah, Oak Park
Cratty Thomas, 279 Oak
Craven Henry, Evanston
Craven Thomas Rev. Evanston
Cravens William D. The Tudor
Crawford Andrew,109 Park av. Lake View
    Sum res. Royalton Heights, St.
    Joseph, Mich.
Crawford A. K. Dr. 3141 South Park av.
Crawford A. W. Hyde Park hotel
Crawford Charles H. 3993 Drexel boul.
Crawford C. J. Leland hotel
Crawford E. W. Mrs. 2001 Michigan av.
Crawford Frank J. 3666 Lake av.
Crawford Frederick E. 6520 Sheridan av.
Crawford George V. 3525 Ellis av.
Crawford George W. 4229 Indiana av.
Crawford Henry, 2000 Calumet av.
Crawford Henry jr. 2329 Calumet av.

Crawford John Mrs. 2103 Clifton
Crawford John H. 2103 Clifton
Crawford John W. Mrs. 18 Sidney ct.
Crawford O. W. 2001 Michigan av.
Crawford Richard C. 566 Division
Crawford William H. Evanston
Crawford William L. 904 Touhy av.
Crawford William R. 2000 Calumet av.
Crawford W. R. La Grange
Crawley Cyrus R. 7712 Emerald av.
Crede Charles, 485 Ashland boul.
Cregar Monroe, Longwood
Cregar P. D. Berwyn
Cregier DeWitt C. 469 Elm
    Sum. res. St. Charles, Ill.
Cregier DeWitt C. jr. 469 Elm
Cregier N. Banks, 524 Garfield av.
Cregier Edward L. Newberry hotel
Cregier Washington R. 469 Elm
Crego David R. 103, 24th
Crego Frank A. Irving Park
Creighton Catherine Mrs. Evanston
Creighton Martha J., M.D. 4217 Ellis av.
Creighton Thomas S. Evanston
Crell Charles A. 77 Bryant av.
Cremin John F. Austin
Crennan Joseph M. 2931 Vernon av.
Creote Clara Miss, Austin
Crepin E. E. 4726 Woodlawn av.
Crerar John, Grand Pacific hotel
Cressler David W. 2630 Wabash av.
Cressler Joseph A. 2630 Wabash av.
Crew Henry, Prof. Evanston
Crews Seth F. Riverside
Crews Seth F. jr. Riverside
Cribben Heury, Oak Park
Cribben W. H. Oak Park
Crie George D. Evanston
Crie Kate B. Miss, Evanston
Crighton James, 227 S. Lincoln
Crilly Daniel F. 3820 Michigan av.
Crilly Frank L. 3820 Michigan av.
Crilly George S. 3808 Calumet av.
Crilly Wm. M. 3816 Michigan av.
Crimmins Nellie Miss, 229, 28th
Crippen A. J. 2027 Indiana av.
Crisand Joseph, 5600 Monroe av.
Crisp John F. Leland hotel
Crissey M. E. Mrs. Julien hotel
Crissman Ira B. Dr. 1686 Barry av.
Crissman Rush E. Dr. 356 N. Clark
Crist Edward, 113 Cass
Crist Edwin Grant, 1651 Briar pl.
Crist Emma Mrs. 7120 Eggleston av.
Crist William D. 7120 Eggleston av.
Criswell James F. 163 S. Wood
Critchell John, 6955 Yale
Critchell J. H. 6955 Yale
Critchell Nellie M. Miss, 6955 Yale
Critchell Robert M. 4338 Ellis av.
Critchell Robert S. 4455 Greenwood av.
Critchfield George W. 576 Lasalle av.
Crittenden Chas. R. D. Rev. 2698 Com-
    mercial (L.V.)
Crittenden Frank T. 1761 Oakdale av.
Crittenden Henry C. 1658 Briar pl.

Crocker Albert H. 588 Lasalle av.
Crocker Benjamin S. 510 W. Adams
Crocker Charles W. Wilmette
Crocker Hubert D. 6020 Edgerton av.
Crocker James R. Evanston
Crocker John T. 14 Chalmers pl.
Crocker Louise Mrs. 435 Lasalle av.
Crocker Percy O. Wilmette
Crocker Ralph R. 6020 Edgerton av.
Crocker William, 2013 Indiana av.
Crockett D. U. 3769 Lake av.
Crockett R. L. Oak Park
Croft Albert E. 3616 Rhodes av.
Croft Edgar H. 210½, 37th
Croft F. L. 6749 Perry av.
Croft F. W. 6749 Perry av.
Croft Herbert J. 210½, 37th
Croft Horace I. 210½, 37th
Croft Nathaniel, 210½, 37th
Crofton R. E. A. Col. Fort Sheridan
Crofut Charles H. 6110 Princeton av.
Cromelien D. 4749 Calumet av.
Cromer Jeremiah C. Rev. 1161 Millard av.
    Sum. res. Macatawa Park, Mich.
Cromwell Caroline Mrs. 3025 Prairie av.
Cromwell Charles, 3025 Prairie av.
Cromwell William Mrs. 7000 Sherman
Crone Charles E. 4106 Vincennes av.
    Sum. res. Spring Lake, Wis.
Cronholm N. N. 3039 Groveland av.
Cronin Albert J. 4430 Prairie av.
Cronin Harry A. 4232 Langley av.
Cronkhite Harriet Miss, Hotel Imperial
Cronkrite B. F. 4436 Evans av.
Crooke William D. Mrs. Hinsdale
Crooker Ernest P. 85, 20th
Crooker William W. 3131 Forest av.
Cropper George E. 46°., 45th
Crosby Amanda Mrs. Riverside
Crosby Arthur A. 307, 53d (H.P.)
Crosby A. C. Mrs. 317 Erie
Crosby Benjamin F. 720 W. Adams
Crosby Charles H. 4453 Emerald av.
Crosby Chauncey H. Riverside
Crosby David K. 720 W. Adams
Crosby Eugene C. Hinsdale
Crosby Frederick W. 301 Huron
Crosby George H. 7220 Yale
Crosby J. G. 3042 Groveland av.
Crosby M. H. Mrs. 2582 Commercial
    (L.V.)
Crosby Thomas F. 797 Warren av.
Crosby William S. 604 Division
Crosby W. W. 6414 Ellis av.
Crose George G. Austin
Crose H. Boyd Austin
Crosley John L. 767 Larrabee
Cross Albert M. Mayfair
Cross A. J. 74 Bellevue pl.
Cross Clarence L. Riverside
Cross Edwin, M.D. 1436 Wrightwood av.
Cross Helen Mrs. 235 Michigan av.
Cross H. A. Dr. 560, 55th
Cross James E. 1406 Millard av.
Cross J. E. Mrs. 2354 Calumet av.
Cross Jesse M. Rev. Mayfair

Cross L. P. Mrs. 5806 Washington av.
Cross Moulton J. 561 Division
Cross R. W. 219, 46th (H.P.)
Cross Thomas jr. Ridgeland
Crossette Charles H. Hinsdale
Crossette William E. 3141 Rhodes av.
Crossley Henry, The Tudor
Crossman Abner, 60 Woodland Park
Crossman A. B. 448 N. Normal Parkway
Crossman F. M. Arlington Heights
Crothers Robert, 6 Langley av.
Crouch Albert W. 15, 46th
Crouch Robert B. 2923 Michigan av.
Crouch Thomas, 15, 46th
Crounse S. H. Oak Park
Crouse D. H. 2231 Prairie ae.
Crouse John N. Dr. 2231 Prairie av.
Crow J. C. 853 Jackson boul.
Crow J. W. 7728 S. Sangamon
Crow Martha Foote Mrs. 2978 Indiana av.
Crowe Frank, 365 W. Congress
Crowe Genevieve Miss, 365 W. Congress
Crowe Martin Mrs. 3138 Wabash av.
Crowe M. S. Evanston
Crowell Henry P. 134 Pine
Crowell Sarah E. Miss, Auditorium
Crowley A. E. 359, 41st
Crowley Edward F. Austin
Crowley William F. Newberry hotel
Croy Simeon W. The Tudor
Cruickshank Geo. B. 2944 Groveland av.
Cruikshank C. E. 671 Park av.
Cruit Robert, LaGrange
Crumbaugh Frederick, 3323 Forest av.
Crumbaugh Lucius B. 909 Pullman bldg.
Crummey James B. 646 Chestnut, Eng.
Crump L. M. Hyde Park hotel
Crump William R. H. 4314 Berkeley av.
Crump W. H. 606 W. Congress
Cruse George O. Sherman house
Crutcher H., M.D. 6036 Oglesby av.
Cruttenden Thomas S. 5003 Madison av.
Cruzen Ralph E. 408 Washington boul.
Cubley Edwin J. 1265 Wolcott
Cudahy Michael, 3138 Michigan av.
    Sum. res. Mackinac Island
Cudahy John, 3254 Michigan av.
    Sum. res. Mackinac Island
Cudell Adolph, 418 N. State
Culbertson James A. Kenilworth
Culbertson Wm. New Hotel Holland
Cullen E. W. 503 W. Congress
Cullen James K. 668 Winthrop av.
Cullen John, 65 The Yale
Cullerton Walter, Auditorium hotel
Culliton C. W. Mrs. 6711 Honore
Culloton Thomas P. 399 Sheffield av.
Cullum A. S. 539, 67th, Eng.
Culmer G. C. K. Hyde Park hotel
Culmer G. F. Hyde Park hotel
Culver Alvin. H. Glencoe
Culver Belden F. 821 The Plaza
Culver Frank H. 461 Elm
Culver George N. Mrs. Virginia hotel
Culver G. W. Mrs. 461 Elm
Culver Harry N. Glencoe

Culver Helen Miss, 31 Ashland boul.
Culver Morton, Glencoe
Culver Morton T, Glencoe
Cumett Grace Miss, 1911½ Diversey
Cummings Andrew, 2978 Wabash av.
Cummings Charles C. 670 Lasalle av.
Cummings Columbus R. 1641 Indiana av.
Cummings D. Mark, 65 Cedar
Cummings Ed. S. 874 Walnut
Cummings E. Mrs. Ridgeland
Cummings E. A. Ridgeland
Cummings Frank A. 143, 39th
Cummings F. D. 1044 Garfield boul.
Cummings George, Clifton house
Cummings Geo. B. Highland Park
Cummings John O. Highland Park
Cummings Joseph Mrs. Evanston
Cummings J. P. Mrs. 1641 Indiana av.
Cummings Martin, 3823 Vincennes av.
Cummings Morris C. 670 Lasalle av.
Cummings Norman P. 4958 Forrestville av.
Cummings Samuel, Park Ridge
Cummings Susan Mrs. 306, 30th
Cummings Walter D. 143, 39th
Cummings William, The Tudor
Cummings William A. 4837 Forrestville av.
Cummings William C. 1044 Garfield boul.
Cummings William H. The Tudor
Cummings W. 343 Park av.
Cummins Atwood, 98, 37th
Cummins B. F. Hotel Windermere
Cummins James S. 126, 47th
Cummins Joseph, 4104 Prairie av.
Cummins Wilham G. Dr. 423 Erie
Cumnock Robert L. Prof. Evanston
Cunliffe Owen H. C. 42, 39th
Cunning John N. 120 DeKalb
Cunningham Catherine Miss, 3249 Groveland av.
Gunningham Hugh, 131 Park av.
Cunningham James E. 3024 Michigan av.
Cunningham John A. Winnetka
Cunningham Michael, 567 W. Adams
Cunningham M. Mrs. 3024 Michigan av.
Cunningham M. E. Mrs. 59 Park av.
Cunningham Peter Mrs. 708 N. Wells
Cunningham Sarah L. Miss, 708 N. Wells
Cunningham Secor, 3545 Michigan av.
       Sum. res. Highland Park
Cunningham Thomas, 6020 Indiana av.
Cunningham Thomas, Hyde Park hotel
Cunningham Thos. S. 4456 Sidney av.
Cunningham V. L. 5734 Kimbark av.
Cunningham William, 6020 Indiana av.
Cunningham Wm. H. 4707 Vincennes av.
Cunningham William B. 3249 Groveland av.
Cure Gustave, 2970 Vernon av.
Curlett Lewis K. Irving Park
Curran D. B. 4059 Lake av.
Curran John M. Evanston
Curran Mary A. Mrs. 42 Bellevue pl.
Curran O. P. 4059 Lake av.
Curran Samuel H. 4059 Lake av.

Curran William, 841 W. Monroe
Currey Arthur L. Evanston
Currey Eliza F. Mrs. Evanston
Currey J. Seymour, Evanston
Currier A. D. 235 Michigan av.
Currier Charles L. 4725 Kimbark av.
Currier C. L. jr. 4725 Kimbark av.
Currier Emily Mrs. Oak Park
Currier E. B. Miss, 4725 Kimbark av.
Currier E. K. Mrs. 6738 Wright
Currier J. H. Revere house
Curry Jacob O. 4439 Greenwood av.
Curry Lewis M. Oak Park
Curry Morton M. Evanston
       Summer res. Channel Lake, Ill.
Curtice Louis, Hotel Imperial
Curtin P. C. Mrs. 60 Wisconsin
Curtis A. C. Mrs. 367 Marshfield av.
Curtis B. 230 Loomis
Curtis Charles H. 409 Washington boul.
Curtis Charles H. 416 Center
Curtis Cornelius, 7437 Nutt av.
Curtis D. H. 409 Washington boul.
Curtis Edmund A. 1149 Millward av.
Curtis Edward S. 579 Burling
Curtis Edward W. 1035 Kenmore av.
Curtis Edward W. jr. 1035 Kenmore av.
Curtis Eugene A., M.D. 900, 70th (H.P.)
Curtis F. A. Mrs. 416 Center
Curtis George H. 2027 Michigan av.
Curtis George P. 409 Washington boul.
Curtis Henry, 171, 51st (H.P.)
Curtis Henry M. 1612 Indiana av.
Curtis H. Rowland, Maywood
Curtis Julia Miss, 3246 Lake Park av.
Curtis J. C. Lexington hotel
Curtis J. F. 5033 Madison av.
Curtis J. F. L. 5033 Madison av.
Curtis J. H. 34 Bellevue pl.
Curtis J. H. Dr. 367 Marshfield av.
Curtis J. Lafayette, 3819 Michigan av.
Curtis Lester, M.D. 35 University pl.
Curtis Nelson H. 660 Washington boul.
Curtis O. 305 Webster av.
Curtis Russell H. 276 Oak
Curtis Samuel C. Hotel Metropole
Curtis Samuel I. 395 W. Monroe
Curtis Walter W. Dr. 78, 50th
Curtis William G. 3709 Lake av.
Curtis W. C. Oak Park
Curtiss Charles C. 446 Chestnut
Curtiss George H. 4422 Oakenwald av.
Curtiss James M. 260, 51st (H.P.)
Curtiss Richard S. Dr. 2545 Indiana av.
Curts Lewis Rev. Evanston
Cusack Edward J. 747 Kenmore av.
Cushing Anna F. Miss, Evanston
Cushing Charles H. Hinsdale
Cushing Edward T. 4820 Greenwood av.
Cushing Frederick W. Highland Park
Cushing F. J. Irving Park
Cushing Geo. H., M.D. Elmhurst
Cushing George W. Evanston
Cushing N. S. Mrs. Lombard
Cushing Otis, Hinsdale
Cushing W. T. 69 Flournoy

Cushman J. C. Highland Park
Cushman Thomas W. Irving Park
Custard Morris B. 4722 Evans av.
Custer Jacob R. 3928 Grand boul.
Custer Samuel, 678 Sedgwick
Cuthbert Carrie Mrs. 4830 Greenwood av.
Cuthbert Ernest, 3631 Prairie av.
Cuthbert William, 4830 Greenwood av.
Cutler Alonzo J. 528 Chestnut, Eng.
Cutler C. Henry, 4801 Kenwood av.
Cutler C. N. 517 Washington boul.
Cutler Frank T. 517 Washington boul.
Cutler J. B. 5545 Monroe av.
Cutler William H. Evanston
Cutter C. G. Hotel Groveland
Cutter George, Kenilworth
Cutter Henry W. K. 6516 Harvard
Cutter John M. 2207 Calumet av.
Cutting C. H. Virginia hotel
Cutting Starr W. Prof. 5616 Ellis av.
Cutts A. D. Mrs. Evanston
Cutts T. B. 411 Belden av.
Cuyler James B. 818 North Park av.
Cuyler William H. 105 Winchester av.
Cyrus J. M. 158 Park av.

DABB CHARLES W. Clifton house
Dabney J. P. 608 Division
Dadie John, 665 W. Monroe
Daegling A. V. 5556 Jefferson av.
Daemicke P. J. 425, 57th
Daggett Frederick F. 3651 Ellis Park
Daggett Harry E. 121, 21st
Daggett J. F. LaGrange
Daggett William F. Austin
Daggitt Joseph, Glencoe
Daggy John J. 3716 Langley av.
Daggy Peter, 3716 Langley av.
Dagrow Lee L. Riverside
Dahl Henry L. 634 Lasalle av.
Dahlberg Alfred Dr. 4546 Evans av.
Dahmke John J. A. 1022 Park av.
Dahms Edward J. Evanston
Dainty A. H. 600 Dearborn av.
Dakin Clarence L. 6939 Yale
Dakin Florence A. Miss, Evanston
Dakin F. C. Dr. Evanston
Dakin Harry W. Evanston
Dakin Richard L. Evanston
Dakin R. H. Park Ridge
Dal J. Dr. 142 Evergreen av.
Dal J. W., M.D. 499 N. Robey
DaLacy W. L. Oak Park
Dale Caroline H. Miss, 904 W. Adams
Dale Charles J. 2706 N. Paulina
Dale Fred, 1840 Belmont av.
Dale George T. 95, 37th
Dale Henry C., M.D. 95, 37th
Dale H. S. 904 W. Adams
Dale James 445 Seminary av.
Dale Jane E. Miss, Winnetka
Dale Jeannette Miss, 904 W. Adams
Dale John T. Winnetka
Dale Mary W. Mrs. Evanston
Dale Samuel E. 1832 Belmont av.
Dale Walter, 1832 Belmont av.

Daley George R. 296 Claremont av.
Dalgleish Charles H. Hotel Groveland
Dally A. Harry, 4118 Lake av.
Dally Samuel, 4118 Lake av.
Dalton Ernest, 1136 Winthrop av.
Dalton James, 1429 Michigan av.
Dalton James P. 2938 Michigan av.
Dalton John E. 627 Austin av.
Dalton Samuel, 1136 Winthrop av.
Daly Andrew P. 359 Bowen av.
Daly Henry P. 807 Touhy av.
Daly J. Miss, 86 Lincoln av.
Daly L. F. 583 W. Adams
Daly Minnie Miss, 3000 Michigan av.
Dalzell James, 5624 Monroe av.
Dalzell Walter, 5624 Monroe av.
Dame M. Lela Mrs. 107, 37th
Dameier Charles W. 4329 Prairie av.
Dammerau Frank C. 12 Lincoln pl.
Damon Orrison B., M.D. 274 Park av.
Damsel William E. Evanston
Damsel William H. Avenue house, Evanston
Dana Arthur D. 3433 South Park av.
Dana A. P. Mrs. 4960 Drexel boul.
Dana Charles Mrs. 2539 Indiana av.
Dana Charles D. 44 Astor
Dana Harry C. Hinsdale
D'Ancona Abraham, 3317 Michigan av.
D'Ancona Alfred E. 3317 Michigan av.
D'Ancona August, 4822 Langley av.
D'Ancona Clarence P. 3317 Michigan av.
D'Ancona Edward N. 3317 Michigan av.
Dandliker R. A. Morgan Park
Dandy John M. 3606 Ellis Park
Dandy William M. 48 Loomis
Dane S. E. Mrs. Riverside
Danek Jacob Mrs. 228B Fremont
Danforth D. F. 6 Pelham flats
Danforth Frank L. 4462 Berkeley av.
Danforth Isaac N., M.D. 903 W. Monroe
        Sum. res. Lake Bluff, Ill.
Danforth Jerome J. Hinsdale
Danforth Martin G. Hinsdale
Dangerfield Frederick 212 The Plaza
Daniel James S. 6426 Stewart av.
Daniel William H. 6617 Harvard
Daniels Alexander M. 5131 Hibbard av.
Daniels Alfred, 194 Bowen av.
Daniels Charles, 727 Fullerton av.
Daniels Edwin F. 4447 Greenwood av.
Daniels George M. Rev. LaGrange
Daniels Henry E. C. Evanston
Daniels Herman, 4831 St. Lawrence av.
Daniels John B. 5131 Hibbard av.
Daniels S. 341 Oakwood boul.
Daniels Walter A. 141 Buena av.
Daniels William R. 1314 Washington boul.
Daniels W. R. 305 Park av.
Dankert William E. Norwood Park
Danks E. Ada Miss, 1311 Michigan av.
Danks Fred F. 1311 Michigan av.
Danks Isaiah, 1311 Michigan av.
Danks William N. 1643 Briar pl.
Dann Obed, 142 Ashland boul.
Danne Emil, 7116 Wentworth av.

Danne Louis, 6237 Oglesby av.
Danner J. Julien hotel
Danner W. E. 7546 Union av.
Danz Albert J. 1286 Washington boul.
Danz Charles A. 1286 Washington boul.
Danz Margaret Mrs. 1286 Washington boul.
Danziger Abraham, 3407 Prairie av.
Danziger Benjamin, 3407 Prairie av.
Danziger Edward, 2945 Indiana av.
Danziger Emanuel, 3407 Prairie av.
Danziger H. Mrs. 3407 Prairie av.
Danziger Louis, 1923 Indiana av.
Danziger Samuel S. 2945 Indiana av.
Danziger Sarah Mrs. 2945 Indiana av.
Darby Benjamin L. 280 Robertson av.
Darby John, 280 Robertson av.
Dare Benjamin F. Ridgeland
Darling Bessie Miss, Hyde Park hotel
Darling Chas. Barton, The Arizona
Darling Ira C. Mrs. Hyde Park hotel
Darling James G. Evanston
Darling J. B. Dr. Austin
Darlington Henry C. 542 Englewood av.
Darlington Henry P. 4650 Drexel boul.
Darlington Herbert, LaGrange
Darlington W. M. 634, 62d
Darlow James, 5202 Kimbark av.
Darnell Riley, 403, 64th (H.P.)
Darrow Alden S. 326, 60th
Darrow Alexander H.149 S. Campbell av.
Darrow Caroline H. Mrs. 326, 60th
Darrow Clarence S. 4219 Vincennes av.
Darrow Geo. W. 145 Oakwood boul.
Darrow Mary A. Mrs. 2613 Indiana av.
Dart Frank, 4743 Langley av.
Dart F. S. Dr. 284 W. Randolph
Dart J. W. Evanston
Dasenbrook Charles H. 213 Fremont
Dash Charles J. 3632 Vernon av.
DaShiell Charles E. 6528 Perry av.
Dashiell V. W. 316 Marshfield av.
Date John S. Austin
Date Sydney S. 817 Washington boul.
Dau J. J. 164, 47th (H.P.)
Daube Abraham, 3402 Forest av.
Daube Eli, 3402 Forest av.
Daube Jo ph, 3402 Forest av.
Daube Leopold, 3212 Vernon av.
Daube Louis, 3402 Forest av.
Daube M. Jacob, 3805 Prairie av.
Dauchy George K. 359 Lasalle av.
Danchy Otis B. 359 Lasalle av.
Dauchy Samuel O. 359 Lasalle av.
Daugherty Joseph W. 43 Hamilton av.
Daul F. X. 866 Walnut
Dauman S. E. Miss, 5526 Cornell av.
Dausch P. Mrs. 1731 Belmont av.
Davenport Edward A. 446 W. Congress
Davenport Charles W. 508 Belden av.
Davenport C. E. Miss, 710 W. Adams
Davenport Don B. Wilmette
Davenport Elizabeth Mrs.2924 Groveland av.
Davenport Elizabeth Mrs. Wilmette
Davenport John L. 3537 Indiana av.

Davenport Nora S., M.D. 446 W.Congress
Davenport Wm. C. 191, 54th
David Cyrenies A., M.D. 325 Belden av.
David Joseph B. 943 W. Monroe
David Rilla A. Miss, 325 Belden av.
Davidson Alice S. Miss, Highland Park
Davidson F. B. 225 S. Oakley av.
Davidson George M. Oak Park
Davidson Harlan P. Col. Highland Park
Davidson H. E. 422 N. State
Davidson H. W. Mayfair
Davidson James A. 953 Jackson boul.
Davidson John A. 2128 Calumet av.
Davidson Joseph C. Austin
Davidson J. E. Mrs. 390 N. State
Davidson J. O. 153, 42d
Davidson K. Mrs. Leland hotel
Davinson Malvina Mrs. 422 N. State
Davidson Royal P. Maj. Highland Park
Davidson Sarah S. Mrs. 2453 Michigan av.
Davidson S. Frank, LaGrange
Davidson Walter, Hinsdale
Davidson William B. 409 Jackson boul.
Davidson W. B. 6212 Oglesby av.
Davie George F. 6350 Yale
Davies Ann Mrs. 3146 Vernon av.
Davies B. M. 4028 Grand boul.
Davies Colby, Evanston
Davies Charles Francis, 3757 Prairie av.
Davies C. A. 656 W. Adams
Davies Edward C. 276 Irving av.
Davies Edwin C. K. Ridgeland
Davies J n G. 1253 N. Clark
Davies IohA. 3736 Ellis av.
Davies L. J. Lake Forest
Davies Thomas, 581, 52d
Davies Thomas, 3223 Rhodes av.
Davies Will T. 4444 St. Lawrence av.
Davies W. J. 276 Irving av.
Davis Andrew, Lakeside
Davis Annie M. Mrs. Evanston
Davis Arthur, 57 E. Pearson
Davis A. B. 4100 Ellis av.
Davis A. J. 1102 Washington boul.
Davis A. P. 271 Fremont
Davis Benjamin, 692 Washington boul.
Davis Charles E. Evanston
Davis Charles E. 7201 Yale
Davis Charles G. 728 W. Adams
Davis Charles W. 689 W. Harrison
Davis Chester B. 3762 Lake av.
Davis C. A. Mrs. 4406 Ellis av.
Davis C. G. Dr. 705 W. Adams
    Sum. res. Juanita Springs, Colo.
Davis C. N. 415 Lasalle av.
Davis Edgar F. Hinsdale
Davis Edward A. 1312 W. Adams
Davis Edward A. 290 Bissell
Davis Edward H. 150 Pine
Davis Effa V. Dr. 508 W. Adams
Davis Elisha T. Park Ridge
Davis Ernest A. 3517 Grand boul.
Davis E. R. Rev. 464 W. Adams
Davis E. V. 7905 Union av.
Davis Fannie Alcot Mrs. 686 North Park av.

Davis Frank B. 5041 Washington av.
Davis F. H. Dr. Berwyn
Davis Frank L. 44 Bryant av.
Davis Frank R. 6618 Lafayette av.
Davis Frank S. 4346 Berkeley av.
Davis George, 3517 Grand boul.
Davis George H. 3517 Grand boul.
Davis George M. Austin
Davis George R. 692 Washington boul.
     Sum. res. Fox Lake, Wis.
Davis George W. 71, 33
Davis George W. 4204 Lake av.
Davis Graham, 4347 Oakenwald av.
Davis G. N. Norwood Park
Davis Harry G. 4227 Champlain av.
Davis Henry H. 7024 Eggleston av.
Davis Horace G. 3658 Vincennes av.
Davis H. H. 1473 Wellington
Davis H. I. Dr. 3269 Cottage Grove av.
Davis H. M. 148 N. State
Davis Irving, 260 Warren av.
Davis James A. 2317 Indiana av.
Davis James C. 621, 60th, Eng.
Davis James G. 4347 Oakenwald av.
Davis James H. 6943 Perry av.
Davis Jedediah R. 3113 Michigan av.
Davis John, 4850 Woodlawn av.
Davis John A. Mrs. The Arizona
Davis John T. Evanston
Davis J. E. Oak Park
Davis J. E. Wilmette
Davis J. M. 3000 Indiana av,
Davis J. S. 31 The Yale
Davis J. T. Hyde Park hotel
Davis K. B. Mrs. 3425 Vernon av.
Davis Lewis H. 1458 Michigan av.
Davis Lillian C. Mrs. 3139 Michigan av.
Davis Louis L. 45 S. Robey
Davis L. D. 3322 Vernon av.
Davis L. J. Dr. 67 Warren av.
Davis Martin S. 2808 Michigan av.
Davis Mortimer A. 3517 Grand boul.
Davis M. G. 241 Oakwood boul.
Davis M. M. Mrs. 2342 Indiana av.
Davis M. R. 377 Dearborn av.
Davis M. T. Mrs. River Forest
Davis Nathan, 3133 Wabash av.
Davis Nathan S. Dr. 291 Huron
Davis Nathan S. j. Dr. 326 Superior
Davis Nellie T. Miss, Riverside
Davis P. I. Irving Park
Davis Richard L. 485 Dearborn av.
Davis R. L. 1817 Aldine av.
Davis Samuel, Park Ridge
Davis Simon S. jr. 35th se. cor. Ellis av.
Davis Sue B. Mrs. 4311 Langley av.
Davis Susan E. Mrs. Evanston
Davis S. Clarence, Evanston
Davis S. E. 3623 Ellis Park
Davis S. J. Mrs. Hinsdale
Davis Thomas, 1009 Warren av.
Davis Thomas F. Capt. Fort Sheridan
Davis T. A. Dr. 987 Jackson boul.
Davis Walter, 214, 31st
Davis Wilbur Rude, 3113 Michigan av.
Davis William C. 39 Stone
34

Davis William, 3562 Forest av.
Davis William E., 7214 Webster av. Eng.
Davis William H. 3816 Ellis av.
Davis Wilson H., M.D. 3423 Indiana av.
Davis W. Claude, Evanston
Davis W. Crosbie Dr. La Grange
Davis W. Edgar, Austin
Davis W. F. Oak Park
Davis W. G. Austin
Davis W. J. 163 Eugenie
Davison Belle Miss, 10 Scott
Davison Benjamin F. 1031 Wilcox av.
Davison Charles, M.D. 955 Jackson boul.
Davison J. C. 815 Pullman bldg.
Davison Martha Mrs. 955 Jackson boul.
Davison Wm. M. W., M.D. 658 Walnut
Davol H. N. Miss, 408 Superior
Davy B. C. Mrs. 380 Erie
Davy Edward W. 43 St. James pl.
Davy H. G. 380 Erie
Daw H. H. 452 Dayton
Daw H. P. 510 Webster av.
Dawes Chester M. 501 N. State
Dawley B. W. Wellington hotel
Dawley C. P. 415, 57th
Dawson Arthur, 1741 Wrightwood av.
Dawson Arthur C. Prof. Lake Forest
Dawson Edwin A. Evanston
Dawson George E. 100, 24th
Dawson Henry G. 607 Pine Grove av.
Dawson James M. 3829 Vernon av.
Dawson Julia A. Mrs. 100, 24th
Dawson Martin, Tremont house
Dawson William R. 605 Pine Grove av.
Day Albert M. Lake Forest
Day Arthur H. Glencoe
Day Charles C. 3918 Langley av.
Day Charles L. Glencoe
Day Charles M. 3918 Langley av.
Day C. A. Irving Park
Day E. C. Chicago Beach hotel
Day Francis H. 36th ne. cor. Cottage
    Grove av.
Day Fred F. 3413 Calumet av.
Day George A. Evanston
Day George R. 2606 Prairie av.
Day Harry O. 4727 Langley av.
Day Henrietta E. Mrs. Evanston
Day Hiram Rev. Glencoe
Day H. N. Dr. 5495 Madison av.
Day John E. 4726 Champlain av.
Day Joseph L. Auditorium hotel
Day Julia L. Mrs. 4145 Langley av.
Day L. A. L. Dr. 3232 Groveland av.
Day M. M. 3034 Groveland av.
Day Robert W. 64 Park av.
Day R. H. 2120 Michigan av.
    Sum. res. St. Joe, Mich.
Day Sullivan, 413 Center
Day Theodore P. 6559 Harvard
Day Thomas, 6744 Perry av.
Day T. G. 5555 Monroe av.
Day V. E. Miss, 3641 Ellis av.
Day W. B. 3034 Groveland av.
Day W. W. Mrs. 4147 Langley av.
Dayan Louis F. Dr. 179, 53d

Dayton Arthur G. 435 S. Leavitt
Dayton Charles, 6341 Oglesby av.
Dayton H. A. 1117 Early av.
Dayton M. E. 6341 Oglesby av.
Dayton W. C. 281 Fremont
Dayton William M. 255 Park av.
Deacon C. B. 446 Belden av.
Deacon Frederick A. 446 Belden av.
Deacon John C. 145 Ashland boul.
Deacon J. E. 6657 Harvard av.
Deacon M. E. Mrs. 446 Belden av.
Deam Henry D. 3624 Ellis Park
Dean Annie Mrs. 468, 50th
Dean Amos C. 329, 34th
Dean A. F. 764 W. Adams
Dean Bradley 267 W. Adams
Dean Charles A. 286 Webster av.
Dean Charles R. Evanston
Dean Edwin B. Rev. Wilmette
Dean Frank P. The Ashland
Dean Harvey, Hinsdale
Dean John E. 3259 Indiana av.
Dean J. Clark, 329, 34th
Dean Marvin A. Evanston
Dean M. B. 545 Farwell av.
Dean M. C. 267 W. Adams
Dean M. E. Mrs. 4565 Lake av.
Dean M. L. Mrs. 265 Chestnut
Dean O. W. 376 S. Oakley av.
Dean Richmond, 121, 55th
Dean Robert L. Hinsdale
Dean Robert M. Hinsdale
Dean Silas A. 6346 Honore
Dean Thaddeus, Auditorium hotel
Dean Thomas A. 3420 Prairie av.
Dean Thomas A. 4119 Vincennes av.
Dean Walter M. 764 W. Adams
Dean William O. Evanston
Deane Albert L. 4520 Woodlawn av.
Deane Charles E. 307 N. Clark
Deane Eloise A. Mrs. 198 S. Robey
Deane John M. 198 S. Robey
DeaneLillie Miss, 4520 Woodlawn av.
Deane Margaret Miss, 4520 Woodlawn av.
Deane Mary F. Mrs. 569, 51st
Deane Ruthven, 504 N. State
Dearborn Asa, Riverside
Dearborn D. Frank, 189 Dearborn av.
Dearborn Robert T. Dr. Riverside
Deardoff Porter, 4401 Oakenwald av.
Deardorff Jacob, 485 Washington boul.
Dearing J. H. 706 Pullman bldg.
Dearlove George, 972 Jackson boul.
Dearlove Mary A., M.D. 972 Jackson
  boul.
DeArmond William W. Ridgeland
DeBeck Frank B. 25 Best av.
DeBeck W. L. 25 Best av.
DeBennette L. Mrs. 3601 Vincennes av.
DeBerard Charles J. Norwood Park
DeBey B. Mrs. 6837 Perry av.
DeBrazza Count. Lakota hotel
DeBruyn George, Hotel Metropole
DeCamp A. 225 Warren av.
DeCamp Herbert C. 415 Dearborn av.
DeCamp H. E. LaGrange

DeCamp Rena Miss, Hyde Park hotel
DeCamp W. H. Oak Park
deCampi Eliodoro, 316 Centre av.
Decker A. Dr. 506 N. Wells
Decker A. B. 99, 33d
Decker Edwin J. 1102 Millard av.
Decker Henry H. 17 Ashland av.
Decker H. J. 668 Kenmore av.
Decker H. P. 2434 Commercial (L.V.)
Decker Jacob E. Austin
Decker W. S. 430 Warren av.
DeClercq Geo. E. W. 1472 W. Monroe
DeClercq Marion Mrs. Evanston
DeClerque Henry, 501 Lasalle av.
De Clerque Raben Eliza Mrs. 501 La-
  salle av.
DeCoudres A. M. Evanston
Dederick Louis, 804 Bryan av.
Dee Arthur W. Evanston
Dee George W. 3746 Forest av.
Dee William E. 3746 Forest av.
Dee William H. Mrs. Evanston
Dee W. J. Lexington hotel
Dee W. M. Mrs. 3746 Forest av.
Deecken Frederick, 1716 Frederick
Deering Charles W. Evanston
Deering James E. 67 Cedar
Deering Joseph H. 706 Pullman bldg.
Deering William, Evanston
Deethmann C. H. 4839 Madison av.
Deeves Griffen H. Chicago AthleticAsso.
Defebaugh James E. 4103 Indiana av.
DeFlow Annie Miss, 4212 Ellis av.
Defoe Lewis, 391, 40th
Defoe Thomas, 391, 40th
DeForest Geo. V. 300 Marshfield av.
Defrees J. H. Hotel Windermere
DeGan Emma Miss, River Forest
DeGan Joseph, River Forest
DeGarmo L. Edward, 361, 65th, Eng.
Degen Isaac, 3811 Langley av.
Degen Mina Mrs. 30 Bryant av.
Degenhardt C. 106 Seeley av.
Degenhardt F. E. 106 Seeley av.
deGignac A. L. Austin
Degge E. John, Lexington hotel
Deggles John W. 211 N. State
DeGolyer Nelson, Evanston
DeGolyer Watts, Riverside
DeGraff A. Mrs. 2222 Calumet av.
DeGraff P. S. 4047 Ellis av.
DeHaye John, Wilmette
DeHorvath Jul. 7614 Union av.
Deimel Joseph, 3141 Calumet av.
Deimel Rudolph, 3141 Calumet av.
Deitsch R. Mrs. 3529 Calumet av.
Deitcher John, Jefferson Park
DeJankovitz M. Mrs. 7614 Union av.
Deknatel Frederick H. Evanston
DeKoven John, 402 Dearborn av
Delafield Charles Mrs. 4333 Ellis av.
Delafield F. S. Virginia hotel
Delafield Walter Rev. 4333 Ellis av.
Delamater Ettie M. Miss, 5241 Madison
  av
Delamater M. L. Mrs. Evanston

Delamater N. B. Dr. 50 Oakwood av.
Delamater Samuel, 5241 Madison av.
DeLand Adelbert, 6445 Sheridan av.
DeLand Elliott, Washington Heights
DeLand Walter, Washington Heights
DeLand W. P. J. 4128 Berkeley av.
Delaney Daniel, 479 W. Adams
Delaney Henry, Evanston
Delaney Thomas F. 4223 Wabash av.
DeLang F. C. Glencoe
DeLang Frederick C. 480 Fullerton av.
     Sum. res. Glencoe, Ill.
Delano Eben A. 905 W. Adams
Delano Edward C. 59 Aberdeen
Delano F. A. 1933 Indiana av.
DeLano Henry A. Rev. Evanston
Delany Martin A. 537 Cleveland av.
DeLap R. C. 504 Webster av.
DeL'Armitage Arabella Root Mme. 4726
     Kenwood av.
DeL'Armitage Robert B. 4726 Kenwood
     av.
Delaware A. S. 510, 63d (H.P.)
Delbridge John B. 65, 37th
DeLee Joseph B. Dr. 3722 Forest av.
DeLee Morris, 3722 Forest av.
DeLee Solomon T. 3722 Forest av.
Delenoy William A. Hotel Normandie
Delihant John Q. Mrs. 296 Webster av.
Dell Joseph, 643 W. Monroe
Dellano E. F. 300 Chestnut
Delmarle O. J. 3802 Lake av.
DeLoss H. H. Evanston
DeLuce C. E. Mrs. 628 Jackson boul.
DeLuce E. C. Mrs. 36 Walton pl.
DeMaid George W. 4200 Berkeley av.
DeMar Willis C. 3712 Ellis av.
Demarest R. C. 823 Jackson boul.
deMarion Marie Biro Mme. 3411 Indiana
     av.
DeMary Jane Mrs. 170, 36th
Dembufsky Max, 3657 Grand boul.
Dement Henry D. Oak Park
Dement Isaac S. 108, 36th
Dement R. S. 3523 Grand boul.
Demers Phedime, 719, 60th (Eng.)
DeMille John C. Lexington hotel
DeMiller Sophia Mrs. 360 Webster av.
Deming Charles, 181 S. Hoyne av.
Deming Everett B. 1671 Alexander av.
Deming Gail E. 147 S. Sacramento av.
Deming Henry H., M.D. 4350 Green-
     wood av.
Deming O. L. River Forest
Deming William B. 181 S. Hoyne av.
Demling Frank J. 5856 Wabash av.
Demmler Karl, 516 North av.
DeMoe Earl W. 1334 Wilton av.
Demorest C. S. 435 Belden av.
Dempsey John, 947, 72d pl. (H. P.)
Dempsey Samuel H. 75 Throop
Dempster Charles W. 2936 Prairie av.
Dempster Wesley, 2936 Prairie av.
DeMuth Benjamin F. 4500 Greenwood av.
Denahy E. W. Sherman house
Deneen Chas. S. 617, 61st, Eng.

Dengler G. 512 Webster av.
Denham Charles, 306, 49th
Denig Lewis A. Elmhurst
Denison Andrew J. 167 Cass
Denison Ephriam H. Highland Park
Denison Franklin, 5316 Cornell av.
Denison Henry H. Highland Park
Denison H. S. Chicago Beach hotel
Denison J. C. 558 62d, Eng.
Denison Margaret Mrs. 167 Cass
Deniston Albert J. 3230 Rhodes av.
Denmark August, Hinsdale
Dennehy Charles Mrs. 429 N. State
Dennehy Thomas C. 429 N. State
Dennett C. R. Mrs. 152 S. Oakley av.
Dennie A. A. Capt. 32 Delaware pl.
Dennis Charles H. 334 Hampden ct.
Dennis C. S. 5120 Kimbark av.
Dennis Edward L. 5473 Cornell av.
Dennis E. Mrs. 3829 Lake av.
Dennis Frederick J. 1229 Washington
     boul.
Dennis George, 4554 Emerald av.
Dennis George E. 6926 Vernon av.
Dennis George J., Dr. Lakota hotel
Dennis Henry, 41, 53d
Dennis H. Miss, Hotel Metropole
Dennis James F. Glencoe
Dennis James J. Mrs. Glencoe
Dennis J. M. 6147 Sheridan av.
Dennis Waldo E. 13 St. James pl.
Dennis William, Berwyn
Dennison Charles G. Hinsdale
Dennison F. A. 4053 Lake av.
Dennison William H. Hinsdale
Denniston J. M. Lexington hotel
Denny Nathan R. 3735 Vincennes av.
Denny William A. 3735 Vincennes av.
Denslow Millard S. 620 N. Clark
Densmore E. W. Mrs. 2328 Indiana av.
Densmore James A. Mrs. Winnetka
Densmore J. B. Winnetka
Dent Lewis D. 804, 64th, Englewood
Dent Linda A. Mrs. 804, 64th, Englewood
Dent Thomas, 1823 Prairie av.
Dent Timothy A. Longwood
Denton C. C. 406, 61st, Eng.
Denyes Alfred, 3022 Groveland av.
DePew Henry H., M.D. 1331 Wolcott
D'Episy Frank J. 2729 Michigan av.
D'Episy Lucie Mme. 2729 Michigan av.
Depp Frank, 1163 N. Clark
DePresse Angelo, 67 Madison Park
Derby James D. 4406 Ellis av.
Derby W. M. Mrs. 70, 23d
Derby W. M. jr. 70, 23d
Derbyshire Fred, 3756 Ellis av.
Derham James E., Dr. Washington
     Heights
Derham Milo G. 545 W. Adams
Derickson Emma C. Mrs. Kenilworth
Dering C. L. 4456 Sidney av.
Dering Henry Ray, The Tudor, 43d and
     Ellis av.
Dering J. Kemper, 554, 45th.
DeRivas F. M. Granada hotel

Dernburg Adolph, 4810 St. Lawrence av.
Dernburg Carl, 1341 Michigan av.
Dernham M. Mrs. 508 Lasalle av.
deRoode Holger, 710½ North Park av.
Derrick Morris B. 5932 Honore
Derry J. 1839 Indiana av.
Deschauer Joseph Mrs. 507 Lasalle av.
DesGranges Belle Mrs. 5401 Monroe av.
DeSilva Joseph, Dr. 7112 Eggleston av.
Desjardins Alexis, 310 S. Oakley av.
DeSmet Georges Wm. 1922 Michigan av.
DeSouchet Julius T. 576 Washington
   boul.
DeSouchet Osman C. 576 Washington
   boul.
DeSponer Franz, 1637 Michigan av.
Despres Alfred, 3218 Calumet av.
Despres Anaise Miss, 3218 Calumet av.
Despres Emil M. 3218 Calumet av.
Despres Samuel, 3727 Prairie av.
Dessau Isaac, 3251 Calumet av.
Dessauer Janette Mrs. 88 Evanston av.
DeTeresa A. H. Mrs. 2018 Prairie av.
DeThal P. Chicago Beach hotel
Detmer Henry, 293 Ashland boul.
Detmer Julian F. 293 Ashland boul.
Detmer J. Henry, 293 Ashland boul.
Detmer Martin J. 293 Ashland boul.
Detrick James M. 5514 Ellis av.
Detweiler E. S. Dr. LaGrange
Detwiler George E. Highland Park
Deuel Henry W. 219 Belden av.
Deutsch Frederick, 7816 Bond av.
Deutsch Joseph, 142 Ashland boul.
Deutsch L. 127, 25th
Deutsch Nathan, Hyde Park hotel
Deutsch Simon O. 7816 Bond av.
DeValcourt-Vermont Edgar Count, Ev-
   anston
Devendorf A. S. 689 W. Adams
Devendorf C. A. 689 W. Adams
DeVeney T. F. 3336 Wabash av.
DeVeny S. Charles, M. D. 2542 Indiana
   av.
DeVerna Frank Mrs. 290 Ashland boul.
D'Evers Henry W. 1275 N. Clark
Devin David T. 965 Warren av.
Devine D. A. 1915 Diversey
Devine James A. 289 Huron
Devine William M. 289 Huron
Devine William P. 289 Huron
Devlin Frank A. 3933 Grand boul.
DeVolt E. R. 626 Park av.
Devore Abraham A. 3233 Rhodes av.
Devore Annie Mrs. 109, 37th
Devore John, 858 Larrabee
Devore John A. 65 University pl.
DeVos John, Irving Park
DeVries F. P. Dr. Morgan Park
Dew Charles A. 461 W. Monroe
DeWalsh E. F. 455 Racine av.
Dewar Alexander L. Glencoe
Dewar David F. 7620 Emerald av.
Dewar Hamilton, 4438 Sidney av.
DeWedig Louise Mrs. 3800 Wabash av.
DeWees William W. 168, 32d

Dewes Francis J. Wrightwood av. sw.
   cor. Hampden ct.
Dewey Albert B. 2631 Prairie av.
Dewey Allen A. 4155 Lake av.
Dewey Amariah A. 4155 Lake av.
Dewey Bertha E. Miss, 1839 Indiana av.
Dewey Charles P. 3266 Lake Park av.
Dewey David B. Evanston
Dewey David C. 670 Park av.
Dewey Fred M. LaGrange
Dewey F. J. Dr. 302 S. Oakley av.
Dewey James, Lake Forest
Dewey James R. Dr. 619 Washington
   boul.   Sum. res. Lake Bluff, Ill.
Dewey Jo   Dr. 5418 Greenwood av.
Dewey NhB. 36th ne. cor. Ellis av.
Dewey O. J. LaGrange
Dewey Richard Dr. 3260 Groveland av.
Dewey Walter E. 1839 Indiana av.
Dewey William E. 4316 Langley av.
DeWindt Heyliger A. Winnetka
DeWitt Clyde, 4522 Evans av.
DeWitt Elden C. 545 Dearborn av.
DeWitt F. L. LaGrange
DeWitt William C. Rev. 790 Washing-
   ton boul.
DeWitte Alice Miss, 162, 25th
Dewitz Henry, 3428 Indiana av.
DeWolf Calvin, 4714 Kimbark av.
DeWolf D. C. 3629 Prairie av.
DeWolf J. E.,·M.D. 440 Englewood av.
DeWolf Wallace L. 4621 Woodlawn av.
DeWolf William F. 226 Dearborn av.
DeWolfe Freeman, 621, 59th, Englewood
Dexter Albert F. 3234 Groveland av.
Dexter Charles P. Mrs. 65 Cedar
Dexter C. F. 356 Warren av.
Dexter Edith Miss, 65 Cedar
Dexter Geo. W. 5458 Jefferson av.
Dexter M. C. Mrs. 65 Cedar
Dexter Ransom Mrs. 2920 Calumet av.
Dexter Rosalie Mrs. 3939 Indiana av.
Dexter Wirt Mrs. 1721 Prairie av.
Dey M. H. Julien hotel
Deyo N. R. Mrs. 723 Pullman bldg.
DeYoe E. H. Dr. 789 Warren av.
DeYoung Benjamin R. 2975 Prairie av.
Dezendorf J. Douglas, 2317 Michigan av.
DeZung Caroline Mrs. Wilmette
Dial Grant D. 16 Bellevue pl.
Diamond S. A. 449 Marshfield av.
Diamond Thomas E. 98, 30th
Dibb James M. 4250 St. Lawrence av.
Dibble Charles A. 111 S. Leavitt
Dibble Harvey M. Wilmette
Dibble William E. Wilmette
Dibblee Henry, 1922 Calumet av.
Dice Jacob M. 929 Jackson av.
Dick Albert Blake, 21 Lake Shore Drive
Dick E. E. 894 Winthrop av.
Dick H. E. 4142 Lake av.
Dick Theodore S. Winnetka
Dickason Livingston T. 4940 Ellis av.
Dickenson Carleton, Edison Park
Dicker Edward A. 908 Warren av.
Dickerman Albert E. 506 Morse av.

Dickerman Eunice J. Evanston
Dickerman Fletcher W. Evanston
Dickerman Frances S. Miss, 2115 Indiana
    av.
Dickerman Horace W. Evanston
Dickerson Charles R. 5624 Monroe av.
Dickerson Clarence W. 5735 Madison av.
Dickerson J. Spencer, Evanston
Dickerson John W. 3241 Michigan av.
Dickerson Louise A., M.D. 2317 Indiana
    av.
Dickey E. M. 46 Sidney ct.
Dickey Frank H. 3626 Ellis av.
Dickey F. L. Mrs. 3820 Prairie av.
Dickey James R. 330 Maple, Eng.
Dickey S. D. 81, 43d
Dickinson Albert, 307 N. Clark
Dickinson Baxter A. 445 Englewood av.
Dickinson Belle Miss, Highland Park
Dickinson Charles, 307 N. Clark
Dickinson Charles S. 3431 Vernon av.
Dickinson Clarence, Evanston
Dickinson C. 499 Webster av.
Dickinson D. H. 651 Washington boul.
Dickinson Edward, 1855 Frederick
Dickinson Frances M.D., Oglesby av.
    nw. cor. 61st
Dickinson Frederick, 26 Bryant av.
Dickinson F. F. 6930 Yale
Dickinson George, 2448 South Park av.
Dickinson G. B. 489 Fullerton av.
Dickinson Henry G. Highland Park
Dickinson H. C. 6749 Wentworth av.
Dickinson James S. Mrs. 4528 Lake av.
Dickinson Jennie Miss, 351, 58th
Dickinson John, Evanston
Dickinson John R. 26 Bryant av.
Dickinson John W. 369 Chicago av.
Dickinson J. T. Col. Hotel Metropole
Dickinson Lewis Edward, 286 Huron
Dickinson Louise Miss, 351, 58th
Dickinson Mary E. Mrs. 248 Warren av.
Dickinson M. Miss, 307 N. Clark
Dickinson Nathan, 307 N. Clark
    Sum. res. Lake Geneva, Wis.
Dickinson Oliver P. Chicago Beach ho-
    tel
Dickinson Paul, 499 Webster av.
Dickinson Priscilla Mrs. Evanston
Dickinson S. S. 2100 Wabash av.
Dickinson Wm. The Ontario
Dickinson Wm. 470 Lasalle av.
Dickinson William C. Rev. Evanston
Dickinson William P. 67 Maple
Dickinson Willis P. 52 Bellevue pl.
Dickinson W. W. 489 Fullerton av.
Dicks A. E. Mrs. 812 Pratt av.
Dickson Anna Mrs. 3354 South Park av.
Dickson Henry, Riverside
Dickson Isaac F. 4585 Oakenwald av.
Dickson William T. 3913 Prairie av.
Dickson Wm. W. Mrs. 3921 Langley av.
Dieden Annie Mrs. 362 N. Wells
Diederich Joseph A. 820 Chase av.
Diederich William G. 812 Touhy av.
Diehl George, 1674 Wellington

Diener Traugott C. 489 Ashland boul.
Diener William J. 489 Ashland boul.
Dierkes Alex. 12 Fowler
Diesel Frank, 701 N. Halsted
Diesel John 701 N. Halsted
Diesel Louis, 695 N. Halsted
Diestelow John A. Dr. 936 N. Halsted
Dietrich C. W. LaGrange
Dietrich Henry Dr. 422 Center
Dietrich W. M. LaGrange
Dietrick Samuel, 4405 Champlain av.
Dietz Albert B. Wilmette
Dietz Delia Miss, 656, 63d, Englewood
Dietz Jacob C. 148, 42d
Dietz John G. Wilmette
Dietz Joseph E. Irving Park
Dietz Joseph M. Irving Park
Dietz J. W. 1650 Aldine av.
Dietz Linnie Miss, 656, 63d, Englewood
Dietz William P. 86 Vernon Park pl.
Dietz William H. 7402 Honore
Dietzgen Eugene, 1694 Barry av.
Dietzgen Joseph,   Barry av.
Diffenderfer L. H. 1698s. 6120 Michigan av.
Diffley M. W. 42 Bellevue pl.
Diggs W. J. Granada hotel
Dilg Paul, 291 Seminary av.
Dille S. M. 320, 45th
Dillenbeck A. L. Lakota hotel
Diller Leonora Mrs. 147 Ashland boul.
Dilley Louise Mrs. 1023 W. Monroe
Dilley William, 1023 W. Monroe
Dillie Nathaniel E. 293 S. Leavitt
Dillingham Edwin R. jr. 4500 Calumet av.
Dillman Louis M. 4508 Ellis av.
Dillon Grace C. Miss, 7425 Honore
Dillon I. F. Mrs. 7526 Eggleston av.
Dillon Joseph B. 3137 Rhodes av.
Dillon J. M. Mrs. 224 N. State
Dillon Mary Miss, 823 Pullman bldg.
Dillon Susan Miss, 3848 Vincennes av.
Dillon Thomas A. 49 Astor
Dillon Thomas C. Dr. 3937 Drexel boul.
Dillon Thomas L. 396 Oak
Dillon William, 3727 Forest av.
Dimery Joseph H. 3159 Forest av.
Dimick M. D. La Grange
Dimmick Edward J. 3139 Michigan av.
Dimmick J. Milton, Evanston
Dimock Frank H. 4825 St. Lawrence av.
Dimock Leonard S. Wilmette
Dimock Sarah Mrs. 4825 St. Lawrence av.
Dimon L. A. Miss, 8 Pelham flats
Dingee Mae Miss, Evanston
Dingee Minnie Miss, 2607 N. Ashland av.
Dingee Samuel M. Wilmette
Dingee Samuel S. Wilmette
Dingee Squire, 2607 N. Ashland av.
Dingee Squire jr. 2607 N. Ashland av.
Dingey P. S. 365 Park av.
Dingman C. W. 154 Alexander av.
Dinsmoor Anne J. Miss, Evanston
Dinsmore Lucien Rev. 927 Sheffield av.
Dinsmore Matilda C. Mrs. 2621 Michigan
    av.
Dinwiddie E. C. Miss, Evanston

Dinwiddie J. A. Oak Park
Dinwoody J.A.Dr. 3300 Cottage Grove av.
Dion Delvina Dr. 223 Oakwood boul.
Dion Joseph, 223 Oakwood boul.
Dirks Chris. LaGrange
Disbrow F. W. 6436 Oglesby av.
Disbrow Geo. H. Austin
Dittman A. S. Tracy
Dittmann Henry, 1631 Belmont av.
Dittmann J. Dr. 331 Maple, Englewood
Ditto Joseph B. Riverside
Ditzler Eli H. Hinsdale
Dix Albert H. 319, 41st
Dix W. T. 5471 Monroe av.
Dixon Arthur, 3131 Michigan av.
         Sum. res. Lake Bluff, Ill.
Dixon Arthur A. 3131 Michigan av.
Dixon George E. LaGrange
Dixon George W. 3131 Michigan av.
Dixon John S. 381 Bissell
Dixon J. Arthur, Evanston
Dixon J. T. Dr. Evanston
Dixon Lawrence Belmont, 3212 Calumet
    av.
Dixon L. B. 3212 Calumet av.
Dixon T. S. P. 5225 Jefferson av.
Dixon Thomas J. 3222 Groveland av.
Dixson Albert, Highland Park
Dixson Zella Allen Mrs. 57th cor. Madi-
    son av.
D'Lisle W. H. 42d se. cor. Lake av.
Doan M. G. Mrs. 181 Warren av.
Doane Charles H. 4738 Champlain av.
Doane James A. 522 W. Monroe
Doane John B. Dr. Hinsdale
Doane John E. 1827 Prairie av.
Doane John W. 1827 Prairie av.
     Sum. res. Thompsonville, Conn.
Doane Philip P. S. Oak Park
Doane Thomas H. Newberry hotel
Doane T. H. Oak Park
Doane William W. 4738 Champlain av.
Dobbins Charles E. 4628 Indiana av.
Dobbins Paris H. 4739 Indiana av.
Dobbins Thomas S. 1825 Michigan av.
Dobson H. W. Mrs. 442 Warren av.
Dobson Robert, 442 Warren av.
Dobson William J. 222 Evergreen av.
Docter Albert M. 3151 Rhodes av.
Doctor J. J. 497, 42d pl.
Dodd A. F. Norwood Park
Dodd J. L. Washington Heights
Dodds Jessie B., M.D. 3943 Langley av.
Dodds Robert, M.D. 3943 Langley av.
Dodds Wm. 3311 Cottage Grove av.
Dodds W. E. Dr. 3617 Prairie av.
Dodge A. H. Chicago Beach hotel
Dodge A. P. 860 W. Monroe
Dodge B. L. Oak Park
Dodge Charles W. Evanston
Dodge C   C. Dr. 718 Washington
    boul.hester
Dodge Edmund F. 3117 Forest av.
Dodge E. C. 407, 33d
Dodge George E. P. 1703 Indiana av.
Dodge Harry A. 3925 Grand boul.

Dodge Henry B. 3958 Drexel boul.
Dodge Julia M. Mrs. 3953 Michigan av.
Dodge Norris G. 3925 Grand boul.
Dodge Philo G. Mrs. 3117 Forest av.
Dodge William A. 55 Laflin
Dodge William H. 5325 Washington av.
Dodge W. R. 5325 Washington av.
Dodgshun Charles J. 4441 Berkeley av.
Dodson Florence C. Mrs. 4210 Prairie av.
Dodson John M. 4458 Oakenwald av.
Dodson John M. Dr. 631 W. Jackson
Dodsworth E. C. Mrs. 3722 Ellis av.
Doe Geo. Merrill, 4507 Lake av.
Doe Ormand P. 4507 Lake av.
Doepp William Dr. 57 Wisconsin
Doering Edmund J. Dr. Hotel Metropole
Doerr Charles P. 335, 61st, Englewood
Doerr Jacob F. 4920 Champlain av.
Doerr John P. 4924 Champlain av.
Doerr J. N. Evanston
Doerr William P. 4924 Champlain av.
Doggett Arthur M. 2620 Prairie av.
Doggett Eunice S. Miss, 5617 Monroe av.
Doggett Harry H. 4911 Forestville av.
Doggett Herbert E. L. 2620 Prairie av.
Doggett Joseph B. Mrs. 5617 Monroe av.
Doggett L. B. 2620 Prairie av.
Doggett Mary E. Mrs. 4911 Forestville av.
Doggett Osce J. 2620 Prairie av.
Doggett William F. 4911 Forestville av.
Doggett William L. 2620 Prairie av.
Dohan T. B. 906 Evanston av.
Doherty Archibald L. 435 Belden av.
Doherty John A. 4158 Calumet av.
Doig John P. Wilmette
Doig John S. Wilmette
Doig Malcolm L. Wilmette
Dolan Frank, 7822 Bohn av.
Dolan J. J. 183 Clifton av.
Doland Franklin H. 852 Touhy av.
Dole Arthur, 230, 52d
Dole Charles E. 455 Elm
Dole George S. 337 Dearborn av.
Dole James H. 337 Dearborn av.
Dole John N. 493 W. Congress
Dole Julia F. Miss, 337 Dearborn av.
Dole William P. 1308 Wolcott
Dolese John 3414 Wabash av.
Dolese John jr. 3414 Wabash av.
Doll Louise Miss, 4356 Champlain av.
     Sum. res. Philadelphia, Pa.
Dolle Edward C. F. 429 Washington boul.
Dolling Harry, 6404 Oglesby av.
Dolliver R. H. Rev. Park Ridge
Dolph Henry C. 2541 Wabash av.
Dolph M. J. Mrs. 2541 Wabash av.
Dolph Sarah A. Mrs. 2308 Wabash av.
Dolph William S. 3528 Indiana av.
Domansky Edward G. Mrs. Evanston
Donahoe Daniel, 1040 Jackson boul.
Donahue F. R. 2346 Calumet av.
Donahue T. S. 3604 Lake av.
Donald F. C. Virginia hotel
Donaldson H. Verner, N. State cor. Oak
Donaldson John T. 426 Oak
Donaldson Oliver H. Maywood

Donaldson Robert P. Maywood
Donaldson S. H. Maywood
Donan Simon, Hotel Windermere
Donelson C. P. Dr. 1373 W. Madison
Donelson Dexter P. Evanston
Donelson Katherine 'H. Mrs. French house, Evanston
Donihoo F. J. 910 Lunt av.
Donker Edward, 5625 Washington av.
Donlan John T. 241 Loomis
Donlan J. P. 241 Loomis
Donle W. C. 305 W. Monroe
Donlon Fidele Miss, Hotel Windermere
Donly H. A. Mrs. 261 Oakwood boul.
Donly John G. 261 Oakwood boul.
Donnell James W. Evanston
Donnelley B. S. 4609 Woodlawn av.
Donnelley Reuben H. 90, 47th
Donnelley R. R. 4609 Woodlawn av.
Donnelley T. E. 4609 Woodlawn av.
Donnelly H. Gratton, 435 Washington boul.
Donnelly J. C. Clifton house
Donnelly Thomas N. 3144 South Park av
Donnelly W. R. 5114 Woodlawn av.
Donnersberger Joseph, 3608 Michigan av.
Donoghue Frank, 398 W. Adams
Donoghue M. F. 398 W. Adams
Donohue John W. 2623 Prairie av.
Donohue Michael A. 7754 Union av.
Donohue M. Mrs. 6851 Honore
Donohue Wm. F. 7754 Union av.
Donovan Harry F. 302 Webster av.
Dooley James C. 482 Marshfield av.
Dooling Annie Miss, 3359 Calumet av.
Dooling Ellen Miss, 3359 Calumet av.
Doolittle Edgar M. 2719 Prairie av.
          Sum. res. Lake Geneva, Wis.
Doolittle E. A. 3802 Lake av.
Doolittle F. A. 255 Belden av.
Doolittle James R. Mrs. The Tudor
Doolittle L. H. Mrs. 539, 62d, Englewood
Doolittle Oliver S. 255 Belden av.
Doolittle William A. 471 Morse av.
Doolittle William H. 471 Morse av.
Doolittle W. W. 539, 62d, Englewood
Doran Frank C. 557, 67th, Englewood
Doran George H. Evanston
Doran Margaret Mrs. 596 Park av.
Doran May Miss, 1429 Michigan av.
Dorcey Charles H. 4450 Langley av.
Dorcey E. A. Mrs. 4450 Langley av.
Dorcey Frank E. 4450 Langley av.
Dorchester C. O. Dr. 332 N. Wells
Dore E. F. Mrs. 2730 Prairie av.
Dore Meta Mrs. 368 Ashland boul.
Dore Walter J. 2730 Prairie av.
Doremus A. F. 533 Jackson boul.
Dorland Edwin H., M.D. 4329 Lake av.
Dorn Gay, 224, 63d (H.P.)
Dorn Peter W. Tracy
Dorner Emil A. 632 Lasalle av.
Dorothy William H. 1323 Wilton av.
Dorr George J. 344 S. Paulina
Dorr H. H. 7015 Yale
Dorr Melvin L. 344 S. Paulina

Dorr Nellie E. Mrs. Morton Park
Dorrance Charles J. 189 Dearborn av.
Dorrance E. Allen, 6925 Stewart av.
Dorsett J. L. 1837 Michigan av.
Dorsey L. T. Dr. 77 Pine
Dorsey Nicholas J. Dr. 281 Erie
Dorsey R. M. Oak Park
Dorwin Thomas, 3044 Calumet av.
Dosch August, 3811 Wabash av.
Dostal J. W. Dr. 447, 37th
Doton C W. 425 Lasalle av.
Doty C. Edwin, 5547 Washington av.
Doty Frederick D. 35 Ashland boul.
Doty G. S. 35 Ashland boul.
Doty G. S. jr. 35 Ashland boul.
Doty Harry E. 35 Ashland boul.
Doty John M. 6426 Stewart av.
Doty Levi R. 4711 Kimbark av.
Doty Luther N. 152, 36th
Doty L. D. 3050 Calumet av.
Doty Melville R. 5547 Washington av.
Doty M. W. 407 Marshfield av.
Doty Paul C Austin
Doty Sadie J. Miss, 6426 Stewart av.
Doty Wilson K. 4711 Kimbark av.
Doud Benjamin S. 4064 Michigan Terrace
Doud James M. 4545 St. Lawrence av.
Doud Levi B. 3257 Michigan av.
Doud R. H. 4064 Michigan Terrace
Dougall G. 355 Chicago av.
Dougall Thomas, 47 Cedar
Dougherty Charles L. 4112 Indiana av.
Dougherty F. L. 569, 51st
Dougherty J. E. Mrs. 330 Lasalle av.
Dougherty E. M. 225, 54th pl.
Dougherty P. 187 Osgood
Dougherty P. S., M.D. 401 Garfield boul.
Dougherty T. E. 260 Warren av.
Douglas Alice Miss, 4424 Lake av.
Douglas A. Mrs. 440 Warren av.
Douglas Bernard M. 4406 Berkeley av.
Douglas Clyde, 440 Warren av.
Douglas Edwin S. 4849 Madison av.
Douglas Frank, 5039 Lake av.
Douglas Frank F. Tracy
Douglas Frank L. 5461 Cornell av.
Douglas F. W. 4424 Lake av.
Douglas John M. jr. 99 Astor
Douglas Percy E. Dr. 440 Warren av.
Douglas Robert Mrs. 4849 Madison av.
          Sum. res. White Lake, Mich
Douglas S. E. Sherman house
Douglass C. H. Chicago Beach hotel
Douglass Frank F. 361, 64th, Englewood
Douglass Frank Middleton, Virginia hotel
Douglass G. A. 4216 Berkeley av.
Douglass L. B. 4216 Berkeley av.
Douglass William A. Oak Park
Doul Emile, 3705 Ellis av.
Dousman H. F. 3708 Lake av.
Douthart S. P. 4412 Lake av.
Douthitt A. Mrs. 2825 Indiana av.
Douville H. B. 1276 Wilcox av.
Dovenmuehle Henry C. 1744 Frederick
Dow Albert, 91 Park av.

Dow Benjamin B. 752, 64th, Englewood
Dow Frederick H. Hotel Barry
Dow George L. 642, 60th, Engy
Dow H. E. Hotel Plaza
Dow L. E. 4104 Prairie av.
Dow M. G. Mrs. 5422 Cornell av.
Dow Samuel K. 10 Aldine sq.
Dow Thomas F. 1369 Wilton av.
Dow Walter K. 91 Park av.
Dow William C. 473 Orchard
Dowd Quincy L. Rev. Winnetka
Dowling John M. 137 E. Pearson
Dowling R. A. 3344 Wabash av.
Dowling S. A. Mrs. 3344 Wabash av.
Downe G. E. 4348 Berkeley av.
Downe Harry S. 4500 Lake av.
Downer M. V. Mrs. 3877 Lake av.
Downey John A. 940 S. Central Park av
Downey Omer L. 6915 Oglesby av.
Downey W. Stewart, Dr. 550 Jackson
      boul.
Downing Anna Mrs. 4015 Vincennes av.
Downs Arthur W. 2505 Michigan av.
Downs A. H. 2838 Indiana av.
Downs A. Ogden 4829 Kimbark av.
Downs Charles S. 4829 Kimbark av.
Downs Clarence M. Highland Park
Downs C. M. Dr. 686 Sheffield av.
Downs Ebenezer A. Evanston
Downs Hubert C. 319 Ashland boul.
Downs H. S. Lakota hotel
Downs J. Edward, 319 Ashland boul.
Downs Lewis C. Evanston
Downs L. E. Mrs. 2505 Michigan av.
Downs Lucy Ogden Mrs. 4829 Kimbark
      av.
Downs M. D. Mrs. 880 Warren av.
Downs M. D. jr. 4722 Kenwood av.
Downs William S. Highland Park
Dowst Charles, Evanston
Dowst Samuel M. 7023 Yale
Dox Hamilton B. 359 Dearborn av.
Doyle Austin J. 5201 Drexel av .
Doyle Austin J. jr. 5201 Drexel av.
Doyle Ella Miss, 3000 Indiana av.
Doyle E. T. 91, 44th
Doyle Guy P. Dr. 42, 39th
Doyle Jas. M. 203 S. Wood
Doyle J. 473 Fullerton av.
Doyle J. J. 39 E. Pearson
Doyle P. J. 335 Garfield boul.
Doyle R. W. Mrs. 354 Maple, Englewood
Doyle Thomas E. 272 Superior
Doyle William A. 758 Warren av.
Drake Chester T. 366 Claremont av.
Drake C. G. 6510 Ross av. Englewood
Drake C. St. Clair Dr. 1185 W. Adams
      Sum. res. Macatawa Park, Mich.
Drake David G. 601 The Plaza
Drake F. E. 3158 Prairie av.
Drake Frank, 3304 Vernon av.
Drake George Mrs. Park Ridge
Drake G. V. 510 Jackson boul.
Drake Isaac, 6500 Yale
Drake John A. 716 The Plaza
Drake John B. 2114 Calumet av.

Drake John B. jr. 2114 Calumet av.
Drake J. J. 1657 Briar pl.
Drake Margaret C. Miss 3213 Michigan av
Drake Mary E. Mrs. 5708 Madison av.
Drake Maud Lord Mrs. 2613 Michigan av.
Drake Ralph H. 42, 39th
Drake Thomas D. 239 Dearborn av.
Drake Tracy Corey, 2840 Indiana av.
Drake W. A. Riverside
Drake W. E. LaGrange
Drake W. H. 4822 Lake av.
Drake W. H. Hyde Park hotel
Draper Arthur M. Oak Park
Draper Arthur W. 958 W. Monroe
Draper A. M. Mrs. Oak Park
Draper Frank B. 4101 Grand boul.
Draper F. G. 336 Ontario
Draper Herbert L. Oak Park
Draper H. C. 6606 Perry av.
Draper T. W. 958 W. Monroe
Dray Gail, Chicago Beach hotel
Dray W. S. Mrs. Chicago Beach hotel
Drebing Frank, 3530 Lake av.
Drebing Tina Miss 3530 Lake av.
Dreher Elmore W. 429 Carroll av.
Dreier Carl Mrs. 4744 Lake av.
Dreier Otto A. 408 Belden av.
Drennan Mary K. Mrs. 743 Garfield boul.
Dresden W.W.Prof.376 Washington boul
Dresher Ernest, 710, 42d
Dresler Fred R. 62 Wisconsin
Dresler Reinhold, 62 Wisconsin
Dressel Lous Mrs. 678 Burling
Dresselhaus Henry, 101 Fowler
Dressler Sarah J.Mrs. 2301 N. Ashland av.
Dressler William M. 2301 N. Ashland av.
Drew Charles F. 309, 53d
Drew Charles W. 2216 Michigan av.
Drew Fred L. 296 Erie
Drew G. H. Morgan Park
Drew Henry H. 4322 Berkeley av.
Drew Minerva W. Mrs. 296 Erie
Drew W. C. 4324 Berkeley av.
Dreyer E. S. 2004 Diversey
Dreyfus Jacob, 4454 Ellis av.
Driggs A. C. 225, 28th
Driggs Arthur W. 1815 Indiana av.
Driggs A. W. 517 Warren av.
Driggs George Mrs. 5461 Cornell av.
Dripps Samuel W. 522, 63d
Driscoll J. J. Lexington hotel
Driscoll Michael F. 195, 30th
Driscoll M. J. 253 Ontario
Driver Edward A. Riverside
Driver E. Raymond, Riverside
Driver John N. 6404 Honore
Driver John S. Riverside
Driver Ellen D. Mrs. 23 Roslyn pl.
Drown M. E. Mrs. 6701 Lafayette av.
Drucker Henry, 15 Roslyn pl.
Druecker John, 23 Wisconsin
Druecker Nicholas, J. 1239 Wrightwood
      av.
Druiding A. 276 Bissell
Druliner David L. 93 Bowen av.
Drummond E. A. Grand Pacific hotel

Drummond F. 1837 Michigan av.
Drummond R. A. Mrs. 1122 Washington boul.
Drury Edwin, Wilmette
Drury Frank, Wilmette
Drury Horace G. Wilmette
Drury Myron M. Evanston
Dryer Herschel W. 427 Warren av.
Dryer P. K. Mrs. 427 Warren av.
Drysdale Andrew, 6439 Yale
DuBois Charles D. 1423 Michigan av.
Dubois M. Mrs. 3030 Lake Park av.
DuBreuil William A. 534, 62d, Englew'd
Dubs Rudolph Rev. 635 W. Adams
Dubs R. S. Dr. 579 Seminary av.
Dubuis Oscar F. 674 Park av.
Ducat Arthur C. Downer's Grove
Duck C. G. Evanston
Duck F. R. Mrs. 122 Ashland boul.
Duddleston George, 360 W. Congress
Duder W. H. 7525 Stewart av.
Dudgeon W. H. 5918 Wright, Englewood
Dudley Arthur H. 2613 Indiana av.
Dudley Charles E. Evanston
Dudley E. C., M.D. 1619 Indiana av.
Dudley Heury W. 2613 Indiana av.
Dudley John H. 1619 Indiana av.
Dudley J. G. 401 N. State
Dudley Lewis W. Dr. 2613 Indiana av.
Dudley Mary Mrs. Evanston
Dudley Oscar, 288 Flournoy
Dudley Raymond, 2613 Indiana av.
Dudley R. N. Evanston
Dudley Walter W. 4427 Lake av.
Dudley William H. Prof. Lake Forest
Dudley W. Frank, Evanston
Duehr Ulrich, 491 Dearborn av.
Duell William C. 2953 Michigan av.
        Winter res. Riverside Cal.
Duensing C. H. River Forest
Duer Benjamin F. River Forest
Duff Edward H. Ridgeland
Duff J. A. Rev. 6504 Honore
Duff Sarah Robinson Mrs. Auditorium hotel
Duffield A. Howard, 3020 Groveland av.
Duffield Charles Mrs. 3020 Groveland av.
Duffield William H. 4552 Champlain av.
Duffin Daniel, 535, 44th
Duffy George, 481 W. Adams
Duffy George, 633 W. Monroe
Duffy John J. 3707 Prairie av.
Duffy John M. 244 S. Lincoln
Duffy Joseph J. 253 Osgood
Duffy Joseph J. 435 Washington boul.
Duffy J. Mason, Austin
Duffy Thomas J. 4500 Vincennes av.
Dugan George M. 3840 Ellis av.
Dugan Rees H. 3840 Ellis av.
Duggan J. A. 1839 Indiana av.
Duggan Thomas J. 349 Chicago av.
Dugger J. P. Hotel Groveland
Duhig M. P. 484, 42d pl.
Dullaghan Edward P. 220 Pine
Dullaghan John, 216 Ohio
Dullaghan Stephen M. 220 Pine

Dummer William F. 115 Pine
Dummert Catharine Mrs. 276 Erie
Dumond Margaret Mrs. Evanston
Dumont Charles W. 2231 Michigan av.
Duncan Alexander C. Wilmette
Duncan Charles D. 6532 Perry av.
Duncan D. M.D. 1084 W. Harrison
Duncan Henry, 443 Warren av.
Duncan James W. 3364 Prairie av.
Duncan John A. 774 Jackson boul.
Duncan Joseph, 4047 Indiana av.
Duncan M. L. Evanston
Duncan S. F. Mrs. 3204 Rhodes av.
Duncan Thomas. 148 N. State
Duncan T. C. Dr. 590 W. Adams
Duncan T. W. 3254 Wabash av.
Duncan William, Hinsdale
Duncanson Herbert W. 190 Warren av.
Duncombe C. S. Mrs. 6538 Sheridan av.
Duncombe D. T. 667 Washington boul.
Duncombe H. S. 1538 W. Monroe
Duncombe W. E. 6538 Sheridan av.
Dunderdale C. F. 1031 Evanston av.
Dundore Aaron G. Prof. 368 Orchard
Dunfee Jonathan, Austin
Dungan C. P. Oak Park
Dungan Thomas A. Tracy
D'Unger Giselle Miss, 1837 Michigan av.
D'Unger Robert Dr. Palmer house
Dunham A. H. 837 Warren av.
Dunham Curtis, 6522 Ellis av.
Dunham F. B. Rev. 5737 Madison av.
Dunham George B. Evanston
Dunham George S. Evanston
Dunham German D. 2619 N. Robey
Dunham James S. 29 Bellevue pl.
Dunham John H. Mrs. 233 Michigan av.
Dunham Hannah A. Mrs. Evanston
Dunham Ransom W. Hon. 3870 Lake av.
Dunham Samuel E. 5536 Madison av.
Dunham William F. 934 Sawyer av.
Dunham William H. Evanston
Dunham William M. 4126 Ellis av.
Dunkley C. W. Mrs. 4744 Woodlawn av.
Dunlap Catherine D. Mrs. Evanston
Dunlap Charles M. Evanston
Dunlap C. 6521 Yale
Dunlap C. J. 4950 Vincennes av.
Dunlap Ernest A. 4009 Vincennes av.
Dunlap George A. 4009 Vincennes av.
Dunlap John, 422 Marshfield av.
Dunlap J. 4539 Lake av.
Dunlap W. P. 4950 Vincennes av.
Dunlevy Hulburd, 419 Huron
Dunlevy John C. 419 Huron
Dunlop Alexander, 4037 Ellis av.
Dunlop Joseph K. Oak Park
Dunlop Joseph R. Palmer house
Dunlop Simpson, Oak Park
Dunlop Sydney H. 4037 Ellis av.
Dunn Adam E. Evanston
Dunn D. H. Mrs. 3012 Michigan av.
Dunn Frank, 5045 Michigan av.
Dunn Frank K. 3136 Lake Park av.
Dunn John J. 5045 Michigan av.
Dunn John O. 311 Park av.

Dunn J. Austin, 427, 41st
Dunn J. A. 315 Chestnut, Englewood
Dunn J. Carrington, 174 Ashland boul.
Dunn J. E. Berwyn
Dunn K. E. 6641 Perry av.
Dunn L. M. Mrs. 1 Park av.
Dunn Mary Mrs. 547 W. Monroe
Dunn Nathan B. 174 Ashland boul.
Dunn Robert W. 640 Fullerton av.
Dunn William, 594 Division
      Sum. res. Tacoma, Wash.
Dunn William H. 6641 Perry av. Eng.
Dunn W. A. Dr. Hotel Metropole
Dunn W. P. 640 Fullerton av.
Dunne A. B. Mrs. 3449 Prairie av.
Dunne Edward F. River Forest
Dunne G- E. Mrs. 32 Delaware pl.
Dunne G. R. LaGrange
Dunne Henry M. 747, 66th, Eng.
Dunne James, 398 Ashland boul.
      Sum. res. Delavan Lake
Dunne James Mrs. 233 Hermitage av.
Dunne John M. Rev. 993 S. Central
   Park av.
Dunne Julia Miss, Austin
Dunne Mary Miss, Austin
Dunne Michael Col. 747, 66th, Eng.
Dunne M. 3338 Wabash av.
Dunne M. J. 4901 Madison av.
Dunne Otho F. 233 Hermitage av.
Dunne Richard, Austin
Dunne Romeo O. 233 Hermitage av.
Dunne Thomas Mrs. 4105 Drexel boul.
Dunnigan W. W. 5420 Monroe av.
Dunning Calvin L. 4318 Berkeley av.
Dunning C. Perry, Winnetka
Dunning David S. Jefferson Park
Dunning Louise M. Miss, 411 Bowen av.
Dunning Russell O. Irving Park
Dunning W. C. Mrs. 837 W. Adams
Dunoon David, Evanston
Dunoon George, Evanston
Dunphy John M. 831 Jackson boul.
Dunphy John M. jr. 831 Jackson boul.
Dunshee W. A. 271 Oakwood boul.
Dunstan Basil, 789 W. Monroe
Dunton Mary P. Mrs. Austin
Dunton T. F. 840 W. Adams
Dunton W. B. 437 Belden av.
Dunwell William C. 406 Warren av.
Dunwiddie I. F. Park Ridge
Dupee Arthur, 486 Dearborn av.
Dupee Charles A. 486 Dearborn av.
      Sum. res. Oconomowoc, Wis.
Dupee Cyrus, 2539 Indiana av.
Dupee C. F. Glencoe
Dupee Emeline W. Mrs. Glencoe
Dupee Eugene H. 486 Dearborn av.
Dupee George W. 486 Dearborn av.
Dupee H. M. 4820 Woodlawn av.
Dupee Jo , Hotel Metropole
Dupee Leroy C. 4820 Woodlawn av.
Dupee Walter, Hotel Metropole
Dupuis Alfred G. Oak Park
Dupuis Charles A. Oak Park
Dupuis Fred, Oak Park

Dupuis M. Hotel Normandie
Dupuy George A. 2625 N. Paulina
Dupuy Henrietta Miss, 381 Bissell
Duquette Louis, 1624 Cornelia
Durand Calvin, Lake Forest
Durand Charles E. Mrs. Lake Forest
Durand C. H. 435, 41st
Durand Elliott, 5712 Rosalie ct.
Durand Henry C. Lake Forest
Durand Henry Z. Lake Forest
Durand H. Calvin, Lake Forest
Durand H. S. 537 N. State
Durand Joseph B. Lake Forest
Durand J. M. Hotel Metropole
Durand Scott S. Lake Forest
Durant W. H. 976 Warren av.
Durborow A. C. 543 W. Adams
Durborow A. C. jr. 543 W. Adams
Durborow Clarence E. 543 W. Adams
Durborow Conrad B. 543 W. Adams
Durell Barbara Miss, 447 Elm
Durfee C. S. Miss, 4 Washington pl.
Durgin John C. 1905 Barry av.
Durham Albert, Evanston
Durham Emily Mrs. Evanston
Durham James, 6922 Yale, Englewood
Durham Theron, Oak Park
Durkee Henry R. 212 Goethe
Durkee R. P. H. Virginia hotel
Durno Edwin B. 3629 Vincennes av.
Durno Nettie Miss, 3629 Vincennes av.
Duryee John Mrs. Austin
Duryee Ruhard H. 514 Burling
Duthie James A. 17 St. James pl.
Dutro Charles H. 305, 41st
Dutton Buell B. Morton Park
Dutton Kirk Avery, 1507 Montrose boul.
Dutton L. B. 4209 St. Lawrence av.
Dutton Marshall M. 1507 Montrose boul.
Dutton S. A. Mrs. 3608 Lake av.
Duvall Paul H. Mayfair
Duvall William H. 219 N. Clark
Duvall Robert B. Irving Park
Duvall R. L. 1152 Kenmore av.
Duvivier A. Devin, 3953 Michigan av.
Duvivier Jenny Addison Mrs. 3953 Mich-
   igan av.
Dwen J. G. 3736 Ellis av.
Dwen Robert G. 3736 Ellis av.
Dwiggins Elmer, 132, 47th
Dwiggins Jay, 234, 45th
Dwiggins Zimri, 3638 Michigan av.
Dwight Charles F. Mrs. Evanston
Dwight Charles S. 984 S. Central Park av.
Dwight Charles W. Austin
Dwight Frank A. Austin
Dwight Henry S. 171 Ashland boul.
Dwight John H. Lake Forest
Dwight Solomon H. Austin
Dwight Timothy, Evanston
Dwight Walter T. Evanston
Dwyer Thomas H. 722 N. Wells
Dyar Hugh W. 221 Hampden ct.
Dyas W. G. Dr. 6936 Vernon av.
Dyche David R. Mrs. Evanston
Dyche Frank B. Evanston

Dyche George B. Evanston
Dyche H. B. Mrs. Evanston
Dyche William A. Evanston
Dye C. Nathan, Longwood
Dye Fannie C. Mrs. 510 Burling
Dye Mary I. Riverside
Dye Robert C. Riverside
Dye William B. Longwood
Dyer A. E. 5458 Cornell av.
Dyer C. H. Mrs. Virginia hotel
Dyer C. J. Mrs. 781 N. Clark
Dyer Edward B. 211 Seminary av.
Dyer Edwin, Highland Park
Dyer Ernest E. 781 N. Clark
Dyer George L. New Hotel Holland
Dyer George T. Virginia hotel
Dyer L. C. Mrs. 2512 Wabash av.
Dyer M. W. 223, 42d pl.
Dyke Edward F. 2909 Groveland av.
Dymond Edwin, Jefferson Park
Dymond John H. Jefferson Park
Dymond J. D. 416 N. Normal Parkway
Dymond W. H. 1623 Fulton
Dyrenforth Arthur, 27 Hawthorne pl.
Dyrenforth Douglas, 1923 Deming ct.
Dyrenforth Julius W. 191 Schiller
Dyrenforth Lewis F. Riverside
Dyrenforth L. J. Riverside
Dyrenforth Philip C. 27 Hawthorne pl.
Dyrenforth Wm. H. Evanston

EAGLE JAMES E. 470 Elm
. Eagle J. A. 395 Warren av.
Eagle T. D. 395 Warren av.
Eagle W. H. 395 Warren av.
Eaker Frank E. 3807 Vincennes av.
Eakin R. D. Virginia hotel
Ealy Elijah R. 7730 Eggleston av.
Eames Edward J. 890, 72d (H.P.)
Eames E. O. Berwyn
Eames Fred S. 405 Erie
Eames Henry E. Palmer house
Eames Lester H. Victoria hotel
Earhart W. I. Evanston
Earl E. T. Virginia hotel
Earl Fred C. 7745 Sherman
Earl James F. 7745 Sherman
Earl J. H. 6840 Wentworth av.
Earl Seth C. 4202 Michigan av.
Earle Charles Warrington Mrs. 535 Washington boul.
Earle Frank B. Dr. 535 Washington boul.
Earle H. L. Chicago Beach hotel
Earle John E. Hinsdale
Earle J. G. 401, 40th
Earle Samuel W. 7648 Eggleston av.
Earling Albert J. 3122 Michigan av.
Earling P. R. 5631 Madison av.
Earll J. E. Oak Park
Early Laura M. Mrs. 6351 Stewart av.
Early P. H. 403 Ontario
Earnshaw Charles, 362 Ontario
Earnshaw E. 362 Ontario
Eastburn Arthur G. 4338 Cottage Grove av.

Eastburn Job H. 4338 Cottage Grove av.
Eastburn Lincoln S. 4337 Evans av.
Easter Jacob P. 827 Farwell av.
Easter Joseph H. 827 Farwell av.
Easterly C. J. Hotel Groveland
Eastes J. E. 71, 23d
Eastlake Lewis S.,M.D. 4617 Langley av.
Eastland L. J. 167 Center av.
Eastman Albert N. 494 Jackson boul.
Eastman Barrett, Newberry hotel
Eastman Charles, Winnetka
Eastman Edward P. 494 Jackson boul.
Eastman Frank L. 5534 Cornell av.
Eastman F. L. 105 Loomis
Eastman George L. Oak Park
Eastman Henry A. 494 Jackson boul.
Eastman Joseph, Oak Park
Eastman Kirk J. 891 S. Kedzie av.
Eastman Kirk N. 891 S. Kedzie av.
Eastman Lorenzo D. 1438 Dakin
Eastman Olin C. 1438 Dakin
Eastman Osgood T. Evanston
Eastman Royal A. 290 Colorado av.
Eastman Sidney C. 1807 Frederick
Eastman William, 1369 Perry (L.V.)
Eastman Z. Mrs. 1807 Frederick
Easton Anna Mrs. 761, 63d ct.
Easton Charles L. Chicago Club
Easton Robert, Hinsdale
Eaton Arthur J. Austin
Eaton A. L. The Arizona
Eaton Charles, 5450 Greenwood av.
Eaton Clement L. 5036 Jefferson av.
Eaton David B. Dr. 3147 Indiana av.
Eaton Edric L. 1907 Michigan av.
    Sum. res. Lake Minnetonka
Eaton Ellen V. Mrs. 1809 Frederick
Eaton E. A. Evanston
Eaton E. W. 1447 Fulton
Eaton George A. 4319 Ellis av.
Eaton Harry, Highland Park
Eaton Ira T. 140, 42d
Eaton Isaac I. 4520 Ellis av.
Eaton James E. 558, 61st, Englewood
Eaton Julia E. Miss, Highland Park
Eaton L. B. 271 Michigan av.
Eaton T. W. 1447 Fulton
Eaton Walter W. Edison Park
Eaton William H. 4520 Ellis av.
Eaton W. T. 6620 Harvard
Eaver H. B. 973 Warren av.
Ebbert Wilham H. 4520 Prairie av.
Ebel Henry C. jr. Washington Heights
Ebeling George, Evanston
Eberhardt Max, 436 Ashland boul.
Eberhardt Waldemar, 436 Ashland boul.
Eberhart Franklin S. 263 Oakwood boul.
Eberhart L. 73 Warren av.
Eberlein F. 56 Bellevue pl.
Ebersol Joseph W. 6044 Princeton av.
Ebersold Albert H. 556, 60th, Englewood
Ebersole S. D., M.D. 2340A Indiana av.
Ebert Albert E. 276 Michigan av.
Ebert C. Augustus, 242 Hampden ct.
Ebert George F. 156, 43d
Eckart George, Oak Park

Eckart Harry S. Oak Park
Eckart Robert Dr. 451 Division
Eckart William, 598 Burling
Eckert A. W. 274 Ashland boul.
Eckes John, 520 Burling
Eckes Peter Mrs. 520 Burling
Eckfeldt Laura B. Miss, 4502 Ellis av.
Eckhart B. A. 499 W. Monroe
Eckhart John W. 716 W. Monroe
Eckhoff George J. Norwood Park
Eckle August, 209 Lasalle av.
Eckle August E. 374 Webster av.
Eckles George M. 228' 53d (H.P.)
Eckstadt Annie Miss, 4029 Indiana av.
Ecks'ein Charles, 256 Seminary av.
Eckstein Henry G. 4421 Vincennes av.
Eckstein Louis, 806 Pullman bldg.
Eckstorm P. F. Mrs. 901 Larrabee
Eckstorm Christian A. 901 Larrabee
Ecton W. B. 4326 Prairie av.
Edbrooke W. J. 3965 Drexel boul.
Eddington J. A. Mrs. 422 S. Oakley av.
Eddy Albert, 697 W. Adams
Eddy Albert M. 478 W. Congress
Eddy Alfred D. 3834 Ellis av.
Eddy Arthur J. 1718 Alexander av.
Eddy Augustus N. 1601 Michigan av.
 Sum. res. Manchester-by-the-Sea, Mass.
Eddy Azariah, 788 W. Monroe
Eddy Clarence, 232 Michigan av.
Eddy C. A. 4137 Southport av.
Eddy Devotion C. 705 Fulton
Eddy Frances M. Miss, 4036 Ellis av.
Eddy Frank M. 2317 Mich'igan av.
Eddy Frederick, Austin
Eddy George D. 697 W. Adams
Eddy George S. 788 W. Monroe
Eddy, Henry, 4440 Berkeley av.
Eddy Henry C. 1680 Sheridan rd.
Eddy Lina A. Miss, 478 W. Congress
Eddy M. A. Leland hotel
Eddy M. E. Mrs. Evanston
Eddy M. J. Miss, 116, 43d
Eddy Sara Hershey Mrs. 232 Michigan av.
Eddy Spencer F. 1601 Michigan av.
Eddy Thomas H. 788 W. Monroe
Edelmann Charles F. 167 Cleveland av.
Edelmann F. B. 193 Lincoln av.
Edelmann John Melchoir, 167 Cleveland
 av.
Eden William S. Great Northern hotel
Edenheim S. 315 Lincoln av.
Eder Charles H. 699 N. Clark
Eder Henry, 699 N. Clark
Ederer Edward P. 1735 Roscoe
Ederheimer Max, 4404 Michigan av.
Edes Warren S. LaGrange
Edgar William H. 4240 Champlain av.
Edgar William H. Mrs. 4240 Champlain
 av.
Edgarton A. Lewis, 875 W. Adams
Edgecomb R. F. 4111 Drexel boul.
Edgell Mary E. Mrs. 1371 Washington
 boul.
Edgerly Daniel G. Morton Park
Edgerton B. G. Hinsdale

Edgerton G. H. Dr. 1206 W. Adams
Edgerton Seymour, 5131 Washington av.
Edgeworth A. D. 627 W. Monroe
Edgeworth J. F. 3441 Calumet av.
Edgington J. F. 6551 Yale
Edgren August Rev. Evanston
Edler Alfred F. 639 Fullerton av.
Edler Fred C. LaGrange
Edmanson George, 454 S. Oakley av.
 Sum. res. Buffalo, N. Y.
Edmonds Howard O. 578 Division
Edmonds Timothy W. Evanston
Edmonson John W. 1299 Wilton av.
Edmonson R. E. 3702 Ellis av.
Edmonson Samuel B. 3702 Ellis av.
Edmunds Abraham, Oak Park
Edmunds Gerald O. Dr. 368 Fullerton av.
Edmunds Joseph, 313 Orchard
Edmunds Nelson Dr. 655 W. Adams
Edsall Samuel C. Rev. 1825 Nevada
Edsall Walter W. 389 Ontario
Edson Julius T. Riverside
Edson J. M. 611, 60th, Englewood
Edson W. S. 611, 60th, Englewood
Edwards Alfred R. 345 N. Clark
Edwards Anna G. Mrs. Highland Park
Edwards Arthur, 2818 Indiana av.
Edwards Arthur R. Dr. 2818 Indiana av.
Edwards A. B. 4310 Emerald av.
Edwards B. 686 Fullerton av.
Edwards Case, Granada hotel
Edwards Charles, LaGrange
Edwards Clifton S. Highland Park
Edwards C. E. 469 W. Congress
Edwards C. T. 3953 Michigan av.
Edwards E. 5334 East End av.
Edwards E. D. Mrs. 368 Winthrop av.
Edwards E. J. 4847 Kimbark av.
Edwards E. K. Mrs. 761 Jackson boul.
Edwards E. M. Mrs. 107, 37th
Edwards E. P. 235 Michigan av.
Edwards Frank L. 808 W. Adams
Edwards Harry D. 761 Jackson boul.
Edwards Harry L. Evanston
Edwards Harry L. Hinsdale
Edwards Harry C. 811 Fargo av.
Edwards Henry J. Evanston
Edwards I. V. 146 Park av.
Edwards James T. 44 Woodland Park
Edwards John, 5859 Washington av.
Edwards Joseph B. 808 W. Adams
Edwards J. A. Oak Park
Edwards J. A. 5244 Lexington av.
Edwards J. Frank, 3743 Vincennes av.
Edwards Kate D. Mrs. Evanston
Edwards Mary Mrs. 6008 Princeton av.
Edwards M. 63, 18th
Edwards Thomas 6930 Perry av.
Edwards Thomas C. 307 N. Clark
Edwards T. K. 761 Jackson boul.
Edwards Willard H. Hinsdale
Edwards Wm. H. 379 S. Campbell av.
Edwards W. H. Evanston
Edwards W. S. 538 Jackson boul.
Effinger H. Gerard, 5551 Lexington av.
Effinger John R. Rev. 5551 Lexington av.

Effinger John R. jr. 5551 Lexington av.
Efner Emma E. Mrs. 255 Ohio
Egan Charles W. 444 Dearborn av.
Egan Daniel, Elmhurst
Egan James A. Dr. 145 Park av.
Egan James J. 2915 Groveland av.
Egan Jennie Miss, 626 Dearborn av.
Egan John G. 4165 Lake av.
Egan Lizzie Miss, 444 Dearborn av.
Egan Mary J. Mrs. 451 Dearborn av.
Egan Patrick A. L. Rev. 7750 Emerald
  ·av.
Egan S. E. 626 Dearborn av.
        Sum. res. Lake Genevá, Wis.
Egan Wiley M. 444 Dearborn av.
Egan William E. Wilmette
Egan William T. 15 Linden pl.
Egan W. C. 620 Dearborn av.
        Sum. res. Highland Park, Ill.
Egbert M. B. Mrs. 176, 37th
Egersdorff Theodore F. 3953 Michigan
  av.
Eggers Louis, 3632 Indiana av.
Eggert A. E. 665 Cleveland av.
Eggleston Charles B. 3336 Indiana av.
        Sum. res. St. Clair, Springs
Eggleston Charles E. 3336 Indiana av.
Eggleston M. J. Mrs. 4724 Drexel boul.
Ehle Louis C. Hotel Windermere
Ehlen Frank H. 548 Burling
Ehlers Julius, 22 Beethoven pl.
Ehlert Charles E. 90 Clifton av.
Ehman Charles, 49 Lane pl.
Ehrhart John T. Maywood
Ehrhorn Henry F. 3809 Wabash av.
Ehrich R. Mrs. 590 Dearborn av.
Ehrlich Eugene M. 38 Astor
Ehrlich Henry Dr. 642 Lincoln av.
Ehrlich Moses, 21 Ashland boul.
Ehrlich Samuel, 21 Ashland boul.
Eichbauer Frederick, Evanston
Eichberg David, 543 Lasalle av.
Eichberg Louis R. Dr. 4056 Indiana av.
Eichberg Max, 3644 Grand boul
Eichberg S. 606 Lasalle av.
Eichengreen Mayer H. 736 W. Congress
Eichman Julius I. 4235 St. Lawrence av.
Eiden John, Evanston
Eiffert Jacob A. Grand av. sw. cor. Far-
  well av.
Eigenman Christian,5011 Washington av.
Eigenman Christian jr. 5011 Washington
  av.
Eiker Charles F. 4595 Oakenwald av.
Eilers Paul C. 695 W. Monroe
Einfeldt August, Oak Park
Einstein Arthur M. 3217 Rhodes av.
Einstein Benjamin M. 1628 Prairie av.
Einstein Morris, 1628 Prairie av.
Einstein Morris J. 3704 Ellis av.
Eiseman Max, 4008 Prairie av.
Eiseman M. 4008 Prairie av.
Eiseman Nathan, 4008 Prairie av.
Eiseman Rudolph, 628 Boulevard pl.
Eisenberg J. W. 703 Washington boul.
Eisenberg Morris, 96, 40th

Eisenberg William P. 703 Washington
  boul.
Eisendrath B. Mrs. 3611 Ellis av. ·
Eisendrath B. W. 3264 Vernon av.
Eisendrath Julius, 708 North Park av.
Eisendrath J. N. 4062 Lake av.
Eisendrath Louis, 3402 Calumet av.
Eisendrath Moses S. 449 Lasalle av.
Eisendrath Nathan, 146, 33d
Eisendrath Oscar, 3611 Ellis av.
Eisendrath Sam, 3611 Ellis av.
Eisendrath Sigmund M. 1721 Cornelia
Eisendrath Simeon B. 3611 Ellis av.
Eisendrath S. L. 134, 34th
Eisendrath Wm. N. 3949 Ellis av.
Eisenstadt Gustave, 424 Ashland boul.
Eisenstaedt A. Lincoln, 3408 Forest av.
Eisenstaedt Isadore, 3408 Forest av.
Eisenstaedt Leopold, 3210 Calumet av.
Eisenstaedt Rudolph, 3440 Indiana av.
Eisenstaedt Solomon, M.D. 3702 Forest
  av.
Eisenstaedt Solomon H. 3740 Forest av.
Eisert Henry Mrs. 622 N. Wells
Eisner Edward R. 1745 Deming ct.
Eiszner John, 1487 Washington boul.
Eiszner J. Frank, 1487 Washington boul.
Ela John W. 25 Scott
Ela S. J. Mrs. 3331 Calumet av.
Elcock Edward G. 4912 Michigan av.
Elder P. L. 177 Rush
Elder P. L. jr. 177 Rush
Elder Robert S. 119 Evanston av.
Elderkin George D. Oak Park
Eldred Adeline Mrs. 1082 Victor av.
Eldred W. L. 576, 43d
Eldredge Charles J. 3510 Lake av.
Eldredge C. Mrs. 2916 Indiana av.
Eldredge C. S. Dr. Palmer house
Eldredge E. S. 3510 Lake av.
Eldredge Fred W. 376 Dearborn av.
Eldredge George C. 6 Tower pl.
Eldridge Byron H. LaGrange
Eldridge E. W. 713 Pullman bldg.
Eldridge John, LaGrange
Eldridge Samuel D. Hotel Metropole
Elfelt Walter, Southern hotel
Eliel Alexander B. 4443 Ellis av.
Eliel Eugene D. 4443 Ellis av.
Eliel Gustav, 3538 Ellis av.
Eliel Levi A. 3538 Ellis av.
Eliel M. Mrs. 4443 Ellis av.
Eliel Therese Mrs. 3531 Vernon av.
Eliel Walter R. 4443 Ellis av.
Elkan Henry, 594 Dearborn av.
Elkin Mark, 3226 Rhodes av.
Elkington Charles S. 448 Cleveland av.
Elkington Henry N. 448 Cleveland av.
Elkins Henry K. 1706 Indiana av.
Ellbogen Max, 3700 Forest av.
Ellege William Rev. Morton Park
Ellett Edwin H. 3767 Ellis av.
Ellett Harry L. 3767 Ellis av.
Ellett O. D. Rev. Longwood
Ellias Edward B. 4320 St. Lawrence av.
Ellias Solomon Dr. 4320 St. Lawrence av.

Ellicott Edward, 4438 Ellis av.
Ellicott E. T. Hotel Barry
Ellinger Albert, 342 Lasalle av.
Ellinger G. S. jr. Granada hotel
Ellinger Morris H. 342 Lasalle av.
Ellingwood Finley, M.D. Evanston
Ellinwood Warren J. 108 Park av.
Elliot Frank M. Evanston
Elliot Henry C. 4301 Oakenwald av.
Elliott A. B. 6116 Michigan av.
Elliott A. C. Miss, 4916 Washington av.
Elliott A. J. The Ashland
Elliott D. B. 1851 Frederick
Elliott Edward E. 647 W. Adams
Elliott Edward S. Hotel Windermere
Elliott Elihu N. Dr. 1531 Belmont av.
Elliott Emma M. Mrs. 6349 Stewart av.
Elliott F. A. Oak Park
Elliott George R. 1170 Millard av.
Elliott Henry F. 4850 Langley av.
Elliott Henry M. 423 Orchard
Elliott Horace M. 3218 Indiana av.
Elliott H. P. 4102 Vincennes av.
Elliott James D. 6349 Stewart av.
Elliott John G. 2124 Michigan av.
Elliott J. N. Rev. 439, 60th, Eng.
Elliott Margaret Miss, Riverside
Elliott M. A. Mrs. Oak Park
Elliott M. E. Mrs. Riverside
Elliott Robert M. 1925 Michigan av.
Elliott Theodore P. Austin
Elliott William S. Ridgeland
Elliott W. P. 4455 Berkeley av.
Elliott W. S. 647 W. Adams
Elliott W. S. jr. 763 W. Adams
Ellis A. M. H. Mrs. 2734 Prairie av.
Ellis Benjamin W. 502 Washington boul
Ellis Clifford J. Evanston
Ellis C. D. 7226 Yale
Ellis E. D. 412 Jackson boul.
Ellis George A. Mrs. Riverside
Ellis George H. Evanston
Ellis Jerome A. Riverside
Ellis Joel Mrs. 4341 Grand boul.
Ellis Joel J. Highland Park
Ellis John, LaGrange
Ellis John Rev. Evanston
Ellis John C. 4120 Lake av.
Ellis John F. 412 Jackson boul.
Ellis M. A. Mrs. Austin
Ellis O. W. 200 Oakwood boul.
Ellis Robert 43 University pl.
Ellis William S. 4120 Lake av.
Ellis Winfield S. Highland Park
Ellis W. M. Evanston
Ellison Charles, 99, 33d
Ellison George, 99, 33d
Ellison T. H. Winnetka
Ellithorpe A. B. 144 Ashland boul.
Ells Huron A. 266 Ontario
Ellsworth Charles W. 220 S. Oakley av.
Ellsworth Frank, Hinsdale
Ellsworth James W. 1820 Michigan av.
Ellsworth M. E. 4222 Berkeley av.
Elm Conrad L. 1707 Barry av.
Elmendorf B. S. 1184 Wilcox av.

Elmendorf Willard, 322 Lasalle av.
Elmendorf William A. 322 Lasalle av.
Elmer Howard N. 684 Kenmore av.
Elmer Theodore H. 210 Park av.
Elmers Albert D. 5330 Ellis av.
Elmes Carleton L. 238 Ashland boul.
Elmes Charles F. 238 Ashland boul.
Elmes C. Warren, 238 Ashland boul.
Elmes Mary Mrs. 171 Aberdeen
Elmore S. K. Mrs. 623 Sheridan av. ·
Elmore William B. 218' 40th (H.P.)
Elms B. C. Dr. 229 Lasalle av.
Elmstedt John, Washington Heights
Elphicke Charles W. Evanston
Elsdon James G. 6401 Wright
Elsner Charles F. 86 Fowler
Elsner Samuel, 3118 Groveland av.
Elsom Wright, Ridgeland
Elson Herman, 3441 Wabash av.
Elston Daniel Mrs. 1547 N. Halsted
Elting Victor, 147 Pine
Eltonhead Edward Y. Hotel Metropole
Elwell Albert, 558 Kenwood pl.
Elwell Edward H. 4056 Grand boul.
Elwell W. J. 4323 Oakenwald av.
Ely Aden G. 3725 Vincennes av.
Ely Arthur C. 297 Ontario
Ely Clare A. Mrs. Evanston
Ely C. L. 3725 Vincennes av.
Ely David S. Evanston
Ely Edward S. La Grange
Ely Elizabeth A. Mrs. 3132 Prairie av.
Ely Frank, 344 Michigan av.
Ely George, 228, 37th
Ely Harriet Mrs. 107, 37th
Ely Henry B. 25, 37th
Ely James O. Dr. 1911 Michigan av.
Ely Joseph H. 228, 37th
Ely Oliver C. Greenwood av. ne. cor. 49th
Embleton R. J. 382 Chicago av.
Embree Jesse R. 6631 Harvard
Emerich Martin, Lexington hotel
Emerick David Mrs. 4404 Berkeley av.
Emerson Frank, Austin
Emerson Frank R. 2435 Michigan av.
Emerson George G. 3605 Lake av.
Emerson George W. 351 Chicago av.
Emerson Joseph Prof. Evanston
Emerson Martin W. 4160 Ellis av.
Emerson Ozias P. Austin
Emerson William H. Highland Park
Emery Albin F. Elmhurst
Emery Alfred B. 5200 Washington av.
Emery Benjamin V. 2564 Commercial (L.
    m V.)
Emery Chas H. 6956 Honore, Englewood
Emery Franklin, 124 Seeley av.
Emery George A. 4815 Champlain av.
Emery George E. 372 S. Paulina
Emery James, Elmhurst
Emery Joseph P. 2973 South Park av.
Emery Plato G. 4127 Maple av.
Emery Theodore, 2838 Indiana av.
Emery Theodosia Mrs. Evanston
Emery William O. 862 W. Monroe
Emery William H. Elmhurst

Emerson Sidney T. 3552 Vernon av.
Emigh Galusha, 481 Washington boul.
Emmart Charles M. Dr. 3936 Prairie av.
Emmel Henry G. 500 N. Wells
Emmel Peter, 916 Larrabee
Emmel Robert, 916 Larrabee
Emmel William, 916 Larrabee
Emmerich Charles, 16 Carl
Emmerich Edward, 16 Carl
Emmert J. P. Mrs. 79 Park av.
Emmerton Lena Mrs. 862 Warren av.
Emmet R. S. 426 N. State
Emmons Charles P. 941 Sawyer av.
Emmons C. A. Dr. 5425 Washington av.
Emmons F. A., M.D. 4129 Drexel boul.
      Sum. res. Lake Geneva, Wis.
Emmons F. S. Mrs. 4211 Ellis av.
Emmons R. A. 5425 Washington av.
Emmons S. M. 4461 Ellis av.
Emrich Myer S. 204 Cass
Emrick George M. Dr. 5700 Kimbark av.
Ender Eugene H. 173 Eugenie
Ender H. 90 Lincoln av.
Ender John C. 173 Eugenie
Enders Margaret Miss, 2816 Michigan av.
Endicott Edward M. 3757 Ellis av.
Engalitcheff E. Hotel Metropole
Engberg Elizabeth Mrs. 565 Cleveland av.
Engberg Martin J. 565 Cleveland av.
Engel Albert W. 230 N. State
Engel Bernhard, 3123 Michigan av.
Engel Charles H. 3766 Lake av.
Engel Hattie Miss, 413 Oak
Engel Jacob, 413 Oak
Engel Nathan, 3531 Indiana av.
Engel Samuel, 3334 Forest av.
Engelhard George P. Evanston
Englemann Lily Miss, 3353 Indiana av.
Engelmann Rosa, M.D., 3353 Indiana av.
Enger George, 2706 Michigan av.
Engers Frank W. 39 Menomonee
England Wm. R. 715 Washington boul.
Engle Augustus A. 556 N. State
Engle Charles, 308 Ohio
Engle C. S. 308 Ohio
Engle Edward 460 N. State
Engle F. F. Mrs. 4440 Berkeley av.
Engle Walter J. 556 N. State
Englehard Benjamin, 366 Lasalle av.
Englehard G. P. Evanston
Engleman Emma Miss, 649 Cleveland av.
Englemann C. P. Evanston
English Barney, Evanston
English Charles B. 51 Ray
English F. Mrs. 26 Park av.
English George R. 1921 Deming ct.
English George S. 6600 Lexington av.
English G. P. 38 E. Pearson
English Lee F. 505, 62d, Eng.
English Thomas, 4114 Michigan av.
English William J. Vendome Club hotel
Engstrom C. J. 4124 Drexel boul.
Ennis Alfred, 3150 Lake Park av.
Ennis Callistus S. 3032 W. 41st pl.
Ennis James I. 813 Morse av.

Ennis Jo   E. 463 Bowen av.
Ennis Lawrence M. 954 Turner av.
Ennis Luelus J. 25 Aldine sq.
Ennis Robert B. 5330 Ellis av.
Ennisson Walter J. 942 Turner av.
Enright J. W. 713 Jackson boul.
Enright M. J. 6114 Madison av.
Ensign A. D. 6104 Woodlawn av.
Ensign A. L. Granada hotel
Ensign Frank G. Ridgeland
Ensign Frederick G. Ridgeland
Ensign Harry A. 6104 Woodlawn av.
Ensign Lewis W. Ridgeland
Enslee Charles L., M.D. 754 W. Monroe
Ensminger William H. Dr. 6349 Stewart
      av.
Entwistle Ja   G., M.D. 6336 Harvard
Eoff J. H. Mrs. 5813 Washington av.
Eppenstein Max C. 3254 Wabash av.
Eppenstein S. C. 3254 Wabash av.
Eppinger John A. 4320 St. Lawrence av.
Eppinghausen Charles, 3038 Lake Park av.
Epply W. H. Chicago Beach hotel
Epps Charles L. 346 Chicago av.
Epps Frank P. 4959 Prairie av.
      Sum. res. Milford, N. H.
Eppstein Samuel, 3527 Vernon av.
Epstein C. L. 3122 Wabash av.
Epstein Hugo, 3631 Grand boul.
Epstein J. J. 3317 Vernon av.
Epstein Max, 3631 Grand boul.
Epstein Morris, 3631 Grand boul.
Epstein M. N. 7 Crilly pl.
Epstein Nathan M. 7 Crilly pl.
Erich Johanna Miss, 3046 Lake Park av.
Erich Victor, 3046 Lake Park av.
Erickson Christian E. 92 Fowler
Erickson Ernst A. 92 Fowler
Erickson E. A. 6325 Woodlawn av.
Ericson Albert F. Prof. Evanston
Ericson Edward H. 528 N. Normal Parkway
Ericson Otto C. 356 Burling
Erkins Heury, 4465 Oakenwald av.
Erlanger T. C. 721 W. Adams
Ermeling Lewis R. 2615 N. Robey
Ernst Benjamin C. 60 Oakwood av.
Ernst Charles E. 1754 Deming ct.
Ernst Edward F. Wilmette
Ernst Leo, 84 Astor
Ernst N. H. 3227 Vernon av.
Ernst Otto, 1852 Surf
Ernstein L. 150 S. Oakley av.
Erpelding Amelia Mrs. 1120 Bryan av.
Erpelding George B. 1120 Bryan av.
Erpelding John N. 1120 Bryan av.
Errant Joseph W. 1506 Wrightwood av.
Erskine Albert Mrs. 226 Dearborn av.
Erskine Albert DeW. 226 Dearborn av.
Erskine David M. jr. Highland Park
Erskine Emily L. Miss, Highland Park
Erskine James D. 226 Dearborn av.
Erskine Louis, Highland Park
Erskine Oscar P. 2359 South Park av.
Erstein L. 150 S. Oakley av.
Ervin William C. 3226 Lake Park av.

Ervin W. Edgar Dr. 3000 Indiana av.
Erwin Augusta Mrs. 55 St. James pl.
Erwin O. R. 394 W. Congress
Eschenburg Grant W. 1657 Briar pl.
Eschenburg Herman, 1347 Wolcott
Eschenburg H. A. 669 Lasalle av.
Eschenburg J. W. 669 Lasalle av.
Eschenburg Peter H. 1351 Wolcott
Eschmeyer H. 6801 Lafayette av.
Esdohr Henry, Jefferson Park
Esdohr Herman H. Jefferson Park
Esher Edward B. 234 Winchester av.
Esher J. J. Rev. 745 Jackson boul.
Eskridge Amaroy Miss, Hotel Normandie
Esmay J. P. 1408 Fulton
Espert Frederick jr. 2419 Calumet av.
Espert Frederick Mrs. 2419 Calumet av.
Espert Mary L. Mrs. 2446 Indiana av.
Espert Michael, 3128 Indiana av.
Essick James C. 783 N. Clark
Essick R. M. Evanston
Essig Frederick J. 65 Beethoven pl.
Essig George, 262 Ashland boul.
Esson Charles, 5211 Madison av.
Estee Tully C. Evanston
Estep W. H. 42, 39th
Estes Mabel Clare Miss, LaGrange
Estes St. Louis A. LaGrange
Estey A. F. 749, 63d ct. Englewood
Estey W. H. Mrs. 503 N. State
Etheridge Francis, 4714 Kenwood av.
Etheridge J. H. Dr. 1634 Michigan av.
Ettelson I. 279 Lasalle av.
Ettinger Charles D. 3847 Michigan av.
Ettinger Charles N. 2430 N. Paulina
Ettinger J. M. Edison Park
Ettlinger M. Mrs. 2502 Indiana av.
Ettlinger R. 4232 Indiana av.
Ettlinger Simon. 3402 South Park av.
Eulette Charles H. 6526 Lafayette av.
Eulette Franklin I. 6526 Lafayette av.
Eulette George W. 6526 Lafayette av.
Eulette John N. 6526 Lafayette av.
Eulette T. J. 7105 Webster av. Englewood
Eustace Thomas, 1839 Indiana av.
Eustis Percy S. LaGrange
Eustis Truman W. Hinsdale
Euston Alex. 907 Pullman bldg.
Evald Carl A. Rev. 1662 Barry av.
Evans Albert S. 286 Ohio.
Evans Arthur T. 3408 Michigan av.
Evans A. E. Dr. Palmer house
    Sum. res. Cape May
Evans Bouden C. 608 Chestnut, Eng.
Evans Charles, 1717 Roscoe
Evans Charles H. 4331 Forrestville av.
Evans Charles H. Dr. 730 Warren av.
Evans Clinton B. 3224 Lake Park av.
Evans C. G. 734 W. Madison
Evans D. E. 5412 Madison av.
Evans Ellicott, Union Club
Evans Evan E. 3537 Indiana av.
Evans E. T. 608 Chestnut, Englewood
Evans E. Webster Mrs. 564 Washington boul.
Evans Fillmore M. Highland Park

Evans Fred T. jr. 491 Dearborn av.
Evans George Judge, 452 Elm
Evans George Mrs. 3845 Ellis av.
Evans George H. Norwood Park
Evans George O. 338 Kenmore av.
Evans Harriet E. Mrs. Hinsdale
Evans Henry J. 1271 Washington boul.
    Sum. res. Lake Geneva, Wis
Evans H. B. 4440 Lake av.
Evans H. O. The Renfost.
Evans James Cary, 401 Oak
Evans John D. 3953 Michigan av.
Evans John M. 454 Fullerton av.
Evans J. B. 261 Ontario
Evans J. W. Capt. Hotel Windermere
Evans Louis H. 564 Washington boul.
Evans Lynden, 452 Elm
Evans Maurice. Oak Park
Evans Orrin Lee, 5609 Indiana av.
Evans P. A. Newberry hotel
Evans Raymond O. The Renfost
Evans Robert G. Highland Park
Evans Rothwell H. 608 Chestnut, Eng.
Evans Rush E. 1035 Evanston av.
Evans T. A. Newberry hotel
Evans Walter N. 3309 Forest av.
Evans William D. 1165 Bonney av.
Evans William W. 562 Washington boul.
Evarts Edward S. 6429 Stewart av.
Eveland Charles S. 301 Chicago av.
Eveleth S. H. Austin
Even Theodore, 1799 N. Halsted
Evenden John G. 751 Warren av.
Everard Edward B. 356, 42d
Everest James G. 6611 Yale
Everets E. S. Auditorium hotel
Everet A. H. Mrs. Chicago Beach hotel
Everett A. S. Dr. 816 Walnut
Everett Charles, 7843 Edwards av.
Everett Charles F. Highland Park
Everett Coleman S. 2947 Prairie av.
Everett E. A. 3619 Lake av.
Everett Frank D. Highland Park
Everett Frederick Dr. 402 Center
Everett John C. 2947 Prairie av.
Everett J. D. Oak Park
Everett William, 7426 Nutt av.
Everett William R. 3058 Calumet av.
Everett William S. Judge, 2947 Prairie av.
Everett Wilson G. Highland Park
Everhart George P. 417 Lasalle av.
Everhart Mella Miss, Virginia hotel
Everingham Belle, 4924 Greenwood av.
Everingham Edward L. 4924 Greenwood av.
Everingham G. Sumner, Highland Park
Everingham H. Dick, 4924 Greenwood av.
Everingham Lyman, 4924 Greenwood av.
    Sum. res. Traverse Beach hotel, Traverse City, Mich.
Everingham Mae, 4924 Greenwood av.
Everingham William B. 656 W. Adams
Evernden William, Hinsdale
Evers Thomas W. 42, 39th
Everson Charles, Pullman
Eversz Ernest H. Evanston

Eversz Moritz E. Rev. Evanston
Everts William F. Evanston
Everts W. W. Mrs. 3342 Rhodes av.
Evoy Thomas A. 6324 Woodlawn av.
Ewart A. N. Oak Park
Ewart Edward G. 3231 Rhodes av.
Ewart Julia D. Miss, 2801 Michigan av.
Ewart William D. 2801 Michigan av.
Ewell Martin D. Judge, Evanston
Ewen John M. Evanston
Ewen Warren, Evanston
Ewing Adlai T. 3747 Ellis av.
Ewing Alexander W. 1142 Bonney av.
Ewing John B. Dr. 426 W. Vanburen
Ewing J. A. 862 W. Monroe
Ewing M. L. Mrs. 410 Oak
Ewing Robert H. 1148 Bonney av.
Ewing William G. 3743 Ellis av.
Ex Simon, 332 S. Paulina
Excell Edwin O. 4349 Ellis av.
Excell Robert, 337 Oakwood boul,
Excell Wm. Alonzo, 4349 Ellis av.
Eyer Claredon B. Evanston
Eyre Clarence Preston, 242 Oakwood boul.
Eyster J. M. Mrs. Hotel Metropole

FABER FRED, 692 N. Hoyne av.
Fabian William J. Evanston
Fabyan George, Hotel Metropole
Fadner Fred J. 4559 Evans av.
Fadner Geo. M. 3226 Indiana av.
Fagan A. B. 4160 Ellis av.
Fagersten Lorenzo 143 Garfield boul.
Faherty Michael J. 36 Sidney ct.
Fahrney Peter Dr. 1074 Warren av.
Fahrney W. H. 1074 Warren av.
Fair A. M. Miss, 2222 Calumet av.
Fair George A. 481 Fullerton av.
Fair Joseph B. 2222 Calumet av.
Fair Robert M. 2222 Calumet av.
Fairbank H. W. 6111 Stewart av.
Fairbank Kellogg, 1801 Michigan av.
Fairbank N. K. 1801 Michigan av.
          Sum. res. Lake Geneva, Wis
Fairbank Wallace, 1801 Michigan av.
Fairbanks Arthur B. Oak Park
Fairbanks Chas. D., M.D. 6342 Yale
Fairbanks Geo. Otis, 481 Fullerton av.
Fairbanks Newton H. 4851 St. Lawrence av.
Fairchild Arthur E. 379 Ohio
Fairchild Edward W. 379 Ohio
Fairchild Edward J. Hinsdale
Fairchild Elijah S. Rev. 379 Ohio
Fairchild Meredith H. 379 Ohio
Fairlee Sidney Mrs. 2415 Michigan av.
Fairman Clarence Woodlawn Park
Fairman Daniel B. 6335 Lexington av.
Fairman Frank, 4744 Kenwood av.
Fairman George C. 6436 Oglesby av.
Fairrington Chas. W. 3807 Vincennes av.
Fairrington Warren M. 3807 Vincennes av.
Faith Thomas Dr. 784 Warren av.
Faithorn John N. 3565 Grand boul.
Faithorn John N. jr. 3565 Grand boul.
35

Faithorn Louis, 4332 Berkeley av.
Faithorn Maude Miss, 3565 Grand boul.
Fake Fred L. 81, 47th
Fake Fred L. jr. 81, 47th
Fales David, Lake Forest
Falk H. B. Mrs. 3517 Wabash av.
Falk Louis, Austin
Falk Max I.. 4346 Grand boul.
Falkenau Louis, 1923 Indiana av.
Falkenau Therese Mrs. 1923 Indiana av.
Falkenau Victor, 465 Dearborn av.
Falker Henry, 4433 Drexel boul.
Fall Humphrey, 599 Jackson boul.
Falley George N. Mrs. Evanston
Falley Lewis H. 578 Division
Fallon W. Edward, 757 Kenmore av.
Fallows Samuel Rt. Rev. 967 W. Monroe
Falls Charles, 430½ Belden av.
Falls S. K., M.D. 1028 W. Monroe
Faloon Emma Miss, 946 W. Adams
Faloon Matthew Dr. 946 W. Adams
Falter David B. 3230 Wabash av.
          Sum. res. Mackinac Island
Faucher Lenore Miss, 738 Washington boul.
Fanning Arthur L. Evanston
Fanning Charles A. 1027 Park av.
Fanning Frank J. 2124 Michigan av.
Fanning Isadore Miss, Newberry hotel
Fanning John, Glencoe
Fanning John, 471 Dearborn av.
Fanning T. C. Mrs. 5620 Washington av.
Fansler T. Evanston
Fargo Charles, 2247 Michigan av.
Fargo Charles E. 1840 Calumet av.
Fargo Charles E. jr. 3121 Wabash av.
Fargo E. A. 3716 Lake av.
Fargo Frank M. Highland Park
Fargo F. B. Miss, 2247 Michigan av.
Fargo James L. Oak Park
Fargo Livingston W. 2247 Michigan av.
Fargo Samuel M. 810 The Plaza
Fargo S. W. 2728 Wabash av.
Fargo William H. Evanston
Farish J. I. Virginia hotel
Farish M. A. Mrs. 434 Belden av.
Farley Andrew J. 117, 33d
Farley J. K. 683 Kenmore av.
Farlin J. Whitney Mrs. 64 Lake Shore Drive
Farlin Myron Whitney, 64 Lake Shore Drive
Farmer M. W. Mrs. 7127 Wentworth av.
Farnham E. W. 343 Warren av.
Farnham G. M. Capt. 6200 Sheridan av.
Farnham Louise M. Miss, 3351 Forest av.
Farnham R. E. 2970 Vernon av.
Farnsworth Ann Miss, Wilmette
Farnsworth A. C. 2904 Groveland av.
Farnsworth Charles E. Mayfair
Farnsworth Ernest L. Mayfair
Farnsworth George, 125 Astor
Farnsworth Harriet M. Miss, 468 Washington boul.
Farnsworth James B. Mayfair
Farnsworth Louis A. 140, 38th

Farnum Albert H. 2209 Calumet av.
Farnum E. J., M.D. 435 Washington boul.
Farnum George C. 944 W. Monroe
Farnum Harry W. 2209 Calumet av.
Farnum H. A. Norwood Park
Farnum Ithiel P. 937 W. Monroe
Farnum S. Vinson, Mrs. Evanston
Farnum T. G. 1224 W. Adams
Faron May Miss, 377 Kenmore av.
Farovid James A. 5338 Washington av.
Farquhar Charles, 4444 Evans av.
Farquhar William R. 290 Rush
Farr A. G. 5103 Hibbard av.
Farr A. L. Dr. 138 Lincoln av.
Farr Charles W. 545 Dearborn av.
Farr C. W. Irving Park
Farr Eugene M. 271 Oakwood boul.
Farr George D. 271 Oakwood boul.
Farr George S. Hinsdale
Farr James, Evanston
Farr Marvin A. 4737 Woodlawn av.
Farrand Harriet A. Miss, 654 Washington boul.
Farrar Arthur, Mrs. 505 Washington boul,
Farrar Charles S. Prof. Evanston
Farrar James S. Mrs. 551 Dearborn av.
Farrar J. Hamilton, 488 Webster av.
Farrar Roy, 551 Dearborn av.
Farrar William G. Highland Park
Farrel John E. 569 Orchard
Farrel John S. 569 Orchard
Farrel Wm. J. 569 Orchard
Farrell F. H. Capt. 278 Bissell
Farrell G. H. 440 W. Adams
Farrell James E. 541 Englewood av.
Farrell J. F. 1510 Michigan av.
Farrell Martin, 201, 30th
Farrell Patrick, 3669 Wabash av.
Farrell T. F. 603 Washington boul.
Farrelly James J. 4418 Champlain av.
Farren John, 5112 Wabash av.
Farren John A. Dr. 5112 Wabash av.
Farrington A. P. 4215 Langley av.
Farrington George E. Hotel Barry
Farson Charles T. 360, 40th
Farson Duke M. 1473 Washington boul.
Farson John, Oak Park
Farson M. Elizabeth Miss, 134 Warren av.
Farson Robert B. Virginia hotel
Farwell Arthur L. 369 Chicago av.
Farwell A. B. 4516 Lake av.
Farwell Charles B. Hon. 99 E. Pearson
          Sum. res. Lake Forest
Farwell Elizabeth S. Mrs. 2705 Indiana av.
Farwell Francis Cooley, Lake Forest
Farwell Francis W. 2705 Indiana av.
Farwell George E. 2705 Indiana av.
Farwell Granger, Lake Forest
Farwell Harry S. Avenue house, Evanston
Farwell John A. 2506 Michigan av.
Farwell John A. jr. 2506 Michigan av.
Farwell John H. 4202 Berkeley av.
Farwell John V. 109 E. Pearson
          Sum. res. Lake Forest, Ill.

Farwell John V. jr. Elmhurst
Farwell J. Charles, 4202 Berkely av.
Farwell J. W. 534 W. Monroe
Farwell Marcus A. Mrs. 1343 Michigan av.
Farwell Simeon, Evanston
Farwell Walter, 99 E. Pearson
Farwell W. W. Mrs. 534 W. Monroe
Fass Charles, 22 Maple
Fass Jacob, 3602 Forest av.
Fassett E. P. 4429 Lake av.
Fassett H. S. 831 Warren av.
Patch Edward P. Wilmette
Fauble Virginia M. Miss, 4406 Grand boul.
Faulkner John, Austin
Faulkner R. W. 6947 Perry av.
Faulkner Samuel, 98 Oakwood av.
Faunce Mary E. 124, 47th
Fauntleroy Thos. S. Lake Forest
Faurot Henry, 3343 Armour av.
Faux Richard W. 828 Jackson av.
Favill Henry B. Dr. 138 Pine
Favor M. H. Mrs. 643 W. Adams
Favor Otis S. 1 Madison Park
Favorite Calvin M. Lakota hotel
Fawcett Robert, 6519 Oglesby av.
Fawcett William Rev. 423 Oak
Faxon J. Warren, Oak Park
Faxon Nathaniel, 372 Chestnut
Fay Albert R. 3326 South Park av.
Fay B. W. 148 Park av.
Fay Charles M. 4332 Ellis av.
Fay Charles Norman, 45 Cedar
Fay John, 90 Park av. (L.V.)
Fay John B. 6620 Lafayette av.
Fay John J. jr. 3132 Calumet av.
Fay J. Edward S. 148 Park av.
Fay John Leo. 231 Linden av.
Fay N. C. Mrs. 3326 South Park av.
Fay Ralph M. 14 Bellevue pl.
Faye Charles M. 724 Pullman bldg.
Fayerweather Edward E. Hinsdale
Fazzie Camella Miss, 1486 Graceland av.
Fazzie Frederick F. 1486 Graceland av.
Fearing L. Blanche Miss, 1030 Walnut
Fearn Percy L. 354 Huron
Featherstone Arthur J. 506 LaSalle av.
Featherstone A. Auditorium hotel
Featherstone Edward A. 277 Ashland boul.
Featherstone George F. 1657 W. Monroe
Featherstone Jno. 1231 Washington boul.
Featherstone K. J. W. 515, 45th
Featherstone R. A. Mrs. 277 Ashland boul.
Feehan P. A. Most Rev. North av. se. cor. N. State
Feeser L. C. Miss, The Wellington
Fegenbush Charles M. 3233 Michigan av.
Feibelman A. Mrs. 3716 Lake av.
Feibelman Daniel E. 1837 Michigan av.
Feil William, 5300 Wabash av.
Feilchenfeld Alex, 3523 Calumet av.
Feilchenfeld Arthur, 3523 Calumet av.
Feilchenfeld Bismark, 3523 Calumet av.
Feilchenfeld Isaac E. 3523 Calumet av.
Feilchenfeld S. Rev. 3523 Calumet av.

Felch Barclay Mrs. 7207 Webster av. Eng.
Feldkamp Charles L. 1127 N. Clark
Felix Ben Bates, N. State
Felix B. F. 555 N. State
Felker F. 741, 63d ct. Englewood
Fell Henry C. 138, 38th
Fell Lewis F. 3610 Ellis Park
Fell William S. 188 Bowen av.
Fellows Alfred, 3008 Lake Park av.
Fellows Alfred W. 3008 Lake Park av.
Fellows Byron M. 4555 Forrestville av.
Fellows Charles J. 6601 Yale
Fellows C. Gurnee Dr. 4345 Ellis av.
Fellows Frederick B. 3756 Ellis av.
Fellows G. A. 104 Loomis
Fellows Henry B., M.D. 2969 Indiana av.
Fellows James E. 4449 Ellis av.
Fellows Lee, 530 Cleveland av.
Fels Joseph Lexington hotel
Felsenthal Adolph, 458 Lasalle av.
Felsenthal Albert, 3745 Langley av.
Felsenthal BernhardRev.450W.Randolph
Felsenthal Edwin I. 450 W. Randolph
Felsenthal Eli B. 4108 Grand boul.
Felsenthal Gabriel, 3655 Forest av.
Felsenthal Henry, 3655 Forest av.
Felsenthal Herman, 4510 Ellis av.
Felsenthal Julius, 430 Fulton
Felsenthal L. 3235 South Park av.
Felsenthal Michael, 223 Jackson Park Terrace
Felt Frank B. 5557 Monroe av.
Felthousen Charles I. 1315 W. Monroe
Felton Charles E. The Tudor
Felton George G. 3211 Michigan av.
Felton H. E. Victoria hotel
Felton Walter S. 655 Walnut
Feltus Lyman, 756 Kenmore av.
Fender Francis M. 715, 60th, Englewood
Fenger Christian, Dr. 269 Lasalle av.
Fenlon T. 7001 Yale
Fenn Curtis T. Dr. 6117 Washington
Fenn H. M. Mrs. 3517 Calumet av.
Fenn John J. 6637 Stewart av.
Fenn P. D. Chicago Beach hotel
Fenn William W. Rev. 3517 Calumet av.
Fenner W. H. 31 Walton pl.
Fennimore Richard, 494 W. Monroe
Fennimore William, 494 W. Monroe
Fenton William T. 5209 Madison av.
Fentress James 118 Pine
Fergus Benjamin F. 421 Erie
Fergus G. Slaymaker, 1100 Washington boul.
Fergus Jessie M. Miss, 421 Erie
Fergus John B. 3229 Sheridan rd.
Fergus Robert C. 421 Erie
Fergus Scott, Evanston
Fergus William L. 3229 Sheridan rd.
Ferguson Albert, 5752 Madison av.
Ferguson A. H., M.D. 2950 Indiana av.
Ferguson B. F. 530 Jackson boul.
Ferguson Chas. M. 2007 Michigan av.
Ferguson Clarissa Mrs. 3700 Ellis av.
Ferguson C. J. Mrs. 5752 Madison av.

Ferguson Edward Ashley, 37 Banks Eng.
Ferguson Elbert C. 4551 Ellis av.
Ferguson George Miller 2007 Michigan av.
Ferguson Henry A. 7720 Eggleston av.
Ferguson James H. Southern hotel
Ferguson James L 2007 Michigan av.
Ferguson John F. Evanston
Ferguson John Q. 3700 Ellis av.
Ferguson Julia E. Miss, Evanston
Ferguson Louis A. Evanston
Ferguson L. L. 434 Dearborn av.
Ferguson William G. 4551 Ellis av.
Ferguson W. Edward, 3700 Ellis av.
Ferguson W. G. Morgan Park
Fern G. B. 829 Warren av.
Fernald F. E. Hotel Groveland
Fernald George, Hotel Groveland
Fernald George E. Wilmette
Fernald James W. 4434 Greenwood av.
Fernandez E. M. S. Dr. 263 Bissell
Fernbach Louis, 4045 Ellis av.
Ferns John P. Mrs. 16 Pine
Feron Walter J. 5326 Cornell av.
Ferre John P. 4729 Langley av.
Ferree Albert G. 559, 69th, Eng.
Ferreira Chas. E. 7754 Sherman
Ferrell J. P. 267 S. Lincoln
Ferrier Walter, 410 The Plaza
Ferris A. S. Mrs. 256 Ontario
Ferris C. J. Mrs. 2596 N. Ashland av.
Ferris George W. 887 Sawyer av.
Ferris George W. G. Hotel Groveland
Ferris Georgia A. Miss, 2596 N. Ashland av.
Ferris Henry B. 1749 Oakdale av.
Ferris James W. 4564 Oakenwald av.
Ferris John H. 4564 Oakenwald av.
Ferris John O. Rev. 4364 Forest av.
Ferris Lorina C. Mrs. 277 Ashland boul.
Ferris L. Vernon, Maywood
Ferris L. W. Mrs. 258 Ontario
Ferris Madison H. 119, 21st
Ferris Robert D. 284, 53d (H.P.)
Ferris William J. 4564 Oakenwald av.
Ferris W. B., M.D. 7554 Bond av.
Ferry Abbie F. Mrs. Lake Forest
Ferry Albert D. Evanston
Ferry Charles H. 612 Division
Ferry C. E. Mrs. 464 Fullerton av.
Ferry James W. 336 Dearborn av.
Ferry J. H. Mrs. 336 Dearborn av.
Ferry M. F. 545 Wilson av.
Ferry Wm. H. Mrs. Lake Forest
Ferson Louise Mrs. 235 Michigan av.
Fessenden Benjamin A. Highland Park
Fessenden Charles B. Highland Park
Fessenden Charles F. 699 Washington boul.
Fessenden C. N. 16 Bellevue pl.
Fessenden Susan S. Miss, 466 Elm
Fessler Ada G. Miss, Evanston
Fetherston Edw. B. Dr. 2397 N. Paulina
Fetrow T. C. 28 Woodland Park
Fetter W. H. K. Mrs. 390 Chicago av.
Fey C. Mme. 3353 Indiana av.

Fick B. W. 284 Ashland boul.
Fick Emma Mrs. 284 Ashland boul.
Ficklen Leonard, The Tudor
Ficklen William, The Tudor
Ficklin Joseph C. 489 Dearborn av.
Fiedler August 463 Lasalle av.
Fiedler A. B. 611 Lasalle av.
Fiedler A. B. jr. 611 Lasalle av.
Fiedler Edmund G. 1107 N. Clark
Fiedler Martin A. 92 Hammond
Fiedler Paul O. 1715 Frederick
Field Anna H. Mrs. 26 Ogden av.
Field Arthur C. 250 Dearborn av.
Field Charles, 813 Pullman bldg.
Field Charles, 2641 N. Paulina
Field Charles E. 614 Englewood av.
Field Charles E. 2359 South Park av.
Field Charles G. 5728 Rosalie ct.
Field Charles H. LaGrange
Field Edward I. 4504 Vincennes av.
Fielp Elisha C. 614 Englewood av.
Field Eugene, 1033 Evanston av.
Field Frank, 2641 N. Paulina
Field George Mrs. 2417 Michigan av.
Field George D. 2248 Michigan av.
Field George W. 250 Dearborn av.
Field Harry, 2641 N. Paulina
Field Henry D. 4136 Cottage Grove av
Field Henry P. 52 Bellevue pl.
Field Herman H. 4826 Kimbark av.
Field Hollis W. 4120 Vincennes av.
Field Howard, Evanston
Field H. N. 5752 Washington av.
Field John S. 2248 Michigan av.
Field Joseph C. 347 Oakwood boul.
Field Judson L. 4826 Kimbark av.
Field Marshall, 1905 Prairie av.
Field Marshall jr. 1919 Prairie av.
Field Martha A. Mrs. 2248 Michigan av.
Field Richard I. 250 Dearborn av.
Field Robert L. 614 Englewood av.
Field R. H. Clifton house
Field Samuel G. Hotel Metropole
Field Stanley, 235 Michigan av.
Field Wentworth G. Hotel Metropole
Field William A. 52 Bellevue pl.
Field W. A. 713 Walnut
Field W. T. 5752 Washington av.
Fielder Henry C. Oak Park
Fieldhouse Joseph 114 S. Lincoln
Fielding Edward, 882 S. St. Louis av.
Fielding Howard H. 7631 Union av.
Fifield J. S. 923 W. Monroe
Filer Alanson, Evanston
Filer George R. 550 Washington boul.
Filkins Edward A. 1467 Wellington
Finch Hunter W. 2348 Calumet av.
Finch Joseph C. 1464 Edgecomb ct.
Finch Silas H. 389 Oakwood boul.
Findlay R. 6318 Drexel av.
Finefield Adelia Bly Mrs. 6216 Princeton
    av
Finerty John F. 3562 Grand boul.
    Sum. res. Brown's Lake, Wis
Finkler C. C. 383 Superior
Finkler J. W. 1821 Oakdale av.

Finla son M. 496 W. Congress
Finley Howard, 4215 Ellis av.
Finn Nicholas R. 622 Jackson boul.
Finn P. 622 Jackson boul.
Finnemore Alfred E. 4510 St. Lawrence
    av.
Finneron Samuel, 206 Cass
Finney A. M. 3747 Langley av.
Finney Elmer E. 3747 Langley av.
Finney E. M. Mrs. 3747 Langley av.
Finney George, 631 Cleveland av.
Finney George S. 376 Bowen av.
Finney Harry, 5755 Madison av.
Finney Harry P. 631 Cleveland av.
Finney Henry E. 5755 Madison av.
Finney John, Highland Park
Finney Thomas J. 38 Walton pl.
Finney William H. 621 The Plaza
Firmenich George F. 2323 Michigan av.
Firmenich Joseph, 2323 Michigan av.
Fischback John 1171 N. Clark
Fischel Theo. G. 3000 Michigan av.
Fischer C. W. 1814 Wrightwood av.
Fischer Ernst H. 595 Larrabee
Fischer Frederick, Highland Park
Fischer G. F. 580 Lasalle av.
Fischer Gustave A. Dr. 514 Ashland boul.
Fischer Henry W. 2687 N. Ashland av.
Fischer Otto C. 458 Cleveland av.
Fischer O. F. 1728 Michigan av.
Fischer Reinhold Prof. 501 Lasalle av.
Fischer Siegfried M. 5012 Drexel boul.
Fischer William D. 1170 Washington
    boul.
Fish A. J. 3611 Grand boul.
Fish Edward G. 4021 Indiana av.
Fish Frederick M. 731 Walnut
Fish Joel W. Rev. 731 Walnut
Fish Joseph, 2217 Calumet av.
Fish Mary J.Miss, 1399 Washington boul.
Fish Peter, 440, 45th
Fish Roswell P. 68 Cedar
Fish R. H. 528 W. Madison
Fish Sarah C.Miss,1399 Washington boul.
Fish Selden, 3226 Calumet av.
Fish S. C. 2720 Wabash av.
Fish S. T. 4508 Drexel boul.
Fish Williston, 5114 Madison av.
Fish W. B. 440, 65th, Englewood
Fishburn Eugene H. 422 Huron
Fishburn Randolph E. 422 Huron
Fishell Albert, 3448 Wabash av.
Fishell E. W. 3448 Wabash av.
Fisher Albert, 350 Chestnut, Eng.
Fisher Albert jr. 321 Chestnut, Eng.
Fisher Alice Miss, 4036 Ellis av.
Fisher Alonzo G. 343 Ashland boul.
Fisher Archibald J. 930 Walnut
Fisher Augustus F. 4515 Greenwood av.
Fisher Charles E. 922 Warren av.
Fisher C. C. Mrs. 552 Jackson boul.
Fisher C. E. Dr. Chicago Beach hotel
Fisher C. E. Oak Park
Fisher Elbert C. 87 Rush
Fisher E. A. Judge, 738 Jackson boul.
Fisher Flora S. Mrs. 2417 Michigan av.

Fisher Francis P. 2419 Michigan av.
Fisher Frank P. LaGrange
Fisher Fred G. 87 Rush
Fisher Frederick J. F. Dr. Elmhurst
Fisher George, 3159 South Park av.
Fisher George Mrs. 87 Rush
Fisher George F. 4332 Greenwood av.
    Sum. Res. Lake Beulah, Wis.
Fisher George M. Hotel Metropole
Fisher George P. Higbland Park
Fisher G. F. jr. 4332 Greenwood av.
Fisher G. P. jr. 497 N. State.
Fisher Harry H. 2716 Calumet av.
Fisher Howard, 463 N. State
Fisher Hart C. 4735 Lake av.
Fisher J., Dr. 277 Lasalle av.
Fisher Lucius G. 4036 Ellis av.
Fisher Lucius G. jr. 4036 Ellis av.
Fisher Napoleon C. 436 Kenmore av.
Fisher Nora Miss, 5127 Hibbard av.
Fisher Reynolds, 4734 Kimbark av.
Fisher Sylvester Rev. 47, 37th pl.
Fisher Walter L. 463 N. State
Fisher William E. Norwood Park
Fisher W. A. Dr. 4161 Berkeley av.
Fishleigh John, 1209W.Ravenswood Park
Fisk Charles H. Maynard
Fisk D. B. Mrs. 2100 Calumet av.
Fisk D. M. 2100 Calumet av.
Fisk Franklin P. Evanston
Fisk Franklin W. Rev. 532 W. Adams
Fisk Henry E. 2100 Calumet av.
Fisk Henry E. 532 W. Adams ·
Fisk Herbert F. Prof. Evanston
Fisk Horace E. 474 N. State
Fisk James H. 2977 South Park av.
Fisk Jane M. Mrs. Evanston
Fisk L. E. Mrs. Evanston
Fiske William H. 376 Washington boul.
Fiske Geo. F. Dr. 438 Lasalle av.
Fiske John M. 4318 Oakenwald av.
Fiske William B. 6516 Sheridan av.
Fitch Alfred L. Ridgeland
Fitch Amza L. Oak Park
Fitch Anna W. Mrs. 4840 Langley av.
Fitch A. L. Oak Park
Fitch Beatrice Miss, 3707 Ellis av.
Fitch Charles A. Evanston
Fitch Charles A. 4058 Michigan Terrace
Fitch C. A. 593 W. Monroe
Fitch C. Fred Dr. 296 W. Monroe
Fitch C. M. Dr. 645 W. Monroe
    Sum. res. Twin Lakes, Wis.
Fitch Ellis B. Austin
Fitch E. O. 375 Dearborn av.
Fitch G. W. New Hotel Holland
Fitch Henry S. 2827 Michigan av.
Fitch Jane L. Mrs. 3159 Indiana av.
Fitch J. R. Capt. Evanston
Fitch Margaret S. Mrs. 227 Seminary av.
Fitch Mary A. Miss, 3707 Ellis av.
Fitch Mary J. Mrs. Evanston
Fitch Moses J. 4510 Greenwood av.
Fitch Timothy S. 3707 Ellis av.
Fitch T. D., M.D. 296 W. Monroe
Fitch Walter M. Dr. 645 W. Monroe

Fitch William D. 1065 Washington boul.
Fitch W. B. 6746 Union av.
Fitts E. C. 922 Jackson boul.
Fitts Leverett E. 222 Dearborn av.
Fittz Jane P. Mrs. 354 W. Adams
Fitzek Joseph, 486 N. Wells
Fitzgerald Burt J. 1574 Alexander av.
Fitzgerald Francis W. Dr. 625 S. Kedzie
Fitzgerald Hart J. 7236 Wentworth av.
Fitzgerald Henry J. 11 Astor
Fitzgerald M. F. Miss, 2616 Indiana av.
Fitzgerald Paul, 425 Winthrop av.
Fitzgerald Porter B. 221 Belden av.
Fitzgerald Thomas H.7226Wentworth av.
Fitzgerald William, 2616 Indiana av
Fitzgerald W. H. 2616 Indiana av.
Fitzgibbon Annie Mrs. 3153 Wabash av.
FitzHugh Carter H. Lake Forest
Fitzhugh J. L. Mrs. The Arizona
Fitzpatrick John, 326 Centre av.
Fitzpatrick P. H. 482 W. Congress
Fitzpatrick Sylvester J.4919Vincennes av.
Fitzpatrick William P. 425 S. Leavitt
FitzRandolph E. L. 354 Kenmore av.
Fitzsimmons F. V. 3450 Indiana av.
Fitzsimmons John, 2801 Prairie av.
FitzSimons Chas. 161 Ashland boul.
Fitzsimons Edward M. 23, 37th
Fizette Charles E. 1465 Michigan av.
Flagg Elmer T. 14 Woodland Park
Flagg Luther N. 7216 Jeffery av
Flagg William H. 14 Woodland Park
Flagler Samuel A. Morton Park
Flagler William B. Morton Park
Flanagan Joseph E. 2844 Commercial (L. V.)
Flanders C. A. 289 Webster av.
Flanders George B. 3645 Vincennes av.
Flanders John J. Glencoe
Flanigan James, 418 Kenmore av.
Flanley Patrick H. 525, 60th, Eng.
Flannery D. F. 798 Kenmore av.
Flannery John L. 285 Evanston av.
Flavin Michael D. 3815 Vincennes av.
Fleetwood Anna Mrs. 15 Scott
Fleetwood Charles, 586 Division
Fleetwood Stanley, 15 Scott
Fleetwood W.Webster, 63 The Hampden
    Sum. res. Colfax
Fleischer Charles H. 72 Ewing pl.
Fleischer Gustav A. 225 Evanston av.
Fleischman Henry, 3648 Indiana av.
Fleischmann Joseph, 418 N. State
Fleischer George P. Hinsdale
Fleishman M. S. 3566 Prairie av.
Fleishman S. M. Mrs. 3207 Calumet av.
Flemming Dierdre Miss,4736 Drexel boul.
Fleming Edward, 444 Ashland boul.
Fleming Edward J. 444 Ashland boul.
Fleming E. M. Mrs. 3519 Indiana av.
Fleming Helen Miss, 145 Oakwood boul.
Fleming I. A. 498, 42d pl.
Fleming John C. 5505 Cornell av.
Fleming John M. Dr. 1534 W. Monroe
Fleming John T. 444 Ashland boul.
Fleming Josiah C. 545, 62d, Eng.

Fleming J. D. 291 Rush
Fleming Lloyd, 444 Ashland boul.
Fleming Martha Miss, 143 Oakwood boul.
Fleming Maurice F. 444 Ashland boul.
Fleming M. 344 Michigan av.
Fleming M. 4749 Calumet av.
Fleming Patrick H. 444 Ashland boul.
Fleming Robert H. Mrs. 4003 Drexel boul.
Fleming Robert H. Chicago Club
Fleming Robert J. Lieut. Fort Sheridan
Fleming Sarah Miss, 4736 Drexel boul.
Fleming Sarah Mrs. 442 Marshfield av.
Fleming William, 4736 Drexel boul.
Fleming William J. 4023 Indiana av.
Fleming Wm. J. 654 Cleveland av.
Flentye W. H. 608 Lasalle av.
Flersheim George B. 81, 44th
Flersheim J. P. 81, 44th
Flershem G. T. 3017 South Park av.
    Sum. res. Highwood, Ill.
Flershem Lem Whitney,269 LakeView av.
Flershem L. H. Mrs. 3017 South Park av.
Flershem Rudolph, 2201 Lake View av.
Flesh Bertha S. Mrs. 925 E. Pearson
Fletcher Archibald W. Highland Park
Fletcher D. H. 333, 42d
Fletcher E. A. French house, Evanston
Fletcher Frank A. French house, Evanston
Fletcher Horace, Hotel Imperial
Fletcher Moses M. 719 N. Wells
Flinn Charles B. Oak Park
Flinn F. J. 1719 Belmont av.
Flinn John J. Evanston
Flinn Wm. W. Highland Park
Flint Franklin F. Mrs. Highland Park
Flint Frederick W. 229 Oakwood boul.
Flint Hale L. 5203 Madison av.
Flitcraft A. J. Oak Park
Flitcraft Isaiah, Oak Park
Floersheim Sol. 3532 Calumet av.
Flonacher Edward, 2228 Prairie av.
Flonacher Henry C. 2228 Prairie av.
Flood Frank J. 3121 Vernon av.
Flood John Dr. 297 N. State
Flood J. Ramsay Dr. 5320 Jefferson av.
Flood Robert D. 5320 Jefferson av.
Flood Samuel D. 5320 Jefferson av.
Flood T. H. 3121 Vernon av.
Flood Wm. 276 Oak
Flook Annie Mrs. 6320 Drexel av.
Florance William Mrs. Irving Park
Florsheim Aaron, 4321 Vincennes av.
Florsheim Augustus, 3236 Wabash av.
Florsheim Felix, 3143 Michigan av.
Florsheim J. Mrs. 600 Lasalle av.
Florsheim Moses, 2973 Wabash av.
Florsheim M. S. 3356 South Park av.
Florsheim Norman, 3343 Wabash av.
Florsheim Sidney, 3343 Wabash av.
Florsheim Siegmund, 3143 Michigan av.
Florsheim Simon, 3343 Wabash av.
Floto W. Mrs. 412 Superior
Flower A. 300 W. Monroe
Flower Elliott, 6519 Ellis av.
Flower James M. 361 Superior

Flower Louis B. 361 Superior
Flower Samuel, 3647 Forest av.
Flowers T. E. Mrs. 83 DeKalb
Floyd Frank, 4650 Drexel boul.
Floyd John I. Newberry hotel
Floyd S. A. Mrs. Newberry hotel
Floyd Helen C. Mrs. Highland Park.
Floyd-Jones Linton T. 1837 Michigan av.
Floyd-Jones Thomas, 1837 Michigan av.
Fluke L. H. 6405 Yale
Flynn Fred. 349 Bowen av.
Flynn Patrick J. 411 Garfield boul.
Fockler Irene Miss, Evanston
Fockler Mary Mrs. Evanston
Foehringer Frederick W. 701 Orchard
Foerster Edward R. 4223 Grand boul.
Foerster Otto, 1188 Washington boul.
Fogarty Frank H. 880 Walnut
Fogarty William A. LaGrange
Fogg A. M. Mrs. 4656 Wabash av.
Fogg E. S. 5855 Wabash av.
Fogg M. G. Mrs. 3652 Lake av.
Fogg Simon F. 236 53d (H. P.)
Foley H. N. Mrs. 3756 Ellis av.
Foley Louisa W. Mrs. 612 Washington
    boul.
Foley Walter, LaGrange
Foley William C. 4635 Grand boul.
Folger Harry S. 7620 Wright
Follansbee Blanche D. Miss, 2342 Indiana
    av.
Follansbee Charles Mrs.4545 Greenw'd av.
Follansbee Charles E. 4515 Ellis av.
Follansbee Frank H. 2301 Calumet av.
Follansbee George A. 2342 Indiana av.
Follansbee M. C. 4029 Indiana av.
Follansbee M. D. 2342 Indiana av.
Follette H. A. 3835 Indiana av.
Follette J. B. Mrs. 4339 Oakenwald av.
Follette M. Mrs. 3835 Indiana av.
Follette W. A. 464 Lasalle av.
Follinger John M. 4004 Prairie av.
Folsom Charles A. 226, 41st
Folsom H. V. Miss, 391 Superior
Folsom O. W. 606, 44th
Foltz Fred L. 47 Astor
Folz Carrie Miss, 193 Lincoln av.
Folz Lillian Miss, 193 Lincoln av.
Fonda David B. Dr. Jefferson Park
Fones James J. Irving Park
Fontayne Albert, 3210 Forest av.
Fontayne Albert jr. 3210 Forest av.
Foord Charles C. 4126 Lake av.
Foote Apollos D. 3222 Rhodes av.
Foote Charles B. Evanston
Foote Charles H. 4842 Washington av.
Foote Delevan S. 312 Belden av.
Foote Edgar S. 3824 Ridge av.
Foote Elizabeth Miss, 1634 Prairie av.
Foote Erastus Mrs. 1634 Prairie av.
Foote Erastus jr. 1634 Prairie av.
Foote F. H. 4530 Lake av.
Foote John B. Norwood Park
Foote Mark A. Irving Park
Foote Stanley C. 4806 St. Lawrence av.
Foote William H. 4806 St. Lawrence av.

Foote William K. Dr. 4901 Calumet av.
Foote W. S., M.D. 5830 Washington av.
Forbes Alexander, 24 Aldine sq.
Forbes Allen B. 24 Aldine sq.
Forbes A. M. 650 W. Monroe
Forbes Daniel, 1379 Washington boul.
Forbes George S. 24 Aldine sq.
Forbes H. A. The Ashland
Forbes James Hyde, 525 Englewood av.
Forbes John A. 24 Aldine sq.
Forbes Mary Mrs. 7001 Wentworth av.
Forbes Robert R. 24 Aldine sq.
Forbes William H. 484, 44th pl.
Forbes William R. 4230 Prairie av.
Forbes W. O. 3156 Indiana av.
Forbush Calvin, Evanston
Forbush Harry R. 533 Dearborn av.
Forbush Thomas B. Rev. 533 Dearborn av.
Forbush Wm. Evanston
Forbush William P. 533 Dearborn av.
Force Fayette L. 7450 Nutt av.
Force George, 644 Sedgwick
Forch T. Mrs. 906 Walnut
Ford Charles N. 981 Jackson boul.
Ford Frederick D. LaGrange
Ford George R. Clifton house
Ford George W. 6530 Oglesby av.
Ford Hannah Mrs. 4742 Langley av.
Ford Henry B. 3757 Vincennes av.
Ford H. Richmond 4740 Langley av.
Ford James M. 405 Seminary av.
Ford John, 1420 Michigan av.
Ford John C. 707 W. Monroe
Ford John S. 3918 Lake av.
Ford J. Sawtelle, 5616 Washington av.
Ford L. E. 226 Michigan av.
       Sum. res. Lake Geneva, Wis.
Ford Mary H. Mrs. 3747 Langley av.
Ford M. A. 4126 Berkeley av.
Ford Rita E. Mrs. 3918 Lake av.
Ford Summerfield, 98, 37th
Ford William, 1420 Michigan av.
Ford William H. 549 Washington boul.
Ford William H. 6237 Oglesby av.
Ford William J. Austin
Ford W. M. Granada hotel
Ford W. M. Mrs. Lakota hotel
Fordham Albert C. 737 Washington boul.
Fordham Oliver C. 24 S. Ada
Fordyce Edmund, River Forest
Fordyce Homer G. 5708 Monroe av.
Foreman David H. 3417 Prairie av.
Foreman Edward H. 3358 South Park av.
Foreman Edward P. 4214 Berkeley av.
Foreman Edwin G. 3122 South Park av.
Foreman Frank, 3518 Forest av.
Foreman Gerhard, 2901 Michigan av.
Foreman Grant, Oak Park
Foreman Henry, 3417 Prairie av.
Foreman Henry G. 3245 Rhodes av.
Foreman Isaac H. 3417 Prairie av.
Foreman John, Hotel Groveland
Foreman Joseph Mrs. 3132 Vernon av.
Foreman Milton J. 3132 Vernon av.
Foreman Oscar G. Lakota hotel
Foreman Rudolph 3819 Langley av.

Foreman Samuel H. 3418 Prairie av.
Foresman Hugh A. 5429 Madison av.
Foresman Robert, 5429 Madison av.
Foresman R. B. Rev. 5429 Madison av.
Forgan James B. 460 Elm
Forline H. Hamilton Dr. 5528 Monroe av.
Forman Edward, 2206 Prairie av.
Forman George M. 3716 Lake av.
Forman John Mrs. 5110 Hibbard av.
Formhals O. G. Newberry hotel
Forrest Alfred E. 237 Oakwood boul.
Forrest George D. La Grange
Forrest Joseph K. C. 1043 Wilcox av.
Forrest Thomas L. 419 Center
Forrest T. Lawrence, jr. 419 Center
Forrest William G. 22 Pelham flats
Forrest William S. 3264 Groveland av.
Forrest William H. 3946 Lake av.
Forrester J. G., Dr. 486 Fullerton av.
Forrester J. H. Mrs. 352 Ontario
Forrester Rose Mrs. 3623 Ellis Park
Forrey Frank M. Evanston
Forsinger J. W. 301 Jackson Park Terrace
Forsman Susan T. Mrs. 45, 46th
Forstall Annie Mrs. 440 Dearborn av.
Forster Charles F 5420 Washington av.
Forsyth C. P. Miss, Berwyn
Forsyth George H. 14 Ritchie pl.
Forsyth George W. 1915 Michigan av.
Forsyth Henry L. 703 North Park av.
Forsyth H. H. 14 Ritchie pl.
Forsyth H. H. jr. 14 Ritchie pl.
Forsyth Jacob, 1915 Michigan av.
Forsyth James F. Berwyn
Forsyth James H. 525, 62d, Eng.
Forsyth John J. 1915 Michigan av.
Forsyth Joseph F. Glencoe
Forsyth J. E. 3763 Ellis av.
Forsyth J. G. Mrs. 287 Ontario
Forsyth J. P. Miss, Berwyn
Forsyth Mark J. Mrs. 660 W. Adams
Forsyth Oliver O. 1915 Michigan av.
Forsyth Robert, 307 N. Clark
Forsyth Robert A. jr. 437 Belden av.
Forsyth R. Clarke, Great Northern hotel
Forsyth William B. 4429 Ellis av.
Forsyth W. Holmes 14 Ritchie pl.
Forsyth W. K. 3113 Forest av.
Forsythe Lizzie Miss, Granada hotel
Forsythe Mary Mrs. 7536 Wright
Forsythe Mollie Miss, Granada hotel
Fort James N. 527 Belden av.
Fortier George G. Mrs. Austin
Fortin Alfred, 350, 41st
Fortin George, 408, 41st
Fortin Nelson, 4729 Langley av.
Fortner Elbert C. Dr. 146 DeKalb
Fortune John, 526 Jackson boul.
Fortune Josie Miss, 258 Park av.
Fortune Peter. 258 Park av.
Fortune W. J. 526 Jackson boul.
Forward H. W. 4247 Calumet av.
Foskett Andrew H. 1542 Fulton
Foskett Charles F. Palmer house
Foskett Charles M. 554 Jackson boul.
Foskett Warren E. 6317 Honore

Fosner W. H. LaGrange
Foss Agnes E. Mrs. 4656 Indiana av.
Foss Eliza Mrs. 475 W. Monroe
Foss Fred. D. 447 W. Monroe
Foss George E. 47 Gordon Terrace
Foss George Edmund, 47 GordonTerrace
Foss Geo. W. Mrs. 6340 Wright
Foss Horace B. 475 W. Monroe
Foss John P. 447 W. Monroe
Foster Adelbert M. Evanston
Foster Albert V. Evanston
Foster Alonzo D. Evanston
Foster A. H. Dr. 779 W. Monroe
Foster Benjamin F. Evanston
Foster Blackman N. 21 St. Johns pl.
Foster Charles F. 5420 Washington av.
Foster Charles H. 2428 Indiana av.
Foster Charles H. 3702 Lake av.
Foster Chauncy W. 4324 Prairie av.
Foster Frank S. 6359 Star av.
Foster Freling C. 880 Jackson boul.
Foster F. H. Dr. 73 Lake View av.
Foster F. L. 410 Ashland boul.
Foster George, 398 Belden av.
Foster George A. 2408 Prairie av.
Foster George B. 527 Lasalle av.
Foster George H. Evanston
Foster George P. 1403, 35th
Foster Hannah R. Mrs. 6359 Star av.
Foster Henry A. 526 N. Clark
Foster Henry C. 464 Farwell av.
Foster Henry L. Newberry hotel
Foster H. C. 3802 Lake av.
Foster Jacob T. 4500 Calumet av.
Foster John O. Rev. Evanston
Foster John W. 1176 Washington boul.
Foster John W. Mrs. 143 Oakwood boul.
Foster J. M. Dr. 6315 Yale, Englewood
Foster M. 4414 Langley av.
Foster M. M. Mrs. 2454 Indiana av.
Foster N. S. Mrs. 789 Fullerton av.
Foster O. C. 527 Lasalle av.
Foster R. N. Dr. 553 Jackson boul.
Foster Samuel B. 3923 Grand boul.
Foster Seaward, 158 Honore
Foster Thomas, 215, 48th
Foster Volney W. Evanston
Foster William, 444, 65th, Englewood
Foster William A. 3031 Prairie av.
Foster Wm. Elmore 4957 Prairie av.
Foster William H. 464 Farwell av.
Foster W. M. 2454 Indiana av.
Foulke Edward, 6351 Star av.
Foulke Mary S. Mrs. 4210 Berkeley av.
Foulke William H. 6351 Star av.
Fountain M. A. 19, 33d
Fouse Robert E. 320 N. State
Fouse Sarah Mrs. 320 N. State
Fouts Bertha Mrs. 291 Rush
Fowle Edwin Hunt Evanston
Fowler A. Lester, 1812 Belmont av.
Fowler Benjamin A.4812 St.Lawrence av.
Fowler Bernard, 4561 Lake av.
Fowler Blanche Miss, 4561 Lake av.
Fowler C. E. 87, 44th
Fowler C. E. 610, 78th, Eng.

Fowler C. H. Hotel Barry
Fowler Emeline B. Mrs. Evanston
Fowler Ernest S. Evanston
Fowler E. J. Chicago Beach hotel
Fowler E. W. 295 Irving av.
Fowler Frank T. 695 Washington boul.
Fowler F. A. 4950 Prairie av.
Fowler George J. 295 Irving av.
Fowler Harriet Miss, 4561 Lake av.
Fowler Henrietta Mrs. 6953 Eggleston av.
Fowler H. W. Chicago Beach hotel
Fowler James W. Dr. 201, 25th
Fowler John P. 25 The Yale
Fowler Joseph, 142 Ashland boul.
Fowler J. E. Oak Park
Fowler J. E. jr. Oak Park
Fowler Martha Miss, 4561 Lake av.
Fowler Mary Bland Mrs. 1812 Belmont av.
Fowler Nellie E. Mrs. 450, 45th
Fowler Samuel Stewart, 422 Huron
Fowler Samuel W. 295 Irving av.
Fowler William A. 6417 Sheridan av.
Fowler William F. Dr. 2346 Calumet av.
Fowler William S. Dr. 378 Dearborn av.
Fox Alpheus, 533 S. Normal Parkway
Fox Arthur A. 549 Chestnut, Englewood
Fox A. M. Mrs. 3019 Calumet av.
Fox Bonham M. 3339 Rhodes av.
Fox Charles, Hinsdale
Fox D. F. Rev. 1280 Wilcox av.
Fox Edward H. 3025 Calumet av.
Fox Eliza Mrs. Oak Park
Fox Frank, 448 Marshfield av.
Fox Frank W. Norwood Park
Fox Fred H. 1817 Barry av.
Fox Frederick, 4533 Greenwood av.
Fox F. C. Oak Park
Fox George M. Dr. LaGrange
Fox G. H. 3156 Prairie av.
Fox Harriet A. Miss, 1817 Barry av.
Fox Harriet Magee Dr. 3339 Rhodes av.
Fox Harry E. 5718 Wright
Fox Harry Mrs. 1817 Barry av.
Fox Heman, Hinsdale
Fox J. B. Mrs. 50 Wisconsin
Fox J. V. 50 Wisconsin
Fox Leo, 3355 South Park av.
Fox Orvin L. 124, 47th
Fox Philo N. Mrs. Evanston
Fox Thomas E. 50 Wisconsin
Fox Will A. 533 S. Normal Parkway
Fox William F. 5736 Rosalie ct.
Fox William O. Hinsdale
Fox W. S. 1361 Jackson boul.
Foy Kate M. Miss, 649 W. Harrison
Foy W. E. Great Northern hotel
Fraenkel Theo. O. 2124 Michigan av.
Fraeser Anna E. Miss, 2714 Michigan av.
Frailey M. Mrs. 35, 29th
Frailey William P. 413 Warren av.
Frake James, 625 Fulton
Fraley James B. 4534 Lake av.
Frame Lulu Miss, 3943 Langley av.
Frame Rueben Mrs. 2453 Michigan av.
Framhein Louis W. 325, 24th
France R. E. Mrs. Evanston

Franche Darius C. Hyde Park hotel
Franchere Gabriel, 406 Ashland boul.
Franchere O. J. 222 Loomis
Franchere Tilly Miss, 406 Ashland boul.
Francis Charles R. 1149 W. Adams
Francis Edward, Austin
Francis Edward C. 4510 St. Lawrence av.
Francis Elizabeth G. Mrs. 682 Washington boul.
Francis Frances R. Mrs. 1149 W. Adams
Francis George F. 17 Kemper pl.
Francis George H. 165, 36th
Francis James L. 7757 Sherman
Francis J. R. 40 Loomis
Francis William jr. 183 S. Hoyne av.
Frank A. I. 25 Wisconsin
Frank Daniel, 3129 Vernon av.
Frank David, 3129 Vernon av.
Frank David, 3728 Forest av.
Frank D. L. 3411 Prairie av.
Frank Edwin B. 3058 Calumet av.
Frank Emanuel J. 2321 Michigan av.
Frank Emil, 720 North Park av.
Frank E. Miss, 3624 Calumet av.
Frank Fred G. 3262 Groveland av.
Frank George, 74 Lincoln av.
Frank Henry L. 1608 Prairie av.
Frank Joseph, 2240 Calumet av.
Frank Joseph Mrs. 2321 Michigan av.
        Sum, res. Waukesha, Wis.
Frank Joseph H. 233 Hampden ct.
Frank Jules, 3106 Groveland av.
Frank J. Dr. 17 Lincoln av.
Frank J. G. 735 Warren av.
Frank Louis, 3614 Prairie av.
Frank Louis E. 3219 Michigan av.
Frank L. Mrs. 2923 Wabash av.
Frank Martin, 3844 Lake av.
Frank Max, 3121 South Park av.
Frank Morris, 3129 Vernon av.
Frank P. Mrs. 4154 Berkeley av.
Frank Sigmond, 3411 Prairie av.
Frank S. Mrs. 369 S. Paulina
Frank S. G. 447 Marshfield av.
Frank William B. 3630 Calumet av.
Frakelyn L. A. Mrs. 55 Astor
Frankenthal C. E. 3229 Groveland av.
Frankenthal Emanuel, 3236 Michigan av.
Frankenthal Lester Dr. 3236 Michigan av.
Frankenthal Oscar E. 3236 Michigan av.
Frankfurter Henry, 347 Kenmore av.
Frankland A. E. 263 Bowen av.
Franklin Charles P. 4516 Ellis av.
Franklin Edgar, 3663 Wabash av.
Franklin Henry B. 439 Dearborn av.
Franklin L. Franklin Park
Franklin Percy R. Mrs. 4516 Ellis av.
Franklin S. 433 Marshfield av.
Franklin Trueman, 3438 Indiana av.
Franks H. J. 667 W. Monroe
Franks Jacob, 3549 Prairie av.
Frantz E. C. 529, 60th, Eng.
Franz Hugo, 1649 Barry av.
Franzen M. 39 Lincoln pl.
Frary O. D. 7237 Harvard
Frasch M. Miss, 65 Lincoln av.

Fraser D. R. 599, 41st
Fraser Flora Mrs. 3226 Groveland av.
Fraser James, 505 W. Congress
Fraser Lizzie Miss, 3157 Forest av.
Fraser May C. Miss, 3157 Forest av.
Fraser Norman D. 1237 Washington boul.
Fraser S. M. Mrs. 538 Sunnyside av.
Frasher Edward S. 4552 Oakenwald av.
Frasher John E. L. 4919 Lake av.
Frasher John S. 4919 Lake av.
Frawley M. J. Mrs. 260 S. Campbell av.
Frazer Hamilton, 2930 Groveland av.
Frazer Mary C. Mrs. 3210 Michigan av.
Frazer S. L. 3410 Vernon av.
Frazier Frank P. Evanston
Frazier George E. Morgan Park
Frazier Horace Boyd, Austin
Frear Alexander E. 191 Oakwood boul.
Frear A. Edward, 191 Oakwood boul.
Frederick Frank S. 3019 Calumet av.
Frederick Gilbert Rev. 418, 61st, Eng.
Fredericks Frank, Riverside
Fredericks Frank jr. Riverside
Frederickson E. Mrs. 5215 Washington av.
Frederickson W. J. 5215 Washington av.
Fredrich Albert, 493 Webster av.
Free John H. 306 West ct
Freedman J. Mrs. 2951 Indiana av.
Freehling M. 514 Webster av.
Freehling Solomon, 3604 Prairie av.
Freeman Andrew W. Dr. 6752 Union av.
Freeman Anthony, 678 Fullerton av.
Freeman Arthur B. Dr. 576 Washington boul.
Freeman A. I. The Ontario
Freeman A. W. Mrs. 9 Aldine sq.
Freeman Benjamin, 3560 Vincennes av.
Freeman Charles E. Evanston
Freeman Chester H. 1069 Winona
Freeman C. Antoinette Miss, Evanston
Freeman Clarence B. Dr. Evanston
Freeman Daniel 6641 Honore
Freeman D. B. Dr. 4000 Drexel boul.
Freeman Edgar K. Evanston
Freeman Emma B. Miss, 1069 Winona
Freeman Henry A. Dr. Evanston
Freeman Henry V. 5760 Woodlawn av.
Freeman Isaac, 3560 Vincennes av.
Freeman I. A., Dr. 4438 Berkeley av.
Freeman James C. 1466 Edgecomb ct.
Freeman John, Evanston
Freeman J. L. Oak Park
Freeman Lemuel H. 9 Aldine sq.
Freeman Libbie Miss, 235 Michigan av.
Freeman L. M. Miss, 873 Fulton
Freeman Marie C. Mrs. 231 Hampden ct.
Freeman Mary Miss, 235 Michigan av.
Freeman Mary L. Miss, Evanston
Freeman M. M. 3838 Wabash av.
Freeman Samuel, 3240 Groveland av.
Freeman S. A. 428 Oak
Freeman Theodore, 1831 Barry av.
Freeman Virginia Miss, 13 Scott
Freeman William, 3560 Vincennes av.
Freeman William H. Hinsdale

Freeman Windsor P. Austin
Freer L. C. P. Mrs. 247 Michigan av.
Freet L. H. LaGrange
Freer Natham M. Oak Park
Freer Otto T., M.D. 288 Huron
Frees Benjamin M. Hotel Windermere
Freiberg Frederick, 1217 Michigan av.
Freiberg Julius, 1217 Michigan av.
Freiberger Leopold, 3225 Vernon av.
Freise Emil, 1698 Wellington
French A. J. Miss, 160 Oakwood boul.
French Byron W. 5124 Jefferson av.
French Charles, 2125 Michigan av.
French Charles B. 5124 Jefferson av.
French Charles G. 5238 Woodlawn av.
French Charles W. 5735 Washington av.
French C. J. Dr. The Arizona
French C. O. Chicago Beach hotel
French Edgar, 626 Washington boul.
French Emma Miss, 31 Ashland boul.
French Frederick, 6517 Wharton av.
French Frederick E. Evanston
French Garrie S. 7443 Bond av.
French George G. Lake Forest
French George H. 5422 Cornell av.
French George R. 3866 Lake av.
French George T. 6610 Yale
French G. M. Tracy
French Harriet Mrs. 505 Jackson boul.
French Henry C. 4821 Madison av.
French Henry W. 708 Washington boul.
French H. D. 644 W. Monroe
French John W. Lagrange
French L. M. 4162 Lake av.
French Mary Miss, 149 Ashland boul.
French Orvis, Evanston
French O. Clinton, Evanston
French Rensellaer W. Rev. 301 Winchester av.
French Samuel, M.D. 64. 23d
French Samuel A. 7443 Bond av.
French S. B. 64 Warren av.
French S. T. Evanston
French T. Allen, 1557 Michigan av.
French Walter, 336, 61st, Englewood
French Will A. 4720 Prairie av.
French William B. 4720 Prairie av.
French William H. 149 Ashland boul.
French William L. 102 N. Clark
French W. Harrison, 5435 Washington av.
French W. M. R. Longwood
Frenke F. L. 1516 Wolfram
Frenz E. Miss, 65 E. Pearson
Frenz P. Miss, 65 E. Pearson
Freschl William, 3636 Calumet av.
Fretts George W. 677, 48th (H.P.)
Fretts Levi A. 3743 Vincennes av.
Freudenthal Joseph, 3403 Forest av.
Freudenthal Sam, 835 W. Congress
Freund Abraham L., M. D. 3201 Indiana av.
Freund Charles, 460 N. Wells
Freund E. Prof. Hotel Barry
Freund Gustavus, 3221 Vernon av.
Freund Herman, 460 N. Wells
Freund Otto E. 1225 Morse av.

Freund William, 460 N. Wells
Freund William jr. 107 Sigel
Freymuth William C. River Forest
Freyesleben Ferdinand Dr. 1637 Michigan av.
Freytag Moritz, 700 N. Wells
Frick John G. 428 Oak
Fricke G. H. Dr. Park Ridge
Fricke William G. Oak Park
Fried Leopold, 3404 Indiana av.
Friedlander Edward D. 934 S. Central Park av.
Friedlander G. 355 Ashland boul.
Friedlander James B. 3313 South Park av.
Friedlander Leon, 3323 Vernon av.
Friedlander Samuel, 546 Cleveland av.
Friedley F. B. Judge, 3611 Lake av.
Friedman Abraham B. 3215 Rhodes av.
Friedman E. B. 941 W. Monroe
Friedman H. C. 3602 Prairie av.
Friedman Isaac K. 3602 Prairie
Friedman Jacob, 40 St. James pl.
Friedman Jennie Miss, 633 Washington boul.
Friedman Joseph, 3602 Prairie av.
Friedman Joseph N. 3215 Rhodes av.
Friedman J. H. Mrs. 204 Vernon av.
Friedman Leopold 633 Washington boul.
Friedman Louis, 3601 Indiana av.
Friedman L. J. 3414 South Park av.
Friedman Maurice, 633 Washington boul.
Friedman Monroe J. 155, 33d
Friedman Morris, 622 Washington boul.
Friedman Nathan, 432 Englewood av.
Friedman Nathan, 3215 Rhodes av.
Friedman Oscar J. 3602 Prairie av.
Friedman Pauline Miss, 3601 Indiana av.
Friedman Racie Miss, 4120 Ellis av.
Friedman William, 633 Washington boul.
Friedman William, 3601 Indiana av.
Friemann John, 4033 Southport av.
Friend Alexander, 55 Park av.
Friend Charles, 4324 Calumet av.
Friend Edward, 2623 Calumet av.
Friend Emanuel Dr. 55 Park av.
Friend N. Mrs. 151, 33d
Friend Samuel, 2948 Groveland av.
Friend William Mrs. 2623 Calumet av.
Friese Anna C. Mrs. 1501 Wrightwood av.
Frillman Fritz, 276 Fremont
Frink Charles, 4152 Lake av.
Frink Charles S. Mrs. 214, 31st
Frink Dorothy Miss, 4811 Kimbark av.
Frink George, Austin
Frink George S. 2417 Michigan av.
Frink Henry F. Austin
    Sum. res. Lake Geneva
Frink William H. 6450 Stewart av.
Frisbee P. W. Mrs. 19 Scott
Frisbie Chauncy O. 939 Jackson av.
Frisbie Evelyn Miss, 2952 Prairie av.
Frisbie R. M. Mrs. 763 N. Clark
Fritsch Alphonse, 487 Belden av.
Frische Christopher, 543 Larrabee
Frische Henry W. 543 Larrabee
Fritts D. H. 233 Park av.

Fritts G. B. 106 Park av.
Fritts L. C. Dr. 106 Park av.
Fritze F. A. 1738 York pl.
Fritze George, 513 Jackson boul.
Fritze S. F. 356 Belden av.
Frizelle C. E. 681 Sedgwick
Frobenius E. 494 Fullerton av.
Frommann C. Mrs. 49 Sidney ct.
Frommann Emil H. 49 Sidney ct.
Frosch George W. 6516 Lafayette av.
Frost Abel H. Ridgeland
Frost Albert E. 4835 Langley av.
Frost Charles S. 3330 Indiana av.
Frost David jr. 2647 N. Robey
Frost Edward Inglis, Virginia hotel
Frost Frank H. 2430 Commercial (L.V.)
Frost Frank S. 880 Washington boul.
Frost Horace C. 2604 Indiana av.
Frost L. W. Mrs. 4619 Lake av.
Frost Mahlon S. Virginia hotel
Frost R. Mrs. 224 Marshfield av.
Frost R. Chester, 600, 60th (H.P.)
Frost Walter A. 3400 South Park av.
Frost W. E. 3000 Prairie av.
Frost W. E. 3413 Vernon av.
Frost Ziney J. Austin
Frost Z. J. jr. Austin
Frothingham H. H. Dr. 5200 East End av.
Frothingham James Rev. 527 Kenwood
  Terrace
Frothingham M. F. Miss, 527 Kenwood
  Terrace
Fruer Richard P. 205 Fremont
Fruth A. C. Dr. 170 Oakwood boul.
Fruth D. O. Dr. 3716 Lake av.
Fry George C. 3638 Lake av.
Fry Henry T. 2383 N. Halsted
Fry I. H. 3111 Groveland av.
Fry Thomas E. 297 Belden av.
Frye George V. 218 Park av.
Fuarey Mary W. Mrs. 576A Washington
  boul.
Fuchs Gustav, 307 West ct.
Fuchs G. Rev. 623 Maple, Englewood
Fucik Frank, 813 Sawyer av.
Fucik John, 801 Sawyer av.
Fuess Lewis, 143 Oakwood boul.
Fuhrmann F. Dr. 263 Center
Fulghum William, 367 Bowen av.
Fullem Edward, 1919 Indiana av.
Fullenwider James A. 678 W. Adams
Fullenwider Mary Mrs. 678 W. Adams
Fuller Allon Miss, 4353 Drevel boul.
Fuller Alonzo M. 4832 Ellis av.
Fuller Arthur G. 605 The Plaza
Fuller A. C. Miss, 3 Washington pl.
Fuller Charles G. Dr. Evanston
Fuller Charles H. 370 Warren av.
Fuller Charles R. 7010 Webster av. Eng.
Fuller C. C. 3605 Lake av.
Fuller Egbert C. 432 Dearborn av.
Fuller Frank Hoyt, 4840 Ellis av.
Fuller Frank L. 319 Washington boul.
Fuller Frank R. 20 Astor
Fuller Frederick B. 2825 Michigan av.
Fuller George A. 4353 Drexel boul.

Fuller George W. Mrs. 2831 Prairie av.
    Sum. res. Oconomowoc, Wis.
Fuller Grace Miss, Glencoe
Fuller Grace Beatrice Miss, 4353 Drexel
  boul.
Fuller G. Edward, Hotel Groveland
Fuller Henry Mrs. 2023 Indiana av.
Fuller Henry B. 2831 Prairie av.
Fuller Henry C. 411 Jackson boul.
Fuller Henry M. 325 Dearborn av.
Fuller H. H. 3139 Michigan av.
Fuller John Y. Mrs. 3025 Prairie av.
Fuller Judson M. Oak Park
Fuller J. Ensign, Grand Pacific
Fuller Kate Mrs. 3701 Vincennes av.
Fuller LeRoy W. 2913 Michigan av.
Fuller L. Hulbert Dr. 5600 Monroe av.
Fuller Mary Miss, 2831 Prairie av.
Fuller Melville W. Judge, Washington
  D. C.
Fuller Oliver F. 325 Dearborn av.
    Sum. res. Peekskill, N. Y.
Fuller Percival S. 584 Dearborn av.
Fuller S. R. Hotel Windermere
Fuller William A. 2913 Michigan av.
Fuller W. Warner, 346 Sunnyside av.
Fullerton Charles W. 628 Dearborn av.
Fullerton Charles W. Highland Park
Fullerton J. E. Mrs. 628 Dearborn av.
Fulton Arthur W. 1176 Washington boul.
Fulton A. W. 214, 33d
Fulton Charles E. 502 Belden av.
Fulton Dell Miss, 4524 Lake av.
Fulton Henry A. Hinsdale
Fulton Henry D. 332, 62d, Eng.
Fulton Hugh H. Ridgeland
Fulton James T. 4450 Sidney av.
Fulton Jefferson L. 342 Ashland boul.
Fulton John, 376 Washington boul.
Fulton John A. 4146 Berkeley av.
Fulton Joseph, 5225 Kimbark av.
Fulton J. M. Rev. 35 Bittersweet pl.
Fulton Lester B. 342 Ashland boul.
Fulton T. M. 5344 Jefferson av.
Fulton William A. 4356 Champlain av.
Funck Pierre, 1471 Edgecomb ct.
Funk C. A. Chicago Beach hotel
Funk E. A. Mrs. 148 Dearborn av.
Funk F. A. Mrs. 1533 Fulton
Funke Edward, Austin
Funkhouser M. L. C. 358 Oakwood boul.
Furbeck George W. Oak Park
Furbeck Warren F. Oak Park
Furber Frank I. 41, 46th
Furber Henry J. 235 Michigan av.
Furber Henry J. jr. 235 Michigan av.
Furber William E. 235 Michigan av.
Furey C. L. Granada hotel
Furlong John, Evanston
Furlong John, Ridgeland
Furlong John D. 3024 Lake Park av.
Furlong Walter H. 6942 Yale
Furman James H. Wilmette
Furman Jeanie Miss, Wilmette
Furman Nettie Miss, Wilmette
Furmer Catherine Mrs. 1463 Dakin

Furness Elizabeth M. Miss, 417 Orchard
Furness Grace E. Miss, 417 Orchard
Furness James T. 417 Orchard
Furness Margaret Miss, 417 Orchard
Furness William Eliot 417 Orchard
Furniss Frank B., 310 Park av.
Furst Charles J. 3352 Calumet av.
Furst Conrad, 84 Astor
Furst Edward A. 1818 Frederick
Furst George, 37 Centre av.
Furst Henry, 505 Ashland boul.
Furst Henry jr. 505 Ashland boul.
Furst William C. 428½ LaSalle av.
Furth Ella Miss, 3805 Michigan av.
Furth Julius, 3805 Michigan av.
Furthmann Edmund, 575 Orchard
Fushiki Hideh, 1423 Michigan av.
Futterer Gustav Dr. 716 Fullerton av.
Fyfe George, 1176 Washington boul.
Fyfe Richard Dr. 683 Washington boul.
Fyffe Colin C. H. 604 Division
Fyffe Edith A. H. Dr. 604 Division
Fyffe John L. Evanston
Fyffe William J. 604 Division

GABRIEL F. A. 707 W. Monroe
Gadsden E. H. Mrs. 7708 Stewart av.
Gadsden James S. 949 W. Harrison
Gaensslen M. 20 Lane pl.
Gaensslen Walter, 20 Lane pl.
Gafford S. B. 13 Aldine sq.
Gaffrey James H. 7805 Winneconna av.
Gage Albert S. The Wellington
Gage August N. Wilmette
Gage E. M. 4201 Lake av.
Gage Frank J. Lakeside
Gage Frank N. 4028 Ellis av.
              Sum. res. Gray's Lake
Gage Henry H. Evanston
Gage Henry H. Wilmette
Gage John V. Riverside
Gage Lyman J. 470 N. State
Gage Mary T. Mrs. Morgan Park
Gage M. Mrs. Hotel Metropole
Gage Seth, 325 Michigan av.
Gagnon Edith Miss, 6409 Howard
Gagnon Eva Miss, 6409 Howard
Gahan Thomas, 4914 Michigan av.
Gail George F. 427 Huron
Gaines O. F. 213 S. Hoyne av.
Gaither Otho S. 4455 Champlain av.
Galbraith Stewart, 412 Winthrop av.
Galbraith T. B. 6648 Harvard
Gale Edward R. 4267 Grand av.
Gale E. O. Oak Park
Gale E. Vincent, Oak Park
Gale Fred, 426 Warren av.
Gale Fred M. 426 Warren av.
Gale Lucia Miss, 259 Dearborn av.
Gale Mary E. Miss, 6 Langley pl.
Gale Thomas H. Oak Park
Gale Walter H. Oak Park
Gale Willis H. 3352 Rhodes av.
Galitzki Leo Dr. 21 Best av.
Gall Barbara Mrs. 930 Catalpha
Gall Charles H. 930 Catalpha

Gall George E. 930 Catalpha
Gall John F. Mrs. 930 Catalpha
Gallagher Annie Miss, 3165 Beacon
Gallagher Catharine Mrs. 385 Oak
Gallagher Daniel J. The Ashland
Gallagher Frank H. 3165 Beacon
Gallagher Frank J. 3165 Beacon
Gallagher Jane B. Mrs. 3014 Michigan av.
Gallagher John C. The Ashland
Gallagher M. Mrs. 227 Park av.
Gallagher M. F. 5649 Washington av.
Gallagher William, 227 Park av.
Gallaher Kate Miss, 844 Sherwin av.
Gallauner Edmund L. 4761 38th
Gallaway William C. 152 Dearborn av.
Gallaway William T. 158 Dearborn av.
Gallear David O. 775 Larrabee
Gallery D. J. 260 Lasalle av.
Gallery D. V. 260 Lasalle av.
Gallery J. J. 260 Lasalle av.
Gallion C. H. Hotel Barry
Galloway Albert, 2629 Commercial (L.V.)
Galloway A. J. 3652 Lake av.
Galloway James B. 3652 Lake av.
Gallup Agnes Miss, 456 Elm
Gallup Benjamin E. 1710 Indiana av.
Gallup David L. 456 Elm
Gallup Edward B. 396 S. Paulina
Gallup Howard H. 1718 Indiana av.
Gallup Lila Miss, 456 Elm
Gallup O. D. S. Park Ridge
Gallup Walter L. Evanston
Galoglee Celia Miss, 235 Michigan
Galpin Homer K. 729 W. Monroe
Galpin H. B. 729 W. Monroe
Galt A. T. 550 Dearborn av.
Galvin Carroll D. 5728 Madison av.
Galvin Edward I. 5728 Madison av.
Galvin James, 4322 Indiana av.
Gamble Edwin H. Evanston
Gamble M. E. Mrs. 204 Winchester av.
Gamble Samuel L. Rev. Riverside
Gamble William C. 204 Winchester av.
Gamer Charles L. 1065 N. Clark
Gamer George W. 1065 N. Clark
Gamet A. E. 525 Racine av.
Gamet Clayton E. 525 Racine av.
Gamet Daniel, 527 Racine av.
Gamet E. J. Mrs. 1195 Rokeby
Gane T. F. 425 Lasalle av.
Gann David B. 4617 Vincennes av.
Gannon Anthony T. 187, 37th
Gannon Henry, 187, 37th
Gannon M. V. 5415 Cottage Grove av.
Gannon R. C. 52 Throop
Gannon Thomas Mrs. 341 W. Monroe
Gannon T. Mrs. 3200 Michigan av.
Gans Leopold, 944 Jackson boul.
Gans Samuel, 961 Jackson boul.
Ganse F. W. 249 Belden av.
Ganse H. D. Mrs. 251 Belden av.
Ganse T. DeWitt, 140, 38th
Ganser G. A. 435 Washington boul.
Ganson James T. 1011 Jackson boul.
Ganson John, 1522 W. Monroe
Gant Charles H. Dr. 302 Michigan av.

Gant I. W. Morgan Park
Garceau A. E. Dr. 5207 Madison av.
Garcelon Agnes Miss, Oak Park
Garcelon C. A. 3730 Forest av.
Garcelon D. D. Oak Park
Garcelon Frances Miss, 5729 Washington av.
Gardener Daniel B. Evanston
      Winter res. Jacksonville, Fla.
Gardin John E. Morton Park
Gardiner E. J., M. D. 85 Astor
Gardiner E. M. 753 W. Monroe
Gardiner Frances Hale Mrs. 2200 Prairie av.
Gardiner Frank H., M.D. Forest av. ne. cor 33d
Gardiner John D. Mrs. 2019 Michigan av
Gardner Addison L. 689 W. Monroe
Gardner Alex. 3618 Ellis av.
Gardner A. S. Mrs. Austin
Gardner Burt M. Evanston
Gardner Charles A. LaGrange
Gardner Edgar A. 4120 Berkeley av.
Gardner Ferry A. 361 41st (H. P.)
Gardner Franc, 284 Belden av.
Gardner Frank G. Hotel Normandie
Gardner Fred W. Hotel Normandie
Gardner George Cadogan, 3724 Langley av.
Gardner George C. Hinsdale
Gardner Harry, 457 Bowen av.   •
Gardner Henry A. Hinsdale
Gardner Ida Mrs. 3011 Vernon av.
Gardner James P. 4803 Greenwood av.
Gardner Peter G. LaGrange
Gardner Richard M. 3724 Langley av.
Gardner S. P. Mrs. Hinsdale
Gardner William, 1543 W. Monroe
Gardner William A. 2574 Commercial (L. V.)
Gardner W. H. Granada hotel
Gareau Cesaire, 875 W. Harrison
Garey Willis L. 17 Gordon Terrace
Garibaldi John G. 26 Astor
Garland Austin M. 7636 Union av.
Garland D. F. 2411 Prairie av.
Garland Hamlin, 474 Elm
Garland Helen B. Mrs. Evanston
Garland Maria J. Mrs. Evanston
Garland M. A. Mrs. 2119 Calumet av.
Garland M. H. Dr. 332 Maple, Eng.
Garm John T. 4500 Vincennes av.
Garman A. B. Sherman house
Garner A. M. Mrs. 201 Park av.
Garner I. G. 379 Dearborn av.
Garner . P. Austin
Garner J. H. 716 Pullman bldg.
Garnett Eugene, 3422 Vernon av.
Garnett Eugene, 3604 Grand boul.
Garnett Gwynn Judge, 3604 Grand boul.
Garnett John L. 3422 Vernon av.
Garnett William, 3422 Vernon av.
Garnett William jr. 4215 Champlain av.
Gamsey Charles A. P. Dr. Evanston
Garnsey Daniel G. 3441 Rhodes av.
Garnsey George O. 316 Oakwood boul.

Garrabrandt L. C. Great Northern hotel
Garrabrant Robert C. 5514 Monroe av.
Garraghan Gilbert J. 3424 Prairie av.
Garratt Lyman D. Irving Park
Garretson George, LaGrange
Garretson J. C. Mrs. 31 Roslyn pl.
Garrett Carlton M. 7216 Harvard
Garrett M. A. 7216 Harvard
Garrett T. M. 301 Ontario
Garrett William H. 544 Chestnut, Eng.
Garrigue Rudolph H. 263' 53d (H. P.)
Garrison Marie Harrold Mrs. 3625 Vincennes av.
Garrison Marshall, Evanston
Garrity Blanche de Chantell Miss, 409 Dearborn av.
Garrity Grace Miss, 409 Dearborn av.
Garrity Joseph Dr. 409 Dearborn av.
Garrity Patrick L. 409 Dearborn av.
Garrity Sylvia Miss, 4008 Drexel boul.
Garrott E. Dr. 751 Washington boul.
Garson Joseph M. Lexington hotel
Garstin B. N. 42, 39th
Garth Robert L. 4732 Evans av.
Garthe Henry, 418 Superior
Garthe Sophie Mrs. 418 Superior
Gartlan Helen Miss, 3431 Wabash av.
Gartside J. M. 4329 Drexel boul.
Gartside W. C. 2946 Groveland av.
Gartz Adolph F. 2641 Prairie av.
Garvey John W. 60 Lytle
Garwood Victor, 921 Pullman bldg.
Garwood Wm. C. Evanston
Gary Elbert H. Wheaton
Gary Fannie E. Miss, 369 Ontario
Gary Geo. A. 7523 Stewart av.
Gary Geo. L. Oak Park
Gary John W. 2107 Indiana av.
Gary Joseph E. Judge, 369 Ontario
Gasaway Charles D. 5918 Honore
Gascoigne J. B. Tracy
Gascoigne John, 610, 67th, Eng.
Gaspard Jules M. 5600 Monroe av.
Gaspard Philip H. Newberry hotel
Gasparo Jane Mrs. Austin
Gassette Norman T. Mrs. 90, 21st
Gassette Wirt K. 52 Walton pl.
Gaston J. A. Leland hotel
Gate W. T. 375 S. Paulina
Gately John, 278 S. Oakley av.
Gately Lizzie Miss, 40 Throop
Gately William, 5931 Dickey
Gates Albert J. 4361 Maple av.
Gates A. E. Chicago Beach hotel
Gates A. H. 173 Rush
Gates Caleb F. Wilmette
Gates Charles Horatio Mrs. 24 Walton pl.
Gates Charles M. 3434 Rhodes av.
Gates C. G. 2440 Michigan av.
Gates C. H. 80 Lincoln av.
Gates Eliza L. Mrs. Oak Park
Gates George, 337 Ohio
Gates Henry B. Wilmette
Gates James L. 412 N. Normal Parkway
      Sum. res. East Gloucester, Mass.
Gates John W. 2440 Michigan av.

Gates J. H. 210, 51st (H.P.)
Gates May E. Miss, 2430 Commercial (L. V.)
Gates P. W. Chicago Beach hotel
Gates Ralph, 4457 Ellis av.
Gates Ryerson D. Ridgeland
Gates Walter S. Evanston
Gates William D. Hinsdale
Gates William S., M.D. 1279 Wolcott
Gates William W. Evanston
Gates W. B. Chicago Beach hotel
Gathmann Louis, 26 Lincoln av.
Gatter Christian F. Evanston
Gattie John, 177 N. State
Gatzert August, 3422 Prairie av.
Gatzert Joseph L. 3628 Grand boul.
Gatzert N. Mrs. 2792 Forest av.
Gauer A. H. 347 Rush
Gauer J. A. Mrs. 16 Cedar
Gauer N. J. 347 Rush
Gauger John A. 4241 Drexel boul.
Gauler John, Winnetka
Gault George M. 751 Jackson av.
Gault Thomas B. 751 Jackson av.
Gault T. H. 719 W. Congress
Gaulter Frank J. 6914 Oglesby av.
Gaulter Fred E. 6914 Oglesby av.
Gaulter Mary Mrs. 6914 Oglesby av.
Gavitt Halsey C. Rev. Evanston
Gay Harry, 457 Bowen av.
Gay Henry Lord, 487 Dearborn av.
Gay Joseph R. 9 Scott
Gay O. C. 145 Oakwood boul.
Gaylord Alvin P. 3515 Calumet av.
Gaylord Ann A. Mrs. 3018 Prairie av.
Gaylord Edward L. 3018 Prairie av.
Gaylord Fred, Grand Pacific hotel
Gaylord Henry Mrs. 4942 Ellis av.
Gaylord Mary A. Mrs. 4337 Grand boul.
Gaylord Robert, 3018 Prairie av.
Gaylord Willard S. 1638 Michigan av.
Gaylord Willis S. 1638 Michigan av.
Gaynor James A. 375 Warren av.
Gaynor John, 4816 Grand boul.
Gaynor P. C. 42, 39th
Geary Jarrett C. Dr. 975 Washington boul.
Geary John R. 3010 South Park av.
Geary Thomas F. 3010 South Park av.
Geary William T. 3010 South Park av.
Gebhard Julius, 19 Bradley pl. (L.V.)
Gebhart C. C. 145 Oakwood boul.
Gee Charles Mrs. 241 Lasalle av.
Geer D. S. The Arizona
Geer Ira J. 240 Goethe
Geeting O. F. 299 Lasalle av.
Gegenheimer B. Mrs. 90 Clifton av.
Gehr Arthur C. 392 N. State
Gehr Phebe B. Mrs. 392 N. State
Gehr S. Whipple, 392 N. State
Gehrig Joseph W. 823 Washington boul.
Gehrke Henry F. Austin
Gehrmann Adolph A., M.D. 4420 Langley av.
Gehrmann Theodore A. 4420 Langley av.
Geiger Henry Dr. 591 N. Clark

Geist George F. 4422 Champlain av.
Geist John W. 3746 Wabash av.
Gelner B. C. 2125 Wabash av.
Gelert Johannes, 333 Oak
Gellatly Francis Mrs. Evanston
Geltmacher J. T. 3200 Rhodes av.
Genius Arthur E. Dr. 3000 Michigan av.
Genius Ethel L. Miss, 3000 Michigan av.
Genius Richard M. Dr. 3000 Michigan av.
Gentles H. W. Dr. 157, 53d (H.P.)
Gentry William D., M.D. 776 Touhy av.
George Amos B. 5815 Madison av.
George Augustus C. Mrs. Evanston
George E. J. Dr. 4319 Lake av.
George Isabella M. Mrs. 1100 Washington boul.
George John Kerr, 234 Hampden ct.
George John P. LaGrange
George Marshall W. 4516 Ellis av.
George Milo, 256 Ontario
George Peter, 1823 Aldine av.
George P. W. 356 Chestnut, Englewood
George William E. 621 Lasalle av.
George W. O. 621 Lasalle av.
Geraghty J. L. 276 Park av.
Geraldine Dion, The Tudor
Geraty J. T. 307, 54th (H.P.)
Gerber Emil, 348 Belden av.
Geringer John, 501 Winchester av.
Germain Charles C. Chicago Beach hotel
German W. H., M.D. Morgan Park
Germer E. Mrs. 11 Burton pl.
Gerold Charles A. 1845 Oakdale av.
Gerould F. W. 15 Lane pl.
Gerow Floyd P. 3166 Lake Park av.
Gerrett David B. Clifton house
Gerrish Lory G. 7819 Sherman
Gerry J. L. Hotel Imperial
Gerstenberg Erich, 1773 Deming ct.
Gerstenberg H. Mrs. 864 Larrabee
Gerstetter John C. 822 Winthrop av.
Gerstetter John Mrs. 822 Winthrop av.
Gerten Nicholas, 463 Cleveland av.
Gertenrich John, 211 Belden av.
Gerts George E. Oak Park
Gerts Walter S. Oak Park
Gerwig Frank L. 455 W. Congress
Getchell Edwin F. 2628 Prairie av.
Getchell George W. 3429 Indiana av.
Gettier Nellie Mrs. Riverside
Getty W. B. 1503 George
Getz George F. Lakota hotel
Getz Harry W. 5803 Madison av.
Geudtner Charles P. 1026 Evanston av.
Geudtner Emil H. 372 Webster av.
Geudtner Francis, 1026 Evanston av.
Gfroerer George M., M.D. 439 W. Taylor
Gibbons E. J. 18 Bellevue pl.
Gibbons John Judge, 373, 40th
Gibbons John W. 1760 Frederick
Gibbs C. H. Mrs. Lexington hotel
Gibbs Fletcher B. Oak Park
Gibbs F. C. Hotel Metropole
Gibbs F. E. 191 Irving av.
Gibbs George A. 2014 Indiana av.
Gibbs George I. 2902 Groveland av.

Gibbs H. M. Mrs. Hinsdale
Gibbs James S. 400 Superior
Gibbs May Mrs. 1250 Michigan av.
Gibbs Ora S. Miss, 206 Ashland boul.
Gibbs Orlando F. Evanston
Gibbs Oscar Dr. 1043 W. Adams
Gibbs Platt P. 4820 Kimbark av.
Gibbs T. N. Granada hotel
Gibbs Warren, 2237 Prairie av.
Gibbs William B. Auditorium
Gibson Belle Miss, 745 Washington boul.
Gibson C. H. 722 Pullman bldg.
Gibson Emmet C. 4408 Oakenwald av.
Gibson Gertrude Miss,4339 Oakenwaldav.
Gibson Guy G. 4076 Lake av.
Gibson I. P. Mrs. 4076 Lake av.
Gibson J. H. 3520 Forest av.
Gibson Laura Mrs. 34 Walton pl.
Gibson Milroy H. 3227 South Park av.
Gibson M. Mrs. 5324 Washington av.
Gibson Thomas, 4528 Prairie av.
Gibson William, 2741 N. Robey
Gibson William H. 732 W. Adams
Gibson W. D. Mrs. 745 Washington boul.
Gieldings Frank C. Hyde Park hotel
Giddings E. E. Oak Park
Giest Frederick, 4536 Prairie av.
Giffin William, 7710 Emerald av.
Gifford Archer, Evanston
Gifford C. E. 4637 Drexel boul.
Gifford C. E. jr. 5035 Lake av.
Gifford Electa Miss, 2400 Indiana av.
Gifford Frank B. The Tudor
Gifford Frederic D. 715 Farwell av.
Gifford Herbert W. 3033 Michigan av.
Gifford Ira L. 1518 Dakin
Gifford I. Cushman, 4637 Drexel boul.
Gifford Robert L. 3733 Ellis av.
Gifford William, Highland Park
Gifford William L. Maywood
Gilbert Abby Mrs. 165 S. Robey
Gilbert Albert M. 328 Dearborn av.
Gilbert Almira M. Mrs. 349 N. State
Gilbert Ashley L. Morton Park
Gilbert Augustus E. 3611 Grand boul.
Gilbert Charles B. 4219 Grand boul.
Gilbert Charles C. 331 Hampden ct.
Gilbert Charles T. Morgan Park
Gilbert C. B. Mrs. 91, 37th
Gilbert C. J. Evanston
Gilbert Edward G. 4717 Champlain av.
Gilbert Edwin S. Winnetka
Gilbert Fannie B. Mrs. 3017 Wabash av.
Gilbert Frank, 16 Walton pl.
Gilbert F. E. Miss, 2028 Indiana av.
Gilbert F. L. Granada hotel
Gilbert George, 355 Chicago av.
Gilbert George A. 3356 Calumet av.
Gilbert   g   H. Prof. 534 Washington
  bouLeor e
Gilbert Harry B. 2028 Indiana av.
Gilbert Henry, 3706 Lake av.
Gilbert H. K. 328 Dearborn av.
Gilbert H. M. Chicago Beach hotel
Gilbert H. T. 5234 Woodlawn av.
Gilbert James H. 3336 Calumet av.

Gilbert James H. Austin
Gilbert James R. LaGrange
Gilbert John, 1174 Washington boul.
Gilbert L. J. Leland hotel
Gilbert Matthew P. 1838 Frederick
Gilbert Maud Miss, 2028 Indiana av.
Gilbert Newell D. Austin
Gilbert Sarah A. Mrs. 4201 Grand boul.
Gilbert Wallace B. Austin
Gilchrist James, 2644 Commercial (L.V.)
Gilchrist James M. Mrs. 5400 Washing-
  ton av.
Gilchrist John F. 5400 Washington av.
Gilcreest John, 3729 Prairie av.
Gilday D. 6738 Perry av.
Gile David H. Oa   Park
Giles Albert W. Oak Park
Giles Charles K. Lake Forest
Giles F. S. Hotel Metropole
Giles George T. 418 Warren av.
Giles William A. 2537 Michigan av.
Giles William F. 2537 Michigan av.
Gilfillan Essington N. 3 Pelham flats
Gilkinson C. P. 284 Park av.
Gilkison Jasper G. 6204 Sheridan av.
Gill Charles E. 4553 Ellis av.
Gill George A. 4500 Vincennes av.
Gill Hannah Mrs. Oak Park
Gill James Prof. Kenilworth
Gill James C. Dr. 870 Warren av.
Gill J. T. 979 Jackson boul.
Gill Preston, 4553 Ellis av.
Gill S. C. Mrs. 150 Pine
Gill Winn W. 4433 Berkeley av.
Gillespie Augustine V. 2821 N. Paulina
Gillespie Chas. M. 2953 Prairie av.
Gillespie C. H. 3769 Lake av.
Gillespie Francis J. 2821 N. Paulina
Gillespie George, 239 Park av.
Gillespie John, 282 S. Leavitt
Gillespie John P. 2953 Prairie av.
Gillespie Joseph M. 1801 Indiana av.
Gillespie J. M. 1801 Indiana av.
Gillespie Lottie E. Mrs. 3953 Michigan
  av.
Gillespie Mary A. Miss, Evanston
Gillespie Marie Miss, 404 Center
Gillespie Patrick F. 2953 Prairie av.
Gillespie Robert H. 132 W. Adams
Gillespie Samuel, 404 Center
Gillespie Walter E. 3953 Michigan av.
Gillespie W. C. C. 23 St. Johns pl.
Gillett Charles H. 3915 Vincennes av
Gillett Charles W. 3334 Michigan av.
Gillett Egbert W. 3334 Michigan av.
Gillett Henry, 3017 Vincennes av
Gillett Lillian May Miss, 3334 Michigan
  av.
Gillett Walter C. 979 Kenmore av.
Gillett William K. 842 North Park av.
Gillette Charles N. 4030 Prairie av.
Gillette Edwin F. 306 Michigan av.
    Sum. res. Lake Beulah, Wis.
Gillette E. L. Mrs. 306 Michigan av.
    Sum. res. Lake Beulah, Wis.
Gillette Howard V. 2908 Michigan av.

Gillette H. R. 3604 Lake av.
Gillette James F. 2908 Michigan av.
Gillette Mary Mrs. Fort Sheridan
Gillette Philander, Fort Sheridan
Gillette Robert, Highland Park
Gillette Sarah W. Miss, Evanston
Gillette Thomas S. Evanston
Gillette Truman S. 4030 Prairie av.
Gilliam John, 480 Fullerton av.
Gillingham D. E. 2937 Groveland av.
Gillingham William, 1925 Michigan av.
Gillmann C. F. 816 Larrabee
Gillmann Ida Mrs. 446 Belden av.
Gilmann William, 446 Belden av.
Gillson Louis K. Evanston
Gilman Alvira Mrs. 4816 Langley av.
Gilman Edward R. Riverside
Gilman E. R. Lexington hotel
Gilman Frank, 3605 Lake av.
Gilman George P. 433 Dearborn av.
Gilman George P. jr. 433 Dearborn av.
Gilman Henry K. Riverside
Gilman H. K. Lexington hotel
Gilman John E. Dr. 2419 Indiana av.
Gilman J. H. Col. U.S.A.,Lexington hotel
Gilman Mary Miss, 433 Dearborn av.
Gilman M. E. Miss, 3605 Lake av.
Gilman Stephen W. Evanston
Gilman William, 2453 Michigan av.
Gilman William T. 2419 Indiana av.
Gilmer Thomas L. Dr. 3220 Lake Park av.
Gilmore Anne Mrs. 468 Ashland boul.
Gilmore A. P. Dr. Iroquois club
Gilmore Ephraim, 948 S. Central Park av.
Gilmore John E. LaGrange
Gilmore Mary E. Miss, 50 Hamilton av.
Gilmore Sidney M. 948 S. Central Park av.
Gilmore Thomas W. 3159 Forest av.
Gilmore T. H. 16 Macalister pl.
Gilmore T. W. 50 Hamilton av.
Gilmore William, Oak Park
Gilmore W. J. 4226 Wabash av.
Gilroy Bernard J. Lake Forest
Gilson Florence Miss, 3154 Michigan av.
Gilson T. W. 5617 Madison av.
Gimbel Charles A. 3646 Michigan av.
Gimbel Horace B. 3646 Michigan av.
Gimbel Jacob W. 3646 Michigan av.
Gimbel Moses, 3646 Michigan av.
Gindele Charles W. 3745 Prairie av.
Gindele Frank L. 264 Park av.
Gindele Franz, 264 Park av.
Gindele F. V. 394 Ashland boul.
Gindele Geo. A. 5407 Wabash av.
Gindele George W. 394 Ashland boul.
Girard Alfred C. Maj. Fort Sheridan
Girardin Jules, 5431 Cottage Grove av.
Girling Winthrop Dr. 4200 Berkeley av.
Giroux G. W. 843 Warren av.
Githens Alonzo M. 177, 51st (H.P.)
Githens Herbert A. 177, 51st (H.P.)
Githens Walter L. 5101 Kimbark av.
Gitterman Stephen, Riverside
Given J. S. jr. Auditorium hotel
Given Robert H. jr. 5226 Kimbark av.
Givins Robert C. Lexington hotel

Givins R. S. Lexington hotel
Givins S. Mrs. 1734 Briar pl.
Glade John H. 712 North Park av.
Glaess Hermann, River Forest
Glann N. P. Great Northern hotel
Glaser Byron Z. 3222 South Park av.
Glaser Edward L. 147, 33d
Glaser George, 3240 South Park av.
Glaser Gustave D. 4342 Grand boul.
Glaser J   s, 3222 South Park av.
Glaser LulMrs. 3252 Wabash av.
Glaser Max, 3240 South Park av.
Glaser Victor L. 3252 Wabash av.
Glasner William Angel, 19 Ashland boul.
Glaspell Elizabeth Mrs. 1128 S. Central
　　Park av.
Glaspell Harrison J. 874 Kenmore av.
Glass Cassius M., D.D.S.686 W.Madison
Glass C. L. 3111 Groveland av.
Glass M. J. Mrs. Julian hotel
Glassbrook T. H. 314 Webster av.
Glasscock Edwin R. 2703 N. Ashland av.
Glasser Wendell, 451 Dayton
Glazier Charles C. 2 Pelham flats
Gleason Charles, Evanston
Gleason C. O. Evanston
Gleason Frederic Grant,4802 Madison av.
　　Sum. res. North Lake, Wis.
Gleason M. C. Mrs. 7819 Sherman
Gleason Sarah Miss, 270½ Lasalle av.
Gleason William H. 2339 Michigan av.
Gleeson P. 327 Loomis
Glende Louisa Mrs. Oak Park
Glenney L. M. Mrs. 520 Washington boul.
Glennie Albert E. Union League Club
Glennon Edward T. 67 Bryant av.
Glessner Arthur W. 4630 Greenwood av.
Glessner John J. 1800 Prairie av.
　　Sum. res. The Rocks, Littleton, N. H.
Glessner   . G. M. 1800 Prairie av.
Glick Lipman, 3663 Michigan av.
Glickauf Samuel, 363 Indiana
Glickauf S. 374 Oak
Glidden Annie L. Miss, 718 Washington
　　boul.
Glidden Henry H. 7 46 Union av.
Glogauer Fritz, 744 Kenmore av. ·
Glos Harry L. Elmhurst
Glos Jacob, Elmhurst
Glover D. H. 7130 Eggleston av.
Glover E. C. Oak Park
Glover Fannie M.Miss, 1315 Michigan av.
Glover George H. 1315 Michigan av.
Glover Henry T. 2607 Prairie av.
Glover Ingram F. 687 W. Adams
Glover Lyman B. 3029 Groveland av.
Glover Otis R. 2607 Prairie av.
Glover Samuel C. 6538 Stewart av.
　　Sum. res. Grand Haven, Mich.
Goan Orrin S. LaGrange
Gobel E. F. 230 Ashland boul.
Gobel Harriette M. Miss, 230 Ashland
　　boul.
Gobel H. Elias, 230 Ashland boul.
Godair Floyd J. 3915 Grand boul.
Goddard Leroy A. 3006 Prairie av.

Goddard Lester O. 3630 Lake av.
Goddard Nettie Miss, 513, 62d, Eng.
Goddard Sterling, 3630 Lake av.
Godfrey Julia D. Dr. 1176 Millard av.
Godfrey Walter B. 29 Ashland boul.
Godley E. Mrs. Oak Park
Godman Charles C. 1641 Michigan av.
Godman J. R. 453 Lake av.
Godwin F. W. Hinsdale
Goe D. E. Longwood
Goehner Gustav A. Park Ridge
Goertz Louise Dr. 3661 Wabash av.
Goes Charles B. Tracy
Goes William, Tracy
Goessling Charles F. Evanston
Goessling Henry F. Evanston
Goetz C. Mrs. 3000 Michigan av.
Goetz Frederick, 29 Lane pl.
Goetz Henry, 456 Orchard
Goetz Margaret Miss, 3000 Michigan av.
Goffe Louis K. Evanston
Gogan C. Mrs. 309 Webster av.
Goggin James Judge, 404 Superior
Goggin Mary Miss, 404 Superior
Going Judson F. 221 Fremont
                    Sum. res. Lake Geneva.
Goit Edward J. 4405 Sidney av.
Goit Frank H. 58 Throop
Goit O. W. Mrs. 58 Throop
Golbeck H. D. 1014 Warren av.
Gold Wm. Jason Rev. 1113 Washington
    boul.   Sum. res. Lima, Ind.
Goldbeck Robert Dr. Woodlawn Park
Goldberg H. Mrs. 413 Bowen av.
Goldbery Edward J. 323 Michigan av.
Golden J. H. 543 W. Monroe
Goldenberg Jonas, 3560 Grand boul.
Golder W. Arthur, 686 Washington boul.
            Winter res. Daytona, Fla.
Goldie Robert, 3716 Lake av.
Goldie William, 2966 Vernon av.
Goldie William jr. 3716 Lake av.
Golding J. F. 915 W. Adams
Golding L. W. Mrs. 1831 Frederick
Goldman Max, 4002 Vincennes av.
Goldmark Henry, 5442 Ridgewood ct.
Goldschmidt Adolph, 423 Ashland boul.
Goldschmidt Marion Mrs. 3341 Calumet
    av.
Goldschmidt Moses, 3341 Calumet av.
Goldsmith J. L. 10 Menomonee
Goldsmith Robert F. 283 Webster av.
Goldsmith Samuel, 3137 Vernon av.
Goldsmith S. 401 Cleveland av.
Goldspohn Albert Dr. 519 Cleveland av.
Goldzier Julius. 220 Schiller
Goll Bruno H. 259 Ashland boul.
Goll Bruno H. jr. 259 Ashland boul.
Goll N. J. 6 Chalmers pl.
Goltz Julius A., M.D. Pullman
Gondring Augustus C. 1312 Wrightwood
    av.
Gooch George E. Glencoe
Gooch Hiram A. 4045 Drexel boul.
Good Henry H. 1017 Washington boul.
Good Robert Dr. 384 N. State
36

Goodall H. L. 4443 Emerald av.
Goode A. H. Hotel Barry
Goode Edwin P. 1102 Montana
Goode R. T. 725 Fullerton av.
Goode Thomas, 327 Racine av.
Goodfellow H. Mrs. 2453 Commercial
    (L.V.)
Goodfellow Wm. Rev. 5831 Monroe av.
Goodhart F. E. Virginia hotel
Goodhue Homer, 54 Bryant av.
Goodhue Wayland S. 54 Bryant av.
Gooding C. F. Irving Park
Gooding I. A. Wilmette
Gooding S. Edgar Wilmette
Gooding William S. Wilmette
Goodkind Gustav, 3731 Elmwood pl.
Goodkind Maurice L., M.D. 2948 Indiana
    av.
Goodkind Max Mrs. 3712 Wabash av.
Goodkind William, 278, 32d
Goodman Alexander, 3529 Calumet av.
Goodman A. L. 98 Warren av.
Goodman Chas. 5830 Washington av.
Goodman Daniel Mrs. 3359 Indiana av.
Goodman Frank W. 4163 Lake av.
Goodman Herbert E. 4051 Indiana av.
Goodman H. Mrs. 3333 Wabash av.
Goodman Jacob, 450, 38th
Goodman James, 5030 Washington av.
Goodman James B. Marinette, Wis.
Goodman James S. River Forest
Goodman Joseph, 20 Lincoln av.
Goodman Joseph D. 2704 Indiana av.
Goodman J. B. Lexington hotel
Goodman L. 2951 Indiana av.
Goodman Magnus, 4533 Ellis av.
Goodman Maurice, 3333 Wabash av.
Goodman Milton F. 3426 South Park av.
Goodman Morris, 3250 Vernon av.
Goodman Moses, 3426 South Park av.
Goodman M. A. Mrs. 5810 Washington av.
Goodman Robert B. 5030 Washington av.
Goodman Robert F. 5030 Washington av.
Goodman Solomon, 4827 St. Lawrence av.
Goodman S. 20 Lincoln av.
Goodman Thomas, 460 Fulton
Goodman Thomas C. 4072 Lake av.
Goodman William A. 460 Fulton
Goodman W. O. 5026 Greenwood av.
Goodrich Adams A. 2970 Vernon av.
Goodrich Albert W. 1474 Michigan av.
Goodrich A. E. Mrs. 1474 Michigan av.
Goodrich Barzella, Wilmette
Goodrich Charles Wilson, 322 Superior
Goodrich Edna Miss, 3216 Groveland av.
Goodrich Edson H. 3216 Groveland av.
Goodrich Grant Mrs. 70 Astor
Goodrich G. H. 7436 Bond av.
Goodrich Horace A. 1788 Deming ct.
Goodrich H. C. 737 Washington boul.
Goodrich Julius G. 3824 Calumet av.
Goodrich L. H. 224 Marshfield av.
Goodrich Nathan K. 426 Superior
Goodrich William, 404 Lasalle av.
Goodridge A. E. G. Chicago Athletic
    Assn.

Goodridge A. G. Irving Park
Goodridge Herbert, 832 Warren av.
Goodridge William M. Highland Park
Goodsmith H. M. Dr. 396 Belden av.
Goodsmith William. 396 Belden av.
Goodsmith William P., M.D. 957 N.Clark
Goodspeed Chas. T. 5630 Kimbark av.
Goodspeed Edgar J. 5630 Kimbark av.
Goodspeed G. S. Prof. Hotel Barry
Goodspeed Stephen, 5630 Kimbark av.
Goodspeed Thos. W. Rev. 5630 Kimbark
    av.
Goodwillie Chas. F. 41 Macalister pl.
Goodwillie David, 1146 N. Clark
Goodwillie Douglas M. 295 Ashland boul.
Goodwillie Douglas M. jr. 295 Ashland
    boul.
Goodwillie Edgar N. Ridgeland
Goodwillie Robert J. 350 Ashland boul.
Goodwillie R. W. Oak Park
Goodwillie Willis L. 1146 N. Clark
Goodwin Albert P. 354 Washington boul.
Goodwin Artie Mrs. Lexington hotel
Goodwin Carrie A. Mrs. 634 Boulevard pl.
Goodwin Daniel, 600 N. State
Goodwin Edward D. Evanston
Goodwin Edward S. 3307 Calumet av.
Goodwin Eva Miss, Riverside
Goodwin E. Mrs. 38 Bryant av.
Goodwin E. P. Rev. 354 Washington boul.
Goodwin Frances L. Miss, 6946 Perry av.
Goodwin Henry O. 3307 Calumet av.
Goodwin Hugh, Lexington hotel
Goodwin Hollister E. LaGrange
Goodwin H. F. Rev. Lombard
Goodwin Karl H. 634 Boulevard pl.
Goodwin Lois A. Mrs. 4204 Oakenwald av.
Goodwin L. W. A. Mrs. Oak Park
Goodwin Mabel E.Miss, 634 Boulevard pl.
Goodwin Margaret Mrs. Irving Park
Goodwin W. F. 3303 Forest av.
Googins David S. 4337 Drexel boul.
Googins Henry F. 3247 South Park av.
Googins Joseph B. 4337 Drexel boul.
Gookin Frederick W. 463 Orchard
Gookin Frederick Y. 463 Orchard
Gookins J. F. 103 N. Clark
Goold Edward L. 5142 Washington av.
Goold John E. 2216 Prairie av.
Goold Nathaniel Mrs. 2216 Prairie av.
Gordon Anna A. Miss, Evanston
Gordon A. H. Dr. 207 Chicago av.
Gordon Charles U. 48 Gordon terrace
Gordon Edward K. Hinsdale
Gordon Emma Mrs. Austin
Gordon Frances A. Mrs. 348 Bowen av.
Gordon George O. 4742 Champlain av.
Gordon J. W. Mrs. Hinsdale
Gordon Robert, Hyde Park hotel
Gordon Thomas S. Austin
Gordon William G. Hinsdale
Gore Alfred W. 333 Park av.
Gore Charles W. 5329 Greenwood av.
Gore George P. 1926 Indiana av.
    Sum. res. Lake Beulah, Wis.
Gore James J. Mrs. 2618 Michigan av.

Gore Joel R. Dr. 2606 Prairie av.
Gore Mary S. Mrs. 333 Park av.
Gore Truman D. 4724 Champlain av.
Gores Paul, The Ontario
Gorgas Lawrence D. Dr. 5720 Madison av.
Gorham J. D. Evanston
Gorham Zaidee Miss, 515 Dearborn av.
Gorique Albert, Riverside
Gorman T. Hyde Park hotel
Gorman William H. 1197, 72d (H. P.)
Gormley James H. Oak Park
Gormley John, 439 Belden av.
Gormully Michael, Glencoe
Gormully R. Philip, 459 Dearborn av.
Gorrell William F. 4916 Washington av.
Gorrell W. C. 4916 Washington av.
Gorsline WilliamP.4201 CottageGrove av.
Gorsuch Noah F. 905 Evanston av.
Gorton Anson, 2961 Michigan av.
Gorton Belle L. Miss, 950 Turner av.
Gorton C. H. Tracy
Gorton C. J. 430 Superior
Gorton Edward F. Lake Forest
Gorton Elizabeth Mrs. 950 Turner av.
Gorton Frank S. 2120 Prairie av.
Goss Charles O. 4636 Vincennes av.
Goss Ferdinand 526 Sedgwick
Goss Sam G. 533 Chestnut, Englewood
Goss S. A. Winnetka
Goss S. C. 5475 Ridgewood ct.
Goss W. T. 1545 W. Monroe
Gott John R. Virginia hotel
Gottfried Carl M. 4559 Ellis av.
Gottfried M. 4559 Ellis av.
Gottig C. H. 1820 Wrightwood av.
Gottlieb A. Mrs. 3420 Vernon av.
Gottlieb Jacob, 683 N. Robey
Gottlieb Richard D. 3420 Vernon av.
Gottlieb Rudolph, 667 N. Robey
Gottman Theodore, 265 Belden av.
Gottschalk L. Gaston, 3626 Lake av.
Goudie Margaret R. Miss, 816 W. Adams
Goudie Thomas C. 1361 W. Ravenswood
    Park
Goudy William C. Mrs. 240 Goethe
Goudy William J. 46 Astor
Gould Allen W. Hinsdale
Gould Charles H. Riverside
Gould C. M. Mrs. 3706 Lake av.
Gould C. W., Dr. Irving Park
Gould DeLoss N. 73 Bowen av.
Gould Elwyn B. 1768 Wrightwood av.
Gould E. I. Mrs. 659 Cleveland av.
Gould Frank E. 42 Groveland Park
Gould Frank M. Evanston
Gould George W. 387 N. State
Gould G. T. 135 Park av.
Gould H. J. 42, 39th
Gould Irving L. 659 Cleveland av.
Gould John, Lake Forest
Gould John S. 2310 Calumet av.
Gould J. Clifford, 5327 Madison av.
Gould J. C. 324 W. Monroe
Gould Leonard, 283 Indiana
Gould M. E. Mrs. 177 N. State
Gould M. L. Kenilworth

Gould Samuel A. 413 Belden av.
Gould Samuel S. Ridgeland
Gould S. P. Mrs. Lake Forest
Gould William S. 39th ne. cor. Langley
    av.
Gow J. R. Rev. 275, 52d (H.P.)
Gowan Victor D. 472 Lasalle av.
Goward G. Granada hotel
Gower Henry, 5214 Hibbard av.
Goyette Louise N. Mrs. 3119 Rhodes av.
Grable B. Miss, 4160 Ellis av.
Grabfield Jacob, 1915 Indiana av.
Grabfield Joseph P. Dr. 1915 Indiana av.
Grabfield Max, 1915 Indiana av.
Grabo H. F. Hinsdale
Grace S. J. Miss, 699 W. Monroe
Grace William, 107 Park av. Lake View
Gradle B. 652 Lasalle av.
Grady Edward Mrs. Tracy
Grady Robert L. 4834 Champlain av.
Graeff Adolph, 265 Fremont
Graeff Alfred, 286 Osgood
Graeff Otto, 265 Fremont
Graff E. A. Chicago Beach hotel
Graff H. D. Chicago Beach hotel
Graff J. Linton, 546 Burling
Grafton John J. 3953 Michigan av.
Grafton Murray L. Evanston
Grafton William H. Evanston
Grafton William R. Mrs. Evanston
Graham Andrew J. 1411 Washington boul.
    Sum. res. Lake Geneva, Wis.
Graham A. Mrs. 279 Ontario
Graham A. T. 283 W. Adams
Graham Beekman, Hotel Windermere
Graham Chauncey L. Evanston
Graham David, 455, 63d (H.P.)
Graham David W., Dr. 672 W. Monroe
Graham Dennis C. Mrs. 21 Bryant av.
Graham Dennis C. 21 Bryant av.
Graham Edwin B. Rev. 611, 66th, Eng.
Graham Ella Mrs. 772 W. Monroe
Graham Ernst Robert, 39, 53d (H.P.)
Graham Eugene, 221 Hermitage av.
Graham Frank H. 1211, 56th (H.P.)
Graham Harry R. 4502 Ellis av.
Graham James, Oak Park
Graham James F. Dr. 278 Bissell
Graham James S. New Hotel Holland
Graham John, 221 Hermitage av.
Graham John jr. 181 Park av.
Graham John A. 1530 Sherfdan av.
Graham Kittie Mrs. Sherman house
Graham M. E. Mrs. Riverside
Graham M. L. Mrs. 4724 Evans av.
Graham William J. 4016 Vincennes av.
Graham W. A. S. Evanston
Grainger John, Morgan Park
Gramm Carl T. Dr. Auditorium annex.
Grandin H. M 20 Bellevue pl.
Grandin H. M. 507 Belden av.
Granger Elmer, 754, 63d ct. Englewood
Granger Rodney, 17 Hawthorne pl.
Granger Sarah Mrs. 1065 Warren av.
Granger William S. East ct. se. cor. Bel-
    mont av.

Grannis Albert A. 2916 Indiana av.
Grannis Amos, 2916 Indiana av.
Grannis C. C. Hotel Imperial
Grannis Frank L. 2916 Indiana av.
Grannis George M. 1225 Wolcott
Grannis G. H. Rev. 83, 74th
Grannis Harry A. 2916 Indiana av.
Grannis Mathilda M. ss, 302 Chicago av.
Grannis W. C. D. 2027 Michigan av.
Granquist Edwin E. 640 N. Hoyne av.
Grant Allen P. River Forest
Grant Carlton U. Ravinia
Grant Charles E. 1610 Indiana av.
Grant David C. 6404 Ellis av.
Grant Edward Kendrick, 4205 Grand boul.
Grant Elizabeth S. 451 Bowen av.
Grant Gilbert L. 287 Webster av.
Grant John Mrs. Ravinia
Grant J. C. 814 W. Monroe
Grant J. C. Prof. 1922 Michigan av.
Grant Louis Moen, 1610 Indiana av.
Grant R. S. 524 W. Congress
Grant-Schaefer G. Alfred, Evanston
Grant William C. 1610 Indiana av.
Grant W. H. 554 N. Clark
Granville Austyn W. 3801 Ellis av.
Grass Mathias Mrs. 418 Lasalle av.
Grassie Henry, 663 Washington boul.
Grassie Isaac A. 301 West ct.
Grassie James, The Ashland
Grassie J. Edgar, 818 Warren av.
Grassie L. M. Mrs. 663 Washington boul.
Grassly Charles W. 641 W. Taylor
Gratton E. O. Dr. 243, 65th, Eng.
Graue John George, 422 Superior
Graver James P. 6059 Wentworth av.
Graver Philip S. 6059 Wentworth av.
Graver William, 6059 Wentworth av.
Graver William F. 6059 Wentworth av.
Graves Albert M. 4526 Woodlawn av.
Graves Arthur, 6663 Washington av.
Graves Charles E. 1919 Wrightwood av.
Graves C. H. 240 Bissell
Graves Dwight W. 214 Goethe
Graves Edwin A, LaGrange
Graves Elma Miss, Evanston
Graves E. L. Dr. 810 Warren av.
Graves George A. 3450 South Park av
Graves George M. LaGrange
Graves Grace Miss, Winnetka
Graves Henry E. River Forest
Graves Justin R. Evanston
Graves J. R. 485 Jackson boul.
Graves Kate I. Dr. 5663 Washington av.
Graves Riley M. Winnetka
Graves S. Haughton, 411 Superior
Graves W. M. Calumet Club
Graves W. P. 1644 Jackson boul.
Gray Albert S. Dr. 4401 Berkeley av.
Gray Alice C. Miss, Evanston
Gray Arthur, 351 Ashland boul.
Gray Arthur W. 3524 Forest av.
Gray Augustus R. 2024 Indiana av.
Gray A. W. Dr. 594 W. Congress
Gray B. M. 881 Sawyer av.
Gray Charles H. 2024 Indiana av.

Gray Chas. W. Evanston
Gray C. L. 234 S. Oakley av.
Gray C. W. 1018 Warren av.
Gray Dorothy Miss, Evanston
Gray D. G. 4515 Emerald av.
Gray Edward E. 1922 Belmont av.
Gray Elisha Prof. Highland Park
Gray E. A., Dr. 1808 Wellington
Gray Frank S. Mrs. Oak Park
Gray Franklin D. 2807 Prairie av.
Gray F. M. 327 W. Monroe
Gray George L. 2644 Indiana av.
Gray George M. 3032 Calumet av.
Gray G. W. Rev. Evanston
Gray Henry, 5907 Honore
Gray Henry A. 498 W. Adams.
Gray Howard P. Evanston
Gray H. C. Lexington hotel
Gray Ida Cornelia Miss, Evanston
Gray James R. Morgan Park
Gray Jennie Miss, 2441 Michigan av.
Gray John H. Prof. Evanston
Gray Louis A. 594 W. Congress
Gray Maggie Mrs. 422 Marshfield av.
Gray P. W. 1177 Palmer
Gray Robert W. 290 Rush
Gray T. Drummond, 1423 Edgecomb ct.
Gray Walter J. 5238 Cornell av.
Gray William P. Jefferson Park
Gray W. C. Dr. Oak Park
Gray W. H. 490 Dearborn av.
Gray W. H. Grayland
Gray W. M. Dr. 122 Park av.
Greeley Ethel M. Miss, 60 Bellevue pl.
Greeley Frederick, Winnetka
Greeley Louis M. 60 Bellevue pl.
Greeley L. M. Miss, 60 Bellevue pl.
Greeley Morris L. 295 Belden av.
Greeley M. A. Mrs. 4504 Ellis av.
Greeley Samuel S. 60 Bellevue pl.
Greeley S. H. 4214 Ellis av.
Green Adolphus W. 4935 Greenwood av.
Green Albert P. 416 Bowen av.
Green Albert S. 353, 61st, Englewood
Green Andrew Hugh, 403 Lasalle av.
Green Ann Mrs. 416 Bowen av.
Green Augustus W. 2306 Calumet av.
Green A. E. Mrs. 1138 Washington boul.
Green Benjamin, 1921 Deming ct.
Green Caroline Mrs. 3753 Vincennes av.
Green Charles, 57 Park av.
Green Charles M. Highland Park
Green Charles W. Evanston
Green Edward Craft. 112 Lake Shore drive
Green Eva M. Mrs. 347 Ashland boul.
Green E. C. 6545 Yale
Green Frank B. Highland Park
Green Fred W. 6346 Myrtle av.
Green F. H. Mrs. 102 S. Oakley av.
Green F. P. Morgan Park
Green George, 3743 Langley av.
Green G. H. 496 Jackson boul.
Green Helen R. Miss, Glencoe
Green Henry L. 4320 Ellis av.
Green Henry R. Riverside

Green Henry R. jr. 386 Chestnut
Green H. J. Evanston
Green H. R. Mrs. Highland Park
Green Isadore L. Dr. 315 Lincoln av.
Green Julia A. Miss, 6346 Myrtle av.
Green J. W. 26 Groveland Park
Green J. W. 3152 South Park av.
Green Kenyon Mrs. 414 Bowen av.
Green Lucien H. 4070 Lake av.
Green L. O. Miss, Hotel Groveland
Green Mary Pomeroy Miss, 403 Lasalle av.
Green Nathan, 680 W. Adams
Green Oliver B. 403 Lasalle av.
Green O. S. 409, 41st (H.P.)
Green R. F. 6641 Woodlawn av.
Green Walter H. Glencoe
Green Wilbur F. Dr. Evanston
Green William O. 57 St. Clair
Green William W. 451 Washington boul.
Green W. Mrs. 582 Division
Green W. A. 4720 Kenwood av.
Green W. M. Evanston
Greenacre I. T. Washington Heights
Greenbaum E. C. Hotel Groveland
Greenbaum Selig, 3340 South Park av.
Greenbaum S. Hotel Groveland
Greenburg E. 1380 Jackson boul.
Greene Albert W. 1052 Kenmore av.
Greene Charles K. 3633 Ellis Park
Greene Cyrenius M. Highland Park
Greene C. W. 148 Dearborn av.
Greene D. Russell, 1928 Calumet av.
Greene Edward M. 73 Warren av.
Greene E. R. 943 Park av.
Greene Frank C. Dr. 1928 Calumet av.
Greene Frank R. 90, 21st
Greene Frederick J. 2602 Indiana av.
Greene F. C. Mrs. 4542 Lake av.
Greene F. F. Virginia hotel
Greene H. N. 1928 Calumet av.
Greene Jesse T. 3633 Ellis Park
Greene J. P. 77 Rush
Greene Mary J. Mrs. 111 Warren av.
Greene Mosher T. 1912 Prairie av.
Greene Philip, 148 Dearborn av.
Greene W. B. 4149 Berkeley av.
Greenebaum D. S. 3156 South Park av.
Greenebaum Elias, 1612 Michigan av.
Greenebaum Gus. M. 3230 South Park av.
Greenebaum Henry E. 3337 Michigan av.
Greenebaum Henry N. 578 Dearborn av.
Greenebaum J. E. 3450 Groveland av.
Greenebaum J. M. 1816 Michigan av.
Greenebaum Moses E. 3201 Rhodes av.
　　　　Sum. res. Lake Beulah
Greenebaum Moses S. 5334 Indiana av.
Greenfield Charles W. 728, 50th
　　　　Sum. res. Lake Mills, Wis.
Greenhood Annie E. Mrs. 460 Bowen av.
Greenhoot Bertha Mrs. 3235 Vernon av.
Greenleaf E. B. 3942 Lake av.
Greenleaf Walter G. Riverside
Greenlee Elias C. 942 Jackson boul.
Greenlee Ralph Stebbins, 1691 Sheridan rd.
Greenlee Robert L. 677 W. Monroe

Greenman Guy W. Evanston
Greenough Edward P. Evanston
Greensfelder Adolph, 2512 Michigan av.
Greensfelder Isaac, 2512 Michigan av.
Greensfelder Julius, 2512 Michigan av.
Greensfelder Louis A. Dr. 3000 Indiana av.
Greensfelder Nathan, 2512 Michigan av.
Greenwood A. G. Clifton House
Greenwood Halbert W. 320, 60th (H.P.)
Greer Howard, 1340 Claremont av.
Greer Howard jr. 200 Ashland boul.
Greer Jefferson A. 3139 Michigan av.
Greer Joseph H. Dr. 307 S. Oakley av.
Greer Paul E. 1340 Claremont av.
Gregg Charles O. Riverside
Gregg Douglas C. 757, 63d ct.
Gregg George, 7 Oakland Crescent
Gregg George A. 367 Mohawk
Gregg Joseph, 4533 Lake av.
Gregg Mary E. Dr. 503 Fullerton av.
Gregg Raymond, 3815 Langley av.
Gregg William M. 503 Fullerton av.
Gregorie James L. 1078 Lawndale av.
Gregory Allen, 600 Chestnut, Englewood
Gregory A. W. 4121 Drexel boul.
Gregory Charles E. 4215 Langley av.
Gregory Daniel, 660 W. Monroe
Gregory Edward W. 550, 62d, Englewood
Gregory Elizabeth Mrs. 1638 Prairie av.
Gregory F. A. 4149 Langley av.
Gregory F. A. jr. 4149 Langley av.
Gregory George D. 440 Elm
Gregory Helen B. Miss, 19 Scott
Gregory Jacob H. 4121 Drexel boul.
Gregory James C. 440 Elm
Gregory Louis L. Dr. 514 Evanston av.
Gregory M. S. 8 St. James pl.
Gregory Robert B. 1638 Prairie av.
Gregory Sarah Mrs. 8 St. James pl.
Gregory S. S. 65 Newport av.
Gregory Walter D. 660 W. Monroe
Gregory W. C. Leland Hotel
Gregson George, 275 S. Oakley av.
Gregson William L. 4345 St. Lawrence av.
Gregsten Samuel, 3435 Michigan av.
Greifenhagen O. F. 1911 Deming ct.
Greig Alexander F. 4449 Lake av.
Greig D. W. 1615 Prairie av.
Greig George W. 620 Jackson av.
Greig John, 3818 Langley av.
Greig Mabelle Luille Miss, 4449 Lake av.
Greig Thomas, 365 S. Oakley av.
Greiner Albin Mrs. 732 N. Hoyne av.
Greiner William jr. 63 Lincoln av.
Grepe Hamilton E. Evanston
Grepe J. Stanley Evanston
Gresham Otto, 2931 Indiana av.
Grey Charles F. Evanston
Grey Howard G. Evanston
Grey Jessie Miss, 2010 Prairie av.
Grey John J. 4354 Oakenwald av.
Grey Sophia C. Mrs. Evanston
Grey Walter 2010 Prairie av.
Grey William L. 2010 Prairie av.

Gridley-Gridley Norah Mrs.61 University pl.
Gridley Martin M. Evanston
Gridley Nelson C. Evanston
Griener Wm. Mrs. 916 N. Halsted
Grier James P. Evanston
Grier R. M. Mrs. Evanston
Griesheimer Fred, 366 Lasalle av.
Griesheimer Morris, 508 Lasalle av.
Griesser William, 605 Sheffield av.
Griewisch Fred, 899 N. Clark
Griffeth Abraham L. 2620 Commercial (L.V.)
Griffeth Albright,2620 Commercial(L.V.)
Griffin A. E. 214 Cass
Griffin B. W. Dr. Glencoe
Griffin Felix J. River Forest
Griffin Fred W. 226 S. Hoyne av.
Griffin F. O. 1670 W. Monroe
Griffin H. T. 393 Dearborn av.
Griffin James F. 744 Washington boul.
    Sum. res. Pittsfield, Mass.
Griffin Jas.W.Garfield boul. ne.cor.Laflin
Griffin John, Garfield boul. ne. cor. Laflin
Griffin John C. 5121 Michigan av.
Griffin Joseph A. Evanston
Griffin J. B. 719 Pullman bldg.
Griffin Stephen D. 1310 W. Adams
Griffin Thomas A. Hotel Richelieu
Griffin W. F. 719 Pullman bldg.
Griffin Wm. V. Evanston
Griffin Z. T. 114 S. Lincoln
Griffing Frank B. 66 Bryant av.
Griffing Josephine C.Miss,5461 Cornell av.
Griffith E. H. Mrs. 5656 Washington av.
Griffith E. U. 6939 Yale
Griffith F. A. 6717 Honore
Griffith George D. Highland Park
Griffith George D. Ridgeland
Griffith G. F. Evanston
Griffith Jennie Miss, 339 Ohio
Griffith J. A. Mrs. 603 Jackson boul.
Griffith J. Clarkson, Ridgeland
Griffith J. N. Mrs. Great Northern hotel
Griffith Robert, 1522 Sheridan rd.
Griffiths D. A. 4201 Lake av.
Griffiths Edward H. 4335 Berkeley av.
Griffiths John, 3806 Michigan av.
Griffitts John R. LaGrange
Griffitts William F. LaGrange
Grigg P. C. Berwyn
Griggs Alida M. Mrs. Evanston
Griggs Carolyn A. Miss, Lexington hotel
Griggs George E. 5652 Monroe av.
Griggs John, Evanston
Griggs Samuel C. Lexington hotel
Grimes Samuel M. 4307 Grand av.
Grimes Sylvester J. 4336 Greenwood av.
Grimm E. A. 971 Park av.
Grimsell Fred, 95 Fowler
Grinnell Julius S. 5116 Kimbark av.
Griswold Charles C. 4056 Michigan Terrace
Griswold Edward P. 2331 Indiana av.
Griswold George E. 569 W. Congress
Griswold H. W. 4535 Oakenwald av.

Griswold J. M. Tracy
Griswold M. E. Tracy
Griswold W. P. 5125 Cornell av.
Gritman Charles, Austin
Groesbeck D. E. 3924 Langley av.
Groesbeck Mary L. Mrs. 413 Washington ·
    boul.
Groesbeck S.W.Maj.U.S.A.703 The Plaza
Groetzinger William C.96 Park av.(L.V.)
Groff Carl, Hinsdale
Groh Louis, 148 Garfield boul.
Groh William, 4422 St. Lawrence av.
Groll Philip F. 1722 Oakdale av.
Grommes J. B. 616 Dearborn av.
Gronow Rudolph W. 1475 Perry
Grose A. M. Hyde Park hotel
Grose H. S. 626 Boulevard pl.
Groshon Lottie J. Mrs. 300 Irving av.
Gross Alfred H. 2339 Indiana av.
Gross August 682 N. Wells
Gross Charles, 559 Kenwood pl.
Gross C. W. 5534 S. Peoria
Gross Edgar J. 969 Jackson boul.
Gross Emile M. 5349 Michigan av.
Gross George G. 969 Jackson boul.
Gross Granville, 3164 Lake Park av.
Gross Howard H. 6001 Indiana av.
Gross H. 969 Jackson boul.
Gross Jacob, 1730 Deming ct.
Gross James E. 235 Michigan av.
Gross J. Ellsworth, 3600 Michigan av.
Gross S. E. 48 Lake Shore Drive
Grosscup Peter S.Judge,4259 Grand boul.
Grosse H. C. 518 Fullerton av.
Grosse John, 667 N. Robey
Grosse Mary C. Mrs. 229 Lasalle av.
Grossheider J. 3201 Calumet av.
Grossman Adolph, 3228 Wabash av.
Grossman Edward B. 4043 Ellis av.
Grossman George, 3228 Wabash av.
Grossman Herman 3924 Grand boul.
Grossman Kate Mrs. 3601 Indiana av.
Grossmith Alfred, 6814 Sherman
Grosswiller Albert J. 813 Lunt av.
Grosvenor George B. 1029 Warren av.
Grosvenor Lemuel C. Dr. 185 Lincoln av.
Grosvenor Lorenzo N. Dr. 928 Kenmore
    av.
Grosvenor Wallace F. 185 Lincoln av.
Grout Charles R. 1179 Washington boul.
Grout Frank R. 1179 Washington boul.
Grove Joseph, Berwyn
Grover Chester A. Evanston
Grover Frank R. Evanston
Grover Marguerite P. Miss, Evanston
Groves Dennison F. 3946 Ellis av.
Groves Geo. M. 3946 Ellis av.
Grow Caroline F, Mrs. 756 Washington
    boul.
Grower William F. 20 Pratt pl.
Grubb Emma Miss, 3000 Michigan av.
Grubb Joseph E. 5313 Madison av.
Grubb W. S. Hotel Barry
Gruber M. L. 67 8 Sherman
Grubey Geo. W5 600 Dearborn av.
Grubey W. H. 609 Dearborn av.

Gruenewald B. Mrs. 18 Lincoln pl.
Grundt Harry T. 822 Sherwin av.
Grundy James, Rev. 137 Locust
Grunewald Augustus H. 738 Sedgwick
Grunewald Dorothea Mrs. 738 Sedgwick
Grunewald Frederick L. 269 Belden av.
Grus Wm. 528 Lasalle av.
Grus Wm. jr. 528 Lasalle av.
Grusendorf Edward, 697 N. Hoyne av.
Grusendorf Henry, 697 N. Hoyne av.
Gscheidlen Emily Miss, Hinsdale
Guckenheimer Joseph, 3241 Rhodes av.
Guenther Otto, 321 Webster av.
Guerin C. R. 3004 Prairie av.
Guerin M. Henry, Columbus club
Guerin Thomas E. Columbus club
Guernsey Charles A. 6462 Oglesby av.
Guernsey Mary E. Mrs. 2841 Michigan av.
Guetschaw Anna Miss, 823 Washington
    boul.
Guettel Julius, 3413 Prairie av.
Guettel Mayer, 4344 St. Lawrence av.
Guettel Nathan M. 4344 St. Lawrence av.
Guggenheimer A. S. 1837 Michigan av.
Guhl F. H. 644 Fullerton av.
Guhl Walter F. 644 Fullerton av.
Guilbert Gertrude Miss, Hotel Winde-
    mere
Guilbert James, Norwood Park
Guilbert O. H. Hotel Windemere
Guile William R. 269 Bissell
Guilford F. A. Maywood
Guilford J. A. 609 Washington boul.
Guinea E. M. Mrs. 407 Belden av.
Guion Edward, 3605 Lake av.
Guion G. Murray Gen. 111, 47th
Guion Leroy P. 111, 47th
Gulick George, 208 Dearborn av.
Gump B. F. Highland Park
Gundelfinger Arnold, 508 Lasalle av.
Gunderson Geo.O. 1239 Washington boul.
Gunderson G. Martin, 23 Roslyn pl.
Gunderson S. M. 1239 Washington boul.
Gunderson S. T. 1239 Washington boul.
Gundlach Conrad J. 297 West ct.
Gundrum Ferdinand, 4944 Ellis av.
Gunlock Nettie E. Mrs. 1183 Washington
    boul.   Sum. res. Burlington, Wis.
Gunn A. H. Mrs. Evanston
Gunn Janet, M.D. Riverside
Gunn John A. 576A Washington boul.
Gunn Malcolm Dr. 2101 Calumet av.
Gunn Moses Mrs. 2101 Calumet av.
Gunn Richard G. Evanston
Gunn Walter C. 2101 Calumet av.
Gunnell Francis S. E. Evanston
Gunning Robert J. Lafayette flats
Gunsaulus Frank W.Rev.619, 46th (H.P.)
Gunther Burnell, 1602 Indiana av.
Gunther C. F. 1602 Indiana av.
Gunther E. Mrs. 5145 Wabash av.
Gunther H. Dr. 2 Groveland Park
    Sum. res. Tower Hill, Wis.
Gunther Whitman, 1602 Indiana av.
Gunthorp Walter J. Austin
Gunthorp W. Percy, Austin

Gunton William M. 898 S. Kedzie av.
Gurley Ida B. Miss, Oak Park
Gurley W. W. 527 N. State
Gurnett W. G. 6643 Honore
Gurney Charles H. Lexington Hotel
Gurney C. S. 878 W. Monroe
Gurney T. T. Mrs. 878 W. Monroe
Gustorf Arthur, The Ashland
Gustorf Fred, Oak Park
Gutches J. H. 396 Jackson boul.
Guth Henry, 3412 South Park av.
Guthman Eugene, 2001 Michigan av.
Guthman Max, 482 Warren av.
Guthman Sol. 3333 South Park av.
Guthmann Emil, 3639 Vernon av.
Guthmann R. 3801 Prairie av.
Guthmann Sigmund, 3912 Prairie av.
Guthrie Marian Mrs. 873 W. Adams
Guthrie Ossian, 6200 Oglesby av.
Guthrie Seymour, Riverside
Gutman Nathan S. 1612 Michigan av.
Gutmann E. J. 592 Dearborn av.
Gutmann Joseph, 594 Dearborn av.
Gwin A. C. Miss, 4558 Oakenwald av.
Gwin A. D. Miss, 4558 Oakenwald av.
Gwin Cornelius V. 4558 Oakenwald av.
Gwinn John M. 4908 Washington av.
Gwinn Russell S. 4908 Washington av.
Gwinn William R. 4919 Lake av.
Gwynne E. E. Dr. 407 Center

HAAKE John H. 2505 Commercial (L. V.)
Haas Charles, 3331 South Park av.
Haas Harris, 4711 Evans av.
Haas Sarah Mrs. 2714 Indiana av.
Haas William H. 94 Laflin
Haase E. R. Oak Park
Haass Herman E. 1819 Indiana av.
Habbeler W. H. 3802 Lake av.
Habel L. M. 820 W. Monroe
Haber Morris, 913 W. Adams
Haber M. Mrs. 368 Warren av.
Hacek Joseph jr. 599 Larrabee
Hack John F. 1412 Palmer
Hack William J. 789 W. Monroe
Hacker A. P. Mrs. 305, 53d (H.P.)
Hacker N. W. 305, 53d (H.P.)
Hacker R. C. Evanston
Hackett Karleton, 4956 Washington av.
Hackett W. H. 1131 Dunning
Hackney George, 3963 Drexel boul.
Hackney Henry C. 3537 Michigan av.
Hackney J. J. Hotel Groveland
Hackney William D. 1205, 67th (H.P.)
Hackney W. 1205, 67th (H.P.)
Hadden A. B. 403, 64th, Englewood
Hadduck Benjamin F. 150 Pine
Hadfield A. W. 224 Park av.
Hadfield Frank W. 6619 Honore
Hadley Edwin M. 4214 Ellis av.
Hadley James M. 4214 Ellis av.
Haerle Adolf, 645 Burling
Haerther A. G. Dr. 1621 Roscoe
Haerther William J. 1741 Roscoe
Hafeld Jordan, 3337 Calumet av.

Hafer Henry, 4631 Michigan av.
Hafner C. F. Oak Park
Hafner J. 4340 Langley av.
Hafner Mary Mrs. Oak Park
Hafner William, 195 S. Hoyne av.
Hafner William H. 2427 Wabash av.
Hafner W. H. jr. 2427 Wabash av.
Haft Charles M. 3145 Groveland av.
Hagaman Benjamin, 3133 Calumet av.
Hagan James, 80 S. Oakley av.
Hagan James M. Rev. LaGrange
Hagans C. E. Miss, 3232 Groveland av.
Hagans H. J. Miss, 3232 Groveland av.
Hagans L. A. Mrs. Elmhurst
Hagans W. E. Elmhurst
Hagans W. L. 3232 Groveland av.
Hagar Edward Mc, 77 Pine
Hagar John M. 77 Pine
Hagarty Kate Mrs. Evanston
Hagedon William H. Hotel Barry
Hageman A. J. 4908 Ellis av.
Hageman Frank C. 4909 Forrestville av.
Hageman Frederick C. Dr. 4909 Forrestville av.
Hagenbuck J. H. 5468 Monroe av.
Hagerty John W. 372 Ontario
Hagerty Lincoln A. 17, 39th
Hagerty T. A. 537 Belden av.
Haggard John D. Austin
Haggard Winfield S. 3352 Prairie av.
Haggerman W. 170 Eugenie
Hahn Edmund J. 3626 G boul.
Hahn Emma J. Mrs. 402 69th, Eng.
Hahn Harry W. 3626 Grand boul.
Hahn Herman F. 3626 Grand boul.
Hahn H. S. Dr. 85 Seeley av.
Hahn John F. Evanston
Hahn Mollie Miss, 3142 Vernon av.
Haigh Fred F. 3237 Rhodes av.
Haigh Raymond C. 3237 Rhodes av.
Haigh William, Evanston
Haigh W. M. Rev. 6915 Yale
Haight A. J. 61 DeKalb
Haight Franklin, LaGrange
Haight Rufus J. 6532 Myrtle av.
Haight William P. 611, 60th, Eng.
Haines Charles J. 437½ Elm
Haines E. H. 17, 46th
Haines Fred H. 288 Ashland boul.
Haines Frederick U. 4719 Langley av.
Haines Geo. B. Chicago Athletic Assn.
Haines George R. Mrs. Hotel Windermere
Haines Geo. W. 89 Lincoln av.
Haines Harry S. 299 S. Leavitt
Haines John Allen, 437½ Elm
Haines J. Lakota Hotel
Haines Mary V. Mrs. 288 Ashland boul.
Haines R. Adelaide Mrs. 530 Washington boul.
Haines Tina M. Miss, Evanston
Haines W. S. Dr. 46 Loomis
Hainsworth Frederick, 1079 W. Taylor
Hainsworth Joseph, 905 Warren av.
Hair Benjamin M. 248 Ashland boul.
Hair E. S. Mrs. 4417 Lake av.

Hair James A. 228, 53d (H.P.)
Hair John V. 3982 Vernon av.
Hair Josiah T. 817 Jackson av.
Hair J. S. 5142 Madison av.
Hair J. W. 5142 Madison av.
Hair Samuel G. 4417 Lake av.
Haire John P. 4327 Lake av.
Haiselden George, 338 Fullerton av.
Haiselden J. Harry Dr. 338 Fullerton av.
Hakes Webster, River Forest
Halbach J. F. A. Union League Club
Halbe Charles F. 228 Winchester av.
Halbert Homer V. Dr. 2300 Indiana av.
Hald J. R. 700A Pullman bldg.
Hale Albert B. Dr. 2200 Prairie av.
Hale Charles N. 170 Howe
Hale Clarence B. 215 Ashland boul.
Hale Daniel, Oak Park
Hale E. C. 4833 Kimbark av.
Hale E. J. M. The Wellington
Hale E. M. Dr. 2200 Prairie av.
Hale Frank A. Riverside
Hale Frank E. 719 Washington boul.
Hale Fred C. Norwood Park
Hale George E. 4545 Drexel boul.
Hale George W. 541 Dearborn av.
    Sum. res. Kenosha, Wis.
Hale George W. 4545 Drexel boul.
Hale H. W. 4736 Langley av.
Hale John G. 6200 Oglesby av.
Hale John P. Rev. 4455 Berkeley av.
Hale Mary I. Miss, Evanston
Hale Prescott G. 719 Washington boul.
Hale Stedman H. Evanston
Hale William Gardner Prof. 5833 Monroe av.
Hale W. C. 493 Jackson boul.
Hale W. E. 4545 Drexel boul.
Hales Ansel, 640, 61st, Eng
Hales Burton F. 408 Washington boul.
Haley Thomas H. 243 Michigan av.
Haley William F. Dr. 1260 Wilcox av.
Hall Albert, 169 Rush
Hall Alfred, 222 S. Paulina
Hall Alfred M. Dr. 2 Washington pl.
Hall Amos T. Mrs. 5516 Jefferson av.
Hall Annie Mrs. 3532 Ellis av.
Hall Augustus O. 32 Aldine sq.
Hall A. A. 185 Warren av.
Hall A. E. Mrs. 2944 Vernon av.
Hall A. H. Evanston
Hall A. L. Mrs. 7520 Sheridan av.
Hall A. Percival, 169 Rush
Hall Carrie E. Mrs. 262 Ashland boul.
Hall Charles Berrien, Dr. 5516 Jeff'son av.
Hall Charles W. 120, 49th
Hall Clara Miss, 752 W. Monroe
Hall Clarence B. 1900 Prairie av.
Hall Clifford P. Lake Forest
Hall C. E. 9 Groveland Park
Hall C. F. 2424 N. Paulina
Hall C. H. 55, 20th.
Hall Daniel L. Ridgeland
Hall Edgar A. 1357 Fuiton
Hall Edward R. Evanston
Hall Ella Mrs. 870 W. Monroe

Hall Ernest, Oak Park
Hall Ernest A. Pullman
Hall Ernest R. Evanston
Hall Eugene J. Oak Park
Hall E. H. Mrs. 5420 Cornell av.
Hall E. P. Mrs. 3142 Vernon av.
Hall E. Sherman, 625 Washington boul.
Hall Fayette C. 710 N. Wells
Hall Ferd, LaGrange
Hall Ford P. Highland Park
Hall Frank, 2616 Calumet av.
Hall Frank, 3327 Michigan av.
Hall Frank, Lake Forest
Hall Frank B. 4757 Calumet av.
Hall Fred H. 513 Fullerton av.
Hall F. D. Mrs. Glencoe
Hall F. H. 150 Park av.
Hall George A. Mrs. 2400 Prairie av.
Hall George E. 2602 Prairie av.
Hall Gordon Mrs. 2 Washington pl.
Hall George W. Hinsdale
Hall G. D. Glencoe
Hall Henry A. Kenilworth
Hall Herman J. 5545 Washington av.
Hall H. Newbery Dr. 198 Goethe
Hall Howard E. 136 Park av.
Hall Irving G. 7629 Wright
Hall James T. 4341 Oakenwald av.
Hall John A. 6521 Yale
    Sum. res. Lake Beulah, Wis.
Hall John F. Mrs. 6521 Yale
Hall Joseph G. 259 Lasalle av.
Hall Joseph H. Mrs. 26 Aldine sq.
Hall Julian S. Berwyn
Hall Junius M., Dr. 2 Washington pl.
Hall J. E. Lakota hotel
Hall J. S. Mrs. 625 Washington boul.
Hall Leicester C. Oak Park
Hall Lewis T. 22 Walton pl.
Hall Lorenzo E. Austin
Hall Louis J. 625 Washington boul.
Hall Lucius M. 3663 Wabash av.
Hall L. E. Austin
Hall L. R. 361 Washington boul.
Hall Miller, Oak Park
Hall M. R. 3167 Groveland av.
Hall Newman G. 32 Aldine sq.
Hall Otis O. 4528 Oakenwald av.
Hall O. F. 4224 Grand boul.
Hall O. H. 402 W. Adams
Hall Richard C. Evanston
Hall Robert G. 3259 Vernon av.
Hall Robert J. 4224 Grand boul.
Hall Robert W. 6417 Oglesby av.
Hall Ross C. Ridgeland
Hall Rufus C. 1723 Cornelia
Hall Russell, Austin
Hall R. A. 4461 Oakenwald av.
Hall R. Boylston Mrs. 1000 N. Halsted
Hall R. N. Dr. 339 Warren av.
Hall Shirley C. 870 W. Monroe
Hall S. M. 938 W. Adams
Hall Thomas C. Rev. 425 N. State
Hall T. W. Oak Park
Hall William, 464 W. Adams
Hall William, 6417 Oglesby av.

Hall William A. 32 Aldine sq.
Hall William T. 3519 Calumet av.
Hall W. D. 435 S. Oakley av.
Hall W. D. Oak Park
Hall W. E. 212 S. Wood
Hall W. E. Dr. 9 Groveland Park
Halla Charles, 592 Lasalle av.
Halla G. T. 7734 Union av.
Halla Philip, 391 Orchard
Halla Sage G. Mrs. 19 Kemper pl.
Halladay E. B. Park Ridge
Hallam Alice B. Miss, Evanston
Hallam Charles A. 1248 Washington
    boul.
Hallberg C. S. 1761 Oakdale av.
Hallberg L. G. 405 Huron
Halle Arnold, 3351 Indiana av.
Halle E. G. 403 The Plaza
Halle F. E. 3351 Indiana av.
Halle Louis, 3740 Ellis av.
Halle Robert J. 157 Eugenie
Halleman Andrew H. 268 S. Oakley av.
Hallen Andrew, 82, 25th
Hallenbeck John C. 6508 Stewart av.
Hallenstein B. 144 Warren av.
Haller G. M. Mrs. Lexington hotel
Hallersleben Martha A. Miss, 1217 Michi-
    gan av.
Hallersleben Otilie H. Miss, 1217 Michi-
    gan av.
Hallett A. E. 42, 39th
Hallett Harvey J. 4007 Vincennes av.
Hallett John, 4007 Vincennes av.
Hallett John G. Evanston
Halley Belton, 72, 44th
Halliday George B. 206 S. Lincoln
Halliday John W. Riverside
Hallier H. C. Evanston
Halligan Francis E. 872 Jackson boul.
Hallinan Harry J. 574 Fullerton av.
Hallinan Thomas P. 574 Fullerton av.
Hallinan T. G. 6329 Woodlawn av.
Halliwell A. C. 6817 Perry av.
Hallman Charles W. 532 Greenleaf av.
Hallock Franklin S. 2691 Commercial
    (L.V.)
Hallock J. A. Mrs. Oak Park
Hallock S. J. 266 Garfield av.
Hallowell P. M. LaGrange
Hallowell Sara T. Miss, Palmer house
Halsey E. A. 301 Belden av.
Halsey E. H. 301 Belden av.
Halsey E. S. Mrs. Evanston
Halsey George E. 3625 Ellis av.
Halsey J. J. Prof. Lake Forest
Halsey L. J. Rev. 301 Belden av.
Halsey Nicoll, 3251 Forest av.
Halsey Tappen, 4824 Lake av.
Halstead A. E. Dr. 844 Warren av
Halsted E. J. Mrs. 717 Fulton
Halsted N. Miss, 553 Jackson boul.
Haman O. E. 454 Irving av.
Hamblen L. A. 230 S. Oakley av.
Hambleton C. E. 461 W. Monroe
Hambleton C. J. 558 Dearborn av.
Hambleton Earl L. 129 Buena av.

Hamblin M. J. Mrs. 3218 Vernon av.
Hamblin William B. Riverside
Hamburger I. L. 3340 Forest av.
Hamburger L. M. Iroquois Club
Hamburger M. 5134 Woodlawn av.
Hamburger Sol, 4347 Grand boul.
Hamburgher E. C. 223 Lasalle av.
Hamburgher Ray Miss, 223 Lasalle av.
Hamill Charles D. 2126 Prairie av.
Hamill Charles H. 2126 Prairie av.
Hamill Ernest A. 2637 Prairie av.
Hamill Frederick J. 4758 Champlain av.
Hamill H. M. Mrs. 520 Orchard
Hamill Paul, 2126 Prairie av.
Hamill Robert W. 3716 Lake av.
Hamill Samuel B. Hinsdale
Hamill T. W. 315, 58th (H.P.)
Hamilton Adelbert, Evanston
Hamilton Charles F. 854 Washington
    boul.
Hamilton David G. 2929 Michigan av.
Hamilton Emil, 440 Belden av.
Hamilton E. F. Evanston
Hamilton E. S. Mrs. 4043 Indiana av.
Hamilton Frederick A. The Renfost
Hamilton F. W. 28 Pelham flats
Hamilton George A. 3014 Lake Park av.
Hamilton George A. The Renfost
Hamilton George W. 758 Jackson av.
Hamilton Henry E. Newberry hotel.
Hamilton Henry R. Oak Park
Hamilton I. K. 3230 Michigan av.
Hamilton J. 147 Cass
Hamilton J. B. Dr. U.S.Marine hospital
Hamilton J. Elwood, Oak Park
Hamilton J. H. 5744 Rosalie ct.
Hamilton J. M. 4720 Madison av.
Hamilton M. E. Miss, 233 S. Leavitt
Hamilton Percy C. 1800 Michigan av.
Hamilton W. A. Evanston
Hamilton William J. 94 Fowler
Hamilton W. L. Evanston
Hamlin Frank, 209 Cass
Hamlin Fred R. 2115 Calumet av.
Hamlin Frederick H. 77 Warren av.
Hamlin George A. 3400 Calumet av.
Hamlin George J. 6 Tower pl.
Hamlin Harry L. Auditorium hotel
Hamlin Herbert W. 2115 Calumet av.
Hamlin John A. 2115 Calumet av.
Hamlin L. A. 6514 Lafayette av.
Hamline John H. 1621 Prairie av.
Hamline L. M. 3 Chalmers pl.
Hamline L. P., M.D. Evanston
Hammell L. J. 1259 Wilcox av.
Hammer Alfred, 2967 Indiana av.
Hammer D. Harry, Lakota hotel
Hammermiller Wm. 434 Lasalle av.
Hammerstroem Wm. 333 Burling
Hammett Edward, Wheaton
Hammill Caleb W. Union club
Hammon Charles N. Evanston
Hammon Forest W. 231 Ashland boul.
Hammon G. M. Dr. 683 W. Adams
Hammond C. 532 S. Oakley av.
Hammond C. G. Highland Park

Hammond C. L. 4627 Greenwood av.
Hammond C. N. 365 Ontario
Hammond Edward C. 4105 Maple av.
Hammond Fred, 11 Bellevue pl.
Hammond F. H. 740 Sawyer av.
Hammond G. B. 407 Oak
Hammond Harry H. 1388 Jackson boul.
Hammond Herbert, 4328 Oakenwald av.
Hammond I. B. 360 Dayton
Hammond Jabez, Auditorium hotel
Hammond Jacob B. 4324 St. Lawrence av.
Hammond J. D.,M.D.AuditoriumAnnex
Hammond Katherine Miss, 2220 Calumet av.
Hammond Luther S. 928 W. Adams
Hammond L. D. 928 W. Adams
Hammond L. M. 3539 Prairie av.
Hammond Theodore M.6150 Wharton av.
Hammond T. C. 11 Bellevue pl.
Hammond W. A. 337 Lasalle av.
Hammond W. A. Evanston
Hamontree C. 5904 Michigan av.
Hampstead Edward, Evanston
Hampton James L. 1054 Wilcox av.
Hanaford Charles G. 3834 Calumet av.
Hanauer J. C. Hotel Barry
Hanchett Frank J. 363 Marshfield av.
Hanchett F. B. 553, 62d, Englewood
Hanchett Louis J. 4564 Indiana av.
Hanchette N. H. Park Ridge
Hancock Bradford Mrs. 39 Bellevue pl.
Hancock C. A. 2233 Wabash av.
Hancock C. D. 3223 Wabash av.
Hancock Ellen Dr. 39 Bellevue pl.
Hancock Thomas, 5833 Madison av.
Hancock W. S. 555 Englewood av.
Hand Bayard E. 7120 Yale
Hand John A. 497 Webster av.
Hand John P. Judge, 1069 Chase av.
Hand J. P. 540 Dearborn av.
        Sum. res. Pine Lake
Hand M. Mrs. 499 Dearborn av.
Hand Nicholas, 603 Cleveland av.
Hand O. H. 4835 Langley av.
Hand Peter, 481 Cleveland av.
Hand S. E, Mrs. 4835 Langley av.
Handford John, Evanston
Handke August P. Evanston
Handtmann F. P. Mrs. 5602 Kimbark av.
Handy H. H. 4423 Ellis av.
Hane Cora M. Mrs. 882 Sawyer av.
Hanecy ElbridgeJudge,3116Michigan av.
Hanes John K. 239 Dearborn av.
Haney Conrad Rev. 4514 Lake av.
Hanff Edward, 3209 Prairie av.
Hanford Louise Freer Mrs. Evanston
Hanford M. E. Mrs. 4720 Kenwood av.
Hanford Philander C. Mrs. 2008 Calumet av.
Hankey F. L. Glencoe
Hankey James P. 4539 Oakenwald av.
Hanley Michael, 225 Loomis
Hanlon John J. 399 S. Paulina
Hanlon John W. 399 S. Paulina
Hanlon Leo. J. 399 S. Paulina
Hanlon Martin, 1400 Michigan av.

Hanlon William J. 1409 Michigan av.
Hanna Edmund, 35 Wisconsin
Hanna E. B. Mrs. 35 Wisconsin
Hanna John T. 953 Spaulding av.
Hanna Leroy, 6744 Honore
Hanna Lucy Miss, 227 S. Lincoln
Hanna Sarah Miss, 227 S. Lincoln
Hanna Wm. B. Dr. 455 Washington boul.
Hannah Ella M. Miss, 411 Bowen av.
Hannah F. H. Mrs. Hinsdale
Hannah Helen M. Dr. 3030 Prairie av.
Hannah John S. 407 Superior
Hannah Lucy Miss, 1491 W. Monroe
Hannah Thomas C. Hinsdale
Hannah W. H. 175 N. State
Hannahan J. J. 5949 Princeton av.
Hannan Charles S. 815 The Plaza
Hannan James, 5134 Grand boul.
Hannan James, 4610 Prairie av.
Hannington Walter, 1089 Winona
Hanscom P. L. Oak Park
Hansel . W. Oak Park
Hansel J. W. Mrs. Oak Park
HansellJH. P. 3343 Indiana av.
Hansell J. R. 5444 Ellis av.
Hansen Charles W. 2030 Indiana av.
Hansen C. O. 342 Center
Hansen Harold M. 599 Pine Grove av.
Hansen Henry C. 2678 Charlton av.
Hansen H. C. Oak Park
Hansen O. J. 1725 Wrightwood av.
Hansen Waldemar T. 2030 Indiana av.
Hanson A. H. 4612 Greenwood av.
Hanson Burton, 235 Michigan av.
Hanson Charles H. 3311 Calumet av.
Hanson C. H. 1848 Surf
Hanson David N. 4737 Ellis av.
Hanson F. S. 1720 Michi'n av. Sum. res.
        Island Park, Mackinac Island, Mich.
Hanson Henry, 113 Evergreen av.
Hanson Herman W. 1728 Buckingham pl.
Hanson Hiram A. 3311 Calumet av.
Hanson John P. 24 Ewing pl.
Hanson J. W. Dr. 4402 Lake av.
Hanson Margaret E. Mrs. 300, 53d (H.P.)
Hanson Ole N. Irving Park
Hanson Sarah E. Miss, 51, 31st
Hanson Zenas P. Dr. 306 Washington boul.   Sum. res. Old Orchard, Me.
Hanssen John, 569 Burling
Hapeman Edgar, LaGrange
Hapgood Norman, 710 Fullerton av.
Haradon Hattie E. Miss, Evanston
Harahan J. T. 53, 53d (H.P.)
Harbeck Eugene, 3350 Prairie av.
Harbert Arthur B. Evanston
Harbert Charles H. Evanston
Harbert W. S. Evanston
        Sum. res. Lake Geneva, Wis
Harbridge William, 2969 Groveland av.
Hardcastle Preston, 34 Sidney ct.
Harden H. B. 888 Warren av.
Hardenbrook E. G. 6223 Woodlawn av.
Hardenbrook G. S. 6221 Woodlawn av.
Harder Charles C. 4643 Michigan av.
Hardick A. T. 1017 Jackson boul.

Hardie George, 4845 Madison av.
Hardie George F. Evanston
Hardie T. Melville Dr. 4526 Lake av.
Hardie William T. Evanston
Hardin E. M. Hotel Windemere
Hardin F. A. Rev. 6410 Wright
Hardin I. N. Evanston
Hardin John H. Evanston
Hardin M. D. Gen. 538 N. State
Hardin P. K. 703, 63d (H.P.)
Harding Adelaide L. Mrs. 449 Washington boul.
Harding Amos J. Evanston
Harding A. C. 3155 Rhodes av.
Harding Charles Mrs. 335 Chestnut
Harding Charles F. 235, 45th
Harding C. E. 7715 Sherman
Harding George F. 2536 Indiana av.
Harding George F. jr. 2536 Indiana av.
Harding Hugh, 6106 Michigan av.
Harding Lucien E. Evanston
Harding P. D. Dr. Evanston
Hardman F. W. Evanston
Hardon R. W. Dr. 3010 Calumet av.
Hardy Alice Miss, 1023 St. Louis av.
Hardy A. W. 4438 Berkeley av.
Hardy B. Frank, 2825 Michigan av.
Hardy Charles M. 3916 Ellis av.
Hardy C. A. 2825 Michigan av.
Hardy Francis A. Evanston
Hardy Frank, 4554 Ellis av.
Hardy Guy, 3916 Ellis av.
Hardy Hannah Mrs. Evanston
Hardy Horace F. 705 Burling
Hardy H. Florville, 705 Burling
Hardy Joseph E. 809 Warren av.
Hardy J. M. 259 Belden av.
Hardy K. M. Hotel Barry
Hardy Marcia M. Mrs. 667 Washington boul.
Hardy Silas, Evanston
Hardy Tucker, 705 Burling
Hardy William, 3916 Ellis av.
Hare L. R. Capt. Fort Sheridan
Hare R. W. 3212 Prairie av.
Harford T. W. 4228 Greenwood av.
Hargis Harry, 660 Lasalle av.
Hargreaves George, Riverside
Haring L. W. Berwyn
Harkness E. J. 291, 48th (H.P.)
Harkness L. D. 467 W. Monroe
Harkness N. J. Rev. 58 N. Sheldon
Harlacher G. H. 338 Fullerton av.
Harlan A. W. Dr. 4414 Greenwood av.
Harlan James S. University club
Harlan John Maynard, 41 Banks
Harland Edward, 563 Webster av.
Harless C. D. 4440 Lake av.
Harless W. W. 4440 Lake av.
Harlev William, 907 Sawyer av.
Harley C. A. 3521 Ellis av.
Harley E. P. Mrs. 3521 Ellis av.
Harley Philip B. 518 W. Adams
Harlin Robert Mrs. Oak Park
Harlow Frank, 5601 Washington av.
Harlow George H. 4835 Madison av.

Harlow Jefferson G. 1285 Washington boul.
   Sum. res. Lake Geneva, Wis.
Harman J. Robert, 6420 Stewart av.
Harman William H. 930 Fargo av.
Harman W. M. Oak Park
Harmon Albert C. 600 The Plaza
Harmon Charles J. 373 Ontario
Harmon C. S. 4035 Lake av.
Harmon Edwin C. 373 Ontario
Harmon E. R. Grand av. sw. cor. Morse av.
Harmon Frederick H. 600 The Plaza
Harmon George E. 47th, 46th (H.P.)
Harmon Henry I. 3820 Ellis av.
Harmon H. W. Mrs. 4619 Lake av.
Harmon John C. 4058 Ellis av.
Harmon J. K. 600 The Plaza
Harmon J. W. 4035 Lake av.
Harmon Lydia Miss, 600 The Plaza
Harmon S. 3610 Prairie av.
Harmon Walter R. 373 Ontario
Harmount G. A. Mrs. 2925 Indiana av.
Harmount H. L. 1397 Wolcott
Harms Charles, 1543 Wolfram
Harms William, 225 Fremont
Harned Henry P. 3249 Prairie av.
Harney T. H. 324 Superior
Harpel Charles, 394 Oak
Harpel Charles J. 394 Oak
Harper Alfred E. 444 Champlain av.
Harper C. L. 3029 Vernon av.
Harper E. T. Prof. 730 W. Adams
Harper Fred, 5407 Monroe av.
Harper George, 351 Jackson boul.
Harper Grosvenor A. 377 Dearborn av.
Harper Harry E. 4959 Prairie av.
Harper Hartley D. 619 The Plaza
Harper Hudson W. Evanston
Harper John E. Dr. 3580 Vincennes av.
Harper J. C. 120 Loomis
Harper Lucina Miss, 730 W. Adams
Harper Malcolm C. Evanston
Harper Mary A. Mrs. 2971 Michigan av.
Harper R. F. Prof. Hotel Barry
Harper U. S. Mrs. 464 Elm
Harper Virginia Mrs. Evanston
Harper William Hudson, Evanston
Harper William H. Lakota hotel
   Sum. res. Lake Geneva, Wis.
Harper William R. 5657 Washington av.
Harpham E. L. Evanston
Harpold Elijah C. 1450 Graceland av.
Harpold Harry W. 1450 Graceland av.
Harpole Enoch, 390 Bowen av.
Harpole William, 390 Bowen av.
Harpole Winfield S. 4238 St. Lawrence av
Harps Estella Mrs. 1914 Indiana av.
Harraden Charles H. 55 Campbell Park
Harrah W. C. 475 Belden av.
Harries D. C. Berwyn
Harries H. H. Park Ridge
Harrigan C. P. Dr. 52 Lytle
Harrington A. T. 9 Burton pl.
Harrington F. A. Miss, 6530 Madison av.
Harrington George K. 3832 Calumet av.

Harrington John C. 379 Chestnut
Harrington K. C. Mrs. 370 Oak
Harrington L. B. LaGrange
Harrington Stephen H. Riverside
Harrington William, 756, 63d ct. Eng.
Harris Albert W. 1, 47th pl.
Harris Arthur, 449 W. Congress
Harris A. 325 Loomis
Harris A. F. Dr. 514, 61st, Englewood
Harris A. J. Dr. 279 Warren av.
Harris B. D. Oak Park
Harris B. F. 3762 Lake av.
Harris Charles Taylor, 617, 60th, Eng.
Harris C. M. 53 Warren av.
Harris David J. Pullman
Harris D. H. The Arizona
Harris D. J. 3145 Vernon av.
Harris Elijah T. 604 Washington boul.
Harris F. E. Lieut. Fort Sheridan
Harris George B. 543 N. State
Harris George P. 1272 Washington boul.
Harris Godfrey, 3322 Indiana av.
Harris Graham H. 561 Dearborn av.
Harris G. E. 5223 Madison av.
Harris H. N. 161 S. Paulina
Harris John F. Virginia hotel
Harris Joseph, Lexington hotel
Harris Julius, 383 Dearborn av.
Harris J. 470½ W. Adams
Harris Laura M. Miss, Virginia hotel
Harris Moses, 325 Loomis
Harris M. C. 4950 Vincennes av.
Harris M. H. Rev. 765 Washington boul.
  Sum. res. Green, Me.
Harris M. L. Dr. 459 Lasalle av.
Harris M. R. 95 S. Sangamon
Harris N. Dwight, 4520 Drexel boul.
Harris N. W. 4520 Drexel boul.
Harris Rachel A. Mrs. Virginia hotel
Harris Samuel, 945 Jackson boul.
Harris S. G. 483 Ashland boul.
Harris S. H. 1489 W. Monroe
Harris S. J. 508 Cleveland av.
Harris S. Rush, 200 Rush
Harris Walter E. 6122 Michigan av.
Harris W. L. Mrs. Evanston
Harrison Annie S. Miss, 521 Dearborn av.
Harrison Benjamin F. 3559 Prairie av.
Harrison Carter H. jr. 295 Schiller
Harrison Charles H. Highland Park
Harrison C. Thomas, 1444 Edgecomb ct.
Harrison Elizabeth Miss, 2231 Prairie av.
Harrison E. Mrs. 3030 Groveland av.
Harrison E. C. Mrs. Austin
Harrison E. M. Dr. 7811 Winneconna av.
Harrison George J. 230 Marshfield av.
Harrison Gertrude Miss, 1444 Edgecomb
  ct.
Harrison Henry S. LaGrange
Harrison Jennie Miss, 3658 Vincennes av.
Harrison John, Hotel Imperial
Harrison J. W. 6537 Sheridan av.
Harrison M. E. Miss, 521 Dearborn av.
Harrison P. B. 708 Chestnut, Eng.
Harrison Thomas, 1444 Edgecomb ct.
Harrison Thomas E. 3658 Vincennes av.

Harrison W. K. Dr. Walton pl. sw. cor.
  Rush
Harron Joseph, 3345 Forest av.
Harroun Oscar T. 3660 Sheridan rd.
Harrower O. C. 6714 Sherman
Harrsch R. E. 107 Seminary av.
Harsh I. O. 6929 Eggleston av.
Harsh J. Irving, 6929 Eggleston av.
Harsha Leslie R. 634 Washington boul.
Harsha M. S. Ravinia
Harsha W. M. Dr. 4026 Drexel boul.
Harshberger A. 6626 Yale
Harshberger C. R. 7116 Webster av.
Hart Abe, 4234 Calumet av.
Hart Alexander H. 740 Washington boul.
Hart Andrew J. 6836 South Chicago av.
Hart A. 3650 Michigan av.
Hart Edward, 6951 Oglesby av.
Hart Edward C. Hotel Barry
Hart Eli S. 3716 Lake av.
Hart Emil, 3233 South Park av.
Hart E. O. Evanston
Hart Frank, Sherman house
Hart George A. 415 The Plaza
Hart Harry, 3320 Calumet av.
Hart Harry R. 3650 Michigan av.
Hart Henry N. 1618 Indiana av.
Hart Herbert L. 1618 Indiana av.
Hart Herman, 3652 Prairie av.
Hart H. H. 1326 Millard av.
Hart H. P. 3756 Ellis av.
Hart H. T. Oak Park
Hart H. W. jr. 42d se. cor. Lake av.
Hart Jacob, 470 Ashland boul.
Hart James, 352 Belden av.
Hart James A. 843 W. Adams
Hart Jesse, Riverside
Hart John J. 612 W. Congress
Hart John W. 1118 Washington boul.
Hart J. B. Hotel Metropole
Hart J. P. 145 Ashland boul.
Hart Leo, 3652 Prairie av.
Hart Louis E. 697 W. Monroe
Hart Max, 3127 Michigan av.
Hart Milton R. 3650 Michigan av.
Hart M. G., M.D. 3805 Wabash av.
Hart N. F. 3257 Indiana av.
Hart Robert, 3330 South Park av.
Hart R. 589 Jackson boul.
Harter Maurice F. 4853 Kimbark av.
Harth Jacob, 406 Seminary av.
Hartigan J. G. 4533 Oakenwald av.
Hartigan Thomas J. 305 Bowen av.
Harting P. Fred, 3223 Calumet av.
Hartley Calvin S. 4567 Oakenwald av.
Hartley Virginia Mrs. 341 W. Monroe
Hartley W. R. 268 Erie
Hartman Adolph, 958 N. Clark
Hartman Emanuel, 3361 South Park av.
Hartman Isaac, 4414 Berkeley av.
Hartman Leon, 3351 South Park av.
Hartman L. 3533 Vernon av.
Hartman S. 3307 Vernon av.
Hartman William W. Dr. 432 Winthrop
  av.
Hartman Wilton, Berwyn

Hartman W. J. 218, 74th
Hartmann Charlotte Mrs.468W.Congress
Hartmann J. S. 403 Bowen av.
Hartney Elizabeth L. Miss, 61 Lincoln av.
Hartney Mollie Miss, 61 Lincoln av.
Hartney M. P. 61 Lincoln av.
Hartoch Charles, 346 Belden av.
Hartoch Sigmund, 346 Belden av.
Hartog Jno. H. 4317 Ellis av.
Harts Edwin B. 215 Ashland boul.
Hartshorn J. W. Evanston
Hartsoff A. Dr. Lexington hotel
Hartt Harry, 1746 Roscoe
Hartupee A. W. Dr. 651 W. Adams
Hartwell A. V. 5200 Washington av.
Hartwell C. S. Lexington hotel
Hartwell D. E. 4624 Emerald av.
Hartwell Edwin S. 35 Newport av.
Hartwell E. A. 646 W. Adams
Hartwell E. E. 274 Lasalle av.
Hartwell F. G. 510 W. Congress
Hartwell M. W. 5210 Hibbard av.
Hartwell P. 39 Seeley av.
Hartwig Herman, 1829 Frederick
Hartz Irving T. 4327 Berkeley av.
Hartz W. T. Capt. Fort Sheridan
Harvey Alexander, 7641 Ford av.
Harvey Edwin F. 4336 Ellis av.
Harvey E. C. Mrs. Oak Park
Harvey E. L. D. Mrs. Evanston
Harvey Frank W. 4001 Vincennes av.
Harvey George, 2413 Prairie av.
Harvey George M. 36 Newport av.
Harvey George V. 3244 Groveland av.
Harvey H. F. 4179 Grand av. (R.P.)
Harvey H. M. 307, 66th (H.P.)
Harvey James, Oak Park
Harvey James A. 2342 Calumet av.
Harvey Joel D. Geneva
Harvey John, Morgan Park
Harvey John H. 7242 Euclid av. (H.P.)
Harvey Joseph. Oak Park
Harvey J. R. Virginia hotel
Harvey J. S. 269 W. Adams
Harvey Robert H. 1702 Prairie av.
Harvey S. A. 4336 Ellis av.
Harvey Thomas F. 4341 Calumet av.
Harvey T. W. 1702 Prairie av.
          Sum. res. Turlington, Neb.
Harvey T. W. jr. 1702 Prairie av.
Harvey William B. 325, 63d (H.P.)
Harvey W. G. 4343 Prairie av.
Harvey W. R. Oak Park
Harvey W. S. Dr. 483 W. Adams
Harwood Henry W. 5012 Ellis av.
Harz C. O. 502 Dearborn av.
Harz Emil G. 266 N. State
Harzfeld Edward, 850 Washington boul.
Hasbrook E. F. 1166 Millard av.
Hasbrook J. V. A. 1166 Millard av.
Hasbrouck Alliger,5415 Cottage Grove av.
Hasbrouck Charles A. 3731 Langley av.
Hasbrouck Edwin, 5415 Cottage Grove av.
Hasbrouck Louis, 196 Bowen av.
Hascall Milo S. Gen. Oak Park
Haselhun Henry C. Oak Park

Haseltine Frank R. 145 Oakwood boul.
Haseltine Fred. W, 145 Oakwood boul.
Haseltine L. A. 145 Oakwood boul.
Haskell David F. 4230 Vincennes av.
Haskell Frederick T. 2824 Prairie av.
Haskell F. Mrs. Victoria hotel
Haskell George W. 410 Ontario
Haskell Georgina Miss, 410 Ontario
Haskell J. E. 521 Washington boul.
Haskell J. W. C. 557 Washington boul.
Haskell Lester A. 4239 Vincennes av.
Haskell Loomis P. Dr. Hinsdale
Haskell Reuben L. 4239 Vidcennes av.
Haskell Simeon D. 1501 Michigan av.
Haskell William, 3657 Prairie av.
Haskell William H. 3657 Prairie av.
Haskell W. H. 6911 Yale
Haskell W. L. 491 Dearborn av.
Haskett E. Webb Mrs. 13 Loomis
Haskett R. E. 649 W. Monroe
Haskin Charles G. Evanston
Haskin Edwin, Wilmette
Haskin Henry L. Dr. Highland Park
Haskin James C. 1501 Sheridan rd.
Haskins C. C. 582 W. Congress
Haskins Frank C. 582 W. Congress
Haskins George W. 1491 W. Monroe
Haskins Mary A. Mrs. 949 Warren av.
Haskins R. C. 949 Warren av.
Hass C. T. 466, 50th
Hasselgren Rudolf, 465 Dearborn av.
Hasterlik Charles, 3248 Vernon av.
Hasterlik Henry, 3666 Indiana av.
Hasterlik Ignatz, 3666 Indiana av.
Hasterlik Samuel, 3248 Vernon av.
Hasterlik Simon, 4800 Michigan av.
Hastie Margaret Mrs. 540 Jackson boul.
Hastings Edward P. 2825 Michigan av.
Hastings George L. 4711 Evans av.
Hastings S. M. 221 Seminary av.
Hastings Thomas D. 3359 Wabash av.
Hastreiter George A. 64 Bryant av.
Hatch Allen, Maywood
Hatch B. S. Evanston
Hatch Azel F. 52 Cedar
Hatch Charles W. Austin
Hatch Edwin H. 25 Aldine sq.
Hatch Eugene A. 5716 Washington av.
Hatch Frank C. Prof. 3524 Calumet av.
Hatch George, Maywood
Hatch Henry L. Newberry hotel
Hatch H. D. 295 S. Leavitt
Hatch H. P. 3756 Ellis av.
Hatch James M. Austin
Hatch John C. 25 Aldine sq.
Hatch J. W. 505 W. Monroe
Hatch Lemoine S. 25 Aldine sq.
Hatch Newton, 4836 Langley av.
Hatch Reuben, 821 Washington boul.
Hatch Thomas W. 619 Washington boul.
Hatch Vinal F. 401, 64th, Englewood
Hatch W. H. Oak Park
Hatch W. H. River Forest
Hatcher Isaac G. Oak Park
Hatcher Morris C. Oak Park
Hately John C. 4013 Ellis av.

Hately J. George, 4013 Ellis av.
Hately Walter C. 5132 Kimbark av.
Hatfield James T. Prof, Evanston
Hatfield Marcus P. Dr. 3301 Forest av.
Hatfield R. M. Mrs. Evanston
Hatfield William P. 981 S. Central Park av.
Hatfield William H. LaGrange
Hathaway Charles H. Evanston
Hathaway C. H. 439 Englewood av.
Hathaway C. H. Prof. 148 N. State
Hathaway Henry, 38 Bellevue pl.
Hathaway Elizabeth Mrs. Evanston
Hathaway James N. Dr. Austin
Hathaway J. C. 440 W. Adams
Hathaway J. L. 324 Park av.
Hathaway Stephen J. 4535 Lake av.
Hathaway S. D. 4535 Lake av.
Hathaway William, Evanston
Hatheway E. C. 4517 Woodlawn av.
Hatheway Franklin, 364 Burling
Hatheway O. P. Dr. 1010 W. Monroe
Hatten W. D. Mrs. 7 University pl.
Hatter George W. 3632 Vincennes av.
Hatterman Charles F. Mrs. 336 Fullerton av.
Hatterman O. Mrs. 812 Warren av.
Hatterman William E. Florence ct. nr. Indian boundary rd.
Hattstaedt John J. 212, 51st (H.P.)
Hauck Frederick, 657 Fullerton av.
Hauck Otto W. 657 Fullerton av.
Haugan H. A. 1713 Deming ct.
Haughey Charles T. Lexington hotel
Haughey Elizabeth Mrs. 3012 Michigan av.
Haughey L. C. 3012 Michigan av.
Hauk Charles D. 5611 Washington av.
Hauk C. B. 5611 Washington av.
Hauk G. Miss, Julien hotel
Hausmann Edward, 3401 Indiana av.
Hausmann E. Mrs. 3401 Indiana av.
Haustetter Catherina Mrs. 3297 Beacon
Havemeyer William A. Riverside
Havemeyer W. A. jr. Riverside
Haven Alfred C., M.D. Lake Forest
Haven E. P. 430 Winthrop av.
Haven H. S. Hotel Imperial
Haven Joseph Dr. 90 Warren av.
Haven S. M. Mrs. 430 Winthrop av.
Havens A. E. 895 W. Monroe
Havens Kate Mrs. 895 W. Monroe
Havens T. C. 6115 Woodlawn av.
Haverkampf John L. 389 Ashland boul.
Haveron John, 4539 Greenwood av.
Haviland Grace Mrs. 4060 Ellis av.
Haviland R. C. LaGrange
Hawes A. C. 5520 Monroe av.
Hawes A. H. 6812 Emerald av.
Hawes Henry F. 4504 Vincennes av.
Hawes Kirk Judge, 2235 Calumet av.
Hawes M. A. Mrs, Evanston
Hawes W. H. 768 Jackson boul.
Hawkes Eliza A. B. Mrs. 494 Fullerton av.
Hawkes M. A. 474 Fullerton av.
Hawkes Thomas, Winnetka

Hawkes W. J., M.D. 17 Scott
Hawkins Charles H. 5016 Greenwood av.
Hawkins D. W. 349 Chicago av.
Hawkins Frank P. Highland Park
Hawkins Frederick, 1126 Millard av.
Hawkins George E. Dr. 657 Sedgwick
Hawkins J. J. Mrs. 160 Ashland boul.
Hawkins M. L. Miss, 4049 Lake av.
Hawkins Robert, 348, 69th (H.P.)
Hawkins W. A. 7508 Wright
Hawks M. L. 423 Washington boul.
Hawks Thomas H. 85 Rush
Hawley Charles A. 3515 Grand boul.
Hawley Clark W. Dr. 879 Spaulding av.
Hawley C. C. Mrs. 4455 Oakenwald av.
Hawley C. M. Judge, 5326 Washington av.
Hawley C. W. Oak Park
Hawley E. B. 503 N. State
Hawley E. H. Dr. Evanston
Hawley E. S. 5430 Ridgewood ct.
Hawley F. R. 5430 Ridgewood ct.
Hawley George A. Morgan Park
Hawley George F., M.D. 131 Buena av.
Hawley H. S. 5845 Madison av.
Hawley Joseph E.R.Dr. 3515 Grand boul.
Hawley Julia C. Miss, 131 Buena av.
Hawley N. G. 243 Erie
Hawley Samuel F. 3515 Grand boul.
Hawley William A. Dr. 243 Erie
    Sum. res. South Haven, Mich.
Hawley William E. 3515 Grand boul.
Haws Charles R. 2665 N. Robey
Hawthorne Silas T. 6220 Oglesby av.
Hawthorne William S.Mrs.446 Belden av.
Hawtin F. Walter, Hinsdale
Hawxhurst Arthur, 584 Fullerton av.
Hawxhurst J. M. Evanston
Hay Alexander B. 464 Washington boul.
Hay William Sherman, 205 Warren av.
Haycock Kimball C. 20 Delaware pl.
Hayde James, 1710 Deming ct.
Hayden Albert, 3155 Michigan av.
Hayden A. G. Dr. 520, 63d, Eng.
Hayden Charles E. 3319 Michigan av.
Hayden Charles H. Mrs. 150, 36th
Hayden Frank N. 5545 Monroe av.
Hayden F. A. 3221 Calumet av.
    Sum. res. Fox Lake, Wis.
Hayden George W. Oak Park.
Hayden Horatio H.Mrs.3319 Michigan av.
Hayden H. H. jr. 3319 Michigan av.
Hayden H. S. 3877 Lake av.
Hayden James T. Oak Park
Hayden Joseph H. 4316 Berkeley av.
Hayden Mae E. Miss, 3221 Calumet av.
Hayden O. B. Dr. 520, 63d, Englewood
Hayden William 414 S. Leavitt
Hayden Wm. French house, Evanston
Hayes Cornelius B. 6552 Ellis av.
Hayes D. Fuller 1177 Lawndale av.
Hayes D. H. 6846 Yale
Hayes Frank 831 Washington boul.
Hayes F. Miss, 20 Astor
Hayes F. A. S. LaGrange
Hayes F. H. 317 Ashland boul.
Hayes F. W. C. 4334 Ellis av.

Hayes George A. 1907 Michigan av.
Hayes Harold V. 6240 Oglesby av.
Hayes James, 5039 Washington av.
Hayes James J. 341, 60th, Eng.
Hayes John A. 4225 Michigan av.
Hayes Louis S. 408 Belden av.
Hayes Martha E. Mrs. 3348 Vernon av.
Hayes Mary Mrs. 1007 Warren av.
Hayes Mary R. Miss, 2013 Indiana av.
Hayes Mary V. Miss, 20 Astor
Hayes Michael, 1288 Washington boul.
Hayes M. 2445 Wabash av.
Hayes Nannie V. Miss, 5156 Michigan av.
Hayes P. B. Dr. 1359 Jackson boul.
Hayes Samuel C. 5415 Cottage Grove av.
Hayes Theodore E. 228, 52d (H.P.)
Hayes William, Ridgeland
Hayes W. P. 5156 Michigan av.
Hayford Ernest L. Dr, 843 Jackson boul.
Hayman H. 94 Laflin
Hayman L. B. Dr. 167 Oakwood boul.
Hayne Frederick E. 4354 Greenwood av.
Hayne W. J. Auditorium annex
Hayne W. W. 7404 Webster av. Eng.
Hayner Frank E. 39 N. Sheldon
Hayner Jennie E. Dr. 1386 Fulton
Haynes Charles, 1516 Michigan av.
Haynes Charles F. 3010.Lake Park av.
Haynes Daniel J. 60th sw. cor. Washington av.
Haynes F. T. 7534 Harvard
Haynes George M. 7534 Harvard
Haynes Joseph R. 7534 Harvard
Haynes J. P. 7624 Wright
Haynes M. W. Rev. 618 Englewood av.
Haynes N. S. Rev. 535 Chestnut, Eng.
Haynes Thomas C. 529 Dearborn av.
Haynes Thomas L. 211 Ashland boul.
Haynes Victor L. 60th sw. cor. Washington av.
Haynes W. J. Lakota hotel
Haynes W. Knox, 4243 Champlain av.
Hays Allan M. 279, 53d (H.P.)
Hays M. D. 319, 41st
Hays Wm. H. 1067 S. Central Park av.
Hayt Henry C. 273 Ashland boul.
Hayt Walter V. 3179 Dover
Haythorne William, Austin
Hayward Ambrose D. 35 Bryant av.
Hayward Arthur W. 5418 Washington av.
Hayward Charles, 99 Park av.
Hayward Charles E. 4122 Calumet av.
Hayward Charles E. Mrs. 4446 Woodlawn av.
Haywood Lucy Mrs. 796 W. Monroe
Haywood Peter S. 39 Macalister pl.
Hazell Ezra F. Dr. 980 N. Halsted
Hazelton H. 223 Loomis
Hazen Frank A. 362 S. Campbell av.
Hazen Hannah Mrs. 362 S. Campbell av.
Hazen Henry C. Rev. Oak Park
Hazen S. S. 237 S. Robey
Hazen W. Lee, 6101 Washington av.
Hazlehurst Andrew, Evanston
Hazlehurst Samuel, Winnetka
Hazlitt George H. 39 Campbell Park

Hazlitt George K. 39 Campbell Park
Hazzard Samuel B. Austin
Head Clara E. Mrs. 1729 Alexander av.
Head Franklin H. 2 Banks
Head George A. 610 Washington boul.
Head Gustavus P. Dr. Austin
Head Harry C. 4128 Drexel boul.
Head M. R. Mrs. Austin
Head Paul, 5467 Jefferson av.
Head Richard, 5467 Jefferson av.
Head William J. 87 Rush
Head W. R. 5467 Jefferson av.
Headen Frank, 230 Dearborn av.
Headly Howard, 139 Garfield boul.
Headly T. H. Mrs. 139 Garfield boul.
Heafford Geo. H. 4560 Oakenwald av.
Heaford Henry H. 3634 Vernon av.
Heald James, 285 Webster av.
Heald J. H. Oak Park
Healey Paul J. Hyde Park hotel
Healey Raymond J. Hyde Park hotel
Healey W. P. Hotel Windermere
Healy B. 4414 Emerald av.
Healy Edward B. 4823 Langley av.
Healy G. L. Chicago Athletic Assn.
Healy G. P. A. Mrs. 387 Ontario
Healy James E. Lakota hotel
Healy James J. 1426 Michigan av.
Healy James T. 3230 Indiana av.
Healy John J. 456 Fullerton av.
Healy J. L. 811 Morse av.
Healy M. R. 80 Bryant av.
Healy N. C. Mrs. 818 Greenleaf av.
Healy P. J. 508 Jackson boul.
          Sum res. Lake Geneva, Wis.
Healy Stephen, 3245 Calumet av.
Heap Arnold, 1423 Washington boul.
          Sum. res. Portsmouth, N. H.
Heap William, 733 Washington boul.
Heaphy A. T. Hinsdale
Heard Dwight B. 739 Evanston av.
Hearn H. J. 407 Oak
Heartle L. H. Evanston
Heath Arthur M. 36 Madison Park
Heath A. Judson, 4016 Ellis av.
          Sum. res. Tower Hill
Heath Ernest W. 5744 Rosalie ct.
Heath E. Mrs. 7105 Webster av.
Heath Fred A. Mrs. 825 Kenmore av,
Heath Ira A. 3136 Prairie av.
Heath John, Winnetka
Heath Josie Miss, 255 Ohio
Heath J. M. Hawthorne av. Eng.
Heaton E. S. Hotel Metropole
Heaton H. R. 292 Rush
Hebard Frank H. 235 Winchester av.
Hebard Frederic S. The Ontario
Hebard J. E. Mrs. 3348 Calumet av.
Hebbard Minerva Mrs. Evanston
Hebblethwaite J. L. Evanston
Hebblethwaite Mary Mrs. Evanston
Hebel Otto W. 692 North Park av.
Hebel William, 692 North Park av.
Hebert Alfred Dr. Evanston
Hebert A. W., Dr. Virginia hotel
Hecht Ernest, 642 Fullerton av.

Hecht Frank A. 639 Jackson boul.
Hecht F. Mrs. 455 Lasalle av.
Hecht Maurice 3644 Prairie av.
Hecht Pauline Miss, 639 Jackson boul.
Hecht Samuel, 180 Howe
Hecht Walter, 642 Fullerton av.
Heckerthorne Edna Miss, 265 Michigan
　av.
Heckman Jean J. 4505 Ellis av.
Heckman Wallace, 4505 Ellis av.
Hecox Daisy Miss, Austin
Hecox J. Frink, Austin
Hecox Marion Miss, Austin
Hecox M. Miss, Austin
Hedden H. D. Evanston
Hedden John H. Evanston
Hedenberg James W. 132 Ashland boul.
Hedges Herbert, 75 Bowen av.
Hedges LeRoy C., M.D. 2571 Commer-
　cial (L.V.)
Hedges S. P. Dr. 890 Evanston av.
Heegaard B. Louise Dr. 666 Lasalle av.
Heegaard W. H. 666 Lasalle av.
　　　　Sum. res. Lake Geneva, Wis.
Heeney Frances Miss, 4101 Vincennes av.
Heeney John B. 4101 Vincennes av.
Heermans T. W. Evanston
Hefferan W. S. 4331 Langley av.
Heffron A. D. Washington Heights
Heffron D. S. Rev. Washington Heights
Hefter Albertina Miss, Austin
Hefter Cæsar L. 3531 Wabash av.
Hefter Charles, 490, 42d pl.
Hefter Charles, 3312 Indiana av.
Hefter C. H. 3312 Indiana av.
Hefter Henry, 3312 Indiana av.
Hefter Herman, 350, 42d
Hefter Louis, 3531 Wabash av.
Hefter R. Austin
Hegert W. Mrs. 172 Howe
Heggie Frank M. 1524 Fulton
Heggie William H. Morton Park
Heicher George, 3232 Beacon
Heide Fred sr. 723 N. Wells
Heideman George F. Dr. Elmhurst
Heidenreich E. Lee,524 Kenwood Terrace
Heidleberger E. Mrs. 1724 Diversey
Heidweyer Sigmund, 2973 Wabash av.
Heikes W. F. 4619 Ellis av.
Heiland John 1506 Michigan av.
Heile Adolph, 1834 Barry av.
Heile Charles Dyer, 1834 Barry av.
Heile Louis, 1834 Barry av.
Heilman L. M. Rev. 782 Larrabee
Heilprin Louis, 4409 Berkeley av.
Heiman H. 148 Dearborn av.
Heimann Albert, 530 Garfield av.
Heimann Emanuel N. Rev. 142 Clarence
　av.
Heimbrodt C. 625 Sedgwick
Heimbrodt George, 165 Warren av.
Heimerdinger Henry H. 3153 Forest av.
Heinberg Fred, 1511 Wolfram
Heine Albert, 3604 Forest av.
Heine Herman, 3604 Forest av.
Heine Oscar, 3604 Forest av.

Heineman Julius, 771 N. Clark
Heineman Samuel, Hinsdale
Heineman Theodore A. 1742 Briar pl.
Heinemann Arnold H. 6915 Stewart av.
Heinemann Charles, 625 Cleveland av.
Heinemann Henry E. O. 6915 Stewart av.
Heinemann William, 349 Hampden ct.
Heinemann William jr. 349 Hampden ct.
Heinig Frank. Lakeside
Heinrich M. Mrs. 3804 Indiana av.
Heinrichs C. L. Miss, 420 N. State
Heinrichs H. W. 420 N. State
Heinroth William C. 612 Washington
　boul.
Heinsen John, 625 N. Hoyne av.
Heinz Charles, 28 Evergreen av.
Heinz L. H. 551, 62d, Englewood
Heinze August, 530 Garfield av.
Heinze August, jr. 530 Garfield av.
Heinze Ernest P. 171 Osgood
Heinze E. F. 912 Larrabee
Heinze F. G. 914 Larrabee
Heinze Hermann, 530 Garfield av.
Heinze Max, 530 Garfield av.
Heinze Paul, 1872 Reta
Heinze Victor, 6123 Sheridan av.
Heinze William, 530 Garfield av.
Heisen C. C. 65 Lake Shore Drive
Heisen G. B. 65 Lake Shore Drive
Heitman A. G. Mrs. 4729 Langley av.
Held Paul E. 1849 Belmont av.
Heldman Charles C. 5434 Monroe av.
Helfenstein Charles B. 6230 Oglesby av.
Hellen Benjamin H. 140, 38th
Heller A. 2964 Wabash av.
Heller B. Mrs. 18 Cedar
Heller E. 3152 Wabash av.
Heller Gustav, 3342 Forest av.
Heller I. 930 W. Monroe
Heller John W. 275 S. Lincoln
Heller J. 2964 Wabash av.
Heller Leopold, 3342 Forest av.
Heller M. L. 3656 Forest av.
Heller Rose Miss, 4160 Ellis av.
Heller T. J. New Hotel Holland
Helliwell Robert A. Ridgeland
Hellman F. D. 6830 Lafayette av.
Hellman George A. 426 Elm
Hellman George A. jr. 426 Elm
Hellman Henry B. 1055 N. Clark
Hellmich Anton, 210 Webster av.
Hellstrom Claus, Evanston
Hellyer Frederick, Riverside
Helm D. T. 865 Washington boul.
Helm Henry T. Judge, 6913 Stewart av.
Helm J. W. 1838 Aldine av.
Helm Lynn, Longwood
Helm S. Harvey, Granada hotel
Helmer Edward E. Riverside
Helmer Frank A. 1428 Michigan av.
Helmer Frederick D. 142, 42d
Helmer Harry, 34 Aldine sq.
Helmer Joseph W. 34 Aldine sq.
Helpman M. L. 5407 Madison av.
Hemenway H. B. Dr. Evanston
Hemington Francis, Oak Park

Hemingway A. T. Oak Park
Hemingway Clarence E. Oak Park
Hemingway H. Dr. 136 Park av.
Hemingway H. W., M.D. 6816 Perry av.
Hemingway James A. 573 Division
Hemmelgarn H. 719 Fullerton av.
Hemphill E. F. 4459 Ellis av.
Hemphill William R. 4459 Ellis av.
Hempstead Charles, 387 N. State
Hempstead C. W. Mrs. 508 The Plaza
Hempstead G. C. The Ontario
Hempstead William G. E
Hemsteger John A. Dr.3836 Vincennes av.
Hemstreet W. J. Highland Park
Hench John B. Dr. Hinsdale
Henchman W. H. Chicago Beach hotel
Henderson Agnes Miss, 418 Washington
  boul.
Henderson Alfred S. Highland Park
Henderson A. M. 549 Jackson boul
Henderson B. 450 Belden av.
Henderson Charles M. 1816 Prairie av.
Henderson Chas. R. 51, 53d (H. P.)
Henderson David, Auditorium hotel
Henderson David H. 668 W. Adams
Henderson Edward, 780 Indian Boundary
  Road
Henderson Edward G. Evanston
Henderson Edwin A. 780 Indian Bound-
  ary Road
Henderson E. A. The Renfost
Henderson E. C. Mrs. Austin
Henderson E. F. Hotel Richelieu
Henderson E. J. Mrs. 2921 Indiana av.
Henderson F. H. 450 Belden av.
Henderson Gustav E. Highland Park
Henderson Harold, 4599 Oakenwald av.
Henderson Howard, 4109 Grand boul.
Henderson H. 964 Mayfair
Henderson H. E. Mrs. 4109 Grand boul.
Henderson H. M. 548, 61st, Englewood
Henderson I. W. Oak Park
Henderson JohnC. 1142 Washington boul.
Henderson John F. Lake Forest
Henderson J. A. 293 Rush
Henderson J. P. Dr. 1210 Winthrop av.
Henderson Lightner, 456 Belden av.
Henderson L. D. Dr. Evanston
Henderson N. H. Dr. 4401 Champlain av.
Henderson S. M. 269 Erie
Henderson Walter, 293 Rush
Henderson Wilbur F. 2623 Michigan
Henderson Wilbur S. 2623 Michigan av.
Henderson William, 293 Rush
Henderson William, 467 W. Congress
Henderson William J. 448 Belden av.
Henderson William P. 1620 Wrightwood
  av.
Hendley L. V. Mrs. 2579 N. Ashland av.
Hendrick H. W. 3405 Vernon av.
Hendricks Anna Miss, 3822 Ellis av.
Hendricks Charles A. 140, 65   , Eng.
Hendricks R. J. Union League Club
Hendrickson Ernest, 5510 Cornell av.
Hendrickson J. S. 5510 Cornell av.
Hendrickson Peter, Evanston
37

Henion W. B. 3027 Vernon av.
Henius Max, 2576 Magnolia av.
Henkel Fred.W. E. Dr. 538 Ashland boul.
Henkle Wm. H. 5317 Jefferson av.
Henn Arnold, 4561 Emerald av.
Henne Phillip, 589 Lasalle av.
Henneberry Kate Miss, 4859 Michigan
  av.
Henneberry W. P. 543 Jackson boul.
Hennegen R. H. Oak Park
Hennessey Richard M. 307 Webster av.
Hennessey W. H. 4338 Calumet av.
Hennessy C. M. 4123 Drexel boul.
Hennessy Edward, 282 Irving av.
Hennessy Elizabeth Mrs. 3131 Indiana av.
Hennessy James Mrs. 3243 Forest av.
Hennessy P. J. Col. 315 Superior
Hennessy W. B. 4123 Drexel Boul.
Hennessy W. E. 4123 Drexel boul.
Hennick Charles, Austin
Hennig Otto E. 3137 Rhodes av.
Henning D. Chicago Beach hotel
Henning E. Chicago Beach hotel.
Henning Francis A., M.D. 483 Dearborn
  av.   Sum. res. Delavan, Wis.
Henning Frank F. 283 Evanston av.
Henning John E. 3625 Ellis Park
Henning Kate Dr. Mayfair
Henning Oscar, Mayfair
Henoch L. M. Granada hotel
Henrich Jacob, 699 North Park av.
Henrici F. H. 170 Laflin
Henrici Philip, 48 Lincoln av.
Henricks E. W. Pullman
Henrotin Adolph, 299 Lasalle av.
Henrotin Charles, 376 Ontario
Henrotin Fernand, M. D. 353 Lasalle av.
Henry Albert J. 3960 Langley av.
Henry E. J. 1501 Oakdale av.
Henry Fidelio S. 3656 Grand boul.
Henry George W. 1913 Michigan av.
Henry G. N. 6605 Yale
Henry Harvey R. 3812 Wabash av.
Henry John A. 6601 Stewart av.
Henry J. B. 3000 Indiana av.
Henry L. E. Evanston
Henry R. L. 3656 Grand boul.
Henry William Mrs. 144 Loomis
Henry William J. 3960 Langley av.
Henschen H. Samuel, Evanston
Henschen William, Evanston
Henshaw F. A. 7719 S. Peoria
Henshaw H. H. 30 Campbell Park
Henshaw H. W. 432 N. State
Henson Charles W. 3249 South Park av.
Henson Horace, 3249 South Park av.
Henson H. L. Mrs. 3249 South Park av.
Henson P. S. Rev. 3249 South Park av.
Henson Wilmer Y. 3249 South Park av.
Hentrich C. Mrs. 351 Chicago av.
Hepburn John W. 36th ne. cor. Ellis av.
Heper Charles, 552 Washington boul.
Heper Otto, 66 Hamilton av.
Heppe George, 456 N. Wells
Heppner Henry, 3407 Forest av.
Hequembourg J. E. Dr. 515 Fullerton av.

Herben Stephen J. Evanston
Herbert H. E. 2210 Prairie av.
Herbert John W. 578 Washington boul.
Herbertz Charles, 3412 South Park av.
Herbst Bernard, 689 Sedgwick
Herbst F. Mrs. 3224 Forest av.
Herbst Herman, 517 Dearborn av.
Herbst William, 200, 25th
Hercock Robert J. 4550 Wabash av.
Herdien P. 402 Kenmore av.
Herdman E. D. 135, 37th
Herdman F. E. Winnetka
Hcreley Michael H. 215 Osgood
Hereley M. B. 450 Lasalle av.
Herendeen Charles, Hawthorne av. Eng.
Hereth Frank S. 284 Belden av.
Herhold Fred, 675 N. Robey
Herhold Fred. H. 302 Chicago av.
Herman Henry 3245 Vernon av.
Herman J. J. 3254 Vernon av.
Herman Leon M. 3423 South Park av.
Herman Samuel, 3352 South Park av.
Hermann Joseph, 411 N. Robey
Hermenhous Ernest, 1427 Michigan av.
Hermes P. E. Pullman
Hern George W. 24 Orchard (H.P.)
Heron Addie E. Mrs. 602 Park av.
Heron A. Gilbert, 570 Fullerton av.
Heron Hugh, 2826 Indiana av.
Heron John, 218 Ohio
Heron Presly M. 878 Jackson boul.
Heron Venetia M. G. Mrs. 1316 Washington boul.
Herr A. W. Mrs. 333, 34th
Herr Hiero B. 4469 Lake av.
Herr Isaac, Oak Park
Herr Percy, 4669 Lake av.
Herr Percy B. 4469 Lake av.
Herren Oscar F. 770 Lunt av.
Herrick C. K. 229 Lasalle av.
Herrick D 3409 Prairie av.
Herrick D. C. Oak Park
Herrick E. K. 4144 Indiana av.
Herrick E. Walter, 2018 Prairie av.
Herrick G. P. Mrs. 4217 Ellis av.
Herrick John J. 2221 Prairie av.
Herrick J. B., M.D. 751 Warren av.
Herrick Louise Miss, 2018 Prairie av.
Herrick L. A. Mrs. 2018 Prairie av.
Herrick O. W. Oak Park
Herrick Roswell Z. 4412 Indiana av.
Herrick W. S. Oak Park
Herriman W D. M.D.6307 Woodlawn av.
Herring Hubert C. 181, 53d (H.P.)
Herring Robert H. Evanston
Herring R. H. 7412 Webster av.
Herrman Charles, 206 Webster av.
Herrmann George, 1059 Warren av.
Herrmann Richard Dr. 1102 N. Halsted
Herrnheiser Adele Miss, 3362 Prairie av.
Herron Samuel P. 2602 Indiana av.
Herron S. B. 6446 Wright
Herschman Charles, 3417 Wabash av.
Herschman Henry, 3417 Wabash av.
Hersey . W. 843 W. Adams
Herson John, 4523 Lake av.
    J

Hertell Emily Miss, 51, 53d (H.P.)
Hertle Louis, Evanston
Hertz Henry L. 632 N. Hoyne av.
Herz Arthur, 4720 Evans av.
Herz Joseph, 4720 Evans av.
Herzfeld I. I. Mrs. 2964 Wabash av.
Hervey James F. 2953 Michigan av.
    Winter res. Riverside, Cal.
Hervey Robert, 33, 25th
Herzog Louis P. 30 Bryant av.
Herzog M. Dr. 1510 Lill av.
Herzog Nathan, 847 Warren av.
Herzog Rose Miss, 190, 37th
Herzog S. 419 Washington boul.
Hesing A. C. 3329 Vernon av.
Hesing Washington, 235 Michigan av.
Hesler Alex. Evanston
Hesler Arthur J. Evanston
Hesly Daniel, 1080 Centre, Argyle Park
Hess Chas. E. 604 Lasalle av.
Hess Christopher J. 4431 Ellis av.
Hess Daniel W. Evanston
Hess Ernest, 602 Lasalle av.
Hess Frank W. 611 Lasalle av.
Hess F. A., M.D. 554 Division
Hess George H. 3736 Lake av.
Hess George W. Evanston
Hess Grace E. Miss, Evanston
Hess Herbert, 3654 Prairie av.
Hess Howard A. 4431 Ellis av.
Hess Isaac, 3224 Prairie av.
Hess Jacob, 3130 Prairie av.
Hess John C. Evanston
Hess John V. 121, 21st
Hess Leo, 3135 Indiana av.
Hess L. W. 625 W. Monroe
Hess Magnus A. 420 Ashland boul.
Hess Mary E. Mrs. 43 S. Sheldon
Hess Siegel, 3135 Indiana av.
Hess William E. Evanston
Hess William H. 5226 Kimbark av.
Hess Winter D. Evanston
Hesselroth Lawrence, 1809 Frederick
Hessert Gustav Dr. 267 Erie
Hessert Gustav jr. 27 Arlington pl.
Hesslein J. R. 292 Rush
Hester Charles R. 373 Bowen av.
Hester John J. Ravinia
Hester J. G. 373 Bowen av.
Hester Nancy Henrietta Miss, 373 Bowen av.
Hester W. W. Dr. 3658 Vincennes av.
Heth H. S. 2024 Indiana av.
Heth James B. 2024 Indiana av.
Hetherington Henry J. Bond av. sw. cor. 73d
Hetherington James R. 5321 Washington av.
Hetherington John T. Bond av. sw. cor. 73d
Hetherington J. E. Dr. 1035 Warren av.
Hetich Charles A. 332 Bowen av.
Hettich Albert H. 308 Webster av.
Hettich H. L. 3715 Forest av.
Hettich L. J. 3715 Forest av.
Hettinger J. P. 460 Dayton

Hettler H. H. 37 Hawthorne pl.
Hetzler Herbert G. Hinsdale
Heuchling Theodore W., M.D. 663 La-
salle av.
Heuer August, 1758 Deming ct.
Heuermann Henry W. 168 Fremont
Heurtley Arthur, Oak Park
Heusner Louis D. 3519 Indiana av.
Heusner W. A. 6423 Wright
Hewes D. A. Mrs. 2428 Indiana av.
Süm. res. New Port, R. I.
Hewett A. C. Dr. 491 W. Adams
Hewitt Charles E.Rev.5535 Lexington av.
Hewitt Charles M. Virginia hotel
Hewitt Ephraim, 347, 56th (H.P.)
Hewitt F. H. Mrs. Lake Forest
Hewitt Henry H. 5535 Lexington av.
Hewitt Herbert E. 5535 Lexington av.
Hewitt James, 5040 Washington av.
Hewitt Jerome, 4318 Forrestville av.
Hewitt J. L. Mrs. 3002 Vernon av.
Hewitt William P. Mrs. 527 Jackson boul.
Hewitt W. W. 355 Park av.
Hewlings A. J. 3325 Indiana av.
Hexter Kaufman, 2513 Wabash av.
Hexter Stephen, 6200 Oglesby av.
Heyer Christian F. Hinsdale
Heyer Maria Anna Mrs. 483 Dearborn av.
Süm. res. Delavan, Wis.
Heyl Edward M. Col. U.S.A. Hotel Met-
ropole
Heylmann A. Mrs. 289 Webster av.
Heylmann C. J. Dr. 289 Webster av.
Heyman Emanuel S. 3716 Lake av.
Heyman Henry, 3207 Calumet av.
Heywood Abbie F. Mrs. 6736 Sherman
Heywood E. F. 403 Oak
Heywood Frank S. 24 Scott
Heywood John P. 24 Scott
Heywood Marion B. Miss, 24 Scott
Heywood P. P. 24 S
Heywood R. H. 6736 Sherman
Heywood W. E. 18 Delaware pl.
Heyworth James O. 2902 Michigan av.
Heyworth J. F. Mrs. 2902 Michigan av.
Süm. res. Long Island, N. Y.
Heyworth Lawrence, 2902 Michigan av.
Heyzer Henry P. 4145 Langley av.
Hiatt A. H., M.D. 4024 Drexel boul.
Hibbard A. S. Mrs. 397 Superior
Hibbard E. C. 5406 Madison av.
Hibbard Frederick A. 4223 Grand boul.
Hibbard F. V. S. 1701 Prairie av.
Hibbard Homer N. 5335 Jefferson av.
Hibbard John Mrs. 4223 Grand boul.
Hibbard John D. 4850 Woodlawn av.
Hibbard Lewis B. Highland Park
Hibbard Thomas W. 1219 Wolcott
Hibbard W. B. 4126 Berkeley av.
Hibbard W. G. 1701 Prairie av.
Hibbard W. G. jr. 1701 Prairie av.
Hibbard W. N. Mrs. 5000 Greenwood av.
Hibben James, Evanston
Hick G. C. Evanston
Hickcox P. 111 Loomis
Hickey Charles M. 2712 Calumet av.

Hickey Jackson J. 5746 Wabash av.
Hickey John, 4809 Indiana av.
Hickey Joseph V. 2712 Calumet av.
Hickey Marie Mrs. 5746 Wabash av.
Hickey Michael C. 2712 Calumet av.
Hickey M. A. 138 Garfield boul.
Hickox W. C. 897 W. Monroe
Hicks A. R. 3152 Groveland av.
Hicks Bohn C. 6617 Stewart av.
Hicks Edward L. 148 Dearborn av.
Hicks Ernestine Dr. 806, 63d ct. Eng.
Hicks E. 7039 Webster av.
Hicks Fannie Mrs. 46, 35th
Hicks Frank M. 59 Warren av.
Hicks George I. 735 W. Monroe
Hicks George W. 561 S. Oakley av.
Hicks Henry C. 6615 Stewart av.
Hicks James A. LaGrange
Hicks John G. 4429 Ellis av.
Hicks O. H. Hotel Barry
Hicks Thomas P. 697 Walnut
Hickson H. R. Chicago Beach hotel
Hiebler J. H. Mrs. 428 N. State
Hield George C. Irving Park
Hieronimus F. C. Mrs. 4400 St. Lawrence
av.
Hieronimus Julius, 4400 St. Lawrence av.
Hiestand Henry, 4279 Grand av.
Hiester Alvin C. Dr. 1058 S. Central Park
av.
Higbee Charles E. 292 Marshfield av.
Higbie D. W. 4407 Calumet av.
Higbie Fred. K. 6920 Eggleston av.
Higbie Nathan B. 4417 Indiana av.
Higgie Archibald A. 4933 Ellis av.
Higgie Arthur M. 4933 Ellis av.
Higgie James L. 4933 Ellis av.
Higgie James L. jr. 348 Ogden av.
Higgie M. L. Miss, 4933 Ellis av.
Higgie Noble K. 4933 Ellis av.
Higgins A. E. Dr. LaGrange
Higgins Caroline Mrs. 441 Englewood av.
Higgins Charles, 844 Sherwin av.
Higgins Charles 375 Ontario
Higgins Charles A. 10 St. James pl.
Higgins Charles F. 391 State
Higgins C. C. Dr. 391 N. State
Higgins Edward, 103 Walton pl.
Higgins Henry T. 4514 Emerald av.
Higgins James D. Dr. 928 Walnut
Higgins James E. 253 Rush
Higgins John, 1566 W. Monroe
Higgins John F. 1566 W. Monroe
Higgins John W. 4064 Michigan terrace
Higgins J. D. 253 Rush
Higgins J. Frank, 644 W. Taylor
Higgins L. M. Miss, 555 W. Monroe
Higgins Marion Miss, 145 Oakwood boul.
Higgins M. O. Hotel Windermere
Higgins S. G. Mrs. 143 Oakwood boul.
Higgins Van H. Mrs. 4948 Woodlawn av.
Higgins W. G. 143 Oakwood boul.
Higginson Charles M. Riverside
Higginson D. T. Elmhurst
Higginson George, 175 Goethe
Higginson George jr. 175 Goethe

Higginson G. M. Elmhurst
Higgs I. W. Rev. 32 Evergreen av.
High George H. 63 Lake Shore drive
High George Meeker, 59 Cedar
High James L. 2021 Prairie av.
Highland John Mrs. Evanston.
Highley G. E. 5611 Washington av.
Higinbotham Florence Miss, 2838 Michigan av.
Higinbotham Harry M. 2838 Michigan av.
Higinbotham H. D. 2838 Michigan av.
Higinbotham H. N. 2838 Michigan av.
Higley D. C. 3347 Calumet av.
Higley Wm. K. Prof. 6148 Sheridan av.
Higley W. E. 4623 Greenwood av.
Hiland J. H. 4525 Ellis av.
Hilbourne Harry C. 3751 Forest av.
Hild Charles, 698 Burling
Hild Frederick H. 321 N. Wells
Hild Mary C. Mrs. 321 N. Wells
Hildebrand Lewis K. Hinsdale
Hildebrand William R. 428 Cleveland av.
Hildebrandt Fred H. 256 Seminary av.
Hildebrandt Geo. 613, 67th, Eng.
Hildreth Charles H. 7 Aldine sq.
Hildreth Fred B. 1411 Michigan av.
Hildreth J. H. 746 W. Monroe
Hildreth L. E. Evanston
Hiles Theron L. Mayfair
Hilgard R. C. Mrs. 5429 Cottage Grove av.
Hilger F. R. 2548 Indiana av.
Hill Alonzo H. Irving Park
Hill Azra, Evanston
Hill A. D. 845 Garfield boul.
Hill A. E. 62 The Yale
Hill A. Leonard Mrs. Ravinia
Hill Bert C. 4054 Grand boul.
Hill B. F. Wilmette
Hill Calvin H. Evanston
Hill Caroline Mrs. 288 Ohio
Hill Carrie A. Mrs. 350 Ashland boul.
Hill Carrie E. Miss, 611 Washington boul.
Hill Chauncey B. Austin
Hill Claude C. 1005 Farwell av.
Hill Cyrus F. Mrs. 2537 Michigan av.
Hill C. Edward, 62 The Yale
Hill C. E. Hotel Metropole
Hill Daniel O. 1912 Barry av.
Hill David K. 2559 Michigan av.
Hill Edgar A. 317 Warren av.
Hill Edward, 824 Pullman bldg.
Hill Edward H. 560 Kenwood pl
Hill Edward Niles, 5100 Hibbard av.
Hill Edwin, Forest hotei (R. P.)
Hill Elmer C. 750 N. Park av.
Hill E. D. Mrs. The Arizona
Hill E. J. 7100 Eggleston av.
Hill E. N. Mrs. Evanston
Hill Francis J. 2942 Indiana av.
Hill Frank H. 745 W. Monroe
Hill Frank L. 57 Delaware pl.
Hill Frank M. 620, 61st, Englewood
Hill Fred A. Austin
Hill Fred M. 4054 Grand boul.
Hill Fred W. 7100 Eggleston av.
Hill Frederick W. 3910 Langley av.

Hill Fremont, LaGrange
Hill George, Lombard
Hill George H. 695 Washington boul.
Hill Helen H. Miss, 19 Ashland boul.
Hill Henry H. 261 Ashland boul.
Hill Henry L. Mrs. 2316 Calumet av.
Hill Henry W. 235 Michigan av.
Hill Howard 231 Marshfield av.
Hill Howard Z. Evanston
Hill H. B. Evanston
Hill Irene N. Miss, 350 Ashland boul.
Hill James A. 4054 Grand boul.
Hill James M. Hotel Windermere
Hill James M. Mrs. 3910 Langley av.
Hill James T. 2559 Michigan av.
Hill John jr. Tracy
Hill John C. Rev. Austin
Hill John H. 4156 Berkeley av.
Hill Joseph W. 6427 Woodlawn av.
Hill J. B. Julien hotel
Hill J. Claude, 6510 Oglesby av.
Hill J. J. 3608 Grand boul.
Hill Lysander Judge, Hotel Metropole
Hill Mary M. Mrs. 4156 Berkeley av.
Hill Matson, 3223 Groveland av.
Hill Mattie S. Miss, 628 Dearborn av.
Hill Percy L. Ravinia
Hill Robert Mrs. Forest hotel (R. P.)
Hill Robert J. 4608 Champlain av.
Hill Robert S. 4243 Vincennes av.
Hill Russell D. 2316 Calumet av.
Hill Sarah Mrs. 231 Marshfield av.
Hill S. V. 4505 Indiana av.
Hill Walter, 205 Warren av.
Hill William, 67 University pl.
Hill William T. 1250 Washington boul.
Hill W. P. Lombard
Hill W. R. 4301 Indiana av.
Hillabrant W. D. 2343 Calumet av.
Hillard Charles W. 4819 Kimbark av.
Hillary P. J. 3138 Wabash av.
Hillegas W. R., M.D. 229, 28th
Hiller Felix, Hotel Normandie
Hiller Gustav, 3751 Lake av.
Hiller Henrietta Mrs. Evanston
Hiller L. 3844 Lake av.
Hilliard E. P. Mrs. Longwood
Hilliard L. P. Longwood
Hillinger Philip, 1458 Wolfram
Hillis D. M. 3341 Prairie av.
Hillis N. D. Rev. Evanston
Hillman Benjamin, Lexington hotel
Hillman Charles H. 6146 Oglesby av
Hillman C. W. French house, Evanston
Hillman Edward, Lexington hotel
Hillman G. F. Virginia hotel
Hillman Louis, 2339 N. Halsted
Hillman Louis, Lexington hotel
Hillman Sarah Miss, Lexington hotel
Hills Abigail M. Mrs. 213, 53d (H.P.)
Hills Alfred K. 3009 Vernon av.
Hills Charles F. 271 Oakwood boul.
Hills Edwin E. 3009 Vernon av.
Hills Erasmus O. 3942 Ellis av.
Hills Frank C. Evanston
Hills Frederick D. 213, 53d (H.P.)

Hills Gage, 3009 Vernon av.
Hills James M. 1038 N. Halsted
Hills John N. Chicago Beach hotel
Hills William E. 3942 Ellis av.
Hills W. Scott, 3953 Michigan av.
Hiltabidell Anna Mrs. 792 Jackson boul.
Hiltman J. W. 1037 Evanston av.
Hilton C. C. 684 W. Monroe
Hilton C. C. Lakota hotel
Hilton Edward, Oak Park
Hilton George L. Lakota hotel
Hilton G. V. Dr. 6327 Woodlawn av.
Hilton H. H. 6327 Woodlawn av.
Hilton John Ranney, 5656 Monroe av.
Hilton J. B. Mrs. Evanston
Hilton P. R. 6628 Perry av.
Hilton Walter W. 5656 Monroe av.
Hilton William K. 194, 36th
Hilts Adelaide Mrs. 7126 South Chicago av.
Hiltz Grace Miss, 3027 Groveland av.
Himrod Charles, 18 Wisconsin
Himrod Frank W. 4531 Vincennes av.
Himrod Kirk, 1624 Belmont av.
Himrod P. Miss, 537 Belden av.
Hincelot Ferdinand, 58 Lincoln av.
Hinchliff William, 502 Jackson boul.
Hinckley Abner T. 5408 Washington av.
Hinckley A. T. jr. 5408 Washington av.
Hinckley E. F. 4554 Oakenwald av.
Hinckley E. G. 4400 Berkeley av.
Hinckley F. E. Lake Forest
Hinckley George W. Hinsdale
Hinckley John H. 4519 Woodlawn av.
Hinckley Myron T. LaGrange
Hinckley M. L. Mrs. 2311 Indiana av.
Hinckley O. W. 4417 Champlain av.
Hinckley S. F. Mrs. 646 W. Monroe
Hinckley S. G. 4400 Berkeley av.
Hinckley William B. Hinsdale
Hinckley William S. Hinsdale
Hinde Thomas Woodnut, 118 Astor
        Sum. res. Elkhorn, Ky.
Hindman W. M. Rev. 6914 Perry av.
Hinds Albert jr. 1029 N. Clark
Hinds Charles E. Hinsdale
Hinds E. P. Hinsdale
Hinds E. P. jr. Hinsdale
Hinds O. S. 98 N. Kedzie av.
Hine Cicero, 1109 Winona
Hine Milton, 1109 Winona
Hine M. F. Mrs. 3554 Prairie av.
Hiner J. W. Hyde Park hotel
Hines A. G. Hinsdale
Hines Edward M. 26 Vernon Park pl.
Hines Nannie M. Miss, Evanston
Hines P. 26 Vernon Park pl.
Hingst Charlotte Mrs. 468 W. Congress
Hinisch Carl W. 723 Chase av.
Hinisch William W. Dr. 723 Chase av.
Hinkins J. E. Dr. 5224 Kimbark av.
Hinkins W. A. 143 Lincoln av.
Hinkley Chas. W. 100, 24th
Hinkley James Otis, 3306 Indiana av.
Hinkley Watson S. 92, 26th
Hinman Albert W. Dr. 718 Washington
        boul.

Hinman Benjamin P. Kenilworth
Hinman Benjamin P. jr. Kenilworth
Hinman C. F. 4349 St. Lawrence av.
Hinman C. H. 2947 Indiana av.
Hinman H. C. 292 Indiana
Hinman J   H. 4118 Ellis av.
Hinman James M. 4118 Ellis av.
Hinman S. D. 2604 Prairie av.
Hinners George R. 602 Greenleaf av.
Hinsdale H. K. Evanston
Hinsdale H. W. Evanston
Hinsey J. A. 4233 Calumet av.
Hinson James A. 606 Englewood av.
Hinton Francis, Auditorium annex
Hinz Augusta Dr. 426 Lasalle av.
Hipp W. Harrison Dr. 4501 Wabash av.
Hippach Charles F. 4348 Grand boul.
Hipple E. H. 4337 Grand boul.
Hipple George, 3227 Arlington
Hipple George I. 3227 Arlington
Hipwell W. O. Highland Park
Hirsch Alfred A. 1523 Wolfram
Hirsch A. 3329 South Park av.
Hirsch Edward, 3249 Vernon av.
Hirsch Emil G. Dr. 3612 Grand boul.
Hirsch Fred, 3639 Michigan av.
Hirsch Henry, 353 Oakwood boul.
Hirsch H. J. Lieut. Fort Sheridan
Hirsch Isaac, 353 Oakwood boul.
Hirsch Joseph, 417 Marshfield av.
Hirsch L. K. 436, 37th ct.
Hirsch Morris, 3442 Prairie av.
Hirsch Morris, 3304 Calumet av.
Hirsch M. 353 Oakwood boul.
Hirsch Oscar, 3329 South Park av.
Hirsch Ralph J. River Forest
Hirsch S. Mrs. 635 Fullerton av.
Hirsch William, 3354 Vernon av.
Hirschbein Samuel, 3406 Vernon av.
Hirschfield Herman H. 260 Fremont
Hirschl A. J. 6054 Sheridan av.
Hirsh Arthur, 3633 Vernon av.
Hirsh Augustus, 4544 Emerald av.
Hirsh Dwight S. 3427 Michigan av.
Hirsh Emanuel, 3018 Groveland av.
Hirsh Harry S. 3427 Michigan av.
Hirsh Jacob, 3430 Michigan av.
Hirsh Joseph M. 3633 Vernon av.
Hirsh Manuel, 4117 Grand boul.
Hirsh Morris G. 4117 Grand boul.
Hirsh Morris M. 3437 Michigan av.
Hirsh Solomon, 3427 Michigan av.
        Sum. res. Mackinac Island, Mich.
Hirsh Solomon, 4117 Grand boul.
Hirsh Solomon J. 3430 Michigan av.
Hirshfield Rosa Mrs. 2637 N. Ashland av.
Hirshman Leon, 3339 Indiana av.
Hirt John, 617 N. Wells
Hislop F. George, 6619 Hope av.
Hiss Nelson, Hotel Metropole
Hitch E. V. 255 Ontario
Hitchcock Alvirus N. Ridgeland
Hitchcock Annie Mrs. 4741 Greenwood
        av.
Hitchcock Charles, 4298 N. Clark
Hitchcock Charles A. Austin

Hitchcock Charles A. jr. Austin
Hitchcock David, 1191 S. Central Park av.
Hitchcock E. J. 787 W. Monroe
Hitchcock Frank A. Riverside
Hitchcock H. H. 618, 65th
    Sum. res. Pistaqua Bay, Ill.
Hitchcock James A. 203 Park av.
Hitchcock John M. 165 Howe
Hitchcock Lemuel, 3845 Ellis av.
Hitchcock Luke Dr. 4613 Drexel boul.
Hitchcock L. Hotel Windermere
Hitchcock Mary E. Mrs. 195 Oakwood
    boul.
Hitchcock M. M. Berwyn
Hitchcock Roderick M. 1222 Wright-
    wood av.
Hitchcock Romyn, 152, 36th
Hitchcock R. A. Lexington hotel
Hitchcock S. A. Mrs. 787 W. Monroe
Hitchcock Wm. 195 Oakwood boul.
Hitchcock W. D. Evanston
Hitchens R. K. 5463 Washington av.
Hitchings Louis B. 175 Evanston av.
Hitt Herman U. 4120 Calumet av.
Hitt Isaac R. Evanston
Hitt Isaac R. jr. Evanston
Hitt John, 384 Oak
Hitt W. J. Tracy
Hitt W. M. 4330 Berkeley av.
Hittel John B. 1746 Wrightwood av.
Hixon W. L. 391 Warren av.
Hixson A. Mrs. 411 Dearborn av.
Hixson Cassius C. 3953 Michigan av.
Hjortsberg Max Mrs. 387 Lasalle av.
Hoadley A. E. Dr. 683 Washington boul.
Hoadley J. H. 3641 Prairie av.
Hoadley J. M. 608, 44th
Hoag Frank D. 6338 Drexel av.
Hoag H. C. Mrs. Evanston
Hoag H. R. Morgan Park
Hoag Junius C. Dr. 58, 43d
Hoag Marie F. Miss, 1101 Washington
    boul.
Hoag William G. Evanston
Hoag W. J. 532 Chestnut, Englewood
Hoagland A. J. 6638 Stewart av.
Hoagland Edward K. 1146 Washington
    boul.
Hoagland Elisha H. 1146 Washington
    boul.
Hoagland Jay S. 1146 Washington boul.
Hoagland John R. 5069 Lake av.
Hoagland William, 23 Oakwood av.
Hoagland W. R. 99, 33d
Hoar Edward, Hinsdale
Hoard Charles D. 3162 Groveland av.
Hoard E. W. Oak Park
Hobart H. M. Mrs. 481 Belden av.
Hobart H. R. 5110 East End av.
Hobb J. N. 4455 Berkeley av.
Hobbs James B. 343 Lasalle av.
    Sum. res. Lake Bluff, Ill.
Hobbs J. O. Dr. 452 Jackson boul.
Hobbs William F. 6221 Lexington av.
Hobler Edward G. Austin
Hobon A. J. 442 Belden av.

Hobson B. L. 497 Fullerton av.
Hoch James J. 1849 Belmont av.
Hoch William jr. 437 Belden av.
Hochbaum Henry, 2337 N. Paulina
Hodge   J. 762 Washington
    boulAlexander
Hodge A. T. 462 Morse av.
Hodge J. M. Hyde Park hotel
Hodge S. Morris, Austin
Hodge Thomas, 462 Morse av.
Hodge W. M. 3760 Lake av.
Hodges Almeda Mrs. Hinsdale
Hodges Charles H. 89 Astor
Hodges C. W. 4445 Langley av.
Hodges L. M. Hinsdale
Hodges Walter E. Riverside
Hodgeson I. jr. Chicago Athletic Assn.
Hodgkins J. 6706 Wentworth av.
Hodgson Joseph, 311 Webster av.
Hodgson J. H. 311 Webster av.
Hodgosn J. S. Mrs. Hotel Metropole
Hodgson J. T. River Forest
Hodnett Thos. P. Rev. 345 Walnut
Hodson J. G. Maywood
Hodson Walter D. 7201 Webster av.
Hoefeld Albert, 3635 Vernon av.
Hoefeld Philipene Miss, 3835 Vincennes
    av.
Hoefner Frank, 681 North Park av.
Hoelscher Edward C. 1319 Wash'n boul.
Hoelscher Herman M. 1319 Washington
    boul.
Hoelscher J. H. Dr. 298 Webster av.
Hoelter H. L. Rev. 527 Ashland boul.
Hoeppner Emil, 327 Maple, Englewood
Hoerlein H. A. 3310½ Rhodes av.
Hoes James H. Austin
Hoey M. H. 6546 Union av.
Hofeld Felix S. 651 Fullerton av.
Hofeld Jordan, 3337 Calumet av.
Hoefeld Sam A. 651 Fullerton av.
Hoff Charles W. 435, 61st (H.P.)
Hoff Herman, Evanston
Hoffert Isaac, 888½ W. Adams
Hoffheimer Nathan, 3616 Prairie av.
Hofflund Alexander, 408 Kenmore av.
Hoffman Edward, 3154 South Park av.
Hoffman Emil, Norwood Park
Hoffman F. A. jr. Elmhurst
Hoffman George W. Oak Park
Hoffman Harry, 4008 Drexel boul.
Hoffman Harry V. 89, 18th
Hoffman Henry A. Evanston
Hoffman Herbert, Morton Park.
Hoffman H. J. 390 Warren av.
Hoffman John Mrs. 1067 Warren av.
Hoffman John L. 1067 Warren av.
Hoffman John W. Evanston
Hoffman Julius, Norwood Park
Hoffman J. Jos. 3764 Indiana av.
Hoffman J. M. 1765 Oakdale av.
Hoffman Otto E. H. Norwood Park
Hoffman William, Evanston
Hoffman William D. 1641 Briar pl.
Hoffman William O. 3660 Michigan av.
Hoffmann Arthur, 5474 Greenwood av.

Hoffmann B. 1273 N. Clark
Hoffmann Charles G. 428 Ashland boul.
Hoffmann G. A. Mrs. 428 Ashland boul.
Hoffmann Henry, 563 Burling
Hoffmann Herman H. 1273 N. Clark
Hoffmann Hugo, 5474 Greenwood av.
Hoffstadt Gus, 217, 32d
Hofheimer Ernst, 2946 Prairie av.
Hofheimer Zach. 342 Lasalle av.
Hofman Henry, 744 W. Monroe
Hofman Moritz, 744 W. Monroe
Hofman Samuel, 744 W. Monroe
Hofmann Elizabeth M. Mrs. 234 Cass
Hofmann Gustav, 2007 Surf
Hogan H. F. 6763 South Chicago av.
Hogan Joseph, 4306 Greenwood av.
Hogan M. W. 970 Jackson boul.
Hogan Thomas, Elmhurst
Hogan Thomas S. 970 Jackson boul.
Hoge G. C. Winnetka
Hoge Holmes, Evanston
Hogey J. H. 3123 Vernon av.
Hoggins John, 77 Centre av.
Hogl C. R. Evanston
Hogue Eugene, Auditorium hotel
Hohlfeld Charles, 877 Spaulding av.
Hohmann John, Oak Park
Hohmann W. A. Miss, 256 Ontario
Hoig William F. 303 Huron
Hoit Charles S. 3916 Lake av.
Hoit George B. The Tudor
Hoit J. P. 3916 Lake av.
Hoit W. P. 292, 41st
Hoke George R. Evanston
Hoke John F. 67 University pl.
Holabird R. G. Evanston
Holabird William A. Evanston
Holbrook A. P. Oak Park
Holbrook A. W. Mrs. 19, 35th
Holbrook Benjamin, 6409 Stewart av.
Holbrook Benjamin jr. 6409 Stewart av.
Holbrook Edmond S. 4441 Champlain
  av.
Holbrook Francis D. Dr. Lincoln Park
  Sanitarium
Holbrook F. A. Evanston
Holbrook F. W. 1740 Addison av.
Holbrook Graves, Oak Park
Holbrook J. H. 3921 Prairie av.
Holbrook J. L. 32, The Yale
Holbrook O. J. LaGrange
Holbrook William G. 1740 Addison av.
Holcomb B. T. Evanston
Holcomb D. N. 2610 Commercial (L.V.)
Holcomb Herbert W. Hinsdale
Holcomb William H. Hinsdale
Holcomb William H. jr. Hinsdale
Holcomb W. B. Mrs. 2610 Commercial
  (L.V.)
Holden Charles C. P. 20 Aberdeen
Holden Charles N. 1841 Wellington
Holden Charles R. 66 Ogden av.
Holden C. N. Mrs. 681 W. Monroe
Holden Elizabeth Mrs. 802 W. Monroe
Holden Ezra, 4526 Oakenwald av.
Holden E. Wallace 4526 Oakenwald av.

Holden F. H. 363 Bowen av.
Holden George, 365, 34th
Holden Henry P. 639 W. Adams
Holden H. G. Mrs. 263 Ontario
Holden Harry R. Evanston
Holden I. H. 88 Centre av.
Holden Jane Mrs. 639 W. Adams
Holden John T. Fort Sheridan
Holden Josephine Miss, The Wellington
Holden J. S. 112 S. Lincoln
Holden N. B. 586 W. Congress
Holden Warren F. 1033 Warren av.
Holden Walter S. 81 S. Robey
Holden William H. 500 W. Monroe
Holder F. W. 3333 Calumet av.
Holdom Jesse, 3324 Vernon av.
Holdredge Charles B. Oak Park
Holdsworth J. J. 620 Lasalle av.
Hole Leonard H. Western Springs
Holenberg C. P. 456 Cleveland av.
Holenshade J. C. 770 Warren av.
Holgate Thomas F. Prof. Evanston
Holinger A. 170 Eugenie
Holladay B. D. Miss, 536 Dearborn av.
Holladay B. E. 1802 Michigan av.
Holladay Jesse, 536 Dearborn av.
Holland Amelia Mrs. 747 Sedgwick
Holland Harry L. 3000 Michigan av.
Holland John, 1176 Washington boul.
Holland John F. 2124 Michigan av.
Holland J. Edmund, 403 N. State
Holland J. J. 5213 Washington av.
Holland J. P. 600, 67th Englewood
Holland Philo L., M.D. 4608 Lake av.
Holland S. C. 11 University pl.
Holland S. J. Hyde Park hotel
Holland William E. 5523 Madison av.
Holland W. E. V. 56 Throop
Hollander Meyer J. 3443 Wabash av.
Hollett R. P. Evanston
Holley L. G. Oak Park
Holley S. A. Mrs. Oak Park
Hollinger Theodore T. Evanston
Hollingshead John, Evanston
Hollingshead Thomas C. Evanston
Hollingsworth Rachel E. Dr. 6356 Stewart
  av.
Hollis F. Irving Park
Hollis Henry L. 3004 Prairie av.
Hollis J. F. Irving Park
Hollister Harry D. 4313 Cottage Grove av
Hollister H. M. Oak Park
Hollister John H., M.D. 3430 Rhodes av.
Hollister M. E. Judge, 3430 Rhodes av.
Hollister W. C. 372 Webster av.
Holloway Charles, 302 Bowen av.
Holloway George A. 3436 Prairie av.
Holloway George F. Oak Park
Holloway Mary S. Mrs. 302 Bowen av.
Hollstein Albert M. 2240 Michigan av.
Hollstein G. M. 2240 Michigan av.
Holly William T. 566 Kenwood pl.
Holman Alfred L. 2115 Indiana av.
Holman Daniel F. 804 W. Monroe
Holman Edward, 4514 Ellis av.
Holman E. E. Dr. 6314 Harvard

Holman Harriet Miss, 2455 Michigan av.
Holman I. W. Hy Park hotel
Holman Maria H. Miss, 2455 Michigan av.
Holman Mary A. Mrs. 2455 Michigan av.
Holman Theo. 4514 Ellis av.
Holmberg Ch. Washington Heights
Holmes Albert W. Jefferson Park
Holmes Bayard, M.D. 104, 40th
Holmes Charles Mrs. 749 W. Monroe
Holmes Charles W. 4320 St. Lawrence av.
Holmes C. B. 4222 Berkeley av. .
Holmes C. N. 5027 Lake av.
Holmes David, Highland Park
Holmes David E. Rev. 3233 Indiana av.
Holmes Edward B. 281 Ashland boul.
Holmes Edward I. 3233 Indiana av.
Holmes Emil A. 172 Evergreen av.
Holmes E. Burton, 229 Michigan av.
Holmes E. L. Dr. 530 W. Adams
Holmes Frank F. 965 Warren av.
Holmes Fred, 3823 Vernon av.
Holmes F. W. 154 Loomis
Holmes George D. 23 Scott
Holmes George E. Kenilworth
Holmes George J. 687 Washington boul.
Holmes George P. Mrs. 687 Washington
　　boul.　Sum. res. Malden, Mass.
Holmes Harvey A. 281 Ashland boul.
Holmes Hiram, 4320 Emerald av.
Holmes Ira, 229 Michigan av.
Holmes Ira G. 229 Michigan av.
Holmes Jacob L. 880' 72d (H.P.)
Holmes Louis H. LaGrange
Holmes Marc S, 4432 Berkeley av.
Holmes Marshall, 436 N. Normal Park-
　　way
Holmes Mary C. Mrs. 153, 25th
Holmes Mary E. Mrs. Oak Park
Holmes Mary E. Mrs. 3233 Indiana av.
Holmes Mary J. Miss, 44 Scott
Holmes Morris G. Evanston
Holmes M. Mrs. 475, 42d (H.P.)
Holmes Oliver W. 373 Ashland boul.
Holmes Ralph H. LaGrange
Holmes Rud lph W. Dr. 530 W. Adams
Holmes R. Co Virginia hotel
Holmes W. C. 42, 39th
Holroyd E. A. 448 W av.
Holroyd E. E. Dr. 88 Washington boul.
Holst Martin, 1219 Wilton av.
Holt A. E. 7209 Jeffrey av.
Holt A. L. Mrs. Lake Forest
Holt Charles S. 1931 Calumet av.
Holt D. R. Lake Forest
Holt Edgar, 235 Michigan av.
Holt George H. Lake Forest
Holt Granville M. 5316 Lexington av.
Holt L. W. Mrs. 2918 Groveland av.
Holt Mary E. Mrs. 3716 Forest av.
Holton Anna Mrs. Auditorium annex
Holton Charles C. 426 Center
　　Winter res. San Mateo, Florida
Holton Ethan A. 426 Center
　　Winter res. San Mateo, Florida
Holton Frank G. Riverside
Holton F. E. Irving Park

Holton George D. 4345 Drexel boul.
Holton T. J. 6405 Oglesby av.
Holton William B. 4124 Ellis av.
Holverscheid Caroline Mrs. Hinsdale
Holverscheid Henry, Hinsdale
Holway W. H. The Arizona
Holyoke William E. Rev. 1170 Washing-
　　ton boul.
Holzheimer Eda Mrs. 3538 Ellis av.
Holzwarth E. Mrs. 616 Fullerton av.
Homan Gus, 6749 Union av.
Homer George W. River Forest
Hommes F. J. 448 Belden av.
Homrig Charles A. 100 Flournoy
Honberger F. H. Dr. 3808 Indiana av.
Honkamp Fred, 3747 Prairie av.
Honkamp Lawrence, 4208 Vincennes av.
Honore Adrian C. 2103 Michigan av.
Honore B. L. 701 The Plaza
Honore Frank L. 3646 Indiana av.
Honore Harry H. jr. 2702 Michigan av.
Honore H. H. 2103 Michigan av.
Honore Lockwood, 2103 Michigan av.
Honore N. K. 2103 Michigan av.
Honsinger Brainard, LaGrange
Honsinger Emanuel Dr. 318 Park av.
Hood C. Todd, Dr. 992 W. Adams
Hood James, 485 Bowen av.
Hood John D. 485 Bowen av.
Hood L. S. Mrs. Hotel Metropole
Hood Thomas, 701 Washington boul.
Hood Thomas C. Austin
Hoof George W. 526 Leland av.
Hoof John C. 1290 Wolcott
Hook George A. 4200 Langley av.
Hook William W. 272 Erie
Hooke A. C. 4430 Berkeley av.
Hooker Francis B. 49, 46th
Hooker George, 300 Webster av.
Hooker H. M. 569 Washington boul.
Hooker J. L. Mrs. Oak Park
Hooker LeRoy Rev. 3017 Vernon av.
Hooker Stephen G. 300 Webster av.
Hooley Robert, Revere house
Hooley R. M. Mrs. 17 Delaware pl.
Hoon John M. 3447 Prairie av.
Hooper Edwin E. 85 Seeley av.
Hooper Henry, M.D. 541 N. State
Hooper H. E. 819 Pullman bldg.
Hooper J. K. 6640 Perry av.
Hoopes J. H. Oak Park
Hoops Charles H. 2957 Michigan av.
Hoops Thomas, 145 Oakwood boul
Hoops William H. 4105 Drexel boul.
Hoover C. A. Mrs. 354 Kenmore av.
Hoover George K. Rev. Evanston
Hoover George Percy, 1832 Oakdale av.
Hoover Laura Miss, 2714 Calumet av.
Hoover Thomas W. LaGrange
Hopkins A. Grant Dr. 1469 Wellington
Hopkins A. S. 5207 Kimbark av.
Hopkins Buel R. 4527 Forrestville av.
Hopkins Charles, 4545 Lake av.
Hopkins Charles R. 3255 Groveland av.
Hopkins E. jr. 66 Warren av.
Hopkins Forest B. 328 Warren av.

Hopkins Francis A. 4036 Prairie av.
Hopkins F. H. Hotel Metropole
Hopkins George E. Evanston
Hopkins George L. Evanston
Hopkins H. G. 371 Bowen av.
Hopkins I. H. Dr. 2715 Wabash av.
Hopkins John P. Hon. Pullman
Hopkins J. Mrs. 328 Warren av.
Hopkins J. A. Chicago Beach hotel
Hopkins J. E. 4545 Lake av.
Hopkins Louis M. 32 Bryant av.
Hopkins M. F. Mrs. 2813 Calumet av.
Hopkins M. P. Mrs. 469 Fullerton av.
Hopkins Robert, 4545 Lake av.
Hopkins R. S. 3556 Prairie av.
Hopkins Sumner, 3237 Forest av.
Hopkins William B. 1686 Barry av.
Hopkins William H. 4814 Champlain av.
Hopkins William P. Evanston
Hopkins W. 4814 Champlain av.
Hopkins W. C. Mrs. 6936 Vernon av.
Hopkinson Mary Mrs. 451 Washington
  boul.
Hopper S. L. 468 Fullerton av.
Hoppin B. E. 6636 Wentworth av.
Hopping Allie M. Mrs. Irving Park
Hopson E. J. Hotel Imperial
Hopson Frances H.Miss, Hotel Imperial
Hopson Joseph A. Hotel Imperial
Horan Edward, 1494 Washington boul.
Horan M. 318 Loomis
Hord Charles S. 4762 Lake av.
Hord George M. 4762 Lake av.
Hord Lillian, 4762 Lake av.
Horine M. W. Dr. 333 Ohio
Horn Herman E. 486 N. Wells
Horn John, 771 Touhy av.
Horn John C. 89 Ewing pl.
Horn M. A. Mrs. 102 Flournoy
Hornbaker W. R. 4343 Prairie av.
Hornbeck William P. Pullman
Horne F. W. Chicago Beach hotel
Horner Albert, 1705 Michigan av.
Horner Angel, 1705 Michigan av.
Horner Charles, 1705 Michigan av.
Horner Henry Mrs. 1705 Michigan av.
Horner Isaac, 1705 Michigan av.
Horner Joseph, 1839 Michigan av.
Horner Maurice L. 3133 Michigan av.
Horney Isaac V. 519 Lasalle av.
Horney William E. 519 Lasalle av.
Horning J. J. 6323 Wentworth av.
Hornsby J. A. 2485 Commercial (L.V.)
Hornstein Leon, 900 Jackson boul.
Hornthal Louis, 56 Bryant av.
Horr George B. 4445 Sidney av.
Horswell Geo. H. Prof. Evanston
Horton Ballister F. 3135 Forest av.
Horton Benjamin P. Oak Park
Horton C. J. 4200 Berkeley av.
Horton Emily Mrs. Ridgeland
Horton F. The Ontario
Horton Henry, Lake Forest
Horton H. B. Oak Park
Horton H. E. Tracy
Horton Jere, Austin

Horton J. M. 122 Ashland boul.
Horton Margaret E. Mrs. 3050 Lake
  Park av.
Horton O. H. Judge, LaGrange
Horton Richard, LaGrange
Horton Sara Miss, 18 Aldine sq.
Horwitz Bernard, 4448 St. Lawrence av.
Horwitz R. Mme. 2500 Indiana av.
Hosbury John, 292 Bowen av.
Hosford Morton A. 4216 Berkeley av.
Hosford Schiller, 300 The Plaza
Hosick Henry M. 852 North Park av.
Hosking A. 822 Jackson boul.
Hosking Ben. T. 726 W. Monroe
Hoskins Benjamin, 6032 Oglesby av.
Hoskins John, LaGrange
Hoskins John M. 1052 Washington boul.
Hoskins Murray G. 1, 31st .
Hoskins William, LaGrange
Hosmer A. B. Dr.Walton pl.sw.cor.Rush
Hosmer Edwin D. 108 Pine
Hosmer E. Miss, 382 Lasalle av.
Hosmer F. B. Mrs. 483 Fullerton av.
Hosmer J. W. 44 Bellevue pl.
Hosmer N. 14 Lincoln av.
Hosmer R. W. 382 Lasalle av.
Hosmer W. H. 2933 Groveland av.
Hosmer W. J. Wilmette
Hossack I. Barbara Miss, Evanston
Hossack John Mrs. Evanston
Hoswell Wm. B. Longwood
Hotaling George W. 140, 65th, Eng.
Hotchkin B. L. Dr. 733 Kenmore av.
Hotchkin C. Marion, 3006 Prairie av.
Hotchkin C. W. 4950 Prairie av.
Hotchkin John L. 5642 Monroe av.
Hotchkiss Charles T. 152 N. Clark
Hotchkiss Everett S. Mayfair
Hotchkiss E. D. Evanston
Hotchkiss Freelon, Riverside
Hotchkiss George W. Evanston
Hotchkiss Hariette Miss, Riverside
Hotchkiss Isabella S., M.D. Riverside
Hotchkiss S. R. Evanston
Hotz Christoph, 301 W. Adams
Hotz Clara J. Miss, 301 W. Adams
Hotz F. C., M.D. 473 Dearborn av.
Hotz Robert S. 301 W. Adams
Hough Albert J. 3737 Ellis av.
Hough Charles H. 3737 Ellis av.
Hough C. R. 7601 Wright
Hough Edward M. 516 W. Adams
Hough George J. Evanston
Hough George W. Prof. Evanston
Hough O. S. Mrs. 3737 Ellis av.
Hough Sheldon L. Hinsdale
Hough W. C. 4615 Woodlawn av.
Houghteling Eliza S. Mrs. 2215 Michigan
  av.
Houghteling J. L. 27 Banks
Houghton Alice Mrs. 4201 Ellis av.
Houghton Olive A. 660 Lasalle av.
House D. P. 4422 Prairie av.
Housel B. Franklin Evanston
Housel C. C. 437 Center
Houston Alexander S. 3953 Michigan av.

Houston Elizabeth E. Mrs. Evanston
Houston Fedo L. 1508 Michigan av.
Houston Frank B. 314 Oakwood boul.
Houston George T. 4318 Grand boul.
Houston Grace G. Mrs. 2596 N. Ashland av.
Houston J. S. 314 Oakwood boul.
Houston J. W. Mrs. 314 Oakwood boul.
Hovey A. H. Morgan Park
Hovey George H. Chicago Beach hotel
Hovey T. A. 4515 Emerald av.
Hovey Wm. C. 417 Belden av.
Hovey W. A. Glencoe
Howard Allen L. 4100 Indiana av.
Howard B. Frank, 983 Jackson boul.
Howard Charles, 6558 Stewart av.
Howard Cornelia Mrs. 1219 W. Ravenswood Park
Howard C. D. Mrs. Evanston
Howard C. H. Gen. Glencoe
Howard Daniel 25, 35th
Howard Emma Miss, 5528 Monroe av.
Howard E. G., M.D. Highland Park
Howard E. L. Evanston
Howard Frank E. Evanston
Howard Frank L. Oak Park
Howard Fred, 4409 Michigan av.
Howard George, 3428 Michigan av.
Howard George, LaGrange
Howard Gertrude A. Miss, 5528 Monroe av.
Howard Granville H. 4350 Oakenwald av.
Howard Harold A. 477 Dearborn av.
Howard Harriet Miss, Newberry hotel
Howard Harrison P. 4820 Langley av.
Howard H. Benton, Oak Park
Howard H. E. 405 Bowen av.
Howard H. R. Miss, Newberry hotel
Howard John Corse, 219 N. State
Howard John J. 32, 42d
Howard Joseph H. 4801 Kimbark av.
Howard J. H. Oak Park
Howard Margaret D. Mrs. 4227 Champlain av.
Howard Martin, 504 Fullerton av.
Howard Matilda C. Mrs. 4820 Langley av.
Howard M. C. Miss, Oak Park
Howard O. McG. Glencoe
Howard Robert T. 321 Belden av.
Howard S. N. 6440 Ellis av.
Howard Thomas, 488 Evanston av.
Howard William D. 4448 St. Lawrence av.
Howard William H. 488 Evanston av.
Howard W. I. Mrs. 353, 60th, Englewood
Howard W. M. 353, 60th, Eng.
Howe Abbie L. Miss, 363 Bowen av.
Howe Arthur T. 798 Kenmore av.
Howe A. O. Dr. 1728 Michigan av.
Howe Charles, 3967 Lake av.
Howe C. M. Elmhurst
Howe Douglas H. 665 Cleveland av.
Howe Dwight N. 4144 Berkeley av.
Howe F. A. 3931 Grand boul.
Howe H. Waldo, 2403 South Park av.
Howe Julia C. Mrs. 622 Washington boul.
Howe Julia R. Dr. 679 N. Wells

Howe M. K. Hotel Windermere
Howe Noble Hill, 42 Woodland Park
Howe Samuel J. 4948 Forrestville
Howe Silas, 4459 Ellis av.
Howe S. E. O. Mrs. 39 University pl.
Howe S. Ferd. 243 Michigan av.
Howe Thad H. 15, 39th
Howe W. A. 405, 41st
Howe W. B. 1009 Jackson boul.
Howe W. G. 107, 37th
Howell Benjamin R. 6538 Stewart av.
Howell Cornelius DuB. 779 Jackson boul.
Howell C. H. 7828 Edwards av.
Howell C. J. Rev. LaGrange
Howell E. P. The Arizona
Howell Frank J. 4449 Sidney av.
Howell Frederick G. Glencoe
Howell Horace, 4461 Oakenwald av.
Howell J. C. LaGrange
Howell Laurentine H. Austin
Howell Louis B. 4528 Forrestville av.
Howell S. R. 3258 Forest av.
Howell Thomas S. 4528 Forrestville av.
Howell Wilson, Evanston
Howells Theodora W. Miss, 441 Dearborn av.
Hower M. Otis, 192 Dearborn av.
Howes A. E. Mrs. Oak Park
Howes Seth B. Lexington hotel
Howie W. M. Rev. 4726 Evans av.
Howland Arthur H. Evanston
Howland E. A. 3917 Langley av.
Howland E. C Mrs. 3917 Langley av.
Howland F. B. 5926 Honore
Howland George Carter, 5735 Washington av.
Howland H. A. 425, 42d pl.
Howland H. I. 510 Webster av.
Howland Jennie Mrs. Oak Park
Howland J. E. Mrs. 510 Webster av.
Howland Lucius A. Riverside
Howland Martha Mrs. Evanston
Howland Sarah Mrs. 2602 Prairie av.
Howland T. H. 4836 Evans av.
Howland Walter M. 482 N. State
Howland William I. 365 Superior
Hoxie John R. Lakota hotel
Hoyer Edward J. 229 N. State
Hoyer Frederick A. 422 Belden av.
Hoyer W. C. The Tudor
Hoyle John V. B. Austin
Hoyne Frank G. 3243 Groveland av.
Hoyne James T. 3208 Prairie av.
Hoyne Temple S., M. D. 1833 Indiana av.
Hoyne Thomas M. 3369 Calumet av.
Hoyt Alfred L. Dr. 4620 Greenwood av.
Hoyt Alfred W., Dr., 4620 Greenwood av.
Hoyt A. E. Oak Park
Hoyt Charles S. Rev. Oak Park
Hoyt Douglass, 235 Michigan av.
Hoyt E. 5752 Madison av.
Hoyt Frank W. 543 Flournoy
Hoyt Fred J. 374 Dearborn av.
Hoyt George W. 5210 Hibbard av.
Hoyt Henry W. 5114 Jefferson av,

Hoyt H. W. Mrs. 2723 Prairie av.
    Sum. res. Charlevoix, Mich.
Hoyt J. Q. 48, 24th
Hoyt Lou Mrs. 6400 Star av.
Hoyt Louis P. 3695 Lake av.
Hoyt L. G. 3756 Ellis av.
Hoyt N. Landon, 370 Dearborn av.
Hoyt Phelps B. 370 Dearborn av.
Hoyt S. C. Mrs. Oak Park
Hoyt William M. 370 Dearborn av.
    Sum. res. Winnetka
Hubbard A. E. Mrs. Evanston
Hubbard Charles W. 3005 Vernon av.
Hubbard Daniel B. 6356 Oglesby av.
Hubbard DeWitt P. Winnetka
Hubbard D. J. 6522 Harvard, Englewood
Hubbard Edna R. Miss, 5403 Madison av.
Hubbard George A. 122, 67th, Englewood
Hubbard Gilbert, 5403 Madison av.
Hubbard Gurdon S. jr. Riverside
Hubbard Harry A. 2001 Michigan av.
Hubbard Harry M. 387 Lasalle av.
Hubbard Heman H. 222 Irving av.
Hubbard Horace S. 3048 Calumet av.
Hubbard H. E. Mrs. 5335 Cornell av.
Hubbard James M. 39, 33d
Hubbard James S. 707 W. Congress
Hubbard John M. 3843 Vincennes av.
Hubbard John M. jr. 3754 Wabash av.
Hubbard John N. Evanston
Hubbard John Wells Mrs. 42 Sidney ct.
Hubbard Joseph D. 36 Bellevue pl.
Hubbard L. M. 55 Laflin
Hubbard S. H. 36 Walton pl.
Hubbard T. M. Evanston
Hubbard Will, Avenue house, Evanston
Hubbard W. H. 82 Astor
Hubbart Joseph, Evanston
Hubbart J. Roy, Evanston
Hubbell Charles W. 3221 Rhodes av.
Hubbell J. P. 111, 47th
Hubbell Orin, Berwyn
Hubbell Sarah Mrs. Maywood
Huber Julius H. 76 Maple
Huck Henry, 575 Dearborn av.
Huck Louis C. 575 Dearborn av.
Huckins Guy, 6804 Emerald av.
Huckins Sarah Mrs. 4021 Indiana av.
Hucksoll D. C. 290 Ashland boul.
Hucksoll E. W. 290 Ashland boul.
Huddilston John H. Prof. Evanston
Huddlestone George W. 903 W. Adams
Hudler H. 566 Fullerton av.
Hudnall Walter, 4524 Lake av.
Hudson Charles H. Hinsdale
Hudson Edward, 3201 Wabash av.
Hudson Edward jr. 3201 Wabash av.
Hudson E. J. Mrs. Evanston
Hudson P. S. 6560 Harvard
Hudson R. 466 Racine av.
Hudson Thomas J. 5112 Hibbard av.
Hudson William, 437 Evanston av.
Hudson William J. Riverside
Huebner H. Mrs. 949 Sawyer av.
Huestis Isaac N. Jefferson Park
Huey A. S. Hotel Windermere

Huey J. S. 28 Woodland Park
Huff Atwood H. 225 Belden av.
Huff H. Miss, 6430 Woodlawn av.
Huff H. M. LaGrange
Huff O. N. Dr. 5 Washington pl. ·
Huffaker T. S. Dr. 245, 43d
Hugel Louis P. 1776 Wrightwood av.
Huggett J. C. 5911 Honore
Huggins Charles W. 492, 42d
Hughes Carroll C. 776 Touhy av.
Hughes Charles, 5831 Madison av.
Hughes C. C. Mrs. Vincennes rd. cor.
    75th
Hughes Eugene A. 6158 Oglesby av.
Hughes E. H. Evanston
Hughes E. J. 3240 Lake Park av.
Hughes Frank, Hinsdale
Hughes Geo. C. Wilmette
Hughes G. B. 6841 Prairie av.
Hughes Hugh W. Lombard
Hughes John L. 6 Groveland Park
Hughes Joseph Dr. Lexington hotel
Hughes J. B. Riverside
Hughes J. O. Dr. Norwood Park
Hughes J. S. Rev. 510, 65th, Eng.
    Sum. res. Macatawa, Mich.
Hughes L. Mrs. 719 W. Congress
Hughes Robert E. 6158 Oglesby av.
Hughes Thomas J. 502 Belden av.
Hughes William M. 5927 Indiana av.
Hughes William T. 3240 Lake Park av.
Hughes W. E. Oak Park
Hughitt Marvin, 2828 Prairie av.
Hughitt Marvin jr. 2828 Prairie av.
Hughson George F. 5117 Woodlawn av.
Hughson M. B. 348 Maple, Englewood
Huguenin Daniel, 551 Lasalle av.
Huguenin James R. 551 Lasalle av.
Huguenin Philip, 551 Lasalle av.
Huguenin William P. 4450 Oakenwald av.
Huiskamp Herman J. Palmer house
Huiskamp J. B. Chicago Athletic Assn.
Huizinger A. H. Rev. 8 Chalmers pl.
Hulbert Alvin, 194 Park av.
Hulbert E. B. Prof. Hotel Barry
Hulbert T. H. Hotel Metropole
Hulbert William M. Austin
Hulburd Charles H. 423 N. State
Hulburd Joel H. Maywood
Huleatt Hugh, 434 W. Adams
Hulin William, 468 Elm
Huling Edward B. 3930 Grand boul.
Huling Edward C. 3930 Grand boul.
Huling Walter C. 4449 Evans av.
Hull Addie Adams Mrs. 3000 Indiana av.
Hull Andress B. Evanston
Hull Arthur E. 1812 Michigan av.
Hull Charles B. 306 West ct.
Hull Cyrus A. 1337 Dunning.
Hull David J. Riverside
Hull DeLos, Oak Park
Hull Gaylord S. 74, 35th
Hull Henry D. Riverside
Hull Morton B. 2626 Prairie av.
Hull Oliver W. 3000 Indiana av.
Hull P. A. 3221 South Park av.

Hull Tracy D. Highland Park
Hull T, Frank, 1043 N. Clark
Hull Walter Scott, 176, 39th
Hullinger H. C. 3731 Ellis av.
Hulsmann Henry, Oak Park
Hultin A. E. 1456 Wellington
Humble H. G. Mrs. Highland Park
Humble Margaret A. Mrs. 4425 Vincennes av.
Hume John H. 237 Dearborn av.
Hume Sumner W. 7212 Jeffery av.
Humiston H. 82 Park av.
Humiston Samuel A. 4202 Drexel boul.
          Sum. res. Swampscott, Mass.
Humiston William H. 82 Park av.
Humlid John N. 392 Webster av.
Hummel Goswin, 667 Sedgwick
Hummel Louis, 1694 Wellington
Humphrey A. B. Evanston
Humphrey A. H. LaGrange
Humphrey A. O. LaGrange
Humphrey Charles I. 4341 Ellis av.
Humphrey E. B. 1810 Frederick
Humphrey E. H. 51 Warren av.
Humphrey E. L. 408 Superior
Humphrey Horace B. Oak Park
Humphrey J. River Forest
Humphrey S. J. Rev. Oak Park
Humphrey T. M. Mrs. 2953 Groveland av.
Humphreys Henry H. Capt. Ft. Sheridan
Humphreys Joseph F. 4312 Emerald av.
Humphreys J. B. Tracy
Huncke Carl, 320 Webster av.
Hunerberg Fred W. 4630 Grand boul.
Hunkins M. F. Mrs. 184 Pine
Hunn A. M. Mrs. 213, 53d (H. P.)
Hunneman Nellie Mrs. 273, 52d (H. P.)
Hunneman William, 665 Lasalle av.
Hunnewell W. B. 2125 Wabash av.
Hunt Albert B. 1034 Kenmore av.
Hunt A. Lucas, 2241 Calumet av.
Hunt Charles H. Mrs. 134 Rush
Hunt Clara Miss, 2241 Calumet av.
Hunt Clement M. 2241 Calumet av.
Hunt Clyde de V. 106 Astor
Hunt C. H. 5101 Hibbard av.
Hunt Daniel T. 2317 Michigan av.
Hunt D. W. 943 Park av.
Hunt Egar E. 883 W. Monroe
Hunt Edward S. 59 Flournoy
Hunt Eugene, 139, 34th
Hunt E Hamilton, Evanston
          Sum. res. Chautauqua, N. Y.
Hunt E. Hamilton jr. Evanston
Hunt Ferd S. 878 Fulton
Hunt Florence Mrs. M. D. 235 Michigan av.
Hunt Frederick R. Dr. Austin
Hunt George, Riverside
Hunt George E., Rev. Tracy
Hunt George S. 983 Warren av.
Hunt George W. 5222 Woodlawn av.
Hunt Haines E. 105 Winchester av.
Hunt Homer C. Evanston
Hunt H. H. Mrs. Oak Park
Hunt H. M. 143 Oakwood boul.

Hunt H. W. Mrs. 5101 Hibbard av.
Hunt James A. Winnetka
Hunt Jarvis, Virginia hotel
Hunt John E. Ridgeland
Hunt John L. Evanston
Hunt John Percival, Evanston
Hunt John R. Austin
Hunt Julius, 4132 Berkeley av.
Hunt J. N. 842 W. Adams
Hunt J. Spafford Dr. 878 Fulton
Hunt Manning, 727, 63d ct. Englewood
Hunt Nancy D. Mrs. Evanston
Hunt Robert W. 588 Division
Hunt Rodney, Oak Park
Hunt S. H. 4243 Drexel boul.
Hunt S. Wade, Evanston
Hunt William B., Dr. 76, 50th (H. P.)
Hunt W. F. 5126 East End av.
Hunter Clinton, Hotel Windermere
Hunter C. L. 32 Groveland Park
Hunter Edgar J. 4357 Indiana av.
Hunter Ethel Miss, 5125 Jefferson av.
Hunter E. S. 34 Groveland Park
Hunter E. W. Dr. Southern hotel
Hunter G. Leland, Granada hotel
Hunter Hugh D. 346 Washington boul. ⌐
Hunter James M. 1541 W. Adams
Hunter John, 947 S. Central Park av.
Hunter John W. 6343 Wright
Hunter J. D. Dr. Lexington hotel
Hunter J. W. 4955 Prairie av.
Hunter Maria P. Mrs. 5517 Washington av.
Hunter Robert Mrs. 5125 Jefferson av.
Hunter R. J. O. 5125 Jefferson av.
Hunter Thomas B. 4955 Prairie av.
Hunter Thomas M. Austin
Hunter William, Wilmette
Hunter William C. Oak Park
Hunter William W. Mrs. 4415 Oakenwald av.
Hunter W. B. Wilmette
Hunter W. C. LaGrange
Hunter W. W. 4665 Lake av.
Hunting Charles F. Irving Park
Hunting C. Fred, Mayfair
Huntington Collins F. 3627 Ellis av.
Huntington P. E. Mrs. Oak Park
Huntley E. L. 456 Belden av.
Huntley Florence Mrs. Leland hotel
Huntley Silas, 3336 Calumet av.
Hupp James M. 23 St. Johns pl.
Hurd Abner, LaGrange
Hurd A. 780 Warren av.
Hurd A. Haynes, LaGrange
Hurd A. R. Mrs. 423 Ashland boul.
Hurd Charles A. 1918 Barry av.
Hurd Charles E. 1918 Barry av.
Hurd C. D. 4304 Emerald av.
Hurd D. Frederick, 108, 43d
Hurd H. B. Evanston
Hurd James D. 4446 Woodlawn av.
Hurd Sadie Miss, Newberry hotel
Hurd Stephen N. 257, 49th
Hurd Walter W. 1918 Barry av.
Hurdle A. Lansing, 97 Park av.
Hurford S. R. Glencoe

Hurlburd H. A. 162 Park av.
Hurlburt Frazier W. 4727 Langley av.
Hurlburt R. F. Mrs. 17 Delaware pl.
Hurlbut A. E. 478 Belden av.
Hurlbut Charles H. Evanston
Hurlbut C. J. 320 Lasalle av.
Hurlbut C. P. 6325 Oglesby av.
Hurlbut Harmon, 5338 Washington av.
Hurlbut Horace E. 586 Dearborn av.
Hurlbut Horace R. 615, 66th, Englewood
Hurlbut H. A. Mrs. 389 Ontario
Hurlbut H. H. 478 Belden av.
Hurlbut J. B. 525 Cleveland av.
Hurlbut J. H. Evanston
Hurlbut Samuel E. Evanston
Hurlbut S. E. Miss, 389 Ontario
Hurlbut Vincent L. Dr. Grand Pacific
    hotel
Hurlbutt Wells H. jr. 5620 Ellis av.
Hurley Clara Mrs. 84 Seeley av.
Hurley Frank J. Austin
Hurley T. D. 3221 Prairie av.
Hurney Frank J. 4916 Forrestville av.
Hurst Charles A. 1221 Wolcott
Hurst Fred C. Jefferson Park
Hurxthal R. A. 215 S. Hoyne av.
Husche C. 1732 Deming ct.
Huse J. B. Evanston
Huson A. B. Mrs. 5910 Indiana av.
Hussander Arthur F. 593 Burling
Hussander A. F. 614 Orchard
Hussander L. F. 29 Hall
Hussander Peter J. Mrs. 576 Burling
Hussey Augustus. 6340 Drexel av.
Hussey William P. 320 Hampden ct.
Husted F. T. Morgan Park
Husted J. H. 5438 Monroe av.
Huston George, 7659 Wright
Huston Phil W. Austin
Huszagh Rudolph D. 1270 Washington
    boul.
Hutchens George W. Evanston
Hutchens O. B. Evanston
Hutchings W. A. 301 Park av.
Hutchins Albert E. 4004 Ellis av.
Hutchins A. V. Dr. 964 W. Monroe
Hutchins A. W. 4578 Oakenwald av.
Hutchins C. S. Lakota hotel
Hutchins Earl A. 630 Chestnut, Eng.
Hutchins E. E. 1279 Palmer
Hutchins E. R. 133 Astor
    Sum. res. Cotuit, Mass.
Hutchins Herbert, 410, 61st
Hutchins James C. 4812 Ellis av.
Hutchins N. E. Mrs. 630 Chestnut, Eng.
Hutchinson Arthur, 3011 Prairie av.
Hutchinson B. P. Mrs. 2703 Prairie av.
Hutchinson Charles Mrs. 3011 Prairie av.
Hutchinson Charles L. 2709 Prairie av.
Hutchinson D. B. 162 Ashland boul.
Hutchinson Edward W. 7530 Brooks
Hutchinson Florence C. Miss, 3145
    Indiana av.
Hutchinson George A. 330 Ashland boul.
Hutchinson George C. 330 Ashland boul.
Hutchinson John Mrs. 3145 Indiana av.

Hutchinson Jonas, 3043 Groveland av.
Hutchinson J. William, 3011 Prairie av.
Hutchinson M. A. Mrs. Riverside
Hutchinson M. S. Mrs. Riverside
Hutchinson O. K. 385 Dearborn av.
Hutchinson O.K.A.Mrs.385 Dearborn av.
Hutchinson Robert B. Glencoe
Hutchinson Thomas, 3920 Vincennes av.
Hutchinson W. A. Oak Park
Hutchinson W. W. Mrs. Riverside
Hutchison A. A. 6559 Harvard
Hutchison Francis 664 W. Adams
Hutchison James, 6559 Harvard
Hutchison James A. Mrs. 299 Erie
Hutchison J. F. 664 W. Adams
Hutchison N. Miller, Evanston
Hutchison Stanton, 299 Erie
Huth F. D. 2440 N. Paulina
Huth Isabella Mrs. 2440 N. Paulina
Hutt George J. 3741 Forest av.
Hutt Louis, 3200 South Park av.
Hutton Blanche M. Miss, 46 Roslyn pl.
Hutton John B. Rev. 451 S. Normal
    Parkway
Hutton Wm. 202 Racine av.
Huyck J. H. 855 W. Adams
Hyams Henry, 2935 Prairie av.
Hyde Benjamin, 234 Hampden ct.
Hyde Charles Cheney, 2409 Michigan av.
    Sum. res. Yale Univ.,New Haven,Conn.
Hyde Charles E. 601 Jackson boul.
Hyde Charles W. Hotel Normandie
Hyde C. A. Hotel Barry
Hyde Dorothea Mrs. 521 Garfield boul.
Hyde Edward A. Evanston
Hyde Frank D. 800 S. Lawndale av.
Hyde F. D. 296 Ohio
Hyde F. M. LaGrange
Hyde Harry Morrow, 2034 Indiana av.
Hyde James C. 884 Sawyer av.
Hyde James Nevins Dr. 2409 Michigan av
    Sum. res. The Barnacle, Prouts
    Neck, Me.
Hyde J. D. 7125 Euclid av. (H.P.)
Hyde Maggie W. Mrs. 7141 Webster av.
Hyers George A. 3532 Lake av.
Hyers S. A. 5543 Monroe av.
Hyland J. J. 1007 Park av.
Hyland J. S. 1240 Southport av.
Hyland M. W. 1009 Park av.
Hyman Albert, 4329 Vincennes av.
Hyman Ben R. 375, 42d
Hyman Charles E. 417 Bowen av.
Hyman Clara Miss, 4350 Grand boul.
Hyman David, 4329 Vincennes av.
Hyman David A. 4350 Grand boul.
Hyman Edward S. 3826 Vernon av.
Hyman Frances Miss, 3257 Vernon av.
Hyman Henry, 2839 Indiana av.
Hyman H. S. 144, 50th (H.P.)
Hyman Joseph, 3257 Vernon av.
Hyman Robert W. jr. 5495 Cornell av.
Hyman S. Mrs. 3631 Forest av.
Hyndman C. D. Highland Park
Hynes W. J. Granada hotel
Hypes W. Finley, Evanston

IBSEN J. H. 3716 Wabash av.
Ickes J. Roy, 435 Washington boul.
Ide Charles B. Evanston
Ide George B. Evanston
Ide George O. Mrs. Evanston
Ide Helen M. Miss, Evanston
Ide H. P. 383 Elm
Ide William K. Evanston
Igle Otto, 2667 N. Ashland av.
Igle Theodore T. 2667 N. Ashland av.
Iglehart C. A. Morgan Park
Iglehart Elizabeth Mrs. Morgan Park
Iglehart N. G. Evanston
Ihne F. H. Dr. 1731 Belmont av.
Ilett Edward P. 642 W. Adams
Ilett William Mrs. 642 W. Adams
Ilette W. C. 4427 Prairie av.
Iliff John W. 4166 Drexel boul.
Iliff William H. 684 W. Adams
Illing Robert, 1635 Brompton av.
Illingworth G. M. Dr. 227 Belden av.
Ilse Frank, 4437 Champlain av.
Ilse John C. 4448 Champlain av.
Indermille T, F. 6618 Lafayette av.
Inderrieden John B. 553 N. State
Inderrieden John L. 553 N. State
Inderrieden Joseph S. 553 N. State
Ingalls Augustus R. 430 Kenmore av.
Ingalls Emerson, Oak Park
Ingalls E. A. Mrs. 430 Kenmore av.
Ingalls F. A. 4216 Berkeley av.
Ingalls Grant, Oak Park
Ingalls John G. Oak Park
Ingalls Mary E. Mrs. Oak Park
Ingalls Robert S. Oak Park
Ingalls S. R. Dr. U. S. Marine hospital
Ingals E., M.D. 34 Throop
Ingals E. Fletcher Dr. 507 W. Adams
Ingersoll George B. 6918 Wright
Ingersoll George W. Oak Park
Ingersoll G. M. Mrs. 747 Warren av.
Ingersoll Jay, 401 Sheffield av.
Ingersoll N. B. 3756 Ellis av.
Ingham H. H. 435 Washington boul.
Ingham S. G. Mrs. 435 Washington boul.
Ingledew Lumley, 3427 Indiana av.
Ingledew Lumley jr. 3427 Indiana av.
Ingles Laurin, Lexington hotel
Inglis Clara Miss, 493 Dearborn av.
Inglis James, 192, 53d (H.P.)
Inglis John, 192, 53d (H.P.)
Inglis John, Morgan Park
Inglis P. L. 4504 Vincennes av.
Inglis William, 493 Dearborn av.
    Sum. res. Crab Apple Island, Fox
    Lake
Ingman L. S. Dr. Oak Park
Ingraham F. E. Mrs. Oak Park
Ingraham Granville S. Mrs. 5520 Washing-
    ton av.
    Winter res. Pass Christian, Miss.
Ingraham G. Foster, Oak Park
Ingraham H. F. Mrs. Oak Park
Ingraham S. C. Evanston
Ingraham W. P. 7929 Reynolds av.
Ingraham W. W. 1174 Millard av.

Ingram Charles H. 116, 43d
Ingram Edward L. 296 Irving av.
Ingram George R. 296 Irving av.
Ingram James, 7731 Wright
Ingram J. E. 619 Jackson boul.
Ingram J. S. Oak Park
Ingram Lawrence T. 6018 Washington av.
Ingram Robert J. Austin
Ingram W. W. 6018 Washington av.
Ingwersen Charles H. 3748 Forest av.
Ingwersen Ella C. Miss, 4239 Michigan
    av.
Ingwersen E. H. 4144 Prairie av.
Ingwersen G. J. 4239 Michigan av.
Ingwersen H. C. 4239 Michigan av.
Ingwersen J. H. 3844 Calumet av.
Ingwersen Marvin, 3748 Forest av.
Ingwersen T. H. 4120 Prairie av.
Ingwersen W. B. 4417 Indiana av.
Inman David, Highland Park
Innes Marion M. Miss, 3010 Prairie av.
Innis Katharine C. Miss, 4 Aldine sq.
Insull Martin J. 2211 Prairie av.
Insull Samuel, 2211 Prairie av.
Iott Franck C. Evanston
Iott George H. Evanston
Iott Lewis, Evanston
Iott M. B. Evanston
Ireland Clement E. 868 Larrabee
Ireland D. J. 609 Maple, Eng.
Ireland Francis M. 609 Maple, Eng.
Ireland Louis E. Dr. 32 Woodland Park
    Sum. res. Asbury Park, N. J.
Ireland Sidnev R. 687 Sedgwick
Irey James C. Dr. 414 Washington boul.
Irion Daniel Prof. Elmhurst
Irish H. C. Mrs. Hinsdale
Irish William W. 856 Washington boul.
Irons Agnes Mrs. 4346 Langley av.
Irons James Mrs. 495 W. Adams
Irvin E. Hugh, 6420 Oglesby av.
Irvin James, 3738 Langley av.
Irvin Washington J. 2566 N. Ashland av.
Irvin William, 50 Oakwood boul.
Irvin William J. Newberry hotel
Irvine Frank R. Hinsdale
Irvine Hugh, 6420 Oglesby av.
Irvine Robert, 823 Morse av.
Irvine William, 5039 Jefferson av.
Irving Robert A. 376 Dearborn av.
Irwin A. de H. Miss, 58 Cedar
Irwin Bernard J. D. Col. U. S. A. 58
    Cedar
Irwin Charles D. 2300 Calumet av.
    Sum. res. Nyack on Hudson, N. Y.
Irwin C. H. Hotel Barry
Irwin Edward A. 4802 Lake av.
Irwin E. L. Mrs. Park Ridge
Irwin Henry L. 4802 Lake av.
Irwin John, 505 Dearborn av.
Irwin John B. 505 Dearborn av.
Irwin John C. 4802 Lake av.
Irwin J. L. Dr. 180 Dearborn av.
Irwin Mary Miss, 4547 Lake av.
Isaacs L. J. Dr. 3136 South Park av.
Isaacs M. C. 3143 Forest av.

Isaacs M. J. 3136 South Park av.
Isaacs Walter S. 4952 Vincennes av.
Isbell Wells, 237 Dearborn av.
Isbester John H. Evanston
Isbester Richard T. Dr. 636 Washington boul.
Isbester Tunis, Evanston
Isgrig Margaret I. Miss, Austin
Isham A.E. Miss, 1 Tower pl.
Isham Edward S. 1 Tower pl.
    Sum. res. Ormsby Hill, Manchester,Vt.
Isham Edward S. jr. 1 Tower pl.
Isham Frances Miss, 1 Tower pl.
Isham George S., M.D. 64 Bellevue pl.
Isham H. P. 10 Tower pl.
Isham Ira D. Dr. 2415 Wabash av.
Isham I. N. 4342 Greenwood av.
Isham Pierrepont, 1923 Prairie av.
    Sum. res. "Ormsby Hill," Manchester, Vt.
Isham Pierrepont Mrs. 10 Tower pl.
Isham Ralph, 381 Lasalle av.
Isham R. N., M.D. 321 Dearborn av.
    Sum. res. Lake Geneva
Ismon Rennie H. 4443 Langley av.
Ismond R. E. 343 Bowen av.
Israel Bernhard, 3740 Grand boul.
Israel C. H. Lafayette flats
Israel W. L. Lafayette flats
Israel W. R. Berwyn
Ivens Henry, Ridgeland
Iverson Chester L. LaGrange
Iverson Edward, 3113 Prairie av.
Iverson Ralph W. LaGrange
Ives Allen D. 4762 Lake av.
Ives Benjamin, Chicago Beach hotel
Ives Florence H. Mrs. 268 Chestnut
Ives F. B. Dr. 3220 Vernon av.
Ives J. H. 4724 Kenwood av.
Ives S. H. Mrs. 2712 Michigan av.
Izard E. M. Union Club

JACK ALBERT, 51 Hamilton av.
    Jack D. T. 294 Park av.
Jack Frank E. 6257 Dickey
Jackman Emma L. Mrs. 509 Burling
Jackman E. S. 688 Winthrop av.
Jackman J. A. jr. 5338 Washington av.
Jackman S. S. 447 Seminary av.
Jackman Wilbur S. 6916 Perry av.
Jackson Abram, 121 Laflin
Jackson Arthur S. 37 Aldine sq.
    Sum. res. Lake Geneva
Jackson A. Reeves Mrs. 569, 51st (H.P.)
Jackson Charles H. 649 W. Adams
Jackson Charles W. 441, 66th, Englewood
Jackson Charles W. 7007 Perry av.
Jackson Chas M. 512 Byron
Jackson Daniel Mrs. 674 Fullerton av.
Jackson Darius C. 3740 Elmwood pl.
Jackson Dwight P. Oak Park
Jackson D. C. Mrs. 3740 Elmwood pl.
Jackson D. W. 2967 Vernon av.
Jackson E. Oak Park
Jackson Frank P. 31 Newport av.
Jackson Frank R. 1431 King pl

Jackson F. W. 4623 Ellis av.
Jackson George, 7524 Harvard
Jackson George, Hotel Normandie
Jackson George C. Mrs. 39, 53d (H.P.)
Jackson G. W. 19 N. Sacramento av.
Jackson Harriet Mrs. 1578 Lill av.
Jackson Harry H. 37 Aldine sq.
    Sum. res. Lake Geneva
Jackson Hattie Miss, 4430 Ellis av.
Jackson Henry G. Rev. 649 W. Adams
Jackson Horace, Hinsdale
Jackson Howard B. 3740 Elmwood pl.
Jackson Huntington W. Auditorium annex
Jackson H. B. 6445 Grace av.
Jackson H. C. The Arizona
Jackson H. H., M.D. 780 W. Monroe
Jackson H. N. 4538 Lake av.
Jackson James, 7621 Union av.
Jackson John L. 1587 W. Adams
Jackson J. Mason, 5726 Monroe av.
Jackson J. P. Mrs. 5506 Monroe av.
Jackson Kate A. Miss, Evanston
Jackson Leigh H. 121 Laflin
Jackson L. 5140 Wabash av.
Jackson L. B. Great Northern hotel
Jackson Mary Mrs. 1853 Frederick
Jackson Nat. 36th se. cor. Ellis av.
Jackson Noyes, 3851 Ellis av.
Jackson Oliver, 4430 Ellis av.
Jackson Oliver A. 4430 Ellis av.
Jackson Oliver B. 243 Michigan av.
Jackson Paul, 4430 Ellis av.
Jackson Sarah E. Mrs. Riverside
Jackson S. K. 6 Langley pl.
Jackson Thomas M. River Forest
Jackson William C. 37 Aldine sq.
Jackson William S. 994 Millard av.
Jackson William S. 37 Aldine sq.
    Sum. res. Lake Geneva.
Jackson Willis G. 939 W. Adams
Jackson W. W. 1 Wellington pl.
Jackson Zadoc O. 1060 S.Central Park av.
Jacobi Stella E. Dr. 822 W. Madison
Jacobs Adolph, 4150 Lake av.
Jacobs B. F. 2201 Calumet av.
Jacobs C. F. 149 Evanston av.
Jacobs C. R. 627 W. Adams
Jacobs Franklin L.1172 Washington boul.
Jacobs Frederick H. 1438 Cornelia
Jacobs Harry L. 942 Park av.
Jacobs Henry C. 4119 Grand boul.
Jacobs Leon J. 3449 Indiana av.
Jacobs Montefiore M. 138, 38th
Jacobs Victor, 438 Ashland boul.
Jacobs William B. 65 Bryant av.
Jacobs William V. Col. 1163, 72d (H.P.)
Jacobsen R. C. French house, Evanston
Jacobson Augustus Col. Union Club
Jacobson August, 389 S. Oakley av.
Jacobson D. 26 Lincoln av.
Jacobson Frank, 197, 30th
Jacobson Herman, 182 Howe
Jacobson Louis, 428 Marshfield av.
Jacobson Morris, 477, 42d pl.
Jacobus J. S. 4314 Greenwood av.

Jacoby Horatio J. 3241 Indiana av.
Jacques Susan Mrs. 156 Dearborn av.
Jacques S. L. 147, 42d
Jacquish L.. C. 283 Irving av.
Jaeger Caroline Mrs. 399 N. State
Jaeger George J. 345 Lasalle av.
Jaeger H. F. 399 N. State
Jaeger Philip, 345 Lasalle av.
        Sum. res. Pistaker Lake
Jaeschke Adolph L. Mrs. 296 Ohio
Jaeschke G. A. 296 Ohio
Jaffray Robert M. 1467 Wellington
Jager E. C. 442 Garfield av.
Jager Frank, 740 Sedgwick
Jaggard W. W., M.D. 2910 Indiana av.
Jagoe James H. Evanston
Jaicks Andrew, River Forest
James Charles G. 4460 Oakenwald av.
James C. F. Mrs. 7022 Vernon av.
James Edward A. 3259 Groveland av.
James Frank N. 432 Belden av.
James Fred S. 1635 Sheridan rd.
James F. W. 438 Englewood av.
James George W. 5422 Ridgewood ct.
James Henry, Dr. 845 Garfield boul.
James J. D. 226 Oakwood boul.
James Lizzie P. Dr. 5759 Rosalie ct.
James Thomas B. 5211 Hibbard av.
James William H. 5745 Princeton av.
James W. P. 1635 Sheridan rd.
James W. S. 6400 Lexington av.
Jameson Charles C. Lieut. Fort Sheridan
Jameson Eliza D. Mrs. 5316 Cornell av.
Jameson Jennie M. Mrs. 426, 34th
Jameson Mary F. Mrs. 426, 34th
Jamieson C. W. Mrs. 34 29th
Jamieson David, Evanston
Jamieson Egbert, 38 Newport av.
Jamieson Elizabeth Miss, 36th nw. cor.
    Ellis av.
Jamieson Malcolm M. 50 Newport av.
Jamieson Thomas N. 3907 Vincennes av.
Jampolis Robert R. Austin
Janery W. W. 7047 Honore
Janes Jesse D. 6104 Stewart av.
Janes John J. 2242 Michigan av.
Janes William E. 1144 Washington boul.
Janisch T. C. 623, 61st, Englewood
Janney James W. 4729 Greenwood av.
Jannotta Alfredo A. Sig. 816 The Plaza
Janssen Theodore G. 2929 Groveland av.
January Emma D. Mrs. 15 Scott
Jaques Eustace, Virginia hotel
Jaques W. K.. M.D. 4334 Ellis av.
Jaquish Ben M, 545 W. Adams
Jaquish Louis C. 283 Irving av.
Jaquith Edwin P. Walton pl. sw. cor.
    Rush   Sum. res. Rockford, Me.
Jaquith O. C. 3802 Lake av.
Jaros F. W. 2458 South Park av.
Jarrett John R. Hinsdale
Jarvis Ada B. Mrs. 153, 25th
Jarvis W. Bancroft, 6050 Park End av.
Jarvis W. H. Hotel Barry
Jauncey William, 631 W. Monroe
Jay Charles A. 7737 Sherman

Jay Frank W., M. D. 2510 Indiana av.
Jay Herbert, 7737 Sherman
Jay Milton, M.D. 2510 Indiana av.
Jaycox Elbert E. Evanston
Jaycox William B. Evanston
Jayne E. L. 5414 Madison av.
Jaynes C. R. 5007 Wabash av.
Jeanneret C. 555 Webster av.
Jeanneret C. W. 557 Webster av.
Jeanneret Harry G. 555 Webster av.
Jefferson B. H. 63 The Hampden
        Sum. res. Colfax
Jefferson Mary Miss, 227 Ohio
Jefferson Ralph J. 3829 Lake av.
Jefferson Ralph. S. Highland Park
Jefferson W. J. 3829 Lake av.
Jefferson W. T. 3829 Lake av.
Jeffery Allen, Evanston
Jeffery Edward T. 1919 Michigan av.
Jeffery Harry B. 3141 South Park av.
Jeffery John B. 3141 South Park av.
Jeffery Thomas B. 3133 Malden
Jeffrey Robert, G. 7807 S. Green
Jeffrey Thompson, 7807 S. Green
Jelke John F. 165 Eugenie
Jellison Linnie M. Miss, 4440 Lake av.
Jellyman Joseph, 6210 Sheridan av.
Jenison Edward S. 4356 Ellis av.
Jenkins Anna E. Miss, Evanston
Jenkins B. D. Miss, Oak Park
Jenkins Charles, 4064 Michigan terrace
Jenkins Charles E. Oak Park
Jenkins Charles W. 329 Michigan av.
Jenkins George, 643 Burling
Jenkins George H. 4441 Sidney av.
Jenkins George R. 3989 Drexel boul.
Jenkins George R. Evanston
Jenkins Harry D. 2548 Indiana av.
Jenkins John E. 2625 Prairie av.
Jenkins M. G. Miss, 224 Ashland boul.
Jenkins Oliver E. 505 Lasalle av.
Jenkins Robert E. 3989 Drexel boul.
Jenkins Robert M. 5203 Jefferson av.
Jenkins Sam. R. 5414 Madison av.
Jenkins Sidney M. 22 Aldine sq.
Jenkins T. R. Calumet club
Jenkins V. B. Mrs. 2548 Indiana av.
Jenkins William P. Austin
Jenkins Wilton A. 329 Michigan av.
Jenkins W. H. 5203 Jefferson av.
Jenkinson Wm. 410, 64th, Eng.
Jenks A. B. 3756 Lake av.
Jenks B. F. 79 Park av.
Jenks Charles L. 3756 Lake av.
Jenks Charles L. 5739 Washington av.
Jenks Charles W. 705 The Plaza
Jeuks John G. 3137 Forest av.
Jenks L. F. Mrs. Auditorium hotel
Jenks Parker A. 3179 Malden
Jenks S. A. 416 Belden av.
Jenks S. L. Mrs. 420, 41st
Jenks W. B. Mrs. 3137 Forest av.
Jenks W. S. 63, 18th
Jenner Ophelia C. Mrs. 4231 St. Lawrence
    av.
Jenness E. J. 5752 Madison av.

Jenney George H. 68 Newport av.
Jenney William L. B. 60 Bittersweet pl.
Jennings A. E. Mrs. 4811 Langley av.
Jennings Charles A. 1209 Wolcott
Jennings Charles P. 304, 54th (H. P.)
Jennings D. Ferguson, Sherman house
Jennings Edwin B. 4811 Langley av.
Jennings E. B. Lexington hotel
Jennings George F. 7534 Union av.
Jennings George M. Mrs. 7534 Union av.
Jennings G. F. Lexington hotel
Jennings G. T. Hotel Windermere
Jennings John T. W. Evanston
Jennings Joseph, Maywood
Jennings J. E. 834 Warren av.
Jennings Louis H. 1046 Bryan av.
Jennings Maud Miss, 3144 Cottage Grove
    av.
Jennings M. C., M.D. 7417 South Chicago
    av.
Jennings Rufus P. 7 Madison Park
Jennison Edwin S. 1855 Frederick
Jennison Floyd E. 229 S. Oakley av.
Jennison N. Edward, LaGrange
Jepson E. 442 Dayton
Jerauld John, Evanston
Jerman Charles A. 433, 57th (H.P.)
Jernberg Reinert A. Rev. 734 Washing-
    ton boul.
Jernegan Charles, Evanston
Jernegan Mary Miss, Evanston
Jerome Charles C. 3431 South Park av.
Jerome Frank, 966 W. Jackson
Jerrems Arthur W. 38 Aldine sq.
Jerrems William G. 38 Aldine sq.
Jerrems William G. jr. Mrs.Hinsdale
Jervis Frank I. Mrs. 18 Sidney ct.
Jessup Robert Dr. 4589 Oakenwald av.
Jessurum Albert E. Stamford hotel
Jett George A. Dr. 516 W. Monroe
Jevne C. 640 Lasalle av.
Jevne Henry M. 640 Lasalle av.
Jewell Albert G. 4319 Forrestville av.
Jewell Edwin S. 4319 Forrestville av.
Jewell H. L. Oak Park
Jewell Ira H. 230 Irving av.
Jewell Omar H. 230 Irving av.
Jewell W. J. 197 S. Hoyne av.
Jewett Edward A. 4809 Madison av.
Jewett Edward R. 1866 Melrose
Jewett Fred L. 3266 Lake Park av.
Jewett George N. Evanston
Jewett Harry M. 3266 Lake Park av.
Jewett John N. 412 Dearborn av.
Jewett Nellie Miss, 2300 Indiana av.
Jewett Samuel R. 467 N. State
Job Frederick W. Riverside
Johson C. Frank, 93, 41st
Jocelyn Franklin C. 4415 Drexel boul.
Joel Moses, 3319 Vernon av.
John James, 812 Winthrop av.
Johns Hepburn, 414 The Plaza
Johns James W. Riverside
Johnson Alfred B. Austin
Johnson Andrew, Oak Park
Johnson Andrew P. 695 N. Robey
    38

Johnson Anton, 102 Fowler
Johnson Archibald, 155 S. Robey
Johnson Arthur H. French house, Evan-
    ston
Johnson A. A. Austin
Johnson A. Blanche Miss, 10 Hawthorne
    pl.
Johnson A. C. 901 Walnut
Johnson A. G. Dr. 237 N. Clark
Johnson A. J. Mrs. 196 Evergreen av.
Johnson Burton, 1774 Wrightwood av.
Johnson B. Arthur, Mayfair
Johnson Calvin C. 4534 Forrestville av.
Johnson Catherine Mrs. Evanston
Johnson Charles E. 497 Dearborn av.
Johnson Charles H. 832 Sherwin av.
Johnson Charles J. 7620 Bond av.
Johnson Charles W. 345 Rush
Johnson Christopher, 1405 N. Halsted
Johnson C. A. 5319 Madison av.
Johnson C. N. Dr. 743 North Park av.
Johnson C. Porter, 624 Rosenmerkel
Johnson Daniel, 1684 Barry av.
Johnson Dudley A. 5802 Jackson av.
Johnson D. W. Forest hotel (R.P.)
Johnson Edward, 5000 Jefferson av.
Johnson Edward H. Ridgeland
Johnson Elmo J. 1330 Washington boul.
Johnson Enos H. LaGrange
Johnson Ernest C. 382 Huron
Johnson Ernest V. Great Northern hotel
Johnson E. E. 3739 Vernon av.
Johnson E. H. 408 Warren av.
    Sum. res. Twin Lakes, Wis.
Johnson E. L. Mrs. Lexington hotel
Johnson E. S. 408 Warren av.
    Sum. res. Twin Lakes, Wis.
Johnson E. T. Oak Park
Johnson Frank A. 3807 Langley av.
Johnson Frank E. 3640 Lake av.
Johnson Frank S. Dr. 2521 Prairie av.
Johnson Franklin Prof. Hotel Barry
Johnson Frederick C. Evanston
Johnson Fremont L. Austin
Johnson F. R. 3533 Indiana av.
Johnson George Hazen, LaGrange
Johnson George J. Rev. 7740 S. Green
Johnson G. Douglas Mrs. 3731 Langley
    av.
Johnson Harriet Miss, 2927 Indiana av.
Johnson Helen M. Mrs. 1110 Washington
    boul.
Johnson Herrick Rev. 1070 N. Halsted
Johnson Hiram B. 3707 Vincennes av.
Johnson Hosmer A. 2223 Prairie av.
Johnson H. B. 5473 Cornell av.
Johnson H. C. 215, 42d pl.
Johnson H. J. Mrs. 4552 Woodlawn av.
Johnson H. N. B. Miss, Hotel Groveland
Johnson Jacob, 390 Oak
Johnson James Gibson Rev. 7 Ritchie pl.
Johnson James H. 965 W. Monroe
Johnson Jennie Miss, 832 Sherwin av.
Johnson John B. 1439 Dakin
Johnson John H. 271 Lasalle av.
Johnson John H. 275 Belden av.

Johnson John H. 437 Belden av.
Johnson John M. 470 Cleveland av.
Johnson John M. 1341 Wolcott
Johnson Jonas, 420A Belden av.
Johnson Joseph, 1512 Perry
Johnson Joslyn, 170 Ashland boul.
Johnson Julius A. 359, 65th, Englewood
Johnson J. D. Mrs. 772 Warren av.
Johnson J. E. Berwyn
Johnson J. F. Mrs. 6945 Yale, Englewood
Johnson J. L. 705 Warren av.
Johnson J. M. 6606 Yale, Englewood
Johnson Kolben, 703 N. Hoyne av.
Johnson Lottie E. Miss, 3025 Indiana av.
Johnson L. Miss, 3,-3 Prairie av.
Johnson L. G. 3612 Pike av.
Johnson McMillan A. 207 Lake View av.
Johnson M. 1749 Deming ct.
Johnson Nels, 1844 Surf
Johnson Olen H. Evanston
Johnson Oliver K. 247 Michigan av.
Johnson Peter C. Hinsdale
Johnson Rebecca A. Mrs. 906 W. Monroe
Johnson Roy, Winnetka
Johnson Roy D. 3602 Lake av.
Johnson R. C. Kenilworth
Johnson R. S. Mrs. 848 Washington boul.
Johnson Samuel, Leland hotel
Johnson Samuel A. 142, 42d
Johnson Spencer, 3422 Prairie av.
Johnson S. B. 581 W. Adams
Johnson S. B. Mrs. Oak Park
Johnson Thomas S. Riverside
Johnson T. S. Oak Park
Johnson Walter L. 3241 Groveland av.
Johnson William, 666 N. Hoyne av.
Johnson William, 50 Oakwood av.
Johnson William C. 3921 Indiana av.
Johnson Wm. H. 72 Maple
Johnson William S. 451 Washington boul.
Johnson William Z. 419 Ashland boul.
Johnson Willis F. 10 Hawthorne pl.
Johnson W. A. Hinsdale
Johnson W. E. W. 615, 61st, Englewood
Johnson W. H. Glencoe
Johnson W. O. 5548 Monroe av.
Johnson W. P. 4433 Ellis av.
Johnson W. S. 4409 Calumet av.
Johnson W. S. Dr. 5332 Washington av.
Johnston Agnes E. Miss, 26 Aldine sq.
Johnston A. C. Irving Park
Johnston A. S. Hinsdale
Johnston A. W. 487½ Jackson boul.
Johnston D. 5484 East End av.
Johnston D. I. 287 Park av.
Johnston E. P. 739 W. Monroe
Johnston Fred. 6537 Lafayette av.
Johnston Fred H. 26 Aldine sq.
Johnston George F. 4244 St. Lawrence av.
Johnston G. H. 1304 W. Adams
Johnston Howard Agnew Rev. 489 Bowen av.
Johnston H. Morris, 1636 Prairie av.
Johnston H. McB. 1636 Prairie av.
Johnston I. D. 126 Seeley av.
Johnston James, 3228 Groveland av.

Johnston James B. 442, 65th, Eng.
Johnston James L. Evanston
Johnston James W. 1 Aldine sq.
Johnston John, 379 Dearborn av.
Johnston John jr. 487 Dearborn av.
Johnston John W. Oak Park
Johnston J. Frank, 26 Aldine sq.
Johnston J. J. 792 Jackson boul.
Johnston J. Milton, Irving Park
Johnston J. Montgomery, 26 Aldine sq.
Johnston Mervyn E. Hotel Windermere
Johnston Morris L. 1636 Prairie av.
Johnston Samuel T. 332, 61st, Eng.
Johnston Shepard Mrs, 65 Warren av.
Johnston Thomas T. Evanston
Johnston Victoria M. Miss, 26 Aldine sq.
Johnston William, 896 W. Adams
Johnston William, Hinsdale
Johnston William J. Evanston
Johnston William M. 4044 Ellis av.
Johnston W. S. Mrs. 87 Rush
Johnstone A. Ralph Dr. 4458 Cottage Grove av.
Johnstone Frederick, 5515 Woodlawn av.
Johnstone Martha Miss, Lakota hotel
Johnstone Stewart C. 4158 Calumet av.
Johnstone Stuart Dr. Hotel Metropole
Johnstone Thatcher W. 314 N. State
Johnstone Thomas W. 314 N. State
Johonnot R. F. Rev. Oak Park
Joice J. K. 3834 Vincennes av.
Joly John W. Mrs. Evanston
Jonas Isidor, 426 Ashland boul.
Jonas James M. 471 Bowen av.
Jonas Martin, 471 Bowen av.
Jones Alex J. 828, 71st pl. (H. P.)
Jones Alfred L. 3559 Vincennes av.
Jones Alfred T. Oak Park
Jones Arthur B. Evanston
Jones Arthur G. 4824 Lake av.
Jones Arthur R. 558 Kenwood pl.
Jones A. D. 4830 Langley av.
Jones A. E. Mrs. Evanston
Jones A. H. Oak Park
Jones A. L. 7355 Wright
Jones A. W. 790 Walnut
Jones Belle H. Miss, 2953 Michigan av. Winter res. Riverside, Cal.
Jones Ben. C. Highland Park
Jones Benjamin B. 3222 Beacon
Jones B. W. 4830 Langley av.
Jones Charles, 3707 Vincennes av.
Jones Charles E. 217½ Belden av.
Jones Charles E. 582 W. Madison
Jones Charles F. 448 Belden av.
Jones Charles J. 208, 31st
Jones Charles S., M.D. 170 Oakwood boul.
Jones Charles W. 6514 Yale, Englewood
Jones Clara A. Miss, 3559 Vincennes av.
Jones Cyrus W. Riverside
Jones C. E., M.D. Austin
Jones C. S. Julien hotel
Jones Daniel A. Mrs. 2140 Calumet av.
Jones David B. 62 Astor
Jones David P. 944 Park av.
Jones Dayton E. 6939 Perry av.

Jones DeWitt C. 695 W. Monroe
Jones Edward 6337 Wharton av.
Jones Edward S. 6727 Wentworth av.
Jones Edward W. 2326 Indiana av.
Jones Edwin L. 3830 Calumet av.
Jones Elliott C. Wilmette
Jones Emma A. Mrs. 4324 Greenwood av.
Jones E. Lee, 480 Dearborn av.
Jones E. Mrs. 944 Park av.
Jones Fernando, 1834 Prairie av.
Jones Florence Miss, 22 Astor
Jones Ford, 134 Park av.
Jones Frank Herbert, 4542 Oakenwald av.
Jones Frank L. 555 W. Monroe
Jones Frank M. 368 Warren av.
Jones Fred A. 7141 Webster av. Eng.
Jones Fred H. 695 W. Monroe
Jones F. B. Capt. Fort Sheridan
Jones F. F. 307 S. Hoyne av.
Jones F. H. 4542 Oakenwald av.
Jones F. W. 6324 Yale, Englewood
Jones George I. 667 Kenmore av.
Jones George P. 935 Kenmore av.
Jones Graham, 1834 Prairie av.
Jones Graham P. 935 Kenmore av.
Jones G. Edwin, 43, 22d
Jones G. Herbert, 56 Woodland Park
Jones Harry P. 555 W. Monroe
Jones Harry P. 6324 Yale
Jones Harry W. 317 Washington boul.
Jones Helen Snow Miss, 480 Dearborn av.
Jones Henry D. 136, 53d (H.P.)
Jones Henry F. 345 Chicago av.
Jones Herbert D. 1127 N. Clark
Jones Hiram J. 134 Park av.
Jones Hugh W. Evanston
Jones H. A. 4901 Calumet av.
Jones H. J. 821 Pullman bldg.
Jones Isabella L. Mrs. 2326 Indiana av.
Jones Jenkin Lloyd Rev. 3939 Langley av.
Jones John D. 107, 37th
Jones John H. 3830 Calumet av.
Jones John H. 4422 Ellis av.
Jones John L. 46 Bryant av.
Jones John M. Austin
Jones Joseph, 489, 42d (H.P.)
Jones Josiah Dr. Morgan Park
Jones Julian C. 542 N. Normal Parkway
Jones J. D. Mrs. 286 Ohio
Jones J. Edmund, 449, 36th
Jones J. Howard, 555 W. Monroe
Jones J. I. Oak Park
Jones J. M. W. 480 Dearborn av.
      Sum. res. Lake Geneva, Wis.
Jones J. Russell, 2108 Michigan av.
Jones J. S. Lakota hotel
Jones Katherine Miss, Evanston
Jones Lewis, 282 Seminary av.
Jones Lewis T. 666 W. Adams
Jones L. Munger Mrs. 248 Oakwood boul.
Jones Mahata Mrs. 317 Washington boul.
Jones Mary Miss, 149 Ashland av.
Jones Maxwell M. 4721 Langley av.
Jones Milton, 612 Orchard av.

Jones M. Augusta Mrs. Evanston
Jones M. J. Dr. 5415 Cottage Grove av.
Jones M. Katherine Miss, 480 Dearborn av.
Jones M. T. 199, 25th
Jones Nettie Ward Mrs. Oak Park.
Jones N. B. Mrs. 652 W. Adams
Jones N. M. Oak Park
Jones N. S. The Wellington
Jones N. T. 4237 Wabash av.
Jones Otis, 5859 Washington av.
Jones Rachel A. Mrs. Oak Park
Jones Richard B. 6642 Lafayette av.
Jones Robert Mrs. Hinsdale
Jones Samuel J. Dr. 47 Madison Park
Jones Sarah Mrs. 569 Lasalle av.
      Sum. res. Burlington, Wis.
Jones Sarah M. Miss, 569 Lasalle av.
Jones Steven B. 1001 Wilcox av.
Jones S. B. Evanston
Jones Thomas D. 62 Astor
Jones Thomas H. 54 Throop
Jones Vina N. Mrs. 4945 Lake av.
Jones Walter S. 3601 Vincennes av.
Jones Warner E. 44, 53d (H.P.)
Jones William, 4534 Greenwood av.
Jones William H. Evanston
Jones William M. 4830 Madison av.
Jones William M. jr. 4830 Madison av.
Jones William O. Evanston
Jones W. Jarvis, 2328 Calumet av.
Jones W. R. 1857 Melrose
Jones W. S. Oak Park
Joralmon John S. Rev. Norwood Park
Jordan Addie M. Mrs. 225 S. Oakley av.
Jordan Ambrose L. Austin
Jordan Anna M. Miss, Austin
Jordan Bud, 3802 Lake av.
Jordan Cady M. 603 Jackson boul.
Jordan Carl W. 614 Evanston av.
Jordan Charles A. 261 Fremont
Jordan Charles F. 6314 Stewart av.
Jordan Collins H. 603 Jackson boul.
Jordan Ella M. Miss, 225 S. Oakley av.
Jordan Franklin E. 15, 39th
      Sum. res. Hackley Park, Mich.
Jordan Frederick G. 322 Ashland boul.
Jordan Ida Mrs. 614 Evanston av.
Jordan James W. 5209 Hibbard av.
Jordan J. F. 3802 Lake av.
Jordan M. Helles, Riverside
Jordan Richard W. 3559 Vincennes av.
Jordan Scott, 499 Jackson boul.
Jordan Thomas, 187 Cass
Jordan William E. Evanston
Jordan W. C. Irving Park
Jordon George B. Russell, Windermere
Jorgenson Julia Miss, 148 Dearborn av.
Jorgesson F. C. Park Ridge
Joseph Albert, 303, 42d
Joseph Carl, 3404 Vernon av.
Joseph Charles, 3406 Forest av.
Joseph Henry M. 3131 Vernon av.
Joseph Herbert L. 3131 Vernon av.
Joseph Jacob, 3529 Grand boul.
Joseph J. M. 3333 Vernon av.

Joseph M. 481 Bowen av.
Joseph M. B. 481 Bowen av.
Joseph Samuel L. 3133 Vernon av.
Joseph Sigmund L. 3529 Grand boul.
Joseph Simon Mrs. 3131 Vernon av.
Josephi C. A. Mrs. 3130 South Park av.
Josephi E. A. 3258 Vernon av.
Joslin Alexander D. 1503 Michigan av.
Joslyn R. Waite, Evanston
Josselyn Benjamin W. Evanston
Josselyn H. R. 800 W. Adams
Josselyn William H. Evanston
Jourdan Edward F. Hinsdale
Jouve August, 568 Division
Jouvenat Charles, 3543 Grand boul.
Joy Frank L. Wilmette
Joy William, 541 Lasalle av.
Joycc George A. Lagrange
Joyce Harry, 412 Centre
Joyce Patrick Mrs. 412 Centre
Jucker John, 903 Larrabee
Judah Noble B. 2701 Prairie av.
Judd Charles J. 812 W. Monroe
Judd Corban E. Evanston
Judd Edward J. 3522 Calumet av.
Judd Edward S. 2223 Sheridan rd.
Judd E. P. Mrs. 507 Fullerton av.
Judd Frederick F. 6351 Yale
Judd George Mrs. Evanston
Judd H. Worthington,321,64th, Eng.
Judd James S. Evanston
Judd John S. Evanston
Judd Marvin, 6551 Lafayette av.
Judd Norman W. Evanston
Judd S. Corning, 47 Astor
Judge Thomas F. 244 S. Lincoln
Judkins Putnam R. 416 Washington boul.
Judson C. E. Chicago Athletic Assn.
Judson E. A. Mrs. 771 W. Adams
Judson Frank P. Evanston
Judson Harry B. Evanston
Judson H. P. Prof. Hotel Barry
Judson J. S. A. Hotel Normandie
Judson Mary M. Mrs. 3366 South Park
    av.
Judson William B. 4231 Michigan av.
    Sum. res. Harbor Point, Mich.
Judson William H. Evanston
Juergens Alfred, Oak Park
Juergens Charles, River Forest
Juergens Frederick, River Forest
Juergens Paul, 488 Lasalle av.
Juergens Wilhelmine Mrs. Oak Park
Juergens William F. 488 Lasalle av.
Jukes Arthur G. 619 Cleveland av.
Julin A. V. 869 Larrabee
Julin C. F. 1741 Briar pl.
June Frank H. Oak Park
June Jennie Mrs. Oak Park
June Susie Miss, Oak Park
Jung Magdalene Mrs. 110 Garfield boul.
Jung Peter, 365 Burling
Jungblut Fred G. 755 Sedgwick
Junge August 3810 Wabash av.
Justice B. M. 462 Dayton
Justice Maibelle Miss, 160 Ashland boul.

KABELL LEO, 962 N. Clark
    Kaderly Bertha Miss, Evanston
Kaeff J. N. Hotel Metropole
Kaehler Frederick, 1744 Roscoe
Kaehler Peter F. 1305 Wolcott
Kaeseberg Ehregott, 771 N. Clark
Kaestner Charles, 923 Jackson boul.
Kahler Conrad, 280 S. Homan av.
Kahler John J. 280 S. Homan av.
Kahn C. S. Lexington hotel
Kahn Dietrich 45 Grant pl.
Kahn Felix, 2951 Michigan av.
Kahn Flora M. Mrs. 3710 Groveland av.
Kahn Harry, 3211 Wabash av.
Kahn Harry, 419 Ashland boul.
Kahn Henry, 3633 Forest av.
Kahn Jacob, 220, 42d
Kahn Joseph, 415 S. Paulina
Kahn Julius, 422 Belden av.
Kahn J. 3211 Wabash av.
Kahn Leopold, 3255 Indiana av.
Kahn Louis, 3211 Wabash av.
Kahn Mark, 2951 Michigan av.
Kahn M. 422 Belden av.
Kahn Sigmund, 4335 Ellis av.
Kahn S. H. 4431 Berkeley av.
Kaiser Alexander, 220 Park av.
Kaiser Henry R. 200, 44th
Kaiser M. L. 3148 Prairie av.
Kaiser Sol, 4406 Michigan av.
Kalb E. William, 105 Evanston av.
    Sum. res. Silver Lake, Wis.
Kaler Emma P. Mrs. Evanston
Kales Frances Mrs. 586 Dearborn av.
Kales J. D. Dr. 586 Dearborn av.
Kales William R. 586 Dearborn av.
Kallman A. Mrs. 2962 Groveland av.
Kalteich Otto, 327 Maple, Englewood
Kammerer F. G. 4626 Woodlawn av.
Kammerer W. S. Riverside
Kane Catherine Mrs. 1712 Diversey
Kane George B. 356 Ashland boul.
Kane Joseph A. Irving Park
Kane Theo. Miss, 310 Ashland boul.
Kane Thomas, 310 Ashland boul.
    Sum. res. Waukegan
Kane William D. 356 Ashland boul.
Kane William H. 709 W. Monroe
Kann J. Mrs. Washington Heights
Kanner Rosa Miss, 568 Division
Kanter Louis, 2621 Wabash av.
Kanter M. 2621 Wabash av.
Kanter Samuel C. 2625 Wabash av.
Kantney Theodore, 462 N. Clark
Kantrowitz G. A. 3607 Prairie av.
Kappes Chas. R. 491 Fullerton av.
Kappes J. Henry, 491 Fullerton av.
Karatasky Celia Mrs. 4122 Berkeley av.
Karcher Louis, 448 Washington boul.
Karger Lessing, 3661 Michigan av.
Karger Samuel I. 3661 Michigan av.
Karger Simon, 3661 Michigan av.
Karls Theodore, 1049 N. Clark
Karnes Geo. 3708 Ellis av.
Karnes Wm. 3708 Ellis av.
Karpen Adolf L. 420 Ashland boul.

Karpen Adolph, 669 Fullerton av.
Karpen Benns, 71 Potomac av.
Karpen Solomon, 1736 Wrightwood av.
Karst Frederick A., M.D. 636 Sedgwick
Kasehagen F. W. 1170 N. Halsted
Kasehagen Leo. 1523 Grace
Kasper Adam J. Evanston
Kasper J. 157½ Eugenie
Kasper Peter J. Evanston
Kasper W. V. 157½ Eugenie
Kasson C. Valette 148 Astor
Kasson Dexter N. Mrs. 631 Jackson boul.
Kasson Frances Miss, 148 Astor
Kasten Herman A. 1727 Frederick
Kastler A. P. 553 Lasalle av.
Kastrup O. Oak Park
Kates Geo. A. 3525 Calumet av.
Katz Aber L. 3147 South Park av.
Katz Caroline Mrs. 2819 Calumet av.
Katz Eli, 194 Center
Katz George A. 2819 Calumet av.
Katz Henry, 2247 Calumet av.
Katz Henry, 2819 Calumet av.
Katz J. P. 3147 South Park av.
Katz Samuel H. 2247 Calumet av.
Katzauer Isaac, 293, 34th
Kaub C. L. Mrs. 11 Lane pl.
Kauffman Fred, Lexington hotel
Kauffman Samuel, Evanston
Kaufman Benjamin H. The Wellington
Kaufman Charles, 3626 Prairie av.
Kaufman Henry, 344, 37th
Kaufman Herman B. Dr. 44 N. Clark
Kaufman H. 516 Dearborn av.
Kaufman Lewis, 2951 Michigan av.
Kaufman Louis, 3229 South Park av.
Kaufman Louis, 3315 Vernon av.
Kaufman Moritz, 555 Seminary av.
Kaufman M. 553 Cleveland av.
Kaufman Philip, 36½ St. John's pl.
Kaufman W. H. Lakota hotel
Kaufmann Gustav G. 549 Burling
Kauimann Joseph, 3533 Calumet av.
Kaufmann Nathan A. 3933 Michigan av.
Kauffmann Benj. 3704 Ellis av.
Kavana Luke J. Oak Park
Kavanagh Charles J. 962 W. Monroe
Kavanagh Marcus Judge, Columbus club
Kavanagh M. A. Mrs. 962 W. Monroe
Kavanagh M. R. LaGrange
Kavanagh Thomas W. 936 Fargo av.
Kay V. W. Mrs. 2205 Calumet av.
Kayzer Samuel, Auditorium hotel
Kean James, Evanston
Kean Samuel A. Evanston
Keane Laura J. Miss, 565 Division
Keane M. J. 565 Division
Kearney J. J. 485, 42d pl.
        Sum. res. Mackinac Island
Kearney Thomas, 3803 Michigan av.
Kearns I. F. 35 Lane pl.
Kearsley Mary J. Dr. Austin
Keasel George E. 1808 Frederick
Keater F. C. Rev. Winthrop av. nr. Hollywood
Keating Edward C. 4331 Greenwood av.

Keating Edward C. jr. 4331 Greenwood av.
Keating Edward F. Longwood
Keating James E. 1177 Washington boul.
Keating John H. 4331 Greenwood av.
Keating Michael, 3143 Vernon av.
Keats Arthur S. 10 Fowler
Keats James, 10 Fowler
Keays Charles H. Rev. 2645 N. Ashland av.
Keck William T. 6100 Michigan av.
Kedzie John H. Evanston
Kedzie Margaret F. Miss, Evanston
Kee James W. 1804 Barry av.
Keebler A. C. 4530 Oakenwald av.
Keebler Edward F. 3833 Forest av.
        Sum. res. LaPorte, Ind.
Keebler Nettie Miss, 4530 Oakenwald av.
Keedy D. V. 6334 Oglesby av.
Keefe A. J. 295 S. Leavitt
Keefe E. 423 Garfield av.
Keefe E. F. Dr. 423 Garfield av.
Keefe James E. Dr. River Forest
Keefe J. Mrs. 3560 Prairie av.
Keefe Mary A. Mrs. 605 Jackson boul.
Keefe T. H. 209, 28th
Keefer George D. Oak Park
Keefer Louis, 3910 Prairie av.
Keegan J. Mrs. 2948 Prairie av.
Keeler Charles F. 1468 Michigan av.
Keeler Edw. A. Mayfair
Keeler E. A. Mrs. 4400 Greenwood av.
Keeler Fred, 2022 Indiana av.
Keeler Frederick, 31, 29th
Keeler Hervey E. 3660 Sheridan rd.
Keeler Homer D. LaGrange
Keeler Horatio Dr. 3541 Prairie av.
Keeler James H. 4534 Woodlawn av.
Keeler Luther C. Winnetka
Keeler Warren, 505 Lasalle av.
Keeler William B. Col. 6200 Sheridan av.
Keeler W. P. 6818 Wright
Keeley Clara Miss, 2829 Prairie av.
Keeley E. S. 213 The Plaza
Keeley E. M. 2829 Prairie av.
Keeley Thomas F. 2829 Prairie av.
Keeling Francis, 446 Elm
Keelyn J. E. Evanston
Keen Edwin H. Mrs. 97, 44th
Keen George, 186 Pine
Keen George, Hotel Metropole
Keen Susan Mrs. 97, 44th
Keen William B. jr. Hotel Metropole
Keenan Horace M. 4420 Prairie av.
Keenan Joseph L. 4042 Michigan av.
Keenan P. H. 4136 Cottage Grove av.
Keenan Walter F. 6224 Sheridan av.
Keenan William E. 4042 Michigan av.
Keenan Wilson T. 4042 Michigan av.
Keene Ethel Miss, Hotel Windermere
Keene Joseph, 6959 Perry av.
Keene W. B. jr. Hotel Windermere
Keener W. T. 507 W. Monroe
Keeney J. Franklin, 2622 Michigan av.
Keep Albert, 2010 Michigan av.
Keep Chauncey, 2825 Prairie av.

Keep Frances Miss, 387 Dearborn av.
Keep Frederick A. 387 Dearborn av.
Keep Henry, 2014 Michigan av.
Keep William B. Hotel Richelieu
Keep William F. 387 Dearborn av.
Keepers Wm. E. Hotel Barry
Keeran Norris C. 630, 62d, Englewood
Keeton Theodore A., M.D. 538 Sunnyside
    av.
Kehl Charles H. 301 Chicago av.
Kehl Robert E. 602, 67th, Englewood
Kehoe John E. 315 Bowen av.
Kehoe Martin C. 336 Oakwood boul.
Kehoe Rossiter Mrs. 4200 Ellis av.
Kehr Cyrus, Lakeside
Kehr W. L. 742 W. Monroe
Keighin David, Ridgeland
Keil L. E. 6539 Perry av.
Keil Moritz, 352 Burling
Keiller Addie C. Mrs. 3754 Forest av.
Keily William E. 225, 28th
Keim E, T. 5429 Cottage Grove av.
Keim Isaac, 3347 Prairie av.
Keim Jacob, 3146 Calumet av.
Keir Edward, 447 Belden av.
Keirnan Thomas S. 230 Homan av.
Keith Abijah Mrs. 387 Lasalle av.
Keith Alice Miss, 1808 Prairie av.
Keith D. W. 2601 Prairie av.
Keith Edson, 1906 Prairie av.
Keith Edson jr. 2110 Prairie av.
    Sum. res. Charlevoix, Mich.
Keith Elbridge B. 1900 Prairie av.
Keith Elbridge G. 1900 Prairie av.
    Sum. res. Charlevoix, Mich.
Keith Ernest W., M.D. 5317 Washing-
    ton av.
Keith Henry A. Evanston
Keith James E. 1211 Palmer
Keith J. G. Capt. 522 Jackson boul.
Keith J. L. Miss, 2601 Prairie av.
Keith Morgan L. Mrs. 2714 South Park av.
Keith N. E. Hinsdale
Keith O. R. 1808 Prairie av.
Keith Walter W 1906 Prairie av.
Keith W. Scott, 708 Pullman bldg.
Kelby Rilla Miss, 3322 Michigan av.
Kelby Walter B. 6 Oakland Crescent
Kellam John H. Evanston
Kellar Stanley E. 614, 65th, Eng.
Keller Fred Mrs. 534 Lasalle av.
Keller George, 133 Dearborn av.
Keller Henry, 3407 Indiana av.
Keller Jacob, 3619 Ellis av.
Keller James S. 5714 Washington av.
Keller Louis, 36,9 Ellis av.
Keller Philip, 3759 Vernon av.
Keller Rosa Miss, 228B. Fremont
Keller Theodore C. 220, 46th
Kelley Addison D. 3159 Michigan av.
Kelley Annie S. Miss, 3232 Lake Park av.
Kelley Asa P. Mrs. 2244 Calumet av.
Kelley Charles B. 4860 Washington av.
Kelley David, 3159 Michigan av.
Kelley George H. Evanston
Kelley Harrison, 2927 Indiana

Kelley James W. D. 3232 Lake Park av.
Kelley J. Frank, 3232 Lake Park av.
Kelley L. A., D.D.S. 302 Garfield boul.
Kelley Maud M. Miss, 2801 Prairie av.
Kelley Pearce C. 623 Englewood av.
Kelley William E. 2129 Calumet av.
    Summer res. Shelter Island
Kelley William R. 2129 Calumet av.
Kelley W. D. 3232 Lake Park av.
Kelley W. V. Chicago Beach hotel
Kelling J. F. Mrs. 4238 Wabash av.
Kellner George W. 744 Sedgwick
Kellogg Edgar H. 42, 53d
Kellogg Edward R. Dr. 24 Orchard (H.P.)
    Sum. res. Delavan Lake, Wis.
Kellogg Emma C. Miss, 85 Rush
Kellogg E. B. 42, 53d
Kellogg E. B. Mrs. 157, 42d
Kellogg Frank P. 2449 Indiana av.
Kellogg Henry H. 27 E. Pearson
Kellogg Henry H. Evanston
Kellogg James B. 524, 62d, Englewood
Kellogg James L. 1819 Aldine av.
Kellogg Julius F. Mrs. Evanston
Kellogg Lizzie B. Mrs. 4585 Oakenwald
    av.
Kellogg Mary F. Mrs. 163, 36th
Kellogg Milo G. 135, E. 47th
Kellogg Milton, 312 S. Hoyne av.
Kellogg Myron L. LaGrange
Kellogg Norman W. 17, 46th (H.P.)
Kellogg O. G. Oak Park
Kellogg Sarah H. Mrs. 1923 Prairie av.
Kellogg William, Evanston
Kellogg William F. 3727 Ellis av.
Kellogg William R. Irving Park
Kellogg W. R. 409 Warren av.
Kelly Daniel J. 344 Michigan av.
Kelly D. F. 290 Lasalle av.
Kelly Elizabeth Mrs. 1276 Washington
    boul.
Kelly Gertrude E. Mrs. 1131 Wilcox av.
Kelly G. W. 6564 Harvard, Englewood
Kelly Hiram Mrs. 2716 Prairie av.
Kelly H. L. D. 3002 Groveland av.
Kelly James, Winnetka
Kelly James J. 423, 67th, Eng.
Kelly John, 4202 Vincennes av.
Kelly J. William, Evanston
Kelly Margaret Miss, 4354 Grand boul.
Kelly Morton W. 81 Macalister pl.
Kelly M. A. Mrs. 162 Park av.
Kelly R. H. Mrs. 9 Aldine sq.
Kelly S. H. Dr. Austin
Kelly Thomas, 3949 Prairie av.
Kelly Thomas, 3449 Wabash av.
Kelly T. L. 3002 Groveland av.
Kelly William A. 1131 Wilcox av.
Kelsey Chauncey, 137, 56th (H.P.)
Kelsey C. M. 507 Pullman bldg.
Kelsey George H. The Arizona
Kelsey H. N. Evanston
Kelsey H. S. 416 Lasalle av.
Kelsey J. A. Hotel Metropole
Kelsey William S. 3756 Ellis av.
Kelso Charles G. L. 5101 Kimbark av.

Kelso Hugh A. 4930 Vincennes av.
Kelso H. A. jr. 4930 Vincennes av.
Kelso May Donnally Mrs. 4930 Vincennes av.
Kelso W. M. Hotel Barry
Kemble Charles C. 7112 Rhodes av.
Kemeys Edward, 7209 Euclid av. (H.P.)
Kemp N. C. Dr. 4226 Indiana av.
Kemp Peter, Ridgeland
Kemper Alfred C. 12 Carl
Kemper Bernard H. Sherman house
Kemper Edward H. 629 Fullerton av.
Kempf Theodore, 152, 36th
Kempster Samuel W. LaGrange
Kendall Albert O. 6341 Stewart av.
Kendall Benjamin W. 2638 Prairie av.
Kendall Eben L. 7522 Eggleston av.
Kendall Robert B. Evanston
Kendall Robert R. Evanston
Kendall Susie D. Miss, Evanston
Kendig H. J. 3004 Prairie av.
Kendig John A. J. 207 S. Hoyne av.
Kendrick A. M. 302, 41st
Kendrick James G. 277 Orchard
    Sum. res. Middletown, Ky.
Kenfield E. D. Morgan Park
Kenfield Fred S. 192, 36th
Kenfield H. J. 192, 36th
Kenfield Sophia S. Mrs. 192, 36th
Kenly David Franklin, 372 Lasalle av.
Kenly F. Corning, 372 Lasalle av.
Kenly William K. 459 Lasalle av.
Kenna E. D. Lakota hotel
Kennard Alexander D. 53 Madison Park
Kennard A. A. 53 Madison Park
Kennard J. Spencer Rev. 11 Chalmers pl.
Kennedy Alexander D. 1030 Warren av.
Kennedy A. H. Hotel Windermere
Kennedy Burr A. 1220 Wolcott
Kennedy B. T. 264 Webster av.
Kennedy D. J. Oak Park
Kennedy Fred P. 5919 Indiana av.
Kennedy F. J. 3000 Michigan av.
Kennedy George, 470 Cleveland av.
Kennedy Harry C. Evanston
Kennedy H. H. 3328 South Park av.
Kennedy John, 5147 Wabash av.
Kennedy John C., M.D. 1313 Michigan av.
Kennedy Joseph B. 4015 Indiana av.
Kennedy J. Edward, Auditorium hotel
Kennedy Madison B. 3656 Michigan av.
    Sum. res. "Bitter Sweet," Galway, N. Y.
Kennedy Marie Miss, Hinsdale
Kennedy P. A. B. 15 Pelham flats
Kennedy R. G. Oak Park
Kennedy Theo. W. 6740 Union av.
Kennedy Vernon Shaw, 3524 Michigan av.
Kennedy William, 1286 Wilton av.
Kennedy William B. 5938 Honore
Kennedy William D. 326 Cedar, Eng.
Kennett B. M. Miss, 353 Bissell
Kennett Francis J. Hotel Metropole
Kenney James H. Evanston
Kennicott Cass L. 4050 Ellis av.
Kennicott J. W. Mrs. 401 N. State

Kennicott Lynn S. 4050 Ellis av.
Kennicott Marie A. Mrs. 4802 Madison av.
Kennicott Ransom, 4050 Ellis av.
Kenny J. S. 372 Ontario
Kenny Mary Mrs. 1180 Washington boul.
Kenny R. 372 Ontario
Kenny William R. Highland Park
Kenny William S. 3235 Rhodes av.
Kent Ada M. Mrs. 5756 Monroe av.
Kent E. L. Miss, 2000 Calumet av.
Kent Fred I. 6536 Harvard
Kent Helen M. Mrs. 6536 Harvard
Kent Henry R. 715½ Washington boul.
Kent H. L. 6536 Harvard
Kent J. F. 5756 Monroe av.
Kent Luman B. 4024 Prairie av.
Kent Sidney A. 2944 Michigan av.
    Sum. res. Suffield, Conn.
Kent Thomas, 3203 Calumet av.
Kent William, 5112 Kimbark av.
Kent W. D. 450 W. Congress
Kent William M. 36c S. Sacramento av.
Kenyon Dexter E. 155, 42d (H.P.)
Kenyon Geo. Z. T. 726, 64th, Englewood
Kenyon S. C. 244 Garfield boul.
Kenyon Theodore, 755, 66th, Englewood
Keogh Chester H. 4346 Drexel boul.
Keogh Eugene, 90 Centre av.
Keogh F. J. 403 S. Robey
Keogh James B. 4346 Drexel boul.
Keogh John Blanchfield, 4200 Ellis av.
Keogh John W. 4346 Drexel boul.
Keogh William H. 4346 Drexel boul.
Keough James, 306 Marshfield av.
Keough William, 1790 W. 22d
Keough W. C. H. 1790 W. 22d
Keown C. S. 4338 Greenwood av.
Kepler J. W. Granada hotel
Kepner Delina Mrs. 4027 Vincennes av.
Keppler Frederick, 5442 Ellis av.
Keppler Karl F. 1330 Wilton av.
Keppler O. K. Evanston
Kerber Henry, 3253 Calumet av.
Kerber W. L. 3236 South Park av.
Kerby James 1817 W. 22d
Kerfoot Charles A. 3253 Michigan av.
Kerfoot C. Stewart, 348 Dearborn av.
Kerfoot Samuel H. 136 Rush
    Sum. res. Dells of the Wisconsin River
Kerfoot Samuel H. jr. 27 Pine
Kerfoot William D. 348 Dearborn av.
Kerkhoff W. H. Oak Park
Kerlin E. I., M.D. 576 Fullerton av.
Kerlin Lizzie M. Miss, 576 Fullerton av.
Kerlin Melissa A. Miss, 576 Fullerton av.
Kern Charles, 4030 Grand boul.
Kern Jacob J. 100 Johnson
Kerns B. F. Dr. 3142 Groveland av.
Kerr Anna J. Miss, 549 W. Vanburen
Kerr F. Austin, 3953 Michigan av.
Kerr George B. 4104 Vincennes av.
Kerr Henry, 307 S. Campbell av.
Kerr Henry H. Evanston
Kerr Jessie Miss, 4101 Drexel boul.
Kerr John L. The Arizona
Kerr J. Brainerd, 549 W. Vanburen

Kerr Luella Miss, 5415 Cottage Grove av.
Kerr Rebecca Miss, 649 W. Monroe
Kerr Robert J. 1323 Washington boul.
Kerr Robert M. 65 E. Pearson
Kerr R. H. 5324 Washington av.
Kerr Samuel, 1323 Washington boul.
Kerr William R. 5126 Washington av.
Kerrison Henry W. LaGrange
Kersey Charles A. Dr. 4714 Evans av.
Kersten George Judge, 368 Mohawk
Kersteter Charles, 230, 54th pl.
Kerwin Henry, 555 Washington boul.
Kerwin Mary E. Miss, 332 Dearborn av.
Kerwin Michael W. 332 Dearborn av.
Kesler Arthur E. 321, 61st, Eng.
Kesler M. R. Mrs. 321, 61st, Eng.
Kesler S. C. Mrs. 321, 61st, Eng.
Kesner A. L. 4418 Prairie av.
Kesner Jacob L. 3545 Grand boul.
Kesner Louis, 3918 Calumet av.
Kessel Julius, Hotel Imperial
Kessler John C. 23 Crilly pl.
Kester John R. 3024 Lake Park av.
Kester P. J. Dr. 340 S. Campbell av.
Kester Reese B. Rev. 4800 St. Lawrence
    av.
Ketcham Frank D. 399 Ashland boul.
Ketcham J. C. 31·Roslyn pl.
Ketcham James P. 399 Ashland boul.
Ketcham J. B. Lexington hotel
Ketcham M. W. Oak Park
Ketcham W. N. Irving Park
Ketcham W. P. 395 Ashland boul.
Ketchum David W. Evanston
Kett Harry Francklyn 3552 Prairie av.
Kettelle George H. 200 The Plaza
Kettelle G. H. Mrs. 200 The Plaza
Kettle R. A. Hotel Metropole
Kettlestrings F. W. Oak Park
Kettlestrings Joseph W. Oak Park
Kettlestrings Orrin R. Oak Park
Kettlestrings W. N. Oak Park
Keuthan Belle Mrs. 219 S. Hoyne av.
Kevan A. A. 5015 Madison av.
Kewley J. R. Dr. 3115 Wabash av
Key John R. 357 Ontario
Keyes A. Belcham, M.D. 30 Walton pl.
Keyes D. H. 29, 33d
Keyes Eben W. 6436 Oglesby av.
Keyes E. T. 594 Cleveland av.
Keyes Herbert A. LaGrange
Keyes Lucy Mrs. 594 Cleveland av.
Keyes Rollin A. Kenilworth
Keys John W. 495, 45th (H.P.)
Keys T. Frank, M.D. 5226 Washington
    av.
Kidd Charles P. 989 Jackson boul.
Kidd William E. Dr. Oak Park
Kidder Albert F. Elmhurst
Kidder Daniel S. Evanston
Kidder Harriette S. Mrs. Evanston
Kidder Henry M. Evanston
Kidder Henry M. Col. Virginia hotel
Kidder W. C. Walton pl. sw. cor. Rush
Kidston James, LaGrange
Kiefer Louis C. 2555 N. Ashland av.

Kienzle William F. 2614 N. Paulina
Kilbourn Frederick H. 1010 Warren av.
Kilbourne Edwin D. 305, 41st
Kilbourne Louise B. Mrs. 305, 41st
Kilbourne L. Bernard, 4020 Ellis av.
Kilbourne M. J. Mrs. 3601 Vincennes av.
Kilbourne Walter F. 305, 41st
Kilcrane Frank J. 1093 W. Monroe
Kiie A. B. 534 Englewood av.
Kiley John, 847 Jackson boul.
Kilgore C. Mrs. Oak Park
Kilgore J. C. 533 Englewood av.
Kilgour Arthur W. 495 Bowen av.
Kilgour Harry B. 495 Bowen av
Kilgour Joseph T. 4804 St. Lawrence av.
Kilgour Mary Mrs. 495 Bowen av.
Killen E. Greble, 225 Michigan av.
Killough Charles H. 1810 Michigan av.
Kilmer Anna Dr. 5735 Indiana av.
Kilmer Elmer E. 5735 Indiana av.
Kilmore John W. 457 Warren av.
Kilpatrick Charles, 166 Park av.
Kilpatrick William, 166 Park av.
Kimball Alma L. Miss, 2612 Michigan av
Kimball A. S. 644 W. Monroe
Kimball Charles F. 479 Washington boul.
Kimball C. Fred, 235 Michigan av.
Kimball Daniel W. Ridgeland
Kimball Dorr A. Evanston
Kimball Edward A. 5020 Woodlawn av.
Kimball Edward D. 3737 Ellis av.
Kimball Elizabeth P. Mrs. Ridgeland
Kimball Elvira Mrs. 5020 Woodlawn av.
Kimball Ernst M. 644 W. Monroe
Kimball Eugene S. 4523 Greenwood av.
Kimball George F. 3341 Michigan av.
Kimball H. D. Rev. Oak Park
Kimball Josiah E. 3522 Michigan av.
Kimball Louise E. Miss, 2612 Michigan
    av.
Kimball Mae Miss, 5538 Cornell av.
Kimball Mark Mrs. Lakota hotel
Kimball Martha B. Miss, 3522 Michigan
    av.
Kimball R. H. Dr. Evanston
    Winter res. Pasadena, Cal.
Kimball S. B. 644 W. Monroe
Kimball S. H. Oak Park
Kimball Thomas, 780 Jackson boul.
Kimball Weston G. 2030 Indiana av.
Kimball William P. Oak Park
Kimball W. W. 1801 Prairie av.
Kimbark Charles A. 60 Lake Shore Drive
Kimbark D. Avery, Evanston
Kimbark Edward H. Evanston
Kimbark Eliza U. Mrs. Evanston
Kimbark Eugene U. Evanston
Kimbark George C. Riverside
Kimbark Grace Miss, 60 Lake Shore
    Drive
Kimbark Marie Miss, 60 Lake Shore
    Drive
Kimbark Seneca D. 60 Lake Shore Drive
    Sum. res. Bear Lake, Mich.
Kimbark Walter, 60 Lake Shore Drive
Kimbell Spencer S. Irving Park

Kimberley Samuel A. French house, Evanston
Kimberly F. N. 5713 Rosalie ct.
Kimberly L. R. 418 Warren av.
Kimmell Theodore A. Dr. 2613 Michigan av.
Kimmelstiel Jacob S. 3650 Grand boul.
Kimmey Fred L. Morgan Park
Kindt J. W. 1723 Deming ct.
King Alfred G. Evanston
King Alice G. Miss, 159 Rush
King Allen H. Mrs. 192 Ashland boul.
King Amos B. 4118 Grand av. (R.P.)
King Andrew J. 492, 42d
. King Anna Mrs. 5417 Washington av.
King A. N. Clifton house
King Carlton, 2317 Michigan av.
King Charles B. 159 Rush
King Charles G. 159 Rush
King Charles H. 4536 Forrestville av.
King Charles H. 232 Warren av.
King C. C. Mrs. 286 Belden av.
King Edward, Oak Park
King Edward A. 923 Pratt av.
King Emma A. Miss, 4185 Grand av. (R.P.)
King E. A. Mrs. 3645 Vernon av.
King Fannie Miss, 4824 Lake av.
King Francis, 5 Tower pl.
King Geo. E. 4445 Ellis av.
King Harry V. 6428 Myrtle av.
King Henry B. Winnetka
King Henry W. 151 Rush
King Henry W. 10 Scott
King Hoyt, 3555 Ellis av.
King James, Elmhurst
King James B. 2317 Michigan av.
King James C. Sherman house
King James L. 2317 Michigan av.
King Jenuie Miss, 232 Warren av.
King Jessie Miss, 4118 Grand av. (R.P.)
King John A. 276 Ashland boul.
King John C. 459 S. Leavitt
King John F. Evanston
King Josie Miss, 4540 Oakenwald av.
King J. G. 6428 Myrtle av.
King Laura A. Mrs. 4060 Ellis av.
King L. A. Miss, 300 Lasalle av.
King L. L. Miss, 300 Lasalle av.
King Mary J. Mrs. Evanston
King McIlwain, Hotel Barry
King Molesworth, 3139 Wabash av.
King M. C. Hotel Barry
King M. H. Morgan Park
King M. L. Mrs. 448 Cleveland av.
King Philo R. 552 Dearborn av.
King Ralph W. 5417 Washington av.
King Richard S. 6401 Star av.
King Rockwell, 63 Hawthorne pl.
King Rufus, 277 Park av.
King Sallie C. Miss, Hotel Metropole
King Sarah C. Mrs. 483 Jackson boul.
King S. B. 5417 Washington av.
King Thomas C. Glencoe
King Tillie Miss, 4540 Oakenwald av.
King T. E. 4203 Lake av.
King Ulric, 224 Ashland boul.

King Vere B. 3645 Vernon av.
King William 277 Park av.
King William H. Winnetka
King W. H. Mrs. 4726 Kenwood av.
King W. O. 23, 23d
Kingman Abbie M. Mrs. 4130 Ellis av.
Kingman Carrie T. 306 Chestnut
Kingman Charles H. 2255 Calumet av.
Kingsbury Byron, Ridgeland
Kingsbury Ezra W. Capt. 11 University pl.
Kingsbury H. I. Miss, 2943 Indiana av.
Kingsbury John W. 11 University pl.
Kingsland Phillip S. 105, 37th
Kingsley Clara Miss, Evanston
Kingsley Frank W. Prof. Mayfair.
Kingsley Homer H. Evanston
Kingwill John F. 17, 43d
Kingwill J. H. 84 Loomis
Kinkaid Albert H. 6500 Myrtle av.
Kinkaid Alexander M. Dr. 7311 Yale
Kinkaid C. F. 7106 Yale
Kinkaid J. S. Mrs. 7106 Yale
Kinnally Cornelius F. 129 Garfield boul.
Kinnally John, 129 Garfield boul.
Kinnare F. T. 874 Walnut
Kinnear M. Miss, 3700 Lake av.
Kinney Corydon B. 7729 Sherman
Kinney F. W. 226 Belden av.
Kinney J. Frederick, Evanston
Kinney Louise L. Mrs. Evanston
Kinney W. H. Wilmette
Kinsella Annie F. Miss, 4110 Indiana av.
Kinsella Daniel P. 1512 Wrightwood av
Kinsella Francis D. 4110 Indiana av.
Kinsella John J. 4110 Indiana av.
Kinsella Joseph F. 1512 Wrightwood av
Kinsella J. Edward, 4110 Indiana av.
Kinsella M. Jennie Miss, 4110 Indiana av.
Kinsella Thomas J. Mrs. 1512 Wrightwood av.
Kinslow B. E. 4463 Ellis av.
Kinsman Charles, 2940 Lake Park av.
Kinzie Arthur M. Riverside
Kinzie John H. Riverside
Kiolbassa Peter, 144 W. Division
Kip A. L. Highland Park
Kiper Herman, 32 Sidney ct.
Kiper Julius, 1743 Wrightwood av.
Kipp C. M. 1436 Michigan av.
Kipp Frank S. Oak Park
Kipp Mary E. Mrs. Oak Park
Kippax J. R., M.D. 3154 Indiana av.
Kirby A. H. Dr. Elmhurst
Kirby Thomas, 4613 Champlain av.
Kirby William, 4731 St. Lawrence av.
Kirchberg E. 345 W. Monroe
Kirchberger Siegfried H. 3552 Ellis av.
Kircher Charles G. Elmhurst
Kirchhoff Herman, Ridgeland
Kirchhoff Hermann, 631 N. Hoyne av.
Kirchhoff H. A. 436 Lasalle av.
Kirchner Gustav A. 389 Elm
Kirchstein Herman Mrs. 649 Fullerton av.
Kirk Alfred, 4229 Oakenwald av.
Kirk Arthur, Evanston

Kirk Charles S. 557 N. State
Kirk Charles Wright, Highland Park
Kirk Edgar White 3132 Prairie av.
Kirk Elizabeth Mrs. 2667 Commercial
   (L.V.)
Kirk E. jr. 6716 Wentworth av.
Kirk Henry J. 6230 Sheridan av.
Kirk James S. Mrs. Evanston
Kirk John B. Evanston
Kirk John W. Hinsdale
Kirk Milton W. Evanston
Kirk Rufus L. Wilmette
Kirk S. S. Miss, 424 Chicago av.
Kirk Wallace, 61 Cedar
Kirk W. T. Virginia hotel
Kirkham C. H. 14 Bellevue pl.
Kirkham Francis M. 7713 Union av.
Kirkland John W. 161 Rush
Kirkland Joseph Mrs. 161 Rush
Kirkland Lloyd G. 1065 Chase av.
Kirkland Robert, 5841 Madison av.
Kirkle James, 241 Park av.
Kirkman A. T. Evanston
Kirkman Marshall M. Evanston
Kirkman Minnie S. Miss Evanston
Kirkman William Bruce, Evanston
Kirkpatrick D. H. 883 S. Kedzie av.
Kirkpatrick John, Oak Park
Kirkpatrick John A. Dr. 331, 43d
Kirkwood Allan S. 1 Vanburen
Kirkwood A. J. 1830 Wellington
Kirtland B. F. Evanston
Kirtland Charles B. 1547 Michigan av.
Kirton David M. 9 Crilly pl.
Kirton James, Oak Park
Kiser John W. 716 Washington boul.
Kissam Frederick G. 462 N. Clark
Kissell Emma Mrs. 269 Bowen av.
Kistner John H. Washington Heights
Kitchell Helen M. Miss, Evanston
Kitchen A. M. 467 Bowen av.
Kitchen J. B. Union Club
Kitchin A. W. 4741 Langley av.
Kitching Cyrus, 603, 65th (H.P.)
Kitson Samuel Mrs. 259 Dearborn av.
Kittredge HiramC.1177Washington boul.
Kittredge H. F. Leland hotel
Kittredge L. A. Leland hotel
Kittridge George A. 235 Michigan av.
Kjellberg Emil Dr. 3000 Indiana av.
Klaim Leon, 2970 Vernon av.
Klais J. G. 223 Belden av.
Klaner E. G. Mrs. 596 Lasalle av.
Klaner Fred, 389 Orchard
Klapp Eugene, 296 Ohio
Klapp Wm. H. Walton pl. sw. cor. Rush
Klappenbach Alexander, 170 Fremont
Klassen Jacob 49, 30th
Klauber E. C. 3158 Wabash av.
Klee Abram, 575 Lasalle av.
Klein Carl Dr. 398 N. Wells
Klein Fred, 107 Seminary av.
Klein George J. 305 Chestnut
Klein Gottlieb, Washington Heights
Klein Henry P. 1824 Belmont av.
Klein Leon, 481 Ashland boul.

Klein Leon, 3151 Forest av.
Klein Mayer, 3742 Wabash av.
Klein Nathan, 3218 Prairie av.
Klein Philip Rev. 569 Cleveland av.
Klein Simon, 364 Ashland boul.
Klein Sol. 474 Ashland boul.
Klein S. 3218 Prairie av.
Klein Wendell, Winnetka
Kleine Frederick, 524 Orchard
Kleine Henry, 1220 N. Clark
Kleine Louis H. 524 Orchard
Kleinert Adolph, 3922 Prairie av.
Kleinhaus M. 3756 Ellis av.
Kleppinger A. S. 6100 Michigan av.
Kley Henry T. 739 N. Hoyne av.
Kley Marguerite Mrs. 325 Cedar, Engle-
   wood
Kline George R. Evanston
Kline G. Ebert, 4201 Ellis av.
Kline Henry C. 888 S. Kedzie av.
Kline Joseph, 3430 Calumet av.
Kline Julius, 3430 Calumet av.
Kline Lee, 4201 Ellis av.
Kline Samuel J. 4511 Grand boul.
Kline Sol, 3430 Calumet av.
Klineofen Louisa Mrs. 2339 N. Halsted
Klinetop Chas. W. Dr. 3058 Calumet av.
Klinger William, 3525 Wabash av.
Klinger W. Mrs. 3525 Wabash av.
Klingman C. 4861 Lake av.
Klock Frank B. River Forest
Klock John H. Evanston
Klock W. W. 1613 Fulton
Klopfer Henry, 3407 Calumet av.
Klotz Robert, 676 N. Wells
Klueter Julius, 5430 Monroe av.
Kluge Frank M. 865 St. Louis av.
Kluge William, 871 St. Louis av.
Knab George D. Clifton house
Knaggs Robert, Evanston
Knapp Charles H. 5112 Jefferson av.
Knapp Charles H. 2811 Michigan av.
Knapp C. A. Miss, 5112 Jefferson av.
Knapp C. S. Mrs. 5112 Jefferson av.
Knapp E. L. Dr. 388 N. Clark
Knapp George O. 69, 48th
Knapp George S. 5112 Jefferson av.
Knapp George W. Rev. 3913 Prairie av.
Knapp H. P. 5324 Madison av.
Knapp H. S. Evanston
Knapp John A. 3612 Prairie av.
Knapp J. D. Miss, 5112 Jefferson av.
Knapp J. N. Evanston
Knapp J. V. Mrs. 411 Oak
Knapp Kemper K. 411 Oak
Knapp R. R. 62 Wisconsin
Knapp Thomas, 3706 Lake av.
Knapp W. A. 2928 Groveland av.
Knauer Edmund, 1474 N. Clark
Knauer Herman, Oak Park
Knauer Peter, 289 Seminary av.
Knecht John, 526 Burling
Kneeland L. D. 1 Groveland Park
Knefel Paul F. 4215 Calumet av.
Kneisly John L. 1136 Washington boul.
Knickerbocker, Charles K. 4045 Ellis av.

Knickerbocker John J. 271 Oakwood boul.
Knickerbocker Marion Louise Miss, 4045 Ellis av.
Knickerbocker R. M. Mrs. 4045 Ellis av.
Kniffin LeGrand, 600 Park av.
Knight Anna W. Mrs. 5100 Hibbard av
Knight Clarence A. 3322 Calumet av.
Knight C. A. Lexington hotel
Knight C. J. 4335 Lake av.
Knight Frederick J. 3761 Lake av.
Knight Hale, 2429 N. Paulina
Knight Henry, Vendome Club hotel
Knight J. B. 4738 Woodlawn av.
Knight Marion Mrs. 620, 62d, Eng.
Knight M. G. Rev. Chicago Beach hotel
Knight Newell C. Evanston
Knight Samuel, 435 Lake av.
Knight Stephen C. 3336 Rhodes av.
Knight T. D. Hyde Park hotel
Knight William H. Hinsdale
Knight William J. 276 Michigan av.
Knight William S. Lexington hotel
Knight William M. 1825 Barry av.
Knights C. H. 6617 Harvard
Knipschild Frank A. 462 Dayton
Knisely George F. 1364 Washington boul.
Knisely Harry C. Hinsdale
Knisely John A. 3241 Michigan av.
Knisely Richard W. 970 Park av.
Kniskern Charles A. 4849 Greenwood av.
Kniskern Warren B. 4849 Greenwood av.
Knokes P. B. Mrs. 632 W. Monroe
Knoop Ernst H. 195 Burling
Knorr Chas. A. 5319 Jefferson av.
Knott F. J. Oak Park
Knott Henry A. 1657 Sheridan rd.
Knowles George W. 261 Warren av.
Knowles Jerry, 3123 Forest av.
Knowles J. C. 261 Warren av.
Knowlton Edward R. Austin
Knowlton Frank B. 323 Michigan av.
Knox Charles M. 535 W. Adams
Knox George G. 535 W. Adams
Knox John, 1021 Jackson boul.
Knox Loren H. Evanston
Knox Loren L. Rev. Evanston
Knox Mary E. Miss, 535 W. Adams
Knox Reuben, Evanston
Knox Resegu C. Dr. 930 Lunt av.
Knox S. Fred. Highland Park
Knox T. M. 159 Eugenie
Knox Wesley L. Evanston
Koach A. H. Granada hotel
Kober George C. 433 Center
Koch Albert, 904 Walnut
Koch C. R. E., Dr. 4537 Greenwood av.
Koch Edward, 210 The Plaza
Koch F. Mrs. Elmhurst
Koch G. Charles, 230 Cass
Koch John, 208, 28th
Koch John, 385 Evanston av.
Koch Nicholas, 454 Lasalle av.
Kochersperger DanielH. 3987Drexel boul.
Kochersperger Harvie L. 3845 Langley av.
Kochersperger John P. 24, 145 Oakwood boul.

Kochi C. Hotel Barry
Kochs Amelia Miss, 15 Lincoln av.
Kochs Theodore A. 15 Lincoln av.
Koechel Henry C. 1229 Grace
Koehler Frederick Mrs. 579 Orchard
Koehler Herman R. 4351 Indiana av.
Koehler Otto, 859 Walnut
Koehn Louis F. jr. 2558 Commercial (L. V.)
Koehsel Fred H. 4446 Indiana av.
Koelling Carl, 241 Hampden ct.
Koelling John, 241 Hampden ct.
Koenig John, 1473 Wellington
Koenig Joseph A. 33 Macalister pl.
Koenigsberg Lizzie M. Mrs. 2949 Michigan av.
Koenker Henry, 451 N. Clark
Koerner C. Rev. 521 Lasalle av.
Koester George F. 2671 Commercial (L. V.)
Koetser Horace J. Hotel Imperial
Kohl Charles E. 2826 Michigan av.
Kohler Albert W. Clifton house
Kohler Franklin W. 252, 51st (H. P.)
Kohler G. A. Edward, 252, 51st (H. P.)
Kohlsaat Anna M. Miss, 505 W. Adams
Kohlsaat Bertha F. Miss, 505 W. Adams
Kohlsaat C. C. Judge, 239 Ashland boul.
    Sum. res. Lake Geneva, Wis.
Kohlsaat E. W. 231 Ashland boul.
Kohlsaat H. H. 2978 Prairie av.
    Sum. res. Oconomowoc, Wis.
Kohlsaat Philemon B. 271 Ashland boul.
Kohn Abe, 2240 Calumet av.
Kohn Albert W. 2614 Indiana av.
Kohn Alfred, 3241 Vernon av.
Kohn Alfred D. 3340 Michigan av.
Kohn David A. 3340 Michigan av.
Kohn Edwin D. 3232 Groveland av.
Kohn Emanuel J. 3223 Michigan av.
    Sum. res. Lake Geneva, Wis.
Kohn Harry D. 2208 Prairie av.
Kohn Henrietta A. Miss, 3541 Ellis av.
Kohn H. A. 2240 Calumet av.
Kohn H. S. Mrs. 3205 Indiana av.
Kohn Isaac A. 3541 Ellis av.
Kohn Johanna Mrs. 181 Howe
Kohn John, Oak Park
Kohn Joseph A. 2018 Calumet av.
Kohn Katie Mrs. 428 Lasalle av.
Kohn Louis, 17 Crilly pl.
Kohn Louis A. 3541 Ellis av.
Kohn Louis H. 3205 Indiana av.
Kohn Morris, 2959 Groveland av.
Kohn Simon, 2959 Groveland av.
Kohn Simon A. 3541 Ellis av.
Kohn Simon H. 3205 Indiana av.
Kohn Theresa Miss, 1717 Michigan av
Kohtz L. O. 650 Fullerton av.
Kolb Adam, 1241 Washington boul.
Kolb Oscar E. 1241 Washington boul.
Koll E. Evanston
Kollenberg C. 17 Sidney ct.
Kollmorgen H. 516 Webster av.
Komans C. M. Mrs. 234 Cass
Koons M. E. Mrs. 1059 N. Clark

Koontz N. B. 4216 Oakenwald av.
Kopf Charles F. Morgan Park
Kopf P. 4743 Indiana av.
Kopperl J. I. 2924 Lake Park av.
Korn George W. 5217 Kimbark av.
Korsoski Dora Mrs. B201 Indiana av.
Korssell Claus Dr. 113 Garfield boul.
Korte Edward, 6851 Honore
Kortum Max, 693 Burling
Kotz Charles, 525 Burling
Kotzenberg Charles Mrs. 1001 Garfield boul.
Kowalski J. H. 3763 Vernon av.
Kozminski Charles Mrs. 3346 Vernon av.
Kozminski Maurice W. 3346 Vernon av.
Kraft Irving, Walton pl. sw. cor. Rush
Kraft Oscar H. 208 Seminary av.
Kraft Walter G. Oak Park
Kramer A. F. 2914 Prairie av.
Kramer Charles A. L. 987 Warren av.
Kramer F. 2914 Prairie av.
Kramer F. C. 385 Orchard
Kramer Joseph A. 3744 Forest av.
Kramer Wm. E. Dr. 1380 N. Clark
Kranz Jo 284 Huron
Kranz Nicholas F. Evanston
Kranz Susie Miss, Evanston
Kraus Adolph, 230A Fremont
Kraus Adolph, 4315 Drexel boul.
Kraus Harry, 504 W. Congress
Kraus Martin J. 855 Lawndale av.
Kraus Rose Mrs. 284 Ohio
Kraus S. 427 Marshfield av.
Krause Edmund R. 53 St. James pl.
Krause E. F. H. 148, 50th
Krause J. W. Mrs. 1611 Cornelia
Krause Margaret Mrs. 6215 Michigan av.
Krauss Alexander, 444 Belden av.
Krauss Justus M. 89, 33d
Krebaum C. R. Mrs. 807 Touhy av.
Kreer John G. 539 Lasalle av.
Kreer John J. 539 Lasalle av.
Kreicker William, 207 Fremont
Kreidler William A. 295 Belden av.
Kreis Gus A. Austin
Kreissl F. Dr. 2929 Groveland av.
Krembs Moritz, 346 Belden av.
Kremer C. E. Lakota hotel
Kretlow Emma Miss, 401 Webster av.
Kretlow Louis Prof. 401 Webster av.
Kretschmar Howard, 583 Lasalle av.
Kretzinger George W. Austin
Kretzinger Joseph, Austin
Kreutzberg John A. 2312 N. Paulina
Kreutzinger Edward, 726 Fullerton av.
Kreye Paul Dr. 454 North av.
Kriechbaum E. G. Mrs. 289 Lasalle av.
Krieger G. Dr. 3242 Vernon av.
Kriegh Katherine D. Miss, 10 Scott
Kriegsman William G. 302 Winchester av.
Kriete C. L. Mrs. 73 Lincoln av.
Krigger G. K. Mrs. 420 Park av.
Kroeger John jr. Auditorium annex
Kroening Albert, 557 Garfield boul.
Kroening August E. Dr. 557 Garfield boul.
Kroeschell Albert, 354 Bissell

Kroeschell Charles, 209 Belden av.
Kroeschell Herman, 354 Bissell
Kroeschell Herman A. Mrs. 207 Belden av.
Kroeschell Otto, 450 Dayton
Kroeschell William L. 457 Dayton
Kroff R. J. 824 Warren av.
Krohn Frank, Hinsdale
Krohn Philip Rev. 8 Best av.
Krohner Jacob, Washington Heights
Kron F. J. 382 Bissell
Krontha Benjamin, 3600 Forest av.
Kropf Oswald F. 689 N. Robey
Krost Joseph Dr. 323 Center
Kroth Louis, 294 Lincoln av.
Krouskup Walter, 3809 Wabash av.
Krout Mary H. Miss, 670 Lasalle av.
Krueger Antoinetta Mrs. 3247 Beacon
Krueger John W. Park Ridge
Krueger Theodore, 3247 Beacon
Krum Charles L. 5222 Jefferson av.
Krum Iretus R. 648 W. Monroe
Krus Perry, 2719 Commercial (L.V.)
Krusemarck Charles, M.D. 2729 Indiana av.
Kubin Otto, 515 Winchester av.
Kuecken Charles, 407 Orchard
Kuecken William, 407 Orchard
Kuehl George, 165 Center
Kuehne Angelica Mrs. 3555 Vincennes av.
Kuehne Clemens, 3555 Vincennes av.
Kuehne Otto, 3555 Vincennes av.
Kuetchar M. R. Winnetka
Kugemann W. Emil, 4348 Berkeley av.
Kuh Abraham, 3141 Michigan av.
Kuh Edwin J. Dr. 3125 Michigan av.
Kuh Henry, 3360 Prairie av.
Kuh Isaac, 3320 Indiana av.
Kuh Julius S. 3141 Michigan av.
Kuh Sidney Dr. 3320 Indiana av.
Kuhlmey Albert, 496 Dearborn av.
Kuhnert L. C. 5610 Washington av.
Kuhns E. Louis, Hotel Windemere
Kulms John M. 4016 Indiana av.
Kultchar M. Richard, Winnetka
Kummer John, 345 Ashland boul.
Kundstadter Sigmund, 355 Bowen av.
Kune Julian, 6637 Lafayette av.
Kunkel Michael, 498 Seminary av.
Kunreuther Johanna Mrs. 471 Lasalle av.
Kuntz P. 3977 Drexel boul.
Kunz Frank. Wilmette
Kunz S. Dr. 381 Mohawk
Kunze Louis G, 697 Sedgwick
Kuppenheimer Albert B. 2956 Michigan av.
Kuppenheimer Bernhard, 2956 Michigan av.
Kuppenheimer Jonas, 3634 Prairie av.
Kuppenheimer Louis B. 1913 Indiana av.
Kurts George E. Austin
Kurtz Charles E. Dr. 4460 Berkeley av.
Kurtz Joseph, 7343 Wright
Kurz Adolph, 3237 South Park av.
Kurz Benne Mrs. 3237 South Park av.
Kurz Louis, 956 N. Clark
Kussel Christian, 721 N. Wells

Kussner Albert J. 3813 Forest av.
Kussner Lawrence, 3813 Forest av.
Kyle William F. 663 W. Harrison
Kytka Gertrude L. Mrs. 1423 Michigan
    av.

L ABES A. 1718 Gary pl.
    LaBounte M. J. 3655 Grand boul.
Lacey Edward S. Evanston
Lacey W. H. 563 W, Vanburen
Lackersteen Mark H., M.D. 4014 Ellis av.
Lackey Charles R. Oak Park
Lackey Robert A. Oak Park
Lackey R. M. Dr. Oak Park
Lackey Walter E. Berwyn
Lackner Ernest Dr. 3201 Calumet av.
Lackner Francis, 579 Dearborn av.
Lacy Daniel, Austin
Lacy Hattie E. Dr. 579 Albany av.
Lacy Nattie Mrs. Austin
Lacy Sara Miss, 903 W. Adams
Ladd Elwood G. 4434 St. Lawrence av.
LaFayette Henrietta W. Mrs. 176, 39th
Lafferty W. J. 6412 Sheridan av.
Laffrinier Sarah Mrs. 1448 Dakin
Laflin Albert S. Auditorium hotel
Laflin Arthur K. 1614 Michigan av.
Laflin George H. 1614 Michigan av.
Laflin John P. 2305 Calumet av.
Laflin Lycurgus, Auditorium hotel
Laflin Matthew, 2335 Michigan av.
    Sum. res. Waukesha. Wis.
Lagergren C. G. Prof. Morgan Park
Laib Samuel, 4154 Berkeley av.
Lain W. H. 6707 Perry av.
Laing A. C. 1159 W. Congress
Laing Cuthbert W. Col. 265 Michigan av.
Laing David.R. 265 Michigan av.
Laing Harold A. 2449 Indiana av.
Laing Howard E. 2449 Indiana av.
Laing Isaiah F. River Forest
Laing John R. 3819 Vincennes av.
Laing M. C. Mrs. River Forest
Laing M. J. Mrs. 1131 Dunning
Latng William G. 3819 Vincennes av.
Laird Orlando P. Longwood
Lake Amy Miss, Evanston
Lake Charles E. 1698 Alexander av.
Lake Charles H. 1698 Alexander av.
Lake Clifford, 621, 78th, Eng.
Lake Frank C. 3756 Ellis av.
Lake Fred I. 1698 Alexander av.
Lake I. L. 1702 Michigan av.
Lake James K. 161 S. Robey
Lake Jessie Miss, Evanston
- Lake Marcus, 4049 Ellis av.
Lake Richard C. Evanston
Lake W. H. 4049 Ellis av.
Lakey Amos, 487, 42d
Lally George H. Leland hotel
Lally John, 5700 Monroe av.
Lalor Margaret Miss, Hinsdale
Lalor Willard A. Hinsdale
Lamb Augustus D. 3925 Michigan av.
Lamb Benjamin B. 3925 Michigan av.
Lamb Charles A. 497 Jackson boul.

Lamb Foster W. 107 S. Hoyne av.
Lamb Frank H. 495 Jackson boul.
Lamb Frank M. 518 Fulton
Lamb Frederick R. 5326 Cornell av.
Lamb John, 92 Laflin
Lamb L. L. Pullman
Lamb Marie Mrs. 4635 Emerald av.
Lamb M. L. Mrs. 4 Pelham flats
Lamb William, 108 S. Leavitt
Lamb W. J. 317 Lincoln av.
Lambach William F. 339 Burling
Lamberson D. Harvey, Evanston
Lamberson Frank, Evanston
Lamberson Josie M. Miss, Evanston
Lamberson S. B. 6024 Park End av.
Lambert C. A., M.D. 6839 Honore
Lambert J. A. Maywood
Lamberton Hull, 4074 Lake av.
Lamberton John F. 415 Kenmore av.
Lamm Abraham, The Wellington
Lamm Arthur G. 3603 Prairie av.
Lamm Edgar, 3603 Prairie av.
Lamm Joseph C. 3405 Forest av.
Lamm S. C. Mrs. 3603 Prairie av.
Lammert Charles F. 330 Marshfield av.
LaMonte Frank A. 261 Bowen av.
LaMonte R. P. Hotel Windermere
Lamoreaux Manning D. 1205 Washington
    boul. Sum. res. North Fairfield, O.
Lampert Henry, 324 Webster av.
Lamplugh E. J. Mrs. 4327 Oakenwald av.
Lamport F. W. 401 Oak
Lamport Nancy Mrs. 547 W. Monroe
Lamson Lorenzo J. 3720 Grand boul.
Lamson S. Warren, 3991 Ellis av.
Lamson W. H. 1185 W. Adams
Lanagan David, 280 Ohio
Lancaster C. L. Lexington hotel
Lancaster Eugene A. 2703 Prairie av.
Lancaster John, 4322 St. Lawrence av.
Lancaster R. Mrs. 4129 Drexel boul.
Landauer Herman, 3735 Ellis av.
Lande Solomon, 88 Park av. (L.V.)
Landergren B. A. E. 333 Ohio
Landis Edmund M. Dr. 1115 N. Clark
Landis Joseph, 688 W. Monroe
Landis Perry, Evanston
Landis Roland R. Hinsdale
Landis William, Hinsdale
Landman P. Mrs. 3764 Indiana av.
Landon Albert W. 4628 Prairie av.
Landon H. J. Miss, 370 Dearborn av.
Landsberg Maurice, 3731 Vincennes av.
Landt Charles C. 4200 Drexel boul.
Lane Albert G. 430 W. Adams
Lane Arthur E. 145 Ashland boul.
Lane Arthur M. Irving Park
Lane A. H., M.D. 305 Division
Lane Chas. E. 307, 56th (H.P.)
Lane C. B. Mrs. 541 W. Adams
Lane C. H. Lexington Hotel
Lane C. W. 6042 Princeton av.
Lane Eben, 2116 Michigan av.
Lane Ella Miss, Evanston
Lane Francis B. 237 Marshfield av.
Lane F. G. Miss, 2116 Michigan av.

Lane George, 312 Indiana
Lane Hannah Miss, Evanston
Lane H. M. Hyde Park hotel
Lane Ida M. Miss, 4815 Lake av.
Lane Irene Miss, Evanston
Lane James, 19 Lane pl.
Lane James R. 683 W. Adams
Lane Jennie E. Mrs. 3250 Rhodes av.
Lane John, 4801 Lake av.
Lane John A. The Tudor
Lane John J. 904 S. Kedzie av.
Lane Joseph, 35 Newport av.
Lane Joseph G. 3528 Ellis av.
Lane Josie Miss, 464 W. Adams
Lane J. C. Evanston
Lane Maurice T. Evanston
Lane M. A. 464 W. Adams
Lane P. E. 6626 Harvard
Lane Sallie Miss, 464 W. Adams
Lane Wm. H. 541 W. Adams
Lane W. C. 6642 Princeton av.
Lanehart John W. 720 Grace
Lang Annie Mrs. 3017 Calumet av.
Lang August Mrs. 2293 Commercial (L.V.)
Lang Emma Miss, 73 Bowen av.
Lang F. C. 323 Hampden ct.
Lang George F. 1071 Kenmore av.
Lang G. 4322 Grand boul.
Lang Otto, 3028 Lake Park av.
        Sum. res. Oshkosh, Wis.
Lang William, 914 Warren av
Langan Bartley Mrs. 294 Superior
Langan John B. Walton pl. sw. cor. Rush
Langbein Ferdinand, 4226 Calumet av.
Langbein Sigfried, 624 Washington boul.
Langdon C. F. Lakota hotel
Langdon Richard B. 3528 Ellis av.
Lange Charles, Riverside
Lange Henry J. 4844 Langley av.
Lange Leonard A. 439 W. Congress
Lange Louis, 925 Kenmore av.
Lange Paul W. 1723 Cornelia
Langell Bliss, Evanston
Langford Ed. G. 6750 Wentworth av.
Langford Geo. C. 6750 Wentworth av.
Langford Thomas, Austin
Langhenry Godfred, 46 Beethoven pl.
Langhorne Maurice, 316 Washington
        boul.
Langle Harry, The Renfost
Langlois Ellen E. Mrs. Evanston
Langworthy Lyman B. 422 Kenwood
        Terrace
Lanphere Edwin O. 5642 Washington av.
Lanphere L. J. Mrs. 67th cor. Oglesby av.
Lansing M. S. 102 Loomis
Lansing Odell E. Hampden flats
Lansing Roscoe U. Hampden flats
Lansingh Killian V. R. 5109 Kimbark av.
Lansingh V. R. 5109 Kimbark av.
Lanterman Etta E. Mrs. 964 S.Cen.Pk.av
Lanterman Lucius, 1023 S . Louis av.
Lanz C. W. 6632 Shermant
Lanz George, 780 Sedgwick
Laparle Wm. B. 704 Warren av.
Lapham Arden B. jr. 5714 Washington av.

Lapham Arthur C. 17 Ashland boul.
Lapham A. B. 5714 Washington av.
Lapham Chester E. 17 Ashland boul.
Lapham C. W. 85, 47th
Lapham E. F. 4323 Lake av.
Lapham E. N. 3601 Vincennes av.
Lapham Joseph B. Chicago Beach hotel
Lapham Marshall, 425 Oak
Lapham Valentine, 3953 Michigan av.
Lapointe D. A. 1335 Fulton
Lapp Peter, 235 Michigan av.
Large Josephine Miss, 320 Superior
Larimer Joseph M. Evanston
Larkin Edna Miss, 1728 Michigan av.
Larkin Edward, Evanston, Eng.
Larkin F. A. Dr. Julien hotel
Larkin John A. 317 Chestnut, Eng.
Larkin J. J. Dr. 466 Ashland boul.
Larkins John P. 36 Park av.
Larkins Robert, 6439 Star av.
Larned Albert H. 50, 24th
Larned Ezra R. 50, 24th
Larned Frances Miss, Virginia hotel
Larned F. M. 803 Pullman bldg.
Larned Mary J. Mrs. Virginia hotel
Larned Walter C. Lake Forest
Larned William E. 3724 Lake av.
La Rocque Leo A. 52 Vernon Park pl.
Larrabee Anna Miss, 1628 Indiana av.
Larrabee Caroline R. Miss, 405 Dearborn
        av.
Larrabee Charles R. 405 Dearborn av.
Larrabee Edw A. Rev. 405 Dearborn av.
Larsen Martin, 483 Webster av.
Larsen Otis R. Evanston
Larson Charles J. 7749 Sherman
Larson F. E. Irving Park,
Lartz William C. C. 287 Park av.
Lashar John A. 6542 Stewart av.
LaShelle Clarence M. Vendome Club
        hotel
Lasher Charles W. 1900 Wellington
Lasher Wm. S. Highland Park
Lasier David S. The Tudor
Laskey Stephen, 1710 Indiana av.
Lateer Ellenor S. Mrs. 4512 Prairie av.
Latham Ellis C. Wilmette .
Latham Harry H. Wilmette
Latham Hattie Miss, Wilmette
Latham Hubbard, Wilmette
Latham James Fanning, 4552 Lake av.
Latham Val A. Dr. 277 S. Lincoln
Lathrop Bryan, 77 Bellevue pl.
Lathrop Charles D. Chicago Beach hotel
Lathrop Ebenezer Dr. 7526 Eggleston av.
Lathrop Edward B. 4436 Ellis av.
Lathrop F. A. Forest hotel (R.P.)
Lathrop Geo. B. 410 Oak
Lathrop John L. 410 Oak
Lathrop Joseph, 410 Oak
Lathrop May Miss, Austin
Latimer Charles E. Lake Forest
Latimer Walter H. 6404 Ellis av.
Latshaw H. C. Berwyn
Latta Anna Miss 265 Michigan av.
Latta Ulysses G. Dr. 3858 Ellis av.

Lattan Louis F. Dr. Austin
Latter James H. 4530 St. Lawrence av.
Latus H. C. 955 Park av.
Laubenheimer E. Mrs. 828 Chase av.
Laubenstein George H. LaGrange
Lauer N. A. 5855 Indiana av.
Laughlan H. D. Great Northern hotel
Laughlin John L. 65, 37th
Laughton M. B. Miss, 373 Superior
Lauman Charles N. 185 Rush
Lauman George V. 185 Rush
Lauman J. G. Mrs. 185 Rush
Launder D. 3557 Vernon av.
Laurence William J. Dr. 4 Langley pl.
Laurine Robert, Mayfair
Lausten Andrew C. 93 Fowler
Lausten Charles, 93 Fowler
Lausten William H. 93 Fowler
Lauth J. P. 345 Elm
Lave J. T. Dr. 5330 Greenwood av.
Lavery George L. The Tudor, Ellis av.
    cor. 43d
Lavery W. J. 4058 Lake av.
Lavigne Theodore Mrs. Evanston
Lavinia W. B. 2953 Groveland av.
Law Anna E. Miss, Wilmette
Law Francis B. Wilmette
Law Ida I. Miss, Wilmette
Law Robert, 1620 Prairie av.
Law Robert, 5120 East End av.
Law Robert H. 1620 Prairie av.
Law Robert O. 2976 South Park av.
Law William, Tracy   .
Law William jr. 6643 Harvard
Lawler John, 3619 Indiana av.
Lawler Joseph H. 357 S. Paulina
Lawler Michael, 3619 Indiana av.
Lawler Michael jr. 3619 Indiana av.
Lawlor Eleanor Miss, 38 Ray
Lawrence Albert H. 462 N. Clark
Lawrence Anson M. 4513 Woodlawn av.
Lawrence Bradford A. Norwood Park
Lawrence Charles H. Evanston
Lawrence C. B. Mrs. 1807 Barry av.
Lawrence Dwight, 57 Lake Shore Drive
Lawrence Edward F. 57 L   Shore Drive
Lawrence Eliza Mrs. 437 S. Oakley av.
Lawrence Harrison H. 6949 Stewart av.
Lawrence James A. 3306 Indiana av.
Lawrence H. C. Evanston
Lawrence J. Frank, Grand Pacific
Lawrence Lydia A. Mrs. 1423 Michigan
    av.
Lawrence Mabel Miss, Evanston
Lawrence Marvin A. 521, 62d, Englewood
Lawrence Philip E. Evanston
Lawrence Preston K. 1438 Cornelia
Lawrence William E. Riverside
Lawrence Wm. M. Rev. 492 W. Monroe
    Sum. res. Hamilton, N. Y.
Lawrie Henry, 4140 Berkeley av.
Lawrie John, 6820 Lafayette av.
Lawrie William, 4140 Berkeley av.
Laws F. B. Chicago Athletic Assn.
Lawson Frank B. 4153 Langley av.
Lawson I. 290 Lasalle av.

Lawson John N. 1535 Aldine av.
Lawson Lawrence O. Capt. Evanston
Lawson Victor F. 317 Lasalle av.
Lawson William C. 5211 Washington av
Lawther T. D. 117, 21st
Lawton Charles T. 4737 Kenwood av.
Lawton Lyndon C. Mrs. 4438 Greenwood
    av.
Lawton R. Mrs. 4438 Greenwood av.
Lawton Thomas Dr. Hinsdale
Lay A. Tracy, 321 Michigan av.
        Sum. res. Highland Park
Lay Charles C. 3963 Ellis av.
Lay Frederick C. 3963 Ellis av.
Lay G. Miss, Ridgeland
Lay Robert D. 3963 Ellis av.
Layton Frederick, 6911 Stewart av.
Layton H. B. Evanston
Layton L. C. Mrs. 3753 Vernon av.
Layton R. P. Tracy
Lazare E. Mrs. 471 Lasalle av.
Lazarus C. 3202 Vernon av.
Lazarus Harry, 3606 Prairie av.
Lazarus S. 443 S. Paulina
Lazear H. Y. 6716 Perry av.
Lazear Wm. W. Dr. 3146 Vernon av.
Lazell Herbert C. 4605 Emerald av.
Lazelle F. Mrs. 5331 Greenwood av.
Lea S. H. 17 St. James pl.
Leach Cephas H. 523 Greenleaf av.
Leach Charles H. 6219 Sheridan av.
Leach Dewitt C. 2965 Michigan av.
Leach E. C. 6907 Yale
Leach F. W. Oak Park
Leach Julia A. Mrs. Highland Park
Leach Thomas A. 1497 W. Adams
Leadbeater W. J. 3224 South Park av.
League William, 1493 Fulton
Leahy Dennis, Lakota hotel
Leahy Ja   e , 3431 Wabash av.
Leahy M. Mrs. M.D., 6648 Wentworth av
Leak T. J. Rev. Dr. 2519 Indiana av.
Leake Charles W. Dr. 2454 Indiana av.
Leake John B. 6704 Union av.
Leake Joseph B. Gen. 218 Cass
Leaming Jeremiah, 3869 Ellis av.
Leaming Joseph F. Highland Park
Learned Edwin J. Lake Forest
Learned E. P. 825 Larrabee
Learned Richard, 825 Larrabee
Learned Samuel J. Mrs. Lake Forest
Leask Arthur, 328 Hampden ct.
Leatherbee George H. Hotel Metropole
Leavell Edward O. 887, 69th (H.P.)
Leavens Julia P. Miss, 296, 43d (H.P.)
Leavenworth Alida Miss, 594 Division
Leavitt C. F. 148, 37th
Leavitt Herbert B. 4935 Forrestville av.
Leavitt Sheldon, M.D. 148, 37th
Leavitt Wellington, 3512 Calumet av.
LeBaron Wm. Naperville
LeBarron Frances Miss, 391½ Park av.
Lebensberger Lafayette, 3251 Vernon av.
Lebold Rose Miss, 2513 Wabash av.
Lebolt J. Y. 3348 Prairie av.
Lebolt L. E. 3348 Prairie av.

Lebolt M. H. 3348 Prairie av.
Leckie Adelaide Miss, 4565 Lake av.
Leckie Archibald S. LaGrange
Leckie Evelyn Mrs. 4306 Calumet av
Leckie William H. 4819 Prairie av.
Ledden Thomas Capt. 1010 Warren av.
Ledden Thomas H. 1010 Warren av.
Lederer Charles,18 Sidney ct.
Lederer Emanuel, 3313 Forest av.
Lederer Isaac S. 4444 Langley av.·
Lederer Nathan, 368 Winthrop av.
Lederer Sigmund M. 191 Laflin
Lederle George A. Palmer house
Ledgerwood Angus J. C. 824 Jackson boul.
Ledward T. C. Mrs. 6630 Harvard
Ledyard Guy C. 3143 Calumet av.
Ledyard Guy C. jr.,3143 Calumet av.
Lee Anna Wells Miss, 4241 Grand boul.
Lee Bertha Miss, Oak Park
Lee Blewett, Granada hotel
Lee Charles R. 3945 Lake av.
Lee Christian, 302 The Plaza
Lee C. D. 5830 Washington av.
Lee D. P. 322 Warren av.
Lee Edward Mrs. 142 Garfield boul.
Lee Elmer, Dr. Palmer house
Lee E. E. 17 Walnut
Lee Frederick W. 4001 Grand boul.
Lee George F. 3804 Calumet av.
Lee George N. 3, 31st
Lee George P. 4241 Grand boul.
Lee Henry R. 7248 Vernon av.
Lee James F. 1853 W. 22d
Lee James W. Rev. Mayfair
Lee Jesse M. Capt. U. S. A. 428 N. State
Lee Joel Mrs. 1010 Washington boul.
Lee John B. 28 Walton pl.
Lee J. Francis, Southern hotel
Lee J. Lewis, Riverside
Lee Philip P. Evanston
Lee R. H. 4421 Prairie av.
Lee Thomas B. 3943 Prairie av.
Lee Walter H. Hotel Windermere
Lee Wm. H. Evanston
Lee William H. LaGrange
Lee W. J. 85 Seminary av.
Leeb Heury, 284 Ohio
Leebrick Arthur C. 1050 Washington boul.
Leech C. E. Morgan Park
Leech Wm. H. 36th ne. cor. Cottage Grove av.
Leeds Robert R. Evanston
Leedy John C. 834 Walnut
Leedy R. M. Mrs. 834 Walnut
Leekley Annie E. Mrs. 1330 Washington boul.
Leekley Charlotte A. Miss, 1330 Washington boul.
Leekley Harlow A. 1330 Washington boul.
Leeming Chas. W., 4545 Grand boul.
Leeming Frank, 4545 Grand boul.
Leeming John, M.D. 3400 Indiana av.
Sum. res. Harbor Springs, Mich,
Leeming R, W. 3400 Indiana av,

Lees M. E. Mrs. 4545 St. Lawrence av.·
Leeson T. V. Hotel Groveland
Leet John M. 1423 W. Monroe
Lefens Thies J. 2626 Michigan av.
Sum. res. Lake Geneva
LeFevre J. J. 1132 Wilcox av.
Leffingwell Frank P. 190, 36th
Leffingwell George M. Evanston
Leffingwell W. B. Evanston
LeFurgy Ludlow R. 5033 Madison av.
Leger Edward, 3234 South Park av.
Leger Harry B. 3234 South Park av.
Leggett John Dr. 1373 Washington boul.
Leggett Thomas Mrs. 1373 Washington boul.
Legner William, 89 Ewing pl.
Lehman Herman, 3926 Grand boul.
Lehman Louis B. 3657 Grand boul.
Lehman William, 3523 Vernon av.
Lehmann Alfred A. 1624 Indiana av.
Lehmann Edmund, 1624 Indiana av.
Lehmann E. J. Mrs. 309 Michigan av.
Sum. res. 1326 N. Clark
Lehmann Fred. 1624 Indiana av.
Lehmann Marie Mrs. 1624 Indiana av.
Lehmann Oscar A. 1624 Indiana av.
Lehmpuhl Frank, 1707 Briar pl.
Lehner John H. 548 Chestnut, Englewood
Lehrberg Gustav, 3423 Forest av.
Leib Alexander S. 185, 36th
Leicht Andrew E. 5 Lake View av.
Leicht Edward A. 11 Lake View av.
Leicht Stella Miss, 5 Lake View av.
Leiferman William C. 307 Irving av.
Leigh E. B. 3321 Armour av.
Leighton George W. 1837 Michigan av.
Leimer Frederick J., M.D. 45 Wisconsin
Leis J. W. Hyde Park hotel
Leiter Joseph, 4 Tower pl.
Sum. res. Lake Geneva
Leiter Levi Z. 4 Tower pl.
Sum. res. Lake Geneva
Leiter T. Benton, 4 Tower pl.
Leith J. S. Evanston
Leland Charles W. 4651 Drexel boul.
Leland Edward F. Hotel Normandie
Leland Frank, 538, 67th Englewood
Leland Henry A. 3316 Forest av.
Leland M. B. Mrs. 5234 Woodlawn av.
Leland Nina B. Mrs. 3447 Prairie av.
Leland P. S. Forest hotel (R. P.)
Leland Samuel, 6620 Oglesby av.
Leland Warren F. 4651 Drexel boul.
Lelewer David, 3835 Vincennes av.
Leman Henry W. 337 Dearborn av.
Lemay W. G. 798 Walnut
LeMessurier John, Glen Ellyn
Lemker H. L. Dr. 797 N. Wells
Lemoine Edwin S. jr. 7241 Yale
Lemon Adelaide Mrs. 691½ W. Adams
Lemon George S. 691½ W. Adams
Lemon Henry M. 927 Jackson boul.
Lemon Herbert L. 691½ W. Adams
Lemon Ida Z. Mrs. 730, 64th, Englewood
Lemon O. M. 582 Lasalle av.
LeMoyne Frank J. 412 Chicago av,

LeMoyne Louis V. 412 Chicago av.
LeMoyne William M. 412 Chicago av.
Lempkey Adeline Mrs. 83 S. Lincoln
Lendrum Alexander, Austin
Lenehan Joseph H. 4534 Forrestville av.
Leng Charles, 371 Mohawk
Lengacher Jacob, 277 Fremont
Lengacher Oscar F. 277 Fremont
L'Engle William J. 2340 Calumet av.
Lenham N. L. 683 W. Monroe
Lenington Norman G. 718, 61st, Eng.
Lenke August, 93 Ewing pl.
Lennard Amos L. Dr. 3848 Vincennes av.
Lennard Lewis L. 3848 Vincennes av.
Lenox E. S. Virginia hotel
Lenox John P. Oak Park
Lenox, J. F. Oak Park
Lenox M. A. Mrs. Oak Park
Lentes Nicholas E., M.D. 945 Lincoln av.
Leon Leonard M. 2939 Prairie av.
Leonard Alice G. Miss, Lake Forest
Leonard Arthur G. 2501 Michigan av.
Leonard Charles C. 399, 46th (H P.)
Leonard Charles E. Auditorium hotel
Leonard Ettie E. Mrs. Evanston
Leonard George A. 2501 Michigan av.
Leonard G. Russell, Hotel Windermere
Leonard James Mrs. 3668 Michigan av.
Leonard James G. Prof. 47 Park av.
Leonard J. H. 338 Burling
Leonard Louisa Mrs. 446 Elm
Leonard Mark T. Hyde Park hotel
Leonard M. 6600 Ellis av.
Leonard O. A. Mrs. Oak Park
Leonard P. 252 Oakwood boul.
Leonard Simeon F. 551 W. Monroe
Leonard Thomas J. 575 Boulevard pl.
Leonard William G. 25, 37th
Leonard William H. 6354 Lexington av.
Leopold Alfred F. 3339 Michigan av.
Leopold Bertha Mrs. 4122 Ellis av.
Leopold Charles 3601 Prairie av.
Leopold Edward F. 1467 Michigan av.
Leopold Henry, 3244 Rhodes av.
Leopold Henry F. 1467 Michigan av.
Leopold Henry F. 4201 Ellis av.
Leopold Joseph, 4122 Ellis av.
Leopold Louis, 4346 Grand boul.
Leopold Maurice, 4346 Grand boul.
Leopold Max, 3639 Prairie av.
Leopold Nathan F. 2901 Michigan av.
Leopold Ralph M. 3828 Vernon av.
Leopold Samuel F. 3339 Michigan av.
Lepman David, 2961 Groveland av.
Lepman Louis, 233, 32d
Leppel Maurice, 3706 Forest av.
Leppel S. 3706 Forest av.
Leppelman Louise Mrs. 4544 Michigan av.
Lepper G. A. 7 University pl.
Lerch Peter, 22 Wisconsin
Lermit L. H. Chicago Beach hotel
Lerow George L. 2691 N. Ashland av.
LeRoy Joseph M. 4028 Grand boul.
LeRoy Stuyvesant jr. 290 Ohio
LeRoy W. G. Dr. Lombard
39

Lesch Henry, 6522 Wharton av.
Lesen Belle Mrs. 3414 South Park av.
Leserman Jacob, 3242 Prairie av.
Lesh L. B. Barrett house
Lesher Wm. T. 1037 Walnut
Leslie Amy Miss, Clifton house
Leslie Arthur M. Evanston
Leslie Belle Miss, 4404 Ellis av.
Leslie George A. 7810 Sherman
Leslie George H. Winnetka
Leslie Jane Mrs. Oak Park
Leslie John H. 3344 Rhodes av.
Leslie Norman B. Evanston
Leslie Oliver G. Berwyn
Leslie Robert, Berwyn
Leslie Walter, Hinsdale
Lessey Edgar N. 619, 78th, Eng.
Lester Charles, 208 S. Lincoln
Lester Charles H. Hotel Metropole
Lester Franklin Mrs. 3145 Groveland av.
Lester Frederick A. 597 Cleveland av.
Lester Henry V. Virginia hotel
      Sum. res. Hartland, Wis.
Lester Leon M. 3145 Groveland av.
Lester W. 1007 Jackson boul.
Letsche Richard, 1940 Oakdale av.
Letterman E. R. 416 Jackson boul.
Letton Harold, 4846 Kimbark av.
Letton T. W. 4846 Kimbark av.
Leusman F. A. Dr. 270 Huron
LeVally John R. 4424 Ellis av.
Levi A. Mrs. 3758 Indiana av.
Levi Carl, Stamford hotel
Levi David, 3758 Indiana av.
Levi David, 3725 Langley av.
Levi Emanuel Mrs. 3266 Vernon av.
Levi Henry, 3758 Indiana av.
Levi Henry C. 4425 Drexel boul.
Levi Jacob, 3651 Michigan av.
Levi Julius, 3834 Wabash av.
Levi Leon, 3266 Vernon av.
Levi Walter C. 3266 Vernon av.
Levie Charles M. 3125 Vernon av.
Levie Jerome M. 3125 Vernon av.
Levie M. Mrs. 3125 Vernon av.
Levie Oliver M. 3125 Vernon av.
Levin Andrew, 754, 60th, Englewood
Levin Henry, Winnetka
Levin Hyman, 538 Lunt av.
Levine A. 916 W. Monroe
Levinson Max, 1456 Fulton
Levis H. H. 209 Seminary av.
Levis John M. 6427 Sheridan av.
Levison Albert, 3131 Indiana av.
Levison M. M. 2814 Indiana av.
Levy Alex. H. Auditorium annex
Levy Benjamin S. 3301 Forest Sv.
Levy David A. 3435 Calumet av.
Levy Dila Mrs. 1705 Michigan av.
Levy D. R. 3000 Michigan av.
Levy E. Mrs. 3732 Langley av.
Levy E. E. 3608 Prairie av.
Levy Harry, 492 N. Hoyne av.
Levy Harry, 713 N. Wells
Levy Henrietta Miss, 3645 Grand boul.
Levy Hyman, 3409 Wabash av.

Levy Isidore, 158 Fremont
Levy I. G. 32 Bryant av.
Levy J. E. 3238 Vernon av.
Levy Louis, 419 Ashland boul.
Levy Marcus, 184 Howe
Levy Max, 158 Fremont
Levy Morris F. 210 Ohio
Levy Samuel, 920 W. Monroe
Levy Simon, 247 Lasalle av.
Levy Sol. M. 3645 Grand boul.
Levy William, 3338 Vernon av.
Levy Wolf, 210 Ohio
Lew Charles H. Austin
Lew F. M. 1244 Wilcox av.
Lewald Frank, 3249 Rhodes av.
Lewey J. M. 2413 uth Park av.
Lewis Abner M. 37 Ashland boul.
Lewis Adolph, 2028 Indiana av.
Lewis Albert W. 6415 Lexington av.
Lewis Arthur B. Mayfair
Lewis Augustus I. 50 Lincoln av.
Lewis A. F. Mrs. 346 Dearborn av.
Lewis B. F. 6340 Stewart av.
Lewis Cassius M. 5838 Rosalie ct.
Lewis Charles Ray, 4140 Ellis av.
Lewis Charles W. 374 W. Adams
Lewis C. George, Evanston
Lewis C. M. Mrs. 507 W. Monroe
Lewis David R. Evanston
Lewis Denslow, M.D. 217, 53d (H.P.)
Lewis Emma M. Miss, 507 W. Monroe
Lewis E. B. 18 Bellevue pl.
Lewis E. H. 4357 Lake av.
Lewis E. J. 92 Park av.
Lewis E. N. Hyde Park hotel
Lewis Frank F. Evanston
Lewis Frederick, 522 Webster av.
Lewis F. C. 5504 Cornell av.
Lewis F. H. Evanston
Lewis George, 86 Vernon Park pl.
Lewis George A. 18 Bellevue pl.
Lewis George E. 374 W. Adams
Lewis George F. Hinsdale
Lewis George G. 520 Dearborn av.
Lewis George R. 107, 37th
Lewis Harriet M. Mrs. 466 Cleveland av.
Lewis Henry B. 6012 Indiana av.
Lewis Henry F., M.D. 4426 Lake av.
Lewis Henry Z. 1126 Washington boul.
Lewis H. C. Hyde Park hotel
Lewis H. M. 30 S. Wood
Lewis Irving J. 466 Cleveland av.
Lewis Isaac J. 3335 Indiana av.
Lewis I. Giles, 4573 Lake av.
Lewis James F. 4435 Ellis av.
Lewis John, Oak Park
Lewis John C. 4140 Ellis av.
Lewis Joseph B. 56, 47th
Lewis Joseph K. Evanston
Lewis J. A. Oak Park
Lewis J. E. 21 Lane pl.
Lewis Leslie 5605 Madison av.
Lewis Lyman, 6537 Perry av.
Lewis Mamie A. Miss, 2428 Indiana av.
Lewis Martin, Evanston
Lewis Martin O. Evanston

Lewis Mary Miss, Oak Park
Lewis Minnie Miss, 5945 Princeton av.
Lewis M. D. Mrs. 678 Lasalle av.
Lewis Nathan B. Evanston
Lewis Parker M. 4206 Michigan av.
Lewis R. J. 357 Racine av.
Lewis S. T. 537 Englewood av.
Lewis Thomas H. Evanston
Lewis Thomas W. 328 Lasalle av.
Lewis Walter R. B. 6415 Lexington av.
Lewis William, 5427 Jefferson av.
Lewis William, Hyde Park hotel
Lewis William B. 499 N. State
Lewis William E. 626 Orchard
Lewis William G. 5100 Madison av.
Lewis William H. French house, Evanston
Lewis W. R. Dr. Oak Park
Leyenberger Charles, 4314 Oakenwald av.
Leyman Louise Mrs. 36th ne.cor.Ellis av.
Leyonmarck John H. 4049 Ellis av.
Libbey Fred A. 14 Marquette Terrace
Libby Arthur A. 3357 Michigan av.
    Winter res. Pasadena, Cal.
Libby Cyrus, 79 Pine
Libby C. Perly, 3358 Michigan av.
Libby Mabel V. Miss, 3357 Michigan av.
Libby Pearl G. Miss, 3357 Michigan av.
Libby Prudence E. Mrs. 734 Washington boul.
Libby Una Miss, 3358 Michigan av.
Liberman Henry, 4953 Prairie av.
Liberman Jacob Mrs. 206, 37th
Liberty George H. 4345 Indiana av.
Lichstern Isaac, 3346 Forest av.
Lichtenberger C. Mrs. 488 Dearborn av.
Lichtenberger C. G. 441 W. Congress
Lichtenheim Anthony, 2723 Wabash av.
Lichtenstadt Harry, 3212 Michigan av.
Lichtenstadt Philip, 3212 Michigan av.
Lichtenstadt Susie Miss, 3212 Michigan av.
Lichtenwalter Wm. 6920 Wright
Lichter Mary B. Miss, 3135 Rhodes av.
Lichtner William, 6633 Yale
Lichtstern Adolph J. 3736 Michigan av.
Lichtstern Bernard Mrs.3740Michigan av.
Lichtstern Isaac, 3346 Forest av.
Liday Thomas E. 266 Ontario
Liddell A. Richard, 76 Throop
Liddell Emilie W. Miss, 76 Throop
Liddell R. H. 76 Throop
Lidell M. I. Mrs. 679 Fullerton av.
Lidgerwood J. M. Chicago Athletic Assn.
Lidgerwood R. E. 820 Pullman bldg.
Lidster Ralph E. 325, 61st, Eng.
Lidy Grace Miss, 2809 Indiana av.
Liebenstein Albert, Hyde Park hotel
Liebenstein A. Mrs. 3150 Calumet av.
Liebenstein A. M. 3150 Calumet av.
Liebenstein Charles, 3238 Wabash av.
Liebhart Frank C. Chicago Athletic Assn.
Liebher Maurice, 3756 Ellis av.
Liebling Emil, 22 Astor
Liebman Herman, 505 Webster av.

Liebmann Jacob, 1725 Deming ct.
Liese Frederick, 49 Elaine
Ligare Ashbel G. Glencoe
Ligare George G. Glencoe
Lightcap Eliza A. Glencoe
Lightfoot S. E. Mrs. 366 S. Campbell av.
Lightner James, 152, 36th •
Lightner Milton C. Highland Park
Lilienfeld T. 149, 33d
Lilienfeld Wm. 3649 Prairie av.
Lilienthal S. N. Mrs. 5415 Cottage Grove
  av.
Lilja H. Mrs. 475 Belden av.
Lilja John R. 479 Belden av.
Liljencrantz G. A. M. 3808 Elmwood pl.
Lill George, 1205 Seminary pl.
Lill James, Evanston
Lill Wm. W. 1205 Seminary pl.
Lilley George W. Vendome Club hotel
Lillybridge Phœbe Mrs. 4810 Champlain
  av.
Limbocker W. G. 540, 59th, Eng.
Lincoln Augustus A. Hinsdale
Lincoln Charles, Evanston
Lincoln Edward T. 5425 Jackson av.
Lincoln Isaac jr. Mrs. 4462 Oakenwald av.
Lincoln John L. 322 Superior
Lincoln John L. jr. 322 Superior
Lincoln M. C. Mrs. Irving Park
Lincoln Robert T. Chicago Club
Lincoln Walter D. 5425 Jackson av.
Lind Sylvester Mrs. Lake Forest
Lindauer Benjamin, 3312 Calumet av.
Lindauer Julius B. 3312 Calumet av.
Lindauer Meyer E. 3225 Wabash av.
Lindauer S. 3420 South Park av.
Lindblom Lenore Miss, 678 Lasalle av.
Lindblom Robert, 678 Lasalle av.
Linden Frank L. 4335 Oakenwald av.
Linden James, 4625 Lake av.
Lindenthal Henry M. 13 Crilly pl.
Linderborg Augusta Dr. 431 Centre
Lindgren C. J. Austin
Lindgren Jennie Miss, Evanston
Lindgren John R. Evanston
Lindheimer Jacob, 3717 Vincennes av.
Lindheimer Max L. 3313 Vernon av.
Lindholm Maurice S. 593 N. Robey
Lindley I. C. Auditorium annex
Lindley William O. Auditorium annex
Lindman John J. 4824 Kimbark av.
Lindman O. F. 4731 Ellis av.
Lindon George, 1616 W. Adams
Lindop Frank R. Ridgeland
Lindop John Mrs. Ridgeland
Lindquist Frederick A. 303 S. Leavitt
Lindsay David J. 5465 Washington av.
Lindsay D. E. Mrs. 3962 Langley av.
Lindsay Henry, 243 Michigan av.
Lindsay J. Clarence Dr. 3628 Prairie av.
Lindsay Thomas E. LaGrange
Lindsey Andrew, Austin
Lindsey William, 1 Crilly pl.
Lineaweaver Albert, 4201 Ellis av.
Lines David J. 2972 South Park av.
Lines Edward C. 1255 N. Clark

Lines Frank B. 5809 Washington av.
Ling John, Wilmette
Lingle Samuel B. 3144 Vernon av.
Liumgton Chas. M. 644 Washington boul
Link George T. 464 W. Adams
Link John E. 4227 St. Lawrence av.
Linn George W. 1850 Frederick
Linn Harry C. Mrs. 926 Jackson boul.
Linn William A. Evanston
Linn William R. 2709 Michigan av. *
Linn W. Scott Mrs. 2631 Michigan av.
Linneen David F. 3419 South Park av.
Linneen P. H. 3419 South Park av.
Linneen William P. 3419 South Park av.
Linnell Angeline M. Mrs. Evanston
Linney Elizabeth D. Mrs. 718½ W. Adams
Linquist Gussie Miss, 310 Mansfield av.
Linscott A. N. 4000 Drexel boul.
Linscott Harry F. 4000 Drexel boul.
Linscott John F. 2965 Groveland av.
Linsenbarth Frank, 518 Dearborn av.
Linsley F. Mrs. Hinsdale
Linsley M. G. Hotel Metropole
Linsley Theron H. Hinsdale
Linsley Thomas H. Evanston
Linthicum Charles C. 2412 Commercial
  (L.V.)
Lintz William H. 4642 Evans av.
Lipe Charles C. Dr. 3208 Prairie av.
Lipe Fred W. Lexington hotel
Lipe Raymond, 4437 Champlain av.
Lipkau Eugene, 654 Fullerton av.
Lipman Abraham, 4413 Ellis av.
Lipman August, 4413 Ellis av.
Lipman Meyer, 3531 Indiana av.
Lippincott George H. Evanston
Lipsey Andrew G. Riverside
Lipsey James H. Riverside
Liscombe Frederick A. 4744 Champlain
  av.
Lish John Mrs. 280 Seminary av.
Lissenden Stephen, Austin
List Edward, 420 The Plaza
Listenwalter E. 5448 Cornell av.
Lister Walter, 312 Park av.
Listman Charles F. 4840 Kimbark av.
Liston D. Grant, 4327 Prairie av.
Liston Robert, 4327 Prairie av.
Lit J. S. 861 W. Monroe
Litchfield I. W. 927 W. Adams
Litchfield Wirt, Elmhurst
Litchfield Wm. H. Elmhurst
Litt Samuel J. 394 Bowen av.
Little Arthur W. Rev. Evanston
Little A. Eugene Mrs. 1462 Perry
Little Charles J. Rev. L.L.D. Evanston•
Little E. M. Mrs. 629 W. Adams
Little Francis B. 177 Warren av.
Little Frank, River Forest
Little George W. 4923 Lake av.
Little James H. 1052 Washington boul.
Little John Mrs. 403, 65th Englewood
Little Joseph Dr. 592 Division
Little Mary Miss, 2900 Prairie av.
Little Mary J. Mrs. 604 Washington boul.
Little Seward H. 1125 Chase av.

Little S. M. 416 Washington boul.
Little William P. 1462 Perry
Little William T. 1122 Morse av.
Little W. H. 205, 46th
Littlefield A. S. 609 Division
Littlefield S. H. 891 Winthrop av.
Littlejohn Wiley J. Evanston
Littler Robert M. 751 Walnut
Litts C. C. 7751 Wright
Lively Frank L. Irving Park
Livermore Charles F. 4338 Oakenwald av.
Livermore C. Frederick 2346 Calumet av.
Livermore D. E. 3231 Prairie av.
Livesey Anna Mrs. Irving Park
Livesey John K. 2681 N. Paulina
Livezey Emma Miss, Hotel Barry
Livezey Sadie Miss, Hotel Barry
Livingston Aaron, 3730 Langley av.
Livingston Charles, 3800 Indiana av.
Livingston C. G. 3632 Prairie av.
Livingston David, 3632 Prairie av.
Livingston Emanuel, 3730 Langley av.
Livingston Gustav, 3730 Langley av.
Livingston G. W. 145 S. Leavitt
Livingston Hannah Mrs. 3708 Wabash
  av.
Livingston Howard W. 3835 Calumet av.
Livingston Isaac, 3632 Prairie av.
Livingston John, 3400 South Park av.
Livingston John L. 622 Washington boul.
Livingston Kittie Miss, Evanston
Livingston Louis, 3710 Wabash av.
Livingston Milton, 3730 Langley av.
Livingston M. L. Mrs. 3835 Calumet av.
Livingston Nathan, 3708 Wabash av.
Livingston Sam. 3730 Langley av.
Livingston Sigmund, 3708 Wabash av.
Livingston Thomas, 3835 Calumet av.
Livingston Van Rensselaer, 248, 57th
  (H.P.)
Livingstone Archie T. 358, 40th
Livingstone John K. 358, 40th
Livingstone Thomas B. 358. 40th
Llewellyn Edward H. 463 W. Monroe
Llewellyn Henry S. Dr. LaGrange
Llewellyn Joseph C. LaGrange
Llewington S. Mrs. 235 Michigan av.
Lloyd Edward Lieut. Fort Sheridan
Lloyd Edwin T. 3843 Langley av.
Lloyd Evan, 4458 Cottage Grove av.
Lloyd E. Starr, 3319 Calumet av.
Lloyd E. S. 2510 N. Paulina
Lloyd F. L. The Ashland
Lloyd George E. Mrs. 505 W. Congress
Lloyd Henry D. Winnetka
Lloyd Henry L. Riverside
Lloyd H. C. Kenilworth
Lloyd H. R. Riverside
Lloyd James, Glencoe
Lloyd John E. 499 N. State
Lloyd Llewellyn H. Glencoe
Lloyd Louis, 712 W. Adams
Lloyd Mary Miss, 6900 Anthony av.
Lloyd Ray N. 2585 Commercial (L. V.)
Lloyd Robert C. 2585 Commercial (L.V.)
Lloyd R. W. 282 Erie

Lloyd William A. Rev. 2585 Commercial
  (L. V.)
Lloyd William G. Austin
Lloyd William W. 2585 Commercial (L.
  V.)
Loag Mary E. Mrs. Evanston
Loag Robert, Evanston
Loba Jean F. Rev. Evanston
Lobanoff Paul F. 778 Sedgwick
Lobdell C. N. 462 N. Clark
Lobdell C. W. 3861 Lake av.
Lobdell Edwin L. 38 Ray
  Sum. res. Highland Park
Lobdell Harry H. 3991 Ellis av.
Lobdell Isaac D. M. Mrs. 1688 Alexander
  av.
Lobdell J. H. 6212 Woodlawn av.
Lobdell Marion Miss, 3861 Lake av.
Lobdell Mervin H. 3704 Elmwood pl.
Lober William H. Austin
Lobig Peter P. 330 Huron
Lockart E. A. Mrs. 524 Chestnut, Eng.
Locke Clinton Rev. Dr. 2825 Indiana av.
Locke John M. 603 The Plaza
Locke Joseph L. 247 Winchester av.
Locke Josephine Miss, 613 The Plaza
Locke William J. 247 Winchester av.
Lockett Oswald, 3151 Calumet av.
Lockey Isaac, 3143 Prairie av.
Lockie Thomas J. Dr. 163 Racine av.
Lockwood C. F. Oak Park
Lockwood F. E. 443 Belden av.
Lockwood F. H. Dr. 200 Cass
Lockwood Henry, Chicago Beach hotel
Lockwood Henry C. Hinsdale
Lockwood I. LeGrand, 325 Chestnut, Eng.
Lockwood James R. 200 Cass
Lockwood T. A. 455, 63d (H. P.)
Lockwood Walter, 1142 Cornelia
Lockwood Walter, 1677 Barry av.
Locy Wm. A. Prof. Lake Forest
Loding Katherine Mrs. 1201 W. Monroe
Lodor Charles H., M.D. 3134 Indiana av.
Loeb Adolph, 528 Dearborn av.
Loeb Adolph, 3622 Grand boul.
Loeb Albert H. 4048 Indiana av.
Loeb A. S. 224, 40th (H. P.)
Loeb Emanuel, 4525 Vincennes av.
Loeb Jacob M. 3924 Prairie av.
Loeb Jacob W. 412 Lasalle av.
Loeb Jacques, 6460 Oglesby av.
Loeb Johanna Mrs. 3924 Prairie av.
Loeb Julius, 3920 Prairie av.
Loeb Leo A. 3401 Calumet av.
Loeb Samuel J. 3127 Vernon av.
Loeb Sidney, 3924 Prairie av.
Loeb Wm. 412 Lasalle av.
Loeber I. G. 451 W. Congress
Loebman Fred, 678 N. Wells
Loebman Gust, 678 N. Wells
Loebstein H. S. Mrs. 3532 Calumet av.
Loeffel Peter, 66 Wisconsin
Loehde William H. 641 Sheffield av.
Loehr Justus, 25 Hall
Loesch F. J. 46 Lincoln pl.
Loescher Martin, 245 Sheffield av.

Loeser Daniel, 275 Lasalle av.
Loeser Julius, 355 Marshfield av.
Loeser Ludwig, 3449 Indiana av.
Loew Alexander Dr. 3237 Michigan av.
Loew Ignace, 3237 Michigan av.
Loewenstein EmanuelL.3316 Calumet av
Loewenstein Harry, 3309 Calumet av.
Loewenstein Jacob, 3309 Calumet av.
Loewenstein L. 3316 Calumet av.
Loewenstein Sidney, 3316 Calumet av.
Loewenthal B. 267 Warren av.
Loewenthal B. 1829 Indiana av.
Loewenthal Edmund, 445 Dearborn av.
Loewenthal Julius, 732 W. Monroe
Loewenthal Julius W. 1829 Indiana av.
Loewy Louis, Austin
Loftis Samuel T. A. 4338 Greenwood av.
Logan C. A., M.D. Tremont house
Logan Floyd T. 7 The Yale
Logan Frank G. 2919 Prairie av.
Logan Theron 6533 Stewart av.
Logan V. M. Mrs. 3519 Indiana av.
Logeman John, Perry sw. cor. Cosgrove
   av.
Logeman John H. Perry sw. cor. Cos-
   grove av.
Loker George T. 3140 South Park av.
Loker Harry A. 3140 South Park av.
Lomax George, 1840 Indiana av.
   Sum. res. Fox Lake, Ill.
Lomax George jr. 1840 Indiana av.
Lombard Benjamin F. Mrs. Evanston
Lombard Ernest B. 1819 Indiana av.
Lombard Isaac G. 1819 Indiana av.
Lombard Josiah L. 2001 Prairie av.
Lombard Thomas R. Granada hotel
Lonergan J. N. Mrs. 565 W. Adams
Long Carrie Miss, 3233 Rhodes av.
Long Charles, 3530 Wabash av.
Long C. A. Winnetka
Long Emma Miss, 65 University pl.
Long Eugene C. 4905 Lake av.
Long E. Miss, Lakota hotel
Long H. C. Mrs. 6550 Sheridan av.
Long James H. 4735 Kimbark av.
Long James T. Evanston
Long Joel B. Evanston
Long John Mrs. 3509 Wabash av.
Long John B. 3520 Wabash av.
Long John Conant, 5538 Washington av.
Long John H. 7748 S. Sangamon
Long John T. 291 Webster av.
Long John T. Evanston
Long J. B. Lakota hotel
Long Lee, 3530 Wabash av.
Long Louis, 3530 Wabash av.
Long Mary C. Mrs. Evanston
Long Patrick J. 751 Garfield boul.
Long R. H. Capt. 204, 74th
Long Sidney, 3530 Wabash av.
Longenecker Joel M. 4125 Vincennes av.
Longevin Genevieve Miss, 3655 Grand
   boul.
Longfellow Frank M. Mayfair
Longhurst William, 96, 31st

Longini Abraham, 1626 Prairie av.
Longini M. 3441 Prairie av.
Longley A. W. Auditorium annex
Longmire Rowland Mrs. 5221 Jefferson
   av.
Longstreet Aaron 788 Washington boul.
Longwell Henry E. 901 Evanston av.
Lonsdale Catherine Mrs. Newberry ho-
   tel
Lonsdale Samuel G. 747 W. Adams
Look Henry S. Highland Park
Loomis Augustus H. 403 Jackson boul.
Loomis Edwin C. 171, 51st (H.P.)
Loomis Eugene E. 6531 Yale
Loomis E. Beach Dr. 145 S. Robey
Loomis E. D. Sherman house
Loomis Frank S. 4105 Grand boul.
Loomis Frank W. 203 Greenleaf av.
Loomis Fred S. Evanston
Loomis Harriet J. Mrs. 2235 Michigan av.
Loomis Henry P. Dr. 6426 Madison av.
Loomis Henry S. Hinsdale
Loomis Hermon M. 3429 Michigan av.
   Sum. res. Lima, Ind.
Loomis Howard G. 5004 Washington av.
Loomis H. N. Chicago Beach hotel
Loomis John E. 651½ Washington boul.
Loomis John M. Col. 55 Lake Shore drive
Loomis Mason B. Evanston
Loomis Philip A. 403 Jackson boul.
Loomis Robert T. Virginia hotel
Loomis Thomas T. jr. 1458 Fulton
Loose J. L. Chicago Beach hotel
Loper W. Harvey 3605 Ellis av.
Loranger J. A. 4429 Calumet av.
Lord Alonzo B. Evanston
Lord Andrew D. 7120 Stewart av.
Lord Andrew H. 142 DeKalb
Lord Benjamin W. Evanston
Lord D. M. 5450 Cornell av.
Lord Edgar A. 1839 Indiana av.
Lord Edward A. Evanston
Lord Elizabeth S. Miss, Oak Park
Lord Frank E. Evanston
Lord Fred. W. River Forest
Lord F. H. 5045 Washington av.
Lord George S. Evanston
Lord James F. 1901 Indiana av.
Lord John B. 5119 Jefferson av.
Lord Lucinda S. Mrs. River Forest
Lord L. N. 148 N. State
Lord Nathaniel, Oak Park
Lord Parley A. LaGrange
Lord PercyA. Evanston
Lord P. R. Mrs. Oak Park
Lord Thomas, Evanston
Lord William B. 385 W. Adams
Lord William S. Evanston
Lorenz Frederick A. 5733 Kimbark av.
Lorimer George, 5538 Cornell av
Loring A. M. Virginia hotel
Loring J. B., M.D. 238 Park av.
Loring M. A. Clifton house
Loring Stella Dyer Mrs. 2535 Prairie av.
Lorins J. Brown Dr. 238 Park av.
Lorwill L. J. Mrs. Oak Park

Loss C. E. Walton pl. sw. cor. Rush
Loth Sidney A. 2240 Michigan av.
Lothholtz R. 31 Lake View av.
Lothrop Loring, 518 Faye
Lott James P. 4021 Vincennes av.
Lotz Adolph, 1824 Aldine
Lotz Carl, 1833 Frederick
Lotz W. H. Mrs. 26 Linden pl.
Loucks Charles N. Irving Park
Louderback DeL. H. 519 Dearborn av.
Louderback S. A. Mrs. 60 Wisconsin
Louderback William J. 60 Wisconsin
Louer A. S. 232, 32d
Lough Matthew, Lake Forest
Loughridge Charles, 4728 Greenwood av
Lounsbury James A. 1691 Sheridan rd.
Lovdall N. Harry, 1549 Lill av.
Lovdall Thomas H. 1549 Lill av.
Lovdall Thomas I. 1549 Lill av.
Love C. F. 4471 Lake av.
Love George, 113 Cass
Love George H. The Arizona
Love H. M. 381 Oak
Love James Mrs. 114, 43d
Love J. M. Mrs. 150 Pine
Love Sidney C. 150 Pine
Love William S. 7506 Honore
Lovedale F. M. Mrs. 791 Warren av.
Loveday L. E, Mrs. 5217 Madison av.
Lovedridge Frederick, 41, 53d (H.P.)
Lovejoy D. S. 258 Ashland boul.
Lovejoy George M. 613 Boulevard pl.
Lovejoy John M. Oak Park
Lovejoy W. W. Oak Park
Loveland Chas. L. Hinsdale
Loveland W. L. Oak Park
Lovell Henry A. 3657 Indiana av.
Lovelock G. M. 357 S. Oakley av.
Lovely John Mrs. 187 S. Oakley av.
Loveridge L. L. 1837 Michigan av.
Lovett L. M. Oak Park
Lovett Mary Mrs. Oak Park
Lovewell C. H. Dr. 6058 Wentworth av.
Lovewell C. H. jr. 6058 Wentworth av.
Lovi Henry. 972 Warren av.
Low Anson, 112, 45th
Low A. G. Mrs. Norwood Park
Low Charles H. 86 Bryant av.
Low D. S. 3721 Ellis av.
Low E. G. 3610 Ellis Park
Low James A. Norwood Park
Low James E. Dr. 410 Washington boul.
Low James E. Evanston
Low John M. 4547 Ellis av.
Low John W. Evanston
Low Joseph H. Dr. 2450 Indiana av.
Low Julia R. Dr. 4756 Kenwood av.
Low J. W. 61 Park av.
Low Mary C. Mrs. 86 Bryant av.
Low S. A. 514 Jackson boul.
Low William H. 4756 Kenwood av.
Low Wilson H. Kenilworth
Lowden Frank O. Lexington hotel
Lowden Samuel, 283 S. Leavitt
Lowdermilk A. W. 2728 Wabash av.
Lowdermilk H. E. Mrs. 2728 Wabash av.

Lowe Charles S. 512 Greenleaf av.
Lowe Henry E. 4548 Lake av.
Lowe Jesse, 499 Dearborn av.
Lowe John W. 216 Dearborn av.
Lowe Perley, 599 Washington boul.
Lowe William, 3611 Grand boul.
Lowell A. D. Dr. 4773 N. Clark
Lowell George C. 78 Centre av.
Lowell George K. 4213 Ellis av.
Loweil Lucerne D. Jefferson Park
Lowell Wallace A. 351, 41st
Lowenbach Joseph, 3340 South Park av.
Lowenbach Wm. L. 3340 South Park av.
Lowenberg Isaac, 1341 Michigan av.
Lowenheim Fred, 720 North Park av.
Lowenthal Adolph S. 2544 Michigan av.
Lowenthal Louis Dr. Washington Heights
Lowery Marion Miss, Hotel Windermere
Lowman Charles O. Park Ridge
Lowrey H. J. 698 Kenmore av.
Lowrey William K. Hotel Barry
Lowrie Ada M. Miss, 13 Scott
Lowrie Wesley M. 378 Dearborn av.
Lowry Butler, 47 Roslyn pl.
Lowry Robert H. Dr. 26 St. Johns pl.
Lowry William, 279 Superior
      Sum. res. Platte Centre, Neb.
Lowy Edward, 3626 Ellis av.
Lozo Alex, 522 Byron
Lubeke William F. 1782 Oakdale av.
Luby W. H. Mrs. 3720 Wabash av.
Lucas C. Y. 953 Warren av.
Lucas James V. Rev. 1230 Palmer
Lucas Robert G. 37 Wisconsin
Luce A. S. 472 Elm
Luce C. C. Oak Park
Luce Frank M. 587 Dearborn av.
      Sum. res. Marion, Mass.
Luce Fred, Oak Park
Luce F. A. 472 Elm
Luce James P. River Forest
Luce Theodore M. 295 Belden av.
Luce W. C. 3802 Lake av.
Luck C. J. 349 S. Paulina
Ludden C. Mrs. 3748 Wabash av.
Ludden John H. 3748 Wabash av.
Ludden Viola H. Dr. 315, 67th, Eng.
Luders H. J. 217 S. Leavitt
Ludington E. N. 4831 Kenwood av.
Ludington M. K. Mrs. Oak Park
Ludington Nelson Mrs. Auditorium an-
      nex
Ludington Rowland S. Oak Park
Ludlam Edward M. P. Dr. 699 Washing-
      ton boul.
Ludlam Jacob W. Evanston
Ludlam Mary Mrs. Evanston
Ludlam Reuben Dr. 1823 Michigan av.
Ludlam Reuben jr. Dr. 1823 Michigan av.
Ludlow Charles G. 1617 Montrose boul.
Ludlow Cynthia Mrs. 222 The Plaza
Ludlow Fred D. 222 The Plaza
Ludwig C. H. Dr. 600 Lincoln av.
Ludwig Martha Miss, 600 Lincoln av.
Ludwig Roscoe F. Dr. LaGrange
Luedders John, 419 Robinson av.

Lueder Arthur, Elmhurst
Lueder John Prof. Elmhurst
Lufkin Daniel I. 2505 Michigan av.
Lufkin William W. 476 Ashland boul.
Luken William M. 587 W. North av.
Lukey William, Evanston
Lukins J. E. Hyde Park hotel
Lull A. E. Mrs 307 N. Clark
Lull Newton, 307 N. Clark
Lull Richard Dr. 1276 W. Adams
Lum Mary H. Mrs. 3810 Langley av.
Lum Walter H. 3810 Langley av.
Lumbard E. C. Oak Park
Lumbard F. H. Oak Park
Lumbard Heury, Oak Park
Lumley C. G. Dr. 3412 Prairie av.
Lumley C. M. Mrs. 296 Irving av.
Lumm E. E. Miss, 113 Cass
Lumsden A. E. 4058 Michigan Terrace
Lunceford Charles D. 2678 Evanston av.
Lund Adolph, 4443 Sidney av.
Lund Arthur H. 4736 Langley av.
Lund Charles E. 4727 Langley av.
Lund E. M. Hotel Barry
Lund F. M. Miss, Lakota hotel
Lundberg John C. 376 Washington boul.
Lundgren A. L., M.D. 2713½ Indiana av.
Lundgren S. A., M.D. 600, 59th, Eng.
Lundie John, 7126 Euclid av. (H.P.)
Lundy Ayres D. LaGrange
Luneau E. Mrs. 1837 Michigan av.
Lunham Robert T. 4234 Prairie av.
Lunsford Louis, Oak Park
Lunsford Todd, Oak Park
Lunt E. M. Fvanston
Lunt E. Sidney, 4245 Drexel boul.
        Sum. Res. Bayside, Mass.
Lunt George, Evanston
Lunt Nina Grey Miss, Evanston
Lunt Orrington, Evanston
Lusch H. B. 536 Orchard
Lusche Frederick C. Austin
Lusk Charles D. 529, 47th
Lusk James W. Austin
Lusk William, Riverside
Lussky E. A. 156, 50th, (H.P.)
Lussky G. Hermann 156, 50th, (H.P.)
Lutkin Peter C. Evanston
Lutrell W. A. Morgan Park
Lutz C. H. Mrs. 4227 Champlain av.
Lutz Harriette Miss, 1728 Alexander av.
Lutz M. E. Mrs. Lexington hotel
Luxton Minnie Clay Miss, 68, 24th
Lydon Harry C. 2952 Indiana av.
Lydon M. B. 2952 Indiana av.
Lydon William A. 2952 Indiana av.
Lydston G. Frank Dr. 758 W. Adams
Lydston James A. Dr. 1556 W. Adams
Lyford Harry B. 2919 Groveland av.
Lyford Louis H. 12 Maple
Lyford Oliver, 2968 Lake Park av.
Lyford Oliver S. 2968 Lake Park av.
Lyford Will H. 2921 Groveland av.
Lyke John W. 1175 Wilcox av.
Lyman Benjamin K. 314 Walnut
Lyman Charles G.Capt.Auditorium hotel

Lyman David, LaGrange
Lyman David B. LaGrange
Lyman E. W. Oak Park
Lyman Francis O. Winnetka
Lyman George Frederick, 1295 W. Congress
Lyman Henry M. Dr. 200 Ashland boul.
Lyman James, 247 Seminary av.
Lyman Jesse P. 5344 Washington av.
Lyman John Chester Dr. 2 Washington pl.
Lyman J. Grant Dr. Lexington hotel
Lyman M. J. Hotel Barry
Lyman M. J., M.D. 6401 Stewart av.
Lyman N. W. 3228 Calumet av.
Lyman Otis S. LaGrange
Lyman R. L. Oak Park
Lyman Wilfred C. 314 Walnut
Lyman Wilfred C. jr. 314 Walnut
Lyman W. C. Mrs. Hotel Groveland
Lynas Thomas R. 3156 Vernon av.
Lynch Alban B. 381 Orchard
Lynch Andrew G. 556 Dearborn av.
Lynch Andrew M. 4220 Grand boul.
Lynch C. R. 475 Marshfield av.
Lynch E. W. Mrs. Chicago Beach hotel
Lynch Helen M. Dr. Highland Park
Lynch James, 592 W. Adams
Lynch James C. 7410 Wright
Lynch John W. Mrs. Highland Park
Lynch J. A. 44 Burton pl.
Lynch J. B. 556 Dearborn av.
Lynch J. D. 44 Burton pl.
Lynce Margaret Mrs. 3449 Prairie av.
Lynch Richard W. Evanston
Lynch Thomas, 251 Dearborn av.
Lynde S. A. 398 Ontario
Lynn Anna V. Mrs. 2825 Michigan av.
Lynn Charles F. 7432 Bond av.
Lynn James R. jr. 3756 Ellis av.
Lyon C. E. P. Chicago Beach hotel
Lyon Daniel A. LaGrange
Lyon D. J. Judge, 3428 Forest av.
Lyon Edward, 462 N. Clark
Lyon F. D. 2223 Calumet av.
Lyon George M. 381 Superior
Lyon Howard N., M.D. 39 Bellevue pl.
Lyon Hugh H. 4955 Prairie av.
Lyon John B. 262 Michigan av.
Lyon John F. 923 Sawyer av.
Lyon Joseph M. LaGrange
Lyon M. Mrs. 548, 61st, Englewood
Lyon Mary P. Mrs. 209 S. Leavitt
Lyon Ray C. 275 Bissell
Lyon Richard S. 500 W. Adams
Lyon Samuel, 5620 Monroe av.
Lyon S. 334 Warren av.
Lyon Thomas R. 72 Astor
        Sum. res. Ludington, Mich.
Lyon William C. 262 Michigan av.
Lyons Eugene R. Granada hotel
Lyons E. H. Hotel Metropole
Lyons George, 7 Burton pl.
Lyons Hattie Miss, 3756 Lake av.
Lyons James, Leland hotel
Lyons Joseph L. 3648 Forest av.

Lyons J. A. 437 Englewood av.
Lyons J. L. Ridgeland
Lyons R. G. Hotel Barry
Lyser Samuel, 3336 Prairie av.
Lystad Hans J. 22 Arlington pl.

McADAM Charles V. 394 S. Oakley av.
McAdam J. V. 394 S. Oakley av.
McAdam May R. Miss, 394 S. Oakley av.
McAdam Peter, 1158 W. Congress
McAdams Andrew, 316, 53d
McAdams E. L. 1302 W. Adams
McAdams John Q. 4839 Vincennes av.
McAdow F. H. 6353 Yale
McAfee Charles H. 1044 S. Central Park av.
McAllaster Howard, Winnetka
McAllister W. K. Mrs. 2454 N. Paulina
McAndrews Jas. jr. 890 Washington boul.
McAndrews James C. 890 Washington boul.
McAndrews Joseph R. 890 Washington boul.
McArdle Edward J. 5203 Michigan av.
McArdle Patrick L. 5203 Michigan av.
McArthur Archibald, Riverside
McArthur A. F. Hotel Metropole
McArthur Cuthbert, 879 Sawyer av.
McArthur James, 3913 Prairie av.
McArthur James Mrs. 3848 Lake av.
McArthur John, 504 W. Monroe
McArthur John jr. 504 W. Monroe
McArthur J. H. Maj. 2813 Indiana av.
McArthur L. L., M. D. 4247 Drexel boul.
McArthur Robert X. 516 The Plaza
McArthur Warren, 4852 Kenwood av.
McAuley Daniel R. Austin
McAuley John T. 3412 Vernon av.
McAuley M. Mrs. 958 Warren av.
McAuley M. L. Miss, 3313 Calumet av.
McAuley Tillie Miss, 1110 Washington boul.
McAuliff Cornelius, 50 Wisconsin
McAvoy Charles P. 423 Huron
McAvoy Frank Mrs. 363 Park av.
McAvoy J. H. Mrs. 171 Goethe
McAvoy Thomas F. 4550 Vincennes av.
McBean Archibald J. F. 2921 Indiana av.
McBean Archie J. 2227 Prairie av.
McBean Duncan S. 3640 Prairie av.
McBean George B. 2227 Prairie av.
McBean James G. 3326 Vernon av.
McBean John, 2227 Prairie av.
McBean LeRoy H. 3326 Vernon av.
McBirney Hugh 1736 Prairie av.
McBirney Hugh J. 1625 Prairie av.
McBride J. W. 93, 33d
McCabe Charles, Lombard
McCabe Charles R. 177 Lincoln av.
McCabe Francis J. 1456 Wrightwood av.
McCabe James, Hotel Windermere
McCabe James F. Edison Park
McCabe John J. 177 Lincoln av.
McCabe Robert R. Evanston
McCabe Sarah H. Mrs. 3000 Michigan av.
McCagg Caroline Miss, 67 Cass

McCagg E. B. 67 Cass
McCain Frank J. Riverside
McCall Harry E. 3018 Michigan av.
McCall Henry, 3018 Michigan av.
McCall Irving G. Hyde Park hotel
McCall James, 6336 Harvard, Englewood
McCall S. F. Virginia hotel
McCall Warner B. Austin
McCalla Mary A. Mrs. 162, 25th
McCallan H. A. 4557 Lake av.
McCallay Daniel, 3328 Michigan av.
Sum. res. Middletown, O.
McCallay Edwin L. 3328 Michigan av.
McCalley Emma Mrs. 4818 Evans av.
McCallery Daniel, 3328 Michigan av.
Sum. res. Middletown, O.
McCallum Alpheus, Austin
McCallum Douglas, 1341 Palmer
McCallum Joseph, Evanston
McCallum Walter C. 6659 Honore
McCallum Wm. B. 4204 Michigan av.
McCandless A. W. Dr. 6407 Sheridan av.
McCann Daniel, Evanston
McCann R. W. New Hotel Holland
McCann S. A. Mrs. Oak Park
McCann Thomas, 965 Jackson boul.
McCarrell Albert F. Evanston
McCarthy Alex J. 1638 N. Halsted
McCarthy Eugene J. 938 Walnut
McCarthy James J. Austin
McCarthy John 448 Marshfield av.
McCarthy John F. 237 Loomis
McCarthy J. Hotel Metropole
McCarthy J. G. 282 Park av.
McCarthy M. H. 4224 Oakenwald av.
McCarthy Veronica Mrs. 37, 33d
McCarthy Wm. Dr. 519 W. Congress
McCartney Harry G. 3348 Rhodes av.
McCartney James, Berwyn
McCartney Joseph A. 4014 Drexel boul.
McCartney Joseph A. jr. 4014 Drexel boul.
McCarty C. H. Dr. 5500 State
McCarty W. W. 3983 Drexel boul.
McCasky Isaac W. 790 W. Monroe
McCauley Frank, 554 Dearborn av.
McCauley James I. 728, 63d ct. Eng.
McCauley James J. Evanston
McCauley J. W. 531 Jackson boul.
McCauley T. N. 1001 Jackson boul.
McCaull George M. Austin
McCausland A. J. Newberry hotel
McCausland Samuel G. 4448 Wabash av.
McChesney James F. 727 Fullerton av.
McChesney J. B. 101, 37th
McChesney J. D. Pullman
McChesney M. H. 6542 Sheridan av.
McClanahan E. B. Mrs. Lake Forest
McClary Nelson A. Oak Park
McClaughery A. C. 7 Wellington pl.
McCleary B. J. 3625 Vernon av.
McCleary Edward B. 185 Oakwood boul.
McCleery Robert, 622 N. Clark
McClellan Archibald, 67, 37th
McClellan E. Mrs. Hotel Metropole
McClellan Fuller, 2023 Indiana av.

McClellan George A. 6519 Yale
McClellan Henry W. 2023 Indiana av.
    Sum. res. Tower Hill, Mich.
McClellan J. J. Hotel Windermere
McClelland J. S. 2804 Michigan av.
McClelland Thomas S. 417 Superior
McClelland Will S. 2804 Michigan av.
McClelland W. A. 2710 Calumet av.
McClintock H. J. Riverside
McClintock James, Hinsdale
McClintock William H. LaGrange
McClintock W. D. Prof. 5745 Madison av.
McClintock W. K. Chicago Beach hotel
McCloud E. C. Mrs. Riverside
McCloud Roy M. Riverside
McCloy H. 3131 Groveland av.
McCluer Charles W. 34 College pl.
McCluer J. L. 3528 Indiana av.
McCluer Wm. B. University Club
McClure Alexander W. 429 Washington
   boul.
McClure Fitzhenry, 5471 Jefferson av.
McClure James G. K. Rev. Lake Forest
McClure John S. 197 Oakwood boul.
McClure V. C. Dr. 259 Warren av.
McClure W. Morgan Park
McClurg Aaron H. 730 Washington boul.
    Sum. res. Pittsburgh, Pa.
McClurg Alex. C. 125 Lake Shore Drive
McClurg Lowrie, 255 Dearborn av.
McCollough Calvin G. Dr. 4705 Evans av.
McComas Duke, 2967 Groveland av.
McComas Eugene, 2967 Groveland av.
McComas Rufus F. 2967 Groveland av.
McComas R. F. Mrs. 2967 Groveland av.
McCombs A. L. 94, 37th
McConnel George M. Winnetka
McConnel Robert B. Winnetka
McConnell Alexander, Evanston
McConnell Benj. F. 36 Hawthorne pl.
McConnell C. H. 4417 Ellis av.
McConnell Dean Miss, 5478 Greenwood
   av.
McConnell Edward D. 60 Hawthorne pl.
McConnell Edward P. 4359 Lake av.
McConnell E. D. 5425 Cottage Grove av.
McConnell Harriet A. Mrs. 5478 Green-
   wood av.
McConnell Horace C. 3623 Grand boul.
McConnell James S. 4359 Lake av.
McConnell John, 60 Hawthorne pl.
McConnell J. H. The Ontario
McConnell Luther, 531 Dearborn av.
McConnell L. W. 531 Dearborn av.
McConnell S. M. 2727 Wabash av.
McConnell S. P. Judge, 429 Huron
McConnell Washington A. Oak Park
McConnell Willard M. 5478 Greenwood av.
McConnell W. S. 2727 Wabash av.
McConville Edward 4316 Emerald av.
McConville Mary Mrs 4316 Emerald av.
McCook Charles M. Kenilworth
McCord Alvin C. Union League Club
McCord David W. Riverside
McCord Herbert A. 400, 65th, Eng.
McCord J. C. 3401 Wabash av.

McCord William B. Dr. 291, 55th (H.P.)
McCorkle Charles W. 496 Fullerton av.
McCorkle C. R. Lexington hotel
McCorkle J. H. 963 Jackson boul.
McCormack T. E. 919 Spaulding av.
McCormick Alexander A. 266 Erie
McCormick Anna Miss, 518, 67th, Eng.
McCormick Anne F. Mrs. 4407 Green-
   wood av.
McCormick A. J. Evanston
McCormick A. Y. Dr. 6400 Harvard
McCormick Charles T. A. 53 Astor
McCormick Cyrus Hall, 321 Huron
McCormick Cyrus H. Mrs. 135 Rush
McCormick C. M. 3833 Ellis av.
McCormick Elizabeth D. Miss, 124 Rush
McCormick Frank P. 355 S. Oakley av.
McCormick George J. 3616 Grand boul.
McCormick Henrietta H. Miss, 124 Rush
McCormick John, 3616 Grand boul.
McCormick John A. 2942 Groveland av.
McCormick J. B. Wilmette
McCormick J. H. 355 S. Oakley av.
McCormick Leander J. Virginia hotel
    Sum. res. Lake Forest
McCormick Martha E. Miss, 2301 N.
   Ashland av.
McCormick, Robert S. 101 Cass
McCormick R. Hall, 124 Rush
    Sum. res. Lake Forest
McCormick W. G. 157 Rush
McCornack A. W. 400, 67th, Eng.
McCortney John Howard, 634 Boulevard
   pl.
McCoull Neil, Riverside
McCourtie Arnold B. 1197 Washington
   boul.   Sum. res. Lake Bluff
McCourtie Martha M. Mrs. 1195 Wash-
   ington boul.
McCoure R. E. The Arizona
McCoy Albert L. 440, 65th, Eng.
McCoy Charles B. 2352 Prairie av.
McCoy Daniel C. Rev. Hinsdale
McCoy Fred B. 3004 Michigan av.
McCoy F. A. Mrs. 3004 Michigan av.
McCoy James S. 1187 Wilton av.
McCoy George, LaGrange
McCoy John, 3443 Prairie av.
McCoy M. Max, 3815 Lake av.
McCoy T. H. 3815 Lake av.
McCoy William, 221 S. Sangamon
McCracken Charles A. S. 7111 Yale, Eng.
McCracken Frank G. 4406 Langley av.
McCracken George, 19 Bryan pl.
McCracken H. S. 734, 64th, Englewood
McCracken James B. 7030 Wright
McCracken Margaret Mrs. 4406 Langley
   av.
McCracken S. G. Dr. Winnetka
McCrea Chas. M. 607 Washington boul.
McCrea Willey S. 122 Pine
McCready E. W. Oak Park
McCreary Anna A. Mrs. 1313 Michigan
   av.
McCreary Jonas E. 331 S. Paulina
McCredie William, Hinsdale

McCreery M. Mrs. 3000 Indiana av.
McCreight S. L. Dr. 458 Marshfield av.
McCulloch Catharine Waugh Mrs. Evanston
McCulloch Frank, Evanston
McCulloh Thomas, 5130 Hibbard av.
McCulloh Thomas G. 5130 Hibbard av.
McCullough Allen, 5627 Michigan av.
McCullough Calvin G. Dr. 4705 Evans av.
McCullough Hiram R. 3332 Indiana av.
McCullough John R. Dr. 37 Park av.
McCullough J. C. Washington heights
McCullough W. W. 6519 Yale
McCully John, 905 W. Monroe
McCune Eugene C. 45 Bryant av.
McCurdy D. E. 3645 Prairie av.
McCurdy E. G. 3827 Vernon av.
McCurdy F. G. Hotel Normandie
McCurdy George L. 3647 Prairie av.
McCurdy William B. 4546 St. Lawrence av.
McDaid L. P. Mrs. 57 St. James pl.
McDaneld Daniel H. 2682 N. Paulina
McDaniel Alexander, Wilmette
McDaniel J. Lyman, 4201 Ellis av.
McDaniel M. Delaplame, 4201 Ellis av.
McDaniels D. L. Oak Park
McDermid John J. 17, 22d
McDermitt E. H. Mrs. 1050 Evanston av.
McDermitt J. H. Miss, 1050 Evanston av.
McDermott J. 3402 Wabash av.
McDermott Michael, 3528 Wabash av.
McDevitt James, 4211 Lake av.
McDoel W. Henry, 3232 Michigan av.
McDonagh P. J. 7465 Bond av.
McDonald Ashley, 393 W. Adams
McDonald A. Y. Mrs. 1686 Barry av.
McDonald Charles B. 6345 Stewart av.
McDonald Edward V., M.D. 5604 Madison av.
McDonald George H. LaGrange
McDonald Harley C. LaGrange
McDonald Harry J. 280 Fullerton av.
McDonald James, 1690 Barry av.
McDonald James, Highland Park
McDonald James A. 2948 Groveland av.
McDonald James W. 4015 Vincennes av.
McDonald John, 26 The Yale
McDonald John, 280 Fullerton av.
McDonald Joseph N. 280 Fullerton av.
McDonald J. Newberry hotel
McDonald J. A. 1741 Wrightwood av.
McDonald J. B. 738 W. Monroe
McDonald J. J. 452 N. Normal Parkway
McDonald Lizzie Miss, 632 Washington boul.
McDonald Louis A. 6730 Rhodes av.
McDonald Malcolm Mrs. 393 Jackson boul.
McDonald Malcolm jr. 393 Jackson boul.
McDonald Richard D. 1837 Michigan av.
McDonald Wm. H. V. 5604 Madison av.
McDonell John A. Dr. 471 Washington boul.
McDonnell E. Miss, 163, 30th
McDonnell Harriet Miss, 163, 30th
McDonnell John J. 440 Ashland boul.

McDonnell William, 461 Kenmore av.
McDonough J. S. Fort Sheridan
McDougal Anna Wood Mrs. Riverside
McDougald A. W. 489 W. Adams
McDougall Alexander, 7114 Eggleston av.
McDougall Esther A. Mrs. 4156 Ellis av.
McDougall John D. 7114 Eggleston av.
McDougall William, 4156 Ellis av.
McDowell Charles E. 5471 Lexington av.
McDowell Charles H. 365 Jackson boul.
McDowell Hanson, Evanston
McDowell Irving, Evanston
McDowell Jacob, 189 Oakwood boul.
McDowell John H. Wilmette
McDowell J. E. 6307 Oglesby av.
McDowell Malcolm, Evanston
McDowell Mary E. Miss, Evanston
McDowell R. P. 189 Oakwood boul.
McDowell S. L. Mrs. 5910 Indiana av.
McDowell W. A., M.D. 35, 46th
McDuffee Henry H. 196, 36th
McEldowney Howard, 7310 Harvard
McElevey W. B. Hyde Park hotel
McElherne Daniel J. 203 Centre av.
McElligott Thomas G. 4516 Indiana av.
McElroy James, 4210 Prairie av.
McElroy James E. 4235 Grand boul.
McElroy J. E. Mrs. Chicago Beach hotel
McElwee Robert H. 400 Ontario
McEnerney James, 4553 Wabash av.
McEnerny Isabel Miss, 4338 Calumet av.
McEnerny John T. 56 Lytle
McEnerny Thomas, 861 S. Central Park av.
McEntee Charles S. 294 Erie
McEvoy Stephen, Maywood
McEwan P. A. 1800 Indiana av.
McEwen Alfred, 512 Lasalle av.
McEwen Eleanor Mrs. 512 Lasalle av.
McEwen John, 512 Lasalle av.
McEwen John jr. 512 Lasalle av.
McEwen Paul J. 512 Lasalle av.
McEwen W. M. Irving Park
McFadden George E. Hawthorne av. Auburn Park
McFadden J. Revere house
McFadon Robert D. Mrs. 183 Rush
McFadon William, 181 Rush
McFarland Charles H. Evanston
McFarland Charles I. 6122 Stewart av.
McFarland F. W. 290 Marshfield av.
McFarland John C. 6635 Honore
McFarland John H. 4001 Drexel boul.
McFarland Lizzie A. Mrs. 6122 Stewart av.
McFarland L. G. Mrs. 3749 Ellis av.
McFarland Thomas W. 6635 Honore
McFarland William W. Austin
McFarlane Helen Miss, 1928 Belmont av.
McFarlane Henry W. Austin
McFarlane Hugh, 1928 Belmont av.
McFarlane Hugh F. Highland Park
McFarlin John, Winnetka
McFarlin M. 3047 Groveland av.
McFarlin W. W. 3047 Groveland av.
McFatrich J. B. Dr. 3408 Prairie av.

McGary C. J. 6108 Washington av.
McGaughey John A. Dr. 4820 Langley av.
McGee Harry L. 1927 Indiana av.
McGee H. Mrs. 275 Bissell
McGee Myron, 1927 Indiana av.
McGee Virginia Mrs. 445 Washington boul.
McGee Wilford J. 1927 Indiana av.
McGee William E. Hinsdale
McGenniss C. B. Mrs. 2514 Prairie av.
McGill David B. LaGrange
McGill George F. LaGrange
McGill James K. 821 W. Adams
McGill James P., M.D. 4553 Forrestville av.
McGill Judith W. Mrs. Evanston
McGill J. A., M.D. 4938 Drexel boul.
McGill J. M. 4547 Lake av.
McGill Thomas B. 7226 Euclid av. (H.P)
McGill Virginia H. Mrs. 7226 Euclid av. (H.P.)
McGill Wm. 7226 Euclid av.
McGillen John, 535 Cleveland av.
McGinnis W. G. Edison Park
McGinty John B. 6341 Wright, Englewood
McGlashon William H. 295 Belden av.
McGonigle Thomas J. 549 Garfield boul.
McGoorty J. P. 6107 Madison av.
McGoorty P. F. 6446 Madison av.
McGovern John, 416 S. Wood
McGovern Wm. J. 5904 Michigan av.
McGowan J. D. Dr. 3946 Drexel boul.
McGowen Edward J. 6731 Lafayette av.
McGrath Charles H. 585 Dearborn av.
McGrath George B. 7138 Euclid av. (H. P.)
McGrath John J. 394 S. Paulina
McGrath John J. 585 Dearborn av.
McGrath John J. jr. 585 Dearborn av.
McGrath J. P. 60 Union Park pl.
McGrath Maurice J. 7138 Euclid Av. (H. P.)
McGraw Daniel T. 3416 Prairie av.
McGraw James, 927 W. Adams
McGregor D. P. LaGrange
McGregor Gardner, 4434 Ellis av.
McGregor G. L. Great Northern hotel
McGregor James, Oak Park
McGregor James R. Oak Park
McGregor J. B. 5738 Monroe av.
McGregor M. E. 6210 Michigan av.
McGregor William, 692 W. Monroe
McGrew A. H. 6926 Oglesby av.
McGrew J. H. LaGrange
McGuire Daniel, 43 Roslyn pl.
McGuire John F. 59 St. James pl.
McGuire W. A. 309 Webster av.
McGunnegle G. K. Capt. Fort Sheridan
McGunnegle I. R. Mrs. Fort Dearborn
McGurrin Edward, 229 Oak
McHatton Margaret Mrs. 4417 Lake av.
McHenry A. C. Mrs. 1815 Indiana av.
McHenry E. S. Mrs. 4060 Ellis av.
McHenry William E. Hotel Imperial
McHie George E. 704 Pullman bldg.
McHugh C. R. Oak Park

McHugh Felix E. 1195 Wilton av.
McHugh Mary Miss, 1313 Michigan av.
McHugh P. Chicago Athletic Assn.
McIlvaine John D. 453 Evanston av.
McIlvaine J. S. Mrs. 356 Ontario
McIlvaine Wm. B. 502 N. State
McIlvaine William D. 610 The Plaza
McIlvane W. D. Oak Park
McIndoe Hugh, 14 Bishop ct.
McInnerney T. H. Lakota hotel
McIntire Frances Mrs. 4332 Ellis av.
McIntosh Alexander, 5412 Ellis av.
McIntosh Francis W. 597 N. Robey
McIntosh Jennie Miss, Hotel Barry
McIntosh John F. 524 W. Congress
McIntosh J. M. Hotel Barry
McIntosh Mary Miss, Hotel Barry
McIntyre A. 385 Ontario
McIntyre Charles W. Dr. 3035 South Park av.
McIntyre Frank M. 7000 Sherman
McIntyre J. Lawrence, 344 Dearborn av.
McIntyre P. J. 3756 Forest av.
McKallor H. L. Mrs. River Forest
McKay Aaron M. 2624 N. Paulina
McKay Alexander A. Union League Club
McKay Augustus F. 402 N. Normal Parkway
McKay E. E. Dr. LaGrange
McKay Henry, 59 Lincoln av.
McKay J. M. 290 Ohio
McKay J. R. 290 Ohio
McKay Margaret Mrs. 201 The Plaza
Sum. res. Lombard, Ill.
McKay M. Mrs. LaGrange
McKay Norah Miss, 59 Lincoln av.
McKeand Archibald, 3626 Calumet av.
McKeand Clarence A. 3626 Calumet av.
McKeand Edward C. 3626 Calumet av.
McKeand Harry A. 3626 Calumet av.
McKeand John, 6426 Harvard, Englewood
McKechney John, 288 Ohio
McKechney John, jr. 288 Ohio
McKee F. R. 422 S. Leavitt
McKee George W. 6040 Park End av.
McKee Harry, 698 Walnut
McKee William H. 412 W. Monroe
McKeeby Sanford, Hyde Park hotel
McKeever Buell, 3900 Lake av.
McKeever John A. Tracy
McKeever J. L. 3900 Lake av.
McKelvey C. A. 6624 Perry av.
McKelvey Elizabeth Mrs. 449, 65th, Eng.
McKelvey S. P. 877 Walnut
McKenna Frank B. Lieut. Ft. Sheridan
McKenna John J. 4807 Wabash av.
McKenney James S. 7120 Harvard, Eng.
McKenzie Daniel, 435 Washington boul.
McKenzie Geo. M. 1238 N. Clark
McKenzie William C. Ravinia
McKenzie William L. Ravinia
McKeon Edward, 316 The Plaza
McKeough John, 3133 Rhodes av.
McKewin Hugh W. 474 W. Adams
McKey Harriet Mrs. 5116 Hibbard av.
McKey Henry Mrs. 5136 Kimbark av.

McKey Richard M. 5116 Hibbard av.
McKey William D. 5114 Hibbard av.
McKibbin C. B. 172 Oakwood boul.
McKibbin Samuel M. 4506 Emerald av.
McKillip David D. 156 Oakwood boul.
McKillip M. H. Dr. 1706 Michigan av.
McKindley D. M. Langley av. cor. 48th
McKindley Harriet M. Miss, 541 Dearborn av.
McKindley Isabelle H. Miss, 541 Dearborn av.
McKindley James, 258 Michigan av.
McKindley Wm. Mrs. 3660 Michigan av.
McKinley Wm. Brown, 19 Scott
McKinlock George A. 1619 Prairie av.
McKinlock John, Lakota hotel
McKinlock John, M. D. Lakota hotel
McKinlock Walter C. 14 Groveland Park
McKinlock William H. 3218 Michigan av.
McKinney A. M. 4201 Oakenwald av.
McKinney Frederick W. 553 Dearborn av.
McKinney George, Winnetka
McKinney James, 137, 37th
McKinney Samuel P. Dr. 810 Warren av.
McKinney William, Winnetka
McKinney Emily Miss, Hinsdale
McKinnie P. Leon Dr. Evanston
McKinnon D. C. Morgan Park
McKinnon Richmond P. Morgan Park
McKittrick Joseph L. Wilmette
McKnight C. H. 5 Washington pl.
McKnight George F. Hawthorne av. Auburn Park
McKnight Sanford C. Hawthorne av. Auburn Park
McLachlan J. C. Mrs. 6361 Wright
McLagan Charles A. 026 Stewart av.
McLagan Charles J. Stewart av.
McLain Andrew J. 24202 Michigan av.
McLain Charles R. 757. 66th, Eng.
McLain Clarence C. LaGrange
McLain Mary E. Mrs. 2430 Michigan av.
McLain William, 2430 Michigan av.
McLain William, 4532 Oakenwald av.
McLain William T. 3702 Lake av.
McLain W. D. Mrs. 3702 Lake av.
McLane H. H. Mrs. 3005 Vernon av.
McLane James A. 3005 Vernon av.
McLaren John, 339 Ashland boul.
McLaren J. Loomis, 339 Ashland boul.
McLaren Wm. E. Rt. Rev. 64 Astor
    Sum. res. Point Pleasant, N. J.
McLaren W. A. 64 Astor
McLarsth Kenneth, Austin
McLauchlan John, 2421 N. Paulina
McLaughlin Albert, LaGrange
McLaughlin George D. 97 Rush
McLaughlin James, Riverside
McLaughlin Jennie Miss, 285½ Lasalle av.
McLaughlin Juliette Miss, 4014 Drexel boul
McLaughlin P. H. 1551 W. Monroe
McLaughlin Reita Miss, 285½ Lasalle av.
McLaughlin W. F. 97 Rush
McLaury T. G. Mrs. 4555 Ellis av.
McLean Charles A. 2836 Indiana av.

McLean Charles F. 2836 Indiana av.
McLean Frederick W. 1448 Dakin
McLean Guy M. Dr. Pullman
McLean James, 5476 Cornell av.
McLean John, M. D. Pullman
McLean J. W. 224 Belden av.
McLean Peter, 579 Burling
McLean William A. 4001 Grand boul.
McLean William H. 161 Dearborn av.
McLean William S. 158 S. Leavitt
McLeish Andrew, Glencoe
McLeish John F. 378 W. Adams
McLellan William Rev. Berwyn
McLelland John, 3756 Ellis av.
McLenahan M. B. LaGrange
McLennan Christopher, 573, 51st (H.P.)
McLennan J. A. 3105 Calumet av.
McLennan Kenneth, 5, 36th
McLennan Kenneth S. 530 Park av.
McLeod Henry C. 62 Cedar
McLeod Peter R. 431 S. Oakley av.
McLeod Robert, 2124 Michigan av.
McLester George W. 1852 Jackson boul.
McLinden Edwin, 917 Sawyer av.
McLinden John J. Mrs. 305 Racine av.
McLindon F. Mrs. 163 S. Wood
McMahan Charles L. 4621 Lake av.
McMahan Florence L. Miss, 4577 Oakenwald av.
McMahan Robert W. Dr. 4577 Oakenwald av.
McMahan Una Miss, 4577 Oakenwald av.
McMahon A. J. 3542 Vernon av.
McMahon Frank T. Dr. 4445 Michigan av.
McMahon James, Evanston
McMahon James A. 500 Jackson boul.
McMahon John, 1389 Washington boul.
McMahon J. P. 359 S. Paulina
McMahon Mary Miss, The Wellingtou
McMahon Patrick, 3542 Vernon av.
McMahon S. P. LaGrange
McManus B. F. Washington Heights
McManus Patrick, 4840 Grand boul.
McMaster William I. 915 Fargo av.
McMath James C. 242 Hampden ct.
McMehan David D. 1040 Chase av.
McMichael Addie L. Miss, 3400 Prairie av.
McMichael James G. 42, 39th
McMichael L. D., M. D. 3400 Prairie av.
McMichael O. W. Dr. 4200 Calumet av.
McMichael S. B. 4200 Calumet av.
McMillan Adelaide Miss, 933 W. Monroe
McMillan A. F. 5404 Ridgewood ct.
McMillan Carroll S. 4139 Grand av.
McMillan E. Erskine, 987 W. Adams
McMillan E. M. Newberry hotel
McMillan James, 152 S. Hoyne av.
McMillan Libbie J. Miss, 715½ Washington boul.
McMillan Louis S. 933 W. Monroe
McMillan Neil, 464 Bowen av.
McMillan Robert S. 2513 Michigan av.
McMillan William, 568 Kenwood pl.
McMillan William M. 568 Kenwood pl.
McMillen Sarah C. Mrs. 316 Lasalle av.

McMillen William F. Rev. 513 Washington av.
McMillin G. W. 6441 Sheridan av.
McMinn Hugh, 42, 39th
McMorrine Cath. Mrs. 769 Washn. boul.
McMullan Floy Miss, Newberry hotel
McMullen Charles B. 282 Erie
McMullen David S. Evanston
McMullen D. Y. 303 Lasalle av.
McMullen K. J. Miss, 4808 Lake av.
McMullen Robert, 276 S. Oakley av.
McMullen Robert A. 276 S. Oakley av.
McMullen Roger B. Evanston
McMullen William J. 3945 Prairie av.
McMullin F. R. 729 W. Adams
McMullin James C. 729 W. Adams
McMurdy Robert, 4853 Kimbark av.
McMurray Albert M. 244, 53d (H.P.)
McMurray Charles H. 244, 53d (H.P.)
McMurray George N. 244, 53d (H.P.)
McMurray G. T. Mrs. 244, 53d (H.P.)
McMurtry John G. 2450 Prairie av.
McMurtry John G. jr. 2450 Prairie av.
McMynn J. C. Oak Park
McNab John, Evanston
McNab Malcom, 6751 Emerald av.
McNair Washington, 4341 Emerald av.
McNally Andrew, 824 North Park av.
McNally Fred G. 836 North Park av.
McNally James, 410 N. State
McNally John, 601 Garfield av.
McNally William J. 171 Ashland boul.
McNamara F. W. Dr. Columbus club
McNamara J. H. 951 Spaulding av.
McNamee Edith R. Mrs. Morton Park
McNaught David W. Ridgeland
McNaughten E. P. 910 Larrabee
McNaughton Guy, 168 Fremont
McNaughton James, 3531 Indiana av.
McNaughton James C. 168 Fremont
McNeal D. W., M.D. 6700 Stewart av.
McNeal S. D. Austin
McNeil Chester, 528 Greenleaf av.
McNeil Halmer E. 4558 Oakenwald av.
McNeil Malcolm, 448 Lasalle av.
McNeil William, 9 Wisconsin
McNeill Archibald, 3154 Michigan av.
McNeill A. C. Hotel Metropole
McNeill Benjamin F. 715 W. Monroe
McNeill Malcolm Prof. Lake Forest
McNeill Malcom, 2001 Michigan av.
McNeill Malcom jr. 2001 Michigan av.
McNeill Rivers, 118 S. Oakley av.
McNeill Thomas H. 925 Jackson boul.
McNellis Charles J. 276 Marshfield av.
McNellis M. 318 Loomis
McNett C. S. Irving Park
McNiff Margaret S. Dr. 1048, 75th (H. P.)
McPhelim Edward J. Hotel Groveland
McPherran A. Mrs. 5648 Madison av.
McPherran Benjamin, 5648 Madison av.
McPherran Edward H. 3601 Vincennes av.
McPherran Samuel H. 5648 Madison av.
McPherson Arthur, Highland Park
McPherson Chester J. 4062 Michigan Terrace

McPherson H. H. 1 Park av.
McPherson J. C. Oak Park
McPherson L. E. 3537 Indiana av.
McPherson S. J. Rev. 2804 Prairie av.
McQuigg W. 168 Howe
McRae Alexander K. 506 The Plaza
McRae William M. 735 W. Vanburen
McReynolds Geo. S. 2203 Calumet av.
McReynolds M. W. 380 Erie
McRoberts J. J. 4430 Emerald av.
McRoy George G. 5426 Madison av.
McRoy J. T. 3250 Rhodes av.
McSchooler E. Berwyn
McShane James C. Lexington hotel
McSorley John, 449 Marshfield av.
McTerney Patrick, 1814 Michigan av.
McVeigh C. F. 4220 Calumet av.
McVicker James H. 1842 Michigan av.
McVicker O. Violia Miss, 3953 Michigan av.
McVicker W. B. 3953 Michigan av.
McVoy Eugene J. 440 Lasalle av.
McVoy John Mrs. 440 Lasalle av.
McVoy John A. 440 Lasalle av.
McWatters W. H. 5740 Monroe av.
McWhinney I. Mrs. 5540 Cornell av.
McWilliams Charles D. Evanston
McWilliams James, 2573 N. Paulina
McWilliams J. G. 3945 Lake av.
McWilliams L. 3961 Lake av.
McWilliams S. A. Dr. 3456 Michigan av.
Maas Fred, 345 Hampden ct.
Maas Moses 537 Lasalle av.
Maas Philip, 345 Hampden ct.
Mabie C. E. 1837 Michigan av.
Mabrey Harriet Mrs. 57 Cedar
MacAdams Edward J. River Forest
Macalister C. B. Miss, 3630 Grand boul.
MacArthur Archibald, Riverside
MacArthur Arthur F. 2000 Indiana av.
MacArthur Florence B. M , Riverside
MacArthur R. D., M.D. 4144 Dearborn av.
Macauley John, 750 North Park av.
MacBurney James A. Irving Park
MacCarty Chas. S. 769 Washington boul.
MacCoun John T. 3953 Michigan av.
MacCracken W. P Dr. 4327 Greenwood av.
MacDonald Albert E. 449 Washington boul.
MacDonald A. R. Lombard
MacDonald Charles A. 367 S. Robey
Macdonald Chas. A. 1563 Sheridan road.
Macdonald Charles Blair, 374 Ontario
MacDonald Cornelius J. 15, 39th
MacDonald Chas. H. 3236 Rhodes av.
Macdonald Cyrus B. 726 Farwell av.
Macdonald C. A. Buena Park
Macdonald David W. Riverside
MacDonald Donald A. 1452 Michigan av.
Macdonald George M. 729 Farwell av.
Macdonald Godfrey, Lakota hotel
MacDonald Grace G. Mrs. 3601 Vincennes av.
MacDonald Henry E. Dr. 1255 Michigan av.

Macdonald H. K. 270 Lasalle av.
Macdonald James, Evanston
MacDonald James M. 2829 Indiana av.
MacDonald John, 3804 Wabash av.
MacDonald J. H. 92 Loomis
MacDonald M. B. Mrs. 3601 Vincennes
  av.
MacDonald P. S., M. D. 2829 Indiana av.
MacDonald Raymond J. 2829 Indiana av.
MacDonald Sarah B. Mrs. 15, 39th
MacDonald W. J. Oak Park
Mace Alfred C. 4336 Berkeley av.
MacEdward James, Lagrange
Macfarland Henry J. 1923 Michigan av.
Macfarlane Henry J. 3945 Ellis av.
MacFarlane John W. 3945 Ellis av.
MacGill A. D. 1069 Warren av.
Mack Charles R. Wilmette
Mack Egbert B. 365 Ohio
Mack E. Mrs. 4306 Calumet av.
Mack Frances D. Mrs. 347, 62d (H.P.)
Mack F. D. 347, 62d (H.P.)
Mack G. H. 310, 53d (H.P.)
Mack Julian W. 4242 Langley av.
Mack M. 1712 Diversey
Mackay Alexander, 560 N. State
Mackay David S. 147 Dearborn av.
Mackay F. 857 Jackson boul.
MacKay Joseph E. Evanston
MacKelvey James A. Rev. 1076 Wash-
  ington boul.
  Sum. res. Coulterville, Ill.
MacKenzie Frederick, 4341 Grand boul.
Mackenzie George S. 680 W. Monroe
Mackenzie John K. 2825 Indiana av.
MacKenzie J. F. 5628 Monroe av.
Mackey B. Palmer, 193 Bowen av.
Mackey F. J. 3214 Michigan av.
Mackey Spoor, 3860 Lake av.
Mackie Arthur Mrs. 1458 Wrightwood av.
Mackie Charles, 511 W. Monroe
  Sum. res. Fox Lake, Ill.
Mackie John D. 337 Racine av.
Mackin John, 251 Lake View av.
Mackin Margaret Miss, Austin
Macklem Wm. 6636 Harvard, Englewood
Macklin Charles G. 2754 Commercial (L.
  V.)
MacLachlan J. W. Dr. 244, 57th (H.P.)
MacLachlan Wm. F. 878 Washington
  boul.
MacLean Alexander W. Wilmette
MacLean Arthur A. 411 Huron
Maclean George A. Riverside
Maclean John D. Austin
MacLean Thomas A. 4058 Michigan Ter-
  race
Maclear W. H. Evanston
MacLeod Gordon 200, 44th
MacLeod Murdock, 288 Marshfield av.
MacMahon John, 5132 Wabash av.
MacMartin R. Dr. Grand Pacific hotel
MacMillan Duncan, 7855 Winneconna av.
MacMillan Hugh, 424 Superior
MacMillan Lincoln, 7855 Winneconna av.
MacMillan Newton, 3960 Drexel boul.

MacMillan T. C. 816 W. Adams
MacNaughtan David, Austin
MacNeal Arthur Dr. Berwy
Macomber F. B. 196 Warren av.
Macomber Levi F. 196 Warren av.
Macomber Wesson, 3334 Vernon av.
MacPhetridge Euclid, 6546 Stewart av.
MacRae Kate E. Dr. 4577 Lake av.
MacRae Norman, 4577 Lake av.
MacVeagh Eames, 103 Lake Shore drive
MacVeagh Franklin, 103 Lake Shore drive
Madden Edgar M. New Hotel Holland
Madden Flora Mrs. 2955 Groveland av.
Madden F. H. 5222 Woodlawn av.
Madden Hannah C. Mrs. 3543 Michigan
  av.
Madden James A. 331 Hampden ct.
Madden Mark F. 331 Hampden ct.
Madden Martin B. 3563 Forest av.
Madden M. S. 331 Hampden ct.
Maddock Henry S. Evanston
Maddox L. Miss, Hotel Metropole
Madeira C. W. Mrs. Morgan Park
Madigan M. D. 1298 Wilcox av.
Madison Gerritt W. 4242 St. Lawrence
  av.
Madison John R. Irving Park
Madison John T. Grayland
Madison P. Chester Dr. 387 S. Leavitt
Madlener F. 17 Lake View av.
Madlung W. F. 6845 Union av.
Magee Charles J. 382 Claremont av.
Magee Ethel J. Miss, 289, 53d
Magee George, 4319 Berkeley av.
Magee Henry W. 7722 Union av.
Magee John J. 5810 Rosalie ct.
Magee Joseph, 16 Gilpin pl.
Magee M. E. Mrs. 4319 Berkeley av.
Magee Robert H. 3530 Lake av.
Mages George C. 727 N. Hoyne av.
Magevney Philip J. 12 Menomonee
Maggart James M. 216 Ohio
Magie Edward A. 40 Ray
Magie Frank O. 40 Ray
Magie William A. 40 Ray
Magill G. L. 3024 Calumet av.
Magill H. W. Lakota hotel
Magill J. C. 733 W. Adams
Magill Matthew E. 3813 Forest av.
Magill M. G. Hotel Groveland
Magill S. E. 6014 Sheridan av.
Magill T. W. Vendome Club hotel
Magill William C. Evanston
Maginnis P. J. Mrs. 1852 Diversey
Magner James, 1337 Michigan av.
Magnus Albert, 1932 Barry av.
Magnus Arthur J. 473 Elm
Magnus August, 522 Dearborn av.
Magnus August C. 487 W. Monroe
Magnus John, 16 Cedar
Magnus Rudolph R. 4560 Oakenwald av.
Magoon C. C. Washington Heights
Magoon C. H. 679 W. Adams
Magoon Henry A. 679 W. Adams
Magruder B. D. Judge, 7 Washington pl.
Magruder Carrie A. Mrs. Evanston

Magruder H. Latham, 7 Washington pl.
Maguire Mary F. Mrs. 70 Astor
Mahaffey Jessie M. Mrs. 3934 Michigan
  av.
Mahan H. W. 5532 Monroe av.
Mahan I. S. Mrs. 5551 Monroe av.
Mahan James L. 2404 Prairie av.
Mahanna Bradley, The Tudor
Maher Albert J. 312, 65th Terrace
Maher Daniel W. 1121 N. Clark
Maher Edward 450, 65th, Eng.
Maher F. R. Mrs. 655 W. Adams
Maher George W. Kenilworth
Maher John, 4549 Vincennes av.
Maher Mark H. 2438 Michigan av.
Maher Philip, 3426 Indiana av.
Maher Theophile, 220 Woodlawn Terrace
Maher Walter S. 220 Woodlawn Terrace
Maher Walter S. 5812 Michigan av.
Mahin J. Lee, 352 Ontario
Mahnke Louis H. 820 Garfield boul.
Mahon James A. 2604 Indiana av.
Mahoney John A. 479 Seminary av.
Mahony Michael F. 174 Fremont
Maidment Edward, 148 N. State
Main William B. 5237 Jefferson av.
Main W. Fred, 1242 Washington boul.
Mair Charles A. Auditorium annex
Mair Henry B. Newberry hotel
Makeever Sanford, Chicago Beach hotel
Malcolm James, 46 Best av.
Malden Peachey, 3030 Michigan av.
Maley Thos. E. Col. 6516 Ross av.
Malkow Fred. 6353 Harvard
Mallen H. W. 1444 W. Monroe
Mallernee Henry J. 1215 Wolcott
Mallers Edward B. 36 Groveland Park
Mallers John B. 36 Groveland Park
Mallette J. P. 7216 Yale
Malley William C. 6111 Woodlawn
Mallin John A. Ridgeland
Mallory Charles A. 5156 Grand boul.
            Winter res. Indian River
Mallory DeWitt C. 4809 Madison av.
Mallory Edward E. 120 S. Kedzie av.
Mallory E. B. 1684 Sheridan rd.
Mallory James L. 342 Warren av.
Mallory S. A. The Renfost
Mallory William H. 4439 Prairie av.
Malone E. T. Oak Park
Malone G. Beecher Dr. 226 Ontario
Maloy Alfred J. Dr. LaGrange
Maloy Sarah E. Dr. LaGrange
Maltby Adolphus W. 819 The Plaza
Maltby George K. 56 The Yale
Maltby J. A. Mrs. 368 Ontario
Maltman Alexander S. 75 Lake View av.
Maltman Stewart A. 75 Lake View av.
Mamerow George, Irving Park
Manahan F. D. Granada hotel
Manasse Louis, 4367 Oakenwald av.
Manasse Nathan, 4808 Kimbark av.
Manchester Ida Mrs. 560 Division
Mandel Emanuel, 3400 Michigan av.
Mandel Emma S. Mrs. 254, 37th
Mandel Frank, 3400 Michigan av.

Mandel Frank S. 3206 Michigan av.
Mandel Fred, LaGrange
Mandel Fred L. 1932 Calumet av.
Mandel Leon, 1932 Calumet av.
            Sum. res. Long Branch, N. J.
Mandel Leonard J. 3206 Michigan av.
Mandel Robert I. 1932 Calumet av.
Mandel Simon, 3206 Michigan av.
Mandelbaum Clara Mrs. 3726 Forest av.
Mandelbaum M. H. 3726 Forest av.
Mandeville C. 235 Lasalle av.
Mandeville C. E. Rev. 6410 Stewart av.
Mandeville Edward E. Riverside
Mandeville S. 148 N. State
Mandl Bernard, 445 Dearborn av.
Maney James A. Lieut. Fort Sheridan
Mangler William, 473 Sedgwick
Manheimer J. C. 3149 Forest av.
Manheimer Louis, Lexington hotel
Manheimer William, 3149 Forest av.
Manierre Charles E. Dr. 552 Lasalle av.
Manierre George, 61 Bellevue pl.
Manierre Kate Miss, 100, 24th
Manierre William R. 399 Superior
Manington John, 6426 Sheridan av.
Manley Elizabeth Mrs. Evanston
Manley George W. 53 Ray
Manlove W. R. 3402 Indiana av.
Manly R. Mrs. 118 S. Leavitt
Mann Almeda Miss, 2927 Indiana av.
Mann Amasa, 418, 61st, Eng.
Mann A. C. 6125 Indiana av.
Mann Charles W. 545 W. Adams
Mann Freeman A. 2600 N. Ashland av.
Mann Henry N. 358 Ohio
Mann Henry V. Winnetka
Mann James R. 334 Oakwood boul.
Mann Joseph B. Auburn Park
Mann J. E. Hotel Metropole
Mann O. H.,M.D., Evanston
            Sum. res. Okobojo Valley, S. D.
Mann Robert R. Evanston
Mann Simon F. 732, 64th, Eng.
Mann William A. J., M. D. 48, 43d
Mann William B. 4 Gordon Terrace
Mann William B. Dr. Evanston
Mann William G. Judge, 4428 Grand boul.
Manners Robert R. 201, 25th
Manney Solon W. Riverside
Mannhardt Emil, 399 Orchard
Mannheimer M. Mrs. 1822 Indiana av.
Mannierre Charles E. Dr. 552 Lasalle av.
Manning George W. 214, 42d (H.P.)
Manning H. S. 5725 Rosalie ct.
Manning John L. 7752 S. Peoria
Manning J. A. Dr. 2912 Prairie av.
Manning J. R. 387 N. State
Manning L. B. Mrs. 216, 28th
Manning Mary Fuller Mrs. The Berk-
            shire Sum. res. Washington, D. C.
Manning O. H. 3431 Michigan av.
Manning Randolph, Riverside
Manning William F. 216, 28th
Manning William J. 3242 Calumet av.
Manny Emeline Mrs. Evanston
Manny F. Hermann, Evanston

Manny Harvey H. Dr. 317 Belden av.
Manny H. A. Miss. 3807 Vincennes av.
Manny James H. 317 Belden av.
Manny J. H. Mrs. 5, 31st
Mansar Jacob, 5127 Woodlawn av.
Mansfield Clara D. Mrs. Evanston
Mansfield Isaac R. 999 Warren av.
Mansfield R. 1837 Michigan av.
Manson Frank M. 49 Astor
Manson William, 3233 Vernon av.
Manson William O. 49 Astor
Mansure E. L. 45, 46th
Mantellini G. Prof. Stamford hotel
Mantonya L. B. 374 Dearborn av.
Manvel Allen Mrs. 22 Lake Shore Drive
   Sum. res. Waldemeer, Long Beach, Me.
Manvel J. 3010 Calumet av.
Many Robert, Oak Park
Many Sidney G. 115 S. California av.
Manz Jacob, 562 Burling
Manz Paul, 562 Burling
Maple William H. 29 Campbell Park
Marazzi G. Count, Chicago Beach hotel
Marble Andrew J. 244 Dearborn av.
Marble C. E. River Forest
Marble Henry E. 361 S. Oakley av.
Marble Oliver W. 4829 Vincennes av.
Marble Walter H. Dr. 733 Grace
Marble W. E. 788 Jackson boul.
Marchand G. L. 490, 42d
Marchant Charles H. Wilmette
Marchant Stuart F. 221, 46th (H. P.)
Marchant Susanna F. Mrs. Ridgeland
Marcus A. I. 276, 32d
Marcus Julius, 439 Warren av.
Marcuse Dora Mrs. 237, 32d
Marcuse Jessie H. Miss, 102 Hammond
Marcuse L. 102 Hammond
Marcusson H. H. 938 Park av.
Marcusson Jacob W. Rev. 429 Carroll av.
Marcusson W. B. Dr. 429 Carroll av.
Marcy George E. 4442 Berkeley av.
Marcy Oliver Prof. Evanston
Marden Bertha Miss, 456 Dayton
Marden Dora Miss, 456 Dayton
Marden Julia, Miss, 456 Dayton
Marden Louis, 456 Dayton
Marder Clarence, 4750 Woodlawn av.
Marder John, 4750 Woodlawn av.
Marder John W. 4750 Woodlawn av.
Margerun William, Winnetka
Marggraf Oscar, 416 Superior
Marguerat Eugene, M.D. 700 W. Monroe
Marienthal George, 3134 Forest av.
Marion Esther Mrs. 52 Oakwood av.
Maritzen A. 1722 Diversey
Marix Arthur T. Hotel Normandie
Mark Anson, 290 Ashland boul.
Mark Clayton, 289 Ashland boul.
Mark Julius, 236 Lunt av.
Markee F. D. Chicago Beach hotel
Markee Wm. Allen, 5031 Madison av.
Markey James, 907 Farwell av.
Markey James B. 907 Farwell av.
Markham Frank H. 3403 Calumet av.
Markham M. C. 115, 33d

Markham R. David, 696 North Park av.
Markle Albert M.Dr. 4236 St.Lawrence av.
Markley John A. 2125 Calumet av.
Markoe Frank, 42, 35th
Marks Charles. 331, 34th
Marks Clarence W. 3121 Michigan av.
Marks Edward C. 2501 Wabash av.
Marks Elizabeth Mrs. 2501 Wabash av.
Marks Harry M. 3434 Michigan av.
Marks Joseph E. P. 2501 Wabash av.
Marks Julius M. Phoenix club
Marks Kossuth, 2501 Wabash av.
Marks Louis, 129, 25th
Marks Louis C. 331, 34th
Marks Louis J. 2501 Wabash av.
Marks Mary W. Miss, Oak Park
Marks Morton L. Elmhurst
Marks M. M. 331, 34th
Marks R. P. 235 Michigan av.
Marks Samuel J. 377, 45th (H. P.)
Marks Simon L. 3613 Prairie av.
Marks William J. 21 Bryant av.
Marley Luther C. 4546 Lake av.
Marmaduke Jesse D. 4127 Southport av.
Marquardt C. D. 9 Madison Park
Marquardt G. W. r. 425 Lasalle av.
Marquis A. N.   Washington boul.
Marquis David   Rev. 1 Chalmers pl.
Marquis Geo. P256M.D. 1 Chalmers pl.
Marr John, 1028 Park av.
Marr R. I. 88 Park av.
Marr Thomas, 402, 65th, Eng.
Marr William, 1028 Park av.
Marrenner Edward, 3227 Groveland av.
Marrenner Edward S. 3227 Groveland av.
Marrh Helen Miss, 4339 Oakenwald av.
Marriner Robert G. Dr. 2227 Calumet av.
Marriott Abe R. Austin
Mars George H. Wilmette
Marsh Alfred H. Tracy
Marsh Charles A. 5639 Washington av.
                     Sum. res. Antioch, Ill
Marsh Charles H. Park Ridge
Marsh Charles L. 60 Bittersweet pl.
Marsh C. G. Oak Park
Marsh Charles T. 616 W. Monroe
Marsh C. V. 4900 Washington av.
Marsh Emma A. Mrs. 3641 Ellis Park
Marsh E. P. Tracy
Marsh Fred A. 5639 Washington av.
Marsh Fred H. 3008 Groveland av.
Marsh F. A. 801 Pullman bldg.
Marsh George, 1406 W. Monroe
Marsh George B. Mrs. Evanston
Marsh George S. Evanston
Marsh George W. 2300 Indiana av.
Marsh Henry W. 454 Elm
Marsh Hiram C. LaGrange
Marsh James P. 3222 Michigan av.
Marsh John S. Dr. 4613 Woodlawn av.
Marsh John W. 12 Aldine sq.
Marsh John W. 12 Aldine sq.
Marsh Jonathan P. 1328 Washington boul.
Marsh J. Gorton, 5639 Washington av.
Marsh Marshall S. Evanston

Marsh Ossian B. LaGrange
Marsh Philo, Evanston
Marsh T. J. Mrs. 454 Elm
          Sum. res. Lake Geneva
Marsh William D. Evanston
Marsh William H. 4634 Vincennes av.
Marsh W. P. Evanston
Marshall Albert, 5400 Jefferson av.
Marshall Alexander, 22 Bellevue pl.
Marshall Alvah, 1824 Surf
Marshall A. J. Mrs. 30 Hawthorne pl.
Marshall Benjamin H. 4730 Drexel boul.
Marshall Caleb H. 4730 Drexel boul.
Marshall Charles H. 302' 48th (H. P.)
Marshall Edward T. 566 Washington boul.
Marshall Frank, 444 Englewood av.
Marshall Fred D., M.D., 731 Jackson boul.
Marshall Geo. A. 61 Laflin
Marshall George E. 30 Hawthorne pl.
Marshall Geo. E. 6600 Lafayette av.
Marshall Harry L. 608 Washington boul.
          Sum. res. Fox Lake, Ill.
Marshall Hattie N. Miss, 2426 Indiana av.
Marshall Ira E. Dr. 576 Washington
          boul.
Marshall Irvin, 1824 Surf
Marshall James D. 525 Jackson boul.
Marshall John I. The Renfost
Marshall John S. Dr. 48 Groveland Park
Marshall Joseph A. LaGrange
Marshall Joseph B. 4561 Oakenwald av.
Marshall Judith L. Mrs. 2109 Prairie av.
Marshall J. J. New Hotel Holland
Marshall J. M. 5400 Jefferson av.
Marshall J. W. 6748 Union av.
Marshall Margaret Mrs. 7620 Eggleston
          av.
Marshall Medora Estes Mrs. LaGrange
Marshall Philip L. 4738 Woodlawn av.
Marshall Randall E. 566 Washington
          boul.
Marshall Stanley, 3521 Grand boul.
Marshall Sylvester, 4341 Indiana av.
Marshall Thomas H. 96 Fowler
Marshall Waldo H. 7620 Eggleston av.
Marshall William, 239 Dearborn av.
Marshall William, 1824 Surf
Marshall Wm. L. Capt. U.S.A. Hyde Park
          hotel
Marshall W. R. Evanston
Marston A. W. 2501 N. Haisted
Marston James D. 318, 61st, Englewood
Marston Louis H. 4852 Calumet av.
Marston Robert H. 225, 28th
Marston Thomas B. 225, 28th
Martell William H. 4530 St. Lawrence av.
Marten R. B. Auditorium hotel
Martens C. F. 536 W. Adams
Martens Louis, 424 Ashland boul.
Marthens Chester M. LaGrange
Martin Addie T. Miss, 4527 Vincennes av.
Martin Alexander C. 195 S. Campbell av.
Martin Alfred V. Kenilworth
Martin Arthur, Austin
Martin A. W. 418 Jackson boul.
Martin Benjamin F. 445 Washington boul,
40

Martin B. F. Rev. Berwyn
Martin Chester H. 4527 Vincennes av.
Martin Cornelius K. Mrs. 5471 Jefferson
          av.
Martin C. E. Irving Park
Martin Daniel R. Pullman
Martin Edward Byam Mrs. 30 Walton pl.
Martin Edward B. 360 Belden av.
Martin Ellen A. Miss, Lombard
Martin Eunice A. Miss, 507 W. Monroe
Martin E. B. 1074 Jackson boul.
Martin E. E. Granada hotel
Martin E. L. Mrs. 712 W. Monroe
Martin E. P. Ridgeland
Martin E. T. 304 Woodlawn Terrace
Martin Florence Miss, 4527 Vincennes av.
Martin Frank C. 601, 65th, Eng.
Martin Frank J. 6602 Lafayette av.
Martin F. S. 16 Burton pl.
Martin Franklin H., M. D. 3210 Lake
          Park av.
Martin George H. 4340 Ellis av.
Martin George S. 2810 Michigan av.
Martin George W. 45 The Yale
Martin G. A. 1020 Park av.
Martin G. H. 4403 Ellis av.
Martin Henry Mrs. Kenilworth
Martin Henry F. 201 Fremont
Martin Horace H. 307 N. Clark
Martin Hugh, 3972 Vincennes av.
Martin H. P. Oak Park
Martin Ida Mrs. 55 St. James pl.
Martin James, 661 Park av.
Martin James A. Austin
Martin John H. 4400 Indiana av.
Martin John L. 5800 Rosalie ct.
Martin John T. 3534 Wabash av.
Martin Joseph, 190 N. State
Martin Julius H. Austin
Martin Earl, 2578 Commercial (L.V.)
Martin J. Edward, 601, 65th, Eng.
Martin J. Motte, 3160 Lake Park av.
Martin J. P. Col., U.S.A. Chicago Beach
          hotel
Martin J. W. Dr. 465 Warren av.
Martin Nicholas, 3246 Forest av.
Martin Robert G. 605, 65th, Eng.
Martin Robert L. 719 W. Vanburen
Martin Robert P. 4400 Indiana av.
Martin Robert T. 2810 Michigan av.
Martin Samuel K. 2600 Michigan av.
Martin Samuel K. jr, 2600 Michigan av.
Martin S. Mrs. Hotel Groveland
Martin S. E. W. Mrs. 656 W. Monroe
Martin Thomas J. 213 Dearborn av.
Martin Wallace R. 4400 Indiana av.
Martin William, 540 W. Adams
Martin William J. 4314 Forrestville av.
Martin William P. 365 Ontario
Martin Wilson O. 4160 Ellis av.
Martin Wilton B. 2600 Michigan av.
Martin W. J. Dr. 800 W. Adams
Martine James E. 331 Hampden ct.
Martyn Carlos Rev. 4033 Vincennes av.
Martyn Edward J. 112 Astor
Martyn R. Delos, 4450 Berkeley av.

Marum Edmund P. 235, 66th pl. (H.P.)
Marvin William, 2974 Indiana av.
Marx Ella L. Mrs. 484, 42d pl.
Marx Hattie Miss 3658 Michigan av.
Marx Marcus, 3658 Michigan av.
Marx Zero, 628 Fullerton av.
Mashek V. F. 40 Loomis
Maslin C. E. Miss, 2034 Indiana av.
Maslin J. C. 2034 Indiana av.
Mason Albert G. 5426 Jefferson av.
Mason A. C. Chicago Beach hotel
Mason A. O. 3723 Prairie av.
Mason Carlisle, 176 Ashland boul.
Mason Charles D. Evanston
Mason Charles F. 49 Astor
Mason Charles S. 508 Cornell av.
Mason Charles T. ⁎ Rosalie ct.
Mason D. W. 3032 Wabash Av.
Mason Edna Mrs. 88 Lincoln av.
Mason Edward G. 1200 Michigan av.
Mason Edward H. 1200 Michigan av.
Mason Edward T. 448 W. Adams
Mason Fred, 323 Belden av.
Mason F. G. Dr. 477 W. Congress
Mason George, 511 W. Monroe
Mason George Allen, 3032 Wabash av.
Mason George A. 145 S. Leavitt
Mason George A. 747 Kenmore av.
Mason George T. 55, 33d
Mason Hattie Miss, 5332 Washington av.
Mason Henry B. 29 Delaware pl.
Mason Henry E. 296 Ohio
Mason Hugh, 369 Jackson boul.
Mason H. L. 557 Dearborn av.
Mason Ira J. 323 Belden av.
Mason James Mrs. Austin
Mason James A. 907 W. Monroe
Mason John A. C. Union club
Mason J. N. Longwood
Mason J. R. Oak Park
Mason Leonard B. 5524 Monroe av.
Mason Lewis J. 29, 37th
Mason Lucy Miss, Evanston
Mason M. Louise Mrs. 22 Bellevue pl.
Mason O. C. Evanston
Mason P. B. Clifton house
Mason Richard Mrs. Evanston
Mason Roswell, 113 Cass
Mason R. J. 489 Jackson boul.
Mason Sheridan, 303 Schiller
Mason Stephen C. 6651 Stewart av.
Mason Travers J. The Tudor
Mason William A. 303 Schiller
Mason Wm. E, 1479 Washington boul.
　　Sum. res. Waukegan, Ill.
Mason William R. 13, 43d (H.P.)
Mason W. T. 1503 Wellington
Massey Albert H. 4208 Oakenwald av.
Massey C. V. Dr. 1607 Diversey
Massey Thomas C. 435 Kenmore av.
Massey Wilfred, 24 St. James pl.
Massman John Dr. Austin
Masters Arthur W. 85 Park av.
Masters G. A. Park Ridge
Masters J. S. Oak Park
Masterson Edwin F. 3825 Vernon av.

Masterson Robert, 4444 Wabash av.
Math John B. 7518 Ellis av.
Mather A. C. 531 N. State
Mather Charles S. 456 N. Normal Parkway
Mather Frank, 152, 36th
Mather Henry H. Dr. 7847 Wright
Mather J. H. 625 Jackson boul.
Mather Robert, 4432 Ellis av.
Mather William H. 1024 N. Clark
Mather W. B. 7211 Yale
Mathers Albert, 461 Warren av.
Matheson Robert, 2410 N. Paulina
Mathew H. A. C. 4363 Lake av.
Mathews Allen A. Dr. Oak Park
Mathews Alvah B. 47 Greenleaf av.
Mathews Clara Louise Miss, 2532 Indiana av.
Mathews Frederick W. 2532 Indiana av.
Mathews George W. 2532 Indiana av.
Mathews George W. Lakota hotel
Mathews Henry B. 1336 Washington boul.
Mathews Henry B. jr. 1336 Washington boul.
Mathews John F. 4613 Champlain av.
Mathews S. Prof. Hotel Barry
Mathews S. S. Rev. The Rosalie, 57th
Mathews T. Erskine, 2637 N. Robey
Mathews W. S. B. Evanston
Mathison George W. 335 Hampden ct.
Mathison O. A. 4638 Indiana av.
Mathison Soren, 2126 Indiana av.
Matile Herman O. Hinsdale
Matkin John I. 4201 Lake av.
Matkin Louise J. Mrs. 4201 Lake av.
Matkin Otho F. 4201 Lake av.
Matrau B.F.Rev. 512 N.Normal Parkway
Matson A. P. Clark, Forest hotel (R.P.)
Matson C. R. 609 Cleveland av.
Matson N. Mrs. Lombard
Matter Martin, M.D., 3117 Wabash av.
Mattern L. 408 Belden av.
Mattern O. C. 597 Ogden av.
Mattes Peter, 417 Belden av.
Matteson Arthur E., D.D.S. 3822 Langley av.
Matteson C. F., Dr. 50, 35th
Matteson H. H. Prof. Oak Park
Matteson Joseph Dr. 3166 Groveland av.
Matteson Jean McN. Miss, Evanston
Matteson Milo D. 1401 Dunning
Matteson Murray G.,D.D.S. 3822 Langley av.
Matteson William P. Evanston
Matthei Charles A. 368 Ashland boul.
Matthei Gustave P. 368 Ashland boul.
Matthei Philip H., M.D. 57 Wisconsin
Matthei William Mrs. 368 Ashland boul.
Matthei William H. 368 Ashland boul.
Matthews A. E. 508 Belden av.
Matthews Chas. E. 4830 Kenwood av.
Matthews Charles E. 1665 W. Monroe
Matthews Charles H. Evanston
　　Sum. res. Kenosha, Wis,
Matthews C. H. Tremont house

Matthews Edwin Scott, 401 The Plaza
Matthews Elizabeth A. Mrs. 721 Washington boul.
Matthews Frank W. 513 The Plaza
Matthews Henry M. 4216 Prairie av.
Matthews John B. Austin
Matthews John T. 1165 Washington boul.
Matthews O. A. 520, 60th, Englewood
Matthews Pascal P. Hinsdale
Matthews Walter C. Austin
Matthews William H. 1155 W. Vanburen
Matthias Charles, 4206 Michigan av.
Matthias Mary M. Mrs. 4206 Michigan av.
Matthiessen C.H. 4917 Drexel boul.
Matthiessen E. A. 567 Dearborn av.
    Sum. res. Cornwall on Hudson, N Y.
Matthiessen Frank, 4440 Ellis av.
Matthiessen Frederick W. jr. 573, 51st (H.P.)
Matthius John D. Rev. Evanston
Mattison Fitch C. E., M.D., 229, 42d pl.
Mattocks Walter, Lexington hotel
Matz Evelyn Miss, 431 Oak
Matz Herman L. 431 Oak
Matz Otto H. 431 Oak
Matz Rudolph. 460 Dearborn av.
Mauch Charles 581 Burling
Maull L. V. Mrs. 3979 Drexel boul.
Maull W. C. Mrs. 174 Oakwood boul.
Maulsby Richmond S. 14 Bishop ct.
Mauran Charles J. 2441 Michigan av.
Mauran Charles S. 2441 Michigan av.
Maurer, William, 4136 Prairie av.
Maus Frederick K. 584 Dearborn av.
Maus James R. LaGrange
Maverick Manton, 3532 Ellis av.
Mavor John, LaGrange
Mavor William, 166 Oakwood boul.
MaWhinney Elgin Dr. 4558 Evans av.
Maxfield George W. 3537 Michigan av.
Maxfield J. C. Mrs. 183 S. Oakley av.
Maxfield O. S. Mrs. 414 S. Leavitt
Maxham H. S. Mrs. Pullman
Maxwell Charles E. 3427 Michigan av.
Maxwell D. G. 538 Cleveland av.
Maxwell E. E. 3980 Lake av.
Maxwell E. J. Mrs. 418 Center
Maxwell Harry Ward, 731 Fullerton av.
Maxwell Henry B. 365 Ashland boul.
Maxwell James, 367 Ashland boul.
Maxwell James W. 599 N. Clark
Maxwell John E. A. LaGrange   ·
Maxwell J. W. 3978 Lake av.
Maxwell M. J. Mrs. 4208 Berkeley av.
Maxwell R. F. 468 Fullerton av.
Maxwell William, 164 Ashland boul.
Maxwell William J. 941 Jackson av.
Maxwell William S.Dr.3017 Michigan av.
Maxwell W. Mrs. 538 Cleveland av.
Maxwell W. J. Revere house
May Benjamin W. 4535 Greenwood av.
May B. A. Winnetka
May C. A. Mrs. 1351 Wolcott
May D. 374 S. Paulina
May George G. 457 Cleveland av.

May Horatio N. 147 Astor
May Jacob Mrs. 3207 Calumet av.
May James, 5235 Kimbark av.
May James F. 252, 51st (H.P.)
May James R. 174 Warren av.
May John A. 2728 Wabash av.
May John V. 19 Crilly pl.
May Marion jr. 259 Dearborn av.
May Mary Mrs. 212 Cass
May Max, 5422 Jackson av.
May O. J. Julien hotel
May Stephen D. 84, 25th
May T. E. Hotel Windermere
May W. L. Mrs. 1177 Washington boul.
May Yetta Miss 322 Marshfield av.
Maydwell B. B., M.D. 14 Menomonee
Mayer Adolph E. 2693 Charlton av.
Mayer Albert, 337 Burling
Mayer Augusta Mrs. 337 Burling
Mayer Bernard, 3442 Vernon av.
Mayer Clara Mrs. 2343 Michigan av.
Mayer Daniel, 4116 Ellis av.
Mayer David, 20 Groveland Park
Mayer David, 378 Oakwood boul.
Mayer David, 3233 Calumet av.
Mayer David, 3251 Prairie av.
Mayer Edgar J. 3213 Wabash av.
Mayer Edward, 3250 Wabash av.
Mayer Edwin L. 2509 Wabash av.
Mayer Harry L. 3250 Wabash av.
Mayer Henry, 3563 Prairie av.
Mayer Isaac H. 3548 Ellis av.
Mayer Isaac M. 4527 Ellis av.
Mayer Jacob, 3560 Vernon av.
Mayer Jacob, 3866 Lake av.
Mayer John A. 1704 Belmont av.
Mayer John C. 30 St. Johns pl.
Mayer Joseph, 3250 Wabash av.
Mayer Joseph, 3752 Wabash av.
Mayer J. A. 37 Lincoln pl.
Mayer Kate A. Mrs. 510 Cleveland av.
Mayer Lee, 3250 Wabash av.
Mayer Leo D. 3213 Wabash av.
Mayer Leopold, 3170 Groveland av.
Mayer Levy, 2112 Prairie av.
Mayer Louis, 2509 Wabash av.
Mayer Minnie C. Mrs. 1347 Michigan av.
Mayer Morris, 3247 Rhodes av.
Mayer Morris, 4234 Calumet av.
Mayer Moses E. 3233 Calumet av.
Mayer M. H. 3229 Wabash av.
Mayer Nathan, 3233 Calumet av.
Mayer Nathan, 3107 Groveland av.
Mayer Otto W. 549 Burling
Mayer R. Mrs. 4527 Ellis av.
Mayer Toby, 378 Oakwood boul.
Mayer William J. 347 Ashland boul.
Mayhew A. M. 614 Orchard
Mayhew L. D. Hotel Windermere
Mayhew Thomas, 1919 Wrightwood av,
Maynard Alfred C. Winnetka
Maynard Charles W. Maywood
Maynard Edwin, Winnetka
Maynard E. Percy, Winnetka
Maynard E. W. 443, 64th, Englewood
Maynard George L. 6410 Harvard

Maynard L. P. 6410 Harvard
Maynard Preston C. 802 Pullman bldg.
Maynard R. K. Oak Park
Mayo E. A. French House, Evanston
Mayo George A. 557 Division
Mayo John B. 2312 Calumet av.
　　Sum. res. Manchester by the Sea
　　Mass.
Mayo Lewis B. 3836 Calumet av.
Mayo Oswin Mrs. 456 Bowen av.
Mayou J. S. 356, 56th
Maypole William T. 185 Park av.
Mayr Walter A. 505 The Plaza
Meacham Charles S. Oak-Park
Meacham C. H. Mrs. Oak Park
Meacham C. O. Mrs. 2458 Michigan av.
Meacham F. D. 469 Jackson boul.
Mead Aaron B. 632 Washington boul.
　　Sum. res. Charlevoix, Mich.
Mead Edwin R. 41 Newport av
Mead E. Allen 41 Newport av.
Mead George A. 1621 Prairie av.
Mead G. A. Hotel M　　p
Mead Harry A. 3605 Lakeav.
Mead Lydia Miss, Oak Park
Mead Morton E. 4429 Berkeley av.
Mead M. A. Chicago Beach hotel
Mead William G. Mrs. 2971 Prairie av.
Mead Wilson L. 26 Delaware pl.
Meade James, Garfield boul.ne.cor.Laflin
Meader Martin C. 1282 Palmer
Meadowcroft Frederick, 718 The Plaza
Meadowcroft Walter, 23 Astor
Meadowcroft William, 23 Astor
Meadows Frederick W. Austin
Meads Albert H. 4444 Berkeley av.
Meagher James F. 4205 Grand boul.
Meaker Guy L. Evanston
Meaker John W. Evanston
Meaker John W. jr. Evanston
Mealiff Frank H. 7831 Winneconna av.
Means Elizabeth T. Mrs. 4752 Champ-
　　lain av.
Mears Charles, 345 Ohio
Mears Charles H. Evanston
Mears Frank, 152, 36th
Mears L. Byron, LaGrange
Mears Nathan, 87 Cass
Mecartney H. S. Virginia hotel
Meckes F. W. 6601 Lafayette av.
Meckling Jonas S. 606 Washington boul.
Mecum C. H. 4560 Oakenwald av.
Medbery Myra Mrs. 3612 Ellis Park
Medill Joseph, 101 Cass
Medill S. J. Mrs. Hotel Metropole
Mee David D. 222 Evergreen av.
Mee Edward, 222 Evergreen av.
Meech George A. Morgan Park
Meech M. G. Mrs. 545 Dearborn av.
Meech William T. 6450 Stewart av.
Meehan H. W. Hotel Barry
Meek Frank. Tracy
Meek J. W. Dr. 6351 Honore
Meek S. Mason, 186 Park av.
Meek Thomas M. 186 Park av.
Meeker Arthur B. 2107 Calumet av. .

Meeker A. B. 2209 Prairie av.
Meeker Charles W. 4337 Forestville av.
Meeker Elizabeth Mrs. 2602 Prairie av.
Meeker George W. 442 Chestnut
Meeker J. W. 6108 Washington av.
Meeker William D. 215 Fremont
Meerhoff Charles E. Dr. 1746 Wright-
　　wood av.
Mehagan Charles H. 5553 Monroe av.
Mehring Frederick, Evanston
Mehring George, 219 S. Oakley av.
Mehrle Caroline Mrs. 146 Lincoln av.
Mehrle Henry A. 146 Lincoln av.
Mehrle H. W. 146 Lincoln av.
Mehrle Richard O. 146 Lincoln av.
Meinel E. C. 1555 W. Monroe
Meinel F. A. 1555 W. Monroe
Meinel William, 1555 W. Monroe
Meinrath Ariel, Virginia hotel
Meiselbar Henry, 19 Park av.
Meister J. S. 114 S. Oakley av.
Meiswinkel Richard A. 1181 N. Clark
Melander Louis M. 521 Lasalle av.
Melander S. P. 252 Ontario
Melchard R. J. Mrs. Hawthorne av. Au-
　　burn Park
Melcher Charles W. 169, 53d (H.P.)
Melcher Grace G. Mrs. 3012 Michigan av.
Melcher Richard, 4342 Langley av.
Melchior Edward, 363 Mohawk
Meleney George B. 4 Aldine sq.
Meleney Henry E. Mrs. 4 Aldine sq.
　　Sum. res. Melrose, Mass.
Melhuish Frank, 1703 Michigan av.
Melhuish Henry, 1703 Michigan av.
Melick Walter J. LaGrange
Melin C. L. Mrs. Oak Park
Mellen Gertrude Miss. 587 Dearborn av
Mellen Harvey H. 540 Jackson av.
Mellen William S. Mrs. 587 Dearborn av.
Meller George, 1741 Deming ct.
Mellinger Jam　H. Dr. 915 Walnut
Mellinger Walter E. 917 Walnut
Mellish E. J. Dr. 307 Belden av.
Mellor Davis G. 240 Hampden ct.
Mellor E. N. Mrs.Riverside
Mellor Viria E. Miss, Riverside
Melody Mary Miss, 447 Belden av.
Melody Thomas R. 3118 Prairie av.
Meloy Edward S. 4427 Champlain av.
Meloy J. Y. 149 S. Paulina
Meloy W. T. Rev. 149 S. Paulina
Melville A. B. Oak Park
Melville Geo. W. Oak Park
Melvin A. S. jr. Dr. Oak Park
Memhard John, 1669 W. Monroe
Memory Wm. 411 Huron
Mendel Albert, 4348 Ellis av.
Mendel Max, 3651 Grand boul.
Mendelsohn Abram, 21 Scott
Mendelsohn Jacob, 21 Scott
Mendelsohn Jacob S. 4202 Calumet av.
Mendelsohn Joseph J. 717 Pine Grove av.
Mendelsohn Louis, 21 Scott
Mendelsohn Max S. 4202 Calumet av.
Mendelsohn Samuel S. 4202 Calumet av.

Mendelsohn Simon, 4202 Calumet av.
Mendelsohn Sol, 420 Warren av.
Mendelson R. Mrs. 503 Lasalle av.
Mendenhall James D. 485, 65th (H.P.)
Mendenhall W. J. 391 Warren av.
Mendsen Edward, Evanston
Mendsen George, 529½ Jackson boul.
Mendsen John F. 712 Washington boul.
Menefee James T. 3821 Forest av.
Menge A. 530 Ashland boul.
Menge Frederick Dr. 154, 42d
Menge Frederick A. 154, 42d
Menge William, 530 Ashland boul.
Menger W. S. 33 Surrey ct.
Menhennitt F. W. 4810 St. Lawrence av.
Menn Rudolph Dr. 547 N. Clark
Mercer Byron, Norwood Park
Mercer Fielding L. 1828 W. 22d
Mercer F. W. Dr. 2600 Calumet av.
Mercer Louis P. Rev. 220. 48th
Merceret Henry J. 419 Oak
Merchant George W. 7804 Sherman
Merchant John F. Grayland
Mercier J. T. Hyde Park hotel
Merckle Henry Dr. 1528 Michigan av.
Meredith L. Mrs. 307 Lake, Oak Park
Meredith William, 1520 W. Monroe
Meredith William T. Austin
Meredith W. M. Austin ·
Mergentheim Aaron D. 1509 Michigan av.
Mergentheim B. 3918 Prairie av.
Mergentheim David, 1509 Michigan av.
Mergentheim Ella Miss, 3918 Prairie av.
Mergler Marie J., M.D. 156, 25th
Meriam James L. 955 S. Central Park av.
Merigold Wm. A. 3984 Lake av.
Meriman Kate A. Mrs. Evanston
Meriman Ralph, 3749 Ellis av.
Merimee Edward J. 32 Bryant av.
Merker Paul, 1700 Wellington av.
Merki George, 130 Garfield boul.
Merki Louis, 130 Garfield boul.
Merki Maitland J. 130 Garfield boul.
Merle W. F. 451 Warren av.
Merrell E. R. 335 Chestnut, Englewood
Merriam Charles W. 3975 Ellis av.
Merriam Frank A. 44 Woodland Park
Merriam Jane W. Mrs. 5754 Monroe av.
Merriam John W. Auditorium hotel
Merriam Joseph W. 591 Lasalle av.
Merriam J. W. Lakota hotel
Merriam J. W. 4202 Michigan av.
Merriam R. B. 70 Warren av.
Merriam William A. 4241 St. Lawrence
av.
Merriam William F. Mrs. Evanston
Merrick Albert W. Oak Park
Merrick Edward C. 2567 N. Robey
Merrick Frederick L. 4318 Greenwood av.
Merrick George G. Mrs. Oak Park
Merrick George P. Evanston
Merrick Levi C. 3741 Grand boul.
Merrick M. M. Austin
Merrick Zella Miss, 3741 Grand boul.
Merrilies John, Lakeside
Merrilies Oscar L. Lakeside

Merrilies William, Lakeside
Merrill Alba W. 3350 Rhodes av.
   Sum. res. Higgins Lake, Mich.
Merrill Anthony F. 258, 51st
Merrill Benjamin W. 630 N. Clark
Merrill Charles B. 876 W. Adams
Merrill Charles H. 514 W. Adams
Merrill Fred B., M.D. 358 Racine av.
Merrill Fred G. 465 Washington boul.
Merrill Frederick L. 514 W. Adams
Merrill George B. 1122 Washington boul.
Merrill Hattie Miss, Hinsdale
Merrill Henry H. 4148 Berkeley av.
Merrill H. W. Dr. Maywood
Merrill J. C. F. Hinsdale
Merrill M. G. Mrs. 465 Washington boul.
Merrill Nathan F. 1401 Washington boul.
Merrill Orson E. 4148 Berkeley av.
Merrill Stephen M. Rev. 876 W. Adams
Merrill William F. 466 Elm
Merriman Andrews T. Evanston
Merriman Andrews T. jr. Evanston
Merriman C. C. 1910 Surf.
Merriman E. L. Oak Park
Merriman Henry P. Dr. 2239 Michigan av.
Merriman John W. 3753 Prairie av.
Merriman Minnie Miss, Oak Park
Merritt Charles J. 201, 36th
Merritt Charles. T. 3601 Vincennes av.
Merritt Edwin B. 1178 Washington boul.
Merritt Frederick, 401 N. State
Merritt H. B. 487 Fullerton av.
Merritt L. B. Miss, 4826 Greenwood av.
Merritt Wesley, 43d nr. Drexel boul.
Merritt W. H. 4432 Lake av.
Merry Charles E. Forest Hotel (R.P.)
Merryweather George, 202 Goethe
Mersereau William R. Highland Park
Mershon Stephen L. Evanston
Mertens H. E. 1456 Wrightwood av.
Mertens Robert, 7626 Ford av.
Merwin G. S. 35 Woodland Park
Merwin O. H. Evanston
Merwin P. B. Mrs. 621 Washington boul.
Merz August 435 Marshfield av.
Merz Edward G. 646 Lasalle av.
Merz E. E. 433 Marshfield av.
Merz Gottlieb 646 Lasalle av.
Meserole N. W. Virginia hotel
Mesny Phillip DeQ. 4325 Greenwood av.
Messenger Flora Mrs. 221, 29th
Messer Charles, 4040 Ellis av.
Messer E. L. 630 W. Congress
Messer Lucy W. Mrs. 4040 Ellis av.
Messer L. W. 5729 Washington av.
Messersmith George, 1644 Wellington av.
Messing Aaron J. Rev. Dr. 3446 Wabash av.
Messing Herman J. 3446 Wabash av.
Messing Sigmund J. 3446 Wabash av.
Messinger Celestia D. Dr. 435 Washington boul.
Messinger Charles T. 1920 Wellington
Messinger E. D., M.D. 435 Washington
boul.
Messinger W. D. 548 Jackson boul.
Messner Mary Miss, 1686 Barry av.

Metcalf E. S. 6956 Wallace
Metcalf Guido, 6956 Wallace
Metcalf Herbert C. Hotel Windermere
Metcalf John S. Evanston
Metcalf Merton P. 4025 Indiana av.
Metcalf Ralph, 3829 Langley av.
Metcalf Thomas, Hotel Windermere
Metcalfe Arthur R. Oak Park
Metcalfe Walter, 6930 Yale
Methven Benjamin F. 393, 41st
Methven Huston F. 3835 Ellis av.
Methven Samuel L. 3835 Ellis av.
Methven Sarah A. Mrs. 3835 Ellis av.
Methven Walter J. 3835 Ellis av.
Mettler I. V. 4544 Lake av
Mettler John K. LaGrange
Mettler L. Harrison Dr. 4544 Lake av.
Metz F. W. 157 S. Wood
Metz H. J. 3404 Forest av.
Metz Samuel, 328 Park av.
Metzger Celestine Miss, 3444 Indiana av.
Metzger Charles, 5602 Kimbark av.
Metzger George W. 23 Bryan pl.
Metzger Herman, 1222 Seminary pl.
Metzger H. E. 762 W. Adams
Metzger William, 5602 Kimbark av.
Metzger William G. 860 Washington boul.
Metzler Jacob, 601 Lasalle av.
Metzler John J. 1049 N. Halsted
Meurer F. 475 Cleveland av.
Mevelle Charles W. 4019 Vincennes av.
Mevelle Mary C. Mrs. 4019 Vincennes av.
Meyer Alexander, 151 Winchester av.
Meyer Alice Mrs. 4203 Ellis av.
Meyer Amelia Mrs. 3709 Ellis av.
Meyer A. 2009 Prairie av.
Meyer Balthasar I. Dr. 60 Fowler
Meyer Carl, 2009 Prairie av.
Meyer Carl H. 1734 Deming ct.
Meyer Charles E. 8 Fowler
Meyer Christian B. 1812 Barry av.
Meyer C. G. 543 Lasalle av.
Meyer Estella Miss, 3831 Ellis av.
Meyer E. F. 2009 Prairie av.
Meyer Fred, 3624 Grand boul.
Meyer Gust, 1727 Belmont av.
Meyer Herman, 1049 N. Clark
Meyer H. A. 462 Warren av.
Meyer H. L. 219 Belden av.
Meyer H. W. 1734 Deming ct.
Meyer Isaac, 2964 Groveland av.
Meyer Isaac, 3806 Indiana av.
Meyer Jacob, 654 Lasalle av
Meyer John, 460 W. Congress
Meyer John B. 1812 Barry av.
Meyer John M. 3831 Ellis av.
Meyer J. P. 677 Kenmore av.
Meyer J. S. 2703 Wabash av.
Meyer Louis B. 3139 Vernon av.
Meyer L. M. Mrs. 71 Maple
Meyer Martin, 3624 Grand boul.
Meyer Mary C. Miss, 132 Pine
Meyer Meyer, 2712 Wabash av.
Meyer Moses, 392 Dayton
Meyer M. A. 3253 Vernon av.
Meyer M. A. Mrs. 2009 Prairie av.

Meyer Peter, 19 Carl
Meyer Sigmund, 3139 Vernon av.
Meyer W. 42 St. James pl.
Meyering Harry, 260 Superior
Meyering Louis 363 Superior
Meyers H. M. 862 Warren av.
Meyers Leo, 3183 Malden
Meyers L. E. Grand Pacific hotel
Meyers L. H. 3928 Prairie av.
Meyne William, 482 N. Robey
Meyrick Charles W. Evanston
Meysenburg Carr, 141 Astor
Meysenburg Edward A. 187 Rush
Meysenburg Otto W. 141 Astor
Michael B. F. 3139 Indiana av.
Michaels Charles D. 528 Fulton
Michaels Isaac, 3236 Vernon av.
Michaels S. A. Mrs. 528 Fulton
Michaelsen Valdemar, 593 N. Clark
Michaelson George, 4427 Ellis av.
Michelet Charles J. Wilmette
Michelet W. E. Dr. Wilmette
Michelson Albert A. Prof. 125, 51st
    (H.P.)
Michelson Halvor, 62 Fowler
Michener Jas. Hart, L   g   hotel
Michener Wm. W. 4705 Woodlawn av.
Michie James W. 3233 Michigan av.
Mick Frank E. 6618 Wright
Mick J. F. 6361 Wright
Mickel Max, 113 Evergreen av.
Mida Lée, 4226 Grand boul.
Mida Walter, 4226 Grand boul.
Mida William, 4226 Grand boul.
Middagh Floyd, 7640 Bond av.
Middaugh Henry C. Hinsdale
Middendorf George, 6565 Harvard
Middlebrook George S. Grand boul. se.
    cor. 40th
Middleton Allen, 4335 Emerald av.
Middleton Bessie Miss, 3322 Michigan
    av.
Middleton Edward Rev. Austin
Middleton Ella Miss, 345 Ohio
Middleton George, 3322 Michigan av.
    Sum. res. Waukesha, Wis.
Middleton Harvey, Pullman
Middleton John, Highland Park
Middleton J. W. Oak Park
Middleton Merle, 64 Cedar
Middleton Robert H. 4734 Langley av.
Middleton Robert J. 4734 Langley av.
Middleton Thomas, 140, 36th
Midgley John W. 242 Ashland boul.
Midlam Arthur S. 4064 Michigan Terrace
Midler W. Irving, 6501 Oglesby av.
Miehle John jr. 493 Dearborn av.
Miers Hannah Miss, 3333 Wabash av.
Mies John, 332 Cedar, Englewood
Miesse Leon, Dr. 4642 Evans av.
Mifflin Charles A. 240, 53d (H.P.)
Mihills Merrick A. Highland Park
Miksch Aaron J. 940 W. Monroe
Milan Edward, 5405 Wabash av.
Milburn E. L. Irving Park
Milbury Emma Mrs. 3002 Lake Park av.

Milchrist Thomas E. 6 Aldine sq.
Milchrist William A. 6 Aldine sq.
Miles Clara B. Miss, 5129 Jefferson av.
Miles C. L. 882 W. Monroe
Miles E. M. Evanston
Miles Fred. S. 3231 Forest av.
Miles F. B. Mrs. 3231 Forest av.
Miles George S. 305 Irving av.
Miles Herbert D. 3231 Forest av.
Miles Hazen T. 296½ Illinois
Miles Holton F. 5311 Madison av.
Miles James, 1727 Frederick
Miles James H. 3802 Lake av.
Miles Joseph S. 1265 Palmer
Miles J. H. Mrs. 5129 Jefferson av.
Miles Marion Miss, 2339 Michigan av.
Miles Moses T. 1 Madison Park
Miles S. B. 945 W. Monroe
Miles Thomas D. 5129 Jefferson av.
Miles T. H. 4054 Mogan Terrace
Miles William E. 262hCommercial (L.V.)
Miley G. W. 583 W. Congress
Miley L. E. Dr. 789 Warren av.
Milhening Joseph, Evanston
Milholland T. J. 374 Webster av.
Milhous L. C. Mrs. 4418 Prairie av.
Millar Allan P. 289 Ontario
Millar Anna Miss, 2400 Indiana av.   •
Millar Earl B. 289 Ontario
Millar Frank W. 4433 Berkeley av.
Millar John, 22, 46th
Millar John, 27 Surrey ct.
Millar Maury O. Wilmette
Millard Evart L. Highland Park
Millard E. Mrs. Park Ridge
Millard Frank R. 435 Washington boul.
Millard George M. 3719 Vincennes av.
Millard J. L. Granada hotel
Millard Laura M. Mrs. 1153 Lawndale av.
Millard Roxanna Mrs. 3719 Vincennes
     av.
Millard R. C. Mrs. 3641 Ellis av.
Millard S. M. Highland Park
Millard Wallace D. 3641 Ellis av.
Millard William, Highland Park
Millard W. K. Irving Park
Miller Aaron, 743 Garfield boul.
Miller Adam, M.D. 172 Ashland boul.
Miller Adam, 1720 Deming ct.
Miller Albert, 649 Fullerton av.
Miller Amos C. Riverside
Miller A. Mrs. 3348 Rhodes av.
Miller A. C. Prof. Hotel Barry
Miller A. L. 3605 Lake av.
Miller A. P. 6541 Perry av.
Miller A. W. 865 S. Kedzie av.
Miller Benjamin, Evanston
Miller Brice A. 46 Roslyn pl.
Miller B. C. 936 W. Adams
Miller Charles B. 3122 Calumet av.
Miller Charles C. 4510 St. Lawrence av.
Miller Charles F. 591 Cleveland av.
Miller Charles Homer, 3705 Vincennes av.
Miller Charles K. 544 N. State
Miller Charles L. 3609 Ellis av.
Miller Charles L. 3717 Langley av.

Miller Charles P. 24 St. James pl.
Miller Charles P. 2941 Calumet av.
Miller Clara F. Mrs. 4752 Champlain av.
Miller C. Oak Park
Miller C. J. The Ontario
Miller David W. 479 Belden av.
Miller Davis W. 6218 Michigan av.
Miller DeLaskie, M.D. 446 Chestnut
Miller D. A. Oak Park
Miller Edgar M. 6345 Greenwood av.
Miller Edward P. 5751 Rosalie ct.
Miller Elissette Mrs. 3146 Calumet av.
Miller Emanuel D. 1138 Washington
     boul.
Miller Emily Huntington Mrs. Evanston
     Sum. res. Chautauqua, N. Y.
Miller Eva S. Mrs. 2339 Commercial
Miller E. B. Mrs. Oak Park
Miller E. H. 2031 Groveland av.
Miller Frank W. 3960 Langley av.
Miller Franklin A. 4817 Madison av.
Miller Fred, 1720 Deming ct.
Miller Fred L. 1765 Oakdale av.
Miller F. A. Hyde Park hotel.
Miller F. C. Avenue house, Evanston
Miller F. J. 5410 Madison av.
Miller George, 5476 Cornell av.
Miller George, Lexington hotel
Miller George L. Lakota hotel
Miller George L. Hinsdale
Miller George S. 2410 Prairie av.
Miller George S. Hinsdale
Miller George W., M.D. 6634 Honore
Miller G. C. 6352 Drexel av.
Miller Harry A. 3203 Rhodes av.
Miller Harry W. 2409 South Park av.
Miller Henry F. Mrs. 5528 Monroe av.
Miller Henry G. 27 Delaware pl.
Miller Henry L. 3733 Langley av.
Miller Henry T. 637 Fullerton av.
Miller Hugh M. 42 39th
Miller Humphreys H. C. Evanston
Miller Isaac H. 2931 Groveland av.
Miller James, Evanston
Miller James A. Lake Forest
Miller James A. Lake Forest
Miller James C. 444 Belden av.
Miller James C. 4200 Vincennes av.
Miller James H. Winnetka
Miller Jay D. Oak Park
Miller John, 236 Pine
Miller John, 385 Elm
Miller John A. Evanston
Miller John B. River Forest
Miller John G. 22 Bellevue pl.
Miller John G. 2807 Michigan av.
Miller John J. Austin
Miller John P. 10 Lane pl.
Miller John S. 4810 Kenwood av.
Miller Joseph M. 5552 Monroe av.
Miller J. F. Kenilworth
Miller Kuni Mrs. 4620 Evans av.
Miller Lanson D. Austin
Miller Lillie P. Mrs. The Arizona
     Sum. res. Brighton Heights, New
     Brighton, S. I.

Miller Louis K. 3146 Calumet av.
Miller Lucas L. 392 Washington boul.
Miller L. P. Mrs. 5556 Monroe av.
Miller Marcus A. 1438 Cornelia
Miller Maynard, The Ontario
Miller Milton B. 3122 Calumet av.
Miller M. G. Austin
Miller M. J. Mrs. 4627 Lake av.
Miller Nicholas C. 418, 40th
Miller Philip C. 453 Englewood av.
Miller Ralph, Glencoe
Miller Raymond J. 5552 Monroe av.
Miller Robert Mrs. 490 Fullerton av.
Miller Robert B. 11 Groveland Park
Miller Robert B. 3228 Lake Park av.
Miller Rollin W. Evanston
Miller Roswell, 2959 Michigan av.
Miller R. B. Dr. 170 Oakwood boul.
Miller R. C. Miss, Oak Park
Miller R. P. Oak Park
Miller Sidney C. Oak Park
Miller S. F. 237, 29 h
Miller Thomas, 25, 46th (H.P.)
Miller Thomas, Riverside
Miller Thomas E. 569 Lasalle av.
        Sum. res. Burlington, Wis.
Miller Thomas H. 2439 Wabash av.
Miller Thomas H. jr. 2439 Wabash av.
Miller Thomas L. Austin
Miller Truman W., M. D. 1071 N. Clark
Miller T. E. Evanston
Miller Waldo F. 322 Warren av.
Miller Walter E. 4106 Lake av.
Miller Walter H. 551 Englewood av.
Miller William, 1283 Palmer
Miller William C. 3158 Prairie av.
Miller Wm. G. 254 Warren av.
Miller William G. Evanston
Miller William M. 4723 Champlain av.
Miller William T. Oak Park
Miller William W. 3336 Michigan av.
        Sum. res. Petoskey, Mich.
Miller William Yates, 3336 Michigan av.
Miller W. B. 4424 St. Lawrence av.
Miller W. B. Leland hotel
Miller W. D. Granada hotel
Miller W. J. 451 Bowen av.
Millerd Clarence N. Mrs. 3150 Indiana av.
Millerd Norman A. Rev. 1153 Lawndale
    av.
Millet Louis J. 248 Oak
Milligan A. R. Mrs. 2604 Indiana av.
Milligan C. F. Hyde Park hotel
Milligan E. J. 187 Oakwood boul.
Milligan Frank, Oak Park
Milligan George D. 4356 Oakenwald av.
Milligan George E. 2678 N. Paulina
Milligan H. F. Rev. 195, 37th
Milligan J. G. Capt. 2947 Indiana av.
Milligan Patience Mrs. 2768 N. Paulina
Milliken J. D. 3015 Vernon av.
Milliken Walter L. Hotel Windermere
Millington J. W. 710 Jackson boul.
Millis C. D. 1038 N. Clark
Millner W. W. 2107 Michigan av.
Milnamow J. F. Austin

Milloy John, 552 Washington boul.
Mills Abbott L. Chicago Beach hotel
Mills A. J. 6321 Oglesby av.
Mills Charles, 412 Cleveland av.
Mills Daniel W. 1510 Washington boul.
Mills Frederick N. 3152 Vernon av.
Mills F. O. 3907 Prairie av.
Mills Geo. F. 1043 Early av.
Mills George P. 6328 Drexel av.
Mills George P. Evanston
Mills Harry, 4827 Madison av.
        Sum. res. Grand Haven
Mills Henry, 4344 Oakenwald av.
Mills H. K. Hotel Barry
Mills Jennie M. Miss, 3152 Vernon av.
Mills John, 3953 Michigan av.
Mills John N. Rev. Evanston
Mills John R. Evanston
Mills John W. 504 Jackson av.
Mills J. M. 3118 Vernon av.
Mills J. P. Dr. 518 W. Adams
Mills Katherine L. Miss, 3152 Vernon av.
Mills Luther Laflin, Graceland av. cor.
    N. Halsted
Mills Mary Miss, 506 Lasalle av.
Mills Mary E. Mrs. 8 Groveland Park
Mills Mary J. Mrs. Wilmette
Mills M. E. 4344 Oakenwald av.
Mills S. B. 367 Park av.
Mills Walter, 367 Park av.
Mills Walter Thomas Mrs. Oak Park
Mills W. K. 407 Belden av.
Millspaugh Chas. F. Dr. 7352 Bond av.
Milne Frank M. Evanston
Milne George H. 3248 Groveland av.
Milne James H. 3248 Groveland av.
Milner D. E. Mrs. 4349 Oakenwald av.
Milner Ja   T. 507 W. Congress
Milner Louisa Miss, 5465 Washington av.
Milnor Lloyd, 441 Elm
Miloslawsky Wolf, 456 Cleveland av.
Milroy Peter, 453 Irving av.
Milsted T. G. 109 Park av. (L. V.)
Milton Thomas, Riverside
Minard A. J. Hotel Barry
Minard F. H. Hotel Barry
Minchin Thomas, 57 E. Pearson
Minchrod Ada B. Miss, 3210 Wabash av.
Minchrod S. 3210 Wabash av.
Minckler P. E. Dr. 5314 Washington av.
Minden Marcy F. 3635 Vernon av.
Mineah A. Miss, 247 Dearborn av.
        Sum. res. Dryden, N. Y.
Mineah M. A Miss, 247 Dearborn av.
Minehart L. T. 118 Flournoy
Miner E. F. Mrs. 160 Oakwood boul.
Miner Floy H. Miss, 147 Ashland boul.
Miner F. L. 3002 Vernon av.
Miner George B. Riverside
Miner James A. 719 The Plaza
Miner James B., M. D., 3130 Indiana av.
Miner Maud Miss, 160 Oakwood boul.
Minges John H. 14 Bishop ct.
Miniter M. 12 Gilpin pl.
Minkler Ward S. 172 Ashland boul.
Minnemeyer Edward G. 2036 Indiana av.

Minor Anderson, LaGrange
Minor F. E. Dr. 6409 Harvard
Minor Josephine Mrs. 232 Michigan av.
Minot C. 5440 Monroe av.
Minter Wm. P. 4511 Wabash av.
Minton W. L. 1144 Bonney av.
Minzesheimer L. F. 2704 Indiana av.
Misch George A. 1761 Wrightwood av.
Misner E. D. Mrs. Evanston
Mitchel Otto W. 4148 Ellis av.
Mitchell Abraham, 538 Byron
Mitchell Albert J. 6536 Ross av.
Mitchell Anna Belle Miss, Hinsdale
Mitchell A. J. 717 W. Adams
Mitchell A. W. 3142 Lake Park av.
Mitchell A. W. jr. 3142 Lake Park av.
Mitchell A. W. Hinsdale
Mitchell Bertrand H. 4001 Grand boul
Mitchell Charles H. 575 W. Congress
Mitchell Charles H. 6700 Perry av.
Mitchell Charles P. Evanston
Mitchell Clifford, Dr. 5515 Woodlawn av.
Mitchell David C. 3142 Lake Park av.
Mitchell D. D. Lieut. Fort Sheridan
Mitchell D. E. 6210 Princeton av.
      Winter res. Daytona, Fla.
Mitchell D. J. 4001 Grand boul.
Mitchell D. W. 45 Macalister pl.
Mitchell Edward G. Hinsdale
Mitchell Eliza Mrs. Oak Park
Mitchell Frank D. Ellis av. cor 56th
Mitchell Frederick A. 638 Washington
      boul.
Mitchell Frederick R. 6643 Stewart av.
Mitchell F. D. Evanston
Mitchell F. H. LaGrange
Mitchell George H. Hinsdale
Mitchell George R. 5340 Cornell av.
Mitchell Grant, Hinsdale
Mitchell Guy H. 2004 Calumet av.
Mitchell Harley B. LaGrange
Mitchell Henry H. 3524 Wabash av.
Mitchell Herbert S. LaGrange
Mitchell Jennie Mrs. 4427 Champlain av.
Mitchell John D. 4001 Grand boul.
Mitchell John J. 5012 Woodlawn av.
Mitchell John S. 509 W. Adams
Mitchell John T. 330 Lasalle av.
Mitchell Jonathan C. 3838 Lake av.
Mitchell J. Sidney Dr. 2954 Prairie av.
      Sum. res. Nantucket, Mass.
Mitchell Lewis H. 163 S. Robey
Mitchell Lucien C. 3020 Indiana av.
Mitchell L. A. 3402 Indiana av.
Mitchell L. B. 50 Astor
Mitchell Malcom C. 3157 Calumet av.
Mitchell Mary Mrs. 4553 Ellis av.
Mitchell Morris, 3524 Wabash av.
Mitchell Nancy D. Miss, 3020 Indiana av.
Mitchell Nancy J. Mrs. 247 Winchester av.
Mitchell N. Adelaide Miss, Hinsdale
Mitchell R. 695 Jackson boul.
Mitchell Thomas H. 6454 Lexington av.
Mitchell Walter B. 2007 Indiana av.
Mitchell William, 1199 Wilton av.
Mitchell William A. R. 714 Pullman bldg.

Mitchell William H. 2004 Calumet av.
Mitchell William H. 5941 Princeton av.
Mitchell Wm. K. 6642 Yale
Mitchell Zaidee Miss, 56 The Yale
Mitton Alice Miss, 563 Division
Mix Ira J. 3251 Indiana av.
Mix James, 1718 Indiana av.
Mix James T. 1718 Indiana av.
Mix Mary Mrs. Hinsdale
Mix M. W. 2210 Prairie av.
Mixer N. M. Berwyn
Mize Eliza Mrs. 907 Evanston av.
Mize William J. 267 Chestnut
Moak Will B. 6924 Stewart av.
Moberly E. E. 191, 30th
Moderwell Erastus C. Hampden flats
Moderwell Louisa F. Miss, Hampden flats
Moderwell Mary W. Miss, Hampden flats
Modica Frank B. 1440 Cornelia
Modin J. A. 1554 Aldine
Modjeski Ralph, 1117 N. Clark
Moe Bernt, 48 Scott
Moeckel Aug. 456 Dayton
Moeller C. C. 402 Lasalle av.
Moeller E. C. River Forest
Moerdyke Peter Rev. 446 Marshfield av.
Moerecke Frederick, 485 Fullerton av.
Moerecke Otto C. 485 Fullerton av.
Moerecke William, 485 Fullerton av.
Moffat Albert, 464 W. Adams
Moffat Edward R. 37 Surrey ct.
Moffat F. S. Morgan Park
Moffatt Annie Mrs. 3521 Wabash av.
Moffett A. S. Mrs. The Arizona
Moffett J. A. 29 Woodland Park
Moffett Samuel A. 73 Park av.
Moffett Walter H. 73 Park av.
Moffett William B. 73 Park av.
Moffitt R. H. Dr. 601 Garfield boul
Mogg Clayton W. 539 S. Normal Parkway
Mogg J. J. 539 S. Normal Parkway
Mogg Millard E. 539 S. Normal Parkway
Mogg M, F. 4358 Berkeley av.
Mohler John A. The Renfost
Mohr Carl M. 21 Linden pl.
Mohr John, 707 N. Robey
Mohr Joseph, 707 N. Robey
Moles F. R. 58 Evergreen av.
Molinelli A. Evanston
Moll Carl, 1427 Washington boul.
Moll Edward, 336 Lasalle av.
Moll J. B. 501 Fullerton av.
Mollan Arabella Mrs. 403 S. Oakley av.
Mollan Charles G. 403 S. Oakley av.
Mollan John F. 403 S. Oakley av.
Molloy E. J. 990 Warren av.
Monaghan J. J. 1817 Aldine av.
Monahan Charles P. 292 Huron
Monahan John J. 507, 79th, Eng.
Monahan Joseph J. 551 Dearborn av.
Monahan T. J. Hotel Metropole
Monash C. P. 3846 Prairie av.
Moncur George A. LaGrange
Mondou Paul, Highland Park
Mondschein Charles A. 559, 65th, Eng.
Mondschein Wm. F. 559, 65th, Eng.

Mondschein William H. 559, 65th, Eng.
Monett Elliot T. 378 Dearborn av.
Money W. R. 286, 42d (H.P.)
Monfort Catherine M. Mrs. 230, 65th, Eng.
Monheimer Isa, 3305 Calumet av.
Monheimer Levi, 1709 Michigan av.
Monheimer L. Mrs. 3252 Wabash av.
Monheimer Milton L. 3252 Wabash av .
Monin Lewis C. Dr. 4206 Michigan av.
Monk John S. Irving Park
Monrad J. H. Winnetka
Monroe B. F. 3962 Langley av.
Monroe C. W. 148 Dearborn av.
Monroe Emiline Mrs. 7120 Eggleston av.
Monroe George G. Dr. 712, 69th (H.P.)
Monroe Harriet S. Miss, 484 Dearborn av.
Monroe Henry S. 484 Dearborn av.
·Monroe J. Allen jr. 4442 Emerald av.
Monroe J. A. 4442 Emerald av.
Monroe Lucy B. Miss, 484 Dearborn av.
Monroe M. A. Mrs. 326 Marshfield av.
Monroe William. Auditorium hotel
Monroe William F. 326 Marshfield av.
Monroe William S. 484 Dearborn av.
Monroe Wilmer D. 7120 Eggleston av.
Montague Gilbert, 3346 Prairie av.
Montfort M. J. Mrs. 933 W. Monroe
Montfort William, 933 W. Monroe
Montgomery B. Miss, 8 Pelham flats
Montgomery Charles P. 3424 Vernon av.
Montgomery E. H. Mrs. 3142 Groveland av.
Montgomery Frederick D. 497 Dearborn av.
Montgomery F. M. Riverside
Montgomery George F. 4421 Ellis av.
Montgomery George W. Chicago club
Montgomery Hugh W. 424 Elm
Montgomery H. M. S. 4729 Woodlawn av.
Montgomery John R. 407 N. State
Montgomery J. A. Rev. LaGrange
Montgomery L. H. Dr. 6 Washington pl.
Montgomery M. V. 1317 Wolcott
Montgomery Palmer A. Highland Park
Montgomery Thomas, 3200 Indiana av.
Montgomery W. A. 407 N. State
Montgomery W. A. D. Dr. 180 N. State
Montgomery W. T. Dr. 567 W. Congress
Montrose J. W. Dr. 36th ne. cor. Cottage Grove av.
Mooar J. C. River Forest
Moody C. H. 229 Loomis
Moody Frank A. 777 Washington boul.
Moody John A. 4404 Champlain av.
Moody J. Byron, La Grange
Moody Mollie E. Miss, 777 Washington boul.
Moody M. T. Hotel Barry
Moody Samuel B. LaGrange
Moody Susan I. Miss, 4404 Champlain av.
Moody Thomas P. 3031 Michigan av.
Moody William, Oak Park
Moody W. J. Mrs. 157 Aberdeen
Moog David, 3738 Wabash av.
Moone W. D. 211, 28th
Mooney S. H. 248 Warren av.

Mooney W. H. 6059 Oglesby av.
Moore Abram J. Dr. 754 Fullerton av.
Moore Alexander P. 8 Aldine sq.
Moore Arthur G. Austin
Moore A. S. 2458 Wabash av.
Moore Birney J. Evanston
Moore Carey F. Rev. Hinsdale
Moore Carlton W. Evanston
Moore Charles B. 1322 Jackson boul.
Moore Clarence E. 8 Aldine sq.
Moore Charles M. 5723 Ingleside av.
Moore C. B. 3000 Michigan av.
Moore C. H. 340 Chestnut, Eng.
Moore C. J. 6635 Yale
Moore C. W. 5506 Monroe av.
Moore Daniel G., M.D. 643 N. Hoyne av.
Moore David, 6733 Lafayette av.
Moore D. F. Oak Park
Moore Edward, 255 Ontario
Moore Edward, 472 Kenwood Terrace
Moore Edward A. 3412 Calumet av.
Moore Edward F. 3412 Calumet av.
Moore Edwin White, 27 Delaware pl.
Moore E. 148 N. State
Moore E. B. Austin
Moore Frank A. B. 486 Kenmore av.
Moore Fred W. 5317 Washington av.
Moore F. 3706 Lake av.
Moore F. F. 6652 Harvard
Moore George B. 3350 Wabash av.
Moore George H. Evanston
Moore George N. Longwood
Moore Gurdon G. Virginia hotel
Moore Hattie B. Miss, 472 Kenwood Terrace
Moore H. E. Wilmette
Moore James, 4503 Indiana av.
Moore James, Evanston
Moore James H. 190 Warren av.
Moore James H. 5319 Washington av.
Moore James J. 408 Chestnut
Moore James S. Riverside
Moore Jennie A. Miss, 3639 Grand boul.
Moore Jesse C. Evanston
Moore John, 6510 Yale
Moore John W. 3905 Vincennes av.
Moore Joseph L. Morton Park
Moore Josiah, Lake Forest
Moore Julia A. Mrs. Evanston
Moore Julia A. Mrs. 817 S. Lawndale av.
Moore Julian C. 720 W. Adams
Moore J. F. 390 S. Oakley av.
Moore J. Gillespie, 88, 25th
Moore J. Hobart Judge, Lakota hotel
Moore Lawrence C. 6071 Edgerton av.
Moore Lewis T. 4403 Lake av.
Moore Logan F. 441, 57th (H.P.)   •
Moore Lindley M. Dr. 337, 42d
Moore Malcomb T. Dr. Jefferson Park
Moore Mary Mrs. 6418 Myrtle av.
Moore Mary J. Miss, 3650 Vincennes av.
Moore Mead, 284 Ashland boul.
Moore M. C. Mrs. 339, 33d
Moore M. H. Mrs. 710 W. Adams
Moore N. G. Oak Park
Moore Orin, Evanston

Moore Robert C. 4405 Lake av.
Moore Samuel R. 3257 Groveland av.
Moore Sarah B. Mrs. 314 Belden av.
Moore Sarah F. Mrs. Hinsdale
Moore Sophia E. Mrs. 3650 Vincennes av.
Moore Stewart, 7525 Eggleston av.
Moore S. D. Mrs. 340 Chestnut, Englewood
Moore S. E. 207, 28th
Moore S. H. 6801 Perry av.
Moore S. M. 4733 Woodlawn av.
Moore Thomas, 346 Sunnyside av.
Moore Thomas, Sheridan club
Moore Will H. 5132 Washington av.
Moore William A. Morton Park
Moore William ... 817 S. Lawndale av.
Moore William H. 2922 Michigan av.
Moore William H. 4419 Champlain av.
Moore William J. 5400 Ellis av.
Moore Wyllys, M.D. Hampden flats
Moore W. A. Morton Park
Moore W. Blanchard, 4247 Calumet av.
Moore W. L. 1837 Michigan av.
Moore W. O. H. 871 Warren av. ·
Mooreland Frederick S. 3012 Michigan av.
Moorhouse William H. 3741 Grand boul.
        Sum. res. Oconomowoc, Wis.
Moorhouse William R. 3741 Grand boul.
Moos J. B. 1814 Oakdale av.
Mora A. R. Park Ridg
Moran Hugh P. 263, 30th
Moran K. Mrs. 4233 Calumet av.
Moran J. P. 4320 Forrestville av.
Moran R. H. 337 Marshfield av.
Moran T. A. Judge, 4710 Vincennes av.
Morava John, 4449 Langley av.
Morava W. 5621 Monroe av.
Morden William J. 1508 Michigan av.
More Clair E. 453 Washington boul.
More R. Wilson, 652 W. Adams
More S. Miss, 652 W. Adams
Morehead E. L. Dr. 422 Ashland boul.
Morehouse Clifton J. 359' 65th, Eng.
        Sum. res. Sharon, N. Y.
Morehouse George C. 4719 Kenwood av.
Morehouse Louis P. 4719 Kenwood av.
Morey Arthur G. 1740 Diversey av.
Morey A. E. Oak Park
Morey Charles J. 1740 Diversey
Morey Henry C. Mrs. 542 Jackson boul.
Morey John, 76, 50th (H.P.)
Morey Lindley A. 1058 Washington boul.
Morey R. E. Mrs. 73, 30th
Morford Arthur, Riverside
Morford Thomas T. Riverside
Morgan Annie Miss, 3834 Lake av.
Morgan Arthur, Evanston
Morgan B. E. Mrs. 58 Park av.
Morgan Charles Dr. 4024 Michigan Terrace
Morgan C. 6956 Webster av. Englewood
Morgan C. A. 1921 Indiana av.
Morgan C. K. 482, 42d pl.
Morgan C. P. Mrs. 3506 Lake av.
Morgan E. Mrs. 58 Park av.
Morgan F. T. 51 N. Sheldon
Morgan F. W. 1093 Washington boul.

Morgan George C. jr. LaGrange
Morgan George T. 4306 Calumet av.
Morgan G. Cadogan, 389 W. Adams
Morgan G. C. 482, 42d pl.
Morgan G. F. 338 Bowen av.
Morgan Harry Mrs. Hyde Park hotel
Morgan Henry I. 635 W. Adams
Morgan H. A. 6565 Yale
Morgan H. H. Oak Park
Morgan H. S. 44 Sidney ct.
Morgan Isabel Mrs. 3316 Indiana av.
Morgan James, 5200 East End av.
Morgan John A. 636 Englewood av.
Morgan John R. 4024 Michigan Terrace
Morgan J. U. 5607 Madison av.
Morgan Kendrick E. 1808 Frederick
Morgan Mae Miss, 1918 Barry av.
Morgan Marie J. Mrs. 494 Fullerton av.
Morgan M. J. Mrs. 3834 Lake av.
Morgan N. G. Mrs. 361 Washington boul.
Morgan N. H. 310, 30th
Morgan Otho H. Capt. Highland Park
Morgan T. Herbert, 2595 N. Ashland av.
Morgan William, 5313 Madison av.
Morgan William A. Lake Forest
Morgan William H., M.D. 34, 29th
Morgan William P. 3131 Indiana av.
        Sum. res. Highland Park
Morgan W. H., M.D. 454 Jackson boul.
Morgan W. T. The Ontario
Morganroth N. 382 Oakwood boul.
Morgenthau George L. Dr. 3327 Calumet av.
Morgenthau J. C. 3009 Groveland av.
Morgenthau Lewis, 3327 Calumet av.
Morgenthau Max, 599 Dearborn av.
Morganthau Mengo, 3412 Wabash av.
Morgenthau Milton, 3327 Calumet av.
Morgenthau Maximilian, 599 Dearborn av.
Morgenthau Selma Miss, 3327 Calumet av.
Morgenthau Sidney, 3327 Calumet av.
Morice Frank H. 4153 Langley av.
Moring G. Race, 244, 57th (H.P.)
Moring Walter F. Mrs. 244, 57th (H.P.)
Morison G. S. 51 Delaware pl.
Morley Alverson E. 3257 Indiana av.
Morley Annie Mrs. Oak Park
Morley F. C. 1227 W. Adams
Morley J. H. Oak Park
Morley Robert L. 869 Winthrop av.
Morley Thomas, Oak Park
Morley William R. Wilmette
Morper J. C. 395 Evanston av.
Morper Lawrence J. 395 Evanston av.
Morper Nicholas, Evanston
Morrell E. C. Mrs. Oak Park
Morrell E. E. Oak Park
Morrell George R. Oak Park
Morrell John, Evanston
Morrill Allan A. 5209 Kimbark av.
Morrill Charles E. 275, 53d (H.P.)
Morrill C. A. 404 Belden av.
Morrill DeWitt C. 1457 N. Clark
Morrill Donald L. 1809 Frederick
Morrill Fred P. Newberry hotel

Morrill Frederick K. 2907 Groveland av.
Morrill John W. Austin
Morrill Wesley, 2907 Groveland av.
Morrill William M. 387 Oakwood boul.
Morris Albert D. 635 Fullerton av.
Morris Charles, 4416 Oakenwald av.
Morris Charles E. Evanston
Morris C. W. Berwyn
Morris D. I. 703 North Park av.
Morris Edward, Lakota hotel
Morris Ernest A. 3183 Malden
Morris Frank M. 568, 43d (H.P.)
Morris Frederick T. 2486 N. Paulina
Morris Henrietta K. Dr. 14 Loomis
Morris Henry, 3756 Indiana av.
Morris Herbert N. 2453 Indiana av.
Morris H. I. 270 Belden av.
Morris Ira, 2453 Indiana av.
Morris James C. 14 Loomis
Morris John, Evanston
Morris John, Lexington hotel
Morris John S. Hotel Groveland
Morris Joseph O. 383 Superior
Morris J. L. Dr. 14 Loomis
Morris Louis, 3756 Indiana av.
Morris L. A. Mrs. 65 Warren av.
Morris Miles H. 1157 N. Clark
Morris M. E. Mrs. 957 Park av.
Morris Nelson, 2453 Indiana av.
Morris Orville M. Hinsdale
Morris Thomas G. Oak Park
Morris T. G. jr. Oak Park
Morris William D. 1157 N. Clark
Morris W.George, 1356 Washington boul.
Morrison Annie L.Miss,4740 Kimbark av.
Morrison Arthur J. 3987 Drexel boul.
Morrison A. D. 7142 Harvard
Morrison Belle Miss, 147 Ashland boul.
Morrison Charles E. 4024 Ellis av.
Morrison David, Highland Park
Morrison Ernest W. 26 Delaware pl.
Morrison Ezekiel, 4024 Ellis av.d
Morrison Franc C. Miss, 472, 42
Morrison Fred H. 147 Ashland boul.
Morrison F. H. 922 W. Adams
Morrison George S. 49 Delaware pl.
Morrison G. H. Mrs. Winnetka
Morrison H. E. Mrs. Chicago Beach hotel
Morrison H. W. Mrs. Winnetka
Morrison John C. 299, 53d (H.P.)
Morrison John W. 3950 Prairie av.
Morrison J. D. 206 Seminary av.
Morrison J. E. Mrs. 157, 42d
Morrison J. H. Oak Park
Morrison J. J. 455 Marshfield av.
Morrison J. P. Dr. 4437 Ellis av.
Morrison Kate Miss, 147 Ashland boul.
Morrison M. Eugene, 350 Burling
Morrison Richard W. 455 Marshfield av.
Morrison R. C. 338 Oakwood av.
Morrison Theo.N. Rev. 260 Ashland boul.
Morrison Wm. M. 3548 Vernon av.
Morrison W. R. 508 Fullerton av.
Morrow Arthur W. Dr. 713 Washington
  boul.
Morrow Charles B. 713 Washington boul.

Morrow Charles W. Dr. 721, 63d (H.P.)
Morrow J. R. 271 Oakwood boul.
Morrow Louis R. 1722 York pl.
Morrow Mary Mrs. 640 Cleveland av.
Morrow Robert, 1722 York pl.
Morrow Robert J. 640 Cleveland av.
Morrow William H. 214, 31st
Morse A. L. Mrs. 4532 Lake av.
Morse Bert 595 Dearborn av.
Morse B. F. 386 Warren av.
Morse Charles H. 284, 48th
Morse Charles J. Evanston
Morse Charles L. Evanston
Morse Chauncey D. 4231 St. Lawrence av.
Morse Clarence T. 4812 Kimbark av.
Morse C. E. Rev. 657 S. Ashland av.
Morse C. H. 3761 Lake av.
Morse C. T. Chicago Beach hotel
Morse Eliza R. Dr. 4353 Berkeley av.
Morse Elizabeth W. Mrs. 586 Division
Morse Ella V. Mrs. Evanston
Morse Elmira Miss, Evanston
Morse E. S. Mrs. Evanston
Morse Francis E. 3659 Grand boul.
Morse Francis G. 2119 Michigan av.
Morse Gertrude Miss, 657 S. Ashland av.
Morse H. A. Hyde Park hotel
Morse Irving, Evanston
Morse John H. Evanston
Morse John W. 3840 Vincennes av.
Morse Joseph L. Evanston
Morse J. C. 297 Ontario
Morse J. F. 3659 Grand boul.
Morse Ransom J. 595 Dearborn av.
Morse Sarah C. Mrs. Evanston
Morse William R. 543 W. Monroe
Morse W. D. 595 Dearborn av.
Mortenson Alfred, 290 Lasalle av.
Mortimer Albert E. 282 S. Leavitt
Mortimer Chas. J. 1271 Washington boul.
Mortimer Frank G.1261 Washington boul.
Mortimer William E. 1261 Washington
  boul.
Mortimer William H. 556 Jackson boul.
Morton Augusta Miss, 85, 33d
Morton C. C. 4450 Oakenwald av.
Morton C. M. Oak Park
Morton Evan J. Mayfair
Morton E. C. 2007 Michigan av.
Morton F. B. Mrs. 2968 Indiana av.
Morton George, Riverside
Morton George C. Mrs. 1800 Michigan av.
Morton H. E. Mrs. 646 W. Monroe
Morton James B. F. 501 Jackson av.
Morton James F. 501 Jackson av.
Morton James W. 7519 Goldsmith av.
Morton Jay, 4347 Ellis av.
Morton Joy, 15 Groveland Park
Morton Mandred A. 2968 Indiana av.
Morton Mark, 3635 Ellis av.
Morton Oliver T. 150 Pine
Morton O. P. Mrs. 144 Pine
Morton Paul, 47, 49th
Mosby Ethel Miss, 42, 35th
Mosby William, 42, 35th
Moseback William, 2333 Michigan av.

Moseley Alexander W. Evanston
Moseley Bryant, 3659 Indiana av.
Moseley Carleton, 6149 Sheridan av.
Moseley George D. Evanston
Moseley M. Drue Miss, Lakeside
Mosely George H. 4833 Langley av.
Moseley George VanHorn, Evanston
Mosely Thomas C. 4833 Langley av.
Moser G. W. Oak Park
Moses Adolph, 3325 South Park av.
Moses Albert 3732 Langley av.
Moses Charles A. LaGrange
Miss Emma Miss, Evanston
Moses Evan, Evanston
Moses I. S. Dr. 58 Bryant av.
Moses Joseph W. 3325 South Park av.
Moses M. R. 4156 Calumet av.
Moses Saul, 736 N. Hoyne av.
Moses T. G. Oak Park
Mosher Belle Miss, 276 Warren av.
Mosher C. D. 6455 Wharton av.
Mosher E. H. 226, 74th (H.P.)
MosherLouise Miss, 327 Bowen av.
Mosher W. H. 276 Warren av.
Mosier Alison E. 4545 St. Lawrence av.
Mosley Charles E. 694 The Plaza
Moss Earl C. 314 Lasalle av.
Moss Edith Helen Miss, 4700 Greenwood
av.
Moss E. S. 6210 Princeton av.
Moss Jesse L. Lake Forest
Moss Jessie S. Mrs. 4619 Ellis av.
Moss Leopold, 69, 22d
Moss Lester. Austin
Moss L. A. 6829 Anthony av.
Moss Milton, 4619 Ellis av.
Moss M. F. 3735 Prairie av.
Moss M. S. Mrs. 6210 Princeton av.
Moss Robert E. Mrs. 314 Lasalle av.
Moss S. J. 330, 41st
Moss Wm. Lathrop, 4700 Greenwood av.
Mosser Joseph F. 6734 Union av.
Mossler Aaron, 751 North Park av.
Mossler G. Miss, 3226 Prairie av.
Mossler S. 3226 Prairie av.
Mostyn E. J. Mrs. 5415 Cottage Grove av.
MothyM. J., M. D. 3438 Indiana av.
Moth Richard S. Winnetka
Mothershead A. M. 536 Orchard
Motlong F. A. Miss, Austin
Mott Abbie Mrs. 638 Washington boul.
Mott E. H. Mrs. 2421 Indiana av.
Mott Harcourt, Evanston.
Mott John M. 1832 Oakdale av.
Mott John R. Oak Park
Mott Merritt H. Evanston.
Mott Robins S. N. Clark cor. Thome av.
Mouat A. J. 221 Fremont
Mouat Elizabeth Mrs. 1027 Warren av.
Mouat Lawrence, 4313 Maple av.
Moulding Sarah Mrs. 957 N. Clark
Moulding Thomas C. 957 N. Clark
Moulton C. L. 5527 Monroe av.
Moulton D. A. 1907 Deming ct.
Moulton E. R. Prof. Hotel Windermere
Moulton F. I. 5228 Jefferson av.

Moulton George M. 2119 Calumet av.
Moulton John B. 322, 60th, Englewood
Moulton Joseph T. 1 Groveland Park
Moulton J. W. 521 The Plaza
Moulton Richard G. Prof. 56th cor. Cor-
nell av.
Moulton William A. 5 Aldine sq.
Moulton William C. 465 Dearborn av.
Mountain John, 409 Huron
Mouns A. jr. 1081 Warren av.
Mowatt James, 4812 Vincennes av.
Mowbray George W. 3713 Ellis av.
Mowen S. J. 4246 Drexel boul.
Mowray H. C. Granada hotel
Moxley P. A. 15 Seeley av.
Moxley W. J. 445 W. Congress
Moyer Charles D. 253 Ohio
Moyer Herbert P. 541 Jackson boul.
Moyer H. Clayton, 541 Jackson boul.
Moyer H. F. 318, 45th
Moyer H. N. Dr. 434 W. Adams
Moyer Levi N. Wilmette
Moyer M. N. 541 Jackson boul.
Moyer William L. 5 Madison Park
Moyer W. 434 W. Adams
Moyer W. J. 434 W. Adams.
Moylan Mary E. Mrs. 4201 St. Law-
rence av.
Muchmore John F. 888 Winthrop av.
Mudd Frank X. Austin
Mudge Daniel A. Evanston
Mudie R. A. Oak Park
Muehlbauer A. 579 N. Clark
Muehleisen Robert, 5349 Michigan av.
Muehlke Charles V. 948 Pratt av.
Muehlmann C. G. 3815 Rhodes av.
Mueller A. O. 4412 Ellis av.
Mueller Carl, 1047 N. Halsted
Mueller Charles, 1635 N. Halsted
Mueller C. E. R. 262 Ohio
Mueller Emma Mrs. 833 N. Clark
Mueller Fred C. 70 Ewing pl.
Mueller Herman, 73 Ewing pl.
Mueller Herman, 221 Waubun av.
Mueller Hermann, 621 Cleveland av.
Mueller H. 778 Sedgwick
Mueller Ida Mrs. Ridgeland
Mueller J H. 240 Winchester av.
Mueller Matthias, 1218 Seminary pl.
Mueller Oscar, 485 Belden av.
Mueller Oscar F. 778 Sedgwick
Mueller William, 3118 Calumet av.
Mueller William jr. 2322 Indiana av.
Muench Fred, 461 Lasalle av.
Muench Louis, 12 Belden pl.
Mugridge D. J. 3802 Lake av.
Mugridge Harry, 42, 39th
Muhlke Catharine Mrs. 307 N. State
Muhlke George F. 307 N. State
Muhlke H. C. 297 N. State
Muhlke Joseph H. 299 N. State
Muir F. D. Chicago Beach hotel
Muir George W. Evanston
Muir James B. 844 W. Adams
Muir John T. Maywood
Muir Robert B. Austin

Muir S. 4044 Prairie av.
Muirhead Geo. 6331 Wentworth av.
Mulcahy Frank J. Hotel Normandie
Muldoon J. J. Dr. 277 Superior
Muletz S. A. Miss, Pullman
Mulfinger J. L., M.D. 936 Jackson boul.
Mulford Edward A. 30 Aldine sq.
Mulford Leonard S. 661 Pine Grove av.
Mulford Mary L. Mrs. Evanston
Mulford Suzanne Miss, Evanston
Mullaly John E. 353 Marshfield av.
Mullaney M. 353 Ashland boul.
Mullaney T. F. 353 Ashland boul.
Mullen Dora Miss, 377 Dearborn av.
Mullen Frederick 4446 Greenwood av.
Mullen James, 4446 Greenwood av.
Mullen John 377 Dearborn av.
Mullen R. G. 4142 Berkeley av.
Mullen T. F. 377 Dearborn av.
Mullen William H. 377 Dearborn av.
Mullen William J. 6534 Oglesby av.
Mullendore A. Mrs. 6818 St. Lawrence av.
Muller Charles G. 1860 Surf
Muller J. Dr. 362 N. Wells
Muller Louis, Hinsdale
Mullholland Miss, Virginia hotel
Mullien A. W. 36th, ne. cor. Ellis av.
Mulligan Allie Miss, 190 Pine
Mulligan Marian A. Mrs. 190 Pine
Mulliken Alfred Henry, 19 Lake Shore Drive
Mulliken Charles H. Virginia hotel
Mullin Ambrose P. Austin
Mullin Jennie Mrs. 485 Lasalle av.
Mullin John, 1220 Washington boul.
Mullmann Paul, Evanston
Mulvane Elizabeth Miss,4022 Grand boul.
Mulvane P. I. Dr. 4022 Grand boul.
Mulvey Arthur B. 5130 Cornell av.
Mulvey Junius Mrs. 5130 Cornell av.
Mumford Wm. R. 293 Walnut
Mumford W. O. 6617 Yale
Muncey Frederick A. 15 St. Johns pl.
Munch H. C. 4328 Langley av.
Munday John W. 6534 Yale
Mundie James B. 27 Gordon Terrace
Mundie William B. 27 Gordon Terrace
Mundy Norris H. Riverside
Mundy Norris W. Riverside
Munford L. G. 1501 Michigan av.
Munger Albert A. 308 Ohio
Munger A. Page, 195 Oakwood boul.
Munger Charles L. 3915 Langley av.
Munger D. S. 86 Loomis
Munger Edwin A. 3307 Rhodes av.
Munger Frank S. 195 Oakwood boul.
Munger Harriet E. Mrs. 248 Oakwood boul.
Munger Henry H. 2818 Calumet av.
Munger H. B. 248 Oakwood boul.
Munger Kittie Mrs. 34 College pl.
Munger L. A. Mrs. 195 Oakwood boul.
Munger Mary E. Mrs. 4213 Ellis av.
Munger O. L. 5412 Washington av.
Munger Pliny F. 5212 Lexington av.
Munger Rollin H. 889 Jackson boul.

Munhall W. D. Auditorium annex
Munn Daniel W, LaGrange
Munn Noel S. 2223 Calumet av.
Munro C. P. 244 Grand av.
Munro Elizabeth C. Miss, 218, 37th
Munro William, Auditorium annex
Munroe Daniel, 725 W. Monroe
Munroe Frank L. River Forest
Munroe Walter H. 821 Jackson boul.
Munsell F. B. 224, 42d
Munsell Gurden Mrs. Evanston
Munsell W. W. Evanston
Munson Charles Mrs. 1276 Washington boul.
Munson Charles A. Victoria hotel
Munson Charles W. 1276 Washington boul.
Munson Frank W. 107, 75th (H.P.)
Munson Fred A. 2388 N. Paulina
Munson Frederick W. 458 Fulton
Munson F. 107, 75th (H.P.)
Murch Charlotte Miss, 14 Bryant av.
Murdoch Jane Miss, 2130 Prairie av.
Murdoch Thos. 2130 Prairie av.
Murdock E. B. Dr. 752 W. Adams
Murdock William H. 4122 Vincennes av.
Murdow Arthur H. Dr. Glencoe
Murdow Edward, Glencoe
Murdow Thomas H. Glencoe
Murison A. Mrs. 1612 Indiana av.
Murison A. J. 7408 Webster av. Eng.
Murison Charles E. 2028 Indiana av.
Murison George W. 1612 Indiana av.
Murphey B. F. Mrs. 2911 Prairie av.
Murphey F. E. 2911 Prairie av.
Murphey J. A. jr. LaGrange
Murphey L. E. 732 N. Wells
Murphy Austin J. 1181 Washington boul.
Murphy A. J. 472 W. Congress
Murphy C. 873 Larrabee
Murphy D. 450 Lasalle av.
Murphy D. J. 2666 N. Paulina
Murphy D. P. Mrs. 1067 Washington boul.
Murphy Edward J. 3744 Wabash av.
Murphy Edward J. 1020 W. Adams
Murphy E. C. 4728 Langley av.
Murphy Francis, 1020 W. Adams
Murphy Francis T. 3707 Prairie av.
Murphy F. H. Mrs. Hotel Metropole
Murphy Hiram P. 1181 Washington boul.
Murphy H. T. Dr. 2304 Cottage Grove av.
Murphy James D. 1067 Washington boul.
Murphy James K. 2502 Michigan av.
Murphy James S. 535, 44th
Murphy Jeremiah, 235 Loomis
Murphy John A. 5430 Washington av.
Murphy John B. 4359 St. Lawrence av.
Murphy John C. Evanston
Murphy John D. 745 Warren av.
Murphy John E. 535 E. 44th
Murphy John H. 1191 Wilton av.
Murphy John P. 3744 Wabash av.
Murphy Joseph A. Judge, Lakota hotel
Murphy Joseph G. 1067 Washington boul.
Murphy J. B., M.D. 44 Throop
          Sum. res. Leland, Ill.

Murphy Michael W. 2964 Prairie av.
Murphy P. M. 6316 Drexel av.
Murphy Richard J. 4615 Vincennes av.
Murphy Thomas, 3744 Wabash av.
Murphy Thomas J. 3744 Wabash av.
Murray Alexander, 711 Fulton
Murray Allen F. 326 Oakwood boul.
Murray A. Gordon, LaGrange
Murray Charles, 205, 47th
Murray Charles R. 713, 60th, Eng.
Murray Clara Mrs. 276 Michigan av.
Murray C. C. Austin
Murray C. H. 25 St. James pl.
Murray Donald Mrs. 460 Elm
Murray Donald, LaGrange
Murray D. L. The Arizona
Murray Edward P. 3517 Indiana av.
Murray Ella Mrs. 3728 Langley av.
Murray E. B. 386 Oakwood boul.
Murray E. D. Hotel Barry
Murray E. D. jr. 386 Oakwood boul.
Murray Fanny Mrs. Ridgeland
Murray Frank G. Austin
Murray George R. Austin
Murray Harold G. Austin
Murray George W. Tracy
Murray Harry W. 3170 Malden
Murray Henry T. 2432 Prairie av.
Murray James S. Evanston
Murray Jean Miss, 205, 47th
Murray Jennie Miss, 386 Oakwood boul.
Murray John, 450 Jackson boul.
Murray John J. 285 Park av.
Murray John S. 4469 Oakenwald av.
Murray Joseph R. 503 W. Congress
Murray J. F. 62 Park av.
Murray Leverett W. Mrs. Riverside
Murray Martha Miss, 412 Oak
Murray Mary Mrs. 503 W. Congress
Murray M. Frank, Austin
Murray O. E. Rev. 350 Chestnut, Eng.
Murray P. J. 6559 Sherman
Murray Thomas H. 5761 Washington av.
Murray Thomas P. 40 Bryant av.
Murray Thomas W. B. Hinsdale
Murray William, 4629 Champlain av.
Murray W. H. Evanston
Murrell George A. Hinsdale
Musgrave Albert F. 435 Washington boul.
Musgrave Harrison, 3004 Prairie av.
Musgrave Mae Miss, 3004 Prairie av.
Musgrave M. S. Mrs. 3004 Prairie av.
Musick J. T. Dr. 762, 63d ct. Englewood
Musselwhite J. 3519 Vernon av.
        Sum. res. Coldwater, Mich.
Mussenden James A. 4205 St. Lawrence
    av.
Mussey Charles E. Mrs. 13 Chalmers pl.
Musson Charles S. Wilmette
Muther Laurence, Oak Park
Myer Alida L. Miss, Evanston
Myer Benjamin, 3842 Prairie av.
Myer Fred, 3345 Prairie av.
Myer Henry, 3419 Forest av.
Myer Moses, 3345 Prairie av.
Myer William A. 2609 Indiana av.

Myers Albert T. 726, 63d ct. Eng.
Myers Charles A. 915 Sawyer av.
Myers E. B. 5126 Kimbark av.
Myers F. N. Evanston
Myers Garson, 148, 42d
Myers George L. 148 N. State
Myers Gertrude Miss, 7343 Wright
Myers Hattie Mrs. 342 Fullerton av.
Myers Herman, 4148 Ellis av.
Myers Jacob H. 3724 Forest av.
Myers John, 1010 W. Monroe
Myers Julia A. Mrs. 1925 Michigan av.
Myers J. B. 640 W. Monroe
Myers J. G. Mrs. 3222 South Park av.
Myers L. 3712 Forest av.
Myers L. P. Mrs. Chicago Beach hotel
Myers Madge Miss, 3846 Lake av.
Myers M. A. 4358 Oakenwald av.
Myers M. C. Chicago Beach hotel
Myers Samuel M. Highland Park
Myers S. H. 445 Marshfield av.
Myers Theodore B. 4301 Oakenwald av.
Myers Willis V. 4417 Berkeley av.
Mygatt W. R. Chicago Beach hotel
Myren Gustave, 516 Boulevard pl.
Myrick W. F. Mrs. 2967 Vernon av.

NACEY PATRICK, 4501 Indiana av.
    Nachbour Joseph F. 699 Washing-
    ton boul.
Naden Thomas M. Oak Park
Nafis Abraham T. Evanston
Naghten Frank A. 1659 W. Monroe
Naghten James J. 1659 W. Monroe
Naghten John, 1659 W. Monroe
Naghten John J. 1220 Washington boul.
Naghten M. J. 106 Walton pl.
Nagle A. F. Evanston
Nagle Margaret Mrs. 353 Winchester av.
        Sum. res. Denver, Colo.
Nagle W. H. 353 Winchester av.
        Sum. res. Denver, Colo.
Nain E. C. Mrs. 97 Warren av.
Nally E. J. 3601 Vincennes av.
Nance H. I. Dr. 4562 Wabash av.
Nance W. O., M.D. 302 Garfield boul.
Napier E. J. 3 Groveland Park
Naramore M. O. Evanston
Nash Charles T. 329 Ashland boul.
Nash E. W. 762 Warren av.
Nash George, Evanston
Nash H. H. Mrs. Lakota hotel
Nash Joseph Mrs. 4547 Prairie av.
Nash O. W. Dunning
Nash Richard, 3252 South Park av.
Nash Samuel J. 4802 Vincennes av.
Nash Thomas C. 715 W. Adams
Nash William, 15 Newport av.
Nash W. T. 4808 Vincennes av.
Nason C. E. 6832 Perry av.
Nason Edward W. 6500 Myrtle av.
Nast Alexander D. 3653 Michigan av.
Nast Esther Mrs. 3653 Michigan av.
Nast Samuel 3653 Michigan av.
Nathan Adolph, 5016 Drexel boul.
Nathan Albert, 103 Walton pl.

Nathan Herman, 1904 Indiana av.
Nathan Pauline Mrs. 103 Walton pl.
Nathan Samuel, 3914 Prairie av.
Nathanson Martin, 525 Dearborn av.
Nathanson N. Mrs. 525 Dearborn av.
Nau Louis, 469 Warren av.
Nau Otto F. 709 North Park av.
Naugle Edward E. LaGrange
Nawn George H 162 Oakwood boul.
Nay N. N. 6527 Stewart av.
Neafus George A. 3756 Ellis av.
Neagle F. C. 1005 Park av.
Neahr George H. 3155 Calumet av.
Neahr Melvin J. 3155 Calumet av.
Neal Charles A. 4334 Prairie av.
Neal John A. Auditorium annex
Neal John P. 4125 Berkeley av.
Neal Juan A. Mrs. Auditorium annex
Neal S. S. Evanston
Neale Alice M. Miss, 25 Scott
Neary Nicholas J. 273 Superior
Neather J. Pearce, 93, 33d
Neather Kittie Miss, 93, 33d
Nebeker Mary F. Mrs. 327, 42d
Nechvatal Anton F. 36 Burlington
Neebes George, 3602 Grand boul.
Neebes William J. 3602 Grand boul.
Neebes William J. jr. 3602 Grand boul.
Needham Erwin B. Hinsdale
Needham George J. 1330 Millard av.
Needham G. S. 1161 Millard av.
Neel Carr B. 3718 Ellis av.
Neel Louise Miss, 3718 Ellis av.
Neel Samuel R. 3718 Ellis av.
Neeler H. G. 273½ Lasalle av.
Neely Arthur C. Oak Park
Neely Charles G. Evanston
Neely Edwin R. LaGrange
Neely F. Tennyson, Auditorium hotel
Neely I. M. Dr. Evanston
Neely John C. 2619 Indiana av.
Neely John C. jr. 2619 Indiana av.
Neely Joseph C. 72 Centre av.
Neely Robert, 72 Centre av.
Neely W. I. 3122 Forest av.
Neemes John C. 4736 Madison av.
Neeson S. J. Mrs. 4227 St. Lawrence av.
Nef J. U. Prof. Hotel Windermere
Neff Aaron W. 1060 Washington boul.
Neff James, 349 Ashland boul.
Negley E. L. 505 N. Clark
Neil W. F. 3538 Michigan av.
Neill Charles W. 2731 Calumet av.
Neill Henry Rev. Highland Park
Neils Annie Mrs. Hotel Groveland
Neilson James D. 552, 61st, Englewood
Neilson James H. 3845 Ellis av.
Neimeyer William G. The Tudor
Neimz Arthur R. 27 Bradley pl. (L.V.)
Neist Julius, Ravinia
Neiswanger Joseph E. 2964 Vernon av.
Nell B. T. 3440 South Park av.
Nellegar John B. 4526 Greenwood av.
Nellis Aaron, 4212 Ellis av.
Nellis Adelaide L. Mrs. 1924 Michigan av.

Nellis Clark F. Longwood
Nellis Frank E. 159½ Eugenie
Nellis James, 3140 Calumet av.
Nelson Andrew, 64 Wisconsin
Nelson A. 4950 Prairie av.
Nelson Celia A. Mrs. 630 Greenleaf av.
Nelson C. L. 5413 Madison av.
Nelson Daniel T., M.D. 2400 Indiana av.
Nelson E. Austin
Nelson E. Case, Evanston
Nelson Francis C. 2400 Indiana av.
Nelson Gustav, 426 Winthrop av.
Nelson H. 717 Pullman bldg.
Nelson H. P. Dr. 605 W. Vanburen
Nelson John, Oak Park
Nelson John E. 53 Ray
Nelson John F. Capt. 142 Garfield boul.
Nelson John L. 3516 Wabash av.
Nelson Louise Mrs. 314 Garfield boul.
Nelson Murry, 1623 Indiana av.
Nelson Nicholas J. 3516 Wabash av.
Nelson Oliver C. 2430 Indiana av.
Nelson Oliver R. 2618 Wabash av.
Nelson P. E. 650 Orchard
Nelson Samuel, 248, 57th (H.P.)
Nelson Thomas E. 3516 Wabash av.
Nelson Walter C. 5120 Jefferson av.
Nelson William D. 12 Chalmers pl.
Nelson William P. Lakota hotel
Nesbett George H. 569, 51st (H.P.)
Nesbitt Mary Miss, 48, 35th
Nessler Samuel C. 3518 Wabash av.
Nessling Samuel C. 4167 Grand boul.
Nester Arthur, Hotel Groveland
Nester Timothy, Hotel Groveland
Nestierode A. L. 4938 Ellis av.
Netcher Charles, 4427 Drexel boul.
Nethercot S. G. 688 North Park av.
Nethercot William, 688 North Park av.
Netterstrom Charles M. 1535 Aldine av.
Nettleton B. P. Pullman
Nettleton E. F. Oak Park
Neu Bernard, 66, 18th
Neubarth Theodore R. Mrs. 13 Astor
Neubauer Adolph. 2303 Wabash av.
Neuberg A. E. 3408 Indiana av.
Neuberger Ferdinand, 3406 Indiana av.
Neuburger Jacob M. 4733 Kenwood av.
Neuburger John M. 4733 Kenwood av.
Neuman Adeline Mrs. 3250 Vernon av.
Neumann Alexander, 3018 Groveland av.
Neumann Barbara Mrs. 3666 Indiana av.
Neumann David, 3018 Groveland av.
Neumann I. D. 3206 Forest av.
Neumann Julius Prof. 3206 Forest av.
Neumann Louis, 3018 Groveland av.
Neumann Maier, 3233 South Park av.
Neumann M. D. Lexington hotel
Neumeister J. G. 33 Sidney ct.
Nevers Edward, 682 Washington boul.
Nevers Roderick, 29 Madison Park
New Byron W. 2809 Indiana av.
Newberger Eli M. 3706 Ellis av.
Newberger Louis, 3213 Vernon av.
Newbern William E. 4540 St. Lawrence av.

Newberry J. S. Mrs. 2910 Indiana av.
Newberry Robert T. 406 Superior
Newberry Walter C. Gen. 399 Erie
Newberry W. F. 4415 Ellis av.
Newbre C. H. 437, 46th
Newburger E. Newton, 3706 Ellis av.
Newburger Frank D. 3706 Ellis av.
Newburger G. Mrs. 3706 Ellis av.
Newburger James M. 3706 Ellis av.
Newburger William S. 3706 Ellis av.
Newburgh Leo B. 3239 South Park av.
Newbury Charles D. 221, 29th
Newbury George G. Hotel Metropole
Newbury L. E. Mrs. Glencoe
Newbury M. L. Mrs. 3827 Ellis av.
Newby Aaron J. 573, 51st (H.P.)
Newcomb Abbie T. Mrs. 7614 Wright
Newcomb George W. 236 Warren av.
Newcomb Herbert D. 7614 Wright
Newcomb John C. 37 Seeley av.
Newcomb William H. 236 Warren av.
Newcomer G. W. Great Northern hotel
Newell Allen G. 1923 Michigan av.
Newell A. B. 444 Chestnut
Newell Byron H. 148 Dearborn av.
Newell Charles B. 2580 N. Ashland av.
Newell Charlotte C. Mrs. 354 Washington
    boul.
Newell D. R. Mrs. 435 Washington boul.
Newell Elizabeth Mrs. 4020 Ellis
Newell F. V. 921 W. Monroe
Newell Hulda H. Miss, Evanston
Newell James B. 2580 N. Ashland av.
Newell James W. Mrs. 2580 N. Ashland
    av.
Newell John Mrs. 348 Ontario
Newell Lester C. Hinsdale
Newell Robert C., M.D. Austin
Newell Sarah H. Mrs. Evanston
Newell S. B. Mrs. 311 Belden av.
Newell William S. 2580 N. Ashland av.
Newell W. A. Chicago Beach hotel
Newfield M. 532 Cleveland av.
Newgard Henry, 4117 Lincoln av. (R.P.)
Newgarden Geo. J. Dr. Fort Sheridan
Newgass M. Mrs. 911 W. Monroe
Newhall Arthur T. 366, 49th
Newhall Benjamin, Glencoe
Newhall Franklin, Glencoe
Newhall Gilbert jr. Austin
Newhall Hiram H. 4736 Champlain av.
Newhall Sylvan, Glencoe
Newhaus George, 467 Bowen av.
Newhouse August, 3000 Cottage Grove av.
Newhouse A.S. Mrs. Chicago Beach hotel
Newhouse Leopold, 438 N. State
Newhouse Max, 438 N. State
Newitt Carlton C. Pullman
Newkirk Garrett Dr. 205, 44th
Newkirk George, 498 Fullerton av.
Newkirk McCurdy C. 317 Superior
Newlin George E. 15 Astor
Newman Augustus, 1710 Addison av.
Newman Burns L. 403 Warren av.
Newman Charles W. 523 Orchard
    Sum. res. Silver Lake

Newman Elias R. 2755 N. Paulina
Newman Elizabeth W. Mrs. Evanston
Newman George B 1838 Frederick
Newman Gustav R. 527 Orchard
Newman Henry, 768 Touhy av.
Newman H. P. Dr. Highland Park
Newman Jacob, 3333 Wabash av.
Newman Jacob jr. 3615 Ellis av.
Newman John A. Mrs. 529 Orchard
Newman J. B. LaGrange
Newman Lilly Miss, 3440 South Park av.
Newman Morris, 4043 Ellis av.
Newman M. A , D.D.S. 4640 Langley av
Newman Nelden A. Evanston
Newman William H. 249, 49th
Newman William L. 909 Jackson boul.
Newmark Louis, 3210 Wabash av.
Newsome G. S. The Arizona
Newton Albert I. 2606 Indiana av.
Newton Arthur W. 3811 Vincennes av.
Newton Asahel, 222 S. Oakley av.
Newton A. S. Mrs. 2606 Indiana av.
Newton Charles E. 812 Washington boul.
Newton Charles W. 3031 Prairie av.
Newton Edward, Pullman
Newton Edward F. 3201 South Park av.
Newton Geo. W., M.D. 460 Dearborn av
Newton Gertrude Miss, 487 W. Adams
Newton G. W. Mrs. 487 W. Adams
Newton G. W. Dr. 878 W. Adams
Newton Henry, 159 Locust
Newton H. S. 95 Warren av.
Newton Jarvis O. 2511 Michigan av.
Newton Louis, 3826 Langley av.
Newton Lyman M. 2511 Michigan av.
Newton Peter A. 4500 Prairie av.
Newton Robert C. 514 W. Adams
Newton William G. 2606 Indiana av.
Neymann A. M. 168 Locust
Niblack William C. 125, 47th
Niblock Charles B. 421, 48th
Niblock Harry C. 1907 Deming ct.
Nichol John, 4717 Kenwood av.
Nicholas E. T. 6348 Lexington av.
Nicholas F. C. 272, 61st (H.P.)
Nicholas Howard E. 4617 Vincennes av.
Nicholas Sarah F. Mrs. 507 W. Monroe
Nicholes Anna E. Miss, 318 Chestnut,
    Englewood
Nicholes C. W. 3435 Michigan av.
Nicholes I. Elsworth, 318 Chestnut,
    Englewood
Nicholes S. Grace Miss, 318 Chestnut,
    Englewood
Nicholes Willard D. 318 Chesnut, Engle-
    wood
Nichols Aaron S. 3853 Ellis av.
Nichols Amos Dr. 728 W, Monroe
Nichols Andrew M. 5218 Jefferson av.
Nichols Ariel Miss, 3749 Ellis av.
Nichols A. J. Dr. 728 W. Monroe
Nichols Charles H. 3630 Grand boul.
Nichols C. M. 4453 Berkeley av.
Nichols D. B. Morgan Park
Nichols Edgar H. 361, 65th, Eng.
Nichols Edwin C. Maywood

41

Nichols Elizabeth J. Miss, 650 Washington boul.
Nichols Emery J. 3813 Michigan av.
Nichols Emily Miss, 2325 Michigan av.
Nichols Eugene M. 624 Lunt av.
Nichols E. R. 113 Cass
Nichols Francis H. 493 Fullerton av.
Nichols Frank M. 1525 W. Monroe
Nichols Franklin, 2342 Calumet av.
Nichols Frederick W. Evanston
Nichols George, 7565 Bond av.
Nichols George E. Julien hotel
Nichols George P. Riverside
Nichols George R. 327 Ashland boul.
Nichols Harrison P. Maywood
Nichols Harry H. Maywood
Nichols Helen S. Mrs. Maywood
Nichols H. N. 706 Pullman bldg.
                 Sum. res. Denver
Nichols Horace W. 4430 Sidney av.
Nichols Isaac W. 547 W. Monroe
Nichols John F. Mrs. Lexington hotel
Nichols J. C. Dr. 7045 Yale
Nichols J. J. 6610 Harvard
Nichols Lewis B. 3637 Vincennes av.
Nichols Myron W. 5127 Lexington av.
Nichols M. S. 3817 Forest av.
Nichols Sarah Mrs. 657 W. Adams
Nichols Spencer J. 3830 Calumet av.
Nichols Washington A. Lake Forest
Nichols William C. 493 Fullerton av.
Nichols W. H. 505 W. Monroe
Nicholson E. L. Mrs. Hotel Metropole
Nicholson H. W. 1447 Edgecomb ct.
Nicholson James, 168, 34th
Nicholson J. T. 4901 Lake av.
Nicholson J. W. 3238 Forest av.
Nicholson S. 6328 Ellis av.
Nicholson Thomas, 168, 34th
Nicholson W. A. 4901 Lake av.
Nickelsen Adolph, 493 Belden av.
Nickerson Albert E. 1192 Wash'ton boul.
Nickerson Benjamin R. 3921 Langley av.
Nickerson Edward J.Dr. 2728 Wabash av.
Nickerson Freeman, 3442 Wabash av.
Nickerson Henry H. 516, 67th, Eng.
Nickerson J. C. 3440 Wabash av.
Nickerson J. F. Hotel Barry
Nickerson J. T. 30, 44th
Nickerson Roland C. 317 Erie
Nickerson Samuel M. 317 Erie
Nickerson Wilbur, 3440 Wabash av.
Nicol James, 917 Evanston av.
Nicolet Arthur J. 31, 37th
Nicolet Will H. 31, 37th
Nichergall P. A. 227 Irving av.
Niehoff C. Louis, 370 Dayton
Nielsen Charles, 314 Garfield boul.
Nielsen N. J. Dr. 39 Ray
Niemann Chas. H. 1325 Wrightwood av.
Niemeyer William, 628 N. Wells
Niese George N. 241 Hampden ct.
Nightingale Augustus F. 2175 Sheridan
     rd.   Sum. res. Lake Geneva, Wis.
Nightingale Harry, 2175 Sheridan rd.
Niles H. G. jr. Hotel Barry

Niles Jo n W., M.D. 355 Dearborn av.
Niles MbC. Oak Park
Niles Sidney S. Oak Park
Niles Smith, Oak Park
Nims C. K. 3300 Vernon av.
Nims O. L. 3300 Vernon av.
Nissen John P. 1742 Wrightwood av.
Nix Charles H. 38 St. James pl.
Nixon Charles E. 741 N. Clark
Nixon Netta Miss, 28 St. James pl.
Nixon Oliver W. 741 N. Clark
Nixon William Penn, 743 N. Clark
Nixon W. K. 156 Rush
Nixon W. W. K. 156 Rush
Noake W. H. Oak Park
Noakes Edward W. Riverside
Noble Alfred, 302 Belden av.
Noble Charles P. 307 West ct.
Noble Edwin J. 6621 Harvard
Noble Frank H. 6459 Dickey
Noble Frederic P. 532 Washington boul.
Noble Frederick A. Rev. 532 Washington
     boul.
Noble F. L. Hotel Normandie
Noble George W. Hinsdale
Noble H. A. 1752 Wrightwood av.
Noble L. C. 451, 65th, Englewood
Noble M. Mrs. 533 Englewood av.
Noblett Edward J. 421, 67th, Englewood
Nockin B. J. 695 North Park av.
Nockin J. M. 459 Irving av.
Noel L. H. 282 Seminary av.
Noelle Joseph B. 4108 Maple av.
Nohe Augustus W. 947 Clifton Park av.
Nohe Frank C. 947 Clifton Park av.
Nolan Arra Miss, 395 Superior
Nolan George W. 1364 Washington boul.
Nolan John H. 4941 Drexel boul.
Nolan W. J Dr. 285 Loomis
Noll Charles F. 364 S. Paulina
Nolte George H. 443 Dayton
Nonnast Louis F. 1774 Deming ct.
Nonweiler Francis H. 7224 Vernon av.
Noonan Edward T. 398 Washington boul.
Noonan Mary H. Mrs. 398 Washington
     boul.
Noonan P. 4730 Champlain av.
Norawa Elizabeth Mrs. 4355 Grand av.
Norcom Philip D. 3658 Vincennes av.
Norcott John, 4833 Madison av.
Norden Aaron Rev. 716 Sedgwick
Norden Felix A. 716 Sedgwick
Norden Henry A., M.D. 716 Sedgwick
Nordenholt George, Oak Park
Nordling Ernest A. Lake Forest
Norfolk G. S. Mrs. 535 Lasalle av.
Norman Charles E. 4335 Ellis av.
Norman Frederick, Wilmette
Norman James, 6647 Perry av.
Norman Richard, 4116 Ellis av.
Norman S. G. Mrs. 4335 Ellis av.
Norris B. F. Auditorium annex
Norris Charles S. 2302 N. Paulina
Norris Charlotte Mrs. 18 Delaware pl.
Norris Frank Y. Evanston
Norris J. M. 7140 Yale

Norris Robert A. 18 Delaware pl.
Norris W. H. Oak Park
Norris W. W. 347 Troy
North Hudson D. Riverside
North H. M. Julien hotel
North Robert L. 1859 Aldine (L.V.)
North Robert L. jr.1850 Aldine (L.V.)
North William S. 26 Walton pl.
Northam Jay V. 3006 Groveland av.
Northcote Amyas S. Hon. 3 Tower pl.
Northcott E. M. Dr. 1003 Jackson boul.
Northcott William P. 1112 Lawndale av.
Northen John, 425 Seminary av.
Northen Thomas, 425 Seminary av.
Northrop Clark T. 7201 Webster av. Eng.
Northrop Henry H. 6519 Sheridan av.
Northrop Howard G. 150, 50th (H.P.)
Northrop John W. Hotel Imperial
Northrup George W. jr. 5735 Monroe av.
Northrup Theodore G. 6416 Oglesby av.
Northrup W. M. 498, 42d pl.
Northup Charles Maj. 4407 Sidney av.
Northup C. J. 4716 Kenwood av.
Northup James H. 3725 Forest av.
Northup Milton, 4407 Sidney av.
Northup Willet, 4543 Ellis av.
Northway F. H. Mrs. 254 Warren av.
Northway Harry Earl, 308 S.Campbell av.
Northway W. R. 937 Jackson boul.
Norton A. L. 104 Warren.av.
Norton Charles L. Lockport, Ill.
Norton Delmon W. Chicago Beach hotel
Norton Dennis, 4459 Oakenwald av.
Norton Edmund, Highland Park
Norton Edwin, Maywood
Norton E. H. 6846 Wentworth av.
Norton Fay, 5137 Michigan av.
Norton G. S. 122, 49th
Norton G. W. Mrs. 1510 Michigan av.
Norton H. L. The Ontario
Norton H. M. 5620 Washington av.
Norton H. N. Oak Park
Norton James H. 2453 Commercial (L.V.)
Norton James S. 560 Dearborn av.
Norton Jesse R. Hyde Park hotel
Norton John E. 5137 Michigan av.
Norton Joseph, 2673 N. Robey
Norton J. H. 604 Division
Norton J. Witham, 140, 77th
Norton Lawrence A. Austin
Norton Lemuel D. Evanston
Norton Leonard R. 4114 Grand boul.
Norton Leverett J. Lakeside
Norton L. K. Mrs. The Wellington
Norton M. Miss, 1822 Indiana av.
Norton Oliver W. 4815 Lake av.
Norton Thomas J. 4919 Vincennes av.
Norton Thomas M. 4352 Calumet av.
Norton Thomas S. 4212 Calumet av.
Norton Warren Mrs. 301 Huron
Norwood F. W. 4945 Lake av.
Noth Frederick, 2979 Indiana av.
Nourse B. F. 2900 Groveland av.
Nourse Edwin R. 515, 67th, Englewood
Nourse Georgia Anna Miss, 346 Racine
    av.

Nourse Henry O. 4029 Vincennes av.
Nourse H. N. Mrs. 5932 Honore
Nourse John A. 4820 Prairie av.
Nourse William G. 346 Racine av.
Nowak Frank, 6564 Yale
Nowlen Addison J. Irving Park
Nowlin Lewis, 4342 Ellis av.
Noyes Charles, 844 Washington boul.
Noyes Charles F. 314 Belden av.
Noyes Clara M. Miss, 5315 Washington
    av.
Noyes David A. 310 The Plaza
Noyes Edmund Dr. Evanston
                    Sum. res. Delavan, Wis.
Noyes Ellen E. Mrs. Evanston
Noyes E. B. 81 Warren av.
Noyes E. E. 5315 Washington av.
Noyes E. H. 5117 Jefferson av.
Noyes George E. Evanston
Noyes Harry B. Oak Park
Noyes Henry C. 3809 Langley av.
Noyes Herbert, 305 The Plaza
Noyes John T. 378 Erie
Noyes LaVerne W. 76 Rush
Noyes Mary M. Mrs. 5315 Washington av.
Noyes M. Oak Park
Noyes M. C. 3819 Ellis av.
Noyes M. Paul, Evanston
Noyes Thomas S. Evanston
Noyes T. J. Evanston
Noyes W. A. Oak Park
Noyes W. S. 5101 Lake av.
Nudd Ira P. Mrs. 1610 Indiana av.
Nugeut Alice Miss, 190 Pine
Nunamaker Frank, Julien hotel
Nusbaum A. E. 3600 Lake av.
Nusbaum Emanuel, 3600 Lake av.
Nusley N. M. 435 Washington boul.
Nussbaum Daniel B. 4407 Greenwood av
Nussbaum Max, 537 Lasalle av.
Nutsford William G. 3648 Wabash av.
Nutt John Dr. Glencoe
Nutt W. F. Dr. 497, 43d (H.P.)
Nutting Samuel E. Ridgeland
Nutting William W. 80 Throop
Nuveen Margaret Mrs. Irving Park
Nycum J. 233 Oakwood boul.
Nye George H. Austin
Nye G. W. 263 Lasalle av.
Nye James W. Hotel Windermere
Nye William J. 1527 W. Monroe
Nye W. A. 3408 Vernon av.
Nyman Fay, 507 Dearborn av.
Nyman Fred, 507 Dearborn av.
Nyman John C. 507 Dearborn av.
Nyman John E. 507 Dearborn av.

O'BRIEN CAPT. 21 Bellevue pl.
    O'Brien Edward, 103 N. Clark
O'Brien Frank, 4018 Grand boul.
O'Brien H. Dr. 6826 Yale
O'Brien H. J. 4027 Indiana av.
O'Brien James C. 525 W. Congress
O'Brien James F. 4018 Grand boul.
O'Brien John, 4523 Prairie av.
O'Brien J. W. Mrs. Highland Park

O'Brien Margaret V. Miss, 2966 Indiana av.
O'Brien Martin, 28 Linden pl.
O'Brien Mary J. Miss, 2966 Indiana av.
O'Brien Thomas D. 3440 Vernon av.
O'Brien Thomas E. 57 Grant pl.
O'Brien Thomas F. 406 Jackson boul.
O'Brien William V. 499 Dearborn av.
O'Brien W. H. 1871 Nevada
O'Bryan A. P. 635 Boulevard pl.
O'Bryne Charles C. Dr. 105 Winchester av.
O'Callaghan James, 4235 Vincennes av.
O'Callaghan John, 681 Fulton
O'Callaghan John R. 4235 Vincennes av.
O'Callahan H. Miss, Hyde Park hotel
O'Connell A. J. 85 MacAlister pl.
O'Connell Dennis, 3418 Prairie av.
O'Connell John Mrs. 532 Lasalle av.
O'Connell John J. 532 Lasalle av.
O'Connell R. Mrs. 3631 Vernon pl.
O'Connell Theo. W. 85 Macalister pl.
O'Connell Thomas, 85 Macalister pl.
O'Connell Thomas F. 85 Macalister pl.
O'Connell William J. 532 Lasalle av.
O'Connell W. Herbert, 457 Bowen av.
O'Connor Francis H. 108 Hammond
O'Connor Jeremiah Mrs. Ridgeland
O'Connor John, 3565 Forest av.
O'Connor Louis H. Austin
O'Connor P. J. Rev. 658 Jackson boul.
O'Day F. C. 487 Lasalle av.
O'Donnell Charles, 400 Jackson boul.
O'Donnell Eleanor Miss, 6506 Lafayette av.
O'Donnell Frank, 416 Superior
O'Donnell James V. 1327 Wilton av.
O'Donnell J. J. 1633 Roscoe
O'Donnell Patrick, 1327 Wilton av.
O'Donnell Robert E. 127 Clarence av.
O'Donnell Simon, 3720 Wabash av.
O'Dwyer Robert, 1006 Washington boul.
O'Grady J. M. 71 Lake View av.
O'Hara E. R. 6602 Perry av.
O'Hara John, 2458 Prairie av.
O'Hara John jr. 2458 Prairie av.
O'Hare Joseph, 2334 Michigan av.
O'Kane William C. 3555 Ellis av.
O'Keefe John, The Arizona
O'Laughlin James, 1053 W. Superior
O'Laughlin John, Austin
O'Leary Arthur J. 4013 Drexel boul.
O'Leary David P. Evanston
O'Leary D. 429 Marshfield av.
O'Leary John Mrs. Evanston
O'Malley Austin, 274 Webster av.
O'Malley P. 1884 Diversey
O'Neal Joseph F. Dr. 167, 67th, Eng.
O'Neil Emma N. Miss, 7733 Emerald av.
O'Neil Helen B. Miss, 6020 Indiana av.
O'Neil J. F. 164 Walnut
O'Neil Arthur W. 4418 St. Lawrence av.
O'Neill A. D. 107 Park av.
O'Neill A. D. jr. 107 Park av.
O'Neill Bernard, 3953 Michigan av.
O'Neill John Mrs. 2963 Wabash av.

O'Neill John, 5900 Wabash av.
O'Neill Louis, 27 Newport av.
O'Neill William E. 3517 Indiana av.
O'Reilly Edward Rev. Lake Forest
O'Reilly Eugene, 3215 Michigan av.
O'Reilly Eugene F. 3215 Michigan av.
O'Reilly Geo. B. 2525 Wabash av.
O'Riley J. D. Granada hotel
O'Rourke John, 3032 Indiana av.
O'Shaughnessy Michael, 3207 Dover
O'Sullivan J. Dr, 268, 55th (H.P.)
O'Sullivan M. 6633 Drexel av.
Oakes Rebecca M. Miss, 625 Washington boul.
Oakey Alfred J. Dr. 515, 65th, Eng.
          Sum. res. Madison, Wis.
Oakley Annie Miss, 4700 Drexel boul.
Oakley Bertha Miss, 4700 Drexel boul.
Oakley Carrie L. Miss, 165 Locust
Oakley Carson M. Mrs. 4700 Drexel boul.
Oakley Horace S. Ontario hotel
Oakley H. L. The Ontario
Oakley James W. 4700 Drexel boul.
Oakley William C. 165 Locust
Oakman T. C. 361 Dearborn av.
Oaks J. F. Dr. 443 Englewood av.
Oaks K. Oak Park
Oaks W. W. Oak Park
Oakshette J. C. Dr. Hotel Normandie
Ober Adolph, 881 Fulton
Ober Charles K. Evanston
Oberfelder Max, 3916 Prairie av.
Oberfelder Tobias, 3648 Grand boul.
Oberholtzer S. Eber Mrs. 485 Lasalle av.
Obermann A. 53 Astor
Oberndorf Fred, 3553 Vernon av.
Oberndorf Henry, 3352 Vernon av.
Oberndorf Herman, 3128 Prairie av.
Oberndorf Joseph, 3352 Vernon av.
Oberndorf Lewis 892 W. Adams
Oberndorf Louis, 3352 Vernon av.
Oberndorf Max L. 892 W. Adams
Oberndorf M. L. 892 W. Adams
Oberne George, 1147 N. Clark
Oberne George N. 1147 N. Clark
Ochsner Albert G., M.D. 710 Sedgwick
Ockerlund S. E. 237 Wilson av.
Ocorr Henry, 6328 Honore
Odell H. C. 867 W. Monroe
Odell J. A. 4531 Ellis av.
Odell J. J. P. 483 N. State
Odell L. J. 4529 Ellis av.
Odell Mary A. Mrs. River Forest
Odell R. S. River Forest
Odell William R. 383 Superior
Odlin Elizabeth M. Mrs. 3226 South Park av.
Oehne Theodore, 5401 Ellis av.
Oestereicher Leopold, 624 Washington boul.
Oestereicher Theresa Mrs. 624 Washington boul.
Officer Alexander, Kenilworth
Officer Julia E. Miss, Newberry hotel
Offield Charles K. 379 Ashland boul.
Ogden Althea Miss, 46, 35th

Ogden Bernon, 111 Lake Shore Drive
Ogden Charles P. 1636 Michigan av.
Ogden E. J. Dr. 1636 Michigan av.
Ogden E. Russell, M. D. 1800 Indiana av.
Ogden G. G. 7761 Wright
Ogden Mahlon D. Mrs. 111 Lake Shore
    Drive   Sum. res. Pittsfield, Mass.
Ogden M. D. Dr. Palmer house
Ogden M. H. Mrs. 682 Park av.
Ogden William P. 5807 Rosalie ct.
Ogilvie George W. Walton pl. s.w. cor.
    Rush
Ogle George A. 3304 Rhodes av.
Ohlerking John H. 516 Washington boul.
Ohlheiser J. T. 4322 Ellis av.
Ohls John, Hinsdale
Ohm Charles Mrs. 406 Belden av.
Ohm Curt, 406 Belden av.
Ohnstein Max, 460 Bowen av.
Okes Joseph D. 161 S. Oakley av.
Okeson W. H. Irving Park
Olbrich Stephen J. Austin
Olcese Louis, Oak Park
Olcott E. W. Dr. 287 S. Oakley av.
Oldberg Oscar, 7808 Union av.
Oldfather George W. Winnetka
Oldfield A. Alfonzo Mrs. 95 Evanston
Olds A. F. Dr. Oak Park
Olds A. W. 810 North Park av.
Olds Edwin R. 686, 65th (H.P.)
    Sum. res. Fairmount, N.D.
Olds Lee, Hotel Windermere
Olds S. J. Mrs. 7620 Bond av.
Olds Walter Judge, Hotel Windermere
Oleson C. W. Dr. Lombard
Olff Lee, 129 Ontario
Olin Harvey C. 5213 Hibbard av.
Olin Nora L. Miss, 5213 Hibbard av.
Olinger Fred E. 3505 Indiana av.
Olinger Jean Prosper, 3505 Indiana av.
Olinger John P. 3505 Indiana av.
    Sum. res. Waukesha, Wis.
Oliphant David, Austin
Oliphant S. F. 335 Lasalle av.
Oliphant Walter, 896 St. Louis av.
Oliphant William B. 419 Marshfield av.
Oliver Andrew J. 270 Marshfield av.
Oliver David, 849 W. Monroe
Oliver Francis S. Evanston
Oliver Frederick S. Evanston
Oliver George, 1424 W. Monroe
Oliver George A. P. Hyde Park hotel
Oliver James B. Hyde Park hotel
Oliver John Mrs. 24 S. Homan av.
Oliver John jr. 1531 W. Monroe
Oliver J. M. 514 W. Congress
Oliver N. Ellis Dr. 1373 N. Clark
Oliver Richard, Hyde Park hotel
Oliver T. T., M.D. 2306 Indiana av.
Oliver William G. 1543 W. Monroe
Oliver W. D. 4461 Lake av.
Oliver W. G. French house, Evanston
Olmstead A. T. 7833 Eggleston av.
Olmstead E. 11 Groveland Park
Olmstead E. L. Mrs. 4429 Berkeley av.
Olmstead W. A. 5642 Madison av.

Olmsted Florence Miss, Palmer house
Olmsted Henry F. Evanston
Olmsted J. F. 6501 Harvard, Englewood
Olmsted O. M. Vendome Club
Olmsted William B. Evanston
Olsen Marie A. Dr. 312 N. State
Olson A. Z. 1048 Garfield boul.
Olson C. 1048 Garfield boul.
Olson Ella Miss, 3250 South Park av.
Olson N. F. 166 Locust
Olson Olof G. 3532 Vernon av.
Olson O. Evanston
Omohundro Riley C. 3559 Vincennes av.
Omohundro William.R. 3559 Vincennes av.
    Sum. res. Lake Geneva, Wis.
Onahan W. J. 37 Macalister pl.
Onderdonk Andrew, Virginia hotel
Onderdonk James L. 344 Michigan av.
Onderdonk William H. Evanston
Ong Louis B. 868 W. Adams
Onsom O. M. Ft. Sheridan
Oothout John, 1249 Michigan av.
Opdyke Edwin, 780, 71st pl. (H.P.)
Opdyke R. H. 83, 20th
Oppenheim W. S. Iroquois Club
Oppenheimer Abraham Mrs.435 S.Paulina
Oppenheimer Beckie Mrs. 210 Ohio
Oppenheimer B. Hotel Imperial
Oppenheimer Moses, 3313 Forest av.
Opper Philip, 3347 South Park av.
Oppermann Emil L. 502 Belden av.
Oran James C. Austin
Orb John A. 3211 Calumet av.
Orchard John G. Evanston
Orcutt M. J. Mrs. Oak Park
Orde George F. Glencoe
Orde Mark, Glencoe
Orelup Amasa, 3148 Groveland av.
Orem H. C. Julien hotel
Orendorff Charles B. 68, 24th
Organ Rollin B. 4019 Indiana av.
Oriel Frank H. Ridgeland
Ormerod H. L. 42, 39th
Ormsbee Adelaide G. Mrs. 117 S. Leavitt.
Ormsby L., L. Mrs. 825 Kenmore av.
Orr Charles B. 3218 Rhodes av.
Orr Claire A. Prof. 738 W. Adams
Orr C. Fred, Evanston
Orr Frank B, 4450 Ellis av.
    Sum. res. Mackinac Island
Orr J. G. Park Ridge
Orr Millard T. 2348 Calumet av.
Orr Robert E. Evanston
Orr Robert M. 194 Oakwood boul.
Orr Samuel C. Lake Forest
Orrell William F. Irving Park
Orschel I. 3255 Wabash av.
Ortengren John R. Park Ridge
Orth William S. 398 N. Wells
Ortmann Rudolph,, 460 Dearborn av.
Ortmayer Andrew, 496 Dearborn av.
Ortmayer Carl G. 4557 Ellis av.
Orton Esther M. Mrs. 445 Washington
    boul.
Orton Thomas, 4043 Ellis av.
Ortseifen Adam 514, 46th

Orvis C. A. 80 Bryant av.
Orvis C. B. 344 Michigan av.
Orvis Edith E. 2443 Prairie av.
Orvis Josephine E. Miss, 457 Washington
)oul.
Orvis Margaret E. Mrs. Evanston
Orvis Orland D. 2443 Prairie av.
Orwig H. I. Winnetka
Osborn A. C. Irving Park
Osborn A. D. Oak Park
Osborn Charles M. 4 Chalmers pl.
Osborn Charles M. jr. 4 Chalmers pl.
Osborn Chauncey V. 114 Flournoy
Osborn Clark D. 254, 47th
Osborn Eugene E. Evanston
Osborn E. H. Mrs. 4222 Berkeley av.
Osborn F. C. 4737 Kimbark av.
Osborn Hartwell, Evanston
Osborn Henry A. 839 W. Adams
Osborn John, 5726 Madison av.
Osborn John Mrs. 590 W. Adams
Osborn P. 548 N. Normal Parkway
Osborn Susan Mrs. 839 W. Adams
Osborne E. F. 5140 Madison av.
Osborne Frank Sayer, 4455 Grand boul.
Osborne Henry S. 4455 Grand boul.
Osborne O. B. 729 Kenmore av.
Osborne Phebe A. Mrs. 4455 Grand boul.
Osborne Thos. O. Gen. Lakota hotel
Osbornson E. A. 1553 Fulton
Oscamp Clemens, 2701 N. Robey
Osgood Albert M. 51 Seeley av.
Osgood Albert T. 51 Seeley av.
Osgood Edwin, Oak Park
Osgood Edwin S. Austin
Osgood Everett W. Winnetka
Osgood Frederick C. Hotel Groveland
Osgood Fred S. Austin
Osgood George B. 51 Seeley av.
Osgood Harry S. 51 Seeley av.
Osgood Henry H. 802 Winthrop av.
Osgood John D. 272 Irving av.
Osgood M. A. Mrs. 4612 Greenwood av.
Osgood Stacy W. Winnetka
Osgood Sarah J. Mrs. 649 Washington
  boul.
Osgood William P. Austin
Osgood W. F. 635 Walnut
Osher Joseph, 4927 Michigan av.
Osman Eaton G. 5107 Kimbark av.
Osmun Damel C. 17 Aldine sq.
Ostatag William, 478 Fullerton av.
Osterman D. 3408 Vernon av.
Ostey Lawrence, 220 Warren av.
Ostheimer S. 4422 Berkeley av.
Ostling E. J. 2292 N. Ashland av.
Ostrander B. Mrs. Winnetka
Ostrander Dempster 23, 35th
Ostrander E. A. Evanston
Ostrander J. W. 1077 W. Monroe
Ostrom J. A. Hotel Windermere
Oswald F. A. 256 Warren av.
Oswald J. W. Dr. 344 Belden av.
Otis A. Mrs. 4504 Lake av.
Otis Charles T. 2033 Prairie av.
Otis Chas. D. 3028 Lake Park av. .

Otis Ephraim A. 294 Huron
Otis F. R. 2033 Prairie av.
Otis George A. 7156 Euclid av. (H.P.)
Otis George C. 1544 Fulton
Otis George L. 1710 Michigan av.
Otis Henry A. LaGrange
Otis Henry B. 3028 Lake Park av.
Otis James, 1722 Michigan av.
Otis Joseph E. 1730 Prairie av.
Otis Joseph E. jr. 2832 Prairie av.
Otis Lucius B. 2458 Michigan av.
Otis Lucius J. 2033 Prairie av.
Otis Marion Miss, 294 Huron
Otis Philo A. 1722 Michigan av.
Otis Ralph C. 1730 Prairie av.
Otis Thomas G. 4508 Lake av.
Otis William A. 26 Delaware pl.
Otis X. L. Mrs. 1906 Michigan av.
Ott John 626 N. Robey
Ott Katherine Mrs. 591 Washington boul.
Ott Oran, 591 Washington boul.
Ott William C. 5146 Jefferson av.
Ottenheimer Henry L. 2815 Indiana av.
Ottenheimer Leopold, 2815 Indiana av.
Ottenheimer Louis S. 2815 Indiana av.
Otterson G. C. 1015 Winona
Ottie William E. 1192 Washington boul.
Ottman P. M. 139 Garfield boul.
Ottman William B. 5732 Rosalie ct. ·
Otto A. T. Hotel Barry
Otto Edward Dr. 1643 Belmont av.
Otto Emil Prof. Elmhurst
Ottofy Louis Dr. New Hotel Holland
Otton Edmond G. 6116 Sheridan av.
Oughton A. R. 6429 Grace av.
Oughton Charles M. Dr. 5410 Jefferson av.
Outerbridge W. G. 375 Marshfield av.
Outhet John C. 399 W. Monroe
Outhet R. M. 399 W· Monroe
Ovenshine S. Lieut. Col., Fort Sheridan
Overbagh Franklin, Evanston
Overbaugh Edgar M. 6415 Stewart av.
Overlock Frank F. 163 Winchester av.
Overman Charles R. 2413 Michigan av.
  Sum. res. "Fairoaks," Umkwona-
  go, Wis.
Overman H. C. 6340 Madison av.
Overman Linnaeus E. 2413 Michigan av.
Overman W. C. 6340 Madison av.
Overmeyer John B. 118 Ashland boul.
Overstreet H. E. Oak Park
Oviatt Frank F. 148 N. State
Ovitt A. W. 818 Walnut
Owen Alfred, 7320 Harvard
Owen Charles S. Morgan Park
Owen Ernest Dale, 3710 Ellis av.
  Sum. res. Marquette, Mich.
Owen E. H. Oak Park
Owen George H. 6505 Harvard
Owen George H. Oak Park
Owen James R. 1902 Michigan av.
Owen John P. 3207 Rhodes av.
Owen Kate Mrs. 3519 Indiana av.
Owen K. R. 497 Dearborn av.
Owen Malcolm D. Lakota hotel
Owen M. E. Mrs. 91 Lincoln av.

Owen Ole, 3519 Indiana av.
Owen T. G. 347½ S. Hoyne av.
Owen Wm. 415 Maple, Englewood
Owen William, 7320 Harvard
Owen William D. 2155 Sheridan rd.
Owen William R. Oak Park
Owens Ann Mrs. 2973 Indiana av.
Owens Anna Mrs. The Renfost
Owens F. E. Mrs. 6241 Sheridan av.
Owens Guy, 6241 Sheridan av.
Owens J. E. Dr. 1806 Michigan av.
Owens Marie G. Miss, 1806 Michigan av.
Owens P. Miss, 4049 Lake av.
Owens Robert Mrs. 50 Loomis
Owings Francis P. 3150 Michigan av.
Owings F. P. 3150 Michigan av.
Owings L. P. Mrs. 51 Warren av.
Owsley Frederic D. Dr. 412 Erie
Owsley George K. 245 Ashland boul.
Owsley Harry B. 142 Astor
Owsley Heaton, 408 Erie•
Owsley Henrietta Mrs. 245 Ashland boul.
Owsley J. Guy, 245 Ashland boul.
Owsley L. S. 3004 Prairie av.
Oxnam William B. 435 Englewood av.
Ozias Eli R. 1172 Washington boul.

PABST HERMAN, 55 Delaware pl.
    Pacaud A. D. 5101 Kimbark av.
Pacaud A. Lincoln, 5101 Kimbark av.
Pack William F. River Forest
Packard A. T. 112 Seeley av.
Packard B. S. Leland hotel
Packard Edward A. 3208 Lake Park av.
Packard Frank I. Evanston
Packard George W. 49 Ray
Packard James B. Mrs. 632 Washington
    boul.
Packard James D. 3523 Grand boul.
Packard Marcus A. O. 39 Woodland Park
Packard Oscar M. 2712 Charlton av.
Packard S. B. Mrs. 3846 Lake av.
Packard S. W. Oak Park
Packer Charles Mrs. 3361 Calumet av.
Packer Charles P. 4747 Lake av.
Packer John F. LaGrange
Padan Robert S. 513, 62d, Englewood
Paddleford Fred A. 3843 Vincennes av.
Paddock A. L. Mrs. Evanston
Paddock C. E. Dr. 2600 Indiana av.
Paddock Eliza Mrs. 1425 Michigan av.
Paddock George L. 5451 Cornell av.
Paddock M. L. 532 Sunnyside av.
Paddock Wilburn E. 1425 Michigan av.
Paddock William E. Evanston
Paddon A. A. 4591 Oakenwald av.
Paddon Herbert M. 5205 Madison av.
Paden Joseph E. Evanston
Paepcke Herman, 628 Lasalle av.
Page Alice W. Miss, 2126 Prairie av.
Page Charles, Evanston
Page Charles G. 5524 Madison av.
Page Charles T. 6562 Stewart av.
Page C. E. 4551 Champlain av.
        Sum. res. Mukwanago, Wis.
Page DeWitt W. Evanston

Page Eleanor H. Miss, 2126 Prairie av.
Page E. C. 3902 Lake av.
Page E. E. Dr. 369 Washington boul.
Page Fred H. River Forest
Page Harlan, River Forest
Page H. E. River Forest
Page H. J. 3902 Lake av.
Page James C. 438, 38th
Page James M. 21 N. Ashland av.
Page J. B. Hinsdale
Page May Miss, 368 Ontario
Page M. E. jr. 446 Garfield av.
Page Ralph, 4747 Kimbark av.
Page R. C. Highland Park
Page William R. 4747 Kimbark av.
Page Willis H. 3235 South Park av.
Pagin Frank S. 61 Walton pl.
Pagin L. A. LaGrange
Pague Samuel S. Lieut. Fort Sheridan
Paige Alonzo W. Tremont house
Paige A. W. Chicago Beach hotel
Paige E. R. 303 Irving av.
        Winter res. Pass Christian, Miss.
Paige W. R. 1645 Roscoe
Pain Charles E. 519 Burling
Paine B. F. 236, 45th
Paine C. D. Oak Park
Paine Lyman M. 4224 Langley av.
Paine Romeyn M. Dr. 47 Newport av.
Paine S. M. Miss, 5555 Monroe av.
Painter Charles S. 4830 Madison av.
Painter Edward J. 126, 33d
Painter Jo ph A. 985 Walnut
Painter WseV. Rev. 259 Park av.
Pajeau Joseph, 4345 Grand boul.
Pallett Frank S. Wilmette
Palm Dorothea Miss, 438 Warren av.
Palm Warren S. 633, 62d
Palmer A. E. Dr. 721 Lincoln av.
Palmer A. G. Evanston
Palmer Byron S. Dr. 631 Wash'ton boul.
Palmer Charles H. 6547 Stewart av.
Palmer Charles H. 7741 Sherman
Palmer Charles M. 3917 Grand boul.
Palmer Charles M. 496, 42d
Palmer C. B. Franklin, Evanston
Palmer C. E. Virginia hotel
Palmer Ed, LaGrange
Palmer Edwin B. Highland Park
Palmer Ernest E. 820 Walnut
Palmer Eugene P. Hotel Metropole
Palmer E. E. 820 Walnut
Palmer F. A. Auditorium hotel
Palmer George R. 5006 Ellis av.
Palmer George W. 2628 Wabash av.
Palmer G. E. 886 Warren av.
Palmer Harriet Mrs. 3917 Grand boul.
Palmer Henry E. The Tudor
Palmer Hiram, 6830 Sherman
Palmer Honore, 100 Lake Shore Drive
Palmer H. L. 513 Burling
Palmer John B. Dr. 3824 Rhodes av.
Palmer John F. Riverside
Palmer John J. 3822 Rhodes av.
Palmer John Mayo, 3252 Rhodes av.
Palmer John S. 4325 Berkeley av.

Palmer John W. Oak Park
Palmer L. A. Mrs. 496, 42d
Palmer L. H. Mrs. 464 W. Adams
Palmer Mamie Miss, Hotel Metropole
Palmer Milton J. 4124 Grand boul.
Palmer McA. Lieut. Ft. Sheridan
Palmer M. C. Mrs. 3021 Vernon av.
Palmer Percival B. 5006 Ellis av.
Palmer Percy W. 3635 Prairie av.
Palmer Potter, 100 Lake Shore Drive
Palmer Potter jr. 100 Lake Shore Drive
Palmer Robert B. 240 Bissell
Palmer Robert F. 518 The Plaza
Palmer Silas, 452 Warren av.
Palmer S. K. Chicago Beach hotel
Palmer Thomas D. Dr. 691 Washington
    boul.
Palmer Truman G. Irving Park
    Winter res. Los Angeles, Cal.
Palmer T. G. Irving Park
Palmer Violet N. Miss, 721 Lincoln av.
Palmer William F. Prof. Lake Forest
Palmer Wm. H. 295, 53d
Palmer W. C. B. 493 W. Monroe
Palmer W. E. 6733 Vincennes av.
Palmer W. W. The Arizona
Palmeter DeWitt C. 293 Park av.
Paltzer Charles A. 3117 Prairie av.
Pam Alexander, 733 W. Monroe
Pam Hugo, 733 W. Monroe
Pam Max, 733 W. Monroe
Pancoast J. Cameron, 2346 Calumet av.
Pancoast Rachael A. I. Mrs. 2346 Calumet
    av.
Pank C. Waller, 943 Park av.
Pank J. Henry, 683 Fullerton av.
Panushka John W. Wilmette
Panushka William, Wilmette
Paoli Gerhard C. Dr. 1834 Frederick
Papin F. Sidney Mrs. 2926 Michigan av.
Paradise M. C. 872 W. Adams
Parcells Frank, Lake Forest
Pardee Charles A. Mrs. 1358 Millard av.
Pardee F. 23 Seeley av.
Pardee F. J. 5415 Cottage Grove av.
Pardee Harry T. 307 N. Clark
Pardee K. C. 541 Cottage Grove av.
Pardee Luther Rev. Austin
Pardee M. F. 624 Lasalle av.
Pardee Theron Mrs. 307 N. Clark
Parden H. Hotel Barry
Pardey H. W. 1058 Warren av.
Pardridge Anson, 4157 Langley av.
Pardridge A. J. 3200 Michigan av.
Pardridge C. A. 3200 Michigan av.
Pardridge C. E. 5163 Wabash av.
Pardridge C. W. 3200 Michigan av.
Pardridge Edward W. 2022 Indiana av.
Pardridge Edwin, 2808 Prairie av.
Pardridge Florence Miss, 2808 Prairie av.
Pardridge Frank R. 2808 Prairie av.
Pardridge Fred C. 2808 Prairie av.
Pardridge May A. Miss, 3200 Michigan av.
Pardridge M. L. Mrs. 3945 Lake av.
Pardridge Williard, Hotel Metropole
Parent Arthur M. Pullman

Paris Frederick R. 4339 Lake av.
Parish Charles P. 4717 Kimbark av.
Parish Harry F. 4828 Kimbark av.
Parish I. H. Mrs. 5338 Washington av.
Parish J. A. Mrs. Lakota hotel
Parish Lillian H. Mrs. 3025 Groveland av.
Parish Lucile M. Miss, 3025 Groveland av.
Parish Lucius W. Irving Park
Parish Rosamond P. Mrs. 4721 Kimbark
    av.
Parish S. M. 2956 Groveland av.
Parish William F. 4828 Kimbark av.
Parish William F. jr. 4828 Kimbark av.
Parish William H. 5918 Indiana av.
Park August V. Dr. 4411 Calumet av.
    Sum. res. Lake Bluff, Ill.
Park A. J., M.D. 3200 Vernon av.
Park C. F. Hotel Barry
Park George H. Austin
Park Harvey S. 4 Langley pl.
Park James E. 1304 W. Adams
Park James S. 3224 Calumet av.
Park Richard H. 1843 Michigan av.
Park Shubael 3718 Ellis av.
Parke Edward J. Mrs. 4338 Greenwood av.
Parke G. W. 237 Warren av.
Parke John E. 5311 Washington av.
Parker Albert O. 248, 53d (H. P.)
Parker Anna M., M.D. 53 Warren av.
Parker Austin H. 248, 53d (H. P.)
Parker A. A. 1836 Michigan av.
Parker A. F. Mrs. 4737 Lake av.
Parker A. H., M.D. Evanston
Parker A. H. jr. Evanston
Parker A. K. Rev. 43½ Seeley av.
Parker Byron J. 5822 Rosalie ct.
Parker Brainerd M. 248, 53d (H. P.)
Parker Charles F. LaGrange
Parker Charles W. Evanston
Parker C. C. Mrs. 268 Erie
Parker Dorus B. 265 Hermitage av.
Parker Edward A. 729 Fullerton av.
Parker Ella G. Miss, 555 Dearborn av.
Parker E. A. 4340 Berkeley av.
Parker E. Harry, Evanston
Parker Frank A. 1836 Michigan av.
Parker Frank W. 6640 Honore
Parker Fred A. 624 W. Congress
Parker F. W. 3430 Vernon av.
Parker George, 1922 Barry av.
Parker George G. 501 W. Jackson
Parker George H. Mrs. Mayfair
Parker G. H. Mrs. Evanston
Parker Harley, 609 Garfield boul.
Parker Harry E. River Forest
Parker Harry M. Evanston
Parker Helen M., M.D. 53 Warren av.
Parker Henry O. Norwood Park
Parker Hiland H. 553 Dearborn av.
Parker Hilon A. Tracy
Parker Horace B. LaGrange
Parker James, 437 Warren av.
Parker James H. Virginia hotel
Parker James K. Winnetka
Parker James O. Winnetka
Parker Jay D. 609 Garfield boul.

Parker John, 227 Winchester av.
Parker John, 6617 Stewart av.
Parker John D. 31 Aldine sq.
Parker John D. Dr. 609 Garfield boul.
Parker John F. 3667 Michigan av.
Parker J. Grafton, 4418 Oakenwald av.
Parker J. Grafton jr. 4418 Oakenwald av
Parker J. J. 4737 Lake av.
Parker J. J. jr. 4737 Lake av.
Parker Leander D. Evanston
Parker Leonard A. 5474 Jefferson av.
Parker Lillian M. Miss, Evanston
Parker L. C. 162 Park av.
Parker Lewis W. Evanston
Parker Mary Mrs. 6617 Stewart av.
Parker Mary A. J. Mrs. 1457 N. Clark
Parker Maud D. Mrs. Evanston
Parker Mortimer B. 248, 53d (H. P.)
Parker N. A. 248, 53d (H. P.)
Parker O. L. Mrs. 501 Jackson boul.
Parker Phineas Mrs. 4310 Oakenwald av.
Parker Robert P. Oak Park
Parker Robert W. 5550 Washington av.
Parker R. D. 2034 Indiana av.
Parker R. F. Mrs. 2034 Indiana av.
Parker R. M. 358 Ontario
Parker Samuel M. 6200 Oglesby av.
Parker Samuel W. Grand Pacific hotel
Parker Sidney, Tracy
Parker Thomas, 4540 Greenwood av.
Parker Thomas, jr. 555 Dearborn av.
Parker William, 3014 South Park av.
Parker William A. 173 Goethe
Parker William C. 3667 Michigan av.
Parker William C. 7002 Prairie av.
Parker William W. Dr. Irving Park
Parker W. B. Oak Park
Parkes Charles T. Mrs. 51 Lincoln av.
Parkes C. Herbert, 51 Lincoln av.
Parkes Elizabeth Miss, 377 Dearborn av.
Parkes John C. 135 Seminary av.
Parkes John C. jr. 135 Seminary av.
Parkhill Charles E. 4338 Berkeley av.
Parkhurst Alton, Evanston
Parkhurst Emogene Dr. Evanston
Parkhurst George L. Evanston
Parkhurst Hiram S. 42, 35th
Parkhurst H. W. 47, 77th
Parkhurst J. J. Evanston
Parkhurst M. M. Rev. Evanston
Parkhurst William S. Mrs. 5136 Kimbark
    av.
Parkhust A. W. 435 Washington boul.
Parkin Henry J. Evanston
Parkins Geo. B. 5526 Jefferson av.
Parkinson Joseph G. 4805 Lake av.
Parkinson Robert H. 69 Bellevue pl.
Parkison Edwin J., M.D. 6923 Stewart av.
Parks George H. Austin
Parks Samuel S. 1543 Fulton
Parliament S. 3331 Calumet av.
Parmelee Charles, 344 Michigan av.
Parmelee Edward D. 296 Ohio
Parmelee Frank, Grand Pacific hotel
Parmelee John W. Auditorium hotel
Parmly Henry C. 3811 Grand boul.

Parmly Samuel P. 3811 Grand boul.
Parmly Samuel P. jr. 3811 Grand boul.
Parnell James E. Revere house
Parr Alexander Mrs. Wilmette
Parr E. S. Wilmette
Parr George R. Wilmette
Parr John C. Glencoe
Parr John H. 3715 Langley av.
Parrette Ella Miss, 2441 Indiana av.
Parrott John E. 42, 39th
Parrotte J. L. 4525 Vincennes av.
Parrotte Walter Lee, 444 Bowen av.
Parry Henry, 438, 57th (H.P.)
Parry John C. Glencoe
Parshall Ross T. 23 Bellevue pl.
Parshall R. F. Rev. 770 W. Monroe
Parshall T. W. 6416 Sheridan av.
Parsons Amelia S. Mrs. 5550 Washington
    av.
Parsons C. D. Oak Park
Parsons E. D. Oak Park
Parsons Harry, M.D. 2584 Commercial
    (L.V.)
Parsons John C. Mrs. 5714 Madison av.
Parsons J. B. 206 Goethe
Parsons J. C. 5714 Madison av.
Parsons O. M. 3015 Groveland av.
Parsons R. L. 5473 Cornell av.
Parsons William H. 437 Dearborn av.
Parsons William R. Dr. 4506 Emerald av.
Parsons W. A. Austin
Parsons W. E. Sherman house
Parsons W. R. Irving
Partridge Lyman H. 8 Ballouhy av.
Partridge N. A. 5614 Madison av.
Pashley Alfred F. 5100 Hibbard av.
Pashley S. C. 906 Walnut
Patch G. M. Oak Park
Patchen J. J. 6246 Woodlawn av.
Patchen Sarah A. Miss, Highland Park
Pate David S. The Wellington
Patera F. J., M. D. 675 W. Taylor
Paterson Alex C. 160 Ashland boul.
Paterson Andrew, Evanston
Paterson Edwin L. 415, 67th, Englewood
Paterson Jas. W. Fay av. nr. Pratt av.
Paterson John L. Fay av. nr. Pratt av.
Patoille Joseph, 2677 N. Robey
Patrick Benjamin F. jr. 4412 Berkeley av.
Patrick Charles B. Austin
Patrick Clarence E. Oak Park
Patrick C. E. 39th ne. cor. Langley av.
Patrick Herbert E. 1120 Washington boul.
Patrick H. E. Oak Park
Patrick Hugh T. Dr. 426 N. State
Patrick Joseph H. 3833 Wabash av.
Patrick J. W. 509 W. Congress
Patrick Mary A. Mrs. 3833 Wabash av.
Patrick M. L. Mrs. Austin
Patrick R. W. Oak Park
Patrick Zorah E., M.D. 25 Woodland
    Park
Patricolo A. Prof. Stamford hotel
Patten Aramenta M. Mrs. 420, 40th
Patten A. Mrs. 306 Warren av.
Patten J. A. 306 Warren av.

Patterson August L. 365 Oakwood boul.
Patterson A. L. 384 Warren av.
Patterson A. S. Hotel Imperial
Patterson A. W. 683 W. Monroe
Patterson Charles A. 384 Warren av.
Patterson Charles I. 508 Belden av.
Patterson Charles L. 235 Michigan av.
Patterson Charles T. 1060 Warren av.
Patterson C. Earl, 4309 Calumet av.
Patterson C. Edgar, 640 Boulevard pl.
Patterson D. R. 7131 Webster av. Eng.
Patterson Edgar, 4524 Lake av.
Patterson Eliza Mrs. 6847 Yale
Patterson Frank D. 4309 Calumet av.
Patterson Frank E. 4232 Wabash av.
Patterson Frank H. 3739 Ellis av.
Patterson Frederick J. 424 Belden av.
Patterson George C. 256 Fremont
Patterson George K. 640 Boulevard pl.
Patterson George M. Evanston
Patterson James C. 43 Campbell Park
Patterson James W. 591 W. Monroe
Patterson John, 3670 Wabash av.
Patterson John E. 1214 Jackson boul.
Patterson John H. Newberry hotel
Patterson J. B. 273 Belden av.
Patterson J. H. Evanston
Patterson L. A. 6356 Harvard
Patterson L. C. Mrs. 640 Boulevard pl.
Patterson Mary M. Mrs. 4350 Oakenwald av.
Patterson M. P. Mrs. 3739 Ellis av.
Patterson Robert H. 556 Englewood av.
    Winter res. Rock Ledge, Fla.
Patterson Robert W. Mrs. Evanston
Patterson Robert W. jr. 166 Astor
Patterson R. M. Clifton house
Patterson S. A. Mrs. 265 Warren av.
Patterson S. E. 124 Flournoy
Patterson S. E. Mrs. 591 W. Monroe
Patterson S. P. 384 Warren av.
Patterson Theodore H. 194, 37th
Patterson T. E. Hotel Metropole
Patterson Walter D. 911 Spaulding av.
Patterson W. A. 6927 Wentworth av.
Patterson W. R. 5730 Monroe av.
Patterson W. R. Oak Park
Pattison Edmo, 3639 Grand boul.
Pattison J. L. 498 Jackson boul.
Pattison Rufus P. 314 The Plaza
Pattison Thomas, Oak Park
Pattison Thomas Col. 275 S. Hoyne av.
Patton A. Chicago Beach hotel
Patton Edward A. Forest hotel (R.P.)
Patton Frank F. 3611 Lake av.
Patton Grace Mrs. 3611 Lake av.
Patton H. D. 198 Oakwood boul.
Patton J. M. Dr. 237 S. Hoyne av.
Patton N. S. Oak Park
Patton Robert Hunter, 5728 Rosalie ct.
Patton Robert W. 307 N. Clark
Patzack Frank, 717 N. Robey
Patzer F. H. Rev. Washington Heights
Paul Annie Mrs. 229 S. Leavitt
Paul Chas. R. Chicago Athletic Assn.
Paul Edgar T. Wilmette

Paul Eltham R. Evanston
Paul Frank M. Wilmette
Paul H. F. Riverside
Paul Jennette E. Miss, 3805 Langley av,
Paul John C. 1414 Roscoe
Paul Joseph, 69 Walton pl.
Paul Mary Miss, 4950 Greenwood av.
Paul Ph. D., Dr. 343 N. Clark
Paulin Fred C. Morgan Park
Paullin George W. Evanston
Pauling Edward G. 25 Astor
Paulsen Theodore C. 465 Irving av.
Paulsen William A. 50 Scott
Pavey M. E. Union Club.
Paxson D. C. 4532 Champlain av.
Paxson John W. 4310 Indiana av.
Paxton Frank, 235 Lasalle av.
Paxton P. P. Virginia hotel
Payen Cecile E. Miss, 4751 Calumet av.
Payen C. Mrs. 4751 Calumet av.
Payen Juliette Miss, 4751 Calumet av.
Payn Eli, 632 W. Congress
Payne Alfred Mrs. Hinsdale
Payne Ann Miss, Hinsdale
Payne A. M. Mrs. 32 Walton pl.
Payne Bruce C. 4831 Langley av.
Payne D. A. Dr. 110 S. Oakley av.
Payne E. H. 3250 South Park av.
Payne James, 534 Evanston av.
Payne John Barton, 3230 Groveland av.
Payne Leroy, 2322 Indiana av.
    Sum. res. Chebanse, Ill.
Payne Lewis, 5216 Jefferson av.
Payne Robert E. 4130 Ellis av.
Payne Wm. C. Hinsdale
Payne William M. 1601 Prairie av.
Payne William R. 236 S. Western av.
Paynter Henry M. 3821 Forest av.
Paysen Fred, 56 Evergreen av.
Payson Edward, Oak Park
Payson George Mrs. 454 Dearborn av.
Payson George S. 88 Astor
Payson Joseph R. 1262 Wilcox av.
Payson J. R. jr. Oak Park
Payson S. Clifford, 480 N. State
Payton C. B. 7700 Bond av.
Peabody Earl W. 5747 Madison av.
Peabody F. B. 426 Dearborn av.
Peabody F. F. Evanston
Peabody F. Stuyvesant, Evanston
Peabody Hiram B. 2968 Michigan av.
Peabody James, 5747 Madison av.
Peabody James B. 644 W. Adams
Peabody J. A. 644 W. Adams
Peabody Selim H. 4200 Berkeley av.
Peachy J. R. 4460 Berkeley av.
Peacock Albert, M.D. 277, 55th (H.P.)
Peacock Alice M. Miss, 872 Michigan av.
Peacock Charles S. 191, 32d
Peacock C. D. 1713 Indiana av.
Peacock C. D. jr. 2000 Indiana av.
Peacock Elijah P. 921 Sawyer av.
Peacock George C. 287 Michigan av.
Peacock Mrs. 287 Michigan av.
Peacock Joseph F. 1138 Wilcox av.
Peacock Joseph J. 1138 Wilcox av.

Peacock Robert, 3668 Wabash av.
Peacock Samuel R. Dr. 277, 55th (H.P.)
Peacock William H. 1375 N. Halsted
Peak Frank H. 435 Belden av.
Peake Frederick, 315 Flournoy
Peale Charles M. 4416 St. Lawrence av.
Peale Fred, 4338 Berkeley av.
Peale George M. 4338 Berkeley av.
Peale George M. jr. 4338 Berkeley av.
Peale Joseph A. 507 Warren av.
Peale R. S. Chicago Beach hotel
Pearce Charles F. 5754 Monroe av.
Pearce Eugene T. 4410 Langley av.
Pearce Frank I. 3627 Grand boul.
        Sum. res. Fox Lake
Pearce John F. 548, 62d, Englewood
Pearce J. Irving, Sherman house
Pearce John Irving jr. Sherman house
Pearce Mary Miss, Evanston
Pearce Myron, Sherman house
Pearce Myron A. 2728 Indiana av.
Pearce Myron L. 2548 Prairie av.
Pearce Ray A. 4410 Langley av.
Pearce Robert T. 3627 Grand boul.
Pearce Thomas A. 3801 Michigan av.
Pearce William H. Ridgeland
Peare Frederick J. 993 Millard av.
Peare George R. 763, 63d ct. Eng.
Peare Richard M. jr. 52 Campbell Park
Pearne W. Dillaye, 6044 Princeton av.
Pearsall Albert L. Hinsdale
Pearson Andrew, 149, 42d
Pearson Arthur L. 509 Jackson boul.
Pearson Charles W. Prof. Evanston
Pearson Eugene H. 357 Ashland boul.
Pearson Frank, 6320 Oglesby av.
Pearson Haynie R. 513 W. Adams
Pearson John L. Oak Park
Pearson J. H. 509 Jackson boul.
Pearson N. P. Dr. 462 N. Clark
Pearson R. N. 518 W. Monroe
Pearson Walter B. 1371 Washington boul.
Pearson W. H. 9 University pl.
Pearsons D. K. Dr. Hinsdale
Pearsons Harry P. Evanston
Pearsons Henry A. Evanston
Pearsons John A. Evanston
Pease Albert E. 364 Park av.
Pease B. M. Mrs. 275 Warren av.
Pease Daniel, Fort Sheridan
Pease Edward H. 4 Washington pl.
Pease Edwin B. 275 Warren av.
Pease Erastus S. Austin
Pease Frank B. Berwyn
Pease Fred N. 1837 Michigan av.
Pease F. O. Dr. 3701 Ellis av.
Pease George D. 649 Washington boul.
Pease Hiram L., M. D. 7530 Greenwood
        av.
Pease James, 1623 Belmont av.
Pease Laura S. Mrs. 1093 Winona
Pease Loring A. 3239 Michigan av.
Pease Philander P. 1729 Alexander av.
Pease Philander P. jr. 1729 Alexander av.
Pease Sarah B. Mrs. 143 Oakwood boul.
Pease Thomas H. 364 Park av.

Pease Walstein C. 1847 Belmont av.
Pease Werdell S. 1093 Winona
Peaslee E. S. 37, 33d
Peaslee L. M. Mrs. 37, 33d
Peasley James C. 309 Huron
Peasley W. S. Chicago Beach hotel
Peats Alfred, Chicago Beach hotel
Peavey Charles T. Hotel Windermere
Pebbles A. W. Oak Park
Pebbles Frank M. Oak Park
Pebbles H. R. Oak Park
Peck Allen S. LaGrange
Peck A. H. Dr. 721 N. Wells
Peck A. W. 326 Webster av.
Peck Buda M. Miss, 1826 Michigan av.
Peck Charles, 6110 Oglesby av.
Peck Charles H. 42, 39th
Peck Clarence I. 2254 Michigan av.
Peck Comfort E. Dr. 55 Pine
Peck D. P. The Tudor
Peck Eva J. Miss, 4330 Greenwood av.
Peck Ferdinand W. 1826 Michigan av.
        Sum. res. Oconomowoc, Wis.
Peck Ferdinand W. jr. 1826 Michigan av.
Peck F. L. Mrs. 35 Park av.
Peck George R. 65 Bellevue pl.
Peck Henry, Lombard
Peck Henry M. 2973 Michigan av.
Peck H. S. Mrs. 3200 Vernon av.
Peck Jerome T. 327, 61st, Englewood
Peck John W. Mrs. 3222 Vernon av.
Peck O. D. Glencoe
Peck Peter H. 7624 Union av.
Peck P. F. W. Mrs. 2254 Michigan av.
        Sum. res. Oconomowoc, Wis.
Peck Remeo, Longwood
Peck R. T. Mrs. Virginia hotel
Peck Staunton B. 3812 Calumet av.
Peck Walter L. Lexington hotel
        Sum. res. Oconomowoc, Wis.
Peck W. Eugene, 391 Orchard
Peckham Charles L. 7150 Euclid av.(H.P.)
Peckham Charles V. 449 Kenmore av.
Peckham W. E. 1469 Palmer
Pedrick Isaac H. 2419 Michigan av.
Peebles Arthur S. 5126 East End av.
Peebles Milicent S. Mrs. 3122 Michigan
        av.
Peebles William S. 5126 East End av.
Peek Walter, 361 Lasalle av.
Peeke E. W. 3404 Wabash av.
Peeke William H. jr. 2728 Calumet av.
Peeples C. M. Chicago Beach hotel
Peeples John M. Chicago Beach hotel
Peerstone C. S. Mrs. 376 Lasalle av.
Peet Henry J. 1701 Sheridan rd.
Peirce A. H. Chicago   Assn.
Peirce Blanford R. 422 Vincennes av.
Peirce D. A. 5464 Washington av.
Peirce Fred D. 479 S. Leavitt
Peirce Luther H. 1904 Surf
Peirce W. H. H. 5025 Lake av.
Peiro Frank L. Dr. 236 Sunnyside av.
Peiser Samuel C. 3348 Forest av.
Pellet Clarence S. Oak Park
Peloubet Jarvis, 1019 Washington boul.

Peloubet Louis G. 1019 Washington boul.
Pelouze Wm. Nelson, Lakota hotel
　　Sum. res. Oconomowoc, Wis.
Pelouze W. N. Col. Lakota hotel
Peltzer Otto, 412 Belden av.
Pence A. M. 550 N. State
Pendarvis R. E. 1413 Lexington av.
Pendleton Amos P. 193, 30th
Pendleton Bradford H. Evanston
Pendleton Edmund, 3338 Calumet av.
Pendry James H. 6416 Stewart av.
Penepacker Samuel, 7738 Sherman
Penfield E. W. 2456 Prairie av.
Penfield Fred W. 849, 72d pl. (H.P.)
Penfield H. D. 2456 Prairie av.
Penfield John Mrs. 849, 72d pl. (H.P.)
Penfield John H. 849, 72d pl. (H.P.)
Penfield Truman, 610 Dearborn av.
Penhallegon James, 6715 Honore
Penhallow William P. 33, 37th
Penniman Frank C. 4420 Champlain av.
Pennington Charles R. 4012 Drexel boul.
Pennington Fred A. 5722 Washington av.
Pennington H. F. 5722 Washington av.
Pennington H. F. jr. 5722 Washington av.
Pennington J. M. 7241 Harvard
Pennington Lewis E. 4366 Oakenwald av.
Pennington M. P. 7241 Harvard
Pennington Richard 3539 Michigan av.
　　Sum. res. Desplaines, Ill.
Pennington Thomas C. 4012 Drexel boul.
Pennoyer George M. 4037 Ellis av.
Pennoyer James C. 3244 Lake Park av.
Penny A. W. Park Ridge
Penny Charles H. Park Ridge
Penny Elizabeth Mrs. 82 Seeley av.
Penny Frank O. 82 Seeley av.
Pentecost R. Graham Evanston
Peppard John A. 4957 Prairie av.
Pepper Charles M. 5038 Washington av.
Perce Charles F. 1034 Wilcox av.
Perce H. Wallace, 509 Dearborn av.
Perce LeGrand W. 509 Dearborn av.
Perce Margaret A. Mrs. 1034 Wilcox av.
Percival Francis W. 1398 Palmer
Percy Louisa Mrs. 451 S. Oakley av.
Perekhan J. S. Dr. 2406 Prairie av.
Peres Hardwick, Stamford hotel
Perfect Florence M. Miss, 6537 Harvard
Perfitt L. The Arizona
Periam Jonathan, 526 Englewood av.
Perine Josiah W. 2818 Calumet av.
Perine Margaret S. Mrs. 2818 Calumet av.
Perkey Samuel Dr. 393 S. Leavitt
Perkins Amos H. 211 Ohio
Perkins Barclay W. LaGrange
Perkins B. Chapman, LaGrange
Perkins Charles 663 Washington boul.
Perkins Charles G. 508 The Plaza
Perkins Dwight H. 3929 Indiana av.
Perkins Emma L. Miss, 1165 S. Central
　　Park av.
Perkins Frank G. 224, 53d (H. P.)
Perkins Frederick W. 2223 Calumet av.
Perkins George B. 5526 Jefferson av.
Perkins George P. 49, 46th

Perkins George W. W. 139 Park av.
Perkins Harry W. Rev. Hinsdale
Perkins Henry S. Prof. 642 W. Monroe
Perkins H. F. 426 Superior
Perkins Janet R. Miss, 1616 Indiana av.
Perkins J. A. Mrs. 330 Oakwood boul.
Perkins Marion H. Mrs. 3029 Indiana av.
Perkins Robert. Berwyn
Perkins Sarah H. Mrs. Hinsdale
Perkins Vincent H. 129 E. Pearson
Perks Charles 4506 Emerald av.
Perley E. E. Hyde Park hotel
Perren Charles, 978 W. Adams
Perren Christopher Rev. 978 W. Adams
Perren Frederick, 978 W. Adams
Perrett Joseph C. 698 W. Adams
Perrigo A. B. 2956 Wabash av.
Perrill A. C. 1619 W. Monroe
Perrin William R. 3354 Rhodes av.
Perrish J. P. Virginia hotel
Perry A. J. 922 W. Adams
Perry Charles N. 3228 South Park av.
Perry C. H. Evanston
Perry C. H. Mrs. 28 Walton pl.
Perry David P. 344 Oakwood boul.
Perry E. O. Hotel Metropole
Perry F. B. 5210 Washington av.
Perry Henry G. Rev. priest Epis. ch. 79
　　N. Oakley av. nr. Fulton
Perry Howard E. 3140 Calumet av.
Perry Isaac N. 2900 Prairie av.
Perry James M. 3207 Indiana av.
Perry Lewis S. Grand Pacific hotel
Perry Louis M. Evanston
Perry L. P. Mrs. 5482 East End av.
Perry Margaret Miss, 287 Michigan av.
Perry Nelson W. Riverside
Perry P. J. 2384 N. Paulina
Perry R. T. 152, 36th
Perry S. A. Hotel Barry
Perry S. O. New Hotel Holland
Perry Thomas O. 1025 Park av.
Perry William N. Evanston
Perryman Jesse E. 4 Langley pl.
Persch Charles F. 2685 N. Paulina
Pershing James F. 6018 Sheridan av.
Person David Van Ness, 3242 Rhodes av.
Peters　　　　　H. 560 Washington
　　boul Alexander
Peters Andrew, 301 Schiller
Peters Benjamin F. 339, 60th, Eng.
Peters C. V. L. 262 Warren av.
Peters Frank, 29 St. James pl.
Peters Frank M. 29 St. James pl.
Peters Harry 36th, ne. cor. Ellis av.
Peters Harry V. Mayfair
Peters Henry G. LaGrange
Peters Homer H. 442, 64th, Eng.
Peters Joseph G. 428 W. Adams
Peters Robert C. 31 Best av.
Peters Roswell A. Chicago Club
Peters R. H. 267 Lasalle av.
Peters U. G. 499 W. 16th
Peters William M. 519 The Plaza
Petersen Adelaide Miss, 601 Dearborn av.
Petersen Alice Mrs. 2126 Indiana av.

Petersen Emil, 249 Lasalle av.
Petersen Emil, 603 Dearborn av.
Petersen Fred A. 579 Seminary av.
Petersen Freda Miss, 603 Dearborn av.
Petersen George L. 595 Pine Grove av.
Petersen Hermann, 601 Dearborn av.
Petersen Hugo T. 603 Dearborn av.
Petersen James, 603 Cleveland av.
Petersen Julius, 275 Ashland boul.
Petersen Victor J. 1750 Oakdale av.
Peterson Andrew, Union League Club
Peterson Frank T. 259 Burling
Peterson Franz, 557 Division
Peterson Henry E. C. 334 Hampden ct.
Peterson James A. Irving Park
Peterson Kate B. Dr. Irving Park
Peterson Morris, Ridgeland
Peterson Peter, 3747 Forest av.
Peterson P. 641 Fullerton av.
Peterson P. S. Rose Hill
Peterson William A. Rose Hill
Peterson W. F. 341 Garfield boul.
Petesch Charlotte Miss, 3267 Beacon
Petesch E. W. 3267 Beacon
Petesch M. H. Oak Park
Petrie Charles S. 17 Ewing pl.
Petrie Elmer D. Tracy
Petrie K. E. Miss, 65 E. Pearson
Petrie William J. Rev. 700 Fullerton av.
Pettee F. L. Hotel Barry
Pettee William H. 1572 W. Monroe
Pettengill A. A. Mrs. 640 Fullerton av.
Pettengill W. H. 507 Belden av.
Petterson Rudolph, Winnetka
Pettet Amanda Mrs. 519 Englewood av.
Pettet Anna May Miss, 519 Englewood
    av.
Pettet Freeman E. 519 Englewood av.
Pettet J. Dr. 656, 63d Eng.
Pettet Ormsby E. 656, 63d Eng.
Pettibone Amos, 316 Belden av.
Pettibone Asa G. 235 Michigan av.
Pettibone C. J. 468 Warren av.
Pettibone F. B. 1220 Wilcox av.
Pettibone Howard C. 147 Ashland boul.
    Sum. res. Evanston
Pettibone P. F. 159 Warren av.
Pettibone R. F. 155 Warren av.
Pettibone R. S. 155 Warren av.
    Sum. res. Macatawa Park, Holland,
    Mich.
Pettibone W. H. 2943 Indiana av.
Pettigrew Earl A. 2703 N. Robey
Pettigrew John A. 525 Belden av.
Pettis Catherine A. Miss, Evanston
Pettit Frank E. 208, 44th
Pettit William B. 270 Michigan av.
Pettitt Edward K. 2672 N. Paulina
Pettitt Robert W. 1741 Briar pl.
Pettitt William J. 2672 N. Paulina
Pew O. S. 148 Dearborn av.
Peyraud F. C. 56 Lytle
Peyser F. Mrs. 4060 Lake av.
Peyton Richard F. 200, 36th
Peyton Richard F. jr. 200, 36th
Peyton T. Dade, 200, 36th

Pfaelzer Bernhard, 3609 Vernon av.
Pfaelzer David, 430 Fulton
Pfaelzer David, 3403 Prairie av.
Pfaelzer David J. 4512 Vincennes av.
Pfaelzer E. 3843 Calumet av.
Pfaelzer Louis, 430 Fulton
Pfaff John L. 4519 Lake av.
Pfaff J. Lincoln, 3529 Ellis av.
Pfaff W. A. 4519 Lake av.
Pfahler C. B. 6557 Yale
Pfau J. Louis jr. 203 Warren av.
Pfeifer Josephine D. Miss, Chicago
    Beach hotel
Pfeiffer Anton 270 Garfield av.
Pfeiffer Christian R. 486 Bowen av.
Pfeiffer Christopher, 70 Lincoln av.
Pfeil Charles H. 1344 Wilton av.
Pfirshing Joseph, 3001 Groveland av.
Pfister William C. 268 Fremont
Pflaum Harry, 455 N. Wells
Pflaum Manna Miss, 258, 37th
Pfuderer W. F. Berwyn
Phalen Albert, 430 Belden av.
Phalen Frank J. 49 Astor
Phalen Michael W. 49 Astor
Phalen William J. 49 Astor
Phelizot George, 573 Division
Phelizot Kate Mrs. 573 Division
Phelon William, 619 Jackson boul.
Phelon W. P., M. D. 619 Jackson boul.
Phelps A. Hollie, 373 Burling
Phelps C   A. Mrs. 469 Washington
    boul. harles
Phelps Charles B. 3004 Prairie av.
Phelps C. E. 107, 37th
Phelps Edward J. 3906 Lake av.
Phelps Erskine M. 1703 Indiana av.
Phelps E. H. Lexington hotel
Phelps E. Louis, 373 Burling
Phelps George B. jr. 2822 Prairie av.
Phelps George D. 373 Burling
Phelps Gregor W. Ridgeland
Phelps Hannah Mrs. 307 Lake, Oak Park
Phelps Harlow W. 743 Touhy av.
Phelps Harriet A. Mrs. 5311 Washington
    av.
Phelps Herbert L. 610 Chestnut, Eng.
Phelps John M. 3004 Prairie av.
Phelps Joseph A. Park Ridge
Phelps Julia Miss, 469 Washington boul.
Phelps Mark, 470½ W. Adams
Phelps Minnie A. Miss, Evanston
Phelps Minnie A. Mrs. 834 St. Louis av.
Phelps O. B. Mrs. 2427 Indiana av.
Phelps Paul J. 317 The Plaza
Phelps S. V. Mrs. Ridgeland
Phelps Wm. 756, 63d ct, Englewood
Phelps William W. Mrs. 2518 Prairie av.
Phelps W. H. 3331 Vernon av.
Phelps W. R. Oak Park
Philbin John J. 251 Lake View av.
Philbrick Charles, 3907 Prairie av.
Philbrick George A. Austin
Philbrick M. E. Miss, 674 Fullerton av.
Philipshorn Max, 89, 32d
Philleo Susan H. Mrs. 205 The Plaza

Phillips Abraham, 424 Lasalle av.
Phillips Andrew J. 54, 35th
Phillips Bezaleel W. 3236 Lake Park av.
Phillips Carrie L. Miss, 4730 Drexel boul.
Phillips Charles W. 569 Division
Phillips Charles H. 175, 47th
Phillips Daisy Miss, 2829 Calumet av.
Phillips D. T. Dr. 3000 Michigan av.
Phillips Edmund R. 4730 Drexel boul.
Phillips E. A. Dr. 380 S. Robey
Phillips Francis V. LaGrange
Phillips Fred L. Austin
Phillips Frederick W. 56, 35th
Phillips Harry W. Mrs. 2621 Michigan av
Phillips Henry,·5511 Cornell av.
Phillips Henry A. Dr. 844 W. Adams
Phillips Irene B. Mrs. Evanston
Phillips James, 5943 Michigan av.
Phillips James M. 5338 Washington av.
Phillips John F. 578 Washington boul.
Phillips John F. Longwood
Phillips Joseph S. 424 Lasalle av.
Phillips J. A. 5339 Cornell av.
Phillips J. C. 935 Walnut
Phillips J. D., M.D. 164 Throop
Phillips J. S. jr. 424 Lasalle av.
Phillips N. A. 335 Warren av.
Phillips O. C. French house, Evanston
Phillips Theodore Mrs. 569 Division
Phillips Thomas W. Hinsdale
Phillips T. S. Mrs. 347 Dearborn av.
Phillips William, 176 Throop
Phillips William, 3027 Groveland av.
Phillips William A., M.D. Evanston
Phillips W. A. Rev. 142 Locust
Phillipson Joseph, 487 S. Paulina
Phillipson Ralph, 29 Wisconsin
Philo E. B. Mrs. LaGrange
Philpot Albert D. 5328 Jefferson av.
Philpot Brian, 2922½ Groveland av.
Philpot Brian F. 2922¼ Groveland av.
Phinney T. W. Great Northern hotel
Phipps Luther H. Dr. 2647 Charlton av.
Phipps Warren, 2403 South Park av.
Phister Walter B. 4049 Ellis av.
Phoenix Charles R. Austin
Phyall William G. The Arizona
Piatt Abner, 4356 Calumet av.
Picard Arthur, 305 Loomis
Picard Charles T. 305 Loomis
Picard Napoleon, 427 W. Congress
Picher E. W. Mrs. Evanston
Pick Albert jr. 4417 Michigan av.
Pick Charles, 3532 Wabash av.
Pick Gustav, 209 Fremont
Pickands Heury S. Auditorium annex
Pickering A. H. 4483 Oakenwald av.
Pickering Philander, 2413 Michigan av.
    Sum. res. Mukwonago, Wis.
Pickett Charles C. Hinsdale
Pickett Elizabeth Mrs. River Forest
Pickett John D. River Forest
Pickett Joseph D. River Forest
Pickett William, 3745 Vernon av.
Pickett W. S. Mrs. 3745 Vernon av.
Pickham J. D. 19 Vernon Park pl.

Pierce Addison S. 4209 Calumet av.
Pierce Arthur H. 2979 Prairie av.
Pierce Asahel Mrs. 457 Bowen av.
Pierce A. B. Mrs. 3116 South Park av.
Pierce Carl H. 1630 Indiana av.
Pierce Charles B. 3342 Prairie av.
Pierce Charles F. 1630 Indiana av.
    Sum. res. Martha's Vineyard, Mass.
Pierce Cora B. Mrs. 720 Jackson boul.
Pierce C. L. 5488 East End av.
Pierce C. W. 3813 Prairie av.
Pierce Delia Mrs. 4726 Woodlawn av.
Pierce D. A. 5464 Washington av.
Pierce Eva Miss. Hotel Windermere
Pierce F. J. Oak Park
Pierce George W. 4233 St. Lawrence av.
Pierce George W. 4847 Grand boul.
Pierce Grace Miss, 3813 Prairie av.
Pierce Herbert A. 4209 Calumet av.
Pierce H. D. Oak Park
Pierce James D. 6655 Stewart av.
Pierce James H. 266 Erie
Pierce M. F. Mrs. 271 Oakwood boul.
Pierce Nathan F. 4524 St. Lawrence av.
Pierce Norval Dr. 369 Elm
Pierce Octavius, 3953 Michigan av.
Pierce Osborn J. 44 Hamilton av.
Peirce R. H. 5426 Monroe av.
Pierce Warren H. 18 Bellevue pl.
Pierce William B. Mrs. 4736 Lake av.
Pierce William C. Sherman house
Pierce William F. 457 Bowen av.
Pierce William L. 5724 Washington av.
Pierce W. E. 881 S. Kedzie av.
Pierpont Henry V. 1805 Barry av.
Pierson Emily D. Mrs. Evanston
Pierson Herman W. Dr. 6351 Stewart av.
Pierson I. W. 1535 W. Adams
Pierson John C. Wilmette
Pierson Lcora Miss, 3826 Calumet av.
Pierson Louis J. Wilmette
Pieser Isaac, 3708 Wabash av.
Pieser Jacob Mrs. 3404 Forest av.
Fieser M. Mrs. 2923 Wabash av.
Pieters Henry, 375 Dearborn av.
Pietsch Charles F. 305 Huron
Pietsch Otto E. 2271 N. Ashland av.
Pietsch William, 538 Burling
Pifer Erwin H. 289 S. Leavitt
Piggott E. J. 774 Walnut
Piggott Samuel, 268 Garfield av.
Pigman W. G. Mrs 339 Lasalle av.
Pigott George, 504 Englewood av.
Pike Albert, 2548 Indiana av.
Pike B. E. Groveland hotel
Pike Charles Bond, 2101 Prairie av.
Pike Charles S. 3908 Ellis av.
Pike Eugene Rockwell, 2101 Prairie av.
Pike Eugene S. 2101 Prairie av.
Pike L. Miss, Hotel Metropole
Pike M. B. Hotel Metropole
Pike Samuel. 3908 Ellis av.
Pike S. W. Mrs. 6416 Madison av.
Pike William Wallace, 2101 Prairie av.
Pillinger Harry, Austin
Pillinger William A. Austin

Pillsbury Harriet Mrs. 1279 Wolcott
Pillsbury Ossian D. 59 Bryant av.
Pillsbury William F. Oak Park
Pilsbury John, M.D. 5101 Kimbark av.
Pinckard Charles P., M.D. Chicago Beach hotel
Pinckney M. W. Hotel Barry
Pincoffs Maurice, 323 Lasalle av.
Pincoffs P. A. 375 Dearborn av.
Pine Albert B. 6653 Yale
Pine Isaac S. 306 Lunt av.
Pine James A. W. Hotel Windermere
Pine M. B. Dr. 63 Walton pl.
Pine Theodore, Hotel Imperial
Pingree Merrill G., M.D. 554, 45th (H.P.)
Pinkerton William A. 196 Ashland boul.
Pinkham Arthur C. Evanston
Pinney Daniel, River Forest
Pinney H. J. Hotel Imperial
Pinney Lorenzo S. Austin
Pinney Lucy Spencer, Miss Evanston
Pinney L. Mrs. 4341 Grand boul.
Pinney W. E. Mrs. 4948 Woodlawn av.
Pinter Lizzie Miss, 280 Belden av.
Pipe E. W. Mrs. 4359 Lake av.
Piper Allen A. 1920 Indiana av.
Piper Anson, 1920 Indiana av.
Piper A. S. Mrs. 1920 Indiana av.
Piper C. E. Berwyn
Piper Henry, 617 N. Wells
Piper Otis, Berwyn
Piper Richard J., M.D. 633 W. Monroe
Piper Richard U. Dr. 2930 Lake Park av.
Piratzky Alma E. Miss, 352 Ashland boul.
Piratzky Robert H. 352 Ashland boul.
Pischczak John Dr. 3506 Lake av.
Pischel Frederick J. 466 Cleveland av.
Pitcher A. D. 99 Warren av.
Pitcher E. D. Irving Park
Pitcher H. R. Mrs. Oak Park
Pitcher Lewis W. 2725 Prairie av.
Pitkin Edward H. Ridgeland
Pitkin George, 3438 Rhodes av.
Pitkin George W. 459 Washington boul.
Pitkin H. E. Lexington hotel
Pitkin H. E. 848 Warren av.
Pitkin Lorraine J. Mrs. 668 Kenmore av.
Pitkin May Miss, Ridgeland
Pitkin Roger S. 616 Washington boul.
Pitkin Stephen G. 224 Schiller
Pitner L. C. Evanston
Pitt H. N. Dr. 418 Hermitage av.
Pitt H. T. 2114 Indiana av.
Pitt Willis W. 2114 Indiana av.
Pittaway James, 6955 Webster av. Eng.
Pittman Clement K. Evanston
Pittman S. Kemp Evanston
Pitts M. L. Mrs. The Newberry
Pixley F. S. Granada hotel
Place D. S. Gault house
Place Frank A. 467 W. Monroe
Place Lewis N. 1058 Wilcox av.
Place N. Beecher, 1058 Wilcox av.
Plamondon Ambrose, 36 Throop
Plamondon Alfred D. 3424 Wabash av.
Plamondon Charles A. 413 W. Monroe

Plamondon George, 84 Centre av.
Plank John Oliver, 3716 Lake av.
   Sum. res. Junior Lake on Plank's Farm, Necedah, Wis.
Plank John O. jr. 3716 Lake av.
Plant Albert M. 4361 Emerald av.
Plantz Walter M. 934 W. Vanburen
Plato C. E. Mrs. 4420 Prairie av.
Platt Carlos C. W. 4453 Berkeley av.
Platt C. H. Leland hotel
Platt Henry Russell, 4853 St. Lawrence av.
Platt John, Austin
Platt Jarve, 1724 York pl.
Platt Lucius C. Lake Forest
Platt L. K. Mrs. 718 The Plaza
Platt N. E. Sherman house
Platt Philander T. 1120 S. Central Park av.
Platt S. A. Miss, 463 W. Randolph
Plattenburg C. B., D.D.S. 721 W. Monroe
Plattenburg C. S. A. 721 W. Monroe
Plattenburg Elizabeth Mrs. 721 W. Monroe
Platter David E. 1551 Alexander av.
Plautz C. Herman, 731 N. Hoyne av.
Playford Robert W. jr. 4715 Champlain av.
Plecker James H. Dr. 422 Wash'ton boul.
Plew James E. 542, 59th, Eng.
Plimley Annie E. Mrs. 6952 Webster av. Eng.
Plimpton Grace Miss, Highland Park
Plochman M. C. Evanston
Plotke Fred, 202 Webster av.
Plotke Nathan M. 411 Cleveland av.
Plum Carl, 6946 Stewart av.
Plum Henry W. Lombard
Plum William R. Lombard
Plumb George, Austin
Plumb Glenn E. 690 W. Monroe
Plummer George W. 810 Washington boul.
   Sum. res. Tyrone, Pa.
Plummer Jonathan W. Glencoe
Plummer John T. Glencoe
Plummer Joseph P. Glencoe
Plummer Ralph W. 810 Washington boul.
Plummer S. C. Dr. 4304 Lake av.
Plumsted James T. 4154 Lake av.
Pode J. S. Mrs. Riverside
Podolski Theodore, 4337 Ellis av.
Podrasnik Louis A. 799 W. Monroe
Pogue George N. 4206½ Berkeley av.
Pohlman Theodore, 1261 Wolcott
Poillon H. C. Chicago Beach hotel
Poillon William, Chicago Beach hotel
Poinier Edward W. 107 DeKalb
Poinier Isaac P. 107 DeKalb
Poirier Henry N. 4425 Vincennes av.
Poitras B. C. Mrs. 4335 Oakenwald av.
Polacheck Leo 185, 25th
Polachek Henry H. 4302 Greenwood av.
Polachek M. 929 W. Monroe
Polack A. M. 3862 Prairie av.
Pole Robert G. Austin
Polglase Thomas R. Riverside
Polhemus W. E. 4540 St. Lawrence av.
Polkey Samuel, 3564 Vernon av.
Pollack David M. 3254 Rhodes av.

Pollak August, 4514 Oakenwald av.
Polak Bertha Mrs. 2714 Indiana av.
Pollak Henry, 3632 Vincennes av.
Pollak Herman J. 413 Bowen av.
Pollard Emma Mrs. 734, 68th, Eng.
Pollard Jerome B. 4464 Berkeley av.
Pollard M. Mrs. 3831 Lake av.
Polley John C. 209 Ashland boul.
Polley John C. jr. 209 Ashland boul.
Pollock Albert, 3547 Grand boul.
Pollock Arthur, 3547 Grand boul
Pollock Bernard, 3547 Grand boul.
Pollock Louis E. Hyde Park hotel
Pollock W. J. Hinsdale
Pollow Henry R. 130 Clarence av.
Pomeroy Augusta Mrs. 217 Winchester av.
Pomeroy D. W. 2721 Indiana av.
Pomeroy Harris, 307 Huron
Pomeroy James F. 696 North Park av.
Pomeroy Joseph, 517 W. Congress
Pomeroy Sterling, 120, 66th, Eng.
Pond Alexander W. 596 Division
Pond A. B. 817 Pullman bldg.
Pond H. S. Mrs. 573, 51st (H.P.)
Pond I. K. 817 Pullman bldg.
Pond Walter E. 325 Ashland boul.
Pond Walter M. 325 Ashland boul.
Pontious LeRoy, 2923 Indiana av.
Pontious W. H. Dr. Park Ridge
Pool A. W. Miss, 4722 Woodlawn av.
Poole Abram, 89 Pine
Poole C. Clarence Evanston
Poole Isaac Dr. Evanston
Poole John, 1635 Michigan av.
Sum. res. Muskoca, Can.
Poole Oscar E. Lakeside
Poole P. R. Mrs. 377 Dearborn av.
Poole William F. Mrs. Evanston
Poole W. Frederick, Evanston
Poole W. H. Morgan Park
Pooler Frederick S. Evanston
Pooley R. H. Rev. Oak Park
Poor F. A. 4800 Grand boul.
Poor Irby W. 503 W. Adams
Poor John E. Evanston
Poor J. Harper, 60 Cedar
Pope Charles, 18 Lake Shore drive.
Sum. res. Lake Geneva, Ill.
Pope Charles Mrs. Virginia hotel
Pope Charles B. Mrs. 2835 Michigan av.
Pope Charles E. 5218 Hibbard av.
Pope Edgar, 4551 Champlain av.
Pope George A. 793 W. Monroe
Pope George G. 3363 South Park av.
Pope Henry A. 4317 Berkeley av.
Pope Henry Pierce, 3363 South Park av.
Pope I. H. Miss, Evanston
Pope James B. 857 Jackson boul.
Pope Lydia Miss, 4551 Champlain av.
Pope Mary Miss, Evanston
Pope Polly Miss, 3998 Ellis av.
Pope Samuel I. 793 W. Monroe
Pope William J. 487 W. Monroe
Pope W. A. 5528 Madison av.
Poppelbaum Gustav A. 7630 Union av.

Poppenhusen Conrad H. Evanston
Poppenhusen H. C. Mrs. Evanston
Popper E. H. 1727 York pl.
Popper Leonard, 351 Dayton
Porter Albert B. 150 Berkeley av.
Porter A. R. 5220 East End av.
Porter Clarence, 75 Lincoln av.
Porter C. P. 508 Belden av.
Porter Duff, 4160 Ellis av.
Porter Edward C. Oak Park
Porter Elizabeth Mrs. 3200 Rhodes av.
Porter Flora D. Mrs. 6336 Drexel av.
Porter Frank, 585 W. Congress
Porter Frank L. 7024 Yale
Porter Fred W. Mrs. 7117 Wentworth av.
Porter Frederick D. 5470 Jefferson av.
Porter F. D., M.D. 1594 N. Halsted
Porter F. F. 402 Chestnut, Eng.
Porter F. W. 5617 Washington av.
Porter George J. M. 6510 Lexington av.
Porter George M. 3751 Langley av.
Porter Gilbert E. 5538 Cornell av.
Porter G. M. 10 Pelham flats
Porter Henry A. 5470 Jefferson av.
Porter H. C. Clifton house
Porter H. H. 311 Erie
Sum. res. Lake Geneva
Porter H. J. 433 Elm
Porter James F. 789 Fullerton av.
Porter James W. 789 Fullerton av.
Porter John Albert, 4160 Ellis av.
Porter Joseph D. 4804 St. Lawrence av.
Porter Julia F. Mrs. 789 Fullerton av.
Porter Lansing L. Evanston
Porter Lucy G. Mrs. Riverside
Porter Mary A. Mrs. 592 Cleveland av.
Porter Pacificus B. M.D. 1362 Wolcott
Porter Parker C. River Forest
Porter Placidus P. 1362 Wolcott
Porter Rogers, 3417 South Park av.
Porter Washington, 4943 Lake av.
Porter Wilfred L. 3751 Langley av.
Porter William 6946 Perry av.
Porter William B., Dr. 7849 Wright
Porter William D. Evanston
Porter William P. Hotel Metropole
Porter William W. 10 Pelham flats
Porter W. B. Berwyn
Porterfield J. F. 42, 39th
Portman August F. 377 Kenmore av.
Portman Edward C. 378 Kenmore av.
Portman Max P. 1297 Wilton av.
Post Charles B. 5423 Ridgewood ct.
Post Charles N. 305 Ashland boul.
Post Henry R. Evanston
Post H. D. 98, 40th
Post John A. 499 N. State
Post Junius S. 305 Ashland boul.
Post Loring W. Wilmette
Post L. D. Mrs. Evanston
Post Sylvester J. 1293 Wilton av.
Post William C. LaGrange
Posta Frank, 612 S. Lawndale av.
Postlewait S. C. 106 Flournoy
Potter Allen L. 4421 Champlain av.
Potter Augustus E. 4421 Champlain av.

Potter Augustus L. 4421 Champlain av.
Potter A. H. 42, 39th
Potter Charles E. Oak Park
Potter C. L. 4202 Michigan av.
Potter D. W. 3995 Drexel boul.
Potter Edwin A. 4832 Madison av.
Potter E. A. Revere house
Potter E. C. 4800 Ellis av.
Potter Frank P. 147 Ashland boul.
Potter F. E. Evanston
Potter G. Douglas, 315 Hampden ct.
Potter Irving B. 4421 Champ ain av.
Potter L. T. Dr. The Arizona
Potter Mary E. Mrs. 7120 Harvard
Potter N. L. Mrs. 4058 Michigan Terrace
Potter Orrin W. 130 Lake Shore Drive
    Sum. res. Lake Geneva, Ill.
Potter Orson 515, 67th, Englewood
Potter Philip, 3002 Lake Park av.
Potter Sarah S. Mrs. 1102 Washington
    boul.
Potter Selah R. 1102 Washington boul.
Potter T. R., M.D. 3960 Drexel boul.
Potter T. R. Dr. 3555 Ellis av.
Potter William C. 2969 Michigan av.
Potter W. H. 6045 Oglesby av.
Potter W. L. 480 Belden av.
Pottle William, 1687 Alexander av.
Potts James M. C. Dr. 1127 N. Clark
Potvan Lucine M. Miss, Hotel Winder-
    mere
Potwin Annie E. Miss, 507 Fullerton av.
Potwin Harry A. Austin
Potwin Henry, Austin
Potwin Homer, 109 S. Oakley av.
Potwin Mary E. Mrs. 109 S. Oakley av.
Potwin William S. 389 Dearborn av.
Poucher Barent G. Evanston
Poucher Morris R. Evanston
Poulkney F. Berwyn
Poulson William E. 3116 South Park av.
Pound Alfred N. 3841 Elmwood pl.
Pound N. D. Pullman
Pound Thomas A. 3841 Elmwood pl.
Pound William, 3841 Elmwood pl.
Powell A. V. 5220 Washington av.
Powell B. Mrs. 353 Oakwood boul.
Powell Charles B. Wilmette
Powell Clifford, 4313 Drexel boul.
Powell C. W. 4313 Drexel boul.
    Sum. res. Bay View, Mich.
Powell Edward, 43 Macalister pl.
Powell Edward L. 43 Macalister pl.
Powell Edwin C. 4754 Langley av.
Powell Elias D. 371 S. Oakley av.
Powell Francis M. Austin
Powell F. R. 4818 Evans av.
Powell Geo. J. 43 Macalister pl.
Powell G. Walter, 797 Kenmore av.
Powell Harry C. Hotel Groveland
Powell H. Eyre, Hotel LaVita
Powell Isaac, 329 Michigan av.
Powell John, Oak Park
Powell Joseph, 5201 Madison av.
Powell May B. Mrs. 515, 62d, Eng.
Powell Medford, Evanston
42

Powell Myron H. 797 Kenmore av.
Powell M. W. 2709 Indiana av.
Powell Samuel, 2424 Indiana av.
Powell Samuel, 2548 Commercial (L.V.)
Powell William H. 43 Macalister pl.
Power Frank M. 1574 Lill av.
Power Mortimer, Wilmette
Power M. J. 99½ Pine
Powers Arthur N. Evanston
Powers A. C. 148 Dearborn av.
Powers D. J. 77 Lincoln av.
Powers Earl S. Mrs. Evanston
Powers Eliza J. Mrs. 3807 Indiana av.
Powers E. L. 2600 Prairie av.
Powers Frank A. 1719 Deming ct.
Powers George E. French house, Evan-
    ston
Powers H. J. 580 Lasalle av.
Powers L. D. 3833 Calumet av.
Powers M. R. Evanston
Powers Ordell H. 4800 St. Lawrence av.
Powers Orville M. 5416 Jefferson av.
Powers Sarah F. Miss, French house,
    Evanston
Powers William P. 23 Arlington pl.
Powers William S. 428 Oak
Powers W. H. The Arizona
Praetorius G. G. Dr. 65 Clifton av.
Prall Johnson S. Highland Park
Prall Wm. George, Ridgeland
Pratt A. M. Mrs. 762 Walnut
Pratt Chester M. Evanston
Pratt Clayton A. 267, 47th
Pratt Clinton B. 4115 Drexel boul.
Pratt C. A. Mrs. 376 Lasalle av.
Pratt D. J. 6611 Yale
Pratt Elbert S. 400 S. Leavitt
    Sum. res. Nantasket, Mass.
Pratt Elizabeth A. Miss, Evanston
Pratt E. H. Dr. Virginia hotel
Pratt George H. 456 Fullerton av.
Pratt George L. 4115 Drexel boul.
Pratt George O. LaGrange
Pratt Grafton H. 5422 Monroe av.
Pratt Harry E. 400 S. Leavitt
Pratt Harry P., M.D. 762 Walnut
Pratt Jacob C. LaGrange
Pratt James F. 767 Jackson av.
Pratt Joel, 804 Greenleaf av.
Pratt John T. 3210 Vernon av.
Pratt Joseph G. 5422 Monroe av.
Pratt L. 267, 47th
Pratt Marcus M. Evanston
Pratt Mary C. Miss, 1837 Michigan av.
Pratt Mary R. Mrs. Evanston
Pratt M. E. Mrs. Kenilworth
Pratt M. Elizabeth, 5422 Monroe av.
Pratt Nelson D. Lake Forest
Pratt Ralph E. 4122 Grand boul.
Pratt Rodney K. 267, 47th
Pratt Roxana Mrs. 3815 Ellis av.
Pratt Sarah Wilder Mrs. 2919 Indiana av
Pratt S. A. Mrs. 672 W. Monroe
Pratt William E. Lake Forest
Pray S. M. 4102 Lake av.
Preasant Charles, 1326 N. Clark

Preasant Tillie Miss, 1326 N. Clark
Preble Earl, 673 Park av.
Preble Eben C. 848, 72d pl. (H.P.)
Preble Glenwood, 6800 Perry av.
Preble R. A. Mrs. 6800 Perry av.
Preble R. B., M.D. 1907 Deming ct.
Preis John P. 66 Hamilton av.
Prendergast R. Judge, 534 Jackson boul.
Prendergast Thomas J. 5303 Wabash av.
Prentice Allen T. 42 Scott
Prentice Chalmer M., M.D. 4670 Lake av.
Prentice Edward Dr. 2703 Michigan av.
Prentice E. Parmelee, 10 Tower pl.
Prentice H. L. Mrs. 5822 Wabash av.
Prentice Leon H. Hotel Windermere
Prentice Sartell, 10 Tower pl.
Prentiss A. M. 198 Oakwood boul.
Prentiss B. C. 695 W. Adams
Prentiss Carroll C. 931 Belle Plaine av.
Prentiss Jo   H. 383 Lasalle av.
Prentiss Lewis M. 292 Ashland boul.
Prentiss Lewis R. 292 Ashland boul.
Prentiss Norman A. Rev. Evanston
Prentiss William, Evanston
Prentiss William P. 4250 St. Lawrence av.
Prenzlauer Herman, 34 Bryant av.
Prescott Albert Mrs. 1145 Kenmore av.
Prescott Charles H. 1125 Lunt av.
Prescott Elmer E. Dr. 214 Park av.
Prescott Eva. L. Mrs. Hotel Windermere
Prescott Howard S. LaGrange
Prescott Mary A. Miss, 58 Astor
Press Adam J. jr. 66 Lincoln av.
Press A. J. 66 Lincoln av.
Press Hubert C. N. 723 N. Wells
Press W. G. 6154 Sheridan av.
Pressprich Otto jr. 356 Racine av.
Presstman Evelyn Eugenia Mrs. 1525 N.
　Halsted
　　　　Sum. res. Lake Geneva, Wis.
Prest C. C. 316, 45th
Prest Harry R. 316. 45th
Prestley James P. Dr. 126 Flournoy
Preston Daniel H. Hinsdale
Preston David A. 639, 61st, Eng.
Preston Emma Miss, 589 Dearborn av.
Preston E. B. 19 Delaware pl.
Preston Franklin W. 4435 Berkeley av.
Preston F. H. 7130 Harvard
Preston J. R. 52 Hamilton av.
Preston Marguerite Miss, 19 Delaware pl.
Preston W. D. 2320 Indiana av.
Pretyman William, 846 Hollywood av.
Pribyl Emma S. Mrs. 877 W. Monroe
Price Abner, 2219 Prairie av.
Price Benjamin O. 725 Washington boul.
Price Benjamin P. Palmer house
Price Cornelius, 1826 Indiana av.
Price David A. 792 Washington boul.
Price Delia Miss, 1826 Indiana av.
Price Ed R. 6748 Perry av.
Price Elizabeth Miss, 5554 Woodlawn av.
Price Eugenia Miss, 2505 Michigan av.
Price E. V. Leland hotel
Price Frank, 499 Fullerton av.
Price Frank A. Jefferson Park

Price F. A. 3769 Lake av.
Price George W. 725 Washington boul.
Price Henry W. 5040 Washington av.
Price Ira M. Prof. Morgan Park
Price James A. Mrs. Washington Heights
Price James S. 1826 Indiana av.
Price John P. Austin
Price J. A. Evanston
Price J. C. Riverside
Price Lee, Auditorium annex
Price Leopold, 4339 Forrestville av.
Price M. Wallace. 1826 Indiana av.
Price Oscar J. Dr. 538 W. Adams
Price P. Bird, 1556 Fulton
Price Robert P. Austin
Price Samuel C. 1826 Indiana av.
Price William H. 1556 W. Monroe
Price William H. Bankes, Virginia hotel
Price W. D. Jefferson Park
Price W. H. 824 W. Monroe
Price W. P. Oak Park
Prickett George W. 4439 Lake av.
Pride Joseph F. Evanston
Pridham D. J. Oak Park
Pridmore Wm. A. 5756 Kimbark av.
Priebe Gustav C. 1721 Cornelia
Priestman John, M.D. 3401 Vernon av.
Primley J. P. Lakota hotel
Prince Frederick H. 109 Hammond
Prince Lawrence H. Dr. 1348 N. Halsted
Prindiville Carlton H. 17 Lane pl.
Prindiville Charles, 407 Elm
Prindiville James Winslow, 3356 Rhodes
　av.　Sum. res. Higgins Lake, Mich
Prindiville John, 388 N. State
Prindiville John R. 3400 Vernon av.
Prindiville Louis A. 36 Cedar
Prindiville Marguerite Miss, 407 Elm.
Prindiville Redmond 388 N. State
Prindiville Thomas W. 407 Elm
Prindle Ebenezer, Evanston
Prindle E. A. Mrs 472 Elm
Prindle Jason R. Evanston
Pringle Robert, 229, 28th
Pringle William O. 229, 28th
Prins R. J. 3636 Calumet av.
Printy J. A. Dr. 598 Lincoln av.
Prior Thomas W. 278 Irving av.
Prior W. A. 3348 Vernon av.
Pritchard M. A. Chicago Beach hotel
Probasco Hannah Mrs. 422 Kenwood
　Terrace
Probst Arthur O. 42 Sidney ct.
Probst Jerome, 1718 Melrose
Proby James W. 109, 47th
Proby Jennie L. Miss, 109, 47th
Proby Walter Mrs. 109, 47th
Proctor Charles, Lake Forest
Proctor Richard, Lake Forest
Prophet Edward, 227, 29th
Prophet Margaret Mrs. 227, 29th
Prosch Emil, 731, 60th, Eng.
Prosch Frank, 731, 60th, Eng.
Prothero James H., M.D., 3953 Michigan
　av.
Proudfit James M. 314, 41st

• Proudfit W. S. 314, 41st
Proudfoot Lawrence A. 413 The Plaza
Prouty Carlton, Winnetka
Prouty Chas. B. 681 Fullerton av.
Prouty Henry W. 272 Ashland boul.
Prouty Merrick F. Winnetka
Prouty S. D. Sherman house
Provost Henry Mrs. 3978 Lake av.
Prudden H. B. 442 Belden av.
Pruitt Andrew J. 280 Osgood
Prussing Charles Mrs. 353 Lasalle av.
Prussing Eugene E. 25 Delaware pl.
Prussing George C. 588 Dearborn av.
Prussing John W. 62 Wisconsin
Pruyn Charles E. Oak Park
Pruyn Charles P., M.D. 371, 40th
Pruyn John R. The Ontario
Pruyn Samuel S. Oak Park
Pryor Gilbert C. 915 Farwell av.
Pudor J. F. Oak Park
Puff Fred, 706 North Park av.
Puffer Edwin R. Riverside
Pugh Charles, 6411 Honore
Pugh James A. Winnetka
Pugh Oliver C. 517, 65th, Eng.
Pugh Robert H. 4062 Michigan Terrace
Pugsley S. P. 1855 Melrose
Pulford Emma L. Mrs. 3953 Michigan
   av.
Pulham Charles, 4341 Indiana av.
Pullen John, Oak Park
Pullen William, Evanston
Pullman Florence Miss, 1729 Prairie av.
Pullman George M. 1729 Prairie av.
Pullman William C. 504 W. Adams
Pullman W. Sanger, 1729 Prairie av.
Pulsifer Charles W. 19, 23d
Pulsifer Fred K. Hotel Metropole
Pulver Arthur W. 414 Kenmore av.
Pulver C. Gertrude Miss, Hinsdale
Pulver Frances L. Mrs. Hinsdale
Punnett E. K. 85 Rush
Purcell C. A. Oak Park
Purcell William A. 4022 Indiana av.
Purcell W. H. 370 Lasalle av.
Purchase H. S. 461 Jackson boul.
Purdon Thomas, 558 Burling
Purdy Charles S. 27 Aldine sq.
Purdy Charles W. Dr. 57, 20th
Purdy C. F. Oak Park
Purdy Fred A. 7820 Bond av.
Purdy John H. 27 Aldine sq.
Purdy Warren G. 4811 Lake av.
Purdy W. A. Tracy
Purdy W. Fred, 4811 Lake av.
Purington Charles S. 1825 Michigan av.
Purington D. V. 2141 Calumet av.
Purington George E. 245 Lasalle av.
Purinton G. L. 6521 Harvard
Purinton H. G. 7664 Bond av.
Purple Theo. H. 22 St. James pl.
Purple William B. 3747 Ellis av.
Pursell Jennie Mrs. 4319 Lake av.
Pursell Peter H. Dr. 1240 E. Ravenswood
   Park
Purves Thomas C. LaGrange

Purvis John, Austin
Purvis Joseph, Oak Park
Pusey Charles M. Dr. 761, 71st pl. (H.P.)
Pusey W. A. Dr. Chicago Beach hotel
Pusheck Charles A. Dr. 330 Lasalle av.
Pusheck Edna Miss, 330 Lasalle av.
Pushman H. F. 920 Pullman bldg.
Puster R. J. 1638 W. Adams
Puterbaugh Franklin P. 4013 Indiana av.
Puterbaugh Samuel G. 459 Bowen av.
Putnam Albert C. Oak Park
Putnam A. A. 362 Ontario
Putnam A. M. Mrs. 734 W. Madison
Putnam Francis Victor, 2728 Wabash av.
Putnam Frank A. 272 Bowen av.
Putnam Frank H. Oak Park
Putnam John A. 362 Ontario
Putnam Julia B. Mrs. Oak Park
Putnam J. R. 4815 Kenwood av.
Putnam M. E. Mrs. Oak Park
Putnam P. H. 695 Jackson boul.
Putnam S. H. 425 Garfield boul.
Putney John S. 4138 Berkeley av.
Puttkammer Ernst, 3748 Forest av.
Pyatt Frank, 414 Washington boul.
Pye Josiah R. 459 Washington boul.
Pynchon Edwin M.D. 3728 Wabash av.
Pynchon George M. Union club
Pyott A. 296 Marshfield av.
Pyott David, 624 Jackson boul.
Pyott D. A. 628 Jackson boul.
Pyott George W. 291 Ashland boul.
Pyott James M. 291 Ashland boul.
Pyott James M. jr. 291 Ashland boul.
Pyott William E. 291 Ashland boul.

QUACKENBOS H. M. 364, 41st
   Quales Niles T. Dr. 52 Fowler
Qualey John A. 1503 Wellington
Qualey Thos. J. 2714 Calumet av.
Quan Henry W. 384 Erie
Quan James E. 384 Erie
Quan T. Albert, 384 Erie
Quan William J. 384 Erie
Quarles Edward C. 2236 Wabash av.
Quayle Thomas, Ridgeland
Queeny Edward J. 4228 Calumet av.
Quick George A. 2900 Michigan av.
Quick John H. S. 2900 Michigan av.
   Sum. res. Holderness, N. H.
Quick R. Frank, 4036 Prairie av.
Quick Thad. H. 756 Washington boul.
Quick William F. 2900 Michigan av.
Quigg David, 5037 Madison av.
Quigg John F. 555, 60th, Eng.
Quimby Benjamin F. 4812 S.Lawrence av.
Quimby B. F. 5749 Madison av.
Quincey T. S. 472, 42d
Quincy Charles F. 412 N. State
Quine William E., M. D. 3160 Indiana av.
Quinlan Anna C. Miss, Evanston
Quinlan Arthur D. 3019 Michigan av.
Quinlan Charles E. Evanston
Quinlan Charles H. Dr. Evanston
Quinlan Charles S. Evanston
Quiulan Cornelius, 832 W. Monroe

Quinlan D. B. 3015 Calumet av.
Quinlan Edward B. Evanston
Quinlan Edward J. 3019 Michigan av.
Quinlan Edward J. jr. 3019 Michigan av.
Quinlan Ellen Mrs. 3162 Lake Park av.
Quinlan George H. Evanston
Quinlan James M. 3019 Michigan av.
Quinlan Jane H. Miss, Evanston
Quinlan Jennie S. Miss, Evanston
Quinlan J. D. Dr. Evanston
Quinlan Sophie E. Miss, Evanston
Quinlan Thomas A. 1194 Sheffield av.
Quinlan William A. 3019 Michigan av.
Quinn Anna Miss, 4018 Grand boul.
Quinn Bernard, 354 S. Paulina
Quinn Catherine Miss, 4018 Grand boul.
Quinn Charles, 4112 Prairie av.
Quinn John, 6502 Oglesby av.
Quinn J. T. 196 Webster av.
Quinn May C. Mrs. Evanston
Quinn William B. 4112 Prairie av.
Quinn William E. Pullman
Quirk Bartholomew, 1383 Washington boul.
Quirk Daniel Mrs. 273 Superior
Quirk James, 1128 Washington boul.
Quirk James P. Dr. 1128 Washington boul.
Quitman Philip, 257 Dearborn av.

RABB LAURA MRS. 193, 54th pl. (H. P.)
Raber Philip W. 3932 Grand boul.
Raber Philip W. Mrs. 475, 42d
Race Ambrosia Miss, Irving Park
Race A. E. 7733 Sherman
Race Frank L. Austin
Race Jane M. Miss, Irving Park
Race Luther E. Austin
Race Richard T. Irving Park
Race Stephen A. Irving Park
Race Warren B. Irving Park
Racey Harry J. Riverside
Rache Charles Mrs. 353 Chicago av.
Raddin Charles S. Evanston
Raddin H. Augusta Mrs. Evanston
Radford J. W. Morton Park
Radford William, Riverside
Radle John N. 6550 Stewart av.
Radtke R. C. 1233 Wrightwood av.
Rae Harry Heisel, 427 Erie
Rae Robert Col. 427 Erie
Rae R. jr. 7100 Webster av. Englewood
Raeder Henry W. Evanston
Rafferty T. E. Evanston
Raftery Edwin, 3769 Lake av.
Raftree Michael L. Hinsdale
Raggio C. A. 3219 South Park av.
Raggio John G. 3219 South Park av.
Ragor Andrew, 430 Ashland boul.
Ragor E. Mrs. 19 Macalister pl.
Ragor Joseph A. 430 Ashland boul.
Rahlfs George, 33 Ewing pl.
Rahlfs George jr. 33 Ewing pl.
Rahn John C. Prof. Elmhurst
Rainbow R. L. 2027 Indiana av.

Rainey W. G. Lake Forest
Rainier Frank E. 937 Turner av.
Raiser Charles, 500 Seminary av.
Ralph Charles W. 880 Washington boul.
Ralston F. C. 1526 Fulton
Ralston Henry M. 2955 Indiana av.
Ralston James, 3817 Wabash av.
Ralston J. S. Oak Park
Ralston Robert W. Mrs. Lake Forest
Ramcke John C. 91 Seminary av.
Ramm C. 60 Lincoln av.
Ramond P. Clifton house
Ramsay Richard, Austin
Ramsay Zatham B. Austin
Ramsdell E. 6149 Sheridan av.
Ramsey Walter, 3222 Vernon av.
Ramsey W. W. 6605 Harvard
Ranck D. A. 41 Roslyn pl.
Rand Charles E. 3937 Lake av.
Rand Charles W. Great Northern hotel
Rand Grace Miss, Lombard
Rand H. C. Lombard
Rand H. S. Lombard
Rand John C. 715 The Plaza
    Sum. res. Avenue house, Evanston
Rand Wm. H. 3937 Lake av.
Randall A. S. Mrs. 179 Evanston av.
Randall Benjamin G. 4625 Ellis av.
Randall Charles H. 2624 Calumet av.
Randall Clarence A. 2624 Calumet av.
Randall Frank C. 624 Boulevard pl.
Randall George, Hotel Normandie
Randall Louis E. 1190 Jackson boul.
Randall Milo B. 4625 Ellis av.
Randall Palmer L. 4353 Berkeley av.
Randall Thomas D. 2624 Calumet av.
Randall T. P. 179 Evanston av.
Randall Wm. L. Evanston
Randall William V. Mrs. 167, 36th
Randall W. G. Virginia hotel
Randell Hattie E. Mrs. Ridgeland
Randle Charles H. 300, 53d (H.P.)
Randolph Fletcher, 442 Belden av.
Randolph Isham, Riverside
Randolph Jackson F. 410 Bowen av.
Randolph Laura L. Dr. 4154 Cottage Grove av.
Randolph Lilian Miss, 3743 Langley av.
Randolph P. C. Miss, Riverside
Randolph Richard Dr. 4154 Cottage Grove av.
Randolph Robert J. 4449 Sidney av.
Randolph Ruth F. Miss, 410 Bowen av.
Randolph S. M. 866 Sawyer av.
Randt W. C. Evanston
Rang Eugene A. 654 W. Adams
Rang Henry, 654 W. Adams
Range George Prof. Elmhurst
Ranger John N. Dr. 651 Park av.
Rankin Andrew C., M.D. Pullman
Rankin C. W. 405 S. Western av.
Rankin David M. Dr. 686 North Park av.
Rankin Frederick, Pullman
Rankin George, Oak Park
Rankin Ida T. Mrs. Indiana av. nw. cor. 63d
Rankin James, 313 Jackson boul.

Rankin James A. 7052 Yale.
Rankin John, Oak Park
Rankin Thomas, 280 Seminary av.
Rankin William, 313 Jackson boul.
Rankin William T. 4714 Langley av.
Rannenberg George, Hotel Groveland
· Rannenberg Henry W: Hotel Groveland
Ranney F. G. 5201 Hibbard av.
Ranney G. A. 36 Ray.
Ranney H. C. 36 Ray
Ranney John S. Dr. 323 Michigan av.
Ranney William A. 3343 South Park av.
Ransford Frank, 5738 Monroe av.
Ransford Thomas F. 165 Locust
Ransom Albert, 45 Campbell Park
Ransom Homer J. Evanston
Ransom Robert W. 142, 36th
Ransom R. 7211 Webster av. Englewood
Ransom William H. Oak Park
Ransom William S. 4400 Greenwood av.
Ransome Ernest L. 495 Fullerton av.
Raper Mary M. Mrs. 97, 51st (H.P.)
Rapley F. H. Chicago Beach hotel
Rapp August, Pullman
Rapp Charles F. Tremont house
Rapp John H. 654 N. Hoyne av.
Rapp Lee S. 50 Park av.
Rapp Lillian May Miss, 50 Park av.
Rapp L. L. Mrs. 4323 Oakenwald av.
Rapp R. T. 6906 Anthony av.
Rapp Walter A. 2631 Michigan av.
Rapp William, 220 Cass
Rapp Wm. J. 220 Cass
Rappal Frederick J. 3917 Prairie av.
Rappal Frederick J. jr. 3917 Prairie av.
Rappal Lawrence L. 3917 Prairie av.
Rappleye N. B. 3636 Prairie av.
Rardon James J. 559 Dearborn av.
Rardon Wm. J. 1804 Deming ct.
Rasch Theodore, 7859 Bond av.
Rasch T. H. 7859 Bond av.
Raster Edwin, 391 Jackson boul.
Raster Herman Mrs. 391 Jackson boul.
Raster Walter, 391 Jackson boul.
Ratcliffe W. A. Evanston
Rathbone P. D. 599 W. Harrison
Rathborne Joseph, 37, 22d
Rathborne Robert W. 5213 Kimbark av.
Rathborne William W. 207 Cass
Rathbun Nathan W. 4043 Ellis av.
Rathje Louis, 754 Englewood av.
Ratledge Charles, Longwood
Ratledge Frederick, 6826 Anthony av.
Ratte Herman F. Dr. 36, 35th
Rattle Anna M. Miss, Oak Park
Rattle O. J. Oak Park
Rattle T. S. Oak Park
Rattray William G. 1156 Lawndale av.
Rattray William H. 263 Bissell
Ratty Mary Mrs. 296 Superior
Ratzek H. 227 Lasalle av.
Ratzel C. M. Palmer house
Rau Henry, Wilmette
Rauch Albert, 344 Burling
Rauch E. Dr. 547 W. Monroe
Rauch Wm. A. 344 Burling

Ravenal Chas. T. 410 Oak
Rawle John, 472 Ashland boul.
Rawleigh Ava F. Miss, 727 Washington boul.
Rawleigh J. Harry, 731 Washington boul.
Rawleigh J. T. 727 Washington boul.
Rawlings J. N. Riverside
Rawll George J. 502 Winthrop av.
Rawson Adrian A. 308 S. Campbell av.
Rawson Albert E. 1465 Michigan av.
Rawson Charles A. 5854 Rosalie ct.
Rawson C. A. Mrs. Hinsdale
Rawson F. H. 4945 Ellis av.
Rawson G. A. Dr. The Wellington
Rawson Hart, 5854 Rosalie ct.
Rawson S. W. 4945 Ellis av.
Ray A. M. 198 Warren av.
Ray A. S. Oak Park
Ray B. F. 5127 Hibbard av.
Ray Edward C. Rev. 495 Bowen av.
Ray Edward O. 747 Warren av.
Ray Frank D. Granada hotel
Ray Frank D. jr. Granada hotel
Ray Frank H. Hotel Groveland
Ray Frederick A. 2548 Indiana av.
Ray Horton S. Granada hotel
Ray John M. 3505 Indiana av.
Ray Julia A. Mrs. 48 Bellevue pl.
Ray P. A. Mrs. Oak Park
Ray William E. 466 Fulton
Ray William F: Austin
Rayfield Ernest, The Arizona
Raymond Addie M. Miss, Hinsdale
Raymond Albert, 919 Jackson boul.
Raymond A. N. Hotel Metropole
Raymond Charles, Evanston
Raymond Chas. H. Hinsdale
Raymond C. L. 2239 Calumet av.
Raymond Edwin H. 3814 Calumet av.
Raymond E. F. Evanston
Raymond Frederick D. Evanston
Raymond George, 915 Jackson boul.
Raymond George W. Hinsdale
Raymond Harry S. 3847 Calumet av.
Raymond H. Hotel Metropole
Raymond H. V. 307 Indiana
Raymond Ida E. Miss, Evanston
Raymond James N. 2001 Michigan av
Raymond J. H. Evanston
Raymond Kathryn K. Miss, Evanston
Raymond L. B. Virginia hotel
Raymond Margaret P. Miss, 360, 65th, Englewood
          Sum. res. Bay Shore, L. I.
Raymond Miner Rev. Evanston
Raymond M. B. Mrs. 3139 Michigan av.
Raymond Sam B. Virginia hotel
Raymond Sherwood, 3814 Calumet av.
Raymond Thomas, 307 Indiana
Raymond William M. Evanston
Raymond William W. Virginia hotel
Raymond W. R. 3304 Vernon av.
Rayner J. B. 2311 Indiana av.
          Sum. res. Saratoga Springs, N. Y.
Rayner Peter K. 1269 Wolcott
Raynolds James D. Riverside

Rea l. H. 4348 Ellis av.
Rea Robert L. Dr. 272 Huron
Read E. O. Mrs. 271 Oakwood boul.
Read Gardner, Evanston
Read Jay J. 808 Farwell av.
Read J. P. Hotel Imperial
Read J. V. Oak Park
Read Nelton T. 4033 Drexel boul.
Read Opie, 4343 Calumet av.
Reade Philip Capt. Walton pl. sw. cor. Rush
Reading Edgar Mrs. 3750 Langley av.
Reading Edgar M. Dr. 3748 Langley av.
Reagan Nannie Mrs. Winnetka
Ream F. K. 197 S. Hoyne av.
Ream Norman B. 1901 Prairie av.
Rearden Henry H. Austin
Reardon John H. 424 Oak
Rearick Ella E. Miss, 1364 Washington boul.
Reasner Marie E. Dr. 215 Schiller
Reckitt Ernest, 732, 63d ct. Englewood
Record Milton L. Evanston
Record Nelson B. 4239 Grand boul.
Rector Charles E. 208 Goethe
Rector Edward, 4411 Berkeley av.
Rector George W. Tracy
Reddick G. W. Prof. Highland Park
Reddish E. Mrs. 348 Ashland boul.
Reddon W. B. 2427 Indiana av.
Reddy James M. 3244 Indiana av.
Redell Richard F. 435 Dearborn av.
Reder Peter, 453 Winchester av.
Redfern Joseph N. Hinsdale
Redfern Samuel, 2124 Michigan av.
Redfield Anson P. 287 S. Leavitt
Redfield B. B. 6422 Yale
Redfield Chandler S. Evanston
Redfield D. Walter, 819 Chase av.
Redfield George E. Evanston
Redfield James G. 4274 Forest av.
Redfield Joseph B. 621 Washington boul
Redfield Sarah G. Mrs. 819 Chase av.
Redheffer J. C. 1247 Wrightwood av.
Redington Edward D. Evanston
Redington William H. 1848 Barry av.
Redlich Alexander E. 375 N. Clark
Redlich Henry O. Dr. 375 N. Clark
Redman G A. 6946 Union av.
Redmond Francis, 225, 28th
Redway Florence A. Miss, 10 Groveland Park
Reece Alonzo N. 4558 Ellis av.
Reed Alanson Henry, Chicago Beach hotel
Reed A. C. Oak Park
Reed Belle Mrs. 470½ W. Adams
Reed Carlos L. 333 Maple, Englewood
Reed Charles A. 5409 Jefferson av.
Reed Charles C. 685 W. Adams
Reed Charles L. 4342 Champlain av.
Reed Charles S. 5409 Jefferson av.
Reed Chester B. 4130 Lake av.
Reed Christie Miss, Lombard
Reed C. B. Dr. 560 Burling
Reed C. E. 853 Walnut

Reed Daisy H. Mrs. 6638 Stewart av.
Reed David, 558 Jackson boul.
Reed David W. 225, 28th
Reed Edwin H. Evanston
Reed E. C. Mrs. Evanston
Reed E. H. 4758 Lake av.
Reed Frank, 4434 Berkeley av.
Reed Frank F. Riverside
Reed Frank J. 4560 Oakenwald av.
Reed Fred Mrs. 392 W. Adams
Reed George F. Park Ridge
Reed George J. 409 Belden av.
Reed Geo. M. 7425 Honore
Reed George W. 333 Maple, Englewood
Reed George W. 1521 George
Reed Herbert H. 820 Lunt av.
Reed Horace Mrs. 2505 Michigan av.
Reed Hugh T. Lieut. Hotel Windermere
Reed H. V. 41 Seeley av.
Reed James A. S. 411 S. Oakley av.
    Winter res. St. Augustine, Fla.
Reed James H., M.D., 1254 Michigan av.
Reed John, Hinsdale
Reed John S. Mrs. 126 Cass
Reed J. T. Lombard
Reed Lawrence J. 1383 Washington boul.
Reed Lewis M. 467 W. Monroe
Reed Mary A. Mrs.1234 Washington boul..
Reed Mary E. Mrs. 333 Maple, Eng.
Reed Mary T. Mrs. 464 W. Adams
Reed Morey L. Dr. 320 Bowen av.
Reed Myrtle Miss, 41 Seeley av.
Reed M. D. Mrs. Riverside
Reed P. A. Mrs. 654 Cleveland av.
Reed Robert J. 382 Bissell
Reed R. C. New Hotel Holland
Reed William Mrs. 488 Belden av.
Reed William, Irving Park
Reed William H. 4130 Lake av.
Reed William J. 382 Bissell
Reed William Kelsey, 3038 Groveland av.
Reed W. Albert, 333 Maple, Englewood
Reedy Ellen Miss, 2547 Commercial (L. V.)
Reedy Louis J. 341, 53d (H. P.)
Reedy William I. 733 Roscoe
Reeme Josiah B. Lexington hotel
Reen Charles W. 459 North av.
Rees Cuyler D. 2620 Commercial (L. V.)
Rees John F. 2819 Calumet av.
Reese C. H. 6449 Wright
Reese Harvey H. Evanston
Reese Theodore, Evanston
Reese Theodore F. Evanston
Reessing George W. 469 Dearborn av
Reeve George B. 848 North Park av.
Reeve James, 5904 Michigan av.
Reeves A. H. 6524 Yale
Reeves Joshua, 619 Jackson boul.
Reeves L. Claude, 2704 Michigan av.
Reeves William O. 2704 Michigan av.
Reeves W. N., M. D., 2704 Michigan av.
Regan K. M. Miss, 333 Ohio
Regan Levi T. 609, 66th, Englewood
Regensburg D. 4611 Ellis av.

Regensburg Fannie Miss, 4203 Grand boul.
Regensburg Henry, 4203 Grand boul.
Regensburg Henry L. 432 Lasalle av.
Regensburg O. H. 4203 Grand boul.
Regensburg Samuel H. 4237 Michigan av.
Regester Robert F. 1383 Palmer
Rehfeld Max, 1450 Wrightwood av.
Rehm Frank, 619 Dearborn av.
Rehm Jacob, 619 Dearborn av.
Rehm William H. 619 Dearborn av.
Rehtmeyer Herman, 533 Cleveland av.
Rehwoldt Ernest H. Irving Park
Reichelt J. A. 340 Warren av.
Reichenfeld Adolph Mrs. 3655 Prairie av.
Reichwald W. G. 271 Racine av.
Reid Alan LeRoy, Chicago Beach hotel
Reid A. W. 3756 Ellis av.
Reid David F. Southern hotel
Reid Elizabeth Miss, 5420 Washington av
Reid George W. 1929 Calumet av.
Reid G. B. 98 Warren av.
Reid Harry M. 3228 Prairie av.
Reid Hugh T. Mrs. Chicago Beach hotel
Reid John, Newberry hotel
Reid John F. 3228 Prairie av.
Reid John G. Mrs. 1657 Briar pl.
Reid J. G. Dr. 4710 Madison av.
Reid J. H. The Arizona
Reid M. K. Mrs. The Arizona
Reid Simon S. Mrs. Lake Forest
Reid William H. 2013 Prairie av.
Reid William H. jr. 534 Englewood av.
Reid W. W. 57 Delaware pl.
Reidell B. 924 Warren av.
Reifschneider Charles L. Austin
Reifsnider Charles, Oak Park
Reifsnider J. F. 1324 Wrightwood av.
Reigart H. P. 510 W. Adams
Reiley Talitha C. Mrs. Evanston
Reiling H. J. 3601 Vincennes av.
Reilly E. S. Mrs. 2956 Indiana av.
Reilly Frank, 1837 Michigan av.
Reilly Frank W. Dr. 2034 Indiana av.
Reilly James J. 2409 Prairie av.
Reilly John J. 2956 Indiana av.
Reilly Leigh, 2034 Indiana av.
Reilly Robert Kennicott, 2034 Indiana av.
Reilly Rudolphe Ransom, 2034 Indiana av.
Reily Daniel, 216 Park av.
Reimann G. L. 73 Grant pl.
Reimers Charles D. Evanston
Reimers J. J. Evanston
Reinach Jacob, 2712 Indiana av.
Reinach Louis Mrs. 1815 Frederick
Reiner Emma Mrs. 4422 Prairie av.
Reinganum Lena Miss, 375, 42d
Reinganum Settie Miss, 375, 42d
Reinhard Abraham, 153, 33d
Reinke A. H. 36 Cedar
Reiss L. W. 3248 Rhodes av.
Reiss Otto, 447 Lasalle av.
Reiss William, 3248 Rhodes av.
Reissig Charles Mrs. Riverside
Reitler Charles, 3147 Rhodes av.

Reitler Joseph, 3255 Wabash av.
Reitermann Charles Dr. Austin
Remick Helen A. Mrs. 3537 Indiana av.
Remien Charles H. 35 E. Pearson
Remien Charles H. jr. 35 E. Pearson
Remington Carver, The Ontario
Remington Franklin, 63 E. Pearson
Remmen Nils E. Dr. 134 Evergreen av.
Remmer E. Mrs. 4827 Lake av.
Remmer Oscar, 4552 Oakenwald av.
Remwick Walter H. 2428 Indiana av.
Remy Curtis H. Evanston
Rend Joseph P. 153 Ashland boul.
Rend William P. 153 Ashland boul.
Rendtorff Johanna Miss, 3247 Beacon
Rennacker E. F. 366 Warren av.
Rennard L. W. 3733 Ellis av.
Rennebaum Chas. E. Dr. 482 N. Clark
Rennels E. E. Mrs. 707 W. Adams
Renner Julius A. 969 Washington boul.
Renners George W. 682 North Park av.
Rennison George T. Evanston
Renshaw William, 4439 Ellis av.
Rentz August, Riverside
Renwick Edward A. 1754 Sheridan rd.
Repka August, Riverside
ReQua Charles H. 3629 Grand boul.
ReQua Charles W. 2454 Michigan av.
ReQua Harry L. Highland Park
ReQua Stephen F. Evanston
ReQua William B. 2454 Michigan av.
Retter J. M. Dr. Oak Park
Retterer Jacob, 533 Cleveland av.
Reum Oscar A. 260 Racine av.
Reusch Ferdinand, 2646 Charlton av.
Reuter Henry, 1145 Washington boul.
Revell Alex. H. 577 Lasalle av.
Revell Alice Miss, 577 Lasalle av.
Revell D. J. 639 Fullerton av.
Revell Emma M. Mrs. Evanston
Revell Fleming H. Evanston
Revell J. T. 639 Fullerton av.
Revell Margaret Mrs. 639 Fullerton av.
Rew Frances Miss, 4536 Lake av.
Rew Francis E. 4536 Lake av.
Rew George C. 4536 Lake av.
Rew Henry C. 2619 Prairie av.
Rew Irwin, 2619 Prairie av.
Rexinger Frederick, 4929 Champlain av.
Reynolds Asa Q. 574 Boulevard pl.
Reynolds A. R. Dr. Lakota hotel
Reynolds Benjamin, Riverside
Reynolds B. P. Dr. Lombard
Reynolds Charles Rev. 334 Cedar, Eng.
Reynolds Charles K. Hotel Windermere
Reynolds C. M. 6334 Wright
Reynolds C. N. 3333 Calumet av.
Reynolds Daniel M. 1122 Washington boul.
Reynolds Edgar W. Irving Park
Reynolds Elizabeth Miss, The Renfost
Reynolds Elon H. 3810 Elmwood pl.
Reynolds Frank D. Evanston
Reynolds Frank G. 6929 Stewart av.
        Winter res. Manville, Tex.
Reynolds Frank W. 3233 Indiana av.

Reynolds Frederic L. Evanston
Reynolds Frederick M. 5803 Rosalie ct.
Reynolds F. H. Irving Park
Reynolds F. M. Dr. Oak Park
Reynolds George A. Hotel Groveland
Reynolds George B. Evanston
Reynolds George H. 4158 Lake av.
Reynolds George W. Berwyn
Reynolds G. W. Dr. 315 Webster av.
Reynolds G. W. Dr. 335 Washington boul.
Reynolds Henry J., M.D. The Renfost
Reynolds James D. Riverside
Reynolds James H. Evanston
Reynolds Jane Mrs. 1089 S. Central Park
  av.
Reynolds J. E. Dr. 460 S. Oakley av.
Reynolds J. J. 16 Bellevue pl.
Reynolds J. P. 468 Lasalle av.
Reynolds K. C. Mrs. 3233 Indiana av.
Reynolds Lewis, 947 Mayfair
Reynolds Marc, Southern hotel
Reynolds M. V. Mrs. 3241 Groveland av.
Reynolds O. 3158 Lake Park av.
Reynolds Russell, Hotel Windermere
Reynolds William J. 4518 Champlain av.
Reynolds William J. Oak Park
Reynolds W. H. Mrs. 5520 Washington
  av.
Rhea Foster A. Union Club
Rhea John C. 7450 Nutt av.
Rhea Prema Miss, 1188 Washington boul.
Rhea Sarah J. Mrs. Lake Forest
Rheinstrom Abram 3939 Indiana av.
Rhoades C. H. The Arizona
Rhode E. Mrs. 151 Goethe
Rhode John C. W. 339 N. Clark
Rhode Otto, 151 Goethe
Rhode Paul J. C. 339 N. Clark
Rhode Rudolph E. 151 Goethe
Rhodes Charles W. 269 Erie
Rhodes George, Evanston
Rhodes George L. Lakota hotel
Rhodes J. Edwin, Dr. 506 W. Adams
Rhodes J. Foster, Lakota hotel
Rhodes J. H. 5037 Lake av.
Rhodes Katharine Miss, 269 Erie
Rhodes William 269 Erie
Rice Arthur T. 187 S. Campbell av.
Rice Calvin F. Evanston
Rice Charles B. Highland Park
Rice Charles W. 36th ne. cor. Ellis av.
Rice C. H. 5727 Madison av.
Rice C. H. Mrs. 549 W. Vanburen
Rice Elliott S. 5530 East End av.
Rice Emily S. Mrs. 72 Astor
Rice Emma L. S. Mrs. Evanston
Rice Ervin A. 6646 Perry av.
Rice E. P. Dr. 183 S. Oakley av.
Rice E. S. Mrs. 157 S. Oakley av.
Rice Frank H. 871 W. Monroe
Rice Frank L. Chicago Athletic Assn.
Rice F. Willis, Lexington hotel
Rice George A. 187 S. Campbell av.
Rice George D. Mrs. Oak Park
Rice George W. 1025 Warren av.
Rice Henry, 1023 Warren av.

Rice H. Arthur, 1520 Washington boul.
Rice I. Preston, 5132 Washington av.
Rice James H. 1321 Michigan av.
Rice John F. Highland Park
Rice John H. Oak Park
Rice Louis S. Evanston
Rice Lucien J. 6454 Stewart av.
Rice Millard W. Irving Park
Rice Myron B. Riverside
Rice N. B. Dr. 584 W. Adams
Rice P. H. 3312 Wabash av.
Rice Rebecca S. Miss, 481 Dearborn av.
Rice Roland P. 6104 Stewart av.
Rice Sidney W. 3937 Ellis av.
Rice Squire Rev. 6104 Stewart av.
Rice The . F. 5554 Woodlawn av.
Rice Thomas B. . 2 Warren av.
Rice Thomas J. 723 Washington boul.
Rice William B. 768 Chestnut, Eng.
Rice William H. Evanston
Rice W. A. Oak Park
Rich Albert D. Riverside
Rich A. D. 6500 Harvard
Rich Christopher. 1210 Wolcott
Rich Elmer A. 113 S. Sangamon
Rich Evert, 445, 65th, Englewood
  Sum. res. Whitehall, Mich.
Rich Frederick W. M.D. Riverside
Rich Harry S. 405 Warren av.
Rich Irving H. The Arizona
Rich M. Byron, 3254 South Park av.
Richard H. W. 5813 Monroe av.
Richards Annette S. Dr. 821 Warren av.
Richards Charles D. Ridgeland
Richards Charles R. 4104 Indiana av.
Richards Charles W. 813 Washington boul.
Richards Emily S. Mrs. Oak Park
Richards George A. Evanston
Richards G. E., M. D. 44½ Bellevue pl.
Richards Herbert V. 77 Bryant av.
Richards Isaac D. 4132 Calumet av.
Richards John T. 3432 Rhodes av.
Richards Julia Mrs. 283 W. Adams
Richards J. P. Rev. 821 Warren av.
Richards J. T. 3438 Vernon av.
Richards J. W. 2426 Indiana av.
Richards Kate Miss, 3, 31st
Richards Lincoln, Oak Park
Richards Maurice G. Evanston
Richards Moses J. 485 Washington boul.
Richards N. B. 215 S. Lincoln
Richards O. K. 2426 Indiana av.
Richards Ransom, 4104 Indiana av.
Richards Robert, 116, 45th
Richards Seaman P. Riverside
Richards William B. 231 Winchester av.
Richards William P. Dr. 1446 Dakin
Richardson Anna Ives Mrs. Riverside
Richardson A. P. 47 Bellevue pl.
Richardson Cecila Mrs. 237 Warren av.
Richardson Charles, 420 Ashland boul.
Richardson Charles A. Oak Park
Richardson C. B. Oak Park
Richardson Daniel E. Riverside
Richardson D. D. Dr. 3312 Cottage Grove
  av.

Richardson Edwin C. 3841 Calumet av.
  Sum. res. Antioch, Ill., Channel Lake
Richardson E. Perrin, 1338 Washington
  boul.
Richardson Francis M.,M.D. 633 Garfield
  boul.
Richardson F. M. 1622 Briar pl.
Richardson George P. 172 Oakwood boul.
Richardson Gordon M. 1338 Washington
  boul.
Richardson Harry B. Oak Park
Richardson John C. Newberry hotel
Richardson J. A. 11½ University pl.
Richardson J. G. Mrs. 6704 Lafayette av.
Richardson J. E. 468 S. Oakley av.
Richardson J. R., M. D. 479, 42d pl.
Richardson Levant M. 1810 Frederick
Richardson L. A. Mrs. 328 Lasalle av.
Richardson L. B. Morton Park
Richardson Merrick A. 1212 Washington
  boul.
Richardson M. Arthur, 1212 Washington
  boul.
Richardson O. S. 117 Buena av.
Richardson Orlo D. 3825 Forest av.
Richardson Orlo W. 3825 Forest av.
  Sum. res. Antioch, Ill., Channel Lake
Richardson Rebecca A. Miss, Elmhurst
Richardson Rose Miss, 4528 Oakenwald
  av.
Richardson R. J. Lakota hotel
Richardson R. W. Lakota hotel
Richardson Samuel H. 5735 Rosalie ct.
Richardson Samuel M. 1810 Frederick
Richardson T. R. 191 Laflin
Richardson William, 2742 N. Paulina
Richardson William W. 4410 Langley av.
Richardson W. C. B. 117 Buena av.
Richardson W. H. 5824 Jefferson av.
Richardson W. J. Sherman house
Richberg John C. 2335 Indiana av.
           Sum. res. Woodstock, Vt.
Richey A. D. Irving Park
Richey Charles G. Austin
Richey F. L. Irving Park
Richey John R. Austin
Richey M. M. 7817 Reynolds av.
Richey Thomas G. Austin
Richie Bruce E. Hinsdale
Richman Jacob, 4335 Langley av.
Richman Nathaniel P. 4245 Grand boul.
Richmond Charles H. Mrs. Evanston
Richmond C. W. LaGrange
Richmond Frederick S. Evanston
Richmond William, 3742 Ridge av.
Richmond W. C. Glencoe
Richolson B. F. 107 Loomis
Richter August F. 1928 Wellington av.
Richter Paul K. 3729 Ellis av.
Rick John G. 946 W. Harrison
Rickards William T. Evanston
Rickcords Frances L. Mrs. 301 Ashland
  boul.
Rickcords George E. 572 Dearborn av.
Ricker Fred, 7222 Euclid av. (H.P.)
Ricker Jewett E. 401 Superior

Ricketts C. Lindsay, 238, 67th, Eng.
Rickey J. W. 5809 Rosalie ct.
Rickey N. F. Mrs. Evanston
Rickey Pardon C. Evanston
Ricklefs Charles G. 391 Ashland boul.
Riddell Annie Miss, 433 Elm
Riddell David R. 2556 Wabash av.
Riddiford William H. 1056 Washington
  boul.
Riddle F. A. 512 Jackson boul.
Rider E. R. Oak Park
Rider M. Mrs. 3624 Ellis av.
Rider William H. 3624 Ellis av.
Riderburg S. W. 908 N. Washtenaw
Ridgaway Henry B. Rev. Evanston
Ridgway G. 248 Ashland boul.
Ridgway James V. Hinsdale
Ridgway William, 213 Ashland boul.
Ridlon John Dr. 2309 Calumet av.
Riebe Gustav, 1853 Barry av.
Riedle Frank, 5837 Washington av.
Riegelman A. 2920 Groveland av.
Riegert E. 74 Racine av.
Rieke Henry, 1705 Deming ct.
Riel Gustav, 1161 N. Clark
Riel John G. 531 Winchester av.
Rieman M. 4325 Drexel boul.
Rieper Henry, 632 N. Hoyne av.
Riesenfeld S. S. 3114 South Park av
Rieser Samuel M. 4559 Evans av.
Rietz Alexander, 926 Walnut
Rietz August, 449 Ashland boul.
Rietz August W. 545 Dearborn av.
Rietz Charles F. 303 Pine Grove av.
Rietz Edward G. W. 724 Washington
  boul.
Rietz Frederick, 307 Pine Grove av.
Rietz Harry F. 449 Ashland boul.
Riford Seth, 1232 Wilcox av.
Riggle Albert W. 321, 61st, Eng.
Riggle Charles F. 1043 Lawndale av.
Riggle Ozias A. 1043 Lawndale av.
Riggs F. L. The Ashland
Riggs George W. 225, 61st (H.P.)
Riggs L. C. The Ashland
Rigler G. W. 6826 Lafayette av.
Rigney John J. 1124 Washington boul.
Riley Ann Mrs. 2511 Indiana av.
Riley A. A. Lexington hotel
Riley Charles J. 6034 Indiana av.
Riley Frank, 3000 Michigan av.
Riley J. W. 5443 Madison av.
Riley Thomas, 3000 Michigan av.
Rilling C. W. 14 Bishop ct.
Rinder Frederick Rev. 929 Sheffield av.
Rinderer Peter 1717 Frederick
Rines Charles, Newberry hotel
Ring A. W. 1732 Buckingham pl.
Ring Daniel M. 382 Bissell
Ring H. H. 180 Warren av.
Ringer Jacob, 3024 Vincennes av.
Ringer Philip, 3024 Vincennes av.
Ringo Alvin L. 6545 Wentworth av.
Rinn George P. 580 Lasalle av.
Rinn Jacob, Evanston
Rinn Philip, 615 Lasalle av.

Rintelman Anton H. 596 Lasalle av.
Rintoul Robert, 3727 Yake av.
Riordan D. J. Rev. 4036 Wabash av.
Ripley B. W. 783 Washington boul.
   Sum. res. Harvard Club, Lake Geneva, Wis.
Ripley Charles H. 1521 Aldine av.
Ripley Edward P. Riverside
Ripley Edwin S. Hinsdale
Ripley Gordon, Oak Park
Ripley John A. Hinsdale
Ripley John T. 281 W. Adams
Ripley J. T. Oak Park
Ripley William, 783 Washington boul.
Ripley J. L. 1677 Barry av.
Risdon Ambrose, 3307 Forest av.
Rising Charles L. 272 Ashland boul.
Rising Frederick H. 272 Ashland boul.
Rispin R. E. 32 Delaware pl.
Risser A. F. Mrs. 3251 South Park av.
Ristine George W. 3335 South Park av.
Ristow William, 664 Evanston av.
Ritchie Frank, Evanston
Ritchie James B. 331 Chestnut
Ritchie Robert H. 5127 Hibbard av.
Ritchie Sarah Mrs. 5408 Washington av
Ritchie Thomas, 430 Lasalle av.
Ritchie Thomas, jr. 430 Lasalle av.
Ritchie Thomas W. 5127 Hibbard av.
Ritchie William, 4543 St. Lawrence av.
Ritchie William C. Mrs. 5127 Hibbard av.
Ritchie W. Edward 99 Madison Park
Ritsher Edward C. 1698 Wellington
Rittenhouse Louis P. 358 S. Paulina
Rittenhouse Moses F. 3340 Prairie av.
Rittenhouse T. A. 205, 46th
Rittenhouse Wm. Dr. 479 S. Leavitt
Ritter Andrew, 3018 Wabash av.
Ritter August, 36 Sigel
Ritter Henry A. 62 Wisconsin
Ritter Jacob F. 3411 Wabash av.
Ritter John H. 1010 Washington boul.
Ritter M. M., M. D. 3000 Michigan av.
Ritterband Moses M. 4208 Prairie av.
Rivenburgh A. M.,D.D.S. 3351 Calumet av.
Rivenburgh Eugene L. Dr. Mayfair
Rivenburgh H. 1279 Palmer
Rives Hallie Miss, 3405 Vernon av.
Rix George K. 281 Bissell
Rixon Albert W. 4142 Lincoln av. (R.P.)
Rixon Hans C. 4142 Lincoln av. (R.P.)
Roach Fred L. 462 Orchard
Roach John M. 462 Orchard
Roach J. B. 4500 Vincennes av.
Robb Wilson J. Maywood
Robbin Eugene Vincent, 57 Cedar
Robbins Burnett W. 2354 N. Halsted
Robbins Burr, 2354 N. Halsted
Robbins E. F. 2934 Indiana av.
Robbins George B. Hinsdale
Robbins Henry S. 414 N. State
Robbins James A. 2973 Indiana av.
Robbins Walter R. 218, 37th
Robe Margaret Mrs. Evanston
Roberg Oscar B. 145 Cleveland av.

Roberson John P. 5311 Washington av.
Roberts Albert L. Austin
Roberts Alonzo, 420 Washington boul.
Roberts A. A. Mrs. 1837 Michigan av.
Roberts B. T. Morgan Park
Roberts Charles, 217 Fremont
Roberts Charles A. 1383 Washington boul
Roberts Charles S. 2320 Indiana av.
Roberts Charles S. 5761 Madison av.
Roberts Clark, Jefferson Park
Roberts Clifford M. Dr. Hinsdale
Roberts C. E. Oak Park
Roberts C. J. 6558 Yale
Roberts Dwight J. Dr. Hinsdale
Roberts Emma L. Miss, Evanston
Roberts E. L. Tracy
Roberts Flora Miss, 25 University pl.
Roberts Frank E. Maywood
Roberts Frank H. 4147 Langley av.
Roberts George O. 4731 St. Lawrence av.
Roberts Gertrude Miss, 25 University pl.
Roberts Grant J. Dr. 695 Lincoln av.
Roberts G. S. Oak Park
Roberts G. W. Highland Park
Roberts Homer, Evanston
Roberts Jennie Miss, 605 W. Monroe
Roberts John, 219 S. Hoyne av.
Roberts John, 4210 Langley av.
Roberts John A. G. 2543 N. Ashland av.
Roberts John P. 307 N. Clark
Roberts John T. 30 Woodlawn Park
Roberts J. A. 2305 N. Paulina
Roberts J. C. Mrs. 2320 Indiana av.
Roberts J. E. 1693 Alexander av.
Roberts J. H. Mrs. 310, 30th
Roberts Lydia Mrs. Maywood
Roberts L. C. Austin
Roberts Mary J. Mrs. 7748 Sherman
Roberts Melissa S. Mrs. 2808 Prairie av.
Roberts Melville T. 4608 Prairie av.
Roberts Roscoe L. Jefferson Park
Roberts Samuel, 6638 Stewart av.
Roberts T. E. Dr. Oak Park
Roberts T. S., M.D. 4416 Oakenwald av.
Roberts Walter A. 2305 N. Paulina
Roberts Walter C. Dr. Maywood
Roberts Willard A. 4748 Champlain av.
Roberts William, 255 Oakwood boul.
Roberts William G. 4103 Grand boul.
Roberts William H. Tracy
Roberts Wilmer K. 1167 Lunt av.
Roberts W. G. Oak Park
Robertson Alex, The Ontario
Robertson Alexander S. 332 Marshfield av.
Robertson A. P. Chicago Beach hotel
Robertson Frederick C. N. 4316 Greenwood av.
Robertson George E. 5642 Monroe av.
Robertson Gordon S, 4212 Drexel boul.
Robertson Howard, Austin
Robertson James Dr. 338, 44th .
Robertson James G. Evanston
Robertson Janet Miss, 4623 Drexel boul.
Robertson John, 1477 Fulton

Robertson John Blair, 4212 Drexel boul.
Robertson John W.,363 Kenmore av.
Robertson J. D., D.D.S. 755 Jackson boul.
Robertson J. Roy, 19. 33d
Robertson J. W. 3238 Groveland av.
Robertson Luanna Miss, Morgan Park
Robertson Thomas, 332 Marshfield av.
Robertson William A. Oak Park
Robertson William H. Evanston
Robeson T. J. Dr. 2608 Calumet av.
Robie G. T 7124 Yale
Robie John F. R. 298 Erie
Robins George, 96 Loomis
Robins G. E. 4343 Berkeley av.
Robinson Albert R. Hinsdale
Robinson Annette Miss,210 Ashland boul.
Robinson A. E. 5406 Jefferson av.
Robinson A. G. 6957 Yale
Robinson Charles F. 3958 Langley av.
Robinson Charles O. 4406 Oakenwald av.
Robinson Clayton H. 663 Washington
    boul.
Robinson C. 5406 Jefferson av.
Robinson C. W. 4206 Ellis av.
Robinson Daniel Capt. Highland Park
Robinson Daniel B. Lakota hotel
Robinson David, 3727 Langley av.
Robinson D. A. Grand Pacific hotel
Robinson Edward H. 2354 N. Paulina
Robinson Elisha A. 210 Ashland boul.
Robinson Ethel Miss, 698 Fullerton av.
Robinson E. D. Austin
Robinson E. H. 738, 63d ct. Eng.
Robinson Frank L. 6343 Yale, Englewood
Robinson Fred Byron Dr.Isabella hotel
Robinson George G. 874 W. Adams
Robinson Geo. W. 176, 37th
Robinson Helen Miss, 434 W. Adams
Robinson H. H. Lakota hotel
Robinson H. P. 570 Division
Robinson H. T. Mrs. 1641 Indiana av.
Robinson Ithamer A. Austin
Robinson James S. 348 S. Oakley av.
Robinson John R. 3341 Indiana av.
Robinson J. B. Lakota hotel
Robinson J. C. 5142 Lexington av.
Robinson J. K. Lakota hotel
Robinson J. W. 7409 Bond av.
Robinson Lena Miss, Lakota hotel
Robinson Lester H. 27 Park av.
Robinson Martha Miss, 210 Ashland boul.
Robinson M. J. Mrs. 6500 Perry av.
Robinson M. W. 698 Fullerton av.
Robinson Samuel, Evanston
Robinson Stephen L. 489 Belden av.
Robinson S. W. Park Ridge
Robinson Thomas, 119 Honore
Robinson Thomas S. 2453 Prairie av.
Robinson Walter B. 698 Fullerton av.
Robinson William Colin, 188, 54th
Robinson William H. Ridgeland
Robinson WilliamW.603 Chestnut,Eng.
Robinson W. B. 192, 40th
Robinson W. H. 192, 40th
Robinson W. H. Rev. 6636 Wright
Robinson W. L. 5214 Cornell av.

Robinson W. W. 603 Chestnut, Eng.
Robison C. H. Mrs. Maywood
Robison John A., M.D. 297 Ashland boul.
Robison J. T. 4756 Lake av.
Robson John, 2637 Michigan av.
Robyn William, 350 Bowen av.
Roche E. H. 179 Rush
Roche Frank J. 2320 Calumet av.
Roche John A. 4605 Drexel boul.
Roche Martin, 3614 Grand boul.
Roche O. H. Lexington hotel
Roche P. J. 2320 Calumet av.
Roche William C. 2320 Calumet av.
Rochlitz J. W. Hotel Imperial
Rock Daniel J. 1219 Lill av.
Rock J. F. Hotel Normandie
Rockfeller George R. 3732 Calumet av.
Rockwell C. B. Dr. 5401 Madison av.
Rockwell Fletcher W 3146 Lake Park av.
Rockwell Gordon C. Dr. 5401 Madison
    av.
Rockwell Helen Mrs. 2101 Prairie av.
Rockwell Irwin E. 901 Pratt av.
Rockwell Thos. H.,M.D. 4467 Oakenwald
    av.
Rockwell W. F. Oak Park
Rockwood Frank B. Elmhurst
Rockwood Frederick S. Elmhurst
Rockwood George, 929 Jackson boul.
Rockwood Harry, Lakota hotel
Rockwood Harvey, Elmhurst
Rockwood Sprague S. Elmhurst
Rockwood W. H. Lakota hotel
Rodatz Jacob, 6337 Wright
Roddin E V. Chicago Athletic assn.
Rodgers Alexander, 363 Hermitage av.
Rodgers E. P. 362 Bowen av.
Rodgers George W. 6400 Oglesby av.
Rodgers John L. 6400 Oglesby av.
Rodgers R. E. L. Dr. 6400 Oglesby av.
Rodiger William, 660 W. Monroe
Rodman Samuel, 113 Cass
Rodman Thos. J. Lake Forest
Roe Albert J. Dr. 4507 Lake av.
Roe Charles, 4507 Lake av.
Roe Charles E. Oak Park
Roe Charles J. 348 Burling
Roe Charles S. 701 Pullman bldg.
Roe Edward, 4507 Lake av.
Roe E. W. Dr. 627 W. Monroe
Roe George W. 298 Erie
Roe Joseph A. 60 Park av.
Roecker Henry L. 481, 42d pl.
Roehl Carl, 1518 N. Halsted
Roehl Edward E. 3751 Lake av.
Roehling George, 1840 Frederick
Roehrig C. H. 148 Dearborn av.
Roelle Emma Miss, 473 Sedgwick
Roemheld Julius, 536 W. Adams
Roemheld J. E. The Arizona
Roesch Frederick, M.D. 769 Larrabee
Roesing Bernard, 328 W. Monroe
Rogan J. B. 899 W. Adams
Rogan W. E. 348 Oakwood boul.
Rogan W. J. 691 W. Adams
Rogers Adolphus D. 361, 65th Eng.

Rogers Albert W. 2211 Sheridan rd.
Rogers Bennajah C. 1129 Kenmore av.
Rogers Bernard F. 80 Buena av.
Rogers Bradford H. 2629 N. Ashland av.
Rogers Charles M. 952 Jackson boul.
Rogers Charles W. 301 West ct.
Rogers Clara H. Miss, Evanston
Rogers C. A. Evanston
Rogers C. D. 5501 Cornell av.
Rogers Edward K. 370 Ontario
Rogers Ernest J. Evanston
Rogers E. M. Mrs. 23 Roslyn pl.
Rogers E. R. Mrs. 6565 Yale
Rogers Frank D. 1313 W. Adams
Rogers Fred S. 1611 Cornelia
Rogers Frederick W. H. 2584 Commer-
  cial (L.V.)
Rogers F. D. Dr. 6106 Michigan av.
Rogers George H. Lombard
Rogers Geo. Mills, Walton pl. sw. cor.
  Rush
Rogers George W. 2575 N. Ashland av.
Rogers George W. Wilmette
Rogers Harry L. 1092 Millard av.
Rogers Henrietta L. Miss, Evanston
Rogers Henry. 2924 Groveland av.
Rogers Henry B. Mrs. 4569 Lake av.
Rogers Henry C. 361, 65th, Eng.
Rogers Henry J. 410 The Plaza
Rogers Henry Wade, Pres. L.L.D.Evans-
  ton
Rogers H. M. Berwyn
Rogers H. W. 320 Lasalle av.
Rogers James C. Oak Park
Rogers James C. Evanston
Rogers John A. 76 Buena av.
Rogers John B. 481 Fulton
Rogers John G. Mrs. Western Springs
Rogers John J. 4750 Champlain av.
Rogers Joseph Dr. 910 W. Monroe
Rogers Joseph M. 76 Buena av.
Rogers Joseph M. jr. 76 Buena av.
Rogers J. Gamble, 76 Buena av.
Rogers J. W. 229 S. Lincoln
Rogers J. W. R. LaGrange
Rogers L. D., M.D. 441 Dearborn av.
Rogers Mary B. Mrs. 359 Ontario
Rogers M. 5425 Cottage Grove av.
Rogers Robert M. 127, 51st (H.P.)
Rogers Robert M. jr. 127, 51st (H.P.)
Rogers Rusha H. Miss, Evanston
Rogers R. N. 16 St. James pl.
Rogers Samuel S. Ridgeland
Rogers Sarah K. Mrs. Evanston
Rogers Sarah N. Mrs. Evanston
Rogers S. M. Miss, 320 Lasalle av.
Rogers T. P. 1092 Millard av.
Rogers W. H. 3942 Lake av.
Rogerson Aspden, Evanston
Rogerson E. J. 88 Loomis
Rogerson John E. 377 Bissell
Rogerson Joseph, 414 Warren av.
Rohde H. F. 6707 Wentworth av.
Rohn Alfred, 1018 Park av.
Rohn Robert F. 108 Seeley av.
Rohn R. 108 Seeley av.

Rohr F. W., M.D. 457 Lasalle av.
Rohu William C. Dr. 267 Ohio
Rojahn Frederick C. 161 S. Lincoln
Roland John G. 540 Cleveland av.
Roland Lorenzo B. 24 St. James pl.
Roler E. O. F., M.D. Lexington hotel
Roles Frances A. Miss, 804 Bryan av.
Rolf A. A. 4459 Oakenwald av.
Rolfe Charles A. 1558 Alexander av.
Rolfe Clark C. 358, 65th, Englewood
Rolfe F. S. 4039 Indiana av.
Rolfe Lucy M. C. Mrs. 358, 65th, Engle-
  wood
Rolfe V. Mrs. 1047 N. Clark
Roll I. E. 5748 Monroe av.
Roll N. B. Miss, 724, 44th
Rolle J. C. 421 Garfield boul.
Rollin J. Chicago Beach hotel
Rollins C. E. 427 Washington boul.
Rollins Georgie L. Miss, 3640 Indiana av.
Rollins G. E. Dr. 3640 Indiana av.
Rollins G. A. Clifton house
Rollins John, 3640 Indiana av.
Rollo C. E. Hotel Holland
Rollo Louis C. 911 W. Adams
Rollo William E. 463 Washington boul.
Rollo W. F. 901 W. Adams
Roloson Robert W. 2109 Prairie av.
Roloson W. L. Lexington hotel
Romaine J. H. 3627 Prairie av.
Roman D. B. Mrs. 812 W. Adams
Romig Samuel V. Dr. 727 Morse av.
Rommeiss Emma Miss, 4504 Greenwood
  av.
Rommeiss Pauline Miss, 4504 Greenwood
  av.
Ronalds James Mrs. Austin
Roney Charles J. 2506 Indiana av.
Roney Henry B. 2506 Indiana av.
Roney Irene B. Mrs. 2506 Indiana av.
Roney Thomas C. 4504 Vincennes av.
Rood Amos D. Evanston
Rood Dudley H. 726 W. Adams
Rood Dwight H. Hawthorne av. Eng.
Rood E. Harris, Hawthorne av. Eng.
Rood George L. 3535 Calumet av.
Rood Golden E. 3966 Langley av.
Rood James, Evanston
Rood James jr. Evanston
Rood James W. 2450 Prairie av.
Rood John H. 4334 Ellis av.
Rood John W. 726 W. Adams
Rood Louis, 2450 Prairie av.
Rood M. A. Mrs. 726 W. Adams
Rood Will C. 303 Park av.
Roof Albert E. 268 Lasalle av.
Rooker W. E. R. 7554 Bond av.
Rooks Edwin S. 636 Park av.
Rooney Thomas E. 407 Marshfield av.
Rooney Thomas F. 407 Marshfield av.
Roop H. T. Dr. 235 S. Campbell av.
Roos Edward, 534 Ashland boul.
Roos Mathias, 5160 Wabash av.
Roos Otto A. 534 Ashland boul.
Roos W. F. Virginia hotel
Roosevelt Wilton C. 2233 Prairie av.

Root Benjamin W. 3236 Calumet av.
Root Charles P. 6011 Madison av.
Root Chester L. 4023 Prairie av.
Root Clarence J. 5534 Washington av.
Root D. E. 3700 Lake av.
Root Eliza H. Dr. 489 W. Monroe
Root E. T. 5200 Cornell av.
Root Frances A. Miss, 5200 Cornell av.
Root Frank K. 35, 22d
Root Fred K. 5725 Washington av.
Root Frederick W. 5323 Cornell av.
Root James P. 5534 Washington av.
Root Jerome, 489 W. Monroe
Root John W. Mrs. 484 Dearborn av.
Root J. Sherman, 489 W. Monroe
Root L. B. Mrs. 3712 Ellis av.
Root Sally G. Mrs. River Forest.
Root Walter R. Kenilworth
Root William, Hawthorne av. Auburn
  Park
Root William J. 1454 Michigan av.
Root William T. Hawthorne av. Auburn
  Park
Root Z. D. Park Ridge
Roper E. U. 1013 N. Halsted
Roper Jessie Miss, 6037 Oglesby av.
Roper John, 4021 Ellis av.
Roper John, 6037 Oglesby av.
Ropp Silas, Irving Park
Rosa George W. 64 Ogden av.
Rosa Harrison, 379 Dearborn av.
Rosback Fred P. 739, 60th, Eng.
Rosche George F. Prof. Elmhurst
Rose Ambrose, 1077 Washington boul.
Rose Annie M. Miss, Hotel Imperial
Rose B. H. New Hotel Holland
Rose Chas. G. 6908 Vernon av.
Rose C. 734, 63d ct. Eng.
Rose C. W. Mrs. 23 University pl.
Rose David Dr. 960 S. Central Park av.
Rose Edward, 3241 Wabash av.
Rose Estelle Miss, Evanston
Rose E. Mrs. 5038 Washington av.
Rose F. E. 2623½ Wabash av.
Rose George A. 738 Washington boul.
Rose George E. Hotel Imperial
Rose Gertrude Seymour Miss, 3000 Indi-
  ana av.
Rose G. A. Lexington hotel
Rose H. H. Lexington hotel
Rose John, 738 Washington boul.
Rose L. C. Lexington hotel
Rose L. C. Mrs. Lexington hotel
Rose Russell C. 6337 Woodlawn av.
Rose William H. 1077 Washington boul.
Rose W. H. 71 Seeley av.
Rose W. R. 5316 Jackson av. (H.P.)
Roseboom Evelyn M. Miss, 1828 Barry av.
Roseboom J. H. 386 Lasalle av.
Roseboom William L. 1828 Barry av.
Rosekrans E. M. Dr. 3756 Ellis av.
Rosekrans S. G. 3756 Ellis av.
Rosenbaum Joseph, 2229 Calumet av.
Rosenbaum Morris, 3311 Michigan av.
Rosenbaum Samuel, 3440 Vernon av.
Rosenbaum William, 3267 Vernon av.

Rosenberg Abraham, 4440 Emerald av.
Rosenberg A. Mrs. 12 Menomonee
Rosenberg Benjamin, 3606 Prairie av.
Rosenberg Bernhard, 3414 Vernon av.
Rosenberg Jacob, 1620 Michigan av.
Rosenberg Julius L. 2901 Michigan av.
Rosenberg J. C. 12 Menomonee
Rosenberg Oscar, 3363 Calumet av.
Rosenberg Philip, 735 N. Hoyne av.
Rosenberg S. Clifton house
Rosenberger Julius Mrs. 3744 Forest av.
Rosenblatt Aaron, 3138 Calumet av.
Rosenblatt Aaron, 3650 Prairie av.
Rosenblatt Benj. H. 4047 Ellis av.
Rosenblatt H. M. 3345 South Park av.
Rosenfeld David, 3363 Indiana av.
Rosenfeld Emma Mrs. 432 Washington
  boul.
Rosenfeld Harry, 2026 Prairie av.
Rosenfeld Levi Mrs. 2026 Prairie av.
Rosenfeld Louis J. 3363 Indiana av.
Rosenfeld Maurice, 1620 Michigan av.
Rosenfeld Maurice B. 3363 Indiana av.
Rosenfeld Sidney, 432 Washington boul.
Rosenfeldt S. Mrs. 264 Webster av.
Rosenfels Samson W. 2957 Groveland av.
Rosenfield Hannah Mrs. 246 Schiller
Rosenfield Henry, 4432 Prairie av.
Rosenfield Isaac, 3428 South Park av.
Rosenfield Louis, 3338 Vernon av.
Rosenfield Morris S. 3405 Calumet av.
Rosenheim Benjamin S. 4432 Prairie av.
Rosenheim Emanuel, 3022 South Park av.
Rosenheim Morris P. 3402 Forest av.
Rosenheim U. 3255 Wabash av.
Rosenow C. G. Evanston
Rosenstein Irving W. 2428 Indiana av.
Rosenthal Aaron E. 3639 Vincennes av.
Rosenthal Alex, 4523 Ellis av.
Rosenthal B. Mrs. 3213 South Park av.
Rosenthal B. J. Hotel Metropole
Rosenthal C. S. 344 Ohio
Rosenthal Elias, 3564 Grand boul.
Rosenthal Emil R. 4120 Ellis av.
Rosenthal E. A. 3210 Indiana av.
Rosenthal E. H. 448 Warren av.
Rosenthal F. 4523 Ellis av.
Rosenthal Henry S. 3564 Grand boul.
Rosenthal H. 445 Marshfield av.
Rosenthal Isaac, 3519 Indiana av.
Rosenthal James, 6046 Edgerton av.
Rosenthal Joseph, 3223 Vernon av.
Rosenthal Julius, 3247 Wabash av.
Rosenthal J. Dr. 3409 Prairie av.
Rosenthal Lessing, 3247 Wabash av.
Rosenthal Louis, 2725 South Park av.
Rosenthal Lubin L. 3564 Grand boul.
Rosenthal Maier, 244 Schiller
Rosenthal Moritz, 2713 Indiana av.
Rosenthal N. 2725 South Park av.
Rosenthal Oscar, 3415 Prairie av.
Rosenthal Samuel, 3265 Vernon av.
Rosenthal Samuel, 4549 Prairie av.
Rosenthal S. M. Mrs. 432 Lasalle av.
Rosenwald Julius, 3152 Calumet av.
Rosenwald Morris S. 3342 South Park av.

Rosenwald S. 3342 South Park av.
Roser E. A. Oak Park
Rosing Edward, 4522 Greenwood av.
Rosing Hannah Mrs. 5238 Jefferson av.
Rosing Kate Miss, 5238 Jefferson av.
Ross Alex M. 1849 Barry av.
Ross Arthur J. 1849 Barry av.
Ross A. S. 233 S. Paulina
Ross Bessie G. Miss, 428 Washington bl.
Ross Catherine Miss, 475 Bowen av.
Ross Charles B. 4442 Sidney av.
Ross Christina M. Miss, 475 Bowen av.
Ross C. E. 115 Seeley av.
Ross Edward F. Chicago Athletic Assn.
Ross Ernest T. 241 Winchester av.
Ross E. L. 319 Lincoln av.
Ross Fletcher R. Dr. 3838 Calumet av.
Ross George, 539 Jackson boul.
Ross George F. 23 Scott
Ross George H. 606 The Plaza
Ross George P. 468 Elm
Ross George P. Hotel Windermere
Ross George W. 505 W. Adams
Ross H. R. Evanston
Ross James L. 3604 Vernon av.
Ross John C. Hinsdale
Ross Joseph P. Mrs. 428 Washington boul.
Ross J. C. 503 W. Adams
Ross J. S. Mrs. Riverside
Ross J. W. 7817 Winneconna av.
Ross J. W. Oak Park
Ross J. W. Dr. 925 Warren av.
Ross Lewin W. H. 1864 Barry av.
Ross L. H. River Forest
Ross Minerva R. Mrs. 4539 Lake av.
Ross M. J. Mrs. 3756 Ellis av.
Ross N. E. Mrs. 574 Boulevard pl.
Ross Oliver S. 4221 Lake av.
Ross Ovington, 468 Elm
Ross Robert E. 428 Washington boul.
Ross Robert S. 475 Bowen av.
Ross Walter W. 2632 Prairie av.
Ross Warner C. 4442 Sidney av.
Ross William A. 4045 Ellis av.
Ross William . 574 Boulevard pl.
Ross William J. 4539 Lake av.
Ross W. C. 3231 Wabash av.
Rossbach Fred L. 750 Fullerton av.
Rossiter E. M. Mrs. Austin
Rossiter Gilbert, Lake Forest
Rossiter Harold, Austin
Rossiter J. S. 528 Orchard
Rossiter Will, 12 Maple
Rossman Ceylon Dr. LaGrange
Rossman Palmer, Oak Park
Roster Joseph, 5488 East End av.
Roszelle Allie D. Mme. 6636 Stewart av.
Roth Charles, 173 Lincoln av.
Roth J. 318 Webster av.
Roth Marshall L. Hinsdale
Roth Matilda Miss, 173 Lincoln av.
Roth Solo W. 1029 Walnut
Rothbarth Paul, 467 Dearborn av.
Rothermel S. A. Oak Park
Rothschild Abram M. 3725 Michigan av.
Rothschild Benjamin, 427 Carroll av.

Rothschild Benjamin, 2633 Michigan av.
Rothschild C. E. 3340 Rhodes av.
Rothschild D. 27 Lincoln av.
Rothschild Emanuel, 2459 Michigan av.
Rothschild Emil, 3742½ Forest av.
Rothschild Fannie Miss, Hotel Metropole
Rothschild Fred, 54, 53d (H.P.)
Rothschild F. 3413 Forest av.
Rothschild Isaac D. 3635 Forest av.
Rothschild Joseph, 586 W. Adams
Rothschild J. A. Mrs. 2633 Michigan av.
Rothschild Leo. J. 2633 Michigan av.
Rothschild Lewis, Barrett hotel
Rothschild Maurice 427 Carroll av.
Rothschild M. L. 3347 South Park av.
Rothschild M. M. Mrs. Hotel Metropole
Rothschild S. M. 3635 Forest av.
Rothschild William, 3926 Indiana av.
Rothschild William L. 3635 Forest av.
Rothschild W. S. 3938 Lake av.
Rothwell Arnold S. LaGrange
Rothwell C. R. 4140 Lake av.
Rothwell Harry L. LaGrange
Rothwell Harry R. LaGrange
Rothwell R. E. LaGrange
Roulet William, 7726 Eggleston av.
Roulston Robert J. 540 Chestnut, Eng.
Rounds Charles H. Austin
Rounds Fred C. Austin
Rounds T. C. Mrs. Oak Park
Rounds William H. Austin
Rounds W. P. Austin
Roundy Daniel C. Dr. Evanston
Roundy Frank C. 447 Irving av.
Roundy William N. Evanston
Rounsavell G. 1847 Wellington
Rounsavell Isabella Mrs. 1847 Wellington
Rounsevell Lucinda Mrs. 2724 Indiana av.
Rounseville R. C. Palmer house
Rountree Harrison H. 1913 Deming ct.
Rouse John Rev. 2212 Prairie av.
Rouse J. E. 1546 Alexander av.
Roush C. F. 278 Bowen av.
Roush E. C. 447 Warren av.
Rowan Charles, 1566 W. Monroe
Rowan James, 1761 Oakdale av.
Rowan P. J. Dr. 372 W. Adams
Rowan Thomas G. 881, 73d (H. P.)
Rowe Charles H. Mrs. Evanston
Rowe F. S. Mrs. 4800 Lake av.
Rowe James A. Evanston
Rowe James L. 511 Fullerton av.
Rowe M. A. Mrs. 6713 Wright, Englewood
Rowe N. Dr. 3011 Wabash av.
Rowe W. H. Hotel Barry
Rowland E. B. Hotel Barry
Rowland E. F. Vendome club hotel
Rowland Ivan R. 445 Washington boul.
Rowland F. W. Miss, 91 Laflin
Rowland Harriett A. Mrs. Evanston
Rowlands David W. 56 Wisconsin
Rowlands H. O. Rev. 586 Lasalle av.
Rowlands William D. 56 Wisconsin
Rowley C. R. Dr. 6316 Drexel av.
Rowley Fanny M. Dr. Oak Park
Rowley Francis H. Rev. Oak Park

Rowley Grace A. Dr. Tracy
Rowley H. Y. 3845 Vincennes av.
Rowley Martin S. 4543 Ellis av.
Rowley S. T. 42 The Yale
Rowley Wm. Rev. Irving Park
Roy John H. 514 W. Adams
      Sum. res. Long Branch
Roy J. E. Rev. Oak Park
Royal Charles B. Oak Park
Royal George, Oak Park
Royal George jr. Oak Park
Royce C. C. Oak Park
Royce E. A. Dr. 721 Washington boul.
Royce Henry F. 1501 Michigan av.
Royer J. C. F. 40, 44th
Roys Cyrus D. 2937 Michigan av.
      Sum. res. Morehouse Place, Elkhart, Ind.
Rozet George H. 340 Lasalle av.
Ruarc C. Mrs. 3131 Indiana av.
Rubel Benj. F. 3341 Wabash av.
Rubel Charles D. 3737 Prairie av.
Rubel Frank D. 3228 Rhodes av.
Rubel Isaac, 3341 Wabash av.
Rubel Isaac, 2714 Indiana av.
Rubel Isaac F. 3432 Michigan av.
Rubel Isidor A. 4213 Vincennes av.
Rubel Levi G. 3927½ Vincennes av.
Rubel L. L. 3745 Vernon av.
Rubel May G. Mrs. 492, 42d pl.
Rubel Milton, 3432 Michigan av.
Rubel Reuben, 3432 Michigan av.
Rubel Rose Miss, 3432 Michigan av.
Rubel Simon L. 3409 Forest av.
Ruben Charles, 4236 Calumet av.
Ruben M. 4236 Calumet av.
Ruben Solomon. 3549 Prairie av.
Rubens Charles, 373 Park av.
Rubens Harry, 581 Lasalle av.
Rubens Lee, 4346 St, Lawrence av.
Rubens Louis, 373 Park av.
Rubidge H. A. 550 N. Normal Parkway
Rubinkam Nathaniel I. Rev. Ph.D. 301, 56th (H.P.)
Rubins Barbara E. Mrs. Morton Park
Rubins Chas. C. Morton Park
Rubins Harry W. Morton Park
Rubins Willis F. Morton Park
Rubovits Edward, 5732 Washington av.
Rubovits Frank E. 5732 Washington av.
Rubovits Toby, 3712 Wabash av
Rucker B. C. Mrs. Austin
Ruddick Charles H. 468 Washington boul.
      Sum. res. Covina, Cal.
Rudert Emil, 5215 Kimbark av.
Rudolph Charles, 283 Lasalle av.
Rudolph Emil, 45 Roslyn pl.
Rudolph Franklin, 283 Lasalle av.
Rudolph Joseph, 283 Lasalle av.
Rudowsky Emma Miss, 141 Lincoln av.
Rueb Edward, 273 Irving av.
Rueckheim F. W. 4201 Vincennes av.
Rueckheim Louis, 4226 Vincennes av.
Ruehl Harry A. 503 Ashland boul.
Ruehl Louis A. 535 Winchester av.
Ruehl L. H. 24 Park st.

Ruehl William, 503 Ashland boul.
Ruehl William G. 445 Winchester av.
Ruehlow Edward, 54 Wisconsin
Ruel George H. Winnetka
Ruethling Henry, 417 Oak
Ruff Albert E. 251, 61st (H. P.)
Ruff Joseph, 3036 Lake Park av.
Ruff Louis P. 251, 61st (H. P.)
Ruffner Frank W. 3607 Ellis Park
Ruffner Will R. 3607 Ellis Park
Ruger A. E. 718 W. Adams
Ruger Thomas H. Gen. Auditorium hotel
Rugg Arthur H. 5338 Washington av.
Rugg George H. 4126 Calumet av.
Rugg John J. 7504 Stewart av.
Ruggles A. Roberta, 33 Roslyn pl.
Ruggles Charles C. 3820 Lake av.
Ruggles Charles R. 299 Ashland boul.
Ruggles C. E. 886 S. Kedzie av.
Ruggles D. M. 520 Dearborn av.
Ruggles Georgia S. Dr. 2211 Michigan av.
Ruggles O. W. 33 Roslyn pl.
Ruggles Paulina C. Mrs. 4434 Greenwood
      av.
Ruggles W. L. Dr. Maywood
Ruhe Edward W. 4750 Langley av.
Rule Charles D. 4314 Berkeley av.
Rumble F. L. 3756 Ellis av.
Rummel Edward Mrs. 1413 N. Halsted
Rumpf W. H. Dr. 87, 18th
Rumsey George D. 607 Division
Rumsey Israel P. Lake Forest
Rumsey Julian M. 313 Huron
Rumsey Julian S. Mrs. 313 Huron
Rumsey J. Franck, Lake Forest
Rumsey Olive Miss, 478 Elm
Rumsey S. Edward, Washington Heights
Runals Clarence L. 1838 Frederick
Rundell A. B. Mrs. 1139 Washington boul.
Rundell Miller H. 1139 Washington boul.
Runge H. D. 79 Ewing pl.
Runnels John F. Dr. 178 Seminary av.
Runnells John S. 350 Dearborn av.
Rush Alfred H. Tracy
Rush D. G. Dr. 576 Lasalle av.
Rush Edwin F., M.D., 369, 44th
Rush G. Fred, 5748 Kimbark av.
Rushton Joseph Rev. 6511 Ellis av.
Rushton Joseph A. 6511 Ellis av.
Rusk John Rev. 647 Fullerton av.
Rusk Nellie B. Miss, 647 Fullerton av.
Russ Alamando B. 181, 37th
Russ Bert S. 346 Ashland boul.
Russ Charles L. 181, 37th
Russ Fred H. 2458 South Park av.
Russ J. S. 3530 Lake av.
Russ Lewis, 346 Ashland boul.
Russegue G. M. 7352 Bond av.
Russell Albert, 6357 Stewart av.
Russell Alfred, 596 W. VanBuren
Russell A. R. 93, 44th
Russell B. M. Tracy
Russell Catherine Mrs. 794 W. Monroe
Russell C. C. 4212 Berkeley av.
Russell Edgar F. Isabella hotel
Russell Edmund A. 2541 Michigan av.

Russell Edward F. Wilmette
Russell Edward P. 28 Delaware pl.
Russell Edward W. 85 Rush
Russell Frank 85 Rush
Russell F. C. 1268 Jackson boul.
Russell Harris, 4214 Ellis av.
Russell Henry F. 102 N. Clark
Russell Homer D. 264, 51st (H.P.)
Russell Hubert M. 708 The Plaza
Russell H. Clay, Morgan Park
    Sum. res. Oconomowoc, Wis.
Russell H. J. 6933 Honore
Russell H. T. Revere house
Russell Isaac Mrs. Ravinia
Russell John M. 183 Cass
Russell Lena L. Miss, Wilmette
Russell Lizzie M. Miss, 525 W. Monroe
Russell L. H. Chicago Beach hotel
Russell Martin J. 5409 Washington av.
Russell Mary B. Mrs. 3847 Langley av.
Russell Mary D. Miss, Morgan Park
Russell M. J. Mrs. Oak Park
Russell O. C. Mrs. Leland hotel
Russell Perley A. 1254 Wrightwood av.
Russell Robert, 4425 Vincennes av.
Russell Robert, Lake Forest
Russell Samuel P. 650 Chestnut, Eng.
Russell William H. 3126 Calumet av.
Russell William H. Highland Park
Rust D. H. 170 Eugenie
Rust Henry A. 1 Aldine sq.
Rust John J. 4721 Langley av.
Rust Josephine E. Miss, 1221 Pratt av.
Rust Julia A. Miss, 4625 Ellis av.
Rust J. W. 4007 Vincennes av.
Rust Mary C. Miss, 1 Aldine sq.
Rusy A. F. 635 Sawyer av.
Rutan Frank C. 3548 Vincennes av.
Ruth A. L. Mrs. 380 Oakwood boul.
Ruth Fannie Mrs. 160 Park av.
Ruth John A. 160 Park av.
Ruth Linus C. Hinsdale
Ruth Samuel S. 235 S. Oakley av.
Ruth VanBuren, 3852 Ellis av.
Ruthenberg Erich B., M.D., 1817 Belmont av.
Ruthenberg Otto A. 1817 Belmont av.
Rutherford Alice Mrs. 824 W. Monroe
Rutherford C., M.D. 631 Fullerton av.
Rutlinger William, 360 Webster av.
Rutt M. B. 581 W. Adams
Rutter David, 410 Ontario
Rutter Lynn R. 410 Ontario
Ruxton William, Oak Park
Ryan Albert W. Hotel Groveland
Ryan Andrew J. 106 Gilpin pl.
Ryan Charles L. Hotel Groveland
Ryan Edwin J. 3938 Grand boul.
Ryan George J. 1373 Washington boul.
Ryan Helen Mrs. 92 Park av. Lake View
Ryan John F. 2525 Indiana av.
Ryan J. Longwood
Ryan J. C. 393, 41st
Ryan J. W. Hotel Groveland
Ryan Kate Miss, Hotel Groveland
Ryan M. W. 40 Throop

Ryan Oswald E. Hotel Groveland
Ryan Patrick F. 1399 Washington boul.
Ryan Philip, Vendome Club hotel
Ryan P. J. 3938 Grand boul.
Ryan W. H 639 Fullerton av.
Rydell J. S. 335, 24th
Ryder A. Mrs. 3016 Prairie av.
Ryder Chauncey F. Hinsdale
Ryder C. E. Mrs. 2606 Indiana av.
Ryder E. Hotel Metropole
Ryder Fred L. 4433 Champlain av.
Ryder J. F. 7850 Bond av.
Ryder S. A. 1506 Michigan av.
Ryer B. F. 799 W. Monroe
Ryerson Arthur, 59 Bellevue pl.
Ryerson Edward L. 31 Banks
    Sum. res. Edgewood, Conn.
Ryerson John A. 141 Pine
Ryerson Martin Mrs. Auditorium hotel
Ryerson Martin A. 4851 Drexel boul.
Ryland Alfred K.Mrs.4400 Greenwood av.
Rynearson James L. 5735 Rosalie ct.
Ryther F. F. 6641 Wright
Ryther Gates A. 6638 Wright

SAALFELD EDWARD A. 3177 Dover
    Sabin Albert, Hinsdale
Sabin Albert R. 794 W. Adams
Sabin Stewart B. 1278 W. Adams
Sabin William, Wilmette
Sackerman Esther Mrs. 192, 25th
Sackett Charles L. LaGrange
Sackett Edward B. 2969 Michigan av.
Sackett Frank V. La Grange
Sackett H. R., M. D. 47, 26th
Sackley James A. 1268 Washington boul.
Sacriste Louis J. LaGrange
Sadler Ernest L. 1525 Fulton
Sadler Ralph H. Hayes, Virginia hotel
Sadtler W. A. Rev. 6100 Michigan av.
Saehn August, 523 Cleveland av.
Saehn Joachim, 523 Cleveland av.
Safford Allen B. 15 Ashland boul.
Safford Bigelow T. 708 Washington boul.
Safford Charles L. 6401 Emerald av.
Safford C. H. Mrs. 708 Washington boul.
Safford H. D. 6434 Honore
Safford James B. 83, 20th
    Sum. res. Batavia, N. Y
Safford Lewis B. 708 Washington boul.
Safford N. C. Mrs. 438 Warren av.
Safford W. H. 6436 Honore
Sage Arthur D. 83, 43d
Sage C. F. 17, 40th (H.P.)
Sage J. C. Rev. Berwyn
Sage Rufus H. 269 Seminary av.
Sage William G. 17, 40th
Sage William M. 17, 40th
Sagendorph Frank E. 888 W. Adams
Sager W. D. 293 Claremont av.
Sailsbury R. D. Prof. 5540 Monroe av.
Sainte Croix A. R. Granada hotel
Saley Met L. 452 Dayton
Salinger David H. 4531 Vincennes av.
Salisbury Darius B. 694 Jackson boul.
Salisbury Jerome H. Dr. 982 W. Adams

Salisbury William H. 568 Washington boul. Sum. res. North Andover, Mass.
Salisbury W. D. Chicago Beach hotel
Salisbury W. M. Walton pl. s.w. cor. Rush
Salladay John W. 2475 Commercial (L.V.)
Sallee H. M. Mrs. 2330 Indiana av.
Sallsbury E. H. Hyde Park hotel
Salmon Chas. 6826 Perry av.
Salmon William W. 410 Ashland boul.
Salmonson Alexander, 4131 Lincoln av. (R.P.)
Salmonson Morris, 4131 Lincoln av. (R.P.)
Salomon August J. 3744 Grand boul.
Salomon A. D. 767 Jackson boul.
Salomon Gottfried S. Dr. 628 W. Monroe
Salomon Joseph, 767 Jackson boul.
Salomon Levi, 313, 41st
Salomon Louis H. 3744 Grand boul.
Salomon Moses, 767 Jackson boul.
Salomon M. Mrs. 628 W.'Monroe
Salomon S. 767 Jackson boul.
Salomon William, 767 Jackson boul.
Salt Mark H. 155 S. Oakley av.
Saltar John jr. 155 S. Oakley av.
Salter F. 6557 Perry av.
Salter George B. Dr. Hotel Barry
Salter George W. 1225 Wilcox av.
Saltonstall Brayton, 2518 Prairie av.
Saltsman E. 3350 Calumet av.
Sammis Fred H. 4210 Berkeley av.
Sammons E. Hudson Dr. 51, 31st
Sammons T. J. 330 Warren av.
Sample Alexander A. 169 Dearborn av.
Sample B. T. Mrs. 551, 60th, Eng.
Sampson Anna E. Miss, 1843 Michigan av.
Sampson Charles H. 67, 37th
Sampson Henry C. Highland Park
Sampson Julia Miss, 40 Sidney ct.
Sampson J. C. 4576 Oakenwald av.
Sampson Nels, Norwood Park
Sampson W. H. 4576 Oakenwald av.
Samson Clark B. 429 Washington boul.
Samson Henry J. 1203 Seminary pl.
Samuel Edward M. 55 Astor
Samuels Daniel V. 103, 37th
Samuelson Charles A. 175, 24th pl.
Sanborn Benjamin S. Evanston
Sanborn Emily A. Mrs. 3120 Calumet av.
Sanborn George E. Glencoe
Sanborn G. C. Austin
Sanborn Joseph B. Winnetka
Sanborn Kate Mrs. Riverside
Sanborn Sherburn, 485 N. State
Sanborn Victor C. LaGrange
Sanborn W. R. Oak Park
Sanborne E. J. Mrs. Oak Park
Sanchez Frank J. 324 Burling
Sandberg Charles, 463 Dearborn av.
Sandberg George, 463 Dearborn av.
Sandberg Karl F. M. Dr, 140 Evergreen av.
Sandberg Nels J. 463 Dearborn av.
Sandherg Fred W. Oak Park
Sander D. 424 Cleveland av.

Sanders Albert D. Evanston
Sanders Alvin H. 1491 Washington boul.
Sanders A. Mrs. 2959 Wabash av.
Sanders H. B. Dr. 3245 Forest av.
Sanders H. P. Oak Park
Sanders John P. 2959 Wabash av.
Sanders J. F. 289, 53d
Sanders J. H. Oak Park
Sanders W. H. Mrs. 3245 Forest av.
Sanderson George C., M. D. 508 Webster av.
Sanderson William J. 4341 St. Lawrence av.
Sandmeyer Henry, 339 Oakwood boul.
Sandmeyer Louis A. 6500 Myrtle av.
Sands A. J. 680 Park av.
Sands Lizzie Miss, 16 Burton pl.
Sands Obadiah, 511 Jackson boul.
Sanford Edward H. New Hotel Holland
Sanford Ella R. Miss, New Hotel Holland Sum. res. Morris, Ill.
Sanford Frank E. LaGrange
Sanford H. F. 1630 Barry av.
Sanford H. T. 4209 Oakenwald av.
Sanford J. E. 6539 Yale
Sanford Merritt E. 5656 Washington av.
Sanford M. S. Miss, 1757 Oakdale av.
Sanford Thomas, 4209 Oakenwald av.
Sanford Wm. C. Dr. 157 Eugenie
Sang Orr, 4112 Grand boul.
Sanger Frederick W. 5401 Cornell av.
Sanger M. C. Mrs. 5401 Cornell av.
Sansome Frederick J. 6213 Stewart av.
Sard Grange Mrs. 2250 Michigan av.
Sard William H. 2250 Michigan av.
Sargeant Charles S. 6200 Sheridan av.
Sargeant Elicia F. Mrs. 80 Bryant av.
Sargeant Mary L. Miss, 464 W. Adams
Sargeant Samuel C. 80 Bryant av.
Sargent Alleta E. Mrs. 947 Clifton Park av
Sargent Benjamin C. Evanston
Sargent Celia Miss, Evanston
Sargent E. H. 4822 Kenwood av.
Sargent Fitz William, 1807 Barry av.
Sargent George H. Evanston
Sargent George M. Evanston
Sargent John, 587 W. Congress
Sargent John S. 8 Aldine sq.
Sargent J. R. W. Lexington hotel
Sargent Walter F. 6800 Perry av.
Sargent Welland F. 5316 Jefferson av.
Sargent William D. Evanston
Satterlee Frank W. Dr. LaGrange
Satterlee John C. 1342 Fulton
Satterthwaite C. Mrs. 2728 Wabash av.
Sattler D. 26 Vernon Park pl.
Sattler D. S. 26 Vernon Park pl.
Sattley Winfield Newell, 4349 Grand boul.
Sauer Albert F. 40, 35th
Sauer Dittmar, 1448 Sheridan rd.
Saunders Austin, 1143 N. Clark
Saunders E. J. Miss, 183 Cass
Saunders Henry, 587 Jackson boul.
Saunders H. 815 Warren av.
Saunders Parker, 6534 Stewart av.
Saunders Thomas H. 815 Warren av.

Saunders Vida A., M.D. 3024 Indiana av.
Saunders Walter P. 6534 Stewart av.
Saunders Will I. 1143 N. Clark
Saur P. B. Mrs., M.D. 4201 Ellis av.
Sauter C. Frank, 541 Cleveland av.
Sauter C. J. 541 Cleveland av.
Sauter Emma Miss, 202 Center
Sauter Joseph A. 227 Fremont
Sauter L. E. 541 Cleveland av.
Sauve Henry B. 4500 Vincennes av.
Sauveur Albert, 4613 Ellis av.
Savage C. H. Auditorium hotel
Savage Edward P. 1377 N. Halsted
Savage Francis W. 1377 N. Halsted
Savage Frank M. Evanston
Savage George S. 4825 St. Lawrence av.
Savage Geo. W. Mayfair
Savage G. S. F. Rev. Dr. 628 Washington
     boul.
Savage Henry G. Evanston
Savage James C. Wilmette
Sawe Henry J. LaGrange
Sawin D. W. Mrs. 2954 Calumet av.
Sawin George, Elmhurst
Sawin J. S. 736 W. Adams
Sawyer Amory W. 5311 Washington av.
Sawyer A. Miss, Lexington hotel
Sawyer A. D. Mrs. 433 Maple, Eng.
Sawyer A. P. Dr. 875 Warren av.
Sawyer Benjamin, 1309 Wolcott
Sawyer Carlos P. 454 W. Adams
Sawyer Charles A. 1640 Indiana av.
Sawyer Charles B. 1640 Indiana av.
Sawyer Charles S. 169 Centre av.
Sawyer D. G. 454 W. Adams
Sawyer Edward W. Dr. 3733 Vincennes av.
          Sum. res. Geneva Lake, Wis.
Sawyer Eugene W. Dr. 4355 Oakenwald
     av.
Sawyer Francis A. Mrs. 150 Pine
          Sum. res. Magnolia, Mass.
Sawyer Frank S. 1309 Wolcott
Sawyer Franklin, 75 Park av.
Sawyer George S. Oak Park
Sawyer Harry C. 94 Park av. (L.V.)
Sawyer H. 875 Warren av.
Sawyer H. B. Hotel Windermere
Sawyer Jo   Y. 1309 Wolcott
Sawyer Leander, 484 Fullerton av.
Sawyer L. N. 305 Lasalle av.
Sawyer M. M. Mrs. 4550 Vincennes av.
Sawyer Robert F. 75 Park av.
Sawyer Sidney, 301 Ontario
Sawyer Ward B. Evanston
Sax Charles, 3608 Prairie av.
Saxe Charles P. LaGrange
Saxe De Forest W. 1331 Michigan av.
Saxe Edward J. Riverside
Saxton Hester B. Mrs. The Arizona
Sayer G. J. 93 Ewing pl.
Sayer James P. 6831 Anthony av.
Sayer Rockwell, 3633 Prairie av.
Sayers B. W. 54 Bellevue pl.
Sayers Henry, 1609 Indiana av.
Sayle J. H. 1028 Park av.
Sayler Carl E. 446 Belden av.

Sayler H. L. 7134 Euclid av. (H.P.)
Sayler Walter, Irving Park
Saylor Charles L. 342 Maple, Englewood
Saylor H. G. 152 N. Clark
Sayre C. E. 1246 Michigan av.
Sayre Virginia Miss, 222 Ashland boul.
Sayward Maria H. Miss, 171 Ashland boul.
Scaife H. W. Dr. 975 Millard av.
Scales Caroline C. Mrs. Evanston
Scales Frank Judge, 234 S. Leavitt
Scales John C. 1383 N. Halsted
Scammon A. E. Miss, 81, 47th
Scammon J. Young Mrs. 5810 Monroe av.
Scanlan Kickham, 85 Ewing pl.
Scanlan Thomas, 6228 Oglesby av.
Scarborough E. E. Mrs. 3926 Prairie av.
Scarborough H. 3926 Prairie av.
Scarrett William R. Rev. Longwood
Scarritt E. B. Mrs. 772 W. Monroe
Scatchard William jr. Austin
Scates Charles, 235 Michigan av.
Scates Walter, 4109 Indiana av.
Schaad C. P. 83 Lincoln av.
Schaaf Adam, 617 Jackson boul.
Schaaf John, 617 Jackson boul.
Schaar C. L. 3554 Vernon av.
Schaberg Charles W. 232, 52d (H.P.)
Schack Arthur P. 1837 Michigan av.
Schackford Samuel, Winnetka
Schaefer C. Bryant, 574 Flournoy
Schaefer Frederick C. Dr. 582 Washing
     ton boul.
Schaefer Konrad Dr. 574 Flournoy
Schaefer L. B. 24 Lane pl.
Schaefer Otto, 914 Pullman bldg.
Schaefer P. J. Wilmette
Schaeffer Christian H. 50 Oakwood av.
Schafer Emil, 1089 Warren av.
Schafer Frank, 1089 Warren av.
Schafer John A. 1089 Warren av.
Schafer J. 762 Warren av.
Schafer Louis, 1089 Warren av.
Schafer Louis H. 631 North Park av.
Schaffner Abraham, 3721 Forest av.
Schaffner Charles, 1906 Indiana av.
Schaffner Fannie Mrs. 3721 Forest av.
Schaffner Herman Mrs. 3217 Wabash av.
Schaffner Joseph, 3306 Calumet av.
Schaffner Louis, 656 Fullerton av.
Schaffner Rachael Miss, 3306 Calumet av.
Schaller G. J. Dr. 515 Cleveland av.
Schaller Henry, 695 Fullerton av.
Schamberg L. 3255 Wabash av.
Schantz O. M. Morton Park
Schapper Ferdinand C. 1832 Frederick
Scharff John P. Evanston-
Scharff W. Mrs. Evanston
Schatz William W. 627 Englewood av.
Schau Clara E. Miss, 147 N. Wells
Schaub Frank J. 234 Hampden ct.
Schaub W. L. 3423 Vernon av.
Schauffler Charles E. Highland Park
Schauweker J. 4549 Greenwood av.
Scheibel Mary Miss, 3456 Michigan av.
Schell Edwin Dr. Berwyn
     Sum. res. Thousand Islands, N. Y.

Schell Frank, 5648 Michigan av.
Schell Louis, 5401 Ellis av.
Schell T. Mrs. 5401 Ellis av.
Schellenberg F. L. 161 Center
Scheppers V. Mrs. 87 Lincoln av
Scherenberg JennieV.Mrs.1953 Deming ct
Scherer Andrew, 383 N. State
Scherer Henry, 443 Ashland boul.
Scherer Louis H. 443 Ashland boul.
Scherr B. Mrs. 427 Cleveland av.
Schevers Arnold J. 343, 60th, Englewood
Schick Albert H. 606 Burling
Schick Charles E. 1751 Frederick
Schick William, 1751 Frederick
Schick William R. 606 Burling
Schiess John C. 1745 Deming ct.
Schiff Henrietta Mrs. 527 Dearborn av.
Schiffer August, 4160 Ellis av.
Schiller Arthur, 4331 Berkeley av.
Schilling Annie Miss, 68 Lincoln av.
Schilling August M. 3026 Lake Park av.
Schilling George F. 4436 Berkeley av.
Schilling John, 68 Lincoln av.
Schilling Minnie Miss, 68 Lincoln av.
Schilling William, 68 Lincoln av.
Schimberg Peter, Evanston
Schimel Charles, 4023 Vincennes av.
Schimpferman W. H. The Wellington
Schindler Albert, 3158 Groveland av.
Schindler Alfred, 3158 Groveland av.
Schintz Theodore, 838 North Park av.
Schirmer Alfred Dr. 401 Marshfield av
Schirmer Gustav, M.D. 625 W. Taylor
Schlacks Charles H. 5924 Wabash av.
Schlacks John, 3725 Prairie av.
Schlecht Catherine Mrs. Austin
Schlecht C. F. Austin
Schlecht Oscar G. Austin
Schlegel Frank, 4858 Evans av.
Schleiter Oscar, 3849 Lake av.
Schlesinger George, 98, 36th
Schlesinger Leopold 2805 Michigan av.
Schlesinger Louis, 309 Belden av.
Schlesinger Max, 3255 Wabash av.
Schlesinger Morris, 637 N. Hoyne av.
Schlesinger Sigmund, 3321 Vernon av.
Schlesinger S. Dr. 457 N. Wells
Schlesinger Theodore R. 637 N. Hoyne av.
Schlick E. R. 455 Dearborn av.
Schlieper Fred. A. 7711 Sherman
Schloesser A. G. Dr. 1741 Gary pl.
Schloesser Rudolph, 265 Lake View av.
Schloss Benjamin 1. 3421 Wabash av.
Schloss Isaac, 3421 Wabash av.
Schloss Samuel B. 3421 Wabash av.
Schlossman Henry S. 3643 Forest av.
Schlytern Charles E. 680 N. Oakley av.
Schmall J. Mrs. 420 N. State
Schmaltz Joseph, 3315 South Park av.
Schmaltz Joseph H. 3430 Michigan av.
Schmaltz M. J. Mrs. 3315 South Park av.
Schmaltz Nathan J. 3315 South Park av.
Schmeling Robert, 720 Fullerton av.
Schmid George, 70 Maple
Schmid Godfrey, 70 Maple
Schmid J. W. 666 Racine av.

Schmid Richard G. 1642 Barry av.
Schmidlap Charles E. 7646 Emerald av.
Schmidt Albert G. 398 Garfield av.
Schmidt A. C. 163 Howe
Schmidt Carl, 503 Webster av.
Schmidt Elizabeth Miss, 5001 Lake av.
Schmidt Ernest, M.D. 424 N. State
Schmidt E. C. 172 Lasalle av.
Schmidt Fred M. 424 N. State
Schmidt F. J. 1159 N. Clark
Schmidt F. Lewis, 6829 Anthony av.
Schmidt F. W. 12 Lincoln pl.
Schmidt Geo. J. 61 Howe
Schmidt G. M. 4408 Lake av.
Schmidt Herman G. Highland Park
Schmidt Hugo W. 12 Lincoln pl.
Schmidt J. 172 LaSalle av.
Schmidt Kaspar G. 756 Sedgwick
Schmidt Leonard 450 N. State
Schmidt Oscar F. 4321 Lake av.
Schmidt Otto L. Dr. 3323 Michigan av.
Schmidt Richard E. 7535 Ford av.
Schmidt William, 1738 Deming ct.
Schmidt William Prof. 3157 Indiana av.
Schmidt William D. 3310½ Rhodes av.
Schmitt Anthony, 4537 Drexel boul.
Schmitt Charles S. 36 Astor
Schmitt Eugene, 4537 Drexel boul.
Schmitt Frank P. jr. 221 Hampden ct.
Schmitt F. P. 36 Astor
    Sum. res. North Conway, N. H.
Schmitt Henry L. 1207 Rokeby
Schmitt Henry W. Austin
Schmitt Herman, Morgan Park
Schmitz Michael, 7839 Bond av.
Schmitz M. 545 Larrabee
Schmitz N. J. 545 Larrabee
Schmoll Hugo, 341 Orchard
Schnadig Jacob, 214, 42d pl,
Schnadig Joseph B. 298, 42d
Schnadig Joseph M. 3213 South Park av.
Schneewind Benjamin, 3019 Vernon av.
Schneewind Harry, 3100 Groveland av.
Schneider A. Mrs, 1511 N. Halsted
Schneider Carl, 1650 Aldine av.
Schneider Daniel, 381 N. Wells
Schneider George, 2000 Michigan av.
Schneider Henry, 5944 Dickey
Schneider Joseph H. 5944 Dickey, Eng.
Schneider Otto C. 356 Lasalle av.
Schneider P. Mrs. Austin
Schneider Samuel, 519 Cleveland av.
Schneider S. N., M.D. 238 Dearborn av.
Schneider William, 140 Garfield boul.
Schnering Julius, 3246 Lake Park av.
Schniglau Charles R. 1855 Barry av.
Schnitzer David, 300 Bissell
Schnur Jacob, 3221 Wabash av.
Schobinger John J. Prof. Morgan Park
Schock Frederick R. Austin
Schock Louise Miss, Austin
Schoellkopf Henry, 298 Chicago av.
Schoellkopf Henry jr. 298 Chicago av.
Schoen G. Mrs. 15 Newport av.
Schoen John, 555 Cleveland av.
Schoen Joseph M. 85 Seminary av.

Schoenberger G. K. 567 Division
Schoenbrun Irving, 3137 Wabash av.
Schoenbrun L. 3137 Wabash av.
Schoenbrun Sampson, 3137 Wabash av.
Schoenfeld J. 360 Oakwood boul.
Schoenfeld Lillie Miss, 4355 Calumet av.
Schoeninger Adolph, 1825 Melrose
Schoenman Byron, 4509 Grand boul.
Schoenman Charles S. 4509 Grand boul.
Schoenman C. Mrs. 4509 Grand boul.
Schoenman Emil L. 4509 Grand boul.
Schoenstedt Fred'k C. 511 Ashland boul.
Schoenthaler Frank C. 1350 Bryn Mawr
   av.
Schoenthaler Joseph A. 894 Turner av.
Schoepflin Adolph, 19 Carl
Schofield J. T. Mrs. 363 Lasalle av.
Schofield Pearl Miss, 213 Park av.
Schofield William E. 363 Lasalle av.
Scholbe Martin A. 771 Larrabee
Scholer E. C. Dr. 886 Lincoln av.
Scholes Parker, 809 Jackson av.
Scholes Robert M. 749 Chase av.
Scholle Henry E. 6627 Woodlawn av.
Schomer Henry, 192 Mohawk .
Schonlau Charles, 1932 Oakdale av.
Schott Louis 467½ Lasalle av.
Schotte Charles, 491 Webster av.
Schoyer Ernest A. 4624 Greenwood av.
Schrader A. 514 North av.
Schrader Otto, 54 Beethoven pl.
Schrader Theodor, 73 Maple
Schrader William L. 528 Cleveland av.
Schrader W. H. Dr. 3974 Drexel boul.
Schram Bernhard, 3337 Prairie av.
Schram David L. 3337 Prairie av.
Schram Louis, 1 Park av.
Schram Sam Mrs. 3402 South Park av.
Schrauder Fred. 3638 Indiana av.
Schreiber Frank P. 724 N. Hoyne av.
Schreiber Thor, Evanston
Schrenk August Mrs. 414 Lasalle av.
Schrimski Isaac Mrs. 3813 Vincennes av
Schrimski Israel, 3813 Vincennes av.
Schrock John D. 440 Belden av.
Schroder Albert, 2718 Calumet av.
Schroder F. F. The Renfost
Schroder Jacob, 2718 Calumet av.
Schroder Milton, 2718 Calumet av.
Schroeder Arthur, 1661 N. Halsted
Schroeder Carl S. Wilmette
Schroeder Fred C. Evanston
Schroeder Fritz, Evanston
Schroeder Henry, 613 N. Hoyne av.
Schroeder Louis, 1816 Frederick
Schroeder William A. Evanston
Schroeder W. E. Dr. 4323 Prairie av.
Schroter Frederick J. 2407 Prairie av.
Schroyer Charles A. Oak Park
Schryver Allen L. 995 S. Kedzie av.
Schub C. H. 648 Washington boul.
Schubert John C. 1821 Indiana av.
Schuchat Henry, 452 W. Congress
Schuchat I. 452 W. Congress
Schueck H. 720 N. Wells
Schuhmann David H. 5334 Cornell av.

Schuhmann Hermann, 5334 Cornell av.
Schuhmann H. H. Dr. 3247 Groveland av.
Schuldt J. 72 Ewing pl.
Schuler E. F. Chicago Beach hotel.
Schulte Francis J. 5031 Jefferson av.
Schultz Albert, 580 Lasalle av.
Schultz Alexander J. 859 W. Monroe
Schultz Charles H. 42, 39th
Schultz C. F. 1417 Ogden av.
Schultz Edward, 1157 N. Clark
Schultz Henry, 1765 Wrightwood av.
Schultz James M. 859 W. Monroe
Schultz Martin, 580 Lasalle av.
Schultz Minnie Miss, 290 Ashland boul.
Schultz R. E. 6337 Woodlawn av.
Schultz S. C. Mrs. 859 W. Monroe
Schultz Theodore, Jefferson Park
Schulz Matthias, 720 N. Robey
Schulz Paul, 526, 65th ct. Eng.
Schumacher Bowen W. Highland Park
Schumann Charles, 481 Cleveland av.
Schumann George P. Mrs. 669 Lasalle av.
Schumm Margaret Mrs. 472 Cleveland av.
Schupp A. Mrs. 1022 N. Halsted
Schureman Jacob L. 427 Chestnut. Eng.
Schureman Jacob L. jr. 427 Chestnut, Eng.
Schuster Charles, 3255 Wabash av.
Schutt Louis, 727 N. Wells
Schutt Louis jr. 727 N. Wells
Schuttler Peter, 287 W. Adams
Schuyler Daniel J. 3427 Vernon av.
Schuyler Daniel J. jr. 3427 Vernon av.
Schuyler Frederick J. Hinsdale
Schuyler John R. Winnetka
Schwab Alfred C. 2901 Michigan av.
Schwab Charles H. 1709 Michigan av.
Schwab Henry C. 1709 Michigan av.
Schwab Jerome C. 1709 Michigan av.
Schwabacher Henry, jr. 3420 Wabash av.
Schwabacher Henry H. 3133 Michigan av.
Schwabacher Julius, 3133 Michigan av.
Schwabacher Morris, 1931 Indiana av.
Schwahn Catherine Mrs. 3224 Vernon av.
Schwautke Fred, 3549 Ellis av.
Schwartz Albert, 3353 Indiana av.
Schwartz Fanny Miss, 77 Bowen av.
Schwartz Gustavus A. Auditorium annex
Schwartz J. C. 3532 Vernon av.
Schwartz W. B. 3531 Indiana av.
Schwarz Albert, 3261 Vernon av.
Schwarz Albert, 880 W. Adams
Schwarz B. Mrs. 279 W. Adams
Schwarz Edmund F. 5233 Kimbark av.
Schwarz Edward, 880 W. Adams
Schwarz George F. 325 Hampden ct.
Schwarz G. B. 462 Racine av.
Schwarz Herbert E. 6901 Grant pl. Eng.
Schwarz H. Mrs. 4510 Ellis av.
Schwarz I. G. 3232 Wabash av.
Schwarz John J. 420 Lasalle av.
Schwarz K. O. Dr. 87, 18th
Schwarz Leigh Dr. 6901 Grant pl. Eng.
Schwarz M. 3261 Vernon av.
Schwarz Peter M. 567 Lasalle av.
Schwarz P. L. August, 100 Park av. (L.V.)
Schwarz Rose Mrs. 420 Lasalle av.

Schwarz Theodore, Higbland Park
Schwarz Wilhelmina Mrs. 420 Lasalle av.
Schweisthal Felix J. 1390 N. Halsted
Schweitzer A. 631 Fullerton av.
Schwender John, Hotel Metropole
Schwender Margaret Mrs. 524 Garfield
    av.
Schwennesen H. P. 1235 Grace
Schwerdt John H. Riverside
Schwind Henry S. 1341 Palmer
Schycker Moritz Dr. 4625 Evans av.
Scobe M. C. 371 Bowen av.
Scobey Zephania D. 7816 Eggleston av.
Scofield Augusta Mrs. 922 Jackson boul.
Scofield F. M. Chicago Beach hotel
Scofield G. S. Hyde Park hotel
Scofield Isaac I. 3707 Vincennes av.
Scofield J. W. 3232 Forest av.
Scofield L. K. 4532 Lake av.
Scollay Elizabeth Mrs. 4060 Ellis av.
Scotford L. K. 6431 Harvard
Scott Agnes J. Mrs 3160 Groveland av.
Scott Alfred F. 110 Warren av.
Scott A. G. 6754 Lafayette av.
Scott Charles F. Evanston
Scott C. H. Lexington hotel
Scott C. W. New Hotel Holland
Scott Edward Hamilton,2714 Michigan av.
    Sum. res. Rosalie Villa, Ontario, Can.
Scott Edwin D. 4132 Lake av.
Scott Edwin J. 108, 43d
Scott E. Norman, 136 Pine
Scott Frank E. 374 Dearborn av.
Scott Frank H. 15 Roslyn pl.
Scott George, Lakeside
Scott George A. H. 4343 Grand boul.
Scott George M. Riverside
Scott Hugh M. Rev. 520 W. Adams
Scott James W. 184 Pine
Scott John B. 408 Ashland boul.
Scott John E. Evanston
Scott John W. Evanston
Scott J. E. G. 7207 Webster av.
Scott J. M. 267 Bissell
Scott J. William, Evanston
Scott Lancaster F. Dr. 741 Grace
Scott Lewis B. 424 Cuyler
Scott Martha Miss, Lakeside
Scott Mary Mrs. Riverside
Scott Mary Avis Miss, 5046 Woodlawn av.
Scott M. B. Mrs. 4132 Lake av.
Scott Robert D. Rev. 279 Seminary av.
Scott Robert L. Evanston
Scott Robert S. Lakeside
Scott R. S. Hotel Metropole
Scott T. P. Julien hotel
Scott Walter A. Virginia hotel
Scott Walter G. 136 Pine
Scott Willard Rev. 216, 42d pl.
Scott William, 159 S. Leavitt
Scott William C. Ridgeland
Scott William D. 4356 Berkeley av.
Scott William H. 4132 Lake av.
Scott Winfield, 204 The Plaza
Scott W. A. LaGrange
Scott W. H. 3158 Prairie av.

Scott W. M. Evanston
Scovel Bernard, 3745 Ellis av.
Scovel Robert A. 3847 Ellis av.
Scovell John C. 883 Winthrop av.
Scovil Melvine M. Mrs. 2408 Prairie av.
Scovill C. F. Hyde Park hotel
Scoville Amasa U. Riverside
Scoville D. S. 1450 Perry
Scoville E. M. Mrs 886 W. Adams
Scoville Henry T. Evanston
Scoville Hiram H. 886 W. Adams
Scoville John S. 4424 Ellis av.
Scoville Melvin S. Evanston
Scrafford M. J. 173 Ashland boul.
Scranton George E. Hotel Barry
Scranton H. T. 4154 Lake av.
Scranton Mary E. Mrs. Evanston
Scribner Belle G. Miss, 426 Warren av.
Scribner Jesse, 4313 Ellis av.
Scribner Sanford A. 226 Ashland boul.
Scribner W. R. 5338 Washington av.
Scripps George B. Evanston
Scripps Grace L. Miss. Evanston
Scruggs Finley, 3953 Michigan av.
Scudder Clarence O. Evanston
Scudder J. Arnold, 106 Pine
Scudder William M. Mrs. 106 Pine
Scull Harry, Hotel Barry
Scully Agnes L. Miss, 812 Washington
    boul.
Scully Alexander B. 812 Washington
    boul.
Scully Daniel Mrs. 350 Warren av.
Scully D. B. 730 W. Adams
Scully John B. 1534 W. Monroe
Scully Maurice H. 811 Washington boul.
Scully Michael, 811 Washington boul.
Scully Rose Mrs. 811 Washington boul.
Scupham William C. 69 Grant pl.
Sea Sidney W. 3340 Vernon av.
Seabrook A. J. Berwyn
Seabury Charles, Oak Park
Sealor Thomas, 463 W. Congress
Seaman John A. Oak Park
Seaman Leopold, 3317 Calumet av.
Seamour Harriet L. Miss, Evanston
Search C. F. Oak Park
Searing Aaron B. Oak Park
Searing George S. 381 Dearborn av.
Searle G. D. 39 Roslyn pl.
Searles Aaron M. 236 S. Oakley av.
Searles Willard G. 236 S. Oakley av.
Sears Amos G. 1035 N. Clark
Sears Charles B. 2124 Michigan av.
Sears John B. Kenilworth
Sears Joseph, Kenilworth
Sears Nathaniel C. Judge, 2429 N.Paulina
Sears Peter C. 71 Park av.
Sears William H. H. Kenilworth
Sears William R. 304 Erie
Seaton Chauncey E. 3360 Calumet av.
Seaton Elwin D. 7526 Eggleston av.
Seaton Samuel G. LaGrange
Seavens E. M. Mrs. Evanston
Seaverns George A. 2819 Michigan av.
    Sum. res. Oconomowoc

Seaverns George A. jr. 3831 Michigan av.
    Sum. res. Oconomowoc
Seaverns H. H. 5403 Wabash av.
Seaverns J. S. 1352 Palmer
Seaverns William S. 148, 46th
Seavert George R. Austin
Seavey Daniel H. Evanston
Seavey E. D. Mrs. 404 Orchard
Seavey Juliet M. Mrs. 404 Orchard
Seavey Thomas B. 4626 Champlain av.
Seavey Thomas B.6722 Rhodes av.
Seavey W. C. 253 Belden av
Seba John, 5 Lake View av.
Sebastian Don B. 4409 Ellis av.
Sebastian John, 4409 Ellis av.
    Sum. res. Martha's Vineyard
Seckel Adolph, 19 Sidney ct.
Seckel Albert, Riverside
Sekel Elise Mrs. Riverside
Secrist J. M. Tracy
Sedgwick Earl P. 1442 Cornelia
Sederholm Edward T. 1629 Fulton
Sedgwick Edwin H. 4524 Ellis av.
Seebaum J. A. 435 Racine av.
Seeberger Anthony F. 2017 Michigan av.
Seeberger Charles D. 1827 Michigan av.
Seeberger Louis A. Riverside
Seeboeck William C. E. 87 Rush
Seeger Eugene, 1186 N. Clark
Seegers Charles, 1944 Oakdale av.
Seegers George F. 1944 Oakdale av.
Seeglitz Albert G. Dr. 445 North av.
Seeley Hulda L. Miss, 318 Park av.
Seeley T. P., M.D. 289 W. Monroe
Seeley Walter G. 3725 Forest av.
Seelye A. H. 2108 Prairie av.
Seelye Frank R. Evanston
Seelye Henry E. Evanston
Seemuller H. E. Hotel Groveland
Sefton John L. The Ashland
Segersten Gustav, 1656 Belmont av.
Seib William J. 2964 Vernon av.
Seidel Clara Miss, 527 Ashland boul.
Seidel Jacob Rev. 527 Ashland boul.
Seidel R. 1723 Belmont av.
Seifert Edward, 1721 Briar pl.
Seifert J. K. 4219 Lake av.
Seifert M. J. 485 N. Robey
Seiffe William. 1459 Dakin
Seigmund Fred, 401 Cleveland av.
Seiler Alfred, 312 Webster av.
Seiler John, 312 Webster av.
Seinworth John E. 6932 Vernon Park
Seipp Conrad Mrs. 3300 Michigan av.
    Sum. res. Lake Geneva, Wis.
Seipp William C. 533 N. State
Seitz Earl M. 3449 Prairie av.
Seixas Hyman L. Palmer house
Selfridge Harry Gordon, 182 Rush
Seligman L. B. 3605 Prairie av.
Sell Henry T. Rev. 7657 Wright
Selleck A. C. 45 Seeley av.
Selleck William R. 4222 Grand boul.
Selleck Wm. E. Union League Club
Sellers Alfred H. 3420 Michigan av.
Sellers Frank H. 3420 Michigan av.

Sellers John M. 514 Lasalle av.
Sellers Morris, 514 Lasalle av.
Sellinger Thomas J. 2704 Evanston av.
Selz Emanuel F. 1717 Michigan av.
Selz J. Harry, 3329 Michigan av.
Selz Morris, 1717 Michigan av.
Semper Louis, 1241 W.Ravenswood Park
Semper Louis H. 1452 Perry
Sempill Walter M. 721 Chase av
Senn Emanuel J. M. D.,180 Dearborn av.
Senn Nicholas, M.D., 532 Dearborn av.
Sennott Thomas W. 328 Marshfield av.
Senour William F. 3735 Forest av.
Sercomb Albert L. 321 Lake View av.
Sergeant F. E. Hotel Groveland
Sergel Charles H. 2317 Michigan av.
Sergel L. J. 6912 Perry av.
Serrell Wallace L. 4806 St. Lawrence av.
Servatius Joseph H. 820 Lunt av.
Servoss C. A. 727 Fullerton av.
Sessions Frank M. 228, 54th pl. (H.P.)
Sessions Heury H. Pullman
Sethness Charles O. Irving Park
Settergren C. G. 6840 Union av. Eng.
Servant Helen Mrs. 3953 Michigan av,
Sewall Edmund O. 1337 Palmer
Seward M F. Miss, 2223 Prairie av.
Sewell Alfred B. Evanston
Sewell Alfred L. Evanston
Sewell Barton, 129, 51st (H.P.)
Sexton Austin O. 3287 Malden
Sexton Edith Mrs. Hotel Imperial
Sexton George, 561 Lasalle av.
Sexton Henry M. 3058 Calumet av.
Sexton James A. 561 Lasalle av.
    Sum. res. Lake Bluff
Sexton John, 11 Lane pl.
Sexton John, 202 Cass
Sexton John M. L. 1459 Michigan av.
Sexton Joseph, 561 Lasalle av.
Sexton P. J. 1340 Michigan av.
Seyfarth Edward, 218 Warren av.
Seyfried George N. Austin
Seymour Edwin O. Lakota hotel
Seymour Frank C. 67, 37th
Seymour Harry C. 23 Bittersweet pl.
Seymour H. F. 6504 Myrtle av.
Seymour H. Vernon, 35 Roslyn pl.
Seymour H. W. 4615 Ellis av.
Seymour John P. 4350 Oakenwald av.
Seymour J. A. 6843 Wentworth av.
Seymour J. P. 6843 Wentworth av.
Seymour Lynden A. Norwood Park
Seymour Mayhew A. 23 Bittersweet pl.
Seymour Ralph C. 4350 Oakenwald av.
Seymour Robert, Oak Park
Seymour Thomas H. Norwood Park
Seymour William, 5117 Hibbard av.
Seymoure Harry A. 3000 Indiana av.
Shackelford Collins, Evanston
Shackleford Charles, 384 W. Adams
Shaddinger Washington M. Lexington hotel
Shafer J. J. Auditorium hotel
Shaffer H. R. 327 W. Monroe
Shaffer John C. Evanston

Shaffer Mary Dr. 2033 Wabash av.
Shaffner Addison E. 263 W. Adams
Shaffner Benjamin E. 307 Schiller
Shaffner Jennie E. Mrs. 3122 Rhodes av.
Shaffner Phillip B. 1429 Michigan av.
    Sum. res. Newport, R. I.
Shailer Robert A. 5822 Washington av.
Shakman Adolph, 508 Dearborn av.
    Sum. res. Spring Lake, Mich.
Shand J. C. 4730 Kenwood av.
Shandrew W. E. 145 Oakwood boul.
Shankland Edward C. 4808 Champlain av.
Shankland Ralph M. 41, 46th
Shanklin Ernest A. 49 Roslyn pl.
Shanklin Robert F. 209 Cass
Shannessy Joseph J. 445 Hermitage av.
Shannon F. H. 516 W. Monroe
Shannon G. W. 39th ne. cor. Langley av.
Shannon J. S. Mrs. Hinsdale
Shannon Osborne J. 3716 Forest av.
Shannon Oscar M. Riverside
Shannon R. S. 516 W. Monroe
Shantz Jane Mrs. Wilmette
Sharon T. W. 6624 Wright
Sharp Edward F. 464 Elm
Sharp George, Oak Park
Sharp George P. Oak Park
Sharp James S. 407 Huron
Sharp Joseph S. Mrs. 464 Elm
Sharp J. P. Oak Park
Sharp Louis L. 145, 36th
Sharp Robert, 145, 36th
Sharp S. Hyde Park hotel
Sharp Thomas, 739 Washington boul.
Sharp William N. Oak Park
Sharp W. H. 6659 Perry av. Englewood
Sharp W. L. 6730 Lafayette av.
Sharpe A. J. The Renfost
Sharpe Caswell A. Oak Park
Sharpe Ernest R. 1201, 56th (H.P.)
Sharpe William, 226 N. State
Sharpneak Lile, 3316 Indiana av.
Shatford J. D. Hotel Windermere
Shattock C. A. Miss, 405 Oak
Shattock Henry E. 402 Belden av.
Shattuck Charles L. 3426 Michigan av.
Shattuck Geo. B. 5300 Woodlawn av.
Shattuck L. Brace 5300 Woodlawn av.
Shauer Gustave G. 2809 Indiana av.
Shaughnessy J. E. 4749 Champlain av.
Shaughnessy Thomas, 740 W. Monroe
Shaul Julia Mrs. 5460 Washington av.
Shaul Nelson, 3252 South Park av
Shaver Charles H. 6209 Madison av.
Shaver Fred D. 308 West ct.
Shaw Albert, 144 Ashland boul.
Shaw Alf M. 4126 Lake av.
Shaw Archibald, 2968 Prairie av.
Shaw A. D. Austin
Shaw D. Lee M.D. 591 W. Congress
Shaw Edward R. 130, 47th (H.P.)
Shaw Edward S. Hinsdale
Shaw E. B. 385 Ashland boul.
Shaw E. M. Miss, Hinsdale
Shaw George C. Evanston
Shaw George C. Highland Park

Shaw George M. 3035 Washington av.
Shaw Gilbert B. 3423 Michigan av.
    Sum. res. Lake Geneva
Shaw Harry B. 502 Belden av.
Shaw H. B. Grand Pacific
Shaw James W. Hinsdale
Shaw Jennie A. Mrs. 384 Bissell
Shaw John, 2968 Prairie av.
Shaw John, 4450 St. Lawrence av.
Shaw John F. Ridgeland
Shaw John W. Hinsdale
Shaw Joseph, 279 Fremont
Shaw Joseph S. 81 Bryant av.
Shaw K. A. Mrs. 97 Loomis
Shaw Louis B. 298, 38th
Shaw Mark W. Evanston
Shaw Maude Alison Miss, Hotel Imperial
Shaw Robert, 385 Ashland boul.
Shaw Sarah J. Mrs. Evanston
Shaw Theodore A. 2124 Calumet av.
Shaw Theodore A. jr. 2124 Calumet av.
Shaw T. J., M.D. 591 W. Congress
Shaw William A. 1080 Washington boul.
Shaw William A. 4741 Kenwood av.
Shaw William S. 130, 47th (H.P.)
Shaw William W. 385 Ashland boul.
Shaw Willis, 2424 Wabash av.
Shaw W. A. 97 Loomis
Shaw W. C. 6722 Wright, Englewood
Shaw W. H. Grand Pacific hotel
Shawan J. E. 229, 28th
Shay Thomas J. 419 Superior
Shayne John T. 3856 Lake av.
Shayne Ray M. 3856 Lake av.
Shea John D. Capt. 3752 Wabash av.
Shea John E. 5515 Madison av.
Sheahan George H. 385 Superior
Sheahan James B. 3238 Calumet av.
Sheahan J. S. 420 Chicago av.
Sheahan James W. Mrs. 385 Superior
Sheahan William D. 385 Superior
Shean H. E. 6028 Park End av
Shearburn George W. River Forest
Shearer Frederick E. Rev. 206 The Plaza
Shearer William W. 4601 Emerald av.
Shears G. F., M.D. 3130 Indiana av.
Sheckler E. G. 308 Webster av.
Shedd A. F. French House, Evanston
Shedd Charles B. 3015 Prairie av.
Shedd Edward A. 3015 Prairie av.
Shedd E. T. 3233 Forest av.
Shedd Henry S. Evanston
Shedd John G. 4628 Ellis av.
Shedd William J. 7138 Vernon av.
Sheehan James, Winnetka
Sheehan James A. 160 Winchester av.
Sheehy J. J. 1240 Southport av.
Sheer E. L. Mrs. 360, 65th, Eng.
Shefler Connell B. 4420 Ellis av.
Sheibley N. K. 870 Sawyer av.
Sheldon Amy B. Mrs. 4223 Langley av.
Sheldon Catherine A. Mrs. 672 W. Adams
Sheldon D. Henry, 143 Oakwood boul.
Sheldon Edward Mrs. 55 Madison Park
Sheldon Emily Mrs. 22 Lake Shore Drive
Sheldon Frank P, Evanston

Sheldon George W. 96 Astor
Sheldon Grace R. Mrs. 3 Oakland Crescent
Sheldon Henry I. 363 Erie
Sheldon H. D. 672 W. Adams
Sheldon May L. Miss, Evanston
Sheldon M. L. Mrs. 162 Oakwood boul.
Sheldon O. M. Mrs. 44, 35th
Sheldon Theodore, 33 Bellevue pl.
        Sum. res. Lake Geneva, Wis.
Sheldon William T. Riverside
Shellberg John A. 1844 Reta
Shellenbach T. Julien hotel
Shellman W. H. 4353 Berkeley av.
Shepard Albert A. Austin
Shepard Annie E. Mrs. Morton Park
Shepard A. L. 13 S. Lincoln
Shepard Charles C. 121, 51st (H.P.)
Shepard Charles F. 1195 Lawndale av.
Shepard Charles G. 190 Bowen av.
Shepard Daniel Mrs. 5526 Madison av.
Shepard Ellen B. Mrs. 17, 39th
Shepard Frank, 322 Oakwood boul.
Shepard George P. 222, 61st (H.P.)
Shepard George W. 3235 Indiana av.
Shepard Henri E. 3347 Michigan av.
Shepard Henry M. Judge, 4445 Grand boul.
Shepard Henry O. 691½ Washington boul.
Shepard H. V. Irving Park
Shepard Jason H. 3347 Michigan av.
Shepard Joseph, 2724 Michigan av.
Shepard J. A. 4415 Oakenwald av.
Shepard Laura J. Miss, 3347 Michigan av.
Shepard Levi, 347 Park av.
Shepard William L. 222, 61st (H.P.)
Shephard John Mrs. 1069 Winona
Shephard Lenox B. 4146 Berkeley av.
Shepherd Charles C. 66th pl. cor. Hope
    av.
Shepherd C. S. 150, 33d
Shepherd Edward S. 392 W. Adams
Shepherd John, 416 Washington boul.
Shepler Milton S. 240 Ohio
Shepley E. A. 113 Cass
Sheppard Louise Miss, 2811 Prairie av.
Sheppard Robert D.Rev.LL.D. Evanston
Sheppard R. Loring, Evanston
Sheppard S. Mrs. 510 Jackson boul.
Sheppard Thomas H. Mrs. 2811 Prairie av.
Sheppard W. S. 5100 Hibbard av.
Sherborne Thomas P. 2728 Wabash av.
Sherburne E. A. 4744 Woodlawn av.
Sherer J. C. 6440 Ellis av.
Sherer L. S. Mrs. 6411 Oglesby av.
Sherer William G. 39 University pl.
Sheridan Albert D. 4580 Oakenwald av.
Sheridan James W. 390 Ashland boul.
Sheridan Millard J. 4351 Calumet av.
Sheridan Robert Mercer Mrs. 9 Scott
Sheridan W. A. Oak Park
Sheridan W. G. Continental hotel
Sherlie James B. 53, 53d (H.P.)
Sherlock George W. Riverside
Sherlock Joseph, Winnetka
Sherman Andrew T. Wilmette
Sherman A. S. Miss. Chicago Beach hotel

Sherman Bessie W. Mrs. Riverside
Sherman Bradford, 463 W. Randolph
Sherman B. W. 3985 Drexel boul.
Sherman Charles D. Riverside
Sherman Charles K. 361 Oakwood boul.
Sherman Charles M. Union Club
Sherman C. B. Mrs. Evanston
Sherman C. C. Irving Park
Sherman Edwin, Evanston
Sherman E. B. Judge, 3985 Drexel boul.
Sherman Frank, Evanston
Sherman Frank C. 3724 Ellis av.
Sherman Fred J. Grayland
Sherman Fred P. 568 Boulevard pl.
Sherman Fred S. 545 N. State
Sherman Harry B. 407 Dearborn av.
Sherman H. A. Mrs. 229 Michigan av.
Sherman H. M. Mrs. 3316 Indiana av.
Sherman I. N. W. 361 Oakwood boul.
Sherman James M. 18 Park av.
Sherman John jr. Mrs. 225 S. Leavitt
Sherman John B. 2100 Prairie av.
Sherman John D. 4433 Lake av.
Sherman John J. 343 Oakwood boul.
Sherman J. M. 18 Park av.
Sherman Lodema Mrs. 2400 Prairie av.
Sherman Lucius B. 4634 Lake av.
Sherman Mark R. 24, 44th
Sherman Martha E. Mrs. Evanston
Sherman Penoyer L. 4634 Lake av.
Sherman Penoyer L. jr. 4634 Lake av.
Sherman Roger, 4634 Lake av.
Sherman Rollin, 133 S. Morgan
Sherman Samuel, 4634 Lake av.
Sherman S. S. 545 N. S
Sherman Ward B. 3724 Ellis av.
Sherman William Wallace, 2942 Indiana
    av.
Sherman W. M. 387 W. Harrison
Sherman W. B. 361 Oakwood boul.
Shermer Elizabeth Mrs. 3616 Ellis Park
Sherry M. R. M. 576 Washington boul.
Sherwin Augustus G. 1471 W. Monroe
Sherwin A. B. 1471 W. Monroe
Sherwin E. J. 143 Oakwood boul.
Sherwin James P. 3308 Calumet av.
Sherwin Joseph, 4615 Vincennes av.
Sherwin N. K. Mrs. 260 Ontario
Sherwin V. P. 3308 Calumet av.
Sherwood A. B. 2968 Vernon av.
Sherwood E. N. Mrs. Glencoe
Sherwood Francis R. Dr. Clifton house
Sherwood F. D. Morgan Park
Sherwood Grace Miss, 2118 Michigan av.
Sherwood Henry M. 2118 Michigan av.
Sherwood Jesse, 6328 Harvard
Sherwood John B. 530 W. Monroe
Sherwood Julia R. Mrs. 713 W. Adams
Sherwood J. 6328 Harvard
Sherwood Marc, 825 Warren av.
Sherwood Nehemiah, 4712 Madison av.
Sherwood Philip, 105, 37th
Sherwood P. N. Glencoe
Sherwood Smith J. 105, 37th
Sherwood William H. 3258 Groveland av.
        Sum. res. Chautauqua, N. Y.

Sherwood William M. 557, 65th, Eng.
Sherwood W. J. 952 W. Adams
Shewell Susan C. Mrs. Hinsdale
Shibley Elizabeth O. Miss, Winnetka
Shields Alexander, Evanston
Shields C. J. 89 Loomis
Shields James F. 4529 Vincennes av.
Shields James H. Highland Park
Shields John E. 570 Kenwood pl.
Shields J. W. 3913 Prairie av.
Shields Lillian Miss, 89 Loomis
Shields Michael, 573 Dearborn av.
Shields R. P. 6521 Stewart av.
Shiells Hugh, 3723 Forest av.
Shillaber Chas. E. 6124 Washington av.
    Sum. res. Diamond Lake, Cassopo-
    lis, Mich.
Shillaber Robert, 6124 Washington av.
Shilton Clara E. Mrs. 278 Belden av.
Shimmin R. E. 535 Jackson boul.
Shinn Lucy Mrs. 53 University pl.
Shinners Patrick H. 364 Ohio
Shinnick Harold C. 148 Dearborn av.
Shipley Joseph E. 1499 Washington boul.
Shipley J. Chesire 1499 Washington boul.
Shipman Daniel B. 1828 Prairie av.
Shipman S. V. 269 Warren av.
Shippen Kathleen M.Miss,425 Lasalle av.
Shippey Charles W. 243 Michigan av.
Shipton J. A. Lieut. Fort Sheridan
Shire Adolph, 557 Jackson boul.
Shirey Blanche Mrs. 87, 33d
Shirk E. W. Chicago Beach hotel
Shirk George M. 5716 Rosalie ct.
Shirra Jane Mrs. 171, 51st, (H.P.)
Shissler Louis, 1827 Wabash av.
Shively David R. 1822 Frederick
Shively L. W. Chicago Beach hotel
Shiverick Asa Frank, 264, 51st, (H.P.)
Shniedewend Paul, 345, 44th
Shockey Ella Miss, 4122 Grand boul.
Shockey E. S. 1748 Wrightwood av.
Shoemaker Alva V. 4632 Vincennes av.
Shoemaker Charles W. 519 Jackson boul.
Shoemaker Clarence D. 202 Fremont
Shoemaker John, 518, 60th, Eng.
Shoemaker M. L. Virginia hotel
Shoemaker Walter, 519 Jackson boul.
Shoemaker William, 7470 Bond av.
Shoemaker Westley C. Riverside
Shoenberger G. K. 567 Division
Shoeneman Samuel, 3428 Indiana av.
Shogren Lida Miss. 3749 Ellis av.
Shogren S. E. 250, 64th (H.P.)
Sholes C. G. 5704 Madison av.
Sholes E. 819 Warren av.
Sholes Zalmoa G. Austin
Shoninger Bernard, 418 Bowen av.
Shoninger Joseph, 3239 Vernon av.
Shoninger Saul, 4216 Calumet av.   ·
Shonts Theodore P. 612 The Plaza
Shoot W. E. Oak Park
Shope S. P. Judge, Sherman house
Shores Georgie Miss, 2607 N. Ashland av.
Shorey A. V. Mrs. 3601 Vincennes av.
Shorey Daniel L. 5520 Woodlawn av.

Shorey Paul Prof. 5516 Woodlawn av.
Short Adam, 207 S. Leavitt
Short B. J. 360 Park av.
Short E. G. Morgan Park
Short F. J. Morgan Park
Short James H. 2338 Michigan av.
Short James M. 360 Park av.
Short Joseph, 1310 Wilcox av.
Shortall John G. 1600 Prairie av.
Shortall John L. 1604 Prairie av.
Shotwell E. H. Mrs. 180 Goethe
Shourds Clayton B. 108, 45th
Shourds Henry A. 4117 Berkeley av.
Shourds James L. 108, 45th
Showalter John W. 514 W. Congress
Shoyer F. A. Mrs. 151 S. Hoyne av.
Shoyer Samuel, 3646 Grand boul.
Shriner Charles H. 3223 Calumet av.
Shriver L. P. 3180 Arlington
Shrock M. J. Mrs. 1130 N. Halsted
Shubert Alphonso B. The Ontario
Shubert Mary Mrs. 1221 Wolcott
Shuey William H. Oak Park
Shufeldt Helen Mrs. 4210 Oakenwald av.
Shufeldt James M. 4437 Lake av.
Shufeldt W. B. E. 2244 Calumet av.
Shufelt Alma H. Miss, 2631 Prairie av.
Shugart J. D., M.D. 667 Jackson boul.
Shull May E. Miss, 519 Jackson boul.
Shults A. W. 5429 Cottage Grove av.
Shultz Louis A. Dr. 338, 63d (H. P.)
Shuman Edwin L. Evanston
Shuman George L. 261 Ashland boul.
Shuman Jessie J. Miss, Evanston
Shuman Percy L. 150 Pine
Shuman R. Roy, Evanston
Shuman W. C. Evanston
Shumway Edward G. 4549 Ellis av.
Shumway E. B. Miss, 286, 37th
Shumway Mary R. Mrs. Evanston
Shumway Phillip R. Evanston
Shurly Bert. 4360 Oakenwald av.
Shurly E. R. P. 4360 Oakenwald av.
Shurtleff B. M. Austin
Shurtleff Wilford C. Wilmette
Shute G. A. Miss, 3236 Prairie av.
Shute G. H. Edison Park
Shute John W. 3641 Vincennes av.
Shute W. B. Hawthorne av. Eng.
Shutterly Eugene E. Dr. Evanston
Shutterly John . Evanston
Shutterly John J. jr. Evanston
Shutts Adelbert J. 1710 Wellington
Shutts John, 1710 Wellington
Sibell Edward A. Mrs. Riverside
Sibell George H. Riverside
Sibley Albert, Oak Park
Sibley Charles A. Oak Park
Sibley Dennis E. 3318 Indiana av.
Sibley E. S. 6039 Edgerton av.
Sibley G. M. 3028 Vernon av.
Sibley Ira G. Austin
Sibley James W. 3318 Indiana av.
Sibley J. A. 3028 Vernon av.
Sibley Sylvester Mrs. 4613 Woodlawn
    av.

Sibley Sylvester Chase, 4613 Woodlawn av.
Sicard Ernest, Park Ridge
Sickel John T. 3004 Prairie av.
Sickles William A. Evanston
Sidley Fred K. 3823 Ellis av.
Sidley William K. 3823 Ellis av.
Sidley William P. 3823 Ellis av.
Sidway H. T. 4349 Oakenwald av.
Sidway L. B. 4349 Oakenwald av.
Sidwell George H. 265 Oakwood boul.
Sidwell Reuben L. 3408 Wabash av.
Sieber F. A. Dr. 424 Belden av.
Sieck William, 1737 Deming ct.
Siefert Martha Miss, 500 N. Wells
Sieg Charles H. 200 Oakwood boul.
Sieg Emily L. Miss, 3924 Langley av.
Sieg Sarah H. Mrs. 3924 Langley av.
Siegel Ferdinand, 3642 Michigan av.
Siegel Henry, Lakota hotel
Siegel Joseph, 3519 Indiana av.
Siegel Sylvan, Hotel Metropole
Siegmund B. 610 The Plaza
Siegmund Emilie, Dr. 823 N. Clark
Sieh J. C. 1108 Millard av.
Siem J. E. Mrs. 408 Dearborn av.
Sierks Henry, 36 S. Wood
Sievers Alexander, 117 Park av.
Sievers Louis, 117 Park av.
Sigler S. 6434 Dickey
Sigler Wm. 6434 Dickey
Silberhorn John J. 4969 Lake av.
Silberhorn William H. Morgan Park
Silberman Adolph, 4066 Lake av.
Silberman Sigmund, 3141 Vernon av.
Silk L. Mrs. 565 W. Adams
Silke Alice E. Mrs. 3307 Rhodes av.
Sill Robert T. 27 St. Johns pl.
Sills Edward P. 4327 Oakenwald av.
Sills W. H. 4416 Berkeley av.
Silsbee Joseph Lyman, 1328 Hollywood av.
Silsby E. W. LaGrange
Silva C. C. P. Dr. 281 Warren av.
Silva C. P. Morgan Park
Silva F. P. Morgan Park
Silver Geo. M. D. 67, 23d
Silverman Charles, 1915 Indiana av.
Silverman E. 533 Lasalle av.
Silverman Lazarus, 2213 Calumet av.
    Sum. res. Mayfair, Ill.
Silverman Leon, 1119 Bonney av.
Silverman Simon, 3913 Grand boul.
Silverstone Morris, 921 W. Monroe
Silverthorne Albert E. 2410 Prairie av.
Silvester Charles F. 4721 Langley av.
Silvey Edward, 3834 Ellis av.
Simes A. H. 221 Seminary av.
Simon James C. 3805 Forest av.
Simmons Alexander, 2951 Groveland av.
Simmons Charles E, Oak Park
Simmons C. H. 635 Jackson boul.
Simmons E. B. Mrs. Evanston
Simmons E. G. Mrs. 513, 62d, Eng.
Simmons Francis T. 48 Gordon Terrace
Simmons Frank A. 513, 62d, Eng.
Simmons Herbert DeVere, Evanston

Simmons Howard L. Oak Park
Simmons H. W. 5027 Madison av.
Simmons I. Mrs. Oak Park
Simmons John J. 92, 21st
Simmons J. W. 4227 Berkeley av.
Simmons Park E. Evanston
Simmons T. H. 736 Warren av.
Simms E. G. Dr. 4223 Lake av.
Simon Benjamin 397 S. Paulina
Simon Benjamin F. 2243 Calumet av.
Simon Bernhart, 3740 Langley av.
Simon Bertha Miss, 2243 Calumet av. ·
Simon Charles E. 43 Hall
Simon Charles W. 25 Lane pl.
Simon C. Mrs. 25 Lane pl.
Simon David S. 1915 Indiana av.
Simon George, 2565 N. Ashland av.
Simon Henry, 946 Jackson boul.
Simon Henry E. 2565 N. Ashland av.
Simon Jennie Miss, 2243 Calumet av.
Simon John G. 25 Lane pl.
Simon J. H. 405 S. Paulina
Simon Leopold, 2243 Calumet av.
Simon Martha W. Miss, 2243 Calumet av.
Simon Robert M. 2565 N. Ashland av.
Simon Sidney, 3538 Vernon av.
Simon Simon, 2565 N. Ashland av.
Simonds Edwin F. 132, 50th (H.P.)
Simonds Gilbert, 3042 Lake Park av.
Simonds Harriett N. Mrs. 1431 Montrose boul.
Simonds Nathaniel M. 19 Ashland boul.
Simonds Ossian C. 1431 Montrose boul.
Simons A. L. 3429 South Park av.
Simons Charles B. 3708 Langley av.
Simons C. J., M.D. 284, 32d
Simons Franklin P. 6629 Yale
Simons F. P. 284, 32d
Simons Harry, 3429 South Park av.
Simons Henry, 523 W. Congress
Simons H. 3639 Forest av.
Simons I. N. 3933 Ellis av.
Simons Leonard, 3933 Ellis av.
Simons Louis E. 3933 Ellis av.
Simons Mark, 3339 Forest av.
Simons Munro N. 1110 Early av.
Simons Robert, 3933 Ellis av.
Simonson Charles F. 4001 Vincennes av.
Simonson Julius, 3219 Rhodes av.
Simpson Andrew, Evanston
SimpsonAnnaSard Mrs. 2250 Michigan av.
Simpson B. F. Mrs. Morgan Park
Simpson D. J. Lakota hotel
Simpson George, 3818 Calumet av.
Simpson George Rev. Oak Park
Simpson George B. 1020 Morse av.
Simpson George W. 4422 Ellis av.
Simpson George W. 6326 Stewart av.
Simpson Howard Sard, 2250 Michigan av.
Simpson Irwin Dr. 5034 Washington av.
Simpson Jerome W. Riverside
Simpson John Dr. 548 Cleveland av.
Simpson Joseph A. 4422 Ellis av.
Simpson Joseph B. Hyde Park hotel
Simpson Joseph G. 5813 Washington av.
Simpson J. W. 4337 Berkeley av.

Simpson Marcus D. L. Gen. Riverside
Simpson P. L. 6413 Drexel av.
Simpson Samuel D. 106 DeKalb
Simpson T. D. Oak Park
Simpson William, 333 Cedar, Eng.
Simpson Wm. A. 5616 Washington av.
Simpson W. J. Irving Park
Sims S. Chapman, 3802 Lake av.
Sincere Edward, 3303 Vernon av.
Sincere E,. M.D. 2974 Wabash av.
Sincere Louis, 4150 Lake av.   .
Sinclair A. E. Mrs. 6545 Perry av.
Sinclair Charles E. 1491 Perry
Sinclair Cyrus H. 411 Center
Sinclair James C. 3221 Calumet av.
Sinclair Jane Mrs. Glencoe
Sinclair Julia Mrs. 2577 Commercial (L. V.)
Sinclair J. G. Dr. 4101 Grand boul.
Sinclair M. A. Mrs. Oak Park
Sinclair R. O. Mrs. 56 The Yale
Sinclair R. W. Mrs. 404 W. Adams
Singer Adolph L. 574 Washington boul.
Singer Arthur J. 2520 Indiana av.
Singer Charles G. 48 Park av.
        Sum. res. "Adirondacks."
Singer Edward T. Union League Club
Singer Eva Mrs. 3255 Wabash av.
Singer Horace M. Lexington hotel
        Win. res. Pasadena, Cal.
Singer H. A. Mrs. 48 Park av.
Singer W. H. Wellington hotel
Singler Henry R. Morgan Park
Singler Joseph A. Morgan Park
Singler N. Mrs. Morgan Park
Singleton William F. Evanston
Sinks Adolph, 3839 Vincennes av.
Sinks B. H. 3839 Vincennes av.
Sinsheimer S. 7 Crilly pl.
Sinsheimer S. 318 Centre av.
Sipe Henry P. 1066 Clifton Park av.
Sipp James D. Riverside
Sisloff Charles T. 4721 Langley av.
Sisson C. T. 145 Ashland boul.
Sisson Frederick M. 837 Warren av.
Sisson L.E.Mrs. 559 Chestnut,Englewood
Sisson Marietta Miss 3525 Grand boul.
Sisson Stella H. Miss, 145 Ashland boul.
Siter Clare M. Miss, Evanston
Sites George L.Highland Park
        Win. res. Evergreen, Alabama
Sittig E. A. 15 Sidney ct.
Sittig William A. 221 Hampden ct.
Sivett Leonard Mrs. 321 Belden av.
Sizer W. B. 4347 Lake av.
Skaggs J. H. 4449 Evans av.
Skeele John W. 4337 Lake av.
Skeeles Harry B. 5138 Wabash av.
Skeeles T. B. 5138 Wabash av.
Skeen Joseph C. 30 Park av.
Skeer Charles H. 681 Washington boul.
Skeer George M. 681 Washington boul.
Skeer J. D. Dr. 681 Washington boul.
Skelton John W. 143 S. Hoyne av.   .
Skelton L. L. 382 Dr. W. Monroe
Skelton Raphael M, 1641 Michigan av.

Skene Edward P. 5460 Jefferson av.
Skidmore George C. 145 Oakwood boul.
Skidmore Ida Miss. 438 Warren av.
Skiff F. J. V. Prof. Hotel Windermere
Skiles H. P. Dr. 963 W. Monroe
Skillen E. S. 3917 Langley av.
Skillin Thomas J. Oak Park
Skillman Abraham D. 838 W. Adams
Skillman Fred B. Dr. 838 W. Adams
Skinkle Eugene T. 6510 Ross av.
Skinner Anna E. Mrs. 969 Washington boul.
Skinner E. Miss, 100 Rush
Skinner E. F. 197, 44th (H.P.)
Skinner E. H. 197, 44th (H.P.)
        Sum. res. Escambia, Fla.
Skinner E. S. 5338 Washington av.
Skinner Frank H. Dr. 912 Sheffield av.
Skinner F. Miss, 100 Rush
Skinner John B. 159 Cass
Skinner N. A. 735 W. Adams
Skinner O. Ainsworth, 4133 Berkeley av.
Slack Charles H. 395 W. Adams
Slack M. Eveline Miss, 145 Oakwood boul.
Slack W. H. 633 W. Monroe
Sladden Sidney C. 545 Dearborn av.
Slade C. B. 4331 Evans av.
Slade Dana, 1105 Millard av.
Slade Dana jr. Hinsdale
Slade Heury, 292 Ohio
Slade Jonathan, 292 Ohio
Slade Robert, 214 Marshfield av.
Slade Samuel, 236 Oakwood boul.
Slafter J. G. 3135 Forest av.
Slagle R. E. The Arizona
        Sum. res. Hobart, N. Y.
Slater H. J. Lexington hotel
Slattery Edward, 4048 Indiana av.
Slattery M. J. 435 Washington boul.
Slattery T. W. 741 W. Monroe
Slaught Arthur W. Dr. 4712 Wabash av.
Slaught H. E. 440, 64th, Englewood
Slaughter Arthur O. 3142 Michigan av.
Slaughter Arthur O. jr. 3142 Michigan av.
Slaughter Gabriel F. 1653 Sheridan rd.
Slavik Frank, 510 Ashland boul.
Slavik Frank jr. 510 Ashland boul.
Slavik Henry A. 510 Ashland boul.
Slavik William M. 510 Ashland boul.
Slavin J. H. Mrs. 67 Bryant av.
Slayback Charles, 2930 Groveland av.
Slaymaker Harry M. Evanston
Slaymaker Henry S. Evanston
Slayter J. Howard Dr. 466 Erie
Slayton Henry L. 25 Waverly pl.
Slayton Joseph W. 2151 Sheridan rd.
Slayton Sarah Mrs. 5919 Indiana av.
Sleeper James M. Ridgeland
Sleicher J. M. Dr. 3960 boul.
Slimmer Jacob, 561 Kenwood pl.
Sloan Alice A. Mrs. 2115 Prairie av.
Sloan Ambrose B. 4329 Berkeley av.
Sloan C. E. Mrs. 697 Chestnut, Eng.
Sloan Daniel, 366 Mohawk

Sloan David, 742, 67th, Englewood
Sloan Edgar C. 330 Dayton
Sloan George S. 223 Marshfield av.
Sloan Howard J. 223 Marshfield av.
Sloan Junius R. 824 W. Adams
Sloan J.Richard, 607 Chestnut, Englewood
Sloan True L. Hotel Windermere
Sloan William H. 279 S. Oakley av.
Sloan Wolsey A. 607 Chestnut, Englewood
Sloat George W. 435 Washington boul.
Sloate C. J. Mrs. Winnetka
Slocum Benjamin D. 3327 Indiana av.
Slocum D. M. 4128 Ellis av.
Slocum J. 88, 26th
Slocum J. E. 2253 South Park av.
Slocum J. F. 181 Park av.
Slocum Louis T. M. 446 Kenmore av.
Slocum L. W. LaGrange
Slocum Mary E. Mrs. 2253 South Park av.
Slocum Robert S. Hinsdale
Slocum Walter F. 88, 26th
Sloman Marcus I. 3146 Rhodes av.
Slonaker J. W. Dr. Wilmette
Slosson Anson H. 63 Clarkson av.
Slosson J. W. 942 Jackson boul.
Slyder A. F. 3243 Vernon av.
Smale James S. Mrs. 78, 44th
Smale Robert, 520 W. Monroe
Smale W. R. 520 W. Monroe
Small Albion W. 5731 Washington av.
    Sum. res. Waterville, Me.
Small Edward A. Mrs. Highland Park
Small H. N. Dr. 538 W. Vanburen
Small H. W. Maywood
Small L. A. Mrs. 652 W. Monroe
Smalley A. L. Rev. 63 The Yale
Smalley Charles, 5758 Rosalie ct.
Smalley J. H. Mrs. 277 Lasalle av.
Smalley J. H. jr. 277 Lasalle av.
Smart D. R. 6701 Stewart av.
Smart John, 3133 Prairie av.
Smart Joseph, 3133 Prairie av.
Smart Joseph jr. 3133 Prairie av.
Smart J. N. Mrs. 5477 Cornell av.
Smead S. F. 935 Sherwin av.
Smedley J. E. Dr. 313 Chicago av.
Smeenk Warner, 5838 Rosalie ct.
Smeeth Alfred T. 882 Washington boul.
Smeeth E. Mrs. 882 Washington boul.
Smeeth George S. 882 Washington boul.
Smiddy Pierce, 134, 30th
Smiddy Richard P. 134, 30th
Smiley E. Samuel Lieut. Ft. Sheridan
Smiley Hiram F. Dr. Hawthorne av. Eng.
Smiley Marvin Dight, Hawthorne av. Eng.
Smillie J. Oliver, 907 Jackson boul.
Smillie Thomas B. 907 Jackson boul.
Smillie William, 907 Jackson boul.
Smith Abe S. 6711 Perry av. Englewood
Smith Abner, 15 Aldine sq.
Smith Adelbert W. 1404 Fulton
Smith Agnes D. Mrs. 21 Bellevue pl.
Smith Agnes F. Miss, Evanston
Smith Albert L. 60 Oakwood av.

Smith Alexander, 2601 N. Robey
Smith Alfred H. 5311 Madison av.
Smith Alfred T. 217 Vilas av.
Smith Alice M. Miss, 665 Cleveland av.
Smith Alonzo D. 359 Ashland boul.
Smith Alpheus M. 4365 Greenwood av.
Smith Alpheus W. 5712 Monroe av.
Smith Amos R. 10 Ritchie pl.
    Sum. res. Harbor Point, Mich.
Smith Andrew L. 326, 57th
Smith Arthur B. 738 W. Adams
Smith Arthur W. Oakland hotel
Smith A. Mrs. 199 S. Wood
Smith A. A. Mrs. 9 Astor
Smith A. C. Mrs. 7127 Yale
Smith A. F. 663 W. Monroe
Smith A. J. 5039 Lake av.
Smith A. K. Dr. 249 Park av.
Smith A. L. 475 Cleveland av.
Smith A. P. Mrs. Highland Park
Smith A. W. Dr. 1544 W. Monroe
Smith Ben M. 924 Fargo av.
Smith Benjamin M. 376 Warren av.
Smith Benjamin F. 107, 37th
Smith Blanche R. Mrs. 3627 Ellis Park
Smith Burton, Lexington hotel
Smith Burton M. 177 Park av.
Smith Byron L. 2140 Prairie av.
    Sum. res. Lake Forest
Smith B. Mrs. 519 Burling
Smith B. Mrs. 110 Warren av.
Smith B. P. 455 Marshfield av.
Smith Calvin, 6704 Lafayette av.
Smith Calvin S. 3982 Lake av.
Smith Carl, 15 Wisconsin
Smith Caroline Dr. 520 Hibbard av.
Smith Catharine Miss, 514 N. Clark
Smith Charles, 7413 Wright
Smith Charles A. Prof. Lake Forest
Smith Charles D. F. Judge, 469 Washington boul.
Smith Charles E. Evanston
Smith Charles Frederic, 21 Walton pl.
Smith Charles F. 3645 Indiana av.
Smith Charles Gilman Mrs. 2220 Calumet av.
Smith Charles H. 953 Warren av.
Smith Charles H. 4328 Berkeley av.
Smith Charles H. 6505 Yale
Smith Charles Mather, 19 Walton pl.
Smith Charles P. 5311 Madison av.
Smith Charles R. 2942 Indiana av.
Smith Charles S. Dr. Kenilworth
Smith Chauncey H. 4515 Lake av.
Smith Christopher C. 6710 Stewart av.
Smith Clara Mrs. 3532 Calumet av.
Smith Clarence E. 912 Walnut
Smith Cres. 4001 Drexel boul.
Smith Correl, Oak Park
Smith C. Alfred, 1256 Wrightwood av.
Smith C. D. 6352 Stewart av.
Smith C. F. 317 Maple, Englewood
Smith C. F. Dr. Hotel Imperial
Smith C. F. Mrs. Irving Park
Smith C. H. 4501 Drexel boul.
Smith C. H. 1085 Millard av.

Smith C. L. 3248 Wabash av.
Smith C. Middleton, 4013 Drexel boul.
Smith C. M. 93 Seeley av.
Smith C. M. 1757 Oakdale av.
Smith C. Stoddard Dr. 2 Oakland crescent
Smith C. W. 5496 East End av.
Smith Daniel Freeman Rev. Evanston
Smith David C. 534, 67th Eng.
Smith David J. Granada hotel
Smith Delavan, Lake Fores.
Smith Dexter A. M.D. Mayfair
Smith Donald, Hinsdale   *
Smith Douglas, 275, 46th
Smith Dunlap, 1924 Wellington
Smith D. C. 6352 Stewart av.
Smith D. G. Mrs. 177 Park av.
Smith Earnest H. Dr. Austin
Smith Eben Byron 5413 Washington av.
Smith Edgar C. 1047 Kenmore av.
Smith Edgar D. Dr. 305 Division
Smith Edna Miss, Hyde Park hotel
Smith Edward E. 158, 51st (H.P.)
Smith Edward L. 699 Evanston av.
Smith Edward L. Lexington hotel
Smith Edward Page, 10 Ritchie pl.
Smith Edwin B. 5530 Cornell av.
Smith Edwin M. 3147 Vernon av.
Smith Edwin M. Dr. 305 Division
Smith Eli 3147 Vernon av.
Smith Ellen C. Miss, 4407 Lake av.
Smith Emily J. Miss, 323 Oakwood boul.
Smith Emmet L. 525, 43d (H.P.)
Smith Ernest Fitzgerald, 440 Chestnut
          Sum. res. Black Walnut, Pa.
Smith Ernest S. 749 Touhy av.
Smith Espy L. Dr. 974 W. Polk
Smith Eugene 1149 Jackson boul.
Smith Eva Mrs. 785 N. Clark
Smith E. A. Mrs. Evanston
Smith E. B. 11 Lincoln pl.
Smith E. B. LaGrange
Smith E. C. 3138 Wabash av.
Smith E. C. Miss, Avenue house, Evanston
Smith E. D. Mrs. 3212 Calumet av.
Smith E. E. Dr. 5484 Cornell av.
Smith E. H. Miss, 360 Lasalle av.
Smith E. J. Evanston
Smith E. K. Fort Sheridan
Smith E. U. 7043 Webster av. Englewood
Smith Fannie Miss, Hotel Metropole
Smith Frances A. Mrs. 6738 Wright
Smith Frances B. Miss, 970 Washington boul.
Smith Francis A. 7336 Stewart av.
Smith Francis Drexel, 19 Walton pl.
Smith Frank A. 6912 Vernon av.
Smith Frank E. Evanston
Smith Frank J. 6438 Oglesby av.
Smith Frank M. 3995 Drexel boul.
Smith Frank R. Mrs. 295 Oak
Smith Frank W. 5539 Cornell av.
Smith Franklin P. Hotel Metropole
Smith Fred A. 377 Superior   ·
Smith Fred A. 4203 Ellis av.
Smith Fred L. Mrs. 3845 Ellis av.

Smith Fred M. 4345 Ellis av.
          Sum. res. Fox Lake
Smith Fred S. 285 Irving av.
Smith Fred U. 399, 33d
Smith Fred W. 4725 Grand boul.
Smith Frederick A. Capt. U.S.A. 5816 Rosalie ct.
Smith Frederick A. B. 4515 Lake av.
Smith Frederick B. 15 Bellevue pl.
Smith Frederick C. Auditorium annex
Smith Frederick W. 3756 Ellis av.
Smith Frederick W. Evanston
Smith F. A. Hotel Metropole
Smith F. C. LaGrange
Smith F. Carey, 156 Dearborn av.
Smith F. Hewitt, Oak Park
Smith F. Stewart, 429, 42d pl.
Smith George, 1637 Indiana av.
Smith George A. Evanston
Smith George A. Riverside
Smith George B. 42 Aldine sq.
Smith George E. 40, 39th
Smith George E. Hinsdale
Smith George E. 6525 Yale
Smith George Hall, 1637 Indiana av.
Smith George H. Evanston
Smith George P. 3316 Indiana av.
Smith George R. Avenue house, Evanston
Smith George S. Evanston
Smith George T. 4717 Grand boul.
Smith George W. Evanston
Smith George W. Mayfair
Smith George W. 514 N. State
          Sum. res. Mackinac Island, Mich.
Smith George W. Oak Park
Smith Gilbert A. Evanston
Smith Gilman W. 860 Warren av.
Smith Grace T. Miss, 3342 Rhodes av.
Smith Granger, Waukegan
Smith G. M. Mrs. 208, 44th
Smith G. S. Dr. 1742 Diversey
Smith Hadleigh W. 5119 Wabash av.
Smith Harry B. 488 Belden av.
Smith Harry D. 42 Aldine sv.
Smith Harry E. 1441 Dakin
Smith Henry, 699 Evanston av.
Smith Henry C. Mrs. 4203 Ellis av.
Smith Henry D. 42 Aldine sq.
Smith Henry L. 2670 Charlton av.
Smith Henry W. 3826 Vincennes av.
Smith Herbert E. Riverside
Smith Herbert Sanborn, Evanston
Smith Horace S. 4727 Greenwood av.
Smith Howard L. 3601 Vincennes av.
Smith Howard P, 4203 Ellis av.
Smith H. A. 615, 78th, Eng.
Smith H. D. 346 Park av.
Smith H. J. 60th sw. cor. Washington av.
Smith H. King, 742 Washington boul.
Smith H. K. Oak Park
Smith H. M. 159 Locust
Smith H. W. Mrs. 376 Oak
Smith Ilestine S. 3028 Michigan av.
Smith Ishi, 527, 65th, Eng.
Smith Isidore G. Mrs. 6217 Woodlawn av.

Smith Jacob B. 5247 Lexington av.
Smith Jacob P. 5222 Lexington av.
Smith Jacob S. 4500 Ellis av.
Smith James, 93 Seeley av.
Smith James, 95, 51st (H.P.)
Smith James 3227 Wabash av.
Smith James B. 3412 Calumet av.
Smith James G. 93 Seeley av.
Smith James H. 1823 Nevada
Smith James Jay, 3339 Vernon av.
Smith James M. 573 Boulevard pl.　·
Smith James M. 4130 Drexel boul.
Smith Janet Mrs. Evanston
Smith Jedediah H. 533 Morse av.
Smith Jennie E. Dr. 665 Sedgwick
Smith Jerome A. Evanston
Smith Jesse E. 932 Morse av.
Smith John, 141, 37th
Smith John, 3830 Prairie av.
Smith John A. 562, 67th, Eng.
Smith John E. S. Gen. 376 Warren av.
Smith John T. 697 Orchard
Smith John U. 534, 67th, Englewood
Smith John W. 3742 Grand boul.
Smith John W. 7721 Union
Smith John W. C. 333 Ohio
Smith John Y. 435 Washington boul.
Smith Jonathan, 230, 74th
Smith Joseph S. 3141 Prairie av.
Smith Joseph W. Riverside
Smith Joshua, 2448 Prairie av.
Smith Julia Holmes, M. D. 492 Lasalle av
Smith Julian, 22 Hamilton av.
Smith J. Miss, Hotel Metropole
Smith J. C. 1456 Michigan av.
Smith J. C. Gen. 65 Sibley
Smith J. C. jr. 65 Sibley
Smith J. Eugene, 280 Irving av.
Smith J. Frank, 19 Chalmers pl.
Smith J. F. 89 Warren av.
Smith J. Hubert, 872 W. Harrison
Smith J. H. 306, 41st
Smith J. K. Dr. 88, 26th
Smith J. Louis, 6847 Honore
Smith J. Monroe, Evanston
Smith J. O. Lakota hotel
Smith J. O. Winnetka
Smith J. O. Mrs. 2300 Indiana av.
Smith J. Parker, 1503 Michigan av.
　　　Sum. res. Lake Geneva, Wis.
Smith J. W. Oak Park
Smith Kate G. Mrs. 3000 Indiana av.
Smith Kinney, 514 N. State
Smith Lawrence W. 10 Ritchie pl.
Smith LeGrand, Virginia hotel
Smith LeGrand Rev. 377 S. Paulina
Smith Lewis M. 172 Oakwood av.
Smith Lillie J. Miss, 360 Lasalle av.
Smith Lloyd J. 115 Evanston av.
Smith Lucina F. Mr. 360, 65th Eng.
Smith Lutellus, 6049 Oglesby av.
Smith Luther, 4145 Langley av.
Smith Luther L. Evanston
Smith L. Mrs. 4324 Prairie av.
Smith L. G. Chicago Beach hotel
Smith L. K. 5247 Lexington av.

Smith L. LaRue, 6421 Stewart av.
Smith L. L. The Wellington
Smith L. M. 6049 Oglesby av.
Smith L. N. 294 Webster av
Smith L. P. Mrs. 27 Bellevue pl.
Smith Margaret Mrs. 742 Washington
　　boul.
Smith Margaret H. Miss, Evanston
Smith Maria E. Mrs. 3020 Indiana av.
Smith Mark L. 1742 Diversey
Smith Marvin E., M.D. 23 Bellevue pl.
Smith Mary E. Miss, Evanston
Smith Mary Rozet Miss, 19 Walton pl.
Smith Melancthon, Mrs. 335, 53d (H.P.)
Smith Monroe A. 688 North Park av.
Smith Moses Rev. Glencoe
Smith M. Miss, 314 Lasalle av.
Smith M. J. Mrs. Hotel Windermere
Smith Nathan, 220, 46th
Smith N. E. 6549 Yale
Smith N. P. 824 Pullman bldg.
Smith Orange A. 418 S. Leavitt
Smith Oliver N. 339, 61st, Englewood
Smith Orrin L. Dr. 453, 47th
Smith Orson, 41 Bellevue pl.
Smith Oscar M. 2682 Evanston av.
Smith Oscar R. 569 Warren av.
Smith O. C. Lexington hotel
Smith Percy, 4021 Indiana av.
Smith Perry H. Mrs. 150 Pine
　　　Sum. res. Magnolia, Mass.
Smith Perry H. jr. 385 Ontario
Smith Peter Mrs. 2237 Michigan av.
Smith Peter, 267 Park av.
Smith Philander Mrs. Oak Park
Smith Philip R. 16 St. James pl.
Smith Pliny B. 2222 Michigan av.
Smith Proctor, Mrs. 4457 Oakenwald av.
Smith Ralph, Evanston
Smith Raymond F, Evanston
Smith Reginald G. 665 Cleveland av.
Smith Robert, 6, Sibley
Smith Robert J. 3659 Ashland boul.
Smith Robert P. 5247 Lexington av.
Smith Robert S. 5101 Kimbark av.
Smith Robert S. 6636 Stewart av
Smith Ruth A. Miss, 65 Sibley
Smith R. Earl, 359 Ashland boul.
Smith R. E. 569 Warren av.
Smith R. S. 441, 64th, Eng.
Smith Sabin, 492 Lasalle av.
Smith Samuel H. 61 Sibley
Smith Sewell, 6217 Woodlawn av.
Smith Shea, 3971 Ellis av.
Smith Sherman W. 682 Walnut
Smith Sidney Judge, Hotel Metropole
Smith Sidney W. Hotel Metropole
Smith Spencer R. Prof. Austin
Smith Stuart, 435 Washington boul.
Smith Susan Mrs. Winnetka
Smith S. C. 2935 Vernon av.
Smith S. E. 3826 Vincennes av.
Smith S. Fred, 2300 Indiana av.
Smith S. G. Mrs. 2300 Indiana av.
Smith S. H. 3248 Wabash av.
Smith S. L. Austin

Smith S. P. New Hotel Holland
Smith S. T. Hyde Park hotel
Smith Theo. Hotel Metropole
Smith Thomas B. 3854 Lake av.
Smith Thomas C. 231 Oakwood boul.
Smith Thomas P. 4731 Grand boul.
Smith Thomas P. jr. 4822 Kenwood av.
Smith T. D. 757 Walnut
Smith T. H. 4407 Lake av.
Smith T. M., D.D.S. 98 Lincoln av.
Smith Uzziel P. 5812 Rosalie ct.
Smith Viola M. Miss, 288 Lasalle av.
Smith Walter Prof. Lake Forest
Smith Walter B. Evanston
Smith Walter H. 1690 Barry av.
Smith Walter O. 403, 65th, Eng
Smith Willard A. 3256 Rhodes av.
Smith Willard C. 732 Chestnut, Eng.
Smith William, Evanston
Smith William, Oak Park
Smith William Mrs. Evanston
Smith William A. Austin
Smith William D. 360 Lasalle av.
Smith William E. 3260 Rhodes av.
Smith William F. 3307 Rhodes av.
Smith William Henry, Lake Forest
Smith William H. Oak Park
Smith William H. 665 Sedgwick
Smith William H. Hotel Groveland
Smith William H. Ridgeland
Smith William J. 6540 Yale
Smith William M. 357 Dearborn av.
Smith William M. 1742 Diversey
Smith William P. 468 W. Adams
Smith William R. 1128 S.Central Park av.
Smith William R. Lieut. Fort Sheridan
Smith William Sooy Gen. Maywood
Smith William T. 4328 Berkeley av.
Smith Willis, 6950 Perry av.
Smith Wyllys K. Hinsdale
Smith W. A. Dr. Morgan Park
Smith W. B. 436 Warren av.
Smith W. B. 6352 Stewart av.
Smith W C. Oak Park
Smith W. D. 21 Linden pl.
Smith W. H. 509 W. Adams
Smith W. J. Mrs. Hotel Metropole
Smith W. L. 5740 Monroe av.
Smith W. P. Mrs. Oak Park
Smith W. S. Oak Park
Smith W. S. 3442 Wabash av.
Smith W. Treese, 1617 Sheridan rd.
Smith W. T. Oak Park
Smith W V. 909 Spaulding av.
Smithman C. E. Hotel Imperial
Smithson H. L. 2454 Indiana av.
Smithson William S. 2458 Indiana av.
Smoot Kenneth R. Highland Park
Smyth Hill C. 235 Marshfield av.
       Sum. res. St. Joseph, Mich
Smyth Hugh P. Rev. Evanston
Smyth John G. 1905 George av.
Smyth John M. 300 W. Adams
Smyth J. P. Dr. 4500 State
Smyth Martin R. 1905 George av.
Smyth Thomas, 440 Englewood av.

Smyth Thomas M. 300 W. Adams
Smyth William J. 83, 43d
Smythe Emily M. Mrs. 3431 Indiana av.
Smythe Ida N. Mrs. 2458 Indiana av.
Smythe L. E. Miss, Hyde Park hotel
Smythe William E. 469 Washington boul.
Snapp Charles D. 6919 Yale
Sneed A. A. Mrs. Evanston
Snell Amos J. Mrs. 425 Washington boul.
Snell Harry J. 157 S. Oakley av.
Snell Theodore, 42 Throop
Snell William C. 93, 26th
Snell William L. 301 Claremont av.
Snider Alonzo, 229 Marshfield av.
Snider George S. 4429 St. Lawrence av.
Snider Harriet Miss, 229 Marshfield av.
Snider Henry K. Evanston
Sniffen Eeward D. 573, 51st (H.P.)
Sniffen E. D. 5826 Washington av.
Snively Thaddeus A. Rev. 714 The Plaza
Snoddy Lot Dr. Hotel Imperial
Snook Verner V. 316 Washington boul.
Snow Albert E. 3365 Indiana av.
Snow A. J. 2351 Calumet av.
Snow Edgar M. Highland Park
Snow E. G. Mrs. 455 Marshfield av.
Snow E. M. Chicago Beach hotel
Snow George, ·15 N. Elizabeth
Snow Helen E. Miss, 85 Rush
Snow Leslie E. Mrs. Longwood
Snow Taylor A. Austin
Snow William B. 5103 Hibbard av.
Snow William H. 627 W. Adams
Snowden Gertrude Miss, 367 Oakwood
    boul.
Snowdon Richard W 4831 Madison av.
Snowhook P. W. 4629 Woodlawn av.
Snowhook William B. 4629 Woodlawn av.
Snydacker Alf. M. 2441 Wabash av.
Snydacker Emanuel F. 2522 Michigan av.
Snydacker Godfrey Mrs.2522 Michigan av.
Snydacker Joseph G. 2522 Michigan av.
Snydacker Joseph L. 95, 32d
Snydacker Louis Mrs. 95, 32d
Snydacker Morris L. 95, 32d
Snyder Alice Miss, 7051 Webster av. Eng.
Snyder Charles C. Rev. Riverside
Snyder Claude S. 718½ W. Adams
Snyder E. D. LaGrange
Snyder Frank M. 3532 Ellis av.
Snyder F. P. Hotel Metropole
Snyder Jacob, 471 Farwell av.
Snyder John C. 376 Washington boul.
Snyder John S. 3532 Ellis av.
Snyder John S. Highland Park
Snyder J. H. 6441 Star av.
Snyder Karl F. Riverside
Snyder Leonard C. 6738 Perry av.
Snyder Omer C. Dr. 42 Scott
Snyder Oscar W. 233 Irving av.
Snyder O. W. F. Dr. 4206 Drexel boul.
Snyder Thomas D. 7031 Webster av.Eng.
Snyder W. J. 308 The Plaza
Soames Arthur F. 2804 Calumet av.
Soames John, 2804 Calumet av.
Soden George A. 5206 Kimbark av.

Soden J. Stephen, 4220 Ellis av.
Soderberg John, 144 Lincoln av.
Solberg Albert F. 694 W. Monroe
Solbery Caroline Mrs. 685 W. Adams
Solger Parry K. Riverside
Sollitt John, 515 Jackson boul.
Sollitt Oliver, 4020 Prairie av.
    Sum. res. Sunset Cottage, Fox Lake
Sollitt Ralph T. 4545 Forrestville av.
Sollitt Sumner, 4020 Prairie av.
Sollitt Thomas, 4020 Prairie av.
Sollitt William, 1257 Washington boul.
Solomon Charles H. 434 Wash'ton boul.
    Sum. res. Lake Geneva, Wis.
Solomon Frederick M. 3400 Forest av.
Solomon Harry C. 3255 Indiana av.
Solomon H. 4060 Lake av.
Solomon Julius, 1217 Wrightwood av.
Solomon Julius I. 3805 Michigan av.
Solomon L. H. 3744 Grand boul.
Solomon M. F. Mrs. 580 Lasalle av.
Solomon W. 3411 Forest av.
Soltow Frank, 135 S. California av.
Somers Agnes L. Miss, Riverside
Somers E. L. Hotel Barry
Somers Frank W. 3802 Lake av.
Somers G. Horace Dr. 505 W. Adams
Somers Joseph, Hotel Imperial
Somerville Robert, Riverside
Somes Chas. H. Hotel Groveland
Somes Frederick M. Hotel Groveland
Somes Will W. Hotel Groveland
Sommer Maximilian, 4450 St. Lawrence
    av.
Sommers E. L. Hotel Barry
Sommers Harry G. 99, 33d
Sommers James R. 650, 62d, Eng.
Sommers Robert, 147 Evanston av.
Sommers William A. 3721 Vincennes av.
Sommers W. C. 5100 Hibbard av.
Sondheimer Edward A. 2619 Michigan av.
Sondheimer Emanuel 2619 Michigan av.
Sondheimer Henry, 2619 Michigan av.
Sondheimer Max, 2619 Michigan av.
Sonnenberg Samuel, 3717 Vincennes av.
Sonnenschein Leopold, 226 Fremont
Sonnenschein L. 20 St. Johns pl.
Sonnenschein Rose Mrs. 3756 Ellis av.
Sontag Fritz, 46 Wisconsin
Sontag Henry Mrs. Evanston
Soper Alexander C. 3998 Ellis av.
Soper B. J. 4862 Washington av.
Soper Henry M. 1644 Jackson boul.
Soper Horace W. 4004 Drexel boul.
Soper James Mrs. Riverside
Soper James P. 503 Jackson boul.
Soper N. D. Cottage Grove av. nw. cor.
    41st
Sorenson T. P. The Ashland
Sorg Adolph jr. 92 Park av.
Sorrick George A. Prof. Elmhurst
Sosman Joseph S. 570 W. Congress
    Sum. res. Lake Bluff, Ill.
Sottmann Henry, 208 Seminary av.
Sottrup Anna D. Mrs. 83, 20th
Souder Charles H. L. Dr. 6951 Stewart av.

Souder Ellen Starr Dr. 6951 Stewart av.
Soule Charles Babson, 549 W. Vanburen
Soule S. L. 2438 Indiana av.
Southard Albert B. 4595 Oakenwald av.
Southard B. D. The Renfost
Southard Calvin N. 7644 Emerald av.
Southard Charles H. 4334 Berkeley av.
Southard Edward C. 1725 Belmont av.
Southard Mary L. Mrs. 1725 Belmont av.
Southard Nellie Estella Miss, 1725 Bel-
    mont av.
Southgate R. H. Auditorium hotel
Southwell Henry E. 469 N. State
Southwick Sylvanus H. 173, 37th
Southwood Edward, Riverside
Southworth D. A. 230, 45th
Southworth H. E. 3213 Groveland av.
Southworth M. S. Mrs. Oak Park
Sowers Isaac M. Newberry hotel
Spach A. B. Dr. 6629 Harvard
Spackman J. M. Ridgeland
Spafford John I. 197 Winchester av.
Spafford William C. 657 47th
Spahn Lewis, 356 Ontario
Spain Henry, 213 Fremont
Spalding A. G. 4924 Woodlawn av.
Spalding Charles R. 518 Byron (L.V.)
Spalding Charles W. 520 Byron (L.V.)
Spalding C. F. 204 Goethe
Spalding C. W. 522 Byron
Spalding Harriet I. Mrs. 4637 Greenwood
    av.
Spalding Heman Dr. 3141 Rhodes av.
Spalding Jesse, 1637 Prairie av.
Spalding Jessie Miss, 1637 Prairie av.
Spalding Joel J. Evanston
Spalding Keith, 4924 Woodlawn av.
Spalding Merrill 1214 Lill av.
Spalding Stewart, 495 N. State
Spangenberg Charles, 1837 Reta
Spangenberg Henry L. 1272 Wolcott
Spangenberg William E. 338 Dayton
Spangler R. E. 858 Warren av.
Sparks George, 42, 39th
Sparling Ellis H. Dr. 6737 Yale
Sparr A. 408 Jackson boul.
Sparre Charles, 730 Sedgwick
Sparrow William S. Mrs. 6144 Sheridan av.
Spaulding Ella Mrs. 1806 Indiana av.
Spaulding F. M. Oak Park
Spaulding Howard H. Kenilworth
Spaulding S. G. Mrs. 2518 Michigan av.
Spaulding Wm. Mrs. 1826 Michigan av.
Spear Albert A. 2451 Michigan av.
Spear Charles E. Hinsdale
Spear Elbridge B. Evanston
Spear E. Raymond, Hinsdale
Spear Frank R. 209 Ashland boul.
Spear Harry E. 97, 51st (H.P.)
Spear James D. 1067 N. Clark
Spear W. H. 97, 51st (H.P.)
Spears J. H. 876 S wyer av.
Specht Adolph W. 6542 Stewart av.
Specht Caroline Miss, 490 Fullerton av.
Speed A. C. 4450 Oakenwald av.
Speed E. E. 481 Fulton

Speed Henry B. 21 The Yale
Speed Kellogg, 21 The Yale
Speer Harry V. 3435 Michigan av.
Speer Henry C. 5104 Jefferson av.
Speidel Laurence H. Lake Forest
Spelz Frederick W. 1620 N. Clark
Spelz John Mrs. 1620 N. Clark
Spence Elizabeth E. Mrs. 3538 Lake av.
Spence Florence Miss, 7726 Eggleston
    av.
Spence Robert T. T. 390 Lasalle av.
Spence W. B. 879 Spaulding av.
Spencer Albert A. 2300 Indiana av.
Spencer A. P. 4311 Oakenwald av.
Spencer Bennett W. Evanston
Spencer Caroline A. Mrs. 797 Kenmore
    av.
Spencer Charles H. 6140 Sheridan av.
Spencer Charles S. 4801 St. Lawrence av.
Spencer Clinton J. Highland Park
Spencer C. F. A. 6106 Woodlawn av.
Spencer Earl W. 5108 Hibbard av.
Spencer Ellen Mrs. 2454 N. Paulina
Spencer George W. 6150 Oglesby av.
Spencer G. G.7110 Webster av Englewood
Spencer Irving Rev. 28 Clybourn av.
Spencer John, 448 Bowen av.
Spencer J. B. Wilmette
Spencer Lloyd G. 100 Warren av.
Spencer Robert, Evanston
Spencer Sarah Mrs. Evanston
Spencer Thomas H. Highland Park
Spencer Waldo H. 256, 64th (H.P.)
Spencer William E. 4736 Lake av.
Spencer William H. Evanston
Spencer W. Frank, 85 Park av.
Spencer Zeno C. 917 Chase av.
Sperbeck E. M. 144 Loomis
Sperry George A. Revere house
Sperry James A. 1274 Wilcox av.
Speyer Julius, 547 Burling
Speyer Julius, 4216 Calumet av.
Spicer A. J. Mrs. 165 S. Robey
Spicer George A. 35th se. cor. Ellis av.
Spicer James R. Forest hotel (R.P.)
Spicer May C. Miss, Evanston
Spicer V. K. 404 Erie
Spiegel Hamlin M. 4415 Berkeley av.
Spiegel Joseph, 3344 South Park av.
Spiegel J, 3235 Groveland av.
Spiegel M. J. 3344 South Park av.
Spiegel S. M. 3344 South Park av.
Spieker Harry E. 138 Garfield boul.
Spiel H. Mrs. 16 Sidney ct.
Spielmann August, 3 Crilly pl.
Spielmann Charles, 2586 N. Paulina
Spielmann Jacob, 11 Crilly pl.
Spielmann Jacob, 2586 N. Paulina
Spielmann Peter, 2586 N. Paulina
Spier William, 3643 Vernon av.
Spiering Louis C. 3539 Michigan av.
Spiering Theodore B. 3539 Michigan av.
Spiering Theresa Mrs. 3539 Michigan av.
Spierling Ernest J. 6421 Lexington av.
Spies Joseph, 4411 Lake av.
Spiesberger L. 386 N. State
44

Spills J. C. 35 Lincoln av.
        Sum. res. Davenport, Ia.
Spilman Gilbert Trufant, 59 Cedar
Spilman T. J. Mrs. 59 Cedar
Spining Charles P. Evanston
Spink A. E. 68 Madison Park
Spinney Ellery C. Mrs. 4007 Drexel boul.
Spiridon L. deB. Hotel Normandie
Spitz Henry, 3637 Forest av.
Spitz Herman, 949 Spaulding av.
Spitz Samuel, 3421 Prairie av.
Spitzer Jacob, 4212 Wabash av.
Spitzer Joseph S. 3756 Ellis av.
Spoehr Charles A. 1088 Evanston av.
Spofford George W.1520Washington boul.
Spofford Percy M. 1520 Washington boul.
Spooner F. E. Chicago Beach hotel
Spooner Harriet F. Mrs. 184, 36th
Spooner Henry H. Ridgeland
Spooner Louis C. 328 Fullerton av.
Spooner Thomas F. 184, 36th
Spooner William, Oak Park
Spoor George H. 435 Belden av.
Spoor John A. 12 Ritchie pl.
Sporlein Ida Mrs. 3555 Vincennes av.
Sprague Albert 2d, 2700 Prairie av.
Sprague Albert A. 2710 Prairie av.
Sprague A. J. Dr. 549, 37th
Sprague Charles W. 2330 Michigan av.
Sprague Edwin W. Longwood
Sprague E. E. Mrs. 162 Ashland boul.
Sprague E. M. Hotel Barry
Sprague Frederick W. 537 Dearborn av.
Sprague Harold Mrs. 2330 Michigan av.
Sprague Herbert A. 122, 33d
Sprague H. J. Mrs. 2596 N. Ashland av.
Sprague Levi, 122, 33d
Sprague Otho S. A. 2700 Prairie av.
Sprague Ralph William, 666 Lasalle av.
Sprague T. W. Hotel Windermere
Sprague William, 537 Dearborn av.
Spray J. C. Dr. 725 Turner
Spread Henry F. Mrs. 580 Evanston av.
Spreine Sophia Mrs. 909 Sawyer av.
Spring Charles E. 1025 Warren av.
Spring C. A. jr. 448 Dearborn av.
Spring Josephine Mrs. 1025 Warren av.
Springer Adele Miss, 78, 44th
Springer A. E. Miss, 3819 Prairie av.
Springer Charles E. 3819 Prairie av.
Springer Edward B. Hotel Barry
Springer Edward L. 3819 Prairie av.
Springer Frank G. 3801 Forest av.
Springer George A. 3819 Prairie av.
        Sum. res. Oak Lodge, Old Mission,
        Mich.
Springer George W. Wilmette
Springer Georgiana Miss, 78, 44th
Springer Gertrude Miss, 3819 Prairie av.
Springer I. 435 Washington boul.
Springer James Mrs. 2240 Calumet av.
Springer James D. 458 Elm
Springer Lewis B. Wilmette
Springer Lorin C. 4832 Langley av.
Springer Milton C. Mrs. Wilmette
Springer S. The Ashland

Springer Theodore, 376 Dearborn av.
Springer T. G. 425 Lasalle av.
Springer Warren, 1635 Prairie av.
Sprinks H. E. Mrs. Bcrwyn
Sproehnle A. W. 4343 Ellis av.
Sproehnle F. M. 28 Groveland Park
Sprœsser Alfred F. Dr. 1271 N. Halsted
Sproul E. W. 6500 Yale
Sproule Alfred L. Evanston
Spruance Harmon, 2400 South Park av.
Spruance L. J. C. 2400 South Park av.
Spry George E. 482 Washington boul.
Spry John Mrs. 481 W. Monroe
Spry John C. jr. 363 Ashland boul.
Spry Samuel A. 481 W. Monroe
Spurgeon R. H. 968 Park av.
Spurlock Henry B. 253 Dearborn av.
Spurlock P. A. Mrs. 253 Dearborn av.
Spurr Edward W. 617 The Plaza
Squair Alexander, 4536 Prairie av.
Squair Francis, 4228 Oakenwald av.
Squibb Frederic J. 519 Dearborn av.
Squire C. H. 1725 Belmont av.
Squire Mary Miss, 308 Belden av.
Squirer William, LaGrange
Squires Charles, 4522 Greenwood av.
Squires Harry W. Morton Park
Squires Homer A. 231 Webster av.
Staab Joseph, 26 Lincoln pl.
Stacey Annie N. Miss, Evanston
Stacey H. C. 5436 Monroe av.
Stacey Thomas I. Evanston
Stacey William, Evanston
Stackpole George M. 345, 61st, Englewood
Stacy C. P. 1857 Frederick
Stacy E. L. 198 Oakwood boul.
Stacy M. A. 174 Oakwood boul.
Stadden Burton W. 3628 Vernon av.
Stade George Mrs. 725 Fullerton av.
Stafford Juniata Miss, 97 Walton pl.
Stafford J. B. 1005 Jackson boul.
Stafford Stephen R. Capt. Fort Sheridan
Stafford William Y. Newberry hotel
Stafford W. H. Longwood
Stafford W. Walter M.D. 2334 Indiana av.
Stagg J. L. Hotel Metropole
Stagg L. R. Hotel Metropole
Stagg Robert, Park Ridge
Stahl Edward L. Dr. 377 S. Campbell av.
Stahl George W. 4800 Kimbark av.
Staiger C. M. 712 Fullerton av.
Staley David W. 339 Lasalle av.
Staley Thos. J. 339 Lasalle av.
Stallman G. Harry, 342 Washington boul.
Stamm Andrew, 99 Macalister pl.
Stamm J. Carl Dr. 99 Macalister pl.
Stamm William, 99 Macalister pl.
Stamsen Joseph, 236 Bissell
Stamsen Paul, 478 Ashland boul.
Stanbro Solon D. 287 Ashland boul.
Stanbury G. H. 208 Cass
Stancliff H. Prof. Evanston
Standart George G. 5029 Lake av.
Standinger E. Miss, 436 Lasalle av.
Standish Albert H. Oak Park
Standring Frank C. 6351 Lexington av.

Standring James H. 6351 Lexington av.
Standring Thomas J. 6351 Lexington av.
Standring Walter, 6351 Lexington av.
Stanford Arthur L. Evanston
Stanford George E. Evanston
Stanford G. W. 781 W. Monroe
Stanford Louisa C. Mrs. Evanston
Stanley Caroline E. Mrs. 571 Dearborn av.
Stanley Cornelia C. Mrs. Lake Forest
Stanley Frank E. 596 Jackson boul.
Stanley Frank K. Dr. 6314 Stewart av.
Stanley Frank W. 565 N. State
Stanley Fred G. 22 Bellevue pl.
Stanley Giles A. 220 Ohio
Stanley Harriet E. Miss, 571 Dearborn av.
Stanley Hiram M. Lake Forest
Stanley John S. 3616 Ellis Park
Stanley P. E. 67 Bellevue pl.
Stanley William O. 3731 Forest av.
Stannard Frank D. Dr. 354 W. Adams
Stannard George A. LaGrange
Stannard George P. LaGrange
Stannard Harry W. 354 W. Adams
Stannard Helen J. Mrs. 354 W. Adams
Stannard James M. LaGrange
Stansbury Charles W. Park Ridge
Stansbury J. A. Dr. 342 W. Monroe
Stanton Edgar, Highland Park
Stanton George W. 442 Warren av.
Stanton Harry S. Longwood
Stanton Henry L. Longwood
Stanton James Mrs. Longwood
Stanton R. T. 305 Racine av.
Stanton S. Cecil, M.D. Park Ridge
Stanton William A. 2720 Wabash av.
Stanton W. H. 5156 Grand boul.
    Winter res. Indian River
Stanwood E. W. 1537 Fulton
Stanwood Thaddeus P. Evanston
Staples John M. 3 Campbell Park
Staples John N. 3 Campbell Park
Stapp David H. 5722 Kimbark av.
Starbird Beecher E. 5201 Jefferson av.
Starbird Lorenzo W. 5201 Jefferson av.
Starbird Rupert N. 5201 Jefferson av.
Starbuck Henry F. 6 Groveland Park
Starbuck J. M. 4053 Lake av.
Starbuck W. H. 4101 Drexel boul.
Starck Phil A. 567 Kenwood pl.
    Sum. res. Pine Lake, Ind.
Stark Adolph, 242 Hampden ct.
Stark Andrew, 974 Warren av.
Starkel Louis T. 43 Menomonee
Starkey Horace M., M.D. 3300 Indiana av.
Starkey M. Ella Miss, 3300 Indiana av.
Starkie Martha Miss, 512 Dearborn av.
Starkweather Charles H. 2016 Calumet av.
Starkweather G. Fillmore, 2501 Magnolia
    av.
Starkweather R. E. Auditorium hotel
Starr A. P. 3433 South Park av.
Starr Charles E. 3840 Langley av.
Starr Eliza Allen Miss, 299 Huron
Starr J. C. 2707 Wabash av.
Starr J. C. Mrs. Glencoe
Starr Mary Mrs. 3840 Langley av.

Starr Merritt, Winnetka
Starr Robert M. 3840 Langley av.
Starr Western, 2707 Wabash av.
Starr William E. Glencoe
Starrett D. A. 578 W. Congress
Starrett Julius, 3658 Prairie av.
Starrett Ralph, Oak Park
Starrett Theodore, 4918 Ellis av.
Starring Henry Mrs. 66 Lake Shore Drive
Starring Mason B. 66 Lake Shore drive
Stattman Caroline Mrs. 338 Kenmore
Stauffer Benj. F. 276 Michigan av.
Stave Mary E. Mrs. 2779 N. Paulina
Staver H. C. 6446 Yale
St. Clair Samuel M. Irving Park
Steam David N. 625 Boulevard pl.
Stearns Allan T. 4355 Grand av.
Stearns Anna Mrs. 524 Garfield av.
Stearns Edward, Evanston
Stearns Edward F. 3508 Ellis av.
Stearns Evelyn H. Miss, Evanston
Stearns E. G. 626 Jackson boul.
Stearns Frank E. 6106 Stewart av.
Stearns George, 29, 35th
Stearns George R. 313 Michigan av.
Stearns G. W. 5830 Washington av.
Stearns John K. 476 N. State
Stearns J. W. 352 Chicago av.
Stearns Marcus, 29, 35th
Stearns Marcus C. Mrs. 313 Michigan av.
Stearns Richard I. 313 Michigan av.
Stearns Willard P. 436 Belden av.
Stearns W. H. Oak Park
Stearns W. M., M.D. 5830 Washington av.
Stebbings C. E. Park Ridge
Stebbings Horace P., M.D. 6033 Indiana av.
Stebbings Horace R. 6015 Indiana av.
Stebbings Walter L. 6015 Indiana av.
Stebbins A. Y. 840 W. Monroe
Stebbins Don C. 335, 61st, Englewood
Stebbins Henry S. 2829 Michigan av.
Stebbins Leonard C. Union League club
Stecher Martin D. 639 N. Robey
Stedman C. E. Oak Park
Stedman D. B. 3716 Lake av.
Stedman E. M. Capt. 3716 Lake av.
Stedman E. M. jr. 3716 Lake av.
Stedman Josiah, 3716 Lake av.
Stedman H. T. Oak Park
Steel Benjamin R. 21 Best av.
Steel Charles S. 212, 28th
Steele Bernard Mrs. 3123 Calumet av;
Steele Charles D. 4121 Berkeley av.
Steele Clara S. Miss, 294 Belden av.
Steele D. A. K., M. D. 2920 Indiana av.
Steele Frances M. Mrs. 4020 Drexel boul.
Steele Frederick M. 3815 Ellis av.
Steele G. F. 294 Belden av.
Steele Henry B. 3119 Calumet av.
Steele James, Evanston
Steele James H. 360 Burling
Steele James N. 4520 Lake av.
Steele James W. 1812 Belmont av.
Steele Jos. H. 4648 Vincennes av.
Steele Julius, 4818 Lake av.

Steele Maurice 3123 Calumet av.
Steele Max, 3901 Lake av,
Steele Robert Dr. 928 Walnut
Steele Samuel B. 3123 Calumet av.
Steele W. F. Chicago Beach hotel
Steen Belle Miss, 871 W. Monroe
Steen Erasmus D. 193, 54th pl. (H. P.)
Steere Frederick, 7455 Honore
Steere George S. Hotel Metropole
Steere Gilbert D. 138 Garfield boul,
Steere Jerome D. 9 Wellington pl.
Steers Jonas, Highland Park
Steever J. G. 4718 Madison av.
Steffens Charles M. 7657 Ford av.
Steffens M. J. 55, 22d
Steger John V. 178, 37th
Steger Robert W. Dr. Great Northern hotel
Stehman H. B. Dr. 635 W. Congress
    Sum. res. Wheaton, Ill.
Stein Adolph, 369 Ashland boul.
Stein Barbara Mrs. 537 W. Adams.
Stein Carl, 23 Lincoln pl.
Stein Charles, 2443 Wabash av.
Stein Charles, 2914 Prairie av.
Stein Charles, 294 Ashland boul.
Stein David A. 3313 Vernon av.
Stein Ignatz, 251 Ashland boul.
Stein Israel, 2945 Indiana av.
Stein Joseph, 616 W Congress
Stein Joseph, 4525 Prairie av.
Stein Lawrence, 3652 Michigan av.
Stein Louis, 3652 Michigan av.
    Sum. res. Mackinac Island
Stein O. J. Dr. 25, 47th (H.P.)
Stein Phillip Judge, 44 Loomis
Stein Rose K. Miss, 369 Ashland boul,
Stein Sigmund, 3362 Forest av.
Stein Sydney, 537 W. Adams
Stein S. Arthur, 537 W. Adams
Stein William D. 3342 Calumet av.
Steinbeiss Charles, 266 Fremont
Steinberg J. 355 Chicago av.
Steiner Jacob, 3517 Wabash av.
Steiner John H. 2226 Prairie av.
    Sum. res. Cataract, Ind.
Steinfeld Ben, 3209 Rhodes av.
Steinfeld Harry, 401 Cleveland av.
Steniger Simon, 3936 Lake av.
Steinke Albert, 4143 Berkeley av.
Steinman William Mrs. 375 Marshfield av.
Steinmann E. A. 350 Oakwood boul.
Steinmann L. E. 350 Oakwood boul.
Steinmetz Conrad, 3231 South Park av.
Steinmetz Henry D. 3231 South Park av.
Steinmetz John H. 3231 South Park av.
Stelle Alexander, 3027 Michigan av.
    Sum. res. Lake George, N. Y.
Stelle E. E. Mrs. 582 Lasalle av.
Stelling F. S. 4759 Madison av.
Stellwagen J. 974 Jackson boul.
Stemp Edward, 529, 66th, Englewood
Stenbeck Caroline Mrs. 1842 Aldine av.
Stender Mathias C. 4516 Cottage Grove av.
Stennett W. H., M.D. Oak Park

Stensland Paul O. 140 Evergreen av.
Stenson James Mrs. 2704 Calumet av.
Stenson Nellie Miss, 2704 Calumet av.
Stephan C. Mrs. Austin
Stephan Emanuel L. Austin
Stephan Traugott F. Austin
Stephens Alonzo, 1255 Wolcott
Stephens Armstead H. Rev. 1442 Cornelia
Stephens Blanche Miss, 3308 Wabash av.
Stephens George H. 435 Washington boul.
Stephens Henry N. 380 Oakwood boul.
Stephens J. 655 W. Adams
Stephens Louisa Brier Miss, 2713 Prairie v.
Stephens Louisa B. Mrs. 2713 Prairie av.
Stephens L. Miss, 330 Dayton
Stephens R. D. 2713 Prairie av.
Stephens William G. 2570 N. Ashland av.
Stephens W. C. Ridgeland
Stephenson Charles A. Hotel Groveland
Stephenson Elizabeth Miss, 4819 Prairie av.
Stephenson F. B. Virginia hotel
Stephenson F. W. 5733 Madison av.
Stephenson L. S. Evanston
Stephenson Thomas Rev. Lake Forest
Steppelman William, 278 S. Leavitt
Sterl Alexander Dr. Riverside
Sterling Charles J. The Arizona
Sterling Herbert T. 3509 Wabash av,
Sterling William H. 5137 Kimbark av.
Stern Aaron, 1639 Michigan av.
Stern Albert, 172 Eugenie
Stern Amson, 3424 Calumet av.
Stern Daniel, 413 Dearborn av.
Stern Daniel S. 4207 Grand boul.
Stern D. H. Dr. 307 Chicago av.
Stern Frank J. 16 Lane pl.
Stern Henry, 2915 Prairie av.
Stern H. 3529 Vernon av.
Stern Julius, 6626 Sheridan av.
Stern Louis, 592 Dearborn av
Stern Max, 222 Schiller
Stern Max, 481 Bowen av.
Stern Morris L. Mrs. 413 Dearborn av.
Stern M. 3633 Grand boul.
Stern Oscar M. 126, 25th
Stern Raphael, 3346 South Park av.
Stern Samuel, 2963 Prairie av.
Stern S. 3255 Wabash av.
Stern Tobias, 318, 37th
Sternberger W. L. 2939 Groveland av.
Sterne George M. 222, 65th, Eng.
Sterrett Adelbert W. 6829 Union av.
Sterrett M. G. 5533 Cornell av.
Stetson John C. 4328 Prairie av.
Stetson Wellington, Austin
Stettauer Charles S. 2026 Prairie av.
Stettauer David, 2026 Prairie av.
Stettauer James, 2026 Prairie av.
Stettheimer Joseph C. 3242 Groveland av.
Stettinius E. R. Hotel Windermere
Stettler Cornelia S. Dr. 181 Dearborn av.
Steveley John F. 756 Washington boul.
Steveley Lucius A. 756 Washington boul.
Stevens A. B. Washington Heights

Stevens A. C. 5470 Ridgewood ct.
Stevens Belle Miss, 3819 Michigan av.
Stevens Charles A. 197, 36th
Stevens Charles L. 1010 Washington boul.
Stevens Charles N. 4752 Langley av.
Stevens Charles P. Evanston
Stevens C. 63 E. Pearson
Stevens C. Nelson, Evanston
Stevens David M. 6557 Yale
Stevens Edmund H. 4752 L   g   av.
Stevens Edward D. 164, 36th an ley
Stevens Elizabeth Mrs. 346 Oakwood boul.
Stevens Eva Miss, 730 W. Adams
Stevens E. F. 6756 Wright
Stevens E. M. Mrs. 657 W. Congress
Stevens Frank K. Evanston
Stevens Frank L. 2939 Michigan av.
Stevens Fred H. LaGrange
Stevens Frederick D. 2560 N. Paulina
Stevens Frederick W. Prof. Lake Forest
Stevens F. E. 6900 Anthony av.
Stevens F. G. The Arizona
Stevens F. R. Mrs. 4164 Lake av.
Stevens George L. Evanston
Stevens George M. 21 Best av.
Stevens George W. Mrs. 408 Superior
Stevens Gertrude L. Miss, 276 Ashland av.
Stevens G. H. 119 Lincoln av.
Stevens Harry D. 408 Superior
Stevens Harry S., Evanston
Stevens Hezekial B. Evanston
Stevens Ira Ellsworth, Oak Park
Stevens H. D. 408 Superior
Stevens I. T. Mrs. 726 Warren av.
Stevens James W. 483 Bowen av.
Stevens Jacob W. 4752 Langley av.
Stevens Jerome P. 6816 Perry av.
Stevens John M. 29 Best av.
Stevens John K. 690 Washington boul.
Stevens John S. 1152 Jackson boul.
Stevens John V. Dr. Evanston
Stevens John W. 305 Racine av.
Stevens Joshua, 7640 Sherman
Stevens Lester W. Hotel Groveland
Stevens Lillie B. Miss, Oak Park
Stevens Lorina Mrs. 276 Ashland boul.
Stevens Louis K. 1010 Washington boul.
Stevens Louise Mrs. 2004 Calumet av.
Stevens L. W. Hotel Groveland
Stevens Plowdon, 521 W. Adams
Stevens Ralph C. 164, 36th
Stevens Robert W. 1010 Washington boul.
Stevens Russell H. 5432 Jefferson av.
Stevens R. G. Mrs. 338, 44th
Stevens Sidney W. 408 Superior
Stevens Silas C. Continental hotel
Stevens Sylvanus H. 5432 Jefferson av.
Stevens S. H. jr. 5432 Jefferson av.
Stevens S. Ross, 42 Sidney ct.
Stevens Theron Fay, 4647 Vincennes av.
Stevens Thomas A. 4114 Indiana av.
Stevens William C. 4647 Vincennes av.
Stevens William E. Riverside
Stevens William T. Hinsdale
Stevens W. A. Dr. 2631 Wabash av.
Stevenson Arthur H. 3528 Prairie av.

Stevenson Alexander F. Col. 378 Lasalle av.
Stevenson Donald M. 170, 36th
Stevenson Elizabeth Mrs. 4339 Ellis av.
    Sum. res. Babylon, L. I.
Stevenson Elizabeth B. Miss, 4339 Ellis av.
Stevenson F. B. 1226 Wilcox av.
Stevenson George D. 6847 Union av.
Stevenson John, 820 North Park av.
Stevenson J. R. Rev. 8 Chalmers pl.
Stevenson J. S. Park Ridge
Stevenson Morton J. Evanston
    Sum. res. Spring Lake, Wis.
Stevenson Robert, 525 Lasalle av.
Stevenson Sarah Hackett, M.D. 322 N. State
Stevenson W. S. River Forest
Stevers Martin D. Mrs. Norwood Park
Stevison J. H. 5407 Jefferson av.
Steward Frank M., M.D. 133 Garfield boul.
Steward J. F. 1068 Kenmore av.
Steward W. T. Hinsdale
Stewart Abbie H. Mrs. Hinsdale
Stewart Alexander, 5753 Madison av.
Stewart Alexander M. 226 Warren av.
Stewart Alice Mrs. 7620 Wright
Stewart Andrew Dr. 464 W. Adams
Stewart Angus 1086 Early av.
Stewart Archibald A. 1022 Washington boul.
Stewart A. W. 676 Fullerton av.
Stewart Benjamin F. 3528 Calumet av.
Stewart Catherine Miss, 575 Cleveland av.
Stewart Charles, 151, 42d
Stewart Charles A. 1285 Wolcott
Stewart Charles C. 5753 Madison av.
Stewart Charles F. Dr. 219, 31st
Stewart Charles H. 1285 Wolcott
Stewart Elizabeth S. Miss, 171, 51st (H. P.)
Stewart Ella B. Miss, 2339 Commercial (L. V.)
Stewart Ettie Miss, 575 Cleveland av.
Stewart E. F. Mrs. 5720 Madison av.
Stewart Edward L. 426 Jackson boul.
Stewart Frank, Tracy
Stewart F. F. Evanston
Stewart George A. Austin
Stewart George R. 575 Cleveland av.
Stewart George W. 1076 Washington boul.
Stewart Graeme, 13 Ritchie pl.
Stewart G. Grant, North Evanston
Stewart Harry J. Dr. 1076 Washington boul.
Stewart Henry Dr. 194 Oakwood boul.
Stewart Henry C. 1110 Washington boul.
Stewart Henry E. Austin
Stewart John, 226 Warren av.
Stewart John F., Evanston
Stewart John P. 226 Warren av.
Stewart John W. Evanston
Stewart Josephine M. Mrs. Walton pl. sw. cor. Rush
Stewart J. 807 Warren av.

Stewart Marcellus K. 4316 Champlain av.
Stewart Nellie E. Mrs. 6532 Myrtle av.
Stewart Ramsey H. 575 Cleveland av.
    Sum. res. Lake Geneva Wis.
Stewart R. M. 226 Warren av.
Stewart Samuel J. 6420 Sheridan av.
Stewart S. J. 821 Warren av.
Stewart William, 194 Oakwood boul.
Stewart William, 623 Dearborn av.
Stewart William Mrs. 879 St. Louis av.
Stewart William H. 6119 Oglesby av.
Stewart William J. Dr. 1076 Washington boul.
Stewart William S. 20, 46th
Stewart W. C. Evanston
Stewart W. R. jr. Hotel Groveland
St. Hiliare J. 143 Oakwood boul.
Stibbs John H. Gen. 234 Irving av.
Stibbs Thomas, 234 Irving av.
Stich George F. 2505 Michigan av.
Stickney C. Hyde Park hotel
Stickney Edward S. Mrs. 162 Rush
    Sum. res. New London, Conn.
Stickney George A. The Arizona
Stickney Lester P. 151 Dearborn av.
Stickney William H. 415 Center
Stickney W. Frank, Mayfair
Stid P. C. Mrs. 7409 Bond av.
Stiefel Samuel, 2522 Wabash av.
Stieglitz Gustaf, 1704 Diversey
Stieglitz Julius Dr. 5479 Lexington av.
Stiles Archer C. 335 Hampden ct.
Stiles Charles H. 1035 Lunt av.
Stiles C. L. LaGrange
Stiles George N. 2325 Michigan av.
Stiles George S. 1804 W. 22d
S i Israel N. 5824 Rosalie ct.
Stiles osiah, 2325 Michigan av.
Stiles J. S. 1804 W. 22d
Stiles J. S. jr. 1806 W. 22d
Stiles Lawrence G. 401 Kenmore av.
Stiles Lucy Goddard Miss, 2325 Michigan av.
Still E. A. Lakota hotel
Stillians Daniel C. Dr. 572 N. Hoyne av.
Stillman Loran A., M.D. 1311 Michigan av.
Stillwell John, 1843 Barry av.
Stimmel C. Harold, 4112 Maple av.
Stimmel Mark G. 4112 Maple av.
Stimpson James M. Maywood
Stinson A. C. 5738 Monroe av.
Stinson Cornelia Miss, 4450 Drexel boul.
Stinson Henry, 4450 Drexel boul.
Stinson James, 4450 Drexel boul.
Stinson Margaret Miss, 4450 Drexel boul.
Stires E. M. Rev. Lexington hotel
Stirlen John, 152, 36th
Stirling J. Carolus, 296, 6th (H.P.)
Stirling William R. 1616 Prairie av.
Stitely Albert C. 515 The Plaza
Stitt Charles F. Riverside
Stitt Lucy L. Mrs. 37 Lane pl.
St. John Alpheus B. 438, 65th, Englewood
St. John A. R. Mrs. 3224 Calumet av.
St. John E. 5, 87 Rush
St. John Esther Miss, 2003 Indiana av.

St. John Fred, 539 W. Monroe
St. John L. Dr. 539 W. Monroe
St. John S. A. Mrs. 378 Dearborn av.
Stobo Robert, 4556 Ellis av.
Stock Ernst, 1648 Belmont av.
Stock George B. 7832 Sherman
Stockdale Curtis V. 291 Ontario
Stockdale M. E. Mrs. 57 Delaware pl.
Stockdale R. F. Park Ridge
Stockham Alice B. Dr. Evanston
Stockham William H. Evanston
Stockton Diantha Mrs. 3767 Ellis av.
Stockton John L. Highland Park
Stockton Joseph Gen. 1932 Diversey
Stockton Josephine Miss, 85 Rush
Stockton Ward, 374 Dearborn av.
Stockton Wm. E. Evanston
Stockwell John R. Norwood Park
Stockwell J. G. Sherman house
Stoddard George B. 5216 Washington av.
Stoddard Horace H. 103 Warren av.
Stoddard James A. 6525 Harvard
Stoddard John, 508 Webster av.
Stoddart Lucy B. Mrs. 2317 Michigan av.
Stoker Eugene L. Evanston
Stokes Amy J. Miss, Evanston
Stokes Charles A. Austin
Stokes Charles F. 332 Oakwood boul.
Stokes Charles J. Evanston
Stokes Chauncey M. 1180 Washington
    boul.
Stokes C. M. Mrs. 332 Oakwood boul.
Stokes Edward H. Evanston
Stokes Edward J. 135 Pine
Stokes E. T. Evanston
Stokes Frederick C. Evanston
Stokes Harry T. Evanston
Stokes S. L. Miss, 135 Pine
Stokes T. Oliver, 1102 Lawndale av.
Stolba Fred, 450 S. Paulina
Stolba J. A. 88 Lincoln av.
Stoll Samuel D. 445 Belden av.
Stoll W. F. 780 Racine av.
Stolp Byron C., M. D. Wilmette
Stoltz J. 627 Englewood av.
Stolz Joseph Rabbi, 410 Warren av.
Stone Albert D. 4215 Ellis av.
Stone A. J. 431 Washington boul.
Stone A. L. 3419 Prairie av.
Stone Burke, 459 Bowen av.
Stone Calvin Mrs. 86 N. Ada
Stone Carl D. 2505 Michigan av.
Stone Charles D. 3546 Ellis av.
Stone Charles D. 3832 Elmwood pl.
Stone Charles H. 442 Ashland boul.
Stone Cynthia L. Miss,5001 Lake av.
Stone C. B. 1186 W. Congress
Stone C. J. 360 Mohawk
Stone D. B. Oak Park
Stone E. B. 661 Jackson boul.
Stone Foster, 191 Oakwood boul.
Stone Frank B. 5627 Monroe av.
Stone Fred K. 86 N. Ada
Stone F. A. 433, 60th, Eng.
Stone F. P. 754 Washington boul.
Stone F. Paul, 4402 Lake av.

Stone F. R. 6755 Union av.
Stone George F. Evanston
Stone George N. 3317 Forest av.
Stone George T. 7100 Rhodes av.
Stone George W. 3933 Prairie av.
Stone George W. Evanston
Stone G. W. 3411 Vernon av.
Stone Harry W. 3411 Vernon av.
Stone Henry B. 45 Bellevue pl.
Stone Herbert S. Glencoe
Stone Horatio O. 3439 Michigan av.
Stone H. O. Mrs. 2035 Prairie av.
Stone Irving I. 1397 Palmer
Stone James D. 2724 Michigan av
Stone John N. 1486, 68th (H.P.)
Stone John R. Park Club
Stone Kenneth 191 Oakwood boul.
Stone Leander Mrs. 3352 Indiana av.
Stone Lucy E. Mrs. 5627 Monroe av.
Stone Luther Mrs. 2013 Michigan av.
Stone Lysander E. 813 The Plaza
Stone L. W. 4316 Michigan av.
Stone Melville E. Glencoe
Stone Morton Rev. LaGrange
Stone M. M. Mrs. LaGrange
Stone Nat. 3359 Forest av.
Stone Robert FS 2035 Prairie av.
Stone R. J. 969 . Central Park av.
Stone S. W. Mrs. Oak Park
Stone S. W. 246, 47th
Stone William, Pullman
Stone William C. 1617 Sheridan rd.
Stone Willis C. Dr. 482 Bowen av.
Stone W. B. 7650 Bond av.
Stonehill Charles A. 417 Bowen av.
Stonehill G. L. 3153 Calumet av.
Stoner Della Miss, 1837 Michigan av.
Stoner H. F. Oak Park
Stoner T. K. Oak Park
Stonestreet George D. Evanston
Stookey Orren V. 4427½ Champlain av.
Storck Charles, M.D. 356 Webster av.
Storck William H. 356 Webster av.
Storer Addison H. 3813 Langley av.
Storer C. A. 18 Bellevue pl.
Storer George B. 3813 Langley av.
Storer Rex S. 3813 Langley av.
Storer Willis D. Dr. 1402 Wrightwood
    av.
Storey C. W. 504 Jackson boul.
Storey Edward H. Riverside
Storey E. Camille Mrs. 2011 Prairie av.
Storey Fred C. 524 W. Congress
Storey Henry C. 166 Ashland boul.
Storey J. B. 200 Park av.
Storke Albert F. Dr. Oak Park
Storm Charles H. 229, 42d pl.
Storrow John M. 6520 Lexington av.
Storrs D. W. 6732 Wentworth av.
Story Allan C. 4506 Prairie av.
Story Charles A. 2832 Vernon av.
Story Charles M. 421 Washington boul.
Story H. 6410 Oglesby av.
Stott J. Wilber, 3632 Vincennes av.
Stouffer Anna L. 2253 South Park av.
Stouffer C. R. 3231 Vernon av.

Stoughton O. W. 1826 Indiana av.
Stoughton Willis G. 609 Winthrop av.
Stout A. M. Dr. 348 S. Oakley av.
Stout B. F. Oak Park
Stout Melancthon Dr. 3806 Langley av.
Stout R. C. Mrs. Hotel Normandie
Stout Stanley S. Clifton house
Stover Ira, 626 Washington boul.
Stow J. R. Mrs. The Tudor
Stowe Bond, M.D. 4060 Ellis av.
Stowell C. G. 459 Dayton
Stowell F. B. 6352 Myrtle av.
Stowell Ida M. Miss, 2633 Indiana av.
Stowell James H., M.D. 2633 Indiana av.
Stowell John D. 3351 Forest av.
Stowell Nelson F. 7715 Goldsmith av.
Strachan James, 6008 Princeton av.
Strachan James jr. 6008 Princeton av.
Strackbein J. W. 90 Park av.
Strader Florence I. Miss, 2428 Michigan av.
Strader Jacob, 2428 Michigan av.
Strader J. E. 462 Bowen av.
Strader J. Louis, 2428 Michigan av.
Straessle Benedict 163 Center
Strahorn Robert, 152, 47th
Straight George W. 1075 Lawndale av.
Straight H. J. Oak Park
Straight L. C. 3329 Indiana av.
Straight M. M. Mrs. 7528 Wright
Strain James C. 1013 Jackson boul.
Strait JosephineS.Mrs.4462 Oakenwald av.
Straith-Miller Fred, 195, 36th
Straith-Miller Harriet, 195, 36th
Stransky E. J. 3118 South Park av.
Strasburger Abbie Mrs. 23 Crilly pl.
Strassburger Ed, 3624 Calumet av.
Strassheim Christopher, 397 Orchard
Strassheim Henry, 1736 Roscoe
Stratford Henry K., M.D. Austin
Stratton Charles J. 1708 Barry av.
Stratton Charles M. New Hotel Holland
Stratton Oliver R. 4223 Langley av.
Straub Arthur M. 6403 Oglesby av.
Straub Effie T. Dr. 922 N. Clark
Straub S. W. 6403 Oglesby av.
Straus Aaron, 3531 Vernon av.
Straus B. F. 3914 Calumet av.
Straus David, 942 W. Adams
Straus Eli M. 2509 Indiana av.
Straus Frederick W. 3440 Michigan av.
Straus Jacob, 4339 Grand boul.
Straus Leo, 2955 Prairie av.
Straus Morton E. 2509 Indiana av.
Straus M. Hotel Groveland
Straus Simeon, 3943 Ellis av.
Straus Simon W. 3223 South Park av.
Straus S. L. 3914 Calumet av.
Strauss Albert L. 1838 Michigan av.
Strauss A. 3337 Wabash av.
Strauss A. S. Lexington hotel
Strauss Clara L.K. Miss, 622 Washington boul.
Strauss Emanuel Mrs. 3332 Forest av.
Strauss Frank R. 3255 Wabash av.
Strauss Henry, 322, 37th

Strauss Henry X. 3337 Wabash av.
Strauss Jacob, 3425 South Park av.
Strauss Jacob N. 3263 Vernon av.
Strauss Jacob W. 850 Washington boul.
Strauss Jennie Miss, 1838 Michigan av.
Strauss J. N. 3263 Vernon av.
Strauss Leo, 631 North Park av.
Strauss Leon A. 3337 Wabash av.
Strauss Leopold, 1838 Michigan av.
    Sum. res. Oconomowoc, Wis.
Strauss Louis E. 3425 South Park av.
Strauss Maurice, 4319 Vincennes av.
Strauss Michael, 5488 East End av.
Strauss Milton A. 3337 Wabash av.
Strauss Milton L. 3238 South Park av.
Strauss N. 3305 Forest av.
Strauss Raphael, 3332 Forest av.
Strauss Samuel, 3332 Forest av.
Strauss Solomon, 3153 Calumet av.
Strauss S. 202 Oakenwald boul.
Strauss S. L. 2962 Groveland av.
Strausser Frank, 522 W. Congress
Straut Elizabeth A. Mrs. Grand Pacific
Straw A. W. Mrs. 225, 28th
Straw J. I. 111 Flournoy
Strawbridge Charles H. 4026 Grand boul
Strawbridge William, 4026 Grand boul.
Strawn Abner, 4126 Lake av.
Strawn Silas H. 4126 Lake av.
Strayer Thomas A. Park Ridge
Street Arthur Wray, 4756 Kenwood av.
Street A. W. 462 Dayton
Street Charles A. 34 Astor
Street C. A. LaGrange
Street C. R. 847 Warren av.
Street Henry C. Highland Park
Street Harry L. 34 Astor
Street John L. 462 Dayton
Street J. H. Miss, Highland Park
Street Richard, 734 W. Adams
Street Richard H. Highland Park
Street Richard J. Highland Park
Street Richard P. Highland Park
Street William D. C. 302 Schiller
Streeter Allen R. Union League Club
Streeter David L. Union League Club
Streeter D. D. Chicago Beach hotel
Streeter Herbert A. Evanston
Streeter Herbert C. Evanston
Streeter John W. Dr. 2646 Calumet av.
Strehl Benjamin C. 397, 50th (H.P.)
Strehl William R. 9 Wisconsin
Streich Fred O. 876 Warren av.
Streich H. F. 715 Washington boul.
Streight John, 2712 Michigan av.
Strelitz David, 4351 Oakenwald av.
Strelitz S. Mrs. 4351 Oakenwald av.
Strelitz Victor, 4351 Oakenwald av.
Strelitzer Julius, 3229 Rhodes av.
Strell George W. 339 Park av.
Stretz Theodore Dr. 24 Beethoven pl.
Strickland E. Mrs. 106, 36th
Strickland Kathrine Miss, 106, 36th
Strickland W. J. 4547 Wabash av.
Striker Edmund H. 1505 Wellington
Stringfield C. Pruyn Dr. 300, 31st

Stringheld F. M. Dr. 4102 Cottage Grove av.
Strobel Charles L. 476 Elm
Stroble Theodore, 375 Bissell
Stroker H. W. 845 Warren av.
Strom Axel, Austin
Stromberg Charles J. 1528 Wolfram
Stromberg Christian G. 1525 Wolfram
Stromberg C. 494 Webster av.
Stromberg John S. 1542 Sheridan rd.
Stronach Robert Prof. 2 The Yale
Strong Albert B. Dr. 533 W. Monroe
Strong Amzi W. 1853 Frederick
Strong Calvin A. Wilmette
Strong Carrie M. Miss, 373 Superior
Strong Charles E. Mrs. 532 W. Monroe
Strong Charles R. 290, 48th (H. P.)
Strong D. O. 290, 48th
Strong Edward B. 313 Superior
Strong Eliza B. Mrs. Evanston
Strong E. J. 598 Division
Strong John W. Evanston
Strong Joseph H. 2528 Indiana av.
Strong Marion Mrs. Lexington hotel
Strong Mary M. Mrs. Mayfair
Strong Ullman, 425 Huron
Strong William E. 371 Superior
Strong William W. 453 Washington boul.
Strong W. B. Great Northern hotel
Strong W. E. Mrs. 802 The Plaza
Strotz Charles N. 349 Hampden ct.
Strotz Nicholas, 658 Lasalle av.
Stroud E. H. 401 N. State
Strouss Aaron, 3349 Forest av.
Strouss Emil, 3349 Forest av.
Strouss Joseph, 3349 Forest av.
Strouss Levi, 3349 Forest av.
Strube H. 6820 Sherman
Struble Henry, River Forest
Struckmann Henry G. Elmhurst
Stryker E. M. Mrs. 4627 Lake av.
Stryker James M. 4627 Lake av.
Stryker Stephen W. Col. 574 Division
Stuart A. W. 7121 Wentworth av.
Stuart Charles, Hinsdale
Stuart Charles B. Mrs. 4445 Grand boul.
Stuart Charles E. Highland Park
Stuart Charles U. 290 Rush
Stuart Elizabeth Mrs. Evanston
Stuart Ernest B. 211 Fremont
Stuart Geo. 6940 Perry av.
Stuart James A. 3836 Ellis av.
Stuart John C. Newberry hotel
Stuart John F. Hinsdale
Stuart Kate Mrs. 4447 Langley av.
Stuart Lewis Prof. Lake Forest
Stuart Milton R. 6920 Oglesby av.
Stuart Owen, Park Ridge
Stuart Robert, 5206 Madison av.
Stubbs Edwin J. 305 Loomis
Stubbs F. Gurney Dr. 3203 South Park av.
Stubbs Jabez B. 3261 Groveland av.
Stubbs James B. 3411 Calumet av.
Stubbs James E. Dr. 3203 South Park av.
Stubbs James H. 3411 Calumet av.
Stubbs William, 3411 Calumet av.

Stubbs William Dr. 6428 Stewart av.
Stubbs William C. Highland Park
Stubinger Geo. L. Dr. 100 Racine av.
Stucker Barbara Mrs. 319 Lincoln av.
Stuckert A. M. Pine, nw. cor. Huron
Stuckert Lily Miss, Pine, nw. cor. Huron
Stuckert Mary Coleman Mrs. Pine, nw. cor. Huron
Studebaker J. F. Mrs. Hotel Metropole
Studebaker Peter E. 1612 Prairie av.
Studebaker W. F. Auditorium hotel
Studley Fred J. 537 Division
Studley Mary E. Mrs. 297 Warren av.
Stuedle Emil, Elmhurst
Stults P. M. 287, 79th (H. P.)
Stumer Abe R. 4404 Grand boul.
Stumer A. N. 4404 Grand boul.
Stumer Louis M. 4404 Grand boul.
Stumer M. 4404 Grand boul.
Stump H. E. 416 Chicago av.
Stumpoffski C. H. Kenilworth
Stumpoffski R. Mrs. Kenilworth
Sturdevant George W. 3000 Michigan av.
Sturdy J. F. 4838 Evans av.
Sturgeon Robert E. 3623 Ellis Park
Sturges Albert, 1712 Prairie av.
Sturges A. M. Mrs. 755, 63d ct. Englew'd
Sturges Benton, 2917 Prairie av.
Sturges Charles A. 3643 Vincennes av.
Sturges Charles M. River Forest
Sturges E. Spencer, 4429 Ellis av.
Sturges Frank, Elmhurst
Sturges George Mrs. 107 Pine
Sturges James D. 511 Webster av.
Sturges J. E. Sherman house
Sturges Lee, Elmhurst
Sturges Marion D. Miss, 107 Pine
Sturges M. A. Miss, 4201 Grand boul.
Sturges Rosalie Miss, 107 Pine
Sturges Solomon 1712 Prairie av.
Sturges Washington, 1712 Prairie av.
Sturges William N. Kenilworth
Sturgis Charles J. 32 Banks
Sturm Adolph, 13 Lane pl.
Sturm Adolph, 515 N. Wells
Stursberg H. Hotel Barry
Sturtevant C. D. Oak Park
Sturtevant Edwin, 2950 Calumet av.
Sturtevant Ezra T. 275 Ontario
Sturtevant Fred, 862 W. Monroe
Sturtevant F. H. Mrs. Oak Park
Sturtevant H. D. 320 Hampden ct.
Sturtevant John W. Hotel Groveland
Sturtevant Laurence M. LaGrange
Stut John, 114 Evergreen av.
Stype Sebastian, Ravinia
Subert Bermann, 806 Washington boul.
Subert Charles, 806 Washington boul.
Subert Max, 806 Washington boul.
Suders Henry, 1619 Huron
Suesman Albert L. 478 Ashland boul.
Suesman Asa B. 478 Ashland boul.
Sugg Edward, G. 608 The Plaza
Sugg Eugene, 1610 Diversey
Sugg George 1610 Diversey
Sullivan Albert W. 4830 Kimbark av.

Sullivan Alexander, 378 Oak
Sullivan Alice Mrs. 147 Pine
Sullivan Charles L. 93, 33d
Sullivan Cornelius, Riverside
Sullivan DanielH., M.D., 3807 Indiana av.
Sullivan David, 4823 Langley av.
Sullivan Dennis W. 445 Garfield av.
Sullivan Edward J. Riverside
Sullivan Ella Miss, 1726 Diversey av.
Sullivan Francis P. 539 Greenleaf av.
Sullivan Ida Mrs 7008 St. Lawrence av.
Sullivan James Mrs. 4024 Grand boul.
Sullivan James B. Mrs. 113 Cass
Sullivan James J. 868 Washington boul.
Sullivan Jeremiah, 3241 Prairie av.
Sullivan John E. Riverside
Sullivan Joseph W. 1214 Kenmore av.
Sullivan J. H. 712 The Plaza
Sullivan J. W. 1214 Kenmore av.
Sullivan Louis H. 4573 Lake av.
Sullivan Margaret Mrs. 485, 42d pl.
Sullivan M. 163 Cass
Sullivan Patrick H. 4319 Prairie av.
Sullivan Roger C. 842 Walnut
Sullivan Samuel J. 4304 Greenwood av.
Sullivan Thomas E. 3149 Prairie av.
Sullivan T. C. Col. U. S. A. Granada
      hotel
Sullivan William K. 1083 Washington
      boul.
Sullivan William M. 247 Osgood
Sulzberger Sol. L. 3311 South Park av.
Sulzberger Sophia Mrs. 3424 South Park
      av.
Sulzer Jane N. Mrs. 2288 N. Paulina
Sulzer M. Mrs. 1306 Perry
Sumerfield C. Mrs. 3514 Calumet av.
Sumerfield George C. 3260 Vernon av.
Summerfield John, 2411 South Park av.
Summerfield Louis, 3019 Vernon av.
Summerfield Louise M. Miss, 405 W.
      Monroe
Summers Bertrand S. 14 Astor
Summers C. H. Fort Sheridan
Summers C. H. 14 Astor
Summers Leland L. 14 Astor
Summers William W. 151 Lytle
Summy Clayton F. 25 -ane pl.
Sumner B. Mrs. Hotel Metropole
Sumner E. C. Mrs. 4049 Lake av.
Sumner Richard B. Mrs. 3811 Grand boul.
Sumner W. A.Julien hotel
Sumney John Dr. 517, 62d, Englewood
Sumpter Henry, 1268 Wolcott
Sunderland George, 3732 Forest av.
Sunderland Isaac T. Indiana av. cor. 63d
Sundermeaer William, 267 Park av.
Sundin John, 4424 Evans av.
Sunny B. E. 138 Astor
Surghnor V. H. 85, 20th
Sutfin E. I. 363 S. Oakley av.
Sutherland D. W. Tracy
Sutherland George, 7408 Honore
Sutherland H. G. Mrs. 2023 Indiana av.
Sutherland Ralph E. 500 Englewood av.
Sutherland S. M. 500 Englewood av.

Sutherland William J. Auditorium hotel
Sutherland W. E. Hotel Groveland
Sutliff M. Mrs. 96, 30th
Sutter Adolph, 3601 Lake av.
Sutter Clarence B. 3603 Lake av.
Sutter Edward A. 4469 Oakenwald av.
Sutter Edwin A. 3601 Lake av.
Sutter Jacob, 3603 Lake av.
Sutter Raymond C. 3603 Lake av.
Sutter Victor, 240 Oakwood boul.
Sutter Victor Mrs. 240 Oakwood boul.
Sutter Walter C. 3603 Lake av.
Sutton E. T. French house, Evanston
Sutton Fred 424 Chicago av.
Sutton George E. 4323 Forrestville av.
Sutton Harry B. 203 Fremont
Sutton Isaac T. 7301 Bond av.
Sutton Jonathan K. 203 Fremont
Sutton J. Wilbur, 285½ Lasalle av.
Sutton Thomas, 234 S. Leavitt
Sutton William H. 2621 Calumet av.
Sutton W. W. Winnetka
Suydam John D. Oak Park
Swabacher Isa,d3311 Rhodes av.
Swadkins Alfre , 1849 Melrose
Swafford J. W. 996 W. Monroe
Swain A. D. 595 W. Monroe
Swain Charles, 1776 Wrightwood av.
Swain Edgar D., M.D. 105, 45th
Swain J. W. 634 Boulevard pl.
Swain Oliver D. Dr. Glencoe
Swan C. J. Dr. 2223 Calumet av.
Swan James, 3148 Michigan av.
Swan James H. 4740 Kimbark av.
Swan Olivia Shailer Mrs.1819 Michigan av.
Swan S. N. 3415 Calumet av.
Swan William F. Evanston
Swander Alexander F. 418 S. Paulina
Swanitz A. W. 4563 Lake av.
Swank C. W., M.D. 307 Division
Swannell Frederick O. 311 Belden av.
Swannell William, 551 Dearborn av.
Swanson Andrew A. Evanston
Swanson Anna Mrs. 619 Fullerton av.
Swanson Charles J. 663 Orchard
Swanson H. A. 1031 N. Clark
Swanson S. A. 720 Fullerton av.
Swanzey H. A. 508 Englewood av.
Swart J. H. 24 Ritchie pl.
Swart M. E. 3306 Indiana av.
Swartchild S. 282 Ohio
Swarth August C. 1715 Wrightwood av.
Swarthout Clara Miss, 1143 N. Clark
Swartley Hannah Mrs. Oak Park
Swartout Charles R. Wilmette
Swarts H. L. 3241 Wabash av.
Swarts Seymour, 413 Marshfield av.
      Sum. res. Brown's Park, Wis.
Swartz George E. 1837 Michigan av.
Swartz I. Honora Miss, 17 Park av.
Swartz J. 377 S. Hoyne av.
Swartz J. E. 644 Jackson boul.
Swartz Thomas Benton M.D. 3737 Forest
      av.
Swasey Jas. A. D.D.S. 3017 Michigan av
      Sum. res. Buchanan, Mich.

Swatek Matthew J. 606 Dearborn av.
Swayer Edmund, 50 Scott
Swazey E. A. Mrs. 4324 Ellis av.
Swazey Louise Miss, 260 Ashland boul.
Swearingen Otho D. 1575 Lill av.
Sweeney John M. 1837 Michigan av.
Sweep C. E. 3714 Langley av.
Sweet Ada C. Miss, 1850 Aldine
Sweet Albert L. 241 Ashland boul.
Sweet Charles A. 241 Ashland boul.
Sweet Charles S. Oak Park·
Sweet Cora F. Mrs. Oak Park
Sweet Dexter B. 4200 Oakenwald av.
Sweet E. C. Dr. 613 W. Monroe
Sweet E. D. L. Oak Park
Sweet Frank, 3845 Ellis av.
Sweet Hiram, 2940 Prairie av.
Sweet John A. 381 Warren av.
Sweet John W. 1231 Pratt av.
Sweet Samuel H. 2940 Prairie av.
Sweet W. H. Lexington hotel
Sweetland Dana W. Highland Park
Sweetland John T. 6335 Woodlawn av.
Sweetman William G. Wilmette
Sweger A. 2425 Wabash av.
Swenie D. J. 36 Pearce
Swenie J. J. 667 Fulton
Swenson A. Mrs. 975 Warren av.
Swenson M. 4531 Greenwood av.
Swett Frank W. 23 Hamilton av.
Swett Frederick C. 2 Madison Park
Swett Wm. O. 5006 Washington av.
Swett Wm. O. jr. 5006 Washington av.
Swift Albert O. 538 Greenleaf av.
Swift A. R. 6757 Wentworth av.
Swift Brown F. 52 Loomis
Swift Charles, 529 Maple, Eng.
Swift Charles H. 4452 Emerald av.   ·
Swif E. F. Lakota hotel.
Swift E. S. 529 Maple, Eng.
Swift Frank R. 108 Dekalb
Swift Frederick, 225 Dearborn av.
Swift George B. 52 Loomis
          Sum. res. Fox Lake, Ill.
Swift Gustavus F. 4452 Emerald av.
Swift Harry A. 164, 39th
Swift Herbert B. 52 Loomis
Swift H. C. 6757 Wentworth av.
Swift Lemuel J. 14 Aberdeen
Swift L. F. 5046 Woodlawn av.
Swift Mary Mrs. 538 Greenleaf av.
Swift Monroe A. 677 Park av.
Swift M. Lewis, 4458 Ellis av.
Swift Otis P. 164, 39th
Swift P. H. Rev. 307, 41st (H.P.)
Swift Rodney B. 1205 W. Monroe
Swift William H. 1838 Indiana av.
Swigart C. F. 280 Park av.
Swigart George W. 477 48th
Swigart R. B. 4136 Prairie av.
Swigert C. P. 575 Boulevard pl.
Swinarton James H. 3842 Ellis av.
Swinborne Charles C. 46, 35th
Swinford W. Riley, 1053 N. Clark
Swinscoe George E. Austin
Swisher·Stephen G. La Grange

Swissler W. F. 455 W. Congress
Switzer Edward M. 20 Ritchie pl.
Switzer Martha J. Mrs. Evanston
Syer E. W. 4458 Sidney av.
          Sum. res. Niagara
Sykes C. A. Mrs. 322 The Plaza
Sykes J. W. 782 Warren av.
Sykes Leon, 465 Warren av.
Sylvester Richard T. 3549 Ellis av.
Sylvester Simeon E. 3549 Ellis av.
Syme John Q. Hotel Windemere
Syme Margaret H. Miss, 367 Mohawk
Symeson J. H. 6631 Drexel av.
Symonds E. K. 794 W. Adams
Symonds Stillman F. 1152 Lawndale av.
Synon Anna W. Miss, 2964 Prairie av.
Synon J. H. 649 W. Harrison
Synwolt Edward W. 568 Burling
Synwolt Henry E. 577 Burling

TABB MAMIE MISS, 3405 Vernon av.
      Taber F. M. 152 N. Clark
Taber Sydney R. Lake Forest
Taberner W. W. 4729 Champlain av.
Tabor C. H. 7111 Eggleston av.
Tabor E. L. 2714 Calumet av.
Tafel G. 3958 Langley av.
Tafft Harriet Miss, 4558 Oakenwald av.
Taft Archibald W. 4257 Grand boul.
Taft Harry L. 3014 Michigan av.
Taft Ina B. Miss, 3014 Michigan av.
Taft Lorado, 86, 20 Vanburen
Taft Olivia M. Miss, 401, 64th (H.P.)
Taft Oren B. 3014 Michigan av.
Taft William H. 401, 64th (H.P.)
          Sum. res. Three Springs Farm,
          White Cloud, Ia.
Tagert Adelbert H., M.D. 846 W. Monroe
Taggart John, 1321 Wolcott
Tagg Edwin C. 1054 W. Monroe
Tahl Edwin V. LaGrange
Tait John, 3614 Grand boul.
Tait John G. 4916 Forrestville av.
Tait J. A. Miss, 145 Oakwood boul.
Tait M. M. Miss, 145 Oakwood boul.
Talbel F. B. Prof. Hotel Barry
Talbot Eliza Mrs. 426 N. State
Talbot Eugene S. Dr. Oak Park
Talbot Florence Miss, Oak Park
Talbot Frederick M. 1825 Indiana av.
Talbot Joseph G. 61 Bryant av.
Talbot J. Francis, 570 Washington boul.
Talbot J. F. 1823 Aldine av.
Talbot Laura Miss, 426 N. State
Talbot Marion Miss, Kelly Hall, University of Chicago
Talbot Thomas D. Evanston
Talbott R. H. Hyde Park hotel
Talcott E. A. Mrs. 433 W. Monroe
Talcott H. H. Des Plaines
Talcott Lester A. 52, 53d (H.P.)
Talcott Marshall D. 243 Ashland boul.
Tallert H. Mrs. 2971 Groveland av.
Tallmadge H. Mrs. 4731 Ellis av.
Tallmadge John H. 500 Fulton
Tallmadge Louis C. Evanston

Tallman Amanda Mrs. 601 W. Monroe
Tallman T. P. Palmer house
Tallmam W. D. 601 W. Monroe
Tallman W. L. Dr. Great Northern hotel
Talman John B. 2241 Irving av. (L.V.)
Tamblyn Wm. L. 4136 Michigan av.
Tanner C. J. 2342 Prairie av.
Tanner Ely J., M.D. Irving Park
Tanner John R. Grand Pacific Hotel
Tappan A. K. 700 Jackson boul.
Tapper George, 31 Bryan pl.
Tapson John L. 732 Washington boul.
Tapson William L. 732 Washington boul
Tarbox C. S. Hotel Barry
Tarnow Charles, Riverside
Tarr Herbert J. 205 Lincoln av.
Tarr Herbert J. jr. 205 Lincoln av.
Tarr William W. Dr. 205 Lincoln av.
Tarrant Robert, 72 Park av.
Tascott James B. 132 Ashland boul.
Tascott William E. Mrs. 3619 Lake av.
Tash John D. 66th sw. cor. Sheridan av.
Tate J. Emery 3821 Vernon av.
Tatge John, 516 Ashland boul.
Tatge Wm. H. 6438 Dickey
Tatham Robert L. 689 Washington boul.
Taubmann John, 72 Racine av.
Tausig J. Mrs. 685 N. Robey
Taussig Samuel, 162 Evanston av.
Taussig William, 1318 Washington boul.
Taylor Abner, Auditorium hotel
Taylor Albert H. Wilmette
Taylor Amory E. 5131 Hibbard av.
Taylor Anna B. Dr. 2402 N. Paulina
Taylor Anna M. Miss, 298 Bowen av.
Taylor A. K. Morgan Park
Taylor Bayard E. 829 Walnut
Taylor Benjamin, 291 Rush
Taylor Burton J. 2402 N. Paulina
Taylor Calvin F. 710 Washington boul.
    Sum. res. Waukesha, Wis.
Taylor Catherine Mrs. 4617 Ellis av.
Taylor Channing, Oak Park
Taylor Charles A. Mrs. 272 Warren av.
Taylor Charles S. Dr. 512 W. Adams
Taylor Charles W. 569, 51st (H.P.)
Taylor Charles W. 733 Chestnut, Eng.
Taylor Cora E. Dr. 6356 Stewart av.
Taylor Cortland C. Wilmette
Taylor D. L. 4321 Lake av.
Taylor D. S. Auditorium annex
Taylor Edward M. 309, 56th (H.P.)
Taylor E. F. Mrs. 426 Kenmore av.
Taylor E. H. 1039 Evanston av.
Taylor E. S. Evanston
Taylor E. Wiley, 551 Jackson boul.
Taylor Franklin C. 359 Dearborn av.
Taylor Fred M. 663 Park av.
Taylor Frederick P. 2452 Prairie av.
Taylor F. C. 493 Jackson boul.
Taylor George H. 35 E. Pearson
Taylor George H. 254 Ashland boul.
Taylor George H. 2621 Michigan av.
Taylor George O. Dr. Highland Park
Taylor Graham Prof. 397 W. Monroe
Taylor Granville P. 23 Marquette Terrace

Taylor Hart, 1039 Evanston av.
Taylor Henry A. Oak Park *
Taylor Henry C. 309, 56th (H.P.)
Taylor Henry P. 291 Rush
Taylor Homer S. Kenilworth
Taylor Horace P. 5622 Madison av.
Taylor Howard S. Rev. 6356 Stewart av.
Taylor H. Fish Miss, 3960 Drexel boul.
Tavlor H. Newton Miss, 3960 Drexel boul.
Taylor H. N. 359 N. State
Taylor James, 5229 Jefferson av.
Taylor James E. 2954 Calumet av.
Taylor John, 339 Maple, Englewood
Taylor John S. 254 Ashland boul.
Taylor John S. 672 Park av.
Taylor Jonah R. 3535 Indiana av.
Taylor Jos. W. 730, 63d ct. Eng.
Taylor Josephine Mrs. 241 Dearborn av.
Taylor Julia H. Mrs. 1039 Evanston av.
Taylor J. C. Granada hotel
Taylor J. G. 4714 Evans av.
Taylor J. Howard, 184, 37th
Taylor J. Mitchell. Dr. 184, 37th
Taylor J. S. Mrs. Riverside
Taylor J. S. L. 879 Warren av.
Taylor J. V. French   , Evanston
Taylor J. W. 57, 37thhouse
Taylor J. W. 416 Lasalle av.
Taylor Lewis S. 4060 Michigan Terrace
Taylor Louis D. Ridgeland
Taylor Louis S. Riverside
Taylor Louise M. Mrs. Lake Forest
Taylor Mary C. Mrs. 339 Bowen av.
Taylor M. P. 3643 Indiana av.
Taylor Peter, Evanston
Taylor Robert F. Col. 39 Flournoy
Taylor Robert J. 24 Waverley pl.
Taylor Rodney L. Mrs. 344 S. Paulina
Taylor Ruth Miss, 69 Laflin
Taylor R. G. Tracy
Taylor Samuel, 2 Campbell Park
Taylor Samuel C. Dr. 2402 N. Paulina
Taylor Samuel G. 610 Division
Taylor Susan Miss, 298 Bowen av.
Taylor S. G. jr. Elmhurst
Taylor S. R. Mrs. 462 Dayton
Taylor Thomas jr. 32 Astor
Taylor Thomas H. Wilmette
Taylor Walter G. 4726 Kenwood av.
Taylor William, Evanston
Taylor William A. Lake Forest
Taylor William N. 426 Kenmore av.
Taylor Woodbury M. Mrs. 3628 Vernon
    av.
Taylor W. 521 Belden av.
Taylor W. A. 879 Warren av.
Taylor W. A. Mrs. 423 Oak
Taylor W. F. 672 Park av.
Taylor W. H. 69 Laflin
Taylor W. H. Oak Park
Teal Norman Dr. 360, 44th
Teall Edward M. 522 W. Adams
Teare John, M.D. 1246 N. Clark
Tebbetts Charles H. 1837 Michigan av.
Tebbetts Frank M., M.D. 439 W. Taylor
Tebbetts J. C. 1383 Millard av.

Teed Herbert G. 4307 Oakenwald av.
Teefy Armand F. 158 Lasalle av.
Teehan Michael J. 201 Dearborn av.
Teel George W. 228, 42d
Teele Horace G. Austin
Teeple F. W. 2 Ogden front
Tegtmeyer William O. 1833 Belmont av.
Tehle Walter, 525 Winchester av.
Telfer R. G. 3129 Groveland av.
Telford John H. 5622 Madison av.
Teller James H. 4315 Berkeley av.
Teller John G. 6850 Union av.
Telling H. I. 519 Belden av.
Telling John, 519 Belden av.
Telling John E. 519 Belden av.
Tempel Anton, 599 Larrabee
Tempel Frank, 696 N. Wells
Tempel John, 499 N. Clark
Temple Alice Miss, 2943 Calumet av.
Temple A. S. Mrs. 37 63½ Ellis av.
Temple Christian, 511 Lasalle av.
Temple Grace E. Miss, 2943 Calumet av.
Temple John F. 2943 Calumet av.
Temple J. J. Dr. 435 Belden av.
Temple Mary Miss, 511 Lasalle av.
Temple M. D. 639 Washington boul.
Temple M. F. Mrs. 6937 Stewart av.
Temple Norris D. 639 Washington boul.
Temple Thomas S. 3705 Ellis av.
Temple-Vriedberg R. 163, 34th
Templeton David C. 5806 Washington av.
Templeton Hugh, 551 W. Van Buren
Templeton James E. 921 Evanston av.
Templeton James Stuart,921 Evanston av.
Templeton M. Miss, 326 Ashland boul.
Templeton Thomas, 326 Ashland boul.
Templeton William T. Oak Park
Templeton W. Oak Park
TenBroeke C. O. Morgan Park
TenBroeke Jane Mrs. 5630 Kimbark av.
TenEyck T. Major, 5704 Madison av.
Tennant J. Mrs. 1436 Michigan av.
Tennant Robert G. 1126 Winthrop av.
Tenney D. K. 3120 Calumet av.
    Sum. res. Jefferson, N. H
Tenney Horace K. 4827 Kenwood av.
Tenney John G. 1245 Wrightwood av.
Tenney J. Frank, 433 Warren av.
Tenney L. S. Dr. 144 Oakwood boul.
Tenney Mary S. Miss, 3120 Calumet av.
Tennis O. B. 2411 Michigan av.
Terhune Edgar, Wellington hotel
Terhune James R. 3042 Groveland av.
Terpenny W. J. 541 Maple, Englewood
Terriberry W. M. 1531 W. Monroe
Terriere D. E.6440 Wright
Terrill A. S. 2444 Commercial (L.V.)
Terrill W. E. Oak Park
Terry Albert C. 4217 Grand boul.
Terry Byron Z. 4217 Grand boul.
Terry Charles S. 9 Burton pl.
Terry F. S. Oak Park
Terry George N. The Renfost
Terry George S. 5540 Monroe av.
Terry M. S. Evanston
Terry Sarah K. Mrs. 7329 Stewart av.

Terry Sidney D. 7329 Stewart av.
Terry Washington I. 191, 54th (H.P.)
Teter George H. Oak Park
Tetu Alfred L. 421 Superior
Teven Joseph, 1316 Wrightwood av.
Tewes Henry, 1730 Waveland av.
Tewksbury C. S. 7037 Honore
Tewksbury George W. Auditorium annex
Tewksbury J. H. 645 Washington boul.
Tewksbury L. Mrs. Hotel Metropole
Tewksbury W. W. 7037 Honore
Thacher Chester I. Dr. 51 Aberdeen
Thacher George W. 507 W. Monroe
Thacher John M. Hotel Metropole
Thacher Sarah A. Miss, Hotel Metropole
Thacher William M. 4717 Champlain av.
Thacher William W. 245 Oakwood boul.
Thacher W. H. 3423 South Park av.
Thackaberry M. L. 378 Dearborn av.
Thacker Albert H. 4109 Drexel boul.
Thacker C. Edward, 4111 Drexel boul.
Thacker J. Frank, 4504 Greenwood av.
Thacker J. Robert, 4111 Drexel boul.
Thacker L. Mrs. 246 Oakwood boul.
Thackray Henry, 3852 Ellis av.
Thain J. A. 3152 Prairie av.
Thain R. S. Oak Park
Thamer George R. 59 Racine av.
Tharp E. H. 4343 Lake av.
Thatcher David A. River Forest
Thatcher David C. Mrs. River Forest
Thatcher David W. River Forest
Thatcher Fred S. River Forest
Thatcher George L. River Forest
Thatcher Luella B. Mrs. 546 Jackson boul.
Thatcher Raymond K. 336 Flournoy
Thaw Anna C. Miss, 85 Rush
Thayer A. G. Mrs. Hyde Park hotel
Thayer A. J. Evanston
Thayer Carl H. Hinsdale
Thayer Charles A. 703 W. Harrison
Thayer Charles H., Dr. 3302 Indiana av.
Thayer C. G. Hyde Park hotel
Thayer C. H. Hyde Park hotel
Thayer Electa L. Mrs. 10 Groveland Park
Thayer F. A. 171 Ashland boul.
Thayer George H. Norwood Park
Thayer Gilbert Mrs. Morgan Park
Thayer Henry A. 4108 Ellis av.
Thayer Henry J. 3830 Lake av.
    Sum. res. Delavan Lake, Wis.
Thayer Herbert, Hinsdale
Thayer H. A. Edison Park
Thayer H. E. Mrs. Morgan Park
Thayer H. N. Morgan Park
Thayer John H. 580 Lasalle av.
Thayer Julia H. Miss, 629, 78th, Eng.
Thayer Myrtle W. Mrs. 41 Aldine sq.
Thayer M. Ellen Miss, 3953 Michigan av.
Thayer Nathaniel C. 5813 Indiana av.
Thayer Selden, 6511 Honore
Thayer William, Hinsdale
Thearle Ernest A. 6947 Stewart av.
Thearle Fred G. jr. 457 Englewood av.
Thearle F. G. 601, 62d, Englewood
Thearle H. B. 6613 Harvard

Thein Jacob, 551 Cleveland av.
Theobald J. Harry, 3245 South Park av.
Theurer Joseph C. 1809 Indiana av.
Thiele August, 495 Marshfield av.
Thiele Edward, 495 Marshfield av
Thiele Louis, 495 Marshfield av.
Thielepape Theodore C. 69 Grant
Thies Wilhelm Dr. 195 Fremont
Thiesing Mary Mrs. 1683 Barry av.
Thin Robert, 4515 Woodlawn av.
Thoman Erwin M. Newberry hotel
Thoman LeRoy D. 1123 N. Clark
Thoman Melissa M. Miss, 1123 N. Clark
Thomas Addison C. 4806 Champlain av.
Thomas Albert R. 4212 Oakenwald av.
Thomas Alfred A. 691 Kenmore av.
Thomas Alfred E., M.D. 3148 Indiana av.
Thomas Ambrose L. 60 Woodland Park
Thomas A. 4625 Lake av.
Thomas A. Mrs. 500, 42d pl. (H.P.)
Thomas A. L., M.D. 3029 Indiana av.
Thomas A. S. 3029 Indiana av.
Thomas Benjamin, 4942 Ellis av.
Thomas Benjamin W. 1842 Indiana av.
Thomas B. H. Virginia hotel
Thomas Catherine Mrs. 3756 Ellis av.
Thomas Charles S. 408 Park av.
Thomas Christopher P. Evanston
Thomas Clara R. Miss, Lake Forest
Thomas Cyrus, 4223 St. Lawrence av.
Thomas C. G. 434, 45th (H.P.)
Thomas C. L. 7236 Yale
Thomas C. P. Oak Park
Thomas D. R. 61 University pl.
Thomas Edith Miss, 7236 Yale
Thomas Edward S. 4204 Ellis av.
Thomas E. C. 946 W. Monroe
Thomas E. C. Mrs. 535 W. Monroe
Thomas E. R. Evanston
Thomas E. W. LaGrange
Thomas Frank H. 60 Woodland Park
Thomas Frederic M. 1926 Indiana av.
   Sum. res. Lake Beulah, Wis.
Thomas F. A. 20 Walton pl.
Thomas George, 4368 Oakenwald av.
Thomas George C. Mayfair
Thomas George O. Evanston
Thomas George W. Mayfair
Thomas GranvilleS.Dr.2930 LakePark av.
Thomas G. W. 3029 Lake av.
Thomas Hampden F. 4558 Oakenwald av.
Thomas Harriet E. Miss, 4625 Lake av.
Thomas Henry, Lombard
Thomas Herbert A. Evanston
Thomas Hiram W. Rev. LL.D. 535 W.
   Monroe
Thomas Horace H. 256 Ontario
Thomas Horatio, Irving Park
Thomas H. M., M.D. 34 Throop
Thomas H. N. 462 North Clark
Thomas John, Lombard
Thomas John A. 4423 Vincennes av.
Thomas John G. 6213 Stewart av.
Thomas John W. 144 Ashland boul.
Thomas J. Mrs. 4440 Sidney av.
Thomas J. B. Chicago Beach hotel

Thomas J. C. 3981 Drexel boul.
Thomas J. H. Evanston
Thomas J. M. Evanston
Thomas J. P. 3029 Indiana av.
Thomas Leonidas, Irving Park
Thomas Leslie D. 244, 47th (H.P.)
Thomas Levi H., M.D. 3824 Ridge av.
Thomas Marion, 174 Ashland av.
Thomas Mary E. Mrs. 4284 Forest av.
Thomas Mary W. Dr. 2930 Lake Park av.
Thomas Mattie Miss, 3029 Indiana av.
Thomas M. Bross Prof. Lake Forest
Thomas M. P. Mrs. Austin
Thomas M. St. P. 553 Dearborn av.
Thomas R. H. The Ashland
Thomas R. M. 5511 Madison av.
Thomas Theodore, 43 Bellevue
Thomas William, 889 W. Congress
Thomas William H. 59 University pl.
Thomas William K. 61 Warren av.
Thomas William K. jr. 61 Warren av.
Thomas William S. 4204 Ellis av.
Thomas W. F. 1343 Jackson boul.
Thomason Frank D. 539, 60th, Eng.
Thomasson Nelson, 427 N. State
Thombs T. Mrs. 6647 Harvard
Thome Arthur G. Dr. 239 Lincoln av.
Thome Hattie S. 239 Lincoln av.
Thome Leo, 1628 Diversey
Thome M. 1628 Diversey
Thome Victoria Miss, 1628 Diversey
Thomlinson John, 71 Lincoln av.
Thomlinson John jr. 7720 Emerald av.
Thompson A. B. Mrs. 2478 Commercial
   (L.V.)
Thompson Benjamin F. C. 285 Dearborn
   av.
Thompson Charles B. 4744 Champlain av.
Thompson Charles F. 4305 Ellis av.
Thompson Charles H. 526 Garfield av.
Thompson Charles M. Dr. 3017 Michigan
   av.
Thompson Charles W. 3813 Michigan av.
Thompson Charles W. 2346 Calumet av.
Thompson C. C. 1425 Michigan av.
Thompson C. F. jr. 3350 South Park av.
Thompson C. M. 143 Oakwood boul.
Thompson David, 3516 Calumet av.
Thompson David D. Evanston
Thompson David O. 4313 Wabash av.
Thompson Dot Mrs. 376 Washington
   boul.
Thompson D. S. 6522 Lafayette av.
Thompson D. S. Mrs. 3431 Indiana av.
Thompson Edwin, 252 W. Congress
Thompson E. F. 523 Belden av.
Thompson E. L. 348 Ashland boul.
Thompson E. W. 948 Jackson boul.
Thompson Fanchon H. Miss, 2346 Cal
   umet av.
Thompson Frank, River Forest
Thompson Fred W. 2346 Calumet av.
Thompson F. S. 6522 Lafayette av.
Thompson Gale, Lakota hotel
Thompson George, 1844 Reta
Thompson George, 6800 Sherm

Thompson George C. Mrs. 6144 Michigan av.
Thompson George G. 681 North Park av.
Thompson George K. Newberry hotel
Thompson George L. 6629 Wentworth av.
Thompson Glenn D. 455, 63d (H.P.)
Thompson G. A. Berwyn
Thompson G. S. Berwyn
Thompson Helen Miss, Berwyn
Thompson Hiram J. 290 Belden av.
Thompson Hiram P. 846 Washington boul.
Thompson H. S. LaGrange
Thompson James H. 3141 Indiana av.
Thompson Jay J. Dr. 681 Fullerton av.
Thompson Jennie Ward Mrs. Evanston
Thompson John, Austin
Thompson John A. 214 Wilson av.
Thompson John D. Virginia hotel
Thompson John F. 3726 Langley av.
        Sum. res. Lake Geneva
Thompson John H. Mrs. 285 Dearborn av.
Thompson John W. Evanston
Thompson J. B. 7301 Yale
Thompson Leverett, 2246 Michigan av.
Thompson Lewis C. 627, 66th, Eng.
Thomqson L. Miss, Berwyn
Thompson Mark M. 805 W. Monroe
Thompson Mary H. Miss, M.D. 638 Jackson boul.
Thompson Mary W. Mrs. 3953 Michigan av.
Thompson Merritt W. Dr. 685 N. Robey
Thompson Milford J. Clifton house
Thompson M. A. 6639 Wright
Thompson M. G. Mrs. Lakota hotel
Thompson N. S. Mrs. Evanston
Thompson Orville Van, 78 Center av.
Thompson O. R. 6758 Sherman
Thompson Pamilla W. Miss, 2926 Michigan av.
Thompson Payson, 285 Dearborn av.
Thompson Peter Mrs. 42 Evergreen av.
Thompson P. Julien hotel
Thompson Richard S. 5406 East End av.
Thompson Robert, 263 Seminary av.
Thompson Robert J. 1723 Cornelia
Thompson R. D. LaGrange
Thompson Samuel, 6346 Harvard
Thompson Samuel B. Hotel Normandie
Thompson Samuel R. 6346 Harvard
Thompson Slason, 328 Superior
Thompson S. C. LaGrange
Thompson S. D. 722 W. Monroe
Thompson S. D. Hotel Normandie
Thompson Thomas C. 1219 Wolcott
Thompson Thomas P. 2189 W. Monroe
Thompson Watts C. 285 Dearborn av.
Thompson William, 252 W. Congress
Thompson William, 1270 Wolcott
Thompson William A. Riverside
Thompson William H. Oak Park
Thompson William H. The Tudor
Thompson William H. jr. 4457 Emerald av.
Thompson William K. Newberry hotel

Thompson William W. Austin
Thompson W. A. Southern hotel
Thompson W. H. Lakota hotel
Thompson W. N. 2300 South Park av.
Thomsen Peter F. Jefferson Park
Thomson Alexander M. 4032 Ellis av.
Thomson B. A. L. 1236 George
Thomson E. B. Mrs. Morgan Park
T mson George R. 2809 Commercial ho(L.V.)
Thomson H. C. M. 5206 Cornell av.
Thomson James, 1718 Belmont av.
Thomson James C. 180 Goethe
Thomson Laura Miss, 982 W. Adams
Thomson Robert B. Morgan Park
Thomson William H. 408 Elm
Thorn Francis, Highland Park
Thornburgh H. L. 464 Jackson boul.
Thorndyke J. Edward, Austin
Thorne A. P. Berwyn
Thorne Charles H. 4544 Greenwood av.
Thorne Charles S. Winnetka
Thorne George A. 90, 47th (H.P.)
Thorne George R. 90, 47th (H.P.)
Thorne Jacob, 4217 Vincennes av.
Thorne James Ward, 90, 47th (H.P.)
Thorne Robert J. 90, 47th
Thorne Stephen, 164 Warren av.
Thorne Wm. C. 140, 47th (H.P.)
Thorne William J. 4438 Berkeley av.
Thorne W. H. 371 Superior
Thornton A. 475 Fullerton av.
Thornton Charles S. 7600 Stewart av.
Thornton D. Mrs. Lexington hotel
Thornton Edward C. LaGrange
Thornton E. A. 475 Fullerton av.
Thornton E. L. 475 Fullerton av.
Thornton Harry S. 3662 Wabash av.
Thornton H. G. Hotel Windermere
Thornton R. L. 1854 Frederick
Thornton Solon, 7600 Stewart av.
Thorp David L. Evanston
Thorp Frank H. LaGrange
Thorpe Frank L. 401 Belden av.
Thorpe H. H. Mrs. Hotel Imperial
Thorpe J. W. 18 Sidney ct.
Thorpe Samuel Mrs. 1011 N. Halsted
Thorsen James B. 16 Madison av.
Thorson Soren D. 619 N. Hoyne av.
Thorwart Henry, 578 N. Clark
Thrall Nelson C. 3139 Michigan av.
Thrall Samuel E. 4620 Woodlawn av.
Thrall W. A. 4620 Woodlawn av.
Thresher David, 524 Washington boul.
Thresher William E. 524 Washington boul.
Thrift Merton B. 276 Michigan av.
Throckmorton Howard, The Plaza
Thule Charles H. 4644 Evans av.
Thumser Elizabeth Miss, 258 Warren av.
Thumser William W. 258 Warren av.
Thunack Julius H. 667 Pine Grove av.
Thurber Edward C. 261 Bowen av.
Thurber Elias C. 528 Washington boul.
Thurber George, 285 Webster av.
Thurber George S. 26 Delaware pl.

Thurber Wm. E. Austin
Thurber W. Scott, 3161 Groveland av.
Thurston Emeline C. Mrs. 4434 Grand
  boul.
Thurston E. H., M.D. 3018 Indiana av.
Thurston Frank W. 4434 Grand boul.
Thurston Hollis M. 329 Ashland boul.
Thurston John C. 4131 Berkeley av.
Thurston N. B. Mrs. 4412 Indiana av.
Thurston Stephen R. Lombard
Thwaite George R. 6940 Oglesby av.
Thyng Laura A. Miss, 2968 Lake Park av.
Tibbits Flora V. W. Mrs. The Arizona
Tibbits Frank H. The Arizona
Tibbitts Henry S. 915 Sawyer av.
Tibbles Charles E. 6138 Stewart av.
Tice Edwin S. 190, 54th (H.P.)
Tichenor A. L. Mrs. 5109 Kimbark av.
Tichenor Kate R. Mrs. 2428 Michigan av.
Tichenor Myron H. 6636 Perry av.
Tichenor W. A. Dr. 492 W. Adams
Tidholm August, 7056 Perry av.
Tiedemann J. 299 N. State
Tiedt John, 1267 N. Halsted
Tiedt Oscar A. Dr. 1267 N. Halsted
Tiernan John, Evanston
Tiernan Michael, Evanston
Tierney Thos. J. 408 S. Wood
Tiffany E. Mrs. 164 S. Wood
Tiffany George S. Hinsdale
Tiffany Henry S. 3742 Ellis av.
Tiffany Horace P. 620, 60th, Englewood
Tiffany H. C. Mrs. 3742 Ellis av.
Tiffany Joel Mrs. Hinsdale
Tiffany L. Scott, 11, 43d
Tiffany Mary J. Miss, 620, 60th, Eng.
Tiffany M. A. Mrs. Austin
Tifft Henry, 492 Dearborn av.
Tigan T. J. Evanston
Tilden B. E. 753, 63d ct. Eng.
Tilden B. F. 6134 Sheridan av.
Tilden Edward, 4612 Emerald av.
Tilden J. B. Mrs. 3142 Michigan av.
Tilden W. A Oak Park
Tilden W. D. Chicago Beach hotel
Tilghman William, Evanston
Tilley Robert, M.D. Lexington hotel
Tillinghast Henry C. Evanston
Tillinghast William, Julien hotel
Tillmann Charles F. 1314 N. Clark
Tillmann Mathias J. 1314 N. Clark
Tillotson E. W. 140, 38th
Tillotson Miles D. 938 Park av.
Tillotson Wm. S. 1081 Washington boul.
Tilt Joseph E. 543 Evanston av.
Tilton Catherine P. Miss, 627 Dearborn
Tilton C. J. 82 Centre av.
Tilton H. H. 360 Ontario
Tilton J. Neal, LaGrange
Tilton Lucretia J. Mrs. 627 Dearborn av.
Timberlake Margaret Mrs. 730 W.Adams
Timm Hugo, 16 Cedar
Timmerman Bernhard, Julien hotel
Timmerman Christian H. 600 Englewood
  av.
Timms F. M. 605, 65th, Englewood

Tindall John W. 652 Walnut
Tinkham C. A. 638 Fullerton av.
Tinley Charles, 6901 Wentworth av.
Tinsley John H. 7420 Brooks av.
Tinsley John W. 7420 Brooks av.
Tinsman H. E. 6436 Yale
Tipman George B. 4532 Woodlawn av.
Tipman Jesse 4532 Woodlawn av.
Tipton Louis Campbell, 270 Huron
Tisdale Laura J. Mrs. 6436 Sheridan av.
Titcomb Arthur B. 638 Fullerton av.
Titcomb S. B. 638 Fullerton av.
Titcomb William C. 1750 Wrightwood av.
Titlow Kate A. Miss, 216 Ohio
Titus Alfred C. Mrs. 258, 37th
Titus Calvin W. 4211 Ellis av.
Titus George, 527 Jackson boul.
Titus G. P. 4627 Lake av.
Titus Joseph F. 4211 Ellis av.
Titus Mary A. Mrs. 811 Farwell av.
Titus S. M. Miss, 4211 Ellis av.
Titus Virgil E. Austin
Titus William H. 811 Farwell av.
Tobey C. Harry, 4837 Kenwood av.
Tobey C. H. M. 4831 Kenwood av.
Tobey E. M. Miss, 4839 Kenwood av.
Tobey E. P. 2231 Calumet av.
Tobey Fannie A. Miss, 356 Warren av.
Tobey Frank B. 448 W. Adams
  Sum. res. Nobscussett, Cape Cod
Tobey Frank D. 2450 Indiana av.
Tobey Heury S. 4037 Indiana av.
Tobey Howard V. 635 Fullerton av.
Tobey John A. 3953 Michigan av.
Tobey Thomas, 3706½ Ellis av.
Tobias Arthur W. Longwood
Tobias D. J. 743 W Monroe
Tobias George J. Dr. 850 W. Monroe
Tobin A. W. 5813 Monroe av.
Tobin B. F. 55, 33d
Tobin C. O. Mrs. 5813 Monroe av.
Tobin F. M. 7362 Bond av.
Tobin Samuel C. 4721 Kimbark av.
Todd Charles C. Oak Park
Todd Edward E. 315 Park av.
Todd George W. 232 Belden av.
Todd James A. 2339 Michigan av.
Todd James F. Dr. 2447 Prairie av.
Todd John Jackson, 87 Rush
Todd J. A. 2339 Michigan av.
Todd L. M. 232 Belden av.
Todd William, Oak Park
Toles Wilfred C. Irving Park
Tollakson T. 128 Evergreen av.
Tollason Nettie Miss, Hotel Barry
Tolley Elmer W. 3833 Ellis av.
Tolley Harry R. 3833 Ellis av.
Tolley W. A. 3833 Ellis av.
Tolman Albert H. 5468 Monroe av.
Tolman Cyrus F. Rev. 41 University pl.
Tolman D. H. 538 Dearborn av.
Tolman Edgar B. 5660 Madison av.
Tolman Elmer E. 538 Dearborn av.
Tolman H. L. Evanston
Tolman John A. 4727 Ellis av.
Tolman Judson A. 3804 Prairie av.

Tolman Samuel A. 2031 Prairie av.
Tolson Benjamin F. Dr. 351 Indiana
Tomaso Salvatore, 3267 Beacon
Tomblin Ira, 491 Jackson boul.
Tomhagen John A. Dr. 1516 Dunning
Tomlin Allan R. 205 Cass
Tomlin Harry P. 205 Cass
Tomlins Wm. L. Evanston
Tomlinson E. S. Oak Park
Tomlinson Horace S. 4553 Emerald av.
Tomlinson Isaac, Oak Park
Tomlinson John L. 3946 Prairie av.
Tomlinson Joseph S. 2920 Indiana av.
Tomlinson J. 1837 Michigan av.
Tomlinson L. O. 3946 Prairie av.
Tomlinson Rockwell N. 4553 Emerald av.
Tomlinson W. M. Dr. 533 W. Adams
Tompkins George K. Irving Park
Tompkins Hiram, 2311 Indiana av.
     Sum. res. Saratoga Springs, N. Y.
Tompkins James Rev. Oak Park
Tompkins Mary W. Mrs. Oak Park
Tompkins Roy J. Oak Park
Tompkins S. L. 301, 53d (H.P.)
Tompkins Selah R. H. Lieut. Fort Sher-
     idan
Tonk Albert E. Evanston
Tonk Max, 592 Fullerton av.
Tonnas H. A. Mrs. 40 Buena Park Ter-
     race
Toohy Joseph B. 866 Walnut
Tooker Robert N., M.D. 263 Dearborn av.
     Sum. res. Fox Lake, Ill.
Tooker Robert N. jr. 263 Dearborn av.
Toolen A. J. 4434 Lake av.
Tope J. W. Dr. Oak Park
Topliff William B. Evanston
Toppan George L. Evanston
Toppan James S. Lakota hotel
     Sum. res. Newburyport, Mass.
Toppan Wm. R. 340 Oakwood boul.
Topping A. M. Mrs. 4425 Berkeley av.
Topping Jeannette Miss, River Forest
Torofsky David, 512 Ashland boul.
Torofsky Mark, 428 Marshfield av.
Torrence Joseph T. Gen. 88 Bellevue pl.
Torrey R. A. Rev. 440 N. State
Totten Harry, Winnetka
Totten Harry B. Glencoe
Totten Susan Mrs. Winnetka
Touhy Edmund R. 5008 N. Clark
Touhy Joseph, 5008 N. Clark
Touhy Patrick L. 5008 N. Clark
Touhy Stephen, 5008 N. Clark
Tourtellotte Fred J. 3432 Vernon av.
Tourtellotte F. W. 3432 Vernon av.
Tourtelot Elie C. Pullman
Tousey C. A. 171, 51st (H. P.)
Tousey George H. Chicago Beach hotel
Tousey Thomas E. 171, 51st (H. P.)
Tower Arthur, Evanston
Tower J. B. 24 Orchard (H. P.)
Towers Albert B. 1821 Aldine
Towers C. G. Oak Park
Towers J. M. 6949 Webster av. Eng.
Towle Eliza J. Mrs. Evanston

Towle Helen Maude Miss, Oak Park
Towle Henry S. Oak Park
Towle John R. 6244 Sheridan av.
Towler E. H. 4343 Prairie av.
Towler E. T. 3809 Prairie av.
Towler Thomas Rev. 4950 Prairie av.
Towles Wm. B. 911 Sawyer av.
Town Nelson H. 4433 Sidney av.
Towne Arthur F. Evanston
Towne Edward Owings, 103 N. Clark
Towne Henry, 528 W. Monroe
Towne Julia R. Mrs. Evanston
Towne Margaret Miss, Lombard
Towne Willis H. 602 Lincoln av.
Towner Henry A. 306 Schiller
Townsend Abram R. 4344 Greenwood av.
Townsend Charles D. 27 Ashland boul.
Townsend Copeland, Hotel Metropole
Townsend E. D. Hotel Barry
Townsend Frederick B. 2233 Sheridan rd.
Townsend G. B. 13 Seeley av.
Townsend Helen Miss, Hotel Barry
Townsend James J. 27 Ashland boul.
Townsend John E. Lake Forest
Townsend John J. 27 Ashland boul.
Townsend John J. jr. 27 Ashland boul.
Townsend Lucy Mrs. 6841 Anthony av.
Townsend Perry S. Hinsdale
Townsend Wm. M. 7827 Reynolds av.
Townsend W. R. Oak Park
Towslee Edwin C. Newberry hotel
Towsley A. W. 14 Astor
Toynton F. E. Tremont house
Tracey Edward, River Forest
Tracy David M. Irving Park
Tracy Joseph P. 507 Leland av.
Tracy Lucretia P. Mrs. 2559 Michigan av.
Traer Glennwood W. 4463 Lake av.
Trahan Frank, Evanston
Traill Richard H. Austin
Trainer William E. 4326 Berkeley av.
Trainor Joanna Mrs. 6518 Wharton av.
Tramel George, 525, 62d, Englewood
Trask Frederick M. 469 Fullerton av.
Trask G. F. 3308 Wabash av.
     Sum. res. Clarendon Springs, Vt.
Traub Adolph, 282 Erie
Traver F. C. 215½ S. Wood
Trayner John, 4426 Grand boul.
Treacy Hugh T. 3952 Indiana av.
Treacy Thomas H. 3952 Indiana av.
Treadway James M. 4500 Vincennes av.
Treadwell H. Mrs. The Renfost
Treat Charles P. 372 Lasalle av.
Treat Francis H. 234 Hampden ct.
Treat Harry W. 2724 Michigan av.
Treat H. J. Dr. 626 W. Monroe
Treat Robert, Hinsdale
Treat R. B. Dr. 247 W. Madison
Treat S. A. Lakota hotel
Trebilcock Albert, 527, 67th, Englewood
Tredwell John, 6314 Stewart av.
Tree Arthur M. 94 Cass
Tree Lambert, 94 Cass
Treer Frederick W. 1701 Wellington
Trego Charles H. 3931 Ellis av.

Trego C. T. 3935 Lake av.
Trego Frank, 3935 Lake av.
Trego William T. 3935 Lake av.
Trelease John, 2433 N. Paulina
Treleaven W. N. 1242 Wilcox av.
Treloar Gustav B. Evanston
Tremaine J. E. Dr. 5318 Jefferson av.
Tremaine Matthew O.4841 Forrestville av.
Tremaine Myron J. 5318 Jefferson av.
Tremaine O. G. Dr. 145 Oakwood boul.
Trench Daniel G. 210 S. Lincoln
Trench Richard R. 455, 47th
Trenter Jacob P. 594 Walnut
Trenton J. R. 6927 Honore
Tresselt Dorothea Mrs. 297 Lincoln av.
Tressler A. R. 148 Dearborn av.
Trestrail May Anderson Mrs. 220, 40th
  (H. P.)
Trevette George F. 473 Irving av.
Trienens Joseph, 305 S. Oakley av.
Trigg Thomas, 871 St. Louis av.
Triggs Charles W. 913 Spaulding av.
Triggs John, 913 Spaulding av.
Triller J. Edward, 7614 Wright
Trimingham Anna E. Miss, 5517 Madison
  av.
Trimingham Ralph N. Oak Park
Trimmer John R. 578 N. Adams
Trimmer Wm. A. 578 W. Adams
Trine John G. Dr. 3621 Ellis Park
Tripp Arnold, 596 Dearborn av.
Tripp D. K. Granada hotel
Tripp F. A. 2705 N. Paulina
Tripp George A. 5022 Greenwood av.
Tripp Herman, 409 Marshfield av.
Tripp M. W. Mrs. 3159 South Park av.
Tripp Robinson Dr. 2030 Indiana av.
Trissal Frank M. 4744 Evans av.
Tristram J. E. Oak Park
Troendle Victor, 1161 N. Clark
Troost William, 417 Dearborn av.
Trorlicht S. K. Mrs. 493 Belden av.
Trott Walter C. 3811 Michigan av.
Trotter A. H. 4921 Madison av.
Trotter D. W. Grand Pacific
Trotter Fred E. Evanston
Trotter Richard G. Evanston
Trout Edgar W. River Forest
Trout Elizabeth, M.D. River Forest
Trout George W. 1564 Fulton
Trowbridge Cornelia R. Miss, 27 Dela-
  ware pl.
Trowbridge Cornelius M. 4338 Oakenwald
  av.
Trowbridge C. W. 800B Pullman bldg.
Trowbridge George M. 27 Delaware pl.
Trowbridge J. H. Mrs. 27 Delaware pl.
Trowbridge Oliver R. 2410 Commercial
  (L.V.)
Trowbridge Wm. A. 2577 Commercial
  (L.V.)
Trowbridge W. L. 9 St. James pl.
Troxell B. F. 3847 Ellis av.
Troxell Thomas G. Capt. Highland Park
Troxell William R. Evanston
Troy L. L. 882 W. Monroe
45

Troyer Joseph H. 3158 Lake Park av.
Troyer L. Mrs. 621 Lasalle av.
Truax Charles H. 2654 N. Paulina
Truax Galloway, M.D. 2736 N. Paulina
Truax Henry A. Mrs. 1103 S. Central Park
  av.
Truax J. Mrs. 3627 Vernon av.
Trude Alfred Percy, 4960 Drexel boul.
Trude A. S. 4960 Drexel boul.
Trude Charlotte Mrs. 4313 L   g   av.
Trude Frank M. Dr. 4313 Langley av.
Trude Frederick H. 5106 Hibbard av.
Trude George A. 4960 Drexel boul.
Trude Mark W. 4313 Langley av.
Trude Samuel H. 216, 33d
Trudeau Eugene J. Mrs. 1165 S. Central
  Park av.
True Albert W. 320 Marshfield av.
True A. S. 217 Loomis
True Charles H. 7127 Wentworth av.
True Charles J. 320 Marshfield av.
True Ella P. Miss, 320 Marshfield av.
True Ella W. Mrs. 323, 61st, Eng.
True John R. 1784 Oakdale av.
True M. A. 711 W. Adams
True M. E. Miss, 320 Marshfield av.
Trueheart C. T. New Hotel Holland
Truman J. H. Mrs. 27 St. James pl.
Truman Orville M. 4619 Woodlawn av.
Trumbull George Mrs. 4016 Lake av.
Trumbull Henry, 4008 Lake av.
Trumbull Herman J. 6557 Sheridan av.
Trumbull James L. Mrs. 1719 Michigan av.
Trumbull J. H. 4026 Lake av.
Trumbull Lyman, 4008 Lake av.
Trumbull Morris, 4544 Oakenwald av.
Trumbull Perry, 873 Kenmore av.
Trumbull Walter Mrs. 4008 Lake av.
Trunkey Addison J. Mrs. 3834 Lake av.
Trusdale W. H. 188 Pine
Trussell H. M. Berwyn
Tryon LeRoy C. Irving Park
Tryon Mary Mrs. 1065 Warren av.
Tubbs F. H. 725 Fullerton av.
Tubbs M. J. Mrs. 340 Maple, Eng.
Tuchband Julius, 745½ North Park av.
Tuck Alice L. Miss, 3017 Michigan av.
Tuck Calvin, 3017 Michigan av.
Tucker Fred W. 3517 Ellis av.
Tucker Frederick J. 1854 Frederick
Tucker Helen L. Miss, 1321 Michigan av.
Tucker Horace, 3517 Ellis av.
Tucker H. E. Mrs. 238 Dearborn av.
Tucker H. S. Dr. 464, 42d
Tucker James I. Dr. 52, 35th
Tucker Jessie M. Mrs. 39 Bryant av.
Tucker Joseph F. Grand Pacific hotel
Tucker J. C. 3755 Lake av.
Tucker J. L. Oak Park
Tucker Luther K. 688 W. Monroe
Tucker Malcolm, Ravinia
Tucker Stephen, 6746 Sherman
Tucker William R. 757 W. Adams
Tucker W. A. 1839 Indiana av.
Tucker W. S. 757 W. Adams
Tuerk Albert, 1027 Centre (L.V.)

Tufts E. L. 3817 Forest av.
Tufts Henry S. 1859 Oakdale av.
Tufts J. H. 7154 Euclid av. (H.P.)
Tugwell Richard J. 593 Walnut
Tuley M. F. Judge, 5135 Washington av.
　　Sum. res. Pine Lake, Wis.
Tull E. E. Dr. 428 Warren av.
Tull J. D. Rev. 428 Warren av.
Tuller R. B. Dr. 877 W. Monroe
Tuller W. G. 71 Lake View av.
Tully A. Melville, M.D. 216 Dearborn av.
Tully E. M. Mrs. 21, 35th
Tully Gerald T. Mrs. 4325 Greenwood av.
Tully John W. 21, 35th
Tuohy David W. 4138 Ellis av.
Tuohy James D. 4138 Ellis av.
Tuohy John D. 4138 Ellis av.
Tuohy J. W. Mrs. 46 Loomis
Tuohy Stephen P. 4138 Ellis av.
Tuppler Purda Miss, 446 Belden av.
Turbin Louis M. Dr. 6049 Madison av.
Turck Fenton B. Dr. 100 The Plaza
Turk Joseph, 473 Ashland boul.
Turnbull John, New Hotel Holland
Turner A. A. 4330 Oakenwald av.
Turner Charles C. Austin
Turner Charles W. 503 Leland av.
Turner C. Heber, Austin
Turner Edward A. 227, 47th (H.P.)
Turner Edward H. 4929 Greenwood av.
Turner Edward S. Evanston
Turner E. E. 76 Walton pl.
Turner Frank D. 1784 Wrightwood av.
Turner F. E. 7240 Webster av. Eng.
Turner Harry M. 182 Bowen av.
Turner Henry, 418 Belden Av.
Turner Henry L. Walton pl. sw. cor. Rush
Turner James W. La Grange
Turner John, Evanston
Turner John W. 3761 Vernon av.
Turner J. C. Mrs. Lexington hotel
Turner J. Lyle, 3601 Ellis Park
Turner Laurin H. 4929 Greenwood av.
Turner Margaret Mrs. 4323 Berkeley av.
Turner Miles L. Evanston
Turner Otis E. Oak Park
Turner S. A. Mrs. 182 Bowen av.
Turner Thomas, 285 W. Adams
Turner Thomas M. 3601 Ellis Park
Turner Thomas M. jr. 3601 Ellis Park
Turner V. C. 112 Lake Shore Drive
Turner Walter E. Evanston
Turner Walter I. Evanston
Turner William H. Palmer house
Turner W. F. 2976 South Park av.
Turner W. M. Fvanston
Turney J. E. Oak Park
Turney W. F. 377 Dearborn av.
Turnley Parmenas T. Col. Highland Park
Turrill John F. 24 Madison Park
Turrill L. B. 24 Madison Park
Tuska Leo, 3237 Michigan av.
Tuteur Edwin B., M.D. 3553 Prairie av.
Tuteur I. Mrs. 3553 Prairie av.
Tuthill F. H. 352 Maple, Englewood.

Tuthill Joseph D. Dr. 294 S. Oakley av.
Tuthill Richard S. Judge, 532 Jackson boul
Tuthill Sophia R. Mrs. 146 DeKalb
Tuttle Charles F. 6620 Oglesby av.
Tuttle Clarence A. 3207 Michigan av.
Tuttle C. P. Mrs. 463 Irving av.
Tuttle Emerson B. Chicago club
Tuttle Frederick B. 2022 Michigan av.
Tuttle Henry N. Lake Forest
Tuttle H. E. Mrs. 634 Park av.
Tuttle John A. S. 5330 Jefferson av.
Tuttle Lucius D. 3652 Vincennes av.
Tuttle O. H. Dr. 634 Park av.
Tuttle Sterling D. Dr. 634 Park av.
Tuttle W. Fay, 5330 Jefferson av.
Tuttle W. H. Berwyn
Tuttle W. P. Lakota hotel
Tweedie Herbert, 7525 Goldsmith av.
Twells P. S. 42, 39th
Twick William, 935 Catalpha
Twitchell J. O. 229, 28th
Twitty Edward Mrs. 650 W. Adams
Twitty Walter G. 834 W. Monroe
Twohig J. W. 55 N. Ada
Twyford Harry B. 503 The Plaza
Twyman Joseph, 5759 Madison av.
Tyler Albert S. 44 Woodland Park
Tyler Frederick C. 4045 Grand boul.
Tyler Harvey A. Dr. 939 W. Monroe
Tyler John H. 437 Irving av.
Tyler Rosina Mrs. 4564 Oakenwald av.
Tyler Sarah M. Mrs. 14 Woodland Park
Tyler W. H. 908 W. Monroe
Tyler William M. Austin
Tyner A. H. 3140 Calumet av.
Tyng Dudley A. 79 Pine
Tyrrell Albert H. 857 Jackson boul.
Tyrrell Charles T. 585 Washington boul.
Tyrrell Fred S. 585 Washington boul.
Tyrrell John, 3328 Indiana av.
Tyrrell John A. Mrs. 585 Washington boul.
Tyrrell Patrick, 1096 Early av.
Tyson Howard N. Wilmette
Tyson Russell, 319 Superior
Tyson Will S. French house, Evanston

UDELL S. R. Chicago Beach hotel
　　Ufen Emil, 6552 Ellis av.
Uhlemann Richard G. 369 Burling
Uhlendorf Lebrecht, 3525 Wabash av.
Uhlmann Fred. 3126 South Park av.
Uhrig Joseph, 6560 Yale
Uhrlaub Adolph, 284 Ohio
Uhrlaub John C. 250 Lasalle av.
Uihlein Edward G. 34 Ewing pl.
Ullery F. B. Dr. 3946 Drexel boul.
Ullman Daniel, 2962 Prairie av.
Ullman E. H. Great Northern hotel
Ullman Gustave S. 2712 Indiana av.
Ullman Jacob, 2712 Indiana av.
Ullman Louis, 3255 Wabash av.
Ullman N. J. 3332 Vernon av.
Ullman Percy G. 4506 Ellis av.
Ullmann Albert I. Oak Park
Ullmann Frederic, 282, 48th (H.P.)
Ullmann H. J. Oak Park

Ullrich Albert H. Evanston
Ullrich Louis Mrs. 3214 Rhodes av.
Ullrich Michael, 587 Lasalle av.
Ullrich William A. 3214 Rhodes av.
Ulm J   W. 3158 Prairie av.
UlrichoAn Louis, 1928 Oakdale av.
Ulrich Bartow A. 1928 Oakdale av.
Ulrich Bartow A. jr. 1928 Oakdale av.
Ulrich Edwin C. 69 University pl.
Ulrich J. A. 79 Warren av.
Ulrich Raymond, M.D. 202 Center
Ulrich Russell, 305 Schiller
Umlauf Louis C. 2501 N. Halsted
Umlauf V. Q. Mrs. 2501 N. Halsted
Umlauf William, 2501 N. Halsted
Umsted Frank A. 7048 Stewart av.
Umsted George, 7048 Stewart av.
Umsted Harry C. 7048 Stewart av.
Umstot William H. 3756 Ellis av.
Underhill A. J. 7535 Honore
Underhill E. Mrs. 5316 Greenwood av.
Underwood Arthur W. Evanston
Underwood Benjamin F. 825 W. Adams
Underwood C. A. 489 Dearborn av.
Underwood E. M. 3662 Michigan av.
Underwood George W.2973South Park av.
Underwood H. G. 415 Marshfield av.
Underwood H. M. 415 Marshfield av.
Underwood J. Platt 4016 Lake av.
Underwood P. L. 3022 Prairie av.
Underwood Sidney L. 5327 Cornell av.
Underwood S. F. 5327 Cornell av.
Underwood T. Mrs. Lakota hotel
Underwood William A. 3846 Vincennes
    av.
Underwood William H.3846 Vincennes av.
Underwood William T. Lakota hotel
Unger M. 431 Warren av.
Unna A. J. Mrs. 3362 Prairie av.
            Sum. res. Belmar, N. J.
Unna Julius A. 3362 Prairie av.
Unold George D. LaGrange
Unold John, LaGrange
Updike Charles M. 320, 37th
Updike Fred P. 4202 Michigan av.
Updike F. D. Oak Park
Updike Harry S. 6048 Edgerton av.
Updike Mary Mrs. 4200 Michigan av.
Upham Abel P. 3218 Groveland av.
Upham E. P. Oak Park
Upham Frank, Oak Park
Upham Frank A. 3568 Vincennes av.
Upham Fred W. 393 Dearborn av.
Upham J. Mrs. 272 Erie
Upham J. Frank, 272 Erie
Upham Louise Miss, 272 Erie
Upman Frank, 5602 Monroe av.
Upp Walter, 3233 Indiana av.
Upson Irwin F. Dr. 382 N. Clark
Upton Cassius A. LaGrange
Upton George P. 2427 South Park av.
Upton L. C. 332 Bowen av.
Upton Timothy Mrs. 3638 Indiana av.
Urann Mary Mrs. Evanston
Ure Daisy D. Mrs. 550 Burling
Ure John F. 5138 N. Clark

Ure Robert H. 88 Park av.
Urion Alfred R. 79 Bowen av.
Ustick John T. 6143 Stewart av.
Utley C. W. 16 Lincoln av.
Utley H. B. 853 W. Monroe
Utley W. P. Oak Park
Utt Frank M. 3756 Ellis av.
Utting William, 1063 W. Madison
Utz A. L. 4632 Vincennes av.

VAIL CHARLES A. 2439 Commercial
    (L.V.)
Vail Charles M. H. 2403 N. Paulina
Vail Edith W. Miss, Hotel Metropole
Vail Ellen P. Mrs. 2129 Calumet av.
Vail Frank, 272 Erie
Vail Henry S. Highland Park
Vail John D. 6616 Harvard
Vail John D. jr. 6825 Yale
Vail Lizzie Miss, 674 Lasalle av.
Vail U. G. 6616 Harvard
Vaile E. O. Oak Park
Vale H. E. 6429 Wright
Valentine Alastair I. 4351 Lake av.
Valentine A. J. Mrs. 4351 Lake av.
Valentine Belle Mrs. 124 Loomis
Valentine C. C. The Renfost
Valentine Edward H. 449 N. State
Valentine E. Archibald, 171 Goethe
Valentine Gordon, 4342 Ellis av.
Valentine G. F. 124 Loomis
Valentine James C. Dr. 2340 Prairie av.
Valentine John, 449 N. State
Valentine Kimball E. The Renfost
Valentine Norman F. 726 W. Adams
Valentine P. A. 4351 Lake av.
Valentine R. H. Washington Heights
Valentine Sara L. Dr. 2340 Prairie av.
Valentine Theodore, 5546 Madison av.
Valentine Watts, The Renfost
Valisi Cesare, 276 Michigan av.
Valisi Giuseppe, 276 Michigan av.
Vallas W. H. 593 Park av.
Vallens Eugene, 3617 Ellis av.
Vallette Frank H. Hamilton club
VanAckeren Frederick Dr. 954 N. Clark
VanAllen Benjamin T. 17 Chalmers pl.
VanAllen Kittie Mrs. 433 S. Oakley av.
VanAllen Martin, 1245 Palmer
Vanalstine M. A. Mrs. Evanston
VanAnda C. A. Dr. Evanston
VanAnden Charles A. 3135 Rhodes av.
VanArsdale John R. Mrs. Evanston
VanArsdale MartinV.B.Rev.518,67th,Eng
VanArsdale William T. Evanston
VanBaalen I. 861 W. Monroe
VanBenschoten Chas. W. 3540 Ellis av.
VanBenschoten George W. 3540 Ellis av.
VanBenschoten Samuel, Evanston
VanBenschoten William C. Evanston
VanBenthuysen William, 103 Evanston
    av.
VanBezey Cornelius, 423 Winchester av.
Van Bezey James, 425 Winchester av.
VanBokkelen Ross C. 4558 Oakenwald
    av.

VanBuren Augustus, 413 Washington boul.
VanBuren Barent Col. 1183 Washington boul.
VanBuren Edgar R. 380 Dayton
VauBuren Henry Mrs. 1364 Washington bou .
    Sum. res. Merrickville, Ont. Can.
Vance George P. 2781 N. Paulina
Vance Thomas H. Lombard
Vance William L. Evanston
VanCleave James R. B. 329 Michigan av.
VanCourtBenjamin P.Forest hotel(R.P.)
VanCraenenbroeck Joseph, 5506 Monroe
VanDalson Edward, 3534 Rhodes av.
VanDeMark E. 961 Park av.
VanDenbergh H. T. 97, 37th
VanDenburgh Nathan, 1837 Reta
VanDerburgh A. C. 4114 Elhs av.
Vandercook Charles R. Austin
Vandercook Emma Mrs. Evanston
Vandercook Henry R. 3237 Forest av.
Vandercook John D. Austin
Vanderkloot A. 4248 Wabash av.
Vanderkloot M. L. Austin
Vanderlip C. L. Mrs. 5126 Madison av.
Vanderlip Frank A. 5126 Madison av.
Vanderploeg H. 6837 Perry av.
Vanderpoel John H. Tracy
VanDeursen Charles S. 612, 62d, Eng.
VanDeusen Arthur S. Evanston
Van de Venter E. Miss, Hyde Park hotel
VanDoozer B. R., M.D. 4318 Prairie av.
VanDoozer Fred R. 42, 39th
VanDoren Chas. L. 7529 Eggleston av.
VanDriesen G.C.Mrs.2976 South Park av.
VanDuyn Marion Mrs. 2548 Indiana av.
VanDuyne A. C. The Renfost
Vane Atwood Mrs. 5200 Kimbark av.
Vane Augustus S. 5200 Kimbark av.
VanEps F. S. Auditorium annex
VanEps George A. Mrs. Evanston
VanEvera DeWitt, 2636 Commercial (L. V.)
VanEvery Joseph J. Evanston
VanHagen George E. 3630 Vernon av.
VanHagen Isaac, 3630 Vernon av.
VanHamm Francis R. 786 Jackson boul.
VanHarlingen Henry C. Mayfair
VanHoff Anna Miss, 36 Aldine sq.
VanHoosen Bertha Dr. 489, 42d
VanHorn James H. 1491 Perry .
VanHorn Joseph, 7009 Yale
VanHorn Washington, 1491 Perry
VanHousen B. T. 477 W. Adams
VanHousen Harry L. 47 Park av.
VanHouten George N. 6616 Oglesby av.
VanIngen J. Wm. Rev. 1429 Michigan av.
VanInwagen Arthur. 5 Ritchie pl.
VanInwagen Fred, Hinsdale
VanInwagen James, 3 Ritchie pl.
    Sum. res. " Negawni," Lake Geneva, Wis.
VanInwagen James jr. 5 Ritchie pl.
VanInwegen Clarence P. 5731 Madison av.
VanInwegen George, Riverside.

VanKeuren C. W. Oak Park
VanKeuren Edward, Oak Park
VanKeuren M. J. Mrs. 592 Division
VanKeuren W. J. Oak Park
VanKirk Charles B. 4754 Greenwood av.
VanKirk SarahA.Mrs.4754 Greenwood av.
VanKirk Stephen, 329 Bowen av.
VanKleeck Wm. V. R. 37 St. James pl.
VanLiew Frederick Mrs. Hinsdale
VanLiew Lewis C. Hinsdale
VanLoan Abraham, Fort Sheridan
VanLoon Nellie Miss, 914 Warren av.
VanMatre W. N. 1472 W. Monroe
VanNess Carrie Mrs. Irving Park
VanNess Frank C. Wilmette
VanNess Gardiner, Irving Park
VanNess Lester T. Irving Park
VanNest J. M. 482, 42d pl.
VanNostrand John J. 4737 Champlain av.
VanOlinda Jane Mrs. 4545 Greenwood av.
VanOlinda W. F. 968 W. Monroe
VanOsdel F. M. 699 W. Jackson
VanOsdel J. M. Mrs. 2310 Indiana av.
VanOsdel J. M. 699 W. Jackson
VanOsdel Martha Miss, 2310 Indiana av.
VanOstrand Archibald E. Irving Park
VanPatten Andrew L. Dr. 408 Bowen av.
VanPelt Ryan T. Dr. Lexington hotel
VanRiper Louis O. Higbland Park
VanSands Robert, 839 W. Congress
Vansant John R. Newberry hotel
VanSchaack Cornelius P. 21, 23d
VanSchaack Peter, 37, 22d
VanSchaack Robert H. 3604 Michigan av.
VanSchaick A. G. Mrs. Highland Park
VanSickel Charles, 271 Irving av.
VanSicklen N. H. 7436 Bond av.
VanSiclen Alexander, Austin
VanSlyck Clara A. Mrs. 2946 Indiana av.
VanTuyl Edward A., M.D. Riverside
VanTuyl Margaret Miss, Riverside
Vantwood Elsie, 114 Evergreen av.
VanUxem James L. 4965 Lake av.
VanValkenberg F. P. Mrs. 174 Oakwood boul.
VanValkenburgh E. T. Mrs. 44 Cedar
VanVliet A. H. 4350 Berkeley av.
VanVliet G. D. Oak Park
VanVliet Leonard S. Oak Park
VanVliet Thornton, 351, 58 (H.P.)
VanVlissingen James H. 2441 Indiana av.
VanVlissingen Peter, 532 Garfield av.
VanVoorhis C. E. Evanston
VanVoorhis Frank, 3222 Rhodes av.
VanWagenen E. C. 42, 39th
VanWinkle A. L. 3236 Prairie av.
VanWinkle David, 3236 Prairie av.
VanWoert G. E. 4465 Ellis av.
VanZandt George, 883 W. Monroe
VanZandt G. Dr. 293 Washington boul.
VanZandt G. W. 938 W. Monroe
VanZandt G. C. 938 W. Monroe
Vanzwoll A. H. 273 Warren av.
Vanzwoll G. M. 43 Seeley av.
Vanzwoll Henry B. 273 Warren av.
Varena Alida Miss, 1925 Michigan av.

Varges Charles, 276 Belden av.
Varges Mae Miss, 276 Belden av.
Varian Alfred R. 637 Fullerton av.
Varney W. H. Maywood
Varnum Charles A. Capt. Fort Sheridan
Varnum Clark, 510 The Plaza
Varrell M. 3404 South Park av.
Varty Albert, 378 Chicago av.
Vasey Robert W. 4260 Grand av.
Vattman Edward J. Rev. Fort Sheridan
Vaughan Alexander, 678 Wash'ton boul.
Vaughan Arthur J. 4139 Langley av.
Vaughan Charles E. 517 Englewood av.
Vaughan Elmer E. Dr. 156 Center
Vaughan James, 922 W. Adams
Vaughan J. B. Mrs. 754 Fullerton av.
Vaughan J. C. 310 Marshfield av.
Vaughan Mary C. Mrs. 179, 37th
Vaughan Mary E. Miss, 425 Warren av
Vaughan Phillips C. Dr. 695 Lincoln av.
Vaughan Sanford S. 678 Washington boul.
Vaughan W. C. Hotel Barry
Vaughn J. S. 6156 Madison av.
Vaughn Thomas F. 4346 Greenwood av.
Vaux Frederick T. 387 N. State
Vawter William A. 455 Kenmore av.
Veasey Edwin C. 4454 Oakenwald av.
Veeder Albert H. 4842 Vincennes av.
Veeder Albert H. jr. 4842 Vincennes av.
Veeder Coles, 510 W. Monroe
Veeder Henry, 440, 64th, Englewood
Vehmeyer C. H. 6416 Harvard
Vehmeyer F. C. 6500 Lafayette av.
Vehmeyer Henry F. 4552 Forrestville av.
Vehon Joseph, 918 W. Monroe
Vehon Louis, 3824 Vernon av.
Vehon Morris, 918 W. Monroe
Vehon Simon, 238 Winchester av.
Vehon William H. 848 W. Monroe
Veirs B. W. 179 Park av.
Veitch Wilberforce, 1842 Indiana av.
Velie Stephen, 276 Belden av.
Vent C. F. 89, 44th
Verbeck Scott F., M.D. Evanston
Verdier T. T. Tracy
Vergho Charles, 1312 Wrightwood av.
Vergho Charles jr. 1312 Wrightwood av.
Vergho Joseph B. 375 Marshfield av.
Verhalen Stephen J. 523 Sheffield av.
Verity W. P. Dr. 450 Garfield av.
Vermilyea Samuel E. Austin
Vernon David, 833 W. Monroe
Vernon Harvey C. 1200 W. Adams
Vernon William W. 18 St. James pl.
VerNooy Charles B. 6220 Sheridan av.
Vernor George W. 3822 Calumet av.
Vesterborg Peter H., M.D. 584, 37th
Vette John F. 178 Loomis
Vetter Thomas, The Renfost
Vial George M. LaGrange
Vial Joseph, LaGrange
Vial Samuel, LaGrange
Vickers C. Belle Mrs. 713 Washington boul.
Vickers John A. D. The Tudor
Vickery James T. 1204 Wabash av.

Vickery John R. 1204 Wabash av.
Vickery Thomas G. 1204 Wabash av.
Victor H. Peter 1639 Belmont av.
Vider Olaf, 525 Garfield av.
Viele Lewis, 4110 Ellis av.
Vierbuchen William, Palmer house
Vierling Clara J. Miss, 3760 Indiana av.
Vierling Frank C. 2347 Michigan av.
Vierling Louis, 3760 Indiana av.
Vierling Robert, 3760 Indiana av.
Viets John B. 143 Oakwood boul.
Vigeant Gregory, 23 Scott
Vigneron Eugene, D.D.S. 6449 Myrtle av.
Viguers William N. Evanston
Vilas Albert H. Oak Park
Vilas Albert M. Oak Park
Vilas Charles H. Dr. Union Club
Vilas D. S. 2927 Groveland av.
Vilas Henry C. Riverside
Viles James Jr. 2932 Indiana av.
Vilim Joseph Prof. Riverside
Vinal Frederick, 5205 Hibbard av.
Vincent Harry, 380 Erie
Vincent J. Russell, 3824 Ellis av.
Vincent S. A. Mrs. 3269 Groveland av.
Vincent William A. 43 Banks
Vining George C. 3726 Elmwood pl.
Vinnedge Allen R. 446 Dearborn av.
Vinnedge Mahlon A. 446 Dearborn av.
Vistendahl H. 1837 Michigan av.
Vocke Fred W. 520 Lasalle av.
Vocke Henry, 827 Larrabee
Vocke Wm. 520 Lasalle av.
Voge Richard, 819 St. Louis av.
Vogel Ethel F. Mrs. 520 Washington boul.
Vogel Frank E. 3642 Michigan av.
Vognild Erik L. 632 N. Robey
Vogt R. F. Hotel Windermere
Voigtmann Frank, 2717 Charlton av.
Voigts Henry, Evanston
Volger Frederick, 385 Mohawk
Volkmann Jacob, 401 Sheffield av.
Volland George J. 2505 Michigan av.
Vollmer A. F. Mrs. 52, 24th
Vollmer Herman, 685 Fullerton av.
VonBachelle Rudolph, 447 S. Paulina
VonGigch H. S. 3012 Michigan av.
VonGlahn August, 719 Fullerton av.
VonHelmott Charles, 1469 Wellington
VonHermann E. 203, 30th
VonHofsten Hugo O. 5545 Woodlawn av.
VonKetel Mary A. Mrs. 636 Washington boul.
VonMasow F.Miss, 5731 Washington av.
VonPlaten Maurice, 1328 Washington boul.   Sum. res. Petoskey, Mich.
VonReichert Baroness, 4119 Drexel boul.
VonReinholts G. Stamford hotel
VonUntzer Maria Baroness, 2032 Calumet av.
Voorhees George L. Austin
Voorhees John W. 47 Campbell Park
Voorhees Martha Mrs. Norwood Park
Vopicka Charles J. 507 Winchester av.
Vorderbrugge L. 68 Lincoln av.

Vorics Charles, 4211 Lake av.
Vorics Harry F. 4211 Lake av.
Voris C. A. Mrs. 308 Belden av.
Voris Floy T. 308 Belden av.
Vosbrink George P. 4749 Champlain av.
Vosburg Homer J. Rev. 535 S. Normal
    Parkway
Vosburgh Cyrus A. 237 S. Leavitt
Vosburgh John, 4437 Champlain av.
Vosburgh W. R. Oak Park
Vose Frederick P. Evanston
Vose L. D. 4160 Ellis av.
Vose William M. R. Evanston·
Voshell William R. 436 Elm
Votaw C. W. Prof. 437, 61st (H.P.)
Voute Henry C. Hampden ct.
Vowell Stewart B. Evanston
Vreeland B. H. 5843 Indiana av.
Vrooman George H. 97 Loomis
Vynne Harold R. 3249 Groveland av.

WACHOB ISAAC S. Oak Park
    Wachsmuth F. H. 7 Groveland Park
Wachsmuth H. F. 7 Groveland Park
Wachsmuth L. C. 7 Groveland Park
Wacker Charles H. 714 North Park av.
    Sum. res. Lake Geneva.
Waddell Alexander M. Oak Park
Waddell E. S. Mrs. Evanston
Waddill George C. Major, 65 Lake Shore
    Drive
Wade Carrie Miss, Elmhurst
Wade Carter Dr. Evanston
Wade Charles, Elmhurst
Wade Harry C. The Tudor
Wade Henry J. Austin
Wade Henry P. The Tudor
Wade James J. 5234 Michigan av.
Wade John, 3532 Ellis av.
Wade John Mrs. 3736 Langley av.
Wade Joseph D. 5101 Kimbark av.
Wade Katherine Miss, 5234 Michigan av.
Wade M. L. 3849 Ellis av.
Wade R. V. 345 Rush
Wade S. W. Mrs. 5545 Washington av.
Wade Thomas P. 5234 Michigan av.
Wadhams Frederick E. Dr. 238, 53d (H.
    P.)
Wadhams H. P. Iroquois club
Wadhams John A. Irving Park
Wadington John, Hinsdale
Wadlow Esther Mrs. 5330 Greenwood av.
Wadsworth Charles F. Oak Park
Wadsworth Edward R. 3416 Michigan av.
Wadsworth Frank R. Oak Park
Wadsworth G. F. 7231 Yale
Wadsworth G. H. 433 Englewood av.
    Sum. res. Sharon Springs, N. Y.
Wadsworth Herbert 319 The Plaza
Wadsworth James, 6317 Lexington av.
Wadsworth S. F. Mrs. Oak Park
Wadsworth Tertius W. 407 Erie
Wagar M. H. 6549 Perry av.
Wager Ella R. Mrs. 5520 Washington av.
Wagg Howard N. 1161 N. Clark
Waggener Albert H. 6404 Honore

Waggener Maggie A. Miss, 4732 Evans av.
Waggener Robert G. 40 Buena Park Ter-
    race
Waggner L. J. Evanston
Waggoner Irving H. 145 Oakwood boul.
Waggoner J. Fred, 437, 57th (H.P.)
Wagner Anna E. Mrs. 7523 Stewart av.
Wagner Charles F. Mrs. 698 North Park av.
Wagner Charles P. 7523 Stewart av.
Wagner David C. Tracy
Wagner Edwin L. 4458 Oakenwald av.
Wagner Ernest J. 4335 Oakenwald av.
Wagner Ernst F. 567 Burling
Wagner E. W. Granada hotel
Wagner F. E. 3802 Lake av.
Wagner George, 6211 Woodlawn av.
Wagner Henry W. 1215 Wilton av.
Wagner Herman D. Ridgland
Wagner John H. 6910 South Park av.
Wagner Julius, 171 Eugenie
Wagner Theodore, Granada hotel
Wagner W. L. Union League Club
Wagner W. R. Oak Park
Wahl Albert, 417 Washington boul.
Wahl Joseph, 2523 Indiana av.
Wahl Julius, 6919 Calumet av.
Wahl Robert, 1030 Winthrop av.
Waide W. A. Hotel Groveland
Waidner F. A. 300 Chicago av.
Wain John, 737 W. Adams
Wainwright Chas. 6721 Union av.
Wait George A. 2122 N. Halsted
Wait Henry H. 4919 Madison av.
Wait Horatio L. 4919 Madison av.
Wait Isaac, Winnetka
Wai, Isabella Miss, 4939 Lake av.
Wait James J. 4919 Madison av.
Wait N. A. Miss, 4939 Lake av.
Wait W yland W. 124 Ashland boul.
Wait Wilber, 4552 Ellis av.
Wait William, Winnetka
Wait W. L. 346 Sunnyside av.
Waite C. B. Junge, Oglesby av. nw. cor.
    61st
Waite Horace F. 7 Astor
Waite Lucy Dr. Oglesby av. nw. cor. 61st
Waite William W. Hinsdale
Waixel David, 3267 Vernon av.
Waixel Henry, 3420 Wabash av.
Waixel Isaac H. 3420 Wabash av.
Waixel Moses, 3630 Michigan av.
Waixel M. Sol. 3630 Michigan av.
Waixel Sol H. 3420 Wabash av.
Wakefield Annie B. Mrs. Newberry hotel
Wakefield James G. Austin
Wakefield J. A. Virginia hotel
Wakefield N. R. 830 N. Wabash av.
Wakeley F. O. 103 DeKalb
Wakeley Lucius W. 134, 50th (H.P.)
Wakem Emily Miss, 149 Pine
Wakem J. Wallace Highland Park
Wakeman A. V. H. Mrs. 35, 53d (H.P.)
Walbank E. J. Mrs. 5538 Monroe av.
Walbank Kenneth S. 5538 Monroe av.
Walbank Robert T. River Forest
Walbridge Anna Miss, 7127 Yale

Walbridge Henry B. 7127 Yale
Walbridge W. H. LaGrange
Walbridge W. P. LaGrange
Walburn Albert W. 211, 48th (H. P.)
Walch Robert H. 504 The Plaza
Walcott Aaron F. 812 Warren av.
Walcott Chester P. Evanston
Walcott L. Miss, 281 Warren av.
Walden S. D. 6544 Harvard
Waldhauser Joseph, 186 N. Clark
Waldmeyer Joseph R., M. D. 570 Fullerton av.
Waldo George E. 194 N. State
Waldo J. A. B. 227 Ontario
Waldo J. B. 227 Ontario
Waldo Otis H. 4437 Sidney av.
Waldron C. L. Mrs. 558 Kenwood pl.
Waldron Edward Harvey, 2028 Michigan av.
Waldron Henry S. 558 Kenwood pl.
Waldron John J. Evanston
Waldron Louis K. 532 Garfield av.
Waldron Lydia M. Mrs. Newberry hotel
Waldschmidt August W. 735 Sedgwick
Waldschmidt Charles, 735 Sedgwick
Walduck Charles W. 1243 Wilcox av.
Wales Albert H. Dr. 4308 Ellis av.
Wales Frederick M. Dr. 4308 Ellis av.
Wales H. W. jr. 4308 Ellis av.
Wales Marion F. Miss, Virginia hotel
Walker Aldace F. 256 Dearborn av.
          Sum. res. Rutland, Vt.
Walker Alfred E. Hinsdale
Walker Annie C. Miss, 345 Dearborn av.
Walker Arthur H. Hotel Windermere
Walker Athalia A. Mrs. Hinsdale
Walker Augustus E. Mrs. 4800 Kenwood av.
Walker A. H. Lexington hotel
Walker A. J. 719 W. Monroe
Walker A. W. LaGrange
Walker B. A. Hotel Metropole
Walker Charles Cobb, 2027 Prairie av.
Walker Charles H. LaGrange
Walker Charles M. 392 Lasalle av.
Walker Charles M. La Grange
Walker Clarence M. 4346 Michigan av.
Walker C. Mrs. 401 N. State
Walker C. F. Oak Park
Walker C. Hayward, LaGrange
Walker C. M. L. Riverside
Walker Dudley, LaGrange
Walker Edwin 2612 Michigan av.
Walker Edwin C. Hotel Metropole
Walker Edwin F. Evanston
Walker Emery S. 459 Lasalle av.
Walker E. L. 4454 Woodlawn av.
Walker E. S. 3421 Vernon av.
Walker E. S. Austin
Walker Francis H. Evanston
Walker Francis W. 3541 Grand boul.
          Sum. res. Lake Geneva, Wis.
Walker F. Albert, Evanston
Walker F. A. 4454 Woodlawn av.
Walker F. E. 4454 Woodlawn av.
Walker George, Oak Park

Walker George C. 228 Michigan av.
          Sum. res. Lake Geneva, Wis.
Walker George H. Oak Park
Walker George L. 891 Warren av.
Walker G. Albert, Oak Park
Walker George R. 10 Aldine sq.
Walker G. B. Hotel Barry
Walker G. B. Mrs. 3580 Vincennes av.
Walker Harry, 3030 Michigan av.
Walker Harry L. Dr. 434 Dearborn av.
Walker Henry C. 4346 Michigan av.
Walker Henry H. Grand Pacific hotel
Walker Henry K. Hinsdale
Walker Henry M. Evanston
Walker Henry S. Evanston
Walker Henry W. 4346 Michigan av.
Walker Herbert, 79 Pine
Walker Hester E. Mrs. Evanston
Walker H. LaGrange
Walker H. Edwin, 4346 Michigan av.
Walker H. H. Hotel Metropole.
Walker H. Winston, Hotel Groveland
Walker James H. 345 Dearborn av.
Walker James H. jr. 345 Dearborn av.
Walker James M. 1720 Prairie av.
Walker James R. 1726 Prairie av.
Walker James T. Hotel Imperial
Walker James W. 442 Dayton
Walker John, 576 W. Adams
Walker John B. Dr. 247 Park av.
Walker J. Brandt, 3154 Michigan av.
Walker J. C. Victoria hotel
Walker J. R. LaGrange
Walker Lizzie M. Miss, Hinsdale
Walker Martha A. Mrs. 39 Bryant av.
Walker Mary A. Mrs. 4247 Drexel boul.
Walker Mathew H. LaGrange
Walker Mathias, 4102 Ellis av.
Walker Moses B. LaGrange
Walker Peter Mrs. Virginia hotel
Walker Porter J. Morgan Park
Walker Ralph S. 3030 Michigan av.
Walker Robert J. 3030 Michigan av.
Walker Robert P. 3716 Lake av.
Walker R. G. Dr. 95 Aberdeen
Walker Samuel J. Dr. 462 Elm
Walker Samuel J. Mrs. 462 Elm
Walker Stephen C. jr. 752 Fullerton av.
Walker Stephen L. 891 Warren av.
Walker Sydney Dr. 299, 47th
Walker S. P. Mrs. 294 W. Monroe
Walker S. S. Mrs. Oak Park
Walker Thomas H. 3153 Prairie av.
Walker Tott L. Mrs. 464 W. Adams
Walker William B. 2027 Prairie av.
Walker Wm. Ernest, 462 Elm
Walker William F. Rev. 678 Sheffield av.
Walker William H. 4435 Evans av.
Walker William J. 891 Warren av.
Walker William P. 875 Walnut
Walker William R. 3159 South Park av.
Walker William Smith, 183 Cass
          Winter res. Jacksonville, Fla.
Walker Wirt D. 1720 Prairie av.
Walker W. J. Mrs. 3159 South Park av.
Walker W. L. Rev. 680 Sheffield av.

Walker W. S. Dr. 521 Racine av.
Wall F. J. Arizona flats
Wall Henry B. 62 Woodland Park
Wall William H. LaGrange]
Wallace Andrew, 3439 Vernon av.
Wallace Clyde H. 4322 Ellis av.
Wallace C. W. Mrs. Auditorium hotel
Wallace Edwin, Clifton house
Wallace Frank P. Austin
Wallace Fred H. Dr. 333 Ohio
Wallace George M. Ontario hotel
Wallace George W. R. LaGrange
Wallace Harold U. 4315 Ellis av.
Wallace H. R. Dr. 116, 43d
Wallace James Mrs. 2619 N. Paulina
Wallace Jas. F. Mrs. 4240 Champlain av.
Wallace John, 313 Lincoln av.
Wallace John C. 4322 Ellis av.
Wallace John F. 4315 Ellis av.
Wallace J. D. 458 Jackson boul.
Wallace Martin R. M. Judge, 3817 Michi-
    gan av.
Wallace Matthew, 56 Lytle
Wallace M. Mrs. 3421 Indiana av.
Wallace M. Edith Miss, Austin
Wallace M. G. Oak Park
Wallace Norman B. Austin
Wallace Peter Rev. 4100 Lake av.
Wallace P. 3609 Prairie av.
Wallace Thomas, Mrs. Evanston
Wallace T. D. Rev. 205 Warren av.
Wallace William, Evanston
Wallace William, Irving Park
Wallace Wm. A. 1330 Washington boul.
Wallace W. G. Oak Park
Wallace W. W. 415 Washington boul.
Wallach J. Frederick, 3216 Lake Park av.
Wallen Charles, 1810 Wellington
Waller Belle L. Miss, River Forest
Waller Charles, 462 N. Clark
Waller Chas. S. 625 Lasalle av.
Waller David F. Mrs. 35 Bellevue pl.
Waller Edward, 356 Dearborn av.
Waller Edward Mrs. 356 Dearborn av.
Waller Edward C. River Forest
Waller E. Mrs. 3105 Groveland av.
Waller Henry, 739 Washington boul.
Waller Henry, River Forest
Waller James B. 1711 Sheridan rd.
Waller James B. Mrs. Evanston av. sw.
    cor. Buena av.
Waller John D. Dr. Oak Park
Waller Lilly L. Miss, River Forest
Waller M. E. Miss, 35 Bellevue pl.
Waller Robert A. 1665 Sheridan rd.
Waller William, 40 Banks
Wallin Charles C. 535 Dearborn av.
Wallin H. J. Dr. 3402 South Park av.
Wallin Peter, 7850 Bond av.
Wallin Thomas S. 535 Dearborn av.
Walling Willoughby Dr. 4127 Drexel boul.
Wallingford Henry J. Evanston
Wallingsford J. Miss, Hotel Metropole
Wallingsford J. M. Hotel Metropole
Wallis Obed W. 709 Washington boul.
Walliser Henry F. 54 Best av.

Walls C. Bruce Dr. 144 S. Kedzie av.
Walls Emma Miss, 4334 Greenwood av.
Walls Frank X. Dr. 21 Park av.
Walls James R. 4334 Greenwood av.
Walls Mercy L. Mrs. 4334 Greenwood av.
Walls Thomas, 21 Park av.
Walls Wyllis Worden,, 5625 Washington
    av.
Wallwork Edward L. 426, 42d pl. (H.P.)
Walmsley A. H. Irving Park
Walmsley James, Norwood Park
Walmsley Mabel Miss, Chicago Beach
    hotel
Walmsley Wm. LaGrange
Walmsley W. H. Chicago Beach hotel
Walpole Elizabeth Mrs. 713 North Park
    av.
Walrath Hamilton M. Evanston
Walrath William B. Evanston
Walsh Angeline C. Miss, 3312 Wabash av.
Walsh Charles, 421 The Plaza
Walsh David, 512 Ashland boul.
Walsh Dennis 682 Fulton
Walsh Edward J. 1614 N. Halsted
Walsh Edward R. 276 Michigan av.
Walsh James, 306 Superior
Walsh James T. Norwood Park
Walsh John E. Dr. 4758 Langley av.
Walsh John F. 353 Bissell
Walsh John R. 2133 Calumet av.
Walsh John W. 503 W. Congress
    Sum. res. Fox Lake
Walsh John W. 4243 Calumet av.
Walsh Lawrence J. 1529 Wrightwood av
Walsh L. J. 592 W. Adams
Walsh Michael Mrs. 2511 Indiana av.
Walsh M. A. Miss, 4725 Lake av.
Walsh M. A. Mrs. 1314 Dunning
Walsh Richard, 4441 Ellis av.
Walsh Richard S. 4921 A Champlain av.
Walsh Thomas D. 4101 Indiana av.
Walsh Thos. J. 512 Ashland boul.
Walsh William, 3131 Wabash av.
Walsh William C. River Forest
Walshe Robert J. 2339 Calumet av.
Walter Alfred M. 2729 Prairie av.
Walter A. M. Mrs. 71 Laflin
Walter Grove E. Irving Park
Walter Henry, Evanston
Walter J. C. Mrs. 2729 Prairie av.
Walters A. E. Oak Park
Walters Fred M. Evanston
Walters G. W. Evanston
Walters J. C. 6621 Yale
Walters M. E. Wilmette
Walters L. M. 1570 W. Monroe
Walters. L. P. Dr. Hotel Barry
Walther A. F. 532 N. Normal Parkway
Walther F. E. 1806 Wellington
Walther Fred H. 516, 65th ct. Eng.
Walton Charles, 528 Sunnyside av.
Walton Chas. A. 874, 71st pl. (H.P.)
Walton Clyde C. 874, 71st pl. (H. P.)
Walton E. L. Miss, Hinsdale
Walton Frederick J. Rev. 7106 Yale

Walton Henry H. 874, 71st pl. (H. P.)
Walton L. A. 6542 Lafayette av.
Walton R. French, LaGrange
Walton Seymour, 1261 Wilton av.
Walton S. B. 4740 Drexel boul.
Walton Thomas B. 1462 E. Ravenswood
　Park
Walworth Charles M. 23 Marquette Ter-
　race
Walworth N. H. Mrs. Evanston
Walworth S. E. Mrs. 303 Park av.
Wambald H. A. Leland hotel
Wampler A. J. 4156 Lake av.
Wampold Leo, 3229 Michigan av.
Wampold Louis, 3229 Michigan av.
Wangeman Hugo, 6435 Stewart av.
Wangersheim Carrie Mrs. 720 North Park
　av.
Wangersheim L. 204 Warren av.
Wann Catharine L. Mrs. 433 S. Oakley av.
Wann William O. 397 S. Leavitt
Wanner Andrew F. 657 Burling
Wanner Edward A. 808 The Plaza
Wanzer Clarence H. Austin
Wanzer Edwin T. Austin
Wanzer Elias, Austin
Wanzer James M. 917 W. Monroe
Wanzer Sidney, 3022 Wabash av.
Wanzer William B. 305, 30th
Wanzer W. G. Oak Park
Ward Albert J. 274 Fullerton av.
Ward A. Montgomery, 4700 Kimbark av.
　Sum. res. Oconomowoc, Wis.
Ward Carlos J. Oak Park
Ward Charles W., M. D., 3449 Indiana av.
Ward Cyrus J. 933 Sawyer av.
Ward Dennis, 1109 N. 59th, Argyle Park
Ward Edmund C. 627 Jackson boul.
Ward Edward P. Dr. Lake Forest
Ward George R. T. 4726 Kimbark av.
Ward George T. 3930 Prairie av.
Ward James H. 524 Jackson boul.
Ward James R. 1911½ Diversey
Ward John S. 6500 Honore
Ward Joseph F. Evanston
Ward J. L. Oak Park
Ward L. C. Mrs. Evanston
Ward Morris E. Lakota hotel
Ward M. E. Mrs. 319 Park av.
Ward Oscar H. 189, 54th pl. (H. P.)
Ward·O. E. French House, Evanston
Ward O. S. 1455 Fulton
Ward O. V. S. Mrs. 1701 Prairie av.
Ward Spencer, 316 Leland av.
Ward S. D. 3536 Ellis av.
Ward Thomas A. Park Ridge
Ward William H. Riverside
Warde John J. 427 Oak
Warde R. Cuttriss, 919 Pullman bldg.
Wardell Charles F. Riverside
Wardell Richard J. Riverside
Wardell Sophia H. Mrs. 1019 Washing-
　ton boul.
Warden Theodore G. 3601 Ellis av.
Warder Benton, 78 Ogden av.
Warder John B. Oak Park

Warder William H. Dr. 149, 42d (H. P.)
Wardlow John, 812 Kenmore av.
Wardner S. J. Mrs. 4108 Lake av.
Wardrop Walter, 146, 54th (H. P.)
Wardrop Walter jr. 146, 54th (H. P.)
Wardwell Clara Miss, 2532 Indiana av.
Wardwell Robert D. 1359 Jackson boul.
Ware Charles, Kenilworth
Ware C. E. 5100 Hibbard av.
Ware C. W. 150 Pine
Ware Elisha C. 5131 Jefferson av.
　Sum. res. Charlevoix, Mich
Ware Frederic D. 5147 Cornell av.
Ware J. H. 5480 Cornell av.
Ware Lyman Dr. 1620 Prairie av.
Ware L. A. Mrs. 4712 Madison av.
Ware Orlando, 161 Eugenie
Ware Robert M. Riverside
Wares Jerome F. The Arizona
Warfield Edwin A. 4325 Ellis av.
Warfield Edwin A. jr. 4325 Ellis av.
Waring Henrietta H. Miss, 491 W. Adams
Warne H. D. 304 Belden av.
Warne S. S. 304 Belden av.
Warner Aaron N. 320 Oakwood boul.
Warner Addison Raynsford, 2022 Indiana
　av.
Warner Albert R. 2124 Michigan av.
Warner Augustus, 503 Dearborn av.
Warder A. F. 1837 Michigan av.
Warner Chester, 635 Washington boul.
Warner Cuthbert, 511 Leland av.
Warner C. H. 3261 Groveland av.
Warner Ezra J. Lake Forest
Warner E. Percy, Hotel Windermere
Warner E. P. 402 Belden av.
Warner Frank A. Evanston
Warner F. 3165 Groveland av.
Warner F. R. Mrs. 2022 Indiana av.
Warner George L. 5120 Hibbard av.
Warner Harry D. 2022 Indiana av.
Warner Henry D. Mrs. 2940 Indiana av.
Warner J. F. Mrs. 1566 W. Monroe
Warner J. M. 6339 Yale
Warner J. M. Julien hotel
Warner M. M. 357 Park av.
Warner Paul B. 527 Belden av.
Warner Sheldon W. Hotel Groveland
Warner Sidney H. 1635 W. Adams
Warner William C. Oak Park
Warner W. C. Winnetka
Warrell Arthur M. 85, 20th
Warren Allyn D. 4310 Oakenwald av.
Warren Aubrey, Lake Forest
Warren Charles A. 5930 Dickey
Warren Charles C. Hinsdale
Warren Clinton J. 801 The Plaza
Warren Cyrus T. Hinsdale
Warren C. D. 4310 Oakenwald av.
Warren C. Frederick, 3946 Prairie av.
Warren C. M. Mrs. 4342 Greenwood av.
Warren C. R. Dr. 1037 W. Madison
Warren Edith Miss, Riverside
Warren Emma S. Miss, 4206 Ellis av.
Warren Everett M. 4808 Lake av.
Warren E. A. Mrs. Evanston

Warren E. J. Dr. 417 Lasalle av.
Warren Frederick A. 349 Dearborn av.
Warren F. H. 3730 Lake av.
Warren James A. 4 Wellington pl.
Warren John P. S. Lake Forest
Warren J. Latham, Berwyn
Warren L. D. 2909 Prairie av.
Warren May H. Dr. 94 Lincoln av.
Warren Nathan H. Hinsdale
Warren Paul, Union Club
Warren Robert Mrs. 5 Groveland Park
Warren Wallace Mrs. 210, 37th
Warren William, 4206 Ellis av.
Warren William Mrs. Lake Forest
Warren William C. 4808 Lake av.
Warren William H. 87 Astor
Warren William S. 437 Elm
Warren William S. 928 Greenleaf av.
Warren W. E. Dr. 94 Lincoln av.
Warrington George. 1706 Alexander av.
Warrington Henry, 127 Park av.
Warrington James N. 127 Park av.
Warrington William H. 127 Park av.
Wartman John, 531 Winchester av,
Warvelle George W. 654 W. Monroe
Washburn Albert T. Dr. Mayfair
Washburn Charles, 438 Englewood av.
Washburn Charles L. Hinsdale
Washburn Elmer, 4559 Woodlawn av.
Washburn E. A. Morgan Park
Washburn H. C. 438 Englewood av.
Washburn J. S. 5484 Monroe av.
Washburn William, 542 Cleveland av.
Washburn William D. 3309 Rhodes av.
Washburn William W. Morgan Park
Washburne Elihu B. 154 Astor
Washburne George F. Dr. 197, 47th
Washburne Hempstead, 154 Astor
Washburne John B. 1470 E. Ravenswood
  Park
Washburne Oscar, 197, 47th
Washburne R. H. 324, 41st
Washington Hermann B. 1847 Melrose
Washington Irving, 214 Sunnyside av.
Washington Lloyd, 1842 Indiana av.
Wasmansdorff Otto, 549 Cleveland av.
Wasmansdorff Wm.G.1456 Wellington
Wassall Jos. W. Dr. 296 Ohio
Wasserman David, 3742 Forest av.
Waterbury Elbert M. 6446 Stewart av.
Waterbury Fordyce H. 4406 Sidney av.
Waterbury Ivan C. 5475 Ridgewood ct.
Waterbury John C. Evanston
Waterbury T. Granada hotel
Waterbury W. A. 2949 Michigan av.
Waterhouse Allan, 343 Warren av.
Waterhouse Charles F. Dr. 4326 Langley
  av.
Waterhouse Darius, 6636 Stewart av.
Waterloo B. Southern hotel
Waterloo Stanley, Hotel Imperial
Waterman Arba N. 40 Groveland Park
Waterman A. H. 701 W. Monroe
Waterman Ella Warren Mrs. 5810 Ros-
  alie ct.
Waterman E. L. 441 Seminary av.

Waterman H. B. Rev. Oak Park
Waterman John A. 3929 Vincennes av.
Waterman Richard, 26 Scott
Waterman Richard jr. 26 Scott
Waterman S. A. Dr. 730, 79th, Eng
Waterman William, 5810 Rosalie ct.
Waters Allen, 6350 Harvard
Waters Charles E. 571 Washington boul.
Waters Charles W. 571 Washington boul.
Waters Fannie T. Mrs. 669 W. Monroe
Waters Frank P. 16 Aldine sq.
Waters Frank S. 377 Warren av.
Waters Harry C. 4906 Washington av.
Waters H. S. Chicago Athletic Assn.
Waters John E. Hotel Windermere
Waters Lisle Cummins Dr. 669 W. Mon-
  roe
Waters Thomas J. 367 S. Paulina
Waters Willey B. 587 Washington boul.
Wathier Joseph P. 545 W. Monroe
Watkins Carrie B. Miss, 4037 Indiana av.
Watkins Carrie Louise, 258 Ashland boul.
Watkins D. L. 258 Ashland boul.
Watkins E. M. 333 Rush
Watkins E. T. 148 Rush
Watkins George, 4206 Oakenwald av.
Watkins Jesse M. 1810 Oakdale av.
Watkins J. O. 50 Loomis
Watkins Maurice, 3752 Lake av.
Watkins M. Mrs. 3833 Calumet av.
Watkins T. J. Dr. 3625 Indiana av.
Watkins Vine A. 2643 Michigan av.
Watkins William, 4328 St. Lawrence av.
Watkins William W. 3536 Lake av.
Watriss Franklin, Virginia hotel
Watrous Christopher, 528 N. State
Watry Joseph Dr. 868 Larrabee
Watry Nicholas, 1668 Wellington
Watson Alexander, Riverside
Watson Benjamin A. 286, 37th
Watson B. R. Chicago Beach hotel
Watson Catherine Mrs. 271 Irving av.
Watson C. E. Mrs. 5762 Rosalie ct.
Watson Edward H. Highland Park
Watson E. A. 444 Englewood av.
Watson Frank, 3403 Indiana av.
Watson Frederick A. 333 Rush
Watson Frederick J. River Forest
Watson George A. Wilmette
Watson George B. 6515 Yale
Watson George W. 3403 Indiana av:
Watson G. E. 8 Wellington pl.
Watson Howard, 643 W. Monroe
Watson I. A. 319 S. Robey
Watson James, Wilmette
Watson James B. Forest hotel (R.P.)
Watson James D. 32, 29th
Watson James S. 413 Warren av.
Watson James V. 3539 Michigan av.
Watson John G. 290 Rush
Watson John P. 4203 St. Lawrence av.
Watson Julia M. Mrs. Evanston
Watson J. F. Lexington hotel
Watson Lewis H., M.D., 297 Indiana
Watson Margaret A. Mrs. 2686 Charlton
  av.

Watson Mary Mrs. Hotel Windermere
Watson M. D. Hotel Windermere
Watson Orson H. 2686 Charlton av.
Watson Richard G. Lake Forest
Watson Richard H. Mrs. 219 Belden av.
Watson R. H. Evanston
Watson Samuel E. 4830 Evans av.
Watson Samuel J. Dr. 849 Turner av.
Watson Thomas, Wilmette
Watson Thomas, 3409 Calumet av.
Watson Thomas jr. Hotel Windermere
Watson Thomas H. 3409 Calumet av.
Watson Thomas H Evanston
Watson Thomas W. Wilmette
Watson T. K. Mrs. 3731 Langley av.
Watson T. Merrill, 615, 60th, Eng.
Watson Walter G. Highland Park
Watson William jr. Union League Club
Watson Wm. John, Oak Park
Watson William J. 2640 Prairie av.
Watson W. M. 1705 Wellington
Watt Archibald M. 55 Union Park pl.
Watt George F. 350 Ashland boul.
Watt G. F. Mrs. 350 Ashland boul.
Watt Hugh, 55 Union Park pl.
Watt James B. 3213 Groveland av.
Watt Reuben J. 7305 Wright
Watt Robert, Lakeside
Watt R. G. Julien hotel
Watt Sara E. Miss, 2577 Commercial
  (L.V.)
Watt William E. 4453 Emerald av.
Watte Joseph M. 615 Cleveland av.
Watterman H. H. Morgan Park
Watters Juliette Mrs. 474 Elm
Watters Owen J. Dr. 361 Chestnut
Watterson D. Mrs. 11 Bellevue pl.
Watterson M. P. Ridgland
Watts E. S. Oak Park
Watts George C. 4726 Langley av.
Watts G. Frank, 4448 Sidney av.
Watts Jeremiah, 7735 Wright
Watts Robert, 4726 Langley av.
Waugh James F. 4335 Emerald av.
Waugh Susie Mrs. Evanston
Waugh William F. Dr. 5539 Monroe av.
Waughop Arthur B. 3842 Calumet av.
Waughop James F. 4207 Ellis av.
Waughop J. W. 2457 Prairie av.
Way E. C. 800A Pullman bldg.
Way Henry J. Dr. 460 S. Oakley av.
Way Kate Miss, 1923 Deming ct.
Way W. Irving, 1923 Deming ct.
Wayman T. E. Granada hotel
Wayne Harry L. Hinsdale
Wayne Thomas D. 209 S. Leavitt
Wayt Edward, Austin
Wayte Alfred, 5204 Cornell av.
Wayte John Mrs. Morgan Park
Weadley J. L. 662 Lasalle. av.
Weadley William, 662 Lasalle av.
Weage C. A. Oak Park
Wean Frank L. 6951 Yale
Wear Charles A. 5517 Washington av.
Weare Charles A. 697 Washington boul.
Weare Portus B. Morton Park

Weare William W. Morton Park
Weart E. N. 7040 Yale
Weart Garret V. 6800 Sherman
Weart James G. Winnetka
Weary Charles A. Wilmette
Weary Edwin D. 5832 Washington av.
Weatherbee George, 148 Dearborn av.
Weatherhead E. Mrs. 469 Jackson boul.
Weatherson C. 3739 Prairie av.
Weatherstone William W. LaGrange
Weaver Arthur C. 686½ Wash'ton boul.
Weaver Charles H. 686½ Wash'ton boul.
Weaver Charles M. 104 S. Hoyne av.
Weaver Charles S. Lake Forest
Weaver C. A. 5127 Cornell av.
Weaver Edith S. Mrs. 882 Wash'ton boul.
Weaver Henry E. 4742 Drexel boul.
Weaver Homer W. Evanston
Weaver John VanA. 369 Chicago av.
Weaver Mary M. Mrs. Highland Park
Weaver Uri. 1173 Washington boul.
Weaver William A. Austin
Webb Charles, 3907 Michigan av.
Webb Edward L. Dr. 703 Greenleaf av.
Webb Emma Miss, 875 W. Monroe
Webb E. L. Miss, Julien hotel
Webb Frank R., M.D. 3907 Michigan av.
Webb George L. Chicago Beach hotel
Webb G. D. Oak Park
Webb Job, 884 W. Adams
Webb J. B. Oak Park
Webb J. E. 780 Racine av.
Webb Thomas A. 3543 Michigan av.
Webb T. E. Mrs. 191, 32d
Webb William J., M. D. 376 Division
Webbe William E. 5831 Washington av.
  Sum. res. Sister Lakes, Mich.
Webber Charles M. 150 Astor
Webber Edward R. Wilmette
Webber Joseph T. 5729 Princeton av.
Webber Samuel T. 7812 Sherman
Weber Andrew, 280 Belden av.
Weber Bernard F. 2546 N. Ashland av.
Weber Charles A. 1287 Wilton av.
Weber Charles F. 1640 Barry av.
Weber David, 4412 Wabash av.
Weber George, 7738 Wright
Weber George W. 337½ Mohawk
Weber Henry, 7738 Wright
Weber Herman, 462 Lasalle av.
Weber H. R. Dr. 403 Belden av.
Weber John, 151 Osgood
Weber J. T. 399 Belden av.
Weber Louis, 515 N. Clark
Weber Samuel L. Dr. 143, 35th
Weber Stephen B. 307 N. Clark
Weber T. F. 319 Lincoln av.
Weber William H. Hotel Groveland
Weber William H. 7732 Wright
Weber W. J. Rev. 200 Center
Webner John T. 997 Warren av.
Webster A. G. 148 Dearborn av.
Webster Catherine Mrs.4140 Berkeley av.
Webster Charles L. Dr. 215 Loomis
Webster Chas. R. Evanston
Webster Charles W. 2034 Indiana av.

Webster Clarence A. LaGrange
Webster C. O. Hotel Windermere
Webster Edward F. Evanston
Webster Edward H. Dr. Evanston
Webster Emma Miss, 148 Dearborn av.
Webster E. Carleton 4738 Evans av.
Webster E. L. Fort Sheridan
Webster E. P. 176, 37th
Webster Frank B. 2034 Indiana av.
Webster George, 638 W. Adams
Webster George H. 2821 Prairie av.
Webster George H. jr. 2821 Prairie av.
Webster George W., M.D. 1922 Indiana av.
Webster G. A. Chicago Beach hotel
Webster H. D. L. Rev. 793 Washington boul.
    Winter res. Tarpon Springs, Fla.
Webster Jerusha A. Mrs. 638 W. Adams
Webster John C. Dr. 820 Jackson boul.
Webster J. P. Dr. 441 Englewood av.
Webster Lewis D. Virginia hotel
Webster Martha Mrs. Evanston
Webster Nathaniel B. 156 S. Leavitt
Webster Percy F. 4207 Oakenwald av.
Webster Ralph W. 5745 Losalie ct.
Webster Stephen O. 645 Washington boul.
Webster Stuart, 2821 Prairie av.
Webster S. L. Mrs. Evanston
Webster Thos. H. 116 Flournoy
Webster Towner K. Evanston
Webster Willett A. Evanston
Webster William G. 23 Roslyn pl.
Webster Wm. V. 759 W. Adams
Webster W. Dix, 68, 53d (H.P.)
Wechsler Phil, Lakota hotel
Weckler William H. 1506 Wolfram
Wedeles Anna Mrs. 3216 Calumet av.
Wedeles Barbetta Miss, 4920 Ellis av.
Wedeles Celia Mrs. 4920 Ellis av.
Wedeles Edward, 3216 Calumet av.
Wedeles Isaac, 3127 Calumet av.
Wedeles Sigmund, 3216 Calumet av.
Wedeles Solomon, 4920 Ellis av.
Wedgewood Benj. F. 107, 37th
Weed Julia G. Miss, Winnetka
Weed J. E. 420, 63d, Eng.
Weed W. A. Mrs. 4024 Michigan Terrace
Weeden Elnathan S. Evanston
Weeks Benjamin F. Evanston
Weeks Charles D. 4812 St. Lawrence av.
Weeks Clinton, Longwood
Weeks Eugene A. 4812 St. Lawrence av.
Weeks Gilbert M. 568 W. Congress
Weeks Harvey T. 568 W. Congress
Weeks Horace S. Hinsdale
Weeks J. B. Irving Park
Weeks J. G. 1521 Michigan av.
Weeks McD. Lieut. Ft. Sheridan
Wegeforth T. C. H. 1033 Warren av.
Wegener George A. 978 Millard av.
Wegener George A. jr. 978 Millard av.
Wegg David S. 510 N. State
Wegg J. Mrs. 510 N. State
Wegmann Julius, 571 N. Clark
Wehmer Minnie Miss, 1837 Michigan av.

Wehrli Christiana Mrs. 176, 37th
Weibezahn Nellie M. Miss, 2710 Michigan av.
Weichmann Mary Mrs. 467 Dearborn av.
Weick Louis E. 451 Cleveland av.
Weide Lilian B. Miss, 4850 Greenwood av.
Weidig George, 365 Ontario
Weidner Otto J. 60 Wisconsin
Weigle Mahlie E. Miss, 100 Park av. (L. V.)
Weigle William G. 663 Orchard
Weigley Fillmore, 238 Honore
Weigley Frank S. 66 Astor
Weigley Wellington, 315 Park av.
Weil Albert M.D. 3025 Indiana av.
Weil A. Lexington hotel
Weil A. 318 Marshfield av.
Weil Carl H. Hotel Groveland
Weil Eugene S. 3445 Prairie av.
Weil E. R. 449 Lasalle av.
Weil H. 322 Marshfield av.
Weil H. Mrs. Hotel Metropole
Weil Jacob, 2703 Wabash av.
Weil Julius E. 3342 South Park av.
Weil J. H. 3255 Wabash av.
Weil L. Hotel Metropole
Weil L. H. Mrs. 531½ Burling
Weil Morris, 3336 South Park av.
Weil Solomon, 26 Fowler
Weil S. Mrs. 227 Lasalle av.
Weil Theodore, 4201 Ellis av.
Weiland Emma Mrs. 3601 Vincennes av.
Weilhart C. E., M.D., 3709 Ellis av.
Weill Marc, 522 W. Congress
Weill Maurice, 3138 South Park av.
Weinberg Adolph, 30 St. James pl.
Weinberg Max, 3443 Wabash av.
Weinberg Moses A. 3414 Calumet av.
Weinberger A. F. 27 Ewing pl.
Weinberger Emanuel, 7 Lincoln pl.
Weinberger Felix, 27 Ewing pl.
Weinberger George A. 27 Ewing pl.
Weinhardt H. 76 Ewing pl.
Weinmann Oscar, 885 Spaulding av.
Weinschenk Lucius, 2963 Groveland av.
Weinschenk M. 2963 Groveland av.
Weinsheimer Alfred S. 3028 Calumet av.
Weinsheimer W. J. 339 Blackstone
Weir John, 744, 64th, Englewood
Weir Robert, 6323 Yale
Weirick C. A. Dr. Lincoln Park Sanitarium
Weise George, 3410 Wabash av.
Weiskopf A. 3624 Vernon av.
Weiss Frederick W. 5918 Honore
Weiss George A. 540 N. State
Weiss Henry W. Hinsdale
Weiss John H. 4419 Drexel boul.
Welch Albert, 4540 Oakenwald av.
Welch John W. Evanston
Welch Leon C. 4454 Oakenwald av.
Welch P. H. Dr. Columbus club
Welch Seymour C. Lake Forest
Welch William M. 548 Morse av.
Welch W. H. 4540 Oakenwald av.
Welcher M. E. Mrs. 463 Cleveland av.

Welchli Fred. 71 Laflin
Welcker H. E. Dr. 458 North av.
Welcker Paul R. Dr. 435 Center
Weld H. J. Miss, 4160 Ellis av.
Welden T. J. Edison Park
Weldon E. Mrs. 276 Marshfield av.
Welge Frederick, Austin
Welisch Ernest, Hotel Groveland
Weller F. Montrose Dr. 3130 Forest av.
Wellers Meta Miss, 214, 31st
Welles E. P. 600 Division
Welles Fred W. 600 Division
Welles F. L. 536 Jackson boul.   ·
Welles Katherine Miss, 536 Jackson boul.
Welles M. W. 600 Division
Welling D. 6740 Perry av.
Welling John C. 4950 Greenwood av.
Wellington Arthur G. 5503 Cornell av.
Wellington Charles W. W. Mrs. 299
    Huron
Wellington Cyrus, 726 Washington boul.
Wellington Gertrude G., M.D. 726 Wash-
    ington boul.
Wellington L. W. Virginia hotel
Wells Addison E. 204 Ashland boul.
Wells Arthur B. 476 N. State
Wells Arthur G. 3558 Grand boul.
Wells Arthur S. 4519 St. Lawrence av.
Wells A. B. Miss, Oak Park
Wells Brenton R. 4853 Lake av.
Wells Catharine J., M.D. 3024 Indiana av.
Wells Charles B. Mrs. Austin
Wells Chloe B. Mrs. Evanston   ·
Wells C. E. Evanston
Wells C. H. Oak Park
Wells C. W. 4537 Lake av.
Wells D. Gordon, 49 Ray
Wells D. W. 841 Warren av.
Wells Edgar, 2947 Indiana av.
Wells Edgar L. 4724 Evans av.
Wells Edward F. M.D. 4571 Lake av.
Wells Edwin S. Lake Forest
Wells Edwin S. jr. Lake Forest
Wells Florence Miss, 1495 Fulton
Wells Frank, 19 Groveland Park   ·
Wells Franklin C. Dr. 359 Warren av.
Wells Fred A. 6704 Stewart av.
Wells George H. Evanston
Wells George V. 4803 St. Lawrence av.
Wells George W. 6832 Lafayette av.
Wells Grace S. Mrs. Evanston
Wells G. S. Park Ridge
Wells Horace E. 636 Boulevard pl.
Wells H. G. Norwood Park·
Wells James T. 1920 Indiana av.
Wells Judd E. 477 W. Congress
Wells J. G. Irving Park
Wells J. Q. Mrs. Riverside
Wells Louise Miss, 4853 Lake av
Wells Michael B. 4571 Lake av.
Wells Moses A. 313 W. Monroe
Wells Moses D. 2550 Michigan av.
        Sum. res. Lakeville, Conn.
Wells O. A. 4418 Prairie av.
Wells R. A. 4724 Evans av.
Wells Samuel, Tracy

Wells Samuel R. 2458 Indiana av.
        Sum. res. Waukegan
Wells S. K. Evanston
Wells Theodore B. 215 Winchester av.
Wells Thomas E. 4725 Vincennes av.
Wells Warren A. 146 Ashland boul.
Wells William L. Evanston .
Wells William W. 89 Warren av.
Wells Willis J. 3753 Ellis av.
Wells W. H. Mrs. 462 Washington boul.
Welsh Blanton C. Lieut. Fort Sheridan
Welsh Matthew, 719 Garfield boul.
Welter Bela, 3766 Indiana av.
Welter Sigmund, 3766 Indiana av.
Welton Charles G. 1857 Melrose
Welton George H. 1857 Melrose
Welty Duncan O. 1855 Frederick
Wenban Albert C. 3150 Groveland av.
Wendell Edward E. 3107 Forest av.
Wendell Emanuel V. 4418 Langley av.
Wendell James A. Evanston
Wendell Melville J. 4441 Evans av.
Wendell M. Lexington hotel
Wenderoth Charles J. Auditorium annex
Wenderoth Frank, Auditorium annex
Wenter Frank, 475 Ashland boul.
Wentworth Edward C. 3802 Prairie av.
Wentworth George O. 97 Park av.
Wentworth Moses J. 465 Elm
Wentworth William C. Evanston
Wentworth Wm. W. Dr. 230, 65th, Eng.
Wentz Albert D. 1870 Reta
Wentz J. A. 7330 Webster av. Eng.
Werkmeister M. 3329 Vernon av.
Wermuth William C. Dr. 277 Bissell
Werneburg Alex. E. 6738 Honore
Werneburg F. William, 6738 Honore
Wernecke O. G. Dr. 258 Loomis
Wernecke Richard, 1629 Brompton av.
Wernecke William, 1629 Brompton av.
Werner Ernest, 2979 Indiana av.
Werno Charles, 427 Cleveland av.
Werno Henry, LaGrange
Werst Jonas Z. 526 W. Adams
Wertheimer Abraham, 3564 Prairie av.
Wertheimer B. J. 3219 Wabash av.
Wescott Cassius D. Dr. 1280 W. Adams
Wesencraft Jane Mrs. Riverside
        Winter. res. Orlando, Fla.
Wesencraft Lotta Mrs. Riverside
Wesley Charles, Evanston
Wessels Frederick J. 5328 Madison av.
Wessels George F. 5328 Madison av.
Wessels Robert S. 5328 Madison av.
Wessling Fred G. 439 Belden av.
Wessling George H. 1454 Edgecomb ct.
West Charles, 945 Mayfair
West Edward F. 67, 37th   ·
West E. A. 434 W. Adams
West Fannie E. Mrs. 365 Ashland boul.
West Francis T. 4560 Oakenwald av.
West Frederick T. 613 Division
        Sum. res. Pittsfield, Mass.
West George A. 4215 Langley av.
West George E. 4054 Michigan Terrace
West George N. Dr. Hotel Barry

West James J. 228, 53d (H. P.)
West James R. Lakeside
West John, 577 Division
West John, Evanston
West Joseph, 120 Seeley av.
West North, 110 S. Hoyne av.
West Roy O. 624 Rosenmerkel, Eng.
West Stephen A. Oak Park
West Stephen G. Dr. 858 W. Monroe
West William H. 4348 Grand boul.
West William K. 406 N. State
Westcott Alvin, 415 Bowen av.
Westcott Charles, Maywood
Westcott Oliver J. Maywood
Westenberger J. 2962 Groveland av.
Westerfield Charles I. 6721 Honore
Westerfield Frank M. Wilmette
Westerfield Henry D. Wilmette
Westerfield W. C. Mrs. 553, 62d, Eng.
Westervelt Douglas, 66, 21st
Westervelt John I. D. 4023 Prairie av.
Westfall Charles K. Rev. 267 Park av.
Westfall E. W. Mrs. 504 Jackson boul.
Westgate William R. 6728 Rhodes av.
Westlake Isabelle E. Miss, 3203 Calumet
    a .
Westlake J. A. 237, 29th
Weston Alonzo, 821 Washington boul.
Weston E. B., M. D. 3975 Drexel boul.
Weston John W. 410 Washington boul.
Weston M. 219 S. Oakley av.
Weston M. E. Miss, 3975 Drexel boul.
Weston Olive E. Mrs. 4852 Kenwood av.
Weston Uriah W. 261 Fremont
Weston Walter, S. Austin
Westover George Frederic, 140 Astor
Westrup Sarah V. Dr. Oak Park
Wetherell Albert P. 3020 Calumet av.
Wetherell Charles C. 1737 Wrightwood av.
Wetherell George F. 459 Jackson boul.
Wetherell George F., M. D. 164 Oakwood
    boul.
Wetherell O. D. 3020 Calumet av.
    Sum. res. Lake Geneva, Wis.
Wetherill J. N. Palmer house
Wethrell Edward H. 369 Elm
Wethrell James B. 369 Elm
Wethrell S. J. Mrs. 369 Elm
Wetmore Chas. O. 445 Washington boul.
Wetmore Ethelbert R. 28 Linden pl.
Wetmore Justin J. 569, 51st (H. P.)
Wetmore Shirley Mrs. 4821 Champlain
    av.
Wettengel A. 4154 Berkeley av.
Wetterer Herman, 563 Lasalle av.
Wetzel S. W. Oak Park
Wetzler W. 503 Lasalle av.
Weyburn Elbert D. 6352 Oglesby av.
Weyburn Ned C. 6352 Oglesby av.
Weyl A. Mrs. 767 Larrabee
Weyl Daniel 342 Center
Whalen Chas. J. Dr. 237 N. Clark
Whalen C. H. 210 Cass
Whaley John J. Dr. 551 Dearborn av.
Whaples J. L. Oak Park
Wharton Ann Mrs. 168, 67th, Englewood

Wharton George C. 425 Lasalle av.
Wharton O. T. 425 Lasalle av.
Wheat C. L. LaGrange
Wheat V. H. Mrs. 91, 43d
Wheatley James B. 5100 Hibbard av.
Wheaton A. C. 191, 78th (H. P.)
Wheaton F. S. Morgan Park
Wheaton Lloyd Mrs. 111 Warren av.
Wheaton Norville, 4221 Oakenwald av.
Whedon C. A. Mrs. Evanston
Whedon James P. Virginia hotel
Wheeler Albert G. 4617 Ellis av.
Wheeler Arthur, 2962 Michigan av.
Wheeler Arthur D. 19 Bellevue pl.
    Sum. res. Lake Forest
Wheeler A. W. 5139 Washington av.
Wheeler Calvin T. 518 N. State
Wheeler Carlton R. 4156 Ellis av.
Wheeler Charles C. 1116 Kenmore av.
Wheeler Charles C. 457 Washington boul.
Wheeler Charles H. 2125 Prairie av.
Wheeler Charles H. 7749 Emerald av.
Wheeler Charles M. 457 Washington boul.
Wheeler Charles P. Evanston
Wheeler C. Gilbert, Lexington hotel
Wheeler C. S. 5413 Ridgewood ct.
Wheeler C. W. Auditorium annex
Wheeler D. L. 60 Wisconsin
Wheeler Edward R. 815 Kenwood av.
Wheeler Emily F. Prof. Woman's Col-
    lege, Evanston
Wheeler Eugene, 2962 Michigan av.
Wheeler Ezra I. Mrs. 400 Dearborn av.
Wheeler E. F. 152, 36th
Wheeler E. M. Mrs. 3525 Ellis av.
Wheeler E. S. Oak Park
Wheeler Frances W. Dr. Evanston
Wheeler Francis T. 3416 Michigan av.
Wheeler Frank S. 217 The Plaza
Wheeler Fred C. 713 The Plaza
Wheeler Frederick S. 4815 Kenwood av.
Wheeler F. Chicago Beach hotel
Wheeler F. A., 5814 Wentworth av.
Wheeler F. W. 6311 Sheridan av.
Wheeler George A. Evanston
Wheeler George Henry, 1812 Prairie av.
Wheeler G. K. 1837 Michigan av.
Wheeler Henry, 347, 60th, Eng.
Wheeler Henry L. Dr. 1812 Prairie av.
Wheeler Henry N. 2520 Indiana av.
Wheeler Hiram Mrs. 2962 Michigan av.
Wheeler H. A. Gen. 652 W. Monroe
Wheeler I. M. Mrs. 3002 Vernon av.
Wheeler John, 3208 Lake Park av.
Wheeler John A. Dr. Irving Park
Wheeler J. H. 4542 Lake av.
Wheeler J. K. 3525 Ellis av.
Wheeler Kittredge Rev. 716 W. Adams
Wheeler Lewis E. Lexington hotel
Wheeler L. C. Mrs. 39, 22d
Wheeler Lotta Miss, 4614 Woodlawn av.
Wheeler Martin L. 4616 Woodlawn av.
Wheeler Meyer, 3615 Ellis Park
Wheeler M. V. Mrs. 41, 46th
Wheeler N. C. 6518 Sheridan av.
Wheeler O. Mrs. 3756 Ellis av.

Wheeler Ralph H. Dr. 251, 35th
Wheeler Sarah E. Mrs. 1851 Oakdale av.
Wheeler S. H. 15 Walton pl.
Wheeler Thomas J. 778 W. Monroe
Wheeler W. W. 138 Park av. •
Wheelhouse Elizabeth Mrs. 1425 Michigan av.
Wheelock Edwin D. 55 Madison Park
Wheelock Everett B. Wilmette
Wheelock Harry B. 3810 Indiana av.
Wheelock Ruth M. Miss, Riverside
Wheelock Sylvester, 967 Jackson boul.
Wheelock Seymour A. Wilmette
Wheelock William G. 936 BellePlaine av.
Wheelock William W. 104 Centre av.
Whelan Bion Dr. The Renfost
Whelpley Richard T. 515 Dearborn av.
Wherry Elwood M. Rev. River Forest
Whetston Charles P. 298 Irving av.
Whidden George F. 891 W. Adams
Whipple Charles B. 4739 Kenwood av.
Whipple Eugene W. 6657 Stewart av.
Whipple E. A. 3716 Elmwood pl.
Whipple Henry, Evanston
Whipple H. E. Mrs. 4600 Ellis av.
Whipple John H. 662 Fulton
Whipple John P. 5121 Washington av.
Whipple Rodney M. 5121 Washington av.
Whitacre C. C. 4835 Madison av.
Whitaker A. E. 343, 41st
Whitaker E. L. Mrs. 2453 Prairie av
Whitaker H. O. Mrs. 4307 Oakenwald av.
Whitbeck F. M. Lexington hotel
Whitcomb Adele Miss, 64, 24th
Whitcomb A. J. Park Ridge
Whitcomb A. O. 463 Irving av.
Whitcomb E. P. Miss, Evanston
Whitcomb E. W. 7116 Yale
Whitcomb George D. 197, 44th (H.P.)
Whitcomb George P. 64, 24th
Whitcomb H. J. 47 Seeley av.
Whitcomb J. C. 47 Seeley av.
Whitcomb Oscar E. 359 S. Oakley av.
Whitcomb Rodney S. 493 W. Monroe
Whitcomb W. C. The Arizona
White Alexander, 34 Lincoln pl.
White Alexander, 806 Washington boul.
White Anna M. Mrs. 667 Washington
   boul.
White A. H. 423 Irving av.
White A. H. Mrs. 3816 Ellis av.
White A. J. 1760 Wrightwood av.
White A. J. 3842 Elmwood pl.
White A. P. 525 W. Monroe
White A. S. 4830 Lake av.
White Bessie M. Miss, Oak Park
White Beverly T. 483 Belden av.
White Burton F. 832 Washington boul.
White B. C. Chicago Beach hotel
White B. H. Hotel Barry
White B. S. 3850 Lake av.
White Carl, Hotel Barry
White Carlos F. River Forest
White Catherine Mrs. 133 Garfield boul.
White Charles Dr. 380 Lasalle av.
White Charles F. 4614 Woodlawn av.

White Charles J. 417 Jackson boul.
White Charles M. 107 Evanston av.
White Charles M. River Forest
White Charles R. Oak Park
White C. B. Lakota hotel
White C. E. 451, 41st (H.P.)
White C. H. 1731 Wabash av.
White David, 6701 Lafayette av.
White Edmund R. LaGrange
White Edward G. 483 Belden av.
White Edward S. 2654 Commercial(L.V.)
White Elizabeth Miss, Evanston
White Elizabeth C. Mrs. 3126 Calumet av.
White Elizabeth V. Miss, 520 Winchester
   av.
White Ellen C. Miss, 520 Winchester av.
White E. J. Mrs. 73 Seeley av.
White E. Norton, 758, 67th, Englewood
White Frank, 230 Woodlawn terrace
White Frank A. 154, 50th (H.P.)
White Friend A. 832 Washington boul.
White F. F. Mrs. 1193 Lawndale av.
White George B. 4539 Oakenwald av.
White George E. 381 Washington boul.
White George H. Austin
White George W. Virginia hotel
White G. Frank, 3627 Vernon av.
White G. J. Dr. 7536 Bond av.
White Halsey B. G. 667 Washington boul
White Harley C. 4402 Ellis av.
White Harry 2426 Wabash av.
White Herman T. 4429 Evans av.
White Horace F. Oak Park
White Hugh A. Mrs. Evanston
White H. G. Hotel Groveland
White H. W. Hotel Barry
White James, 1831 Oakdale av.
White James A. 148 N. State
White James J. 993 Wilcox av.
White John, 520 Winchester av.
White John D. 161 Locust
White John E. Evanston
White John H. 345 Park av.
White John T. 202 Oakwood boul.
White John W. 13 Lincoln av.
White John W. Dr. 260. 64th (H.P.)
White J. A. Rev. Lakeside
White Kate A. Miss, 2505 Michigan av.
White Luelle Mrs. 3647 Michigan av.
White L. 230 Woodlawn terrace
White Marie M. D. 3146 Indiana av.
White Martha M. Mrs. 1188 Bonney av.
White Maude Miss, 6701 Lafayette av.
White Nelson A. 729 Fullerton av.
White Peter Mrs. 3953 Michigan av.
White P. T. Hyde Park hotel
White Randall H. Judge, 2512 Wabash av.
White Robert, 1732 Wrightwood av.
White Rufus A. Rev. 6550 Lafayette av.
White Samuel K. LaGrange
White Selden F. Evanston
White Thomas, 620 Washington boul.
White Thomas H. Tracy
White Thomas M. 520 Winchester av.
White William, 133 Garfield boul.
White William, 728 Sedgwick

White William F. 221 The Plaza
White William F. 4340 Oakenwald av.
White William J. 5110 Hibbard av.
White William M. 4402 Ellis av. ·
White William R. 263 Warren av.
White William S. Dr. 833 Washington boul.
White W. C. 2624 Wabash av.
White W. G. Mrs. Evanston
White W. T. Miss, 263 Warren av.
White W. W. 912 Evanston av.
Whitefield George W. Dr. Evanston
Whitefield John Rev. Evanston
Whiteford David, 804 Warren av.
Whitehall Alexander L. 627, 61st, Eng.
Whitehead Edward J. Austin
Whitehead Elisha P. 2965 Prairie av.
Whitehead Harry W. Evanston
Whitehead Percy D. Chicago Athletic Assn.
Whitehead Thomas J. Evanston
Whitehead William M. Lexington hotel
Whitehouse F. Meredyth 158 Rush
Whitehouse S. S. 3965 Ellis av.
Whitely Arthur, Evanston
Whitely C. J. Mrs. Evanston
Whiteman Sarah C. Mrs. 4748 Champlain av.
Whiteside J. H. 1473 W. Monroe
Whiteside William H. Mrs. 9 Scott
Whiteside W. H. 6527 Yale
Whiteside W. S. 5544 Monroe av.
Whitfield Albert, 5423 Washington av.
Whitfield Fred, Evanston
Whitfield George W. Dr. 5423 Washington av.
    Sum. res. Pueblo, Col.
Whitfield Joseph H. Evanston
Whitfield Thomas, 2437 Indiana av.
Whitfield William, Evanston
Whitford Henry E., M.D. 427, 67th, Eng.
Whitford Mary Mrs. 223 Marshfield av.
Whitgreave C. T. 3234 Vernon av.
Whiting A. C. 2417 South Park av.
Whiting A. T. 44 Cedar
Whiting B. Miss, Hotel Metropole
Whiting C. F. The Wellington
Whiting C. H. Hotel Metropole
Whiting C. H. 5721 Rosalie ct.
Whiting David, 3568 Grand boul.
Whiting E. T. Mrs. Hotel Metropole
Whiting Fannie Miss, 4823 Lake av.
Whiting Frederick G. 3154 Lake Park av.
Whiting Herbert L. 2417 South Park av.
Whiting John F. 3568 Grand boul.
Whiting L. Miss, Hotel Metropole
Whiting Robert, 3568 Grand boul.
Whiting Walter P. 1851 Barry av.
Whitley Arthur H. 617, 62d, Eng.
Whitley C. Mrs. 464, 42d
Whitley John, 6334 Yale
Whitley S. E. 403, 64th, Eng.
Whitlock A. E. Park Ridge
Whitlock Charles, Park Ridge
Whitlock Harold H. Evanston
Whitlock J. L. Evanston

Whitlock Royal J. Evanston
Whitman Anna Mrs. 191 54th (H. P.)
Whitman Arthur T. 6534 Lafayette av.
Whitman Charles O. Prof. 223, 54th (H. P.) .
Whitman Freeman F. 1295 Washington boul.
Whitman George B. 436 W. Adams
Whitman H. B. Evanston
Whitman John M. 1295 Washington boul.
Whitman J. H. 2950 Calumet av. ‹ ʼ
Whitman Lucius O. 277 S. Lincoln
Whitman Russell, 406 Erie
Whitmarsh Charles F. 6538 Madison av.
Whitmarsh J. C. 352 Chicago av.
Whitmer L. W. Dr. 1508 Aldine av.
Whitney Charles A. La Grange
Whitney Clarence J. 1571 Lill av.
Whitney C. P. 1220 Winthrop av.
Whitney Duane P. Evanston
Whitney E. H. Mrs. Evanston
Whitney Frank, Lakeside
Whitney F. E. Mrs. Auditorium annex
Whitney George, Lakeside
Whitney George B. 48 Gordon Terrace
Whitney George W. Mrs. 4723 Woodlawn av.
Whitney Guilford M. Evanston
Whitney G. M. 685 W. Monroe
Whitney Henry S. Dr. 1164 W. Adams
Whitney H. E. Hotel Groveland
Whitney H. H. Leland hotel
Whitney John B. 5486 Washington av.
Whitney J. B. 5486 Washington av.
Whitney J. C. Lexington hotel
Whitney J. D. C. 453 Belden av.
Whitney J. E. Mrs. 4130 Drexel boul.
Whitney Kate A. Mrs. 1220 Winthrop av.
Whitney M. J. Mrs. 6246 Lexington av.
Whitney M. M. Mrs. 4738 Lake av.
Whitney T. Deykes, 48 Gordon Terrace
Whiton L. K. Lexington hotel
Whiton W. S. Lexington hotel
Whitridge Phillip R. Virginia hotel
Whitson John M. Hinsdale
Whitson John M. jr. Hinsdale
Whittemore Charles L. Evanston
Whittemore F. K. Grand Pacific hotel
Whittlesey H. L. 5433 Madison av.
Whittlesey N. H. Oak Park
Whitworth Lawrence, Newberry hotel
Whyland B. 3262 Vernon av.
Whyland C. A. 3142 South Park av.
Wiard Hiram D. Rev. 352 Belden av.
Wichert Henry, 1649 Barry av.
Wicke William, Oak Park
Wicker Charles G. 4043 Ellis av.
Wicker Henry C. Virginia hotel
Wickersham D. Lemoyne, Irving Park
Wickersham Herman B. 23 Scott
Wickersham Joseph R. Irving Park
Wickersham S. Dr. Great Northern hotel
Wickes Roscoe L. Evanston
Wickes Thomas H. 3647 Grand boul.
Wicks Charles, Winnetka
Wicks John Rev. 1615 Grace

Wicks John E. P. 1615 Grace
Widerstrom Hannah Miss, 405 Oak
Wieboldt William A. 1836 Surf
Wiemer John A. 3505 Indiana av.
Wienhoeber Ernest, 656 Lasalle av.
Wies August, 4831 Vincennes av.
Wies Charles, 4831 Vincennes av.
Wiese John, 580, 37th
Wigeland Andrew G. 1273 Wilton av.
Wigeland Minnie Miss, 521 Belden av.
Wigfall T. B. 1029 N. Clark
Wiggin Edward G. 3239 Rhodes av.
Wiggin Twing B. Dr. 690 Ione pl.
Wiggins John B. 3823 Elmwood pl.
Wigginton James, Evanston
Wiggs George W. 3647 Michigan av.
Wight Andrew Mrs. 295, 42d (H.P.)
Wight B. W. 5463 Ridgewood ct.
Wight Edwin W. 3827 Ellis av.
Wight Eli Dr. 853 Warren av.
Wight Josiah W. 3827 Ellis av.
Wight P, B. 289, 42d (H.P.)
Wightman Charles R. Evanston
Wightman Joseph, Evanston
Wigley W. A. 1158 W. Jackson
Wigmore John Heury Prof. Evanston
          Sum. res, Cambridge, Mass.
Wignall Thomas M. 162 Walnut
Wikoff Bernard D. Austin
Wilber E. J. 6200 Woodlawn av.
Wilber Edwin J. jr. 6340 Madison av.
Wilber J. D. 5710 Madison av.
Wilber M. D. 5708 Madison av.
Wilber W. H. Mrs. 247 Michigan av.
Wilbur Anne B. Mrs. 1564 Fulton
Wilbur Benjamin, 72 Bellvue pl.
Wilbur C. M. 48, 35th
Wilbur George W. 1055 N. Halsted
Wilbur Helen P. Mrs. 258 Ontario
Wilbur Josephine M. Miss, Evanston
Wilbur J. B. 72 Bellevue pl.
Wilbur J. H. Evanston
Wilce Edwin P. Mrs. 361 Ashland boul.
Wilce E. Harvey, 708 W. Harrison
Wilce George C. 708 W. Harrison
Wilce Thomas, 708 W. Harrison
Wilce Thomas E. 708 W. Harrison
Wilcox Arthur E. 333 Warren av.
Wilcox A. P. Mrs. 59, 77th
Wilcox Beatrice Miss, 5101 Kimbark av.
Wilcox Belle Mrs. Grayland
Wilcox Charles E. 16 Chalmers pl.
Wilcox Charles H. 59, 77th
Wilcox Charles S. 176, 37th
Wilcox Cyrus S. Mrs. 6361 Lexington av.
Wilcox C. H. The Ashland
Wilcox F. W. 19 N. Ada
Wilcox George, 415 Warren av.
Wilcox George G. Avenue house, Evanston
Wilcox Harry M. 246 Oakwood boul.
Wilcox H. E. 176, 37th
Wilcox Jewett, 4762 Lake av.
Wilcox J. Chicago Beach hotel
Wilcox J. H. 2972 Indiana av.
Wilcox L. 4338 Ellis av.
46

Wilcox Margaret A. Mrs. 176, 37th
Wilcox M. L. Mrs. 1721 Cornelia
Wilcox Robert B. 285 W. Adams
Wilcox Thomas H. Newberry hotel
Wilcox T. B. The Ontario
Wilcox Wesley W. 3012 Vernon av.
Wilcox William D. Irving Park
Wilcox William E. 289 South Leavitt
Wilcox William L. Dr. Irving Park
Wilcox Willis P. 3650 Calumet av.
Wilcox W. B. Mrs. 285 W. Adams
Wilcox W. W. Mrs. 415 Warren av.
Wild Harrison M. 830 Morse av.
Wild Max E. 118 Wisconsin
Wild Theodore, M. D. 697 N. Robey
Wild Theodore jr. 697 N. Robey
Wild Thomas S. 813 Morse av.
Wilde Allan C. 3625 Vincennes av.
Wilder Edwin D. 298 Park av.
Wilder Edwin P. B. Dr. 189, 25th
Wilder E. A. Miss, 2919 Indiana av.
Wilder E. L. Mrs. 293 Chicago av.
Wilder Frank L. 4206 Ellis av.
Wilder F. M. Mrs. 2515 Wabash av.
          Sum. res. Ann Arbor, Mich.
Wilder F. N. Morgan Park
Wilder G. J. Dr. 6320 Wentworth av.
Wilder H. 4338 Greenwood av.
Wilder H. H. Washington Heights
Wilder John E. Evanston
Wilder M. H. Mrs. Evanston
Wilder T. Edward, Elmhurst
Wilder Walter L. 4206 Ellis av.
Wilder William H. Dr. 4002 Ellis av.
Wildman H. G. Dr. 4467 Lake av.
Wile David J. 4823 Kimbark
Wile Edwin W. 3639 Vincennes av.
Wile Jacob, M. D., 3537 Indiana av.
Wiley Edward N. 4733 Woodlawn av.
          Sum. res. Charlevoix, Mich
Wiley Frederick L. 4816 Langley av.
Wiley George W. 3023 Calumet av.
Wiley Lyman A. 4709 Woodlawn av.
Wiley O. G. 420 Belden av.
Wiley Rollin F. 6617 Hope av.
Wiley Sterling P. The Arizona
Wiley Willard R. 4811 Kimbark av.
Wilbartz William, 616 W. Congress
Wilk Fred L. 470 W. Division
Wilkens J. Anthony, Vendome hotel
Wilkie August, 1938 Wrightwood av.
Wilkie A. C. Southern hotel
Wilkie D. H. 580 Warren av.
Wilkin James S. Dr. 764 Walnut
Wilkin John L. 676 W. Monroe
Wilkins Charles H. 41 Aldine sq.
Wilkins Daniel Mrs. 4407 Calumet av,
Wilkins D. W. 4163 Lake av.
Wilkins Edwin P. 41 Aldine sq.
Wilkins Emma Miss, 410 Lasalle av.
Wilkins F. L. Rev. 935 W. Adams
Wilkins Joseph R. 564 Division
Wilkins Myrtilla Mrs. 41 Aldine sq.
Wilkins S. Grafton, 5128 Washington av.
Wilkins Walter M. Dr. 703 Greenleaf av,
Wilkins William A. 41 Aldine sq,

Wilkins W. S. 410 Lasalle av.
Wilkins W. W. 3530 Indiana av.
Wilkinson Charles D. 213 S. Campbell av.
Wilkinson Dudley P. 163 Rush
Wilkinson Dudley P. jr. 163 Rush
Wilkinson Frederick, 7660 Bond av.
Wilkinson Harry, 4413 Berkeley av.
Wilkinson Harry C. 7305 Yale
Wilkinson Jerome B. 5411 Jefferson av.
Wilkinson John, 482 Lasalle av.
Wilkinson J. P. Miss, 4413 Berkeley av.
Wilkinson William C. 361, 58th (H. P.)
Wilkinson William E. Rev. Evanston
Wilkinson William S. Newberry hotel
Will Chas. J. C. 257 Oakwood boul.
Will Charles L. 4211 Vincennes av.
Will George Mrs. 201 Fremont
Willard A. J. Winnetka
Willard Charles E. The Tudor
Willard C. P. Union Club
Willard E. R. Evanston
Willard Frances E. Miss, Evanston
Willard Frank E. Longwood
Willard Gardner G. 5528 Madison av.
Willard George, 262, 53d (H. P.)
Willard George R. 262, 53d (H. P.)
Willard G. E. Dr. 470, 44th
Willard Harry G. 4730 Kimbark av.
Willard Henry Rev. 5555 Woodlawn av.
Willard I. Geneva Miss, 4647 Vincennes
    av. Sum. res. Harbor Springs, Mich.
Willard John Rev. 643 Washington boul.
Willard M. L. 5528 Madison av.
Willard Norman P. 5555 Woodlawn av.
Willard P. H. Mrs. 5528 Madison av.
Willard Rose Dr. 5555 Woodlawn av.
Willard Samuel Dr. 865 Jackson boul.
Willard Wells Capt. U. S. A. Granada
    hotel
Willard William G. Dr. 544 Washington
    boul.
Willard W. F. 182 Cass
Willcox Alfred B. 512 Washington boul.
Willcox G. Buckingham Prof. D. D. 512
    Washington boul.
Willden John G. 4512 Prairie av.
Wille Louis, Evanston
Willems Peter, 396 Lasalle av.
Willets Joseph H. 2804 Indiana av.
Willett A. T. 164, 25th
Willett James R. 434 Jackson boul.
Willey Albert, 671 W. Monroe
Willey C. L. 2732 Calumet av.
Willey C. L. 2732 Calumet av.
Williams Aaron, 289 S. Oakley av.
Williams Albert H. 42d, se. cor. Lake av.
Williams Albert P. 550 Burling
Williams Alice Miss, 1844 George av.
Williams Andrew L. 122 Goethe
Williams Ann Mrs. 6533 Stewart av.
Williams Anna Miss, 1837 Michigan av.
Williams Annie E. Miss, 289 S. Oakley av.
Williams Arthur L. 6453 Woodlawn av.
Williams Augustus W. Rev. 731 Morse av.
Williams A. 2834 Prairie av.
Williams A. F. 166, 25th

Williams Ben, 5220 Jefferson av
Williams B. 278 Belden av.
Williams Carrie E. Miss, 1425 Michigan
    av.
Williams Charles, Evanston
Williams Charles A. Dr. 5141 Kimbark av.
Williams Charles H. Dr. LaGrange
Williams Charles T. 4206 Berkeley av.
Williams Christopher L. Evanston
Williams Clarence T. Hotel Normandie
Williams Clifford, 3253 Forest av.
Williams C. L. Oak Park
Williams C. M. Mrs. Lombard
Williams C. R. 771 W. Adams
Williams Daniel H. Dr. 3034 Michigan av.
Williams Daniel W. 4316 Langley av.
Williams David, 1820 Wellington
Williams Day, 4206 Berkeley av.
Williams Dixon C. 1261 Wilton av.
Williams Edward C. 505 W. Congress
Williams Edwin C. Dr. 4405 Ellis av.
Williams Ellen H. Miss, 2914 Groveland av.
Williams E. J. Evanston
Williams E. S. Rev. 147 Ashland boul.
Williams E. T. 4600 Ellis av.
Williams Fitzallen B. 3566 Vincennes av.
Williams Frank B. 3566 Vincennes av.
Williams Frank J. Evanston
Williams Frank N. 1728 Briar pl.
Williams Frederick N. Stamford hotel
Williams George A. 346 Washington boul.
Williams George H. Hinsdale
Williams George H. 637 Jackson boul.
Williams George J. 1921 Wrightwood av.
Williams George P. Rev. 6712 Emerald av.
Williams George T. 4724 Drexel boul.
Williams Grant 4724 Drexel boul.
Williams Gwendolyn Miss, 2246 Michigan
    av.
Williams G. W. 224 Seminary av.
Williams Helen R. Miss, 1844 George av.
Williams Helen S. Dr. 6621 Stewart av.
Williams Homer A. 1101 Wash'ton boul.
Williams Hugh Blake Dr. 2210 Michigan
    av.
Williams Hugh S. Rev. 6621 Stewart av.
Williams H. Mrs. 2246 Michigan av.
Williams H. B. 94, 37th
Williams H. E. 2246 Michigan av.
Williams H. F. 522 Dearborn av.
Williams H. J. 4660 Michigan Terrace
Williams H. P. Evanston
Williams H. R. 435 Washington boul.
Williams Ida Miss, 668 W. Adams
Williams Isaac B. 14 Bellevue pl.
Williams Jabez W. Oak Park
Williams Jacob, 3670 Indiana av.
Williams James B. Dr. 20 Ewing pl.
Williams James Davy, 3670 Indiana av.
Williams Jennie B. Mrs. 245 Oakwood
    boul.
Williams John A. Evanston
Williams John C. Evanston
Williams John E. 1473 W. Monroe
Williams John E. Evanston
Williams John H. 213 S. Leavitt.

Williams John Milton Rev. 597 Cleveland av.
Williams John M. Evanston
Williams John Q. Evanston
Williams John R. 4600 Ellis av.
Williams Joseph H. S. Winnetka
Williams J. Charles, Evanston
Williams J. D. 47 Warren av.
Williams J. F., M.D. 427 Center
Williams J. W. Irving Park
Williams Laura Miss, 1836 Calumet av.
Williams Lawrence M. 396 Ontario
Williams Lucas R. 1901 Wrightwood av.
Williams Lucian M. 18 St. James pl.
Williams Luther, 4539 Oakenwald av.
Williams Marcus R. 846 North Park av.
Williams Mary E. Mrs. 1425 Michigan av.
Williams M. B. 35, 33d
Williams M. D. 1651 W. Monroe
Williams M. E. Mrs. 363 Ontario
Williams Nathan, Evanston
Williams Newton P. Evanston
Williams Nony R. Mrs. 595 Washington boul.
    Sum. res. "Briarwood," Lake Geneva, Wis.
Williams Norman, 1836 Calumet av.
Williams Norman A. 1651 W. Monroe
Williams Robert A. 641 W. Adams
Williams Rudolph, 258 Ontario
Williams R. C. Lieut. Fort Sheridan
Williams Samuel H. 1819 Aldine av.
Williams Sydney, 167 Rush
Williams Simeon B. The Ontario
Williams Stalham L. 593 Jackson boul.
Williams Stalham L. jr. 593 Jackson boul.
Williams S. T. Hotel Metropole
Williams Thomas D. LaGrange
Williams T. C. jr. 3831 Ellis av.
Williams T. H. 358, 41st
Williams Waldo A. 3566 Vincennes av.
Williams William, Austin
Williams Wm. Carver Dr. 4206 Berkeley av.
Williams William J. S. Newberry hotel
Williams William L. Evanston
Williams W. E. 765 W. Adams
Williamson Caroline L. Miss, 3230 Michigan av.
Williamson E. 4846 Washington av.
Williamson George T. 5008 Greenwood av.
Williamson Harry Dr. 3703 Ellis av.
Williamson H. Y. 507 W. Monroe
Williamson John, 45 Macalister pl.
Williamson J. A. Gen. U. S. A. Granada hotel
Williamson J. W. Dr. 152, 36th
Williamson M. W. 314 Jackson boul.
Williamson Thos. F. 4214 Vincennes av.
Williamson Wm. Longwood
Williamson W. G. 949 Jackson boul.
Willing Evelyn Pierrepont Miss, 110 Rush
Willing Henry J. 110 Rush
Willing Mary J. Mrs. 54, 20th
Willis Alice Mrs. 1054 Washington boul.
Willis Edwin E. Evanston

Willis F. C. New Hotel Holland
Willis George E. 695 Burling
Willis George S. 769 N. Clark
Willison E. C. 508 Belden av.
Williston Alfred D. 1115 Early av.
Williston Edward B. Col. U.S.A. 501 The Plaza
Williston Martin L. Rev. Elmhurst
Willits George Spencer, 369 Erie
    Sum. res. Bar Harbor
Willits J. E. Mrs. 223 S. Campbell av.
Willits Ward W. 223 S. Campbell av.
Willmarth Edward L. 4001 Grand boul.
Willner L. J. Lakota hotel
Willner Moses, 3715 Ellis av.
Willoughby A. V. Ravinia
Willoughby Charles L. 1714 Michigan av.
Willoughby J. B. 104 Warren av.
Willoughby J. D., M.D. Chicago Beach hotel
Wills John, 31 Aldine sq.
Wills William E. 679 Fullerton av.
Willsie L. Miss, Evanston
Willson C. C. 4524 Lake av.
Willson H. T. 4524 Lake av.
Willson John, 33 Wisconsin
Wilmanns Arnold D. 487 Cleveland av.
Wilmarth H. M. Mrs. Auditorium annex
Wilmarth Thomas W. 3733 Forest av.
Wilmarth T. S. Hyde Park hotel
Wilmerding Charles Henry, 45 Cedar
Wilmeroff Carl A. River Forest
Wilmeroth Charles W. Avenue house, Evanston
Wilmersdorf Maurice, 3343 Prairie av.
Wilming John B. Evanston
Wilmot Alta E. Miss, 7700 Union av.
Wilmot Maud Miss, 1712 Diversey
Wilmot Samuel A. Evanston
Wilms L. M. Mrs. 533 S. Normal Parkway
Wilson Adelaide Miss, 4613 Drexel boul.
Wilson Archibald R. 3662 Michigan av.
Wilson Arthur B. 445, 64th, Eng.
Wilson A. H. Oak Park
Wilson A. T. 4630 Indiana av.
Wilson B. M. Virginia hotel
Wilson Charles, 401 N. State
Wilson Charles A. 5454 Washington av.
Wilson Charles B. 116 S. Leavitt
Wilson Charles S. 290 Rush
Wilson Charles W. Austin
Wilson C. Bruce, 866 W. Adams
Wilson C. H. 190, 45th
Wilson C. L. 4584 Oakenwald av.
Wilson Elizabeth Miss, 21 Aldine sq.
Wilson Elvira L. Mrs. Evanston
Wilson Emma L. Miss, 1371 Washington boul.
Wilson Ethel Edwin, 4210 Calumet av.
Wilson E. Crane, 4613 Drexel boul.
Wilson E. J. Mrs. 1624 Cornelia
Wilson E. L. 320, 41st
Wilson Frank I. 1287 Washington boul.
Wilson Frank J. Irving Park
Wilson Frank R. 1624 Cornelia
Wilson Fred J. Evanston

Wilson F. Cortez, 123 Park av.
Wilson George, 4432 Langley av.
Wilson George A.S.3521 Vernon av.
Wilson George C. 4801 Lake av.
Wilson George H. Rev. Hinsdale
Wilson George L. Oak Park
Wilson George W. 341 Park av.
Wilson George W. Hinsdale
Wilson Gilbert. 5496 Monroe av.
Wilson G. M. 129, 51st (H.P.)
Wilson Harry E. 4432 Langley av.
Wilson Harry G. 3935 Ellis av.
Wilson Henry, 4630 Indiana av.
Wilson Henry B. 4346 Langley av.
Wilson Henry K. 2922 Prairie av.
Wilson H. S. 2330 Indiana av.
Wilson Horatio R. 4547 Grand boul.
Wilson Hugh M. 331 Hampden ct.
Wilson Hugh R. Evanston
Wilson I. C. 901 Sawyer av.
Wilson Jacob H. 936 S. Central Park av.
Wilson James W. Austin
Wilson John jr. 425 Marshfield av.
Wilson John Mrs. Virginia hotel
Wilson John B. 4519 Oakenwald av.
Wilson John C. 710 Turner av.
Wilson John F. 2019 Michigan av.
Wilson John H. Evanston
Wilson John H. Mrs. 220 Dearborn av.
Wilson John P. 564 Dearborn av.
Wilson John R. 434 N. State
Wilson John R. 657 Lasalle av.
Wilson John S. Col. Evanston
Wilson Joseph H. 165 Warren av.
Wilson Joseph M. 93, 32d
Wilson Justice, 578 Fullerton av.
Wilson J. 148 N. State
Wilson J. A. 288 Irving av.
Wilson J. F. Oak Park
Wilson J. H. 160 Ashland boul.
Wilson J. H. 971 Park av.
Wilson J. H. 3648 Wabash av.
Wilson J. H. 4405 Calumet av.
Wilson J. W. 42, 39th
Wilson Lee, 862 W. Adams
Wilson Louis W. 21 Aldine sq.
Wilson Lucy L. 619 Washington boul.
Wilson Luke I. 4613 Drexel boul.
Wilson Lyman, 1615 Prairie av.
Wilson L. 238 Belden av.
Wilson L. H. 4339 Oakenwald av.
Wilson L. M. Mrs. 4106 Drexel boul.
Wilson Maggie V. Miss, 102 Ashland boul.
Wilson Marshall J. 2922 Prairie av.
Wilson Mary Mrs. 3535 Wabash av.
Wilson Mary A. Miss, Park Ridge
Wilson Mary C. Mrs. 4816 Grand boul.
Wilson Milton H. 2917 Michigan av.
Wilson Moses, 4210 Calumet av.
Wilson Nina Miss, 259 Lasalle av.
Wilson Olin T. 7736 Sherman
Wilson Proctor M. 1163 N. Clark
Wilson P. E. Oak Park
Wilson Robert C. Dr. 106, 43d
Wilson Robert F. 4733 St. Lawrence av.
Wilson R. A. 3619 Lake av.

Wilson R. J. 201, 46th
Wilson R. L. 4455 Oakenwald av.
Wilson Samuel A. 3242 South Park av.
Wilson Samuel C. Hinsdale
Wilson Samuel G. Lake Forest
Wilson Samuel R. Irving Park
Wilson Solon D. 4051 Ellis av.
Wilson Stephen, 1214 Lill av.
Wilson Stephen R. 102 Dekalb
Wilson S. Frank, Evanston
Wilson Theodore I. 766 Warren av.
Wilson Thomas, 12 Campbell Park
Wilson Thomas E. 4210 Calumet av.
Wilson Thomas H. Austin
Wilson Thomas S., U. S. N. 320, 41st
Wilson Walter H. 2532 Prairie av.
Wilson William, 525 N. Clark
Wilson William C. Evanston
Wilson William G. Mrs. 3920 Lake av.
Wilson William J. 192 Ashland boul.
Wilson William R. 1313 Michigan
Wilson William White Rev. 21 Aldine sq.
Wilson W. M. 4551 Woodlawn av.
Wilson W. N. 217 Belden av.
Wilt Charles T. 344 Dayton
          Sum. res. Petoskey, Mich.
Wilt Charles T. jr. 290 Garfield av.
Wilt Elmer E. 344 Dayton
Wiltberger L. J. Mrs. Oak Park
Wimermark Arvid H.Dr.57 Cleveland av.
Wimersted M. Mrs. Austin
Wimersted Oscar T. Austin
Wimond Mark, Evanston
Winans Frank E. Evanston
Winchell F. Albert, Evanston
Winchell Harley C. Evanston
Winchell Harriet E, Miss, 414 Washington boul.
Winchell Louis E. 3116 Lake Park av.
Winchell N. P. 3946 Prairie av.
Winchell S. Robertson Prof. Evanston
Wincher W. P. 12 Maple
Winchester Andrew, 47 Warren av.
Winchester C. J. Highland Park
Winchester F. C. Highland Park
Winchester Lucius W.654 Washburne av.
Windes Thomas G. Winnetka
Windes Zel F. 1784 Wrightwood av.
Windett Arthur W. 2522 Calumet av.
Windett Victor, 2522 Calumet av.
Windheim John C. 1817 Frederick
Windmuller Levi, 555 Lasalle av.
Windrow Mia Miss, 233 Lasalle av.
Windrow Sven Dr. 233 Lasalle av.
Windsor Henry H. 4446 Berkeley av.
Windsor Herbert T. Riverside
Windsor James A. 1039 Lawndale av.
Windsor Walter Mrs. 756 Washington boul.
Winegardner William H.7544 Emerald av.
Wineman E. M. 6957 Calumet av.
Wineman Jacob R. 2544 Michigan av.
Wineman Joseph M. 2544 Michigan av.
Wineman Marx, 2544 Michigan av.
Wineman Milton R. 2544 Michigan av.
Wineman Simon R. 2544 Michigan av.

Winer John K. Dr. 95 Evanston av.
Wing Daniel, Maywood
Wing Elbert Dr. 55, 33d
Wing Henry, Maywood
Wing Luman R. Evanston
Wing Peter G. Austin
Wing Russell M. Judge, Evanston
Wing Samuel C. 3347 Calumet av.
Wing Thomas W. 1880 Diversey
Wingate Mary E. Mrs. Oak Park
Wingate M. D. Miss, 649 W. Monroe
Winger E. B. 532 Kenwood Terrace
Wingert John, Edison Park
Wingreen Anna Miss, 238 Pine
Wingren Eric Rev. Norwood Park
Wink Charles G. 894 S. Kedzie av.
Wink Henry, 2546 Cottage Grove av.
Winkelman F. A. 387 Warren av.
Winklebeck Andrew, 3012 Michigan av.
Winklebeck H. C. 3012 Michigan av.
Winkler John W. 4328 Prairie av.
Winn C. S. 2600 Indiana av.
Winn J. C. 632 Jackson boul.
Winn William E. Evanston
Winne Archibald, 3534 Ellis av.
Winne Frank N. Evanston
Winne John, 3534 Ellis av.
Winne William N. D. 55 St. Clair
Winship Charles A. 271 Huron
Winship Frederick A. 443 Lasalle av.
Winship Joseph C. Winnetka
Winslow Albert H. 1651 Briar pl.
Winslow A. D. 1627 Sheridan rd.
Winslow Charles S. 43 Cedar
Winslow Chas. W. 4748 Kenwood av.
Winslow Emma C. Mrs. 1562 Fulton
Winslow E. D. 1629 Sheridan rd.
Winslow Francis A. 239 Hampden ct.
Winslow George W.Dr. 3012 Michigan av.
Winslow James M. 1337 Michigan av.
Winslow J. H. Mrs. 2940 Prairie av.
Winslow Rapsima B.Mrs.6341 Stewart av.
Winslow R. W. Mrs. Hotel Windermere
Winslow W. P. Oak Park
Winslow William H. River Forest
            Sum. res. Tower Hill, Wis.
Winslow Zebedee R. 1337 Michigan av.
Windstandley J. B. 3555 Ellis av.
Winston Bertram M. 383 Superior
Winston Dudley, 99 Pearson
Winston Edward M. 6051 Madison av.
Winston Frederick H. 369 Superior
Winston Frederick S. 378 Ontario
Winston Marie Miss, 369 Superior
Winston Thomas Dr. 6051 Madison av.
Winter E. J. 414 S. Oakley av.
Winter Frank F. 642 Washington boul.
Winter   L. Miss, 642 Washington
   bouGrace
Winter Hugh A. 642 Washington boul.
Winter Joanna O. Mrs. 419 Warren av.
Winter Julius A. 414 S. Oakley av.
Winter Mary S. Dr. 1245 Michigan av.
Winter Robert W. 414 S. Oakley av.
Winterbotham J. Russell Mrs. 2215 Mich-
   igan av.

Wintermeyer J. C. 504 W. Congress
Winters Eric, 3315 Forest av.
Winters John A. 281 Sunnyside av.
Winters Thomas H. 6643 Lafayette av.
Wintersteen Lambert S. LaGrange
Wintrode Frank C. 4800 St. Lawrence av.
Wire George E. Dr. Evanston
Wire Nancy B. Mrs. Evanston
Wire William C. Evanston
            Sum. res. Fisk's, Wis.
Wirt William B. Lexington hotel
Wirth F. 140 Center
Wirts Stephen M. Chicago View hotel
Wischemeyer Henry, 132 Pine
Wischover John, 664 Evanston av.
Wisdom Edward, 683½Washington boul.
Wisdom Edward jr. 683½ Washington
   boul.
Wisdom Harry E. 683½ Washington boul.
Wisdom T. B. 6439 Yale
Wisdom W. J. New Hotel Holland
Wise Albert, 260, 37th
Wise Clift B. 4456 Berkeley av.
Wise Homer, Hotel Windermere
Wise H. A. 3605 Lake av.
Wise Julius Dr. 3756 Ellis av.
Wise Kate A. Mrs. 896 W. Adams
Wise William C. Dr. 567, 42d
Wiseman Lucy D. Mrs. 6351 Stewart av.
Wiser Clinton B. 321, 49th
Wisiner J. E. Hotel Metropole
Wisner Albert, 4825 Drexel boul.
Wisshack Geo. F. 149 Warren av.
Wiswall A. Morgan Park
Wiswall Charles E. Evanston
Wiswell Jane W. Mrs. 2417 Michigan av.
Witbeck John H. 2841 Michigan av.
            Sum. res. Delavan, Wis.
Withrow Bonnie Miss, 627 Dearborn av.
Withrow Harrison Dr. 5816 Washington
   av.
Withrow John L. Rev. 149 Ashland boul.
Withrow J. F. 627 Dearborn av.
Withrow Thomas F. 627 Dearborn av.
Witkowski E. 497 Lasalle av.
Witkowski Isadore, 497 Lasalle av.
Witkowsky Conrad, 2802 Prairie av.
Witkowsky David, 3256 Vernon av.
Witkowsky David, 3364 Calumet av.
Witkowsky Esther Miss, 3364 Calumet av.
Witkowsky James, 2802 Prairie av.
Witkowsky Leopold, 3364 Calumet av.
Witkowsky M. D. 3202 Indiana av.
Witkowsky Samuel D. 4204 Calumet
Witkowsky S. 614 W. Congress
Witmer Mary A. Miss, Lakeside
Witt Andrew, 3806 Vincennes av.
Witt Peter H. 3806 Vincennes av.
Witte Ernest, LaGrange
Witte Joachim C. 1427 Washington boul.
Witters Gilbert, 464 Lasalle av.
Witters Gilbert, Oak Park
Wittman A. I. 731 Fullerton av.
Wittmeyer Gustave, 35 Best av.
Wittmeyer Gustave jr. 35 Best av.
Wittstein Alfred H. 46 Scott

Wittstein August, 46 Scott
Wittstein Charles T. 46 Scott
Wittstein Emma Miss, 46 Scott
Witty John A. 2908 Commercial (L.V.)
Witwer T. Wilbur 6724 Union av.
Wixon C. Frank. 101, 37th
Wixon F. A. 101, 37th
Woelffer Charles. 758 North Park av.
Wohlgemuth Julius, 176, 37th
Wohlgemuth Lina Mrs. 166, 37th
Wolbach J. S. 3211 Wabash av.
Wolcott Eben E. Dr. Lagrange
Wolcott Francis E. A. 4535 Ellis av.
Wolcott Frank H. 6417 Sheridan av.
Wolcott James G. LaGrange
Wolcott Maria C. Mrs, Evanston
Wolcott Mary S. Mrs. 1067 N. Clark
Wolcott Peter C. Rev. Highland Park
Woley Edwin R. 3302 Rhodes av.
Woley Henry P. Dr. 3302 Rhodes av.
Wolf Ada Mrs. 3616 Prairie av.
Wolf Alphonse S. 698 W. Monroe
Wolf A. H. 3939 Ellis av.
Wolf Benjamin, 698 W. Monroe
Wolf Bernhard, 3561 Prairie av.
Wolf Fred W. 504 Lasalle av.
Wolf Gabriel, 83, 32d
Wolf Henry, 454 Marshfield av.
Wolf Henry M. 3939 Ellis av.
Wolf John P. 85, 33d
Wolf Joseph, The Wellington
Wolf J. Mme. 1927 Indiana av.
Wolf Leon, 624 Fullerton av.
Wolf Leopold, 3247 Vernon av.
Wolf L. J. 2912 Groveland av.
Wolf Max, 3255 Wabash av.
Wolf Morris E. 698 W. Monroe
Wolf Moses, 3939 Ellis av.
Wolf M. W. 3156 Wabash av.
Wolf Peter, 15, 33d
Wolf Samuel, 454 Marshfield av.
Wolf Simon, 698 W. Monroe
Wolf S. 4440 Berkeley av.
Wolf Thomas L. 534 Sunnyside av.
Wolf Victorine Mrs. 4154 Ellis av.
Wolfe Aretas W. 5934 Princeton av.
Wolfe Hattie E. Miss, 158 Lasalle av.
Wolfe H. C. 4449 Evans av.
Wolfe Ida M. Miss, Morton Park
Wolfe Joseph G.Dr. 322 Centre av.
Wolfe J. Stephenson 5934 Princeton av.
Wolfe Lottie Miss, Morton Park
Wolfe Mary Mrs. Morton Park
Wolfe Moses 53, 32d
Wolfe Oswald F. Morton Park
Wolfe Solomon 4416 Langley av.
Wolfe William O. 6547 Drexel av.
Wolfenstetter J. 321 Park av.
Wolff Benjamin, 453 Dearborn av.
Wolff C. J. 831 W. Monroe
        Sum. res. Channel Lake, Ill.
Wolff George, 715 Fullerton av.
Wolff Isaac, 4333 Forrestville av.
Wolff John F. 797 W. Monroe
Wolff Ludwig, 1319 Washington boul.
Wolff Ludwig jr. 1319 Washington boul.

Wolff L. 652 Fullerton av.
Wolff L. Miss, 7100 Webster av.
Wolff L. G. 3437 Calumet av.
Wolff M. 453 Dearborn av.
Wolff Nathan, 453 Dearborn av.
Wolff Otto A. 653 Pine Grove av.
Wolff Peter F. 3834 Langley av.
Wolff Samuel, 453 Dearborn av.
Wolff William, 3546 Forest av.
Wolff W. F. 735 Fulton
Wolfinger C. I. Irving Park
Wolfner Rudolph 4544 St. Lawrence av.
Wolfolk James A. Winnetka
Wolford F. H. 4541 Champlain av.
Wolford Jacob A. 552 N. State
Wolfsohn Carl, 2502 Indiana av.
Wolgamott Geo. W. Dr. 826 Warren av.
Wollensak J. F. 362 Lasalle av.
Wollner Otto, 397 S. Paulina
Wolseley Henry W. 4456 Ellis av.
Wolter Peter, 144 Garfield boul.
Wolter Peter jr. 144 Garfield boul.
Woltersdorf Arthur F. 360 Ashland boul.
Woltersdorf Ernest, 461 Irving av.
Woltersdorf Louis, 360 Ashland boul.
Woltz Fred, 244 Hampden ct.
Woltz J. 143 Lincoln av.
Wood Alonzo C. 989 W. Congress
Wood Andrew J. 802 W. Monroe
Wood A. L. Mrs. 535 Orchard
Wood A. Wilder, Oak Park
Wood Caroline Miss, 5420 East End av.
Wood Caroline C. Miss, Oak Park
Wood Casey A. Dr. 1800 Michigan av.
Wood Charles, Ridgeland
Wood Charles B. 5420 East End av.
Wood C. J. 156 Dearborn av.
Wood C. S. Dr. Oak Park
Wood David Ward, 533, 62d, Eng.
Wood D. W. Park Ridge
Wood Edith Miss, 2604 Prairie av.
Wood Edmond A. 620 Englewood av.
Wood Edward D. 535 Orchard
Wood Edward G. 141 Park av.
Wood Elinor P. Miss, 405 Dearborn av.
Wood Emily Mrs. Austin
Wood Eneas A. 4436 Vincennes av.
Wood Erwin E. Mrs. 2952 Prairie av.
Wood E. W. Dr. Oak Park
Wood Frank, 5313 Cornell av.
Wood Frank C. Oak Park
Wood Frank F. 4819 Kimbark av.
Wood Fred T. Evanston
Wood F. M. 143 Oakwood boul.
Wood Frederick W. 5436 Jefferson av.
Wood George, 4540 Prairie av.
Wood George A. Dr. 4016 Michigan av.
Wood George E. 2801 Prairie av.
Wood Glen Mrs. Lake Forest
Wood Harriet Miss, 5420 East End av.
Wood Henry C. 321 The Plaza
Wood Horace E. R. 5440 Jefferson av.
Wood Horatio F., M. D. 1728 Michigan
        av.
Wood Ida M. Miss, 2904 Prairie av.
Wood Ira C. 608 Division

Wood Irene E. Miss, 188, 36th
Wood James, 4016 Michigan av.
Wood James Mrs. 5307 Lexington av.
Wood James A. 3650 Calumet av.
Wood Jane Mrs. 188, 36th
Wood John, 1089 S. Central Park av.
Wood John Clinton, 4534 Forrestville av.
Wood John E. 3259 Indiana av.
Wood John H. 4300 Michigan av.
Wood John H. 5806 Rosalie ct.
Wood Julia Miss, 5420 East End av.
Wood J. C. 42, 39th
Wood J. H. Col. 721 W. Adams
Wood J. M. The Arizona
Wood Lenore Miss, 2604 Prairie av.
Wood Leslie, Oak Park
Wood Milton R. 2904 Prairie av.
Wood M. M. Berwyn
Wood O. F. 943 Sawyer av.
Wood Peter P. 535 Orchard
Wood Ralph, 535 Orchard
Wood R. E. Julien hotel
Wood Samuel E. Dr. 3924 Michigan av.
Wood Samuel Kay, 3924 Michigan av.
Wood Silas L. 804 W. Monroe
Wood S. Ella Miss, 3924 Michigan av.
Wood Thomas R. 5436 Jefferson av.
Wood Walpole, 766 Warren av.
Wood Webster, 5420 East End av.
Wood Wm. Fairfax, 212, 32d
Wood William G. 141 Park av.
Wood William G. Mayfair
Wood William H. 4354 Calumet av.
Wood William H. Dr. 936 N. Halsted
Wood William H. Oak Park
Wood William L. 2771 N. Paulina
Wood William R. Rev. 6231 Sheridan av.
Wood W. F. 3646 Vincennes av.
Wood W. H. LaGrange
Wood W. H. Hotel Metropole
Wood W. W. Oak Park
Woodard Willard Mrs. 703 Jackson boul.
Woodbridge Eugene M. 344 Ohio
Woodbridge John, 5 Chalmers pl.
Woodbridge John R. Evanston
Woodbridge J. E. The Ontario
Woodbridge Laura K. Mrs. 451 S. Oakley av.
Woodbury De Wilton B. 4314 Langley av.
Woodbury Fitz Allan, 340 Chestnut, Eng.
Woodbury George W. Oak Park
Woodbury Leonard P. 4060 Ellis av.
Woodbury Lorenzo D. Austin
Woodbury Louis E. 1425 Edgecomb ct.
Woodbury Sidney H. Austin
Woodbury William H. Dr. 611 Washington boul.
Woodbury W. H. 1425 Edgecomb ct.
Woodbury W. R. Mrs. Austin
Woodcock Arthur, 2419 Michigan av.
Woodcock L. T. 810 W. Monroe
Woodcock Thomas J. Mrs. Hinsdale
Woodford Archibald T. Winnetka
Woodford Charles A. 3438 Wabash av.
Woodford George Col. Grand Pacific
Woodford O. F. Mrs. 3438 Wabash av.

Woodford P. R. Evanston
Woodhead J. E. 468 W. Randolph
Woodland Fred B. 355 Oakwood boul.
Woodland George, 355 Oakwood boul.
Woodle Edward R. 5729 Madison av.
Woodley George, Evanston
Woodley Harry R. 452 Irving av.
Woodley T. E. 55 Laflin
Woodman F. F. Hotel Windermere
Woodman Jennie Miss, 44, 35th
Woodman T. F. Hotel Windermere
Woodrough Rufus L. 150 Pine
Woodruff Amos H. 456 Washington boul.
Woodruff Charles A. Riverside
Woodruff Charles E. 4857 Kimbark av.
Woodruff C. B. 6645 Yale
Woodruff C. E. Capt. Fort Sheridan
Woodruff Edward, 4831 Madison av.
Woodruff E. Fort Sheridan
Woodruff Fred D. Maywood
Woodruff F. E. Ft. Sheridan
Woodruff James S. 545 Dearborn av.
Woodruff John B., M.D. 941 S. Homan av.
Woodruff Joseph B. 2937 Indiana av.
Woodruff Joseph S. 29 University pl.
Woodruff Mary E. Mrs. 3164 Groveland av.
Woodruff Samuel, Maywood
Woodruff W. G. 3756 Ellis av.
Woods Antoinette L. Mrs. 2728 Wabash av.
Woods Don C. 7742 Sherman
Woods F. Marion 1218 Washington boul.
Woods Isaac L. 537 65th, Eng.
Woods John P. 900 Walnut
Woods J. L. Major, Pullman
Woods M. M. Mrs. 5809 Washington av.
Woods M. R. Mrs. 91, 44th
Woods W. J. Chicago Beach hotel
Woodson Emily A. Mrs. Evanston
Woodson E. M. 235 Michigan av.
Woodward Alfred W., M.D. 130 Ashland boul.
Woodward Charles, 148 Dearborn av.
Woodward Cyrus H. 7108 Vincennes av.
Woodward Edwin A. 1814 Wrightwood av.
Woodward Eliza Mrs. French house, Evanston
Woodward Ellen L. Mrs. Evanston
Woodward E. E. L. Mrs. 1917 Diversey
Woodward Harriet V. Miss, Lexington hotel
Woodward James L. Mrs. Chicago Beach hotel
Woodward Joseph, 415 Dearborn av.
Woodward Julius K. Mrs. 415 Dearborn av.
Woodward M. S. 4548 Oakenwald av.
Woodward R. E. Dr. 2231 Wabash av.
Woodward Theron R. Lexington hotel
Woodward T. H. Chicago Beach hotel
Woodward William E. 4791 Oakenwald av.
Woodward W. H. 542 Monroe av.
Woodward W. H. Berwyn
Woodwell Gertrude Mrs. 7 Burton pl.

Woodworth B. 80 Seeley av.
Woodworth George B. Evanston
Woodworth James A. Highland Park
Woodworth John C. 6315 Honore
Woodworth Plumer M. Dr. 1246 N. Clark
Woodworth R. N. 6620 Yale
Woodworth W. S. 6542 Lafayette av.
Woodyatt Clara L. Mrs. Evanston
Wooler August, 7524 Bond av.
Wooley John, 5535 Cornell av.
Woolf B. 434 Warren av.
Woolf E. 434 Warren av.
Woolf Harry, 375 Ashland boul.
Woolf Isaac, 3305 Michigan av.
Woolfolk Alexander M. Col. Evanston
Woolfolk Clinton S. Evanston
Woollacott John Mrs. 17 Roslyn pl.
Woollen Frank P. 1860 Melrose
Woolley A. Mrs.223 Jackson Park terrace
Woolley Clarence, Virginia hotel
Woolley C. E. 4952 Vincennes av.
Woolley C. M. Virginia hotel
Woolley E. A. Mrs. 3000 Indiana av.
Woolley Frances C. Mrs. 222 Sheridan rd.
Woolley Verner S. 2229 Sheridan rd.
Wooster Clarence K. Hotel Windermere
Wooster E. D. Hotel Barry
Worcester Francis, 465 Lasalle av.
Worcester Theodore, 465 Lasalle av.
Work A. S. Hotel Metropole
Work George R. Virginia hotel
Work George Z. Virginia hotel
Work Henry, Hotel Windermere
Worley Brice, 4419 Ellis av.
Worley John, Austin
Worman William S. Winnetka
Wormer Isabelle Mrs. 3541 Calumet av.
Wormser D. 3215 South Park av.
Wormser Louis, 3215 South Park av.
Wormser M. 4325 Prairie av.
Worrall B. H. 277 S. Lincoln
Worster Asa, Oak Park
Worswick T. J. Oak Park
Worth Richard F. Dr. 1064 S. Central
Park av.
Worth William H. 435 Washington boul.
Worth W. H. 1066 S. Central Park av.
Worthington Edward Stanley, 405 Erie
Worthington Elizabeth Mrs. Highland
Park
Worthington E. E. Lakota hotel
Worthington G. H. Oak Park
Worthington James L. Oak Park
Worthington J. Franklin 78, 50th (H.P.)
Worthington R. S. Oak Park
Worthy John, 304 Superior
Wragg George, 416, 57th (H.P.)
Wray Frank J. Austin
Wray James T. Evanston
Wray R. C. S. Austin
Wrenn George L. Rev. Highland Park
Wrenn H. A. 3252 South Park av.
Wrenn John H. 2917 Prairie av.
Wrenn W. B. 3252 Vernon av.
Wright Albert H. Evanston
Wright Alfred J. The Tudor

Wright Andrew J. Evanston
Wright Augustine W. 322 Ashland boul.
Wright A. L. Mrs. Oak Park
Wright A. M. 406 The Plaza
Wright A. M. Mrs. 111 Loomis
Wright A. W. 3354 Wabash av.
Wright Charles, Pullman
Wright Charles E. Evanston
Wright Charles F. Dr. 4311 Berkeley av.
Wright Charles H. 3716 Lake av.
Wright Charles S. 645, 61st, Eng.
Wright Charles W. 290 Park av.
Wright Chester Mrs. 1050 S. Central Park
av.
Wright Christopher, 678 W. Monroe
Wright Clarence H. Dr. 647 Washington
boul.
Wright C. K. Mrs. Pullman
Wright C. Walter, LaGrange
Wright Ebenezer, 645, 61st, Eng.
Wright Edgar A. 31 Best av.
Wright Edward, 14 Astor
Wright Edward J. 4335 Ellis av.
Wright E. G. 5900 Michigan av.
Wright E. J. H. 1079 W. Taylor
Wright Frances E. A. Miss, Hinsdale
Wright Frank, 113 Cass
Wright Frank G. 4422 Lake av.
Wright Frank L. Oak Park
Wright Frank P. 647 Washington boul.
Wright Frank S. 467 Jackson boul.
Wright Gabriel K. Hinsdale
Wright George, 4422 Lake av.
Wright George, Hinsdale
Wright George Mrs. 4017 Vincennes av.
Wright George A. 4225 Oakenwald av.
Wright George E. 4257 Grand boul.
Wright George F. 22 Walton pl.
Wright George F. Mrs. 22 Walton pl.
Wright George P. Irving Park
Wright George W. 4017 Vincennes av.
Wright Harriet B. Miss, 2930 Lake Park
av.
Wright Henry G. 517 Greenleaf av.
Wright Henry M. 4819 Madison av.
Wright H. C. 5900 Michigan av.
Wright H. M. 3963 Ellis av.
Wright H. M. Evanston
Wright H. T. Virginia hotel
Wright James, 1805 Indiana av.
Wright James, 3921 Grand boul.
Wright James G. 36 Woodlawn Park
Wright Johanna V. D. Mrs. 3136 Lake
Park av.
Wright John, 346 Burling
Wright John C. 174 Fremont
Wright John E. 290 Park av.
Wright John E. 647 Washington boul.
Wright John F. 388 W. Adams
Wright Joseph, 4119 Grand boul.
Wright J. Joseph 36 Woodland Park
Wright Josephine L. Miss, 1093 Wash-
ington boul.
Wright Julian V. 54, 20th
Wright J. M. 1800 Indiana av.
Wright Lyman D. 4321 Berkeley av.

Wright L. R. Hotel Imperial
Wright Mamie Miss, 3963 Ellis av.
Wright Martha Miss, 1805 Indiana av
Wright Nathaniel T. 2941 Michigan av.
Wright Newton D. Evanston
Wright Peter R. 682½ Washington boul.
Wright P. L. 3012 Michigan av.
Wright Reuben, 4343 Berkeley av.
Wright S. H. 4812 Lake av.
Wright Thomas, Wilmette
Wright Thomas A. 3601 Michigan av.
Wright Thomas M. 7334 Stewart av.
Wright T. S. Mrs. 4432 Lake av.
Wright Walter C. 4742 Monroe av.
Wright Warren, 4400 Lake av.
Wright William H. Mrs. Evanston
Wright William L. 3341 Forest av.
Wright William M. 4400 Lake av.
Wright William V. D. 3136 Lake Park av
Wright Wilmer, 1911 Michigan av.
Wright Winslow Mrs. 1839 Indiana av.
Wright W. H. 961 Park av.
Wright W. M. 345 Warren av.
Wright W. Parker, 4236 Prairie av.
Wrightson Hugh 2433 Commercial(L.V.)
Wrigley Thomas, Oak Park
Wrigley Walter, 1016 Washington boul.
Wrigley William jr. 422 The Plaza
Wrisley A. B. Lombard
Wrisley George A. 2478 Commercial
    (L.V.)
Wrixon Thomas W. 1548 Sheridan rd.
Wuichet L. 814 Pullman bldg.
Wulff Henry, Jefferson Park
Wulff Robert, Irving Park
Wullweber Otto L. 1151 Seminary av.
Wunder Frank A. 2211 Michigan av.
Wurtele Joseph G. Riverside
Wurts Charles Pemberten, 216 The Plaza
Wurzberger L. M. 3232 South Park av.
Wurzburger Jonas, 333 Burling
Wurzburger Louis Mrs. 333 Burling
Wyatt F. O. 7 Chalmers pl.
Wyatt Robert L. 390 Washington boul.
Wyatt S. W. 3232 Calumet av.
Wyatt William W. 327 Bowen av.
Wyckoff F. B. 7110 Yale
Wyckoff W. H. Evanston
Wyckoff W M. Evanston
Wycoff Eva Emmet Miss, 236 Sunnyside
    av.
Wycoff John, 236 Sunnyside av.
Wygant Alonzo, 537 Jackson boul.
Wygant Bernard 131 Park av.
Wylde Edward, Hinsdale
Wyles Susan O. Mrs. 6530 Madison av.
Wyles William, Sherman house
Wylie David, 9 St. James pl.
Wylie George W. 6348 Stewart av.
Wylie W. F. 4214 Oakenwald av.
Wyman C. E. 1495 Fulton
Wyman Edward F. Evanston
Wyman Franklin, 5420 Ridgewood ct.
Wyman Harry J. 12 Hamilton av.
Wyman James D. Austin
Wyman J. H. 6457 Dickey

Wyman Richard F. Mrs. Evanston
Wyman Richard H. Evanston
Wyman R. L. 525 W. Monroe.
Wyman Walter C. Evanston
Wyman W. D. 4362 Oakenwald av.
Wyman W. L. Austin
Wyne William B. 1010 Washington boul.
Wynkopp H. T. Mrs. 267 Winchester av.
Wynn Edwin, 507 W. Monroe
Wynne John, 496 Lasalle av.
Wynne J. Edward, 8 Burton pl.
Wynne Madeline G. Mrs. 9 Ritchie pl.

YAGER WILLIAM A. 2243 Michigan
    av.
Yagle W. F. 185 Burling
Yakel John A. 4220 Ellis av.
Yale J. A. 369 Chicago av.
Yale J. L. 9 Ritchie pl.
Yale Rachel Mrs. Austin
Yardley Thomas W. 588 Division
Yarnell John K. 4551 Evans av.
Yarr Bartel, 811 Washington boul.
Yates Millard F. 999 Wilcox av.
Yates Nettie A. Mrs. 663 W. Monroe
Yates Thomas, 6952 Webster av. Eng.
Yeates William W. 4232 Prairie av.
Yeomans Clara Dr. 1048, 75th (H. P.)
Yeomans George G. 4167 Berkeley av.
Yerkes Charles S. Oak Park
Yerkes Charles T. 3201 Michigan av.
Yetman C. E. Oak Park
Yocum John L. 2306 Indiana av.
Yoe C. C. Virginia hotel
Yoe Lucian G. 476 Dearborn av.
Yoe Peter L. 476 Dearborn av.
Yondorf A. 583 Lasalle av.
Yondorf Charles, 2547 Indiana av.
Yondorf David, 190, 32d
Yondorf Maude Miss, 2960 Prairie av.
Yondorf Simon, 2960 Prairie av.
York Alice Miss, 4101 Grand boul.
York Anna Miss, 4101 Grand boul.
York Edna Miss, 1837 Michigan av.
York H. Mrs. 1837 Michigan av.
York John, 43 Centre av.
York John B. 43 Centre av.
York John H. 181, 25th
York J. Devereux, 614 Division
York William S. 4101 Grand boul.
Yorke W. H. Oak Park
Yorty John, Mayfair
Yott Frank, 1856 Barry av.
Young A. N. Evanston
Young Benjamin J. 4207 Indiana av.
Young B. Bicknell, 531 Belden av.
Young Caryl, 1704 Michigan av.
Young Caryl B. 1704 Michigan av.
Young Cecile Miss, 2032 Calumet av.
Young Charles L. Longwood
Young C. H. Mrs. 3319 Calumet av.
Young D. J. 3736 Forest av.
Young Edith G. Miss, 341 Washington
    boul.
Young Edward A. 341, 62d (H. P.)
Young Edward C. Longwood

Young Elbert S. 5406 Ellis av.
Young Ella Mrs. 235 Michigan av.
Young E. L. Granada hotel
Young E. L. Mrs. 327 Warren av.
Young Frank, 227, 52d (H. P.)
Young Frank O. Blue Island
Young Frank W. 676 W. Adams
Young F. S. 736 W. Adams
Young George, 7330 Yale
Young George H. Mrs. Austin
Young George W. Auditorium annex
Young Harry, 4207 Indiana av.
Young Harry P. Oak Park
Young Henry G. 4032 Prairie av.
Young Henry M. 3004 Prairie av.
Young James, Evanston
Young James, 664 Evanston av.
Young James N. Tracy
Young James T. 4240 Indiana av.
Young John Mrs. 447 W. Congress
Young John, 461 Warren av.
Young John M. 6642 Harvard
Young J. E. 71 Park av.
Young J. S. Dr. 341 Washington boul.
Young Kimball, The Ontario
Young Late Miss, 531 Belden av.
Young Linn H. 3953 Michigan av.
Young Louis, 1207 Wilton av.
Young Luther C. 4124 Drexel boul.
Young L. E. Mrs. 243 Michigan av.
Young Marie A. Mrs. 4307 Oakenwald av.
Young Martha E. Mrs. 708, 42d
Young Mary Miss, 18 Waverly pl.
Young Max, 254, 61st (H. P.)
Young Mazzucato Mme. 531 Belden av.
Young Nellie Miss, The Ontario
Young Nelson, 5140 Indiana av.
Young N. L. 435 Washington boul.
Young Otto, 2032 Calumet av.
Young Ulrich, 227, 52d (H. P.)
Young William, 2032 Calumet av.
Young William S, 427 Evanston av.
Young W. D. 797 Warren av.
Young W. W. 4465 Lake av.
Youngblood R. N. 735 Chestnut, Eng.
Youngdahl Alfred J. 376 Washington boul.
Younglove Ira S. 3104 Calumet av.
Younglove Truman G. 3570 Vincennes av.
Younglove W. W. Mrs. 522 Fullerton av.
Yuille George A. 240, 61st (H.P.)
Yung Emil, 1137 Lunt av.
Yunker August, Hotel Imperial

ZAHRINGER CHARLES T. 4420 Champlain av.
Zander Aug. 239 Bissell
Zander E. W. 2749 N. Robey
Zang William, Evanston
Zarbell Iver C. 4132 Ellis av.
Zaun G. F. Dr. 122 Seminary av.
Zearing James R. Dr. 3600 Michigan av.
Zeddies F. W. 4504 Vincennes av.

Zeese Albert, 95 Buena av.
Zeese Alexander, 95 Buena av.
Zeiger Gebhardt W. 1103 N. Clark
Zeis Jacob H. 6814 Union av.
Zeisler Adolph, 307 Chicago av.
Zeisler Joseph Dr. 2932 Lake Park av.
Zeisler Sigmund, 568 Division
Zeiss C. Morgan Park
Zeiss Henry C. F. 11 Aldine sq.
Zeitner Julius H. 2303 Commercial (L.V.)
Zelie Lucina C. Mrs. 2518 Prairie av.
Zellar Susan Mrs. 3716 Lake av.
Zeller Andrew P. 6428 Stewart av
Zellmann William, 542 Lasalle av.
Zeltner John E. 4422 Prairie av.
Zemansky H. W. 3233 Indiana av.
Zemansky Nathan J. 3233 Indiana av.
Zeno William A., M.D. 497 Cleveland av.
Zenos Andrew C., Rev. 2 Chalmers pl.
Zernitz John P. 690 Fullerton av.
Zernitz Julius C. 690 Fullerton av.
Zernitz J. D. 690 Fullerton av.
Zeublin Charles Prof. 6052 Sheridan av.
Zeublin John E. 6052 Sheridan av.
Zeug Ferdinand, 2922 Groveland av.
Ziegfeld Carl, 501 W. Adams
Ziegfeld F. Dr. 501 W. Adams
Ziegfeld F. jr. 501 W. Adams
Ziegfeld William, 501 W. Adams
Ziegler Herman, Tracy
Ziegler John S. 602 Lunt av.
Ziesing August, 2569 N. Ashland av.
Ziesing Helene Miss, 2569 N.Ashland av.
Zilla John Rev. Elmhurst
Zimmerman Arnold W. Tracy
Zimmerman ClintonS.HotelWindermere
Zimmerman George E. 271 Fremont
Zimmerman Gustav A. 683 Sedgwick
Zimmerman Harold, 197 Fremont
Zimmerman John S. 200 Warren av.
Zimmerman Joseph, Hinsdale
Zimmerman J. E. 6640 Oglesby av.
Zimmerman Milton T. 528, 61st, Eng.
Zimmerman Wm. 5621 Washington av.
Zimmermann John, 509 W. Adams
Zimmermann Wm. F. 526 Fullerton av.
Zinn Frank H. 1225 Wilcox av.
Zinn George E. Dr. 518 Washington boul.
Zipf Edward 166 Fremont
Zipf Oscar R. Riverside
Zitt J. Henry, 1159 N. Clark
Zitzewitz Herman, 3283 Beacon
Zoller Walter G. 171 Ashland boul.
Zollmann Gustav Rev. 419 Winthrop av.
Zollmann John, 419 Winthrop av.
Zook David L. Highland Park
Zorge Robert J. 74 Maple
Zscheck G. S. 148 S. Oakley av.
Zuckerman S. Mrs. 77 Bowen av.
Zuetell William, Edison Park
Zulfer Anton G. 4438 Prairie av.
Zwetow Samuel R. 439 Winchester av.

La Ferté

CHICAGO:
- - - 2121 Michigan Avenue - - -

PARIS:
- - - 10 Rue Louis le Grand - - -

Milliners,.....

Gown and

Habit=Makers.

Ozonate Lithia Water

EXCELS IN THE TREATMENT OF RHEUMATISM, GOUT AND URIC ACID

Because "Lithia Ozonate," combined with "White Rock Spring Water" is the most active and searching solvent for Uric Acid (the attested cause of Gout and Rheumatism) in the group of Lithias.

From the many testimonials of its merit and efficiency, we mention only a few:

Dr. D. R. Brower.	Dr. Lackerstein.
" E. F. Ingals.	" J. E. Rhodes.
" E. Pynchon.	" C. F. Ely.
Dr. Sarah Hackett Stevenson.	

FOR SALE BY ALL DRUGGISTS

AND

White Rock Spring Company

**55 MEAGHER STREET
CHICAGO**

Send For Circular　　　　　　　　**Telephone Canal-212**

NTH.

SUBURBAN LIST.

E BLUE BOOK.

THE NAMES OF THE PROMINENT
HOLDERS OF THE SUBURBS OF
ICAGO WITHIN A RADIUS OF
TWENTY-FIVE MILES.

SUBURBAN LIST.

AUSTIN.

NORTH CENTRAL AVENUE.

221 Dr. & Mrs. R. C. Newell
225 Mr. & Mrs. N. B. Wallace
225 Miss M. Edith Wallace
225 Frank P. Wallace
227 Mr. & Mrs. John S. Date & dr.
243 Mr. & Mrs. G. W. Church
243 Mrs. E. C. Harrison
303 Mr. & Mrs. Charles S. Castle
303 Mr. & Mrs. Edward Church
307 Mr. & Mrs. Stephen Lissenden
311 Mr. & Mrs. Andrew Lindsey
317 Mr. & Mrs. Wm. P. Jenkins
319 Mr. & Mrs. Edward Francis
325 Mr. & Mrs. Geo. B. Cogdal
337 Mr. & Mrs. Frank L. Race
339 Mr. & Mrs. Frank Emerson
339 Mr. & Mrs. Francis Canfield
405 Dr. & Mrs. Geo. B. Charles & dr.
431 Mrs. A. S. Gardner & dr.
435 Mr. & Mrs. Geo. W.Cone & drs.
529 Mr. & Mrs. Russell Hall & dr.

---

116 Mr. & Mrs. J. J. McCarthy.&drs.
126 Mr. & Mrs. Edward A. Adams & dr.
136 Mrs. Rachel Yale
216 Mr. & Mrs. Frederick W. Meadows
218 Mr. & Mrs. A. L. Jordan
218 Henry W. McFarlane
222 Mr. & Mrs. A. C. Collins
234 Mr. & Mrs. Virgil E. Titus
238 Mr. & Mrs. E. G. Hobler
238 Mrs. Emily Wood
238 Mrs. Chas. B. Wells
308 Mrs. M. L. Patrick & drs.
308 Charles B. Patrick
324 Mr. & Mrs. G. L. Voorhees
408 Mr. & Mrs. Wm. Amerson & dr

418 Mrs. Mary P. Dunton
418 Gilbert Newhall jr.

SOUTH CENTRAL AVENUE.

111 Mr. & Mrs. T. P. Elliott & dr.
117 Mr. & Mrs. Arthur Eaton
123 Mr. & Mrs. George M. Davis
231 Mr. & Mrs. M. M. Merrick
231 Mr. & Mrs. B. F. Buck
301 Mr. & Mrs. Edward R. Knowlton
305 Mr. & Mrs. Z. J. Frost jr.
309 Mr. & Mrs. H. E. Stewart
313 Mr. & Mrs. Edward Andrew
317 Mr. & Mrs. C. F. Bonney
317 Mrs. E. A. Bonney
317 Lester Moss
325 Mr. & Mrs. Geo.A. Philbrick
333 Mrs. W. R. Woodbury
333 Sidney H. Woodbury
403 Mr. & Mrs. T. A. Snow

---

108 Mr. & Mrs. R. R. Jampolis
112 Mrs. Andrew J. Bassett
122 Mr. & Mrs. J. W. Bennett
226 Mr. & Mrs. W. E. Thurber
230 Miss Marion Hecox
230 Miss M. Hecox
230 Miss Daisy Hecox
230 J. Frink Hecox
312 Mr. & Mrs. Jacob J. Walser
324 Mr. & Mrs. Thomas Cihlar
400 Mr. & Mrs. E. J. Nelson

CHICAGO AVENUE.

5437 Mr. & Mrs. Paul G. Biggs
5437 Mr. & Mrs. Bert P. Biggs
5513 Mr. & Mrs. Thomas Langford
5515 Mr.&Mrs.Chas.W.Blatherwick
5708 Mr. & Mrs. Edwin Blackman

ERIE STREET

5801 Mr. & Mrs. Orval G. Blair
5728 Mr. & Mrs. F. L. Johnson
5904 Mr. & Mrs. S. D. McNeal

SOUTH FRANKLIN AVENUE.

121 Mr. & Mrs. Harry Pillinger
135 Rev. & Mrs. E. Middleton
315 Mr. & Mrs. Fred Eddy
319 Mr. & Mrs. Jos. H. Barnett
415 Mr. & Mrs. A. D. Shaw
515 Mr. & Mrs. Charles C. Turner
  Receiving day Wednesday
515 Mrs. Anna E. Bradford
  Receiving day Wednesday
212 Alex. Lendrum
320 Mr. & Mrs. G. W. Kretzinger
420 Mr. & Mrs. Alfred B. Johnson

SOUTH HOWARD AVENUE.

117 Mr. & Mrs. Gus A. Kreis
123 Mr. & Mrs. John O'Laughlin
221 Mr. & Mrs. Wellington Stetson
221 Mrs. Emma Gordon
303 Mr. & Mrs. John Worley
329 Mr. & Mrs. F. H. Alden
329 Dr. S. H. Kelly
329 A. B. Johnson.
322 Mr. & Mrs. C. Heber Turner
  & drs.
326 Mrs. F. Butler

INDIANA STREET.

5411 Mr. & Mrs. B. M. Shurtleff
5411 Ira G. Sibley
5437 Mr. & Mrs. E. S. Osgood & dr.
5437 Wm. P. Osgood
5437 Fred S. Osgood
5437 Mrs. E. H. Bryan
5437 Mrs. M. P. Thomas

MIDWAY PARK.

5715 Mrs. E. M. Rossiter & dr.
5715 Harold Rossiter
5715 Mr. & Mrs. Henry J. Wade
5735 Mr. & Mrs. E. J. Whitehead
cor. Prairie Mr. & Mrs. F. C. Beeson
cor. Franklin Mr. & Mrs. Edw. Funke
5915 Mr. & Mrs. Jos. C. Davidson
5919 Mr. & Mrs. Jas. G. Wakefield
5923 Mr. & Mrs. Wm. J. Ford
5927 Mr. & Mrs. Wm. H. Rounds
5927 Charles H. Rounds
5927 William P. Rounds

5927 Fred C. Rounds
5927 Mr. & Mrs. Erastus S. Pease
5939 Mr. & Mrs. Daniel R. McAuley
5953 Mr. & Mrs. Charles H. Lew
  Receiving day Wednesday

OHIO STREET.

5411 Mr. & Mrs. Thos. H. Wilson
5517 Mr. & Mrs. M. Frank Murray
5517 Chas. C. Murray
5517 Frank G. Murray
5517 George R. Murray
5517 Harold G. Murray
5521 Mrs. C. C. Carlton
5521 Lewis F. Carlton
5521 Mr. & Mrs. S. J. Crafts
5531 Mr. & Mrs. N. M. Bassett & drs.
5641 Dr. Mary J. Kearsley
5641 Miss Margaret I. Isgrig
5641 Mr. & Mrs. Paul C. Doty
5641 Rev. Luther Pardee
5719 Mr. & Mrs. T. R. Coates
5719 G. R. Coates
5723 Mr. & Mrs. O. P. Emerson
5727 Mr. & Mrs. R. C. S. Wray
5737 Dr. & Mrs. Chas. Reiterman
5739 Mr. & Mrs. Samuel E. Vermilyea
5803 Mrs. Catherine Schlecht & dr.
5803 Oscar G. Schlecht
5809 Mr. & Mrs. Lawrence A. Norton
5809 Miss Isabel Bulckens
5809 Miss Louise Bulckens
5809 Miss Sarah Colby
5815 Mr. & Mrs. L. E. Hall
5905 Mr. & Mrs. Alpheus McCallum

5700 Mr. & Mrs. L. E. Race
cor. Prairie av. Miss Louise M.
  Schock
5916 Mr. & Mrs. Charles R. Phoenix
5930 Mr. & Mrs. Bernard D. Wikoff
5946 Mr. & Mrs. John Thompson
5946 W. W. Thompson
cor. Austin av. Mr. & Mrs. A. P. Mullin
  Receiving day Wednesday

ONTARIO STREET.

5703 Mr. & Mrs. Charles A. Hitchcock
5703 Charles A. Hitchcock jr.
5729 Mr. & Mrs. L. S. Pinney & drs.
5901 Mr. & Mrs. W. P. Freeman & dr.
5903 Mrs. John Duryee
5917 Mr. & Mrs. Axel Strom

5921 Mr. & Mrs. Henry F. Gehrke
5941 Mr. & Mrs. Wm. A. Weaver

5706 Mr. & Mrs. Percy V. Castle
5710 Mr. & Mrs. R. H. Trail
5722 Mrs. M. Wimersted
5722 Mr. & Mrs. Chas. J. Brown
5722 Oscar T. Wimersted
5722 Mr. & Mrs. H. W. Schmitt
5726 Mrs. P. Schneider
5800 Dr. & Mrs. John Massman
5820 Mr. & Mrs. Thomas L. Miller
5822 Mr. & Mrs. S. H. Dwight
5822 Mr. & Mrs. Chas. W. Dwight
5822 Frank A. Dwight
5902 Mr. & Mrs. W. F. Dagget
5914 Mr. & Mrs. Richard Ramsey & drs.
5914 Zatham B. Ramsey
5948 Mr. & Mrs. John Faulkner

NORTH PARK AVENUE.

225 M. G. Miller
214 Dr. & Mrs. Earnest H. Smith
214 Mrs. M. A. Tiffany
232 Dr. & Mrs. J. A. Campbell
416 Mr. & Mrs. E. D. Robinson
458 Mr. & Mrs. Howard Robertson

SOUTH PARK AVENUE.

113 Mr. & Mrs. John R. Bowes
119 Mr. & Mrs. E. B. Moore
123 Mrs. Nattie Lacy
123 Daniel Lacy
127 Mr. & Mrs. John B. Matthews
127 Mr. & Mrs. W. C. Matthews
131 Mr. & Mrs. H. M. Alexander & drs.
131 Charles A. Alexander
135 Mr. & Mrs. George H. Parks
135 Phil. W. Huston
205 Mr. & Mrs. George Plumb
209 Mr. & Mrs. Wm. H. Lober
213 Mr. & Mrs. C. R. Vandercook
217 Mr. & Mrs. J. D. Vandercook
221 Mr. & Mrs. W. W. McFarland
227 Mr. & Mrs. Joseph Kretzinger
313 Mr. & Mrs. Chas. W. Wilson
313 Mrs. E. C. Henderson
313 W. M. Meredith
317 Mr. & Mrs. Arthur A. Crafts
317 Miles B. Crafts
321 Mr. & Mrs. Frank J. Wray
331 Mr. & Mrs. R. J. Ingram & dr.
339 Mrs. G. G. Fortier
47

401 Rev. Louis A. Campbell
413 Mr. & Mrs. J. V. B. Hoyle
413 Mr. & Mrs. F. X. Mudd
425 Mr. & Mrs. Henry H. Rearden
425 Mrs. M. A. Ellis
527 Mr. & Mrs. John F. Cremin
527 James Carroll
531 Mr. & Mrs. Fred'k C. Lusche
535 Mr. & Mrs. J. Mason Duffy
553 Mr. & Mrs. Simon Callaghan

118 Mr. & Mrs. John Purvis & drs.
128 Mr. & Mrs. Geo. A. Stewart
128 W. A. Parsons
138 Mr. & Mrs. R. P. Price
138 John P. Price
200 Mr. & Mrs. Geo. H. White & dr.
206 Mr. & Mrs. F. E. Bartelme
210 Mr. & Mrs. J. W. Lusk
226 Mr. & Mrs. Henry Potwin&drs.
226 Harry A. Potwin
304 Mr. & Mrs. Edwin E. Bush

NORTH PINE AVENUE.

237 Mrs. C. A. Black
239 Rev. & Mrs. John C. Hill & dr.
239 Chauncey B. Hill
315 G. A. Kreis
401 Mr. & Mrs. Warner B. McCall
409 Dr. & Mrs. Frederick R. Hunt
415 Mr. & Mrs. Newell D. Gilbert
441 Mr. & Mrs. Stephen J. Olbrich
519 William M. Tyler
521 Mr. & Mrs. Ellis B. Fitch
536 Mr. & Mrs. L. H. Howell
537 Mr. & Mrs. Jonathan Dunfee & dr
214 Mr. & Mrs. R. Hefter
314 Miss Albertina Hefter
540 Mr. & Mrs. Peter G. Wing

SOUTH PINE AVENUE.

109 Mr. & Mrs. Louis Loewy
113 J. P. Garner
123 Mr. & Mrs. A. A. Shepard
123 Albert A. Shepard
127 Samuel B. Hazzard
127 Mrs. B. C. Rucker
211 Mr. & Mrs. L. H. O'Connor
215 Mr. & Mrs. C. D. Gammon
221 Mr. & Mrs. Charles Hennick
227 Mrs. Jane Gasparo & dr.
301 Mr. & Mrs. David Oliphant
303 Mr. & Mrs. Wm. Scatchard jr.
305 Mr. & Mrs. Wm. N. Burns

307 Rev. & Mrs. Jos. F. Bartlett
307 Harry A. Bartlett
307 Mrs. Geo. H. Young
309 Mr. & Mrs. J. D. Haggard
311 Mr. & Mrs. Wm. T. Meredith &
     dr.
317 Mr. & Mrs. Wm. Haythorn & dr.
325 Mr. & Mrs. Jere Horton
345 Mr. & Mrs. Louis F. Lattan
cor. Washington boul. Mr. & Mrs.
     Horace Boyd Frazier

118 Dr. & Mrs. C. E. Jones
330 Mr. & Mrs. J. D. MacLean &dr.
334 Mr. & Mrs. E. S. Walker & dr.
338 Mr. & Mrs. Zalmon G. Sholes
cor. Washington boul. Mr. & Mrs.
     Robert B. Muir

POPLAR AVENUE.
431 A. L. Roberts

NORTH PRAIRIE AVENUE.
cor. Midway Park Mr. & Mrs. F. R.
     Schock

SOUTH PRAIRIE AVENUE.
119 Mrs. C. Stephan & drs.
119 Emanuel L. Stephan
119 Traugott F. Stephan
123 Mr.& Mrs.David MacNaughtan
123 Miss F. A. Motlong
127 Mr. & Mrs. Kenneth McLaroth
209 Mr. & Mrs. Richard Burke
209 Rev. & Mrs. R. H. Burke
209 Miss Margaret Mackin
215 Mrs. James Mason & dr.
221 Mr. & Mrs. Edwin F. Crowley
225 Mr. & Mrs. Thomas M. Hunter
313 S. H. Eveleth
543 Mr. & Mrs. Wm. A. Smith
547 Richard Dunne
547 Miss Julia Dunne
547 Miss Mary Dunne
549 Mr. & Mrs. Geo. E. Kurts

124 Mr. & Mrs. W.P. Gunthorp
124 Walter J. Gunthorp
202 Miss Anna M. Jordan
202 Mr. & Mrs. Walter S. Weston
202 Mr. & Mrs. Lorenzo D. Wood-
     bury
214 Mr. & Mrs. James C. Oran
234 Mr. & Mrs. Thos. G. Richey
234 Charles G. Richey

234 John R. Richey
234 George H. Ackerman
234 A. A. Johnson
316 Mr. & Mrs. Julius M. Blanchard
558 Mr. & Mrs. Lanson D. Miller
558 Miss May Lathrop

ROBINSON AVENUE.
54 Mrs. H. L. Bortree
54 M. R. Bortree
84 Mr. & Mrs. Franklin S. Bortree
94 Mr. & Mrs. H. W. Bortree
201 Mr. & Mrs. E. R. Case
209 Dr. & Mrs. J. B. Darling & dr.
405 Mr. & Mrs. Frank J. Hurley
419 John Luedders

SOUTH BOULEVARD.
5636 Mr. & Mrs. H. F. Frink
5636 Miss Clara Creote
5640 Mr. & Mrs. Geo. Frink
5646 Mr. & Mrs. John J. Miller
5800 Mr. & Mrs. James H. Hoes
5802 Mr. & Mrs. Geo. H. Disbrow
5804 Mr. & Mrs. A. L. deGignac
5816 Mr. & Mrs. Robert G. Pole
5820 Mr. & Mrs. A. B. Clark
5900 Mr. & Mrs. Charles A. Stokes
5904 Mr. & Mrs. Charles Gritman
5916 Mr. & Mrs. Geo. R. Seavert
5918 G. H. Nye & drs.
5936 Mr. & Mrs. Geo. G. Crose
5936 H. Boyd Crose

SUPERIOR STREET.
5625 Mr. & Mrs. Jacob E. Decker
5811 Mr. & Mrs. Chas. L. Reif-
     schneider
5915 Mr. & Mrs. John M. Jones
5915 Mr. & Mrs. H. R. Buck
5929 Mr. & Mrs. F. L. Phillips

5900 Mr. & Mrs. Edwin T. Wanzer
5900 Mr. & Mrs. Elias Wanzer
5900 Clarence H. Wanzer
5936 Mr. & Mrs. Geo. N. Seyfried

SOUTH WALLER AVENUE.
113 Mr. & Mrs. Julius H. Martin&dr.
113 Arthur Martin
117 Mr. & Mrs. Wm. G. Lloyd
121 Mr. & Mrs. E. P. Chapell
121 Mr. & Mrs. George E. Chapell
121 H. O. Campbell

125 Prof. & Mrs. Spencer R. Smith
129 Mr. & Mrs. J. E. Thorndyke
201 Dr. & Mrs. Henry Stratford
201 Mr. & Mrs. Stanley C. Crafts
201 Edward Wayt
201 Mr. & Mrs. Wm. F. Ray
215 Mr. & Mrs. Wm. B. Conklin
217 Mr. & Mrs. Wm. M. Hulbert
223 Mr. & Mrs. John R. Hunt
305 James D. Wyman
305 W. L. Wyman
309 Mr. & Mrs. I. A. Robinson
333 Mrs. L. Crane & dr.
335 Mr. & Mrs. A. R. Marriott
349 Mr. & Mrs. David Brown
401 Mr. & Mrs. Fred A. Hill

112 Dr. & Mrs. G. P. Head
112 Mrs. M. R. Head
116 Mr. & Mrs. Arthur G. Moore
116 Mr. & Mrs. S. Morris Hodge
128 Mr. & Mrs. James M. Hatch
128 Mr. & Mrs. C. W. Hatch
128 Mr. & Mrs. Geo. M. McCaull
128 Thomas W. Hatch
132 Mr. & Mrs. M. L. Vanderkloot
206 Mr. & Mrs. Wm. A. Pillinger
316 Mr. & Mrs. Charles Arnold

316 Mr. & Mrs. Irving L. Arnold
316 Mrs. James Ronalds

WALNUT AVENUE.

117 Mr. & Mrs. Thomas J. Cavey
137 Mr. & Mrs. Horace G. Teele
345 F. M. Powell
525 William Williams
120 Mr. & Mrs. Geo. F. Barton
120 Mr. & Mrs. Wm. W. Thompson
124 Mr. & Mrs. Fred Welge
124 Mr. & Mrs. S. L. Smith

WASHINGTON BOULEVARD.

5307 Alexander Van Siclen
5433 Mr. & Mrs. Clayton E. Crafts
5433 William C. Crafts
5915 Mr. & Mrs. Edwin F. Abbott
5600 Mr. & Mrs. Walter G. Beeson

WILLOW AVENUE.

218 Mr. & Mrs. Wallace B. Gilbert
218 James H. Gilbert
229 Mr. & Mrs. Jas. W. Wilson & dr.
229 John Platt
121 H. O. Campbell
303 Mr. & Mrs. Perley D. Castle
315 Mr. & Mrs. George E. Swinscoe

BERWYN.

Mr. & Mrs. F. I. Abbott
Mr. & Mrs. L. Abbott
Mr. & Mrs. George H. Anderson
Mr. & Mrs. I. J. Archer
Mr. & Mrs. G. W. Ashby
Mr. & Mrs. C. A. Bader
Mr. & Mrs. C. C. Baldwin
Mr. & Mrs. Charles Blanden
Mr. & Mrs. Charles Bliss
Mr. & Mrs. Wirt Burch
Dr. F. S. Carpenter
Mr. & Mrs. P. D. Cregar
Dr. & Mrs. F. H. Davis
Mr. & Mrs. William Dennis
Mr. & Mrs. J. E. Dunn
Mr. & Mrs. E. O. Eames
Miss C. P. Forsyth
Miss J. P. Forsyth
Mr. & Mrs. James F. Forsyth
Mr. & Mrs. P. C. Grigg
Mr. & Mrs. Joseph Grove
Mr. & Mrs. Julian S. Hall
Mr. & Mrs. L. W. Haring
Mr. & Mrs. D. C. Harries

Mr. & Mrs. Wilton Hartman
Mr. & Mrs. M. M. Hitchcock
Mr. & Mrs. Orin Hubbell
Mr. & Mrs. W. R. Israel
Mr. & Mrs. J. E. Johnson
Mr. & Mrs. Walter E. Lackey
Mr. & Mrs. H. C. Latshaw
Mr. & Mrs. Robert Leslie
Oliver G. Leslie
Dr. & Mrs. Arthur MacNeal
Rev. & Mrs. B. F. Martin
Mr. & Mrs. James McCartney
Rev. & Mrs. William McLellan
Mr. & Mrs. E. McSchooler
Mr. & Mrs. N. M. Mixer
Mr. & Mrs. C. W. Morris
Mr. & Mrs. Frank Pease
Mr. & Mrs. Robert Perkins
Mr. & Mrs. W. F. Pfuderer
Mr. & Mrs. C. E. Piper
Mr. & Mrs. Otis Piper
Mr. & Mrs. W. B. Porter
Mr. & Mrs. F. Poulkney
Mr. & Mrs. George W. Reynolds

Mr. & Mrs. H. M. Rogers
Rev. & Mrs. J. C. Sage
Dr. & Mrs. Edwin Schell
Mr. & Mrs. A. J. Seabrook
Mrs. H. E. Sprinks & drs.
Mr. & Mrs. G. A. Thompson
Mr. & Mrs. G. S. Thompson
Miss Helen Thompson

Miss L. Thompson
Mr. & Mrs. A. P. Thorne
Mr. & Mrs. H. M. Trussell
Mr. & Mrs. W. H. Tuttle
Mr. & Mrs. J. Latham Warren
Mr. & Mrs. M. M. Wood
Mr. & Mrs. W. H. Woodward

BROOKDALE.

ADDISON AVENUE.

7034 Mr. & Mrs. H. C. W. Cowdery
　　& dr.

OGLESBY AVENUE.

6915 Mr. & Mrs. O. L. Downey
6951 Mr. & Mrs. Edwart Hart & dr.
7015 Mr. & Mrs. S. S. Baker
————
6914 Mrs. Mary Gaulter & dr.
6914 Fred E. Gaulter

6914 Frank J. Gaulter
6920 Mr. & Mrs. M. R. Stuart
6926 Mr. & Mrs. A. H. McGrew
6940 Mr. & Mrs. Geo. R. Thwaite

SEVENTIETH STREET.

900 Dr. & Mrs. Eugene A. Curtis

SIXTY-NINTH STREET.

855 Mrs. L. K. Bloss & dr.
855 Harry H. Bloss
887 Mr. & Mrs. E. O. Leavell

BRYN MAWR.

EUCLID AVENUE.

7125 Mr. & Mrs. J. D. Hyde & dr.
7137 Mr. & Mrs. H. J. Cassady
7149 Mr. & Mrs. Chas. A. Barker
7209 Mr. & Mrs. Edward Kemeys
　　Receiving day Tuesday

7120 Mr. & Mrs. M. I. Beck
7126 Mr. & Mrs. George Best
　　Receive Saturday evg.
7126 John Lundie
7134 Mr. & Mrs. H. L. Sayler
　　Receiving day Tuesday
7138 Mr. & Mrs. Maurice J. McGrath
7138 George B. McGrath
7140 Mr. & Mrs. S. T. Bowen
7150 Charles L. Peckham
7154 Mr. & Mrs. J. H. Tufts
7156 Mr. & Mrs. George A. Otis
7206 Mr. & Mrs. George Canfield
7210 Mr. & Mrs. George Clingman
7222 Mr. & Mrs. Fred Ricker
7226 Mrs. Virginia H. McGill
　　Receiving day Tuesday
7226 Mr. & Mrs. Thos. Bayton Mc-
　　Gill
7226 Mr. & Mrs William McGill
7242 Mr. & Mrs. John Harvey

JEFFERY AVENUE.

7209 Mr. & Mrs. Alfred E. Holt
7251 Mr. & Mrs. C. S. Cleaver
7251 C. A. Cleaver
7251 P. F. Cleaver
7251 Miss Mary Cleaver

7212 Mr. & Mrs. S. W. Hume
7216 Mr. & Mrs. L. N. Flagg

KENWOOD TERRACE.

422 Mrs. Hannah Probasco
422 Mr. & Mrs. Lyman B. Lang-
　　worthy
440 Mr. & Mrs. George C. Bour
　　Receiving day Thursday
468 Mr. & Mrs. Evans Blake
472 Miss Hattie B. Moore
472 Edward Moore
472 Mr. & Mrs. F. F. Bour
　　Receiving day Tuesday
524 Mr. & Mrs. E. Lee Heidewich
532 Mr. & Mrs. E. B. Winger
527 Rev. & Mrs. J. Frothingham
527 Miss M. F. Frothingham
　　Receives Tuesday & Friday
567 Mr. & Mrs. Phil A. Starck
　　Receiving day Wednesday

CHELTENHAM.

BOND AVENUE.

7839 Mr. & Mrs. Michael Schmitz
7859 Mr. & Mrs. T. H. Rasch
7859 Theodore Rasch

7816 Mr. & Mrs. Frederick Deutsch
7816 Simon O. Deutsch
7816 Miss Pauline Deutsch
7820 Mr. & Mrs. Fred A. Purdy
    & dr.
7822 Mr. & Mrs. Frank Dolan
7850 Mr. & Mrs. Peter Wallin
7850 Luke Clark
7850 Mr. & Mrs. J. F. Ryder

EDWARDS AVENUE.

7828 Mr. & Mrs. C. H. Howell
7843 Mr. & Mrs. Charles Everett
7918 Mr. & Mrs. C. N. Camp

REYNOLDS AVENUE.

7817 Mr. & Mrs. M. M. Richey
7827 Mr. & Mrs. Wm. M. Townsend
7929 Mr. & Mrs. W. P. Ingraham

SEVENTY-EIGHTH STREET.

191 Mr. & Mrs. A. C. Wheaton

SEVENTY-NINTH STREET.

287 Mr. & Mrs. P. M. Stults

EDISON PARK.

Mr. & Mrs. A. A. Ames
Mr. & Mrs. Carleton Dickenson
Mr. & Mrs. W. W. Eaton
Mr. & Mrs. J. M. Ettinger
Mr. & Mrs. James F. McCabe
Mr. & Mrs. W. G. McGinnis

Mr. & Mrs. G. H. Shute
Mr. & Mrs. H. A. Thayer
Mr. & Mrs. T. J. Welden
Mr. & Mrs. John Wingert
Mr. & Mrs. William Zuetell

ELMHURST.

Prof. & Mrs. C. J. Albert
Dr. & Mrs. F. H. Bates
Mr. & Mrs. Cyrus Bentley
Rev. & Mrs. August Berens
Prof. Chas. Bouer
Mr. & Mrs. John Boyd & dr.
Prof. & Mrs. Herman Brodt
Mr. & Mrs. A. S. Brownell
Col C. Page Bryan
Mr. & Mrs. Thos. B. Bryan
Mr. & Mrs. John R. Case
Mr. & Mrs. H. A. Christy
Mr. & Mrs. George H. Cushing
Mr. & Mrs. L. A. Denig & drs.
Mr. & Mrs. Daniel Egan
Mr. & Mrs. James Emery
Mr. & Mrs. W. H. Emery & dr.
Mr. & Mrs. A. F. Emery
Mr. & Mrs. J. V. Farwell jr.
Dr. & Mrs. F. J. T. Fisher
Mr. & Mrs. Harry L. Glos
Mr. & Mrs. Jacob Glos
Mrs. L. A. Hagans
Wilbur E. Hagans
Dr. & Mrs. Geo. F. Heideman
Mr. & Mrs. D. T. Higginson

G. M. Higginson
Mr. & Mrs. F. A. Hoffman, jr.
Mr. & Mrs. Thomas Hogan
Mr. & Mrs. C. M. Howe
Prof. & Mrs. Daniel Irion
Mr. & Mrs. James King
Mr. & Mrs. Albert F. Kidder
Dr. A. H. Kirby
Mr. & Mrs. C. G. Kircher
Mrs. F. Koch
Wirt Litchfield
Wm. H. Litchfield
Arthur Lueder
Prof. & Mrs. John Lueder
Mr. & Mrs. M. L. Marks
Prof. & Mrs. Emil Otto
Prof. & Mrs. John C. Rahn
Prof. George Range
Miss Rebecca A. Richardson
Mr. & Mrs. Frederick S. Rockwood
Mr. & Mrs. F. B. Rockwood & dr.
Harvey Rockwood
Sprague S. Rockwood
Prof. & Mrs. Geo. F. Rosche
Mr. & Mrs. George Sawin
Prof. & Mrs. George A. Sorrick

Mr. & Mrs. H. G. Struckmann
Mr. & Mrs. Emil Stuedle
Mr. & Mrs. Frank Sturges & drs.
Mr. & Mrs. Lee Sturges
Mr. & Mrs. S. G. Taylor jr.

Charles Wade
Miss Carrie Wade
Mr. & Mrs. T. Edward Wilder
Rev. & Mrs. M. L. Williston
Rev. John Zilla

EVANSTON.

ASBURY AVENUE.

921 Mr. & Mrs. Charles Page
939 Mr. & Mrs. T. J. Tigan
1025 Mr. & Mrs. O. D. Angole
1035 Mr. & Mrs. Edw. D. Goodwin
1321 Mr. & Mrs. W. H. Cutler
1501 Mr. & Mrs. Geo. A. Bennett
1501 Edward F. Hamilton
1513 Mr. & Mrs. Francis A. Hardy
1583 Mr. & Mrs. Walter T. Dwight
1713 Mr. & Mrs. H. K. Hinsdale
1713 Miss Lilian Burgard
1723 Mr. & Mrs. H. W. Hinsdale
1733 Mr. & Mrs. Chas. H. Chandler
1733 H. E. Chandler
1735 Mr. & Mrs. Harvey H. Reese
1745 Mr. & Mrs. Henry W. Raeder
1825 Mr. & Mrs. Charles J. Morse
1847 Mr. & Mrs. Willard Bennett
1849 Mr. & Mrs. Chas. J. Gilbert

902 Mr. & Mrs. T. E. Miller
906 Mr. & Mrs. J. N. Doerr
922 Mr. & Mrs. F. H. Lewis
926 Mr. & Mrs. Geo. T. Rennison
928 Mr. & Mrs. W. A. Ratcliffe
930 Mr. & Mrs. John F. King
1026 Mr. & Mrs. E. T. Stokes
1042 Mr. & Mrs. O. K. Keppler
sw. cor. Crain Mr. & Mrs. F. Stuyvesant Peabody
1204 Mr. & Mrs. C. O. Gleason
1204 Charles Gleason
1232 Mr. & Mrs. C. K. Pittman
1302 Mr. & Mrs. W. J. Battams
1314 Mr. & Mrs. Hartwell Osborn
1318 Mr. & Mrs. John H. Morse
1318 Irving Morse
1326 Mr. & Mrs. Leighton Turner &
  drs.
1326 Walter I. Turner
1326 Miles L. Turner
1334 Mr. & Mrs. Milton L. Record
1404 Mr. & Mrs. Thomas H. Beebe
1404 Archibald A. Beebe
1410 Mr. & Mrs. Stephen J. Herben
1416 Mr. & Mrs. John Freeman
1416 Charles E. Freeman

1416 Edgar K. Freeman
1454 Mr. & Mrs. Dorr A. Kimball
1460 Mr. & Mrs. Charles W. Buckley
1512 Mr.& Mrs.Edward Hampstead
1570 Dr. & Mrs. Wm. Bell Mann
1570 Robert R. Mann
1570 Mrs. Irene B. Phillips
1570 Mrs. Sarah Bailey
1570 Mr. & Mrs. George N. Jewett
1574 Mrs. M. A. Hawes
1704 Mr. & Mrs. John Dickinson
1720 Mr. & Mrs. E. A. Hyde
1724 Mr. & Mrs. H. G. Savage
1724 Frank M. Savage
1734 Mr. & Mrs. Birney J. Moore
1734 Mr. & Mrs. Orin Moore
1734 Mrs. Marion De Clercq
1742 Mr. & Mrs. Herman D. Cable
1812 Mr. & Mrs. J. H. Raymond &
  dr.
1812 E. F. Raymond
1828 Mr. & Mrs. F. S. Brown
1840 Mr. & Mrs. C. J. Stokes & drs.
1840 Frederick C. Stokes
1906 Mr. & Mrs. W. R. Troxell
1912 Mr. & Mrs. E. A. Ostrander
1912 Miss E. P. Whitcomb
1918 Mr. & Mrs. Fred J. Wilson
1920 Mr. & Mrs. M. S. Crowe

ASHLAND AVENUE.

1628 Mr. & Mrs. H. H. DeLoss

BENSON AVENUE.

517 Mr. & Mrs. H. C. Hallier
521 Mr. & Mrs. Frank Trahan
909 Mr. & Mrs. N. Morper
911 Mr. & Mrs. H. DeVere Simmons
913 Mr. & Mrs. F. W. Brown
939 Mr. & Mrs. W. H. Robertson
  & dr.
939 James G. Robertson
943 Mr. & Mrs. E. E. Bradley
947 Dr. & Mrs. Wilbur F. Green
1001 Rev. D. F. Smith

1001	Miss M. E. Smith	416	Miss Katherine Jones
1001	Miss M. H. Smith	836	Mr. & Mrs. A. G. Palmer
1001	Miss Agnes F. Smith	836	Mrs. Ward H. Case
1007	Mr. & Mrs. E. Koll	838	Mr. & Mrs. Arthur G. Baker
1015	Mr. & Mrs. Geo. W. Hotchkiss	838	William Hathaway
1015	Miss Elma Graves	928	Mr. & Mrs. T. Fansler
1019	Mr. & Mrs. F. D Mitchell	930	Mrs. J. W. Joly
1019	Mrs. E. W. Pither	930	Mrs. Theodore Lavigne
1019	Mrs. C. A. Whedon	934	Mr. & Mrs. H. B. Layton
1023	Mr. & Mrs. W. M. Ellis & dr.	938	Mr. & Mrs. James Hibben
1029	Mr. & Mrs. Alex. Shields	938	Mrs. H. E. Day
1035	Mr. & Mrs. C. C. Ash	944	Mr. & Mrs. J. H. Butler & dr.
1137	Mr. & Mrs. M. C. Plochman	1002	Mr. & Mrs. Proctor Cooley
1203	Mr. & Mrs. G. H. Kelley	1006	Mr. & Mrs. Geo. W. Hutchens
1203	Miss Hattie E. Haradon	1010	Mrs. Ella V. Morse
1205	Mr. & Mrs. O. B. Hutchens	1010	Mrs. Sarah Morse
1207	Mr. & Mrs. F. S. Pooler	1010	Miss May C. Spicer
1207	Mrs. J. M. Fisk	1018	Mr. & Mrs. G. W. Stone
1209	Mr. & Mrs. E. L. Howard	1022	Mrs. E. S. Halsey & drs.
1215	Mr. & Mrs. W. M. Turner	1028	Mr. & Mrs. W. L. Williams
1219	Mr. & Mrs. James J. McCauley	1034	Mrs. W. H. Dee & drs.
1223	Mr. & Mrs. Wilbur E. Coe	1034	Arthur W. Dee
1227	Mr. & Mrs. A. D. Sanders	1036	Miss Elizabeth Ayres
1301	Mr. & Mrs. N. D. Wright	1036	Miss Julia Ferguson
1301	Mrs. G. Munsel	1040	Mr. & Mrs. James E. Low
1301	Charles E. Wright	1040	Mrs. D. E. Barker
1301	Mr. & Mrs. J. A. Price	1040	Miss R. A. Barker
1301	Mrs. A. E. Jones	1106	Mr. & Mrs. R. H. Watson
1305	Mr. & Mrs. Fritz Schroeder	1112	Mr. & Mrs. G. H. Brown
1305	Fred C. Schroeder	1124	Mr. & Mrs. Geo. B. Woodworth
1305	William A. Schroeder	1134	Mr. & Mrs. Henry Voigts
1311	Mr. & Mrs. Wm. Carney	1138	Rev. & Mrs. John Ellis
1315	Rev. & Mrs. J. H. Alling & drs.	1146	Mr. & Mrs. Fred Whitfield
1317	Mr. & Mrs. William Haigh	1206	Mr. & Mrs. John McNab & drs.
1321	Mr. & Mrs. Geo.M. Leffingwell		
1325	Mr. & Mrs. H. B. Hill & dr.	1212	Mr. & Mrs. Edwin H. Gamble
1329	Mrs. J. B. Hilton & dr.	1218	Mr. & Mrs. H. L. Boltwood
1335	Mr. & Mrs. R. C. Hacker	1226	Mr. & Mrs. Frank Barhydt
1401	Mr. & Mrs. J. G. Darling	1230	Mr. & Mrs. O. L. Baskin
1401	Mrs. M. J. Switzer	1238	Mr. & Mrs. B. W. Josselyn & dr.
1403	Rev. & Mrs. Thos. Craven & dr.		
		1238	William H. Josselyn
1403	Henry Craven	1244	Mr. & Mrs. N. B. Barlow
1405	Mrs. Virginia Harper & dr.	1304	Mr. & Mrs. W. W. Munsell
1407	Mr. & Mrs. John W. Strong	1312	Mr. & Mrs. R. N. Dudley
1411	Mrs. Martha Howland & drs.	1322	Mrs. E. S. Bliss & drs.
1411	Arthur H. Howland	1322	Mrs. E. B. Strong
1413	Mr. & Mrs. Charles Wesley	1326	Mr. & Mrs. George M. Patterson
1419	Mr. & Mrs. J. R. Graves & dr.		
1423	Mr. & Mrs. J. H. Kenney & dr.	1404	Mr. & Mrs. David Jamieson
1427	Mr. & Mrs H. B. Stevens	1408	Mr. & Mrs. Charles G. Neely
1431	Mr. & Mrs. H. S. Stevens	1418	Mrs. M. W. Dale & dr.
1453	Mr. & Mrs. Samuel Kauffman	1422	Mr. & Mrs. C. E. VanVoorhis
1455	Mr. & Mrs. C. G. Rosenow	1426	Mr. & Mrs. F. E. Potter
1459	Rev. & Mrs. George C. Booth	1430	Mrs. Hannah Hardy & drs.
1615	John H. Klock	1430	Silas Hardy

1432 Mr. & Mrs. George Woodley
1432 Mrs. S. N. Rogers
1464 Mrs. Mary Hebblethwaite&dr.

CENTRAL STREET.

1425 Mr. & Mrs. Lewis Blanchard
2121 Mr. & Mrs. John F. Stewart
2209 Dr. & Mrs. Finley Ellingwood

2106 Rev. & Mrs. A. E. Burrows
2106 Dr. & Mrs. J. T. Dixon
2218 Mr. & Mrs. John W. Brown
2218 Richard Brown
2218 Mrs. R. E. France
2624 Mr. & Mrs. Geo. A. Richards
2624 Mr. & Mrs. M. G. Richards

CHICAGO AVENUE.

317 W. C. Van Benschoten
507 Mr. & Mrs. Jacob Rinn & dr.
725 Mr. & Mrs. Guilford M. Whitney
807 Mr. & Mrs. W. S. B. Mathews & drs.
817 Mr. & Mrs. Heary C. Stone
835 Miss Fannie E. Blye
933 Rev. & Mrs. Wm.E.Wilkinson
941 Mr. & Mrs. O. F. Gibbs & drs.
1011 Mr. &.Mrs. Myron M. Drury
1023 Mr. & Mrs. J. M. Brown & dr.
1027 Rev. & Mrs. J. O. Foster
1039 Mr. & Mrs. T. H. Watson & drs.
1143 Mrs. Hannah Adams
1201 Dr. & Mrs. Thomas S. Bond
1201 John R. Mills
1209 Mrs. John O'Leary & dr.
1209 D. P. O'Leary
1211 Mr. & Mrs. W. L. Gallup
1215 Mr. & Mrs. E. H. Parker
1217 Dr. & Mrs. C. B. Freeman
1235 Mr. & Mrs. Chas. K. Ober
1239 Mr. & Mrs. John E. White&dr.
1239 Mrs. Alida M. Griggs
1243 Mr. & Mrs. G. C. Hick
1249 Mr. & Mrs. J. T. Wray
1301 Mr. & Mrs. H. G. Ransom
1303 Rev. & Mrs. W. C. Dickinson & dr.
1303 Clarence Dickinson
1307 Mr. & Mrs. Henry Whipple
1311 Mr. & Mrs. Geo. H. Smith & drs.
1311 Mr. & Mrs. Rollin W. Miller
1315 Mrs. E. L. D. Harvey

1319 Mr. & Mrs. Lewis Babbitt
1323 Mr. & Mrs. Richard B. Carr
1323 Richard B. Carr jr.
1323 Clyde M. Carr
1327 Mr. & Mrs. P. R. Woodford
1403 Mr. & Mrs. W. F. Dudley
1405 Mrs. N. S. Thompson & drs.
1405 Mrs. V. T. Collins
1411 Mr. & Mrs. George Dunoon
1415 Mr. & Mrs. Homer Roberts
1419 Mr. & Mrs. Samuel VanBen-
      schoten
1505 Mr. & Mrs. Lemuel J. Arthur
1509 Mr. & Mrs. J. J. Reimers & dr.
1509 Charles D. Reimers
1509 J. Arthur Dixon
1515 Mr. & Mrs. W. C. Wilson
1515 John H. Wilson
1519 Mr. & Mrs. James Kean
1619 Dr. & Mrs. C. H. Quinlan
1619 Miss Sophie E. Quinlan
1619 Miss Anna C. Quinlan
1619 Miss Jeannie S. Quinlan
1619 Charles E. Quinlan
1619 George H. Quinlan
1619 Edward B. Quinlan
1703 Prof. & Mrs. Oliver Marcy
1703 Mrs. Annie M. Davis
1709 Dr. & Mrs. M. C. Bragdon
1717 Mr. & Mrs. Isaac R. Hitt
1717 Mr. & Mrs. Isaac R. Hitt jr.
1723 Mr. & Mrs. Wm. Griswold Burt
1735 Mr. & Mrs. Frank Gould & dr.
1735 Frank M. Gould
1745 Mr. & Mrs. J. W. Campbell
1803 Mr. & Mrs. A. E. Dunn
1815 Mrs. R. M. Hatfield
1815 Mr. & Mrs. S. A. Kean & dr.
1817 Mr. & Mrs. H. M. Walker
1817 Mrs. Sarah H. Newell
1817 Miss H. H. Newell
1831 Rev. & Mrs. Jean F. Loba
      Receiving day Tuesday
1837 Mrs. M. J. Ball

640 E. R. Willard
1130 Miss Clara H. Rogers
1130 Miss Rusha H. Rogers
1138 Mr. & Mrs. Marvin A. Dean
1138 Mr. & Mrs. Wm. J. Canfield
1144 Mr. & Mrs. J. Wightman & dr.
1202 Prof.& Mrs. S. R.Winchell&dr.
      Receiving day, Friday
1202 Harley C. Winchell
1208 Mr. & Mrs. B. H. Pendleton

1218 Mr. & Mrs. John A. Childs
1220 J. J. Shutterly & drs.
1220 Dr. E. E. Shutterly
1220 John J. Shutterly jr.
1234 Dr. & Mrs. Frank M. Brewer
1234 Dr. & Mrs. Frank B. Brewer
1234 C. S. Brewer
1312 Mr. & Mrs. A. C. Bird & dr.
1312 Miss Alberta Bird
1312 George H. Lippincott
1318 Mr. & Mrs. A. L. Sewell
1318 Alfred B. Sewell
1326 Mrs. Caroline C. Scales
1332 Dr. & Mrs. Edw. H. Webster
1402 Mr. & Mrs. A. L. Belknap
1402 Fred W. Belknap
1406 Mr. & Mrs. Warren Ewen
1410 Mr. & Mrs. B. D. Caldwell
1414 Mr. & Mrs. B. S.Sanborn &drs.
1420 Dr. & Mrs. E. P. Clapp
1420 Mrs. A. E. Clapp
1430 Mr. & Mrs. W. L. Wells & dr.
1434 Mr. & Mrs. W. F. Everts & dr.
1468 Mrs. Earl S. Powers
1468 Mr. & Mrs. J. H. Patterson
1468 William G. Hoag
1468 Roscoe L. Wickes
1468 Hamilton E. Grepe
1468 William Corlies
1468 Henry H. Kerr
1468 Miss Alice B. Hallam
1614 Dr. & Mrs. P. D. Harding
1614 Mrs. H. D. Clifford
1616 Prof & Mrs. Henry Cohn
Receive Wednesday 3 to 5 p. m.
1618 Mr. & Mrs. W. E. Clifford&dr.
1624 Mr. & Mrs. Lucius W. Conkey
1628 Dr. & Mrs. A. B. Clayton
Receiving day Wednesday
1632 Mrs. W. M. Chapin & drs.
1632 Frederick S. Chapin
1632 Gardner Read
1634 Mr. & Mrs. Geo.D.Stonestreet
1634 Mr. & Mrs. Frederick Arnd
1634 J. N. Crampton
1634 William Zaug
1636 Prof. & Mrs. J. Scott Clark
1640 Mr. & Mrs. W. H. Judson &dr.
1640 Mr. & Mrs. Frank P. Judson
1640 Harry W. Whitehead
1640 Fred E. Trotter
1640 William Tilghman
1714 Mr. & Mrs. J. A. Pearsons
1718 Mr. & Mrs. H. A. Pearsons
1718 Harry P. Pearsons
1724 Capt. & Mrs. J. R. Fitch & dr.

1724 Mrs. S. C. Bragdon
1728 Miss Frances E. Willard
1728 Miss Anna A. Gordon
1728 Mrs. Mary Fockler
1728 Miss Irene Fockler
1730 Mr. & Mrs. O. H. Merwin
1732 Mrs. E. M. Seaverns
1738 Mr. & Mrs. W. H. Onderdonk
Receiving day Tuesday
1744 Dr. & Mrs. H. B. Hemenway
1802 Mr. & Mrs. C. A. Rogers
1802 Miss Henrietta L. Rogers
1808 Col. & Mrs.A.M.Woolfolk&dr.
1808 Clinton S. Wolfolk
1810 Mr. & Mrs. Chas. E. Smith
1812 Mr. & Mrs. Charles P. Mitchell
 & drs.
1816 Mrs. M. H. Wilder
1824 Mr. & Mrs. George T. Cook
1830 T. P. Ballard
1834 Mrs. K. D. Edwards & dr.
1838 Mrs. Joseph Cummings
1838 Mrs. Daniel Bonbright

CHURCH STREET.

423 Mr.& Mrs. H. H. C. Miller &
 dr.
615 Mr. & Mrs. Wm. C. Wentworth
619 Mrs. Minerva Hebbard & dr.
625 Mr. & Mrs. W.F.Merriam & dr.
625 Mr. & Mrs. Joseph F. Pride
625 Mr. & Mrs. William Boyd
629 Mr. & Mrs. S. W. Gilman
707 Mr. & Mrs. Andrew Simpson
713 Mrs. Emma Vandercook & dr.
715 Mr. & Mrs. G. E. Redfield &
 drs.
715 Miss Celia Sargent
1121 Mr. & Mrs. John F. Hahn
1321 Mr.& Mrs. Benjamin M.Butler
1327 Mr. & Mrs. Duane P. Whitney
1327 Mrs. E. H. Whitney
1333 Mr. & Mrs. G. W. P. Atkinson
1333 G. Clarence Atkinson
1333 Pearce Atkinson
1333 Miss Marguerite P. Grover
1333 Miss Mary Pearce
1415 Mr. & Mrs. Henry S. Shedd

408 Mr. & Mrs. William Deering &
 dr.
612 Mr. & Mrs. John Morris
614 Mrs. W. L. Harris & dr.
618 Mr. & Mrs. F. H. Manny
618 Robert E. Orr

618 Mrs. Emeline Manny
1016 H. F. Olmsted
1016 W. B. Olmsted
1104 Mr. & Mrs. N. P. Williams
1106 Mr. & Mrs. P. C. Lutkin
1106 Mrs. R. Carman
1106 A. R. Carman
1114 Mr. & Mrs. A. J. McCormick
1122 Mr. & Mrs. E. P. Greenough
1122 George R. Hoke
1318 Mr. & Mrs. T. C. Lewis & dr.
    Receiving day Tuesday
cor. Judson av. Mr. & Mrs. C. B.
    Congdon
cor. Judson av. Miss L. Willsie

CLARK STREET.

615 Mr. & Mrs. J. L. Morse & drs
615 Charles L. Morse
621 Mrs. Catherine Creïghton
710 N. Miller Hutchinson

DAVIS STREET.

305 Mr. & Mrs. E. S. Lacey & drs.
307 Mr. & Mrs. H. M. Boice
309 Mr. & Mrs. A. O. Bosworth
315 Mr. & Mrs. Isaac Bailey
321 Mr. & Mrs. Wm. Wallace & dr.
331 Dr. J. D. Quinlan & dr.
331 Miss Jane H. Quinlan
331 Charles S. Quinlan
515 Dr. G. W. Whitefield
515 Rev. & Mrs. John Whitefield
ne. cor. Chicago av. Avenue House
    Mr. & Mrs. Charles G. Ayars
    D. E. Bradley
    Mr. & Mrs. C. E. H. Brelsford
    C. W. Cranshaw
    Mr. & Mrs. W. H. Damsel & dr.
    Mr. & Mrs. H. S. Farwell
    W. A. Hamilton
    Will Hubbard
    Fred C. Miller
    Miss E. C. Smith
    George R. Smith
    Mr. & Mrs. Geo. G. Wilcox & dr.
    Mr. & Mrs. C. W. Wilmerworth
se. cor. Sherman William T. Balding
803 E. J. Williams
1007 Mr. & Mrs. B. C. Sargent
1013 Mrs. Talitha C. Reiley
1105 Mrs. James Ayars
1105 H. M. Ayars
1127 Mr. & Mrs. J. J. Parkhurst
1127 Mr. & Mrs. R. W. Lynch

1221 Dr. & Mrs. R. H. Kimball
1221 Miss Grace E. Hess
1223 Mr. & Mrs. A. F. Towne
1309 Mrs. M. A. Van Alstine & dr.
1309 Mr. & Mrs. Clyde M. Carr
1315 Mr. & Mrs. H. J. Wallingford
1323 Mr. & Mrs. Chas. F. Dwight
1323 Mrs. E. A. Chapman

    ————

204 Mrs. Geo. Carleton Cassard &
    dr. *Receiving day Thursday*
204 George Carleton Cassard
210 Mr. & Mrs. E. E. Willis
210 Miss Helen M. Kitchell
cor. Forest av. Mr. & Mrs. H. R.
    Wilson & dr.
404 Mr. & Mrs. L. H. Boutelle & dr.
410 Mr. & Mrs. James Rood & dr.
410 Mr. & Mrs. James Rood jr.
422 Rev. & Mrs. M. Raymond
422 Wm. M. Raymond
438 William C. Garwood
502 Mr. & Mrs. D. B. Gardener &
    drs.
502 Miss Lucy Spencer Pinney
502 Mr. & Mrs. Ernest J. Rogers
520 Mr. & Mrs. N. B. Lewis
520 Miss Nannie M. Hines
520 Mrs. Emily D. Pierson
522 Mr. & Mrs. Geo. D. Corson
522 Mrs. Ettie E. Leonard & dr.
522 Miss Anne J. Dinsmoor
524 Mr. & Mrs. J. B. Wilming
810 Dr. & Mrs. O. H. Mann
1016 Mr. & Mrs. Edw. Mendsen
1106 Mr. & Mrs. L. C. Pitner
1206 Mr. & Mrs. Harry B. Judson
1206 Richard G. Trotter
1300 Mr. & Mrs. W. S. Candee & dr.
1300 Dr. & Mrs. A. B. Clark & drs.
1300 Mr. & Mrs. J. A. Wendell & dr.
1300 Dr. & Mrs. L. D. Henderson
1300 Mr. & Mrs. B. S. Hatch
1300 Mrs. Benj. F. Lombard
1300 Miss Mary A. Gillespie
1300 G. Alfred Grant-Schaefer
1306 Dr. & Mrs. John H. Burchmore
1316 Mr. & Mrs. Chas. W. Elphicke
1318 R. Waite Joslyn
1318 A. B. Humphrey
1318 Miss Suzanne Mulford

DEMPSTER STREET.

217 Mr. & Mrs. Wm. Liston Brown
217 Miss Harriet L. Seamour

221 Mr. & Mrs. C. P. Wheeler
227 Mr. & Mrs. I. N. Hardin & drs.
227 John H. Hardin
231 Mrs. C. L. Woodyatt
513 Mr. & Mrs. F. F. Stewart&drs.
515 Mr. & Mrs. George W. Hess
515 Mrs. K. A. Meriman
519 Mr. & Mrs. J. M. Thomas
519 Samuel Robinson
523 Mr. & Mrs. F. N. Myers
607 Mrs. William R. Grafton & dr.
607 William H. Grafton
607 Murray L. Grafton

cor. Forest av. Mr. & Mrs. Daniel
     H. Burnham
318 Mr. & Mrs. A. D. Foster
318 Mr. & Mrs. John A. Miller
416 Mrs. William Smith
416 William Smith
910 Mr. & Mrs. George B. Ide
1016 Mrs. W. Scharff
1016 John P. Scharff
1020 Mr. & Mrs. J. R. Crocker
1024 Mr. & Mrs. John West
1028 Mrs. L. E. Fisk
1028 J. E. Baker
1028 M. J. Blackwell
1028 L. S. Stephenson
1028 L. E. Henry

EMERSON STREET.

711 Mrs. H. C. Hoag
711 Mrs. L. D. Post & drs.
717 Mr. & Mrs. Andrew Paterson
725 Mr. & Mrs. H. H. Gage
729 Mr. & Mrs. E. S. Weeden

718 Prof. & Mrs. Chas. Horswell
724 Mr. & Mrs. Edw. F. Webster
724 Mrs. Martha Webster
724 Malcolm C. Harper
726 Mr. & Mrs. Chas. P. Stevens &
     dr.
726 Mr. & Mrs. C. Nelson Stevens
730 Mr. & Mrs. T. M.Hubbard&dr.
730 Mrs. A. E. Hubbard
732 Mr. & Mrs. Irvin E. Clapp

EVANSTON AVENUE.

809 Mr. & Mrs. J. C. Murphy
809 Miss Margaret Carroll
925 Mr. & Mrs. John Jerauld
1117 Mr. & Mrs. Edward S. Clark
1129 Mr. & Mrs. James A. Rowe

1311 Mr. & Mrs. F. C. Johnson
1311 Mrs. James Stanton
1311 Mr. & Mrs. James Lill
1315 Mrs. Emma P. Kaler
1315 Mr. & Mrs. J. B. Calligan
1319 Mr. & Mrs. Wm. E. Chambers
1319 Mrs. Judith W. McGill
1325 Mr. & Mrs. C. O. Scudder
1325 Mrs. Mary Beyer

1306 Mr. & Mrs. F. R. Carver
1406 Mr. & Mrs. J. N. Knapp
1418 Mr. & Mrs. Louis Wille
1428 Mr. & Mrs. J. C. Waterbury

FOREST AVENUE.

653 Mr. & Mrs. Wm. Pullen & drs.
703 Mr. & Mrs. Frank I. Packard
707 Mr. & Mrs. W. A. Webster
733 Mr. & Mrs. W. M. R. Vose
733 Frederick P. Vose
739 Mr. & Mrs. E. A. Downs
739 Lewis C. Downs
805 Mr. & Mrs. J. B. Bright
817 Mrs. Elizabeth Hathaway&dr.
817 Charles H. Hathaway
821 Mr. & Mrs. J. G. Hallett
829 Mrs. George N. Falley & dr.
843 Mr. & Mrs. E. R. Thomas
843 Mr. & Mrs. A. B. Adair
1005 Mrs. H. C. Poppenhusen
1005 Conrad H. Poppenhusen
1015 Mr. & Mrs. W. M. Green
1015 Mr. & Mrs. David Bonnell
1127 Mr. & Mrs. W. V. Griffin
1133 Mr. & Mrs. John L. Fyffe
1139 Mr. & Mrs. W. D. Hitchcock
     & dr.
1143 Mr. & Mrs. James W. Donnell
1305 Dr. & Mrs. Charles G. Fuller
1305 Miss Elizabeth White
1331 Mr. & Mrs. W. H. Bartlett
1509 Mr. & Mrs. E. R. T. Armstrong
     & dr.
1513 Mrs. Louisa C. Stanford & dr.
1513 Arthur L. Stanford
1513 George E. Stanford

522 Mr. & Mrs. Peter Hendrickson
534 Rev. & Mrs. Geo. K. Hoover
630 Mr. & Mrs. Wm.H. Dyrenforth
708 Mr. & Mrs. George Nash
708 Herbert Arnison
726 Mrs. Catherine Johnson
730 Mr. & Mrs. W. C. Brown

736 Mr. & Mrs.Collins Shackelford
740 Mr. & Mrs. Charles H. Cowper
746 Mr. & Mrs. O. F. Carpenter
806 Mr. & Mrs. R. H. Wyman
932 Mr. & Mrs. John E. Poor
1006 Mr.& Mrs. Geo. W. Andrew
1010 Mr. & Mrs. Franklin Overbagh
1014 Mrs. S. J. Shaw & dr.
1014 George C. Shaw
1014 Mark W. Shaw
1020 Mr. & Mrs. W. G. Miller
1026 Mr. & Mrs. W. A. Sickles.
1232 Mrs. Richard Mason & drs.
1232 Charles D. Mason
1236 Mrs. Richard F. Wyman
1236 Walter C. Wyman
1240 Stewart B. Vowell
1314 J. R. Lindgren
1314 Miss Jenny Lindgren
1318 Mr. & Mrs. D. P. Donelson
1324 Mr. & Mrs. W. T. Rickards&dr.
1332 Mrs. M. E. Eddy
1404 Mr. & Mrs. Frank P. Frazier
1414 Mr. & Mrs. F. P. Crandon&drs.
1418 Mr. & Mrs. George Bancroft
1418 Allen R. Bancroft
1418 J. H. Bradbury jr.
1422 Mr. & Mrs. B. F. Weeks & dr.
1426 Mrs. E. E. Houston & drs.
1432 Mr. & Mrs. D. S. Cook
1508 Mr.& Mrs. Charles F. Grey&dr.
1608 Mr. & Mrs. Franklin G. Beach
1622 Mr. & Mrs. Curtis H. Remy

FOSTER STREET.

617 Prof. & Mrs. James T. Hatfield
617 Mrs. E. A. Smith & dr.
621 Mr. & Mrs. Horace W. Dick-
    erman
721 Mr. & Mrs. W. N. Perry & dr.
813 Mrs. H. P. Bissett & dr.
813 C. N. Bissett
720 Mr. & Mrs. R. M. Essick

GREENLEAF AVENUE.

827 Mr. & Mrs. Chas. T. Bartlett
1020 Mr. & Mrs. Geo. L. Parkhurst

GREENWOOD BOULEVARD.

235 Mr. & Mrs. W. A. Hammond
239 Mrs. Charles H. Rowe & dr.
415 Mr. & Mrs. C. H. Harbert
421 Mrs. W. G. White
421 Selden F. White

nw. cor. Hinman av. French House
Mr. & Mrs. A. T. Andreas
Charles Arnd
Mr. & Mrs. Benj. Bayless
Chas. T. Bayless
Geo. W. Bayless
Mr. & Mrs. W. C. Brooks
Mr. & Mrs. Louis F. Brown
Miss Minnie F. Brown
Mrs. Margaret Cassard & dr.
Mrs. K. H. Donelson
Mr & Mrs. Frank A. Fletcher
William Hayden
Mr. & Mrs. C. W. Hillman
R. C. Jacobsen
Arthur H. Johnson
Mr. & Mrs. S. A. Kimberley
W. H. Lewis
Mr. & Mrs. E. A. Mayo
Mr. & Mrs. W. G. Oliver
Mr. & Mrs. O. C. Phillips
George E. Powers
Miss Sarah F. Powers
A. F. Shedd
Mr. & Mrs. E. F. Sutton
Mr. & Mrs. J. V. Taylor
Will S. Tyson
Mr. & Mrs. O. E. Ward
Mrs. Eliza Woodward
1007 Mr. & Mrs. Thomas W. Bell
1007 Mr.& Mrs. Charles T. Boynton
1015 Dr. F. C. Dakin
1015 Richard L. Dakin
1015 Harry W. Dakin
1015 Miss Florence A. Dakin
1021 Mr. & Mrs. M. R. Powers
1021 Arthur N. Powers
1027 Mr. & Mrs. D. A. Coe
1317 Mr. & Mrs. John A. Briggs
1319 Mr.& Mrs. R.H. Aishton & drs.
1327 Dr. & Mrs. C. A. Van Anda &
    dr.
_____

nr. the Lake Mr.&Mrs. J.W. Camp-
    bell
J. McDougal Campbell
Coler Campbell
228 Mr. & Mrs. F. F. Peabody
320 Mr. & Mrs. James S. Murray
404 Mr. & Mrs. C. L. Williams &dr.
408 Mr. & Mrs. F. D. Raymond
412 Mr. & Mrs. Edward C. Carter
416 Dr. & Mrs. H. A. Freeman
422 Mr. & Mrs. E. L. Harpham
428 Mr. & Mrs. Joseph Hubbart
428 J. Roy Hubbart

518 Mr. & Mrs. Geo. L. Toppan
526 Mr. & Mrs. Frank N. Winne
528 Mr. & Mrs. George L. Stevens
618 Mrs. John Highland
1004 Mr. & Mrs. Gilbert A. Smith
1014 Mrs. E. N. Hill
1014 Volney W. Foster
1014 Albert V. Foster
1022 Mr. & Mrs. A. J. Wright
1022 Mr. & Mrs. C. H. Mears
1028 Mr. & Mrs. Fleming H. Revell
1104 Mr. & Mrs. W. O. Dean
1104 Charles R. Dean
1224 Mr. & Mrs. S. E. Hurlbut
1224 Charles H. Hurlbut
1228 Mr. & Mrs. J. L. Whitlock & dr.
1228 Harold H. Whitlock
1228 Royal J. Whitlock
1410 Rev. & Mrs. J. D. Matthius

GROVE STREET.

405 Mr.& Mrs.Robt.B.Kendall&dr.
405 Miss Susie D. Kendall
405 Robert R. Kendall
411 Mr. & Mrs. W. M. Scott & dr.
411 Charles F. Scott
413 Mrs. Seth Bullock & dr.
817 T. J. Noyes & dr.
907 Dr. & Mrs. Scott F. Verbeck
913 Mr. & Mrs. David Dunoon
1017 Mr. & Mrs. D. S. McMullen
1017 Mr.& Mrs. Roger B. McMullen
1027 Mrs. M. H. Bass
1027 George A. Bass
1027 Perkins B. Bass
1027 James K. Bass
1223 Mr. & Mrs. Tunis Isbester
1223 John H. Isbester

802 Mr. & Mrs. James Moore
922 Mr. & Mrs. Guy W. Greenman
1020 Mrs. Susan E. Davis & dr.
1020 W. Claude Davis
1020 John T. Davis
1020 S. Clarence Davis
1022 Mr. & Mrs. George B. Scripps'
1022 Miss Grace L. Scripps
1024 Mrs. Chas. H. Richmond &dr.
1024 Frederick S. Richmond
1024 Louis K. Comstock
1026 Mr. & Mrs. John Turner
1028 Mr. & Mrs. Andrew Hazlehurst
1030 Mr.&Mrs. Wm. G. Hemstead
1102 Mr. & Mrs. Howard Z. Hill
1112 Rev. & Mrs. A. W. Little

HAMILTON AVENUE.

323 Mr. & Mrs. Osgood T. Eastman
323 Miss Addie T. Chapman
cor. Michigan av. Judge Elliott Anthony
Mr. & Mrs. C. E. Anthony
George D. Anthony

318 Mr. & Mrs. E. F. Wyman
324 Mr. & Mrs. Jas. G. Campbell
428 Mr. & Mrs. A. L. Cayzer
428 J. D. Gorham

HAMLIN STREET.

617 Prof. & Mrs. Thos. F. Holgate
627 Prof. & Mrs. Henry Crew

HARRISON STREET.

2101 Mr. & Mrs. John W. Branch
2101 Mrs. G. H. Parker
2509 Mr. & Mrs. Jas. L. Johnston
2513 J. S. Leith
2515 Mr. & Mrs. John Q. Williams
2519 Mr. & Mrs. Albert Billingslea
2519 Claude Billingslea
2519 Edward Billingslea
2711 Mr. & Mrs. Fred M. Walters
2725 Mr. & Mrs. Fred T. Wood

2020 Mr. & Mrs.AndrewA.Swanson
2130 Mr. & Mrs. John Anderson
sw. cor. Hartrey rd. Mr. & Mrs. C. Hellstrom
2306 Mr. & Mrs. Charles R. Hogle
2316 Dr. & Mrs. Carter Wade
2318 Mr. & Mrs. Jas. H. Jagoe
2322 Mr. & Mrs. Charles A. Fitch
2410 Mr. & Mrs. Harcourt Mott
2410 Merritt H. Mott
2410 Mrs. Hannah A. Dunham
2514 Mr. & Mrs. Edward J. Dahms
2520 Count & Countess Edgar de Valcourt-Vermont
Receiving day Monday
2526 Mr. & Mrs. Frank Y. Norris
2602 Mr. & Mrs. Morris G. Holmes
2622 Mr. & Mrs. Frederick S.Oliver
2720 Mr. & Mrs. Sam'l A. Wilmot

HARTZELL STREET.

2311 Mr. & Mrs. John G. Brown

2210 Mrs. M. E. Orvis
2210 John C. Williams

2408 Mr. & Mrs. G. Grant Stewart
2408 Mrs. Margaret Dumond
2414 Mr. & Mrs. Wm. H. Burke
2418 Mr. & Mrs. Wm. Henschen &
     dr.
2418 H. Samuel Henschen

HINMAN AVENUE.

639 Mrs. Maud D. Parker
639 Miss Lillian M. Parker
641 Mr. & Mrs. A. C. Bearup
649 Mr. & Mrs. E. H. Hughes
703 J. G. Cowling
707 Mr. & Mrs. John E. Williams
713 Mrs. C. A. Ely & dr.
713 Mr. & Mrs. James C. Rogers
715 Mr. & Mrs. J. H. Wilbur
715 Miss Josephine M. Wilbur
715 Mrs. Henrietta Hiller
715 Miss Tina M. Haines
723 Mr. & Mrs. Frederick Mehring
743 Mr. & Mrs. J. C. Lane
747 Mr. & Mrs. M. O. Naramore
747 Judge M. D. Ewell
817 Rev. & Mrs. Lewis Curts
827 Mr. & Mrs. W. P. Marsh
831 Mr. & Mrs. William E. Hess
831 J. C. Hess
837 Mr. & Mrs. J. Milhening
845 Mr. & Mrs. O. H. Johnson
911 Mr. & Mrs. Geo. F. Hardie
915 Mr. & Mrs. A. H. Hall
919 Mr. & Mrs. H. L. Tolman &
     dr.
927 Mr. & Mrs. Charles Dowst
1017 Mr. & Mrs. Stephen F. ReQua
1043 Mr. & Mrs. A. C. Pinkham
1109 Mr.&Mrs. E. S. Taylor & dr.
1109 Miss Evelyn H. Stearns
1109 Edward Stearns
1111 Evan Moses /
1111 Miss Emma Moses
1111 Miss Bertha Kaderly
1123 Mr. & Mrs. H. R. Ross
1203 Mrs. Martha E. Sherman
1203 Mr. & Mrs. Edwin Sherman
1205 James Miller & drs. ·
1205 Benjamin Miller
1211 Mrs. Francis Gellatly
1221 Mr. & Mrs. Thaddeus P. Stan-
     wood
1225 Mr. & Mrs. Arthur B. Jones
1229 Mr. & Mrs. H. A. Keith
1229 Mrs. C. D. Howard
1229 Frank E. Howard

1235 Mr. & Mrs. G. H. Wells & drs.
1241 Mr. & Mrs. Edw. H. Buehler
     & dr.
1241 William Buehler
1247 Mr. & Mrs. A. D. Ferry
1247 Mrs. L. L. Kinney
1247 J. F. Kinney
1311 Mr. & Mrs. J. S. Currey
1319 Mr. & Mrs. Wm. H. Lee
1323 Mr. & Mrs. F. A. Holbrook
1323 Harry R. Holden
1323 Mrs. Jennie Ward Thompson
1327 Mr. & Mrs. L. R. Wing
1405 Mr. & Mrs. N. C. Gridley
1405 M. M. Gridley
1417 Mr. & Mrs. A. N. Young
1427 Mr. & Mrs. Albert R. Barnes
1433 Mr.&Mrs.Simeon Farweil&drs.
1503 Mr. & Mrs. H. P. Williams ·
1507 Mr. & Mrs. John E. Wilder
1507 Mr. & Mrs. J. H. Hurlbut
1513 Mr. &Mrs. W.E. Stockton & dr.
1519 Prof. & Mrs. Jos. Emerson&dr.
1521 Mr. & Mrs. G. P. Engelhard
1605 Mrs. Mary R. Shumway
1605 Miss S. H. Brayton, M. D.
1605 P. R. Shumway
1617 Mr. & Mrs. Chas. H. Aldrich
1625 Mr. & Mrs. H. C. Kennedy
1625 Mrs. S. K. Rogers
1625 Prof. & Mrs. John H. Gray
1625 Mr. & Mrs. S. T. French
1625 Dr. Alfred Hebert
1625 Thomas Beard
1625 E. J. Smith
1625 S. K. Wells
1631 Mr.&Mrs. Louis C. Tallmadge
1639 Dr. & Mrs. A.H. Parker & drs.
1639 E. Harry Parker
1639 Charles W. Parker
1639 A. H. Parker jr.
1711 Dr. & Mrs. W. A. Phillips
1719 Mr.&Mrs. Wm. D. Marsh &dr.
1719 Charles Williams
1725 Mr.&Mrs. Joseph F.Ward &dr.
1733 Mr. & Mrs. Frederick Arnd &
     dr.
1745 Prof. & Mrs. C. F. Bradley
1745 Arthur L. Brown
1805 Mr.& Mrs. Charles W.Meyrick
1805 Miss H. Lane
1805 Mr. & Mrs. W. H. Brown
1813 Mrs. C. J. Whitely & dr.
1813 Arthur Whitely
1813 Miss Kate A. Jackson
1813 Mrs. Jane H. Ball

1819 Mr. & Mrs. Nelson DeGolyer
1823 Mr.&Mrs. Charles W. Deering

646 Mr. & Mrs. Frank E. Winans
652 Mrs. G. A. VanEps & dr.
700 Mr. & Mrs. W. H. Booth
706 Mr. & Mrs. Medford Powell
710 Mr. & Mrs. F. D. Reynolds
716 Mrs. Thomas Wallace
716 Mrs. A. A. Sneed
729 Mr. & Mrs. W. L. Tomlins &dr.
730 Mr. & Mrs. Timothy Dwight & dr.
740 Mr. & Mrs. L. L. Smith
746 Mrs. A. H. Gunn
746 Richard G. Gunn
804 Mr. & Mrs. W. L. Knox
828 Mr. & Mrs. J. M. Dimmick
828 Miss Henrietta Cowles
832 Mr. & Mrs. J. H. Thomas & dr.
832 George O. Thomas
904 Mr. & Mrs. H. C. Lawrence
904 Philip E. Lawrence
906 Mr. & Mrs. Paul Benson & dr.
918 Mr. & Mrs. W. H. Blake
922 Mr. & Mrs. G. B. Treloar
922 Mrs. Matilda Ashton
926 Mr. & Mrs. C. H. McFarland
926 Mrs. Wm. L. Church
930 Mrs. M. L. Delamater
930 Mrs. E. D. Misner
932 Mr. & Mrs. F. W. Nichols
936 Mr. & Mrs. E. E. Jaycox
1004 Mr.&Mrs.JohnW.Burdsal & dr.
1004 George B. Burdsal
1004 John W. Burdsal jr.
1012 Mrs. Frances A. Burdsal & dr.
1014 Mr. & Mrs. Wm. Taylor
1016 Mr. & Mrs. Wm. S. Burling
1030 Dr. E. H. Hawley
1040 Mr. & Mrs. C. H. Perry
1042 Mr. & Mrs. Wm. N. Viguers & dr.
1134 Mr. & Mrs. W.C.Stewart & dr.
1134 W. L. Hamilton
1142 Mr. & Mrs. R. P. Hollett
1142 Mrs. A. C. George
1202 Mr. & Mrs. F. E. French
1206 Mrs. Mary Ludlam
1206 J. W. Ludlam
1216 Mr. & Mrs. J. Chas. Williams & drs.
1220 Mr. & Mrs. Adelbert M. Foster
1224 Mr. & Mrs. Philo Marsh
1228 Mr. & Mrs. E. O. Hart
1232 Mr. & Mrs. Orvis French

1236 Mr. & Mrs. Frank Ritchie
1240 Mr. & Mrs. John Hollingshead
1240 Thomas C. Hollingshead
1240 Ralph.Smith
1246 Mr. & Mrs. H. A. Streeter
1246 R. Cortland Burkholder
1302 Mr. & Mrs. O. C. Mason & dr.
1306 Mr. & Mrs. George S. Marsh
1310 Mr. & Mrs. J. J. Charles
1314 Mr. & Mrs. E. F. Carpenter
1314 Mrs. E. C. Reed
1318 Mr. & Mrs. Wm. B. Topliff
1322 Charles H. Lawrence
1322 Miss Mabel Lawrence
1328 E. A. Lord & dr.
1328 Alonzo B. Lord
1328 P. A. Lord
1328 Frank E. Lord
1328 Mrs. S. L. Webster
1332 Mr. & Mrs. Wm. D. Porter
1334 Mr. & Mrs. Marshall S. Marsh
1334 Mrs. E. A. Eaton
1334 Mrs. George B. Marsh
1408 Mr. & Mrs. Walter Lee Brown
1414 Mr. & Mrs. O. C. French
1416 Mr. & Mrs. Amos J. Harding
1422 Mr. & Mrs.AndressB.Hull&dr.
1426 Mrs. J. H. Bayliss & dr.
1502 Mr. & Mrs. G.M.Sargent & dr.
1502 Mrs. Emily Durham
1502 William D. Sargent
1502 George H. Sargent
1508 Mr. & Mrs. C. B.Cleveland&dr.
1602 Mr. & Mrs. J. C. Shaffer
1610 Mr. & Mrs. Edward R. Hall
1612 Rev. & Mrs. M. M. Parkhurst & dr.
1614 Mr. & Mrs. Walter M. Anthony
1624 Mrs. Francis Bradley & drs.
1624 Burt M. Gardner
1632 Rev. & Mrs. Frank M. Bristol
1632 Mrs. Angeline B. Bristol
1714 Rev.& Mrs. HenryB.Ridgaway
1714 Miss Estella Rose
1726 Mrs. L. C. Ward & drs.
1726 Miss Sara W. Gillette
1746 Mr. & Mrs. J. M. Williams&drs.
1746 Nathan Williams
1804 Prof. & Mrs. R. L. Cumnock
1810 Mr. & Mrs. Charles J. Connell
1812 Mr. & Mrs. Edw. Hotchkiss & dr.
1812 Mr. & Mrs. E. D. Hotchkiss
1812 Stewart R. Hotchkiss
1818 Mr. & Mrs. A. M. DeCoudres

1824 W. L. Randall
1824 Mr. & Mrs. E. M. Board
1830 Mr. & Mrs.GeorgeF.Stone&dr.
1832 Mr. & Mrs. Wiley J. Littlejohn
1838 Mr. & Mrs. G. B. Reynolds

INGLESIDE PARK.

Mr. & Mrs. H. K. Snider
Mr. & Mrs. W. W. Catlin
Mr. & Mrs. Wilson Howell

JUDSON AVENUE.

543 Mr. & Mrs. E. R. Bradford
635 Mr. & Mrs. David W. Ketchum
723 Mr. & Mrs Robert R. Leeds
723 Mr. & Mrs. H. S. Walker & dr.
723 F. Albert Walker
745 Mr. & Mrs. H. E. Seelye & drs.
807 Mr. & Mrs. John W. Byam
Receiving day Wednesday
813 Mr. & Mrs. C. E. Dudley
813 Mrs. Mary Dudley
817 Mr. & Mrs. Chas. F. Goessling
817 Mrs. Eliza F. Currey
817 Henry F. Goessling
831 F. H. Brammer
821 Miss Matilda Brammer
835 Mr. & Mrs.J. Monroe Smith
835 Raymond F. Smith
839 Mr. & Mrs. C. L. Graham & dr.
1007 Mr. & Mrs. C. N. Hammon
1013 Mr. & Mrs.C. Frederick Orr
1013 Mrs. Mary J. Fitch
1021 Rev. & Mrs. John Nelson Mills
Receiving day Thursday
1027 Mr. & Mrs. George Rhodes
1027 Mrs. Maria C. Wolcott
1031 Mr. & Mrs. W. H. Spencer & dr.
1031 Bennett W. Spencer
1031 George J. Albee
1119 Mr. & Mrs. Wm. H. Rice & dr.
1139 Mr. & Mrs. Richard C. Hall
1143 Mr. & Mrs. F. W. Cleveland & dr.
1205 Mr. & Mrs. A. Rogerson
1207 Mr. & Mrs. John W. Meaker
1207 John W. Meaker jr.
1207 Guy L. Meaker
1211 Dr. & Mrs. Edmund Noyes
1211 Mrs. Chloe B. Wells
1213 Mr. & Mrs. R. H. Herring
1213 Mr. & Mrs. Newell C. Knight
1225 Mr. & Mrs. E. A. Dawson
1229 Prof. & Mrs. H. H. Kingsley

1235 Mr. & Mrs. Perry Landis
Receiving day Wednesday
1235 Miss Ada G. Fessler
1241 Mr. & Mrs. John Griggs & dr.
1241 Mrs. Alida L. Myer
1247 Mr. & Mrs. W. E. Burden
1323 Rev. & Mrs. Moritz E. Eversz
1323 Ernest H. Eversz
1325 Mr. & Mrs. H. D. Baker
1325 Frank M. Milne
1327 Mrs. M. J. King & dr.
1329 Mr. & Mrs. L. L. Knox
1329 L. H. Knox
1405 Mr. & Mrs. John E. Scott
1405 John William Scott
1405 Robert L. Scott
1405 Mrs. John Hossack
1405 Miss I. B. Hossack
1411 Mr. & Mrs. E. S. Turner
1411 Mr. & Mrs. W. E. Turner
1415 Mr. & Mrs. W. H.Murray&drs.
1419 Mr. & Mrs. Geo. B. Dunham
1419 William H. Dunham
1419 George S. Dunham
1423 Judge & Mrs. R. M. Wing
1431 Mr. & Mrs. Colby Davies
1433 Mr. & Mrs. A. T. Nafis
1615 Mr. & Mrs. H. B. Cragin & dr.
1621 Mr. & Mrs. Thos. J. Whitehead
1621 Mr. & Mrs. Geo. A. Calkins
1625 Prof. & Mrs. H. F. Fisk
1629 Mr. & Mrs. T. S. Creighton
1637 Mr. & Mrs. John M. Ewen
1637 Mrs. R. W. Patterson

612 Mr. & Mrs. Ernest S. Fowler
612 Mrs. E. B. Fowler
634 Mr. & Mrs. J. H. Harshman
638 Mr. & Mrs. Geo. L. Hopkins
638 Mr. & Mrs. Geo. E. Hopkins
638 William P. Hopklns
716 Mr. & Mrs. W. H. Fargo
724 Mr. & Mrs. F. R. Seelye
730 E. S. Bowers
730 Mrs. M. L. Bowers
828 Mr. & Mrs. G. W. Adams & dr.
828 Mr. & Mrs. H. J. Parkin
832 Mr. & Mrs. J. H. Reynolds & dr.
832 Frederic L. Reynolds
840 Mr. & Mrs. F. A. Winchell
846 Mr. & Mrs. Christian F. Gatter
904 Mr. & Mrs. Wm. T. Hardie
926 Mr. & Mrs. Alexander Clark
932 Mr. & Mrs. A. H. Ullrich
Receiving day Tuesday

938 Mr. & Mrs. David L. Thorp &
  dr.
1008 Mr. & Mrs. George Campbell
1008 Miss Georgie C. Anderson
1012 Dr. & Mrs. D. C. Roundy
1012 W. N. Roundy
1012 James Young
1016 Mr. & Mrs. Walter B. Smith
1016 Mr. & Mrs. W. P. Matteson
1016 Mr. & Mrs. T. W. Edmonds
1028 Mr. & Mrs. B. D. Baldwin
  Receiving day Thursday
1040 Mr. & Mrs. W. E. Church &
  drs.
1040 Rollin Church
1048 Mrs. E. E. Noyes ·
1048 Mr. & Mrs. George E. Noyes
1048 Thomas S. Noyes
1048 M. Paul Noyes
1102 Mrs. Eliza U. Kimbark
1102 Edward H. Kimbark
1102 D. Avery Kimbark
1114 Mr. & Mrs. Chester P. Walcótt
1130 Mr. & Mrs. Ernest R. Hall
1134 Mr. & Mrs. Chas. H. Betts
1138 Mr. & Mrs. N. W. Brooks
1200· Mr. & Mrs. S. Frank Wilson
1208 Mr. & Mrs. A. T. Merriman &
  dr. *Receiving day Wednesday*
1208 Andrews T. Merriman jr.
1208 Mr. & Mrs. Peter Taylor
1212 Mr. & Mrs. J. M. Hawxhurst
1212 Mr. & Mrs. W. H. Crawford
1216 Mr. & Mrs. T. W. Heefmans
1226 Mr. & Mrs. Geo. F. Griffith
1228 Mr. & Mrs. L. E. Hildreth
1228 Miss Mary L. Barrie
1232 Mr. & Mrs. Frank A. Warner &
  drs.
1242 Mr. & Mrs. Wm. R. Adams
1242 Richard K. Adams
1246 Mr. & Mrs. A. M. Leslie
1246 Norman B. Leslie
1304 Mr. & Mrs. Wm. L. Vance
1310 Stedman H. Hale
1310 Miss Mary I. Hale
1314 Mr. & Mrs. S. L. Mershon
1316 Mrs. Mary C. Long & drs.
1318 Mr. & Mrs. Jos. E. MacKay
1322 Mr. & Mrs. E. H. Hunt
1322 E. H. Hunt jr.
1322 John Percival Hunt
1326 Mr. & Mrs. C. S. Burch
1412 Mr. & Mrs. W. S. Harbert &
  drs.
1412 Arthur B. Harbert
48

1418 Eltham R. Paul & dr.
1422 Mr.& Mrs. F. K. Stevens
1422 Miss Elmira Morse
1424 Mrs. Sarah L. Babcock & drs.
1574 Mrs. Nancy B. Wire
1574 Mr. & Mrs. William C. Wire
1574 Dr. George E. Wire
1704 Mr. & Mrs. C. B. Congdon
1704 Miss L. Willsie
1722 Dr. & Mrs. L. P. Hamline
1742 Mr. & Mrs. Orrington Lunt &
  dr.
1742 George Lunt.
1742 Miss Nina Gray Lunt
1742 Miss Ida Cornelia Gray
1742 Miss Dorothy Gray

KEDZIE AVENUE.

221 Mr. & Mrs. Alfred G. King

LAKE STREET.

211 Mr. & Mrs. G. G. Calkins
215 Mr. & Mrs. Michael Tiernan
  & dr.
215 John Tiernan
225 Mr. & Mrs. Frank M. Elliot
329 Mr. & Mrs. H. G. Grey
615 Mr. & Mrs. W. M. Wyckoff &
  drs.
615 W. H. Wyckoff
901 Mr. & Mrs. Henry T. Scovill
901 Melvin S. Scovill
907 Mr. & Mrs. J. L. Hebblethwaite
1015 Mr. & Mrs. W. A. S. Graham
1323 Mr. & Mrs. B. G. Poucher

216 Mr. & Mrs. Alexander Hesler
  & dr.
216 Arthur J. Hesler
222 Mr. & Mrs. Stewart Clark
408 Mr. & Mrs. B. F. Adams
412 Mr. & Mrs. George P. Merrick
416 Miss I. H. Pope
416 Miss Mary Pope
502 Mr. & Mrs. H. E. C. Daniels &
  dr.
512 Mrs. J. R. Towne
512 Mr. & Mrs. E. D. Redington &
  dr.
610 Mr. & Mrs. J. E. Paden
910 Mr. & Mrs. P. P. Lee & drs.
1002 Mr. & Mrs. Lucien E. Harding

1010 Mr. & Mrs. Chas. P. Spining
1012 Mr. & Mrs. George S. Baker
1016 Mrs. R. M. Grier
1016 James P. Grier
1026 Rev. Hugh P. Smyth
1026 Rev. Thomas M. Burke
1270 Mr. & Mrs. H. N. Kelsey

LAKE SHORE AVENUE.

1012 Mr. & Mrs. J. Stanley Grepe

LEE STREET.

510 E. T. Bond & dr.
516 Mr. & Mrs. Frank R. Bissell
521 Mr. & Mrs. Amos D. Rood & drs.
521 Mrs. Carrie A. Magruder
531 Mr. & Mrs. John Morrell
1017 Mr. & Mrs. G. A. Smith
1017 Mrs. Mary Urann
1017 Mrs. Mary R. Pratt
1021 Mr. & Mrs. Geo. S. Smith
1021 Miss Lucy Mason

MADISON AVENUE.

715 Mr. & Mrs. Charles A. Barton
719 Mr. & Mrs. D. D. Thompson
827 Mr. & Mrs. John F. Ferguson
833 Mr. & Mrs. Wm. A. Linn

826 Mr. & Mrs. Marshall Garrison & dr.
830 Mr. & Mrs. Chas. W. Green & dr.
834 Mr. & Mrs. Ford J. Allen
834 Mrs. Margaret Robe & dr.

MAPLE AVENUE.

1039 Mr. & Mrs. W. J. Andrews
1107 Mr. & Mrs. C. P. Englemann
1111 Mr. & Mrs. Wm. H. Damsel
1111 Mr. & Mrs. Marcus M. Pratt
1113 Mr. & Mrs. H. M. Wright
1113 Albert H. Wright
1203 Mrs. Mary A. Childs & dr.
1203 E. W. Childs
1211 Mr. & Mrs. Robert Spencer
1213 Mr. & Mrs. J. A. Williams
1213 Frank J. Williams
1217 Mr. & Mrs. Wm. Bruce Kirkman
1217 Mr. & Mrs. Malcolm McDowell

1217 Miss Mary E. McDowell
1217 Hanson McDowell
1217 Irving McDowell
1223 Mr. & Mrs. C. E. Morris
1223 Mrs. Mary E. Scranton
1227 Mr. & Mrs. C. B. Eyer
1231 Mr. & Mrs. J. A. Smith & dr.
1231 Frederick W. Smith
1235 Mr. & Mrs. A. W. Cooper
1239 Mr. & Mrs. James Steele
1313 Mr. & Mrs. Joseph K. Lewis
1319 Mr. & Mrs. J. A. Battelle
1333 Mr. & Mrs. James K. Armsby jr.
1337 Volney W. Foster
1403 Mr. & Mrs. Towner K. Webster
1411 Charles E. Davis
1415 Mr. & Mrs. James Macdonald
1421 Mr. & Mrs. N. G. Iglehart
1425 Mrs. Helen M. Ide & dr.
1425 William K. Ide
1425 Charles B. Ide
1433 Mr. & Mrs. J. N. Hubbard
1453 Mr. & Mrs. Reuben Knox
1459 Mr. & Mrs. Joseph K. Lewis
1459 Mr. & Mrs. Frank A. Burgess
1509 Rev. & Mrs. H. A. DeLano
1553 Mr. & Mrs. J. W. Thompson
1553 F. W. Hardman
1559 Mr. & Mrs. Charles Aikin

1030 Mr. & Mrs. A. L. Fanning
1116 Mr. & Mrs. James Farr
1122 Mr. & Mrs. C. W. Gray
1128 Mr. & Mrs. J. S. Judd
1128 Norman W. Judd
1128 Herman J. S. Judd
1128 Corban E. Judd
1202 Mr. & Mrs. Albert F. McCarrell
1202 Mr. & Mrs. Francis S. Oliver
1208 Mr. & Mrs. Morris R. Poucher
1208 Mr. & Mrs. David Jamieson
1214 Mr. & Mrs. J. M. Larimer
1220 Mrs. James C. Connor
1224 Mr. & Mrs. L. L. Porter
1224 Mr. & Mrs. T. B. Carter
1232 Mr. & Mrs. N. Arthur Coble
1232 J. H. Kellam
1236 Mr. & Mrs. John Handford & dr.
1242 C. O. Boring
1242 Mrs. M. Augusta Jones
1246 Mr. & Mrs. L. D. Parker
Receiving day Thursday

1246 Harry M. Parker
1316 Mr. & Mrs. Holmes Hoge
1406 Mr. & Mrs. Arthur W. Underwood
1420 Mr. & Mrs. H. D. Hedden & dr.
1420 John H. Hedden
1422 Mr. & Mrs. Louis K. Goffe
1428 Mr. & Mrs. Thomas Bates
1454 Mr. & Mrs. E. H. Reed & dr.
1454 James H. Reed
1458 Mr. & Mrs. A. L. Butler
1458 James S. Judd
1460 Mr. & Mrs.John R.Woodbridge
1500 Mr. & Mrs. F. A. Aplin
1506 Mr. & Mrs. D. B. Dewey
1512 Mrs. E. B. Simmons & dr.
1512 Park E. Simmons
1516 Mrs. James K. Armsby
1516 George N. Armsby
1516 Miss Maria Anderson
1562 Mr. & Mrs. H. J. Edwards
1576½ Mr. & Mrs. E. Prindle

MICHIGAN AVENUE.

943 Mr. & Mrs. Clarence C. Poole
  Receiving day Friday
943 Mrs. Wm. F. Poole
943 W. Frederick Poole
1037 Mr. & Mrs. Henry Delaney
1107 Mrs. Catharine D. Dunlap
1107 Charles M. Dunlap
1107 George D. Crie
1107 Miss Kate B. Crie

1110 Mr. & Mrs. Robert S. Clark
1110 Mrs. Theodosia Emery
1110 Mrs. W. L. Breckinridge
1116 Mr. & Mrs. J. S. Dickerson
1122 Mr. & Mrs. T. S. Gillette
1130 Mr. & Mrs. Chas. P. Coffin
1130 John Coffin
1134 Mr. & Mrs. Tully C. Estee
1134 Mrs. Anne W. Tower
1134 Mr. & Mrs. Arthur Tower
1144 Mr. & Mrs. Charles Jernegan
1144 Miss Mary Jernegan
1210 Mr. & Mrs. W. H. Stockham
cor. Lincoln pl. Mr. & Mrs. O. M. Carson

MONROE AVENUE.

735 Mr. & Mrs. Wm. Hoffman
903 Mr. & Mrs. Frank Sherman
903 Mrs. W. H. Wright
913 Mr. & Mrs. W. S. Gates

913 William W. Gates
919 Mr. & Mrs. Arthur Morgan

840 Mr. & Mrs. Nicholas F. Kranz
840 Miss Susie Kranz

OAK AVENUE.

1115 Mr. & Mrs. James Wigginton
1217 Mr. & Mrs. Thos. E. Connor
1219 Mr. & Mrs. J. M. Bond
1223 Mr. & Mrs. Daniel McCann
1505 Mr. & Mrs. Andrew J. Brown
1563 Mr. & Mrs. A. H. Childs
1567 Mr. & Mrs. E. C. Nelson
1571 Mr. & Mrs. GeorgeH.Iott & dr.
1575 Mr. & Mrs. A. L. Sproule
1615 M. P. Aiken
1615 Miss Rose T. Aiken
1621 Mr. & Mrs. W. S. Lord
1621 Mrs. H. A. Rowland
1625 Mr. & Mrs. F. H. Walker
1625 Edwin F. Walker
1629 Mr. & Mrs. C. B. F. Palmer
1633 Mr. & Mrs. James M. Barnes
1633 Mr. & Mrs. Chas. H. Burkitt

1240 Mr. & Mrs. Howard Field
1304 Mr. & Mrs. Thos. A. Buckner
1456 C. George Lewis
1456 Mrs. Catharine D. Dunlap
1456 Martin O. Lewis
1456 Martin Lewis & dr.
1456 Thomas H. Lewis
1462 Mr. & Mrs. C. H. Matthews
1500 Mr. & Mrs. Wm. A. Holabird
1500 R. G. Holabird
1504 Mr. & Mrs. David R. Lewis
1504 J. William Kelly
1554 Mr. & Mrs. L. K. Gillson
1560 Mr. & Mrs. J. W. Low
1566 Mr. & Mrs. H. C. Hunt & drs.
1566 John L. Hunt
1570 Mr.&Mrs.TheodoreReese&drs.
1570 Theodore F. Reese
1570 Mrs. Emma M. Revell
1614 Mr. & Mrs. Daniel W. Hess
1618 Mr. & Mrs. W. F. Hypes
1622 Mr. & Mrs. C. B. Foote
1720 Justin L. Bray

ORRINGTON AVENUE.

1631 Mr.&Mrs. George R. Kline&dr.
1631 Dr. Frances W. Wheeler
1633 Mrs. Mary E. Loag & drs.
1633 Robert Loag
1639 Mr. & Mrs. C. P. Thomas & drs.

1639 Mrs. Ada L. Burt
1715 Mr. & Mrs. J. B. Huse
1723 Chas. D. McWilliams
1725 Mr. & Mrs. H. S. Maddock
1727 Mr. & Mrs. F. Eichbauer & dr.
1731 Mrs. E. W. Newman & dr.
1731 Nelden A. Newman
1735 Dr. & Mrs. J. V. Stevens
1735 George A. Day
1737 Mr. & Mrs. Allen Jeffery
1805 Mrs. E. J. Hudson
1815 Mrs. Catharine S. Clow & drs.
1819 Alton Parkhurst
1819 Dr. Emogene Parkhurst
1823 Prof. & Mrs. Charles S. Farrar
1827 Rev. & Mrs. N. D. Hillis
1923 Mr. & Mrs. Otis R. Larsen
1925 Mrs. F. A. Bradley
1931 Mr. & Mrs. Edwin H. Towle
1931 Miss Clara Kingsley
1943 Mr. & Mrs. R. R. McCabe & drs.
1945 Mr. & Mrs. Louis S. Rice
1945 Mrs. Emma L. S. Rice & dr.
1945 Mrs. S. Vinson Farnum
2001 S. Wade Hunt
2001 Mrs. Nancy D. Hunt
2001 Prof. H. Stancliff
2003 Mr. & Mrs. Geo. W. Muir
    Receiving day Thursday
2131 Mr. & Mrs. Geo. H. Moore & dr.
    Receiving day Friday
2131 Carleton W. Moore
2243 Frank McCulloch
2243 Mrs. Catharine Waugh McCulloch *Receiving day Monday*
2243 Mrs. Susie Waugh

1610 Dr. & Mrs. J. C. Bennett
1708 Mrs. Emily A. Woodson
1708 Mr. & Mrs. John J. Waldron
1710 Mr. & Mrs. Alanson Filer
1712 Mr. & Mrs. Wm. Lukey
1714 Mrs. Clara D. Mansfield
1714 Miss C. Antoinette Freeman
1714½ Dr. & Mrs. Wm. Bradley
1716 Mr. & Mrs. James McMahon
1740 Mrs. E. J. Towle & dr.
1740 Prof. J. H. Huddilston
1800 Mrs. Emily H. Miller
1800 Prof. Emily F. Wheeler
1800 Miss Mary L. Freeman
1906 Mrs. Eliza.C. Barber
1906 Arthur E. Barber
1906 Miss Emma L. Roberts
1918 Mr. & Mrs. H. M. Walrath & dr.

1918 William B. Walrath
1918 John M. Curran
1922 Mr. & Mrs. Jos. A. Griffin
1926 Mr. & Mrs. John W. Welch & dr.
1930 Mr. & Mrs. H. Sanborn Smith
1934 Mrs. J. J. Spalding & drs.
1934 Miss Catharine A. Pettis
1936 Mrs. Ellen E. Langlois
2010 Chester A. Grover
2018 Mrs. Julia A. Moore & dr.
2020 Mr. & Mrs. T. T. Hollinger
2024 M . & Mrs. Wm. E. Jordan & drs.
2032 Mr. & Mrs. Chas. S. Raddin
2034 Mrs. H. A. Raddin & drs.
2102 Mr. & Mrs George P. Mills
2106 Mr. & Mrs. C. J. Ellis
2112 Mr. & Mrs. C. L. Whittemore
2112 Mrs. Elvina L. Wilson
2118 Mrs. Olive Beason & drs.
2118 Mr. & Mrs. Wm. S. Blair
2306 Prof. & Mrs. A. F. Ericson & drs.
2422 Mrs. Julius F. Kellogg
2422 Mr. & Mrs. Wm. Kellogg

PRAIRIE AVENUE.

2611 Mr. & Mrs. J. W. Stewart & dr.
2615 Col. & Mrs. John S. Wilson
2675 Mr. & Mrs. Herman Hoff

REBA PARKWAY.

715 Dr. Arthur W. Cooper
715 Edward M. Cooper
715 Miss E. Cooper
715 Mr. & Mrs. A. J. Cooper
727 Mr. & Mrs. C. S. Redfield
829 Mr. & Mrs. George Colling
911 Mr. & Mrs. R. B. Burbans

714 Mr. & Mrs. M. T. Lane
714 Miss Irene Lane
714 Miss Ella Lane
722 Mr. & Mrs. W. B. Leffingwell
802 Mr. & Mrs. John G. Beazley
810 Mr. & Mrs. W. E. Brothers
814 Mr. & Mrs. Charles Lincoln
826 Mr. & Mrs. F. F. Lewis & dr.

RIDGE AVENUE.

319 Mr. & Mrs. A. J. Kasper
365 Mrs. James S. Kirk
365 Mr. & Mrs. Arthur Kirk

515 Mrs. H. Sontag & drs.
521 Mr. & Mrs. Joseph Berry
545 Mr. & Mrs. P. J. Kasper
707 Mr. & Mrs. John W. Hoffman
731 Mr. & Mrs. Henry Walter
739 Mr. & Mrs. Peter Schimberg
921 Dr. & Mrs. A. B. Stockham
1139 Mr. & Mrs. N. R. Marshall
1139 Mrs. C. G. Duck
1205 Mr. &Mrs. Osro A. Crain
1205 Miss Clare M. Siter
1247 Mrs. P. N. Fox & dr.
1407 Mrs. Hugh A. White
1429 Mr. & Mrs. M. M. Kirkman &
     dr.
1429 A. T. Kirkman
1429 Mrs. S. Spencer
1453 Mr. & Mrs. Howard P. Gray
1453 Miss Alice C. Gray
1461 Mr. & Mrs. Charles Raymond
1461 Miss I. E. Raymond
1461 Miss Kathryn K. Raymond
1501 Mr. & Mrs. Frank P. Sheldon
1501 Miss Mae Dingee
1501 Miss May L. Sheldon
1509 Mr. & Mrs. W. J. Fabian
1555 Mr. & Mrs. Morton Butler
1563 Mr. & Mrs. Geo. D. Moseley
1563 Mr. & Mrs. Geo. VanHorn
     Moseley •
1563 Alex W. Moseley
1579 Dr. & Mrs. Isaac Poole
1585 Mrs. J. R. VanArsdale & dr.
1585 William T. VanArsdale
2237 Mr. & Mrs. S. C. Ingraham
2237 Mrs. Helen B. Garland
2237 Mrs. Mary L. Mulford

---

826 Mr. & Mrs. Henry A. Hoffman
906 Mr. & Mrs. Morton M. Curry
     Receiving day Friday
930 Mr. & Mrs. George A. Wheeler
938 Mr. & Mrs. J. W. Hartshorn
1046 Mrs. Charles Crain & dr.
1046 George H. Crain
1142 Mr. & Mrs. H. Cheatle & dr.
1220 Mr. & Mrs. D. A. Mudge
1230 Mr. & Mrs. William H. Jones
1246 Mr. & Mrs. H. C. Tillinghast
1246 Mrs. C. S. Morse
1314 Mr. & Mrs. Augustine C. Buell
1326 Mr. & Mrs. Charles Comstock
     & drs.
1326 Alphonso S. Comstock
1332 Mr. & Mrs. Wm. H. Jones

1332 Mr. & Mrs. Wm. O. Jones
1332 Hugh W. Jones
1408 Mrs. Julia M. Watson & dr.
1408 Mrs. Priscilla Dickinson
1426 Mr. & Mrs. Milton W. Kirk
1456 Mr. & Mrs. John B. Kirk
1462 Mr. & Mrs. George W. Smith
1462 Mrs. Janet Smith
1514 Mr. & Mrs. J. H. Kedzie & dr.
1558 Mr. & Mrs. George S. Lord &
     dr.
1572 Mr. & Mrs. H. B. Hurd
1608 Mr. & Mrs. W. Blanchard & dr.
1608 Mrs. George Judd
1612 Mr. & Mrs. Louis-Hertle
1620 Mr. & Mrs. Thomas Lord & drs.
1620 Benjamin W. Lord
1628 Mr. & Mrs. Lewis Iott
1628 Frank C. Iott
1628 M. B. Iott & drs.
1632 Mr. & Mrs. Calvin F. Rice &
     dr.
1708 Richard C. Lake
1708 Miss Jessie Lake
1708 Miss Amy Lake

RIDGE PLACE.

919 Mrs. May C. Quinn
927 Mr. & Mrs. F. E. Atwood
931 Mr.&Mrs. R. GrahamPentecost
935 Mr. & Mrs. Bliss Langill

926 Mr. & Mrs. Thor Schreiber

SHERIDAN ROAD.

551 Mr. & Mrs. D. H. Lamberson
     & dr.
551 Miss Josie M. Lamberson
se. cor. Keeney av. Mrs. E. G. Do-
     mansky
707 Rev. & Mrs. W. H. Burns
     Receiving day Friday
707 W. Foster Burns
721 Dr. & Mrs. P. L. McKinnie
721 Mrs. Sophia C. Grey
929 Mr. & Mrs. J. T. Long
929 John T. Long
929 Joel B. Long
2235 Prof.& Mrs. Geo. W. Hough
2235 George J. Hough
2625 Mr. & Mrs. Isaac R. Hitt jr.
2625 Edward A. Birch
2703 Mr. & Mrs. E. G. Henderson

2703 Mrs. Catharine N. Barlow
2703 Miss Ida Bell Brook

706 Mr. & Mrs. M. J. Stevenson
Receiving day Thursday
926 Mr. & Mrs. Chas. R. Webster
Receiving day Monday
1014 Dr. & Mrs. Edward F. Baker
1124 Rev. & Mrs. G. W. Gray
1124 Mr. & Mrs. Frank L. Borton
1138 Mr. & Mrs. Herbert A. Thomas
1138 Mr. & Mrs. Daniel H. Seavey
1204 Mr. & Mrs. W. R. Condict
1204 Wallace R. Condict jr.
1224 Mr. & Mrs. Wm. Hudson Harper
1430 Rev. & Mrs. Robt. D. Sheppard
1430 R. Loring Sheppard
1632 Mr. & Mrs. Eugene E. Osborn
1640 Mr. & Mrs. Edwin F. Brown
1806 Mr. & Mrs. L. D. Norton
1806 Mrs. Louise Freer Hanford
1818 Mr. & Mrs. Wm. B. Bogert
1830 Mr. & Mrs. Wm. E. Paddock
1830 Miss Minnie A. Phelps
1834 Capt. & Mrs. L. O. Lawson
1882 Mrs. D. R. Dyche
1882 Mrs. H. B. Dyche
1882 Frank B. Dyche
1882 William A. Dyche
1882 George B. Dyche
1888 Mrs. Caroline M. Bennett & dr.
1888 Charles S. Bennett
1892 Mr. & Mrs. F. W. Dickerman
1892 Mrs. Eunice J. Dickerman
1892 Mr. & Mrs. C. E. Wiswall
1896 Mr. & Mrs. W. J. Johnston
1908 Mr. & Mrs. Calvin H. Hill
1914 Mr. & Mrs. George H. Foster
1930 Prof. & Mrs. C. W. Pearson
1936 Mr. & Mrs. Eugene E. Barnard
1936 Mr. & Mrs. M. R. Barnard & drs.
1958 Pres. & Mrs. Henry Wade Rogers
Receiving day Saturday
1960 Prof. & Mrs. J. H. Wigmore
1960 Ward B. Sawyer
2016 Rev. & Mrs. Chas. J. Little & dr.
2206 M . & Mrs. J. G. Orchard & dr.
2238 Prof. & Mrs. Robert Baird

SHERIDAN SQUARE.

sw. cor. Keeney av. Mrs. John C. Bundy
Mr. & Mrs. Lewis W. Parker

SHERMAN AVENUE.

925 Mr. & Mrs. Robert Birdsall
925 William Y. Birdsall
1403 Mr. & Mrs. J. C. Moore & dr.
1409 Miss E. C. Dinwiddie
1431 Rev. & Mrs. August Edgren
1853 Mr. & Mrs. Alex. McConnell & drs.
1857 Mr. & Mrs. Eugene L. Stoker
1921 Dr.&Mrs.C. A. P. Garnsey&dr.
1925 David S. Ely & dr.
1943 Mr. & Mrs. W. H. Edwards
2011 Mr. & Mrs. E. B. Spear
2015 Mrs. Hester E. Walker & dr.
2031 Mrs. Ellen L. Woodward

822 Mr. & Mrs. Jos. J. Van Every
826 Mrs. A. D. Cutts & drs.
828 Mr. & Mrs. Chester M. Pratt
1202 Dr. & Mrs. I. M. Neely & dr.
1218 Mr. & Mrs. DeWitt W. Page & dr.
1224 Mr. & Mrs. S. S. Neal & dr.
1506 Mr. & Mrs. A. L. Currey
1508 Mr. & Mrs. Frank R. Grover
1716 Mr.& Mrs.Thomas T. Johnston
1724 Mrs. N. F. Rickey
1724 Pardon C. Rickey
1724 Mr. & Mrs. John S. Metcalf
1862 Mr. & Mrs. Louis M. Perry
1910 Mr. & Mrs. A. J. Thayer
1928 Mr. & Mrs. Jos. McCallum &dr.
1928 Miss Kittie Livingston
1938 Mr. & Mrs. Charles B. Atwell
1938 Mr. & Mrs. Henry H. Kellogg
1942 Mrs. Elizabeth Stuart & drs.
2040 Mr. & Mrs. F. M. Forrey
2040 Mrs. C. A. Churcher
2044 Mr. & Mrs. E. M. Lunt
2122 Mr. & Mrs. Wm. Prentiss
Receiving day Thursday
2122 Mrs. Elizabeth Manley
2130 Mr. & Mrs.W.C. Shuman & dr.
2130 Edwin L. Shuman
2130 Miss Jessie J. Shuman
2130 R. Roy Shuman

UNIVERSITY PLACE.

615 Mr. & Mrs. G. W. Cushing
615 Miss Anna F. Cushing

619 Mrs. Harriette S. Kidder
619 Mr. & Mrs. M. S. Terry
625 Mr. & Mrs. E. B. Case
625 Rev. & Mrs. N. A. Prentiss
645 Mrs. N. H. Walworth

---

620 Mr. & Mrs. T. D. Talbot
630 Prof. and Mrs. Geo. A Coe

WASHINGTON AVENUE.

903 Mr. & Mrs. Paul Mullmann
907 Mr. & Mrs. A. P. Handke
915 Mr. & Mrs. F. S. Capron & drs.
1125 Mr. & Mrs. A. Molinelli
1203 Mr. & Mrs. A. H. Bodine

---

802 Mr. & Mrs. Mason B. Loomis
802 Mr. & Mrs. Fred S. Loomis
808 Mr. & Mrs. Wm. Whitfield
808 Joseph H. Whitfield
808 Henry Caralan
810 Mr. & Mrs. J. T. W. Jennings
812 Mr. & Mrs. Edward F. Capron
818 Mr. & Mrs. W. E. Winn
822 Mr. & Mrs. Albert Durham & dr.
834 Mr. & Mrs. John Furlong & dr.
904 Mr. & Mrs. G. W. Walters
922 Mr. & Mrs. Mark Wimond
1202 Mr. & Mrs. C. E. Wells
1208 Mr. & Mrs. O. Olson
1310 Mr. & Mrs. Edward H. Stokes
1310 Harry T. Stokes
1310 Miss Amy J. Stokes
1314 Mr. & Mrs. Axel Carlson
1330 Adelbert Hamilton

WESLEY AVENUE.

1413 Mr. & Mrs. J. P. Boutelle
1415 Mr. & Mrs. Archer Gifford
    Receiving day Wednesday
1427 Mr. & Mrs. H. W. Weaver
1427 Mrs. A. M. Linnell
1515 Mr. & Mrs. Geo. Ebeling
    Receiving day Thursday
1735 Mr. & Mrs. Chas. A. Wightman
1805 Mr. & Mrs. Wm. Stacey & dr.
1805 Miss Annie N. Stacey
1805 Thomas I. Stacey
1811 Mrs. Maria J. Garland
1815 Jacob Bodine

1815 Mr. & Mrs. Jacob Bodine jr.
1837 Mr. & Mrs. Geo. W. Paullin

---

926 Mr. & Mrs. Charles W. Dodge
930 Mrs. Kate Hagarty
944 Mr. & Mrs. F. E. Smith
1414 Mrs. Joseph Brown
1418 Mr. & Mrs. A. S. VanDeusen
1432 Mr. & Mrs. William C. Magill
1456 Mr. & Mrs. F. H. DeKnatel
1584 Mr. & Mrs. Wm. F. Swan & dr.
1612 Mr. & Mrs. J. A. Comstock
1622 Mr. & Mrs. Jason R. Prindle
1632 Mr. & Mrs. George R. Jenkins
1632 Miss Anna E. Jenkins
1632 Miss Elizabeth A. Pratt
·1702 Mr. & Mrs. E. A. Coburn
1708 Mr. & Mrs. Thos. H. Linsley
1720 Mr. & Mrs. Louis A. Ferguson
1802 Mr. & Mrs. J. E. Keelyn
1810 H. S. Slaymaker & dr.
1810 Harry M. Slaymaker
1818 Mr. & Mrs. George H. Ellis
    Receiving day Thursday

WHEELER AVENUE.

641 Mr. & Mrs. B. F. Kirtland
645 Mr. & Mrs. E. M. Miles
649 Mr. & Mrs. Foster H. Biggs
653 Mrs. G. S. Wells
653 Mrs. C. B. Sherman
803 Mr. & Mrs. Wm. F. Singleton
815 Mr. & Mrs. T. C. Rafferty
833 Mr. & Mrs. L. J. Waggner
835 Mr. & Mrs. S. B. Jones
839 Mr. & Mrs. Frank C. Hills
845 Mr. & Mrs. J. E. Byus

---

712 Mr. & Mrs. H. S. Knapp
712 Mrs. E. S. Waddell
716 Mr. & Mrs. H. B. Whitman
720 Mr. & Mrs. Robert Knaggs
724 Mr. & Mrs. B. T. Holcomb
742 Mr. & Mrs. W. H. Maclear
742 Mrs. A. L. Paddock
806 Mr. & Mrs. Calvin Forbush
806 Mrs. E. A. Warren
806 William Forbush
814 Mr. & Mrs. John J. Flinn
822 Mr. & Mrs. Albert E. Tonk
828 Mr. & Mrs. Geo. W. Burchard

FORT SHERIDAN.

Maj. & Mrs. C. M. Bailey
Lieut W. H. Bertsch
Lieut. & Mrs. W. F. Blauvelt
Lieut. & Mrs. W. N. Blow jr.
Mrs. G. Bohl
Mr. & Mrs. S. Breakwell
Lieut E. P. Brewer
Capt. & Mrs. H. R. Brinkerhoff
Lieut. & Mrs. R. L. Bush
Capt. & Mrs. A. Capron
Capt. E. S. Chapin
Capt. & Mrs. C. H. Conrad
Capt. G. A. Cornish
Lieut J. Cotter
Col. & Mrs. R. E. A. Crofton
Capt. & Mrs. T. F. Davis
Lieut. & Mrs. R J. Fleming
Mrs. Mary Gillette
Philander Gillette
Maj. & Mrs. A. C. Girard
Capt. & Mrs. L. R. Hare
Lieut. F. E. Harris
Capt. & Mrs. W. T. Hartz
Lieut. H. J. Hirsch
Mr. & Mrs. John T. Holden
Capt. & Mrs. H. H. Humphreys
Lieut. & Mrs. C. C. Jameson
Capt. & Mrs. F. B. Jones
Lieut. & Mrs. E. Lloyd

Lieut. J. A. Maney
Mr. & Mrs. J. S. McDonough
Capt. G. K. McGunnegle
Mrs. I. R. McGunnegle
Lieut. Frank B. McKenna
Lieut. & Mrs. D. D. Mitchell
Dr. & Mrs. Geo. J. Neugarden
Mr. & Mrs. O. M. Onsom
Lieut-Col. & Mrs. S. Ovenshine
Lieut. & Mrs. S. S. Pague
Lieut. & Mrs. McA. Palmer
Mr. & Mrs. D. Pease
Lieut. J. A. Shipton
Lieut. E. S. Smiley
Mr. & Mrs. E. K. Smith
Lieut. Wm. R. Smith
Capt. & Mrs. S. R. Stafford
Mr. & Mrs. C. H. Summers & drs.
Lieut. S. R. H. Tompkins
Mr. & Mrs. Abraham VanLoan
Capt. & Mrs. C. A. Varnum
Chaplain E. J. Vattman
Mr. &. Mrs. E. L. Webster
Lieut. McD. Weeks
Lieut. & Mrs. B. C. Welsh
Lieut. & Mrs. R. C. Williams
Capt. & Mrs. C. E. Woodruff
Mr. & Mrs. E. Woodruff
Mr. & Mrs. F. E. Woodruff

GLENCOE.

Mrs. John Aken
Thomas Allen
Mr. & Mrs. James P. Brewster
Benjamin Brewster
C. E. Browne & dr.
Mr. & Mrs. G. J. Case
Mr. & Mrs. G. V. Clementi
Mr. & Mrs. J. E. Colburn
Mr. & Mrs. Lewis H. Cox
Harry N. Cox
William H. Cox
Mr. & Mrs. R. D. Coy
Mr. & Mrs. Harry N. Culver
Alvin H. Culver
Mr. & Mrs. Morton Culver & drs.
Morton T. Culver
Mr. & Mrs. Joseph Daggitt
Mr. & Mrs. Arthur H. Day
Mr. & Mrs. C. L. Day
Rev. & Mrs. Hiram Day
Mr. & Mrs. John L. Day
Mr. & Mrs. F. C. DeLang

Mrs. J. J. Dennis
James F. Dennis
Mr. & Mrs. A. L. Dewar
Mrs. E. W. Dupee & dr.
C. F. Dupee
Mr. & Mrs. John Fanning
J. J. Flanders & dr.
Mr. & Mrs. Joseph F. Forsyth & drs.
Miss Grace Fuller
Mr. & Mrs. G. E. Gooch
Mr. & Mrs. Michael Gormully
Miss Helen R. Green
Walter H. Green
Dr. & Mrs. B. W. Griffin
Mrs. F. D. Hall & dr.
Mr. & Mrs. G. D. Hall
Mr. & Mrs. F. L. Hankey
Mr. & Mrs. W. A. Hovey
Gen. & Mrs. C. H. Howard & dr.
O. McG. Howard
Mr. & Mrs. Frederick G. Howell
Mr. & Mrs. S. R. Hurford

Mr. & Mrs. R. B. Hutchinson
Mr. & Mrs. W. H. Johnson
Mr. & Mrs. T. C. King
Mr. & Mrs. Ashbel G. Ligare
Mr. & Mrs. George G. Ligare
Mrs. Eliza A. Lightcap
Mr. & Mrs. James Lloyd
Mr. & Mrs. L. H. Lloyd
Mr. & Mrs. Andrew McLeish
Mr. & Mrs. Ralph Miller
Mr. & Mrs. Thomas H. Murdow & dr.
Edward Murdow
Dr. Arthur H. Murdow
Mrs. L. E. Newbury & dr.
Mr. & Mrs. Benjamin Newhall
Franklin Newhall
Mr. & Mrs. Sylvan Newhall
Mr. & Mrs. George F. Orde
Mr. & Mrs. Mark Orde

Dr. & Mrs. John Nutt
Mr. & Mrs. John C. Parry
Mr. & Mrs. O. D. Peck
Receiving day Friday
Mr. & Mrs. John T. Plummer
Mr. & Mrs. J. P. Plummer
Mr. & Mrs. J. W. Plummer & dr.
Mr. & Mrs. W. C. Richmond
George E. Sanborn
Mrs. E. N. Sherwood
Mr. & Mrs. P. N. Sherwood & dr.
Mrs. Jane Sinclair
Rev. & Mrs. Moses Smith
Mrs. J. C. Starr
William E. Starr
Herbert S Stone
Mr. & Mrs. Melville E. Stone
Receiving day Monday
Dr. & Mrs. O. D. Swain
Mr. & Mrs. Harry B. Totten

GRAND CROSSING.

BROOKS AVENUE.

7420 Mr. & Mrs. John W. Tinsley
7420 John H. Tinsley
7530 Mr. & Mrs. E. W. Hutchinson

COTTAGE GROVE AVENUE.

7214 Mr. & Mrs. J. B. Ashford
7235 Mr. & Mrs. A. S. Bradt
7235 Mr. & Mrs. S. B. Bradt

ELLIS AVENUE.

7518 Mr. & Mrs. John B. Math

GREENWOOD AVENUE.

7510 Dr. & Mrs. Geo. H. Chapman
7530 Dr. Hiram L. Pease

NUTT AVENUE.

7425 Mr. & Mrs. James Beynon

7437 Mr. & Mrs. Cornelius Curtis & dr.

7426 Mr. & Mrs. William Everett
7450 Mr. & Mrs. John C. Rhea & dr.
7450 F. L. Force
7520 Mr. & Mrs. Arthur J. Bassett

SEVENTY-FIRST STREET.

874 Mr. & Mrs. H. H. Walton
874 Charles A. Walton
874 Clyde C. Walton

SEVENTY-FIFTH STREET.

1048 Dr. & Mrs. M. S. McNiff
1048 Dr. & Mrs. C. Yeomans

SOUTH CHICAGO AVENUE.

7126 Mrs. A. Hilts
7417 Dr. & Mrs. M. C. Jennings

GRAYLAND.

Mr. & Mrs. Samuel A. Bobb
Mr. & Mrs. W. H. Gray
Mr. & Mrs. J. T. Madison

Mr. & Mrs. John F. Merchant & dr.
Mr. & Mrs. Fred J. Sherman
Mrs. Belle Wilcox

HIGHLAND PARK.

Mr. & Mrs. George G. Adams
Mrs. Anna M. Allen
Mr. & Mrs. William H. Alley

Mr. & Mrs. James F. Anderson
Mr. & Mrs. James C. Anderson
Mr. & Mrs. John W. Atkinson

Dr. & Mrs. R. H. Babcock
Mr. & Mrs. Charles H. Baker
Mrs. M. H. Baker & dr.
Milton H. Baker jr.
Mr. & Mrs. Wm. C. Barrett
Dr. & Mrs. Lloyd M. Bergen
Mr. & Mrs. S. R. Bingham
Mr. & Mrs. G. D. Boulton & dr.
Mr. & Mrs. Arthur M. Boyington
Mr. & Mrs. George B. Boyington
Mr. & Mrs. W. W. Boyington & drs.
Mr. & Mrs. Edgar S. Boynton
Mr. & Mrs. Wm. E. Brand
Mr. & Mrs. M. R. Brock
Mr. & Mrs. Edward H. Brown
Mr. & Mrs. Francis C. Brown
Mr. & Mrs. Frank A. Burgess
Mr. & Mrs. August S. Campbell
Miss Anna A. Carver
Mr. &. Mrs. Henry C. Carver
J. Winchester Carver
Mr. & Mrs. H. H. Chandler & dr.
Edwin W. Chandler
Mr. & Mrs. E. W. Chase
Mr. & Mrs. W. Fred Childs
Mr. & Mrs. Theodore M. Clark
Mr. & Mrs. Daniel Cobb
John D. Cobb
Miss M. L. Cobb
Mr. & Mrs. Schuyler M. Coe
Dr. & Mrs. J. E. Colburn
Dr. & Mrs. Theodore H. Conger
Mr. & Mrs. F. W. Corey
Mr. & Mrs. Geo. B. Cummings
Receiving day Thursday
Mr. & Mrs. John O. Cummings
Frederick W. Cushing
Mr. & Mrs. J. C. Cushman & dr.
Col. & Mrs. H. P. Davidson
Miss Alice S. Davidson
Maj. & Mrs. R. P. Davidson
Mr. & Mrs. E. H. Denison
Mr. & Mrs. Henry H. Denison
Mr. & Mrs. George E. Detwiler & drs.
Miss Belle Dickinson
Mr. & Mrs. Henry G. Dickinson
Mr. & Mrs. Albert Dixson
Clarence Downs
Mr. & Mrs. William S. Downs
Mr. & Mrs. Edwin Dyer
Mr. & Mrs. Harry Eaton
Miss Julia E. Eaton
Mrs. Anna G. Edwards & dr.
Mr. & Mrs. Clifton S. Edwards
Mr. & Mrs. Winfield S. Ellis
Joel J. Ellis

Mr. & Mrs. Wm. H. Emerson
Mr. & Mrs. David M. Erskine jr.
Mr. & Mrs. Louis Erskine
Miss Emily L. Erskine
Mr. & Mrs. Filmore Evans
Mr. & Mrs. Robert G. Evans
Mr. & Mrs. Frank D. Everett & dr.
Charles F. Everett
Mr. & Mrs. Wilson G. Everett
Mr. & Mrs. G. S. Everingham
Mr. & Mrs. Frank M. Fargo
Mr. & Mrs. William G. Farrar
Mr. & Mrs. Benjamin Fessenden
Charles B. Fessenden
Mr. & Mrs. John Finney & drs.
Mr. & Mrs. Frederick Fischer
Mr. & Mrs. George P. Fisher
Mr. & Mrs. A. W. Fletcher
Mr. & Mrs. William W. Flinn
Mrs. F. F. Flint & drs.
Mrs. Helen C. Floyd & drs.
Mr. & Mrs. Charles W. Fullerton
Mr. & Mrs. William Gifford
Mr. & Mrs. Robert Gillette
Mr. & Mrs. Wm. M. Goodridge & dr.
Prof. & Mrs. Elisha Gray & drs.
Mr. & Mrs. Charles M. Green
Mr. & Mrs. F. B. Green
Mrs. H. R. Green
Mr. & Mrs. Cyrenius M. Greene
Mr. & Mrs. Geo. D. Griffith
Mr. & Mrs. B. F. Gump
Mr. & Mrs. Ford P. Hall
Mr. & Mrs. C. G. Hammond & dr.
Mr. & Mrs. Chas. H. Harrison
Dr. & Mrs. Henry L. Haskin
Mr. & Mrs. F. P. Hawkins
Mr. & Mrs. W. J. Hemstreet
Mr. & Mrs. Alfred S. Henderson
Mr. & Mrs. Gustav E. Henderson
Mr. & Mrs. Lewis B. Hibbard
Mr. & Mrs. W. O. Hipwell & dr.
Mr. & Mrs. David Holmes & dr.
Dr. E. G. Howard
Mr. & Mrs. Tracy D. Hull & dr.
Mrs. H. G. Humble
Mr. & Mrs. C. D. Hyndman
Mr. & Mrs. David Inman
Mr. & Mrs. Ralph S. Jefferson
Mr. & Mrs. Ben C. Jones
Mr. & Mrs. W. R. Kenny
A. L. Kip
Mr. & Mrs. Chas. Wright Kirk
Mr. & Mrs. S. Fred Knox
Mr. & Mrs. William S. Lasher
Mrs. J. A. Leach & dr.

Mr. & Mrs. Joseph Leaming
Milton C. Lightner
Mr. & Mrs. H. S. Look
Dr. Helen M. Lynch
Mrs. J. W. Lynch
Mr. & Mrs. James McDonald
Mr. & Mrs. Arthur McPherson
Mr. & Mrs. W. R. Mersereau
Mr. & Mrs. John Middleton & dr.
Mr. & Mrs. Merrick A. Mihills & dr.
    Receiving day Wednesday
Evart L. Millard
Mr. & Mrs. S. M. Millard & dr.
Mr. & Mrs. William Millard
Mr. & Mrs. Paul Mondou
Mr. & Mrs. P. A. Montgomery
Capt. & Mrs. O. H. Morgan & dr.
Mr. & Mrs. David Morrison
Samuel M. Myers
Rev. & Mrs. Henry Neill
Dr. & Mrs. H. P. Newman
Mr. & Mrs. Edmund Norton
    Receiving day Wednesday
Mrs. J. W. O'Brien & dr.
Mr. & Mrs. R. C. Page
Mr. & Mrs. E. B. Palmer & dr.
Miss Sarah A. Patchen
Miss Grace Plimpton
Mr. & Mrs. J. S. Prall
J. T. Raffen & drs.
Prof. & Mrs. G. W. Reddick
Mr. & Mrs. Harry L. Requa
Mr. & Mrs. C. B. Rice
Mr. & Mrs. John F. Rice
Mr. & Mrs. G. W. Roberts
Capt. & Mrs. Daniel Robinson & dr.
Mr. & Mrs. W. H. Russell & dr.
Mr. & Mrs. H. C. Sampson
Mr. & Mrs. Chas. E. Schauffler
Mr. & Mrs. Herman G. Schmidt
Mr. & Mrs. B. W. Schumacher

Mr. & Mrs. Theodore Schwarz
Mr. & Mrs. George C. Shaw
Mr. & Mrs. James H. Shields
Mr. & Mrs. G. L. Sites
Mr. & Mrs. Edward A. Small
Mrs. A. P. Smith
Mr. & Mrs. K. R. Smoot
    Receiving day Wednesday
Mr. & Mrs. Edgar M. Snow
Mr. & Mrs. J. S. Snyder
Clinton J. Spencer
Mr. & Mrs. T. H. Spencer
Mr. & Mrs. Edgar Stanton
Mr. & Mrs. Jonas Steers
Mr. & Mrs. John L. Stockton
Mr. & Mrs. Henry C. Street
Mr. & Mrs. R. P. Street
Richard H. Street
Miss J. H. Street
Mr. & Mrs. R. J. Street
Mr. & Mrs. C. E. Stuart
Mr. & Mrs. Wm. C. Stubbs
Mr. & Mrs. Dana W. Sweetland
Dr. & Mrs. George O. Taylor
Mr. & Mrs. Francis Thorn & dr.
Capt. & Mrs. Thomas G. Troxell
Col. & Mrs. P. T. Turnley & dr.
Mr. & Mrs. H. S. Vail
Mr. & Mrs. L. O. Van Riper
Mrs. A. G. VanSchaick & drs.
Mr. &. Mrs. J. Wallace Wakem
Mr. & Mrs. Edward H. Watson
Mr. & Mrs. Walter G. Watson
Mrs. Mary W. Weaver
F. C. Winchester
C. J. Winchester
Rev. & Mrs. P. C. Wolcott
Mr. & Mrs. J. A. Woodworth & dr.
Mrs. Elizabeth Worthington & dr.
Rev. & Mrs. George L. Wrenn & dr.
Mr. & Mrs. David L. Zook

HINSDALE.

Mr. & Mrs. C. A. Allen
J. E. Allen
Mrs. Sarah R. Andrews
Mrs. Anson Ayres
Frank E. Ayres
Mr. & Mrs. W. H. Babcock
Mr. & Mrs. Frederick P. Bagley
Mr. & Mrs. E. D. Baker
Mr. & Mrs. James H. Ballagh
Mr. & Mrs. Wm. T. Barr
Mr. & Mrs. O. P. Bassett
Miss Emma Bates

Mr. & Mrs. George Beach
Mr. & Mrs. Randolph R. Beam
Mr. & Mrs. E. L. Benton
Mr. & Mrs. C. D. Bird
Mr. & Mrs. W. L. Blackman
Mr. & Mrs. George W. Blayney
Mr. & Mrs. J. A. Blood
Mr. & Mrs. G. M. Bogue
Elias Bogue
Mr. & Mrs. J. H. Bradley
Mrs. E. L. Bradley
Ralph R. Bradley

Mr. & Mrs. Sidney H. Breese
Mr. & Mrs. Lafayette Briggs
Mr. & Mrs. Wm. A. Brooks
Mr. & Mrs. John Burton
Mr. & Mrs. George H. Burtt
Frederick P. Burtt
Mr. & Mrs. G. N. Burtt
Mr. & Mrs. I. S. Bush
Mr. & Mrs. John Campbell
Mr. & Mrs. Fred J. Candee
Mr. & Mrs. Henry W. Candee
Mr. & Mrs. W. B. Carleton
Mr. & Mrs. Byron B. Carter
Mr. & Mrs. John W. Cary
Paul V. Cary
Mr. & Mrs. Robert A. Childs
Receiving day Thurday
Mr. & Mrs. R. W. Clarke
Mrs. Helen E. Coffeen
Mr. & Mrs. Wm. Coffeen
Mrs. S. A. Colburn & dr.
Harry Colburn
William Colburn
Miss Blanche E. Cole
Harry A. Cole
Mr. & Mrs. William H. Cole
Mr. & Mrs. W. O. Cole
Mr. & Mrs. S. T. Collins
Mr. & Mrs. Lawrence P. Conover
Mrs. A. A. Convis & dr.
J. E. Convis
Mr. & Mrs. Owen D. Cook
Mr. & Mrs. H. H. Cooke
Mr. & Mrs. D. A. Courter
Mr. & Mrs. W. D. Crooke
Mr. & Mrs. E. C. Crosby
Mr. & Mrs. C. H. Crossette
Mr. & Mrs. C. H. Cushing
Mr. & Mrs. Otis Cushing
Mr. & Mrs. Harry C. Dana
Mr. & Mrs. Jerome J. Danforth
Mr. & Mrs. Martin G. Danforth
Mr. & Mrs. Walter Davidson
Mr. & Mrs. Edgar F. Davis
Mrs. S. J. Davis & dr.
Mr. & Mrs. Harvey Dean
Robert L. Dean
Mr. & Mrs. R. M. Dean
Mr. & Mrs. August Denmark
Mr. & Mrs. C. G. Dennison
W. H. Dennison
Mr. & Mrs. Eli H. Ditzler
Dr. John B. Doane
Mr. & Mrs. William Duncan
Mr. & Mrs. John E. Earle
Robert Easton

Mr. & Mrs. B. G. Edgerton
Mr. & Mrs. Harry L. Edwards
Mr. & Mrs. Willard H. Edwards
Mr. & Mrs. Frank Ellsworth
Mr. & Mrs. Truman W. Eustis
Mrs. Harriet E. Evans
Mr. & Mrs. William Evernden
E. J. Fairchild
Mr. & Mrs. George S. Farr
Mr. & Mrs. E. E. Fayerweather
Mr. & Mrs. George P. Fleisher
Mr. & Mrs. Charles Fox & dr.
Mr. & Mrs. Heman Fox
Mr. & Mrs. William O. Fox
Mr. & Mrs. William H. Freeman
Mr. & Mrs. H. A. Fulton
Mr. & Mrs. Henry A. Gardner
George C. Gardner
Mrs. S. P. Gardner
Mr. & Mrs. William D. Gates
Mrs. H. M. Gibbs
Mr. & Mrs. F. W. Godwin
Mr. & Mrs. Edward K. Gordon
Mrs. J. W. Gordon
Mr. & Mrs. William G. Gordon
Mr. & Mrs. Alten W. Gould
Mr. & Mrs. H. F. Grabo
Carl Groff
Miss Emily Gscheidlen
Mr. & Mrs. George W. Hall
Mr. & Mrs. S. B. Hamill
Mrs. F. H. Hannah & dr.
Mr. & Mrs. Thomas C. Hannah
Dr. & Mrs. L. P. Haskell & dr.
Mr. & Mrs. F. W. Hawtin
Mr. & Mrs. A. T. Heaphy
Mr. & Mrs. Samuel Heineman
Dr. & Mrs. J. B. Hench
Mr. & Mrs. Herbert G. Hetzler
Mr. & Mrs. C. F. Heyer
Mr. & Mrs. L. K. Hildebrand
Mr. & Mrs. Charles E. Hinds
Mr. & Mrs. E. P. Hinds
E. P. Hinds jr.
Mr. & Mrs. George W. Hinckley
Mr. & Mrs. Wm. B. Hinckley
Mr. & Mrs. Wm. S. Hinckley
Receiving day Thursday
Mr. & Mrs. A. G. Hines
Mr. & Mrs. Edward Hoar & dr.
L. M. Hodges
Wm. H. Holcomb & dr.
Mr. & Mrs. Wm. H. Holcomb jr.
Herbert W. Holcomb
Mrs. Almeda Hodges & dr.
Mrs. Caroline Holverscheid

Mr. & Mrs. Henry Holverscheid
Mr. & Mrs. Sheldon L. Hough
Mr. & Mrs. Chas. Hudson
Mr. & Mrs. Frank Hughes
Mrs. H. C. Irish
F. R. Irvine
Mr. & Mrs. Horace Jackson
Mr. & Mrs. John R. Jarrett & dr.
Mrs. W. G. Jerrems jr.
Mr. & Mrs. P. C. Johnson
Mr. & Mrs. W. A. Johnson
Mr. & Mrs. A. S. Johnston
Mr. & Mrs. William Johnston
Mrs. Robert Jones
E. F. Jourdan
Mr. & Mrs. A. E. Keith
Miss Marie Kennedy
Mr. & Mrs. J. W. Kirk
Mr. & Mrs. W. H. Knight
Mr. & Mrs. Harry C. Knisely
Mr. & Mrs. Frank Krohn
W. A. Lalor
Miss Margaret Lalor
Roland R. Landis
Mr. & Mrs. William Landis
Dr. & Mrs. Thomas Lawton
Mr. & Mrs. Walter Leslie
Mr. & Mrs. George F. Lewis
Mr. & Mrs. A. A. Lincoln
Mrs. F. Linsley
Mr. & Mrs. T. H. Linsley
Mr. & Mrs. Henry C. Lockwood
Mr. & Mrs. Henry S. Loomis
Mr. & Mrs. Chas. L. Loveland
Mr. & Mrs. J. McClintock
Rev. & Mrs. D. C. McCoy
Mr. & Mrs. Wm. McCredie & dr.
Mr. & Mrs. Hugh F. McFarlane
Mr. & Mrs. W. E. McGee
Miss Emily McKinnie
Herman O. Matile
Pascal P. Matthews
Miss Hattie Merrill
J. C. F. Merrill
Mr. & Mrs. H. C. Middaugh
George L. Miller
Mr. & Mrs. Geo. S. Miller & drs.
Mr. & Mrs. A. W. Mitchell
Miss Anna Belle Mitchell
Edward G. Mitchell
Mr. & Mrs. George H. Mitchell
Grant Mitchell
Miss N. Adelaide Mitchell
Mrs. Mary Mix
Rev. C. F. Moore
Mrs. Sarah F. Moore

Mr. & Mrs. Orville M. Morris
Mr. & Mrs. L. Muller
Mr. & Mrs. James Murray
Mr. & Mrs. Thos. W. B. Murray
Mr. & Mrs. G. A. Murrell
Mr. & Mrs. E. B. Needham
Mr. & Mrs. Lester C. Newell
Mr. & Mrs. George W. Noble
John Ohls
Mr. & Mrs. J. B. Page
Mrs. Alfred Payne
Miss Ann Payne
Mr. & Mrs. A. L. Pearsall
Mr. & Mrs. D. K. Pearsons
Rev. Harry W. Perkins
Mrs. Sarah H. Perkins
Mr. & Mrs. T. W. Phillips
Mr. & Mrs. Chas. C. Pickett
Mr. & Mrs. W. J. Pollock
Mr. & Mrs. D. H. Preston
Mrs. Frances L. Pulver
Miss C. Gertrude Pulver
Mr. & Mrs. M. L. Raftree
Mrs. C. A. Rawson
Miss Addie M. Raymond
Mr. & Mrs. Chas. A. Raymond
Mr. & Mrs. George W. Raymond
J. N. Redfern
Mr. & Mrs. John Reed
Mr. & Mrs. Bruce E. Richie
Mr. & Mrs. James V. Ridgway
Edwin S. Ripley
Mr. & Mrs. J. A. Ripley
Mr. & Mrs. George B. Robbins
Dr. & Mrs. C. M. Roberts
Dr. Dwight J. Roberts
Mr. & Mrs. Albert R. Robinson
Mr. & Mrs. John C. Ross
Mr. & Mrs. M. L. Roth
Mr. & Mrs. L. C. Ruth
Chauncey F. Ryder
Mr. & Mrs. Albert Sabin & drs.
Mr. & Mrs. F. J. Schuyler
Mr. & Mrs. J. S. Shannon
Mr. & Mrs. Edward S. Shaw
Miss E. M. Shaw
James W. Shaw
Mr. & Mrs. J. W. Shaw & dr.
Mrs. Susan C. Shewell
Mr. & Mrs. Dana Slade jr.
Mr. & Mrs. John C. Slocum
Mr. & Mrs. Donald Smith
Mr. & Mrs. Geo. E. Smith
W. K. Smith
Mr. & Mrs. Chas. E. Spear
Mr. & Mrs. E. Raymond Spear

Mr. & Mrs. W. T. Stevens
Mr. & Mrs. W. T. Steward
Mrs. Abbie H. Stewart
Charles Stuart
Mr. & Mrs. J. F. Stuart & dr.
Mr. & Mrs. C. H. Thayer
Herbert Thayer
Mr. & Mrs. William Thayer & dr.
G. S. Tiffany
Mrs. Joel Tiffany
Mr. & Mrs. P. S. Townsend
Robert Treat
Mr. & Mrs. Fred VanInwagen
Mrs. Frederick VanLiew & drs.
L. C. VanLiew
Mr. & Mrs. John Wadington
Mr. & Mrs. Wm. W. Waite
Mrs. Athalia A. Walker
Mr. & Mrs. A. E. Walker
Mr. & Mrs. H. K. Walker & drs.
Miss Lizzie M. Walker

Miss E. L. Walton
Mr. & Mrs. C. C. Warren
Mr. & Mrs. C. T. Warren
Mr. & Mrs. Nathan H. Warren
Mr. & Mrs. Charles L. Washburn
H. L. Wayne
Mr. & Mrs. Horace S. Weeks & dr.
Mr. & Mrs. Henry W. Weiss
Mr. & Mrs. J. M. Whitson
J. M. Whitson jr.
Mr. & Mrs. George H. Williams
Mr. & Mrs. George W. Wilson&drs.
Rev. & Mrs. G. H. Wilson
S. C. Wilson
Mrs. Thos. J. Woodcock & drs.
Miss Frances E. A. Wright
George Wright
Mr. & Mrs. G. K. Wright
Mr. & Mrs. Edward Wylde
Mr. & Mrs. Joseph Zimmerman

IRVING PARK.

Mr. & Mrs. H. E. Adams
J. Albert Allison
Mr. & Mrs. C. F. Barstow
Mrs. H. D. Barstow
Dr. Rhoda Barstow-Pike
G. H. Bauer
A. V. Berry
Mr. & Mrs. C. F. Bixel
Mr. & Mrs. D. W. Blair
Mr. & Mrs. G. C. Blair
Mr. & Mrs. Louis Boche
Mr. & Mrs. Louis J. Boerlin
Miss Emma E. Brown
Dr. F. I. Brown
Mr. & Mrs. W. H. Brown
Mr. & Mrs. D. L. Buzzell
Mr. &. Mrs. F. W. Calais & dr.
Mrs. George Calhoun
Mr. & Mrs. S. C. Chetham
Mrs. Sophia A. Christensen
S. J. Christensen
Mr. & Mrs. C. P. Coggeshall
Mr. & Mrs. James W. Converse
Mr. & Mrs. C. A. Cook
Mr. & Mrs. F. L. Cook
Mr. & Mrs. Theron W. Cookingham
Miss Marietta Coon
Mr. & Mrs. F. A. Crego
Mr. & Mrs. Louis K. Curlett
Mr. & Mrs. F. J. Cushing
Mr. & Mrs. T. W. Cushman & dr.

Mr. & Mrs. P. I. Davis
Mr. & Mrs. C. A. Day
Mr. & Mrs. John De Vos
Mr. & Mrs. J. E. Dietz & dr.
Mr. & Mrs. J. M. Dietz
Mr. & Mrs. R. O. Dunning
Mr. & Mrs. Robert Duvall
Mr. & Mrs. C. W. Farr
Mrs. Wm. Florance
Mr. & Mrs. J. J. Fones
Mr. & Mrs. M. A. Foote
Mr. &. Mrs. L. D. Garratt
Mr. & Mrs. C. F. Gooding
Mr. & Mrs. A. G. Goodridge
Mrs. Margaret Goodwin
Dr. & Mrs. C. W. Gould
Mr. & Mrs. Ole N. Hanson
Mr. & Mrs. George C. Hield
Mr. & Mrs. A. H. Hill
F. Hollis
J. F. Hollis
Mr. & Mrs. F. E. Holton & dr.
Mr. & Mrs. C. F. Hunting
Mr. & Mrs. A. C. Johnston
Mr. & Mrs. J. Milton Johnston
W. C. Jordan
Joseph A. Kane
Mr. & Mrs. W. R. Kellogg
W. N. Ketcham
Mr. & Mrs. Spencer S. Kimbell
Mr. & Mrs. Arthur M. Lane

F. E. Larson
Mrs. M. C. Lincoln
Mr. & Mrs. F. L. Lively
Mrs. Anna Livesey
Mr. & Mrs. Charles N. Loucks
Mr. & Mrs. J. A. MacBurney
Mr. & Mrs. John R. Madison
Mr. & Mrs. George Mamerow
Mr. & Mrs. Chas. E. Martin
Mr. & Mrs. W. M. McEwen
Mr. & Mrs. C. S. McNett
Mr. & Mrs. E. L. Milburn
Mr. & Mrs. W. K. Millard
Mr. & Mrs. J. S. Monk
Mr. & Mrs. A. J. Nowlen & dr.
Mrs. Margaret Nuveen
W. H. Okeson
Mr. & Mrs.. Wm. F. Orrell
A. C. Osborn
Mr. & Mrs Alonzo W. Paige
Albert Paige
F. W. Paige
Mr. & Mrs. T. G. Palmer
Receive Thursday
Mr. & Mrs. Lucius W. Parish
Dr. & Mrs. Wm. W. Parker
Mr. & Mrs. W. R. Parsons
Mr. & Mrs. J. A. Peterson
Dr. Kate B. Peterson
Mr. & Mrs. E. D. Pitcher
R. T. Race
Mr. & Mrs. S. A. Race
Mr. & Mrs. W. B. Race
Miss Ambrosia Race
Miss Jane M. Race
Mr. & Mrs. Wm. Reed
Ernest H. Rehwoldt
Mr. & Mrs. E. W. Reynolds
F. H. Reynolds
Millard W. Rice

A. D. Richey
F. L. Richey
Silas Ropp
Rev. & Mrs. Wm. Rowley
Mr. & Mrs. Walter Sayler
Mr. & Mrs. Chas. O. Sethness
Mr. & Mrs. H. V. Shepard
Mr. & Mrs. C. C. Sherman
Mr. & Mrs. W. J. Simpson
Mrs. C. F. Smith
Mr. & Mrs. S. M. St. Clair
Dr. & Mrs. E. J. Tanner
Mr. & Mrs. Horatio Thomas
Mr. & Mrs. Leonidas Thomas
Mr. & Mrs. W. C. Toles
George K. Tompkins & drs.
Devid M. Tracy
Mr. & Mrs. LeRoy C. Tryon
Mrs. Carrie VanNess
Gardiner VanNess
L. T. VanNess
Mr. & Mrs. A. E. VanOstrand
Mr. & Mrs. John A. Wadhams
Mr. & Mrs. William Wallace
Mr. & Mrs. A. H. Walmsley
Mr. & Mrs. Grove E. Walter
Mr. & Mrs. J. B. Weeks
Mr. & Mrs. J. G. Wells
Dr. & Mrs. John A. Wheeler
Mr. & Mrs. J. R. Wickersham
& dr.
Mr.&Mrs. D. Lemoyne Wickersham
Mr. & Mrs. Wm. D. Wilcox
Dr. & Mrs. W. L. Wilcox
Mr. & Mrs. J. W. Williams
F. J. Wilson
S. R. Wilson
Mr. & Mrs. C. I. Wolfinger
Mr. & Mrs. Geo. P. Wright
Mr. & Mrs. Robert Wulff

JEFFERSON PARK.

Mr. & Mrs. Hubert W. Butler
Mr. & Mrs. John Deitcher
Mr. & Mrs. David S. Dunning
Mr. & Mrs. Edwin Dymond
Mr. & Mrs. John H. Dymond
Mr. & Mrs. Henry Esdohr
Mr. & Mrs. Herman H. Esdohr
Dr. David B. Fonda
Mr. & Mrs. Win P. Gray
Mr. & Mrs. Albert W. Holmes
Mr. & Mrs. Isaac N. Huestis

Mr. & Mrs. Fred C. Hurst
Mr. & Mrs. L. D. Lowell
Dr. & Mrs. Malcomb T. Moore
Receiving day Thursday
Mr. & Mrs. Frank A. Price
Mr. & Mrs. W. D. Price
Mr. & Mrs. Clark Roberts
Roscoe L. Roberts
Mr. & Mrs. Theodore Schultz
Mr. & Mrs. Peter F. Thomsen
Mr. & Mrs. Henry Wulff & drs.

KENILWORTH.

Mrs. Mary Keys Babcock & drs.
Mr. & Mrs. S. S. Barry & dr.
Mr. & Mrs. Edward F. Bideleux
Mr. & Mrs. L. Brinckerhoff
Mr. & Mrs. John W. Brooks
Mr. & Mrs. Franklin P. Burnham
Mr. & Mrs. J. Y. Calahan
Mr. & Mrs. M. L. Coffeen
Mr. & Mrs. J. A. Culbertson
          Receive Friday
Mr. & Mrs. George Cutter
Mrs. E. C. Derickson
Prof. & Mrs. James Gill
M. L. Gould
Mr. & Mrs. Henry A. Hall
Mr. & Mrs. B. P. Hinman & dr.
B. P. Hinman jr.
Mr. & Mrs. George E. Holmes
Mr. & Mrs. R. C. Johnson
Mr. & Mrs. Rollin A. Keyes
Mr. & Mrs. H. C. Lloyd

Mr. & Mrs. Wilson H. Low
Mr. & Mrs. George W. Maher
Mr. & Mrs. A. V. Martin & dr.
Mrs. Henry Martin
Mr. & Mrs. C. M. McCook
Mr. & Mrs. J. F. Miller
Mr. & Mrs. Alex Officer
Mrs. M. E. Pratt
Mr. & Mrs. Walter R. Root
Mr. & Mrs. Joseph Sears
John B. Sears
Mr. & Mrs. Wm. H. H. Sears
Dr. & Mrs. Charles S. Smith
Mr. & Mrs. Howard H. Spaulding
C. H. Stumpoffski
Mrs. R. Stumpoffski
Mr. & Mrs. William N. Sturges
          Receiving day Tuesday
Mr. & Mrs. Homer S. Taylor & dr.
Mr. & Mrs. Charles Ware

LAGRANGE.

Mr. & Mrs. Frank E. Abbott
Mr. & Mrs. John T. Allison
Mr. & Mrs. Llewellyn W. Arnold
Mr. & Mrs. Wm. H. Arnold
Mr. & Mrs. A. B. Ashley & dr.
Mr. & Mrs. Clarence M. Babbitt
W. H. Baker
Mr. & Mrs. M. T. Baldwin
Mr. & Mrs. W. K. Balfour
Mr. & Mrs. J. C. Banks
Mr. & Mrs. H. Bearse
Mr. & Mrs. F. E. Beatty
H. B. Beatty
Mr. & Mrs. J. T. Beatty
Mrs. S. J. Beatty
Mr. & Mrs. W. R. Beatty
Mr. & Mrs. F. W. Beecroft
Mr. & Mrs. Theodore L. Bergen
Mr. & Mrs. Paul Bessems
Mrs. Edwin R. Bishop & dr.
William S. Bishop
Mr. & Mrs. G. W. Blakelidge
Mr. & Mrs. L. P. Blakely
Mr. & Mrs. Levi Blakeslee & dr.
Mr. & Mrs. Walter H. Blick
Mr. & Mrs. Emile K. Boisot
Mr. & Mrs. Frank L. Borwell
Mr. & Mrs. Oscar T. Bourgeois
Mr. & Mrs. John Bowers
Mr. & Mrs. Joseph B. Bowles

Mr. & Mrs. W. F. Brabook jr.
Mr. & Mrs. J. O. Bracken
Mr. & Mrs. Edward C. Brainard
Mr. & Mrs. Charles L. Breed
George M. Briggs
Mr. & Mrs. N. E. Briggs
Mr. & Mrs. John M. Brown & dr.
Mr. & Mrs. L. Cass Brown
Mr. & Mrs. Josiah M. Browne
Mr. & Mrs. Malcolm J. Browne
Mr. & Mrs. Willis W. Browne
Mr. & Mrs. J. A. Brydon
Mr. & Mrs. A. O. Buckius
Mr. & Mrs. W. I. Bunker
Mr. & Mrs. Mark Burget
Mr. & Mrs. H. Burkholder & drs.
H. P. Burkholder
Mr. & Mrs. W. R. Burleigh
Dr. & Mrs. L. Bush
Mr. & Mrs. E. B. Bushnell
Rev. & Mrs. H. A..Bushnell
Mr. & Mrs. Fred H. Butler
Mr. & Mrs. B. Cadwallader
Mr. & Mrs. E. S. Cadwell
Dr. & Mrs. W. Carey
Mr. & Mrs. B. J. Carpenter
Mr. & Mrs. Charles C. Carpenter
Mr. & Mrs. Miron J. Carpenter
Mr. & Mrs. Egbert Chase
Mr. & Mrs. Bertram M. Chattell

Mr. & Mrs. Clarence C. Cheney
Mr. & Mrs. Theo. D. Christopher
J. Irving Christopher
Mr. & Mrs. F. H. Churchill
Mr. & Mrs. John V. Clark
 Receiving day Thursday
Mr. & Mrs. N. C. Clark
Mr. & Mrs. W. Irving Clark
Mr. & Mrs. Ed A. Clarke
Mr. & Mrs. J. L. Clough
Mr. & Mrs. P. M. Coates
Mr. & Mrs. R. W. Coates
Mr. & Mrs. W. J. Cobb
Mr. & Mrs. J. A. Connell
Mr. & Mrs. Edwin G. Cooley
Mr. & Mrs. Sidney Coolidge
B. E. Cooper
Mr. & Mrs. Henry N. Cooper
J. Edward Cooper
Mr. & Mrs. George J. Corey
 Receive Tuesday and Friday
Ray Webster·Corey
Mr. & Mrs. F. D. Cossitt
Mr. & Mrs. F. D. Cossitt jr.
Mr. & Mrs. W. H. Council
Mr. & Mrs. M. C. Covell
Mr. & Mrs. W. R. Crawford
Mr. & Mrs. Robert Cruit
Mr. & Mrs. J. F. Daggett
Rev. & Mrs. Geo. M. Daniels
Mr. & Mrs. Herbert Darlington
Mr. & Mrs. S. Frank Davidson
Dr. W. Crosbie Davis
Mr. & Mrs. H. E. DeCamp
Dr. & Mrs. E. S. Detweiler
Mr. & Mrs. Fred M. Dewey
Mr. & Mrs. O. J. Dewey
Mr. & Mrs. F. L. DeWitt
Mr. & Mrs. C. W. Dietrich
Mr. & Mrs. W. M. Dietrich
Mr. & Mrs. M. D. Dimick & dr.
Mr. & Mrs. Chris Dirks
Mr. & Mrs. George E. Dixon
Mr. & Mrs. W. E. Drake
Mr. & Mrs. G. R. Dunne
Mr. & Mrs. W. S. Edes
Mr. & Mrs. Fred C. Edler
Mr. & Mrs. Charles Edwards
Mr. & Mrs. B. H. Eldridge
Mr. & Mrs. John Eldridge
Mr. & Mrs. John Ellis
Edward S. Ely
Miss Mabel Clare Estes
St. Louis A. Estes
Mr. & Mrs. P. S. Eustis
Mr. & Mrs. C. H. Field & drs.

Mr. & Mrs. Frank F. Fisher
Mr. & Mrs. Wm. A. Fogarty
Walter Foley
Mr. & Mrs. F. D. Ford
Mr. & Mrs. George D. Forrest
Mr. & Mrs. W. H. Fosner
Dr. G. M. Fox & dr.
Mr. & Mrs. L. H. Freer
Mr. & Mrs. John W. French
Charles A. Gardner
Mr. & Mrs. P. G. Gardner
Mr. & Mrs. George Garretson
Mr. & Mrs. J. P. George & dr.
Mr. & Mrs. James R. Gilbert
Mr. & Mrs. J. E. Gilmore
Mr. & Mrs. Orrin S. Goan
Mr. & Mrs. H. E. Goodwin & dr.
Mr. & Mrs. Edwin A. Graves
George M. Graves
Mr. & Mrs. J. R. Griffitts
Mr. & Mrs. W. F. Griffitts
Rev. James M. Hagan
Mr. & Mrs. Franklin Haight
Mr. & Mrs. Ferd Hall
P. M. Hallowell
Mr. & Mrs. Edgar Hapeman
Mr. & Mrs. L. B. Harrington
Mr. & Mrs. Henry S. Harrison
Mr. & Mrs. Edward P. Hatch
Mr. & Mrs. W. H. Hatfield
Mr. & Mrs. R. C. Haviland
Mr. & Mrs. F. A. S. Hayes
Mr. & Mrs. James A. Hicks
Dr. & Mrs. A. E. Higgins
Mr. & Mrs. Fremont Hill
Mr. & Mrs. Myron T. Hinckley
Mr. & Mrs. O. J. Holbrook
Mr. & Mrs. L. H. Holmes & dr.
 Receiving day Thursday
Ralph H. Holmes
Mr. & Mrs. Thomas W. Hoover
Mr. & Mrs. Brainard Honsinger
Judge & Mrs. O. H. Horton
Richard Horton
Mr. & Mrs. John Hoskins
Mr. & Mrs. William Hoskins
Mr. & Mrs. Geo. Howard
Rev. & Mrs. Charles J. Howell
Mr. & Mrs. John C. Howell & dr.
Mr. & Mrs. H. M. Huff
Mr. & Mrs. A. H. Humphrey
A. O. Humphrey
Mr. & Mrs. W. C. Hunter
Mr. & Mrs. Abner Hurd & drs.
Mr. & Mrs. A. Haynes Hurd
Mr. & Mrs. F. M. Hyde

49

Mr. & Mrs. C. L. Iverson
Mr. & Mrs. R. W. Iverson
Mr. & Mrs. N. E. Jennison
Mr. & Mrs. E. H. Johnson
Mr. & Mrs. Geo. H. Johnson & dr.
Mr. & Mrs. Geo. A. Joyce
Mr. & Mrs. M. R. Kavanagh
Mr. & Mrs. H. D. Keeler
Mr. & Mrs. M. L. Kellogg
Mr. & Mrs. S. W. Kempster
Mr. & Mrs. Henry W. Kerrison
Mr. & Mrs. H. A. Keyes
Mr. & Mrs. James Kidston
Mr. & Mrs. Charles Lang
Mr. & Mrs. G. H. Laubenstein
Mr. & Mrs. Archibald S. Leckie
Mr. & Mrs. W. H. Lee
Mr. & Mrs. Thomas E. Lindsay
Dr. & Mrs. H. S. Llewellyn
Mr. & Mrs. Joseph C. Llewellyn
Mr. & Mrs. P. A. Lord
Dr. & Mrs. R. F. Ludwig & dr.
Mr. & Mrs. Ayres D. Lundy
David Lyman
Mr. & Mrs. D. B. Lyman
Mr. & Mrs. O. S. Lym
Mr. & Mrs. C. B. Lyoran
Mr. & Mrs. D. A. Lyon
Mr. & Mrs. J. M. Lyon
Mr. & Mrs. W. H. McClintock
George McCoy
Mr. & Mrs. G. H. McDonald
Mr. & Mrs. Harley C. McDonald
Mr. & Mrs. D. B. McGill
Mr. & Mrs. G. F. McGill
Mr. & Mrs. D. P. McGregor
Mr. & Mrs. J. H. McGrew
Dr. & Mrs. E. E. McKay
Mrs. M. McKay
Mr. & Mrs. C. C. McLain
Mr. & Mrs. Albert McLaughlin
Mr. & Mrs. M. B. McLenahan
Mr. & Mrs. S. P. McMahon
Mr. & Mrs. James Mac Edward
A. J. Maloy M.D.
Dr. Sarah E. Maloy
Mr. & Mrs. Fred Mandell
Mr. & Mrs. Hiram C. Marsh
Mr. & Mrs. O. B. Marsh
Capt. Joseph A. Marshall
Mrs. Medora Estes Marshall
Receiving day Thursday 3 to 6 p. m.
Mr. & Mrs. Chester M. Marthens
Mr. & Mrs. J. R. Maus
Mr. & Mrs. John Mavor
Mr. & Mrs. J. E. A. Maxwell

Mr. & Mrs. L. Byron Mears & dr.
Mr. & Mrs. W. J. Melick
Mr. & Mrs. J. K. Mettler
Mr. & Mrs. A. Minor
Mr. & Mrs. F. H. Mitchell
Mr. & Mrs. Harley B. Mitchell
Mr. & Mrs. H. S. Mitchell
Mr. & Mrs. George A. Moncur
Rev. & Mrs. J. A. Montgomery &
    dr.
Mr. & Mrs. J. Byron Moody
Mr. & Mrs. S. B. Moody
Mr. & Mrs. Geo. C. Morgan jr.
Charles A. Moses
Mr. & Mrs. Daniel W. Munn
Mr. & Mrs. John A. Murphey jr.
Mr. & Mrs. A. G. Murray
Mr. & Mrs. Donald Murray
Mr. & Mrs. Edward E. Naugle
Mr. & Mrs. E. R. Neely
J. B. Newman
Mr. & Mrs. J. C. Osborne
Mr. & Mrs. Henry A. Otis
Mr. & Mrs. J. F. Packer
Mr. & Mrs. L. A. Pagin
Ed. Palmer
Mr. & Mrs. H. B. Parker
Mr. & Mrs. C. F. Parker
Mr. & Mrs. A. S. Peck
Mr. & Mrs. B. C. Perkins
Mr. & Mrs. B. W. Perkins
Mr. & Mrs. Henry G. Peters
Mr. & Mrs. Francis V. Phillips
Mrs. E. B. Philo & drs.
Mr. & Mrs. William C. Post
Mr. & Mrs. G. O. Pratt
Jacob C. Pratt
Mr. & Mrs. Howard S. Prescott
Mr. & Mrs. Thomas C. Purves
Mr. & Mrs. C. W. Richmond & dr.
J. W. R. Rogers
C. Rossman
Arnold S. Rothwell
Harry L. Rothwell
Mr. & Mrs. H. R. Rothwell
R. E. Rothwell
Mr. & Mrs. C. L. Sackett
Frank V. Sackett
Mr. & Mrs. L. J. Sacriste
Mr. & Mrs. V. C. Sanborn
Mr. & Mrs. Frank E. Sanford
Dr. & Mrs. F. W. Satterlee
Charles P. Saxe
Mr. & Mrs. W. A. Scott
Mr. & Mrs. S. G. Seaton
Mr. & Mrs. E. W. Silsby

Mr. & Mrs. L. W. Slocum
Mr. & Mrs. E. B. Smith
Mr. & Mrs. F. C. Smith
Mr. & Mrs. E. D. Snyder
Mr. & Mrs. Wm. Squirer
Mr. & Mrs. George A. Stannard
G. P. Stannard
James M. Stannard
Mr. & Mrs. Fred H. Stevens
Mr. & Mrs. C. L. Stiles
Rev. & Mrs. Morton Stone
Mrs. M. M. Stone
Mr. & Mrs. C. A. Sreet
Mr. & Mrs. Laurence M. Sturtevant
Mr. & Mrs. Stephen G. Swisher
Mr. & Mrs. Edwin V. Tahl
E. W. Thomas
H. S. Thompson
Mr. & Mrs. R. D. Thompson
S. C. Thompson
Edward C. Thornton
Mr. & Mrs. F. H. Thorp
Mr. & Mrs. J. Neal Tilton
Mr. & Mrs. James W. Turner
Mr. & Mrs. John Unold
Mr. & Mrs. C. A. Upton
Mr. & Mrs. George M. Vial
Mr. & Mrs. Joseph Vial
Samuel Vial & drs.
Mr. & Mrs. W. H. Walbridge

W. P. Walbridge
Mr. & Mrs. A. W. Walker
Mr. & Mrs. Chas. H. Walker & dr.
Charles M. Walker
Mr. & Mrs. C. Hayward Walker
Dudley Walker
J. R. Walker
Mr. & Mrs. Moses B. Walker
Mr. & Mrs. M. H. Walker
Mr. & Mrs. William H. Wall
Mr. & Mrs. G. W. R. Wallace
Mr. & Mrs. Wm. Walmsley
Mr. & Mrs. R. F. Walton
Mr. & Mrs. James P. Weatherstone
Mr. & Mrs. Wm. W. Weatherstone
Mr. & Mrs. C. A. Webster
Mr. & Mrs. Henry Werno
C. L. Wheat
Mr. & Mrs. Edmund R. White
Mr. & Mrs. S. K. White
Mr. & Mrs. C. A. Whitney
Dr. & Mrs. C. H. Williams
Mr. & Mrs. T. D. Williams
Rev. & Mrs. J. H. Windsor & dr.
Mr. & Mrs. L. S. Wintersteen
Mr. & Mrs. E. Witte
Eben E. Wolcott
Mr. & Mrs. James G. Wolcott
Mr. & Mrs. J. H. Wolcott
Mr. & Mrs. C. W. Wright

LAKE FOREST.

Mr. & Mrs. F. C. Aldrich
Mr. & Mrs. F. W. Alex
Mr. & Mrs. Frederick H. Anderman
Mr. & Mrs. James Anderson & drs.
Miss J. L. Axtell
Mr. & Mrs. Robert Bell
Mr. & Mrs. Samuel Blackler
Prof. & Mrs. W. R. Bridgman
Miss Annie Brown
Mr. & Mrs. W. P. Butler
Mr. & Mrs. Edgar S. Calvert
Mr. & Mrs. Frank Calvert
Mr. & Mrs. Edward F. Chapin
Mr. & Mrs. A. W. Cobb
Mr. & Mrs. Henry Ives Cobb
Dr. & Mrs. John M. Coulter
Mr. & Mrs. L. J. Davies
Prof. Arthur C. Dawson
Mr. & Mrs. A. M. Day & drs.
Mr. & Mrs. James Dewey
Prof. Wm. H. Dudley

Mr. & Mrs. Calvin Durand & dr.
    Receiving day Monday
Mrs. Chas. E. Durand
Henry Z. Durand
H. Calvin Durand
Mr. & Mrs. Henry C. Durand
Mr. & Mrs. Joseph B. Durand & drs.
Scott Durand
Mr. & Mrs. J. H. Dwight
Mr. & Mrs. David Fales & dr.
Mr. & Mrs. Frank C. Farwell
Mr. & Mrs. Granger Farwell
Mr. & Mrs. T. S. Fauntleroy
Mrs. Abbie F. Ferry
Madame Wm. H. Ferry
Mr. & Mrs. Carter H. Fitz Hugh
Mr. & Mrs. G. G. French
Mr. & Mrs. Charles K. Giles
Mr. & Mrs. Bernard J. Gilroy
Mr. & Mrs. E. F. Gorton
Mr. & Mrs. John Gould

Mrs. S. P. Gould & dr.
Clifford P. Hall
Mr. & Mrs. Frank G. Hall
Prof. & Mrs. J. J. Halsey
Dr. & Mrs. Alfred C. Haven
   Receiving day Friday
Mr. & Mrs. J. F. Henderson
Mrs. F. H. Hewitt
Mr. & Mrs. F. E. Hinckley
Mr. & Mrs. D. R. Holt & dr.
Mrs. A. L. Holt
George H. Holt
Mr. & Mrs. Henry Horton & dr.
Mr. & Mrs. Walter C. Larned
Mr. & Mrs. Charles E. Latimer & dr.
E. J. Learned
Mrs. S. J. Learned & drs.
Miss Alice G. Leonard
Mrs. Sylvester Lind
Prof. & Mrs. Wm. A. Locy
Mr. & Mrs. Matthew Lough
Mrs. E. B. McClanahan
Rev. & Mrs. James G. K. McClure
Prof. Malcolm McNeill
Mr. & Mrs. James A. Miller
Mr. & Mrs. Josiah Moore & drs.
Mr. & Mrs. Wm. A. Morgan
Mr. & Mrs. Jesse L. Moss
Mr. & Mrs. W. A. Nichols
E. A. Nordling
Rev. Edward O'Reilly
Mr. & Mrs. S. C. Orr
Prof. & Mrs. Wm. F. Palmer
Mr. & Mrs. Frank Parcells
Mr. & Mrs. L. C. Platt & drs.
Mr. & Mrs. N. D. Pratt & dr.
Wm. E. Pratt
Mr. & Mrs. Charles Proctor
Mr. & Mrs. Richard Proctor

Mr. & Mrs. W. G. Rainey & dr.
Mrs. Robert W. Ralston
Mrs. Simon S. Reid & drs.
Mrs. Sarah J. Rhea
Thomas J. Rodman
Mr. & Mrs. Gilbert Rossiter
J. Franck Rumsey
Mr. & Mrs. Israel P. Rumsey & drs.
Mr. & Mrs. Robert Russell
Mr. & Mrs. Byron L. Smith
Prof. & Mrs. Charles A. Smith
Delavan Smith
Prof. Walter Smith
William Henry Smith
Mr. & Mrs. L. H. Speidel
Mrs. Cornelia C. Stanley & drs.
Hiram M. Stanley
Rev. and Mrs. Thomas Stephenson
Prof. & Mrs. F. W. Stevens
Prof. Louis Stuart
Mr. & Mrs. Sydney R. Taber
Mrs. Louise M. Taylor & drs.
William A. Taylor
Prof. & Mrs. M. B. Thomas
Miss Clara R. Thomas
Mr. & Mrs. J. E. Townsend
Mr. & Mrs. Henry Tuttle
Dr. & Mrs. E. P. Ward
Mr. & Mrs. Ezra J. Warner & dr.
Mrs. William Warren
John P. S. Warren
Aubrey Warren
Mr. & Mrs. Richard G. Watson
Mr. & Mrs. C. S. Weaver
Mr. & Mrs. S. C. Welch
Mr. & Mrs. Edwin S. Wells
Edwin S. Wells jr.
Mr. & Mrs. Samuel G. Wilson
Mrs. Glen Wood & dr.

LAKESIDE.

Mr. & Mrs. Andrew Davis
Mr. & Mrs. Frank J. Gage
Mr. & Mrs. Frank Heinig
Mr. & Mrs. Cyrus Kehr
Mr. & Mrs. John Merrilies & dr.
O. L. Merrilies
William Merrilies
Miss M. D. Moseley
Mr. & Mrs. L. J. Norton
Mr. & Mrs. O. E. Poole

George Scott
Mr. & Mrs. Robert S. Scott
Miss Martha Scott
Mr. & Mrs. Robert Watt
Mr. & Mrs. James R. West & dr.
Rev. & Mrs. J. A. White
Mr. & Mrs. Frank Whitney
Mr. & Mrs. George Whitney
Miss Mary A. Witmer

LOMBARD.

Mrs. P. Albee & dr.
Mr. & Mrs. A. H. Andrews
Miss Bertha M. Andrews

Mr. & Mrs. Charles O. Chapin
Mr. & Mrs. Isaac Claflin
Mr. & Mrs. W. Claflin

Mrs. N. S. Cushing
Rev. H. F. Goodwin
Mr. & Mrs. George Hill
Mr. & Mrs. W. P. Hill & dr.
Receiving day Thursday
Mr. & Mrs. Hugh W. Hughes
Dr. & Mrs. W. G. Leroy & dr.
A. R. Macdonald
Charles McCabe
Miss Ellen A. Martin
Mrs. N. Matson
Dr. & Mrs. C. W. Oleson
Mr. & Mrs. Henry Peck
Mr. & Mrs. H. W. Plum
Mr. & Mrs. W. R. Plum

Mr. & Mrs. H. S. Rand
Mrs. H. C. Rand
Miss Grace Rand
J. T. Reed
Miss Christie Reed
Dr. & Mrs. B. P. Reynolds
Mr. & Mrs. George H. Rogers
Henry Thomas
John Thomas
Mr. & Mrs. S. R. Thurston
Miss Margaret Towne
Dr. & Mrs. Louis M. Turbin
Mr. & Mrs. T. H. Vance
Mrs. C. M. Williams
A. B. Wrisley & dr.

LONGWOOD.

Mr. & Mrs. Wm. Ashton
William Ashton jr.
Edward Baker
Mr. & Mrs. H. H. Belding
Mr. & Mrs. E. W. Bennett
Mr. & Mrs. Albert Biggs
Mr. & Mrs. E. H. Bosler
Mr. & Mrs. Oliver G. Burnham
Dr. & Mrs. C. S. Burr
Mr. & Mrs. H. R. Caberey
Mr. & Mrs. Chas. P. Campbell
Mr. & Mrs. D. C. Campbell
Mr. & Mrs. Char. W. Capper
Mr. & Mrs. Henry Capper
Mr. & Mrs. John S. Capper
Mr. & Mrs. F. S. Church
Cleveland E. Church
William T. Church
Mr. & Mrs. C. M. Clark
Dr. & Mrs. F. M. Clement
Mr. & Mrs. C. J. Corse
Mr. & Mrs. Monroe Cregar
Mr. & Mrs. T. A. Dent
Mr. & Mrs. C. Nathan Dye
William B. Dye
Rev. & Mrs. O. D. Ellett
Mr. & Mrs. W. M. R. French

Mr. & Mrs. D. E. Goe
Mr. & Mrs. Lynn Helm
Mrs. E. P. Hilliard
Mr. & Mrs. L. P. Hilliard
Mr. & Mrs. Wm. B. Hoswell
Mr. & Mrs. Edward F. Keating
Mr. & Mrs. O. P. Laird
Mr. & Mrs. J. N. Mason
Mr. & Mrs. George R. Moore
Mr. & Mrs. C. F. Nellis
Mr. & Mrs. Romeo Peck
Mr. & Mrs. John F. Phillips
Mr. & Mrs. C. Ratledge
Mr. & Mrs. J. Ryan
Rev. & Mrs. Wm. R. Scarrett
Mrs. Leslie E. Snow
Mr. & Mrs. Edwin W. Sprague
Mr. & Mrs. W. H. Stafford
Mr. & Mrs. Harry S. Stanton
Mr. & Mrs. Henry L. Stanton
Mr. & Mrs. Arthur W. Tobias
Mr. & Mrs. Clinton Weeks
Mr. & Mrs. F. E. Willard
Mr. & Mrs. Wm. Williamson
Mr. & Mrs. Charles L. Young
Mr. & Mrs. Edward C. Young

MAYFAIR.

Mr. & Mrs. P. E. Baird
Dr. & Mrs. Eisen Bockius
Albert M. Cross
Rev. & Mrs. J. M. Cross
Mr. & Mrs. A. W. Davidson
Mr. & Mrs. Charles E. Farnsworth
Ernest L. Farnsworth
Mr. & Mrs. J. B. Farnsworth
Dr. Kate Henning

Mr. & Mrs. Oscar Henning
Mr. & Mrs. Theron L. Hiles
Mr. & Mrs. Everett S. Hotchkiss
Mr. & Mrs. C. Fred Hunting
Mr. & Mrs. B. A. Johnson
Mr. & Mrs. Edw. A. Keeler
Mr. & Mrs. Frank W. Kingsley
Mr. & Mrs. Robert Laurine
Rev. James W. Lee

Mr. & Mrs. Arthur B. Lewis
Mr. & Mrs. Frank M. Longfellow
Mr. & Mrs. Evan J. Morton
Mrs. George H. Parker
Mr. & Mrs. H. V. Peters
Dr. & Mrs. E. L. Rivenburgh
Mr. & Mrs. George W. Savage
Dr. & Mrs. Dexter Smith
Mr. & Mrs. G. W. Smith
Mr. & Mrs. W. Frank Stickney
Mrs. Mary M. Strong & drs.
Mr. & Mrs. Geo. C. Thomas
G. W. Thomas
Mr. & Mrs. Harry C. Van Harlingen
Dr. Albert T. Washburn
Mr. & Mrs. W. G. Wood
Mr. & Mrs. John Yorty

MAYWOOD.

Mr. & Mrs. Abel Akin
Mr. & Mrs. H. F. Akin
Mr. & Mrs. Geo. L. Bacon
Clyde E. Barrett
Mrs. Thomas Bishop
Mr. & Mrs. J. Bohlander
Mr. & Mrs. E. S. Bryan
Mr. & Mrs. Charles W. Bullard
Mr. & Mrs. C. H. Burnett & dr.
Mr. & Mrs. B. F. Chamberlain
Mrs. Elizabeth Clark
Mr. & Mrs. Harry Clark
Dr. & Mrs. I. Clendenen & dr.
H. Rowland Curtis
Oliver H. Donaldson
Robert P. Donaldson
Mr. & Mrs. S. H. Donaldson
Mr. & Mrs. John T. Ehrhart
Mr. & Mrs. L. Vernon Ferris
Mr. & Mrs. Chas H. Fisk
Mr. & Mrs. Wm. L. Gifford
Mr. & Mrs. F. A. Guilford
Allen Hatch
Mr. & Mrs. George Hatch
Mr. & Mrs. J. G. Hodson
Mrs. Sarah Hubbell
Mr. & Mrs. Joel H. Hulburd
Mr. & Mrs. Joseph Jennings
Mr. & Mrs. J. A. Lambert
Mr. & Mrs. Chas. W. Maynard
Mr. & Mrs. Stephen McEvoy
Dr. & Mrs. H. W. Merrill
Mr. & Mrs. John T. Muir
Receiving day Wednesday
Edwin C. Nichols
Mr. & Mrs. Harry H. Nichols
Mrs. Helen S. Nichols
Mr. & Mrs. H. P. Nichols
Mr. & Mrs. Edwin Norton
Mr. & Mrs. Wilson J. Robb
Mr. &. Mrs. F. E. Roberts
Mrs. Lydia Roberts
Dr. & Mrs. Walter C. Roberts
Mrs. C. H. Robison
Dr. & Mrs. W. L. Ruggles
Mr. & Mrs. H. W. Small & dr.
Gen. & Mrs. Wm. Sooy-Smith
Mr. & Mrs. James M. Stimpson & dr.
Mr. & Mrs. W. H. Varney & dr.
Mr. & Mrs. Charles Westcott
Mr. & Mrs. Oliver J. Westcott
Mr. & Mrs. Daniel Wing & dr.
Henry Wing
Fred D. Woodruff
Mr. & Mrs. Samuel Woodruff

MORGAN PARK.

Prof. & Mrs. G. Anderson
Mr. & Mrs. Joseph Anderson & dr.
Miss Sarah B. Anderson
Rev. & Mrs. W. F. Atchison
Mr. & Mrs. A. J. Atwater
Mr. & Mrs. Edgar Ayres
Mr. & Mrs. I. S. Blackwelder
Receiving day Friday
Mr. & Mrs. H. J. Bohn
Receiving day Wednesday
Mr. & Mrs. J. J. Borland
Mr. & Mrs. W. F. Brabrook
Rev. & Mrs. H. W. Brown
Mr. & Mrs. F. M. Brunson
Mr. & Mrs. I. S. Burgess
Mr. & Mrs. S. P. Cady
Mr. & Mrs. Ernest L. Caldwell
Prof. & Mrs. Geo. N. Carman
Prof. & Mrs. W. J. Chase
Mrs. George R. Clarke
Mr. & Mrs. H. R. Clissold
Mr. & Mrs. Geo. G. Coldwell
Dr. & Mrs. W. H. Cowen
Prof. & Mrs. Robt. H. Cornish
Mr. & Mrs. John T. Cowles
Mr. & Mrs. R. A. Dandliker
Dr. & Mrs. F. P. DeVries
Mr. & Mrs. G. H. Drew

Mr. & Mrs. W. G. Ferguson
Mr. & Mrs. George E. Frazier
Mrs. Mary T. Gage & dr.
Mr. & Mrs. I. W. Cant
Dr. & Mrs. W. H. German
Mr. & Mrs. Chas. T. Gilbert
Mr. & Mrs. John Grainger
Mr. & Mrs. James R. Gray
Mr. & Mrs. F. P. Green
Mr. & Mrs. John Harvey & drs.
Mr. & Mrs. G. A. Hawley
Mr. & Mrs. A. H. Hovey & drs.
Mr. & Mrs. F. T. Husted
Mr. & Mrs. C. A. Iglehart
Mrs. Elizabeth Iglehart & drs.
Mr. & Mrs. John Inglis & dr.
Dr. Josiah Jones
Mr. & Mrs. E. D. Kenfield
Mr. & Mrs. M. H. King
Mr. & Mrs. Fred L. Kimmey
Mr. & Mrs. Charles F. Kopf & dr.
Prof. & Mrs. C. G. Lagergren
Mr. & Mrs. Chas. E. Leech
Receiving day Monday
Mr. & Mrs. W. A. Lutrell & dr.
Mr. & Mrs. W. McClure
Mr. & Mrs. D. C. McKinnon
Richmond P. McKinnon
Mrs. C. W. Madeira & dr.
Mr. & Mrs. G. A. Meech
Mr. & Mrs. F. S. Moffat
Col. & Mrs. T. S. Moffatt
Mr. & Mrs. D. B. Nichols & dr.
Mr. & Mrs. Charles S. Owen
Mr. & Mrs. Fred C. Paulin
Mr. & Mrs. W. H. Poole
Receiving day Tuesday

Prof. & Mrs. Ira M. Price
Mr. & Mrs. B. T. Roberts
Miss Luanna Robertson
Mr. & Mrs. H. Clay Russell
Receiving day Thursday
Miss Mary D. Russell
Mr. & Mrs. H. Schmitt & drs.
Prof. & Mrs. John J. Schobinger
Mr. & Mrs. F. B. Sherwood
Mr. & Mrs. E. G. Short
Mr. & Mrs. F. J. Short
Mr. & Mrs. Wm. H. Silberhorn
Mr. & Mrs. C. P. Silva
Mr. & Mrs. F. P. Silva
B. F. Simpson
Dr. & Mrs. W. A. Smith
Henry R. Singler
Joseph A. Singler
Mrs. N. Singler & drs.
Mr. & Mrs. A. K. Taylor
Mr. & Mrs. C. O. Ten Broeke
Mrs. Gilbert Thayer
Mrs. H. E. Thayer & dr.
H. W. Thayer
Mr. & Mrs. Robert B. Thomson
Mrs. E. B. Thomson
Mr. & Mrs. Porter J. Walker
Mr. & Mrs. E. A. Washburn
Mr. & Mrs. William W. Washburn
Mr. & Mrs. H. H. Watterman
Mrs. John Wayte
Mr. & Mrs. F. S. Wheaton
Mr. & Mrs. F. N. Wilder
Mr. & Mrs. A. Wiswall & dr.
Mr. & Mrs. C. Zeiss

MORTON PARK.

Mr. & Mrs. John H. Behrens
H. E. Blowney
Mr. & Mrs. William Brown
Mr. & Mrs. Lot Brown
Mr. & Mrs. Charles Bruce
Mr. & Mrs. George W. Bushnell
Mr. & Mrs. William H. Clarkson
Mr. & Mrs. J. F. Corris
Dr. & Mrs. J. H. Coulter
Mrs. Nellie E. Dorr
Mr. & Mrs. Buell B. Dutton
Mr. & Mrs. D. G. Edgerly
Rev. & Mrs. William Ellege
Mr. & Mrs. S. A. Flagler
William B. Flagler
Mr. & Mrs. J. E. Gardin

Mr. & Mrs. Ashley L. Gilbert
Mr. & Mrs. William H. Heggie
Herbert Hoffman
Mrs. Edith R. McNamee
Joseph L. Moore
Mr. & Mrs. W. A. Moore
Mr. & Mrs. J. W. Radford
Mr. & Mrs. L. B. Richardson
Mrs. Barbara E. Rubins
Charles C. Rubins
Harry W. Rubins
Willis F. Rubins
O. M. Schantz
Mrs. Annie E. Shepard
Mr. & Mrs. Harry W. Squiers
Rev. & Mrs. E. W. Watson

Mr. & Mrs. Portus B. Weare
Mr. & Mrs. William W. Weare
Miss Ida M. Wolfe

Miss Lottie Wolfe
Mrs. Mary Wolfe
Oswald F. Wolfe

NORWOOD PARK.

Mr. & Mrs. Jean E. C. Agnass
Mr. & Mrs. B. L. Anderson
Mr. & Mrs. C. A. Baird
Mr. & Mrs. D. M. Ball
Dr. Mary E. Bennett
Mr. & Mrs. Edward W. Buss
Mr. & Mrs. John P. Campbell
Mr. & Mrs. F. A. Cleaveland
Mr. & Mrs. F. B. Cleaveland
Mr. & Mrs. William E. Dankert
Mr. & Mrs. G. N. Davis
Mr. & Mrs. Charles J. DeBerard
Mr. & Mrs. A. F. Dodd
Mr. & Mrs. George J. Eckhoff & dr.
Mr. & Mrs. George H. Evans
Mr. & Mrs. H. A. Farnum
Mr. & Mrs. William E. Fisher
Mr. & Mrs. John B. Foote
Mr. & Mrs. F. W. Fox
Mr. & Mrs. James Guilbert
Mr. & Mrs. Fred C. Hale

Mr. & Mrs. Emil Hoffman
Julius Hoffman
Mr. & Mrs. Otto E. H. Hoffman
Dr. & Mrs. J. O. Hughes & dr.
Rev. & Mrs. John S. Joralmon
Mr. & Mrs. B. A. Lawrence
Mrs. A. G. Low
Mr. & Mrs. James A. Low
Mr. & Mrs. Byron Mercer
Mr. & Mrs. Henry O. Parker
Mr. & Mrs. Nels Sampson
Lynden A. Seymour
Mr. & Mrs. T. H. Seymour
Mrs. M. D. Stevers
Mr. & Mrs. John R. Stockwell
Mr. & Mrs. G. H. Thayer
Mrs. Martha Voorhees
Mr. & Mrs. James Walmsley & drs.
Mr. & Mrs. James T. Walsh & dr.
Mr. & Mrs. H. G. Wells
Rev. & Mrs. Eric Wingren

OAK PARK.

ANN STREET.

321 Wm. H. Shuey
321 Mrs. Hannah Gill & dr.
325 Mr. & Mrs. J. L. Whaples
331 Mr. & Mrs. A. W. Pebbles & drs.
331 H. R. Pebbles
337 Mr. & Mrs. Frank M. Pebbles

BELLEFORTE AVENUE.

718 Mr. & Mrs. C. P. Dungan
721 Mr. & Mrs. A. Burgess
723 Mr. & Mrs. Wm. H. Smith
729 Mr. & Mrs. C. G. Towers
733 Mr. & Mrs. D. B. Stone

THE BOULEVARD.

205 Mr. & Mrs. R. W. Goodwillie
205 Mrs. Rachel A. Jones
323 Mr. & Mrs. B. L. Dodge & dr.
329 Mr. & Mrs. D. O. Barto
335 Mr. & Mrs. G. S. Roberts & dr.
345 Mr. & Mrs. Scott Brown
355 Henry Lumbard & dr.
355 E. C. Lumbard
365 Mr. & Mrs. D. D. Garcelon

365 Miss Agnes Garcelon
417 Mrs. E. J. Sanborne & dr.
421 Mrs. E. C. Morrell
421 George R. Morrell
433 Mr. & Mrs. Charles Reifsnider
609 Mr. & Mrs. G. H. Worthington
617 Mr. & Mrs. A. B. Fairbanks
625 Mr. & Mrs. Edward Hilton
633 W. H. Norris & dr.
633 Mrs. Eliza Mitchell

314 Dr. & Mrs. Albert F. Storke
340 Mr. & Mrs. F. J. Knott & dr.
344 Mrs. S. A. McCann
344 Mr. & Mrs. G. D. VanVliet
346 Mr. & Mrs. A. N. Ewart
348 Mr. & Mrs. C. H. Wells
350 Mr. & Mrs. E. R. Rider
412 Edward Van Keuren & drs.
412 W. J. Van Keuren
412 C. W. Van Keuren
424 Mr. & Mrs. Fred Barnard
512 Mr. & Mrs. A. L. Fitch & dr.
518 Mr. & Mrs. Frank L. Howard
518 Mr. & Mrs. Thomas Wrigley
522 Mr. & Mrs. J. W. Ross

806 Mr. & Mrs. R. B. Wallace
814 Mr. & Mrs. Norman C. Betts
814 Mr. & Mrs. John D. Suydam
818 Mr. & Mrs. F. W. Leach
820 Mr. & Mrs. H. G. Bentley
902 Mrs. S. W. Stone
902 Mrs. J. B. Putnam
902 Mrs. Mary E. Holmes
1002 Frank S. Kipp
1002 W. G. Adams
1002 Mrs. Mary E. Kipp
1010 Mr. & Mrs. L. J. Kavana
1010 Mrs. J. W. Hansel & dr.
1010 Mr. & Mrs. W. P. Price
1010 Mr. & Mrs. R. M. Dorsey
1020 E. Jackson & dr.

CEDAR STREET

315 Mr. & Mrs. J. E. Earll
323 Fred W. Sandberg
328 Dr. Fanny M. Rowley

CHICAGO AVENUE.

209 Mr. & Mrs. Graves Holbrook
219 Mr. & Mrs. C. F. Abbott
305 Mr. & Mrs. W. L. DaLacy
313 Mr. & Mrs. H. C. Hansen
403 Mrs. Mary Hafner & dr.
409 Mr. & Mrs. C. F. Hafner
421 Mr. & Mrs. S. W. Griggs
425 Mr. & Mrs. J. A. Edwards

300 Mr. & Mrs. Geo. Nordenholt
306 Mr. & Mrs. A. B. Melville
322 Mr. & Mrs. Walter Gale
324 Mr. & Mrs. Thos. H. Gale
330 Mr. & Mrs. Robert P. Parker
424 Mrs. A. L. Wright & drs.
428 Mr. & Mrs. W. R. Sanborn
432 Mr. & Mrs. W. G. Kraft
436 Mr. & Mrs. T. J. Worswick

CLINTON AVENUE.

115 Mr. & Mrs. J. H. Hoopes
117 Mr. & Mrs. J. B. Webb
207 Mr. & Mrs. F. Q. Ball
207 T. W. Hall
221 Mr. & Mrs. George H. Teter
227 Mr. & Mrs. Geo. D. Elderkin
237 Mr. & Mrs. W. A. Rice
245 Mr. & Mrs. Fred Comley
251 Mr. & Mrs. Louis Olcese
301 Mr. & Mrs. C. E. Yetman
309 Rev. & Mrs. H. B. Waterman
Receiving day Wednesday

309 Prof. H. H. Matteson
325 Mr. & Mrs. W. G. Wallace
325 Mr. & Mrs. G. D. Webb
335 Mr. & Mrs. Frank H. June
339 Mr. & Mrs. S. C. Miller
Receiving ·day Tuesday

110 Mr. & Mrs. L. S. VanVliet & drs.
112 Mrs. P. R. Lord
112 Miss Elizabeth S. Lord
118 Mr. & Mrs. C. M. Morton & dr.
120 Mr. & Mrs. Robert Seymour
126 Mr. & Mrs. W. A. Hutchinson
126 Miss E. Clement
134 Mr. & Mrs. R. L. Crockett
200 Mr. & Mrs. Arthur Heurtley
200 R. L. Crampton
202 Mr. & Mrs. J. S. Ralston
204 Mr. & Mrs. Henry C. Haselhun
206 Mr. & Mrs. J. C. McPherson
208 Mrs. M. A. Elliott
208 F. A. Elliott
210 Mr. & Mrs. Isaac N. Connard
210 Miss Lydia Mead
216 Mr. & Mrs. J. V. Read
220 Mr. & Mrs. E. L. Merriman
220 Miss Minnie Merriman
220 Mr. & Mrs. J. Elwood Hamilton
222 Mr. & Mrs. J. L. Tucker
222 H. L. Jewell
228 Mr. & Mrs. C. F. Walker
228 George H. Walker
230 Mr. & Mrs. Miller Hall
234 Mr. & Mrs. W. D. Hall
240 Mr. & Mrs. J. L. Freeman
300 Mr. & Mrs. E. F. Bodey
308 Mrs. T. C. Rounds
308 Mr. & Mrs. C. W. C. Chandler
312 Mrs. Emily Currier & drs.
320 Mr. & Mrs. Chas. G. Burton

SOUTH EAST AVENUE.

121 Mrs. George D. Rice
121 John H. Rice
125 Mr. & Mrs. Charles L. Bliss
131 Mr. & Mrs. J. R. Payson jr.
209 Mr. & Mrs. Alfred T. Jones
213 Mr. & Mrs. A. C. Putnam
217 Mr. & Mrs. A. Armitage
221 Mr. & Mrs. Wm. John Watson
221 Miss Alice J. Colburn
305 Mr. & Mrs. M. T. Carey
315 Mr. & Mrs. W. R. Townsend & dr.
323 Mrs. M. E. Putnam & dr.
323 Frank H. Putnam
329 Mrs. E. C. Harvey

329 William H. Cheal
333 Mr. & Mrs. Geo. l.. Wilson
335 Mr. & Mrs. W. G. Wanzer
339 Mr. & Mrs. J. H. Gormley & dr.
415 Mr. & Mrs. W. R. Comstock
419 Mr. & Mrs. R. A. Mudie
423 Mr. & Mrs. F. C. Wood
cor. Lake Antoine J. Bedard

ELIZABETH COURT.

1 Mr. & Mrs. Edward Payson
3 Mr. & Mrs. J. Fred Butler
5 Mr. & Mrs. C. L. Williams

2 Mr. & Mrs. Giles F. Belknap
4 Mr. & Mrs. A. C. Reed
8 Rev. & Mrs. J. E. Roy

ELIZABETH STREET.

120 Mr. & Mrs. J. D. Andrews
323 Mr. & Mrs. John G. Ingalls
325 Rowland S. Ludington
325 Mrs. M. K. Ludington

EUCLID AVENUE.

305 Mr. & Mrs. Edwin Osgood
309 Mr. & Mrs. Geo. W. Melville
315 Mr. & Mrs. A. L. Bostedo & dr.
319 Mrs. Eliza L. Gates
405 Mr. & Mrs. M. G. Wallace
413 Mr. & Mrs. T. S. Rattle
421 Mr. & Mrs. C. E. Roberts & drs.
433 Mr. & Mrs. Paul Blatchford
715 Mr. & Mrs. Fred G. Baker
308 Mr. & Mrs. C. A. Sharpe
308 N. M. Freer
422 Mr. & Mrs. P. E. Wilson
430 Mr. & Mrs. J. R. Mason
434 Mr. & Mrs. Joseph Harvey

SOUTH EUCLID AVENUE.

111 Mr. & Mrs. John Nelson
115 Mr. & Mrs. James Graham
115 Wm. F. Pillsbury
127 C. F. Lockwood
131 Mr. & Mrs. A. H. Jones
131 Mr. & Mrs. A. C. Bruner
131 Miss Lillie B. Stevens
143 Mr. & Mrs. H. M. Hollister
209 Mr. & Mrs. Gilbert Witters
213 Mr. & Mrs. Geo. W. Woodbury
221 Mr. & Mrs. David S. Baldwin
221 Dr. Charles M. Baldwin
225 Rev. & Mrs. Geo. Simpson
225 T. D. Simpson

227 Mr. & Mrs. A. C. Neely
229 Mr. & Mrs. W. E. Shoot
233 Mr. & Mrs. T. G. Moses
237 Mr. & Mrs. R. Colekin jr.
301 Dr. & Mrs. L. H. Baker & drs.
309 Mr. & Mrs. J. E. Turney & dr.
317 Mr. & Mrs. G. M. Patch
321 Mr. & Mrs. W. H. Cribben
325 Mr. & Mrs. A. E. Walters
329 Mr. & Mrs. F. J. Pierce

230 Mr. & Mrs. Charles E. Jenkins
230 Miss B. D. Jenkins
314 Mrs. Catherine Austin & drs.
316 Mr. & Mrs. Willis A. Austin

FOREST AVENUE.

403 Mr. & Mrs. R. K. Bickford
Receiving day Wednesday
409 Mr. & Mrs. James T. Hayden
409 George W. Hayden
415 Mr. & Mrs. Albert H. Vilas & dr.
415 Albert M. Vilas
419 Mr. & Mrs. Henry D. Dement
& drs.
419 Mrs. L. W. A. Goodwin
423 Mr. & Mrs. A. B. Searing & dr.
427 Mr. & Mrs. F. D. Updike
431 Mr. & Mrs. E. C. Cook & dr.
505 Mr. & Mrs. Gordon Ripley
509 Mr. & Mrs. Chas. Seabury
513 Mr. & Mrs. D. L. McDaniels
521 Mrs. Frank S. Gray
529 Mr. & Mrs. N. G. Moore
529 Mrs. S. S. Walker
603 Mr. & Mrs. H. N. Norton
623 Mr. & Mrs. R. L. Boyd & dr.
625 Mr. & Mrs. John Kirkpatrick
627 Mr. & Mrs. C. R. McHugh
717 Dr. & Mrs. A. F. Olds

214 Mr. & Mrs. John Powell
214 Mr. & Mrs. Palmer Rossman
220 Mr.& Mrs.N.H.Whittlesey & dr.
224 Mr. & Mrs. Channing Taylor
230 Rev. & Mrs. R. H. Pooley
234 Mr. & Mrs. J. W. Smith
234 W. T. Smith
300 Mr. & Mrs. F. C. Fox
306 R. G. Kennedy
302 Mr. & Mrs. Chas. R. White
304 Mr. & Mrs. W. H. Hatch
306 Rev. & Mrs. C. P. Anderson
306 J. L. Anderson
404 Mr. & Mrs. F. W. Cook
406 Mr. & Mrs. Lawrence Muther

412 Mr. & Mrs. J. D. Everett
412 Mrs. M. S. Southworth
412 D. A. Miller
422 Mr. & Mrs. James L. Fargo
426 Mr. & Mrs. Chas. B. Holdredge
430 Mr. & Mrs.George Walker
430 G. Albert Walker
508 Mr. & Mrs. C. A. Purcell
518 Mr. & Mrs. P. L. Hanscom
518 Mrs. Emily C. Bridges
528 Mr. & Mrs. W. M. Harman & dr.
606 Mr. & Mrs. Edward King & dr.
Receiving day Monday
612 Mr. & Mrs. I. W. Henderson
cor. Chicago av. Mr & Mrs. Frank
L. Wright

GROVE AVENUE.

221 Mr. & Mrs. Albert M. Butz
221 W. T. Miller
221 Miss R. C. Miller
225 Mr. & Mrs. Norman S. Patton
231 Mr. & Mrs. J. F. Cleveland
231 Miss Kate Bradley
237 Mr. & Mrs. Wm. Spooner & dr.
311 Mr. & Mrs. O. C. Blackmer
311 Mrs. Mary E. Wingate & dr.
315 Rev. & Mrs. S. J. Humphrey &
dr.
435 Mr. & Mrs. E. O. Vaile
439 Mr. & Mrs. Henry R. Hamilton
443 Mr. & Mrs. W. H. Noake
449 Mr. & Mrs. Albert H. Standish
455 Mr. & Mrs. Isaac Tomlinson &
dr.
467 Mr. & Mrs. Fred Dupuis & dr.
467 Alfred G. Dupuis
467 Charles A. Dupuis
503 Mr. & Mrs. C. F. Purdy
503 Mr. & Mrs. J. C. McMynn
503 W. F. Rockwell
503 Miss Bessie M. White
509 Mr. & Mrs. James Kirton
515 Mr. & Mrs. Lewis M. Curry
525 Mr. & Mrs. Thomas Morley
529 Dr. & Mrs. C. S. Wood
529 Dr. Sarah V. Westrup

238 Mr. & Mrs. S. H. Kimball
302 Mr. & Mrs. W. H. Taylor
306 Mr. & Mrs. Thomas Pattison
316 Mr. & Mrs. A. J. Cheney
322 Mrs. G. D. Conklin
322 W. F. Conklin
322 H. T. Hart

328 Mr. & Mrs. Joseph Eastman
402 Mr. & Mrs. C. S. Yerkes
402 Nathaniel Lord
440 Mr. & Mrs. Theron Durham
442 Mr. & Mrs. Wm. Ransom
446 Mr. & Mrs. A. Wilder Wood &
dr.
446 Leslie Wood
446 Miss Bertha Lee
456 Mr. & Mrs. W. D. McIlvane
472 Mr. & Mrs. Geo. D. Keefer
476 Mr. & Mrs. I. E. Brown
478 Mr. & Mrs. J. S. Masters
538 Mr. & Mrs. E. H. Andrews

SOUTH GROVE AVENUE.

103 Mrs. F. H. Sturtevant
103 Chester D. Sturtevant
103 Mr. & Mrs. S. M. Wetzel
103 Mrs. W. P. Smith & dr.
103 Mrs. P. E. Huntington
123 W. T. Templeton & dr.
123 Mr. & Mrs. H. H. Morgan
133 Mr. & Mrs. H. D. Pierce
139 Mr. & Mrs. J. A. Seaman
209 Mr. & Mrs. J. I. Jones
213 Mrs. Wilhelmine Juergens & dr.
213 Alfred Juergens
215 Mr. & Mrs. J. F. Pudor
215 Miss M. C. Howard
219 Mrs. A. M. Draper
219 Herbert L. Draper
219 Arthur M. Draper
223 Mr. & Mrs. O. B. Barker
231 Mr. & Mrs. C. A. Weage & dr.
Receiving day Wednesday
235 Mr. & Mrs. C. R. Blanchard &
drs.
237 Mr. & Mrs. J. Carruthers
317 Mr. & Mrs. R. W. Patrick
317 Mr. & Mrs. C. B. Richardson
321 Mr. & Mrs. W. R. Vosburgh
323 Mr. & Mrs. Fletcher B. Gibbs
331 Mr. & Mrs. Horace F. White

102 Mr. & Mrs. A. A. Adair & dr.
110 Mr. & Mrs. Carlos J. Ward
110 Mrs. Nettie Ward Jones
110 Miss Mary W. Marks
116 Mr. & Mrs. John L. Pearson
120 Mr. & Mrs. Andrew Johnson
140 Mr. & Mrs. E. S. Tomlinson
218 Mr. & Mrs. Geo. W. Smith
226 Mr. & Mrs. Dwight P. Jackson
230 Mr. & Mrs. W. L. Loveland

234 Mr. & Mrs. I. G. Hatcher & drs.
234 Morris C. Hatcher
308 Mr. & Mrs. C. A. Richardson
312 Mr. & Mrs. Isaac W. Brown
324 Mr. & Mrs. Nelson A. McClary

HOLLEY COURT.

107 Mr. & Mrs. J. S. Ingram & drs.
107 Mrs. E. B. Borwell
115 Mr. & Mrs. Robert Many
115 Mrs. Eliza Fox
119 Mr. & Mrs. Charles A. Schroyer
114 Mr. & Mrs. Wm. H. Thompson

HOME AVENUE.

229 Mr. & Mrs. W. R. Harvey & dr.
239 Mr. & Mrs. A. H. Wilson
241 Mr. & Mrs. Abraham Edmunds
    & drs.
245 Mr. & Mrs. A. P. Holbrook
247 Mr. & Mrs. James Harvey
249 Mr. & Mrs. S. H. Crounse & drs.
305 Mr. & Mrs. Joseph Purvis
317 Mr. & Mrs. Joseph C. Skeen
321 Mr. & Mrs. J. L. Worthington
325 Mr. & Mrs. E. T. Johnson
325 T. S. Johnson
337 Mr. & Mrs. A. F. Banks
341 Mr. & Mrs. John Hohmann
345 Mr. & Mrs. Dwight Jackson
345 Mr. & Mrs. J. H. Sanders
345 H. P. Sanders
401 Mrs. M. A. Lenox
401 John P. Lenox
401 J. F. Lenox

100 Dr. & Mrs. L. S. Ingman
102 Mr. & Mrs. M. W. Ketcham
104 Mrs. C. Kilgore
106 Mr. & Mrs. C. F. Search
108 Mr. & Mrs. Clarence S. Pellett
110 Mr. & Mrs. Correl Smith
110 Mr. & Mrs. Charles Cox
118 Mr. & Mrs. E. A. Roser
126 Mr. & Mrs. Warren F. Furbeck
    Receiving day Wednesday
126 George W. Furbeck
210 Mr. & Mrs. R. S. Thain & dr.
    Receive Friday eve.
212 Wm. Todd
212 Charles C. Todd
216 Mr. & Mrs. W. Templeton
226 Mr. & Mrs. E. P. Upham & dr.
226 Frank Upham
232 Mrs. George G. Merrick & drs.

232 Albert W. Merrick
244 Mr. & Mrs. W. E. Terrill
248 Mr. & Mrs. W. H. Stearns
326 Mr. & Mrs. C. S. Burton
330 Mr. & Mrs. O. Kastrup
332 Mr. & Mrs. Wm. Wicke
338 Mr. & Mrs. C. A. Blaurock & drs.

KENILWORTH AVENUE.

217 Louis Lunsford
239 Mr. & Mrs. E. V. Gale
    Receiving day Wednesday
303 Mr. & Mrs. C. G. Marsh
309 Mr. & Mrs. F. W. Bicknell & dr.
309 E. Dean Bicknell
309 W. W. Bicknell
309 Miss A. B. Wells
319 Dr. & Mrs. W. C. Gray
327 Mr. & Mrs. J. M. Baker
331 Mr. & Mrs. W. H. Kerkhoff
345 Mr. & Mrs. John Rankin & drs.
345 George Rankin
409 Mr. & Mrs. D. J. Kennedy
417 Mr. & Mrs. W. A. Douglass
429 Mr. & Mrs. J. K. Dunlop
453 Mr. & Mrs. W. B. Chambèrlain
533 Mr. & Mrs. Horace B. Humph-
    rey
533 Mrs. Walter Thomas Mills
539 Mr. & Mrs. John R. Mott

114 Grant Foreman
234 Mr. & Mrs. Geo. L. Eastman
324 Mr. & Mrs. N. M. Jones
400 Mr. & Mrs, W. J. MacDonald
408 Mr. & Mrs. Charles E. Potter
422 Mr. & Mrs. H. B. Horton & drs.
422 Benjamin P. Horton
428 Mr. & Mrs. F. M. Spaulding & dr.
434 Mr. & Mrs. H. P. Young
438 Mr. & Mrs. S. A. Rothermel
444 Mr. & Mrs. W. C. Smith
448 Mr. & Mrs. W. B. Parker
452 Mr. & Mrs. E. C. Glover
468 Mr. & Mrs. W. H. Yorke
482 Mr. & Mrs. Richard Beard & drs.

LAKE STREET.

217 Mrs. H. W. Austin & dr.
217 H. W. Austin
307 Mrs. L. Meredith & dr.
307 Mrs. Hannah Phelps
309 Mrs. S. A. Holley
309 E. E. Giddings
321 Robert S. Ingalls

321 Mrs. Mary E. Ingalls
321 Grant Ingalls
333 Mr. & Mrs. G. E. Gerts & drs.
    Receiving day Wednesday
333 Walter S. Gerts
347 Mr. & Mrs. E. O. Gale
401 Mr. & Mrs. Simpson Dunlop
515 J. H. Dinwiddie
515 Ralph Starrett

---

200 L. M. Lovett
320 Mrs. C. H. Meacham & dr.
324 Dr. & Mrs. E. S. Talbot
324 Miss Florence Talbot
332 Mrs. Philander Smith
332 Mr. & Mrs. W. E. Blackstone
332 Andrew P. Blackstone
332 James H. Blackstone
348 Rev. & Mrs. Charles S. Hoyt
348 Mrs. S. C. Hoyt
350 Dr. & Mrs. J. W. Tope
356 Dr. & Mrs. John D. Waller
358 Mr. & Mrs. C. E. Bolles
364 Mr. & Mrs. L. G. Holley
368 Mr. & Mrs. S. W. Packard
416 Mr. & Mrs. Luther Conant & dr.
416 William C. Conant
422 Mr. & Mrs. M. T. Cole & dr.
428 Mr. & Mrs. George J. Bliss & dr.
432 Mr. & Mrs. O. D. Allen & drs.
440 Dr. & Mrs. N. H. Aspinwall & dr.
440 Mr. & Mrs. Charles E. Simmons
440 Mrs. I. Simmons
440 Howard L. Simmons
454 Mr. & Mrs. J. L. Ward & dr.
502 Dr. & Mrs. J. M. Retter

LINDEN AVENUE.

303 Dr. & Mrs. W. H. Stennett
303 Mrs. M. Covert
317 Mr. & Mrs. George M. Davidson
335 Mr. & Mrs. J. H. Howard & dr.
335 H. Benton Howard
409 Mr. & Mrs. Wm. P. Kimball

---

302 Mrs. S. F. Wadsworth
302 Charles F. Wadsworth
302 Frank R. Wadsworth
320 Mr. & Mrs. O. L. Bicknell
334 Mr. & Mrs. T. F. Bliss

MAPLE AVENUE.

105 Mrs. Jennie June
105 Miss Susie June
111 Mr. & Mrs. John B. Warder
117 Mr. & Mrs. T. F. Bradshaw

121 Mr. & Mrs. W. A. McConnell
125 Mr. & Mrs. C. S. Meacham
125 Dr. William E. Kidd
201 Mr. & Mrs. Josiah Cratty
211 Mr. & Mrs. E. D. L. Sweet
211 Mrs. Cora F. Sweet
211 Charles S. Sweet
217 Mr. & Mrs. T. G. Morris & dr.
217 T. G. Morris jr.
227 Mr. & Mrs. Charles Roe
235 Mr. & Mrs. George Sharp
235 Dr. & Mrs. H. W. Bassett
237 Mr. & Mrs. Harry A. Angel
239 Mrs. Emily S. Richards
239 Lincoln Richards
241 Gen. & Mrs. Milo S. Hascall
    Receiving day Thursday
303 Mr. & Mrs. Stephen A. West
309 Mr. & Mrs. J. E. Tristram & dr
321 Mr. & Mrs. Frank Milligan
329 John P. Burnham
329 Mrs. M. J. Orcutt & dr.
337 Mr. & Mrs. Amza L. Fitch
341 Mr. & Mrs. E. D. Parsons
401 Mr. & Mrs. W. R. Patterson
405 Otis E. Turner
405 Mr. & Mrs. H. K. Smith & dr.
409 Alexander Austin & dr.
409 Charles W. Austin
409 Mrs. S. B. Johnson
419 William Ruxton
425 Mr. & Mrs. S. R. Ainslie
521 Mr. & Mrs. H. E. Overstreet
525 Mr. & Mrs. H. F. Stoner
525 T. K. Stoner
527 Mr. & Mrs. J. F. Wilson & dr.
529 Mr. & Mrs. L. D. Brown
609 Mr. & Mrs. A. J. Flitcraft
617 Mr. & Mrs. Isaiah Flitcraft

---

120 Mrs. M. J. Russell
120 Dr. & Mrs. W. R. Lewis
126 Mr. & Mrs. J. W. Middleton & dr.
126 Mr. & Mrs. B. F. Stout
200 Mr. & Mrs. Sidney S. Niles
210 Mr. & Mrs. G. A. Bodenschatz
216 Mr. & Mrs. W. R. Owen
226 Mr. & Mrs. E. S. Conway
234 Mr. & Mrs. A. W. Bryant
242 Mr. & Mrs. William Beye
252 Mr. & Mrs. C. B. Flinn
308 Mr. & Mrs. B. D. Harris
334 Mrs. Hannah Swartley & dr.
340 Mr. & Mrs. William Gilmore
344 Mrs. E. B. Miller & dr.
344 R. P. Miller

400 Mr. & Mrs. G. W. Moser
400 Mrs. Jane Leslie
414 Mr. & Mrs. J. T. Ripley
520 Mr. & Mrs. J. A. Lewis
530 Mr. & Mrs. Albert Sibley

MARION STREET.

103 Dr. & Mrs. A. S. Melvin jr.
115 Mr. & Mrs. Robert A. Lackey
115 Dr. & Mrs. R. M. Lackey
115 Charles R. Lackey
115 Dr. Allen A. Mathews
127 Mr. & Mrs. E. W. Hoard
127 Mrs. B. Congdon
127 Miss Ida B. Gurley
513 Mr. & Mrs. Jay D. Miller
519 James McGregor & dr.
519 James R. McGregor
525 Mr. & Mrs. W. N. Kettlestrings

---

122 Dr. & Mrs. E. W. Wood
122 K. Oaks & dr.
122 W. W. Oaks
228 Mr. & Mrs. C. Miller
228 Mr. & Mrs. John Kohn
238 Mr. & Mrs. C. E. Stedman
238 H. T. Stedman
246 Mr. & Mrs. Maurice Evans & drs.
524 Mr. & Mrs. J. W. Johnston & dr.
604 Mr. & Mrs. August Einfeldt

OAK PARK AVENUE.

307 Mr. & Mrs. O. W. Herrick & dr
333 Mr. & Mrs. H. S. Towle & dr.
333 Miss Helen Maude Towle
405 Mr. & Mrs. E. W. Lyman & dr.
405 R. L. Lyman
417 Mr. & Mrs. T. H. Doane
417 Philip P. S. Doane
425 Mr. & Mrs. George Eckart
433 Mr. & Mrs. C. B. Ayers & dr.
    Receiving day Thursday
439 Mr. & Mrs. Ernest Hall
439 Leicester C. Hall
443 Mr. & Mrs. R. H. Hennegen
447 Mr. & Mrs. G. W. Ingersoll
507 Mr. & Mrs. J. W. Kettlestrings
507 F. W. Kettlestrings
507 Orrin R. Kettlestrings
519 Mr. & Mrs. W. J. Cooke & dr.
605 Mr. & Mrs. A. E. Morey
643 Mr. & Mrs. C. D. Paine
643 Mrs. M. A. Sinclair

238 Mr. & Mrs. C. P. Thomas & dr.
238 Mr. & Mrs. Geo. W. Hoffman
308 Mr. & Mrs. Wm. H. Wood
308 Miss Caroline C. Wood
308 Mrs. F. E. Ingraham
308 G. Foster Ingraham
308 Mrs. Robert Harlin
324 Mr. & Mrs. H. J. Straight & drs
332 Mr. & Mrs. George Clapp & dr.
408 Mr. & Mrs. W. R. Phelps
416 Mr. & Mrs. H. A. Cole
420 Mr. & Mrs. W. S. Herrick
424 Mr. & Mrs. John Lewis
424 Miss Mary Lewis
432 Mr. & Mrs. Wm. C. Warner
500 Mr. & Mrs. A. T. Hemingway & dr.
500 Clarence E. Hemingway
520 Mr. & Mrs. W. R. Wagner
608 Mr. & Mrs. C. S. Beattie
    Receiving day Wednesday
620 Mr. &. Mrs. J. W. Palmer
620 Mrs. J. L. Hooker

SOUTH OAK PARK AVENUE.

103 Mr. & Mrs. E. S. Watts
107 Mr. & Mrs. Henry Cribben
113 Mr. & Mrs. Henry A. Caldwell
117 Mr. & Mrs. E. H. Owen
125 Mr. & Mrs. C. A. Sibley
125 Mrs. H. R. Pitcher
129 Mr. & Mrs. F. C. Caldwell
133 Mr. & Mrs. O. G. Kellogg
141 Mr. & Mrs. C. C. Royse
141 Mrs. E. Godley
209 Mr. &. Mrs. William Smith
211 Mr. & Mrs. Geo. Royal
211 Mr. & Mrs. Geo. Royal jr.
211 Charles B. Royal
231 Mr. & Mrs. C. H. Ackert
239 Mr. & Mrs. John Farson
333 Mr. & Mrs. John C. Clark

---

108 Mr. & Mrs. L. A. Gilbert
112 Mr. & Mrs. Edward C. Porter
118 Mr. & Mrs. W. A. Robertson
124 Mr. & Mrs. Jabez W. Williams & dr.
126 J. D. Bancroft & dr.
132 Mr. & Mrs. W. A. Tilden
136 Mr. & Mrs. C. B. S. Conyne
144 Dr. & Mrs. T. E. Roberts
200 Mr. & Mrs. E. J. Hall
208 Mr. & Mrs. N. Board
210 Mr. & Mrs. A. S. Ray
210 Mrs. P. A. Ray

214 Mr. & Mrs. G. M. Clayberg
224 Mr. & Mrs. Isaac Herr
228 Mr. & Mrs. E. F. Burton
310 Mr. & Mrs. Daniel Hale & drs.
316 Mrs. Annie Morley
316 J. H. Morley

ONTARIO STREET.

316 Mr. & Mrs. Emerson Ingalls
316 Mr. & Mrs. E. F. Nettleton

PARK PLACE.

121 Mr. & Mrs. Smith Niles
129 Mr. & Mrs. M. C. Niles & dr.

PEASE COURT.

301 Mr. & Mrs. C. C. Luce & drs.
301 Fred Luce
310 Rev. & Mrs. H. D. Kimball
325 Mr. & Mrs. Wm. Moody
330 William C. Hunter
331 Mr. & Mrs. C. W. Hawley

PLEASANT STREET.

323 Rev. & Mrs. James Tompkins
323 Roy J. Tompkins
329 Mrs. H. H. Hunt & dr.
329 Rodney Hunt
335 Mr. & Mrs. C. B. Albro
341 Mr. & Mrs. J. A. Baldwin

316 Mr. & Mrs. J. H. Heald
324 Rev. & Mrs. R. F. Johonnot
332 Mr. & Mrs. M. Noyes
332 W. A. Noyes

PRAIRIE AVENUE.

125 Mr. & Mrs. F. H. Lumbard
203 Mr. & Mrs. Albert W. Giles
209 Mr. & Mrs. Samuel S. Pruyn
209 Charles E. Pruyn
217 Mrs. L. J. Lorwill
217 Tod Lunsford
243 Mr. & Mrs. J. W. Faxon

108 Mr. & Mrs. M. H. Petsch
110 Mrs. J. A. Hallock & dr.
114 Mr. & Mrs. W. E. Hughes
114 Mrs. Mary W. Tompkins
122 Mr. & Mrs. Miles Crandall
122 A. E. Hoyt
130 Mr. & Mrs. W. G. Roberts
134 Mr. & Mrs. George L. Gary
134 W. S. Smith
138 Mr. & Mrs. E. S. Wheeler

142 Mr. & Mrs. J. H. Morrison
210 Mr. & Mrs. A. D. Osborn
214 Mr. & Mrs. Henry Hulsmann
214 Mrs. Louisa Glende
232 Mr. & Mrs. C. E. Fisher
232 Mr. & Mrs. Geo. F. Holloway
238 Mr. & Mrs. Henry C. Fielder
242 Mr. & Mrs. I. S. Wachob

SCOVILLE AVENUE.

636 Mr. & Mrs. F. E. Ballard

SUPERIOR STREET.

709 Mr. & Mrs. D. C. Herrick
721 Mr. & Mrs. Edward Cook & dr.

WASHINGTON BOULEVARD.

316 Mr. & Mrs. H. P. Martin
317 Mr. & Mrs. J. E. Fowler & dr.
   Receiving day Tuesday
317 J. E. Fowler jr.
318 Mr. & Mrs. Francis Hemington
318 Mr. & Mrs. Thos. M. Naden

WESLEY AVENUE.

103 Mr. & Mrs. W. H. DeCamp
115 Mr. & Mrs. Edwin T. Malone
121 Mr. & Mrs. W. A. Sheridan
131 Mr. & Mrs. F. H. Smith
201 Mr. & Mrs. H. J. Ullmann
209 Mrs. L. J. Wiltberger
   Receiving day Wednesday
213 Mr. & Mrs. R. N. Trimingham
217 Mr. & Mrs. DeLos Hull
   Receiving day Thursday
225 Mr. & Mrs. A. H. Adams
229 Mr. & Mrs. F. S. Terry
231 Mr. & Mrs. F. P. Armbruster
301 Mrs. L. B. Castle & dr.
315 Mr. & Mrs. J. E. Davis
405 Mrs. Laura Ashelman & drs.

122 Mr. & Mrs. A. E. Branch
124 Mr. & Mrs. W. C. Curtis
218 Mr. & Mrs. Geo. H. Owen
218 D. J. Pridham
234 Mr. & Mrs. E. E. Morrell
300 Mr. & Mrs. Ira Ellsworth Stevens
300 Mr. & Mrs. Wm. G. Fricke

WISCONSIN AVENUE.

117 Mr. & Mrs. J. P. Sharp
117 William N. Sharp

117 George P. Sharp
203 Mr.& Mrs. James C.Rogers & dr.
223 Mr. & Mrs. R. S. Worthington
223 Mr.& Mrs. Harry B. Richardson
229 Miss Anna M. Rattle
229 O. J. Rattle
235 Mrs. A. E. Howes & drs.
235 Rev. & Mrs. H. C. Hazen
241 Mr. & Mrs. E. R. Haase
245 Mrs. C. D. Parsons & dr.
249 Herman Knauer & dr.
329 Mr. & Mrs. Harry B. Noyes
337 Mr. & Mrs. F. C. S. Calhoun
339 Mr. & Mrs. Henry E. Patrick
339 Clarence E. Patrick
341 Mr. & Mrs. Geo. F. Cook & dr.
341 Mrs. E. V. Bronson
413 Mr. & Mrs. Judson M. Fuller

116 Mr. & Mrs. Andrew O. Butler
116 Frank M. Butler
252 Mr. & Mrs. George S. Sawyer
256 Mr. & Mrs. J. F. Claflin
256 Mack A. Claflin
264 Mr. & Mrs.W.W. Lovejoy & drs.
264 John M. Lovejoy

308 Mr. & Mrs. A. C. Childs
308 Mrs. O. A. Leonard
312 Mr. & Mrs. D. H. Gile
316 Mr. & Mrs. Fred Gustorf & drs.
320 Mr. & Mrs. D. F. Moore
324 Mr. & Mrs. E. B. Bartlett
328 Rev. & Mrs. Francis H. Rowley
328 Mrs. F. J. Babcock
332 Mr. & Mrs. H. A. Taylor
340 Mr. & Mrs. W. P. Utley
340 Mrs. Jennie Howland & dr.
410 Mrs. Mary Lovett
410 Mrs. W. C. Brown
414 Mr. & Mrs. W. W. Wood
416 Mr. & Mrs. R. K. Maynard
420 Mr. & Mrs. John Pullen
424 Mr. & Mrs. J. M. Allen
428 Mr. & Mrs. John Breitling

WOODBINE AVENUE.

736 Mr. & Mrs. H. S. Eckart
736 Mrs. C. L. Melin
738 Mr. & Mrs. J. W. Hansel
740 Dr. & Mrs. F. M. Reynolds
740 William J. Reynolds

PARK MANOR.

ANTHONY AVENUE.

6825 Mrs. Garris Cochran
6825 Miss Annie Colt
6829 Mr. & Mrs. L. A. Moss
6829 Mr. & Mrs. F. Lewis Schmidt
6831 Mr. & Mrs. James P. Sayer
6841 Mrs. Lucy Townsend

6826 Mr. & Mrs. F. Ratledge
6900 Mr. & Mrs. F. E. Stevens
    Receiving day Tuesday
6900 Miss Mary Lloyd
6902 Mr. & Mrs. John A. Bowman
6906 Mr. & Mrs. R. T. Rapp

CALUMET AVENUE.

6919 Mr. & Mrs. Julius Wahl
6957 Mr. & Mrs. E. M. Wineman

PRAIRIE AVENUE.

6747 Mr. & Mrs. J. T. Bingham
6829 John M. Cameron
6841 Mr. & Mrs. G. B. Hughes

7002 Mr. & Mrs. W. C. Parker

RHODES AVENUE.

6720 Mr. & Mrs. J. G. Coats
6722 Mr. & Mrs. Thos. B. Seavy
6728 Mr. & Mrs. W. R. Westgate
6730 Mr. & Mrs. Louis A. McDonald
7100 Mr. & Mrs. Geo. T. Stone
7112 Mr. & Mrs. C. C. Kemble
    Receiving day Thursday

SEVENTY-SECOND STREET.

1163 Col. & Mrs. Wm. V. Jacobs
1197 Mr. & Mrs. W. H. Gorman

SIXTY-SEVENTH STREET.

1205 Mr. & Mrs. W. D. Hackney

SIXTY-EIGHTH STREET.

1486 Mr. & Mrs. J. N. Stone

SOUTH CHICAGO AVENUE.

6763 Mr. & Mrs. Hugh F. Hogan

6836 Mr. & Mrs. Andrew J. Hart

SOUTH PARK AVENUE.

6814 Mr. & Mrs. Benj. F. Bowman
6910 Mr. & Mrs. John H. Wagner

ST. LAWRENCE AVENUE.

6818 Mrs. A. Mullendore
6818 Mr. & Mrs. Fred W. Bucholz
7008 Mrs. Ida Sullivan

VERNON AVENUE.

6909 Mr. & Mrs. C. R. Babeuf

6908 Mr. & Mrs. Chas. G. Rose
6912 Mr. & Mrs. Frank A. Smith

6926 Mr. & Mrs. Geo. E. Dennis
6932 Mr. & Mrs. J. E. Seinwerth
6936 Dr. William G. Dyas
6936 Mrs. W. C. Hopkins
7022 Mrs. C. F. James
7108 Mr. & Mrs. James Callahan
7138 Mr. & Mrs. Wm. J. Shedd
7224 Mr. & Mrs. F. H. Nonweiler
7232 Mr. & Mrs. R. G. Barrett jr.
7248 Mr. & Mrs. Henry R. Lee

VINCENNES AVENUE.

6733 Mr. & Mrs. W. E. Palmer

7108 Mr. & Mrs. C. H. Woodward

PARK RIDGE.

Mrs. A. O. Austin & dr.
Mr. & Mrs. F. G. Barnard
Dr. Annette Bennett
Capt. & Mrs. William P. Black
W. E. Blaikie
Mr. & Mrs. W. W. Burns
Mr. & Mrs. J. H. Butler
Mr. & Mrs. Robert Cade
Mr. & Mrs. Geo. C. Chittendon
Mr. & Mrs. A. W. Cochran
Mr. & Mrs. Samuel Cochran
Mr. & Mrs. Samuel Cummings & dr.
Mr. & Mrs. R. H. Dakin
Mr. & Mrs. E. T. Davis
Mr. & Mrs. Samuel Davis
Rev. & Mrs. R. H. Dolliver
Mrs. George Drake & drs.
Mr. & Mrs. I. F. Dunwiddie
Dr. & Mrs. G. H. Fricke
Mr. & Mrs. O. D. S. Gallup
Mr. & Mrs. Gustave A. Goehner
Mr. & Mrs. E. B. Halladay
Mr. & Mrs. N. H. Hanchette
Mr. & Mrs. H. H. Harries
Mrs. E. L. Irwin
Mr. & Mrs. F. C. Jorgesson
Mr. & Mrs. John W. Krueger
Mr. & Mrs. Charles O. Lowman
Mr. & Mrs. Chas. H. Marsh

Mr. & Mrs. G. A. Masters
Mrs. E. Millard
Mr. & Mrs. A. R. Mora
Mr. & Mrs. J. G. Orr
Mr. & Mrs. John R. Ortengren
Mr. & Mrs. A. W. Penny
Charles H. Penny
Mr. & Mrs. Joseph A. Phelps
Dr. & Mrs. W. H. Pontious
Mr. & Mrs. George F. Reed
Mr. & Mrs. S. W. Robinson
Mr. & Mrs. Z. D. Root
Mr. & Mrs. Ernest Sicard
Mr. & Mrs. Robert Stagg
Mr. & Mrs. Chas. W. Stansbury
Dr. & Mrs. S. C. Stanton
Mr. & Mrs. C. E. Stebbings
Mr. & Mrs. J. S. Stevenson
Mr. & Mrs. R. F. Stockdale
Mr. & Mrs. Thomas A. Strayer
Mr. & Mrs. Owen Stuart & drs.
Mr. & Mrs. Thomas A. Ward
Mr. & Mrs. G. S. Wells
Mr. & Mrs. A. J. Whitcomb
Mr. & Mrs. A. E. Whitlock
Mr. & Mrs. C. Whitlock
Miss Mary A. Wilson
Mr. & Mrs. D. W. Wood

PARKSIDE.

SIXTY-NINTH STREET.

348 Mr. & Mrs. Robt. Hawkins
712 Dr. & Mrs. Geo. G. Monroe

SEVENTY-FIRST PLACE.

761 Dr. & Mrs. Chas. M. Pusey

879 Mr. & Mrs. James Chalmers

780 Mr. & Mrs. Edwin Opdyke
828 Mr. & Mrs. Alex. J. Jones
874 Mr. & Mrs. Henry H. Walton
874 Mrs. Nancy Cameron

SEVENTY-SECOND STREET.

880 Mr. & Mrs. Jacob L. Holmes
890 Mr. & Mrs. Edward J. Eames

SEVENTY-SECOND PLACE.

849 Mrs. John Penfield & dr.
849 Fred W. Penfield
849 John H. Penfield

943 Mr. & Mrs. J. W. Andrews
947 Mr. & Mrs. John Dempsey

---

848 Mr. & Mrs. E. C. Preble
856 Mr. & Mrs. Wm. P. Adams

SEVENTY-THIRD STREET.

881 Mr. & Mrs. Thos. G. Rowan

PULLMAN.

ARCADE ROW.

1 Mr. & Mrs. Charles Wright&drs.
2 Dr. & Mrs. J. A. Goltz
3 M . & Mrs. D. R. Martin
3 Carlton C. Newitt
6 William E. Quinn
9 Dr. & Mrs. A. C. Rankin
9 Fred Rankin
9 Mr. & Mrs. P. E. Hermes
10 Mr. & Mrs. B. P. Nettleton
11 Mr. & Mrs. E. C. Tourtelot
12 Mr. & Mrs. E. W. Henricks
12 Hon. John P. Hopkins

FLORENCE BOULEVARD.

(111th street.)
1 Mr. & Mrs. H. H. Sessions
1 Mr. & Mrs. David J. Harris
1 Mrs. H. S. Maxham

2 Mr. & Mrs. H. Middleton
3 Dr. & Mrs. John McLean
3 Dr. Guy M. McLean
4 Mr. & Mrs. Edward F. Bryant
5 Mr. & Mrs. W. P. Hornbeck
5 Miss S. A. Muletz
7 Mr. & Mrs. A. Rapp

HOTEL FLORENCE.

Robert M. Burns
Charles Everson
Ernest A. Hall
Mr. & Mrs. L. L. Lamb
Mr. & Mrs. J. D. McChesney
Mr. & Mrs. Edward Newton
Mr. & Mrs. Arthur M. Parent
N. D. Pound
Mr. & Mrs. Wm. Stone
Major & Mrs. J. L. Woods
Mrs. C. K. Wright & dr.

RAVINIA.

O. F. Bentley
Mr. & Mrs. W. R. Boerner
Gustav R. Boerner
Mr. & Mrs. Levi M. Comstock
Carlton U. Grant
Mrs. John Grant
Mr. & Mrs. M. S. Harsha
Mr. & Mrs. John J. Hester
Mrs. A. Leonard Hill

Percy L. Hill
Mr. & Mrs. W. C. McKenzie
Mr. & Mrs. W. L. McKenzie
Mr. & Mrs. Julius Neist
Mrs. Isaac Russell
Mr. & Mrs. Sebastian Stype
Mr. & Mrs. Malcolm Tucker
Mr. & Mrs. A. V. Willoughby

RIDGELAND.

BOULEVARD.

1324 Mr. & Mrs. F. H. Oriel

CUYLER AVENUE.

220 John Carne & dr.
226 Mr. & Mrs. Edgar W. Carne
    Receiving day Tuesday
230 Mr. & Mrs. Gregor W. Phelps
230 Mrs. S. V. Phelps

236 Mr. & Mrs. Frank Borwell
242 Mr. & Mrs. Hiram Coombs
313 Mr. & Mrs. Herman Kirchhoff
319 Mr. & Mrs. David Keighin
320 Mr. & Mrs. Morris Peterson

EAST AVENUE.

124 Mr. & Mrs. E. G. Corneau
130 Mr. & Mrs. J. D. Colwell

138 Mr. & Mrs. William S. Elliott
216 Mr. & Mrs. G. D. Bills
234 Mr. & Mrs. Edward H. Pitkin
234 Miss May Pitkin

HARVEY AVENUE.

121 Mr. & Mrs. W. H. Robinson
141 Mr. & Mrs. James Barbeau
201 Mr. & Mrs. Edward H. Johnson
205 Mr. & Mrs. John F. Shaw
205 Mrs. Fanny Murray
213 Mr. & Mrs. J. A. Clark
235 Mr. & Mrs. John A. Mallin
239 Mr. & Mrs. John Furlong
245 Mr. & Mrs. John L. Lyons
        Receiving day Tuesday
329 Mr. & Mrs. Thomas Quayle
330 Mr. & Mrs. Almon Chapman
330 Mr. & Mrs. M. P. Watterson

LOMBARD AVENUE.

241 Mr. & Mrs. E.A. Cummings & dr.
        Receiving day Tuesday
241 Mrs. E. Cummings
247 Dr. & Mrs. Francis B. Clarke
311 Mr. & Mrs. Samuel S. Gould
216 Mr. & Mrs. R. A. Helliwell
224 Mr. & Mrs. Wright Elsom
252 Mr. & Mrs. Edgar N.Goodwillie
310 Mr. & Mrs. Farmer D. Bayless
310 William H. Smith
312 Mr. & Mrs. Benj. F. Dare

OGDEN AVENUE.

121 Mr. & Mrs. H. H. Fulton
131 Mrs. Susanna F. Marchant &
        drs.
131 Mrs. Elizabeth P. Kimball
135 Mr. & Mrs. S. D. Attridge
300 Mr. & Mrs. E. P. Martin
311 Mr. & Mrs. Louis D. Taylor
313 Mr. & Mrs. W. Hayes
317 Mr. & Mrs. Thomas Cross jr.
332 Mr. & Mrs. J. M. Spackman
421 Mr. & Mrs. George D. Griffith
214 Mr. & Mrs. C. L. Ames & dr.
214 A. H. Frost
226 Mr. & Mrs. Henry H. Spooner
234 Rev. & Mrs. Wm. Bartlett
324 Mr. & Mrs. A. N. Hitchcock

RIDGELAND AVENUE.

223 Mrs. Hattie Randell
226 Mr. & Mrs. Alfred Budde

233 Mr. & Mrs. Edwin C. K. Davies
245 Mr. & Mrs. George Butters
301 Mr. & Mrs. F. G. Ensign & drs.
301 Frank G. Ensign
301 Lewis W. Ensign
311 Mr. & Mrs. Charles H. Ballard
324 Mr. & Mrs. Wm. C. Scott & drs.

SCOVILLE AVENUE.

135 Mr. & Mrs. A. L. Fitch
137 Mr. & Mrs. E. H. Duff
141 Mr. & Mrs. S. S. Rogers
221 Mr. & Mrs. Walter G. Bentley
229 Mr. & Mrs. George J. Charlton
241 Mr. & Mrs. S. E. Nutting
241 M. Erwin Bruce
309 Mr. & Mrs. Ross C. Hall
311 Mr. & Mrs. John J. Cleary
315 Mr. & Mrs. Daniel L. Hall
323 Mrs. Ida Mueller
325 Mr. & Mrs. J. M. Sleeper
325 Mrs. Emily Horton

214 Mrs. Jeremiah O'Connor & drs.
220 Mr. & Mrs. R. D. Gates
400 Mr. & Mrs. B. Kingsbury
408 Mr. & Mrs. W. G. Prall
412 Mr. & Mrs. John E. Hunt

TAYLOR AVENUE.

215 Miss G. Lay
215 Mr. & Mrs. W. W. DeArmond
219 Mr. & Mrs. Edwin D. Brink
222 Mr. & Mrs. David W.McNaught
223 Mr. & Mrs. Daniel W. Kimball
227 Mr. & Mrs. Charles Wood
233 Mr. & Mrs. Cookson M. Wright

218 Mr. & Mrs. T. H. Butler
252 Mr. & Mrs. W. H. Pearce
nw. cor. Cedar, Mr. & Mrs. Peter
        Kemp
nr. Cedar, Mr. & Mrs. Herman D.
        Wagner
nr. Cedar, Mr. & Mrs. Henry Ivens

WASHINGTON BOULEVARD.

1112 Mr. & Mrs. J. C. Griffith
1112 G. D. Griffith
1226 Mr. & Mrs. Charles D. Rich-
        ards
n.w. cor. Ogden av. Mr. & Mrs.
        Frank R. Lindop
n.w. cor.Ogden av.Mrs.John Lindop

RIVER FOREST.

ASHLAND AVENUE.

Rev. & Mrs. Elwood M. Wherry
& drs.
319 Mr. & Mrs. S. E. Baker
319 Benjamin F. Duer
339 Mr. & Mrs. Frank D. Butler

316 Mr. & Mrs. O. M. Barr
318 Mr. & Mrs. C. C. Collins

AUVERGNE PLACE.

Mr. & Mrs. Joseph D. Pickett & drs.
Receiving day Thursday
John D. Pickett
Mrs. Elizabeth Pickett
Henry Waller
Miss Lilly L. Waller
Miss Bell L. Waller
Mr. & Mrs. Edward C. Waller & dr.
Receiving day Thursday
Mr. & Mrs. W. H. Winslow
Receiving day Wednesday

CENTRAL AVENUE

56 Mr. & Mrs. Chas. M. Sturges
358 Mrs. H. L. McKallor
362 Mr. & Mrs. Felix J. Griffin

FOREST AVENUE.

239 Mr. & Mrs. Henry Struble
281 Mr. & Mrs. Daniel Pinney
293 Mr. & Mrs. E. C. Moeller
295 Mr. & Mrs. J. E. Adams
299 Mr. & Mrs. Geo. W. Shearburn
337 Mr. & Mrs. Wm. C. Walsh
343 Mr. & Mrs. C. Juergens
347 Mr. & Mrs. F. Juergens
357 Mr. & Mrs. J. T. Hodgson

244 Mr. & Mrs. Geo. W. Homer
322 Mr. & Mrs. A. P. Grant
486 Mr. & Mrs. Henry E. Graves

FRANKLIN AVENUE.

348 Mr. & Mrs. Frank L. Munroe
348 Miss Mary Cadman

GALE AVENUE.

97 Mr. & Mrs. P. C. Porter
121 Mr. & Mrs. H. E. Page

114 Mr. & Mrs. H. E. Parker
cor. Hawthorne av. Mr. & Mrs. Frank
Thompson

GROVE STREET.

87 Mr. & Mrs. B. F. Disbrow
97 Mr. & Mrs. C. E. Marble
113 Mr. & Mrs. E. F. Dunne
145 Mr. & Mrs. W. H. Hatch

32 Mr. & Mrs. Charles J. Barnard.
36 Mr. & Mrs. Herman Glaess
sw. cor. Vine Mr. & Mrs. W. S. Stevenson
s.w. cor. Vine Mr. & Mrs. Wm. F Pack

KEYSTONE AVENUE.

245 Dr. Elizabeth Trout & dr.
245 Edgar W. Trout
253 Mr. & Mrs. F. N. Boyer
253 Mrs. K. D. Buell
253 Mrs. M. T. Davis
281 D. W. Thatcher & dr.
281 Mr. & Mrs. J. C. Mooar
305 Mr. & Mrs. Webster Hakes
315 Mr. & Mrs. Wm. T. Barbour
353 Mr. & Mrs. E. J. MacAdams
363 Mr. & Mrs. W. C. Freymuth

254 Mr. & Mrs. R. S. Odell
254 Mrs. Mary A. Odell
296 Carl A. Wilmeroff
306 Mr. & Mrs. G. W. Clark
340 Mr. & Mrs. Ralph J. Hirsch
344 Mr. & Mrs. Jacob A. Cost

LAKE STREET.

396 Mr. & Mrs. James P. Luce

LATHROP AVENUE.

317 Mr. & Mrs. L. G. Bostedo
317 Edmund Fordyce
321 Mr. & Mrs. John Ahern
333 Mr. & Mrs. John F. Barrett
333 Joseph DeGan
333 Miss Emma DeGan

OAK AVENUE.

261 Mr. & Mrs. J. Humphrey
299 Mr. & Mrs. Edw. Tracy & dr.

270 Mr. & Mrs. George L. Thatcher
272 Mr. & Mrs. O. L. Deming

PARK AVENUE.

350 Mr. & Mrs. Brunot Bailey
350 Mrs. Sally G. Root

354 Mr. & Mrs. Isaiah F. Laing
354 Mrs. M. C. Laing & dr.

THATCHER AVENUE.

263 Mr. & Mrs. L. H. Ross
269 Mrs. David C. Thatcher
269 Mr. & Mrs. Frank Little
269 Fred S. Thatcher
273 Mr. & Mrs. Andrew Jaicks
275 Mr. & Mrs. F. B. Klock
283 Dr. & Mrs. James E. Keefe
293 Mr. & Mrs. J. B. Miller
122 Mr. & Mrs. Harlan Page
122 Fred H. Page
130 Mr. & Mrs. Frederick J. Watson

130 Miss Jeannette Topping
238 Mr. & Mrs. C. H. Duensing
256 Mr. & Mrs. John W. Bronghton
Receiving day Thursday
256 H. E. Broughton
260 Mr. & Mrs. Robert T. Walbank
272 Mr. & Mrs. D.A.Thatcher & dr.
278 Mr. & Mrs. Jas. S. Goodman
278 Mrs. Thomas Brown
278 Miss Alma L. Brown
284 Mrs. Lucinda S. Lord
284 Fred W. Lord
290 Mr. & Mrs. R. C. Brown
310 Mr. & Mrs. T. M. Jackson
356 Mr. & Mrs. Chas. M. White
356 Carlos F. White

RIVERSIDE.

Rev. & Mrs. George Davis Adams
Mr. & Mrs. Charles E. Allen
Harry K. Allen
Mrs. Sarah C. Allen
Mr. & Mrs. A. F. Ames
Mr. & Mrs. James S. Andrews
Mr. & Mrs. H. M. Avers
Carlton S. Badger
Mr. & Mrs. H. H. Badger
Mr. & Mrs. Edward Badger
Mr. & Mrs. John Balfour
Harry Balfour
Walter E. Balfour
A. C. Barnes
Mr. & Mrs. Albert W. Barnum
Mr. & Mrs. W. H. Barnum
Receiving day Thursday
Mr. & Mrs. Walter N. Bates
Mr. & Mrs. C. B. Beach
Mr. & Mrs. M. H. E. Beckley
Mr. & Mrs. George W. Beisel
Mrs. Louise Blayney & dr.
Mr. & Mrs. Thomas C. Blayney
Mr. & Mrs. Edgar B. Bliss
Mr. & Mrs. Arthur P. Bowen
Mr. & Mrs. Charles C. Boyles & dr.
Charles D. Boyles
Thomas D. Boyles
Mr. & Mrs. Street Bradley
Edward L. Bradley
Dr. S. L. Breckenridge
Clarence S. Brown
Mr. & Mrs. John J. Bryant
John J. Bryant jr.
Miss H. S. Campbell
Mr. & Mrs. W. J. Campbell & drs.
Mr. & Mrs. D. W. Carhart

Charles Chambers
Mr. & Mrs. George Chambers
Dudley Chase
Mr. & Mrs. H. G. Chase
Mr. & Mrs. Henry I. Chase
Philander F. Chase
Mrs. & Mrs. Harry G. Chester
Dr. & Mrs. S. V. Clevenger & dr.
Dr. & Mrs. J. L. Congdon
Mrs. Carrie Congdon & drs.
Dr. W. R. Congdon
Mr. & Mrs. Thomas M. Conpropst
Dr. George Coryell
Mr. & Mrs. A. D. Craig
Mr. & Mrs. James Christie
Mr. & Mrs. Seth F. Crews & dr.
Seth F. Crews jr.
Mr. & Mrs. Chauncey H. Crosby
Mrs. Amanda Crosby
Mr. & Mrs. C. L. Cross
Mr. & Mrs. Lee L. Dagron
Mrs. S. E. Dane
Miss Nellie T. Davis
Asa Dearborn
Dr. & Mrs. Robert T. Dearborn
Mr. & Mrs. Watts DeGolyer & dr.
Receiving day Wednesday
Mr. & Mrs. H. M. Dickson
Mr. & Mrs. Joseph Bell Ditto
W. A. Drake
Mr. & Mrs. E. A. Driver
Mr. & Mrs. J. S. Driver
E. Raymond Driver
Mr. & Mrs. Robert C. Dye
Mrs. Mary I. Dye
Mr. & Mrs. L. F. Dyrenforth
L. J. Dyrenforth

Mr. & Mrs. J. T. Edson
Mrs. M. E. Elliott
Miss Margaret Elliott
Mrs. George A. Ellis
Jerome A. Ellis
Mr. & Mrs. Frank Fredericks & dr.
Frank Fredericks jr.
Mr. & Mrs. John V. Gage
Rev. Samuel L. Gamble
Mrs. Nellie Gettier
Mr. & Mrs. H. K. Gilman
E. R. Gilman
Mr. & Mrs. Stephen Gitterman
Miss Eva Goodwin
Mr. & Mrs. A. Gorique
Mr. & Mrs. Chas. H. Gould
Mrs. M. E. Graham
Mr. & Mrs. Henry R. Green
Mr. & Mrs. Walter G. Greenleaf
Receiving day Wednesday
Mr. & Mrs. Charles O. Gregg
Mr. & Mrs. Seymour Guthrie
Frank A. Hale
John W. Halliday & drs.
Mr. & Mrs. W. B. Hamblin
Mr. & Mrs. Thomas C. Hannah
Mr. & Mrs. George Hargreaves
Mr. & Mrs. S. H. Harrington & dr.
Mr. & Mrs. Jesse Hart
Mr. & Mrs. W. A. Havemeyer & dr.
W. A. Havemeyer jr.
Mr. & Mrs. F. Hellyer & dr.
Mr. & Mrs. E. E. Helmer
Mr. & Mrs. C. M. Higginson
Mr. & Mrs. Frank A. Hitchcock
Mr. & Mrs. Walter E. Hodges
Mr. & Mrs. Frank G. Holton
Mr. & Mrs. Freelon Hotchkiss
Dr. I. S. Hotchkiss
Miss Hariette Hotchkiss
Mr. & Mrs. L. A. Howland
Mr. & Mrs. Gurdon S. Hubbard jr.
Mr. & Mrs. Wm. J. Hudson & drs.
Mr. & Mrs J. B. Hughes
Mr. & Mrs. David J. Hull
Henry D. Hull
Mr. & Mrs. George Hunt
Mrs. M. A. Hutchinson
Mrs. M. S. Hutchinson
Mrs. W. W. Hutchinson
Mrs. Sarah E. Jackson
Frederick W. Job
Mr. & Mrs. James W. Johns
Mr. & Mrs. Thomas S. Johnson
Mr. & Mrs. Cyrus M. Jones
Mr. & Mrs. M. Helles Jordan

Mr. & Mrs. W. S. Kammerer
George Chandlin Kimbark
Mr. & Mrs. A. M. Kinzie
John H. Kinzie
Mr. & Mrs. Charles Lange
Mr. & Mrs. Wm. E. Lawrence
J. Lewis Lee
Mr. & Mrs. A. Lipsey
Mr. & Mrs. James H. Lipsey
Mr. & Mrs. Henry R. Lloyd
Mr. & Mrs. Wm. Lusk
Mr. & Mrs. Archibald McArthur
Receive Tuesday & Sunday
Miss Florence B. McArthur
Mr. & Mrs. Frank J. McCain
Mr. & Mrs. H. J. McClintock
Mrs. E. C. McCloud
Mr. & Mrs. Neil McCoull
Receiving day Thursday
Roy M. McCloud
Mr. & Mrs. David W. McCord
Mrs. Anna Wood McDougal & dr.
James B. McLaugblin
Mr. & Mrs. David W. MacDonald
Mr. & Mrs. George A. Maclean
Receiving day Tuesday
Mr. & Mrs. E. E. Mandeville
Mr. & Mrs. S. W. Manney
Mr. & Mrs. Randolph Manning
Mrs. E. N. Mellor
Miss Vivia E. Mellor
Mr. & Mrs.. Amos C. Miller
Mr. & Mrs. Thomas Miller & dr.
George B. Miner
F. M. Montgomery
Mr. & Mrs. James S. Moore
Arthur Morford
Mr. & Mrs. T. T. Morford
Mr. & Mrs. George Morton
Mr. & Mrs. Norris W. Mundy
Norris H. Mundy
Mrs. Leverett W. Murray
Mr. & Mrs. George P. Nichols
Mr. & Mrs. E. W. Noakes
Mr. & Mrs. H. D. North
Mr. & Mrs. John F. Palmer
Mr. & Mrs. H. F. Paul
Nelson W. Perry
Mrs. J. S. Pode
Mr. & Mrs. Thomas R. Polglase & dr.
Mrs. Lucy G. Porter
Mr. & Mrs. J. C. Price
Edwin R. Puffer
Mr. & Mrs. H. J. Racey
Mr. & Mrs. William Radford

Mr. & Mrs. Isham Randolph
Miss P. C. Randolph
Mr. & Mrs. J. N. Rawlings
Mr. & Mrs. James D. Raynolds
Mr. & Mrs. Frank F. Reed
Mrs. M. D. Reed
Mrs. Charles Reissig
Mr. & Mrs. Aug. Rentz
Mr. & Mrs. August Repka
Mr. & Mrs. Benj. Reynolds
Mr. & Mrs. Myron B. Rice
 Receiving day Thursday
Dr. & Mrs. Frederick W. Rich
Albert D. Rich
Mr. & Mrs. S. P. Richards & dis.
Mr. & Mrs. D. E. Richardson
Mrs. Anna Richardson
Mr. & Mrs. Edward P. Ripley & drs
Mrs. J. S. Ross
Mrs. Kate Sanborn
Mr. & Mrs. Edward J. Saxe
Mr. & Mrs. John H. Schwerdt
George M. Scott
Mrs. Mary Scott
Mr. & Mrs. A. U. Scoville
Mr. & Mrs. Albert Seckel
Mrs. Elise Seckel
Mr. & Mrs. Louis A. Seeberger
Mr. & Mrs. Oscar M. Shannon
Mr. & Mrs. Wm. T. Sheldon
Mr. & Mrs. George W. Sherlock
Mr.&Mrs.Charles D. Sherman&drs.
Mrs. Bessie W. Sherman
Mr. & Mrs. W. C. Shoemaker
Mrs. E. A. Sibell
 Receiving day Thursday
George H. Sibell
Gen. & Mrs. M. D. L. Simpson
 Receiving day Thursday
Jerome W. Simpson
Mr. & Mrs. J. D. Sipp
Mr. & Mrs. George A. Smith

Mr. & Mrs. Herbert E. Smith
Mr. & Mrs. J. W. Smith & drs.
Revd& Mrs. Charles C. Snyder & r.
Karl F. Snyder
Mr. & Mrs. P. K. Solger
Miss Agnes L. Somers
Mr. & Mrs. Robert Somerville
Mrs. James Soper
Mr. & Mrs. Edward Southwood&dr.
Dr. & Mrs. Alexander Sterl
Mr. & Mrs. Wm. E. Stevens
Mr. & Mrs. C. F. Stitt
Mr. & Mrs. Edward H. Storey
Mr. & Mrs. Cornelius Sullivan&drs.
Edward J. Sullivan
John E. Sullivan
Mr. & Mrs. Charles Tarnow & dr.
Mrs. J. S. Taylor & drs.
Louis S. Taylor
Mr. & Mrs. Milton Thomas
Mr. & Mrs. W. A. Thompson
Mr. & Mrs. George Van Inwegen
Dr. & Mrs. E. A. VanTuyl
Miss Maggie Van Truyl
Mr. & Mrs. H. C. Vilas
Prof. & Mrs. Joseph Vilim
Mr. & Mrs. C. M. L. Walker
Mr. & Mrs. Wm. H. Ward
Mr. & Mrs. C. F. Wardell
R. J. Wardell
Mr. & Mrs. Robert M. Ware
Miss Edith Warren
Mr. & Mrs. Alexander Watson
Mrs. J. Q. Wells
Mrs. Jane Wesencraft
Mrs. Lotta Wesencraft
Miss Ruth M. Wheelock
Mr. & Mrs. Herbert T. Windsor
Mr. & Mrs. Charles A. Woodruff
Mr. & Mrs. Joseph G. Wurtele
Mr. & Mrs. Oscar R. Zipf
 Receiving day Wednesday

TRACY.

Daniel Barnard
Mr. & Mrs. E. A. Barnard
Miss Alice L. Barnard
Miss Elizabeth Barnard
Mr. & Mrs. John Barwick
Mr. & Mrs. James A. Beach
Mr. & Mrs. J. L. Clark
Mr. & Mrs. W. G. Coulter
Mr. & Mrs. Cornelius Cox & dr.
Mr. & Mrs. A. S. Dittman & dr.

Mr. & Mrs. P. W. Dorn
Mr. & Mrs. Frank F. Douglas
Mr. & Mrs. T. A. Dungan
Mr. & Mrs. G. M. French
Mr. & Mrs. J. B. Gascoigne
Mr. & Mrs. Charles B. Goes
Mr. & Mrs. Wm. Goes
Mr. & Mrs. C. H. Gorton & dr.
Mrs. Edward Grady
Mrs. J. M. Griswold & drs.

Mr. & Mrs. M. E. Griswold
Mr. & Mrs. John Hill jr.
Mr. & Mrs. W. I. Hitt
Mr. & Mrs. H. E. Horton & dr.
  Receiving day Tuesday
Mr. & Mrs. J. B. Humphreys
Rev. & Mrs. George E. Hunt
Mr. & Mrs. William Law   .
R. P. Layton & drs.
Mr. & Mrs. Alfred H. Marsh
Mr. & Mrs. E. P. Marsh & drs.
Mr. & Mrs. J. A. McKeever
Mr. & Mrs. Frank Meek
Mr. & Mrs. George W. Murray
H. A. Parker & dr.
Mr. & Mrs. Sidney Parker
Mr. & Mrs. E. D. Petrie
Mr. & Mrs. W. A. Purdy

Mr. & Mrs. George W. Rector
Mr. & Mrs. E. L. Roberts
Mr. & Mrs. W. H. Roberts
Dr. Grace A. Rowley
Mr. & Mrs. Alfred H. Rush
Mr. & Mrs. B. M. Russell
J. M. Secrist
Mr. & Mrs. Frank Stewart
Mr. & Mrs. D. W. Sutherland
Mr. & Mrs. R. G. Taylor
Mr. & Mrs. J. H. Vanderpoel
Mr. & Mrs. T. T. Verdier & dr.
Mr. & Mrs. D. C. Wagner
Mr. & Mrs. Samuel Wells
Mr. & Mrs. T. H. White
Mr. & Mrs. James M. Young
Mr. & Mrs. Herman Ziegler
Mr. & Mrs. Arnold W. Zimmerman
  & dr.

WASHINGTON HEIGHTS.

Mr. & Mrs. C. H. L. Ahrens & dr.
Mrs. Emily Baker
Mrs. Mary Baker & dr.
L. G. Brown
Rev. & Mrs. P. H. Budach
Mr. & Mrs. John E. Clarke
Prof. John W. Clarke
Mr. & Mrs. J. B. Clarke
Mr. & Mrs. J. F. Clausson
Mr. & Mrs. Elliott DeLand & dr.
Walter DeLand
Dr. & Mrs. James E. Derham
Mr. & Mrs. J. L. Dodd
Henry C. Ebel jr.
Mr. & Mrs. John Elmstedt
Mr. & Mrs. I. T. Greenacre
Mr. & Mrs. A. D. Heffron

Rev. & Mrs. D. S. Heffron & dr.
Mr. & Mrs. Ch. Holmberg
Mrs. J. Kann & dr.
Mr. & Mrs. John H. Kistner
Mr. & Mrs. Gottlieb Klein & dr.
Jacob Krohner
Dr. & Mrs. Louis Lowenthal
Mr. & Mrs. C. C. Magoon
Mr. & Mrs. J. C. McCullough
Mr. & Mrs. B. F. McManus
Rev. & Mrs. F. H. Patzer
Mrs. James A. Price
Mr. & Mrs. S. Edward Rumsey
Mr. & Mrs. A. B. Stevens & dr.
Mr. & Mrs. R. H. Valentine
Mr. & Mrs. H. H. Wilder

WILMETTE.

Mr. & Mrs. J. G. Anderson
Mr. & Mrs. John Arndt
Rev. & Mrs. Hugh Atchinson
Mr. & Mrs. M. E. Barker
Mr. & Mrs. F. W. Barnes
Mr. & Mrs. George Barry & drs.
George F. Barry
Mr. & Mrs. Ralph E. Beebe
Mr. & Mrs. John S. Belknap
Mrs. J. McD. Benight
Mr. & Mrs. Frank Berry
Mr. & Mrs. J. A. Bockius & dr.
Mr. & Mrs. R. Bodinghouse
Mr. & Mrs. S. E. Bradley

Mr. & Mrs. Leland Breeze & drs.
Mr. & Mrs. C. H. Brethvold
Mr. & Mrs. J. D. Brown & dr.
Edward A. Burge
Mr. & Mrs. Charles Carhart
Mr. & Mrs. C. O. Carlson
Mr. & Mrs. M. T. Carter & drs.
Mr. & Mrs. R. W. Chappell & dr.
Mr. & Mrs. W. A. Chatterton
Dr. & Mrs. A. S. Childs & dr.
Mr. & Mrs. C. S. Clark
Mr. & Mrs. John B. Clay
Mr. & Mrs. Alonzo P. Convis
Mr. & Mrs. C. D. Cramer

Mr. & Mrs. H. A. Crane & drs.
Mr. & Mrs. Willis E. Crane & drs.
Mr. & Mrs. C.. W Crocker & dr.
Mr. & Mrs. P. O. Crocker
Mr. & Mrs. Don B. Davenport
Mrs. Elizabeth Davenport
Mr. & Mrs. J. E. Davis
Rev. & Mrs. E. B. Dean
Mr. & Mrs. John DeHaye
Mrs. Caroline DeZeng
Mr. & Mrs. W. E. Dibble
Mr. & Mrs. Harvey M. Dibble
Mr. & Mrs. Albert Dietz
Mr. & Mrs. J. G. Dietz
L. S. Dimock
Mr. & Mrs. S. M. Dingee & dr.
S. S. Dingee
Mr. & Mrs. J. P. Doig & drs.
John S. Doig
Malcomb Doig
Mr. & Mrs. Edwin Drury & dr.
Mr. & Mrs. Frank Drury
Mr. & Mrs. H. G. Drury & dr.
Mr. & Mrs. A. C. Duncan
W. E. Egan
Mr. & Mrs. Edward F. Ernst
Miss Ann Farnsworth
Mr. & Mrs. Edward P. Fateh
Mr. & Mrs. G. E. Fernald
J. H. Furman
Miss Jeanie Furman
Miss Nettie Furman
Mr. & Mrs. A. N. Gage
Mr. & Mrs. Henry H. Gage
Mrs. Caleb F. Gates & dr.
Mr. & Mrs. Henry B. Gates
Mrs. I. A. Gooding & dr.
S. E. Gooding
W. S. Gooding
Mr. & Mrs. Barzelli Goodrich
Mr. & Mrs. Edwin Haskin
Mr. & Mrs. W. J. Hosmer
Mr. & Mrs. George C. Hughes & dr.
Mr. & Mrs. William Hunter
Mr. & Mrs. W. B. Hunter
Mr. & Mrs. E. C. Jones
Mr. & Mrs. F. L. Joy
Mr. & Mrs. W. H. Kinney
Mr. & Mrs. Rufus L. Kirk
Mr. & Mrs. Frank Kunz
Mr. & Mrs. E. C. Latham
Miss Hattie Latham
Mr. & Mrs. Hubbard Latham
Mr. & Mrs. H. H. Latham
Francis B. Law
Miss Anna E. Law

Miss Ida I. Law
Mr. & Mrs. John Ling
Charles R. Mack
Mr. & Mrs. A. W. MacLean & dr.
Mr. & Mrs. Chas. H. Marchant
Mr. & Mrs. George H. Mars
Mr. & Mrs. J. B. McCormick
Mr. & Mrs. Alex. McDaniel
Mr. & Mrs. J. H. McDowell
Mr. & Mrs. J. L. McKittrick
Mr. & Mrs. Chas. J. Michelet
Dr. & Mrs. W. E. Michelet
Mr. & Mrs. M. O. Millar
Mrs. Mary J. Mills
Mr. & Mrs. H. E. Moore
Mr. & Mrs. W. R. Morley
Mr. & Mrs. L. N. Moyer
Mr. & Mrs. C. S. Musson
Frederick Norman
Mr. & Mrs. F. S. Pallett
Mr. & Mrs. William Panushka & dr.
John W. Panushka
Mrs. Alexander Parr & dr.
E. S. Parr
George R. Parr
Mr. & Mrs. Edgar T. Paul
Mr. & Mrs. Frank M. Paul
Mr. & Mrs. J. C. Pierson
Mr. & Mrs. L. J. Pierson
Mr. & Mrs. Loring W. Post
Mr. & Mrs. Mortimer Power
Mr. & Mrs. Henry Rau
Mr. & Mrs. George W. Rogers & dr.
Edward F. Russell
Miss Lena L. Russell
Mr. & Mrs. William Sabin
Mr. & Mrs. James C. Savage & dr.
Mr. & Mrs. P. J. Schaefer
Mr. & Mrs. Carl S. Schroeder
Mrs. Jane Shantz & dr.
Mr. & Mrs. A. T. Sherman
Mr. & Mrs. W. C. Shurtleff
Dr. & Mrs. J. W. Slonaker
Mr. & Mrs. J. B. Spencer
G. W. Springer
Mr. & Mrs. L. B. Springer
Mrs. M. C. Springer & dr.
Dr. & Mrs. B. C. Stolp
Mr. & Mrs. Calvin A. Strong
Mr. & Mrs. Charles Swartout
Mr. & Mrs. Wm. G. Sweetman
Mr. & Mrs. Albert H. Taylor
Mr. & Mrs. Cortland C. Taylor
Mr. & Mrs. Thos. H. Taylor
Mr. & Mrs. Howard N. Tyson
Mr. & Mrs. Frank C. VanNess

Mr. & Mrs. M. E. Walters
Mr. & Mrs. James Watson
Mr. & Mrs. George A. Watson
Mr. & Mrs. Thomas Watson & dr.
Mr. & Mrs. Thomas W. Watson
Mr. & Mrs. C. A. Weary & dr.

Mr. & Mrs. E. R. Webber
Mr. & Mrs. F. M. Westerfield
Mr. & Mrs. H. D. Westerfield
Mr. & Mrs. E. B. Wheelock
Mr. & Mrs. S. A. Wheelock & dr.
Thomas Wright & dr.

WINDSOR PARK.

BOND AVENUE.

7301 Mr. & Mrs. Isaac T. Sutton
7409 Mrs. P. C. Stid
7409 Mr. & Mrs. J. W. Robinson
7443 Mr. & Mrs. Samuel A. French
7443 Mr. & Mrs. Garrie S. French
nr. 75th Alexander Craig
7465 Mr. & Mrs. P. J. McDonagh
7565 Mr. & Mrs. George Nichols
 & dr.
sw. cor. 73d Mr. & Mrs. Henry J.
 Hetherington
sw. cor. 73d John T. Hetherington
7352 Mr. & Mrs. G. M. Russegue
7352 Dr. & Mrs. Chas. F. Millspaugh
7362 Mr. & Mrs. F. M. Tobin
7432 Mr. & Mrs. Chas. F. Lynn&dr.
7436 Mr. & Mrs. G. H. Goodrich
7442 Mrs. J. M. Bacon
7456 Mr. & Mrs. N. H. VanSicklen
7470 Mr. & Mrs. Wm. Shoemaker
7524 Mr. & Mrs. August Wooler
7536 Dr. & Mrs. G. J. White
7554 Dr. & Mrs. W. B. Ferris
7554 W. E. Rooker
7554 Frederick M. Barnes
7620 Mr. & Mrs. Charles J. Johnson
7620 Mrs. S. J. Olds
7640 Mr. & Mrs. Floyd Middagh
7650 Mr. & Mrs. Wellington B.
 Stone
7660 Mr.&Mrs.Frederick Wilkinson
7664 Mr. & Mrs. H. G. Purinton
7700 Mr. & Mrs. C. B. Payton

FORD AVENUE.

7535 Mr. & Mrs. R. E. Schmidt
7641 Mr. & Mrs. Alexander Harvey
7657 Mr. & Mrs. Charles M. Steffens
7626 Mr. & Mrs. Robert Mertens
7636 Mr. & Mrs. Thomas D. Bentley
7636 Thomas D. Bentley jr.

SEVENTY-THIRD.

nw. cor. Lake av. Mr. & Mrs. Harry
 K. Childs

SEVENTY-FOURTH.

83 Rev. & Mrs. G. H. Grannis
 Receiving day Tuesday
204 Capt. & Mrs. R. H. Long & dr.
218 Mr. & Mrs. W. J. Hartman
226 Mr. & Mrs. E. H. Mosher
230 Mr. & Mrs. Jonathan Smith &
 drs.

SEVENTY-FOURTH PLACE.

225 Byron Boyden

SEVENTY-FIFTH.

107 Mr. & Mrs. F. Munson & drs.
 Receiving day Thursday
107 Frank W. Munson

SEVENTY-SEVENTH.

47 Mr. & Mrs. H. W. Parkhurst
47 Mrs. R. S. Crandall
59 Mr. & Mrs. Charles H. Wilcox
59 Mrs. A. P. Wilcox
140 Dr. J. Witham Norton

WINNETKA.

Mr. & Mrs. John Alles
Mr. & Mrs. John Alles jr.
Mr. & Mrs. Chars. C. Arnold
Mr. & Mrs. George Baker & dr.
Mrs. S. C. Bartlett
 Receiving day Wednesday
J. H. Batchelder
Robert Y. Baxter
Mr. & Mrs. Chas. Guy Bolte
Mr. & Mrs. J. Edwin Bradstreet

Miss Lizzie Brock
Col. & Mrs. J. E. Buckbee & dr.
Julian E. Buckbee jr.
Miss Minnie H. Butler
Mrs. H. E. Calrow & dr.
Mr. & Mrs. J. G. Calrow
Mr. & Mrs. A. B. Capron & dr.
Mr. & Mrs. Charles W. Cole
Mr. & Mrs. F. K. Copeland
Lowell Copeland

Mr. & Mrs. Thomas Copelin
J. A. Cunningham
Mr. & Mrs. J. T. Dale
Miss Jane E. Dale
Mrs. J. A. Densmore & dr.
Mr. & Mrs. J. B. Densmore
Mr. & Mrs. H. A. de Windt
Mr. & Mrs. T. S. Dick & drs.
Rev. & Mrs. Q. L. Dowd
Mr. & Mrs. C. P. Dunning
Mr. & Mrs. Charles Eastman
T. H. Ellison
Mr. & Mrs. John Gauler
Mr. & Mrs. E. S. Gilbert
Mr. & Mrs. S. A. Goss
Miss Grace Graves
Mr. & Mrs. R. M. Graves & dr.
Mr. & Mrs. Frederick Greeley
Mr. & Mrs. Thomas Hawkes & dr.
Mr. & Mrs. Samuel Hazlehurst
Mr. & Mrs. John Heath
Mr. & Mrs. F. E. Herdman
Mr. & Mrs. G. C. Hoge
Mr.&Mrs. DeWitt P. Hubbard & dr.
Mr. & Mrs. James A. Hunt
Mr. & Mrs. Roy Johnson
Mr. & Mrs. Luther C. Keeler & drs.
James Kelly
Mr. & Mrs. H. B. King
Mr. & Mrs. William H. King
Mr. & Mrs. Wendell Klein
Mr. & Mrs. M. R. Kultchar
Mr. & Mrs. George H. Leslie
Mr. & Mrs. Henry Levin
Mr. & Mrs. H. D. Lloyd
Mr. & Mrs. C. A. Long
Mr. & Mrs. Francis O. Lyman
Mr. & Mrs. H. V. Mann
Mr. & Mrs. William Margerun
Mr. & Mrs. B. A. May & drs.
Alfred C. Maynard
Edwin Maynard
E. Percy Maynard
Mr. & Mrs. Howard McAllaster
Mr. & Mrs. G. M. McConnel & dr.
Mr. & Mrs. Robert B. McConnel
 Receiving day Tuesday
Dr. S. G. McCracken
Mr. & Mrs. John McFarlin
Mr. & Mrs. George McKinney

William McKinney
Mr. & Mrs. James H. Miller
Mr. & Mrs. J. H. Monrad
Mrs. G. H. Morrison
Mrs. H. W. Morrison
R. S. Moth
Mr. & Mrs. G. W. Oldfather
Mr. & Mrs. H. I. Orwig
E. W. Osgood
Mr. & Mrs. S. W. Osgood
Mrs. B. Ostrander
Mr. & Mrs. J. O. Parker & drs.
James K. Parker
Mr. & Mrs. Rudolph Petterson & dr.
Mr. & Mrs. C. B. Powell
Mr. & Mrs. Carlton Prouty
Mr. & Mrs. M. F. Prouty
Mr. &. Mrs. J. A. Pugh
Mrs. Nannie Reagan & dr.
Mr. & Mrs. G. H. Ruel
Mr. & Mrs. Jos. B. Sanborn
Mr. & Mrs. Samuel Schackford
Mr. & Mrs. John R. Schuyler
Mr. & Mrs. James Sheehan
Joseph Sherlock
Miss Elizabeth O. Shibley
Mrs. C. J. Sloate & drs.
Mr. & Mrs. J. O. Smith & dr.
Mrs. Susan Smith & drs.
Mr. & Mrs. Merritt Starr
Mr. & Mrs. W. W. Sutton
Mr. & Mrs. C. S. Thorne & drs.
Mr. & Mrs. H. Totten
Mrs. Susan Totten
Harry Totten
Miss Susan Totten
Isaac Wait
Mr. & Mrs. William Wait
Mr. & Mrs. W. C. Warner
Mr. & Mrs J. G. Weart
Miss Julia G. Weed
Mr. & Mrs Charles Wicks
Mr. & Mrs. Thomas G. Windes
A. J. Willard
Mr. & Mrs. J. H. S. Williams
Mr. & Mrs. J. C. Winship
Mr. & Mrs. James A. Wolfolk
Mr. & Mrs. A. T. Woodford
Mr. & Mrs. W. S. Worman

R. R. Donnelley & Sons Co.

PART EIGHTH.

SHOPPING GUIDE.

THE BLUE BOOK.

*CONTAINING A SELECTED LIST OF PROMINENT
FIRMS AND INDIVIDUALS OF CHICAGO,
ARRANGED UNDER THEIR PROPER
PROFESSIONAL AND BUSI-
NESS HEADINGS;
ALSO DIAGRAMS OF THE THEATERS.*

Ladies' Shopping Guide.

EMBRACING NAMES AND ADDRESSES OF RELIABLE AND PROMI-
NENT FIRMS AND INDIVIDUALS, CLASSIFIED UNDER
APPROPRIATE BUSINESS HEADINGS AND
PROFESSIONS.

Analytical Chemists.
Mathison Soren, R. Ph. 2126 Indiana av. Tel. South-172

Antique Goods.
VAN MINDEN J. 3220 Graves pl.

Architects.
DeHorvath Jul, 119 Dearborn

Architectural Sculptors.
SCHMIDT & STAAK, 200 N. Wells

Art.
(Fine.)

Art Galleries.
Art Institute, The, Lake Front opposite Adams st.

Art—High Class Works.
ANDERSON ART CO. 172 N. Clark
THURBER W. SCOTT, 210 Wabash av.

Art Leaded Glass.
FLANAGAN & BIEDENWEG, 450-452 Wabash av.

Art Needle Work.

Art, Painters.
(Fancy and Ornamental.)
CAPLAIN K. A. MRS. 451 W. Madison

Art Schools.

HENRY KOENKER.   *DANIEL SCHNEIDER.*

KOENKER & SCHNEIDER,

BAKERY, CONFECTIONERY.

*ALL ORDERS FOR FANCY CAKES, ICE CREAM,
CHARLOTTE RUSSE, ETC., PROMPTLY ATTENDED TO.*

TELEPHONE NORTH-792.

*451 NORTH CLARK STREET,
NEAR DIVISION STREET.*

Art, Wood Carving School.

ART WOOD CARVING SCHOOL
Suite 42 Athenaeum, 18-26 Van Buren St.
Class and private lessons in Artistic
Wood Carving. Medal and Diploma
awarded at World's Fair.
MISS M. L. BENTLEY. Principal.

Artistic Picture Frames.

LIVINGSTONE T. B. 44 and 46
W. Quincy

Artificial Limbs.

SHARP & SMITH, 73 Randolph

Artists.

MRS. FRANC HAWES-ALLORE,

....Artist....

SUITE 40, THE POTOMAC,

Michigan Avenue, s. w. cor. 30th.

WILLARD G. SEARLES,
Portraits in Crayon, Monochrome and
...Water Colors...
Studio, 79 Athenæum Building,
26 Van Buren Street.

MATILDA VANDERPOEL,
...LESSONS IN...
Drawing and Painting
...DECORATING. .
Dinner and Menu Cards
STUDIO, 47 ATHENÆUM,

Artists.
(Miniature.)

MISS MAGDA M. HEUERMANN.
Studio 1107 Auditorium Tower.
Instruction in China Painting and
Pyrography. Miniatures on
Ivory a Specialty.

MISS CECILE E. PAYEN
Miniature Artist

STUDIO 1106, AUDITORIUM TOWER
CONGRESS STREET ENTRANCE

Artists.
(Portra.ts, Etc.)

ALTA E. WILMOT,
....ARTIST AND TEACHER....
Portraits, Home Interiors,
Room 1308 The Auditorium Tower.

Awnings for Rent.

Awnings, **Carpet Coverings, Chairs,
Tables, Step Carpets, Carriage
Men and Calcium Lights Furnished
for Weddings, Receptions, etc.**

GEO. M. COOK,

3742 Cottage Grove Avenue
TELEPHONE OAKLAND-977.

Awnings and Tents.

CARPENTER GEO. B. & CO. 208
South Water

Bakers and Confectioners.

KOENKER & SCHNEIDER, 451
N. Clark

Bank and Office Fittings.

**CHICAGO INTERIOR DECO-
RATING CO.** 149 and 150 Michigan
av.

Banks.

GLOBE SAVINGS BANK, Cor,
Dearborn and Jackson

CHICAGO CALCIUM LIGHT CO.

▲ ▲ ▲

PRIVATE THEATRICALS LIGHTED
With all Modern Stage Effects.

Colored Lights for Tableaux,
Masquerades, Lawn Parties, etc.

▲ ▲ ▲

84 MARKET STREET. Telephone Main-4322.

Baths.

MASSAGE
By Mrs. Folke-Kjellberg,
47 TO 51 CENTRAL MUSIC HALL
(See Page xviii.)

Baths, Electro-Thermal.

Auditorium Electro-Thermal Bath Rooms
J. Mitchell Taylor, M. D.
Electricity in all forms applied in
Nervous and Chronic Diseases. Ladies'
dept. in charge of Mrs. Mary S. Halloway, Suite 35 Auditorium Bldg., Wabash Avenue entrance.

Bicycles.
OVERMAN WHEEL CO. 287
Wabash av.

Billiard and Pool Tables.

Brunswick-Balke-Collender Co.
263 & 265 WABASH AVE.
BILLIARD TABLES FOR PRIVATE
RESIDENCES A SPECIALTY.

Birds.
Kaempfer Fred, 217 Madison

Book Cases.
YOST CIRCULAR CASE CO. 266
S. Jefferson

Bookbinders.
Geiger J. J. 440 N. Wells
Ringer P. & Co. 108 and 110 Randolph

Books.
(Foreign.)
KOELLING & KLAPPEN-
BACH, 100 and 102 Randolph
51

Brushes, Carpet Sweepers and Dusters.

BRUSHES
OF EVERY DESCRIPTION
DILLEY'S BRUSH STORE
172 E. Adams St., Rand-McNally Bldg.
CARPET SWEEPERS REPAIRED.

• **Business Colleges.**
JONES BUSINESS COLLEGE,
582 W. Madison, cor. Ashland boul.

Butter and Eggs.

CHARLES CREAMERY CO.
41 N. State Street,
Sells Finer Butter than any other
Dealer and Gives Full Weight.
Telephone Main-600.

Cabinet Makers.
VISCONTI F. 2920 Cottage Grove av.

Calcium Lights.
CHICAGO CALCIUM LIGHT
CO. 84 Market
Frankenstein Sam, 30 S. Market. Tel.
Main-1672

Carpenters and Builders.

A. H. ANDERSON & CO.
Carpenters and
Builders . . .
64 N. State Street, cor. Illinois Street
All Kinds of Repairing.
Screens and Screen Doors Made to Order
...Weather Strips and Glazing...

DR. A. R. SOMMERVILLE,

COMPLEXION SPECIALIST.

Wrinkles, Pockmarks, and all Facial Blemishes removed.

The skin entirely renewed by Electricity.

Twenty years' experience.

Room 38, McVicker's Theatre Building.

Carpet Cleaners.

BEDELL GEORGE MRS. 265 N. Clark
BEECROFT & CO. 103, 105 and 107 W. Monroe
COOK GEORGE M. 3742 Cottage Grove av.
GREAT AMERICAN STEAM CARPET & LACE CLEANING WORKS, Nicholas Auw, prop. 141, 20th. Tel. South-803
HOERLEIN H. A. 3104 and 3106 Cottage Grove av. Tel. South-647

Carpets and Rugs.
Steamed, Renovated and Laid.

WILSON & CO.
403 and 405 N. Clark Street.

Lace Curtains Cleaned. ————★

Carpetings, Curtains and Rugs.
(Exclusively.)
RICHARDSON O. W. & CO. 315 to 321 Wabash av. opposite "The Auditorium"

Carriages and Buggies.
COLUMBUS BUGGY CO. 381 to 385 Wabash av.
MILBURN WAGON CO. 521 to 531 Wabash av.

Caterers.
FISH R. H. 528 W. Madison
JOHNSON E. H. 973 W. Madison. Tel. West-69
MORSE F. G. 2119 Michigan av. Tel. South-459
RODLEY W. W. 3035 Indiana av. Tel. South-15. Branch Office 228 N. State
WERNER A. 2112 Michigan av.

Cemeteries.
ROSE HILL CEMETERY, office 90, 161 Lasalle

Chairs, Globes, Folding Beds, Etc.
ANDREWS A. H. & CO. 215 Wabash av.

Chimney Tops and Repairing.
KING MOLESWORTH, 3139 Wabash av.

China, Glass, Etc.
PITKIN & BROOKS, 105 State

China, Glass and Queensware.
BURLEY & COMPANY, 145 and 147 State

China Repairing.
OTAKI H. M. 1517 Michigan av.

Chiropodists.

MISS AMAROY ESKRIDGE, CHIROPODIST.
711, 34 Washington Street.
Reference by permission:
Dr. Sarah Hackett Stevenson;
Drs. Henry T. Byford, J. E. Stubbs, Venetian Building;
Dr. Otto Schmidt, Schiller Bldg.

Dr. Maximilian Pincus,
Surgeon Chiropodist.

SUITE 53, 207 STATE ST. COR. ADAMS.
Hours: 9 a. m to 6 p. m. Sunday, 12 m. to 1 p. m. Patients treated at residence, if desired.

REIS I. J. 28, 125 State

Church Furniture.
(Manufacturers and Designers.)
CHICAGO INTERIOR DECORATING CO. 149 and 150 Michigan av.

Delsarte Corsets.

and...

Waists

═══

ARTISTIC
AND
HYGIENIC
NOVELTIES

═══

Delsarte Strophium.   *New Delsarte Short Hip.*

Endorsed by leading Costumers of the centres of fashion, Teachers of Physical Culture, School of Acting and Dancing, Physicians and Nurses.

PROFITABLE LINE FOR AGENTS TO SELL.

Delsarte Mfg. Co.,   44 E. Madison St., Chicago.

MISS HARRIET R. HOWARD, Mgr.

The American Dancing Academy,

A. RITTER, Instructor.

205 E. Madison Street,

Private lessons every Tuesday and Saturday, at Academy, 1 to 6 p. m., or at your Residence at any hour.   **Chicago.**

Special Attention Given to Private Dancing Clubs.

Corsets.
(Manufacturers.)
DELSARTE MNFG. CO. 44 Madison

GRISWOLD CORSETS.
HIGH GRADE CORSETS TO MEASURE.
J. B. PUTNAM,
Corset and Hair Parlors
Columbus Memorial Bldg.,
103 State Srreet.

Curiosity Shop.
BURGHOFFER J. J. G. 1549 Michigan av.

Dancing Academies.
AMERICAN DANCING ACADEMY, A. Ritter, instructor, 205 Madison
McKEE H. MR. & MRS. 1249 and 1251 W. Madison, and Siegler's Hall. Residence 698 Walnut

LINDLEY MURRAY MOORE,

::: Dentist :::

MASONIC TEMPLE, SUITE 205

CROWN AND BRIDGE WORK
A SPECIALTY.

STATE AND RANDOLPH

Decorative Art.
PUTNAM A. M. MRS. 730 W. Madison

Decorators.

ALMINI COMPANY

•• **Interior Decorators, General Painters, etc.**
434 Wabash Ave. Tel. Harrison-265

CHICAGO INTERIOR DECO-RATING CO. 149 and 150 Michigan av.
CRANDALL FRANK A. 2210 and 2212 Indiana av. Tel. South-1. "The Hallman Wall Cleaner"
CRANDALL R. A. CO. 2127 Michigan av. Tel. South-230.
CROSSMAN & LEE, 1303 Michigan av.
NELSON W. P. & CO. 193 Wabash av.

ROSS & WHITE,
PAINTERS AND DECORATORS,
Dealers in Wall Paper, Paints, Oils, Glass, etc.
Tel. Oakland-50. 4221 Lake Ave.

Decorators and Wall Paper.

D. NORTON & SON,

Dealers in **WALL PAPER**
Also Plain and Decorative Painting, etc.
1311 Wabash Av. | Tel. South-431.

Dentists.

A. BROM ALLEN, D.D.S.

Suite **710 Venetian Bldg**, **34 and 36 Washington St.**
Hours, 9 a. m. to 5 p. m.

BROWN & ELY, 1911 Michigan av.
DENNIS GEORGE J. Michigan av. cor. 31st
DUNN J. AUSTIN, 901 Marshall Field bldg.
ERVIN W. EDGAR, Norwood Flats, 3000 Indiana av.

Carl Theodor Gramm, M. D.

---DENTIST---
Suite 1003, Columbus Memorial Bldg.
Telephone Main-3886.

GUNTHER H. ALFRED, 3300 Cottage Grove av.

DR. W. W. LAZEAR,

...Dentist...
3506 Indiana Avenue.
'Phone Oakland-15.

MARSHALL JOHN S. M.D., 1003, 36 Washington, hours 9 a.m. to 4 p.m.

LOUIS E. IRELAND, M.D.S., D.D.S.
Secretary
Metropolitan Dental Association,
96 State Street, Suite 501.

MOORE LINDLEY MURRAY, 205 Masonic Temple

DR. M. A. NEWMAN,

DENTIST,
Masonic Temple, Suite 1101.
Telephone Main-3826.

NOYES EDMUND, 65 Randolph
PALMER J. B. 32, 34 Monroe

Dentists—continued.

PECK A. H., M.D., 65 Randolph

PITT H. N. 209 and 210, 577 W. Monroe

ALEX. M. RIVENBURG, D. D. S.

58 STATE STREET.

. . . .   Hours: 9 a. m. to 5 p. m.

SALOMON GODFREY S. DR.
1004 to 1006 Masonic Temple

DR. GEORGE B. SALTER,

= = Dentist = =

Suite 827-829, Marshall Field Building.
Telephone Main-3846.

SWAIN EDGAR D. 65 Randolph,
hours 9 a.m. to 4 p. m.

Philadelphia Dental Parlors,
210 State Street.

We have all the Modern Electrical
Devices for Painless Dentistry.
Gold Crowns, 22 K, $4. H. J. TARR, Mgr.

J. HAMILTON THURSTON,
DENTIST

711 Venetian Bldg. Hours P. M. The
Harcourt, 57th cor. Madison Av. 9 to 12
a.m. After March 1, '95, Reliance Bldg.

DR. I. F. UPSON, Dentist.

Suite 825 . . . . .
Marshall Field Building,
31 Washington Street

DR. FREDERICK M. WALES
.:.DENTIST...

Hours, 9 until 4. Office and Residence
"The Tudor," 4308 Ellis Avenue.
Telephone Oakland-821,

WHITMORE CHARLES C. 1208
Champlain bldg.

DR. A. W. ZIEGLER,
DENTIST.

Room 1310 Champlain Building,
Cor. State and Madison Sts.
Hours, 12 m. to 5.30 p m.   Tel. Main-933

ZINN GEO. E. 580 W. Madison

Mme. L. McDonald

Gowns and Mantles

Perfect Style and Perfect Fit Guaranteed at Reasonable Prices . . . . .

.... Of Every Description.

607 No. Clark St., Chicago.

Dermatologists.

FACIAL BLEMISHES! The only Medical Institute in the West for the treatment of Birth Marks, Red Nose, Red Veins, Pimples, Moles, Black Heads, Scars, Pitting, Powder Marks, Acne, Eczema, Lupus, Oily Skin, Barbers' Itch, Superfluous Hair on Ladies' Faces destroyed. Skin Diseases Cured. Special attention given to the treatment of the above conditions of the skin. I treat only the face. **DR. WHITING**, Physician, 1132 MASONIC TEMPLE, CHICAGO.

Detective Agencies.

BERRY'S DETECTIVE AGENCY, 829-830 Chicago Stock Exchange
MOONEY & BOLAND AGENCY, The, Security bldg.

Diamond Setters.

C. W. TERNAND & CO.

Fine Diamond Work.
Remounting and Resetting a Specialty
1008–1009 Champlain Building,
N. W. Cor. State and Madison.

Diamonds.

J. J. G. BURGHOFFER,

OPALS AND UNSET PRECIOUS STONES

1549 MICHIGAN AVE.

CHAMBERS J. B. & CO. Clark and Madison

Dressmakers.

FARRON J. A. MRS. 3903 Michigan av. Flat C

MRS. L. FOY,

Dresses and Tea Gowns

Made to order on short notice.
405 State Street.

D. W. HAWKINS   MISS LULU HAWKINS
HAWKINS and DAUGHTER,
Ladies' Tailoring, also Evening, Dinner and Reception Dresses.
Room 26, 125 State.

MISS ANNA HIRSH,

Fashionable Dress Making

1620 Orrington Ave., Evanston.

Mrs. Dora C. James

- - MODISTE - -

4856 N. CLARK ST., - ROGERS PARK

McDONALD MME. 607 N. Clark

MRS. M. McLAUGHLIN,
IMPORTER

Fine Dresses and Garments

3029 Michigan Avenue,
CHICAGO.

MELHUISH,

Ladies' Tailor and Furrier,

1703 Michigan Ave.

REYNOLDS A. S. 2101 Michigan av.

Dressmakers—continued.

MME. SWARTHOUT,

Ladies' Tailor,

Suite 1218 Masonic Temple.

THOMAS A. R. MME. 1831 Michigan av.

MME J. WOLF,
DRESSMAKER,
1927 INDIANA AVENUE.

Druggists.
RHODE R. E. 504 N. Clark

Zahn Emil A. 1801 Wabash av.

Dyers and Scourers.
AUW NICHOLAS, 141, 20th. Tel South-803

JOHN P. HOEVER,
WELLS STREET STEAM DYE HOUSE,
Ladies' Silk, Satin and Woolen Dresses, Shawls, Sacks, etc., Dyed or Cleaned in a Superior Manner.
546 Wells Street.

Parisian Steam Dye and Cleaning Works, 1025 W. Madison
SOUTH SIDE STEAM DYE WORKS, Henry Wink, prop. 2546 Cottage Grove av.

Electricians.
Tel. Main-3669.   Established 1882.
HENRY NEWGARD,
Electrical Construction and Repairing. Rooms 23 and 24, 88 La Salle St. Speaking Tubes.

Electro Therapy.
ELECTRO-THERAPEUTIC & SURGICAL INSTITUTE, 609 Masonic Temple

Murray Mathews

··· FEMALE EMPLOYMENT

130 No. Clark Street,	**2205 Michigan Ave.,**
Telephone North–869.	Telephone South–63.
MRS. WILLIS, Forelady	MISS JENNIE CULVER, Forelady.

ESTABLISHED. 5 YEARS. (FORMERLY 147 No. CLARK ST.)

Acquainted with over 10,000 working girls and nearly all the employers of female help in Chicago and surrounding country, occupy two large stor s, employ seven office assistants; my Foreladies are long experienced, and expert in judging fitness and places. I personally acquaint myself with each applicant, and every order. By dealing with my offices you will get honorable, conscientious and fair treatment, or better still, get what you want. I recognize nobody as competitors in my line of business.

R. R. DONNELLEY & SONS CO.

Printers

140-146 Monroe Street Chicago

Telephone Main-610

Electropoise.

NATIONAL ELECTROPOISE CO. 20 and 21, 34 Monroe

Elocution.

MME. A. D. ROSZELLE,
READER, AND TEACHER OF THE DELSARTE SYSTEM OF ELOCUTION, AND DRAMATIC ART . . . .
6636 STEWART AVENUE, FLAT 2.

Elocutionists.

Hall Eva True Mrs. 259 Lasalle av.
MR. & MRS. W. W. MILLNER, 76, 243 Wabash av.
SOPER H. M. 26 Vanburen

Employment Agencies.

MATHEWS MURRAY, 130 N. Clark; tel. North-869; and 2205 Michigan av. Tel. South-63

John Russell

FEMALE EMPLOYMENT

TEL.
NORTH 958   **147 NORTH CLARK STREET**

Cooks, Maids and General Servants (with references) promptly supplied for city or suburbs.

Employment Agencies –con'd.

MRS. C. OTTINGER,
SUCCESSOR TO MRS. STORM
EMPLOYMENT AGENCY,
Ladies supplied with competent help
of all nationalities.
3035 Indiana Ave.   Tel. South-15.

RUSSELL JOHN, 147 N. Clark

Engravers.
(Wedding Invitations, Announcements
and Calling Cards.)
CHILDS S. D. & CO. 140 and 142
Monroe

Wedding Invitations and Calling
::::Cards::::
WM. FREUND & SONS,
155 State Street.

| Wedding Invitations and::::: Embossing | PHENIX ENGRAVING COMPANY |

W. E. PECKHAM, MANAGER

Take
Elevator   185 Wabash Ave.

WEDDING and CALLING CARDS
LATEST FORMS
AND LOWEST PRICES
WIGGINS, SOCIETY ENGRAVER
44 MADISON ST., CHICAGO

Engravings, Etchings, Etc.
KEPPEL FREDERICK & CO.
1 Vanburen

Entertainments.

| SLAYTON LYCEUM BUREAU | PRIVATE AND PUBLIC ENTERTAINMENTS FURNISHED Central Music Hall. |

Family Hotel.
Lakeside, Mrs. Irving A. Leonard,
prop. 1839 Indiana av.

Fire Places.
(Built, Cleaned and Repaired.)
KING MOLESWORTH, 3139 Wabash av.

Florists.
ART FLORAL CO. 3911 Cottage
Grove av. Branch, 6, 43d

JOHN BLANCK,
FLORIST,
160-164 E. 43RD ST   TEL. OAKLAND-39.
CHOICE CUT FLOWERS,
PALMS, FERNS AND BEDDING PLANTS.

CHICAGO FLORAL CO. Weston
& Newitt, props. 38th and Grand
Boulevard
EAGLE ED. & CO. 129, 53d, and
4683 Lake av.

FRIEDMAN,
FLOWERS   FLOWERS
JACKSON & MICHIGAN AVE.
Telephone Harrison-380.

GALLAGHER FLORAL CO. 163
Wabash av. and 185 Michigan av.
GLEN FLORAL CO. 458½ W. Madison
GLOEDE W. H. & SON, 1602 W.
Madison
KIDWELL J. F. 3810 to 3824 Wentworth av. Tel. Yards-694

A. McADAMS,

SUCCESSOR TO

J. GOODE & CO.,

Florist, Etc.

53d STREET, CORNER KIMBARK AVENUE.

Plants,   Bouquets,

Shrubs,   Wreaths, Table

Hardy Roses,   Decoration and

and Vines.   Floral Designs.

CUT ROSES A SPECIALTY.

Telephone Oakland-863.

McADAMS A. 53d cor. Kimbark av.
MUIR SAMUEL, 3530 Michigan av.

C. A. SAMUELSON,
FLORIST.
Tel. South-411. 2129 Michigan Avenue.
Choice Cut Flowers.
Long Stem Roses a Specialty.

SCHILLER H. 899 and 730½ W.
Madison

Furnace Repairs.
ROOD GEORGE L. 79 Lake

Furniture.
(Special Designs.)
CHICAGO INTERIOR DECO-
RATING CO. 149 and 150 Michigan
av.

Gas and Electric Light'Fixtures.
WILMARTH T. W. CO. 225 and
227 State

Gas and Gasoline Stoves.
(Manufacturers.)
CLARK GEO. M. & CO. 161 Su-
perior

Glass, Cut and Fancy.
Pairpoint Mnfg. Co. 224 Wabash av.

Glassware.
BOHNER GEORGE CO. THE,
83 and 85 Wabash av.

Gold and Silver Plated Ware.
Pairpoint Mnfg. Co. 224 Wabash av.

Gout and Rheumatic Cure.
BROWN BENJAMIN DR. GOUT
& RHEUMATIC CURE, 2123
Michigan av.

Grocers.

E. A. GARDNER,
DEALER IN
GROCERIES AND MEATS.
66, 43D ST., COR. GREENWOOD AV.
TELEPHONE OAKLAND-535.

Grocers, Fancy.
JEVNE C. & CO. 110-112 Madison,
109-111 Wabash av.
STANTON & CO. 54 Madison

Gymnasiums.
YOUNG MEN'S CHRISTIAN
ASSN. 153 Lasalle

PROF. LABRET'S

PARIS HAIR STORE

MME. UNDERHILL, Manager.

Manicuring at Very Reasonable Charges.
For Ladies Only.   **131, 22d Street.**

Hair Goods.

UNDERHILL R. B. MRS. 3 The
Clinton, 1423 Michigan av.

CENTRAL MUSIC HALL HAIR STORE.

E. BURNHAM.

Hair Goods. Hair Dressing.
Ladies' Turkish Baths.
71 and 73 State St.

J. B. PUTNAM'S

CORSET AND HAIR PARLORS
Columbus Memorial Building.
ALICE L. KLINE, Mgr. Hair Dept.
Hair Goods, Hair Dressing, Shampoo-
ing Manicuring.
Griswold Corsets. 103 STATE STREET.

Hair Preparations,
(Shampoo, Bleaches, Dyeing.)
GOOD J. L. 1324 Indiana av.

Harness and Horse Furnishings.
FENTON J. H. CO. THE, 267-269
Wabash av.

Harps.
ERARD'S HARP, Lyon, Potter &
Co. Sole Agts. 174 and 176 Wabash
av.

Hospitals.
STREETER HOSPITAL, 2646 Calumet av.

Hotels.
HOTEL WINDERMERE, 56th
and Cornell av.
THE WELLINGTON, Wabash av.
and Jackson

House Cleaners.

ESTABLISHED 1891.

WM. J. WICKS,

Contractor and House Cleaner.
Fine Residence Cleaning a Specialty.
966 West Madison St. Tel. West-819.
110 and 112 West Washington St.
Tel. Main-4361.

Ice Dealers.

KNICKERBOCKER ICE CO. 134
Vanburen. See page 38
LINCOLN ICE CO. 18 Marine bldg.
Lake ne. cor. Lasalle
SMITH JAS. P. & CO. 145 Monroe.
See adv. opposite page
WASHINGTON ICE CO. 175 Dear-
born

Ices, Ice Creams, Etc.

REID ICE CREAM CO, THE, 15
and 17 Madison, branch, 4545 State

Insect Exterminators.

OSMUN LEE B. & CO. 213 and 215
State

Interior Decorations.

CHICAGO INTERIOR DECO-
RATING CO. 149 and 150 Michigan
av.

Interior Decorator.

CRANDALL FRANK A. 2210 and
and 2212 Indiana av. Tel. South-1.
" The Hallman Wall Cleaner "

Interior Decorators.

BARRY & KIPP, 362 Wabash av.
CRANDALL R. A. CO. 2127 Michi-
gan av. Tel. South-230
ECKART BROS. & CO. 442 to 452
Wabash av.
MAXWELL S. A. & CO. 134 and 136
Wabash av.

Interior Finish.

CHICAGO INTERIOR DECO-
RATING CO. 149 and 150 Michigan
av.

Iron Works.

Smith F. P. Wire and Iron Works, 96
Lake cor. Dearborn

JAMES P. SMITH & CO.,

ESTABLISHED 1855.

Wholesale and Retail ICE
...DEALERS IN...

145 East Monroe Street.

TELEPHONE MAIN-410.

Jewelers.

CHAMBERS J. B. & CO. Clark and Madison

EDWARD J. HOYER,
Diamonds, Watches and Jewelry
Repairing, Engraving, Diamond
...Setting...
228 North State Street.

PEACOCK CHARLES D. 96 and 98 State

ESTABLISHED 1885.

C. W. TERNAND & CO.
MANUFACTURING JEWELERS
Fine Diamond Work
1008–1009 CHAMPLAIN BUILDING,
N. W. Cor. State and Madison Sts.
Repairing Neatly Done.

Kindergarten.
CHICAGO KINDERGARTEN
COLLEGE, 10 Vanburen

Kindergarten Supplies.
CHARLES THOMAS CO. 211 and 213 Wabash av.

Kindergarten Training School.
CHICAGO FROEBEL ASSN. 274 Wabash av.

Ladies' Physician and Nurse.
LYONS ANNIE MRS. 3803 Michigan av.
Ladies' Tailors.

Rosenfeld & Co.

Ladies' Tailoring
Riding Habits......
and Fine Dressmaking

3363 Indiana Ave.

D. P. SHAW, Manager.   TELEPHONE SOUTH-585.
JAS. E. PLEW, Asst. Manager.
E. A. WOODWARD, Treasurer, 60 Wabash Avenue.

THE OFFICE TOILET SUPPLY CO.
INCORPORATED 1885.

**Furnishers of Clean Towels and Toilet Supplies.
Fine Laundry and Hand Work of all Kinds Done on Short Notice.**

1448 WABASH AVENUE.

· Ladies'. Tailors—continued.

MAY CLARK STINCHFIELD
Ladies' Fine Tailoring.
Parlors 1004 and 1005 Champlain Bldg.
N. W. Cor. State and Madison Sts.

MESDAMES TAGGERT AND WINEBROD
Fashionable Dressmaking,
Also Cloaks and Wraps of all Kinds.
Suites 35 and 36, 247 State, cor. Jackson
...Take Elevator...

, **Lamps, Shades, Etc.**
BOHNER GEORGE CO., THE,
83 and 85 Wabash av.

Laundries.
CLEAVER'S LAUNDRY, A. W.
Cleaver & Co. props. 103 to 107, 38th
GARFIELD LAUNDRY, 1349 W.
Madison
O. T. S. CO. LAUNDRY, 1448 Wabash av. . E. Plew, mngr. Tel.
South-585Jas
Olson's Hand Laundry, hand work a
specialty, 276 N. Clark.

Libraries, Circulating.
COBB'S LIBRARY, 132 Wabash av.

Livery, Boarding and Carriages.
DREXEL STABLES, 171-173, 43d

Livery and Boarding Stables.
**METROPOLE CLUB LIVERY
AND BOARDING STABLES,**
73-75, 26th
OAKENWALD LIVERY, Geo. F.
Ebert, agt. 158 E. 43d. Tel. Oakland-
39

Magazines.
ARTS, THE, 1408 Auditorium Tower

Mandolin Orchestras.
**VALISI'S MANDOLIN OR-
CHESTRA,** 21, 241 Wabash av.
VARALLO BROS. 616 Schiller bldg.

Mandolin School.
VALISI'S MANDOLIN SCHOOL,
21, 241 Wabash av.

Manicure and Shampooing.
Vickers C. B. Mrs. 713 Washington
boul.

Manicures.

MISS BLANCHARD
MANICURING PARLORS
McVICKER'S THEATRE BLDG.
... ROOM 32 ...

Mantels and Grates.
**CHICAGO INTERIOR DECOR-
ATING CO.** 149 and 150 Michigan av.

Marble and Mosaic.
**CERAMIC MOSAIC, TILE AND
MARBLE CO.** 46 to 50 Jackson

Massage

JOHN HEDLUND, M. D.
460 N. CLARK ST.
Massage. "Swedish Movements,"
Electricity and Hydro-Therapeutics

Massage, Baths, Etc.
LAGERQUIST EMMA MISS, 12,
240 Wabash av. and 28 Jackson
Massage and Swedish Move-
ments.

BATHS With Electricity or
Massage for Medical
Purposes. **MRS. FOLKE-KJELL-
BERG,** 47 to 51 Central Music Hall.
(See Page xviii.)

HIGHEST GRADE
OF EXCELLENCE

Robes Fabrique a la Mode Francaise

MADAME COOK

(Formerly the fashionable parlors of MADAME ROY.)

**Evening Costumes and
Tailor Made Gowns...
A Specialty**

GRACEFUL CURVES
DELICATE OUTLINES
BEAUTIFIED FORMS
Obtained only by the
French Method..·

874 WEST MADISON STREET

We also show the most beautiful effects in the highest style of the **MILLINERY ART**, in which **Madame Pearce** is the designer, whose productions are marvels of exquisite grace and loveliness. No two designs alike.

We invite the **Members** of **The West Side Woman's Club** to make our store their headquarters in the matter of dress, as we produce exclusive and correct designs in **Imported Millinery and Stylish Gowns.**

Mattresses and Feathers, Renovators.

Loeser John, 2032 Wabash av. and 1914 State

Medical Electricity and Massage,

WILLIAM YATES, Established 1879.
Electrician, Masseur, Chiropodist.
3034 Wabash Ave., Chicago, Ill,
Mrs. Yates administers treatment to Ladies Treatment at Patient's Residence when desired. Telephone South-108.

Medical Gymnastics and Massage.

WIEMER JOHN A. 3505 Indiana av. tel. Oakland-85

Merchant Tailors.

ESTABLISHED 1853.
THE EDWARD ELY CO.
Merchant Tailors.
Ely Bldg., 165 Wabash Ave.
**CUSTOM-MADE SHIRTS
A SPECIALTY.**

Metaphysicians.

MRS. L. V. COMER

METAPHYSICIAN

Office Hours: - - - 9 a.m. to 1 p.m.

2009 Indiana Ave.

Milk Depots.
BOWMAN DAIRY CO. 68 and 70 N. State, 3514 Rhodes av., 607, 63d (L.), 73 Loomis, 1247 Belmont av.

Milliners.
Cook W. L. 874 W. Madison

MISS A. B. KENYON,
FINE MILLINERY,
676 WEST MADISON STREET,
CHICAGO.

MME. MURDOCH,
Fine Millinery and Dress Making,
634 N. Clark St. (Near Plaza.)

F. H. SAMMIS,

Mineral Springs.

CHIPPEWA SPRING CO. 620 S. Halsted

Mineral Waters.

ALLOUEZ MINERAL SPRING CO. J. Frank Hoeffel, sole agent, 131 Adams

LONDONDERRY LITHIA SPRING WATER CO. Edwin E. Hills, sole agent, 70 State. Tel. Main-4471

SILURIAN MINERAL SPRING CO. 157 Wabash av. tel. Main-2571

WAUKESHA HYGEIA MINERAL SPRING CO. 1908 Wabash av. tel. South-929

WHITE ROCK MINERAL SPRING CO. O. W. Hinckley, mngr. 55 Meagher. Tel. Canal-212

Modistes.

BARBER & HENDERSON, 418 Washington boul.

Cook W. L. 874 W. Madison

FEY C. MME. 3353 Indiana av.

LA FERTE, 2121 Michigan av.

TALLEY A. M. MRS. 2232 Indiana av.

Monuments.

GEISSLER R. 540 Wabash av.

MITCHELL GEO. H. 24 Adams, room 20, 2d door e. of Wabash av.

Mosaic Flooring.

SAMMIS F. H. 159 Lasalle

Mosaic Floors in All Designs.

CHICAGO INTERIOR DECORATING CO. 149 and 150 Michigan av.

Mosaic and Marble.

CERAMIC MOSAIC, TILE AND MARBLE CO. 46 to 50 Jackson

Columbian College of Music

VAN BUREN STREET
BETWEEN MICHIGAN AND WABASH AVENUES

MAX BENDIX,
A. D. DUVIVIER, } Directors.
W. C. E. SEEBOECK,

MOST COMPLETE COLLEGE OF MUSIC IN THE WEST

Students may enter at any time. Address all communications to

THOS. C. LOMBARD, Secretary

Music Colleges.
COLUMBIAN COLLEGE OF MUSIC, 26 VanBuren

Music Publishers and Dealers.

NATIONAL MUSIC CO.
General Depot, 215-221 Wabash Ave.
Retail, "The Leader." State & Adams.
Headquarters 6c. Sheet Music.

SUMMY CLAYTON F. 174 and 176 Wabash av.

Music Schools.

Hugo Schmoll's School of Music.
Competent Teachers for Vocal and Instrumental Departments
Suite, 614-616 Schiller Bldg.
Residence, 341 Orchard St.

Music Teachers.
BENEDICT HATTIE MISS, piano, 24 Adams and 2415 Indiana av.

MRS. IDA LEPELLE CLASON,
Contralto, Soloist and
Teacher of Singing.
Room 56, Kimball Hall Building.

ANGELO DE PROSSE,
...Teaches...
BEGINNERS, as well as ADVANCED PUPILS in PIANO.
52 Kimball Hall, 243 Wabash Ave.

FREDERIC GRANT GLEASON,
TEACHER OF
PIANO, ORGAN, HARMONY, COMPOSITION AND ORCHESTRATION.
74 Auditorium Bldg.
52

MATHEWS W. S. B. 1402-05 Auditorium tower.

Mrs. Adeline Louise Nellis,
VOICE TEACHER. Best and most successful Method known. Voices trained for Choirs, Concert & Opera.
Suite 65, Stevens Art Building,
24-26 East Adams Street.

MISS STELLA H. SISSON,
Teacher of Piano.
Studio, Kimball Hall.

FRANK F. WINTER,
TEACHER OF
...VIOLIN...
642 Washington Boulevard,
Bet. Lincoln and Robey Sts.

Music Teachers.
(Mandolin and Banjo.)
HAZEN W. L. 74 Kimball Hall

Music and French.
MORTON ALBINA MRS. 2457 Michigan av.

Musical Colleges.

THE AMERICAN CONSERVATORY OF MUSIC.
J. J. HATTSTAEDT, Director,
WEBER MUSIC HALL,
.....Wabash Ave. and Jackson St.

CHICAGO CONSERVATORY OF MUSIC AND DRAMATIC ART.
SAMUEL KAYZER, DIRECTOR.
Auditorium Bldg.
Wabash Ave., Cor. Congress

THE CHICAGO
PARLOR ENTERTAINMENT BUREAU ~~~~

Is prepared to furnish the best of talent for concerts, public and private receptions, musicales, banquets, weddings, lodge and council entertainments, dinner parties and all occasions. Male and lady quartettes, vocal and instrumental soloists, mandolin orchestras, readers, zither soloists and others. Call or address

TEL. MAIN-2196   **HENRY F. STEINBACH, Manager,**   505 Masonic Temple.

Musical Colleges—continued.

Chicago National College of Music
26 VAN BUREN STREET.
H. S. PERKINS, Director.

Goldbeck College of Music
DR. ROBERT GOLDBECK
and PROF. THOMAS MOORE. Directors
Office, **79 KIMBALL HALL,**
243 Wabash Ave.

Gottschalk Lyric School
ISABELLA BUILDING
46 AND 48 VANBUREN ST.
Vocal, Instrumental, Dramatic
IN ALL ITS BRANCHES
L. G. GOTTSCHALK,
Send for Catalogue.   DIRECTOR.

The Kelso School of Musical and Dramatic Art
Kimball Hall, 243 Wabash Ave., Chicago
MR. H. A. KELSO, JR., and
MRS. MAY DONNALLY KELSO, Directors

Musical Entertainments.
Chicago Parlor Entertainment Bureau,
505 Masonic Temple.

Musical Instruments.
CHURCH JOHN CO. THE, 200 to 206 Wabash av.
LYON, POTTER & CO. 174 and 176 Wabash av.
LYON & HEALY, Wabash av. sw. cor. Adams
MAHAN J. L. 308 Wabash av.

PRES. OSBORN,
Pianos and Musical Merchandise
211 WABASH AVE., 3rd floor.
SPECIALTIES: Bargain Pianos for Cash. Renting, Fine Tuning, Polishing.

Musical Schools.
VARALLO BROS. 616 Schiller bldg.

Oculists and Aurists.
Bettman Boerne, 1008 to 1012, 34 and 36 Washington, hours 10 a.m. to 1 p.m. and 4 to 5 p.m.
Buffum J H. 905, 34 Washington, Venetian bldg. Hours 9 to 12 a.m. 3 to 5 p.m. Residence 366 Ontario
Camfield B. A. 1202 Champlain bldg. hours 9:30 a.m. to 4:30 p.m. Sundays 11 to 1:30. Tel. Main-752
Coleman W. Franklin, M.D., M.R.C.S., Eng. 1109 Venetian bldg. 36 Washington. Hours 9:30 a.m. to 12:30 p.m., 4:30 to 5:30 p.m.
Foster F. H. 813, 34 Washington; hours 9 to 1 and 3 to 5 p.m. Residence 73 Lake View av.
FOWLER W. S. DR. 38 Madison. Hours 9 to 12 a.m., 3 to 6 p.m.

Established A.D. 1862.
DR. J. B. WALKER,
OCULIST AND AURIST
247 Park Ave. Office, 85 Washington St
11 to 4. Sunday, 12 to 2.

Old Gold and Silver.
Dee Thomas J. 67 Washington

Optical Goods.
J. M. & A. C. Johnston Optical Co.
Scientific Manufacturing Opticians,
912 MASONIC TEMPLE.
Oculists' Prescriptions a Specialty.
Spectacles, Opera Glasses, &c., &c.

MANASSE L. 88 Madison

Orchestras—continued.

**H A Z E N ' S MANDOLIN OR-
CHESTRA,** 74 Kimball Hall
VARALLO BROS. 616 Schiller bldg.

Organs.

KIMBALL W. W. CO. 243 to 245
Wabash av.

Organs and Pianos.

**CHICAGO COTTAGE ORGAN
CO.** 215 Wabash av.
LYON & HEALY, Wabash av. sw.
cor. Adams ·

Oysters, Fish and Canned Goods.

BOOTH A. PACKING CO. Lake
and State
        Painters.   −   ·
CRANDALL FRANK A. 2210 and
2212 Indiana av.   Tel. South-1. "The
Hallman Wall Cleaner"
CRANDALL R. A. CO. 2127 Michigan av. tel. South-230

Painters and Decorators.

BARRY & KIPP, 362 Wabash av.
NELSON W. P. & CO. 193 Wabash av.

Photographer, Amateur.

THE KOMBI, Alfred C Kemper,
mnfr. 208 Lake

Photographers.

ROOT W. J. 79, 243 Wabash av.

J. W. TAYLOR,
Owings Bldg.
LANDSCAPE PHOTOGRAPHER.
INTERIORS OF RESIDENCES
a Specialty.

VARNEY G. W. 3937 Drexel Boulevard

P hotographic Supplies.

**≡≡≡BOSTON≡≡≡
PHOTOGRAPHIC FINISHING CO.**
96 STATE STREET.
Photo Supplies for Amateurs, Develop-
ing and Printing, Mounting in Albums
and on Glass a Specialty.

DOUGLASS & SHUEY CO. 111
State
WALMSLEY, FULLER & CO.
134 and 136 Wabash av.

Phrenologists.

PROF. THAYER,
Chicago's practical and reliable

PHRENOLOGIST

52 years experience, 18 years in Chicago·
113 E. Madison Street.

Physicians.

DR. FALOON,
Specialist.
Cancer and Kidney Diseases,
Cancer permanently cured, no knife,
plaster or electricity. 44 years experi-
ence. Consultation and book free.
MC VICKER'S THEATER BUILDING.

·**DR. O. W. F. SNYDER,** ·
Obesity Specialist,
Suite 1 to 4 McVicker's Theatre,
Madison St., near State,
Office Hours: 9 a. m. to 5 p. m.

Physicians and Surgeons.

Babcock Elmer E. 3239 Indiana av.
until 8:30 a.m., 12 to 1:30 p.m. and 6
to 7:30 p.m. Tel. South-76
Brower Daniel R., M.D. 1201, 34 Washington; hours 10:30 a.m. to 2:30 p. m;
Tel. Main-3834. Residence 597 Jackson boul. until 8 a. m. and 7 to 7:30
p.m. Tel. West-85.

TEL. SOUTH-575
DR. W. BONNAR,
Office and Residence, 300 Thirty-First St.
N. W. COR. WABASH AVE.
Office Hours, until 10 a. m.; 1 to 2.30
p. m.; 6 to 8.00 p. m.

BUCHANAN WALTER W. 1318
Wabash av. Tel. South-85.
Byford Henry T. 803, 36 Washington,
hours 9 to 12 a.m. except Wednesday
and Saturday. Tel. Main-5156, residence 3021 Calumet av.
Dinwoody J. A. 3300 Cottage Grove av.;
hours 9 to 11 a.m., 1 to 3 and 6 to 8
p.m. Tel. South-310
Doyle G. P. Dr. The Cambridge.
Hours 12 to 3 p.m. Tel. Oakland-872
Ferguson A. H. M.D. Surgeon. Venetian bldg. 36 Washington; hours 1
to 4 p. m. Tel. Main-3834; residence
2950 Indiana av.; hours 8 to 10 a.m.
Tel. South-108
GROSVENOR LEMUEL C. 185
Lincoln av.; office hours 8 to 10 a.m.,
3 to 5 p.m. and evenings. Tel. North-
692. Consulting physician and ob-
stetrician
Hemsteger J. A., M.D. 3836 Vincennes
av.
Johnson Frank S. Dr. 2521 Prairie av.;
hours 11 a.m. to 1 p.m. Tel. South-
239
JOHNSTONE STUART, M.D. 709
Venetian bldg. 11 to 3

DR. EDWARD R. KELLOGG,
Surgery, Nose, Throat and Ear; also
Facial Blemishes removed.
1108 Masonic Temple. Phone Main-5871
Residence, 24 Orchard St. cor. Oak-
enwald Ave. Phone Oakland-20.

MILES FRANKLIN DR. 1315
Masonic Temple

Morrow C. W. 63d ne. cor. Cottage
Grove av.
Palmer A. E., M.D. 721 Lincoln av.;
hours until 9:30 a.m., 1 to 2 and 6 to
7:36 p.m. Tel. LakeView-211

Dr. Helen P. Phillips.
Famous Home Treatment for Ladies.
Hours: 1 to 4 p.m,
"Argyle," Suite B, Michigan Blvd. and
Jackson St. Treatment, **$5 a Month,**
Medicines included.

Reed Morey L., M.D. 320 Bowen av.
Ruggles Georgia S., M.D. 2211 Michigan av.
Shears G. F., M. D. 3130 Indiana av.;
hours 8 to 9 a. m. 1 to 2 and 6:30 to
7:30 p. m. Tel. South-358
Stearns W. M., M. D. ear, nose and
throat, 813 Marshall Field & Co.
bldg.; hours 9 to 12 a. m., 3 to 5 p. m.

GERTRUDE G. WELLINGTON, M. D.
Residence: 726 Washington Boulevard.
Office hours, 3 to 6 p. m.

Office: Room 7, Central Music Hall.
Office hours, 9 to 11 a. m.
Office Telephone, Main-2642.
Office, after Feb. 1, '95 in Reliance Bldg.
S. W. cor. State and Washington.

Piano Music Furnished for Dancing.
OWEN KATE MRS. 3519 Indiana
av.

Piano Stools and Scarfs.

Specialty of high-grade Stools,
Grand Piano Covers and Scarfs,
Braiding and Embroidering
of all kinds.

JAS. H. WILSON & CO., 90-98 Market St.

 *PIANOS*
ORGANS

.AND A FULL LINE OF

Musical Merchandise, Small Musical Instruments,

Music Books and Sheet Music.

308 Wabash Ave., Auditorium Building.

Pianos.

CHASE BROTHERS PIANO CO.
219 and 221 Wabash av.
CHICAGO COTTAGE ORGAN
CO. 215 Wabash av.
COLBY PIANOS, Julius N. Brown,
western mngr. 327 Wabash av.
CROSS R. W. & CO. 22 Vanburen

 The EVERETT PIANO.

THE JOHN CHURCH COMPANY,
General Factors, 200-206 Wabash Ave.

KIMBALL W. W. CO. 243 to 253
Wabash av.
LYON & HEALY, Wabash av. sw.
cor. Adams
MAHAN J. L., 308 Wabash av.
NEW ENGLAND PIANO CO. 262
and 264 Wabash av.
RINTELMAN PIANO CO. 165
Wabash av.

SCHAEFFER PIANO CO. 42, 24
Adams

SHONINGER PIANOS.
First-Class in every respect.
Durability Guaranteed.
B. Shoninger Co.
182-84 Wabash Avenue.
Telephone Main-3622.

THE THOMPSON MUSIC CO.
SOHMER PIANOS
261 Wabash Ave. Tel, Harrison-63.

Pianos and Organs.
ESTEY & CAMP, 233 State and 49
Jackson
LYON, POTTER & CO. 174 and 176
Wabash av.

Picture Frames.
NEWCOMB-MACKLIN CO. 307-9
Wabash av.

Plaiting, Pinking, Button Holes, Etc.
Fowler John E. 253 W. Madison

--Peter Willems,-----

PLUMBER, GASFITTER

and SEWER BUILDER.

Telephone North-484.   **254 North Clark St.**

Plumbers and Gasfitters.

TELEPHONE SOUTH-670.
FITZSIMMONS & CO.
Plumbers, Gas Fitters and Sewer Builders
Jobbing a Specialty.
3450 Indiana Avenue.

WILLEMS PETER, 254 N. Clark

Porcelain Paintings.
(High Class Art.)
ENS & GREINER, 241 Wabash av.

Portrait Artists.
SHOGREN S. E. 250, 64th (H.P.)

Precious Stones.
Essig Frederick J. 115 State

Printers.
Almberg S. Th. 290 N. Wells

Railroads.
CHICAGO. MILWAUKEE & ST. PAUL RY. ticket office 209 Clark
CHICAGO, ROCK ISLAND & PACIFIC RY. depot Vanburen cor. Sherman, ticket office 104 Clark

Restaurants.
FRENCH RESTAURANT, 77 and 79 S. Clark

Restaurant Bismarck!
180-182 Randolph St.
Excellent Meals served at any time.
Finest Ladies' Cafe and Restaurant.
Best Imported Wines and Beer.
SPECIALTY :
Muenchner Pschorr Brau.

Rheumatism and Gout Cure.
BROWN BENJAMIN DR. GOUT
& RHEUMATIC CURE, 2123
Michigan av.

Roofers.
POWELL M. W. CO. 334 Dearborn

Saddles, Harness, Etc.
(Riding.)
FENTON J. H. CO., THE, 267-269
Wabash av.

Sanitariums.
FORSYTH REST CURE, Berwyn, Ill.
PENNOYER SANITARIUM CO.
Kenosha, Wis.

Savings Banks.
GLOBE SAVINGS BANK, cor.
Dearborn and Jackson

Schools and Academies.
ASSOCIATION EVENING COL-
LEGE, Young Men's Christian
Assn. 153 Lasalle
CHICAGO ACADEMY OF DRA-
MATIC ART, 28, 241 Wabash av.
COLUMBIA SCHOOL OF ORA-
TORY AND PHYSICAL CUL-
TURE, 24 Adams
JONES BUSINESS COLLEGE,
582 W. Madison cor. Ashland boul.

L. SCHUTT GERMAN-ENGLISH
ACADEMY,
621 & 623 Wells St.

Sea Shells.

SHELLS, Minerals, Corals, Fossils, Birds' Eggs, Indian Relics, etc. Taxidermy in all its branches. Illustrated Catalogue by mail 10 cents. **J. M. WIERS, 357 W. Van Buren St., Chicago.**

Sewing Machines.
Fowler John E. 253 W. Madison

WHEELER & WILSON
═No. 9═
185-87 WABASH   **Tel. Main-2643**

Shirt Makers.

Established 1853.
THE EDWARD ELY CO.
SHIRT MANUFACTURERS
AND TAILORS.
Ely Bldg., 165 Wabash Ave.

Show Cases.
YOST CIRCULAR CASE CO. 266
, S. Jefferson

Silversmiths.
Rugg Frank E. 524, 94 and 96 State

Stained Glass.
FLANAGAN & BIEDENWEG,
57 to 63 Illinois

M. W. POWELL COMPANY

Roofing and Paving

**PATENT
TILE
ROOFING**

**FLAX and WOOL FELT and
ACTINOLITE ROOFING**

Phone Harrison-354

334 Dearborn Street.

Frank E. Rugg

SILVERSMITH

**GOLD, SILVER
AND NICKEL PLATER**

AND JEWELER

All kinds of BRONZES repaired and rebronzed. All kinds of SILVER
and PLATED WARE repaired and refinished. Satisfaction Guaranteed.

Room 524, 94 and 96 STATE STREET.

Stamping Patterns.

EMBROIDERY STAMPING CO.
45 Randolph

Stationers.

PETTIBONE P. F. & CO. 48 and
50 Jackson

**THAYER & JACKSON STA-
TIONERY CO.** 245 and 247 State

Steamship Agencies.

**COMPAGNIE GENERALE
TRANSATLANTIQUE,** 164 Randolph

Steamship Agencies.
(Ocean.)

WHITE STAR LINE,
N. Anderson, G'l W'n Agt. 54 S. Clark

Steamship Agencies.
(Ocean Lines.)

HAMBURG AMERICAN LINE,
C. Ramm, West. Agt. 125 Lasalle

**INTERNATIONAL NAVIGA-
TION COMPANY,** 32 S. Clark

**NORTH GERMAN LLOYD
STEAMSHIP CO.** 80-82, 5th-av.

Stone Seal Engravers.

Stecher M. D. 24, 70 Madison

Tailors, Merchant.

DEFOE & CO. 14 Jackson

ESTABLISHED 1853.

THE EDWARD ELY CO.
Merchant Tailors.
Ely Bldg., 165 Wabash Ave.
**CUSTOM-MADE SHIRTS
A SPECIALTY.**

Taxidermists.

Kaempfer Fred, 217 Madison

Temperature Regulators.

GAY & CULLOTON, 52 N. Clark

Tents and Awnings.

CARPENTER GEO. B. & CO. 208
South Water

Tile.
(For Floors and Walls.)

**CERAMIC MOSAIC, TILE AND
MARBLE CO.** 46 to 50 Jackson

Tile Ceramic Mosaics.
(For Floors and Halls.)

**CHICAGO INTERIOR DECOR-
ATING CO.** 149 and 150 Michigan
av.

Tinsmiths and Furnaces.

RAYMOND BEHER, TIN, COPPER and SHEET IRON WORK,

Furnaces, Stoves, Hotel and Restaurant Work. Job-Work and Repairing promptly attended to.
No. 8 RUSH ST., COR. KINZIE.

Toys, Games and Novelties.
SCHWARZ TOY BAZAAR, 231 State

Trunks and Valises.
Lynch James C. 135 Randolph

Trusses, Elastic Stockings, Etc.
SHARP & SMITH, 73 Randolph

Upholsterers.
Hawkins B. 3448 Indiana av.

Tel. West-366.
L. MENHART, Fine Upholstering,
585 W. MADISON STREET.

PHILLIPS & FELDMAN, 827 and 829 W. Madison
Walker W. H. 2258 Indiana av.

Upholsterers and Decorators.

W. BAKER, QUANTICK & CO. Decorators and .....Upholsterers, **2228 INDIANA AVE.**

Upholsterers and Drapers.
HOERLEIN H. A. 3104 and 3106 Cottage Grove av. Tel. South-647
Violins. (Antique and Modern.)
PELZ ROBERT, 185 and 187 Wabash av.

Vocal Teachers.

CHARLES W. CLARK, Voice Culture,

BARITONE SOLOIST 47, 243
CONCERT AND ORATORIO WABASH AVE.

Cohen Kate Miss, 60, 243 Wabash av.
DUNN L. M. MRS. "Ingleside," 1 Park av.

EVA EMMETT WYCOFF,
Concert and Oratorio Soprano,
VOCAL TEACHER.
60, 243 Wabash Avenue.

Wall Paper.

CRANDALL FRANK A. 2210 and 2212 Indiana av. Tel. South-1. "The Hallman Wall Cleaner."

CRANDALL R. A. CO. 2127 Michigan av. Tel. South-230

LARTZ WALL PAPER CO., THE, 45 to 49 Randolph

J. G. McCARTHY COMPANY
...WALL PAPER...
PAINTING AND DECORATING
202 Washington Boulevard, cor. Green
TELEPHONE WEST-929. CHICAGO

MAXWELL S. A. & CO. 134 and 136 Wabash av.

NELSON W. P. & CO. 193 Wabash av.

Wall Paper Cleaners.

Peerless Wall Paper Cleaning Co. The, 40 S. May

ROBERTSON BROS. 244 Warren av.

Watch Repairing.

...C. FRANZ...
FINE WATCH REPAIRING
A SPECIALTY.
57 Washington St., Rooms 37 38.

Watches.

CHAMBERS J. B. & CO. Clark and Madison

Waukesha Water.

SILURIAN MINERAL SPRING CO. 157 Wabash av. Tel. Main-2571

WAUKESHA HYGEIA MINERAL SPRING CO. 1908 Wabash av. Tel. South-929

Wedding Invitations.

Wedding and Calling Cards.
WM. FREUND & SONS,
FINE STATIONERY.
155 State Street.

Window Shades.

CRANDALL FRANK A. 2210 and 2212 Indiana av. Tel. South-1. "The Hallman Wall Cleaner."

Wines.

BROCTON WINES, 1227 Masonic Temple

Wines, High Grade.
(Importers.)

CAUBERT EUGENE & CO. 19-21 Wabash av.

Wire and Iron Works.

BARBEE WIRE AND IRON WORKS, 44 and 46 Dearborn

SMITH F. P. WIRE & IRON WKS, 96 Lake, cor. Dearborn

Wood Carpets.

MOORE E. B. & CO. 50 Randolph

PART NINE

· DIAGRAMS

OF

PLACES OF AMUSEMENT

SHOWING POSITION OF BOXES AND SEATS BY NUMBER AND SECTION

ASSOCIATION AUDITORIUM

AUDITORIUM

CENTRAL MUSIC HALL

CHICAGO OPERA HOUSE

HAVLIN'S THEATRE   *COLUMBIA THEATRE*

HAYMARKET THEATRE

HOOLEY'S THEATRE

LINCOLN THEATRE

McVICKER'S THEATRE

SCHILLER THEATRE

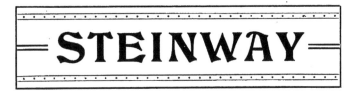
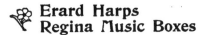

ASSOCIATION AUDITORIUM.

10 Arcade Court.

Under the management of
THE YOUNG MEN'S CHRISTIAN ASSOCIATION, of Chicago.

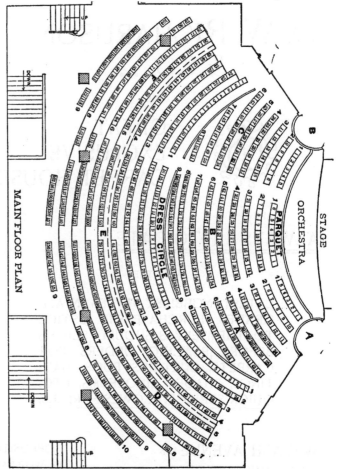

LA SALLE STREET and ARCADE COURT.

FOYER

834

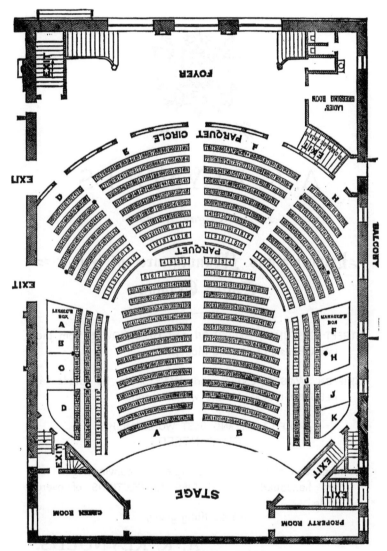

CENTRAL MUSIC HALL.

Maison Rein,

A. R. REYNOLDS

2101 Michigan Avenue

==Importer and Manufacturer of Smart== Tailor Gowns

STREET COSTUMES, RECEPTION and BALL GOWNS from the latest Parisian Cuts and Models.

CHIFFON WAISTS, CAPES and JACKETS, to be made at REDUCED PRICES for the winter months.

PERFECT FIT AND BEST WORKMANSHIP
.....GUARANTEED.....

An Inspection of my work and style will convince you we are headquarters for LADIES' CONFECTIONS of every style.......

Respectfully yours,

A. R. REYNOLDS.

CHICAGO OPERA HOUSE.

DAVID HENDERSON, Manager. .....**Fire Proof.**

American Extravaganza Company and Duquesne Theatre, Pittsburg.
NEW YORK OFFICE, 1404 BROADWAY.

WM. MUELLER, JR.   GEO. F. EBERT,
        Proprietor.   Agent.

 akenwald

Stables

Livery
    Boarding and
        Sale Stable

.....158 Forty-Third Street.....
CHICAGO

TELEPHONE OAKLAND-39

The Columbia

The Leading Theatre of Chicago.

AL. HAYMAN, New York.
WILL DAVIS, Chicago.
Proprietors and Managers.

MONROE AND DEARBORN STS.

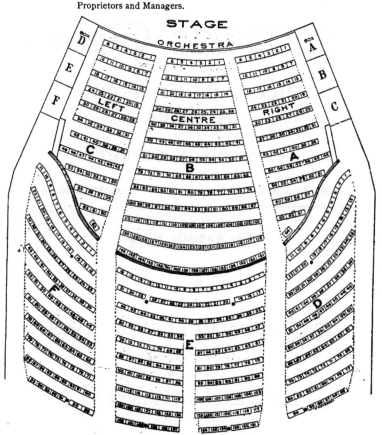

Presents Only Highest Class Attractions.

839

M. W. DIFFLEY

Established 1875

Importer and Dealer in Reliable High Grade.... **Cigars**

Pipes and Smokers' Articles

72 MADISON STREET

Branch, 67 Van Buren Street   **Telephone Main-3666**

GRAND OPERA HOUSE.

Clark St., Opp. Court House.

HARRY L. HAMLIN, - - Manager.

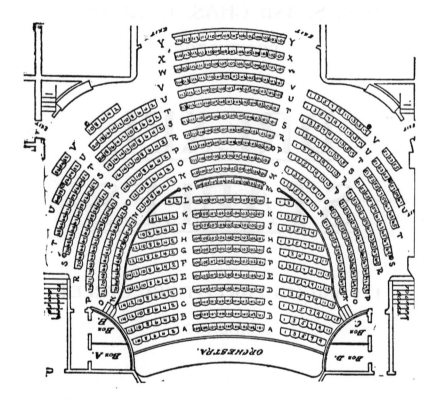

Every Night. Matinees, Wednesdays and Saturdays.

841

Telephone Oakland-51.

WM. S. AND CHAS. E. ADAMS,

PROPRIETORS

DREXEL

STABLES

171 AND 173 FORTY-THIRD STREET

CHICAGO

**CARRIAGES, LIGHT LIVERY
AND BOARDING**

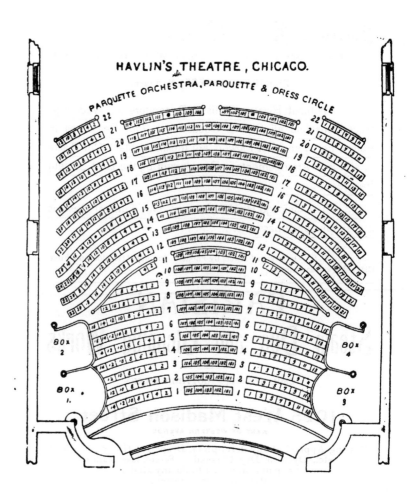

HAVLIN'S THEATRE, CHICAGO.

PARQUETTE ORCHESTRA, PARQUETTE & DRESS CIRCLE

The Haymarket.

The Handsome Theatre of the World.

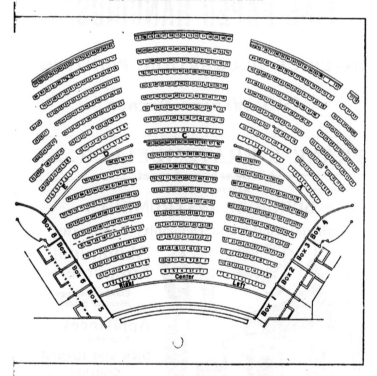

WEST MADISON STREET, BETWEEN UNION AND HALSTED STREETS.

WILL J. DAVIS, Proprietor and Manager.

th Side Ticket Offices at Lyon & Healy's, Adams and Wabash Ave., and Bob Bayley's 155 State.

845

W.P. NELSON Co.

TELEPHONE MAIN-2716

FINE PAPER HANGINGS,

INTERIOR DECORATION, PAINTING

193 WABASH AVENUE.

846

HOOLEY'S THEATRE.

"THE PARLOR HOME OF COMEDY."

MRS. R. M. HOOLEY, Lessee.   HARRY J. POWERS, Manager.

"Hooley's has become to Chicago like Daly's and the Lyceum of New York rolled into one—more than that—like six of the best comedy houses in their combined essence."—*Chicago Tribune.*

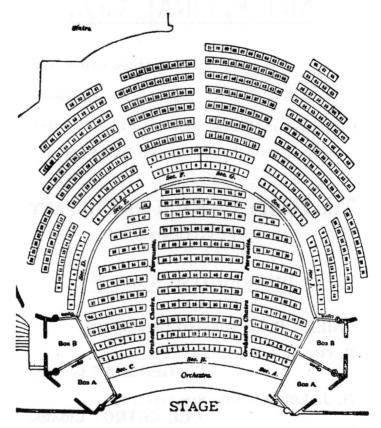

84

848

RANDOLPH STREET, OPPOSITE THE CITY HALL.

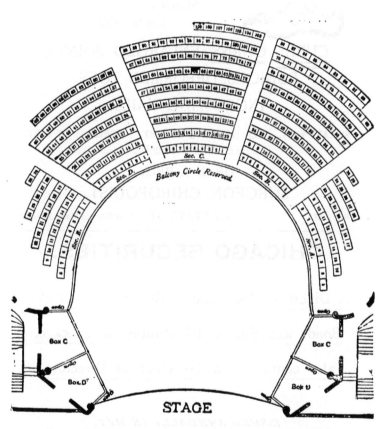

Open all the Year. Playing only the leading attractions.

CHICAGO SECURITIES.

A Digest of Information Relating to Stocks,

Bonds and Financial Institutions of Chicago,

also containing a Directory of Directors.

ISSUED ANNUALLY IN MAY.

CHICAGO DIRECTORY CO.,

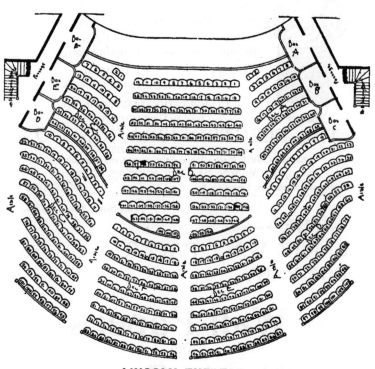

LINCOLN THEATRE.

McVICKER'S THEATRE.

Thirty-eighth year under same management.

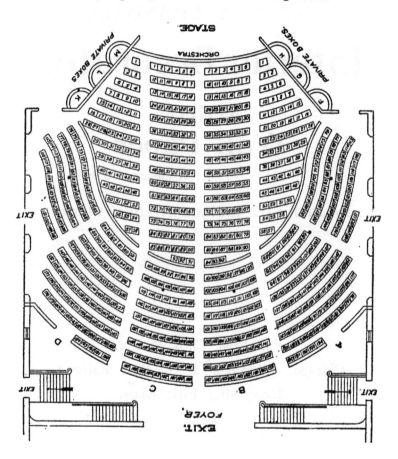

854

SCHILLER THEATRE.

Thos. W. Prior, Manager.

Chicago's Handsomest Play House, Randolph Street, Between Clark and Dearborn Streets.
The only absolutely Fire Proof Theatre in the City. The Highest and Finest Theatre Building in the World.

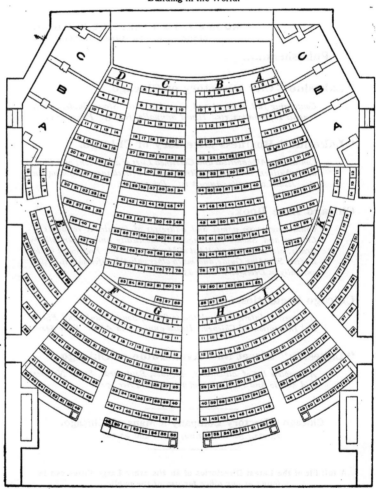

Chicago Directory Company....

ROOMS 2, 3 & 4 LAKESIDE BUILDING
CLARK, S. W. COR. ADAMS STREETS.

Publishers......

"Lakeside" City Directory of Chicago.

Containing full, General and Classified Lists, Street Guide, Miscellaneous Information, etc. Issued annually, July 15. Price, $7.50.

"Lakeside" Business Directory of Chicago.

Containing Alphabetical and Classified Lists of all Persons and Firms doing business in Chicago; Street Guide. Miscellaneous Information, etc. Issued annually, August 1st. Price, $2.50.

Chicago Blue Book.

Coutaining 25,000 names and addresses of Prominent residents of Chicago and Suburbs, arranged alphabetically and numerically by streets; also containing full list of Members of all the Prominent Clubs, Ladies' Shopping Guide, and much other valuable information. Issued annually in December. Price $3.

Chicago Securities.

A Digest of Information relative to Stocks, Bonds, Banks and Financial Institutions of Chicago. Issued annually in April. Price $2.00.

"Lakeside" Street and Ave. Guide of Chicago.

A complete list of all Streets, Avenues, Boulevards, Street Numbers and how to find them. Issued annually. Price 25 cts.

Chicago Directory Company's Maps of Chicago.
25 cts., 50 cts., $1.00, $2.00 and $3.00.

A full file of the Latest Directories of all the other Large Cities can be found at our office for use of the public.

857

NELSON CO.

GLOBE
SAVINGS BANK

DEARBORN AND MONROE STREETS, CHICAGO

Lightning Source UK Ltd.
Milton Keynes UK
UKHW02f0725160818
327336UK00008B/295/P